CONO19
B80

D0764238

Canadian Constitutional Law

Fourth Edition

THE CONSTITUTIONAL LAW GROUP

Executive Editors

Patrick Macklem
University of Toronto

Carol Rogerson
University of Toronto

Editors

Joel Bakan
University of British Columbia

Jean Leclair
Université de Montréal

John Borrows
University of Victoria

Ian Lee
University of Toronto

Sujit Choudhry
University of Toronto

Richard Moon
University of Windsor

Robin Elliot
University of British Columbia

R.C.B. Risk
University of Toronto

Jean-François Gaudreault-DesBiens
University of Toronto

Kent Roach
University of Toronto

Donna Greschner
University of Saskatchewan

Bruce Ryder
Osgoode Hall Law School

Patricia Hughes
University of Calgary

David Schneiderman
University of Toronto

Lorraine Weinrib
University of Toronto

2010
EMOND MONTGOMERY PUBLICATIONS
TORONTO, CANADA

Copyright © 2010 Emond Montgomery Publications Limited.

NOTICE & DISCLAIMER: All rights reserved. No part of this publication may be reproduced in any form by any means without the written consent of Emond Montgomery Publications. Emond Montgomery Publications and all persons involved in the creation of this
publication disclaim any warranty as to the accuracy of this publication and shall not be
responsible for any action taken in reliance on the publication, or for any errors or omissions contained in the publication. Nothing in this publication constitutes legal or other
professional advice. If such advice is required, the services of the appropriate professional
should be obtained.

Emond Montgomery Publications Limited
60 Shaftesbury Avenue
Toronto ON M4T 1A3
http://www.emp.ca/lawschool

Printed in Canada.
Reprinted January 2014.

We acknowledge the financial support of the Government of Canada through the Canada
Book Fund for our publishing activities.

Acquisitions editor: Peggy Buchan
Copy and production editor: Nancy Ennis
Proofreader: Cindy Fujimoto
Permissions editor: Jennifer Blackmore

Library and Archives Canada Cataloguing in Publication

   Canadian constitutional law / the Constitutional Law Group ; executive editors,
Patrick Macklem ... [et al.]; editors, Joel Bakan ... [et al.].—4th ed.

ISBN 978-1-55239-332-1

   1. Constitutional law—Canada—Cases. I.   Macklem, Patrick.   II.   Bakan, Joel.
III. Constitutional Law Group

KE4219.C35 2009   342.71   C2009-903687-8

Preface to the Fourth Edition

This edition continues our efforts to make *Canadian Constitutional Law* a truly national project—one that benefits from an editorial team rich with regional, linguistic, and scholarly diversity. The fourth edition remains true to the structure and purposes of previous editions, and especially to our shared commitment to the idea that understanding constitutional history is critical to comprehending the present and future of Canadian constitutional law. Like its predecessor, this edition reaches back in time to the earliest colonial encounters between Aboriginal peoples and European colonies, and to conflicts between European empires over territorial and sovereign control of the continent. We have made significant changes to several chapters, including Chapter 8, Interpreting the Division of Powers; Chapter 9, Peace, Order, and Good Government; Chapter 14, Aboriginal Peoples and the Constitution; Chapter 19, Freedom of Religion; Chapter 22, Life, Liberty, and Security of the Person; and Chapter 23, Equality Rights. Other chapters have been updated thoroughly to reflect recent developments in constitutional jurisprudence and scholarship.

Despite its commitment to constitutional history, this edition continues to have a flexible design, so that different teachers can use it to teach constitutional law in different ways. Each part is designed to be relatively free-standing; the book can operate as a reader for a course on any combination of issues relating to federalism, Aboriginal rights, and the Charter. Those who wish to underscore the historical dimensions of the field (and have the hours to do so!) may want to follow the order of the chapters; others can bypass the early chapters and commence with contemporary issues and approaches.

We wish to thank our publisher, Paul Emond, and his staff, especially Peggy Buchan, Nancy Ennis, and Cindy Fujimoto, for their institutional dexterity in publishing this edition so quickly. We also wish to thank our academic colleagues and student readers for their constructive comments on the previous edition.

Patrick Macklem
Carol Rogerson
October 2009

Acknowledgments

A book of this nature borrows heavily from other published material. We have attempted to request permission from, and to acknowledge in the text, all sources of such material. We wish to make specific references here to the authors, publishers, journals, and institutions that have generously given permission to reproduce in this text works already in print. If we have inadvertently overlooked an acknowledgment or failed to secure a permission, we offer our sincere apologies and undertake to rectify the omission in the next edition.

The Advocate. A. Petter, "Immaculate Deception: The Charter's Hidden Agenda" (1987), 45 *The Advocate* 857.

Butterworths. W.R. Lederman, "Classification of Laws and the British North America Act," in *Continuing Canadian Constitutional Dilemmas* (Toronto: Butterworths, 1981).

Canada Law Book Inc. K. Roach, *Constitutional Remedies in Canada* (Aurora, ON: Canada Law Book, 1994). Reproduced from *Constitutional Remedies in Canada* (1994) by Kent Roach, with the permission of Canada Law Book, A Division of The Cartwright Group Ltd. (1-800-263-3269, www.canadalawbook.ca).

Canadian Bar Association. R. Elliot, "References, Structural Argumentation, and the Organizing Principles of Canada's Constitution" (2001), 80 *Canadian Bar Review* 67.

Canadian Bar Association. B. Laskin, "Note on the Queen v. Klassen" (1959), 37 *Canadian Bar Review* 630.

Canadian Bar Association. A. Petter, "Federalism and the Myth of the Federal Spending Power" (1989), 68 *Canadian Bar Review* 448.

Canadian Bar Association. P. Russell, "The Political Purposes of the Canadian Charter of Rights and Freedoms" (1983), 61 *Canadian Bar Review* 30.

Canadian Bar Association. F.R. Scott, "The Consequences of the Privy Council Decisions" (1937), 15 *Canadian Bar Review* 485.

Canadian Bar Association. F.R. Scott, "Some Privy Counsel" (1950), 28 *Canadian Bar Review* 780.

Canadian Bar Association. H.E. Smith, "The Residue of Power in Canada" (1926), 4 *Canadian Bar Review* 432.

Canadian Bar Association. W.S. Tarnopolsky, "The Equality Rights in the Canadian Charter of Rights and Freedoms" (2001), 46 *Canadian Bar Review* 533.

Canadian Journal of Women and the Law. D. Pothier, "Connecting Grounds of Discrimination to Real People's Real Experiences" (2001), 13 *Canadian Journal of Women and the Law* 37.

Canadian Political Science Association. A. Cairns, "The Judicial Committee and Its Critics" (1971), 4 *Canadian Journal of Political Science* 301.

Caribbean Law Review. L. Weinrib, " 'Limitations on Rights' in a Constitutional Democracy" (1996), 6 *Caribbean Law Review* 428.

Carswell. K. Swinton, *The Supreme Court and Canadian Federalism: The Laskin-Dickson Years* (Scarborough, ON: Carswell, 1990). Reprinted by permission of Carswell, a division of Thomson Reuters Limited.

Constitutional Forum. P.W. Hogg, "The Charter Revolution: Is It Undemocratic?" (2001-2), 1 *Constitutional Forum* 1.

Government of Québec. Report of the Commission de consultation sur les pratiques d'accommodement relieés aux differences culturelles. G. Bouchard and C. Taylor, *Building the Future: A Time for Reconciliation* (Government of Québec, 2008).

Harcourt Brace Canada. A. Prentice et al., *Canadian Women: A History* (Toronto: HBJ-Holt Canada, 1988). Reprinted by permission of Harcourt Brace & Company Canada, Limited.

Hart Publishing. P. Macklem, "Social Rights in Canada," in D. Barak-Erez and E. Gross, eds., *Exploring Social Rights: Between Theory and Practice* (Oxford: Hart Publishing, 2007).

Human Rights Research and Education Centre at the University of Ottawa. W.S. Tarnopolsky, "The Equality Rights," in Walter S. Tarnopolsky and Gerald-A. Beaudoin, eds., *The Canadian Charter of Rights and Freedoms* (Ottawa: Human Rights Research and Education Centre at the University of Ottawa, 1982).

Institute of Intergovernmental Relations. K.G. Banting, "The Past Speaks to the Future: Lessons from the Postwar Social Union," in H. Lazar, ed. *Non-Constitutional Renewal* (Kingston, ON: Institute of Intergovernmental Relations, 1998).

Irwin Law. K. Roach, *The Supreme Court on Trial: Judicial Activism or Democratic Dialogue* (Toronto: Irwin Law, 2001).

William Kaplan. W. Kaplan, *State and Salvation: The Jehovah's Witnesses and Their Fight for Civil Rights* (Toronto: University of Toronto Press, 1989).

McGill Law Journal. P. Macklem, "First Nations Self-Government and the Borders of the Canadian Legal Imagination" (1991), 36 *McGill Law Journal* 382. This article first appeared in the *McGill Law Journal*.

McGill Law Journal. D. Réaume and L. Green, "Education and Linguistic Security in the Charter" (1989), 34 *McGill Law Journal* 777. This article first appeared in the *McGill Law Journal*.

McGill Law Journal.   B. Ryder, "The Demise and Rise of the Classical Paradigm in Canadian Federalism: Promoting Autonomy for the Provinces and First Nations" (1991), 36 *McGill Law Journal* 309. This article first appeared in the *McGill Law Journal*.

McGill Law Journal.   C. Sheppard, "Of Forest Fires and Systemic Discrimination: A Review of *British Columbia (Public Service Employee Relations Commission) v. BCGSEU*" (2001), 46 *McGill Law Journal* 533. This article first appeared in the *McGill Law Journal*.

McGill-Queen's University Press.   A. Cairns, *Charter Versus Federalism: The Dilemmas of Constitutional Reform* (Kingston, ON: McGill-Queen's University Press, 1992).

Osgoode Hall Law Journal.   S. Choudhry, "Bill 11, the Canada Health Act, and the Social Union: The Need for Institutions" (2000), 38 *Osgoode Hall Law Journal* 39.

Osgoode Hall Law Journal.   R. Moon, "Justified Limits on Expression: The Collapse of the General Approach to Limits on Charter Rights" (2002), 40 *Osgoode Hall Law Journal* 337.

Osgoode Society.   John Saywell, *The Lawmakers: Judicial Power and the Shaping of Canadian Federalism* (Toronto: Osgoode Society for Canadian Legal History and University of Toronto Press, 2004) 4-12. Reprinted by permission of the Osgoode Society for Canadian Legal History and the author.

Ottawa Law Review.   B.J. Hibbitts, "A Bridle for Leviathan: The Supreme Court and the Board of Commerce" (1989), 21 *Ottawa Law Review* 65.

Oxford University Press.   W. Bogart, *Courts and Country* (Toronto: Oxford University Press, 1994).

Peter Lang.   P.A. Coulombe, *Language Rights in French Canada* (New York: Peter Lang, 1995).

Public Works and Government Services.   Canada, Royal Commission on Aboriginal Peoples, *Report*, vol. 2, *Restructuring the Relationship* (Ottawa: Queen's Printer, 1996).

Public Works and Government Services.   Report of the Special Joint Committee of the Senate and the House of Commons, *A Renewed Canada* (Ottawa: Queen's Printer, 1992).

Queen's Law Review.   R. Simeon, "Criteria for Choice in Federal Systems" (1982-83), 8 *Queen's Law Review* 131.

Revue of Constitutional Studies.   L.E. Weinrib, "Canada's Charter of Rights: Paradigm Lost?" *Revue of Constitutional Studies* (forthcoming).

South African Law Times.   W.P.M. Kennedy, "Our Constitution in the Melting Pot" (1934), *South African Law Times* 156.

G. Stevenson.   G. Stevenson, *Unfulfilled Union*, 3d ed. (Montreal: McGill-Queen's University Press, 1989).

Supreme Court Law Review.   S. Choudhry, "So, What Is the Real Legacy of Oakes? Two Decades Proportionality Analysis Under the Canadian Charter's Section 1" (2006), 35 *Supreme Court Law Review* 501.

Supreme Court Law Review.   M.E. Gold, "The Mask of Objectivity: Politics and Rhetoric in the Supreme Court of Canada" (1985), 7 *Supreme Court Law Review* 462.

Supreme Court Law Review.   P. Macklem, "Developments in Employment Law: The 1990-91 Term" (1992), 3 *Supreme Court Law Review* (2d) 227.

P.E. Trudeau.   P.E. Trudeau, "A Canadian Charter of Human Rights, January '68," in Anne Bayefsky, *Canada's Constitution Act 1982 and Amendments: A Documentary History* (Toronto: McGraw-Hill Ryerson, 1989).

University of British Columbia Law Review.   J. Leclair, "The Elusive Quest for the Quintessential 'National Interest'" (2005), 38 *University of British Columbia Law Review* 353.

University of British Columbia Press.   R. Moon, "Government Support for Religious Practice," in R. Moon, ed., *Law and Religious Pluralism in Canada* (Vancouver: UBC Press, 2008). Reprinted with permission of the Publisher © University of British Columbia Press 2008. All rights reserved by the Publisher.

University of Toronto Law Journal.   S. Choudhry, "Recasting Social Canada: A Reconsideration of Federal Jurisdiction Over Social Policy" (2002), 52 *University of Toronto Law Journal* 163. Reprinted by permission of University of Toronto Press Incorporated (www.utpjournals.com).

University of Toronto Law Journal.   V. MacDonald, "Judicial Interpretation of the Canadian Constitution" (1935), 1 *University of Toronto Law Journal* 260. Reprinted by permission of University of Toronto Press Incorporated (www.utpjournals.com).

University of Toronto Law Journal.   S.R. Moreau, "The Wrongs of Unequal Treatment" (2004), 54 *University of Toronto Law Journal* 291. Reprinted by permission of University of Toronto Press Incorporated (www.utpjournals.com).

University of Toronto Law Journal.   D. Schneiderman, "Harold Laski, Viscount Haldane, and the Law of the Canadian Constitution in the Early Twentieth Century" (1998), 48 *University of Toronto Law Journal* 521. Reprinted by permission of University of Toronto Press Incorporated (www.utpjournals.com).

University of Toronto Law Journal.   L. Weinrib, "Of Diligence and Dice: Reconstituting Canada's Constitution" (1992), 42 *University of Toronto Law Journal* 207. Reprinted by permission of University of Toronto Press Incorporated (www.utpjournals.com).

University of Toronto Press.   P. Macklem, *Indigenous Difference and the Constitution of Canada* (Toronto: University of Toronto Press, 2001). Reprinted with permission of the publisher.

University of Toronto Press.   J.R. Mallory, *Social Credit and the Federal Power in Canada* (Toronto: University of Toronto Press, 1976). Reprinted with permission of the publisher.

University of Toronto Press.   R. Moon, *The Constitutional Protection of Freedom of Expression* (Toronto: University of Toronto Press, 2000). Reprinted with permission of the publisher.

University of Toronto Press.   K. Norrie, R. Simeon, and M. Krasnick, *Federalism and the Economic Union* (Toronto: University of Toronto Press, 1986). Reprinted with permission of the publisher.

University of Toronto Press.   D. Pothier, "Connecting Grounds of Discrimination to Real People's Real Experiences" (2001), 13 *Canadian Journal of Women and the Law* 37. Reprinted with permission of the publisher.

University of Toronto Press.   A. Silver, *The French-Canadian Idea of Confederation, 1864-1900* (Toronto: University of Toronto Press, 1982).

University of Toronto Press.   R. Simeon and I. Robinson, *State, Society and the Development of Canadian Federalism* (Toronto: University of Toronto Press, 1990).

Westview Press.   Pages 1, 4-6, and 12-17 from *Liberalism Divided: Freedom of Speech and the Many Uses of State Power* by Owen Fiss. Copyright © 1996 by Westview Press. Reprinted by permission of Westview Press.

Les éditions Yvon Blais.   A. Braën, "Language Rights," in Michel Bastarche, André Braën, Emmanuel Didier, and Pierre Foucher, eds., *Language Rights in Canada* (Montreal: Les éditions Yvon Blais, 1987).

Short Table of Contents

PART FIVE   RIGHTS

Detailed Table of Contents

PART FIVE   RIGHTS

Table of Cases

A page number in boldface type indicates that the text of the case or a portion thereof is reproduced. A page number in lightface type indicates that the case is quoted briefly or discussed by the author. Cases mentioned within excerpts are not listed.

Introduction to Canadian Constitutional Law

CHAPTER ONE

Introduction

Welcome to the study of constitutional law. We believe it is an important and fascinating subject, and we hope that you will come to appreciate its place in understanding both our system of law and our political culture. Constitutional law expresses conceptions about social organization that affect all aspects of our lives and, in particular, our lives as members of a political society. Because of its general application over time and in diverse contexts, constitutional law also expresses deep social oppositions—between, for instance, honouring community commitments and respecting individual autonomy. Constitutional law embodies nothing less than the challenge of finding the means to live together in mutual respect. Having said this much, our purposes in the remainder of the chapter are modest: we plan to describe the subject and this book briefly, expecting that lectures and classroom discussions will provide detail to issues and themes addressed in this introduction only on a general level.

It seems sensible now to turn to a description of the subject "constitutional law." We hesitate, though, to provide a definition lest it be too wide, too narrow, or too vague. Erring on the side of vagueness, and reminding you of our sense that constitutional law broadly engages the organization of our social life, we suggest that the constitution of a society is an assortment of important rules, principles, and practices relating to the governance of society.

In this light, constitutions may address several different subjects and relationships. Typically, they deal with the structures, procedure, and powers of governmental institutions and the nature and scope of individual rights and responsibilities in the face of public power. Often, they also address relations between collectivities and between collectivities and governments, such as the relationship between Aboriginal peoples and the Canadian state. In some countries, the constitution may also include protection for individual rights against the exercise of private power or impose economic and social obligations on the state—for example, a right to housing or a broader social charter.

Most of these subjects and relationships find expression, in one form or another, in particular provisions of the Canadian Constitution. Constitutional provisions perform several different kinds of functions. In many cases, they establish legally enforceable obligations. They also serve to ground judicial decisions concerning the constitutionality of the exercise of power. Finally, constitutional provisions also perform a significant symbolic role, setting out the fundamental values and aspirations of a country.

It is important to note that in many countries, including Canada, the term "constitution" is used in at least two senses. Generically, it refers to all the rules by which a country has chosen to govern itself, regardless of where those rules might be found. On this understanding, a constitution can include rules found in ordinary statutes and the common law. The term can also be used to refer to a particular document or set of documents that has been given special legal significance. In Canada, we have a set of documents called "the Constitution of Canada." The provisions of these documents have the character of "the supreme law of Canada," and they can be changed only in accordance with rules that themselves are prescribed in one of them.

If this is a preliminary definition of constitutions, what then is "constitutional law"? In brief, constitutional law is an open-ended set of rules, principles, and practices that represent efforts to identify, define, and reconcile competing rights, responsibilities, and functions of governments, communities, and individuals. Any attempt to provide a more complete definition at this point raises an even more difficult question: what is law? Responding to the first question—what is constitutional law—is a central task of this book. We hope that it will also provide some insight into the nature of law itself.

THE ELEMENTS OF THE CANADIAN CONSTITUTION

The Canadian Constitution involves a unique combination of five major features: parliamentary democracy, federalism, individual and group rights, Aboriginal rights, and the principle of constitutionalism. These five features of the Canadian Constitution interact with each other in complex ways. Occasionally, they complement each other; more often, they are in conflict.

The heart of our constitutional structure, parliamentary democracy, ensures that our general laws are made by elected legislative bodies. These legislative bodies also confer extensive authority on executive bodies (cabinets), whose members are formally accountable to the legislature for the administration of the laws. While elected representatives make law, the ultimate meaning of their actions is assessed by the courts and by administrative tribunals.

Federalism is the division of government along territorial lines. In Canada, the federal Parliament possesses the power to enact laws over matters of national concern, whereas provincial legislatures possess the power to enact laws in relation to matters of local concern. As you will discover, the distinction between matters of national and local concern is hotly contested and often changes over time.

Rights, the third feature of our Constitution, are claims that citizens, as individuals and as members of particular communities, have against the state: rights to democratic government—for example, rights to vote and to annual sessions of a legislature—and rights to conduct their lives as they choose—for example, the right to freedom of religion.

The fourth feature, Aboriginal rights, are rights recognized by the Constitution as belonging to Aboriginal peoples in the light of the fact that they lived on the continent in organized societies before European contact. The precise nature and scope of such rights are still being worked out by the courts.

The principle of constitutionalism refers to the fact that governmental action, including legislation enacted by Parliament and the provincial legislatures, can be held by the courts to be "of no force or effect" if the courts find that action to be inconsistent with a provision of the Constitution of Canada.

Other features perhaps ought to be included among these basic elements of the Constitution. One is the rule of law, a concept difficult indeed to define. It suffices at this point to say that it is an expectation that governments will exercise power according to law and not in an arbitrary manner. Another is the collection of constitutional conventions, which are not laws in the strict sense of legally enforceable rules, but nonetheless form part of the Canadian constitutional order. Still another is the principle of judicial independence.

For centuries, legislative supremacy has been a central principle of the British constitution: a statute made by the British Parliament is supreme, meaning that no other institution—be it the monarch or the courts—can legally modify it or circumscribe its application. Parliament can, in theory, make statutes about whatever it wishes, in whatever terms it wishes, and the courts are obligated to enforce its dictates. Because British colonial constitutions were made in the model of the British Constitution, legislative supremacy has been a feature of Canadian legislatures since their establishment as colonial legislative bodies, although colonial legislative supremacy was tempered by imperial power. Since the birth of Canada, legislative supremacy has also been tempered by the principle of federalism, which ensured that Parliament and the provincial legislatures were supreme only when they were exercising powers conferred on them by the Constitution. Moreover, legislative supremacy was significantly modified by the 1982 enactment of the *Canadian Charter of Rights and Freedoms* (the Charter), which will be described at greater length below.

THE SOURCES OF THE CANADIAN CONSTITUTION

Constitutions come in different shapes and forms. Some, like the US Constitution, are primarily a single, comprehensive document. Others, including the Canadian Constitution, are made up of a variety of sources, often generated over a long period.

One such source is the common law, which is law created by judges, first in Great Britain and more recently in Canada. It is, for example, a source of Canadian rules for the recognition of Aboriginal rights and the law of parliamentary privilege. It also provides a measure of protection for individual rights, through presumptions for the interpretation of statutes, which we shall describe later, and the law governing the actions of government officials, boards, and tribunals. Other constitutional rules are found in ordinary statutes, which differ from the common law insofar as they are created by legislatures and can modify and indeed overrule common law rules. For example, the Supreme Court of Canada is created by a federal statute, the *Supreme Court Act*, RSC 1985, c. S-26, but is still considered to be part of the fabric of the Canadian Constitution.

Conventions are another part of our Constitution. Conventions are rules that have developed from government practice over time and that are enforced not by the courts but by political sanction. Despite the fact that conventions, by definition, are not legally enforceable, they often lie at the heart of constitutional tradition. For example, the principle of responsible government, whereby the executive in the House of Commons or a provincial legislature is chosen from the party or parties with the greatest support in the House, is a constitutional convention with deep roots in Canadian constitutional history, but it is not legally binding on government.

Some of our most significant constitutional documents are the result of actions by the British Crown and the British Parliament. The Royal Proclamation of 1763 is one example. Issued by the Crown after the British conquest of the French colony of New France, it continues to be an important source of constitutional protection of Aboriginal rights. Similarly, the *Quebec Act*, enacted by the British Parliament in 1774, allowed French civil law to continue to exist in Quebec despite conquest. Another important British statute is the *British

North America Act, 1867 (renamed the *Constitution Act, 1867* in 1982), which created the new country of Canada in 1867, federally uniting the colonies of New Brunswick, Nova Scotia, and Canada, which was divided into Ontario and Quebec. It gave the new dominion a constitution, in the words of the preamble, "similar in Principle to that of the United Kingdom." By conferring on provincial legislatures powers to pass laws in relation to property and civil rights, and local and private matters, the *British North America Act, 1867* also acknowledged Quebec's aspiration to retain its civil law tradition.

As other provinces joined Confederation, they became bound by the *British North America Act*. However, terms of union varied somewhat for the different provinces—for example, the *Manitoba Act, 1870* provided for settlement of Métis land claims and protection of the French language; the 1873 Terms of Union guaranteed a steam ferry link for Prince Edward Island; the three prairie provinces were not given the same jurisdiction as the other provinces over their natural resources (until a constitutional amendment in the Natural Resources Transfer Agreements in 1930); and for Newfoundland there were not only special provisions dealing with denominational schools, but a guarantee that oleomargarine could continue to be manufactured and sold in the province, unless the province agreed to restrictions on manufacture and sale by the federal Parliament.

A reading of the *British North America Act* makes clear that it was drafted to provide a measure of self-government for a British colony. Much was left unsaid about the operation of parliamentary institutions and structures—for example, there was no reference to the prime minister's office or the cabinet—since these were regulated by convention in the British Constitution. There was no mechanism to change the Act domestically (save for a provision allowing the provinces to change their own provincial constitutions in s. 92(1)); there was no explicit provision for Canada to create treaties of its own and thus no process to implement such treaties; and there was not even provision for a Canadian supreme court in the Act, although s. 101 did confer the power on the federal Parliament to create a general court of appeal.

FROM COLONY TO INDEPENDENT NATION STATE

As Canada grew in population and in international stature, it moved gradually toward independence from the United Kingdom. The end of its status as a colony was formally recognized by the British Statute of Westminster in 1931 (found in RSC 1985, Appendix II, No. 27), which provided that no further British statute would apply to Canada unless enacted at the request and with the consent of Canada. Canadian legislative bodies were also given the power to repeal or amend imperial statutes applicable to Canada. This aspect of the Statute of Westminster repealed an earlier British statute, the *Colonial Laws Validity Act, 1865* (28 & 29 Vict., c. 63 (UK)), which had invalidated any colonial law in conflict with an imperial law extending to the colony, with one exception. Section 7(1) of the Statute of Westminster preserved the special status of the *British North America Act*. By this exception, the role of the British Parliament in the amendment of the most significant parts of the Canadian Constitution was maintained, although any changes had to be made at the request and with the consent of Canada.

In 1949, another badge of colonial status was removed when appeals to the Judicial Committee of the Privy Council were abolished. From the very beginnings of the colonies, an appeal to England—to the Privy Council—was the apex of the colonial judicial structure. Whether to abolish this route of appeal was debated occasionally after Confederation, especially when the Supreme Court was created in 1875. But while the kinds of cases that could be appealed were restricted several times, the Privy Council remained in place until 1949, and, as the next few chapters demonstrate, the British law lords had a large impact on the evolution of the Canadian Constitution.

From the early 1960s, there was increasing pressure for constitutional reform in Canada, spurred largely by the demands of Quebec, but with growing sympathy for change in many other parts of Canada. Advocates of change took primary aim at the *British North America Act*. Its status as a British act was an irritant, if not an affront, to many Canadians who wished to see the Act "patriated," thus ending the last vestige of colonial status. To do this, however, required agreement on a domestic amending formula—a difficult task indeed, as demonstrated by the history of failed attempts over many decades.

There were demands, as well, to change various parts of the *British North America Act*: to rearrange the powers and functions of the federal and provincial governments, to reform the Senate and replace it with a body more representative of the regional diversity of Canada, to give the Supreme Court of Canada constitutional status, to provide constitutional protection for individual rights, and to give constitutional recognition to the rights of the Aboriginal peoples of Canada.

In 1982, a number of these objectives were achieved. In the *Canada Act, 1982* (UK), c. 11, the British Parliament passed an Act that stated, in s. 2, that "No Act of the Parliament of the United Kingdom passed after the *Constitution Act, 1982* comes into force shall extend to Canada as part of its law." Thus, from April 17, 1982 (the date on which the *Constitution Act, 1982* was proclaimed), the newly renamed *Canadian Constitution Acts* were patriated.

The *Constitution Act, 1982* introduced fundamental changes to Canada's Constitution. Foremost is the protection for individual and group rights in the *Canadian Charter of Rights and Freedoms*, which has given a significant new role to the courts in overseeing the legality of governmental action. Equally important, the Act also recognizes and affirms existing Aboriginal and treaty rights in s. 35(1). It also implements a set of complex amending formulae, described in more detail below, and has altered the distribution of powers in relation to natural resources. Last, it qualifies legislative supremacy as a basic element of the Constitution. In brief, s. 52 of the Act declares that the Constitution is "the supreme law of Canada, and any law that is inconsistent with the provisions of the Constitution is ... of no force or effect." Sections 2 to 23 guarantee certain fundamental rights, such as freedom of expression, but s. 33(1) declares that Parliament or the legislature of any province may "override" some of these rights by enacting a statute expressly specifying the legislature's intention to make it effective notwithstanding those rights.

The *Constitution Act, 1982* is the last major amendment to the Constitution to date but, for some, the changes were insufficient. Most significant, the government of Quebec did not agree to this set of constitutional amendments, which had failed to address Quebec's traditional demands, such as controls on the federal spending power and increased powers for the Quebec legislature. Many in Quebec demanded further reforms to address their concerns with the deficiencies of the Canadian Constitution. In an effort to win Quebec's support, the provincial premiers and the prime minister agreed on the Meech Lake Accord in 1987. The Accord was a set of proposed constitutional amendments, including, among other matters, the recognition of Quebec as a distinct society and Canada as a country with two linguistic groups, controls on the federal spending power, a mechanism to constitutionalize federal–provincial immigration agreements, and changes to the amending formulas. The Accord died in 1990 because it did not have the necessary support in all the provincial legislatures by the expiry of the three-year time limit for some of the changes, as required by the Constitution's amending formula.

Pressure for further reform came from a number of sources: Quebeckers, angered and disappointed by the rejection of the Accord; Aboriginal peoples demanding express constitutional recognition of the inherent right to self-government; and westerners committed to Senate reform. Again, a package of constitutional amendments was agreed upon by First Ministers and Aboriginal leaders. Far more comprehensive than the Meech Lake Accord, it included much of that document plus detailed provisions dealing with Aboriginal rights, a new elected Senate, and changes to the distribution of powers. This package, known as the Charlottetown Accord, was rejected by a majority of voters in a national referendum in 1992.

Despite public sentiment to the contrary, constitutional reform does not seem to go away, especially with the strong commitment of many Quebeckers to a different relationship between Quebec and the other provinces, whether in the form of independence for Quebec or a new form of sovereignty association, and with continued insistence by Aboriginal peoples for explicit constitutional recognition of ancestral territories and Aboriginal rights of self-government.

PERSPECTIVES ON THE CONSTITUTION

Much of the stuff of constitutional law involves disagreement over the meaning and relative weight that ought to be accorded to various sources of the Canadian Constitution. For example, in 1867, the *British North America Act* was viewed by many from within Quebec as a protection of its distinctive culture, and viewed from within Ontario as a means of nation-building or as a means of opening up the west. For many Aboriginal peoples, the Royal Proclamation signifies a fundamental commitment to recognize and respect the territory and autonomy of Aboriginal nations. The transfer of natural resources to the western provinces in 1930 may represent to a westerner the affirmation of a value of equality of the provinces. And for some, the Charter is a strong guarantee of universal individual rights, creating a new "citizen's constitution," while for others it is a continuation of the Canadian tradition of respect for group rights and community values.

Differing perspectives on the Constitution also emerge from disagreement over the function of constitutional law. Some scholars emphasize constitutional law's relation to economic ordering, and examine its relation to the distribution of economic entitlements to individuals, communities, and political jurisdictions, as well as its capacity to facilitate the maximization of efficient allocations of goods and resources. Others focus on the nature and effect of constitutional rights as instruments of defining individual and collective identities, in the light of political struggles over such matters as gender, race, and Aboriginality. Additional perspectives on the Constitution emerge from its relation to democratic participation and accountability. On the one hand, the Constitution expresses basic democratic aspirations; on the other hand, it is interpreted and enforced primarily by courts, which are not democratically accountable in the same way as elected officials. And, of course, constitutional law implicates basic principles of justice, both in the process of interpreting general constitutional provisions and in terms of assessing the justice of particular constitutional outcomes.

CONSTITUTIONAL CHANGE

Some constitutions are quite flexible. In Britain, for example, the doctrine of legislative supremacy meant that Parliament could modify the Constitution by enacting an ordinary statute, although social expectations greatly restricted what was politically possible. Other constitutions are more rigid, specifying special procedures for amendment on the theory that the Constitution is a form of supreme law more fundamental than other laws. Since it sets out the basic rules of governance, it should only be subject to change by special mechanisms that ensure broad consensus.

In Canada, the supremacy of the Constitution Acts is established in s. 52 of the *Constitution Act, 1982*, while special rules for constitutional amendment are found in Part V of that document. Part V requires different configurations of federal and provincial legislative approval depending on the subject matter of the amendment. The general formula, set out in s. 38, requires the approval of the federal Parliament and at least two-thirds of the provincial legislatures representing at least 50 percent of the population. Section 41 provides that other amendments, such as changes to the amending formula itself, require the approval of Parliament and all the provincial legislatures. Still other configurations are needed for other types of amendments.

Constitutional change by formal amendment is difficult and time-consuming, given the high degree of consensus required by the various amending formulae. However, there are other mechanisms by which the Constitution evolves. An important one that you will encounter in this book is judicial interpretation of the Constitution. An extensive case law exists that explains and applies the words of the Constitution, often in ways never contemplated by the original drafters, and this case law is a large part of the material for the study of constitutional law. In addition, there are other, less formal ways in which our constitutional arrangements evolve. The use of taxation and spending powers, for example, has substantially altered the distribution of functions between the federal and provincial governments in various periods of Canadian history.

Should constitutions be difficult to change? This question raises fundamental issues and tensions in constitutional law. Stability and change are values that we cherish, yet they often conflict, in both our personal and our political lives. The tension between stability and change is also reflected in constitutional interpretation. Written constitutions codify discrete exercises of deliberate self-determination and aim to enshrine deeply held beliefs about political society and to impose constraints and obligations on governments. Citizens want and expect the Constitution to endure, both as a public symbol and as a guide and limit for political conduct. We expect that our Constitution entitles us, for example, to periodic elections, responsible government, and freedom of expression, both now and in the future. Therefore, we tend to expect that it will not be changed, or will not be changed except for extraordinary reasons and with extraordinary justification.

Yet constitutional change is inevitable and, in many cases, desirable. The original framers of any constitution cannot foresee the needs of generations to come. Moreover, values viewed by the framers as fundamental may be understood differently or no longer seem worthy of constitutional respect. In such circumstances, why should the framers beliefs prevail? Perhaps each generation should have a right to determine its own future—but if that is true, why do we make the rules for constitutional change so rigid?

Thus, changing social and economic conditions may make constitutional provisions seem inappropriate, and put the preference for stability in tension with the desire for change. Thinking about these questions ultimately requires thinking about the sources of legitimacy of constitutions, an issue that runs through this book.

THE LAWYER'S ROLE

What is a lawyer's interest in constitutions? What is his or her particular contribution to thinking about a constitution or administering one? More to the point, what is distinctive about a constitutional law course? We are sure that lawyers have interests and contributions that are often different from those of political scientists or economists, and we are equally sure that these interests are diverse. This diversity makes them difficult to describe, but one large theme is an interest in courts. Counsel argue cases in courts and predict what courts will do; judges, of course, decide cases, and consider earlier cases (precedents) when they decide; drafters of statutes, contracts, and policy take into account what meaning courts will give to the language they use; and scholars synthesize, analyze, and assess the work of the courts.

This interest in the judiciary can obscure the lives of people who for economic or social reasons do not appear in courts, the effects of judicial decisions on everyday life, and the important work of other legal institutions. As well, it can tempt one into assuming that courts are the only institutions that matter, and it can inhibit thinking about their limitations. Therefore, while many important decisions about our Constitution are assigned to courts, lawyers and law students in particular should consider the appropriateness of this responsibility—what values are furthered and what values are frustrated by assigning primary responsibility to the judiciary to act as guardians of our constitutional destiny?

Intimately related to the legitimacy of the judicial function is the fact that the words of constitutional documents are often open to many meanings, and courts are often called upon to decide which of these meanings is to prevail—a job that is usually called interpretation. Indeed, constitutions are often drafted in very general terms to allow for some degree of flexibility and change. For example, in the next chapter, which is an introduction to constitutional interpretation, the central reading is the "*Persons*" case, in which the issue before the judiciary was whether the reference to "person" in the *Constitution Act, 1867* included women. Other examples appear throughout the book. Section 91(27) of the *Constitution Act, 1867* gives the federal government the power to legislate in relation to "the Criminal Law." Does this permit legislation restricting abortions, or requiring labels on foodstuffs to disclose their contents? Section 7 of the *Canadian Charter of Rights and Freedoms* guarantees the right to "life, liberty and security of the person." Does this give individuals a right to choose an abortion, a right to medical services, or a right to commit suicide? In answering these questions, judges are faced with the difficult task of determining the meaning of highly contested concepts, sometimes holding invalid the actions of elected legislators who hold broad public support. Inevitably, this calls into question the legitimacy of what judges do, a question that will be considered at great length in later chapters.

Moreover, in answering questions of this kind, the courts are often faced with the tension between stability and change. After a constitution is made, problems arise that could not have been foreseen or understood by its makers: can answers to these problems be grounded in the constitution and, if so, are they deserving of constitutional status? As well, social and economic contexts may change, and interpretations that were appropriate for one time may appear antiquated in another era. How do, and should, courts go about answering these questions? What kinds of reasoning are permitted, and what kinds not? What, if any, are the standards of a "good" answer or a "right" answer? These questions, too, will run through the materials that follow.

Many of the issues that have been touched upon in this introductory overview of the Canadian Constitution and the nature of constitutional law are dealt with by the Supreme Court of Canada in the *Quebec Secession Reference*, a portion of which is reproduced below. The *Secession Reference* raises many complex issues about the nature of constitutional interpretation and the relationship between law and politics that we will return to in subsequent chapters. It is included here primarily for the Court's discussion of the historical evolution of the Canadian Constitution and its articulation of the four principles that structure it.

Reference re Secession of Quebec
[1998] 2 SCR 217, 161 DLR (4th) 385

THE COURT (Lamer CJC, L'Heureux-Dubé, Gonthier, Cory, McLachlin, Iacobucci, Major, Bastarache, and Binnie JJ):

I. Introduction

[1] This Reference requires us to consider momentous questions that go to the heart of our system of constitutional government. The observation we made more than a decade ago in *Reference re Manitoba Language Rights*, [1985] 1 SCR 721 (*Manitoba Language Rights Reference*), at p. 728, applies with equal force here: as in that case, the present one "combines legal and constitutional questions of the utmost subtlety and complexity with political questions of great sensitivity." In our view, it is not possible to answer the questions that have been put to us without a consideration of a number of underlying principles. An exploration of the meaning and nature of these underlying principles is not merely of academic interest. On the contrary, such an exploration is of immense practical utility. Only after those underlying principles have been examined and delineated may a considered response to the questions we are required to answer emerge.

[2] The questions posed by the Governor in Council by way of Order in Council PC 1996-1497, dated September 30, 1996, read as follows:

> 1. Under the Constitution of Canada, can the National Assembly, legislature or government of Quebec effect the secession of Quebec from Canada unilaterally?

2. Does international law give the National Assembly, legislature or government of Quebec the right to effect the secession of Quebec from Canada unilaterally? In this regard, is there a right to self-determination under international law that would give the National Assembly, legislature or government of Quebec the right to effect the secession of Quebec from Canada unilaterally?

3. In the event of a conflict between domestic and international law on the right of the National Assembly, legislature or government of Quebec to effect the secession of Quebec from Canada unilaterally, which would take precedence in Canada?

. . .

III. Reference Questions

A. Question 1

Under the Constitution of Canada, can the National Assembly, legislature or government of Quebec effect the secession of Quebec from Canada unilaterally?

(1) Introduction

[32] As we confirmed in *Reference re Objection by Quebec to a Resolution to amend the Constitution*, [1982] 2 SCR 793, at p. 806, "The *Constitution Act, 1982* is now in force. Its legality is neither challenged nor assailable." The "Constitution of Canada" certainly includes the constitutional texts enumerated in s. 52(2) of the *Constitution Act, 1982*. Although these texts have a primary place in determining constitutional rules, they are not exhaustive. The Constitution also "embraces unwritten, as well as written rules," as we recently observed in the *Provincial Judges Reference* [*Reference re Provincial Court Act and Public Sector Pay Reduction Act (PEI)*, [1997] 3 SCR 3] at para. 92. Finally, as was said in the *Patriation Reference* [*Reference re Amendment of the Constitution of Canada* (1981), [1981] 1 SCR 753] at p. 874, the Constitution of Canada includes

> the global system of rules and principles which govern the exercise of constitutional authority in the whole and in every part of the Canadian state.

These supporting principles and rules, which include constitutional conventions and the workings of Parliament, are a necessary part of our Constitution because problems or situations may arise which are not expressly dealt with by the text of the Constitution. In order to endure over time, a constitution must contain a comprehensive set of rules and principles which are capable of providing an exhaustive legal framework for our system of government. Such principles and rules emerge from an understanding of the constitutional text itself, the historical context, and previous judicial interpretations of constitutional meaning. In our view, there are four fundamental and organizing principles of the Constitution which are relevant to addressing the question before us (although this enumeration is by no means exhaustive): federalism; democracy; constitutionalism and the rule of law; and respect for minorities. ...

(2) Historical Context: The Significance of Confederation

[33] In our constitutional tradition, legality and legitimacy are linked. The precise nature of this link will be discussed below. However, at this stage, we wish to emphasize only that our constitutional history demonstrates that our governing institutions have adapted and changed to reflect changing social and political values. This has generally been accomplished by methods that have ensured continuity, stability and legal order.

[34] Because this Reference deals with questions fundamental to the nature of Canada, it should not be surprising that it is necessary to review the context in which the Canadian union has evolved. To this end, we will briefly describe the legal evolution of the Constitution and the foundational principles governing constitutional amendments. Our purpose is not to be exhaustive, but to highlight the features most relevant in the context of this Reference.

[35] Confederation was an initiative of elected representatives of the people then living in the colonies scattered across part of what is now Canada. It was not initiated by Imperial fiat. In March 1864, a select committee of the Legislative Assembly of the Province of Canada, chaired by George Brown, began to explore prospects for constitutional reform. The committee's report, released in June 1864, recommended that a federal union encompassing Canada East and Canada West, and perhaps the other British North American colonies, be pursued. A group of Reformers from Canada West, led by Brown, joined with Étienne P. Taché and John A. Macdonald in a coalition government for the purpose of engaging in constitutional reform along the lines of the federal model proposed by the committee's report.

[36] An opening to pursue federal union soon arose. The leaders of the maritime colonies had planned to meet at Charlottetown in the fall to discuss the perennial topic of maritime union. The Province of Canada secured invitations to send a Canadian delegation. On September 1, 1864, 23 delegates (five from New Brunswick, five from Nova Scotia, five from Prince Edward Island, and eight from the Province of Canada) met in Charlottetown. After five days of discussion, the delegates reached agreement on a plan for federal union.

[37] The salient aspects of the agreement may be briefly outlined. There was to be a federal union featuring a bicameral central legislature. Representation in the Lower House was to be based on population, whereas in the Upper House it was to be based on regional equality, the regions comprising Canada East, Canada West and the Maritimes. The significance of the adoption of a federal form of government cannot be exaggerated. Without it, neither the agreement of the delegates from Canada East nor that of the delegates from the maritime colonies could have been obtained.

[38] Several matters remained to be resolved, and so the Charlottetown delegates agreed to meet again at Quebec in October, and to invite Newfoundland to send a delegation to join them. The Quebec Conference began on October 10, 1864. Thirty-three delegates (two from Newfoundland, seven from New Brunswick, five from Nova Scotia, seven from Prince Edward Island, and twelve from the Province of Canada) met over a two and a half week period. Precise consideration of each aspect of the federal structure preoccupied the political agenda. The delegates approved 72 resolutions, addressing almost all of what subsequently made its way into the final text of the *Constitution Act,*

1867. These included guarantees to protect French language and culture, both directly (by making French an official language in Quebec and Canada as a whole) and indirectly (by allocating jurisdiction over education and "Property and Civil Rights in the Province" to the provinces). The protection of minorities was thus reaffirmed.

[39] Legally, there remained only the requirement to have the Quebec Resolutions put into proper form and passed by the Imperial Parliament in London. However, politically, it was thought that more was required. Indeed, Resolution 70 provided that "The Sanction of the Imperial and *Local Parliaments* shall be sought for the Union of the Provinces, on the principles adopted by the Conference." (Cited in J. Pope, ed., *Confederation: Being a Series of Hitherto Unpublished Documents Bearing on the British North America Act* (1895), at p. 52 (emphasis added).)

[40] Confirmation of the Quebec Resolutions was achieved more smoothly in central Canada than in the Maritimes. In February and March 1865, the Quebec Resolutions were the subject of almost six weeks of sustained debate in both houses of the Canadian legislature. The Canadian Legislative Assembly approved the Quebec Resolutions in March 1865 with the support of a majority of members from both Canada East and Canada West. The governments of both Prince Edward Island and Newfoundland chose, in accordance with popular sentiment in both colonies, not to accede to the Quebec Resolutions. In New Brunswick, a general election was required before Premier Tilley's pro-Confederation party prevailed. In Nova Scotia, Premier Tupper ultimately obtained a resolution from the House of Assembly favouring Confederation.

[41] Sixteen delegates (five from New Brunswick, five from Nova Scotia, and six from the Province of Canada) met in London in December 1866 to finalize the plan for Confederation. To this end, they agreed to some slight modifications and additions to the Quebec Resolutions. Minor changes were made to the distribution of powers, provision was made for the appointment of extra senators in the event of a deadlock between the House of Commons and the Senate, and certain religious minorities were given the right to appeal to the federal government where their denominational school rights were adversely affected by provincial legislation. The British North America Bill was drafted after the London Conference with the assistance of the Colonial Office, and was introduced into the House of Lords in February 1867. The Act passed third reading in the House of Commons on March 8, received royal assent on March 29, and was proclaimed on July 1, 1867. The Dominion of Canada thus became a reality.

[42] There was an early attempt at secession. In the first Dominion election in September 1867, Premier Tupper's forces were decimated: members opposed to Confederation won 18 of Nova Scotia's 19 federal seats, and in the simultaneous provincial election, 36 of the 38 seats in the provincial legislature. Newly-elected Premier Joseph Howe led a delegation to the Imperial Parliament in London in an effort to undo the new constitutional arrangements, but it was too late. The Colonial Office rejected Premier Howe's plea to permit Nova Scotia to withdraw from Confederation. As the Colonial Secretary wrote in 1868:

> The neighbouring province of New Brunswick has entered into the union in reliance on having with it the sister province of Nova Scotia; and vast obligations, political and commercial, have already been contracted on the faith of a measure so long discussed and so solemnly adopted. ... I trust that the Assembly and the people of Nova Scotia will not be

surprised that the Queen's government feel that they would not be warranted in advising the reversal of a great measure of state, attended by so many extensive consequences already in operation. ...

(Quoted in H. Wade MacLauchlan, "Accounting for Democracy and the Rule of Law in the Quebec Secession Reference" (1997), 76 *Can. Bar Rev.* 155, at p. 168.)

The interdependence characterized by "vast obligations, political and commercial," referred to by the Colonial Secretary in 1868, has, of course, multiplied immeasurably in the last 130 years.

[43] Federalism was a legal response to the underlying political and cultural realities that existed at Confederation and continue to exist today. At Confederation, political leaders told their respective communities that the Canadian union would be able to reconcile diversity with unity. It is pertinent, in the context of the present Reference, to mention the words of George-Étienne Cartier (cited in the *Parliamentary Debates on the subject of the Confederation* (1865), at p. 60):

Now, when we [are] united together, if union [is] attained, we [shall] form a political nationality with which neither the national origin, nor the religion of any individual, [will] interfere. It was lamented by some that we had this diversity of races, and hopes were expressed that this distinctive feature would cease. The idea of unity of races [is] utopian—it [is] impossible. Distinctions of this kind [will] always exist. Dissimilarity, in fact, appear[s] to be the order of the physical world and of the moral world, as well as in the political world. But with regard to the objection based on this fact, to the effect that a great nation [can]not be formed because Lower Canada [is] in great part French and Catholic, and Upper Canada [is] British and Protestant, and the Lower Provinces [are] mixed, it [is] futile and worthless in the extreme. ... In our own Federation we [will] have Catholic and Protestant, English, French, Irish and Scotch, and each by his efforts and his success [will] increase the prosperity and glory of the new Confederacy. ... [W]e [are] of different races, not for the purpose of warring against each other, but in order to compete and emulate for the general welfare.

The federal–provincial division of powers was a legal recognition of the diversity that existed among the initial members of Confederation, and manifested a concern to accommodate that diversity within a single nation by granting significant powers to provincial governments. The *Constitution Act, 1867* was an act of nation-building. It was the first step in the transition from colonies separately dependent on the Imperial Parliament for their governance to a unified and independent political state in which different peoples could resolve their disagreements and work together toward common goals and a common interest. Federalism was the political mechanism by which diversity could be reconciled with unity.

[44] A federal–provincial division of powers necessitated a written constitution which circumscribed the powers of the new Dominion and Provinces of Canada. Despite its federal structure, the new Dominion was to have "a Constitution similar in Principle to that of the United Kingdom" (*Constitution Act, 1867*, preamble). Allowing for the obvious differences between the governance of Canada and the United Kingdom, it was nevertheless thought important to thus emphasize the continuity of constitutional principles, including democratic institutions and the rule of law; and the continuity of the

exercise of sovereign power transferred from Westminster to the federal and provincial capitals of Canada.

[45] After 1867, the Canadian federation continued to evolve both territorially and politically. New territories were admitted to the union and new provinces were formed. In 1870, Rupert's Land and the Northwest Territories were admitted and Manitoba was formed as a province. British Columbia was admitted in 1871, Prince Edward Island in 1873, and the Arctic Islands were added in 1880. In 1898, the Yukon Territory and in 1905, the provinces of Alberta and Saskatchewan were formed from the Northwest Territories. Newfoundland was admitted in 1949 by an amendment to the *Constitution Act, 1867*. The new territory of Nunavut was carved out of the Northwest Territories in 1993 with the partition to become effective in April 1999.

[46] Canada's evolution from colony to fully independent state was gradual. The Imperial Parliament's passage of the *Statute of Westminster*, 1931 (UK), 22 & 23 Geo. 5, c. 4, confirmed in law what had earlier been confirmed in fact by the Balfour Declaration of 1926, namely, that Canada was an independent country. Thereafter, Canadian law alone governed in Canada, except where Canada expressly consented to the continued application of Imperial legislation. Canada's independence from Britain was achieved through legal and political evolution with an adherence to the rule of law and stability. The proclamation of the *Constitution Act, 1982* removed the last vestige of British authority over the Canadian Constitution and re-affirmed Canada's commitment to the protection of its minority, aboriginal, equality, legal and language rights, and fundamental freedoms as set out in the *Canadian Charter of Rights and Freedoms*.

[47] Legal continuity, which requires an orderly transfer of authority, necessitated that the 1982 amendments be made by the Westminster Parliament, but the legitimacy as distinguished from the formal legality of the amendments derived from political decisions taken in Canada within a legal framework which this Court, in the *Patriation Reference*, had ruled was in accordance with our Constitution. It should be noted, parenthetically, that the 1982 amendments did not alter the basic division of powers in ss. 91 and 92 of the *Constitution Act, 1867*, which is the primary textual expression of the principle of federalism in our Constitution, agreed upon at Confederation. It did, however, have the important effect that, despite the refusal of the government of Quebec to join in its adoption, Quebec has become bound to the terms of a Constitution that is different from that which prevailed previously, particularly as regards provisions governing its amendment, and the *Canadian Charter of Rights and Freedoms*. As to the latter, to the extent that the scope of legislative powers was thereafter to be constrained by the *Charter*, the constraint operated as much against federal legislative powers as against provincial legislative powers. Moreover, it is to be remembered that s. 33, the "notwithstanding clause," gives Parliament and the provincial legislatures authority to legislate on matters within their jurisdiction in derogation of the fundamental freedoms (s. 2), legal rights (ss. 7 to 14) and equality rights (s. 15) provisions of the *Charter*.

[48] We think it apparent from even this brief historical review that the evolution of our constitutional arrangements has been characterized by adherence to the rule of law, respect for democratic institutions, the accommodation of minorities, insistence that governments adhere to constitutional conduct and a desire for continuity and stability.

We now turn to a discussion of the general constitutional principles that bear on the present Reference.

(3) Analysis of the Constitutional Principles

(a) Nature of the Principles

[49] What are those underlying principles? Our Constitution is primarily a written one, the product of 131 years of evolution. Behind the written word is an historical lineage stretching back through the ages, which aids in the consideration of the underlying constitutional principles. These principles inform and sustain the constitutional text: they are the vital unstated assumptions upon which the text is based. The following discussion addresses the four foundational constitutional principles that are most germane for resolution of this Reference: federalism, democracy, constitutionalism and the rule of law, and respect for minority rights. These defining principles function in symbiosis. No single principle can be defined in isolation from the others, nor does any one principle trump or exclude the operation of any other.

[50] Our Constitution has an internal architecture, or what the majority of this Court in *OPSEU v. Ontario (Attorney General)*, [1987] 2 SCR 2, at p. 57, called a "basic constitutional structure." The individual elements of the Constitution are linked to the others, and must be interpreted by reference to the structure of the Constitution as a whole. As we recently emphasized in the *Provincial Judges Reference*, certain underlying principles infuse our Constitution and breathe life into it. Speaking of the rule of law principle in the *Manitoba Language Rights Reference, supra*, at p. 750, we held that "the principle is clearly implicit in the very nature of a Constitution." The same may be said of the other three constitutional principles we underscore today.

[51] Although these underlying principles are not explicitly made part of the Constitution by any written provision, other than in some respects by the oblique reference in the preamble to the *Constitution Act, 1867*, it would be impossible to conceive of our constitutional structure without them. The principles dictate major elements of the architecture of the Constitution itself and are as such its lifeblood.

[52] The principles assist in the interpretation of the text and the delineation of spheres of jurisdiction, the scope of rights and obligations, and the role of our political institutions. Equally important, observance of and respect for these principles is essential to the ongoing process of constitutional development and evolution of our Constitution as a "living tree," to invoke the famous description in *Edwards v. Attorney-General for Canada*, [1930] AC 124 (PC), at p. 136. As this Court indicated in *New Brunswick Broadcasting Co. v. Nova Scotia (Speaker of the House of Assembly)*, [1993] 1 SCR 319, Canadians have long recognized the existence and importance of unwritten constitutional principles in our system of government.

[53] Given the existence of these underlying constitutional principles, what use may the Court make of them? In the *Provincial Judges Reference, supra*, at paras. 93 and 104, we cautioned that the recognition of these constitutional principles (the majority opinion referred to them as "organizing principles" and described one of them, judicial independence, as an "unwritten norm") could not be taken as an invitation to dispense with the written text of the Constitution. On the contrary, we confirmed that there are

compelling reasons to insist upon the primacy of our written constitution. A written constitution promotes legal certainty and predictability, and it provides a foundation and a touchstone for the exercise of constitutional judicial review. However, we also observed in the *Provincial Judges Reference* that the effect of the preamble to the *Constitution Act, 1867* was to incorporate certain constitutional principles by reference, a point made earlier in *Fraser v. Public Service Staff Relations Board*, [1985] 2 SCR 455, at pp. 462-63. In the *Provincial Judges Reference*, at para. 104, we determined that the preamble "invites the courts to turn those principles into the premises of a constitutional argument that culminates in the filling of gaps in the express terms of the constitutional text."

[54]   Underlying constitutional principles may in certain circumstances give rise to substantive legal obligations (have "full legal force," as we described it in the *Patriation Reference, supra*, at p. 845), which constitute substantive limitations upon government action. These principles may give rise to very abstract and general obligations, or they may be more specific and precise in nature. The principles are not merely descriptive, but are also invested with a powerful normative force, and are binding upon both courts and governments. "In other words," as this Court confirmed in the *Manitoba Language Rights Reference, supra*, at p. 752, "in the process of Constitutional adjudication, the Court may have regard to unwritten postulates which form the very foundation of the Constitution of Canada." It is to a discussion of those underlying constitutional principles that we now turn.

(b) Federalism

[55]   It is undisputed that Canada is a federal state. Yet many commentators have observed that, according to the precise terms of the *Constitution Act, 1867*, the federal system was only partial. See, e.g., K.C. Wheare, *Federal Government* (4th ed., 1963), at pp. 18-20. This was so because, on paper, the federal government retained sweeping powers which threatened to undermine the autonomy of the provinces. Here again, however, a review of the written provisions of the Constitution does not provide the entire picture. Our political and constitutional practice has adhered to an underlying principle of federalism, and has interpreted the written provisions of the Constitution in this light. For example, although the federal power of disallowance was included in the *Constitution Act, 1867*, the underlying principle of federalism triumphed early. Many constitutional scholars contend that the federal power of disallowance has been abandoned (e.g., P.W. Hogg, *Constitutional Law of Canada* (4th ed., 1997), at p. 120).

[56]   In a federal system of government such as ours, political power is shared by two orders of government: the federal government on the one hand, and the provinces on the other. Each is assigned respective spheres of jurisdiction by the *Constitution Act, 1867*. … It is up to the courts "to control the limits of the respective sovereignties." … In interpreting our Constitution, the courts have always been concerned with the federalism principle, inherent in the structure of our constitutional arrangements, which has from the beginning been the lodestar by which the courts have been guided.

[57]   This underlying principle of federalism, then, has exercised a role of considerable importance in the interpretation of the written provisions of our Constitution. In the *Patriation Reference, supra*, at pp. 905-9, we confirmed that the principle of federalism runs through the political and legal systems of Canada. Indeed, Martland and Ritchie JJ, dissenting in the *Patriation Reference*, at p. 821, considered federalism to be

"the dominant principle of Canadian constitutional law." With the enactment of the *Charter*, that proposition may have less force than it once did, but there can be little doubt that the principle of federalism remains a central organizational theme of our Constitution. Less obviously, perhaps, but certainly of equal importance, federalism is a political and legal response to underlying social and political realities.

[58] The principle of federalism recognizes the diversity of the component parts of Confederation, and the autonomy of provincial governments to develop their societies within their respective spheres of jurisdiction. The federal structure of our country also facilitates democratic participation by distributing power to the government thought to be most suited to achieving the particular societal objective having regard to this diversity. The scheme of the *Constitution Act, 1867*, it was said in *Re the Initiative and Referendum Act*, [1919] AC 935 (PC), at p. 942, was

> not to weld the Provinces into one, nor to subordinate Provincial Governments to a central authority, but to establish a central government in which these Provinces should be represented, entrusted with exclusive authority only in affairs in which they had a common interest. Subject to this each Province was to retain its independence and autonomy and to be directly under the Crown as its head.

More recently, in *Haig v. Canada*, [1993] 2 SCR 995, at p. 1047, the majority of this Court held that differences between provinces "are a rational part of the political reality in the federal process." It was referring to the differential application of federal law in individual provinces, but the point applies more generally. ...

[59] The principle of federalism facilitates the pursuit of collective goals by cultural and linguistic minorities which form the majority within a particular province. This is the case in Quebec, where the majority of the population is French-speaking, and which possesses a distinct culture. This is not merely the result of chance. The social and demographic reality of Quebec explains the existence of the province of Quebec as a political unit and indeed, was one of the essential reasons for establishing a federal structure for the Canadian union in 1867. The experience of both Canada East and Canada West under the *Union Act, 1840* (UK), 3-4 Vict., c. 35, had not been satisfactory. The federal structure adopted at Confederation enabled French-speaking Canadians to form a numerical majority in the province of Quebec, and so exercise the considerable provincial powers conferred by the *Constitution Act, 1867* in such a way as to promote their language and culture. It also made provision for certain guaranteed representation within the federal Parliament itself.

[60] Federalism was also welcomed by Nova Scotia and New Brunswick, both of which also affirmed their will to protect their individual cultures and their autonomy over local matters. All new provinces joining the federation sought to achieve similar objectives, which are no less vigorously pursued by the provinces and territories as we approach the new millennium.

(c) Democracy

[61] Democracy is a fundamental value in our constitutional law and political culture. While it has both an institutional and an individual aspect, the democratic principle was also argued before us in the sense of the supremacy of the sovereign will of a people, in

this case potentially to be expressed by Quebecers in support of unilateral secession. It is useful to explore in a summary way these different aspects of the democratic principle.

[62] The principle of democracy has always informed the design of our constitutional structure, and continues to act as an essential interpretive consideration to this day. A majority of this Court in *OPSEU v. Ontario, supra,* at p. 57, confirmed that "the basic structure of our Constitution, as established by the *Constitution Act, 1867,* contemplates the existence of certain political institutions, including freely elected legislative bodies at the federal and provincial levels." As is apparent from an earlier line of decisions emanating from this Court, including *Switzman v. Elbling,* [1957] SCR 285, *Saumur v. City of Quebec,* [1953] 2 SCR 299, *Boucher v. The King,* [1951] SCR 265, and *Reference re Alberta Statutes,* [1938] SCR 100, the democracy principle can best be understood as a sort of baseline against which the framers of our Constitution, and subsequently, our elected representatives under it, have always operated. It is perhaps for this reason that the principle was not explicitly identified in the text of the *Constitution Act, 1867* itself. To have done so might have appeared redundant, even silly, to the framers. As explained in the *Provincial Judges Reference, supra,* at para. 100, it is evident that our Constitution contemplates that Canada shall be a constitutional democracy. Yet this merely demonstrates the importance of underlying constitutional principles that are nowhere explicitly described in our constitutional texts. The representative and democratic nature of our political institutions was simply assumed.

[63] Democracy is commonly understood as being a political system of majority rule. It is essential to be clear what this means. The evolution of our democratic tradition can be traced back to the *Magna Carta* (1215) and before, through the long struggle for Parliamentary supremacy which culminated in the English *Bill of Rights* of 1689, the emergence of representative political institutions in the colonial era, the development of responsible government in the 19th century, and eventually, the achievement of Confederation itself in 1867. "[T]he Canadian tradition," the majority of this Court held in *Reference re Provincial Electoral Boundaries (Sask.),* [1991] 2 SCR 158, at p. 186, is "one of evolutionary democracy moving in uneven steps toward the goal of universal suffrage and more effective representation." Since Confederation, efforts to extend the franchise to those unjustly excluded from participation in our political system—such as women, minorities, and aboriginal peoples—have continued, with some success, to the present day.

[64] Democracy is not simply concerned with the process of government. On the contrary, … democracy is fundamentally connected to substantive goals, most importantly, the promotion of self-government. Democracy accommodates cultural and group identities: *Reference re Provincial Electoral Boundaries,* at p. 188. Put another way, a sovereign people exercises its right to self-government through the democratic process. In considering the scope and purpose of the *Charter,* the Court in *R v. Oakes,* [1986] 1 SCR 103, articulated some of the values inherent in the notion of democracy (at p. 136):

> The Court must be guided by the values and principles essential to a free and democratic society which I believe to embody, to name but a few, respect for the inherent dignity of the human person, commitment to social justice and equality, accommodation of a wide variety of beliefs, respect for cultural and group identity, and faith in social and political institutions which enhance the participation of individuals and groups in society.

[65] In institutional terms, democracy means that each of the provincial legislatures and the federal Parliament is elected by popular franchise. These legislatures, we have said, are "at the core of the system of representative government": *New Brunswick Broadcasting, supra*, at p. 387. In individual terms, the right to vote in elections to the House of Commons and the provincial legislatures, and to be candidates in those elections, is guaranteed to "Every citizen of Canada" by virtue of s. 3 of the *Charter*. Historically, this Court has interpreted democracy to mean the process of representative and responsible government and the right of citizens to participate in the political process as voters ... and as candidates ... . In addition, the effect of s. 4 of the *Charter* is to oblige the House of Commons and the provincial legislatures to hold regular elections and to permit citizens to elect representatives to their political institutions. The democratic principle is affirmed with particular clarity in that s. 4 is not subject to the notwithstanding power contained in s. 33.

[66] It is, of course, true that democracy expresses the sovereign will of the people. Yet this expression, too, must be taken in the context of the other institutional values we have identified as pertinent to this Reference. The relationship between democracy and federalism means, for example, that in Canada there may be different and equally legitimate majorities in different provinces and territories and at the federal level. No one majority is more or less "legitimate" than the others as an expression of democratic opinion, although, of course, the consequences will vary with the subject matter. A federal system of government enables different provinces to pursue policies responsive to the particular concerns and interests of people in that province. At the same time, Canada as a whole is also a democratic community in which citizens construct and achieve goals on a national scale through a federal government acting within the limits of its jurisdiction. The function of federalism is to enable citizens to participate concurrently in different collectivities and to pursue goals at both a provincial and a federal level.

[67] The consent of the governed is a value that is basic to our understanding of a free and democratic society. Yet democracy in any real sense of the word cannot exist without the rule of law. It is the law that creates the framework within which the "sovereign will" is to be ascertained and implemented. To be accorded legitimacy, democratic institutions must rest, ultimately, on a legal foundation. That is, they must allow for the participation of, and accountability to, the people, through public institutions created under the Constitution. Equally, however, a system of government cannot survive through adherence to the law alone. A political system must also possess legitimacy, and in our political culture, that requires an interaction between the rule of law and the democratic principle. The system must be capable of reflecting the aspirations of the people. But there is more. Our law's claim to legitimacy also rests on an appeal to moral values, many of which are imbedded in our constitutional structure. It would be a grave mistake to equate legitimacy with the "sovereign will" or majority rule alone, to the exclusion of other constitutional values.

[68] Finally, we highlight that a functioning democracy requires a continuous process of discussion. The Constitution mandates government by democratic legislatures, and an executive accountable to them, "resting ultimately on public opinion reached by discussion and the interplay of ideas" (*Saumur v. City of Quebec, supra*, at p. 330). At both the federal and provincial level, by its very nature, the need to build majorities necessitates

compromise, negotiation, and deliberation. No one has a monopoly on truth, and our system is predicated on the faith that in the marketplace of ideas, the best solutions to public problems will rise to the top. Inevitably, there will be dissenting voices. A democratic system of government is committed to considering those dissenting voices, and seeking to acknowledge and address those voices in the laws by which all in the community must live.

[69] The *Constitution Act, 1982* gives expression to this principle by conferring a right to initiate constitutional change on each participant in Confederation. In our view, the existence of this right imposes a corresponding duty on the participants in Confederation to engage in constitutional discussions in order to acknowledge and address democratic expressions of a desire for change in other provinces. This duty is inherent in the democratic principle which is a fundamental predicate of our system of governance.

(d) Constitutionalism and the Rule of Law

[70] The principles of constitutionalism and the rule of law lie at the root of our system of government. The rule of law, as observed in *Roncarelli v. Duplessis*, [1959] SCR 121, at p. 142, is "a fundamental postulate of our constitutional structure." As we noted in the *Patriation Reference, supra*, at pp. 805-6, "[t]he 'rule of law' is a highly textured expression, importing many things which are beyond the need of these reasons to explore but conveying, for example, a sense of orderliness, of subjection to known legal rules and of executive accountability to legal authority." At its most basic level, the rule of law vouchsafes to the citizens and residents of the country a stable, predictable and ordered society in which to conduct their affairs. It provides a shield for individuals from arbitrary state action.

[71] In the *Manitoba Language Rights Reference, supra*, at pp. 747-52, this Court outlined the elements of the rule of law. We emphasized, first, that the rule of law provides that the law is supreme over the acts of both government and private persons. There is, in short, one law for all. Second, we explained, at p. 749, that "the rule of law requires the creation and maintenance of an actual order of positive laws which preserves and embodies the more general principle of normative order." It was this second aspect of the rule of law that was primarily at issue in the *Manitoba Language Rights Reference* itself. A third aspect of the rule of law is, as recently confirmed in the *Provincial Judges Reference, supra*, at para. 10, that "the exercise of all public power must find its ultimate source in a legal rule." Put another way, the relationship between the state and the individual must be regulated by law. Taken together, these three considerations make up a principle of profound constitutional and political significance.

[72] The constitutionalism principle bears considerable similarity to the rule of law, although they are not identical. The essence of constitutionalism in Canada is embodied in s. 52(1) of the *Constitution Act, 1982*, which provides that "[t]he Constitution of Canada is the supreme law of Canada, and any law that is inconsistent with the provisions of the Constitution is, to the extent of the inconsistency, of no force or effect." Simply put, the constitutionalism principle requires that all government action comply with the Constitution. The rule of law principle requires that all government action must comply with the law, including the Constitution. This Court has noted on several occasions that with the adoption of the *Charter*, the Canadian system of government was transformed

to a significant extent from a system of Parliamentary supremacy to one of constitutional supremacy. The Constitution binds all governments, both federal and provincial, including the executive branch … . They may not transgress its provisions: indeed, their sole claim to exercise lawful authority rests in the powers allocated to them under the Constitution, and can come from no other source.

[73] An understanding of the scope and importance of the principles of the rule of law and constitutionalism is aided by acknowledging explicitly why a constitution is entrenched beyond the reach of simple majority rule. There are three overlapping reasons.

[74] First, a constitution may provide an added safeguard for fundamental human rights and individual freedoms which might otherwise be susceptible to government interference. Although democratic government is generally solicitous of those rights, there are occasions when the majority will be tempted to ignore fundamental rights in order to accomplish collective goals more easily or effectively. Constitutional entrenchment ensures that those rights will be given due regard and protection. Second, a constitution may seek to ensure that vulnerable minority groups are endowed with the institutions and rights necessary to maintain and promote their identities against the assimilative pressures of the majority. And third, a constitution may provide for a division of political power that allocates political power amongst different levels of government. That purpose would be defeated if one of those democratically elected levels of government could usurp the powers of the other simply by exercising its legislative power to allocate additional political power to itself unilaterally.

[75] The argument that the Constitution may be legitimately circumvented by resort to a majority vote in a province-wide referendum is superficially persuasive, in large measure because it seems to appeal to some of the same principles that underlie the legitimacy of the Constitution itself, namely, democracy and self-government. In short, it is suggested that as the notion of popular sovereignty underlies the legitimacy of our existing constitutional arrangements, so the same popular sovereignty that originally led to the present Constitution must (it is argued) also permit "the people" in their exercise of popular sovereignty to secede by majority vote alone. However, closer analysis reveals that this argument is unsound, because it misunderstands the meaning of popular sovereignty and the essence of a constitutional democracy.

[76] Canadians have never accepted that ours is a system of simple majority rule. Our principle of democracy, taken in conjunction with the other constitutional principles discussed here, is richer. Constitutional government is necessarily predicated on the idea that the political representatives of the people of a province have the capacity and the power to commit the province to be bound into the future by the constitutional rules being adopted. These rules are "binding" not in the sense of frustrating the will of a majority of a province, but as defining the majority which must be consulted in order to alter the fundamental balances of political power (including the spheres of autonomy guaranteed by the principle of federalism), individual rights, and minority rights in our society. Of course, those constitutional rules are themselves amenable to amendment, but only through a process of negotiation which ensures that there is an opportunity for the constitutionally defined rights of all the parties to be respected and reconciled.

[77] In this way, our belief in democracy may be harmonized with our belief in constitutionalism. Constitutional amendment often requires some form of substantial consensus

precisely because the content of the underlying principles of our Constitution demand it. By requiring broad support in the form of an "enhanced majority" to achieve constitutional change, the Constitution ensures that minority interests must be addressed before proposed changes which would affect them may be enacted.

[78] It might be objected, then, that constitutionalism is therefore incompatible with democratic government. This would be an erroneous view. Constitutionalism facilitates—indeed, makes possible—a democratic political system by creating an orderly framework within which people may make political decisions. Viewed correctly, constitutionalism and the rule of law are not in conflict with democracy; rather, they are essential to it. Without that relationship, the political will upon which democratic decisions are taken would itself be undermined.

(e) Protection of Minorities

[79] The fourth underlying constitutional principle we address here concerns the protection of minorities. There are a number of specific constitutional provisions protecting minority language, religion and education rights. Some of those provisions are, as we have recognized on a number of occasions, the product of historical compromises. As this Court observed in *Reference re Bill 30, An Act to amend the Education Act (Ont.)*, [1987] 1 SCR 1148, at p. 1173, and in *Reference re Education Act (Que.)*, [1993] 2 SCR 511, at pp. 529-30, the protection of minority religious education rights was a central consideration in the negotiations leading to Confederation. In the absence of such protection, it was felt that the minorities in what was then Canada East and Canada West would be submerged and assimilated. ... Similar concerns animated the provisions protecting minority language rights, as noted in *Société des Acadiens du Nouveau-Brunswick Inc. v. Association of Parents for Fairness in Education*, [1986] 1 SCR 549, at p. 564.

[80] However, we highlight that even though those provisions were the product of negotiation and political compromise, that does not render them unprincipled. Rather, such a concern reflects a broader principle related to the protection of minority rights. Undoubtedly, the three other constitutional principles inform the scope and operation of the specific provisions that protect the rights of minorities. We emphasize that the protection of minority rights is itself an independent principle underlying our constitutional order. The principle is clearly reflected in the *Charter*'s provisions for the protection of minority rights. ...

[81] The concern of our courts and governments to protect minorities has been prominent in recent years, particularly following the enactment of the *Charter*. Undoubtedly, one of the key considerations motivating the enactment of the *Charter*, and the process of constitutional judicial review that it entails, is the protection of minorities. However, it should not be forgotten that the protection of minority rights had a long history before the enactment of the *Charter*. Indeed, the protection of minority rights was clearly an essential consideration in the design of our constitutional structure even at the time of Confederation ... . Although Canada's record of upholding the rights of minorities is not a spotless one, that goal is one towards which Canadians have been striving since Confederation, and the process has not been without successes. The principle of protecting minority rights continues to exercise influence in the operation and interpretation of our Constitution.

[82] Consistent with this long tradition of respect for minorities, which is at least as old as Canada itself, the framers of the *Constitution Act, 1982* included in s. 35 explicit protection for existing aboriginal and treaty rights, and in s. 25, a non-derogation clause in favour of the rights of aboriginal peoples. The "promise" of s. 35, as it was termed in *R v. Sparrow*, [1990] 1 SCR 1075, at p. 1083, recognized not only the ancient occupation of land by aboriginal peoples, but their contribution to the building of Canada, and the special commitments made to them by successive governments. The protection of these rights, so recently and arduously achieved, whether looked at in their own right or as part of the larger concern with minorities, reflects an important underlying constitutional value.

[The Court went on to apply these constitutional principles to the secession context, ruling that while unilateral secession would be unconstitutional, a clear expression by the people of Quebec of their will to secede from Canada would impose a reciprocal obligation on all parties to Confederation to negotiate constitutional changes to respond to that desire. This portion of the judgment is reproduced in Chapter 12, Instruments of Flexibility in the Federal System, which deals with, among other issues, constitutional amendment.]

Answers to questions 1 and 2: No; not necessary to answer question 3.

NOTES

1. Quebec refused to appear in the proceedings before the Court, alleging that the Court lacked the jurisdiction to consider a matter that was fundamentally political in nature, and that was for the population of Quebec to decide for itself. However, the Court did wish to hear all sides of the legal argument, and as a consequence, appointed a lawyer to make arguments on Quebec's behalf. The Court acted pursuant to s. 53(7) of the *Supreme Court Act*, RSC 1985, c. S-26, which provides that in the case of references (discussed below, note 2):

> The Court may, in its discretion, request any counsel to argue the case with respect to any interest that is affected and with respect to which counsel does not appear ... .

A lawyer acting in this capacity is known as an *amicus curiae*, which literally means "a friend of the Court." It is relatively rare for the Court to appoint an *amicus curiae*.

2. The *Quebec Secession Reference* came before the Court through a special process known as the reference procedure, discussed below in Chapter 2, Judicial Review and Constitutional Interpretation. The essence of a reference is that it asks the Court to give an advisory opinion on important legal questions that may or may not have arisen in the context of concrete disputes between interested parties, without the benefit of findings of fact made at trial. The *amicus curiae* argued, by way of a preliminary objection challenging the jurisdiction of the Court to hear the case, that the Court should decline to answer the reference questions because they were political in nature, and hence incapable of legal resolution. The Court rejected this argument as follows:

[26] Though a reference differs from the Court's usual adjudicative function, the Court should not, even in the context of a reference, entertain questions that would be inappropriate to answer. However, given the very different nature of a reference, the question of the appropriateness of answering a question should not focus on whether the dispute is formally adversarial or whether it disposes of cognizable rights. Rather, it should consider whether the dispute is appropriately addressed by a court of law. ... [T]he circumstances in which the Court may decline to answer a reference question on the basis of "non-justiciability" include:

  (i) if to do so would take the Court beyond its own assessment of its proper role in the constitutional framework of our democratic form of government or

 (ii) if the Court could not give an answer that lies within its area of expertise: the interpretation of law.

[27] As to the "proper role" of the Court, it is important to underline, contrary to the submission of the *amicus curiae*, that the questions posed in this Reference do not ask the Court to usurp any democratic decision that the people of Quebec may be called upon to make. The questions posed by the Governor in Council, as we interpret them, are strictly limited to aspects of the legal framework in which that democratic decision is to be taken. ... The legal framework having been clarified, it will be for the population of Quebec, acting through the political process, to decide whether or not to pursue secession. As will be seen, the legal framework involves the rights and obligations of Canadians who live outside the province of Quebec, as well as those who live within Quebec.

[28] As to the "legal" nature of the questions posed, if the Court is of the opinion that it is being asked a question with a significant extralegal component, it may interpret the question so as to answer only its legal aspects; if this is not possible, the Court may decline to answer the question. In the present Reference the questions may clearly be interpreted as directed to legal issues, and, so interpreted, the Court is in a position to answer them.

Do you agree with the Court's reasoning? What was the effect of the judgment on "any democratic decision that the people of Quebec may be called upon to make"? Do you think the Court confined itself to a consideration of the legal aspects of the reference questions, or did it address the extralegal components of those questions as well? If it did, was it justified in doing so? If it did not, should it have? Why? How?

3. The Court's use, in the *Secession Reference*, of "unwritten" constitutional principles to generate legally enforceable constitutional obligations has generated both confusion and controversy about their use. While the use of such principles to guide the interpretation of existing provisions in the written text of the Constitution is relatively uncontroversial, particular concern has been voiced about the use of such principles to ground free-standing constitutional obligations that might be used by courts to invalidate legislation. This issue, and constitutional interpretation more generally, are dealt with in Chapter 2, Judicial Review and Constitutional Interpretation.

4. The implications of the *Secession Reference* for constitutional amendment are discussed further in Chapter 12, Instruments of Flexibility in the Federal System.

A BRIEF TOUR OF WHAT IS TO FOLLOW

Last, we come to a brief description of this book, beginning with a caveat. It is designed to be an introduction to constitutional law. Being realistic about how much anyone can cover in such a course, we have compiled a set of materials that is far from comprehensive. Inevitably, lots of topics, approaches, and questions have been omitted. We have included most of what we think is important or useful, and can only hope that our readers will not disagree greatly with our choices. As well, at several points we have taken care to permit teachers to omit parts, or to change the order of the materials, to suit their purposes.

A chapter introducing judicial review and constitutional interpretation, including some of the unique procedural aspects of constitutional litigation, follows this introduction. Next comes a long part, entitled Federalism and containing 10 chapters, which can be divided into two sections: history and modern federalism. These two sections are not as different from each other as the above names might suggest, because law is usually shaped in one way or another by an accumulation of past experience. Users of this book may follow the book as it is arranged; others may find it preferable to introduce the interpretation of the distribution of powers in the Canadian federal system by working through one or more cases in Chapter 8, Interpreting the Division of Powers.

After the part that deals with Canadian federalism, there is a short part, consisting of a single chapter on the judicial function. This chapter examines the constitutional implications of describing in Part VII of the *Constitution Act, 1867* the powers relating to and characteristics of the judicial branch. Canadian constitutional law does not contain a highly elaborated scheme of separated governmental functions but, on the other hand, neither does it completely ignore the need to define and protect the diverse roles of constitutionally recognized institutions. This part explores the place of specialized institutional functions in the design of our Constitution.

The next part, on Aboriginal peoples, integrates a number of otherwise discrete areas of law, including the common law of Aboriginal title, the distribution of legislative authority as it affects Aboriginal peoples, and constitutional recognition of Aboriginal and treaty rights.

The final part is dedicated to the role of rights in the Canadian Constitution. It is dominated by the *Canadian Charter of Rights and Freedoms*, although it begins with a chapter tracing other rights-protecting mechanisms in our constitutional structure. The treatment of the Charter begins with two chapters introducing basic and pervasive themes in Charter interpretation, followed by a chapter reviewing the scope of the Charter's application. The remaining chapters are about selected rights—for example, the right to freedom of expression and the right to equality. There is little material on Charter rights in the criminal justice system; because this material draws so heavily on criminal law and the law of evidence, we felt it was more effectively studied in those courses. We conclude with a chapter about enforcing Charter rights, which primarily focuses on remedies, but also deals with other procedural aspects of Charter litigation.

CHAPTER TWO

Judicial Review and Constitutional Interpretation

The purpose of this chapter is twofold: first, to introduce the institution of judicial review; and second, to identify and provide a very brief discussion of some of the issues to which that institution gives rise. Those issues include the legitimacy of judicial review under Canada's Constitution; how courts determine the meaning to be given to the provisions of the Constitution that come before them when the power of judicial review is triggered—that is, the issue of constitutional interpretation; how the power of judicial review is triggered—that is, how constitutional issues get to court; and a few of the procedural issues that can arise in constitutional cases.

I. JUDICIAL REVIEW AND THE LEGITIMACY ISSUE

Judicial review is a term that can be used to describe more than one judicial function. For the purposes of this casebook, it refers to the power of the courts in Canada to determine, when properly asked to do so, whether action taken by a governmental body or legal actor—the Parliament of Canada, for example, or a member of the RCMP—is or is not in compliance with our Constitution, and, if they find that it is not, to declare it to be unconstitutional. (The notion that governmental action has to comply with the requirements of the Constitution in order to be valid has become known as the principle of constitutionalism: see *Reference re Secession of Quebec*, [1998] 2 SCR 217, 161 DLR (4th) 385, excerpted in Chapter 1, Introduction.) In the United States, at least in the early years of its existence, there was real doubt in the minds of some as to whether the power of judicial review existed under the American constitution. That doubt was only removed by the famous case of *Marbury v. Madison*, 5 US 137 (1803), in which the Supreme Court held that the power did exist. In Canada, by contrast, there seemed from the very beginning to be relatively little doubt that this power existed (although some arguments were initially made that constitutional compliance was meant to be secured by the disallowance power). As you will see in Chapter 4, The Late Nineteenth Century: The Canadian Courts Under the Influence, Canadian courts called upon in the 1870s to rule on the constitutionality of action taken by the newly created federal and provincial governments had no difficulty with the notion that they had the authority to do so. In their view, they were simply being asked to interpret and give effect to one of a number of Imperial statutes—in this instance, the *British North America Act, 1867*—that they were accustomed to having come before them.

Since 1982, the power of judicial review has been given recognition in the text of our Constitution. Section 52(1) of the *Constitution Act, 1982*, which is applicable to the entire Constitution, provides that "[t]he Constitution of Canada is the supreme law of Canada, and any law that is inconsistent with the provisions of the Constitution is, to the extent of the inconsistency, of no force or effect." In addition, s. 24(1) of the *Canadian Charter of Rights and Freedoms* provides that "[a]nyone whose rights or freedoms, as guaranteed by this Charter, have been infringed or denied may apply to a court of competent jurisdiction to obtain such remedy as the court considers appropriate and just in the circumstances."

In one sense, the fact that the power of judicial review is a longstanding and accepted tradition in Canada, and has recently been given textual recognition in our Constitution, resolves the question of the legitimacy of that power. In another sense, however, it does not. If legitimacy is understood to refer not only to whether the power exists at all, but also to the basis upon which the power is exercised, it is not resolved simply by pointing to tradition or to s. 52(1) of the *Constitution Act, 1982*. There may be some instances in which it will be generally agreed that the text of the Constitution makes it clear that governmental action of a particular kind is unconstitutional. In these instances, the court's decision will be seen to be legitimate because it is firmly grounded in that text. But such instances will be very rare, in part because governments are not in the habit of taking action that clearly violates the text of the Constitution and in part because, in the cases that do get into the courts, the meaning of the text of the Constitution—which text is usually formulated in general language—is seldom clear. In the overwhelming majority of cases, both the challenger and the government will be able to make plausible arguments, grounded directly or indirectly in the text of the relevant parts of the Constitution, in support of their respective positions. These cases, particularly those in which the courts rule that the impugned governmental action is unconstitutional, implicate this other—and for practical purposes more important—understanding of the question of the legitimacy of judicial review.

In recent years, our courts have been asked in a number of cases to declare legislation unconstitutional, not on the ground that that legislation was in conflict with one or more provisions of the text of the Constitution, but on the ground that it was in conflict with one or more of the "organizing or underlying principles of the Constitution." It will be recalled that in *Reference re Secession of Quebec*, excerpted in Chapter 1, Introduction, the Supreme Court of Canada said that federalism, democracy, the rule of law, and the protection of minorities should all be understood to have the character of an "organizing" or "underlying" principle of our Constitution. In other cases, the Court has ascribed that status to judicial independence and the separation of powers. Is it open to our courts—that is, legitimate for them—to rely on democracy, the rule of law, or judicial independence as a basis for striking legislation down without also having to find a basis in the text of the Constitution for doing so? That question was at least partially addressed in the following case, decided by the Supreme Court in 2005.

British Columbia v. Imperial Tobacco Canada Ltd.
[2005] 2 SCR 473, 2005 SCC 49, 257 DLR (4th) 193

[The *Tobacco Damages and Health Care Costs Recovery Act*, SBC 2000, c. 30 ("the Act"), authorized an aggregate action by the government of British Columbia against a manufacturer of tobacco products for the recovery of health care expenditures incurred by the government in treating a population of individuals exposed to those products. Liability under the Act hinged on that population of individuals having been exposed to tobacco products because of the manufacturer's breach of a duty owed to persons in British Columbia, and on the government having incurred health care expenditures in treating disease in those individuals caused by such exposure. The Act provided for special evidentiary and procedural rules to be applied in such an aggregate action. These rules were intended to make it easier for the government to succeed in its action than the evidentiary and procedural rules applied in common law tort actions would have. The Act was also made retroactive to at least the 1950s.

The appellant tobacco manufacturers, each of which was sued by the government pursuant to the Act, challenged its constitutional validity on three different grounds. One was based in the division of powers between Parliament and the provincial legislatures, and the other two in the underlying principles of judicial independence and the rule of law. The BC Supreme Court concluded that the Act was unconstitutional on the first ground, holding that the Act failed to respect territorial limits on provincial legislative jurisdiction. That court rejected the arguments based on the other two grounds. The BC Court of Appeal allowed the government's appeal from the first holding, finding that the Act's pith and substance was "Property and Civil Rights in the Province" within the meaning of s. 92(13) of the *Constitution Act, 1867*, and that the extraterritorial aspects of the Act, if any, were incidental to it. The Court of Appeal also found that the Act did not offend judicial independence or the rule of law. The tobacco manufacturers then appealed to the Supreme Court of Canada.]

MAJOR J (McLachlin CJC and Bastarache, Binnie, LeBel, Deschamps, Fish, Abella, and Charron JJ concurring):

[Justice Major agreed with the Court of Appeal that the Act was within provincial legislative jurisdiction under s. 92(13) of the *Constitution Act, 1867*. He then proceeded to deal with the challenges based on judicial independence and the rule of law.]

B. Judicial Independence

[44] Judicial independence is a "foundational principle" of the Constitution reflected in s. 11(d) of the *Canadian Charter of Rights and Freedoms*, and in both ss. 96-100 and the preamble to the *Constitution Act, 1867* ... . It serves "to safeguard our constitutional order and to maintain public confidence in the administration of justice." ...

[45] Judicial independence consists essentially in the freedom "to render decisions based solely on the requirements of the law and justice" ... . It requires that the judiciary be left free to act without improper "interference from any other entity" ... —i.e., that the

executive and legislative branches of government not "impinge on the essential 'authority and function' … of the court" … .

[46] Security of tenure, financial security and administrative independence are the three "core characteristics" or "essential conditions" of judicial independence … . It is a precondition to judicial independence that they be maintained, and be seen by "a reasonable person who is fully informed of all the circumstances" to be maintained … .

[47] However, even where the essential conditions of judicial independence exist, and are reasonably seen to exist, judicial independence itself is not necessarily ensured. The critical question is whether the court is free, and reasonably seen to be free, to perform its adjudicative role without interference, including interference from the executive and legislative branches of government. …

[48] The appellants submit that the Act violates judicial independence, both in reality and appearance, because it contains rules of civil procedure that fundamentally interfere with the adjudicative role of the court hearing an action brought pursuant to the Act. They point to s. 3(2), which they say forces the court to make irrational presumptions, and to ss. 2(5)(a), 2(5)(b) and 2(5)(c), which they say subvert the court's ability to discover relevant facts. They say that these rules impinge on the court's fact-finding function, and virtually guarantee the government's success in an action brought pursuant to the Act.

[49] The rules in the Act with which the appellants take issue are not as unfair or illogical as the appellants submit. They appear to reflect legitimate policy concerns of the British Columbia legislature regarding the systemic advantages tobacco manufacturers enjoy when claims for tobacco-related harm are litigated through individualistic common law tort actions. That, however, is beside the point. The question is not whether the Act's rules are unfair or illogical, nor whether they differ from those governing common law tort actions, but whether they interfere with the courts' adjudicative role, and thus judicial independence.

[50] The primary role of the judiciary is to interpret and apply the law, whether procedural or substantive, to the cases brought before it. It is to hear and weigh, in accordance with the law, evidence that is relevant to the legal issues confronted by it, and to award to the parties before it the available remedies.

• • •

[52] It follows that the judiciary's role is not, as the appellants seem to submit, to apply only the law of which it approves. Nor is it to decide cases with a view simply to what the judiciary (rather than the law) deems fair or pertinent. Nor is it to second-guess the law reform undertaken by legislators, whether that reform consists of a new cause of action or procedural rules to govern it. Within the boundaries of the Constitution, legislatures can set the law as they see fit. "The wisdom and value of legislative decisions are subject only to review by the electorate" … .

[53] In essence, the appellants' arguments misapprehend the nature and scope of the courts' adjudicative role protected from interference by the Constitution's guarantee of judicial independence. To accept their position on that adjudicative role would be to recognize a constitutional guarantee not of judicial independence, but of judicial governance.

[54] None of this is to say that legislation, being law, can never unconstitutionally interfere with courts' adjudicative role. But more is required than an allegation that the content of the legislation required to be applied by that adjudicative role is irrational or

unfair, or prescribes rules different from those developed at common law. The legislation must interfere, or be reasonably seen to interfere, with the courts' adjudicative role, or with the essential conditions of judicial independence. As McLachlin CJ stated in *Babcock* [*v. Canada (Attorney General)*, [2002] 3 SCR 3], at para. 57:

> It is well within the power of the legislature to enact laws, even laws which some would consider draconian, as long as it does not fundamentally alter or interfere with the relationship between the courts and the other branches of government.

[55] No such fundamental alteration or interference was brought about by the legislature's enactment of the Act. A court called upon to try an action brought pursuant to the Act retains at all times its adjudicative role and the ability to exercise that role without interference. It must independently determine the applicability of the Act to the government's claim, independently assess the evidence led to support and defend that claim, independently assign that evidence weight, and then independently determine whether its assessment of the evidence supports a finding of liability. The fact that the Act shifts certain onuses of proof or limits the compellability of information that the appellants assert is relevant does not in any way interfere, in either appearance or fact, with the court's adjudicative role or any of the essential conditions of judicial independence. Judicial independence can abide unconventional rules of civil procedure and evidence.

[56] The appellants' submission that the Act violates the independence of the judiciary and is therefore unconstitutional fails for the reasons stated above.

C. Rule of Law

[57] The rule of law is "a fundamental postulate of our constitutional structure" ... that lies "at the root of our system of government" (*Reference re Secession of Quebec*, [1998] 2 SCR 217, at para. 70). It is expressly acknowledged by the preamble to the *Constitution Act, 1982*, and implicitly recognized in the preamble to the *Constitution Act, 1867* ... .

[58] This Court has described the rule of law as embracing three principles. The first recognizes that "the law is supreme over officials of the government as well as private individuals, and thereby preclusive of the influence of arbitrary power" ... . The second "requires the creation and maintenance of an actual order of positive laws which preserves and embodies the more general principle of normative order" ... . The third requires that "the relationship between the state and the individual ... be regulated by law ... .

[59] So understood, it is difficult to conceive of how the rule of law could be used as a basis for invalidating legislation such as the Act based on its content. That is because none of the principles that the rule of law embraces speak directly to the terms of legislation. The first principle requires that legislation be applied to all those, including government officials, to whom it, by its terms, applies. The second principle means that legislation must exist. And the third principle, which overlaps somewhat with the first and second, requires that state officials' actions be legally founded. ...

[60] This does not mean that the rule of law as described by this Court has no normative force. As McLachlin CJ stated in *Babcock*, at para. 54, "unwritten constitutional principles," including the rule of law, "are capable of limiting government actions." ... But the government action constrained by the rule of law as understood in *Reference re*

Manitoba Language Rights [[1995] 1 SCR 721] and *Reference re Secession of Quebec* is, by definition, usually that of the executive and judicial branches. Actions of the legislative branch are constrained too, but only in the sense that they must comply with legislated requirements as to manner and form (i.e., the procedures by which legislation is to be enacted, amended and repealed).

[61] Nonetheless, considerable debate surrounds the question of what *additional* principles, if any, the rule of law might embrace, and the extent to which *they* might mandate the invalidation of legislation based on its content. P. W. Hogg and C. F. Zwibel write in "The Rule of Law in the Supreme Court of Canada" (2005), 55 *UTLJ* 715, at pp. 717-18:

> Many authors have tried to define the rule of law and to explain its significance, or lack thereof. Their views spread across a wide spectrum. ... T.R.S. Allan, for example, claims that laws that fail to respect the equality and human dignity of individuals are contrary to the rule of law. Luc Tremblay asserts that the rule of law includes the liberal principle, the democratic principle, the constitutional principle, and the federal principle. For Allan and Tremblay, the rule of law demands not merely that positive law be obeyed but that it embody a particular vision of social justice. Another strong version comes from David Beatty, who argues that the "ultimate rule of law" is a principle of "proportionality" to which all laws must conform on pain of invalidity (enforced by judicial review). In the middle of the spectrum are those who, like Joseph Raz, accept that the rule of law is an ideal of constitutional legality, involving open, stable, clear, and general rules, even-handed enforcement of those laws, the independence of the judiciary, and judicial review of administrative action. Raz acknowledges that conformity to the rule of law is often a matter of degree, and that breaches of the rule of law do not lead to invalidity. ...

[62] This debate underlies Strayer JA's apt observation in *Singh v. Canada (Attorney General)*, [2000] 3 FC 185 (CA), at para. 33, that "[a]dvocates tend to read into the principle of the rule of law anything which supports their particular view of what the law should be."

[63] The appellants' conceptions of the rule of law can fairly be said to fall at one extreme of the spectrum of possible conceptions and to support Strayer JA's thesis. They submit that the rule of law requires that legislation: (1) be prospective; (2) be general in character; (3) not confer special privileges on the government, except where necessary for effective governance; and (4) ensure a fair civil trial. And they argue that the Act breaches each of these requirements, rendering it invalid.

[64] A brief review of this Court's jurisprudence will reveal that none of these requirements enjoy constitutional protection in Canada. But before embarking on that review, it should be said that acknowledging the constitutional force of anything resembling the appellants' conceptions of the rule of law would seriously undermine the legitimacy of judicial review of legislation for constitutionality. That is so for two separate but interrelated reasons.

[65] First, many of the requirements of the rule of law proposed by the appellants are simply broader versions of rights contained in the Charter. For example, the appellants' proposed fair trial requirement is essentially a broader version of s. 11(d) of the Charter, which provides that "[a]ny person charged with an offence has the right ... to ... a fair

and public hearing." But the framers of the Charter enshrined that fair trial right only for those "charged with an offence." If the rule of law constitutionally required that all legislation provide for a fair trial, s. 11(d) and its relatively limited scope (not to mention its qualification by s. 1) would be largely irrelevant because *everyone* would have the unwritten, but constitutional, right to a "fair ... hearing." (Though, as explained in para. 76, the Act provides for a fair trial in any event.) Thus, the appellants' conception of the unwritten constitutional principle of the rule of law would render many of our written constitutional rights redundant and, in doing so, undermine the delimitation of those rights chosen by our constitutional framers. That is specifically what this Court cautioned against in *Reference re Secession of Quebec*, at para. 53:

> Given the existence of these underlying constitutional principles, what use may the Court make of them? In [*Reference re Remuneration of Judges of the Provincial Court of Prince Edward Island*], at paras. 93 and 104, we cautioned that *the recognition of these constitutional principles ... could not be taken as an invitation to dispense with the written text of the Constitution. On the contrary, we confirmed that there are compelling reasons to insist upon the primacy of our written constitution.* A written constitution promotes legal certainty and predictability, and it provides a foundation and a touchstone for the exercise of constitutional judicial review. [Emphasis added.]

[66] Second, the appellants' arguments overlook the fact that several constitutional principles other than the rule of law that have been recognized by this Court—most notably democracy and constitutionalism—very strongly favour upholding the validity of legislation that conforms to the express terms of the Constitution (and to the requirements, such as judicial independence, that flow by necessary implication from those terms). Put differently, the appellants' arguments fail to recognize that in a constitutional democracy such as ours, protection from legislation that some might view as unjust or unfair properly lies not in the amorphous underlying principles of our Constitution, but in its text and the ballot box. See *Bacon v. Saskatchewan Crop Insurance Corp.* (1999), 180 Sask. R 20 (CA), at para. 30; Elliot [Robin Elliot, "References, Structural Argumentation, and the Organizing Principles of Canada's Constitution" (2001), 80 *Can. Bar Rev.* 67], at pp. 141-42; Hogg and Zwibel, at p. 718; and Newman ["The Principles of the Rule of Law and Parliamentary Sovereignty in Constitutional Theory and Litigation" (2005), 16 *NJCL* 175], at p. 187.

[67] The rule of law is not an invitation to trivialize or supplant the Constitution's written terms. Nor is it a tool by which to avoid legislative initiatives of which one is not in favour. On the contrary, it requires that courts give effect to the Constitution's text, and apply, by whatever its terms, legislation that conforms to that text.

[68] A review of the cases showing that each of the appellants' proposed requirements of the rule of law has, as a matter of precedent and policy, no constitutional protection is conclusive of the appellants' rule of law arguments.

[Justice Major then proceeds to review a series of cases in which, he says, the Supreme Court of Canada rejected arguments very similar if not identical to those made under the rule of law rubric in this case. He concludes by holding that the Act is valid.]

NOTES AND QUESTIONS

1. While the Court in *Imperial Tobacco* rejected the challenges to the Act based on both judicial independence and the rule of law, it did so for different reasons. In the case of judicial independence, Justice Major appeared to accept that, in some circumstances, it is open to the courts to strike down legislation on the ground that the legislation conflicts with that principle, but was of the view that this was not one of those circumstances. In the case of the rule of law, he appeared to hold that in no circumstances is it open to courts to strike down legislation on the ground that the legislation conflicts with that principle. If that interpretation of Justice Major's reasoning is correct, does he provide a persuasive basis on which to draw such a distinction?

2. Not long after the Supreme Court decided *Imperial Tobacco*, Chief Justice McLachlin gave a public lecture in New Zealand in the course of which she suggested that it was open to the courts in Canada, in at least some circumstances, to use the underlying principles of our Constitution, including the rule of law, to invalidate legislation. No reference was made in the text of the lecture to the decision in *Imperial Tobacco*. (See B. McLachlin, "Unwritten Constitutional Principles: What Is Going On?" (2006), 4 *NZJ Public & International Law* 147.)

3. For a case in which a lower court relied on unwritten constitutional principles to invalidate governmental action, albeit not legislative action but an administrative decision, see *Lalonde v. Ontario (Commission de restructuration des services de santé)* (2001), 56 OR (3d) 505, 208 DLR (4th) 577 (CA). In *Lalonde*, the unwritten principle of respect for and protection of minorities was used to invalidate a decision of Health Services Restructuring Commission to substantially reduce health services provided by Ontario's sole francophone hospital.

4. For further discussion of the use of unwritten constitutional principles, see R. Elliot, "References, Structural Argumentation, and the Organizing Principles of Canada's Constitution" (2001), 80 *Canadian Bar Review* 67.

The Supreme Court had occasion to revisit the rule of law as a possible independent basis for striking down legislation in the following case, which also had its origins in British Columbia.

British Columbia (Attorney General) v. Christie
[2007] 1 SCR 873, 2007 SCC 21, 280 DLR (4th) 528

[British Columbia's *Social Service Tax Amendment Act (No. 2)*, 1993, SBC 1993, c. 24, imposed a 7 percent tax on the purchase price of legal services within the province, ostensibly to fund legal aid there. Dugald Christie, a lawyer who worked with poor and low-income people in Vancouver, challenged the constitutionality of the legal service tax, claiming that the net effect of the tax was to make it impossible for some of his low-income clients to retain him to pursue their claims. His "access to justice" argument relied, in part, on the fundamental constitutional principle of "the rule of law" as referred to in the preamble to the *Constitution Act, 1982*. The chambers judge found that the tax breached a fundamental constitutional right to access to justice for low-income persons

and declared it unconstitutional to that extent. The majority of the Court of Appeal upheld that decision. The Supreme Court of Canada allowed the appeal of the BC attorney
general and set aside the order declaring the legal services tax to be unconstitutional.]

BY THE COURT (McLachlin CJC and Bastarache, Binnie, LeBel, Deschamps, Fish, Abella,
Charron, and Rothstein JJ):

· · ·

[10] The respondent's claim is for effective access to the courts which, he states, necessitates legal services. This is asserted not on a case-by-case basis, but as a general right.
What is sought is the constitutionalization of *a particular type of* access to justice—access
aided by a lawyer where rights and obligations are at stake before a court or tribunal ... .
In order to succeed, the respondent must show that the Canadian constitution mandates
this particular form or quality of access. The question is whether he has done so. In our
view, he has not.

[11] We take as our starting point the definition of the alleged constitutional principle offered by the majority of the Court of Appeal ... —the right to be represented by a
lawyer in court or tribunal proceedings where a person's legal rights and obligations are
at stake, in order to have effective access to the courts or tribunal proceedings.

[12] We will first discuss what the proposed right entails. We will then ask whether
the right, thus described, is prescribed by the constitution.

[13] This general right to be represented by a lawyer in a court or tribunal proceedings where legal rights or obligations are at stake is a broad right. It would cover almost
all—if not all—cases that come before courts or tribunals where individuals are involved.
Arguably, corporate rights and obligations would be included since corporations function as vehicles for individual interests. Moreover, it would cover not only actual court
proceedings, but also related legal advice, services and disbursements. Although the respondent attempted to argue otherwise, the logical result would be a constitutionally
mandated legal aid scheme for virtually all legal proceedings, except where the state
could show this is not necessary for effective access to justice.

[14] This Court is not in a position to assess the cost to the public that the right
would entail. No evidence was led as to how many people might require state-funded legal services, or what the cost of those services would be. However, we do know that many
people presently represent themselves in court proceedings. We also may assume that
guaranteed legal services would lead people to bring claims before courts and tribunals
who would not otherwise do so. Many would applaud these results. However, the fiscal
implications of the right sought cannot be denied. What is being sought is not a small,
incremental change in the delivery of legal services. It is a huge change that would alter
the legal landscape and impose a not inconsiderable burden on taxpayers.

[15] The next question is whether the constitution supports the right contended
for. ...

· · ·

[18] [One] argument is that the right to have a lawyer in cases before courts and tribunals dealing with rights and obligations is constitutionally protected, either as an aspect of the rule of law, or a precondition to it.

[19] The rule of law is a foundational principle. This Court has described it as "a fundamental postulate of our constitutional structure" ... that "lie[s] at the root of our system of government" .... It is explicitly recognized in the preamble to the *Constitution Act, 1982*, and implicitly recognized in s. 1 of the Charter, which provides that the rights and freedoms set out in the Charter are "subject only to such reasonable limits *prescribed by law* as can be demonstrably justified in a free and democratic society." And, as this Court recognized in *Reference re Manitoba Language Rights*, [1985] 1 SCR 721, at p. 750, it is implicit in the very concept of a constitution.

[20] The rule of law embraces at least three principles. The first principle is that the "law is supreme over officials of the government as well as private individuals, and thereby preclusive of the influence of arbitrary power" .... The second principle "requires the creation and maintenance of an actual order of positive laws which preserves and embodies the more general principle of normative order" .... The third principle requires that "the relationship between the state and the individual ... be regulated by law" ....

[21] It is clear from a review of these principles that general access to legal services is not a currently recognized aspect of the rule of law. However, in *Imperial Tobacco* [*British Columbia v. Imperial Tobacco Canada Ltd.*, [2005] 2 SCR 473], this Court left open the possibility that the rule of law may include additional principles. It is therefore necessary to determine whether general access to legal services in relation to court and tribunal proceedings dealing with rights and obligations is a fundamental aspect of the rule of law.

[22] Before examining this question, it is important to note that this Court has repeatedly emphasized the important role that lawyers play in ensuring access to justice and upholding the rule of law: .... This is only fitting. Lawyers are a vital conduit through which citizens access the courts, and the law. They help maintain the rule of law by working to ensure that unlawful private and unlawful state action in particular do not go unaddressed. The role that lawyers play in this regard is so important that the right to counsel in some situations has been given constitutional status.

[23] The issue, however, is whether *general* access to legal services in relation to court and tribunal proceedings dealing with rights and obligations is a fundamental aspect of the rule of law. In our view, it is not. Access to legal services is fundamentally important in any free and democratic society. In some cases, it has been found essential to due process and a fair trial. But a review of the constitutional text, the jurisprudence and the history of the concept does not support the respondent's contention that there is a broad general right to legal counsel as an aspect of, or precondition to, the rule of law.

[24] The text of the Charter negates the postulate of the general constitutional right to legal assistance contended for here. It provides for a right to legal services in one specific situation. Section 10(b) of the Charter provides that everyone has the right to retain and instruct counsel, and to be informed of that right "on arrest or detention." If the reference to the rule of law implied the right to counsel in relation to all proceedings where rights and obligations are at stake, s. 10(b) would be redundant.

[25] Section 10(b) does not exclude a finding of a constitutional right to legal assistance in other situations. Section 7 of the Charter, for example, has been held to imply a right to counsel as an aspect of procedural fairness where life, liberty and security of the person are affected: .... But this does not support a general right to legal assistance whenever a matter of rights and obligations is before a court or tribunal. ... [T]he Court

[has taken] pains to state that the right to counsel outside of the s. 10(b) context is a case-specific multi-factored enquiry ... .

[26] Nor has the rule of law historically been understood to encompass a general right to have a lawyer in court or tribunal proceedings affecting rights and obligations. The right to counsel was historically understood to be a limited right that extended only, if at all, to representation in the criminal context: ... .

[27] We conclude that the text of the constitution, the jurisprudence and the historical understanding of the rule of law do not foreclose the possibility that a right to counsel may be recognized in specific and varied situations. But at the same time, they do not support the conclusion that there is a general constitutional right to counsel in proceedings before courts and tribunals dealing with rights and obligations.

NOTES AND QUESTIONS

1. An important step in the Court's reasoning in this case was the inference drawn that "the logical result" of accepting that the right claimed by Mr. Christie was constitutionally protected "would be a constitutionally mandated legal aid scheme for virtually all legal proceedings." Was the Court correct to draw this inference?

2. Where does the decision in *Christie* leave us in relation to the viability of using the rule of law as an independent basis on which to strike down legislation? The decision in *Imperial Tobacco* appeared to have closed the door to using the rule of law in this way. Has the decision in *Christie* reopened that door? If so, how wide?

Underlying the questions about the legitimacy of judicial review is a concern that it can result in the actions of democratically elected representatives of the people being declared of no force or effect by appointed judges. If court decisions that strike down legislation are not firmly grounded in the text of the Constitution, from where does the authority to make them come? How can the rendering of such decisions be said to be compatible with our longstanding and deep commitment to the principle of democratic self-government? Bear these questions in mind as you work your way through the many readings that follow. As you will see, some of the judges and scholars whose writings you will come across challenge the proposition that judicial review is antidemocratic. Others accept that it is, or at least can be, and suggest approaches that courts can take to the exercise of the power of judicial review—often called theories of judicial review—that will eliminate or at least minimize the incompatibility between judicial review and democratic values. Still others take the position that that incompatibility should not trouble our courts.

Note that the legitimacy issue did not dominate discussions of judicial review under the *British North America Act, 1867* in the latter part of the 19th century and the first part of the 20th. This was primarily because the legal culture then was such that those who commented on the courts' performance in the area of constitutional law—most of which dealt with federalism issues—either did not think in terms of the legitimacy of judicial review as an issue the way we do now or, if they did, were less willing than commentators today to raise it. But it may also have been because those commentators were more willing to accept that the courts really were doing what they claimed to be doing—giving effect to the text of that constitutional instrument. This did not mean that those commentators never questioned the decisions the courts rendered in that area; as you will see from the readings in Chapters 4 through 6, some of them did, and with considerable vigour. It simply means that those criticisms were not explicitly formulated in terms that challenged the legitimacy of those decisions.

In recent decades, a number of constitutional scholars have questioned the legitimacy of the courts' use of the power of judicial review in particular contexts. One of these scholars, Paul Weiler, in his book *In the Last Resort* (Scarborough, ON: Carswell/Methuen, 1974), went so far as to question the wisdom of using the courts to resolve disputes about the division of legislative jurisdiction between Parliament and the provincial legislatures. In his view, such disputes were better resolved through federal–provincial negotiations and the operation of the democratic process. Another scholar, Peter Hogg, author of *Constitutional Law of Canada*, 4th ed. (Scarborough, ON: Carswell, 1997), the leading textbook in this area, has long been an advocate of having courts exercise restraint in their handling of federalism disputes.

The legitimacy issue has, by contrast, featured prominently in literature that relates to the *Charter of Rights and Freedoms* from the time it was first enacted—this is reflected in some of the readings in Chapter 16, The Advent of the Charter. It is also a recurring theme in many of the later chapters that deal with the Charter.

The special role of the courts in constitutional review is related to certain constitutional protections for the courts and the judiciary, in particular with respect to judicial independence, which is dealt with in Chapter 13, The Judicial Function.

II. CONSTITUTIONAL INTERPRETATION

Important to any consideration of the legitimacy of judicial review is the question of *how* judges interpret a written constitution, particularly in the overwhelming majority of cases in which the meaning of the relevant text is unclear. What sources of guidance are judges entitled to employ? What sources of guidance do they, in fact, employ? What weight do they give to particular sources? These are questions that are explored throughout this book in the context of a broad range of readings, some taken from decisions rendered by the courts and others from scholarly commentary. An excerpt from a recent article by Robin Elliot provides a brief introduction to the subject, as do excerpts from the reasons for judgment of both the Supreme Court of Canada and the Judicial Committee of the Privy Council in a famous Canadian constitutional case known as the "*Persons*" case.

R. Elliot, "References, Structural Argumentation, and the Organizing Principles of Canada's Constitution"
(2001), 80 *Canadian Bar Review* 67, at 72-74 (footnotes and citations omitted)

[In this article, Professor Elliot examines the increasing use in recent years by the Supreme Court of Canada of a kind of interpretive argument that has come to be called "structural argumentation," and some of the issues that that form of argumentation raises in the Canadian context. He begins his analysis by providing a summary of six different forms of argumentation identified by an American scholar Philip Bobbitt in his book *Constitutional Fate: Theory of the Constitution* (New York: Oxford University Press, 1982), and suggests that all of them have been used at one time or another by the courts here. As you will see, each of these forms of argumentation relies on a different source of interpretive guidance. You will encounter most of the cases he refers to as you work your way through this casebook, and the citations have therefore been omitted.]

The first of these ... forms of argumentation is labelled *historical*. By historical argumentation, Professor Bobbitt means "argument that marshals the intent of the draftsmen of the Constitution and the people who adopted the Constitution." This form of argumentation has been a good deal less popular in Canada than in the United State, where it forms the basis of a theory of judicial review, known as "originalism," to which a number of American constitutional scholars and at least one current member of the Supreme Court of the United States, Justice Scalia, subscribe. However, it is clearly a legitimate form of argumentation in this country as well, in relation to both the *Constitution Act, 1867* and the *Constitution Act, 1982*. And while it generally is viewed as having little persuasive force, it can on occasion play quite a significant role in the resolution of disputes about the proper meaning to be given to a provision of the Constitution. For example, in *R v. Prosper*, the Supreme Court placed considerable weight on the fact that the drafters of the Charter chose not to constitutionalize a right to state-funded counsel under section 10 when it decided not to read such a right into section 10(b).

Textual argument comes next. This, says Professor Bobbitt, is "argument that is drawn from a consideration of the present sense of the words of the provision [in question]." Examples of its use in Canada are not difficult to find. One that comes quickly to mind is the interpretation given by the Privy Council in both the *Radio Reference* and the *Labour Conventions Reference* to section 132 of the *Constitution Act, 1867*, relating to the power of Parliament to implement treaty obligations. Because section 132 had been formulated in terms of the power to implement obligations towards foreign countries arising under treaties between the Empire and such foreign countries, the Privy Council was quick to hold that it had no application in relation to obligations undertaken towards foreign countries in treaties that Canada itself had entered into with those countries. Another more recent example is provided by *Société des Acadiens v. Association of Parents*, in which Beetz J for the majority of the Supreme Court held that the right in section 19(2) of the Charter to *use* either English or French in the courts of New Brunswick did not include the right to be understood in the language chosen.

Third comes *doctrinal* argument, or argument from previously decided cases, which is also clearly accepted in Canada. In fact, it is probably fair to say that it is the predominant form of argumentation here. Examples of it abound—there is the definition of section 91(2) ["regulation of trade and commerce"] of the *Constitution Act, 1867* in *Citizens Insurance v. Parsons*, there is the analytical framework for freedom of expression cases under the Charter prescribed by *Irwin Toy v. Quebec*, and there is the analytical framework for section 1 of the Charter established in *R v. Oakes*, to name but three.

Next on the list comes *prudential* argument, or "argument about costs and benefits," or simply "practical argument." This is the form of argumentation that is used in the context of the final component of the proportionality test under section 1 of the Charter prescribed by *Oakes*, in which the question is in effect whether or not society loses more than it gains as a result of the impugned governmental action. But this form of argumentation can also be found in the federalism context, for example, in the tests devised in *General Motors v. City National Leasing* and *R v. Crown Zellerbach* respectively for the second branch of section 91(2) of the *Constitution Act, 1867* and the national concern branch of Parliament's residual power. In both of these tests, explicit consideration is given to the question of whether or not the legislative initiative is one that can be effectively pursued at the provincial level, or whether, by contrast, the initiative is one that can only be effectively undertaken at the national level. In other words, the court is concerned about how best the governmental task in question can be performed—the very stuff of practical or prudential argument.

The fifth of these ... forms of argumentation discussed by Professor Bobbitt is *ethical* argumentation, by which he means "constitutional argument whose force relies on a characterization of American institutions and the role within them of the American people"; elsewhere he describes it as "an appeal to the American ethos: not necessarily what we are, but perhaps what we think we are, and thus how we think about ourselves and our society ... ." This form of argumentation may be peculiarly American. But it is possible that it too finds at least some resonance within our jurisprudence. For example, the concern underlying the admonition in Chief Justice Dickson's reasons for judgment in *Edwards Books* that, "in interpreting and applying the Charter I believe that the courts must be cautious to ensure that it does not simply become an instrument of better situated individuals to roll back legislation which has as its object the improvement of the condition of less advantaged persons," can be said to be what we might like to think of as an important part of the Canadian ethos. This admonition has ... now been formalized in the principle that the courts in exercising their power of judicial review the Charter should show considerable deference to Parliament and the provincial legislatures when they [are asked to review] action that can be said to further the interests of vulnerable groups within Canadian society.

That brings us to *structural* argumentation. This form of argumentation, Bobbitt says, is based on "inferences from the existence of constitutional structures and the relationships which the Constitution ordains among these structures." "Structural arguments," he goes on to say, "are largely factless and depend on deceptively simple logical moves from the entire Constitutional text rather than from one of its parts." We will be exploring in some detail the use of this form of argumentation in Canada later in this paper. Suffice it to say here that it is clearly accepted as a legitimate form of argumentation in this country.

[Professor Elliot then examines the use of structural argumentation in the Canadian context. The two main examples he gives of cases in which this form of argumentation is used are *Reference re Provincial Court Judges*, [1997] 3 SCR 3, 150 DLR (4th) 577, in which the Court held that the true constitutional basis of the principle of judicial independence was the preamble to the *Constitution Act, 1867*, and *Reference re Secession of Quebec*, [1998] 2 SCR 217, 161 DLR (4th) 385, in which the Court invoked four of the organizing principles of our Constitution—federalism, democracy, the rule of law, and the protection of minorities—to resolve the issue of the constitutionality of secession by a province. The former case is discussed in Chapter 13, The Judicial Function; the latter in Chapter 1, Introduction.]

NOTES AND QUESTIONS

1. Professor Bobbitt argues that the six different forms of argumentation that he identifies and discusses in the American context are the *only* viable forms of argumentation for purposes of determining the meaning of the American constitution. Are these six forms of argumentation the only viable ones for purposes of determining the meaning of Canada's constitution? If not, what other forms of argumentation are also viable? What about arguments that are based on a particular community's collective memory of events that were foundational to its existence, such as an argument that Quebec is a distinct society within Canada in part because unique cultural and legal traditions have survived in Quebec despite the conquest of New France? Are such arguments historical arguments? Ethical arguments? What is a court to do when the forms of argumentation yield conflicting answers, or when history is remembered differently by different communities? We explore these questions at greater length in Chapter 3, From Contact to Confederation. Keep these questions about constitutional interpretation in mind when you read through the decisions of the courts that are excerpted in this and later chapters.

2. Also consider as you read through the decisions in this book whether particular forms of argumentation feature more prominently in some historical periods than others, or in cases dealing with certain kinds of constitutional issues.

The excerpts from the judgments of the Supreme Court of Canada and Privy Council in the *"Persons"* case that follow provide a good opportunity to explore the differing approaches that courts and judges can take to the task of interpreting provisions of the Constitution. Some commentators have said that Lord Sankey's reasons for judgment in this case represented a dramatic departure from the approach to constitutional interpretation that had previously been taken by these two courts. That earlier approach, it is said, was grounded in the conviction that the *British North America Act* was no different from other statutes that they were asked to construe and should therefore be interpreted in the same way that those other statutes were interpreted. See if you can find support for this view of Lord Sankey's judgment in his reasoning. These two decisions are preceded by a reading that provides some historical background.

A. Prentice et al., *Canadian Women: A History*
(Toronto: HBJ-Holt Canada, 1988), at 207-8, 282-83 (footnotes omitted)

In spite of obstacles and disagreements, women continued to campaign for the suffrage. The turning point in the long battle finally came in 1916, when the vigorous suffrage campaign waged by western women culminated in their enfranchisement in Manitoba, Alberta, and Saskatchewan. A year later British Columbia and Ontario followed suit, and women in Nova Scotia, New Brunswick, and Prince Edward Island won the vote in 1918, 1919, and 1922 respectively. In all cases, except New Brunswick and Ontario, the right to vote was accompanied by the right to hold office; New Brunswick women became eligible to hold office in 1934 and Ontario women in 1919. Only Quebec and the British colony of Newfoundland held back and refused to grant the vote to women.

At the federal level, women's franchise was achieved in three phases. The *Military Voters Act* in 1917 gave the vote to women nurses serving in the war. Later that year the *Wartime Elections Act* extended the franchise to wives, widows, mothers, sisters, and daughters of those, alive or deceased, who had served or were serving in the Canadian or British military or naval forces. This act, designed to help re-elect Borden's Union government and endorse its mandate for conscription, drew both praise and outrage from suffrage advocates. Support came primarily from people who, in the wartime context, believed in the superiority of the Anglo-Saxon race and saw the vote as a way of reshaping society according to their values. Opponents, like the Victoria and Regina Local Councils of Women, both of which passed resolutions protesting the law, also saw the vote as an instrument for achieving social change, but objected to the act's discriminatory provisions, maintaining that valid change could only be achieved when all women acquired equal political rights with men. Their political objective was finally met in 1918 with the passage of the federal *Women's Franchise Act*, which gave the vote to every women who was over the age of twenty-one and a British subject, and who possessed the same qualifications as men required for the provincial franchise. Canadian women had achieved the franchise before women in Great Britain and, as far as the federal government was concerned, in the United States as well. The following year the federal government enacted legislation enabling women to be elected to the House of Commons. ...

A campaign of great symbolic significance that was visibly initiated and led to a successful conclusion by women was the action taken to gain Senate appointments for women. At issue was the exclusion of women from the upper house; some reform women also believed that the Senate could be used as a platform from which to exert influence on public policy. In 1919 the first conference of the Federated Women's Institutes of Canada, presided over by Judge Emily Murphy, passed a resolution requesting that the prime minister appoint a woman senator. Surely women, now voters and eligible for election to the lower house of Parliament, ought to be among those "persons" who, if qualified, could be summoned to serve in the Senate. The National Council of Women and the Montreal Women's Club renewed the request, settling on Judge Murphy as their candidate. But the governments of both Arthur Meighen and Mackenzie King stalled, apologetically pointing out that women were precluded from eligibility under the terms of the *British North America Act* of 1867. After eight years of requests, refusals, and lack of progress, Murphy got together with four other prominent women, including Nellie McClung, Louise McKinney, and Irene Parlby, all of whom had served in the Alberta legislature, to mount a legal challenge. The fifth petitioner, Henrietta Muir Edwards, was very well known in women's organizations for her many years of service as convenor of laws for the National Council of Women. These women used an obscure section of the *Supreme Court Act* to petition the government for an Order-in-Council directing the Supreme Court to rule on the constitutional question of whether the term "qualified persons" in section 24 of the *BNA Act* included women, and therefore whether women were eligible to be summoned to the Senate. The Supreme Court ruling in April 1928 held that the term "qualified persons" did not include women. The five petitioners then asked the government to allow an appeal of the judgement to the Judicial Committee of the Privy Council in England, at that time the highest court of appeal on questions related to Canadian law. The government agreed and the appeal was heard. On October 18, 1929, the Judicial Committee unanimously reversed the judgement of the Supreme Court of Canada and held that the word "persons" in section 24 of the *BNA Act* did (in 1929) include women as well as men. Unfortunately, Emily Murphy was never invited to sit in the Senate; being a well known Conservative, she was passed over by Mackenzie King in favour of Liberal Cairine Wilson, who was appointed the first woman senator in 1930. Even when the Conservatives returned to office later that year, and a Senate vacancy was created in 1931 by the death of a Catholic senator from Edmonton, Murphy was once again denied a seat, this time because she was a Protestant. Two years later, Emily Murphy died without achieving the appointment for which she had fought so long and hard. In 1935 a second woman, Iva Fallis, was named to the Senate.

Montreal-born Cairine Wilson had not achieved the same recognition from the general public and the women's movement as Murphy, but she had devoted her married life to social and charitable reform causes, and more importantly from the point of view of the Senate appointment, to Liberal party politics after 1921. An active volunteer with the Red Cross, Victorian Order of Nurses, Presbyterian Women's Missionary Society, Salvation Army, YWCA, and the Ottawa Welfare Bureau, Wilson was a founder of the National Federation of Liberal Women. As a senator, she involved herself in divorce legislation, immigration, and the League of Nations. She was president of the Canadian League of Nations Society, and also one of the few Canadians to protest the government's restrictive immigration policies, which prevented the entry of Jews fleeing Nazi persecution in the 1930s.

Reference re Meaning of the Word "Persons" in Section 24 of the British North America Act, 1867
[1928] SCR 276, 4 DLR 98

ANGLIN CJC (Mignault, Lamont, and Smith JJ concurring): By Order of the 19th of October, 1927, made on a petition of five ladies, His Excellency the Governor in Council was pleased to refer to this court "for hearing and consideration" the question:

Does the word "Persons" in section 24 of the *British North America Act, 1867* include female persons?

... The *British North America Act, 1867*, does not contain provisions in regard to the Senate corresponding to its sections 41 and 52, which, respectively, empower the Parliament of Canada from time to time to alter the qualifications or disqualifications of persons to be elected to the House of Commons and to determine the number of members of which that House shall consist. Except in regard to the number of Senators required to constitute a quorum (s. 35), the provisions affecting the constitution of the Senate are subject to alteration only by the Imperial Parliament. ...

It should be observed that, while the question now submitted by His Excellency to the court deals with the word "Persons," section 24 of the *BNA Act* speaks only of "qualified Persons"; and the other sections empowering the Governor General to make appointments to the Senate (26 and 32) speak, respectively, of "qualified Persons" and of "fit and qualified Persons." The question which we have to consider, therefore, is whether "female persons" are qualified to be summoned to the Senate by the Governor General; or, in other words—Are women eligible for appointment to the Senate of Canada? ...

In considering this matter we are, of course, in no wise concerned with the desirability or the undesirability of the presence of women in the Senate, nor with any political aspect of the question submitted. Our whole duty is to construe, to the best of our ability, the relevant provisions of the *BNA Act, 1867*, and upon that construction to base our answer.

Passed in the year 1867, the various provisions of the *BNA Act* (as is the case with other statutes, *Bank of Toronto v. Lambe* (1887), 12 AC 575 at 579) bear to-day the same construction which the courts would, if then required to pass upon them, have given to them when they were first enacted. If the phrase "qualified persons" in s. 24 includes women to-day, it has so included them since 1867. ...

"In deciding the question before us," said Turner LJ, in *Hawkins v. Gathercole* (1855), 6 DeG M & G 1, 43 ER 1129, "we have to construe not merely the words of the Act of Parliament but the intent of the Legislature as collected, from the cause and necessity of the Act being made, from a comparison of its several parts and from foreign (meaning extraneous) circumstances so far as they can be justly considered to throw light upon the subject."

Two well-known rules in the construction of statutes are that, where a statute is susceptible of more than one meaning, in the absence of express language an intention to abrogate the ordinary rules of law is not to be imputed to Parliament (*Wear Commissioners v. Adamson* (1876), 1 QBD 546 at 554); and, "as they are framed for the guidance of the people, their language is to be considered in its ordinary and popular sense," per Byles J, in *Chorlton v. Lings* (1868), LR 4 CP 374.

Two outstanding facts or circumstances of importance bearing upon the present reference appear to be

> (a) that the office of Senator was a *new* office first created by the *BNA Act*. It is an office, therefore, which no one apart from the enactments of the statute has an inherent or common law right of holding, and the right of any one to hold the office must be found within the four corners of the statute which creates the office, and enacts the conditions upon which it is to be held, and the persons who are entitled to hold it; (*Beresford-Hope v. Sandhurst* (1881), 131 Mass. 371, per Lord Coleridge CJ);
>
> (b) that by the common law of England (as also, speaking generally, by the civil and the canon law: *foeminae ab omnibus officiis civilibus vel publicis remotae sunt*) women were under a legal incapacity to hold public office, "referable to the fact" (as Willes J said in *Chorlton v. Lings*), "that in this country in modern times, chiefly out of respect to women, and a sense of decorum, and not from their want of intellect, or their being for any other such reason unfit to take part in the government of the country, they have been excused from taking any share in this department of public affairs."

The same very learned judge had said, at p. 388:

Women are under a legal incapacity to vote at elections. What was the cause of it, it is not necessary to go into: but, admitting that fickleness of judgment and liability to influence have sometimes been suggested as the ground of exclusion, I must protest against its being supposed to arise in this country from any underrating of the sex either in point of intellect or worth. That would be quite inconsistent with one of the glories of our civilization, the respect and honour in which women are held. This is not a mere fancy of my own, but will be found in Selden, de Synedriis Veterum Ebraeorum, in the discussion of the origin of the exclusion of women from judicial and like public functions, where the author gives preference to this reason, that the exemption was founded upon motives of decorum, and was a privilege of the sex (*honestatis privilegium*): Selden's Works, vol. 1, pp. 1083-1085. Selden refers to many systems of law in which this exclusion prevailed, including the civil law and the canon law, which latter, as we know, excluded women from public functions in some remarkable instances. With respect to the civil law, I may add a reference to the learned and original work of Sir Patrick Colquhon (*sic*) on the Roman Law, vol. 1, c. 580, where he compares the Roman system with ours, and states that a woman "cannot vote for members of parliament, or sit in either the House of Lords or Commons."

[Anglin CJC then cited further cases on women's common law legal incapacity.]

Prior to 1867 the common law legal incapacity of women to sit in Parliament had been fully recognized in the three provinces—Canada (Upper and Lower), Nova Scotia and New Brunswick, which were then confederated as the Dominion of Canada.

Moreover, paraphrasing an observation of Lord Coleridge CJ, in *Beresford-Hope v. Sandhurst, supra* at 370, it is not also perhaps to be entirely left out of sight, that in the sixty years which have run since 1867, the questions of the rights and privileges of women have not been, as in former times they were, asleep. On the contrary, we know as a matter of fact that the rights of women, and the privileges of women, have been much discussed, and able and acute minds have been much exercised as to what privileges ought to be conceded to women. That has been going on, and surely it is a significant fact, that never from 1867 to the present time has any woman ever sat in the Senate of Canada, nor has any suggestion of women's eligibility for appointment to that House until quite recently been publicly made.

Has the Imperial Parliament, in sections 23, 24, 25, 26 and 32 of the *BNA Act*, read in the light of other provisions of the statute and of relevant circumstances proper to be considered, given to women the capacity to exercise the public functions of a Senator? Has it made clear its intent to effect, so far as the personnel of the Senate of Canada is concerned, the striking constitutional departure from the common law for which the petitioners contend, which would have rendered women eligible for appointment to the Senate at a time when they were neither qualified to sit in the House of Commons nor to vote for candidates for membership in that House? Has it not rather by clear implication, if not expressly, excluded them from membership in the Senate? Such an extraordinary privilege is not conferred furtively, nor is the purpose to grant it to be gathered from remote conjectures deduced from a skilful piecing together of expressions in a statute which are more or less precisely accurate. (*Nairn v. University of St. Andrews*, [1909] AC 147 to 161.) When Parliament contemplates such a decided innovation it is never at a loss for language to make its intention unmistakable. "A judgment," said Lord Robertson in the case last mentioned, at pp. 165-6: "is wholesome and of good example which puts forward subject-matter and fundamental constitutional law as guides of construction never to be neglected in favour of verbal possibilities."

There can be no doubt that the word "persons" when standing alone *prima facie* includes women. (Per Loreburn LC, *Nairn v. University of St. Andrews*.) It connotes human beings—the criminal and the insane equally with the good and the wise citizen, the minor as well as the adult. Hence the propriety of the restriction placed upon it by the immediately preceding word "qualified" in ss. 24 and 26 and the words "fit and qualified" in s. 32, which exclude the criminal and the lunatic or imbecile as well as the minor, who is explicitly disqualified by s. 23(1). Does this requirement of qualification also exclude women?

[In answering his question, Anglin CJC went on to deal with the rule of statutory interpretation found in *Lord Brougham's Act, 1850*, which read as follows: "Be it enacted that in all Acts words importing the Masculine Gender shall be deemed and taken to include Females, and the Singular to include the Plural, and the Plural the Singular, unless the contrary as to Gender or Number is expressly provided."]

"Persons" is not a "word importing the masculine gender." Therefore, *ex facie*, *Lord Brougham's Act* has no application to it. It is urged, however, that that statute so affects the word "Senator" and the pronouns "he" and "his" in s. 23 that they must be "deemed and taken to include Females," "the contrary" not being "expressly provided."

The application and purview of *Lord Brougham's Act* came up for consideration in *Chorlton v. Lings, supra*, where the Court of Common Pleas was required to construe a statute (passed, like the *British North America Act*, in 1867) which conferred the parliamentary franchise on "every man" possessing certain qualifications and registered as a voter. The chief question discussed was whether, by virtue of *Lord Brougham's Act*, "every man" included "women." Holding that "women" were "subject to a legal incapacity from voting at the election of members of Parliament," the court unanimously decided that the word "man" in the statute did not include a "woman." Having regard to the subject-matter of the statute and its general scope and language and to the important and striking nature of the departure from the common law involved in extending the franchise to women, Bovill CJ declined to accept the view that Parliament had made that change by using the term "man" and held that

> this word was intentionally used expressly to designate the male sex; and that it amounts to
> an express enactment and provision that every man, as distinguished from women, possess-
> ing the qualification, is to have the franchise. In that view, *Lord Brougham's Act* does not ap-
> ply to the present case, and does not extend the meaning of the word "man" so as to include
> "women." (386-87)

. . .

In our opinion *Chorlton v. Lings* is conclusive against the petitioners alike on the question of the common law incapacity of women to exercise such public functions as those of a member of the Senate of Canada and on that of their being expressly excluded from the class of "qualified persons" within s. 24 of the *BNA Act* by the terms in which s. 23 is couched (*New South Wales Taxation Commissioners v. Palmer*, [1907] AC 179 at 184), so that *Lord Brougham's Act* cannot be invoked to extend those terms to bring "women" within their purview.

We are, for these reasons, of the opinion that women are not eligible for appointment by the Governor General to the Senate of Canada under s. 24 of the *British North America Act, 1867*, because they are not "qualified persons" within the meaning of that section. The question submitted, understood as above indicated, will, accordingly, be answered in the negative.

[Duff J delivered a concurring judgment in which he rejected the idea that the common law disabilities of women established a rule of interpretation for the *BNA Act*. He found that the language of the Act as a whole did not give rise to a general presumption that the legislative and executive powers it conferred should be interpreted to preclude women from public office, but rather that they be interpreted to provide for adaptation over time. He reasoned, for example, that once women had been allowed to sit in the House of Commons, the principle of responsible government would require that the term "persons" in s. 11 of the Act dealing with the constitution of the Privy Council—that is, the cabinet—be interpreted to include women. He concluded, however, that the provisions in the *BNA Act* with respect to the Senate were intended to create a chamber whose constitution would in all respects be fixed and determined by the Act itself. Hence the rules for appointment would not be open to adaptation over time, and women were ineligible for appointment.]

Edwards v. Canada (Attorney General)
[1930] AC 123, 1 DLR 98 (PC)

LORD SANKEY LC: By s. 24 of the *British North America Act, 1867*, it is provided that "The Governor General shall from time to time, in the Queen's name, by instrument under the Great Seal of Canada, summon qualified persons to the Senate; and, subject to the provisions of this Act, every person so summoned shall become and be a member of the Senate and a senator."

The question at issue in this appeal is whether the words "qualified persons" in that section include a woman, and consequently whether women are eligible to be summoned to and become members of the Senate of Canada.

Of the appellants, Henrietta Muir Edwards is the Vice-President for the Province of Alberta of the National Council of Women for Canada; Nellie L. McClung and Louise C. McKinney were for several years members of the Legislative Assembly of the said Province; Emily F. Murphy is a police magistrate in and for the said Province; and Irene Parlby is a member of the Legislative Assembly of the said Province and a member of the Executive Council thereof.

[An account of the judgments of the Supreme Court of Canada is omitted.]

Their Lordships are of opinion that the word "persons" in s. 24 does include women, and that women are eligible to be summoned to and become members of the Senate of Canada.

In coming to a determination as to the meaning of a particular word in a particular Act of Parliament it is permissible to consider two points—namely: (i) The external evidence derived from extraneous circumstances such as previous legislation and decided cases. (ii) The internal evidence derived from the Act itself. As the learned counsel on both sides have made great researches and invited their Lordships to consider the legal position of women from the earliest times, in justice to their argument they propose to do so and accordingly turn to the first of the above points—namely: (i) The external evidence derived from extraneous circumstances.

[Lord Sankey then reviewed the history of the exclusion of women from public offices from before the time of the Roman Empire through to the early part of the 20th century. In the course of this review, he noted that the courts in England had recently held that women were not entitled either to sit in the House of Lords or to become barristers or solicitors.]

The passing of *Lord Brougham's Act* in 1850 does not appear to have greatly affected the current of authority. Section 4 provided that in all acts words importing the masculine gender shall be deemed and taken to include female unless the contrary as to gender is expressly provided.

The application and purview of that Act came up for consideration in *Chorlton v. Lings* (1868), LR 4 CP 374, where the Court of Common Pleas was required to construe a statute passed in 1861, which conferred the parliamentary franchise on every man possessing certain qualifications and registered as a voter. The chief question discussed was whether by virtue of *Lord Brougham's Act* the words "every man" included women. Bovill CJ, having regard to the subject-matter of the statute and its general scope and language and to the important and striking nature of the departure from the common law involved in extending the franchise to women, declined to accept the view that Parliament had made that change by using the term "man" and held that the word was intentionally used expressly to designate the male sex. Willes J said: "It is not easy to conceive that the framer of that Act, when he used the word 'expressly,' meant to suggest that what is necessarily or properly implied by language is not expressed by such language."

Great reliance was placed by the respondents to this appeal upon that decision, but in our view it is clearly distinguishable. The case was decided on the language of the *Representation of the People Act, 1867*, which provided that "every man" with certain qualifications and "not subject to any legal incapacity" should be entitled to be registered as a voter. Legal incapacity was not defined by the Act, and consequently reference was necessary to the common law disabilities of women. ...

No doubt in any code where women were expressly excluded from public office the problem would present no difficulty, but where instead of such exclusion those entitled to be summoned to or placed in public office are described under the word "person" different considerations arise.

The word is ambiguous, and in its original meaning would undoubtedly embrace members of either sex. On the other hand, supposing in an Act of Parliament several centuries ago it had been enacted that any person should be entitled to be elected to a particular office it would have been understood that the word only referred to males, but the cause of this was not because the word "person" could not include females but because at common law a woman was incapable of serving a public office. The fact that no woman had served or has claimed to serve such an office is not of great weight when it is remembered that custom would have prevented the claim being made or the point being contested.

Customs are apt to develop into traditions which are stronger than law and remain unchallenged long after the reason for them has disappeared.

The appeal to history therefore in this particular matter is not conclusive.

As far back as *Stradling v. Morgan* (1560), 75 ER 305 it was laid down that extraneous circumstances may be admitted as an aid to the interpretation of a statute, and in *Herron v. Rathmines and Rathgar Improvement Commissioners*, [1892] AC 498 Lord Halsbury LC said: "The subject matter with which the legislature was dealing, and the facts existing at the time with respect to which the legislature was legislating, are legitimate topics to consider in ascertaining what was the object and purpose of the legislature in passing the Act," but the argument must not be pushed too far, and their Lordships are disposed to agree with Farwell LJ in *Rex v. West Riding of Yorkshire County Council*, [1906] 2 KB 676, "although it may, perhaps, be legitimate to call history in aid to show what facts existed to bring about a statute, the inferences to be drawn therefrom are extremely slight": see Craies, Statute Law, 3d ed., p. 118.

Over and above that, their Lordships do not think it right to apply rigidly to Canada of to-day the decisions and the reasons therefor which commended themselves, probably rightly, to those who had to apply the law in different circumstances, in different centuries, to countries in different stages of development. Referring therefore to the judgment of the Chief Justice and those who agreed with him, their Lordships think that the appeal to Roman law and to early English decisions is not of itself a secure foundation on which to build the interpretation of the *British North America Act* of 1867. ...

Their Lordships now turn to the second point—namely, (ii) the internal evidence derived from the Act itself.

Before discussing the various sections they think it necessary to refer to the circumstances which led up to the passing of the Act.

The communities included within the Britannic system embrace countries and peoples in every stage of social, political and economic development and undergoing a continuous process of evolution. His Majesty the King in Council is the final Court of Appeal from all these communities, and this Board must take great care therefore not to interpret legislation meant to apply to one community by a rigid adherence to the customs and traditions of another. ...

The *British North America Act* planted in Canada a living tree capable of growth and expansion within its natural limits. The object of the Act was to grant a Constitution to Canada. "Like all written constitutions it has been subject to development through usage and convention": Canadian Constitutional Studies, Sir Robert Borden (1922), p. 55.

Their Lordships do not conceive it to be the duty of this Board—it is certainly not their desire—to cut down the provisions of the Act by a narrow and technical construction, but rather to give it a large and liberal interpretation so that the Dominion to a great extent, but within certain fixed limits, may be mistress in her own house, as the Provinces to a great extent, but within certain fixed limits, are mistresses in theirs. "The Privy Council, indeed, has laid down that Courts of law must treat the provisions of the *British North America Act* by the same methods of construction and exposition which they apply to other statutes. But there are statutes and statutes; and the strict construction deemed proper in the case, for example, of a penal or taxing statute or one passed to regulate the affairs of an English parish, would be often subversive of Parliament's real intent if applied to an Act passed to ensure the peace, order and good government of a British Colony": see Clement's Canadian Constitution, 3d ed., p. 347.

The learned author of that treatise quotes from the argument of Mr. Mowat and Mr. Edward Blake before the Privy Council in *St. Catherine's Milling and Lumber Co. v. The Queen* (1888), 14 AC 46 at 50: "That Act should be on all occasions interpreted in a large, liberal and comprehensive spirit, considering the magnitude of the subjects with which it purports to deal in very few words." With that their Lordships agree, but as was said by the Lord Chancellor in *Brophy v. Attorney-General of Manitoba*, [1895] AC 202, the question is not what may be supposed to have been intended, but what has been said.

It must be remembered, too, that their Lordships are not here considering the question of the legislative competence either of the Dominion or its Provinces which arise under ss. 91 and 92 of the Act providing for the distribution of legislative powers and assigning to the Dominion and its Provinces their respective spheres of Government. Their Lordships are concerned with the interpretation of an Imperial Act, but an Imperial Act which creates a constitution for a new country. Nor are their Lordships deciding any question as to the rights of women but only a question as to their eligibility for a particular position. No one, either male or female, has a right to be summoned to the Senate. The real point at issue is whether the Governor General has a right to summon women to the Senate. ...

Such being the general analysis of the Act, their Lordships turn to the special sections dealing with the Senate.

It will be observed that s. 21 provides that the Senate shall consist of seventy-two members, who shall be styled senators. The word "member" is not in ordinary English confined to male persons. Sect. 24 provides that the Governor General shall summon qualified persons to the Senate.

As already pointed out, "persons" is not confined to members of the male sex, but what effect does the adjective "qualified" before the word "persons" have?

In their Lordship's view it refers back to the previous section, which contains the qualifications of a senator. ...

Their Lordships agree with Duff J when he says; "I attach no importance to the use of the masculine personal pronoun in s. 23 ..." and refer to s. 1 of the *Interpretation Act, 1889*, which in s. 1, sub-s. 2, provides that words importing the masculine gender shall include females.

The reasoning of the Chief Justice would compel their Lordships to hold that the word "persons" as used in s. 11 relating to the constitution of the Privy Council for Canada was limited to "male persons," with the resultant anomaly that a woman might be elected a member of the House of Commons but could not even then be summoned by the Governor General as a member of the Privy Council. ...

Looking at the sections which deal with the Senate as a whole (ss. 21-36) their Lordships are unable to say that there is anything in those sections themselves upon which the Court could come to a definite conclusion that women are to be excluded from the Senate.

So far with regard to the sections dealing especially with the Senate—are there any other sections in the Act which shed light upon the meaning of the word "persons"?

Their Lordships think that there are. For example, s. 41 refers to the qualifications and disqualifications of persons to be elected or to sit or vote as members of the House of Assembly or Legislative Assembly, and by a proviso it is said that until the Parliament of Canada otherwise provides at any election for a member of the House of Commons for the district of Algoma in addition to persons qualified by the law of the Province of Canada to vote every male British subject aged twenty-one or upwards being a householder shall have a vote. This section shows a distinction between "persons" and "males." If persons excluded females it would only have been necessary to say every person who is a British subject aged twenty-one years or upwards shall have a vote.

Again in s. 84, referring to Ontario and Quebec, a similar proviso is found stating that every male British subject in contradistinction to "person" shall have a vote.

Again in s. 133 it is provided that either the English or the French language may be used by any person or in any pleadings in or issuing from any court of Canada established under this Act and in or from all of any of the courts of Quebec. The word "person" there must include females, as it can hardly have been supposed that a man might use either the English or the French language but a woman might not.

If Parliament had intended to limit the word "persons" in s. 24 to male persons it would surely have manifested such intention by an express limitation, as it has done in ss. 41 and 84. The fact that certain qualifications are set out in s. 23 is not an argument in favour of further limiting the class, but is an argument to the contrary, because it must be presumed that Parliament has set out in s. 23 all the qualifications deemed necessary for a senator, and it does not state that one of the qualifications is that he must be a member of the male sex. ...

A heavy burden lies on an appellant who seeks to set aside a unanimous judgment of the Supreme Court, and this Board will only set aside such a decision after convincing argument and anxious consideration, but having regard: (1) To the object of the Act— namely, to provide a constitution for Canada, a responsible and developing State; (2) that the word "person" is ambiguous, and may include members of either sex; (3) that there are sections in the Act above referred to which show that in some cases the word "person" must include females; (4) that in some sections the words "male persons" are expressly used when it is desired to confine the matter in issue to males; and (5) to the provisions of the *Interpretation Act*; their Lordships have come to the conclusion that the word "persons" in s. 24 includes members both of the male and female sex, and that, therefore, the question propounded by the Governor General should be answered in the affirmative, and that women are eligible to be summoned to and become members of the Senate of Canada, and they will humbly advise His Majesty accordingly.

NOTES

1. The procedure by which the *Edwards* case got to court was the reference, a procedure often used in Canada in constitutional litigation. That procedure is invoked when the federal Cabinet refers a question to the Supreme Court of Canada for an opinion, or a provincial Cabinet sends a question to the provincial Court of Appeal. The reference power is discussed further below, in this chapter.

2. The approach to constitutional interpretation taken by Lord Sankey in *Edwards* has not always prevailed in Canadian constitutional law. As we noted in the introductory chapter, there is a real tension between the desire for stability and the desire for change in constitutional interpretation. While the Privy Council spoke of "living trees" in *Edwards*, a few years later it emphasized the value of stability in the following passage from *AG Canada v. AG Ontario (Labour Conventions)*, [1937] AC 326, at 354:

> While the ship of state now sails on larger ventures and into foreign waters she still retains the watertight compartments which are an essential part of her original structure.

As you proceed through the cases in this book, the tensions between stability and change—between "living trees" and "watertight compartments"—will emerge regularly, whether in disputes about federalism or the interpretation of the Charter.

3. A detailed examination of the *Persons* case can be found in R.J. Sharpe and P.I. McMahon, *The Persons Case: The Origins and Legacy of the Fight for Legal Personhood* (Toronto: University of Toronto Press for the Osgoode Society for Canadian Legal History, 2007).

III. TRIGGERING JUDICIAL REVIEW AND PROCEDURAL ISSUES

This section will provide a very brief overview of the ways in which constitutional issues reach the courts for adjudication. Constitutional litigation addresses broad issues of public concern but is conducted within the basic framework developed for the litigation of private law claims. This section outlines a number of special rules and procedures developed to accommodate the particular requirements of public law. Further reading on all of the issues touched on here can be found in B. Strayer, *The Canadian Constitution and the Courts*, 3d ed. (Toronto: Butterworths, 1988); P. Hogg, *Constitutional Law of Canada*, 4th ed. (Scarborough, ON: Carswell, 1997) (looseleaf); and R.J. Sharpe and K. Roach, *The Charter of Rights and Freedoms*, 3d ed. (Toronto: Irwin Law, 2005), Chapter 7.

A. How Do Constitutional Issues Get to Court?

1. Ordinary Litigation and the Rules of Standing

Constitutional disputes reach the courts in a variety of ways. Sometimes constitutional issues are raised in the course of ongoing civil or criminal proceedings. In civil cases between private parties, one party may challenge the validity of a law that the other party relies on. In the context of a prosecution, the accused might raise a constitutional challenge to the provision that is the basis of the criminal or penal charges. In other cases, an independent action may be commenced by someone seeking a declaration that a particular law is invalid on constitutional grounds.

The rules of standing determine who has a sufficient interest in a legal issue to raise it before a court. Historically, the common law standing rules required that an individual's own interests be directly affected by the law that he or she challenges in a way that is different from the impact on the public at large (the "special prejudice" test). These rules were intended to prevent "officious intermeddlers" from clogging the courts as well as to ensure a concrete factual context for the adjudication of disputes. The traditional common law rules of standing are typically satisfied in the situation where a law is being challenged on federalism or Charter grounds in the course of ongoing legal proceedings. This, however, is not necessarily the case where an independent action is commenced seeking a declaration that a law is unconstitutional, and it is in that context that the issue of standing generally arises.

The traditional common law rules of standing would preclude private citizens from bringing constitutional challenges in the public interest because that role was the exclusive preserve of the attorney general, at the federal or provincial level, as the chief law office of the Crown. But in a series of cases, the Supreme Court of Canada significantly broadened the rules of standing in constitutional cases, creating a new category of "public interest standing" to be granted at the discretion of the courts: see *Thorson v. AG Canada (No. 2)*, [1975] 1 SCR 138, 43 DLR (3d) 1; *Nova Scotia Board of Censors v. McNeil*, [1976] 2 SCR 265, 55 DLR (3d) 632; and *Minister of Justice of Canada v. Borowski*, [1981] 2 SCR 575, 130 DLR (3d) 588. A fourth case, *Finlay v. Minister of Finance of Canada*, [1986] 2 SCR 607, 33 DLR (4th) 321, extended the rules for public interest standing to non-constitutional, public law issues.

The test for standing was summarized by Martland J writing for the majority in *Borowski* (at SCR 598):

> [T]o establish status as a plaintiff in a suit seeking a declaration that legislation is invalid, if there is a serious issue as to its invalidity, a person need only to show that he is affected by it directly or that he has a genuine interest as a citizen in the validity of the legislation and that there is no other reasonable and effective manner in which the issue may be brought before the Court.

These rules recognize the special significance of constitutional issues and the private citizen's interest in ensuring that governments act within constitutional bounds. In *Canadian Council of Churches v. Canada*, [1992] 1 SCR 236, 88 DLR (4th) 193, the Court applied the test to a public interest group's challenge to a number of provisions contained in the new *Immigration Act*, which had not yet come into force. The Court determined there was ample opportunity for refugee claimants to challenge the various provisions and it refused standing to the group, which had demonstrated a strong commitment to fairness in the immigration and refugee process. The Court expressed concern that the interest group's challenge was too expansive and that it would lack factual underpinning as to the actual operation of the provisions in question.

Note that the rules of standing have been applied somewhat differently in the Charter context than in the federalism context; see Chapter 25, Enforcement of Rights. In that chapter there is also a discussion of the related issue of jurisdiction. That is the issue of which courts and other adjudicative bodies, such as administrative tribunals, have competence to deal with constitutional issues and to order remedies for breach of the rules of the Constitution.

2. The Reference Procedure

Constitutional issues may also reach the courts—as in the "*Persons*" case—by means of a process initiated by the executive arm of government, known as the reference procedure. Under this procedure, governments may refer important legal questions, including constitutional issues, directly to an appellate court for an advisory opinion. The provincial cabinets are empowered under provincial legislation to send reference questions to provincial appellate courts. The federal cabinet sends its reference questions directly to the Supreme Court of Canada. The technical term for this type of judicial review is "abstract review," in contrast to "concrete review" of litigation initiated by private parties.

The federal reference power is found in s. 53 of the *Supreme Court Act*, RSC 1985, c. S-26. It reads, in part:

References by Governor in Council

53(1) The Governor in Council may refer to the Court for hearing and consideration important questions of law or fact concerning

(a) the interpretation of the *Constitution Acts*;

(b) the constitutionality or interpretation of any federal or provincial legislation;

(c) the appellate jurisdiction respecting educational matters, by the *Constitution Act, 1867*, or by any other Act or law vested in the Governor in Council; or

(d) the powers of the Parliament of Canada, or of the legislatures of the provinces, or of the respective governments thereof, whether or not the particular power in question has been or is proposed to be exercised.

Section 53 goes on to provide that the Court has a duty to answer the questions posed. Nonetheless, the Supreme Court has on occasion invoked discretionary authority to refuse to answer a reference question—for example, where the question lacks sufficient legal content, is ambiguous or imprecise, or where the information submitted to the Court is inadequate.

In *Reference re Same-Sex Marriage*, [2004] 3 SCR 698 (paras. 61 to 71), 246 DLR (4th) 193, the Court refused to answer the question whether an opposite-sex requirement for marriage was consistent with the Charter. The Court set out the "unique combination of factors" supporting this refusal. The same-sex couples who had initiated the litigation in the provincial courts had secured declarations of their entitlement to marry. They had relied on the finality of the judgments and acquired rights entitled to protection when they entered into marriages on the basis of these rulings. A Supreme Court advisory opinion to the contrary in a reference would not dislodge those rights but would undermine them unfairly. In addition, answering this question would not ensure uniformity of provincial law on the question. Further, the Court clearly believed that it was inappropriate for the federal government to bring this reference question to the Court when it had not taken the opportunity to appeal the constitutional question to the Supreme Court for a legal determination after it lost at the appellate court level.

Section 53 also stipulates that, if the interests of provincial governments are engaged by a reference question, notice must be given as well as the right to be heard. In addition, provision is made for the appointment by the Court of an *amicus curiae* in respect of "any interest that is affected and with respect to which counsel does not appear." The Court made use of this power in *Reference re Secession of Quebec*, [1998] 2 SCR 217, 161 DLR (4th) 385 (found in Chapter 1, Introduction) to ensure that the "interest" of the government of Quebec was represented when it refused to participate in the proceeding.

There is parallel legislation in each province that empowers the provincial cabinet to initiate references to its court of appeal. Appeals from the appellate court rulings in reference cases are allowed as of right—that is, without seeking permission—to the Supreme Court of Canada.

The reference procedure departs from the common law requirement that courts consider legal issues in the context of concrete disputes between interested parties who are best situated to make the most pertinent arguments and present the relevant facts. The US Constitution requires a "case or controversy" for the Supreme Court to hear a case for this reason. However, jurisdiction akin to the Canadian arrangements is a common feature of modern constitutions.

To its detractors, the reference procedure politicizes the judiciary by requiring consideration of hypothetical issues. However, reference cases are often mounted to formalize, expedite, or consolidate proceedings raising the same or similar challenges. In these instances, the issue may be so important that the provincial or federal government in question wants to have carriage of the case, or to shift the cost from private parties to the state. In addition, the reference procedure affords a variety of ways to bring the factual nexus to the courts.

The reference procedure provides a relatively quick mechanism for obtaining a definitive answer on a question of constitutional validity because it bypasses the trial level proceeding. The government that has carriage of the case can ensure expeditious preparation when the importance of the case warrants. In some cases the reference procedure is invoked to obtain a determination of validity before a particular piece of legislation comes into force in order to avoid the complications and costs of reliance on an unconstitutional law.

Reference cases produce advisory opinions that do not carry the precedential weight of decisions made in the context of ordinary litigation. In practice, however, reference cases are considered as authoritative as other court judgments. Perhaps the strongest indication of the important role of the reference procedure is the fact that reference cases have not only been numerous, but many have delineated significant areas of constitutional theory and doctrine.

The importance of references in Canada is illustrated by the following passage from B. Strayer, *The Canadian Constitution and the Courts*, 3d ed. (Toronto: Butterworths, 1988), at 311:

> One of the most distinctive features of Canadian judicial review is its frequent resort to the constitutional reference. This frequency can be demonstrated by a survey of the leading cases: those reaching the Privy Council up to 1949, the Supreme Court of Canada thereafter, decided from 1867 to 1981. Of 282 cases involving constitutional issues, 77 had their origins in a constitutional reference while 205 involved concrete cases. Nor does the fact that over a quarter of the leading decisions were given in such proceedings reveal the full significance of constitutional references. In terms of impact on the political, social, and economic affairs of the country, the decisions in these cases have had an effect far beyond their numerical proportion.

For an in-depth study of the reference proceduere, see François Chevrette and Gregoire Charles N. Webber, "L'utilisation de la procédure d'avis consultatif devant la Cour suprême du Canada: Essai de typologie" (2003), 82 *Can. Bar Rev.* 757.

B. Notice Requirements

Governments have an interest in defending constitutional challenges to their legislation. The early case of *Russell v. The Queen* (1882), 7 AC 829 (PC) (found in Chapter 4, The Late Nineteenth Century: The Canadian Courts Under the Influence) is often cited as an example of a significant constitutional decision made with no governmental participation. In response to this concern, constitutional notice requirements have been in place since the late 19th century. These stipulations, included in legislation dealing with the rules of litigation practice, require litigants to notify the affected attorneys general of any constitutional issues raised in the courts.

The Supreme Court of Canada considered the consequences of failing to provide such notice in *Eaton v. Brant County of Education*, [1997] 1 SCR 241, 142 DLR (4th) 385:

> [53] ... I am inclined to agree with the opinion ... that the provision is mandatory and failure to give the notice invalidates a decision made in its absence without a showing of prejudice. It seems to me that the absence of notice is in itself prejudicial to the public interest. I am not reassured that the Attorney General will invariably be in a position to explain after the fact what steps might have been taken if timely notice had been given. As a result, there is a risk that in some cases a statutory provision may fall by default.
>
> [54] There is, of course, room for interpretation of s. 109 [*Courts of Justice Act*, RSO 1990, c. C.43] and there may be cases in which the failure to serve a written notice is not fatal either because the Attorney General consents to the issue's being dealt with or there has been a *de facto* notice which is the equivalent of a written notice. It is not, however, necessary to express a final opinion on these questions in that I am satisfied that under either strand of authority the decision of the Court of Appeal is invalid. No notice or any equivalent was given in this case and in fact the Attorney General and the courts had no reason to believe that the Act was under attack. Clearly, s. 109 was not complied with and the Attorney General was seriously prejudiced by the absence of notice.

If the Attorney General is already a party to the litigation, the notice provisions serve to provide the details of the particular constitutional claim and the time and place for the hearing. If the issue arises in private litigation, the notice provisions provide this information as well as the opportunity to participate in the litigation as intervenors, who may make written and oral submissions on the constitutional issues and have carriage of any appeal. If the intervention takes place at the trial level, the intervening attorney general may be permitted to submit evidence as well. (The general arrangement for non-governmental intervention is discussed further below.)

In each province, constitutional notice requirements apply to provincially administered courts and, in some cases, administrative boards and tribunals as well. Although the provincial legislation varies, the general approach is to require litigants raising a constitutional issue to notify the federal Attorney General and the Attorney General of the province in question. In Ontario, the notice requirements are found in s. 109 of the *Courts of Justice Act*, RSO 1990, c. C.43:

Notice of constitutional question

109(1) Notice of a constitutional question shall be served on the Attorney General of Canada and the Attorney General of Ontario in the following circumstances:

1. The constitutional validity or constitutional applicability of an Act of the Parliament of Canada or the Legislature, of a regulation or by-law made under such an Act or of a rule of common law is in question.

2. A remedy is claimed under subsection 24(1) of the *Canadian Charter of Rights and Freedoms* in relation to an act or omission of the Government of Canada or the Government of Ontario.

Note the broad reach of Ontario's notice requirement. It extends to challenges to legislation, regulations, bylaws, and the common law. It applies to questions of general validity as well as to applicability of the impugned provision in the particular context.

For constitutional cases reaching the Supreme Court of Canada on appeal, the procedural requirements combine the distillation of the constitutional issue with the notice function. See s. 60 of the *Rules of the Supreme Court of Canada*, SOR/2002-156, as amended:

> 60(1) Within 30 days after leave to appeal has been granted or after the filing of a notice of appeal in an appeal for which leave is not required, an appellant, respondent or attorney general shall make a motion to the Chief Justice or a judge to have a constitutional question stated if that appellant, respondent or attorney general intends to raise a question of
>
> (a) the constitutional validity or the constitutional applicability of a law of Canada or of a province or of regulations made under them,
>
> (b) the inoperability of a law of Canada or of a province or of regulations made under them, or
>
> (c) the constitutional validity or the constitutional applicability of a common law rule.

C. Parties and Intervenors

Constitutional issues often affect the interests of a wide range of persons and groups. Apart from constitutional references, which envision broad participation by interested and affected parties, participation in constitutional litigation is, as a starting point, confined to the parties to the litigation. In cases where a private party has commenced a court proceeding to directly challenge a piece of legislation (or a regulation promulgated under statute or an executive order), the attorney general, or another cabinet minister or government official or body, will be the respondent. As noted earlier, when an attorney general intervenes in litigation between private parties pursuant to a notice of constitutional question, he or she takes on the status of intervenor and may make written or oral submissions on the constitutional issues.

Other interested and affected persons and groups may apply to the Court to be allowed to participate as intervenors under the applicable procedural rules. At the Supreme Court of Canada, for example, intervention is governed by ss. 55-59 of the *Rules of the Supreme Court of Canada*, SOR/2002-156, as amended. Section 55 provides: "Any person interested in an application for leave to appeal, an appeal or a reference may make a motion for intervention to a judge." The judge, in granting intervention, may "impose any terms and conditions and grant any rights and privileges that the judge may determine, including whether the intervener is entitled to adduce further evidence or otherwise to supplement the record" (s. 59(b)). The intervenor is not allowed to present oral argument, unless authorized by the judge as per s. 59(2), nor can the intervenor introduce new issues, unless ordered by the judge as per s. 59(3). Since the adoption of the Charter, intervention by public interest groups has become a common feature of constitutional litigation. In some instances, cases have attracted a large number of intervenors.

Where constitutional issues arise in the course of private litigation or in the context of a criminal or penal prosecution, a request for intervention requires the court to balance a variety of considerations. These include, on the one hand, concerns about unfairness to the parties or the accused, the cost to all participants of additional participants, and any delay in resolving the specific dispute. On the other hand, the court will consider the potential usefulness of the intervenor's contribution to full consideration of the constitutional issue. In reference cases, where private interests are not exclusively at stake, intervention raises fewer concerns. The courts may nonetheless place some limits on the number of intervenors to avoid repetition and irrelevancy, or require intervenors to work together on their submissions.

PART TWO

Federalism

CHAPTER THREE

From Contact to Confederation

For decades, many Canadian jurists have assumed that Canada was born after the British conquest of New France and the assertion of Great Britain's sovereignty over the territory of what is now Canada. For example, Bora Laskin, who later became Chief Justice of Canada, wrote in the introductory sentence of his 1969 Hamlyn Lecture that "[m]ore than two hundred years have passed since English law and English legal institutions were rooted *in a yet unborn Canada*" (emphasis added). (B. Laskin, *The British Tradition in Canadian Law* (London: Stevens & Sons, 1969), at 1.) Jurists such as Laskin essentially believed that Canada's constitutional history either started with the Treaty of Paris of 1763, by which the French Crown ceded to the British Crown all of its rights over the territory of Canada, or, alternatively, with the creation of Canada as a confederation of colonies in 1867.

Such accounts often fail to acknowledge the presence of legal orders in North America prior to the imposition of British rule. Aboriginal peoples exercised law-making authority over territory and persons prior to European contact. And contact led to the establishment of French colonies—again, with law-making authority over territory and persons—on the continent. These legal orders expressed and produced diverse legal and constitutional norms that structured the economic, social and political affairs of their citizens. They also interacted with each other and, later, with British North American colonial legal orders. A complex web of often competing narratives invested these legal orders, and their interaction, with constitutional significance. Some of these narratives diverge in important respects from those that inform and perhaps dominate contemporary constitutional discourse. But some nonetheless have become ingrained in the collective memory of various communities across Canada, and continue to influence constitutional debates—sometimes directly affecting constitutional argument and interpretation.

What is the distinction between "history" and "memory" and how can that distinction improve our understanding of constitutional law? How does memory influence the creation and evolution of "imagined communities," to use an expression coined by B. Anderson (*Imagined Communities: Reflections on the Origin and Spread of Nationalism*, 2d and rev. ed. (New York: Verso, 1991)). To what extent can constitutional law be described as an intellectual tool by which an imagined community is institutionalized? According to J.-F. Geaudreault-DesBiens:

> At the heart of the Canadian constitutional debate lies a clash of stories about Canada's history. Far from reflecting a universally shared understanding of the meaning of Canada's founding historical events, these stories reflect instead divergent collective memories. This raises the question of the distinction that must be drawn between "history" and "memory." History refers to an intellectual undertaking which attempts to look at past events from an allegedly objective

standpoint and to view these events as unmediated material facts. In contrast, memory describes a subjective interpretation of past events, that has been elaborated over a long period of time and that sheds light on contemporary events, while at the same time being fed by those events. While history has more to do with the research of "hard facts," memory is related to the manner in which a community remembers and interprets its past, and, ultimately, to the manner in which it perceives itself. It crystallizes the community's particular remembrance of things past, to [paraphrase Proust]. ... [from "The Quebec Secession Reference and the Judicial Arbitration of Conflicting Narratives About Law, Democracy, and Identity" (1999), *Vermont Law Review* 793 at 796].

In this chapter, we provide an overview of some of the main features of these prior legal orders, the constitutional narratives that account for their presence, and the events marking their interaction, before turning to the events of 1867. Perhaps contrary to popular understandings, Canada's constitutional evolution was not a tranquil and incremental process of development, but one that had its share of tragedies, collective traumas, and major conflicts. Canada is not a young country—the very word "Canada" is of Aboriginal origins—which is why it is worth looking at what happened before 1867, most notably to determine the extent to which Canada was—and is—constituted by events that occurred before the formal confederation of British North American colonies in 1867. As we shall see, while not being entirely determined by these events, contemporary Canada cannot be abstracted from those events—or the competing constitutional narratives to which they gave rise.

I. PRE-CONTACT, CONTACT, AND THE MYTH OF TERRA NULLIUS

Prior to European contact, Aboriginal peoples lived in North America in organized societies exercising law-making authority over territory and persons since time immemorial. While the laws of these societies did not conform, formally or substantively, to European models of legality, they were laws nevertheless. (It bears noting that European models of legality are of relatively recent origins, essentially linked to the emergence of the nation-state in the sixteenth century. Before this time, the law in much of Europe was customary, and it was only in the twelfth century, with the rediscovery of Rome's Corpus Juris Civilis, that the idea of "written law" was rekindled.) Legal anthropologist Alain Bissonnette puts it this way:

> One must recognize a juridical character to any rule of social conduct that is rendered obligatory by the members of a given group. Native law is a traditional form of law; it is oral and unwritten. It has not been enacted by a supreme authority; it is customary. It reflects a cosmocentric view of the world which, in turn, is not reflected in dominant Western law. [A. Bissonnette, "Les droits des peuples autochtones: d'hier à demain" (Étude réalisée pour la Commission royale sur les peuples autochtones, juin 1992), at 5 (translation).]

Based mainly on oral traditions and customs, as well as being inspired by radically different views of the relationship between human beings and the world, Aboriginal legal orders that existed at the time of contact belonged to the family of what anthropologists now call traditional legal systems. The commonalities among them should not obscure their differences. Some were more formalized—or at least more cognizable to European legal consciousness—than others, such as the legal order governing the Iroquois nations, which eventually culminated into a confederacy of nations. Given their diversity, and the scarce data that is available, it is impossible to give a full account of all the Aboriginal legal orders that existed at the time of contact. And relying on their existence in a judicial context today raises complex evidentiary problems given that they are based in oral, rather than written, legal traditions. (For more discussion of the rules of evidence in the context of constitutional claims of Aboriginal rights, see *Delgamuukw v. British Columbia*, [1997] 3 SCR 1010; 153 DLR (4th) 193, excerpted in chapter 14, Aboriginal Peoples and the Constitution.)

In chapter 14, we examine the contemporary constitutional status of Aboriginal lands and peoples in some detail. In the remainder of this section, we want only to draw your attention to the fact that European nations asserting sovereignty over the lands newly "discovered" in the Americas justified their claims by relying upon what is known as the doctrine of *terra nullius*.

P. Macklem, *Indigenous Difference and the Constitution of Canada*
(Toronto: University of Toronto Press, 2001), at 113-15 (footnotes omitted)

The initial distribution of sovereignty over North America among European powers was generated not by a single decision-making authority, but by and through a series of acts of mutual recognition by European powers. Each colonizing power viewed itself and others as entitled to claim sovereignty to territory if it could establish a valid claim according to rules and principles that governed European colonial practice. According to "the doctrine of discovery," sovereignty could be acquired over unoccupied territory by discovery. Sovereignty over occupied territory could be acquired only by conquest or cession. However, international law deemed North America to be unoccupied, or terra nullius, for the purposes of distributing sovereignty. European settlement thus vested sovereignty in settling nations despite an indigenous presence. Because North America was treated as vacant, neither conquest nor cession was necessary to transfer sovereignty from Aboriginal nations to European powers.

International law deemed North America to be terra nullius under the doctrine of discovery because European powers viewed Aboriginal nations as insufficiently Christian or insufficiently civilized to justify recognizing them as sovereign over their lands and people. An Aboriginal nation did not constitute "a legal unit in international law" [*Cayuga Indians (Great Britain) v. United States* (1926), 6 RIAA 173, at 176]. [I]n the words of Chief Justice Marshall [of the United States Supreme Court, in *Johnson v. M'Intosh*, 21 US (8 Wheat.) 543, at 573 (1823)], "the character and religion of [North America's] inhabitants afforded an apology for considering them as a people over whom the superior genius of Europe might claim an ascendancy. The potentates of the old world found no difficulty in convincing themselves that they made ample compensation to the inhabitants of the new, by bestowing on them civilization and Christianity, in exchange for unlimited independence."

The doctrine of *terra nullius* has had a lasting impact on Western juridical and political thought (see, generally, M. Morin, *L'usurpation de la souveraineté autochtone: Le cas des peuples de la Nouvelle-France et des colonies anglaises de l'Amérique du Nord* (Montréal: Boréal, 1997). One of its underlying assumptions was that Aboriginal societies were essentially lawless societies.

Although the influence of the *terra nullius* doctrine cannot be underestimated, in what was known as "Indian policy" in both England and France, practical reason often prevailed. For example,

> The law of the Prairie West, according to the Hudson's Bay Company Royal Charter of 1670, was the law of England insofar as it applied to those people in Prince Rupert's Land who did not live under the authority of other previously established nations in the regions. While never expressed officially, the Company in practice accepted the rule of aboriginal law for domestic concerns of native people. [L.A. Knafla, "From Oral to Written Memory: The Common Law Tradition in Western Canada," in L.A. Knafla, ed., *Law and Justice in a New Land: Essays in Western Canadian Legal History* (Scarborough, ON: Carswell, 1986), at 35.]

In other words, even under a legal regime not naturally receptive to the existence of Aboriginal legal orders, there was still room for some degree of Aboriginal self-government. That paradoxical logic also inspired the numerous treaties that were concluded between the French and British Crowns and different Aboriginal nations.

As will be seen in chapter 14, Aboriginal Peoples and the Constitution, contemporary Canadian constitutional law today recognizes that what is now Canada was not in fact *terra nullius* when the Europeans began to assert territorial sovereignty over North America. It also recognizes that treaties between Aboriginal nations and the Crown possess constitutional significance. What might constitutional recognition of Aboriginal legal orders mean for the future of the Canadian constitutional order?

II. NEW FRANCE: CANADA'S FIRST EUROPEAN CONSTITUTIONAL REGIME

France was the first European nation to establish a colony, New France, on Canadian territory. New France here is understood as comprising different administrative divisions, such as Acadie, Canada (now Quebec), and Louisiane. Although Jacques Cartier claimed sovereignty over Canada on behalf on the French Crown in 1534, it was only in the early seventeenth century that the first settlements were established in Acadie (now Nova Scotia) and in Canada.

The colony of New France was created at a time when the King of France personally ruled his kingdom with the assistance of a Council placed under his direction. Recent historiography shows that the King's powers were not in truth absolute and that his authority in a practical sense depended upon the continuing support of the nobility in all of his kingdom's regions. But what was the legal regime of New France? In addition to the rules governing the monarchy itself, colonial laws included royal ordinances and edicts, rulings made by the Council, customary laws governing private relations, and seigniorial rights. Concepts of Roman law and Canon law in its Gallican interpretation also were sources of law. Even though the King of France was vested with very broad constitutional prerogatives, which encompassed legislative, executive, administrative, and judicial authority, the only way for him to exercise fully his sovereignty over his kingdom and his colonies was to delegate the exercise of some of his authority to colonial authorities. Thus, officials acting on his behalf in New France were mere delegates of the King and did not possess any original jurisdiction.

Initially, the Governor of New France exercised a virtually monopolistic jurisdiction, the scope of which was reduced as colonial institutions slowly took shape, a process that culminated in 1663, the year of a major administrative reform in the colony. After a brief period under the co-administration of the Compagnie des Cent-Associés, which had been granted ownership of the colony, and of a Governor presented by the Compagnie to the King, a Council was created in 1647 and was made responsible for the regulation of the fur trade and the control of public finances. It was also given responsibility to ensure the public good in the colony. This Council was composed of the Governor, a representative of the clergy, and, from 1657 to 1663, four councillors elected by the inhabitants of the colony. In 1663, however, it was abolished and replaced by the Sovereign Council ("Conseil souverain"), which was to last until the end of the French regime in 1760, its name changing to Superior Council ("Conseil supérieur") in 1703.

The creation of this Council, based on similar arrangements in some French provinces, heralded a period of significant institutional changes in New France. First, the King, then Louis XIV, regained the ownership of the colony from the Compagnie des Cent-Associés and eventually placed it under his direct administration; second, he delegated to the Sovereign Council the powers of the former Council, granted police powers to it, and made it the ultimate appellate court of the colony, exercising jurisdiction over civil and criminal cases. There was no real separation of legislative, executive, and judicial authority in the colony, which was the state of affairs in most European countries at the time. In fact, Montesquieu's *Esprit des lois*, in which the famous jurist-philosopher advocated the separation between these branches, was not published until 1748, twelve years before the end of New France. And it was not until much later that this idea was implemented in France and elsewhere.

At the end of the French regime, there were three major institutional actors whose responsibilities and prerogatives sometimes overlapped, partly because of the terms and conditions of the royal delegation under which they were working, and partly because of the absence of a separation between the branches of the state. These actors were the Council, the Governor, and the Intendant. While all of them were vested with executive powers, it was the Intendant who, practically, ended up exercising most of these powers. Under the terms of his mandate, which included military and Indian affairs, the Intendant was responsible for justice, police, and finances. Although the Governor exercised concurrent jurisdiction over "general police," the broad jurisdiction conferred upon the Intendant meant that, in practice, the Intendant was responsible for everything that touched upon agriculture, trade, industry, professions, health, public safety and order, and education.

Legislative authority was exercised by the King in France, and the edicts and ordinances that applied there applied in the colony as well. Officials such as the Governor and the Intendant were responsible for applying and enforcing these laws. However, the terms of their respective mandates allowed them to adapt metropolitan laws to the sometimes different situations that existed in the colony, and to enact local legislation called "ordinances." This legislative power also fell under the responsibility of the Intendant, a responsibility that he mostly exercised alone, except for ordinances concerning important issues in which the Council was called upon to participate. The Council, though its "droit de remonstrance," could also ask the King to introduce changes in the ordinances enacted by the King himself.

This account of legislative authority points to the absence of an assembly composed of elected representatives of the inhabitants of the colony, except for the period between 1657 and 1663, as mentioned above. Indeed, formal institutions where representative democracy could be practised did not exist in New France. But from the beginning to the end of the French regime, public meetings where the inhabitants of the different cities of the colony could express their views were called on a relatively frequent basis by colonial officials. The need to hold such meetings arose out of practical necessity. Given its large territory and widely dispersed population, New France required the collaboration and the input of the inhabitants of the colony for its effective administration. In 1700, Intendant Bochart de Champigny even proposed to metropolitan authorities, albeit unsuccessfully, to formalize the existence of these meetings. While the inhabitants of the colony could express their views in such meetings, they could only do so on issues that had been previously identified by colonial officials. Moreover, while votes were sometimes taken, they could never constitute "decisions" since they had no binding legal effect on colonial officials. Another impediment to the effectiveness of these informal consultations was the absence in the colony of recognized rights to freedom of association and to petition colonial officials.

Finally, the exercise of judicial power in New France was characterized by the involvement of non-judicial actors. At the end of the French regime, the Superior Council, as the ultimate appellate tribunal in the colony, could hear civil and criminal appeals from lower courts in Québec, Montréal, and Trois-Rivières. The Governor, the Intendant, the Bishop, and the Attorney General for the colony were among the seventeen councillors. In addition to being members of a judicial body, the Superior Council, the Governor and the Intendant could also directly adjudicate cases. On the one hand, the Governor could always review the rulings of the Council, which he did a few times when he believed that a denial of justice had occurred. On the other hand, being responsible for the administration of justice in the colony, the Intendant could adjudicate on cases raising the application of his own ordinances in respect to police and financial affairs and his rulings could only be appealed to the King's Council. The Intendant could also rule on alleged crimes against the safety of the state, review decisions taken by all judicial bodies, and even decide to hear cases already brought before courts of competent jurisdiction. This has led two commentators to describe the Intendant's judicial competence as follows:

> Relying on contemporary criteria presently applied in respect of the administration of justice, one could say that he [the Intendant] was vested with exclusive jurisdiction over the review of administrative action, could act as a "small claims" judge, in addition to which he had concurrent jurisdiction to hear cases that ordinary courts were competent to hear. [J.-Y. Morin, "L'évolution constitutionnelle du Canada et du Québec de 1534 à 1867," in J.-Y. Morin and J. Woehrling, *Les Constitutions du Canada et du Québec du régime français à nos jours*, vol. 1, Études (Montreal: Thémis, 1994), at p. 19 (translation).]

The above discussion summarizes Morin, *supra*, at 9-27. See also G. Lanctôt, *L'administration de la Nouvelle-France* (Montréal: Éditions du Jour, 1971).

As the colonists eventually adapted their way of life to the difficult conditions of New France, most notably through interaction with Aboriginal peoples, their identity began to change, and they soon started to define themselves as "Canadiens," as opposed to "Français." They were the first people in the Canadian territory to define themselves as "Canadians."

This self-definition as unhyphenated "Canadians" lasted long after the birth of Canada as a federation in 1867, since it took some time for the population of British descent to define itself as "Canadian." When they did, the ancient "Canadiens" increasingly became known as "French-Canadians."

III. FROM ACADIA TO NOVA SCOTIA: THE GENESIS OF THE MARITIMES

It was in Acadia that the clash between the French and the British North American empires first entailed major legal consequences. As early as 1689, sporadic conflicts had plagued relations between the two empires in Europe and in North America. The year of 1710 saw the fall of Port Royal (now Annapolis Royal) to an expedition of New Englanders. Three years later, this victory was confirmed in the Treaty of Utrecht, under which France yielded Acadia and Newfoundland to Great Britain, but maintained its control over Cape Breton (then called "Isle royale") where it founded Louisbourg in 1720, Prince Edward Island (then called "Isle Saint-Jean"), and other islands in the Gulf of St. Lawrence. It also kept the St. Lawrence valley.

For the French population of Acadia, and its Aboriginal allies, the Treaty of Utrecht heralded a period of significant change. Given their cultural ties and geographical proximity with the remaining French North American colonies, the inhabitants of the new British colony of Nova Scotia were required in 1713 to take an oath of allegiance, which they did on the condition that they would not have to bear arms against France. That condition was accepted by British authorities. The Acadians then came to be referred to as the "French neutrals." Despite the establishment of a military government in Nova Scotia and immigration from Great Britain, British authorities were still faced, in mid-eighteenth century, with a problem in their Maritime colony: most of its inhabitants were not of British origin, and their population was expanding. By then, the Acadians considered themselves a people, distinct from both the French and the English. The Acadians had carved for themselves a relatively comfortable niche within the British colony of Nova Scotia, and their society felt secure enough to envisage the future with confidence. This was to last until the late 1740s, when conflict between the two empires resumed.

Fearing that the Acadians, despite their oath, could be tempted to support France in this new conflict, British authorities decided to strengthen their hold on Nova Scotia by promoting the settlement of the colony with migrants whose loyalty could not be questioned—that is, British and non-British Protestants. Despite meetings with colonial authorities, and even the agreement of some Acadian communities to take an unqualified oath, British authorities decided to deport the Acadians. That decision was implemented in the last months of 1755: "The reality, even if it had been fully expected, would have been psychologically stunning. Settlements burnt, cattle driven off, lives now entirely at the command of the soldiery; within days the Acadians were turned from a free and flourishing people into a crowd of refugees." (N.E.S. Griffiths, *The Contexts of Acadian History, 1686-1784* (Montreal/Kingston: McGill-Queen's University Press, 1992), at 91.)

The deportation, which would continue until 1762, saw between 12,000 and 18,000 Acadians uprooted from what are now Nova Scotia, New Brunswick, and Prince Edward Island. Thousands died due to diseases contracted on board ships, or because the vessels they were on sank. This led France to accuse England of having committed genocide. Eventually, the

Acadians who wanted to return home were permitted to do so in 1764, only to realize that their former lands were now occupied by British settlers. As for the Mi'kmaq, even though they had most often sided with the French, they "had never stopped considering themselves the rightful tenants of the land" (Griffiths, *supra*, at 82) and entered into discussions with the British that eventually culminated in the signing of treaties (for a judicial interpretation of these treaties, see *R v. Marshall*, [1999] 3 SCR 456; 179 DLR (4th) 193, an excerpt of which appears in chapter 14, Aboriginal Peoples and the Constitution).

Interpretations abound as to the reasons why the deportation was ordered. For example, an early commentator, Édouard Richard, was of the view that "the deportation, in the minds of its chief authors, was neither a justifiable act nor a deed of cruelty pure and simple, but a means of acquiring wealth by despoiling the Acadians of their cattle and lands" (*Acadia: Missing Links of a Lost Chapter in American History*, vol. 1 (New York: Home Book Co. and Montreal: John Lovell & Son, 1895), at 264). One thing is certain. The deportation of the Acadians was not an isolated incident, but rather the result of a public policy carried out as a part of Great Britain's plan to build its North American empire:

> The policy in this case was followed systematically for years, and it would be a gross error to see in the expulsion the result of a sudden excess of violence—a monstrous fit of bad temper on the part of Lawrence and his colleagues, and foreign to the British government. No—the dispersal continued into 1762 and was neither incidental nor accidental. [G. Frégault, *Canada: The War of the Conquest*, M. Cameron, trans. (Toronto: Oxford University Press, 1969), at 186.]

Legal and political events before and after the deportation reveal that empire-building lay at the heart of the decision. In August 1754, Lieutenant Governor Charles Lawrence had informed the Board of Trade and Plantations in London—the authority responsible for overseeing the colonies—that the Acadians' loyalty was more dubious than ever and that he was of the view that they either had to take an unconditional oath or leave the colony.

This raised the question of the legal status of the Acadians in the colony. As described by Frégault, *supra*, at 174:

> The fact was ... that after the Treaty of Utrecht the Acadians could continue to live in the province only on condition that they become subjects of Great Britain, and in order to acquire this status, they must take the oaths required by the British authorities. It was therefore most important to consider to what extent they could be treated as British subjects if they refused to take the oaths, and whether refusal to do so would not cancel their titles to their property. ...
>
> The Lords of Trade were unwilling to commit themselves, but their statements sufficed to authorize the principle of massive deportation: if the Acadians had not the status of British subjects they had no right to the land they were cultivating, for it was British land; and if they had no right to the land, it would not be illegal to dislodge them from it. It would require only the decision of a colonial magistrate to give this reasoning the force of law.

That colonial magistrate would be Jonathan Belcher, Chief Justice of Nova Scotia, who was asked by Lawrence to clarify the Acadians' legal status and the nature of their title, if any, to their lands. On July 28, 1755, the same day that the final decision to deport the Acadians was taken, Belcher released an opinion in which he relied on legal technicalities to conclude that the law not only authorized but *required* the deportation. He reasoned that because Cornwallis, then lieutenant governor of the colony, had been instructed by London to request once again that the Acadians take an unqualified oath to the British Crown, a demand to which they responded negatively in 1749, the Acadians had impliedly declared their intention not to become British subjects. The instruction to Cornwallis also stated that the persons refusing to take the oath would not be eligible to retake it should they wish to, because such a profession of faith would not be reliable. Belcher concluded that given the Acadians' prior refusal to take the oath, the government of the colony had lost the legal power to reoffer them the opportunity to take it. In his view, their deportation and the taking of their lands was therefore required by law.

Belcher added that to illegally allow them to take the oath would also threaten the survival of Nova Scotia, both at the military level and at the socio-economic level. According to Belcher, the Acadians had behaved since the Treaty of Utrecht in an unsubmissive manner, and, with the help of the Mi'kmaq who were allied with the French, had consistently plotted against the British Crown. Having acted with "perfidy and treacheries" in the past, the Chief Justice argued that they could only act in the same way in the future. Moreover, not deporting them would mean refusing to take advantage of the fall of Beauséjour, these advantages being the weakening of the "Sauvages'" power and of the repression of the insolence of the French inhabitants. To this military threat was coupled a socio-economic one. Belcher considered that the "surplus" of French inhabitants in the colony (5,000 more Acadians than settlers of British descent) would compromise the effective settlement of the colony. For him, the overall threat that they represented forced the British inhabitants to live in fortified burghs, thereby preventing them from cultivating land and earning their living—thus supporting Édouard Richard's economic interpretation of the deportation referred to above.

After having given the law's formal sanction to the deportation of the Acadians in his capacity as Chief Justice of Nova Scotia, Jonathan Belcher was later appointed lieutenant governor of Nova Scotia and dutifully carried out the last segments of the deportation policy up to 1762. However, Chief Justice Belcher's opinion did not end the law's role, or his own, in the deportation. Despite his legal opinion and assurances received from colonial authorities, the new British owners of the lands confiscated from the Acadians legitimately feared what would happen if the former Acadian owners of their lands were to return to Nova Scotia and challenge their successors' title to these lands. To alleviate these fears, Belcher, acting as a member of the legislative assembly of Nova Scotia, tabled a bill entitled an *Act for the Quieting of Possessions to the Protestant Grantees of the Lands formerly occupied by the French Inhabitants, and for preventing vexatious Actions relating to the same*, which was eventually adopted as SNS 1758-1759, 30 Geo. II, c. 3. The Bill affirmed that the

> Province of Nova Scotia or Acadie, and the property thereof, *did always of right belong to the Crown of England, both by priority of discovery and ancient possession*, and that no grant of property to any of the lands or territories belonging thereto, is of any validity, or can give the possessor thereof any legal right or title to any part thereof, unless derived from thence. [Emphasis added.]

The preamble was followed by a narrative of the reasons for the deportation, its justification, and the subsequent grant by the Crown of Great Britain of lands formerly "occupied" by Acadians to "settlers" who came to Nova Scotia from New England.

Practically speaking, the Act purported to bar any lawsuit "for the recovery of any of the lands, ... by virtue of any former right, title, claim, interest, or possession of any of the former French inhabitants, or by virtue of any right, title, claim, or interest, holden under or derived from them, by grant, deed, will, or in any other manner whatsoever." The Act literally rewrote the history of Nova Scotia, rendering it uninhabited territory "discovered" by the British, and therefore a colony of settlement and not of conquest. A French presence of 151 years (1604-1755) was symbolically erased by the law—not to mention the Act's attitude toward the Mi'kmaq nation, whose members it refers to as "Indian Savages." This legal rewriting of history was judicially reiterated in the case of *The King v. McLaughlin* (1830), 1 NBR 218. Once Great Britain extended its rule over the entire region after 1763, the territory of Nova Scotia was divided in three different colonies: Nova Scotia; Prince Edward Island, created in 1769; and New Brunswick, created in 1784 after the influx of Loyalists fleeing the American revolution.

How would you characterize the law's role in the deportation of Acadians? What is or ought to be the present constitutional status of the Acadians in Canada? Was the deportation an "act of war" justifiable in the context in which it took place? How would the deportation be characterized by today's standards?

IV. THE EXPANSION AND CONSOLIDATION OF BRITISH NORTH AMERICA: FROM THE CONQUEST OF NEW FRANCE TO THE CONSTITUTIONAL ACT, 1791

In September of 1759, an event of extraordinary historical importance took place in the capital of New France, Quebec. That event, which lasted only a few minutes, was a battle that opposed British and French troops in a field known as the Plains of Abraham. The outcome of that battle changed Canada forever, as the British forces prevailed over the French. The following year, the city of Montreal also capitulated to the British. The days of New France were over.

The 1759 Articles of Capitulation of Quebec provided that "the inhabitants shall be preserved in the possession of their houses, goods, effects and privileges" (Article II), and that "the free exercise of the roman religion is granted, likewise safeguards to all religious persons" (Article VI). The 1760 Articles of Capitulation of Montreal granted the continued operation of local French law: "The French and Canadians shall continue to be governed according to the custom of Paris, and the laws and usages established for this country" (Article XLII). As regards Aboriginal nations who may have joined with the French against the English, the 1760 Articles provided that "The Savages of Indian allies of his Most Christian Majesty, shall be maintained in the lands they inhabit, if they chuse to remain there; they shall not be molested on any pretence whatsoever, for having carried arms, and served his most Christian Majesty; they shall have, as well as the French, liberty of religion, and shall have their missionaries" (Article XL). (A. Shortt and A.G. Doughty, *Documents Relating to the Constitutional History of Canada*, 2d and rev. ed., part I (Ottawa: King's Printer, 1918), at 5-6, 33-34.)

This state of affairs was confirmed in 1763 with the Treaty of Paris that ended the seven-year war between Great Britain and France. Article IV of the Treaty of Paris similarly provided that: "His Britannick Majesty, on his side, agrees to grant the liberty of the Catholick religion to the inhabitants of Canada: he will, in consequence, give the most precise and effectual orders, that his new Roman Catholick subjects may profess the worship of their religion according to the rites of the Romish church, as far as the laws of Great Britain permit." (Shortt and Doughty, *supra*, at 115.) However, at that time, British laws severely restricted the rights of Roman Catholics, who were prohibited from participating in government.

A few months after the Treaty of Paris, the King of Great Britain issued a proclamation establishing a government for the newly conquered colony. It is in that Royal Proclamation of October 3, 1763 (RSC 1985, app. II, no. 1) that the entity called "Quebec" makes its first appearance in a constitutional instrument. Two elements of that Proclamation are worth mentioning here. First, the Proclamation contained a pledge to create a legislative assembly in the province which, together with the Governor and his Council, could make laws, statutes, and ordinances for "the Public Peace, Welfare and good Government of our said Colonies." By making the pledge to establish a general assembly, the King lost the prerogative to legislate for the colony by means of proclamation, that prerogative being divested to Parliament (*Campbell v. Hall*, (1774) Lofft 655, 98 ER 848). Second, British imperial law provided that the laws of a conquered colony were to continue until altered by the conqueror. This was reflected in the Articles of Capitulation of 1759 and 1760, above. The Proclamation overrode this rule and imposed on the colony the laws of England in civil and criminal cases.

The Proclamation also contained a number of provisions concerning Aboriginal peoples, some of which are still relevant today (see, e.g., s. 25 of the *Canadian Charter of Rights and Freedoms*). Among other things, the Proclamation provided that "Nations or Tribes of Indians with whom We are connected, and who live under our Protection, should not be molested or disturbed in the Possession of such Parts of our Dominions and Territories as, not having been ceded or purchased by Us, are reserved to them, or any of them, as their Hunting Grounds," and that "lands and territories not included within the limits of [the governments created under the Royal Proclamation, including that of Quebec], or within the limits of the territory granted to the Hudson's Bay Company ..." be reserved under the King's protection and dominion for the use of the Indians. Not only were these lands reserved, but they could not be purchased or settled, or taken by British subjects, without the Crown's consent and prior issuance of a licence. Practically, that meant that the Crown alone possessed the initial right to acquire these lands.

With respect to Quebec, the Proclamation introduced the British "Test Oath," which forced Roman Catholics to abjure central tenets of their faith if they wanted to participate in government. As well, the King imposed English laws in all matters. The imposition of laws unknown to the inhabitants of the colony soon proved to be counter-productive, especially in civil and commercial matters. Here is what Governor Guy Carleton had to say about that issue in 1767:

> [L]aws, ill adapted to the Genius of the Canadians, to the situation of the Province, and to the Interests of Great Britain, unknown, and unpublished were introduced to their Stead; A Sort of Severity, if I remember right, never before practiced by any Conqueror, even where the People, without Capitulation, submitted to His Will and Discretion. How far this Change of Laws, which Deprives such Numbers of their Honors, Privileges, Profits, and Property, is conformable to the Capitulation of Montreal, and Treaty of Paris; How far this Ordinance, which affects the Life, Limb, Liberty, and Property of the Subject, is within the Limits of the Power His Majesty has been pleased to Grant to the Governor and Council; How far this Ordinance, which in a Summary Way, Declares the Supreme Court of Judicature shall Judge all Cases Civil and Criminal

by Laws unknown and unpublished to the People, is agreeable to the natural Rights of Man-
kind, I humbly submit; This much is certain, that it cannot long remain in Force, without a
General Confusion and Discontent. [Letter by Guy Carleton to Lord Shelburne, in Shortt and
Doughty, *supra*, at 289-90.]

Carleton noted the resilience of French law despite a few years under another legal system:
"[t]he people notwithstanding continue to regulate their Transactions by Their Ancient
Laws, tho' unknown and unauthorised in the Supreme Court, where most of these Transactions would be declared Invalid" (letter by Guy Carleton to Lord Shelburne, *supra*).

The Proclamation's prohibition of the taking of Indian lands angered American settlers,
as it was perceived as unjustly inhibiting the progress and the expansion of these colonies.
Some have argued that this prohibition played a role in fuelling revolutionary sentiments in
the American colonies. Resentment increased after the enactment in 1774 of the *Quebec Act*
(RSC 1985, app. II, no. 1), which extended the territory of Quebec well beyond the St. Lawrence Valley, that is, up to the Ohio Valley. As a result, the American colonies became effectively surrounded, which was seen as an affront to their settlers.

The *Quebec Act* also restored French laws, referred to as the "Laws of Canada," in "all Matters of Controversy, relative to Property and Civil Rights." In matters respecting the criminal
law, because the "Certainty and Lenity of the Criminal Law of England, and the Benefits and
Advantages resulting from the Use of it, have been sensibly felt by the Inhabitants, from an
Experience of more than Nine Years during which it has been uniformly administered ... the
same shall continue to be administered and shall be observed as the Law in the Province of
Quebec." The pleadings of Guy Carleton, supported by petitions from the "Canadiens," had
prevailed over the counter-petitions of the British merchants based in Canada and of the Attorney General of the Province, all of whom opposed restoration of French civil law. While
the Act heralded the return of the civilian tradition in Canada, it is also notable for its repeal
of the requirement that all persons appointed to the council of the colony take an oath in
which they abjure the dogma of transubstantiation. In practice, that requirement, based on
imperial public law introduced in the colony, prevented all Catholics and, consequently,
most of the French inhabitants, from taking part in the administration of the colony.

The *Quebec Act* was enacted at a crucial moment. It constitutes one of the most important
moments in Canada's constitutional history not only for what it actually accomplished, but
also because of what it provoked. First, as it was seen as an affront to American colonists, it
contributed to the American Revolution. In turn, this event led to the exodus of numerous
loyalists to Nova Scotia and Quebec, forever changing the visage of these colonies, especially
of the latter. From a colony inhabited by an essentially French Catholic population ruled by
an English Protestant minority, the colony of Quebec became a locus of religious, ethnic,
and linguistic competition. Second, the *Quebec Act* did not provide for the creation of a
legislative assembly, despite the pledge made by the King in 1763. This became a major concern after the emigration of American loyalists to Canada in the aftermath of the revolution.
Indeed, all the British colonies from which they had emigrated had legislative assemblies at
the end of the seventeenth century. The absence of such was cruelly resented from the moment they arrived in Canada.

Changes in the socio-demographic composition of the population of the province of
Quebec, as well as pressures for the creation of a legislative assembly, thus paved the way for

a major constitutional change, which came about with the *Constitutional Act, 1791* (RSC 1985, app. II, no. 3). The two main features of the *Constitutional Act, 1791* were the division of Quebec into two distinct provinces, and the creation of legislative assemblies for both provinces. The province of Quebec was divided into Upper Canada, located west of the Ottawa River and north of Lake Ontario, where most of the Anglo-Protestant Loyalists had settled, and Lower Canada, where the huge majority of the population remained Franco-Catholic. Both provinces were granted a legislative assembly, the members of which were to be elected by the population, and a legislative council, the members of which were appointed. The creation of these legislative assemblies, twenty-eight years after the pledge made by the King in the Royal Proclamation of 1763, heralded the beginning of an era marked by a quest for self-government.

V. TROUBLES IN THE COLONIES: THE QUEST FOR SELF-GOVERNMENT, THE REBELLIONS, AND THE UNION ACT OF 1840

Conflicts between the legislative assemblies and the legislative councils erupted in both Canadas soon after the enactment of the *Constitutional Act, 1791*. Laws voted by the legislative assemblies were opposed by the legislative councils, monies appropriated for certain purposes by the assemblies were spent for other purposes by the councils, and members of the councils constantly placed themselves in conflicts of interest. In sum, the executive branch of the state was completely unaccountable to the legislative branch and could systematically disregard its will. As well, there was no separation between the judiciary and the executive branches of government, with judges commonly being appointed to the legislative council.

The problems were roughly the same in both Canadas. But the specific linguistic and religious fabric of Lower Canada increased the acrimony between the legislative council, essentially composed of English Protestants, and the legislative assembly, where the majority of members were French Catholics. The quest for self-government and for responsible government, and the particular problem that was posed by the existence in Lower Canada of a French-speaking majority that perceived itself as forming a "Canadian nation," led some members of the British colonial elite to entertain ideas about the union of the Canadas. According to them, such a union would have reinforced the power of the executive, strengthened London's grip over the colony, eased the defence of the colonies (which were potential military targets for the United States), eliminated the inconvenience of having to deal with an assembly controlled by a majority of French speakers, and, ultimately, facilitated the assimilation of the French population of Lower Canada. While such projects, proposed in the early decades of the nineteenth century, did not immediately materialize, petitions in favour of responsible government emanating from both Canadas remained ignored by London. This led to a radicalization of the democrats in the two colonies, who were already influenced by republican ideas coming from the United States and, to a lesser extent, from France. London's insensitivity to their demands eventually led to armed rebellions in the two colonies in 1837-38, which were crushed, with particular ferocity in Lower Canada, by the British army.

Even though republican ideas enjoyed some popularity in both Canadas, they never appealed to a large enough segment of the population to significantly put in question British rule. The situation was once again more complex in Lower Canada, where the Catholic clergy, well aware of the anti-clerical tone of republicanism in France, took every possible step to ensure that the French population became immunized against the "corruption of liberalism" and submitted to the British Crown. That the overall population lent little concrete support to the rebellion movements led by Mackenzie in Upper Canada and by Papineau in Lower Canada seems to be evidence of a relatively weak penetration of the republican creed beyond a certain intellectual elite. This is not to say, however, that the larger population in both colonies did not support the principle of responsible government.

In the aftermath of the rebellions, Lord Durham was sent to Canada to examine the situation and to report to the Colonial Office and the Imperial Parliament. After five months in Canada, he tabled a report in which he proposed the legislative union of the two Canadas and the institution of responsible government. Durham acknowledged the existence of a Canadian nationality at the core of which were the French language and the Catholic religion. But he also saw in it the source of an irresolvable clash of "races" as well as an obstacle to the progress of a truly British colony. Given Anglo-Saxons' "superior knowledge, energy, enterprise and wealth," it was a "vain endeavour to preserve a French-Canadian nationality in the midst of Anglo-American colonies and states" (*The Report of the Earl of Durham* (London: Methuen 1902), at 169). Having characterized the French inhabitants of Lower Canada as members of an inferior race, he recommended the erasure of their nationality, not only through informal means such as an increased British immigration, but also through formal means such as a legislative union where the British citizens would eventually form the majority. This new majority would be largely unfettered. "The colonists may not always know what laws are best for them, or which of their countrymen are the fittest for conducting their affairs; but at least they have a greater interest in coming to a right judgment on these points, and will take greater pains to do so." Durham therefore recommended that "internal government of the colony" be placed "in the hands of the colonists themselves" save for the money bills, which would originate with the executive council, and a few other matters that "affect their relations with the mother country" (*Durham Report, supra*, at 169 and 181). On the political and constitutional theory underlying Durham's report, see Janet Ajzenstat, *The Political Thought of Lord Durham* (Montreal and Kingston: McGill-Queen's University Press, 1988).

Responding in part to Durham's suggestions, in 1840 the Imperial Parliament passed the *Union Act* (RSC 1985, app. II, no. 4), which united Lower and Upper Canada into a new entity called United Canada. Going beyond what Lord Durham had asked for, the *Union Act, 1840* provided that the parliamentary representation of Upper Canada (now Canada-West) and Lower Canada (now Canada-East) would be equal, in violation of the democratic principle of representation by population. (In 1840, the population of Canada-East was still higher than that of Canada-West.) Moreover, the *Union Act* merged the public debts of the former Upper and Lower Canadas, despite the fact that the debt of the former was much higher than that of the latter. The Act also declared English as the sole language of the legislative assembly, a provision that soon proved to be practically unenforceable. However, the civil law tradition continued to prevail in Canada-East, at least in matters of private law. Furthermore, the legislative council of the new province of Canada remained unelected and, contrary to what Durham had proposed, responsible government was not instituted. It was granted only in 1846. Fiercely opposed in Lower Canada, the unitary regime instituted by the *Union Act* soon proved to be extremely difficult to administer, as ethnic and religious disputes were reinforced by economic rivalries between Canada-East and Canada-West.

VI. CONFEDERATION

The failure of the *Union Act, 1840* was only one of the many complex factors that led to the proposal that the British North American colonies form a confederation, a proposal that became a reality with the enactment of the *British North America Act, 1867* (RSC 1985, app. II, no. 5). The first excerpt below describes the circumstances leading up to Confederation, as well as some of the strategic and economic factors at play. The next reading examines the reactions of French-Canadians to the proposed confederation.

G. Stevenson, *Unfulfilled Union*
5th ed. (Toronto: Gage Publishing, 1989), at 22-33 (footnotes omitted)

The event we call "Confederation" arose from a convergence of internal and external circumstances, and probably no single factor can explain it. Its complexity is enhanced by the fact that it simultaneously did three things, none of which would have been possible without the others. It reorganized the internal government of "Canada" in the pre-Confederation sense of Ontario and Quebec; it united this entity with New Brunswick and Nova Scotia; and it provided for the expansion of the federalized state westward to the Pacific. In the process of doing so it paved the way for economic development, and ended a potentially dangerous power vacuum in the northern part of North America.

The Internal Difficulties of the Province of Canada

On the recommendation of Lord Durham's report, the Province of Canada was established in 1841 by uniting the two colonies of Lower and Upper Canada. The distinction between the civil law of the lower province and the common law of the upper one was retained. Also, despite a brief attempt to impose unilingualism (one of Durham's recommendations), the status of the French language was eventually recognized. At about the same time, the principle was established that the government was dependent on the confidence and support of the elected lower house of the legislature.

In spite of these developments, the governing of both English-speaking and French-speaking Canadians within a unitary or at least a quasi-unitary state proved difficult, and discontent increased on both sides. ...

Each section of the province harboured the belief that it was being constrained and dictated to by the other. Since they were of roughly equal size and had equal representation in Parliament, such a belief was equally plausible on both sides. Once the western half became the more populous, its residents found the equal representation of the two sections to be an intolerable affront to liberal principles, although the injustice of it had somehow managed to escape their notice when they were a minority.

Ethnic and religious antagonisms were exacerbated by many of the issues which came before the legislature, and were reinforced by divergences of economic interest between the sections. Farmers and businessmen in the western part of the province, like their counterparts in the larger western hinterland of a later date, resented the commercial hegemony of Montreal and the measures that were taken with the aim of funneling their commerce through that city.

For all of these reasons it became increasingly difficult to construct governments that could retain the confidence of the lower house. By about 1857 things were widely believed to be approaching an impasse, and the territorial expansion of Canada began to be viewed as a possible means of escape from its difficulties, although this probably would not have been considered had not economic motives (which will be considered subsequently) pointed in the same direction. Expansion might be either eastward, to include the other British colonies on the Atlantic seaboard, or westward, to absorb the inland fur-trading empire of the Hudson's Bay Company, with each half of the Province of Canada tending to prefer the alternative that corresponded to its own point of the compass. Expansion in both directions at once might satisfy both sections, permit federalism (a separate government for each section with a central government over both) while avoiding the dangers of a double-headed monstrosity, and enable French-speaking Canadians to accept representation by population in the lower house at the same time as the more onerous conventions of the existing system could be safely eliminated.

Strategic and Economic Motives

The change that took place in the new decade was the emergence of an external threat to the security of British North America. …

The threat, of course, came from the United States. British relations with the government in Washington had deteriorated during the American Civil War, a situation for which the British were more to blame than the Americans (and for which the Canadians bore little if any responsibility), but which exposed Canada to the threat of an American invasion in the event of war. By 1864 it was apparent that the industrial North would win the war and incorporate the southern states back into the union, presenting the British Empire with a very powerful and unfriendly opponent. Another source of danger inherent in the outcome of the Civil War was the removal of the controversy over slavery from the agenda of American politics. Previously that controversy had prevented the United States from expanding northward, since to do so would have upset the delicate balance between slave states and free states. This obstacle to the annexation of Canada had now disappeared. Although the British government had discouraged efforts toward Confederation until 1864, it reversed itself in that year for reasons of military defence and security. A united British North America, especially one tied together by railways, would be more defensible and could bear a larger share of the costs of its own defence. In particular, the port of Halifax with its British naval base could be used to send British troops to Canada even when the St. Lawrence was frozen, and without the necessity of crossing American soil.

The American threat also made the need for Confederation more apparent to the colonists themselves, or at least to those who were exposed to it. …

All historians of Confederation have emphasized, and with good reason, the decisive role of capitalist entrepreneurs and their interests in bringing about Confederation.

There were few countervailing interests at a time when the working class was largely dis-enfranchised, the salaried middle class hardly existed, and prominent politicians were directly involved in railways, banks, and insurance companies to an extent that would seem scandalous today. Confederation was no different from contemporaneous nation-building ventures elsewhere or from the formation of the United States a century before with respect to the decisive role played by the entrepreneurial class. ...

Montreal had been the chief Canadian stronghold of merchant capital in the heyday of British mercantilism before 1849, and it was still the largest city and leading economic centre, as it remained for some time. The Bank of Montreal was the dominant financial institution and included the government of the Province of Canada among its customers. The Montreal bourgeoisie, and their political spokesmen, like Galt and Cartier, were particularly interested in uniting with the Maritimes and building the Intercolonial Rail-way, which would funnel more trade through their city.

Toronto, although then much smaller than Montreal, was rising rapidly as an eco-nomic centre. Its importance in the Confederation movement has been emphasized by J.M.S. Careless in his biography of George Brown. A number of Toronto businessmen, including Brown, had recently organized the Bank of Commerce as a counterweight to the Bank of Montreal. Manufacturing was also developing in and around the city and the production of railway locomotives in Toronto had begun as early as 1853, long before it began in most European countries. Toronto businessmen had little interest in the Mari-times, but looked with increasing enthusiasm toward the West, which they viewed as potentially a vast extension of Toronto's agricultural hinterland in Upper Canada. ...

This complex of interests was tied together by the Great Coalition of 1864. George Brown, the spokesman for Toronto business, joined forces with John A. Macdonald, whose political allies included Cartier and Galt, the spokesmen for Montreal business. Brown accepted expansion to the east, Cartier accepted expansion to the west, and Mac-donald accepted federalism, despite serious reservations (even though he had been a long-time supporter of uniting the colonies). Macdonald's preference for a unitary state, which he called a "legislative union," was consistent with his relative detachment from specifically regional interests, part of the secret of his political success. However, a federal union was the only kind that could possibly be acceptable to French Canadians or Mari-timers, and Brown shrewdly understood that a federal state would be "capable of gradual and efficient expansion in future years." The United States had convincingly demonstrat-ed that federalism was ideally suited to facilitate the westward course of empire. ...

An additional economic motive for Confederation, which the Maritimes shared with the Province of Canada, was provided by the expectation that the United States would terminate its reciprocal trade agreement with the colonies, as it actually did in 1866. This forced all the colonies to reorient their trade on an east-west rather than a north-south basis. It threatened to end the arrangements by which Canada had used American sea-ports for its trade with Britain during the winter months. It also meant that Maritime fishermen could no longer fish in American waters, and would need help to defend their own waters from American encroachments. ...

The Terms of Union

The terms of what became Canada's constitution reflected both the diversity of interests and motives behind Confederation and the ideological preferences of the colonial politicians who attended the conferences at Quebec in 1865 and London in 1866. Prominent among these motives were enthusiasm for "a Constitution similar in Principle to that of the United Kingdom," a phrase which appears in the preamble to the *British North America Act*, and a desire to avoid what were considered the undesirable aspects of the American constitution. John A. Macdonald in particular was obsessed with the belief, a somewhat superficial one for a man so shrewd in other respects, that the American Civil War might have been avoided if the American constitution had granted only limited and specified powers to the individual states, rather than leaving them with all powers not granted to the federal government. He acknowledged that the political circumstances in 1787 had probably left the Americans with no alternative, but he was determined to avoid the same mistake himself.

Fortunately for Macdonald, circumstances were more propitious for him than they had been for Alexander Hamilton, whose views on federalism and on other political subjects had been very similar to his own. The forces of agrarian radicalism were much weaker in British North America than they had been in the thirteen colonies, and their political representatives, being on the opposition benches, were excluded from the conferences that drafted Canada's constitution. Canada also lacked any equivalent of the southern plantation owners, who had opposed the centralization desired by the Federalist merchants. In addition, there were no vested interests attached to provincial autonomy in what became Ontario and Quebec, since the governments of those provinces did not exist between 1841 and 1867. It was both easy and logical to give specifically defined powers to those governments which were to be established, while leaving the general, unspecified, or "residual" power with the government that already existed, that of Canada.

Only in the Maritimes did Macdonald have to deal with already existing governments that would have to be enticed into accepting a completely new level of government superior to themselves. Even there he was aided by discreet pressure from London and the fact that some of the Maritimers, like Charles Tupper, shared his preference for a centralized regime. The chief concerns of the Maritime delegates at the conferences were provincial revenues and representation in the Senate, rather than the division of legislative powers. The demands for provincial legislative powers came mainly from the French Canadians, for whom the establishment of a Quebec legislature was the major attraction of Confederation. The powers which they demanded for that legislature were mainly related to social institutions, education, the family, and the legal system. Even the celebrated provincial jurisdiction over "property and civil rights," expressly designed to protect Quebec's legal system by repeating a phrase first used in the *Quebec Act* of 1774, at first included the qualifying phrase "excepting portions thereof assigned to the General Parliament." These words were removed at the last moment by the British Colonial Office.

The stated preference for "a Constitution similar in Principle to that of the United Kingdom" combined a widely shared sentiment with more pragmatic and mundane considerations. Access to British capital and markets was essential to the economic objectives of Confederation, and British assistance would be needed to defend Canada against the United States. A firm assertion of loyalty to British principles might encourage pro-Canadian sentiments in the United Kingdom, where they were not particularly strong. Many influential people in the United Kingdom believed that the colonies were economically worthless and a source of friction with the United States, and that they should be encouraged to sever their connection with Britain.

British principles also had certain implications for the constitution itself. Monarchy, which is based on the principle that political authority flows from the top downward, had never before been combined with federalism, and in a sense they were logically incompatible. However, it suited the kind of union that Macdonald and most of his colleagues wanted to create. Ottawa would be subordinate to London and the provinces would be subordinate to Ottawa, with a British governor general in Ottawa and a federally appointed lieutenant-governor in each province, each of whom would have the power to "reserve" legislation for the final decision of the government that had appointed him. Both London and Ottawa could disallow the acts of the level of government immediately below them, even though such acts had received the assent of the governor general or lieutenant-governor. The judicial system revealed similar hierarchical notions. Ottawa would appoint the judges of the provincial courts, and it was understood, although not stated, that the final court of appeal would be the Judicial Committee of the (Imperial) Privy Council, which already exercised that function for all of the colonies.

The heart of any federal constitution is the division of legislative powers. In the Quebec and London resolutions, and in the *BNA Act* (which followed their provisions quite closely), powers were allocated so that the central government could carry out the major objectives of Confederation. For reasons already referred to, Parliament was given all legislative powers not specifically assigned to the provincial legislatures. The Quebec Resolutions described this as a power to make laws for "the peace, welfare, and good government of Canada," consciously or unconsciously recalling the "general welfare" clause of the United States constitution. Regrettably, the Colonial Office later changed this to "Peace, Order, and good Government," contributing to a lasting myth that the Fathers of Confederation were less "liberal," whatever that may mean, than their American counterparts.

The federal government was given unlimited power to tax and borrow, the latter being particularly important at a time when colonial governments depended on the London bond market. Tariff and commercial policy would also be under its control, as would the banking system and the currency, the postal service, weights and measures, and patents and copyrights. Jurisdiction over agriculture (and immigration) was shared with the provinces, while, at the London Conference, fisheries were placed under federal jurisdiction, for reasons already discussed. For the sake of uniformity the criminal law was placed under federal control, a departure from American practice that perhaps reflected Macdonald's experience as a defence counsel in criminal cases.

The provisions for transportation, an essential part of the economics of Confederation, were complex. The federal government was given jurisdiction over navigation and shipping, and was also required to begin building the Intercolonial Railway within six months of the union and to complete it as quickly as possible. Macdonald originally proposed to list all the means of interprovincial communication that were placed under federal authority, but roads and bridges were excluded at the suggestion of Leonard Tilley, the Premier of New Brunswick. This still left the federal government with steamships, railways, canals, telegraphs, and other works and undertakings connecting two or more provinces, and with steamships connecting Canada with other countries. Parliament could also assume jurisdiction over "works" entirely within one province by declaring them to be for the general advantage of Canada. In the legislative debates on the Quebec Resolutions, Macdonald cited the Welland Canal between Lake Erie and Lake Ontario as an example of the "works" that would fall under this provision.

The provinces were given responsibility for the administration of justice, apart from criminal procedure, and the organization of the courts. They would also be responsible for municipal institutions, which were well developed in the Province of Canada although not in the Maritimes. The enumerated provincial responsibilities included those matters which were then viewed as defining the distinctiveness of French Canada: education, the family, social institutions, and the law relating to "property and civil rights." The prospect of provincial control over such matters was welcomed by the French Canadian clergy, who undoubtedly foresaw that they would be able to exercise considerable influence over Quebec's provincial legislature. Religious minorities whose rights to separate educational systems were already assured "by law," would be protected from provincial interference with those rights. This provision protected the Protestant anglophones of Quebec and the Roman Catholics—mainly Irish at that time—of Ontario. Its applicability elsewhere was less clear; a few years after Confederation, New Brunswick succeeded in abolishing its Roman Catholic separate school system on the grounds that the latter existed only by custom, and not by law.

The provincial governments were given certain powers over economic matters, which proved important later on. They shared jurisdiction over agriculture with the federal government, could borrow on their own credit, could incorporate companies "for provincial objects," and controlled roads, bridges, and whatever other "works" were not under federal jurisdiction.

The provinces were also given ownership of natural resources and the power to legislate concerning the public lands and the timber on those lands. With hindsight these provisions would appear to have been seriously mistaken, if the intention was to ensure the preponderance of the federal government. However, mineral resources, apart from Nova Scotia's coal, were then of little importance, and the timber trade, which had dominated British America for fifty years, was declining by the 1860s, the victim both of its own failure to conserve the resource on which it was based and of British and American actions that restricted its access to markets.

The fact that provincial powers and revenues were, by design, so closely associated with this declining industry may explain Macdonald's confident belief that the provincial level of government would also decline in importance. The future apparently belonged to agriculture, commerce, manufacturing, and the opening of the West, all of which would be mainly or exclusively under federal jurisdiction. …

The terms of union clearly embodied a very centralist concept of federalism, which was perpetuated after 1867 when most of the politicians who had drafted the terms pursued their careers at the federal level, where they dominated Canadian politics for some time. The chief among them, of course, was John A. Macdonald, the principal author of the Quebec Resolutions and the *BNA Act*. As Prime Minister from 1867 until 1873, and again from 1878 until his death in 1891, Macdonald continued to expound the views that had inspired his constitutional draftsmanship, while at the same time he attempted to put them into practice. The Macdonaldian version of federalism, although it was increasingly challenged in the last years of Macdonald's life, thus enjoyed a more or less official status at the outset.

Macdonald was well aware, as was every other knowledgeable observer of Canadian life, that the new Dominion was a fragile and artificial creation whose impressive constitutional facade contrasted with a very limited degree of social and economic integration. He did not, however, consider the diversity of Canadian society and the persistence of local attachments to be an argument in favour of political decentralization. On the contrary, it was precisely these circumstances that made a strong central government essential. As a Hamiltonian conservative, Macdonald believed that the state could and should play an autonomous and creative role, rather than merely reflecting the social diversity that lay beneath it.

A. Silver, *The French-Canadian Idea of Confederation, 1864-1900*
(Toronto: University of Toronto Press, 1982), at 33-50 (footnotes omitted)

When French Lower Canadians were called on to judge the proposed confederation of British North American provinces, the first thing they wanted to know was what effect it would have on their own nationality. Before deciding whether or not they approved, they wanted to hear "what guarantees will be offered for the future of the French-Canadian nationality, to which we are attached above all else." ... [C]oncern for the French-Canadian nationality had geographical implications, ... Canadians in the 1860s generally considered French Canada and Lower Canada to be equivalent. When French Canadians spoke of their *patrie*, their homeland, they were invariably referring to Quebec. Even the word *Canada*, as they used it, usually referred to the lower province, or, even more specifically, to the valley of the St. Lawrence, that ancient home of French civilization in America, whose special status went back to the seventeenth century. ...

Throughout the discussion of Confederation, between 1864 and 1867, there ran the assumption that French Canada was a geographical as well as an ethnic entity, forming, as the *Revue Canadienne* pointed out optimistically, "the most considerable, the most homogeneous, and the most regularly constituted population group" in the whole Confederation. ...

It followed from this question that provincial autonomy was to be sought in the proposed constitution as a key safeguard of the interests of French Canada. "We must never forget," asserted the *Gazette de Sorel*, "that French Canadians need more reassurance than the other provinces for their civil and religious immunities. ..." But since French Canada was a province, its immunities were to be protected by provincial autonomy; hence, "this point is important above all for Lower Canada. ..."

On this key issue, French Canadians felt themselves to have different interests from those of other British North Americans. Thus, Cartier's organ [Cartier's newspaper, *La Minerve*]:

> The English ... have nothing to fear from the central government, and their first concern is
> to ensure its proper functioning. This is what they base their hopes upon, and the need for
> strong local governments only takes second place in their minds.
>
> The French press, on the contrary, feels that guarantees for the particular autonomy of
> our nationality must come before all else in the federal constitution. It sees the whole system
> as based on these very guarantees. ...

A confederation would be a fine thing, but only "if it limited as much as possible the rights of the federal government, to general matters, and left complete independence to the local governments." ...

While most papers did not go so far as to support the provincial sovereignty which that last implied, they did opt for co-ordinate sovereignty:

> The federal power will be sovereign, no doubt, but it will have power only over certain gen-
> eral questions clearly defined by the constitution.
>
> This is the only plan of confederation which Lower Canada can accept. ... The two levels
> of government must both be sovereign, each within its jurisdiction as clearly defined by the
> constitution.

What, after all, could be simpler than that each power, federal or provincial, should have complete control of its own field?

> Isn't that perfectly possible without having the local legislatures derive their powers from
> the central legislature or vice versa? Isn't it possible for each of these bodies to have perfect
> independence within the scope of its own jurisdiction, neither one being able to invade the
> jurisdiction of the other?

To be sure, the fathers of Confederation were aware that French Canadians would reject complete centralization. John A. Macdonald told the Assembly that though he would have preferred a legislative union, he realized it would be unacceptable to French Canadians. Nevertheless, he felt the Quebec Resolutions did not provide for a real federalism, but would "give to the General Government the strength of a legislative and administrative union." They represented "the happy medium" between a legislative and a federal union, which, while providing guarantees for those who feared the former, would also give "us the strength of a Legislative union." In short, he appeared to understand the Quebec scheme to provide for the closest thing possible to a legislative union, saving certain guarantees for the French Canadians' "language, nationality and religion."

This interpretation was hotly rejected by French Canadians of both parties, including those who spoke for Macdonald's partner, Cartier:

> Whatever guarantees may be offered here, Lower Canada will never consent to allowing its
> particular interests to be regulated by the inhabitants of the other provinces. ... We want a
> solid constitution ... but we demand above all perfect freedom and authority for the prov-
> inces to run their own internal affairs.

Let there be no mistake about it: anything close to a legislative union "cannot and will not be accepted by the French-Canadian population." A centralized union would be fatal to the French-Canadian nationality. The *Courrier de St-Hyacinthe*, in fact, summed up the whole French-Canadian position when it said:

> But whatever guarantees they decide to offer us, we cannot accept any union other than a federal union based on the well-understood principles of confederations.

. . .

There was agreement between Bleus and Rouges [the major political groups] that the autonomy of a French-Canadian Lower Canada was the chief thing to be sought in any new constitution. Accordingly, the Confederation discussion revolved around whether or not the Quebec plan achieved that aim. As far as the opposition was concerned, it did not. The Rouges maintained that this was an "anglicizing bill," the latest in a line of attempts to bring about the "annihilation of the French race in Canada," and thus realize Lord Durham's wicked plans. And it would achieve this goal because it was not really a confederation at all, but a legislative union in disguise, a mere extension of the Union of 1840. "It is in vain," cried C.-S. Cherrier at a Rouge-sponsored rally, "that they try to disguise it under the name of confederation. ... This *quasi* legislative union is just a step toward a complete and absolute legislative union."

. . .

In answering all [the] opposition arguments, the Bleus certainly did not attempt to defend the notion of a strong or dominant central government. But, they maintained, that was not at all what British North America was going to get. Lower Canada, liberated from the forced Union of 1840, would become a distinct and autonomous province in a loose and decentralized Confederation—that was the real truth of the matter.

The defenders of Confederation refuted the opposition's arguments one after another. Did the Rouges speak of Rep by Pop? Why, any schoolboy ought to see the difference between Rep by Pop, which the Bleus had opposed as long as the legislative union remained, and a "confederation which would give us, first of all, local legislatures for the protection of our sectional interests, and then a federal legislature in which the most populous province would have a majority *only in the lower house*." As long as there was only a single legislature for the two Canadas, Rep by Pop would have put "our civil law and religious institutions at the mercy of the fanatics." But Confederation would eliminate that danger by creating a separate province of Quebec with its own distinct government:

> We have a system of government which puts under the exclusive control of Lower Canada those questions which we did not want the fanatical partisans of Mr. Brown to deal with. ...
>
> Since we have this guarantee, what difference does it make to us whether or not Upper Canada has more representatives than we in the Commons? Since the Commons will be concerned only with general questions of interest to all provinces and not at all with the particular affairs of Lower Canada, it's all the same to us, as a nationality, whether or not Upper Canada has more representation.

This was central to the Bleu picture of Confederation: all questions affecting the French-Canadian nationality as such would be dealt with at Quebec City, and Ottawa would be "powerless, if it should want to invade the territory reserved for the administration of the local governments." As for the questions to be dealt with at Ottawa, they might divide men as Liberals and Conservatives, but not as French and English Canadians. "In the [federal] Parliament," said Hector Langevin, "there will be no questions of race, nationality, religion or locality, as this Legislature will only be charged with the settlement of the great general questions which will interest alike the whole Confederacy and not one locality only." Cartier made the same point when he said that "in the questions which will be submitted to the Federal parliament, there will be no more danger to the rights and privileges of the French Canadians than to those of the Scotch, English or Irish." Or, as his organ, *La Minerve*, put it, Ottawa would have jurisdiction only over those matters "in which the interests of everyone, French Canadians, English, or Scotch, are identical." For the rest—for everything which concerned the French Canadians *as* French Canadians— for the protection and promotion of their national interests and institutions, they would have their own province with their own parliament and their own government.

· · ·

[I]n the federal alliance thus formed, Quebec was to be the French-Canadian country, working together with the others on common projects, but always autonomous in the promotion and embodiment of the French-Canadian nationality. "Our ambitions," wrote a Bleu editor, "will not centre on the federal government, but will have their natural focus in our local legislature; this we regard as fundamental for ourselves." This was, no doubt, an exaggerated position, like the statement of de Niverville in the Canadian legislature, but what it exaggerated was the general tendency of the Confederationist propaganda. It underlined the Quebec-centredness of French Canada's approach to Confederation, and the degree to which French Quebec's separateness and autonomy were central to French-Canadian acceptance of the new régime.

Though much the *Constitution Act, 1867* was the product of negotiations between Canadian and Maritime political leadership, once the principal negotiators headed to London to finalize the draft resolutions, the text was altered under the influence of the British Colonial Office. The following extract traces the salient changes to the distribution of legislative power from the initial draft to the final text.

**J. Saywell, *The Lawmakers: Judicial Power and the
Shaping of Canadian Federalism***
(Toronto: Osgoode Society for Canadian Legal History and
University of Toronto Press, 2004), at 4-12 (footnotes omitted)

Although the political reconstruction of the colonies had long been discussed, by 1864 "such was the opposition between the two sections of the province, such was the danger of impending anarchy," said John A. Macdonald, that some solution was imperative. When the ninth ministry in a decade tottered to its fall in the spring of 1864, ancient animosities were set aside as George Brown agreed to a coalition with Macdonald and George-Étienne Cartier, whose purpose was to seek a federal union of all British North America or, that failing, a federal union of the Canadas.

• • •

By the end of August the federal scheme was sufficiently well developed to be placed before the Maritime delegations who coincidentally had gathered at Charlottetown to discuss Maritime union. Press reports suggest that the proposed distribution of legislative powers anticipated the enumerations that would emerge in the Quebec Resolutions. The Canadians were also emphatic that the federal government would possess the residual power. When E.B. Chandler of New Brunswick proposed the reverse at Quebec, Charles Tupper interjected:

> I have heard Mr. Chandler's argument with surprise. Powers undefined must rest somewhere. Those who were at Charlottetown will remember that it was fully specified that all the powers not given to the Local should be reserved to the Federal Government. This was stated as being a prominent feature of the Canadian scheme, and it was said then that it was desirable to have a plan contrary to that adopted by the United States. It was a fundamental principle laid down by Canada and the basis of our deliberations.

Publicly, Macdonald stated in a speech at Halifax after the conference that all the dangers inherent in the American system would be avoided "if we can agree upon forming a strong central government—a great central legislature—a constitution for a Union which will have all the rights of sovereignty except those given to the local governments."

The Maritimers were at least sufficiently intrigued to give further consideration to the Canadian proposal for a broader federal union. For two weeks in October 1864, delegates from the four colonies put the finishing touches on what was essentially a Canadian agreement. Apart from some debate over the location of the residual authority, even the wisdom of adding the enumerations to the federal residual authority, there was surprisingly little discussion about the distribution of legislative jurisdiction. There seemed to be general agreement with the principles Macdonald outlined when the conference opened that the "primary error" in the American constitution must be reversed "by strengthening the General Government and conferring on the provincial bodies only such powers as may be required for local purposes. All sectional prejudices and interests can be legislated by local legislatures" while the minority would be protected "by having a powerful central government." But "great caution" was necessary for "the people of every section must feel they are protected, and by no overstraining of central authority should such guarantees be overridden." The constitution would be based on an imperial act, and "any question as to overriding sectional matters determined by '[i]s it legal or not?' The judicial tribunals of Great Britain would settle any such difficulties should they occur."

What became the first version of sections 91 and 92 of the 1867 constitution emerged in the Quebec Resolutions as follows:

> 29. The General Parliament shall have power to make Laws for the peace, welfare and good Government of the Federated Provinces (saving the Sovereignty of England), and especially Laws respecting the following subjects:—[then followed a list of subjects, numbers 1 through 36, much like those in section 91 and including what became section 94]
>
> 37. And Generally respecting all matters of a general character, not specially and exclusively reserved for the Local Governments and Legislatures.

• • •

43. The Local Legislatures shall have power to make Laws respecting the following subjects [then followed a list similar to that in section 92 and including the following subjects]:

15. Property and civil rights, excepting those portions thereof assigned to the General Parliament.

18. And generally all matters of a private or local nature, not assigned to the General Parliament.

The heads of the two sections are distinct, with the federal government's enumerations unqualified and prefaced by the word "especially" but the tails are identical in providing a home for matters either general or local not otherwise captured by the preceding enumerations and not to be found among those reserved for the other jurisdiction. (The so-called "sovereignty" of the central government apparently was to be found in the head with the traditional enacting clause in which the imperial government had conveyed legislative power to colonial legislatures, although Macdonald seemed to find it in the tail or more generally in the breadth and importance of federal jurisdiction.)

The debate on the Quebec Resolutions in the Canadian Legislative Assembly in 1865 casts less light than shadow on precisely what had been accomplished, perhaps because amendments were prohibited: it was all or nothing. Macdonald maintained that the federal government had "all the great subjects of legislation. We have conferred on them, not only specifically and in detail, all the powers which are incident to sovereignty, but we have expressly declared that all subjects of general interest not distinctly and exclusively conferred upon the local governments and local legislatures, shall be conferred upon the General Government and Legislature." The 37th subsection, he added, "confers on the General Legislature the general mass of sovereign legislation … This is precisely the provision which is wanting in the Constitution of the United States."

Although Macdonald maintained that they had "avoided all conflict of jurisdiction and authority," Christopher Dunkin found the opposite: "Do we follow the American example, and give so much to the Union and the rest to the provinces; or so much to them, and the rest to it? Either rule would be plain; but this plan follows neither. It simply gives a sort of special list for each; making much common to both, and as to much more, not showing what belongs to either." Antoine-Aimé Dorion concluded that federal jurisdiction was not limited by the 29th section and there was "not a word in these resolutions" to prevent the federal government from legislating within provincial jurisdiction "because all the sovereignty is vested in the General Government, and there is no authority to define its functions and attributes and those of the local governments.

It remained for Joseph Cauchon to lecture Dorion, the future chief justice of Quebec, as well as Macdonald, on the nature of sovereignty in the new federation. If sovereignty existed, "it must be in the Constitution. If it is not to be found there, it is because it does not exist." In the proposed federation "there will be no absolute sovereign power, each legislature having its distinct and independent attributes, not proceeding from one to the other by delegation, either from above or from below. The Federal Parliament will have legislative sovereign power in all questions submitted to its control in the Constitution. So also the local legislatures will be sovereign in all matters which are specially assigned to them." And, as in the United States, disputes between them would be settled by the courts.

After six weeks of partisan debate in February and March 1865, the Quebec Resolutions were approved by a vote of forty-five to fifteen in the Legislative Council and ninety-one to thirty-three in the Assembly. It was not until December 1866, however, that the delegates from Canada, New Brunswick, and Nova Scotia were able to meet in London to draft the final resolutions for submission to the imperial government. On Boxing Day 1866, after three weeks of work and play, but with the Quebec Resolutions virtually unchanged, Macdonald sent the London Resolutions to Lord Carnarvon, the colonial secretary, to be embodied in an act creating the Canadian federation.

From the outset, the Colonial Office, the *Times*, the *Edinburgh Review*, and the *Economist* were sharply critical of the proposed federation. What Canada needed, they agreed, was, if not a legislative union, at least a highly centralized federation. "The hinge of the whole matter is, I think, this: Has the Central Power complete control over the Local Powers?" wrote Edward Cardwell, the colonial secretary, on receipt of the Quebec Resolutions. "If not," he privately warned the governor general, "anarchy is to be apprehended as the result, sooner or later." Assuming that Quebec was the obstacle to a more complete "fusion," he wondered whether it was not "possible to recognize more pointedly the difficulty about Lower Canada: and to provide in more express terms for the autonomy of the French population in all such respects as the Union with Scotland provided for the independence of Worship, Tribunal etc etc." Cardwell continued to believe that "Lower Canada would have a better guarantee, & not a worse, for her specialities if they are specifically enacted in the new Constitution Act: and the general scheme would be free from the numerous imperfections, which at present attach to it."

The greatest imperfection was provincial jurisdiction over property and civil rights. As discussion on the drafts began late in January 1867, Cartier and Hector Langevin were summoned to a meeting to face Lord Carnarvon, the new colonial secretary, Lord Monck, the governor general, and senior officials of the Colonial Office in a futile attempt to get them to agree to some special guarantees for their distinct society, presumably in return for some weakening of provincial jurisdiction over property and civil rights (or conceivably even its removal from the provincial enumerations). As Langevin wrote to his wife: "L'effort est fait, la victoire nous reste." All that remained was the diplomacy of drafting.

Shortly after receiving the Quebec Resolutions, Cardwell had set Sir Francis Reilly, "our best draughtsman," to work on a bill. Reilly was instructed to "get rid of some of the ambiguities" and was unquestionably made aware that Cardwell and the cabinet wanted "the Local Legislatures to dwindle down towards the Municipal as much as possible." Lord Carnarvon, who succeeded Cardwell in the summer of 1866, informed Cardwell (and certainly Reilly) that "my foremost object wd. be to strengthen, as far as is practicable, the central govt. against the exclusive power or encroachments of the local administration." Reilly had completed most of his first draft before the London Conference began in December 1866.

Reilly radically altered the structure of what became section 91. At its head he placed the now familiar enacting clause, an unambiguous assertion of residual legislative jurisdiction:

It shall be lawful for Her Majesty, Her Heirs and Successors, by and with the Advice and Consent of the Houses of Parliament of the United Colony, to make laws for the Peace,

Order and good Government of the United Colony and of the several Provinces, in relation
to all Matters not coming within the Classes of Subjects by this Act assigned exclusively to
Provincial Legislation.

He followed this with a declaratory clause:

and for greater Certainty, but not so as to restrict the Generality of the foregoing Terms of
this Section, it is hereby declared that the Legislative Authority of the Parliament of the
United Colony extends to all Matters coming within the Classes of Subjects next hereinafter
enumerated; that is to say …

The federal enumerations remained largely as they were in the resolutions. However,
Reilly made two significant changes in the provincial enumerations. He removed the limitation on "property and civil rights"—"excepting those portions thereof assigned to the
General Parliament" (which had been in the resolutions)—and completely eliminated
the enumeration "matters of a local or private nature." Obviously well aware of the enormous potential of the breadth of property and civil rights with the qualification removed,
Reilly added a very emphatic deeming clause at the end of what became section 91:

And any Matter coming within any of the Classes of Subjects enumerated in this Section
shall not be deemed to come within the Subject of Property and Civil Rights comprised in
the enumeration of the Classes of Subjects by this Act assigned exclusively to Provincial
Legislation.

After receiving the London Resolutions, Reilly touched up his draft and sent it to Carnarvon on 17 January 1867.

For two weeks, draft followed draft. "The difficulties, the suggestions, the amendments during the last week have been endless," Carnarvon informed the prime minister
on 6 February. Three days later, the draughtsmen, Reilly and the colonial attorneys general, finished what Sir Joseph Pope called the "final draft." The enacting and declaratory
clauses remained as in Reilly's draft; the deeming clause, which had been in and out, was
in to protect against an interpretation of property and civil rights which could encroach
on the federal enumerations; and matters "local and private," which had been in and out,
was out. However, it was not until six o'clock on 12 February, when Carnarvon moved
first reading in the House of Lords, that the real final draft was completed. "Oh! Si tu
savais, si tu savais," Langevin exclaimed to his brother when the bill finally went to Parliament, for it had been necessary to "y revoir, y revoir encore, et puis revoir quand d'autres
y avaient vu ou y avaient mis la main."

In the three days after 9 February, three unquestionably interrelated changes were
made to sections 91 and 92. Provincial jurisdiction over "generally matters of a merely
local and private nature" had reappeared without the qualification in the Quebec and
London resolutions but with the addition of the word "merely." Provincial jurisdiction
over property and civil rights was listed without qualification. There were, however, two
critically important additions and alterations in section 91. The exclusivity and paramountcy of the federal enumerations had been reinforced in the declaratory clause by
the addition of italicized words:

> ... and for greater certainty, but not so as to restrict the Generality of the foregoing Terms of this Section, it is hereby declared that (*notwithstanding anything in this Act*) the exclusive Legislative Authority of the Parliament of Canada extends to all Matters coming within the Classes of Subjects next hereinafter enumerated ...

The second was an alteration in the application of the deeming clause, which had previously been used to protect against property and civil rights. The draftsmen obviously believed that the reinforced declaratory clause adequately protected all federal enumerations against all provincial enumerations, including property and civil rights. Although it may not have been necessary, they used the deeming clause as an additional safeguard—with the singular "Class" and the words "comprised in" unchanged—to refer explicitly to "Class of Matters of a local or private Nature comprised in the Enumerations of the Classes of Subjects assigned exclusively to the Legislatures of the Provinces." No other plausible conclusions about the purpose and the interrelationship of the new provisions of the act can be reached on the basis of the drafting history and the language used.

The drafting in London had provided a structural coherence, or logic, to the relationship between sections 91 and 92. Moreover, Reilly had also created a sequential approach to determining the appropriate home for federal or provincial legislation. The Quebec Resolutions had given each jurisdiction power to make laws "respecting subjects" at the head of their respective sections and also "generally respecting all matters" of either a general or local nature at the tail. In his first draft Reilly had empowered governments to make laws "in relation to matters," not subjects, "coming within" the enumerated powers which he categorized as "Classes of Subjects." The sequence was first to identify the matter and then determine the "class of subjects" within which it came. Only at that stage might the relationship of sections 91 and 92 be critical in the allocation of jurisdiction.

Reilly and his Canadian associates in London had also made the exclusivity of the legislative jurisdiction of both levels of government much clearer than in the Quebec Resolutions. Within their allocated sphere, however they might be determined, both were autonomous and supreme. Jurisdictionally, coordinate or classical federalism was written into the constitution. The provision, based on the imperial model but with an undefined purpose, that the federal government could disallow provincial legislation qualified that legislative autonomy, but it could be exercised only at the discretion of the executive and was thus a matter of politics or policy, not of law, and its use was not justiciable. It would be the function of the courts to police the boundaries separating provincial and federal legislative jurisdiction.

NOTES

1. Was the Canada created by the *British North America Act, 1867* a true federal state? That depends, of course, on the attributes that a country must possess in order for it to qualify for that designation. What those attributes are, or should be, is a matter that scholars of federalism have debated for a long time. One view is that they include the following: (1) a division of legislative powers between two independent orders of government of coordinate (or equal) status, one national and the other regional; (2) which division of powers cannot

be altered by the unilateral action of either order; and (3) which division of powers is protected and enforced by an impartial and independent arbiter. Assuming for the sake of argument that those are the appropriate attributes, did the Canada of 1867 possess them? If not, in what respects did it fall short?

2. When you have finished reading the remaining chapters of Part II of this casebook, ask yourself whether the Canada of today is any closer to being a true federal state (as defined in note 1) than the Canada of 1867.

3. Paul Romney emphasizes that *general* residual authority was allocated to both levels of government in the Quebec Resolutions. Only after the text went through several drafts was local residuary authority restored to the provinces in s. 92(16). Without this history in mind, the final text left the impression that the federal government alone had residual authority. This was not the intention of the framers, Romney maintains, although, as you will see in the chapters that follow, the place where residual authority resides becomes a matter of some controversy. See P. Romney, *Getting It Wrong: How Canadians Forgot Their Past and Imperilled Confederation* (Toronto: University of Toronto Press, 1999), at 100-2.

A NOTE ON QUEBEC'S CIVIL CODE

Recall that in the 1760 *Articles of Capitulation* of Montreal, *supra*, local laws and customs were preserved "according to the custom of Paris." The *Coutume de Paris* has been described as Quebec's first civil code:

> Although no more than the body of customary law applicable to Paris and its environs, it had in fact attained in France, by the end of the sixteenth century, the status of the preeminent French custom. It was, in effect, a "common law" (*droit commun coutumier*) of Northern France and, as such, a logical choice for extension to a colony, even though the majority of the population in Canada came from areas other than Paris itself. In its final written redaction of 1580, however, it was far from providing a complete body of law. [J.E.C. Brierly and Roderick A. Macdonald, eds., *Quebec Civil Law: An Introduction to Quebec Private Law* (Toronto: Emond Montgomery, 1993), at 8.]

The *Royal Proclamation of 1763* imposed British civil and criminal law in the new colony of Quebec. To the extent that it was intended to displace Canadian laws and customs, it was described as "impossible [to do], as it would be injurious." (See W.P.M. Kennedy and Gustave Lanctot, *Reports on the Law of Quebec 1767-1770* (Ottawa: F.A. Acland, 1931), at 64.) The *Quebec Act* of 1774 restored what were then called the "Laws of Canada," in "all Matters of Controversy, relative to Property and Civil Rights." As it evolved over the years, the diversity of sources associated with civil law in Quebec gave rise to what Durham called

> a patch-work of the results of the interference, at different times, of different legislative powers, each proceeding on utterly different and generally incomplete views, and each utterly regardless of the other. The law itself is a mass of incoherent and conflicting laws, part French, part English, and with the line between each very confusedly drawn. [Report of the Earl of Durham (London: Methuen, 1902), at 81.]

It was this mélange of laws and customs, with its diversity of influences, that was codified in the first *Civil Code of Lower Canada* of 1866. The *Civil Code* encapsulates the legal principles to be accorded to persons, property, and civil obligations, subjects that in English-speaking Canada are ordinarily associated with the "private law" or "common law."

This is how Professor J.E.C. Brierly described the pre-codification situation in "Quebec's Civil Law Codification: Viewed and Reviewed" (1968), *McGill Law Journal* 521, at 538-40:

> The bulk of the *droit civil*, apart from the superimposition on specific points of provincial or imperial legislation drawn on many points from English law, was made up of French *ancien droit*, such as it existed during the latter part of the eighteenth century prior to the French political revolution of 1789 and the legal changes brought about by the *Code civil* of 1804. Lower Canada's legal system was denied any continuing nourishment, so to speak, from the legal system of the country which was the seat of the tradition that had produced it; the source from which it sprang was stopped off by the transformation of the uncodified *ancien droit* into a modern code, and the consequential change in the viewpoint of French legal writers. "[T]he old laws still in force in Lower Canada," the preamble [to the 1857 *Act to Provide for Codification*] states, "are no longer reprinted or commented upon in France, and it is becoming more and more difficult to obtain copies of them, or of the commentaries upon them."
>
> With respect, first of all, to the "old laws," it has already been intimated that the *Coutume de Paris*, probably the single most important *statut* of the private law of Lower Canada, had never been the object of any legislative action on the part of governmental authorities. Its only publication in a quasi-official form occurred in the 1770's, when a committee was entrusted with the task of establishing (but only in French) an *Abstract* of those parts of the *Coutume* received and practised in Lower Canada during the time when the colony was ruled by France. ...
>
> • • •
>
> The lack of re-publication, revision or translation of relevant legislative materials and the absence of judicial reports during the first part of the century also explain, in large part, the want of systematic doctrinal works dealing with such sources as living law in their Canadian context. The point made by the preamble as to the difficulty of obtaining relevant French commentaries would certainly have been applicable, for example, to the work of de Ferrière whose *Commentaire sur la Coutume de Paris*, the classic writing on the subject, had not been re-published since the end of the eighteenth century; on the other hand, Pothier, also a standard author, had been re-edited many times during the first part of the nineteenth century. It is not surprising therefore that other works, even those principally treating the new *Code civil* and only incidentally dealing with the former law, those for example of Maleville and Merlin published in the early 1800's, had some currency before the courts of Lower Canada.
>
> But all these, while undoubtedly the classic explanations of the *ancien droit* or of many of its principles as contained in the new French Code, were not written with the growing complexities of the Canadian scene in mind; their rarity, if such indeed were the case, was exceeded by their increasing unsuitability to the difficulties and immediate needs of local society. At this level, and not surprisingly in view of the absence of organized structures for the teaching of law, there was no doctrinal production, in either quantity or quality, able to accomplish the work of systematization that might normally have been expected, to some degree at least, to have emerged from the responsible exercise of legislative authority. There was no Canadian Pothier to synthesize this confused body of uncodified law.

That codification of Lower Canada's civil law came about alongside the push toward Confederation is not entirely coincidental. George-Étienne Cartier, Attorney General for

Canada East and one of the fathers of Confederation, is credited with having spearheaded the effort. By the time the Code was adopted, the general outlines of the Confederation scheme were sufficiently well known that the drafters steered clear of some obvious federal subjects. As Thomas McCord noted in the first English-language edition of the Code:

> In view of a union of the British American provinces, the codification of our laws is perhaps better calculated than any other available means to secure to Lower Canada an advantage which the proposed plan of confederation appears to have already contemplated, that of being the standard of assimilation and unity, and of entering into new political relations without undergoing disturbing alterations in her laws or institutions. [T. McCord, *The Civil Code of Lower Canada Together With a Synopsis of the Changes in the Law Effected by the Civil Code of Lower Canada*, 2d ed. (Montreal: Dawson 1870), at i-ii.]

Keep in mind, however, that while enabling legislation establishing a commission to draft the Code was introduced in 1857, the first meeting of the framers occurred in Charlottetown in 1864 (though constitutional reform had been proposed since the 1850s). Brierly maintains that political factors were only one among a number of influences precipitating codification:

> It is probably also true to say that, as the plan for the Canadian political union took shape, the codification of the civil law came to be looked upon, more and more, in the light of its "political" significance ... . There is however no evidence to support the proposition that the *idea* of codification itself was born with such considerations in mind. [Brierly, above, at 528-29.]

Mere months before Confederation, nevertheless, codification "imposed a simple, written, organized, revised, unified and universal civil law across what in 1867 became the province of Quebec" (B. Young, *The Politics of Codification: The Lower Canadian Civil Code of 1866* (Montreal and Kingston: McGill-Queen's University Press, 1994), at 178). This process crystallized, practically and symbolically, Quebec's status as a mixed legal jurisdiction and Canada's status as a bijural federation. For an examination of the legal and cultural challenges facing bijuralism and mixity in Canada and the role of law as an identification marker, see: J.-F. Gaudreault-DesBiens, *Les solitudes du bijuridisme au Canada: Essai sur les rapports de pouvoir entre les traditions juridiques et la résilience des atavismes identitaires* (Montreal: Éditions Thémis, 2007). Whatever the motivations for codification, it was a prescient exercise and its significance in future constitutional confrontations is immeasurable.

As you read the cases that follow, consider to what degree the *Civil Code* represents a convenient compendium of laws typically falling within the provincial enumeration called "property and civil rights." Do the subjects covered by Quebec's *Civil Code* serve as a proxy for jurisdiction for all provinces over such private law matters? Might they also have been intended to serve as a model for "the standard of assimilation and unity" represented by Confederation and embodied in the promise of s. 94, which provides for the federal uniformity of laws respecting property and civil rights for those provinces outside Quebec that provide their consent?

CHAPTER FOUR

The Late Nineteenth Century: The Canadian Courts Under the Influence

This chapter deals with the period from Confederation to about 1900. During this period, Canada experienced a dramatic expansion to the east, west, and north. In 1870, two British territories to the west and north of Ontario and Quebec, Rupert's Land and the North-Western Territory, were admitted to Canada and, as territories, were made subject to the jurisdiction of Parliament. In the same year, the province of Manitoba was established by Parliament out of part of Rupert's Land, and the remainder of that territory and the North-Western Territory was renamed the Northwest Territories. British Columbia joined Confederation the following year, and Prince Edward Island joined Confederation in 1873.

Also during this period, for the first time, judges and scholars faced the task of interpreting the *British North America (BNA) Act*. In retrospect, the decisions they had to make involved two large and overlapping topics: the general nature of Canadian federalism, especially decisions about the nature of the provincial legislatures and executives, and the division of legislative powers. Both are included here, although the second is our primary concern and the first appears only briefly, in the middle of the chapter. The chapter concludes with a description of the establishment of Manitoba in the aftermath of a rebellion by the Métis people, and a subsequent constitutional dispute over religious education in the province.

One element of the context needs to be described. Within a few years after Confederation, a struggle for power began between the Dominion, led throughout most of this period by Sir John A. Macdonald and the Conservatives, and the provinces, led by Ontario and its Liberal premier, Oliver Mowat. This story has come to be known as the story of "provincial rights." The name is a wonderful example of the effective use of words: the provinces appropriated powerful constitutional words, evoking the glories of centuries of British constitutional history by claiming to be fighting for their "liberty" or their "rights." On the discourse of rights in the late nineteenth century, see Richard Risk and Robert C. Vipond, "Rights Talk in Canada and Right Feeling of the People" (1996), 14 *Law and History Review* 1.

The reasons for the struggle are debatable. Some historians, perhaps most, explain it as a product of political opportunism by the provinces and inconsistent with the agreement at Confederation; others, understanding Confederation differently, see it as a continuation of a long tradition of local autonomy. Whatever the reasons, a wide range of issues were involved, including the financial terms of Confederation, the location of the boundary between Ontario and Manitoba, the nature of the provincial legislatures, the powers of the

provincial executives, the use of the disallowance power, and the division of legislative powers. The contest took place on a wide range of battlegrounds, including newspapers, election
platforms, legislatures, and courts. By 1900, Ontario and Mowat had triumphed. The results
in the courts were a measure of that triumph—the provinces won most of the cases, by far.

The Canadian courts began to hear challenges to statutes on division-of-powers grounds
in the late 1860s, and the legitimacy of their function was soon challenged in a New Brunswick case, *R v. Chandler* (1868), 1 Hannay 556, 12 NBR 556. If legislative supremacy was a
fundamental constitutional principle, how could courts review statutes and declare them to
be void? W.J. Ritchie, Chief Justice of New Brunswick, responded:

> We must recognize the undoubted legislative control of the British Parliament, and give full
> force and effect to the statute of the Supreme Legislature, and ignore the Act of the subordinate,
> when, … they are repugnant and in conflict. … The constitution of the Dominion and the
> Provinces is now, to a great extent, a written one, and where under the terms of the *Union Act*
> the power to legislate is granted to be exercised exclusively by one body, the subject so exclu-
> sively assigned is as completely taken from the others, as if they had been expressly forbidden
> to act on it; and if they do legislate beyond their power, or in defiance of the restrictions placed
> on them their enactments are no more binding than rules or regulations promulgated by any
> other unauthorized body.

That is, courts would interpret the *BNA Act* to determine whether it gave the power to
enact the statute. That courts would have the final say about the scope of constitutional authority seems, in hindsight, inevitable and inescapable. Yet some politicians and judges took
issue with this judicial role, particularly in New Brunswick in the early 1870s, believing that
judicial review under the *BNA Act* was inconsistent with the notion of legislative supremacy
enshrined in the Act. Instead, some thoughtful voices believed that the power of disallowance was the only means of controlling legislative activity beyond the jurisdiction of the
provinces (see below, "Note: The Power of Disallowance"). These debates in New Brunswick
suggest that judicial review in Canada was not inevitable. Chief Justice Ritchie's views, however, quickly took hold in the Canadian legal imagination, and thereafter judicial review was
so firmly established that it needed little or no explanation or justification. This history is
discussed in Gordon Bale, *Chief Justice William Johnstone Ritchie: Responsible Government
and Judicial Review* (Ottawa: Carleton University Press, 1991), ch. 10.

The decisions of provincial courts of appeal could be appealed to the Supreme Court of
Canada, which was established in 1875, and from provincial courts of appeal or from the
Supreme Court to the Privy Council. Eventually, and no later than 1900, the Privy Council
came to be dominant, not only in the sense that it was the final court of appeal, but, as well,
in the sense that it determined the outcomes and doctrine with little or no restraint or respect for the Canadian courts. It became the oracle to which Canadian lawyers and courts
deferred for more than half a century, thereby providing one of the meanings of our ambiguous subtitle.

Citizens Insurance Company v. Parsons
(1881), 7 AC 96 (PC); aff'g. (1880), 4 SCR 215

[In 1876 Ontario enacted legislation about fire insurance policies that specified a set of standard conditions, which were "deemed to be a part of every policy of fire insurance" made in the province and which were to be "printed on every such policy with the heading 'Statutory Conditions.'" An insurer could vary or omit any of these conditions, if it added the variations or omissions to the policy, "in conspicuous type and in ink of a different colour."

Parsons brought an action on two fire insurance policies, written by two different insurers, to recover compensation for losses caused by a fire in his hardware store. Several issues were raised, but the central one was whether the Ontario legislation was valid. The insurers' refusal to pay was based on Parsons's failure, at the time the policies were made, to disclose information required by conditions in the policies. Parsons claimed that the conditions were void because they did not comply with the legislation, and the insurers argued that the legislation was *ultra vires*.

This dispute was between private parties, Parsons and the insurance companies, but, nonetheless, Mowat participated by arguing Ontario's position at the Supreme Court and by preparing a thorough analysis for the benefit of Parson's counsel in the Privy Council. He participated in this sort of way in other cases throughout this period, and this effort may have been one of the reasons for his success.

In the trial court and the Ontario Court of Appeal the plaintiff's claim succeeded and the insurers' challenge was dismissed. The insurers appealed to the Supreme Court of Canada, which affirmed by a majority of four to two. Because the insurer appealed again, to the Privy Council, the decision of the Supreme Court was of little or no use as a precedent in arguing subsequent cases and it did not become part, even a small part, of the fabric of the doctrine. Nonetheless, we have included some parts of its judgments here, and we have done the same throughout this part for other judgments of Canadian courts that suffered the same fate.]

RITCHIE CJC: Is, then, such legislation as this with respect to the contract of insurance beyond the power of local legislation? I think at the outset I may affirm with confidence that the *BNA Act* recognizes in the Dominion constitution and in the provincial constitutions a legislative sovereignty, if that is a proper expression to use, as independent and as exclusive in the one as in the other over the matters respectively confided to them, and the power of each must be equally respected by the other, or *ultra vires* legislation will necessarily be the result. ...

The Act now under consideration is not, in my opinion, a regulation of trade and commerce; it deals with the contract of fire insurance, as between the insurer and the insured. That contract is simply a contract of indemnity against loss or damage by fire, whereby one party, in consideration of an immediate fixed payment, undertakes to pay or make good to the other any loss or damage by fire, which may happen during a fixed period to specified property, not exceeding the sum named as the limit of insurance. ...

I think the power of the Dominion parliament to regulate trade and commerce ought not to be held to be necessarily inconsistent with those of the local legislatures to regulate property and civil rights in respect to all matters of a merely local and private nature, such as matters concerned with the enjoyment and preservation of property in the province, or matters of contract between parties in relation to their property or dealings, although the exercise by the local legislatures of such powers may be said remotely to affect matters connected with trade and commerce, unless, indeed, the laws of the provincial legislatures should conflict with those of the Dominion parliament passed for the general regulation of trade and commerce. I do no think the local legislatures are to be deprived of all power to deal with property and civil rights, because parliament, in the plenary exercise of its power to regulate trade and commerce, may possibly pass laws inconsistent with the exercise by the local legislatures of their powers—the exercise of the powers of the local legislatures being in such a case subject to such regulations as the Dominion may lawfully prescribe.

I scarcely know how one could better illustrate the exercise of the power of the local legislatures to legislate with reference to property and civil rights, and matters of a merely local and private nature, than by a local Act of incorporation, whereby a right to hold or deal with real or personal property in a province is granted, and whereby the civil right to contract and sue and to be sued as an individual in reference thereto is also granted. If a legislature possesses this power, as a necessary sequence, it must have the right to limit and control the manner in which the property may be so dealt with, and as to the contracts in reference thereto, the terms and conditions on which they may be entered into, whether they shall contain conditions for the protection or security of one or other or both the parties, or that they may be free to deal as may be agreed on by the contracting parties without limit or restriction. ...

I am happy to say I can foresee, and I fear, no evil effects whatever, as has been suggested, as likely to result to the Dominion from this view of the case. On the contrary, I believe that while this decision recognizes and sustains the legislative control of the Dominion parliament over all matters confided to its legislative jurisdiction, it, at the same time, preserves to the local legislatures those rights and powers conferred on them by the *BNA Act*, and which a contrary decision would, in my opinion, in effect, substantially, or, to a very large extent, sweep away.

GWYNNE J dissenting: ... It seems to me to be difficult to conceive what greater assertion of jurisdiction to regulate trade and commerce there could be, than is involved in the assumption and exercise of the right to prescribe by Act of the legislature in what manner only, by what form of contract only, by what persons only, and subject to what conditions only, particular trades, or a particular trade, may be carried on, and to prohibit their being carried on otherwise than is prescribed by the Act. If this may be done in one trade, obviously it may be done in every trade, and so all trades must be subject to the will of the legislature having jurisdiction so to legislate as to whether it shall be carried on at all or not. As to the Act under consideration, if it be open to the construction put upon it by the courts below, it seems to me to be impossible to conceive any stronger instance of the assertion of supreme sovereign legislative power to regulate and control the trade of fire insurance and of fire insurance companies, if the business of those companies be a trade. Now, among all the items enumerated in s. 92, it is observable that not one of them in terms indicates the slightest intention of conferring upon the local legislatures the power to interfere in any matter relating to trade or commerce, or in any matter which in any manner affects any commercial business of any kind, ...

Within this Dominion the right of exercise of National Sovereignty is vested solely in Her Majesty, the Supreme Sovereign Head of the State, and in the Parliament of which Her Majesty is an integral part; these powers are, within this Dominion, the sole administrators and guardians of the Comity of Nations. To prevent all possibility of the local legislatures creating any difficulties embarrassing to the Dominion Government, by presuming to interfere in any matter affecting trade and commerce, and by so doing violating, it might be, the Comity of Nations, all matters coming within those subjects are placed under the exclusive jurisdiction of the Dominion parliament; that the Act in question does usurp the jurisdiction of the Dominion parliament, I must say I entertain no doubt. The logical result of a contrary decision would afford just grounds to despair of the stability of the Dominion. The object of the *BNA Act* was to lay in the Dominion Constitution the foundations of a nation, and not to give to provinces carved out of, and subordinated to, the Dominion, anything of the nature of a national or *quasi* national existence. ...

[Henry J, with whom Strong J concurred, and Fournier J wrote similar judgments; Taschereau J dissented. Throughout this period, Gwynne J was the member of the court most sympathetic to the Dominion and Sir John A. Macdonald's vision of Confederation.

The insurer appealed to the Privy Council.]

SIR MONTAGUE SMITH: The scheme of this legislation, as expressed in the first branch of s. 91, is to give to the dominion parliament authority to make laws for the good government of Canada in all matters not coming within the classes of subjects assigned exclusively to the provincial legislature. If s. 91 had stopped here, and if the classes of subjects enumerated in s. 92 had been altogether distinct and different from those in s. 91, no conflict of legislative authority could have arisen. The provincial legislatures would have had exclusive legislative power over the sixteen classes of subjects assigned to them, and the dominion parliament exclusive power over all other matters relating to the good government of Canada. But it must have been foreseen that this sharp and definite distinction had not been and could not be attained, and that some of the classes of subjects assigned to the provincial legislatures unavoidably ran into and were embraced by some of the enumerated classes of subjects in s. 91; hence an endeavour appears to have been made to provide for cases of apparent conflict; and it would seem that with this object it was declared in the second branch of the s. 91, "for greater certainty, but not so as to restrict the generality of the foregoing terms of this section" that (notwithstanding anything in the Act) the exclusive legislative authority of the parliament of Canada should extend to all matters coming within the classes of subjects enumerated in that section. With the same object, apparently, the paragraph at the end of s. 91 was introduced, though it may be observed that this paragraph applies in its grammatical construction only to s. 92(16).

Notwithstanding this endeavour to give pre-eminence to the dominion parliament in cases of a conflict of powers, it is obvious that in some cases where this apparent conflict exists, the legislature could not have intended that the powers exclusively assigned to the provincial legislature should be absorbed in those given to the dominion parliament. Take as one instance the subject "marriage and divorce," contained in the enumeration of subjects in s. 91; it is evident that solemnization of marriage would come within this general description; yet "solemnization of marriage in the province" is enumerated among the classes of subjects in s. 92, and no one can doubt, notwithstanding the general language of s. 91, that this subject is still within the exclusive authority of the legislatures of the provinces. So "the raising of money by any mode or system of taxation" is enumerated among the classes of subjects in s. 91; but, though the description is sufficiently large and general to include "direct taxation within the province, in order to the raising of a revenue for provincial purposes," assigned to the provincial legislatures by s. 92, it obviously could not have been intended that, in this instance also, the general power should override the particular one. With regard to certain classes of subjects, therefore, generally described in s. 91, legislative power may reside as to some matters falling within the general description of these subjects in the legislatures of the provinces. In these cases it is the duty of the Courts, however difficult it may be, to ascertain in what degree, and to what extent, authority to deal with matters falling within these classes of subjects exists in each legislature, and to define in the particular case before them the limits of their respective powers. It could not have been the intention that a conflict should exist; and, in order to prevent such a result, the two sections must be read together, and the language of one interpreted, and, where necessary, modified, by that of the other. In this way it may, in most cases, be found possible to arrive at a reasonable and practical construction of the language of the sections, so as to reconcile the respective powers they contain, and give effect to all of them. In performing this difficult duty, it will be a wise course for those on whom it is thrown, to decide each case which arises as best they can, without entering more largely upon an interpretation of the statute than is necessary for the decision of the particular question in hand.

The first question to be decided is, whether the Act impeached in the present appeal falls within any of the classes of subjects enumerated in s. 92, and assigned exclusively to the legislatures of the provinces; for if it does not, it can be of no validity, and no other question would then arise. It is only when an Act of the provincial legislature prima facie falls within one of these classes of subjects that the further questions arise, viz., whether, notwithstanding this is so, the subject of the Act does not also fall within one of the enumerated classes of subjects in s. 91, and whether the power of the provincial legislature is or is not thereby overborne.

The main contention on the part of the respondent was that the Ontario Act in question had relation to matters coming within the class of subjects described in s. 92(13), viz., "Property and civil rights in the province." The Act deals with policies of insurance entered into or in force in the province of Ontario for insuring property situate therein against fire, and prescribes certain conditions which are to form part of such contracts. These contracts, and the rights arising from them, it was argued, came legitimately within the class of subject, "Property and civil rights." The appellants, on the other hand, contended that civil rights meant only such rights as flowed from the law, and gave as an instance the status of persons. Their Lordships cannot think that the latter construction is the correct one. They find no sufficient reason in the language itself, nor in the other parts of the Act, for giving so narrow an interpretation to the words "civil rights." The words are sufficiently large to embrace, in their fair and ordinary meaning, rights arising from contract, and such rights are not included in express terms in any of the enumerated classes of subjects in s. 91.

It becomes obvious, as soon as an attempt is made to construe the general terms in which the classes of subjects of ss. 91 and 92 are described, that both sections and the other parts of the Act must be looked at to ascertain whether language of a general nature must not by necessary implication or reasonable intendment be modified and limited. In looking at s. 91, it will be found not only that there is no class including, generally, contracts and the rights arising from them, but that one class of contracts is mentioned and enumerated, viz., "18, bills of exchange and promissory notes," which it would have been unnecessary to specify if authority over all contracts and the rights arising from them had belonged to the dominion parliament.

The provision found in s. 94 of the *British North America Act*, which is one of the sections relating to the distribution of legislative powers, was referred to by the learned counsel on both sides as throwing light upon the sense in which the words "property and civil rights" are used. By that section the parliament of Canada is empowered to make provision for the uniformity of any laws relative to "property and civil rights" in Ontario, Nova Scotia, and New Brunswick, and to the procedure of the Courts in these three provinces, if the provincial legislatures choose to adopt the provision so made. The province of Quebec is omitted from this section for the obvious reason that the law which governs property and civil rights in Quebec is in the main the French law as it existed at the time of the cession of Canada, and not the English law which prevails in the other provinces. The words "property and civil rights" are, obviously, used in the same sense in this section as in s. 92(13), and there seems no reason for presuming that contracts and the rights arising from them were not intended to be included in this provision for uniformity. If, however, the narrow construction of the words "civil rights," contended for by the appellants were to prevail, the dominion parliament could, under its general power, legislate in regard to contracts in all and each of the provinces and as a consequence of this the province of Quebec, though now governed by its own Civil Code, founded on the French law, as regards contracts and their incidents, would be subject to have its law on that subject altered by the dominion legislature, and brought into uniformity with the English law prevailing in the other three provinces, notwithstanding that Quebec has been carefully left out of the uniformity section of the Act.

It is to be observed that the same words, "civil rights," are employed in the Act of 14 Geo. 3, c. 83, [the *Quebec Act* of 1774] which made provision for the Government of the province of Quebec. Sect. 8 of that Act enacted that His Majesty's Canadian subjects within the province of Quebec should enjoy their property, usages, and other civil rights, as they had before done, and that in all matters of controversy relative to property and civil rights resort should be had to the laws of Canada, and be determined agreeably to the said laws. In this statute the words "property" and "civil rights" are plainly used in their largest sense; and there is no reason for holding that in the statute under discussion they are used in a different and narrower one.

The next question for consideration is whether, assuming the Ontario Act to relate to the subject of property and civil rights, its enactments and provisions come within any of the classes of subjects enumerated in s. 91. The only one which the Appellants suggested as expressly including the subject of the Ontario Act is s. 91(2), "the regulation of trade and commerce."

A question was raised which led to much discussion in the Courts below and this bar, viz., whether the business of insuring buildings against fire was a trade. This business, when carried on for the sake of profit, may, no doubt, in some sense of the word, be called a trade. But contracts of indemnity made by insurers can scarcely be considered trading contracts, nor were insurers who made them held to be "traders" under the English bankruptcy laws; they have been made subject to those laws by special description. Whether the business of fire insurance properly falls within the description of a "trade" must, in their Lordships' view, depend upon the sense in which that word is used in the particular statute to be construed; but in the present case their Lordships do not find it necessary to rest their decision on the narrow ground that the business of insurance is not a trade.

The words "regulation of trade and commerce," in their unlimited sense are sufficiently wide, if uncontrolled by the context and other parts of the Act, to include every regulation of trade ranging from political arrangements in regard to trade with foreign governments, requiring the sanction of parliament, down to minute rules for regulating particular trades. But a consideration of the Act shews that the words were not used in this unlimited sense. In the first place the collocation of s. 91(2) with classes of subjects of national and general concern affords an indication that regulations relating to general trade and commerce were in the mind of the legislature, when conferring this power on the dominion parliament. If the words had been intended to have the full scope of which in their literal meaning they are susceptible, the specific mention of several of the other classes of subjects enumerated in s. 91 would have been unnecessary; as, s. 91(15), banking; s. 91(17), weights and measures; s. 91(18), bills of exchange and promissory notes; s. 91(19), interest; and even s. 91(21), bankruptcy and insolvency.

"Regulation of trade and commerce" may have been used in some such sense as the words "regulations of trade" in the *Act of Union between England and Scotland* (6 Anne, c. 11), and as these words have been used in Acts of State relating to trade and commerce. Article V of the *Act of Union* enacted that all the subjects of the United Kingdom should have "full freedom and intercourse of trade and navigation" to and from all places in the United Kingdom and the Colonies; and Article VI enacted that all parts of the United Kingdom from and after the Union should be under the *same* "prohibitions, restrictions, and *regulations of trade.*" Parliament has at various times since the Union passed laws affecting and regulating specific trades in one part of the United Kingdom only, without its being supposed that it thereby infringed the Articles of Union. Thus the Acts for regulating the sale of intoxicating liquors notoriously vary in the two kingdoms. So with regard to Acts relating to bankruptcy, and various other matters.

Construing therefore the words "regulation of trade and commerce" by the various aids to their interpretation above suggested, they would include political arrangements in regard to trade requiring the sanction of parliament, regulation of trade in matters of inter-provincial concern, and it may be that they would include general regulation of trade affecting the whole dominion. Their Lordships abstain on the present occasion from any attempt to define the limits of the authority of the dominion parliament in this direction. It is enough for the decision of the present case to say that, in their view, its authority to legislate for the regulation of trade and commerce does not comprehend the power to regulate by legislation the contracts of a particular business or trade, such as the business of fire insurance in a single province, and therefore that its legislative authority does not in the present case conflict or compete with the power over property and civil rights assigned to the legislature of Ontario by s. 92(13).

Having taken this view of the present case, it becomes unnecessary to consider the question how far the general power to make regulations of trade and commerce, when competently exercised by the dominion parliament, might legally modify or affect property and civil rights in the provinces, or the legislative power of the provincial legislatures in relation to those subjects; ...

On the best consideration they have been able to give to the arguments addressed to them and to the judgments of the learned judges in Canada, their Lordships have come to the conclusion that the Act in question is valid. ...

Appeal dismissed.

Much of the remaining material in this chapter is about challenges to legislation about liquor. In the late nineteenth century, people drank, debated drinking, and regulated drinking. Local governments had regulated taverns for decades before Confederation, and had powers to impose temperance measures, such as limitations on the numbers of taverns. Fees for tavern licences and taxes on the import and manufacture of liquor were important sources of government revenue, and tavern licences were a major source of patronage and political loyalty, especially for Mowat's government. After the late 1860s, campaigns for temperance and prohibition became one of the most powerful and divisive social and political movements of the late nineteenth and early twentieth centuries. All of this concern and conflict produced a multitude of challenges to statutes, thereby providing the other meaning of our ambiguous subtitle.

The parts of the story that concern us here begin in the 1870s, when pressure from temperance groups mounted. Two statutes were enacted that made the political stakes much higher than they had been before. The first was the *Liquor License Act*, SO 1876, c. 26, known commonly as the *Crooks Act*, which was enacted by Ontario in 1876 and which will be described later in this chapter. The second was the *Canada Temperance Act*, SC 1878, c. 16, enacted in 1878 by the Dominion, which enabled local option across the nation. A majority of voters in any city or county could opt to prohibit retail sales of liquor. More precisely, the effect of a vote for local option was to prohibit sales, except for sales of quantities over specified minimums by brewers, distillers, and wholesale traders, as long as they had "good reason to believe" that the liquor would be taken "forthwith" from the city or county. Anyone who sold liquor in violation of this prohibition was liable, on summary conviction, to a fine of fifty dollars for the first offence and one hundred for the second. In *Russell*, a private citizen began a criminal prosecution under the Act against Russell, a tavern owner, for selling liquor in violation of its terms.

Russell v. The Queen
(1882), 7 AC 829 (PC)

SIR MONTAGUE SMITH: … The general scheme of the *British North America Act* with regard to the distribution of legislative powers, and the general scope and effect of ss. 91 and 92, and their relation to each other, were fully considered and commented on by this Board in the case of the *Citizens Insurance Company v. Parsons* (1881), 7 AC 96 (PC). According to the principle of construction there pointed out, the first question to be determined is, whether the Act now in question falls within any of the classes of subjects enumerated in s. 92, and assigned exclusively to the Legislatures of the Provinces. If it does, then the further question would arise, viz., whether the subject of the Act does not also fall within one of the enumerated classes of subjects in s. 91, and so does not still belong to the Dominion Parliament. But if the Act does not fall within any of the classes of subjects in s. 92, no further question will remain, for it cannot be contended, and indeed was not contended at their Lordships' bar, that, if the Act does not come within one of the classes of subjects assigned to the Provincial Legislatures, the Parliament of Canada had not, by its general power "to make laws for the peace, order, and good government of Canada," full legislative authority to pass it.

Three classes of subjects enumerated in s. 92 were referred to, under each of which, it was contended by the appellant's counsel, the present legislation fell. These were:—

> 9. Shop, saloon, tavern, auctioneer, and other licenses in order to the raising of a revenue for provincial, local, or municipal purposes.
> 13. Property and civil rights in the province.
> 16. Generally all matters of a merely local or private nature in the province.

With regard to the first of these classes, s. 92(9), it is to be observed that the power of granting licenses is not assigned to the Provincial Legislatures for the purpose of regulating trade, but "in order to the raising of a revenue for provincial, local, or municipal purposes."

The Act in question is not a fiscal law; it is not a law for raising revenue; on the contrary, the effect of it may be to destroy or diminish revenue; indeed it was a main objection to the Act that in the city of Frederickton it did in point of fact diminish the sources of municipal revenue. It is evident, therefore, that the matter of the Act is not within the class of subject No. 9, and consequently that it could not have been passed by the Provincial Legislature by virtue of any authority conferred upon it by that sub-section. …

Next, their Lordships cannot think that the *Temperance Act* in question properly belongs to the class of subjects, "Property and Civil Rights." It has in its legal aspect an obvious and close similarity to laws which place restrictions on the sale or custody of poisonous drugs, or of dangerously explosive substances. These things, as well as intoxicating liquors, can, of course, be held as property, but a law placing restrictions on their sale, custody, or removal, on the ground that the free sale or use of them is dangerous to public safety, and making it a criminal offence punishable by fine or imprisonment to violate these restrictions, cannot properly be deemed a law in relation to property in the sense in which those words are used in s. 92. What Parliament is dealing with in legislation of this kind is not a matter in relation to property and its rights, but one relating to public order and safety. That is the primary matter dealt with, and though incidentally the free use of things in which men may have property is interfered with, that incidental interference does not alter the character of the law. Upon the same considerations, the Act in question cannot be regarded as legislation in relation to civil rights. In however large a sense these words are used, it could not have been intended to prevent the Parliament of Canada from declaring and enacting certain uses of property, and certain acts in relation to property, to be criminal and wrongful. Laws which make it a criminal offence for a man wilfully to set fire to his own house on the ground that such an act endangers the public safety, or to overwork his horse on the ground of cruelty to the animal, though affecting in some sense property and the right of a man to do as he pleases with his own, cannot properly be regarded as legislation in relation to property or to civil rights. Nor could a law which prohibited or restricted the sale or exposure of cattle having a contagious disease be so regarded. Laws of this nature designed for the promotion of public order, safety, or morals, and which subject those who contravene them to criminal procedure and punishment, belong to the subject of public wrongs rather than to that of civil rights. They are of a nature which fall within the general authority of Parliament to make laws for the order and good government of Canada, and have direct relation to criminal law, which is one of the enumerated classes of subjects assigned exclusively to the Parliament of Canada. It was said in the course of the judgment of this Board in the case of the *Citizens Insurance Company of Canada v. Parsons*, that the two sections (91 and 92) must be read together, and the language of one interpreted, and, where necessary, modified by that of the other. Few, if any, laws could be made by Parliament for the peace, order, and good government of Canada which did not in some incidental way affect property and civil rights; and it could not have been intended, when assuring to the provinces exclusive legislative authority on the subjects of property and civil rights, to exclude the Parliament from the exercise of this general power whenever any such incidental interference would result from it. The true nature and character of the legislation in the particular instance under discussion must always be determined, in order to ascertain the class of subject to which it really belongs. In the present case it appears to their Lordships, for the reasons already given, that the matter of the Act in question does not properly belong to the class of subjects "Property and Civil Rights" within the meaning of ss. 92(13). ...

It was lastly contended that this Act fell within s. 92(16)—"Generally all matters of a merely local or personal nature in the province."

It was not, of course, contended for the appellant that the Legislature of New Brunswick could have passed the Act in question, which embraces in its enactments all the provinces; nor was it denied, with respect to this last contention, that the Parliament of Canada might have passed an Act of the nature of that under discussion to take effect at the same time throughout the whole Dominion. Their Lordships understand the contention to be that, at least in the absence of a general law of the Parliament of Canada, the provinces might have passed a local law of a like kind, each for its own province, and that, as the prohibitory and penal parts of the Act in question were to come into force in those counties and cities only in which it was adopted in the manner prescribed, or, as it was said, "by local option," the legislation was in effect, and on its face, upon a matter of a merely local nature. ...

Their Lordships cannot concur in this view. The declared object of Parliament in passing the Act is that there should be uniform legislation in all the provinces respecting the traffic in intoxicating liquors, with a view to promote temperance in the Dominion. Parliament does not treat the promotion of temperance as desirable in one province more than in another, but as desirable everywhere throughout the Dominion. The Act as soon as it was passed became a law for the whole Dominion, and the enactments of the first part, relating to the machinery for bringing the second part into force, took effect and might be put in motion at once and everywhere within it. It is true that the prohibitory and penal parts of the Act are only to come into force in any county or city upon the adoption of a petition to that effect by a majority of electors, but this conditional application of these parts of the Act does not convert the Act itself into legislation in relation to a merely local matter. The objects and scope of the legislation are still general, viz., to promote temperance by means of a uniform law throughout the Dominion.

The manner of bringing the prohibitions and penalties of the Act into force, which Parliament has thought fit to adopt, does not alter its general and uniform character. Parliament deals with the subject as one of general concern to the Dominion, upon which uniformity of legislation is desirable, and the Parliament alone can so deal with it. There is no ground or pretence for saying that the evil or vice struck at by the Act in question is local or exists only in one province, and that Parliament, under colour of general legislation, is dealing with a provincial matter only. It is therefore unnecessary to discuss the considerations which a state of circumstances of this kind might present. The present legislation is clearly meant to apply a remedy to an evil which is assumed to exist throughout the Dominion, and the local option, as it is called, no more localises the subject and scope of the Act than a provision in an Act for the prevention of contagious diseases in cattle that a public officer should proclaim in what districts it should come in effect, would make the statute itself a mere local law for each of these districts. In statutes of this kind the legislation is general, and the provision for the special application of it to particular places does not alter its character.

Their Lordships having come to the conclusion that the Act in question does not fall within any of the classes of subjects assigned exclusively to the Provincial Legislatures, it becomes unnecessary to discuss the further question whether its provisions also fall within any of the classes of subjects enumerated in s. 91. In abstaining from this discussion, they must not be understood as intimating any dissent from the opinion of the Chief Justice of the Supreme Court of Canada and the other Judges, who held that the Act, as a general regulation of the traffic in intoxicating liquors throughout the Dominion, fell within the class of subject, "the regulation of trade and commerce," enumerated in that section, and was, on that ground, a valid exercise of the legislative power of the Parliament of Canada.

In the result, their Lordships will humbly recommend Her Majesty to affirm the judgment of the Supreme Court of Canada, and with costs.

Appeal dismissed with costs.

The next major case was *Hodge v. The Queen* (1883), 9 AC 117 (PC), which was decided by the Privy Council about a year and a half after *Russell*. It was a challenge to Ontario's *Crooks Act*, which was mentioned, briefly, earlier. The Act transferred the powers over liquor licensing from the municipalities to newly created Boards of License commissioners, appointed and controlled by the provincial government, and added powers to enable the boards to limit the numbers of licences. The control over the commissioners greatly increased the government's patronage powers, which Mowat used openly and shrewdly to encourage loyalty to the provincial Liberal party.

Hodge v. The Queen
(1883), 9 AC 117 (PC); aff'g. (1882), 7 OAR 246;
rev'g. (1881), 46 UCQB 141 (Ont. HC)

[Hodge, a tavern keeper, was charged with permitting billiards to be played in his tavern, contrary to the regulations made by the licence commissioners for Toronto. He challenged the Act on two grounds: first, it conflicted with the Dominion power over trade and commerce; and second, the provincial legislature could not delegate law-making powers to the Boards of Commissioners. This second argument was based on the fact that the Canadian legislatures were created by the British Parliament. They were therefore delegates and not sovereign legislatures, and they were therefore limited by the common law maxim *delegatus non potest delegare*. Translated, this phrase means "a delegate may not delegate." It presumes that an individual (or institution) who is given responsibility to do something may not transfer the responsibility to another individual (or institution) unless there is something in the grant of power or the context that permits the transfer.

Another tavern keeper, Frawley, was charged with operating his tavern without any licence at all. He was convicted and, because it was his second offence, sentenced to imprisonment with hard labour. He challenged this sentence, and raised a third ground: the province could not impose imprisonment with hard labour as a punishment, because s. 92(15) of the *BNA Act*, which gave the provinces power to impose punishment for enforcing their laws, spoke only of imprisonment. These two cases were consolidated, and have become known by Hodge's name alone.

The trial judge was persuaded by the argument about delegation, but the Court of Appeal and the Privy Council dismissed all three grounds. The second and third grounds are not directly relevant to our major topic, the division of powers, but they prompted important responses about the nature of the provincial legislatures and about interpretation.

The Court of Appeal gave its decision a week before *Russell* was decided, and said that the argument about regulation of trade and commerce was hopeless. About the delegation argument, Burton J said that the British Parliament was sovereign, but its sovereignty was "a power existing in name only, and one which it would never attempt to exercise." The provincial legislatures had "plenary powers of legislation within their respective spheres as large and ample as those of the Imperial Parliament itself," and their authority was "the same character as that of the Imperial Parliament" (at 278 OAR). Considering the third argument, about hard labour, Spragge J called for a liberal interpretation, and said at 271 OAR:

an instrument conferring a constitution should not by interpretation lose its character as the fundamental organic law of a Government and be brought to the level of an ordinary private statute, to be expounded with the technical and literal precision which would be appropriate to a penal code.

Hodge appealed, and argued that *Russell* gave the Dominion comprehensive control over liquor.]

LORD FITZGERALD: … The appellants contended that the legislature of Ontario had no power to pass any Act to regulate the liquor traffic; that the whole power to pass such an Act was conferred on the Dominion Parliament, and consequently taken from the provincial legislature, by s. 91 of the *British North America Act, 1867*; and that it did not come within any of the classes of subjects assigned exclusively to the provincial legislatures by s. 92. The class in s. 91 which the *Liquor License Act, 1877*, was said to infringe was s. 91(2), "The Regulation of Trade and Commerce," and it was urged that the decision of this Board in *Russell v. The Queen* (1882), 7 AC 829 (PC) was conclusive that the whole subject of the liquor traffic was given to the Dominion Parliament, and consequently taken away from the provincial legislature. It appears to their Lordships, however, that the decision of this tribunal in that case has not the effect supposed, and that, when properly considered, it should be taken rather as an authority in support of the judgment of the Court of Appeal.

The sole question there was, whether it was competent to the Dominion Parliament, under its general powers to make laws for the peace, order, and good government of the Dominion, to pass the *Canada Temperance Act, 1878*, which was intended to be applicable to the several Provinces of the Dominion, or to such parts of the Provinces as should locally adopt it. It was not doubted that the Dominion Parliament had such authority, under s. 91 unless the subject fell within some one or more of the classes of subjects, which by s. 92 were assigned exclusively to the legislatures of the Provinces. …

It appears to their Lordships that *Russell v. The Queen*, when properly understood, is not an authority in support of the appellant's contention, and their Lordships do not intend to vary or depart from the reasons expressed for their judgment in that case. The principle which that case and the case of the *Citizens Insurance Company* illustrate is, that subjects which in one aspect and for one purpose fall within s. 92, may in another aspect and for another purpose fall within s. 91.

Their Lordships proceed now to consider the subject matter and legislative character of ss. 4 and 5 of the *Liquor License Act of 1877*. That Act is so far confined in its operation to municipalities in the province of Ontario, and is entirely local in its character and operation. It authorizes the appointment of License Commissioners to act in each municipality, and empowers them to pass, under the name of resolutions, what we know as by-laws, or rules to define the conditions and qualifications requisite for obtaining tavern or shop licenses for sale by retail of spirituous liquors within the municipality; for limiting the number of licenses; for declaring that a limited number of persons qualified to have tavern licenses may be exempted from having all the tavern accommodation required by law, and for regulating licensed taverns and shops, for defining the duties and powers of license inspectors, and to impose penalties for infraction of their resolutions.

These seem to be all matters of a merely local nature in the Province, and to be similar to, though not identical in all respects with, the powers then belonging to municipal institutions under the previously existing laws passed by the local parliaments.

Their Lordships consider that the powers intended to be conferred by the Act in question, when properly understood, are to make regulations in the nature of police or municipal regulations of a merely local character for the good government of taverns, & c., licensed for the sale of liquors by retail, and such as are calculated to preserve, in the municipality, peace and public decency, and repress drunkenness and disorderly and riotous conduct. As such they cannot be said to interfere with the general regulation of trade and commerce which belongs to the Dominion Parliament, and do not conflict with the provisions of the *Canada Temperance Act*, which does not appear to have as yet been locally adopted. ...

Their Lordships are, therefore, of opinion that, in relation to ss. 4 and 5 of the Act in question, the legislature of Ontario acted within [ss. 92(8), (15), and (16) of] the *Imperial Act of 1867*, and that in this respect there is no conflict with the powers of the Dominion Parliament.

Assuming that the local legislature had power to legislate to the full extent of the resolutions passed by the License Commissioners, and to have enforced the observance of their enactments by penalties and imprisonment with or without hard labour, it was further contended that the Imperial Parliament had conferred no authority on the local legislature to delegate those powers to the License Commissioners, or any other persons. In other words, that the power conferred by the Imperial Parliament on the local legislature should be exercised in full by that body, and by that body alone. The maxim *delegatus non potest delegare* was relied on.

It appears to their Lordships, however, that the objection thus raised by the appellants is founded on an entire misconception of the true character and position of the provincial legislatures. They are in no sense delegates of or acting under any mandate from the Imperial Parliament. When the *British North America Act* enacted that there should be a legislature for Ontario, and that its legislative assembly should have exclusive authority to make laws for the Province and for provincial purposes in relation to the matters enumerated in s. 92, it conferred powers not in any sense to be exercised by delegation from or as agents of the Imperial Parliament, but authority as plenary and as ample within the limits prescribed by s. 92 as the Imperial Parliament in the plenitude of its power possessed and could bestow. Within these limits of subjects and area the local legislature is supreme, and has the same authority as the Imperial Parliament, or the Parliament of the Dominion, would have had under like circumstances to confide to a municipal institution or body of its own creation authority to make by-laws or resolutions as to subjects specified in the enactment, and with the object of carrying the enactment into operation and effect.

. . .

If, as their Lordships have decided, the subjects of legislation come within the powers of the provincial legislature, then s. 92(15) of the *British North America Act*, which provides for "the imposition of punishment by fine, penalty, or imprisonment, for enforcing any law of the Province made in relation to any matter coming within any of the classes of subjects enumerated in this section," is applicable to the case before us, and is not in conflict with s. 91(27); under these very general terms, "the imposition of punishment by imprisonment for enforcing any law," it seems to their Lordships that there is imported an authority to add to the confinement or restraint in prison that which is generally incident to it—"hard labour"; in other words, that "imprisonment" there means restraint by confinement in a prison, with or without its usual accompaniment, "hard labour." ...

Their Lordships do not think it necessary or useful to advert to some minor points of discussion, and are, on the whole, of opinion that the decision of the Court of Appeal of Ontario should be affirmed, and this appeal dismissed, with costs, and will so humbly advise Her Majesty.

Appeal dismissed.

The holdings about the second and the third arguments in *Hodge* need comment. The second of the arguments was, ultimately, about the nature of the provincial legislatures and its outcome was one of the important decisions about the nature of Canadian federalism. Because it is now so well established, what the Privy Council said may seem to be no more than an elegant statement of the obvious, but in the late 1870s and early 1880s the topic was passionately debated and one of the battlegrounds of the contest about provincial rights. Even entire books were devoted to the question whether the provincial legislatures were parliaments, like the British Parliament, or merely bodies created by the *BNA Act*, with no more powers than it specifically gave them, more like municipal governments than parliaments, and severed from their own histories and from the majesty of the British Parliament. At stake were the inherent privileges of a parliament, such as a power to punish for contempt, and the power of a glorious name.

The arguments invoked basic constitutional law and the terms of the *BNA Act*. One of the fundamental principles of the Constitution was the sovereignty of parliament, and the dominant legal theory held that in each nation there must be one sovereign and only one. How, then could both the Dominion and the provinces be sovereign, and how could law-making power be divided within one nation? In part, this question was answered by avoiding it: neither could be the sovereign of Canada, because Canada was a colony; the British Parliament was the sovereign, and it had enacted the *BNA Act*. The terms of the *BNA Act* were far from clear. It used the word "Parliament" for the Dominion and the word "legislatures" for the provinces; was there a difference? It gave the Dominion a power to disallow provincial legislation, and how could provinces be said to be made in the model of the British Parliament if their statutes could be made nullities by the will of the Dominion? As well, arguably, it gave the residue of legislative power to the Dominion, which seemed to mark a difference from the United States and the claims the states had made to sovereignty.

The crux of the resolution in *Hodge* was that the Dominion and the provinces were equal in kind, and each supreme within their spheres. (Note the use of the word "supreme" and not "sovereign," which acknowledged sovereignty of the British Parliament and denoted a relative power: the Dominion and the provinces were, legally, supreme over other institutions within their jurisdiction.) It was a major triumph for Mowat, who had argued for it in the Ontario Court of Appeal. Not only were the Dominion and the provinces supreme within their spheres of jurisdiction, the jurisdictional lines between them could be easily discerned. This mode of argument—that social and political life could be legally classified and categorized—was common to the legal thought of the nineteenth century.

Next, we turn to the fate of the third argument in *Hodge*. The Privy Council ignored Spragge J's plea in the Ontario Court of Appeal for a liberal interpretation and, a few years later, it made a more express statement of its contrary interpretive approach in *Bank of Toronto v. Lambe* (1887), 12 AC 575 (PC). The issue was whether taxes imposed by Quebec on specified kinds of commercial corporations were direct taxes and, therefore, valid under s. 92(2) (direct taxation within the province). Lord Hobhouse said, at 579, "Questions of this class have been left for the decision of the ordinary Courts of Law which must treat the provisions of the Act in question [the *BNA Act*] by the same methods of construction and exposition which they apply to other statutes." These "methods of construction and exposition"— that is, the prevailing attitudes toward statutory interpretation—are well illustrated by the first paragraph of the leading English text in the late nineteenth century: Maxwell, *On the Interpretation of Statutes* (London: William Maxwell, 1875):

> Statute law is the will of the Legislature; and the object of all judicial interpretation of it is to determine what intention is either expressly or by implication conveyed by the language used, … When the intention is expressed, the task is one simply of verbal construction; but when, as occasionally happens, the statue expresses no intention on a question to which it gives rise, and on which some intention must necessarily be imputed to the Legislature, the interpreter has to determine it by inference grounded on legal principles.

The "legal principles" to which Maxwell referred were largely derived from the common law and, whatever else they included, they did not permit consideration of the history of a country, the beliefs of its peoples, or its apparent needs.

NOTE ON THE McCARTHY ACT REFERENCE

Understanding the *McCarthy Act Reference* requires returning to June 1882, a few weeks before *Russell* was decided and a Dominion election campaign was underway. Macdonald was outraged that Mowat had a stranglehold on patronage and, when asked in Yorkville about Ontario's *Crooks Act* (the Act that was upheld in *Hodge* late in the following year), he said it was

> not worth the paper it was written on … If he carried the country, as he would [do], he would tell Mr. Mowat—that little tyrant, who had attempted to control public opinion by taking hold of every office, from that of a Division Court bailiff to a tavern-keeper—that he would get a Bill passed at Ottawa returning to the municipalities the power taken away from them by the *License Act*.

When *Russell* was decided, Macdonald concluded that it gave the Dominion exclusive power over liquor licensing. The Speech from the Throne at the opening of Parliament in February 1883 promised that legislation would be introduced "in order to prevent the unrestrained sale of intoxicating liquors, and to regulate the granting of shop, saloon and tavern licenses." When pressed by Edward Blake, who was the leader of the opposition, an eminent lawyer, and a champion of provincial rights, Macdonald spoke confidently about *Russell*:

It is quite clear to every lawyer, and any man who is not a lawyer, who reads that judgment, that the very reasons on which the Privy Council decided ... are the reasons showing that the Provincial legislature had not a right to deal with that subject under the *Crooks Act*, except as a matter of revenue.

A month later, when Macdonald asked for a special committee to investigate and to prepare legislation, Blake gave Macdonald a long lecture about reading *Russell* and about provincial rights. He pointed out that s. 92(8), which had been the major ground for provincial arguments about the police power and local matters, had not been considered in *Russell*, and argued that the history of the distinctive cultures of the colonies and the pre-Confederation legislation should be considered when interpreting the *BNA Act*. He also claimed that there was a crucial difference between prohibition and regulation, and pointed to recent decisions, especially the Ontario Court of Appeal's decision in *Hodge*.

Blake's lecture had no effect on Macdonald, and, in May, Parliament enacted the *McCarthy Act*. Whatever benevolent impulses Macdonald might have felt toward Ontario's municipalities had disappeared. The Act established licensing requirements for hotel, saloon, shop, vessel, and wholesale sales to be administered by the Dominion and the Conservative party. It was quickly referred to the Supreme Court, which decided in early 1885 that it was *ultra vires*, except for wholesale sales and sales on vessels. On appeal, the Privy Council held that it was *ultra vires* entirely. Like the result in *Hodge*, the result was hardly startling—the Dominion could hardly have been permitted to regulate bedding and stables in hotels. Unfortunately, in accordance with the prevailing practice about references, no written reasons were given.

Lawyers had a lot of trouble reconciling *Russell* and *Hodge*, and the result in the *McCarthy Act Reference* didn't help. As well, some decisions of the Canadian courts on related issues compounded the confusion. The most difficult issue, and also the most pressing politically, was the division of powers to prohibit liquor. *Russell* remained a secure authority permitting Dominion prohibition. The provinces had equally secure and exclusive authority to regulate taverns for police purposes. A distinction between prohibition and regulation may now seem to be implicit in these propositions, and it had been expressly made by *Hodge* in terms of purposes, but this kind of analysis was not widely understood and accepted. The most difficult and pressing question was whether the provinces had power to prohibit. Was the power given by *Russell* exclusive? Any prediction would have been precarious, and a confident one would have been foolhardy. *Russell*'s language and the general structure of spheres of exclusive power seemed to some lawyers to say that it was, but the claim of the provinces to govern their own social and moral lives was strong. The Supreme Court had said little— and much of what it had said was vague, at best—and the provincial courts were divided.

Mowat resolved to confront federal power in 1890 by enacting a statute (SC 1890, c. 56) that, by s. 18, gave municipalities power to impose prohibition in the same terms that had existed at Confederation—which was a power to prohibit only retail sales. In 1893, when the opposition in Ontario introduced a bill calling for total prohibition, Mowat responded with an amendment that called for a plebiscite on New Year's Day, 1894. The result was a large majority for prohibition, but Mowat then claimed that the jurisdictional uncertainties must be resolved before the government could act. By agreement with the Dominion government, seven questions were referred to the Supreme Court; the first six were abstract questions about the powers to prohibit sales, manufacturing, and import, and the seventh asked whether the 1890 Act was valid.

A majority of the Supreme Court held that the provinces had no power at all to impose prohibition. The judges who denied the power relied on s. 91(2), and here Gwynne J made his last stand. He began by describing the understandings at Confederation in detail, quoting extensively from speeches and presenting a vision of a powerful Dominion that might have been written by Sir John A. Macdonald, and concluded with a warning that to give control of trade to the local legislatures would deny the intent of the framers and imperil Confederation. An appeal was taken to the Privy Council.

Lord Watson delivered the decision of the Privy Council. As the following excerpt makes clear, not a lot is known about him, though his impact on Canadian constitutional law was formidable (from David Schneiderman, "A.V. Dicey, Lord Watson, and the Law of the Canadian Constitution in the Late Nineteenth Century" (1998), 16 *Law and History Review* 495, at 510-12):

> Born in 1827 in Covington, County of Lanark, Scotland, Watson received his education at the Universities of Edinburgh and Glasgow and was admitted to the bar as advocate in 1851. For the first ten years of his career, he "was practically one of the unemployed" at the Scottish bar, his career "practically a failure." Throughout his adult life Watson was a staunch Tory, and there seems to be little doubt that his rise to the highest ranks of the judiciary was facilitated by his conservative connections. There were few Scottish lawyers in the Conservative Party in 1874, according to the author of Watson's obituary in *The Times*. Thus "it was probably more the accident of his politics than knowledge of his merits which led to his appointment" that year as Solicitor General of Scotland. By then "altogether exceptional at the Scottish bar," reports the *Dictionary of National Biography*, Disraeli was warranted in "rewarding [Watson for] his conservatism." Watson went on to serve as Lord Advocate (the chief law officer of Scotland) and Dean of the Faculty of Advocates (head of the Scottish Bar) while representing the constituency of the Universities of Glasgow and Aberdeen for an undistinguished four years. At the age of fifty-two, Watson was appointed Lord of Appeal in Ordinary, entitling him to a life peerage (as Baron Watson of Thankerton), a seat in the House of Lords, and another on the Judicial Committee of the Privy Council. It was in this last capacity that he earned the title of judicial overseer of the empire. In the words of Richard Burdon (later Viscount) Haldane, Watson "was an imperial judge of the very first order ... one of the greatest lawyers that ever sat upon the British Bench."
>
> By the time of his death in 1899, Watson had distinguished himself not only as a great judge of Scots law but also of the English common law and, for our purposes, of the law of the colonies of the British Empire. According to *The Times*, "it may be doubtful whether in the Victorian era any one has contributed in equal degree to the sum total of British and Imperial jurisprudence." His judicial temperament was described as simple, plain spoken, and inquisitive: "He never wrote a judgement without the greatest consideration, or without consulting every source of information open to him." His one fault (if he had one) was his habit of interrupting counsel too often during argument. Of the particular details of Watson's life, we know little. As was said of him in tribute: "Lives spent in keen intellectual activity are often devoid of outward incident."

AG Ontario v. AG Canada (The Local Prohibition Reference)
[1896] AC 348 (PC); rev'g. (1895), 24 SCR 170

LORD WATSON: … The seventh question raises the issue, whether, in the circumstances which have just been detailed, the provincial legislature had authority to enact s. 18. In order to determine that issue, it becomes necessary to consider, in the first place, whether the Parliament of Canada had jurisdiction to enact the *Canada Temperance Act*; and, if so, to consider in the second place, whether, after that Act became the law of each province of the Dominion, there yet remained power with the Legislature of Ontario to enact the provisions of s. 18.

The authority of the Dominion Parliament to make laws for the suppression of liquor traffic in the provinces is maintained, in the first place, upon the ground that such legislation deals with matters affecting "the peace, order, and good government of Canada," within the meaning of the introductory and general enactments of s. 91 of the *British North America Act*; and, in the second place, upon the ground that it concerns "the regulation of trade and commerce," being No. 2 of the enumerated classes of subjects which are placed under the exclusive jurisdiction of the Federal Parliament by that section. These sources of jurisdictions are in themselves distinct, and are to be found in different enactments.

It was apparently contemplated by the framers of the *Imperial Act* of 1867 that the due exercise of the enumerated powers conferred upon the Parliament of Canada by s. 91 might, occasionally and incidentally, involve legislation upon matters which are *prima facie* committed exclusively to the provincial legislatures by s. 92. In order to provide against that contingency, the concluding part of s. 91 enacts that "any matter coming within any of the classes of subjects enumerated in this section shall not be deemed to come within the class of matters of a local or private nature comprised in the enumeration of the classes of subjects by this Act assigned exclusively to the legislatures of the provinces." It was observed by this Board in *Citizens' Insurance Co. of Canada v. Parsons* (1881), 7 AC 96 at 108 (PC) that the paragraph just quoted "applies in its grammatical construction only to s. 92(16)." The observation was not material to the question arising in that case, and it does not appear to their Lordships to be strictly accurate. It appears to them that the language of the exception in s. 91 was meant to include and correctly describes all the matters enumerated in the sixteen heads of s. 92, as being, from a provincial point of view, of a local or private nature. It also appears to their Lordships that the exception was not meant to derogate from the legislative authority given to provincial legislatures by these sixteen sub-sections, save to the extent of enabling the Parliament of Canada to deal with matters local or private in those cases where such legislation is necessarily incidental to the exercise of the powers conferred upon it by the enumerative heads of clause 91. That view was stated and illustrated by Sir Montague Smith in *Citizens' Insurance v. Parsons* and [several other cases].

The general authority given to the Canadian Parliament by the introductory enactments of s. 91 is "to make laws for the peace, order, and good government of Canada, in relation to all matters not coming within the classes of subjects by this Act assigned exclusively to the legislatures of the provinces"; and it is declared, but not so as to restrict the generality of these words, that the exclusive authority of the Canadian Parliament extends to all matters coming within the classes of subjects which are enumerated in the clause. There may, therefore, be matters not included in the enumeration, upon which the Parliament of Canada has power to legislate, because they concern the peace, order, and good government of the Dominion. But to those matters which are not specified among the enumerated subjects of legislation, the exception from s. 92, which is enacted by the concluding words of s. 91, has no application: and, in legislating with regard to such matters, the Dominion Parliament has no authority to encroach upon any class of subjects which is exclusively assigned to provincial legislatures by s. 92. These enactments appear to their Lordships to indicate that the exercise of legislative power by the Parliament of Canada, in regard to all matters not enumerated in s. 91, ought to be strictly confined to such matters as are unquestionably of Canadian interest and importance, and ought not to trench upon provincial legislation with respect to any of the classes of subjects enumerated in s. 92. To attach any other construction to the general power which, in supplement of its enumerated powers, is conferred upon the Parliament of Canada by s. 91, would, in their Lordships' opinion, not only be contrary to the intendment of the Act, but would practically destroy the autonomy of the provinces. If it were once conceded that the Parliament of Canada has authority to make laws applicable to the whole Dominion, in relation to matters which in each province are substantially of local or private interest, upon the assumption that these matters also concern the peace, order, and good government of the Dominion, there is hardly a subject enumerated in s. 92 upon which it might not legislate, to the exclusion of the provincial legislatures.

In construing the introductory enactments of s. 91, with respect to matters other than those enumerated, which concern the peace, order, and good government of Canada, it must be kept in view that s. 94, which empowers the Parliament of Canada to make provision for the uniformity of the laws relative to property and civil rights in Ontario, Nova Scotia, and New Brunswick does not extend to the province of Quebec; and also that the Dominion legislation thereby authorized is expressly declared to be of no effect unless and until it has been adopted and enacted by the provincial legislature. These enactments would be idle and abortive, if it were held that the Parliament of Canada derives jurisdiction from the introductory provisions of s. 91, to deal with any matter which is in substance local or provincial, and does not truly affect the interest of the Dominion as a whole. Their Lordships do not doubt that some matters, in their origin local and provincial, might attain such dimensions as to affect the body politic of the Dominion, and to justify the Canadian Parliament in passing laws for their regulation or abolition in the interest of the Dominion. But great caution must be observed in distinguishing between that which is local and provincial, and therefore within the jurisdiction of the provincial legislatures, and that which has ceased to be merely local or provincial, and has become matter of national concern, in such sense as to bring it within the jurisdiction of the Parliament of Canada. An Act restricting the right to carry weapons of offence, or their sale to young persons, within the province would be within the authority of the provincial legislature. But traffic in arms, or the possession of them under such circumstances as to raise a suspicion that they were to be used for seditious purposes, or against a foreign State, are matters which, their Lordships conceive, might be competently dealt with by the Parliament of the Dominion.

The judgment of this Board in *Russell v. The Queen* (1882), 7 AC 829 (PC) has relieved their Lordships from the difficult duty of considering whether the *Canada Temperance*

Act of 1886 relates to the peace, order, and good government of Canada, in such sense as to bring its provisions within the competency of the Canadian Parliament. In that case the controversy related to the validity of the *Canada Temperance Act* of 1878; and neither the Dominion nor the Provinces were represented in the argument. It arose between a private prosecutor and a person who had been convicted, at his instance, of violating the provisions of the Canadian Act within a district of New Brunswick, in which the prohibitory clauses of the Act had been adopted. But the provisions of the Act of 1878 were in all material respects the same with those which are now embodied in the *Canada Temperance Act* of 1886; and the reasons which were assigned for sustaining the validity of the earlier, are, in their Lordships' opinion, equally applicable to the later Act. It therefore appears to them that the decision in *Russell v. The Queen* must be accepted as an authority to the extent to which it goes, namely, that the restrictive provisions of the Act of 1886, when they have been duly brought into operation in any provincial area within the Dominion, must receive effect as valid enactments relating to the peace, order, and good government of Canada.

That point being settled by decision, it becomes necessary to consider whether the Parliament of Canada had authority to pass the *Canada Temperance Act* of 1886 as being an Act for the "regulation of trade and commerce" within the meaning of s. 91(2). If it were so, the Parliament of Canada would, under the exception from s. 92 which has already been noticed, be at liberty to exercise its legislative authority, although in so doing it should interfere with the jurisdiction of the provinces. The scope and effect of s. 91(2) were discussed by this Board at some length in *Citizens' Insurance Co. v. Parsons*, where it was decided that, in the absence of legislation upon the subject by the Canadian Parliament, the Legislature of Ontario had authority to impose conditions, as being matters of civil right, upon the business of fire insurance, which was admitted to be a trade, so long as those conditions only affected provincial trade. Their Lordships do not find it necessary to reopen that discussion in the present case. The object of the *Canada Temperance Act* of 1886 is, not to regulate retail transactions between those who trade in liquor and their customers, but to abolish all such transactions within every provincial area in which its enactments have been adopted by a majority of the local electors. A power to regulate, naturally, if not necessarily, assumes, unless it is enlarged by the context, the conservation of the thing which is to be made the subject of regulation. In that view, their Lordships are unable to regard the prohibitive enactments of the Canadian statute of 1886 as regulations of trade and commerce. They see no reason to modify the opinion which was recently expressed on their behalf by Lord Davey in *Municipal Corporation of the City of Toronto v. Virgo*, [1896] AC 88 at 93 (PC) in these terms: "Their Lordships think there is marked distinction to be drawn between the prohibition or prevention of a trade and the regulation or governance of it, and indeed a power to regulate and govern seems to imply the continued existence of that which is to be regulated or governed."

The authority of the Legislature of Ontario to enact s. 18 of [the 1890 Act] was asserted by the appellant on various grounds. The first of these, which was very strongly insisted on, was to the effect that the power given to each province by s. 92(8) to create municipal institutions in the province necessarily implies the right to endow these institutions with all the administrative functions which had been ordinarily possessed and exercised by them before the time of the Union. Their Lordships can find nothing to support that contention in the language of s. 92(8), which, according to its natural meaning, simply gives provincial legislatures the right to create a legal body for the management of municipal affairs. Until confederation, the Legislature of each province as then constituted could, if it chose, and did in some cases, entrust to a municipality the execution of powers which now belong exclusively to the Parliament of Canada. Since its date a provincial Legislature cannot delegate any power which it does not possess; and the extent and nature of the functions which it can commit to a municipal body of its own creation must depend upon the legislative authority which it derives from the provisions of s. 92 other than s. 92(8).

Their Lordships are likewise of opinion that s. 92(9) does not give provincial legislatures any right to make laws for the abolition of the liquor traffic. It assigns to them "shop, saloon, tavern, auctioneer and other licences, in order to the raising of a revenue for provincial, local or municipal purposes." It was held by this Board in *Hodge v. The Queen* (1883), 9 AC 117 (PC) to include the right to impose reasonable conditions upon the licencees which are in the nature of regulation; but it cannot, with any show of reason, be construed as authorizing the abolition of the sources from which revenue is to be raised.

The only enactments of s. 92 which appear to their Lordships to have any relation to the authority of provincial legislatures to make laws for the suppression of the liquor traffic are to be found in ss. 92(13) and (16), which assign to their exclusive jurisdiction, (1.) "property and civil rights in the province," and (2.) "generally all matters of a merely local or private nature in the province." A law which prohibits retail transactions and restricts the consumption of liquor within the ambit of the province, and does not affect transactions in liquor between persons in the province and persons in other provinces or in foreign countries, concerns property in the province which would be the subject-matter of the transactions if they were not prohibited, and also the civil rights of persons in the province. It is not impossible that the vice of intemperance may prevail in particular localities within a province to such an extent as to constitute its cure by restricting or prohibiting the sale of liquor a matter of a merely local or private nature, and therefore falling prima facie within s. 92(16). In that state of matters, it is conceded that the Parliament of Canada could not imperatively enact a prohibitory law adapted and confined to the requirements of localities within the province where prohibition was urgently needed. ...

It is not necessary for the purposes of the present appeal to determine whether provincial legislation for the suppression of the liquor traffic, confined to matters which are provincial or local within the meaning of ss. 92(13) and (16), is authorized by the one or by the other of these heads. It cannot, in their Lordships' opinion, be logically held to fall within both of them. In s. 92, ss. (16) appears to them to have the same office which the general enactment with respect to matters concerning the peace, order, and good government of Canada, so far as supplementary of the enumerated subjects, fulfils in s. 91. It assigns to the provincial legislature all matters in a provincial sense local or private which have been omitted from the preceding enumeration, and, although its terms are wide enough to cover, they were obviously not meant to include, provincial legislation in relation to the classes of subjects already enumerated.

In the able and elaborate argument addressed to their Lordships on behalf of the respondents it was practically conceded that a provincial legislature must have power to deal with the restriction of the liquor traffic from a local and provincial point of view, unless it be held that the whole subject of restriction or abolition is exclusively committed to the Parliament of Canada as being within the regulation of trade and commerce. In that case the subject, in so far at least as it had been regulated by Canadian legislation, would, by virtue of the concluding enactment of s. 91, be excepted from the matters committed to provincial legislatures by s. 92. Upon the assumption that s. 91(2) does not embrace the right to suppress a trade, Mr. Blake maintained that, whilst the restriction of the liquor traffic may be competently made matter of legislation in a provincial as well as a Canadian aspect, yet the Parliament of Canada has, by enacting the *Canada Temperance Act* of 1886, occupied the whole possible field of legislation in either aspect, so as completely to exclude legislation by a province. That appears to their Lordships to be the real point of controversy raised by the question with which they are at present dealing; and, before discussing the point, it may be expedient to consider the relation in which Dominion and provincial legislation stand to each other.

It has been frequently recognised by this Board, and it may now be regarded as settled law, that according to the scheme of the *British North America Act* the enactments of the Parliament of Canada, in so far as these are within its competency, must override provincial legislation. But the Dominion Parliament has no authority conferred upon it by the Act to repeal directly any provincial statute, whether it does or does not come within the limits of jurisdiction prescribed by s. 92. The repeal of a provincial Act by the Parliament of Canada can only be effected by repugnancy between its provisions and the enactments of the Dominion; and if the existence of such repugnancy should become a matter of dispute, the controversy cannot be settled by the action either of the Dominion or of the provincial legislature, but must be submitted to the judicial tribunals of the country. In their Lordships' opinion the express repeal of the old provincial Act of 1864 by the *Canada Temperance Act* of 1886 was not within the authority of the Parliament of Canada. ...

In like manner, the express repeal, in the *Canada Temperance Act* of 1886, of liquor prohibitions adopted by a municipality in the province of Ontario under the sanction of provincial legislation, does not appear to their Lordships to be within the authority of the Dominion Parliament.

The question must next be considered whether the provincial enactments of s. 18 to any, and if so to what, extent come into collision with the provisions of the *Canadian Act* of 1886. In so far as they do, provincial must yield to Dominion legislation, and must remain in abeyance unless and until the Act of 1886 is repealed by the parliament which passed it.

The prohibitions of the *Dominion Act* have in some respects an effect which may extend beyond the limits of a province, and they are all of a very stringent character. ...

On the other hand, the prohibitions which s. 18 authorizes municipalities to impose within their respective limits do not appear to their Lordships to affect any transactions in liquor which have not their beginning and their end within the province of Ontario. ...

It thus appears that, in their local application within the province of Ontario, there would be considerable difference between the two laws; but it is obvious that their provisions could not be in force within the same district or province at one and the same time. In the opinion of their Lordships the question of conflict between their provisions which arises in this case does not depend upon their identity or non-identity, but upon a feature which is common to both. Neither statute is imperative, their prohibitions being of no force or effect until they have been voluntarily adopted and applied by the vote of a majority of the electors in a district or municipality. In *Russell v. The Queen* it was observed by this Board, with reference to the *Canada Temperance Act* of 1878, "The Act as soon as it was passed became a law for the whole Dominion, and the enactments of the first part, relating to the machinery for bringing the second part into force, took effect and might be put in motion at once and everywhere within it." No fault can be found with the accuracy of that statement. *Mutatis mutandis*, it is equally true as a description of the provisions of s. 18. But in neither case can the statement mean more than this, that, on the passing of the Act, each district or municipality within the Dominion or the province, as the case might be, became vested with a right to adopt and enforce certain prohibitions if it thought fit to do so. But the prohibitions of these Acts, which constitute their object and their essence, cannot with the least degree of accuracy be said to be in force anywhere until they have been locally adopted.

If the prohibitions of the *Canada Temperance Act* had been made imperative throughout the Dominion, their Lordships might have been constrained by previous authority to hold that the jurisdiction of the Legislature of Ontario to pass s. 18 or any similar law had been superseded. In that case no provincial prohibitions such as are sanctioned by s. 18 could have been enforced by a municipality without coming into conflict with the paramount law of Canada. For the same reason, provincial prohibitions in force within a particular district will necessarily become inoperative whenever the prohibitory clauses of the Act of 1886 have been adopted by that district. But their Lordships can discover no adequate grounds for holding that there exists repugnancy between the two laws in districts of the province of Ontario where the prohibitions of the Canadian Act are not and may never be in force. ...

Their Lordships, for these reasons, ... are of opinion that the Ontario Legislature had jurisdiction to enact s. 18, subject to this necessary qualification, that its provisions are or will become inoperative in any district of the province which has already adopted, or may subsequently adopt, the second part of the *Canada Temperance Act* of 1886.

[Lord Watson went on to hold that, in the absence of conflicting federal legislation, a province possesses the jurisdiction to prohibit the manufacture of liquor within the province if the manufacture was carried on in such a way as to make its prohibition a merely local matter in the province, but that it lacks the jurisdiction to prohibit the importation of liquor.]

Appeal allowed.

NOTE: THE NATURE OF FEDERALISM

What did lawyers understand about the basic nature of federalism in the late nineteenth century? We begin with an excerpt from the leading English text, *Introduction to the Study of the Law of the Constitution*, by A.V. Dicey (London: Macmillan, 1885), at 131, 132, and 161-62, which we use because it was the dominant statement of the constitutional faiths of English and Canadian lawyers during the late nineteenth century.

A federal state is a political contrivance intended to reconcile national unity and power with the maintenance of "state rights." The end aimed at fixes the essential character of federalism. For the method by which federalism attempts to reconcile the apparently inconsistent claims of national sovereignty and of state sovereignty consists of the formation of a constitution under which the ordinary powers of sovereignty are elaborately divided between the common or national government and the separate states. The details of this division vary under every different federal constitution, but the general principle on which it should rest is obvious. Whatever concerns the nation as a whole should be placed under the control of the national government. All matters which are not primarily of common interest should remain in the hands of the several States.

From the notion that national unity can be reconciled with state independence by a division of powers under a common constitution between the nation on the one hand and the individual States on the other, flow the three leading characteristics of completely developed federalism— the supremacy of the constitution—the distribution among bodies with limited and co-ordinate authority of the different powers of government—the authority of the Courts to act as interpreters of the constitution.

After a lengthy analysis of these three characteristics, Dicey made some general comments, "of more than merely legal interest," about federalism, including this observation about "legalism":

Federalism, lastly, means legalism—the predominance of the judiciary in the constitution—the prevalence of a spirit of legality among the people.

That in a confederation like the United States the Courts become the pivot on which the constitutional arrangements of the country turn is obvious. Sovereignty is lodged in a body which rarely exerts its authority and has (so to speak) only a potential existence; no legislature throughout the land is more than a subordinate law-making body capable in strictness of enacting nothing but by-laws; the powers of the executive are again limited by the constitution; the interpreters of the constitution are the judges. The Bench therefore can and must determine the limits to the authority both of the government and of the legislature; its decision is without appeal; the consequence follows that the Bench of judges is not only the guardian but also at a given moment the master of the constitution.

Doubtless, Canadians shared the essence of these beliefs. They may, though, have differed in emphasis. Consider this paragraph from D.A. O'Sullivan's *Government in Canada: The Principles and Institutions of Our Federal and Provincial Constitutions* (Scarborough, ON: Carswell, 1887), at 7-8.

A federal union then means two perfectly independent co-ordinate powers in the same state. The powers of each are equally sovereign and neither are derived from the other. The state governments are not subordinate to the general government, nor the general government to the state governments. They are co-ordinate governments standing on the same level and deriving their powers from the same sovereign authority. In their respective spheres neither yields to the other. Each is independent in its own work; incomplete and dependent on the other for the complete work of government.

Arguably, O'Sullivan's beliefs are, in contrast to Dicey's, marked by an emphasis on the autonomy of the provinces and the federal government: they are mutually exclusive spheres of power, separated by sharp boundaries. If this perception is correct, perhaps a large part of the reason is that visions of federalism were a fighting ground in the struggle for power between the provinces and the federal government. O'Sullivan's model is aggressive, and it expresses the eventual triumph of the provinces.

NOTE: THE COMPACT THEORY

Next, we turn to the compact theory. Its foundation was its claim about the way the Dominion had been created: the colonies had made a compact, ratified by the British Parliament, creating the Dominion and conferring powers and property and, after Confederation, they continued to exist as the new provinces. One of the first sustained expressions of this theory was by T.J.J. Loranger, a Quebec judge, in a series of pamphlets that were published as a book early in 1883: *Letters Upon the Interpretation of the Federal Constitution* (Quebec, 1884). He began by declaring that the French nation in Quebec was threatened by centralizing tendencies in the early judgments of the Supreme Court about the *BNA Act*.

> During the past century of British rule, the French race in Canada has been through many political crises and has fought many political battles. It has, however, come out triumphant, and averted the dangers which threatened it.
>
> The antagonism resulting from different institutions, traditions, languages and religious beliefs—irresistible when people of various origins dwell in the same territory—which influences them sometimes without their knowledge and often against their will, has made the position of this race an exceptional one in the midst of the Anglo-Saxon population of the Confederation.
>
> The rivalry of races is the same as that which existed under former regimes, but is on a larger scale. ...
>
> French-Canadians should, under the new regime as they did under the old, see with jealous care to the maintenance of their national rights, the preservation of their political autonomy, combat and prevent any aggression that may disturb these guarantees.

Loranger then set out the elements of the "federal compact":

> 1. In constituting themselves into a confederation, the provinces did not intend to renounce, and in fact never did renounce their autonomy. This autonomy with their rights, powers and prerogatives they expressly preserved for all that concerns their internal government; by forming themselves into a federal association, under political and legislative aspects, they formed a central government, only for interprovincial objects, and, far from having created the provincial powers, it is from these provincial powers that has arisen the federal government, to which the provinces have ceded a portion of their rights, property and revenues.
> 2. At the time of Confederation, all legislative and executive power, legal attributes, public property and revenues that are now the appanagé of the central government and of the provinces, belonged to the latter. The federal compact did not create a single new power. The part now belonging to the federal government was taken from the jurisdiction of the provinces.

In the early 1880s, the provincial rights advocates began to use the compact as support for a wide range of their claims. Although Loranger used it to defend the French-Canadians, it was embraced by politicians and common law lawyers (and many of the central individuals were both) as well. One claim, which during the twentieth century has become the best-known, was that the *BNA Act* could not be amended without the consent of each of the parties: the provinces. Other claims, though, loomed larger in the 1880s, all of them directed at interpretation of the *BNA Act*. For example, the provinces were entitled to government property not clearly allocated to the Dominion and to all legislative powers not specifically granted to the Dominion—the residue of legislative power. As well, their lieutenant governors had the stature and powers they possessed before Confederation.

In Quebec, the compact has continued to be a powerful part of constitutional beliefs, but its hold among common law lawyers began to fade in the late 1880s. Although it has been resurrected several times since, it had little direct influence on the law. One major reason is that, so far as it is an account of what happened at Confederation, it was vulnerable to the simple claim that it was fundamentally inaccurate. More interesting is another possible reason, one based on beliefs about interpretation. The compact was derived from the history of making the *BNA Act*, but the prevailing beliefs about interpretation (demonstrated, for example, by the Privy Council in *Hodge*) were at odds with considering history of this kind.

This incompatibility is demonstrated in the leading constitutional text, A.F.H. Lefroy, *The Law of Legislative Power in Canada* (Toronto: Law Book and Publishing, 1897-1898). Lefroy's first proposition declared that the *BNA Act* was the "sole charter" for determining the rights of the Dominion and the provinces. Given the basic understandings of sovereignty, constitutions, and interpretation, this principle was both basic and inescapable, but it was an assertion about both the origins of the nation and the interpretation of its constitution that excluded any consideration of a compact. The second proposition was that the *BNA Act*, because it was founded on the Quebec resolutions, "must be accepted as a treaty of union between the provinces" but, once enacted, it became a "wholly new point of departure." The contrast between the two branches seemed to acknowledge a compact, but only as an historical event, irrelevant to interpretation. In this light, the compact foundered because it was at odds with the dominant common law thought.

NOTE: THE POWER OF DISALLOWANCE

The power of disallowance did not sit well with the compact theory of federalism or a conception of legislative supremacy within exclusive spheres of jurisdiction. The power, as expressed in ss. 59 and 90 of the *Constitution Act, 1867*, entitles the Governor General, acting on the advice of the federal cabinet, to reserve for up to one year and then disallow (or veto) any enactment of the provincial legislatures. A similar power is exercisable as between the Crown and the Canadian parliament, but this is not the focus of discussion here. The subordination of provincial power to federal did not fit well with an understanding of Canadian federalism premised on equality of federal and provincial authority.

The following excerpt from W.P.M. Kennedy illustrates the uses to which the power was put in the years immediately after Confederation (from *The Constitution of Canada: An Introduction to Its Development and Law* (London: Oxford University Press, 1922), at 415-21):

We can well understand a principle of disallowance where a constitutional question arises, or where dominion or imperial interests are threatened by a provincial Act; but it would be safer if the decision in such cases were left to the courts as in the United States, since in a federation differences on Constitutional law must frequently arise. The resolution of the problem of *intra vires* or *ultra vires* ought not to be left to the minister of justice. This tends to make him too supreme, and to detract from the character of the supreme court of Canada or of the privy council. For many years, however, after 1867 the dominion government considered it was justified in disallowing provincial Acts which appeared unjust or oppressive—through, for example, interference with vested rights without compensation, or through the impairing of contractual obligations. Provincial Acts were disallowed under these principles.

It appears early to have been a working convention of the Canadian constitution that, as the courts would deal with legislation *ultra vires* of the provinces, the power of disallowance was intended to cover cases outside legal review. In other words, the power of disallowance was inserted in the *British North America Act* to cover, in general terms, unjust, confiscatory, or *ex post facto* legislation, against which there are express safeguards in the constitution of the United States. ...

Whatever other motives—if any—which may have been at work during that period, it is clear that there is a certain consistency of purpose in dealing with provincial legislation which appeared to hurt private property, to invalidate contracts, or to be contrary to what were known as "sound principles of legislation." It lies outside the discussion to search for or to examine motives which political writers have suggested. All that can be said here is that the constitutional power of disallowance was consistently used during these years to protect those spheres of provincial civil life which are protected explicitly or by implication in the constitution of the United States.

By the mid-twentieth century, the federal power of disallowance fell into disuse. The federal government offered it up for negotiation in the rounds of constitutional reform in 1987 (Meech Lake) and again in 1992 (Charlottetown). The legal text of the Charlottetown Accord proposed that this federal power be repealed. Though the constitutional proposals failed, Canadians likely will see the power return as a subject in whatever future constitutional negotiations may be conducted.

THE MANITOBA SCHOOLS QUESTION

The province of Manitoba entered Canada in 1870 on terms intended to guarantee denominational education rights to Roman Catholics. Population growth in the years following made the province overwhelmingly Protestant and English speaking. This enabled the Protestant majority to sweep away all denominational control and impose a non-sectarian public school system (or what were called the old Protestant schools "thinly disguised"). The Roman Catholic minority were forced to choose between sending their children to Protestant schools or bearing the burden of paying for both public and separate schools.

The context that gave rise to this controversy is set out in the following excerpt from Gordon Bale, "Law, Politics and the Manitoba School Question: Supreme Court and Privy Council" (1985), 63 *Canadian Bar Review* 461, at 466-73:

Confederation of 1867 stretched only from the Atlantic to Lake Superior, but the vision of a transcontinental nation was clearly enunciated in section 146 of the Constitution Act, 1867 in its provision for the admission of Newfoundland, Prince Edward Island, British Columbia, Rupert's Land and the North-western Territory into the union. The dream of a dominion stretching from sea to sea was threatened by the westward expansion of the United States and its purchase of Alaska from Russia in 1867, and Sir John A. Macdonald appreciated that continuing to haggle with the Hudson's Bay Company jeopardized the Canadian transcontinental dream. In 1869, George-Etienne Cartier and William McDougall, dispatched to London, purchased Rupert's Land for one and a half million dollars and gave a guarantee that five per cent of the land in the fertile belt would continue to belong to the Hudson's Bay Company.

The Canadian government failed to assure the local inhabitants that their rights would be respected. When surveyors sent to the Red River appeared to disregard completely the river-strip holding of the Metis, Riel and a party of armed horsemen broke up the survey party. Riel then organized the Metis, prevented Lieutenant-Governor-designate William McDougall from entering, seized Fort Garry and put down an attempted overthrow by Dr. John Schultz, the leader of the Canadians in the Red River. On December 29, 1869, Riel assumed the presidency of the provisional government. In February 1870 another bungled effort was made to unseat Riel, and Thomas Scott was captured. Scott was tried before a court-martial presided over by Ambrose Lepine, adjutant general in the provisional government, and a jury of six Metis; he was found guilty, and on March 4, 1870 was taken outside the walls of Fort Garry and shot by a firing squad. The execution of this Orangeman fuelled anti-Catholic feeling in Ontario.

Macdonald was appalled by the events because they revealed Canadian impotence to both Americans and Metis. The formal transfer of Rupert's Land to Canada was to have occurred on December 1, 1869; Macdonald now had the date postponed. As he was reluctant to seek permission to send troops through the United States, he had no alternative but to negotiate with Riel and await the spring. Donald A. Smith, the Hudson's Bay Commissioner in Montreal, travelled to the Red River in the winter of 1869-70. Smith persuaded Riel to state the demands of his provisional government and to choose delegates to send to Ottawa. Many of the Metis demands were agreed to by Macdonald and Cartier and were incorporated in the Manitoba Act. On July 15, 1870, the transfer of the whole northwest to Canada occurred and simultaneously Manitoba became a new province. On that day the new Lieutenant-Governor, Adams G. Archibald, left Port Arthur, accompanied by a force of 1,200 British and Canadian soldiers under Colonel Garnet Wolseley, who navigated the old voyageur route to Fort Garry. Canada's introduction to the West was thus marred by its association with military force.

A census taken in 1871 revealed that there were 5,720 French-speaking Half-breeds or Metis, 4,080 English-speaking Half-breeds or "country-born" and only 1,600 White settlers. Two provisions of the Manitoba Act reflect the approximately equal balance between French-speaking Roman Catholics and English-peaking Protestants. Section 22 of the Manitoba Act provided that the legislature might exclusively enact laws relating to education, subject to three provisions, of which the first was:

> Nothing in any Law shall prejudicially affect any right or privilege with respect to Denominational Schools which any class of persons have by Law or practice in the Province at the Union.

Section 23 provided that either English or French could be used in the legislature or in any courts, and Acts of the legislature were to be printed and published in both languages. The religious compromise, in the form of the denominational educational guarantee upon which Canada was founded, was thus projected westward. It should, however, be emphasized that Manitoba was to be a province like Quebec, not one like Ontario, Nova Scotia and New Brunswick. The language guarantee of section 23 of the Manitoba Act was virtually identical to that contained in section 133 of the Constitution Act, 1867. Section 133 accorded equal status to English and French in Parliament and the federal courts, but then provided that such equal status would prevail only in Quebec and not in the other original provinces. ...

The linguistic and religious guarantees of the Manitoba Act were appropriate for a province which was almost equally balanced between Francophones and Anglophones and between Roman Catholics and Protestants. The subsequent demographic changes in Manitoba in the 1870s and 1880s were enormous. The population increased almost fourteen fold in twenty years. There had been a large influx of Protestant and English-speaking settlers, particularly from Ontario. The Manitoba of 1890 was therefore strikingly different in composition from the Manitoba of 1870. The census of 1891 revealed that Manitoba had a population of 152,500, of which only 20,571 or thirteen per cent were Roman Catholics, and only 9,949 or seven per cent were French Canadians. ...

In 1890, the Department of Education Act was passed by the Manitoba Legislature. Section 18 provided that the existing Board of Education and Superintendents of Education were to cease to hold office and were to "deliver over to the Provincial Secretary all records, books, papers, documents and property of every kind belonging to said Boards." The Catholic section of the Board ceased to exist and its property was compulsorily acquired without compensation. The Public Schools Act then provided for free non-sectarian education to be paid for by an assessment of all ratepayers, Protestant and Catholic, in each municipality. The Manitoba legislature at the same session also passed the Official Language Act, which, in spite of section 23 of the Manitoba Act, 1890, made English the sole official language. ...

In *Barrett v. City of Winnipeg* (1891), 1 SCR 374, Mr. Barrett challenged the levy issued by the City of Winnipeg on the assessed value of his property in order to support the new public school system. Barrett argued that this prejudicially affected denominational school rights of Roman Catholics by requiring them to contribute twice: to free public schools, to which they could not, in good conscience send children, and to Roman Catholic Schools. In the lower courts, the judges of the Trial Division and Manitoba Court of Queen's Bench split along denominational lines. On appeal, the Supreme Court of Canada reversed these decisions and eschewed the appearance of sectarian allegiance. The Court held the Public Schools Act *ultra vires*. Chief Justice Ritchie wrote:

Does it not prejudicially, that is to say injuriously, disadvantageously, which is the meaning of the word "prejudicially," affect them when they are taxed to support schools of the benefit of which, by their religious belief and the rules and principles of their church, they cannot conscientiously avail themselves, and at the same time by compelling them to find means to support schools to which they can conscientiously send their children, or in the event of their not being able to find sufficient means to do both to be compelled to allow their children to go without either religious or secular instruction? In other words, I think the Catholics were directly prejudicially affected by such legislation, but whether directly or indirectly the local legislature was powerless to affect them prejudicially in the matter of denominational schools which they certainly did by practically depriving them of their denominational schools and compelling them to support schools the benefit of which Protestants alone can enjoy.

On appeal to the Judicial Committee of the Privy Council, the case was joined to that of Mr. Logan, who mischievously sought similar relief on behalf of Anglicans in Winnipeg as was accorded to Roman Catholics. In *City of Winnipeg v. Barrett; City of Winnipeg v. Logan*, [1892] AC 445, the Board reversed the decision of the Supreme Court. According to Lord MacNaghten:

> Catholics and members of every other religious body in Manitoba are free to establish schools throughout the province; they are free to maintain their schools by school fees or voluntary subscriptions; they are free to conduct their schools according to their own religious tenets without molestation or interference. No child is compelled to attend a public school. No special advantage other than the advantage of a free education in schools conducted under public management is held out to those who do attend. But then it is said that it is impossible for Roman Catholics, or for members of the Church of England (if their views are correctly represented by the Bishop of Rupert's Land, who has given evidence in Logan's case), to send their children to public schools where the education is not superintended and directed by the authorities of their Church, and that therefore Roman Catholics and members of the Church of England who are taxed for public schools, and at the same time feel themselves compelled to support their own schools, are in a less favourable position than those who can take advantage of the free education provided by the Act of 1890. That may be so. But what right or privilege is violated or prejudicially affected by the law? It is not the law that is in fault. It is owing to religious convictions which everybody must respect, and to the teaching of their Church, that Roman Catholics and members of the Church of England find themselves unable to partake of advantages which the law offers to all alike.

After the Privy Council's decision, the federal cabinet chose to refer six questions to the Supreme Court of Canada. The questions, in sum, asked whether the Roman Catholic minority could appeal to the federal cabinet because a right or privilege in relation to education had been affected by the 1890 Act. In *Brophy v. Attorney-General of Manitoba* (1894), 22 SCR 577, the Supreme Court of Canada, following the lead of the Privy Council in *Barrett* split three to two, ruling against the Roman Catholic minority. Chief Justice Strong, writing for the majority, held that the Governor-General in Council (the federal cabinet) had no remedial authority it could exercise in this case. It could not be suggested that the Province of Manitoba did not have the right to repeal rights and privileges conferred under statute:

> [T]here is, it seems to me, much force in the consideration, that whilst it was reasonable that the organic law should preserve vested rights existing at the union from spoliation or interference, yet every presumption must be made in favour of the constitutional right of a legislative body to repeal the laws which it has itself enacted. No doubt this right may be controlled by a written constitution which confers legislative powers, and which may restrict those powers and make them subject to any condition which the constituent legislators may think fit to impose. A notable instance of this is, as my brother King has pointed out, afforded by the constitution of the United States, according to the construction which the Supreme Court in the well known

"*Dartmouth College* case" put upon the provision prohibiting the state legislatures from passing laws impairing the obligation of contracts. It was there held, with a result which has been found most inconvenient, that a legislature which had created a private corporation could not repeal its own enactment granting the franchise, the reason assigned being that the grant of the franchise of a corporation was a contract. This has in practice been got over by inserting in such acts an express reservation of the right of the legislature to repeal its own act. But, as it is a *prima facie* presumption that every legislative enactment is subject to repeal by the same body which enacts it, every statute may be said to contain an implied provision that it may be revoked by the authority which has passed it, unless the right of repeal is taken away by the fundamental law, the overriding constitution which has created the legislature itself. The point is a new one, but having regard to the strength and universality of the presumption that every legislative body has power to repeal its own laws, and that this power is almost indispensable to the useful exercise of legislative authority since a great deal of legislation is of necessity tentative and experimental, would it be arbitrary or unreasonable, or altogether unsupported by analogy, to hold as a canon of constitutional construction that such an inherent right to repeal its own acts cannot be deemed to be withheld from a legislative body having its origin in a written constitution, unless the constitution itself, by express words, takes away the right. I am of opinion that in construing the Manitoba Act we ought to proceed upon this principle and hold the legislature of that province to have absolute powers over its own legislation, untrammelled by any appeal to federal authority, unless we find some restriction of its rights in this respect in express terms in the constitutional act.

In a startling reversal in tone from the *Logan* and *Barrett* decisions, the Privy Council in *Brophy* ([1895] AC 209) found that the rights and privileges of Roman Catholics existing before 1890 had been affected. According to Lord Herschell:

> Contrast the position of the Roman Catholics prior and subsequent to the Acts from which they appeal. Before these passed into law there existed denominational schools, of which the control and management were in the hands of Roman Catholics, who could select the books to be used and determine the character of the religious teaching. These schools received their proportionate share of the money contributed for school purposes out of the general taxation of the province, and the money raised for these purposes by local assessment was, so far as it fell upon Catholics, applied only towards the support of Catholic schools. What is the position of the Roman Catholic minority under the Acts of 1890? Schools of their own denomination, conducted according to their views, will receive no aid from the State. They must depend entirely for their support upon the contributions of the Roman Catholic community, while the taxes out of which State aid is granted to the schools provided for by the statute fall alike on Catholics and Protestants. Moreover, while the Catholic inhabitants remain liable to local assessment for school purposes, the proceeds of that assessment are no longer destined to any extent for the support of Catholic schools, but afford the means of maintaining schools which they regard as no more suitable for the education of Catholic children than if they were distinctively Protestant in their character.
>
> In view of this comparison it does not seem possible to say that the rights and privileges of the Roman Catholic minority in relation to education which existed prior to 1890 have not been affected.

Before the federal government could enact remedial legislation under s. 22(3), the federal election of 1896 intervened. The Liberal leader, Wilfrid Laurier, had maintained that a strategy of "conciliation" rather than one of confrontation with the province was the only approach which could restore any measure of rights to the minority. Voluntary concessions, he maintained, would better secure the minority's interests than interfere with provincial rights. In his famous speech on second reading of the remedial bill in the House of Commons, Laurier declared that if it were to become law, "while it would afford no protection whatever to the suffering minority in Manitoba, it would be a most violent wrench of the principles upon which our constitution is based." This remedy of interfering in local legislation, Laurier observed, "has never been applied and probably never can be applied without friction, disturbance and discontent." In the ensuing election campaign, the Church threw its support behind the Conservatives, led by Sir Charles Tupper. Laurier, nevertheless, carried the election, even in the Catholic province of Quebec.

Once in office, Laurier reached his negotiated settlement with the province of Manitoba. Religious teaching could be carried on at the end of the school day; at least one Roman Catholic teacher would be employed in urban and rural schools, where the average attendance exceeded a certain number; and where ten pupils spoke the French language "or any language other than English, as their native language, the teaching of such pupils shall be conducted in French, or such other language, and English upon a bilingual system." According to Laurier's biographer, O.D. Skelton, in essence, "the agreement left the system of public schools intact, but secured for the minority distinct religious teaching, and, where numbers warranted, teachers of their own faith and the maintenance of the French tongue. The language clause was framed in general terms by the provincial authorities in order to make it apply to the German Mennonites as well as to the French Catholics. (*Life and Letters of Sir Wilfrid Laurier*, vol. 2 (Toronto: Oxford University Press, 1921), at 17.)

CHAPTER FIVE

The Early Twentieth Century: The Beginnings of Economic Regulation

This chapter continues the story of federalism into the early twentieth century. In 1898, the Yukon Territory was carved out of the western corner of the Northwest Territories, and, in 1905, Alberta and Saskatchewan were created out of the Northwest Territories' southern expanse. During this period, regulation of the economy expanded, and this is the subject of most of the cases in this chapter. The dominant personality is Lord Richard Burdon Haldane. Because it is unclear whether his decisions in the 1920s were his own contribution or a faithful elaboration of the earlier doctrine, especially the decisions of Lord Watson, an excerpt from his assessment of Lord Watson, written in 1899, is an appropriate beginning.

Lord R.B. Haldane, "Lord Watson"
(1899), 11 *Juridical Review* 278, at 279-81

He was an Imperial judge of the very first order. The function of such a judge, sitting in the supreme tribunal of the Empire, is to do more than decide what abstract and familiar legal conceptions should be applied to particular cases. His function is to be a statesman as well as a jurist, to fill in the gaps which Parliament has deliberately left in the skeleton constitutions and laws that it has provided for the British Colonies. The Imperial legislature has taken the view that these constitutions and laws must, if they are to be acceptable, be in a large measure unwritten, elastic, and capable of being silently developed and even altered as the Colony develops and alters. This imposes a task of immense importance and difficulty upon the Privy Council judges, and it was this task which Lord Watson had to face when some fifteen years ago he found himself face to face with what threatened to be a critical period in the history of Canada. Lord Carnarvon's *Confederation Act of 1867*, which had given separate legislatures and executives to the Provinces, had by no means completely defined the relations of these legislatures and their Lieutenant-Governors to the Parliament and Governor-General of the Dominion. Two views were being contended for. The one was that, excepting in such cases as were specially provided for, a general principle ought to be recognised which would tend to make the Government of Ottawa paramount, and the Governments of the Provinces subordinate. The other was that of federalism through and through, in executive as well as legislative concerns, whenever the contrary had not been expressly said by the Imperial Parliament. The Provincial Governments naturally pressed this latter view very strongly. The Supreme Court of Canada, however, which had been established under the *Confederation Act*, and was originally intended by all parties to be the practically final Court of Appeal for Canada, took the other view. Great unrest was the result, followed by a series of appeals to the Privy Council, … I happened to be engaged in a number of these cases, and had to give assistance as I could to the various Prime Ministers of the Provinces who came over to argue in person. Lord Watson made the business of laying down the new law that was necessary his own. He completely altered the tendency of the decisions of the Supreme Court, and established in the first place the sovereignty (subject to the power to interfere of the Imperial Parliament alone) of the legislatures of Ontario, Quebec and the other Provinces. He then worked out as a principle the direct relation, in point of exercise of the prerogative, of the Lieutenant-Governors to the Crown. In a series of masterly judgments he expounded and established the real constitution of Canada. The liquor laws, the Indian reserve lands, the title to regalia, including the precious metals, were brought before a Judicial Committee, in which he took the leading part, for consideration as to which of the rival claims to legislate ought to prevail. Nowhere is his memory likely to be more gratefully preserved than in those distant Canadian Provinces whose rights of self-government he placed on a basis that was both intelligible and firm.

The major cases in this section were decided in the 1920s, but a short look at two earlier ones gives some perspective for assessing the degree of continuity. The first, *Montreal v. Montreal Street Railway*, [1912] AC 333, 1 DLR 681 (PC), involved a challenge to a section of the *Dominion Railway Act* that regulated through traffic on all provincial railways that crossed Dominion railways. In the Privy Council, Lord Atkinson expressed concern about provincial autonomy:

> If the Parliament of Canada had power to make laws applicable to the whole Dominion in relation to matters which in each province are substantially of local or private interest, upon the assumption that these matters also concern the peace, order, and good government of the dominion, there is hardly a subject upon which it might not legislate to the exclusion of provincial legislation. The same considerations appear to their Lordships to apply to two of the matters enumerated in s. 91, namely the regulation of trade and commerce (at 344).

The second case, *AG Canada v. AG Alberta (The Insurance Reference)*, [1916] 1 AC 589, aff'g. 48 SCR 260, considered the *Dominion Insurance Act*, which sought to regulate large insurance companies carrying on business across the country. Section 4 prohibited any person or corporation from undertaking the business of insurance without a licence, although this prohibition did not include a corporation incorporated by a province and carrying on business wholly within the province that created it.

In the Supreme Court, a majority of four to two held the Act *ultra vires*. In the Privy Council, Lord Haldane agreed. He said at 595 AC that the Act "deprives private individuals of their liberty to carry on the business of insurance." As regards the federal authority to make laws for the peace, order, and good government of Canada, Haldane considered *Russell v. The Queen* (1882), 7 AC 829 (PC) as having illustrated the principle, "now well established, but [which] nonetheless ought to be applied with great caution, that subjects which in one aspect and for one purpose fall within the jurisdiction of the provincial Legislatures may in another aspect and for another purpose fall within Dominion legislative jurisdiction." He considered *Russell* and *Hodge v. The Queen* (1883), 9 AC 117 (PC), and said at 596 AC:

> Their Lordships think that as the result of these decisions it must now be taken that the authority to legislate for the regulation of trade and commerce does not extend to the regulation by a licensing system of a particular trade in which Canadians would otherwise be free to engage in the provinces.

Undoubtedly, Lord Haldane admitted, "the business of insurance is a very important one, which has attained to great dimensions in Canada. But this is equally true of other highly important and extensive forms of business in Canada which are to-day freely transacted under provincial authority."

In the context of his discussion of the federal peace, order, and good government power, Lord Haldane held that a potential new aspect arises when a matter has attained "great dimensions," but called for "great caution" before finding that a matter has this kind of double aspect. Was Lord Haldane reading *Hodge* too narrowly? Was Lord FitzGerald in that case articulating a double aspect doctrine only in the context of peace, order, and good government or was he contemplating its application to federal enumerations more generally? Recall that Lord FitzGerald referred to both *Russell* and *Citizens Insurance Company v. Parsons* (1881), 7 AC 96, as illustrating this rule.

The background of the next case, *Reference re The Board of Commerce Act, 1919 & The Combines and Fair Prices Act, 1919*, [1922] 1 AC 191, 60 DLR 513 (PC); aff'g. (1920), 60 SCR 456, 54 DLR 354, is described in B.J. Hibbitts, "A Bridle for Leviathan: The Supreme Court and The Board of Commerce" (1989), 21 *Ottawa Law Review* 65, at 67-72:

> The Great War had been like no other conflict in history. The struggle had been one not merely of armies, but of entire nations harnessed to the single goal of victory. Governments had been forced to make unprecedented military and economic commitments to sustain their strategies and, indeed, themselves. When the guns finally fell silent it was discovered that along with millions of men, women and children had perished an entire world.
>
> Canada had been spared the ravages of the fighting, but it nonetheless emerged in 1918 profoundly changed. Among the more obvious and important consequences of the war had been a phenomenal expansion of government and a concomitant increase in the extent of governmental intervention in the daily economic life of the citizenry. This is not to suggest that prior to 1914 the Canadian state or economy could have been adequately described in terms of laissez-faire; on the contrary, Canada had been remarkable for the tendency of governments throughout its history to direct the course of economic and national development from above and to control or indeed displace private enterprise in the public interest. Traditional Canadian conceptions of the state had nonetheless proven inadequate to meet the challenges posed by a total war in the twentieth century. Within a few months of the outbreak of hostilities the Borden Government had moved to mobilize the capacity of the nation in a more efficient manner.
>
> … McGill's Stephen Leacock voiced the thoughts of many when he wrote in 1917:

The war has brought with it a new conception of society ... It has shown us in concrete form, in the shape of the war machine itself, a vast economic organization drawn to a scale never before imagined. The co-ordination of resources rendered necessary by the war, the united efforts made in production, manufacture and transport, suggest bound-less possibilities for a time of peace. ...

By this point it was already apparent that it would be peace, not the war, that would ultim-ately pose the greater danger to Canadian prosperity and economic well-being. The scale of the existing conflict presaged the extent of the disruption that would follow an armistice. Hundreds of thousands of men would return from the Front looking for work. Entire industries which had grown up during the conflict and which had fueled the economic growth of the period—munitions being an obvious example—would atrophy or collapse almost overnight. Consumer demand patterns would change as the expectations and desires of the populace returned to what they had been in peacetime. Canadian trade abroad stood to suffer to the extent that for-eign buyers would no longer need to depend as heavily on Canadian supplies of both raw ma-terials and manufactured goods; at the same time it was feared that Canadian concerns would be exposed to competition from foreign—including, ironically, German—cartels.

In this context organization and co-operation became business bywords. Only through effi-cient combinations of plant and capital and/or co-ordination of marketing strategies did the country's commercial leaders believe that Canada's prosperity could be preserved.

... [M]any businessmen desired the creation of a forum in which they could work out their own disputes in an expeditious and effective manner. That serious disputes existed there could be no doubt. Manufacturers and retailers differed on the issue of resale price agreements; wholesalers and retailers differed on methods and terms of product distribution; farmers' co-operatives complained that many manufacturers refused to deal with them under threat of boycott by retailers, and that they were having difficulty buying from wholesalers as the latter refused to grant the "co-ops" retail standing. Again, the court system was perceived to be inad-equate—litigation (assuming that commercial grievances represented valid causes of action in the first place) was expensive and, as noted above, businessmen were not convinced that judges had the commercial sensitivity required in the circumstances. In this context, business looked to the state to provide it with an institution which could, by its decisions, not only mute public criticism of its co-ordinative efforts, but could also facilitate post-war commerce by resolving the differences that created friction and disruption within the business community itself. In addition, many small businessmen hoped that such a tribunal would protect them from dis-crimination and other so-called unfair practices engaged in by the monopolistic "big interests" against which their own trade associations could be but a partial defence.

Such problems became more pressing as businessmen and consumers alike found them-selves swept along by a rapidly rising cost of living. Wholesale and retail prices had skyrocketed during the war.

... In the face of this inflation, embittered members of the public accused businessmen of having conspired to suppress competition that would have kept prices down, and of having made undue profits in the process. In an atmosphere of increasing urgency exacerbated by widespread labour unrest (in particular the Winnipeg General Strike), the Government decid-ed in May 1919 to appoint a special Parliamentary committee to look into the problem and re-port as soon as possible. This committee, chaired by Conservative MP George Nicholson, sat through the month of June, hearing witnesses from government, business, labour and consumer groups. Reporting on July 5, it suggested that the allegations of profiteering were generally without foundation: "[i]ndividual cases of high profits have been discovered, but these are probably no more numerous or excessive than during ordinary times of peace." Prices were high, but reasons for the wartime increases were to be found less in unfair or exploitative business practices than in consumers' wasteful buying and the general industrial expansion due to munitions making. Recognizing the need to act or at least be seen to act, a majority of the Committee nonetheless suggested that the Government establish a Board of Commerce which would continue and extend the investigative work of the Committee. … Casting about for policy alternatives and becoming increasingly desperate in the last days of the Parliamentary session, the Government embraced the Committee recommendation and introduced implementing legislation even before the Committee's final report had been officially released. Not coincidentally, one suspects, the proposals appeared to offer a means by which the Government could satisfy the expressed needs of consumers and businessmen alike. The former would get a commission which in appropriate circumstances could act to limit profits and to a certain extent fix prices so as to stabilize and perhaps even reduce the cost of living; the latter would get their businessman's court which could legitimize business associations and co-ordinative practices while providing a forum for dispute settlement. Two Bills were in fact brought into the House: the first, the *Board of Commerce Bill*, setting up the Board of Commerce more or less along the lines proposed, and the second, the *Combines and Fair Prices Bill*, essentially setting out its powers.

Reference re The Board of Commerce Act, 1919 &
The Combines and Fair Prices Act, 1919
[1922] 1 AC 191, 60 DLR 513 (PC); aff'g. (1920), 60 SCR 456, 54 DLR 354

[The *Board of Commerce Act*, 1919, 9 & 10 Geo. 5, Dom., c. 37 and the *Combines and Fair Prices Act*, 1919, 9 & 10 Geo. 5, Dom., c. 45 were enacted in July 1919. The general objective was to restrict two sorts of perceived abuses: first, combines, monopolies, and mergers; and, second, taking unfair profits, or hoarding "necessaries of life," including food and clothing, for the purpose of unfairly increasing prices. The board had extensive powers to investigate and to make orders, including orders to cease formation or operation of combines and orders to repay unfair profits. A violation of an order of the board was an indictable offence, for which the penalty was a fine not exceeding $1,000 for each day of the offence or imprisonment for a term not exceeding two years.

The board began to work with great enthusiasm, making investigations and orders about prices, but almost immediately it encountered resistance. An order about profit margins for retail sales of clothing led to protests by irate merchants, and the board reacted by arranging a reference to the Supreme Court to determine whether it had constitutional authority to make orders of this kind. Some preliminary procedural wrangling followed, caused largely by the court's dissatisfaction with the abstract form of the questions in the reference. Eventually the questions were reformulated, and the court was asked whether the board had power to make a specific order setting profit margins for clothing prices in Ottawa. This depended upon the validity of the *Combines and Fair Prices Act*, which gave the board its powers.

The Supreme Court divided equally, three to three. Anglin J, writing for himself and Fitzpatrick and Mignault JJ, would have upheld the statute, relying primarily on s. 91(2):

> Effective control and regulation of prices so as to meet and overcome in any one province what is generally recognized to be an evil—"profiteering"—an evil so prevalent and so insidious that in the opinion of many persons it threatens to-day the moral and social well-being of the Dominion—may thus necessitate investigation, inquiry and control in other provinces. It may be necessary to deal with the prices and the profits of the growers or other producers of raw material, the manufacturers, the middlemen and the retailers. No one provincial legislature could legislate so as to cope effectively with such a matter and concurrent legislation of all the provinces interested is fraught with so many difficulties in its enactment and in its administration and enforcement that to deal with the situation at all adequately by that means is, in my opinion, quite impracticable (at 467 SCR).

He did, though, say that the statute could also be upheld under p.o.g.g. Although it dealt with property and civil rights, it did so "in an aspect" (at 467 SCR) that was not local or private. As well, he would have upheld the provisions about hoarding necessities under s. 91(27) (the criminal law power).

Opposed to Anglin were Idington, Duff, and Brodeur JJ. Idington J began his discussion of s. 91(2) by speaking of "the old forlorn hope, so many times tried, unsuccessfully" (at 488 SCR). Regulation of prices in a "tailor shop, or the corner grocery" (at 488 SCR) came within s. 92(13) and, if the statute were valid, "Is there any sumptuary or socialistic conception of organized society which could not be made to fall within the power of Parliament by the same process of reasoning. … Our *Confederation Act* was not intended to be a mere sham, but an instrument of government intended to assign to the provincial legislatures some absolute rights, and these were supposed to be more precious than those over property and civil rights" (at 489 SCR). Turning to p.o.g.g., he spoke of "the remarkable legislation now in question" (at 490 SCR), and said it could not include a power to affect "property and civil rights … save in the extreme necessity begotten of war conditions, or in manifold ways that do not touch provincial rights" (at 491 SCR). Duff J began by considering s. 91(2), and separated the board's powers about hoarding and unfair profits. The powers about hoarding were too broad because they extended to hoarding by anyone, not only traders: "For example, it applies to accumulations by the house-holder of articles produced by the house-holder himself, the small farmer's pork and butter, as well as to his cordwood" (at 500 SCR). The powers about unfair profits did not fail in the same way, but they did not come within the general principles specified by the cases.

> I have indicated the principle which in my opinion is deducible from *Parson's Case* (1881), 7 AC 96 (PC), namely that section 91(2) does not authorize an enactment by the Dominion Parliament regulating in each of the provinces the terms of the contracts of a particular business or trade, for the reason (put very broadly) that such legislation involves an interposition in the transactions of individuals in the provinces, within the sphere of property and civil rights and local undertakings …
>
> I cannot discover any principle consistent with these conclusions, upon which an enactment delegating to a commission the authority to regulate the terms of particular contracts of individual traders in a specified commodity according to the views of the board as to

what may be fair between the individual trader and the public in each transaction, can be sustained as an exercise of that power; and if such legislation could not be supported when the subject dealt with is a single commodity, or the trade in a single commodity, or a single group of commodities, how can jurisdiction be acquired so to legislate by extending the scope of the legislation and bringing a large number of specified trades or commodities within its sweep? (at 503-04 SCR)

Duff J then considered p.o.g.g., and said at 507-8 SCR:

[W]here a subject matter is from a provincial point of view comprehended within the class of subjects falling under "property and civil rights," properly construed (*ex hypothesi* such matter could not fall strictly within any of the classes of subjects enumerated in s. 91) it is incompetent to the Dominion in exercise of the authority given by the introductory clause to legislate upon that matter either alone or together with subjects over which the Dominion has undoubted jurisdiction as falling neither within s. 92 nor within the enumerated heads of s. 91; and legislation which in effect has this operation cannot be legitimised by framing it in comprehensive terms embracing matters over which the Dominion has jurisdiction as well as matters in which the jurisdiction is committed exclusively to the provinces.

Nor do I think it matters in the least that the legislation is enacted with the view of providing a remedy uniformly applicable to the whole of Canada in relation to a situation of general importance to the Dominion. The ultimate social economic or political aims of the legislator cannot I think determine the category into which the matters dealt with fall in order to determine the question whether the jurisdiction to enact it is given by s. 91 or s. 92. The immediate operation and effect of the legislation, or the effect the legislation is calculated immediately to produce must alone, I think, be considered.

Both Idington and Duff JJ also rejected the arguments based on s. 91(27). The Dominion appealed to the Privy Council.]

VISCOUNT HALDANE: ... The first question to be answered is whether the Dominion Parliament could validly enact such a law. Their Lordships observe that the law is not one enacted to meet special conditions in wartime. It was passed in 1919, after peace had been declared, and it is not confined to any temporary purpose, but is to continue without limit in time, and to apply throughout Canada. No doubt the initial words of s. 91 of the *British North America Act* confer on the Parliament of Canada power to deal with subjects which concern the Dominion generally, provided that they are not withheld from the powers of that Parliament to legislate, by any of the express heads in s. 92, untrammelled by the enumeration of special heads in s. 91. It may well be that the subjects of undue combination and hoarding are matters in which the Dominion has a great practical interest. In special circumstances, such as those of a great war, such an interest might conceivably become of such paramount and overriding importance as to amount to what lies outside the heads in s. 92, and is not covered by them. The decision in *Russell v. The Queen* (1882), 7 AC 829 (PC), appears to recognize this as constitutionally possible, even in time of peace; but it is quite another matter to say that under normal circumstances general Canadian policy can justify interference, on such a scale as the statutes in controversy involve, with the property and civil rights of the inhabitants of the Provinces.

It is to the Legislatures of the Provinces that the regulation and restriction of their civil rights have in general been exclusively confided, and as to these the Provincial Legislatures possess quasi-sovereign authority. It can, therefore, be only under necessity in highly exceptional circumstances, such as cannot be assumed to exist in the present case, that the liberty of the inhabitants of the Provinces may be restricted by the Parliament of Canada, and that the Dominion can intervene in the interests of Canada as a whole in questions such as the present one. For, normally, the subject-matter to be dealt with in the case would be one falling within s. 92. Nor do the words in s. 91, the "Regulation of trade and commerce," if taken by themselves, assist the present Dominion contention. It may well be, if the Parliament of Canada had, by reason of an altogether exceptional situation, capacity to interfere, that these words would apply so as to enable that Parliament to oust the exclusive character of the Provincial powers under s. 92.

In the case of Dominion companies their Lordships in deciding the case of *John Deere Plow Co. v. Wharton*, [1915] AC 330 (PC), expressed the opinion that the language of s. 91(2) could have the effect of aiding Dominion powers conferred by the general language of s. 91. But that was because the regulation of the trading of Dominion companies was sought to be invoked only in furtherance of a general power which the Dominion Parliament possessed independently of it. Where there was no such power in that Parliament, as in the case of the *Dominion Insurance Act*, it was held otherwise, and that the authority of the Dominion Parliament to legislate for the regulation of trade and commerce did not, by itself, enable interference with particular trades in which Canadians would, apart from any right of interference conferred by these words above, be free to engage in the Provinces. This result was the outcome of a series of well-known decisions of earlier dates, which are now so familiar that they need not be cited.

For analogous reasons the words of s. 91(27) do not assist the argument for the Dominion. It is one thing to construe the words "the criminal law, except the constitution of courts of criminal jurisdiction, but including the procedure in criminal matters," as enabling the Dominion Parliament to exercise exclusive legislative power where the subject matter is one which by its very nature belongs to the domain of criminal jurisprudence. A general law, to take an example, making incest a crime, belongs to this class. It is quite another thing, first to attempt to interfere with a class of subject committed exclusively to the Provincial Legislature, and then to justify this by enacting ancillary provisions, designated as new phases of Dominion criminal law which require a title to so interfere as basis of their application. ...

As their Lordships have already indicated, the jurisdiction attempted to be conferred on the new Board of Commerce appears to them to be *ultra vires* for the reasons now discussed. It implies a claim of title, in the cases of non-traders as well as of traders, to make orders prohibiting the accumulation of certain articles required for every-day life, and the withholding of such articles from sale at prices to be defined by the Board, whenever they exceed the amount of the material which appears to the Board to be required for domestic purposes or for the ordinary purposes of business. The Board is also given jurisdiction to regulate profits and dealings which may give rise to profit. The power sought to be given to the Board applies to articles produced for his own use by the householder himself, as well as to articles accumulated, not for the market but for the purposes of their own processes of manufacture by manufacturers. The Board is empowered to in-

quire into individual cases and to deal with them individually, and not merely as the result of applying principles to be laid down as of general application. This would cover
such instances as those of coal mines and of local Provincial undertakings for meeting
Provincial requirements of social life.

Legislation setting up a Board of Commerce with such powers appears to their Lordships to be beyond the powers conferred by s. 91. They find confirmation of this view in
s. 41 of the *Board of Commerce Act*, which enables the Dominion Executive to review and
alter the decisions of the Board. It has already been observed that circumstances are
conceivable, such as those of war or famine, when the peace, order and good Government of the Dominion might be imperilled under conditions so exceptional that they
require legislation of a character in reality beyond anything provided for by the enumerated heads in either s. 92 or s. 91 itself. Such a case, if it were to arise would have to be
considered closely before the conclusion could properly be reached that it was one which
could not be treated as falling under any of the heads enumerated. Still, it is a conceivable
case, and although great caution is required in referring to it, even in general terms, it
ought not, in the view their Lordships take of the *British North America Act*, read as a
whole, to be excluded from what is possible. For throughout the provisions of that Act
there is apparent the recognition that subjects which would normally belong exclusively
to a specifically assigned class of subject may, under different circumstances and in another aspect, assume a further significance. Such an aspect may conceivably become of
paramount importance, and of dimensions that give rise to other aspects. This is a principle which, although recognized in earlier decisions, such as that of *Russell v. The Queen*,
both here and in the Courts in Canada, has always been applied with reluctance, and its
recognition as relevant can be justified only after scrutiny sufficient to render it clear that
the circumstances are abnormal. In the case before them, however important it may
seem to the Parliament of Canada that some such policy as that adopted in the two Acts
in question should be made general throughout Canada, their Lordships do not find any
evidence that the standard of necessity referred to has been reached, or that the attainment of the end sought is practicable, in view of the distribution of legislative powers
enacted by the *Constitution Act*, without the co-operation of the Provincial Legislatures.
It may well be that it is within the power of the Dominion Parliament to call, for example,
for statistical and other information which may be valuable for guidance in questions
affecting Canada as a whole. Such information may be required before any power to regulate trade and commerce can be properly exercised, even where such power is construed in a fashion much narrower than that in which it was sought to interpret it in the
argument at the Bar for the Attorney-General for Canada. But even this consideration
affords no justification for interpreting the words of s. 91(2), in a fashion which would,
as was said in the argument on the other side, make them confer capacity to regulate
particular trades and businesses.

For the reasons now given their Lordships are of opinion that the first of the questions
brought before them must be answered in the negative. As a consequence the second
question does not arise. …

Appeal dismissed.

A revised measure regulating anti-competitive conduct was upheld in *Proprietary Articles Trade Association v. AG Canada*, [1931] AC 310, reproduced in Chapter 6, The 1930s: The Depression and the New Deal.

Fort Frances Pulp and Paper Company v. Manitoba Free Press Company
[1923] AC 695, 3 DLR 629 (PC)

[This case dealt with regulation of prices for newsprint. It shared the social and economic background of the *Board of Commerce* case but it involved different legislation. In 1914, the Dominion enacted the *War Measures Act*, 5 Geo. 5, c. 2, which gave the government power to do whatever it considered "necessary or advisable for the security, defense, peace, order and welfare of Canada." This power was limited to the existence of "real or apprehended war, invasion, insurrection" and a proclamation by the government was to be conclusive evidence that these conditions existed. Under the *War Measures Act*, the government regulated prices of newsprint in a series of different administrative arrangements. Most important was the creation, in 1917, of the Paper Controller, who made the initial decisions, and the Paper Control Tribunal, which heard appeals. On December 24, 1919, the Controller made an order about prices up to December 31 and ordered the Fort Frances Company to repay whatever it had received from the Manitoba Free Press in excess of these prices. The Tribunal confirmed this order on July 8, 1920. When Fort Frances refused to pay, the Manitoba Free Press brought an action in Ontario. A trial judgment allowing the claim was affirmed by the Ontario Court of Appeal and the defendant appealed directly to the Privy Council.]

VISCOUNT HALDANE: ... It is clear that in normal circumstances the Dominion Parliament could not have so legislated as to set up the machinery of control over the paper manufacturers which is now in question. The recent decision of the Judicial Committee in the *Board of Commerce Case*, [1922] 1 AC 191 (PC), as well as earlier decisions, show that as the Dominion Parliament cannot ordinarily legislate so as to interfere with property and civil rights in the Provinces, it could not have done what the two statutes under consideration purport to do had the situation been normal. But it does not follow that in a very different case, such as that of sudden danger to social order arising from the outbreak of a great war, the Parliament of the Dominion cannot act under other powers which may well be implied in the constitution. The reasons given in the *Board of Commerce Case* recognize exceptional cases where such a power may be implied.

In the event of war, when the national life may require for its preservation the employment of very exceptional means, the provision of peace, order and good government for the country as a whole may involve effort on behalf of the whole nation, in which the interests of individuals may have to be subordinated to that of the community in a fashion which requires s. 91 to be interpreted as providing for such an emergency. The general control of property and civil rights for normal purposes remains with the Provincial Legislatures. But questions may arise by reason of the special circumstances of the national emergency which concern nothing short of the peace, order and good government of Canada as a whole.

The overriding powers enumerated in s. 91, as well as the general words at the commencement of the section, may then become applicable to new and special aspects which they cover of subjects assigned otherwise exclusively to the Provinces. It may be, for example, impossible to deal adequately with the new questions which arise without the imposition of special regulations on trade and commerce of a kind that only the situation created by the emergency places within the competency of the Dominion Parliament. It is proprietary and civil rights in new relations, which they do not present in normal times, that have to be dealt with; and these relations, which affect Canada as an entirety, fall within s. 91, because in their fullness they extend beyond what s. 92 can really cover. The kind of power adequate for dealing with them is only to be found in that part of the constitution which establishes power in the State as a whole. For it is not one that can be reliably provided for by depending on collective action of the Legislatures of the individual Provinces agreeing for the purpose. That the basic instrument on which the character of the entire constitution depends should be construed as providing for such centralised power in an emergency situation follows from the manifestation in the language of the Act of the principle that the instrument has among its purposes to provide for the State regarded as a whole, and for the expression and influence of its public opinion as such. This principle of a power so implied has received effect also in countries with a written and apparently rigid constitution such as the United States, where the strictly federal character of the national basic agreement has retained the residuary powers not expressly conferred on the Federal Government for the component States. The operation of the scheme of interpretation is all the more to be looked for in a constitution such as that established by the *British North America Act*, where the residuary powers are given to the Dominion Central Government, and the preamble of the statute declares the intention to be that the Dominion should have a constitution similar in principle to that of the United Kingdom.

Their Lordships, therefore, entertain no doubt that however the wording of ss. 91 and 92 may have laid down a framework under which, as a general principle, the Dominion Parliament is to be excluded from trenching on property and civil rights in the Provinces of Canada, yet in a sufficiently great emergency such as that arising out of war, there is implied the power to deal adequately with that emergency for the safety of the Dominion as a whole. The enumeration in s. 92 is not in any way repealed in the event of such an occurrence, but a new aspect of the business of Government is recognized as emerging, an aspect which is not covered or precluded by the general words in which powers are assigned to the Legislatures of the Provinces as individual units. Where an exact line of demarcation will lie in such cases it may not be easy to lay down a priori, nor is it necessary. For in the solution of the problem regard must be had to the broadened field covered, in case of exceptional necessity, by the language of s. 91, in which the interests of the Dominion generally are protected. As to these interests the Dominion Government, which in its Parliament represents the people as a whole, must be deemed to be left with considerable freedom to judge.

The other point which arises is whether such exceptional necessity as must be taken to have existed when the war broke out, and almost of necessity for some period subsequent to its outbreak, continued through the whole of the time within which the questions in the present case arose.

When war has broken out it may be requisite to make special provision to ensure the maintenance of law and order in a country, even when it is in no immediate danger of invasion. Public opinion may become excitable, and one of the causes of this may conceivably be want of uninterrupted information in newspapers. Steps may have to be taken to ensure supplies of these and to avoid shortage, and the effect of the economic and other disturbance occasioned originally by the war may thus continue for some time after it is terminated. The question of the extent to which provision for circumstances such as these may have to be maintained is one on which a Court of law is loath to enter. No authority other than the central Government is in a position to deal with a problem which is essentially one of statesmanship. It may be that it has become clear that the crisis which arose is wholly at an end and that there is no justification for the continued exercise of an exceptional interference which becomes *ultra vires* when it is no longer called for. In such a case the law as laid down for distribution of powers in the ruling instrument would have to be invoked. But very clear evidence that the crisis had wholly passed away would be required to justify the judiciary, even when the question raised was one of *ultra vires* which it had to decide, in overruling the decision of the Government that exceptional measures were still requisite. In saying what is almost obvious, their Lordships observe themselves to be in accord with the view taken under analogous circumstances by the Supreme Court of the United States, and expressed in such decisions as that in October, 1919, in *Hamilton v. Kentucky Distilleries Co.*, 251 US 146.

When then, in the present instance, can it be said that the necessity altogether ceased for maintaining the exceptional measure of control over the newspaper print industry introduced while the war was at its height? At what date did the disturbed state of Canada which the war had produced so entirely pass away that the legislative measures relied on in the present case became *ultra vires*? It is enough to say that there is no clear and unmistakable evidence that the Government was in error in thinking that the necessity was still in existence at the dates on which the action in question was taken by the Paper Control Tribunal. No doubt late in 1919 statements were made to the effect that the war itself was at an end. For example, in the Order in Council made at Ottawa on December 20, 1919, it is stated that it must "be realised that although no proclamation has been issued declaring that the war no longer exists, actual war conditions have in fact long ago ceased to exist, and consequently existence of war can no longer be urged as a reason in fact for maintaining these extraordinary regulations as necessary or advisable for the security of Canada."

The Order in Council then goes on to say that in consequence of the armistice of November, 1918, the Expeditionary Force had since been withdrawn and demobilised, and the country generally is devoting its energies to re-establishment in the ordinary avocations of peace. In these circumstances, it states, the Minister of Justice considers that the time has arrived when the emergency Government legislation should cease to operate. This was in December, 1919. The Order then goes on to declare repealed all Orders and Regulations of the Governor in Council which depend for their sanction upon s. 6 of the *War Measures Act, 1914*, and repeals them as from January 1, 1920. But from this repeal it expressly excepts, among other Orders and Regulations specified, those relating to paper control, which are to remain in force until the end of another session of Parliament.

It will be observed that this Order in Council deals only with the results following from the cessation of actual war conditions. It excepts from repeal certain measures concerned with consequential conditions arising out of war, which may obviously continue to produce effects remaining in operation after war itself is over.

Their Lordships find themselves unable to say that the Dominion Government had no good reason for thus temporarily continuing the paper control after actual war had ceased, but while the effects of war conditions might still be operative. ...

Appeal dismissed.

NOTES

The Board of Commerce, too, was entangled in the regulation of the price of newsprint, although later and in a different way. Early in 1920, as part of the dismantling of wartime controls, the Dominion assigned the Board of Commerce the functions of the Paper Controller and it inherited a quarrel with Price Brothers, one of the large pulp and paper firms. Shortly afterward, the Board declared newsprint to be a necessity and set a maximum price that was well below the market price in the United States. Price Brothers refused to comply, and the Board sought to enforce its order. This quarrel led to another case, *Reference re Price Brothers* (1920), 60 SCR 265, 54 DLR 286, in which two issues of interpretation were raised. The first involved the *War Measures Act*, and here the question was whether it authorized the appointment of the Paper Controller even though armistice had been declared three months before the appointment. The second of these two issues involved the phrase "necessary of life" in the *Combines and Fair Prices Act*: was newsprint a "necessary"? A majority of the Supreme Court decided both issues against the Board, and no appeal was taken.

In the article that appears in the discussion preceding the *Board of Commerce* case, Hibbitts argues that the case is a watershed in the attitudes of Canadian judges toward economic regulation, and his argument may be useful in considering explanations of the cases throughout the 1920s and 1930s (at 97-102):

The outright split in the *Reference* and the variations in approach which had been evident in *Price Brothers* reflected philosophical and conceptual differences among members of the Supreme Court going far beyond the level of disagreements as to the *vires* of particular legislation or the jurisdiction of a particular Board. Beneath the veneer afforded by the circumstances of the cases, the Court was divided on such fundamental issues as the appropriate functions of the state, the rights of the individual, the nature of Canadian federalism, the role of the courts and the task of law. The divisions, granted, were not always hard and fast and sometimes individuals appeared inconsistent. The Board of Commerce decisions nonetheless made it clear that the Judges of the Court were not altogether of one mind. Regarded in a broader context, the decisions further suggested that far from being a static institution, the Court in this period was in the process—albeit by now in the last stages—of a transformation which was having an important impact on its behaviour, and in particular on its relationship with government.

Ultimately, the differences among the members of the Court were differences about values— in particular, the respective worths of Man (the individual) and the state (the community). Idington, Duff and Brodeur JJ, for instance, were very much animated by faith in the capacity of individuals to advance and benefit themselves and society and by a concomitant concern for their rights. In the *Board of Commerce Reference*, these things had revealed themselves directly as an aversion to compulsion of the individual by the state and a willingness to confine the power and discretion of state instrumentalities so as to limit the potential extent of that compulsion. Similar considerations had encouraged the same men to deny federal authority over such undertakings in favour of provincial jurisdiction. ...

Justices Anglin, Davies and Mignault had been rather less concerned with such rights and provincial autonomy. Their judgments contained no paeons to the state, but they had nonetheless been prepared to allow the legislature and its instrumentalities a greater degree of "interference" in the lives and business of the citizenry. In sum, they seemed less convinced of the individual's social omnipotence and omnicompetence, more concerned with the efficient solution of important social problems and more prepared to defer to authority purporting to be engaged in such solution. ...

It may be argued that the inconsistencies in approach manifest among members of the Supreme Court in the Board of Commerce cases reflected a confrontation within the Court between two competing visions of law; one newly dominant, the other in decline. The dominant vision—that shared by Idington, Duff and Brodeur JJ—had been imported to Canada from late nineteenth century England, and was the more modern of the two. The other view of law—arguably apparent in the judgments of Anglin, Davies and Mignault JJ, but even in them somewhat qualified by aspects of the dominant vision—was more traditional, being principally a philosophic holdover from the colonial past.

Toronto Electric Commissioners v. Snider
[1925] AC 396, 2 DLR 5 (PC); rev'g. [1924] 2 DLR 761 (CA)

[Here the Privy Council considered the validity of the *Industrial Disputes Investigation Act*, enacted by the Dominion in 1907. It applied to mining, transportation, and communications undertakings, as well as public service utilities, and it was limited to those with more than ten employees. It enabled an employee or an employer in a dispute about the conditions of work to apply to the Minister of Labour for the appointment of a Board of Conciliation and Investigation. If a Board was appointed, a strike or lockout was prohibited, and the function of this Board was to inquire into the dispute and to attempt to effect a settlement. If a settlement was reached, it had the effect of an order of a court; if no settlement was reached, the Board was to report to the Minister, who was to make the report public. In 1914, Ontario enacted a similar statute.

A Board was appointed to inquire into a dispute between the Toronto Electric Commissioners and some of its employees, and the Commissioners sought an injunction, alleging that the Act was *ultra vires*. The Ontario Court of Appeal, reversing the trial court, dismissed the claim. Ferguson JA, with whom Mulock CJO and Magee and Smith JJA concurred, wrote the judgment for the majority. He avoided relying on p.o.g.g., because he felt that its limits were not clearly settled. The Act, though, was valid under s. 91(2) and s. 91(27). About s. 91(2), Ferguson JA said, "It cannot be disputed that to deprive the City of Toronto of electric power on which it depends for light, heat and power is to disturb and hinder the national trade and commerce and to endanger public peace, order

and safety. ... Industrial disputes are not now regarded as matters concerning only a disputing employer and his employees. It is common knowledge that such disputes are
matters of public interest and concern, and frequently of national and international importance" (at 785-86).

Hodgins JA dissented. For p.o.g.g., he saw two distinct grounds, emergency and "matters of 'general Canadian interest and importance,'" an expression borrowed from Lord
Watson. The Act was not a response to an emergency. Instead, it dealt with "the normal
working of industrial relations, which often require time and patience and some restraint, to afford protection against dislocation or disturbance in the usual conduct of
business as between employer and employees. It [was] essentially a sedative measure, and
not in any way designed to meet a serious emergency." He held the other branch of
p.o.g.g. could not support the Act, because it "plainly invades the specified domain of
provincial legislation" (at 769) even though the subject of labour relations was one that
should, "in the interest of the whole community ... be dealt with by some national measure" (at 769). In conclusion, he said that s. 91(27) did not support the Act, because it was
"substantially in relation to property and civil rights" (at 778). The Commissioners appealed to the Privy Council.]

LORD HALDANE: [A description of the legislation and the dispute is omitted. Lord Haldane's description was inaccurate in one respect—it asserted that the legislation applied
to "industrial disputes between any employer in Canada and any one or more of his
employees."]

Their Lordships are of opinion that, on authority as well as on principle, they are today precluded from accepting the arguments that the *Dominion Act* in controversy can
be justified as being an exercise of the Dominion power under s. 91 in relation to criminal law. What the *Industrial Disputes Investigation Act*, which the Dominion Parliament
passed in 1907, aimed at accomplishing was to enable the Dominion Government to appoint anywhere in Canada a Board of Conciliation and Investigation to which the dispute between an employer and his employees might be referred. The Board was to have
power to enforce the attendance of witnesses and to compel the production of documents. It could under the Act enter premises, interrogate the persons there, and inspect
the work. It rendered it unlawful for an employer to lock-out or for a workman to strike,
on account of the dispute, prior to or during the reference, and imposed an obligation on
employees and employers to give thirty days' notice of any intended change affecting
wages or hours. Until the reference was concluded neither were to alter the conditions
with respect to these. It is obvious that these provisions dealt with civil rights, and it was
not within the power of the Dominion Parliament to make this otherwise by imposing
merely ancillary penalties. The penalties for breach of the restrictions did not render the
statute the less an interference with civil rights in its pith and substance. The Act is not
one which aims at making striking generally a new crime. Moreover, the employer retains under the general common law a right to lock-out, only slightly interfered with by
the penalty. In this connection their Lordships are therefore of opinion that the validity
of the Act cannot be sustained. ...

Nor does the invocation of the specific power in s. 91 to regulate trade and commerce
assist the Dominion contention.

[A discussion of cases, especially *Parsons*, is omitted.]

It is, in their Lordships' opinion, now clear that, excepting so far as the power can be invoked in aid of capacity conferred independently under other words in s. 91, the power to regulate trade and commerce cannot be relied on as enabling the Dominion Parliament to regulate civil rights in the Provinces.

A more difficult question arises with reference to the initial words of s. 91, which enable the Parliament of Canada to make laws for the peace, order and good government of Canada in matters falling outside the Provincial powers specifically conferred by s. 92.

[Another discussion of cases, especially *Russell*, is omitted.]

It appears to their Lordships that it is not now open to them to treat *Russell v. The Queen* (1882), 7 AC 829 (PC) as having established the general principle that the mere fact that Dominion legislation is for the general advantage of Canada, or is such that it will meet a mere want which is felt throughout the Dominion, renders it competent if it cannot be brought within the heads enumerated specifically in s. 91. Unless this is so, if the subject matter falls within any of the enumerated heads in s. 92, such legislation belongs exclusively to Provincial competency. No doubt there may be cases arising out of some extraordinary peril to the national life of Canada, as a whole, such as the cases arising out of a war, where legislation is required of an order that passes beyond the heads of exclusive Provincial competency. Such cases may be dealt with under the words at the commencement of s. 91, conferring general powers in relation to peace, order and good government, simply because such cases are not otherwise provided for. But instances of this, as was pointed out in the judgment in *Fort Frances Pulp and Power Co. v. Manitoba Free Press*, [1923] AC 695 (PC) are highly exceptional. Their Lordships think that the decision in *Russell v. The Queen* can only be supported to-day, not on the footing of having laid down an interpretation, such as has sometimes been invoked of the general words at the beginning of s. 91, but on the assumption of the Board, apparently made at the time of deciding the case of *Russell v. The Queen*, that the evil of intemperance at that time amounted in Canada to one so great and so general that at least for the period it was a menace to the national life of Canada so serious and pressing that the National Parliament was called on to intervene to protect the nation from disaster. An epidemic of pestilence might conceivably have been regarded as analogous. It is plain from the decision in the *Board of Commerce* case, [1922] 1 AC 191 (PC) that the evil of profiteering could not have been so invoked, for Provincial powers, if exercised, were adequate to it. Their Lordships find it difficult to explain the decision in *Russell v. The Queen* as more than a decision of this order upon facts, considered to have been established at its date rather than upon general law. ...

As the result of consideration, their Lordships have come to the conclusion that they ought humbly to advise the Sovereign that the appeal should be allowed, and that judgment should be entered for the appellants for the declaration and injunction claimed.

Appeal allowed.

The Board's decision to strike down the federal *Industrial Disputes Investigation Act* came as no great surprise to some commentators, even though the Act had been in continuous operation for 19 years previously. The following excerpt helps to explain why Lord Haldane saw labour relations as more appropriately the subject of provincial regulation (from David Schneiderman, "Harold Laski, Viscount Haldane, and the Law of the Canadian Constitution in the Early Twentieth Century" (1998), 48 *University of Toronto Law Journal* 521, at 558-59):

> Labour at first opposed the scheme [in *Snider*]. It came around to support the Act, submitted counsel for Snider, Mr. Duncan, in oral argument, because labour saw the "justice" in supporting a national scheme that dealt with the subject satisfactorily "from a Labour point of view." The same could not be expected of the provinces acting severally. Federal authority was justified, argued Duncan, not only because social conditions had changed so dramatically that regulation of industrial relations was a national priority, but also because of the fear that collective action by labour could "be very quickly turned into an attack on the State"—always an imminent [sic] emergency.
>
> Lord Haldane could find no authority for the Act in the federal trade and commerce power because it was not invoked in aid of another power conferred independently of section 91(2); nor could he find support under the federal criminal law power. As for pogg, Haldane resisted the conclusion that the Act arose out of some "extraordinary peril to the national life of Canada, as a whole." As in the case of the evil of "profiteering," which was the target of federal legislation in *Board of Commerce*, provincial powers "if exercised, were adequate" to the task of regulating labour relations.
>
> Not only did the structure and interpretation of the 1867 Act compel the conclusion that the provinces had this authority, but Haldane made clear during oral argument that he preferred that authority rest with the provinces, for reasons having to do with the ethical superiority of local government: "In all those labour disputes the stopping of a strike depends a good deal on whether the Minister can get alongside the men, and whether he knows them, and can talk as familiar friends; you have a better chance of that if you are all local men than if you are spread over a huge Dominion." Haldane went so far as to describe each province as "a country by itself," as an "independent State, ... cut into expressly by the enumerations of section 91." ... Perhaps the better interpretation of Haldane's understanding of Canadian constitutional law is this: citizenship in a federal polity is advanced by favouring autonomous local government over centralized state authority, save for those rare instances when the polity itself is under threat.

NOTE: LORD HALDANE AND THE TRADE AND COMMERCE POWER

Citizens Insurance Company v. Parsons (1881), 7 AC 96, found in Chapter 4, The Late Nineteenth Century: The Canadian Courts Under the Influence, had suggested a narrow reading of the scope of the federal trade and commerce power. In the series of decisions discussed in this chapter, Lord Haldane further reduced this power to one available only "in aid of" another federal enumeration. The federal trade and commerce power alone had no independent authority; it could only be used to tip the balance in favour of the federal government under some other independent enumeration. Yet, in *Parsons*, Sir Montague Smith admitted that the federal power under s. 91(2) extended to international and interprovincial trade. Could it have been that Lord Haldane intended to deny even this authority to the federal government? Professor Alexander Smith suggests that it was a "Procrustean adjustment" to proscribe the power relating to the "general regulation of trade" to a subsidiary role. "If it was intended to apply to all components of the commerce clause, including international and interprovincial trade," Smith wrote, then it is remarkable indeed" (see Alexander Smith, *The Commerce Power in Canada and the United States* (Toronto: Butterworths, 1963), at 115). In the following case, Justice Anglin expresses a similar concern. Justice Duff, for the majority, seems to acknowledge that the federal government continues to have authority to regulate foreign trade, but holds that it does not have authority to intermingle regulation of foreign trade with trade taking place entirely within provincial boundaries.

The King v. Eastern Terminal Elevator Co.
[1925] SCR 434, 3 DLR 1; aff'g. [1924] Ex. CR 167

[Early in the twentieth century, exports of grain grown on the prairies became a major element of Canada's economy. Typically, the grain was delivered by farmers to local elevators and, from them, transported by rail to elevators in Winnipeg. From Winnipeg, it went, again by rail, to elevators in Port Arthur or Fort William (now Thunder Bay) and then to markets in Canada and abroad. The entire industry was governed by the *Canada Grain Act*, 1912, 9-10 Geo. 5, c. 40, which created the Board of Grain Commissioners and gave it extensive regulatory powers.

One of the purposes of the Act was to facilitate commercial transactions, especially international transactions, by requiring all prairie grain shipped through elevators to be cleaned, weighed, and graded, and by providing certificates of weights and grades, upon which buyers could rely. The railway cars were inspected at Winnipeg, to determine the kind of grain, its grade and weight, and the percentage of "dockage"—extraneous grain and foreign matter. When the grain arrived in Port Arthur or Fort William, the elevators issued certificates of weight and grade, which were used in commercial transactions, and warehouse receipts, which were traded on the Winnipeg Grain Exchange.

This case involved a quarrel between farmers and terminal grain elevators in Port Arthur and Fort William. The quarrel was about the arrangements established by the Act for compensating the terminal elevators for storing and cleaning the grain. These arrangements were complex. If the dockage was over three percent of the weight of the grain delivered, it was returned to the shipper (with a small deduction for waste), and the shipper paid a fee for storage and cleaning. If it was under three percent, it was a "surplus," and was retained by the elevator, in lieu of a separate fee. The elevators screened this surplus, and sold the marketable grain it contained.

In 1919, in response to complaints that the terminal elevators were making unfair profits from the surpluses, s. 95(7) was added. It provided that each elevator could retain only a limited amount of the surplus: one-quarter percent of the total grain it received. The remainder was to be sold, and the proceeds paid to the Board and used for administrative costs.

The Board brought this action against the Eastern Terminal Company, one of the terminal elevators, after it refused to pay, and the Company claimed that s. 95(7) was *ultra vires*. The trial judge, Maclean J agreed. Even though the Act as a whole might be valid because "the export of Canadian grain was a matter of national concern," and "a primary industry of great magnitude" (at 177 Exch.), s. 95(7) was not necessarily incidental. Considering the legislative history, especially the concern for unfair profits, the limitation to terminal elevators, and the fact that the Board had a power to impose fees to pay its expenses, it was "an attempt to regulate profits" (at 178 Exch.), and not an imposition of a tax. The Board appealed.]

ANGLIN CJC dissenting: … Assuming that the *Canada Grain Act* as a whole is *intra vires* of Parliament, ss. 7 of s. 95 seems to me to be defensible as an incidental enactment designed to promote the attainment of the purposes of the Act. It not only provides for the obtaining of revenue from persons and corporations instrumental and beneficially interested in the carrying out of the scheme which it sanctions, and to be applied towards the cost of working it, but it furnishes, perhaps, the best possible security that one of the main operations for which the Act provides, namely, the cleaning of the grain so that it will actually conform to the grade and quality called for by the Government certificate based on its prior inspection, will be honestly and efficiently carried out. …

The object of Parliament in enacting the *Canada Grain Act* was, in my opinion, to provide for the economical expeditious and profitable export and marketing abroad of what is to-day the most valuable product of Canada—the most important subject of its trade and commerce—its greatest source of wealth. The scheme of the Act is the constitution and regulation of machinery to effectuate that purpose. It provides, as only the Dominion Parliament can, for the control and handling of the grain from the moment it leaves the hands of the grower—practically always in one of the Western Provinces—until its shipment in Ontario or one of the eastern provinces for the foreign market accompanied by a government certificate of its grade and quality, upon the acceptance of which in that market the Canadian shipper can depend. No single province could legislate to cover this field. Concurrent legislation by all the provinces interested, if practicable (which I doubt), would be ineffectual to accomplish the purpose. Dominion legislation is required. Apart from the fact that a provincial certificate would not carry the weight and authority attaching to a certificate issued under Dominion sanction, the necessary control over transit and handling in different provinces and ultimate shipment could not be exercised under provincial legislation.

I regard the subject matter of the *Canada Grain Act*, therefore, as lying outside the scope of the powers entrusted to the legislatures by the sixteen heads of provincial legislative jurisdiction contained in s. 92.

[Anglin CJC discussed the Privy Council decisions and, when he came to Lord Haldane's description of *Russell* in *Snider*, he said, at 438, "I should indeed be surprised if a body so well informed as their Lordships had countenanced such an aspersion on the fair fame of Canada, even though some hard driven advocate had ventured to insinuate it in argument." He continued the discussion of the cases and came to Lord Haldane's account of trade and commerce, again in *Snider*, and said:]

With the utmost respect, I fail to appreciate the reasoning on which this view is based. If neither the power conferred by the general language of s. 91, nor the power under

s. 1(2), to regulate trade and commerce, taken independently, warrants Dominion legislation which trenches on the provincial field, if both powers are subject in this respect to the like restriction, I find rather elusive and difficult to understand the foundation for the view that legislation authorized only by the former may be so helped out by the latter that invasion of the provincial domain may thus be justified. But the decisive authority of the judgments which have so determined cannot now be questioned in this court. I defer to it. …

But for their Lordships' emphatic and reiterated allocation of "the regulation of trade and commerce" to this subordinate and wholly auxiliary function, my inclination would have been to accord to it some independent operation, such as was indicated in *Parsons' Case* (1881), 7 AC 96 (PC), and within that sphere, however limited, to treat it as appropriating exclusively to the Dominion Parliament an enumerated subject of legislative jurisdiction with consequences similar to those which attach to the other twenty-eight enumerative heads of s. 91. It is incontrovertible and readily apprehended that the subject matter of head No. 2 must be restricted as was indicated in *Parsons' Case*, of which the authority has been frequently recognized in later decisions of the Judicial Committee. But that it should be denied all efficacy as an independent enumerative head of Dominion legislative jurisdiction—that it must be excluded from the operation of the concluding paragraph of s. 91, except for the subsidiary and auxiliary purposes indicated in recent decisions—these are propositions to which I find it difficult to accede. …

But apart from any assistance afforded by s. 91(2), I would uphold the *Canada Grain Act* as a statute of which the subject matter lies outside all of the subject matters enumeratively entrusted to the provinces under s. 92, in which case, said Lord Haldane in the *Insurance Reference*, [1916] 1 AC 588 (PC), "the Dominion Parliament can legislate effectively as regards a province." …

In my view not only is the grain trade of Canada a matter of national concern and of such dimensions as to affect the body politic of the Dominion, but the provisions of the *Canada Grain Act*, with some possible exceptions, deal with matters which, as envisaged by that legislation, do not come within that class of matters of a local or private nature … assigned exclusively to the legislatures of the provinces. As to most of them there is, therefore, no encroachment on the provincial domain. …

So regarded the *Canada Grain Act* may, I think, be supported without having recourse to the existence of abnormal conditions involving some extraordinary peril to the national life of Canada, recently indicated as a justification for the invasion by Parliament of the provincial field when legislating under the general power conferred by s. 91. But if there should be in the statute provisions essential to its effective operation for the purpose aimed at which must be regarded as trenching on the provincial domain, and if it should therefore be deemed necessary to meet this test of their validity, I know of nothing more likely to create a national emergency in Canada than a judicial determination that the Dominion Parliament lacks the power to legislate for the regulation of the export grain trade of the country. It cannot be that Parliament must defer legislative action until a national emergency with attendant disaster has developed. To protect the national interest it assuredly may anticipate and ward off such an evil. There is an emergency connected with the movement of the grain crop at the end of each season incontrovertibly greater than any which can be supposed to have existed in 1878 with regard to the liquor traffic.

DUFF J: … The Act is an attempt to regulate, directly and through the instrumentality of Grain Commissioners, the occupations mentioned. It is also an attempt to regulate generally elevators as warehouses for grain, and the business of operating them; and it seems, *ex facie*, to come within the decision of the Judicial Committee, *Attorney General for Canada v. Attorney General for Alberta*, [1916] 1 AG 588 (PC), condemning the *Insurance Act* of 1910 as *ultra vires*.

Mr. Symington, in a very able argument, attempted to support the Act on the ground that the trade in grain is largely an external trade (between seventy and eighty per cent, apparently, of the grain produced in the country is exported); and that the provisions of the Act are, on the whole, an attempt to regulate a branch of external trade, the provisions dealing with local matters being, as a rule, subsidiary and reasonably ancillary to the main purpose of the Act.

It is undeniable that one principal object of this Act is to protect the external trade in grain, and especially in wheat, by ensuring the integrity of certificates issued by the Grain Commission in respect of the quality of grain, and especially of wheat; and the beneficent effect and the value of the system provided by the legislation as a whole is not at all disputed by anybody. I do not think it is fairly disputable, either, that the Dominion possesses legislative powers, in respect of transport (by its authority over Dominion railways, over lines of ships connecting this country with foreign countries, over navigation and shipping); in respect of weight and measures; in respect of trade and commerce, interpreted as that phrase has been interpreted; which would enable it effectively, by properly framed legislation, to regulate this branch of external trade for the purpose of protecting it, by ensuring correctness in grading and freedom from adulteration, as well as providing for effective and reliable public guarantees as to quality. It does not follow that it is within the power of Parliament to accomplish this object by assuming, as this legislation does, the regulation in the provinces of particular occupations, as such, by a licensing system and otherwise, and of local works and undertakings, as such, however important and beneficial the ultimate purpose of the legislation may be.

There are, no doubt, many provisions of this statute which, as they stand, can be sustained; with them we are not concerned at this moment. The particular provision which is sought to be enforced is one of a series of provisions which are designed to regulate elevators and the occupations of those who make it their business to operate elevators. The particular provision, if it stood alone, might, perhaps, be sustained as a tax, but it cannot be separated from its context; it is only one part of a scheme for the regulation of elevators. There is one way in which the Dominion may acquire authority to regulate a local work such as an elevator; and that is, by a declaration properly framed under s. 92(10) of the *BNA Act*. …

There are two lurking fallacies in the argument advanced on behalf of the Crown; first, that, because in large part the grain trade is an export trade, you can regulate it locally in order to give effect to your policy in relation to the regulation of that part of it which is export. Obviously that is not a principle the application of which can be ruled by percentages. If it is operative when the export trade is seventy per cent of the whole, it must be equally operative when that percentage is only thirty; and such a principle in truth must postulate authority in the Dominion to assume the regulation of almost any trade in the country, provided it does so by setting up a scheme embracing the local, as well as the external and interprovincial trade; and regulation of trade, according to the conception of it which governs this legislation, includes the regulation in the provinces of the occupations of those engaged in the trade, and of the local establishments in which it is carried on. Precisely the same thing was attempted in the *Insurance Act* of 1910, unsuccessfully. The other fallacy is (the two are, perhaps, different forms of the same error) that the Dominion has such power because no single province, nor, indeed, all the provinces acting together, could put into effect such a sweeping scheme. The authority arises, it is said, under the residuary clause because of the necessary limits of the provincial authority. This is precisely the view which was advanced in the *Board of Commerce Case*, [1922] 1 AC 191 (PC) and, indeed, is the view which was unsuccessfully put forward in the *Montreal Street Railway Case*, [1912] AC 333 (PC), where it was pointed out that in a system involving a division of powers such as that set up by the *British North America Act*, it may often be that subsidiary legislation by the provinces or by the Dominion is required to give full effect to some beneficial and necessary scheme of legislation not entirely within the powers of either.

In one respect there is a close analogy between this case and the *Montreal Street Railway Case*. The expedient which their Lordships there pointed out as the appropriate one in order to enable the Dominion to acquire the authority it was seeking to exercise, is precisely that by which the Dominion could invest itself with the authority over such elevators as it might be considered necessary to regulate; that is to say, by resorting, as already suggested, to the power conferred by s. 92(10) to assume, through the procedure there laid down, jurisdiction in respect of "local works."

Fortunately, however, to repeat what has been said above, the control possessed by the Dominion over the subject matters mentioned, and especially over transport (both land transport and water transport) and over external trade, would really appear to be amply sufficient to enable the Dominion, by appropriately framed legislation, effectively to secure the essential objects of this statute.

[Mignault J held the Act invalid, for reasons similar to those of Duff J. Rinfret J concurred with Duff J and Idington J agreed with the trial judge, Maclean J.]

Appeal dismissed.

After *King v. Eastern Terminal*, the Dominion adopted the technique suggested by Duff J and acquired regulatory authority by declaring grain elevators to be works for the general advantage of Canada, pursuant to s. 92(10)(c) of the *British North America (BNA) Act*.

———————————————

Before 1925, scholars expressed little concern about the general course of the decisions by the Privy Council. For example, the leading Canadian constitutional scholar in the later nineteenth century, A.F.H. Lefroy, was, generally, utterly respectful and in 1913, when he did dare to criticize one of its decisions, he said that he had never before "seen the smallest loophole for criticism or for doubt as to the correctness of any one of them before this last judgment" ("The Alberta and Great Waterways Railway Case" (1913), 29 *Law Quarterly Review* 285, at 288). Shortly after *Snider*, misgivings began to appear, together with a new attitude toward legal thought and scholarship. The following article was the first substantial mark of these changes.

H.A. Smith, "The Residue of Power in Canada"
(1926), 4 *Canadian Bar Review* 432 (footnotes omitted)

[T]he difficulties of interpretation begin when words are not unambiguous, and it is at this point that our practice has drawn an arbitrary distinction between statutes and all other legal documents. In interpreting an obscure clause in a contract the court will take into consideration the whole of the previous correspondence between the parties and any words or conduct which may throw light upon their intentions. So again, if the words of a will are capable of two or more meanings, evidence is freely admitted to show what was passing in the testator's mind when he wrote those words. In all these cases our law is in accordance with common sense and with the ordinary practice of historical and literary criticism in other branches of learning.

If the application of this rule were extended to the interpretation of statutes it would follow that obscure clauses could be elucidated by studying the debates in Parliament and the considered public utterances of statesmen responsible for the introduction of the new law. ...

Unfortunately an arbitrary rule of English practice has cut off from the judge the light which is available for the historian, and it is now settled law that counsel are not permitted to quote from the proceedings of Parliament in order to explain the meaning of a statute. The same rule operates to exclude the speeches of statesmen outside Parliament, and probably extends to other forms of *contemporanea expositio*. In other words the courts are forbidden to adopt historical methods in solving a historical problem.

The immediate purpose of this rather lengthy introduction is to explain how an arbitrary and unreasonable rule of interpretation has produced the very serious result of giving Canada a constitution substantially different from that which her founders intended that she should have. A study of the available historical evidence gives us a clear and definite idea of what the fathers of Canadian confederation sought to achieve. By excluding this historical evidence and considering the *British North America Act* without any regard to its historical setting the courts have recently imposed upon us a constitution which is different, not only in detail but also in principle, from that designed at Charlottetown and Quebec.

The latest and leading authority upon the meaning of the "peace, order and good government" clause in the Canadian constitution is now the case of *Toronto Electric Commissioners v. Snider*, where the validity of the "*Lemieux Act*" dealing with compulsory industrial arbitration was in question. The judgment delivered by Lord Haldane in this case is now too well-known to need detailed analysis here. Its importance lies in the fact that it definitely relegated the words "peace, order and good government" to the position of a reserve power to be used only in cases of war or similar national emergencies. The real residuary power of legislation in normal times is now held to be contained in the words "property and civil rights," with regard to which the legislative power of the provinces is exclusive. The specific powers enunciated in section 91 are to be treated as exceptions to the general jurisdiction of the provinces to legislate upon property and civil rights. …

I do not think that it is going too far to say that this result is the precise opposite of that which our fathers hoped and endeavoured to attain. …

Upon reading the [Confederation] debates as a whole two points strike the attention. In the first place, no speaker, whether an advocate or an opponent of confederation, seems to have doubted that the Dominion was endowed with a general power to pass all legislation that it might deem to be for the general interest of Canada. Broadly speaking, the distinction between section 91 and section 92 was the distinction between those things that were of general and those that were of merely local importance. The true balance of the constitution is to be found in the opposition between the words "laws for the peace, order, and good government of Canada," in section 91 and the concluding words of section 92—"Generally, all matters of a merely local or private nature in the Province." The detailed enumerations were really intended to be explanatory of these two main principles, subject to the proviso that nothing specifically mentioned in section 91 should be deemed to be of a local or private nature. …

The second point that will strike the student of these debates is that nobody even thought of the modern idea that the words "peace, order, and good government" were intended to provide a kind of reserve power to be used only in the event of war, pestilence, or similar national calamities. So far as I am aware, this doctrine begins with the judgment in *Re the Board of Commerce Act*. The encroachment upon the sound and lucid doctrine of *Russell v. The Queen* began much earlier, but it did not at first amount to a denial of the main principle of Confederation.

[Here, Smith quoted the famous passage from the *Local Prohibition Reference* about "national concern."]

In these words we have a clear recognition of the true test of jurisdiction, as laid down by the statesmen of 1867.

Canadian historians, political scientists, and lawyers have spilled a lot of ink trying to explain the decisions of the Privy Council, especially the judgments of Lords Watson and Haldane. Here are two of the best-known efforts.

J.R. Mallory, *Social Credit and the Federal Power in Canada*
(Toronto: University of Toronto Press, 1976), at 48-49 and 55-56
(footnotes omitted)

What is the explanation of [the *Board of Commerce* case] and the trend of interpretation which it represents? Lord Haldane's reasoning, although elaborate, is not always easy to follow. An important element in the arguments appears to be the repeated view that the Act in question represented something altogether abnormal, and outside the range and scope of the functions of government as properly conceived. There are two aspects of the judgment which support this explanation.

The first arises from the nature of the agency itself, as is evident from the above quotation. The board, which is an agency enjoying rather wide discretionary powers and considerable independence of Parliament, is a very common device in Canada, particularly for dealing with problems of administration where the matter is technical in character, or where political pressure in the execution of policy is unlikely to serve any useful purpose. The independent administrative agency has been unpopular in England because it has tended to usurp functions of both Parliament and the judiciary. At no time was it in greater disrepute in legal circles than in the period which followed the dismantling of much of the war-created machinery of government in the early twenties. The fact that the decisions of the Board of Commerce were subject to review and alteration by the executive, rather than by Parliament, created in the English mind the illusion of concentrated state power of an emergency character. Thus the independent board, controlled only by the executive, appeared in the light of contemporary anxiety to transcend the words of sections 91 and 92 altogether.

The second explanation of Lord Haldane's judgment reinforces the first. Throughout the judgment there is the clear assumption that the eradication of hoarding and undue combination was scarcely an activity which should commend itself to the sense of propriety of a national parliament. Such matters, indeed, might be causes of local annoyance, and perhaps occasionally might be dealt with by local governments, but to pretend in ordinary times that hoarding and market-rigging were the proper subject for the attention of a national government suggested that they must be a cloak for some unwarranted extension of the proper sphere of the state.

Lord Haldane's decision in the *Snider* case is of the same order. There he took the almost incredible step of finding that a statute, which had been in force for nineteen years without serious question, was *ultra vires* the Parliament of Canada. In fact, his judgments follow a consistent pattern of nineteenth-century liberalism. This is, admittedly, not easy to explain since his philosophical outlook was scarcely Benthamite and his political sympathies were openly with the British Labour party. But the judgments, with their painstaking inability to be sympathetic to the intention of the legislature and their disastrous effect on novel functions and novel methods of government, remain. ...

Increasingly, constitutional case-law had become a reflection of conflict over the major issues of economic and social policy. If they are looked at in this way, one-half of the important leading cases in Canadian constitutional law involved an attempt by the state to interfere with the free disposal by individuals of their property. The results of this constant litigious pressure against limitation of the freedom of action of the individual are imposing. In one-half of the cases the plea of *ultra vires* was successful in defeating the intention of the legislature. It is impossible to avoid the conclusion that the resulting spheres of authority of the Dominion and the provinces are the incidental outcome of a clash between individualism and collectivism.

Thus, only on the surface has this struggle been a conflict between two conceptions of federalism. Basically it has been a dialectic of two sets of ideas. These ideas in turn, as we have seen, have been set in conflict by two forces. One force has been the current of world opinion over the last half century. The other has been the change in the nature of the Canadian economy. The assumptions of *laissez-faire* and individual self-help fitted the facts of frontier life. With greater diversification, a growth of scale in enterprise, an

increase in urbanization, and an increase in economic interdependence which was accompanied by a growth of group consciousness, collective wants became more important
and individual freedom of action so limited as to destroy the validity of the old individualistic assumptions.

The extension of the franchise, the granting of provincial stature to the prairies, and
the opening up of new areas and new kinds of economic activity gave a measure of political power to groups which did not benefit directly from the old national policy. The
clash in interest and in ideas took place through the party system in elections and in the
legislatures, and resulted in legislation which was a concession to the newly emerged interests. The struggle was continued in the courts where the interests which felt themselves inconvenienced by these restrictions on their freedom of action were able to enlist
the aid of a judicial theory of interpretation and legislative propriety which found ways
of nullifying the effect of undesirable legislation.

A. Cairns, "The Judicial Committee and Its Critics"
(1971), 4 *Canadian Journal of Political Science* 301 (footnotes omitted)

[After quoting from Lord Haldane's praise of Lord Watson, Cairns argued that "there can
be no doubt that Watson and Haldane consciously fostered the provinces in Canadian
federalism, and by so doing helped to transform the highly centralist structure originally
created in 1867." Later, in making a defence or justification of the Privy Council, he said,
"The most elementary justification of the Privy Council rests on the broad sociological
ground that the provincial bias which pervaded so many of its decisions was in fundamental harmony with the regional pluralism of Canada. ... From the vantage point of a
century of constitutional evolution the centralist emphasis of the Confederation appears
increasingly unrealistic."]

[After Confederation t]he provinces, which had initially been endowed with functions
of lesser significance, found that their control of natural resources gave them important
sources of wealth and power, and extensive managerial responsibilities. By the decade of
the twenties, highways, hydro-electric power, a host of welfare functions, and mush-
rooming educational responsibilities gave them tasks and burdens far beyond those anticipated in 1867. By this time the centralizing effect of the building of the railways and
the settlement of the west was ended by the virtual completion of these great national
purposes.

As the newer provinces west of the great lakes entered the union, or were created by
federal legislation, they quickly developed their own identities and distinct public purposes. Their populations grew. Their economies expanded. Their separate histories
lengthened. Their governmental functions proliferated, and their administrative and
political competence developed. They quickly acquired feelings of individuality and a
sense of power which contributed to the attenuation of federal dominance in the political
system.

Only in special, unique, and temporary circumstances—typically of an emergency
nature—has the federal system been oriented in a centralist direction. The focus of so

many Canadian academic nationalists on the central government reflected their primary concern with winning autonomy from the United Kingdom. An additional and less visible process was also taking place. Canadian political evolution has been characterized not only by nation-building, but by province-building. Further, it is too readily overlooked that with the passing of time Canada became more federal. In 1867 there were only four provinces in a geographically much more compact area than the nine provinces which had emerged by 1905, and the ten by 1949. If a province is regarded as an institutionalized particularism the historical development of Canada has been characterized by expansion which has made the country more heterogeneous than hitherto.

In response to this increasingly federal society the various centralizing features of the *BNA Act* fell into disuse, not because their meaning was distorted by the courts, but because they were incompatible with developments in the country as a whole. In numerous areas, decentralizing developments occurred entirely on Canadian initiative, with no intervention by the Judicial Committee. The powers of reservation and disallowance were not eroded by the stupidity or malevolence of British judges but by concrete Canadian political facts. The failure to employ section 94 of the *BNA Act* to render uniform the laws relating to property and civil rights in the common law provinces was not due to the prejudice of Lords Watson and Haldane, but to the utopian nature of the assumptions which inspired it, and the consequent failure of Canadians to exploit its centralizing possibilities.

The preceding analysis of Canadian federalism makes it evident that the provincial bias of the Privy Council was generally harmonious with Canadian developments. A more detailed investigation provides added support for this thesis.

At the time when Privy Council decisions commenced to undermine the centralism of Macdonald there was a strong growth of regional feeling. During the long premiership of Oliver Mowat, 1872-96, Ontario was involved in almost constant struggle with Ottawa. The status of the lieutenant governor, the boundary dispute with Manitoba and the central government, and bitter controversies over the federal use of the power of disallowance constituted recurrent points of friction between Ottawa and Ontario. Friction was intensified by the fact that with the exception of the brief Liberal interlude from 1873 to 1878 the governing parties at the two levels were of opposed partisan complexion, and by the fact that Mowat and Macdonald were personally hostile to each other. The interprovincial conference of 1887, at which Mowat played a prominent part, indicated the general reassertion of provincialism. The "strength and diversity of provincial interests shown by the conference," in the words of the *Rowell-Sirois Report*, "indicated that, under the conditions of the late nineteenth century, the working constitution of the Dominion must provide for a large sphere of provincial freedom." Nationalism had become a strong political force in Quebec in reaction to the hanging of Riel and the failure of the newly opened west to develop along bicultural and bilingual lines. Nova Scotia was agitated by a secession movement. The maritime provinces generally were hostile to the tariff aspects of the National Policy. Manitoba was struggling against federal railway policies. British Columbia was only slowly being drawn into the national party system after the belated completion of the CPR in 1885. It was entering a long period of struggle with the Dominion over Oriental immigration. In addition, the late eighties and early nineties constituted one of the lowest points of national self-confidence in Canadian history. It was a period in which the very survival of Canada was questioned. By the late 1890s, when economic conditions had markedly improved, a new Liberal government, with provincial sympathies, was in office. The year of the much criticized *Local Prohibition* decision was the same year in which Laurier assumed power and commenced to wield federal authority with much looser reins than had his Conservative predecessors. "The only means of maintaining Confederation," he had declared in 1889, "is to recognize that, within its sphere assigned to it by the constitution, each province is as independent of control by the federal Parliament as the latter is from control by the provincial legislatures."

The Privy Council clearly responded to these trends in a series of landmark decisions in the eighties and nineties.

Cairns's sociological explanation accords well with P.E. Trudeau's observations (at the time, Trudeau was a law professor at the Université de Montréal) that the Privy Council rulings had the effect of forestalling the separation of Quebec from Canada: "[I]t should perhaps be considered that if the law lords had not leaned in that [provincial] direction, Quebec separatism might not be a threat today; it might be an accomplished fact." See P.E. Trudeau, *Federalism and the French Canadians* (Toronto: Macmillan, 1968), at 198. The literature offers many other explanations, including the Privy Council's concern about the preservation of the British Empire, its reluctance to make a vague phrase such as p.o.g.g. a major power, its attitudes toward Home Rule for Ireland (which was one of the searing domestic political issues in England), and its desire to preserve its own power; Lord Haldane's affection for Hegelian philosophy (he was an amateur philosopher of some substance); and the possibility that the Privy Council interpreted the *BNA Act* correctly, after all.

Another candidate is the power of ideas about federalism in lawyers' and judges' minds. Here, recall the passage from Dicey near the end of Chapter 4, The Late Nineteenth Century: The Canadian Courts Under the Influence. According to Dicey, federalism gives rise to a spirit of legalism in which "no legislature throughout the land is more than a subordinate law-making body capable in strictness of enacting nothing but by-laws." Might this model have contributed to the reasoning and results of the courts in the late nineteenth century? Another version of federalism may have been at work in the Haldane era. It is described in the following excerpt from David Schneiderman, "Harold Laski, Viscount Haldane, and the Law of the Canadian Constitution in the Early Twentieth Century" (1998), 48 *University of Toronto Law Journal* 521, at 529-38 and 543-46:

> "Federalistic feeling" was described as "curiously widespread" in Britain in the early part of the twentieth century. … [The theory of political pluralism] merged these economic and political streams, attacking the all-absorptive state and promoting the inherent worthiness of group associations. … [Political scientist Harold Laski was one of the leading figures of the British political pluralist movement.] Laski believed that citizens derived meaning and identity from the plurality of groups with which they were associated. The individual was portrayed as a complex of multiple loyalties and belongings with many forms of association competing for his or her allegiance. He described the individual as "a point towards which a thousand associations converge." Whether we will it or not, he wrote, we are all a "bundle of hyphens." …
>
> If the state had no privileged existence over group life, it could not legitimately attempt to absorb or control the diverse allegiances of its citizens. Each of these associations—"the club,

trade-union, church, society, town, country, university"—has a "group-life, a group-will, to en rich the imagination." English law treated organized groups largely as incapable of having an existence independent of the state—group life was contingent upon, rather than independent of, state recognition. ...

The modern state was in need of more, not less, decentralization. To consider Ottawa or Washington as reserves of nascent power capable of resolving conflict by simple generalizable solutions was to risk local stagnation. Centralized government, wrote Laski, "cannot grasp ... the genius of place: ... To multiply the centres of authority is to multiply the channels of discussion and so promote the diffusion of healthy and independent opinion." In contrast, the vices of centralized government for Laski were numerous:

> It is so baffled by the very vastness of its business as necessarily to be narrow and despotic and over-formal in character. It tends to substitute for a real effort to grapple with special problems an attempt to apply wide generalisations that are in fact irrelevant. It involves the decay of local energy by taking real power from its hands. It puts real responsibility in a situation where, from its very flavour of generality, an unreal experiment is postulated. It prevents the saving grace of experiment. It invites the congestion of business.

 . . .

For the pluralists, then, self-government was exercised preferably at local levels where the implications of social policy choices could be felt and better understood. The object of the pluralist state was to partition power along these lines so that the diversity of group life could be given expression. Functional devolution along territorial and non-territorial lines not only facilitated the expression of individual moral development through participation in associational life, it also created a "corporate sense of responsibility" or "training in self-government." Like Hegel (and Mill), Laski believed that local self-government was "educative in perhaps a higher degree, at least contingently, than any other part of government." This training in self-government would lead, ultimately, to connections being made between associational life and "the general background of social life." ...

In a highly decentralized society, what role remained for the national state? On this, Laski moved from a position of radical polyarchy in 1915 to one of centralized authority for the performance of key public functions in 1925. For just as associations had social functions to fulfil, so did the state. "The state exists as the most adequate means we have yet invented for the promotion of an end we deem good," admitted Laski. ...

[Lord Haldane befriended Laski and wrote, in his review of Laski's 1922 book *The Foundation of Sovereignty and Other Essays*, that Laski] had "achieved a remarkable success" with this book. Regarding the personality of associations, Laski had "no difficulty in showing that the reluctance of our jurisprudence to treat an association as a person that can be made responsible in law has given rise to many obscurities and difficulties." Haldane contrasted the monistic with the pluralistic view of the state and concluded that the doctrine of political pluralism "is an ethical ideal" greatly superior to the monistic state. It is those "institutions which have genuine popular power expressed in them that become organs of ethical ideals and of true citizenship, and so the superiority of the pluralistic State becomes evident," wrote Haldane. Decentralization, therefore, was "essential." Haldane also could agree with Laski's desire to remodel government from time to time, not only in the direction of devolution, but also in the other direction:

"In wartime, a highly centralized control may be essential. In peacetime it may be politically and ethically very undesirable." …

The true nature of state sovereignty, then, was not revealed in the arguments of either the monists or the pluralists. The "real source of sovereignty," according to Haldane, was "general opinion," which lay behind the institutional apparatus of state and society. Acknowledging merit in the monist case, Haldane argued that the minds that constitute the general will cohere into a "unitary and monistic" form represented by the state, though this is not the exclusive vehicle of public opinion. Its "forms of expression may be diverse," Haldane conceded to the pluralists. The true source of sovereignty, though, was constituted neither wholly in the state nor in group life; rather, it could be found in "public opinion," which he equated with the general will. …

The distribution of sovereignty to organizational groups did not exclude the general will "which may manifest itself as supreme, and may arm Govt. with extended authority on occasion." The general will, as an expression of homogeneous opinion, could emerge to supersede the heterogeneity of sovereignty in such extreme circumstances. Ernest Barker, in his modified defence of the pluralists, agreed: "If it comes to a pinch, we shall forget that we are anything but citizens."

CHAPTER SIX

The 1930s: The Depression and the New Deal

Early in the 1930s, the Privy Council decided three cases that seemed to signal a shift in both results and manner of reasoning. Recall that in the *Persons* case, decided in 1929 and reproduced in Chapter 2, Judicial Review and Constitutional Interpretation, Lord Sankey spoke of a "living tree" and the need for a "large and liberal interpretation," even though he also took pains to point out that the issue there was not the division of powers.

Proprietary Articles Trade Association v. AG Canada
[1931] AC 310, 2 DLR 1 (PC); aff'g. [1929] 2 SCR 409, 2 DLR 802

[A reference was made to determine whether the *Dominion Combines Investigation Act* and s. 498 of the *Criminal Code* were valid. Section 498 of the Code prohibited participation in an agreement to restrain competition. The *Combines Investigation Act* made it a criminal offence to participate in a combine, and defined a combine as an agreement or merger that limited competition or increased prices to the detriment of the public. It also created a commission to administer the Act, with powers to investigate, and it gave the government power to reduce tariffs that protected a combine. The Proprietary Articles Trade Association was permitted to participate in the reference, presumably because the commission had found that it had participated in a combine.

Both the Supreme Court and the Privy Council held that both statutes were valid. In the Supreme Court, Duff J, writing for himself and Rinfret and Smith JJ, discussed the Dominion's criminal law power. He began by quoting from the judgment of the Privy Council in *AG Ontario v. Hamilton Street Railway*, [1903] AC 524 (PC), where Lord Halsbury said, at 529 AC that s. 91(27) gave the Dominion power over "the criminal law in its widest sense." Duff J quickly added, at 412 SCR, the reservation that some limitation was needed to respect the "constitutional autonomy of the provinces." Then, turning to s. 498, he said, at 415 SCR, it "aims at suppressing certain practices calculated, in the view of Parliament, to limit competition and produce the evil of high prices. [The prohibited conduct is] dealt with from that point of view and that point of view only." In response to an argument that s. 91(27) extended only to offences that were offences at Confederation or offences that were criminal "in their very nature" (and here the reference was obviously to Lord Haldane's judgment in the *Board of Commerce Reference*), he said, at 415 SCR:

It is difficult to understand upon what justification the Dominion Parliament can be denied the power under s. 91 to declare any act to be a crime which, in its opinion, is such a violation of generally accepted standards of conduct as to deserve chastisement as a crime. The views of the community as to what deserves punishment change from generation to generation. Practices calculated to imperil health and safety, or to prejudice the moral standards of the community may become, in the course of a few years, so widely prevalent as to create a general demand for the abatement and prevention of them by State action in the sphere of the Criminal Law. Other acts, once within the scope of the Criminal Law, may, in the course of time, come to be regarded as outside the proper domain of State interference. It is difficult to understand on what principle the court is to review the decisions of Parliament in seeking to adapt the Criminal Law to successive phases of public opinion in such matters.

The primary parts of the *Combines Investigation Act* were valid on the same ground. Newcombe J, writing for himself and Mignault and Lamont JJ, reasoned in much the same way.]

LORD ATKIN: "Criminal law" means "the criminal law in its widest sense": *Attorney-General for Ontario v. Hamilton Street Ry. Co.* It certainly is not confined to what was criminal by the law of England or of any Province in 1867. The power must extend to legislation to make new crimes. Criminal law connotes only the quality of such acts or omissions as are prohibited under appropriate penal provisions by authority of the State. The criminal quality of an act cannot be discerned by intuition; nor can it be discovered by reference to any standard but one: Is the act prohibited with penal consequences? Morality and criminality are far from co-extensive; nor is the sphere of criminality necessarily part of a more extensive field covered by morality—unless the moral code necessarily disapproves all acts prohibited by the State, in which case the argument moves in a circle. It appears to their Lordships to be of little value to seek to confine crimes to a category of acts which by their very nature belong to the domain of "criminal jurisprudence"; for the domain of criminal jurisprudence can only be ascertained by examining what acts at any particular period are declared by the State to be crimes, and the only common nature they will be found to possess is that they are prohibited by the State and that those who commit them are punished. Their Lordships agree with the view expressed in the judgment of Newcombe J [1929] SCR 409 that the passage in the judgment of the Board in the *Board of Commerce* case [1922] 1 AC 191 at 198-199 to which allusion has been made, was not intended as a definition. In that case their Lordships appear to have been contrasting two matters—one obviously within the line, the other obviously outside it. For this purpose it was clearly legitimate to point to matters which are such serious breaches of any accepted code of morality as to be obviously crimes when they are prohibited under penalties. The contrast is with matters which are merely attempts to interfere with Provincial rights, and are sought to be justified under the head of "criminal law" colourably and merely in aid of what is in substance an encroachment. ...

The view that their Lordships have expressed makes it unnecessary to discuss the further ground upon which the legislation has been supported by reference to the power to legislate under s. 91(2), for "The regulation of trade and commerce." Their Lordships merely propose to disassociate themselves from the construction suggested in argument of a passage in the judgment in the *Board of Commerce* case under which it was contended that the power to regulate trade and commerce could be invoked only in furtherance of a general power which Parliament possessed independently of it. No such restriction is properly to be inferred from that judgment. The words of the statute must receive their proper construction where they stand as giving an independent authority to Parliament over the particular subject-matter.

Their Lordships are of opinion that the Supreme Court of Canada were right in answering both questions in the negative, and that this appeal should be dismissed, and they will humbly advise His Majesty accordingly.

Appeal dismissed.

Reference re the Regulation and Control of Aeronautics in Canada
[1932] AC 54, 1 DLR 58 (PC); rev'g. [1930] SCR 663, [1931] 1 DLR 13

[After World War I, a convention about aeronautics was made by the peace conference, and ratified by Canada and by the King on behalf of the British Empire. The Canadian Parliament enacted legislation and regulations implementing this convention and regulating aeronautics in a comprehensive way, including licensing of pilots, aircraft, and commercial services and regulations for navigation and safety. A reference was made to the Supreme Court to determine the validity of this legislation. It held, in a series of divided judgments, that the subject of aeronautics was, generally, one for the provinces but that the Dominion had paramount, although not exclusive, authority to implement the convention under s. 132.]

LORD SANKEY LC: ... Before discussing the several questions individually, it is desirable to make some general observations upon ss. 91 and 92, and 132. ...

Under our system decided cases effectively construe the words of an Act of Parliament and establish principles and rules whereby its scope and effect may be interpreted. But there is always a danger that in the course of this process the terms of the statute may come to be unduly extended and attention may be diverted from what has been enacted to what has been judicially said about the enactment.

To borrow an analogy; there may be a range of sixty colours, each of which is so little different from its neighbour that it is difficult to make any distinction between the two, and yet at the one end of the range the colour may be white and at the other end of the range black. Great care must therefore be taken to consider each decision in the light of the circumstances of the case in view of which it was pronounced, especially in the interpretation of an Act such as the *British North America Act*, which was a great constitutional charter, and not to allow general phrases to obscure the underlying object of the Act, which was to establish a system of government upon essentially federal principles. Useful as decided cases are, it is always advisable to get back to the words of the Act itself and to remember the object with which it was passed.

Inasmuch as the Act embodies a compromise under which the original Provinces agreed to federate, it is important to keep in mind that the preservation of the rights of minorities was a condition on which such minorities entered into the federation, and the foundation upon which the whole structure was subsequently erected. The process of interpretation as the years go on ought not to be allowed to dim or to whittle down the provisions of the original contract upon which the federation was founded, nor is it legitimate that any judicial construction of the provisions of ss. 91 and 92 should impose a new and different contract upon the federating bodies.

But while the Courts should be jealous in upholding the charter of the Provinces as enacted in s. 92 it must no less be borne in mind that the real object of the Act was to give the central Government those high functions and almost sovereign powers by which uniformity of legislation might be secured on all questions which were of common concern to all the Provinces as members of a constituent whole.

[A discussion of cases, which concluded with Lord Haldane's judgment in *Fort Frances Pulp and Paper Company v. Manitoba Free Press Company*, [1923] AC 695, 3 DLR 629 (PC), excerpted in Chapter 5, The Early Twentieth Century: The Beginnings of Economic Regulation, is omitted.]

It is obvious, therefore, that there may be cases of emergency where the Dominion is empowered to act for the whole. There may also be cases where the Dominion is entitled to speak for the whole, and this not because of any judicial interpretation of ss. 91 and 92, but by reason of the plain terms of s. 132, where Canada as a whole, having undertaken an obligation, is given the power necessary and proper for performing that obligation.

During the course of the argument, learned counsel on either side endeavoured respectively to bring the subject of aeronautics within s. 91 or s. 92. Thus, the appellant referred to s. 91(2) (the regulation of trade and commerce); s. 91(5) (postal services); s. 91(9) (beacons); s. 91(10) (navigation and shipping). Their Lordships do not think that aeronautics can be brought within the subject navigation and shipping, although undoubtedly to a large extent, and in some respects, it might be brought under the regulation of trade and commerce, or the postal services. On the other hand, the respondents contended that aeronautics as a class of subject came within s. 92(13) (property and civil rights in the Provinces) or s. 92(16) (generally all matters of a merely local and private nature in the Provinces). Their Lordships do not think that aeronautics is a class of subject within property and civil rights in the Provinces, although here again, ingenious arguments may show that some small part of it might be so included.

In their Lordships' view, transport as a subject is dealt with in certain branches both of s. 91 and of s. 92, but neither of those sections deals specially with that branch of transport which is concerned with aeronautics.

Their Lordships are of opinion that it is proper to take a broader view of the matter rather than to rely on forced analogies or piecemeal analysis. They consider the governing section to be s. 132, which gives to the Parliament and Government of Canada all powers necessary or proper for performing the obligations towards foreign countries arising under treaties between the Empire and such foreign countries. As far as s. 132 is concerned, their Lordships are not aware of any decided case which is of assistance on the present occasion. It will be observed, however, from the very definite words of the section, that it is the Parliament and Government of Canada who are to have all powers necessary or proper for performing the obligations of Canada, or any Province thereof. It would therefore appear to follow that any Convention of the character under discussion necessitates Dominion legislation in order that it may be carried out. ... [W]e think that the Dominion Parliament not only has the right, but also the obligation, to provide by statute and by regulation that the terms of the Convention shall be duly carried out. With regard to some of them, no doubt, it would appear to be clear that the Dominion has power to legislate, for example, under s. 91(2), for the regulation of trade and commerce, and under s. 91(5) for the postal services, but it is not necessary for the Dominion to piece together its powers under s. 91 in an endeavour to render them co-extensive with its duty under the Convention when s. 132 confers upon it full power to do all that is legislatively necessary for the purpose.

To sum up, having regard (a) to the terms of s. 132; (b) to the terms of the Convention which covers almost every conceivable matter relating to aerial navigation; and (c) to the fact that further legislative powers in relation to aerial navigation reside in the Parliament of Canada by virtue of s. 91(2), (5), and (7), it would appear that substantially the whole field of legislation in regard to aerial navigation belongs to the Dominion. There may be a small portion of the field which is not by virtue of specific words in the *British North America Act* vested in the Dominion; but neither is it vested by specific words in the Provinces. As to that small portion it appears to the Board that it must necessarily belong to the Dominion under its power to make laws for the peace, order and good government of Canada. Further, their Lordships are influenced by the facts that the subject of aerial navigation and the fulfilment of Canadian obligations under s. 132 are matters of national interest and importance; and that aerial navigation is a class of subject which has attained such dimensions as to affect the body politic of the Dominion.

For these reasons their Lordships have come to the conclusion that it was competent for the Parliament of Canada to pass the Act and authorize the Regulations in question, and that questions 1, 3 and 4, which alone they are asked to answer, should be answered in the affirmative. ...

Appeal allowed.

Reference re Regulation and Control of Radio Communication in Canada
[1932] AC 304 (PC); aff'g. [1931] 4 DLR 865 (SCC)

[In the late 1920s, the Dominion government entered into a series of international agreements about radio, the major one created in 1927, in Washington. After enacting legislation to implement these agreements, the government made a reference asking, generally, whether it had the power to regulate radio. In the Supreme Court, the conventions and s. 132 were barely mentioned and a majority of three to two held that the Dominion had power under p.o.g.g.]

VISCOUNT DUNEDIN: The learned Chief Justice and Rinfret J expressed their regret that at the time of delivering judgment they had not had the advantage of knowing what was the conclusion reached by this Board on the question referred as to aviation. It is however unnecessary to speculate as to what would have been the result had the learned judges known as we know now that the judgment of this Board (*In re Regulation and Control of Aeronautics in Canada*, [1932] PC 54 (PC), delivered on October 22, 1931) settled that the regulation of aviation was a matter for the Dominion. It would certainly only have confirmed the majority in their opinions. And as to the minority, though it is true that reference is made in their opinions to the fact that as the case then stood aviation had been decided not to fall within the exclusive jurisdiction of the Dominion, yet had they known the eventual judgment it is doubtful whether that fact would have altered their opinion. For this must at once be admitted; the leading consideration in the judgment of the Board was that the subject fell within the provisions of s. 132 of the *British North America Act, 1867*, which is as follows: "The Parliament and Government of Canada shall have all powers necessary or proper for performing the obligations of Canada or of any Province thereof as part of the British Empire towards foreign countries arising under treaties between the Empire and such foreign countries." And it is said with truth that, while as regards aviation there was a treaty, the convention here is not a treaty between the Empire as such and foreign countries, for Great Britain does not sign as representing the Colonies and Dominions. She only confirms the assent which had been signified by the Colonies and Dominions who were separately represented at the meetings which drafted the convention. But while this is so, the aviation case in their Lordships' judgment cannot be put on one side. ...

This idea of Canada as a Dominion being bound by a convention equivalent to a treaty with foreign powers was quite unthought of in 1867. It is the outcome of the gradual development of the position of Canada vis-à-vis to the mother country, Great Britain, which is found in these later days expressed in the *Statute of Westminster*. It is not, therefore, to be expected that such a matter should be dealt with in explicit words in either s. 91 or s. 92. The only class of treaty which would bind Canada was thought of as a treaty by Great Britain, and that was provided for by s. 132. Being, therefore, not mentioned explicitly in either s. 91 or s. 92, such legislation falls within the general words at the opening of s. 91 which assign to the Government of the Dominion the power to make laws "for the peace order and good government of Canada in relation to all matters not coming within the classes of subjects by this Act assigned exclusively to the legislatures of the Provinces." In fine, though agreeing that the Convention was not such a treaty as is defined in s. 132, their Lordships think that it comes to the same thing. ...

The result is in their Lordships' opinion clear. It is Canada as a whole which is amenable to the other powers for the proper carrying out of the convention; and to prevent individuals in Canada infringing the stipulations of the convention it is necessary that the Dominion should pass legislation which should apply to all the dwellers in Canada.

At the same time, while this view is destructive of the view urged by the Province as to how the observance of the international convention should be secured, it does not, they say, dispose of the whole of the question. They say it does not touch the consideration of inter-Provincial broadcasting. Now, much the same might have been said as to aeronautics. It is quite possible to fly without going outside the Province, yet that was not thought to disturb the general view, and once you come to the conclusion that the convention is binding on Canada as a Dominion, there are various sentences of the Board's judgment in the aviation case which might be literally transcribed to this. The idea pervading that judgment is that the whole subject of aeronautics is so completely covered by the treaty ratifying the convention between the nations, that there is not enough left to give a separate field to the Provinces as regards the subject. The same might at least very easily be said on this subject, but even supposing that it were possible to draw a rigid line between inter-Provincial and Dominion broadcasting, there is something more to be said. It will be found that the argument for the Provinces really depends on a complete difference being established between the operations of the transmitting and the receiving instruments.

[A discussion of s. 92(10)(a) is omitted.]

The argument of the Province really depends on making, as already said, a sharp distinction between the transmitting and the receiving instrument. In their Lordships' opinion this cannot be done. Once it is conceded, as it must be, keeping in view the duties under the convention, that the transmitting instrument must be so to speak under the control of the Dominion, it follows in their Lordships' opinion that the receiving instrument must share its fate. Broadcasting as a system cannot exist without both a transmitter and a receiver. The receiver is indeed useless without a transmitter and can be reduced to a nonentity if the transmitter closes. The system cannot be divided into two parts, each independent of the other. ...

As their Lordships' views are based on what may be called the pre-eminent claims of s. 91, it is unnecessary to discuss the question which was raised with great ability by Mr. Tilley—namely, whether, if there had been no pre-eminent claims as such, broadcasting could have been held to fall either within "property and civil rights," or within "matters of a merely local or private nature."

Upon the whole matter, therefore, their Lordships have no hesitation in holding that the judgment of the majority of the Supreme Court was right, and their Lordships will therefore humbly advise His Majesty that the appeal should be dismissed.

Appeal dismissed.

The Great Depression devastated Canada, and the rest of the capitalist world, between the late 1920s and the late 1930s. Some measure of its impact can be suggested by numbers: in 1933, the worst year of the Depression, 33 percent of non-agricultural workers were unemployed and, taking 1929 as a base, national output had fallen 30 percent, personal incomes had fallen almost 50 percent, and prices had fallen 18 percent—and far further in export markets. On the prairies, drought and crop failure compounded the economic decline; crop yield fell from 23.5 bushels of wheat per acre in 1928 to 6.4 bushels in 1937 and farm income fell from $450 million to $100 million in 1931. In the cities, thousands sought "dole" after prospects for work disappeared. For the governments, the cost of providing assistance fell most heavily on the municipalities and provinces, which were the least able to bear it, and by 1934, in the metropolitan Toronto area, every municipality except Forest Hill and Swansea was bankrupt.

When the Depression began, the Liberals and MacKenzie King were in power in Ottawa. In 1930, the Conservatives, led by R.B. Bennett, swept to power, aided somewhat by King's pronouncement in Parliament that he would not give any Conservative provincial govern-ment "a five-cent piece" for relief. Bennett, like King, offered little more than traditional measures: manipulation of the tariff, a balanced budget, and hard work. The *Unemployment Relief Act*, SC 1930, c. 1, enacted first in 1930, provided a modest amount for public works and for direct relief—the dole—but in 1932, the aid for public works was terminated in an effort to balance the budget. Bennett had little comprehension, let alone sympathy, for the radical proposals for increased public spending made by J.M. Keynes in the *Atlantic Monthly* in 1932. In 1932, as well, the Department of National Defence began a program of work camps for single men and, by 1935, there were 200 of these camps through which 170,000 men had passed.

In 1934, Bennett's government enacted the *Farmers' Creditors Arrangements Act*, SC 1934, c. 53 to protect farmers from their creditors and the *Natural Products Marketing Act*, SC 1934, c. 57 to regulate the marketing of agricultural products. (As well, legislation creat-ed the *Canadian Radio Broadcasting Commission Act*, SC 1932, c. 51 and the Bank of Can-ada, but neither were at stake in the constitutional conflict that followed.)

The Depression continued, apparently unabated. The Conservatives were threatened with losses in provincial general elections and federal byelections and a divisive and theatri-cal inquiry into commercial abuses—the "Price Spreads" inquiry. Late in 1934, Bennett, who had been a powerful and autocratic leader, seemed to be faltering but, in January 1935, he reappeared and, with little warning to his cabinet, let alone consultation, he dramatically promised a "new deal" in a series of radio broadcasts. (The phrase "new deal" was taken from President Roosevelt's "fireside chats" in the United States; Bennett did not use the phrase but it has become the common label.) Bennett likely did not have a comprehensive and concrete program in mind when he spoke, although he promised regulation of hours of work, wages, and working conditions; social insurance against sickness, industrial accidents, and unemployment; expansion of the regulation of agricultural products; and an agricul-tural credit program. Shortly afterward, six statutes were enacted, all of which fell far short of Bennett's promises. The *Limitation of Hours Work Act*, SC 1935, c. 63; the *Weekly Rest in Industrial Undertakings Act*, SC 1935, c. 4; and the *Minimum Wages Act*, SC 1935, c. 44 were all, explicitly, based on International Labour Organization conventions and enacted to fulfill treaty obligations. They established, respectively, maximum hours of work, a weekly day of rest, and administrative arrangements for specifying a minimum wage, although the scope of each of them was sharply limited. The *Employment and Social Insurance Act*, SC 1935, c. 38 established unemployment insurance for industrial workers; an amendment to the *Criminal Code*, SC 1935, c. 56 prohibited specified commercial practices; and the *Dominion Trade and Industry Commission Act*, SC 1935, c. 59 established a commission to regulate competition and a federal trademark—the Canada Standard.

As the following excerpt suggests, neither the Bennett or King governments substantially improved the conditions of working and unemployed individuals.

R. Simeon and I. Robinson, *State, Society, and the Development of Canadian Federalism*
(Toronto: University of Toronto Press, 1990), at 78-80 (references omitted)

Aside from substantial increases in federal transfers, "charity" to which the provinces had no legal claim and which could not be expected to last beyond the economic emergency, the Bennett government did remarkably little in the early depression years. Increased subsidies were made to the railways and the coal industry, and a variety of price support schemes were undertaken for wheat producers, but Bennett launched no dramatic policy initiatives like those in Roosevelt's America.

Prime Minister Bennett's reticence cannot plausibly be traced to a keen sense of provincial rights, or of the sociological realities underlying the legal doctrine. When, in 1935, he finally decided that a major departure from conventional economic policies was necessary, he did not bother to consult his own cabinet ministers, much less the provincial governments. Nor was Prime Minister Bennett one for worrying about the details of the constitutional division of powers. He seems to have been confident that constitutional grounds for his "New Deal" legislation could be found within the BNA Act.

The principal reason for the relative lack of federal initiative in the early years of the Depression seems to have been that Bennett believed the crisis could be remedied by the policies he campaigned for in 1930: the restoration of access to foreign markets for Canadian goods through Imperial preferences and the use of Canadian tariffs. Nor did provincial governments press forcefully for the federal government to undertake more radical programs in these early years. They were focussing on the immediate task of meeting their burgeoning relief commitments and their principal interest in the federal government was increased tax room, larger grants, or both. This focus on fiscal arrangements meant that in the first phase of the Depression there was relatively little intergovernmental discussion of fundamental reform to the federal constitution. As in 1927, so in 1931, the Dominion-Provincial Conference discussed the amending formula only because the issue had to be dealt with as part of the Statute of Westminster.

By 1935 the situation had greatly changed. Prime Minister Bennett's radio speeches of that spring had proclaimed the necessity of major changes in national economic and social institutions. These changes, his legislative program implied, had to be brought about primarily by the federal government. This entailed a clear challenge to the existing federal order. Bennett's defeat in the 1935 federal election left King with the dilemma of what to do with the Bennett New Deal. Unlike Bennett, King was highly sensitive to provincial objections (especially from Quebec and Ontario) that the legislation constituted a major encroachment on provincial jurisdiction. One of King's first acts upon being restored to power was to refer all of Bennett's proposed legislation to the Supreme Court of Canada.

King then sought to determine whether a consensus on constitutional reform could be found at the Dominion-Provincial Conference of December 1935. He was open to proposals to extend federal authority to regulate wages, working conditions and combines in restraint of trade, but advocated no specific amendments. King preferred to concentrate on the preliminary problem of securing agreement to an amendment formula.

A committee of the conference was assigned the task of exploring the latter issue. Premier Taschereau, who had opposed any discussion of an amendment formula in 1927, now proved receptive to the idea in the twilight hours of his regime. Still, the participants were a long way from agreement on a concrete formula at the end of the conference and it was agreed that federal and provincial officials should immediately begin to meet with a view to developing such a formula.

The conference of 1935 was remarkably conciliatory considering the economic stress facing both orders of government, and there was considerable optimism that an amending formula would soon be found. By February 1936 federal Minister of Justice Ernest Lapointe and the provincial Attorneys-General had, with the exception of New Brunswick, reached agreement on a formula: unanimous consent of all legislatures would be required for amendments touching on such crucial areas of the constitution as the educational rights of religious minorities. For other areas, such as social policy, the consent of parliament and two thirds of the legislatures, representing at least 55 percent of the Canadian population, would be sufficient. It was a major advance, but New Brunswick could not be induced to agree to it. King refused to act without unanimous consent, and the recommendations were shelved. Soon federal-provincial conflict began to escalate. The moment for constitutional reform based on unanimous provincial consent had passed.

The King government did take some initiatives. It negotiated a formal trade agreement with the United States within weeks of taking office. The Bank of Canada, which Bennett had established in 1934 as a "banker's bank," was nationalized, but the federal control thus acquired was not used to go beyond the easy money policy already established under its first Governor, Graham Towers. A National Employment Commission was created with the aim of coordinating the administration of relief expenditures and recommending measures to create employment opportunities. But when the Commission took up the views of Keynes in 1937 and urged the federal government to run a major budget deficit, King balked.

During the 1930s, the three major Canadian constitutional scholars were Vincent Macdonald, dean of the Faculty of Law at Dalhousie University; W.P.M. Kennedy, chair of the Honour School of Law at the University of Toronto; and Frank Scott, a member of the Faculty of Law at McGill University and, as well, a major Canadian poet, a founder of the Co-operative Commonwealth Federation (CCF), and a crusader for civil liberties. These scholars shared beliefs about Canada, its constitution, and legal reasoning: Canada had become an independent nation, her economy and social structure had changed fundamentally, and only a strong Dominion government could respond adequately to the Depression. They were passionately critical of the decisions of the Privy Council, and they feared that the *British North America (BNA) Act* was becoming more and more inadequate, despite the hopes suggested by the cases in the early 1930s.

Their beliefs about interpretation of the *BNA Act* were an expression of new approaches to legal reasoning and scholarship, which had arisen around the turn of the twentieth century in the United States, under the banners of "sociological jurisprudence" and "realism." The function of the courts was to determine the intent, or purpose, of the legislature but the words of a text, especially a constitutional text, often did not express this intent and, therefore, sometimes history and current social needs were necessary sources for determining meaning. These scholars read the *BNA Act* as making the federal government dominant and giving it power to legislate about matters of general importance. The Act gave the provinces specific powers to legislate about local matters; the remaining powers went to the Dominion. The p.o.g.g. clause was the sole grant of power in s. 91, and the enumerations were examples. Beginning in the late 1920s, the three scholars berated the Privy Council for betraying this design, for its "literal" approach (its belief that interpretation should be limited to the words alone), and for its failure to respect both the text and evidence of the understandings of Confederation. The article by Smith near the end of Chapter 5, The Early Twentieth Century: The Beginnings of Economic Regulation, is representative of much of their writing in the early 1930s. Some excerpts from articles by Kennedy and Macdonald, written a few years later as their despair mounted, follow.

W.P.M. Kennedy, "Our Constitution in the Melting Pot"
(1934), *South African Law Times* 156

Before the depression, the federal government, with the "generous" permission and approval of the provinces, had already undertaken to assist in old age pensions. The subject-matter is purely and solely provincial; but "What's the constitution," said the provinces, "when will the Dominion pay?" The example and procedure were unfortunate perhaps; but, as the issues may show, perhaps creative. Then came the crash. Unemployment—a purely provincial subject-matter—increased by leaps and bounds. There was no work; firm after firm went down; economic life was atrophied. Unemployment insurance—a purely provincial subject-matter—though suggested time after time by the "traitors," etc., was now too late. Then the whole problem of industrial control came to the front in a manner never before experienced—fair competition, hours of labour, rates of wages, minimum wages for *men*, marketing organizations, the capitalisation of companies, mass-production—all provincial subject-matters, but now erected, before the impelling forces of a world agony, into questions of vital national importance. Once again the Dominion stepped beyond its field to spend millions upon millions on unemployment—a provincial subject-matter. Nor was this the end. Province after province, especially in the west, faced bankruptcy, a repudiation of its obligations. Once again the Dominion stepped in with vast funds to prevent the crash. The Prime Minister, however, began to scent dangers, such as financial aid to the provinces without financial control of the federal money given to their aid. A Dominion provincial conference suggested constitutional changes. ... The provinces stood firm on their " rights," but next day they came hat in hand to almost demand the continuance of the federal relief. ...

It will no longer be possible to look on the *British North America Act* as a sacred instrument. The persistent forces of national tragedy—poverty, hunger, employment, possible bankruptcies, contracting trade, lower wages, miserable market prices, narrowed credit, lowering value of money—have all combined to rob "1867" of the glamour of romance. We do not dispute the creative work of that year any more than we dispute the creative work of Noah; but we see it at long last in its proper and just setting. .... We are now face to face with this issue: Shall we continue as a loose league of "sovereign" provinces, which the unfortunate judgments of the Privy Council had almost made us, surviving *legally* in order to break *culturally* and *economically*. Or shall we boldly face the problem that a nation of vast potential wealth and possibilities and of many remarkable achievements shall not be sacrificed at a constitutional altar erected in a far-off pioneer past, itself creatively barren by judicial obscurantism?

V. Macdonald, "Judicial Interpretation of the Canadian Constitution"
(1935), 1 *University of Toronto Law Journal* 260, at 282-84

The constitution of to-day, as it exists in enactment and construction, it is generally agreed, is ill-adapted in many important respects to our new status within the empire, to our present social and economic organization and needs, and to prevailing political theories which indicate the propriety or necessity of a greater degree of national control over, and governmental intervention in, matters of social welfare and business activity. New political facts, such as our greater autonomy in intraempire matters, new legal facts, such as our increased legislative capacity under the Statute of Westminster, 1931, emergent conditions arising out of the present economic depression, and a new philosophy of government—all these make up a background vastly different from that against which the act was projected in 1867, or that which conditioned the decisions of the past.

Much has been written and spoken elsewhere of the inability of the Canadian constitution to meet the social, economic, and political needs of to-day and of the necessity for its revision. However, it is not necessary to traverse this familiar ground, for the point at the moment is that great problems affecting the social and economic life of the country demand legislative capacity and solution. The second great fact at the moment is that effective solution of these contemporary problems is, in part, handicapped, and, in part, rendered impossible by (a) the terms of the act of 1867, and (b) previous decisions thereon, which, together, withhold jurisdiction where it is necessary that jurisdiction should be, divide jurisdiction where unity of jurisdiction is essential, and, in other cases, paralyse action because of doubt as to jurisdiction where certainty of jurisdiction is vital. Thus, it is not inaccurate to say that the constitutionality of many of the statutes which constituted the effort of the Dominion administration of the day (1934-5) to put through a great programme of social and economic reform is shrouded in doubt. ...

And so, born of the knowledge that new and unusual conditions demanded, in some matters, a unity of action, and, in others, a certainty of jurisdiction denied by the terms of the act or by its judicial interpretation, there came into being among the Canadian people the strong conviction, ... that the constitution must be revised. ...

Whether amended or not, the Canadian constitution will continue to be a written instrument requiring interpretation by a supreme judicial authority. When the task of revising the constitution is approached, the question as to the identity of the body which will be charged with its interpretation in the years to come must bulk large. Up to now this has been the judicial committee of the privy council, and, inevitably, the question must arise as to whether it shall continue to be entrusted with the ultimate power of interpretation.

The New Deal did not save Bennett, and, as described by Simeon and Robinson, *supra*, King and the Liberals came to power in the general election of 1935. King quickly referred all six statutes to the Supreme Court, together with the *Farmers' Creditors Arrangements Act* and the *Natural Products Marketing Act*. Six members of the Supreme Court heard arguments in the reference on Bennett's New Deal legislation early in 1936 and gave their decision on June 17. The results were complicated: the court unanimously upheld two of the statutes, the *Farmers' Creditors Arrangements Act* and the *Criminal Code* amendments. They were also unanimous in declaring both the *Dominion Trade and Industry Commission Act* and the *Natural Products Marketing Act ultra vires*, and they declared the *Employment and Social Insurance Act ultra vires* by a margin of four to two. Last, they divided three to three on the three International Labour Organization statutes—the *Limitation of Hours Work Act*, the *Weekly Rest in Industrial Undertakings Act*, and the *Minimum Wages Act*. On appeal, the Privy Council declared all the statutes *ultra vires*, except the *Farmers' Creditors Arrangements Act*, the amendments to the *Criminal Code*, and the Canada Standard provisions of the *Dominion Trade and Industry Commission Act*.

AG Canada v. AG Ontario (Labour Conventions)
[1937] AC 326, 1 DLR 673 (PC);
on appeal from [1936] SCR 461, 3 DLR 673

[This was a reference about the validity of the *Limitation of Hours Work Act*, which set eight hours a day and 48 hours a week as maximum hours of work; the *Weekly Rest in Industrial Undertakings Act*, which required a rest period of at least 24 consecutive hours for industrial workers; and the *Minimum Wages Act*, which gave the Governor in Council power to establish minimum wages. In 1919, Canada signed the Treaty of Peace as a member of the British Empire to secure humane conditions for workers. In 1930, the International Labour Organization of the League of Nations adopted conventions about hours of work, minimum wages, and days of rest. In March and April 1935, the Dominion government ratified these conventions and, in June, enacted these three statutes expressly to implement its treaty obligations.

In argument before the Supreme Court, the Dominion relied primarily on s. 132 (the treaty power). The provinces, fearing a threat to their autonomy, all opposed use of this power to permit the Dominion to legislate about subjects that would normally be within s. 92. Only Ontario stressed the possibility that, in the depression, p.o.g.g. could support the legislation but its invitation went largely unanswered by the Dominion.

The six-member court split equally and, in all the judgments, the treaty power was the dominant issue. Duff CJC, writing for himself and Davis and Kerwin JJ, would have upheld the statutes. He began by demonstrating that the rapid development of Canada's independence gave the Dominion power to enter into international obligations. Then, relying greatly on the *Radio* and *Aeronautics* references, he held that the treaty came within s. 132, which gave the Dominion exclusive power to implement its terms even though the subject matter might otherwise come within s. 92. As well, he asserted that p.o.g.g. gave the Dominion the same power to implement treaties that did not come within s. 132. The other three court members, Rinfret, Crocket, and Cannon JJ, held that, because the conventions had been adopted by Canada on her own behalf, they did not come within s. 132 and, distinguishing the *Radio* and *Aeronautics* references, they held that p.o.g.g. did not give the Dominion power. Rinfret J agreed about s. 132, but then shifted to a different ground and held that provincial consent was necessary for the validity of a treaty if its subject came under s. 92. All three were sensitive to the threat to provincial autonomy represented by an exclusive Dominion power to make and implement treaties. For example, Cannon J said, at 721 DLR:

> The framers of our Constitution, and the Privy Council by their recent judgments in the *Radio* and *Aviation* cases never intended to plant in its bosom the seeds of its own destruction. If such interference with provincial rights by way of international agreements is admitted as *intra vires* of the central Government, we may as well say that we have in Canada a Confederation in name, but a legislative union in fact. Uniformity is not in the spirit of our Constitution. We have not a single community in this country. We have nine commonwealths, several different communities. This is the fact embodied in the law. It may be wise or unwise, according to the preferences and predilection of every one, but this is the basis of our Constitution. Diversity is the basis of our Constitution. The federative system was adopted in order to give to the Provinces their autonomy and to secure, specially in Quebec, the rights to their own customs as crystallized in their civil law.]

LORD ATKIN: … Their Lordships, having stated the circumstances leading up to the reference in this case, are now in a position to discuss the contentions of the parties which were summarized earlier in this judgment. It will be essential to keep in mind the distinction between (1.) the formation, and (2.) the performance, of the obligations constituted by a treaty, using that word as comprising any agreement between two or more sovereign States. Within the British Empire there is a well-established rule that the making of a treaty is an executive act, while the performance of its obligations, if they entail alteration of the existing domestic law, requires legislative action. Unlike some other countries, the stipulations of a treaty duly ratified do not within the Empire, by virtue of the treaty alone, have the force of law. If the national executive, the government of the day, decide to incur the obligations of a treaty which involve alteration of law they have to run the risk of obtaining the assent of Parliament to the necessary statute or statutes. To make themselves as secure as possible they will often in such cases before final ratification seek to obtain from Parliament an expression of approval. But it has never been suggested, and it is not the law, that such an expression of approval operates as law, or that in law it precludes the assenting Parliament, or any subsequent Parliament, from refusing to give its sanction to any legislative proposals that may subsequently be brought before it. Parliament, no doubt, as the Chief Justice points out, has a constitutional control over the executive: but it cannot be disputed that the creation of the obligations undertaken in treaties and the assent to their form and quality are the function of the executive alone. Once they are created, while they bind the State as against the other contracting parties, Parliament may refuse to perform them and so leave the State in default. In a unitary State whose Legislature possesses unlimited powers the problem is simple. Parliament will either fulfil or not treaty obligations imposed upon the State by its executive. The nature of the obligations does not affect the complete authority of the Legislature to make them law if it so chooses. But in a State where the Legislature does not possess absolute authority, in a federal State where legislative authority is limited by a constitutional document, or is divided up between different Legislatures in accordance with the classes of subject-matter submitted for legislation, the problem is complex. The obligations imposed by treaty may have to be performed, if at all, by several Legislatures; and the executive have the task of obtaining the legislative assent not of the one Parliament to whom they may be responsible, but possibly of several Parliaments to whom they stand in no direct relation. The question is not how is the obligation formed, that is the function of the executive; but how is the obligation to be performed, and that depends upon the authority of the competent Legislature or Legislatures. ...

The first ground upon which counsel for the Dominion sought to base the validity of the legislation was s. 132. So far as it is sought to apply this section to the conventions when ratified the answer is plain. The obligations are not obligations of Canada as part of the British Empire, but of Canada, by virtue of her new status as an international person, and do not arise under a treaty between the British Empire and foreign countries. This was clearly established by the decision in the *Radio* case, [1932] AC 304 (PC), and their Lordships do not think that the proposition admits of any doubt. It is unnecessary, therefore, to dwell upon the distinction between legislative powers given to the Dominion to perform obligations imposed upon Canada as part of the Empire by an Imperial executive responsible to and controlled by the Imperial Parliament, and the legislative powers of the Dominion to perform obligations created by the Dominion executive responsible to and controlled by the Dominion Parliament. While it is true, as was pointed out in the *Radio* case, that it was not contemplated in 1867 that the Dominion would possess treaty-making powers, it is impossible to strain the section so as to cover the uncontemplated event. A further attempt to apply the section was made by the suggestion that while it does not apply to the conventions, yet it clearly applies to the Treaty of Versailles itself, and the obligations to perform the conventions arise "under" that treaty because of the stipulations in Part XIII. It is impossible to accept this view. No obligation to legislate in respect of any of the matters in question arose until the Canadian executive, left with an unfettered discretion, of their own volition acceded to the conventions, a novus actus not determined by the treaty. For the purposes of this legislation the obligation arose under the conventions alone. It appears that all the members of the Supreme Court rejected the contention based on s. 132, and their Lordships are in full agreement with them.

If, therefore, s. 132 is out of the way, the validity of the legislation can only depend upon ss. 91 and 92. Now it had to be admitted that normally this legislation came within the classes of subjects by s. 92 assigned exclusively to the Legislatures of the Provinces, namely—property and civil rights in the Province. This was in fact expressly decided in respect of these same conventions by the Supreme Court in 1925. How, then, can the legislation be within the legislative powers given by s. 91 to the Dominion Parliament? It is not within the enumerated classes of subjects in s. 91: and it appears to be expressly excluded from the general powers given by the first words of the section. It appears highly probable that none of the members of the Supreme Court would have [ruled in favour of federal jurisdiction under s. 91] had it not been for the opinion of the Chief Justice that the judgments of the Judicial Committee in the *Aeronautics* case, [1932] AC 54 (PC) and the *Radio* case constrained them to hold that jurisdiction to legislate for the purpose of performing the obligation of a treaty resides exclusively in the Parliament of Canada. Their Lordships cannot take this view of those decisions. The *Aeronautics* case concerned legislation to perform obligations imposed by a treaty between the Empire and foreign countries. Section 132, therefore, clearly applied, and but for a remark at the end of the judgment, which in view of the stated ground of the decision was clearly obiter, the case could not be said to be an authority on the matter now under discussion. The judgment in the *Radio* case appears to present more difficulty. But when that case is examined it will be found that the true ground of the decision was that the convention in that case dealt with classes of matters which did not fall within the enumerated classes of subjects in s. 92 or even within the enumerated classes in s. 91. Part of the subject-matter of the convention, namely—broadcasting, might come under an enumerated class, but if so it was under a heading "Inter-provincial Telegraphs," expressly excluded from s. 92. Their Lordships are satisfied that neither case affords a warrant for holding that legislation to perform a Canadian treaty is exclusively within the Dominion legislative power.

For the purposes of ss. 91 and 92, i.e., the distribution of legislative powers between the Dominion and the Provinces, there is no such thing as treaty legislation as such. The distribution is based on classes of subjects; and as a treaty deals with a particular class of subjects so will the legislative power of performing it be ascertained. No one can doubt that this distribution is one of the most essential conditions, probably the most essential condition, in the inter-provincial compact to which the *British North America Act* gives effect. If the position of Lower Canada, now Quebec, alone were considered, the existence of her separate jurisprudence as to both property and civil rights might be said to depend upon loyal adherence to her constitutional right to the exclusive competence of her own Legislature in these matters. Nor is it of less importance for the other Provinces, though their law may be based on English jurisprudence, to preserve their own right to legislate for themselves in respect of local conditions which may vary by as great a distance as separate the Atlantic from the Pacific. It would be remarkable that while the Dominion could not initiate legislation, however desirable, which affected civil rights in the Provinces, yet its Government not responsible to the Provinces nor controlled by Provincial Parliaments need only agree with a foreign country to enact such legislation, and its Parliament would be forthwith clothed with authority to affect Provincial rights to the full extent of such agreement. Such a result would appear to undermine the constitutional safeguards of Provincial constitutional autonomy.

It follows from what has been said that no further legislative competence is obtained by the Dominion from its accession to international status, and the consequent increase in the scope of its executive functions. It is true, as pointed out in the judgment of the Chief Justice, that as the executive is now clothed with the powers of making treaties so the Parliament of Canada, to which the executive is responsible, has imposed upon it responsibilities in connection with such treaties, for if it were to disapprove of them they would either not be made or the Ministers would meet their constitutional fate. But this is true of all executive functions in their relation to Parliament. There is no existing constitutional ground for stretching the competence of the Dominion Parliament so that it becomes enlarged to keep pace with enlarged functions of the Dominion executive. If the new functions affect the classes of subjects enumerated in s. 92 legislation to support the new functions is in the competence of the Provincial Legislatures only. If they do not, the competence of the Dominion Legislature is declared by s. 91 and existed *ab origine*. In other words, the Dominion cannot, merely by making promises to foreign countries, clothe itself with legislative authority inconsistent with the constitution which gave it birth.

But the validity of the legislation under the general words of s. 91 was sought to be established not in relation to the treaty-making power alone, but also as being concerned with matters of such general importance as to have attained "such dimensions as to affect the body politic," and to have "ceased to be merely local or provincial," and to have "become matter of national concern." It is interesting to notice how often the words used by Lord Watson in *Attorney-General for Ontario v. Attorney-General for the Dominion*, [1896] AC 348 (PC) have unsuccessfully been used in attempts to support encroachments on the Provincial legislative powers given by s. 92. They laid down no principle of constitutional law, and were cautious words intended to safeguard possible eventualities which no one at the time had any interest or desire to define. The law of Canada on this branch of constitutional law has been stated with such force and clarity by the Chief Justice in his judgment in the reference concerning the *Natural Products Marketing Act*, dealing with the six Acts there referred to, that their Lordships abstain from stating it afresh. The Chief Justice, naturally from his point of view, excepted legislation to fulfil treaties. On this their Lordships have expressed their opinion. But subject to this, they agree with and adopt what was there said. They consider that the law is finally settled by the current of cases cited by the Chief Justice on the principles declared by him. It is only necessary to call attention to the phrases in the various cases, "abnormal circumstances," "exceptional conditions," "standard of necessity" (*Board of Commerce* case, [1922] 1 AC 191 (PC)), "some extraordinary peril to the national life of Canada," "highly exceptional," "epidemic of pestilence" (*Snider's* case, [1925] AC 396 (PC)), to show how far the present case is from the conditions which may override the normal distribution of powers in ss. 91 and 92. The few pages of the Chief Justice's judgment will, it is to be hoped, form the *locus classicus* of the law on this point, and preclude further disputes.

It must not be thought that the result of this decision is that Canada is incompetent to legislate in performance of treaty obligations. In totality of legislative powers, Dominion and Provincial together, she is fully equipped. But the legislative powers remain distributed, and if in the exercise of her new functions derived from her new international status Canada incurs obligations they must, so far as legislation be concerned, when they deal with Provincial classes of subjects, be dealt with by the totality of powers, in other words by co-operation between the Dominion and the Provinces. While the ship of state now sails on larger ventures and into foreign waters she still retains the watertight compartments which are an essential part of her original structure. The Supreme Court was equally divided and therefore the formal judgment could only state the opinions of the three judges on either side. Their Lordships are of opinion that the answer to the three questions should be that the Act in each case is *ultra vires* of the Parliament of Canada, and they will humbly advise His Majesty accordingly.

Appeal allowed.

AG Canada v. AG Ontario (The Employment and Social Insurance Act)
[1937] AC 355, 1 DLR 684 (PC); aff'g. [1936] SCR 427, 3 DLR 673

[Out of a fund created by the joint contributions of workers and employers, the federal *Employment and Social Insurance Act* provided for compulsory insurance against unemployment for workers. The subject of unemployment insurance had been included, also, in the International Labour Organization conventions but, although these conventions were described in the preamble, Bennett chose not to make the Act an explicit implementation of the international obligation, perhaps because he did not want to present opponents with the temptation to remind Canadians that relief assistance was closely associated with unemployment insurance in the Conventions.

The Supreme Court, by a majority of four to two, held the Act invalid. The majority, Rinfret, Cannon, Crocket, and Kerwin JJ, shared substantially the same grounds: the Act dealt with property and civil rights, because it dealt with insurance, which Rinfret said had always been a provincial matter, and because it regulated contracts and employment. It was, therefore, in its "pith and substance," within s. 92 and it was not a response to an emergency that might be justified by p.o.g.g. Duff CJC, with whom Davis J concurred, dissented, essentially because he characterized the Act differently: it was, in essence, a taxation measure, justified under s. 91(3). Part of his reasoning was the proposition that there was no constitutional restriction against the Dominion spending public money for the benefit of individuals.]

LORD ATKIN: A strong appeal was made on the ground of the special importance of unemployment insurance in Canada at the time of, and for some time previous to, the passing of the Act. On this point it … is sufficient to say that the present Act does not purport to deal with any special emergency. It founds itself in the preamble on general world-wide conditions referred to in the Treaty of Peace: it is an Act whose operation is intended to be permanent: and there is agreement between all the members of the Supreme Court that it could not be supported upon the suggested existence of any special emergency. Their Lordships find themselves unable to differ from this view.

It only remains to deal with the argument which found favour with the Chief Justice and Davis J, that the legislation can be supported under the enumerated heads, 1 and 3 of s. 91 of the *British North America Act, 1867*: (1.) The public debt and property, namely (3.) The raising of money by any mode or system of taxation. Shortly stated, the argument is that the obligation imposed upon employers and persons employed is a mode of taxation: that the money so raised becomes public property, and that the Dominion have then complete legislative authority to direct that the money so raised, together with assistance from money raised by general taxation, shall be applied in forming an insurance fund and generally in accordance with the provisions of the Act.

That the Dominion may impose taxation for the purpose of creating a fund for special purposes, and may apply that fund for making contributions in the public interest to individuals, corporations or public authorities, could not as a general proposition be denied. Whether in such an Act as the present compulsion applied to an employed person to make a contribution to an insurance fund out of which he will receive benefit for a period proportionate to the number of his contributions is in fact taxation it is not necessary finally to decide. It might seem difficult to discern how it differs from a form of compulsory insurance, or what the difference is between a statutory obligation to pay insurance premiums to the State or to an insurance company. But assuming that the Dominion has collected by means of taxation a fund, it by no means follows that any legislation which disposes of it is necessarily within Dominion competence.

It may still be legislation affecting the classes of subjects enumerated in s. 92, and, if so, would be *ultra vires*. In other words, Dominion legislation, even though it deals with Dominion property, may yet be so framed as to invade civil rights within the Province, or encroach upon the classes of subjects which are reserved to Provincial competence. It is not necessary that it should be a colourable device, or a pretence. If on the true view of the legislation it is found that in reality in pith and substance the legislation invades civil rights within the Province, or in respect of other classes of subjects otherwise encroaches upon the provincial field, the legislation will be invalid. To hold otherwise would afford the Dominion an easy passage into the Provincial domain.

It follows that the whole Act must be pronounced *ultra vires*, and in accordance with the view of the majority of the Supreme Court their Lordships will humbly advise His Majesty that this appeal be dismissed.

Appeal dismissed.

AG British Columbia v. AG Canada (The Natural Products Marketing Act)
[1937] AC 377, 1 DLR 691 (PC); aff'g. [1936] SCR 398, 3 DLR 622

[The purpose of the *Natural Products Marketing Act* was to establish regulation of natural products for the benefit of producers and, especially, to establish effective marketing arrangements and to impose pooling to equalize prices in particular products and areas. The Act was limited to products for which the principal market was outside the province of production, and products that were, in some part, exported.

In the Supreme Court, the Act was unanimously declared invalid. Duff CJC, writing for the Court, considered s. 91(2) and p.o.g.g. separately and, for each, he discussed the Privy Council decisions at length, on the assumption that his contribution was to summarize them and announce their consequences. About s. 91(2), after discussing *Parsons*, the *Insurance Reference*, and *Montreal Street Railway*, he said, at 629 DLR:

> It would appear to result from these decisions that the Regulation of Trade and Commerce does not comprise, in the sense in which it is used in s. 91, the regulation of particular trades or occupations or of a particular kind of business such as the insurance business in the Provinces, or the regulation of trade in particular commodities or classes of commodities in so far as it is local in the provincial sense; while, on the other hand, it does embrace the regulation of external trade and the regulation of interprovincial trade and such ancillary legislation as may be necessarily incidental to the exercise of such powers.

After discussing other cases, including *Hodge* and the *Local Prohibition Reference*, he said, at 631 DLR:

The enactments in question, therefore, in so far as they relate to matters which are in substance local and provincial are beyond the jurisdiction of Parliament. Parliament cannot
acquire jurisdiction to deal in the sweeping way in which these enactments operate with
such local and provincial matters by legislating at the same time respecting external and
interprovincial trade and committing the regulation of external and interprovincial trade
and the regulation of trade which is exclusively local and of traders and producers engaged
in trade which is exclusively local to the same authority (*The King v. Eastern Terminal Elevator Co.*, [1925] 3 DLR 1).

It should also be observed that these enactments operate by way of the regulation of
dealings in particular commodities and classes of commodities. The regulations contemplated are not general regulations of trade as a whole or regulations of general trade and
commerce within the sense of the judgment in *Parsons*'s case.

Then, after discussing *Board of Commerce* and *Snider*, and distinguishing the *Radio*
and *Aeronautics* references, he concluded, at 633 DLR:

There is one further observation which, perhaps, ought not to be omitted although it may be
a mere corollary of what has already been said. Legislation necessarily incidental to the exercise of the undoubted powers of the Dominion in respect of the Regulations of Trade and
Commerce is competent although such legislation may trench upon subjects reserved to the
Provinces by s. 92, but it cannot, we think, be seriously contended that sweeping regulation
in respect of local trade, such as we find in this enactment, is, in the proper sense, necessarily
incidental to the regulation of external trade or interprovincial trade or both combined.

For p.o.g.g., he began, at 635 DLR:

The initial clause of s. 91 has been many times considered. There is no dispute now that the
exception which excludes from the ambit of the general power all matters assigned to the
exclusive authority of the Legislatures must be given its full effect. Nevertheless, it has been
laid down that matters normally comprised within the subjects enumerated in s. 92 may, in
extraordinary circumstances, acquire aspects of such paramount significance as to take
them outside the sphere of that section.

Next, after pointing out that his reference was to the *Local Prohibition Reference*, he
added, at 636 and 638 DLR:

It seems to us right, if these two sentences are to be properly understood, that they should
be read with the preceding sentences; and experience seems to show that there has been a
disposition not to attend to the limits implied in the carefully guarded language in which
the Board expressed itself.

... As we have said, Lord Watson's language is carefully guarded. He does not say that
every matter which attains such dimensions as to effect the body politic of the Dominion
falls thereby within the introductory matter of s. 91. But he said that "some matters" may attain such dimensions as to affect the body politic of the Dominion and, as we think the sentence ought to be read having regard to the context, in such manner and degree as may
"justify the Canadian Parliament in passing laws for their regulation or abolition. ..." So, in
the second sentence, he is not dealing with all matters of "national concern" in the broadest

sense of those words, but only those which are matter of national concern "in such sense" as to bring them within the jurisdiction of the Parliament of Canada.

The application of the principle implicit in this passage must always be a delicate and difficult task. ...

A discussion of *Russell, Board of Commerce, Fort Frances*, and *Snider* followed, after which he asserted that the *Radio* and *Aeronautics* references were not a "new point of departure" (at 643 DLR). He concluded, at 644 DLR, "consistently with these decisions, we do not see how it is possible that the argument now under discussion can receive effect."]

LORD ATKIN: There can be no doubt that the provisions of the Act cover transactions in any natural product which are completed within the Province, and have no connection with inter-provincial or export trade. It is therefore plain that the Act purports to affect property and civil rights in the Province, and if not brought within one of the enumerated classes of subjects in s. 91 must be beyond the competence of the Dominion Legislature. It was sought to bring the Act within the class (2) of s. 91—namely, The Regulation of Trade and Commerce. Emphasis was laid upon those parts of the Act which deal with inter-provincial and export trade. But the regulation of trade and commerce does not permit the regulation of individual forms of trade or commerce confined to the Province. In his judgment the Chief Justice says [1936] SCR 412: "The enactments in question, therefore, in so far as they relate to matters which are in substance local and provincial are beyond the jurisdiction of Parliament. Parliament cannot acquire jurisdiction to deal in the sweeping way in which these enactments operate with such local and provincial matters by legislating at the same time respecting external and inter-provincial trade and committing the regulation of external and inter-provincial trade and the regulation of trade which is exclusively local and of traders and producers engaged in trade which is exclusively local to the same authority: *The King v. Eastern Terminal Elevator Co.*, [1925] SCR 434."

Their Lordships agree with this, and find it unnecessary to add anything. There was a further attempt to support the Act upon the general powers to legislate for the peace, order and good government of Canada. Their Lordships have already dealt with this matter in their previous judgments in this series and need not repeat what is there said. The judgment of the Chief Justice in this case is conclusive against the claim for validity on this ground. ...

The Board were given to understand that some of the Provinces attach much importance to the existence of marketing schemes such as might be set up under this legislation: and their attention was called to the existence of Provincial legislation setting up Provincial schemes for various Provincial products. It was said that as the Provinces and the Dominion between them possess a totality of complete legislative authority, it must be possible to combine Dominion and Provincial legislation so that each within its own sphere could in co-operation with the other achieve the complete power of regulation which is desired. Their Lordships appreciate the importance of the desired aim. Unless and until a change is made in the respective legislative functions of Dominion and Province it may well be that satisfactory results for both can only be obtained by co-operation.

But the legislation will have to be carefully framed, and will not be achieved by either party leaving its own sphere and encroaching upon that of the other. In the present case their Lordships are unable to support the Dominion legislation as it stands. They will therefore humbly advise His Majesty that this appeal should be dismissed.

Appeal dismissed.

The remaining New Deal cases can be dealt with briefly. We deal first with *AG British Columbia v. AG Canada*, [1937] AC 368 (PC), var'g. [1936] 3 DLR 593 (SCC). The amendments to the *Criminal Code* prohibited two kinds of conduct: (1) selling goods at prices that discriminated among competitors, and (2) selling goods at prices designed to eliminate competitors. In the Supreme Court, a majority of four held both provisions valid. Duff CJC, writing for himself and Rinfret, Davis, and Kerwin JJ, said at 594-95:

> We see no good reason for denying the authority of Parliament, under subdivision 27 of s. 91 of the *BNA Act*, to pass these enactments. ...
>
> Whatever doubt may have previously existed, none can remain since the decision of the Judicial Committee in *Proprietary Articles Trade Ass'n. v. A-G Can.*, [1931] 2 DLR 1, 55 Can. CC 241, that, in enacting laws in relation to matters falling within the subject of the Criminal Law, as these words are used in s. 91, Parliament is not restricted by any rule limiting the acts declared to be criminal acts to such as would appear to a Court of law to be "in their own nature" criminal. The jurisdiction in relation to the criminal law is plenary; and enactments passed within the scope of that jurisdiction are not subject to review by the Courts.

He added that some limits were needed to avoid permitting the Dominion to exclude the provinces entirely, but these limits were not relevant here. The dissenters, Crocket and Cannon JJ, believed that the first prohibition was invalid because it was not, in its nature, a prohibition of criminal conduct. According to Crocket J, what it prohibited was a private wrong and not a "danger to the community" (at 597). The Privy Council affirmed the Supreme Court's decision. Lord Atkin said, at 375, "Their Lordships agree that this case is covered by the decision of the Judicial Committee in the *Proprietary Articles* case. ... The only limitation on the plenary power of the Dominion to determine what shall or shall not be criminal is the condition that Parliament shall not in the guise of enacting criminal legislation in truth and substance encroach on any of the classes of subjects enumerated in s. 92. It is no objection that it does in fact affect them."

Next, we come to the fate of the *Dominion Trade and Industry Commission Act*, which was decided in *AG Ontario v. AG Canada*, [1937] AC 405; [1937] 1 DLR 702 (PC), var'g. [1936] SCR 607. The Act included two major parts: (1) it authorized administrative approval for agreements among businesses to restrict undue competition, and (2) it established a national trademark, "Canada Standard," to be used to identify products that complied with standards to be set by the Dominion. The Supreme Court unanimously found both parts invalid and, again, Duff CJC wrote the judgment. For the first part, he relied on his judgment in the *Natural Products Marketing Reference*. For the second, his reasoning was that the standard was not a trade mark, but a "civil right of an entirely novel character. ... Generally speaking, ... Parliament possesses no competence to create a civil right of a new kind ..." (at 609). The Privy Council agreed about the first part but not the second. Lord Atkin declared that it could be upheld under s. 91(2):

> There could hardly be a more appropriate form of the exercise of this power than the creation and regulation of a uniform law of trade marks. But if the Dominion has power to create trade mark rights for individual traders, it is difficult to see why the power should not extend to that which is now a usual feature of national and international commerce—a national mark. It is perfectly true, as is said by the Chief Justice, that the method adopted in s. 18 is to create a civil right of a novel character. ...
>
> But there seems no reason why the legislative competence of the Dominion Parliament should not extend to the creation of juristic rights in novel fields, if they can be brought fairly within the classes of subjects confided to Parliament by the constitution (at 417-18).

Last of all, we can dispose of the *Farmers' Creditors Arrangements Act* briefly: it established administrative boards with powers to impose compromises or extensions of farmers' obligations to their debtors, and in *AG British Columbia v. AG Canada*, [1937] AC 391; [1937] 1 DLR 695 (PC), aff'g. [1936] SCR 610, both the Supreme Court and the Privy Council upheld it under s. 91(21), the Dominion's power to legislate about bankruptcy and insolvency.

King saw the "New Deal" cases as an excuse for further federal inactivity, as discussed in the following excerpt from Simeon and Robinson, *State, Society, and the Development of Canadian Federalism, supra*, at 81-83 (references omitted):

> The effect of the Privy Council's decisions, in Mallory's opinion, was "practically to paralyse the Dominion as an agency for regulating economic activity ... the Dominion had practically no jurisdiction over labour, prices, production, and marketing except in wartime." King was now able to blame the constitution for federal inaction. Many accepted this explanation and there was much argument among reformers such as Scott concerning the conservative politics of the old men on the Privy Council.
>
> Yet, ... King had other options, including constitutional reform and court-packing. Moreover, if he had supported the Bennett legislation, he could have implemented it, awaiting such private challenges to its constitutional status as might arise. If these measures had improved the national economy, or were believed to have done so, the public outcry against their abolition by a foreign court would have backed his demands for constitutional change. This was the strategy being followed at this time by the Social Credit government in Alberta, with growing popular support despite its constitutional defeats. But King did none of these things; instead, he immediately referred the Bennett legislation to the courts. As Mallory observes: "Under such circumstances, it is unlikely that the Court would be led to believe that the government was strongly attached to the legislation."
>
> Why was King against the federal government playing the sort of extended economic and social role implied by Bennett's legislation? It was not because King was an inflexible fiscal conservative. By 1938, albeit with some misgivings, he had been persuaded to undertake a moderately expansionary budget on the Keynesian grounds advocated by the National Employment Commission and his Minister of Labour, Norman Rogers. Nor can King plausibly be portrayed as a libertarian intent upon maintaining a minimal state. In the same year that King accepted

the desirability of running a deficit, he refused to utilize the federal power of disallowance to strike down Duplessis' "Padlock Law."

The best explanation for the King government's relative inactivity during the Depression, and his willingness to expand federal social and economic policy thereafter, is not to be found either in the federal constitution or in King's ideas of economics or justice. It is that the first priority of King and his Liberals, for both ideological and party self-interest reasons, was national unity. As long as there was no clear English-speaking majority position on the appropriate role of the state, electoral politics left King with room to manoeuvre. In this context, King preferred to avoid the kind of economic and social policy initiatives that Taschereau denounced in 1935. To his conscience and his diary King justified his refusal to disallow or refer the Padlock Law to the courts, in spite of his personal opposition to it, by arguing that "in the last resort, the unity of Canada was the test by which we would meet all these things."

King's inclinations were reinforced by the election of a Quebec government, less than a year after his own re-election in 1935, which was a more militant, if still conservative, defender of provincial rights than its Liberal predecessors. But King's strategy of minimal federal activity, informed by his conviction that the principal threat to national unity lay in French-English conflict, was much less effective under conditions of economic crisis than it had been in the 1920s. For while federal inaction minimized the potential for new federal-provincial conflicts related to language, it provoked increasing criticism from those who saw the nation primarily through the lenses of region and class.

These elements argued that only the federal government possessed the fiscal resources and technical expertise to implement progressive social and economic policies. These policies involved redistribution between individuals and regions which could only be achieved in accordance with national conceptions of collective welfare and fairness. Provincial governments, given their accountability to sub-national political communities, could not be expected to take a national perspective on such issues. Poorer provinces, whatever their progressive aims, were hampered by inadequate resources and limited ability to assert claims on the rich, given the mobility of capital. Accordingly, it was deemed essential that the federal government expand its jurisdiction.

Even before the 1937 decisions by the Privy Council, a growing number of English Canadian intellectuals had begun to attack the federal system as a major impediment to the adoption of progressive policies. Foremost among them had been Norman Rogers, who had first argued that federalism had become a "dead hand" in 1931. Upon entering national politics, Rogers carried his views into King's cabinet. Leading figures within the League for Social Reconstruction and the CCF echoed this conclusion, although there was considerable difference of opinion as to who should be blamed for the constitutional failure. F.R. Scott stressed the culpability of the Privy Council, while Frank Underhill argued that the deeper source of stalemate was class-based opposition to "the substitution of government power in place of private wealth." Still, all agreed that the solution to both economic and constitutional crisis lay in a centralization of federal powers. Harold Laski, reflecting widely-held views among the Social Democratic left, went further, declaring that federalism was obsolete, a luxury which could no longer be afforded because it denied governments effective control over the forces of "giant capitalism."

We now return to the constitutional scholars. When the Privy Council decisions were announced, their criticisms turned to despair. Two such examples are manifestos written by Kennedy and Scott for a symposium in the *Canadian Bar Review*: W.P.M. Kennedy, "The British North America Act: Past and Future" (1937), 15 *Canadian Bar Review* 393 and F.R. Scott, "The Consequences of the Privy Council Decisions" (1937), 15 *Canadian Bar Review* 485. Here is part of Kennedy's reaction at 398-99:

> We must no longer live in the vain world of delusion that the Judicial Committee will do for the Act what the Supreme Court of the United States has been able to do, in a wide manner, since the days of John Marshall, for perhaps the most rigid formal constitution in the world. ... As we read the recent judgments we must be convinced that the Judicial Committee has no intention whatever, in any substantial or fundamental matter, of acting as a constituent assembly for Canada. We would have faced this issue long ago had we not too largely believed that constitutional and legal wisdom never really crossed the Atlantic.
>
> For, I submit, we must now face issues. The federal "general power" is gone with the winds. It can be relied on at the best when the nation is intoxicated with alcohol, at worst when the nation is intoxicated with war; but in times of sober poverty, sober financial chaos, sober unemployment, sober exploitation, it cannot be used, for these, though in fact national in the totality of their incidents, must not be allowed to leave their legal water-tight provincial compartments; the social lines must not obliterate the legal lines of jurisdiction—at least this is the law, and it killeth. ...
>
> The time has come to abandon tinkering with or twisting the *British North America Act*—a curiosity belonging to an older age. At long last we can criticize it, as the stern demands of economic pressure have bitten into the bastard loyalty which gave to it the doubtful devotion of primitive ancestor worship. We must seek machinery to do in Canada certain things: (i) to repeal the *BNA Act in toto*; (ii) to rewrite completely the constitution; (iii) to provide reasonable and sane and workable constituent machinery; (iv) to abolish all appeals to the Judicial Committee. I submit that every one of these things is necessary; and above all we must get rid of all the past decisions of the Judicial Committee, for they will hang round the necks of the judiciary, if appeals are abolished, in that uncanny stranglehold with which *stare decisis* seems doomed to rob the law of creative vitality.

Scott was equally passionate, and his article concluded in this way at 491-94:

> Turning from the legal to the economic consequences of the decisions, it is obvious that they leave this country even more helpless than she was in 1929 to deal with the problems created by a changing economic system. The depression came, revealing gross injustices and inefficiencies in the body economic; the Stevens Committee and the Royal Commission on Price Spreads disclosed evils crying out for remedy; a considerable attempt was made to provide a system of controls and palliatives on a national scale. This attempt has failed because the constitution could not, in the hands of the judiciary at the moment interpreting it, adapt itself to the new requirements. ...
>
> If the whole trend of world developments is wrong and all government interference in economic matters is an obstacle to progress, then Canada will benefit from her constitutional impasse, but should the reverse be true, should the need of the hour be increasingly to bring an intelligent and conscious direction to economic affairs, then Canada has suffered a national

set-back of grievous proportions. A federal government that cannot concern itself with questions of wages and hours and unemployment in industry, whose attempts at the regulation of trade and commerce are consistently thwarted, which has no power to join its sister nations in the establishment of world living standards, and which cannot even feel on sure ground when by some political miracle it is supported in a legislative scheme by all the provinces, is a government wholly unable to direct and to control our economic development.

The history of recent cases dealing with the control of trade and commerce in Canada shows a fairly consistent attitude in the courts against control, an attitude which overrides any feeling for or against provincial autonomy. ...

It would seem that even without special mention in the *British North America Act*, the doctrines of *laissez-faire* are in practice receiving ample protection from the courts. ...

One lesson, it is to be hoped, will be learned again from these decisions. The Privy Council is our final court of appeal. Its interpretations of the Canadian constitution vitally affect the political, social and economic destinies of eleven million Canadians. Such a court should be staffed with men fully qualified to understand the spirit which infuses the *British North America Act*, and the environment in which it must be made to work. Unfortunately it is only too evident that judges of this type rarely sit upon the Judicial Committee. ...

To imagine that we shall ever get consistent and reasonable judgments from such a casually selected and untrained court is merely silly. To continue using it under the circumstances is costly sentimentality. ... No alterations to the *British North America Act* will ever achieve what Canadians want them to achieve if their interpretation is left to a non-Canadian judiciary.

Scott was particularly concerned that there had been complete cooperation between the federal government and the provinces in the implementation of the *Natural Products Marketing Act*, writing at 489-91:

Another important consequence of these holdings is the doubt they cast upon the possibility of Dominion-Provincial co-operation as an escape from constitutional difficulties. Hitherto it has been thought that whatever problem there might be with regard to legislative jurisdiction, the difficulty could be overcome by joint action by all the legislatures. If the Dominion added all its powers to those already possessed by the provinces, surely, it seemed, anything and everything might be accomplished. On several occasions the Privy Council and the Supreme Court of Canada have suggested that this is a proper method of procedure. In the very decisions under review Duff CJ, discussing the *Natural Products Market Act*, quoted from the judgment in the *Board of Commerce Case* and said that such a scheme of regulation as set up by the Marketing Boards was not practicable "without the co-operation of the provincial legislatures"; while the Privy Council tempered their destruction of the Dominion treat-making power with the helpful reminder that "It must not be thought that the result of this decision is that Canada is incompetent to legislate in performance of treaty obligations. In totality of legislative powers, Dominion and Provincial together, she is fully equipped."

Nevertheless, in the judgment on the *Marketing Act* in the Supreme Court there was no consideration whatever of the fact that every province in Canada had co-operated with the Dominion in setting up Marketing Boards, and had enacted special legislation to provide for this co-operation. Ten legislatures in Canada had acted to attain an end unanimously desired, yet the key-statute was declared *ultra vires* and the whole structure destroyed. The *Dominion Act* by section 12 provided that if any parts of the Act were *ultra vires*, none of the other provisions should be inoperative on that account, but should be considered as separate enactments; and the provincial statutes were intended to supply any legislative power lacking in the Dominion. In the Privy Council Lord Atkin, after repeating the empty formula that "satisfactory results" for both Dominion and Provinces "can only be obtained by co-operation," went on to warn that "the legislation will have to be very carefully framed, and will not be achieved by either party leaving its own sphere and encroaching upon that of the other. In the present case their Lordships are unable to support the Dominion legislation as it stands. They will therefore humbly advise His Majesty that this appeal should be dismissed."

Thus the courts take the view that even where there is complete co-operation between all Canadian legislatures, each one contributing its share of legislative capacity, still the scheme thus established will be destroyed, if, perchance, one legislature has made a slip in the wording of its contributory statute and has in fact included some subject matter beyond its jurisdiction. Instead of considering that this mistake is rectified by the other supporting statutes, it may be looked upon as fatal. So co-operation between the Dominion and the provinces, as in the case of the marketing legislation, may be of no use whatever in the way of overcoming constitutional difficulties, and leaves the courts as free as before to set aside legislation of which they disapprove. This legalistic straining at technicalities will do little to enhance the prestige of the courts. The *Dominion Marketing Act* was not an isolated statute, but was part of a national scheme and should have been interpreted as such.

Another example of the dismay among Canadian lawyers is a document that has come to be known as the O'Connor Report (Ottawa: Senate, "Report ... [the O'Connor Report]" (1939)). In 1938, W.F. O'Connor, Counsel to the Senate, was directed to examine Confederation, the *BNA Act*, and the Act's interpretation by the Privy Council. His report, submitted in 1939, is long and does not lend itself easily to being represented by quotations and, therefore, a summary must suffice, even though it cannot capture the tone of anger and frustration that O'Connor sustained throughout almost 150 pages.

O'Connor analyzed ss. 91 and 92 and the Privy Council decisions at great length, presenting a comprehensive account of their structure. After quoting extensively from the debates at Confederation, he claimed that the *BNA Act* made "two grand divisions" of legislative powers: general and local. The first 15 subsections of s. 92 granted powers over specified local subjects to the provinces and s. 92(16) was a grant of power over residual local subjects. Section 91 assigned the residue of legislative power to the Dominion; its opening words were the sole grant and they gave the Dominion exclusive and paramount power. The effect of the "notwithstanding clause" (beginning "and for greater certainty") was to extend the exclusivity given by the opening words to the enumerations, which were simply examples, and the effect of the deeming clause (beginning, "And any matter") was to exclude from s. 92(16) any local element of the enumerated subjects.

O'Connor claimed that this design had been "repealed by judicial legislation," particularly by Lords Watson and Haldane. The Privy Council had been guilty of "demonstrable error" and "serious and persistent deviation." The path of error began in *Parsons*, in its reading of the closing words of s. 91. *Russell* represented a proper understanding of the structure and a sensible determination of aspects, but the path of error was resumed in *Tennant v. Union Bank*, [1894] AC 41 (PC), where Lord Watson said, "[Section] 91 expressly declares that 'notwithstanding anything in this Act,' the legislative authority of the Parliament of

Canada shall extend to all matters coming within the enumerated classes, which plainly indicates that the legislation of that Parliament, so long as it strictly relates to these matters, is
to be of paramount authority." O'Connor argued that this reading divided the enumerated
subjects in s. 91 from the opening grant of power and gave them both independent stature
and priority.

This misreading was continued in Lord Watson's "extraordinary" decision in *The Local
Prohibition Reference*, which struck s. 91 "the deadliest blow it has received." The opening
grant of power in s. 91, its sole grant of power, was limited to "extraordinary circumstances
only, and without exclusiveness or paramountcy." This interpretation "paralysed many essential law-making activities of the Dominion" and the result was "an undeniable partial
breakdown of the general scheme of Confederation." During the twentieth century, Lord
Haldane's decisions "exceeded those of Lord Watson in their emasculatory effect upon the
Dominion's authority." "If only this fatal error in construction could be undone, nothing
much need be done in order to restore the *BNA Act* to that state of reasonable satisfactori-
ness in which it was before the fatal error was committed." Lord Watson and Lord Haldane
were the villains of Canadian federalism.

O'Connor's intensive, detailed analysis of the structure of ss. 91 and 92 was a substantially
new kind of undertaking. Prior to his report, the furthest scholars had gone in this direction
had been to make claims of the kind that Smith had made in 1926 in the note that appears
near the end of Chapter 5, The Early Twentieth Century: The Beginnings of Economic Regulation: the p.o.g.g. power had been diminished and supplanted by s. 92(13). O'Connor's analysis quickly became authoritative and set the terms for discussion for about 30 years. For
example, Kennedy used an elegant summary in an article in 1943 ("The Interpretation of the
British North America Act" (1943), 8 *Cambridge Law Journal* 146) and Bora Laskin took the
analysis as settled in a comprehensive and fierce attack on the Privy Council in 1947 ("Peace,
Order and Good Government Re-examined" (1947), 25 *Canadian Bar Review* 1054).

Competing assessments of the Privy Council began to appear in the 1950s, expressing
different visions of Canadian federalism and representing different parts of the country. The
first came from Quebec. In 1951, Louis-Philippe Pigeon, later to become a member of the
Supreme Court, wrote about provincial autonomy ("The Meaning of Provincial Autonomy"
(1951), 29 *Canadian Bar Review* 1126), beginning with the claim that provincial autonomy
had been an important element of the debates and the agreements preceding Confederation,
and had been established in the terms of the *BNA Act*, especially in the opening words of
s. 91, which excluded the subjects assigned to the provinces from the grant of power to the
Dominion. He concluded (at 1133, 1134, and 1135):

> Just as freedom means for the individual the right of choosing his own objective so long as it is
> not illegal, autonomy means for a province the privilege of defining its own policies ... .
>
> [T]he courts have consistently refused to allow any particular clause of the *BNA Act* to be
> construed in a way that would enable the federal Parliament to invade the provincial sphere of
> action outside of emergencies ... .
>
> A great volume of criticism has been heaped upon the Privy Council and the Supreme
> Court on the ground that their decisions rest on a narrow and technical construction of the
> *BNA Act*. This contention is ill-founded. The decisions on the whole proceed from a much
> higher view ... . [T]hey recognize the implicit fluidity of any constitution by allowing for emer-

gencies and by resting distinctions on questions of degree. At the same time they firmly uphold the fundamental principle of provincial autonomy: they staunchly refuse to let our federal constitution be changed gradually, by one device or another, to a legislative union. In doing so, they are preserving the essential condition of the Canadian confederation.

Another perspective was given by William Lederman, from Queen's University, who had grown up in the West. In a series of articles beginning in 1965, he argued that at the heart of Canada was a balanced federalism—a balance between unity and diversity and between a strong Dominion and autonomous provinces. The "equilibrium points" of this balanced federalism had been made by courts, especially the Privy Council, and Lord Watson was "the greatest of the Privy Council judges concerned with the Canadian constitution." ("Unity and Diversity in Canadian Federalism: Ideals and Methods of Moderation" (1975), 53 *Canadian Bar Review* 597, as reprinted in W. Lederman, *Continuing Canadian Constitutional Dilemmas* (Toronto: Butterworths, 1981), 285, at 291 and 294.) A villain of the 1930s had become a hero.

The most appropriate ending for this chapter is the following poem, written by Frank Scott in 1950.

F.R. Scott, "Some Privy Counsel"
(1950), 28 *Canadian Bar Review* 780

"Emergency, emergency," I cried, "give us emergency,
This shall be the doctrine of our salvation.
Are we not surrounded by emergencies?
The rent of a house, the cost of food, pensions and health, the unemployed,
These are lasting emergencies, tragic for me"
Yet ever the answer was property and civil rights,
And my peace-time troubles were counted as nothing.
"At least you have an unoccupied field," I urged,
"Or something ancillary for a man with four children?
Surely my insecurity and want affect the body politic?"
But back came the echo of property and civil rights.
I was told to wrap my sorrows in water-tight compartments.
"Please, please," I entreated, "look at my problem.
I and my brothers, regardless of race, are afflicted.
Our welfare hangs on remote policies, distant decisions,
Planning of trade, guaranteed prices, high employment—
Can provincial fractions deal with this complex whole?
Surely such questions are now supra-national!"
But the judges fidgeted over their digests
and blew me away with the canons of construction.

"This is intolerable," I shouted, "this is one country;
Two flourishing cultures, but joined in one nation.
I demand peace, order and good government.
This you must admit is the aim of Confederation!"
But firmly and sternly I was pushed to a corner
And covered with the wet blanket of provincial autonomy.
Stifling under the burden I raised my hands to Heaven
And called out with my last and expiring breath
"At least you cannot deny I have a new aspect?
I cite in my aid the fresh approach of Lord Simon!"
But all I could hear was the old sing-song,
this time in Latin, muttering *stare decisis*.

CHAPTER SEVEN

Federalism and the Modern Canadian State

In the materials that follow, we examine the judicial interpretation of some of the major heads of federal and provincial power since 1949. We begin with materials that pick up the story from the last chapter and then go on to discuss the modern principles that govern interpretation of the division of powers. Then we continue with an examination of the peace, order, and good government; trade and commerce; criminal law; and property and civil rights powers. The materials are by no means comprehensive. Over the past few decades, many major areas of federal–provincial dispute came before the court, and we have had to be selective, leaving out, for example, disputes over control of broadcasting and telecommunications.

From the early 1970s, the Supreme Court of Canada played an increasingly active role in adjudication of disputes between the federal and provincial governments, although constitutional cases of this type were never a large part of the court's docket. K. Swinton, in *The Supreme Court and Canadian Federalism: The Laskin-Dickson Years* (Scarborough, ON: Carswell, 1990), states that the court decided 158 cases raising distribution of powers issues between 1970 and 1989. The court was especially active in the period from 1976 through 1983, reaching a "high" of 14 cases in 1976-77 (at 8).

This activity occurred in a period in which federal–provincial relations were often quite acrimonious as a result of disputes about constitutional reform and natural resource policy as well as disagreements over such matters as the administration of justice and broadcasting. Some of the cases began as references generated by governments; others were the result of corporate or individual challenges to legislative action.

In recent years, the court's involvement in federalism disputes has decreased, in part because many federal and provincial disputes have arisen in response to fiscal arrangements and harmonization of functions, which are being worked out in political, rather than judicial, arenas.

Before turning to the cases in the following chapters, the excerpt below gives the political context within which modern federalism disputes have been decided.

K. Norrie, R. Simeon, and M. Krasnick, *Federalism and the Economic Union*
(Toronto: University of Toronto Press, 1986), at 49-59 (footnotes omitted)

Evolution of the Division of Powers

A reborn Father of Confederation might have great difficulty recognizing his handiwork
if he tried to get a grasp on the role that the different orders of government play today.
He would, perhaps, be struck most by the expansion in the activities of both orders of
government, each now operating across a vastly broader range of economic, social, and
cultural life than was imagined in 1867. Many of the responsibilities he had assigned to
the provinces were, at the time, primarily carried out by private religious and charitable
institutions. Today, now they are the domain of governments, and often the federal
government as much as (or even more than) the provincial governments. He would also
be struck by how much the bulkheads he had built to separate federal and provincial
powers into watertight compartments had been broken down. He would find few areas
indeed in which both levels of government were not active; and he would, of course, find
governments doing things that he and his colleagues had not even contemplated. All
these new activities have, however, been fitted into the capacious, elastic pockets of the
original *BNA Act.* ...

The most striking development is in the increase in shared, overlapping jurisdiction.
A vast range of governmental functions are now concurrent, *de facto* if not *de jure*. This
is a result of four distinct processes. First is the projection of federal concerns and interests into areas once reserved primarily for the provinces, largely, but not entirely, through
the device of the spending power. The most obvious are the fields of social security and
social policy, generally beginning with a few small shared-cost programs in the early
years of the century, followed by old-age pensions in 1927, then extended during the
depression era and after. They increased to a flood after World War II. The federal government has become primarily responsible for both defining and financing the Canadian
welfare state in the name of national standards, national citizenship, and redistribution
across regions and individuals. Some programs, such as family allowances, were undertaken directly by the federal government. Others, such as unemployment insurance and
pensions, were transferred to it through constitutional amendment. In others, notably
health care and education, the chief device has been transfers between levels of government. Federal and provincial programs in social policy now intersect each other at virtually every point.

The federal government has also projected itself into other areas that were previously
predominantly provincial, notably economic development, with such joint projects as
the Trans-Canada Highway and later with the massive range of programs to promote
regional development. To a somewhat lesser extent, the provinces have projected themselves into areas thought to be of predominantly federal concern. For example, if part of
the rationale of Confederation was that Ottawa would be the main economic actor, with
the provinces reserved mainly to cultural and social matters, today provinces engage in
a wide range of economic policies to promote their development, including, on occasion,
engaging in explicit provincial fiscal policies or demand management policies. Provinces
have also become involved in many international activities. These include provincial

representation abroad and a host of trade promotion activities. As international trade policy becomes increasingly focussed on the reduction of non-tariff barriers, provinces are becoming increasingly involved, partly because many of the practices at issue are within provincial jurisdiction, and partly because constitutional interpretation has meant that the federal power to implement treaties does not extend into provincial jurisdiction. Again, the examples can be multiplied. ...

[O]verlapping has increased massively in the field of revenue-raising. In the early years of Confederation, the revenue fields cultivated by the federal government and the provinces overlapped little, the provinces relying on direct taxing, and the federal government relying primarily on the tariff, which was not available to the provinces. Today, both levels rely heavily on the same fields, especially the corporate and personal income tax. ...

[C]oncurrency has been encouraged by the growth of new policy areas that fall outside any of the categories that were set out in the *BNA Act*. Many of these emerging problems could fall equally plausibly into a number of clauses of ss. 91 and 92, virtually inviting each level of government in. In some cases, it was possible for courts to find an existing power into which to fit the new responsibility; in others, the advantage tended to fall to whichever level of government first occupied the field and defined its terms. Such new areas are frequently subjects of intense federal–provincial conflict, a kind of competitive expansionism, which subsides as a rough division of labour is worked out among them. Numerous new fields cut across jurisdictional lines: the environment, consumer protection, manpower training, and many others. As Stevenson [G. Stevenson, "The Division of Powers in Canada: Evolution and Structure," in *Division of Powers and Public Policy*, vol. 61 (Toronto: University of Toronto Press, 1985)] notes, between 1959 and 1984, both the Alberta cabinet and the federal cabinet nearly doubled in size, and many of the new portfolios that each added, such as environment and manpower, overlapped directly.

For all these reasons, concurrency, overlapping, and shared responsibilities are fundamental features of Canadian federalism as in all other federations. A second broad development, which is both cause and consequence of increased concurrency, is the breakdown of a clear rationale, or set of criteria, for determining how responsibilities should be allocated. Two such rationales were built into the *BNA Act*. On one hand was a broad distinction between "local" and "national," the former to be provincial and the latter federal. But society and economy are now so interwoven that such a distinction cannot carry us very far. If we can agree that, to use Stevenson's example, defence is a national responsibility and garbage collection a local one, we can find exceptions even here. Defence may be a national concern, but the location of defence facilities or of plants to build equipment are decidedly local. Garbage collection may be local, but its larger effects, such as pollution, may well be interprovincial, national, and even international.

In other less extreme examples, the distinction is impossible to make. Education is the classic example. While in many respects it is, as the Constitution suggests, undeniably local, in other respects it is undeniably national—intimately related to the quality and character of the workforce and to the development of pan-Canadian attitudes and values. The same is true for many federal responsibilities. Transportation again is a classic example. It is certainly national, but in a country as vast and diverse as ours, its local manifestations and impacts are critical. Hence, a case could be made both for federal involvement in education (which has happened in post-secondary education funding, funding of research activities, and support for minority-language education programs) and for provincial involvement in transportation (which has been done through provincial ownership of railways in British Columbia and Ontario, through provincial administration of interprovincial trucking, and through provincial involvement in highways, to name but a few).

Another way to think of the weakness of the national/local distinction is to use the economist's terms of spillovers and externalities. A host of provincial actions can have effects on citizens and governments outside a province's borders. A host of federal programs—taxing, spending and regulations—can spill over to affect provincial programs and priorities. Similarly, competing views of community can lead to widely varying conceptions of what is appropriately national or provincial. Thus, an expansive view of the supremacy of the national community, and of the federal government as its essential instrument, can lead to a virtually open-ended assertion of the national significance of local-level activities and hence of an essentially unlimited scope for the potential exercise of federal power. Conversely, a strongly held provincialist view justifies an equally unlimited projection of provincial interests into national affairs. Quebec nationalism, of course, erodes the distinction by seeing the nation as Quebec, again justifying an almost unlimited claim to jurisdiction.

A second distinction of government roles found in the *BNA Act* is between economic matters on one hand and sociocultural matters on the other, with the former primarily federal and the latter primarily provincial—though, as we have seen, the federal government was from the start allocated important powers here too. This distinction has also broken down. On one hand, the concern with the national community and with increasing Canada's international autonomy has not only led the federal government to be the architect of the welfare state, as discussed above, but has also led it into many areas of cultural and symbolic importance: multiculturalism, the CBC, the Canada Council, and others. By the same token, provinces have recognized that preservation of a distinct society and culture is impossible without the maintenance of a strong economy, and thus they have become much more interested in economic matters.

No other broad-brush simple rationale appears to offer any better guide to deciding what should legitimately be federal and what should be provincial. The complexity of the modern division of powers mirrors this lack of consensus on the fundamental federal and provincial roles. One can, however, push this argument too far. Chaotic and complex as it may be, the Constitution does provide broad boundaries to the abilities of each level of government to act in an entirely unrestrained way. Supreme Court decisions frequently draw such lines, and they have important effects on subsequent developments. Moreover, some broad agreement on general roles does seem to exist, as Richard Johnston [R. Johnston, *Public Opinion and Public Policy in Canada* (Toronto: University of Toronto Press, 1986)] shows in his Commission monograph. Few would disagree that defence and foreign affairs are overwhelmingly federal responsibilities. Few would deny that while the provinces are indeed important economic actors, the federal government is primarily responsible for broad macroeconomic management: for fiscal policy, monetary policy, and the like. Few would deny an overarching federal responsibility for the major redistributive programs, both for individuals and for regions, nor would they challenge the federal government's responsibility for interregional trade and commerce or for transportation.

Indeed, in these areas the call seems to be generally not for increased provincial juris-diction but for a greater degree of regional sensitivity, whether through consultation with provincial governments or in the internal operations of the national government. A simi-lar listing for provincial government roles might be more controversial, but it would probably include education, social services, and most of the detailed regulation of indi-vidual and commercial life encompassed in "property and civil rights." ...

What accounts for these changes in the operating division of powers? The proximate causes lie in the changing roles that governments play in advanced industrial societies such as Canada. Especially in the postwar period, federal institutions were required to adapt to new roles for the state and to new relationships between the state and society. The story of the evolution of the division of powers is essentially the story of how this was done, within the context of the institutions we had inherited and the ways in which the courts had understood them. However, these changes in the role of government were themselves the product of other forces, which also therefore must be understood as "causes" of shifts in the division of powers. These include such broad trends as the in-creasing and changing importance of international influences in shaping the Canadian society and economy, the increased politicization of society, and the changing expecta-tions and demands of citizens.

Moreover, to say that the division of powers had to respond to changing roles for the state does not necessarily explain how it did so. In particular, it does not explain how these new responsibilities would be allocated among governments, whether they would fall primarily to provincial governments or to the national government, or whether they would be shared. In order to answer this question, we shall return to the larger perspec-tives of functional federalism, democracy, and community that we outlined in Part I. All three are required to understand the Canadian pattern.

That pattern has been distinctive in some important ways. While increased overlap-ping and concurrency has been common to all federal states as they respond to the same pressures for the growth of government, in most cases the result has been a considerable degree of centralization. The major new responsibilities fell to the central governments, even though they were often delivered through complex mechanisms of intergovern-mental transfers. Canadian commentators (at least virtually all English-speaking ones) on the events of the 1930s, in which federal institutions were seen so clearly and tragi-cally to have failed, argued that decentralized federalism was inherently incapable of undertaking the responsibilities that economic and social developments were forcing on the modern state. The "dead hand" of the Constitution (aided and abetted by the Judicial Committee of the Privy Council) had to be removed. The division of powers had to be reworked to reflect the new responsibilities of government.

Events during and immediately after World War II seemed to indicate that this was precisely what was happening. The Rowell-Sirois Commission reported in 1940, recom-mending federal jurisdiction over pensions and unemployment insurance and full fed-eral jurisdiction over personal and corporate income taxes. All provinces agreed to a 1940 amendment transferring responsibility for unemployment insurance to the federal government. During the war, the fiscal and bureaucratic capacities of the federal govern-ment increased tremendously, and this dominance extended into the years following. Toward the end of the war, the government's white paper on incomes and employment embraced both freer trade and a responsibility for managing the entire economy, a role that would fall to Ottawa. At the end of the war, the government also released its proposals for postwar federalism, the so-called Green Book proposals, which were discussed with the provinces at a series of Reconstruction Conferences. They, too, envisioned a greatly enhanced role for the federal government, including extension of welfare state policies and control over the income tax system.

The larger, wealthier provinces rejected the Green Book proposals. However, most of the elements of the proposals were achieved over the next two decades in a piecemeal series of federal–provincial agreements: tax rental agreements, grants for health care, culminating in the *Hospital Insurance and Diagnostic Services Act, 1957* and the *Medical Care Act, 1966*; grants for post-secondary education, leading to federal assumption of half the operating costs of all post-secondary institutions in 1967; grants to assist the provinces in social welfare, culminating in the Canada Assistance Plan, 1968; and developments in pensions, including the establishment of the federal old-age security pension in 1951, the Canada and Quebec pension plans in 1964, the guaranteed income supplement, and so on.

Equally remarkable was the persistence and vitality of federalism. In only a few cases were responsibilities formally transferred to the federal level. In most cases, the federal government was to achieve its goals through shared-cost programs, with the provinces retaining a major role in program design and delivery. The fiscal centralization of the immediate postwar period was steadily relaxed. The provincial shares of taxing, spending, and government employment rose at a considerably faster rate than federal spending throughout most of this period. The strength and self-confidence of provincial governments increased, along with their budgets. Thus, predictions that the provinces would wither away, to become little more than municipalities, able merely to weave minor variations on national themes, were proved to be decidedly premature. All this was reflected in the shifting division of powers.

As the state adopted new roles, expectations of federalism pulled in somewhat different directions. Most thinking in the postwar period held that the efficiency and effectiveness of public policy implied the need for increased centralization, or federal authority. There are a number of strands to this argument. The new Keynesian economics stressed the need for the state to manipulate overall levels of taxing and spending in order to smooth out aggregate demand in the economy. Many assumed that this would be more feasible if one single authority was able to determine aggregate levels of taxation, borrowing, and expenditure, rather than if independent actions of 11 governments had to be coordinated. Most provinces were clearly too small to operate their own fiscal policy; any provincial effort was likely to be dissipated in spillovers to other jurisdictions. Without control over their money supply, the provinces' capacity to engage in stabilization policy was further limited. The Canadian commitment to freer international trade in the post-War era also increased the importance of international economic relations in domestic policy-making, a development that was also assumed by many to require wider federal authority. More generally, it was felt that the private economic actors with which governments would have to interact, and which they would have to regulate, were increasingly transcending provincial boundaries. National and international corporations and unions were felt to be beyond the reach of most provincial governments. If the economy itself was becoming organized on a national basis, then the political system should be organized more nationally as well.

Similar reasoning applied to the development of the welfare state. Individual provinces, it was felt, lacked the resources to put the new policies in place, though often they had acted as the pioneers, as Saskatchewan had done with public health care. It was also difficult for the provinces to pursue progressive redistributive policies, since in a society with mobile capital and labour, the wealthy could easily move to areas of low spending and low taxes, and the less well-off could do the reverse. Provincial provision of services such as post-secondary education would probably be less than was desirable for national purposes, since provinces would fear that graduates trained at their expense might move elsewhere on graduation. The more integrated and tight-knit the society, the more inhibiting such interdependencies could be and, as the Saskatchewan health care example shows, the more each level of government would require the assistance of the other to meet its goals. The expansion was therefore complementary as often as competitive.

There thus was a powerful functionally based rationale for a broader federal role; or, if not, for a high degree of federal involvement in provincial policy. By the 1970s, such functional arguments had attenuated somewhat. Perhaps the chief reason was that with the fundamental economic management policies well established, it was possible to turn more attention to the virtues of decentralization in terms of policy experiment, innovation, and the like. By the 1970s there was also growing disquiet about the efficacy and desirability of some of the postwar policies; they were now less able to command broad support. In particular, the limitations of such policies, especially for some regions, had become more apparent. Keynesian economics had indeed appeared to promote national growth, but it was not clear that it had done much to alleviate underlying regional disparities. Thus, a new set of issues was arising for which, at least for some interests, centralization was not the obvious solution.

If the logic of functionalism was broadly centralizing, the logic of democracy was more complicated. The postwar period was characterized by increased citizen expectations and demands on governments, and by the proliferation of interest groups. Both phenomena were simultaneously cause and consequence of the growth of governments. As Hugh G. Thorburn [H.G. Thorburn, *Interest Groups in the Canadian Federal System: The Relationships Between Canadian Governments and Interest Groups* (Toronto: University of Toronto Press, 1985), at 59-66] has demonstrated in his study of interest groups, the organization and strategies of such groups was greatly influenced by the federal political structure and by the division of powers. Groups tended to organize around those governments which had the prime responsibility for matters of greatest concern to them. For example, provincial ownership of oil and gas resources led companies in these fields to orient themselves primarily toward the provincial governments. However, federalism also required many groups, such as labour, to orient themselves to both levels, often stretching their resources very thin and rendering it difficult for groups to develop coherent national policies.

At the same time, the groups also helped shape the evolution of federalism. They greatly stimulated the development of jurisdictional overlap and policy interdependence, for neither interest groups nor citizens were likely to consult ss. 91 and 92 before articulating their demands. The call was for action by government generally, and both orders of government were often anxious to respond, especially in the newly emerging areas of public concern.

Finally, community concerns also pulled in both directions. It was widely felt in the postwar period that the searing collective experiences of the depression and the war had greatly strengthened the sense of a Canadian national community. Shared sacrifice and the increased linkages among citizens was producing a stronger national consciousness, one that was focussed on the federal government, for it had been the prime instrument of the war effort and alone seemed capable of putting in place the new public agenda. The commitment to the welfare state embodied an idea of social rights and national standards which should apply to citizens wherever they lived. A stronger national consciousness legitimized federal policies that were designed to foster it. No longer did it seem justified that we should tolerate large differences in the level and quality of public services simply because of the province of residence. It was widely thought that the processes of economic development in an advanced industrial society were likely to erode the importance of identities rooted in territory and culture, and to strengthen those related to one's status in the economic system, for example as worker, manager, or farmer. This, too, was predicted to undermine the salience of provincial identities and to strengthen those at the national level.

Nevertheless, the support for regional communities had by no means disappeared, especially in Quebec. In their response to the Rowell-Sirois Report (which itself had restrained its recommendations out of a recognition of the value of provincial diversity) and to the federal Green Book proposals, dissenting provinces were able to make strong appeals to values such as provincial autonomy. In the 1950s, Quebec's Tremblay Commission was able to articulate a province-centred view of federalism which attacked the essentials of the thrust for postwar centralization. The strength of such feelings ensured that in the assumption of new roles, the answer would not simply be a wholesale transfers of responsibilities from the provinces to the federal government, however logical this might seem on functional grounds. Instead, many of these functions would be carried out by the provinces. In other cases, ways would be found to introduce them in a manner consistent with the maintenance of federalism and of provincial responsibility, primarily through the development of the techniques that came to be known as cooperative federalism.

As we shall discuss later at greater length, by the 1970s federal and provincial governments were articulating highly divergent and competing views of the character of the Canadian communities and their relations to the two orders of government. This competitive state-building also promoted increased overlap and *de facto* concurrency, since each of the competing visions tended to be predicated not on a functional division of powers, as suggested by ss. 91 and 92, but on a global view of the dominance of one or other level of community. In the pursuit of such visions, it was legitimate to deploy the full range of public policy—economic, social, and cultural. From this perspective, nothing was easily excluded from the purview of any government; no easy dividing line could be drawn. So in Quebec, for example, by the 1960s the issue was not whether there should be a welfare state but under whose auspices it should be organized. Thus, while in the postwar period the muting of regional consciousness had limited fundamental debate over the division of powers in favour of a search for cooperative mechanisms, by the

1960s the division of powers was at the heart of federal–provincial conflict, as each government explored the limits of its "jurisdictional potential."

As the preceding comment suggests, changes in the division of powers were not automatic reflections of a changing society and economy. They were developed and articulated by and through the governments in the federal system, each utilizing the resources allocated to it by the Constitution. Thus, we must also understand change in the operating division of powers through the internal dynamics of governments themselves. As they sought to master their own environments, and respond to electoral and other incentives, they were increasingly led to intervene in areas occupied by other governments and to use policy instruments that had previously been largely monopolized by the others. As we have seen, the terms of the *BNA Act* were permissive: a government could almost always find a legitimate constitutional peg on which to hang its desired programs. This was made possible both by the fact that many new areas did not fall neatly into any one category and by the presence of open-ended authority in areas such as the spending or the taxing power.

NOTE

With increasing levels of activity by federal and provincial governments and the resulting interdependency, executive federalism became an important institution of Canadian political life. The term "executive federalism" describes the relationships between elected and appointed officials representing federal and provincial governments. Through consultation and negotiations in a wide variety of policy areas, these actors have often reshaped the allocation of functions under the Constitution's distribution of powers, as interpreted by the courts. Further discussion of the intergovernmental relations that characterize modern federalism is found in G. Stevenson, "Federalism and Intergovernmental Relations," in M. Whittington and G. Williams, eds., *Canadian Politics in the 1990's*, 3d ed. (Scarborough, ON: Nelson Canada, 1990), 380 99. Intergovernmental agreements will be dealt with further in Chapter 12, Instruments of Flexibility in the Federal System.

CHAPTER EIGHT

Interpreting the Division of Powers

This chapter contains an overview of the general principles relied upon in the judicial interpretation of the division of powers. The structure of the chapter follows the three types of arguments that can be used to challenge statutes on the ground of division of powers.

The first kind of argument involves a challenge to the *validity* of a statute on the grounds that it is in its dominant characteristic (or "pith and substance") in relation to a matter beyond the enacting legislature's jurisdiction and thus within the exclusive jurisdiction of the other level of government. Challenges to the validity of a statute can be made equally against either federal or provincial statutes.

The second kind of argument seeks to limit the *applicability* of valid statutes. Even if a statute is within the enacting legislature's jurisdiction, it may have to be limited in its application (or "read down") so as not to touch matters at the core of the other level of government's areas of exclusive jurisdiction. This doctrine, known as interjurisdictional immunity, has been used far more often by the courts to limit the applicability of provincial statutes to protect the exclusivity of federal heads of power than to limit the applicability of federal statutes to protect the exclusivity of provincial heads of power. However, in a recent decision, the Supreme Court of Canada affirmed that the logic underlying the doctrine means that it can be used to protect the core areas of jurisdiction of both orders of government.

The third kind of argument seeks to limit the *operability* of provincial statutes. Even if a provincial law is valid, and even if it is applicable, it will be rendered inoperative if it conflicts with a valid federal statute that also applies to the same facts. This doctrine, known as the federal paramountcy rule, works against the operation of provincial statutes to protect the primacy of federal policies embodied in valid federal legislation.

Before turning to an examination of arguments based on validity, applicability, and operability, the chapter begins with an excerpt from a Richard Simeon article discussing the fundamental values that shape and animate debates about the federal form of government. The interpretation of the division of powers is an exercise that is inevitably deeply influenced by judicial conceptions of the appropriate weight to be given to the values Simeon discusses. For example, a judge's conception of the relative importance of national and local communities will likely influence his or her choice of either a broad or narrow approach to the scope and meaning of competing federal and provincial heads of power. The weight a judge attaches to a concern about functional efficiency may influence the degree to which he or she is willing to tolerate overlapping schemes of federal and provincial regulation. An appreciation of the underlying values discussed by Simeon is necessary to grasp the normative dynamics that drive debates about the proper interpretation of the division of powers.

I. VALUES INFORMING THE INTERPRETATION OF THE
DIVISION OF POWERS

R. Simeon, "Criteria for Choice in Federal Systems"
(1982-83), 8 *Queen's Law Journal* 131, at 131-37, 141-43, and 148-55
(footnotes omitted)

[F]ederalism is not an end in itself, not something which can be inherently "balanced" or "unbalanced." Federalism (and its many variations in the view taken here) is valued or criticized because it is felt to promote (or constrain) other important values, and is believed to have certain kinds of effects.

Federalism, as a doctrine, is thus often associated with a number of other political values, such as liberty or pluralism; federalism as a set of institutions is felt to enhance the likelihood of approximating these values in practice. Moreover, if this is true, then it should also be true that proposals for change in a federal system like Canada's can be judged by whether they serve or block these wider values, and perhaps even that if we had clear normative criteria in mind we should be able to deduce proposals for reform from them. ...

In this paper, we will examine the links between federalism and three distinct bodies of theory, each of which provides a different vantage point for assessing a federal system.

Federalism can be evaluated first from the perspective of *community*. Here the question is: what implications do different forms of federalism have for different images of the ideal or preferred community with which people identify and to which they feel loyalty? Linguistic dualism and regional diversity have made this perspective the overwhelming focus of both practitioners and students of Canadian federalism, especially since the 1960s. Second, federalism can be evaluated from the perspective of democratic theory: does federalism promote democracy; do different conceptions of democracy generate different images of the good federal system? ...

Third, federalism can be assessed from the vantage point of functional effectiveness: does it enhance or frustrate the capacity of government institutions to generate effective policy and respond to citizen needs?

Debates about federalism take place both within and between each perspective. Proponents of each standpoint ask very different questions and have quite different criteria for judgement. Indeed the debate is often confused simply because the combatants talk past each other. But there is also vigorous debate within each of these traditions: between localists and universalists in community terms; between majoritarians and protectors of minority rights in democratic terms; between proponents of economies of scale and of the pathologies of size among the functionalists.

The relative emphasis among the three perspectives tends to vary considerably from country to country and time to time. Thus, if Canadians have been preoccupied with accommodating rival conceptions of community, Americans have—with the major exception of the Civil War period—debated federalism overwhelmingly in terms of its implications for democracy. Australians and Germans have emphasized the functional dimension—though the establishment of the Bonn republic sought the restoration of federalism as one means to diffuse power and thus inhibit the reemergence of totalitarianism. In Canada, while community has been central, English-Canadian academics of the thirties concentrated largely on federalism and effective government, rather than federalism and community. The economic crisis of the present and the (at least temporary) setting aside of the constitutional debate, suggests that attention is turning back to the preoccupations characteristic of the thirties. ...

[P]olitical values are nested in institutional forms. Constitutional doctrines have important educative values. They privilege some concepts of sovereignty, legitimacy, representation and the like over others and thus make them easier to defend or harder to attack. At a more empirical level, they entrench some kinds of interests over others, and structure the incentives within which political actors work. ...

Conceptions of Community

The first set of criteria asks what conception of the political *community* is to be embodied in political arrangements. Federalism is thus assessed largely in terms of its ability to defend and maintain a balance between regional and national political communities. Conflict arises out of competing models of community: between a vision of a single pan-Canadian community, a vision of a union of ten provincial communities and a vision of two distinct national communities, each with full sovereignty. Within the perspective of community, moreover, is the controversy about whether the communities in Canada are to be defined largely in political terms, or in terms of the relationship of linguistic and ethnic communities. In the present context, the competing images of community can be summarized in terms of a conflict between three drives: country-building, province-building, and two-nation or Quebec nation-building. Federalism itself represents, from this point of view, a dynamic balance between regional and national communities, reflected in the relationship between federal and provincial governments. The tension threatens the federal system itself when residents of different parts of the country hold fundamentally clashing conceptions of the balance; or when residents of one or more regions develop a conception of community in which their identification or links with other regions and the central government become weak.

The criterion of community asks concerning which set of people do we assert a common citizenship, maintain a common loyalty, maintain a common set of obligations one to another, or maximize values such as equity, growth or wealth? Who is entitled to share, as of right, in the resources of the group? What set of people do we regard as "us"? When an Albertan or a New Brunswicker says "we," whom does he include? What is "the appropriate space dimension for the resolution of value conflict?"

In this sense everyone belongs to multiple communities, ranging from family, to city, to province, to country, to humanity in general. And most of the time these identities are not incompatible. For some purposes the relevant community will be defined broadly, for others narrowly. Indeed federalism is predicated on just this sort of division in the minds of citizens.

Nor, of course, need communities be territorial or geographic—they can equally be communities such as religious groups or classes. Here however, we are concerned primarily with territorially defined communities, though religious, ethnic and indeed economic communities have to a large extent coincided with territorial divisions and have given them much of their force. Moreover, we are concerned with provincially-bounded communities, even though communities defined intra and supra-provincially exist in many parts of Canada. We focus on nation and province because it is these communities which have been institutionalized, and which have governments with the capacity to define and articulate community interests. Each sense of community has a governmental spokesman possessing a wide range of resources. For this reason, arguments about political community in Canada tend to focus on the relative role and power of federal and provincial authorities. More than most other successful federations, Canadian history has turned on such questions and on shifts in the political strength of each conception. From the immediate post-war period, perhaps the high-water mark of country-building, we have seen a resurgence of both province and Quebec nation-building, and it is this, rather than either a crisis of democracy, or of functionalism, that called into question the Canadian political regime since the 1960s. ...

The Functional Perspective

The second set of criteria may be labelled *functional*. Here the focus is not on regions, communities or rival national and provincial states. Rather, federal and provincial governments are seen to be different elements within a single system. Together—either through independent action, or through various forms of cooperation—they are responsible for governing the country and for satisfying the needs of citizens. Powers are allocated, at least in principle, not according to what different communities need to express and protect themselves but rather according to a division of labour criterion: which level can most efficiently and effectively carry out any given responsibility of contemporary government? The system as a whole is evaluated in terms of its ability to respond to the needs of citizens—to provide them with the mix of public policies which they prefer. And citizen interests in terms of economic and social goals—as consumers, workers, businessmen, homeowners, etc.—are held to be more important to them than their interests as members of territorially-defined communities. Does the federal system facilitate or frustrate governmental responsiveness, does it promote or block desires for more effective economic planning, control over foreign ownership, environmental protection, a fair welfare system, or any other set of objectives? Does it impose unacceptably high delays or uncertainties in decision-making, or impose heavy organizational and decision costs?

If the community perspective is the domain of sociologists, the functional perspective is that of the economists and public administrators. If the primary orientation of community theorists is collectivist, the functionalist perspective tends to be individualist. And if advocates of each model of community often take for granted or ignore the policy or efficiency implications of different proposals, functional theorists equally tend to leave unexamined the scope of the community across which values like equity, redistribution, growth or welfare are to be maximized. Most writers in this perspective tend to reject debate in terms of community as illegitimate: it is seen either as a sterile competition among political elites, or as rivalry among vague collectivities. As Pierre Trudeau and his colleagues said in a 1964 manifesto, "An Appeal for Realism in Politics":

> To use nationalism (English or French-Canadian) as a yardstick deciding politics and priorities is both sterile and retrograde. Overflowing nationalism distorts one's vision of reality, prevents one from seeing problems in their true perspective, falsifies solutions and constitutes a classic diversionary tactic for politicians caught by the facts. …

The constitutional problem, then, is to allocate powers and erect machinery that maximizes the capacity of governments collectively to satisfy citizen needs. And the question is whether there exists a body of theory which can provide criteria to suggest how this can be done.

Arguments about the functional ineffectiveness of the federal system abound. Some argue the system is ineffective because it is too *decentralized*. For example, it is suggested that the Canadian common market—and hence the rational allocation of resources—has been substantially eroded by a wide variety of provincial actions. Businessmen argue that they are hampered by differing provincial regulations in such areas as consumer protection. It is often argued that the proportion of taxing and spending power in the hands of the provinces vitiates the federal capacity to manage the economy, or to develop effective national planning. Social Democrats have traditionally argued that federalism has slowed down development of the Canadian welfare state, or that it permits small vulnerable provinces to be easily manipulated by external capital.

But there are also functionally derived arguments that the system is too *centralized*. They include the view that no remote central government can adequately take into account the interests of all sectors and regions. The federal decision-making apparatus is overloaded and hence ineffective.

Finally, many functionalist arguments focus on the costs of the sharing and overlapping of responsibilities among governments. Such sharing, it is suggested, imposes unacceptably high decision costs. The costs to citizens are in the form of delay, uncertainty, and the difficulty of knowing who is responsible or to whom to direct demands. Citizens are burdened by buck-passing between governments, and by the petty competition between them. Governments themselves face the costs of coordinating policies among themselves—in time, money and the diversion of bureaucratic talent—from the *substance* of policy to the *procedures* of developing it. The sharing of powers and the process of federal-provincial bargaining, it is argued, freezes out interest groups and contributes to the "overgovernment" of Canadian society. Functionalist critiques thus come from all parts of the ideological spectrum. They can lead either to centralization or to decentralization, and they usually embody an implicit conception of community. …

Most of the theorizing in this vein deals with the economic functions of government. It is also much influenced by an individualist market-oriented approach which neglects or assumes away some important problems. While enunciating criteria, few of the economic models provide clear guides to the most appropriate division of powers. …

This is in part because as Bernard Dafflon puts it:

> … it is impossible to make any pronouncements that will generally govern the economic policies of federalism without falling back on value judgements about what should be the "correct" nature of the federal relation.

These include value judgements about *whose* values are to be optimized. Terms like "efficiency" and "effectiveness" or even "coordination" always contain the implicit "for whom," "in whose eyes." A set of programs coordinated from one perspective may be quite uncoordinated from another.

One of the most important lessons of the functional perspective is that not all interests are defined in territorial terms; the interests of workers vs. owners, producers vs. consumers, farmers vs. factory workers and so on may be more important, and may be neglected in a political regime predicated on the centrality of territory or region. Here, abstract criteria are of little help. What is necessary is assessment of the underlying nature of political, economic and cultural cleavages, and the territorial distribution of interests. Which kinds of interests are benefited by greater provincial power; which would gain by greater federal power? "Who benefits" from greater centralization or greater decentralization is not a question that can be answered in the abstract; nor are benefits and costs distributed equally across all groups. It is a much more political question, in which the interests of different groups, their distribution across the country, [and] the relative influence they can bring to bear on each level of government are all crucial to the determination.

Functionalist theorists have tended to discuss the allocation of powers in terms of watertight compartments; overlapping, except in the eyes of some public choice theorists, is held to be inefficient, costly, and perverse. Yet overlapping jurisdictions characterize all federations, and theorists must take into account the political forces which have led to this situation. Most issues have both local and national dimensions, so their assignment to one or other level will inevitably result in inefficiencies. As Dafflon says, "For multi-level problems, single level problem solving structures are unlikely to be optimal." ...

The Democratic Perspective

The third perspective is that of democratic theory. It asks: what are the consequences of alternative federal arrangements for different conceptions of democracy—for participation, responsiveness, liberty and equality? There are several strands to such arguments. The first approach is primarily concerned with protecting citizens *from* governments; it stresses preservation of liberty and of minority rights against oppression by the majority. The classic defence of federalism as it emerged in the United States suggests that its fundamental purpose is to minimize the possibility of tyranny, especially majority tyranny, by ensuring that power would be fragmented among competing governmental authorities. It is thus part of the complex ideas of Madisonian liberalism, along with the division of powers, checks and balances, a constitutional Bill of Rights, and so on. In this view federalism is a device to place limits on government, in part by ensuring that "ambition" will be checked by ambition, and in part by ensuring that diverse jurisdictions will offer different packages of services from which mobile individuals can choose. This approach tends to argue for considerable decentralization and makes a virtue out of divided jurisdiction and competing governments. A minority tyrannized over by a local majority can seek redress at another level, as blacks faced with discriminatory state policies were able to do by turning to Washington or, to some extent, as French-Canadians were able to do by turning to the provincial government. ...

There are several problems with this approach. It places an excessive faith in the capacity of institutions to prevent tyranny. And if the goal of federalism is more *limited* government overall, many contemporary critics conversely suggest it is associated with *too much* government. Finally, the reverse of protection of minorities is the frustration of majorities. Federalism does not resolve the classic problem of majority versus minority rights.

A second strand of democratic theorizing stresses the advantages of smaller units in terms of governmental responsiveness and citizen participation. In Montesquieu's view:

> In a large republic, the common good is subject to a thousand considerations; it is subordinated to various exceptions; it depends on accidents. In a small republic, the public good is more strongly felt, better known and closer to each citizen; abuses are less extensive, and consequently less protected.

Smaller units are likely to be more homogeneous, so a clear majority interest is more likely to emerge. The political weight of an individual citizen is greater if he is one of a small rather than a large number. Political leaders are more sensitive to public opinion with small constituencies. The advantage of a decentralized federal system, then, is that it maximizes opportunities for effective citizen participation.

Again, there are difficulties. In order for communities to be homogeneous, or for individuals to have a real chance of exercising influence, the units probably need to be a great deal smaller than provinces: we would be talking about decentralization to the neighbourhood, or the factory, as in the federalism of Prudhon. The opportunity to participate in a small unit may also pose a difficult dilemma: one may be able to achieve influence, but that may be negated by the inability of the unit itself to achieve one's goal because it lacks the resources: system responsiveness and system capacity are inversely related. This is a strong argument for a multi-level system of government, such as federalism.

Thus, "democratic" views of federalism support both a high degree of decentralization and of overlapping between governments. But democratic theory also produces important critiques of federalism. Most prominent recently in Canada is the argument that the Canadian pattern of "executive federalism" in which relations between governments are conducted primarily through the negotiations of political executives limits citizen participation and effectiveness in many ways. Confusion about which level of government is responsible for what makes rational intervention difficult. The mixing of responsibilities reduces accountability and allows governments to pass the buck. The secrecy of the process has similar effects and freezes out interest groups. The dominance of executives strengthens the role of bureaucrats as against politicians, and cabinets as against legislatures and opposition parties. Citizens' interests, it is argued, get lost in governmental competition for status and power. ...

The second critique of federalism is that it frustrates majority rule; indeed, it does so almost by definition. It does so by denying a level of government the jurisdiction or resources to achieve certain ends, or by providing inadequate mechanisms for joint decision-making. This concern, of course, is quite different from those advanced by Madisonian liberals. The difference is well-illustrated by those who oppose an entrenched *Bill of Rights* on the grounds that it infringes on legislative sovereignty. Again, the critical prior question is: which majorities? Within what community is majority rule to prevail? Thus it has often been argued that federalism has frustrated *national* majorities. ...

A related argument, advanced by Porter and others, is that the federal structure, by fragmenting groups and institutionalizing the territorial dimension of politics, has inhibited the emergence of national majorities or of majorities and minorities based on non-regional cleavages, such as class. Both these views argue for more centralization.

But on the other hand, one can argue that federalism has frustrated provincial majorities. This may be either because the national government has forced on them policies which they dislike—as in the view that tariff policy frustrates the West, that national welfare state initiatives were repugnant to a Catholic majority in Quebec, as the Tremblay Report argued, or, most clearly, that national measures to appropriate the revenues from natural resources directly attack the right of a local majority to them. Or it may be because the lack of provincial resources and jurisdiction are held to frustrate provincial attempts to pursue their own goals. This is a central argument of the PQ: Quebec cannot achieve its goals in economic, social or cultural policy so long as Ottawa controls so many of the levels of policy-making. More generally, majority rule in Canada as a whole implies inevitably that Central Canada outweighs the East and West, and that English-Canadians predominate over French-Canadians. If regional and ethnic identities are the most salient divisions, and if political issues divide the country on these lines, then the doctrine of majority rule is a major threat to national unity. ...

Thus arguments from majority rule depend crucially on prior conceptions of community. They also depend on the territorial distribution of political cleavages. If most interests are distributed evenly across the whole country, dividing it horizontally rather than vertically, then the argument for aggregation at the national level is strong. If, on the other hand, opinions are sharply divided by region, which implies that a majority in each region is likely to have a different preference, then a strong argument can be made for provincial responsibility. Indeed the "democratic" version of containing spillovers is the idea that political boundaries should be aligned with the distribution of preferences, so that each region is as homogeneous as possible: each unit could then enact its preferences without either imposing them on others or being vetoed by others. This is a fundamental justification of federalism. It is, however, hard to make operational, and does not deal with the problem of the distribution of rewards across units, "conflicts of claim." ...

NOTES AND QUESTIONS

1. Important as these underlying values can be to the resolution by judges of the federalism disputes that come before them, it is rare for a judge to openly acknowledge that he or she has based a particular decision on one or more of those values. Why do you suppose that is the case?

2. For examples of cases in which judges *have* openly acknowledged the influence of a particular value in resolving a federalism issue, see the reasons for judgment of Justice Ritchie in *Re Nova Scotia Board of Censors v. McNeil*, [1978] 2 SCR 662, 84 DLR (3d) 1 (excerpted in Chapter 11, Criminal Law) (community); Justice Estey in *Dominion Stores Ltd. v. The Queen*, [1980] 1 SCR 844, 106 DLR (3d) 581 (the subject of a note in Chapter 10, Economic Regulation) (functional efficiency); and Justice Lamer (as he then was) in *Starr v. Houlden*, [1990] 1 SCR 1366, 68 DLR (4th) 641 (democracy).

3. In *Starr v. Houlden*, Justice Lamer said that one of the relevant considerations in characterizing legislation for division of powers purposes is "what Professor Hogg refers to at p. 323 [of his textbook, *Constitutional Law of Canada* 2d ed. (1985)] as a 'concept of federalism' comprised of the enduring values in the allocation of power between the two levels of government." The "enduring values" to which Hogg refers in his text are those discussed by Professor Simeon in the article excerpted above.

4. For an analysis of the impact that the nature of a particular head of power in ss. 91 and 92 can have on the preference shown by a court for one of Simeon's criteria of choice over another (as well as on the use of the double aspect and necessarily incidental doctrines considered below), see J. Leclair, "L'impact de la nature d'une compétence législative sur l'étendue du pouvoir conféré dans le cadre de la Loi constitutionnelle de 1867" (1994), 24 *Revue juridique Thémis* 661-719. See also J. Leclair, "The Supreme Court's Understanding of Federalism: Efficiency at the Expense of Diversity" (2003), 28 *Queen's Law Journal* 411-53, for another examination of federalism's normative dimensions.

II. VALIDITY: CHARACTERIZATION OF LAWS

A. Pith and Substance

K. Swinton, *The Supreme Court and Canadian Federalism:*
The Laskin-Dickson Years
(Scarborough, ON: Carswell, 1990), at 24-30 (footnotes omitted)

The Anatomy of Constitutional Interpretation

Sections 91 and 92 of the Constitution Act, 1867

To understand the nature of [constitutional] argument ... it is necessary to begin with sections 91 and 92 of the *Constitution Act, 1867*, for any legal argument must be grounded in the constitutional document. Every federal system requires a distribution of legislative powers between the national and regional governments, and sections 91 and 92 perform that function in Canada. Section 91 sets out a list of 30 classes of subjects which are said to fall exclusively within federal legislative competence. The federal classes of subjects cover a wide range, from "sea coast and inland fisheries," ... to the more frequently litigated "regulation of trade and commerce" in section 91(2) and "the criminal law" in section 91(27). The provinces similarly have "exclusive" jurisdiction over classes of subjects, 15 in number, among which the most important is "property and civil rights in the Province" in section 92(13).

There has been longstanding academic controversy over the status of the federal classes of subjects because of the opening words of section 91, referred to as the "peace, order and good government" or p.o.g.g. power. Some commentators have argued that the federal classes are illustrative only, with the federal government's legislative power "general" in scope, unlimited by anything except the list of provincial powers. Others assert that the classes are an independent source of federal power, and the opening words serve only to give the federal government a residuary power to deal with matters not expressly assigned to provincial or federal jurisdiction. Bora Laskin, as a professor, took the first position—that section 91 was a grant of general power to the federal Parliament—while others, such as Professors Lysyk and Lederman, have maintained that the federal classes of subjects are express grants of power which have primary interpretive force. In fact, the courts do give primary effect to the enumerated powers, using the opening words of section 91 only in limited circumstances.

The classes in sections 91 and 92, while numerous, are not exhaustive of the scope of governmental activity. The terms chosen to describe the grants of power were thought to cover the major areas of governmental activity in 1867, but over time, government has inevitably engaged in new areas of regulation, as the changing society and economy presented problems for public policy not contemplated over one hundred years ago. As a result, when a court is presented with a constitutional challenge to legislation, it will decide whether the impugned legislation falls within the provincial or federal sphere through consideration of the enumerated classes and, as well, the power contained in the opening words of section 91, which comes into play when a legislative matter is not covered by the enumerated powers. For example, aeronautics has been held to be a federal matter under the p.o.g.g. power, as it is a matter that was not allocated by the original distribution of powers (for obvious technological reasons).

In deciding the validity of a law, a court engages in a process of classification to determine whether the law comes within a federal or provincial class of powers. Generally, the argument is framed in terms of competing federal and provincial classifications. ...

Choosing Between Competing Classifications

How does the court choose between these competing classifications? The process is far from mechanistic, for it requires considerations both about the impugned legislation and the meaning of the constitution's language. It can, however, be broken down into three steps, as Professor Abel ["The Logic of 91 and 92," in A. Abel, *Laskin's Canadian Constitutional Law*, 4th ed., rev. (Scarborough, ON: Carswell, 1975), at 97] suggested: identification of the "matter" of the statute, delineation of the scope of the competing classes, and then a determination of the class into which the challenged statute falls. While Abel criticized the tendency of judges and academics to collapse this process by describing the matter of the statute in the terms of the classes, such action is inevitable, for the exercise of determining the "matter" or predominant feature of the statute is affected by the ultimate objective of linking the statute to the classes of subjects in the constitution. Nevertheless, Abel's exercise is useful to illustrate the type of questions which a judge, consciously or subconsciously, works through in characterizing legislation in Canadian constitutional law.

In determining the meaning or matter of legislation (Abel's first step), a court looks to a variety of aids. Obviously, the starting place is the statutory context. ...

In addition to the statutory context, a court may look to the purpose of the legislation, as illustrated by its legislative history or by government reports identifying a problem which triggered the legislation. The effects of the legislation may also be relevant. ...

The ultimate decision as to the meaning or matter of the legislation is not uncontroversial, for some judges give greater weight to effects, others to purpose, in deciding meaning, and there has been little discussion of when they will adopt one approach as opposed to the other. The dominant form of inquiry is into purpose—that is, to the problem underlying the legislation which the legislature is trying to address. Inevitably, the focus on purpose or effects turns, in part, on judicial attitudes of deference to legislatures and concerns about the balance of powers in the federal system. Deference to the legislature's avowed purpose, without attention to the effects of the legislation on the other level of government, permits governments to expand their areas of responsibility.

If one turns to the second stage of Abel's inquiry, the scope of the classes of legislative subjects, one finds that, once again, the judges have discretion. Despite the reference to the "exclusivity" of the classes in sections 91 and 92, there is opportunity for extensive overlapping regulation, because the constitution confers jurisdiction to make laws regarding certain classes of subjects, rather than jurisdiction over facts, persons or activities. Similar laws may fit within both federal and provincial heads of power. For example, the federal Parliament can make misleading advertising a crime under its criminal law power, but the provinces may give a civil remedy for the same conduct or even penalize it under their jurisdiction over property and civil rights in section 92(13) of the constitution. The courts often uphold such legislation using the "double aspect doctrine," whereby they acknowledge that some laws may have both federal and provincial purposes. While the Fathers of Confederation may have wished for exclusivity of legislative powers or "watertight compartments" between federal and provincial governments, it became clear early in the interpretation of the constitution that there must be some overlap or entanglement between federal and provincial regulation, for provincial and federal governments often have good reasons, that can be supported by their distinct heads of legislative power, for dealing with the same activity. Even if the courts of an earlier era might have preferred a classical federal system with watertight compartments, they could never ignore the aspect doctrine and, as governments became increasingly interventionist in the second half of the twentieth century, there was a need for more frequent resort to this doctrine, as the opportunities for overlap between the regulation of the two levels of government expanded.

The court's discretion in defining the scope of classes is not unlimited, for precedent plays an important role in constitutional adjudication. ...

History, as well, may play a part in the definition of class boundaries, for some judges look to the meaning of words or practices in 1867 to guide them in interpreting the scope of the classes today.

Precedent and history may assist the courts in defining the classes of powers, but they do not fix the boundaries of classes nor show whether a law should come within one class rather than another. Often, the court's ultimate decision about boundaries and the matters within them is guided by federalism concerns—by beliefs about the optimal balance of power between the federal and provincial governments. In Professor Lederman's words [in "Classification of Laws and the British North America Act," excerpted later in this chapter], the courts should reach their decisions by weighing the values of uniformity and diversity and by following "widely prevailing beliefs." Absent such beliefs, he says that judges should do the following:

> In the making of these very difficult relative-value decisions, all that can rightly be required
> of judges is straight thinking, industry, good faith, and a capacity to discount their own

prejudices. No doubt it is also fair to ask that they be men of high attainment, and that they be representative in their thinking of the better standards of their times and their countrymen.

Many would challenge Lederman's premise that there are widely held beliefs on the proper allocation of power in a federal system. Indeed, the constitutional reform debates of the 1960s and 1970s are strong evidence to support the conclusion that there is no one predominant view of the proper allocation of powers in a federal system; rather, there are competing perspectives of the ideal system, with views about the proper distribution of legislative powers shaped by the individual's belief in other values promoted or protected by federalism, such as a stronger national or regional community responsive to the country's needs or loyalties, or increased economic efficiency.

W.R. Lederman, "Classification of Laws and the British North America Act"
in W.R. Lederman, *Continuing Canadian Constitutional Dilemmas*
(Toronto: Butterworths, 1981), at 236-43 (footnotes omitted)

Usually systems for the classification of laws result from the meditations of jurists and derive what authority they have from the prestige of their respective authors. But it is otherwise with a federal constitution which of necessity contains a complete and authoritative system for the classification of laws as the basis of its allocation of law-making powers between the different legislatures concerned. In the *BNA Act* such rules are found primarily in the well-known sections 91 and 92. These contain respectively enumerations of federal and provincial law-making powers. It is important to realize that these enumerated "subjects" or "matters" are classes of laws, not classes of facts. It is impossible for instance to look at a set of economic facts and say that the activity is trade and commerce within section 91(2) and therefore any law concerning it must be federal law. Rather, one must take a specific law (either actual or proposed) which is relevant to those facts and then ask if that rule is classifiable as a trade or commercial law. The Act very wisely recognizes this necessity in the wording of section 91(2). It does not say just "trade and commerce," it says rather "the regulation of trade and commerce," meaning of course "laws regulating trade and commerce."

The same can be said of all the enumerated classes in both sections 91 and 92. Some of them are obviously classes of laws on their face for they speak of rights, institutions, relations, or operations which have necessarily to be created or provided for by appropriate laws, e.g. taxation, legal tender, patents of invention and discovery, copyrights, marriage and divorce, criminal law, incorporation, municipal institutions, solemnization of marriage, and property and civil rights. The wording used for certain other classes makes them seem classes of fact, but these they cannot be. They must be read as the "trade and commerce" clause is worded: thus "seacoast and inland fisheries" truly means "laws regulating seacoast and inland fisheries." Similarly with such classes or categories as postal service, defence, banking, insolvency, and local works and undertakings. The late Chief Justice Harvey of Alberta seems to have put his finger on the point here being made when he said, in a recent case concerned with "banking" in section 91(15): "The word is used as the Statute [the *BNA Act*] says as describing a subject for legislation, not a definite object." We do not look just for banking as a matter of economic fact, we must look for regulation of banking as a matter of law. ...

II. The Application of Sections 91 and 92 of the BNA Act

Certain of the essential principles for the interpretation of the *BNA Act* now require consideration in detail in light of the foregoing analysis. In the first place the categories of laws enumerated in sections 91 and 92 are not in the logical sense mutually exclusive; they overlap or encroach upon one another in many more respects than is usually realized. To put it another way, many rules of law have one feature that renders them relevant to a provincial class of laws and another feature which renders them equally relevant logically to a federal class of laws. It is inherent in the nature of classification as a process that this should be so, and hence the concluding words of section 91 represent aspiration for the unattainable. It will be recalled that they read as follows: "And any Matter coming within any of the classes of subjects enumerated in this Section shall not be deemed to come within the Class of Matters of a local or private Nature comprised in the Enumeration of the Classes of Subjects by this Act assigned exclusively to the Legislatures of the Provinces." Over eighty years of judicial interpretation have demonstrated conclusively the impossibility of such mutual exclusion. ...

For a simple illustration, take the well-known rule that a will made by an unmarried person becomes void if and when he marries. Is this a rule of "marriage" (s. 91(26)) or of "property and civil rights" (s. 92(13))? In England and the common law provinces of Canada it occurs in the respective "*Wills Acts*," and its validity in Canada as provincial law has not been challenged. This would suggest it is deemed a rule of "property and civil rights" for constitutional purposes. Yet if we turn to Private International Law (which has similar problems of classification) we find English and Canadian courts in agreement that this provision about marriage voiding a pre-nuptial will is to be deemed a matrimonial law for purposes of Private International Law. Obviously, this rule could in addition be classed as testamentary or successive. In truth it is logically quite correct to classify it as matrimonial or successive or testamentary or as concerning property and civil rights. It is any or all of these things. The decision as to which classification is to be used for a given purpose has to be made on non-logical grounds of policy and justice by the legal authority with the duty and power of decision in that respect. The criteria of relative importance involved in such a decision cannot be logical ones, for logic merely displays to us as of equivalent logical value all the possible classifications. ...

How then do we determine the several features of a law by any one of which or by any combination of which it may be classified? This question takes us back to the question of the true meaning of the challenged law. In many of the cases we are told that it all depends on what is determined to be the "subject-matter" of the rule. Presumably this phraseology coupling "subject" and "matter" comes from the wording of the opening parts of sections 91 and 92, which speak of "exclusive Legislative Authority" extending "to all Matters coming within the Classes of Subjects next hereinafter enumerated" (s. 91), and "Laws in relation to Matters coming within the Classes of Subjects next hereinafter enumerated" (s. 92). As has been pointed out, what is really being dealt with is power to enact *laws coming within the classes of laws next hereinafter enumerated*, and the *BNA Act* could well be more concisely and clearly phrased in that way. "Subjects" and "matters" simply refer to meaning. Everything in a rule of law is "subject-matter" of it. "Subject-matter" can only refer to all features of its fact-category and the rights and duties prescribed. You must construe meaning before you can talk of subject-matter, and you only know what is subject-matter when you have settled meaning.

Further, in other cases a false antithesis is set up between the subject-matter of a rule on the one hand and its object or purpose on the other. For instance, Dr. MacRae states: "The Court, having regard to the language used in sections 91 and 92, has to find what the 'matter' is which is being legislated in relation to and in doing this it must look, not merely at the subject-matter of the legislation (in the sense of the thing legislated about), but also at the object or purpose of the legislation. In other words, it has to look not merely at the thing legislated *about*, but the object or purpose legislated *for*." This sounds plausible, but is not as helpful as it seems. In addition to speaking of the object or purpose of a rule, we may also speak of its intention and of its effects or consequences. But all these words lead us back to the one primary problem, the full or total meaning of the rule. There is an essential unity here that defies these grammatical attempts at separation. A rule of law expresses what should be human action or conduct in a given factual situation. We assume enforcement and observance of the rule and hence judge its meaning in terms of the consequences of the action called for. It is the effects of observance of the rule that constitute at least in part its intent, object, or purpose. Certainly the total meaning of the rule cannot be assessed apart from these effects. ...

It should be noted that the problem of the colourable statement cannot be dealt with except in accordance with the foregoing analysis of total meaning. A colourable law is one which really means something more than or different from what its words seem at first glance to say. A law may have been so worded as to make it seem that it has only provincially classifiable features of meaning, and only when the effects of it (if enforced) are assessed can one ascertain a fuller or different meaning which supplies federally classifiable features. ...

The matter of intention also causes some confusion at this point. It is virtually impossible to find determinate human intenders behind most statutes. The examination of Hansard would not be nearly as helpful as many jurists suggest, though it might have some value. On the whole, the position is as the Privy Council itself has stated it: "The question is, not what may be supposed to have been intended, *but what has been said*." Here, as in other departments of the law, it has to be taken that ordinary consequences are intended consequences. Ordinary consequences are those reasonably informed men would expect as effects of the course of conduct the rule prescribes. The word intention, with or without adjectives such as "real," "true," or "essential," could well be completely dispensed with. It is superfluous, and at best represents a pseudo-subjective approach to meaning. ...

Nevertheless, while all the effects of a particular rule are features of its meaning, it by no means follows that all are equally important. Let us suppose that the federal Government proposes to enact a heavy tax on the consumers of liquor. It can be seen that enforcement of the law will (a) bring in some revenue and (b) reduce consumption of liquor, which in turn will gladden the hearts of members of the WCTU, facilitate the diversion of more alcohol to the manufacture of explosives, and put some marginal distillers out of business. These are all effects of the law and features of its meaning by which, severally or in combination, it may be classified in different ways. Which of the logically possible classifications is to prevail? As this law would put certain distillers in the provinces out of business it is a law concerning "Property and Civil Rights in the Provinces." But in a time of national peril there would be little difficulty in deciding that country-wide diversion of alcohol to the manufacture of explosives was its most important object, purpose, effect, or feature of meaning. Thus this circumstance would be the crucial feature of meaning for purposes of the division of legislative powers, and the law would be deemed a law of the national emergency class allotted to the central Parliament.

This suggests the main thesis of this essay: *That a rule of law for purposes of the distribution of legislative powers is to be classified by that feature of its meaning which is judged the most important one in that respect.* The thesis so stated points to the heart of the problem of interpretation, i.e. whence come the criteria of relative importance necessary for such a decision? In this inquiry, the judges are beyond the aid of logic, because logic merely displays the many possible classifications, it does not assist in a choice between them. If we assume that the purpose of the constitution is to promote the well-being of the people, then some of the necessary criteria will start to emerge. When a particular rule has features of meaning relevant to both federal and provincial classes of laws, then the question must be asked, Is it better for the people that this thing be done on a national level, or on a provincial level? In other words is the feature of the challenged law which falls within the federal class more important to the well-being of the country than that which falls within the provincial class of laws? Such considerations as the relative value of uniformity and regional diversity, the relative merits of local versus central administration, and the justice of minority claims, would have to be weighed. Inevitably, widely prevailing beliefs in the country about these issues will be influential and presumably the judges should strive to implement such beliefs. Inevitably there will be some tendency for them to identify their own convictions as those which generally prevail or which at least are the right ones. On some matters there will not be an ascertainable general belief anyway. In the making of these very difficult relative-value decisions, all that can rightly be required of judges is straight thinking, industry, good faith, and a capacity to discount their own prejudices. No doubt it is also fair to ask that they be men of high professional attainment, and that they be representative in their thinking of the better standards of their times and their countrymen.

Furthermore, our judges need all the assistance they can be afforded by the provision of data relevant for their constitutional decisions. ... [It is true that] Canadian judges do not have to consider the substantive merit of a challenged law ... ; indeed they are accustomed to labour the point that they are not concerned with whether such a law is good or bad, necessary or unnecessary.

They say in effect that the malady and its proper cure are not their concern, rather that they have to ask only, Who is to be the physician? Yet does not the choice of physician depend to an important degree on the nature of the malady and of the proposed remedy? Admittedly if the challenged law is logically classifiable in only one way there is no problem, but the main thesis here is that such a situation will be rare, and that often so far as logic is concerned the challenged law will have features of meaning relevant to both federal and provincial classes of laws. Then our judges cannot be content simply to ask, Who is to be the physician? They must rather ask, Who is the better physician to prescribe in this way for this malady? ...

Lest a false impression of complete uncertainty and fluidity be conveyed by the foregoing, the importance of the rules of precedent that obtain in our courts should be remembered. However open logically the classification of a given type of law may have been when first it was considered by the highest court, that decision will in all probability foreclose the question of the correct classification should the same type of law come up again. ...

[F]requently there will be new laws, both federal and provincial, which the precedents on classification will not touch decisively or concerning which indeed there may be conflicting analogies. Thus in spite of the principles of precedent the full-blown problem of classification described earlier is often with us. Therefore, it is not merely those who would make or amend the federal constitution who must ask themselves and each other, What is truly of national concern and what is truly of provincial concern for purposes of law? Within the limits set by the terms of particular laws being challenged before them from time to time, the judges frequently confront this question *just as starkly as did the original constitution-makers themselves*. Further, as conditions change with the years, the relative importance of various classifiable features of particular laws may change as well. For instance the motor vehicle has brought to highway traffic today an interprovincial and international character undreamed of forty years ago; hence regulation of highway-using enterprises is now to be regarded to some extent in a new light. Another way to put this point is to say that changed economic and social conditions and a different moral climate will give to present or proposed laws new features of meaning by which they may be classified and may also alter judgments on the relative importance of their several classifiable features. ... The authority of appropriate precedents then will remove much of the uncertainty just described as implicit in the process of classification but inevitably much unpredictability will remain. The principles of stare decisis are important in our courts, but the degree of certainty and predictability their operation can provide is often much overestimated or misconceived.

The Supreme Court of Canada's general approach to questions of validity in the federalism context was summarized by Lamer J (as he then was) writing for a majority of the Court in *Starr v. Houlden*, [1990] 1 SCR 1366, 68 DLR (4th) 641, at 657 DLR:

> I begin with a few general comments on the approach to division of powers issues. The first step in judicial review in the context of division of powers is to identify the "matter" of the law ... This is done by looking for the dominant feature of the law, or to use the term of art, its "pith and substance." Professor Hogg in *Constitutional Law of Canada* (2d ed. 1985), at pp. 318-19, notes that pith and substance is determined by examining both the purpose and effect of the law. In undertaking the characterization of a law the Court must consider the legislative scheme, judicial precedent and what Professor Hogg refers to at p. 323 as a "concept of federalism" comprised of the enduring values in the allocation of power between the two levels of government. Once the matter or pith and substance of a law has been identified, it is necessary to assign it to a specific head of power under either s. 91 or s. 92 of the *Constitution Act, 1867*.

The *Morgentaler* case, which is excerpted below, was decided by the Supreme Court a few years after *Starr v. Houlden*. It illustrates the kinds of factors a court can take into account in determining the "matter" or the "pith and substance" of a law.

R v. Morgentaler
[1993] 3 SCR 463, 107 DLR (4th) 537

SOPINKA J (Lamer CJC, La Forest, L'Heureux-Dubé, Gonthier, Cory, McLachlin, Iacobucci, and Major JJ concurring): The question in this appeal is whether the Nova Scotia *Medical Services Act*, RSNS 1989, c. 281, and the regulation made under the Act, NS Reg. 152/89, are *ultra vires* the province of Nova Scotia on the ground that they are in pith and substance criminal law. The Act and regulation make it an offence to perform an abortion outside a hospital.

Between October 26 and November 2, 1989, the respondent performed 14 abortions at his clinic in Halifax. He was charged with 14 counts of violating the *Medical Services Act*. He was acquitted at trial after the trial judge held that the legislation under which he was charged was beyond the province's legislative authority to enact because it was in pith and substance criminal law. This decision was upheld by the Nova Scotia Court of Appeal. The Crown appeals from the Court of Appeal's decision with leave of this Court.

Facts and Legislation

In January 1988, this Court ruled that the *Criminal Code* provisions relating to abortion were unconstitutional because they violated women's *Charter* guarantee of security of the person: *R v. Morgentaler*, [1988] 1 SCR 30 (*Morgentaler (1988)*). At the same time the Court reaffirmed its earlier decision that the provisions were a valid exercise of the federal criminal law power: *Morgentaler v. The Queen*, [1976] 1 SCR 616 (*Morgentaler (1975)*). The 1988 decision meant that abortion was no longer regulated by the criminal law. It was no longer an offence to obtain or perform an abortion in a clinic such as those run by the respondent. A year later, in January 1989, it was rumoured in Nova Scotia that the respondent intended to establish a free-standing abortion clinic in Halifax. Subsequently, the respondent publicly confirmed his intention to do so.

On March 16, 1989, the Nova Scotia government took action to prevent Dr. Morgentaler from realizing his intention. The Governor in Council approved two identical regulations ... which prohibited the performance of an abortion anywhere other than in a place approved as a hospital under the *Hospitals Act*. At the same time it made a regulation ... denying medical services insurance coverage for abortions performed outside a hospital. These regulations are referred to collectively as the "March regulations." ...

... [A] court challenge to the March regulations was still outstanding on June 6, 1989, when the Minister of Health and Fitness introduced the *Medical Services Act* for first reading. The Act progressed rapidly through the legislature. It received third reading and Royal Assent on June 15, the last day of the legislative session. The relevant portions of the Act are as follows:

2. The purpose of this Act is to prohibit the privatization of the provision of certain medical services in order to maintain a single high-quality health-care delivery system for all Nova Scotians. *not true*

3. In this Act,

(a) "designated medical service" means a medical service designated pursuant to the regulations … .

4. No person shall perform or assist in the performance of a designated medical service other than in a hospital approved as a hospital pursuant to the Hospitals Act.

5. Notwithstanding the *Health Services and Insurance Act*, a person who performs or for whom is performed a medical service contrary to this Act is not entitled to reimbursement pursuant to that Act.

6(1) Every person who contravenes this Act is guilty of an offence and liable upon summary conviction to a fine of not less than ten thousand dollars nor more than fifty thousand dollars … . *prohibition*

7. Notwithstanding any other provision of this Act, where designated medical services are being performed contrary to this Act, the Minister may, at any time, apply to a judge of the Supreme Court for an injunction, and the judge may make any order that in the opinion of the judge the case requires.

8(1) The Governor in Council, on the recommendation of the Minister, may make regulations

(a) after consultation by the Minister with the Medical Society of Nova Scotia, designating a medical service for the purpose of this Act … .

The Medical Society was consulted after the passage of the Act, and a list of medical services was finalized. On July 20, 1989, the *Medical Services Designation Regulation*, NS Reg. 152/89, was made, designating the following medical services for the purposes of the Act:

(a) Arthroscopy

(b) Colonoscopy (which, for greater certainty, does not include flexible sigmoidoscopy)

(c) Upper Gastro-Intestinal Endoscopy

(d) Abortion, including a therapeutic abortion, but not including emergency services related to a spontaneous abortion or related to complications arising from a previously performed abortion

(e) Lithotripsy

(f) Liposuction

(g) Nuclear Medicine

(h) Installation or Removal of Intraocular Lenses

(i) Electromyography, including Nerve Conduction Studies

The March regulations were revoked on the same day … . Item (d) of the new regulation continued the March regulations' prohibition of the performance of abortions outside hospitals. Section 5 of the Act continued the denial of health insurance coverage for abortions performed in violation of the prohibition.

Despite these actions, Dr. Morgentaler opened his clinic in Halifax as predicted. … He was charged with 14 counts of unlawfully performing a designated medical service, to wit, an abortion, other than in a hospital approved as such under the *Hospitals Act*, contrary to s. 6 of the *Medical Services Act*. ...

When the case proceeded to trial in June 1990, Dr. Morgentaler did not dispute that he had performed the abortions as alleged. He argued, instead, that the Act and the regulation were inconsistent with the Constitution of Canada and consequently of no force or effect, on the grounds that they violate women's *Charter* rights to security of the person and equality and that they are an unlawful encroachment on the federal Parliament's exclusive criminal law jurisdiction. He also argued that the regulation was an abuse of discretion by the provincial cabinet and therefore in excess of its jurisdiction. ...

Analysis

A. General

The appellant argued that the *Medical Services Act* and the regulation are valid provincial legislation enacted pursuant to the province's legislative authority over hospitals, health, the medical profession and the practice of medicine. It relies particularly on heads (7), (13), and (16) of s. 92 of the *Constitution Act, 1867*, which give the province exclusive legislative authority over [hospitals, property and civil rights, and generally all matters of a merely local or private nature] ... .

The ground on which the legislation is challenged is head (27) of s. 91, which reserves "The Criminal Law ..." to Parliament. On the basis of the analysis that follows I conclude that the *Medical Services Act* and *Medical Services Designation Regulation* are criminal law in pith and substance and consequently *ultra vires* the province of Nova Scotia. The appeal must therefore be dismissed. ...

B. Classification of Laws

(1) "What's the 'Matter'?"

(Classification of a law for purposes of federalism involves first identifying the "matter" of the law and then assigning it to one of the "classes of subjects" in respect to which the federal and provincial governments have legislative authority under ss. 91 and 92 of the *Constitution Act, 1867*. This process of classification is "an interlocking one, in which the *British North America Act* and the challenged legislation react on one another and fix each other's meaning": B. Laskin, "Tests for the Validity of Legislation: What's the 'Matter'?" (1955), 11 *UTLJ* 114, at p. 127. Courts apply considerations of policy along with legal principle; the task requires "a nice balance of legal skill, respect for established rules, and plain common sense. It is not and never can be an exact science": F.R. Scott, *Civil Liberties and Canadian Federalism* (1959), at p. 26.)

A law's "matter" is its leading feature or true character, often described as its pith and substance: *Union Colliery Co. of British Columbia v. Bryden*, [1899] AC 580 (PC), at p. 587; see also *Whitbread v. Walley*, [1990] 3 SCR 1273, at p. 1286. There is no single test for a law's pith and substance. The approach must be flexible and a technical, formalistic approach is to be avoided. ... While both the purpose and effect of the law are relevant considerations in the process of characterization ... , it is often the case that the legislation's dominant purpose or aim is the key to constitutional validity. ...)

(2) Purpose and Effect

(A) "LEGAL EFFECT" OR STRICT LEGAL OPERATION

Evidence of the "effect" of legislation can be relevant in two ways: to establish "legal effect" and to establish "practical effect." The analysis of pith and substance necessarily starts with looking at the legislation itself, in order to determine its legal effect. "Legal effect" or "strict legal operation" refers to how the legislation as a whole affects the rights and liabilities of those subject to its terms, and is determined from the terms of the legislation itself. … Legal effect is often a good indicator of the purpose of the legislation … , but is relevant in constitutional characterization even when it is not fully intended or appreciated by the enacting body. …

The analysis of pith and substance is not, however, restricted to the four corners of the legislation (see, e.g., *Reference re Anti-Inflation Act*, [1976] 2 SCR 373, at pp. 388-89). Thus the court "will look beyond the direct legal effects to inquire into the social or economic purposes which the statute was enacted to achieve," its background and the circumstances surrounding its enactment … and, in appropriate cases, will consider evidence of the second form of "effect," the actual or predicted practical effect of the legislation in operation … . The ultimate long-term, practical effect of the legislation will in some cases be irrelevant. …

(B) THE USE OF EXTRINSIC MATERIALS

In determining the background, context and purpose of challenged legislation, the court is entitled to refer to extrinsic evidence of various kinds provided it is relevant and not inherently unreliable: *Reference re Residential Tenancies Act, 1979*, [1981] 1 SCR 714, at p. 723, *per* Dickson J. This clearly includes related legislation (such as, in this case, the March regulations and the former s. 251 of the *Criminal Code*), and evidence of the "mischief" at which the legislation is directed: *Alberta Bank Taxation Reference*, [*Reference re Alberta Legislation; AG Alberta v. AG Can.*, [1939] AC 117 (PC)], at pp. 130-33. It also includes legislative history, in the sense of the events that occurred during drafting and enactment; as Ritchie J, concurring in *Reference re Anti-Inflation Act, supra*, wrote at p. 437, it is "not only permissible but essential" to consider the material the legislature had before it when the statute was enacted.

The former exclusionary rule regarding evidence of legislative history has gradually been relaxed (*Reference re Upper Churchill Water Rights Reversion Act*, [1984] 1 SCR 297, at pp. 317-19), but until recently the courts have balked at admitting evidence of legislative debates and speeches. Such evidence was described by Dickson J in *Reference re Residential Tenancies Act, 1979, supra*, at p. 721 as "inadmissible as having little evidential weight," and was excluded in *Reference re Upper Churchill Water Rights Reversion Act, supra*, at p. 319, and *Attorney General of Canada v. Reader's Digest Association (Canada) Ltd.*, [1961] SCR 775. The main criticism of such evidence has been that it cannot represent the "intent" of the legislature, an incorporeal body, but that is equally true of other forms of legislative history. Provided that the court remains mindful of the limited reliability and weight of Hansard evidence, it should be admitted as relevant to both the background and the purpose of legislation. Indeed, its admissibility in constitutional cases to aid in determining the background and purpose of legislation now appears well established. …

I would therefore hold, as did Freeman JA in the Court of Appeal, that the excerpts from Hansard were properly admitted by the trial judge in this case. In a nutshell, this evidence demonstrates that members of all parties in the House understood the central feature of the proposed law to be prohibition of Dr. Morgentaler's proposed clinic on the basis of a common and almost unanimous opposition to abortion clinics *per se*. ...

(3) Scope of the Applicable Heads of Power

The issue we face in the present case is whether Nova Scotia has, by the present legislation, regulated the place for delivery of a medical service with a view to controlling the quality and nature of its health care delivery system, or has attempted to prohibit the performance of abortions outside hospitals with a view to suppressing or punishing what it perceives to be the socially undesirable conduct of abortion. The former would place the legislation within provincial competence; the latter would make it criminal law.

(A) THE CRIMINAL LAW

Section 91(27) of the *Constitution Act, 1867* gives the federal Parliament exclusive legislative jurisdiction over criminal law in the widest sense of the term. ...

[Sopinka J's discussion of the criminal law cases is omitted. Criminal law is defined, for the purposes of the division of powers, as any law that has as its dominant characteristic the prohibition of an activity, subject to penal sanctions, for a public purpose such as peace, order, security, health, or morality.]

(B) PROVINCIAL HEALTH JURISDICTION

The provinces have general legislative jurisdiction over hospitals by virtue of s. 92(7) of the *Constitution Act, 1867*, and over the medical profession and the practice of medicine by virtue of ss. 92(13) and (16). Section 92(16) also gives them general jurisdiction over health matters within the province. ...

In addition, there is no dispute that the heads of s. 92 invoked by the appellant confer on the provinces jurisdiction over health care in the province generally, including matters of cost and efficiency, the nature of the health care delivery system, and privatization of the provision of medical services.

(C) THE REGULATION OF ABORTION

In the UK and Canada, the prohibition of abortion with penal consequences has long been considered a subject for the criminal law. As early as the mid-nineteenth century, with the adoption of legislation imitating *Lord Ellenborough's Act* (UK), 43 Geo. 3, c. 58, through the time of Confederation and up to the 1969 amendments to the *Criminal Code* which introduced the relieving portion of s. 251 ... , the criminal law in Canada prohibited abortions with penal consequences; before the introduction of the relieving portion of s. 251 there was no such thing as a non-criminal abortion. As Dickson J (as he then was) said in *Morgentaler (1975)*, *supra*, at p. 672, "since Confederation, and indeed before, the law of Canada has regarded as criminal, interference with pregnancy, however early it may take place. ..."

The two *Morgentaler* decisions focus attention on the purpose or concern of abortion legislation to determine if it is truly criminal law: Is the performance or procurement of abortion prohibited as socially undesirable conduct? Is protecting the state interest in the foetus or balancing the interests of the foetus against those of women seeking abortions a primary objective of the legislation? Is the protection of the woman's health only an ancillary concern? And are other provincial concerns such as the establishment of hospitals or the regulation of the medical profession or the practice thereof merely incidental?

It is not necessary for the purposes of this appeal to attempt to delineate the scope of provincial jurisdiction to regulate the performance of abortions. Suffice it to say that any provincial jurisdiction to regulate the delivery of abortion services must be solidly anchored in one of the provincial heads of power which give the provinces jurisdiction to legislate in relation to such matters as health, hospitals, the practice of medicine and health care policy.

C. Application of the Principles to the Case at Bar

An examination of the terms and legal effect of the *Medical Services Act* and the *Medical Services Designation Regulation*, their history and purpose and the circumstances surrounding their enactment leads to the conclusion that the legislation's central purpose and dominant characteristic is the restriction of abortion as a socially undesirable practice which should be suppressed or punished. Although the evidence of the legislation's practical effect is equivocal, it is not necessary to establish that its immediate or future practical impact will actually be to restrict access to abortions in order to sustain this conclusion.

(1) Legal Effect: The Four Corners of the Legislation

Starting with the terms of the legislation, the *Medical Services Act* makes it an offence subject to significant fines (s. 6) to perform abortions or other services designated by the *Medical Services Designation Regulation* outside a hospital approved as such under the *Hospitals Act* (s. 4). It is impossible to tell from the legislation itself whether this amounts to a total prohibition of abortion (which all parties concede would be *ultra vires* the province), since extrinsic evidence is necessary to establish that abortions are available in Nova Scotia hospitals. The Act also denies public health insurance coverage for the performer and recipient of such services (s. 5), and provides for injunctive relief against violations of its terms (s. 7). It is entitled "*An Act to Restrict the Privatization of Medical Services*," and its purpose is expressed to be the prohibition of the privatization of certain medical services in order to maintain a single high-quality health care delivery system in the province (s. 2). ...

The majority in the Court of Appeal conceded that the province had the legislative authority to pass a law in the present form. I acknowledge that the legislation has the legal effect of preventing privatization by prohibiting the private (i.e., outside a hospital) provision of the designated services. But the legislation expressly prohibits the performance of abortions in certain circumstances with penal consequences, a subject, as I have said, traditionally regarded as part of the criminal law. ... The present legislation, prohibiting traditionally criminal conduct, is therefore of questionable validity on its face ... .

(2) Beyond the Four Corners

(A) DUPLICATION OF CRIMINAL CODE PROVISIONS

Once the legal effect of legislation is ascertained, it can be compared with that of any relevant legislation passed by the other level of government. ... Provincial legislation has been held invalid when it employs language "virtually indistinguishable" from that found in the *Criminal Code* ... . However, even when the legal effect of federal and provincial legislation is virtually identical this does not necessarily determine validity, since the provinces can enact provisions with the same legal effect as federal legislation provided this is done in pursuit of a provincial head of power ... . The duplication of *Criminal Code* language may raise an inference that the province has stepped into the realm of the criminal law; the more exact the reproduction, the stronger the inference that this is the dominant purpose of the enactment.

The guiding principle is that the provinces may not invade the criminal field by attempting to stiffen, supplement or replace the criminal law ... or to fill perceived defects or gaps therein ... . The legal effect of s. 251 and the present legislation, each taken as a whole, is quite different: among other things, s. 251 made it an offence for a woman to obtain an abortion, and prescribed the burdensome "therapeutic abortion committee" system and the "life or health" criterion for a legal abortion, none of which are present in the Act and regulation; and the present legislation prohibits other services besides abortion and directly concerns public health insurance coverage. Freeman JA was clearly right, however, that in so far as it prohibits abortion clinics the legal effect of the medical services legislation is completely embraced by s. 251 and, had the latter provision not been struck down, the present legislation would have been redundant in that respect. Section 251 is now, of course, inoperative. The absence of operative federal legislation does not enlarge provincial jurisdiction, though. It simply means that if the provincial legislation is found to be *intra vires*, no problem of paramountcy arises.

In my opinion the overlap of legal effects between the now defunct criminal provision and the Nova Scotia legislation is capable of supporting an inference that the legislation was designed to serve a criminal law purpose. It is a piece in the puzzle which along with the other evidence may demonstrate the true purpose of the legislation.

(B) BACKGROUND AND SURROUNDING CIRCUMSTANCES

The events leading up to and including the enactment of the Act and regulation do not support the appellant's assertions that the pith and substance of the legislation relate to provincial jurisdiction over health. On the contrary, they strengthen the inference that the impugned Act and regulation were designed to serve a criminal law purpose.

(I) THE COURSE OF EVENTS   *The legislation's special reaction to Dr.*

It is clear that the catalyst for government action was the rumour and later announcement of Dr. Morgentaler's intention to open his clinic. The Crown concedes this. The respondent was clearly, as the trial judge concluded, a "mischief" against which the legislation was directed. The government knew of Dr. Morgentaler's intention to open a clinic by some time in January 1989. It responded with the March regulations, which prohibited abortions outside hospitals and "de-insured" such services. ... The March regulations

were the first response to Dr. Morgentaler's announcement, and the subsequent legislation was the continuation and consolidation of that response. Together they constituted
a hastily devised plan aimed directly at ridding the province of Dr. Morgentaler and his
proposed clinic. The course of events suggests that this purpose was the principal purpose of the legislation and contributes to the impression that privatization and quality
assurance were only incidental concerns at best.

not concern privatization though claimed in S2

(II) HANSARD

I have reviewed the evidence of the legislative debates on the *Medical Services Act*, and
have concluded that they give a clear picture of what the members of the House, both
government and opposition, saw as being in issue. ...

The Hansard evidence demonstrates both that the prohibition of Dr. Morgentaler's
clinic was the central concern of the members of the legislature who spoke, and that
there was a common and emphatically expressed opposition to free-standing abortion
clinics *per se*. The Morgentaler clinic was viewed, it appears, as a public evil which should
be eliminated. The concerns to which the appellant submits the legislation is primarily
directed—privatization, cost and quality of health care, and a policy of preventing a two-
tier system of access to medical services—were conspicuously absent throughout most
of the legislative proceedings. ...

The appellant argues that even if the object of the legislation was to suppress free-
standing abortion clinics on grounds of public morals, this is not fatal to provincial jurisdiction. Although there has been some recognition of a provincial "morality" power, it is
clear that the exercise of such a power must be firmly anchored in an independent provincial head of power ... .

While legislation which authorizes the establishment and enforcement of a local standard of morality does not *ipso facto* "invade the field of criminal law" (see *Nova Scotia
Board of Censors v. McNeil*, [[1978] 2 SCR 662], at pp. 691-92), it cannot be denied that
interdiction of conduct in the interest of public morals was and remains one of the classic
ends of the criminal law ... .

In view of the foregoing, there is a strong inference that the purpose of the legislation
and its true nature relate to a matter within the federal head of power in respect of criminal law. In order to determine whether this is its dominant purpose or characteristic, it
is necessary to compare the above indicia of federal subject matter with indications of
provincial objectives.

(III) SEARCHING FOR PROVINCIAL OBJECTIVES

At trial the appellant presented evidence that the Act's objectives were to prevent privatization and the consequent development of a two-tier system of medical service delivery,
to ensure the delivery of high-quality health care, and to rationalize the delivery of medical services so as to avoid duplication and reduce public costs. ... [T]his evidence was
not established at trial to have been the basis for the impugned legislation. Indeed, Kennedy Prov. Ct. J considered the evidence and found that any privatization concerns were
"incidental to the paramount purpose of the legislation." ...

First, as to the health and safety of women and the argument that the in-hospital requirement was enacted because of a concern over quality assurance, there is no evidence

in the record to indicate that abortions performed in clinics like Dr. Morgentaler's pose any danger to the health of women. Counsel conceded that the quality of medical service in free-standing abortion clinics is comparable to that available in hospitals. ...

Second, the government did not express concerns about privatization in relation to this legislation or the March regulations until the Act was moved for second reading. ...

Third, it is significant that there is no evidence of any prior study or consultation regarding the cost-effectiveness or quality of medical services delivered in private clinics. ...

The lack of prior study or consultation is not raised to show that the province acted indiscreetly or ineffectually in pursuing provincial objectives, but rather to indicate that the evidence simply does not support the submission that these provincial objectives were the basis for the legislative action in question.

Another factor I consider relevant is that the "cost-effectiveness" rationale appears to be divorced from reality. Dr. Morgentaler's clinic will not represent a direct increase in the cost to the province of the provision of health care services. ...

A fifth consideration is the list of designated medical services itself. There is no apparent link between the different services. The only common denominator suggested by the appellant is that the government anticipated that these services might be attractive to private facilities. The appellant argued at trial and maintained before us, however, that the government's policy was to oppose the performance of any and all surgical procedures outside hospital. If that were the case, one might wonder why the Act did not prohibit the performance of surgical procedures generally outside a hospital. Designating nine apparently unrelated procedures does not accomplish this purpose.

If the means employed by a legislature to achieve its purported objectives do not logically advance those objectives, this may indicate that the purported purpose masks the legislation's true purpose. In *Westendorp v. The Queen*, [[1983] 1 SCR 43], Laskin CJ held that it was specious to regard a by-law which prohibited street prostitution as relating to control of the streets, since if that were its true purpose, "it would have dealt with congregation of persons on the streets or with obstruction, unrelated to what the congregating or obstructing persons say or otherwise do" (at p. 51). Here, one would expect that if the province's policy were to prohibit the performance of any surgical procedures outside hospitals, the legislation would have simply done so.

Finally, although I put little weight on this factor, I agree with both courts below that the relatively severe penalties provided for by the Act are relevant to its constitutional characterization. Section 6(1) of the Act prescribes fines of $10,000 to $50,000 for each infraction of the Act. Kennedy Prov. Ct. J and Freeman JA considered the relative severity of the fines as one indication that the fines were not simply measures to enforce a regulatory scheme, but penalties to punish abortion clinics as inherently wrong. Of course, s. 92(15) of the *Constitution Act, 1867* allows the provinces to impose punishment to enforce valid provincial law, and the mere addition of penal sanctions to an otherwise valid provincial legislative scheme does not make the legislation criminal law ... . However, the unusual severity of penalties may be taken into account in characterizing legislation ... .

D. Conclusion

(1) Pith and Substance

This legislation deals, by its terms, with a subject historically considered to be part of the criminal law—the prohibition of the performance of abortions with penal consequences. It is thus suspect on its face. Its legal effect partially reproduces that of the now defunct s. 251 of the *Criminal Code*, in so far as both precluded the establishment and operation of free-standing abortion clinics. Its legislative history, the course of events leading up to the Act's passage and the making of NS Reg. 152/89, the Hansard excerpts and the absence of evidence that privatization and the cost and quality of health care services were anything more than incidental concerns, lead to the conclusion that the *Medical Services Act* and the *Medical Services Designation Regulation* were aimed primarily at suppressing the perceived public harm or evil of abortion clinics. ... The primary objective of the legislation was to prohibit abortions outside hospitals as socially undesirable conduct, and any concern with the safety and security of pregnant women or with health care policy, hospitals or the regulation of the medical profession was merely ancillary. This legislation involves the regulation of the place where an abortion may be obtained, not from the viewpoint of health care policy, but from the viewpoint of public wrongs or crimes ... ‹

... I find unpersuasive the argument that this legislation is solidly anchored in s. 92(7), (13) or (16) of the *Constitution Act, 1867*. There is nothing on the surface of the legislation or in the background facts leading up to its enactment to convince me that it is designed to protect the integrity of Nova Scotia's health care system by preventing the emergence of a two-tiered system of delivery, to ensure the delivery of high-quality health care, or to rationalize the delivery of medical services so as to avoid duplication and reduce public health care costs. Any such objectives are clearly incidental to the central feature of the legislation, which is the prohibition of abortions outside hospitals as socially undesirable conduct subject to punishment. ...

Appeal dismissed.

NOTES AND QUESTIONS

1. The characterization of a law's pith and substance is a crucial step in the determination of its constitutional validity. Yet as Swinton noted above, the choice between competing characterizations of a law is not a "mechanistic" exercise. Lederman also emphasized that logic cannot be determinative: it "merely displays the many possible characterizations, it does not assist in a choice between them." The choice between competing characterizations will inevitably be influenced by background understandings of federalism and the values described by Simeon that ought to be furthered by a federal constitutional design. What values do you think influenced Sopinka J's characterization of the *Medical Services Act* as invalid criminal law rather than a valid law in relation to medical services? Were these values ones that ought to influence the interpretation of the division of powers?

2. If the province had evidence that the medical procedures listed in the Act posed greater dangers when performed outside of hospitals, would the result have been different? If not, what other sorts of evidence do you think would have been necessary to ground the Act in provincial jurisdiction?

3. Sopinka J declared the *Medical Services Act ultra vires* the Nova Scotia legislature even though, on its face, the Act appeared to deal exclusively with a matter within provincial legislative competence: the delivery of medical services. In essence, Sopinka J determined that the title of the Act, its stated purpose, and its terms masked its real purpose: punishing the provision of abortion services as a public evil. When the courts determine that legislation on its face addresses matters that are within its jurisdiction, but in pith and substance it is directed at matters outside its jurisdiction, they normally say the legislation is "colourable." In its recent decision in *Reference re Firearms Act (Can.)*, [2000] 1 SCR 783, 185 DLR (4th) 577, the Supreme Court of Canada provided the following description of the colourability doctrine in the context of a broader discussion of the way in which a law's effects are taken into account in the characterization process:

> [18] Determining the legal effects of a law involves considering how the law will operate and how it will affect Canadians. ... Within its constitutional sphere, Parliament is the judge of whether a measure is likely to achieve its intended purposes; efficaciousness is not relevant to the Court's division of powers analysis ... . Rather, the inquiry is directed to how the law sets out to achieve its purpose in order to better understand its "total meaning".... . In some cases, the effects of the law may suggest a purpose other than that which is stated in the law .... . In other words, a law may say that it intends to do one thing and actually do something else. Where the effects of the law diverge substantially from the stated aim, it is sometimes said to be "colourable."

In a puzzling portion of the *Morgentaler* judgment not reproduced above, Sopinka J stated that the colourability doctrine was not relevant to his analysis. Arguably, his judgment is a classic example of a court not allowing a legislature to covertly regulate a matter through colourable legislation when it lacks jurisdiction to regulate that matter openly. Why would he not have thought it appropriate to apply the colourability doctrine?

4. Sopinka J canvassed a wide range of evidence in reaching his conclusion that the dominant characteristic of the *Medical Services Act* was the criminal suppression of the provision of abortion services. He considered the text of the legislation, the events leading up to its enactment, the related policy documents prepared by the government, statements made in the legislature, the law's effects, and the plausibility of its stated purpose. While these kinds of evidence are all relevant to characterizing a law's pith and substance, and therefore should be considered, courts are not always as receptive to them as Sopinka J was in *Morgentaler*.

For example, contrast the Supreme Court's ruling in *Walter v. AG Alberta*, [1969] SCR 383. At issue was the validity of Alberta legislation, the *Communal Property Act*, that strictly regulated communal ownership of land. The legislation was enacted in response to public hostility to Hutterites who held land communally in accordance with their religious beliefs. The law was challenged on the grounds that its dominant characteristic was the punishment of a religious minority. Martland J, writing for the Court, upheld the law on the grounds that its pith and substance was a provincial matter, the regulation of property ownership. In doing so, Martland J focused on the legislative text, scarcely paying any heed to the legislative history, the social facts, or the absence of a plausible *intra vires* legislative purpose. What considerations would lead a judge to favour the more deferential approach to judicial review taken by Martland J in *Walter* over the more searching review undertaken by Sopinka J in *Morgentaler*?

5. *Morgentaler* exemplifies two common features of division-of-powers litigation in which the validity of legislation is called into question. One is the tendency of the opposing lawyers to present to the court two very different characterizations of the impugned legislation, one of which will provide the court with a basis on which to strike it down and the other of which will provide the court with a basis on which to uphold it. The second is a willingness on the part of courts to accept that their job is simply to choose between those two opposing characterizations. In that case, Dr. Morgentaler's lawyer argued that the appropriate characterization of the *Medical Services Act* was "[prohibiting] the performance of abortions outside hospitals with a view to suppressing or punishing what it perceives to be the socially undesirable conduct of abortion," while the government's lawyer argued that it was "[regulating] the place for delivery of a medical service with a view to controlling the quality and nature of its health care delivery system," and Justice Sopinka defined the issue as being which of the two characterizations the Court should accept. While it may be inevitable that the opposing lawyers would approach such cases in this way, it is not inevitable that the courts should understand their role in terms of simply choosing between the two options presented to them. It is clearly open to them to come up with their own characterization. Assuming it is not inevitable, do you think it is advisable for the courts to understand their role in such limited terms?

Given the passage of time since the *Constitution Act, 1867* was enacted, it is rare nowadays for there to be any serious dispute about the scope and meaning of the competing heads of power in federalism cases in which the validity of legislation is called into question. Most such cases therefore turn on which characterization of the impugned legislation—which "pith and substance" or "matter"—the court accepts. However, courts are still on occasion asked to define the scope and meaning of one of the heads of power in s. 91 or 92. That occurred in a recent reference by the Quebec government to the Quebec Court of Appeal that ended up in the Supreme Court of Canada, *Reference re Employment Insurance Act (Can.), ss. 22 and 23*, which is excerpted below. The specific head of power at issue in that case was s. 91(2A), which grants jurisdiction to Parliament over "Unemployment Insurance." Section 91(2A) was added to the list of heads of power in s. 91 in 1940 after the Privy Council had struck down the *Employment and Social Insurance Act*, a federal statute enacted in 1934 as part of Canada's "New Deal" and which represented the first attempt to provide unemployment insurance to Canadian workers. The Privy Council held that the statute invaded provincial jurisdiction over "Property and Civil Rights" in s. 92(13). (This decision, *AG Canada v. AG Ontario (The Employment and Social Insurance Act)*, [1937] AC 355, is excerpted in Chapter 6, "The 1930s: The Depression and the New Deal.")

Reference re Employment Insurance Act (Can.), ss. 22 and 23
[2005] 2 SCR 669, 2005 SCC 56, 258 DLR (4th) 243

[At issue in this case was the validity of the maternity and parental benefit provisions of the *Employment Insurance Act*, SC 1996, c. 23, enacted in 1971 and 1984 respectively. The position of the Quebec government was that these provisions were directed at supporting families with children, and therefore fell within s. 92(13), "Property and Civil Rights" and/or s. 92(16), "Generally all Matters of a Merely Local or Private Nature in the Province." The position of the federal government was that the provisions were directed at providing replacement income for working mothers and parents when their employment is interrupted as a result of the birth or adoption of a child, and fell within "Unemployment Insurance" in s. 91(2A). The Quebec Court of Appeal accepted the argument of the Quebec government and struck down the impugned provisions, and the federal government appealed.

Justice Deschamps, writing for a unanimous panel of seven members of the Supreme Court, allowed the federal government's appeal and upheld the impugned provisions. She began her analysis by characterizing the provisions as being "in pith and substance [mechanisms] for providing replacement income when an interruption of employment occurs as a result of the birth or arrival of a child." She then addressed the question of whether or not s. 91(2A) could be understood broadly enough to support provisions so characterized.]

DESCHAMPS J (McLachlin CJC and Binnie, LeBel, Fish, Abella, and Charron JJ concurring):

2.1 Principles of Interpretation

. . .

[9] At the first stage of the [division of powers] analysis, in order to identify the head of power, the Court takes a progressive approach to ensure that Confederation can be adapted to new social realities. The Court has on numerous occasions cited the "living tree" metaphor, and we need not revisit it here: *Reference re Same-Sex Marriage* [[2004] 3 SCR 698], at para. 29. While the debates or correspondence relating to the constitutional amendment are relevant to the analysis as regards the context, they are not conclusive as to the precise scope of the legislative competence. They reflect, to a large extent, the society of the day, whereas the competence is essentially dynamic ... . In giving them predominant weight, the Quebec Court of Appeal adopted an original intent approach to interpreting the Constitution rather than the progressive approach the Court has taken for a number of years.

[10] A progressive interpretation cannot, however, be used to justify Parliament in encroaching on a field of provincial jurisdiction. To derive the evolution of constitutional powers from the structure of Canada is delicate, as what that structure is will often depend on a given court's view of what federalism is. What are regarded as the characteristic features of federalism may vary from one judge to another, and will be based on political rather than legal notions. The task of maintaining the balance between federal and provincial powers falls primarily to governments. If an issue comes before a court, the court must refer to the framers' description of the power in order to identify its essential components, and must be guided by the way in which courts have interpreted the power in the past. In this area, the meaning of the words used may be adapted to modern-day realities, in a manner consistent with the separation of powers of the executive, legislative and judicial branches.

[11] Some heads that set forth narrow powers leave little room for interpretation. Other, broader, heads result in legislation that can have several aspects.

. . .

2.3.1 Background

[37] When the Privy Council declared the *Employment and Social Insurance Act* to be unconstitutional, there was no doubt that, *prima facie*, measures relating to insurance, and in particular measures relating to contracts of employment, were in relation to property and civil rights and were within the exclusive competence of the provincial legislatures ... . Because the UIA [*Unemployment Insurance Act*], 1940 essentially reiterated the provisions of the *Employment and Social Insurance Act*, it cannot be denied that it affected contracts of employment or insurance relating to those contracts. This means that when the Constitution was amended, a portion of the jurisdiction over property and civil rights was detached so that the aspects relating to unemployment insurance could be assigned to Parliament.

[38] There can be no doubt that a public unemployment insurance plan, in addition to the fact that it concerns insurance relating to contracts of employment, is also a social measure. Characterizing it in this way does not mean, however, that it can be associated exclusively with any one head of power. The term "social measure" has a number of aspects that may be associated just as validly with property and civil rights as with unemployment insurance. For instance, no one would deny that employment insurance benefits paid to workers who are laid off as a result of bankruptcy are in the nature of unemployment insurance. The measure, which affects property and civil rights, is undeniably social in nature, but it is also in the nature of unemployment insurance. To begin the analysis by classifying the maternity benefits provision as a social measure and to conclude from this that it is a matter under provincial jurisdiction is tantamount to evading a review of the scope of the constitutional amendment. The question that must be asked in order to determine the head of power to which maternity benefits relate is whether the provision, in pith and substance, falls within the jurisdiction assigned by the constitutional amendment.

[39] The Attorney General of Quebec submits that the jurisdiction over unemployment insurance is limited by the parameters defined in the early legislation. Under those Acts, to be entitled to benefits, insured persons had to have lost their employment involuntarily, and had to be capable of and available for work. In so arguing, the Attorney General of Quebec equates the field of jurisdiction assigned by s. 91(2A) of the *Constitution Act, 1867* to the initial exercise of the federal power. This approach is inappropriate in more than one respect, the most obvious being that the eligibility requirements established in the scheme of the UIA, 1940 may be modified, provided that the scheme still represents a valid exercise of the jurisdiction over unemployment insurance. Thus, no one would think of questioning the right to modify the eligibility requirements to calculate insurable periods in hours rather than weeks. Such a modification would plainly make the scheme more accessible to part-time workers, but it would in no way change the fundamental nature of unemployment insurance. The question is therefore not the way in which Parliament initially exercised its jurisdiction, but the scope of its jurisdiction over unemployment insurance.

[40] While the views of the framers are not conclusive where constitutional interpretation is concerned, the context in which the amendment was made is nonetheless relevant. If the objectives of the framers are taken as a starting point, it will be easier to determine the scope of the jurisdiction that was transferred, and then to determine how it may be adapted to contemporary realities.

2.3.2 Circumstances of the Transfer of Jurisdiction

[41] In a letter sent to each of the provincial premiers on November 5, 1937, then Prime Minister W.L. Mackenzie King asked whether their provinces would agree to jurisdiction over unemployment insurance being assigned to Parliament. The letter contains an outline of the justification cited by the federal government at that time:

> My dear Premier:
>
> My colleagues and I are convinced that a national system of unemployment insurance would contribute materially to individual security and industrial stability throughout Canada, and would assist in mitigating the distress incident to any recurrence of widespread unemployment.
>
> A strong recommendation with respect to national control of employment offices, based upon a full investigation of the unemployment situation throughout the Dominion, has been submitted to the government by the National Employment Commission. We share the opinion that a national employment service within federal jurisdiction is a necessary complement of any plan of national unemployment insurance.

On May 13, 1940, Quebec agreed to the federal request.

· · ·

[43] In essence, the purpose of the transfer of jurisdiction was to equip Canada with the tools it needed to mitigate the effects of anticipated unemployment by providing certain classes of unemployed persons with benefits and by setting up job search centres. The transfer of jurisdiction was to be a tool for internal organization involving both short-term relief measures, namely benefits, and medium-term measures, namely job placement services for the unemployed.

[44] … The nature of unemployment has changed as prevailing conditions in Canada, and the needs of Canadians, have changed. Parliament must adapt its actions to new circumstances, in a manner consistent with the limits resulting from the constitutional division of powers. In a case such as this, where a specific power has been detached from a more general power, the specific power cannot be evaluated in relation to the general power, because any evolution would then be regarded as an encroachment. Rather, it is necessary to consider the essential elements of the power and to ascertain whether the impugned measure is consistent with the natural evolution of that power.

2.3.3 Essential Elements of Unemployment Insurance

[45] On the one hand, no constitutional head of power is static. On the other hand, the evolution of society cannot justify changing the nature of a power assigned by the Constitution to either level of government. …

[46] In constitutional interpretation, the essential elements of a power are deter-mined by adopting a generous reading of the words used, taken in their strictly legal context. The interpretation may also be expanded by having regard to relevant historical elements.

[47] The jurisdiction over unemployment insurance must be interpreted progres-sively and generously. It must be considered in the context of a measure that applies throughout Canada and the purpose of which, according to the intention of the framers of the constitutional amendment, is to curb the destitution caused by unemployment and provide a framework for workers' re-entry into the labour market.

[48] With these principles and objectives in mind, four characteristics that are es-sential to a public unemployment insurance plan can be identified:

(1) It is a public insurance program based on the concept of social risk
(2) the purpose of which is to preserve workers' economic security and ensure their re-entry into the labour market
(3) by paying temporary income replacement benefits
(4) in the event of an interruption of employment.

[49] These four characteristics do not take into account the way a plan may have been implemented over the years, but allow changes in the labour market to be taken into consideration. Thus, the social risks associated with unemployment may vary from one period to another, and the way that the needs of the plan are calculated may be revised. Social policy choices are part of the exercise of the jurisdiction. They do not define what it is.

[50] Having defined the essential characteristics of a public unemployment insurance plan, I will now address two specific objections raised by the Attorney General of Que-bec. He submits, first, that maternity benefits are granted in respect of a voluntary ab-sence from work and cannot be regarded as relating to insurance. He also asserts that the individuals who receive maternity benefits are not unemployed, because they are not available for work.

2.3.4 Maternity Benefits as an Insurance Measure

[51] In *Martin Service Station* [*Martin Service Station Ltd. v. Minister of National Rev-enue* (1976), [1977] 2 SCR 996], at p. 1004, Beetz J accepted that Parliament's jurisdiction over unemployment insurance is qualified by an insurance aspect. Citing that principle, the Attorney General of Quebec submits that an interruption of work due to maternity cannot be insured against, because no risk is involved. He defines a risk as [TRANSLA-TION] "a fortuitous event the materialization [of which cannot] depend exclusively on the will of the parties, and in particular on the will of the insured."

[52] While I do not dispute that this narrow definition of the word "risk" is often used in private insurance plans, I am of the view that it cannot be used to exclude mater-nity from any unemployment insurance plan.

[53] The Attorney General's argument based on the absence of risk reflects the argu-ments addressed by this Court in *Brooks v. Canada Safeway Ltd.*, [1989] 1 SCR 1219, at pp. 1237-38. In that case, the Court had to decide whether pregnancy could be covered

by an insurance plan even though it did not involve an accident or illness. The employer submitted that it was excluded because it was a voluntary condition. The employer's argument was not accepted. Dickson CJ wrote the following:

> It seems indisputable that in our society pregnancy is a valid health-related reason for being absent from work. It is to state the obvious to say that pregnancy is of fundamental importance in our society. Indeed, its importance makes description difficult. To equate pregnancy with, for instance, a decision to undergo medical treatment for cosmetic surgery—which sort of comparison the respondent's argument implicitly makes—is fallacious. If the medical condition associated with procreation does not provide a legitimate reason for absence from the workplace, it is hard to imagine what would provide such a reason. Viewed in its social context pregnancy provides a perfectly legitimate health-related reason for not working and as such it should be compensated by the Safeway plan. In terms of the economic consequences to the employee resulting from the inability to perform employment duties, pregnancy is no different from any other health-related reason for absence from the workplace. [pp. 1237-38]

[54] In our times, having a child is often the result of a deliberate act decided on by one or both parents. There are many facets to pregnancy, however. Despite all the technological progress that has been made, conception does not result from a mathematical calculation that can be used to determine when or even if it will occur. In addition, the benefit derived from procreation extends beyond the benefit to the parents. Children are one of society's most important assets, and the contribution made by parents cannot be overstated. If pregnancy may be regarded as an insurable risk in private insurance plans, as was held in *Brooks*, then *a fortiori* it may be so regarded in a public plan.

[55] The approach taken by the Attorney General of Quebec therefore disregards the collective impact of the parents' decision and the social role of a public insurance plan. Apart from the fact that it is perfectly legitimate for a commercial insurer to agree to insure pregnant women against the loss of employment income, it must be acknowledged that the public nature of the unemployment insurance plan provides even greater justification for the decision to have all contributors assume together the risk of the loss of women's earnings that is associated with maternity. Just as the marginalization of seasonal workers cannot justify excluding them, ... protection against the loss of earnings that results from maternity is a social policy decision. Even though some people may see a tenuous connection with the concept of insurable risk in the strict sense, the jurisdiction in relation to unemployment is in the nature of social insurance. This means that the concept of risk may be understood in the social, and not the actuarial, sense. S. Ledoux provides a helpful analysis of the main characteristics of a social insurance plan and the concept of risk that applies to such a plan in *L'influence du droit constitutionnel dans l'émergence et l'évolution du droit aux prestations de maternité, d'adoption et parentales au sein de la Loi sur l'assurance-chômage* (1991), at p. 76:

> [TRANSLATION] Social insurance is the application, on a much larger scale, of the principle of pooling that has long been the basis of insurance. Social insurance [is] a special technique of organizing provision collectively by securing contributions from various groups for *a need that cannot be left safely to individuals' or families' own resources*. [L.C. Marsh, *Report on*

Social Security for Canada (1943), at pp. 10 and 15] *The primary objective of social insurance is therefore to reduce individuals' economic insecurity by promising them compensation in relation to social risks.* [L. Poulin Simon, *Les assurances sociales pour une sécurité du revenu des salariés* (1981), at p. 7] [Emphasis added.]

[56] The decision to offer women the possibility of receiving income replacement benefits when they are off work due to pregnancy is therefore a social policy decision that is not incompatible with the concept of risk in the realm of insurance, and that can moreover be harmoniously incorporated into a public unemployment insurance plan.

2.3.5 Maternity Benefits as an Unemployment Protection Measure

[57] The Attorney General of Quebec also argues that pregnancy cannot be characterized as an unemployment situation because a pregnant woman is not capable of and available for work. This argument cannot be accepted either.

[58] The Depression and war that led to the realization that a national unemployment insurance plan was necessary ended a long time ago, but unemployment itself endures. The nature of unemployment has changed, however. The unemployment that was foreseen in the 1930s was expected to result from the end of war-related production activities. It was conjunctural unemployment. But unemployment can also relate to the period between the time when a person loses one job and the time when he or she is hired for another job, apart from any structural constraint in a particular industry. ...

[59] The labour market also experiences technological unemployment, that is, unemployment brought about by technological change. Whether unemployment is conjunctural, structural, frictional or technological, the interruption of employment will undeniably be regarded as an unemployment situation regardless of the nature of the unemployment.

[60] The eligibility requirements for benefits under the UIA, 1940 have been expanded to take the new realities into account. Availability for employment does not necessarily mean that there are realistic chances of finding employment. Seasonal unemployment provides a clear illustration of this reality. While the first legislation excluded all employment in agriculture, forestry, fishing and hunting (UIA, 1940, First Schedule, Part II), there can now be no question regarding the public plan's support in relation to these economic activities, which are vital to Canada but are subject to constraints over which employers and employees have no control.

[61] The expressions "unemployed person," "unemployed" and "unemployment" have a variety of meanings. For example, according to the *Nouveau Petit Robert* (2003), at p. 431, a "*chômeur*" [unemployed person] is a person who is involuntarily deprived of employment; the word "*chômé*" [unemployed] relates to a requirement to stop working; and the word "*chômage*" [unemployment], in its ordinary sense, means an interruption of work resulting from a lack of employment. However, that dictionary also gives a more modern definition, which refers simply to an interruption of work. *Merriam-Webster's Collegiate Dictionary* (10th ed. 1994), at p. 1290, defines the expression "unemployment insurance" as follows: "social insurance against involuntary unemployment that provides unemployment compensation for a limited period to unemployed workers."

[62] The ordinary meaning fits easily into the early unemployment insurance legislation. Stable, permanent employment was indeed the rule at that time. However, the eli-

gibility rules in those statutes do not define the limits of Parliament's jurisdiction. Today, interruptions of employment have multiple causes. Lengthy layoffs, when a worker is entitled to be recalled, and temporary or part-time employment are only a few examples of situations indicating a need to reflect on the concept of unemployment. The idea of a "lack of employment" or of a situation being involuntary is not a reliable guide. The modern meaning, which simply requires that there be an interruption of employment, is a better reflection of the contemporary reality of the workplace and more readily incorporates the meaning given to the other words that derive from the same root.

[63] Furthermore, some new kinds of benefits have been considered by the courts, and in each case this Court has interpreted the provisions liberally. For example, a provision that discriminated against fishers was held to be invalid: *Attorney General of Canada v. Silk*, [1983] 1 SCR 335. In another case, teaching contracts were construed so as not to interfere with an entitlement to maternity benefits: *Dick v. Deputy Attorney General of Canada*, [1980] 2 SCR 243.

[64] A review of the circumstances surrounding the inclusion of interruptions of employment due to illness offers a helpful parallel. The possibility of making benefits available to contributors who were sick was studied prior to the enactment of the UIA, 1940: *Report of the Royal Commission on Dominion-Provincial Relations* (1940) (Rowell-Sirois Report), vol. II, at pp. 25, 31 and 40. This suggests at the very least that, despite the fact that the contributor would not be available for work, such benefits did not at the time appear to be antinomic to unemployment insurance. From this perspective, the obligations to seek employment and to be capable of working are regarded as mechanisms for screening applications and providing an incentive to return to the labour market, and not as essential characteristics of the constitutional power.

[65] The requirement that a claimant seek or be available for employment, which is inapplicable in the case of maternity benefits, is sometimes unrealistic. For example, seasonal workers or people working in remote regions will often be unsuccessful if they seek work during their periods of interruption of earnings. The nature of unemployment varies from one period to another, from one region to another and from one group to another, but the reality remains the same. These are workers who are not receiving their employment income.

[66] The extent of the protection required by Canadian society changes with the needs of the labour force. A growing portion of the labour force is made up of women, and women have particular needs that are of concern to society as a whole. An interruption of employment due to maternity can no longer be regarded as a matter of individual responsibility. Women's connection to the labour market is well established, and their inclusion in the expression "unemployed persons" is as natural an extension as the extension involving other classes of insured persons who lose their employment income. To limit a public unemployment insurance plan, from a constitutional perspective, to cases in which contributors are actively seeking employment or are available for employment would amount to denying its social function. The social nature of unemployment insurance requires that Parliament be able to adapt the plan to the new realities of the workplace. Some eligibility requirements derive from the essence of the unemployment concept, while other requirements are, rather, mechanisms that reflect a social policy choice linked to the implementation of the plan.

2.3.6 Conclusion with Respect to the Identification of the Head of Power

[67] The Attorney General of Quebec submits that the social program under which maternity benefits are paid is, in pith and substance, a measure to assist families. While that is an undeniable effect, it is not the pith and substance of the program. The EIA [*Employment Insurance Act*, SC 1996, c. 23] governs the entitlement to benefits: it entitles pregnant women to receive benefits when they sustain an interruption of earnings. However, not all the various aspects of interruptions of work associated with maternity relate to unemployment insurance. Maternity leave is not governed by the EIA. Parliament does not grant female workers either maternity leave or job security. Because the provinces have a general power in relation to civil rights, it is the provinces that are responsible for establishing most of the rules that are needed to protect the jobs of pregnant women. Those rules are provided for in provincial statutes, and are often incorporated into individual contracts of employment and collective labour agreements. ...

[68] In pith and substance, maternity benefits are a mechanism for providing replacement income during an interruption of work. This is consistent with the essence of the federal jurisdiction over unemployment insurance, namely the establishment of a public insurance program the purpose of which is to preserve workers' economic security and ensure their re-entry into the labour market by paying income replacement benefits in the event of an interruption of employment.

[Justice Deschamps then went on to hold that parental benefits could also be supported by s. 91(2A).]

NOTES AND QUESTIONS

1. Was Justice Deschamps correct to use the original conception of unemployment insurance invoked by the government of Quebec as merely the starting point for her analysis of the scope of s. 91(2A) instead of as a binding constraint? Does it make sense for judges to say that the original intent of the drafters is an appropriate source of guidance in the interpretation of a constitutional provision, but then give it such little weight?

2. The Supreme Court of Canada had occasion to consider the constitutionality of several other provisions of the *Employment Insurance Act*, SC 1996, c. 23 in *Confederation des syndicates nationaux v. Canada (Attorney-General)*, 2008 SCC 68. The provisions under attack dealt with a broad range of issues, including the addition of new benefits (wage subsidies, earnings supplements, self-employment assistance, job-creation partnerships, and skills, loans and grants); rate-setting mechanisms; the accumulation of surpluses; and the allocation of surpluses to the federal government's Consolidated Revenue Fund. All but one of the provisions was upheld (the one exception was a rate-setting mechanism that was held to offend s. 53 of the *Constitution Act, 1867*, which prescribes a special process for the levying of taxes). In his analysis of the constitutionality of the provisions creating the new benefits, Justice LeBel, writing for a unanimous court, invoked the judgment in the *Employment Insurance Act Reference* in support of the following propositions (at para. 30):

In [the] analysis of the content of legislative powers, changes in the way such powers are exercised and in the interplay of the powers assigned to the two levels of government often raise difficult problems. The solutions that must be applied when exercising powers change where new problems must be addressed. However, the evolution of society cannot serve as a pretext for changing the nature of the division of powers, which is a fundamental component of the Canadian federal system. The power in question must be interpreted generously, but in a manner consistent with its legal context, having regard to relevant historical elements (*Reference*, at paras. 45-46; H. Brun, G. Tremblay and E. Brouillet, *Droit constitutionnel*, 5th ed. (2008), at 201-2).

3. For another example of a recent case in which the meaning and scope of a head of power was at issue, see *Same-Sex Marriage Reference*, [2004] 3 SCR 698, 2004 SCC 79, 246 DLR (4th) 193. One of the four questions put to the Supreme Court of Canada in that case required it to decide whether the term "marriage" in s. 91(26), which grants jurisdiction over "Marriage and Divorce" to Parliament, had to be understood today as it would have been in 1867, and as therefore meaning the union of a man and a woman. The Court, invoking the image of Canada's constitution as a "living tree," unanimously rejected such an interpretive approach and held that it was open to Parliament today to redefine marriage to include unions between people of the same sex. The Court made the following statement about "progressive" interpretation of the heads of power in ss. 91 and 92 (at para. 23):

> A large and liberal, or progressive, interpretation ensures the continued relevance and, indeed, legitimacy of Canada's constituting document. By way of progressive interpretation our Constitution succeeds in its ambitious enterprise, that of structuring the exercise of power by the organs of the state in times vastly different from those in which it was crafted. For instance, Parliament's legislative competence in respect of telephones was recognized on the basis of its authority over interprovincial "undertakings" in s. 92(10)(a) even though the telephone had yet to be invented in 1867: *Toronto (City) v. Bell Telephone Co.* (1904), [1905] AC 52 (Ontario PC). Likewise, Parliament is not limited to the range of criminal offences recognized by the law of England in 1867 in the exercise of its criminal law power in s. 91(27): *Proprietary Articles Trade Assn. v. Canada (Attorney General)*, [1931] AC 310 (Canada PC), at p. 324.

(See also *Ward v. Canada (Attorney General)*, [2002] 1 SCR 569, 2002 SCC 17, 210 DLR (4th) 42, dealing with Parliament's power over "Sea Coast and Inland Fisheries" in s. 91(12). This case is discussed further in Chapter 11, Criminal Law.)

B. Double Aspect Doctrine

W.R. Lederman, "Classification of Laws and the British North America Act"
in W.R. Lederman, *Continuing Canadian Constitutional Dilemmas* (Toronto: Butterworths, 1981), at 243-45 (footnotes omitted)

Having explored the main problem of interpretation regarding our constitutional division of legislative powers, we may now attend in detail to the particular doctrines developed by the judges to facilitate the making of the necessary decisions. In the case of many, if not most, particular laws, the overlapping of federal and provincial categories of laws logically relevant is inevitable, no matter how often the *BNA Act* cries "exclusive." The courts have dealt with this overlapping in a number of ways. For one thing, they have

limited the generality of the classes of laws in sections 91 and 92 by the so-called principle of "mutual modification," and have thus eliminated some of the encroachment of one
upon the other. For example, consider the relation of the federal class, "regulation of
trade and commerce," with the provincial class, "property and civil rights." Trade and
commerce is carried on in articles in which persons have property and in respect of
which they have civil rights. Obviously, in the logical sense there is here a wide overlapping. However, speaking generally, the courts have said that "regulation of trade and
commerce" is to be reduced in generality and read as "regulation of interprovincial and
international trade and commerce." Likewise, "property and civil rights" is to be rendered "property and civil rights except those involved in interprovincial and international trade and commerce." By these operations the overlapping of the literal words of the
statute is reduced and some additional degree of exclusiveness is imparted to federal and
provincial classes of laws. The reading of sections 91 and 92 as a whole certainly makes
it clear that some of this rewording is necessary.

Nevertheless, in spite of all that can or should be done by mutual modification, some
overlapping inevitably remains. Where this occurs, either one of two things has then
been done. First, the nature of the challenged law relevant to a provincial class of powers
has been completely ignored as only an "incidental affectation" of the provincial sphere,
and the law concerned has been classed only by that feature of it relevant to a federal
class of laws. Thus, in spite of the logical overlap the decision is made that only the federal Parliament has power to enact the challenged law. Obviously this decision involves a
judgment that the provincial feature of the law is quite unimportant relative to its federal
feature. On the other hand if the federal feature be deemed quite unimportant relative to
the provincial feature, then the converse decision would be made.

But if the contrast between the relative importance of the two features is not so sharp,
what then? Here we come upon the double-aspect theory of interpretation, which constitutes the second way in which the courts have dealt with inevitable overlapping categories. When the court considers that the federal and provincial features of the challenged
rule are of roughly equivalent importance so that neither should be ignored respecting
the division of legislative powers, the decision is made that the challenged rule could be
enacted by either the federal Parliament or a provincial legislature. In the language of the
Privy Council, "subjects which in one aspect and for one purpose fall within section 92,
may in another aspect and for another purpose fall within section 91." Clearly this decision raises some further problems. Under such principles of interpretation there may
well be both a valid federal law and a valid provincial law directed to the same persons
concerning the same things, but requiring from them different courses of conduct and
thus having certain differing effects. Now if these different courses of conduct and effects
are merely cumulative and not conflicting, then both rules may operate. But, if the two
rules call for inconsistent behaviour from the same people, they are in conflict or collision and both cannot be obeyed. In these circumstances the courts have laid it down that
the federal rule is to prevail and the provincial one is inoperative and need not be observed. The suspension of the provincial law continues so long as there is a federal law
inconsistent in the sense explained. This is known as the doctrine of "Dominion paramountcy." Thus, it is a principle of our constitution that in the event of collision between
a federal law and a provincial law each valid under the double-aspect theory, the federal

features of the former law are considered in the last analysis more important than the provincial features of the latter. At this ultimate point of conflict, presumably the federal classes and features relevant to them are deemed the more important simply because they have a national as opposed to a sectional reference. At any rate, "Dominion paramountcy" is said to be called for by the concluding words of section 91, quoted earlier.

In the following excerpt from *Multiple Access*, Dickson J (as he then was) relies upon Lederman's understanding of the operation of the double aspect doctrine to find a double aspect over regulation of insider trading in the securities of federally incorporated companies.

Multiple Access Ltd. v. McCutcheon
[1982] 2 SCR 161, 138 DLR (3d) 1

[The Ontario *Securities Act*, RSO 1970, c. 426 prohibited insider trading in shares trading on the Toronto Stock Exchange. The *Canada Corporations Act*, RSC 1970, c. C-32 had almost identical provisions, applicable to corporations incorporated under federal law.

Insider trading is the purchase or sale of corporate securities by someone who has information about the value of the shares not available to other shareholders or to members of the general public. Insider trading is usually carried out by officers or employees of a company who know that the values of the shares will go up or down when information is released by the company or some other source. Shareholders who are not privy to the confidential information are at a disadvantage in this kind of trading. The insider-trading prohibitions protect such shareholders by regulating the marketplace in shares and also by enabling them to initiate proceedings against alleged insider traders.

Such a shareholder action was initiated against insiders of Multiple Access Inc., a federally incorporated company, with respect to trades on the Toronto Stock Exchange. The allegation was that these insiders took the opportunity to buy shares in the company, relying on their knowledge that the Canadian Radio-television and Telecommunications Commission would soon announce the grant of a licence to the company.

The shareholder initiated the proceeding under the Ontario *Securities Act* and the Ontario Securities Commission took carriage of the case. The respondents, the alleged insider traders, argued that the Ontario statute could not validly apply to their case because the regulation of the trading in shares of federally incorporated companies falls within exclusive federal jurisdiction. In the alternative, they relied on the doctrine of paramountcy to assert that the Ontario provisions were rendered inoperative, in the case of alleged insider trading in the shares of a federally incorporated company, by the provisions of the *Canada Corporations Act* that deal with the issue. This latter argument was advantageous to the alleged insider traders because the limitation period for initiating an action under the federal statute had already elapsed.

The Supreme Court's approach to the paramountcy issue is discussed in section IV of this chapter, below. Before reaching the paramountcy issue, the Court had to find that the relevant provisions of the *Canada Corporations Act* and the Ontario *Securities Act* were both valid and that both applied to trading in Ontario in the shares of a federally incorporated company. The Court's analysis of these issues, which relies heavily on the double aspect doctrine, is reproduced below. The majority held that both statutes were valid and applicable on the facts. Three dissenting judges, Estey, Beetz, and Chouinard JJ, decided that the federal provisions were invalid. The dissenters characterized the legislation as the regulation of securities transactions falling within provincial jurisdiction over property and civil rights, rather than as regulation of the functional aspects of a federally incorporated company.]

DICKSON J (Laskin CJC, Martland, Ritchie, McIntyre, and Lamer JJ concurring): ... I should like to turn now to the first constitutional question, namely, are ss. 100.4 and 100.5 of the *Canada Corporations Act ultra vires* the Parliament of Canada in whole or in part? ...

... [T]here may be a temptation to regard the insider trading provisions of the *Canada Corporations Act* as redundant having regard to the almost identical provisions found in the Ontario legislation applicable to federal companies as well as Ontario companies. Any such temptation should be resisted. The validity of the federal legislation must be determined without heed to the Ontario legislation. Further, a number of the provinces have not yet enacted insider trading legislation. Striking down the federal legislation would leave federal companies, having head offices in those provinces, and their shareholders, without the double protection, which Ontario shareholders now enjoy. A declaration of invalidity of the federal act would create a potential gap in the present regulatory schemes that might be exploited by the unprincipled.

I turn now to the main question. Does the "matter" (or pith and substance) of the insider trading provisions of the federal act fall within a "class of subject" (or head of power) allocated to Parliament? ... Sections 100.4 and 100.5 put teeth into s. 100 of the Act. Viewed in isolation it can no doubt be argued that their matter is the trading in securities. Viewed in context, however, they are, in my opinion, company law. They fit properly and comfortably into Part I of the *Canada Corporations Act*. The provisions deal with obligations attached to the ownership of shares in a federal company, which extend to shareholders, officers and employees of such companies, a subject matter that is not within the exclusive jurisdiction of provincial legislatures. The provisions are also directed to the relationship between management and shareholders of federal companies. Their enactment by Parliament is in the discharge of its company law power.

It has been well established ever since *John Deere Plow Co. v. Wharton*, [1915] AC 330 (PC) that the power of legislating with reference to the incorporation of companies with other than provincial objects belonged exclusively to the Dominion Parliament as a matter covered by the expression "the peace, order and good government of Canada" ... . The power of Parliament in relation to the incorporation of companies with other than provincial objects has not been narrowly defined. The authorities are clear that it goes well beyond mere incorporation. It extends to such matters as the maintenance of the company, the protection of creditors of the company and the safeguarding of the interests of the shareholders. It is all part of the internal ordering as distinguished from the commercial activities ... . Insider malfeasance affects, directly and adversely, corporate powers, organization, internal management. It affects also financing because shareholders and potential shareholders must be assured the company's affairs will be scrupulously and fairly conducted; otherwise the raising of capital, clearly an element of company law, will be inhibited. ...

Because "[t]he language of [ss. 91 and 92] and of the various heads which they contain obviously cannot be construed as having been intended to embody the exact disjunctions of a perfect logical scheme" (*John Deere Plow Co. v. Wharton, supra*, at p. 338 per Viscount Haldane), a statute may fall under several heads of either s. 91 or s. 92. For example, a provincial statute will often fall under both s. 92(13), property and civil rights and s. 92(16), a purely local matter, given the broad generality of the language. There is, of course, no constitutional difficulty in this. The constitutional difficulty arises, however, when a statute may be characterized, as often happens, as coming within a federal as well as a provincial head of power. "To put the same point in another way, our community life—social, economic, political, and cultural—is very complex and will not fit neatly into any scheme of categories or classes without considerable overlap and ambiguity occurring. There are inevitable difficulties arising from this that we must live with so long as we have a federal constitution" (Lederman, "The Concurrent Operation of Federal and Provincial Laws in Canada" (1963), 9 *McGill LJ* 185). As Professor Ziegel has stated "[s]ecurities legislation clearly has a double character" ("Constitutional Aspects of Canadian Companies" in *Canadian Company Law* (1967), Chapter 5, at p. 167) and, "there is no simple dichotomy between legislation of a company law character and legislation affecting property and civil rights in the province. Viewed in its proper social and economic context the legislation may well have a double character" (at pp. 192-93).

I incline to the view that the impugned insider trading provisions have both a securities law and a companies law aspect and would adopt as the test for applying the double aspect doctrine to validate both sets of legislative provisions, that formulated by Professor Lederman ... .

[Dickson J then quotes from the Lederman excerpt from "Classification of Laws and the British North America Act," found above.]

The double aspect doctrine is applicable, as Professor Lederman says, when the contrast between the relative importance of the two features is not so sharp. When, as here, the corporate-security federal and provincial characteristics of the insider trading legislation are roughly equal in importance there would seem little reason, when considering validity, to kill one and let the other live.

Although the application of the double aspect doctrine has been most prevalent in the highway traffic field there is ample precedent for its use in the field of provincial securities regulations. ... Concurrent matters or fields have been recognized, among others, in the realms of temperance, insolvency, highways, trading stamps and aspects of Sunday observance. ...

[Dickson J went on to discuss whether the provisions of the Ontario *Securities Act* were rendered inapplicable to insider trading in the securities of federally incorporated companies under the doctrine of interjurisdictional immunity and/or inoperative by the overlapping provisions of the *Canada Corporations Act* under the federal paramountcy

doctrine. He held that neither doctrine applied. The latter portion of his judgment is reproduced in section IV of this chapter, below.]

NOTES

1. The double aspect doctrine has its origins in the case of *Hodge v. The Queen* (1883), 9
AC 117 (PC), found in Chapter 4, The Late Nineteenth Century: The Canadian Courts Under
the Influence, where the Privy Council said, in reference to legislation regulating the liquor
trade, "subjects which in one aspect and for one purpose fall within sect. 92, may in another
aspect and for another purpose fall within sect. 91." Where such dual aspects are found to
exist, overlapping federal and provincial laws are permitted.

2. Not every case in which a court is asked to consider the double-aspect doctrine is analyzed in the manner in which Lederman proposed. In fact, in most such cases, application
of the doctrine entails the court evidencing a willingness to characterize very similar federal
and provincial enactments in different ways and in such a manner as to permit the court to
uphold both aspects as valid. However, *Multiple Access* is not the only case in which the Supreme Court has adopted Lederman's approach to the application of the doctrine. *Law Society of British Columbia v. Mangat*, [2001] 3 SCR 113, 2001 SCC 67, 205 DLR (4th) 577 is
another. At issue in *Mangat* was a provision of the federal *Immigration Act*, RSC 1985, c. I-2,
that permitted non-lawyers to represent clients in proceedings before the Immigration and
Refugee Board, and a provision of the BC *Legal Profession Act*, SBC 1987, c. 25, which prohibited non-lawyers from engaging in the practice of law. After quoting from Lederman,
Gonthier J, writing for the Court, stated (at para. 50) that "[b]oth the federal and provincial
features of the challenged provisions are of equivalent importance, and so neither should be
ignored in the analysis of the division of powers. Parliament must be allowed to determine
who may appear before tribunals it has created, and the provinces must be allowed to regulate the practice of law as they have always done." The double aspect doctrine applied since
there were roughly equivalent federal and provincial aspects to the regulation of legal representation in immigration matters.

3. In addition to the regulation of trading in securities and the regulation of legal representation in immigration matters, the double aspect doctrine has been applied to a wide
range of subject matters including highway traffic, the moral regulation of films and videos,
nude dancing, gaming, temperance, support and custody in divorce proceedings, interest
rates, and insolvency. The double aspect doctrine has been invoked frequently in relation to
laws regulating public order, safety, and morality. (For a very recent example of this tendency, see *Chatterjee v. Ontario (Attorney General)*, 2009 SCC 19, 304 DLR (4th) 513, discussed
in Chapter 11, Criminal Law, in which the Supreme Court upheld provincial legislation
providing for the forfeiture of the proceeds of unlawful activity.) The result has been that
"legislative power is concurrent ... over much of the field which may loosely be thought of
as criminal law" (P. Hogg, *Constitutional Law of Canada*, 4th ed., looseleaf (Scarborough,
ON: Carswell, 1997), at 18-30). In other contexts, however, the courts have shown no inclination to invoke the double aspect doctrine and thus give effect to concurrency of legislative
power. For example, courts have insisted that jurisdiction to pass laws in relation to the regulation of trade, or in relation to labour relations, is exclusive rather than concurrent. The
double aspect doctrine has played virtually no role in these areas.

4. The courts' willingness to employ the double aspect doctrine and other doctrinal tools is very much shaped by context and has varied both over time and between subject matters. Compare, for example, the attitude of Dickson J to overlap and the duplication of regulatory regimes in *Multiple Access*, excerpted both above and in section IV, below, with Beetz J's approach in *Bell #2*, excerpted in section III, below. In *Multiple Access* Dickson J demonstrates a willingness to create areas subject to concurrent federal and provincial regulatory authority. In *Bell #2*, Beetz J, on the other hand, is troubled by the complexities and inefficiencies accompanying concurrent jurisdiction. Because federal laws prevail over provincial laws in the case of conflict, he also expressed concern that using the double aspect doctrine to expand areas of concurrent jurisdiction is to expand areas where the provinces are subordinate to the federal government. For these reasons, he suggested that the double aspect doctrine should be used "with great caution"; it should be invoked only "where the multiplicity of aspects is real and not merely nominal."

C. Necessarily Incidental

The pith and substance doctrine results in a law being upheld if its dominant characteristic falls within the classes of subject matter allocated to the jurisdiction of the enacting government. This means that a law may have an impact on matters outside the enacting legislature's jurisdiction, so long as these effects remain secondary or incidental features of the legislation rather than its most important feature. For example, the former abortion provision of the *Criminal Code* was a valid exercise of the federal criminal law power, even though the provision had a range of important effects on provincial matters such as hospitals, health, and the medical profession. These effects were considered incidental to the provision's dominant characteristic: the punishment of abortion on moral grounds.

An extension of the idea of incidental effects is the ancillary doctrine (sometimes called the "necessarily incidental" doctrine). The ancillary doctrine is used in cases where the provision being challenged is part of a larger scheme of legislation. When the impugned provision is examined in isolation, it appears to intrude into the jurisdiction of the other level of government. However, if the larger scheme of which the impugned provision is part is constitutionally valid, the impugned provision may also be found valid because of its relationship to the larger scheme. This will depend on how well the offending provisions are integrated into the valid legislative scheme. If they are not closely related, they will be severed and declared invalid. If they are closely related, they will be deemed "necessarily incidental" to the valid scheme and the law as a whole will be upheld. In this way, the necessarily incidental doctrine, like the pith and substance doctrine, permits governments to intrude substantially on the other level of government's jurisdiction, so long as the most important features of their laws remain within jurisdiction.

An early attempt to use the doctrine, albeit unsuccessfully, is found in *The King v. Eastern Terminal Elevator Co.*, [1925] SCR 434, 3 DLR 1, Chapter 5, The Early Twentieth Century: The Beginnings of Economic Regulation, in which the federal government attempted to uphold the validity of certain provisions in the *Canada Grain Act* regulating grain elevators by arguing that such regulation was necessarily incidental to larger purposes of the Act as a whole—that is, the regulation of the interprovincial and international trade in grain.

An extensive modern analysis of the necessarily incidental doctrine, which recognizes the balancing exercise involved in applying it, is found in the judgment of Dickson CJC in *General Motors*, below.

General Motors of Canada Ltd. v. City National Leasing
[1989] 1 SCR 641, 58 DLR (4th) 255

[City National Leasing (CNL) brought a civil action against General Motors (GM) alleging that it suffered losses as a result of a discriminatory pricing policy that constituted a kind of anti-competitive behaviour prohibited by the *Combines Investigation Act*. The civil action was authorized by s. 33.1 of the Act. GM argued that s. 33.1 was beyond the jurisdiction of Parliament because the creation of civil causes of action falls within provincial jurisdiction in relation to "property and civil rights."

The *General Motors* ruling is notable for its holding that the *Combines Investigation Act* (now the *Competition Act*) is a valid exercise of the federal power over the "general regulation of trade" (see Chapter 10, Economic Regulation). It is also notable for setting out the general approach to the necessarily incidental doctrine. When the constitutional challenge is focused on a single provision of a larger legislative scheme, how is the constitutional validity of the challenged provision to be determined? The excerpts below address this issue.]

DICKSON CJC (Beetz, McIntyre, Lamer, La Forest, and L'Heureux-Dubé JJ concurring): ... [I]n circumstances such as exist in the case at bar, it will normally be necessary to consider both the impugned provision and the Act as a whole (or a significant part of it) when undertaking a constitutional analysis. ... The first step should be to consider whether and to what extent the impugned provision can be characterized as intruding into provincial powers. If it cannot be characterized as intruding at all, i.e., if in its pith and substance the provision is federal law, and if the act to which it is attached is constitutionally valid (or if the provision is severable or if it is attached to a severable and constitutionally valid part of the act) then the investigation need go no further. In that situation both the provision and the act are constitutionally unimpeachable. If, as may occur in some instances, the impugned provision is found to be constitutionally unimpeachable while the act containing it is not, then the act must be assessed on it own. In these instances, it is clear that the claim of invalidity should originally have been made against the act and not against the particular provision. In most cases like the present, however, it will be concluded that the impugned provision can be characterized, *prima facie*, as intruding to some extent on provincial powers: the question is to what extent. I emphasize that in answering this initial question the court is considering the provision on its own and not assessing the act; thus the answer it reaches does not provide a conclusion with respect to the ultimate constitutional validity of the provision. The purpose is merely to ascertain the degree to which the provision could be said to intrude on provincial powers, so that this intrusion can be weighed in light of the possible justification for the section.

Such a justification will result from the impugned provision's relationship to valid legislation. Thus the next step in the process is to ascertain the existence of valid legislation. …

The final question is whether the provision can be constitutionally justified by reason of its connection with valid legislation. As Laskin CJ remarked in *MacDonald v. Vapour Canada*, [1977] 2 SCR 134, 66 DLR (3d) 1, inclusion of an invalid provision in a valid statute does not necessarily stamp the provision with validity. Here the court must focus on the relationship between the valid legislation and the impugned provision. Answering the question first requires deciding what test of "fit" is appropriate for such a determination. By "fit" I refer to how well the provision is integrated into the scheme of the legislation and how important it is for the efficacy of the legislation. The same test will not be appropriate in all circumstances. In arriving at the correct standard the court must consider the degree to which the provision intrudes on provincial powers. The case law, to which I turn below, shows that in certain circumstances a stricter requirement is in order, while in others, a looser test is acceptable. For example, if the impugned provision only encroaches marginally on provincial powers, then a "functional" relationship may be sufficient to justify the provision. Alternatively, if the impugned provision is highly intrusive vis a vis provincial powers then a stricter test is appropriate. A careful case by case assessment of the proper test is the best approach.

In determining the proper test it should be remembered that in a federal system it is inevitable that, in pursuing valid objectives, the legislation of each level of government will impact occasionally on the sphere of power of the other level of government; overlap of legislation is to be expected and accommodated in a federal state. Thus a certain degree of judicial restraint in proposing strict tests which will result in striking down such legislation is appropriate. I reiterate what I said on this general theme (although in a slightly different context) in *OPSEU v. Ontario (Attorney General)*, [1987] 2 SCR 2, at p. 18:

> The history of Canadian constitutional law has been to allow for a fair amount of interplay and indeed overlap between federal and provincial powers. It is true that doctrines like inter-jurisdictional and Crown immunity and concepts like "watertight compartments" qualify the extent of that interplay. But it must be recognized that these doctrines and concepts have not been the dominant tide of constitutional doctrines: rather they have been an undertow against the strong pull of pith and substance, the aspect doctrine and, in recent years, a very restrained approach to concurrency and paramountcy issues.

The above comments also emphasize that the question in this appeal of how far federal legislation may validly impinge on provincial powers is one part of the general notion of the "pith and substance" of legislation; i.e., the doctrine that a law which is federal in its true nature will be upheld even if it affects matters which appear to be a proper subject for provincial legislation (and vice versa). On p. 334 of his book *Constitutional Law of Canada* (2nd ed. 1985), Professor Hogg explains this in the following way:

> The pith and substance doctrine enables a law that is classified as "in relation to" a matter within the competence of the enacting body to have incidental or ancillary effects on matters outside the competence of the enacting body.

I emphasize that these comments should not be seen as altering the balance of constitutional powers. Both provincial and federal governments have equal ability to legislate in ways that may incidentally affect the other government's sphere of power. I quote from Professor Hogg again, where at p. 336 he states: "I think it is plain both on principle and on authority that the provincial enumerated powers have exactly the same capacity as the federal enumerated powers to affect matters allocated to the other level of government."

In the present appeal, the appellant focuses its attack on a particular section of the Act. The issue is not whether the Act as a whole is rendered *ultra vires* because it reaches too far, but whether a particular provision is sufficiently integrated into the Act to sustain its constitutionality. In numerous cases courts have considered the nature of the relationship which is required, between a provision which encroaches on provincial jurisdiction and a valid statute, for the provision to be upheld. In different contexts courts have set down slightly different requirements, *viz*: "rational and functional connection" in *Papp v. Papp*, [1970] 1 OR 331, *R v. Zelensky*, [1978] 2 SCR 940, and *Multiple Access Ltd. v. McCutcheon*, [1982] 2 SCR 161; "ancillary," "necessarily incidental" and "truly necessary" in the *Regional Municipality of Peel v. MacKenzie* (1982), 139 DLR (3d) 14; "intimate connection," "an integral part" and "necessarily incidental" in *Northern Telecom Ltd. v. Communications Workers of Canada*, [1980] 1 SCR 115; "integral part" in *Clark v. Canadian National Railway Co.*, [1988] 2 SCR 680; "a valid constitutional cast by the context and association in which it is fixed as a complementary provision" in *Vapor Canada, supra*; and "truly necessary" in *R v. Thomas Fuller Construction Co. (1958) Ltd.*, [1980] 1 SCR 695. I believe the approach I have outlined is consistent with the results of this jurisprudence. These cases are best understood as setting out the proper test for the particular context in issue, rather than attempting to articulate a test of general application with reference to all contexts. Thus the tests they set out are not identical. As the seriousness of the encroachment on provincial powers varies, so does the test required to ensure that an appropriate constitutional balance is maintained. In surveying past jurisprudence it is to be expected that some example of patterns between the appropriate test of fit, and the head of power under which the federal legislation is valid, will be found. Such patterns exist not only because of a possible degree of similarity between the federal legislation which falls under any one head of power, but also for the reason that certain federal heads of power, for example, s. 92(10), are narrow and distinct powers which relate to particular works and undertakings and are thus quite susceptible to having provisions "tacked-on" to legislation which is validated under them, while other federal heads of power, for example, trade and commerce, are broad and therefore less likely to give rise to highly intrusive provisions.

The steps in the analysis may be summarized as follows: First, the court must determine whether the impugned provision can be viewed as intruding on provincial powers, and if so to what extent (if it does not intrude, then the only possible issue is the validity of the act). Second, the court must establish whether the act (or a severable part of it) is valid. ... If the scheme is not valid, that is the end of the inquiry. If the scheme of regulation is declared valid, the court must then determine whether the impugned provision is sufficiently integrated with the scheme that it can be upheld by virtue of that relationship. This requires considering the seriousness of the encroachment on provincial powers, in order to decide on the proper standard for such a relationship. ... I note that in certain

cases it may be possible to dispense with some of the aforementioned steps if a clear answer to one of them will be dispositive of the issue. For example, if the provision in question has no relation to the regulatory scheme then the question of its validity may be
quickly answered on that ground alone. The approach taken in a number of past cases is
more easily understood if this possibility is recognized.

Does Section 31.1 Encroach on Provincial Powers?

The first step, therefore, in assessing the validity of s. 31.1 of the *Combines Investigation
Act* is to determine whether the impugned provision can be seen as encroaching on
provincial powers, and if so, to what extent. As s. 31.1 creates a civil right of action it is
not difficult to conclude that the provision does, on its face, appear to encroach on provincial power to some extent. The creation of civil actions is generally a matter within
provincial jurisdiction under s. 92(13) of the *Constitution Act, 1867*. This provincial
power over civil rights is a significant power and one that is not lightly encroached upon.
In assessing the seriousness of this encroachment, however, three facts must be taken
into consideration. The first is that s. 31.1 is only a remedial provision; its purpose is to
help enforce the substantive aspects of the Act, but it is not in itself a substantive part of
the Act. By their nature, remedial provisions are typically less intrusive vis-à-vis provincial powers. The second important fact is the limited scope of the action. Section 31.1
does not create a general cause of action; its application is carefully limited by the provisions of the Act. The third relevant fact is that it is well-established that the federal government is not constitutionally precluded from creating rights of civil action where such
measures may be shown to be warranted. This Court has sustained federally-created civil
actions in a variety of contexts … .

In sum, the impugned provision encroaches on an important provincial power; however, the provision is a remedial one; federal encroachment in this manner is not unprecedented and, in this case; encroachment has been limited by the restrictions of the Act.

[Dickson CJC turned to the second stage of the analysis and concluded that the *Combines Investigation Act* constituted a scheme of regulation validly enacted by Parliament
pursuant to its power to enact laws in relation to trade and commerce; see the portion of
the judgment found in Chapter 10, Economic Regulation.]

The Validity of Section 31.1 of the Combines Investigation Act

Having found that the *Combines Investigation Act* contains a regulatory scheme, valid
under s. 91(2) of the Constitution, the only issue remaining to be addressed is the constitutional validity of s. 31.1. As I have already noted, mere inclusion in a valid legislative
scheme does not *ipso facto* confer constitutional validity upon a particular provision. The
provision must be sufficiently related to that scheme for it to be constitutionally justified.
The degree of relationship that is required is a function of the extent of the provision's intrusion into provincial powers. I have already discussed this issue and concluded that
s. 31.1 intrudes, though in a limited way, on the important provincial power over civil
rights. In this light, I do not think that a strict test, such as "truly necessary" or "integral,"

is appropriate. On the other hand, it is not enough that the section be merely "tacked on" to admittedly valid legislation. The correct approach in this case is to ask whether the provision is functionally related to the general objective of the legislation, and to the structure and the content of the scheme. A similar test has been applied in other cases, as I have noted, and I think it is also the proper test for the circumstances of this appeal. ...

I am of the opinion that the necessary link between s. 31.1 and the Act exists. Section. 31.1 is an integral, well-conceived component of the economic regulation strategy found in the *Combines Investigation Act*. Even if a much stricter test of fit were applied—for instance, one of "necessarily incidental"—s. 31.1 would still pass the test. Under the test of "functionally related" the section is clearly valid.

[Dickson CJC noted that s. 31.1 is a remedy bounded by the parameters of the Act; it does not create an open-ended private right of action. He also relied on the fact that s. 31.1 is integrated into the purpose and underlying philosophy of the Act: privately initiated and conducted proceedings can help fulfill the objectives of the legislation.]

For these reasons, I conclude that s. 31.1 is an integral part of the *Combines Investigation Act* scheme regulating anti-competitive conduct. The relationship between the section and the Act easily meets the test for the section to be upheld. This finding should not be interpreted as authority for upholding all provisions creating private civil action that are attached to a valid trade and commerce regulatory scheme or any other particular type of scheme. Section 31.1 is carefully constructed and restricted by the terms of the *Combines Investigation Act*. ...

Appeal dismissed.

NOTES

1. The approach to the necessarily incidental doctrine described by Dickson CJC is equally applicable when a provision of a provincial law that is part of a larger scheme of regulation is challenged on the grounds that it encroaches on a federal area of jurisdiction. For example, in *Global Securities Corp. v. British Columbia (Securities Commission)*, [2000] 1 SCR 494, 185 DLR (4th) 439, the Supreme Court upheld s. 141(1)(b) of the *British Columbia Securities Act*, a provision that empowers the BC Securities Commission (BCSC) to make orders requiring brokers registered in the province to produce records in their control "to assist in the administration of the securities laws of another jurisdiction." The BCSC entered into an agreement with the US Securities and Exchange Commission (SEC) to provide each other with mutual assistance in investigating violations of their respective jurisdictions' securities laws. Pursuant to a request from the SEC, which was investigating possible violations of US law, the BCSC ordered Global Securities to produce records in its possession. The company refused to produce some of the requested records, and sought a declaration that s. 141(1)(b) was in pith and substance in relation to the enforcement of foreign laws, and was thus *ultra vires*. The Court disagreed, finding that the impugned provision was in pith and substance

part of a reciprocal arrangement in relation to the uncovering of violations of local securities laws, and thus within provincial jurisdiction over "property and civil rights."

In reaching this conclusion, Iacobucci J, writing for the Court, identified two dominant
purposes of the impugned provision: the first was the goal of obtaining reciprocal cooperation from other securities regulators and the second was the uncovering of violations of
foreign law by brokers registered in British Columbia. He went on to note that had the provision been found to lie outside provincial jurisdiction on the ground that it was primarily
concerned with assisting in the enforcement of foreign law, it would have been saved by the
ancillary or necessarily incidental doctrine articulated by the Court in *General Motors*. The
impugned section, he said, "is a part of a valid legislative scheme, namely, the *Securities Act*.
Moreover, even assuming that the most rigorous version of the ancillary doctrine applies, I
believe that s. 141(1)(b) is 'necessarily incidental' to the *Securities Act* and would therefore
also uphold it under the ancillary doctrine." (See also *Kitkatla Band v. BC*, [2002] 2 SCR 146,
2002 SCC 31, 210 DLR (4th) 577, in which the Court upheld a provision of BC's *Heritage
Conservation Act* that specifically referred to aboriginal artifacts.)

2. You will by now have noted that the word "incidental" is used by the courts in two different contexts in this area of the law—in the term "incidental effects" in the context of the pith
and substance doctrine and in the term "necessarily incidental" in the context of the doctrine
of that name. If you are unclear as to the differences between these two uses of the word, it
might be helpful for you to think of "incidental effects" as simply another way of saying "not
the dominant feature" of the impugned legislation. It is a way of acknowledging that the impugned legislation has an "aspect" or "feature" that connects it to a head of power assigned to
the other order of government than the one that enacted it, but that connection is not considered fatal to its validity. By contrast, "incidental" in the context of the necessarily incidental
doctrine refers to the relationship between the part of a statute that is under challenge and the
rest of that statute. (If you do not find this attempt at distinguishing between the two uses to
be helpful, just substitute "ancillary doctrine" for "necessarily incidental doctrine" wherever
you see the latter term; while the language is obviously different, the meaning is the same.)

3. While the approach to the necessarily incidental doctrine outlined by Justice Dickson
in *General Motors* suggests that that doctrine is to be applied whenever the validity of a single part of a larger whole is called into question, the Court has not always applied the doctrine in such circumstances, and has instead applied a standard pith and substance analysis.
For example, the doctrine was not applied in either the *Employment Insurance Reference* or
Multiple Access, both excerpted above, even though the challenge in both cases was to small
components of large statutes. The Court has not explained why it has not been consistent in
this regard.

B. Ryder, "The Demise and Rise of the Classical Paradigm in Canadian Federalism: Promoting Autonomy for the Provinces and First Nations"
(1991), 36 *McGill Law Journal* 309, at 309-14 and 380-81 (footnotes omitted)

In [*OPSEU v. AG Ontario*, [1987] 2 SCR 2, at 18] Chief Justice Dickson remarked that
"[t]he history of Canadian constitutional law has been to allow for a fair amount of interplay and indeed overlap between federal and provincial powers." This is an accurate

description of only part of our constitutional jurisprudence. It may be that, in the post-World War II era, judicial interpretation of the constitution has gradually moved away from a "classical" view of the distribution of powers, that allowed for little overlap and interplay of provincial and federal powers, towards the more flexible "modern" federalism described by the Chief Justice. But this movement, from what I will call the classical paradigm to the modern paradigm in Canadian federalism, has been neither consistent nor steady. Indeed, both approaches have been invoked by the courts at all stages of our history of constitutional judicial review. Nevertheless, the larger trend does emerge from a study of the cases. One can say, at least, that the modern paradigm has replaced the classical paradigm as the dominant approach to the judicial interpretation of the division of powers. ...

The classical and modern paradigms represent different judicial approaches to defining "exclusivity" of federal and provincial powers, and thus of preserving provincial autonomy. The classical paradigm is premised on a "strong" understanding of exclusivity: there shall be no overlap or interplay between federal and provincial heads of power. The heads of power in the federal and provincial lists should not be interpreted literally, but should be "mutually modified" in light of the subjects accorded to the jurisdiction of the other level of government so as to avoid overlapping responsibilities as much as possible. Each level of government must act within its hermetically sealed boxes of jurisdiction, or "watertight compartments" ("compartiments étanches"). Any spillover effects on the other level of government's jurisdiction will not be tolerated. Such legislative spillover must be contained, either by ruling such laws *ultra vires*, or by "reading them down" so that they remain strictly within the enacting legislature's jurisdiction. ...

The modern paradigm, on the other hand, is premised on a weaker understanding of exclusivity. Instead of seeking to prohibit as much overlap as possible between provincial and federal powers, the modern approach to exclusivity simply prohibits each level of government from enacting laws whose dominant characteristics ("pith and substance") is the regulation of a subject matter within the other level of government's jurisdiction. Exclusivity, on this approach, means the exclusive ability to pass laws that deal predominantly with a subject matter within the enacting government's catalogue of powers. If a law is in pith and substance within the enacting legislature's jurisdiction, it will be upheld notwithstanding that it might have spillover effects on the other level of government's jurisdiction. And if a problem of national or international dimensions is functionally beyond the capacity of a province to regulate effectively, it will be allocated to federal jurisdiction. In these ways, the modern paradigm, to borrow Dickson CJ's words, allows for a "fair amount of interplay and indeed overlap between federal and provincial powers." ...

The weakness of the classical paradigm is that in a complex, interdependent world, social problems do not fit so neatly into jurisdictional boxes. Virtually any piece of legislation can be cut down by a holding of *ultra vires* if the classical paradigm is invoked in all its vigour. In addition, the watertight compartments metaphor can give rise to a legislative vacuum by hiving off parts of interconnected phenomena, granting jurisdiction over part to the federal government and part to the provinces. In this way, effective regulation of the whole is left to the unpredictable fate of attempts at inter-governmental cooperation. In sum, the classical paradigm is the course of judicial activism, because it puts more stringent constraints on legislation enacted by both levels of government. And, by creating legislative vacuums, it compromises the principle of exhaustiveness.

The modern paradigm is the course of judicial restraint; it avoids the deregulatory tendencies of the classical paradigm by maximizing the ambit of the legislative powers available to the federal and provincial governments alike. However, the weakness of the modern paradigm is that it can be employed in a manner that compromises provincial autonomy. By allowing legislation to have spillover effects on the other government's areas of jurisdiction, it creates areas of social life subject to overlapping or concurrent powers. Where overlapping federal and provincial laws come into conflict, the rule of federal paramountcy provides that the federal law prevails, rendering the provincial law inoperative to the extent of the conflict. Thus, the modern paradigm, by extending the areas subject to concurrent powers, extends the potential for federal dominance inherent in the paramountcy rule. Carried to its logical extreme, the modern paradigm would make a mockery of provincial autonomy. ...

An analysis of the case law interpreting the constitutional division of powers indicates that the doctrinal techniques of what I have called the classical and modern paradigms have been utilized by the courts at all stages of our constitutional history. Most scholars have associated the use of these paradigms with particular time periods and courts—the classical paradigm is frequently associated with the pre-World War II Privy Council era, and the modern paradigm with the Supreme Court of Canada's post-war jurisprudence. I have suggested that it is more fruitful to map the use of the two paradigms by reference to differing judicial attitudes to regulation in different areas of social life. The deregulatory bias of the classical paradigm has been applied to legislation that is viewed as interfering with the operation of free markets; the judicial tolerance of the modern paradigm has been applied to legislation perceived to deal with issues of morality or social order ... . These broad tendencies in the doctrinal structure of Canadian federalism can be traced from the early days following Confederation through to the present day.

Most Canadian scholars have been partisans of either the classical or the modern paradigm as the only appropriate approach to defining the meaning of exclusivity in the division of powers. The classical paradigm has been defended by jurists such as Jean Beetz as the best means of preserving an authentic federalism with equally autonomous provincial and federal governments. Others, such as Peter Hogg, have defended the judicial restraint inherent in the modern paradigm as the appropriate interpretive posture of an unaccountable judiciary. I have argued that the task of federal interpretation should not be approached as an either/or choice between the two paradigms. Both the classical and the modern paradigms are legitimate attempts to give real meaning to exclusivity and to the democratic principle of exhaustiveness. Each has an important role to play.

III. APPLICABILITY: THE INTERJURISDICTIONAL IMMUNITY DOCTRINE

This section deals with another of the basic interpretive doctrines employed by the courts in division of powers cases, that of interjurisdictional immunity. Currently, the pith and substance, ancillary, and double aspect doctrines, which were explored above, result in a fair amount of overlapping jurisdiction. Legislation enacted by one level of government, as long as it can be characterized in relation to a matter assigned to that level of government, is allowed to have an incidental effect on matters assigned to the other level of government. (If both levels of government have enacted laws applicable to the same subject matter, any conflict between the two will be resolved by the doctrine of federal paramountcy, which will be discussed in section IV, below.)

The doctrine of interjurisdictional immunity constitutes something of a departure from this tendency of the pith and substance doctrine to create overlapping jurisdiction, and is instead a doctrine that emphasizes exclusivity of jurisdiction. It typically comes into play in situations where a generally worded provincial law is clearly valid in most of its applications, but in some of its applications it arguably overreaches, affecting a matter falling within a core area of federal jurisdiction. On an application of the normal pith and substance doctrine, one might expect the conclusion in such cases to be that the effect on the federal matter is incidental to a valid provincial law and therefore acceptable. However, the doctrine of interjurisdictional immunity protects certain matters that fall within federal jurisdiction from the impact or interference of otherwise valid provincial laws. To put it another way, in those circumstances where the doctrine of interjurisdictional immunity applies, provincial laws are not allowed to have an effect on matters falling within core areas of federal jurisdiction, and there is no double aspect to the matter regulated.

When the interjurisdictional immunity doctrine is invoked, the courts will "read down" provincial (or federal) statutes to protect the core of exclusive federal (or provincial) powers from encroachment. Reading down is a technique of interpretation used to save statutes from constitutional challenge: the words of the statute are interpreted to apply only to matters within the enacting body's jurisdiction. It is often, but not exclusively, used in conjunction with the doctrine of interjurisdictional immunity.

The accepted wisdom is that the doctrine of interjurisdictional immunity originated in cases involving federally incorporated companies and federally regulated undertakings. In *John Deere Plow Co. v. Wharton*, [1915] AC 330 (PC); *Great West Saddlery v. The King*, [1921] 2 AC 91 (PC); and *AG Manitoba v. AG Canada*, [1929] AC 260 (PC), the Privy Council held that valid provincial laws would have to be restricted in their application if they would have the effect of impairing the status or essential powers of a federally incorporated company. And in *Toronto v. Bell Telephone Co.*, [1905] AC 52, the Privy Council applied similar reasoning in support of its holding that provincial legislation could not impair or sterilize the operations of an interprovincial communications undertaking. (This accepted wisdom has recently been questioned. See R. Elliot, "Interjurisdictional Immunity after Canadian Western Bank and Lafarge Canada Inc.: The Supreme Court Muddies the Doctrinal Waters—Again" (2008), 43 *Supreme Court Law Review* (2d) 433.)

Whatever the true origins of the doctrine, it has come to be an accepted—if still somewhat contentious—feature of the law of Canadian federalism and, as the cases excerpted and discussed below make clear, has been applied by the Supreme Court of Canada in a broad range of different areas.

McKay v. The Queen
[1965] SCR 798, 53 DLR (2d) 532

[The appellants displayed a sign on their house in support of a candidate during the period of a federal election campaign. They were convicted of violating a municipal bylaw that prohibited the display of all signs in a residential area, except for certain specified exceptions, such as real estate signs and trespassing or safety signs. The appellants did not challenge the validity of the bylaw, only its application in the circumstances. Their conviction before a Justice of the Peace was quashed in the High Court, but then restored by the Court of Appeal.]

CARTWRIGHT J (Taschereau CJC, Abbott, Judson, and Spence JJ concurring): ... In framing those portions of the by-law with which we are concerned the Council has not enumerated the classes of signs the display of which on residential property is prohibited. It has taken the permissible course of forbidding the display of all signs except those few described in [the regulation]. It results from this that the words of prohibition are extremely wide.

In construing the by-law two rules of construction are of assistance. The first is that conveniently expressed in the maxim, *Verba generalia restringuntur ad habilitatem rei vel personae* (Bac. Max. reg. 10) Broom's Legal Maxims, 10th ed., 438. The rule was regarded as already well established when *Stradling v. Morgan* (1560), 1 Plowd. 199, 75 ER 308 was decided in 1560 and it is scarcely necessary to quote authority in support of it. It is expressed as follows in Maxwell on Interpretation of Statutes, 11th ed., at pages 58 and 59:

> It is in the interpretation of general words and phrases that the principle of strictly adapting the meaning to the particular subject-matter with reference to which the words are used finds its most frequent application. However wide in the abstract, they are more or less elastic, and admit of restriction or expansion to suit the subject-matter. While expressing truly enough all that the legislature intended, they frequently express more in their literal meaning and natural force; and it is necessary to give them the meaning which best suits the scope and object of the statute without extending to ground foreign to the intention. It is, therefore, a canon of interpretation that all words, if they be general and not express and precise, are to be restricted to the fitness of the matter. They are to be construed as particular if the intention be particular, that is, they must be understood as used with reference to the subject-matter in the mind of the legislature, and limited to it. ...

The second applicable rule of construction is that if an enactment, whether of Parliament or of a legislature or of a subordinate body to which legislative power is delegated, is capable of receiving a meaning according to which its operation is restricted to matters within the power of the enacting body it shall be interpreted accordingly. An alternative form in which the rule is expressed is that if words in a statute are fairly susceptible of two constructions of which one will result in the statute being *intra vires* and the other will have the contrary result the former is to be adopted. ...

A municipal corporation which drives its legislative power from an act of the Provincial Legislature, of course, cannot have power to enact a provision which would be *ultra vires* of that legislature.

In the case at bar the learned Justice of the Peace and the Court of Appeal have given effect to the by-law as if it provided:

> During an election to Parliament no owner of property in an R2 zone in Etobicoke shall display on his property any sign soliciting votes for a candidate at such election.

I cannot think that it was the intention of the Council to so enact or that it was the intention of the Legislature to empower it to do so. Such an enactment would, in my opinion, be *ultra vires* of the provincial legislature. The power of the legislature to enact such a law, if it exists, must be found in s. 92 of the *British North America Act*. It is argued for the respondent that it falls within head 13, "Property and Civil Rights in the Province." Whether or not the right of an elector at a federal election to seek by lawful means to influence his fellow electors to vote for the candidate of his choice is aptly described as a civil right need not be discussed; it is clearly not a civil right in the province. It is a right enjoyed by the elector not as a resident of Ontario but as a citizen of Canada.

A political activity in the federal field which has theretofore been lawful can, in my opinion, be prohibited only by Parliament. ...

If by-law 11737 is construed as it has been by the learned Justice of the Peace and by the Court of Appeal, it does not merely affect, it destroys the right of the appellants to engage in a form of political activity in the federal field which has heretofore been possessed and exercised by electors without question. ...

In my opinion, the legislature has no power to enact a prohibition of the sort which by-law 11737, as construed by the Court of Appeal, contains as such a prohibition would be a law in relation to proceedings at a federal election and not in relation to any subject-matter within the provincial power. As was said by Lord Watson in *Union Colliery v. Bryden*, [1899] AC 580 at 588:

> The abstinence of the Dominion Parliament from legislating to the full limit of its powers, could not have the effect of transferring to any provincial legislature the legislative power which had been assigned to the Dominion by s. 91 of the Act of 1867.

While that case dealt with an attempted invasion by the provincial legislature of a field exclusively reserved to Parliament by head 25 of s. 91 of the *British North America Act*, the subject matter of elections to Parliament appears to me to be from its very nature one which cannot be regarded as coming within any of the classes of subjects assigned to the legislatures of the provinces by section 92. As to this I agree with the following statement of Taschereau J, as he then was, in *Valin v. Langlois* (1879), 3 SCR 1 at 71:

> It is admitted, and is beyond doubt, that the Parliament of Canada has the exclusive power of legislation over Dominion controverted elections. By the *lex Parliamentaria*, as well as by the 41st, 91st, and 92d sections of the *British North America Act*, this power is as complete as if it was specially and by name contained in the enumeration of the federal powers of section 91, just as promissory notes, Insolvency, & c., are. ...

It is scarcely necessary to add that, just as the legislature cannot do indirectly what it cannot do directly, it cannot by using general words effect a result which would be beyond its powers if brought about by precise words. An enactment in general words which, if literally construed, would bring about such a result is one to which the maxim, *Verba generalia restringuntur ad habilitatem rei vel personae*, is peculiarly applicable.

Earlier in these reasons I have stated that counsel for the appellants did not question the validity of the by-law or of the enabling provincial legislation. I should make it plain that this admission on his part depended upon the acceptance of his argument that on its proper construction the by-law did not prohibit the display of the sign in regard to which the appellants were convicted. It was implicit in his argument that if the by-law should be construed so as to prohibit that display it would be *pro tanto* invalid.

For these reasons I agree with the conclusion of Hughes J that on its proper construction by-law number 11737 does not prohibit the display of the sign displayed by the appellants during the period mentioned in the charge against them. ...

MARTLAND J (Fauteux, Ritchie, and Hall JJ concurring) dissenting: ... I cannot find in any of these provisions [of the *Canada Elections Act*] any recognition by Parliament, express or implied, of an overriding right to erect anywhere a sign for purposes of political propaganda.

Subsections (3) and (4) of s. 49 contain prohibitions against the supplying and use of certain kinds of election propaganda on polling day, and during certain other periods.

Section 71 requires printed advertisements, handbills, placards, posters or dodgers having reference to an election to carry the name and address of the printer and publisher.

Section 100 is the only one of the provisions mentioned which contains enabling, rather than restrictive, provisions. It deals with the posting of official notices required under the Act. It authorizes their posting in certain ways and in certain places. It is significant that subs. (2) contains the words "notwithstanding the provisions of any law of Canada or of a province or of any municipal ordinance or by-law," thereby recognizing that, in the absence of the authority of this section, even the posting of official notices in certain places might properly be forbidden by a provincial statute or a municipal by-law.

In my opinion there is nothing in the provisions of the by-law relating to the erection of signs which runs counter to any of the provisions of the *Canada Elections Act*.

It is, however, contended that, even though Parliament has not legislated on this subject, the field of proceedings at federal elections is one of federal jurisdiction and cannot be affected by provincial legislation, even though it is so affected only incidentally. ...

Undoubtedly the federal Parliament can legislate and has legislated respecting federal elections. To the extent that it has legislated, such legislation governs and would override any provincial enactment which ran counter to it. The point which I make is that there is no general field of legislation on this subject assigned to the federal Parliament under an enumerated class in s. 91 to which the proviso at the conclusion of that section can attach.

That being so, in my opinion, provincial legislation in relation to the use of property, which, in its pith and substance, is in relation to property and civil rights in the province, and which is of general application, is not only valid, but can apply even though, incidentally, it may affect the means of propaganda used by an individual or by a political party during a federal election campaign. ...

This, I think, is an answer to the suggestion that, if the municipality could not have enacted a by-law aimed exclusively at federal election signs, then a general by-law could not be applicable to them. The essential feature of the by-law in question here is that it is of general application and, admittedly, valid.

[Martland J then deals with the appellants' second argument, that the exercise of the right of freedom of expression in a federal election was a matter which could only be regulated by the federal government. This argument rests upon three cases, *Saumur v. City of Quebec*, *Switzman v. Elbling*, and *Reference re Alberta Statutes*, found in Chapter 15, Antecedents of the Charter, which deal with a doctrine known as the "Implied Bill of Rights."]

In each of these cases some of the reasons have recognized the existence of fields of federal legislative jurisdiction in relation to freedom of religion (*Saumur*) and freedom of speech (*Switzman*). In each of these cases this view was expressed in relation to legislation which the judges expressing that view had found not to fall within any head of s. 92. ...

Assuming ... the existence of federal legislative powers in the field of freedom of religion and freedom of discussion, there is no case as yet which has ruled that provincial legislation not directed at those fields, but validly enacted in relation to property and civil rights, cannot, incidentally, effect any curtailment of the same. ...

Freedom of discussion is not an unlimited right to urge views, political or other, at any time, in any place, and in any manner. It is a freedom subject to law, and, depending on the nature of the legislation involved, may be subject to certain restrictions, whether federal or provincial. ...

Furthermore, ... I would not accept the proposition that, because a by-law of general application incidentally prevented a particular form of political propaganda from being used in a particular area, this constituted a substantial interference with the working of the parliamentary institutions of Canada.

In my opinion the appeal fails and should be dismissed with costs.

Appeal allowed.

NOTES AND QUESTIONS

1. Does this case prevent the province or municipality from engaging in *any* regulation of federal election signs? The McKays' sign was 14 inches by 16 inches. What if they had lived at an intersection and had erected a large billboard on their lawn that made it difficult for drivers to see approaching traffic?

2. Since the advent of the Charter, there is much less need to rely on federalism principles, such as interjurisdictional immunity, to protect rights like freedom of expression, and in recent years courts have declined to use the doctrine in that context; see *Ontario Public Service Employees' Union v. AG Ontario*, [1987] 2 SCR 2, 41 DLR (4th) 1.

3. The analytical approach taken by Justice Cartwright (as he then was) in support of his holding that the municipal bylaw could not be applied to the McKays was very different from the approach taken in the earlier (and, as you will see, later) cases involving federally

incorporated companies and federally regulated undertakings. Instead of asking whether application of the bylaw would impair or sterilize the integrity of federal elections, he asked whether the bylaw, had it been targeted specifically at signs erected during the course of federal election campaigns, would have been valid. Which of the two approaches do you think is the better one?

4. It should be noted that the courts have held that valid statutes may be inapplicable to certain fact situations, and the doctrine of reading down invoked, outside of the context of interjurisdictional immunity. For example, reading down is a common technique employed to prevent a statute from being found to violate the *Charter of Rights and Freedoms*.

In *Commission du salaire minimum v. Bell Telephone Co. of Canada (Bell #1)*, [1966] SCR 767, 59 DLR (2d) 145, the issue was whether the Quebec *Minimum Wage Act* could apply to Bell Telephone, an undertaking within exclusive federal jurisdiction pursuant to ss. 92(10)(a) and (c). The Act gave the Commission du salaire minimum the power to regulate matters such as minimum wages, working hours, and working conditions. When the Commission sought to impose a levy on Bell Canada, the company refused to pay it, contending that the statute could not apply to it because of its undisputed status as a federally regulated undertaking. The Court held that a Quebec minimum wage law could not apply to Bell or other federally regulated undertakings operating in the province, even though no federal minimum wage law existed at the time. Martland J, the author of the dissenting judgment in *McKay*, now writing for the Court, stated the rule as follows:

> [A]ll matters which are a vital part of the operation of an interprovincial undertaking as a going concern are matters which are subject to the exclusive legislative control of the federal parliament.

Because, in his view, issues related to employment contracts, such as rates of pay and hours of work, qualified as vital parts of the management and operation of an undertaking, it followed that the Quebec minimum wage law could not apply to federal undertakings.

Martland J's ruling initiated a significant doctrinal change by broadening the test for interjurisdictional immunity applicable to federal undertakings. In earlier cases, the courts had applied the same test for federally incorporated companies and federal undertakings— namely, the "sterilization" or impairment test. On this test, a valid provincial law could apply to federal undertakings or federally incorporated companies so long as it did not impair their status or essential powers. After *Bell #1*, a valid provincial law could not apply to federal undertakings if it affected a vital part of their operation or management. This test created a larger area of immunity for federal undertakings.

The doctrine of interjurisdictional immunity has been controversial, both because—at least until recently—it appeared to extend to the federal government an exclusivity of jurisdiction not available to the provinces and because, in its emphasis on exclusivity of jurisdiction, it seems at odds with the tendency of modern federalism to allow considerable overlap between federal and provincial powers. The following excerpt from the concurring reasons of Dickson CJC in *Ontario Public Service Employees' Union v. AG Ontario*, [1987] 2 SCR 2, 41 DLR (4th) 1, at 17 SCR, captures this criticism:

However, even though the doctrine of interjurisdictional immunity has arguably expanded since its company law origins, it is, in my opinion, not a particularly compelling doctrine. Professor Hogg has offered two strong reasons to doubt its value (*Constitutional Law of Canada*, 2d ed. (Scarborough, ON: Carswell, 1985), 331). The first, doctrinal, reason is:

> The theory behind the results [in the cases in which the doctrine has been applied] appears to be that federal heads of power not only confer power on the federal Parliament, but also operate "defensively to deny power to the provincial Legislatures." In my view, this theory is inconsistent with the basic pith and substance doctrine—that a law "in relation to" a provincial matter may validly "affect" a federal matter. And, indeed, for every case asserting an interjurisdictional immunity there are dozens which deny such an immunity by application of the pith and substance doctrine.

The second, policy, reason is:

> From a policy standpoint, the immunity of federal undertakings seems unnecessary, because the federal Parliament can, if it chooses, easily protect undertakings within federal jurisdiction from the operation of provincial laws by enacting appropriate laws which will be paramount over conflicting provincial laws.

> I favour both of these arguments of caution about the scope of the interjurisdictional immunity doctrine. The history of Canadian constitutional law has been to allow for a fair amount of interplay and indeed overlap between federal and provincial powers. It is true that doctrines like interjurisdictional and Crown immunity and concepts like "watertight compartments" qualify the extent of that interplay. But it must be recognized that these doctrines and concepts have not been the dominant tide of constitutional doctrines; rather they have been an undertow against the strong pull of pith and substance, the double aspect doctrine and, in recent years, a very restrained approach to concurrency and paramountcy issues.

The doctrine of interjurisdictional immunity remains controversial today. While the Supreme Court of Canada, speaking through Justice Beetz, appeared to reject Justice Dickson's criticisms of it in the next case excerpted, *Bell Canada v. Quebec (Commission de la santé et de la securité du travail (Bell #2)*, it has resurrected them in two recent cases, *Canadian Western Bank v. Alberta* and *BC v. Lafarge Canada Inc.*, the first of which is excerpted below.

As you read the cases that follow, note the doctrinal choices that typically face the court. One option is to allow the provincial law to apply to the federal undertaking or other federal matter until the federal government enacts conflicting legislation, which will then have priority by virtue of the doctrine of paramountcy. The other is to apply the doctrine of interjurisdictional immunity to the federal undertaking or other federal matter, with the result that the provincial law is not applicable, even if the federal government has not legislated on the matter. Think about the implications of each of these choices. What values are furthered by each choice?

Note the result of the application of the doctrine of interjurisdictional immunity—in many cases, where the provincial law in issue is drafted in general terms and is of broad application, the entire provincial law is not found invalid; it is only found *inapplicable* to the federal undertaking or other federal matter. Because the provincial laws in issue in these cases appear so clearly to fall within provincial jurisdiction in most of their applications, their validity is assumed. Invalidation is not considered an option. Rather, it is the applicability of the law in particular circumstances that is at issue. When the interjurisdictional immunity doctrine is invoked, the courts will interpret, or read down, generally worded provincial statutes so that they do not apply to matters that fall within the core of exclusive federal powers.

Bell Canada v. Quebec (Commission de la santé et de la sécurité du travail) (Bell #2)
[1988] 1 SCR 749, 51 DLR (4th) 161

[This case was one in a trilogy that dealt with the application of provincial health and safety laws to federal undertakings. The companion cases were *Alltrans Express Ltd. v. British Columbia (Workers' Compensation Board)*, [1988] 1 SCR 897, 43 DLR (4th) 424, which dealt with the applicability of provincial regulations requiring the wearing of safety boots to an interprovincial and international trucking business, and *Canadian National Railway Co. v. Courtois*, [1988] 1 SCR 868, 51 DLR (4th) 271, which dealt with the ability of a provincial inspector to inquire into a railway accident that caused death and serious injury to workers. The case reproduced here dealt with the application to Bell Canada of a Quebec law giving a right to protective reassignment to a pregnant worker. Beetz J's views on federalism are discussed in the Swinton excerpt found in Chapter 9, Peace, Order, and Good Government.]

BEETZ J (Dickson CJC, Lamer, Wilson, Le Dain, and La Forest JJ concurring): ... To facilitate an understanding of the judgments of the lower courts and the arguments put forward by the parties, I think it is best to summarize at the outset the rules which have so far been applied by the courts and in accordance with which this Court must resolve the question stated at the start of these reasons and presented by the three appeals. These rules are well known and most of them need only be stated in the form of propositions: a more critical study of them can be made when it comes time to apply them to the circumstances of the case at bar, namely the classification of the impugned legislation.

PROPOSITION ONE

General legislative jurisdiction over health belongs to the provinces ... . This jurisdiction has historically been seen as resting with the provinces under s. 92(16) of the *Constitution Act, 1867*, "Generally all Matters of a merely local or private Nature in the Province," although the considerable dimensions of this jurisdiction were probably not foreseen in 1867.

PROPOSITION TWO

In principle, labour relations and working conditions fall within the exclusive jurisdiction of the provincial legislatures: these matters fall into the class of subjects mentioned in s. 92(13) of the *Constitution Act, 1867*, "Property and Civil Rights in the Province": *Toronto Electric Commissioners v. Snider*, [1925] AC 396 ("*Snider*").

PROPOSITION THREE

Notwithstanding the rule stated in proposition two, Parliament is vested with exclusive legislative jurisdiction over labour relations and working conditions when that jurisdiction is an integral part of its primary and exclusive jurisdiction over another class of subjects, as is the case with labour relations and working conditions in the federal undertakings covered by ss. 91(29) and 92(10)a., b. and c. of the *Constitution Act, 1867*, that is undertakings such as Alltrans Express Ltd., Canadian National and Bell Canada. It follows that this primary and exclusive jurisdiction precludes the application to those undertakings of provincial statutes relating to labour relations and working conditions, since such matters are an essential part of the very management and operation of such undertakings, as with any commercial or industrial undertaking: *Reference re Minimum Wage Act of Saskatchewan*, [1948] SCR 248 (the "*Postal Service Case 1948*"); *Reference re Industrial Relations and Disputes Investigation Act*, [1955] SCR 529 (the "*Stevedoring Case*"); *Commission du salaire minimum v. Bell Telephone Co. of Canada*, [1966] SCR 767 ("*Bell Canada 1966*"). This third proposition reflects, at least in part, a constitutional theory which commentators who have criticized it have called the theory of "interjurisdictional immunity." I will return to this below.

It should however be noted that the rules stated in this third proposition appear to constitute only one facet of a more general rule: works, such as federal railways, things, such as land reserved for Indians, and persons, such as Indians, who are within the special and exclusive jurisdiction of Parliament, are still subject to provincial statutes that are general in their application, whether municipal legislation, legislation on adoption, hunting or the distribution of family property, provided however that the application of these provincial laws does not bear upon those subjects in what makes them specifically of federal jurisdiction: *Canadian Pacific Railway Co. v. Corporation of the Parish of Notre Dame de Bonsecours*, [1899] AC 367 ("*Bonsecours*"); *Natural Parents v. Superintendent of Child Welfare*, [1976] 2 SCR 751 ("*Natural Parents*"); *Dick v. The Queen*, [1985] 2 SCR 309; *Derrickson v. Derrickson*, [1986] 1 SCR 285.

PROPOSITION FOUR

Several years before the exclusive legislative jurisdiction of Parliament over the working conditions and management of federal undertakings was recognized and established, the Judicial Committee of the Privy Council had held that provincial workmen's compensation schemes were applicable to federal undertakings: *Workmen's Compensation Board v. Canadian Pacific Railway Co.*, [1920] AC 184 ("*Workmen's Compensation Board*").

· · ·

What was held by the Judicial Committee in *Workmen's Compensation Board* to be applicable to a federal undertaking was the compensatory scheme established by the statute at issue in that case.

PROPOSITION FIVE

Proposition five is the double aspect theory, which appears to have been stated for the first time in *Hodge v. The Queen* (1883), 9 App. Cas. 117, at p. 130: "… subjects which in one aspect and for one purpose fall within sect. 92, may in another aspect and for another purpose fall within sect. 91."

It follows from this theory that two relatively similar rules or sets of rules may validly be found, one in legislation within exclusive federal jurisdiction, and the other in legislation within exclusive provincial jurisdiction, because they are enacted for different purposes and in different legislative contexts which give them distinct constitutional characterizations. ...

However, in *Attorney-General for Canada v. Attorney-General for Alberta*, [1916] 1 AC 588, Viscount Haldane issued a warning about the double aspect theory. This is what he said about this theory, at p. 596: ... [it] is now well established, but none the less ought to be applied only with great caution ... .

The reason for this caution is the extremely broad wording of the exclusive legislative powers listed in ss. 91 and 92 of the *Constitution Act, 1867* and the risk that these two fields of exclusive powers will be combined into a single more or less concurrent field of powers governed solely by the rule of paramountcy of federal legislation. Nothing could be more directly contrary to the principle of federalism underlying the Canadian Constitution: see Laskin's *Canadian Constitutional Law* (5th ed. 1986), vol. 1, at p. 525.

The double aspect theory is neither an exception nor even a qualification to the rule of exclusive legislative jurisdiction. Its effect must not be to create concurrent fields of jurisdiction, such as agriculture, immigration and old age pensions and supplementary benefits, in which Parliament and the legislatures may legislate on the same aspect. On the contrary, the double aspect theory can only be invoked when it gives effect to the rule of exclusive fields of jurisdiction. As its name indicates, it can only be applied in clear cases where the multiplicity of aspects is real and not merely nominal. ...

I think it is quite impossible to distinguish the circumstances of the case at bar from those of *Bell Canada 1966*. The working conditions and labour relations as well as the management of federal undertakings such as Bell Canada, are matters falling within the classes of subject mentioned in s. 91(29) of the *Constitution Act, 1867*, and consequently fall within the exclusive legislative jurisdiction of the Parliament of Canada.

Moreover, as I indicated at the start of these reasons, the exclusivity rule approved by *Bell Canada 1966* does not apply only to labour relations or to federal undertakings. It is one facet of a more general rule against making works, things or persons under the special and exclusive jurisdiction of Parliament subject to provincial legislation, when such application would bear on the specifically federal nature of the jurisdiction to which such works, things or persons are subject. ...

2. Criticism of Bell Canada 1966

Bell Canada 1966 has been criticized by certain commentators: see, for example, "Interjurisdictional Immunity in Canadian Federalism," by Professor Dale Gibson (1969), 47 *Can. Bar Rev.* 40, at pp. 53-57; "The Supreme Court and the Law of Canadian Federalism," by Professor Paul c. Weiler (1973), 23 *UTLJ* 307, at pp. 340-43 and 363; *Constitutional Law of Canada* (2d ed. 1985), by Professor Peter W. Hogg, at pp. 329-32 and 465-66.

These analyses have much in common and I think it will suffice to consider the comments of Professor Hogg, which are in greater detail and more recent. [Hogg's comments are found in the excerpt from *Ontario Public Service Employees' Union v. AG Ontario*, discussed after *McKay*, above.]

... This analysis gives rise to several observations.

The first is that the criticism says nothing of the close study by Martland J in *Bell Canada 1966* of the relevant provisions of ss. 91 and 92 of the *Constitution Act, 1867*.

The second observation is that this analysis does not address the essential question raised and answered by Martland J: the critics refrain from defining the content of the exclusive legislative authority of Parliament over federal undertakings. This is necessary because the effect of s. 91(29) and the exceptions in s. 92(10) is to create exclusive classes of subject, those of federal undertakings, to which a basic, minimum and unassailable content has to be assigned to make up the matters falling within these classes. Martland J considered that the management of these undertakings and their labour relations are matters which are part of this basic and unassailable minimum, as these matters are essential and vital elements of any undertaking. How is it possible to disagree with this? How can the exclusive power to regulate these undertakings not include at least the exclusive power to make laws relating to their management? Additionally, just as the management of the undertaking and working conditions determined by agreement or by operation of law are parts of the same whole in labour law, how can the exclusive power to legislate as to management of an undertaking not include the equally exclusive power to make laws regarding its labour relations? To deny this, as the critics have done, is to strip the exclusive federal power of its primary content and transform it simply into a power to make ancillary laws connected to a primary power with no real independent content, apart from the power to regulate rates and the availability and quality of services such as telephone services or railway services. The latter undoubtedly fall within the exclusive classes of subject represented by such federal undertakings, but there is nothing in the constitutional provisions, rules or precedents to indicate that the exclusive legislative authority of Parliament must or may be confined to so narrow a field. Indeed, rates and the availability and quality of services are inseparable from the wage scale that the undertaking must pay, the availability of its manpower, leave, vacation—in short, working conditions. This is why in *Bell Canada 1966* Martland J refers at p. 772 to rates and services in their relation to wages, and it is why he comes back to this at p. 777 in arriving at his conclusions.

Professor Hogg writes that the theory which is the basis of *Bell Canada 1966* not only confers a power on Parliament but operates defensively to deny the power of the Legislature. In my view, and I say so with the greatest respect, this theory does not confer on Parliament any power that it does not already have, since it is an integral and vital part of its primary legislative authority over federal undertakings. If this power is exclusive, it is because the Constitution, which could have been different but is not, expressly specifies this to be the case; and it is because this power is exclusive that it pre-empts that of the legislatures both as to their legislation of general and specific application, in so far as such laws affect a vital part of a federal undertaking. The exclusivity rule is absolute and does not allow for any distinction between these two types of statute. However, the pith and substance doctrine does require a distinction to be made between these two types of statute, as well as between laws of general application and their application to particular institutions. General legislation on the management and working conditions of undertakings is legislation on matters falling within the property and civil rights class. But particular legislation on the management of federal undertakings and their working conditions, like that in the *Canada Labour Code*, is legislation on matters falling within an exclusively federal class of subjects, that of federal undertakings. The particular effect of general provincial laws that would result from their application to federal undertakings would, in the case at bar, constitute an encroachment on the exclusive jurisdiction of Parliament.

…

This principle appears to have been omitted in the criticism of *Bell Canada 1966* offered by Professor Hogg. Yet this line of reasoning explains the nature of the exclusive federal power given that working conditions and labour relations cannot be divorced from the management of a federal undertaking.

In one of the foregoing passages, Professor Hogg contrasts exclusive powers with "concurrent" powers. This can only be a way of speaking. Professor Hogg likely intends to refer to the overlapping of federal and provincial legislation which may result from the exercise of an ancillary power by Parliament or the application of the double aspect theory; however, as I said at the start of these reasons, these are not concurrent powers such as the fields of agriculture or immigration. …

That leaves the "policy" argument, according to which it would always be open to Parliament to protect federal undertakings against provincial statutes by an exercise of its so-called ancillary power and the application of the paramountcy of federal legislation.

I must say that I find very little merit in such an argument, both in general terms and when invoked in the particular field of occupational health and safety.

It is an argument which relies on a spirit of contradiction between systems of regulation, investigation, inspection and remedial notices which are increasingly complex, specialized and, perhaps inevitably, highly detailed. A division of jurisdiction in this area is likely to be a source of uncertainty and endless disputes in which the courts will be called on to decide whether a conflict exists between the most trivial federal and provincial regulations, such as those specifying the thickness or colour of safety boots or hard hats.

Furthermore, in the case of occupational health and safety, such a twofold jurisdiction is likely to promote the proliferation of preventive measures and controls in which the contradictions or lack of coordination may well threaten the very occupational health and safety which are sought to be protected.

Federalism requires most persons and institutions to serve two masters; however, in my opinion an effort must be made to see that this dual control applies as far as possible in separate areas. With all due respect for the opposite view, therefore, I think that the decision in *Bell Canada 1966* is correct.

[Beetz J turned to a consideration of the double aspect doctrine, which he characterized as permitting Parliament and a province to "enact two relatively similar rules provided they are legislating for different purposes and on the basis of different aspects." After examining the relevant provisions of the *Quebec Act* and the *Canada Labour Code*, he concluded that "both legislators are pursuing exactly the same objective by similar techniques and means." Since the "legislators have legislated *for the same purpose and in the same aspect*," the double aspect doctrine did not apply. Labour relations and the management of federal undertakings fall within the exclusive jurisdiction of Parliament. To allow provincial law to apply concurrently, Beetz J argued, would strip the exclusivity of federal power of any distinct or meaningful content.

He concluded that the provincial law had to be read down so as not to apply to federally-regulated undertakings such as Bell Canada. Following the approach in *Bell #1*, he stated that "in order for the inapplicability of provincial legislation rule to be given effect, it is sufficient that the provincial statute which purports to apply to the federal undertaking affects a vital or essential part of that undertaking, without necessarily going as far as impairing or paralyzing it." Since the working conditions and management of an undertaking are vital or essential parts of the undertaking, it follows that the *Quebec Act* could not apply to them.]

Appeal dismissed.

NOTES AND QUESTIONS

1. In *Bell #2*, Beetz J rests his defence of the interjurisdictional immunity doctrine on a strong understanding of the exclusivity of federal powers. Because federal powers are exclusive, Beetz J argued, and because this rule is "absolute," the application of valid provincial laws is pre-empted. Note that the pith and substance, ancillary, and double aspect doctrines rest on a weaker view of exclusivity, one that understands exclusivity as the exclusive ability to enact legislation that has as its dominant characteristic the subject matter in question.

2. The doctrine of interjurisdictional immunity has not been applied to all areas of exclusive federal power. It has, however, been applied to a broad range of them, including, as we have seen, federal elections, telecommunications undertakings, interprovincial railways and trucking undertakings, as well as to the postal service, banking, aeronautics, navigation and shipping, the military, Aboriginal peoples and lands, the RCMP, federal parks, and even criminal procedure. In *Ordon Estate v. Grail*, [1998] 3 SCR 437, 166 DLR (4th) 193, the doctrine was described in general terms as one that can be used to protect any exclusive federal power. In their judgment for the Court, Iacobucci and Major JJ wrote (at para. 81) that "[t]he principal question in any case involving exclusive federal jurisdiction is whether the provincial statute trenches, either in its entirety or in its application to specific factual contexts, upon a head of exclusive federal power. Where a provincial statute trenches upon exclusive federal power in its application to specific factual contexts, the statute must be read down so as not to apply to those situations." They went on to hold that maritime negligence law is a "core element" of federal jurisdiction over navigation, and thus is an area that is immune from the operation of provincial statutes.

3. One issue that had remained unresolved after *Bell #2* was whether provincial environmental regulations would be applicable to federal undertakings. Arguably, such regulations could involve matters central to the operation and management of federal undertakings. The issue reached the Supreme Court of Canada in *R v. Canadian Pacific Ltd.*, [1995] 2 SCR 1031, 125 DLR (4th) 385. The case involved a railway that had conducted a controlled burn of dry grass and weeds on its railway right-of-way. A large amount of smoke was produced that created a nuisance for nearby residents and the railway was charged with unlawful discharge of a contaminant under the Ontario *Environmental Protection Act*. In very brief oral reasons the Supreme Court of Canada found the provincial legislation to be applicable to

the railway, a federal undertaking. The Court simply relied upon a nineteenth-century case, *Canadian Pacific Railway Co. v. Corporation of the Parish of Notre Dame de Bonsecours*, [1899] AC 367 (PC), in which the Privy Council had ruled that a railway was required to comply with a municipal order requiring it to clear a blocked drainage ditch on its right-of-way that was causing damage to adjacent land. Is the ruling in *Canadian Pacific* consistent with the rulings in *Bell #1* and *Bell #2*?

4. In *Irwin Toy Ltd. v. Quebec (AG)*, [1989] 1 SCR 927, 58 DLR (4th) 577, a majority of the Court pulled back on the scope of immunity the *Bell #2* ruling had conferred on federal undertakings and other federally regulated enterprises. The case involved a Quebec law prohibiting advertisers from directing advertisements at persons under thirteen years of age. An advertiser argued that the law was *ultra vires* to the extent that it applied to television advertising and thereby affected a vital part of the management of broadcast undertakings. A narrow 3 to 2 majority of the Supreme Court rejected this argument and upheld the application of the provincial law to television advertisers. In doing so, the majority introduced a refinement to the doctrine of interjurisdictional immunity. The majority acknowledged that advertising is a vital part of the operation of a broadcast undertaking. Following the reasoning in *Bell #2*, this acknowledgment should have led to the conclusion that the Quebec legislation would have to be read down so that it would not apply to federally regulated broadcast undertakings. The majority (in an opinion written jointly by Dickson CJC, Lamer, and Wilson JJ), perhaps troubled by the negative impact that *Bell #2*'s approach could have on Quebec's ability to pursue distinctive cultural policies, avoided the result apparently dictated by *Bell #2*. They did so by introducing a new wrinkle into the jurisprudence. They ruled that the "vital part" test properly determines the scope of the interjurisdictional immunity doctrine when a provincial law applies *directly* to a federal undertaking. However, the narrower sterilization or impairment test should be followed when a provincial law applies *indirectly* to the undertaking. Since the provincial law at issue did not apply directly to broadcasters (it affected them indirectly through the prohibitions directed at advertisers), the majority applied the impairment test. The majority concluded that the law did not go so far as to impair or sterilize the operation of broadcast undertakings, and therefore it could validly apply to them.

The majority did not explain why the test should be different depending on whether the legislation directly or indirectly achieves its effects. One is left with the impression that the distinction was an unprincipled one, apparently produced by the majority's desire to loosen the constraints imposed by the interjurisdictional immunity doctrine without overruling *Bell #2*. See D. Gibson, Comment (1990), 69 *Canadian Bar Review* 339.

The Supreme Court of Canada had occasion to consider the doctrine of interjurisdictional immunity in two recent cases, *Canadian Western Bank v. Alberta*, [2007] 2 SCR 3, 2007 SCC 22, 281 DLR (4th) 125 and *British Columbia (Attorney General) v. Lafarge Canada Inc.*, [2007] 2 SCR 86, 2007 SCC 23, 281 DLR (4th) 54. In both cases, the doctrine was invoked by federally regulated undertakings, banks in the first and a port authority in the second. In each case, the Court declined to apply the doctrine, and for essentially the same reason—application of the provincial legislation at issue was held not to encroach on a core area of federal legislative jurisdiction. In *Canadian Western Bank*, promoting "peace of mind" insurance was held not to fall within the core of Parliament's jurisdiction over banking; in *Lafarge Canada*, permitting a cement batching plant to be built on land owned by the port authority was held not to fall within the core of Parliament's jurisdiction over navigation and shipping. In each case, therefore, there was no bar to applying the provincial legislation at issue—regulating the business of insurance in the first and regulating land use within a particular municipality in the second—to the claimants.

While it was not necessary for the Court to make any general comments on the doctrine in either of these two cases, it nevertheless chose to do so, and the bulk of those comments were made in *Canadian Western Bank*. As you will see from the majority reasons for judgment of Justices Binnie and LeBel in that case, excerpted below, the comments were wide-ranging and varied. Justices Binnie and LeBel affirmed the doctrine's legitimacy and acknowledged that the doctrine works to protect the exclusivity of both provincial and federal jurisdiction—an issue on which there had been some uncertainty. However, they also resurrected the critiques of the doctrine made by Chief Justice Dickson in *OPSEU*, tightened up the test that has to be met in order for the doctrine to be applicable, and expressed a preference for relying on the doctrine of federal paramountcy over the doctrine of interjurisdictional immunity to resolve federalism disputes once the validity of the impugned legislation has been established.

Canadian Western Bank v. The Queen in Right of Alberta
[2007] 2 SCR 3, 2007 SCC 22, 281 DLR (4th) 125

BINNIE and LeBEL JJ (McLachlin CJC and Fish, Abella, and Charron JJ concurring):

(2) The Doctrine of Interjurisdictional Immunity and its Sources

[33] Interjurisdictional immunity is a doctrine of limited application, but its existence is supported both textually and by the principles of federalism. The leading modern formulation of the doctrine of interjurisdictional immunity is found in the judgment of this Court in *Bell Canada* [*v. Québec (Commission de la santé et de la sécurité du travail)*, [1988] 1 SCR 749], where Beetz J wrote that "classes of subject" in ss. 91 and 92 must be assured a "basic, minimum and unassailable content" (p. 839) immune from the application of legislation enacted by the other level of government. Immunity from such intrusion, Beetz J observed in the context of a federal undertaking, is

> an integral and vital part of [Parliament's] primary legislative authority over federal undertakings. If this power is exclusive, it is because the Constitution, which could have been different but is not, expressly specifies this to be the case; and it is because this power is exclusive that it pre-empts that of the legislatures both as to their legislation of general and specific application, in so far as such laws affect a vital part of a federal undertaking. [p. 840]

[34] The doctrine is rooted in references to "exclusivity" throughout ss. 91 and 92 of the *Constitution Act, 1867*. The opening paragraph of s. 91 refers to the "*exclusive* [l]egislative [a]uthority of the Parliament of Canada" in relation to matters coming within the listed "[c]lasses of [s]ubjects" including "Banking, Incorporation of Banks, and the

Issue of Paper Money" (s. 91(15)). If that authority is truly exclusive, the reasoning goes, it cannot be invaded by provincial legislation even if the federal power remains unexercised ... . Equally, s. 92 (headed "*Exclusive* Powers of Provincial Legislatures") is introduced by the words "In each Province the Legislature may *exclusively* make Laws in relation to Matters coming within the Classes of Subjects next herein-after enumerated," including "Property and Civil Rights in the Province" (s. 92(13)) and "Generally all Matters of a merely local or private Nature in the Province" (s. 92(16)). The notion of exclusivity and the reciprocal notion of non-encroachment by one level of legislature on the field of exclusive competence of the other gave rise to Lord Atkin's famous "watertight compartments" metaphor, where he wrote of Canadian federalism that "[w]hile the ship of state now sails on larger ventures and into foreign waters she still retains the watertight compartments which are an essential part of her original structure" (*Attorney-General for Canada v. Attorney-General for Ontario*, [1937] AC 326 (PC), at p. 354). Its modern application expresses a continuing concern about risk of erosion of provincial as well as federal competences (*Bell Canada (1988)*, at p. 766). At the same time, the doctrine of interjurisdictional immunity seeks to avoid, when possible, situations of concurrency of powers (Laskin CJ, in *Natural Parents v. Superintendent of Child Welfare*, [1976] 2 SCR 751, at p. 764).

(3) The Dominant Tide of Constitutional Interpretation Does Not Favour Interjurisdictional Immunity

[35] Despite the efforts to find a proper role for the doctrine, the application of interjurisdictional immunity has given rise to concerns by reason of its potential impact on Canadian constitutional arrangements. In theory, the doctrine is reciprocal: it applies both to protect provincial heads of power and provincially regulated undertakings from federal encroachment, and to protect federal heads of power and federally regulated undertakings from provincial encroachment. However, it would appear that the jurisprudential application of the doctrine has produced somewhat "asymmetrical" results. Its application to federal laws in order to avoid encroachment on provincial legislative authority has often consisted of "reading down" the federal enactment or federal power without too much doctrinal discussion, e.g., *Attorney General of Canada v. Law Society of British Columbia*, [1982] 2 SCR 307, *Dominion Stores Ltd. v. The Queen*, [1980] 1 SCR 844, and *Labatt Breweries of Canada Ltd. v. Attorney General of Canada*, [1980] 1 SCR 914. In general, though, the doctrine has been invoked in favour of federal immunity at the expense of provincial legislation: Hogg, at p. 15-34.

[36] A view of federalism that puts greater emphasis on the legitimate interplay between federal and provincial powers was championed by the late Chief Justice Dickson, who described the doctrine of interjurisdictional immunity as "not ... particularly compelling" (*OPSEU v. Ontario (Attorney General)*, [1987] 2 SCR 2, at p. 17):

> The history of Canadian constitutional law has been to allow for a fair amount of interplay and indeed overlap between federal and provincial powers. It is true that doctrines like interjurisdictional and Crown immunity and concepts like "watertight compartments" qualify the extent of that interplay. But it must be recognized that these doctrines and concepts have not been the dominant tide of constitutional doctrines; rather they have been an undertow

against the strong pull of pith and substance, the aspect doctrine and, in recent years, a very restrained approach to concurrency and paramountcy issues. [p. 18]

This statement was reproduced in Dickson CJ's judgment (for a unanimous bench that included Beetz J) in *General Motors* [*City National Leasing Ltd. v. General Motors of Canada Ltd.* [1989] 1 SCR 641], at p. 669.

[37] The "dominant tide" finds its principled underpinning in the concern that a court should favour, where possible, the ordinary operation of statutes enacted by *both* levels of government. In the absence of conflicting enactments of the other level of government, the Court should avoid blocking the application of measures which are taken to be enacted in furtherance of the public interest. ...

[38] In our view, the sweeping immunity argued for by the banks in this appeal is not acceptable in the Canadian federal structure. The argument exposes the dangers of allowing the doctrine of interjurisdictional immunity to exceed its proper (and very restricted) limit and to frustrate the application of the pith and substance analysis and of the double aspect doctrine. The latter have the ability to resolve most problems relating to the validity of the exercise of legislative powers under the heads of power applicable to the activities in question.

[Justices Binnie and LeBel then provide an overview of the early cases involving federally incorporated companies and federally regulated undertakings that are said to have given rise to the doctrine, as well as some of the later cases in which the scope of the doctrine was extended to other areas, including certain "activities" falling within exclusive federal jurisdiction. They suggest that application of the doctrine to protect federal "activities" from the reach of provincial legislation poses special problems.]

[41] ... In *Ordon Estate v. Grail*, [1998] 3 SCR 437, in the course of considering federal jurisdiction over maritime law, the Court acknowledged that the doctrine could potentially apply to all "activities" within Parliament's jurisdiction. See also *McKay v. The Queen*, [1965] SCR 798, where the issue was the applicability of a municipal sign law to a federal activity, namely a federal election; *OPSEU, per* Beetz J, at p. 30; and *Scowby v. Glendinning*, [1986] 2 SCR 226, *per* La Forest J, at p. 257.

[42] While the text and logic of our federal structure justifies the application of interjurisdictional immunity to certain federal "activities," nevertheless, a broad application of the doctrine to "activities" creates practical problems of application much greater than in the case of works or undertakings, things or persons, whose limits are more readily defined. A broad application also appears inconsistent, as stated, with the flexible federalism that the constitutional doctrines of pith and substance, double aspect and federal paramountcy are designed to promote. ... It is these doctrines that have proved to be most consistent with contemporary views of Canadian federalism, which recognize that overlapping powers are unavoidable. Canadian federalism is not simply a matter of legalisms. The Constitution, though a legal document, serves as a framework for life and for political action within a federal state, in which the courts have rightly observed the importance of co-operation among government actors to ensure that federalism operates flexibly.

[43] Excessive reliance on the doctrine of interjurisdictional immunity would create serious uncertainty. It is based on the attribution to every legislative head of power of a "core" of indeterminate scope—difficult to define, except over time by means of judicial interpretations triggered serendipitously on a case-by-case basis. The requirement to develop an abstract definition of a "core" is not compatible, generally speaking, with the tradition of Canadian constitutional interpretation, which favours an incremental approach. While it is true that the enumerations of ss. 91 and 92 contain a number of powers that are precise and not really open to discussion, other powers are far less precise, such as those relating to the criminal law, trade and commerce and matters of a local or private nature in a province. Since the time of Confederation, courts have refrained from trying to define the possible scope of such powers in advance and for all time ... . For example, while the courts have not eviscerated the federal trade and commerce power, they have, in interpreting it, sought to avoid draining of their content the provincial powers over civil law and matters of a local or private nature. A generalized application of interjurisdictional immunity related to "trade and commerce" would have led to an altogether different and more rigid and centralized form of federalism. It was by proceeding with caution on a case-by-case basis that the courts were gradually able to define the content of the heads of power of Parliament and the legislatures, without denying the unavoidable interplay between them, always having regard to the evolution of the problems for which the division of legislative powers must now provide solutions.

[44] Moreover, as stated, interjurisdictional immunity means that despite the absence of law enacted at one level of government, the laws enacted by the other level cannot have even incidental effects on the so-called "core" of jurisdiction. This increases the risk of creating "legal vacuums" ... . Generally speaking, such "vacuums" are not desirable.

[45] Further, a broad use of the doctrine of interjurisdictional immunity runs the risk of creating an unintentional centralizing tendency in constitutional interpretation. As stated, this doctrine has in the past most often protected federal heads of power from incidental intrusion by provincial legislatures. The "asymmetrical" application of interjurisdictional immunity is incompatible with the flexibility and co-ordination required by contemporary Canadian federalism. Commentators have noted that an extensive application of this doctrine to protect federal heads of power and undertakings is both unnecessary and "undesirable in a federation where so many laws for the protection of workers, consumers and the environment (for example) are enacted and enforced at the provincial level" [P.W. Hogg, *Constitutional Law of Canada* (loose-leaf ed.), at p. 15-30]. The asymmetrical effect of interjurisdictional immunity can also be seen as undermining the principles of subsidiarity, i.e. that decisions "are often best [made] at a level of government that is not only effective, but also closest to the citizens affected" (*114957 Canada Ltée (Spraytech, Société d'arrosage) v. Hudson (Town)*, [2001] 2 SCR 241, 2001 SCC 40, at para. 3).

[46] Finally, the doctrine would seem as a general rule to be superfluous in that Parliament can always, if it sees fit to do so, make its legislation sufficiently precise to leave those subject to it with no doubt as to the residual or incidental application of provincial legislation. As we shall see, sufficient confirmation of this can be found in the history and operation of the doctrine of federal paramountcy.

[47] For all these reasons, although the doctrine of interjurisdictional immunity has a proper part to play in appropriate circumstances, we intend now to make it clear that the Court does not favour an intensive reliance on the doctrine, nor should we accept the invitation of the appellants to turn it into a doctrine of first recourse in a division of powers dispute.

D. A More Restricted Approach to Interjurisdictional Immunity

(1) Impairment Versus Affects

[48] Even in situations where the doctrine of interjurisdictional immunity is properly available, we must consider the level of the intrusion on the "core" of the power of the other level of government which would trigger its application. In *Bell Canada (1988)*, Beetz J wrote, at pp. 859-60:

> In order for the inapplicability of provincial legislation rule to be given effect, it is sufficient that the provincial statute which purports to apply to the federal undertaking *affects a vital or essential part of that undertaking, without necessarily going as far as impairing or paralyzing it*. [Emphasis added.]

... We believe that the law as it stood prior to *Bell Canada (1988)* better reflected our federal scheme. In our opinion, it is not enough for the provincial legislation simply to "affect" that which makes a federal subject or object of rights specifically of federal jurisdiction. The difference between "affects" and "impairs" is that the former does not imply any adverse consequence whereas the latter does. ... It is when the adverse impact of a law adopted by one level of government increases in severity from "affecting" to "impairing" (without necessarily "sterilizing" or "paralyzing") that the "core" competence of the other level of government (or the vital or essential part of an undertaking it duly constitutes) is placed in jeopardy, and not before.

[49] In *Irwin Toy Ltd. v. Quebec (Attorney General)*, [1989] 1 SCR 927, Dickson CJ and Lamer and Wilson JJ observed in passing that a distinction could be drawn between the *direct* application of provincial law (where the operative verb is "affects") and the *indirect* application (where the operative verb may still be "impairs") (p. 957). This further exercise in line drawing signalled a measure of dissatisfaction with the "affects" test without doing anything about it. At this point, we should complete the reassessment begun in *Irwin Toy* and hold that, in the absence of impairment, interjurisdictional immunity does not apply.

(2) Identification of the "Basic, Minimum and Unassailable" Content of a Legislative Power

[50] One of the important contributions of *Bell Canada (1988)* was to limit the scope of the doctrine to the "basic, minimum and unassailable content" (p. 839) sometimes referred to as the "core" of the legislative power in question. (By "minimum," we understand that Beetz J meant the minimum content necessary to make the power effective for the purpose for which it was conferred.) This is necessary, according to Beetz J, to give effect to what he called "the principle of federalism underlying the Canadian Constitution" (p. 766). Thus, the success of the appellants' argument in this appeal depended in

part on locating the promotion of "peace of mind" insurance at the core of banking. For the reasons already discussed, and particularized below, we do not believe that this aspect of the appellants' argument can be sustained.

(3) The Vital or Essential Part of an Undertaking

[51] In the exercise of their legislative powers, federal and provincial legislators bring into existence "undertakings." The appellant banks are "federal undertakings" constituted pursuant to the s. 91(15) banking power. In *Bell Canada (1988)*, Beetz J spoke of interjurisdictional immunity in relation to "essential and vital elements" of such undertakings (pp. 839 and 859-60). In our view, some text writers and certainly the appellants have been inclined to give too wide a scope to what should be considered "vital or essential" to a federal undertaking. We believe that Beetz J chose his words carefully and intended to use "vital" in its ordinary grammatical sense of "[e]ssential to the existence of something; absolutely indispensable or necessary; extremely important, crucial" (*Shorter Oxford English Dictionary* (5th ed. 2002), vol. 2, at p. 3548). The word "essential" has a similar meaning, e.g. "[a]bsolutely indispensable or necessary" (vol. 1, at p. 860). The words "vital" and "essential" were not randomly chosen ... . What is "vital" or "essential" is, by definition, not co-extensive with every element of an undertaking incorporated federally or subject to federal regulation. In the case of federal undertakings, Beetz J referred to a "general rule" that there is *no* interjurisdictional immunity, provided that "the application of [the] provincial laws does not bear upon those [federal] subjects *in what makes them specifically of federal jurisdiction*" (*Bell Canada (1988)*, at p. 762 (emphasis added)). In the present appeal, for example, the appellants' argument inflates out of all proportion what could reasonably be considered "vital or essential" to their banking undertaking. The promotion of "peace of mind" insurance can hardly be considered "absolutely indispensable or necessary" to banking activities unless such words are to be emptied of their ordinary meaning.

[52] In this respect, following the sage common law adage that it is wise to look at what the courts do as distinguished from what they say, a useful approach to understanding the limited scope of the doctrine of interjurisdictional immunity in respect of undertakings is to see how it has been applied to the facts. A comparison between *Bell Canada (1988)* and the present case is instructive. In *Bell Canada (1988)*, the Court concluded that the application of a provincial Act respecting occupational health and safety could not apply to a federal telephone undertaking because such application would "enter directly and massively into the field of working conditions and labour relations ... and ... management and operation" of the federal utility (p. 798). Amongst other things, the provincial Act would impose "a system of partial co-management of the undertaking by the workers and the employer" (p. 810), thereby regulating the federal undertaking in a manner not sanctioned by Parliament. To the same effect is *Canadian National Railway Co. v. Courtois*, [1988] 1 SCR 868, released concurrently with *Bell Canada (1988)*, where the same provincial Act was declared inapplicable to a federally regulated railway (p. 890). In the third case of the 1988 trilogy, *Alltrans Express Ltd. v. British Columbia (Workers' Compensation Board)*, [1988] 1 SCR 897, the Court held that the preventative (as distinguished from compensatory) aspects of the BC provincial *Workers Compensation Act*

could not apply to an interprovincial and international trucking undertaking because to do so would intrude on the management of the federally regulated undertaking, including the "BC Board's power to order an employer to close down all or part of the place of employment to prevent injuries" (p. 911). These cases may usefully be contrasted with *Canadian Pacific Railway Co. v. Corporation of the Parish of Notre Dame de Bonsecours*, [1899] AC 367 (PC), where it was held *not* to be vital or essential for the federal government to regulate the clearance of trash and debris from the ditch on the south side of the railway undertaking's roadbed. (See also *Ontario v. Canadian Pacific Ltd.*, [1995] 2 SCR 1028.) Yet it seems that clearing debris from the roadbed is at least as essential to the operations of a rail service as is selling optional "peace of mind" insurance to bank borrowers.

[53] Nor do the other authorities relied on by the appellants, in our view, justify their expansive view of the elements that are vital and essential to their banking operations. It is simply not credible, in our view, to suggest that the promotion of "peace of mind" insurance is "absolutely indispensable or necessary" to enable the banks to carry out their undertakings in what makes them specifically of federal jurisdiction.

E. The Interjurisdictional Immunity Case Law Relied on by the Appellants

[Justices Binnie and LeBel review many of the prior cases in which either the Privy Council or the Supreme Court had been asked to apply the doctrine for the purpose of showing that the existing jurisprudence supports their view that what is "vital and essential"—or truly "core" to an area of federal legislative jurisdiction—has to be understood narrowly.]

(7) Conclusion

[67] In our view, the above review of the case law cited by the appellants, the respondent and interveners shows that not only *should* the doctrine of interjurisdictional immunity be applied with restraint, but with rare exceptions it *has* been so applied. Although the doctrine is in principle applicable to all federal and provincial heads of legislative authority, the case law demonstrates that its natural area of operation is in relation to those heads of legislative authority that confer on Parliament power over enumerated federal things, people, works or undertakings. In most cases, a pith and substance analysis and the application of the doctrine of paramountcy have resolved difficulties in a satisfactory manner.

[Justices Binnie and LeBel then discuss the appropriate approach to take to the doctrine of federal paramountcy, which is the subject of the next section of this chapter. Before they apply this approach, however, they express their view on the question of the order in which courts should consider the doctrines of interjurisdictional immunity and federal paramountcy after they have satisfied themselves that the impugned legislation is valid on the basis of the pith and substance doctrine. Prior to this case, it was understood that the doctrine of interjurisdictional immunity should always be applied first.]

G. Order of Application of the Constitutional Doctrines

. . .

[77] Although our colleague Bastarache J takes a different view on this point, we do not think it appropriate to *always* begin by considering the doctrine of interjurisdictional immunity. To do so could mire the Court in a rather abstract discussion of "cores" and "vital and essential" parts to little practical effect. As we have already noted, interjurisdictional immunity is of limited application and should in general be reserved for situations already covered by precedent. This means, in practice, that it will be largely reserved for those heads of power that deal with federal things, persons or undertakings, or where in the past its application has been considered absolutely indispensable or necessary to enable Parliament or a provincial legislature to achieve the purpose for which exclusive legislative jurisdiction was conferred, as discerned from the constitutional division of powers as a whole, or what is absolutely indispensable or necessary to enable an undertaking to carry out its mandate in what makes it specifically of federal (or provincial) jurisdiction. If a case can be resolved by the application of a pith and substance analysis, and federal paramountcy where necessary, it would be preferable to take that approach, as this Court did in *Mangat* [*Law Society of British Columbia v. Mangat*, [2001] 3 SCR 113].

[78] In the result, while in theory a consideration of interjurisdictional immunity is apt for consideration after the pith and substance analysis, in practice the absence of prior case law favouring its application to the subject matter at hand will generally justify a court proceeding directly to the consideration of federal paramountcy.

[Justices Binnie and LeBel then proceed to apply the doctrine of federal paramountcy. They conclude that there is no conflict between the provincial and federal legislation at issue and that the provincial legislation can therefore operate in relation to the banks in Alberta that wish to promote "peace of mind" insurance to their customers. This part of the decision is discussed further in the next section of this chapter, which deals with the doctrine of paramountcy.]

NOTES AND QUESTIONS

1. Justice Bastarache concurred in the result in *Canadian Western Bank*, but did not agree with the new approach to the doctrine of interjurisdictional immunity outlined by Justices Binnie and LeBel. His view of the doctrine, which is a much more positive one that would have left the doctrine more or less in the state it was in prior to these two cases, is developed in his concurring reasons for judgment in *British Columbia (Attorney General) v. Lafarge Canada Inc.*, [2007] 2 SCR 86, 2007 SCC 23, 281 DLR (4th) 54.

2. In their reasons for judgment in *Lafarge Canada*, Justices Binnie and LeBel suggest that the doctrine of interjurisdictional immunity "should not be used where, as here, the legislative subject matter (waterfront development) presents a double aspect" (para. 4). If that suggestion is to be taken seriously, what room, if any, will be left for the doctrine?

3. A number of scholars have commented on the new approach to the doctrine taken by Justices Binnie and LeBel in these two cases, not all of them favourably. See L. Edinger, "Back

to the Future with Interjurisdictional Immunity: Canadian Western Bank v. Alberta and British Columbia v. Lafarge Canada Inc." (2008), 66 *The Advocate* 553; P.W. Hogg and R. Godil, "Narrowing Interjurisdictional Immunity" (2008), 42 *Supreme Court Law Review* (2d) 623; J.G. Furey, "Interjurisdictional Immunity: The Pendulum Has Swung" (2008), 42 *Supreme Court Law Review* (2d) 597; and R. Elliot, "Interjurisdictional Immunity after Canadian Western Bank and Lafarge Canada Inc.: The Supreme Court Muddies the Doctrinal Waters—Again" (2008), 43 *Supreme Court Law Review* (2d) 433.

IV. OPERABILITY: THE PARAMOUNTCY DOCTRINE

Federal systems require a mechanism for dealing with the overlap of and conflict between national and regional laws. In some federal constitutions, the rules are provided expressly by the constitutional document. In Canada, however, the Constitution is silent on the issue, with three specific exceptions. Section 95 of the *Constitution Act, 1867* recognizes agriculture and immigration as areas of concurrent jurisdiction and provides that provincial laws shall have effect only to the extent that they are not "repugnant" to any Act of Parliament. Similarly, s. 92A, added by constitutional amendment in 1982, confers on provincial legislatures a concurrent power to enact laws in relation to the export of natural resources to other provinces, subject to the paramountcy of federal legislation in the case of conflict. Section 94A, added by constitutional amendments in 1951 and 1964, provides for concurrency in relation to old-age pensions and supplementary benefits (including survivors' and disability benefits), but provides a form of provincial paramountcy by stating that no federal law "shall affect the operation of any law present or future of a provincial legislature in relation to any such matter." But for most subjects of legislation, including all of those listed in ss. 91 and 92, no paramountcy rule is specified in the Constitution.

The absence in the Constitution of a general set of rules for dealing with conflict between federal and provincial laws may be explained by the belief of the drafters, in 1867, that overlap would not occur given the exclusivity of subject matters in ss. 91 and 92, or that any problems of conflict between federal and provincial laws would be solved in the political arena through the federal Parliament's exercise of the declaratory power in s. 92(10)(c) or the powers of reservation and disallowance. A judicially created rule filled the gap—the doctrine of federal paramountcy, modelled on the rule found in s. 95. It provides that in cases of conflict between federal and provincial laws, the federal law is paramount and the provincial law is *inoperative* to the extent of the conflict.

Note that if a conflict is found to exist by the application of the paramountcy rule, the provincial law is not declared invalid. Its operation is merely suspended to the extent that it conflicts with federal legislation. If the federal legislation is repealed, the conflict disappears and the provincial law may once again be applied.

The key issue in paramountcy cases is whether a conflict exists between federal and provincial laws. How should courts go about defining the necessary conflict? The Supreme Court of Canada struggles with that question in the cases that follow. A narrow reading of conflict allows both the federal and provincial laws to operate unless it is impossible for those subject to, or responsible for giving effect to, the two legislative schemes to comply with both. This approach is referred to as the "express conflict" or "impossibility of dual compliance" test. It has as its focus the individuals, corporations, or legal decision makers who must tailor their behaviour to the legislative dictates. A broader reading of conflict holds a valid provincial law inoperative whenever it has an impact on a matter already regulated by a valid federal law. The broader approach is referred to as the "covering the field" test or the "negative implication" doctrine. The idea underlying this approach is that Parliament, by legislating in a particular area, has enacted a code that was intended to be complete and thus by implication was intended to oust the operation of any provincial laws. Another possibility is to define the necessary conflict as an incompatibility of legislative policies or objectives. This approach has as its focus the intention of the legislature that enjoys the benefit of the paramountcy rule, here the federal Parliament. What values are furthered by each of these rules?

While support for the covering-the-field test can be found in some older cases, the Supreme Court tended, until the past couple of decades, to define conflict narrowly, and therefore to leave a great deal of room for the concurrent operation of federal and provincial statutes. That narrow approach was exemplified by a series of cases dealing with highway traffic offences decided in the 1960s and 1970s, in which the Court upheld provincial statutes that impose different standards and consequences for driving offences than those set out in the *Criminal Code*. The rejection of a broad definition of conflict in favour of an "impossibility of dual compliance" test, implicit in cases like *Ross*, below, was explicitly confirmed by the Supreme Court in 1982 in what was for a number of years considered the leading case, *Multiple Access v. McCutcheon*, excerpted following *Ross*, below. However, in some of the more recent cases, notably *Bank of Montreal v. Hall* and *Rothmans, Benson & Hedges v. Saskatchewan*, also excerpted below, the Court has adopted a broader approach, with the result that more provincial legislation than was the case before is now at risk of being declared inoperative in the face of overlapping federal legislation.

Ross v. Registrar of Motor Vehicles
[1975] 1 SCR 5, 42 DLR (3d) 68

[In 1972, under s. 234 of the *Criminal Code*, Ross was convicted of driving while impaired. In cases where an accused had been convicted of certain motor vehicle offences under the Code, including offences under s. 234, s. 238(1) of the Code allowed a trial judge to make, in addition to any other punishment, "an order prohibiting the accused from driving a motor vehicle in Canada, at all times or at such times and places as may be specified in the order ... during any period not exceeding three years." Section 238(2) provided that a copy of any order made under subsection (1) was to be sent to the Registrar of Motor Vehicles for the province that had issued the accused's driver's licence. The judge sentencing Ross ordered that "[t]he accused shall be prohibited from driving for a period of six months except Monday to Friday, 8:00 a.m. to 5:45 p.m. in the course of employment and going to and from work." The order further provided that Ross's driver's licence was not to be suspended and that the Registrar of Motor Vehicles be advised of the order.

The Registrar of Motor Vehicles in the province of Ontario, where Ross resided, nonetheless suspended his licence for three months in accordance with s. 21 of the Ontario *Highway Traffic Act*. That section provided that the licence of any person convicted of an offence under any of several sections of the *Criminal Code*, including s. 234, was thereupon suspended for a period of three months for the first offence, and six months where personal injury, death, or damage to property occurred in connection with the offence.

Ross instituted an action claiming a declaration that s. 21 of the *Highway Traffic Act* was inoperative because of its conflict with s. 238 of the *Criminal Code* and that the suspension of his driver's licence was of no effect. The Registrar of Motor Vehicles and the provincial attorney general responded by requesting a declaration that s. 238(1) of the *Criminal Code* was *ultra vires*. The constitutional issues raised were sent to the Supreme Court for determination. The Supreme Court was required to deal with three issues: (1) was the provincial legislation—that is, s. 21 of the *Highway Traffic Act*—valid; (2) was the federal legislation—that is, s. 238(1) of the *Criminal Code*—valid; and (3) if both pieces of legislation were valid, was there a conflict between the two provisions requiring the application of the rule of federal paramountcy, with the result that the provincial legislation would be inoperative.]

PIGEON J (Abbott, Martland, Ritchie, and Dickson JJ concurring): ... In 1941, a substantially similar question concerning the validity and effect of provincial motor vehicle legislation was raised in the case of *Provincial Secretary of Prince Edward Island v. Egan*, [1941] SCR 396, [1941] 3 DLR 305 [in which] this Court ... unanimously [determined] that the operation and validity of provincial legislation suspending driving licences upon conviction of certain offences under the *Criminal Code* remained unaffected by the enactment, by the Parliament of Canada, of a provision for the making of orders prohibiting a convicted person from driving a motor vehicle during a period not exceeding three years. This enactment was s-s. (7) of s. 285 of the *Criminal Code* then in force. ...

Duff CJC said (at p. 310 DLR):

> Primarily, responsibility for the regulation of highway traffic, including authority to prescribe the conditions and the manner of the use of motor vehicles on highways and the operation of a system of licences for the purpose of securing the observance of regulations respecting these matters in the interest of the public generally, is committed to the local Legislatures.
>
> Sections 84(1)(a) and (c) are enactments dealing with licences. The Legislature has thought fit to regard convictions of the classes specified as a proper ground for suspending the licence of the convict. Such legislation, I think, is concerned with the subject of licensing, over which it is essential that the Province should primarily have control. In exercising such control it must, of course, abstain from legislating on matters within the enumerated subjects of s. 91. Suspension of a driving licence does involve a prohibition against driving; but so long as the purpose of the provincial legislation and its immediate effect are exclusively to prescribe the conditions under which licences are granted, forfeited, or suspended, I do not think, speaking generally, it is necessarily impeachable as repugnant to s. 285(7) of the *Criminal Code* in the sense above mentioned.
>
> It is, of course, beyond dispute that where an offence is created by competent Dominion legislation in exercise of the authority under s. 91(27), the penalty or penalties attached to that offence, as well as the offence itself, become matters within that paragraph of s. 91 which are excluded from provincial jurisdiction.

There is, however, no adequate ground for the conclusion that these particular enactments (s. 84(1)(a) and (c)) are in their true character attempts to prescribe penalties for the offences mentioned, rather than enactments in regulation of licences. ...

The provisions of the *Criminal Code* presently in force concerning the making of orders prohibiting a person from driving are in s. 238.

[There follows a discussion of amendments made to the *Criminal Code* provision in 1972 that allowed the judge to make orders allowing a person to drive intermittently; before the amendment, the legislation had been interpreted as allowing only an order for a single, continuous period.]

The direction that Ross' operator's licence was not to be suspended shows that the judge who made the prohibitory order considered not only that the prohibition may be limited as to time and place, but also that the person to whom the order is directed should enjoy the right to drive at a specified time and place, irrespective of provincial legislation concerning the suspension of driving privileges. In terms, the *Criminal Code* merely provides for the making of prohibitory orders limited as to time and place. If such an order is made in respect of a period of time during which a provincial licence suspension is in effect, there is, strictly speaking, no repugnancy. Both legislations can fully operate simultaneously. It is true that this means that as long as the provincial licence suspension is in effect, the person concerned gets no benefit from the indulgence granted under the federal legislation. But, is the situation any different in law from that which was considered in the *Egan* case, namely, that due to the provincial legislation, the right to drive was lost by reason of the conviction, although the convicting magistrate had made no prohibitory order whatsoever?

Reference was made in this case to s. 5(1) of the *Criminal Code* which reads:

5(1) Where an enactment creates an offence and authorizes a punishment to be imposed in respect thereof,

(a) a person shall be deemed not to be guilty of that offence until he is convicted thereof; and

(b) a person who is convicted of that offence is not liable to any punishment in respect thereof other than the punishment prescribed by this Act or by the enactment that creates the offence.

It should now be taken as settled that civil consequences of a criminal act are not to be considered as "punishment" so as to bring the matter within the exclusive jurisdiction of Parliament. ...

In *O'Grady v. Sparling*, [1960] SCR 804, 25 DLR (2d) 145, the question of repugnancy between *Criminal Code* provisions and provincial motor vehicle legislation was considered by the full Court. The problem was whether provincial legislation making it an offence to drive "without due care and attention" was repugnant to s. 221(1) (now s. 233(1)) of the *Criminal Code*. It was determined that the federal enactment did not make a crime of inadvertent negligence and provincial legislation making any negligence in driving an offence was valid. Only the two dissenting judges considered that "by necessary implication," the *Criminal Code* said not only what kinds or degrees of negligence shall be punishable, but also what kinds or degrees shall not. In other words, the majority decided that Parliament did not implicitly permit conduct which did not come within the description of the *Criminal Code* offence. Therefore, the legislation could validly prohibit such conduct under penalty as long as this was done for a proper provincial purpose. This was reaffirmed in *Mann v. The Queen*, [1966] SCR 238, 56 DLR (2d) 1. ...

In my view, it should be said in the present case that Parliament did not by the amendments to s. 238 of the *Criminal Code* purport to deal generally with the right to drive a motor vehicle after a conviction for certain offences. The only change effected was that a larger area of discretion was given to the convicting magistrate. Instead of being authorized only to make an order prohibiting driving for a definite length of time not exceeding the period stated, the magistrate was empowered to issue an order limited as to time and place. No authorization was given to make an order such as made in the present case, directing that the licence of the person convicted be not suspended. It seems clear to me that this order was made by an inferior Court completely without jurisdiction and is to be ignored.

On my view of the enactment, I can see no reason for which it could be considered as going beyond Parliament's competence. Apparently, the contention that Parliament thereby invaded provincial jurisdiction was advanced solely on the basis that s. 238 might operate to prevent the application of provincial legislation either of itself or by virtue of orders made thereunder.

It may be of some interest to observe that under the Australian constitution, a principle was developed to determine whether a field of legislation is to be considered as occupied by federal legislation so as to exclude or make inoperative State legislation. The rule was stated by Dixon J, in *Ex p. McLean* (1930), 43 CLR 472 at p. 483, in the following statement that was subsequently approved by the Privy Council (*O'Sullivan v. Noarlunga Ltd.*, [1957] AC 1 at p. 28):

> The inconsistency does not lie in the mere co-existence of two laws which are susceptible of simultaneous obedience. It depends upon the intention of the paramount legislature to express by its enactment, completely, exhaustively, or exclusively, what shall be the law governing the particular conduct or matter to which its attention is directed. When a Federal statute discloses such an intention, it is inconsistent with it for the law of a State to govern the same conduct or matter.

Of course, if we were to apply that rule, it would have to be said that Parliament did not purport to state exhaustively the law respecting motor driving licences, or the suspension or cancellation for driving offences. Therefore, the question whether this could validly be done by Parliament does not arise.

For those reasons, I would answer the questions of law stated in the order of the Supreme Court of Ontario by stating that s. 21 of the *Highway Traffic Act* is valid and operative legislation, and that s. 238 of the *Criminal Code* (as amended), is also valid. I would make no order as to costs as none were demanded.

JUDSON J dissenting in part: ... Turning now to the questions submitted, I am not in any doubt about the answer to the first two questions. Section 21 of the *Highway Traffic Act* is valid provincial legislation, and s. 238(1) of the *Criminal Code*, either in its original form or as amended in 1972, is within the powers of the Parliament of Canada. This was clearly decided in *Provincial Secretary of Prince Edward Island v. Egan*. The difficulty arises with respect to the third question, whether s. 21 of the *Highway Traffic Act* is rendered inoperative by s. 238(1) of the *Criminal Code*. The order made by the convicting Court permits intermittent driving. In s. 21 of the *Highway Traffic Act* there is an automatic and complete suspension of the licence for a stated period.

In the *Ross* case, the *Criminal Code*, as applied, and the provincial statute, s. 21 of the *Highway Traffic Act*, are in direct conflict and the federal legislation must prevail. This situation did not arise in the *Egan* case, where there was no order for the suspension of the licence made by the convicting magistrate. The power of the Province to impose an automatic suspension must give way to an order for punishment validly made under the *Criminal Code* and to that extent the provincial suspension is inoperative. ...

SPENCE J dissenting in part: ... I have come to the conclusion that I agree with the views expressed by Mr. Justice Judson. ...

By the enactment of s. 238(1) in its amended form in 1972, Parliament has stipulated the penalties attached to the offence of, *inter alia*, impaired driving, and therefore the matters specified are excluded from provincial jurisdiction.

For the reasons outlined by my brother Judson, after the enactment of s. 238(1) in its present form and when that section is used by the Court sentencing an accused person upon conviction for one of the offences dealt with therein, the subject-matter of the order made by that Court within its jurisdiction cannot be affected by the provision of the provincial statute dealing with suspension of licences and particularly s. 21 of the *Highway Traffic Act*. ...

I would therefore dispose of the *Ross* appeal in the fashion proposed by my brother Judson.

Judgment accordingly.

Multiple Access Ltd. v. McCutcheon
[1982] 2 SCR 161, 138 DLR (3d) 1

[The facts of this case are set out in more detail in the excerpt reproduced in section II.B, above. Briefly, the case involved federal and Ontario statutes regulating insider trading in securities. The Ontario *Securities Act*, RSO 1970, c. 426 prohibited insider trading in shares trading on the Toronto Stock Exchange. The *Canada Corporations Act*, RSC 1970, c. C-32 had almost identical provisions, applicable to corporations incorporated under federal law. A shareholder action was initiated against insiders of Multiple Access Inc., a federally incorporated company, with respect to trades on the Toronto Stock Exchange. The shareholder initiated the proceeding under the Ontario *Securities Act* and the Ontario Securities Commission took carriage of the case. The respondents, the alleged insider traders, argued that the Ontario statute could not validly apply to their case because the regulation of the trading in shares of federally incorporated companies falls within exclusive federal jurisdiction. In the alternative, they relied on the doctrine of paramountcy to assert that the Ontario provisions were rendered inoperative, in the case of alleged insider trading in the shares of a federally incorporated company, by the provisions of the *Canada Corporations Act* that deal with the issue. This latter argument was advantageous to the alleged insider traders because the limitation period for initiating an action under the federal statute had already elapsed.

The trial judge ruled that the federal and provincial laws could operate concurrently, but both the Divisional Court and the Court of Appeal took the view that the provincial law was inoperative by virtue of the doctrine of paramountcy. In the extract of the case reproduced in section II(C), above, a majority of the Supreme Court relied upon the double aspect doctrine to hold that both statutes were valid and applicable to trading in Ontario in the shares of federally incorporated companies. The majority then turned to the paramountcy issue: was the Ontario legislation rendered inoperative to the extent that it overlapped with the virtually identical provisions of the federal Act? Three dissenting judges decided that the federal provisions were invalid and thus did not reach the paramountcy issue.

The paramountcy issue usually requires judges to determine the degree of overlap and/or conflict between federal and provincial statutes that differ in at least some aspects. This case is distinctive in that the two pieces of legislation regulated insider trading in virtually identical ways. The question, therefore, was whether duplicate legislation could operate at both the federal and provincial levels, or, was duplication a kind of conflict that should give rise to federal paramountcy? As you consider the issue, bear in mind the criteria outlined by Simeon at the outset of this chapter that are likely to influence judicial interpretation of the division of powers. What values could be invoked in favour of letting both laws stand? What values could be invoked in favour of using paramountcy to eliminate duplication and overlap?]

DICKSON J (Laskin CJC, Martland, Ritchie, McIntyre, and Lamer JJ concurring): Having found ss. 100.4 and 100.5 of the *Canada Corporations Act* to be *intra vires* the Parliament of Canada, and ss. 113 and 114 of the Ontario *Securities Act* to be *intra vires* the Legislature of Ontario, there remains but to respond to the third and final question. Are ss. 113 and 114 of the Ontario Act suspended and rendered inoperative in respect of corporations incorporated under the laws of Canada? This is the issue Mr. Justice Henry faced at trial [65 DLR (3d) 577] ... .

He said [at 580-81]:

It is common ground that the corporate plaintiff is a federally incorporated company, that it was competent to Parliament and the Legislature to enact respectively these provisions so that each is *intra vires*.

There was no dispute between counsel that the two sets of provisions are for all material purposes identical, with the exception that if proceedings are taken under the federal provisions, the agency that will have carriage of the proceedings is the director of the corporations branch of the federal Department of Consumer and Corporate Affairs, whereas if proceedings are undertaken under the provincial *Securities Act*, the Ontario Securities Commission has carriage of the proceedings. It was also not a matter of dispute that if both sets of provisions are in operation together, both would apply to the circumstances of this case.

Although the appellant argues, weakly, that there are minor differences in the legislation, Henry J found an identity of purpose, conduct and remedy. Does mere duplication constitute "the conflict" required by the paramountcy doctrine in order to render a provincial statutory provision inoperative? This is the issue upon which Mr. Justice Henry at trial and Mr. Justice Morden in the Divisional Court parted ways. The same difference of opinion is reflected by the commentators.

Mr. Justice Henry chose a more narrow and if I may say so, more modern, test of conflict with the concomitant result of leaving to the provinces ample legislative room. He adopted the test propounded by Mr. Justice Martland in *Smith v. The Queen*, [1960] SCR 776 at 800:

> It may happen that some acts might be punishable under both provisions and in this sense that these provisions overlap. However, even in such cases, there is no conflict in the sense that compliance with one law involves breach of the other. It would appear, therefore, that they can operate concurrently.

Parenthetically, and interestingly, the test adopted by Martland J in *Smith v. The Queen* was the very test propounded by the Attorney-General of Canada in *Smith*. If one refers to the factum of the federal Attorney-General in *Smith*, prepared by W.R. Jackett and S. Samuels, one will find the following passage (at p. 8):

> It might happen that the same facts might be punishable under both provisions. In this sense they overlap. However there is no conflict in the sense that compliance with one law involves breach of the other. That being so, it is submitted that they can live together and are not only both valid but are operative concurrently.

… On the basis of the "overwhelming weight of recent authority" Mr. Justice Henry found that the two sets of statutory provisions could "live together and operate concurrently." Any "diseconomies" resulting from the proliferation of laws and administration were inherent in the federal system. Double liability would be avoided by "cooperation between administrators and the ordinary supervision of the courts over duplication of proceedings before them."

Mr. Justice Henry and Professor Hogg are of one mind. Professor Hogg writes:

> There is no reason why duplication should be a case of inconsistency once the negative implication or covering the field test is rejected. On the contrary, duplication is "the ultimate in harmony." The argument that it is untidy, wasteful and confusing to have two laws when only one is needed reflects a value which in a federal system often has to be subordinated to that of provincial autonomy. Nor does the latter value disappear when provincial law merely duplicates federal law, because the suspension of a provincial law may create a gap in a provincial scheme of regulation which would have to be filled by federal law—a situation as productive of untidiness, waste and confusion as duplication.

[P.W. Hogg, *Constitutional Law of Canada* (Scarborough, ON: Carswell, 1977), at 110.] …

Morden J adopts the older and more prevalent view of the commentators that "The authorities establish one of the implications of Dominion paramountcy to be that provincial duplicative legislation is suspended and inoperative. Simple duplication by a province is not permitted": Lederman, "The Concurrent Operation of Federal and Provincial Laws in Canada" (1963), 9 *McGill LJ* 185 at p. 195; see also B. Laskin, *Laskin's Canadian Constitutional Law* (Scarborough, ON: Carswell, 1975), at p. 117: "If member and federal measures are substantial duplicates, every situation covered by one is likewise covered by the other and there is no provincial room left, given full operation of the federal law." Morden J finds [78 DLR (3d) 1, at 709] that "Resort to one statute, from a practical point of view, precludes the other from having any application."

The conflict between the reasons of Mr. Justice Henry and the reasons of Mr. Justice Morden lies in large measure upon the opinion of the latter that the paramountcy doctrine became applicable because a plaintiff could resort to one set of provisions only and, having done so, there would be no scope for the other to have operational effect. That is unquestionably an important consideration but it is not, in my view, conclusive. The provincial legislation merely duplicates the federal; it does not contradict it. The fact that a plaintiff may have a choice of remedies does not mean that the provisions of both levels of government cannot "live together" and operate concurrently. In the *Smith* case the provincial and federal provisions were virtually identical in substance, and the law authorities could prosecute the proscribed conduct as a provincial offence or as a federal offence under the *Criminal Code*.

... [T]here is no true repugnancy in the case of merely duplicative provisions since it does not matter which statute is applied; the legislative purpose of Parliament will be fulfilled regardless of which statute is invoked by a remedy-seeker; application of the provincial law does not displace the legislative purpose of Parliament.

The respondents strenuously support Mr. Justice Morden's reasons in this court. Counsel for the respondent McCutcheon argues: "Where two actions are brought under the federal and provincial legislation against the insider, either concurrently or *seriatum*, the Court will not permit both to proceed to judgment. Both pieces of legislation cannot operate concurrently in that resort to one precludes resort to the other. The legislation under which one action is commenced operates to prevent the application of the other. In such case, the two statutes meet and are in conflict." I am not of that opinion.

With Mr. Justice Henry I would say that duplication is, to borrow Professor Lederman's phrase, "the ultimate in harmony." The resulting "untidiness" or "diseconomy" of duplication is the price we pay for a federal system in which economy "often has to be subordinated to ... provincial autonomy" (Hogg, at p. 110). Mere duplication without actual conflict or contradiction is not sufficient to invoke the doctrine of paramountcy and render otherwise valid provincial legislation inoperative.

The following passage from Professor Lederman's article "The Concurrent Operation of Federal and Provincial Laws in Canada," *supra*, at p. 199 (fn. 39), is apposite:

> As Dr. J.A. Corry has pointed out, our country is increasingly moving away from the older classical federalism of "watertight compartments" with provincial legislatures and federal parliament carefully keeping clear of one another. We seem to be moving towards a co-operative federalism. "The coordinate governments no longer work in splendid isolation

from one another but are increasingly engaged in cooperative ventures in which each relies heavily on the other." See J.A. Corry, "Constitutional Trends and Federalism," in the volume of essays *Evolving Canadian Federalism* (Durham, NC, USA, 1958), p. 96. The multiplication of concurrent fields is one of the facets of this trend.

In principle, there would seem to be no good reason to speak of paramountcy and preclusion except where there is actual conflict in operation as where one enactment says "yes" and the other says "no"; "the same citizens are being told to do inconsistent things"; compliance with one is defiance of the other. The courts are well able to prevent double recovery in the theoretical and unlikely event of plaintiffs trying to obtain relief under both sets of provisions. The fact that a court must authorize proceedings under the Ontario Act provides a safeguard against double recovery if the company has already proceeded under the federal Act. In addition the court at the final stage of finding and quantifying liability could prevent double recovery if in fact compensation and an accounting had already been made by a defendant. No court would permit double recovery.

I find that ss. 113 and 114 of the *Securities Act* of Ontario are not suspended or rendered inoperative in respect of corporations incorporated under the laws of Canada by ss. 100.4 and 100.5 of the *Canada Corporations Act*. ...

Appeal allowed.

NOTES AND QUESTIONS

1. The impossibility of dual compliance referred to in *Multiple Access* may arise when one considers the obligations imposed by laws on legal decision makers charged with their enforcement. For example, in *M & D Farm Ltd. v. Manitoba Agricultural Credit Corp.*, [1999] 2 SCR 961, 176 DLR (4th) 585, at issue was whether a conflict existed between a stay of proceedings issued pursuant to federal law and an order authorizing the commencement of foreclosure proceedings pursuant to provincial legislation. The creditor could comply with both laws by refraining from initiating proceedings until the stay was lifted, but once it sought to initiate foreclosure proceedings, an impossibility of dual compliance arose. A court cannot simultaneously give effect to a stay of enforcement proceedings and a right to initiate foreclosure proceedings against the debtor. The Supreme Court held that "we have here an 'express contradiction' within the extended meaning of the relevant jurisprudence. The doctrine of federal paramountcy is triggered." See also *Crown Grain Co. v. Day*, [1908] AC 504 (PC) (provincial law that purported to make Court of Appeal ruling "final and conclusive" rendered inoperative by federal law providing for a right of appeal to the Supreme Court).

2. The fact situation in *Multiple Access* involved duplicative legislation where there was no policy conflict between the federal and provincial schemes. Are the reasons adopted by the Court for favouring an "express contradiction" test compelling in situations where the overlapping federal and provincial laws differ in their objectives? Does *Multiple Access* mean that even in cases where the federal and provincial laws differ, the courts are not to consider policy conflict in determining paramountcy, but are only to ask whether a citizen can comply with both? See the *Bank of Montreal v. Hall* case, which follows.

3. How should the courts deal with overlapping penal legislation? For example, how should the courts deal with a case where an individual could be prosecuted for an offence under the federal *Criminal Code* and under provincial regulatory legislation? This might happen in the case of a death in a workplace accident. Should the court consider principles of criminal law, such as double jeopardy? What is the effect of s. 11(h) of the *Canadian Charter of Rights and Freedoms*? See *R v. Wigglesworth*, [1987] 2 SCR 541, 45 DLR (4th) 235.

Bank of Montreal v. Hall
[1990] 1 SCR 121, 65 DLR (4th) 361

[Hall, a farmer, contracted loans from a bank and in return granted the bank a security interest on a piece of farm machinery pursuant to what was then s. 88 of the federal *Bank Act*, now s. 178 of RSC 1985, c. B-1. Hall defaulted on his loan and the bank, pursuant to the provisions of the *Bank Act*, seized the piece of machinery and brought an action to enforce its real property mortgage loan agreement. The bank did not follow the procedures established in the *Limitation of Civil Rights Act*, RSS 1978, c. L-16. Under s. 27 of that Act, failure to give the requisite notice of intention to seize resulted in the termination of the security interest and the release of the debtor from further obligations. The parties applied to the Court of Queen's Bench of Saskatchewan for a determination of the question of whether the bank was required to comply with the *Limitation of Civil Rights Act* in enforcing a security interest under the *Bank Act*. The chambers judge determined that the bank did not have to comply with the provincial legislation. The Saskatchewan Court of Appeal reversed. On further appeal to the Supreme Court of Canada, the issue of the constitutional validity of the relevant provisions of both the federal and provincial Acts was raised, as well as the issue of whether the security interest created under the *Bank Act* could be subjected to the procedures for enforcement of security interests prescribed in the provincial legislation.

The judgment of the court was delivered by La Forest J. He dealt first with the issue of the validity of the federal and provincial laws. Sections 19 to 36 of the *Limitation of Civil Rights Act* came within property and civil rights and were thus *intra vires* the provincial legislature. He then concluded that ss. 178 and 179 of the *Bank Act* were also *intra vires* the federal government. The banking power was found to empower Parliament not only to create the security interest but also to define the methods for realization and enforcement of that security interest. In reaching this conclusion, La Forest J reviewed the history of the s. 178 security interest that showed that its creation was predicated on the pressing need to provide, on a nationwide basis, for a uniform security mechanism so as to facilitate access to capital by producers of primary resources and manufacturers. Such a security interest, precisely because it freed borrower and lender from the obligation to defer to a variety of provincial lending regimes, facilitated the ability of banks to realize on their collateral. This, in turn, translated into important benefits for the borrower— lending became less complicated and more affordable. La Forest J reasoned from this that the definition of the precise manner in which a bank is permitted to realize on its s. 178 security interest cannot be viewed as a mere appendage or gloss inseparable from the legislative scheme. To sunder from the *Bank Act* the legislative provisions defining realization and, as a consequence, to purport to oblige the banks to contend with all the idiosyn-crasies and variables of the various provincial schemes for realization and enforcement, would be tantamount to defeating the specific purpose of Parliament in creating the *Bank Act* security interest.

Having concluded that both pieces of legislation were valid, La Forest J then went on to deal with the issue of paramountcy and whether the provincial legislation was ren-dered inoperative because of a conflict with the federal legislation. In reaching the con-clusion that there was a conflict, La Forest J appears to depart somewhat from the narrow understanding of conflict articulated in *Multiple Access*. What values does La Forest J in-voke, or what values could be invoked, in favour of his approach? What values could have been invoked in favour of an approach to paramountcy that would have upheld the Saskatchewan legislature's attempt to provide greater financial security to farmers?]

LA FOREST J (Wilson, L'Heureux-Dubé, Sopinka, and Cory JJ concurring): ... Do ss. 178 and 179 of the *Bank Act* conflict with ss. 19 to 36 of the *Limitation of Civil Rights Act* so as to render inoperative ss. 19 to 36 in respect of security taken pursuant to s. 178 by a chartered bank?

The decision of this Court in *Multiple Access Ltd. v. McCutcheon*, [1982] 2 SCR 161, 138 DLR (3d) 1, has delimited the circumstances that will justify application of the doc-trine of paramountcy, whereby otherwise validly enacted provincial legislation will be held to be inoperative to the extent that it conflicts with federal legislation. In a widely quoted passage, Dickson J, as he then was, espoused the view that the doctrine of para-mountcy would only need to be invoked in instances where it is impossible to comply with both legislative enactments. ...

Multiple Access Ltd. v. McCutcheon was a case involving duplicative federal and prov-incial legislation. This Court rejected the view that such enactments could not operate concurrently simply because resort to the one would preclude resort to the other. On the contrary, Dickson J, borrowing the phrase coined by Professor Lederman in his seminal article "The Concurrent Operation of Federal and Provincial Laws in Canada" (1963), 9 *McGill LJ* 185, expressed the view that in a federal system such legislation was expressive of the "ultimate in harmony." In the following excerpt Dickson J provides a cogent and succinct rationale for this view, at pp. 189-90 SCR:

> ... there is no true repugnancy in the case of merely duplicative provisions since it does not matter which statute is applied; the legislative purpose of Parliament will be fulfilled regardless of which statute is invoked by a remedy-seeker; application of the provincial law does not dis-place the legislative purpose of Parliament.

[Emphasis added.]

On the basis of these principles, the question before me is thus reducible to asking whether there is an "actual conflict in operation" between the *Bank Act* and the *Limita-tion of Civil Rights Act* in the sense that the legislative purpose of Parliament stands to be displaced in the event that the appellant bank is required to defer to the provincial legis-lation in order to realize on its security. This calls for an examination of the provincial legislation.

As is apparent from s. 20, the purpose of ss. 21 to 35 of the *Limitation of Civil Rights Act* is to prescribe, in a comprehensive manner, the procedure which a secured creditor must follow in Saskatchewan in order to take possession of his security. Failure to follow the prescribed procedure results in the imposition of a sweeping penalty provision; s. 27 provides, in these circumstances, for the determination of the security agreement and the release of the debtor from all liability. I shall assume for the purposes of this appeal that the Court of Appeal correctly interpreted the provision as applying to federally created securities.

The most salient feature of the procedure set out in ss. 21 to 35 of the Act, as I understand it, is that it is designed to ensure that a judge determine the terms and conditions under which a creditor may repossess and seize articles. Section 33 makes this clear. It is a judge who is to decide if, when, and under what circumstances the pledged article is to be returned to the secured party.

The contrast with the comprehensive regime provided for in ss. 178 and 179 of the *Bank Act* could not be more striking. The essence of that regime, it hardly needs repeating, is to assign to the bank, on the taking out of the security, right and title to the goods in question, and to confer, on default of the debtor, an *immediate* right to seize and sell those goods, subject only to the conditions and requirements set out in the *Bank Act*.

On a comparison of the two enactments, can it be said that there is an "actual conflict in operation" between them, giving that phrase the meaning above described? I am led inescapably to the conclusion that there is. The *Bank Act* provides that a lender may, on the default of his borrower, seize his security, whereas *The Limitation of Civil Rights Act* forbids a creditor from immediately repossessing the secured article on pain of determination of the security interest. There could be no clearer instance of a case where compliance with the federal statute necessarily entails defiance of its provincial counterpart. The necessary corollary to this conclusion is that to require the bank to defer to the provincial legislation is to displace the legislative intent of Parliament. As the dissenting judge, Wakeling J, put it in the Court of Appeal, at pp. 34-35:

> The provincial legislation obviously intends that the unqualified right of seizure granted to the bank is to be restricted. It does so by saying a bank may exercise the right of seizure given by s. 178(3) but only by leave of a judge, who will apply criteria formulated by the Province as to when and under what circumstances seizure can take place.

I do not think it is open to a provincial legislature to qualify in this way a right given and defined in a federal statute; see *Attorney-General for Alberta and Winstanley v. Atlas Lumber Co.*, [1941] SCR 87, *per* Duff CJ, at p. 95.

I am not, with respect, dissuaded from this conclusion by the reasoning of the majority in the Court of Appeal to the effect that requiring a bank to defer to the provisions of the *Limitation of Civil Rights Act* would, in any given instance, have, in all likelihood, the sole effect of delaying the bank's ability to take possession of its security. As Sherstobitoff JA put it, at p. 40:

> The *Limitations of Civil Rights Act* simply requires that a creditor give notice to a debtor before seizure of property so as to enable the debtor to make application to the court. The application and resulting order may have the effect of delaying the taking of possession by the

creditor. It does not affect the amount of the indebtedness or liability for payment of same except in cases of noncompliance with the terms of the Act so as to bring s. 27 into play. Put simply, it requires the Bank to follow certain procedures before realizing upon its security, and nothing more.

The reasoning of the majority on this point cannot be determinative of the question of paramountcy. Such a view, with respect, rests on a misinterpretation of what was said in *Multiple Access Ltd. v. McCutcheon*. For, as we have seen, dual compliance will be impossible when application of the provincial statute can fairly be said to frustrate Parliament's legislative purpose. In this instance, as I have already noted, Parliament's legislative purpose in defining the unique security interest created by ss. 178 and 179 of the *Bank Act* was manifestly that of creating a security interest susceptible of uniform enforcement by the banks nationwide, that is to say a lending regime *sui generis* in which, to borrow the phrase of Muldoon J in *Canadian Imperial Bank of Commerce v. R* (1984), 52 CBR 145, at p. 159, the "bank obtains and may assert its right to the goods and their proceeds against the world, *except as only Parliament itself may reduce or modify those rights*" [emphasis added]. This, of course, is merely another way of saying that Parliament, in its wisdom, wished to guard against creating a lending regime whereby the rights of the banks would be made to depend solely on provincial legislation governing the realization and enforcement of security interests.

I can only conclude that it was Parliament's manifest legislative purpose that the sole realization scheme applicable to the s. 178 security interest be that contained in the *Bank Act* itself. Again, as I pointed out earlier, I am firmly of the view that the security interest and realization procedure must, in essence, be viewed as a single whole in that both components of the legislation are fully integral to Parliament's legislative purpose in creating this form of financing. In other words, a s. 178 security interest would no longer be cognizable as such the moment provincial legislation might operate to superadd conditions governing realization over and above those found within the confines of the *Bank Act*. To allow this would be to set at naught the very purpose behind the creation of the s. 178 security interest.

Accordingly, the determination that there is no repugnancy cannot be made to rest on the sole consideration that, at the end of the day, the bank might very well be able to realize on its security if it defers to the provisions of the provincial legislation. A showing that conflict can be avoided if a provincial Act is followed to the exclusion of a federal Act can hardly be determinative of the question whether the provincial and federal acts are in conflict, and, hence, repugnant. That conclusion, in my view, would simply beg the question. The focus of the inquiry, rather, must be on the broader question whether operation of the provincial Act is compatible with the federal legislative purpose. Absent this compatibility, dual compliance is impossible. Such is the case here. The two statutes differ to such a degree in the approach taken to the problem of realization that the provincial cannot substitute for the federal.

I have dealt with this case on the basis of paramountcy to meet the arguments put forward by counsel. But the issue can, I think, be answered more directly. At the end of the day, I agree with counsel for the Attorney General of Canada that this is simply a case where Parliament, under its power to regulate banking, has enacted a complete code that at once defines and provides for the realization of a security interest. There is no room left for the operation of the provincial legislation and that legislation should, accordingly, be construed as inapplicable to the extent that it trenches on valid federal banking legislation.

In response to the third question, then, I would hold that ss. 19 to 36 of *The Limitation of Civil Rights Act*, if interpreted to include a s. 178 security, conflict with ss. 178 and 179 of the *Bank Act* so as to render ss. 19 to 36 inoperative in respect of the security taken pursuant to s. 178 by a chartered bank. To put it another way, ss. 19 to 36 of *The Limitation of Civil Rights Act* are inapplicable to security taken pursuant to ss. 178 and 179 of the *Bank Act*.

Appeal allowed.

NOTES AND QUESTIONS

1. The decision in *Hall* is difficult to reconcile with a number of earlier cases that upheld provincial laws requiring compliance with more stringent standards than their federal counterparts. For example, in *Ross, supra*, the Court held that drivers could comply with the more severe provincial licence suspension by not driving at all. Similarly, as Professor Hogg has pointed out, it was possible for a bank to comply with both laws in *Hall*: "The federal statute did not forbid the bank from serving a notice giving the debtor a last chance to pay, and such a notice could have been served without any breach of the federal statute. The sole effect of compliance with the provincial law would be to delay the bank in realizing its security. There was no express contradiction (or actual conflict in operation), because both laws could be complied with by following the more stringent provincial law." (P.W. Hogg, *Constitutional Law of Canada*, 4th ed., looseleaf (Scarborough, ON: Carswell, 1997), at 16-5.) After *Hall*, it appeared that the "conflict in operation" referred to in *Multiple Access* that is necessary to give rise to federal paramountcy can be satisfied by either an impossibility of dual compliance or an incompatibility of legislative purposes.

2. At the end of his judgment in *Bell #2*, above, Beetz J inserted an *obiter dicta* suggesting that "a practical and functional incompatibility" between two legal regimes should be sufficient to give rise to federal paramountcy. Beetz J held that the interjurisdictional immunity doctrine prevented the application of Quebec health and safety legislation to federal undertakings. Therefore, a paramountcy issue did not arise. If it had arisen, he would have held the provincial law inoperative. As he explained,

> ... a procedural conflict may suffice to render the provincial act inoperative if the conflict is irreconcilable or if, as the majority held, it leads to a deadlock. The mere duplication of two enactments certainly does not make the Act inoperative: *Multiple Access Ltd. v. McCutcheon*, [1982] 2 SCR 161, 138 DLR (3d) 1. However, in view of the difference between the mechanisms resulting in re-assignment in both statutes, between the rights conferred on workers under the two schemes, between the types of danger which give rise to the right, between the procedures and the avenues of appeal, I am inclined to think as did the majority on the Court of Appeal that there is a practical and functional incompatibility between the two groups of provisions.

3. What values influence the choice between the broader test of paramountcy favoured by La Forest J in *Hall* and Beetz J in *Bell #2*, and the narrower approach favoured by Dickson J in *Multiple Access*? Which of the "criteria of choice" identified by Simeon at the outset of this chapter would you invoke in favour of each approach?

4. The *Hall* "incompatibility of legislative purposes" approach to paramountcy was followed in *Law Society of British Columbia v. Mangat*, 2001 SCC 67, 205 DLR (4th) 577. The case involved a conflict between a provision of the BC *Legal Profession Act* that prohibits non-lawyers from appearing as counsel for a fee and provisions of the federal *Immigration Act* that permit non-lawyers to appear as counsel before the Immigration and Refugee Board. (The federal legislation made provision for regulations to be made concerning the appearance of persons other than members of a provincial bar before immigration tribunals, but no such regulations had been promulgated.) Gonthier J, writing for the Court, found that both laws were valid: the regulation of legal representation in immigration proceedings had a double aspect. Turning to the paramountcy issue, Gonthier J concluded as follows:

> In this case, there is an operational conflict as the provincial legislation prohibits non-lawyers to appear for a fee before a tribunal but the federal legislation authorizes non-lawyers to appear as counsel for a fee. At a superficial level, a person who seeks to comply with both enactments can succeed either by becoming a member in good standing of the Law Society of British Columbia or by not charging a fee. Complying with the stricter statute necessarily involves complying with the other statute. However, following the expanded interpretation given in cases like *M & D Farm* and *Bank of Montreal, supra,* dual compliance is impossible. To require "other counsel" to be a member in good standing of the bar of the province or to refuse the payment of a fee would go contrary to Parliament's purpose in enacting ss. 30 and 69(1) of the *Immigration Act.* In those provisions, Parliament provided that aliens could be represented by non-lawyers acting for a fee, and in this respect it was pursuing the legitimate objective of establishing an informal, accessible (in financial, cultural, and linguistic terms), and expeditious process, peculiar to administrative tribunals. Where there is an enabling federal law, the provincial law cannot be contrary to Parliament's purpose. Finally, it would be impossible for a judge or an official of the IRB to comply with both acts.

5. The *Hall* approach was also applied in *114957 Canada Ltée (Spraytech, Société d'arrosage) v. Hudson (Town)*, [2001] 2 SCR 241, 2001 SCC 40, 200 DLR (4th) 419. At issue was a municipal bylaw that restricted the use of pesticides to specified locations for specified purposes. The Court ruled that the bylaw was not rendered inoperative by the federal *Pest Control Products Act.* The federal Act regulates which pesticides can be registered for manufacture or use in Canada. L'Heureux-Dubé J, writing the principal judgment for four members of the Court, characterized the federal law as permissive legislation that does not purport to exhaustively regulate pesticides. In these circumstances, she ruled, there is no conflict that gives rise to federal paramountcy. There is no impossibility of dual compliance, L'Heureux-Dubé J wrote, nor does the bylaw displace or frustrate the purpose of the federal legislation. LeBel J, in his concurring judgment for three members of the Court, appeared to take a narrower view of the federal paramountcy rule. Citing *Multiple Access* and ignoring *Hall*, he stated that "the basic test remains the impossibility of dual compliance" in the sense that "compliance with one set of rules would require breach of the other."

6. Note that in the second to last paragraph of his reasons in *Hall*, La Forest J suggests a way of resolving the case other than through the paramountcy doctrine. The passage is somewhat cryptic and is open to differing interpretations. Is La Forest J simply talking about applying the old "covering the field" test of paramountcy? Or is he applying the doctrine of interjurisdictional immunity to find the provincial law inapplicable to the realization of security interests held by banks? If the latter, the provincial law would be "read down" so as not to apply to banks' security interests, and no issue of paramouncty would arise.

The latter interpretation appears to have been followed by a majority of the Supreme Court of Canada in *Husky Oil Operations Ltd. v. MNR*, [1995] 3 SCR 453, 128 DLR (4th) 1, one of many cases which involve the operation of provincial legislation in bankruptcy situations. The majority judgment of Gonthier J held that validly enacted provincial legislation, in that case the Saskatchewan *Workers' Compensation Act*, cannot apply to bankruptcies if it would have the effect of subverting the order of priorities for creditors' claims set out in the federal *Bankruptcy Act*. Quoting the second to last paragraph of La Forest J's judgment in *Hall*, above, Gonthier J emphasized that his conclusion was based on applicability (interjurisdictional immunity), not operability (paramountcy).

As Iacobucci J pointed out in dissent, Gonthier J's analysis is not easy to reconcile with established understanding of these two doctrines. Arguments based on applicability (interjurisdictional immunity) protect the core of exclusive areas of federal jurisdiction from provincial encroachment, whether or not Parliament has actually passed legislation in the area. Arguments based on operability (paramountcy) protect existing federal legislative policies from being disrupted by conflicting provincial legislation. There are two ways to understand Gonthier J's ruling in *Husky Oil* that are consistent with the jurisprudence. He could be saying that the establishment of the priority of claims is a matter that falls at the core of federal jurisdiction in relation to bankruptcy, and therefore is a matter immune from the application of valid provincial laws. This immunity would arise without regard to the terms of federal laws. Or he could be saying that provincial laws affecting priorities in bankruptcy can validly apply and need not be read down, but they are rendered inoperative to the extent that they conflict with the *Bankruptcy Act*. Either way, the priority of creditors' claims is determined exclusively by federal legislation. Does it matter whether the irrelevance of provincial law results from inapplicability or inoperability?

The confusion generated by *Husky Oil* is apparent in the lower court rulings in *Law Society of British Columbia v. Mangat, supra*. Some of the lower court judges relied on interjurisdictional immunity, others on paramountcy, to prevent the BC *Legal Profession Act* from interfering with provisions of the *Immigration Act* that permit non-lawyers to appear before the Immigration and Refugee Board. Writing for the Court, Gonthier J seemed to acknowledge that the Court had perhaps given too much encouragement to the use of the interjurisdictional immunity doctrine. He noted that "the more supple paramountcy doctrine," not interjurisdictional immunity, is the appropriate doctrine when dealing with alleged operational conflicts between valid provincial and federal laws. (It will be recalled that Justice Gonthier's views in this regard were subsequently adopted by Justices Binnie and LeBel in their majority reasons for judgment in *Canadian Western Bank*, excerpted above.) The difficulty that remains in the jurisprudence, however, is determining when the Court will employ the double aspect and other doctrines to permit overlap and potential conflict to arise, and when it will employ the interjurisdictional immunity and other doctrines to eliminate any potential paramountcy issue.

Rothmans, Benson & Hedges Inc. v. Saskatchewan
[2005] 1 SCR 188, 2005 SCC 13, 250 DLR (4th) 411

MAJOR J (McLachlin CJC and Major, Bastarache, Binnie, LeBel, Deschamps, Fish, Abella, and Charron JJ concurring): [1] The question on this appeal is whether Saskatchewan legislation, and in particular s. 6 of *The Tobacco Control Act*, SS 2001, c. T-14.1, is sufficiently inconsistent with s. 30 of the federal *Tobacco Act*, SC 1997, c. 13, so as to be rendered inoperative pursuant to the doctrine of federal legislative paramountcy. At the end of the hearing, the Court concluded that that question should be answered in the negative and allowed the appeal, with reasons to follow.

I. Facts

[2] In 1997, Parliament enacted the *Tobacco Act*. Section 4 of the statute speaks to its purpose as follows:

> 4. The purpose of this Act is to provide a legislative response to a national public health problem of substantial and pressing concern and, in particular,
>
> (a) to protect the health of Canadians in light of conclusive evidence implicating tobacco use in the incidence of numerous debilitating and fatal diseases;
>
> (b) to protect young persons and others from inducements to use tobacco products and the consequent dependence on them;
>
> (c) to protect the health of young persons by restricting access to tobacco products; and
>
> (d) to enhance public awareness of the health hazards of using tobacco products.

[3] Section 19 of the *Tobacco Act* prohibits the promotion of tobacco products and tobacco product-related brand elements, except as authorized elsewhere in the *Tobacco Act* or its regulations. Section 18 of the *Tobacco Act* defines "promotion" as:

> ... a representation about a product or service by any means, whether directly or indirectly, including any communication of information about a product or service and its price and distribution, that is likely to influence and shape attitudes, beliefs and behaviours about the product or service.

[4] The provisions that follow s. 19 both prohibit specific types of tobacco product promotion, and permit other types of promotion that s. 19 would otherwise prohibit. Among those provisions, s. 30(1) provides that, "[s]ubject to the regulations, any person may display, at retail, a tobacco product or an accessory that displays a tobacco product-related brand element." Section 30(2) further provides that retailers may post signs indicating the availability and price of tobacco products.

[5] On March 11, 2002, *The Tobacco Control Act* came into force in Saskatchewan. Section 6 of that Act bans all advertising, display and promotion of tobacco or tobacco-related products in any premises in which persons under 18 years of age are permitted.

[6] The respondent sued the appellant in the Saskatchewan Court of Queen's Bench, seeking two forms of relief: a declaration that s. 6 of *The Tobacco Control Act* is inoperative in light of s. 30 of the *Tobacco Act*, and a declaration that ss. 6 and 7 of *The Tobacco Control Act* are of no force and effect in light of s. 2(b) of the *Canadian Charter of Rights and Freedoms*. The respondent applied pursuant to Rule 188 of The Queen's Bench Rules of Saskatchewan for a summary determination by the court as to whether s. 6 of *The Tobacco Control Act* is inoperative in light of s. 30 of the *Tobacco Act* by virtue of the doctrine of federal legislative paramountcy.

. . .

III. Analysis

[11] The doctrine of federal legislative paramountcy dictates that where there is an inconsistency between validly enacted but overlapping provincial and federal legislation, the provincial legislation is inoperative to the extent of the inconsistency. *Multiple Access Ltd. v. McCutcheon*, [1982] 2 SCR 161, is often cited for the proposition that there is an inconsistency for the purposes of the doctrine if it is impossible to comply simultaneously with both provincial and federal enactments. Dickson J (as he then was) wrote, at p. 191:

> In principle, there would seem to be no good reasons to speak of paramountcy and preclusion except where there is actual conflict in operation as where one enactment says "yes" and the other says "no"; "the same citizens are being told to do inconsistent things"; compliance with one is defiance of the other. ...

[12] However, subsequent cases indicate that impossibility of dual compliance is not the sole mark of inconsistency. Provincial legislation that displaces or frustrates Parliament's legislative purpose is also inconsistent for the purposes of the doctrine. In *Bank of Montreal v. Hall*, [1990] 1 SCR 121, at p. 155, La Forest J wrote:

> A showing that conflict can be avoided if a provincial Act is followed to the exclusion of a federal Act can hardly be determinative of the question whether the provincial and federal acts are in conflict, and, hence, repugnant. That conclusion, in my view, would simply beg the question. The focus of the inquiry, rather, must be on the broader question whether operation of the provincial Act is compatible with the federal legislative purpose.

See also *Spraytech* [*114957 Canada Ltée (Spraytech, Société d'arrosage) v. Hudson (Town)*, [2001] 2 SCR 241], at para. 35, and *Law Society of British Columbia v. Mangat*, [2001] 3 SCR 113, 2001 SCC 67, at paras. 69-70.

[13] This concern about frustration of Parliament's legislative purpose may find its roots in *McCutcheon*, in which Dickson J stated, at p. 190:

> ... [T]here is no true repugnancy in the case of merely duplicative provisions since it does not matter which statute is applied; *the legislative purpose of Parliament will be fulfilled regardless of which statute is invoked by a remedy-seeker; application of the provincial law does not displace the legislative purpose of Parliament.* [Emphasis added.]

[14] In my view, the overarching principle to be derived from *McCutcheon* and later cases is that a provincial enactment must not frustrate the purpose of a federal enactment, whether by making it impossible to comply with the latter or by some other means. In this way, impossibility of dual compliance is sufficient but not the only test for inconsistency.

[15] It follows that in determining whether s. 6 of *The Tobacco Control Act* is sufficiently inconsistent with s. 30 of the *Tobacco Act* so as to be rendered inoperative through the paramountcy doctrine, two questions arise. First, can a person simultaneously comply with s. 6 of *The Tobacco Control Act* and s. 30 of the *Tobacco Act*? Second, does s. 6 of *The Tobacco Control Act* frustrate Parliament's purpose in enacting s. 30 of the *Tobacco Act*?

[16] Before answering those questions, it is necessary to examine the character of s. 30 of the *Tobacco Act*.

[17] Read in the context of the *Tobacco Act* as a whole, it is clear that the purpose and effect of s. 30 is to define with greater precision the prohibition on the promotion of tobacco products contained in s. 19. Specifically, it serves to exclude from the wide net of s. 19 promotion by way of retail display. In this way, it is like ss. 22(2), 26(1) and 28(1) of the *Tobacco Act*, which also exclude from the s. 19 prohibition certain types of tobacco product promotion that it might otherwise capture. This demarcation of the s. 19 prohibition represents a measured approach to protecting "young persons and others from inducements to use tobacco products," one of the purposes of the *Tobacco Act* set out in s. 4.

[18] However, in demarcating the scope of the s. 19 prohibition through s. 30, Parliament did not grant, and could not have granted, retailers a positive entitlement to display tobacco products. That is so for two reasons.

[19] First, like the *Tobacco Products Control Act*, SC 1988, c. 20, before it, the *Tobacco Act* is directed at a public health evil and contains prohibitions accompanied by penal sanctions. Accordingly, and as the Saskatchewan courts correctly concluded in light of this Court's decision in *RJR-MacDonald Inc. v. Canada (Attorney General)*, [1995] 3 SCR 199, it falls within the scope of Parliament's criminal law power contained in s. 91(27) of the *Constitution Act, 1867*. It might be noted that no argument was made regarding the possibility that the legislation was adopted under the "peace, order, and good government" clause of s. 91, nor could any have been made, given the concessions on the basis of which this chambers motion proceeded. As the criminal law power is essentially prohibitory in character, provisions enacted pursuant to it, such as s. 30 of the *Tobacco Act*, do not ordinarily create freestanding rights that limit the ability of the provinces to legislate in the area more strictly than Parliament. This limited reach of s. 91(27) is well understood: see, for example, *O'Grady v. Sparling*, [1960] SCR 804; *Ross v. Registrar of Motor Vehicles*, [1975] 1 SCR 5; and *Spraytech*.

[20] Second, it is difficult to imagine how granting retailers a freestanding right to display tobacco products would assist Parliament in providing "a legislative response to a national public health problem of substantial and pressing concern" (*Tobacco Act*, s. 4). To put it slightly differently, an interpretation of s. 30 as granting retailers an entitlement to display tobacco products is unsupported by, and perhaps even contrary to, the stated purposes of the *Tobacco Act*.

[21] I do not accept the respondent's argument that Parliament, in enacting s. 30, intended to make the retail display of tobacco products subject only to its own regulations.

In my view, to impute to Parliament such an intention to "occup[y] the field" in the absence of very clear statutory language to that effect would be to stray from the path of judicial restraint in questions of paramountcy that this Court has taken since at least *O'Grady* (p. 820).

A. Impossibility of Dual Compliance

[22] It is plain that dual compliance is possible in this case. A retailer can easily comply with both s. 30 of the *Tobacco Act* and s. 6 of *The Tobacco Control Act* in one of two ways: by admitting no one under 18 years of age on to the premises or by not displaying tobacco or tobacco-related products.

[23] Similarly, a judge called upon to apply one of the statutes does not face any difficulty in doing so occasioned by the existence of the other. The judge, like this Court, can proceed on the understanding that *The Tobacco Control Act* simply prohibits what Parliament has opted not to prohibit in its own legislation and regulations.

[24] For an impossibility of dual compliance to exist, s. 30 of the *Tobacco Act* would have to require retailers to do what s. 6 of *The Tobacco Control Act* prohibits—*i.e.*, to display tobacco or tobacco-related products to young persons.

B. Frustration of Legislative Purpose

[25] Section 6 of *The Tobacco Control Act* does not frustrate the legislative purpose underlying s. 30 of the *Tobacco Act*. Both the general purpose of the *Tobacco Act* (to address a national public health problem) and the specific purpose of s. 30 (to circumscribe the *Tobacco Act*'s general prohibition on promotion of tobacco products set out in s. 19) remain fulfilled. Indeed, s. 6 of *The Tobacco Control Act* appears to further at least two of the stated purposes of the *Tobacco Act*, namely, "to protect young persons and others from inducements to use tobacco products" (s. 4(b)) and "to protect the health of young persons by restricting access to tobacco products" (s. 4(c)).

[26] The conclusion that s. 6 of *The Tobacco Control Act* does not frustrate the purpose of s. 30 of the *Tobacco Act* is consistent with the position of the Attorney General of Canada, who intervened in this appeal to submit that the *Tobacco Act* and *The Tobacco Control Act* were enacted for the same health-related purposes and that there is no inconsistency between the two provisions at issue. While the submissions of the federal government are obviously not determinative of the legal question of inconsistency, there is precedent from this Court for bearing in mind the other level of government's position in resolving federalism issues: ... .

IV. Conclusion

[27] There is no inconsistency between s. 6 of *The Tobacco Control Act* and s. 30 of the *Tobacco Act* that would render the former inoperative pursuant to the doctrine of federal legislative paramountcy. ...

Appeal allowed.

NOTES AND QUESTIONS

1. In *Canadian Western Bank v. Alberta*, [2007] 2 SCR 3, 2007 SCC 22, 281 DLR (4th) 125, excerpted above, the Supreme Court of Canada was unanimous in rejecting a claim that the Alberta legislation regulating the promotion of insurance, even if it was not rendered inapplicable to banks under the doctrine of interjurisdictional immunity, was rendered inoperative in relation to banks under the doctrine of federal paramountcy. The banks argued that "the federal *Bank Act* authorizes the banks to promote insurance, subject to enumerated restrictions, and that these enactments are comprehensive and paramount over those of the province" (para. 98). Justices Binnie and LeBel for the majority, and Justice Bastarache writing separately, held that neither the impossibility of the dual-compliance test nor the frustration of the federal purpose test was satisfied in the circumstances of that case.

2. By contrast, in *British Columbia (Attorney General) v. Lafarge Canada Inc.*, [2007] 2 SCR 86, 2007 SCC 23, 281 DLR (4th) 54, Justices Binnie and LeBel, writing for a majority of six, held that the provincial legislation there at issue—a municipal zoning and development bylaw—conflicted with and was thus rendered inoperative by the provisions of the *Canada Marine Act*, which authorized the Vancouver Port Authority to regulate land use on property it owned. In their view, both tests for finding a conflict were satisfied. The impossibility of the dual-compliance test was said to be satisfied because "[i]f the Ratepayers had succeeded in persuading the City to seek an injunction to stop the Lafarge project from going ahead without a city permit, the judge could not have given effect both to the federal law (which would have led to a dismissal of the application) and the municipal law (which would have led to the granting of an injunction)" (para. 82). The frustration of the federal purpose test was said to be satisfied because "the [*Canada Marine Act*] has authorized the VPA to make its decision about the project and has enabled Lafarge to proceed on the basis of that authorization" (para. 84). Do you agree with the majority's application of these tests in that case? In relation to the second, has the majority not substituted the intention to cover the field test for the frustration of the federal purpose test?

3. At various times in Canadian discussions of constitutional reform, it has been suggested that the allocation of functions between federal and provincial governments be altered by changing the rules of paramountcy. Often, the suggestion is to define areas where the provincial laws will be paramount. David Milne, in "Equality or Asymmetry: Why Choose?" in R.L. Watts and D.M. Brown, eds., *Options for a New Canada* (Toronto: University of Toronto Press, 1991), at 285, calls this the "CPP" solution, referring to s. 94A of the *Constitution Act, 1867*. He advocates this change to achieve asymmetry in the distribution of powers, allowing a province like Quebec to assert jurisdiction in areas where other provinces are content to have the federal government continue to take the primary role.

Consider the wording of s. 94A. Does it give rise to the same doctrine of paramountcy as the court has developed in the cases that you have read? Contrast the wording with s. 95 of the *Constitution Act, 1867*. If you were a lawyer for the Quebec government, which wording would you prefer and why? Consider which wording is more likely to keep the federal government from giving grants to individuals or institutions in an area of provincial jurisdiction, such as health care.

4. For further discussion of the doctrine of paramountcy, see W. Lederman, "The Concurrent Operation of Federal and Provincial Laws in Canada" (1963), 9 *McGill Law Journal*

185; E. Colvin, "Legal Theory and the Paramountcy Rule" (1979), 25 *McGill Law Journal* 82; E. Colvin, Case Comment on *Multiple Access v. McCutcheon* (1983), 17 *University of British Columbia Law Review* 347; B. Crawford, "Case Comment on *Bank of Montreal v. Hall*" (1991), 70 *Canadian Bar Review* 142; and R. Elliot, "Safeguarding Provincial Autonomy from the Supreme Court's New Federal Paramountcy Doctrine: A Constructive Role for the Intention to Cover the Field Test?" (2007), 38 *Supreme Court Law Review* (2d) 629.

CHAPTER NINE

Peace, Order, and Good Government

NOTE ON THE HISTORICAL DEVELOPMENT OF THE P.O.G.G. POWER

This chapter continues the story of the federal peace, order, and good government power since the 1930s. The distinguishing feature of the modern interpretation of the p.o.g.g. power has been the re-emergence of the national concern doctrine, first introduced by Lord Watson in the *Local Prohibition* case, Chapter 4, The Late Nineteenth Century: The Canadian Courts Under the Influence, in a form that allows for federal legislation in situations of national concern apart from emergencies.

The national concern doctrine was given its modern formulation by Viscount Simon in *AG Ontario v. Canada Temperance Federation*, [1946] AC 193, [1946] 2 DLR 1 (PC), at 5-6 DLR:

> In their Lordships' opinion, the true test must be found in the real subject matter of the legislation: if it is such that it goes beyond local or provincial concern or interests and must from its inherent nature be the concern of the Dominion as a whole (as, for example, in the *Aeronautics Case* and the *Radio Case*), then it will fall within the competence of the Dominion Parliament as a matter affecting the peace, order and good government of Canada, though it may in another aspect touch on matters specially reserved to the provincial legislatures. War and pestilence, no doubt, are instances; so, too, may be the drink or drug traffic, or the carrying of arms. In *Russell v. The Queen,* Sir Montague Smith gave as an instance of valid Dominion legislation a law which prohibited or restricted the sale or exposure of cattle having a contagious disease. Nor is the validity of the legislation, when due to its inherent nature, affected because there may still be room for enactments by a provincial legislature dealing with an aspect of the same subject in so far as it specially affects that Province.

In that case the doctrine was used to uphold the federal government's 1927 re-enactment of the *Canada Temperance Act*. Viscount Simon reaffirmed the validity of *Russell* and also rejected the suggestion that *Russell* was based upon a finding that intemperance constituted a national emergency in 1878:

> It is to be noticed that the Board in *Snider's* case nowhere said that *Russell v. The Queen* was wrongly decided. What it did was to put forward an explanation of what it considered was the ground of the decision, but in their Lordships' opinion the explanation is too narrowly expressed. True it is that an emergency may be the occasion which calls for the legislation, but it is the nature of the legislation itself, and not the existence of emergency, that must determine whether it is valid or not.

Viscount Simon also expanded the scope of the p.o.g.g. power by recognizing, at 7 DLR, the power to legislate for the prevention of an emergency:

> To legislate for prevention appears to be on the same basis as legislation for cure. A pestilence has been given as an example of a subject so affecting, or which might so affect, the whole Dominion that it would justify legislation by the Parliament of Canada as a matter concerning the order and good government of the Dominion. It would seem to follow that if the Parliament could legislate when there was an actual epidemic it could do so to prevent one occurring and also to prevent it happening again.

The national concern doctrine, as set out in *Canada Temperance Federation*, was applied to validate federal legislation in two cases decided by the Supreme Court in the 1950s and 1960s. Both suggested an expansive reading of the doctrine.

In *Johannesson v. Rural Municipality of West St. Paul*, [1952] 1 SCR 292, [1951] 4 DLR 609, a case involving a challenge to a municipal by-law controlling the location of airports, the majority of the court referred to the doctrine as supporting exclusive federal legislative jurisdiction with respect to the whole field of aeronautics. (Recall that the justification for federal jurisdiction over aeronautics relied upon in the *Aeronautics Reference*, [1932] AC 54, [1932] 1 DLR 58 (PC), Chapter 6, The 1930s: The Depression and the New Deal, was the treaty power found in s. 132 of the *Constitution Act, 1867*. This justification was no longer available since Canada's international obligations with respect to aeronautics were found in a treaty signed by Canada itself, rather than by Britain on Canada's behalf.) There were five judgments in the Supreme Court of Canada supporting the result, with substantially similar reasoning. The judgment of Locke J, at 633 DLR, offered the following reasons to justify granting exclusive jurisdiction over aeronautics to the federal government:

> It is … desirable … that some of the reasons for the conclusion that the field of aeronautics is one exclusively within Federal jurisdiction should be stated. There has been since the First World War an immense development in the use of aircraft flying between the various provinces of Canada and between Canada and other countries. There is a very large passenger traffic between the provinces and to and from foreign countries, and a very considerable volume of freight traffic not only between the settled portions of the country but between those areas and the northern part of Canada, and planes are extensively used in the carriage of mails. That this traffic will increase greatly in volume and extent is undoubted. While the largest activity in the carrying of passengers and mails east and west is in the hands of a government controlled company, private companies carry on large operations, particularly between the settled parts of the country and the North and mails are carried by some of these lines. The maintenance and extension of this traffic, particularly to the North, is essential to the opening up of the country and the development of the resources of the nation. It requires merely a statement of these well recognized facts to demonstrate that the field of aeronautics is one which concerns the country as a whole. It is an activity, which to adopt the language of Lord Simon in the *Attorney General for Ontario v. Canada Temperance Federation*, must from its inherent nature be a concern of the Dominion as a whole. The field of legislation is not, in my opinion, capable of division in any practical way. If, by way of illustration, it should be decided that it was in the interests of the inhabitants of some northerly part of the country to have airmail service with centres of population to the south and that for that purpose some private line, prepared to undertake such carriage, should

be licensed to do so and to establish the southern terminus for their route at some suitable place in the Municipality of West St. Paul where, apparently, there is an available and suitable field and area of water where planes equipped in a manner enabling them to use the facilities of such an airport might land, it would be intolerable that such a national purpose might be defeated by a rural municipality, the Council of which decided that the noise attendant on the operation of airplanes was objectionable.

In *Munro v. National Capital Commission*, [1966] SCR 663, 57 DLR (2d) 753, the Supreme Court unanimously upheld the *National Capital Act*, RSC 1985, c. N-3, on the basis of the federal peace, order, and good government power. The Act created a National Capital Commission to "prepare plans for and assist in the development, conservation and improvement of the National Capital Region in order that the nature and character of the seat of the Government of Canada may be in accordance with its national significance." The case arose when Munro's property in the Township of Gloucester was expropriated under the Act in the course of establishing a Green Belt outside the City of Ottawa. This expropriation was part of a master plan for the development of the National Capital Region around Ottawa, partly in Ontario and partly in Quebec. Munro argued that the federal legislation was a form of planning and zoning legislation similar to that covered by provincial *Planning Acts*. Cartwright J, who delivered the judgment of the Court, argued first that the national concern doctrine had been adopted by the Court in *Johannesson* and, second, that the development of the National Capital Region under the Act was a "single matter of national concern."

In another case, the opening words of s. 91 were relied on to uphold a federal law without mention of the national concern doctrine, giving rise to the implication, first suggested in the *Radio Reference*, that s. 91 also authorizes federal legislation in relation to subject matters not explicitly assigned to either level of government. In *Jones v. AG New Brunswick*, [1975] 2 SCR 182, 45 DLR (3d) 583, at issue was the constitutionality of the federal *Official Languages Act*, which provided for the equal status of French and English in federal institutions. Laskin CJC, for a unanimous Court, upheld the legislation on the basis that federal institutions are "clearly beyond provincial reach," and, as such, fall within the opening words of s. 91 because "of the purely residuary character of the legislative power thereby conferred."

There was still some uncertainty about the scope of the peace, order, and good government power following these cases, especially the reach of the national concern doctrine. In the case that follows, the *Reference re Anti-Inflation Act*, the Supreme Court was asked to determine the constitutionality of federal wage and price controls that applied in areas traditionally within provincial jurisdiction. The Act was drafted in a manner that allowed the federal government to argue its validity under either the national dimensions doctrine or the emergency doctrine. Were it to succeed under the former, there would be a substantial accretion to the federal government's power to deal with matters of economic regulation. Therefore, the case was seen as a potential turning point in constitutional law, with five provinces and several labour organizations intervening.

The leading judgments in the case, those of Justices Laskin and Beetz, are informed by the very different views of Canadian federalism and the interpretation of the division of powers that each of them had articulated in their earlier careers as legal academics. The background and prior writings of each are described by Professor Katherine Swinton in the excerpt that follows.

K. Swinton, *The Supreme Court and Canadian Federalism:*
The Laskin-Dickson Years
(Scarborough, ON: Carswell, 1990), at 219-25, 240-41, and 260-65
(footnotes omitted)

Laskin's Centralist Vision

A study of the approaches to federal–provincial disputes by members of the Supreme
Court of Canada in recent years must begin with Bora Laskin. Not only was he a leading
academic constitutional lawyer before he joined the judiciary; in his 19 years as a judge,
he played a predominant role in decisions on the distribution of powers under the *Constitution Act, 1867*. ...

It is often difficult to articulate, with any degree of certainty, the views of a particular
judge on a range of federalism issues. Laskin, while prolific in his judicial writing, was
highly formal in his judicial style in constitutional cases, obscuring the policy aspect of
his decisions behind a recitation of cases and consideration of precedent. While this style
would obscure the views of some judges, the outcomes in the wide range of cases in
which Laskin wrote are revealing, as are some of the statements found in his judgments.
Invaluable, as well, as a guide to his thinking, is his academic writing on constitutional
law. From 1941 to 1965, he was a professor at either Osgoode Hall Law School or the
University of Toronto, and in that period he wrote several articles and case comments, as
well as his casebook on constitutional law, which cast additional light on his attitudes
towards federalism as well as his views on judging. Obviously, some of the academic's
beliefs were reshaped by his judicial experience, but many of his early views on the constitution remained with him throughout his career. ...

Safeguarding Federal Jurisdiction

Laskin the academic had firm views on the way in which the then *British North America
Act* should be interpreted, and these beliefs were later applied in his judgements. His approach invited results favouring a strong central government. For example, he believed
that the opening words of section 91, the "peace, order and good government" clause,
constituted the "general power," while the enumerated powers in section 91 were illustrative only. This approach had not been adopted by the Privy Council, which had given
primacy to the enumerated powers and relegated the opening words to a residuary position. While Laskin disliked the Privy Council approach, he felt that its error would not
have been that serious if the Court had properly applied the aspect doctrine, which, in
his opinion, it did not. Indeed, he was highly critical of the Privy Council's treatment of
the aspect doctrine, which focussed on the subject matter of legislation, allocating particular concrete subjects to the federal or provincial governments as "fields" of law-
making. In contrast to this "territorial" or boundary driven approach, Laskin felt that a
court should focus on the object or purpose of legislation, asking whether the law had a
federal or provincial "aspect," with the result that concrete subjects like the wheat trade,
for example, might be regulated by both levels of government—albeit from different aspects as permitted by the classes of law-making powers set out in sections 91 and 92 of
the constitution. Because of this view of the aspect doctrine, Laskin particularly disliked

the "trenching doctrine" or the "necessarily incidental doctrine," which seemed to imply that one government could legislate on a subject normally within the jurisdiction of the other level of government *if* the measure was "necessarily incidental" to effective regulation within its own sphere. This, he felt, was unnecessary "embroidery" on the aspect doctrine, for, as he said of the trenching doctrine:

> Its use to explain a privileged encroachment on provincial legislative authority is purely gratuitous because once a court is satisfied that impugned legislation carries a "federal" aspect, no invasion of provincial legislative authority exists.

Once again, there is a rejection of the territorial approach to jurisdiction which would fence off subjects for exclusive federal or provincial jurisdiction.

If we turn from the structure of inquiry to its substance, we find that, in Laskin's opinion, the federal government was the logical institution to deal with important problems, and he decried the results of Privy Council jurisprudence for the following reason:

> [H]as provincial autonomy been secured? In terms of positive ability to meet economic and social problems of interprovincial scope, the answer is not. A destructive negative autonomy exists, however, which has as a corollary that the citizens of a province are citizens of the Dominion for certain limited purposes only.

Consistent with this confidence in the efficacy of national regulation, Laskin believed that problems once local in nature could take on a federal aspect, as they became more complex or spilled over provincial borders. He believed that the courts should interpret the constitution so as to recognize this evolutionary potential. Thus, in judicial review under the constitution, a court should take a flexible view of the instrument, interpreting it so as to allow effective governmental responses to important problems of public policy. In his constitutional law casebook, a leading teaching and research tool for many years, he emphasized that the process of constitutional adjudication requires creativity by the judge:

> That is not to say that the process is mechanical or that there are logically-discoverable essences which go to make up a class of subject. The distribution of legislative power must surely be envisaged as an instrumental or operating scheme. ...

The words suggest an adherence to the sociological school of jurisprudence, which emphasizes the importance of applying law to serve social needs.

Perhaps this response to the Privy Council's jurisprudence is not surprising. Laskin was a young man in the 1930s, a time of great economic and social upheaval in Canada, and his constitutional philosophy seems to have been shaped by his personal experience, growing up in Northern Ontario as the son of an immigrant family. In the period of his youth, progressive thinkers advocated strong federal government to meet the problems of the Depression through economic planning. The provinces, because of their lack of financial resources, were seen as unable to provide adequate social and economic benefits, while business interests opposed to novel forms of government regulation could use the division of jurisdiction between national and provincial governments to challenge legislative intervention in the economy, thus often undermining progressive measures. Not surprisingly, Laskin saw the wisdom of a strong federal government in this period, a view that remained with him until his death. ...

Beetz's Classical Federalism

... The contrast in the constitutional visions of these two men [Bora Laskin and Jean Beetz] is one of the most interesting in the Court's history, perhaps in part because it has been so easy to trace through debates in their judgements which had their roots in the academic writings of their previous careers. While Laskin espoused a view of federalism that favoured the existence of a strong central government and called for flexibility in the interpretation of the constitution, Beetz seemed to search for principles and rules to confine the exercise of judicial discretion. Overall, he was much more protective of provincial rights and, as a consequence, cautious about departing from precedents which provided safeguards for provincial autonomy. It would be misleading, however, to describe Beetz in one-dimensional terms—as the Quebec nationalist constantly on guard for the province's interests. His vision of the constitution was indeed guided by a concern for provincial autonomy, a value which he embedded in Canadian traditions and the language of the constitutional document, but his reading of that document was influenced by a classical vision of the federal system, which demanded respect for the autonomy of the federal, as well as the provincial governments in the areas of jurisdiction which the constitution allocated to each. In contrast to the functional approach to interpretation espoused by Laskin (which seemed to lend itself to the expansion of the central power), Beetz preferred a more conceptual approach to the interpretation of the constitution which would preserve exclusive areas of jurisdiction for both levels of government. ...

Beetz the Academic

Like Laskin, Beetz began his career as a professor of law. Educated at the University of Montreal and Oxford, where he studied as a Rhodes Scholar, he returned to teach law at the University of Montreal and, for a period, served as dean of the law faculty. His academic expertise in constitutional law was enriched by a period of service at the federal level as Assistant Secretary to the federal cabinet and later as Special Counsel to the Prime Minister of Canada for constitutional matters from 1968 through 1971. Two years later he was appointed to the Quebec Court of Appeal and, in 1974, to the Supreme Court of Canada.

Beetz was not a prolific scholar in his professorial days, although two of his articles are, in retrospect, revealing about his views on the constitution, the one dealing with the interpretation of the *British North America Act* and the other with the constitutional protection of civil liberties through the implied Bill of Rights doctrine.

A Québécois Point of View

The first article, dealing with the changing attitudes of Quebec towards the constitution, was written in 1965, when Quebec was in the midst of the turmoil of the Quiet Revolution, and federal and provincial politicians were trying to renegotiate the terms of the constitution in light of the demands of Quebec and, to a lesser extent at that time, some of the other provinces. The article discussed issues of constitutional interpretation, as well as Quebec's political agenda in federal–provincial relations over the years. In my overview of the article, I shall concentrate on the interpretive issues, although the political discussion is equally interesting and perceptive.

Beetz began with the historical proposition that the *British North America Act* was a document designed to protect the French-speaking minority of Quebec from majority domination in certain areas important to the preservation of the Francophone culture—specifically religion, language, laws, and education. Control over education was important to the province of Quebec in order to protect its religious, linguistic and cultural tradition, while civil law was felt to be intimately connected with individual capacity to act. Once these areas of jurisdiction were designated for provincial governments, it became important, from a Québécois point of view, that the constitution be interpreted in a manner sympathetic to provincial competence. Noting that there are various methods of interpreting legislation, depending on the type of statute and the style of drafting, Beetz characterized the *British North America Act* as a "document paradoxal": its status as a fundamental law, difficult to amend and designed to last indefinitely, suggests the need for a liberal interpretation to allow the document to evolve with changing circumstances, yet the Act was drafted in the technical and detailed manner of a statute to which one would normally give a restrictive interpretation, for it lacks the statement of general principles which one would expect to find in a constitution.

Beetz felt that the nature and style of the *British North America Act* had an impact on the subsequent interpretation of the document, fostering competing schools of interpretation of sections 91 and 92—the one supportive of the decisions of the Privy Council, because that body treated the opening words of section 91 as residuary and subordinate and gave primacy only to the federal enumerated powers over the provincial powers; the second critical of that institution because of the reduced role for the federal residuary power (and, thus, the circumscription of federal action).

In an interesting footnote, Beetz expressed his personal opinion that the Privy Council's interpretation was correct, given the contradictions of the text. He explained that the federal enumerated powers must be of primary importance in interpretation in order to limit the reach of the provincial powers. …

While some critics of Beetz's judicial work have described him as mechanistic and unduly conceptual, the charge is unfair if it implies that he had no conception of the creative nature of judging. Beetz, like Laskin, clearly acknowledged that judges have a considerable amount of discretion in interpreting the distribution of powers in the constitution. …

While many of the cases brought before the Privy Council could have been differently decided, he noted that it has been in Quebec's interest to emphasize the immutability of the constitution, since the Privy Council jurisprudence was so favourable to minority interests. As a result, the Quebec approach to the constitution has emphasized the importance of *stare decisis* and has rejected the functional approach of the realist scholars, which would rest support for a particular piece of legislation on the basis of its ability to meet existing needs and which would allocate power according to the importance of the problem to be addressed. Instead, in Quebec, there has been a preference for analytical jurisprudence, with concentration on the development of concepts, rather than a functional or relativist approach. Thus, there was a distrust of the "national dimensions" approach to the peace, order and good government clause of section 91, because that doctrine would

allow matters traditionally within provincial jurisdiction to take on a national importance warranting federal action. A Québécois would prefer the emergency interpretation
of the peace, order, and good government power, because it leads only to a temporary
suspension of the constitution, rather than a permanent transfer of power to the federal
government based on the importance of the problem to be addressed. ...

Those like F.R. Scott, who advocated national power to deal with important problems,
were described as using political and functional reasons, rather than legal argument, in
an effort to alter the constitution in favour of the federal government.

Along with the national dimensions power, Québécois were also concerned about the
increasing tendency to find concurrent powers between federal and provincial governments, for this seemed inconsistent with the constitution's reference to "exclusivity" of
legislative powers. Concurrency seems problematic because it gives a wider zone for the
supremacy of federal laws, through the operation of the paramountcy doctrine (although
it is acknowledged that the precise impact on provincial autonomy depends on the test
devised to determine whether federal and provincial laws conflict).

Finally, Beetz expressed disquiet about the attitudes of many English Canadian jurists.
For example, the views of William Lederman were troublesome because of his emphasis
on "quantitative criteria" to aid in the determination of validity. Lederman's work, which
has been described elsewhere in this book, appears to have disturbed Beetz because of
the argument that the courts should decide who is the "best physician" to deal with a
given problem. The work of Professor Bora Laskin was also seen to be disturbing because
of his emphasis on the degree of judicial intuition in constitutional interpretation. It is
interesting that Beetz conceded that these two authors might have correctly described
the constitutional interpretation process; nevertheless, their approach disturbed him,
because it could create confusion between law and political science and undermine the
analytical and conceptual approach which should, in his opinion, underlie the law. And,
for the Québécois, it was clearly important to preserve the legal approach, in that it
would provide the best protection for Quebec's identity.

Beetz went on to examine Quebec's attitude towards state action under the constitution, commenting on the transformation from a fixation on the parts of the constitution
which could protect Quebec culturally and linguistically—the powers over education
and civil law—to the use of the constitution to advance Quebec economically. The power
to legislate over property and civil rights then becomes important not because it permits
the preservation of the civil law of Quebec, but because it gives the province jurisdiction
over labour relations, industrial development, transportation, and commerce in general
within its territory. Quebec's special debt to the Privy Council for the expansion of the
property and civil rights power is acknowledged ... .

The spirit of Quebec in the 1960s described by Beetz is quite familiar, capturing Quebec's nationalism and its government's wariness of federal encroachment on provincial
jurisdiction. In this newly activist Quebec state, the Canadian constitution was a problematic document, because Québécois were (and are) inevitably concerned about the
"law of centralization" which seems to operate in federal systems. While that process may
have been slower in Canada than in other federal countries, the language of the Canadian constitution would allow for much greater centralization without any formal amendment. This could occur through the overruling of past decisions or interpretation of

heads of power hitherto little explored. Most obviously, the judges could use existing doctrine to expand federal jurisdiction ... .

Reference re Anti-Inflation Act
[1976] 2 SCR 373, 68 DLR (3d) 452

[The *Anti-Inflation Act*, SC 1974-75-76, c. 75 established a system of price, profit, and income controls. The Act applied to private sector firms with more than 500 employees, members of designated professions, construction firms with more than 20 employees, and other private sector firms declared to be of strategic importance to the scheme. The Act was also binding on the federal public sector, but applicable to the public sector of each province only if an agreement was made between the federal government and the government of the province.

The long title and preamble of the Act were as follows:

An Act to provide for the restraint of profit margins, prices, dividends and compensation in Canada

WHEREAS the Parliament of Canada recognizes that inflation in Canada at current levels is contrary to the interests of all Canadians and that the containment and reduction of inflation has become a matter of serious national concern;

AND WHEREAS to accomplish such containment and reduction of inflation it is necessary to restrain profit margins, prices, dividends and compensation. ...

The Governor in Council directed a reference to the Supreme Court of Canada to determine whether the Act was *ultra vires* and whether the Ontario agreement, purporting to make the Act applicable to the Ontario public sector, was valid. Seven judges (the Chief Justice, Judson, Spence, Dickson, Ritchie, Martland, and Pigeon JJ) held that the Act was supportable under the p.o.g.g. power as emergency or "crisis" legislation, while two (Beetz and de Grandpré JJ) held it was not. The Court divided differently on the question of whether the existence of an emergency was essential to the Act's validity. Five (Ritchie, Martland, Pigeon, Beetz, and de Grandpré JJ) held that it was, rejecting a national dimensions argument; four (Laskin CJC, Judson, Spence, and Dickson JJ) left open the questions of whether the legislation was supportable under the national dimensions test.]

LASKIN CJC (Judson, Spence and Dickson JJ concurring): ... The Attorney-General of Canada having the carriage of the Reference, included in the case (1) the Order of Reference and the annexes thereto; (2) the federal Government's White Paper, entitled "Attack on Inflation," being the policy statement of the Minister of Finance tabled in the House of Commons on October 14, 1975, as a prelude to the introduction of the Bill, which became the *Anti-Inflation Act*, and to the Guidelines promulgated thereunder; and (3) the monthly bulletin of Statistics Canada for October, 1975, containing, *inter alia*, various consumer price indices showing the index position for certain periods up to and including September of 1975. Leave was given in the order for directions of April 6, 1976, to other interested parties to file additional materials, and the Canadian Labour Congress included as

an appendix to its factum an untitled study by Professor Richard G. Lipsey, now a professor of economics at Queen's University, Kingston, Ontario, in which he dealt with (1) the
harm caused by inflation, (2) Canadian inflationary experience, (3) the state of the Canadian economy in 1975, and (4) various policy options in dealing with inflation, among
them a prices and incomes policy. Telegrams from a large number of economists supporting the analysis made by Professor Lipsey were also submitted by the Canadian Labour Congress. The Attorney-General of Canada, following the filing of Professor
Lipsey's study and as permitted by the order for directions, filed in answer a transcript of
a speech delivered on September 22, 1975, by the Governor of the Bank of Canada, Mr.
Gerald Bouey. The Attorney-General of Ontario filed, after the permitted period for
submitting answering material, a comment, prepared by the Ontario Office of Economic
Policy, on the 1975 Economic Environment and the Anti-Inflation Programme, designed
to show the need for national action; and it also submitted a critique of Professor Lipsey's
study, directed to the emphases of that study and to its interpretation of the historical
context in which the federal anti-inflation programme was instituted. ...

In order to assess how relevant and, if relevant, what weight should be assigned to the
extrinsic material, it is necessary to examine the ambit of the legislative power under
which the *Anti-Inflation Act* was enacted. It is my opinion that only in such a context can
the Court be urged, whether through a doctrine of judicial notice or through an adaptation to constitutional purposes of the rules in *Heydon's Case* [that is, the rule that legislation is to be interpreted in light of its purpose or the mischief at which it was aimed], to
consider extrinsic materials as bearing on the validity of challenged legislation. It may
well be that in most situations it is unnecessary to go beyond the terms of the impugned
legislation to determine its validity. Yet, even where this has been deemed sufficient
Courts have thought it proper to consider the operation and effect of the legislation as
providing a key to its purpose, especially where the allegation is that the legislation has
been cast in a colourable form. ...

[N]o general principle of admissibility or inadmissibility can or ought to be propounded by this Court, and ... questions of resort to extrinsic evidence and what kind of
extrinsic evidence may be admitted must depend on the constitutional issues on which
it is sought to adduce such evidence. *flexible approaches*

[A review of cases is omitted.]

The present case is ... one in which federal legislation is challenged as involving unconstitutional regulation, and I am of the opinion that extrinsic material, bearing on the
circumstances in which the legislation was passed, may be considered by the Court in
determining whether the legislation rests on a valid constitutional base. There is no issue
in this case as to the meaning of the terms of the legislation nor, in my opinion, is there
any issue as to the object of the legislation. As will appear from what follows, the arguments of the proponents and the opponents of the *Anti-Inflation Act* turn substantially
on whether the social and economic circumstances upon which Parliament can be said
to have proceeded in passing the Act were such as to provide support for the Act in the
power of Parliament to legislate for the peace, order and good government of Canada.

The extrinsic material proffered in this case was directed to this question and may, hence, be properly considered thereon.

… Simply put, the *Anti-Inflation Act* is supported by the Attorney-General of Canada under the opening words of s. 91 of the *British North America Act*, 1867 as being a law for the peace, order and good government of Canada in relation to matters not coming within the classes of subjects assigned exclusively to the Legislatures of the Provinces. There are two prongs to this assertion and they relate to two lines of judicial decision which have both given substance and placed limitation on the so-called general power of Parliament. Fully spelled out, this general power, which is operative outside of the powers assigned to the provincial Legislatures, is also fed by a catalogue of enumerated federal powers which are declared to be paramount to and thus diminish the scope of provincial legislative authority. Among the federal enumerated powers that are material here are the powers in relation to the regulation of trade and commerce, in relation to currency and coinage, in relation to banking and the issue of paper money, in relation to interest, in relation to the raising of money by any mode or system of taxation and in relation to the borrowing of money on the public credit, *i.e.*, of Canada … .

[A lengthy discussion of the case law has been omitted.]

The Attorney-General of Canada, supported by the Attorney-General of Ontario, put his position in support of the *Anti-Inflation Act* on alternative bases. He relied, primarily, on the *Canada Temperance Federation* case, contending that the Act, directed to containment and reduction of inflation, concerned a matter which went beyond local or private or provincial concern and was of a nature which engaged vital national interests, among them the integrity of the Canadian monetary system which was unchallengeably within exclusive federal protection and control. He urged, in the alternative, that there was an economic crisis amounting to an emergency or exceptional peril to economic stability sufficient to warrant federal intervention, and, if not an existing peril, there was a reasonable apprehension of an impending one that justified federal intervention through the legislation in question which was designed to support measures and policies of a fiscal and monetary character which were undoubtedly within Parliament's legislative authority.

. . .

Since there was, in general, a concession by those opposing the legislation that it would be valid if it were what I may call crisis legislation, and since the proponents of the legislation urged this as an alternative ground on which its validity should be sustained, it appears to me to be the wise course to consider first whether the *Anti-Inflation Act* can be supported on that footing. If it is sustainable as crisis legislation, it becomes unnecessary to consider the broader ground advanced in its support [that is, as legislation in relation to a matter of national concern], and this because, especially in constitutional cases, Courts should not, as a rule, go any farther than is necessary to determine the main issue before them.

The competing arguments on the question whether the Act is supportable as crisis legislation raised four main issues: (1) Did the *Anti-Inflation Act* itself belie the federal contention because of the form of the Act and, in particular, because of the exclusion of the provincial public sector from its imperative scope, notwithstanding that it is framed as a temporary measure albeit subject to extension of its operation? (2) Is the federal contention assisted by the preamble to the statute? (3) Does the extrinsic evidence put before the Court, and other matters of which the Court can take judicial notice without extrinsic material to back it up, show that there was a rational basis for the Act as a crisis measure? (4) Is it a tenable argument that exceptional character could be lent to the legislation as rising beyond local or provincial concerns because Parliament could reasonably take the view that it was a necessary measure to fortify action in other related areas of admittedly federal authority, such as that of monetary policy?

I have referred to the first of these issues earlier in these reasons. It goes to the form of the *Anti-Inflation Act* and to the question whether the scope of the compulsory application of the *Anti-Inflation Act* may be taken to indicate that the Parliament of Canada did not act through any sense of crisis or urgency in enacting it. I note that the federal public service, a very large public service, is governed by the Act and the Guidelines, that private employers of five hundred or more persons are subject to the Act and Guidelines, that the construction industry is particularly dealt with by making those who employ twenty or more persons in that industry subject to the Act and Guidelines and that the Act and Guidelines apply also to persons in various professions, including architects, accountants, dentists, engineers, lawyers, doctors and management consultants. Again, the Act provides for bringing within the Act and Guidelines businesses, irrespective of numbers employed, which are declared by Order in Council to be of strategic importance to the containment and reduction of inflation in Canada. Having regard to the enormous administrative problems which the programme entails, the coverage is comprehensive indeed in its immediately obligatory provisions. What is left out of compulsory coverage is the provincial public sector, including the municipal public sector, but provision is made for bringing this area into the programme under the Guidelines by agreements under s. 4(3) or s. 4(4) or s. 5.

I do not regard the provisions respecting the provincial public sector as an indicator that the Government and Parliament of Canada were not seized with urgency or manifested a lack of any sense of crisis in the establishment of the programme. Provincial governmental concern about rising inflation and concurrent unemployment was a matter of public record prior to the inauguration of the programme, and this Court was provided with copies of agreements that eight of the ten Provinces had made with the federal Government for the application therein of the federal Guidelines. Only British Columbia and Saskatchewan had not entered into agreements. With private industry and private services bound to the extent that they are, and with the federal public service also bound, I see it as a reasonable policy from the standpoint of administration to allow the Provinces to contract into the programme in respect of the provincial public sector under their own administration if this was their preference rather than by simply accepting, as they could, the federal administration. Since the "contracting in" is envisaged on the basis of the federal Guidelines the national character of the programme is underlined.

One of the submissions made by counsel [opposing the legislation] concerned provincial co-operation, but it was put in terms of an objection to the validity of the federal legislation, the proposition being that inflation was too sweeping a subject to be dealt with by a single authority, *i.e.*, the federal Parliament, and that the proper constitutional approach, at least as a first approach, was through federal–provincial co-operation in terms of their respective powers under the respective enumerations in ss. 91 and 92. If this is meant to suggest that Parliament cannot act in relation to inflation even in a crisis situation, I must disagree. No doubt, federal–provincial co-operation along the lines suggested might have been attempted, but it does not follow that the federal policy that was adopted is vulnerable because a co-operative scheme on a legislative power basis was not tried first. Co-operative federalism may be consequential upon a lack of federal legislative power, but it is not a ground for denying it.

I appreciate that Viscount Haldane espoused co-operative federalism in the *Board of Commerce* case (see 60 DLR 513 at pp. 519-20, [1922] 1 AC 191 at p. 201) but that was to relieve against a lack of federal power. Moreover, when he came to consider the propriety of the federal legislation in the *Fort Frances* case, he noted that the situation that had to be dealt with "is not one that can be reliably provided for by depending on collective action of the Legislatures of the individual Provinces agreeing for the purpose" (see [1923] 3 DLR 629 at pp. 633-4, [1923] AC 695 at p. 704).

The Attorney-General of Canada ... emphasized the words [in the preamble] "that the containment and reduction of inflation has become a matter of *serious* national concern" and as well the following words that "to accomplish such containment and reduction of inflation it is *necessary* to restrain profit margins, prices, dividends and compensation" (the italicized words were especially emphasized). I do not regard it as telling against the Attorney-General's alternative position that the very word "emergency" was not used. Forceful language would not carry the day for the Attorney-General of Canada if the circumstances attending its use did not support the constitutional significance sought to be drawn from it. Of course, the absence of any preamble would weaken the assertion of crisis conditions, and I have already drawn attention to the fact that no preamble suggesting a critical economic situation, indeed no preamble at all was included in the legislation challenged in the *Board of Commerce* case.

The preamble in the present case is sufficiently indicative that Parliament was introducing a far-reaching programme prompted by what in its view was a serious national condition. The validity of the *Anti-Inflation Act* does not, however, stand or fall on that preamble, but the preamble does provide a base for assessing the gravity of the circumstances which called forth the legislation.

This brings me to the third of the four issues above-mentioned, namely, the relevancy and weight of the extrinsic evidence and the assistance to be derived from judicial notice. When, as in this case, an issue is raised that exceptional circumstances underlie resort to a legislative power which may properly be invoked in such circumstances, the Court may be asked to consider extrinsic material bearing on the circumstances alleged, both in support of and in denial of the lawful exercise of legislative authority. In considering such material and assessing its weight, the Court does not look at it in terms of whether it provides proof of the exceptional circumstances as a matter of fact. The matter concerns social and economic policy and hence governmental and legislative judgment. It may be that the existence of exceptional circumstances is so notorious as to enable the Court, of its own motion, to take judicial notice of them without reliance on extrinsic material to inform it. Where this is not so evident, the extrinsic material need go only so far as to persuade the Court that there is a rational basis for the legislation which it is attributing to the head of power invoked in this case in support of its validity.

There is before this Court material from Statistics Canada, upon which the Court is justified in relying, which, proceeding from a base of 100 in 1971, shows that the purchasing power of the dollar dropped to 0.78 by September, 1974, and to 0.71 in September, 1975. On the same base, the cost of living index rose to 127.9 by September, 1974, and to 141.5 by September, 1975, with food, taken alone, and weighted at 28% of all the items taken into calculation, showing a rise to 147.3 in September, 1974, and 166.6 in September, 1975. These are figures from the Consumer Price Index monitored by Statistics Canada, and I note that Professor Lipsey in his study states that "the measure [of inflation] that is of most direct relevance to the person in the street is the rate of inflation of the CPI." He defines inflation as "a monetary phenomenon in the sense that a rise in the price level is the same thing as a fall in the value of money (*i.e.*, a fall in its purchasing power)." What the Consumer Price Index shows, and Professor Lipsey himself relies on its figures, is that for the first time in many years Canada had a double digit inflation rate for successive years, *i.e.*, in 1974 and 1975, the index rising 10.9% in 1974 above its reading for 1973 and being 10.8% higher in 1975 than it was in 1974. Some monthly drops slightly below double digit rises do not materially affect the relevance of the annual figures.

There have been inflationary periods before in our history but, again referring to Professor Lipsey's study, "the problem of the coexistence of high unemployment and high inflation rates was not, however, encountered before the late 1960's." These twin conditions continued to the time that the Government and Parliament acted in establishing its prices and incomes policy under the *Anti-Inflation Act* and Guidelines, and were the prime reason for the policy.

Among the submissions in opposition to the contention of crisis was an assertion that the Government and Parliament did not act upon the phenomenon of concurrent rising inflation and rising unemployment when they were first discerned, nor even after they began to persist. I do not see that this is an answer to the issue if those conditions were still apparent when Parliament chose to act. Its judgment as to the appropriate time for intervening as it did may be open to political or economic contestation, but I cannot agree that by waiting for some time before acting the Government and Parliament can be said by the Court to have disentitled themselves to reply upon the power to legislate as Parliament did for the peace, order and good government of Canada.

There is another consideration that arises from the submissions, particularly those of the Canadian Labour Congress, in opposition to the validity of the *Anti-Inflation Act* as a measure justified by crisis circumstances. The consideration I refer to is based on Professor Lipsey's study and on his conclusion that the policy adopted in the *Anti-Inflation Act* is not one that can, on the basis of experience elsewhere and on his appraisal as an economist, be expected to reduce the rate of inflation by more than one to two per cent. The answer to this submission is simple, and it is an answer that has been consistently given by the Courts, namely, that the wisdom or expediency or likely success of a particular policy expressed in legislation is not subject to judicial review. Hence, it is not for the Court to say in this case that because the means adopted to realize a desirable end, *i.e.*, the containment and reduction of inflation in Canada, may not be effectual, those means are beyond the legislative power of Parliament.

I would not exclude the possibility that the means chosen to deal with an alleged evil may be some indicator of whether that evil exists as a foundation for legislation. Professor Lipsey is candid enough to say in his study that whether "a problem is serious enough to be described as a crisis must be partly a matter of judgment." The general question to which his study is directed is, to use his words, "could an economist say that the Canadian economy faced an economic crisis, or was in a critical situation, in October 1975?" He answers this question in the negative on the basis, *inter alia*, of comparative assessment of different periods, and he is supported in this view by many other economists. The Court cannot, however, be concluded by the judgment of an economist, distinguished as he is in the opinion of his peers, on a question of the validity of the exercise of the legislative power invoked in this case. The economic judgment can be taken into account as an element in arriving at an answer to the question whether there is a rational basis for the governmental and legislative judgment exercised in the enactment of the *Anti-Inflation Act*. It cannot determine the answer.

In my opinion, this Court would be unjustified in concluding, on the submissions in this case and on all the material put before it, that the Parliament of Canada did not have a rational basis for regarding the *Anti-Inflation Act* as a measure which, in its judgment, was temporarily necessary to meet a situation of economic crisis imperilling the well-being of the people of Canada as a whole and requiring Parliament's stern intervention in the interests of the country as a whole. That there may have been other periods of crisis in which no similar action was taken is beside the point.

The rationality of the judgment so exercised is, in my view, supported by a consideration of the fourth of the issues which I enumerated above. The fact that there had been rising inflation at the time federal action was taken, that inflation is regarded as a monetary phenomenon and that monetary policy is admittedly within exclusive federal jurisdiction persuades me that the Parliament of Canada was entitled, in the circumstances then prevailing and to which I have already referred, to act as it did from the springboard of its jurisdiction over monetary policy and, I venture to add, with additional support from its power in relation to the regulation of trade and commerce. The Government White Paper refers to a prices and incomes policy as one element in a four-pronged programme of which the first engages its fiscal and monetary authority; and although the White Paper states that the Government rejects the use of severe monetary and fiscal restraints to stop inflation because of the alleged heavy immediate cost in unemployment and foregone output, it could seek to blend policies in those areas with a prices and incomes policy under the circumstances revealed by the extrinsic material.

Since no argument was addressed to the trade and commerce power I content myself with observing only that it provides the Parliament of Canada with a foothold in respect of "the general regulation of trade affecting the whole dominion," to use the words of the Privy Council in *Citizens Ins. Co. of Canada v. Parsons* (1881), 7 App. Cas. 96 at p. 113. The *Anti-Inflation Act* is not directed to any particular trade. It is directed to suppliers of commodities and services in general and to the public services of governments, and to the relationship of those suppliers and of the public services to those employed by and in them, and to their overall relationship to the public. With respect to some of such suppliers and with respect to the federal public service, federal legislative power needs no support from the existence of exceptional circumstances to justify the introduction of a policy of restraint to combat inflation.

The economic interconnection with other suppliers and with provincial public services, underlined by collective bargaining conducted by, or under the policy umbrella of trade unions with Canada-wide operations and affiliations, is a matter of public general knowledge of which the Court can take judicial notice. The extrinsic material does not reveal any distinction in the operation and effect of inflation in respect of those economic areas which are ordinarily within and those ordinarily outside of effective federal regulatory control. In enacting the *Anti-Inflation Act* as a measure for the peace, order and good government of Canada, Parliament is not opening an area of legislative authority which would otherwise have no anchorage at all in the federal catalogue of legislative powers but, rather, it is proceeding from legislative power bases which entitle it to wage war on inflation through monetary and fiscal policies and entitle it to embrace within the *Anti-Inflation Act* some of the sectors covered thereby but not all. The circumstances recounted above justify it in invoking its general power to extend its embrace as it has done.

For all the foregoing reasons, I would hold that the *Anti-Inflation Act* is valid legislation for the peace, order and good government of Canada and does not, in the circumstances under which it was enacted and having regard to its temporary character, invade provincial legislative jurisdiction. ...

BEETZ J (de Grandpré J concurring) dissenting: ... The control and regulation of local trade and of commodity pricing and of profit margins in the provincial sectors have consistently been held to lie, short of a national emergency, within exclusive provincial jurisdiction. ...

The same is true generally of the contract of employment, including wages, whether concluded on an individual basis or collectively in the context of labour relations. ...

The *Anti-Inflation Act*, therefore, and the Guidelines directly and ostensibly interfere with classes of matters which have invariably been held to come within exclusive provincial jurisdiction, more particularly property and civil rights and the law of contract. They do not interfere with provincial jurisdiction in an incidental or ancillary way, but in a frontal way and on a large scale. *Prima facie*, the *Anti-Inflation Act* is *pro tanto ultra vires* of the Parliament of Canada which, under s. 91 of the Constitution, cannot make laws in relation to matters "coming within the classes of subjects by this Act assigned exclusively to the Legislatures of the Provinces." ...

I

The first submission made by counsel for Canada and for Ontario is that the subject-matter of the *Anti-Inflation Act* is the containment and the reduction of inflation. This subject-matter, it is argued, goes beyond local provincial concern or interest and is from its inherent nature the concern of Canada as a whole and falls within the competence of Parliament as a matter affecting the peace, order and good government of Canada. It was further submitted that the competence of Parliament over the subject of inflation may be supported by reference to the following heads of s. 91 of the Constitution: [ss. 91(2), (3), (4), (14), (15), (16), (19), and (20)].

... If the first submission is to be accepted, then it must be conceded that the *Anti-Inflation Act* could be compellingly extended to the provincial public sector. Parliament has not done so in this case as a matter of legislative policy but, it could decide to control and regulate at least the maximum salaries paid to all provincial public servants notwithstanding any provincial appropriations, budgets and laws. Parliament could also regulate wages paid by municipalities, educational institutions, hospitals and other provincial services as well as tuition or other fees charged by some of these institutions for their services. Parliament could occupy the whole field of rent controls. Since in time of inflation there can be a great deal of speculation in certain precious possessions such as land or works of arts, Parliament could move to prevent or control that speculation not only in regulating the trade or the price of those possessions but by any other efficient method reasonably connected with the control of inflation. For example Parliament could presumably enact legislation analogous to mortmain legislation and even extend it to individuals. Parliament could control all inventories in the largest as in the smallest undertakings, industries and trades. Parliament could ration not only food but practically everything else in order to prevent hoarding and unfair profits. One could even go further and argue that since inflation and productivity are greatly interdependent, Parliament could regulate productivity, establish quotas and impose the output of goods or services which corporations, industries, factories, groups, areas, villages, farmers, workers, should produce in any given period. Indeed, since practically any activity or lack of activity affects the gross national product, the value of the Canadian dollar and, therefore, inflation, it is difficult to see what would be beyond the reach of Parliament. Furthermore, all those powers would belong to Parliament permanently; only a constitutional amendment could reduce them. Finally, the power to regulate and control inflation as such would belong to Parliament to the exclusion of the Legislatures if, as is contended, that power were to vest in Parliament in the same manner as the power to control and regulate aeronautics or radio communication or the power to develop and conserve the national capital (*Aeronautics, Radio, Johannesson* and *Munro* cases): the Provinces could probably continue to regulate profit margins, prices, dividends and compensation if Parliament saw fit to leave them any room; but they could not regulate them in relation to inflation which would have become an area of exclusive federal jurisdiction.

Such are the constitutional imports of the first submission in terms of the so-called subject-matter of inflation.

Its effects on the principles which underlie the distribution of other powers between Parliament and the Legislatures are even more far-reaching assuming there would be much left of the distribution of powers if Parliament has exclusive authority in relation to the "containment and reduction of inflation."

If the first submission is correct, then it could also be said that the promotion of economic growth or the limits to growth or the protection of the environment have become global problems and now constitute subject-matters of national concern going beyond local provincial concern or interest and coming within the exclusive legislative authority of Parliament. It could equally be argued that older subjects such as the business of insurance or labour relations, which are not specifically listed in the enumeration of federal and provincial powers and have been held substantially to come within provincial jurisdiction have outgrown provincial authority whenever the business of insurance or labour

have become national in scope. It is not difficult to speculate as to where this line of reasoning would lead: a fundamental feature of the Constitution, its federal nature, the distribution of powers between Parliament and the provincial Legislatures, would disappear
not gradually but rapidly.

I cannot be persuaded that the first submission expresses the state of the law. It goes
against the persistent trend of the authorities. It is founded upon an erroneous characterization of the *Anti-Inflation Act*. As for the cases relied upon by counsel to support the
submission, they are quite distinguishable and they do not, in my view, stand for what
they are said to stand.

[After canvassing the case law, Beetz J concluded that the state of the law was "totally incompatible with the first submission."]

This submission is predicated upon the proposition that the subject-matter of the
Anti-Inflation Act, its pith and substance, is inflation or the containment and reduction
of inflation.

To characterize a law is but to give a name to its content or subject-matter in order to
classify it into one or the other of the classes of matters mentioned in s. 91 or s. 92 of the
Constitution. These classes of matters are themselves so many labels bearing a more or
less specific name, except the general power of Parliament to make laws in relation to
matters not coming within the classes of matters exclusively assigned to the Provinces—a
label specific only in a negative way—and except the power of the Provinces in relation
to all matters of a merely local or private nature—a label unspecific except mainly with
regard to dimensions. This leaves some forty-six specific labels, thirty-one of which are
in the federal list and fifteen of which are in the provincial list.

But there are in language a great many expressions other than those used for the labels
in the federal and the provincial lists. Those innumerable other expressions, often
broader and more extensive than those of s. 91 and s. 92, may, apart from any issue of
colourability, be employed in the title of a statute or to describe a statute. The expressions
"inflation" or "the containment and reduction of inflation" are of that nature. Needless to
say, their use in the title of a statute or as an attempt to characterize a statute does not
suffice by far in disposing of the characterization or in taking the matter with which in
fact they deal outside the ambit of provincial jurisdiction. It is necessary to look at the
reality of the matter or of the matters with which in effect they deal.

> It is possible to invent such matters by applying new names to old legislative purposes. There
> is an increasing tendency to sum up a wide variety of legislative purposes in single, compre-
> hensive designations. Control of inflation, environmental protection, and preservation of
> the national identity or independence are examples.
>
> Many matters within provincial jurisdiction can be transformed by being treated as part
> of a larger subject or concept for which no place can be found within that jurisdiction. This
> perspective has a close affinity to the notion that there must be a single, plenary power to
> deal effectively and completely with any problem. The future of the general power, in the
> absence of emergency, will depend very much on the approach that the courts adopt to this
> issue of characterization.

"Sir Lyman Duff and the Constitution," by Professor Gerald Le Dain QC, as he then was, 12 *Osgoode Hall Law Journal* 261 (1974) at p. 293. (See also "Unity and Diversity in Canadian Federalism: Ideals and Methods of Moderation," by Professor W.R. Lederman QC, 53 *Can. Bar Rev.* 596 (1975). I am much indebted to these two articles.)

The "containment and reduction of inflation" can be achieved by various means including monetary policies, a federal field; the reduction of public expenditures, federal, provincial and municipal; and the restraint of profits, prices and wages, a federal or a provincial field depending on the sector.

I have no reason to doubt that the *Anti-Inflation Act* is part of a more general programme aimed at inflation and which may include fiscal and monetary measures and Government expenditure policies. I am prepared to accept that inflation was the occasion or the reason for its enactment. But I do not agree that inflation is the subject-matter of the Act. In order to characterize an enactment, one must look at its operation, at its effects and at the scale of its effects rather than at its ultimate purpose where the purpose is practically all-embracing. If for instance Parliament is to enact a tax law or a monetary law as a part of an anti-inflation programme no one will think that such laws have ceased to be a tax law or a monetary law and that they have become subsumed into their ultimate purpose so that they should rather be characterized as "anti-inflation laws," an expression which, in terms of actual content, is not meaningful. They plainly remain and continue to be called a tax law or a monetary law, although they have been enacted by reason of an inflationary situation. When the Bank of Canada changes its rate of interest, it must obviously take inflation into account; even if inflation is the main reason for such a measure, this measure will still be characterized by everyone as a central banking measure relating to interest. The same would also be said of a measure relating to the issue of currency; although it may have been dictated by inflationary trends, it remains a measure relating to currency, coinage or the issue of paper money. Similarly, the *Anti-Inflation Act* is, as its preamble states, clearly a law relating to the control of profit margins, prices, dividends and compensation, that is, with respect to the provincial private sector, a law relating to the regulation of local trade, to contract and to property and civil rights in the Provinces, enacted as part of a programme to combat inflation. Property and civil rights in the Provinces are, for the greater part, the pith and substance or the subject-matter of the *Anti-Inflation Act*. According to the Constitution, Parliament may fight inflation with the powers put at its disposal by the specific heads enumerated in s. 91 or by such powers as are outside of s. 92. But it cannot, apart from a declaration of national emergency or from a constitutional amendment, fight inflation with powers exclusively reserved to the Provinces, such as the power to make laws in relation to property and civil rights. This is what Parliament has in fact attempted to do in enacting the *Anti-Inflation Act*.

The authorities relied upon by Counsel for Canada and Ontario in support of the first submission are connected with the constitutional doctrine that became known as the national concern doctrine or national dimension doctrine.

[There follows a discussion of the *Russell* and *Local Prohibition* cases, *Citizens Insurance Co. v. Parsons*, *John Deere Plow Co. v. Wharton*, and the *Aeronautics*, *Radio*, *Canada Temperance*, *Japanese Canadians*, *Johannesson*, and *Munro* cases. The *Russell* case was the most problematic for Beetz J, who described it as a "special case" and as an "exceptional" case. He also noted that the Privy Council came close to characterizing the legislation as criminal law (at 521-23 DLR).]

In my view, the incorporation of companies for objects other than provincial, the regulation and control of aeronautics and of radio, the development, conservation and improvement of the National Capital Region are clear instances of distinct subject-matters which do not fall within any of the enumerated heads of s. 92 and which, by nature, are of national concern.

I fail to see how the authorities which so decide lend support to the first submission. They had the effect of adding by judicial process new matters or new classes of matters to the federal list of powers. However, this was done only in cases where a new matter was not an aggregate but had a degree of unity that made it indivisible, an identity which made it distinct from provincial matters and a sufficient consistence to retain the bounds of form. The scale upon which these new matters enabled Parliament to touch on provincial matters had also to be taken into consideration before they were recognized as federal matters: if an enumerated federal power designated in broad terms such as the trade and commerce power had to be construed so as not to embrace and smother provincial powers (*Parsons'* case) and destroy the equilibrium of the Constitution, the Courts must be all the more careful not to add hitherto unnamed powers of a diffuse nature to the list of federal powers.

The "containment and reduction of inflation" does not pass muster as a new subject matter. It is an aggregate of several subjects some of which form a substantial part of provincial jurisdiction. It is totally lacking in specificity. It is so pervasive that it knows no bounds. Its recognition as a federal head of power would render most provincial powers nugatory.

I should add that inflation is a very ancient phenomenon, several thousand years old, as old probably as the history of currency. The Fathers of Confederation were quite aware of it. *The framer donot want to put it in.*

It was argued that other heads of power enumerated in s. 91 of the Constitution and which relate for example to the regulation of trade and commerce, to currency and coinage, to banking, incorporation of banks and the issue of paper money may be indicative of the breadth of Parliament's jurisdiction in economic matters. They do not enable Parliament to legislate otherwise than in relation to their objects and it was not argued that the *Anti-Inflation Act* was in relation to their objects. The Act does not derive any assistance from those powers any more than the legislation found invalid in the *Board of Commerce* case.

For those reasons, the first submission fails.

II

The second submission made in support of the validity of the *Anti-Inflation Act* is that the inflationary situation was in October of 1975, and still is such as to constitute a national emergency of the same significance as war, pestilence or insurrection and that there is in Parliament an implied power to deal with the emergency for the safety of Canada as a whole; that such situation of exceptional necessity justified the enactment of the impugned legislation.

Before I deal with this second submission I should state at the outset that I am prepared to assume the validity of the following propositions:

- the power of Parliament under the national emergency doctrine is not confined to war situations or to situations of transition from war to peace; an emergency of the nature contemplated by the doctrine may arise in peace time;
- inflation may constitute such an emergency;
- Parliament may validly exercise its national emergency powers before an emergency actually occurs; a state of apprehended emergency or crisis suffices to justify Parliament in taking preventive measures including measures to contain and reduce inflation where inflation amounts to state of apprehended crisis.

In order to decide whether the *Anti-Inflation Act* is valid as a national emergency measure, one must first consider the way in which the emergency doctrine operates in the Canadian Constitution; one must find, in the second place whether the *Anti-Inflation Act* was in fact enacted on the basis that it was a measure to deal with a national emergency in the constitutional sense.

In referring to the emergency doctrine, the Judicial Committee has sometimes used expressions which would at first appear to indicate that there is no difference between the national dimension or national concern doctrine and the emergency doctrine, the latter being but an instance of the first, or that the distribution of powers between Parliament and the provincial Legislatures is not altered by a state of emergency, or again that when Parliament deals with a matter which in normal times would be an exclusively provincial matter, it does so under a federal aspect or in a new relation which lies outside of s. 92 of the Constitution.

. . .

I disagree with the proposition that the national concern or national dimension doctrine and the emergency doctrine amount to the same. Even if it could be said that "where an emergency exists it is the emergency which gives the matter its dimension of national concern or interest" (Le Dain, *op. cit.*, p. 291) the emergency does not give the matter the same dimensions as the national concern doctrine applied for instance in the *Aeronautics* case or in the *Munro* case.

The national concern doctrine illustrated by these cases applies in practice as if certain heads such as aeronautics or the development and conservation of the national capital were added to the categories of subject-matters enumerated in s. 91 of the Constitution when it is found by the Courts that, in substance, a class of subjects not enumerated in either s. 91 or s. 92 lies outside the first fifteen heads enumerated in s. 92 and is not of a merely local or private nature. Whenever the national concern theory is applied, the effect is permanent although it is limited by the identity of the subject newly recognized to be of national dimensions. By contrast, the power of Parliament to make laws in a great crisis knows no limits other than those which are dictated by the nature of the crisis. But one of those limits is the temporary nature of the crisis.

In my view, the verbal precautions taken by the Judicial Committee in the *Fort Frances* case, pp. 633-5 DLR, pp. 704-6 AC, and in other cases reflect its concern over the fact that a power of such magnitude as the national emergency power had to be inferred. But further passages, some of which are even to be found in the very judgments which in other parts appear to say the contrary, make clear that, in practice, the emergency doctrine operates as a partial and temporary alteration of the distribution of powers between Parliament and the provincial Legislatures. ...

Perhaps it does not matter very much whether one chooses to characterize legislation enacted under the emergency power as legislation relating to the emergency or whether one prefers to consider it as legislation relating to the particular subject-matter which it happens to regulate. But if one looks at the practical effects of the exercise of the emergency power, one must conclude that it operates so as to give to Parliament for all purposes necessary to deal with the emergency, concurrent and paramount jurisdiction over matters which would normally fall within exclusive provincial jurisdiction. To that extent, the exercise of that power amounts to a temporary *pro tanto* amendment of a federal Constitution by the unilateral action of Parliament. The legitimacy of that power is derived from the Constitution: when the security and the continuation of the Constitution and of the nation are at stake, the kind of power commensurate with the situation "is only to be found in that part of the constitution which establishes power in the state as a whole" (Viscount Haldane in the *Fort Frances* case, p. 634 DLR, p. 704 AC).

The extraordinary nature and the constitutional features of the emergency power of Parliament dictate the manner and form in which it should be invoked and exercised. It should not be an ordinary manner and form. At the very least, it cannot be a manner and form which admits of the slightest degree of ambiguity to be resolved by interpretation. In cases where the existence of an emergency may be a matter of controversy, it is imperative that Parliament should not have recourse to its emergency power except in the most explicit terms indicating that it is acting on the basis of that power. Parliament cannot enter the normally forbidden area of provincial jurisdiction unless it gives an unmistakable signal that it is acting pursuant to its extraordinary power. Such a signal is not conclusive to support the legitimacy of the action of Parliament but its absence is fatal. It is the duty of the Courts to uphold the Constitution, not to seal its suspension, and they cannot decide that a suspension is legitimate unless the highly exceptional power to suspend it has been expressly invoked by Parliament. Also, they cannot entertain a submission implicitly asking them to make findings of fact justifying even a temporary interference with the normal constitutional process unless Parliament has first assumed responsibility for affirming in plain words that the facts are such as to justify the interference. The responsibility of the Courts begins after the affirmation has been made. If there is no such affirmation, the Constitution receives its normal application. Otherwise, it is the Courts which are indirectly called upon to proclaim the state of emergency whereas it is essential that this be done by a politically responsible body.

We have not been referred to a single judicial decision, and I know of none, ratifying the exercise by Parliament of its national emergency power where the constitutional foundation for the exercise of that power had not been given clear utterance to. And, apart from judicial decisions, I know of no precedent where it could be said that Parliament had attempted to exercise such an extraordinary power by way of suggestion or innuendo.

The use of the national emergency power enables Parliament to override provincial laws in potentially every field: it must be explicit.

This is not to say that Parliament is bound to use ritual words. Words such as "emergency" are not necessarily required and they may indeed be used in a non-constitutional sense since Parliament can enact emergency or urgent legislation in fields *prima facie* coming within its normal authority. ...

What is required from Parliament when it purports to exercise its extraordinary emergency power in any situation where a dispute could arise as to the existence of the emergency and as to the constitutional foundation of its action, is an indication, I would even say a proclamation, in the title, the preamble or the text of the instrument, which cannot possibly leave any doubt that, given the nature of the crisis, Parliament in fact purports to act on the basis of that power. The Statutes of Canada and the Canada Gazette contain several examples of laws, proclamations and Orders in Council which leave room for no doubt that they have been enacted pursuant to the exceptional emergency power of Parliament, or issued or passed under the authority of an Act of Parliament enacted by virtue of that power. Those dealing with wartime or post-wartime conditions usually present no difficulty given the global aspect of modern warfare, the total conscription of activities which it is susceptible to impose upon nations, and the general recognition of the factual situation. ...

The *Anti-Inflation Act* fails in my opinion to pass the test of explicitness required to signal that it has been enacted pursuant to the national emergency power of Parliament.

The preamble has been much relied upon:

> WHEREAS the Parliament of Canada recognizes that inflation in Canada at current levels is contrary to the interests of all Canadians and that the containment and reduction of inflation has become a matter of serious national concern;
>
> AND WHEREAS to accomplish such containment and reduction of inflation it is necessary to restrain profit margins, prices, dividends and compensation;

The words "a matter of serious national concern" have been emphasized.

I remain unimpressed.

The death penalty is a matter of national concern. So is abortion. So is the killing or maiming of innumerable people by impaired drivers. So is the traffic in narcotics and drugs. One can conceive of several drastic measures, all coming within the ordinary jurisdiction of the Parliament of Canada, and which could be preceded by a preamble reciting that a given situation had become a matter of serious national concern. I fail to see how the adding of the word "serious" can convey the meaning that Parliament has decided to embark upon an exercise of its extraordinary emergency power.

· · ·

There is nothing in the rest of the Act and in the Guidelines to show that they have been passed to deal with a national emergency. There is much, on the other hand, within the Act and the Guidelines, in terms of actual or potential exemptions which is inconsistent with the nature of a global war launched on inflation considered as a great emergency. It would not be within our province to judge the efficacy and wisdom of the legislation if it were truly enacted to deal with an extraordinary crisis but its lack of comprehensiveness may be indicative of its ordinary character.

[Beetz J reviewed the various exemptions under the Act and the optional application to the provincial public sector by provincial consent.]

It may be argued that those exemptions and options were put into the Act and the Guidelines in order to make their administration lighter and easier or as a matter of federal–provincial comity. Still, a situation of national emergency does not, at first sight, lend itself to opting in and opting out formulae nor to large scale exemptions.

We have been invited to go outside the Act and the Guidelines and consider extrinsic evidence and take judicial notice of facts of public knowledge.

It is a fact for instance that provincial Governments were seriously concerned about rising inflation and that eight of the ten Provinces have entered into agreements with the Government of Canada for the application of the federal guidelines. But I cannot regard that concern and these agreements as a recognition that Parliament was acting under its national emergency power when it enacted the *Anti-Inflation Act*. Only Parliament, or under a law of Parliament, the Government of Canada, can assume responsibility for declaring a state of national emergency; it would be delicate and probably unwarranted for the Courts to count Provinces and to evaluate the degree of provincial support in such a matter. ...

We were provided with a wealth of extrinsic material the consideration of which, it was expected, would enable us to make a finding of fact as to whether or not inflation had reached a level which justified Parliament's reliance on its extraordinary power or as to whether or not there was a rational basis for Parliament to judge that it could rely upon that power. I do not reach that point, of course, since I hold the view that Parliament did not rely upon its extraordinary power. It seems to me, however, that, if we are entitled to look at extrinsic material such as a policy statement tabled in the House of Commons by the Minister of Finance, statistics, an economic study, a speech delivered by the Governor of the Bank of Canada, it is not improper for us to read Hansard in this case, in order not to construe and apply the provisions of the *Anti-Inflation Act*, but to ascertain its constitutional pivot. A perusal of the debates reveals that between October 14, 1975, when the policy statement was tabled—the *Anti-Inflation Bill* C-73 was read for the first time in the Commons on October 16, 1975—and the third reading and the passing of the Bill in the Senate on December 10, 1975, the question was raised repeatedly in both Houses and in Committee as to what was the constitutional foundation of the Bill and as to whether it was not necessary expressly to declare a state of emergency in order to insure its constitutionality. The replies vary but slightly; their general tenor is to the effect that Parliament has jurisdiction to pass the bill as drafted under the peace, order and good government power—which is rather unrevealing—in addition to other specific federal powers enumerated in s. 91 of the Constitution.

. . .

Reliance upon those statements is not essential to my conclusions. However, they reinforce my opinion that the *Anti-Inflation Act* was enacted in this form because it was believed, erroneously, that Parliament had the ordinary power to enact it under the national concern or national dimension doctrine, that is, a basis which coincides identically with the first submission made to us by counsel for Canada. Parliament did not purport to enact it under the extraordinary power which it possesses in time of national crisis.

The *Anti-Inflation Act* is in my opinion *ultra vires* of Parliament in so far at least as it applies to the provincial private sector; but severability having not been pleaded by counsel for Canada, I would declare the Act *ultra vires* of Parliament in whole.

[Ritchie J, with Martland and Pigeon JJ concurring, agreed with Beetz J that the national concern doctrine could not apply here. He went on to find that the legislation was justified under the national emergency doctrine, relying on the Act's preamble and the government's White Paper to show that Parliament was motivated "by a sense of urgent necessity created by highly exceptional circumstances." In his view, the opponents of the legislation had failed to show by "very clear evidence that an emergency had not arisen when the statute was enacted."]

NOTE: THE ANTI-INFLATION CASE AND EXTRINSIC EVIDENCE

The significance of the *Anti-Inflation* case has been vigorously debated. Some regretted the narrow reading of the federal power (see A. Abel, "The Anti-Inflation Judgment: Right Answer to the Wrong Question" (1976), 26 *University of Toronto Law Journal* 409), while others decried the generous reading of the emergency power (see P. Patenaude, "The Anti-Inflation Case: The Shutters Are Closed But the Back Door Is Wide Open" (1977), 15 *Osgoode Hall Law Journal* 397). One significant aspect of the case was the introduction and use of extrinsic evidence. Indeed, Peter Hogg has commented, in "Proof of Facts in Constitutional Cases" (1976), 26 *University of Toronto Law Journal* 386, at 404:

> The *Anti-Inflation Reference* constitutes a clear precedent for the admission of social-science briefs in constitutional cases where legislative facts are in issue. Despite the court's silence on this aspect of the decision, it may prove in the long run to be the most influential point of the case.

The Supreme Court of Canada elaborated on its approach to extrinsic evidence in constitutional cases in *Reference re Residential Tenancies Act*, [1981] 1 SCR 714, 123 DLR (3d) 554. The extract that follows is from the judgment of Dickson J, at 560-63 DLR, writing for the Court:

> Professors Whyte and Lederman correctly point out in c. 4 of their work on *Canadian Constitutional Law* (1977), that a classification process is at the heart of judicial determination of the distribution or limitation of primary legislative powers. That process joins logic with social fact, value decisions and the authority of precedents. A Court faces particular difficulty in a constitutional reference when only the bare bones of the statute arrive for consideration. The Chief Justice of this Court made this point in the "chicken and egg" reference, *AG Man. v. Manitoba Egg & Poultry Ass'n et al.* (1971), 19 DLR (3d) 169, [1971] SCR 689. There is normally a dearth of relevant facts from which to draw logical inferences, determine social impact, make value decisions and select governing precedents. As Whyte and Lederman note, p. 229, "the challenge of *ultra vires* raises a need for evidence of facts of social context and legislative effect."
>
> In my view a Court may, in a proper case, require to be informed as to what the effect of the legislation will be. The object or purpose of the Act in question may also call for consideration

though, generally speaking, speeches made in the Legislature at the time of enactment of the measure are inadmissible as having little evidential weight.

It now seems reasonably clear that Royal Commission reports and the reports of parliamentary committees made prior to the passing of a statute are admissible to show the factual context and purpose of the legislation. ...

Although admittedly a far different case from the present, in *Reference re Anti-Inflation Act* (1976), 68 DLR (3d) 452, [1976] 2 SCR 373, this Court admitted extrinsic evidence relating to the then prevailing level of inflation, including the White Paper tabled in the House by the Minister of Finance. I think it can be taken from the conduct of the *Anti-Inflation Reference* and the use of extrinsic materials by the members of the Court in that case that the exclusionary rule expressed *obiter* by Rinfret CJC in *Reference re Wartime Leasehold Regulations*, [1950] 2 DLR 1, [1950] SCR 124, can no longer be taken as a correct statement of the law. We should be loath, it seems to me, to enunciate any inflexible rule governing the admissibility of extrinsic materials in constitutional references. The effect of such a rule might well be to exclude logically relevant and highly probative evidence. It is preferable, I think, to follow the practice adopted in the *Anti-Inflation Reference* and give timely directions establishing the evidence or extraneous materials to be admitted to serve the ends of the Court in the particular reference.

Generally speaking, for the purpose of constitutional characterization of an Act we should not deny ourselves such assistance as Royal Commission reports or Law Reform Commission reports underlying and forming the basis of the legislation under study, may afford. The weight to be given such reports is, of course, an entirely different matter. They may carry great, little, or no weight, but at least they should, in my view, generally be admitted as an aid in determining the social and economic conditions under which the Act was enacted: ... The mischief at which the Act was directed, the background against which the legislation was enacted and institutional framework in which the Act is to operate are all logically relevant ... .

A constitutional reference is not a barren exercise in statutory interpretation. What is involved is an attempt to determine and give effect to the broad objectives and purpose of the Constitution, viewed as a "living tree," in the expressive words of Lord Sankey in *Re s. 24 of the BNA Act*, [1930] 1 DLR 98, [1930] AC 124 *sub nom. Edwards et al. v. A-G Can.*, [1929] 3 WWR 479. Material relevant to the issues before the Court, and not inherently unreliable or offending against public policy should be admissible, subject to the proviso that such extrinsic materials are not available for the purpose of aiding in statutory construction ... .

The remainder of the *Residential Tenancies* case is found in Chapter 13, The Judicial Function. You will note that the one restriction Dickson J left on the admissibility of extrinsic evidence was speeches made in the legislature at the time of the enactment of the impugned law. Even this restriction has since been lifted, as indicated in the following passage from Sopinka J's reasons for the court in *R v. Morgentaler*, [1993] 3 SCR 463, at 484-85, 107 DLR (4th) 537, at 553:

The main criticism of [legislative debates and speeches] has been that [they] cannot represent the "intent" of the legislature, an incorporeal body, but that is equally true of other forms of legislative history. Provided that the court remains mindful of the limited reliability and weight of Hansard evidence, it should be admitted as relevant to both the background and the purpose of legislation. Indeed, its admissibility in constitutional cases to aid in determining the background and purpose of legislation now appears well established ... . I would adopt the following passage from Hogg [*Constitutional Law of Canada*, 3d ed. (Scarborough, ON: Carswell, 1992)], as an accurate summary of the state of the law on this point:

> In determining the "purpose" of a statute in this special sense, there is no doubt as to the propriety of reference to the state of law before the statute and the defect in the law (the "mischief") which the statute purports to correct. These may be referred to under ordinary rules of statutory interpretation. Until recently, there was doubt about the propriety of reference to parliamentary debates (Hansard) and other sources of the "legislative history" of the statute. The relevance of legislative history is obvious: it helps to place the statute in its context, gives some explanation of its provisions, and articulates the policy of the government that proposed it. Legislative history has usually been held inadmissible in Canada under ordinary rules of statutory interpretation. But the interpretation of a particular provision of a statute is an entirely different process from the characterization of the entire statute for purposes of judicial review. There seems to be no good reason why legislative history should not be resorted to for the latter purpose, and, despite some earlier authority to the contrary, it is now established that reports of royal commissions and law reform commissions, government policy papers and even parliamentary debates are indeed admissible. [At pp. 15-14 to 15-15, footnotes omitted.]

The remainder of the *Morgentaler* decision, in which the court relied extensively on evidence from Hansard, is found in Chapter 8, Interpreting the Division of Powers.

NOTE: EMERGENCY LEGISLATION AFTER THE ANTI-INFLATION REFERENCE

The federal Parliament enacted new legislation to deal with national emergencies in 1988 (the *Emergencies Act*, RSC 1985, c. 22 (4th Supp.), enacted SC 1988, c. 29). The following note contains a brief description of its contents.

The statute defines a national emergency as

> 3. ... an urgent and critical situation of a temporary nature that
> (a) seriously endangers the lives, health or safety of Canadians and is of such proportions or nature as to exceed the capacity or authority of a province to deal with it, or
> (b) seriously threatens the ability of the Government of Canada to preserve the sovereignty, security and territorial integrity of Canada
> and that cannot be effectively dealt with under any other law of Canada.

The law contains provisions dealing with different types of emergencies, including public welfare, public order, international, and war emergencies. Of special interest to us are the public welfare emergencies (including those caused by real or imminent fires, floods, disease, accident, or pollution amounting to a national emergency). While the federal Cabinet (Governor in Council) can declare an emergency, the declaration must concisely describe the state of affairs constituting the emergency and it must be confirmed by Parliament. As well, the declaration cannot be made without prior consultation with affected provincial governments and an agreement by the provincial Cabinet that the province is unable to deal with the situation. Thus, the legislation seems to reflect Beetz J's concern about "signals" in

Anti-Inflation. For a more detailed review of the legislation, see Peter Rosenthal, "The New Emergencies Act: Four Times the War Measures Act" (1991), 20 *Manitoba Law Journal* 563.

After reading this summary, do you think the courts would interfere with a declaration of a public welfare emergency in relation to a matter within provincial jurisdiction?

NOTE: THE NATIONAL CONCERN DOCTRINE AFTER ANTI-INFLATION

While five judges appeared to give a narrow reading to the national concern doctrine in *Anti-Inflation*, the doctrine emerged again in two further cases: *R v. Hauser*, [1979] 1 SCR 984, 98 DLR (3d) 193 and *Schneider v. The Queen*, [1982] 2 SCR 112, 139 DLR (3d) 417. In *R v. Crown Zellerbach Ltd.*, [1988] 1 SCR 401, 49 DLR (4th) 161, reproduced below, Le Dain J summarizes these cases in light of their role in the formulation of the federal p.o.g.g. power at 180-82 DLR:

> In *Hauser*, a majority of the Court (Martland, Ritchie, Pigeon and Beetz JJ) held that the constitutional validity of the *Narcotic Control Act* rested on the peace, order and good government power of Parliament rather than on its jurisdiction with respect to criminal law. Pigeon J, who delivered the judgment of the majority, said that the principal consideration in support of this view was that the abuse of narcotic drugs, with which the Act dealt, was a new problem which did not exist at the time of Confederation, and that since it did not come within matters of a merely local or private nature in the province it fell within the "general residual power" in the same manner as aeronautics and radio. ...
>
> In *Schneider*, in which the Court unanimously held that the *Heroin Treatment Act* of British Columbia was *intra vires*, Dickson J (as he then was), with whom Martland, Ritchie, Beetz, McIntyre, Chouinard and Lamer JJ concurred, indicated, with particular reference to the national concern doctrine and what has come to be known as the "provincial inability" test, why he was of the view that the treatment of heroin dependency, as distinct from the traffic in narcotic drugs, was not a matter falling within the federal peace, order and good government power. He referred to the problem of heroin dependency as follows at pp. 131-32:
>
>> It is largely a local or provincial problem and not one which has become a matter of national concern, so as to bring it within the jurisdiction of the Parliament of Canada under the residuary power contained in the opening words of the *BNA Act, 1867* (now, *Constitution Act, 1867*).
>>
>> There is no material before the Court leading one to conclude that the problem of heroin dependency as distinguished from illegal trade in drugs is a matter of national interest and dimension transcending the power of each province to meet and solve its own way. It is not a problem which "is beyond the power of the provinces to deal with" (Professor Gibson (1976-77), 7 *Man. LJ* 15, at p. 33). Failure by one province to provide treatment facilities will not endanger the interests of another province. The subject is not one which "has attained such dimensions as to affect the body politic of the Dominion" (*In re Regulation and Control of Aeronautics in Canada*, [1932] AC 54, at p. 77). It is not something that "goes beyond local provincial concern or interests and must from its inherent nature be the concern of the Dominion as a whole (as, for example, in the *Aeronautics* case and the *Radio* case)" per Viscount Simon in *Attorney-General for Ontario et*

al v. Canada Temperance Foundation et al., [1946] AC 193, at p. 205. See also *Johannesson v. Rural Municipality of West St. Paul*, [1952] 1 SCR 292; *Munro v. National Capital Commission*, [1966] SCR 663; *Re CFRB and Attorney General for Canada*, [1973] 3 OR 819. Nor can it be said, on the record, that heroin addiction has reached a state of emergency as will ground federal competence under residual power.

I do not think the subject of narcotics is so global and indivisible that the legislative domain cannot be divided, illegal trade in narcotics coming within the jurisdiction of the Parliament of Canada and the treatment of addicts under provincial jurisdiction.

[Note that the Court revisited the issue of the validity of the *Narcotics Control Act* under the division of powers in *R v. Malmo-Levine; R v, Caine*, [2003] 3 SCR 571, 2003 SCC 74, 233 DLR (4th) 415, discussed in the notes at the end of this chapter.]

R v. Crown Zellerbach Canada Ltd.
[1988] 1 SCR 401, 49 DLR (4th) 161

LE DAIN J (Dickson CJC, McIntyre, and Wilson JJ concurring): The question raised by this appeal is whether federal legislative jurisdiction to regulate the dumping of substances at sea, as a measure for the prevention of marine pollution, extends to the regulation of dumping in provincial marine waters. In issue is the validity of s. 4(1) of the *Ocean Dumping Control Act*, SC 1974-75-76, c. 55, which prohibits the dumping of any substance at sea except in accordance with the terms and conditions of a permit, the sea being defined for the purposes of the Act as including the internal waters of Canada other than fresh waters. ...

2(2) For the purposes of this Act, "the sea" means
(a) the territorial sea of Canada;
(b) the internal waters of Canada other than inland waters;
(c) any fishing zones prescribed pursuant to the *Territorial Sea and Fishing Zones Act*;
(d) the arctic waters within the meaning of the *Arctic Waters Pollution Prevention Act*;
(e) any area of the sea adjacent to the areas referred to in paragraphs (a) to (d) as may be prescribed;
(f) any area of the sea, under the jurisdiction of a foreign state, other than internal waters; and
(g) any area of the sea, other than the internal waters of a foreign state, not included in the areas of the sea referred to in paragraphs (a) to (f).
(3) For the purposes of paragraph (2)(b),"inland waters" means all the rivers, lakes and other fresh waters in Canada and includes the St. Lawrence River as far seaward as the straight lines drawn
(a) from Cap des Rosiers to the western-most point of Anticosti Island; and
(b) from Anticosti Island to the north shore of the St. Lawrence River along the meridian of longitude sixty-three degrees west.

[Section 13(1) sets out the offence of contravening ss. 4-6 of the Act and specifies the penalty.]

I

The general purpose of the *Ocean Dumping Control Act* is to regulate the dumping of substances at sea in order to prevent various kinds of harm to the marine environment. The Act would appear to have been enacted in fulfillment of Canada's obligations under the Convention on the Prevention of Marine Pollution by Dumping of Wastes and other Matter, which was signed by Canada on December 29, 1972. That is not expressly stated in the Act, but there are several references to the Convention in the Act.

The concerns of the Act are reflected in the nature of the prohibited and restricted substances in Schedules I and II and in the factors to be taken into account by the Minister of the Environment in granting permits to dump, which are set out in ss. 9 and 10 of the Act and in Schedule III. What these provisions indicate is that the Act is concerned with marine pollution and its effect on marine life, human health and the amenities of the marine environment. There is also reference to the effect of dumping on navigation and shipping and other legitimate uses of the sea. ...

The respondent carries on logging operations on Vancouver Island in connection with its forest products business in British Columbia and maintains a log dump on a water lot leased from the provincial Crown for the purpose of log booming and storage in Beaver Cove, off Johnstone Strait, on the northeast side of Vancouver Island. The waters of Beaver Cove are *inter fauces terrae*, or as put in the stated case, "Beaver Cove is of such size that a person standing on the shoreline of either side of Beaver Cove can easily and reasonably discern between shore and shore of Beaver Cove." On August 16 and 17, 1980 the respondent, using an 80-foot crane operating from a moored scow, dredged woodwaste from the ocean floor immediately adjacent to the shoreline at the site of its log dump in Beaver Cove and deposited it in the deeper waters of the cove approximately 60 to 80 feet seaward of where the woodwaste had been dredged. The purpose of the dredging and dumping was to allow a new A-frame structure for log dumping to be floated on a barge to the shoreline for installation there and to give clearance for the dumping of bundled logs from the A-frame structure into the waters of the log dump area. The woodwaste consisted of waterlogged logging debris such as bark, wood and slabs. There is no evidence of any dispersal of the woodwaste or any effect on navigation or marine life. At the relevant time the only permit held by the respondent under the Act was one issued on or about July 28, 1980, effective until July 25, 1981, to dump at a site in Johnstone Strait some 2.2 nautical miles from the place where the woodwaste was dumped.

[The company was charged under s. 13(1)(c) with violating s. 4(1) of the Act. The trial judge found s. 4(1) *ultra vires* and dismissed the charges. An appeal to the BC Court of Appeal was dismissed.]

II

As the constitutional question indicates, the issue raised by the appeal is the constitutionality of the application of s. 4(1) of the Act to the dumping of waste in waters, other than fresh waters, within a province. The respondent concedes, as it must, that Parliament has jurisdiction to regulate dumping in waters lying outside the territorial limits of any province. It also concedes that Parliament has jurisdiction to regulate the dumping of substances in provincial waters to prevent pollution of those waters that is harmful to fisheries, if the federal legislation meets the test laid down in the *Fowler v. The Queen*, [1980] 2 SCR 213 and *Northwest Falling Contractors Ltd. v. The Queen*, [1980] 2 SCR 292 cases. It further concedes, in view of the opinion expressed in this Court in *Interprovincial Co-operatives Ltd. v. The Queen*, [1976] 1 SCR 477, that Parliament has jurisdiction to regulate the dumping in provincial waters of substances that can be shown to cause pollution in extra-provincial waters. What the respondent challenges is federal jurisdiction to control the dumping in provincial waters of substances that are not shown to have a pollutant effect in extra-provincial waters. The respondent contends that on the admitted facts that is precisely the present case. The respondent submits that in so far as s. 4(1) of the Act can only be read as purporting to apply to such dumping it is *ultra vires* and, alternatively, that it should be read, if possible, so as not to apply to such dumping. In either case the appeal must fail. The Attorney General of British Columbia, who supported the attack on s. 4(1), as applied to the dumping of waste in Beaver Cove, and with whom the Attorney General of Quebec agreed, made a similar submission that s. 4(1) should be read down so as not to apply to dumping in provincial waters. He submitted that the constitutional question should be answered as follows:

> Section 4(1) of the *Ocean Dumping Control Act* is constitutionally inapplicable to marine waters within a province and, therefore, the definition of "the sea" in s. 2(2) of the Act must be read to exclude from the term "internal waters of Canada" in paragraph (b) those internal waters which are within a province.

In this Court ... [the attorney general of Canada's] principal submission in this court was that the control of dumping in provincial marine waters, for the reasons indicated in the Act, was part of a single matter of national concern or dimension which fell within the federal peace, order and good government power. He characterized this matter as the prevention of ocean or marine pollution.

. . .

The respondent, on the other hand, contends that by its terms the Act is directed at dumping which need not necessarily have a pollutant effect. It prohibits the dumping of *any* substance, including a substance not specified in Sch. I or II, except in accordance with the terms and conditions of a permit. In my opinion, despite this apparent scope, the Act, viewed as a whole, may be properly characterized as directed to the control or regulation of marine pollution, in so far as that may be relevant to the question of legislative jurisdiction. The chosen and perhaps only effective, regulatory model makes it necessary, in order to prevent marine pollution, to prohibit the dumping of any substance without a permit. Its purpose is to require a permit so that the regulatory authority may determine before the proposed dumping has occurred whether it may be permitted upon certain terms and conditions, having regard to the factors or concerns specified in ss. 9 and 10 of the Act and Sch. III. The Act is concerned with the dumping of substances which may be shown or presumed to have an adverse effect on the marine environment. The Minister and not the person proposing to do the dumping must be the judge of this, acting in accordance with the criteria or factors indicated in ss. 9 and 10 and Sch. III of the Act. There is no suggestion that the Act purports to authorize the prohibition of dumping without regard to perceived adverse effect or the likelihood of such effect on the marine environment. The nature of the marine environment and its protection from adverse effect from dumping is a complex matter which must be left to expert judgment.

I agree with Schmidt Prov. Ct. J and the British Columbia Court of Appeal that federal legislative jurisdiction with respect to seacoast and inland fisheries is not sufficient by itself to support the constitutional validity of s. 4(1) of the Act because that section, viewed in the context of the Act as a whole, fails to meet the test laid down in *Fowler* and *Northwest Falling*. While the effect on fisheries of marine pollution caused by the dumping of waste is clearly one of the concerns of the Act it is not the only effect of such pollution with which the Act is concerned. A basis for federal legislative jurisdiction to control marine pollution generally in provincial waters cannot be found in any of the specified heads of federal jurisdiction in s. 91 of the *Constitution Act, 1867*, whether taken individually or collectively.

IV

It is necessary then to consider the national dimensions or national concern doctrine (as it is now generally referred to) of the federal peace, order and good government power as a possible basis for the constitutional validity of s. 4(1) of the Act, as applied to the control of dumping in provincial marine waters.

[After an overview of the p.o.g.g. doctrine, Le Dain J gave the following summary.]

From this survey of the opinion expressed in this Court concerning the national concern doctrine of the federal peace, order and good government power I draw the following conclusions as to what now appears to be firmly established:

1. The national concern doctrine is separate and distinct from the national emergency doctrine of the peace, order and good government power, which is chiefly distinguishable by the fact that it provides a constitutional basis for what is necessarily legislation of a temporary nature; *new doctrine.*

2. The national concern doctrine applies to both new matters which did not exist at Confederation and to matters which, although originally matters of a local or private nature in a province, have since, in the absence of national emergency, become matters of national concern;

3. For a matter to qualify as a matter of national concern in either sense it must have a singleness, distinctiveness and indivisibility that clearly distinguishes it from matters of provincial concern and a scale of impact on provincial jurisdiction that is reconcilable with the fundamental distribution of legislative power under the Constitution;

4. In determining whether a matter has attained the required degree of singleness, distinctiveness and indivisibility that clearly distinguishes it from matters of provincial concern it is relevant to consider what would be the effect on extra-provincial interests of a provincial failure to deal effectively with the control or regulation of the intra-provincial aspects of the matter. *test, what if*

This last factor, generally referred to as the "provincial inability" test and noted with apparent approval in this Court in *Labatt Breweries of Canada Ltd. v. AG Can.*, [1980] 1 SCR 914, 110 DLR (3d) 594, *Schneider v. The Queen*, [1982] 2 SCR 112, 139 DLR (3d) 417, and *R v. Wetmore*, [1983] 2 SCR 284, 2 DLR (4th) 577, was suggested, as Professor Hogg acknowledges, by Professor Gibson in his article, "Measuring 'National Dimensions'" (1976), 7 *Man. LJ* 15, as the most satisfactory rationale of the cases in which the national concern doctrine of the peace, order and good government power has been applied as a basis of federal jurisdiction. As expounded by Professor Gibson, the test would appear to involve a limited or qualified application of federal jurisdiction. As put by Professor Gibson at pp. 34-35:

> By this approach, a national dimension would exist whenever a significant aspect of a problem is beyond provincial reach because it falls within the jurisdiction of another province or of the federal Parliament. It is important to emphasize however that the entire problem would not fall within federal competence in such circumstances. Only that aspect of the problem that is beyond provincial control would do so. Since the "P.O. & G.G." clause bestows only residual powers, the existence of a national dimension justifies no more federal legislation than is necessary to fill the gap in provincial powers. For example, federal jurisdiction to legislate for pollution of interprovincial waterways or to control "pollution price-wars" would (in the absence of other independent sources of federal competence) extend only to measures to reduce the risk that citizens of one province would be harmed by the non-co-operation of another province or provinces.

To similar effect, he said in his conclusion at p. 36:

> Having regard to the residual nature of the power, it is the writer's thesis that "national dimensions" are possessed by only those aspects of legislative problems which are beyond the ability of the provincial legislatures to deal because they involve either federal competence or that of another province. Where it would be possible to deal fully with the problem by co-operative action of two or more legislatures, the "national dimension" concerns only the risk of non-co-operation, and justifies only federal legislation addressed to that risk.

This would appear to contemplate a concurrent or overlapping federal jurisdiction which, I must observe, is in conflict with what was emphasized by Beetz J in the *Anti-Inflation Act Reference*, [1976] 2 SCR 373—that where a matter falls within the national concern doctrine of the peace, order and good government power, as distinct from the emergency doctrine, Parliament has an exclusive jurisdiction of a plenary nature to legislate in relation to that matter, including its intra-provincial aspects.

As expressed by Professor Hogg in the first and second editions of his *Constitutional Law of Canada*, the "provincial inability" test would appear to be adopted simply as a reason for finding that a particular matter is one of national concern falling within the peace, order and good government power: that provincial failure to deal effectively with the intra-provincial aspects of the matter could have an adverse effect on extra-provincial interests. In this sense, the "provincial inability" test is one of the indicia for determining whether a matter has that character of singleness or indivisibility required to bring it within the national concern doctrine. It is because of the interrelatedness of the intra-provincial and extra-provincial aspects of the matter that it requires a single or uniform legislative treatment. The "provincial inability" test must not, however, go so far as to provide a rationale for the general notion, hitherto rejected in the cases, that there must be a plenary jurisdiction in one order of government or the other to deal with any legislative problem. In the context of the national concern doctrine of the peace, order and good government power, its utility lies, in my opinion, in assisting in the determination whether a matter has the requisite singleness or indivisibility from a functional as well as a conceptual point of view.

V

Marine pollution, because of its predominantly extra-provincial as well as international character and implications, is clearly a matter of concern to Canada as whole. The question is whether the control of pollution by the dumping of substances in marine waters, including provincial marine waters, is a single, indivisible matter, distinct from the control of pollution by the dumping of substances in other provincial waters. The *Ocean Dumping Control Act* reflects a distinction between the pollution of salt water and the pollution of fresh water. The question, as I conceive it, is whether that distinction is sufficient to make the control of marine pollution by the dumping of substances a single, indivisible matter falling within the national concern doctrine of the peace, order and good government power.

Marine pollution by the dumping of substances is clearly treated by the Convention on the Prevention of Marine Pollution by Dumping of Wastes and other Matter as a distinct and separate form of water pollution having its own characteristics and scientific considerations. This impression is reinforced by the United Nations Report of the Joint Group of Experts on the Scientific Aspects of Marine Pollution, Reports and Studies No. 15, *The Review of the Health of the Oceans* (UNESCO 1982) (hereinafter referred to as the "UN Report"), which forms part of the materials placed before the Court in the argument. It is to be noted, however, that, unlike the *Ocean Dumping Control Act*, the Convention does not require regulation of pollution by the dumping of waste in the internal marine waters of a state. Article III, para. 3, of the Convention defines the "sea" as "all marine waters other than the internal waters of the States." The internal marine waters of a state are those which lie landward of the baseline of the territorial sea, which is determined in accordance with the rules laid down in the United Nations Convention on the Law of the Sea (1982). The limitation of the undertaking in the Convention, presumably for reasons of state policy, to the control of dumping in the territorial sea and the open sea cannot, in my opinion, obscure the obviously close relationship, which is emphasized in the UN Report, between pollution in coastal waters, including the internal marine waters of a state, and pollution in the territorial sea. Moreover, there is much force, in my opinion, in the appellant's contention that the difficulty of ascertaining by visual observation the boundary between the territorial sea and the internal marine waters of a state creates an unacceptable degree of uncertainty for the application of regulatory and penal provisions. This, and not simply the possibility or likelihood of the movement of pollutants across that line, is what constitutes the essential indivisibility of the matter of marine pollution by the dumping of substances.

There remains the question whether the pollution of marine waters by the dumping of substances is sufficiently distinguishable from the pollution of fresh waters by such dumping to meet the requirement of singleness or indivisibility. In many cases the pollution of fresh waters will have a pollutant effect in the marine waters into which they flow, and this is noted by the UN Report, but that report, as I have suggested, emphasizes that marine pollution, because of the differences in the composition and action of marine waters and fresh waters, has its own characteristics and scientific considerations that distinguish it from fresh water pollution. Moreover, the distinction between salt water and fresh water as limiting the application of the *Ocean Dumping Control Act* meets the consideration emphasized by a majority of this Court in the *Anti-Inflation Act* reference—that in order for a matter to qualify as one of national concern falling within the federal peace, order and good government power it must have ascertainable and reasonable limits, in so far as its impact on provincial jurisdiction is concerned.

For these reasons I am of the opinion that s. 4(1) of the *Ocean Dumping Control Act* is constitutionally valid as enacted in relation to a matter falling within the national concern doctrine of the peace, order and good government power of the Parliament of Canada, and, in particular, that it is constitutional in its application to the dumping of waste in the waters of Beaver Cove. I would accordingly allow the appeal, set aside the judgments of the Court of Appeal and Schmidt Prov. Ct. J and refer the matter back to the Provincial Court judge.

LA FOREST J (Beetz and Lamer JJ concurring) dissenting: … I start with the proposition that what is sought to be regulated in the present case is an activity wholly within the province, taking place on provincially owned land. Only local works and undertakings are involved, and there is no evidence that the substance made subject to the prohibition in s. 4(1) is either deleterious in any way or has any impact beyond the limits of the province. It is not difficult, on this basis, to conclude that the matter is one that falls within provincial legislative power unless it can somehow be established that it falls within Parliament's general power to legislate for the peace, order and good government of Canada.

Peace, Order and Good Government

There are several applications of the peace, order and good government power that may have relevance to the control of ocean pollution. One is its application in times of emergency. The federal Parliament clearly has power to deal with a grave emergency without regard to the ordinary division of legislative power under the Constitution. The most obvious manifestation of this power is in times of war or civil insurrection, but it has in recent years also been applied in peacetime to justify the control of rampant inflation; see *Re: Anti-Inflation Act, supra*. But while there can be no doubt that the control of ocean pollution poses a serious problem, no one has argued that it has reached such grave proportions as to require the displacement of the ordinary division of legislative power under the Constitution.

A second manner in which the power to legislate respecting peace, order and good government may be invoked in the present context is to control that area of the sea lying beyond the limits of the provinces. The federal government may not only regulate the territorial sea and other areas over which Canada exercises sovereignty, either under its power to legislate respecting its public property, or under the general power respecting peace, order and good government under s. 91 (*Reference re Offshore Mineral Rights of British Columbia*, [1967] SCR 792) or under s. 4 of the *Constitution Act, 1871* (UK), 34 & 35 Vict., c. 28. I have no doubt that it may also, as an aspect of its international sovereignty, exercise legislative jurisdiction for the control of pollution beyond its borders; see *Reference re Newfoundland Continental Shelf*, [1984] 1 SCR 86.

In legislating under its general power for the control of pollution in areas of the ocean falling outside provincial jurisdiction, the federal Parliament is not confined to regulating activities taking place within those areas. It may take steps to prevent activities in a province, such as dumping substances in provincial waters that pollute or have the potential to pollute the sea outside the province. Indeed, the exercise of such jurisdiction, it would seem to me, is not limited to coastal and internal waters but extends to the control of deposits in fresh water that have the effect of polluting outside a province. Reference may be made here to *Interprovincial Co-operatives Ltd. v. The Queen, supra*, where a majority of this Court upheld the view that the federal Parliament had exclusive legislative jurisdiction to deal with a problem that resulted from the depositing of a pollutant in a river in one province that had injurious effects in another province. This is but an application of the doctrine of national dimensions triggering the operation of the peace, order and good government clause.

It should require no demonstration that water moves in hydrologic cycles and that effective pollution control requires regulating pollution at its source. That source may, in fact, be situated outside the waters themselves. It is significant that the provision of the *Fisheries Act* upheld by this Court in *Northwest Falling Contractors Ltd. v. The Queen, supra*, as a valid means of protecting the fisheries not only prohibited the depositing of a deleterious substance in water, but *in any place* where it might enter waters frequented by fish. Given the way substances seep into the ground and the movement of surface and ground waters into rivers and ultimately into the sea, this can potentially cover a very large area. Indeed, since the pollution of the ocean in an important measure results from aerial pollution rather than from substances deposited in waters, similar regulations could be made in respect of substances that so pollute the air as to cause damage to the ocean or generally outside the provinces. ...

I should add that considerable administrative flexibility goes with the exercise of these powers. Thus considerable administrative control is given federal authorities by a power given by s. 33(4) of the *Fisheries Act* to exempt some pollutants in specified quantities in certain areas, subject to prescribed conditions. I see no reason why similar provisions could not be devised to control the pollution of the ocean.

The power above described can be complemented by provisions made pursuant to the criminal law power. Thus specific provisions prohibiting the deposit of particular substances could be devised in a manner similar to the prohibitions in the *Food and Drugs Act*, RSC 1970, c. F-27. The combination of the criminal law power with its power to control pollution that has extra-provincial dimensions gives the federal Parliament very wide scope to control ocean pollution. While it would not be proper for me to enter into

the validity of the provisions of the *Clean Air Act*, SC 1970-71-72, c. 47, which were upheld in *Re Canada Metal Co. and The Queen* (1982), 144 DLR (3d) 124 (Man. QB), those
provisions do indicate that a combination of the general federal legislative power and the
criminal power could go a long way towards prohibiting the pollution of internal waters
as well as those in territorial waters and the high seas.

In fact, as I see it, the potential breadth of federal power to control pollution by use of
its general power is so great that, even without resort to the specific argument made by
the appellant, the constitutional challenge in the end may be the development of judicial
strategies to confine its ambit. It must be remembered that the peace, order and good
government clause may comprise not only prohibitions, like criminal law, but regulation.
Regulation to control pollution, which is incidentally only part of the even larger global
problem of managing the environment, could arguably include not only emission standards but the control of the substances used in manufacture, as well as the techniques of
production generally, in so far as these may have an impact on pollution. This has profound implications for the federal–provincial balance mandated by the Constitution. The
challenge for the courts, as in the past, will be to allow the federal Parliament sufficient
scope to acquit itself of its duties to deal with national and international problems while
respecting the scheme of federalism provided by the Constitution.

These considerations underline the importance of linking the prohibition to the purpose sought to be achieved. At times, that link can readily be inferred, for example in the
case of dumping noxious fluid into coastal waters. In other cases, such as the depositing
of noxious solid material inland, cogent proof will be required. ...

However widely one interprets the federal power to control ocean pollution along the
preceding line of analysis, it will not serve to support the provision impugned here, one
that, as in the *Fowler* case, *supra*, is a blanket prohibition against depositing any substance in waters without regard to its nature or amount, and one moreover where there
is, in Martland J's words, at p. 226 of that case, "no attempt to link the proscribed conduct
to actual or potential harm" to what is sought to be protected; in *Fowler*, the fisheries,
here, the ocean. As in *Fowler*, too, there is no evidence to indicate that the full range of
activities caught by the provision cause the harm sought to be prevented. ...

Here, Parliament may undoubtedly prohibit the dumping of anything into federal
waters, but unless a more comprehensive theory for applying the national dimensions
doctrine can be found, prohibitions against dumping substances into provincial waters
must be linked to some federal power.

Why Parliament should have chosen to enact a prohibition in such broad terms is a
matter upon which one is left to speculate. It may be that, in view of the lack of knowledge
about the effects of various substances deposited in water, it may be necessary to monitor
all such deposits. We have no evidence on the extent to which it is necessary to monitor all
deposits into the sea to develop an effective regime for the prevention of ocean pollution.
A system of monitoring that was necessarily incidental to an effective legislative scheme
for the control of ocean pollution could constitutionally be justified. But here not only was
no material advanced to establish the need for such a system, the Act goes much further
and prohibits the deposit of any substance in the sea, including provincial internal waters.
If such a provision were held valid, why would a federal provision prohibiting the emission of any substance in any quantity into the air, except as permitted by federal authorities,

not be constitutionally justifiable as a measure for the control of ocean pollution, it now being known that deposits from the air are a serious source of ocean pollution? ...

Counsel for the appellant did not, of course, frame the issue in the manner in which I have thus far discussed it. I have examined it in this way, however, to show that on a more traditional approach to the underlying issues than he suggests Parliament has very wide powers to deal with ocean pollution, whether within or outside the limits of the province, but that even if one stretches this traditional approach to its limits, the impugned provision cannot constitutionally be justified. It requires a quantum leap to find constitutional justification for the provision, one, it seems to me, that would create considerable stress on Canadian federalism as it has developed over the years. What he argues for, we saw, is that the dumping of any substance in the sea beginning, apparently, from the coasts of the provinces and the mouths of provincial rivers falls exclusively within the legislative jurisdiction of Parliament as being a matter of national concern or dimension even though the sea-bed is within the province and whether or not the substance is noxious or potentially so.

Le Dain J has in the course of his judgment discussed the cases relating to the development of the "national concern or dimension" aspect of the peace, order and good government clause, and I find it unnecessary to review that development in any detail. It is sufficient for my purpose to say that this development has since the 1930s particularly been resorted to from time to time to bring into the ambit of federal power a number of matters, such as radio (*In re Regulation and Control of Radio Communication in Canada*, [1932] AC 304), aeronautics (*Johannesson v. Municipality of West St. Paul*, [1952] 1 SCR 292), and the national capital region (*Munro v. National Capital Commission*, [1966] SCR 663), that are clearly of national importance. They do not fit comfortably within provincial power. Both in their workings and in their practical implications they have predominantly national dimensions. Many of these subjects are new and are obviously of extraprovincial concern. They are thus appropriate for assignment to the general federal legislative power. They are often related to matters intimately tied to federal jurisdiction. Radio (which is relevant to the power to regulate interprovincial undertakings) is an example. The closely contested issue of narcotics control (*cf. R v. Hauser*, [1979] 1 SCR 984, and *Schneider v. The Queen*, [1982] 2 SCR 112, *per* Laskin CJC) is intimately related to criminal law and international trade.

The need to make such characterizations from time to time is readily apparent. From this necessary function, however, it is easy but, I say it with respect, fallacious to go further, and, taking a number of quite separate areas of activity, some under accepted constitutional values within federal, and some within provincial legislative capacity, consider them to be a single indivisible matter of national interest and concern lying outside the specific heads of power assigned under the Constitution. By conceptualizing broad social, economic and political issues in that way, one can effectively invent new heads of federal power under the national dimensions doctrine, thereby incidentally removing them from provincial jurisdiction or at least abridging the provinces' freedom of operation. ...

What was there [in *Anti-Inflation*] said by Beetz J seems to me to apply, *a fortiori*, to the control of the environment, a subject more germane to the present issue. All physical activities have some environmental impact. Possible legislative responses to such activities cover a large number of the enumerated legislative powers, federal and provincial.

To allocate the broad subject-matter of environmental control to the federal government under its general power would effectively gut provincial legislative jurisdiction. ...

To allocate environmental pollution exclusively to the federal Parliament would, it seems to me, involve sacrificing the principles of federalism enshrined in the Constitution. As Professor William R. Lederman indicated in his article "Unity and Diversity in Canadian Federalism: Ideals and Methods of Moderation" (1975), 53 *Can. Bar Rev.* 597, at p. 610, environmental pollution "is no limited subject or theme, [it] is a sweeping subject or theme virtually all-pervasive in its legislative implications." If, he adds, it "were to be enfranchised as a new subject of federal power by virtue of the federal general power, then provincial power and autonomy would be on the way out over the whole range of local business, industry and commerce as established to date under the existing heads of provincial powers." And I would add to the legislative subjects that would be substantially eviscerated the control of the public domain and municipal government. Indeed as Beetz J in *Reference Re Anti-Inflation Act* (1976), 68 DLR (3d) 452 at p. 458, stated of the proposed power over inflation, there would not be much left of the distribution of power if Parliament had exclusive jurisdiction over this subject. For similar views that the protection of environmental pollution cannot be attributed to a single head of legislative power, see P.W. Hogg, *Constitutional Law of Canada* (2nd ed. 1985), at pp. 392 and 598; Gérald A. Beaudoin, "La protection de l'environnement et ses implications en droit constitutionnel" (1977), 23 *McGill LJ* 207.

It is true, of course, that we are not invited to create a general environmental pollution power but one restricted to ocean pollution. But it seems to me that the same considerations apply. I shall, however, attempt to look at it in terms of the qualities or attributes that are said to mark the subjects that have been held to fall within the peace, order and good government clause as being matters of national concern. Such a subject, it has been said, must be marked by a singleness, distinctiveness and indivisibility that clearly distinguishes it from matters of provincial concern. In my view, ocean pollution fails to meet this test for a variety of reasons. In addition to those applicable to environmental pollution generally, the following specific difficulties may be noted. First of all, marine waters are not wholly bounded by the coast; in many areas, they extend upstream into rivers for many miles. The application of the Act appears to be restricted to waters beyond the mouths of rivers (and so intrude less on provincial powers), but this is not entirely clear, and if it is so restricted, it is not clear whether this distinction is based on convenience or constitutional imperative. Apart from this, the line between salt and fresh water cannot be demarcated clearly; it is different at different depths of water, changes with the season and shifts constantly; see *UN Report*, op. cit., at p. 12. In any event, it is not so much the waters, whether fresh or salt, with which we are concerned, but their pollution. And the pollution of marine water is contributed to by the vast amounts of effluents that are poured or seep into fresh waters everywhere (*ibid.*, at p. 13). There is a constant intermixture of waters; fresh waters flow into the sea and marine waters penetrate deeply inland at high tide only to return to the sea laden with pollutants collected during their incursion inland. Nor is the pollution of the ocean confined to pollution emanating from substances deposited in water. In important respects, the pollution of the sea results from emissions into the air, which are then transported over many miles and deposited into the sea; see *UN Report*, p. 15; *IJC* [International Joint Commission] *Report*, op. cit., at

p. 22. I cannot, therefore, see ocean pollution as a sufficiently discrete subject upon which to found the kind of legislative power sought here. It is an attempt to create a federal pollution control power on unclear geographical grounds and limited to part only of the causes of ocean pollution. Such a power then simply amounts to a truncated federal pollution control power only partially effective to meet its supposed necessary purpose, unless of course one is willing to extend it to pollution emanating from fresh water and the air, when for reasons already given such an extension could completely swallow up provincial power, no link being necessary to establish the federal purpose.

This leads me to another factor considered in identifying a subject as falling within the general federal power as a matter of national domain: its impact on provincial legislative power. Here, it must be remembered that in its supposed application within the province the provision virtually prevents a province from dealing with certain of its own public property without federal consent. A wide variety of activities along the coast or in the adjoining sea involves the deposit of some substances in the sea. In fact, where large cities like Vancouver are situated by the sea, this has substantial relevance to recreational, industrial and municipal concerns of all kinds. As a matter of fact, the most polluted areas of the sea adjoin the coast; see *UN Report*, op. cit., at pp. 3-4. Among the major causes of this are various types of construction, such as hotels and harbours, the development of mineral resources and recreational activities (*ibid.*, at p. 3). These are matters of immediate concern to the province. They necessarily affect activities over which the provinces have exercised some kind of jurisdiction over the years. Whether or not the "newness" of the subject is a necessary criterion for inventing new areas of jurisdiction under the peace, order and good government clause, it is certainly a relevant consideration if it means removing from the provinces areas of jurisdiction which they previously exercised. As I mentioned, pollution, including coastal pollution, is no new phenomenon, and neither are many of the kinds of activities that result in pollution.

A further relevant matter, it is said, is the effect on extra-provincial interests of a provincial failure to deal effectively with the control of intra-provincial aspects of the matter. I have some difficulty following all the implications of this, but taking it at face value, we are dealing here with a situation where, as we saw earlier, Parliament has extensive powers to deal with conditions that lead to ocean pollution wherever they occur. The difficulty with the impugned provision is that it seeks to deal with activities that cannot be demonstrated either to pollute or to have a reasonable potential of polluting the ocean. The prohibition applies to an inert substance regarding which there is no proof that it either moves or pollutes. The prohibition in fact would apply to the moving of rock from one area of provincial property to another. I cannot accept that the federal Parliament has such wide legislative power over local matters having local import taking place on provincially owned property. The prohibition in essence constitutes an impermissible attempt to control activities on property held to be provincial in *Reference Re Ownership of the Bed of the Strait of Georgia and Related Areas*, [1984] 1 SCR 388. It may well be that the motive for enacting the provision is to prevent ocean pollution, but as Beetz J underlines in *Re: Anti-Inflation Act, supra*, Parliament cannot do this by attempting to regulate a local industry, although it can, of course, regulate the activities of such an industry that fall within federal power, whether such activities are expressly encompassed within a specific head of power, *e.g.*, navigation, or affect areas of federal concern, *e.g.*, health under the criminal law power, or cause pollution to those parts of the sea under federal jurisdiction. But here the provision simply overreaches. In its terms, it encompasses activities—depositing innocuous substances into provincial waters by local undertakings on provincial lands—that fall within the exclusive legislative jurisdiction of the province.

Finally, it was argued that the provision might be read down to apply to federal waters only, but I do not think this is possible. One need only look at the broad definition of "the sea" in ss. 2(2) and (3) to appreciate the comprehensive reach of the Act. Besides, it is well known that many bays and other internal bodies of waters in Canada fall within the limits of the provinces. Many of the federal internal waters are located in the Arctic and have been expressly dealt with by the federal government. ...

I would dismiss the appeal with costs and reply to the constitutional question in the affirmative.

Appeal allowed.

NOTES AND QUESTIONS

1. Do you agree with Justice Le Dain's conclusion that marine pollution is sufficiently indivisible to constitute a matter of national concern? Consider the views expressed in the following article.

Jean Leclair "The Elusive Quest for the Quintessential 'National Interest'"
(2005), 38 *UBC Law Review* 353-72, at 360-66 (footnotes omitted)

[A]lthough Justice Le Dain asserts that a matter must be both functionally and conceptually indivisible to be of a national dimension, his own application of the test is limited to an examination of the first dimension of indivisibility. By emphasizing functional indivisibility, he seems to forget that the purpose of the national interest doctrine is not to confer [on] Parliament a property right over a particular matter, but rather a power to regulate in relation to such a matter. In *Crown Zellerbach*, the Court had to decide whether marine pollution was a matter of national interest. Justice Le Dain concluded that it was, based on the fact that it was difficult to ascertain "by visual observation the boundary between the territorial sea and the internal marine waters of a state," and because marine pollution "... has its own characteristics and scientific considerations that distinguish it from fresh water pollution." Justice Le Dain limited his inquiry to the functional, if not the physical, dimension of the indivisibility criterion. However, as correctly underlined by the dissenting Justice La Forest, "it is not so much the waters, whether fresh or salt, with which we are concerned, but their pollution." Justice La Forest had previously emphasized that "... effective pollution control requires regulating pollution at its source." In other words, a conceptual approach to indivisibility was required, as Parliament had claimed the exclusive power to regulate the sources of marine pollution ... .

Had Justice Le Dain conducted a careful analysis of the legislative means necessary to regulate the wide range of polluting activities, he would have recognized that treating marine pollution as a matter of national interest would greatly affect provincial spheres of enumerated powers. Indeed, the exclusive authority to regulate the sources of marine pollution is a *carte blanche* to regulate every conceivable activity known to humankind, be they inter- or intra-provincial in nature. ...

... [I]t appears that judges who are willing to address the issue of conceptual indivisibility do not apply it to the matter claimed to be of national dimension, but rather to the legislative means employed to regulate it.

[The example given to illustrate this problematic use of the concept of indivisibility is a finding that the entire subject of tobacco use is a matter of national concern because the provinces are incapable of efficiently controlling advertising originating outside the province.]

However, this interpretation is most erroneous. The conceptual indivisibility test must be applied using the approach of Justice Beetz in *Anti-Inflation*; that is, to the matter said to be of national interest (tobacco use), and not to the legislative means employed to ensure its regulation (control of advertising). In other words, the conceptual indivisibility of a particular matter should hinge upon whether the totality of legislative means necessary for its overall regulation amounts to an important invasion of provincial spheres of power. Otherwise, the central government could adopt a law said to be confined to a very limited aspect of a particular trade, argue successfully that it was sufficiently indivisible to qualify as a matter of national interest and, after having established its "... exclusive jurisdiction of a plenary nature to legislate in relation to that matter", Parliament could select, this time in all impunity, any other legislative means it would find appropriate to adopt. ...

[In addition,] Justice Le Dain's functional test is extremely obscure. Recall that in order to determine the existence of indivisibility, one must "consider what would be the effect on extra-provincial interests of a provincial failure to deal effectively with the control or regulation of the intra-provincial aspects of the matter." Is Justice Le Dain referring to political incapacity, political unwillingness, or legal inability to deal with a problem? ...

Notwithstanding the problems described above, the most troubling aspect of Justice Le Dain's test is that it gives the impression that Canada's federal system was designed to achieve functional efficiency to the exclusion of other normative concerns. Functional efficiency, though important, has never been the sole normative concern of our federal regime. In reality, Canadian federalism has been much more preoccupied with establishing a just and coherent balance between the legitimate demands of both national and regional communities. As the Court itself underlined in [the] *Secession [Reference]*:

> The federal–provincial division of powers was a legal recognition of the diversity that existed among the initial members of Confederation, and manifested a concern to accommodate that diversity within a single nation by granting significant powers to provincial governments. The *Constitution Act, 1867* was ... the first step in the transition from colonies separately dependent on the Imperial Parliament for their governance to a unified and independent political state in which different peoples could resolve their disagreements and work together toward common goals and a common interest. Federalism was the political mechanism by which diversity could be reconciled with unity.

Justice Le Dain's functional approach, with its obviously centralist slant, is impervious to this need for diversity. By unduly favouring federal exclusivity to the detriment of federal/provincial concurrency, Justice Le Dain also puts into jeopardy federalism's capacity to promote "... democratic participation by distributing power to the government thought to be most suited to achieving the particular societal objective having regard to th[e] diversity [of the component parts of Confederation]." Moreover, by placing the interests of the national community before those of the regions, Justice Le Dain's centralist approach could very well hamper, in certain circumstances, Quebec's ability to exercise "... the considerable provincial powers conferred by the *Constitution Act, 1867* in such a way as to promote [its] language and culture."

2. What are the implications of the Court's ruling that ocean pollution is a matter of national concern for provincial jurisdiction over pollution in provincial marine waters? This is a matter of ongoing debate and confusion. At one point Le Dain J states:

> [Professor Gibson's articulation of the provincial inability test as a basis for federal jurisdiction would] appear to contemplate a concurrent or overlapping federal jurisdiction which, I must observe, is in conflict with what was emphasized by Beetz J in the *Anti-Inflation Act Reference*, [1976] 2 SCR 373—that where a matter falls within the national concern doctrine of the peace, order and good government power, as distinct from the emergency doctrine, Parliament has an exclusive jurisdiction of a plenary nature to legislate in relation to that matter, including its intra-provincial aspects.

However, he later appears to contradict this in the following statement:

> The "provincial inability" test must not, however, go so far as to provide a rationale for the general notion, hitherto rejected in the cases, that there must be a plenary jurisdiction in one order of government or the other to deal with any legislative problem.

Why wouldn't the general trends in modern federalism that permit significant regulatory overlap through the use of the double aspect and necessarily incidental doctrines also apply to matters of national concern under p.o.g.g. and thus allow the province to regulate pollution in provincial marine waters? For further discussion, see Sujit Choudhry, "Recasting Social Canada: A Reconsideration of Federal Jurisdiction Over Social Policy" (2002), 52 *University of Toronto Law Journal* 163, extracted below.

3. The "provincial inability" test relied on by the Court in *Crown Zellerbach* is a major conceptual development in modern federalism. It has been used by the Court to structure the development of not only the national concern branch of the p.o.g.g. power, but also the general trade branch of s. 91(2), the trade and commerce power. See *General Motors of Canada Ltd. v. City National Leasing*, [1989] 1 SCR 641, found in Chapter 10, Economic Regulation, where the Court shifted the constitutional basis of federal competition legislation from s. 91(27) to the second branch of s. 91(2). The case laid out a list of five factors (non-exhaustive, and not all required) to assess whether legislation could be justified under this head of jurisdiction. Without explicit reference to *Crown Zellerbach* or to Professor Gibson's article, the Court invoked the idea of provincial inability to define and circumscribe the federal government's power to regulate intraprovincial economic activity—a core area of provincial jurisdiction under s. 92(13)—and, on the facts, found that the provinces were unable to effectively regulate anti-competitive activity within their borders.

Despite the centrality of the provincial inability test, there are many questions about its meaning. The following excerpt sheds some light on how to understand the concept of "provincial inability."

**Sujit Choudhry, "Recasting Social Canada: A Reconsideration of
Federal Jurisdiction Over Social Policy"**
(2002), 52 *University of Toronto Law Journal* 163, at 227, 234-245 (footnotes omitted)

[T]he provincial inability test reflects the Dickson court's central contribution, and its major legacy, to the enduring problem of legal federalism. The basic intuition underlying the test is that the federal government can act only in those circumstances in which the provinces are unable to act. Although the Court provided little in the way of theoretical explanation to justify this principle, the test is consistent with at least the following account of the nature of the Canadian political community. Canada consists not of one political community but, rather, of a multiplicity of political communities, which often disagree on questions of public policy but which nevertheless have come together and have created common institutions with the power to act on matters of common interest. To the question of when matters are of common interest, the answer provided by the Dickson court is those subject-matters where the provinces are unable to act alone—that is, when pursuing their self-interest requires them to act together. On this conception, the Canadian federation is imagined as a scheme for mutual advantage. In my view, this is a rather impoverished vision of the Canadian political community; indeed, I have argued elsewhere that Canada is a community of fate, bound together not simply by convenience and self-interest but also through shared accomplishments and history that can sustain rather thick bonds of social solidarity. But, assuming that federalism is a scheme of mutual advantage, the provincial inability test provides a rational way to allocate jurisdiction between the provinces and the federal government.

But what does the provincial inability test mean? The best place to begin is with the Dickson court's various formulations of the test. ...

Properly understood, the statements of the Court [in *Crown Zellerbach* and *General Motors*] set out not one but *three* circumstances that can be described as situations of provincial inability. I term these (1) negative extra-provincial externalities, (2) collective action problems, and (3) true provincial inability. I now discuss each in turn.

1. Negative Extra-Provincial Externalities

"Externality" is a term used by economists to describe situations in which an entity (a person, a corporation) does not bear all of the costs, or receive all of the benefits, of decisions they take. In cases of negative externalities, some or all of the costs of a decision are borne by another entity; in cases of positive externalities, some or all of the benefits of a decision are received by another party. The basic idea behind an externality is that the disjuncture between the entity that makes a decision and the entities that bear the costs or receive the benefits of a decision means that that decision is made differently than it would be where the costs and benefits were strictly private. In cases of negative externalities, because costs can be shifted onto other entities, an entity may engage in more of an externality-causing activity than they otherwise would. The opposite is true for positive externalities.

Although externalities are often used to describe the decisions of, and the incentives operating on, private economic actors, they can also be used to examine the decisions of governments. Governments can make decisions that impose costs on other governments. In a federation, a province can externalize the costs of its public policies onto other provinces, or onto the federal government. A case study of the former can be found in *Interprovincial Co-Operatives Ltd. v. Dryden Chemicals Ltd.* [[1976] 1 SCR 477]. In that case, two companies, one operating in

Saskatchewan, the other in Ontario, operated chlor-alkali plants close to rivers that flow into Manitoba. The allegation was that both companies discharged mercury into these rivers, which then carried the mercury into Manitoba, where it was ingested by fish. According to the Manitoba government, the mercury ultimately had a negative impact upon the commercial fishery by rendering fish unfit for human consumption.

… [B]oth *Crown Zellerbach* and *General Motors* clearly contemplated that this kind of scenario would count as an example of provincial inability. But, on further reflection, we find that "provincial inability" is a bit of a misnomer. Consider the legal position of Manitoba. Because of the territorial limits on provincial jurisdiction, Manitoba lacked the legal power to regulate mercury discharges in waters outside its borders. Manitoba, therefore, was clearly unable to regulate pollution that harmed interests within the province. As the Court said, it was "impossible to hold that … Manitoba can … require the shutting down of plants erected and operated in another province." But no one seriously doubted that Ontario and Saskatchewan possessed jurisdiction to regulate the mercury discharges; the operative assumption throughout the judgment was that mercury discharges were legal under Ontario and Saskatchewan law. At most, we can say that those provinces were not unable but merely *unwilling* to regulate these discharges.

In sum, the most that can be said is that the affected province, Manitoba, was unable, but not that no province was able, to regulate mercury discharges. There was no provincial inability as such. Nonetheless, in *Crown Zellerbach* and *General Motors*, the Court considered that this scenario warranted shifting jurisdiction to the federal government. And, indeed, this was the holding of the plurality (*per* Ritchie J) in *Interprovincial Co-operatives*. Why did the Court reach this conclusion? One obvious solution would have been a negotiated or cooperative arrangement whereby Saskatchewan and Ontario regulated industries within their borders for Manitoba's benefit. The Court must have reasoned that because of the incentives at play, there were reasons to doubt that bilateral or multilateral bargains to address inter-provincial spillovers would be easy to achieve. If so, federal jurisdiction under the national dimensions doctrine was premised on the risk of inter-provincial non-cooperation. And this is exactly what Gibson said, in passages quoted with approval by Le Dain J in *Crown Zellerbach*.

The idea that extra-provincial negative externalities should ground federal jurisdiction over subject-matters under the national concern doctrine is a dominant theme in the case law. …

2. Collective Action Problems

… Two types of collective action problems exist in federations, both of which have been relied on as reasons by the Supreme Court to vest jurisdiction over certain subject-matters with the federal government. First, there are inter-provincial collective action problems, which are particularly important in the area of redistribution … . Some of the passages [from *Crown Zellerbach* and *General Motors*] invoke collective action problems of this sort, either explicitly or implicitly. The key phrase is in *General Motors*, where Dickson CJ states that "the failure to include one or more provinces or localities in a legislative scheme would jeopardize the successful operation of the scheme in other parts of the country." … Dickson CJ does not discuss provincial inability *per se*. Rather, what seems to do the work here is the fact that for certain types of regulatory regimes to be effective, they must be national in scope, and that the possibility of an inter-provincial solution—one negotiated by, agreed to, and implemented by all the provinces—is either unrealistic or infeasible. The premise of this argument, as is the case with negative externalities, is that provinces are constitutionally able to regulate an area of socio-economic policy but for some reason are un-willing to, creating the risk of inter-provincial non-cooperation.

Consider two examples of inter-provincial collective action problems. The first is the prob-lem of races to the bottom … . Although the risk of a race to the bottom can occur whenever provinces adopt redistributive policies, a similar risk is created by any public policy that in-creases the cost of doing business. Labour standards of various kinds—minimum wage laws, workplace health and safety standards—are a prominent example. The basic point here is intui-tively clear: that all provinces must buy into a coordinated regime of environmental or labour regulation or the scheme fails, because if one province is non-compliant, the rational response of other provinces would be to compete by adopting lax public policies.

The second example of an inter-provincial co-ordination problem arises in the case of pub-lic goods. A public good is a good that is non-rival and non-exclusive. The marginal cost of providing *non-rival goods* to an additional consumer is zero. *Non-exclusive goods* are goods that it is impossible to exclude people from consuming. The classic example of a public good is na-tional defence: the cost of providing the benefits of national defence to an additional resident is zero, and it is impossible to exclude some residents from the benefits of national defence. The relevant point here is that persons can benefit from non-exclusive goods without contributing to their cost. Non-exclusive goods, then, confer positive externalities on entities other than those who produce them—that is, the benefits of consumption are not captured fully by the entity that bears the costs of generating those goods. The problem created by public goods, and non-exclusive goods more generally, is that potential beneficiaries have an incentive to *free ride*—that is, to consume those goods without contributing to the cost of producing them. The inability of the producer to fully capture the benefits of consumption means that that good will be produced at lower levels than it would were the benefits entirely internalized. As with nega-tive externalities, the analysis that applies to private economic entities can also be applied to governments. Provincial governments can enact public policies that confer benefits on resi-dents of other provinces who do not shoulder the costs of those policies. And the inability of provincial governments to fully capture the benefits of public investment creates the incentive to under-produce the relevant good.

In these two cases, can it really be said that there is no constitutional inability? In an import-ant sense, an inability does exist, because the territorial limits on provincial jurisdiction (a) render provinces that want a uniform policy for the federation as a whole constitutionally un-able to enact such a policy and (b) render provinces that provide non-exclusive goods unable to coerce non-residents into making financial contributions toward the cost of providing those goods. However, as is true of negative externalities, although the provinces that desire a certain policy may be unable to adopt it, it is not the case that no province can adopt the policy. Again, the problem is one of provincial unwillingness, not provincial inability.

In addition to inter-provincial collective action problems, there are also *federal-provincial collective action problems*. In a system of divided jurisdiction, some policy concerns straddle the division of powers between the provinces and the federal government, rendering either level of government constitutionally incapable of regulating the problem alone. … [In such cases one] solution [as in the case of agricultural marketing boards] has been to enact a system of inter-locking federal and provincial statutes (eleven in total) that together regulate the scheme in a comprehensive fashion … . But should one province hold out and not cooperate, the creation of a [comprehensive scheme] would be impossible. Again, in a sense, there are constitutional inabilities at play, because the governments that wish to adopt a national ... scheme are consti-tutionally disabled from doing so. But the fact that some governments, even collectively, lack the requisite jurisdiction to adopt a policy for the entire federation does not mean that there is a provincial inability, since hold-out provinces possess the constitutional capacity to cooperate but decline to do so. ...

3. True Provincial Inability

Finally, there are cases of true provincial inability, where provinces really are constitutionally incapable of regulating subject-matters, even if willing to do so. In particular, provinces are con-stitutionally incapable of regulating activity in parts of Canada that lie outside the ten provinces, namely the Yukon and Northwest Territories, Nunavut, the territorial sea, and the continental shelf. The province's constitutional incapacity arises from the territorial limits on provincial jurisdiction, which are laid down by s. 92. Because of the assumption that the division of pow-ers distributes legislative authority exhaustively between the provincial and federal govern-ments, the corollary of the territorial limits on provincial jurisdiction is that jurisdiction over these parts of Canada goes to the federal government. The constitutional pegs for this alloca-tion of jurisdiction are the little-used "gap" branch of POGG ... .

... [I]nvoking the national dimensions branch of POGG as a reason to grant the federal government jurisdiction here is redundant because the subject-matter (*e.g.*, the continental shelf) already lies under federal jurisdiction. So the national dimensions test must be an *addi-tional* reason to assign subject-matters to POGG. And if this is true, then the provincial inabil-ity test, oddly enough, must mean something other than true provincial inability, in the way that I have described.

4. Some have suggested that the national concern doctrine is similar to the doctrine of subsidiarity in the European Union. According to that doctrine, powers should be distrib-uted between the centre and the regions according to the principle that decisions should be made at the lowest level of government that is reasonably possible. More specifically, article 3b of the 1992 Maastricht Treaty states that outside its areas of exclusive competence, "the Community shall take action in accordance with the principle of subsidiarity, only if and in so far as the objectives of the proposed action cannot be sufficiently achieved by the Mem-ber States and can therefore, by reason of the scale or effects of the proposed action, be bet-ter achieved by the Community."

Not surprisingly, there is debate as to whether "sufficiently achieved" focuses only on the issue of inability on the part of lower levels of government or whether it includes consider-ation of the efficacy of action by that level as well. This debate occurs overwhelmingly in the political rather than the judicial sphere.

Many in Europe see subsidiarity as a brake on the process of federalization that preserves the sovereignty of the member states. Is it appropriate to invoke the doctrine of subsidiarity within Canada to guide in the interpretation of the national concern doctrine?

5. One factor influencing the majority's finding that marine pollution is a matter of na-tional dimension was the presence of international regulation of the problem. Does this suggest an indirect relaxation of the constraints on federal jurisdiction imposed by the *La-bour Conventions* case, found in Chapter 6, The 1930s: The Depression and the New Deal?

6. It is interesting to contrast Canadian federal power to address matters on the inter-national agenda with the federal power in Australia. The Australian constitution gives explicit

legislative jurisdiction over "external affairs" to the federal Parliament (*Commonwealth of Australia Constitution Act*, 1900, s. 51(xxix)), and the High Court of Australia has interpreted this aspect of the division of powers expansively. The two leading cases on this issue concern land use conflicts between, on the one hand, the proposed natural resource projects of state governments and, on the other, the Commonwealth of Australia's commitments to preserve certain lands under the United Nations Convention for the Protection of the World Cultural and Natural Heritage. In *Commonwealth of Australia v. Tasmania* (1983), 158 CLR 1, 46 ALR 625 (the *Tasmanian Dam* case), the High Court upheld a federal statute prohibiting the state of Tasmania from constructing a hydroelectric dam that would have threatened lands listed on the United Nations World Heritage List. A majority of the Court held that s. 51(xxix) confers on the federal government the legislative authority to implement any treaty obligation irrespective of whether it possesses a traditionally "international" subject matter.

This decision was followed in *Queensland v. Commonwealth of Australia* (1989), 167 CLR 232, 86 ALR 519, in which the state of Queensland challenged a federal proclamation prohibiting forestry operations in a World Heritage rain forest area. Writing for the majority, Chief Justice Mason stated at 525 ALR:

> The existence of Australia's international duty is determined by the inclusion of the property in the World Heritage List consequent on Australia's nomination of the property for inclusion in the List, for the listing of the property determines its status for the international community. There is no suggestion of bad faith either in the nomination or in the listing. As the inclusion of the property in the List is conclusive of its status in the eyes of the international community, it is conclusive of Australia's international duty to protect and conserve it. Its inclusion is therefore conclusive of the constitutional support for the proclamation of 15 December 1988 and of the satisfaction of paras (b), (c) and (d) of s. 6(2).

For further reading on the constitutional law of international agreements in Australia, see Cheryl Saunders, "Articles of Faith or Lucky Breaks?" (1995), 17 *Sydney Law Review* 150.

NOTE: JURISDICTION OVER THE ENVIRONMENT

There is still much uncertainty about the scope of federal jurisdiction over the environment. The case that follows dealt with federal jurisdiction over environmental assessment, while the notes that follow consider the federal role with respect to the regulation of toxic substances and activities harmful to the environment.

Friends of the Oldman River Society v. Canada (Minister of Transport)
[1992] 1 SCR 3, 88 DLR (4th) 1

[The Environmental Assessment and Review Process Guidelines, SOR/84-467 issued under the federal *Department of the Environment Act*, RSC 1985, c. E-10 required all federal departments and agencies that have a decision-making authority for any proposed activity that may have an environmental effect on an area of federal responsibility to screen the proposal to determine whether it may give rise to any potentially adverse environmental effects. If the proposal could have serious adverse environmental effects, there must be public review by an environmental assessment panel.

The Alberta government proposed to construct a dam on the Oldman River to create a storage reservoir. Various procedures were used to consider the environmental impacts. Approval for the project was obtained from the federal Minister of Transport under the *Navigable Waters Protection Act*, RSC 1985, c. N-22, but the Minister did not subject the project to an environmental assessment.

The Society brought an action to quash the decision of the Minister of Transport and to compel that Minister and the Minister of Fisheries and Oceans to comply with the Guidelines. The action was dismissed at trial, but was successful at the Federal Court of Appeal.

The Supreme Court of Canada dismissed an appeal, with Stevenson J dissenting on certain issues. Only the reasons of La Forest J, speaking for the whole court on the constitutional issue, are reproduced.]

LA FOREST J (Lamer CJC, L'Heureux-Dubé, Sopinka, Gonthier, Cory, McLachlin, and Iacobucci JJ concurring): ...

Alberta argues that Parliament has no plenary jurisdiction over the environment, it being a matter of legislative jurisdiction shared by both levels of government, and that the *Guidelines Order* has crossed the line which circumscribes Parliament's authority over the environment. The appellant Ministers argue that in pith and substance the *Guidelines Order* is merely a process to facilitate federal decision-making on matters that fall within Parliament's jurisdiction—a proposition with which the respondent substantially agrees.

The substance of Alberta's argument is that the *Guidelines Order* purports to give the Government of Canada general authority over the environment in such a way as to trench on the province's exclusive legislative domain. Alberta argues that the *Guidelines Order* attempts to regulate the environmental effects of matters largely within the control of the province and, consequently, cannot constitutionally be a concern of Parliament. In particular, it is said that Parliament is incompetent to deal with the environmental effects of provincial works such as the Oldman River Dam.

I agree that the *Constitution Act, 1867* has not assigned the matter of "environment" *sui generis* to either the provinces or Parliament. The environment, as understood in its generic sense, encompasses the physical, economic and social environment touching several of the heads of power assigned to the respective levels of government. ...

I earlier referred to the environment as a diffuse subject, echoing what I said in *R v. Crown Zellerbach Canada Ltd.*, [1988] 1 SCR 401, to the effect that environmental control, as a subject matter, does not have the requisite distinctiveness to meet the test under the "national concern" doctrine as articulated by Beetz J in *Reference re Anti-Inflation Act*, [1976] 2 SCR 373. Although I was writing for the minority in *Crown Zellerbach*, this opinion was not contested by the majority. The majority simply decided that marine pollution was a matter of national concern because it was predominantly extra-provincial and international in character and implications, and possessed sufficiently distinct and separate characteristics as to make it subject to Parliament's residual power.

· · ·

It must be noted that the exercise of legislative power, as it affects concerns relating to the environment, must, as with other concerns, be linked to the appropriate head of power, and since the nature of the various heads of power under the *Constitution Act, 1867* differ, the extent to which environmental concerns may be taken into account in the exercise of a power may vary from one power to another. For example, a somewhat different environmental role can be played by Parliament in the exercise of its jurisdiction over fisheries than under its powers concerning railways or navigation since the former involves the management of a resource, the others activities. The foregoing observations may be demonstrated by reference to two cases involving fisheries. In *Fowler v. The Queen*, [1980] 2 SCR 213, the Court found that s. 33(3) of the *Fisheries Act* was *ultra vires* Parliament because its broad prohibition enjoining the deposit of "slash, stumps or other debris" into water frequented by fish was not sufficiently linked to any actual or potential harm to fisheries. However, s. 3(2), prohibiting the deposit of deleterious substances *in any place* where they might enter waters frequented by fish, was found *intra vires* Parliament under s. 91(12) in *Northwest Falling Contractors Ltd. v. The Queen*, [1980] 2 SCR 292.

The provinces may similarly act in relation to the environment under any legislative power in s. 92. Legislation in relation to local works or undertakings, for example, will often take into account environmental concerns. What is not particularly helpful in sorting out the respective levels of constitutional authority over a work such as the Oldman River dam, however, is the characterization of it as a "provincial project" or an undertaking "primarily subject to provincial regulation" as the appellant Alberta sought to do. That begs the question and posits an erroneous principle that seems to hold that there exists a general doctrine of interjurisdictional immunity to shield provincial works or undertakings from otherwise valid federal legislation. ... What is important is to determine whether either level of government may legislate. One may legislate in regard to provincial aspects, the other federal aspects. Although local projects will generally fall within provincial responsibility, federal participation will be required if the project impinges on an area of federal jurisdiction as is the case here. ...

Appeal dismissed.

NOTE: OTHER DEVELOPMENTS

1. More recently, there has been litigation concerning the federal government's power to regulate toxic substances under the peace, order, and good government clause. The *Canadian Environmental Protection Act* (CEPA) is an effort to regulate toxic substances. CEPA regulates matters as diverse as nutrient contamination, international air pollution, and ocean dumping, and provides for environmental guidelines to be established for Crown corporations and federal departments, agencies, undertakings, and lands. The Act also specifies offences and punishments, mandates an annual minister's report to Parliament, and establishes procedures for a board of review to inquire into the nature and extent of environmental dangers.

The centrepiece of CEPA, however, is its response to toxic substances (CEPA, Part II). Unlike traditional emission regulation, CEPA's treatment of toxic substances involves potentially comprehensive or "life-cycle" regulation. The Act establishes detailed classification procedures, and for those substances designated as toxic, it tracks and regulates every stage of their existence, from creation through to disposal.

In *R v. Hydro-Québec*, [1997] 3 SCR 213, 151 DLR (4th) 32, a majority of the Supreme Court, per La Forest J, upheld the Act as a valid exercise of the federal criminal law power, holding it "unnecessary to deal with the national concern doctrine, which inevitably raises profound issues respecting the federal structure of our Constitution which do not arise with anything like the same intensity in relation to the criminal law power." Lamer CJC and Iacobucci J, dissenting, held that the Act could not be supported under the criminal law power. They added that the Act also failed the test of "singleness, distinctiveness and indivisibility" required by *Crown Zellerbach* because it was not confined to a narrow range of toxic chemical substances such as PCBs that have a severely harmful effect on human health and the environment and whose pollutant effects are diffuse and persist in the environment, but potentially covered a broader range of harmful substances whose effects may be temporary and more local in nature. An extract from *Hydro-Québec* appears in section I of Chapter 11, Criminal Law.

2. Jean Leclair has written extensively on the distribution of legislative authority as it pertains to environmental issues. See Leclair, "L'étendue du pouvoir constitutionnel des provinces et de l'État central en matière d'évaluation des incidences environnementales au Canada" (1995), 21 *Queen's Law Journal* 37-77; Leclair, "Aperçu des virtualités de la compétence fédérale en matière de droit criminel dans le contexte de la protection de l'environnement" (1996), 27 *Revue générale de droit* 137-171; Leclair, "The Supreme Court, the Environment, and the Construction of National Identity" (1998), 4 *Revue d'études constitutionnelles/Review of Constitutional Studies* 372-78.

3. The Supreme Court of Canada revisited the peace, order, and good government clause in *Ontario Hydro v. Ontario (Labour Relations Board)*, [1993] 3 SCR 327, 107 DLR (4th) 457. At issue was the proper jurisdiction—federal or Ontario—to issue a certificate for collective bargaining for employees at Ontario Hydro's nuclear electrical generating stations. In other words, could the federal government regulate nuclear energy under the peace, order, and good government power? A majority of the Court (4 to 3) held that the *Canada Labour Code* applied to employees employed on or in connection with those nuclear facilities. The sources of federal jurisdiction were the declaratory power in s. 92(10)(c) and the peace, order, and good government clause.

With respect to p.o.g.g., La Forest J (L'Heureux-Dubé and Gonthier JJ concurring) stated (at 489-90 DLR):

> There can surely be no doubt that the production, use and application of atomic energy constitute a matter of national concern. It is predominantly extraprovincial and international in character and implications, and possesses sufficiently distinct and separate characteristics to make it subject to Parliament's residual power: see *Reference re Anti-Inflation Act*, [1976] 2 SCR 373; *R v. Crown Zellerbach Canada Ltd.*, [1988] 1 SCR 401. No one seriously disputed this assertion, and my colleagues both agree that this is so. The view of the Attorney-General of Canada is supported by authority in the lower courts: see *Pronto Uranium Mines Ltd. v. Ontario Labour Relations Board*, [1956] OR 862 (HC), at p. 869; and *Denison Mines Ltd. v. Attorney General of Canada*, [1973] 1 OR 797 (HC), at p. 808. The strategic and security aspects of nuclear power in relation to national defence and the catastrophe and near catastrophe associated with its

peaceful use and development at Chernobyl and Two Mile Island, bespeak its national character and uniqueness.

The appellants, we saw, argue, however, that the distinct aspects over which atomic energy rises to the national level are those concerned with health and safety. But this very argument is self-defeating. With the inherent potential dangers associated with nuclear fission, industrial safety—indeed the safety of people hundreds of miles from a nuclear facility—is necessarily dependent on the personnel who operate the facility. A strike, and indeed mere carelessness, could invite disaster. As the Attorney-General of Canada put it: "The whole purpose of federal regulation of nuclear electrical generating plants would be frustrated if Parliament could not govern the standards and conditions of employment of the individuals who operate the plant, both for their own safety, and for that of the general public."

Quite apart from this doomsday scenario, what was said in the context of a work subject to the declaratory power applies equally to a work over which Parliament has jurisdiction under its general power in relation to matters of national concern. Labour relations are an integral part of that jurisdiction. I observe that this approach had been adopted in *Pronto, supra*.

Lamer CJC wrote separate concurring reasons upholding federal jurisdiction. In dissent, Iacobucci J stated (Sopinka and Cory JJ concurring) at 524-25 DLR:

> In summary, while Parliament has jurisdiction over atomic energy under the national concern branch of the p.o.g.g. power, that jurisdiction does not extend to the labour relations between Ontario Hydro and those of its employees employed in the nuclear electrical generating stations. The federal government does not require control over labour relations at Ontario Hydro's nuclear facilities for the exercise of jurisdiction over atomic energy. In other words, the labour relations at issue in this case are not part of the single, distinctive and indivisible matter identified as atomic energy. This is not to say, however, that Parliament, where circumstances warrant, may not, in exercising its valid jurisdiction over nuclear energy, enact legislation which has an impact on the labour relations of Ontario Hydro's employees under either the national concern branch or the national emergency branch of the power to legislate for the peace, order and good government of Canada.

4. In *R v. Malmo-Levine; R v. Caine*, [2003] 3 SCR 571, 2003 SCC 74, 233 DLR (4th) 415, the Court dealt with the issue of the validity of the prohibition of possession of marijuana in the *Narcotic Control Act*, SC 1960-61, c. 35 (NCA). Recall that in *R v. Hauser*, [1979] 1 SCR 984, 98 DLR (3d) 193, discussed above in the notes after the *Anti-Inflation* case, a majority of the Court upheld the *Narcotics Control Act* as a valid exercise of the national concern branch of the p.o.g.g. power. In *Malmo Levine*, the Court revisited that issue and concluded that the prohibition on marijuana possession was a valid exercise of the criminal law power, making consideration of the broader issue of Parliament's residual power to deal with narcotics in general or marijuana in particular under p.o.g.g. unnecessary. Gonthier and Binnie JJ (who attracted the support of all members of the Court on the division of powers issue) wrote:

> [71] The Attorney General of Canada contends that the control of narcotics is a legislative subject matter that "goes beyond local or provincial concern and must, from its inherent nature, be the concern of the Dominion as a whole." He puts his position as follows:

The importation, manufacture, distribution, and use of psychoactive substances are matters having an impact on the country as a whole, and which can only be dealt with on an integrated national basis. Additionally, the international aspects are such that these matters cannot be effectively addressed at the local level.

[72] We do not exclude the possibility that the NCA might be justifiable under the "national concern" branch on the rationale adopted in *R v. Crown Zellerbach Canada Ltd.*, [1988] 1 SCR 401, at p. 432, where we held that concerted action amongst provincial and federal entities, each acting within their respective spheres of legislative jurisdiction, was essential to deal with Canada's international obligations regarding the environment. In our view, however, the Court should decline in this case to revisit Parliament's residual authority to deal with drugs in general (or marihuana in particular) under the POGG power. If, as is presently one of the options under consideration, Parliament removes marihuana entirely from the criminal law framework, Parliament's continuing legislative authority to deal with marihuana use on a purely regulatory basis might well be questioned. The Court would undoubtedly have more ample legislative facts and submissions in such a case than we have in this appeal. Our conclusion that the present prohibition against the use of marihuana can be supported under the criminal law power makes it unnecessary to deal with the Attorney General's alternative position under the POGG power, and we leave this question open for another day.

Gonthier and Binnie JJ referred to the speculation by some commentators that in *Hauser* the majority strained to locate the *Narcotics Control Act* under the p.o.g.g. power because of uncertainty about whether the federal Crown had the authority to prosecute criminal law offences, an uncertainty that was subsequently resolved in favour of the federal Crown.

CHAPTER TEN

Economic Regulation

I. THE CONSTITUTION AND THE ECONOMY

In this chapter, we focus on the Constitution and the economy, largely through an examination of the federal power to regulate trade and commerce in s. 91(2) and the provincial power over property and civil rights in s. 92(13). These powers are not exhaustive of the heads of power affecting economic policy. Obviously, taxation powers are also important, as is the federal criminal law power in some circumstances—for example, in the area of product safety standards. The latter is discussed in more detail in Chapter 11, Criminal Law, as well as in the note on the *Labatt* case, below. Moreover, the federal government has powers to regulate aspects of the economy through such enumerated powers as banking, interest, copyright, and patents, as well as its jurisdiction over interprovincial and international transportation. Finally, s. 121 of the *Constitution Act, 1867* protects the free movement of goods across provincial borders.

In recent years, there has been much concern about the respective roles of federal and provincial governments in economic regulation, especially in light of the pressures on the Canadian economy from an increasingly competitive global marketplace. At times, the debate focuses on the need for a stronger federal legislative role to deal with transnational issues—for example, through negotiation and implementation of international trade agreements, such as the North American Free Trade Agreement (NAFTA). However, much of the public debate has focused on the need to create a stronger economic union in Canada, through the removal of barriers to the mobility of goods, services, labour, and capital. On the one hand, concern has been expressed about unfair discrimination against factors of production from other provinces and territories—that is, a call for "negative integration." On the other hand, some have also expressed a desire for greater harmonization of standards across the country—for example, in the recognition of occupational qualifications or greater similarity in environmental or consumer safety standards—that is, a need for greater "positive integration." As you read the materials that follow, keep these distinctions in mind and ask yourself whether the existing distribution of powers can and should address both of these policy concerns.

This chapter starts with an excerpt from *Black and Co. v. Law Society of Alberta*, a mobility rights case under s. 6 of the *Charter of Rights and Freedoms*. This section, which was the culmination of efforts at constitutional reform to strengthen the economic union, guarantees labour mobility across provincial and territorial boundaries. As indicated at the end of this chapter, subsequent efforts at constitutional reform have failed.

In *Black*, La Forest J, for the majority, discussed the relationship between the Constitution and the economic union. While much of his discussion is about individual rights, note as well the reference to economic integration as a goal of federalism at the time of Confederation.

Black and Co. v. Law Society of Alberta
[1989] 1 SCR 591, 58 DLR (4th) 317

[This case involved a challenge to a rule of the Law Society of Alberta prohibiting partnerships between resident and non-resident lawyers, a rule enacted to prevent the Toronto-based law firm McCarthy and McCarthy from opening a branch office in Calgary. The Supreme Court concluded that the rule violated s. 6(2)(b) of the Charter and could not be upheld as a reasonable limit under s. 1 of the Charter. Section 6(2)(b) guarantees a citizen or permanent resident the right to pursue the gaining of a livelihood in any province. Section 6(3) subjects these rights to laws or practices of general application in force in a province other than those that discriminate among persons primarily on the basis of province of present or previous residence.]

LA FOREST J (Dickson CJC and Wilson J concurring): ... A discussion of the scope and effect of s. 6(2)(b) in the context of this case is enhanced by a brief review of the history of the protection of interprovincial mobility in Canada.

A dominant intention of the drafters of the *British North America Act, 1867* (now the *Constitution Act, 1867*) was to establish "a new political nationality" and, as the counterpart to national unity, the creation of a national economy: D. Creighton, *British North America Act at Confederation: A Study Prepared for the Royal Commission on Dominion– Provincial Relations* (1939), Appendix 2, at p. 40 (Ottawa: King's Printer, 1940). The attainment of economic integration occupied a place of central importance in the scheme. "It was an enterprise which was consciously adopted and deliberately put into execution": Creighton, *supra*; see also *Lawson v. Interior Tree Fruit & Vegetable Committee*, [1931] SCR 357, [1931] 2 DLR 193 at pp. 206-7. The creation of a central government, the trade and commerce power, s. 121 and the building of a transcontinental railway were expected to help forge this economic union. The concept of Canada as a single country comprising what one would now call a common market was basic to the Confederation arrangements and the drafters of the *British North America Act, 1867* attempted to pull down the existing internal barriers that restricted movement within the country.

Section 121 of the *Constitution Act, 1867* was one of the pillars of the Confederation scheme for achieving the economic union sought by the Fathers of Confederation. ... Rand J in *Murphy v. CPR Co.*, [1958] SCR 626, 15 DLR (2d) 145 at p. 150, commented on the scope of s. 121:

> Apart from matters of purely local and private concern, this country is one economic unit;
> in freedom of movement its business interests are in an extra-provincial dimension, and,
> among other things, are deeply involved in trade and commerce between and beyond
> Provinces.

The word "free" in the context of s. 121 was held to mean "without impediment related to the traversing of a provincial boundary."

Echoes of these sentiments can be found in Laskin J's (as he then was) decision in *A-G Man. v. Manitoba Egg & Poultry Ass'n.*, [1971] SCR 689, 19 DLR (3d) 169. Laskin J asserted at p. 190 that,

... to permit each Province to seek its own advantage, so to speak, through a figurative sealing of its borders to entry of goods from others would be to deny one of the objects of Confederation, evidenced by the catalogue of federal powers and by s. 121, namely, to form an
economic unit of the whole of Canada. ...

Before the enactment of the Charter, however, there was no specific constitutional
provision guaranteeing personal mobility, but it is fundamental to nationhood, and even
in the early years of Confederation there is some, if limited, evidence that the courts
would, in a proper case, be prepared to characterize certain rights as being fundamental
to, and flowing naturally from a person's status as a Canadian citizen. In *Union Colliery
Co. of BC v. Bryden*, [1899] AC 580, the Privy Council dealt with the validity of a British
Columbia enactment that prohibited people of Chinese origin or descent from being
employed in mines. The Privy Council found the provision to be *ultra vires* the provincial
legislature and thus illegal. Lord Watson based his reasons on s. 91(25) of the *British
North America Act, 1867*, which gives exclusive legislative authority over "naturalization
and aliens" to the Parliament of Canada. "Naturalization," it was held at p. 586, includes
"the power of enacting ... what shall be the rights and privileges pertaining to residents
in Canada after they have been naturalized." Provincial interference with a resident's
right to live and work in the province was thus not permitted; see also *Cunningham v.
Homma*, [1903] AC 151 at p. 157.

It was left to Rand J in *Winner v. SMT (Eastern) Ltd.*, [1951] SCR 887, [1951] 4 DLR
529, to spell out the full implications of the *Bryden* case for Canadian citizenship. Rand J
makes it clear that Canadian citizenship carries with it certain inherent rights, including
some form of mobility right. The essential attributes of citizenship including the right to
enter and the right to work in a province, he asserted, cannot be denied by the provincial
legislatures. And he extended this right for practical purposes to other residents of Canada. He thus put it at pp. 558-9:

> What this implies is that a Province cannot, by depriving a Canadian of the means of work-
> ing, force him to leave it: it cannot divest him of his right or capacity to remain and to en-
> gage in work there: that capacity inhering as a constituent element of his citizenship status
> is beyond nullification by provincial action. The contrary view would involve the anomaly
> that although British Columbia could not by mere prohibition deprive a naturalized for-
> eigner of his means of livelihood, it could do so to a native-born Canadian. He may, of
> course, disable himself from exercising his capacity or he may be regulated in it by valid
> provincial law in other aspects. But that attribute of citizenship lies outside of those civil
> rights committed to the Province, and is analogous to the capacity of a Dominion corpora-
> tion which the Province cannot sterilize.
>
> It follows, *a fortiori*, that a Province cannot prevent a Canadian from entering it except,
> conceivably, in temporary circumstances, for some local reason as, for example, health.
> With such a prohibitory power, the country could be converted into a number of enclaves
> and the "union" which the original Provinces sought and obtained disrupted. In a like posi-
> tion is a subject of a friendly foreign country; for practical purposes he enjoys all the rights
> of the citizen.

Such, then, is the national status embodying certain inherent or constitutive characteristics, of members of the Canadian public, and it can be modified, defeated or destroyed, as
for instance by outlawry, only by Parliament.

During the constitutional exercise culminating in the enactment of the Charter, there
was a wave of political and academic concern regarding the construction of numerous
barriers to interprovincial economic activity. There was also a strong feeling that the integration of the Canadian economy, which had been only partially successful under the
British North America Act, 1867, should be completed. The federal government in particular was concerned about the growing fragmentation of the Canadian economic
union ... .

These economic concerns undoubtedly played a part in the constitutional entrenchment of interprovincial mobility rights, under s. 6(2) of the Charter. But citizenship, and
the rights and duties that inhere in it are relevant not only to state concerns for the proper structuring of the economy. It defines the relationship of citizens to their country and
the rights that accrue to the citizen in that regard, a factor not lost on Rand J, as is evident
from the passage already quoted. This approach is reflected in the language of s. 6 of the
Charter, which is not expressed in terms of the structural elements of federalism, but in
terms of the rights of the citizen and permanent residents of Canada. Citizenship and
nationhood are correlatives. Inhering in citizenship is the right to reside wherever one
wishes in the country and to pursue the gaining of a livelihood without regard for provincial boundaries. Under Charter disposition, that right is expressly made applicable to
citizens and permanent residents alike. Like other individual rights guaranteed by the
Charter, it must be interpreted generously to achieve its purpose to secure to all Canadians and permanent residents the rights that flow from membership or permanent residency in a united country.

NOTE: THE EXTENT OF INTERNAL TRADE BARRIERS

La Forest J refers to the concern about internal trade barriers in the constitutional discussions prior to the 1982 amendments to the Constitution. These concerns have continued
post-1982, coupled with ongoing debate about the actual significance of these barriers. In
support of its 1991 constitutional proposals with respect to the economic union, the federal
government provided a description of some common internal trade barriers and an estimate of their cost:

> Although a definitive list of internal barriers does not exist, one recent study (by the Canadian
> Manufacturers' Association) argued that there were at least 500 government impediments to
> the mobility of goods, services, people, and capital in Canada. Both the federal and provincial
> governments—acting individually or jointly—are responsible for the laws, practices, and poli-
> cies that create impediments to the operation of a fully integrated national market. For ex-
> ample, the range of impediments created by governments includes:
>
> • procurement practices that favour local suppliers over lower-cost out-of-province
>   suppliers;
> • policies favouring local wine, liquor, and beer industries over out-of-province suppliers;

- agricultural supply marketing boards that regulate the production and prices of various food products including milk, poultry, and eggs;
- regulations that effectively restrict the ability of firms to operate freely across provincial boundaries;
- health, safety, and labelling standards that differ by province;
- hiring policies that favour local residents over those from other provinces;
- standards for professionals and tradespeople that restrict employment opportunities for residents of other provinces; and
- use of provincial limitations on certain financial investments to influence business decisions.

Although it is extremely difficult to measure precisely the overall effect of such barriers on the national economy, efforts to quantify existing costs point to a significant national economic burden.

- The Macdonald Commission cited estimates ranging as high as 1.5 percent of the gross national product (GNP) for the total cost of internal trade barriers for the national economy.
- More recently, the Canadian Manufacturers' Association (CMA) suggested that savings from the elimination of barriers could be as high as $6 billion (just under 1 percent of gross domestic product (GDP)), or almost $1,000 per year for a family of four.

These estimates do not capture the costs associated with new activity that is deterred as a result of the existence of barriers. For example, existence of internal barriers—and the knowledge that new ones can be introduced at any time—can deter Canadian businesses and entrepreneurs from undertaking new investments based on the expectation of access to the whole Canadian market. Similarly, the existence of internal barriers may discourage international investors, who seek to locate their plants in fully integrated markets, from bringing their productive investments to Canada.

From Canada, *Canadian Federalism and Economic Union: Partnership for Prosperity* (Ottawa: Minister of Supply and Services, 1991), at 19.

The purposes of the Charter's mobility rights section were revisited in the *Richardson* case, which is excerpted below. Note a shift in emphasis in the Court's reasons concerning the objectives served by s. 6.

Canadian Egg Marketing Agency v. Richardson
[1998] 3 SCR 157, 166 DLR (4th) 1

[This case concerned the exclusion of egg producers in the Northwest Territories from Canada's national egg marketing scheme. The scheme is the product of interlocking federal and provincial legislation and regulations governing the production and marketing of eggs in Canada. The federal portion of the scheme is administered by the Canadian Egg Marketing Agency. Under the scheme, production and marketing quotas are allocated based on egg production levels in 1972, at which time there was no egg production in the Northwest Territories. Thus, egg producers in the Northwest Territories, like Richardson, are prohibited by law from marketing or exporting eggs interprovincially or internationally. In the course of addressing the claim that the scheme offended s. 6 of the Charter, the Court addressed the larger purposes served by the mobility guarantees.]

IACOBUCCI and BASTARACHE JJ (Lamer CJC, L'Heureux-Dubé, Gonthier, Cory, and Binnie JJ concurring):

. . .

[60] Situated in the Charter, and closely mirroring the language of international human rights treaties, it seems clear then that s. 6 responds to a concern to ensure one of the conditions for the preservation of the basic dignity of the person. The specific guarantee described in s. 6(2)(b) and s. 6(3)(a) is mobility in the gaining of a livelihood subject to those laws which do not discriminate on the basis of residence. The mobility guarantee is defined and supported by the notion of equality of treatment, and absence of discrimination on the ground normally related to mobility in the pursuit of a livelihood (i.e. residence). ... The freedom guaranteed in s. 6 embodies a concern for the dignity of the individual. Sections 6(2)(b) and 6(3)(a) advance this purpose by guaranteeing a measure of autonomy in terms of personal mobility, and by forbidding the state from undermining this mobility and autonomy through discriminatory treatment based on place of residence, past or present. The freedom to pursue a livelihood is essential to self-fulfilment as well as survival. Section 6 is meant to give effect to the basic human right, closely related to equality, that individuals should be able to participate in the economy without being subject to legislation which discriminates primarily on the basis of attributes related to mobility in pursuit of their livelihood.

[61] The terms of s. 6 suggest that this right is not violated by legislation regulating any particular type of economic activity, but rather by the effect of such legislation on the fundamental right to pursue a livelihood on an equal basis with others. Indeed, the provinces and federal government are authorized by virtue of ss. 91 and 92 of the *Constitution Act, 1867* to regulate all manner of economic activity, as defined by *type* of activity. ... [Cooperative federal–provincial] economic legislation, and the growth of divergent regulatory regimes in the provinces, is undoubtedly authorized by the Constitution.

[62] There is, thus, a tension in the purposes and text of ss. 91 and 92 of the *Constitution Act, 1867*, and s. 6 of the Charter. The former sections authorize the development of distinct legal regimes in the provinces, and define the matters, including many integral to the functioning of the economy, under their exclusive jurisdiction; the latter section, however, says that the individual has a right to pursue a livelihood throughout Canada, without discrimination "primarily on the basis of province of present or previous residence."

[63] This tension is heightened when one takes into account the judicial interpretation and legislative history of s. 121 of the *Constitution Act, 1867*. That section reads:

> 121. All Articles of the Growth, Produce, or Manufacture of any one of the Provinces shall, from and after the Union, be admitted free into each of the other Provinces.

. . .

[65] Dissatisfaction in the federal government with the scope of s. 121 and a perceived tendency in the provinces to erect interprovincial trade barriers led to a proposal for a more robust version of the section in the constitutional negotiations leading up to the 1982 amendments ... . In addition to the free movement of persons, this new version of s. 121 would also have expressly protected the mobility of specified factors of economic production which are often integrally related to the gaining of a livelihood by a person: goods, services, and capital. This proposed s. 121 did not purport to confer rights on individuals or groups; rather, it sought to ensure mobility in the pursuit of a livelihood by dramatically limiting any government's right to legislate with respect to the interprovincial mobility of certain factors of economic production. As it turned out, nine of ten provinces rejected this amendment, leaving s. 121 as it is worded today.

[The majority went on to characterize the inclusion of s. 6 in the Charter as reflecting "a human rights objective," holding that "it guarantees the mobility of persons, not as a feature of the economic unity of the country, but in order to further a human rights purpose" (para. 66). The majority could not find that the primary purpose of the scheme was to "discriminate among persons primarily on the basis of province of present ... residence" (the language of s. 6). Evaluating the primary purpose of the law in this context was akin to identifying its "pith and substance." It could not be said that the dominant feature of the legislation was to discriminate against out-of-province producers. Hence, the challenge to the legislation was dismissed.

Justice McLachlin (Major J concurring) offered dissenting reasons. The purpose of the mobility rights guarantee, according to McLachlin J, was to enshrine

> the right of Canadian citizens and permanent residents to pursue a living wherever in the country they choose without undue government interference. It has two purposes, one collective, one individual: (1) to promote economic union among the provinces; and (2) to ensure to all Canadians one of the fundamental incidents of citizenship: the right to travel throughout the country, to choose a place of residence anywhere within its borders, and to pursue a livelihood, all without regard to provincial boundaries. These purposes are related. The individual right of citizens and permanent residents of Canada to reside and pursue the gaining of a living in any province is the private correlative of the collective interest in a unified economy. (para. 122)

For McLachlin J, the exclusion of NWT producers from the national egg marketing scheme "is a senseless and counter-productive impediment to the right of the respondents to pursue their chosen livelihood, egg production, in the province or territory of their choice, the Northwest Territories" (para. 173). Nor could this scheme constitute a reasonable measure demonstrably justified in a free and democratic society and so saved under s. 1. Being the product of historical accident, the infringing aspects of the scheme could not be characterized as a pressing and substantial objective.]

II. PROVINCIAL POWERS OVER ECONOMIC REGULATION

A. General Principles

As indicated in section I, one area of current concern with respect to the constitutional ordering of the economy is the extent to which the provinces are allowed to impose barriers
to the free flow of goods, capital, services, and labour between the provinces in ways that
impair the functioning of the Canadian economic union. This section examines provincial
regulatory powers from that perspective. In the cases that follow, which deal with the marketing of agricultural products, courts struggle with the scope of provincial jurisdiction over
economic regulation under the property and civil rights power, s. 92(13). In each case, the
province had established a scheme to regulate marketing of a product that, at some point,
moved into interprovincial or international trade. A concern for the preservation of the
Canadian economic union and the elimination of unacceptable barriers to trade seems to
underlie the Court's reasoning in some of these cases.

Carnation Co. Ltd. v. Quebec Agricultural Marketing Board
[1968] SCR 238, 67 DLR (2d) 1

MARTLAND J (Fauteux, Abbott, Judson, Ritchie, Hall, and Spence JJ concurring): This is
an appeal from the Court of Queen's Bench for the Province of Quebec, Appeal Side,
which confirmed the judgment given in the Superior Court, upholding the validity of
three decisions of the Quebec Agricultural Marketing Board, hereinafter referred to as
"the Marketing Board." The question in issue before this Court is as to whether, in making
these orders, the Marketing Board had infringed on the exclusive legislative powers of
Parliament under s. 91(2) of the *BNA Act* to regulate trade and commerce. Submissions
on this issue were made on behalf of the Attorney-General of Canada and the Attorney-
General of Alberta, in addition to those represented by the parties to the litigation.

The Marketing Board was created as a corporation by the provisions of the *Quebec
Agricultural Marketing Act*, 1955-56 (Que.), c. 37. It was empowered, *inter alia*, to approve
joint marketing plans, and to arbitrate any dispute arising in the course of carrying out a
joint marketing plan. The Act provided that ten or more producers of agricultural products
in any territory in Quebec could apply to the Marketing Board for approval of a joint plan
for the marketing of one or more classes of farm products in such territory, if such plan
was supported by a vote of at least 75% in number and value of all producers concerned.

On July 25, 1957, the Marketing Board approved the Quebec Carnation Company
Milk Producers' Plan. The administration of the Plan was entrusted to the Quebec Carnation Company Milk Producers' Board. The Plan bound all *bona fide* milk producers
shipping milk and dairy products to any of the plants of the appellant in Quebec. The
Producers' Board had power to negotiate with the buyer (the appellant) for the marketing and sale to it of milk and dairy products from the farms of producers bound by the
Plan. The Plan provided for a board of arbitration, which might be the Marketing Board,
to decide conflicts in the event of a failure to agree with the appellant in the negotiation
or execution of a convention.

Agreement was not reached as to the purchase price of milk to be purchased by the appellant from the producers, pursuant to the Plan. The matter was arbitrated by the Marketing Board which, after hearing evidence for both sides, wrote extensive reasons, and determined a price of $3.07 per 100 pounds, on December 18, 1958. Subsequently, on June 11, 1962, after a further arbitration, the Marketing Board decided on a price of $2.78 per 100 pounds.

It is these three orders of the Marketing Board, which approved the Plan, and which determined the price to be paid by the appellant for milk purchased from producers subject to the Plan, which are the subject of the appellant's attack.

The appellant was incorporated under the *Canadian Companies Act* [later renamed *Canada Corporations Act*, 1964-65, c. 52, s. 2], and has its head office in Toronto. It operates, in Quebec, an evaporated milk plant at Sherbrooke and a receiving station at Waterloo.

During the period concerned, it purchased raw milk from approximately 2,000 farmers, situated mostly in the eastern townships. At the Sherbrooke plant it processes raw milk into evaporated milk. The major part of such production is shipped and sold outside Quebec. Milk received at the Waterloo receiving station, during the relevant period, was either sent to the Sherbrooke plant, for processing, or else skimmed, the butterfat being sold to other manufacturers, and the skim milk being sent to appellant's plant at Alexandria, Ontario, to be processed into skim milk powder. ...

The position taken by the appellant is that the three orders of the Marketing Board are invalid because they enable it to set a price to be paid by the appellant for a product the major portion of which, after processing, will be used by it for export out of Quebec. This, it is contended, constitutes the regulation of trade and commerce within the meaning of s. 91(2) of the *BNA Act*, a field reserved to the Parliament of Canada.

The appellant, in support of this submission, relies upon the reasons of four of the Judges of the Court in the *Reference re Farm Products Marketing Act (Ont.)*, [1957] SCR 198, 7 DLR (2d) 257, which case is hereinafter referred to as "*the Ontario Reference.*" ...

Four of the members of the Court, Kerwin CJC, Rand, J, Locke J and Nolan J, were of the view that a transaction might take place within a Province and yet not constitute an "intraprovincial" transaction which would be subject to provincial control. ...

Counsel for the respondent points out that, as a result of the Reference, there was no majority opinion as to what transactions, completed within a Province, constituted interprovincial trade, and contends that the views expressed by the four Judges were not in harmony with earlier decisions of this Court and of the Privy Council. ...

The validity of provincial legislation governing the marketing of agricultural products was before this Court in *Lawson v. Interior Tree Fruit & Vegetable Committee*, [1931] SCR 357, [1931] 2 DLR 193, which concerned the *Produce Marketing Act* of British Columbia, 1926-27 (BC), c. 54. In holding that Act to be *ultra vires* of the Legislature of British Columbia, Duff J (as he then was), said, at pp. 198-9:

Coming now to the first ground of attack, namely, that the statute constitutes an attempt to regulate trade within the meaning of s. 91(2)—To repeat the general language of s. 10(1), the functions of the committee are "for the purpose of controlling and regulating—the marketing of any product within its authority," and for that purpose the committee is empowered "to determine whether or not and at what time and in what quantity, and from and to what places, and at what price and on what terms the product may be marketed and delivered."

As I have said, the respondent committee has attempted (in professed exercise of this authority)—and in this litigation asserts its right to do so—to regulate the marketing of products into parts of Canada outside British Columbia. It claims the right under the statute to control (as in fact it does) the sale of such products for shipment into the prairie Provinces as well as the shipment of them into those Provinces for sale or storage. The moment his product reaches a state in which it becomes a possible article of commerce, the shipper is (under the committee's interpretation of its powers), subject to the committee's dictation as to the quantity of it which he may dispose of, as to the places from which, and the places to which he may ship, as to the route of transport, as to the price, as to all the terms of sale. I ought to refer also to the provision of the statute which prohibits anybody becoming a licensed shipper who has not, for six months immediately preceding his application for a licence, been a resident of the Province, unless he is the registered owner of the land on which he carries on business as shipper. In a statute which deals with trade that is largely inter-provincial, this is a significant feature. It is an attempt to control the manner in which traders in other Provinces, who send their agents into British Columbia to make arrangements for the shipment of goods to their principals, shall carry out their inter-provincial transactions. I am unable to convince myself that these matters are all, or chiefly, matters of merely British Columbia concern, in the sense that they are not also directly and substantially the concern of the other Provinces, which constitute in fact the most extensive market for these products. In dictating the routes of shipment, the places to which shipment is to be made, the quantities allotted to each terminus *ad quem*, the committee does, altogether apart from dictating the terms of contracts, exercise a large measure of direct and immediate control over the movement of trade in these commodities between British Columbia and the other Provinces. ...

In 1938, the Privy Council dealt with the validity of a British Columbia statute, *The Natural Products Marketing (British Columbia) Act, 1936*, in *Shannon v. Lower Mainland Dairy Products Board*, [1938] AC 708, [1938] 4 DLR 81. This Act enabled the Lieutenant-Governor in Council to set up a central British Columbia Marketing Board, to establish or approve schemes for the control and regulation within the Province of the transportation, packing, storage and marketing of any natural products, to constitute Marketing Boards to administer such schemes, and to vest in those Boards any powers considered necessary or advisable to exercise those functions.

It was held that this statute was, in pith and substance, an Act to regulate particular businesses, entirely within the Province, and was *intra vires* of the provincial Legislature under s. 92(13) of the *BNA Act*. In dealing with the contention that this Act encroached upon s. 91(2) of the *BNA Act*, Lord Atkin said, at pp. 84-5:

> 1. It is sufficient to say upon this point that it is apparent that the legislation in question is confined to regulating transactions that take place wholly within the Province, and are therefore within the sovereign powers granted to the Legislature in that respect by s. 92. Their Lordships do not accept the view that natural products as defined in the Act are confined to natural products produced in British Columbia. There is no such restriction in the Act, and the limited construction would probably cause difficulty if it were sought at some

future time to co-operate with a valid Dominion scheme. But the Act is clearly confined to dealings with such products as are situate within the Province. ...

It is now necessary to consider, in the light of these decisions, the validity of the three orders which are under attack in the present case. The first order, which created the Quebec Carnation Company Milk Producers' Board and empowered it to negotiate, on behalf of the milk producers, for the sale of their products to the appellant, is somewhat analogous to the creation of a collective bargaining agency in the field of labour relations. The purpose of the order was to regulate, on behalf of a particular group of Quebec producers, their trade with the appellant for the sale to it, in Quebec, of their milk. Its object was to improve their bargaining position.

The Producers' Board then undertook, with the appellant, negotiations for the sale to it of that milk. The order provided a machinery whereby the price of milk could be determined by arbitration if agreement could not be reached. In this respect it differs from most provincial legislation governing labour disputes, but there would seem to be no doubt that provincial labour legislation incorporating compulsory arbitration of disputes would be constitutional, unless objectionable on some other ground.

The two subsequent orders of the Marketing Board, under attack, contained the decisions which it reached in determining the proper price to be paid to the producers for milk purchased by the appellant.

Are these orders invalid because the milk purchased by the appellant was processed by it and, as to a major portion of its product, exported from the Province? Because of that fact, do they constitute an attempt to regulate trade in matters of interprovincial concern?

That the price determined by the orders may have a bearing upon the appellant's export trade is unquestionable. It affects the cost of doing business. But so, also, do labour costs affect the cost of doing business of any company which may be engaged in export trade and yet there would seem to be little doubt as to the power of a Province to regulate wage rates payable within a Province, save as to an undertaking falling within the exceptions listed in s. 92(10) of the *BNA Act*. It is not the possibility that these orders might "affect" the appellant's interprovincial trade which should determine their validity, but, rather, whether they were made "in relation to" the regulation of trade and commerce. ...

Thus, as Kerwin CJC, said in the *Ontario Reference*, in the passage previously quoted [7 DLR (2d) at p. 264]: "Once a statute *aims* at 'regulation of trade in matters of interprovincial concern' ... it is beyond the competence of a Provincial Legislature."

I am not prepared to agree that, in determining that aim, the fact that these orders may have some impact upon the appellant's interprovincial trade necessarily means that they constitute a regulation of trade and commerce within s. 91(2) and thus renders them invalid. The fact of such impact is a matter which may be relevant in determining their true aim and purpose, but it is not conclusive.

In the *Lawson* case, where the provincial legislation was found to be unconstitutional, the Committee created by the statute was enabled and purported to exercise a large measure of direct and immediate control over the movement of trade in commodities between a Province and other Provinces. That is not this case.

On the other hand, in the *Shannon* case the regulatory statute was upheld, as it was confined to the regulation of transactions taking place wholly within the Province. It was held that s. 91(2) was not applicable to the regulation for legitimate provincial purposes of particular trades or businesses confined to the Province.

The view of the four Judges in the *Ontario Reference* was that the fact that a transaction took place wholly within a Province did not necessarily mean that it was thereby subject solely to provincial control. The regulation of some such transactions relating to products destined for interprovincial trade could constitute a regulation of interprovincial trade and be beyond provincial control.

While I agree with the view of the four Judges in the *Ontario Reference* that a trade transaction, completed in a Province, is not necessarily, by that fact alone, subject only to provincial control, I also hold the view that the fact that such a transaction incidentally has some effect upon a company engaged in interprovincial trade does not necessarily prevent its being subject to such control.

I agree with the view of Abbott J, in the *Ontario Reference*, that each transaction and each regulation must be examined in relation to its own facts. In the present case, the orders under question were not, in my opinion, directed at the regulation of interprovincial trade. They did not purport directly to control or to restrict such trade. There was no evidence that, in fact, they did control or restrict it. The most that can be said of them is that they had some effect upon the cost of doing business in Quebec of a company engaged in interprovincial trade, and that, by itself, is not sufficient to make them invalid.

Appeal dismissed.

NOTE ON AG MANITOBA v. MANITOBA EGG AND POULTRY ASSOCIATION

AG Manitoba v. Manitoba Egg and Poultry Association, [1971] SCR 689, 19 DLR (3d) 169, commonly referred to as the *Manitoba Egg Reference*, was one of the battles fought in what became known as the interprovincial "chicken and egg war." The following summary is taken from P. Weiler, *In the Last Resort* (Scarborough, ON: Carswell/Methuen, 1974), at 156-57:

> [The "chicken and egg war" was] primarily an engagement fought by the bordering provinces of Ontario and Quebec. Ontario farmers produced an abundance of cheap eggs and Quebec farmers an abundance of cheap chickens. The surplus producers were naturally interested in the market of the consumers in the neighbouring jurisdiction. Equally naturally, the somewhat less efficient producers of each product were not so enamoured of competition within their own bailiwick. When they went to their own government for protection, the response was legislation facilitating the creation of marketing schemes. These provided for the controlled marketing, at fixed prices, of all the chickens sold in Ontario and all the eggs in Quebec, whatever the source. Unfortunately, it appears that the marketing boards became a little greedy and went even further, giving undue preference in marketing to those products coming from within the province. This had particularly adverse effects on farmers in other provinces such as Manitoba, which, as a consistent producer of agricultural surpluses, was the classic innocent and injured bystander in the "chicken and egg war." ...
>
> At this very time, the federal government was attempting to shepherd through Parliament a new *Farm Products Marketing Act* which would endeavour to solve these problems through a complicated process of inter-administrative delegation. Though there appeared to be substantial consensus in favour of the general scheme of the Bill by both federal and provincial ministers of

agriculture, it was being delayed by opposition members who largely represented western farming interests. In the interim, the federal government had carefully resisted many calls to refer the "political" dispute to the Supreme Court of Canada for immediate "legal" resolution.

Unfortunately, Manitoba, which was understandably loath to wait for a political decision on the larger questions, devised a scheme for circumventing the reluctance of the federal Justice Minister. This provincial government manufactured a controversy by initiating a carbon copy of the Quebec scheme, a proposed Order-in-Council which provided for Manitoba control of the marketing of extraprovincial eggs in Manitoba. It then referred these regulations to the Manitoba Court of Appeal for a decision about their constitutionality, under its own provincial reference legislation. When the Manitoba Court of Appeal decided against the constitutional validity of the scheme, the Manitoba government was entitled as of right to appeal this "loss" to the Supreme Court of Canada. In this way, it could achieve a binding decision as to all such schemes which would be authoritative in all the provinces.

The scheme at issue in the reference applied to all eggs marketed within the province of Manitoba, whether or not produced within the province. Complete control over the marketing of eggs in Manitoba was vested in the Manitoba Egg Producers' Marketing Board, the members of which were to be elected by Manitoba producers. In the main judgment in the case, written by Justice Martland (Fauteux CJC, Abbott, Judson, Ritchie, and Spence JJ concurring) the marketing Board's authority was described as follows:

> It is only through the Board, as selling agent, that any eggs may be sold or offered for sale. It has the authority, as already noted, to impose marketing quotas and to prohibit the offering for sale of a particular regulated product to ensure the orderly marketing of the regulated product. No eggs can be sold or offered for sale unless graded, packed and marked by a grading or packing station under contract with the Board. All eggs must be offered for sale to distributors, under contract with the Board, at prices set, from time to time, by the Board.

Justice Martland then turned to the main issue on appeal:

> The issue which has to be considered in this appeal is as to whether the Plan is *ultra vires* the Manitoba Legislature because it trespasses upon the exclusive legislative authority of the Parliament of Canada to legislate on the matter of the regulation of trade and commerce conferred by s. 91(2) of the *BNA Act, 1867*.
>
> When the Privy Council first addressed itself to the meaning of that provision it was stated that it included "regulation of trade in matters of inter-provincial concern": *Citizens Insurance Co. of Canada v. Parsons* (1881), 7 App. Cas. 96 at p. 113. That proposition has not since been challenged. However, the case went on to hold that the provision did not include the regulation of the contracts of a particular business or trade in a single Province.
>
> This limitation on the federal power was reiterated in subsequent decisions of the Privy Council ... .
>
> In [*Shannon et al. v. Lower Mainland Dairy Products Board*, [1938] AC 708; 4 DLR 81] the *Natural Products Marketing (British Columbia) Act, 1936* was held to be *intra vires* the provincial Legislature because it was confined to dealings with such products as were situate within the Province, even though not necessarily produced there. The basis of this decision was that "The pith and substance of this Act is that it is an Act to regulate particular businesses entirely within the Province ..." (at p. 86).

Similarly, this Court upheld, in *Home Oil Distributors Ltd. et al. v. A-G BC*, [1940] SCR 444, 2 DLR 609, provincial legislation authorizing the fixing of wholesale or retail prices for coal or petroleum products sold in British Columbia for use in that Province. This judgment was based upon the decision in the *Shannon* case. ...

The earlier authorities on the matter of provincial marketing regulation were ... reviewed in the judgment of this Court in *Carnation Co. Ltd. v. Quebec Agricultural Marketing Board et al.*, [1968] SCR 238, 67 DLR (2d) 1. ...

Our conclusion was that each transaction and regulation had to be examined in relation of its own facts, and that, in determining the validity of the regulatory legislation in issue in that appeal, the issue was not as to whether it might affect the interprovincial trade of the appellant company, but whether it was made in relation to the regulation of interprovincial trade and commerce. ...

It is my opinion that the Plan now in issue not only affects interprovincial trade in eggs, but that it aims at the regulation of such trade. It is an essential part of this scheme, the purpose of which is to obtain for Manitoba producers the most advantageous marketing conditions for eggs, specifically to control and regulate the sale in Manitoba of imported eggs. It is designed to restrict or limit the free flow of trade between Provinces as such. Because of that, it consti-tutes an invasion of the exclusive legislative authority of the Parliament of Canada over the matter of the regulation of trade and commerce. ...

Justice Laskin (Hall J concurring) expressed concern about answering the reference question in the abstract. There was "no factual underpinning for the issues" that were raised by the reference, he complained. Nevertheless, Justice Laskin proceeded to answer the refer-ence question, holding the proposed scheme to be beyond provincial authority. He first dis-tinguished the earlier holdings of the Court in *Carnation*, *Shannon*, and *Home Oil* on the basis that, unlike the legislation in these earlier cases, the scheme at issue in *Manitoba Egg* was directed at goods coming from outside of the province:

Although the emphasis is on control of the Manitoba producers and distributors in order (as stated in the proposed measures) "to obtain for producers the most advantageous marketing conditions" and "to avoid overproduction," the scheme brings into its grasp "persons" as well as producers, that is, those outside the Province who are either producers or distributors seek-ing to enter the Manitoba market, or those inside the Province who are not themselves produ-cers but who bring in out-of-Province eggs for disposition in Manitoba. This view is reinforced by the provision for indicating the origin of eggs, including eggs other than those produced in Manitoba.

There may be a variety of reasons which impel a Province to enact regulatory legislation for the marketing of various products. For example, it may wish to secure the health of the inhabit-ants by establishing quality standards; it may wish to protect consumers against exorbitant prices; it may wish to equalize the bargaining or competitive position of producers or distribu-tors or retailers, or all three classes; it may wish to ensure an adequate supply of certain prod-ucts. These objects may not all nor always be realizable through legislation which fastens on the regulated product as being within the Province. That is no longer, if it ever was, the test of valid-ity. Just as the Province may not, as a general rule, prohibit an owner of goods from sending them outside the Province, so it may not be able to subject goods to a regulatory scheme upon their entry into the Province. This is not to say that goods that have come into a Province may not, thereafter, be subject to the same controls in, for example, retail distribution to consumers as apply to similar goods produced in the Province.

Assuming such controls to be open to a Province, the scheme before this Court is not so limited. It embraces products which are in the current of interprovincial trade and, as noted at the beginning of these reasons, it embraces them in whatever degree they seek to enter the provincial market. It begs the question to say that out-of-Province producers who come in voluntarily (certainly they cannot be compelled by Manitoba) must not expect to be treated differently from local producers. I do not reach the question of discriminatory standards applied to out-of-Province producers or distributors (that is, the question of a possibly illegal administration of the scheme as bearing on its validity) because I am of opinion that the scheme is on its face an invasion of federal power in relation to s. 91(2).

There are several grounds upon which I base this conclusion. The proposed scheme has as a direct object the regulation of the importation of eggs, and it is not saved by the fact that the local market is under the same regime. Anglin J said in *Gold Seal Ltd. v. Dominion Express Co. and A-G Alta.* (1921), 62 SCR 424, 62 DLR 62 at p. 86, that "It is common ground that the prohibition of importation is beyond the legislative jurisdiction of the Province." Conversely, the general limitation upon provincial authority to exercise of its powers within or in the Province precludes it from intercepting either goods moving into the Province or goods moving out, subject to possible exceptions, as in the case of danger to life or health. Again, the Manitoba scheme cannot be considered in isolation from similar schemes in other Provinces; and to permit each Province to seek its own advantage, so to speak, through a figurative sealing of its borders to entry of goods from others would be to deny one of the objects of Confederation, evidenced by the catalogue of federal powers and by s. 121, namely, to form an economic unit of the whole of Canada ... . The existence of egg marketing schemes in more than one Province, with objectives similar to the proposed Manitoba scheme, makes it clear that interprovincial trade in eggs is being struck at by the provincial barriers to their movement into various provincial markets. If it be thought necessary or desirable to arrest such movement at any provincial border then the aid of the Parliament of Canada must be sought, as was done through Part V of the *Canada Temperance Act*, RSC 1952, c. 30, in respect of provincial regulation of the sale of intoxicating liquor.

I do not find it necessary in this case to invoke s. 121, and hence say nothing about its applicability to the marketing scheme under review.

Paul Weiler ("The Supreme Court of Canada and Canadian Federalism," in J.S. Ziegel, ed., *Law and Social Change* (Scarborough, ON: Carswell, 1973)) has questioned whether it was appropriate for the Court to respond to the *Manitoba Egg Reference* on the basis of the material placed before it:

There was no concrete focus around which the reasoning of the Court could be organized, nor was the factual economic background to the statute depicted. The Manitoba government conspicuously omitted to set out in the Reference the relevant economic background which might well have supported the reasonability of provincial action in the area. Ontario and Quebec, which were vitally interested in sustaining this kind of legislation, did not have an opportunity to present this factual support. Indeed, the questions which the Manitoba government posed to the Court did not focus on what appears to have been the real character of the dispute—the discriminatory application of provincial marketing quotas against out-of-province producers—

and instead required the Court to make a blanket decision about the legality of any such marketing scheme, no matter how favourably it might be applied to extra-provincial products. In
my opinion, the most sensible response would have been a forthright refusal to answer the
questions on the grounds that the dispute was not appropriate for judicial resolution. One
senses that Mr. Justice Laskin, who was especially critical of the abstract character of the Reference, was drawn in this direction, but eventually the legal mystique surrounding issues of federalism overcame his reluctance. The majority opinion proceeded blithely ahead, without any
apparent concern for the complex and inter-related political or economic interests involved in
the dispute, and the Court gave Manitoba the broad legal weapon it was hoping for.

According to Weiler, this resulted in several inadequacies in the Court's reasoning. In his
view, there were no real functional or economic differences between the provincial schemes
at issue in *Carnation* and *Manitoba Egg*:

> In the final analysis, the only difference is that in *Carnation* the wholesale marketing and prices
> of Quebec milk are controlled by Quebec law—whether it is destined for inside or outside
> Quebec—while in the *Manitoba Egg* case, all eggs sold in Manitoba are to be marketed and
> priced under Manitoba controls, whether they come from within or without Manitoba. Yet
> Martland J decided that, "on its own facts," the Manitoba legislation is *in relation to* trade and
> commerce, as well as *affecting* it, and thus unconstitutional. As to the *Carnation* scheme, again
> "on its own facts" he said it merely had some effect on inter-provincial trade, and was valid. If
> there is a difference, which is relevant to the federal division of legislative power, it is not appar-
> ent to me, and certainly not adverted to on the face of the opinion.

Weiler went on to say that:

> The functional problem which the Court is required to face in the case is the degree of latitude
> which a province should be allowed in subjecting the business sector of our society to regula-
> tion within its borders. As a matter of plain, economic facts, the inter-dependent nature of
> business activity in this country is such that almost all provincial regulations will have ramifica-
> tions on citizens and enterprises outside the country, whether or not the legal rule technically
> applies only to purely intra-provincial trade or transactions. Moreover, the citizens of these
> provinces, who are so affected by these regulatory decisions, have no real say in the election of
> the representative governments which make them. Hence the arguments which can be made
> for judicial laissez-faire with respect to democratically-elected parliaments do not have the
> same weight as in many of the other constitutional areas decided by the Court.

NOTES AND QUESTIONS

1. Do you agree with Weiler's argument that the economic consequences of the Manitoba and Quebec schemes were similar? Are the two cases distinguishable?

2. *Manitoba Egg* was followed in *Burns Foods Ltd. v. AG Manitoba*, [1975] 1 SCR 494, 40
DLR (3d) 731, which involved a challenge to a Manitoba hog marketing scheme that required that all hogs slaughtered in the province by processors be purchased from the Hog
Producers' Marketing Board. The scheme applied to hogs brought from other provinces as
well as hogs produced in the province. There was no power to limit the entry of out-of-
province hogs or impose quotas, only a requirement that out-of-province hogs be treated

the same way as in-province hogs. The Supreme Court concluded (Ritchie J dissenting) that because the legislation had the effect of prohibiting processors from purchasing hogs from producers in another province except through the agency of the Board, it was *ultra vires* as in substance an attempt to regulate the interprovincial trade in hogs.

Pigeon J (Fauteux CJC, Abbott, Martland, Judson, and Spence JJ concurring) stated at 739 DLR:

> It was also said that the pith and substance is not to erect any barrier against the free flow of trade but to stabilize the price of hogs in Manitoba. The difficulty is that such regulation by subjecting the price of "imports" to the same regulations as local sales is, of itself, a regulation of the interprovincial trade. The fact that this is presently being done without the features of discrimination present in the *Egg* case (*supra*) cannot make a real difference, not only because discrimination could at any time be established at the discretion of the Board, but also because what is sought to be regulated in all its essential aspects is the trade in hogs between the Packers in Manitoba and hog producers in any other province.

The case discussed in the following note involved the constitutionality of a federal–provincial egg marketing scheme—the same scheme that was at issue in *Canadian Egg Marketing Agency v. Richardson*, excerpted in section I of this chapter, *supra*. The case, *Re Agricultural Products Marketing Act*, is noteworthy for several reasons: first, it seems to indicate a greater degree of judicial deference in reviewing a scheme that imposes barriers to the free movement of goods because of the joint federal–provincial action; second, Pigeon J emphasizes that the "production" stage is *prima facie* provincial jurisdiction; and third, there is discussion in Laskin CJC's reasons of the "common market" clause in s. 121 of the *Constitution Act, 1867*.

NOTE ON RE AGRICULTURAL PRODUCTS MARKETING ACT

Re Agricultural Products Marketing Act, [1978] 2 SCR 1198, 84 DLR (3d) 257 originated in a reference by the lieutenant governor of Ontario to that province's Court of Appeal of a series of questions concerning the validity of certain provisions of the *Agricultural Products Marketing Act*, RSC 1970, c. A-7, the *Farm Products Marketing Agencies Act*, SC 1970-71-72, c. 65, and the *Farm Products Marketing Act*, RSO 1970, c. 162, and of the orders in council and regulations passed pursuant to these statutes. This legislative package constituted a solution worked out, through federal–provincial cooperation, to the problems of regulating the marketing of agricultural products that gave rise to *Manitoba Egg*.

This legislation and a companion agreement (entered into by the federal and ten provincial ministers of agriculture, together with the federal and provincial marketing boards) established a comprehensive program for regulating the marketing of eggs in Canada. The program provided for sharing of the interprovincial and export market by allocating quotas to each province and to each egg producer. The Canadian Egg Marketing Agency (CEMA) administered the plan, with authority to buy and dispose of any surplus production, to impose levies on producers so as to finance its operations, and to authorize local boards to collect the levies on its behalf. Under provincial regulations, the Ontario board set quotas on eggs to be marketed intraprovincially that were identical to the interprovincial and export quotas established under the national program. Ontario egg producers challenged quotas set by the Ontario Farm Products Marketing Board, arguing that provincial quotas could only apply to goods sold within the province and thus these quotas were beyond provincial competence.

A number of other constitutional issues were raised, including the validity of CEMA's surplus disposal program, the authority of Parliament to provide for levies in respect of intra-provincial marketing, and the validity, in the light of s. 121 of the *British North America (BNA) Act*, of a marketing scheme based on provincial boundaries.

The majority judgment was delivered by Pigeon J (Martland, Ritchie, Beetz, and de Grand-pré JJ concurring). He began his analysis by establishing that control of production is *prima facie* a matter falling within provincial jurisdiction:

> In my view, the control of production, whether agricultural or industrial, is *prima facie* a local matter, a matter of provincial jurisdiction. Egg farms, if I may use this expression to designate the kind of factories in which feed is converted into eggs and fowl, are local undertakings subject to provincial jurisdiction under s. 92(10) of the *British North America Act, 1867*, unless they are considered as within the scope of "agriculture" in which case, by virtue of s. 95, the jurisdiction is provincial subject to the overriding authority of Parliament. In my view *Carnation Co. Ltd. v. Quebec Agricultural Marketing Board*, [1968] SCR 238, 67 DLR (2d) 1, is conclusive in favour of provincial jurisdiction over undertakings where primary agricultural products are transformed into other food products. In that case, the major portion of the production was shipped outside the Province) .... In view of the reasons given, the conclusion could not be different even if the whole production had been going into extraprovincial trade.

Justice Pigeon recognized the difficulty of distinguishing between eggs consumed within the province and those destined for out-of-province trade—"any workable control scheme has to be effective with respect to all eggs irrespective of intended disposition." He also acknowledged that, as was held in *Manitoba Egg*, provincial authority cannot extend to the control of extraprovincial trade. However, according to Pigeon J "marketing" does not extend to production and so

> provincial control of production is *prima facie* valid. In the instant case, the provincial regulation is not aimed at controlling the extraprovincial trade. In so far as it affects this trade, it is only complementary to the Regulations established under federal authority. In my view this is perfectly legitimate, otherwise it would mean that our Constitution makes it impossible by federal–provincial co-operative action to arrive at any practical scheme for the orderly and efficient production and marketing of a commodity which all Governments concerned agree requires regulation in both intraprovincial and extraprovincial trade. As early as 1912, it was asserted by the Privy Council that "whatever belongs to self-government in Canada belongs either to the Dominion or to the provinces": *A-G Ont. v. A-G Can.*, [1912] AC 571 at p. 584, 3 DLR 509 at p. 513. I do not overlook the admonition in *AG BC v. A-G Can. et al.; Reference re Natural Products Marketing Act*, [1937] AC 377 at p. 389, [1937] 1 DLR 691 at pp. 694-5, that the legislation has to be carefully framed but, when after 40 years a sincere co-operative effort has been accomplished, it would really be unfortunate if this was all brought to nought. While I adhere to the view that Provinces may not make use of their control over local undertakings to affect extraprovincial marketing, this does not, in my view prevent the use of provincial control to complement federal regulation of extraprovincial trade.

Justice Laskin (Judson, Spence, and Dickson JJ concurring) delivered a separate judgment addressing the claim that the scheme offended s. 121 of the *British North America Act, 1867*. The argument was that the Canadian Egg Marketing Agency, by establishing a fixed quota system for the production of eggs within each province, "effectively prevents the establishment of a single economic unit in Canada with absolute freedom of trade between its constituent parts, which was one of the main purposes of confederation and which is guaranteed by s. 121 of the Constitution." Justice Laskin admitted that s. 121 applied to federal law as it did to provincial law, but that its application may be different

> according to whether it is provincial or federal legislation that is involved because what may amount to a tariff or customs duty under a provincial regulatory statute may not have that character at all under a federal regulatory statute. ... A federal regulatory statute which does not directly impose a customs charge but through a price fixing scheme, designed to stabilize the marketing of products in intraprovincial trade, seeks through quotas, paying due regard to provincial production experience, to establish orderly marketing in such trade cannot, in my opinion, be in violation of s. 121. ...
>
> ... I find nothing in the marketing scheme here that, as a trade regulation, is *in its essence and purpose* related to a provincial boundary. To hold otherwise would mean that a federal marketing statute, referable to intraprovincial trade, could not validly take into account patterns of production in the various Provinces in attempting to establish an equitable basis for the flow of trade. I find here no design of punitive regulation directed against or in favour of any Province. ...

Patrick Monahan (in *Politics and the Constitution: The Charter, Federalism and the Supreme Court of Canada* (Scarborough, ON: Carswell, 1987), at 207-8) argues that the Court in this case did not engage in any sensitive balancing of the issues at stake:

> It would not have been difficult to construct some functional counterargument in favour of the provincial quotas. For instance, it could have been suggested that it was impossible to identify, at the point of production, whether the goods were eventually to be sold locally or interprovincially. Any requirement that separate regimes be established for local as opposed to interprovincial producers would have been unworkable. But Pigeon J did not rely on any such limited, functional argument. Instead, he advanced the sweeping generalization that a province had control over all "production" of eggs. The destination of the eggs was irrelevant. One did not have to inquire whether most or even all of a producer's eggs would eventually leave the province. The only relevant issue was that the province had enacted "production" quotas rather than "marketing" quotas; "marketing does not include production and, therefore, provincial control of production is *prima facie* valid."

This distinction between "marketing" and "production" is reminiscent of American cases in the early twentieth century interpreting Congress' power over interstate commerce. These cases relied on a distinction between "commerce" on the one hand and "manufacture" or "production " on the other. Congress was said to lack power to interfere with production or manufacture, regardless of their importance or interconnection with interstate trade. For instance, in *US v. E.C. Knight Co.*, 156 US 1 (1895), the US Supreme Court held that the *Sherman Antitrust Act* did not prohibit a near monopoly in the manufacture of refined sugar. This was because "commerce succeeds to manufacture and is not part of it." This distinction relieved the Court of the responsibility of determining the impact of this manufacturing monopoly on interstate commerce itself. The attempt to regulate manufacture was absolutely void regardless of how socially desirable or necessary it might have been. The Court reasoned that if the polity was not satisfied with this result, it might amend the Constitution. The judiciary was merely charged with interpreting the Constitution, not with rewriting it.

The US Supreme Court moved away from this rigid formulation of the federal commerce power in the 1930s. This departure was signalled in a series of cases that greatly expanded congressional authority over interstate commerce. See, for example, *NLRB v. Jones & Laughlin Steel Corp.*, 301 US 1 (1937). More recently, the US Supreme Court has imposed some limitations on the federal commerce power. Federal law now must concern the regulation of "economic activity," rather than activity tangentially related to commerce; see *US v. Lopez*, 514 US 549 (1995).

NOTES AND QUESTIONS

1. A dispute arose in Quebec in the 1990s with respect to the labelling of kosher food products. Quebec's *Charter of the French Language* required the labelling of all prepackaged products offered for sale in the province to be in both French and English. (As you will see in Chapter 24, Language Rights, both federal and provincial governments can legislate with respect to language use as a matter ancillary to other heads of power.) Almost all "kosher for Passover" foods sold in Quebec are imported from New York and labelled only in English or English and Hebrew. It would be prohibitively expensive to add French labels, especially with respect to perishable foods, given the small market in Quebec. Could this law be challenged on federalism grounds?

2. Many of the barriers to trade imposed by the provinces are imposed through exercises of the spending power—for example, by letting government contracts; or ownership—for example, by setting conditions for those exploiting provincial resources. Most of these measures are not constrained by the distribution of powers in ss. 91 and 92. To deal with them effectively, one must find other tools, as discussed below.

B. Natural Resources

Jurisdiction over natural resources was one of the most contentious areas of federal–provincial relations through the late 1970s and early 1980s. As the following excerpt from Simeon and Robinson indicates, rapid increases in the world price of oil generated major disputes about appropriate policy responses and government responsibilities within Canada. Not surprisingly, many of the disputes between federal and provincial governments ended up in the courts, sometimes launched by governments, but often initiated by business interests. These disputes involved important questions about the scope of the trade and commerce power similar to those examined in the agricultural products cases in the previous section—questions about the limits that should be placed on provincial economic regulatory powers because of their impact on interprovincial trade. The cases also involved the provincial power to tax within s. 92(2) of the *Constitution Act, 1867*, and the scope of intergovernmental immunity from taxation under s. 125. The decisions of the Supreme Court of Canada were often unpopular in the western provinces, and a constitutional amendment in

1982 added s. 92A to the Constitution to clarify federal and provincial responsibilities over natural resources and to curb the impact of the Court's decisions.

R. Simeon and I. Robinson, *State, Society and the Development of Canadian Federalism*
(Toronto: University of Toronto Press, 1990), at 236-38 (footnotes omitted)

In 1973, the OPEC capped a series of small increases with a quadrupling of prices. In 1979, following the Iranian revolution, there was a further doubling of prices. In Canada, the effect was to "internalize in the form of sharp federal–provincial conflict, the struggle raging internationally between oil importing and exporting countries."

Energy divided Canada regionally as did no other issue. The territorial distribution of energy resources combined with the allocation of ownership, taxing and trade powers to maximize division. "It unveiled with shocking clarity the intergovernmental conflict of interests in Canadian energy politics." This had not been the case before the 1970s. Both federal and provincial governments had agreed on the need to encourage natural resource development and promote exports. With the Borden Line along the Ottawa River, a large part of the Canadian market had been reserved for western oil, which then cost more than imported oil. But now regional conflicts of interest were substantially reduced.

The consuming provinces, led by Ontario, wished to restrain price increases as much as possible to benefit both domestic and industrial users, and to ensure that the revenue gains would be shared widely across the country. Ontario argued that world oil prices bore no particular relation to the costs of production, either in Saudi Arabia or Canada, but rather were merely a reflection of the new market power of the OPEC cartel. Adopting such prices could not, therefore, be justified on efficiency grounds. Lower Canadian oil price increases would dampen inflation and provide a comparative advantage for Canadian industry.

The producing provinces wished to capitalize on their ownership of the resource by retaining full control over its management, by moving as fast as possible to world oil prices, and by capturing the lion's share of increased public revenues. Alberta and the other oil producing provinces argued that, whatever their origins, high energy prices seemed likely to prevail henceforth. Any short-term competitive gains resulting from subsidized oil prices would be more than offset in the long run as Canada's competitors became more efficient energy users. If Canada were totally self-sufficient, now or in the foreseeable future, the picture might be different. But since it was not, and since maintaining prices below world energy prices would discourage new investment in exploration, Canada would have to adapt. It was better to do it now, while competitors faced the same difficulties, than later when the competitors had solved their problems and Canada had not.

The federal government had a far more complex set of conflicting demands to resolve. In response to consumer interests it wanted to limit price increases, but it also wanted a single Canadian price. The greater the discrepancy between domestic and world prices, the greater would be the drain on the federal treasury in the form of subsidies for the imported oil on which the east coast still depended. On the other hand, if the discrepancy were reduced to zero, Ottawa's commitments under the existing equalization system would mushroom. Either way, Ottawa needed a greater share of windfall resource revenues. The federal government had to reconcile several other partly contradictory goals: reducing energy consumption, promoting Canadian ownership in the industry, ensuring security of future supplies, and developing new reserves in the so-called "Canada lands" in the north and off-shore. While necessarily responsive to majority interest, the federal government also saw itself as "the arbiter of provincial interest … the only government able to strike a compromise between producer and consumer interests."

The redistributive stakes were enormous. A 1979 Ontario government paper estimated that a $7 per barrel increase in the price of oil would add $3 billion to the coffers of the producing provinces, while adding 3.2 percent to the Ontario inflation rate and reducing its GPP by 1.5 percent. The revenue bonanza, Ontario argued, was creating massive inequalities in the revenues of provincial governments. By 1980, for example, Alberta's revenues from its own sources were 232 percent of the provincial average. The Ontario paper argued that "the eventual size of fiscal imbalances created by revenue flows of these orders of magnitude is staggering and represents a significant challenge to the flexibility of the central financial arrangements of Confederation." It concluded that "petro-dollars, not constitutional lawyers are rewriting our constitutional system."

The Alberta government responded with a study estimating that between 1974 and 1981 the oil producing region had subsidized the other regions of the country to the tune of about $40 billion. The Economic Council of Canada, with a less immediate stake in the outcome of these statistical battles, estimated that in 1980 alone Canada's less-than-world prices represented between $12 billion and $15 billion in revenues lost to the Alberta government.

Questions of regional redistribution were so large and important that it was impossible not to believe that, in the final analysis, Ottawa's policy decision would be determined primarily by a choice between the conflicting interests of the two competing sectors and regions. Ottawa's preference for below-world prices was interpreted as a victory for the non-producing regions, not only in consequence but also in intent. "Now once again, Canada was calling on the west to … help salvage the viability of the nation. Many in the west felt that too much had been asked in the past and too much was being asked again."

Canadian Industrial Gas and Oil Ltd. v. Government of Saskatchewan
[1978] 2 SCR 545, 80 DLR (3d) 449

MARTLAND J (Laskin CJC, Judson, Ritchie, Spence, Pigeon, and Beetz JJ concurring): The question in issue in this appeal is as to the constitutional validity of certain statutes enacted by the Legislature of the Province of Saskatchewan and Regulations enacted pursuant thereto, to which reference will be made hereafter. Their validity was challenged by the appellant, a corporation engaged in the exploration for, drilling for and production of oil and natural gas in Saskatchewan and owning freehold leases, Crown leases and royalty interests in that Province. The respondents are the Government of the Province of Saskatchewan and the Attorney-General of the Province. The appellant was unsuccessful in seeking to obtain a declaration of their invalidity, both at trial and on appeal to the

Court of Appeal for Saskatchewan. It appeals, with leave, to this Court from the judgment of the Court of Appeal.

The legislation was enacted following the sharp rise in the price of oil on the world market which occurred in 1973. The effect of the legislation has been summarized in the reasons of my brother Dickson, which I have had the advantage of reading. For purposes of convenience I substantially repeat that summary here:

> First, production revenues from freehold lands were subjected to what was called a "mineral income tax." The tax was 100% of the difference between the price received at the well-head and the "basic well-head price," a statutory figure approximately equal to the price per barrel received by producers prior to the energy crisis. The owner's interest in oil and gas rights in producing tracts of less than 1,280 acres were exempted from tax. Deductions approved by the Minister of Mineral Resources were allowed in respect of increases in production costs and extraordinary transportation costs. Provision was made for the Minister to determine the well-head value of the oil where he was of the opinion that oil had been disposed of at less than its fair value.
>
> Secondly, all petroleum and natural gas in all producing tracts within the Province were expropriated and subjected to what was called a "royalty surcharge." Oil and gas rights owned by one person in producing tracts not exceeding 1,280 acres were exempted. Although introduced by Regulation rather than statute, the royalty surcharge is calculated in the same manner as the mineral income tax. For all practical purposes they are the same, save one exception. The well-head value for the purposes of royalty surcharge is the *higher* of the price received at the well-head and the price per barrel listed in the Minister's order.

… The practical consequence of the application of this legislation is that the Government of Saskatchewan will acquire the benefit of all increases in the value of oil produced in that province above the set basic well-head price fixed by the statute and regulations, which is approximately the same as that which existed in 1973 before the increase in world prices for oil. In this connection, there is the important fact that 98% of all crude oil produced in Saskatchewan is destined for export from the Province either to Eastern Canada or the United States of America.

The appellant's attack upon the legislation is made upon two grounds:

1. It is contended that both the mineral income tax and the royalty surcharge constitute indirect taxation, and are therefore beyond the power of the Province to impose, the provincial legislative powers being limited to direct taxation within the province under s-s. 92(2) of the *British North America Act, 1867*.

2. It is contended that the legislation relates to the regulation of interprovincial and international trade and commerce, a matter over which the federal Parliament has exclusive legislative power under s-s. 91(2) of the *British North America Act, 1867*.

[The discussion of the taxation issue has been omitted. Martland J concluded that the mineral income tax and royalty surcharge were an indirect tax and hence not within provincial jurisdiction.]

Regulation of Trade and Commerce

In considering this issue the important fact is, of course, that practically all of the oil to which the mineral income tax or the royalty surcharge becomes applicable is destined for interprovincial or international trade. Some of this oil is sold by producers at the well-head and thereafter transported from the Province by pipeline. Some of the oil is not sold at the well-head, but is produced by companies for their own purposes, and is likewise transported out of the Province by pipeline. In either case the levy becomes applicable. The producer in the first case must, if he is to avoid pecuniary loss, sell at the well-head at the well-head value established. The company which has its own oil production transported from the Province must, if it is to avoid pecuniary loss, ultimately dispose of the refined product at a price which will recoup the amount of the levy. Thus, the effect of the legislation is to set a floor price for Saskatchewan oil purchased for export by the appropriation of its potential incremental value in interprovincial and international markets, or to ensure that the incremental value is not appropriated by persons outside the province. ...

The purpose of the legislation under review was accurately defined by Chief Justice Culliton in the Court of Appeal [(1975), 65 DLR (3d) 79, at 98]:

> There is no doubt in my mind that both the mineral income tax and the royalty surcharge were imposed for one purpose, and one purpose only—to drain off substantial benefits that would have accrued to the producers due to the sudden and unprecedented price of crude oil.

The means used to achieve this end are to compel a Saskatchewan oil producer to effect the sale of the oil at a price determined by the Minister. The mineral income tax is defined as the difference between the basic well-head price and the price at which the oil is sold, but with the important proviso that if the Minister is of the opinion that the oil has been sold at less than its fair value, he can determine the price at which it should have been sold, and that price governs in determining the amount of the tax. The royalty surcharge, as provided under the Regulations requires the payment of the surcharge on oil produced on the basis of the difference between its well-head value, as established by the Minister, less the basic well-head price. In either case the Minister is empowered to determine well-head value of the oil which is produced which will govern the price at which the producer is compelled to sell the oil which he produces. In an effort to obtain for the provincial treasury the increases in the value of oil exported from Saskatchewan which began in 1973, in the form of a tax upon the production of oil in Saskatchewan, the legislation gave power to the Minister to fix the price receivable by Saskatchewan oil producers on their export sales of a commodity that has almost no local market in Saskatchewan. Provincial legislative authority does not extend to fixing the price to be charged or received in respect of the sale of goods in the export market. It involves the regulation of interprovincial trade and trenches upon s-s. 91(2) of the *British North America Act, 1867*.

This is not a case similar to *Carnation Co. Ltd. v. Quebec Agricultural Marketing Board*, [1968] SCR 238, 67 DLR (2d) 1, where the effect of the Regulations was to increase the cost of the milk purchased by Carnation in Quebec and processed there, mostly for sale outside Quebec. The legislation there indirectly affected Carnation's export trade in the sense that its costs of production were increased, but was designed to establish a method for determining the price of milk sold by Quebec milk producers, to a purchaser in Quebec, who processed it there. Here the legislation is directly aimed at the production of oil destined for export and has the effect of regulating the export price, since the producer is effectively compelled to obtain that price on the sale of his product.

For these reasons, in my opinion, the statutory provisions, and the Regulations and orders enacted and made relating to the imposition of the mineral income tax and royalty surcharge, are *ultra vires* of the Legislature of the Province of Saskatchewan. ...

DICKSON J (de Grandpré J concurring) dissenting: ... Before considering in detail the legislation, one or two observations of a general nature are warranted. This Court is sensitive to the freedom of action which must be allowed to the Legislatures to safeguard their legitimate interests as in their wisdom they see fit. It presumes that they have acted constitutionally. The onus of rebutting that presumption is upon the appellant. Before the Court concludes that the Province has transcended its constitutional powers the evidence must be clear and unmistakable; more than conjecture or speculation is needed to underpin a finding of constitutional incompetence. ...

Subject to the limits imposed by the Canadian Constitution, the power of the Province to tax, control and manage its natural resources is plenary and absolute. ...

[Dickson J's analysis of the taxation issue has been omitted. He would have upheld the mineral income tax as a form of direct taxation within the province.]

Counsel for appellant urged the Court to strike down the legislation as an infringement of Parliament's exclusive authority respecting the regulation of trade and commerce. Appellant says:

> ... the tax and surcharge are established in a way which enables the Province of Saskatchewan to control the minimum price at which Saskatchewan crude oil is sold. This control is imposed on a commodity almost exclusively consumed outside of Saskatchewan, either in the Canadian or international marketplace. This imposition of a minimum price by the Province to be passed on to consumers outside of the Province is an interference with the free flow of trade between provinces ... so as to prevent producers in Saskatchewan from dealing unhampered with purchasers outside of Saskatchewan.

... The conceptual tool of "flow" or "current," or "stream" of commerce has been referred to by the Court in a number of subsequent cases, the most recent being *MacDonald v. Vapor Canada Ltd.*, [1977] 2 SCR 134 at 167, 66 DLR (3d) 1 at 27. The real question, unsettled in the jurisprudence, is the determination of when the product enters the export stream marking the start of the process of exportation. American jurisprudence has held that the distinguishing mark of an export product is shipment or entry with a common carrier for transportation to another jurisdiction: *Coe v. Errol*, 116 US 517 at 527; *Richfield Oil Corp. v. State Board of Equalization*, 329 US 69; *Empresa Siderurgica v. Merced Co.*, 337 US 154. Implicit in the argument of the appellant is the assumption that federal regulatory power pursuant to s. 91(2) follows the flow of oil backward across provincial boundaries, back through provincial gathering systems and finally to the well-head. A secondary assumption is that sale at the well-head marks the start of the process of exportation. In the view I take of the case it is unnecessary to reach any conclusion as to the validity of either of these assumptions. It is, however, worth noting that neither American nor Canadian jurisprudence has ever gone that far.

I can find nothing in the present case to lead me to conclude that the taxation measures imposed by the Province of Saskatchewan were merely a colourable device for assuming control of extra-provincial trade. The language of the impugned statutes does not disclose an intention on the part of the Province to regulate, or control, or impede marketing or export of oil from Saskatchewan. "Oil produced and sold" means produced and sold within the Provinces. "Well-head price" by definition means the price at the well-head of a barrel of oil produced in Saskatchewan. The mineral income tax and the royalty surcharge relate only to oil produced within Saskatchewan. The transactions are well-head transactions. There are no impediments to the free movement of goods as were found objectionable in *A-G Man. v. Manitoba Egg & Poultry Ass'n*, [1971] SCR 689, 19 DLR (3d) 169, and in *Burns Foods Ltd. v. A-G Man.*, [1975] 1 SCR 494, 40 DLR (3d) 731.

Nor is there anything in the extraneous evidence to form the basis of an argument that the impugned legislation in its *effect* regulated interprovincial or international trade. The evidence is all to the contrary and that evidence comes entirely from witnesses called on behalf of the appellant. Production and export of oil increased after the legislative scheme was implemented. Sales of oil by the appellant were continued in 1974 as in 1973 and previously. ...

It was contended in argument that the effect was to place a floor price under Saskatchewan oil and thereby interfere with interprovincial trade. So far as mineral income tax is concerned the incidence of taxation is pegged to the price received for the oil at the well-head. Section 4A is an "after-the-event" provision which comes into play only if there was a sale at less than fair value. The emphasis on fair value ensures that the tax will not change the export oil price. The price of oil subject to the tax and the price of oil free of the tax, *i.e.*, from the exempted 1,280-acre tracts, will be the same as the product crosses the provincial border. The ultimate position of consumers is unaffected. The only way in which extra-provincial consumers could have benefited would have been in the event of the Province freezing the price of oil, assuming constitutional competence to do so.

One is free to speculate that, to the extent producers would be prepared to undercut the fair market value of their oil, the legislation discourages them from doing so by virtue of the constant tax liability. The possibility of price-cutting is highly theoretical, unsupported by evidence and in view of the inelasticity of demand for petroleum products, highly unlikely. ...

The Province of Saskatchewan had a *bona fide* legitimate and reasonable interest of its own to advance in enacting the legislation in question, as related to taxation and natural resources, out of all proportion to the burden, if there can be said to be a burden, imposed on the Canadian free trade economic unit through the legislation. The effect, if any, on the extra-provincial trade in oil is merely indirectly and remotely incidental to the manifest revenue-producing object of the legislation under attack. ...

Appeal allowed.

NOTES

1. This case was a controversial one, on both political and jurisprudential grounds. Arne Paus-Jenssen argued that it raised serious questions about the Supreme Court's ability to adjudicate economic issues. In "Resource Taxation and the Supreme Court of Canada: The Cigol Case" (1979), 5 *Canadian Public Policy* 45, at 53, he stated:

> The conclusion to the Court's analysis of the economic impact of the legislation is indeed re-markable and must come as a surprise to people who are familiar with price formation in the North American oil markets. One searches in vain in the majority decision for the process of reasoning which led the Court to conclude that the "real effects" of the legislation were that the provincial taxes determined prices. ...
>
> The Court's lack of understanding of economic issues and the logical errors which it com-mitted, perhaps as result of this, becomes very evident in the relief which it ordered. ... [The tax] is indirect taxation because the producer against which the tax is levied is only "a conduit," the tax is paid by the purchaser of the oil or the consumer. Further, it is an attempt to regulate trade because the purchaser is a consumer. Further, it is an attempt to regulate trade because the purchaser is a non-resident of the province. Thus by the Court's own reasoning the produc-er has not borne the tax; if he had, the Court would have ruled that the tax was direct and therefore valid! Yet in Martland's opinion "the appellant is entitled to judgment against the Government for the recovery of the sums paid ... with interest thereon from dates of payment up to date of repayment, monies which had been collected without legal authority." ... Accord-ing to the Court the producers are now "entitled" to tax monies which by the Court's own rea-soning they have not paid!

2. Are the facts in *CIGOL* distinguishable from those in *Carnation*? Is *CIGOL* more faithful, instead, to the decision in the *Manitoba Egg Reference*? For discussion, see Patrick Monahan, *Constitutional Law* (Concord, ON: Irwin Law, 1997), at 270-71.

3. Saskatchewan ultimately paid CIGOL $3.7 million. To safeguard the over $500 mil-lion collected under the mineral income tax and royalty scheme, it enacted new legislation, The *Oil Well Income Tax Act*, RSS 1978 (Supp.), c. O-3.1, which implemented an income tax on oil well income earned after January 1, 1974. (See William Moull, "Natural Resources: The Other Crisis in Canadian Federalism" (1980), 18 *Osgoode Hall Law Journal* 1, at 25.)

Central Canada Potash Co. Ltd. v. Government of Saskatchewan
[1979] 1 SCR 42, 88 DLR (3d) 609

[Facing possible trade sanctions by the United States arising out of a complaint of dump-ing and a depressed market for potash, Saskatchewan instituted a potash prorationing scheme in 1969. At that time, almost all of its potash was sold outside the province, with about 64 percent marketed in the United States. The scheme was discussed with officials from New Mexico, the only US producer of potash. The scheme and its successors con-trolled production through licences, which prevented Central Canada Potash from ful-filling one of its contracts. The trial judge found the regulations *ultra vires*, while the Court of Appeal upheld their validity. The other issue in the case involving a claim for damages for intimidation is omitted.]

LASKIN CJC (Martland, Ritchie, Spence, Pigeon, Dickson, and Pratte JJ concurring): This appeal, which is here by leave of this Court, concerns (1) the validity of what I may compendiously refer to as a potash prorationing scheme, established pursuant to the *Mineral Resources Act*, RSS 1965, c. 50, as amended. ...

What is evident from the circumstances under which the *Potash Conservation Regulations, 1969* were promulgated, and from the terms of the directives and licences through which the ABC and FP schemes were instituted and administered, is that the Government of Saskatchewan had in view the regulation of the marketing of potash through the fixing of a minimum selling price applicable to the permitted production quotas. The only market for which the schemes had any significance was the export market. There could be no suggestion that the schemes had any relation to the marketing of potash within the Province of Saskatchewan when there was hardly any Saskatchewan market for the mineral. There was no question here of any concluded transactions of sale and purchase in the Province, as was the situation in the *Carnation* case [*Carnation Co. Ltd. v. Quebec Agricultural Marketing Board*, [1968] SCR 238; 67 DLR (2d) 1]. Out of Province and offshore sales were the principal objects of the licences and directives.

The documentary evidence leaves no doubt about this. The first directive fixing the minimum floor price for potash to the producer, f.o.b. the potash plant, dated November 25, 1969, was stated to be for the purpose of determining the demand for it "for reasonable current requirements and current consumption or use within or without Saskatchewan." The first producing licence to Noranda, dated December 12, 1969, required the licensee to comply with "all applicable Acts, regulations, orders and directions governing production, conservation, processing, disposal, marketing, transporting ... ." The second producing licence conditioned its validity on observance of the minimum selling price, f.o.b. the producer's plant in Saskatchewan. Subsequent producing licences did not indicate any change of focus, although they forfeited ministerial control.

A directive of August 24, 1971, to all producers fixed the minimum price f.o.b. vessel, Vancouver. On August 27, 1971, a letter to producers from the Deputy Minister advised of approval given, on certain conditions, to an agreement for delivery of potash to a business organization in France. One of the conditions required that "all potash delivered to Europe from Saskatchewan pursuant to the agreement shall be for consumption in Europe." The new allocation formula prescribed by the directive of June 30, 1972, from which I have already quoted, was concerned with the sharing of production "to meet the market demand." The purpose of Canpotex, to which I have also referred above, was to make it the instrument for offshore sales of Saskatchewan potash.

In all of the foregoing, the Government of Saskatchewan, and its responsible Ministers and their deputies, were acting not under proprietary right but in pursuance of legislative and statutory authority directed to the proprietary rights of others, including the appellant. It was strenuously contended by the respondent Government (and in this they were supported by the intervening Provinces) that the natural resources, the mineral wealth of the Province was subject to provincial regulatory control alone, and that production controls or quotas were peculiarly matters within exclusive provincial legislative authority. Chief Justice Culliton gave force to this point in two concluding paragraphs of his reasons, which he prefaced by saying that "Courts must approach constitutional problems with a sense of realism and practicality." The two paragraphs read as follows [(1977), 79 DLR (3d) 203, at 234-35]:

> It was admitted by all parties that the potash industry of Saskatchewan was facing diffi-
> cult problems, problems which, if not solved, would have a most detrimental effect on the
> industry and on the Province. In these circumstances, the potash industry had a right to
> seek assistance from whatever Government had the power to grant that assistance. Natural
> resources, being exclusively within the provincial jurisdiction, the industry turned to the
> Province. The Province, to protect and conserve the potash industry, implemented con-
> trolled production and established minimum prices in the Province. These programmes did
> assist the industry but at the same time had some effect on areas within Federal jurisdiction.
> However, in pith and substance, they were programmes directed to a matter within Provin-
> cial jurisdiction and thus were valid notwithstanding such ultimate effects.
>
> If I am not right in this conclusion, then it must be said the right to control production
> of potash within the Province and to establish a minimum price at the mine, rests with the
> Parliament of Canada, for the right to do so must rest somewhere. Clearly, in my opinion,
> the Parliament of Canada does not have the power to control the production of potash
> within the Province, or to set a minimum price at the mine. Thus, in my opinion, to hold
> that the prorationing and price stabilization programmes are *ultra vires* the Province, is to
> determine their validity by the ultimate effects of such programmes and not by their true
> nature and character.

It is, of course, true, that production controls and conservation measures with respect to natural resources in a Province are, ordinarily, matters within provincial legislative authority. This Court's reasons in its recent judgment in the *Ontario Egg Reference* (*Refer-ence re Agricultural Products Marketing Act and two other Acts*) [(1978), 84 DLR (3d) 257; 19 NR 361], supports that view. The situation may be different, however, where a Prov-ince establishes a marketing scheme with price fixing as its central feature. Indeed, it has been held that provincial legislative authority does not extend to the control or regula-tion of the marketing of provincial products, whether minerals or natural resources, in interprovincial or export trade. The Saskatchewan Courts recognized this almost fifty years ago in the judgment in *Re Grain Marketing Act, 1931*, [1931] 2 WWR 146, 25 SLR 273. Legislation with this thrust in other Provinces has likewise been struck down: see *Lawson v. Interior Tree Fruit & Vegetable Committee*, [1931] SCR 357, [1931] 2 DLR 193; *Re Sheep and Swine Marketing Scheme (PEI)*, [1941] 3 DLR 569.

The present case reduces itself therefore to a consideration of "the true nature and character" of the prorationing and price stabilization schemes which are before us. This Court cannot ignore the circumstances under which the *Potash Conservation Regula-tions, 1969*, came into being, nor the market to which they were applied and in which they had their substantial operation. In *Canadian Industrial Gas & Oil Ltd. v. Govern-ment of Saskatchewan et al.* (1977), 80 DLR (3d) 449, this Court, speaking in its majority judgment through Martland J said (at p. 464 DLR) that: "Provincial legislative authority does not extend to fixing the price to be charged or received in respect of the sale of goods in the export market." It may properly be said here of potash as it was said there of oil that "the legislation is directly aimed at the production of potash destined for export, and it has the effect of regulating the export price since the producer is effectively compelled to obtain that price on the sale of his product" (at pp. 464-5).

I do not agree with Chief Justice Culliton that the consequence of invalidating the provincial scheme in this case is to move to the Parliament of Canada the power to control production of minerals in the Province and the price to be charged at the mine. There is no accretion at all to federal power in this case, which does not involve federal legislation, but simply a determination by this Court, in obedience to its duty, of a limitation on provincial legislative power. It is true, as he says that (with some exceptions, not relevant here) the *British North America Act, 1867* distributes all legislative power either to Parliament or to the provincial Legislatures, but it does not follow that legislation of a Province held to be invalid may *ipso facto* be validly enacted by Parliament in its very terms. It is nothing new for this Court, or indeed, for any Court in this country seized of a constitutional issue, to go behind the words used by a Legislature and to see what it is that it is doing. It is especially important for Courts, called upon to interpret and apply a constitution which limits legislative power, to do so in a case where not only the authorizing legislation but regulations enacted pursuant thereto are themselves couched in generalities, and the bite of a scheme envisaged by the parent legislation and the delegated regulations is found in administrative directions.

Where governments in good faith, as in this case, invoke authority to realize desirable economic policies, they must know that they have no open-ended means of achieving their goals when there are constitutional limitations on the legislative power under which they purport to act. They are entitled to expect that the Courts, and especially this Court, will approach the task of appraisal of the constitutionality of social and economic programmes with sympathy and regard for the serious consequences of holding them *ultra vires*. Yet, if the appraisal results in a clash with the Constitution, it is the latter which must govern. That is the situation here.

In my opinion, the judgment of the Saskatchewan Court of Appeal on the constitutional question posed for this Court should be set aside and the declaration of invalidity by the trial Judge should be restored. ...

Appeal with respect to constitutional validity allowed;
declaration of invalidity by trial Judge restored.

NOTE ON PROPRIETARY RIGHTS

In the *Potash* case, reference was made to the fact that Saskatchewan was acting in a regulatory capacity rather than as a proprietor.

The original four provinces own the "lands, mines, minerals and royalties" within their borders under s. 109 of the *Constitution Act, 1867*, subject to certain exceptions in s. 108. Analogous provisions were made for the other provinces, except Alberta, Saskatchewan, and Manitoba, as they entered Confederation. Through the 1930 Resource Transfer Agreements (*Constitution Act, 1930*, 21 Geo. V, c. 26 (UK)), the prairie provinces were put in the same position. Pursuant to s. 92(5), provinces can legislate with regard to the management and sale of public lands.

Should a province be able to do things as owner that it cannot implement by legislation? That was the assumption underlying much of Alberta's energy policy during the 1970s. For a discussion, see William Moull, "Natural Resources: Provincial Proprietary Rights, The Supreme Court of Canada, and the Resource Amendment to the Constitution" (1983), 21 *Alberta Law Review* 472.

NOTE ON SECTION 92A

As a result of the constitutional amendments adopted in 1982, s. 92A was added to the *Constitution Act, 1867*, granting the provinces additional powers over natural resources. The Supreme Court of Canada made reference to s. 92A in *Ontario Hydro v. Ontario (Labour Relations Board)*, [1993] 3 SCR 327, 107 DLR (4th) 457. At issue was the proper jurisdiction to issue a certificate for collective bargaining for employees at Ontario Hydro's nuclear electrical generating stations. A majority of the Court held that the Canada Labour Code applied to employees employed on or in connection with those nuclear facilities. The sources of federal jurisdiction were the declaratory power in s. 92(10)(c) and the peace, order, and good government clause. With reference to s. 92A, La Forest J, writing for himself and L'Heureux-Dubé and Gonthier JJ, stated at 487-89 DLR:

> [I]t is useful to examine the backdrop against which s. 92A was passed. In a general sense, the interventionist policies of the federal authorities in the 1970s in relation to natural resources, particularly oil and other petroleum products, were a source of major concern to the provinces. These concerns were by no means minimized by cases such as *Canadian Industrial Gas & Oil Ltd. v. Government of Saskatchewan*, [1978] 2 SCR 545, and *Central Canada Potash Co. v. Government of Saskatchewan*, [1979] 1 SCR 42, which underlined the severe limits on provincial power over resources that are mainly exported out of the province, as well as on the provincial power to tax these resources.
>
> It was to respond to this insecurity about provincial jurisdiction over resources—one of the mainstays of provincial power—that s. 92A was enacted. Section 92A(1) reassures by restating this jurisdiction in contemporary terms, and the following provisions go on, for the first time, to authorize the provinces to legislate for the export of resources to other provinces subject to Parliament's paramount legislative power in the area, as well as to permit indirect taxation in respect of resources so long as such taxes do not discriminate against other provinces.
>
> Most commentators mention only these issues in describing the background against which s. 92A was enacted, but there were others, specifically in relation to the generation, production and exporting of electrical energy, that must have been seen as a threat to provincial autonomy in these areas. In most of the provinces, at least, the generation and distribution of electrical energy is done by the same undertaking. There is an integrated and interconnected system beginning at the generating plant and extending to its ultimate destination. There was authority that indicated that even an emergency interprovincial grid system might effect an interconnection between utilities sufficient to make the whole system a work connecting or extending beyond the province, and so falling within federal jurisdiction within the meaning of s. 92(10)(a) of the *Constitution Act, 1867*; see *British Columbia Power Corp. v. Attorney General of British Columbia* (1963), 44 WWR 65 (BC SC). More important, provincial power commissions supply electrical energy to other provinces and the United States on a "regular and continuing basis,"

which a number of cases in other areas have held to be sufficient to make an integrated under-taking fall within federal legislative competence; see, for example, *Re Tank Truck Transport Ltd.* (1960), 25 DLR (2d) 161 (Ont. HC), aff'd. [1963] 1 OR 272 (CA). There was danger, then, that at least the supply system and conceivably the whole undertaking, from production to export, could be viewed as being a federal undertaking. For a discussion of these problems as they ap-peared in the period preceding the enactment of s. 92A, see G.V. La Forest and Associates, *Water Law in Canada* (1973), at pp. 46 *et seq.*, esp. at pp. 50-51, 53-56. While a number of com-mentators, including myself, did not share this view of the law, the result on the authorities was by no means certain. The express grant of legislative power over the development of facilities for the generation and production of electrical energy (s. 92A(1)(c)), coupled with the legis-lative power in relation to the export of electrical energy offers at least comfort for the position that, leaving aside other heads of power, the development, conservation and management of generating facilities fall exclusively within provincial competence. The nature of provincial electrical generating and distribution systems at the time of the passing of s. 92A must have been appreciated.

What is important to note is that the danger to provincial autonomy over the generation of electrical energy did not arise out of the discretion Parliament had or might in future exercise under its declaratory power. The danger, rather, lay in the possible transformation of these en-terprises into purely federal undertakings by reason of their connection or extension beyond the province. Section 92A ensures the province the management, including the regulation of labour relations, of the sites and facilities for the generation and production of electrical energy that might otherwise be threatened by s. 92(10)(a). But I cannot believe it was meant to inter-fere with the paramount power vested in Parliament by virtue of the declaratory power (or for that matter Parliament's general power to legislate for the peace, order and good government of Canada) over "[a]ll works and undertakings constructed for the production, use and applica-tion of atomic energy." This, as already seen, comprises the management of these facilities, dis-placing any management powers the province might otherwise have had under s. 92A. And a vital part of the power of management is the power to regulate labour relations.

Lamer CJC wrote separate reasons upholding federal jurisdiction. The dissent, written by Iacobucci J, Sopinka and Cory JJ concurring, would have upheld provincial jurisdiction over these workers. With reference to s. 92A, Iacobucci J stated at 520-21 DLR:

This section expressly provides for provincial jurisdiction over the management of electrical generating sites, including those fueled by nuclear reactors. Provincial control over labour rela-tions appears to me to be integral to provincial jurisdiction over the management of nuclear electrical generating facilities. Further, ... Ontario Hydro as a whole is a provincial undertaking.

After reading the whole of s. 92A, consider whether the results in *CIGOL* and *Central Canada Potash* would be different today. Does the amendment significantly increase prov-incial jurisdiction over natural resources?

NOTE ON OFFSHORE MINERALS

The disputes about natural resources between Alberta, Saskatchewan, and the federal government were not the only ones to reach the Supreme Court of Canada. There was much uncertainty, as well, about the respective jurisdiction of the federal government and the coastal provinces to control the exploration for and exploitation of natural resources in coastal waters, especially the continental shelf off Newfoundland once oil was discovered in the Hibernia fields.

A 1967 decision of the Supreme Court of Canada had held that the coastal waters off British Columbia (from the low water mark) were within federal jurisdiction (*Reference re Offshore Mineral Rights of British Columbia*, [1967] SCR 792, 65 DLR (2d) 353). As those waters had not been within the jurisdiction of the colony prior to Confederation, they fell to federal jurisdiction. The federal government had ownership rights over the seabed of the territorial sea off British Columbia under the peace, order, and good government clause, and it had the right to explore for and exploit resources on the continental shelf beyond the territorial sea.

This decision was further discussed in *Re AG Can. and AG BC (Re Strait of Georgia)*, [1984] 1 SCR 388, 8 DLR (4th) 161, which determined that the waters between the mainland of British Columbia and Vancouver Island were within the jurisdiction of the province, since they had been included in the colony of British Columbia at the time of its creation and thus formed part of the province at the time it entered Confederation in 1871.

The dispute involving the continental shelf off Newfoundland was resolved in *Reference re the Seabed and Subsoil of the Continental Shelf Offshore Newfoundland*, [1984] 1 SCR 86, 5 DLR (4th) 385. The Court held that the right to explore for and exploit minerals on the continental shelf was within federal jurisdiction under the peace, order and good government clause in its residual capacity, because Newfoundland had no jurisdiction over this area at the time it entered Confederation in 1949.

III. FEDERAL POWERS OVER ECONOMIC REGULATION

Another focus of concern with respect to the current constitutional framework for economic regulation, in addition to its alleged failure to provide sufficient checks on provincial policies that interfere with the efficient functioning of the economic union, is the constraints that are imposed on concerted federal regulation in the national interest. The cases that follow deal with two major doctrinal developments, after 1960, that opened up the possibility of a much larger federal regulatory role over trade and commerce. First, the courts seemed more willing to apply the "necessarily incidental" doctrine in relation to the trade and commerce power, thus allowing the federal government to regulate some intraprovincial transactions as part of a scheme directed at the regulation of interprovincial or international trade: see *The Queen v. Klassen* and *Caloil Inc. v. AG Canada*. Second, the Supreme Court applied the general regulation of trade doctrine to uphold federal competition legislation: see *General Motors of Canada Ltd. v. City National Leasing*.

A. Regulation of Interprovincial and International Trade

The Queen v. Klassen

(1960), 20 DLR (2d) 406, 29 WWR 369 (Man. CA)

[This case arose as a prosecution under the *Canadian Wheat Board Act*, RSC 1952, c. 44. Section 16(1) prohibited delivery of grain to a grain elevator contrary to the provisions of the Act. Grain could be delivered to an elevator only by its producer, and the quantity of each delivery was to be entered by the elevator operator in the producer's "delivery permit book." The total quantity of grain delivered by a producer in a given year could not exceed the quota established by the Canada Wheat Board for delivery by that producer to that elevator. These detailed recordings were the mechanism by which a quota system was enforced to maintain an orderly international trade in grain. Section 45 of the *Canadian Wheat Board Act* declared that any elevator and many other of the buildings used in the grain trade, including feed mills, were "works for the general advantage of Canada" pursuant to s. 92(10)(c) and s. 91(29) of the *BNA Act*.

Klassen, a resident of the village of Grunthal, Manitoba, and manager and operator of a feed mill (an elevator under the Act) in the town, was charged with failing to record a delivery of 296 bushels of wheat delivered to him by Leppky, of the Village of Niverville, Manitoba. Klassen had purchased the wheat from Leppky and used it as an ingredient in prepared feeds, which he sold to farmers and feeders in his immediate neighbourhood. Klassen's operation was located 10 miles from the nearest railroad; he bought and processed the grain, and then delivered it to its purchaser by truck. It was found as a fact at trial that "the accused has not at any time been engaged in interprovincial or export trade personally, nor so far as the accused is aware have the products of the said mill been used in the interprovincial or export trade."

Klassen was convicted at trial and appealed to the Manitoba Court of Appeal. On appeal, he argued that s. 45 of the *Canadian Wheat Board Act*, which declared all elevators and other buildings used in the grain trade to be works to the general advantage of Canada, was *ultra vires* in respect to his feed mill.

The appeal was dismissed, and leave to appeal to the Supreme Court of Canada was denied.]

ADAMSON CJM:

[Adamson CJM thought that Klassen had conceded the validity of s. 16 in his factum, and that it was therefore unnecessary to consider s. 45. Nonetheless, he made the following comments about s. 16.]

The appellant is in the grain, feed and mill business. He "has not been at any time in interprovincial or export trade personally" but cannot say that some of his products have not been exported. It is clear that if the appellant is to be allowed to purchase wheat without complying with the provisions of s. 16(2) of the Act the quota system and the orderly marketing of grain is to that extent rendered ineffective. Moreover, so far as the facts show, the appellant could (though he has not done so) ship his products out of the province and this would be a contravention of the Act. It is evident that s. 16 of the Act is necessary and incidental in the control of the export of grain. Section 16(2) and s. 45 of the Act are simply the machinery by which the policy and general purposes and provisions of the Act are administered and enforced. ...

TRITSCHLER JA (Schultz JA concurring):

[While s. 45 was not considered, s. 16 was, in the following terms.]

There is no doubt that Part II "affects" property and civil rights in the provinces. It is a serious interference with the intraprovincial business of (among others) the owners of grain and the operators of flour, feed and seed-cleaning mills.

But this interference of Part II may be justified if it is necessarily incidental to the other provisions of the Act dealing with the interprovincial and export trade in grain.

I think that since *Murphy v. CPR*, [1958] SCR 626, 15 DLR (2d) 145, it has been settled that the principal purposes of the Act, *i.e.*, the interprovincial and export marketing of certain grains by the board and the regulation of interprovincial and export trade in such grains is legislation in relation to the regulation of trade and commerce. ...

Our inquiry must, therefore, be whether the questioned interference of Part II is necessarily incidental or ancillary to (in aid of) effective legislation in respect of the general marketing scheme set up for certain grains by the Act.

... [S]crutinizing the Act in its entirety to determine the true nature and character of the controls of Part II and what it is that the Legislature is really doing, I am of the opinion that Part II is not an attempt by Parliament to interfere with or control the business of flour, feed and seed mills within the provinces as an end in itself but that the interference with property and civil rights which results under Part II is incidental and ancillary to the achievement of the purpose of the Act, the pith and substance of which is the provision of an export market for surplus grains, a matter which has undoubtedly assumed a national importance.

The "quota" controls which are established by Part II, and which are the real subject-matter under appeal, have several objects. They regulate the intake of grain into all channels of the marketing system so that currently marketable grains can be received when needed and grain for which there is no present market kept out of the system. The saleable grain must be at the right place at the right time. If the channels become clogged with unmarketable grains the scheme set up by the Act would become unworkable. This necessary interference with the right of individuals to deliver and receive grain into the marketing system must be made to fall as evenly as possible on all and justice demands that delivery opportunity be rationed as equitably as is possible among producers. The scheme ensures this.

But the opponents of the scheme object that these considerations cease to be valid when applied to mills which are turning grains into flour, feed and seed in purely intraprovincial transactions and particularly so where the mill has little or even no storage space. How, it is argued, can such transactions clog the channels of the marketing system? This submission ignores the other but equally essential feature of the controls, the equitable rationing of delivery opportunity and the ensuring that as nearly as may be all producers whose freedom to trade is interfered with by the scheme will get the same price at the same time for the like kind and quantity of grain. If a producer might sell a portion of his crop to a mill for flour, feed or seed and not have it noted on his permit book he would be able to deliver to the other channels of the marketing system grain up to his quota and thus achieve an advantage over less fortunate producers who were not able to get their grains into the local flour, feed and seed outlets. Equality of delivery opportunity is a basic feature of the scheme. As was said by Rand J in *Murphy*'s case, *supra* "The Act operates on the individual by keeping him in effect in a queue." If this be disturbed then, whether or not the channels of the system are clogged, injustice must result and the public acceptance of the scheme endangered. The quotas allowed are not, as was submitted by counsel for the appellant, "for interprovincial and export purposes" but they fix the quantity of grain a producer may deliver into the market system anywhere. It must be kept in mind that the board which is bound to market for producers certain grains in interprovincial and export trade is itself a prospective seller to all in the milling trades. As agent for the producer the board may find itself in competition with its own principal (the producer) and on that ground also controls are justified as ancillary to the scheme. In respect of grains which the board does not sell as agent for the producers— rye and flaxseed—then if storage and transport considerations were not affected the board would doubtless give permission for such grain to enter ordinary trade channels.

It is admitted that the appellant personally has not been engaged in interprovincial or export trade and that so far as he is aware the products of his mill have not been used in such trade. No one can say that the products of his mill will not be so used. If intraprovincial transactions are beyond the control of the Act so far as he is concerned so should they be in respect of every other miller, but there are obvious difficulties about letting into the marketing system even grains which can be proved to have an intraprovincial destination. This also would make the system unworkable. In short, it seems impractical if not impossible to draw distinctions between the appellant and all other handlers (or at least millers) of grain in respect of intraprovincial transactions.

Appellant's counsel has placed his greatest emphasis on the fact that appellant operates his feed mill in a purely local and provincial manner and does not engage in interprovincial or export trade. This is not relevant if it appears, as I think it does, that the Act is not legislation "in relation to" property and civil rights but is legislation which in pith and substance is in relation to trade and commerce and merely "affects" property and civil rights incidentally.

Appeal dismissed.

NOTES

Murphy v. CPR, a 1958 Supreme Court of Canada decision referred to in *Klassen*, involved a BC farmer who went to Manitoba and purchased some grain. When he tried to ship it to British Columbia, the railway refused the shipment on the ground that it was prohibited by s. 32 of the *Canadian Wheat Board Act*, which gave the Canada Wheat Board the exclusive power, subject to exceptions created by regulation, to export grain or to transport it or cause it to be transported interprovincially. Murphy argued that the Act was *ultra vires* because it interfered with property and civil rights in the province. The Court found that s. 32 and the Act as a whole were valid legislation in relation to the regulation of trade and commerce. On the issue of interference with s. 92(13), Locke J, writing for five members of the Court, stated:

> [T]he fact that of necessity [the Act] interferes with property and civil rights in the province of the nature referred to in head 13 of s. 92 is immaterial. For reasons which have been stated in a great number of cases decided in the Judicial Committee as well as in this Court, it has been decided that if a given subject-matter falls within any class of subjects enumerated in s. 91 it cannot be treated as covered by any of those in s. 92. … It is, of course, obvious that it would be impossible for Parliament to fully exercise the exclusive jurisdiction assigned to it by head 2 and many others of the heads of s. 91 without interfering with property and civil rights in some or all of the provinces. …
>
> It is contended for the appellant that the power to regulate trade and commerce under head 2 does not enable Parliament to regulate a particular trade, but this is too broad a statement. The result of the cases in the Judicial Committee dealing with this question appear to me to be most clearly summarized in the judgment of Lord Atkin in *Shannon v. Lower Mainland Dairy Products Board* [[1938] AC 708, at 719, 4 DLR 81, 2 WWR 604], where it was said:
>
> > It is now well settled that [s. 91(2)] does not give the powers to regulate for legitimate provincial purposes particular trades or businesses so far as the trade or business is confined to the province.
>
> The *Canadian Wheat Board Act* controls and regulates not one trade or business but several, including the activities of the producer, the railroads, the elevators and flour and feed mills and, except to a very minor extent, these activities are directed to the export of grain or grain products from the province, activities which the province itself is powerless to control.

B. Laskin, "Note on The Queen v. Klassen"
(1959), 37 *Canadian Bar Review* 630 (footnotes omitted)

The story of the trade and commerce power, traced with some bitterness by O'Connor in his *Report to the Senate on the British North America Act* (1945), 27 *Journal of Comparative Legislation* (3rd) 24, is in my view, the saddest legacy of Privy Council adjudication. …

What, it may properly be asked, were the defects of Privy Council interpretation of section 91(2)? The major one was its consistent refusal to look at an economic or social problem as a whole, and its correlative *a priori* assumption that every problem of trade regulation necessarily had its national and its local aspects which constitutionally had to be separated regardless of resulting violence to a legislative scheme. Strangely enough, this attitude was not reflected or manifested in the transportation cases or in communication issues in general. But when it came to trade or to marketing, federal regulation (according to the Privy Council) could begin only at the point of interprovincial or export movement, and certainly not at the point of production or harvesting. Arguments of functional connection or integration, if made, were rejected.

… This, however, was the very approach which was used in the *Klassen* case and which undergirds its importance.

... In the *Eastern Terminal Elevator* case [*King v. Eastern Terminal Elevator Co.*, [1925] SCR 434, an excerpt of which is found in Chapter 5, The Early Twentieth Century: The Beginnings of Economic Regulation] Duff J spurned, as a "lurking fallacy" the argument in favour of federal power that (to quote his words) "because in large part the grain trade is an export trade you can regulate it locally in order to give effect to your policy in relation to the regulation of that part of it which is export." The learned judge went on to say, somewhat illogically in my submission, that "obviously that is not a principle the application of which can be ruled by percentages. If it is operative when the export trade is seventy percent, of the whole, it must be equally operative when that percentage is only thirty." This is surely a *non-sequitur*, unless one rests on an arbitrary constitutional determination that the local and national market in any product can never be dealt with by a central scheme of regulation. The *Klassen* case has now given a direct rebuff to the proposition advanced by Duff J, and, in so doing, it has taken the line long ago adopted in the United States in dealing with similar marketing problems and exemplified by the judgment of the Supreme Court of the United States in *United States v. Wrightwood Dairy Co.* (1942), 62 SCt. 523 and in *Wickard v. Filburn* (1942), 63 SCt. 82, 317 US 111. In the *Wrightwood* case, the court said that the power of Congress to regulate interstate commerce "extends to those activities intrastate which so affect interstate commerce, or the exertion of the power of Congress over it, as to make regulation of them appropriate means to the attainment of a legitimate end, the effective execution of the granted power to regulate interstate commerce." In the *Wickard* case, in upholding federal regulation of the production of wheat even though intended for home consumption by the producer, the court remarked, in words which are apt to the situation in the *Klassen* case, that "it can hardly be denied that a factor of such volume and variability as home-consumed wheat would have a substantial influence on price and market conditions. This may arise because being in marketable condition such wheat overhangs the market and, if induced by rising prices, tends to flow into the market and check price increases. But if we assume that it is never marketed, it supplies a need of the man who grew it which would otherwise be reflected by purchases in the open market. Homegrown wheat in this sense competes with wheat in commerce. The stimulation of commerce is a use of the regulatory function quite as definitely as prohibitions or restrictions thereon."

It is a fitting characterization of the *Klassen* case to declare, in paraphrase of another sentence in the *Wickard* case, that it has recognized that "questions of the power of Parliament are not to be decided by reference to any formula which would give controlling force to nomenclature such as 'production' and 'indirect' and foreclose consideration of the actual effects of the activity in question upon the regulation of trade and commerce." Not only are "mechanical applications of legal formulas no longer feasible" if the *Klassen* case survives, but we will have to withdraw Idington J's portrait of the federal trade and commerce power as "the old forlorn hope, so many times tried unsuccessfully."

Caloil Inc. v. AG Canada
[1971] SCR 543, 20 DLR (3d) 472

[In 1970, in order to enforce its energy policy, the federal government passed regulations that prevented oil importers from transporting any gasoline across a line running north–south through Ontario and Quebec. The government's aim was to provide a market for western Canadian oil west of the line, and to restrict the sale of imported oil to the eastern half of Canada. When Caloil lost its licence for having violated this provision, it obtained a ruling from the courts that the regulations were unconstitutional, as they invaded provincial jurisdiction over "property and civil rights." Rather than appeal this decision, the federal government passed new legislation and again denied the company a licence. The amended regulations read:

> 20(1) In this section and section 21 "consumption" means the placing of oil in tanks connected to an internal combustion engine for purposes of operating such engine.
>
> (2) Where the Board is of the opinion that importation of oil that is the subject of an application for a licence to import into Canada will be consistent with the development and utilization of Canadian indigenous oil resources, it may issue a licence to import oil for consumption in the area of Canada specified therein, in such quantities, at such times and at such points of entry into Canada as it may consider appropriate.
>
> (3) Any licence issued by the Board pursuant to subsection (2) may be issued on the condition that the oil to be imported will be consumed in the area of Canada specified in the licence.
>
> (4) Where the Board is not reasonably satisfied that the consumption of oil to be imported will be in the area of Canada specified in the application for a licence and that the terms of the licence to be issued will be complied with, it shall not issue a licence.

This action was challenged, but the Supreme Court held the law to be *intra vires*. Pigeon J delivered the main judgment in a unanimous decision, Fauteux CJC, Abbott, Martland, Judson, Ritchie, Hall, Spence, and Laskin JJ concurring. The earlier case was distinguished on the grounds that the new regulations were implicitly limited in scope to imported oil, while the previous ones applied to "any gasoline." Therefore, the new law was a valid regulation of international trade. The following was said about the propriety of schemes regulating such trade affecting local property rights.]

PIGEON J: In the present case, s. 20(2) of the Regulations clearly shows that the policy intended to be implemented by the impugned enactment is a control of the imports of a given commodity to foster the development and utilization of Canadian oil resources. The restriction on the distribution of the imported product to a defined area is intended to reserve the market in other areas for the benefit of products from other Provinces of Canada. Therefore, the true character of the enactment appears to be an incident in the administration of an extra-provincial marketing scheme as in *Murphy v. CPR Co. and A-G Can.*, [1958] SCR 626, 15 DLR (2d) 145. Under the circumstances, the interference with local trade restricted as it is to an imported commodity, is an integral part of the control of imports in the furtherance of an extra-provincial trade policy and cannot be termed "an unwarranted invasion of provincial jurisdiction."

Appeal dismissed.

K. Swinton, *The Supreme Court and Canadian Federalism:*
The Laskin-Dickson Years
(Scarborough, ON: Carswell, 1990), at 141 (footnotes omitted)

While *Caloil* was a welcome development for those who saw the need for a greater federal regulatory role over trade, it permitted federal regulation over trade matters in the
provinces only if such regulation was "necessary" to the effective regulation of interprovincial or international trade. Thus, there was still a requirement that goods move across
provincial borders. The test provided no support for federal regulation of economic
problems where such flow did not exist, or where the Court felt that the regulation of
intraprovincial activity was not necessary to the effective regulation of interprovincial or
international trade. Although Paul Weiler suggested that there were no reasoned limits
to this test and that it would support a wide range of federal legislation, the Supreme
Court proved him wrong. Several years after *Caloil*, in *Dominion Stores*, [1980] 1 SCR
844, 106 DLR (3d) 581, it held that the federal government could not set grading standards for the sale of agricultural produce in a province, even though it could do so for
produce sold interprovincially, for the intraprovincial regulation could not be said to be
"incidental" to the regulation of interprovincial trade.

NOTE ON DOMINION STORES LTD. v. THE QUEEN

In *Dominion Stores Ltd. v. The Queen*, [1980] 1 SCR 844, 106 DLR (3d) 581, Dominion
Stores Ltd. was charged under the *Canada Agricultural Products Standards Act* (CAPSA)
with selling bruised Spartan apples under the trade name "Canada Extra Fancy." The bruised
apples, produced in Ontario and sold within the city of Toronto, did not meet the quality
standards for use of that grade name as required by federal law. The statutory backdrop to
the case was complicated by the fact that Dominion Stores was charged under a part of the
CAPSA that was voluntary. The mandatory provisions of CAPSA applied only to agricultural products that moved in interprovincial and international trade. Wholly intraprovincial
sales could be caught by the law only if the seller voluntarily chose to use the trade name. As
Dominion Stores chose to sell apples within Ontario graded "Canada Extra Fancy," they
were caught by the voluntary provisions and so had to satisfy federal standards. The further
complication for the Court was that the federal law mirrored the requirements of an existing
Ontario law, the *Farm Products and Grades and Sales Act*, which set mandatory grading
standards for intraprovincial sales. The Court was closely divided, ruling 5 to 4 that the federal law was *ultra vires*.

Justice Estey (Martland, Pigeon, Beetz, Estey, and Pratte JJ concurring) wrote for the
majority:

> The allocation of the power with respect to regulation of trade and commerce in this country
> under the *British North America Act* has been settled, until now at least, by *Citizens Insurance Co.*
> *v. Parsons* (1881), 7 App. Cas. 96; *R v. Eastern Terminal Elevator Co.*, [1925] SCR 434; *Lawson*
> *v. Interior Tree, Fruit and Vegetable Committee*, [1931] SCR 357; and *The Attorney-General for*
> *British Columbia v. The Attorney-General for Canada*, [1937] AC 377. Under the interpretation
> placed upon s. 91(2) of the *British North America Act* in these decisions, the power of Parlia-
> ment with reference to the regulation of trade and commerce is limited to trade in the inter-

national and interprovincial sense and Parliament is not empowered thereby to regulate local trade simply as a part of a scheme for the regulation of international and interprovincial trade. ... Consequently, ... I approach the issue raised in this appeal on the basis that the Parliament of Canada may not, in the guise of regulating trade and commerce, reach into the fields allocated to the provinces by s. 92(13) and (16) and regulate trading transactions occurring entirely within the provinces. In actual fact the provinces and Parliament taking the lead from the Privy Council marketing decision of 1937, *supra*, have adopted cooperative and complementary schemes for the marketing of natural products.

A key factor in the reasoning was Justice Estey's view that it was preferable that only provincial law regulate intraprovincial sales. Otherwise, "the wasteful overlapping or double-decking of administration or enforcement" would surely defeat

the constitutional plan designed and constructed in the *British North America Act* and as evolved through the decisions of the Privy Council. ... The federal statute seeks to add another consequence to the same action already proscribed under the Ontario Act. It is said that the result is simply that if the retailer affixes to the apples the "extra fancy" grade identification, he is to be prosecuted under the federal statute (assuming quality does not match the prescribed standards), but if he does not affix the label, he is to be prosecuted under the provincial Act. To that result, my strong preference is for the simple solution that Part I of the federal statute is inapplicable to the local trade here in question, and hence the charge, if any, must be laid under the provincial statute.

The majority judgment distinguished an earlier decision of the Privy Council in *AG Ontario v. AG Canada*, [1937] AC 405 (PC) (the "*Canada Standards*" case), discussed briefly in Chapter 6, The 1930s: The Depression and the New Deal. The Board there upheld a federally created national trade mark called "Canada Standard." Use of the trademark was voluntary, but any user was required to conform to federal product standards. Justice Estey held that there was no comparable statutory scheme in place in that case:

Marketing schemes affecting as they do the process of marketing as such, are in no way comparable in fact or in law with a program for the creation of a property right in the form of a trade mark coupled with a truly voluntary scheme for licensing the users of that trade mark.

Somewhat surprisingly, Justice Estey ended his judgment with a comment to the effect that the interpretation of s. 91(2) on which he had relied, based on Privy Council decisions, might not be the correct description of the federal power, and suggested that the Court on a future occasion might have the opportunity to deal with the interlocking of federal and provincial powers with respect to the local marketing of articles of commerce which have entered the interprovincial and international stream.

Chief Justice Laskin (Ritchie, Dickson, and McIntyre JJ dissenting) upheld the federal standard. It was quite logical, to the dissenting justices, that

the Parliament of Canada, having enacted compulsory grading requirements for agricultural products moving in export and interprovincial trade, should complement those provisions by giving an opportunity to dealers in such products to avail themselves, if they so wished, of the same grade prescriptions for local transactions. It could be a convenience for them and for consumers as well.

NOTE ON THE FEDERAL POWER TO IMPLEMENT
INTERNATIONAL AGREEMENTS

While there have been few cases since *Caloil*, other than *Dominion Stores*, in which the necessarily incidental doctrine has been raised in relation to the trade and commerce power,
one possible area of future litigation arises out of international agreements on trade liberal-
ization—for example, the *North American Free Trade Agreement* (NAFTA) (implemented by
the *North American Free Trade Agreement Implementation Act*, SC 1993, c. 44).

Among NAFTA's provisions are articles incorporated from the Canada-United States Free
Trade Agreement addressed to the listing, pricing, and distribution practices for wines and
distilled spirits. Generally, the underlying concern is the discrimination practised by some
provinces, especially Ontario, against out-of-province wines and spirits. Thus, there are
rules about differential pricing, for example, designed to limit provinces, over time, to "cost-
of-service" differentials in wine pricing. NAFTA also provides, as does the FTA, that the
parties "shall ensure that all necessary measures are taken in order to give effect to its provisions, including their observance, except as otherwise provided in this Agreement, by state
and provincial governments" (art. 105).

As you know from the *Labour Conventions* case, Chapter 6, The 1930s: The Depression
and the New Deal, the federal government can only pass laws implementing treaties where
the subject matter of the treaty is within federal jurisdiction. Could the federal government
bind a recalcitrant province to the NAFTA wine pricing provisions by relying on the trade
and commerce power as developed in *Caloil*?

(Note that the provinces have exercised their discriminatory pricing policy through their
monopoly over liquor sales. A provincial corporation would buy the out-of-province wine
and then impose a higher markup for wines from out of the province. Traditionally, provinces, as owners, have not been bound by s. 91(2) of the Constitution, which has allowed
them to do things as owners that they could not do as regulators.)

B. General Regulation of Trade

K. Swinton, *The Supreme Court and Canadian Federalism:*
The Laskin-Dickson Years
(Scarborough, ON: Carswell, 1990), at 141-44 (footnotes omitted)

[Professor Swinton begins by noting that recent doctrinal developments with respect to
the trade and commerce power, such as the expansion of the necessarily incidental doctrine in *Caloil*, still required that goods move across provincial borders. These developments thus provided no support for federal regulation of economic problems where such
flow did not exist, or where a court believed that the regulation of intraprovincial activity
was not necessary to the effective regulation of interprovincial or international trade.]

As a result, the case law on the trade and commerce power, fixing on the interprovincial or international flow of goods, would not support federal government efforts to regulate problems because of their detrimental impact on national economic health. To permit
such action by the federal government, it was necessary to develop another approach to

the interpretation of the federal and provincial heads of power, and this seemed to emerge with a new doctrinal development in 1976, when the Supreme Court made reference to the federal government's authority over the "general regulation of trade." That doctrine had its origins in *Citizens' Insurance v. Parsons*, where the Privy Council stated that Parliament might have jurisdiction over "general regulation of trade."

For many years, this strand of doctrine was of minimal assistance to federal regulators—invoked only in 1914, in *John Deere Plow Co.*, [1915] AC 330, 18 DLR 353, to support federal regulation of the activities of federally incorporated companies, and twenty years later in the Privy Council's judgment upholding the *Dominion Trade and Industry Act, 1935*. That Act provided for voluntary use of a national trademark, the Canada Standard, when the user of the mark complied with standards for a product established under the federal legislation. After these cases, the general regulation of trade doctrine fell into disuse until Laskin CJC attempted to revive it in *Macdonald v. Vapor Canada*, [1977] 2 SCR 134, 66 DLR (3d) 1, a case involving the validity of a section of the *Trade Marks Act* permitting a civil cause of action by an individual harmed by a "business practice contrary to honest industrial or commercial usage in Canada." While Laskin CJC made extensive reference to the general regulation of trade doctrine, he held it inapplicable in this case because of the private enforcement of the legislation, the lack of any regulatory scheme under public supervision, and the close similarity between the statutory remedy and common law and civil law remedies coming under provincial jurisdiction. All these factors militated against a finding that the section dealt with "general" regulation of trade.

Macdonald did, however, open the door to permit a new justification for federal regulation of economic matters, and the doctrine of general regulation of trade surfaced in several cases following *Macdonald*, and finally was used by the Court to uphold federal competition legislation in 1989. There is an explanation for the Court's initial reluctance to apply the test, which lies in the tension between the general regulation of trade doctrine and the dominant mode of analysis in trade and commerce cases, which emphasizes the need for an interprovincial or international flow of products in order to justify federal regulation of local transactions intertwined with the cross-border flow. The general regulation of trade doctrine does not preclude federal regulation of intraprovincial transactions—provided that there is a sufficiently important national interest to warrant such regulation. However, a judge who looks at a federal scheme from the traditional perspective under the trade and commerce power will be concerned if he or she sees extensive federal regulation of intraprovincial transactions such as contract terms or production standards. Yet if the general regulation of trade doctrine is to be applied, the traditional approach must be discarded, for the court must look beyond the stage at which the regulation is imposed. Instead, the inquiry must be directed to whether the federal measure regulates a national economic problem of interest to the whole country, even if it does so at the stage of production or retailing in a province.

The general regulation of trade test requires the judge to make controversial and difficult decisions about the importance of the national interest at stake and the impact of federal regulation on provincial autonomy in the economic sphere. Indeed, the general regulation of trade doctrine confronts the courts with difficulties similar to those under the national dimensions test of the peace, order and good government clause, since the judges must find some criteria of national interest which leave room for provincial regulation of economic problems, even when those problems are duplicated in more than one province. While the old intra/interprovincial distinction was not altogether satisfactory because it hampered federal initiatives, it had the advantage of clearly recognizing a zone for provincial autonomy in economic regulation. As well, it avoided the problem of judicial balancing of national and provincial interests on a case by case basis in the search for the "national concerns" underlying particular federal measures. Instead, the Court could focus on whether the particular measure under attack dealt with interprovincial or intraprovincial trade—an inquiry that appeared more objective and fact-based than the value-laden inquiry under the general regulation of trade test.

NOTE ON LABATT BREWERIES OF CANADA LTD. v. AG CANADA

The federal *Food and Drugs Act*, RSC 1970, c. F-27 regulated the content of a variety of food and drug products. Section 6 of the Act provided:

> 6. Where a standard has been prescribed for a food, no person shall label, package, sell, or advertise any article in such a manner that it is likely to be mistaken for such food, unless the article complies with the prescribed standard.

The standards were prescribed by regulations passed pursuant to the legislation. At issue in *Labatt Breweries of Canada Ltd. v. AG Canada*, [1980] 1 SCR 914, 110 DLR (3d) 594 were regulations prescribing minimum and maximum alcohol content for beer marketed as "light beer." Labatt Breweries marketed "Special Lite Beer," which exceeded the maximum allowable alcohol content. Labatt challenged the validity of the Act and regulations. The federal government sought to justify the law under the trade and commerce power, and in addition relied on its criminal law and p.o.g.g. powers.

The Court split 6 to 3, finding the Act and regulations, in so far as they applied to malt liquors and light beer, *ultra vires*. With respect to the trade and commerce power, Justice Estey (Martland, Dickson, Pratte, and Beetz JJ concurring) held that the first branch of *Parsons*, giving the federal government power over interprovincial and foreign trade, was not applicable as the impugned regulation was concerned with production and local sale:

> The impugned Regulations in and under the *Food and Drugs Act* are not concerned with the control and guidance of the flow of articles of commerce through the distribution channels, but rather with the production and local sale of the specified products of the brewing industry. There is no demonstration by the proponent of these isolated provisions in the *Food and Drugs Act* and its Regulations of any interprovincial aspect of this industry. The labels in the record reveal that the appellant produces these beverages in all Provinces but Quebec and Prince Edward Island. From the nature of the beverage, it is apparent, without demonstration, that transportation to distant markets would be expensive, and hence the local nature of the production operation.

Nor could federal authority be justified as an exercise of the second branch of *Parsons*, the general trade power. In setting out the scope of this power, Estey J stated that

> What clearly is not of general national concern is the regulation of a single trade or industry ... . [I]t is clear that neither national ownership of a trade or undertaking or even national

advertising of its products will alone suffice to authorize the imposition of federal trade and commerce legislation.

The impugned provisions, wrote Estey J, were concerned "with the production process of a *single industry*" (emphasis added), that was "substantially local in character." The *Food and Drugs Act*, though it covered a substantial portion of Canadian economic activity, was seen as a scheme regulating "one industry or trade at a time, by a varying array of regulations or trade codes applicable to each individual sector" and thus was not, in the result, "a regulation of trade and commerce in the sweeping general sense contemplated in the *Citizens Insurance* case."

Justice Estey could not agree that this was trade mark legislation of the sort upheld as a valid exercise of the trade and commerce power in the *Canada Standards* case, discussed *supra* in the note on *Dominion Stores*, because of the arrogation by Parliament of common names from the language. While suggesting the possibility of a federal "labelling power," he went on to find it of no relevance to this case as labelling legislation typically prescribes no standards for the production or marketing of a product, but only requires the revelation of the contents or conditions of use, etc.

Finally, Estey J found no basis for the legislation in either the criminal law power or the p.o.g.g. power. With respect to the former power, Estey J found that the impugned provisions, which he characterized as involving detailed regulation of the brewing industry, were not directed at the protection of health or the prevention of deception. With respect to the latter, there was no matter of national concern.

Ritchie J wrote a separate judgment, but concurred with Estey J as to the result. Pigeon J dissented (McIntyre J concurring). After stating that the federal Parliament had authority under s. 91(2) to enact laws relating to trade marks, he concluded that the legislation here, as in the *Canada Standards* case, created a "national mark" within the exclusive use of the federal government:

> In my view, the federal enactments under attack provide for no more than what might be called "labelling regulations." These state what specifications must be met if some specific designations are used on food labels. In my view this does not go beyond a proper concept of trade mark legislation.

Chief Justice Laskin also dissented. Though the federal law could be characterized merely as a labelling provision, he preferred to rest his judgment on a broader ground under the authority of the general trade power. In Laskin CJC's view:

> [Parliament] should be able to fix standards that are common to all manufacturers of foods, including beer, drugs, cosmetics and therapeutic devices, at least to equalize competitive advantages in the carrying on of businesses concerned with such products. I find some reinforcement in this view of the scope of the federal trade and commerce power in s. 121 of the *British North America Act, 1867* which precludes interprovincial tariffs, marking Canada as a whole as an economic union.
>
> The operations of Labatt Breweries and of other brewers of beer extend throughout Canada, and I would not attenuate the federal trade and commerce power any further than has already been manifested in judicial decisions by denying Parliament authority to address itself to uniform prescriptions for the manufacture of food, drugs, cosmetics, therapeutic devices in the

way, in the case of beer, of standards for its production and distribution according to various alcoholic strengths under labels appropriate to the governing Regulations.

For discussion of the case, see James C. MacPherson, "Economic Regulation and the British North America Act: Labatt Breweries and Other Constitutional Imbroglios" (1980-81), 5 *Canadian Business Law Journal* 172.

NOTES

1. There are many product standards found in the Food and Drug Regulations, CRC 1978, c. 870. See, for example:

> Meat, Meat By-Products
> B.14.015.[S]. Regular Ground Beef shall be beef meat processed by grinding and shall contain not more than 30 per cent beef fat as determined by the official method.
> B.15.015A.[S]. Medium Ground Beef shall be beef meat processed by grinding and shall contain not more than 23 per cent beef fat as determined by the official method.
> B.14.015B.[S]. Lean Ground Beef shall be beef meat processed by grinding and shall contain not more than 17 per cent beef fat as determined by the official method.
> B.14.015C. No person shall sell ground beef that contains more than 30 per cent beef fat as determined by the official method.

2. While the Supreme Court of Canada found s. 6 of the *Food and Drugs Act ultra vires*, this did not leave the federal government without recourse to enforce product standards. Section 5(1) of the Act provides that "No person shall label, package, treat, process, sell or advertise any food in a manner that is false, misleading or deceptive or is likely to create an erroneous impression regarding its character, value, quantity, composition, merit or safety." A constitutional challenge to this provision was rejected in *R v. Wetmore*, [1983] 2 SCR 284, 2 DLR (4th) 577.

3. During the constitutional talks leading to the 1982 amendments to the Constitution, the federal government at one point proposed the following amendment to s. 91(2) of the then *BNA Act*, which would have given it concurrent powers with the provinces over competition and product standards:

> 1. Add to section 91 the following heads of jurisdiction immediately following head 91.2:
>   2.1 Competition
>   2.2 The establishment of products standards throughout Canada
> 2. Add to section 91 the following new subsections:
>   (2) For greater certainty, "regulation of trade and commerce" in subsection (1) includes the regulation of trade and commerce in goods, services and capital.
>   (3) The authority conferred on Parliament by heads 91(2.1) and 91(2.2) does not render invalid a law enacted by a legislature that is not in conflict with a law of Parliament enacted under either of those heads.

The proposal was never accepted. The amendment with respect to product standards was a response to the Supreme Court of Canada's decision in *Labatt Breweries*. The commentary on this proposal found in A.F. Bayefsky, *Canada's Constitution Act 1982 & Amendments: A*

Documentary History, vol. 2 (Toronto: McGraw-Hill, 1989), at 741 explains the lack of provincial enthusiasm for this proposal:

> While it was recognized that recent court decisions have placed federal jurisdiction in jeopardy, some provinces expressed concern that the proposed modification, in spite of subsection (3) below, might restrict provincial ability to establish standards for products circulating essentially within a province, or standards at a level different from national ones.

4. The issue of the general trade power arose in *AG Canada v. Canadian National Transportation Ltd.*, [1983] 2 SCR 206, 3 DLR (4th) 16. The case involved a challenge to the federal government's ability to initiate prosecutions for offences under the federal *Combines Investigation Act*, RSC 1970, c. C-23. The argument raised was that the prosecution of criminal offences was a power that belonged to the provinces under s. 92(14) respecting the administration of justice within the province. That argument was rejected by the Court.

In analyzing this issue, the Court was required to characterize the legislation. A majority of the court supported the Act under the criminal law power, which had been its traditional basis for support. Dickson J, writing for three members of the Court, would have supported the Act under the trade and commerce power, specifically under branch 2 of *Parsons*, the general trade power, because he believed the provinces had exclusive authority to prosecute criminal offences. In the course of his judgment he discussed, at 61-62 DLR, the constitutional dilemma posed by interpretation of the general trade power and suggested some criteria central to the federal power:

> Every general enactment will necessarily have some local impact and if it is true that an overly literal conception of "general interest" will endanger the very idea of the local, there are equal dangers of swinging the telescope the other way around. The forest is no less a forest for being made up of individual trees. Whatever the constitutional flaws in the *Board of Commerce Act* and *Combines and Fair Prices Act*, they cannot be attributed, as Duff J seems to contend, to the fact that any individual order made by the board would have its effect on a business or trade in the province. Were that the test then no economic legislation could ever qualify under the general trade and commerce power. Such a conception is merely the obverse of the equally unacceptable proposition that economic legislation qualifies under the general trade and commerce rubric merely because it applies equally and uniformly throughout the country.
>
> The reason why the regulation of a single trade or business in the province cannot be a question of general interest throughout the Dominion, is that it lies at the very heart of the local autonomy envisaged in the *Constitution Act, 1867*. That a federal enactment purports to carry out such regulation in the same way in all the provinces or in association with other regulatory codes dealing with other trades or businesses does not change the fact that what is being created is an exact overlapping and hence a nullification of a jurisdiction conceded to the provinces by the Constitution. A different situation obtains, however, when what is at issue is general legislation aimed at the economy as a single integrated national unit rather than as a collection of separate local enterprises. Such legislation is qualitatively different from anything that could practically or constitutionally be enacted by the individual provinces either separately or in combination. The focus of such legislation is on the general, though its results will obviously be manifested in particular local effects any one of which may touch upon "property and civil rights in the province." Nevertheless, in pith and substance such legislation will be addressed to

questions of general interest throughout the Dominion. The line of demarcation is clear between measures validly directed at a general regulation of the national economy and those
merely aimed at centralized control over a large number of economic entities. The regulations
in the *Labatt* case were probably close to the line. It may also well be that, given the state of the
economy in 1920 and the actual mechanics of the legislation, the *Board of Commerce Act* and
the *Combines and Fair Prices Act* amounted simply to an attempt to authorize the issuance of
an unco-ordinated series of local orders and prohibitions.

The issue of the constitutionality of the *Combines Investigation Act* came before the Supreme Court again in the *General Motors* case which follows. Dickson CJC, writing for the
entire Court, drew heavily on his earlier judgment in *Canadian National Transportation* in
upholding the legislation as a general regulation of trade.

General Motors of Canada Ltd. v. City National Leasing
[1989] 1 SCR 641, 58 DLR (4th) 255

DICKSON CJC (Beetz, McIntyre, Lamer, La Forest, and L'Heureux-Dubé JJ concurring): The principal issue in this appeal is the constitutional validity of s. 31.1 of the
Combines Investigation Act, RSC 1970, c. C-23. Section 31.1 creates a civil cause of action
for certain infractions of the *Combines Investigation Act*. It is this fact which makes the
section constitutionally suspect: a civil cause of action is within the domain of the provinces to create. The essential question raised by this appeal is whether s. 31.1 can, nevertheless, be upheld as constitutionally valid by virtue of its relationship with the *Combines
Investigation Act*. Answering this question requires addressing two issues: first, is the Act
valid under the federal trade and commerce power, expressed in s. 91(2) of the *Constitution Act, 1867*; and second, is s. 31.1 integrated with the Act in such a way that it too is
intra vires under s. 91(2).

For the reasons which follow, I have found s. 31.1 to be *intra vires* the federal Parliament. In answering the two aforementioned issues, I have decided, first, that the *Combines
Investigation Act* is valid under the federal trade and commerce power, in particular, it is
valid under the "second branch" of that power, the power over "general" trade and commerce. Second, I have found that s. 31.1 is constitutionally valid by virtue of being functionally related to the Act.

Legislation

Section 31.1 of the Act reads as follows:

31.1(1) Any person who has suffered loss or damage as a result of
    (a) conduct that is contrary to any provision of Part V, or
    (b) the failure of any person to comply with an order of the Commission or a court
  under this Act,
may, in any court of competent jurisdiction, sue for and recover from the person who engaged in the conduct or failed to comply with the order an amount equal to the loss or
damage proved to have been suffered by him, together with any additional amount that the

court may allow not exceeding the full cost to him of any investigation in connection with the matter and of proceedings under this section.

Among the offences covered by Part V of the Act, referred to in s. 31.1(1)(a) above, are those set out in s. 34(1) which reads:

> 34.(1) Every one engaged in a business who
>
> (a) is a party or privy to, or assists in, any sale that discriminates to his knowledge, directly or indirectly, against competitors of a purchaser of articles from him in that any discount, rebate, allowance, price concession or other advantage is granted to the purchaser over and above any discount, rebate, allowance, price concession or other advantage that, at the time the articles are sold to such purchaser, is available to such competitors in respect of a sale of articles of like quality and quantity;
>
> (b) engages in a policy of selling products in any area of Canada at prices lower than those exacted by him elsewhere in Canada, having the effect or tendency of substantially lessening competition or eliminating a competitor in such part of Canada, or designed to have such effect; or
>
> (c) engages in a policy of selling products at prices unreasonably low, having the effect or tendency of substantially lessening competition or eliminating a competitor, or designed to have such effect,
>
> is guilty of an indictable offence and is liable to imprisonment for two years. ...

General Motors of Canada Ltd. ("GM") manufactures automobiles and trucks. City National Leasing ("CNL") leases across Canada fleets of automobiles and trucks in competition with other national fleet leasing companies. CNL purchases the majority of its vehicles from franchised GM dealers, but does not purchase from GM directly. To finance purchases of GM vehicles between 1970 and 1980, CNL received interest rate support, a programme offered by General Motors Acceptance Corporation ("GMAC"). CNL alleges that during that time GM, directly or indirectly, had been paying "preferential" interest rate support to competitors of CNL in respect of competitors' purchases of GM manufactured automobiles and trucks, in addition to the interest rate support available to CNL. It is further alleged that the exclusion of CNL from the preferential interest rate support program from 1970 to 1980 was a practice of price discrimination contrary to s. 34(1)(a) of the Act, giving CNL an action under s. 31.1. CNL claims that it lost profits equivalent to monies saved by its competitors, and that it is entitled to recover from GM damages equivalent to the lost profits and compound interest thereon. CNL also sued GM for breach of contract for damages arising after March 1980. ...

IV

The General Trade and Commerce Power

. . .

The leading case of *Citizens' Insurance Company of Canada v. Parsons* (1881), 7 App. Cas. 96, sets out the most frequently quoted statement of the scope of s. 91(2). Speaking for the Privy Council, Sir Montague Smith noted at p. 112 that if the words trade and commerce were given their ordinary meaning, s. 91(2) conceivably granted very wide-ranging powers to the federal government ... . To limit the breadth of a literal interpretation of s. 91(2), Sir Montague Smith settled upon the following construction, at p. 113:

> Construing therefore the words "regulation of trade and commerce" by the various aids to their interpretation above suggested, they would include political arrangements in regard to trade requiring the sanction of parliament, regulation in matters of inter-provincial concern, and it may be that they would include general regulation of trade affecting the whole dominion.

Sir Montague Smith continued, on the same page:

> Having taken this view of the present case, it becomes unnecessary to consider the question how far the general power to make regulations of trade and commerce, when competently exercised by the dominion parliament, might legally modify or affect property and civil rights in the provinces, or the legislative power of the provincial legislatures in relation to those subjects ... .

In *Canadian National Transportation* [*AG Canada v. Canadian National Transportation, Ltd.*, [1983] 2 SCR 206], at p. 258, I suggested that *Parsons* had established three important propositions with regard to the federal trade and commerce power:

> (i) it does not correspond to the literal meaning of the words "regulation of trade and commerce"; (ii) it includes not only arrangements with regard to international and interprovincial trade but "it may be that ... [it] would include general regulation of trade affecting the whole dominion"; (iii) it does not extend to regulating the contracts of a particular business or trade.

Since *Parsons*, the jurisprudence on s. 91(2) has largely been an elaboration on the boundaries of the two aspects or "branches" of federal power: (1) the power over international and interprovincial trade and commerce; and (2) the power over general trade and commerce affecting Canada as a whole. The first branch has been the subject of considerable constitutional challenge and judicial scrutiny. The second branch, in contrast, has remained largely unexplored, terra incognita. In this appeal, however, it is under this second branch of s. 91(2) that CNL and the Attorney General of Canada seek to uphold s. 31.1.

So far as I can gather, legislation has been upheld under the second branch by a final appellate court on only two occasions. In 1937 the Privy Council upheld a federal scheme creating a national trade mark to be used in conjunction with federally established commodity standards under the general trade and commerce power: *Attorney-General for Ontario v. Attorney-General of Canada* (*Canada Standards Trade Mark*), [1937] AC 405. ... The second occasion was in *John Deere Plow Co. v. Wharton*, [1915] AC 330, where the Privy Council located the regulation of federally incorporated companies within the general branch of s. 91(2), although they also upheld the legislation under the "peace, order and good government" power.

Aside from these two cases, at least until of late, the general trade and commerce power met with consistent rejection by the courts. ...

The treatment of the general trade and commerce power in the cases just mentioned was no doubt strongly influenced by earlier Privy Council decisions on s. 91(2) and in particular what Anglin CJ referred to in *The King v. Eastern Terminal Elevator Co.*, [1925] SCR 434 at p. 441, as "… their Lordships' emphatic and reiterated allocation of 'the regulation of trade and commerce' to … [a] subordinate and wholly auxiliary function … ." As Professor McDonald observed in his article "Constitutional Aspects of Canadian Anti-Combines Law Enforcement" (1969), 47 *Can. Bar Rev.* 161, at p. 189:

> The *British North America Act* was framed with a greater interest in central control than motivated the constitutional fathers to the south. Reaction in the founding provinces to the consequences of decentralized control in the United States has been well documented. The broad and unqualified language of section 91(2) reflected the basic interest that strength from economic unity replace the floundering provincial economies. Yet, as the American courts broadened their commerce clause until it meant essentially what the Fathers of Confederation had sought for Canada, so have the Privy Council and the Canadian courts reacted against the hopes of the framers of their constitution and have decentralized commercial control.
>
> At least until relatively recently the history of interpretation of the trade and commerce power has almost uniformly reinforced the federal paralysis which resulted from a series of Privy Council decisions in the years 1881-1896. The predominant view was that section 91(2) did not in any way go to either general commerce, contracts, particular trades or occupations, or commodities so far as those things might be intraprovincial. The test for the local nature of a transaction was abstractly legal, divorced from commercial effect.

Since 1949 and the abolition of appeals to the Privy Council, the trade and commerce power has, I think it fair to say, enjoyed an enhanced importance in such cases as *Murphy v. Canadian Pacific Railway Co.*, [1958] SCR 626, upholding the validity of the federal *Canadian Wheat Board Act*; *The Queen v. Klassen* (1959), 20 DLR (2d) 406 (Man. CA), upholding the application of the *Canadian Wheat Board Act* to intraprovincial transactions; and *Caloil Inc. v. Attorney General of Canada*, [1971] SCR 543, upholding a federal scheme regulating the movement of imported gasoline. See also *Reference respecting the Agricultural Products Marketing Act*, [1978] 2 SCR 1198.

In examining cases which have considered s. 91(2), it is evident that courts have been sensitive to the need to reconcile the general trade and commerce power of the federal government with the provincial power over property and civil rights. Balancing has not been easy.

· · ·

With respect, in my view, neither the position articulated in *John Deere Plow Co. v. Wharton*, [1915] AC 330, 18 DLR 353, nor that advanced in the *Board of Commerce* (1920), 60 SCR 456, 54 DLR 354, case correctly assesses the balance to be struck between s. 91(2) and s. 92(13). *Wharton* is clearly overly expansive, sweeping all general economic issues into the grasp of s. 91(2). On the other hand, the residual interpretation articulated in the *Board of Commerce* case fails to breathe life into the trade and commerce power and fails to recognize that provincial powers are a subtraction from the federal powers. The true balance between property and civil rights and the regulation of trade and commerce must lie somewhere between an all pervasive interpretation of s. 91(2) and an interpretation that renders the general trade and commerce power to all intents vapid and meaningless.

This Court took the first step towards delineating more specific principles of validity for legislation enacted under the general trade and commerce power in *MacDonald v. Vapor Canada*, [1977] 2 SCR 134, 66 DLR (3d) 1. In that case, s. 7(e) of the *Trade Marks Act*, RSC 1970, c. T-10, was challenged as *ultra vires* Parliament. Section 7 prohibited certain commercial practices, including the making of false and misleading statements to discredit a competitor, passing off goods or services, and making use of false descriptions likely to mislead the public, under the general heading of unfair competition. The impugned subsection was a general catch-all provision, unrelated to the rest of the statute, which prohibited a person from doing "any other act" or adopting "any other business practice contrary to honest industrial or commercial usage in Canada." The respondent, Vapor Canada Ltd., supported by the Attorney General of Canada, argued that s. 7(e) could be sustained as legislation regulating general trade and commerce under s. 91(2).

The Court struck down the provision as *ultra vires*. Chief Justice Laskin, speaking for five members of the Court, proposed three hallmarks of validity for legislation under the second branch of the trade and commerce power. First, the impugned legislation must be part of a general regulatory scheme. Second, the scheme must be monitored by the continuing oversight of a regulatory agency. Third, the legislation must be concerned with trade as a whole rather than with a particular industry. Each of these requirements is evidence of a concern that federal authority under the second branch of the trade and commerce power does not encroach on provincial jurisdiction. By limiting the means which federal legislators may employ to that of a regulatory scheme overseen by a regulatory agency, and by limiting the object of federal legislation to trade as a whole, these requirements attempt to maintain a delicate balance between federal and provincial power. On the basis of these criteria, Laskin CJC then rejected the general trade and commerce power as the constitutional foundation for s. 7(e).

Three members of the Court affirmed the *Vapor Canada* criteria in *A-G Can. v. Canadian National Transportation*, [1983] 2 SCR, 206, 3 DLR (4th) 16. At issue in *Canadian National Transportation* was the authority of the Attorney-General of Canada to conduct prosecutions under the *Combines Investigation Act*. Four members of the Court held that provincial authority over the administration of justice in s. 92(14) of the Constitution did not preclude the federal government from conducting prosecutions of criminal offences. I was of the view that s. 92(14) did preclude the federal government from prosecuting criminal offences—unless the offences could be upheld under a head of power other than s. 91(27). I then took the further position, in which Beetz and Lamer JJ agreed in substance, that the section could be sustained as legislation relating to the general trade and commerce power and thus the federal government was competent to prosecute a violation of s. 32(1) of the *Combines Investigation Act*.

In reaching the conclusion that s. 32(1)(c) of the *Combines Investigation Act* was within the scope of the general trade and commerce power, and writing for the minority of the Court, I adopted Laskin CJC's three criteria in *Vapor Canada*, *supra*, but added two factors that I considered indicia of the valid exercise of the general trade and commerce power: (i) the legislation should be of a nature that the provinces jointly or severally would be constitutionally incapable of enacting; and (ii) the failure to include one or more provinces or localities in a legislative scheme would jeopardize the successful operation of the scheme in other parts of the country. These two requirements, like

Laskin CJC's three criteria, serve to ensure that federal legislation does not upset the balance of power between federal and provincial governments. In total, the five factors provide a preliminary checklist of characteristics, the presence of which in legislation is an indication of validity under the trade and commerce power. These indicia do not, however, represent an exhaustive list of traits that will tend to characterize general trade and commerce legislation. Nor is the presence or absence of any of these five criteria necessarily determinative. As noted in *Canadian National Transportation, supra*, at p. 268:

> The above does not purport to be an exhaustive list, nor is the presence of any or all of these indicia necessarily decisive. The proper approach to the characterization is still the one suggested in *Parsons*, a careful case by case assessment. Nevertheless, the presence of such factors does at least make it far more probable that what is being addressed in a federal enactment is genuinely a national economic concern and not just a collection of local ones.

On any occasion where the general trade and commerce power is advanced as a ground of constitutional validity, a careful case by case analysis remains appropriate. The five factors articulated in *Canadian National Transportation* merely represent a principled way to begin the difficult task of distinguishing between matters relating to trade and commerce and those of a more local nature.

V

Approach to Determining Constitutionality

[What then follows is a long discussion of the appropriate methodology in cases such as this where the impugned provision is part of a larger act. This portion of the judgment has been reproduced in Chapter 8, Interpreting the Division of Powers, in the context of that chapter's examination of the necessarily incidental doctrine. Only the final paragraph, which summarizes the methodology, is left here.]

The steps in the analysis may be summarized as follows: First, the court must determine whether the impugned provision can be viewed as intruding on provincial powers, and if so, to what extent ... . Second, the court must establish whether the act (or a severable part of it) is valid. ... If the scheme is not valid, that is the end of the inquiry. If the scheme of regulation is declared valid, the court must then determine whether the impugned provision is sufficiently integrated with the scheme that it can be upheld by virtue of that relationship. This requires considering the seriousness of the encroachment on provincial powers in order to decide on the proper standard for such a relationship. ...

VI

Does Section 31.1 Encroach on Provincial Powers?

[In a passage reproduced in Chapter 8, Interpreting the Division of Powers, Dickson CJC concludes that the impugned provision, in creating a civil right of action, encroached on provincial powers, but that the encroachment was a limited one.]

VII

The Presence of a Regulatory Scheme in the Combines Investigation Act

The second step in determining the validity of s. 31.1 is to establish whether the Act contains a regulatory scheme. The presence of a well orchestrated scheme of economic regulation is immediately apparent on examination of the *Combines Investigation Act*. The existence of a regulatory scheme is in evidence throughout the entire Act.

The *Combines Investigation Act* is divided into eight parts. Part I creates the Director of Investigation and Research, whose role is to investigate the possibility that companies are engaging in certain forms of anti-competitive conduct specifically proscribed by later parts of the Act. The Director has the power to require the Restrictive Trade Practices Commission, created by Part II of the Act, to conduct hearings into suspected violations of the Act. The Director is also in charge of enforcing the criminal provisions of the Act (Part V) by referring the matter to the Attorney General of Canada, and of enforcing the provisions relating to the civil violations of the Act by the exclusive right to apply to the Restrictive Trade Practices Commission for a remedial order (Part IV.1).

• • •

From this overview of the *Combines Investigation Act* I have no difficulty in concluding that the Act as a whole embodies a complex scheme of economic regulation. The purpose of the Act is to eliminate activities that reduce competition in the marketplace. The entire Act is geared to achieving this objective. The Act identifies and defines anti-competitive conduct. It establishes an investigatory mechanism for revealing prohibited activities and provides an extensive range of criminal and administrative redress against companies engaging in behaviour that tends to reduce competition. In my view, these three components, elucidation of prohibited conduct, creation of an investigatory procedure, and the establishment of a remedial mechanism, constitute a well-integrated scheme of regulation designed to discourage forms of commercial behaviour viewed as detrimental to Canada and the Canadian economy.

VIII

The Validity of the Regulatory Scheme

Having discerned the presence of a regulatory scheme in the *Combines Investigation Act*, it is necessary to consider the validity of the scheme under the general trade and commerce power in light of the criteria established in *Canadian National Transportation*, *supra*. Four criteria remain to be examined: (1) whether the regulatory scheme operates under the oversight of an agency, (2) whether the Act is concerned with trade in general, (3) whether the provinces would be constitutionally capable of enacting combines legislation, and finally, (4) whether the failure to include one or more provinces or localities would jeopardize the successful operation of the *Combines Investigation Act*.

The foregoing review of the *Combines Investigation Act* leaves no doubt that the scheme regulating anti-competitive activities operates under the watchful gaze of a regulatory agency. The regulatory mechanism is carefully controlled by the Director of Investigation and Research and to a lesser degree by the Restrictive Trade Practices Commission. The authority to launch an inquiry into suspected anti-competitive conduct lies with the Director. The Director is required to initiate an inquiry whenever there is reason to believe either that a person has failed to comply with an order of the Commission or where an offence proscribed by the Act has been or is about to be committed, whenever the Minister of Consumer and Corporate Affairs so directs, and on application of six residents of Canada over the age of eighteen. The inquiry is conducted by the Director and his or her staff. If the Director concludes that there has been a violation of Part V of the Act, the Director may refer the matter to the Commission whose role is to hold proceedings and to report the outcome, including any remedial recommendations, to the Minister. It is clear that the Director exercises a significant degree of control over the operation of the *Combines Investigation Act*. In my view, the control over the entire process exercised by the Director and the Commission satisfies the requirement that there be vigilant oversight of the administration of a regulatory scheme.

I am also of the view that the *Combines Investigation Act* meets the remaining three indicia of *Canadian National Transportation*. These criteria share a common theme: all three are indications that the scheme of regulation is national in scope and that local regulation would be inadequate. The Act is quite clearly concerned with the regulation of trade in general, rather than with the regulation of a particular industry or commodity. Ryan J, in upholding the validity of s. 37.1 of the Act, in *Miracle Mart*, [1982] CS 342, 68 CCC (2d) 242, described the Act in terms I agree with. At p. 259 he said:

> … s. 37.1 is part of, as I previously indicated, a complete regulatory scheme aimed at eliminating commercial practices which are contrary to healthy competition *across the country*, and not in a specific place, in a specific business or industry.

[Emphasis in original.] This generality of application distinguishes the Act from the legislation which was found *ultra vires* in *Labatt Breweries of Canada Ltd. v. Attorney General of Canada*, [1980] 1 SCR 914. In that case the legislation regulated a single trade or industry. As I noted earlier, the purpose of the Act is to ensure the existence of a healthy level of competition in the Canadian economy. The deleterious effects of anti-competitive practices transcend provincial boundaries. Competition is not an issue of purely local concern but one of crucial importance for the national economy.

Various factors underlie the need for national regulation of competition in the economy. Professors Hogg and Grover, in "The Constitutionality of the Competition Bill" (1976), 1 *Can. Bus. LJ* 197 at pp. 199-200 (an abridged version of a paper written for the federal government's Department of Consumer and Corporate Affairs) provide a useful discussion of the diverse economic, geographical, and political factors which make it essential that competition be regulated on the federal level:

> It is surely obvious that major regulation of the Canadian economy has to be national. Goods and services, and the cash or credit which purchases them, flow freely from one part of the country to another without regard for provincial boundaries. Indeed, a basic concept of the federation is that it must be an economic union. An over-all national policy is the key to efficiency in the production of goods and services. Each province of the country is differently endowed with national resources, capital, labour and access to consumers. The result is that each province will be able to produce some products or services more efficiently than others. The introduction of an effective competition policy can be seen as one method to

ensure that these differing regional advantages will accrue to the nation as a whole in terms of lower prices, better quality and variety and increased opportunities for Canadians. Any attempt to achieve an optimal distribution of economic activity must transcend provincial boundaries, for, in many respects, Canada is one huge marketplace. ...

The relative unimportance of provincial boundaries has become progressively more obvious as industry has tended to become more concentrated. Improved communications and transportation have increased the mobility of labour, capital and technology, as well as raw materials and the finished product. ...

With respect to businesses which are confined to Canada, with few exceptions, any individual or corporation, including a provincially incorporated corporation, has the capacity to "walk across" provincial boundaries in order to buy or sell, lend or borrow, hire or fire. In the absence of artificial impediments, therefore, the market for goods and services is competitive on a national basis, and provincial legislation cannot be an effective regulator.

Among the materials filed in this appeal by the Attorney-General of Canada was a study prepared by A.E. Safarian for the Government of Canada, entitled "Canadian Federalism and Economic Integration" (1974), which states a similar point at p. 58:

> Competition policy can be used most effectively to support the common market if it is within federal power. With mobility of goods, it is quite unrealistic to attempt to maintain diverse provincial competition policies. The more competitive structure of industry in one or more provinces would tend to impose competitive conditions on the other provinces. In such circumstances, any provincial authority which was more tolerant of monopoly or combinations than other provincial authorities would be forced to resort to protection against interprovincial imports and might be tempted to subsidize interprovincial exports. By contrast, the point of a federal common market is precisely to allow consumers and producers anywhere in Canada free access to supplies and markets across Canada.

It is evident from this discussion that competition cannot be effectively regulated unless it is regulated nationally. As I have said, in my view combines legislation fulfills the three indicia of national scope as described in *Canadian National Transportation*: it is legislation "aimed at the economy as a single integrated national unit rather than as a collection of separate local enterprises," it is legislation "that the provinces jointly or severally would be constitutionally incapable of passing" and "failure to include one or more provinces or localities would jeopardize successful operation" of the legislation "in other parts of the country."

The above arguments also answer the claim of the Attorney General of Quebec that the regulation of competition does not fall within federal jurisdiction in its intraprovincial dimension and thus the Act should be read down so that s. 31.1 only applies to interprovincial trade. Quebec relies on two points to support its position. First, in the Interim Report on Competition Policy of the Canadian Economic Council, the Report which the federal government relies on to show that competition is exclusively federal, there is a passage at p. 108 that recognizes that the provinces have an important role to play in local competition laws:

> We would like to make it emphatically clear that in recommending such a test we intend no implication whatever that the federal government should seek exclusive occupancy of the

field of competition policy under civil law, or that only the federal government is competent to manage competition policy in Canada. On the contrary, while it is clear that a considerable proportion of Canadian economic activity crosses provincial and international boundaries, and would be impossible to subject effectively to any provincial competition policy, we believe that the provinces could play a most useful role in respect of other lines of activity under their existing constitutional powers. Their assumption of such a role would be a most welcome development. If the recommendations of this Report are largely framed in terms of federal legislation, this is because a federal presence is clearly indispensable and the federal government has hitherto been, to all intents and purposes, the sole active occupant of the field. But the door to provincial participation should be left widely ajar. Such activity by the provinces would be in many ways a natural extension of their already considerable activity in the field of consumer protection.

The second point is that provincial law, both Civil Code and common law, already provides some remedies for unfair competition, as in the *Rocois Construction Inc. v. Quebec Ready Mix*, [1985] 2 FC 40, 64 NR 209, case where the suit was brought under art. 1053 of the *Civil Code*, as well as s. 31.1 of the *Combines Investigation Act*. Quebec points out that in the United States, forty-three states have adopted competition acts to combat local restraints on trade, in coordination with the federal government.

The arguments made above offer a response to these points. They make it clear that not only is the Act meant to cover intraprovincial trade, but that it must do so if it is to be effective. Because regulation of competition is so clearly of national interest and because competition cannot be successfully regulated by federal legislation which is restricted to interprovincial trade, the Quebec argument must fail. I also note that, contrary to the view of Marceau J in the Trial Division of the Federal Court in *Quebec Ready Mix, supra*, at p. 208, that the presence of an already existing action in Quebec law does not argue for invalidating federal legislation. I would repeat what I said at p. 175 of *Multiple Access, supra* (which words were also quoted by MacGuigan J in the Court of Appeal's judgment in *Attorney General of Canada v. Quebec Ready Mix, supra*, at p. 78): "The validity of the federal legislation must be determined without heed to the … [provincial] legislation."

On the other hand, competition is not a single matter, any more than inflation or pollution. The provinces too, may deal with competition in the exercise of their legislative powers in such fields as consumer protection, labour relations, marketing and the like. The point is, however, that Parliament also has the constitutional power to regulate intraprovincial aspects of competition.

In sum, the *Combines Investigation Act* is a complex scheme of competition regulation aimed at improving the economic welfare of the nation as a whole. It operates under a regulatory agency. It is designed to control an aspect of the economy that must be regulated nationally if it is to be successfully regulated at all. As Linden J of the Ontario High Court of Justice said, when discussing the Act at p. 32 in *R v. Hoffman-La Roche* (1981), 33 OR (2d) 694, 62 CCC (2d) 118 at p. 191:

> It is part of a legislative scheme aimed at deterring a wide range of unfair competitive practices that affect trade and commerce generally across Canada, and is not limited to a single industry, commodity or area. The conduct being prohibited is generally of national and of international scope. The presence or absence of healthy competition may affect the welfare

of the economy of the entire nation. It is, therefore, within the sphere of the federal Parliament to seek to regulate such competition in the interest of all Canadians.

I am therefore of the view that the *Combines Investigation Act* as a whole is *intra vires* Parliament as legislation in relation to general trade and commerce and I would reiterate the conclusion I reached in *Canadian National Transportation, supra*, at p. 278:

> A scheme aimed at the regulation of competition is in my view an example of the genre of legislation that could not practically or constitutionally be enacted by a provincial government. Given the free flow of trade across provincial borders guaranteed by s. 121 of the *Constitution Act, 1867* Canada is, for economic purposes, a single huge marketplace. If competition is to be regulated at all it must be regulated federally. This fact leads to the syllogism cited by Hogg and Grover, "The Constitutionality of the Competition Bill" (1977), 1 *Can. Bus. LJ* 197, at p. 200:
>
> > ... regulation of the competitive sector of the economy can be effectively accomplished only by federal action. If there is no federal power to enact a competition policy, then Canada cannot have a competition policy. The consequence of a denial of federal constitutional power is therefore, in practical effect, a gap in the distribution of legislative powers.

[Chief Justice Dickson went on to conclude that the necessary link between s. 31.1 and the Act existed. He found that s. 31.1 was "an integral, well-conceived component of the economic regulation strategy found in the *Combines Investigation Act*." He held that this degree of connection clearly satisfied the "functionally related" test (which was deemed to be the proper test given the limited intrusion on provincial powers) and would even have passed the stricter test of "necessarily incidental."]

Appeal dismissed.

NOTES AND QUESTIONS

1. The two criteria that Dickson CJC adds to the those posited by Laskin CJC in *Vapor Canada* for a valid exercise of the general trade power invoke the concept of "provincial inability" that was also central to the Supreme Court of Canada's articulation of the national concern branch of the p.o.g.g. power in *R v. Crown Zellerbach Ltd.*, [1988] 1 SCR 401, decided one year earlier. A discussion of the meaning and implications of the provincial inability test is found in the notes following *Crown Zellerbach* in Chapter 9, Peace, Order, and Good Government.

2. The general regulation of trade doctrine has been discussed as a possible source of federal jurisdiction over securities regulation and the implementation of international trade obligations. For discussion of the trade issue, see Robert Howse, "NAFTA and the Constitution: Does *Labour Conventions* Really Matter Any More?" (1994), 5 *Constitutional Forum* 54.

3. A more balanced approach to the use of the general trade and commerce power has been urged by John Whyte ("Constitutional Aspects of Economic Development Policy" in R. Simeon, ed., *Division of Powers and Public Policy* (Toronto: University of Toronto Press, 1985), at 44-46):

The prime obstacle to national economic regulatory authority is the recognition that there are no manifest dividing lines between the regulation of general trade and the regulation of all aspects of the nation's economic activity. If Parliament may enact legislation which, as in *MacDonald v. Vapor Canada Ltd.*, [[1997], 2 SCR 134] requires persons engaged in any form of business activity to conduct their business affairs according to "honest industrial and commercial usage in Canada," then, so the concern goes, it may enact legislation requiring business to do or desist from doing anything regardless of how small the enterprise, how local its economic impact, how limited its market. The constitutional powers of provinces over "property and civil rights" (the power over contracting) and "matters of merely local and private nature" (the power to develop provincial social and economic environments), would be obliterated. What is needed is a conception of federal power that enables national standards, goals and policies to be pursued while leaving room for provinces to stipulate certain conditions and features for the provincial marketplace.

Let us first state a conception of the Canadian federal state that would support a federal, general economic power and still leave provinces constitutional room to determine their own economic patterns. That conception is expressed in the *Constitution Act, 1867*, and is based on that document's clear concern with nation building—with activities that produce a nation state that despite its illogicality in terms of geography, will function as a single state and as an economically viable whole. This view explains the limited form of economic union represented by s. 121 of the *Constitution Act, 1867* and the special place of interconnecting (or nation-creating) transportation and communication systems created by s-ss. (a), (b) and (c) of s. 92(10). Economic survival and economic viability are implicit aims in the structure of the division of powers. If Canada's economic survival in the last decades of the 20th century demands increased coherence in the governmental shaping of economic activity, then the implicit message of ss. 91 and 92, it is argued, is that the economic regulatory powers to meet this need must be seen to be present. The power, in s. 91(2), of regulation of trade and commerce may mean something limited throughout much of the 1900s; but it can mean something different and more intrusive when there are increased demands for governmental management of economic development.

In this way it might be appropriate to make an analogy between the potential of the federal trade and commerce power and the potential of the peace, order and good government clause. Both heads of power could, by a literal reading of their terms, sustain immense realms of legislative authority. Both heads, out of the need to preserve some scope for provincial autonomy, have been read in limited ways. At times the meaning given to these large general powers has been extremely limited. The peace, order and good government clause has been equated to a federal emergency power, and the trade and commerce power has been held to be auxiliary to other heads of federal power. Yet for both heads there have been other roles recognized; the general trade regulation capacity of s. 91(2) has never been denied at a theoretical level, and the peace, order and good government clause has occasionally sustained legislation in matters of a national dimension.

The analogy is even more direct. The national dimension idea of peace, order and good government is the right idea by which we can understand federal jurisdiction over trade and commerce. When the governmental management of trading activity is in response to a generally experienced need, and when it can be demonstrated that the mechanisms of state involvement in the economy are general mechanisms dependent on national implementation and national coordination, then the general trade idea of trade and commerce will be properly available as constitutional support.

The generality and genuineness of need for national trade regulation are, however, only the background conditions for judicial recognition of substantive content to Parliament's general trade jurisdiction under the trade and commerce power. More precise conditions for this recognition need to be spelled out. These conditions should include, first, the requirement that actual federal regulation be general in conception—that it be directed toward economic goals that transcend the needs of specific economic or industrial sectors. This is not to say that the administration of policies that have been developed to satisfy the general goals cannot entail specific sectoral applications. It is, of course, a truism that even generally expressed standards or proscriptions must be applied in particular instances. The tolerance for sectoral application of general federal trade policies goes further. It would permit regulations and even primary legislation to be expressed in terms of specific industries, occupations or activities, so long as the legislation was clearly relatable to general economic goals or was clearly an application of a general economic strategy.

A second condition for the exercise of federal authority would be the recognition of some form of provincial paramountcy. General federal regulation is tolerable only as long as it does not disrupt established provincial patterns of economic organization. The establishment of a doctrine of provincial immunity from federal trade regulation is based on the great value of provincial trade regimes in the sense that, for many aspects of trading activity and economic regulation, the provinces are best situated to determine what is appropriate for the circumstances and what is likely to be effective. When, through provincial legislation, a pattern of economic activity has been established—for example, the creation of a monopoly within the province, or the allocation, by public authority, of segments of markets to certain traders—federal policies ought not to disrupt those patterns except in the most compelling circumstances.

The third condition follows from the second; provincial paramountcy must itself be set aside in circumstances in which Parliament has expressly determined that its policies must, for compelling reasons of economic health, prevail and be in force in the nation without any exceptions.

The Supreme Court of Canada has had only one further opportunity to consider the general trade power since the *General Motors* decision in 1989—in 2005 in *Kirkbi v. Ritvik Holdings*, in which it upheld a civil remedy for passing-off found in the federal *Trade-marks Act*.

Kirkbi AG v. Ritvik Holdings Inc.
[2005] 3 SCR 302, 2005 SCC 65, 259 DLR (4th) 577

[Kirkbi held the patents for LEGO construction sets. When the patents expired in Canada, Ritvik (which subsequently became Mega Bloks Inc.), a Canadian toy manufacturer, began manufacturing and selling bricks that were interchangeable with LEGO. Kirkbi tried to assert a trademark in the "LEGO *indicia*": the upper surface of the block with eight studs distributed in a regular geometric pattern. When the Registrar of Trademarks refused registration, Kirkbi claimed the LEGO *indicia* as an unregistered mark and sought a declaration that it had been infringed by Ritvik/Mega Bloks pursuant to s. 7(b) of the *Trade-marks Act*. Section 7(b) creates a civil cause of action, essentially codifying the common law tort of passing-off. Ritvik/Mega Bloks challenged the constitutionality of s. 7(b), arguing that the provision was *ultra vires* the legislative competence of Parliament under s. 91(2) of the *Constitution Act, 1867*.]

LeBEL J (McLachlin CJC and Major, Bastarache, Binnie, Deschamps, Fish, Abella, and Charron JJ concurring):

. . .

B. The Constitutionality of Section 7(b) of the Trade-marks Act

[14] In this appeal, the constitutional validity of s. 7(b) of the *Trade-marks Act* arises in the particular context of an unregistered trade-mark. The respondent challenges the constitutional validity of the impugned provision and submits that s. 7(b) of the *Trade-marks Act* is *ultra vires* the legislative competence of the Parliament of Canada because it is not linked or connected in any way to the trade-mark registration scheme in the Act.

(1) Trade and Commerce

[15] The grant of legislative authority to the Parliament of Canada listed in s. 91 of the *Constitution Act, 1867* does not specify that trade-marks are a component of the federal government's power to legislate. Patents and copyrights are explicitly allocated to federal legislative power (s. 91(22) and (23)). Pursuant to s. 91(2), the federal government has exclusive jurisdiction in relation to trade and commerce. In *Citizens Insurance Co. of Canada v. Parsons* (1881), 7 App. Cas. 96, the Judicial Committee of the Privy Council distinguished two branches of federal power under s. 91(2): (1) the power over international and interprovincial trade and commerce, and (2) the power over general trade and commerce affecting Canada as a whole ("general trade and commerce"). This interpretation of s. 91(2), which limits the scope of the federal trade and commerce power to these two branches, is intended to ensure a proper constitutional balance between the otherwise overlapping federal power over trade and commerce (s. 91(2)) and the provincial power over property and civil rights in the province (s. 92(13)): see A.K. Gill and R.S. Jolliffe, *Fox on Canadian Law of Trade-marks and Unfair Competition* (4th ed. 2002), at p. 2-4.

[16] The "general trade and commerce" category requires an assessment of the relative importance of an activity to the national economy as well as an inquiry into whether an activity should be regulated by Parliament as opposed to the provinces. To determine whether a particular issue requires national rather than local regulation, this Court has set out five criteria to be considered. These criteria are integrated into an assessment of whether federal legislation can be supported on the basis of Parliament's authority over general trade and commerce. They reflect principles which help distinguish the federal trade and commerce power from the provincial property and civil rights power. In two comprehensive decisions dealing with the second branch of s. 91(2) (*Attorney General of Canada v. Canadian National Transportation, Ltd.*, [1983] 2 SCR 206; *General Motors of Canada Ltd. v. City National Leasing*, [1989] 1 SCR 641), Dickson CJ adopted and extended the three indicia initially set out by Laskin CJ in *MacDonald v. Vapor Canada Ltd.*, [1977] 2 SCR 134. These requirements "serve to ensure that federal legislation does not upset the balance of power between federal and provincial governments" (*City National Leasing*, at p. 662).

[Reference is then made to the five factors set out in *General Motors*.]

[18] The federal government's power to legislate with respect to trade-marks has never been the target of a direct constitutional challenge. The issue was raised in the Privy Council in a 1937 decision examining the constitutionality of federal trade-mark legislation. The Privy Council judgment relies, albeit implicitly, on the second branch of the trade and commerce powers under s. 91(2) to confirm Parliament's jurisdiction to enact trade-mark legislation: *Attorney-General for Ontario v. Attorney-General for Canada*, [1937] AC 405. Lord Atkin for the Privy Council commented as follows (at p. 417):

> No one has challenged the competence of the Dominion to pass such legislation. If challenged one obvious source of authority would appear to be the class of subjects enumerated in s. 91(2), the Regulation of trade and commerce, referred to by the Chief Justice. There could hardly be a more appropriate form of the exercise of this power than the creation and regulation of a uniform law of trade marks. ...

[19] The constitutionality of specific provisions of the *Trade-marks Act* has been challenged but the validity of the Act as a whole has never been conclusively determined. The courts have implicitly recognized the validity of this federal legislation in several decisions: ... . The constitutionality of the *Trade-marks Act* as a whole is not challenged on this appeal. I will return to the issue of the constitutional foundation for federal trade-mark legislation and will consider the five criteria outlined by Dickson CJ further below.

(2) Determining the Constitutionality of Section 7(b): The Test to Be Applied

[20] In *City National Leasing*, Dickson CJ set out the proper framework for analysis to determine the characterization of an impugned provision for constitutional purposes. He stressed that the mere fact that a provision codifies a civil cause of action does not necessarily make it *ultra vires* the federal government. Although the creation of civil causes of action is generally a matter of property or civil rights in the province, a finding that a provision standing alone, in its pith and substance, intrudes on provincial powers does not determine its ultimate constitutional validity. At the same time, a provision will not be valid merely because the main provisions of an Act are valid. It is necessary to consider both the impugned provision and the Act as a whole when undertaking constitutional analysis. The nature of the relationship between a provision and the statute determines the extent to which the provision is integrated into otherwise valid legislation. If the legislation is valid and the provision is sufficiently integrated within the scheme, it can be upheld by virtue of that relationship: a provision may take on a valid constitutional cast by the context and association in which it is fixed as complementary provision serving to reinforce other admittedly valid provisions (*Vapor Canada*, at pp. 158-59, *per* Laskin CJ).

· · ·

(3) Application to the Facts of This Case

[22] For ease of reference, I reproduce here s. 7 of the *Trade-marks Act*:

7. No person shall
  (a) make a false or misleading statement tending to discredit the business, wares or services of a competitor;
  (b) direct public attention to his wares, services or business in such a way as to cause or be likely to cause confusion in Canada, at the time he commenced so to direct attention to them, between his wares, services or business and the wares, services or business of another;
  (c) pass off other wares or services as and for those ordered or requested;
  (d) make use, in association with wares or services, of any description that is false in a material respect and likely to mislead the public as to
    (i) the character, quality, quantity or composition,
    (ii) the geographical origin, or
    (iii) the mode of the manufacture, production or performance
  of the wares or services; or
  (e) do any other act or adopt any other business practice contrary to honest industrial or commercial usage in Canada. …

(a) Characterization of the Impugned Provision: Does Section 7(b) Encroach on Provincial Powers?

[LeBel J follows the reasoning in *General Motors* to conclude that although the impugned provision, which creates a civil remedy, encroaches on an important provincial power, the intrusion is minimal.]

(b) The Validity of the Federal Trade-marks Act

[28] In the second stage of the analysis, the Court must determine whether the *Trade-marks Act* is a valid exercise of Parliament's general trade and commerce power. The analysis is guided by the five indicia of validity set out above. In *Asbjorn Horgard A/S* [*Asbjorn Horgard A/S v. Gibbs/Nortac Industries*, [1987] 3 FC 544], MacGuigan JA of the Federal Court of Appeal noted that:

All of the criteria of Chief Justice Dickson are verified in the Act: a national regulatory scheme, the oversight of the Registrar of Trade Marks, a concern with trade in general rather than with an aspect of a particular business, the incapability of the provinces to establish such a scheme and the necessity for national coverage. [p. 559]

The parties do not dispute Parliament's constitutional power to regulate registered trade-marks. Rather, it is Parliament's right to create a civil remedy in relation to an *unregistered trade-mark* that is in issue. The respondent's position is that the only regulatory scheme in the *Trade-marks Act* is the scheme governing registered trade-marks. In my view this is an incorrect characterization of the Act. The *Trade-marks Act* establishes a regulatory scheme for both registered and unregistered trade-marks.

[29] The protection of unregistered trade-marks is integral to the legitimacy, legal standards and efficacy of registered trade-marks. The *Trade-marks Act* is clearly concerned with trade as a whole, as opposed to within a particular industry. There is no question that trade-marks apply across and between industries in different provinces. Divided provincial and federal jurisdiction could mean that the provincial law could be changed by each provincial legislature. This could result in unregistered trade-marks that were more strongly protected than registered trade-marks, undermining the efficacy and integrity of the federal Parliament's *Trade-marks Act*. The lack of a civil remedy integrated into the scheme of the Act, applicable to all marks, registered or unregistered, might also lead to duplicative or conflicting and hence inefficient enforcement procedures.

[30] The *Trade-marks Act* includes numerous provisions relating to unregistered trade-marks: "Parliament by sections 1 to 11 of the *Trade Marks Act* has prescribed a regime concerning what constitutes a trade mark and the adoption thereof, whether registered or not" … . The primary difference between registered and unregistered trade-marks under the Act is that the rights of a holder of a registered trade-mark are more extensive: … Registration of a trade-mark gives the registrant the exclusive right to the use throughout Canada of the trade-mark and a right of action to remedy any infringement of that right: ss. 19-20. In addition, in order to exercise those rights, the existence of the mark itself does not have to be established. Registration is evidence enough. Nonetheless, marks remain marks, whether registered or unregistered, because their legal characteristics are the same.

[31] There is no reason to believe that the registration regime under the *Trade-marks Act* was intended to create two separate enforcement regimes. The scheme set out in the *Trade-marks Act* regulates both registered and unregistered trade-marks. It regulates the adoption, use, transfer, and enforcement of rights in respect of all trade-marks. If trade-marks are intended to protect the goodwill or reputation associated with a particular business and to prevent confusion in the marketplace, then a comprehensive scheme dealing with both registered and unregistered trade-marks is necessary to ensure adequate protection. The inclusion of unregistered trade-marks in the regulatory scheme is necessary to ensure the protection of all trade-marks. The *Trade-marks Act* is more than simply a system of registration.

(c) The Extent of Integration

[32] The final step in the analysis is to determine whether the provision is sufficiently integrated into the otherwise valid statute. The inquiry has two parts. First, it is necessary to determine the appropriate test of "fit", namely "how well the provision is integrated into the scheme of the legislation and how important it is for the efficacy of the legislation" (*City National Leasing*, at p. 668). Once the correct standard is determined, the test is applied on a case-by-case basis. If the provision passes this integration test, it is *intra vires* Parliament as an exercise of the general trade and commerce power. If the provision is not sufficiently integrated into the scheme of regulation, it cannot be sustained under the second branch of s. 91(2). …

[33] As outlined above, s. 7(b) of the Act only minimally intrudes into provincial jurisdiction over property and civil rights. It is a remedial provision limited to trade-

marks as defined in the Act (ss. 2 and 6). ... [Section] 7(b) "rounds out" the federal trade-marks scheme. In this regard s. 7(b) is, in its pith and substance, directly connected to the enforcement of trade-marks and trade-names in Canada because it is directed to avoiding confusion through use of trade-marks.

· · ·

[35] The respondent submits that the civil action in s. 7(b) has no functional connection to the registered trade-mark scheme in the *Trade-marks Act*. Having concluded that the Act creates a scheme regulating both *registered* and *unregistered* trade-marks, the functional relation of s. 7(b) to the scheme in the *Trade-marks Act* is apparent. In its pith and substance, s. 7(b) is directly connected to the enforcement of trade-marks and trade-names in Canada: the civil remedy in s. 7(b) protects the goodwill associated with trade-marks and is directed to avoiding consumer confusion through use of trade-marks. As Gill and Jolliffe note: "No provision of s. 7 is more inextricably linked to the overall scheme of the *Trade-marks Act* than is s. 7(b)" (p. 2-22).

[36] Unlike breach of confidence and appropriation of confidential information (s. 7(e)), the passing-off action plays a clear role in the federal scheme. Without this provision there would be a gap in the legislative protection of trade-marks. This would create inconsistencies in the protection of registered and unregistered trade-marks and lead to uncertainty. Section 7(b) is sufficiently integrated into the federal scheme and, in this respect, is significantly different from s. 7(e). I conclude that s. 7(b) lies within the federal government's legislative competence. I will now turn to the issues of interpretation and application of the Act raised by the present appeal.

[The Court went on to dismiss Kirkbi's claim for passing-off under s. 7(b) of the *Trade-marks Act*, finding that the claim was based on the technical or functional characteristics of the LEGO bricks, which could not be the basis of a trademark, whether registered or unregistered.]

IV. STRENGTHENING THE CANADIAN ECONOMIC UNION

As mentioned above, there has been increasing concern about barriers to internal trade, as well as the ability of Canadian governments to respond effectively to economic issues. Various suggestions for reform have been made, some aimed at strengthening protection against barriers, some at the augmentation of federal legislative powers. While many of these suggestions have contemplated changes to the Constitution, either through amendment or judicial interpretation, reform is also possible through intergovernmental arrangements or policy responses to international competition.

A. Constitutional Reform to Reduce Barriers

During the process of constitutional reform, which resulted in the 1982 amendments to the Constitution, the federal government proposed an amendment to the "common market clause" found in s. 121 of the *Constitution Act, 1867* that would have guaranteed, subject to certain exceptions, the movement of persons, goods, services, and capital across provincial borders without discrimination on the basis of province of origin or destination. That proposal was not accepted, and what made its way into the Constitution was the guarantee of mobility rights found in s. 6 of the Charter.

Section 6(1) confers a right on citizens to enter, remain in, and leave Canada, while s. 6(2) is a guarantee of interprovincial mobility for citizens and permanent residents with respect to employment and residency. The leading cases interpreting s. 6 are *Black and Co. v. Law Society of Alberta*, [1989] 1 SCR 591, 58 DLR (4th) 317, and *Canadian Egg Marketing Agency v. Richardson*, [1998] 3 SCR 157, 166 DLR (4th) 1. Both are discussed above in section I of this chapter.

In the constitutional round that culminated in a national referendum on the Charlottetown Accord in October 1992, the federal government pushed for a strengthened s. 121. The following excerpt illustrates the way in which the initial proposal was reformulated by the Special Joint Committee of the Senate and House of Commons on a Renewed Canada (the Beaudoin-Dobbie Committee).

Report of the Special Joint Committee of the Senate and the House of Commons,
A Renewed Canada
(Ottawa: Queen's Printer, 28 February 1992)
(Co-chairs: Hon. G.-A. Beaudoin and D. Dobbie)

The Common Market—Section 121

Section 121 of the *Constitution Act, 1867* would be replaced by the following section. A mechanism for resolving disputes concerning the application of this section is also required, but has not been included in this draft.

Free movement of goods, etc.
    121(1) Canada is an economic union within which goods, services, persons and capital may move freely.

Prohibitions or restrictions
    (2) The Parliament and Government of Canada, the provincial legislatures and governments and the territorial councils and governments shall not by law or practice impose any prohibition or restriction that is inconsistent with subsection (1) and is based on provincial or territorial boundaries if the prohibition or restriction impedes the efficient functioning of the economic union and constitutes a means of arbitrary discrimination or a disguised restriction of trade across provincial or territorial boundaries.

Saving
    (3) Subsection (2) does not invalidate a restriction or prohibition imposed by or under
        (a) a federal law enacted to further the principles of equalization or regional development;
        (b) a provincial or territorial law enacted to reduce economic disparities between regions wholly within a province or territory; or
        (c) a federal, provincial or territorial law enacted for
            (i) public protection, safety or health,

(ii) the establishment and functioning of government-owned corporations exercising monopolies in the public interest, or

(iii) the preservation of existing marketing and supply management systems in the national, provincial or territorial interest, subject to Canada's international commitments.

Federal–provincial agreement

(4) The federal, provincial and territorial governments shall seek agreement on equivalent national standards for mutual implementation to enhance the mobility of persons and to further the well-being of Canadians wherever they live or work in Canada.

No derogation from s. 6 of the Canadian Charter of Rights and Freedoms

(5) Nothing in this section abrogates or derogates from the mobility rights guaranteed by section 6 of the *Canadian Charter of Rights and Freedoms*.

QUESTIONS

1. Would this section be effective to deal with the barriers discussed throughout this chapter? Consider its impact with respect to discrimination in government contracting, diversity in legislated product standards, and marketing board quotas such as those seen in the note on *Re Agricultural Products Marketing Act*, in Section II, above.

2. Consider Robert Howse's criticism of this and other proposals in *Economic Union, Social Justice, and Constitutional Reform: Towards a High But Level Playing Field*, Background Studies of the York University Constitutional Reform Project, Study No. 9 (Toronto: York University Centre for Public Law and Public Policy, 1992), at 1-5 (footnotes omitted):

In the alternative, the study proposes a *political* theory of economic integration. At the core of this theory is a notion of equal economic citizenship, which holds that Canadians should not have their economic opportunities unreasonably impeded on the basis of their place of residence within the federation.

The theory recognizes that equal economic opportunity is consistent with, and indeed *requires*, positive government policies that enhance opportunities for disadvantaged groups and regions, and that address the dislocation costs of economic change—especially where those costs fall disproportionately on particular groups or regions.

Some policies and practices, however, may involve discrimination against out-of-province residents that is largely arbitrary, that may constitute a form of pure protection for politically powerful intraprovincial interests, or, in the case of federal policies, may represent an attempt to buy votes in particular regions or communities. Under a theory of equal economic citizenship, it is such discriminatory and unjustifiably protectionist policies and practices that require strict constitutional scrutiny. In addition, there are other laws and policies that serve legitimate public goals, but could be replaced by policy instruments that are less restrictive of economic mobility, or that do not discriminate so sharply against citizens residing in other provinces or regions of Canada. These laws and policies, as well, should be subject to constitutional review.

This approach differs profoundly from the tone and intent of other, neo-conservative proposals for strengthening the economic union. These proposals proceed from the notion that the Canadian economy is currently over-regulated, or over-governed, and that barriers to economic mobility are undesirable, not because they are discriminatory or unnecessarily harmful to the individual's economic opportunities, but because they interfere with the "magic of the marketplace."

3. Should a revised s. 121 be enforced through the courts or some other institution, perhaps a special tribunal with expertise in economic or social policy matters? See the Agreement on Internal Trade, discussed next.

B. Constitutional Change Through Intergovernmental Cooperation: The Agreement on Internal Trade

In 1994, the federal, provincial, and territorial governments signed a major Agreement on Internal Trade (AIT), a document over 200 pages in length that commits the parties to remove various trade barriers and to increase harmonization in areas such as the environment and occupational qualifications. The general rules commit the parties to reciprocal non-discrimination, prohibit governments from imposing measures that limit the movement of persons, goods, services, or investments across provincial and territorial boundaries, and require governments to ensure that their policies and practices do not have the effect of creating obstacles to trade. The Agreement also recognizes that there are "legitimate objectives" that can limit the application of the previous rules, such as consumer or environmental protection or public health and safety. Such objectives must not be more trade restrictive than necessary to meet the legitimate objective or impair unduly the access of persons, goods, services, and investments that meet the legitimate objective.

The Agreement contains its own dispute settlement procedures, which culminate in mediation and arbitration by a specialized panel, rather than the courts. Should a party fail to comply with a panel decision, other parties can impose sanctions. Finally, the Agreement expressly provides that the contents do not alter the legislative authority of Parliament or the provincial or territorial legislatures (art. 300). A significant decision was issued by a 1998 AIT panel in the MMT case (see www.intrasec.mb.ca). The decision is described in the following excerpt from David Schneiderman, "The Old and New Constitutionalism," in Janine Brodie, ed., *Reinventing Canada: Politics of the 21st Century* (Toronto: Pearson Education Canada, 2003):

> Operating at the level of an intergovernmental agreement, the scheme appears innocuous enough. An AIT panel decision that thwarted the federal government's plans to ban the manganese-based fuel additive MMT, however, should have brought the AIT to greater prominence.
>
> MMT has been blended in gasoline fuel sold in Canada for almost twenty years. Invoking environmental, health, and consumer protection grounds, the federal government moved to prohibit the importation and interprovincial trade in MMT in June 1997. The Ethyl Corporation of Richmond, Virginia, the sole producer of MMT, answered by invoking the investment-protection provisions of the North American Free Trade Agreement (NAFTA), claiming $250 million (US) in damages as compensation for the alleged expropriation of the company's investment interests. [See section IV(D), below, for a more detailed discussion of NAFTA's implications for the Canadian economic union.]

The government of Alberta (supported by three provinces) also filed an AIT complaint against the federal government for prohibiting interprovincial movement of MMT. The decision by an AIT dispute panel ultimately preempted Ethyl's NAFTA claim. The AIT was armed with enough ammunition to force the federal government to back down. By a vote of 4 to 1, the dispute panel held that the federal ban on MMT was inconsistent with the AIT. According to the panel, the scientific evidence concerning the effects of MMT on vehicle emission systems and on the environment was "inconclusive." The panel did concede that there was a "reasonable basis" for the federal government to limit access to MMT in the interests of promoting environmental objectives. But the panel was not willing to give the benefit of the doubt to the federal government in any other respect. The panel, instead, adopted a strict approach to interpretation of the AIT—an approach most favourable to the complaining provinces, oil refiners, and to free trade. By blocking the movement of MMT across provincial borders, the AIT panel concluded, the federal initiative ran afoul of the agreement. One year later, the government of Canada paid Ethyl the sum of $13 million (US), representing legal fees and lost profits, rescinded the legislation, and admitted publicly that the use of MMT poses no environmental or health risks.

Though the scientific evidence of health risks associated with MMT may be ambiguous, Canada remains one of the few countries in the world where MMT is blended into automotive fuel. MMT was banned for 17 years in the United States by the Environmental Protection Agency (EPA). It was not until a court ruled in 1995 that the EPA had no legal authority to consider health issues under the *Clean Air Act*, that MMT legally was available in the states (though it is still banned in California, with the toughest emission standards). Three years later, the Environmental Defence Fund reports that over 75% of US oil refining capacity remains MMT free.

Some have criticized the extent of the Agreement's obligations, arguing that its reach is too modest. Others are concerned that the Agreement is not legally binding because of the principle of parliamentary sovereignty, which is discussed more fully in Chapter 12, Instruments of Flexibility in the Federal System. For further discussion, see the various chapters in Michael Trebilcock and Daniel Schwanen, eds., *Getting There: An Assessment of the Agreement on Internal Trade* (Toronto: C.D. Howe, 1995); David Cohen, "The Internal Trade Agreement: Furthering the Canadian Economic Disunion?" (1995), 25 *Canadian Business Law Journal* 257; and Bryan Schwartz, "Assessing the Agreement on Internal Trade: The Case for A 'More Perfect Union,'" in Douglas M. Brown and Jonathan W. Rose, eds., *Canada: The State of the Federation 1995* (Kingston, ON: Institute for Intergovernmental Relations, 1995), at 189-217.

C. Constitutional Change Through the Courts

While there have been various proposals to strengthen federal authority through constitutional amendment, none has received much support. Nevertheless, a number of commentators have suggested that the Supreme Court would be supportive of a more active federal role in the economy, should the federal government have the political will to act unilaterally in areas such as securities regulation or the setting of professional qualifications.

Support for this view is drawn from the statements of La Forest J in *Hunt v. T & N Plc*, [1993] 4 SCR 289, 109 DLR (4th) 16. In *Hunt*, Quebec legislation prevented the removal of business records from the province for use in judicial proceedings in another province. The Court held that the provincial law was inapplicable to the extent that it prevented the discovery of records in a British Columbia proceeding. Justice La Forest, for the Court, made mention of the Canadian common market, noting that to apply the provincial law would lead to higher transactional costs for interprovincial transactions that would "constitute an infringement on the unity and efficiency of the Canadian market-place, ... as well as unfairness to the citizen" (at 45 DLR). He drew on his earlier reasons in *Morguard Investments Ltd. v. De Savoye*, [1990] 3 SCR 1077, 76 DLR (4th) 256, where he wrote: "the business community operates in a world economy and we correctly speak of a world community even in the face of decentralized political and legal power. Accommodating the flow of wealth, skills and people across state lines has now become imperative" (at 1098 SCR).

In *Hunt* Justice La Forest also affirmed the view that Parliament has the authority to legislate respecting the recognition and enforcement of judgments, an issue "ultimately related to the rights of the citizen, trade and commerce and other federal legislative powers, including that encompassed in the peace, order and good government clause" (at 42 DLR).

For contrasting views on *Hunt*, see Vaughan Black and A. Wayne McKay, "Constitutional Alchemy in the Supreme Court: *Hunt v. T&N Plc*" (1995), 5 *National Journal of Constitutional Law* 79 and Joel Bakan, Bruce Ryder, David Schneiderman, and Margot Young, "Developments in Constitutional Law: The 1993-94 Term" (1995), 6 *Supreme Court Law Review* (2d) 67, at 119-25. Black and McKay applaud the Court for looking "beyond the express text of the constitution to find core values and concepts" of the Canadian constitution. Bakan et al., in contrast, characterize the Court as adopting "neo-liberal themes" in order to justify constitutional interpretation lacking in textual support that is "consistent with, and surely influenced by, the political and economic restructuring resulting from NAFTA."

For contrasting views on the role of the courts in expanding federal jurisdiction, see Robert Howse, *Securing the Canadian Economic Union* (Toronto: C.D. Howe Institute, 1996) and Katherine Swinton, "Courting Our Way to Economic Integration: Judicial Review and Canadian Economic Union" (1995), 25 *Canadian Business Law Journal* 280. Professor Howse concludes that the federal government could take a more active legislative role to deal with provincial trade barriers, while Professor Swinton argues that many of the significant barriers could not be addressed without a major shift in power to the federal level, which the courts would be unlikely to support in light of current case law.

D. Constitutional Change Through International Agreements

Finally, even without formal constitutional change or concerted federal and provincial action, internal trade barriers may be coming down. The effect of international trade agreements to which Canada is a signatory, such as the Uruguay-Round General Agreement on Tariffs and Trade (GATT), now enforced by the World Trade Organization, or the North American Free Trade Agreement (NAFTA) may reduce the ability of governments to erect trade barriers because of international standards and sanctions. For example, the supply management techniques of the marketing boards described earlier in this chapter will have to be modified over the next few years, as the World Trade Organization rules will allow tariffs on agricultural products, but not import controls.

The investment-protection provisions in NAFTA also may have the effect of shifting Canadian constitutionalism further in the direction of removing barriers to economic movement. This may be accomplished by empowering foreign investors to sue for violations of NAFTA's investment chapter. Chapter Eleven commits Canada, Mexico, and the United States to equal treatment (or "non-discrimination") as between foreign investors and resident investors. Foreign investors are entitled to trigger NAFTA's dispute settlement mechanism and may seek damages for state violations of NAFTA obligations. Among other obligations in NAFTA, of particular interest is the rule concerning expropriations. The rule prohibits "direct or indirect" expropriations or measures "tantamount to" expropriation (Art. 1110). The rule has been invoked by a variety of investors from the United States in order to challenge Canadian laws and regulations that, in their view, impact so negatively on an investment interest that they amount to expropriation. There are reports that Ontario's proposed public auto insurance plan (under the NAFTA's predecessor, the Canada-US Free Trade Agreement) and the cancellation of contracts to transfer public property into private hands at Toronto's Pearson Airport triggered threats of litigation. Two large US tobacco manufacturers threatened to challenge a Canadian federal government initiative that would have mandated the plain packaging of cigarettes sold in Canada—all cigarettes sold in Canada would have been packaged in plain, brown paper wrapping. The tobacco companies alleged that this would be a compensable taking of their trade "dress" and trade marks under NAFTA and threatened to sue for hundreds of millions of dollars in compensation (see David Schneiderman, "NAFTA's Takings Rule: American Constitutionalism Comes to Canada" (1996), 46 *University of Toronto Law Journal* 499).

The Ethyl Corporation's challenge of a Canadian ban on the import and export of the toxic gasoline additive MMT has already been discussed in the context of the Agreement on Internal Trade (see Section IV.B, above). The classification of MMT as a "dangerous toxin," Ethyl claimed, amounted to an expropriation under NAFTA. The Canadian federal government settled the Ethyl claim for US$13 million subsequent to losing an interprovincial trade dispute under the non-binding Agreement on Internal Trade. In another dispute, United Parcel Service is claiming $230 million in lost profits as a result of Canada Post cross-subsidizing courier services with profits generated from its publicly funded regular delivery service. Not all disputes emanate from US firms. In a reverse-Ethyl case, Vancouver-based Methanex is suing for losses suffered by the phasing out of the gasoline additive MTBE in the state of California.

The constitutional nature of NAFTA's investment chapter was highlighted in the Separate Opinion of Bryan Schwartz issued by the NAFTA dispute panel in the *S.D. Myers Inc. v. Government of Canada* case (40 *International Legal Materials* 1408, at 1447-92). Trade agreements like NAFTA "have an enormous impact on public affairs in many countries" he wrote. Schwartz likened these agreements to "a country's constitution" in that "[t]hey restrict the ways in which governments can act and they are very hard to change." While governments usually have the right to withdraw with notice, Schwartz admits that this "is often practically impossible to do" because "[p]ulling out of a trade agreement may create too much risk of reverting to trade wars, and may upset the settled expectations of many participants in the economy." Amendment is made no easier, he writes, "just as it is usually very hard to change a provision of a domestic constitution" (para. 34).

For views on the constitution-like features of NAFTA and its constitutional impacts see, for example, David Schneiderman, "Canadian Constitutionalism and Sovereignty After NAFTA" (1994), 5 *Constitutional Forum* 93; David Schneiderman, "Investment Rules and the New Constitutionalism: Interlinkages and Disciplinary Effects" (2000), 25 *Law and Social Inquiry* 757; and Martin J. Wagner, "International Investment, Expropriation and Environmental Protection" (1999), 29 *Golden Gate University Law Review* 465.

CHAPTER ELEVEN

Criminal Law

I. FEDERAL POWERS OVER CRIMINAL LAW

Section 91(27) of the *Constitution Act, 1867* assigns responsibility over criminal law to the federal Parliament, a choice that stands in contrast to that made in the United States and Australia where criminal law is a state responsibility. The choice to make criminal law an area of national rather than local standards gives rise to two issues that will be explored in this chapter: (1) the scope of the federal power, and (2) the extent to which the existence of this federal power has constrained provincial attempts to control local conditions of public order and morality.

On the first issue, the scope of the federal criminal power, Allan Hutchinson and David Schneiderman have commented as follows:

> The federal government's "exclusive" jurisdiction under section 91(27) has always been a difficult and dynamic category of power to circumscribe: its scope is potentially limitless and can subvert the division of powers between the federal and provincial legislatures. With succinct understatement, Justice Estey was close to the mark when he noted [in *Scowby v. Glendinning*, [1986] 2 SCR 226, at 236] that "criminal law is easier to recognize than to define." In seeking to set some guidelines and limits, the courts have tended to swing between unrealistically narrow and broad interpretations. Striking a considered and consistent balance has proved an elusive task for the courts. ["Smoking Guns: The Federal Government Confronts the Tobacco and Gun Lobbies" (1995), 7:1 *Constitutional Forum* 16, at 16]

As Hutchinson and Schneiderman note, s. 91(27) has experienced fairly dramatic shifts in interpretation. You will recall that in *Reference re The Board of Commerce Act*, [1922] 1 AC 191 (PC), found in Chapter 5, The Early Twentieth Century: The Beginnings of Economic Regulation, Lord Haldane interpreted the criminal law power as "enabling the Dominion Parliament to exercise exclusive legislative power where the subject matter is one which by its very nature belongs to the domain of criminal jurisprudence." He gave incest as an example and, applying this restrictive definition, concluded that the federal *Combines and Fair Prices Act* was not an exercise of the criminal law power. Subsequently, in *Proprietary Articles Trade Association v. AG Canada*, [1931] AC 310 (PC), (PATA) found in Chapter 6, The 1930s: The Depression and the New Deal, Lord Atkin rejected a narrow definition of criminal law that would be restricted to matters that, because of their inherent nature, have traditionally fallen within the domain of criminal jurisprudence. He offered instead a very wide definition of criminal law that included all acts that at any particular period of time are prohibited with penal sanctions. Applying this definition, he concluded that the federal *Combines Investigation Act, 1927* was a valid exercise of the criminal law power.

The modern starting point for any discussion of the federal criminal law power is the judgment of Rand J in the *Margarine Reference*, which follows. Concerned with the impact of a purely formal definition of criminal law in a federal system, Rand J emphasizes the need for a criminal purpose, in addition to the formal requirements of prohibition and penalty, in order for a federal law to be upheld as an exercise of the criminal law power.

Reference re Validity of Section 5(a) of the Dairy Industry Act
(Margarine Reference)
[1949] SCR 1, 1 DLR 433

RAND J: His Excellency in Council has referred to this Court the following question: Is section 5(a) of the *Dairy Industry Act*, RSC 1927, chapter 45, *ultra vires* of the Parliament of Canada either in whole or in part and if so in what particular or particulars and to what extent?

The section is as follows:

> 5. No person shall
>
> (a) manufacture, import into Canada, or offer, sell or have in his possession for sale, any oleomargarine, margarine, butterine, or other substitute for butter, manufactured wholly or in part from any fat other than that of milk or cream. ...

The appearance of the provision in a statute dealing comprehensively with the dairy industry and the inclusion of prohibition of importation, the ordinary mode of protection of industry in its ultimate form, are, for this initial purpose, of considerable significance. On the other hand, the scope and importance of agriculture in the economy of this country, the part played by the dairy industry as an essential branch of it, and the desirability of maintaining a market demand for butter to meet the seasonal exigencies of that industry, are beyond controversy. What, then, in that whole background is the true nature of the enactment?

Mr. Varcoe argues that it is simply a provision of criminal law, a field exclusively Dominion, and the issue, I think, depends upon the validity of that contention. In *Proprietary Articles Trade Ass'n v. A-G Can.*, [1931] 2 DLR 1, [1931] AC 310, Lord Atkin rejected the notion that the acts against which criminal law is directed must carry some moral taint. A crime is an act which the law, with appropriate penal sanctions, forbids; but as prohibitions are not enacted in a vacuum, we can properly look for some evil or injurious or undesirable effect upon the public against which the law is directed. That effect may be in relation to social, economic or political interests; and the legislature has had in mind to suppress the evil or to safeguard the interest threatened. ...

Criminal law is a body of prohibitions; but that prohibition can be used legislatively as a device to effect a positive result is obvious; we have only to refer to Adam Smith's *Wealth of Nations* ... to discover how extensively it has been used not only to keep foreign goods from the domestic market but to prevent manufactures in the colonies for the benefit of home industries ... . The Court in its enquiry is not bound by the *ex facie* form of the statute; and in the ordinary sense of the word, the purpose of a legislative enactment is generally evidential of its true nature or subject matter. ... Under a unitary legislature, all prohibitions may be viewed indifferently as of criminal law, but as the cases cited demonstrate, such a classification is inappropriate to the distribution of legislative power in Canada. *competing intrest / local trade / civil right*

Is the prohibition then enacted with a view to a public purpose which can support it as being in relation to criminal law? Public peace, order, security, health, morality: these are the ordinary though not exclusive ends served by that law, but they do not appear to be the object of the parliamentary action here. That object, as I must find it, is economic and the legislative purpose, to give trade protection to the dairy industry in the production and sale of butter; to benefit one group of persons as against competitors in business in which, in the absence of the legislation, the latter would be free to engage in the provinces. To forbid manufacture and sale for such an end is *prima facie* to deal directly with the civil rights of individuals in relation to particular trade within the provinces ... .

The public interest in this regulation lies obviously in the trade effects: it is annexed to the legislative subject-matter and follows the latter in its allocation to the one or other Legislature. But to use it as a support for the legislation in the aspect of criminal law would mean that the Dominion under its authority in that field, by forbidding the manufacture or sale of particular products, could, in what it considered a sound trade policy, not only interdict a substantial part of the economic life of one section of Canada but do so for the benefit of that of another. Whatever the scope of the regulation of interprovincial trade, it is hard to conceive a more insidious form of encroachment on a complementary jurisdiction. ...

[Rand J then went on to conclude that although the prohibition of manufacture, possession, and sale of margarine was *ultra vires* Parliament, the prohibition of importation could be upheld under the federal government's power to regulate foreign trade, and that it could stand on its own apart from the remainder of the legislation. Taschereau, Kellock, and Estey JJ wrote concurring judgments; Locke J concurred in part; Rinfret CJC and Kerwin J dissented.]

Question answered in the affirmative.

The judgment of the Supreme Court of Canada in the *Margarine Reference* was affirmed by the Privy Council: *Canadian Federation of Agriculture v. AG for Quebec*, [1951] AC 179; [1950] 4 DLR 689 (PC).

NOTES

1. Why did it seem so apparent to Rand J that there was no "public" interest informing protection of the dairy industry? Could it not be argued that a healthy dairy industry was an important component of the overall Canadian economy and hence a benefit to all Canadians?

2. Despite the constraint of "a public purpose which can support it as being in relation to criminal law" imposed in *Margarine Reference*, the criminal law power has remained very broad and has been relied upon by the federal government in enacting a vast array of regulatory legislation beyond the *Criminal Code*, including environmental and health and safety

legislation, as well as combines legislation. Apart from the *Margarine Reference* itself, there have been relatively few occasions where federal laws that meet the formal requirements of criminal law—that is, prohibition and penalty—have been found invalid because of the absence of a criminal law purpose. One notable exception is *Boggs v. The Queen*, [1981] 1 SCR 29, 120 DLR (3d) 718, in which Estey J writing for the Court struck down a section of the *Criminal Code* that made it an offence to drive while one's provincial driver's licence was suspended. Licence suspensions could be imposed not only for violations of the *Criminal Code*, but also for breach of various provincial regulations and failure to pay taxes, judgments, and other fees. The Court concluded that there was no discernible community interest in the criminalization of the administration of such provincial regulatory schemes. Some economic regulation enforced by criminal sanctions has also failed the test of criminal purpose. In *Dominion Stores Ltd. v. The Queen*, [1980] 1 SCR 844, 106 DLR (3d) 581, for example, federal legislation creating national grade names and standards for agricultural products, which left the use of the grade names voluntary in intraprovincial trade but made it an offence to not comply with the standards if the grade names were used, was found to be marketing legislation involving no criminal purpose. As well, in *Labatt Breweries of Canada Ltd. v. AG Canada*, [1980] 1 SCR 914, 110 DLR (3d) 594, discussed further in Section III.B of Chapter 10, Economic Regulation, Estey J refused to find federal commodity standards for food valid under the criminal law power, finding no consumer protection purpose as the legislation was not directed either at the adulteration of food or false or misleading advertising or labelling. In that case, the form of the law, dealing as it did with the "detailed regulation of the brewing industry in the production and sale of its product," may also have contributed to the Court's reluctance to characterize the legislation as criminal law.

3. More recently, in *Ward v. Canada (Attorney General)*, 2002 SCC 17, [2002] 1 SCR 569, a regulation enacted under the federal *Fisheries Act*, RSC 1985, c. F-14 that prohibited the sale of young harp seals and hooded seals was found not to be sustainable under the criminal law power because the legislative history suggested that the legislation was enacted to manage the fisheries by eliminating the large-scale killing and commercial hunting of the young seals, not to criminalize their killing or sale. The regulation was upheld, however, under the fisheries power. One very recent example of a federal law failing to satisfy the test of criminal purpose is the decision of the Quebec Court of Appeal in *Reference re Assisted Human Reproduction Act*, 2008 QCCA, 298 DLR (4th) 712, which found several parts of the federal *Assisted Human Reproduction Act*, SC 2004, c. 2, to be *ultra vires*. A discussion of that decision can be found at the end of this section. As in *Labatt Breweries of Canada Ltd. v. AG Canada*, above, there were also problems with the form of the law.

4. In *R v. Malmo-Levine; R v. Caine*, [2003] 3 SCR 571, 2003 SCC 74, 233 DLR (4th) 415, the Court upheld the prohibition of possession of marijuana in the *Narcotic Control Act*, SC 1960-61, c. 35 (NCA) as a valid exercise of the criminal law power by treating the protection of vulnerable groups from self-inflicted harms as a valid public purpose within the meaning of the *Margarine Reference*. It defended this characterization in the following terms:

> [76] The purpose of the NCA fits within the criminal law power, which includes the protection of vulnerable groups: *Rodriguez v. British Columbia (Attorney General)*, [1993] 3 SCR 519, at p. 595.

[77] The protection of vulnerable groups from self-inflicted harms does not, as [the appellant] argues, amount to no more than "legal moralism." Morality has traditionally been identified as a legitimate concern of the criminal law (*Labatt Breweries [of Canada Ltd. v. AG Canada*, [1980] 1 SCR 914, 110 DLR (3d) 594], at p. 933) although today this does not include mere "conventional standards of propriety" but must be understood as referring to societal values beyond the simply prurient or prudish ... . The protection of ... chronic users ... and adolescents who may not yet have become chronic users, but who have the potential to do so, is a valid criminal law objective. In *R v. Hydro-Québec* [[1997] 3 SCR 213], the Court held at para. 131 that "Parliament has for long exercised extensive control over such matters as food and drugs by prohibitions grounded in the criminal law power." ... In our view, the control of a "psychoactive drug" that "causes alteration of mental function" clearly raises issues of public health and safety, both for the user as well as for those in the broader society affected by his or her conduct.

Do you agree?

In three decisions that are excerpted below—*RJR MacDonald Inc. v. Canada (Attorney General)*, *R v. Hydro-Québec*, and *Reference re Firearms Act (Can.)*—the Supreme Court of Canada provides strong confirmation of the broad scope of the federal criminal law power. As you read the cases, note the ways in which the tests of both purpose and form are being applied.

RJR MacDonald Inc. v. Canada (Attorney General)
[1995] 3 SCR 199, 127 DLR (4th) 1

[The *Tobacco Products Control Act*, SC 1988, c. 20 was enacted by Parliament in 1988. The purpose of the Act was set out in s. 3, which states:

> 3. The purpose of this Act is to provide a legislative response to a national public health problem of substantial and pressing concern and, in particular,
> (a) to protect the health of Canadians in the light of conclusive evidence implicating tobacco use in the incidence of numerous debilitating and fatal diseases;
> (b) to protect young persons and others, to the extent that is reasonable in a free and democratic society, from inducements to use tobacco products and consequent dependence on them; and
> (c) to enhance public awareness of the hazards of tobacco use by ensuring the effective communication of pertinent information to consumers of tobacco products.

The Act prohibited all advertising and promotion of tobacco products offered for sale in Canada, with an exemption for advertising of foreign tobacco products in imported publications. As well, the legislation required the display of unattributed health warnings on all tobacco products and precluded manufacturers from putting other information on tobacco products. Violation of the provisions of the Act constituted an offence punishable by way of summary conviction or indictment, with penalties ranging in seriousness from a fine not exceeding $2,000 or six months' imprisonment to a fine not exceeding $300,000 or two years' imprisonment.

Two tobacco companies challenged the constitutionality of the legislation, seeking declarations that the law was *ultra vires* Parliament as an intrusion into provincial jurisdiction over advertising grounded in ss. 92(13) or (16) of the *Constitution Act, 1867* and that it infringed freedom of expression guaranteed by s. 2(b) of the Charter. A majority of the Supreme Court of Canada found the legislation *intra vires* as a legitimate exercise of the criminal law power, but then went on to declare its central provisions of no force and effect as an unjustifiable infringement of freedom of expression. Only those portions of the judgment dealing with the federalism issue are reproduced here. On that issue, the trial judge had found the legislation to be *ultra vires* as it was in relation to the control of advertising, a provincial matter under ss. 92(13) and (16). The Quebec Court of Appeal concluded that the legislation was *intra vires*, finding that although it could not be sustained under the criminal law power, it was a valid exercise of Parliament's power to legislate for the peace, order and good government of Canada in a matter of national concern.]

LA FOREST J (Lamer CJC, L'Heureux-Dubé, Gonthier, Cory, McLachlin, and Iacobucci JJ concurring): ... The criminal law power is plenary in nature and this Court has always defined its scope broadly. ... In developing a definition of the criminal law, this Court has been careful not to freeze the definition in time or confine it to a fixed domain of activity ... . In *Proprietary Articles Trade Association v. Attorney-General for Canada*, [1931] AC 310 (*PATA*), at p. 324, the Privy Council defined the federal criminal law power in the widest possible terms to include any prohibited act with penal consequences. Subsequent to that decision, this Court recognized that the Privy Council's definition was too broad in that it would allow Parliament to invade areas of provincial legislative competence colourably simply by legislating in the proper form ... . [The] necessary adjustment was introduced in *Reference re Validity of Section 5(a) of the Dairy Industry Act*, [1949] SCR 1 (the *Margarine Reference*). Rand J drew attention ... to the need to identify the evil or injurious effect at which a penal prohibition was directed. ...

Taking into account the broad definition of the criminal law developed by this Court, I am satisfied that the Act is, in pith and substance, criminal law ... . From a plain reading of the Act, it seems clear that Parliament's purpose in enacting this legislation was to prohibit three categories of acts: advertisement of tobacco products (ss. 4 and 5), promotion of tobacco products (ss. 6 to 8) and sale of tobacco products without printed health warnings (s. 9). These prohibitions are accompanied by penal sanctions under s. 18 of the Act, which, as Lord Atkin noted in *PATA* ... creates at least a *prima facie* indication that the Act is criminal law. However, the crucial further question is whether the Act also has an underlying criminal public purpose in the sense described by Rand J in the *Margarine Reference*. ...

In these cases, the evil targeted by Parliament is the detrimental health effects caused by tobacco consumption. This is apparent from s. 3, the Act's "purpose" clause ... . Quite clearly, the common thread running throughout the three enumerated purposes ... is a concern for public health and, more specifically, a concern with protecting Canadians from the hazards of tobacco consumption. This is a valid concern. A copious body of evidence was introduced at trial demonstrating convincingly, and this was not disputed by the appellants, that tobacco consumption is widespread in Canadian society and that it poses serious risks to the health of a great number of Canadians. ...

It appears, then, that the detrimental health effects of tobacco consumption are both dramatic and substantial. Put bluntly, tobacco kills. Given this fact, can Parliament validly employ the criminal law to prohibit tobacco manufacturers from inducing Canadians to consume these products, and to increase public awareness concerning the hazards of their use? In my view, there is no question that it can. "Health," of course, is not an enumerated head under the *Constitution Act, 1867*. As Estey J observed in *Schneider v. The Queen*, [1982] 2 SCR 112, at p. 142:

> ... "health" is not a matter which is subject to specific constitutional assignment but instead is an amorphous topic which can be addressed by valid federal or provincial legislation, depending in the circumstances of each case on the nature or scope of the health problem in question.

Given the "amorphous" nature of health as a constitutional matter, and the resulting fact that Parliament and the provincial legislatures may both validly legislate in this area, it is important to emphasize once again the plenary nature of the criminal law power. In the *Margarine Reference* ... Rand J made it clear that the protection of "health" is one of the "ordinary ends" served by the criminal law, and that the criminal law power may validly be used to safeguard the public from any "injurious or undesirable effect." The scope of the federal power to create criminal legislation with respect to health matters is broad, and is circumscribed only by the requirements that the legislation must contain a prohibition accompanied by a penal sanction and must be directed at a legitimate public health evil. If a given piece of federal legislation contains these features, and if that legislation is not otherwise a "colourable" intrusion upon provincial jurisdiction, then it is valid as criminal law. ...

As I have indicated, it is clear that this legislation is directed at a public health evil and that it contains prohibitions accompanied by penal sanctions. Is it colourable? In my view, it is not. Indeed, it is difficult to conceive what Parliament's purpose could have been in enacting this legislation apart from the reduction of tobacco consumption and the protection of public health. ... [I]f Parliament's intent had been to regulate the tobacco industry as an industry, and not merely to combat the ancillary health effects resulting from tobacco consumption, then it would surely have enacted provisions that relate to such matters as product quality, pricing and labour relations ... . [T]here is no evidence in the present cases that Parliament had an ulterior motive in enacting this legislation, or that it was attempting to intrude unjustifiably upon provincial powers under ss. 92(13) and (16). It thus differs from the *Margarine Reference* where the prohibition was not really directed at curtailing a public evil, but was in reality, in pith and substance, aimed at regulating the dairy industry.

Why, then, has Parliament chosen to prohibit tobacco advertising, and not tobacco consumption itself? In my view, there is a compelling explanation for this choice. It is not that Parliament was attempting to intrude colourably upon provincial jurisdiction but that a prohibition upon the sale or consumption of tobacco is not a practical policy option at this time. It must be kept in mind that the very nature of tobacco consumption makes government action problematic. ... Given the addictive nature of tobacco products, and the fact that over one-third of Canadians smoke, it is clear that a legislative prohibition on the sale and use of tobacco products would be highly impractical. ... As legislators in

this country discovered earlier in the century, the prohibition of a social drug such as tobacco or alcohol leads almost inevitably to an increase in smuggling and crime.

However, the mere fact that it is not practical or realistic to implement a prohibition
on the use or manufacture of tobacco products does not mean that Parliament cannot,
or should not, resort to other intermediate policy options. ...

This Court has long recognized that Parliament may validly employ the criminal law
power to prohibit or control the manufacture, sale and distribution of products that present a danger to public health, and that Parliament may also validly impose labelling and
packaging requirements on dangerous products with a view to protecting public health.

[Reference is then made to a number of cases including *R v. Wetmore*, [1983] 2 SCR 284,
2 DLR (4th) 577 in which offences under the federal *Food and Drug Act* of manufacturing drugs under unsanitary conditions and deceptive labelling of drugs were upheld as
criminal law.]

Moreover, in my view ... the federal criminal law power to legislate with respect to
dangerous goods also encompasses the power to legislate with respect to health warnings
on dangerous goods. Since health warnings serve to alert Canadians to the potentially
harmful consequences of the use of dangerous products, the power to prohibit sales
without these warnings is simply a logical extension of the federal power to protect public health by prohibiting the sale of the products themselves. ...

From the foregoing, it is clear that Parliament could, if it chose, validly prohibit the
manufacture and sale of tobacco products under the criminal law power on the ground
that these products constitute a danger to public health. Such a prohibition would be
directly analogous to the prohibitions on dangerous drugs and unsanitary foods or poisons mentioned earlier, which quite clearly fall within the federal criminal law power. In
my view, once it is accepted that Parliament may validly legislate under the criminal law
power with respect to the manufacture and sale of tobacco products, it logically follows
that Parliament may also validly legislate under that power to prohibit the advertisement
of tobacco products and sales of products without health warnings. In either case, Parliament is legislating to effect the same underlying criminal public purpose: protecting
Canadians from harmful and dangerous products. ...

The foregoing considerations, it seems to me, are sufficient to establish that the pith
and substance of the Act is criminal law for the purpose of protecting public health and
that Parliament accordingly has the legislative authority under s. 91(27) of the *Constitution Act, 1867* to enact this legislation. However, I think it right to address directly the
three principal arguments raised by the appellants in support of their submission that the
Act is not valid as criminal law. ...

I. Affinity of the Act with a Traditional Criminal Law Concern

The appellants' first argument is that the Act is not a valid exercise of the criminal law
power because it does not involve conduct having an affinity with a traditional criminal
law concern. The appellants observe that both tobacco consumption and tobacco advertising have always been legal in this country and, on this basis, argue that this legislation
does not serve a "public purpose commonly recognized as being criminal in nature." ...

In my view, this argument fails because it neglects the well-established principle that the definition of the criminal law is not "frozen as of some particular time." ... It has long been recognized that Parliament's power to legislate with respect to the criminal law must, of necessity, include the power to create new crimes. ...

[La Forest J then deals quickly with the second argument that Parliament cannot criminalize an activity ancillary to an "evil" if it does not criminalize the "evil" itself, emphasizing once again that Parliament is allowed to choose a "circuitous path" to accomplish its goals as long as the goals are constitutionally valid. In this case, Parliament's underlying purpose was clearly to eradicate the practice of tobacco consumption.]

III. The Creation of Exemptions Under the Criminal Law Power

The appellants' third argument is that the Act is fundamentally regulatory, not criminal, in nature. In support of this argument, they observe that the Act contains exemptions for publications and broadcasts originating outside Canada. ... The practical effect of these exemptions, the appellants argue, is that the very same act can be legal when committed by one party in Canada but illegal when committed by another.

In my view, this argument fails because it disregards the long-established principle that the criminal law may validly contain exemptions for certain conduct without losing its status as criminal law. As early as 1959, in *Lord's Day Alliance of Canada v. Attorney General of British Columbia*, [1959] SCR 497, this Court held that the *Lord's Day Act*, RSC 1952, c. 171, which prohibited gambling on Sunday, was a valid exercise of the criminal law power despite the fact that s. 6 of that Act created an exemption for provinces which had passed legislation to the contrary. ...

This principle was reiterated in *Morgentaler v. The Queen*, [1976] 1 SCR 616, where this Court addressed the constitutionality of s. 251 of the *Criminal Code*, RSC 1970, c. C-34. Under s. 251(1) of the *Code*, the intentional procurement of a miscarriage was declared to be unlawful. However, under s. 251(4) and (5), Parliament had also created an exemption for miscarriages carried out by qualified medical practitioners where the life of the woman was in danger. Laskin CJ, dissenting in the result but not on this issue, made it clear that the creation of such an exemption did not detract from the validity of the provision as criminal law, at p. 627:

> I need cite no authority for the proposition that Parliament may determine what is not criminal as well as what is, and may hence introduce dispensations or exemptions in its criminal legislation.

. . .

The clear implication of this Court's decisions ... is that the creation of a broad status-based exemption to criminal legislation does not detract from the criminal nature of the legislation. On the contrary, the exemption helps to define the crime by clarifying its contours. In my view, this is precisely what Parliament has done in creating exemptions under the Act. The crime created by Parliament is the advertisement and promotion of tobacco products offered for sale in Canada. Rather than diluting the criminality of these acts, the exemptions to which the appellants refer serve merely to delineate the logical and practical limits to Parliament's exercise of the criminal law power in this context. For example, it is clear that the exemption for foreign media under s. 4(3) was created to avoid both the extraterritorial application of Canadian legislation and the page-by-page censorship of foreign publications at the border. ... Given the fact that foreign tobacco products comprise less than 1 percent of the Canadian market, it is apparent that the exemption has an extremely limited scope. ...

For all the foregoing reasons, I am of the view that the Act is a valid exercise of the federal criminal law power. ...

MAJOR J dissenting (Sopinka J concurring): ... It is undisputed that Parliament may legislate with respect to hazardous, unsanitary, adulterated and otherwise dangerous foods and drugs pursuant to its power to legislate in the field of criminal law.

It follows that Parliament can require manufacturers to place warnings on tobacco products which are known to have harmful effects on health. Manufacturers of tobacco products are under a duty to disclose and warn of the dangers inherent in the consumption of tobacco products. Failure to place warnings on tobacco products can validly constitute a crime, a "public wrong" which merits proscription and punishment and ought to be suppressed as "socially undesirable conduct." ... Section 9 of the *Tobacco Products Control Act* [requiring the display of unattributed health warnings] ... falls within Parliament's power under s. 91(27) of the *Constitution Act, 1867*.

However, I do not agree that Parliament under its criminal law power is entitled to prohibit all advertising and promotion of tobacco products and restrict the use of tobacco trademarks. ...

[Major J then discusses the requirement of a "typically criminal purpose" and refers to cases where that test was not satisfied—the *Margarine Reference*, *Labatt Breweries*, and *Boggs*. (The latter two cases are discussed in the notes after *Margarine Reference*.) These cases are read as standing for the principle that "although Parliament's power to legislate in the field of criminal law is broad, it is subject to constitutional limits."]

A definitive and all-encompassing test to determine what constitutes a "criminal offence" remains elusive but the activity which Parliament wishes to suppress through criminal sanction must pose a significant, grave and serious risk of harm to public health, morality, safety or security before it can fall within the purview of the criminal law power. While there is a range of conduct between the most and less serious, not every harm or risk to society is sufficiently grave or serious to warrant the application of the criminal law.

The heart of criminal law is the prohibition of conduct which interferes with the proper functioning of society or which undermines the safety and security of society as a whole. ... [A] crime is a public wrong involving a violation of the public rights and duties to the whole community, considered as a community, in its social aggregate capacity. Matters which pose a significant and serious risk of harm or which cause significant and serious harm to public health, safety or security can be proscribed by Parliament as criminal.

Consequently, lesser threats to society and its functioning do not fall within the criminal law, but are addressed through non-criminal regulation, either by Parliament or provincial legislatures, depending on the subject matter of the regulation. ...

I agree that criminal law is not frozen in time. ... I disagree that affinity with a traditional criminal law concern has no part to play in the analysis, whether the conduct proscribed by Parliament has an affinity with a traditional criminal law concern is a starting point in determining whether a particular matter comes within federal criminal competence. ...

The objective of the advertising ban and trade mark usage restrictions ... is to prevent Canadians from being persuaded by advertising and promotion to use tobacco products. I respectfully disagree with La Forest J that this type of persuasion constitutes criminal conduct.

Tobacco advertising and promotion may encourage some people to start or to continue to smoke. For that reason, it is viewed by many as an undesirable form of commercial expression. I do not disagree that it may be an undesirable form of expression, but is this undesirability sufficient to make such expression criminal? Does tobacco advertising pose a significant, grave and serious danger to public health? Or does it simply encourage people to consume a legal but harmful product? I cannot agree that the commercial speech at issue poses such a significant, grave and serious danger to public health to fall within the purview of the federal criminal law power. In my opinion, the Act is too far removed from the injurious or undesirable effects of tobacco use to constitute a valid exercise of Parliament's criminal law power. Legislation prohibiting all advertising of a product which is both legal and licensed for sale throughout Canada lacks a typically criminal public purpose and is *ultra vires* Parliament under s. 91(27) of the *Constitution Act, 1867*. ...

Since Parliament has chosen not to criminalize tobacco use, it is difficult to understand how tobacco advertising can somehow take on the character of criminal activity. The Act does not deal in any way with the regulation or prohibition of dangerous products or drugs. The underlying "evil" of tobacco use which the Act is designed to combat remains perfectly legal. Tobacco advertising is in itself not sufficiently dangerous or harmful to justify criminal sanctions. In my view, it is beyond Parliament's competence to criminalize this type of speech where Parliament has declined to criminalize the underlying activity of tobacco use.

On a final note, La Forest J addressed the exemptions contained within the Act, most notably the exemption for foreign periodicals. He concluded that notwithstanding the exemptions, tobacco advertising still constitutes criminal law. I disagree. ... While exemptions do not necessarily take a statute out of criminal law, broadly based exemptions are a factor which may lead a court to conclude that the proscribed conduct is not truly criminal. Both *Morgentaler* (dealing with abortion) and *Furtney* (dealing with gambling) involved conduct which has traditionally been viewed as criminal. The exemptions could not be described as "broadly based." ...

In these appeals, McLachlin J notes that despite the advertising ban, 65 percent of the Canadian magazine market will contain tobacco advertisements, given that the ban applies only to Canadian media and not to imported publications. The exemptions for advertising cannot be seen as being limited in nature because most Canadians will be exposed to advertising for tobacco products in newspapers, magazines and so forth. It is hard to understand how the respondent on the one hand claims that nothing short of a total ban will accomplish the goal of reducing tobacco consumption while at the same time the Act allows a very significant amount of advertising to enter the country. It is difficult to imagine how tobacco advertising produced by the United States or other countries and distributed in Canada through publications somehow becomes criminal when produced and distributed by Canadians. The broadly based exemptions contained in the Act, combined with the fact that the Act does not engage a typically criminal public purpose, leads to the conclusion that the prohibitions on advertising cannot be upheld as a valid exercise of Parliament's criminal law power.

The Act, except for s. 9 and its associated provisions relating to mandatory health warnings on tobacco packaging, cannot be upheld as valid criminal legislation. The Act is a regulatory measure aimed at decreasing tobacco consumption. While Parliament's desire to limit tobacco advertising may be desirable, its power to do so cannot be found in s. 91(27) of the *Constitution Act, 1867.* ...

Appeal allowed.

NOTE: THE REQUIREMENT OF A CRIMINAL FORM

One of the main constraints on the federal criminal law power has been that of form—the standard form of criminal law is a prohibition and penalty enforced by the courts. The presence of regulatory features in a federal law—such as powers of licensing and prior inspection, involvement of an administrative agency exercising discretionary authority in the administration of the law, detailed regulation, and civil remedies—may make the law incapable of being upheld as an exercise of the criminal power. However, in cases where a clear criminal law purpose has been found, courts have allowed some deviation from the strict form of prohibition and penalty. In *RJR MacDonald*, a majority of the Court found that the presence of exemptions did not preclude a finding that the legislation was criminal law. Reference was also made in *RJR* to cases establishing the federal government's undisputed power to regulate unsafe food and products under the criminal law power. In *R v. Cosman's Furniture (1972) Ltd.* (1976), 73 DLR (3d) 312 (Man. CA), for example, detailed regulations setting out standards for the manufacture of babies' cribs and cradles, made pursuant to the federal *Hazardous Products Act* (which made it an offence to manufacture or sell products that did not conform to the safety standards set in the regulations), were found to be a valid exercise of the criminal law power as they were directed at safeguarding the health and security of infants. In *R v. Hydro-Québec*, which follows, the Supreme Court of Canada went even further in finding that a regulatory scheme with a large measure of administrative discretion satisfied the formal requirements of criminal law.

Ancillary civil remedies have also been upheld under the criminal power. In *R v. Zelensky*, [1978] 2 SCR 940, 86 DLR (3d) 179, for example, a provision of the *Criminal Code* authorizing a court to order an accused found guilty of an indictable offence to pay compensation to the victim was upheld, as was a provision allowing courts to make an order prohibiting the repetition of competition offences in *Goodyear Tire and Rubber Co. v. The Queen*, [1956] SCR 303, 2 DLR (2d) 11.

Finally, in some cases a departure from the criminal form of prohibition and penalty has been allowed where the purpose of the law is the prevention of a crime. In *R v. Swain*, [1991] 1 SCR 933, for example, the Supreme Court of Canada found that the provisions of the

Criminal Code that provided for the detention in a provincial mental health institution of persons acquitted of an offence by reason of insanity were *intra vires* the federal government. While acknowledging that the criminal committal provisions were not designed to impose a punishment, the Court nonetheless found that they were a valid exercise of the preventive branch of the criminal law power. The provisions were found only to relate to insane persons whose actions were proscribed by the *Criminal Code*, and were intended to protect society by preventing further dangerous conduct. The protection of society was found to be one of the important aims of the criminal law. (The provisions were, however, found to violate s. 7 of the Charter.)

R v. Hydro-Québec
[1997] 3 SCR 213, 151 DLR (4th) 32

[Hydro-Québec was charged with violation of an interim order made by the federal Minister of the Environment restricting its emissions of PCBs. This order was made under Part II of the Canadian *Environmental Protection Act*, RSC 1985, c. 16 (4th Supp.), which, in short, established a process for regulating the use of toxic substances. In its defence, Hydro-Québec claimed that the two sections of the Act that were crucial to the making of the interim order and hence to the charge, ss. 34 and 35, were *ultra vires*. This claim succeeded throughout the Quebec courts, and the federal government appealed to the Supreme Court. The federal government attempted to support the legislation under both the p.o.g.g. and criminal law powers. A narrow majority of the Supreme Court of Canada, in a judgment written by La Forest J, found that the impugned legislation was a valid exercise of the criminal law power and that it was therefore unnecessary to address the p.o.g.g. arguments. In a dissenting judgment, Lamer CJC and Iacobucci J found no basis for the legislation in either the criminal law or p.o.g.g. powers. Only the portion of their judgment dealing with the criminal law power has been reproduced below; a discussion of their reasoning on the p.o.g.g. power can be found in Chapter 9, Peace, Order, and Good Government, under the heading "Note: Other Developments."

The analysis in both the majority and dissenting reasons involves detailed references to the Act, which is both complex and long. The preamble, which provides some evidence of the government's intentions in enacting the legislation, reads as follows:

> WHEREAS the presence of toxic substances in the environment is a matter of national concern;
>
> WHEREAS toxic substances, once introduced into the environment, cannot always be contained within geographic boundaries;
>
> WHEREAS the Government of Canada in demonstrating national leadership should establish national environmental quality objectives, guidelines and codes of practice;
>
> AND WHEREAS Canada must be able to fulfil its international obligations in respect of the environment ...

The scheme of the legislation was summarized as follows in the dissenting reasons of Lamer CJC and Iacobucci J:

[15] ... Part II of the Act, which contains ss. 34 and 35, is called "Toxic Substances" and deals with the identification and regulation of substances which could potentially pose a risk to the environment and/or to human health. According to s. 11 of the Act, a substance is toxic where "it is entering or may enter the environment" under conditions "having or that may have an immediate or long-term harmful effect on the environment," "constituting or that may constitute a danger to the environment on which human life depends," or "constituting or that may constitute a danger in Canada to human life or health." Section 3 broadly defines a "substance" as "any distinguishable kind of organic or inorganic matter, whether animate or inanimate" and the "environment" as "the components of the Earth." "Harmful effect" and "danger" are not defined.

[16] The Act instructs the Ministers of the Environment and Health to compile and maintain four lists: the Domestic Substances List (DSL), the Non-Domestic Substances List (NDSL), the Priority Substances List (PSL) and the List of Toxic Substances (LTS). The DSL includes all substances in use in Canada since 1986 (some 21,700 substances as of January 1991). The NDSL contains all other substances. ... There is a blanket restriction on importing NDSL substances into Canada until they are approved (s. 26).

[17] Sections 12 and 13 of the Act require the Ministers to compile a "Priority Substances List" specifying those substances to which priority should be given in determining whether or not they should be placed on the List of Toxic Substances. Under s. 15, either the Minister of the Environment or the Minister of Health may conduct investigations with a view to determining whether a given substance is toxic. The Ministers may examine, *inter alia*, the nature of the substance in question, its effects on natural biological processes, the extent to which the substance will persist in the environment, its ability to bio-accumulate, methods of controlling it, and methods of reducing the amount of it used. ...

[18] Once a priority listed substance is found to be toxic within the meaning of s. 11, the Ministers may recommend adding it to the List of Toxic Substances. After a federal–provincial advisory committee (established under s. 6) has been given an opportunity to provide its advice, the Governor in Council may add the substance to the list and bring it under the regulatory control of s. 34.

[19] Section 34 provides for the regulation of substances on the List of Toxic Substances. The Governor in Council is given extensive powers to prescribe regulations dealing with every conceivable aspect of the listed substance, including: the quantity or concentration in which it can be released; the commercial or manufacturing activity in the course of which it can be released; the quantity of that substance that can be manufactured, imported, owned, sold, or used—including total prohibitions on its manufacture, importation, ownership, use or sale—and likewise the manner in and purposes for which it can be manufactured, imported, processed, used, offered for sale or sold; the manner and conditions in which the substance may be advertised, stored, displayed, handled, transported or offered for transport; the manner, conditions, places and method of disposal of the substance; the maintenance of books and records in respect of the substance; and the extent to which reports must be made to the Minister regarding the monitoring of the substance. Section 34(1)(x) allows the Governor in Council to regulate "any other matter necessary to carry out the purposes of this Part."

[20] Where a substance is not on the List of Toxic Substances (or where it is listed, but the Ministers believe that it is not adequately regulated), and where the Ministers believe that immediate action is necessary in respect of that substance, s. 35 allows for the making

of "interim orders" without going through the usual procedure. These orders can contain any regulation which could have been made under s. 34, but they remain in effect for only 14 days unless they are approved by the Governor in Council. Approval can be given only if, *inter alia*, the Ministers have offered to consult with the governments of any affected provinces to see whether they are prepared to take sufficient action to deal with the threat posed by the substance (s. 35(4)). According to s. 35(8), interim orders expire after two years, even if such approval is granted.

· · ·

[22] Finally, the Act prescribes a number of civil and criminal penalties. ...]

LA FOREST J (L'Heureux-Dubé, Gonthier, Cory, and McLachlin JJ concurring): ...

[110] ... [I]n my view, the impugned provisions are valid legislation under the criminal law power—s. 91(27) of the *Constitution Act, 1867*. It thus becomes unnecessary to deal with the national concern doctrine, which inevitably raises profound issues respecting the federal structure of our Constitution which do not arise with anything like the same intensity in relation to the criminal law power. ...

[La Forest J first reviews the manner in which the Court has approached environmental issues under the division of powers.]

[116] The general thrust of [*Friends of the Oldman River Society v. Canada (Minister of Transport)*, [1992] 1 SCR 3] is that the Constitution should be so interpreted as to afford both levels of government ample means to protect the environment while maintaining the general structure of the Constitution. This is hardly consistent with an enthusiastic adoption of the "national dimensions" doctrine. That doctrine can, it is true, be adopted where the criteria set forth in *Crown Zellerbach* [*R v. Crown Zellerbach Canada Ltd.*, [1988] 1 SCR 401] are met so that the subject can appropriately be separated from areas of provincial competence.

[117] I have gone on at this length to demonstrate the simple proposition that the validity of a legislative provision (including one relating to environmental protection) must be tested against the specific characteristics of the head of power under which it is proposed to justify it. For each constitutional head of power has its own particular characteristics and raises concerns peculiar to itself in assessing it in the balance of Canadian federalism. This may seem obvious, perhaps even trite, but it is all too easy ... to overlook the characteristics of a particular power and overshoot the mark or, again, in assessing the applicability of one head of power to give effect to concerns appropriate to another head of power when this is neither appropriate nor consistent with the law laid down by this Court respecting the ambit and contours of that other power. In the present case, it seems to me, this was the case of certain propositions placed before us regarding the breadth and application of the criminal law power. There was a marked attempt to raise concerns appropriate to the national concern doctrine under the peace, order and good government clause to the criminal law power in a manner that, in my view, is wholly inconsistent with the nature and ambit of that power as set down by this Court from a very early period and continually reiterated since, notably in specific pronouncements in the most recent cases on the subject.

The Criminal Law Power

[118] Section 91(27) of the *Constitution Act, 1867* confers the exclusive power to legislate in relation to criminal law on Parliament. The nature and ambit of this power has
recently been the subject of a detailed analytical and historical examination in *RJR-
MacDonald* [*Inc. v. Canada (Attorney General)*, [1995] 3 SCR 199] … where it was again
described, as it has [been] for many years, as being "*plenary in nature*" (emphasis added). … I add that Professor Leclair in an excellent article, "Aperçu des virtualités de la
compétence fédérale en droit criminel dans le contexte de la protection de l'environnement"
(1996), 27 RGD 137, has very recently analysed all the relevant cases and has come to the
same conclusion about the general scope of the criminal law power and its application to
the environment, and in particular the Act here in question.

· · ·

[121] The Charter apart, only one qualification has been attached to Parliament's
plenary power over criminal law. The power cannot be employed colourably. Like other
legislative powers, it cannot, as Estey J put it in *Scowby v. Glendinning*, [1986] 2 SCR 226,
at p. 237, "permit Parliament, simply by legislating in the proper form, to colourably
invade areas of exclusively provincial legislative competence." To determine whether such
an attempt is being made, it is, of course, appropriate to enquire into Parliament's purpose
in enacting the legislation. As Estey J noted in *Scowby*, at p. 237, since the *Margarine Reference* [*Reference re Validity of Section 5(a) of the Dairy Industry Act*, [1949] SCR 1], it has
been "accepted that some legitimate public purpose must underlie the prohibition." …

[122] … [T]he listed purposes [in the *Margarine Reference*] by no means exhaust the
purposes that may legitimately support valid criminal legislation. … [T]his is, of course,
consistent with the view, most recently reiterated in *RJR-MacDonald*, at pp. 259-61, that
criminal law is not frozen in time.

[123] During the argument in the present case, however, one sensed, at times, a tendency, even by the appellant and the supporting interveners, to seek justification solely
for the purpose of the protection of health specifically identified by Rand J. Now I have
no doubt that that purpose obviously will support a considerable measure of environmental legislation, as perhaps also the ground of security. But I entertain no doubt that
the protection of a clean environment is a public purpose within Rand J's formulation in
the *Margarine Reference*, sufficient to support a criminal prohibition. It is surely an "interest threatened" which Parliament can legitimately "safeguard," or to put it another way,
pollution is an "evil" that Parliament can legitimately seek to suppress. Indeed, … it is a
public purpose of superordinate importance; it constitutes one of the major challenges of
our time. It would be surprising indeed if Parliament could not exercise its plenary power over criminal law to protect this interest and to suppress the evils associated with it by
appropriate penal prohibitions.   *Do anything*

[Excerpts from statements by public bodies, both Canadian and international, about the
urgent need to protect the environment are omitted.]

[127] What the foregoing underlines is … that the protection of the environment is
a major challenge of our time. It is an international problem, one that requires action by

governments at all levels. And, as is stated in the preamble to the Act under review, "Canada must be able to fulfil its international obligations in respect of the environment." I am confident that Canada can fulfil its international obligations, in so far as the toxic substances sought to be prohibited from entering into the environment under the Act are concerned, by use of the criminal law power. The purpose of the criminal law is to underline and protect our fundamental values. ... [T]he stewardship of the environment is a fundamental value of our society and ... Parliament may use its criminal law power to underline that value. The criminal law must be able to keep pace with and protect our emerging values. *move from form to a broad*

[128] In saying that Parliament may use its criminal law power in the interest of protecting the environment or preventing pollution, there again appears to have been confusion during the argument between the approach to the national concern doctrine and the criminal law power. The national concern doctrine operates by assigning full power to regulate an area to Parliament. Criminal law does not work that way. Rather it seeks by discrete prohibitions to prevent evils falling within a broad purpose, such as, for example, the protection of health. In the criminal law area, reference to such broad policy objectives is simply a means of ensuring that the prohibition is legitimately aimed at some public evil Parliament wishes to suppress and so is not a colourable attempt to deal with a matter falling exclusively within an area of provincial legislative jurisdiction.

[129] The legitimate use of the criminal law I have just described in no way constitutes an encroachment on provincial legislative power, though it may affect matters falling within the latter's ambit.

...

propriety!

[131] ... [T]he use of the federal criminal law power in no way precludes the provinces from exercising their extensive powers under s. 92 to regulate and control the pollution of the environment either independently or to supplement federal action. The situation is really no different from the situation regarding the protection of health where Parliament has for long exercised extensive control over such matters as food and drugs by prohibitions grounded in the criminal law power. This has not prevented the provinces from extensively regulating and prohibiting many activities relating to health. The two levels of government frequently work together to meet common concerns.

unless there are conflict

The Provisions Respecting Toxic Substances

[133] The respondent, the *mis en cause* and their supporting interveners primarily attack ss. 34 and 35 of the Act as constituting an infringement on provincial regulatory powers conferred by the Constitution. This they do by submitting that the power to regulate a substance is so broad as to encroach upon provincial legislative jurisdiction. That is because of what they call the broad "definition" given to toxic substances under s. 11 ... .

[134] I cannot agree with this submission. As I see it, the argument focusses too narrowly on a specific provision of the Act and for that matter only on certain aspects of it, and then applies that provision in a manner that I do not think is warranted by a consideration of the provisions of the Act as a whole and in light of its background and purpose. I shall deal with the latter first.

[La Forest J then comments that broad wording is unavoidable in environmental protection legislation because of the breadth and complexity of the subject, and has to be kept in mind in interpreting the relevant legislation.]

[135] I turn then to the background and purpose of the provisions under review. Part II does not deal with the protection of the environment generally. It deals simply with the control of toxic substances that may be released into the environment under certain restricted circumstances, and does so through a series of prohibitions to which penal sanctions are attached.

. . .

[138] There was no intention that the Act should bar the use, importation or manufacture of all chemical products, but rather that it should affect only those substances that are dangerous to the environment, and then only if they are not regulated by law.

. . .

[141] The impugned Act appears to me to respond closely to these objectives. ... The subject of toxic substances is dealt with principally in Part II of the Act. It begins, we saw, with s. 11, which has been described as a "definition" in argument. While the provision has some properties of a definition, to speak of it in this way is misleading and does not do full justice to its purpose and function. [The provision is not one that] describes with finality what the defined concept means. Rather, it sets forth that a substance can only be toxic, for the purposes of Part II, if it is entering or may enter the environment in a quantity or concentration or under conditions that result in the detrimental effects on the environment, human life and human health described in paras. (a) to (c). In other words, one cannot look at a phrase like "having or that may have an immediate or long-term harmful effect on the environment" in a manner divorced from the term "toxic" (i.e. "poisonous"; see the *Oxford English Dictionary* (2nd ed. 1989)). As well, the provision underlines that toxic as used in the Act includes substances that are not *per se*, toxic, but that may, when released into the environment in a certain quantity, concentration or condition, become toxic. ...

[142] I add that the determination of whether the various components of s. 11 are satisfied in respect of particular substances is by no means an easy task. Whether substances enter or may enter the environment in a quantity, concentration or conditions sufficient to have the effects set forth in that provision are not matters that are generally known. Rather these are matters that must be ascertained by assessments or tests set forth in s. 15, and in accordance with a procedure that requires consultation with the provinces, the informed community and the general public with a view to determining whether certain substances "are toxic or capable of becoming toxic," to use the expression employed in the provisions of Part II dealing with testing, beginning with the Ministers' weeding out most substances by establishing a priority list of substances to be tested. ... In light of this, it is difficult to believe "toxic" is not given its ordinary meaning in the Act, and that s. 11 is, therefore, simply a drafting tool for the demarcation of those aspects of toxicity that are to be considered in the tests required in the sections that follow.

[143] What the assessments described in Part II are aimed at is the selection of new items to add to the List of Toxic Substances set forth in Schedule I. Thus s. 11 is the first of a series of provisions respecting testing or assessment for toxicity. ...

[A long account of the process of decision making is omitted.]

[146] In summary, as I see it, the broad purpose and effect of Part II is to provide a procedure for assessing whether out of the many substances that may conceivably fall within the ambit of s. 11, some should be added to the List of Toxic Substances in Schedule I and, when an order to this effect is made, whether to prohibit the use of the substance so added in the manner provided in the regulations made under s. 34(1) subject to a penalty. These listed substances, toxic in the ordinary sense, are those whose use in a manner contrary to the regulations the Act ultimately prohibits. This is a limited prohibition applicable to a restricted number of substances. The prohibition is enforced by a penal sanction and is undergirded by a valid criminal objective, and so is valid criminal legislation.

[147] This, in my mind, is consistent with the terms of the statute, its purpose, and indeed common sense. It is precisely what one would expect of an environmental statute—a procedure to weed out from the vast number of substances potentially harmful to the environment or human life those only that pose significant risks of that type of harm. Specific targeting of toxic substances based on individual assessment avoids resort to unnecessarily broad prohibitions and their impact on the exercise of provincial powers. Having regard to the particular nature and requirements of effective environmental protection legislation, I do not share my colleagues' concern that the prohibition originates in a regulation, the breach of which gives rise to criminal sanction. The careful targeting of toxic substances is borne out by practice.

. . .

[149] I turn now to a more detailed examination of the provisions of the Act impugned in the present case, *i.e.* ss. 34 and 35. I mentioned earlier that the testing phase provided for under Part II ends with s. 32. Up to that point, Part II deals with the testing of substances that may be toxic when released into the environment as described in s. 11. The remainder of Part II, beginning with s. 33, however, is no longer addressed at substances that may be toxic in that broad sense. Rather it is more narrowly addressed at substances specifically listed in the List of Toxic Substances in Schedule I of the Act. In particular, s. 34 authorizes the Governor in Council to make regulations setting forth the restrictions imposed on those using or dealing with such substances. ...

[150] ... [Section] 34 precisely defines situations where the use of a substance in the List of Toxic Substances in Schedule I is prohibited, and these prohibitions are made subject to penal consequences. This is similar to the techniques Parliament has employed in providing for and imposing highly detailed requirements and standards in relation to food and drugs, which control their import, sale, manufacturing, labelling, packaging, processing and storing.

. . .

[152] ... [T]his kind of legislation does not constitute an invasion of provincial regulatory power ... . As noted earlier, we are dealing with prohibitions accompanied by penal sanctions, so that we are really not concerned with whether these may incidentally affect property and civil rights but whether the prohibitions are directed at a public evil.

. . .

[154] In *Crown Zellerbach*, I expressed concern with the possibility of allocating legislative power respecting environmental pollution exclusively to Parliament. I would

be equally concerned with an interpretation of the Constitution that effectively allocated to the provinces, under general powers such as property and civil rights, control over the environment in a manner that prevented Parliament from exercising the leadership role expected of it by the international community and its role in protecting the basic values of Canadians regarding the environment through the instrumentality of the criminal law power. ...

[155] Turning then to s. 35, I mentioned that it is ancillary to s. 34. It deals with emergency situations. The provision, it seems to me, indicates even more clearly a criminal purpose, and throws further light on the intention of s. 34 and of the Act generally. It can only be brought into play when the Ministers believe a substance is not specified in the List in Schedule I or is listed but is not subjected to control under s. 34. In such a case, they may make an interim order in respect of the substance if they believe "immediate action is required to deal with a significant danger to the environment or to human life or health." ...

LAMER CJC and IACOBUCCI J dissenting (Sopinka and Major JJ concurring): ...

The Pith and Substance of the Legislation

[30] ... [W]e cannot, with respect, agree with our colleague, La Forest J, that the criteria found in s. 11 are simply a "drafting tool" or that to speak of s. 11 as a definition is "misleading." The purpose of this section is to delineate from the category of "substances" (as defined by s. 3) those particular substances which qualify for regulation under ss. 34 and 35. It does so by specifying that "toxic" substances are, for the purposes of Part II, those which are capable of posing one of the threats listed above. This seems to us a clear statement of Parliament's intentions in this area. ...

[31] Nothing in the Act suggests that "toxic" is to be defined by any criteria other than those given in s. 11. ... If a substance (which can be essentially anything) poses or may pose a risk to human life or health, or to the environment upon which human life depends, or to any aspect of the environment itself, it qualifies as toxic according to the Act and may be made the subject of comprehensive federal regulation.

. . .

[33] In light of these factors, we believe the pith and substance of Part II of the Act lies in the wholesale regulation by federal agents of any and all substances which may harm any aspect of the environment or which may present a danger to human life or health. That is, the impugned provisions are in pith and substance aimed at protecting the environment and human life and health from any and all harmful substances by regulating these substances. It remains to be seen whether this can be justified under any of the heads of power listed in s. 91 of the *Constitution Act, 1867*. In that connection, we will begin by considering s. 91(27), the criminal law power.

The Criminal Law Power

[34] Parliament has been given broad and exclusive power to legislate in relation to criminal law by virtue of s. 91(27). ... This power has traditionally been construed generously. ...

[35] Nevertheless, the criminal law power has always been made subject to two requirements: laws purporting to be upheld under s. 91(27) must contain prohibitions backed by penalties; and they must be directed at a "legitimate public purpose."

· · ·

[38] The next step is therefore to examine the impugned provisions and determine whether they meet these criteria. In our view, they fall short. While the protection of the environment is a legitimate public purpose which could support the enactment of criminal legislation, we believe the impugned provisions of the Act are more an attempt to regulate environmental pollution than to prohibit or proscribe it. As such, they extend beyond the purview of criminal law and cannot be justified under s. 91(27).

[With respect to the requirement of a "legitimate public purpose," Lamer CJC and Iacobucci J find that, given the broad definition of "toxic" in s. 11(a), which does not require a finding of danger to human life or health and could, for example, include a substance which affected groundhogs but had no effect on people, the legislation cannot be supported as relating to health. However, they agree with La Forest J that the protection of the environment is itself a legitimate criminal public purpose, analogous to those cited in the *Margarine Reference*.]

[44] However, we still do not feel that the impugned provisions qualify as criminal law under s. 91(27). While they have a legitimate criminal purpose, they fail to meet the other half of the *Margarine Reference* test. The structure of Part II of the Act indicates that they are not intended to prohibit environmental pollution, but simply to regulate it. As we will now explain in further detail, they are not, therefore, criminal law. ...

[45] Ascertaining whether a particular statute is prohibitive or regulatory in nature is often more of an art than a science.

· · ·

[47] ... [A] criminal law does not have to consist solely of blanket prohibitions. It may, as La Forest J noted in *RJR-MacDonald*, *supra*, at pp. 263-64, "validly contain exemptions for certain conduct without losing its status as criminal law." ... These exemptions may have the effect of establishing "regulatory" schemes which confer a measure of discretionary authority without changing the character of the law, as was the case in *RJR-MacDonald*.

[48] Determining when a piece of legislation has crossed the line from criminal to regulatory involves, in our view, considering the nature and extent of the regulation it creates, as well as the context within which it purports to apply. A scheme which is fundamentally regulatory, for example, will not be saved by calling it an "exemption." As Professor Hogg suggests [P.W. Hogg, *Constitutional Law of Canada*, 3d ed., looseleaf (Scarborough, ON: Carswell, 1992), vol. 1], at p. 18-26, "the more elaborate [a] regulatory scheme, the more likely it is that the Court will classify the dispensation or exemption as being regulatory rather than criminal." At the same time, the subject matter of the impugned law may indicate the appropriate approach to take in characterizing the law as criminal or regulatory.

[49] Having examined the legislation at issue in this case, we have no doubt that it is essentially regulatory in nature, and therefore outside the scope of s. 91(27). In order to

have an "exemption," there must first be a prohibition in the legislation from which that exemption is derived. Thus, the *Tobacco Products Control Act*, SC 1988, c. 20, at issue in *RJR-MacDonald*, *supra*, contained broad prohibitions against the advertising and promotion of tobacco products in Canada.

. . .

[51] In the legislation at issue in this appeal, on the other hand, no such prohibitions appear. ...

[52] [Section 34] is not ancillary to existing prohibitions found elsewhere in the Act or to exemptions to such prohibitions. It is not itself prohibitory in nature.

. . .

[54] Moreover, as Professor Hogg notes, *supra*, at p. 18-24:

> A criminal law ordinarily consists of a prohibition which is to be self-applied by the persons to whom it is addressed. There is not normally any intervention by an administrative agency or official prior to the application of the law. The law is "administered" by law enforcement officials and courts of criminal jurisdiction only in the sense that they can bring to bear the machinery of punishment after the prohibited conduct has occurred.

[55] In this case, there is no offence until an administrative agency "intervenes." Sections 34 and 35 do not define an offence at all: which, if any, substances will be placed on the List of Toxic Substances, as well as the norms of conduct regarding these substances, are to be defined on an on-going basis by the Ministers of Health and the Environment. It would be an odd crime whose definition was made entirely dependent on the discretion of the Executive.

. . .

[57] Moreover, this process is further complicated by the equivalency provisions in s. 34(6) of the Act. Under this provision, the Governor in Council may exempt a province from the application of regulations made under ss. 34 or 35 if that province already has equivalent regulations in force there. This would be a very unusual provision for a criminal law. Provinces do not have the jurisdiction to enact criminal legislation, nor can the federal government delegate such jurisdiction to them: ... Any environmental legislation enacted by the provinces must, therefore, be of a regulatory nature. Deferring to provincial regulatory schemes on the basis that they are "equivalent" to federal regulations made under s. 34(1) creates a strong presumption that the federal regulations are themselves also of a regulatory, not criminal, nature.

[58] ... [In contrast to *RJR-MacDonald*], [t]he impugned provisions in this case ... involve no ... general prohibition. In our view, they can only be characterized as a broad delegation of regulatory authority to the Governor in Council. The aim of these provisions is not to prohibit toxic substances or any aspect of their use, but simply to control the manner in which these substances will be allowed to interact with the environment.

[59] *RJR-MacDonald*, *supra*, may be further distinguished, in our view. The *Tobacco Products Control Act* addressed a narrow field of activity: the advertising and promotion of tobacco products. The impugned provisions here deal with a much broader area of concern: the release of substances into the environment. This Court has unanimously held that the environment is a subject matter of shared jurisdiction, that is, that the Con-

stitution does not assign it exclusively to either the provinces or Parliament: ... A decision by the framers of the Constitution not to give one level of government exclusive control over a subject matter should, in our opinion, act as a signal that the two levels of government are meant to operate in tandem with regard to that subject matter. One level should not be allowed to take over the field so as to completely dwarf the presence of the other. This does not mean that no regulation will be permissible, but wholesale regulatory authority of the type envisaged by the Act is, in our view, inconsistent with the shared nature of jurisdiction over the environment. ...

[60] ... Granting Parliament the authority to regulate so completely the release of substances into the environment by determining whether or not they are "toxic" would not only inescapably preclude the possibility of shared environmental jurisdiction; it would also infringe severely on other heads of power assigned to the provinces. ...

Peace, Order and Good Government

[Only the national concern branch of the p.o.g.g. power was in issue, and the legislation was found to fail the test of "singleness, distinctiveness and indivisibility" from *R v. Crown Zellerbach Canada Ltd.*, [1988] 1 SCR 401 because it was not confined to a narrow range of toxic chemical substances such as PCBs that have a severely harmful effect on human health and the environment, and whose pollutant effects persist in the environment and are diffuse, but potentially covered a broader range of harmful substances whose effects may be temporary and more local in nature.]

Appeal allowed.

NOTES

1. David Beatty is extremely critical of the Court's ruling in *Hydro-Québec*, arguing that it unjustifiably expands the federal government's criminal law power by removing the constraint of prohibition and penalty, and undermines the federal–provincial equilibrium that previous decisions of the Court had established in the environmental area:

> Because the outcome in the case is so congenial with most people's political instincts, it is easy to overlook or forgive the fact that jurisprudentially, *Hydro-Québec* poses a serious threat to the integrity of the country's federal structure and to the rule of law. The decision of the majority puts at risk the federal principle and the idea that both levels of government have a role to play in protecting the environment. If Parliament can justify everything it does under its power to make criminal law, provincial authority over even the local aspects of the environment will depend upon the sufferance of federal officials. Such a sweeping authorization of law making power, combined with a paramountcy rule which gives precedence to federal enactments whenever they conflict with parallel provincial laws, effectively would allow the federal government to dictate to the provinces what their environmental policies would be. As a practical matter it would reverse the Court's earlier rulings on the environment and give the federal government exclusive jurisdiction in the field [David M. Beatty, "Polluting the Law to Protect the Environment" (1998), 9 *Constitutional Forum* 55, at 58.]

Beatty argues that a more principled (and preferable) approach would have been to uphold the legislation under the p.o.g.g. power by demonstrating provincial inability to effectively control the spread of toxic substances.

For a contrasting opinion on *Hydro-Québec*, see Jean Leclair, "The Supreme Court, the Environment, and the Construction of National Identity: *R v. Hydro-Québec*" (1998), 4 *Rev. of Constitutional Studies* 372. Leclair notes that even Quebec environmentalists strongly encourage federal involvement in environmental matters given the general lack of interest shown by the provinces in protection of the environment. Leclair finds no difficulty with the Court's treatment of the criminal law power, arguing that, based on prior jurisprudence, s. 91(27) need not be confined to traditional modes of sanctions so long as the law is aimed at the regulation of "public evils"—that is, conduct that endangers either the safety of the public or the integrity of the environment. On the issue of impact on provincial jurisdiction, he reasons (at 374):

> Such an approach does not preclude the possibility of shared environmental jurisdiction. The provinces can still intervene to protect the environment. Under the criminal law power, Parliament can only prevent evils which offend against certain fundamental values, such as the protection of health and the protection of the environment. A province can regulate the very same activity or conduct, so long as it pursues an objective falling within its constitutional jurisdiction. In so doing, it will not be enacting criminal legislation.

Leclair goes on to express pessimism about the practical effect of the judgment in improving the quality of environmental protection in Canada, recognizing that the federal government may be unwilling to seriously assume its responsibilities to protect the environment. Nevertheless, he argues that even if it fails to accomplish anything for the environment, the *Hydro-Québec* decision is an important one from the perspective of nation building and national identity (at 377-78):

> In recognizing very extensive powers to Parliament in matters such as the protection of health (*Imperial Tobacco*) and the protection of the environment (*Hydro-Québec*), two highly sensitive issues for *all* Canadians, the Court participates in a process of legitimation of the Canadian state and in the construction of national identity. Not only do protection of health and the environment represent two values perceived by many as traditionally and typically "Canadian" values, but they also have the singular ability of enabling us to transcend the issues which constantly divide us (language, ethnic origin, etc.). In other words, they are values about which we can all agree. Thus they operate as symbols of what being Canadian really means. ... In identifying and defining [the "fundamental values of our society"] the Court actively participates in the construction of "Canadian identity."

2. As noted previously, in *R v. Malmo-Levine; R v. Caine*, [2003] 3 SCR 571, 2003 SCC 74, 233 DLR (4th) 415, the Court upheld the prohibition of possession of marijuana in the *Narcotic Control Act* as a valid exercise of the criminal law power. In *obiter*, it added:

> [72] We do not exclude the possibility that the NCA might be justifiable under the "national concern" branch on the rationale adopted in *R v. Crown Zellerbach Canada Ltd.*, [1988] 1 SCR 401, at p. 432, where we held that concerted action amongst provincial and federal entities, each acting within their respective spheres of legislative jurisdiction, was essential to deal with Can-

ada's international obligations regarding the environment. In our view, however, the Court should decline in this case to revisit Parliament's residual authority to deal with drugs in general (or marihuana in particular) under the POGG power. If, as is presently one of the options under consideration, Parliament removes marihuana entirely from the criminal law framework, Parliament's continuing legislative authority to deal with marihuana use on a purely regulatory basis might well be questioned. The Court would undoubtedly have more ample legislative facts and submissions in such a case than we have in this appeal. Our conclusion that the present prohibition against the use of marihuana can be supported under the criminal law power makes it unnecessary to deal with the Attorney General's alternative position under the POGG power, and we leave this question open for another day.

In the light of the Court's decision in *Hydro-Québec*, do you think that Parliament would need to rely on the peace, order, and good government power to deal with marijuana on a regulatory basis?

NOTE: REFERENCE RE FIREARMS ACT (CAN.)

In 1995, the federal government passed new gun control legislation. In addition to banning or restricting the use of certain types of firearms, the *Firearms Act*, SC 1995, c. 39, which amended the existing *Criminal Code* provisions related to firearms, established a comprehensive licensing system for the possession and use of firearms and a national registration system for all firearms. Failure to comply with the licensing and registration requirements was made an offence under the *Criminal Code*. While licensing requirements for the use of certain firearms had for many years been found in Part III of the *Criminal Code*, the new scheme extended the reach of the regulation to all firearms (thus including what are often referred to as "ordinary firearms," such as rifles and shotguns). It also provided for much more detailed regulation of licence conditions, including, for example, the specific locations at which firearms may be stored and used. Under the licensing provisions, applicants with criminal records involving drug offences or violence, or a history of mental illness, could be denied a licence. The national firearms registration system, requiring registration of all firearms, was a completely new addition. Registration of a firearm would not be permitted unless the applicant was licensed to possess that type of firearm. Minister of Justice Allan Rock stated, after the bill passed third reading in the House of Commons:

> This legislation will help us preserve the peaceful character of Canadian society and help the police fight crime and violence. This tough new gun control program will improve public safety and also send a strong message that the criminal misuse of guns will not be tolerated. While recognizing and permitting the legitimate use of firearms in this country, in passing this Bill we are making a fundamental statement about the kind of country we want for our children.

In 1996, the province of Alberta challenged the federal government's power to enact the new gun control law by a reference to the Alberta Court of Appeal. The essence of the challenge was that the scheme was regulatory rather than criminal legislation because of the complexity of the legislation and the discretion given to the chief firearms officer. The province argued that the gun control scheme was indistinguishable from existing provincial property regulation schemes such as automobile and land title registries. The Court of

Appeal upheld the legislation by a 3 to 2 majority, a result confirmed on appeal by the Supreme Court of Canada in *Reference re Firearms Act (Can.)*, [2000] 1 SCR 783, 185 DLR (4th) 577. In a unanimous judgment, the Court found that the gun control law fell within Parliament's jurisdiction over criminal law, thus continuing the trend in the Court's recent judgments toward an expansive interpretation of the criminal law power. The following paragraph provides a summary of the Court's reasons:

> [4] We conclude that the gun control law comes within Parliament's jurisdiction over criminal law. The law in "pith and substance" is directed to enhancing public safety by control-ling access to firearms through prohibitions and penalties. This brings it under the federal criminal law power. While the law has regulatory aspects, they are secondary to its primary criminal law purpose. The intrusion of the law into the provincial jurisdiction over property and civil rights is not so excessive as to upset the balance of federalism.

The Court had little difficulty finding a criminal law purpose:

> [33] Gun control has traditionally been considered valid criminal law because guns are dangerous and pose a risk to public safety. ... The law is limited to restrictions which are di-rected at safety purposes. As such, the regulation of guns as dangerous products is a valid pur-pose within the criminal law power ... .

With respect to the more difficult issue of the requirement of criminal form, the Court focused on the *Criminal Code* prohibition of the possession of firearms without a licence and registration certificate. As a result of this method of analysis, the Court was not re-quired to resort to the necessarily incidental doctrine to uphold the licensing and registra-tion provisions as sufficiently integral to a larger scheme of criminal prohibition:

> [34] The finding of a valid criminal law purpose does not end the inquiry, however. In or-der to be classified as a valid criminal law, that purpose must be connected to a prohibition backed by a penalty. The 1995 gun control law satisfies these requirements. Section 112 of the *Firearms Act* prohibits the possession of a firearm without a registration certificate. Section 91 of the *Criminal Code* (as amended by s. 139 of the *Firearms Act*) prohibits the possession of a firearm without a licence and a registration certificate. These prohibitions are backed by penal-ties: see s. 115 of the *Firearms Act* and s. 91 of the *Code*.

The complex, regulatory nature of the legislation was found not to preclude a finding of criminal prohibition:

> [36] The first objection [of Alberta] is that the *Firearms Act* is essentially regulatory rather than criminal legislation because of the complexity of the law and the discretion it grants to the chief firearms officer. These aspects of the law, the provinces argue, are the hallmarks of regula-tory legislation, not the criminal law ... .
>
> [37] Despite its initial appeal, this argument fails to advance Alberta's case. The fact that the Act is complex does not necessarily detract from its criminal nature. Other legislation, such as the *Food and Drugs Act*, RSC, 1985, c. F-27, and the *Canadian Environmental Protection Act*, RSC, 1985, c. 16 (4th Supp.), are legitimate exercises of the criminal law power, yet highly com-plex. Nor does the Act give the chief firearms officer or Registrar undue discretion. The offences are not defined by an administrative body, avoiding the difficulty identified in the dissenting

judgment in *Hydro-Québec* ... . They are clearly stated in the Act and the *Criminal Code*: no one shall possess a firearm without a proper licence and registration. While the Act provides for discretion to refuse to issue ... a registration certificate under s. 69, that discretion is restricted by the Act. ...

Gun control was distinguished from provincial regulatory schemes for the registration of motor vehicles and land titles because of the inherently dangerous nature of firearms:

[42] [The provincial] argument overlooks the different purposes behind the federal restrictions on firearms and the provincial regulation of other forms of property. Guns are restricted because they are dangerous. While cars are also dangerous, provincial legislatures regulate the possession and use of automobiles not as dangerous products but rather as items of property and as an exercise of civil rights, pursuant to the provinces' s. 92(13) jurisdiction ... .

[43] The argument that the federal gun control scheme is no different from the provincial regulation of motor vehicles ignores the fact that there are significant distinctions between the roles of guns and cars in Canadian society. Both firearms and automobiles can be used for socially approved purposes. Likewise, both may cause death and injury. Yet their primary uses are fundamentally different. Cars are used mainly as means of transportation. Danger to the public is ordinarily unintended and incidental to that use. Guns, by contrast, pose a pressing safety risk in many if not all of their functions. Firearms are often used as weapons in violent crime, including domestic violence; cars generally are not. Thus Parliament views guns as particularly dangerous and has sought to combat that danger by extending its licensing and registration scheme to all classes of firearms. Parliament did not enact the *Firearms Act* to regulate guns as items of property. The Act does not address insurance or permissible locations of use. Rather, the Act addresses those aspects of gun control which relate to the dangerous nature of firearms and the need to reduce misuse.

Finally, in an interesting doctrinal development, the Court explicitly considered the question of whether its holding would upset the federal–provincial balance of power:

[48] ... Alberta and the provincial intervenors submit that this law inappropriately trenches on provincial powers and that upholding it as criminal law will upset the balance of federalism ... [It] is beyond debate that an appropriate balance of power must be maintained between the central and provincial levels of government, as this court affirmed in *Reference re Secession of Quebec*, [1998] 2 SCR 217. ... The question is not whether such a balance is necessary, but whether the 1995 gun control law upsets that balance.

The Court went on to find that the gun control law did not upset the balance of power because its effects on property rights were incidental: the Act did not hinder the ability of the provinces to regulate the property and civil rights aspects of guns, nor did the law precipitate the federal government's entry into a new field given that gun control had been the subject of federal legislation since Confederation.

NOTE: REFERENCE RE ASSISTED HUMAN REPRODUCTION ACT
(QUEBEC COURT OF APPEAL)

In 2004 Parliament enacted the *Assisted Human Reproduction Act*, SC 2004, c. 2, criminaliz-ing a series of technologies and activities relating to assisted reproduction. Section 5 pro-hibits, for example, human cloning, the creation of an *in vitro* embryo for any purpose other than creating a human being, and the creation of hybrids or chimeras for the purpose of transplanting them into a human being or a non-human life form. Sections 6 and 7 reiterate the principle of non-commercialization of the human body by prohibiting any form of pay-ment to surrogate mothers as well as the purchase or sale of ova, sperm, *in vitro* embryos, and human cells or genes. Section 8 prohibits the use or removal of human reproductive materi-al for the purpose of creating an embryo, as well as the use of an *in vitro* embryo without the donor's consent. Finally, s. 9 prohibits the removal or use of ova or sperm of a person under 18 years of age.

The Act goes on to prohibit a second series of activities relating to assisted reproduction except in accordance with the regulations and the authorization of the Assisted Human Re-production Agency of Canada ("the Agency") (ss. 10 to 13). These controlled activities con-sist, *inter alia*, of the manipulation, alteration, or treatment of human reproductive material for the purpose of creating an embryo; the alteration, treatment, or use of an *in vitro* em-bryo; the combination of the human genome with that of another species; and the reim-bursement of expenditures incurred by donors and surrogate mothers. These "controlled activities" target both clinical practice and research in assisted reproduction. Section 13 provides that these controlled activities may only be exercised at a facility that has been li-censed by the the Agency. It establishes a mechanism to collect personal information about people who use assisted reproductive technology and specifies the circumstances in which such information may be disclosed, and establishes a registry to contain this information (ss. 14 to 19).

The Quebec government referred the question of the Act's validity under the *Constitution Act, 1867* to the Quebec Court of Appeal. According to the Attorney General of Quebec, the pith and substance of the impugned provisions is the regulation of all aspects of medical practices related to assisted human reproduction, including health professionals and the health institutions in which those professionals work, the doctor–patient relationship, and civil aspects of medically assisted human reproduction. In the Attorney General's view, those provisions are contrary to the division of powers provided for in the *Constitution Act, 1867* and are, accordingly, invalid. The Attorney General of Canada submitted that the pro-visions in question are valid pursuant to both the power of the Parliament of Canada to make laws in relation to the criminal law and the "double aspect" doctrine, according to which two levels of government may make laws on different aspects of a single field. He added that the purpose of the Act is to protect health, safety, and public morals and that, ac-cordingly, the Act has a valid criminal law purpose.

In *Reference re Assisted Human Reproduction Act*, 2008 QCCA 1167, 298 DLR (4th) 712, the Quebec Court of Appeal held in favour of the province, declaring that the provisions in issue exceed the authority of the Parliament of Canada under the *Constitution Act, 1867*. In its opinion, apart from its outright prohibitions in ss. 5-9, the Act did not serve a valid criminal law purpose:

[137] … In the present case, with the exception of the outright prohibitions, the record reveals no "evil" that needs to be repressed. Rather, it establishes the intent to control the clinical and research aspects of a medical activity in order to create a uniformity that is considered to be desirable. The appropriateness of a single piece of legislation applying to Canada as a whole and regulating a permitted and recognized activity is not a purpose that confers criminal law jurisdiction.

[138] [T]he fundamental and dominant purpose of the impugned part of the Act is the safeguarding of health and not the elimination of an "evil." Consequently, the impugned provisions cannot be characterized as criminal law under the *Constitution Act, 1867*. In this respect, it is relevant to note the comments of Sopinka J in *R v. Morgentaler*, [[1993] 3 SCR 463]:

> The provinces have general legislative jurisdiction over hospitals by virtue of s. 92(7) of the *Constitution Act, 1867*, and over the medical profession and the practice of medicine by virtue of ss. 92(13) and (16). Section 92(16) also gives them general jurisdiction over health matters within the province: *Schneider v. The Queen*, [1982] 2 SCR 112, at p. 137. The Schneider case gives an indication of the watershed between valid health legislation and criminal law. In that case, British Columbia's *Heroin Treatment Act* was held to be *intra vires* because its object was not to punish narcotics addicts, but to treat their addiction and ensure their safety and security. Narcotic addiction was targeted not as a public evil but as a "physiological condition necessitating both medical and social intervention" (at p. 138). *Accordingly, if the central concern of the present legislation were medical treatment of unwanted pregnancies and the safety and security of the pregnant woman, not the restriction of abortion services with a view to safeguarding the public interest or interdicting a public harm, the legislation would arguably be valid health law enacted pursuant to the province's general health jurisdiction.* (Emphasis added.)

> • • •

[140] If the impugned part of the Act was found to be validly enacted under the federal criminal law power, it would follow that few, if any, cutting-edge medical activities would escape such control, since it could be argued that in each case exclusive federal control was necessary to safeguard health, respect ethical standards, and promote a pan-Canadian uniformity of legislation. Indeed, one must ask why work on viruses or nanotechnology, neonatal surgery, and psychosurgy, to name but a few, should not also be overseen by one national agency, given the dangers they present and the ethical problems they raise. What is more, thanks to scientific and technological progress and the development of new material and equipment, what was dangerous yesterday has become common practice today. Organ transplants are an eloquent example.

[141] By definition, medical activities must be decided upon and practiced ethically and be subject to standards that safeguard the health of the patient and the medical services provider. Controlling any one activity through criminal legislation opens the door to doing the same with all the others, thereby neutralizing an essential aspect of provincial jurisdiction in health matters. This does not mean that a particular activity cannot be prohibited and a penalty attached, as is done in sections 5, 6 and 7 of the Act. Health falls primarily within provincial jurisdiction and is not limited to the building and administration of hospitals, clinics, and laboratories; it also includes setting the standards to govern the activities carried out in such places. Redefining assisted reproduction practices as subject matters relating to the criminal law rather than health could create a Trojan horse that would significantly reduce provincial jurisdiction

over health by permitting exhaustive regulation of other fields of medical practice, particularly those that have recently been developed.

In the alternative, the Quebec Court of Appeal also held that the provisions in question were regulatory in nature:

[142] Unlike the situation in the *Firearms Reference* [*Reference re Firearms Act (Can.)*, [2000] 1 SCR 783], the impugned part of the Act seeks essentially to regulate an activity relating to health care. Offences are not actually defined in the Act but depend on the discretion of the government. Admittedly, the statute does create some prohibitions; these do not exist to forbid undesirable activities, however, but to impose standards on establishments and individuals regarding the carrying out of these activities. In short, the offences—or more accurately, the crimes, since offenders are liable to five years' imprisonment—constitute a legal framework that ensures that reproductive activities are carried out in environments that are described and stipulated in the regulations.

[143] It is true that an exemption does not deprive a law of its criminal nature. In the present case, however, the Act does not create exemptions. Indeed, Parliament designed the Act to permit assisted reproduction in Canada while ensuring federal control over it by conferring on the federal government the power to establish practice standards and by creating an agency to oversee the activity. This legislative architecture does not create exceptions to the prohibitions but defines the framework within which the medical practice of assisted reproduction may evolve.

[144] In effect the Act is conceived in the negative, in the form of a prohibition unless the targeted action is carried out in compliance with regulations and by a licence holder. Thus, the prohibition does not target medical activities *per se* (for example, *in vitro* fertilization procedures) but seeks only to create a framework for the activities by imposing licence requirements, defining skill standards for physicians, and creating rules to govern the operation of clinics. The Act also contains a number of other provisions relating to the practice of assisted reproduction, such as a requirement for patient consent, information collection, and the Agency's management of the information collected. Thus, the criminal prohibition is a legal mechanism that confers the power to create provisions governing practice and research in the area of assisted reproduction. In this case, the objective of the prohibition is to ensure compliance with the regulations, not to brand the offender with the stigma of a criminal conviction.

[145] Finally, section 68 of the Act creates an unusual situation in which the same action may be interpreted as a crime in one province but not in another. Specifically, this provision authorizes the federal government to order that the rules stipulated by one province be equivalent to its own. A standard may be equivalent without being identical, however, and since criminal statutes must be given a strict interpretation, it is possible for the prohibition to differ from one province to another. This is certainly a novel situation in the criminal law. It also indicates, once again, that Parliament's objective was not to repress an unlawful activity but to place the power to make regulations to govern assisted reproduction in the hands of the federal government.

Leave to appeal to the Supreme Court of Canada has been granted. In the light of its previous decisions on the criminal law power, how do you think the Court will rule?

II. PROVINCIAL POWER TO REGULATE
MORALITY AND PUBLIC ORDER

In our federal system, Parliament's power over criminal law exists in tension with the need to respond to local conditions of public order and morality, which may vary throughout the country. As noted above, in other federal systems, the local interest in criminal matters has been perceived as so strong that jurisdiction over criminal law matters has been assigned to the states. In Canada, various mechanisms exist for giving recognition to local interests in criminal law matters. First, as a result of s. 92(14) of the *Constitution Act, 1867*, which gives the provincial legislatures jurisdiction over the administration of justice in the province (including provincial policing), combined with federal delegation to the provinces of the power to prosecute *Criminal Code* offences, much of the federal *Criminal Code* is provincially enforced. A degree of responsiveness to local conditions may thus inform decisions about the investigation and prosecution of criminal offences.

Second, in some cases, the federal government itself has, through the mechanism of conditional legislation (discussed further in Chapter 12, Instruments of Flexibility in the Federal System), drafted its criminal laws in ways that allow them to be shaped by the provinces to respond to local conditions. For example, Sunday observance laws were found to be a federal matter under the criminal law power in *AG Ont. v. Hamilton Street Railway*, [1903] AC 524 (PC), which declared provincial legislation on the subject *ultra vires*. However, the federal *Lord's Day Act* recognized the need for responsiveness to local values by following its general prohibition of work on Sunday with an exculpatory clause, "except as provided in any Provincial Act or law." Similarly, the *Criminal Code* prohibition on lotteries is followed by an exemption for provincial lotteries conducted in accordance with terms and licences issued by the lieutenant governor (see *R v. Furtney*, [1991] 3 SCR 1989).

The third way in which local interests in matters of public order and morality may be given expression is through judicial recognition of concurrent provincial jurisdiction in matters that may also be the subject of criminal law. The extent to which this has been allowed and, conversely, the extent to which the federal criminal law power has operated as a brake on provincial attempts to regulate matters of public order and morality, is explored in the materials that follow. Section 92(15) of the *Constitution Act, 1867* allows the provinces to enact penal sanctions, but the power is understood as an "ancillary" one, authorizing the use of penal sanctions to enforce provincial regulatory schemes that are validly anchored elsewhere in the s. 92 list of provincial powers. The cases that follow typically turn on the issue of what constitutes a valid provincial anchor and the extent to which the courts are willing to recognize a double aspect with respect to matters covered by the *Criminal Code*. Just as the criminal law power has proven difficult to define with precision, so too has the scope of the limitation it imposes on provincial powers, and the issue has been the source of ongoing litigation since Confederation as the provinces have attempted to regulate local conditions of public order and morality.

In general, a fair amount of concurrency has been allowed by the courts, following the early precedent set in the battle over liquor regulation detailed in Chapter 4, The Late Nineteenth Century: The Canadian Courts Under the Influence, where the end result was a recognition that both the federal and provincial governments could legislate prohibition. However, from time to time, as in *Westendorp* and *Morgentaler*, below, it has been found that provinces have exceeded their jurisdiction and intruded into the federal criminal law power. As you read these cases, try to think about the factors that make a provincial law vulnerable to attack.

Re Nova Scotia Board of Censors v. McNeil
[1978] 2 SCR 662, 84 DLR (3d) 1

[The Nova Scotia *Theatres and Amusements Act* and the regulations enacted under it established a system for licensing and regulating the showing of films. The regulations required that all films be submitted to the provincial censor board prior to their exhibition, the censor board having an unfettered power to permit or prohibit the showing of the film, or to permit its showing with directed changes. Sanction for breach of the regulations was a monetary penalty and revocation of a theatre owner's licence. After the censor board banned the film *Last Tango in Paris* from public viewing in theatres or other places in the province, McNeil, a private citizen, sought a declaration that the provisions of the Act and the regulations that authorized the ban were *ultra vires* the provincial legislature. The Appeal Division of the Nova Scotia Supreme Court granted the declaration. The Attorney General of Nova Scotia then appealed to the Supreme Court of Canada.]

LASKIN CJC (Judson, Dickson, and Spence JJ concurring) dissenting: ... What is involved [here] is an unqualified power in the Nova Scotia Board to determine the fitness of films for public viewing on considerations that may extend beyond the moral and may include the political, the social and the religious. Giving its assertion of power the narrowest compass, related to the film in the present case, the Board is asserting authority to protect public morals, to safeguard the public from exposure to films, to ideas and images in films, that it regards as morally offensive, as indecent, probably as obscene.

The determination of what is decent or indecent or obscene in conduct or in a publication, what is morally fit for public viewing, whether in films, in art or in a live performance is, as such, within the exclusive power of the Parliament of Canada under its enumerated authority to legislate in relation to the criminal law. This has been recognized in a line of cases in which ... the criminal law power has been held to be as much a brake on provincial legislation as a source of federal legislation. For example, in *Switzman v. Elbling et al.*, [1957] SCR 285, (1957), 7 DLR (2d) 337, the Supreme Court invalidated a provincial statute which not only made it illegal for the possessor or occupier of a house to use or permit it to be used to propagate communism or bolshevism (which were not defined), but also made it unlawful to print, publish or distribute any newspaper or writing propagating or tending to propagate communism or bolshevism. ...

It is beside the point to urge that morality is not co-extensive with the criminal law. Such a contention cannot of itself bring legislation respecting public morals within provincial competence. Moreover, the federal power in relation to the criminal law extends beyond control of morality, and is wide enough to embrace anti-social conduct or behaviour and has, indeed, been exercised in those respects. ...

This is not a case where civil consequences are attached to conduct defined and punished as criminal under federal legislation ... but rather a case where a provincially authorized tribunal itself defines and determines legality, what is permissible and what is

protect art
free expression

not. This, in my view, is a direct intrusion into the field of criminal law. At best, what the challenged Nova Scotia legislation is doing is seeking to supplement the criminal law enacted by Parliament, and this is forbidden ... .

It was contended, however, by the appellant and by supporting intervenants that the Nova Scotia Board was merely exercising a preventive power, no penalty or punishment being involved, no offence having been created. It is true, of course, that no penalty or punishment is involved in the making of an order prohibiting the exhibition of a film, but it is ingenuous to say that no offence is created when a licensee who disobeyed the order would be at risk of a cancellation of his licence and at risk of a penalty and anyone else who proposed to exhibit the film publicly would likewise be liable to a penalty. Indeed, the contention invites this Court to allow form to mask substance and amounts to an assertion that the provincial Legislature may use the injunction or prohibitory order as a means of controlling conduct or performances or exhibitions, doing by prior restraint what it could not do by defining an offence and prescribing *post facto* punishment. ...

It does not follow from all of the foregoing that provincial legislative authority may not extend to objects where moral considerations are involved, but those objects must in themselves be anchored in the provincial catalogue of powers and must, moreover, not be in conflict with valid federal legislation. It is impossible in the present case to find any such anchorage in the provisions of the Nova Scotia statute that are challenged ... . What is asserted, by way of tying the challenged provisions to valid provincial regulatory control, is that the Province is competent to licence the use of premises, and entry into occupations, and may in that connection determine what shall be exhibited in those premises. This hardly touches the important issue raised by the present case and would, if correct, equally justify control by the Province of any conduct and activity in licensed premises even if not related to the property aspect of licensing, and this is patently indefensible. Moreover, what is missing from this assertion by the appellant is a failure to recognize that the censorship of films takes place without relation to any premises and is a direct prior control of public taste. ...

RITCHIE J (Martland, Pigeon, Beetz, and de Grandpré JJ concurring): ... When the Act and the Regulations are read as a whole, I find them to be primarily directed to the regulation, supervision and control of the film business within the Province of Nova Scotia, including the use and exhibition of films in that Province. To this end the impugned provisions are, in my view, enacted for the purpose of reinforcing the authority vested in a provincially appointed Board to perform the task of regulation which includes the authority to prevent the exhibition of films which the Board, applying its own local standards, has rejected as unsuitable for viewing by provincial audiences. This legislation is concerned with dealings in and the use of property (*i.e.*, films) which take place wholly within the Province and in my opinion it is subject to the same considerations as those which were held to be applicable in such cases as *Shannon et al. v. Lower Mainland Dairy Products Board et al.*, [1938] AC 708, 4 DLR 81; *Home Oil Distributors Ltd. et al. v. A-G BC*, [1940] SCR 444, [1940] 2 DLR 609, and *Caloil Inc. v. A-G Can. et al.*, [1971] SCR 543, (1971) 20 DLR (3d) 472.

It will be seen that, in my opinion, the impugned legislation constitutes nothing more than the exercise of provincial authority over transactions taking place wholly within the *ok regulate the morality*

Province and it applies to the "regulating, exhibition, sale and exchange of films" whether those films have been imported from another country or not. ...

Simply put, the issue raised by the majority opinion in the Appeal Division is whether the Province is clothed with authority under s. 92 of the *British North America Act, 1867* to regulate the exhibition and distribution of films within its own boundaries which are considered unsuitable for local viewing by a local board on grounds of morality or whether this is a matter of criminal law reserved to Parliament under s. 91(27). ...

Under the authority assigned to it by s. 91(27), the Parliament of Canada has enacted the *Criminal Code*, a penal statute the end purpose of which is the definition and punishment of crime when it has been proved to have been committed.

On the other hand, the *Theatres and Amusements Act* is not concerned with creating a criminal offence or providing for its punishment, but rather in so regulating a business within the Province as to prevent the exhibition in its theatres of performances which do not comply with the standards of propriety established by the Board. ...

I share the opinion [expressed by Lord Atkin in *Proprietary Articles Trade Association v. AG Canada*, [1931] AC 310] that morality and criminality are far from co-extensive and it follows in my view that legislation which authorizes the establishment and enforcement of a local standard of morality in the exhibition of films is not necessarily "an invasion of the federal criminal field" as Chief Justice MacKeigan thought it to be in this case.

Even if I accepted the view that the impugned legislation is concerned with criminal morality, it would still have to be noted that it is preventive rather than penal and the authority of the Province to pass legislation directed towards prevention of crime is illustrated by the case of *Bedard v. Dawson et al.*, [1923] SCR 681, [1923] 4 DLR 293. ...

As I have already said, however, I take the view that the impugned legislation is not concerned with criminality. The rejection of films by the Board is based on a failure to conform to the standards of propriety which it has itself adopted and this failure cannot be said to be "an act prohibited with penal consequences" by the Parliament of Canada either in enacting the *Criminal Code* or otherwise. This is not to say that Parliament is in any way restricted in its authority to pass laws penalizing immoral acts or conduct, but simply that the provincial Government in regulating a local trade may set its own standards which in no sense exclude the operation of the federal law.

There is, in my view, no constitutional barrier preventing the Board from rejecting a film for exhibition in Nova Scotia on the sole ground that it fails to conform to standards of morality which the Board itself has fixed notwithstanding the fact that the film is not offensive to any provision of the *Criminal Code*; and, equally, there is no constitutional reason why a prosecution cannot be brought under s. 163 of the *Criminal Code* in respect of the exhibition of a film which the Board of Censors has approved as conforming to its standards of propriety. ...

As I have said, I take the view that the legislation here in question is, in pith and substance, directed to property and civil rights and therefore valid under s. 92(13) of the *British North America Act, 1867* but there is a further and different ground on which its validity might be sustained. In a country as vast and diverse as Canada, where tastes and standards may vary from one area to another, the determination of what is and what is not acceptable for public exhibition on moral grounds may be viewed as a matter of a "local and private nature in the Province" within the meaning of s. 92(16) of the *British*

North America Act, 1867, and as it is not a matter coming within any of the classes of subject enumerated in s. 91, this is a field in which the Legislature is free to act. ...

Appeal allowed.

NOTES

1. While upholding most of the Act and regulations as they applied to film censorship, Ritchie J did invalidate one particular regulation (reg. 32), applicable to both films and live performances, which provided that: "No theatre owner ... shall permit any indecent or improper performance in his theatre." Given the similarity of wording, reg. 32 was found to be indistinguishable from the *Criminal Code* provision making it an offence to publicly exhibit an indecent show, with the result that the regulation impermissibly authorized the censor board to define what constituted a *Criminal Code* offence. Is this a satisfactory justification for invalidation? Are the differences between reg. 32 and the rest of the censorship scheme significant, or was Ritchie J perhaps confusing the issues of validity and paramountcy?

2. In *McNeil*, reference is made to an earlier decision delineating the limits imposed on provincial powers by the federal criminal power: *Bedard v. Dawson*, [1923] SCR 681, 4 DLR 293. *Bedard* involved a challenge to Quebec legislation providing for the closure of premises being used as a "disorderly house." The legislation was primarily concerned with premises in respect of which there had been *Criminal Code* convictions for prostitution and gambling. The five members of the Supreme Court of Canada who heard the case upheld the legislation. Some of the judgments emphasized that the law was in relation to property use and drew an analogy to the control of nuisance. Others relied upon the broader ground of a provincial power to suppress conditions favouring the development of crime—hence giving rise to the arguments made in *McNeil* that the scheme of censorship was "preventive" rather than penal. It is also clearly established that provinces can legislate with respect to the civil consequences of crime; for example, provincial highway traffic legislation providing for suspension of a provincial driver's licence after conviction for certain *Criminal Code* offences has been held valid; see *Ross v. Registrar of Motor Vehicles*, [1975] 1 SCR 5, found in Chapter 8, Interpreting the Division of Powers.

3. The pattern of sympathy to provincial interests in regulating local conditions of morality and public order demonstrated by the majority judgment in *McNeil* was continued in *Dupond v. City of Montreal et al.*, [1978] 2 SCR 770, 84 DLR (3d) 420, decided shortly thereafter. In 1969, after a period of numerous public demonstrations, many of which were accompanied by violence, vandalism, and looting, the City of Montreal passed a bylaw prohibiting parades or other gatherings that "endanger tranquillity, safety, peace or public order" in public places and thoroughfares. One section of the bylaw gave the city's executive committee the power to make an ordinance prohibiting public gatherings if there were reasonable grounds to believe that the gatherings would endanger "safety, peace or public order." The penalties provided for violation of the bylaw and ordinance were fines and imprisonment. Acting under the authority of the bylaw, the executive council imposed a prohibition on all public demonstrations for 30 days. Both the bylaw and ordinance were challenged by Dupond, as a ratepayer of the city. Beetz J, writing for a majority of the Court that also included Martland, Judson, Ritchie, Pigeon, and de Grandpré JJ, found that the bylaw and ordinance were

intra vires as a regulation of the municipal public domain, a pre-eminently local matter. In contrasting the challenged enactments with the *Criminal Code* provisions dealing with breach of the peace, Beetz J emphasized the preventive character of the municipal regulations. Laskin CJC, who dissented, Spence and Dickson JJ concurring, viewed the bylaw and ordinance as an *ultra vires* attempt to reinforce the criminal law. He characterized the law as a "mini-criminal code, dealing with apprehended breach of the peace, apprehended violence and the maintenance of public order." In the course of his reasons, Laskin CJC emphasized the Draconian nature of the law in barring all gatherings, even those for innocent purposes, and the striking departure from the basic criminal law principle that the police are expected to enforce the law against violators and not against innocents. He concluded with the comment: "This is the invocation of a doctrine which should alarm free citizens."

4. Laskin CJC's dissenting judgments in both *McNeil* and *Dupond* are informed by a concern to protect civil liberties by means of the federal criminal power. While he failed to gain majority support in these cases, such concerns had in the past, through combined reliance on the federal criminal power and a doctrine called the "Implied Bill of Rights," led to the invalidation of provincial laws viewed as seriously threatening civil liberties: see the cases and materials found in Chapter 15, Antecedents of the Charter, including the *Switzman v. Elbling* case relied upon by Laskin CJC in *McNeil*. Did the enactment of the *Charter of Rights* in 1982 eliminate the need for the indirect use of federalism doctrines to protect civil liberties? For an argument that Laskin CJC's view of the criminal power led him to miss the strong provincial claims to an anchor in s. 92, see K. Swinton, "Bora Laskin and Federalism" (1985), 35 *UTLJ* 353, at 367-72.

In *Westendorp v. The Queen*, which follows, the Supreme Court of Canada reversed the trend established in *McNeil* and *Dupond* and struck down a municipal bylaw regulating public order and morality as an intrusion into the federal criminal law power. How can *Westendorp* be distinguished from *McNeil* and *Dupond*?

Westendorp v. The Queen
[1983] 1 SCR 43, 144 DLR (3d) 259

[Westendorp had been charged with being on a street for the purpose of prostitution in contravention of s. 6.1(2) of By-law 9022 of the City of Calgary. The bylaw dealt generally with the regulation of the use of city streets and included provisions controlling soliciting or carrying on businesses, trades, or occupations on any street. The penalties provided for breach of the provisions of the bylaw (other than s. 6.1) were fines ranging from $20 to $300 and imprisonment for up to 10, 30, 45, or 60 days, according to the gravity of the infractions. In June 1981, city council had amended the bylaw, by means of By-law 25M81, to add s. 6.1, an explicit provision dealing with prostitution, which provided in 6.1(2) that "No person shall be or remain on a street for the purpose of prostitution," and in 6.1(3) that "No person shall approach another person on a street for the purposes of prostitution." The penalties provided for contravention of the provisions of s. 6.1 were fines ranging from $100 to $500 and imprisonment of up to six months.

No person shall — like CC — punish

The recitals that introduced the amendment and explained its necessity referred to the fact that prostitutes "often collect in groups on city streets and attract crowds on city streets, vehicular and pedestrian ... [which] activities are a source of annoyance and embarrassment to members of the public and interfere with their right and ability to move freely and peacefully upon the city streets."

In her defence, Westendorp challenged the constitutionality of s. 6.1 of the bylaw on the ground that it invaded federal authority in relation to criminal law. She was successful at trial, but her acquittal was set aside by the Alberta Court of Appeal, which found no invasion of the criminal law power.]

LASKIN CJC (Ritchie, Dickson, Beetz, Estey, McIntyre, Chouinard, Lamer, and Wilson JJ concurring): ... I have referred, however briefly, to the types of regulations and prohibitions and accompanying penalties which the by-law encompasses beyond s. 6.1. ... [T]here is nothing in the by-law which has any relation to s. 6.1 or to the scale of penalties prescribed for breach of s. 6.1 compared with those in the general penalty provisions of the by-law to which I have referred. Section 6.1 stands as an intruded provision of By-law 9022 which might just as well have been left in its original form in By-law 25M81. In short, there is nothing in By-law 9022 which invigorates s. 6.1 which must stand on its own merit as a valid municipal by-law. ...

It is patent, from a comparison of s. 6.1 with ss. 3, 4 and 5 of the by-law, that s. 6.1 is of a completely different order from its preceding sections and, certainly, from all those succeeding it. It is specious to regard s. 6.1 as relating to control of the streets. If that were its purpose, it would have dealt with congregation of persons on the streets or with obstruction, unrelated to what the congregating or obstructing persons say or otherwise do. As the by-law stands and reads, it is activated only by what is said by a person, referable to the offer of sexual services. For persons to converse together on a street, as did the two women and the police officer here, and to discuss a recent or upcoming sporting event or a concert or some similar event would not attract liability. It is triggered only by an offer of sexual services or a solicitation to that end. There is no violation of s. 6.1 by congregation or obstruction *per se*; the offence arises only by proposing or soliciting another for prostitution. To remain on a street for the purpose of prostitution or to approach another for that purpose is so patently an attempt to control or punish prostitution as to be beyond question. ... There is no property question here, no question even of interference with the enjoyment of public property let alone private property.

Nor can any comparison be made between this case and the judgment of this court in *A-G Can. et al. v. Dupond et al.*, [1978] 2 SCR 770, 84 DLR (3d) 420 which related to a municipal anti-demonstration by-law which was also emphasized as being of a temporary nature. That by-law related plainly to parades and assemblies on the streets, different from s. 6.1 of the present case.

The question remains, however, whether ... there is none the less constitutional scope for the valid enactment of the challenged by-law. This brings me to consider the reasons given by Kerans JA for upholding the by-law. He construed it as an attempt to deal with a public nuisance. This is not how the offence under the by-law is either defined or charged.

What is the P&S of the by-law
Why not double aspect

[Reference is then made to Kerans JA's assessment of the bylaw as "an attempt, by preventative measure, to regulate the activities of the prostitutes and their customers on the streets. It is, as it were, a pre-emptive strike."]

What appears to me to emerge from Kerans JA's consideration of the by-law is to establish a concurrency of legislative power, going beyond any double aspect principle and leaving it open to a Province or to a municipality authorized by a Province to usurp exclusive federal legislative power. If a Province or municipality may translate a direct attack on prostitution into street control through reliance on public nuisance, it may do the same with respect to trafficking in drugs. And, may it not, on the same view, seek to punish assaults that take place on city streets as an aspect of street control!

However desirable it may be for the municipality to control or prohibit prostitution, there has been an over-reaching in the present case which offends the division of legislative powers. I would, accordingly, allow the appeal, set aside the judgment of the Alberta Court of Appeal and restore the acquittal directed by the provincial court judge.

Appeal allowed.

NOTE

A similar bylaw enacted by the City of Montreal was also found *ultra vires*—*Goldwax v. City of Montreal*, [1984] 2 SCR 525, 16 DLR (4th) 667; rev'g. 146 DLR (3d) 460 (Que. CA). Municipalities such as Calgary and Montreal were led to enact anti-prostitution bylaws because of a dissatisfaction with the operation of the existing *Criminal Code* provision prohibiting solicitation in a public place for the purposes of prostitution. As a result of the Supreme Court of Canada's interpretation of the Code provision as requiring that soliciting had to be "pressing or persistent" in order to be a crime (see *Hutt v. The Queen*, [1978] 2 SCR 476, 82 DLR (3d) 95), the control of street prostitution became much more difficult. Some municipalities reacted by imposing more stringent controls on the nuisance aspects of prostitution. When these controls were found to be unconstitutional, as in *Westendorp*, the federal government responded by repealing the existing *Criminal Code* provision and replacing it with one making it an offence to communicate or attempt to communicate with any person in a public place for the purpose of engaging in prostitution. The new Code provision was challenged under the Charter and upheld by the Supreme Court of Canada. See *Reference re ss. 193 and 195.1(1)(c) of the Criminal Code*, [1990] 1 SCR 1123, 56 CCC (3d) 65; the decision contains a detailed review of the history of the legal regulation of prostitution.

———————————

Subsequent cases at the Supreme Court of Canada level continue the general pattern of upholding provincial laws dealing with public order and morality through generous use of the doctrine of double aspect rather than finding them to be an intrusion on the federal criminal law power. Every so often, however, no valid provincial purpose is found and, instead, the provincial law is found to constitute an invalid attempt to duplicate, stiffen, or undermine the operation of the criminal law.

Rio Hotel Ltd. v. New Brunswick (Liquor Licensing Board), [1987] 2 SCR 59, 44 DLR (4th) 663 conforms to the dominant pattern of concurrency. In this case, the Supreme Court of

Canada upheld provisions of the New Brunswick *Liquor Control Act*, RSNB 1978, c. L-10, which gave the Liquor Licensing Board the power to attach conditions to liquor licences regulating and restricting the nature and conduct of live entertainment in licensed premises. On the facts of the case, a licence had been issued to a hotel owner with a condition precluding nude performances. The hotel owner argued that the condition related to public morality and therefore fell within the exclusive jurisdiction of the federal Parliament under s. 91(27), noting that Parliament had enacted numerous provisions in the *Criminal Code* relating directly or indirectly to public nudity. The Supreme Court of Canada confirmed the province's ability to prohibit nude entertainment as part of a liquor licensing scheme notwithstanding the related provisions in the *Criminal Code*. The following is an extract from the main judgment of Dickson CJC, which emphasizes the integration of the provincial prohibition in a comprehensive scheme of regulation and licensing:

> DICKSON CJC (McIntyre, Wilson, and Le Dain JJ concurring): ... The Attorney General of New Brunswick submits that the impugned licence condition is part of a legislative scheme which "has a purpose entirely different from that sought to be served by the criminal law." While the criminal law addresses nudity and obscenity, the licence condition is simply directed toward the types of entertainment available as a marketing device for the sale of liquor within the province. This submission clearly calls into play the "aspect doctrine" ... .
>
> ... I conclude that the provincial legislation which authorizes the impugned licence condition is *intra vires* the Legislature of New Brunswick. The legislation is, as I have stated, *prima facie* related to property and civil rights within the Province and to matters of a purely local nature. The Legislature seeks only to regulate the forms of entertainment that may be used as marketing tools by the owners of licensed premises to boost sales of alcohol. Although there is some overlap between the licence condition precluding nude entertainment and various provisions of the *Criminal Code*, there is no direct conflict. It is perfectly possible to comply with both the provincial and the federal legislation. Moreover, the sanction for breach of the provincially-imposed licence conditions is suspension or cancellation of the liquor licence. No penal consequences ensue for the nude entertainer or for the holder of the licence. Under the relevant *Criminal Code* provisions, the primary object is obviously to punish entertainers and proprietors who breach the prohibitions on public nudity. I cannot say that the federal characteristics of this subject matter are palpably more important than the provincial characteristics. The provincial regulatory scheme relating to the sale of liquor in the Province can, without difficulty, operate concurrently with the federal *Criminal Code* provisions.
>
> I should point out that the instant case is distinguishable from the situation discussed in *Westendorp v. The Queen*, [1983] 1 SCR 43, 144 DLR (3d) 259. In that case, the City of Calgary enacted a by-law purportedly in relation to the use of city streets. In fact, one section of the by-law was a blatant and colourable attempt to punish prostitution. That section was held by this Court to be an "intruded provision" that bore no relation, either in subject-matter or in the scale of penalties, to the remainder of the by-law. In other words, the prostitution provision could not be said to relate to any head of provincial jurisdiction; it was not truly part of a regulatory scheme authorized under s. 92(13) or 92(16) of the *Constitution Act, 1867*. The licence conditions in the instant case are only part of a comprehensive scheme regulating the sale of liquor in New Brunswick. There is no colourable intrusion upon a federal head of jurisdiction. ...

In *R v. Morgentaler*, [1993] 3 SCR 463, 107 DLR (4th) 537, in contrast, the Supreme Court of Canada struck down a provincial law prohibiting the performance of certain designated medical services, in particular abortion, anywhere other than in a hospital. Penal sanctions were imposed for breach of the prohibition. The legislation was enacted in the wake of the Supreme Court of Canada decision in *R v. Morgentaler*, [1988] 1 SCR 30, 44 DLR (4th) 385, found in Chapter 22, Life, Liberty, and Security of the Person, which ruled that the *Criminal Code* provisions relating to abortion were unconstitutional because they violated s. 7 of the Charter. Although the province attempted to uphold its legislation as a valid exercise of its jurisdiction to regulate health and hospitals, the Supreme Court of Canada, like the courts below, concluded that the legislation was in pith and substance in relation to criminal law. Heavy reliance was placed upon excerpts from Hansard which demonstrated that the proposed law was understood to be about preventing the establishment of free-standing abortion clinics that were viewed as a "public evil." The 1993 *Morgentaler* case can be found in Chapter 8, Interpreting the Division of Powers. How is *Morgentaler* distinguishable from *Rio Hotel*? Are there similarities between *Morgentaler* and *Westendorp*? Is it possible to view *Morgentaler* as a case in which issues of rights indirectly influenced the federalism analysis?

In *Chatterjee v. Ontario (Attorney General)*, 2009 SCC 19, 304 DLR (4th) 513, at issue was the constitutionality of Ontario's *Civil Remedies Act*, SO 2001, c. 28 (CRA), which authorizes the forfeiture of proceeds of unlawful activity. The CRA does not require an allegation or proof that any particular person committed any particular crime. Property may be forfeited under the CRA if, on a balance of probabilities, it is demonstrated that the property constituted the proceeds of crime in general without further specificity. The police arrested the appellant for breach of probation and, in a search of his car incidental to the arrest, discovered cash and items associated with the illicit drug trade that also smelled of marijuana, but found no drugs. The appellant was never charged with any offence in relation to the money and items or with any drug-related activity. The Attorney General of Ontario applied under ss. 3 and 8 of the CRA for forfeiture of the seized money as proceeds of unlawful activity. Chatterjee challenged the CRA's constitutionality, arguing that its forfeiture provisions were *ultra vires* the province because they encroach on the federal criminal law power.

The following extract is from the unanimous judgment of Binnie J, which focuses on the ways in which criminal activity adversely affects numerous provincial interests:

> [2] The argument that the CRA is *ultra vires* is based in this case on an exaggerated view of the immunity of federal jurisdiction in relation to matters that may, in another aspect, be the subject of provincial legislation. Resort to a federalist concept of proliferating jurisdictional enclaves (or "interjurisdictional immunities") was discouraged by this Court's decisions in *Canadian Western Bank v. Alberta*, [2007 SCC 23, [2007] 2 SCR 3], and *British Columbia (Attorney General) v. Lafarge Canada Inc.*, 2007 SCC 23, [2007] 2 SCR 86, and should not now be given a new lease on life. As stated in *Canadian Western Bank*, "a court should favour, where possible, the ordinary operation of statutes enacted by *both* levels of government" (para. 37; emphasis in original).
>
> [3] The present appeal provides an opportunity to apply the principles of federalism affirmed in those recent cases. The CRA was enacted to deter crime and to compensate its victims. The former purpose is broad enough that both the federal government (in relation to criminal law) and the provincial governments (in relation to property and civil rights) can validly pursue it. The latter purpose falls squarely within provincial competence. Crime imposes substantial costs on provincial treasuries. Those costs impact many provincial interests, includ-

ing health, policing resources, community stability and family welfare. It would be out of step with modern realities to conclude that a province must shoulder the costs to the community of criminal behaviour but cannot use deterrence to suppress it.

[4] Moreover, the *CRA* method of attack on crime is to authorize *in rem* forfeiture of its proceeds and differs from both the traditional criminal law which ordinarily couples a prohibition with a penalty (see *Reference re Firearms Act (Can.)*, 2000 SCC 31, [2000] 1 SCR 783) and criminal procedure which in general refers to the means by which an allegation of a particular criminal offence is proven against a particular offender. The appellant's answer, however, is that the effect of the *CRA in rem* remedy just adds to the penalties available in the criminal process, and as such the *CRA* invalidly interferes with the sentencing regime established by Parliament. It is true that forfeiture may have *de facto* punitive effects in some cases, but its dominant purpose is to make crime in general unprofitable, to capture resources tainted by crime so as to make them unavailable to fund future crime and to help compensate private individuals and public institutions for the costs of past crime. These are valid provincial objects ... . It cannot reasonably be said that the *CRA* amounts to colourable criminal legislation.

NOTE: PROVINCIAL COMMISSIONS OF INQUIRY AND THE CRIMINAL LAW POWER

Many of the cases examined thus far have involved provincial attempts to regulate public order and morality in areas where the subject matter is (or was at one time) also covered by the *Criminal Code*. Concerns about provincial intrusion on the federal criminal law power may also arise in contexts where provincial laws are seen as potentially undermining the procedural protections offered to an accused under the criminal law. One such context is where a provincial commission of inquiry has been established to examine conduct that has also given rise to a criminal investigation or charges. In contrast to criminal proceedings, where the accused cannot be compelled to testify in either the investigation or the trial, commissions of inquiry have the power to compel testimony (although with the restriction that any evidence given cannot be used against the person giving that evidence in any subsequent proceeding).

The general pattern of the case law has been to find a double aspect with respect to the subject matter of the inquiry, recognizing both federal and provincial jurisdiction for different purposes. Thus, in the majority of cases in which this issue has come before it, the Supreme Court of Canada has upheld provincial commissions of inquiry and sanctioned the granting to them of fairly broad powers of investigation on the basis that the inquiry has a primary purpose other than the investigation of whether a specific crime was committed—such as, for example, determining the extent and causes of a problem, with a view to future prevention. Any impact upon the federal criminal law and criminal procedure has been held to be merely "incidental." (See *Faber v. The Queen*, [1976] 2 SCR 9; *Diorio v. Warden of the Montreal Jail*, [1978] 1 SCR 152; *Keable v. AG Canada*, [1979] 1 SCR 218; *O'Hara v. British Columbia*, [1987] 2 SCR 591.)

In *Starr v. Houlden*, [1990] 1 SCR 1366, 68 DLR (4th) 641, however, the Supreme Court of Canada departed from this pattern and found a commission of inquiry to be an *ultra vires* intrusion on the criminal law power. In *Starr*, a provincial commission of inquiry was set up to investigate allegations of improper financial dealings between provincial government officials and private individuals. The terms of reference as set out in the order-in-council establishing the commission of inquiry were relatively narrow, naming only Patricia Starr, the head of a charitable organization, and Tridel, a real estate development corporation. Criminal investigations were being conducted concurrently. Emphasizing the narrow focus of the commission of inquiry on only two named individuals and the incorporation into the terms of reference of the language of the parallel *Criminal Code* provisions dealing with the conferring of benefits on public officials, a majority of the Supreme Court of Canada characterized the inquiry as being "in substance … a substitute police investigation and preliminary inquiry with compellable accused in respect of a specific criminal offence under s. 121 of the *Criminal Code*." The inquiry was thus found to be *ultra vires* as it related to criminal law and criminal procedure.

The reasons of Lamer J (as he then was), writing for the majority, suggest that the characterization process was influenced by a view of the federal criminal law power as a source of protection for individual rights:

> It is clear … that provinces should be given ample room within their constitutional competence to establish public inquiries aimed at investigating, studying and recommending changes for the better government of their citizens. What a province may not do, and what it has done in this case, is enact a public inquiry, with all its coercive powers, as a substitute for an investigation and preliminary inquiry into specific individuals in respect of specific criminal offences. This is an interference with federal interests in the enactment of and provision for a system of criminal justice as embodied in the *Criminal Code*. The net effect of such an inquiry is to bypass the protection accorded to an individual by the *Criminal Code* and is accordingly *ultra vires* the province.

CHAPTER TWELVE

Instruments of Flexibility in the Federal System

At this point in the materials, you might feel that the provisions relating to the distribution of powers have been interpreted by the courts in a manner that either denies the federal government the authority necessary to deal with important issues of public policy, or that imposes unjustified constraints on the provinces in dealing with issues of significance to them.

However, it is important to be aware that the emphasis in the casebook is on the jurisdiction of federal and provincial governments to enact regulatory laws—or what some might call "command and control" legislation. Before coming to any firm conclusions about the balance of power in the Canadian federal system, one should look beyond the "regulatory" jurisdiction of the federal and provincial governments to a number of policy instruments that have been used to alter the formal distribution of functions and the policy responsibilities of each level of government in many areas. These instruments include taxation, the spending power, public ownership, interdelegation, and intergovernmental agreements. In the materials that follow, you will see that the courts have placed few legal constraints on the use of these instruments, with the result that the actual distribution of functions is quite different from what we have studied so far.

At times, these instruments have permitted significant centralization of some functions. But more recently, with federal attempts to respond to both fiscal pressures and Quebeckers' demands for constitutional change, the federal role has been reduced in many policy areas. For example, as we will see, the spending power has been used both as means of centralization and decentralization.

While the instruments we discuss below have been important in reshaping the Canadian Constitution, they do not reallocate regulatory jurisdiction over policy areas and, as a consequence, are always subject to legislative repeal. Only a constitutional amendment can securely shift the boundaries of federal and provincial regulatory jurisdiction.

Therefore, the chapter ends with a discussion of the amending formulae in the Canadian Constitution. In this section, we also discuss the constitutional framework surrounding the secession of a province, in light of the judgment of the Supreme Court in *Reference re Secession of Quebec*.

463

I. POLICY INSTRUMENTS AND FLEXIBLE FEDERALISM

A. The Spending Power

K.G. Banting, "The Past Speaks to the Future:
Lessons from the Postwar Social Union"
in H. Lazar, ed., *Non-Constitutional Renewal*
(Kingston, ON: Institute of Intergovernmental Relations, 1998), at 39

Introduction

During the postwar years, Canadians built their own version of the welfare state, establishing a new social contract between citizens and the state. This process was underway throughout the western world, as all countries experienced similar pressures to protect citizens from the social insecurities inherent in industrial society. Canada, however, faced the additional challenge of fashioning its social programs in the context of a federal state and society divided along linguistic and regional lines. Constructing the welfare state therefore also involved building what would now be called a *social union*, a set of understandings about the balance between federal and provincial social programs, and a set of intergovernmental arrangements to give those understandings life.

The postwar generation had to decide whether there would be a *pan-Canadian* welfare state or a series of distinctive *provincial* welfare states. The social union that emerged in those years was a compromise between these two poles. The system was significantly more decentralized than that in many other federal systems, including countries such as Australia and the United States, but it did incorporate critical pan-Canadian dimensions. Major social programs operated across the country as a whole and established a set of social benefits that Canadians held in common, irrespective of the region in which they lived. ...

In the postwar social union, the pan-Canadian elements of the welfare state were associated strongly with the role of the federal government. As the political and economic strength of the federal government has declined in recent years, and as our constitutional tensions have grown, the original social union has come under strain. Increasingly, Canadians are being forced back to first principles in social debate. What is the appropriate balance between pan-Canadianism and regional diversity in the construction of the welfare state? If pan-Canadianism is an important value, are there mechanisms other than federal power through which it can be sustained? ...

Federal Instruments

The federal government utilized three critical policy instruments in developing pan-Canadian social programs: the provision of benefits directly to citizens, federal shared-cost programs in areas of provincial jurisdiction, and equalization grants to poorer provinces.

Direct Federal Programs

Although it is sometimes argued casually that social policy generally is a provincial responsibility, the federal government's own jurisdiction in social policy is substantial, especially in the area of income security. During the middle decades of this century, three formal amendments to the constitutional division of powers gave the federal government complete authority over Unemployment Insurance, and substantial authority in the area of pensions. In addition, under the doctrine of the spending power, the federal government claimed an untrammeled right to make payments to individuals, institutions or other governments for any purpose, and argued that such transfers do not represent an invasion of provincial jurisdiction as long as they do not constitute regulation of the sector. Finally, the federal role in taxation constitutes a powerful instrument in redistributive policies, especially with the development of a fuller array of refundable tax credits and benefits.

On these constitutional footings, the federal government developed a significant direct presence in social policy. In 1940, it introduced Unemployment Insurance, which was later complemented by training and other labour market programs. The federal government also established two universal programs: Family Allowances (1944) which were paid to all families with dependent children; and Old Age Security (1951), which provided a basic pension to all elderly Canadians. In the mid-1960s, the federal government enriched pensions with two additional programs: the Canada Pension Plan, a contributory plan providing earnings-related pensions, and the Guaranteed Income Supplement, an income-tested benefit for the elderly poor. Finally, a Spouse's Allowance for younger spouses of pensioners was added in 1975.

These initiatives established a direct federal presence in the lives of Canadians, and made Ottawa the dominant government in income security. Provincial governments delivered Workers' Compensation and social assistance programs; and Quebec chose to operate its own Quebec Pension Plan, which is closely aligned with the Canada Pension Plan operating throughout the rest of the country. Nevertheless, the federal role was dominant. ... [T]he federal government paid out between 70 to 80 percent of all income security dollars directly to Canadians for the entire period from the late 1950s to the early 1990s. ...

Shared-Cost Programs

In other parts of the welfare state, the constitution and political realities pointed to provincial responsibility and delivery. In such areas as health care, social assistance and post-secondary education, the federal government therefore relied on the spending power to make shared-cost grants to provincial governments. Under these programs, Ottawa provided substantial financial support to any province mounting a program that met conditions or standards specified in federal legislation. In this way, the federal government stimulated the expansion of key social services, and established a common framework for program design from coast to coast.

The pan-Canadian nature of these programs turned to a significant degree on the terms and conditions attached to federal funding, especially in their developmental stages. The level of specificity in shared-cost programs varied considerably, both over

time and from program to program. For example, some of the early shared-cost programs, such as the categorical social assistance programs that were the precursors to the
Canada Assistance Plan, did establish relatively detailed conditions, including maximum
shareable benefit levels. However, provincial resistance, especially from Quebec, changed
that practice, and federal conditions became less detailed. Nevertheless, the federal conditions that were attached to shared-cost programs were important in giving broad shape
to provincial programs. ...

Equalization Grants

Federal equalization grants to poorer provinces constituted the third instrument that
sustained pan-Canadianism. These grants were designed to enable the seven poorer
provinces to provide average levels of public services without having to resort to above-
average levels of taxation. Equalization grants have always been unconditional, and in
theory could be used to reduce provincial taxes rather than enhance provincial programs. In practice, however, the equalizing of fiscal capacity among provincial governments led to a more common level of public services generally across the country than
would have been possible if provinces had to rely on their own revenues alone. ...

NOTE ON SHARED-COST PROGRAMS

In the above extract, Banting refers to the ability of the federal government to spend in areas
outside of its jurisdiction. This power is known as the federal spending power (which we
refer to simply as the "spending power," not to be confused with the power of provincial
governments to spend in areas of federal jurisdiction, recently recognized by the Supreme
Court in *Lovelace v. Ontario*, [2000] 1 SCR 950). As Banting notes, the spending power has
been used in connection with three kinds of programs: direct federal programs, equalization grants, and shared-cost programs. Our focus in this note is on the last of these three.

The dominant legal instrument for the exercise of the spending power has been the
shared-cost statute. However, the design of the programs created by these statutes may vary
along a number of different dimensions. Indeed, much of the politics of social policy revolves
around these issues of design. Historically, the level of the grant was set on a shared cost basis,
with the federal and provincial government providing a fixed percentage of funds (usually
50/50). However, in recent years, the federal government has relied instead on a system of
block grants, which are set at a level that is not tied to program expenditures. Closely related
to the level of federal grants is the form of the federal transfer. Again, there has been a shift
over time, from direct cash transfers to a mix of cash transfers and tax points (that is, a
percentage of federal tax revenue). Finally, most shared-cost program grants come with
conditions—for example, the prohibition on residency requirements for the receipt of social
assistance in the *Canada Health Transfer, Canada Social Transfer and Wait Times Reduction
Transfer Regulations* (SOR/2004-62) and the various conditions on the delivery of medical
care set out in the *Canada Health Act*, RSC, 1985, c. C-6 (CHA), both discussed below.
However, this need not be the case; for example, equalization grants are unconditional.

In the area of health insurance, the central pieces of legislation were the *Hospital Insurance
and Diagnostic Services Act*, SC 1957, c. 28 (covering in-patient and out-patient hospital ser-

vices), the 1966 *Medical Care Act*, SC 1966-67, c. 64 (covering non-hospital-based physician services), and, finally, the 1984 *Canada Health Act*, RSC 1985, c. C-6, which consolidated and replaced the earlier two statutes, and which is still in force. The *Canada Health Act* requires provincial health plans to meet five national standards in order to qualify for federal funding: accessibility ("reasonable access to health care without financial or other barriers"), comprehensiveness (coverage of all medically necessary hospital and medical services), universality (coverage of all residents of a province after three months' residency), portability (coverage when temporarily absent from the province), and non-profit public administration. As well, the Act contains specific bans on extra-billing by physicians and user charges by other providers (for example, hospitals) for insured services. The Act contains enforcement machinery for provincial noncompliance, imposing mandatory deductions for violations of the bans on extra-billing and user charges, and vesting a discretion in the federal cabinet to withhold funds from provinces in breach of the five national standards, after consultation with the province in question. (For a detailed discussion of these standards, see S. Choudhry, "The Enforcement of the *Canada Health Act*" (1996), 41 *McGill Law Journal* 461.)

On the income assistance side, the central piece of legislation was the *Canada Assistance Plan* (CAP), SC 1966-67, c. 45, enacted in 1966 (but since repealed, as explained below). The CAP contained a series of national standards for provincial social assistance programs. Central among these was the requirement that provinces provide financial aid or other assistance to "any person in need," in an amount that met the "basic requirements" of that person. Other conditions required that there be no minimum residency requirement for the receipt of social assistance, and that provincial law provide for a right of appeal from decisions regarding social assistance. There was and is no shared-cost statute specifically directed at postsecondary education.

During the first wave of federal policy activism that created the Social Union, federal transfers for health insurance and social assistance were funded on a 50/50 basis. However, these arrangements have been altered in stages, in response to growing fiscal pressures on the federal government. In the health care context, this shift is described in the following passage:

> The story of declining federal funding began in 1977, with the shift away from 50/50 cost-sharing to a block grant (the Established Programs Financing or EPF Grant) consisting of a mixture of cash and tax points, with the cash component tied to an escalator based on growth in per capita Gross National Product (GNP). In 1982, the escalator was applied to the entire EPF entitlement, not just the cash component, making the EPF cash transfer strictly residual. The escalator was then eliminated in stages, first in 1986 (when it was reduced to GNP less 2 per cent), then in 1990 (when the EPF per capita transfer was frozen).

(S. Choudhry, "Bill 11, the Canada Health Act, and the Social Union: The Need for Institutions" (2000), 38 *Osgoode Hall Law Journal* 39, at 62.)

A similar story can be told about federal transfers for social assistance. First came the so-called "cap on CAP." Until 1990, the federal government paid half the costs of social assistance in the provinces. In the 1990 budget, it unilaterally announced a five percent ceiling on the growth of payments to the three "have" provinces: Alberta, British Columbia, and Ontario. Coupled with a recession that increased the numbers on the welfare rolls, the province of Ontario was particularly hard hit, with the federal share of social assistance costs dropping from 50 percent to 28 percent in 1992-93, a reduction of $1.7 billion.

These trends culminated in creation of the CHST in 1995 (by the *Budget Implementation Act*, SC 1995, c. 17, Part V, especially ss. 13 to 23.2). The CHST is a new global block grant (consisting of a mix of cash transfers and tax points) to cover postsecondary education, medicare, and social assistance, that replaced both the EPF and CAP. Because it is a block grant that is not tied to actual program expenditures, it marked the final break with the shared-cost approach to federal shared-cost programs. The cash component of the CHST for 1996-97 was set at $14.7 billion, a $4.2 billion reduction from the 1995-96 total for transfers under the EPF and CAP ($18.5 billion). Moreover, as a quid-pro-quo for reduced federal funding, the CHST eliminated all national standards in the CAP for social assistance programs, except for the prohibition on residency requirements. However, the national standards of the CHA remained.

The CHST has provoked a storm of controversy, in large part because it was announced with neither prior notice to, nor consultation with, the provinces. Equally controversial has been the sharp decline in federal funding that accompanied the introduction of the CHST. In 1997-98, the cash component of the CHST dropped a further $2 billion, to $12.5 billion. Since then, however, the total cash transfer has increased, both by increases to base as well as by one-time supplements. The CHST cash transfer for 2002-3 was $19.1 billion, and is budgeted to increase to $21 billion in 2005-6.

The federal government continues to assert that it makes a larger contribution to provincial social programs than these numbers suggest, for it calculates its contributions to take into account the transfer of tax points to the provinces in 1977 as part of the formula for calculating provincial entitlements to EPF grants. Moreover, the value of those tax points has increased over time due to economic growth, partially offsetting the reduction in cash transfers. Thus, while the tax points were worth $11.4 billion in 1995-96, they were worth $16.1 billion in 2001-2. However, in practical terms, those transfers are irrevocable, and provincial governments accordingly argue that the only current federal contribution is the cash transfer. Whatever the merits of these arguments, the cash transfer is the only means available to the federal government to exert pressure on the provinces to comply with national standards such as those set out above.

THE SPENDING POWER AND THE CONSTITUTION

The spending power has been central to the growth, development, and politics of post-War Canada. However, its constitutional foundations are unclear. The existence of the spending power was announced by Lord Atkin in the *Unemployment Insurance Reference* (*AG Canada v. AG Ontario*) (*The Employment and Social Insurance Act*), [1937] AC 355, found in Chapter 6, The 1930s: The Depression and the New Deal) in the following famous passage:

> That the Dominion may impose taxation for the purpose of creating a fund for special purposes and may apply that fund for making contributions in the public interest to individuals, corporations or public authorities could not as a general proposition be denied. Whether in such an Act as the present, compulsion applied to an employed person to make a contribution to an insurance fund out of which he will receive benefit for a period proportionate to the number of his contributions is in fact taxation, it is not necessary finally to decide. It might seem difficult to discern how it differs from a form of compulsory insurance, or what the difference is between

a statutory obligation to pay insurance premiums to the State, or to an insurance company. But assuming that the Dominion has collected by means of taxation a fund, it by no means follows that any legislation which disposes of it is necessarily within Dominion competence.

It may still be legislation affecting the classes of subjects enumerated in s. 92, and, if so, would be *ultra vires*. In other words, Dominion legislation, even though it deals with Dominion property, may yet be so framed as to invade civil rights within the Province, or encroach upon the classes of subjects which are reserved to Provincial competence. It is not necessary that it should be a colourable device, or a pretence. If on the true view of the legislation it is found that in reality in pith and substance the legislation invades civil rights within the Province or in respect of other classes of subjects otherwise encroaches upon the provincial field, the legislation will be invalid. To hold otherwise would afford the Dominion an easy passage into the Provincial domain.

This brief passage has given rise to a host of interpretive questions. First and foremost is the constitutional source of the spending power. The spending power is not mentioned in s. 91 of the *Constitution Act, 1867*. Commentators have suggested a variety of sources for the spending power: s. 91A (federal jurisdiction over the public debt and property), s. 91(3) (taxation), and s. 106, the authority to make payments out of the Consolidated Revenue Fund. Others have turned to the royal prerogative, or even the legal rule that the Crown possesses the powers of a private person, including the power to spend its monies as it chooses.

But there are other questions as well. In the Supreme Court of Canada's judgment in the *Unemployment Insurance Reference* ([1936] SCR 427), Kerwin J supported the ability of the federal government to spend in areas out of its jurisdiction by making a distinction between spending and "coercive" forms of regulation on the ground that the recipient of a grant, including one with conditions, is free to "decline the gift or ... accept it subject to such conditions." Scholars have questioned the cogency of this distinction, however, given that the Constitution allocates jurisdiction on the basis of subject-matter, not on the basis of policy instrument (a point made by the Privy Council in the *Labour Conventions* case, in the context of treaties; see *AG Canada v. AG Ontario (Labour Conventions)*, [1937] AC 326, found in Chapter 6, The 1930s: The Depression and the New Deal.

Another issue is whether the spending power is subject to any justiciable limits. For example, is federal legislation enacted with the purpose of regulating an area of provincial regulatory jurisdiction *ultra vires*? Alternatively, can the degree of impact of a federal spending statute on areas of provincial jurisdiction rise to such a level as to take that statute out of federal jurisdiction? Lord Atkin's judgment clearly contemplated both kinds of limits on the exercise of the federal spending power.

In most areas of constitutional law, subsequent jurisprudence would be available to answer these questions. However, the spending power is an exception. Consider the following observation:

In the years after the New Deal, the question of the division of powers in relation to social policy almost never came before the Supreme Court. Thus, although handed down over six decades ago, the *UI Reference* decisions are still the leading judgments in the area. The contrast with other areas of public policy is striking. In the post-war period, the Court pronounced on the division of powers in a broad variety of policy contexts—including agricultural marketing, natural resources, inflation controls, the environment and broadcasting, making social policy conspicuous by its absence from the Court's docket. The silence of the Court on social policy is all the more unusual because jurisdictional questions often ended up before the Supreme Court because of intense federal–provincial conflict. In the social policy arena, disputes over the source and scope of federal involvement have been the norm and have often been framed in jurisdictional terms, and yet the courts have rarely been given an opportunity to elaborate upon and clarify the Privy Council's holdings. By contrast, federal–provincial conflicts that raised fundamental questions about the Canadian constitutional order, such as the patriation of the Constitution and the potential secession of Quebec have landed before the Court.

Why did social policy not give rise to litigation under the division of powers? Although federal–provincial relations in this area were often acrimonious, in the end, both the federal and provincial governments likely concluded that the potential costs of a litigation strategy outweighed the potential benefits. The federal government, for example, has consistently asserted the federal spending power is a plenary power that allows it to spend in areas of provincial jurisdiction without constitutional limitation. The risk of bringing the spending power before the courts, however, was that a ruling might have imposed some limits on that power, for example, by holding that extremely intrusive conditions might amount to an unconstitutional attempt regulate matters in provincial jurisdiction. The provinces other than Quebec faced a similar dilemma. Given the existence of vertical fiscal imbalance, they did not oppose the federal spending power in principle, but wanted federal transfers to be unconditional. A court pronouncement, though, might have had the effect of legitimizing intrusive federal conditions. Even Quebec, which opposed even unconditional federal transfers, opted not to litigate, likely because it seemed exceedingly unlikely that its consistent demand—a right to opt-out with compensation—would not be granted by the Court. Not surprisingly, the cases in which the division of powers and social policy was litigated were brought by private parties. The first social policy case brought by a government did not come before the Supreme Court until 1990.

(S. Choudhry, "Recasting Social Canada: A Reconsideration of Federal Jurisdiction Over Social Policy" (2002), 52 *University of Toronto Law Journal* 163, at 198-99 (footnotes omitted).)

As sparse as it is, subsequent case law appears to have departed from some of the limits imposed on the spending power by Lord Atkin. The focus of these cases has been on whether *conditions* attached to grants amount to a federal attempt to legislate in areas of provincial jurisdiction. In *Winterhaven Stables v. Canada* ((1988), 53 DLR (4th) 413 (Alta. CA), leave to appeal to Supreme Court denied (1989), 95 AR 236), the Alberta Court of Appeal considered a constitutional challenge brought by a taxpayer to a number of statutes, including the CAP (since repealed) and the *Federal–Provincial Fiscal Arrangements and Established Programs Financing Act*, 1977, SC 1976-77, c. 10 (which established funding arrangements for the *Canada Health Act*, and has also since been repealed). The Court rejected the challenge. The Court conceded that "the consequence [of legislation authorizing conditional grants to the provinces] is to impose considerable pressure on the provinces to pass complementary legislation or otherwise comply with the conditions of the allocation," and stated that conditions could be attached to grants "so long as the conditions do not amount in fact to a regulation or control of a matter outside of federal authority," thereby suggesting that the effects of some conditions on provincial areas of responsibility could be so significant as to render the federal law *ultra vires*. But the Court also stated that "questions of constitutional validity under ss. 91 and 92 are not resolved by looking at the ultimate probable effect."

The issue was also commented on by the Supreme Court in *Reference re Canada Assistance Plan*, [1991] 2 SCR 525, discussed further below. In that case, the Supreme Court addressed an argument raised by Manitoba that the cap on CAP was unconstitutional because it intruded on provincial jurisdiction. The Court rightly noted this argument was a challenge to the constitutionality of the CAP itself. It rejected Manitoba's submission, stating that the simple fact that a federal spending statute "impacts upon [a] constitutional interest" outside of federal jurisdiction was "not enough to find that a statute encroaches upon the jurisdiction of the other level of government." This statement suggests that the effects of federal spending statutes are constitutionally irrelevant. Moreover, both judgments appeared to assume that the spending power may be deliberately directed at matters lying within provincial jurisdiction. If this is true, then the *Canada Assistance Plan Reference* may have overruled the *Unemployment Insurance Reference*. However, the *Unemployment Insurance Reference* decision was referred to by the Court in the *Canada Assistance Plan Reference*, leaving the matter uncertain.

NORMATIVE CRITIQUES AND DEFENCES OF THE SPENDING POWER

Consider the following criticism of the federal spending power by Andrew Petter ("Federalism and the Myth of the Federal Spending Power" (1989), 68 *Canadian Bar Review* 448), at 463-67:

> There are many values which find voice in the Canadian Constitution but, in terms of the structure of government, the two most fundamental are federalism and responsible government. Although federalism has many forms, at root it implies a division of legislative and executive responsibilities between two orders of government, neither of which is subordinate to the other. Responsible government is a system of representative democracy in which the head of state acts upon the advice of an executive that, in turn, is directly answerable to a democratically elected legislature. Viewed in light of these constitutional values, the debate over the federal spending power takes on new importance. It becomes a debate not just about constitutional doctrine, but about the integrity of the federal system and the preservation of political accountability in Canadian government.
>
> The underlying rationale for federalism is a belief that while some matters are better decided by the national political community, others should be left to regional political communities. Implicit in this belief is a view that, with respect to certain matters, regional governments can better reflect the political attitudes and aspirations of citizens. It is not hard to see why this might be the case. In a country as large and diverse as Canada, the opinions and priorities of the inhabitants of one region may well differ from those of other regions. A system of regional governments is more likely to be responsive to these regional variations than is a single central government. ...
>
> The *raison d'être* of the federal spending power (and of conditional grants in particular) is to permit the federal government to use fiscal means to influence decision-making at the provincial level. In other words, it allows national majorities to set priorities and to determine policy within spheres of influence allocated under the Constitution to regional majorities. Thus, both by design and effect, the spending power runs counter to the political purposes of a federal system. ...

An even more powerful objection to the federal spending power concerns its impact upon responsible government. The organizing principle of responsible government is political accountability: accountability of the executive to the legislature and of the legislature to the electorate. It is this thread of accountability that transforms what would otherwise be a despotic system of government into a democratic one. Yet if a legislature is to be held accountable to the electorate, citizens must have a definite understanding of the scope of that legislature's powers. An electorate that cannot attribute political responsibility to one order of government or the other lacks both the ability to express its political will and the assurance that its will can be translated into action.

By allowing the federal government to use fiscal means to influence provincial policies, the spending power compromises political accountability and thereby weakens the ability of electors to exercise democratic control over government. ...

Petter then discusses a hypothetical example where a province wishes to impose user fees for health care services on high income individuals, but does not because of the fiscal penalties that it would face under the *Canada Health Act*, and continues:

Some may argue that the solution is for citizens to favour such a policy to organize at the national rather than the provincial level. ... Even if citizens, by organizing nationally, were able to convince the federal government to endorse their proposal, that government would be forced to rely solely upon fiscal measures to implement the reform. While such measures probably could be structured so as to compel provincial acquiescence with federal requirements, they could not give the federal government direct regulatory control over the policy. Thus the policy, although well conceived at the federal level, could suffer from incompetence or lack of political support on the part of the provincial authorities charged with its administration.

What the above example shows is that the spending power does not simply shift political responsibility from one order of government to the other; it intersperses responsibility between both orders. The result is to require those advocating a particular reform to fight a battle on two fronts. At the same time, it becomes virtually impossible for citizens to determine which order of government to hold accountable for policies that fail or, for that matter, for ones that succeed.

Consider the following defence by Sujit Choudhry of a strong federal role in redistribution, which is one of the policy goals achieved by exercises of the spending power ("Recasting Social Canada," *supra*, at 219-24):

To fully grasp the difficulties that the pursuit of redistributive goals poses for a federal state, we must define what those redistributive goals actually are. The goal I focus on here is *vertical equity*. Vertical equity refers to the appropriate stance of governments toward interpersonal economic inequality (however measured) prior to and independent of redistributive policies. ...

How does vertical equity operate in a federal state? In federations like Canada ... the concern raised by economists is that this goal is quite difficult to achieve.

The seminal work here is Wallace Oates' *Fiscal Federalism* ... . Oates starts by considering how redistribution would work in a highly decentralized federation, in which the federal government did not exercise any of the traditional functions of the public sector, including redistribution. For the purposes of his analysis, he makes a key assumption—"an absence of restrictions on the movements of goods and services" within the federation, i.e. extensive inter-provincial economic mobility. Oates' central claim is that in a decentralized federation, vertical equity, understood as interpersonal redistribution in order to reduce economic inequality, is very difficult to achieve. To understand why, Oates outlines the normative justification for federalism that emerges from the public choice literature, particularly the work of Charles Tiebout.

Tiebout relies on an economic conception of citizenship, which gives principal importance to the satisfaction of citizens' preferences. Tiebout's focus is on citizens' preferences for goods and services provided by governments, and he argues that systems of government can be compared with one another and assessed by their ability to maximize preference satisfaction. His central point is that federalism can be expected to produce a higher degree of preference satisfaction than would a unitary state, in the following way. Suppose each province provides a package of goods and services that varies along a number of different dimensions. As a simplifying device, assume that the two dimensions that matter most are the level or quantity of those goods and services, and the cost of those services. Each province can be uniquely characterized by where it lies on these two dimensions. One province may offer larger quantities per capita of goods and services (e.g. comprehensive health insurance, publicly funded education through to the post-secondary level) and will charge accordingly. Another province may offer a slightly lower quantity of goods and services (e.g. health insurance covering minimal health needs, and no publicly operated higher education system), but will charge less. Tiebout assumes that citizens are mobile, and that they will migrate to the province which offers them the basket of policies which suits them best. Federalism, then, creates a market for mobile citizens, where federal sub-units compete with one another through packages of goods and services they offer their citizens in exchange for fees to finance those services. ...

A complication arises, though, when one considers how provincial governments charge their residents for publicly provided goods and services. Oates sketches two different pricing options: benefit pricing and pricing on the basis of ability to pay. Under benefit pricing, each provincial resident, regardless of income level, would be charged an identical fee to cover the additional costs of offering goods and services to an additional resident of a province. From the vantage point of vertical equity, the principal problem with a flat benefit tax is that it disproportionately burdens the poor. The obvious solution, then, is to price publicly provided goods and services on the basis of ability to pay, so that those with relatively higher incomes pay more for the same goods and services than those with relatively lower incomes. A provincial income tax system would be the simplest mechanism for this sort of pricing.

Oates argues, though, that provincial governments are limited in their ability to redistribute interpersonally. The difficulty is the prospect of inter-provincial migration, both of higher and lower income persons. Higher income individuals would have an economic incentive to relocate to provinces where they would pay less for publicly provided goods and services, either because those provinces priced on a benefit basis, or adopted forms of income taxation which were less redistributive. Conversely, lower income individuals would have an incentive to move into provinces that finance services in a manner that least disadvantages low income individuals. The result is a cycle of out-migration and in-migration, whereby the departure of the rich and the arrival of the poor increases the proportion of lower income persons in the province, reduces the per capita provincial tax base, and accordingly requires an increase in the provincial income tax rate in order to provide public goods and services at the original level. Each increase in income taxes would in turn cause more higher income persons to leave and more poor persons to immigrate. After a point, the decline in the per capita tax base would force provinces to offer a lower level of goods and services. As a consequence, provinces that redistribute will be constrained in their ability to offer goods and services to their residents. Indeed, Oates goes further, and identifies the same dynamic at work in any provincial effort to achieve vertical equity. Thus, if a province wished to achieve a more egalitarian distribution of income than currently existed, it too would create incentives for higher income individuals, who would bear the burden of this policy, to migrate to jurisdictions with less egalitarian income tax policies. The end result would be a more egalitarian distribution of income, but a decline in per capita income.

One solution would be for provinces interested in redistribution to co-ordinate their public policies so as to make unavailable an attractive exit option within the federation for high-income individuals. Provinces might co-ordinate the structure of provincial income tax regimes, and/or might ensure that they provide comparable levels of goods and services to their residents, acting as a cartel to set a price for their goods and services other than the one which would prevail in the absence of co-ordinated action. High-income individuals would lack the incentive to migrate inter-provincially, because they would be unable to escape redistribution. Inter-provincial co-ordination, though, may be ineffectual, because in some circumstances provinces have strong incentives to defect from a co-ordinated regime of redistribution. Provinces will have an incentive to defect when the benefits foregone exceed the benefits of participating in such a regime. The foregone benefit is the additional tax revenue brought in by each additional high-income individual who migrates to a province from another province in response to an inter-provincial redistribution differential. Provinces benefit from the in-migration of each additional high-income individual as long as the tax yield exceeds the marginal cost of providing goods and services to that person. But provinces will only be able to derive that benefit if other provinces do *not* defect, and adhere to the co-ordinated redistribution regime, thereby creating the incentive for high-income persons to migrate.

The difficulty though, is that each province has the same incentive to defect, and to adopt policies that are less redistributive in nature. Moreover, in response to a defection that has already occurred, a province will have an incentive to defect and adopt less redistribution in order to stem the out-migration of high-income individuals, because failing to do so would leave them in a worse off situation than if they did not respond. Thus, given sufficient incentives, rather than co-operate, provinces will compete on the terrain of redistribution. The net result will be lower rates of redistribution than would have occurred were inter-provincial co-ordination to have been successful. In other words, if left to the provinces alone, Canada risks a redistribution race to the bottom.

Choudhry goes on to argue that the prospect of races to the bottom can serve as the basis of federal regulatory jurisdiction over social policy under the national dimensions/national concern branch of p.o.g.g. Would the existence of federal regulatory jurisdiction over social policy be an effective response to Petter's concerns?

NOTE ON PROPOSED CONSTITUTIONAL AMENDMENTS

The spending power has been the subject of constitutional discussions on a number of occasions. Quebec governments, in particular, have demanded controls on the federal spending power to prevent encroachments on provincial areas of jurisdiction. But others see the federal spending power as an important mechanism for maintaining a social union with common national standards. The following is a proposal on the reform of the spending power found in the 1987 *Meech Lake Accord* and duplicated in the *Charlottetown Accord* in 1992. It would have added a new s. 106A to the *Constitution Act, 1867*, which would have read as follows:

> 106A.(1) The Government of Canada shall provide reasonable compensation to the government of a province that chooses not to participate in a national shared-cost program that is established by the Government of Canada after the coming into force of this section in an area of exclusive provincial jurisdiction, if the province carries on a program or initiative that is compatible with the national objectives.
>
> (2) Nothing in this section extends the legislative powers of the Parliament of Canada or of the legislatures of the provinces.

This provision raised a series of difficult interpretive questions. One was whether it amounted to an explicit recognition of the ability of the federal government to expend monies in areas of provincial jurisdiction. The reference to "national shared cost program ... in an area of exclusive provincial jurisdiction" seems to presuppose this. But how can this position be reconciled with s. 106A(2)? A host of questions surrounded the opt-out with compensation. What was a "national" program—one that operated in every province, or simply one operated by the federal government in some provinces? Section 106A would have only applied, prospectively, to new shared-cost programs. But would it apply to amendments to, or extensions of, existing programs? What amount of compensation would be "reasonable" (on this point, see similar language in s. 41 of the *Constitution Act, 1982*)? What is a "program," and is it different from an "initiative"? What are "national objectives," and in particular, how are they related to the national standards laid down in the *Canada Health Act*? What would it mean for a provincial program to be "compatible" with national objectives? Need that program employ identical means to pursue the same ends, or would it be sufficient if the program pursued the same objectives, by whatever means?

Although s. 106A was never entrenched, the federal government made a promise in the February 1996 Speech from the Throne not to use its spending power to create new shared-cost programs in areas of exclusive provincial jurisdiction without the consent of a majority of the provinces. Provinces choosing not to participate were promised compensation if they established "equivalent or comparable initiatives."

NOTE ON THE ENFORCEMENT OF NATIONAL STANDARDS

The enforcement of the national standards set out in the *Canada Health Act* has been a flash point of federal–provincial controversy. However, Sujit Choudhry suggests that national standards are largely unenforced ("Bill 11, the Canada Health Act, and the Social Union: The Need for Institutions," *supra*, at 51-58):

> Let me begin with two facts. The first is that, despite the explicit bans on user charges and extra-billing—which are remarkably specific in a statute otherwise marked by its use of open-ended language—provinces continue to violate these conditions of federal funding. ... Since these conditions are subject to the mandatory enforcement mechanism, the federal government is

legally obliged to make deductions in federal transfer payments, and it appears that the federal government complies with the *CHA*. [The data show, however, that the total dollar amounts involved are small.] ...

In stark contrast, the discretionary enforcement mechanism, which attaches itself to the important conditions of universality, comprehensiveness and accessibility, has never been used. Juxtaposed against the active use of the mandatory deductions scheme, a casual observer could reasonably conclude that the federal government is actively monitoring provincial compliance with the terms of the *CHA*, and has come to the conclusion that provincial plans meet those national standards. Alternatively, one could conclude that instances of non-compliance have been resolved without the need for financial penalties. ...

However, the reports of the auditor general tell a radically different story. The auditor general has examined the enforcement of the *CHA* on three occasions, in 1987, 1990, and 1999. I focus on the last report, because it is by far the most detailed, and because it repeats many of the concerns advanced in the first two. The auditor general indicated in 1999 that there had been numerous instances of non-compliance in the last five years. Six cases were resolved without the use of financial penalties; the report did not provide any details. However, the auditor general noted that there were other cases of non-compliance that had not been resolved. A number of provinces (which the auditor general did not name) contravened the portability condition, which requires that medical services received outside of a province (including outside of the country) by insured persons temporarily absent from that province be reimbursed at the same rate as inside the province. The portability condition was apparently violated by five provinces with respect to treatment received outside of Canada; in addition, one province violated the condition with respect to treatment received in other provinces. The auditor general also stated, without providing any detail, that "[o]ther examples of suspected non-compliance with the comprehensiveness and accessibility criteria have been the subject of considerable discussion between the federal government and the provinces and territories." These disputes remained unresolved.

The most charitable interpretation of the auditor general's findings to this point of the report is that the federal government has been aware of the extent of provincial non-compliance, has been able to resolve some but not all disputes through negotiation, and has been reluctant to use the powerful financial levers available to it to secure better compliance. However, the report then went on to state that the federal government was largely unaware of the true extent of provincial non-compliance, because it lacked the required information. ...

[T]he federal government's non-enforcement of the *CHA*, along with the failure of political actors and the academic community to highlight the federal government's abdication of its responsibilities, is a national embarrassment. ...

Why the lacklustre federal performance? There would appear to be two reasons why the federal government has failed to aggressively enforce the national conditions spelled out in the *CHA*. The first is a lack of institutional capacity. Information gathering of the kind that is required to gauge provincial compliance with the conditions of accessibility and comprehensiveness, in particular, requires a serious commitment of human and capital resources.

In an earlier article, "The Enforcement of the Canada Health Act," *supra*, at 504-5, Choudhry concludes:

However, it would be a mistake to reduce the federal government's neglect of the *CHA* to a lack of resources. The more fundamental problem is a lack of political will. The auditor general's report made an oblique yet revealing reference to this problem, when it stated that the enforcement of the *CHA* had been tempered by national unity concerns. What the report was referring to was a long history of tense federal–provincial relations surrounding the federal spending power. Particular exercises of the federal spending power have long been regarded as federal impositions by provincial governments (although only one province, Quebec, has ever challenged the constitutionality of federal government expenditures in areas of provincial jurisdiction). The dynamic of fiscal federalism has also been profoundly affected by the dramatic decline in federal transfer payments. ... [T]he legitimacy of the federal enforcement of national standards has been diminished along with its financial involvement. The failure to exercise its discretionary enforcement power accordingly reflects a loss of legitimacy and political capital on the part of the federal government.

In 1999, the federal government, the nine provinces other than Quebec, and the three territories entered signed the Social Union Framework Agreement (SUFA). The goal of SUFA was to provide for a normative framework for federal–provincial relations in the social policy arena. The document contains seven articles of varying specificity, ranging from the extremely general (for example, Article 1's statement that "Canada's social union should reflect and give expression to the fundamental values of Canadians—equality, respect for diversity, fairness, individual dignity and responsibility, and mutual aid and our responsibilities to one another"), to the fairly specific (for example, Article 5's requirement that the federal government "consult with provincial and territorial governments at one year prior to renewal or significant funding changes in existing social transfers to provinces/territories"). Noteworthy is Article 6 ("Dispute Avoidance and Resolution"), which provides for the establishment of dispute settlement machinery for disagreements regarding the interpretation of national standards.

NOTE ON EQUALIZATION

Alongside the shared-cost programs, is the equalization program. Unlike the other federal transfers, equalization is anchored in the text of the Constitution, specifically s. 36(2) of the *Constitution Act, 1982*, which commits "Parliament and the government of Canada ... to the principle of making equalization payments." Equalization payments are designed to enhance the ability of provinces to provide "reasonably comparable levels of public services at reasonably comparable levels of taxation" (s. 36(2)). Equalization payments stood at approximately $10.1 billion in 2001-2. The design of the equalization program differs in two significant respects from the CHST. First, equalization payments are unconditional. This means that funds obtained under equalization can be spent on any manner of provincial program, and that those programs need not comply with national standards. Indeed, equalization payments could be substituted for provincial tax revenues, and therefore allocated to tax freezes or reductions. Because of the greater flexibility that equalization grants afford provincial governments, there have occasionally been calls to roll the CHST and equalization together into a single unconditional block grant. Second, equalization payments are not made to every province, unlike payments under the CHST. Moreover, the level of per capita payments varies from province to province, again unlike the CHST. The level of provincial payments is arrived at by comparing the fiscal capacity of a province (by using a formula that measures its ability to raise revenue from thirty sources, at average tax rates) with the average fiscal capacity of five provinces (British Columbia, Saskatchewan, Manitoba, Ontario, and Quebec). At present, every province other than Ontario and Alberta receives equalization payments, with Newfoundland receiving the highest per capita payments, and British Columbia the lowest.

NOTE ON FEDERAL TAXATION POWERS

The federal power to tax in s. 91(3) of the *Constitution Act, 1867* is virtually unrestricted, despite the Privy Council's judgment in the *Unemployment Insurance Reference*, found in Chapter 6, The 1930s: The Depression and the New Deal. Provinces' powers are more circumscribed, since s. 92(2) limits them to direct taxation within the province (except with respect to natural resources, where indirect taxation is permitted by s. 92A(4)). The meaning of "direct" and "indirect" taxation is explored in the *Canadian Industrial Gas and Oil* case, found in Chapter 10, Economic Regulation. Both federal and provincial governments are immune from the taxes of the other level of government in relation to their lands and property because of s. 125.

B. Intergovernmental Agreements

Federal and provincial governments enter into a wide variety of agreements on matters within their authority. Some of these agreements look like detailed contracts, and may cover matters such as the delivery of services or conditions to be satisfied for the receipt of funds. Others are broad statements of political objectives and obligations, such as an agreement by ministers to develop a common approach to educational standards. Because of this range, there is some uncertainty about the role of the courts in enforcing intergovernmental agreements. The most ambitious intergovernmental agreement in recent times is the Agreement on Internal Trade, described in Chapter 10, Economic Regulation.

The following case deals with the enforceability of intergovernmental agreements in a context where the federal government had unilaterally altered its obligations to certain provinces under the Canada Assistance Plan.

Reference Re Canada Assistance Plan (BC)
[1991] 2 SCR 525, 83 DLR (4th) 297

[Section 4 of the *Canada Assistance Plan*, RSC 1985, c. C-1 authorized the Government of Canada to enter into agreements with provincial governments to pay contributions toward their expenditures on social assistance and welfare. Section 5 of the Plan authorized payments to the provinces pursuant to such agreements, and generally authorized contributions amounting to half of the provinces' eligible expenditures. The Plan (s. 6(2)) specified certain conditions for eligibility of provincial expenditures, but left it to the provinces to decide which programs would be operated and how much money would be spent. Section 8(1) of the Plan provided that agreements would continue in force so long as the relevant provincial law remained in operation, but they could be terminated by consent or on one year's notice from either party (s. 8(2)). Agreements could also be amended by consent (s. 8(2)). The Plan (s. 9(1)) provided for regulations to govern such things as the calculation of eligible costs, but regulations affecting the substance of agreements were ineffective unless passed with the consent of any province affected (s. 9(2)). The Plan was silent as to the authority of Parliament to amend the Plan.

The Government of Canada entered into agreements with each of the provincial governments in 1967. In 1990, the federal government decided to limit its expenditures in order to reduce its budget deficit. Therefore, it decided that payments due to the "have" provinces of Alberta, British Columbia and Ontario (those that do not receive equalization payments) would grow by no more than five percent for the 1991 and 1992 fiscal years.

The government of British Columbia initiated a reference to the British Columbia Court of Appeal to determine whether the federal government could reduce its contributions in this manner. A majority of that court relied on the doctrine of legitimate expectations to find that the federal government was required to obtain British Columbia's consent to the changes to the agreement.]

SOPINKA J (Lamer CJC, La Forest, Gonthier, Cory, McLachlin, and Stevenson JJ concurring): ... In general, the language of the [Canada Assistance] Plan is duplicated in the [federal–provincial] Agreement. But the contribution formula, which actually authorizes payments to the provinces, does not appear in the Agreement. It is only in s. 5 of the Plan. Clause 3(1)(a) of the Agreement provides that "Canada agrees ... to pay to the province of British Columbia the contributions or advances ... that Canada is authorized to pay to that province under the Act and the Regulations." That means, of course, the contributions or advances authorized by s. 5 of the Plan, an instrument that is to be construed as subject to amendment. This is the effect of s. 42(1) of the *Interpretation Act* which states: "Every Act shall be so construed as to reserve to Parliament the power of repealing or amending it, and of revoking, restricting or modifying any power, privilege or advantage thereby vested in or granted to any person. ..."

In my view this provision reflects the principle of parliamentary sovereignty. The same results would flow from that principle even in the absence or non-applicability of this enactment. But since the *Interpretation Act* governs the interpretation of the Plan and all federal statutes where no contrary intention appears, the matter will be resolved by reference to it.

It is conceded that the government could not bind Parliament from exercising its powers to legislate amendments to the Plan. To assert the contrary would be to negate the sovereignty of Parliament. This basic fact of our constitutional life was, therefore, present to the minds of the parties when the Plan and Agreement were enacted and concluded. The parties were also aware that an amendment to the Plan would have to be initiated by the government by reason of the provisions of s. 54 of the *Constitution Act, 1867*. If it had been the intention of the parties to arrest this process, one would have expected clear language in the Agreement that the payment formula was frozen. Instead, the payment formula was left out of the Agreement and placed in the statute where it was, by virtue of s. 42, subject to amendment. In these circumstances the natural meaning to be given to the words "authorized to pay ... under the Act" in clause 3(1)(a) is that the obligation is to pay what is authorized from time to time. The government was, therefore, not precluded from exercising its powers to introduce legislation in Parliament amending the Plan. ...

The contention is that the Agreement could only be amended in accordance with s. 8. This submission fails to take into account that the Agreement which is subject to the amending formula in s. 8 obliges Canada to pay the amounts which Parliament has authorized Canada to pay pursuant to s. 5 of the Plan. Hence, the payment obligations under the Agreement are subject to change when s. 5 is changed. That provision contains within it its own process of amendment by virtue of the principle of parliamentary sovereignty reflected in s. 42 of the *Interpretation Act*.

If this appears to deprive the Agreement of binding effect or mutuality, which are both features of ordinary contracts, it must be remembered that this is not an ordinary contract but an agreement between governments. Moreover, s. 8 itself contains an amending formula that enables either party to terminate at will. In lieu of relying on mutually binding reciprocal undertakings which promote the observance of ordinary contractual obligations, these parties were content to rely on the perceived political price to be paid for non-performance.

The result of this is that the Government of Canada, in presenting Bill C-69 to Parliament, acted in accordance with the Agreement and otherwise with the law which empowers the Government of Canada to introduce a money bill in Parliament. ...

Appeal allowed.

NOTES

1. The exact holding in the *Canada Assistance Plan Reference* is the subject of some dispute. It has been argued, for example, that the judgment stands for one of three propositions:

> First, a narrow reading would hold that the agreement did not specify the levels of payment, leaving this matter to federal legislation. Thus, the agreement was not breached, and the question of legal enforceability was not decided. A second, and slightly broader, reading of the decision would be that the agreement was binding but could be discharged by conflicting legislation. ... Until Parliament or a provincial legislature did enact conflicting legislation, governments would be bound to comply with the terms of the agreement and could be held accountable by a court. The third, and broadest view, however, seems to be that the agreement only created political, not legal, obligations ... .

(S. Choudhry, "The Enforcement of the *Canada Health Act*," *supra*.)

For a case applying the second reading of the judgment, see *Saskatchewan Egg Producers Marketing Board v. Ontario (Min. of Agriculture & Food)*, [1993] OJ No. 434 (Gen. Div.).

2. The issue of the binding nature of intergovernmental agreements has arisen most recently in relation to the 1994 Agreement on Internal Trade, discussed in Chapter 10, Eco-

nomic Regulation. While the Agreement sets out detailed obligations on federal, provincial, and territorial governments, the *Canada Assistance Plan Reference* seems to suggest that a province could refuse to comply with the Agreement or a decision of the dispute settlement process. This is further discussed in K. Swinton, "Law, Politics, and the Enforcement of the Agreement on Internal Trade," in M.J. Trebilcock and D. Schwanen, eds., *Getting There: An Assessment of the Agreement on Internal Trade* (Toronto: C.D. Howe, 1995), at 196. For discussion on intergovernmental agreements more generally, see L. Friedlander, "Constitutionalizing Intergovernmental Agreements" (1994), 4 *National Journal of Constitutional Law* 153.

3. In response to the judgment in the *Canada Assistance Plan Reference*, the *Charlottetown Accord* of 1992 proposed a constitutional amendment to make intergovernmental agreements binding. It read:

> 126A.(1) Where the Government of Canada and the government of one or more provinces or territories enter into an agreement that is approved under this section, no law made by or under the authority of the Parliament of Canada or of any legislature of a province or legislative authority of a territory that is a party to the agreement and has caused it to be approved under this section may amend, revoke or otherwise supersede the agreement while the approval of the agreement remains in force.
>
> (2) An agreement is approved when the Parliament of Canada and the legislature of a province, or the legislative authority of a territory, that is a party thereto have each passed a law that approves the agreement and that includes an express declaration that this section applies in respect of the agreement.
>
> (3) An agreement approved under this section may be amended, revoked or otherwise superseded only in accordance with its terms or by a further agreement approved under this section.
>
> (4) An approval under this section expires no later than five years after it is given, but may be renewed under this section for additional periods not exceeding five years each.

Why does subsection (4) set a time limit of five years on an approval of an agreement? Would this provision be a useful addition to the Constitution?

C. Delegation

Another way in which governments get around the constraints of the distribution of powers is through delegation of functions to the other level of government. Although governments cannot delegate legislative powers directly to one another, various devices allow them to achieve this result by indirect means.

In the *Nova Scotia Interdelegation* case (*AG NS v. AG Can.*, [1951] SCR 31, [1950] 4 DLR 369), the Supreme Court of Canada rejected the argument that the federal Parliament and the provincial legislatures could delegate *legislative* power to one another. The plan of the federal and provincial governments in that case had been to alter their respective legislative authority to regulate employment and indirect taxation in order to establish a public pension scheme. The seven members of the Court each wrote reasons rejecting the possibility of legislative delegation. The following quote from Rinfret CJC captures some of the reasons for the conclusion (at 371 DLR):

The Parliament of Canada and the Legislatures of the several Provinces are sovereign within their sphere defined by the *BNA Act*, but none of them has the unlimited capacity of an individual. They can exercise only the legislative powers respectively given to them by ss. 91 and 92 of the Act, and these powers must be found in either of these sections.

The constitution of Canada does not belong either to Parliament, or to the Legislatures; it belongs to the country and it is there that the citizens of the country will find the protection of the rights to which they are entitled. It is part of that protection that Parliament can legislate only on the subject-matters referred to it by s. 91 and that each Province can legislate exclusively on the subject-matters referred to it by s. 92. The country is entitled to insist that legislation adopted under s. 91 should be passed exclusively by the Parliament of Canada in the same way as the people of each Province are entitled to insist that legislation concerning the matters enumerated in s. 92 should come exclusively from their respective Legislatures.

The Court has since relaxed this position, in that it has permitted extensive delegation between governments through various devices:

1. "administrative delegation," whereby functions are delegated to an official, minister, or administrative tribunal of the other level of government, or to a tribunal created by both levels, as in the *Reference re Agricultural Products Marketing Act*, a note on which can be found in Chapter 10, Economic Regulation;

2. "incorporation by reference" of the laws of the other level of government, as they now exist or as they may be amended from time to time (the latter being known as "anticipatory incorporation by reference"); and

3. "conditional legislation," whereby a law or legislative provision of one government does not come into effect at the other level of government without a certain condition being fulfilled, such as approval by that level's government.

All of these devices are used in the case that follows, which was the most dramatic example of the effectiveness of these devices to circumvent the holding in the *Nova Scotia Interdelegation* case.

Coughlin v. Ontario Highway Transport Board
[1968] SCR 569, 68 DLR (2d) 384

[The federal Parliament enacted the *Motor Vehicle Transport Act*, SC 1953-54, c. 59, which delegated power to provincial highway transport boards to regulate interprovincial trucking, a matter within federal jurisdiction under s. 92(10)(a) of the *Constitution Act, 1867*. The Act read as follows:

2. In this Act,

(a) "extra-provincial transport" means the transport of passengers or goods by means of an extra-provincial undertaking;

(b) "extra-provincial undertaking" means a work or undertaking for the transport of passengers or goods by motor vehicle, connecting a province with any other or others of the provinces, or extending beyond the limits of a province; ...

(g) "local undertaking" means a work or undertaking for the transport of passengers or goods by motor vehicle, not being an extra-provincial undertaking; and

(h) "provincial transport board" means a board, commission or other body or person having under the law of a province authority to control or regulate the operation of a local undertaking.

3.(1) Where in any province a licence is by the law of the province required for the operation of a local undertaking, no person shall operate an extra-provincial undertaking in that province unless he holds a licence issued under the authority of this Act.

(2) The provincial transport board in each province may in its discretion issue a licence to a person to operate an extra-provincial undertaking into or through the province upon the like terms and conditions and in the like manner as if the extra-provincial undertaking operated in the province were a local undertaking. ...

5. The Governor in Council may exempt any person or the whole or any part of an extra-provincial undertaking or any extra-provincial transport from all or any of the provisions of this Act. ...

Coughlin was engaged only in extra-provincial trucking and challenged the constitutionality of the delegation of power to the Ontario Highway Transport Board to issue extra-provincial operating licences. That board was established by the *Public Commercial Vehicles Act*, RSO 1950, c. 304, which authorized the board to regulate intra-provincial trucking.]

CARTWRIGHT CJC (Fauteux, Abbott, Judson, and Spence JJ concurring): ... [A]s matters stand at present the question whether a person may operate the undertaking of an inter-provincial carrier of goods by motor vehicle within the limits of the Province of Ontario is to be decided by a Board constituted by the provincial legislature and which must be guided in the making of its decision by the terms of the statutes of that Legislature and the Regulations passed thereunder as they may exist from time to time.

Mr. Laidlaw argues that in bringing about this result by the enactment of s. 3 of the *Motor Vehicle Transport Act* Parliament has in substance and reality abdicated its power to make laws in relation to the subject of interprovincial motor vehicle carriage and unlawfully delegated that power to the provincial Legislature. ...

It is well settled that Parliament may confer upon a provincially constituted board power to regulate a matter within the exclusive jurisdiction of Parliament. On this point it is sufficient to refer to the reasons delivered in the case of *Prince Edward Island Potato Marketing Board v. H.B. Willis Inc.*, [1952] 2 SCR 392, [1952] 4 DLR 146.

In the case before us the respondent Board derives no power from the Legislature of Ontario to regulate or deal with the interprovincial carriage of goods. Its wide powers in that regard are conferred upon it by Parliament. Parliament has seen fit to enact that in the exercise of those powers the Board shall proceed in the same manner as that prescribed from time to time by the Legislature for its dealings with intraprovincial carriage. Parliament can at any time terminate the powers of the Board in regard to interprovincial carriage or alter the manner in which those powers are to be exercised. Should occasion for immediate action arise the Governor-General in Council may act under s. 5 of the *Motor Vehicle Transport Act*.

In my opinion there is here no delegation of law-making power, but rather the adoption by Parliament, in the exercise of its exclusive power, of the legislation of another body as it may from time to time exist, a course which has been held constitutionally valid by this Court in *Attorney-General for Ontario v. Scott*, [1956] SCR 137, 1 DLR (2d) 433, and by the Court of Appeal for Ontario in *R v. Glibbery*, [1963] 1 OR 232, 36 DLR (2d) 548. …

RITCHIE J (Martland J concurring) dissenting: … In the case of *A-G Ont. v. Winner*, [1954] AC 541, [1954] 4 DLR 657, the Privy Council had decided that it was beyond the legislative powers of a Province (New Brunswick) to prohibit the operator of an interprovincial bus line from carrying passengers from points outside the Province to points within the Province and vice versa on the ground that no Province had jurisdiction to legislate in relation to extra-provincial transport. The matter was succinctly stated by Lord Porter at p. 678 DLR where he said: "… it is for the Dominion alone to exercise either by Act or by Regulation control over connecting undertakings."

It appears to me to be of more than passing interest to note that the *Motor Vehicle Transport Act* (Can.) was assented to by Parliament almost exactly four months after the decision in the *Winner* case had been rendered by the Privy Council and that three months later, at the request of the Province of Ontario, a proclamation was issued "declaring the said act to be in force in the said province."

It seems to me that if it is to be held that s. 3(2) of the *Motor Vehicle Transport Act* is valid federal legislation, then the effect of the decision in the *Winner* case has been effectively nullified in so far as the province of Ontario is concerned. …

In the case of the *Motor Vehicle Transport Act*, direct authority has been given to the local board in each Province "in its discretion to issue a licence to a person to operate an extra-provincial undertaking into or through the province," and the manner in which that discretion is to be exercised is not limited to such provincial Regulations as the Governor in Council may designate but is to be exactly the same as if the extra-provincial undertaking were a "local undertaking." In my view the effect of this legislation is that the control of the regulation of licensing of a "connecting undertaking," is turned over to the provincial authority, and in the Province of Ontario this means that the controlling legislation is the *Ontario Highway Transport Board Act*, RSO 1960, c. 273, and the *Public Commercial Vehicles Act*, RSO 1960, c. 319. …

There can, in my view, be no objection to Parliament enacting a statute in which existing provincial legislation is incorporated by reference so as to obviate the necessity of re-enacting it verbatim, but in providing for the granting of licences to extra-provincial undertakings in the like manner as if they were local undertakings, Parliament must, I think, be taken to have adopted the provisions of the provincial statutes in question as they may be amended from time to time. The result is that the granting of such licences is governed by the *Public Commercial Vehicles Act*, *supra*, pursuant to s. 16 of which the Lieutenant-Governor in Council may make Regulations "… (q) respecting any matter necessary or advisable to carry out effectively the intent and purpose of this Act."

I can only read this as meaning that the licensing Regulations for extra-provincial transport may be governed by decisions made from time to time by the Lieutenant-Governor in Council without any control by, or reference to, the federal authority. This is very different from adopting by reference the language used in a provincial statute and, in my opinion, it means that the control over the regulation of licensing in this field has been left in provincial hands.

It is, of course, true that Parliament can at any time terminate the powers of the provincial Boards to license extra-provincial undertakings, but it seems to me that this would entail repealing s. 3(2) of the *Motor Vehicle Transport Act* and it is the constitutionality of that subsection which is here impugned.

It is also suggested that the Governor in Council might exercise control by acting under s. 5 of the *Motor Vehicle Transport Act* [quoted above]. ...

I do not read this latter section as reserving any power to the Governor in Council to nullify the effect of s. 3(2) of the Act by exempting all extra-provincial transport from its provisions, and I am therefore of opinion that no control was retained by the federal authority over the unlimited legislative powers which it purported to transfer to the Province by the language employed in s. 3(2) of the Act. Presumably, any person or undertaking exempted by the Governor in Council from the provisions of the Act would be without authority to operate in the Province of Ontario, unless and until provision was made for the granting of a federal licence, but this would in no way affect the powers which s. 3(2) purported to confer on the Board to issue licences to persons or undertakings which had not been so exempted.

In my view, therefore, in enacting the *Motor Vehicle Transport Act*, and particularly s. 3(2) and s. 5 thereof, the Parliament of Canada purported to relinquish all control over a field in which Parliament has exclusive jurisdiction under the *BNA Act*, and left the power to exercise control of the licensing of extra-provincial undertakings to be regulated in such manner as the province might from time to time determine. ...

Appeal dismissed.

II. AMENDING THE CONSTITUTION

A. The Canadian Process of Constitutional Amendment

1. Design Issues

Designing an amending formula for a constitution raises many difficult issues. In the Canadian context, two have predominated. The first is the locus of sovereignty—that is, which institutions should be vested with the power of constitutional amendment. Should the power of constitutional amendment be directly vested with citizens, or instead with governments that are accountable to them? If the former, should there be provision for the election of a constituent assembly that would deliberate on constitutional amendments in advance of voting on them, or would ratification by a popular referendum with universal suffrage suffice? If the latter, are legislative assemblies the appropriate governmental institutions, and if so, given the federal nature of our polity, should some combination of legislative assemblies (both provincial and federal) be necessary to achieve constitutional change? Should certain groups, such as Aboriginal peoples in Canada, be required to consent to amendments affecting their rights? As these questions make clear, identifying the locus of sovereignty for constitutional change is parasitic on an underlying conception of the nature of the political community whose terms of association are found in that constitutional document. And to the extent that there is a lack of an agreement on that conception—as is arguably the case in Canada—the process for constitutional amendment becomes a forum through which competing conceptions of the Canadian political community come into conflict.

Closely related to the first issue is a second—the correct balance to be struck between stability and flexibility. On the one hand, a constitution is meant to provide a framework within which the ordinary politics of political communities take place. If this framework were easily subject to change, it would be more difficult for it to provide a set of background rules for political decision making. Moreover, since a constitution often addresses controversial issues, making constitutional change difficult arguably protects political decision making, because it reduces the ability of constitutional politics to crowd out ordinary politics (that is, the politics of nonconstitutional issues). On other hand, should a constitution prove to be too difficult to change, it may be incapable of adapting to responding to the changing nature of the political community, or to fundamental challenges to the constitutional order itself. A constitution that is overly rigid risks becoming illegitimate, a "suicide pact," rather than the foundation for the ongoing existence and functioning of a political order. The balance between stability and flexibility plays out in the level of support required for constitutional change. For example, should there be a super-majority requirement within legislative assemblies? Is a simple majority sufficient for referenda?

2. The Canadian Amendment Process

The process for amending the Canadian Constitution—often referred to as the amending formula—has been a source of ongoing controversy. Until 1982, amendments to the most important parts of the Canadian Constitution required legislation by the Parliament of the United Kingdom. The process was initiated by a joint resolution of the Canadian House of Commons and the Senate. Generally, the agreement of the provinces was sought when amendments affected their rights and interests. However, in 1980, in the face of failure to secure the agreement of the provinces on what would become the *Constitution Act, 1982*, the federal government announced its attention to secure the necessary constitutional amendment without provincial consent.

This federal move prompted a series of constitutional challenges before several provincial courts of appeal that were heard together by the Supreme Court in the 1981 *Patriation Reference (Re Resolution to Amend the Constitution of Canada*, [1981] 1 SCR 753, 125 DLR (3d) 1). The provinces argued that Canadian constitutional practice had crystallized into a legal requirement for provincial consent to constitutional changes affecting provincial interests. The federal government took the position that no such consent was required. Moreover, the provinces made the additional argument that a constitutional convention existed for provincial consent, a position that the federal government rejected as well. The Court held by a 7 to 2 margin that there was no legal requirement of provincial consent. But the Court also held by 6 to 3 that a constitutional convention had been established requiring a "substantial degree" of provincial consent to amendments affecting the provinces' interests.

The decision has been credited with forcing the federal government and the provinces back to the negotiating table, because although the Court acknowledged the legality of a unilateral federal move, it effectively declared that such a move would be illegitimate. The negotiations culminated in an agreement between the federal government and the nine provinces other than Quebec. In a later case brought by the Quebec government challenging whether Quebec's agreement to constitutional change was required for the requirement of "substantial consent," the Court concluded that there was no convention of a "Quebec veto"—that is, Quebec need not be among the provinces granting consent (*Re Objection by Quebec to Resolution to Amend the Constitution*, [1982] 2 SCR 793, 140 DLR (3d) 385).

An important feature of the 1982 constitutional package—which explains why it is referred to as the patriation package—is that it transferred the power for amending the Canadian Constitution from the Parliament in Westminster to Canadian political institutions. As it turns out, there is not a single decision rule for amending the Canadian Constitution. Rather, there are five rules, contained in Part V of the *Constitution Act, 1982*, which purport to apply to different types or categories of amendments:

1. The "general amending formula," or the "7/50 formula," found in s. 38(1), requires the consent of the Parliament of Canada and the legislatures of two thirds of the provinces having at least 50 percent of the population of Canada. No province alone has a veto on amendment, which has been a source of dissatisfaction in Quebec. This procedure is the only one in the Constitution subject to time limits: an amendment cannot be proclaimed until one year after the initiation of the amendment process unless every province has indicated assent or dissent (s. 39(1)), and an amendment dies unless it has received the appropriate degree of support within three years of the start of the process (s. 39(2)). Section 38(3) permits a province to opt out of an amendment derogating from its legislative powers, proprietary rights, or other rights and privileges. If the amendment transfers legislative powers from the provinces in relation to education or cultural matters, the province opting out is also entitled to reasonable compensation (s. 40). Section 38 is the default formula for constitutional amendments; that is, it applies to amendments that do not fall under the other amending formulas. Moreover, s. 42 specifically assigns some amendments to s. 38, for example, "the principle of proportionate representation of the provinces in the House of Commons" (the amendments specified by s. 42 cannot be the subject of opting out).

2. The "unanimity procedure," found in s. 41, requires that consent be provided by Parliament and the legislatures of all the provinces in relation to amendments to the office of the Queen, the Governor General, and the Lieutenant Governor of a province; the minimum number of members to which a province is entitled in the House of Commons as of 1982 (because of the "Senate floor rule" found in s. 51A of the *Constitution Act, 1867*); the general use of the English and French languages; the composition of the Supreme Court of Canada; and any amendment to the amending formulae.

3. The "bilateral procedure," found in s. 43, deals with provisions of the Constitution affecting only some provinces. Where an amendment is in relation to a provision affecting one or more, but not all provinces, only the legislatures of the provinces affected and Parliament need consent to the amendment.

4. The "federal unilateral procedure," in s. 44, allows Parliament alone to make amendments to the federal executive or the House of Commons or Senate (provided
amendments to the Houses of Parliament do not affect their powers or their method
of selection in ways protected by other parts of the amending formulae.) Section 44
replaces the old s. 91(1) of the *Constitution Act, 1867*, which was similarly worded.

5. The "provincial unilateral procedure," in s. 45, replaces the old s. 92(1) of the *Constitution Act, 1867* and permits the province to amend its constitution, provided that
the amendment does not affect matters governed by other amending formulae, such
as the office of the lieutenant governor.

In addition to Part V, s. 35.1 provides that amendments affecting Aboriginal rights or
changes to s. 91(24) of the *Constitution Act, 1867* will be preceded by a constitutional conference of first ministers and representatives of Aboriginal peoples. However, s. 35.1 does
not impose a duty to obtain the consent of Aboriginal peoples.

For further readings on the amending formula, see K. Swinton, "Amending the Canadian
Constitution: Lessons from Meech Lake" (1992), 42 *University of Toronto Law Journal* 139
and P.W. Hogg, "Formal Amendment of the Constitution of Canada" (1992), 55 *Law & Contemporary Problems* 253.

B. Evaluating the Amending Formula

1. Constitutional Amendment After 1982

The amending formula in Part V of the *Constitution Act, 1982* has been used successfully on
ten occasions since 1982. The "7/50" formula has only been used once, to amend the Aboriginal rights provisions in ss. 25 and 35 of the *Constitution Act, 1982*, to add ss. 35(3),
35(4), and 35.1, and to amend s. 25(2). Section 44 has been relied on by Parliament twice.
The *Constitution Act, 1985* (Representation) repealed s. 51(1) of the *Constitution Act, 1867*
(which had been amended many times since 1867) to lay down new rules governing representation in the House of Commons; the *Constitution Act, 1999* (Nunavut) amended the
relevant provisions of the *Constitution Act, 1867* to provide for the appointment of a senator
from Nunavut.

The remaining seven amendments have been made through s. 43, and have all involved
the federal government and one other province. For example, s. 43 was used in 1993 to extend language rights in New Brunswick, by adding s. 16.1 to the *Constitution Act, 1982*. The
most controversial amendments involving s. 43 have concerned denominational school
rights in Newfoundland (three amendments) and Quebec (one amendment). The Newfoundland amendments have all involved changes to Term 17 of the Newfoundland Terms
of Union (which were constitutionalized by the *Newfoundland Act*, 12 & 13 Geo. VI, c. 22
(UK)). Term 17 replaced s. 93 of the *Constitution Act, 1867* with respect to Newfoundland,
and entrenched a set of denominational school rights. In 1987, Term 17 was amended to
extend those rights to Pentecostal schools (Constitution Amendment, 1987). However, in
1997 (Constitution Amendment, 1997 (*Newfoundland Act*)), and again in 1998 (Constitution Amendment, 1998 (*Newfoundland Act*)), Term 17 was amended first to dilute, and then
to remove, the constitutional protection accorded to denominational schools. Both of these

amendments were made after province-wide referenda in which a majority of Newfoundlanders voted in favour of the amendments.

During the Parliamentary debate surrounding the first amendment, a number of religious groups argued that Parliament should not pass the resolution approving the proposed amendment because of the impact on minority rights. Nevertheless, the House of Commons passed the necessary resolution. Is there a federal obligation to enact such a measure, simply if the majority in the province so wishes? Conversely, does the federal Parliament owe a special obligation to protect the denominational school rights of minority groups who are liable to be outvoted in the political process?

The second amendment was challenged in the courts on the ground that the appropriate amending formula was s. 38, not s. 43, since denominational school rights were elements of national citizenship. The challenge was rejected on the grounds that Term 17 only applied to Newfoundland, and hence that s. 43 was the appropriate provision to amend it: *Hogan v. Newfoundland (Attorney-General)* (2000), 183 DLR (4th) 225 (Nfld. CA), leave to appeal denied, 2000 SCC No. 191. The Quebec amendments also abolished denominational school rights in that province by providing, in a new s. 93A, that s. 93 no longer applied to Quebec (Constitutional Amendment, 1999 (Quebec)). A similar constitutional challenge was rejected by the Quebec courts: *Potter c. Québec (Procureur général)*, [2001] JQ No. 5553 (Que. CA). Do you agree with these holdings?

Notwithstanding the numerous amendments that have been made since 1982, there have been two significant failures. These are the Meech Lake Accord and the Charlottetown Accord. Both accords began as efforts to win Quebec's acceptance of the 1982 constitutional amendments. The Meech Lake Accord included constitutional recognition of Quebec as a distinct society, entrenchment of the Supreme Court of Canada and provincial nomination of its justices, an increase in the number of items requiring unanimity under the amending formula, and controls on the federal spending power. Many of these elements reappeared in the Charlottetown Accord, along with changes to the distribution of powers, an entrenched Aboriginal right to self-government, an elected Senate with equal provincial representation, and a guaranteed level of Quebec representation in the House of Commons.

The Meech Lake Accord included items that required unanimous approval (for example, changes to the amending formula), as well as items that could be approved under the general formula in s. 38. As a consequence, the issue of how the different amending formulas would interact was an important one. In theory, the Accord could have been voted upon by legislative assemblies in two ways. The first route would have been to break down the Accord into its constituent components, and to vote on each component separately according to the appropriate amending formula. This approach would have raised the possibility that some aspects of the Accord would have been adopted, but others rejected, an unacceptable political outcome since the package represented a compromise that its proponents believed stood or fell together. The second route was to present the amendments for approval as a package. By implication, the requirements of ss. 38 and 41 applied to the entire package, meaning that unanimous approval (s. 41) was required within three years (s. 38). The Accord died in June 1990, having failed to meet these requirements. The Charlottetown Accord, which was voted down in a national referendum in 1992, also contained a mix of amendments, some requiring approval under s. 38, others under s. 41.

Peter Russell has argued that in the wake of the Meech Lake and Charlottetown accords, the politics of constitutional reform has become a so-called "mega-constitutional" politics (P.H. Russell, *Constitutional Odyssey: Can Canadians Become a Sovereign People?* (Toronto: University of Toronto Press, 1993)). The characteristic feature of mega-constitutional politics is the unwillingness of various constitutional actors to undertake piecemeal or incremental constitutional reform, tackling issues one at a time (for example, Senate reform, the spending power). Instead, complex packages of the sort found in the Meech Lake and Charlottetown accords will be the norm into the foreseeable future. Arguably, one of the legal implications of mega-constitutional politics is that ss. 38 and 41 will apply cumulatively to future packages of constitutional amendments, making amendment extraordinarily difficult.

2. Is Part V Undemocratic?

Alan Cairns has argued that the dominance of governments in the amending formula is inconsistent with popular sovereignty and the "citizens' constitution" enshrined with the Charter of Rights in 1982 (*Charter Versus Federalism: The Dilemmas of Constitutional Reform* (Montreal: McGill-Queen's University Press, 1991), at 6-8):

> In Pierre Trudeau's oft-repeated phrase, the Charter says that the rights of people precede those of governments. The amending formula states that sovereignty resides in a collective of governments that can amend the constitution in terms of their own self-interest and announce their results as a *fait accompli*, assuming that legislatures can be kept under control.
>
> In somewhat different language, the *Constitution Act, 1982*, displays two competing visions of the relation of the constitution to the peoples and governments of Canada. The amending formula presupposes that federalism is the most important constitutional organizing principle, that governments are the major actors in federalism, and that accordingly amendment of the constitution that determines their status and power within federalism is properly a matter for those governments to handle. This "government's constitution" contrasts with the "citizens' constitution" generated by the Charter, which presupposes that the citizen state axis is no less fundamental than the federal–provincial constitutional axis. Accordingly, citizens via the Charter are just as much part of the constitution as are provincial governments by virtue of section 92 of the *Constitution Act, 1867*, allocating law-making power to provincial legislatures. ...
>
> The amending formula defines Canada as a country of governments presiding over and speaking for the national and provincial communities that federalism sustains. Its implicit assumption is that only the cleavages defined by federalism have to be catered to in the amending formula, and they can be represented by governments. The Charter, however, defines Canadians as a single community of rights-bearers, makes only limited concessions to provincialism, and clearly engenders a non-deferential attitude toward those who wield government power. The community message of the Charter contradicts the community message of the amending formula. The Charter, in addition to defining Canadians in terms of rights, also singles out specific categories for particular recognitions and rights—women, official-language minorities, multicultural Canadians, and others. By so doing it states that the federal–provincial cleavage, and the communities derived from it, do not exhaust the constitutionally significant identities that Canadians now possess. Succinctly, the Charter states what the amending formula denies, that "federalism is not enough"—that Canadians are more than a federal people.

Do you agree with Cairns? If so, should there be some guarantee of popular input in the amendment process? Should it come at the stage of formulating an amendment (for example, in the form of a constituent assembly), or at the time of approval (for example, in a referendum)? Cairns' criticism was leveled at the process that led to the negotiation of the Meech Lake Accord, which occurred almost entirely behind closed doors and with minimal input from legislatures (which were presented with the Accord by first ministers as a *fait accompli*), let alone citizens.

However, Patrick Monahan has argued that the process surrounding the Charlottetown Accord illustrates the democratic potential of Part V. Monahan notes that before the formulation of the Charlottetown Accord, the federal government established the Citizens Forum on Canada's Future (chaired by Keith Spicer) in November 1990, and established a joint House–Senate committee to consider proposals for changes to the amending formula (the Beaudoin-Edwards Committee) in December 1990. The federal government's constitutional proposals were then released in September 1991. Initially, these proposals were put before a second joint House–Senate committee (the Beaudoin-Dobbie Committee). However, in response to public demand for greater participation, the federal government convened five conferences held in early 1992, attended by federal and provincial politicians, interest groups' representatives, and ordinary Canadians. The final phase of the Charlottetown process was an intergovernmental negotiation, in which governments and Aboriginal representatives were the sole participants. But after the Accord had been negotiated, it was put to the public in a national referendum, in which it was voted down. See P.J. Monahan, "The Sounds of Silence," in K. McRoberts and P.J. Monahan, eds., *The Charlottetown Accord, the Referendum, and the Future of Canada* (Toronto: University of Toronto Press, 1993), at 222.

Some commentators have argued that resort to a referendum during the Charlottetown process established a constitutional convention of popular ratification of amendments. You may remember from Chapter 1, Introduction, that conventions are not legally binding. In the 1981 *Patriation Reference, supra,* the majority on the convention issue adopted (at 90 DLR) the following passage from Sir W. Ivor Jennings, *The Law and the Constitution*, 5th ed. (London: University of London Press, 1959), at 136,

> We have to ask ourselves three questions: first, what are the precedents; second, did the actors in the precedents believe that they were bound by a rule; and third, is there a reason for the rule? A single precedent with a good reason may be enough to establish the rule. A whole string of precedents without such a reason will be of no avail, unless it is perfectly certain that the persons concerned regarded themselves as bound by it.

Do you think that there is a convention that there should be a referendum before any constitutional amendment? Before a package of major constitutional changes?

3. Constitutional Amendment and Quebec Sovereignty

Quebec governments have pressed for the inclusion of a Quebec veto in the amending formula. To date they have been unsuccessful, except for the list of matters in s. 41 (the unanimity formula), which gives a veto to all the provinces. The Meech Lake and Charlottetown accords would have expanded the list of matters subject to s. 41. Would this have been advisable?

In October 1995, a referendum on sovereignty was narrowly defeated in Quebec (discussed below). This prompted the federal Parliament to enact the *Constitutional Amendments Act*, SC 1996, c. 1, which provides a regional veto—including a veto for Quebec—in the form of a federal government promise not to propose any constitutional amendment without the agreement of the five regions of Canada, except in circumstances where a province affected can exercise a veto or opt out of the amendment. The Act reads:

> 1(1) No Minister of the Crown shall propose a motion for a resolution to authorize an amendment to the Constitution of Canada, other than an amendment in respect of which the legislative assembly of a province may exercise a veto under section 41 or 43 of the *Constitution Act, 1982* or may express its dissent under subsection 38(3) of that Act, unless the amendment has first been consented to by a majority of the provinces that includes:
>
> > (a) Ontario;
> >
> > (b) Quebec;
> >
> > (c) two or more of the Atlantic provinces that have, according to the then latest general census, combined population of at least fifty per cent of the population of all the Atlantic provinces; and
> >
> > (d) two or more of the Prairie provinces that have, according to the then latest general census, combined population of at least fifty per cent of the population of all the Prairie provinces;
> >
> > (e) British Columbia.
>
> (2) In this section,
>
> > "Atlantic provinces" mean the provinces of Nova Scotia, New Brunswick, Prince Edward Island and Newfoundland;
> >
> > "Prairie provinces" means the provinces of Manitoba, Saskatchewan and Alberta.

Does this make the amending formula unnecessarily rigid?

In recent years, discussions of the amending formula have centred on the potential secession of Quebec. This issue has attracted the attention of legal commentators because of the 1995 sovereignty referendum in that province, which rejected sovereignty by an extremely narrow margin. Part of the federal government's response was to convince Quebeckers' that the road to independence would be costly and difficult. In particular, the federal government sought to respond to the view, asserted by some Quebec sovereigntists, that a "yes" vote would automatically effect the legal secession of the province. They did this by asserting that a "yes" vote had no concrete legal effect, and would at best result in a political process of intergovernmental negotiations that might culminate in a package of constitutional amendments that would have to comply with the rules spelled out in Part V to become effective. The centrepiece of this part of the federal strategy—referred to as "Plan B"—was the posing of the following three reference questions to the Supreme Court of Canada on September 30, 1996:

> 1. Under the Constitution of Canada, can the National Assembly, legislature or government of Quebec effect the secession of Quebec from Canada unilaterally?
>
> 2. Does international law give the National Assembly, legislature or government of Quebec the right to effect the secession of Quebec from Canada unilaterally? In this regard, is there a right to self-determination under international law that would give the National Assembly, legislature or government of Quebec the right to effect the secession of Quebec from Canada unilaterally?

3. In the event of a conflict between domestic and international law on the right of the National Assembly, legislature or government of Quebec to effect the secession of Quebec from
Canada unilaterally, which would take precedence in Canada?

The expectation among legal commentators was that the Court would answer the first two
questions in the negative and that, as a consequence, it would decline to answer the third
question. With respect to question 1, it was thought that the Court would simply point out
that although the Constitution contains no provisions governing secession of a province, the
Constitution does not expressly prohibit it, meaning that secession is legally possible. However, what secession requires is a constitutional amendment and, hence, compliance with
the amending formulas in Part V of the *Constitution Act, 1982*. The legal secession of a province from Canada would require many constitutional amendments (for one list, see P. Russell and B. Ryder, *Ratifying a Postreferendum Agreement on Quebec Sovereignty* (Toronto:
C.D. Howe Institute, 1997)). Legal commentators were generally of the view that most of the
required changes would engage amending formulas other than s. 45 (the provincial unilateral procedure), because the required changes would go much further than the constitution
of a province. And since every other amending formula requires the consent of the federal
government, it was thought that the Court would simply hold that a unilateral secession, by
definition, is unconstitutional.

In its judgment, the Supreme Court confounded those expectations. The following extract contains the part of the Court's judgment dealing specifically with the constitutionality
of unilateral secession. The earlier portions of the judgment, in which the Court sets out the
principles of the Canadian Constitution on which it draws to deal with the secession issue,
are found in Chapter 1, Introduction.

Reference re Secession of Quebec
[1998] 2 SCR 217, 161 DLR (4th) 385

THE COURT (Lamer CJC, L'Heureux-Dubé, Gonthier, Cory, McLachlin, Iacobucci, Major, Bastarache, and Binnie JJ): ... [83] Secession is the effort of a group or section of a
state to withdraw itself from the political and constitutional authority of that state, with
a view to achieving statehood for a new territorial unit on the international plane. In a
federal state, secession typically takes the form of a territorial unit seeking to withdraw
from the federation. Secession is a legal act as much as a political one. By the terms of
Question 1 of this Reference, we are asked to rule on the legality of unilateral secession
"[u]nder the Constitution of Canada." This is an appropriate question, as the legality of
unilateral secession must be evaluated, at least in the first instance, from the perspective
of the domestic legal order of the state from which the unit seeks to withdraw. ...

[84] The secession of a province from Canada must be considered, in legal terms, to
require an amendment to the Constitution, which perforce requires negotiation. The
amendments necessary to achieve a secession could be radical and extensive. Some commentators have suggested that secession could be a change of such a magnitude that it
could not be considered to be merely an amendment to the Constitution. We are not
persuaded by this contention. It is of course true that the Constitution is silent as to the

ability of a province to secede from Confederation but, although the Constitution neither expressly authorizes nor prohibits secession, an act of secession would purport to alter the governance of Canadian territory in a manner which undoubtedly is inconsistent with our current constitutional arrangements. The fact that those changes would be profound, or that they would purport to have a significance with respect to international law, does not negate their nature as amendments to the Constitution of Canada.

[85] The Constitution is the expression of the sovereignty of the people of Canada. It lies within the power of the people of Canada, acting through their various governments duly elected and recognized under the Constitution, to effect whatever constitutional arrangements are desired within Canadian territory, including, should it be so desired, the secession of Quebec from Canada. ... By the terms of this Reference, we have been asked to consider whether it would be constitutional in such a circumstance for the National Assembly, legislature or government of Quebec to effect the secession of Quebec from Canada *unilaterally*.

[86] The "unilateral" nature of the act is of cardinal importance and we must be clear as to what is understood by this term. In one sense, any step towards a constitutional amendment initiated by a single actor on the constitutional stage is "unilateral." We do not believe that this is the meaning contemplated by Question 1, nor is this the sense in which the term has been used in argument before us. Rather, what is claimed by a right to secede "unilaterally" is the right to effectuate secession without prior negotiations with the other provinces and the federal government. At issue is not the legality of the first step but the legality of the final act of purported unilateral secession. The supposed juridical basis for such an act is said to be a clear expression of democratic will in a referendum in the province of Quebec. This claim requires us to examine the possible juridical impact, if any, of such a referendum on the functioning of our Constitution, and on the claimed legality of a unilateral act of secession.

[87] Although the Constitution does not itself address the use of a referendum procedure, and the results of a referendum have no direct role or legal effect in our constitutional scheme, a referendum undoubtedly may provide a democratic method of ascertaining the views of the electorate on important political questions on a particular occasion. The democratic principle identified above would demand that considerable weight be given to a clear expression by the people of Quebec of their will to secede from Canada, even though a referendum, in itself and without more, has no direct legal effect, and could not in itself bring about unilateral secession. Our political institutions are premised on the democratic principle, and so an expression of the democratic will of the people of a province carries weight, in that it would confer legitimacy on the efforts of the government of Quebec to initiate the Constitution's amendment process in order to secede by constitutional means. In this context, we refer to a "clear" majority as a qualitative evaluation. The referendum result, if it is to be taken as an expression of the democratic will, must be free of ambiguity both in terms of the question asked and in terms of the support it achieves.

[88] The federalism principle, in conjunction with the democratic principle, dictates that the clear repudiation of the existing constitutional order and the clear expression of the desire to pursue secession by the population of a province would give rise to a reciprocal obligation on all parties to Confederation to negotiate constitutional changes to respond to that desire. The amendment of the Constitution begins with a political process

undertaken pursuant to the Constitution itself. In Canada, the initiative for constitutional amendment is the responsibility of democratically elected representatives of the participants in Confederation. Those representatives may, of course, take their cue from a referendum, but in legal terms, constitution-making in Canada, as in many countries, is undertaken by the democratically elected representatives of the people. The corollary of a legitimate attempt by one participant in Confederation to seek an amendment to the Constitution is an obligation on all parties to come to the negotiating table. The clear repudiation by the people of Quebec of the existing constitutional order would confer legitimacy on demands for secession, and place an obligation on the other provinces and the federal government to acknowledge and respect that expression of democratic will by entering into negotiations and conducting them in accordance with the underlying constitutional principles already discussed.

[89] What is the content of this obligation to negotiate? At this juncture, we confront the difficult inter-relationship between substantive obligations flowing from the Constitution and questions of judicial competence and restraint in supervising or enforcing those obligations. This is mirrored by the distinction between the legality and the legitimacy of actions taken under the Constitution. We propose to focus first on the substantive obligations flowing from this obligation to negotiate; once the nature of those obligations has been described, it is easier to assess the appropriate means of enforcement of those obligations, and to comment on the distinction between legality and legitimacy.

[90] The conduct of the parties in such negotiations would be governed by the same constitutional principles which give rise to the duty to negotiate: federalism, democracy, constitutionalism and the rule of law, and the protection of minorities. Those principles lead us to reject two absolutist propositions. One of those propositions is that there would be a legal obligation on the other provinces and federal government to accede to the secession of a province, subject only to negotiation of the logistical details of secession. This proposition is attributed either to the supposed implications of the democratic principle of the Constitution, or to the international law principle of self-determination of peoples.

[91] For both theoretical and practical reasons, we cannot accept this view. We hold that Quebec could not purport to invoke a right of self-determination such as to dictate the terms of a proposed secession to the other parties: that would not be a negotiation at all. As well, it would be naive to expect that the substantive goal of secession could readily be distinguished from the practical details of secession. The devil would be in the details. The democracy principle, as we have emphasized, cannot be invoked to trump the principles of federalism and rule of law, the rights of individuals and minorities, or the operation of democracy in the other provinces or in Canada as a whole. No negotiations could be effective if their ultimate outcome, secession, is cast as an absolute legal entitlement based upon an obligation to give effect to that act of secession in the Constitution. Such a foregone conclusion would actually undermine the obligation to negotiate and render it hollow.

[92] However, we are equally unable to accept the reverse proposition, that a clear expression of self-determination by the people of Quebec would impose *no* obligations upon the other provinces or the federal government. The continued existence and operation of the Canadian constitutional order cannot remain indifferent to the clear expression of a clear majority of Quebecers that they no longer wish to remain in Canada. This

would amount to the assertion that other constitutionally recognized principles necessarily trump the clearly expressed democratic will of the people of Quebec. Such a proposition fails to give sufficient weight to the underlying constitutional principles that must inform the amendment process, including the principles of democracy and federalism. The rights of other provinces and the federal government cannot deny the right of the government of Quebec to pursue secession, should a clear majority of the people of Quebec choose that goal, so long as in doing so, Quebec respects the rights of others. Negotiations would be necessary to address the interests of the federal government, of Quebec and the other provinces, and other participants, as well as the rights of all Canadians both within and outside Quebec.

[93] Is the rejection of both of these propositions reconcilable? Yes, once it is realized that none of the rights or principles under discussion is absolute to the exclusion of the others. This observation suggests that other parties cannot exercise their rights in such a way as to amount to an absolute denial of Quebec's rights, and similarly, that so long as Quebec exercises its rights while respecting the rights of others, it may propose secession and seek to achieve it through negotiation. The negotiation process precipitated by a decision of a clear majority of the population of Quebec on a clear question to pursue secession would require the reconciliation of various rights and obligations by the representatives of two legitimate majorities, namely, the clear majority of the population of Quebec, and the clear majority of Canada as a whole, whatever that may be. There can be no suggestion that either of these majorities "trumps" the other. A political majority that does not act in accordance with the underlying constitutional principles we have identified puts at risk the legitimacy of the exercise of its rights.

[94] In such circumstances, the conduct of the parties assumes primary constitutional significance. The negotiation process must be conducted with an eye to the constitutional principles we have outlined, which must inform the actions of *all* the participants in the negotiation process.

[95] Refusal of a party to conduct negotiations in a manner consistent with constitutional principles and values would seriously put at risk the legitimacy of that party's assertion of its rights, and perhaps the negotiation process as a whole. Those who quite legitimately insist upon the importance of upholding the rule of law cannot at the same time be oblivious to the need to act in conformity with constitutional principles and values, and so do their part to contribute to the maintenance and promotion of an environment in which the rule of law may flourish.

[96] No one can predict the course that such negotiations might take. The possibility that they might not lead to an agreement amongst the parties must be recognized. Negotiations following a referendum vote in favour of seeking secession would inevitably address a wide range of issues, many of great import. After 131 years of Confederation, there exists, inevitably, a high level of integration in economic, political and social institutions across Canada. The vision of those who brought about Confederation was to create a unified country, not a loose alliance of autonomous provinces. Accordingly, while there are regional economic interests, which sometimes coincide with provincial boundaries, there are also national interests and enterprises (both public and private) that would face potential dismemberment. There is a national economy and a national debt. Arguments were raised before us regarding boundary issues. There are linguistic and

cultural minorities, including aboriginal peoples, unevenly distributed across the country who look to the Constitution of Canada for the protection of their rights. Of course, secession would give rise to many issues of great complexity and difficulty. These would have to be resolved within the overall framework of the rule of law, thereby assuring Canadians resident in Quebec and elsewhere a measure of stability in what would likely be a period of considerable upheaval and uncertainty. Nobody seriously suggests that our national existence, seamless in so many aspects, could be effortlessly separated along what are now the provincial boundaries of Quebec. As the Attorney General of Saskatchewan put it in his oral submission:

> A nation is built when the communities that comprise it make commitments to it, when they forego choices and opportunities on behalf of a nation, ... when the communities that comprise it make compromises, when they offer each other guarantees, when they make transfers and perhaps most pointedly, when they receive from others the benefits of national solidarity. The threads of a thousand acts of accommodation are the fabric of a nation ... .

[97] In the circumstances, negotiations following such a referendum would undoubtedly be difficult. While the negotiators would have to contemplate the possibility of secession, there would be no absolute legal entitlement to it and no assumption that an agreement reconciling all relevant rights and obligations would actually be reached. It is foreseeable that even negotiations carried out in conformity with the underlying constitutional principles could reach an impasse. We need not speculate here as to what would then transpire. Under the Constitution, secession requires that an amendment be negotiated.

[98] The respective roles of the courts and political actors in discharging the constitutional obligations we have identified follows ineluctably from the foregoing observations. In the *Patriation Reference* [*Reference re Amendment of the Constitution, Nos. 1, 2, 3*, [1981] 1 SCR 753], a distinction was drawn between the law of the Constitution, which, generally speaking, will be enforced by the courts, and other constitutional rules, such as the conventions of the Constitution, which carry only political sanctions. It is also the case, however, that judicial intervention, even in relation to the *law* of the Constitution, is subject to the Court's appreciation of its proper role in the constitutional scheme.

· · ·

[100] The role of the Court in this Reference is limited to the identification of the relevant aspects of the Constitution in their broadest sense. We have interpreted the questions as relating to the constitutional framework within which political decisions may ultimately be made. Within that framework, the workings of the political process are complex and can only be resolved by means of political judgments and evaluations. The Court has no supervisory role over the political aspects of constitutional negotiations. Equally, the initial impetus for negotiation, namely a clear majority on a clear question in favour of secession, is subject only to political evaluation, and properly so. A right and a corresponding duty to negotiate secession cannot be built on an alleged expression of democratic will if the expression of democratic will is itself fraught with ambiguities. Only the political actors would have the information and expertise to make the appropriate judgment as to the point at which, and the circumstances in which, those ambiguities are resolved one way or the other.

[101] If the circumstances giving rise to the duty to negotiate were to arise, the distinction between the strong defence of legitimate interests and the taking of positions which, in fact, ignore the legitimate interests of others is one that also defies legal analysis. The Court would not have access to all of the information available to the political actors, and the methods appropriate for the search for truth in a court of law are ill-suited to getting to the bottom of constitutional negotiations. To the extent that the questions are political in nature, it is not the role of the judiciary to interpose its own views on the different negotiating positions of the parties, even were it invited to do so. Rather, it is the obligation of the elected representatives to give concrete form to the discharge of their constitutional obligations which only they and their electors can ultimately assess. The reconciliation of the various legitimate constitutional interests outlined above is necessarily committed to the political rather than the judicial realm, precisely because that reconciliation can only be achieved through the give and take of the negotiation process. Having established the legal framework, it would be for the democratically elected leadership of the various participants to resolve their differences.

· · ·

[104] Accordingly, the secession of Quebec from Canada cannot be accomplished by the National Assembly, the legislature or government of Quebec unilaterally, that is to say, without principled negotiations, and be considered a lawful act. Any attempt to effect the secession of a province from Canada must be undertaken pursuant to the Constitution of Canada, or else violate the Canadian legal order. However, the continued existence and operation of the Canadian constitutional order cannot remain unaffected by the unambiguous expression of a clear majority of Quebecers that they no longer wish to remain in Canada. The primary means by which that expression is given effect is the constitutional duty to negotiate in accordance with the constitutional principles that we have described herein. In the event secession negotiations are initiated, our Constitution, no less than our history, would call on the participants to work to reconcile the rights, obligations and legitimate aspirations of all Canadians within a framework that emphasizes constitutional responsibilities as much as it does constitutional rights.

NOTES

1. *Clear Majority, Clear Question, and the Duty to Negotiate*: Until the judgment, it had been thought that referenda played no role in constitutional amendment. Indeed, an earlier draft of Part V had included an additional formula that would have permitted amendment on the basis of a positive result in a national referendum; this procedure was removed during federal–provincial negotiations. The central holding in the *Secession Reference* is that "a decision of a clear majority of the population of Quebec on a clear question to pursue secession" would trigger a duty to negotiate the required constitutional amendments to give effect to the desire to secede. However, the Court did not define what a "clear majority" or a "clear question" was. Commentators have offered a range of views on both issues. The clear majority requirement has been given varying interpretations: that it imposes a super-majority requirement (for example, 60 percent or two-thirds); that it means a simple majority but with the results free from doubt that could be created, for example, by voting irregularities; or that it means a majority of eligible voters, as opposed to simply a majority of votes cast. What do

you think? On the issue of what a clear question would be, the Court says no more than that the question should be on secession. Would this preclude posing a question that omitted any reference to secession, for example, a question that referred to sovereignty, or to renewed federalism? In this context, consider the question posed to voters in the 1995 referendum:

> "Do you agree that Quebec should become sovereign, after having made a formal offer to Canada for a new economic and political partnership, within the scope of the bill respecting the future of Quebec and of the agreement signed on June 12, 1995?"

Is this question "a clear question to pursue secession"? As well, the Court did not specify who the parties to constitutional negotiations would be—that is, which parties would be under the duty to negotiate. The judgment refers variously to "the other provinces and the federal government," "the representatives of two legitimate majorities," and "participants in Confederation." Does this mean that negotiations would be bilateral (that is, between Quebec and the federal government) or multilateral? If the negotiations are multilateral, would they be limited to representatives of the federal and provincial governments, or would they include Aboriginal peoples?

2. *No Judicial Supervision*: Arguably, the ambiguities in the judgment would not have posed a difficulty if the Court had indicated its future willingness to flesh out the legal framework governing secession, and to supervise both the process and outcome of constitutional negotiations. However, the Court declined to do so, effectively leaving the interpretation and application of the rules of the Canadian Constitution governing secession to "the political actors." Is this the normal division of labour between courts and legislatures in constitutional interpretation? If not, what reasons did the Court give for departing from this norm? Are these reasons convincing? Consider the following explanation offered by Sujit Choudhry and Robert Howse:

> [O]nce we examine the political context surrounding the *Quebec Secession Reference*, it becomes evident that the Court acted in the face of the failure of federal political institutions to face the challenge posed by the referendum process in Quebec to the legitimacy of the Canadian constitutional order ... . Before the reference questions had been issued, it was entirely open to the federal government to lay down principles governing referenda and secession.

(S. Choudhry and R. Howse, "Constitutional Theory and the *Quebec Secession Reference*" (2000), 13 *Canadian Journal of Law & Jurisprudence* 143.)

Both the federal Parliament and the Quebec National Assembly have accepted the Court's invitation to contextualize the constitutional norms regarding secession. See the federal *Clarity Act* (*An Act to give effect to the requirement for clarity as set out in the opinion of the Supreme Court of Canada in the Quebec Secession Reference*, SC 2000, c. 26) and Quebec's *Fundamental Rights Act* (*An Act respecting the exercise of the fundamental rights and prerogatives of the Québec people and the Québec State*, SQ 2000, c. 46). On the question of what constitutes a clear majority, s. 2 of the *Clarity Act* provides as follows:

> 2(1) Where the government of a province, following a referendum relating to the secession of the province from Canada, seeks to enter into negotiations on the terms on which that province might cease to be part of Canada, the House of Commons shall, except where it has determined pursuant to section 1 that a referendum question is not clear, consider and, by resolution,

set out its determination on whether, in the circumstances, there has been a clear expression of a will by a clear majority of the population of that province that the province cease to be part of Canada.

(2) In considering whether there has been a clear expression of a will by a clear majority of the population of a province that the province cease to be part of Canada, the House of Commons shall take into account

(a) the size of the majority of valid votes cast in favour of the secessionist option;

(b) the percentage of eligible voters voting in the referendum; and

(c) any other matters or circumstances it considers to be relevant

(3) In considering whether there has been a clear expression of a will by a clear majority of the population of a province that the province cease to be part of Canada, the House of Commons shall take into account the views of all political parties represented in the legislative assembly of the province whose government proposed the referendum on secession, any formal statements or resolutions by the government or legislative assembly of any province or territory of Canada, any formal statements or resolutions by the Senate, any formal statements or resolutions by the representatives of the Aboriginal peoples of Canada, especially those in the province whose government proposed the referendum on secession, and any other views it considers to be relevant.

(4) The Government of Canada shall not enter into negotiations on the terms on which a province might cease to be part of Canada unless the House of Commons determines, pursuant to this section, that there has been a clear expression of a will by a clear majority of the population of that province that the province cease to be part of Canada.

By contrast, s. 4 of the *Fundamental Rights Act* provides (citations omitted):

When the Québec people [are] consulted by way of a referendum under the *Referendum Act*, the winning option is the option that obtains a majority of the valid votes cast, namely 50% of the valid votes cast plus one.

Do these provisions potentially conflict? How? If they do, do you think the Court will intervene in a subsequent case? Note that the Court did seem to suggest that it would pronounce on the correct amending formula for achieving secession (although the note below raises some questions about this).

3. *Secession Without a Constitutional Amendment?* In the *Secession Reference*, the Court refers to the need for a constitutional amendment to effect secession, states that the constitutional negotiations to secure such an amendment could be unsuccessful, and refuses to speculate on what the consequences of a failure of negotiations would be. However, consider the following paragraph:

[103] To the extent that a breach of the constitutional duty to negotiate in accordance with the principles described above undermines the legitimacy of a party's actions, it may have important ramifications at the international level. Thus, a failure of the duty to undertake negotiations and pursue them according to constitutional principles may undermine that government's claim to legitimacy which is generally a precondition for recognition by the international community. Conversely, violations of those principles by the federal or other provincial governments responding to the request for secession may undermine their legitimacy. Thus, a Quebec

that had negotiated in conformity with constitutional principles and values in the face of unreasonable intransigence on the part of other participants at the federal or provincial level would be more likely to be recognized than a Quebec which did not itself act according to constitutional principles in the negotiation process. Both the legality of the acts of the parties to the negotiation process under Canadian law, and the perceived legitimacy of such action, would be important considerations in the recognition process. In this way, the adherence of the parties to the obligation to negotiate would be evaluated in an indirect manner on the international plane.

Does this passage effectively create a right to unilateral secession after good faith negotiations? If so, can this be squared with the Court's holding that unilateral secession is unconstitutional? Conversely, does it explain the Court's statement that a right to unilateral secession is "the right to effectuate secession without prior negotiations with the other provinces and the federal government," as opposed to the right to secede without prior consent? Does it leave the enforcement of the rules of the Canadian Constitution governing secession to the international community?

PART THREE

The Judiciary

CHAPTER THIRTEEN

The Judicial Function

I. INTRODUCTION

This chapter deals with the place of courts and the judiciary in our constitutional structure. It addresses the structure of the court system in Canada, including the relationship between federal and provincial courts, and the shared responsibility of the federal and provincial governments for its operation; the extent to which Parliament and the provincial legislatures can assign adjudicative functions to bodies other than the superior courts; the principle of judicial independence; and the appointment of judges.

The most obvious, and in some ways most important, constitutional provisions relating to the judiciary are found in Part VII of the *Constitution Act, 1867*, which provides for the appointment of judges to the superior and district courts, as well as for their payment and removal. Together, these provisions are directed at guaranteeing judicial independence. They are also the basis upon which the powers of superior courts are distinguished from those of inferior courts—although this distinction has become increasingly less significant—and upon which certain powers of superior courts are protected from government interference (that is, the idea of a core of constitutionally protected jurisdiction). Finally, these provisions provide the framework for judicial review. Thus, Part VII provides constitutional standards relating to the independence of the judiciary and, through preserving the role of courts, it creates a constitutional separation of powers.

The provisions relating to the judiciary are essential to ensuring maintenance of the rule of law, that is, the principle that public actions, as well as citizens' liabilities and duties to the state, must have a legal basis and are to be determined according to law. The Supreme Court of Canada has inferred the rule of law from the *Constitution Act, 1867*: see the *Manitoba Language Rights Reference*, [1985] 1 SCR 721, 19 DLR (4th) 1 and the *Quebec Secession Reference*, [1998] 2 SCR 217, 161 DLR (4th) 385, the latter of which is found in Chapter 1, Introduction. In both cases, the rule of law was treated as a fundamental constitutional principle. In 1982, a commitment to the rule of law was explicitly acknowledged through the Preamble to the *Canadian Charter of Rights and Freedoms*, which states, in part: "Canada is founded upon ... the rule of law."

II. THE COURT STRUCTURE

Under section 92(14) of the *Constitution Act, 1867*, the provinces are responsible for the administration of justice in the province, including "the Constitution, Maintenance, and Organization of Provincial Courts, both of Civil and Criminal Jurisdiction." These "provincial courts" include both the superior courts, the judges of which are appointed by the Governor General under s. 96 of the *Constitution Act, 1867*, and the inferior courts, the judges of which are appointed by the province under s. 92(4) of the *Constitution Act, 1867*. The nomenclature can be confusing, since the term "provincial courts" is used to refer both to the courts to which the provinces appoint judges (the inferior courts) and to those superior and inferior courts that fall under provincial administrative responsibility by virtue of s. 92(14). The courts of the territories are not encompassed by Part VII of the *Constitution Act, 1867*, but are established by the statutes establishing the territories; see, for example, ss. 31 to 36 of the *Nunavut Act*, SC 1993, c. 28.

Sections 96 to 98 of the *Constitution Act, 1867* set out the manner of and qualifications for appointment to the superior, district, and county courts (all of which may be termed "s. 96 courts"). The judges of the s. 96 courts must be appointed by the Governor General from the bar of the province on whose courts they will sit. Section 99 provides that superior court judges (no specific reference is made to judges of the district and county courts) shall hold office during good behaviour until age seventy-five, but are removable by the Governor General on address of the Senate and House of Commons. Section 100 provides that the salaries and benefits of s. 96 judges are to be determined and paid by Parliament. This combination of provisions regarding appointment, payment, tenure, and process of removal is directed at guaranteeing the independence of what we may call superior court judges, an issue addressed more fully below. Thus we speak of "federally appointed" judges when referring to judges of the superior courts, even though the courts themselves are the responsibility of the provinces.

Sections 97 and 98 also recognize the fact that Canada has both common law and civil law traditions: s. 97 provides that the judges of all provinces except Quebec are to be appointed from among the members of the bar of the province to whose courts they are appointed, but it contemplates that the judges of those provinces might at some point come from any of those provinces, should the laws relating to property and civil rights be made uniform; under s. 98, the Quebec judges are always to be appointed from Quebec, since the Constitution does not contemplate that laws in Quebec and the other provinces will be made uniform.

Under s. 101, Parliament may also constitute, maintain, and organize "a General Court of Appeal for Canada," as well as "additional Courts for the better Administration of the Laws of Canada." These are known as "federal courts." Thus, in 1875 Parliament established the Supreme Court of Canada as a general court of appeal, as well as the Exchequer Court, replaced in 1970 by the Federal Court, which had both trial and appeal divisions. Sections 3 and 4 of the *Federal Courts Act*, RSC 1985, c. F-7, s. 1 (as am. by *Courts Administration Service Act*, SC 2002, c. 8), have modified this structure and there are now the Federal Court of Appeal and the Federal Court (previously the Federal Court Trial Division). Again, the nomenclature is confusing. The judges of both the Supreme Court of Canada and the Federal Court are federally appointed (the terms and conditions of appointment are established by statute). However, with respect to jurisdiction, the Supreme Court of Canada deals with matters arising from both the provincial courts and the Federal Court, while the jurisdiction of the Federal Court itself is established by statute to address matters involving federal institutions or arising out of federal law.

The superior courts have inherent jurisdiction and by provincial and federal statutes may also be given jurisdiction to deal with particular matters. In particular, they always have jurisdiction to deal with constitutional questions, whether those questions are the only issues raised or whether they are raised in the context of another issue. Where the constitutional question is raised in the context of another issue that is properly before an inferior court or a tribunal, the inferior court or tribunal may also have jurisdiction to which the superior court may defer. Similarly, the superior court may defer to the Federal Court when they have concurrent jurisdiction to deal with constitutional issues: *Reza v. Canada*, [1994] 2 SCR 394, 116 DLR (4th) 61. (The jurisdiction of provincial superior courts in constitutional cases is explored further in a note below.)

Inferior courts and tribunals (federal and provincial) find their jurisdiction in their mandating statutes or in other statutes that explicitly grant them jurisdiction in specified matters. Similarly, the Federal Court obtains its jurisdiction from the *Federal Court Act* or from other federal statutes. Because the Federal Court was created by statute, and thus lacks the "inherent" jurisdiction of the provincial superior courts (see *Roberts v. Canada*, [1989] 1 SCR 322, at 331, 57 DLR (4th) 197), the issue of whether it has jurisdiction over a matter, or, conversely, of whether the jurisdiction of the provincial superior courts has been excluded has often been central to litigation involving a federal actor or aspect. (The jurisdiction of the Federal Court will be discussed more extensively in the note below.)

Throughout much of our history the court system in the provinces has been complex; it was inherited from the system in England. Following changes made throughout Canada, however, the system has been simplified. In each province there is a superior trial court and a superior appellate court, as well as a system of provincial (inferior) courts that may include young offender courts, small claims courts, courts dealing with criminal matters and certain civil matters, and other specialized courts, such as those devoted to family violence or commercial matters. These courts deal with both federal and provincial laws, as do the superior courts. Appeals from all the provincial appellate courts (as well as from the Federal Court of Appeal) are taken by right or by leave to the Supreme Court of Canada. Thus the decisions of the Supreme Court have a national or unifying effect on provincial laws and, indeed, it has been said that "[t]he position of the Supreme Court of Canada, with its plenary jurisdiction, at the top of each provincial hierarchy, has the effect of melding the ten provincial hierarchies into a single national system" (Peter W. Hogg, *Constitutional Law of Canada*, 5th ed., looseleaf (Scarborough, ON: Carswell, 2007), at 7-3). Section 6 of the *Supreme Court Act*, RSC 1985, c. S-26, provides that three judges must be appointed from among Quebec superior court jurists or members of the Quebec bar. Similarly, s. 5.4 of the *Federal Courts Act*, RSC 1985, c. F-7, requires that a certain number of judges on the Federal Court and on the Federal Court of Appeal are to be from Quebec. Even so, there has been controversy over the impact of Supreme Court decisions in blurring the distinctiveness among provinces (Quebec and others) that federalism is intended to reflect.

NOTE ON THE FEDERAL COURT OF CANADA AND ITS JURISDICTION

The requirement that federal courts established under s. 101 of the *Constitution Act, 1867* (other than the Supreme Court of Canada) are limited to applying "laws of Canada" has been interpreted to mean that there must be existing federal law to apply to a case. In *Quebec North Shore Paper Company v. Canadian Pacific Ltd.*, [1977] 2 SCR 1054, 71 DLR (3d) 111, the Supreme Court of Canada stated that the mere possibility that Parliament could competently enact legislation in a given area was insufficient to give the Federal Court jurisdiction to try an issue. In this case, CP Ltd. sued Quebec North Shore when the latter breached a contract to build a rail car marine terminal at Baie Comeau, intended for transporting newsprint to the United States. The plaintiff brought the action in the Federal Court, taking the position that the Federal Court had jurisdiction because the subject matter of the contract—international transportation—fell within federal legislative competence by virtue of ss. 92(10) and 91(29) of the *Constitution Act, 1867*. The defendants challenged this, arguing that the proper forum was the Quebec Superior Court. The contract itself provided that it was to be interpreted under the laws of Quebec, where it had been entered into. Laskin CJC, for the Court, stated that the words of s. 101 "[require] that there be applicable and existing federal law, whether under statute or regulation or common law ... upon which the jurisdiction of the Federal Court can be exercised" (at 1065-66 SCR). In this case, he found that there was no federal law and Quebec law could not be considered a law of Canada or transposed into federal law.

As Laskin CJC pointed out, the Federal Court will have jurisdiction not only where a federal statute exists, but also where the matter is one of federal common law. This was confirmed in *Northern Telecom Canada Ltd. v. Communication Workers of Canada*, [1983] 1 SCR 733, at 740, 147 DLR (3d) 1, at 14. As to the content of federal common law, the Court stated in *Quebec North Shore* that the "common law associated with the Crown's position as a litigant ... is federal law in relation to the Crown in right of Canada" (at 1063 SCR). The further content of "federal common law" is not well defined, and the concept is clearly an evolving one. The Federal Court of Appeal has suggested that federal common law is that over which only Parliament can competently legislate—that is, it is common law beyond the competence of the provinces to change (*Associated Metals & Minerals Corp. v. "Evie W" (The)*, [1978] 2 FC 710, at 713-16 (CA)). More recently, the Supreme Court of Canada found in *Roberts v. Canada, supra*, that the law of Aboriginal title is federal common law.

It is also well established that the Constitution Acts are not "laws of Canada" within the meaning of s. 101. In the *Northern Telecom* case, for example, the Court reached this conclusion on the basis that the these enactments are not laws enacted by Parliament (at 745 SCR). The main implication of this interpretation has been that where a federal law is challenged on constitutional grounds, provincial superior courts will retain concurrent jurisdiction over such challenges. However, this interpretation has also caused confusion because it raised the possibility that the Federal Court lacks the jurisdiction to decide certain "purely" constitutional challenges. In *Northern Telecom*, the Court found that the Federal Court of Appeal could decide the constitutionality of legislation as long as the question arose in the context of applying federal law (in that case, federal labour law).

The precise nature of the distinction between cases founded on the Constitution Acts and those founded on federal legislation but that raise constitutional issues has yet to be defined by the courts. Constitutional challenges will, in virtually all cases, rest on acts by federal authorities purportedly authorized by statute or common law. (One conceivable exception is the situation where the signatories of a constitutional document argue over its meaning— for example, the Terms of Union between Prince Edward Island and Canada.) Structurally, all constitutional challenges depend on a tension between the text of a statute and that of the constitution, so it makes little sense in principle to classify constitutional litigation either as primarily about the constitution or as primarily originating in a federal statute or common law. One cannot exist without the other. The elusive action "founded on the Constitution," which ousts Federal Court jurisdiction in matters that appear to relate to existing federal law, may never be captured.

In *Rudolph Wolff & Co. Ltd. v. Canada*, [1990] 1 SCR 695, 69 DLR (4th) 392, the Supreme Court of Canada held that ss. 17(1) and (2) of the *Federal Court Act*, RSC 1970 (2d Supp.), c. 10 and s. 7(1) of the *Crown Liability Act*, RSC 1970, c. C-38 (now the *Crown Liability and Proceedings Act*, RSC 1985, c. C-50, which does not contain an exclusivity provision), providing that actions against the Crown in right of Canada were within the exclusive jurisdiction of the Federal Court, did not contravene s. 15(1) of the Charter. Section 17(1) of the *Federal Courts Act*, RSC 1985, c. F-7, now provides that with some exceptions "the Federal Court has concurrent original jurisdiction in all cases in which relief is claimed against the Crown."

NOTE ON THE JURISDICTION OF PROVINCIAL SUPERIOR COURTS OVER CONSTITUTIONAL ISSUES

Turning to the jurisdiction of the provincial superior courts, it is clear that provincial courts may hear cases that raise constitutional questions about federal laws: *Attorney General of Canada v. Law Society of British Columbia*, [1982] 2 SCR 307, 137 DLR (3d) 1. The *Law Society* case was emphatic on this point, with Estey J quoting from *The Queen v. Thomas Fuller Construction Co. (1958) Ltd. et al.*, [1980] 1 SCR 695, at 713, 106 DLR (3d) 193, at 205-6:

> It must be considered that the basic principle governing the Canadian system of judicature is the jurisdiction of the Superior Courts of the Provinces in all matters federal and provincial. The federal Parliament is empowered to derogate from this principle by establishing additional Courts only for the better administration of the laws of Canada.

And later, in *Law Society*, Estey J wrote (at 17 DLR):

> It is difficult to see how an argument can be advanced that a statute adopted by Parliament for the establishment of a court for the better administration of the laws of Canada can at the same time include a provision that the provincial superior courts may no longer declare a statute enacted by Parliament to be beyond the constitutional authority of Parliament. Sections 17 and 18 of the *Federal Court Act* must, in the view of [the attorney general of Canada], be so construed. In my view Parliament lacks the constitutional authority to so provide. To do so would strip the basic constitutional concepts of judicature of this country, namely, the superior courts of the provinces, of a judicial power fundamental to a federal system as described in the *Constitution Act, 1867*.

The jurisdiction of a provincial superior court to hear a Charter challenge to federal legislation was questioned in *Reza v. Canada, supra*, in which the applicant claimed Convention refugee status upon his arrival in Canada from Iran. He failed to establish this status, and after exhausting the appeal process available to him in the Federal Court under the *Immigration Act* he applied to the Ontario courts for a declaration pursuant to s. 24(1) of the *Charter of Rights and Freedoms* that certain provisions of the Act violated the Charter. The Supreme Court of Canada decided unanimously (at para. 21):

> [W]e agree with Abella JA's conclusion [in dissent in the Ontario Court of Appeal] that there is no basis for interfering [with the motions judge's decision]. ... The Ontario Court (General

Division) and the Federal Court had concurrent jurisdiction to hear the respondent's application but … any judge of the General Division had a discretion to stay the proceedings. Ferrier J [the motions judge] properly exercised his discretion on the basis that Parliament had created a comprehensive scheme of review of immigration matters and the Federal Court was an effective and appropriate forum.

This case clearly affirms the position taken in *Law Society* that provincial superior courts have jurisdiction to hear constitutional challenges to federal law and federal administration. However, the refusal to let the case proceed in the Ontario Court on the ground that a comprehensive review system was established in the Federal Court means the creation of that jurisdiction, in itself, could displace constitutional review by provincial courts. Similarly, the blithe finding that the Federal Court was, in this instance, an effective and appropriate forum may undermine confidence that constitutional review in provincial superior courts will actually be available.

III. SEPARATION OF POWERS AND SECTION 96

Although its literal wording suggests that it is an appointment power, s. 96 of the *Constitution Act, 1867* has, through judicial interpretation, come to play a more significant role than merely locating the authority for controlling the appointment and remuneration of judges. It is also the basis for the claim that the judicial function (at least, the judicial function as performed by superior courts on the English model) cannot be eroded through provincial legislatures, or even Parliament, enacting legislation that assigns such functions to non-court (or executive) decision-making agencies. Perhaps the most important value behind this constitutional restraint is the desire to restrict significant legal adjudication to judges or, in other words, to a group of persons who, by the Constitution, are marked by legal training and security of tenure and pay. In short, the constitutional goal here is to preserve, through institutional design, legalism, or the rule of law.

Yet, when we look at the cases under s. 96, and at the social context of modern government, this purpose is not necessarily well served. The federal appointing power is not exercised "above" politics. There seems to be no danger of the courts' role in legal administration falling into disuse; there is a relentless growth in the number of judges and in court loads. The cases show that legislatures are, in fact, free to assign to non-court administrative agencies responsibility for supervising legal relationships that were formerly governed by superior court adjudication—so long as the adjudicative function has been altered by the legislature through the creation of new administrative law. As for protecting the rule of law, this could be achieved through reading s. 96 to guarantee judicial review by superior courts of non-curial legal administration so that the limits of legislative mandates would always be protected. It may be argued that the rule of law does not seem to require the constitutional preservation of the *original* jurisdiction of superior courts.

The preservation of original jurisdiction for superior courts through the judicial interpretation of s. 96 has been subject to criticism as unduly constraining the provinces in their choice of institutional structure for the administration of provincial laws, thus constituting an unwarranted judicial interference with legitimate legislative choices; see Bora Laskin, "Municipal Tax Assessment and Section 96 of the British North America Act: The Olympia

Bowling Alleys Case" (1955), 33 *Canadian Bar Review* 993 and John Willis, "Section 96 of the British North America Act" (1940), 18 *Canadian Bar Review* 516.

On the other hand, it can be argued that the constitutional entrenchment of original superior court jurisdiction reflects a difference in function between the judiciary and the executive that ought to be respected. Restraining legislatures from assigning original jurisdiction to non-courts could be based on the view that if legislatures wish there to be a new body of law developed by an administrative agency, then legislatures must explicitly identify the directions in which the non-curial agency is to develop the law. Constitutions are, in part, dedicated to creating (or recognizing) basic governmental institutions. Courts are thought to offer disciplined and restrained elaborations of legal rules, while the executive branch and its various elements offer the capacity to develop effective policies and mechanisms for achieving general legislative aims. Legislatures, which create new ordering regimes, give democratic legitimacy to the making of new policies. The roles of each of the branches must reflect the virtues that each represents. For instance, the democracy of legislatures makes them poor instruments for adjudicating between competing claims of right and the legalism of courts makes them poor instruments for devising new ways for achieving legislated policies.

In this way the *Constitution Act, 1867*, in ss. 96 to 101, expresses a more complex theory of separation of powers than has been recognized. As a result of restraining legislative choices over arrangements for primary legal administration, the Constitution also limits the extent to which legislatures can assign, without legislating substantive norms and goals, a law-making function to the executive branch.

NOTE ON JOHN EAST IRON WORKS

The first major case dealing with whether a provincially appointed tribunal could exercise powers that had traditionally been exercised by the superior or s. 96 courts was *Labour Relations Board of Saskatchewan v. John East Iron Works Ltd.*, [1949] AC 134, [1948] 4 DLR 673 (PC). Under the *Trade Union Act, 1944* the province of Saskatchewan established a Labour Relations Board with the power to require, pursuant to s. 5(e), "an employer to reinstate any employee discharged contrary to the provisions of this Act and to pay such employee the monetary loss suffered by reason of such discharge." When John East Iron Works Ltd. terminated the employment of six of its employees, the United Steelworkers of America filed a complaint with the Labour Relations Board that John East had been guilty of an unfair labour practice, asking that the workers be reinstated and compensated. The Board issued orders requiring reinstatement and compensation for five of the employees (one application had been withdrawn during the hearings). On a motion by John East, the Court of Appeal for Saskatchewan quashed the orders of the Board. The Board successfully appealed this decision to the Judicial Committee of the Privy Council. Writing for the Privy Council, Lord Simonds, at DLR 680, characterized the question before the court as "a double one": (1) did the appellant Board exercise a judicial power, and (2) if so, in that exercise was it a tribunal analogous to a superior, district, or county court? Declining to answer the first question, their Lordships turned their attention to the second and considered the ways in which the Board differed from a superior, district, or county court.

Lord Simonds noted several ways in which the Labour Relations Board differed "from the traditional conception of a Court." Although the relief granted related to the individual employee, he noted that others could raise the controversy without the employee's assent "and, it may be, against his will, for the solution of some far-reaching industrial conflict." While the issue could be described as a *lis* and its determination as an exercise of judicial power, it was nevertheless unlike the issues with which superior, county, or district courts dealt in Upper Canada in 1867. The issue was not the employee's contractual rights, but the means by which the policy of collective bargaining "as a road to industrial peace is secured"; this was "a new conception of industrial relations" that did not exist in 1867. Even if this conception of industrial relations had existed in 1867, it might well have been that a representative and expert tribunal system would have been established, and that the question of whether it was desirable that the judges dealing with this matter have the same qualifications as the judges of the superior or other courts (the "assumed justiciable issue") would have been answered in the negative. Lord Simonds also indicated that while it might be acceptable not to have the decisions of a specialized tribunal reviewed by an ordinary court, this immunity had limitations.

The factors identified by Lord Simonds in 1944 appear in the later decisions addressing the s. 96 issue. The increased development of administrative law regimes by the provinces required the Supreme Court of Canada to provide greater guidance on the limits of the provinces and, as it turned out, Parliament's power to grant jurisdiction to courts and tribunals which closely resembled that enjoyed by the superior courts in 1867. Over time, the strictures have been loosened and the tests refined, but there remain core powers of the superior courts that cannot be assigned exclusively to inferior courts and tribunals without undermining the independence of the judiciary and the separation of powers.

The modern test for determining whether the powers accorded a tribunal or inferior court are powers that are to be exercised only by judges appointed by the Governor General is found in *Reference re Residential Tenancies Act*, excerpted below. The case dealt with powers accorded the Residential Tenancy Commission by the Ontario government under the *Residential Tenancies Act, 1979*, legislation designed to redress a perceived imbalance favouring landlords over tenants, particularly at a time of a low vacancy rate. Among its other powers, the Commission was to be given authority to evict tenants from residential premises and to require landlords and tenants to comply with obligations imposed under the Act. The Ontario Cabinet had referred the issue of whether these powers were constitutional to the Ontario Court of Appeal, which concluded that they were not. The attorney general of Ontario appealed to the Supreme Court of Canada. Dickson J (as he then was), speaking for the Court, noted that, along with the attorney general of Canada, organizations representative of tenants and of landlords, as well as community-based clinics and property management associations, intervened in the case. He also referred to the Green Paper released by the Ontario government, which explained that the government was considering the legislation because of the high number of tenants in the province; the need to provide a means other than courts for landlords to exercise their right to obtain an order evicting tenants; the need for an informal system that would permit complainants to represent themselves; and the desire to combine administrative and judicial functions, including mediation and adjudication. He then considered and refined the "s. 96 tests" that had been developed; his formulation of the test is now known as "the *Residential Tenancies* test."

Reference re Residential Tenancies Act
[1981] 1 SCR 714, 123 DLR (3d) 554

DICKSON J (Laskin CJC, Martland, Ritchie, Estey, McIntyre, and Lamer JJ concurring): ... The *Residential Tenancies Act*, 1979 was enacted to implement the recommendations of the Green Paper. As I have said, the Act set up a new tribunal, the Residential Tenancy Commission, to oversee and enforce the obligations of landlords and tenants in Ontario. The tribunal is given wide-ranging powers and functions. Some of these are purely administrative in nature, for example, the Commission is charged with the obligation of informing members of the public as to their rights under the legislation. But by far the most significant role to be played is in the resolution of disputes between landlords and tenants. The mechanism for dispute resolution is triggered "upon application" by either the landlord or the tenant. In one or two circumstances the process is put in motion by application by a third party, e.g., a neighbouring tenant. ...

I do not think it can be doubted that the Courts have applied an increasingly broad test of constitutional validity in upholding the establishment of administrative tribunals within provincial jurisdiction. In general terms it may be said that it is now open to the Provinces to invest administrative bodies with "judicial functions" as part of a broader policy scheme. There will still be situations, however, as in *A-G Que. et al. v. Farrah et al.*, [1978] 2 SCR 638, 86 DLR (3d) 161, where a s. 96 "judicial function" is isolated from the rest of the administrative structure of the relevant legislation. ...

The teaching of *Labour Relations Board of Saskatchewan v. John East Iron Works Ltd.*, [1949] AC 134, *Tomko v. Labour Relations Board (Nova Scotia)*, [1977] 1 SCR 112, and *City of Mississauga v. Regional Municipality of Peel*, [1979] 2 SCR 244 is that one must look to the "institutional setting" in order to determine whether a particular power or jurisdiction can validly be conferred on a provincial body.

The Privy Council in *John East*, *supra*, suggested that the application of s. 96 required a determination as to whether or not the powers being exercised were judicial or administrative and if judicial, whether or not the administrative body was "broadly analogous" to a Superior, District or County Court. *Tomko* added a further dimension. An administrative tribunal may be clothed with power formerly exercised by s. 96 Courts, so long as that power is merely an adjunct of, or ancillary to, a broader administrative or regulatory structure. If, however, the impugned power forms a dominant aspect of the function of the tribunal, such that the tribunal itself must be considered to be acting "like a Court," then the conferral of the power is *ultra vires*.

The jurisprudence since *John East* leads one to conclude that the test must now be formulated in three steps. The first involves consideration, in the light of the historical conditions existing in 1867, of the particular power or jurisdiction conferred upon the tribunal. The question here is whether the power or jurisdiction conforms to the power or jurisdiction exercised by Superior, District or County Courts at the time of Confederation. This temporary segregation, or isolation, of the impugned power is not for the purpose of turning back the clock and restoring *Toronto v. York*, [1938] AC 415, as the governing authority, an approach deplored in *Mississauga*. It is rather the first step in a three step process.

If the historical inquiry leads to the conclusion that the power or jurisdiction is not broadly conformable to jurisdiction formerly exercised by s. 96 Courts, that is the end of the matter. As Rand J noted in *A.E. Dupont et al. v. Inglis et al.*, [1958] SCR 535 at p. 542, 14 DLR (2d) 417 at p. 424: "Judicial power, not of that type [that is, that exercised by s. 96 Courts at Confederation], such as that exercised by inferior Courts, can be conferred on a Provincial tribunal whatever its primary character." If, however, the historical evidence indicates that the impugned power is identical or analogous to a power exercised by s. 96 Courts at Confederation, then one must proceed to the second step of the inquiry.

Step two involves consideration of the function within its institutional setting to determine whether the function itself is different when viewed in that setting. In particular, can the function still be considered to be a "judicial" function? In addressing the issue, it is important to keep in mind the further statement by Rand J in *Dupont v. Inglis* [at 424 DLR, 543 SCR] that "it is the subject-matter rather than the apparatus of adjudication that is determinative." Thus the question of whether any particular function is "judicial" is not to be determined simply on the basis of procedural trappings. The primary issue is the nature of the question which the tribunal is called upon to decide. Where the tribunal is faced with a private dispute between parties, and is called upon to adjudicate through the application of a recognized body of rules in a manner consistent with fairness and impartiality, then, normally, it is acting in a "judicial capacity." To borrow the terminology of Professor Ronald Dworkin, the judicial task involves questions of "principle," that is, consideration of the competing rights of individuals or groups. This can be contrasted with questions of "policy" involving competing views of the collective good of the community as a whole: see Dworkin, *Taking Rights Seriously* (1977), at 82-90 (Duckworth).

If, after examining the institutional context, it becomes apparent that the power is not being exercised as a "judicial power" then the inquiry need go no further for the power, within its institutional context, no longer conforms to a power or jurisdiction exercisable by a s. 96 Court and the provincial scheme is valid. On the other hand, if the power or jurisdiction is exercised in a judicial manner, then it becomes necessary to proceed to the third and final step in the analysis and review the tribunal's function as a whole in order to appraise the impugned function in its entire institutional context. The phrase—"it is not the detached jurisdiction or power alone that is to be considered but rather its setting in the institutional arrangements in which it appears"—is the central core of the judgment in *Tomko*. It is no longer sufficient simply to examine the particular power or function of a tribunal and ask whether this power or function was once exercised by s. 96 Courts. This would be examining the power or function in a "detached" manner, contrary to the reasoning in *Tomko*. What must be considered is the "context" in which this power is exercised. *Tomko* leads to the following result: it is possible for administrative tribunals to exercise powers and jurisdiction which once were exercised by the s. 96 Courts. It will all depend on the context of the exercise of the power. It may be that the impugned "judicial powers" are merely subsidiary or ancillary to general administrative functions assigned to the tribunal (*John East, Tomko*) or the powers may be necessarily incidental to the achievement of a broader policy goal of the Legislature (*Mississauga*). In such a situation, the grant of judicial power to provincial appointees is valid. The scheme is only invalid when the adjudicative function is a sole or central function of the tribunal (*Farrah*) so that the tribunal can be said to be operating "like a s. 96 Court." ...

Implicit throughout the argument advanced on behalf of the Attorney-General of Ontario is the assumption that the Court system is too formal, too cumbersome, too expensive and therefore unable to respond properly to the social needs which the *Residential Tenancies Act*, 1979 is intended to meet. All statutes respond to social needs. The Courts are not unfamiliar with equity and the concepts of fairness, justice, convenience, reasonableness. Since the enactment in 1976 of the legislation assuring "security of tenure" the County Court Judges of Ontario have been dealing with matters arising out of that legislation, apparently with reasonable dispatch, as both landlords and tenants in the present proceedings have spoken clearly against transfer of jurisdiction in respect of eviction and compliance orders from the Courts to a special commission. It is perhaps also of interest that there is no suggestion in the material filed with us that the Law Reform Commission favoured removal from the Courts of the historic functions performed for over 100 years by the Courts. ...

[Dickson CJC applied the test to the provisions at issue that involved the Commission's power to make an eviction order and its power to make a "compliance" order. He explained that "prior to 1867 in Upper Canada the only tribunals which could make ejectment orders were the Court of Queen's Bench, the Court of Common Pleas, and the County Court in limited situations, and that only the Court of Chancery could make orders of specific performance or issue mandatory or prohibitory injunction orders. The settlement of disputes between landlords and tenants, including the termination of tenancies and eviction of tenants, has thus always been within the exclusive jurisdiction of the Superior, District and County Court judges both before and after Confederation."

In considering the second stage of the test, the Chief Justice pointed out that the power to order a remedy would "be exercised in the context of a *lis* between parties ... [and] the task of the Commission will be to determine the respective rights and obligations of the parties according to the terms of the legislation." The Commission was required to analyze the law, apply the law to the facts, make a decision and issue an order, leading Dickson CJC to conclude: "It is difficult to conceive that when so acting the Commission acts otherwise than as a curial tribunal. In substance the tribunal is exercising judicial powers roughly in the same way as they are exercised by the courts." Other processes all reflected judicial procedures. Thus the Commission's judicial powers, when examined in their institutional setting, remained "essentially" judicial powers.

With respect to the third stage of the test, Dickson CJC stated that "the central function of the Commission is that of resolving disputes, in the final resort by a judicial form of hearing between landlords and tenants." The power to mediate was of secondary importance, available only on application by one of the parties, and other powers are either "ancillary" or "bear no relation" to the core power of adjudication.

Accordingly, the impugned provisions were held to be *ultra vires*.]

Appeal dismissed.

NOTES

1. The basic three-step test for determining an infringement of s. 96 as articulated by Dickson J in *Residential Tenancies* has become routine, with some modifications that will be dealt with below. The test has not, however, been without criticism. Peter Hogg, for example, in *Constitutional Law of Canada*, 5th ed., looseleaf (Scarborough, ON: Carswell, 2007), at 7-49, takes the view that while the test

> is no doubt a sound synthesis of the prior case law ... it is not satisfactory as constitutional-law doctrine. Each of the three steps is vague and disputable in many situations, and small differences between the provinces in their history or institutional arrangements can spell the difference between the validity and invalidity of apparently similar administrative tribunals.

See also Robin Elliot, "Rethinking Section 96—From a Question of Power to a Question of Rights," in D.N. Magnusson and D.A. Soberman, eds., *Canadian Constitutional Dilemmas Revisited* (Kingston, ON: Institute of Intergovernmental Relations, 1997). As the subsequent case law shows, there is still room for disagreement over the application of the test. In many of the cases reviewed below, while not disagreeing in the result, various members of the Court apply the different steps of the test in very different ways, in particular the initial historical inquiry. As well, in *Reference re Young Offenders Act (PEI)*, [1991] 1 SCR 252, 77 DLR (4th) 492, discussed further below, two justices questioned whether the latter two branches of the test can be meaningfully applied to an inferior court.

2. In *Re Attorney General of Quebec and Grondin*, [1983] 2 SCR 364, 4 DLR (4th) 605, the Supreme Court of Canada upheld the conferral by the Quebec government of broad powers with respect to leases on a provincial board, the Régie du logement, in contrast to the result in *Reference re Residential Tenancies Act*. In *Grondin*, the historical evidence showed that in Quebec, at the time of Confederation, jurisdiction over relations between lessors and lessees was exercised by inferior courts as well as superior courts. The possibility of different results for similar legislative schemes based on the outcome of the historical inquiry was one aspect of the *Residential Tenancies* test addressed by Wilson J in *Sobeys Stores Ltd. v. Yeomans and Labour Standards Tribunal*, which follows.

Sobeys Stores Ltd. v. Yeomans and Labour Standards Tribunal (NS)
[1989] 1 SCR 238, 57 DLR (4th) 1

WILSON J (Dickson CJC, McIntyre, and Lamer JJ concurring): The respondent Sobeys Stores Limited ("Sobeys") operates a chain of grocery supermarkets in the Atlantic provinces. The appellant Clifford Yeomans was continuously employed by Sobeys from April 16, 1973 until August 6, 1983 when he was dismissed for alleged unsatisfactory performance. At the time of his dismissal he was the manager of a Sobeys outlet in Dartmouth, Nova Scotia. ...

Yeomans complained to the Director of Labour Standards for Nova Scotia that he had been dismissed "without just cause" within the meaning of s. 67A of the Code [*Labour Standards Code*, SNS 1972, c. 10]. On May 22, 1984 the Director ordered that Yeomans be reinstated and that Sobeys pay him $21,242 in lost wages stemming from the unjust dismissal. This decision was upheld by the Labour Standards Tribunal. Sobeys' [direct] appeal to the Appeal Division of the Nova Scotia Supreme Court was allowed. The court held that ss. (2) and (3) of s. 67A of the Code were unconstitutional because they conferred a s. 96 power on a provincially appointed tribunal. ...

[Section 67A of the Code stated that an employee discharged or suspended without just cause may complain to the Director and, if dissatisfied with the Director's decision, may complain to the Tribunal. It further provided:]

> 24(1) The Tribunal in determining any matter under this Act
>   (a) shall decide whether or not a party has contravened this Act; and
>   (b) shall make an Order in writing.
> (2) Where the Tribunal decides that a party has contravened a provision of this Act the Tribunal may order the contravening party to
>   (a) do any act or thing that, in the opinion of the Tribunal, constitutes full compliance with the provision; and
>   (b) rectify an injury caused to the person injured or to make compensation therefor. ...

Appeals from Tribunal decisions are permitted by s. 18(2):

> 18(2) Any party to an order or decision of the Tribunal may, within thirty days of the mailing of the order or decision, appeal to the Appeal Division of the Supreme Court on a question of law or jurisdiction.

[The first stage of analysis undertaken by Wilson J was to ask whether the Labour Standards Tribunal's jurisdiction over unjust dismissal was in broad conformity with the powers of s. 96 courts at the time of Confederation. In the course of this analysis Wilson J considered three problems. The first was the question of how widely the jurisdiction should be characterized.]

In argument before this Court both the Attorney General for Nova Scotia (appellant) and the respondent Sobeys initially characterized the jurisdiction under s. 67A as jurisdiction in relation to the equitable remedy of specific performance of employment contracts. Each argued that such a characterization would be determinative in his favour, the appellant because traditionally the courts did not grant such a remedy and the respondent because the remedy, whether actually granted or not, was equitable and therefore clearly part of the exclusive jurisdiction of superior courts at Confederation. This was not, however, the only characterization offered to the Court. When the argument progressed to the second and third stages of the *Residential Tenancies* test [*Reference re Residential Tenancies Act*, [1981] 1 SCR 714], the same parties suggested broader characterizations such as "unjust dismissal," "employer–employee relations" and "labour standards." Counsel for the other appellant, Yeomans, argued consistently throughout that the jurisdiction was over "master–servant relations." [Hart JA, in the Appeal Division, characterized s. 67A as a provision relating to "unjust dismissal."] ...

The purposes of s. 96 require a strict, that is to say a narrow, approach to characterization at the first stage. Given what I have to say below on concurrent superior/inferior court jurisdiction at Confederation, any other approach would potentially open the door to large accretions of jurisdiction and thereby defeat the purposes of the constitutional provision. I would therefore reject as too broad characterizations of the s. 67A jurisdiction as being in relation to employer/employee relations or labour standards. Having rejected broad characterizations, the court is given a choice between two possible narrow ones, jurisdiction over reinstatement or jurisdiction over unjust dismissal. ...

I would ... resolve the issue by reference to the language and purpose of the *Residential Tenancies* test. At the first stage the search is for "broad conformity" with the powers of s. 96 courts at Confederation. It is a search for analogous, not precisely the same, jurisdiction. Even if I were to accept the appellant's contention that the remedy of reinstatement was outside the purview of s. 96 courts. ... I do not think that should be determinative in s. 96 cases. To do so would be to freeze the jurisdiction of those courts at 1867 by a technical analysis of remedies. It is, in my view, the type of dispute that must guide us and not the particular remedy sought. The question of new remedies for traditional causes of action is better suited to the second and third steps of the *Residential Tenancies* test which are specifically designed to allow the courts to consider new approaches to old problems, approaches which are more responsive to changing social conditions. Thus, the jurisdiction in this case should, in my view, be characterized as jurisdiction in relation to unjust dismissal.

The fact that the different stages of the *Residential Tenancies* test serve different purposes also, in my view, militates against any "broadening" of the characterization as the analysis progresses from one stage to another. The characterization chosen is irrelevant to a consideration at stage two of whether the Tribunal is functioning judicially or not. A broad characterization at the third stage would be equally unnecessary because this aspect of the test requires the courts to view the particular power or jurisdiction within a broad context. Thus, in this case, for example, a broadening of the characterization to "labour standards" would require the court to assess whether such a power or jurisdiction is "so integrated with the valid regulatory regime" (*Residential Tenancies*, p. 736) of labour standards legislation as to take on a different character. The inquiry would have become a teleological one and the *Residential Tenancies* test would be deprived of its essential purpose.

[Wilson J next considered whether the superior court jurisdiction at the time of Confederation must be an exclusive jurisdiction.]

The foregoing leads me to conclude that a certain gloss must be added to the *Residential Tenancies* test. At the first step, the threshold question is whether at Confederation superior courts exercised an exclusive jurisdiction. This test accords with the general principle that inferior court jurisdiction need not be frozen at its pre-Confederation level: see *Re Cour de Magistrat de Quebec*, [1965] SCR 772. If the jurisdiction was exclusive to superior courts, then the inquiry must pass on to the second and third stages of the test. If the jurisdiction was shared, the legislation under challenge may, in some circumstances, be held valid by the historical test.

How much concurrent jurisdiction is necessary for the purposes of the test? It would obviously largely defeat the purpose of s. 96 if a finding of one small aspect of jurisdiction, limited, for example, by subject matter, geography or monetary amount, in an inferior court were sufficient to permit legislatures to oust the jurisdiction of today's superior courts. However, the dangers of this are not as great as they might at first sight appear, given what I have said earlier about the need to characterize the power or jurisdiction relatively narrowly for the purposes of the historical test. Yet they must be borne in mind in fashioning a test of general application. ...

In all cases, however, the inquiry should be directed to the question whether or not the work of the inferior courts at the time of Confederation was broadly co-extensive with that of the superior courts. Only if this standard is met will the history of shared jurisdiction validate the contemporary scheme under the historical test.

(iii) Extent of the Historical Inquiry

... It seems to me that this issue should be resolved by answering a somewhat broader question—does pre-confederation jurisdiction refer to pre-1867 jurisdiction or to jurisdiction in a particular province immediately prior to that province joining confederation? If the former approach is adopted, the courts must consider only the four original confederating provinces (Quebec, Ontario, Nova Scotia and New Brunswick) irrespective of which present-day province is involved in the litigation. If the latter approach is adopted, the test will involve perhaps only one colony, perhaps as many as eight, and a potential chronological span of as many as 72 years, from 1867 to 1949. I note that on all of these points past decisions of this Court have been somewhat inconsistent. ...

In resolving this issue I take as my starting point this Court's decision in *Residential Tenancies*. In describing the historical test Dickson J had this to say at pp. 729 and 734:

> ... the test must now be formulated in three steps. The first involves consideration, *in the light of the historical conditions existing in 1867*, of the particular power or jurisdiction conferred upon the tribunal. The question here is whether the power or jurisdiction conforms to the power or jurisdiction exercised by superior, district or county courts at the time of Confederation. [Emphasis added.]

Although it might be argued that the references to 1867 were the result of the fact that the *Residential Tenancies* case emanated from Ontario, I think the better view is that they were intended to refer generally to the original bargain made in 1867. ...

I would not, however, rest this conclusion purely on an analysis of the language of *Residential Tenancies* but would note two further points. Firstly, the judgment of this Court in *Reference re Section 6 of Family Relations Act*, [1982] 1 SCR 62, 131 DLR (3d) was released only a few months after that in *Residential Tenancies* (January 26, 1982 and May 28, 1981, respectively). The *Family Relations Act* judgment provides clear evidence that the Court at that time thought it necessary to look at jurisdiction at 1867 when the confederation bargain was made. Secondly, in his discussion of the purposes of s. 96 Dickson J made it clear that he saw the provision as one intimately related to the division of powers and to the need to maintain a guaranteed core of superior court jurisdiction. ...

When new provinces joined confederation they accepted the existing constitutional arrangements in ss. 91 and 92 and must, in my view, be taken to have done the same with s. 96.

Once this principle is accepted, it seems to me unavoidable to conclude that the *Residential Tenancies* test of 1867 jurisdiction should be expanded somewhat to include examination of the general historical conditions in all four original confederating provinces. I say this for two reasons. The first is a practical one. While it might make sense to examine only Ontario in an Ontario case (as was done in *Residential Tenancies*) or Quebec in a Quebec case … there would be no reason to choose one or the other in deciding a case emanating from Alberta, Prince Edward Island or elsewhere. The second and more important reason is that implicit in what I have said above is the principle that s. 96 should apply in the same way across the country.

The "strong constitutional basis for national unity, through a unitary judicial system" (*Residential Tenancies*, p. 728) would indeed be undermined by inconsistent results derived from a jurisprudence developed province by province. …

I do not wish to suggest that there must be uniformity of result for all s. 96 challenges to provincial initiatives in a given area. It is entirely possible that different results may emerge from analyzing contemporary schemes in light of the second and third stages of the *Residential Tenancies* test. I am suggesting only that consistency at the level of the historical analysis would seem to be desirable and that it is best achieved by measuring each s. 96 challenge against the same historical yardstick. The test at this stage should be national, not provincial. …

[In case of a tie, as there was in this case, Wilson J stated that the court should "examine jurisdiction in the United Kingdom at the time of Confederation." She held that "jurisdiction over unjust dismissal in the UK in 1867 was the preserve of courts equivalent to Canada's superior, district and county courts. It is, accordingly, not a power or jurisdiction which may be conferred on provincially appointed tribunals today." Given her answer to the historical stage in the test, Wilson J went on to examine the judicial function of the Labour Standards Tribunal. After considering the various submissions, she concluded that "the tribunal [was] acting sufficiently like a court that it [could] not pass this stage of the test." It was not until she examined the institutional setting within which the judicial function was being exercised that she concluded, "[A]lthough the Labour Standards Tribunal exercises a jurisdiction broadly conformable to that of s. 96 courts at the time of Confederation, and although in doing so it performs a judicial function, it does so as a necessarily incidental aspect of the broader social policy goal of providing minimum standards of protection for non-unionized employees."

While La Forest J concurred in the result, he disagreed with the reasoning of Wilson J on the application of the *Residential Tenancies* test. By addressing the policy question first, La Forest J was able to argue that the Labour Standards Tribunal was part of a legislative package whose "underlying social and economic philosophy … could not be in sharper contrast to that which existed at Confederation." This meant that the Tribunal passed the first stage in the *Residential Tenancies* test for reasons not dissimilar to those followed by the Privy Council in *John East*.]

Appeal allowed.

The disagreement in *Sobeys* between Wilson and La Forest JJ with respect to the application of the first stage of the *Residential Tenancies* test is instructive. A similar disagreement can be found in the *Reference re Young Offenders Act (PEI)*, [1991] 1 SCR 252, 77 DLR (4th) 492. In that case, while the Court unanimously endorsed the creation of Youth Courts and the endowing of those courts with the jurisdiction to try young offenders, three conflicting sets of reasons were given in support of this result. While all of the justices sitting agreed that the creation of the Youth Courts involved a novel jurisdiction not protected by s. 96, five of them found that this result followed from the application of the first stage of the *Residential Tenancies* test (although they disagreed among themselves on another matter), while two found that it could not be established until the third stage. As Wilson J recognized in *Sobeys*, the stage at which one reaches a decision can be determined by the language one uses to pose the question at the outset. This was already evident in *John East*, where the characterization of the legislation in terms of labour unions, which did not exist in 1867, instead of in terms of individual contracts of employment, which did, could be seen to have determined the result.

Yet, even in those cases where there is general agreement that the issue can be settled at the first stage, there is still room for disagreement over the application of the test for novel jurisdiction. For example, the question of how to determine a novel jurisdiction became the basis of a disagreement between McLachlin J and Lamer CJC in *Reference re Amendments to the Residential Tenancies Act (NS)*, which follows.

Reference re Amendments to the Residential Tenancies Act (NS)
[1996] 1 SCR 186, 131 DLR (4th) 609

McLACHLIN J (La Forest, L'Heureux-Dubé, Iacobucci, and Major JJ concurring): ... The impugned provisions of the *Residential Tenancies Act*, RSNS 1989, c. 401, contained in *An Act to Amend Chapter 401 of the Revised Statutes, 1989, the Residential Tenancies Act*, SNS 1992, c. 31 (collectively, the "Act") provide a mechanism for the resolution of first- and second-level residential tenancy disputes. The legislation gives the provincially appointed Director of Residential Tenancies and his delegates the power to investigate, mediate and adjudicate disputes between landlords and their residential tenants. It empowers the Director to make orders for compliance, termination, repair and possession. The Director's order may be appealed to the Board, and an order of the Board may be appealed, with leave, to the Appeal Division of the Supreme Court of Nova Scotia on questions of law or jurisdiction. An unappealed order is deemed to be an order of the Board, which in turn may be entered as an order of the court under s. 21 of the Act.

The jurisdiction of the Director and Board is exclusive. All residential tenancy disputes must be determined by the procedure specified in the Act and, except for formally entering orders and its limited appellate jurisdiction, the superior court has no power to determine them. ...

[With respect to the first step of the *Residential Tenancies* test, after surveying the situation in each of the four original provinces, McLachlin J concluded: "In every former colony inferior courts exercised a significant concurrent jurisdiction at or about the time of

Confederation. It follows that the Nova Scotia House of Assembly's conferral of jurisdiction over residential tenancies on a provincially appointed tribunal does not violate s. 96 of the *Constitution Act, 1867."*

In contrast, Lamer CJC, speaking for himself and Sopinka and Cory JJ, held that the regime established by the province constituted an example of "novel jurisdiction." Although landlord–tenant law was not new, the concept of a "residential tenancy was largely a phenomenon of modern and urban society." Lamer CJC noted that there was a very different philosophical approach underlying the *Residential Tenancies Act* that "[had] carved out a distinct branch of landlord–tenant law and developed a complete code to govern the residential tenancy relationship. The relationship [was] no longer based on either land law or the law of contract and tort." The legislation reflected a different social policy than that reflected in traditional landlord–tenant legislation. The Chief Justice not only held that landlord–tenant matters were not "core powers" of s. 96 courts, but also characterized most of the disputes addressed under the legislation as involving "a high volume of repetitive and narrowly defined matters of limited complexity [that were] amply suited to resolution by lay persons applying the rules with fairness and common sense," observing that "[t]hese were the hallmarks of the cases entertained by many pre-Confederation inferior courts."

Although it was not necessary to her disposition of the appeal, McLachlin J also considered the issue of "novel jurisdiction," with the majority of the Court agreeing with her views. She concluded that "the power conferred on provincially appointed officials by the legislation here at issue does not represent a new jurisdiction, but rather simply a reorganization for administrative reasons of a jurisdiction which has been exercised by superior and inferior tribunals in Canada since before Confederation."]

If a power is new, there can be no conflict with s. 96, since it cannot have been within the jurisdiction of the superior courts at the time of Confederation. Section 96 cannot be infringed by the conferral of a jurisdiction that the superior courts never exercised before 1867. The historical inquiry undertaken in the first step of the *Residential Tenancies* test searches for pre-Confederation analogs of the superior court jurisdiction at issue. If none are found, the grant of power is valid: *Labour Relations Board of Saskatchewan v. John East Iron Works, Ltd.*, [1949] AC 134 (PC). In *John East*, the Privy Council held that the modern system of collective bargaining in industrial relations was sufficiently distinct from the traditional 19th century conceptualization of the master–servant relationship, as expressed through individual contracts of employment, to constitute a novel jurisdiction. Similarly, in *Sobeys Stores Ltd. v. Yeomans and Labour Standards Tribunal (NS)*, [1989] 1 SCR 238, 57 DLR (4th) 1, La Forest J held in a concurring minority judgment that a comprehensive regime of new rights and entitlements for unorganized workers amounted to a new jurisdiction. A jurisdiction historically exercised by the superior courts may also cease to be analogous if its current manifestation is animated by a distinctly different organizational or operational principle or philosophy. Hence, the majority of this Court in *Reference Re Young Offenders Act (PEI)*, [1991] 1 SCR 252, 77 DLR (4th) 492, also reasoned that a comprehensive legislative scheme for young offenders, treating a discrete class of individuals differently by emphasizing rehabilitation rather than punishment, constituted a new jurisdiction which could be conferred on youth courts without violating the strictures of s. 96.

In my respectful view, the legislation here at issue does not meet the test for novel jurisdiction set out in these authorities. The powers conferred are clearly analogous to those exercised by the courts in 1867. In *Reference Re Residential Tenancies Act*, [1981] 1 SCR 714, 123 DLR (3d) 554, Dickson J prefaced his judgment with the observation that "[t]he resolution of disputes between landlords and tenants has long been a central pre-occupation of the common law courts" (p. 718 SCR). The purpose of the Act was not to create a new jurisdiction, but "to transfer jurisdiction over a large and important body of law" (p. 747 SCR). Dickson J summarily dismissed the suggestion that a new jurisdiction was involved: "[T]he jurisdiction sought to be transferred is precisely the same as that which was previously, and is presently, exercised by the courts" (p. 748 SCR).

The adjudicative aspects of the legislation in this case are fundamentally similar to those in *Re Residential Tenancies Act* and *Re Attorney General of Quebec and Grondin*, [1983] 2 SCR 364, 4 DLR (4th) 605, although considerably briefer than either the 1979 Ontario Act or other comparable contemporary provincial statutes. If anything, the Act provides a less comprehensive code than the Ontario scheme at issue in *Re Residential Tenancies Act*, which combined administrative provisions for rent review and an advisory bureau with those setting out the judicial functions of the Residential Tenancy Commission.

The legislation here at issue codifies the existing law and establishes an impartial dispute resolution mechanism for landlords and tenants. Both the Director and the Board decide disputes between the parties. The parties present evidence and make submissions. Appeals are allowed and orders can be enforced by the parties as orders of the court. This is exactly the sort of work courts have traditionally done in relation to residential tenancy disputes. One looks in vain for the additional powers that may serve to make new soup of this old broth. Unlike the Director of Labour in *Sobeys*, the Director here does not have "carriage of the action" before the Board. The Director does not enforce standards or advocate on behalf of a group that the legislation protects. The Act proclaims no new policy aims to guide the Director or Board in interpreting and enforcing the Act. Nor does it consolidate and unify a disparate assemblage of statutes in order to present a comprehensive and principled new scheme of protection. Indeed, the 1992 amendments *removed* the Board's previous authority under s. 18(4) of the Act to "provide and disseminate information concerning rental practices, rights and remedies" and to "give advice and direction to landlords and tenants in disputes": *An Act to Amend Chapter 401 of the Revised Statutes, 1989, the Residential Tenancies Act*, s. 8(2).

Lamer CJC in *Reference Re Young Offenders Act* and La Forest J in *Sobeys* identified organizing principles and philosophies in the respective legislative schemes under consideration in those cases which were distinctly different from the conceptual basis for the powers exercised by the courts at the time of Confederation. A rehabilitative regime designed specifically for young offenders can be seen as novel in comparison with the criminal law of the 19th century, which emphasized punishment scaled to the crime regardless of the miscreant's age. Similarly, a labour relations code calculated to extend many of the benefits of collective bargaining to unorganized workers might be construed as creating an innovative jurisdiction, a finding consistent with the conclusion of the Privy

Council in *John East*. By contrast, the legislation here at issue evinces no new defining social purpose capable of transforming traditional s. 96 powers into something so new and different that they defy the search for pre-Confederation antecedents.

The Chief Justice bases his case for novel jurisdiction on the premise that the concept of residential tenancy is "largely a phenomenon of modern and urban society." ... However, while there is little doubt that the process of urbanization has increased the number of residential tenants living in cities, the number of people renting premises as a percentage of the total population appears to have remained relatively constant over the years. Indeed, the respondent cites census figures which show that the proportion of renters actually declined by 4 percent from 1921 to 1991.

More importantly, it is difficult, with respect, to see how the increased urbanization of residential tenancy suffices to transform the subject matter of the jurisdiction. One might make the same argument with respect to crime. There was much less crime at the time of Confederation. Moreover, crime today, unlike then, is largely an urban phenomenon. Does this mean that the powers courts exercise in modern criminal trials are not analogous to the powers courts exercised in criminal trials before 1867? Moreover, the significance of the distinction between urban and agricultural residential leases is difficult to grasp. The legislation applies to both, and bears no evidence of being directed at a peculiarly urban problem. Residential leases may be properly contrasted with commercial leases, but not with rural leases, which often were and are concerned with residential premises. As well, it is clear that residential tenancy disputes arose with enough frequency in urban areas before Confederation to warrant empowering strictly urban courts, like the Halifax City Court, to deal with such disputes. Section 123 of *An Act concerning the City of Halifax*, SNS 1864, 27 Vict., c. 81, was not restricted to commercial leases:

> 123. The city court shall also try and determine in a summary way without a jury, all cases of forcible entry and detainer, and over-holding lands, *houses, and tenements* by the tenants, upon a summons at the suit of the landlord ... [Emphasis added.]

While neither the common law nor statute singled out residential tenancies in 1867, that does not mean they did not exist, or that disputes were not resolved by the ordinary application of the law.

The Chief Justice also suggests that the consolidation of residential tenancy remedies in legislation somehow changes the essential subject matter: "[T]he purpose of the Nova Scotia statute—to provide a complete and comprehensive code to govern residential tenancies—'would have sounded strange to the ears of the legislature of 1867.'" ... So, one might venture, would the notion of a criminal code have sounded strange to 1867 ears; criminal codes were first introduced at the turn of the century and still sound strange to some English ears. Codifying law cannot by definition create a new jurisdiction, since codification necessarily presumes the jurisdiction previously existed. Covering an existing body of law with a new statutory wrapper does not make it novel.

The Chief Justice suggests that the jurisdiction is novel because it moves away from the contractual and leasehold bases of landlord–tenant law, arguing that the legislation at issue "represented a shift towards the policy view that the law respecting residential tenancies should be neither leasehold nor contractual but rather should involve a distinct, comprehensive statutory code governing the residential tenancies relationship." ...

But, as Dickson J cautioned in *Re Residential Tenancies Act*, "[M]ere alteration in rules cannot change the substance of things or prevent the drawing of analogies" (p. 738 SCR). The fact that "different considerations" might guide the Director and Board in the discharge of their adjudicative functions, and the rules governing those responsibilities may have been "altered somewhat since 1867," cannot detract from the inescapable conclusion that the powers at issue "are not merely analogous to those (pre-1867) powers but are the same powers" (p. 737 SCR).

Moreover, the Act does not fundamentally change the leasehold and contractual nature of residential tenancies. The Act does not substitute fundamentally new statutory duties for the principles of contract and property law. The lease still governs the rights and obligations of the parties. The lease is a contract. This contract defines and assigns the rights and obligations of the lessor and lessee, owner and fix-term occupant, two *personae* well known to property law. Disputes are still resolved by interpreting the lease and applying it to the evidence. The legislation simply ensures that certain terms which may or may not have been consensually reached by the parties to the lease are included as a matter of statute. Standardized statutory terms themselves have become well known to property and contract law.

It may also be noted that the vast majority of the terms imposed by the legislation here at issue would have been express or implied in leases of the 19th century: for example, the landlord is held responsible for keeping the premises in a "good state of repair," and the tenant is obliged to maintain the ordinary cleanliness of the interior. Some terms reflect relatively recent innovations of the common law—for example, the obligation to mitigate upon abandonment—but do not represent a doctrinal transmogrification; their incorporation simply mirrors incremental adjustments to the common law of leases. While the fact that the parties cannot contract out of these statutory conditions may represent an attempt to redress the imbalance of power inhering in the landlord–tenant relationship, this does not change the fact that the medium by which this is done is the traditional law of contract and lease. The relationship of landlord to residential tenant continues to be based on property law and the law of contract and tort, whether it is expressed through the common law or in statutes.

Finally, the Chief Justice alludes to the policy goals of the legislation as a basis for inferring novel jurisdiction. Again, the imposition of a few new obligations cannot suffice to create a new jurisdiction; it is difficult to think of a legislative scheme or statute that does not do this. Nor is the fact that the legislation apparently seeks to address a perceived social priority sufficient to create a new jurisdiction; again, most legislative schemes do so. What is required to create a new jurisdiction is a unifying concept or goal, and a sufficiently novel philosophy to belie any analogy with the powers previously exercised by superior courts. The legislation at issue here does not, in my respectful view, meet this test.

I have treated the issue of novel jurisdiction at some length out of a concern that too liberal an application of this concept may trivialize the three-part test for conferring superior court powers on provincially or federally appointed bodies. The factors cited in this case in support of the novel jurisdiction argument have the potential to permit any transfer of s. 96 powers to inferior tribunals. Virtually all types of disputes regulated by the superior courts at the time of confederation can be argued to have become modernized or urbanized. There are few social problems which came before the courts at the time of Confederation which have not been subjected to legislation effecting changes in the property law or contract law by which alone they were once regulated. The subdivision and amalgamation of subjects through codification in more comprehensive legislation, and the proclamation of new goals and priorities, are the routine stuff of every legislative and parliamentary agenda, year after year. If these are the criteria for novel jurisdiction, there must be little that cannot be removed from the s. 96 courts with impunity.

On a theoretical level, reliance on arguments of legislative policy in support of novel jurisdiction may be seen as conflating the first and third steps of the three-part test for infringement of s. 96. As noted, the purpose of the first two steps is to identify whether the law is one which has the potential to deprive the superior courts of the powers the Fathers of Confederation intended them to have. In keeping with this limited purpose, the issue at step one is best confined to an objective comparison of the nature of the powers conferred on the inferior tribunal and the powers exercised by superior courts at the time of Confederation to see if these powers are analogous. If they are, and if they are also shown to be judicial in nature as required by step two, the reviewing court passes to the third stage of the analysis to determine whether the analogous judicial power is transformed by the new legislative and administrative context in such a way that it is no longer a s. 96 power, but rather a power that is ancillary or necessarily incidental to the new scheme or legislative goal: *Re Residential Tenancies Act, supra*. To conclude at the outset that the administrative scheme or legislative goal makes the jurisdiction novel is to decide the entire issue of constitutionality at the first stage, without ever asking whether the power is merely ancillary to the administrative scheme or necessarily incidental to an otherwise valid legislative goal. This is not to say that a jurisdiction which is truly novel, either in the sense that new powers are being exercised or that the legislation reflects an entirely new approach to traditional concerns, should not be validated as insufficiently analogous to the powers exercised by the superior courts before Confederation. It is to say that the three-part test that this Court has scrupulously followed for fifteen years is perfectly capable of ensuring the fulfillment of that objective. ...

I conclude that the powers conferred on the Director of Residential Tenancies and the Residential Tenancies Board by the Act cannot violate s. 96 of the *Constitution Act, 1867* because they were not within the exclusive purview of the superior courts at the time of Confederation. Accordingly, I would allow the appeal and dismiss the cross-appeal. ...

Appeal allowed.

The s. 96 cases examined above have involved limits on the provinces' abilities to assign functions to provincially appointed tribunals and, to a lesser degree, courts. A second strand of s. 96 jurisprudence raises the question of the authority of Parliament to give away superior court jurisdiction, typically the criminal law jurisdiction under s. 91(27) of the *Constitution Act, 1867*. While these cases may appear to be variations of the first line of cases, they should be considered separately, because they involve an assignment of jurisdiction to a court rather than an administrative tribunal. In *McEvoy, Reference re Young Offenders Act (PEI)*, and *MacMillan Bloedel*—all of which are discussed below—the issue was clearly the removal by Parliament of superior court jurisdiction to another court in such a way that the superior courts were liable to being deprived of a jurisdiction they once enjoyed. As will be seen in *McEvoy*, the position adopted by the Supreme Court of Canada is that "Parliament can no more give away federal constitutional powers than a province can usurp them." By interpreting s. 96 to restrict Parliament as well as the provincial legislatures, the Court has affirmed the idea that the Constitution places the superior courts, typically defined in terms of a "core jurisdiction," or, in slightly different terms, an "inherent jurisdiction," outside the reach of ordinary legislative action. While this jurisdiction is said to date, in Canada, from Confederation, it is also said to be the "hallmark" or the "essence" of a superior court. In other words, in the absence of such jurisdiction, or without such powers, there could be no such entity as a court. The idea of a "core jurisdiction" raises, at least by implication, the doctrine of separation of powers.

McEvoy v. Attorney General of New Brunswick and Attorney General of Canada
[1983] 1 SCR 704, 148 DLR (3d) 25

THE COURT (Laskin CJC, Ritchie, Dickson, Beetz, Estey, Chouinard, and Wilson JJ): This is an appeal from a unanimous judgment of the New Brunswick Court of Appeal, delivered by Hughes CJNB, answering in the affirmative three questions put before that court on a reference by the provincial Lieutenant-Governor in Council pursuant to s. 23(1) of the *Judicature Act*, RSNB 1973, c. J-2, as amended. The questions, attached as a schedule to the reference order, are stated to be draft questions directed to determine the constitutional validity of a proposed course of action with respect to the establishment of a unified criminal court in New Brunswick.

The three questions posed to the court in New Brunswick, and the very same questions are now before this court on appeal, read as follows:

> 1. Is it *intra vires* the Parliament of Canada to amend the *Criminal Code* to confer upon a court constituted by the legislature of a province, the judges of which are appointed by the Lieutenant-Governor in Council, exclusive jurisdiction to try all indictable offences under that Act?
>
> 2. Is it *intra vires* the Parliament of Canada to amend the *Criminal Code* to confer upon a court constituted by the legislature of a province, the judges of which are appointed by the Lieutenant-Governor in Council, jurisdiction to try all indictable offences under that Act, if that jurisdiction is concurrent with that of courts whose judges are appointed pursuant to section 96 of the *British North America Act*?
>
> 3. Is it *intra vires* the legislature of a province to constitute a court, the judges of which are appointed by the Lieutenant-Governor in Council, to exercise such jurisdiction in criminal law matters as is conferred upon it by the Parliament of Canada, if the jurisdiction conferred by Parliament is to try all indictable offences under the *Criminal Code*, and is either
>> (a) exclusive; or
>> (b) concurrent with that of courts whose judges are appointed pursuant to section 96 of the *British North America Act*?

It will be noted that questions 1 and 2 relate to the constitutional power of the Parliament of Canada. Only question 3 relates to the powers of the provincial Legislature. The New Brunswick Court of Appeal answered all three questions in the affirmative.

In general terms the issue is whether s. 96 of the *Constitution Act, 1867* is a bar to a plan whereby the federal government and a provincial government would by conjoint action transfer the criminal jurisdiction of provincial superior courts to a new court to be called the "unified criminal court" the judges of which would be provincially appointed. ...

There is no doubt that jurisdiction to try indictable offences was part of the superior court's jurisdiction in 1867; none of the parties suggests otherwise. Nor does anyone argue that inferior courts had concurrent jurisdiction to try indictable offences in 1867. Although this fact is not conclusive (see *Reference re Residential Tenancies Act*, [1981] 1 SCR 714, 123 DLR (3d) 554), none of the other considerations which might save the scheme from the force of s. 96 apply here. The proposed court is obviously a judicial body; its judicial aspect does not change colour when considered in the factual setting in which the court will operate; nor will the court exercise administrative powers to which its adjudicative functions are incidental. The proposed body is clearly and only a criminal court. ...

What is proposed in the New Brunswick proposals is the establishment of a statutory court. As distinguished from what? Certainly not from existing provincial courts which must be fed criminal jurisdiction by federal legislation. No doubt, however, to separate the new court from provincial superior courts. Will that help or advance the matter if functional considerations have to be considered? It has long been the rule that s. 96, although in terms an appointing power, must be addressed in functional terms lest its application be eroded. What then, is the relation between the proposed new statutory court and s. 96? This is the key constitutional issue in the present case and, as we view the matter, the result is to defeat the new statutory court because it will effectively be a s. 96 court.

Sections 96, 97, 98, 99 and 100 are couched in mandatory terms. They do not rest merely on federal statutory powers as does s. 91(27). ...

What is being contemplated here is not one or a few transfers of criminal law power, such as has already been accomplished under the *Criminal Code*, but a complete obliteration of superior court criminal law jurisdiction. Sections 96 to 100 do not distinguish between courts of civil jurisdiction and courts of criminal jurisdiction. They should not be read as permitting the Parliament of Canada through use of its criminal law power to destroy superior courts and to deprive the Governor-General of appointing power and to exclude members of the bar from preferment for superior court appointments.

Parliament can no more give away federal constitutional powers than a province can usurp them. Section 96 provides that "The Governor General *shall* appoint the Judges of the Superior, District, and County Courts in each Province" [emphasis added]. The proposal here is that Parliament transfer the present superior courts' jurisdiction to try indictable offences to a provincial court. The effect of this proposal would be to deprive the Governor-General of his power under s. 96 to appoint the judges who try indictable offences in New Brunswick. That is contrary to s. 96. Section 96 bars Parliament from altering the constitutional scheme envisaged by the judicature sections of the *Constitution Act, 1867* just as it does the provinces from doing so.

The traditional independence of English superior court judges has been raised to the level of a fundamental principle of our federal system by the *Constitution Act, 1982* and cannot have less importance and force in the administration of criminal law than in the case of civil matters. Under the Canadian Constitution the superior courts are independent of both levels of government. The provinces constitute, maintain and organize the superior courts; the federal authority appoints the judges. The judicature sections of the *Constitution Act, 1867* guarantee the independence of the superior courts; they apply to Parliament as well as to the provincial Legislatures.

Both sides of the proposal under review are flawed. Parliament cannot in effect give away the Governor-General's s. 96 appointing power under colour of legislation vesting jurisdiction to try all indictable offences in a provincial court. New Brunswick cannot exercise an appointing power in respect of courts with s. 96 jurisdiction under colour of legislation in relation to the constitution, maintenance and organization of courts with criminal jurisdiction.

Nor is much gained for the proposed new provincial statutory court by providing for concurrent superior court jurisdiction. The theory behind the concurrency proposal is presumably that a provincial court with concurrent rather than exclusive powers would not oust the superior courts' jurisdiction, at least not to the same extent; since the superior courts' jurisdiction was not frozen as of 1867, it would be permissible to alter that jurisdiction so long as the essential core of the superior courts' jurisdiction remained; s. 96 would be no obstacle because the superior court would retain jurisdiction to try indictable offences. With respect, we think this overlooks the fact that what is being attempted here is the transformation by conjunct action of an inferior court into a superior court. Section 96 is, in our view, an insuperable obstacle to any such endeavour.

We wish before ending these reasons to say a word about *Valin v. Langlois* (1879), 3 SCR 1. The case concerned a federal controverted election petition, and federal legislation had assigned authority to try such issues in provincial superior courts. There was no doubt of Parliament's power to make the assignment, when it was concerned with legal issues which fell within its legislative jurisdiction. The issues there were widely canvassed by the court, and particular attention was paid by the New Brunswick Court of Appeal in this case to ascertain views expressed by Taschereau J. He said this at pp. 74-5:

> ... I think that to decide that the Federal Parliament can never or in any way add to or take from the jurisdiction of the Provincial Courts, would be curtailing its powers to an extent, perhaps, not thought of by the Appellant, and that it would destroy, in a very large measure, the rights and privileges which are given to the federal power by sections 91 and 101 of the Act. I take, for one instance, the criminal law. The constitution, maintenance and organization of Provincial Courts of criminal jurisdiction is given to the Provincial Legislatures, as well as the constitution, maintenance and organization of courts of civil jurisdiction, yet, cannot Parliament, in virtue of section 101 of the Act, create new courts of criminal jurisdiction, and enact that all crimes, all offences shall be tried exclusively before these new courts? I take this to be beyond controversy.

> Yet, would not that be altering, diminishing, in fact, taking away all the Provincial Criminal Court's jurisdiction?

With great respect, we do not accept these *obiter* observations as governing the proposed transfer of criminal law power from the provincial superior courts to a new provincial statutory court presided over by a provincial appointee. There is, in our view, a cardinal difference between mere alteration or diminution of criminal jurisdiction and complete exclusion of such jurisdiction. In so far as this latter point was taken by Taschereau J, we find it unacceptable.

It is hardly necessary to say that the proposed provincial scheme is not saved by preserving civil jurisdiction for the provincial superior courts.

We have taken perhaps a limited view of the important issues that are thrown up by the three referred questions but, having decided to address them, we felt it best to consider only those provisions of the Constitution which we think are beyond conjoint provincial and federal action.

We would, therefore, allow the appeal and answer all three questions in the negative. There will be no order as to costs.

Appeal allowed.

NOTE ON SECTION 96 CONSTRAINTS ON PARLIAMENT

Several questions remained unanswered after *McEvoy*. First, does s. 96 prevent Parliament from transferring judicial functions from provincial superior courts to federal courts (also considered superior courts) established by Parliament under s. 101? Second, is it only "wholesale" transfers of superior court powers to inferior courts and tribunals, as in *McEvoy*, that are beyond Parliament's competence? In other words, are "piecemeal," or modest, transfers permissible? (These issues are discussed in R. Elliot, "Case Comment, New Brunswick Unified Criminal Court Reference" (1984), 18 *University of British Columbia Law Review* 127.)

The practice of transferring portions of the jurisdiction to try criminal offences to lower courts was challenged in *Reference re Young Offenders Act (PEI)*, [1991] 1 SCR 252, 77 DLR (4th) 492. The PEI Cabinet had, following the authority given to it by s. 2 of the *Young Offenders Act*, SC 1980-81-82-83, c. 110, designated its provincial court as the Youth Court for the purposes of hearing all cases brought against a young person as defined by the Act. This transfer was held to be valid despite the partial transfer of what was formerly superior court jurisdiction to try criminal cases brought against young persons. *McEvoy* was distinguished on the basis of the novelty of a jurisdiction over offences allegedly committed by young persons—a jurisdiction that, in those terms, did not exist at Confederation. Bur and Kehoe (D.F. Bur and J.K. Kehoe, "Developments in Constitutional Law: The 1990-91 Term" (1992), 3 *Supreme Court Law Review* 403) object to characterizing the jurisdiction transferred to the Youth Court in terms of the current legislative policy (dealing with young persons involved with the criminal justice system) instead of the categories of historical court jurisdiction (serious crimes and less serious crimes). They believe that the Court ought to have restricted Parliament from empowering the transfer of jurisdiction to try serious crimes even when committed by young persons. While properly drawing attention to the potentially determinative effect of adopting modern descriptions of jurisdiction rather than holding to the categories of jurisdiction in place in 1867, they overlook, first, that s. 96 jurisprudence specifically requires courts to give weight to novel policy objectives and, second, that the idea behind the *Young Offenders Act* is to not treat as seriously criminal the acts of young persons, even when seriously harmful.

Reference re Young Offenders Act granted "exclusive jurisdiction" to the youth court to try young offenders. If a jurisdiction is found to be "novel" it is, strictly speaking, no longer appropriate to speak of it as having been transferred. While the idea of a novel jurisdiction precludes the possibility of a transfer, it appears to be possible for a novel jurisdiction to encroach upon the core jurisdiction of a s. 96 court. This situation arose in *MacMillan Bloedel Ltd. v. Simpson*, [1995] 4 SCR 725, 130 DLR (4th) 385. In this case, a young offender was charged with contempt for disobeying an injunction issued by a superior court. He was subsequently tried and convicted in a superior court. On appeal the defence argued that since the contempt did not occur in the face of a superior court the youth should have been tried in a youth court. The point at issue was not the power of the federal government to use its criminal law power to grant jurisdiction to provincial courts but, rather, its power to make a grant of *exclusive* jurisdiction in the case of an offence that was traditionally within the jurisdiction of a superior court. Like *McEvoy* and *Young Offenders*, this case addressed the problem of the independence of the superior courts from the federal government.

Chief Justice Lamer, writing for the majority, argued that there are certain core powers of the superior courts that cannot be removed without a constitutional amendment. Since a grant of "exclusive jurisdiction" has the effect of placing the jurisdiction in question beyond the reach of the superior courts, it effectively reduces the jurisdiction of those courts. It is this reduction of the core jurisdiction that would require a constitutional amendment. As noted above, the idea of a "core jurisdiction" raises, at least by implication, the doctrine of separation of powers. Writing in dissent, Justice McLachlin argued against the idea that there is an immutable core of superior court functions that cannot be transferred. Significantly, she began her remarks by noting, at 406 DLR, that "a strict separation of judicial and legislative powers is not a feature of the Canadian Constitution."

In *MacMillan Bloedel Ltd. v. Simpson*, Lamer CJC affirmed the existence of "the core or inherent jurisdiction of superior courts" in the following passages:

> The superior courts have a core or inherent jurisdiction which is integral to their operations. The jurisdiction which forms this core cannot be removed from the superior courts by either level of government, without amending the Constitution. Without this core jurisdiction, s. 96 could not be said either to ensure uniformity in the judicial system throughout the country or to protect the independence of the judiciary. Furthermore, the power of superior courts to fully control their own process is, in our system where the superior court of general jurisdiction is central, essential to the maintenance of the rule of law itself. (393 DLR)
>
> • • •
>
> In the constitutional arrangements passed on to us by the British and recognized by the preamble to the *Constitution Act, 1867*, the provincial superior courts are the foundation of the rule of law itself. Governance by rule of law requires a judicial system that can ensure its orders are enforced and its process respected. In Canada, the provincial superior court is the only court of general jurisdiction and as such is the centre of the judicial system. None of our statutory

courts has the same core jurisdiction as the superior court and therefore none is as crucial to the rule of law. To remove the power to punish contempt *ex facie* by youths would maim the institution which is at the heart of our judicial system. Destroying part of the core jurisdiction would be tantamount to abolishing the superior courts of general jurisdiction, which is impermissible without constitutional amendment. (402 DLR)

* * *

In light of its importance to the very existence of a superior court, no aspect of the contempt power may be removed from a superior court without infringing all those sections of our Constitution which refer to our existing judicial system as inherited from the British, including ss. 96-101, s. 129, and the principle of the rule of law recognized both in the preamble and in all our conventions of governance. (403-4 DLR)

More recently, in *Cooper v. Canada (Human Rights Commission); Bell v. Canada (Human Rights Commission)*, [1996] 3 SCR 854, 140 DLR (4th) 193, Lamer CJC, concurring in the result but writing his own reasons, stated, at DLR 201-2, that:

One of the defining features of the Canadian Constitution, in my opinion, is the separation of powers. ... There is in Canada a separation of powers among the three branches of government—the legislature, the executive and the judiciary. ... [T]he absence of a strict separation of powers does not mean that the Canadian Constitution does not recognize and sustain some notion of the separation of powers. This is most evident in the Court's jurisprudence on s. 96 of the *Constitution Act, 1867*. Although the wording of this provision suggests that it is solely concerned with the appointment of judges, through judicial interpretation—an important element of which has been the recognition that s. 96 must be read along with ss. 97-100 as part of an integrated whole—s. 96 has come to guarantee the core jurisdiction of the superior courts against legislative encroachment. As I recently noted in *MacMillan Bloedel v. Simpson*, [1995] 4 SCR 725, at 753:

Governance by rule of law requires a judicial system that can ensure its orders are enforced and its process respected.

As this passage makes clear, the existence of the courts is definitional to the Canadian understanding of constitutionalism.

In *Cooper*, Lamer CJC, who notably did not have the support of the Court, would have used this concept of separation of powers to deny administrative tribunals any ability to deal with Charter issues. That issue is discussed more fully in Section III of Chapter 25, Enforcement of Rights.

NOTE ON APPELLATE AND REVIEW JURISDICTION

In many of the s. 96 cases the focus of judicial interest has been on the issue of original jurisdiction, since administrative tribunals and inferior courts are typically established to handle entry level complaints and disputes. Administrative regimes may, however, incorporate bodies with an appellate function and attempts have been made to shield these bodies from review by superior courts through the use of privative clauses. These cases form a third strand of the s. 96 jurisprudence. As already noted, in *John East* Lord Simonds advised caution in this area.

The limit of legislative authority appears to have been set by the decision of the Supreme Court in *Crevier v. Quebec (Attorney General)*, [1981] 2 SCR 220, 127 DLR (3d) 1, which is found below. While it is possible to create an administrative structure that includes a body to hear appeals, this body must be integrated into the overall scheme and it must not be shielded from judicial review (*MacMillan Bloedel Ltd. v. Simpson, supra,* at 417 DLR).

Crevier was preceded by *Attorney General of Quebec v. Farrah*, [1978] 2 SCR 636, 86 DLR (3d) 161. In 1972 the government of Quebec established a transport tribunal under the *Transport Act*. The Act, which created "a regulatory regime in respect of public and private transport," also established the Quebec Transport Commission. The primary role of the Transport Tribunal, which was made up of provincial judges, was defined in s. 58 of the Act as follows:

> 58. The transport tribunal shall also have jurisdiction, to the exclusion of any other court, to hear and dispose of:
>
> (a) in appeal, on any question of law, and decision of the Commission which terminates a matter;
>
> (b) in appeal, decisions of the Commission under section 50;
>
> (c) any matter, by evocation, when the Commission has omitted or neglected to render its decision within six months following the making of the application.

Sections 24 and 72 of the Act prohibited access to judicial review concerning the decisions of the Commission and the Tribunal respectively. Thus, appeals from decisions of the Commission had to be taken before the Tribunal and the decisions of that body could not be appealed in any court. In *Farrah* the Supreme Court ruled on a challenge to the constitutionality of this administrative regime.

As often happens in s. 96 cases, the members of the court agreed in the result, unanimously declaring the Transport Tribunal to be *ultra vires*, but differed on the reasons given for reaching this conclusion. There was, however, general agreement regarding the issues raised in the appeal. The function of the Transport Tribunal was to hear appeals from decisions of the Quebec Transport Commission. Since the Tribunal had no other function it was for all intents and purposes an appellate court. Furthermore, since there was no appeal from decisions of the Tribunal to any other judicial body, the Commission and the Tribunal, when considered together, had both original and final jurisdiction on all of the matters brought before them.

The disagreement among the justices in *Farrah* concerned the ways in which the combination of the Tribunal's jurisdiction with the privative clauses served to make the Tribunal *ultra vires*. Nonetheless, the decision made it clear that a province could not create an administrative body, even within the setting of a larger administrative regime, whose primary or sole function was to exercise a judicial power previously exercised by s. 96 courts, nor could it shield such bodies from judicial review. This point was made even more strongly three years later in *Crevier*, a case which Laskin CJC, writing for a unanimous court, declared to be "no different in principle" from *Farrah*.

Crevier v. Quebec (Attorney General)
[1981] 2 SCR 220, 127 DLR (3d) 1

[The *Professional Code* (Quebec) governed 38 professional corporations in Quebec. Under the Code, each profession was to create a discipline committee that would have jurisdiction over every complaint of an offence under the Code. Each discipline committee was to consist of a chair, who was to be a lawyer, and two other members, who were to be members of the relevant profession. The Code also created a Professions Tribunal consisting of six Provincial Court judges designated by the Chief Judge. An appeal lay to the Professions Tribunal from any decision of a discipline committee. The proceedings before the Professions Tribunal were very formal.

Section 175 of the *Professional Code* said:

> The tribunal may confirm, alter or quash any decision submitted to it and render the decision which it considers should have been rendered in the first place. ...
>
> The tribunal's decision shall be final.

A number of other sections of the *Professional Code* repeated the theme of the unreviewability of decisions of the Professions Tribunal. For example, although Article 33 of the Code of Civil Procedure provided that bodies in Quebec "are subject to the superintending and reforming power of the Superior Court," section 195 said that Article 33 did not apply to decision makers under the *Professional Code*.

Two members of a professional corporation (the corporation for optometrists) were charged with three offences. They were convicted of one of them (practising optometry in a dispensing optician's outlet) and acquitted of the others. They appealed to the Professions Tribunal and the Tribunal decided that the discipline committee had acted beyond its authority in deciding that an offence had been committed. Crevier, on behalf of the optometrists' corporation, sought to have the decision of the Professions Tribunal set aside on the ground that its powers violated s. 96 of the *Constitution Act, 1867*. His application succeeded in Quebec Superior Court, but the Quebec Court of Appeal reversed this decision and upheld the decision of the Professions Tribunal.]

LASKIN CJC (Martland, Ritchie, Dickson, Beetz, Estey, McIntyre, Chouinard, and Lamer JJ concurring): ... The Court of Appeal majority viewed the preclusive words of s. 194 [which shielded the decision of the Professions Tribunal from review] as not touching the power and right of the Superior Court to issue a writ of evocation where there has been a want or excess of jurisdiction. Section 194 itself, however, does not recognize this supervisory authority of the Superior Court. If it did, it would be arguable that so long as the Professions Tribunal was subject to the superintendence of the Superior Court on questions of jurisdiction, it would not be tainted as exercising a power belonging to a s. 96 court by an initial but reviewable conclusion that a Discipline Committee had exceeded its jurisdiction. That is not this case, having regard to the embracive terms of s. 194 of the *Professional Code*. Even if it were otherwise and the supervisory authority of the Superior Court on questions of jurisdiction was expressly preserved, it would still not be a complete answer to a contention that the Professions Tribunal is exercising powers more conformable to those belonging to a s. 96 court than those properly exercisable by a provincial administrative or quasi-judicial tribunal or even a provincial judicial tribunal. ...

Three issues arise from the reasons in the Court of Appeal. The first, which I think may be quickly disposed of, concerns the intimation by Jacques J of a *Tomko* [*Tomko v. Labour Relations Board (Nova Scotia)*, [1977] 1 SCR 112] situation. The Professions Tribunal is given no function other than that of a general tribunal of appeal in respect of all professions covered by the *Professional Code* and it is, therefore, impossible to see its final appellate jurisdiction as part of an institutional arrangement by way of a regulatory scheme for the governance of the various professions. The Professions Tribunal is not so much integrated into any scheme as it is sitting on top of the various schemes and with an authority detached from them, although, of course, exercising that authority in relation to each scheme as the occasion requires. There is no valid comparison with the cease and desist orders which the Labour Relations Board in the *Tomko* case was authorized to issue in its administration of a collective bargaining statute.

I draw support for distinguishing *Tomko* in this assessment of the Professions Tribunal by relying on the recent judgment of this Court in *Reference re Residential Tenancies Act*, [1981] 1 SCR 714. ...

The second issue arising from the reasons of the Quebec Court of Appeal concerns the effect upon s. 96 of a privative clause of a statute which purports to insulate a provincial adjudicative tribunal from any review of its decisions. Is it enough to deflect s. 96 if the privative clause is construed to preserve superior court supervision over questions of jurisdiction, and if (as in this case) such a construction is not open because of the wording of the privative clause, is the clause constitutionally valid? In my opinion, where a provincial Legislature purports to insulate one of its statutory tribunals from any curial review of its adjudicative functions, the insulation encompassing jurisdiction, such provincial legislation must be struck down as unconstitutional by reason of having the effect of constituting the tribunal a s. 96 court. As Judson J noted in *Farrell v. Workmen's Compensation Board*, [1962] SCR 48, at 52, "the restrictions on the legislative power of the province to confer jurisdiction on boards must be derived by implication from the provisions of s. 96 of the *British North America Act*." In the *Farrell* case, there was a preclusive provision against judicial review of Board decisions on questions of law but not on questions of jurisdiction, as distinguished from questions of law, and there was no doubt in that case that the Board had jurisdiction. The conclusion in the *Farrell* case, supported as well in the *Farrah* case, was that there was no constitutional impediment to such a limitation by a province on judicial review.

· · ·

It is true that this is the first time that this Court has declared unequivocally that a provincially-constituted statutory tribunal cannot constitutionally be immunized from review of decisions on questions of jurisdiction. In my opinion, this limitation, arising by virtue of s. 96, stands on the same footing as the well-accepted limitation on the power of provincial statutory tribunals to make unreviewable determinations of constitutionality. There may be differences of opinion as to what are questions of jurisdiction but, in my lexicon, they rise above and are different from errors of law, whether involving statutory construction or evidentiary matters or other matters. It is now unquestioned that privative clauses may, when properly framed, effectively oust judicial review on questions of law and, indeed, on other issues not touching jurisdiction. However, given that s. 96 is in the *British North America Act* and that it would make a mockery of it to treat it in non-functional formal terms as a mere appointing power, I can think of nothing that is more the hallmark of a superior court than the vesting of power in a provincial statutory tribunal to determine the limits of its jurisdiction without appeal or other review. ...

The Court has hitherto been content to look at privative clauses in terms of proper construction and, no doubt, with a disposition to read them narrowly against the long history of judicial review on questions of law and questions of jurisdiction. Where, however, questions of law have been specifically covered in a privative enactment, this Court, as in *Farrah*, has not hesitated to recognize this limitation on judicial review as serving the interests of an express legislative policy to protect decisions of adjudicative agencies from external correction. Thus, it has, in my opinion, balanced the competing interests of a provincial Legislature in its enactment of substantively valid legislation and of the courts as ultimate interpreters of the *British North America Act* and s. 96 thereof. The same considerations do not, however, apply to issues of jurisdiction which are not far removed from issues of constitutionality. It cannot be left to a provincial statutory tribunal, in the face of s. 96, to determine the limits of its own jurisdiction without appeal or review.

The third issue that emerges from the reasons of the Court of Appeal relates to the impact of the *Farrah* [*AG Quebec v. Farrah*, [1978] 2 SCR 636] case. There, as here, the provincial Legislature established a statutory tribunal of appeal.

· · ·

[W]hat the *Farrah* case decided was that to give a provincially-constituted statutory tribunal a jurisdiction in appeal on questions of law without limitation, and to reinforce this appellate authority by excluding any supervisory recourse to the Quebec Superior Court, was to create a s. 96 court. The present case is no different in principle, even though in ss. 162 and 175 of the *Professional Code*, dealing with the appellate authority of the Professions Tribunal, there is no mention of the word "law" or the word "jurisdiction." When regard is had to the privative terms of ss. 194 and 195, added to the fact that by s. 175 the Professions Tribunal's decisions are final, I see no significant distinction between the present case and the *Farrah* case in the fact that in the latter the authority granted to the appeal tribunal was "to the exclusion of any other court." In both cases there was a purported exclusion of the reviewing authority of any other court, whether by appeal or by evocation.

In the result, I would allow the appeal. ...

Appeal dismissed.

IV. THE INDEPENDENCE OF THE JUDICIARY

The institution of judicial review and its place in our constitutional structure was introduced in Chapter 2, Judicial Review and Constitutional Interpretation. Once it is accepted that constitutional norms are enforceable by courts, then the integrity of the constitutional order, as well as of the entire legal order, is dependent on the integrity of the judicial branch. Sections 96 to 101 of the *Constitution Act, 1867* are directed to producing the greatest legitimacy for the judicial branch—sound appointments, a membership skilled in law, and independence from political interference achieved through guaranteed compensation and security of appointment. Arguably, the appointing power in s. 96 was not designed with the idea of producing an independent judicial branch. E.R.A. Edwards in "Section 96: The Historical Rationale" (1984), 42 *The Advocate* 541 suggests that the grant of the appointment power to the federal government was intended as a "quality control" measure. As Edwards explains, at 541: "It was assumed that the brighter lights at the Bar would, in anticipation of judicial preferment, involve themselves in federal rather than provincial politics and hence patronage appointments, which were clearly anticipated, would result in a better quality judiciary if made by the federal authority." However, others have argued that "[i]t was apparently felt that federally appointed, paid and tenured judges would have the independence necessary to impartially apply both federal and provincial law since they would not be solely dependent on either body for their jurisdiction or remuneration" (J.P. McEvoy, "New Brunswick's Residential Tenancies Act: The Constitution and the Rentalsman" (1983), 32 *University of New Brunswick Law Journal* 231, at 234). Estey J, writing for a majority of the Supreme Court of Canada in *Reference re Section 6 of Family Relations Act*, [1982] 1 SCR 62, 131 DLR (3d) 257, at 280-81, provided the following comments on the purpose served by s. 96:

> Behind that simple provision lie many real as well as fanciful theories as to its role and purpose in our Constitution. The generally accepted theory has been that the national appointment of Superior, County and District Court Judges was designed to ensure a quality of independence and impartiality in the courtroom where the more serious claims and issues in the community arise; and an aura of detachment said to be analogous to that of the Royal Justices on Circuit from Westminster is thought to be the aim of the authors of s. 96: see *O. Martineau & Sons Ltd. v. City of Montreal*, [1932] 1 DLR 353 at 359, [1932] AC 113 at 121, where Lord Blanesburg stated:
>
> > ... the section is shown to lie at the root of the means adopted by the framers of the statute to secure the impartiality and independence of the provincial judiciary.

With respect to preserving judicial independence through limiting interference with the terms and conditions of judges' employment, s. 100 of the *Constitution Act, 1867* provides that salaries and benefits be fixed and provided by Parliament. This clearly shields the judiciary from improper encroachment by the executive with respect to pay. The Supreme Court of Canada elaborated on this principle in *Beauregard v. Canada*, [1986] 2 SCR 56, 30 DLR (4th) 481: "[T]he essence of judicial independence for superior court judges is complete freedom from arbitrary interference by *both* the executive and the legislature. Neither the executive nor the legislature can interfere with the financial security of superior court judges" (at 75).

Beauregard considered the constitutional validity of s. 29.1, an amendment to the federal *Judges Act*, RSC 1970, c. J-1, which required newly appointed judges (but not existing judges) to contribute to the cost of their pensions which, on its own, effectively reduced the salaries of those affected. The Supreme Court ruled that s. 100 of the *Constitution Act, 1867* provides for federal jurisdiction over remunerative benefits for superior court judges and preserves Parliament's capacity to modify those benefits (at 80-81). However, this general power to fix the salaries and benefits of superior court judges is not unlimited. For the majority, Dickson CJC wrote: "If there were any hint that a federal law dealing with these matters was enacted for an improper or colourable purpose, or if there was discriminatory treatment of judges *vis-à-vis* other citizens, then serious issues relating to judicial independence would arise and the law might well be held to be *ultra vires* s. 100 of the *Constitution Act, 1867*" (at 77). The amendment at issue in *Beauregard* was found to be untainted by such improper motives and, moreover, was effectively introduced as part of a remuneration package that included substantial salary and pension increases (at 78). As such, it did not offend judicial independence.

NOTE ON THE PROVINCIAL JUDGES REFERENCE

In a series of cases together known as the *Reference re Provincial Court Judges* (or the *Provincial Judges Reference*), [1997] 3 SCR 3, 150 DLR (4th) 577, involving Prince Edward Island, Alberta, and Manitoba, the Supreme Court of Canada addressed the independence of provincial court judges within the context of their financial security. Each of the provinces had in some way imposed a salary reduction on provincial court judges. Prince Edward Island had referred to the Court of Appeal its relevant legislation that reduced the salaries of provincial court judges and public sector employees. In Alberta, three accused had challenged the constitutionality of their trials before provincial court judges who were subject to similar provincial legislation. The provincial court judges themselves challenged Manitoba's equivalent legislation. The cases all invoked section 11(d) of the *Canadian Charter of Rights and Freedoms*, which guarantees to persons charged with an offence the presumption of innocence until found guilty in a fair trial by an independent and impartial tribunal.

Speaking for the majority of the Court (La Forest J dissented vigorously on this point), Lamer CJC considered the impact of the fundamental constitutional principle of judicial independence in light of the "gap" in the Constitution left by the absence of an explicit guarantee of judicial independence with respect to provincial court judges dealing with civil matters:

> [83] ... Notwithstanding the presence of s. 11(d) of the *Charter*, and ss. 96-100 of the *Constitution Act, 1867*, I am of the view that judicial independence is at root an *unwritten* constitutional principle, in the sense that it is exterior to the particular sections of the *Constitution Acts*. The existence of that principle, whose origins can be traced to the *Act of Settlement* of 1701, is recognized and affirmed by the preamble to the *Constitution Act, 1867*. The specific provisions of the *Constitution Acts, 1867 to 1982*, merely "elaborate that principle in the institutional apparatus which they create or contemplate": *Switzman v. Elbling*, [1957] SCR 285, at p. 306, *per* Rand J.
>
> [84] I arrive at this conclusion, in part, by considering the tenability of the opposite position—that the Canadian Constitution already contains explicit provisions which are directed at the protection of judicial independence, and that those provisions are exhaustive of the matter. Section 11(d) of the *Charter*, as I have mentioned above, protects the independence of a wide range of courts and tribunals which exercise jurisdiction over offences. Moreover, since well before the enactment of the *Charter*, ss. 96-100 of the *Constitution Act, 1867*, separately and in

combination, have protected and continue to protect the independence of provincial superior courts ... .

[85] However, upon closer examination, there are serious limitations to the view that the express provisions of the Constitution comprise an exhaustive and definitive code for the protection of judicial independence. The first and most serious problem is that the range of courts whose independence is protected by the written provisions of the Constitution contains large gaps. Sections 96-100, for example, only protect the independence of judges of the superior, district, and county courts, and even then, not in a uniform or consistent manner. Thus, while ss. 96 and 100 protect the core jurisdiction and the financial security, respectively, of all three types of courts (superior, district, and county), s. 99, on its terms, only protects the security of tenure of superior court judges. Moreover, ss. 96-100 do not apply to provincially appointed inferior courts, otherwise known as provincial courts.

Lamer CJC then considered the limitations of the express provisions in achieving the objective of judicial independence, concluding that it has been through judicial interpretation that these provisions have served to protect the judicial role. They do so, however, through reference to an unwritten principle of judicial independence that fills in the gaps of the constitutional text, which he described as follows:

[106] The historical origins of the protection of judicial independence in the United Kingdom, and thus in the Canadian Constitution, can be traced to the *Act of Settlement* of 1701. As we said in *Valente* [*Valente v. The Queen*, [1985] 2 SCR 273], at p. 693, that Act was the "historical inspiration" for the judicature provisions of the *Constitution Act, 1867*. Admittedly, the Act only extends protection to judges of the English superior courts. However, our Constitution has evolved over time. In the same way that our understanding of rights and freedoms has grown, such that they have now been expressly entrenched through the enactment of the *Constitution Act, 1982*, so too has judicial independence grown into a principle that now extends to all courts, not just the superior courts of this country.

[107] I also support this conclusion on the basis of the presence of s. 11(d) of the *Charter*, an express provision which protects the independence of provincial court judges only when those courts exercise jurisdiction in relation to offences. As I said earlier, the express provisions of the Constitution should be understood as elaborations of the underlying, unwritten, and organizing principles found in the preamble to the *Constitution Act, 1867*. Even though s. 11(d) is found in the newer part of our Constitution, the *Charter*, it can be understood in this way, since the Constitution is to be read as a unified whole ... . An analogy can be drawn between the express reference in the preamble of the *Constitution Act, 1982* to the rule of law and the implicit inclusion of that principle in the *Constitution Act, 1867*: *Reference re Manitoba Language Rights* [[1985], 1 SCR 721], at p. 750. Section 11(d), far from indicating that judicial independence is constitutionally enshrined for provincial courts only when those courts exercise jurisdiction over offences, is proof of the existence of a general principle of judicial independence that applies to all courts no matter what kind of cases they hear.

[108] I reinforce this conclusion by reference to the central place that courts hold within the Canadian system of government. In *OPSEU* [*Ontario Public Service Employees' Union v. AG Ontario*, [1987] 2 SCR 2], as I have mentioned above, Beetz J linked limitations on legislative sovereignty over political speech with "the existence of certain political institutions" as part of the "basic structure of our Constitution" (p. 57). However, political institutions are only one

part of the basic structure of the Canadian Constitution. As this Court has said before, there are three branches of government—the legislature, the executive, and the judiciary … . Courts, in other words, are equally "definitional to the Canadian understanding of constitutionalism" (*Cooper v. Canada (Human Rights Commission)*, [1996] 3 SCR 721, at para. 11) as are political institutions. It follows that the same constitutional imperative—the preservation of the basic structure—which led Beetz J to limit the power of legislatures to affect the operation of political institutions, also extends protection to the judicial institutions of our constitutional system. By implication, the jurisdiction of the provinces over "courts," as that term is used in s. 92(14) of the *Constitution Act, 1867*, contains within it an implied limitation that the independence of those courts cannot be undermined.

[109] In conclusion, the express provisions of the *Constitution Act, 1867* and the *Charter* are not an exhaustive written code for the protection of judicial independence in Canada. Judicial independence is an unwritten norm, recognized and affirmed by the preamble to the *Constitution Act, 1867*. In fact, it is in that preamble, which serves as the grand entrance hall to the castle of the Constitution, that the true source of our commitment to this foundational principle is located … .

With respect to the content of the principle of judicial independence, three aspects were identified: financial security, security of tenure, and institutional independence. Given the nature of the issues that generated the references, the particular focus was the process by which judicial remuneration must be determined if the financial security component of the principle is to be respected. The decision established a requirement that governments establish "independent, effective and objective" commissions to make recommendations on a periodic basis relating to the appropriate level of remuneration for the judiciary. Governments are not required to accept these recommendations, but a departure from the recommendations requires a "legitimate" reason. The judicial salary reductions of each of the three provinces involved in the *Reference* were found to be unconstitutional because they had not been preceded by a report of a judicial compensation commission.

The *Provincial Judges Reference* has generated significant criticism. Some take the position that across-the-board public sector salary reductions of the sort at issue in the *Reference* pose no serious threat to judicial independence; see Peter Hogg, *Constitutional Law of Canada*, 5th ed., looseleaf (Scarborough, ON: Carswell, 2007), at 7-14 to 7-18. Others take issue with the method of constitutional interpretation in the case, which, through reliance on the preamble, extended the reach of the principle of judicial independence beyond what was expressly provided for in the text of the Constitution. This methodology was subsequently applied in *Reference re Secession of Quebec*, [1998] 2 SCR 217, 161 DLR (4th) 385, found in Chapter 1, Introduction, and is further discussed in Chapter 2, Judicial Review and Constitutional Interpretation. For a discussion of this aspect of the *Provincial Judges Reference*, see Robin Elliot, "References, Structural Argumentation and the Organizing Principles of Canada's Constitution" (2001), 80 *Canadian Bar Review* 67.

In *Ell v. Alberta*, [2003] 1 SCR 857, 227 DLR (4th) 217, the Supreme Court of Canada held that the principle of judicial independence applied to justices of the peace, but that changing the qualifications to be appointed a justice of the peace did not contravene the principle.

Section 63(2) of the federal *Judges Act*, RSC 1985, c. J-1, provides that the Canadian Judicial Council "may investigate any complaint or allegation made in respect of a judge of a superior court." These complaints may be made by lawyers or parties to a particular case or members of the public. Following a complaint under s. 63(2), the Council will follow an established process to determine whether it should establish an inquiry into or otherwise investigate the complaint. Under s. 63(1), however, the Council is obliged, at the request of the Minister of Justice or a provincial attorney general, to commence an inquiry into whether a judge should be removed from office. *Cosgrove v. Canadian Judicial Council*, [2007] 4 FCR 714, s. 63(1) was challenged as infringing judicial independence. The Federal Court of Appeal held that s. 63(1) was constitutional (although perhaps not necessary). An application for leave to appeal to the Supreme Court of Canada was dismissed (November 29, 2007).

V. THE JUDICIAL APPOINTMENT PROCESS

As explained, s. 96 of the *Constitution Act, 1867* provides that the Governor General appoints superior court judges, while the Lieutenant Governor of a province appoints provincial court judges (judges of the inferior courts) under s. 92(4), in both cases on the advice of the Cabinet. Pursuant to s. 5.2 of the *Federal Courts Act*, the Governor in Council (the Cabinet) makes Federal Court of Appeal and Federal Court appointments. In practice, in both cases, committees have been established to prepare a list of names. In the case of superior court appointments, the provincial or territorial Judicial Appointments Advisory Committee reviews applications and submits a list of names to the federal Minister of Justice who then recommends an individual to the federal Cabinet. The Advisory Committees are composed of representatives of the chief justice of the province or senior judge of the territory, the law society, the Canadian Bar Association, three representatives of the federal Minister of Justice and, in a controversial addition, a representative of the law enforcement community. There is also an Advisory Committee, differently constituted, for the Tax Court of Canada.

Section 4(2) of the *Supreme Court Act*, RS 1985, c. S-26, provides that the judges to that court be appointed by the Governor in Council. In practice, the Prime Minister selects Supreme Court justices on the advice of the Minister of Justice. In recent years, there have been several changes to the process designed to provide for Parliament to play a greater role in Supreme Court appointments. In 2004, an Interim Ad Hoc Committee on the Appointment of Supreme Court Judges, composed of parliamentarians of all parties in Parliament, a representative of the Canadian Judicial Council, and a representative of the Law Society of Upper Canada reviewed the candidacy of two nominees for the Supreme Court (from Ontario) for the purpose of advising the Prime Minister on the suitability of the two nominees for appointment. The process included a public hearing where the Minister of Justice explained the process and the nominees' qualifications, and answered the Committee's questions. This process was "interim" because it was established to ensure that appointments would be made for the commencement of the Court's next sittings. In 2005, the Minister of Justice announced a new process for appointments that reflected the interim process and included consultation with the attorneys general of the relevant provinces or territories and other members of the legal community to develop a "long short list" of potential candidates, to be reduced to three candidates by an advisory committee engaged in its own consultation process. The Minister of Justice would recommend a nominee to the Prime Minister and was to appear before the Justice Standing Committee to explain the selection of the person appointed. Prior to the completion of this process, however, the government was defeated and the new government, while accepting the short list of three candidates, established an Ad Hoc Committee to Review a Nominee for the Supreme Court of Canada composed of parliamentarians before whom the nominee (Justice Rothstein) appeared. These processes recognized that the authority to make the appointment lay with the Governor General on the recommendation of the Prime Minister. Although the government had stated that it would develop a more permanent formal means by which Parliament could review Supreme Court nominees, it had not established this process by the time that the next Supreme Court vacancy occurred. In the event, when the advisory committee was unable to develop a candidate list, the Prime Minister announced the name of the nominee and, subsequently, to make the appointment in a timely way during a period when Parliament had been prorogued, the Prime Minister bypassed the process to confirm the appointment.

These changes, actual and intended, are a response to arguments that there should be greater transparency and broader input into the appointment process. They raise questions such as "What does transparency mean in the context of appointments to the Supreme Court?" and "How can transparency be achieved without impairing the independence of the court and the individual judges?" For some, greater parliamentary involvement in the process is appropriate to ensure that a balance is maintained between the power of the judiciary and the power of Parliament. For others, public hearings risk descent into the kind of ideological questioning and political manoeuvring that often occurs during Senate hearings into appointments to the US Supreme Court. The first test of a more "open" process, the hearing into Justice Rothstein's appointment, did not answer these questions. Because the committee, composed of MPs, was *ad hoc*, the parliamentarians did not have the benefit of parliamentary privilege; everyone was on their best behaviour. For the most part, the questioning was restrained. Justice Rothstein's judicial record did not raise any particular "red flags" for those concerned about so-called activist judicial decision making. If all the current justices were to sit until required to retire at age 75, the earliest new appointment, and the next test of the new process, will not occur until 2013. It is not uncommon for judges to resign for other reasons, however, and the opportunity to assess the process employed and its relationship both to transparency and judicial independence may occur earlier.

PART FOUR

Aboriginal Peoples

CHAPTER FOURTEEN

Aboriginal Peoples and the Constitution

I. INTRODUCTION

There are over one million people of Aboriginal ancestry in Canada today. They are members of indigenous nations that existed before the arrival of the French, British, and other early settlers that initiated the Dominion of Canada. The term "Aboriginal" conceals the great diversity among peoples descended from those who lived in North America prior to the arrival of Europeans. Indigenous peoples are distinguished from one another by different social, cultural, economic, political, and spiritual traditions. Their languages may be as different from one another as English is to Mandarin, or as Hindi is to Hawaiian. Aboriginal peoples in Canada are divided into 12 distinct language families and are further separated into 50 different linguistic groupings. In British Columbia, where six of the language families are located, these differences are often found merely by crossing from one mountain valley into the next.

Despite the diversity that exists among the first peoples of Canada, the text of s. 35(2) of the *Constitution Act, 1982* makes only three distinctions among Aboriginal peoples: the Indian, Inuit, and Métis. While courts have been somewhat sensitive to the greater multiplicity of Aboriginal groups than this section may suggest, the terms Indian, Inuit, and Métis continue to form the predominant classification to describe differences among Aboriginal peoples.

The federal government has maintained the term "Indian" as a category to recognize certain indigenous people as holding status under its *Indian Act*. Thus, the term continues to have legal relevancy, as Indian status entitles its holder to a specific set of rights and obligations set out in treaties, legislation, and other government policies and programs. The status Indian population in Canada is over 700,000. It is a young population (over 51 percent under the age of 25) and is closely divided in residency between reserve (land set aside exclusively for Indians) and off-reserve locations. First Nations people who are not registered by the government under federal procedures are referred to as non-status Indians. There are approximately 200,000 people who fit into this category.

The Inuit are the indigenous peoples of the circumpolar north. Historically known as the Eskimo, they are divided between Alaska, Russia, Greenland, and Canada. Inuit people speak Inuktitut (though there are about 20 different dialects) and they number over 50,000 people in 53 Canadian communities. Most of the Inuit in Canada are found in the Northwest Territories, Quebec, Labrador, and Nunavut, the latter territory being formed in 1999 as a result of a land claim agreement with the Inuit of the eastern Arctic. There is no federal Inuit registry, and thus the status/non-status distinction does not exist in this group.

The origins of the Métis peoples are entwined with the historical fabric of Canada. It was in the Canadian northwest that they first evolved into a new and distinct grouping that eventually affected Aboriginal rights in Canada. The Métis originally formed as the result of nineteenth century unions between male fur traders and Cree women on the Canadian plains; this population of mixed ancestry forged a common culture and ethnic identity. This shared identity led to the creation of the Métis nation that negotiated and fought for recognition when Manitoba and parts of the old North-Western Territory were being ushered into Confederation. While the Métis under Louis Riel achieved some limited success in causing Canada to take account of their rights, for most of the country's history numerous federal administrations treated the group as if they had no distinct rights. For example, the federal government acted as though it had no obligations to the Métis, and largely presumed that they would be assimilated into the general population. At the same time, other Métis groups arose throughout the country as Aboriginal people from different regions of the country married non-native settlers and created distinct political and cultural identities that have legal significance for Aboriginal rights today.

II. COMMON LAW FOUNDATIONS OF CONSTITUTIONAL RECOGNITION

There has been a search for appropriate ways to constitute peaceful relationships between Aboriginal and non-Aboriginal peoples ever since their first encounters in North America, dealt with in Chapter 3, From Contact to Confederation. Chiefs and elders, legislators and judges, fur traders, farmers, and others have all accessed their own particular legal traditions in an attempt to create a workable order between the groups. As a result of these efforts, constitutional law in relation to Aboriginal peoples has become an amalgam of different legal sources. Its doctrines are informed by, *inter alia*, the traditional laws and customs of Aboriginal peoples, French and British colonial practice, executive proclamations, British legislative action, treaties, Privy Council rulings and decisions of the senior appellate courts of the United States and Australia, international law, and various sections of the *British North America Acts* and *Constitution Act, 1982*. As contemporary Canadian legal institutions sort through these various legal orders in answering the questions that come before them, the quest for reconciliation between Aboriginal peoples and the Crown is gaining momentum. The responses generated by this search are changing our understanding of constitutional law in Canada.

Most, if not all, constitutional issues involving Aboriginal peoples occur against the backdrop of Aboriginal rights with respect to land. Before 1982, apart from treaties that establish "reserves" for the exclusive use and enjoyment of Aboriginal peoples, which, generally speaking, are regulated by the federal *Indian Act*, RSC 1985, c. I-5, Anglo-Canadian law conceptualized Aboriginal rights with respect to land as "Aboriginal title"—a common law entitlement that vested in Aboriginal peoples, initially at least, by virtue of the Royal Proclamation of 1763. As noted in Chapter 3, the Royal Proclamation was issued in the aftermath of the Treaty of Paris, in which France ceded what is now Quebec to Great Britain. The Royal Proclamation also declared that lands possessed by Indians throughout British territories in America were reserved for their exclusive use, unless previously ceded to the Crown. Specifically, it stated that

Nations or Tribes of Indians with whom We are connected, and who live under our Protection, should not be molested or disturbed in the Possession of such Parts of our Dominions and Territories as, not having been ceded or purchased by Us, are reserved to them, or any of them, as their Hunting Grounds.

It also stipulated that "lands and territories not included within the limits of [the governments created under the Royal Proclamation, including that of Quebec], or within the limits of the territory granted to the Hudson's Bay Company" be reserved under the King's protection and dominion for the use of the Indians. Not only were these lands reserved, but they could not be purchased, settled, or taken by British subjects without the Crown's consent and prior issuance of a licence. Practically, that meant that the Crown alone possessed the initial right to acquire the indigenous territory to which the Proclamation referred.

Until the Supreme Court of Canada's decision in *Calder v. Attorney General of British Columbia*, [1973] SCR 313, 34 DLR (3d) 145, the Royal Proclamation was generally viewed by the judiciary as the sole Anglo-Canadian legal source of Aboriginal rights. In 1888, for example, the Privy Council in *St. Catherine's Milling & Lumber Co. v. The Queen* (1888), 14 App. Cas. 46, held that Aboriginal title existed in common law because the Royal Proclamation declared that Aboriginal peoples had certain rights to their territory. The Privy Council held further that Aboriginal title was but a burden on the underlying title of the Crown, and gave rise to rights that were merely personal and usufructuary in nature, and that could be extinguished by the exercise of the Crown's sovereign power.

One exception to this conception of the source of Aboriginal rights lay with the famous decision by Monk J in *Connolly v. Woolrich* (1867), 17 RJRQ 75 (Que. SC), discussed below in an excerpt from a report by the Royal Commission on Aboriginal Peoples. As the Royal Commission indicates, *Connolly v. Woolrich* suggests that Aboriginal peoples hold rights to their territory not because of what the Royal Proclamation may have said about the matter, but because Aboriginal rights emanate from Aboriginal legal systems that predate the establishment of colonies on the continent.

Canada, Royal Commission on Aboriginal Peoples, *Report*, vol. 2, *Restructuring the Relationship*
(Ottawa: Queen's Printer, 1996), at 186-90 (footnotes omitted)

In about 1802, a young Quebec lad by the name of William Connolly left his home near Montreal and went west to seek his fortune in the fur trade with the North-West Company. A year or so later, William married a young woman of the Cree Nation, Suzanne by name. Suzanne had an interesting background. She was born of a Cree mother and a French-Canadian father and was the stepdaughter of a Cree chief at Cumberland House, located west of Lake Winnipeg. The union between William and Suzanne was formed under Cree law by mutual consent, with a gift probably given to Suzanne's stepfather. It was never solemnized by a priest or minister. Marriages of this kind were common in the fur trade during that era.

William and Suzanne lived happily together for nearly 30 years and had six children, one of whom later became Lady Amelia Douglas, the wife of the first governor of British

Columbia. William Connolly prospered in the fur trade. He was described by a contemporary as "a veritable *bon garçon*, and an Emeralder of the first order." When the North-West Company merged with the Hudson's Bay Company, he continued on as a chief trader and was later promoted to the position of chief factor.

In 1831, William left the western fur trade and returned to the Montreal area with Suzanne and several of their children. Not long after, however, William decided to treat his first marriage as invalid and he married his well-to-do second cousin, Julia Woolrich, in a Catholic ceremony. Suzanne eventually returned west with her younger children and spent her final years living in the Grey Nuns convent at St. Boniface, Manitoba, where she was supported by William and later by Julia. When William died in the late 1840s, he willed all his property to Julia and their two children, cutting Suzanne and her children out of the estate.

Several years after Suzanne's death in 1862, her eldest son, John Connolly, sued Julia Woolrich for a share of his father's estate. This famous case, *Connolly v. Woolrich*, was fought through the courts of Quebec and was eventually appealed to the Privy Council in Britain before being settled out of court. The judgement delivered in the case sheds a remarkable light on the constitutional status of Aboriginal nations and their relations with incoming French and English settlers.

In support of his claim, John Connolly argued that the marriage between his mother and William Connolly was valid under Cree law and that the couple had been in "community of property," so that each partner to the marriage was entitled to one-half of their jointly owned property. When William died, only his half-share of the property could be left to Julia, with the other half passing automatically to Suzanne as his lawful wife. On Suzanne's death, her children would be entitled to inherit her share of the estate, now in the hands of Julia.

The initial question for the Quebec courts was whether the Cree marriage between Suzanne and William was valid. The lawyer for Julia Woolrich argued that it was not valid. He maintained that English common law was in force in the northwest in 1803 and that the union between Suzanne and William did not meet its requirements. Moreover, he said, in an argument that catered to the worst prejudices of the times, the marriage customs of so-called uncivilized and pagan nations could not be recognized by the court as validating a marriage even between two Aboriginal people, much less between an Aboriginal and a non-Aboriginal person.

The Quebec Superior Court rejected Julia Woolrich's arguments. It held that the Cree marriage between Suzanne and William was valid and that their eldest son was entitled to his rightful share of the estate. This decision was maintained on appeal to the Quebec Court of Queen's Bench.

In his judgement, Justice Monk of the Superior Court stated that he was prepared to assume, for the sake of argument, that the first European traders to inhabit the northwest brought with them their own laws as their birthright. Nevertheless, the region was already occupied by "numerous and powerful tribes of Indians; by Aboriginal nations, who had been in possession of these countries for ages." Assuming that French or English law had been introduced in the area at some point, "will it be contended that the territorial rights, political organization, such as it was, or the laws and usages of the Indian tribes, were abrogated; that they ceased to exist, when these two European nations began to trade with the aboriginal occupants?" Answering his own question in the negative, Justice Monk wrote: "In my opinion, it is beyond controversy that they did not, that so far from being abolished, they were left in full force, and were not even modified in the slightest degree, in regard to the civil rights of the natives."

Justice Monk supported this conclusion by quoting at length from *Worcester v. Georgia*, a landmark case decided in 1832 by the United States Supreme Court under Chief Justice Marshall. Justice Marshall, describing the policy of the British Crown in America before the American Revolution, states:

> Certain it is, that our history furnishes no example, from the first settlement of our country, *of any attempt on the part of the Crown to interfere with the internal affairs of the Indians* farther than to keep out the agents of foreign powers, who, as traders or otherwise, might seduce them into foreign alliances. The king purchased their lands when they were willing to sell, at a price they were willing to take; but never coerced a surrender of them. *He also purchased their alliance and dependence by subsidies; but never intruded into the interior of their affairs, or interfered with their self-government, so far as respected themselves only.* [Emphasis supplied by Justice Monk.]

According to this passage, the British Crown did not interfere with the domestic affairs of its Indian allies and dependencies, so that they remained self-governing in internal matters. Adopting this outlook, Justice Monk concluded that he had no hesitation in holding that "the Indian political and territorial rights, laws, and usages remained in full force" in the northwest at the relevant time. This decision portrays Aboriginal peoples as autonomous nations living within the protection of the Crown but retaining their territorial rights, political organizations and common laws.

A number of lessons can be drawn from *Connolly v. Woolrich*. First, the sources of law and authority in Canada are more diverse than is sometimes assumed. They include the common laws and political systems of Aboriginal nations in addition to the standard range of Euro-Canadian sources.

Second, in earlier times, the history of Canada often featured close and relatively harmonious relations between Aboriginal peoples and newcomers. The fur trade, which played an important role in the economy of early Canada, was based on long-standing alliances between European fur traders and Aboriginal hunters and traders. At the personal level, these alliances resulted in people of mixed origins, who sometimes were assimilated into existing groups but in other cases coalesced into distinct nations and communities, as with the Métis of Red River.

Connolly v. Woolrich demonstrates that newcomers have sometimes found it convenient to forget their early alliances and pacts with Aboriginal peoples and to construct communities that excluded them and suppressed any local roots. Despite these efforts, however, the courts have periodically upheld the original relationship between newcomers and Aboriginal peoples and enforced the rights it embraced. Among these was the right of Aboriginal peoples to conduct their affairs under their own laws, within a larger constitutional framework linking them with the Crown.

The decision in *Connolly v. Woolrich* stands in contrast, then, to the common impression that Aboriginal peoples do not have any general right to govern themselves. It is often thought that all governmental authority in Canada flows from the Crown to Parliament

and the provincial legislatures, as provided in the constitution acts—the basic enactments that form the core of our written constitution. According to this view, since the
constitution acts do not explicitly recognize the existence of Aboriginal governments, the
only governmental powers held by Aboriginal peoples are those delegated to them by
Parliament or the provincial legislatures ... .

This outlook assumes that all law is found in statutes or other written legal instruments. Under this view, if a right has not been enshrined in such a document, it is not a
legal right. At best, it is regarded as only a moral or political right, which does not have
legal status and so cannot be enforced in the ordinary courts. Since the constitution acts
do not explicitly acknowledge an Aboriginal right of self-government, such a right does
not exist as a matter of Canadian law.

However, this view overlooks important features of our legal system. The laws of Canada spring from a great variety of sources, both written and unwritten, statutory and
customary. It has long been recognized, for example, that the written constitution is
based on fundamental unwritten principles, which govern its status and interpretation.
In Quebec, the general laws governing the private affairs of citizens trace their origins in
large part to a body of French customary law, the *Coutume de Paris*, which was imported
to Canada in the 1600s and embodied in the *Civil Code of Lower Canada* in 1866. In the
other provinces, the foundation of the general private law system is English common law,
a body of unwritten law administered by the courts, with its roots in the Middle Ages.
English common law has never been reduced to statutory form, except in partial and
fragmentary ways. Over the years, it has become a supple legal instrument, capable of
being adapted by the courts to suit changing circumstances and social conditions.

Given the multiple sources of law and rights in Canada, it is no surprise that Canadian courts have recognized the existence of a special body of "Aboriginal rights." These
are not based on written instruments such as statutes, but on unwritten sources such as
long-standing custom and practice. ...

The doctrine of Aboriginal rights is not a modern innovation, invented by courts to
remedy injustices perpetrated in the past. ... [T]he doctrine was reflected in the numerous treaties of peace and friendship concluded in the seventeenth and eighteenth centuries between Aboriginal peoples and the French and British Crowns. Aboriginal rights
are also apparent in the *Royal Proclamation of* 1763 and other instruments of the same
period, and in the treaties signed in Ontario, the west, and the northwest during the late
nineteenth and early twentieth century. These rights are also considered in the many
statutes dealing with Aboriginal matters from earliest times and in a series of judicial decisions extending over nearly two centuries. As such, the doctrine of Aboriginal rights is
one of the most ancient and enduring doctrines of Canadian law.

The principles behind the decision in *Connolly v. Woolrich* form the core of the modern Canadian law of Aboriginal rights. This body of law provides the basic constitutional
context for relations between Aboriginal peoples and the Crown and oversees the interaction between general Canadian systems of law and government and Aboriginal laws,
government institutions and territories.

Justice Monk's views in *Connolly v. Woolrich* on the territorial and political rights of Aboriginal peoples initially received little judicial attention in Canada. Indeed, it was only in 1973,

with the decision of the Supreme Court of Canada in *Calder*, above, that Canadian law recognized Aboriginal title as a common law entitlement separate and distinct from the Royal Proclamation of 1763. With Judson and Hall JJ writing the principal judgments, the Court split evenly on the major issue of whether Nisga'a Aboriginal title to ancestral territory had been extinguished by general land enactments in British Columbia. The Court also split on the issue of whether the Royal Proclamation was applicable to indigenous territory in that province. Judson and Hall JJ were in agreement, however, that Aboriginal title existed in Canada (at least where it has not been extinguished by appropriate legislative action) independently of the Royal Proclamation of 1763. Judson J stated expressly that the Proclamation was not the "exclusive" source of Indian title (at 322-23 and 328 SCR, 152-53 and 156 DLR). Hall J said (at 390 SCR, 200 DLR) that "aboriginal Indian title does not depend on treaty, executive order or legislative enactment."

The following case, *Guerin v. The Queen*, builds on the Court's decision in *Calder* and provides an overview of legal developments on the subject. Although it is concerned specifically with the nature and scope of Aboriginal rights to reserve land, it also addresses broader issues relating to the common law of Aboriginal title.

Guerin v. The Queen
[1984] 2 SCR 335, 13 DLR (4th) 321

DICKSON J (Beetz, Chouinard, and Lamer JJ concurring): The question is whether the appellants, the chief and councillors of the Musqueam Indian Band, suing on their own behalf and on behalf of all other members of the band, are entitled to recover damages from the federal Crown in respect of the leasing to a golf club of land on the Musqueam Indian Reserve. Collier J, of the Trial Division of the Federal Court, declared that the Crown was in breach of trust [[1982] 2 FC 385, 10 ETR 61 and 127 DLR (3d) 170; [1982] 2 FC 445 (supplementary reasons)]. He assessed damages at $10,000,000. The Federal Court of Appeal allowed a Crown appeal, set aside the judgment of the Trial Division and dismissed the action [143 DLR (3d) 416, [1983] 2 FC 656].

General

... [R]eference should be made to several of the relevant sections of the *Indian Act*, RSC 1952, c. 149, as amended. Section 18(1) provides in part that reserves shall be held by Her Majesty for the use of the respective Indian bands for which they were set apart. Generally, lands in a reserve shall not be sold, alienated, leased or otherwise disposed of until they have been surrendered to Her Majesty by the band for whose use and benefit in common the reserve was set apart (s. 37). A surrender may be absolute or qualified, conditional or unconditional (s. 38(2)). To be valid, a surrender must be made to Her Majesty, assented to by a majority of the electors of the band, and accepted by the Governor in Council (s. 39(1)).

The gist of the present action is a claim that the federal Crown was in breach of its trust obligations in respect of the leasing of approximately 162 acres of reserve land to the Shaughnessy Heights Golf Club of Vancouver. The band alleged that a number of the terms and conditions of the lease were different from those disclosed to them before the surrender vote and that some of the lease terms were not disclosed to them at all. The band also claimed failure on the part of the federal Crown to exercise the requisite degree of care and management as a trustee. ...

[A review of the facts is omitted.]

Fiduciary Relationship

... In my view, the nature of Indian title and the framework of the statutory scheme established for disposing of Indian land places upon the Crown an equitable obligation, enforceable by the courts, to deal with the land for the benefit of the Indians. This obligation does not amount to a trust in the private law sense. It is rather a fiduciary duty. If, however, the Crown breaches this fiduciary duty it will be liable to the Indians in the same way and to the same extent as if such a trust were in effect.

The fiduciary relationship between the Crown and the Indians has its roots in the concept of aboriginal, native or Indian title. The fact that Indian bands have a certain interest in lands does not, however, in itself give rise to a fiduciary relationship between the Indians and the Crown. The conclusion that the Crown is a fiduciary depends upon the further proposition that the Indian interest in the land is inalienable except upon surrender to the Crown.

An Indian band is prohibited from directly transferring its interest to a third party. Any sale or lease of land can only be carried out after a surrender has taken place, with the Crown then acting on the band's behalf. The Crown ...first took this responsibility upon itself in the Royal Proclamation of 1763 (RSC 1970, App. II, No. 1). It is still recognized in the surrender provisions of the *Indian Act*. The surrender requirement, and the responsibility it entails, are the source of a distinct fiduciary obligation owed by the Crown to the Indians. In order to explore the character of this obligation, however, it is first necessary to consider the basis of aboriginal title and the nature of the interest in land which it represents.

(a) The existence of Indian title

In *Calder et al. v. A-G BC* (1973), 34 DLR (3d) 145, [1973] SCR 313, this court recognized aboriginal title as a legal right derived from the Indians' historic occupation and possession of their tribal lands. ...

In recognizing that the Proclamation is not the sole source of Indian title the *Calder* decision went beyond the judgment of the Privy Council in *St. Catherine's Milling & Lumber Co. v. The Queen* (1888), 14 App. Cas. 46. In that case Lord Watson acknowledged the existence of aboriginal title but said it had its origin in the Royal Proclamation. In this respect *Calder* is consistent with the position of Chief Justice Marshall in the leading American cases of *Johnson and Graham's Lessee v. M'Intosh* (1823), 8 Wheaton 543, 21 US 240, and *Worcester v. State of Georgia* (1832), 6 Peters 515, 31 US 530, cited by Judson and Hall JJ in their respective judgments.

In *Johnson v. M'Intosh* Marshall CJ, although he acknowledged the Royal Proclamation of 1763 as one basis for recognition of Indian title, was none the less of [the] opinion that the rights of Indians in the lands they traditionally occupied prior to European coloniz-ation both predated and survived the claims to sovereignty made by various European nations in the territories of the North American continent. The principle of discovery which justified these claims gave the ultimate title in the land in a particular area to the nation which had discovered and claimed it. In that respect at least the Indians' rights in the land were obviously diminished; but their rights of occupancy and possession re-mained unaffected. Marshall CJ explained this principle as follows, at pp. 573-74:

> The exclusion of all other Europeans, necessarily gave to the nation making the discovery the sole right of acquiring the soil from the natives, and establishing settlements upon it. ... It was a right which all asserted for themselves, and to the assertion of which, by others, all assented.
>
> These relations which were to exist between the discoverer and the natives, were to be regulated by themselves. The rights thus acquired being exclusive, no other power could in-terpose between them.
>
> In the establishment of these relations, the rights of the original inhabitants were, in no instance, entirely disregarded, but were necessarily, to a considerable extent, impaired. *They were admitted to be the rightful occupants of the soil, with a legal as well as just claim to retain possession of it*, and to use it according to their own discretion; but their rights to complete sovereignty, as independent nations, were necessarily diminished, and their power to dis-pose of the soil at their own will, to whomsoever they pleased, was denied by the original fundamental principle, that discovery gave exclusive title to those who made it. [Emphasis is mine.]

The principle that a change in sovereignty over a particular territory does not in gen-eral affect the presumptive title of the inhabitants was approved by the Privy Council in *Amodu Tijani v. Secretary, Southern Nigeria*, [1921] 2 AC 399. That principle supports the assumption implicit in *Calder* that Indian title is an independent legal right which, al-though recognized by the Royal Proclamation of 1763, none the less predates it. ...

It does not matter, in my opinion, that the present case is concerned with the interest of an Indian band in a reserve rather than with unrecognized aboriginal title in tradi-tional tribal lands. The Indian interest in the land is the same in both cases: see *Attorney-General for Quebec v. Attorney-General for Canada*, [1921] 1 AC 401, at pp. 410-11 (the *Star Chrome* case). It is worth noting, however, that the reserve in question here was cre-ated out of the ancient tribal territory of the Musqueam band by the unilateral action of the Colony of British Columbia, prior to Confederation.

(b) The Nature of Indian Title

In the *St. Catherine's Milling* case, *supra*, the Privy Council held that the Indians had a "personal and usufructuary right" [at 54] in the lands which they had traditionally occu-pied. Lord Watson said that "there has been all along vested in the Crown a substantial and paramount estate, underlying the Indian title, which became a plenum dominium whenever the title was surrendered or otherwise extinguished" (at p. 55). He reiterated this idea, stating that the Crown "has all along had a present proprietary estate in the land, upon which the Indian title was a mere burden" (at p. 58). This view of aboriginal title was affirmed by the Privy Council in the *Star Chrome* case. In *Amodu Tijani, supra,* Viscount Haldane, adverting to the *St. Catherine's Milling* and *Star Chrome* decisions, explained the concept of a usufructuary right as a "mere qualification of or burden on the radical or final title of the Sovereign" (p. 403). He described the title of the Sovereign as a pure legal estate, but one which could be qualified by a right of "beneficial user" that did not necessarily take the form of an estate in land. Indian title in Canada was said to be one illustration "of the necessity for getting rid of the assumption that the ownership of land naturally breaks itself up into estates, conceived as creatures of inherent legal principle" [at 403]. Chief Justice Marshall took a similar view in *Johnson v. M'Intosh, supra,* saying, "All our institutions recognize the absolute title of the Crown, subject only to the Indian right of occupancy" (p. 588).

It should be noted that the Privy Council's emphasis on the personal nature of aboriginal title stemmed in part from constitutional arrangements peculiar to Canada. The Indian territory at issue in *St. Catherine's Milling* was land which in 1867 had been vested in the Crown subject to the interest of the Indians. The Indians' interest was "an interest other than that of the Province," within the meaning of s. s. 109 of the *Constitution Act, 1867.* Section 109 provides:

> 109. All Lands, Mines, Minerals, and Royalties belonging to the several Provinces of Canada, Nova Scotia and New Brunswick at the Union, and all Sums then due or payable for such Lands, Mines, Minerals, or Royalties, shall belong to the several Provinces of Ontario, Quebec, Nova Scotia, and New Brunswick in which the same are situate or arise subject to any Trusts existing in respect thereof, and to any Interest other than that of the Province in the same.

When the land in question in *St. Catherine's Milling* was subsequently disencumbered of the native title upon its surrender to the federal government by the Indian occupants in 1873, the entire beneficial interest in the land was held to have passed, because of the personal and usufructuary nature of the Indians' right, to the Province of Ontario under s. 109 rather than to Canada. The same constitutional issue arose recently in this court in *Smith et al. v. The Queen* (1983), 147 DLR (3d) 237, [1983] 1 SCR 554, 47 NR 132 *sub nom. Government of Canada v. Smith,* in which the court held that the Indian right in a reserve, being personal, could not be transferred to a grantee, whether an individual or the Crown. Upon surrender the right disappeared "in the process of release."

No such constitutional problem arises in the present case, since in 1938 the title to all Indian reserves in British Columbia was transferred by the provincial government to the Crown in right of Canada.

· · ·

It appears to me that there is no real conflict between the cases which characterize Indian title as a beneficial interest of some sort, and those which characterize it a personal, usufructuary right. Any apparent inconsistency derives from the fact that in describing what constitutes a unique interest in land the courts have almost inevitably found themselves applying a somewhat inappropriate terminology drawn from general property law. There is a core of truth in the way that each of the two lines of authority has described native title, but an appearance of conflict has none the less arisen because in neither case is the categorization quite accurate.

Indians have a legal right to occupy and possess certain lands, the ultimate title to which is in the Crown. While their interest does not, strictly speaking, amount to beneficial ownership, neither is its nature completely exhausted by the concept of a personal right. It is true that the *sui generis* interest which the Indians have in the land is personal in the sense that it cannot be transferred to a grantee, but it is also true, as will presently appear, that the interest gives rise upon surrender to a distinctive fiduciary obligation on the part of the Crown to deal with the land for the benefit of the surrendering Indians. These two aspects of Indian title go together, since the Crown's original purpose in declaring the Indians' interest to be inalienable otherwise than to the Crown was to facilitate the Crown's ability to represent the Indians in dealings with third parties. The nature of the Indians' interest is therefore best characterized by its general inalienability, coupled with the fact that the Crown is under an obligation to deal with the land on the Indians' behalf when the interest is surrendered. Any description of Indian title which goes beyond these two features is both unnecessary and potentially misleading.

(c) The Crown's Fiduciary Obligation

The concept of fiduciary obligation originated long ago in the notion of breach of confidence, one of the original heads of jurisdiction in chancery. In the present appeal its relevance is based on the requirement of a "surrender" before Indian land can be alienated.

The Royal Proclamation of 1763 provided that no private person could purchase from the Indians any lands that the Proclamation had reserved to them, and provided further that all purchases had to be by and in the name of the Crown, in a public assembly of the Indians held by the governor or commander-in-chief of the colony in which the lands in question lay. As Lord Watson pointed out in *St. Catherine's Milling, supra*, at p. 54, this policy with respect to the sale or transfer of the Indians' interest in land has been continuously maintained by the British Crown, by the governments of the colonies when they became responsible for the administration of Indian affairs, and, after 1867, by the federal government of Canada. Successive federal statutes, predecessors to the present *Indian Act*, have all provided for the general inalienability of Indian reserve land except upon surrender to the Crown, the relevant provisions in the present Act being ss. 37-41.

The purpose of this surrender requirement is clearly to interpose the Crown between the Indians and prospective purchasers or lessees of their land, so as to prevent the Indians from being exploited. This is made clear in the Royal Proclamation itself, which prefaces the provision making the Crown an intermediary with a declaration that "great Frauds and Abuses have been committed in purchasing Lands of the Indians, to the great Prejudice of our Interest and to the great Dissatisfaction of the said Indians ... ." Through the confirmation in the *Indian Act* of the historic responsibility which the Crown has undertaken, to act on behalf of the Indians so as to protect their interests in transactions with third parties, Parliament has conferred upon the Crown a discretion to decide for itself where the Indians' best interests really lie. This is the effect of s. 18(1) of the Act.

This discretion on the part of the Crown, far from ousting, as the Crown contends, the jurisdiction of the courts to regulate the relationship between the Crown and the Indians, has the effect of transforming the Crown's obligation into a fiduciary one. Professor Ernest Weinrib maintains in his article "The Fiduciary Obligation" (1975), 25 *UTLJ* 1, at

p. 7, that "the hallmark of a fiduciary relation is that the relative legal positions are such that one party is at the mercy of the other's discretion." Earlier, at p. 4, he puts the point in the following way:

> [Where there is a fiduciary obligation] there is a relation in which the principal's interests can be affected by, and are therefore dependent on, the manner in which the fiduciary uses the discretion which has been delegated to him. The fiduciary obligation is the law's blunt tool for the control of this discretion.

I make no comment upon whether this description is broad enough to embrace all fiduciary obligations. I do agree, however, that where by statute, agreement, or perhaps by unilateral undertaking, one party has an obligation to act for the benefit of another, and that obligation carries with it a discretionary power, the party thus empowered becomes a fiduciary. Equity will then supervise the relationship by holding him to the fiduciary's strict standard of conduct.

· · ·

Section 18(1) of the *Indian Act* confers upon the Crown a broad discretion in dealing with surrendered land. In the present case, the document of surrender, set out in part earlier in these reasons, by which the Musqueam band surrendered the land to the Crown at issue, confirms this discretion in the clause conveying the land to the Crown "in trust to lease ... upon such terms as the Government of Canada may deem most conducive to our Welfare and that of our people." When, as here, an Indian band surrenders its interest to the Crown, a fiduciary obligation takes hold to regulate the manner in which the Crown exercises its discretion in dealing with the land on the Indians' behalf.

· · ·

The discretion which is the hallmark of any fiduciary relationship is capable of being considerably narrowed in a particular case. This is as true of the Crown's discretion *vis-à-vis* the Indians as it is of the discretion of trustees, agents, and other traditional categories of fiduciary. The *Indian Act* makes specific provision for such narrowing in ss. 18(1) and 38(2). A fiduciary obligation will not, of course, be eliminated by the imposition of conditions that have the effect of restricting the fiduciary's discretion. A failure to adhere to the imposed conditions will simply itself be a *prima facie* breach of the obligation. In the present case both the surrender and the Order in Council accepting the surrender referred to the Crown leasing the land on the band's behalf. Prior to the surrender the band had also been given to understand that a lease was to be entered into with the Shaughnessy Heights Golf Club upon certain terms, but this understanding was not incorporated into the surrender document itself. The effect of these so-called oral terms will be considered in the next section.

(d) Breach of the Fiduciary Obligation

The trial judge found that the Crown's agents promised the band to lease the land in question on certain specified terms and then, after surrender, obtained a lease on different terms. The lease obtained was much less valuable. As already mentioned, the surrender document did not make reference to the "oral" terms. I would not wish to say that those terms had none the less somehow been incorporated as conditions into the surrender. They were not formally assented to by a majority of the electors of the band, nor were they accepted by the Governor in Council, as required by s. 39(1)(b) and (c). I agree with Le Dain J that there is no merit in the appellants' submission that for purposes of s. 39 a surrender can be considered independently of its terms. This makes no more sense than would a claim that a contract can have an existence which in no way depends on the terms and conditions that comprise it.

Nonetheless, the Crown, in my view, was not empowered by the surrender document to ignore the oral terms which the band understood would be embodied in the lease. The oral representations form the backdrop against which the Crown's conduct in discharging its fiduciary obligation must be measured. They inform and confine the field of discretion within which the Crown was free to act. After the Crown's agents had induced the band to surrender its land on the understanding that the land would be leased on certain terms, it would be unconscionable to permit the Crown simply to ignore those terms. When the promised lease proved impossible to obtain, the Crown, instead of proceeding to lease the land on different, unfavourable terms, should have returned to the band to explain what had occurred and seek the band's counsel on how to proceed. The existence of such unconscionability is the key to a conclusion that the Crown breached its fiduciary duty. Equity will not countenance unconscionable behaviour in a fiduciary, whose duty is that of utmost loyalty to his principal.

While the existence of the fiduciary obligation which the Crown owes to the Indians is dependent on the nature of the surrender process, the standard of conduct which the obligation imports is both more general and more exacting than the terms of any particular surrender. In the present case the relevant aspect of the required standard of conduct is defined by a principle analogous to that which underlies the doctrine of promissory or equitable estoppel. The Crown cannot promise the band that it will obtain a lease of the latter's land on certain stated terms, thereby inducing the band to alter its legal position by surrendering the land, and then simply ignore that promise to the band's detriment: see, *e.g.*, *Central London Property Trust Ltd. v. High Trees House Ltd.*, [1947] 1 KB 130; *Robertson v. Minister of Pensions*, [1949] 1 KB 227 (CA).

In obtaining without consultation a much less valuable lease than that promised, the Crown breached the fiduciary obligation it owed the band. It must make good the loss suffered in consequence.

. . .

I would therefore allow the appeal, set aside the judgment in the Federal Court of Appeal and reinstate without variation the trial judge's award, with costs to the present appellants in all courts.

[Estey J, concurring in the result, held that there existed an agency relationship between the band and the Crown, and that the Crown was in breach of agency obligations. Wilson J also wrote a concurring judgment (Ritchie and McIntyre JJ concurring), in which she held the Crown in breach of trust.]

Appeal allowed with costs.

NOTES

1. In *Guerin*, Dickson CJ interpreted *Calder* as deriving common law Aboriginal title from Aboriginal peoples' historic occupation and possession of their ancestral lands. No mention is made of *Connolly v. Woolrich* or the possibility that Aboriginal legal systems might be the source of Aboriginal rights. As you read the cases in the remainder of this chapter, look for instances in which the judiciary treats Aboriginal laws and Aboriginal legal orders to be potential legal sources of Aboriginal rights.

2. The existence of a fiduciary duty arising from the Crown's acceptance of surrenders of Aboriginal lands is potentially positive for First Nations. By holding the Crown to an obligation of good faith in dealing with Indian lands, the duty creates important incentives for the Crown to consider Aboriginal representations and perspectives in its transactions with these lands. However, might the existence of the Crown's fiduciary duty to Aboriginal peoples also run the risk of replicating or creating dependency between the First Nations and the Crown? Could the constant oversight of First Nations' activities by the Crown, to ensure that the Crown's fiduciary duty is being met, create problems for First Nations who want to be more independent and self-sufficient?

III. THE CONSTITUTIONAL ENTRENCHMENT OF ABORIGINAL RIGHTS

Despite the development of a common law framework for Aboriginal rights in Canada, the centuries-long legal history of Aboriginal–Crown relations did not resolve many issues of basic justice and fairness between the parties. In an attempt to remedy this failure, Aboriginal rights were entrenched in Canada's newly patriated *Constitution Act* in 1982, as Part II of that instrument, outside of its *Charter of Rights and Freedoms*. Section 35(1) protects these rights by stating that "the existing aboriginal and treaty rights of the aboriginal peoples of Canada are hereby recognized and affirmed." The problem with this language was that no one was quite sure what Aboriginal rights were existing as of that date, and therefore what, if anything, was being protected. After the failure to define these rights through four high profile First Ministers conferences mandated by s. 37 of the *Constitution Act, 1982* and a nationally negotiated Charlottetown Accord, the task of defining Aboriginal rights passed to the country's highest court.

The following cases analyze the nature and scope of Aboriginal rights recognized and affirmed by s. 35(1).

R v. Sparrow
[1990] 1 SCR 1075, 70 DLR (4th) 385

DICKSON CJC and LA FOREST J (Lamer, Wilson, L'Heureux-Dubé, and Sopinka JJ concurring): This appeal requires this Court to explore for the first time the scope of s. 35(1) of the *Constitution Act, 1982*, and to indicate its strength as a promise to the aboriginal peoples of Canada. Section 35(1) is found in Part II of that Act, entitled "Rights of the Aboriginal Peoples of Canada," and provides as follows:

35.(1) The existing aboriginal and treaty rights of the aboriginal peoples of Canada are hereby recognized and affirmed.

The context of this appeal is the alleged violation of the terms of the Musqueam food fishing licence which are dictated by the *Fisheries Act*, RSC 1970, c. F-14, and the regulations under that Act. The issue is whether Parliament's power to regulate fishing is now limited by s. 35(1) of the *Constitution Act, 1982*, and, more specifically, whether the net length restriction in the licence is inconsistent with that provision.

Facts

The appellant, a member of the Musqueam Indian Band, was charged under s. 61(1) of the *Fisheries Act* of the offence of fishing with a drift net longer than that permitted by the terms of the Band's Indian food fishing licence. The fishing which gave rise to the charge took place on May 25, 1984 in Canoe Passage which is part of the area subject to the Band's licence. The licence, which had been issued for a one-year period beginning March 31, 1984, set out a number of restrictions including one that drift nets were to be limited to 25 fathoms in length. The appellant was caught with a net which was 45 fathoms in length. He has throughout admitted the facts alleged to constitute the offence, but has defended the charge on the basis that he was exercising an existing aboriginal right to fish and that the net length restriction contained in the Band's licence is inconsistent with s. 35(1) of the *Constitution Act, 1982* and therefore invalid.

... On November 24, 1987, the following constitutional question was stated:

Is the net length restriction contained in the Musqueam Indian Band Indian Food Fishing Licence dated March 30, 1984, issued pursuant to the *British Columbia Fishery (General) Regulations* and the *Fisheries Act*, RSC 1970, c. F-14, inconsistent with s. 35(1) of the *Constitution Act, 1982*?

[An account of the arguments of the parties and the regulatory regime is omitted.]

Analysis

We will address first the meaning of "existing" aboriginal rights and the content and scope of the Musqueam right to fish. We will then turn to the meaning of "recognized and affirmed," and the impact of s. 35(1) on the regulatory power of Parliament.

"Existing"

The word "existing" makes it clear that the rights to which s. 35(1) applies are those that were in existence when the *Constitution Act, 1982* came into effect. This means that extinguished rights are not revived by the *Constitution Act, 1982*. ...

Further, an existing aboriginal right cannot be read so as to incorporate the specific manner in which it was regulated before 1982. The notion of freezing existing rights would incorporate into the Constitution a crazy patchwork of regulations. Blair JA in *Agawa* [*R v. Agawa* (1988), 53 DLR (4th) 101, 43 CCC (3d) 266 (Ont. CA)] had this to say about the matter, at p. 214:

Some academic commentators have raised a further problem which cannot be ignored. The *Ontario Fishery Regulations* contained detailed rules which vary for different regions in the province. Among other things, the *Regulations* specify seasons and methods of fishing, species of fish which can be caught and catch limits. Similar detailed provisions apply under the comparable fisheries *Regulations* in force in other provinces. These detailed provisions might be constitutionalized if it were decided that the existing treaty rights referred to in s. 35(1) were those remaining after regulation at the time of the proclamation of the *Constitution Act, 1982*.

As noted by Blair JA, academic commentary lends support to the conclusion that "existing" means "unextinguished" rather than exercisable at a certain time in history. Professor Slattery, "Understanding Aboriginal Rights" (1987), 66 *Can. Bar Rev.* 727, at pp. 781-82, has observed the following about reading regulations into the rights:

> This approach reads into the Constitution the myriad of regulations affecting the exercise of aboriginal rights, regulations that differed considerably from place to place across the country. It does not permit differentiation between regulations of long-term significance and those enacted to deal with temporary conditions, or between reasonable and unreasonable restrictions. Moreover, it might require that a constitutional amendment be enacted to implement regulations more stringent than those in existence on 17 April 1982. This solution seems unsatisfactory.

... The unsuitability of the approach can also be seen from another perspective. Ninety-one other tribes of Indians, comprising over 20,000 people (compared with 540 Musqueam on the reserve and 100 others off the reserve) obtain their food fish from the Fraser River. Some or all of these bands may have an aboriginal right to fish there. A constitutional patchwork quilt would be created if the constitutional right of these bands were to be determined by the specific regime available to each of those bands in 1982.

Far from being defined according to the regulatory scheme in place in 1982, the phrase "existing aboriginal rights" must be interpreted flexibly so as to permit their evolution over time. To use Professor Slattery's expression, in "Understanding Aboriginal Rights," *supra*, at p. 782, the word "existing" suggests that those rights are "affirmed in a contemporary form rather than in their primeval simplicity and vigour." Clearly, then, an approach to the constitutional guarantee embodied in s. 35(1) which would incorporate "frozen rights" must be rejected.

The Aboriginal Right

We turn now to the aboriginal right at stake in this appeal. The Musqueam Indian Reserve is located on the north shore of the Fraser River close to the mouth of that river and within the limits of the City of Vancouver. There has been a Musqueam village there for hundreds of years. This appeal does not directly concern the reserve or the adjacent waters, but arises out of the Band's right to fish in another area of the Fraser River estuary known as Canoe Passage in the South Arm of the river, some 16 kilometres (about 10 miles) from the reserve. The reserve and those waters are separated by the Vancouver International Airport and the Municipality of Richmond.

The evidence reveals that the Musqueam have lived in the area as an organized society long before the coming of European settlers, and that the taking of salmon was an integral part of their lives and remains so to this day. Much of the evidence of an aboriginal right to fish was given by Dr. Suttles, an anthropologist, supported by that of Mr. Grant, the Band administrator. The Court of Appeal thus summarized Dr. Suttles' evidence, at pp. 307-8:

> Dr. Suttles was qualified as having particular qualifications in respect of the ethnography of the Coast Salish Indian people of which the Musqueams were one of several tribes. He thought that the Musqueam had lived in their historic territory, which includes the Fraser River estuary, for at least 1,500 years. That historic territory extended from the north shore of Burrard Inlet to the south shore of the main channel of the Fraser River, including the waters of the three channels by which that river reaches the ocean. As part of the Salish people, the Musqueam were part of a regional social network covering a much larger area but, as a tribe, were themselves an organized social group with their own name, territory and resources. Between the tribes there was a flow of people, wealth and food. No tribe was wholly self-sufficient or occupied its territory to the complete exclusion of others.
>
> Dr. Suttles described the special position occupied by the salmon fishery in that society. The salmon was not only an important source of food but played an important part in the system of beliefs of the Salish people, and in their ceremonies. The salmon were held to be a race of beings that had, in "myth times," established a bond with human beings requiring the salmon to come each year to give their bodies to the humans who, in turn, treated them with respect shown by performance of the proper ritual. Toward the salmon, as toward other creatures, there was an attitude of caution and respect which resulted in effective conservation of the various species.

While the trial for a violation of a penal prohibition may not be the most appropriate setting in which to determine the existence of an aboriginal right, and the evidence was not extensive, the correctness of the finding of fact of the trial judge "that Mr. Sparrow was fishing in ancient tribal territory where his ancestors had fished from time immemorial in that part of the mouth of the Fraser River for salmon" is supported by the evidence and was not contested. The existence of the right, the Court of Appeal tells us, was "not the subject of serious dispute." It is not surprising, then, that, taken with other circumstances, that court should find, at p. 320, that "the judgment appealed from was wrong in … failing to hold that Sparrow at the relevant time was exercising an existing aboriginal right."

In this Court, however, the respondent contested the Court of Appeal's finding, contending that the evidence was insufficient to discharge the appellant's burden of proof upon the issue. It is true that for the period from 1867 to 1961 the evidence is scanty. But the evidence was not disputed or contradicted in the courts below and there is evidence of sufficient continuity of the right to support the Court of Appeal's finding, and we would not disturb it.

What the Crown really insisted on, both in this Court and the courts below, was that the Musqueam Band's aboriginal right to fish had been extinguished by regulations under the *Fisheries Act*.

The history of the regulation of fisheries in British Columbia is set out in *Jack v. The Queen*, [1980] 1 SCR 294, especially at pp. 308 *et seq.*, and we need only summarize it here. ...

[An account of this history is omitted.]

It is this progressive restriction and detailed regulation of the fisheries which, respondent's counsel maintained, have had the effect of extinguishing any aboriginal right to fish. The extinguishment need not be express, he argued, but may take place where the sovereign authority is exercised in a manner "necessarily inconsistent" with the continued enjoyment of aboriginal rights ... . The consent to its extinguishment before the *Constitution Act, 1982* was not required; the intent of the Sovereign could be effected not only by statute but by valid regulations. Here, in his view, the regulations had entirely displaced any aboriginal right. There is, he submitted, a fundamental inconsistency between the communal right to fish embodied in the aboriginal right, and fishing under a special licence or permit issued to individual Indians (as was the case until 1977) in the discretion of the Minister and subject to terms and conditions which, if breached, may result in cancellation of the licence. The *Fisheries Act* and its regulations were, he argued, intended to constitute a complete code inconsistent with the continued existence of an aboriginal right.

At bottom, the respondent's argument confuses regulation with extinguishment. That the right is controlled in great detail by the regulations does not mean that the right is thereby extinguished.

[A discussion of authority is omitted.]

... The test of extinguishment to be adopted, in our opinion, is that the Sovereign's intention must be clear and plain if it is to extinguish an aboriginal right.

There is nothing in the *Fisheries Act* or its detailed regulations that demonstrates a clear and plain intention to extinguish the Indian aboriginal right to fish. The fact that express provision permitting the Indians to fish for food may have applied to all Indians and that for an extended period permits were discretionary and issued on an individual rather than a communal basis in no way shows a clear intention to extinguish. These permits were simply a manner of controlling the fisheries, not defining underlying rights.

We would conclude then that the Crown has failed to discharge its burden of proving extinguishment. In our opinion, the Court of Appeal made no mistake in holding that the Indians have an existing aboriginal right to fish in the area where Mr. Sparrow was fishing at the time of the charge. This approach is consistent with ensuring that an aboriginal right should not be defined by incorporating the ways in which it has been regulated in the past.

The scope of the existing Musqueam right to fish must now be delineated. The anthropological evidence relied on to establish the existence of the right suggests that, for the Musqueam, the salmon fishery has always constituted an integral part of their distinctive culture. Its significant role involved not only consumption for subsistence purposes, but also consumption of salmon on ceremonial and social occasions. The Musqueam have always fished for reasons connected to their cultural and physical survival. As we stated earlier, the right to do so may be exercised in a contemporary manner.

The British Columbia Court of Appeal in this case held that the aboriginal right was to fish for food purposes, but that purpose was not to be confined to mere subsistence. Rather, the right was found to extend to fish consumed for social and ceremonial activities. The Court of Appeal thereby defined the right as protecting the same interest as is reflected in the government's food fish policy.

... [I]t was contended before this Court that the aboriginal right extends to commercial fishing. While no commercial fishery existed prior to the arrival of European settlers, it is contended that the Musqueam practice of bartering in early society may be revived as a modern right to fish for commercial purposes. The presence of numerous interveners representing commercial fishing interests, and the suggestion on the facts that the net length restriction is at least in part related to the probable commercial use of fish caught under the Musqueam food fishing licence, indicate the possibility of conflict between aboriginal fishing and the competitive commercial fishery with respect to economically valuable fish such as salmon. We recognize the existence of this conflict and the probability of its intensification as fish availability drops, demand rises and tensions increase.

Government regulations governing the exercise of the Musqueam right to fish, as described above, have only recognized the right to fish for food for over a hundred years. This may have reflected the existing position. However, historical policy on the part of the Crown is not only incapable of extinguishing the existing aboriginal right without clear intention, but is also incapable of, in itself, delineating that right. The nature of government regulations cannot be determinative of the content and scope of an existing aboriginal right. Government policy can however regulate the exercise of that right, but such regulation must be in keeping with s. 35(1).

In the courts below, the case at bar was not presented on the footing of an aboriginal right to fish for commercial or livelihood purposes. Rather, the focus was and continues to be on the validity of a net length restriction affecting the appellant's food fishing licence. We therefore adopt the Court of Appeal's characterization of the right for the purpose of this appeal, and confine our reasons to the meaning of the constitutional recognition and affirmation of the existing aboriginal right to fish for food and social and ceremonial purposes.

"Recognized and Affirmed"

We now turn to the impact of s. 35(1) of the *Constitution Act, 1982* on the regulatory power of Parliament and on the outcome of this appeal specifically.

Counsel for the appellant argued that the effect of s. 35(1) is to deny Parliament's power to restrictively regulate aboriginal fishing rights under s. 91(24) ("Indians and Lands Reserved for the Indians"), and s. 91(12) ("Sea Coast and Inland Fisheries"). The essence of this submission, supported by the intervener, the National Indian Brotherhood/Assembly of First Nations, is that the right to regulate is part of the right to use the resource in the Band's discretion. Section 35(1) is not subject to s. 1 of the Charter nor to legislative override under s. 33. The appellant submitted that, if the regulatory power continued, the limits on its extent are set by the word "inconsistent" in s. 52(1) of the

Constitution Act, 1982 and the protective and remedial purposes of s. 35(1). This means that aboriginal title entails a right to fish by any non-dangerous method chosen by the aboriginals engaged in fishing. Any continuing governmental power of regulation would have to be exceptional and strictly limited to regulation that is clearly not inconsistent with the protective and remedial purposes of s. 35(1). Thus, counsel for the appellant speculated, "in certain circumstances, necessary and reasonable conservation measures *might* qualify" (emphasis added)—where for example such measures were necessary to prevent serious impairment of the aboriginal rights of present and future generations, where conservation could only be achieved by restricting the right and not by restricting fishing by other users, and where the aboriginal group concerned was unwilling to implement necessary conservation measures. The onus of proving a justification for restrictive regulations would lie with the government by analogy with s. 1 of the Charter.

In response to these submissions and in finding the appropriate interpretive framework for s. 35(1), we start by looking at the background of s. 35(1).

It is worth recalling that while British policy towards the native population was based on respect for their right to occupy their traditional lands, a proposition to which the *Royal Proclamation of 1763* bears witness, there was from the outset never any doubt that sovereignty and legislative power, and indeed the underlying title, to such lands vested in the Crown ... . And there can be no doubt that over the years the rights of the Indians were often honoured in the breach. ... As MacDonald J stated in *Pasco v. Canadian National Railway Co.*, [1986] 1 CNLR 35 (BC SC), at p. 37: "We cannot recount with much pride the treatment accorded to the native people of this country."

For many years, the rights of the Indians to their aboriginal lands—certainly as legal rights—were virtually ignored. The leading cases defining Indian rights in the early part of the century were directed at claims supported by the *Royal Proclamation* or other legal instruments, and even these cases were essentially concerned with settling legislative jurisdiction or the rights of commercial enterprises. For fifty years after the publication of Clement's *The Law of the Canadian Constitution* (3rd ed. 1916), there was a virtual absence of discussion of any kind of Indian rights to land even in academic literature. By the late 1960s, aboriginal claims were not even recognized by the federal government as having any legal status. Thus the Statement of the Government of Canada on Indian Policy (1969), although well meaning, contained the assertion (at p. 11) that "aboriginal claims to land ... are so general and undefined that it is not realistic to think of them as specific claims capable of remedy except through a policy and program that will end injustice to the Indians as members of the Canadian community." In the same general period, the James Bay development by Quebec Hydro was originally initiated without regard to the rights of the Indians who lived there, even though these were expressly protected by a constitutional instrument; see *The Quebec Boundaries Extension Act*, 1912, SC 1912, c. 45. It took a number of judicial decisions and notably the *Calder* case in this Court [*Calder v. AG BC*, [1973] SCR 313, 34 DLR (3d) 145] to prompt a reassessment of the position being taken by government.

In the light of its reassessment of Indian claims following *Calder*, the federal Government on August 8, 1973 issued "a statement of policy" regarding Indian lands. By it, it sought to "signify the Government's *recognition and acceptance* of its continuing responsibility under the *British North America Act* for Indians and lands reserved for Indians," which it regarded "as an historic evolution dating back to the *Royal Proclamation of 1763*, which, whatever differences there may be about its judicial interpretation, stands as a basic declaration of the Indian people's interests in land in this country." (Emphasis added.) See Statement made by the Honourable Jean Chrétien, Minister of Indian Affairs and Northern Development on Claims of Indian and Inuit People, August 8, 1973. The remarks about these lands were intended "as an expression of acknowledged responsibility." But the statement went on to express, for the first time, the government's willingness to negotiate regarding claims of aboriginal title, specifically in British Columbia, Northern Quebec, and the Territories, and this without regard to formal supporting documents. "The Government," it stated, "is now ready to negotiate with authorized representatives of these native peoples on the basis that where their traditional interest in the lands concerned can be established, an agreed form of compensation or benefit will be provided to native peoples in return for their interest." ...

It is clear, then, that s. 35(1) of the *Constitution Act, 1982*, represents the culmination of a long and difficult struggle in both the political forum and the courts for the constitutional recognition of aboriginal rights. The strong representations of native associations and other groups concerned with the welfare of Canada's aboriginal peoples made the adoption of s. 35(1) possible and it is important to note that the provision applies to the Indians, the Inuit and the Métis. Section 35(1), at the least, provides a solid constitutional base upon which subsequent negotiations can take place. It also affords aboriginal peoples constitutional protection against provincial legislative power. We are, of course, aware that this would, in any event, flow from the *Guerin* case [*Guerin v. The Queen*, [1984] 2 SCR 335, 13 DLR (4th) 321], but for a proper understanding of the situation, it is essential to remember that the *Guerin* case was decided after the commencement of the *Constitution Act, 1982*. ...

In our opinion, the significance of s. 35(1) extends beyond these fundamental effects. Professor Lyon in "An Essay on Constitutional Interpretation" (1988), 26 *Osgoode Hall LJ* 95, says the following about s. 35(1), at p. 100:

> ... the context of 1982 is surely enough to tell us that this is not just a codification of the case law on aboriginal rights that had accumulated by 1982. Section 35 calls for a just settlement for aboriginal peoples. It renounces the old rules of the game under which the Crown established courts of law and denied those courts the authority to question sovereign claims made by the Crown.

The approach to be taken with respect to interpreting the meaning of s. 35(1) is derived from general principles of constitutional interpretation, principles relating to aboriginal rights, and the purposes behind the constitutional provision itself. Here, we will sketch the framework for an interpretation of "recognized and affirmed" that, in our opinion, gives appropriate weight to the constitutional nature of these words. ...

The nature of s. 35(1) itself suggests that it be construed in a purposive way. When the purposes of the affirmation of aboriginal rights are considered, it is clear that a generous, liberal interpretation of the words in the constitutional provision is demanded. ...

In *Nowegijick v. The Queen*, [1983] 1 SCR 29, at p. 36 [144 DLR (3d) 193], the following principle that should govern the interpretation of Indian treaties and statutes was set out:

... [T]reaties and statutes relating to Indians should be liberally construed and doubtful expressions resolved in favour of the Indians.

In *R v. Agawa, supra,* Blair JA stated that the above principle should apply to the interpretation of s. 35(1). He added the following principle to be equally applied, at pp. 215-16:

> The second principle was enunciated by the late Associate Chief Justice MacKinnon in *R v. Taylor and Williams* (1981), 34 OR (2d) 360. He emphasized the importance of Indian history and traditions as well as the perceived effect of a treaty at the time of its execution. He also cautioned against determining Indian rights "in a vacuum." The honour of the Crown is involved in the interpretation of Indian treaties and, as a consequence, fairness to the Indians is a governing consideration. ...

... In our opinion, *Guerin,* together with *R v. Taylor and Williams* (1981), 34 OR (2d) 360 (Ont. CA), ground a general guiding principle for s. 35(1). That is, the Government has the responsibility to act in a fiduciary capacity with respect to aboriginal peoples. The relationship between the Government and aboriginals is trust-like, rather than adversarial, and contemporary recognition and affirmation of aboriginal rights must be defined in light of this historic relationship.

We agree with both the British Columbia Court of Appeal below and the Ontario Court of Appeal that the principles outlined above, derived from *Nowegijick, Taylor and Williams* and *Guerin,* should guide the interpretation of s. 35(1). As commentators have noted, s. 35(1) is a solemn commitment that must be given meaningful content. ...

In response to the appellant's submission that s. 35(1) rights are more securely protected than the rights guaranteed by the Charter, it is true that s. 35(1) is not subject to s. 1 of the Charter. In our opinion, this does not mean that any law or regulation affecting aboriginal rights will automatically be of no force or effect by the operation of s. 52 of the *Constitution Act, 1982.* Legislation that affects the exercise of aboriginal rights will nonetheless be valid, if it meets the test for justifying an interference with a right recognized and affirmed under s. 35(1).

There is no explicit language in the provision that authorizes this Court or any court to assess the legitimacy of any government legislation that restricts aboriginal rights. Yet, we find that the words "recognition and affirmation" incorporate the fiduciary relationship referred to earlier and so import some restraint on the exercise of sovereign power. Rights that are recognized and affirmed are not absolute. Federal legislative powers continue, including, of course, the right to legislate with respect to Indians pursuant to s. 91(24) of the *Constitution Act, 1867.* These powers must, however, now be read together with s. 35(1). In other words, federal power must be reconciled with federal duty and the best way to achieve that reconciliation is to demand the justification of any government regulation that infringes upon or denies aboriginal rights. Such scrutiny is in keeping with the liberal interpretive principle enunciated in *Nowegijick, supra,* and the concept of holding the Crown to a high standard of honourable dealing with respect to the aboriginal peoples of Canada as suggested by *Guerin v. The Queen, supra.*

We refer to Professor Slattery's "Understanding Aboriginal Rights," *supra,* with respect to the task of envisioning a s. 35(1) justificatory process. Professor Slattery, at p. 782, points out that a justificatory process is required as a compromise between a "patchwork" characterization of aboriginal rights whereby past regulations would be read into a definition of the rights, and a characterization that would guarantee aboriginal rights in their original form unrestricted by subsequent regulation. We agree with him that these two extreme positions must be rejected in favour of a justificatory scheme.

Section 35(1) suggests that while regulation affecting aboriginal rights is not precluded, such regulation must be enacted according to a valid objective. Our history has shown, unfortunately all too well, that Canada's aboriginal peoples are justified in worrying about government objectives that may be superficially neutral but which constitute *de facto* threats to the existence of aboriginal rights and interests. By giving aboriginal rights constitutional status and priority, Parliament and the provinces have sanctioned challenges to social and economic policy objectives embodied in legislation to the extent that aboriginal rights are affected. Implicit in this constitutional scheme is the obligation of the legislature to satisfy the test of justification. The way in which a legislative objective is to be attained must uphold the honour of the Crown and must be in keeping with the unique contemporary relationship, grounded in history and policy, between the Crown and Canada's aboriginal peoples. The extent of legislative or regulatory impact on an existing aboriginal right may be scrutinized so as to ensure recognition and affirmation.

The constitutional recognition afforded by the provision therefore gives a measure of control over government conduct and a strong check on legislative power. While it does not promise immunity from government regulation in a society that, in the twentieth century, is increasingly more complex, interdependent and sophisticated, and where exhaustible resources need protection and management, it does hold the Crown to a substantive promise. The government is required to bear the burden of justifying any legislation that has some negative effect on any aboriginal right protected under s. 35(1).

In these reasons, we will outline the appropriate analysis under s. 35(1) in the context of a regulation made pursuant to the *Fisheries Act*. We wish to emphasize the importance of context and a case-by-case approach to s. 35(1). Given the generality of the text of the constitutional provision, and especially in light of the complexities of aboriginal history, society and rights, the contours of a justificatory standard must be defined in the specific factual context of each case.

Section 35(1) and the Regulation of the Fisheries

Taking the above framework as guidance, we propose to set out the test for *prima facie* interference with an existing aboriginal right and for the justification of such an interference. ...

The first question to be asked is whether the legislation in question has the effect of interfering with an existing aboriginal right. If it does have such an effect, it represents a *prima facie* infringement of s. 35(1). Parliament is not expected to act in a manner contrary to the rights and interests of aboriginals, and, indeed, may be barred from doing so by the second stage of s. 35(1) analysis. The inquiry with respect to interference begins with a reference to the characteristics or incidents of the right at stake. Our earlier observations regarding the scope of the aboriginal right to fish are relevant here. Fishing rights are not traditional property rights. They are rights held by a collective and are in keeping with the culture and existence of that group. Courts must be careful, then, to avoid the application of traditional common law concepts of property as they develop their understanding of what the reasons for judgment in *Guerin, supra,* at p. 382, referred to as the "*sui generis*" nature of aboriginal rights. ...

While it is impossible to give an easy definition of fishing rights, it is possible, and, indeed, crucial, to be sensitive to the aboriginal perspective itself on the meaning of the rights at stake. For example, it would be artificial to try to create a hard distinction between the right to fish and the particular manner in which that right is exercised.

To determine whether the fishing rights have been interfered with such as to constitute a *prima facie* infringement of s. 35(1), certain questions must be asked. First, is the limitation unreasonable? Second, does the regulation impose undue hardship? Third, does the regulation deny to the holders of the right their preferred means of exercising that right? The onus of proving a *prima facie* infringement lies on the individual or group challenging the legislation. In relation to the facts of this appeal, the regulation would be found to be a *prima facie* interference if it were found to be an adverse restriction on the Musqueam exercise of their right to fish for food. We wish to note here that the issue does not merely require looking at whether the fish catch has been reduced below that needed for the reasonable food and ceremonial needs of the Musqueam Indians. Rather the test involves asking whether either the purpose or the effect of the restriction on net length unnecessarily infringes the interests protected by the fishing right. If, for example, the Musqueam were forced to spend undue time and money per fish caught or if the net length reduction resulted in a hardship to the Musqueam in catching fish, then the first branch of the s. 35(1) analysis would be met.

If a *prima facie* interference is found, the analysis moves to the issue of justification. This is the test that addresses the question of what constitutes legitimate regulation of a constitutional aboriginal right. The justification analysis would proceed as follows. First, is there a valid legislative objective? Here the court would inquire into whether the objective of Parliament in authorizing the department to enact regulations regarding fisheries is valid. The objective of the department in setting out the particular regulations would also be scrutinized. An objective aimed at preserving s. 35(1) rights by conserving and managing a natural resource, for example, would be valid. Also valid would be objectives purporting to prevent the exercise of s. 35(1) rights that would cause harm to the general populace or to aboriginal peoples themselves, or other objectives found to be compelling and substantial.

The Court of Appeal below held, at p. 331, that regulations could be valid if reasonably justified as "necessary for the proper management and conservation of the resource *or in the public interest.*" (Emphasis added.) We find the "public interest" justification to be so vague as to provide no meaningful guidance and so broad as to be unworkable as a test for the justification of a limitation on constitutional rights.

The justification of conservation and resource management, on the other hand, is surely uncontroversial ... . Further, the conservation and management of our resources is consistent with aboriginal beliefs and practices, and, indeed, with the enhancement of aboriginal rights.

If a valid legislative objective is found, the analysis proceeds to the second part of the justification issue. Here, we refer back to the guiding interpretive principle derived from

Taylor and Williams and *Guerin, supra.* That is, the honour of the Crown is at stake in dealings with aboriginal peoples. The special trust relationship and the responsibility of the government vis-à-vis aboriginals must be the first consideration in determining whether the legislation or action in question can be justified.

The problem that arises in assessing the legislation in light of its objective and the responsibility of the Crown is that the pursuit of conservation in a heavily used modern fishery inevitably blurs with the efficient allocation and management of this scarce and valued resource. The nature of the constitutional protection afforded by s. 35(1) in this context demands that there be a link between the question of justification and the allocation of priorities in the fishery. The constitutional recognition and affirmation of aboriginal rights may give rise to conflict with the interests of others given the limited nature of the resource. There is a clear need for guidelines that will resolve the allocational problems that arise regarding the fisheries. We refer to the reasons of Dickson J in *Jack v. The Queen*, [[1980], 1 SCR 294, 100 DLR (3d) 193], for such guidelines.

In *Jack*, the appellants' defence to a charge of fishing for salmon in certain rivers during a prohibited period was based on the alleged constitutional incapacity of Parliament to legislate such as to deny the Indians their right to fish for food. They argued that art. 13 of the British Columbia *Terms of Union* imposed a constitutional limitation on the federal power to regulate. While we recognize that the finding that such a limitation had been imposed was not adopted by the majority of this Court, we point out that this case concerns a different constitutional promise that asks this Court to give a meaningful interpretation to recognition and affirmation. That task requires equally meaningful guidelines responsive to the constitutional priority accorded aboriginal rights. We therefore repeat the following passage from *Jack*, at p. 313:

> Conservation is a valid legislative concern. The appellants concede as much. Their concern is in the allocation of the resource after reasonable and necessary conservation measures have been recognized and given effect to. They do not claim the right to pursue the last living salmon until it is caught. Their position, as I understand it, is one which would give effect to an order of priorities of this nature: (i) conservation; (ii) Indian fishing; (iii) non-Indian commercial fishing; or (iv) non-Indian sports fishing; the burden of conservation measures should not fall primarily upon the Indian fishery.
>
> I agree with the general tenor of this argument. ... With respect to whatever salmon are to be caught, then priority ought to be given to the Indian fishermen, subject to the practical difficulties occasioned by international waters and the movement of the fish themselves. But any limitation upon Indian fishing that is established for a valid conservation purpose overrides the protection afforded the Indian fishery by art. 13, just as such conservation measures override other taking of fish.

The constitutional nature of the Musqueam food fishing rights means that any allocation of priorities after valid conservation measures have been implemented must give top priority to Indian food fishing. If the objective pertained to conservation, the conservation plan would be scrutinized to assess priorities. While the detailed allocation of maritime resources is a task that must be left to those having expertise in the area, the Indians' food requirements must be met first when that allocation is established. The significance of giving the aboriginal right to fish for food top priority can be described as follows. If, in a given year, conservation needs required a reduction in the number of fish to be caught such that the number equalled the number required for food by the Indians, then all the fish available after conservation would go to the Indians according to the constitutional nature of their fishing right. If, more realistically, there were still fish after the Indian food requirements were met, then the brunt of conservation measures would be borne by the practices of sport fishing and commercial fishing. ...

To afford user groups such as sports fishermen (anglers) a priority to fish over the legitimate food needs of the appellants and their families is simply not appropriate action on the part of the Federal government. It is inconsistent with the fact that the appellants have for many years, and continue to possess an aboriginal right to fish for food. The appellants have, to employ the words of their counsel, a "right to share in the available resource." This constitutional entitlement is second only to conservation measures that may be undertaken by federal legislation.

We acknowledge the fact that the justificatory standard to be met may place a heavy burden on the Crown. However, government policy with respect to the British Columbia fishery, regardless of s. 35(1), already dictates that, in allocating the right to take fish, Indian food fishing is to be given priority over the interests of other user groups. The constitutional entitlement embodied in s. 35(1) requires the Crown to ensure that its regulations are in keeping with that allocation of priority. The objective of this requirement is not to undermine Parliament's ability and responsibility with respect to creating and administering overall conservation and management plans regarding the salmon fishery. The objective is rather to guarantee that those plans treat aboriginal peoples in a way ensuring that their rights are taken seriously.

Within the analysis of justification, there are further questions to be addressed, depending on the circumstances of the inquiry. These include the questions of whether there has been as little infringement as possible in order to effect the desired result; whether, in a situation of expropriation, fair compensation is available; and, whether the aboriginal group in question has been consulted with respect to the conservation measures being implemented. The aboriginal peoples, with their history of conservation-consciousness and interdependence with natural resources, would surely be expected, at the least, to be informed regarding the determination of an appropriate scheme for the regulation of the fisheries.

We would not wish to set out an exhaustive list of the factors to be considered in the assessment of justification. Suffice it to say that recognition and affirmation requires sensitivity to and respect for the rights of aboriginal peoples on behalf of the government, courts and indeed all Canadians.

Application to This Case: Is the Net Length Restriction Valid?

The Court of Appeal below found that there was not sufficient evidence in this case to proceed with an analysis of s. 35(1) with respect to the right to fish for food. In reviewing the competing expert evidence, and recognizing that fish stock management is an uncertain science, it decided that the issues at stake in this appeal were not well adapted to being resolved at the appellate court level. ...

According to the Court of Appeal, the findings of fact were insufficient to lead to an acquittal. There was no more evidence before this Court. We also would order a re-trial which would allow findings of fact according to the tests set out in these reasons.

The appellant would bear the burden of showing that the net length restriction constituted a *prima facie* infringement of the collective aboriginal right to fish for food. If an infringement were found, the onus would shift to the Crown which would have to demonstrate that the regulation is justifiable. To that end, the Crown would have to show that there is no underlying unconstitutional objective such as shifting more of the resource to a user group that ranks below the Musqueam. Further, it would have to show that the regulation sought to be imposed is required to accomplish the needed limitation. In trying to show that the restriction is necessary in the circumstances of the Fraser River fishery, the Crown could use facts pertaining to fishing by other Fraser River Indians.

In conclusion, we would dismiss the appeal and the cross-appeal and affirm the Court of Appeal's setting aside of the conviction. We would accordingly affirm the order for a new trial on the questions of infringement and whether any infringement is nonetheless consistent with s. 35(1), in accordance with the interpretation set out here. ...

Appeal and cross-appeal dismissed.

NOTES

1. The Court in *Sparrow* did not provide detailed reasons why fishing was an Aboriginal right. Nor did it address the difficult issue of the scope of protection accorded by s. 35(1) to Aboriginal commercial fishing practices, stating that "[i]n the courts below, the case at bar was not presented on the footing of an aboriginal right to fish for commercial or livelihood purposes." What are the implications of *Sparrow* for an Aboriginal community that seeks to rely on Aboriginal rights as a justification for commercial fishing contrary to federal or provincial law? What if the community in question could point to a historical Aboriginal practice of bartering fish for other commodities?

2. In *Sparrow*, the Court acknowledged that there was no explicit language in s. 35 to authorize an assessment of the legitimacy of any governmental action that might restrict Aboriginal rights. Nevertheless, the Court developed a test that allowed the government to justify the infringement of Aboriginal rights. How did the Court arrive at this proposition, and is its formulation persuasive?

R v. Van der Peet
[1996] 2 SCR 507, 137 DLR (4th) 289

LAMER CJC (La Forest, Sopinka, Gonthier, Cory, Iacobucci, and Major JJ concurring): ...

Statement of Facts

[5] The appellant Dorothy Van der Peet was charged under s. 61(1) of the *Fisheries Act*, RSC 1970, c. F-14, with the offence of selling fish caught under the authority of an

Indian food fish licence, contrary to s. 27(5) of the *British Columbia Fishery (General) Regulations*, SOR/84-248. At the time at which the appellant was charged s. 27(5) read:

> 27.(5) No person shall sell, barter or offer to sell or barter any fish caught under the authority of an Indian food fish licence.

[6] The charges arose out of the sale by the appellant of 10 salmon on September 11, 1987. ... The appellant, a member of the Sto:lo, has not contested these facts at any time, instead defending the charges against her on the basis that in selling the fish she was exercising an existing aboriginal right to sell fish. The appellant has based her defence on the position that the restrictions imposed by s. 27(5) of the Regulations infringe her existing aboriginal right to sell fish and are therefore invalid on the basis that they violate s. 35(1) of the *Constitution Act, 1982*.

· · ·

Analysis

Introduction

[15] I now turn to the question which ... lies at the heart of this appeal: How should the aboriginal rights recognized and affirmed by s. 35(1) of the *Constitution Act, 1982* be defined?

[16] In her factum the appellant argued that the majority of the Court of Appeal erred because it defined the rights in s. 35(1) in a fashion which "converted a Right into a Relic"; such an approach, the appellant argued, is inconsistent with the fact that the aboriginal rights recognized and affirmed by s. 35(1) are *rights* and not simply aboriginal practices. The appellant acknowledged that aboriginal rights are based in aboriginal societies and cultures, but argued that the majority of the Court of Appeal erred because it defined aboriginal rights through the identification of pre-contact activities instead of as pre-existing legal rights.

[17] While the appellant is correct to suggest that the mere existence of an activity in a particular aboriginal community prior to contact with Europeans is not, in itself, sufficient foundation for the definition of aboriginal rights, the position she would have this Court adopt takes s. 35(1) too far from that which the provision is intended to protect. Section 35(1), it is true, recognizes and affirms existing aboriginal *rights*, but it must not be forgotten that the rights it recognizes and affirms are *aboriginal*.

[18] In the liberal enlightenment view, reflected in the American *Bill of Rights* and, more indirectly, in the *Charter*, rights are held by all people in society because each person is entitled to dignity and respect. Rights are general and universal; they are the way in which the "inherent dignity" of each individual in society is respected: *R v. Oakes*, [1986] 1 SCR 103, at p. 136 [26 DLR (4th) 200]; *R v. Big M Drug Mart Ltd.*, [1985] 1 SCR 295, at p. 336 [18 DLR (4th) 321].

[19] *Aboriginal* rights cannot, however, be defined on the basis of the philosophical precepts of the liberal enlightenment. Although equal in importance and significance to the rights enshrined in the *Charter*, aboriginal rights must be viewed differently from *Charter* rights because they are rights held only by aboriginal members of Canadian society. They arise from the fact that aboriginal people are *aboriginal*. As academic commentators have noted, aboriginal rights "inhere in the very meaning of aboriginality." ...

[20] The task of this Court is to define aboriginal rights in a manner which recognizes that aboriginal rights are *rights* but which does so without losing sight of the fact that they are rights held by aboriginal people because they are *aboriginal*. The Court must neither lose sight of the generalized constitutional status of what s. 35(1) protects, nor can it ignore the necessary specificity which comes from granting special constitutional protection to one part of Canadian society. The Court must define the scope of s. 35(1) in a way which captures *both* the aboriginal and the rights in aboriginal rights.

[21] The way to accomplish this task is, as was noted at the outset, through a purposive approach to s. 35(1). It is through identifying the interests that s. 35(1) was intended to protect that the dual nature of aboriginal rights will be comprehended. ... A purposive approach to s. 35(1), because ensuring that the provision is not viewed as static and only relevant to current circumstances, will ensure that the recognition and affirmation it offers are consistent with the fact that what it is recognizing and affirming are "rights." Further, because it requires the court to analyze a given constitutional provision "in the light of the interests it was meant to protect"(*Big M Drug Mart Ltd.*, *supra*, at p. 344), a purposive approach to s. 35(1) will ensure that that which is found to fall within the provision is related to the provision's intended focus: aboriginal people and their rights in relation to Canadian society as a whole.

. . .

General Principles Applicable to Legal Disputes Between Aboriginal Peoples and the Crown

[23] Before turning to a purposive analysis of s. 35(1), however, it should be noted that such analysis must take place in light of the general principles which apply to the legal relationship between the Crown and aboriginal peoples. In *Sparrow* [*R v.*, [1990] 1 SCR 1075, 70 DLR (4th) 385], this Court held at p. 1106 that s. 35(1) should be given a generous and liberal interpretation in favour of aboriginal peoples. ...

[24] This interpretive principle, articulated first in the context of treaty rights, ... arises from the nature of the relationship between the Crown and aboriginal peoples. The Crown has a fiduciary obligation to aboriginal peoples with the result that in dealings between the government and aboriginals the honour of the Crown is at stake. Because of this fiduciary relationship, and its implication of the honour of the Crown, treaties, s. 35(1), and other statutory and constitutional provisions protecting the interests of aboriginal peoples, must be given a generous and liberal interpretation ... . This general principle must inform the Court's analysis of the purposes underlying s. 35(1), and of that provision's definition and scope.

[25] The fiduciary relationship of the Crown and aboriginal peoples also means that where there is any doubt or ambiguity with regards to what falls within the scope and definition of s. 35(1), such doubt or ambiguity must be resolved in favour of aboriginal peoples. In *R v. Sutherland*, [1980] 2 SCR 451, at p. 464 [113 DLR (3d) 374], Dickson J held that paragraph 13 of the Memorandum of Agreement between Manitoba and Canada, a constitutional document, "should be interpreted so as to resolve any doubts in favour of the Indians, the beneficiaries of the rights assured by the paragraph." This interpretive principle applies equally to s. 35(1) of the *Constitution Act, 1982* and should, again, inform the Court's purposive analysis of that provision.

Purposive Analysis of Section 35(1)

[26] When the court identifies a constitutional provision's purposes, or the interests the provision is intended to protect, what it is doing in essence is explaining the rationale of the provision; it is articulating the reasons underlying the protection that the provision gives. With regards to s. 35(1), then, what the court must do is explain the rationale and foundation of the recognition and affirmation of the special rights of aboriginal peoples; it must identify the basis for the special status that aboriginal peoples have within Canadian society as a whole.

. . .

[28] In identifying the basis for the recognition and affirmation of aboriginal rights it must be remembered that s. 35(1) did not create the legal doctrine of aboriginal rights; aboriginal rights existed and were recognized under the common law. ... The pre-existence of aboriginal rights is relevant to the analysis of s. 35(1) because it indicates that aboriginal rights have a stature and existence prior to the constitutionalization of those rights and sheds light on the reasons for protecting those rights.

. . .

[30] In my view, the doctrine of aboriginal rights exists, and is recognized and affirmed by s. 35(1), because of one simple fact: when Europeans arrived in North America, aboriginal peoples *were already here*, living in communities on the land, and participating in distinctive cultures, as they had done for centuries. It is this fact, and this fact above all others, which separates aboriginal peoples from all other minority groups in Canadian society and which mandates their special legal, and now constitutional, status.

[31] More specifically, what s. 35(1) does is provide the constitutional framework through which the fact that aboriginals lived on the land in distinctive societies, with their own practices, traditions and cultures, is acknowledged and reconciled with the sovereignty of the Crown. The substantive rights which fall within the provision must be defined in light of this purpose; the aboriginal rights recognized and affirmed by s. 35(1) must be directed towards the reconciliation of the pre-existence of aboriginal societies with the sovereignty of the Crown.

. . .

[35] The view of aboriginal rights as based in the prior occupation of North America by distinctive aboriginal societies, finds support in the early American decisions of Marshall CJ. Although the constitutional structure of the United States is different from that of Canada, and its aboriginal law has developed in unique directions, I agree with Professor Slattery [Brian Slattery, "Understanding Aboriginal Rights" (1987), 66 *Canadian Bar Review* 727, at 739] both when he describes the Marshall decisions as providing "structure and coherence to an untidy and diffuse body of customary law based on official practice" and when he asserts that these decisions are "as relevant to Canada as they are to the United States."

. . .

[38] The High Court of Australia has also considered the question of the basis and nature of aboriginal rights. Like that of the United States, Australia's aboriginal law differs in significant respects from that of Canada. ... Despite these relevant differences, the

analysis of the basis of aboriginal title in the landmark decision of the High Court in *Mabo v. Queensland [No. 2]* (1992), 175 CLR 1, is persuasive in the Canadian context.

[39] The *Mabo* judgment resolved the dispute between the Meriam people and the Crown regarding who had title to the Murray Islands. The islands had been annexed to Queensland in 1879 but were reserved for the native inhabitants (the Meriam) in 1882. The Crown argued that this annexation was sufficient to vest absolute ownership of the lands in the Crown. The High Court disagreed, holding that while the annexation did vest radical title in the Crown, it was insufficient to eliminate a claim for native title ... .

[40] Brennan J, writing for a majority of the Court ... consider[ed] the nature and basis of aboriginal title:

> *Native title has its origin in and is given its content by the traditional laws acknowledged by and the traditional customs observed by the indigenous inhabitants of a territory.* The nature and incidents of native title must be ascertained as a matter of fact by reference to those laws and customs. ...

This position is the same as that being adopted here. "Traditional laws" and "traditional customs" are those things passed down, and arising, from the pre-existing culture and customs of aboriginal peoples. ... To base aboriginal title in traditional laws and customs, as was done in *Mabo*, is, therefore, to base that title in the pre-existing societies of aboriginal peoples. This is the same basis as that asserted here for aboriginal rights.

[41] Academic commentators have also been consistent in identifying the basis and foundation of the s. 35(1) claims of aboriginal peoples in aboriginal occupation of North America prior to the arrival of Europeans. ...

[42] ... In his comment on *Delgamuukw v. British Columbia* ("British Imperial Constitutional Law and Aboriginal Rights: A Comment on *Delgamuukw v. British Columbia*" (1992), 17 *Queen's LJ* 350), Mark Walters suggests at pp. 412-13 that the essence of aboriginal rights is their bridging of aboriginal and non-aboriginal cultures:

> *The challenge of defining aboriginal rights stems from the fact that they are rights peculiar to the meeting of two vastly dissimilar legal cultures*; consequently there will always be a question about which legal culture is to provide the vantage point from which rights are to be defined. ... [A] morally and politically defensible conception of aboriginal rights will incorporate both legal perspectives. [Emphasis added.]

Similarly, Professor Slattery has suggested that the law of aboriginal rights is "neither English nor aboriginal in origin: it is a form of intersocietal law that evolved from long-standing practices linking the various communities" (Brian Slattery, "The Legal Basis of Aboriginal Title," in Frank Cassidy, ed., *Aboriginal Title in British Columbia: Delgamuukw v. The Queen* (Lantzville, BC: Oolichan Books, 1992), at pp. 120-21) ... .

· · ·

The Test for Identifying Aboriginal Rights in Section 35(1)

[44] In order to fulfil the purpose underlying s. 35(1)—*i.e.*, the protection and reconciliation of the interests which arise from the fact that prior to the arrival of Europeans

in North America aboriginal peoples lived on the land in distinctive societies, with their own practices, customs and traditions—the test for identifying the aboriginal rights recognized and affirmed by s. 35(1) must be directed at identifying the crucial elements of those pre-existing distinctive societies. It must, in other words, aim at identifying the practices, traditions and customs central to the aboriginal societies that existed in North America prior to contact with the Europeans.

[45] In *Sparrow, supra*, this Court did not have to address the scope of the aboriginal rights protected by s. 35(1); however, in their judgment at p. 1099 Dickson CJ and La Forest J identified the Musqueam right to fish for food in the fact that ... participation in the salmon fishery is an aboriginal right because it is an "integral part" of the "distinctive culture" of the Musqueam. This suggestion is consistent with the position just adopted; identifying those practices, customs and traditions that are integral to distinctive aboriginal cultures will serve to identify the crucial elements of the distinctive aboriginal societies that occupied North America prior to the arrival of Europeans.

[46] In light of the suggestion of *Sparrow, supra*, and the purposes underlying s. 35(1), the following test should be used to identify whether an applicant has established an aboriginal right protected by s. 35(1): in order to be an aboriginal right an activity must be an element of a practice, custom or tradition integral to the distinctive culture of the aboriginal group claiming the right.

· · ·

Factors to Be Considered in Application of the Integral to a Distinctive Culture Test

[48] The test just laid out—that aboriginal rights lie in the practices, customs and traditions integral to the distinctive cultures of aboriginal peoples—requires further elaboration with regards to the nature of the inquiry a court faced with an aboriginal rights claim must undertake. I will now undertake such an elaboration ... .

Courts Must Take into Account the Perspective of Aboriginal Peoples Themselves

[49] In assessing a claim for the existence of an aboriginal right, a court must take into account the perspective of the aboriginal people claiming the right. In *Sparrow, supra*, Dickson CJ and La Forest J held, at p. 1112, that it is "crucial to be sensitive to the aboriginal perspective itself on the meaning of the rights at stake." It must also be recognized, however, that that perspective must be framed in terms cognizable to the Canadian legal and constitutional structure. As has already been noted, one of the fundamental purposes of s. 35(1) is the reconciliation of the pre-existence of distinctive aboriginal societies with the assertion of Crown sovereignty. Courts adjudicating aboriginal rights claims must, therefore, be sensitive to the aboriginal perspective, but they must also be aware that aboriginal rights exist within the general legal system of Canada. To quote again Walters, at p. 413: "a morally and politically defensible conception of aboriginal rights will incorporate both [aboriginal and non-aboriginal] legal perspectives." The definition of an aboriginal right must, if it is truly to reconcile the prior occupation of Canadian territory by aboriginal peoples with the assertion of Crown sovereignty over that territory, take into account the aboriginal perspective, yet do so in terms which are cognizable to the non-aboriginal legal system.

[50] ... . [T]he only fair and just reconciliation is, as Walters suggests, one which takes into account the aboriginal perspective while at the same time taking into account the perspective of the common law. True reconciliation will, equally, place weight on each.

Courts Must Identify Precisely the Nature of the Claim Being Made in Determining Whether an Aboriginal Claimant Has Demonstrated the Existence of an Aboriginal Right

[51] Related to this is the fact that in assessing a claim to an aboriginal right a court must first identify the nature of the right being claimed; in order to determine whether a claim meets the test of being integral to the distinctive culture of the aboriginal group claiming the right, the court must first correctly determine what it is that is being claimed. ...

[52] ... The nature of an applicant's claim must be delineated in terms of the particular practice, custom or tradition under which it is claimed; the significance of the practice, custom or tradition to the aboriginal community is a factor to be considered in determining whether the practice, custom or tradition is integral to the distinctive culture, but the significance of a practice, custom or tradition cannot, itself, constitute an aboriginal right.

[53] To characterize an applicant's claim correctly, a court should consider such factors as the nature of the action which the applicant is claiming was done pursuant to an aboriginal right, the nature of the governmental regulation, statute or action being impugned, and the practice, custom or tradition being relied upon to establish the right. In this case, therefore, the Court will consider the actions which led to the appellant's being charged, the fishery regulation under which she was charged and the practices, customs and traditions she invokes in support of her claim.

[54] It should be acknowledged that a characterization of the nature of the appellant's claim from the actions which led to her being charged must be undertaken with some caution. In order to inform the court's analysis the activities must be considered at a general rather than at a specific level. Moreover, the court must bear in mind that the activities may be the exercise in a modern form of a practice, custom or tradition that existed prior to contact, and should vary its characterization of the claim accordingly.

In Order to Be Integral a Practice, Custom or Tradition Must Be of Central Significance to the Aboriginal Society in Question

[55] To satisfy the integral to a distinctive culture test the aboriginal claimant must do more than demonstrate that a practice, custom or tradition was an aspect of, or took place in, the aboriginal society of which he or she is a part. The claimant must demonstrate that the practice, custom or tradition was a central and significant part of the society's distinctive culture. He or she must demonstrate, in other words, that the practice, custom or tradition was one of the things which made the culture of the society distinctive—that it was one of the things that truly *made the society what it was.*

[56] This aspect of the integral to a distinctive culture test arises from fact that aboriginal rights have their basis in the prior occupation of Canada by distinctive aboriginal societies. To recognize and affirm the prior occupation of Canada by distinctive aboriginal

societies it is *to what makes those societies distinctive* that the court must look in identifying aboriginal rights. The court cannot look at those aspects of the aboriginal society that
are true of every human society (e.g., eating to survive), nor can it look at those aspects
of the aboriginal society that are only incidental or occasional to that society; the court
must look instead to the defining and central attributes of the aboriginal society in question. It is only by focusing on the aspects of the aboriginal society that make that society
distinctive that the definition of aboriginal rights will accomplish the purpose underlying s. 35(1). ...

[57] Moreover, the aboriginal rights protected by s. 35(1) have been said to have the
purpose of reconciling pre-existing aboriginal societies with the assertion of Crown sovereignty over Canada. To reconcile aboriginal societies with Crown sovereignty it is necessary to identify the distinctive features of those societies; it is precisely those distinctive
features which need to be acknowledged and reconciled with the sovereignty of the
Crown.

[58] As was noted earlier, Lambert JA erred when he used the significance of a practice, custom or tradition as a means of identifying what the practice, custom or tradition
is; however, he was correct to recognize that the significance of the practice, custom or
tradition is important. The significance of the practice, custom or tradition does not
serve to identify the nature of a claim of acting pursuant to an aboriginal right; however,
it is a key aspect of the court's inquiry into whether a practice, custom or tradition has
been shown to be an integral part of the distinctive culture of an aboriginal community.
The significance of the practice, custom or tradition will inform a court as to whether or
not that practice, custom or tradition can be said to be truly integral to the distinctive
culture in question.

[59] A practical way of thinking about this problem is to ask whether, without this
practice, custom or tradition, the culture in question would be fundamentally altered or
other than what it is. One must ask, to put the question affirmatively, whether or not a
practice, custom or tradition is a defining feature of the culture in question.

*The Practices, Customs and Traditions Which Constitute Aboriginal Rights Are Those
Which Have Continuity with the Practices, Customs and Traditions That Existed
Prior to Contact*

[60] The time period that a court should consider in identifying whether the right
claimed meets the standard of being integral to the aboriginal community claiming the
right is the period prior to contact between aboriginal and European societies. Because
it is the fact that distinctive aboriginal societies lived on the land prior to the arrival of
Europeans that underlies the aboriginal rights protected by s. 35(1), it is to that pre-
contact period that the courts must look in identifying aboriginal rights.

[61] The fact that the doctrine of aboriginal rights functions to reconcile the existence of pre-existing aboriginal societies with the sovereignty of the Crown does not alter
this position. Although it is the sovereignty of the Crown that the pre-existing aboriginal
societies are being reconciled with, it is to those pre-existing societies that the court must
look in defining aboriginal rights. It is not the fact that aboriginal societies existed prior
to Crown sovereignty that is relevant; it is the fact that they existed *prior to the arrival of*

Europeans in North America. As such, the relevant time period is the period prior to the arrival of Europeans, not the period prior to the assertion of sovereignty by the Crown.

[62] That this is the relevant time should not suggest, however, that the aboriginal group claiming the right must accomplish the next to impossible task of producing conclusive evidence from pre-contact times about the practices, customs and traditions of their community. It would be entirely contrary to the spirit and intent of s. 35(1) to define aboriginal rights in such a fashion so as to preclude in practice any successful claim for the existence of such a right. The evidence relied upon by the applicant and the courts may relate to aboriginal practices, customs and traditions post-contact; it simply needs to be directed at demonstrating which aspects of the aboriginal community and society have their origins pre-contact. It is those practices, customs and traditions that can be rooted in the pre-contact societies of the aboriginal community in question that will constitute aboriginal rights.

[63] ... Where an aboriginal community can demonstrate that a particular practice, custom or tradition is integral to its distinctive culture today, and that this practice, custom or tradition has continuity with the practices, customs and traditions of pre-contact times, that community will have demonstrated that the practice, custom or tradition is an aboriginal right for the purposes of s. 35(1).

[64] The concept of continuity is also the primary means through which the definition and identification of aboriginal rights will be consistent with the admonition in *Sparrow, supra*, at p. 1093, that "the phrase ʻexisting aboriginal rightsʼ must be interpreted flexibly so as to permit their evolution over time." The concept of continuity is, in other words, the means by which a "frozen rights" approach to s. 35(1) will be avoided. Because the practices, customs and traditions protected by s. 35(1) are ones that exist today, subject only to the requirement that they be demonstrated to have continuity with the practices, customs and traditions which existed pre-contact, the definition of aboriginal rights will be one that, on its own terms, prevents those rights from being frozen in pre-contact times. The evolution of practices, customs and traditions into modern forms will not, provided that continuity with pre-contact practices, customs and traditions is demonstrated, prevent their protection as aboriginal rights.

[65] I would note that the concept of continuity does not require aboriginal groups to provide evidence of an unbroken chain of continuity between their current practices, customs and traditions, and those which existed prior to contact. It may be that for a period of time an aboriginal group, for some reason, ceased to engage in a practice, custom or tradition which existed prior to contact, but then resumed the practice, custom or tradition at a later date. Such an interruption will not preclude the establishment of an aboriginal right. Trial judges should adopt the same flexibility regarding the establishment of continuity that, as is discussed, *infra*, they are to adopt with regards to the evidence presented to establish the prior-to-contact practices, customs and traditions of the aboriginal group making the claim to an aboriginal right.

[66] Further, I would note that basing the identification of aboriginal rights in the period prior to contact is not inconsistent with the fact that s. 35(2) of the *Constitution Act, 1982* includes within the definition of "aboriginal peoples of Canada" the Métis people of Canada.

[67] Although s. 35 includes the Métis within its definition of "aboriginal peoples of Canada," and thus seems to link their claims to those of other aboriginal peoples under the general heading of "aboriginal rights," the history of the Métis, and the reasons underlying their inclusion in the protection given by s. 35, are quite distinct from those of other aboriginal peoples in Canada. As such, the manner in which the aboriginal rights of other aboriginal peoples are defined is not necessarily determinative of the manner in which the aboriginal rights of the Métis are defined. At the time when this Court is presented with a Métis claim under s. 35 it will then, with the benefit of the arguments of counsel, a factual context and a specific Métis claim, be able to explore the question of the purposes underlying s. 35's protection of the aboriginal rights of Métis people, and answer the question of the kinds of claims which fall within s. 35(1)'s scope when the claimants are Métis. The fact that, for other aboriginal peoples, the protection granted by s. 35 goes to the practices, customs and traditions of aboriginal peoples prior to contact, is not necessarily relevant to the answer which will be given to that question. It may, or it may not, be the case that the claims of the Métis are determined on the basis of the pre-contact practices, customs and traditions of their aboriginal ancestors; whether that is so must await determination in a case in which the issue arises.

Courts Must Approach the Rules of Evidence in Light of the Evidentiary Difficulties Inherent in Adjudicating Aboriginal Claims

[68] In determining whether an aboriginal claimant has produced evidence sufficient to demonstrate that her activity is an aspect of a practice, custom or tradition integral to a distinctive aboriginal culture, a court should approach the rules of evidence, and interpret the evidence that exists, with a consciousness of the special nature of aboriginal claims, and of the evidentiary difficulties in proving a right which originates in times where there were no written records of the practices, customs and traditions engaged in. The courts must not undervalue the evidence presented by aboriginal claimants simply because that evidence does not conform precisely with the evidentiary standards that would be applied in, for example, a private law torts case.

Claims to Aboriginal Rights Must Be Adjudicated on a Specific Rather Than General Basis

[69] Courts considering a claim to the existence of an aboriginal right must focus specifically on the practices, customs and traditions of the particular aboriginal group claiming the right. In the case of *Kruger* [*and Manuel v. The Queen*, [1978] 1 SCR 104, 75 DLR (3d) 434] this Court rejected the notion that claims to aboriginal rights could be determined on a general basis. This position is correct; the existence of an aboriginal right will depend entirely on the practices, customs and traditions of the *particular aboriginal community claiming the right*. As has already been suggested, aboriginal rights are constitutional rights, but that does not negate the central fact that the interests aboriginal rights are intended to protect relate to the specific history of the group claiming the right. Aboriginal rights are not general and universal; their scope and content must be determined on a case-by-case basis. The fact that one group of aboriginal people has an aboriginal right to do a particular thing will not be, without something more, sufficient to demon-

strate that another aboriginal community has the same aboriginal right. The existence of the right will be specific to each aboriginal community.

For a Practice, Custom or Tradition to Constitute an Aboriginal Right It Must Be of Independent Significance to the Aboriginal Culture in Which It Exists

[70] In identifying those practices, customs and traditions that constitute the aboriginal rights recognized and affirmed by s. 35(1), a court must ensure that the practice, custom or tradition relied upon in a particular case is independently significant to the aboriginal community claiming the right. The practice, custom or tradition cannot exist simply as an incident to another practice, custom or tradition but must rather be itself of integral significance to the aboriginal society. Where two customs exist, but one is merely incidental to the other, the custom which is integral to the aboriginal community in question will qualify as an aboriginal right, but the custom that is merely incidental will not. Incidental practices, customs and traditions cannot qualify as aboriginal rights through a process of piggybacking on integral practices, customs and traditions.

The Integral to a Distinctive Culture Test Requires That a Practice, Custom or Tradition Be Distinctive; It Does Not Require That That Practice, Custom or Tradition Be Distinct

[71] The standard which a practice, custom or tradition must meet in order to be recognized as an aboriginal right is *not* that it be *distinct* to the aboriginal culture in question; the aboriginal claimants must simply demonstrate that the practice, custom or tradition is *distinctive*. A tradition or custom that is *distinct* is one that is unique—"different in kind or quality; unlike" (*Concise Oxford Dictionary [of Current English*, 9th ed., ed. Della Thompson (Oxford: Clarendon Press, 1995). A culture with a distinct tradition must claim that in having such a tradition it is different from other cultures; a claim of distinctness is, by its very nature, a claim relative to other cultures or traditions. By contrast, a culture that claims that a practice, custom or tradition is *distinctive*—"distinguishing, characteristic"—makes a claim that is not relative; the claim is rather one about the culture's own practices, customs or traditions considered apart from the practices, customs or traditions of any other culture. It is a claim that this tradition or custom makes the culture *what it is*, not that the practice, custom or tradition is different from the practices, customs or traditions of another culture. The person or community claiming the existence of an aboriginal right protected by s. 35(1) need only show that the particular practice, custom or tradition which it is claiming to be an aboriginal right is distinctive, not that it is distinct.

· · ·

The Influence of European Culture Will Only Be Relevant to the Inquiry if It Is Demonstrated That the Practice, Custom or Tradition Is Only Integral Because of That Influence

[73] The fact that Europeans in North America engaged in the same practices, customs or traditions as those under which an aboriginal right is claimed will only be relevant to

the aboriginal claim if the practice, custom or tradition in question can only be said to exist because of the influence of European culture. If the practice, custom or tradition was an integral part of the aboriginal community's culture prior to contact with Europeans, the fact that that practice, custom or tradition continued after the arrival of Europeans, and adapted in response to their arrival, is not relevant to determination of the claim; European arrival and influence cannot be used to deprive an aboriginal group of an otherwise valid claim to an aboriginal right. On the other hand, where the practice, custom or tradition arose solely as a response to European influences then that practice, custom or tradition will not meet the standard for recognition of an aboriginal right.

Courts Must Take into Account Both the Relationship of Aboriginal Peoples to the Land and the Distinctive Societies and Cultures of Aboriginal Peoples

[74] As was noted in the discussion of the purposes of s. 35(1), aboriginal rights and aboriginal title are related concepts; aboriginal title is a sub-category of aboriginal rights which deals solely with claims of rights to land. The relationship between aboriginal title and aboriginal rights must not, however, confuse the analysis of what constitutes an aboriginal right. Aboriginal rights arise from the prior occupation of land, but they also arise from the prior social organization and distinctive cultures of aboriginal peoples on that land. In considering whether a claim to an aboriginal right has been made out, courts must look at both the relationship of an aboriginal claimant to the land *and* at the practices, customs and traditions arising from the claimant's distinctive culture and society. Courts must not focus so entirely on the relationship of aboriginal peoples with the land that they lose sight of the other factors relevant to the identification and definition of aboriginal rights.

· · ·

Application of the Integral to a Distinctive Culture Test to the Appellant's Claim

[76] The first step in the application of the integral to a distinctive culture test requires the court to identify the precise nature of the appellant's claim to have been exercising an aboriginal right. In this case the most accurate characterization of the appellant's position is that she is claiming *an aboriginal right to exchange fish for money or for other goods*. She is claiming, in other words, that the practices, customs and traditions of the Sto:lo include as an integral part the exchange of fish for money or other goods.

[77] That this is the nature of the appellant's claim can be seen through both the specific acts which led to her being charged and through the regulation under which she was charged. Mrs. Van der Peet sold ten salmon for $50. Such a sale, especially given the absence of evidence that the appellant had sold salmon on other occasions or on a regular basis, cannot be said to constitute a sale on a "commercial" or market basis. These actions are instead best characterized in the simple terms of an exchange of fish for money. It follows from this that the aboriginal right pursuant to which the appellant is arguing that her actions were taken is, like the actions themselves, best characterized as an aboriginal right to exchange fish for money or other goods.

[Lamer CJC then held that the trial judge made no error in justifying an appellate court's substituting its finding of fact. These findings included: (1) prior to contact, exchanges of fish were only "incidental" to fishing for food purposes; (2) there was no "regularized trading system" among the Sto:lo prior to contact; (3) the trade engaged in between the Sto:lo and the Hudson's Bay Company, while certainly of significance to the Sto:lo society of the time, was found by the trial judge to be qualitatively different from that which was typical of the Sto:lo culture prior to contact; and (4) the Sto:lo exploitation of the fishery was not specialized and that suggested that the exchange of fish was not a central part of Sto:lo culture. As a result, Lamer CJC held that the appellant failed to demonstrate that the exchange of fish for money or other goods was an integral part of the distinctive Sto:lo culture that existed prior to contact, and he dismissed the appeal.]

NOTES

1. Justices L'Heureux-Dubé and McLachlin issued dissenting judgments in *Van der Peet*. L'Heureux-Dubé J outlined and critiqued the majority's approach to characterizing the nature and extent of Aboriginal rights under s. 35(1). She advocated describing Aboriginal rights at a fairly high level of abstraction, rather than focusing on the particular Aboriginal practice, custom, or tradition. L'Heureux-Dubé J rejected the majority's approach as overly majoritarian, unduly restrictive, and as misconstruing *Sparrow*'s use of the words "distinctive culture":

> [157] [Section] 35(1) should be viewed as protecting, not a catalogue of individualized practices, traditions or customs, as the Chief Justice does, but the "distinctive culture" of which aboriginal activities are manifestations. Simply put, the emphasis would be on the significance of these activities to natives rather than on the activities themselves.
>
> • • •
>
> [162] … The criterion of "distinctive aboriginal culture" should not be limited to those activities that only aboriginal people have undertaken or that non-aboriginal people have not. Rather, all practices, traditions and customs which are connected enough to the self-identity and self-preservation of organized aboriginal societies should be viewed as deserving the protection of s. 35(1). Further, a generous, large and liberal construction should be given to these activities in order to give full effect to the constitutional recognition of the distinctiveness of aboriginal culture. Finally, it is almost trite to say that what constitutes a practice, tradition or custom distinctive to native culture and society must be examined through the eyes of aboriginal people, not through those of the non-native majority or the distorting lens of existing regulations.

Regarding the period of time necessary for an activity to be recognized as an Aboriginal right, Justice L'Heureux-Dubé adopted what she termed a flexible "dynamic-right" approach in preference to a "frozen-right" approach, which, in her view, overstates the impact of European influence, crystallizes Aboriginal practices as of an arbitrary date, imposes a heavy burden on those claiming an Aboriginal right, and embodies inappropriate and unprovable assumptions about Aboriginal culture and society. To qualify as an Aboriginal right, in her view, an Aboriginal activity must have formed an integral part of the distinctive Aboriginal culture for a substantial continuous period of time. In the instant case, Justice L'Heureux-Dubé distinguished the activity in question from commercial fishing, characterizing it instead as the right to sell, trade, and barter fish for livelihood, support, and sustenance. Fishing for this limited purpose, in her view, formed part of the Sto:lo's distinctive Aboriginal culture and was protected under s. 35(1). L'Heureux-Dubé J would have remitted to trial the questions of extinguishment, *prima facie* infringement, and justification, because she found that there was insufficient evidence before the court to decide these issues.

Justice McLachlin's dissent differed in both reasoning and result. She emphasized the distinction between an Aboriginal right, which is to be broadly conceived and constant over time, and the exercise of that right, which may vary over time and take modern forms. Unlike L'Heureux-Dubé J, she considered the activity in these cases to be undeniably commercial. Nevertheless, she identified the crucial issue to be whether the sale could be defended as the exercise of a basic Aboriginal right to continue a historic use of the resource. Justice McLachlin considered and rejected the "integral part," "dynamic rights," and "integral–incidental" tests, favouring instead an empirical, historical approach to defining Aboriginal rights. Applying this view, she found the Sto:lo to have an Aboriginal right to continue to use the resource, though this use would not extend beyond providing for the traditional sustenance needs in their modern form. McLachlin J also articulated and applied a limited view of justification, by which the Crown may prohibit exploitation of a resource only for conservation and the prevention of harm to others. Subject to these limitations, Aboriginal people would have a priority to fish for food, ceremony, and supplementary sustenance. Finally, in both cases, she found that the Crown failed to justify the regulations at issue.

2.   Requiring Aboriginal rights to manifest continuity with practices, customs, and traditions that existed prior to contact raises conceptual problems with respect to Métis rights recognized by s. 35(1), given that Métis peoples are post-contact communities. See *R v. Powley*, [2003] 2 SCR 207, 230 DLR (4th) 1, an excerpt from which appears later in this chapter, to learn how the Court has addressed this problem.

3.   There were two companion cases to *Van der Peet*. In the first, *R v. NTC Smokehouse*, [1996] 2 SCR 672, 137 DLR (4th) 528, the issue was whether the Sheshaht and Opetchesaht peoples possessed an existing Aboriginal right to exchange fish for money. Lamer CJC (La Forest, Sopinka, Gonthier, Cory, Iacobucci, and Major JJ concurring) affirmed the findings of fact of the trial judge, which did not support the claim that prior to contact the exchange of fish for money was an integral part of the distinctive cultures of the Sheshaht and Opetchesaht peoples. The exchange of fish incidental to social and ceremonial occasions was not a sufficiently central, significant, or defining feature of these societies to be recognized as an Aboriginal right under s. 35(1). L'Heureux-Dubé J dissented on the basis that the evidence showed that the sale, trade, and barter of fish for livelihood purposes was sufficiently significant and fundamental to the culture and social organization of the groups in question to constitute an Aboriginal right, and that the right had not been extinguished prior to 1982. McLachlin J also dissented on the basis that there existed an unextinguished right to sell fish, limited to equivalence with what the Sheshaht and Opetchesaht historically took from the fishery in accordance with Aboriginal law and custom.

In the second companion case, *R v. Gladstone*, [1996] 2 SCR 723, 137 DLR (4th) 648, the Supreme Court of Canada also addressed the application of the justification test outlined in *Sparrow* to laws that unduly interfered with the exercise of Aboriginal commercial fishing rights. Gladstone was a member of the Heiltsuk Band, charged with attempting to sell herring spawn on kelp without a proper licence. His defence to the charge was that he was exercising a pre-existing right to fish for commercial purposes. After his conviction was upheld by both the Supreme Court of British Columbia and the Court of Appeal, the accused appealed to the Supreme Court of Canada. A majority of the Court (La Forest J dissenting) found that there was an Aboriginal right that had not been extinguished, and that there was a *prima facie* infringement. The Chief Justice held the commercial sale or barter of herring spawn on kelp to be an Aboriginal right, since it was found to constitute a central, significant, and defining feature of the culture of the Heiltsuk prior to contact. The majority also found that there was no clean and plain intention to extinguish the right, and therefore that the regulation of the right was *prima facie* an infringement. Lamer CJC then turned to the issue of justification in the following excerpt.

R v. Gladstone
[1996] 2 SCR 723, 137 DLR (4th) 648

LAMER CJC (Sopinka, Gonthier, Iacobucci and Major JJ concurring): ...

Justification

[54] In [*R v.*] *Sparrow* [1990] 1 SCR 1075, 70 DLR (4th) 385], Dickson CJ and La Forest J articulated a two-part test for determining whether government actions infringing aboriginal rights can be justified. ... In this case, where, particularly at the stage of justification, the context varies significantly from that in *Sparrow*, it will be necessary to revisit the *Sparrow* test and to adapt the justification test it lays out in order to apply that test to the circumstances of this appeal.

. . .

[57] Two points of variation are of particular significance. First, the right recognized and affirmed in this case—to sell herring spawn on kelp commercially—differs significantly from the right recognized and affirmed in *Sparrow*—the right to fish for food, social and ceremonial purposes. That difference lies in the fact that the right at issue in *Sparrow* has an inherent limitation which the right recognized and affirmed in this appeal lacks. The food, social and ceremonial needs for fish of any given band of aboriginal people are internally limited—at a certain point the band will have sufficient fish to meet these needs. The commercial sale of the herring spawn on kelp, on the other hand, has no such internal limitation; the only limits on the Heiltsuk's need for herring spawn on kelp for commercial sale are the external constraints of the demand of the market and the availability of the resource. This is particularly so in this case where the evidence supports a right to exchange fish on a genuinely commercial basis; the evidence in this case does not justify limiting the right to harvest herring spawn on kelp on a commercial basis to, for example, the sale of herring spawn on kelp for the purposes of obtaining a "moderate livelihood." ...

[58] The significance of this difference for the *Sparrow* test relates to the position taken in that case that, subject to the limits of conservation, aboriginal rights holders

must be given priority in the fishery. In a situation where the aboriginal right is internally limited, so that it is clear when that right has been satisfied and other users can be allowed to participate in the fishery, the notion of priority, as articulated in *Sparrow*, makes sense. In that situation it is understandable that in an *exceptional* year, when conservation concerns are severe, it will be possible for aboriginal rights holders to be alone allowed to participate in the fishery, while in more ordinary years other users will be allowed to participate in the fishery after the aboriginal rights to fish for food, social and ceremonial purposes have been met.

[59] Where the aboriginal right has no internal limitation, however, what is described in *Sparrow* as an exceptional situation becomes the ordinary: in the circumstance where the aboriginal right has no internal limitation, the notion of priority, as articulated in *Sparrow*, would mean that where an aboriginal right is recognized and affirmed that right would become an exclusive one. Because the right to sell herring spawn on kelp to the commercial market can never be said to be satisfied while the resource is still available and the market is not sated, to give priority to that right in the manner suggested in *Sparrow* would be to give the right-holder exclusivity over any person not having an aboriginal right to participate in the herring spawn on kelp fishery.

· · ·

[61] The basic insight of *Sparrow*—that aboriginal rights holders have priority in the fishery—is a valid and important one; however, the articulation in that case of what priority means, and its suggestion that it can mean exclusivity under certain limited circumstances, must be refined to take into account the varying circumstances which arise when the aboriginal right in question has no internal limitations.

[62] Where the aboriginal right is one that has no internal limitation then the doctrine of priority does not require that, after conservation goals have been met, the government allocate the fishery so that those holding an aboriginal right to exploit that fishery on a commercial basis are given an exclusive right to do so. Instead, the doctrine of priority requires that the government demonstrate that, in allocating the resource, it has taken account of the existence of aboriginal rights and allocated the resource in a manner respectful of the fact that those rights have priority over the exploitation of the fishery by other users. This right is at once both procedural and substantive; at the stage of justification the government must demonstrate both that the process by which it allocated the resource and the actual allocation of the resource which results from that process reflect the prior interest of aboriginal rights holders in the fishery.

[63] The content of this priority—something less than exclusivity but which nonetheless gives priority to the aboriginal right—must remain somewhat vague pending consideration of the government's actions in specific cases. ... [U]nder *Sparrow*'s priority doctrine, where the aboriginal right to be given priority is one without internal limitation, courts should assess the government's actions not to see whether the government has given exclusivity to that right (the least drastic means) but rather to determine whether the government has taken into account the existence and importance of such rights.

[64] That no blanket requirement is imposed under the priority doctrine should not suggest, however, that no guidance is possible in this area, or that the government's actions will not be subject to scrutiny. Questions relevant to the determination of whether

the government has granted priority to aboriginal rights holders are those enumerated in *Sparrow* relating to consultation and compensation, as well as questions such as whether the government has accommodated the exercise of the aboriginal right to participate in the fishery (through reduced licence fees, for example), whether the government's objectives in enacting a particular regulatory scheme reflect the need to take into account the priority of aboriginal rights holders, the extent of the participation in the fishery of aboriginal rights holders relative to their percentage of the population, how the government has accommodated different aboriginal rights in a particular fishery (food *versus* commercial rights, for example), how important the fishery is to the economic and material well-being of the band in question, and the criteria taken into account by the government in, for example, allocating commercial licences amongst different users. These questions, like those in *Sparrow*, do not represent an exhaustive list of the factors that may be taken into account in determining whether the government can be said to have given priority to aboriginal rights holders; they give some indication, however, of what such an inquiry should look like.

· · ·

[69] I now turn to the second significant difference between this case and *Sparrow*. In *Sparrow*, while the Court recognized at p. 1113 that, beyond conservation, there could be other "compelling and substantial" objectives pursuant to which the government could act in accordance with the first branch of the justification test, the Court was not required to delineate what those objectives might be. Further, in delineating the priority requirement, and the relationship between aboriginal rights-holders and other users of the fishery, the only objective considered by the Court was conservation. ...

[70] Considering this question is made more difficult in this case because, as will be discussed below, almost no evidence has been provided to this Court about the objectives the government was pursuing in allocating the herring resource as it did. Absent some concrete objectives to assess, it is difficult to identify the objectives other than conservation that will meet the "compelling and substantial" standard laid out in *Sparrow*. That being said, however, it is possible to make some general observations about the nature of the objectives that the government can pursue under the first branch of the *Sparrow* justification test.

· · ·

[73] Aboriginal rights are recognized and affirmed by s. 35(1) in order to reconcile the existence of distinctive aboriginal societies prior to the arrival of Europeans in North America with the assertion of Crown sovereignty over that territory; they are the means by which the critical and integral aspects of those societies are maintained. Because, however, distinctive aboriginal societies exist within, and are a part of, a broader social, political and economic community, over which the Crown is sovereign, there are circumstances in which, in order to pursue objectives of compelling and substantial importance to that community as a whole (taking into account the fact that aboriginal societies are a part of that community), some limitation of those rights will be justifiable. Aboriginal rights are a necessary part of the reconciliation of aboriginal societies with the broader political community of which they are part; limits placed on those rights are, where the objectives furthered by those limits are of sufficient importance to the broader community as a whole, *equally* a necessary part of that reconciliation.

[74] The recognition of conservation as a compelling and substantial goal demonstrates this point. Given the integral role the fishery has played in the distinctive cultures of many aboriginal peoples, conservation can be said to be something the pursuit of which can be linked to the recognition of the existence of such distinctive cultures. Moreover, because conservation is of such overwhelming importance to Canadian society as a whole, including aboriginal members of that society, it is a goal the pursuit of which is consistent with the reconciliation of aboriginal societies with the larger Canadian society of which they are a part. In this way, conservation can be said to be a compelling and substantial objective which, provided the rest of the *Sparrow* justification standard is met, will justify governmental infringement of aboriginal rights.

[75] Although by no means making a definitive statement on this issue, I would suggest that with regards to the distribution of the fisheries resource after conservation goals have been met, objectives such as the pursuit of economic and regional fairness, and the recognition of the historical reliance upon, and participation in, the fishery by non-aboriginal groups, are the type of objectives which can (at least in the right circumstances) satisfy this standard. *In the right circumstances, such objectives are in the interest of all Canadians and, more importantly, the reconciliation of aboriginal societies with the rest of Canadian society may well depend on their successful attainment.*

. . .

[77] Other than with regards to the first aspect of the government's regulatory scheme, the evidence and testimony presented in this case is insufficient for this Court to make a determination as to whether the government's regulatory scheme is justified. The trial in this case concluded on May 7, 1990, several weeks prior to the release of this Court's judgment in *Sparrow*. Perhaps as a result of this fact, the testimony, evidence and argument presented at the trial simply do not contain the information that is necessary for this Court to assess whether, in allocating the 40,000 tons of herring allotted to the herring fishery, the government has either acted pursuant to a compelling and substantial objective or has acted in a manner consistent with the fiduciary obligation it owes to aboriginal peoples. It is not that the Crown has failed to discharge its burden of demonstrating that the scheme for allocating the 20% of the herring stock was justified; it is simply that the question of whether or not that scheme of allocation was justified was not addressed at trial, at least in the sense necessary for this Court to decide the question of whether, under the *Sparrow* test, it was justified.

. . .

[83] A new trial on the question of justification will remedy this deficiency .... A new trial is not, however, necessary with regards to the first aspect of the government's scheme; the evidentiary record clearly demonstrates that this aspect of the government's scheme was justified. Witnesses testified as to the conservation objectives of setting the stock at 20% and as to the difficulties encountered by the herring fishery when the catch was set at much higher levels, as was the case in the 1960s. Moreover, the defence witness Dr. Gary Vigers testified that "fisheries management is full of uncertainty"; in the context of such uncertainty this Court must grant a certain level of deference to the government's approach to fisheries management.

. . .

[85] In the result, the appeal is allowed and a new trial directed on the issue of guilt or innocence and, with regards to the constitutionality of s. 20(3), on the issue of the justifiability of the government's allocation of herring.

[L'Heureux-Dubé J, in separate reasons, concurred with the Chief Justice. McLachlin J, in separate reasons, would have allowed the appeal to the extent of confirming the existence of an Aboriginal right of the Heiltsuk to sell herring spawn on kelp for sustenance purposes, and would have ordered a new trial to decide whether that right had been infringed, and if so, whether such an infringement had been justified.]

Appeal allowed.

NOTES

1. The justification test for the infringement of Aboriginal rights as modified by *Gladstone* has not been without controversy. McLachlin J warned of this in *Van der Peet* when she observed:

> The extension of the concept of compelling objectives to matters like economic development and regional fairness and the interests of aboriginal fishers ... would negate the very Aboriginal right to fish itself, on the ground that this is required for the reconciliation of Aboriginal rights, and other interests and the consequent good of the community as a whole. This is not limitation required for the responsible exercise of the right, but rather limitation based on the economic demands of non-aboriginal individuals. It is a limitation of a different order than the conservation, harm prevention type of limitation sanctioned in *Sparrow*.

2. Aboriginal rights in Quebec are not treated any differently from the way they are in the rest of the country, despite the historic presence of French sovereignty in the region. In *R v. Côté*, [1996] 3 SCR 139, 138 DLR (4th) 185, Lamer CJC (Sopinka, Gonthier, Cory, McLachlin, Iacobucci, and Major JJ concurring) wrote:

> I do not believe that the intervention of French sovereignty negated the potential existence of aboriginal rights within the former boundaries of New France under s. 35(1). The entrenchment of aboriginal ancestral and treaty rights in s. 35(1) has changed the landscape of aboriginal rights in Canada. As explained in the *Van der Peet* trilogy, the purpose of s. 35(1) was to extend constitutional protection to the practices, customs and traditions central to the distinctive culture of aboriginal societies prior to contact with Europeans. If such practices, customs and traditions continued following contact in the absence of specific extinguishment, such practices, customs and traditions are entitled to constitutional recognition subject to the infringement and justification tests outlined in *Sparrow, supra*, and *Gladstone, supra*.
>
> As such, the fact that a particular practice, custom or tradition continued, in an unextinguished manner, following the arrival of Europeans *but* in the absence of the formal gloss of legal recognition from French colonial law should not undermine the constitutional protection accorded to aboriginal peoples. Section 35(1) would fail to achieve its noble purpose of preserving the integral and defining features of distinctive aboriginal societies if it only protected those defining features which were fortunate enough to have received the legal recognition and

approval of European colonizers. I should stress that the French Regime's failure to recognize legally a specific aboriginal practice, custom or tradition (and indeed the French Regime's tacit toleration of a specific practice, custom or tradition) clearly cannot be equated with a "clear and plain" intention to extinguish such practices under the extinguishment test of s. 35(1). See *Sparrow, supra*, at p. 1099; *Gladstone, supra*, at para. 34.

The respondent's view, if adopted, would create an awkward patchwork of constitutional protection for aboriginal rights across the nation, depending upon the historical idiosyncrasies of colonization over particular regions of the country. In my respectful view, such a static and retrospective interpretation of s. 35(1) cannot be reconciled with the noble and prospective purpose of the constitutional entrenchment of aboriginal and treaty rights in the *Constitution Act, 1982*. Indeed, the respondent's proposed interpretation risks undermining the very purpose of s. 35(1) by perpetuating the historical injustice suffered by aboriginal peoples at the hands of colonizers who failed to respect the distinctive cultures of pre-existing aboriginal societies. To quote the words of Brennan J in *Mabo v. Queensland [No. 2]* (1992), 175 CLR 1 (HC), at p. 42:

> Whatever the justification advanced in earlier days for refusing to recognize the rights and interests in land of the indigenous inhabitants of settled colonies, an unjust and discriminatory doctrine of that kind can no longer be accepted.

3. In *R v. Sappier; R v. Gray*, [2006] 2 SCR 686, 274 DLR (4th) 75, at issue was whether the Maliseet and Mi'kmaq peoples in New Brunswick possessed an Aboriginal right to harvest timber on Crown lands for personal use. In holding for the Maliseet and Mi'kmaq, Bastarache J, for a majority of the Court, held that "an aboriginal right cannot be characterized as a right to a particular resource because to do so would be to treat it as akin to a common law property right" (para. 21). Instead, attention must be paid to the significance of the resource to the community in question:

> [22] [I]n order to grasp the importance of a resource to a particular aboriginal people, the Court seeks to understand how that resource was harvested, extracted and utilized. These practices are the necessary "aboriginal" component in aboriginal rights. ... The goal for courts is, therefore, to determine how the claimed right relates to the pre-contact culture or way of life of an aboriginal society. This has been achieved by requiring aboriginal rights claimants to found their claim on a pre-contact practice which was integral to the distinctive culture of the particular aboriginal community. It is critically important that the Court be able to identify a *practice* that helps to define the distinctive way of life of the community as an aboriginal community. The importance of leading evidence about the pre-contact practice upon which the claimed right is based should not be understated. In the absence of such evidence, courts will find it difficult to relate the claimed right to the pre-contact way of life of the specific aboriginal people, so as to trigger s. 35 protection.
>
> ...
>
> [24] In the present cases, the relevant practice for the purposes of the *Van der Peet* test is harvesting wood. It is this practice upon which the respondents opted to found their claims. However, the respondents do not claim a right to harvest wood for any and all purposes — such a right would not provide sufficient specificity to apply the reasoning I have just described. The respondents instead claim the right to harvest timber for personal uses; I find this characteriza-

tion to be too general as well. As previously explained, it is critical that the Court identify a practice that helps to define the way of life or distinctiveness of the particular aboriginal community. The claimed right should then be delineated in accordance with that practice: see *Van der Peet*, at para. 52. The way of life of the Maliseet and of the Mi'kmaq during the pre-contact period is that of a migratory people who lived from fishing and hunting and who used the rivers and lakes of Eastern Canada for transportation. Thus, the practice should be characterized as the harvesting of wood for certain uses that are directly associated with that particular way of life. The record shows that wood was used to fulfill the communities' domestic needs for such things as shelter, transportation, tools and fuel. I would therefore characterize the respondents' claim as a right to harvest wood for domestic uses as a member of the aboriginal community.

Bastarache J went on to discuss the meaning of "distinctive culture":

[42] ... [T]his Court in *Van der Peet* set out to interpret s. 35 of the Constitution in a way which captures both the aboriginal and the rights in aboriginal rights. Lamer CJ spoke of the "necessary specificity which comes from granting special constitutional protection to one part of Canadian society" (para. 20). It is that aboriginal specificity which the notion of a "distinctive culture" seeks to capture. However, it is clear that "Aboriginality means more than interesting cultural practices and anthropological curiosities worthy only of a museum" (C.C. Cheng, "Touring the Museum: A Comment on *R v. Van der Peet*" (1997), 55 *UT Fac. L Rev.* 419, at p. 434). R.L. Barsh and J. Youngblood Henderson argue that as a result of the *Van der Peet* decision, "'culture' has implicitly been taken to mean a fixed inventory of traits or characteristics" ("The Supreme Court's *Van der Peet* Trilogy: Naive Imperialism and Ropes of Sand" (1997), 42 *McGill LJ* 993, at p. 1002).

[43] Many of these concerns echo those expressed by McLachlin J (as she then was) and by L'Heureux-Dubé J in dissenting opinions in *Van der Peet*. L'Heureux-Dubé J was of the view that "the approach based on aboriginal practices, traditions and customs considers only discrete parts of aboriginal culture, separating them from the general culture in which they are rooted" (para. 150). McLachlin J opined that "different people may entertain different ideas of what is distinctive," thereby creating problems of indeterminacy in the *Van der Peet* test (para. 257).

[44] Culture, let alone "distinctive culture," has proven to be a difficult concept to grasp for Canadian courts. Moreover, the term "culture" as it is used in the English language may not find a perfect parallel in certain aboriginal languages. Barsh and Henderson note that "[w]e can find no precise equivalent of European concepts of 'culture' in Mi'kmaq, for example. How we maintain contact with our traditions is *tan'telo'tlieki-p*. How we perpetuate our consciousness is described as *tlilnuo'lti'k*. How we maintain our language is *tlinuita'sim*. Each of these terms connotes a process rather than a thing" (p. 1002, note 30). Ultimately, the concept of culture is itself inherently cultural.

[45] The aboriginal rights doctrine, which has been constitutionalized by s. 35, arises from the simple fact of prior occupation of the lands now forming Canada. The "integral to a distinctive culture" test must necessarily be understood in this context. As L'Heureux-Dubé J explained in dissent in *Van der Peet*, "[t]he 'distinctive aboriginal culture' must be taken to refer to the reality that, despite British sovereignty, aboriginal people were the original organized society occupying and using Canadian lands: *Calder v. [British Columbia (Attorney General)*, [1973] SCR 313], at p. 328, *per* Judson J, and *Guerin [v. The Queen*, [1984] 2 SCR 335], at p. 379, *per* Dickson J (as he then was)" (para. 159). The focus of the Court should therefore be on the *nature* of

this prior occupation. What is meant by "culture" is really an inquiry into the pre-contact way of life of a particular aboriginal community, including their means of survival, their socialization methods, their legal systems, and, potentially, their trading habits. The use of the word "distinctive" as a qualifier is meant to incorporate an element of aboriginal specificity. However, "distinctive" does not mean "distinct," and the notion of aboriginality must not be reduced to "racialized stereotypes of Aboriginal peoples" (J. Borrows and L.I. Rotman, "The *Sui Generis* Nature of Aboriginal Rights: Does it Make a Difference?" (1997), 36 *Alta. L Rev.* 9, at p. 36).

[46] In post-hearing submissions to the Court of Appeal in the *Sappier* and *Polchies* case, the Crown admitted that gathering birch bark for the construction of canoes or hemlock for basket-making were practices likely integral to the distinctive Maliseet culture (para. 94). But it would be a mistake to reduce the entire pre-contact distinctive Maliseet culture to canoe-building and basket-making. To hold otherwise would be to fall in the trap of reducing an entire people's culture to specific anthropological curiosities and, potentially, racialized aboriginal stereotypes. Instead, the Court must first inquire into the way of life of the Maliseet and Mi'kmaq, pre-contact. As previously explained, these were migratory communities using the rivers and lakes of Eastern Canada for transportation and living essentially from hunting and fishing. The Court must therefore seek to understand how the particular pre-contact practice relied upon relates to that way of life. In the present cases, the practice of harvesting wood for domestic uses including shelter, transportation, fuel and tools is directly related to the way of life I have just described. I have already explained that we must discard the idea that the practice must go to the core of a people's culture. The fact that harvesting wood for domestic uses was undertaken for survival purposes is sufficient, given the evidence adduced at trial, to meet the integral to a distinctive culture threshold.

IV. CONSTITUTIONAL RECOGNITION OF ABORIGINAL TITLE

In *R v. Adams*, [1996] 3 SCR 101, 138 DLR (4th) 657, a majority of the Court held that Aboriginal title was a specific subset of Aboriginal rights recognized and affirmed by s. 35(1) of the *Constitution Act, 1982*. In so doing, the Court elevated Aboriginal title from its common law status to the level of constitutional guarantee. In *Adams*, Lamer CJC (La Forest, Sopinka, Gonthier, Cory, McLachlin, Iacobucci, and Major JJ concurring; L'Heureux-Dubé J concurring in separate reasons) outlined this principle as follows:

> [W]hile claims to aboriginal title fall within the conceptual framework of aboriginal rights, aboriginal rights do not exist solely where a claim to aboriginal title has been made out. Where an aboriginal group has shown that a particular practice, custom or tradition taking place on the land was integral to the distinctive culture of that group then, *even if they have not shown that their occupation and use of the land was sufficient to support a claim of title to the land*, they will have demonstrated that they have an aboriginal right to engage in that practice, custom or tradition. The *Van der Peet* test protects activities which were integral to the distinctive culture of the aboriginal group claiming the right; it does not require that that group satisfy the further hurdle of demonstrating that their connection with the piece of land on which the activity was taking place was of a central significance to their distinctive culture sufficient to make out a claim to aboriginal title to the land. *Van der Peet* establishes that s. 35 recognizes and affirms the rights of those peoples who occupied North America prior to the arrival of the Europeans;

that recognition and affirmation is not limited to those circumstances where an aboriginal group's relationship with the land is of a kind sufficient to establish title to the land.

To understand why aboriginal rights cannot be inexorably linked to aboriginal title it is only necessary to recall that some aboriginal peoples were nomadic, varying the location of their settlements with the season and changing circumstances. That this was the case does not alter the fact that nomadic peoples survived through reliance on the land prior to contact with Europeans and, further, that many of the practices, customs and traditions of nomadic peoples that took place on the land were integral to their distinctive cultures. The aboriginal rights recognized and affirmed by s. 35(1) should not be understood or defined in a manner which excludes some of those the provision was intended to protect.

Moreover, some aboriginal peoples varied the location of their settlements both before and after contact. ... That this is the case may (although I take no position on this point) preclude the establishment of aboriginal title to the lands on which they settled. ...

Finally, I would note that the Court in *Van der Peet* did address itself to this question, holding at para. 74 that:

> Aboriginal rights arise from the prior occupation of land, but they also arise from the prior social organization and distinctive cultures of aboriginal peoples on that land. In considering whether a claim to an aboriginal right has been made out, courts must look at both the relationship of an aboriginal claimant to the land *and* at the practices, customs and traditions arising from the claimant's distinctive culture and society. Courts must not focus so entirely on the relationship of aboriginal peoples with the land that they lose sight of the other factors relevant to the identification and definition of aboriginal rights. ... [Emphasis in original.]

The recognition that aboriginal title is simply one manifestation of the doctrine of aboriginal rights should not, however, create the impression that the fact that some aboriginal rights are linked to land use or occupation is unimportant. Even where an aboriginal right exists on a tract of land to which the aboriginal people in question do not have title, that right may well be site specific, with the result that it can be exercised only upon that specific tract of land. For example, if an aboriginal people demonstrates that hunting on a specific tract of land was an integral part of their distinctive culture then, even if the right exists apart from title to that tract of land, the aboriginal right to hunt is nonetheless defined as, and limited to, the right to hunt on the specific tract of land. A site-specific hunting or fishing right does not, simply because it is independent of aboriginal title to the land on which it took place, become an abstract fishing or hunting right exercisable anywhere; it continues to be a right to hunt or fish *on the tract of land in question.*

As outlined earlier, historically, one of the primary methods to deal with Aboriginal title has been the signing of treaties following the principles outlined and agreed to in the Royal Proclamation of 1763. However, there were places in Canada where these principles were not followed and land was not the subject of treaty promises. These areas include the Maritimes, parts of the north, southern Quebec, and British Columbia. The existence of Aboriginal title is a contemporary issue in these areas. The issue of Aboriginal title has proven to be a particularly charged and high profile issue in British Columbia, bringing into question the issue of property and resource use rights in many parts of the province.

When British Columbia entered Confederation in 1871, Aboriginal people outnumbered non-Aboriginal people by a ratio of 2:1. However, among the very first acts of the newly created provincial legislature was the disenfranchisement of Aboriginal people from voting and the removal of Aboriginal peoples to small reserves. There was also an explicit denial of Aboriginal title, and a disallowance of any attempt by Aboriginal peoples to take up land through pre-emption, as was permitted for newly arriving non-Aboriginal settlers. These actions all took place against the strong objections of numerous First Nations throughout the province, and numerous commissions were set up to deal with their complaints. Unfortunately, these bodies repeatedly failed to address the underlying conflict concerning Aboriginal peoples' pre-existing interest in land and the provincial government's non-recognition of Aboriginal title. The federal government also failed to bring any resolution to this issue under its authority for "Indians and lands reserved for Indians" in section 91(24) of the *British North America Act, 1867*. When, in 1927, it looked as though the Allied Tribes of British Columbia might finally succeed in pressing a case to the Privy Council, the *Indian Act* was amended to make it illegal to raise funds for or hire a lawyer for land claims purposes. As a result, the issue of Aboriginal title in British Columbia did not appear before the courts until the early 1970s in the *Calder* case, and did not receive any treatment under s. 35(1) until the groundbreaking case of *Delgamuukw v. British Columbia*, excerpted below.

Delgamuukw v. British Columbia
[1997] 3 SCR 1010, 153 DLR (4th) 193

LAMER CJC (Cory, Major, and McLachlin JJ concurring):

I. Introduction

[1] This appeal is the latest in a series of cases in which it has fallen to this Court to interpret and apply the guarantee of existing aboriginal rights found in s. 35(1) of the *Constitution Act, 1982*. Although that line of decisions, commencing with *R v. Sparrow*, [1990] 1 SCR 1075 [70 DLR (4th) 385], proceeding through the *Van der Peet* trilogy (*R v. Van der Peet*, [1996] 2 SCR 507 [137 DLR (4th) 289]; *R v. NTC Smokehouse*, [1996] 2 SCR 672 [137 DLR (4th) 528] and *R v. Gladstone*, [1996] 2 SCR 723 [137 DLR (4th) 648]) and ending in *R v. Pamajewon*, [1996] 2 SCR 821; *R v. Adams*, [1996] 3 SCR 101 [138 DLR (4th) 657] and *R v. Côté*, [1996] 3 SCR 139 [138 DLR (4th) 185], have laid down the jurisprudential framework for s. 35(1), this appeal raises a set of interrelated and novel questions which revolve around a single issue—the nature and scope of the constitutional protection afforded by s. 35(1) to common law aboriginal title.

· · ·

II. Facts

· · ·

[7] This action was commenced by the appellants, who are all Gitksan or Wet'suwet'en hereditary chiefs, who, both individually and on behalf of their "Houses" claimed separate portions of 58,000 square kilometres in British Columbia. For the purpose of the

claim, this area was divided into 133 individual territories, claimed by the 71 Houses. This represents all of the Wet'suwet'en people, and all but 12 of the Gitksan Houses. Their claim was originally for "ownership" of the territory and "jurisdiction" over it. (At this Court, this was transformed into, primarily, a claim for aboriginal title over the land in question.) The province of British Columbia counterclaimed for a declaration that the appellants have no right or interest in and to the territory or alternatively, that the appellants' cause of action ought to be for compensation from the Government of Canada. ...

[At the time of trial the Gitksan consisted of approximately 4,000 to 5,000 persons in the watersheds of the north and central Skeena, Nass, and Babine Rivers. The Wet'suwet'en consisted of approximately 1,500 to 2,000 persons mainly in the watersheds of the Bulkley and parts of the Fraser-Nechako River systems. There were also approximately 30,000 non-Aboriginals living in the territory at the time of the trial. There was archeological evidence, which was accepted at trial, that there was some form of human habitation in the territory and its surrounding areas from 3,500 to 6,000 years ago. The trial judge held that the time of direct contact in the claimed territory was approximately 1820.]

V. Analysis

A. Do the Pleadings Preclude the Court from Entertaining Claims for Aboriginal Title and Self-Government?

[73] ... [T]he appellants, 51 Chiefs representing most of the Houses of the Gitksan and Wet'suwet'en nations, originally advanced 51 individual claims on their own behalf and on behalf of their houses for "ownership" and "jurisdiction" over 133 distinct territories which together comprise 58,000 square kilometres of northwestern British Columbia.

[On appeal, that original claim was altered in two ways: (1) replacing the claims for ownership and jurisdiction with claims for Aboriginal title and self-government, and (2) amalgamating the 51 individual claims into two communal claims, one for each nation. Lamer CJC held that there was no formal amendment to the first pleading, but that the trial judge had allowed a *de facto* amendment to permit "a claim for aboriginal rights other than ownership and jurisdiction." As a result, he held that there was no prejudice to the respondents by virtue of the first alteration. However, Lamer CJC held that no such amendment was made with respect to the amalgamation of the individual claims brought by the 51 Gitksan and Wet'suwet'en Houses into two collective claims.]

[77] ... [G]iven the absence of an amendment to the pleadings, he concluded that the respondents suffered some prejudice that prevented the Court from considering the merits of this appeal. The Chief Justice ordered a new trial as the correct remedy for this defect in the pleadings. The remainder of the judgement was dedicated to other reasons why a new trial should be ordered.

B. What Is the Ability of This Court to Interfere with the Factual Findings Made by the Trial Judge?

(1) General Principles

[78] … As a general rule, this Court has been extremely reluctant to interfere with the findings of fact made at trial, especially when those findings of fact are based on an assessment of the testimony and credibility of witnesses. Unless there is a "palpable and overriding error," appellate courts should not substitute their own findings of fact for those of the trial judge.

· · ·

[80] … [W]hile accepting the general principle of non-interference, this Court has also identified specific situations in which an appeal court can interfere with a finding of fact made at trial. … In cases involving the determination of aboriginal rights, appellate intervention is also warranted by the failure of a trial court to appreciate the evidentiary difficulties inherent in adjudicating aboriginal claims when, first, applying the rules of evidence and, second, interpreting the evidence before it. …

[81] The justification for this special approach can be found in the nature of aboriginal rights themselves. I explained in *Van der Peet* that those rights are aimed at the reconciliation of the prior occupation of North America by distinctive aboriginal societies with the assertion of Crown sovereignty over Canadian territory. They attempt to achieve that reconciliation by "their bridging of aboriginal and non-aboriginal cultures" (at para. 42). Accordingly, "a court must take into account the perspective of the aboriginal people claiming the right … while at the same time taking into account the perspective of the common law" such that "[t]rue reconciliation will, equally, place weight on each" (at paras. 49 and 50).

[82] In other words, although the doctrine of aboriginal rights is a common law doctrine, aboriginal rights are truly *sui generis*, and demand a unique approach to the treatment of evidence which accords due weight to the perspective of aboriginal peoples. However, that accommodation must be done in a manner which does not strain "the Canadian legal and constitutional structure" (at para. 49). … In practical terms, this requires the courts to come to terms with the oral histories of aboriginal societies, which, for many aboriginal nations, are the only record of their past.

· · ·

[86] Many features of oral histories would count against both their admissibility and their weight as evidence of prior events in a court that took a traditional approach to the rules of evidence. The most fundamental of these is their broad social role not only "as a repository of historical knowledge for a culture" but also as an expression of "the values and mores of [that] culture." … Dickson J (as he then was) recognized as much when he stated in *Kruger v. The Queen*, [1978] 1 SCR 104, at p. 109 [75 DLR (3d) 434], that "[c]laims to aboriginal title are woven with history, legend, politics and moral obligations." The difficulty with these features of oral histories is that they are tangential to the ultimate purpose of the fact-finding process at trial—the determination of the historical truth. Another feature of oral histories which creates difficulty is that they largely consist of out-of-court statements, passed on through an unbroken chain across the generations of a particular aboriginal nation to the present-day. These out-of-court statements are

admitted for their truth and therefore conflict with the general rule against the admissibility of hearsay.

[87] Notwithstanding the challenges created by the use of oral histories as proof of historical facts, the laws of evidence must be adapted in order that this type of evidence can be accommodated and placed on an equal footing with the types of historical evidence that courts are familiar with.

. . .

[107] The trial judge's treatment of the various kinds of oral histories did not satisfy the principles I laid down in *Van der Peet*. These errors are particularly worrisome because oral histories were of critical importance to the appellants' case. They used those histories in an attempt to establish their occupation and use of the disputed territory, an essential requirement for aboriginal title. The trial judge, after refusing to admit, or giving no independent weight to these oral histories, reached the conclusion that the appellants had not demonstrated the requisite degree of occupation for "ownership." Had the trial judge assessed the oral histories correctly, his conclusions on these issues of fact might have been very different.

[108] In the circumstances, the factual findings cannot stand. However, given the enormous complexity of the factual issues at hand, it would be impossible for the Court to do justice to the parties by sifting through the record itself and making new factual findings. A new trial is warranted, at which the evidence may be considered in light of the principles laid down in *Van der Peet* and elaborated upon here. In applying these principles, the new trial judge might well share some or all of the findings of fact of McEachern CJ.

C. What Is the Content of Aboriginal Title, How Is It Protected by Section 35(1) of the Constitution Act, 1982, and What Is Required for Its Proof?

(1) Introduction

[109] The parties … have … a fundamental disagreement over the content of aboriginal title itself, and its reception into the Constitution by s. 35(1). In order to give guidance to the judge at the new trial, it is to this issue that I will now turn.

[110] … I believe that all of the parties have characterized the content of aboriginal title incorrectly. …

[111] The content of aboriginal title … is a right in land and, as such, is more than the right to engage in specific activities which may be themselves aboriginal rights. … [I]t confers the right to use land for a variety of activities, not all of which need be aspects of practices, customs and traditions which are integral to the distinctive cultures of aboriginal societies. Those activities do not constitute the right *per se*; rather, they are parasitic on the underlying title. However, that range of uses is subject to the limitation that they must not be irreconcilable with the nature of the attachment to the land which forms the basis of the particular group's aboriginal title. This inherent limit … flows from the definition of aboriginal title as a *sui generis* interest in land, and is one way in which aboriginal title is distinct from a fee simple.

(2) Aboriginal Title at Common Law

(a) General Features

[112] … Aboriginal title has been described as *sui generis* in order to distinguish it from "normal" proprietary interests, such as fee simple. However, as I will now develop, it is also *sui generis* in the sense that its characteristics cannot be completely explained by reference either to the common law rules of real property or to the rules of property found in aboriginal legal systems. As with other aboriginal rights, it must be understood by reference to both common law and aboriginal perspectives.

[113] The idea that aboriginal title is *sui generis* is the unifying principle underlying the various dimensions of that title. One dimension is its *inalienability*. Lands held pursuant to aboriginal title cannot be transferred, sold or surrendered to anyone other than the Crown and, as a result, is inalienable to third parties. This Court has taken pains to clarify that aboriginal title is only "personal" in this sense, and does not mean that aboriginal title is a non-proprietary interest which amounts to no more than a licence to use and occupy the land and cannot compete on an equal footing with other proprietary interests: see *Canadian Pacific Ltd. v. Paul*, [1988] 2 SCR 654, at p. 677 [53 DLR (4th) 487].

[114] Another dimension of aboriginal title is its *source*. It had originally been thought that the source of aboriginal title in Canada was the *Royal Proclamation, 1763.* … However, it is now clear that although aboriginal title was recognized by the *Proclamation*, it arises from the prior occupation of Canada by aboriginal peoples. That prior occupation, however, is relevant in two different ways, both of which illustrate the *sui generis* nature of aboriginal title. The first is the physical fact of occupation, which derives from the common law principle that occupation is proof of possession in law. … Thus, in *Guerin* [*Guerin v. The Queen*, [1984] 2 SCR 335] Dickson J described aboriginal title, at p. 376, as a "legal right derived from the Indians' historic occupation and possession of their tribal lands." What makes aboriginal title *sui generis* is that it arises from possession *before* the assertion of British sovereignty, whereas normal estates, like fee simple, arise afterward. This idea has been further developed in *Roberts v. Canada*, [1989] 1 SCR 322, where this Court unanimously held at p. 340 that "aboriginal title predated colonization by the British and survived British claims of sovereignty." … What this suggests is a second source for aboriginal title—the relationship between common law and pre-existing systems of aboriginal law.

[115] A further dimension of aboriginal title is the fact that it is held *communally*. Aboriginal title cannot be held by individual aboriginal persons; it is a collective right to land held by all members of an aboriginal nation. Decisions with respect to that land are also made by that community. This is another feature of aboriginal title which is *sui generis* and distinguishes it from normal property interests.

(b) The Content of Aboriginal Title

[116] Although cases involving aboriginal title have come before this Court and Privy Council before, there has never been a definitive statement from either court on the *content* of aboriginal title. …

[117] Although the courts have been less than forthcoming, I have arrived at the conclusion that the content of aboriginal title can be summarized by two propositions:

first, that aboriginal title encompasses the right to exclusive use and occupation of the land held pursuant to that title for a variety of purposes, which need not be aspects of those aboriginal practices, customs and traditions which are integral to distinctive aboriginal cultures; and second, that those protected uses must not be irreconcilable with the nature of the group's attachment to that land. ...

ABORIGINAL TITLE ENCOMPASSES THE RIGHT TO USE THE LAND HELD PURSUANT TO THAT TITLE FOR A VARIETY OF PURPOSES, WHICH NEED NOT BE ASPECTS OF THOSE ABORIGINAL PRACTICES, CULTURES AND TRADITIONS WHICH ARE INTEGRAL TO DISTINCTIVE ABORIGINAL CULTURES

[118] The respondents argue that aboriginal title merely encompasses the right to engage in activities which are aspects of aboriginal practices, customs and traditions which are integral to distinctive aboriginal cultures of the aboriginal group claiming the right and, at most, adds the notion of exclusivity; i.e., the exclusive right to use the land for those purposes. However, the uses to which lands held pursuant to aboriginal title can be put are not restricted in this way. This conclusion emerges from three sources: (i) the Canadian jurisprudence on aboriginal title, (ii) the relationship between reserve lands and lands held pursuant to aboriginal title, and (iii) the *Indian Oil and Gas Act*, RSC, 1985, c. I-7. ...

(i) CANADIAN JURISPRUDENCE ON ABORIGINAL TITLE

[119] Despite the fact that the jurisprudence on aboriginal title is somewhat underdeveloped, it is clear that the uses to which lands held pursuant to aboriginal title can be put is not restricted to the practices, customs and traditions of aboriginal peoples integral to distinctive aboriginal cultures. In *Guerin*, for example, Dickson J described aboriginal title as an "interest in land" which encompassed "a legal right to occupy and possess certain lands" (at p. 382). The "right to occupy and possess" is framed in broad terms and, significantly, is not qualified by reference to traditional and customary uses of those lands. Any doubt that the right to occupancy and possession encompasses a broad variety of uses of land was put to rest in *Paul* [*Canadian Pacific Ltd. v. Paul*, [1988] 2 SCR 654, 53 DLR (4th) 487], where the Court went even further and stated that aboriginal title was "more than the right to enjoyment and occupancy" (at p. 678). Once again, there is no reference to aboriginal practices, customs and traditions as a qualifier on that right. Moreover, I take the reference to "more" as emphasis of the broad notion of use and possession.

(ii) RESERVE LAND

[120] Another source of support for the conclusion that the uses to which lands held under aboriginal title can be put are not restricted to those grounded in practices, customs and traditions integral to distinctive aboriginal cultures can be found in *Guerin*, where Dickson J stated at p. 379 that the same legal principles governed the aboriginal interest in reserve lands and lands held pursuant to aboriginal title. ...

[121] The nature of the Indian interest in reserve land is very broad, and can be found in s. 18 of the *Indian Act*, which I reproduce in full:

18.(1) Subject to this Act, reserves are held by Her Majesty for the *use and benefit* of the respective bands for which they were set apart ...

(2) The Minister may authorize the use of lands in a reserve for the purpose of Indian schools, the administration of Indian affairs, Indian burial grounds, Indian health projects or, with the consent of the council of the band, *for any other purpose for the general welfare of the band*, and may take any lands in a reserve required for those purposes ... . [Emphasis added.]

The principal provision is s. 18(1), which states that reserve lands are held "for the use and benefit" of the bands which occupy them; those uses and benefits, on the face of the *Indian Act*, do not appear to be restricted to practices, customs and traditions integral to distinctive aboriginal cultures. The breadth of those uses is reinforced by s. 18(2), which states that reserve lands may be used "for any other purpose for the general welfare of the band." The general welfare of the band has not been defined in terms of aboriginal practices, customs and traditions, nor in terms of those activities which have their origin pre-contact; it is a concept, by definition, which incorporates a reference to the present-day needs of aboriginal communities. On the basis of *Guerin*, lands held pursuant to aboriginal title, like reserve lands, are also capable of being used for a broad variety of purposes.

(iii) INDIAN OIL AND GAS ACT

[122] ... The overall purpose of the statute is to provide for the exploration of oil and gas on reserve lands through their surrender to the Crown. The statute presumes that the aboriginal interest in reserve land includes mineral rights, a point which this Court unanimously accepted with respect to the *Indian Act* in *Blueberry River Indian Band v. Canada*, [1995] 4 SCR 344. On the basis of *Guerin*, aboriginal title also encompass[es] mineral rights, and lands held pursuant to aboriginal title should be capable of exploitation in the same way, which is certainly not a traditional use for those lands. This conclusion is reinforced by s. 6(2) of the Act, which provides:

6.(2) Nothing in this Act shall be deemed to abrogate the rights of Indian people or preclude them from negotiating for oil and gas benefits in those areas in which land claims have not been settled.

The areas referred to in s. 6(2), at the very least, must encompass lands held pursuant to aboriginal title, since those lands by definition have not been surrendered under land claims agreements. The presumption underlying s. 6(2) is that aboriginal title permits the development of oil and gas reserves.

• • •

[124] In conclusion, the content of aboriginal title is not restricted to those uses which are elements of a practice, custom or tradition integral to the distinctive culture of the aboriginal group claiming the right. However, nor does aboriginal title amount to a form of inalienable fee simple, as I will now explain.

(c) Inherent Limit: Lands Held Pursuant to Aboriginal Title Cannot Be Used in a Manner That Is Irreconcilable with the Nature of the Attachment to the Land That Forms the Basis of the Group's Claim to Aboriginal Title

[125] The content of aboriginal title contains an inherent limit that lands held pursuant to title cannot be used in a manner that is irreconcilable with the nature of the claimants' attachment to those lands. This limit on the content of aboriginal title is a manifestation of the principle that underlies the various dimensions of that special interest in land—it is a *sui generis* interest that is distinct from "normal" proprietary interests, most notably fee simple.

[126] I arrive at this conclusion by reference to the other dimensions of aboriginal title which are *sui generis* as well. I first consider the source of aboriginal title. As I discussed earlier, aboriginal title arises from the prior occupation of Canada by aboriginal peoples. That prior occupation is relevant in two different ways: first, because of the physical fact of occupation, and second, because aboriginal title originates in part from pre-existing systems of aboriginal law. However, the law of aboriginal title does not only seek to determine the historic rights of aboriginal peoples to land; it also seeks to afford legal protection to prior occupation in the present-day. Implicit in the protection of historic patterns of occupation is a recognition of the importance of the continuity of the relationship of an aboriginal community to its land over time.

[127] ... The relevance of the continuity of the relationship of an aboriginal community with its land here is that it applies not only to the past, but to the future as well. That relationship should not be prevented from continuing into the future. As a result, uses of the lands that would threaten that future relationship are, by their very nature, excluded from the content of aboriginal title.

[128] Accordingly, in my view, lands subject to aboriginal title cannot be put to such uses as may be irreconcilable with the nature of the occupation of that land and the relationship that the particular group has had with the land which together have given rise to aboriginal title in the first place. As discussed below, one of the critical elements in the determination of whether a particular aboriginal group has aboriginal title to certain lands is the matter of the occupancy of those lands. Occupancy is determined by reference to the activities that have taken place on the land and the uses to which the land has been put by the particular group. If lands are so occupied, there will exist a special bond between the group and the land in question such that the land will be part of the definition of the group's distinctive culture. It seems to me that these elements of aboriginal title create an inherent limitation on the uses to which the land, over which such title exists, may be put. For example, if occupation is established with reference to the use of the land as a hunting ground, then the group that successfully claims aboriginal title to that land may not use it in such a fashion as to destroy its value for such a use (e.g., by strip mining it). Similarly, if a group claims a special bond with the land because of its ceremonial or cultural significance, it may not use the land in such a way as to destroy that relationship (e.g., by developing it in such a way that the bond is destroyed, perhaps by turning it into a parking lot).

[129] It is for this reason also that lands held by virtue of aboriginal title may not be alienated. Alienation would bring to an end the entitlement of the aboriginal people to

occupy the land and would terminate their relationship with it. I have suggested above that the inalienability of aboriginal lands is, at least in part, a function of the common law principle that settlers in colonies must derive their title from Crown grant and, therefore, cannot acquire title through purchase from aboriginal inhabitants. It is also, again only in part, a function of a general policy "to ensure that Indians are not dispossessed of their entitlements." ... What the inalienability of lands held pursuant to aboriginal title suggests is that those lands are more than just a fungible commodity. The relationship between an aboriginal community and the lands over which it has aboriginal title has an important non-economic component. The land has an inherent and unique value in itself, which is enjoyed by the community with aboriginal title to it. The community cannot put the land to uses which would destroy that value.

· · ·

[131] [T]he continuity of the relationship between an aboriginal community and its land, and the non-economic or inherent value of that land, should not be taken to detract from the possibility of surrender to the Crown in exchange for valuable consideration. On the contrary, the idea of surrender reinforces the conclusion that aboriginal title is limited in the way I have described. If aboriginal peoples wish to use their lands in a way that aboriginal title does not permit, then they must surrender those lands and convert them into non-title lands to do so. ...

[132] This is not, I must emphasize, a limitation that restricts the use of the land to those activities that have traditionally been carried out on it. That would amount to a legal straitjacket on aboriginal peoples who have a legitimate legal claim to the land. The approach I have outlined above allows for a full range of uses of the land, subject only to an overarching limit, defined by the special nature of the aboriginal title in that land.

(d) Aboriginal Title Under Section 35(1) of the Constitution Act, 1982

[133] ... On a plain reading of the provision, s. 35(1) did not create aboriginal rights; rather, it accorded constitutional status to those rights which were "existing" in 1982. The provision, at the very least, constitutionalized those rights which aboriginal peoples possessed at common law, since those rights existed at the time s. 35(1) came into force. Since aboriginal title was a common law right whose existence was recognized well before 1982 (e.g., *Calder, supra*), s. 35(1) has constitutionalized it in its full form.

· · ·

[136] I hasten to add that the constitutionalization of common law aboriginal rights by s. 35(1) does not mean that those rights exhaust the content of s. 35(1). ... [T]he existence of a particular aboriginal right at common law is not a *sine qua non* for the proof of an aboriginal right that is recognized and affirmed by s. 35(1). Indeed, none of the decisions of this Court handed down under s. 35(1) in which the existence of an aboriginal right has been demonstrated has relied on the existence of that right at common law. The existence of an aboriginal right at common law is therefore sufficient, but not necessary, for the recognition and affirmation of that right by s. 35(1).

[137] The acknowledgement that s. 35(1) has accorded constitutional status to common law aboriginal title raises a further question—the relationship of aboriginal title to the "aboriginal rights" protected by s. 35(1). I addressed that question in *Adams* [*R v.*, [1996] 3 SCR 101], where the Court had been presented with two radically different

conceptions of this relationship. The first conceived of aboriginal rights as being "inherently based in aboriginal title to the land" (at para. 25), or as fragments of a broader claim to aboriginal title. By implication, aboriginal rights must rest either in a claim to title or the unextinguished remnants of title. Taken to its logical extreme, this suggests that aboriginal title is merely the sum of a set of individual aboriginal rights, and that it therefore has no independent content. However, I rejected this position for another— that aboriginal title is "simply one manifestation of a broader-based conception of aboriginal rights" (at para. 25). Thus, although aboriginal title is a species of aboriginal right recognized and affirmed by s. 35(1), it is distinct from other aboriginal rights because it arises where the connection of a group with a piece of land "was of a central significance to their distinctive culture" (at para. 26).

[138] The picture which emerges from *Adams* is that the aboriginal rights which are recognized and affirmed by s. 35(1) fall along a spectrum with respect to their degree of connection with the land. At the one end, there are those aboriginal rights which are practices, customs and traditions that are integral to the distinctive aboriginal culture of the group claiming the right. However, the *"occupation and use of the land"* where the activity is taking place is not *"sufficient to support a claim of title to the land"* (at para. 26 (emphasis in original)). Nevertheless, those activities receive constitutional protection. In the middle, there are activities which, out of necessity, take place on land and indeed, might be intimately related to a particular piece of land. Although an aboriginal group may not be able to demonstrate title to the land, it may nevertheless have a site-specific right to engage in a particular activity. I put the point this way in *Adams*, at para. 30:

> Even where an aboriginal right exists on a tract of land to which the aboriginal people in question do not have title, that right may well be site specific, with the result that it can be exercised only upon that specific tract of land. For example, *if an aboriginal people demonstrates that hunting on a specific tract of land was an integral part of their distinctive culture then, even if the right exists apart from title to that tract of land, the aboriginal right to hunt is nonetheless defined as, and limited to, the right to hunt on the specific tract of land.* [Emphasis added.]

At the other end of the spectrum, there is aboriginal title itself. As *Adams* makes clear, aboriginal title confers more than the right to engage in site-specific activities which are aspects of the practices, customs and traditions of distinctive aboriginal cultures. Site-specific rights can be made out even if title cannot. What aboriginal title confers is the right to the land itself.

[139] Because aboriginal rights can vary with respect to their degree of connection with the land, some aboriginal groups may be unable to make out a claim to title, but will nevertheless possess aboriginal rights that are recognized and affirmed by s. 35(1), including site-specific rights to engage in particular activities. As I explained in *Adams*, this may occur in the case of nomadic peoples who varied "the location of their settlements with the season and changing circumstances" (at para. 27). The fact that aboriginal peoples were non-sedentary, however (at para. 27)

does not alter the fact that nomadic peoples survived through reliance on the land prior to contact with Europeans and, further, that many of the practices, customs and traditions of nomadic peoples that took place on the land were integral to their distinctive cultures.

(e) Proof of Aboriginal Title

(i) INTRODUCTION

[140] ... To date, the Court has defined aboriginal rights in terms of *activities*. As I said in *Van der Peet* (at para. 46):

> [I]n order to be an aboriginal right an *activity* must be an element of a practice, custom or tradition integral to the distinctive culture of the aboriginal group claiming the right. [Emphasis added.]

Aboriginal title, however, is a *right to the land* itself. ...

[141] This difference between aboriginal rights to engage in particular activities and aboriginal title requires that the test I laid down in *Van der Peet* be adapted accordingly. ... Since the purpose of s. 35(1) is to reconcile the prior presence of aboriginal peoples in North America with the assertion of Crown sovereignty, it is clear from this statement that s. 35(1) must recognize and affirm both aspects of that prior presence—first, the occupation of land, and second, the prior social organization and distinctive cultures of aboriginal peoples on that land. To date the jurisprudence under s. 35(1) has given more emphasis to the second aspect. ...

[142] The adaptation of the test laid down in *Van der Peet* to suit claims to title must be understood as the recognition of the first aspect of that prior presence. ...

(ii) THE TEST FOR THE PROOF OF ABORIGINAL TITLE

[143] In order to make out a claim for aboriginal title, the aboriginal group asserting title must satisfy the following criteria: (i) the land must have been occupied prior to sovereignty, (ii) if present occupation is relied on as proof of occupation pre-sovereignty, there must be a continuity between present and pre-sovereignty occupation, and (iii) at sovereignty, that occupation must have been exclusive.

THE LAND MUST HAVE BEEN OCCUPIED PRIOR TO SOVEREIGNTY

[144] In order to establish a claim to aboriginal title, the aboriginal group asserting the claim must establish that it occupied the lands in question at the *time at which the Crown asserted sovereignty over the land subject to the title*. ...

[145] ... [I]n the context of aboriginal title, sovereignty is the appropriate time period to consider for several reasons. First, from a theoretical standpoint, aboriginal title arises out of prior occupation of the land by aboriginal peoples and out of the relationship between the common law and pre-existing systems of aboriginal law. Aboriginal title is a burden on the Crown's underlying title. However, the Crown did not gain this title until it asserted sovereignty over the land in question. Because it does not make sense to speak of a burden on the underlying title before that title existed, aboriginal title crystallized at the time sovereignty was asserted. Second, aboriginal title does not raise the problem of distinguishing between distinctive, integral aboriginal practices, customs and

traditions and those influenced or introduced by European contact. Under common law, the act of occupation or possession is sufficient to ground aboriginal title and it is not necessary to prove that the land was a distinctive or integral part of the aboriginal society before the arrival of Europeans. Finally, from a practical standpoint, it appears that the date of sovereignty is more certain than the date of first contact. It is often very difficult to determine the precise moment that each aboriginal group had first contact with European culture. ... For these reasons, I conclude that aboriginals must establish occupation of the land from the date of the assertion of sovereignty in order to sustain a claim for aboriginal title. McEachern CJ found, at pp. 233-34, and the parties did not dispute on appeal, that British sovereignty over British Columbia was conclusively established by the Oregon Boundary Treaty of 1846. This is not to say that circumstances subsequent to sovereignty may never be relevant to title or compensation; this might be the case, for example, where native bands have been dispossessed of traditional lands after sovereignty.

[146] There was a consensus among the parties on appeal that proof of historic occupation was required to make out a claim to aboriginal title. However, the parties disagreed on how that occupancy could be proved. ... This debate over the proof of occupancy reflects two divergent views of the source of aboriginal title. The respondents argue, in essence, that aboriginal title arises from the physical reality at the time of sovereignty, whereas the Gitksan effectively take the position that aboriginal title arises from and should reflect the pattern of land holdings under aboriginal law. However, as I have explained above, the source of aboriginal title appears to be grounded both in the common law and in the aboriginal perspective on land; the latter includes, but is not limited to, their systems of law. It follows that both should be taken into account in establishing the proof of occupancy.

· · ·

[148] This approach to the proof of occupancy at common law is also mandated in the context of s. 35(1) by *Van der Peet*. In that decision, as I stated above, I held at para. 50 that the reconciliation of the prior occupation of North America by aboriginal peoples with the assertion of Crown sovereignty required that account be taken of the "aboriginal perspective while at the same time taking into account the perspective of the common law" and that "[t]rue reconciliation will, equally, place weight on each." I also held that the aboriginal perspective on the occupation of their lands can be gleaned, in part, but not exclusively, from their traditional laws, because those laws were elements of the practices, customs and traditions of aboriginal peoples: at para. 41. As a result, if, at the time of sovereignty, an aboriginal society had laws in relation to land, those laws would be relevant to establishing the occupation of lands which are the subject of a claim for aboriginal title. Relevant laws might include, but are not limited to, a land tenure system or laws governing land use.

[149] However, the aboriginal perspective must be taken into account alongside the perspective of the common law. Professor McNeil has convincingly argued that at common law, the fact of physical occupation is proof of possession at law, which in turn will ground title to the land: *Common Law Aboriginal Title* (Oxford: Clarendon Press, 1989) at p. 73. ... Physical occupation may be established in a variety of ways, ranging from the construction of dwellings through cultivation and enclosure of fields to regular use of definite tracts of land for hunting, fishing or otherwise exploiting its resources. ... In

considering whether occupation sufficient to ground title is established, "one must take into account the group's size, manner of life, material resources, and technological abilities, and the character of the lands claimed": Brian Slattery, "Understanding Aboriginal Rights," [(1987), 66 *Canadian Bar Review* 727] at p. 758.

[150] In *Van der Peet*, I drew a distinction between those practices, customs and traditions of aboriginal peoples which were "an aspect of, or took place in" the society of the aboriginal group asserting the claim and those which were "a central and significant part of the society's distinctive culture" (at para. 55). The latter stood apart because they "made the culture of the society distinctive ... it was one of the things that truly *made the society what it was*" (at para. 55, emphasis in original). The same requirement operates in the determination of the proof of aboriginal title. As I said in *Adams*, a claim to title is made out when a group can demonstrate "that their connection with the piece of land ... was of a central significance to their distinctive culture" (at para. 26).

[151] ... [I]n the case of title, it would seem clear that any land that was occupied pre-sovereignty, and which the parties have maintained a substantial connection with since then, is sufficiently important to be of central significance to the culture of the claimants. As a result, I do not think it is necessary to include explicitly this element as part of the test for aboriginal title.

IF PRESENT OCCUPATION IS RELIED ON AS PROOF OF OCCUPATION PRE-SOVEREIGNTY, THERE MUST BE A CONTINUITY BETWEEN PRESENT AND PRE-SOVEREIGNTY OCCUPATION

[152] ... Conclusive evidence of pre-sovereignty occupation may be difficult to come by. Instead, an aboriginal community may provide evidence of present occupation as proof of pre-sovereignty occupation in support of a claim to aboriginal title. What is required, in addition, is a *continuity* between present and pre-sovereignty occupation, because the relevant time for the determination of aboriginal title is at the time before sovereignty.

[153] Needless to say, there is no need to establish "an unbroken chain of continuity" (*Van der Peet*, at para. 65) between present and prior occupation. The occupation and use of lands may have been disrupted for a time, perhaps as a result of the unwillingness of European colonizers to recognize aboriginal title. To impose the requirement of continuity too strictly would risk "undermining the very purpose of s. 35(1) by perpetuating the historical injustice suffered by aboriginal peoples at the hands of colonizers who failed to respect" aboriginal rights to land (*Côté, supra*, at para. 53). In *Mabo* [*Mabo v. Queensland* (1992), 107 ALR 1], the High Court of Australia set down the requirement that there must be "substantial maintenance of the connection" between the people and the land. In my view, this test should be equally applicable to proof of title in Canada. ...

[154] I should also note that there is a strong possibility that the precise nature of occupation will have changed between the time of sovereignty and the present. I would like to make it clear that the fact that the nature of occupation has changed would not ordinarily preclude a claim for aboriginal title, as long as a substantial connection between the people and the land is maintained. ...

AT SOVEREIGNTY, OCCUPATION MUST HAVE BEEN EXCLUSIVE

[155] Finally, at sovereignty, occupation must have been exclusive. The requirement for exclusivity flows from the definition of aboriginal title itself, because I have defined aboriginal title in terms of the right to *exclusive* use and occupation of land. Exclusivity, as an aspect of aboriginal title, vests in the aboriginal community which holds the ability to exclude others from the lands held pursuant to that title. The proof of title must, in this respect, mirror the content of the right. Were it possible to prove title without demonstrating exclusive occupation, the result would be absurd, because it would be possible for more than one aboriginal nation to have aboriginal title over the same piece of land, and then for all of them to attempt to assert the right to exclusive use and occupation over it.

[156] As with the proof of occupation, proof of exclusivity must rely on both the perspective of the common law and the aboriginal perspective, placing equal weight on each. ... Exclusivity is a common law principle derived from the notion of fee simple ownership and should be imported into the concept of aboriginal title with caution. As such, the test required to establish exclusive occupation must take into account the context of the aboriginal society at the time of sovereignty. For example, it is important to note that exclusive occupation can be demonstrated even if other aboriginal groups were present, or frequented the claimed lands. Under those circumstances, exclusivity would be demonstrated by "the intention and capacity to retain exclusive control" ... Thus, an act of trespass, if isolated, would not undermine a general finding of exclusivity, if aboriginal groups intended to and attempted to enforce their exclusive occupation. Moreover ... the presence of other aboriginal groups might actually reinforce a finding of exclusivity. For example, "[w]here others were allowed access upon request, the very fact that permission was asked for and given would be further evidence of the group's exclusive control" (at p. 204).

[157] A consideration of the aboriginal perspective may also lead to the conclusion that trespass by other aboriginal groups does not undermine, and that presence of those groups by permission may reinforce, the exclusive occupation of the aboriginal group asserting title. For example, the aboriginal group asserting the claim to aboriginal title may have trespass laws which are proof of exclusive occupation, such that the presence of trespassers does not count as evidence against exclusivity. As well, aboriginal laws under which permission may be granted to other aboriginal groups to use or reside even temporarily on land would reinforce the finding of exclusive occupation. Indeed, if that permission were the subject of treaties between the aboriginal nations in question, those treaties would also form part of the aboriginal perspective. ...

[158] In their submissions, the appellants pressed the point that requiring proof of exclusive occupation might preclude a finding of joint title, which is shared between two or more aboriginal nations. ... I would suggest that the requirement of exclusive occupancy and the possibility of joint title could be reconciled by recognizing that joint title could arise from shared exclusivity. ... There clearly may be cases in which two aboriginal nations lived on a particular piece of land and recognized each other's entitlement to that land but nobody else's. However, since no claim to joint title has been asserted here, I leave it to another day to work out all the complexities and implications of joint title, as well as any limits that another band's title may have on the way in which one band uses

its title lands. ... In my opinion, this accords with the general principle that the common law should develop to recognize aboriginal rights (and title, when necessary) as they were recognized by either *de facto* practice or by the aboriginal system of governance. It also allows sufficient flexibility to deal with this highly complex and rapidly evolving area of the law.

. . .

(f) Infringements of Aboriginal Title: The Test of Justification

[160] The aboriginal rights recognized and affirmed by s. 35(1), including aboriginal title, are not absolute. Those rights may be infringed, both by the federal (e.g., *Sparrow*) and provincial (e.g., *Côté*) governments. ...

[A review of authorities is omitted.]

(iii) JUSTIFICATION AND ABORIGINAL TITLE

[165] ... The general principles governing justification laid down in *Sparrow*, and embellished by *Gladstone*, operate with respect to infringements of aboriginal title. In the wake of *Gladstone*, the range of legislative objectives that can justify the infringement of aboriginal title is fairly broad. Most of these objectives can be traced to the *reconciliation* of the prior occupation of North America by aboriginal peoples with the assertion of Crown sovereignty, which entails the recognition that "distinctive aboriginal societies exist within, and are a part of, a broader social, political and economic community" (at para. 73). In my opinion, the development of agriculture, forestry, mining, and hydro-electric power, the general economic development of the interior of British Columbia, protection of the environment or endangered species, the building of infrastructure and the settlement of foreign populations to support those aims, are the kinds of objectives that are consistent with this purpose and, in principle, can justify the infringement of aboriginal title. ...

[166] The manner in which the fiduciary duty operates with respect to the second stage of the justification test—both with respect to the standard of scrutiny and the particular form that the fiduciary duty will take—will be a function of the nature of aboriginal title. Three aspects of aboriginal title are relevant here. First, aboriginal title encompasses the right to *exclusive* use and occupation of land; second, aboriginal title encompasses *the right to choose* to what uses land can be put, subject to the ultimate limit that those uses cannot destroy the ability of the land to sustain future generations of aboriginal peoples; and third, that lands held pursuant to aboriginal title have an inescapable *economic component*.

[167] The exclusive nature of aboriginal title is relevant to the degree of scrutiny of the infringing measure or action. For example, if the Crown's fiduciary duty requires that aboriginal title be given priority, then it is the altered approach to priority that I laid down in *Gladstone* which should apply. What is required is that the government demonstrate (at para. 62) "both that the process by which it allocated the resource and the actual allocation of the resource which results from that process reflect the prior interest" of the holders of aboriginal title in the land. By analogy with *Gladstone*, this might entail, for example, that governments accommodate the participation of aboriginal peoples in the

development of the resources of British Columbia, that the conferral of fee simples for agriculture, and of leases and licences for forestry and mining reflect the prior occupation of aboriginal title lands, that economic barriers to aboriginal uses of their lands (e.g., licensing fees) be somewhat reduced. This list is illustrative and not exhaustive. ...

[168] Moreover, the other aspects of aboriginal title suggest that the fiduciary duty may be articulated in a manner different than the idea of priority. This point becomes clear from a comparison between aboriginal title and the aboriginal right to fish for food in *Sparrow*. First, aboriginal title encompasses within it a right to choose to what ends a piece of land can be put. The aboriginal right to fish for food, by contrast, does not contain within it the same discretionary component. This aspect of aboriginal title suggests that the fiduciary relationship between the Crown and aboriginal peoples may be satisfied by the involvement of aboriginal peoples in decisions taken with respect to their lands. There is always a duty of consultation. Whether the aboriginal group has been consulted is relevant to determining whether the infringement of aboriginal title is justified. ... The nature and scope of the duty of consultation will vary with the circumstances. In occasional cases, when the breach is less serious or relatively minor, it will be no more than a duty to discuss important decisions that will be taken with respect to lands held pursuant to aboriginal title. Of course, even in these rare cases when the minimum acceptable standard is consultation, this consultation must be in good faith, and with the intention of substantially addressing the concerns of the aboriginal peoples whose lands are at issue. In most cases, it will be significantly deeper than mere consultation. Some cases may even require the full consent of an aboriginal nation, particularly when provinces enact hunting and fishing regulations in relation to aboriginal lands.

[169] Second, aboriginal title, unlike the aboriginal right to fish for food, has an inescapably economic aspect, particularly when one takes into account the modern uses to which lands held pursuant to aboriginal title can be put. The economic aspect of aboriginal title suggests that compensation is relevant to the question of justification as well, a possibility suggested in *Sparrow* and which I repeated in *Gladstone*. Indeed, compensation for breaches of fiduciary duty are a well-established part of the landscape of aboriginal rights: *Guerin*. In keeping with the duty of honour and good faith on the Crown, fair compensation will ordinarily be required when aboriginal title is infringed. The amount of compensation payable will vary with the nature of the particular aboriginal title affected and with the nature and severity of the infringement and the extent to which aboriginal interests were accommodated. Since the issue of damages was severed from the principal action, we received no submissions on the appropriate legal principles that would be relevant to determining the appropriate level of compensation of infringements of aboriginal title. In the circumstances, it is best that we leave those difficult questions to another day.

[A discussion of the Aboriginal right of self-government and the extinguishment of aboriginal title is omitted. A discussion of the relationship between s. 35(1) and the distribution of legislative authority is also omitted but is reproduced later in this chapter.]

[184] For the reasons I have given above, I would allow the appeal in part, and dismiss the cross-appeal. Reluctantly, I would also order a new trial.

• • •

[186] Finally, this litigation has been both long and expensive, not only in economic but in human terms as well. By ordering a new trial, I do not necessarily encourage the parties to proceed to litigation and to settle their dispute through the courts. As was said in *Sparrow*, at p. 1105, s. 35(1) "provides a solid constitutional base upon which subsequent negotiations can take place." Those negotiations should also include other aboriginal nations which have a stake in the territory claimed. Moreover, the Crown is under a moral, if not a legal, duty to enter into and conduct those negotiations in good faith. Ultimately, it is through negotiated settlements, with good faith and give and take on all sides, reinforced by the judgments of this Court, that we will achieve ... a basic purpose of s. 35(1)—"the reconciliation of the pre-existence of aboriginal societies with the sovereignty of the Crown." Let us face it, we are all here to stay.

[La Forest J (L'Heureux-Dubé J concurring) wrote separate reasons agreeing with Lamer CJC's conclusion, but disagreeing with the methodology used to determine the possession of Aboriginal title.]

Appeal allowed (in part) and cross-appeal dismissed.

NOTES AND QUESTIONS

1. In *Delgamuukw*, the Court held that "lands subject to aboriginal title cannot be put to such uses as may be irreconcilable with the nature of the occupation of that land and the relationship that the particular group has had with the land which together have given rise to aboriginal title in the first place." The Court also observed that the inherent limit on Aboriginal title does not amount to "a limitation that restricts the use of the land to those activities that have traditionally been carried out on it. That would amount to a legal straitjacket on Aboriginal peoples who have a legitimate legal claim to the land." How are these two propositions reconciled, especially when it seems as if the determination of what constitutes an inherent limit on the use of Aboriginal title lands will have reference to traditional Aboriginal uses of land?

2. The *Delgamuukw* case set out a test for the proof of Aboriginal title that revolves around the date of the assertion of British sovereignty. The Court wrote: "Because it does not make sense to speak of a burden on the underlying title before that title existed, aboriginal title crystallized at the time sovereignty was asserted." How does Crown sovereignty "crystallize" Aboriginal title? Why should sovereignty be the relevant date for proof of title, and contact be the crucial date for the proof of other Aboriginal rights (as held in *Van der Peet*)? Could other dates be just as appropriately cited for the proof of title or rights; for example, Confederation or the date of a province's union with Canada, or even 1982, when s. 35 was enacted? Furthermore, what is the justification for Crown sovereignty as the measure of Aboriginal rights, and why should Aboriginal peoples have the burden of proof in showing their title or rights when they were there first?

3. In *R v. Marshall; R v. Bernard*, 2005 SCC 43, 2 SCR 220, 255 DLR (4th) 1, the Supreme Court of Canada upheld the convictions of members of the Mi'kmaq nation in Nova Scotia who harvested timber on Crown lands without authorization. In her reasons, McLachlin CJC,

for a majority of the Court, elaborated on Lamer CJC's holding in *Delgamuukw* that one must prove "exclusive" pre-sovereignty "occupation" of the land in order to establish a valid claim of Aboriginal title:

> [56] "Occupation" means "physical occupation." This "may be established in a variety of ways, ranging from the construction of dwellings through cultivation and enclosure of fields to regular use of definite tracts of land for hunting, fishing or otherwise exploiting its resources": *Delgamuukw*, per Lamer CJ, at para. 149.
>
> [57] "Exclusive" occupation flows from the definition of aboriginal title as "the right to *exclusive* use and occupation of land": *Delgamuukw*, per Lamer CJ, at para. 155 (emphasis in original). It is consistent with the concept of title to land at common law. Exclusive occupation means "the intention and capacity to retain exclusive control," and is not negated by occasional acts of trespass or the presence of other aboriginal groups with consent: (*Delgamuukw*, at para. 156, citing McNeil, at p. 204). Shared exclusivity may result in joint title (para. 158). Non-exclusive occupation may establish aboriginal rights "short of title" (para. 159).
>
> [58] It follows from the requirement of exclusive occupation that exploiting the land, rivers or seaside for hunting, fishing or other resources may translate into aboriginal title to the land if the activity was sufficiently regular and exclusive to comport with title at common law. However, more typically, seasonal hunting and fishing rights exercised in a particular area will translate to a hunting or fishing right. This is plain from this Court's decisions in *Van der Peet*, *Nikal*, *Adams* and *Côté*. In those cases, aboriginal peoples asserted and proved ancestral utilization of particular sites for fishing and harvesting the products of the sea. Their forebears had come back to the same place to fish or harvest each year since time immemorial. However, the season over, they left, and the land could be traversed and used by anyone. These facts gave rise not to aboriginal title, but to aboriginal hunting and fishing rights.
>
> • • •
>
> [61] The common law, over the centuries, has formalized title through a complicated matrix of legal edicts and conventions. The search for aboriginal title, by contrast, takes us back to the beginnings of the notion of title. Unaided by formal legal documents and written edicts, we are required to consider whether the practices of aboriginal peoples at the time of sovereignty compare with the core notions of common law title to land. It would be wrong to look for indicia of aboriginal title in deeds or Euro-centric assertions of ownership. Rather, we must look for the equivalent in the aboriginal culture at issue.
>
> [62] Aboriginal societies were not strangers to the notions of exclusive physical possession equivalent to common law notions of title: *Delgamuukw*, at para. 156. They often exercised such control over their village sites and larger areas of land which they exploited for agriculture, hunting, fishing or gathering. The question is whether the evidence here establishes this sort of possession.
>
> [63] Having laid out the broad picture, it may be useful to examine more closely three issues that evoked particular discussion here ... .
>
> [64] The first of these sub-issues is the concept of exclusion. The right to control the land and if necessary to exclude others from using it is basic to the notion of title at common law. In European-based systems, this right is assumed by dint of law. Determining whether it was present in a pre-sovereignty aboriginal society, however, can pose difficulties. Often, no right to exclude arises by convention or law. So one must look to evidence. But evidence may be hard to

find. The area may have been sparsely populated, with the result that clashes and the need to exclude strangers seldom if ever occurred. Or the people may have been peaceful and have chosen to exercise their control by sharing rather than exclusion. It is therefore critical to view the question of exclusion from the aboriginal perspective. To insist on evidence of overt acts of exclusion in such circumstances may, depending on the circumstances, be unfair. The problem is compounded by the difficulty of producing evidence of what happened hundreds of years ago where no tradition of written history exists.

[65] It follows that evidence of acts of exclusion is not required to establish aboriginal title. All that is required is demonstration of effective control of the land by the group, from which a reasonable inference can be drawn that it could have excluded others had it chosen to do so. The fact that history, insofar as it can be ascertained, discloses no adverse claimants may support this inference. This is what is meant by the requirement of aboriginal title that the lands have been occupied in an exclusive manner.

[66] The second sub-issue is whether nomadic and semi-nomadic peoples can ever claim title to aboriginal land, as distinguished from rights to use the land in traditional ways. The answer is that it depends on the evidence. As noted above, possession at common law is a contextual, nuanced concept. Whether a nomadic people enjoyed sufficient "physical possession" to give them title to the land, is a question of fact, depending on all the circumstances, in particular the nature of the land and the manner in which it is commonly used. Not every nomadic passage or use will ground title to land; thus this Court in *Adams* asserts that one of the reasons that aboriginal rights cannot be dependent on aboriginal title is that this would deny any aboriginal rights to nomadic peoples (at para. 27). On the other hand, *Delgamuukw* contemplates that "physical occupation" sufficient to ground title to land may be established by "regular use of definite tracts of land for hunting, fishing or otherwise exploiting its resources" (para. 149). In each case, the question is whether a degree of physical occupation or use equivalent to common law title has been made out.

[67] The third sub-issue is continuity. The requirement of continuity in its most basic sense simply means that claimants must establish they are right holders. Modern-day claimants must establish a connection with the pre-sovereignty group upon whose practices they rely to assert title or claim to a more restricted aboriginal right. The right is based on pre-sovereignty aboriginal practices. To claim it, a modern people must show that the right is the descendant of those practices. Continuity may also be raised in this sense. To claim title, the group's connection with the land must be shown, to have been "of a central significance to their distinctive culture": *Adams*, at para. 26. If the group has "maintained a substantial connection" with the land since sovereignty, this establishes the required "central significance": *Delgamuukw*, per Lamer CJ, at paras. 150-51.

[68] Underlying all these issues is the need for a sensitive and generous approach to the evidence tendered to establish aboriginal rights, be they the right to title or lesser rights to fish, hunt or gather. Aboriginal peoples did not write down events in their pre-sovereignty histories. Therefore, orally transmitted history must be accepted, provided the conditions of usefulness and reasonable reliability set out in *Mitchell v. MNR*, [2001] 1 SCR 911, 2001 SCC 33 [199 DLR (4th) 385], are respected. Usefulness asks whether the oral history provides evidence that would not otherwise be available or evidence of the aboriginal perspective on the right claimed. Reasonable reliability ensures that the witness represents a credible source of the particular people's

history. In determining the usefulness and reliability of oral histories, judges must resist facile assumptions based on Eurocentric traditions of gathering and passing on historical facts.

[69] The evidence, oral and documentary, must be evaluated from the aboriginal perspective. What would a certain practice or event have signified in their world and value system? Having evaluated the evidence, the final step is to translate the facts found and thus interpreted into a modern common law right. The right must be accurately delineated in a way that reflects common law traditions, while respecting the aboriginal perspective.

4. In *Delgamuukw*, Lamer CJC provided an extensive list of activities that could constitute the infringement of Aboriginal title. He wrote that "In my opinion, the development of agriculture, forestry, mining, and hydroelectric power, the general economic development of the interior of British Columbia, protection of the environment or endangered species, the building of infrastructure and the settlement of foreign populations to support those aims, are the kinds of objectives that are consistent with this purpose and, in principle, can justify the infringement of aboriginal title." Do these actions merely infringe Aboriginal title, or could some of these activities be tantamount to an extinguishment of Aboriginal title?

V. TREATY RIGHTS

Section 35(1) of the *Constitution Act, 1982* protects two broad classes of rights: Aboriginal and *treaty* rights. By and large, treaty making in Canada can be divided into three eras: pre-Confederation, post-Confederation, and modern treaties. From 1764 until 1867 there were approximately 375 treaties between the British Crown and First Nations. From 1867 until 1923 there were approximately another 150 treaties between the Crown and indigenous peoples north of the 49th parallel. Finally, starting in 1973 with the James Bay and Northern Quebec Agreement, there have been another 16 so-called modern treaties between First Nations and Canada. Each of these historical eras had its own social, economic, and political distinctiveness that must be considered in order to approach a satisfactory understanding of the treaties signed within these eras. For example, Aboriginal peoples had relatively greater bargaining power prior to Confederation, though this slowly began waning between 1814 and 1867. In the period after Confederation, particularly with the numbered treaties on the prairies, the Crown took a more dominant role in the negotiations, though they never fully succeeded in overwhelming the agency of Aboriginal peoples in this period. Last, in the modern era, First Nations have seen their power somewhat expand relative to the era immediately prior, and thus they have been able to realize a growing influence in the negotiation of treaties.

Patrick Macklem, "First Nations Self-Government and the Borders of the Canadian Legal Imagination"
(1991), 36 *McGill Law Journal* 382, at 428-29 (footnotes omitted)

With respect to the legal status of treaties, treaty rights [prior to 1982 were] imagined in law in such a way as to render them either unenforceable or enforceable only against state inaction. More specifically, judicial attitudes toward the legal status of treaties entered into by native peoples and the Crown historically has involved a shift from an approach that imagines native people as different than, and inferior to, non-native people, toward an approach that imagines native people as the same as non-native people and therefore not worthy of special consideration. The earlier approach viewed agreements between the Crown and native peoples as essentially political agreements not enforceable in a court of law. Traditional international law principles provide that an agreement between two "independent powers" constitutes a treaty binding on the parties to the agreement. Courts viewed native people as "uncivilized" and as belonging to an inferior race and thus agreements between native peoples and the Crown were not binding on the Crown in law. Contemporary jurisprudence has rejected the view that native people are different than, and inferior to, non-native people, with the result being that treaties are elevated from the level of nonbinding political agreement to that of contractual right. Native people are imagined under this approach as possessing legal personality similar to that possessed by non-native people in Canada and therefore capable of entering into binding agreements with the Crown. Because such agreements are not viewed as anything more than contractual agreements with the Crown, despite exhortations by the courts that treaties are "unique," they are seen as subject to legislative authority. Prior to 1982, this had the effect of permitting Parliament to regulate or extinguish existing treaty rights.

With respect to judicial interpretation of the content of treaty guarantees, there has been a shift in the opposite direction, namely, toward the embrace of native difference. More specifically, early judicial pronouncements on the content of treaty guarantees were blind to native cultural difference. Treaty rights historically were rendered concrete and given determinate meaning by reference to Anglo-Canadian public and private law norms and values. The "plain meaning" of a treaty guarantee was determined by a process that accepted without question the legitimacy of basic categories of Anglo-Canadian legal consciousness. This resulted in expansive definitions of the meaning of land surrenders and narrow interpretations of treaty benefits flowing to native people. Recent jurisprudence is more sensitive to native expectations about treaty negotiation and thus is more accommodating of native difference. This shift has resulted in more expansive definitions of treaty benefits to native people, though the meaning of land surrenders effected by treaty continues to be steeped in Anglo-Canadian notions concerning title and transfer.

In *R v. Sioui*, [1990] 1 SCR 1025, 70 DLR (4th) 427, at issue was the constitutionality of actions of members of the Huron nation on the Lorette Indian reserve in Quebec. They were convicted of cutting down trees, camping, and making fires in a provincial park, contrary to provincial legislation. They alleged that they were engaged in ancestral customs and religious rites protected by a treaty entered into by the Huron and the Crown in 1760. In his analysis of the scope of the treaty right, Justice Lamer provided a broad interpretation of the treaty's provision for "the free Exercise of [the Huron] religion [and] their Customs." Because the text of the treaty makes no mention of the territory over which treaty rights may be exercised, Quebec argued that the treaty right did not extend to activities performed in park territory. Justice Lamer held that this issue had to be resolved "by determining the intention of the parties ... at the time it was concluded." He acknowledged the possibility of different interpretations of the parties' common intention and, adding another principle to the interpretive framework articulated in *Simon v. The Queen*, [1985] 2 SCR 387, 24 DLR (4th) 390, stated that the Court must choose "from among the various possible interpretations of the common intention the one which best reconciles the Hurons' interests and those of the conquerer." Justice Lamer was of the opinion that "the rights guaranteed by the treaty could be exercised over the entire territory frequented by the Hurons at the time, so long as the carrying on of the customs and rites is not incompatible with the particular use made by the Crown of this territory."

In *R v. Badger*, [1996] 1 SCR 771, 137 DLR (4th) 324, Cory J for the Supreme Court identified several canons of treaty interpretation that inform contemporary jurisprudence on the subject:

> First, it must be remembered that a treaty represents an exchange of solemn promises between the Crown and the various Indian nations. It is an agreement whose nature is sacred. See *R v. Sioui*, [1990] 1 SCR 1025, at p. 1063 [70 DLR (4th) 427]; *Simon v. The Queen*, [1985] 2 SCR 387, at p. 401 [24 DLR (4th) 390]. Second, the honour of the Crown is always at stake in its dealing with Indian people. Interpretations of treaties and statutory provisions which have an impact upon treaty or aboriginal rights must be approached in a manner which maintains the integrity of the Crown. It is always assumed that the Crown intends to fulfil its promises. No appearance of "sharp dealing" will be sanctioned. See *Sparrow, supra*, at pp. 1107-08 and 1114; *R v. Taylor* (1981), 34 OR (2d) 360 (Ont. CA), at p. 367. Third, any ambiguities or doubtful expressions in the wording of the treaty or document must be resolved in favour of the Indians. A corollary to this principle is that any limitations which restrict the rights of Indians under treaties must be narrowly construed. See *Nowegijick v. The Queen*, [1983] 1 SCR 29, at p. 36 [144 DLR (3d) 193]; *Simon, supra*, at p. 402; *Sioui, supra*, at p. 1035; and *Mitchell v. Peguis Indian Band*, [1990] 2 SCR 85, at pp. 142-43 [71 DLR (4th) 193]. Fourth, the onus of proving that a treaty or aboriginal right has been extinguished lies upon the Crown. There must be "strict proof of the fact of extinguishment" and evidence of a clear and plain intention on the part of the government to extinguish treaty rights. See *Simon, supra*, at pp. 405-06; *Sioui, supra*, at p. 1061; *Calder v. Attorney-General of British Columbia*, [1973] SCR 313, at p. 404 [34 DLR (3d) 145].

To what extent are these canons consistent with the interpretive approach adopted by Lamer J in *Sioui*? To what extent are they consistent with the approach adopted in the following case?

R v. Marshall
[1999] 3 SCR 456, 177 DLR (4th) 513

[Donald Marshall Jr., a Mi'kmaq citizen, was charged with selling 463 pounds of eels for $787.10 without a licence, contrary to federal regulations made pursuant to the *Fisheries Act*. Marshall's defence was that he was entitled to sell the eels by virtue of a treaty right agreed to by the British Crown in 1760. The only issue at trial was whether Marshall had an existing treaty right exempting him from compliance with the federal legislation, thus mandating his acquittal. In 1760-1761, Aboriginal leaders in the Maritimes asked for truckhouses (i.e., trading posts) "furnishing them with necessaries, in Exchange for their Peltry" during negotiations leading up to the treaties. However, the written document recording the treaty contained only the promise by the Mi'kmaq not to "Traffick, Barter or Exchange any Commodities in any manner but with such persons, or the Manager of such Truckhouses as shall be appointed or established by His majesty's Governor." As such, the dispute in this case was over whether this "trade clause," framed in negative terms as a restraint on trade, reflected the grant of the positive right to Mi'kmaq people (like Marshall) to bring the products of their hunting, fishing, and gathering to a truckhouse to trade. The trial judge held that there was no positive right to trade embodied in the trade clause, and thus rejected Marshall's defence that he had a treaty right to catch and sell fish. Marshall appealed, and the Nova Scotia Court of Appeal dismissed his appeal. Marshall then appealed to the Supreme Court of Canada.]

BINNIE J (Lamer CJC, L'Heureux-Dubé, Cory, and Iacobucci JJ concurring):

• • •

[5] ... The starting point for the analysis of the alleged treaty right must be an examination of the specific words used in any written memorandum of its terms. In this case, the task is complicated by the fact the British signed a series of agreements with individual Mi'kmaq communities in 1760 and 1761 intending to have them consolidated into a comprehensive Mi'kmaq treaty that was never in fact brought into existence. The trial judge, Embree Prov. Ct. J, found that by the end of 1761 all of the Mi'kmaq villages in Nova Scotia had entered into separate but similar treaties. Some of these documents are missing. Despite some variations among some of the documents, Embree Prov. Ct. J was satisfied that the written terms applicable to this dispute were contained in a Treaty of Peace and Friendship entered into by Governor Charles Lawrence on March 10, 1760, which ... provides as follows:

> Treaty of Peace and Friendship concluded by [His Excellency Charles Lawrence] Esq. Govr and Comr. in Chief in and over his Majesty's Province of Nova Scotia or Accadia with Paul Laurent chief of the LaHave tribe of Indians at Halifax in the Province of [Nova Scotia] or Acadia.
>
> • • •
>
> And I do further promise for myself and my tribe that we will not either directly nor indirectly assist any of the enemies of His most sacred Majesty King George the Second, his heirs or Successors, nor hold any manner of Commerce traffick nor intercourse with them, but on the contrary will as much as may be in our power discover and make known to His Majesty's Governor, any ill designs which may be formed or contrived against His Majesty's subjects. *And I do further engage that we will not traffick, barter or Exchange any Commodities in any manner but with such persons or the managers of such Truck houses as shall be appointed or Established by His Majesty's Governor at Lunenbourg or Elsewhere in Nova Scotia or Accadia.*

[6] The [emphasized] portion of the document, the so-called "trade clause," is framed in negative terms as a restraint on the ability of the Mi'kmaq to trade with non-government individuals. A "truckhouse" was a type of trading post. The evidence showed that the promised government truckhouses disappeared from Nova Scotia within a few years and by 1780 a replacement regime of government licensed traders had also fallen into disuse while the British Crown was attending to the American Revolution. ...

[7] The appellant's position is that the truckhouse provision not only incorporated the alleged right to trade, but also the right to pursue traditional hunting, fishing and gathering activities in support of that trade. It seems clear that the words of the March 10, 1760 document, standing in isolation, do not support the appellant's argument. The question is whether the underlying negotiations produced a broader agreement between the British and the Mi'kmaq, memorialized only in part by the Treaty of Peace and Friendship, that would protect the appellant's activities that are the subject of the prosecution.

· · ·

Evidentiary Sources

[9] The Court of Appeal took a strict approach to the use of extrinsic evidence when interpreting the Treaties of 1760-61. Roscoe and Bateman JJA stated at p. 194: "While treaties must be interpreted in their historical context, extrinsic evidence cannot be used as an aid to interpretation, in the absence of ambiguity." I think this approach should be rejected for at least three reasons.

[10] Firstly, even in a modern commercial context, extrinsic evidence is available to show that a written document does not include all of the terms of an agreement. Rules of interpretation in contract law are in general more strict than those applicable to treaties, yet Professor Waddams states in *The Law of Contracts* (3rd ed. 1993), at para. 316:

> The parol evidence rule does not purport to exclude evidence designed to show whether or not the agreement has been "reduced to writing," or whether it was, or was not, the intention of the parties that it should be the exclusive record of their agreement. Proof of this question is a pre-condition to the operation of the rule, and all relevant evidence is admissible on it. ...

[11] Secondly, even in the context of a treaty document that purports to contain all of the terms, this Court has made clear in recent cases that extrinsic evidence of the historical and cultural context of a treaty may be received even absent any ambiguity on the face of the treaty. MacKinnon ACJO laid down the principle in *Taylor and Williams* [*R v. Taylor and Williams* (1981), 62 CCC (2d) 227 (Ont. CA)] at p. 236:

> ... if there is evidence by conduct or otherwise as to how the parties understood the terms of the treaty, then such understanding and practice is of assistance in giving content to the term or terms. ...

[12] Thirdly, where a treaty was concluded verbally and afterwards written up by representatives of the Crown, it would be unconscionable for the Crown to ignore the oral terms while relying on the written terms, per Dickson J (as he then was) in *Guerin v. The Queen*, [1984] 2 SCR 335 [13 DLR (4th) 321]. ...

[13] The narrow approach applied by the Court of Appeal to the use of extrinsic evidence apparently derives from the comments of Estey J in *R v. Horse*, [1988] 1 SCR 187 [47 DLR (4th) 526], where, at p. 201, he expressed some reservations about the use of extrinsic materials, such as the transcript of negotiations surrounding the signing of Treaty No. 6, except in the case of ambiguity. ... Lamer J, as he then was, mentioned this aspect of *Horse* in *Sioui* [*R v. Sioui*, [1990] 1 SCR 1025, 70 DLR (4th) 427], ... but advocated a more flexible approach when determining the existence of treaties. Lamer J stated,

at p. 1068, that "[t]he historical context, which has been used to demonstrate the existence of the treaty, may equally assist us in interpreting the extent of the rights contained in it."

[14] Subsequent cases have distanced themselves from a "strict" rule of treaty interpretation, as more recently discussed by Cory J, in *Badger* [*R v. Badger*, [1996] 1 SCR 771; 133 DLR (4th) 324], at para. 52:

> ... when considering a treaty, a court must take into account the context in which the treaties were negotiated, concluded and committed to writing. The treaties, as written documents, recorded an agreement that had already been reached orally and they did not always record the full extent of the oral agreement. ... The treaties were drafted in English by representatives of the Canadian government who, it should be assumed, were familiar with common law doctrines. Yet, the treaties were not translated in written form into the languages (here Cree and Dene) of the various Indian nations who were signatories. Even if they had been, it is unlikely that the Indians, who had a history of communicating only orally, would have understood them any differently. *As a result, it is well settled that the words in the treaty must not be interpreted in their strict technical sense nor subjected to rigid modern rules of construction.* [Emphasis added.]

"Generous" rules of interpretation should not be confused with a vague sense of after-the-fact largesse. The special rules are dictated by the special difficulties of ascertaining what in fact was agreed to. The Indian parties did not, for all practical purposes, have the opportunity to create their own written record of the negotiations. Certain assumptions are therefore made about the Crown's approach to treaty making (honourable) which the Court acts upon in its approach to treaty interpretation (flexible) as to the existence of a treaty (*Sioui*, at p. 1049), the completeness of any written record (the use, e.g., of context and implied terms to make honourable sense of the treaty arrangement: *Simon v. The Queen*, [1985] 2 SCR 387 [24 DLR (4th) 390], and *R v. Sundown*, [1999] 1 SCR 393 [170 DLR (4th) 385]), and the interpretation of treaty terms once found to exist (*Badger*). The bottom line is the Court's obligation is to "choose from among the various possible interpretations of the *common* intention [at the time the treaty was made] the one which best reconciles" the Mi'kmaq interests and those of the British Crown (*Sioui*, per Lamer J, at p. 1069 (emphasis added)). ...

[A discussion of a 1752 Mi'kmaq treaty and the trial judge's factual findings are omitted.]

The 1760 Negotiations

[22] I propose to review briefly the documentary record to emphasize and amplify certain aspects of the trial judge's findings. He accepted in general the evidence of the Crown's only expert witness, Dr. Stephen Patterson, a Professor of History at the University of New Brunswick, who testified at length about what the trial judge referred to (at para. 116) as British encouragement of the Mi'kmaq "hunting, fishing and gathering lifestyle." That evidence puts the trade clause in context, and answers the question whether there was something more to the treaty entitlement than merely the right to bring fish and wildlife to truckhouses.

[23] I take the following points from the matters particularly emphasized by the trial judge at para. 90 following his thorough review of the historical background:

> 1 The 1760-61 treaties were the culmination of more than a decade of intermittent hostilities between the British and the Mi'kmaq. Hostilities with the French were also prevalent in Nova Scotia throughout the 1750's, and the Mi'kmaq were constantly allied with the French against the British.
>
> 2 The use of firearms for hunting had an important impact on Mi'kmaq society. The Mi'kmaq remained dependant on others for gun powder and the primary sources of that were the French, Acadians and the British.
>
> 3 The French frequently supplied the Mi'kmaq with food and European trade goods. By the mid-18th century, the Mi'kmaq were accustomed to, and in some cases relied on, receiving various European trade goods [including shot, gunpowder, metal tools, clothing cloth, blankets, and many other things].
>
> . . .
>
> 6 The British wanted peace and a safe environment for their current and future settlers. Despite their recent victories, they did not feel completely secure in Nova Scotia.

[24] Shortly after the fall of Louisbourg in June 1758, the British commander sent emissaries to the Mi'kmaq, through the French missionary, Father Maillard (who served as translator at the subsequent negotiations), holding out an offer of the enjoyment of peace, liberty, property, possessions and religion. ...

[25] In the harsh winter of 1759-1760, so many Mi'kmaq turned up at Louisbourg seeking sustenance that the British Commander expressed concern that unless their demand for necessaries was met, they would become "very Troublesome" and "entirely putt a Stop to any Settling or fishing all along the Coast" or indeed "the Settlement of Nova Scotia" generally. ... It is apparent that the British saw the Mi'kmaq trade issue in terms of peace, as the Crown expert Dr. Stephen Patterson testified, "people who trade together do not fight, that was the theory." Peace was bound up with the ability of the Mi'kmaq people to sustain themselves economically. Starvation breeds discontent. The British certainly did not want the Mi'kmaq to become an unnecessary drain on the public purse of the colony of Nova Scotia or of the Imperial purse in London, as the trial judge found. To avoid such a result, it became necessary to protect the traditional Mi'kmaq economy, including hunting, gathering and fishing. ...

[26] The trial judge concluded that in 1760 the British Crown entered into a series of negotiations with communities of first nations spread across what is now Nova Scotia and New Brunswick. These treaties were essentially "adhesions" by different Mi'kmaq communities to identical terms because, as stated, it was contemplated that they would be consolidated in a more comprehensive and all-inclusive document at a later date, which never happened. The trial judge considered that the key negotiations took place not with the Mi'kmaq people directly, but with the St. John River Indians, part of the Maliseet First Nation, and the Passamaquody First Nation, who lived in present-day New Brunswick.

[27] The trial judge found as a fact, at para. 108, that the relevant Mi'kmaq treaty did "make peace upon the *same* conditions" (emphasis added) as the Maliseet and Passamaquody. Meetings took place between the Crown and the Maliseet and the Passamaquody on February 11, 1760, twelve days before these bands signed their treaty with the British

and eighteen days prior to the meeting between the Governor and the Mi'kmaq representatives, Paul Laurent of LaHave and Michel Augustine of the Richibucto region, where the terms of the Maliseet and Passamaquody treaties were "communicated" and accepted.

[28] The trial judge found (at para. 101) that on February 29, 1760, at a meeting between the Governor in Council and the Mi'kmaq chiefs, the following exchange occurred:

> His Excellency then Ordered the Several Articles of the Treaty made with the Indians of St. John's River and Passamaquody to be *Communicated* to the said Paul Laurent and Michel Augustine who expressed their satisfaction therewith, and *declar'd that all the Tribe of Mickmacks would be glad to make peace upon the same Conditions.* [Emphasis added.]

Governor Lawrence afterwards confirmed, in his May 11, 1760 report to the Board of Trade, that he had treated with the Mi'kmaq Indians on "the same terms."

[29] The genesis of the Mi'kmaq trade clause is therefore found in the Governor's earlier negotiations with the Maliseet and Passamaquody First Nations. In that regard, the appellant places great reliance on a meeting between the Governor and their chiefs on February 11, 1760 for the purpose of reviewing various aspects of the proposed treaty. The following exchange is recorded in contemporaneous minutes of the meeting prepared by the British Governor's Secretary:

> His Excellency then demanded of them, Whether they were directed by their Tribes, to propose any other particulars to be Treated upon at this time. To which they replied that their Tribes had not directed them to propose any thing further than that *there might be a Truckhouse established, for the furnishing them with necessaries, in Exchange for their Peltry,* and that it might, at present, be at Fort Frederick.
>
> Upon which His Excellency acquainted them *that in case of their now executing a Treaty* in the manner proposed, and its being ratified at the next General Meeting of their Tribes the next Spring, *a Truckhouse should be established at Fort Frederick, agreable to their desire,* and likewise at other Places if it should be found necessary, for furnishing them with such Commodities as shall be necessary for them, in Exchange for their Peltry & and that great care should be taken, that the Commerce at the said Truckhouses should be managed by Persons on whose Justice and good Treatment, they might always depend; and that it would be expected that the said Tribes should not Trafic or Barter and Exchange any Commodities at any other Place, nor with any other Persons. *Of all which* the Chiefs expressed their entire Approbation. [Emphasis added.]

[30] It is true ... that the British made it clear from the outset that the Mi'kmaq were not to have any commerce with "any of His Majesty's Enemies." A Treaty of Peace and Friendship could not be otherwise. ...

[31] At a meeting of the Governor's Council on February 16, 1760 (less than a week later), the Council and the representatives of the Indians proceeded to settle the prices of various articles of merchandise. ...

[32] In furtherance of this trade arrangement, the British established six truckhouses following the signing of the treaties in 1760 and 1761. ... The existence of advantageous terms at the truckhouses was part of an imperial peace strategy. ... The British were concerned that matters might again become "troublesome" if the Mi'kmaq were subjected to

the "pernicious practices" of "unscrupulous traders." The cost to the public purse of Nova Scotia of supporting Mi'kmaq trade was an investment in peace and the promotion of ongoing colonial settlement. The strategy would be effective only if the Mi'kmaq had access both to trade and to the fish and wildlife resources necessary to provide them with something to trade.

· · ·

[35] In my view, all of this evidence, reflected in the trial judgment, demonstrates the inadequacy and incompleteness of the written memorial of the treaty terms by selectively isolating the restrictive trade covenant. Indeed, the truckhouse system offered such advantageous terms that it hardly seems likely that Mi'kmaq traders had to be compelled to buy at lower prices and sell at higher prices. At a later date, they objected when truckhouses were abandoned. The trade clause would not have advanced British objectives (peaceful relations with a self-sufficient Mi'kmaq people) or Mi'kmaq objectives (access to the European "necessaries" on which they had come to rely) unless the Mi'kmaq were assured at the same time of continuing access, implicitly or explicitly, to wildlife to trade.

[A review of Dr. Patterson's comments at trial is omitted.]

[40] In my view, the Nova Scotia judgments erred in concluding that the only enforceable treaty obligations were those set out in the written document of March 10, 1760, whether construed flexibly (as did the trial judge) or narrowly (as did the Nova Scotia Court of Appeal). The findings of fact made by the trial judge taken as a whole demonstrate that the concept of a disappearing treaty right does justice neither to the honour of the Crown nor to the reasonable expectations of the Mi'kmaq people. It is their common intention in 1760—not just the terms of the March 10, 1760 document— to which effect must be given.

Ascertaining the Terms of the Treaty

[41] Having concluded that the written text is incomplete, it is necessary to ascertain the treaty terms not only by reference to the fragmentary historical record, as interpreted by the expert historians, but also in light of the stated objectives of the British and Mi'kmaq in 1760 and the political and economic context in which those objectives were reconciled.

[42] … The appellant asserts the right of Mi'kmaq people to catch fish and wildlife in support of trade as an alternative or supplementary method of obtaining necessaries. The right to fish is not mentioned in the March 10, 1760 document, nor is it expressly noted elsewhere in the records of the negotiation put in evidence. This is not surprising. As Dickson J mentioned with reference to the west coast in *Jack* [*Jack v. The Queen*, [1980] 1 SCR 294, 100 DLR (3d) 193], at p. 311, in colonial times the perception of the fishery resource was one of "limitless proportions."

[43] The law has long recognized that parties make assumptions when they enter into agreements about certain things that give their arrangements efficacy. Courts will imply a contractual term on the basis of presumed intentions of the parties where it is necessary to assure the efficacy of the contract, e.g., where it meets the "officious bystander

test": ... Here, if the ubiquitous officious bystander had said, "This talk about truck-houses is all very well, but if the Mi'kmaq are to make these promises, will they have the right to hunt and fish to catch something to trade at the truckhouses?," the answer would have to be, having regard to the honour of the Crown, "of course." If the law is prepared to supply the deficiencies of written contracts prepared by sophisticated parties and their legal advisors in order to produce a sensible result that accords with the intent of both parties, though unexpressed, the law cannot ask less of the honour and dignity of the Crown in its dealings with First Nations. The honour of the Crown was, in fact, specific-ally invoked by courts in the early 17th century to ensure that a Crown grant was effec-tive to accomplish its intended purpose. ...

[44] An example of the Court's recognition of the necessity of supplying the deficien-cies of aboriginal treaties is *Sioui, supra,* where Lamer J considered a treaty document that stated simply (at p. 1031) that the Huron tribe "are received upon the same terms with the Canadians, being allowed the free Exercise of their Religion, their Customs, and Liberty of trading with the English." Lamer J found that, in order to give real value and meaning to these words, it was necessary that a territorial component be supplied, as follows, at p. 1067:

> The treaty gives the Hurons the freedom to carry on their customs and their religion. No mention is made in the treaty itself of the territory over which these rights may be exercised. There is also no indication that the territory of what is now Jacques-Cartier park was con-templated. However, *for a freedom to have real value and meaning,* it must be possible to exercise it somewhere. [Emphasis added.]

Similarly, in *Sundown, supra,* the Court found that the express right to hunt included the implied right to build shelters required to carry out the hunt. See also *Simon, supra,* where the Court recognized an implied right to carry a gun and ammunition on the way to exercise the right to hunt. These cases employed the concept of implied rights to support the meaningful exercise of express rights granted to the first nations in circumstances where no such implication might necessarily have been made absent the *sui generis* nature of the Crown's relationship to aboriginal people. While I do not believe that in ordinary commercial situations a right to trade implies any right of access to things to trade, I think the honour of the Crown requires nothing less in attempting to make sense of the result of these 1760 negotiations.

Rights of the Other Inhabitants

[45] ... [I]t is ... true that a general right enjoyed by all citizens can nevertheless be made the subject of an enforceable treaty promise.

· · ·

[47] ... The settlers and the military undoubtedly hunted and fished for sport or nec-essaries as well, and traded goods with each other. The issue here is not so much the con-tent of the rights or liberties as the level of legal protection thrown around them. A treaty could, to take a fanciful example, provide for a right of the Mi'kmaq to promenade down Barrington Street, Halifax, on each anniversary of the treaty. Barrington Street is a com-mon thoroughfare enjoyed by all. There would be nothing "special" about the Mi'kmaq

use of a common right of way. The point is that the treaty rights-holder not only has the right or liberty "enjoyed by other British subjects" but may enjoy special treaty protection against interference with its exercise. So it is with the trading arrangement. On June 25, 1761, following the signing of the Treaties of 1760-61 by the last group of Mi'kmaq villages, a ceremony was held at the farm of Lieutenant Governor Jonathan Belcher, the first Chief Justice of Nova Scotia, who was acting in the place of Governor Charles Lawrence, who had recently been drowned on his way to Boston. In reference to the treaties, including the trade clause, Lieutenant Governor Belcher proclaimed:

> The Laws will be like a great Hedge about your Rights and properties, if any break this Hedge to hurt and injure you, the heavy weight of the Laws will fall upon them and punish their Disobedience.

[48] Until enactment of the *Constitution Act, 1982*, the treaty rights of aboriginal peoples could be overridden by competent legislation as easily as could the rights and liberties of other inhabitants. The hedge offered no special protection, as the aboriginal people learned in earlier hunting cases such as *Sikyea v. The Queen*, [1964] SCR 642 [43 DLR (2d) 150], and *R v. George*, [1966] SCR 267 [55 DLR (2d) 386]. On April 17, 1982, however, this particular type of "hedge" was converted by s. 35(1) into sterner stuff that could only be broken down when justified according to the test laid down in *R v. Sparrow*, [1990] 1 SCR 1075 [70 DLR (4th) 385], at pp. 1112 *et seq.*, as adapted to apply to treaties in *Badger, supra*, per Cory J, at paras. 75 *et seq.* The fact the content of Mi'kmaq rights under the treaty to hunt and fish and trade was no greater than those enjoyed by other inhabitants does not, unless those rights were extinguished prior to April 17, 1982, detract from the higher protection they presently offer to the Mi'kmaq people.

The Honour of the Crown

[49] This appeal puts to the test the principle, emphasized by this Court on several occasions, that the honour of the Crown is always at stake in its dealings with aboriginal people. ...

[50] This principle that the Crown's honour is at stake when the Crown enters into treaties with first nations dates back at least to this Court's decision in 1895, *Province of Ontario v. Dominion of Canada and Province of Quebec; In re Indian Claims* (1895), 25 SCR 434. In that decision, Gwynne J (dissenting) stated, at pp. 511-12:

> ... [W]hat is contended for and must not be lost sight of, is that the British sovereigns, ever since the acquisition of Canada, have been pleased to adopt the rule or practice of entering into agreements with the Indian nations or tribes in their province of Canada, for the cession or surrender by them of what such sovereigns have been pleased to designate the Indian title, by instruments similar to these now under consideration to which they have been pleased to give the designation of "treaties" with the Indians in possession of and claiming title to the lands expressed to be surrendered by the instruments, and further that *the terms and conditions expressed in those instruments as to be performed by or on behalf of the Crown, have always been regarded as involving a trust graciously assumed by the Crown to the fulfilment of which with the Indians the faith and honour of the Crown is pledged, and which trust has always been most faithfully fulfilled as a treaty obligation of the Crown.* [Emphasis added.]

[A review of authorities is omitted.]

[52] I do not think an interpretation of events that turns a positive Mi'kmaq trade demand into a negative Mi'kmaq covenant is consistent with the honour and integrity of the Crown. Nor is it consistent to conclude that the Lieutenant Governor, seeking in good faith to address the trade demands of the Mi'kmaq, accepted the Mi'kmaq suggestion of a trading facility while denying any treaty protection to Mi'kmaq access to the things that were to be traded, even though these things were identified and priced in the treaty negotiations. This was not a commercial contract. The trade arrangement must be interpreted in a manner which gives meaning and substance to the promises made by the Crown. In my view, with respect, the interpretation adopted by the courts below left the Mi'kmaq with an empty shell of a treaty promise.

· · ·

The Limited Scope of the Treaty Right

[57] The Crown expresses the concern that recognition of the existence of a constitutionally entrenched right with, as here, a trading aspect, would open the floodgates to uncontrollable and excessive exploitation of the natural resources. Whereas hunting and fishing for food naturally restricts quantities to the needs and appetites of those entitled to share in the harvest, it is argued that there is no comparable, built-in restriction associated with a trading right, short of the paramount need to conserve the resource. ... The ultimate fear is that the appellant, who in this case fished for eels from a small boat using a fyke net, could lever the treaty right into a factory trawler in Pomquet Harbour gathering the available harvest in preference to all non-aboriginal commercial or recreational fishermen. (This is indeed the position advanced by the intervener [of] the Union of New Brunswick Indians.) This fear (or hope) is based on a misunderstanding of the narrow ambit and extent of the treaty right.

[58] The recorded note of February 11, 1760 was that "there might be a Truckhouse established, for the furnishing them with *necessaries*" (emphasis added). What is contemplated therefore is not a right to trade generally for economic gain, but rather a right to trade for necessaries. The treaty right is a regulated right and can be contained by regulation within its proper limits.

[59] The concept of "necessaries" is today equivalent to the concept of what Lambert JA, in *R v. Van der Peet* (1993), 80 BCLR (2d) 75, at p. 126, described as a "moderate livelihood." Bare subsistence has thankfully receded over the last couple of centuries as an appropriate standard of life for aboriginals and non-aboriginals alike. A moderate livelihood includes such basics as "food, clothing and housing, supplemented by a few amenities," but not the accumulation of wealth (*Gladstone*, [*R v. Gladstone*, [1996] 2 SCR 672], at para. 165). It addresses day-to-day needs. This was the common intention in 1760. It is fair that it be given this interpretation today.

· · ·

[61] Catch limits that could reasonably be expected to produce a moderate livelihood for individual Mi'kmaq families at present-day standards can be established by regulation and enforced without violating the treaty right. In that case, the regulations would

accommodate the treaty right. Such regulations would not constitute an infringement that would have to be justified under the *Badger* standard.

Application to the Facts of This Case

[62] The appellant is charged with three offences: the selling of eels without a licence, fishing without a licence and fishing during the close season with illegal nets. These acts took place at Pomquet Harbour, Antigonish County. For Marshall to have satisfied the regulations, he was required to secure a licence under either the *Fishery (General) Regulations*, SOR/93-53, the *Maritime Provinces Fishery Regulations*, SOR/93-55, or the *Aboriginal Communal Fishing Licences Regulations*, SOR/93-332.

[63] All of these regulations place the issuance of licences within the absolute discretion of the Minister. ...

[64] Furthermore, there is nothing in these regulations which gives direction to the Minister to explain how she or he should exercise this discretionary authority in a manner which would respect the appellant's treaty rights. The test for infringement under s. 35(1) of the *Constitution Act, 1982* was set out in *Sparrow, supra*, at p. 1112:

> To determine whether the fishing rights have been interfered with such as to constitute a *prima facie* infringement of s. 35(1), certain questions must be asked. First, is the limitation unreasonable? Second, does the regulation impose undue hardship? Third, does the regulation deny to the holders of the right their preferred means of exercising that right? The onus of proving a *prima facie* infringement lies on the individual or group challenging the legislation.

Lamer CJ in *Adams* [*R v. Adams*, [1996] 3 SCR 101, 138 DLR (4th) 657] applied this test to licensing schemes and stated as follows at para. 54:

> In light of the Crown's unique fiduciary obligations towards aboriginal peoples, *Parliament may not simply adopt an unstructured discretionary administrative regime which risks infringing aboriginal rights in a substantial number of applications in the absence of some explicit guidance*. If a statute confers an administrative discretion which may carry significant consequences for the exercise of an aboriginal right, the statute or its delegate regulations must outline specific criteria for the granting or refusal of that discretion which seek to accommodate the existence of aboriginal rights. In the absence of such specific guidance, the statute will fail to provide representatives of the Crown with sufficient directives to fulfil their fiduciary duties, and the statute will be found to represent an infringement of aboriginal rights under the Sparrow test. [Emphasis added.]

Cory J in *Badger, supra*, at para. 79, found that the test for infringement under s. 35(1) of the *Constitution Act, 1982* was the same for both aboriginal and treaty rights, and thus the words of Lamer CJ in *Adams*, although in relation to the infringement of aboriginal rights, are equally applicable here. There was nothing at that time which provided the Crown officials with the "sufficient directives" necessary to ensure that the appellant's treaty rights would be respected. To paraphrase *Adams*, at para. 51, under the applicable regulatory regime, the appellant's exercise of his treaty right to fish and trade for sustenance was exercisable only at the absolute discretion of the Minister. Mi'kmaq treaty rights were not accommodated in the Regulations because, presumably, the Crown's position was, and continues to be, that no such treaty rights existed. In the circumstances, the purported regulatory prohibitions against fishing without a licence (*Maritime Provinces Fishery Regulations*, s. 4(1)(a)) and of selling eels without a licence (*Fishery (General) Regulations*, s. 35(2)) do *prima facie* infringe the appellant's treaty rights under the Treaties of 1760-61 and are inoperative against the appellant unless justified under the *Badger* test.

[65] Further, the appellant was charged with fishing during the close season with improper nets, contrary to s. 20 of the *Maritime Provinces Fishery Regulations*. Such a regulation is also a *prima facie* infringement, as noted by Cory J in *Badger*, *supra*, at para. 90: "This Court has held on numerous occasions that there can be no limitation on the method, timing and extent of Indian hunting under a Treaty," apart, I would add, from a treaty limitation to that effect.

[66] The appellant caught and sold the eels to support himself and his wife. Accordingly, the close season and the imposition of a discretionary licensing system would, if enforced, interfere with the appellant's treaty right to fish for trading purposes, and the ban on sales would, if enforced, infringe his right to trade for sustenance. In the absence of any justification of the regulatory prohibitions, the appellant is entitled to an acquittal.

Disposition

[67] The constitutional question stated by the Chief Justice on February 9, 1998, as follows: Are the prohibitions on catching and retaining fish without a licence, on fishing during the close time, and on the unlicensed sale of fish, contained in ss. 4(1)(a) and 20 of the *Maritime Provinces Fishery Regulations* and s. 35(2) of the *Fishery (General) Regulations*, inconsistent with the treaty rights of the appellant contained in the Mi'kmaq Treaties of 1760-61 and therefore of no force or effect or application to him, by virtue of ss. 35(1) and 52 of the *Constitution Act, 1982*? Should be answered in the affirmative. I would therefore allow the appeal and order an acquittal on all charges.

[McLachlin and Gonthier JJ dissented.]

Appealed allowed.

NOTES AND QUESTIONS

1. Following the release of the judgment in *R v. Marshall*, there were numerous clashes between Aboriginal and non-Aboriginal fishers in Nova Scotia and New Brunswick. The commercial fishers widely condemned the ruling for its potential to disrupt their livelihoods, while Aboriginal fishers strongly praised it as a means to enhance their access to economic opportunity. In this climate of unrest and instability the West Nova Fishermen's Coalition applied for a rehearing of the case. They wanted "to have the Court address the regulatory authority of the Government of Canada over the east coast fisheries" and requested an order that the Court's earlier judgment be stayed to allow the Crown to justify restrictions on the exercise of Marshall's treaty right. In *R v. Marshall*, [1999] 3 SCR 533, 179 DLR

(4th) 193 (*Marshall No. 2*), the Court dismissed West Nova's application, but in an unprecedented move, it reframed its judgment of only a month earlier. Some commentators observed that the Court's "clarification" arguably had the effect of emphasizing certain aspects of the original judgment at the expense of other elements of the original decision. Some criticized the Court for bowing to public pressure, and compromising its independence, while others applauded it for bringing order to an unstable situation. The gist of the Court's decision is illustrated in the following excerpt. Is this a restatement or a revision?

> THE COURT: ... [20] The September 17, 1999 majority judgment did not rule that the appellant had established a treaty right "to gather" anything and everything physically capable of being gathered. The issues were much narrower and the ruling was much narrower. No evidence was drawn to our attention, nor was any argument made in the course of this appeal, that trade in logging or minerals, or the exploitation of off-shore natural gas deposits, was in the contemplation of either or both parties to the 1760 treaty; nor was the argument made that exploitation of such resources could be considered a logical evolution of treaty rights to fish and wildlife or to the type of things traditionally "gathered" by the Mi'kmaq in a 1760 aboriginal lifestyle. It is of course open to native communities to assert broader treaty rights in that regard, but if so, the basis for such a claim will have to be established in proceedings where the issue is squarely raised on proper historical evidence, as was done in this case in relation to fish and wildlife. Other resources were simply not addressed by the parties, and therefore not addressed by the Court in its September 17, 1999 majority judgment. ...
>
> • • •
>
> [25] With all due respect to the Coalition, the government's general regulatory power is clearly affirmed.
>
> • • •
>
> [35] Despite the limitations on the Court's ability in a prosecution to address broader issues not at issue between the Crown and the defence, the majority judgment of September 17, 1999 nevertheless referred to the Court's principal pronouncements on the various grounds on which the exercise of treaty rights may be regulated. These include the following grounds: ... (a) The treaty right itself is a limited right. The September 17, 1999 majority judgment referred to the "narrow ambit and extent of the treaty right" (para. 57).
>
> • • •
>
> [38] Other limitations apparent in the September 17, 1999 majority judgment include the local nature of the treaties, the communal nature of a treaty right, and the fact it was only hunting and fishing resources to which access was affirmed, together with traditionally gathered things like wild fruit and berries. With regard to the Coalition's concern about the fishing rights of its members, para. 38 of the September 17, 1999 majority judgment noted the trial judge's finding that the Mi'kmaq had been fishing to trade with non-natives for over 200 years prior to the 1760-61 treaties. The 1760-61 treaty rights were thus from their inception enjoyed alongside the commercial and recreational fishery of non-natives. Paragraph 42 of the September 17, 1999 majority judgment recognized that, unlike the scarce fisheries resources of today, the view in 1760 was that the fisheries were of "limitless proportions." ... The Mi'kmaq treaty right to participate in the largely unregulated commercial fishery of 1760 has evolved into a treaty right to participate in the largely regulated commercial fishery of the 1990s. ... [T]he Mi'kmaq treaty right to hunt and trade in game is not now, any more than it was in 1760, a commercial hunt

that must be satisfied before non-natives have access to the same resources for recreational or commercial purposes. The emphasis in 1999, as it was in 1760, is on assuring the Mi'kmaq equitable access to identified resources for the purpose of earning a moderate living. In this respect, a treaty right differs from an aboriginal right which in its origin, by definition, was exclusively exercised by aboriginal people prior to contact with Europeans.

· · ·

[41] The Minister's authority extends to other compelling and substantial public objectives which may include economic and regional fairness, and recognition of the historical reliance upon, and participation in, the fishery by non-aboriginal groups. The Minister's regulatory authority is not limited to conservation. … It is for the Crown to propose what controls are justified for the management of the resource, and why they are justified. In *Gladstone, supra* (cited at para. 57 of the September 17, 1999 majority judgment), the Chief Justice commented on the differences between a native food fishery and a native commercial fishery, and stated at para. 75 as follows:

> Although by no means making a definitive statement on this issue, I would suggest that with regards to the distribution of the fisheries resource after conservation goals have been met, objectives such as the pursuit of economic and regional fairness, and the recognition of the historical reliance upon, and participation in, the fishery by non-aboriginal groups, are the type of objectives which can (at least in the right circumstances) satisfy this standard. In the right circumstances, such objectives are in the interest of all Canadians and, more importantly, the reconciliation of aboriginal societies with the rest of Canadian society may well depend on their successful attainment.

This observation applies with particular force to a treaty right. The aboriginal right at issue in *Gladstone, supra,* was by definition exercised exclusively by aboriginal people prior to contact with Europeans. As stated, no such exclusivity ever attached to the treaty right at issue in this case. … [T]he Court again emphasizes that the specifics of any particular regulatory regime were not and are not before us for decision.

[42] In the case of any treaty right which may be exercised on a commercial scale, the natives constitute only one group of participants, and regard for the interest of the non-natives, as stated in *Gladstone, supra,* may be shown in the right circumstances to be entirely legitimate. Proportionality is an important factor. …

2. Modern treaties have been negotiated and passed into law in the last 35 years, starting with the James Bay and Northern Quebec Agreement in 1975, through the recent *Nisga'a Final Agreement Act* of 2000. These modern land claims agreements are constitutionally protected by virtue of s. 35(3) of the *Constitution Act, 1982,* which reads, "For greater certainty, in subsection (1) "treaty rights" includes rights that now exist by way of land claims agreements or may be so acquired." Should the courts take the same approach to modern treaties as they do with historic treaties? See *R v. Howard,* [1994] 2 SCR 299; 115 DLR (4th) 312.

VI. THE DUTY TO CONSULT

Recall that, in *Delgamuukw*, above, the Court stated (at para. 168):

> There is always a duty of consultation. Whether the aboriginal group has been consulted is relevant to determining whether the infringement of aboriginal title is justified ... . The nature and scope of the duty of consultation will vary with the circumstances. In occasional cases, when the breach is less serious or relatively minor, it will be no more than a duty to discuss important decisions that will be taken with respect to lands held pursuant to aboriginal title. Of course, even in these rare cases when the minimum acceptable standard is consultation, this consultation must be in good faith, and with the intention of substantially addressing the concerns of the aboriginal peoples whose lands are at issue. In most cases, it will be significantly deeper than mere consultation. Some cases may even require the full consent of an aboriginal nation, particularly when provinces enact hunting and fishing regulations in relation to aboriginal lands.

In *Haida Nation v. British Columbia (Minister of Forests)*, [2004] 3 SCR 511, 2004 SCC 73, 245 DLR (4th) 33, the Court gave a strong interpretation of the "duty to consult" and, with it, a renewed emphasis on the principle of the honour of the Crown in all dealings with Aboriginal peoples. In a unanimous judgment, the Court established that the government has a duty to consult with Aboriginal groups whenever government decision making could adversely affect an Aboriginal right or Aboriginal title, and that the duty extended to cases where claims of Aboriginal rights or title had been asserted but not yet proven. On the facts of the case, the Haida Nation challenged the provincial government's unilateral replacements and transfer of tree-farming licences (TFL) over lands to which the Haida claimed Aboriginal title. The replacements and transfer were made over the objections of the Haida. The Court held that the provincial government had a duty to consult with and accommodate the Haida with respect to harvesting timber in [the block of land in issue.

The Court grounded the duty to consult in the principle of "the honour of the Crown":

> [16] The government's duty to consult with Aboriginal peoples and accommodate their interests is grounded in the honour of the Crown. The honour of the Crown is always at stake in its dealings with Aboriginal peoples ... .
>
> [17] The historical roots of the principle of the honour of the Crown suggest that it must be understood generously in order to reflect the underlying realities from which it stems. In all its dealings with Aboriginal peoples, from the assertion of sovereignty to the resolution of claims and the implementation of treaties, the Crown must act honourably. Nothing less is required if we are to achieve "the reconciliation of the pre-existence of aboriginal societies with the sovereignty of the Crown."

Recognizing that the honour of the Crown gives rise to different duties in different contexts, the Court went on to discuss the implications of the principle in the context of negotiating claims to Aboriginal rights and title:

> [25] Put simply, Canada's Aboriginal peoples were here when Europeans came, and were never conquered. Many bands reconciled their claims with the sovereignty of the Crown through negotiated treaties. Others, notably in British Columbia, have yet to do so. The potential rights embedded in these claims are protected by s. 35 of the *Constitution Act, 1982*. The

honour of the Crown requires that these rights be determined, recognized and respected. This, in turn, requires the Crown, acting honourably, to participate in processes of negotiation. While this process continues, the honour of the Crown may require it to consult and, where indicated, accommodate Aboriginal interests.

[26] Honourable negotiation implies a duty to consult with Aboriginal claimants and conclude an honourable agreement reflecting the claimants' inherent rights. But proving rights may take time, sometimes a very long time. In the meantime, how are the interests under discussion to be treated? Underlying this question is the need to reconcile prior Aboriginal occupation of the land with the reality of Crown sovereignty. Is the Crown, under the aegis of its asserted sovereignty, entitled to use the resources at issue as it chooses, pending proof and resolution of the Aboriginal claim? Or must it adjust its conduct to reflect the as yet unresolved rights claimed by the Aboriginal claimants?

[27] The answer, once again, lies in the honour of the Crown. The Crown, acting honourably, cannot cavalierly run roughshod over Aboriginal interests where claims affecting these interests are being seriously pursued in the process of treaty negotiation and proof. It must respect these potential, but yet unproven, interests. The Crown is not rendered impotent. It may continue to manage the resource in question pending claims resolution. But, depending on the circumstances, discussed more fully below, the honour of the Crown may require it to consult with and reasonably accommodate Aboriginal interests pending resolution of the claim. To unilaterally exploit a claimed resource during the process of proving and resolving the Aboriginal claim to that resource, may be to deprive the Aboriginal claimants of some or all of the benefit of the resource. That is not honourable.

The Court dismissed the provincial government's argument that any duty to consult and accommodate Aboriginal interests arose only after there had been a final determination of the scope and content of any Aboriginal right:

[32] The jurisprudence of this Court supports the view that the duty to consult and accommodate is part of a process of fair dealing and reconciliation that begins with the assertion of sovereignty and continues beyond formal claims resolution. Reconciliation is not a final legal remedy in the usual sense. Rather, it is a process flowing from rights guaranteed by s. 35(1) of the *Constitution Act, 1982*. This process of reconciliation flows from the Crown's duty of honourable dealing toward Aboriginal peoples, which arises in turn from the Crown's assertion of sovereignty over an Aboriginal people and *de facto* control of land and resources that were formerly in the control of that people. ...

[33] To limit reconciliation to the post-proof sphere risks treating reconciliation as a distant legalistic goal, devoid of the "meaningful content" mandated by the "solemn commitment" made by the Crown in recognizing and affirming Aboriginal rights and title: *Sparrow* [*R v.*, [1990] 1 SCR 1075, 70 DLR (4th) 385], at p. 1108. It also risks unfortunate consequences. When the distant goal of proof is finally reached, the Aboriginal peoples may find their land and resources changed and denuded. This is not reconciliation. Nor is it honourable.

The Court found that the duty to consult arises when the Crown has knowledge, real or constructive, of the potential existence of the Aboriginal right or title and contemplates conduct that might adversely affect it. As for the exact content of the duty to consult, the Court left much to be determined by developing case law:

[39] The content of the duty to consult and accommodate varies with the circumstances. Precisely what duties arise in different situations will be defined as the case law in this emerging area develops. In general terms, however, it may be asserted that the scope of the duty is proportionate to a preliminary assessment of the strength of the case supporting the existence of the right or title, and to the seriousness of the potentially adverse effect upon the right or title claimed.

[40] In *Delgamuukw* [[1997] 3 SCR 1010; 153 DLR (4th) 193], at para. 168, the Court considered the duty to consult and accommodate in the context of established claims. Lamer CJ wrote:

> The nature and scope of the duty of consultation will vary with the circumstances. In occasional cases, when the breach is less serious or relatively minor, it will be no more than a duty to discuss important decisions that will be taken with respect to lands held pursuant to aboriginal title. Of course, even in these rare cases when the minimum acceptable standard is consultation, this consultation must be in good faith, and with the intention of substantially addressing the concerns of the aboriginal peoples whose lands are at issue. In most cases, it will be significantly deeper than mere consultation. Some cases may even require the full consent of an aboriginal nation, particularly when provinces enact hunting and fishing regulations in relation to aboriginal lands.

. . .

[42] At all stages, good faith on both sides is required. The common thread on the Crown's part must be "the intention of substantially addressing [Aboriginal] concerns" as they are raised (*Delgamuukw* [*supra*], at para. 168), through a meaningful process of consultation. Sharp dealing is not permitted. However, there is no duty to agree; rather, the commitment is to a meaningful process of consultation. As for Aboriginal claimants, they must not frustrate the Crown's reasonable good faith attempts, nor should they take unreasonable positions to thwart government from making decisions or acting in cases where, despite meaningful consultation, agreement is not reached ... .

. . .

[47] When the consultation process suggests amendment of Crown policy, we arrive at the stage of accommodation. Thus the effect of good faith consultation may be to reveal a duty to accommodate. Where a strong *prima facie* case exists for the claim, and the consequences of the government's proposed decision may adversely affect it in a significant way, addressing the Aboriginal concerns may require taking steps to avoid irreparable harm or to minimize the effects of infringement, pending final resolution of the underlying claim. Accommodation is achieved through consultation, as this Court recognized in *R v. Marshall*, [1999] 3 SCR 533, at para. 22: "... the process of accommodation of the treaty right may best be resolved by consultation and negotiation."

On the facts of the case, the Court found that the Crown's obligation to consult the Haida was engaged. The Haida's claims to title and an Aboriginal right to harvest red cedar were supported by a good *prima facie* case, and the province knew that the potential Aboriginal rights and title applied to the block of land in question and could be affected by the decision to replace the TFLs. TFL decisions were found to reflect strategic planning for use of the resource and, potentially, to have a serious impact on Aboriginal rights and title. In the Court's view, for consultation to be meaningful, it must take place at the stage of granting or renewing TFLs. The Court went on to state that the strength of the case for both the Haida's title and their right to harvest red cedar, coupled with the serious impact of incremental strategic decisions on those interests, suggested that the honour of the Crown might also require significant accommodation to preserve the Haida's interest pending resolution of their claims.

Taku River Tlingit First Nation v. British Columbia (Project Assessment Director), [2004] 3 SCR 550, 2004 SCC 74, 245 DLR (4th) 193 was decided at the same time as *Haida Nation*. In this case, the Court determined that the provincial government's duty to consult with the Taku River Tlingit First Nation (TRTFN) was engaged because the proposed action—the construction of a 160 km long road through the group's traditional territory—could significantly and negatively affect the TRTFN. However, the Court went on to hold that the provincial government had consulted and fulfiled its duty to accommodate before approving the reopening of the mine.

This was accomplished through the environmental assessment that was conducted, which included consultation with interested Aboriginal groups including the TRTFN. Not all of the broad concerns of the TRTFN were addressed when the final construction plan was approved. However, the Court was satisfied that the assessment committee had given sufficient attention to the specific issues raised by the TRTFN both in the initial assessment process and when the group brought forward additional concerns after the assessment's report was written. The Court stated explicitly (at para. 22): "The Province was not under a duty to reach agreement with the TRTFN, and its failure to do so did not breach the obligations of good faith that it owed the TRTFN." Furthermore:

> [40] … The Province was not required to develop special consultation measures to address TRTFN's concerns, outside of the process provided for by the *Environmental Assessment Act*, which specifically set out a scheme that required consultation with affected Aboriginal peoples.
>
> • • •
>
> [42] As discussed in *Haida*, the process of consultation may lead to a duty to accommodate Aboriginal concerns by adapting decisions or policies in response. The purpose of s. 35(1) of the *Constitution Act, 1982* is to facilitate the ultimate reconciliation of prior Aboriginal occupation with *de facto* Crown sovereignty. Pending settlement, the Crown is bound by its honour to balance societal and Aboriginal interests in making decisions that may affect Aboriginal claims. The Crown may be required to make decisions in the face of disagreement as to the adequacy of its response to Aboriginal concerns. Balance and compromise will then be necessary.

Mikisew Cree First Nation v. Canada (Minister of Canadian Heritage), [2005] 3 SCR 388, 2005 SCC 69, 259 DLR (4th) 610 involved the Crown "taking up" surrendered lands to build a winter road to meet regional transportation needs. The proposed road would have the effect of reducing the territory over which the Mikisew Cree First Nation would be entitled to exercise its treaty rights to hunt, fish, and trap. The Court found that the Crown had a duty to consult that it had breached.

While the Court found that the Crown had the authority under the treaty to "take up" surrendered lands, it was nevertheless under the obligation to inform itself on the impact its project would have on the exercise by the Mikisew of their treaty hunting, fishing, and trapping rights and to communicate its findings to the Mikisew. The Crown was then required to attempt to deal with the Mikisew in good faith and with the intention of substantially addressing their concerns. On the facts, the Court found that the impacts of the proposed road were clear, established, and demonstrably adverse to the continued exercise of the Mikisew's hunting and trapping rights over the lands in question, and that the duty to consult was thereby triggered.

However, given that the Crown was proposing to build a fairly minor winter road on surrendered lands where the Mikisew treaty rights are expressly subject to the "taking up" limitation, the content of the Crown's duty of consultation in this case was found to lie at the lower end of the spectrum. The Crown was required to provide notice to the Mikisew and to engage directly with them. This engagement was to include providing information about the project, addressing what the Crown knew to be the Mikisew's interests and what the Crown anticipated might be the potential adverse impact on those interests. The Crown was also required to solicit and listen carefully to the Mikisew's concerns and attempt to minimize adverse impacts on its treaty rights.

The Crown was found not to have discharged its obligations when it unilaterally declared that the road realignment would be shifted from the reserve itself to a track along its boundary. It had failed to demonstrate an intention of substantially addressing Aboriginal concerns through a meaningful process of consultation.

VII. MÉTIS RIGHTS

Recall that in *Van der Peet* the Supreme Court of Canada stated that "the history of the Métis, and the reasons underlying their inclusion in the protection given by s. 35, are quite distinct from those of other Aboriginal peoples in Canada." The existence of the Métis in the west prior to Confederation was centrally significant to the economic development and expansion of the east. Without their presence the fur trade would have foundered, and political and economic development on the St. Lawrence River and eastern Great Lakes would have been severely delayed or restricted. The Métis Nation was also an integral part of the process ushering western and northern Canada into Confederation and increasing the wealth of the country by opening up the prairies to agriculture and settlement. These developments could not have occurred without their intercession (see George F.G. Stanley, *The Birth of Western Canada: A History of the Riel Rebellion* (Toronto: University of Toronto Press, 1960)). The Dominion Parliament's unilateral attempt to survey the old North-Western Territory around the Red River in 1869 was strongly resisted by the local Métis settlements. The Métis resisted becoming a part of the Dominion without their participation and consent. Therefore, after blocking the surveyors from their work, and thereby preventing Canada's expansion into this region, the Métis compelled the government of Sir John A. Macdonald to recognize their interests.

In particular, the Red River Métis formed a provisional government that was given authority to negotiate the terms of union with Ottawa and bring the area into Confederation. Representatives of this government travelled to Ottawa, as delegates of the Métis people, to negotiate conditions for western Canada's entry. They brought with them a locally developed bill of rights that expressed their demands. The negotiations were challenging, but an agreement was reached and its terms were embodied in the *Manitoba Act of 1870 (UK)*, 32 & 33 Vict., c. 3. The democratic legitimacy of this process was sealed through the Métis provisional government's acceptance of the agreement before the Dominion and Imperial Parliament's statutory endorsement that made it part of the constitutional law of Canada.

(See the *Constitution Act, 1871 (UK)*, c. 28.) The people of the Métis Nation regard the *Manitoba Act* as embodying a treaty that recognizes and affirms their nation-to-nation relationship with Canada, even though they argue that its provisions concerning land and resources have not been fulfilled: see *R v. Dumont* (1988), 52 DLR (4) 25 (Man. CA); rev'd. *Dumont v. Canada (Attorney General)*, [1990] 1 SCR 279, 67 DLR (4th) 159.

R v. Powley
[2003] 2 SCR 207, 2003 SCC 43, 230 DLR (4th) 1

[Steve Powley and his son Roddy were charged with unlawfully hunting moose and knowingly possessing game hunted in contravention of the *Game and Fish Act*, RSO 1990, c. G-I. They both entered pleas of not guilty. They admitted having killed the moose without a hunting licence. They claimed, however, that as Métis they had an Aboriginal right to hunt for food in the Sault Ste. Marie area and that this right could not be infringed by the government of Ontario without justification. The trial court, Superior Court, and Ontario Court of Appeal agreed with the Powleys.]

THE COURT (McLachlin CJC and Gonthier, Iacobucci, Major, Bastarache, Binnie, Arbour, LeBel and Deschamps JJ): ...

A. The Van der Peet Test

[15] The core question in *Van der Peet* [*R v. Van der Peet*, [1996] 2 SCR 507, 137 DLR (4th) 289] was: "How should the aboriginal rights recognized and affirmed by s. 35(1) of the *Constitution Act, 1982* be defined?" (para. 15, *per* Lamer CJ). Lamer CJ wrote for the majority, at para. 31:

> [W]hat s. 35(1) does is provide the constitutional framework through which the fact that aboriginals lived on the land in distinctive societies, with their own practices, traditions and cultures, is acknowledged and reconciled with the sovereignty of the Crown. The substantive rights which fall within the provision must be defined in light of this purpose; the aboriginal rights recognized and affirmed by s. 35(1) must be directed towards the reconciliation of the pre-existence of aboriginal societies with the sovereignty of the Crown.

[16] The emphasis on prior occupation as the primary justification for the special protection accorded aboriginal rights led the majority in *Van der Peet* to endorse a precontact test for identifying which customs, practices or traditions were integral to a particular aboriginal culture, and therefore entitled to constitutional protection. However, the majority recognized that the pre-contact test might prove inadequate to capture the range of Métis customs, practices or traditions that are entitled to protection, since Métis cultures by definition post-date European contact. For this reason, Lamer CJ explicitly reserved the question of how to define Métis aboriginal rights for another day. He wrote at para. 67:

> [T]he history of the Métis, and the reasons underlying their inclusion in the protection given by s. 35, are quite distinct from those of other aboriginal peoples in Canada. As such, the

manner in which the aboriginal rights of other aboriginal peoples are defined is not neces-sarily determinative of the manner in which the aboriginal rights of the Métis are defined. At the time when this Court is presented with a Métis claim under s. 35 it will then, with the benefit of the arguments of counsel, a factual context and a specific Métis claim, be able to explore the question of the purposes underlying s. 35's protection of the aboriginal rights of Métis people, and answer the question of the kinds of claims which fall within s. 35(1)'s scope when the claimants are Métis. The fact that, for other aboriginal peoples, the protec-tion granted by s. 35 goes to the practices, customs and traditions of aboriginal peoples prior to contact, is not necessarily relevant to the answer which will be given to that question.

[17] As indicated above, the inclusion of the Métis in s. 35 is not traceable to their pre-contact occupation of Canadian territory. The purpose of s. 35 as it relates to the Métis is therefore different from that which relates to the Indians or the Inuit. The con-stitutionally significant feature of the Métis is their special status as peoples that emerged between first contact and the effective imposition of European control. The inclusion of the Métis in s. 35 represents Canada's commitment to recognize and value the distinctive Métis cultures, which grew up in areas not yet open to colonization, and which the fram-ers of the *Constitution Act, 1982* recognized can only survive if the Métis are protected along with other aboriginal communities.

[18] With this in mind, we proceed to the issue of the correct test to determine the entitlements of the Métis under s. 35 of the *Constitution Act, 1982*. The appropriate test must then be applied to the findings of fact of the trial judge. We accept *Van der Peet* as the template for this discussion. However, we modify the pre-contact focus of the *Van der Peet* test when the claimants are Métis to account for the important differences be-tween Indian and Métis claims. Section 35 requires that we recognize and protect those customs and traditions that were historically important features of Métis communities prior to the time of effective European control, and that persist in the present day. This modification is required to account for the unique post-contact emergence of Métis communities, and the post-contact foundation of their aboriginal rights.

(1) Characterization of the Right

[19] The first step is to characterize the right being claimed: *Van der Peet*, *supra*, at para. 76. Aboriginal hunting rights, including Métis rights, are contextual and site-specific. The respondents shot a bull moose near Old Goulais Bay Road, in the environs of Sault Ste. Marie, within the traditional hunting grounds of that Métis community. They made a point of documenting that the moose was intended to provide meat for the winter. The trial judge determined that they were hunting for food, and there is no rea-son to overturn this finding. The right being claimed can therefore be characterized as the right to hunt for food in the environs of Sault Ste. Marie.

[20] We agree with the trial judge that the periodic scarcity of moose does not in it-self undermine the respondents' claim. The relevant right is not to hunt *moose* but to hunt for *food* in the designated territory.

(2) Identification of the Historic Rights-Bearing Community

[21] The trial judge found that a distinctive Métis community emerged in the Upper Great Lakes region in the mid-17th century, and peaked around 1850. We find no reviewable error in the trial judge's findings on this matter, which were confirmed by the Court of Appeal. The record indicates the following: In the mid-17th century, the Jesuits established a mission at Sainte-Marie-du-Sault, in an area characterized by heavy competition among fur traders. In 1750, the French established a fixed trading post on the south bank of the Saint Mary's River. The Sault Ste. Marie post attracted settlement by Métis—the children of unions between European traders and Indian women, and their descendants (A.J. Ray, "An Economic History of the Robinson Treaty Areas Before 1860" (1998) ("Ray Report"), at p. 17). According to Dr. Ray, by the early nineteenth century, "[t]he settlement at Sault Ste. Marie was one of the oldest and most important [Métis settlements] in the upper lakes area" (Ray Report, at p. 47). The Hudson Bay Company operated the St. Mary's post primarily as a depot from 1821 onwards (Ray Report, at p. 51). Although Dr. Ray characterized the Company's records for this post as "scanty" (Ray Report, at p. 51), he was able to piece together a portrait of the community from existing records, including the 1824-25 and 1827-28 post journals of HBC Chief Factor Bethune, and the 1846 report of a government surveyor, Alexander Vidal (Ray Report, at 52-53).

• • •

(3) Identification of the Contemporary Rights-Bearing Community

[24] Aboriginal rights are communal rights: They must be grounded in the existence of a historic and present community, and they may only be exercised by virtue of an individual's ancestrally based membership in the present community. The trial judge found that a Métis community has persisted in and around Sault Ste. Marie despite its decrease in visibility after the signing of the Robinson-Huron Treaty in 1850. While we take note of the trial judge's determination that the Sault Ste. Marie Métis community was to a large extent an "invisible entity" ([1999] 1 CNLR 153, at para. 80) from the mid-19th century to the 1970s, we do not take this to mean that the community ceased to exist or disappeared entirely.

[25] Dr. Lytwyn describes the continued existence of a Métis community in and around Sault Ste. Marie despite the displacement of many of the community's members in the aftermath of the 1850 treaties:

> [T]he Métis continued to live in the Sault Ste. Marie region. Some drifted into the Indian Reserves which had been set apart by the 1850 Treaty. Others lived in areas outside of the town, or in back concessions. The Métis continued to live in much the same manner as they had in the past—fishing, hunting, trapping and harvesting other resources for their livelihood. (Lytwyn Report, at p. 31 (emphasis added); see also J. Morrison, "The Robinson Treaties of 1850: A Case Study," at p. 201.)

[26] The advent of European control over this area thus interfered with, but did not eliminate, the Sault Ste. Marie Métis community and its traditional practices, as evidenced by census data from the 1860s through the 1890s. Dr. Lytwyn concluded from this census data that "[a]lthough the Métis lost much of their traditional land base at Sault Ste. Marie,

they continued to live in the region and gain their livelihood from the resources of the land and waters" (Lytwyn Report, at p. 32). He also noted a tendency for underreporting and lack of information about the Métis during this period because of their "removal to the peripheries of the town," and "their own disinclination to be identified as Métis" in the wake of the Riel rebellions and the turning of Ontario public opinion against Métis rights through government actions and the media (Lytwyn Report, at p. 33).

[27] We conclude that the evidence supports the trial judge's finding that the community's lack of visibility was explained and does not negate the existence of the contemporary community. There was never a lapse; the Métis community went underground, so to speak, but it continued. Moreover, as indicated below, the "continuity" requirement puts the focus on the continuing practices of members of the community, rather than more generally on the community itself, as indicated below.

[28] The trial judge's finding of a contemporary Métis community in and around Sault Ste. Marie is supported by the evidence and must be upheld.

(4) Verification of the Claimant's Membership in the Relevant Contemporary Community

[29] While determining membership in the Métis community might not be as simple as verifying membership in, for example, an Indian band, this does not detract from the status of Métis people as full-fledged rights-bearers. As Métis communities continue to organize themselves more formally and to assert their constitutional rights, it is imperative that membership requirements become more standardized so that legitimate rights-holders can be identified. In the meantime, courts faced with Métis claims will have to ascertain Métis identity on a case-by-case basis. The inquiry must take into account both the value of community self-definition, and the need for the process of identification to be objectively verifiable. In addition, the criteria for Métis identity under s. 35 must reflect the purpose of this constitutional guarantee: to recognize and affirm the rights of the Métis held by virtue of their direct relationship to this country's original inhabitants and by virtue of the continuity between their customs and traditions and those of their Métis predecessors. This is not an insurmountable task.

[30] We emphasize that we have not been asked, and we do not purport, to set down a comprehensive definition of who is Métis for the purpose of asserting a claim under s. 35. We therefore limit ourselves to indicating the important components of a future definition, while affirming that the creation of appropriate membership tests *before* disputes arise is an urgent priority. As a general matter, we would endorse the guidelines proposed by Vaillancourt J and O'Neill J in the courts below. In particular, we would look to three broad factors as indicia of Métis identity for the purpose of claiming Métis rights under s. 35: self-identification, ancestral connection, and community acceptance.

[31] First, the claimant must *self-identify* as a member of a Métis community. This self-identification should not be of recent vintage: While an individual's self-identification need not be static or monolithic, claims that are made belatedly in order to benefit from a s. 35 right will not satisfy the self-identification requirement.

[32] Second, the claimant must present evidence of an *ancestral connection* to a historic Métis community. This objective requirement ensures that beneficiaries of s. 35

rights have a real link to the historic community whose practices ground the right being claimed. We would not require a minimum "blood quantum," but we would require some proof that the claimant's ancestors belonged to the historic Métis community by birth, adoption, or other means. Like the trial judge, we would abstain from further defining this requirement in the absence of more extensive argument by the parties in a case where this issue is determinative. In this case, the Powleys' Métis ancestry is not disputed.

[33] Third, the claimant must demonstrate that he or she is *accepted by the modern community* whose continuity with the historic community provides the legal foundation for the right being claimed. Membership in a Métis political organization may be relevant to the question of community acceptance, but it is not sufficient in the absence of a contextual understanding of the membership requirements of the organization and its role in the Métis community. The core of community acceptance is past and ongoing participation in a shared culture, in the customs and traditions that constitute a Métis community's identity and distinguish it from other groups. This is what the community membership criterion is all about. Other indicia of community acceptance might include evidence of participation in community activities and testimony from other members about the claimant's connection to the community and its culture. The range of acceptable forms of evidence does not attenuate the need for an objective demonstration of a solid bond of past and present mutual identification and recognition of common belonging between the claimant and other members of the rights-bearing community.

· · ·

(5) Identification of the Relevant Time Frame

[36] As indicated above, the pre-contact aspect of the *Van der Peet* test requires adjustment in order to take account of the post-contact ethnogenesis of the Métis and the purpose of s. 35 in protecting the historically important customs and traditions of these distinctive peoples. While the fact of prior occupation grounds aboriginal rights claims for the Inuit and the Indians, the recognition of Métis rights in s. 35 is not reducible to the Métis' Indian ancestry. The unique status of the Métis as an Aboriginal people with post-contact origins requires an adaptation of the pre-contact approach to meet the distinctive historical circumstances surrounding the evolution of Métis communities.

[37] The pre-contact test in *Van der Peet* is based on the constitutional affirmation that aboriginal communities are entitled to continue those practices, customs and traditions that are integral to their distinctive existence or relationship to the land. By analogy, the test for Métis practices should focus on identifying those practices, customs and traditions that are integral to the Métis community's distinctive existence and relationship to the land. This unique history can most appropriately be accommodated by a post-contact but pre-control test that identifies the time when Europeans effectively established political and legal control in a particular area. The focus should be on the period after a particular Métis community arose and before it came under the effective control of European laws and customs. This pre-control test enables us to identify those practices, customs and traditions that predate the imposition of European laws and customs on the Métis.

[38] We reject the appellant's argument that Métis rights must find their origin in the pre-contact practices of the Métis' aboriginal ancestors. This theory in effect would deny to

Métis their full status as distinctive rights-bearing peoples whose own integral practices are entitled to constitutional protection under s. 35(1). The right claimed here was a practice of both the Ojibway and the Métis. However, as long as the practice grounding the right is distinctive and integral to the pre-control Métis community, it will satisfy this prong of the test. This result flows from the constitutional imperative that we recognize and affirm the aboriginal rights of the Métis, who appeared after the time of first contact.

· · ·

[40] The historical record indicates that the Sault Ste. Marie Métis community thrived largely unaffected by European laws and customs until colonial policy shifted from one of discouraging settlement to one of negotiating treaties and encouraging settlement in the mid-19th century. The trial judge found, and the parties agreed in their pleadings before the lower courts, that "effective control [of the Upper Great Lakes area] passed from the Aboriginal peoples of the area (Ojibway and Métis) to European control" in the period between 1815 and 1850 (para. 90). The record fully supports the finding that the period just prior to 1850 is the appropriate date for finding effective control in this geographic area, which the Crown agreed was the critical date in its pleadings below.

(6) Determination of Whether the Practice Is Integral to the Claimants' Distinctive Culture

[41] The practice of subsistence hunting and fishing was a constant in the Métis community, even though the availability of particular species might have waxed and waned. The evidence indicates that subsistence hunting was an important aspect of Métis life and a defining feature of their special relationship to the land ([J. Peterson, "Many Roads to Red River: Métis Genesis in the Great Lakes Region, 1680-1815," in *The New Peoples: Being and Becoming Métis in North America* (Winnipeg: University of Manitoba Press, 1985)], at p. 41; Lytwyn Report, *supra*, at p. 6). A major part of subsistence was the practice at issue here, hunting for food.

· · ·

[43] Dr. Ray emphasized in his report that a key feature of Métis communities was that "their members earned a substantial part of their livelihood off of the land" (Ray Report, *supra*, at p. 56). Dr. Lytwyn concurred: "The Métis of Sault Ste. Marie lived off the resources of the land. They obtained their livelihood from hunting, fishing, gathering and cultivating" (Lytwyn Report, at p. 2). He reported that "[w]hile Métis fishing was prominent in the written accounts, hunting was also an important part of their livelihood," and that "[a] traditional winter hunting area for the Sault Métis was the Goulais Bay area" (Lytwyn Report, at pp. 4-5). He elaborated at p. 6:

> In the mid-19th century, the Métis way of life incorporated many resource harvesting activities. These activities, especially hunting and trapping, were done within traditional territories located within the hinterland of Sault Ste. Marie. The Métis engaged in these activities for generations and, on the eve of the 1850 treaties, hunting, fishing, trapping and gathering were integral activities to the Métis community at Sault Ste. Marie.

[44] This evidence supports the trial judge's finding that hunting for food was integral to the Métis way of life at Sault Ste. Marie in the period just prior to 1850.

(7) Establishment of Continuity Between the Historic Practice and the Contemporary Right Asserted

[45] Although s. 35 protects "existing" rights, it is more than a mere codification of the common law. Section 35 reflects a new promise: a constitutional commitment to protecting practices that were historically important features of particular aboriginal communities. A certain margin of flexibility might be required to ensure that aboriginal practices can evolve and develop over time, but it is not necessary to define or to rely on that margin in this case. Hunting for food was an important feature of the Sault Ste. Marie Métis community, and the practice has been continuous to the present. Steve and Roddy Powley claim a Métis aboriginal right to hunt for food. The right claimed by the Powleys falls squarely within the bounds of the historical practice grounding the right.

(8) Determination of Whether or Not the Right Was Extinguished

[46] The doctrine of extinguishment applies equally to Métis and to First Nations claims. There is no evidence of extinguishment here, as determined by the trial judge. The Crown's argument for extinguishment is based largely on the Robinson-Huron Treaty of 1850, from which the Métis as a group were explicitly excluded.

(9) If There Is a Right, Determination of Whether There Is an Infringement

[47] Ontario currently does not recognize any Métis right to hunt for food, or any "special access rights to natural resources" for the Métis whatsoever (appellant's record, at p. 1029). This lack of recognition, and the consequent application of the challenged provisions to the Powleys, infringe their aboriginal right to hunt for food as a continuation of the protected historical practices of the Sault Ste. Marie Métis community.

(10) Determination of Whether the Infringement Is Justified

[48] The main justification advanced by the appellant is that of conservation. Although conservation is clearly a very important concern, we agree with the trial judge that the record here does not support this justification. If the moose population in this part of Ontario were under threat, and there was no evidence that it is, the Métis would still be entitled to a priority allocation to satisfy their subsistence needs in accordance with the criteria set out in *R v. Sparrow*, [1990] 1 SCR 1075. While preventative measures might be required for conservation purposes in the future, we have not been presented with evidence to support such measures here. The Ontario authorities can make out a case for regulation of the aboriginal right to hunt moose for food if and when the need arises. On the available evidence and given the current licensing system, Ontario's blanket denial of any Métis right to hunt for food cannot be justified.

· · ·

B. The Request for a Stay

[51] With respect to the cross-appeal, we affirm that the Court of Appeal had jurisdiction to issue a stay of its decision in these circumstances. This power should continue to be used only in exceptional situations in which a court of general jurisdiction deems that giving immediate effect to an order will undermine the very purpose of that order or otherwise threaten the rule of law: *Reference re Manitoba Language Rights*, [1985] 1 SCR 721 [74 DLR (4th) 23]. We note that the Powleys' acquittal would have remained valid notwithstanding the stay. It was, however, within the Court of Appeal's discretion to suspend the application of its ruling to other members of the Métis community in order to foster cooperative solutions and ensure that the resource in question was not depleted in the interim, thereby negating the value of the right.

[52] The initial stay expired on February 23, 2002, and more than a year has passed since that time. The Court of Appeal's decision has been the law of Ontario in the interim, and chaos does not appear to have ensued. We see no compelling reason to issue an additional stay. We also note that it is particularly important to have a clear justification for a stay where the effect of that stay would be to suspend the recognition of a right that provides a defence to a criminal charge, as it would here.

Appeal and cross-appeal dismissed.

VIII. DISTRIBUTION OF LEGISLATIVE AUTHORITY

A remaining gap in our review of the Court's treatment of Aboriginal rights is the distribution of governmental powers relative to Aboriginal peoples in Canada's federal system. Before 1982, Parliament and provincial legislatures were viewed as free to pass laws that interfered with the exercise of common law Aboriginal rights, as long as each level of government acted within its sphere of legislative authority. Federal legislative competence in this regard was seen to stem from s. 91(24) of the *Constitution Act, 1867*, which confers on Parliament the authority to pass laws in relation to "Indians, and Lands reserved for the Indians." For example, the federal *Indian Act*, RSC 1985, c. I-5, which provides for the establishment of elected band councils and the management and protection of Indian reserve land, owes its constitutional validity to s. 91(24).

Provincial authority to pass laws affecting Aboriginal peoples is more complicated. While a province, generally speaking, is not entitled to "single out" Aboriginal people (see *R v. Sutherland*, [1980] 2 SCR 451, 113 DLR (3d) 374), a province may, in some circumstances, regulate Aboriginal peoples by "laws of general application." The following excerpt from *Delgamuukw* provides some insight into the scope of "Indians, and Lands reserved for Indians" under s. 91(24) of the *Constitution Act, 1867*.

Delgamuukw v. British Columbia
[1997] 3 SCR 1010, 153 DLR (4th) 193

LAMER CJC (Cory, Major, and McLachlin JJ concurring): ...

E. Did the Province Have the Power to Extinguish Aboriginal Rights After 1871, Either Under Its Own Jurisdiction or Through the Operation of Section 88 of the Indian Act?

. . .

(2) Primary Jurisdiction

[173] Since 1871, the exclusive power to legislate in relation to "Indians, and Lands reserved for the Indians" has been vested with the federal government by virtue of s. 91(24) of the *Constitution Act, 1867.* That head of jurisdiction, in my opinion, encompasses within it the exclusive power to extinguish aboriginal rights, including aboriginal title.

"Lands reserved for the Indians"

[174] I consider the second part of this provision first, which confers jurisdiction to the federal government over "Lands reserved for the Indians." The debate between the parties centred on whether that part of s. 91(24) confers jurisdiction to legislate with respect to aboriginal title. The province's principal submission is that "Lands reserved for the Indians" are lands which have been specifically set aside or designated for Indian occupation, such as reserves. However, I must reject that submission, because it flies in the face of the judgment of the Privy Council in *St. Catherine's Milling* [*St. Catherine's Milling and Lumber Co. v. The Queen* (1888), 14 App. Cas. 46 (PC)]. One of the issues in that appeal was the federal jurisdiction to accept the surrender of lands held pursuant to aboriginal title. It was argued that the federal government, at most, had jurisdiction over "Indian Reserves." Lord Watson, speaking for the Privy Council, rejected this argument, stating that had the intention been to restrict s. 91(24) in this way, specific language to this effect would have been used. He accordingly held that (at p. 59):

> ... the words actually used are, according to their natural meaning, sufficient to include all lands reserved, upon any terms or conditions, for Indian occupation.

Lord Watson's reference to "all lands" encompasses not only reserve lands, but lands held pursuant to aboriginal title as well. Section 91(24), in other words, carries with it the jurisdiction to legislate in relation to aboriginal title. It follows, by implication, that it also confers the jurisdiction to extinguish that title.

[175] The province responds by pointing to the fact that underlying title to lands held pursuant to aboriginal title vested with the provincial Crown pursuant to s. 109 of the *Constitution Act, 1867.* In its submission, this right of ownership carried with it the right to grant fee simples which, by implication, extinguish aboriginal title, and so by negative implication excludes aboriginal title from the scope of s. 91(24). The difficulty with the province's submission is that it fails to take account of the language of s. 109, which states in part that:

109. All Lands, Mines, Minerals, and Royalties belonging to the several Provinces of Canada ... at the Union ... shall belong to the several Provinces ... subject to any Trusts existing in respect thereof, and to any Interest other than that of the Province in the same.

Although that provision vests underlying title in provincial Crowns, it qualifies provincial ownership by making it subject to the "any Interest other than that of the Province in the same." In *St. Catherine's Milling*, the Privy Council held that aboriginal title was such an interest, and rejected the argument that provincial ownership operated as a limit on federal jurisdiction. The net effect of that decision, therefore, was to separate the ownership of lands held pursuant to aboriginal title from jurisdiction over those lands. Thus, although on surrender of aboriginal title the province would take absolute title, jurisdiction to accept surrenders lies with the federal government. The same can be said of extinguishment—although on extinguishment of aboriginal title, the province would take complete title to the land, the jurisdiction to extinguish lies with the federal government.

. . .

"Indians"

[177] The extent of federal jurisdiction over Indians has not been definitively addressed by this Court. We have not needed to do so because the *vires* of federal legislation with respect to Indians, under the division of powers, has never been at issue. The cases which have come before the Court under s. 91(24) have implicated the question of jurisdiction over Indians from the other direction—whether provincial laws which on their face apply to Indians intrude on federal jurisdiction and are inapplicable to Indians to the extent of that intrusion. As I explain below, the Court has held that s. 91(24) protects a "core" of Indianness from provincial intrusion, through the doctrine of interjurisdictional immunity.

[178] It follows, at the very least, that this core falls within the scope of federal jurisdiction over Indians. That core, for reasons I will develop, encompasses aboriginal rights, including the rights that are recognized and affirmed by s. 35(1). Laws which purport to extinguish those rights therefore touch the core of Indianness which lies at the heart of s. 91(24), and are beyond the legislative competence of the provinces to enact. The core of Indianness encompasses the whole range of aboriginal rights that are protected by s. 35(1). Those rights include rights in relation to land; that part of the core derives from s. 91(24)'s reference to "Lands reserved for the Indians." But those rights also encompass practices, customs and traditions which are not tied to land as well; that part of the core can be traced to federal jurisdiction over "Indians." Provincial governments are prevented from legislating in relation to both types of aboriginal rights.

(3) Provincial Laws of General Application

[179] The vesting of exclusive jurisdiction with the federal government over Indians and Indian lands under s. 91(24), operates to preclude provincial laws in relation to those matters. Thus, provincial laws which single out Indians for special treatment are *ultra vires*, because they are in relation to Indians and therefore invade federal jurisdiction. ...

However, it is a well-established principle that (*Four B Manufacturing Ltd.* [*v. United Garment Workers of America*, [1980] 1 SCR 1031, 102 DLR (3d) 385]):

> The conferring upon Parliament of exclusive legislative competence to make laws relating to certain classes of persons does not mean that the totality of these persons' rights and duties comes under primary federal competence to the exclusion of provincial laws of general application.

In other words, notwithstanding s. 91(24), provincial laws of general application apply *proprio vigore* to Indians and Indian lands. …

[180] What must be answered, however, is whether the same principle allows provincial laws of general application to extinguish aboriginal rights. I have come to the conclusion that a provincial law of general application could not have this effect, for two reasons. First, a law of general application cannot, by definition, meet the standard which has been set by this Court for the extinguishment of aboriginal rights without being *ultra vires* the province. That standard was laid down in *Sparrow* [*R v.*, [1990] 1 SCR 1075, 70 DLR (4th) 385] … as one of "clear and plain" intent. In that decision, the Court drew a distinction between laws which extinguished aboriginal rights, and those which merely regulated them. Although the latter types of laws may have been "necessarily inconsistent" with the continued exercise of aboriginal rights, they could not extinguish those rights. While the requirement of clear and plain intent does not, perhaps, require that the Crown "use language which refers expressly to its extinguishment of aboriginal rights" (*Gladstone* [[1996] 2 SCR 723, 137 DLR (4th) 648]), the standard is still quite high. My concern is that the only laws with the sufficiently clear and plain intention to extinguish aboriginal rights would be laws in relation to Indians and Indian lands. As a result, a provincial law could never, *proprio vigore*, extinguish aboriginal rights, because the intention to do so would take the law outside provincial jurisdiction.

[181] Second, as I mentioned earlier, s. 91(24) protects a core of federal jurisdiction even from provincial laws of general application, through the operation of the doctrine of interjurisdictional immunity. That core has been described as matters touching on "Indianness" or the "core of Indianness" … [*Dick v. The Queen*, [1985] 2 SCR 309, 23 DLR (4th) 33]. The core of Indianness at the heart of s. 91(24) has been defined in both negative and positive terms. Negatively, it has been held to not include labour relations (*Four B* [*supra*]) and the driving of motor vehicles (*R v. Francis*, [1988] 1 SCR 1025 [51 DLR (4th) 418]). The only positive formulation of Indianness was offered in *Dick*. Speaking for the Court, Beetz J assumed, but did not decide, that a provincial hunting law did not apply *proprio vigore* to the members of an Indian band to hunt and because those activities were "at the centre of what they do and what they are" (at p. 320). But in *Van der Peet* [*R v. Van der Peet*, [1996] 2 SCR 507], I described and defined the aboriginal rights that are recognized and affirmed by s. 35(1) in a similar fashion, as protecting the occupation of land and the activities which are integral to the distinctive aboriginal culture of the group claiming the right. It follows that aboriginal rights are part of the core of Indianness at the heart of s. 91(24). Prior to 1982, as a result, they could not be extinguished by provincial laws of general application.

(4) Section 88 of the Indian Act

[182] Provincial laws which would otherwise not apply to Indians *proprio vigore*, however, are allowed to do so by s. 88 of the *Indian Act*, which incorporates by reference provincial laws of general application: *Dick* ... . However, it is important to note, in Professor Hogg's words, that s. 88 does not "invigorate" provincial laws which are invalid because they are in relation to Indians and Indian lands (*Constitutional Law of Canada* (3rd ed. 1992), at p. 676; also see *Dick*). What this means is that s. 88 extends the effect of provincial laws of general application which cannot apply to Indians and Indian lands because they touch on the Indianness at the core of s. 91(24). For example, a provincial law which regulated hunting may very well touch on this core. Although such a law would not apply to aboriginal people *proprio vigore*, it would still apply through s. 88 of the *Indian Act*, being a law of general application. Such laws are enacted to conserve game and for the safety of all.

[183] The respondent BC Crown argues that since such laws are *intra vires* the province, and applicable to aboriginal persons, s. 88 could allow provincial laws to extinguish aboriginal rights. I reject this submission, for the simple reason that s. 88 does not evince the requisite clear and plain intent to extinguish aboriginal rights. ... I see nothing in the language of the provision which even suggests the intention to extinguish aboriginal rights. Indeed, the explicit reference to treaty rights in s. 88 suggests that the provision was clearly not intended to undermine aboriginal rights.

NOTES

1. The principles articulated in the *Dick* case referred to in *Delgamuukw* were considered in *Kitkatla Band v. British Columbia*, [2002] 2 SCR 46, 2002 SCC 31, 210 DLR (4th) 577. At issue was the constitutionality of sections of the provincial *Heritage Conservation Act* (HCA), RSBC 1996, c. 187 that allowed the BC Minister of Small Business, Tourism, and Culture to issue permits to "damage, alter, cover or move an aboriginal rock painting or aboriginal rock carving that has historical or archeological value." Representatives of the Kitkatla Band argued that the impugned sections of the HCA were *ultra vires* the province as matters that were in their pith and substance reserved exclusively to Parliament under s. 91(24) of the *Constitution Act, 1867*. The province argued that it had the authority to pass the impugned sections of the HCA under s. 92(13), "Property and Civil Rights." The Court held that the impugned sections of the Act were valid as provincial legislation falling within provincial jurisdiction over property and civil rights in the province, and that the impugned provisions did not single out Aboriginal peoples nor impair their status or condition as Indians. The Court stated that the province was within its jurisdiction to enact this law because the impugned provisions prohibited everyone, not just Aboriginal peoples, from the named acts and required everyone, not just Aboriginal peoples, to seek the minister's permission to commit the prohibited acts. Therefore, they said that the treatment afforded to Aboriginal and non-Aboriginal heritage objects under the Act was the same. The Court noted that any disproportionate effects of the Act on Aboriginal peoples were only due to the fact that Aboriginal peoples produced the largest number of heritage products in the province. Furthermore, the Court wrote that the evidence in the case was quite sparse, and

did not establish that the Act's provisions affected the essential and distinctive values of Indianness. Thus there was no question of paramountcy or interjurisdictional immunity raised in the case. In arriving at this conclusion, Justice LeBel observed (at para. 66):

> [T]he Court must remember the basic assumption that provincial laws can apply to aboriginal peoples; First Nations are not enclaves of federal power in a sea of provincial jurisdiction: see *Cardinal v. Attorney General of Alberta*, [1974] SCR 695 [40 DLR (3d) 553]. The mere mention of the word "aboriginal" in a statutory provision does not render it *ultra vires* the province.

In *Kitkatla,* the Court's unwillingness to conclude, absent evidence, that the Act struck at the core of Indianness suggests that it will not determine what falls within the core of s. 91(24) in the abstract. Jean Leclair notes that "if the Court in *Kitkatla* had resorted to abstraction to define the minimum content of section 91(24), it would have run the risk of recognizing some practices as fundamental under section 91(24) while refusing to recognize the very same practices as aboriginal rights under section 35." He notes further that such an approach "would also have rendered the result of the case applicable to all aboriginal peoples falling under federal jurisdiction whether or not they had established an aboriginal right to the aboriginal heritage object or sites within their traditional territory." (Jean Leclair, "The Kitkatla Decision: Finding Jurisdictional Room to Justify Provincial Regulation of Aboriginal Matters" (2001), 21 *Supreme Court Law Review* (2d) 73, at 88, 90.)

IX. ABORIGINAL RIGHTS OF SELF-GOVERNMENT

Aboriginal peoples organized their affairs and exercised governing authority for millennia prior to the arrival of Europeans and others in North America. These powers of governance varied according to clan and nation, and were suited to the varieties of languages, economies, and cultures represented on the continent. There were alliances, confederacies, powerful families, democracies, and empires. Traditions of governance were often closely connected to the land, and many emphasized the connection of the spiritual, familial, economic, and political spheres. The nature, scope, and existence of these ancient powers are the subject of debate in contemporary Canada. Through negotiation and litigation, many First Nations are attempting to articulate their rights of self-government.

On August 4, 1998, for example, representatives of the federal and provincial governments and the Nisga'a Tribal Council initialed the *Nisga'a Final Agreement* in a ceremony in the Nass Valley. In terms of its legislative and administrative powers, the Nisga'a government will have jurisdiction over a wide range of areas, including culture, language, employment, public works, land use, and marriage. The Nisga'a government will also continue to provide health, child welfare, and education services. Perhaps more important, however, is that the *Nisga'a Agreement* makes provisions for which laws will prevail when a conflict arises between Nisga'a laws and federal and provincial laws. Thus far, the Court has not directly tackled the implications for federalism and the division of powers that s. 35(1) poses if Aboriginal self-government is among the existing rights recognized and affirmed by that section. The Supreme Court has, however, suggested a framework for the recognition of self-government in *R v. Pamajewon*, which follows.

R v. Pamajewon
[1996] 2 SCR 821, 138 DLR (4th) 204

[Pamajewon and his co-accused, each a member of either the Shawanaga First Nation or Eagle Lake Band, were convicted of keeping a common gaming house contrary to s. 201 of the *Criminal Code*. The gaming activities were conducted on reserves, though many of the participants were non-natives. On appeal the band members argued, *inter alia*, that the activities in question were protected as an Aboriginal right under s. 35(1) or as an incident of the inherent right of self-government claimed by the two First Nations. The Ontario Court of Appeal and the Supreme Court of Canada dismissed the appeals.]

LAMER CJC (La Forest, Sopinka, Gonthier, Cory, McLachlin, Iacobucci, and Major JJ concurring): [1] This appeal raises the question of whether the conduct of high stakes gambling by the Shawanaga and Eagle Lake First Nations falls within the scope of the aboriginal rights recognized and affirmed by s. 35(1) of the *Constitution Act, 1982*.

. . .

[21] The appellants appealed on the basis that the Court of Appeal erred in restricting aboriginal title to rights that are activity and site specific and in concluding that self-government only extends to those matters which were governed by ancient laws or customs. The appellant argued further that the Court of Appeal erred in concluding that the *Code* extinguished self-government regarding gaming and in not addressing whether the *Code*'s gaming provisions unjustifiably interfered with the rights recognized and affirmed by s. 35(1) of the *Constitution Act, 1982*.

. . .

[23] The resolution of the appellants' claim in this case rests on the application of the test, laid out by this Court in *R v. Van der Peet*, [1996] 2 SCR 507 [137 DLR (4th) 289], for determining the aboriginal rights recognized and affirmed by s. 35(1) of the *Constitution Act, 1982*. The appellants in this case are claiming that the gambling activities in which they took part, and their respective bands' regulation of those gambling activities, fell within the scope of the aboriginal rights recognized and affirmed by s. 35(1). *Van der Peet*, *supra*, lays out the test for determining the practices, customs and traditions which fall within s. 35(1) and, as such, provides the legal standard against which the appellants' claim must be measured.

[24] The appellants' claim involves the assertion that s. 35(1) encompasses the right of self-government, and that this right includes the right to regulate gambling activities on the reservation. Assuming without deciding that s. 35(1) includes self-government claims, the applicable legal standard is nonetheless that laid out in *Van der Peet*, *supra*. Assuming s. 35(1) encompasses claims to aboriginal self-government, such claims must be considered in light of the purposes underlying that provision and must, therefore, be considered against the test derived from consideration of those purposes. This is the test laid out in *Van der Peet*, *supra*. In so far as they can be made under s. 35(1), claims to self-government are no different from other claims to the enjoyment of aboriginal rights and must, as such, be measured against the same standard.

[25] In *Van der Peet*, *supra*, the test for identifying aboriginal rights was said to be as follows, at para. 46:

> ... [I]n order to be an aboriginal right an activity must be an element of a practice, custom or tradition integral to the distinctive culture of the aboriginal group claiming the right.

In applying this test the Court must first identify the exact nature of the activity claimed to be a right and must then go on to determine whether, on the evidence presented to the trial judge, and on the facts as found by the trial judge, that activity could be said to be (*Van der Peet*, at para. 59) "a defining feature of the culture in question" prior to contact with Europeans.

[26] I now turn to the first part of the *Van der Peet* test, the characterization of the appellants' claim. In *Van der Peet*, *supra*, the Court held at para. 53 that:

> To characterize an applicant's claim correctly, a court should consider such factors as the nature of the action which the applicant is claiming was done pursuant to an aboriginal right, the nature of the governmental regulation, statute or action being impugned, and the practice, custom or tradition being relied upon to establish the right.

When these factors are considered in this case it can be seen that the correct characterization of the appellants' claim is that they are claiming the right to participate in, and to regulate, high stakes gambling activities on the reservation. The activity which the appellants organized, and which their bands regulated, was high stakes gambling. The statute which they argue violates those rights prohibits gambling subject only to a few very limited exceptions (laid out in s. 207 of the *Code*). Finally, the applicants rely in support of their claim on the fact that the "Ojibwa people ... had a long tradition of public games and sporting events, which pre-dated the arrival of Europeans." Thus, the activity in which the appellants were engaged and which their bands regulated, the statute they are impugning, and the historical evidence on which they rely, all relate to the conduct and regulation of gambling. As such, the most accurate characterization of the appellants' claim is that they are asserting that s. 35(1) recognizes and affirms the rights of the Shawanaga and Eagle Lake First Nations to participate in, and to regulate, gambling activities on their respective reserve lands.

[27] The appellants themselves would have this Court characterize their claim as to "a broad right to manage the use of their reserve lands." To so characterize the appellants' claim would be to cast the Court's inquiry at a level of excessive generality. Aboriginal rights, including any asserted right to self-government, must be looked at in light of the specific circumstances of each case and, in particular, in light of the specific history and culture of the aboriginal group claiming the right. The factors laid out in *Van der Peet*, and applied, *supra*, allow the Court to consider the appellants' claim at the appropriate level of specificity; the characterization put forward by the appellants would not allow the Court to do so.

[28] I now turn to the second branch of the *Van der Peet* test, the consideration of whether the participation in, and regulation of, gambling on the reserve lands was an integral part of the distinctive cultures of the Shawanaga or Eagle Lake First Nations. The evidence presented at both the Pamajewon and Gardner trials does not demonstrate that gambling, or that the regulation of gambling, was an integral part of the distinctive cultures of the Shawanaga or Eagle Lake First Nations. In fact, the only evidence presented

at either trial dealing with the question of the importance of gambling was that of James Morrison, who testified at the Pamajewon trial with regards to the importance and prevalence of gaming in Ojibwa culture. While Mr. Morrison's evidence does demonstrate that the Ojibwa gambled, it does not demonstrate that gambling was of central significance to the Ojibwa people. Moreover, his evidence in no way addresses the extent to which this gambling was the subject of regulation by the Ojibwa community. His account is of informal gambling activities taking place on a small-scale; he does not describe large-scale activities, subject to community regulation, of the sort at issue in this appeal.

[29] I would note that neither of the trial judges in these cases relied upon findings of fact regarding the importance of gambling to the Ojibwa; however, upon review of the evidence I find myself in agreement with the conclusion arrived at by Osborne JA when he said first, at p. 400, that there "is no evidence to support a conclusion that gambling generally or high stakes gambling of the sort in issue here, were part of the First Nations' historic cultures and traditions, or an aspect of their use of their land" and, second, at p. 400, that "there is no evidence that gambling on the reserve lands generally was ever the subject matter of aboriginal regulation." I also agree with the observation made by Flaherty Prov. Ct. J in the Gardner trial when he said that

> commercial lotteries such as bingo are a twentieth century phenomena and nothing of the kind existed amongst aboriginal peoples and was never part of the means by which those societies were traditionally sustained or socialized.

[30] Given this evidentiary record, it is clear that the appellants have failed to demonstrate that the gambling activities in which they were engaged, and their respective bands' regulation of those activities, took place pursuant to an aboriginal right recognized and affirmed by s. 35(1) of the *Constitution Act, 1982.*

[L'Heureux-Dubé J concurred in separate reasons.]

Appeal dismissed.

NOTES

1. In *Casimel v. Insurance Corporation of British Columbia* (1993), 106 DLR (4th) 720 (BCCA), the court held that a customary Aboriginal adoption should be treated as a legal adoption. The plaintiffs, Louise Casimel and Francis Casimel, raised their grandson, Ernest Casimel, in a parent–child relationship following a customary adoption acknowledged by the Stellaquo Band of the Carrier People. When Ernest was killed in a motor vehicle accident, his adoptive parents sued his insurance company to claim the benefit owed to dependent parents. (It was determined early on that they were, in fact, dependent on him.) The insurance company claimed that the plaintiffs were not Ernest's parents because the adoption had not followed the procedures set out in provincial adoption legislation, and were therefore not eligible to claim the benefit. The court rejected the insurance company's claim. The court first determined that there was in fact a custom of adoption among the Stellaquo Band and that this custom had been fulfilled by the Casimel family. Second, it held that nothing

in statutory or common law had extinguished or limited the Band's right to establish family connections, including those created by adoption, according to custom; this right remained protected by s. 35 of the *Constitution Act, 1982.* Louise and Francis Casimel, as dependents to and parents by adoption of Ernest, were therefore successful in their claim against the insurance company. Does *Casimel* reinscribe *Connelly v. Woolrich* (1867), 17 RJRQ 75 (Que. SC), as described by the Royal Commission on Aboriginal Peoples in the excerpt at the outset of this chapter, in constitutional terms? Is *Casimel* consistent with *Pamajewon*?

2. More generally, are the Court's holdings in *Delgamuukw* and *Pamajewon* consistent with each other? How might an Aboriginal right of self-government relate to the distribution of legislative authority between Parliament and the provincial legislatures? Consider the following excerpt.

Patrick Macklem, *Indigenous Difference and the Constitution of Canada*
(Toronto: University of Toronto Press, 2001), at 173-80 (footnotes omitted)

The Court's decision in *Pamajewon* should be read in light of its subsequent decision in *Delgamuukw*, in which the Gitksan and Wet'suwet'en nations asserted an Aboriginal right of self-government over lands to which they possessed Aboriginal title. The Court in *Delgamuukw* held that errors of the trial judge made it "impossible ... to determine whether the claim to self-government has been made out." Nonetheless, the Court also held that Aboriginal title confers an exclusive right to use and occupy land for a variety of activities that need not relate to customs, practices or traditions that are integral to the distinctive culture of the Aboriginal nation in question. It held further that "the same legal principles governed the aboriginal interest in reserve lands and lands held pursuant to aboriginal title." In other words, *Delgamuukw* contemplates the very possibility that *Pamajewon* sought to foreclose: a First Nation successfully asserting a broad Aboriginal right to regulate and engage in economic activity on reserve lands unrelated to traditional patterns of territorial use and enjoyment. Viewed together, *Delgamuukw* and *Pamajewon* suggest that the Constitution of Canada recognizes and affirms an inherent Aboriginal right of self-government—specifically, a right to make laws in relation to customs, practices and traditions integral to the distinctive culture of the Aboriginal nation and in relation to the use of reserve lands and lands subject to Aboriginal title.

Whether the Constitution ought to be interpreted as recognizing an Aboriginal right of self-government, however, turns less on what precedent says and more on the distributive justice of recognizing an Aboriginal order of government within the Canadian constitutional order. The legitimacy of the Canadian constitutional order rests in part on the extent to which it protects interests associated with indigenous difference. Because protection of interests associated with prior Aboriginal sovereignty promotes both formal and substantive equality, such interests ought to receive protection in the form of an existing Aboriginal right of self-government. Constitutional recognition of an Aboriginal right of self-government formally acknowledges that Aboriginal nations were and continue to be self-governing despite the establishment of the Canadian state and begins to ameliorate the substantive inequalities that Aboriginal people face in contemporary society by enabling them to exercise greater control over their individual and collective identities.

If interests associated with Aboriginal sovereignty merit constitutional protection in the form of an existing Aboriginal right of self-government, how would an Aboriginal order of government relate to the distribution of power between Parliament and provincial legislatures? The Constitution assigns to provincial legislatures subject-matters over which they enjoy exclusive jurisdiction. Parliament is assigned jurisdiction over different specific subject-matters, as well as residual authority "to make Laws for the Peace, Order, and good Government of Canada." The judiciary generally takes a purposive approach to the delineation of the distribution of legislative authority, and subject-matters are often viewed as possessing both federal and provincial "aspects." A central feature of the distribution of legislative authority in Canada is that both levels of government can regulate the same activity as long as each is acting within its sphere of jurisdiction. This approach permits a great deal of overlap in the exercise of legislative authority. Perhaps the most common example of such overlap is highway traffic legislation, where a federal and a provincial law, for different purposes, can regulate the same activity. In the event of a conflict between a federal and a provincial law, where one law prohibits what the other requires, federal law is paramount. In the absence of conflict, where an individual can obey both federal and provincial laws, the presence of a federal law does not invalidate a provincial law regulating the same or similar conduct.

Regardless of the precise means by which interests associated with Aboriginal sovereignty receive constitutional protection, recognition of Aboriginal governmental authority will throw current law governing the distribution of legislative authority into a state of confusion. For example, both Parliament and provincial legislatures are currently entitled to pass laws regulating Aboriginal people. A fundamental issue surrounding constitutional recognition of Aboriginal governmental authority will be whether and to what extent federal or provincial laws continue to apply to Aboriginal people. Suppose an Aboriginal nation is viewed by agreement, law or constitutional right as possessing jurisdiction to pass laws or otherwise to regulate certain matters that affect community life. To what extent should Aboriginal jurisdiction be exclusive to the Aboriginal nation and to what extent should it be shared with Parliament or a provincial legislature? And which level of government—federal, provincial or Aboriginal—should prevail in the event of a conflict between or among laws regulating subjects that fall within shared jurisdiction?

Pre-existing principles governing the current distribution of legislative authority in Canada can be extended to account for three instead of two levels of government. Traditional principles suggest that the mere fact that a federal law and a provincial law regulate the same subject-matter does not render either unconstitutional as long as each level of government is acting within its sovereign sphere of authority. This approach to the distribution of legislative authority could easily operate in a tri-federal system of government. Subject matters could potentially be regulated by all three levels of government assuming that each acts within its jurisdiction. As long as an individual could conform to all three laws, there would be no conflict and no need to determine which law is paramount. Extending this approach to a tri-federal system would result in a great deal of overlap among federal, provincial, and Aboriginal law. For example, if an Aboriginal community decides to levy a tax on the sale of alcohol already taxed by federal and provincial governments, the purchaser could conform to all three laws by paying all three taxes. The enactment of an Aboriginal tax would not result in a direct conflict among laws, i.e., by which complying with one law necessitates violating another. All three laws could co-exist comfortably, each representing an expression of the sovereign authority of the governing entity by which it was enacted. Other federal, and possibly provincial, laws would continue to apply to Aboriginal people even after an Aboriginal government entered the field with legislation of its own. The judiciary would need to develop principles to address actual conflict between laws but the mere fact of duplication or overlap would not limit the operation of a federal or provincial law.

Alternatively, recognizing an Aboriginal order of government could involve carving out a sphere of exclusive Aboriginal jurisdiction into which no other level of government could enter. Such exclusivity would operate even when no conflict existed between a federal or provincial law and an Aboriginal law, that is, where an individual could conform to both laws by adhering to the stricter prohibition. Although the dominant judicial approach to the current distribution of legislative authority is to permit a great deal of duplication and overlap among federal and provincial laws, a competing approach is to view each sphere of authority as immune from the legislative reach of the other. This approach suggests that some "matters" are exclusively federal and others exclusively provincial. Extended to apply to a tri-federal system, some matters would be exclusively within the jurisdictional domain of Aboriginal governments, beyond the reach of federal or provincial regulation even if such regulation does not actually conflict with Aboriginal law. This approach would entail the identification of an exclusively Aboriginal sphere of jurisdictional authority into which neither Parliament nor provincial legislatures, for whatever reason, could enter. It would suggest, for example, that the taxation of certain economic activity perhaps ought to be viewed as within the exclusive jurisdiction of Aboriginal governments, and that federal and provincial taxes which invade Aboriginal jurisdiction would be unconstitutional, even if they did not actually conflict with Aboriginal law.

A third possibility is to seek a compromise between these two competing approaches to the distribution of legislative authority. Overlap and duplication would in some cases be an appropriate attribute of a tri-federal system. All levels of government would be permitted to regulate certain subject matters, assuming that each could point to a valid legislative purpose and that overlap or duplication did not result in actual conflict. Other matters, however, would be exclusively Aboriginal and beyond the reach of federal or provincial legislative authority. This compromise would involve distinguishing between core and peripheral jurisdiction and maintaining a core of jurisdiction into which neither the federal nor provincial governments could enter. Matters on the periphery of Aboriginal jurisdiction could allow for concurrent regulation, overlap, and duplicative laws.

Although it failed to achieve enough support to produce a constitutional amendment, the *Charlottetown Accord* offers one approach to conceptualizing Aboriginal government as one of three orders of government in Canada. The *Accord* proposed to define a core of Aboriginal jurisdiction. Matters essential or "integral" to an Aboriginal community's ability "to safeguard and develop" its language, culture, economy, identity, institutions and traditions and "to develop, maintain and strengthen" its relationship to its land, water and environment, were to fall within the exclusive jurisdiction of Aboriginal governments. The Royal Commission on Aboriginal Peoples also proposed that Aboriginal governmental authority could be clarified by distinguishing between a core and a periphery. The Commission identified the core of Aboriginal jurisdiction as the authority to make laws in relation to matters of vital concern to the life and welfare of the community, that do not have a major impact on adjacent jurisdictions, and that are not otherwise the object of overarching federal or provincial concern. Such a core would prevent Parliament and provincial legislatures from enforcing against Aboriginal people laws that regulated matters central to Aboriginal identity. Subject to the above principles, Aboriginal governments would have the authority to establish a national constitution, governmental and judicial institutions, and citizenship criteria, and enact laws in relation to education, health, family matters, and certain economic activity as well as aspects of criminal law and procedure. On the other hand, matters that do not fall within the core of Aboriginal jurisdiction could support overlapping and duplicative laws enacted by all three levels of government. Aboriginal authority over matters on the periphery of Aboriginal jurisdiction, such as those that would have a major impact on adjacent jurisdictions, would require intergovernmental agreement.

Assuming that the judiciary would permit some degree of overlap among federal, provincial and Aboriginal laws, which law will be paramount in the event of actual conflict? The current approach is one of federal paramountcy: in the event of an actual conflict between federal and provincial law, where compliance with one results in breach of the other, federal law prevails. Regardless of which reform initiatives usher in an Aboriginal order of government, principles will be necessary to govern conflicts among exercises of legislative authority. If, for example, an Aboriginal community passes a law that requires persons to engage in activity prohibited by an otherwise-applicable federal or provincial law, which law ought to be paramount? Four possibilities present themselves: (a) Aboriginal law is paramount over federal and provincial law; (b) Aboriginal law is paramount over federal but not provincial law; (c) Aboriginal law is paramount over provincial but not federal law; and (d) both federal and provincial law are paramount over Aboriginal law.

The *Charlottetown Accord* also attempted to provide guidance on this issue. It proposed that "[n]o Aboriginal law or any exercise of the inherent right of self-government … may be inconsistent with federal or provincial laws that are essential to the preservation of peace, order and good government in Canada." This provision can be read in at least two different ways. One interpretation is that it said nothing concerning paramountcy; it was directed to the scope of Aboriginal jurisdiction and not to which law was paramount, assuming each was a valid exercise of legislative authority. On this view, an Aboriginal government would not have possessed the authority to pass laws that address matters essential to peace, order and good government in Canada. Instead of providing guidance on the nature of the hierarchy that ought to structure the three orders of government, the *Accord* would have declared Aboriginal laws that regulated matters essential to peace, order and good government in Canada unconstitutional regardless of whether they actually conflicted with federal or provincial legislation.

Another interpretation, however, is that a federal or provincial law essential to the peace, order and good government of Canada is paramount if it conflicts with an otherwise valid exercise of Aboriginal jurisdiction. This interpretation of the *Accord* would have opened the door for partial Aboriginal paramountcy. Aboriginal laws that did not conflict with federal or provincial laws essential to peace, order and good government but which did conflict with other federal or provincial laws would have been paramount over those other laws. The Royal Commission on Aboriginal Peoples proposed another version of this interpretation. In the Commission's view, Aboriginal laws regulating the core of Aboriginal jurisdiction would be paramount over conflicting provincial legislation and paramount over federal legislation if the federal law in question did not serve a compelling and substantial need or was inconsistent with the Crown's fiduciary responsibilities to Aboriginal peoples. Either version is far-reaching: Aboriginal law would be paramount over some or all conflicting provincial laws and paramount over federal laws that do not serve a compelling or substantial need.

How should the Constitution address these concerns? Respecting a core of Aboriginal jurisdiction into which neither the federal nor provincial government can enter is consistent with the reason why the fact of Aboriginal prior sovereignty possesses constitutional significance. It is distributively unjust to constitutionally enshrine the proposition that European settlement of lands previously occupied by Aboriginal people triggers a complete transfer of sovereignty over those lands and peoples to the nation responsible for settlement. European settlement should be regarded in less absolutist terms, as justifying the establishment of states to which non-Aboriginal and Aboriginal people can claim allegiance but not displacing modified forms of Aboriginal governance that maintain and reproduce distinct Aboriginal identities. A just distribution of sovereignty requires a constitutional order that both respects the integrity of Aboriginal governmental authority and reflects the plurality of contemporary Aboriginal allegiances. The extent to which Aboriginal people claim allegiance to their own forms of government as well as governments established by settlement ought to be reflected in a federal structure which recognizes that Aboriginal people possess the authority to make laws in relation to matters that affect their daily lives. Similarly, treating Aboriginal law as paramount over some or all conflicting provincial laws and paramount over federal laws that do not serve a compelling or substantial need conforms to a vision of contemporary Aboriginal governmental authority as a remnant of inherent Aboriginal sovereignty. Despite settlement and the establishment of the Canadian state, Aboriginal law ought to continue to govern Aboriginal people and their lands and, in certain circumstances, ought to be treated as paramount in the event of a conflict with an inconsistent federal or provincial law.

The issue of a more general Aboriginal right of self-government was addressed by the BC Supreme Court in *Campbell v. AG BC* (2000), 189 DLR (4th) 333. The *Campbell* case dealt with the submission that the recently adopted Nisga'a Treaty was inconsistent with the division of powers granted to Parliament and the legislative assemblies of the provinces by ss. 91 and 92 of the *Constitution Act, 1867*. The position taken by the opponents of the treaty was that the Agreement was of no force or effect, to the extent that it purports to provide the Nisga'a government with legislative jurisdiction, or provides that the Nisga'a government may make laws which prevail over federal and provincial laws. Justice Williamson of the BC Supreme Court ruled against the challenge, finding that self-government was a constitutionally protected right within the *Nisga'a Final Agreement*. His summary reasons for decision at the end of the judgment are excerpted below:

[179] … I have concluded that after the assertion of sovereignty by the British Crown, and continuing to and after the time of Confederation, although the right of aboriginal people to govern themselves was diminished, it was not extinguished. Any aboriginal right to self-government could be extinguished after Confederation and before 1982 by federal legislation which plainly expressed that intention, or it could be replaced or modified by the negotiation of a treaty. Post-1982, such rights cannot be extinguished, but they may be defined (given content) in a treaty. The *Nisga'a Final Agreement* does the latter expressly.

[180] I have also concluded that the *Constitution Act, 1867* did not distribute all legislative power to the Parliament and the legislatures. Those bodies have exclusive powers in the areas listed in Sections 91 and 92 (subject until 1931 to the Imperial Parliament). But the *Constitution Act, 1867* did not purport to, and does not end, what remains of the royal prerogative or aboriginal and treaty rights, including the diminished but not extinguished power of self-government which remained with the Nisga'a people in 1982.

[181] Section 35 of the *Constitution Act, 1982*, then, constitutionally guarantees, among other things, the limited form of self-government which remained with the Nisga'a after the assertion of sovereignty. The *Nisga'a Final Agreement* and the settlement legislation give that limited right definition and content. Any decision or action which results from the exercise of this now-entrenched treaty right is subject to being infringed upon by Parliament and the legislative assembly. This is because the Supreme Court of Canada has determined that both aboriginal and treaty rights guaranteed by s. 35 may be impaired if such interference can be justified and is consistent with the honour of the Crown.

[182] The *Nisga'a Final Agreement*, negotiated in full knowledge of the limited effect (a fact accepted by the Nisga'a Nation in these proceedings) of the constitutional promise of s. 35, itself limits the new Nisga'a governments' rights to legislate. In addition, it specifies that in a number of areas, should there be any conflict between Nisga'a laws and federal or provincial laws, federal or provincial laws will prevail.

[183] Thus, the Nisga'a government, subject as it is to both the limitations set out in the treaty itself and to the limited guarantee of s. 35 of the *Constitution Act, 1982*, does not have absolute or sovereign powers. …

• • •

[185] In the RESULT I find the *Nisga'a Final Agreement*, and the settlement legislation passed by Parliament and the Legislative Assembly of the Province of British Columbia, establish a treaty as contemplated by Section 35 of the *Constitution Act, 1982*. The legislation and the Treaty are constitutionally valid. The application for a declaration that the settlement legislation and the Treaty are in part void and of no effect is dismissed.

The preamble to the *Nisga'a Final Agreement* reads as follows:

WHEREAS the Nisga'a Nation has lived in the Nass Area since time immemorial;

   WHEREAS the Nisga'a Nation is an aboriginal people of Canada;

   WHEREAS section 35 of the *Constitution Act, 1982* recognizes and affirms the existing aboriginal and treaty rights of the aboriginal peoples of Canada, which the Courts have stated include aboriginal title;

   WHEREAS the Nisga'a Nation has never entered into a treaty with Canada or British Columbia;

WHEREAS the Nisga'a Nation has sought a just and equitable settlement of the land question since the arrival of the British Crown, including the preparation of the Nisga'a Petition to His Majesty's Privy Council, dated 21 May, 1913, and the conduct of the litigation that led to the decision of the Supreme Court of Canada in *Calder v. the Attorney-General of British Columbia* in 1973, and this Agreement is intended to be the just and equitable settlement of the land question;

WHEREAS Canadian courts have stated that the reconciliation between the prior presence of aboriginal peoples and the assertion of sovereignty by the Crown is best achieved through negotiation and agreement, rather than through litigation or conflict;

WHEREAS the Parties intend that this Agreement will result in this reconciliation and establish a new relationship among them;

WHEREAS this Agreement sets out Nisga'a section 35 rights inside and outside of the area that is identified in this Agreement as Nisga'a Lands;

WHEREAS the Parties acknowledge the ongoing importance to the Nisga'a Nation of the *Simgigat* and *Sigidimhaanak* (hereditary chiefs and matriarchs) continuing to tell their *Ada-awak* (oral histories) relating to their *Angoʼoskw* (family hunting, fishing, and gathering territories) in accordance with the *Ayuuk* (Nisga'a traditional laws and practices);

WHEREAS the Parties intend their relationship to be based on a new approach to mutual recognition and sharing, and to achieve this mutual recognition and sharing by agreeing on rights, rather than by the extinguishment of rights; and

WHEREAS the Parties intend that this Agreement will provide certainty with respect to Nisga'a ownership and use of lands and resources, and the relationship of federal, provincial and Nisga'a laws, within the Nass Area.

Chapter 2 of the Agreement, outlining the general provisions, begins:

This Agreement is a treaty and a land claims agreement within the meaning of sections 25 and 35 of the *Constitution Act, 1982*.

The *Campbell* case, above, lists Nisga'a governmental powers as follows:

[45] The Nisga'a Government has power to make laws in a number of different areas which can be divided generally into two groupings. In the first category, when Nisga'a law conflicts with federal or provincial law, the Nisga'a law will prevail, although in many cases only if it is consistent with comparable standards established by Parliament, the Legislative Assembly, or relevant administrative tribunals.

[46] Generally speaking, the subjects in this category are matters which concern the identity of the Nisga'a people, their education, the preservation of their culture, the use of their land and resources, and the means by which they will make decisions in these areas. As noted, however, some of these areas remain subject to comparable provincial standards. For example, adoption laws must provide for the best interests of the child, just as does the *Adoption Act*, RSBC 1996, c. 5. The provision for Nisga'a control of education is subject to various comparable provincial educational standards.

[47] Other jurisdictions of the Nisga'a government in this category have specific matters carved out and reserved to the Crown, or to laws generally applicable in the subject area. For example, the right to regulate the use and development of Nisga'a Lands rests with the Nisga'a, but rights of way held or required by the Crown are subject to special provisions. The right to

regulate businesses, professions and trades on Nisga'a lands rests with the Nisga'a, but it is subject to provincial laws concerning accreditation, certification and regulation of the conduct of professions and trades.

[48] In the second classification of jurisdiction, when a Nisga'a law conflicts with federal or provincial law, the federal or provincial law will prevail.

[49] The Treaty permits the Nisga'a to establish police services and a police board. Any regimes established pursuant to these provisions require the approval of the provincial cabinet. If the Attorney General of the province is of the opinion that "effective policing in accordance with standards prevailing elsewhere in British Columbia" is not in place, she or he may provide or reorganize policing on the Nisga'a lands, appointing constables or using the provincial police (the RCMP) as a police force.

[50] The Treaty also provides that the Nisga'a Lisims Government may decide to establish a Nisga'a Court. But again, if that course is followed, its structure and procedures, and the method of selecting judges, must be approved by the provincial cabinet. Further, an appeal from a final decision of the Nisga'a Court lies to the Supreme Court of British Columbia. The Court section of the Treaty includes a number of references to the requirement that any Nisga'a court system must operate in accordance with generally accepted principles. For example, a Nisga'a Court and its judges must comply with "generally recognized principles in respect of judicial fairness, independence and impartiality."

[51] The Nisga'a Government has no authority to make criminal law (that power remains with Parliament). Importantly, a person accused of any offence for which he or she may be imprisoned under Nisga'a law has the right to elect to be tried in the Provincial Court of British Columbia rather than a Nisga'a Court. Any provincial court proceedings would be subject to rights of appeal to the Supreme Court of British Columbia or the Court of Appeal.

[52] Labour relations law, or what in the Agreement is called industrial relations, is governed by federal and provincial laws. However, the Nisga'a Lisims Government has a right in some instances to make representations concerning the effect of a particular aspect of labour relations law upon Nisga'a culture.

[53] While the Treaty defines the right of the Nisga'a to harvest fish and aquatic plants in Nisga'a fisheries areas, all the fisheries rights of the Nisga'a are expressly subject to measures that are necessary for conservation and to legislation enacted for the purposes of public health or safety. Nisga'a peoples' harvest of fish is subject to limits set by the federal Minister of Fisheries. Any laws made by the Nisga'a government concerning fish or aquatic plants harvested by the Nisga'a are subject to relevant federal or provincial laws.

[54] The Nisga'a government may make laws concerning assets the Nisga'a Nation, a Nisga'a village or Nisga'a corporation may hold off Nisga'a lands, but in the event of a conflict between such laws and federal or provincial laws of general application, the latter prevail.

[55] Similarly, while the Nisga'a may make laws concerning the sale and consumption of alcohol (intoxicants) on Nisga'a lands, they are subject to federal and provincial laws in the area in the event of conflict.

[56] British Columbia retains the right to licence or approve gambling or gaming facilities on Nisga'a lands, but the Agreement provides that the province will not do so except in accordance with terms established by the Nisga'a government. Such terms, however, must not be inconsistent with federal and provincial laws.

Mitchell v. MNR
[2001] 1 SCR 911, 199 DLR (4th) 385

[In this case, Grand Chief Mitchell, a Mohawk of Akwesasne, claimed an Aboriginal right to cross the border into Canada from the United States without paying customs and excise taxes. His claim was not successful, with the majority concluding that there was insufficient evidence of an ancestral Mohawk practice of trading north of the St. Lawrence river to establish the right. The case is included here for two reasons. The first is the explicit recognition by McLachlin CJC that Aboriginal customary laws were not extinguished by the assertion of British sovereignty. The second is the discussion, in Binnie J's minority concurring judgment, of the sovereignty claims entailed by the Aboriginal right claimed in this case and his contentious incorporation of the doctrine of "sovereign incompatability" into s. 35.]

McLACHLIN CJC (Gonthier, Iacobucci, Arbour, and LeBel JJ concurring):

What Is the Nature of Aboriginal Rights?

[9] Long before Europeans explored and settled North America, aboriginal peoples were occupying and using most of this vast expanse of land in organized, distinctive societies with their own social and political structures. The part of North America we now call Canada was first settled by the French and the British who, from the first days of exploration, claimed sovereignty over the land on behalf of their nations. English law, which ultimately came to govern aboriginal rights, accepted that the aboriginal peoples possessed pre-existing laws and interests, and recognized their continuance in the absence of extinguishment, by cession, conquest, or legislation: see, e.g., the *Royal Proclamation* of 1763, RSC 1985, App. II, No. 1, and *R v. Sparrow*, [1990] 1 SCR 1075, at p. 1103 [70 DLR (4th) 385]. At the same time, however, the Crown asserted that sovereignty over the land, and ownership of its underlying title, vested in the Crown: *Sparrow*, *supra*. With this assertion arose an obligation to treat aboriginal peoples fairly and honourably, and to protect them from exploitation, a duty characterized as "fiduciary" in *Guerin v. The Queen*, [1984] 2 SCR 335 [13 DLR (4th) 321].

[10] Accordingly, European settlement did not terminate the interests of aboriginal peoples arising from their historical occupation and use of the land. To the contrary, aboriginal interests and customary laws were presumed to survive the assertion of sovereignty, and were absorbed into the common law as rights, unless (1) they were incompatible with the Crown's assertion of sovereignty, (2) they were surrendered voluntarily via the treaty process, or (3) the government extinguished them: see B. Slattery, "Understanding Aboriginal Rights" (1987), 66 *Can. Bar Rev.* 727. Barring one of these exceptions, the practices, customs and traditions that defined the various aboriginal societies as distinctive cultures continued as part of the law of Canada ... .

· · ·

Is the Claimed Right Barred from Recognition as Inconsistent
with Crown Sovereignty?

[61] The conclusion that the right claimed is not established on the evidence suffices to dispose of this appeal. I add a note, however, on the government's contention that s. 35(1) of the *Constitution Act, 1982* extends constitutional protection only to those aboriginal practices, customs and traditions that are compatible with the historical and modern exercise of Crown sovereignty. Pursuant to this argument, any Mohawk practice of cross-border trade, even if established on the evidence, would be barred from recognition under s. 35(1) as incompatible with the Crown's sovereign interest in regulating its borders.

[62] This argument finds its source in the doctrine of continuity, which governed the absorption of aboriginal laws and customs into the new legal regime upon the assertion of Crown sovereignty over the region. As discussed above, this incorporation of local laws and customs into the common law was subject to an exception for those interests that were inconsistent with the sovereignty of the new regime ... .

[63] This Court has not expressly invoked the doctrine of "sovereign incompatibility" in defining the rights protected under s. 35(1). In the *Van der Peet* trilogy [*R v. Van der Peet*, [1996] 2 SCR 507, 137 DLR (4th) 289, *R v. NTC Smokehouse Ltd.*, [1996] 2 SCR 672, 137 DLR (4th) 528, *R v. Gladstone*, [1996] 2 SCR 723, 137 DLR (4th) 648], this Court identified the aboriginal rights protected under s. 35(1) as those practices, customs and traditions integral to the distinctive cultures of aboriginal societies ... . Subsequent cases affirmed this approach to identifying aboriginal rights falling within the aegis of s. 35(1) ... and have affirmed the doctrines of extinguishment, infringement and justification as the appropriate framework for resolving conflicts between aboriginal rights and competing claims, including claims based on Crown sovereignty.

[64] The Crown now contends that "sovereign incompatibility" is an implicit element of the *Van der Peet* test for identifying protected aboriginal rights, or at least a necessary addition. In view of my conclusion that Chief Mitchell has not established that the Mohawks traditionally transported goods for trade across the present Canada–US border, and hence has not proven his claim to an aboriginal right, I need not consider the merits of this submission. Rather, I would prefer to refrain from comment on the extent, if any, to which colonial laws of sovereign succession are relevant to the definition of aboriginal rights under s. 35(1) until such time as it is necessary for the Court to resolve this issue.

· · ·

BINNIE J (Major J concurring): [66] I have read the reasons of the Chief Justice and I concur in the result and with her conclusion that even if Mohawks did occasionally trade goods across the St. Lawrence River with First Nations to the north, this practice was not on the evidence a "defining feature of the Mohawk culture" ... or "vital to the Mohawk's collective identity" ... in pre-contact times. There are, however, some additional considerations that have led me to conclude that the appeal must be allowed.

[67] It has been almost 30 years since this Court emphatically rejected the argument that the mere assertion of sovereignty by the European powers in North America was necessarily incompatible with the survival and continuation of aboriginal rights: *Calder v. Attorney-General of British Columbia*, [1973] SCR 313 [34 DLR (3d) 145]. Because not *all* customs and traditions of aboriginal First Nations are incompatible with Canadian

sovereignty, however, does not mean that *none* of them can be in such conflict. The Chief Justice refrains from addressing the sovereignty issue … but she holds, correctly in my view, that "any finding of a *trading* right would also confirm a mobility right" (emphasis added). …

· · ·

[69] [W]e are [thus] left with [the] legitimate concern about the sovereignty implications of the international trading/mobility right claimed by the respondent … . Much of the debate during the 35-day trial implicated this issue, as did much of the argument on appeal to this Court, and I therefore think it desirable to address at least some aspects of the sovereignty controversy.

[70] Counsel for the respondent does not challenge the reality of Canadian sovereignty, but he seeks for the Mohawk people of the Iroquois Confederacy the maximum degree of legal autonomy to which he believes they are entitled because of their long history at Akwesasne and elsewhere in eastern North America. This asserted autonomy, to be sure, does not presently flow from the ancient Iroquois legal order that is said to have created it, but from the *Constitution Act, 1982*. Section 35(1), adopted by the elected representatives of Canadians, recognizes and affirms existing aboriginal and treaty rights. If the respondent's claimed aboriginal right is to prevail, it does so not because of its own inherent strength, but because the *Constitution Act, 1982* brings about that result.

· · ·

[73] In terms of traditional aboriginal law, the issue, as I see it, is whether trading/mobility activities asserted by the respondent not as a Canadian citizen but as an heir of the Mohawk regime that existed prior to the arrival of the Europeans, created a *legal right* to cross international boundaries under succeeding sovereigns. This aspect of the debate, to be clear, is not at the level of *fact* about the effectiveness of border controls in the 18th century. (Nor is it about the compatibility of internal aboriginal self-government with Canadian sovereignty.) The issue is at the level of *law* about the alleged incompatibility between European (now Canadian) sovereignty and mobility rights across non-aboriginal borders said by the trial judge to have been acquired by the Mohawks of Akwesasne by reason of their conduct prior to 1609.

[74] In terms of post-1982 aboriginal law, consideration should be given to whether the international trading/mobility right asserted by the respondent would advance the objective of reconciliation of aboriginal peoples with Canadian sovereignty which, as established by the *Van der Peet* trilogy, is the purpose that lies at the heart of s. 35(1).

· · ·

[125] [T]he respondent's claim … is not just about physical movement of people or goods in and about Akwesasne. It is about pushing the envelope of Mohawk autonomy within the Canadian Constitution. It is about the Mohawks' aspiration to live as if the international boundary did not exist. Whatever financial benefit accrues from the ability to move goods across the border without payment of duty is clearly incidental to this larger vision.

[126] It is true that in *R v. Pamajewon*, [1996] 2 SCR 821 [138 DLR (4th) 204], the Court warned … against casting the Court's aboriginal rights inquiry "at a level of excessive generality." Yet when the claim, as here, can only properly be construed as an international trading and mobility right, it has to be addressed at that level.

[127] In the constitutional framework envisaged by the respondent, the claimed aboriginal right is simply a manifestation of the more fundamental relationship between
the aboriginal and non-aboriginal people. In the Mohawk tradition this relationship is
memorialized by the "two-row" wampum, referred to by the respondent in Exhibit D-13,
at pp. 109 110, and in his trial evidence (trans., vol. 2, at pp. 191-92), and described in
the Haudenosaunee presentation to the Parliamentary Special Committee on Indian
Self-Government in 1983 as follows:

> When the Haudenosaunee first came into contact with the European nations, treaties of
> peace and friendship were made. Each was symbolized by the Gus-Wen-Tah or Two Row
> Wampum. There is a bed of white wampum which symbolizes the purity of the agreement.
> There are two rows of purple, and those two rows have the spirit of your ancestors and mine.
> There are three beads of wampum separating the two rows and they symbolize peace,
> friendship and respect.
>
> These two rows will symbolize two paths or two vessels, travelling down the same river
> together. One, a birch bark canoe, will be for the Indian people, their laws, their customs
> and their ways. The other, a ship, will be for the white people and their laws, their customs
> and their ways. We shall each travel the river together, side by side, but in our own boat.
> Neither of us will try to steer the other's vessel.

(Indian Self-Government in Canada: Report of the Special Committee (1983), back cover)

[128] Thus, in the "two-row" wampum there are two parallel paths. In one path travels the aboriginal canoe. In the other path travels the European ship. The two vessels co-
exist but they never touch. Each is the sovereign of its own destiny.

[129] The modern embodiment of the "two-row" wampum concept, modified to reflect some of the realities of a modern state, is the idea of a "merged" or "shared" sovereignty. "Merged sovereignty" asserts that First Nations were not wholly subordinated to
non-aboriginal sovereignty but over time became merger partners. The final *Report of
the Royal Commission on Aboriginal Peoples*, vol. 2 (*Restructuring the Relationship*
(1996)), at p. 214, says that "Aboriginal governments give the constitution [of Canada] its
deepest and most resilient roots in the Canadian soil." This updated concept of Crown
sovereignty is of importance. Whereas historically the Crown may have been portrayed
as an entity across the seas with which aboriginal people could scarcely be expected to
identify, this was no longer the case in 1982 when the s. 35(1) reconciliation process was
established. The Constitution was patriated and all aspects of our sovereignty became
firmly located within our borders. If the principle of "merged sovereignty" articulated by
the Royal Commission on Aboriginal Peoples is to have any true meaning, it must include at least the idea that aboriginal and non-aboriginal Canadians *together* form a sovereign entity with a measure of common purpose and united effort. It is this new entity,
as inheritor of the historical attributes of sovereignty, with which existing aboriginal and
treaty rights must be reconciled.

[130] The final *Report of the Royal Commission on Aboriginal Peoples*, vol. 2, goes on
to describe "shared" sovereignty at pp. 240-41 as follows:

> Shared sovereignty, in our view, is a hallmark of the Canadian federation and a central feature
> of the three-cornered relations that link Aboriginal governments, provincial governments

and the federal government. These governments are sovereign within their respective spheres and hold their powers by virtue of their constitutional status rather than by delegation. Nevertheless, many of their powers are shared in practice and may be exercised by more than one order of government.

On this view, to return to the nautical metaphor of the "two-row" wampum, "merged" sovereignty is envisaged as a single vessel (or ship of state) composed of the historic elements of wood, iron and canvas. The vessel's components pull together as a harmonious whole, but the wood remains wood, the iron remains iron and the canvas remains canvas. Non-aboriginal leaders, including Sir Wilfrid Laurier, have used similar metaphors. It represents, in a phrase, partnership without assimilation.

· · ·

[133] In the earlier years of the century the federal government occasionally argued that Parliament's jurisdiction under s. 91(24) of the *Constitution Act, 1867* ("Indians, and Lands reserved for the Indians") was plenary. Indians were said to be federal people whose lives were wholly subject to federal "regulation." This was rejected by the courts, which ruled that while an aboriginal person could be characterized as an Indian for some purposes including language, culture and the exercise of traditional rights, he or she does not cease thereby to be a resident of a province or territory. For other purposes he or she must be recognized and treated as an ordinary member of Canadian society. ... In *Gladstone* (at para. 73) and again in *Delgamuukw v. British Columbia*, [1997] 3 SCR 1010 (at para. 165) [153 DLR (4th) 193], Lamer CJ repeats that "distinctive aboriginal societies exist within, and *are a part* of, a broader social, political and economic community, over which the Crown is sovereign" (emphasis added). The constitutional objective is reconciliation not mutual isolation.

[134] The Royal Commission does not explain precisely how "shared sovereignty" is expected to work in practice, although it recognized as a critical issue how "60 to 80 historically based nations in Canada at present, comprising a thousand or so local Aboriginal communities" would "interact with the jurisdictions of the federal and provincial governments" in cases of operational conflict (final report, vol. 2, *supra*, at pp. 166 and 216). It also recognized the challenge aboriginal self-government poses to the orthodox view that constitutional powers in Canada are wholly and exhaustively distributed between the federal and provincial governments ... . There are significant economic and funding issues. Some aboriginal people who live off reserves, particularly in urban areas, have serious concerns about how self-government would affect them ... . With these difficulties in mind perhaps, the Royal Commission considered it to be "essential that any steps toward self-government be initiated by the aboriginal group in question and "respond to needs identified by its members" (*Partners in Confederation: Aboriginal Peoples, Self-Government and the Constitution* (1993), at p. 41). It rejected the "one size fits all" approach to First Nations' self-governing institutions in favour of a negotiated treaty model. The objective, succinctly put, is to create sufficient "constitutional space for aboriginal peoples to be aboriginal" ... . The Royal Commission Final Report, vol. 2, states at p. 214 that:

> Section 35 does not warrant a claim to unlimited governmental powers or to complete sovereignty, such as independent states are commonly thought to possess. As with the federal and provincial governments, Aboriginal governments operate within a sphere of sovereign-

ty defined by the constitution. In short, the Aboriginal right of self-government in section 35(1) involves circumscribed rather than unlimited powers.

[135] It is unnecessary, for present purposes, to come to any conclusion about these assertions. What is significant is that the Royal Commission itself sees aboriginal peoples as full participants with non-aboriginal peoples in a shared Canadian sovereignty. Aboriginal peoples do not stand in opposition to, nor are they subjugated by, Canadian sovereignty. They are part of it.

[136] With this background I return to the point that the respondent does not base his mobility rights in this test case as a Canadian citizen. ...

[137] The respondent's claim ... presents two defining elements. He asserts a trading and mobility right across the international boundary and he attaches this right to his current citizenship not of Canada but of the Haudenosaunee Confederacy with its capital in Onondaga, New York State.

The Legal Basis of the Respondent's Claim

[138] The respondent initially asserted both a treaty right and an aboriginal right but the conceptual distinction between these two sources of entitlement is important. A treaty right is an affirmative promise by the Crown which will be interpreted generously and enforced in a way that upholds the honour of the Crown ... .

[139] The trial court acknowledged that if duty-free provisions had been incorporated into a treaty with the Mohawks, the promise would be enforceable as a s. 35 treaty right. A treaty right is itself an expression of Crown sovereignty.

[140] In the case of aboriginal rights, there is no historical event comparable to the treaty-making process in which the Crown negotiated the right or obligation sought to be enforced. The respondent's claim is rooted in practices which he says long preceded the Mohawks' first contact with Europeans in 1609.

[141] I return to the comment of McLachlin J, dissenting in the result, in *Van der Peet, supra*, at para. 227 that "[t]he issue of what constitutes an aboriginal right must, in my view, be answered by looking at what the law has historically accepted as fundamental aboriginal rights." There was a presumption under British colonial law that the Crown intended to respect the pre-existing customs of the inhabitants that were not deemed to be unconscionable ... .

• • •

[143] Since *Calder, supra*, the courts have extended recognition beyond pre-existing "rights" to practices, customs or traditions integral to the aboriginal community's distinctive culture (*Van der Peet, supra*, at para. 53). The aboriginal rights question, as McLachlin J put it, dissenting in the result, in *Van der Peet*, at para. 248, is traditionally "what laws and customs held sway before superimposition of European laws and customs [?]"

[144] Reference has already been made to the fact that one of several sources of the concept of aboriginal rights, now significantly modified by the more generous principles of constitutional interpretation, is traditional British colonial law. Many of the cases decided by the Judicial Committee of the Privy Council were concerned with rights of property created under a former regime. In *Amodu Tijani v. Southern Nigeria (Secretary)*,

[1921] 2 AC 399, at p. 407, it was confirmed that "A mere change in sovereignty is not to be *presumed* as meant to disturb rights of private owners" (emphasis added). More recently, Lord Denning, speaking for the Privy Council in *Oyekan v. Adele*, [1957] 2 All ER 785, at p. 788, said: "In inquiring ... what rights are recognised, there is one guiding principle. It is this: The courts will *assume* that the British Crown intends that the rights of property of the inhabitants are to be fully respected" (emphasis added). As with the modern law of aboriginal rights, the law of sovereign succession was intended to reconcile the interests of the local inhabitants across the empire to a change in sovereignty.

· · ·

[148] I am far from suggesting that the key to s. 35(1) reconciliation is to be found in the legal archives of the British Empire. The root of the respondent's argument nevertheless is that the Mohawks of Akwesasne acquired under the legal regimes of 18th century North America, a positive *legal right* as a group to continue to come and go across any subsequent international border dividing their traditional homelands with whatever goods they wished, just as they had in pre-contact times. In other words, Mohawk autonomy in this respect was continued but not as a mere custom or practice. It emerged in the new European-based constitutional order as a *legal* trading and mobility *right*. By s. 35(1) of the *Constitution Act, 1982*, it became a constitutionally protected right. That is the respondent's argument.

The Limitation of "Sovereign Incompatibility"

[149] Care must be taken not to carry forward doctrines of British colonial law into the interpretation of s. 35(1) without careful reflection. ...

[150] Yet the language of s. 35(1) cannot be construed as a wholesale repudiation of the common law. The subject matter of the constitutional provision is "existing" aboriginal and treaty rights and they are said to be "recognized and affirmed" not wholly cut loose from either their legal or historical origins. One of the defining characteristics of sovereign succession and therefore a limitation on the scope of aboriginal rights, as already discussed, was the notion of incompatibility with the new sovereignty. Such incompatibility seems to have been accepted, for example, as a limitation on the powers of aboriginal self-government in the 1993 working report of the Royal Commission on Aboriginal Peoples, *Partners in Confederation: Aboriginal Peoples, Self-Government and the Constitution, supra*, at p. 23:

> ... Aboriginal nations did not lose their inherent rights when they entered into a confederal relationship with the Crown. Rather, they retained their ancient constitutions *so far as these were not inconsistent with the new relationship.* [Emphasis added.]

[151] Prior to *Calder, supra*, "sovereign incompatibility" was given excessive scope. The assertion of sovereign authority was confused with doctrines of feudal title to deny aboriginal peoples any interest at all in their traditional lands or even in activities related to the use of those lands. To acknowledge that the doctrine of sovereign incompatibility was sometimes given excessive scope in the past is not to deny that it has any scope at all, but it is a doctrine that must be applied with caution.

[152] I take an illustration from the evidence in this case. The trial judge showed that pre-contact the Mohawks, as a military force, moved under their own command through what is now parts of southern Ontario and southern Quebec. The evidence, taken as a whole, suggests that military values were "a defining feature of the Mohawk [or Iroquois] culture … .

[153] However, important as they may have been to the Mohawk identity as a people, it could not be said, in my view, that pre-contact warrior activities gave rise under successor regimes to a *legal right* under s. 35(1) to engage in military adventures on Canadian territory. Canadian sovereign authority has, as one of its inherent characteristics, a monopoly on the *lawful* use of military force within its territory. I do not accept that the Mohawks *could* acquire under s. 35(1) a legal right to deploy a military force in what is now Canada, as and when they choose to do so, even if the warrior tradition was to be considered a defining feature of pre-contact Mohawk society. Section 35(1) should not be interpreted to throw on the Crown the burden of demonstrating subsequent extinguishment by "clear and plain" measures (*Gladstone, supra*, at para. 31) of a "right" to organize a private army, or a requirement to justify such a limitation after 1982 under the *Sparrow* standard. This example, remote as it is from the particular claim advanced in this case, usefully illustrates the principled limitation flowing from sovereign incompatibility in the s. 35(1) analysis.

[154] In my opinion, sovereign incompatibility continues to be an element in the s. 35(1) analysis, albeit a limitation that will be sparingly applied. For the most part, the protection of practices, traditions and customs that are distinctive to aboriginal cultures in Canada does not raise legitimate sovereignty issues at the definitional stage.

The Alleged Incompatibility Between the Aboriginal Right Disclosed by the Evidence and Canadian Sovereignty

. . .

[158] The question is whether the asserted legal right to the autonomous exercise of international trade and mobility was compatible with the new European (now Canadian) sovereignty and the reciprocal loss (or impairment) of Mohawk sovereignty.

[159] In the resolution of this legal issue, as stated, we are addressing *legal* incompatibility as opposed to *factual* incompatibility. The latter emerged more slowly as assertions of sovereignty gave way to colonisation and progressive occupation of land. …

[160] Control over the mobility of persons and goods into one country is, and always has been, a fundamental attribute of sovereignty. … In other words, not only does authority over the border exist as an incident of sovereignty, the state is expected to exercise it in the public interest. The duty cannot be abdicated to the vagaries of an earlier regime whose sovereignty has been eclipsed … .

[161] The legal situation is further complicated by the fact, previously mentioned, that the respondent attributes his international trading and mobility right not to his status as a Canadian citizen but as a citizen of the Haudenosaunee (Iroquois Confederacy) based at Onondaga, New York. Border conditions in the modern era are vastly different from those in the 18th century. Nevertheless, as stated, borders existed among nations,

including First Nations. They were expressions of sovereign autonomy and then, as now, compelled observance.

. . .

[163] … In my view, therefore, the international trading/mobility right claimed by the respondent as a citizen of the Haudenosaunee (Iroquois) Confederacy is incompatible with the historical attributes of Canadian sovereignty.

[164] The question that then arises is whether this conclusion is at odds with the purpose of s. 35(1), i.e. the reconciliation of the interests of aboriginal peoples with Crown sovereignty? In addressing this question it must be remembered that aboriginal people are themselves part of Canadian sovereignty as discussed above. I agree with Borrows [J. Borrrows, "Uncertain Citizens: Aboriginal Peoples and the Supreme Court" (2001), 80 *Can. Bar Rev.* 15], at p. 40, that accommodation of aboriginal rights should *not* be seen as "a zero-sum relationship between minority rights and citizenship; as if every gain in the direction of accommodating diversity comes at the expense of promoting citizenship" (quoting W. Kymlicka and W. Norman, eds., *Citizenship in Diverse Societies* (2000), at p. 39). On the other hand, the reverse is also true. Affirmation of the sovereign interest of Canadians as a whole, including aboriginal peoples, should not necessarily be seen as a loss of sufficient "constitutional space for aboriginal peoples to be aboriginal" (Greschner [D. Greschner, "Aboriginal Women, the Constitution and Criminal Justice," [1992] *UBC L Rev. (Sp. ed.)* 338], at p. 342). A finding of distinctiveness is a judgment that to fulfill the purpose of s. 35, a measure of constitutional space is required to accommodate particular activities (traditions, customs or practices) rooted in the aboriginal peoples' prior occupation of the land. In this case, a finding against "distinctiveness" is a conclusion that the respondent's claim does not relate to a "defining feature" that makes Mohawk "culture what it is" (*Van der Peet*, at paras. 59 and 71 (emphasis in original deleted)); it is a conclusion that to extend constitutional protection to the respondent's claim finds no support in the pre-1982 jurisprudence and would overshoot the purpose of s. 35(1). In terms of sovereign incompatibility, it is a conclusion that the respondent's claim relates to national interests that all of us have in common rather than to distinctive interests that for some purposes differentiate an aboriginal community. In my view, reconciliation of these interests in this particular case favours an affirmation of our collective sovereignty.

Implications for Internal Aboriginal Self-Government

[165] In reaching that conclusion, however, I do not wish to be taken as either foreclosing or endorsing any position on the compatibility or incompatibility of *internal* self-governing institutions of First Nations with Crown sovereignty, either past or present. I point out in this connection that the sovereign incompatibility principle has not prevented the United States (albeit with its very different constitutional framework) from continuing to recognize forms of *internal* aboriginal self-government which it considers to be expressions of residual aboriginal sovereignty. The concept of a "domestic dependent nation" was introduced by Marshall CJ in *Cherokee Nation v. Georgia*, 30 US (5 Pet.) 1 (1831), at p. 17, as follows:

... It may well be doubted whether those tribes which reside within the acknowledged boundaries of the United States can, with strict accuracy, be denominated foreign nations. They may, more correctly, perhaps, be denominated domestic dependent nations.

[166] More recently, in *United States v. Wheeler*, 435 US 313 (1978), the United States Supreme Court, *per* Stewart J, described the applicable US doctrine at pp. 322, 323 and 326:

> The powers of Indian tribes are, in general, "*inherent powers of a limited sovereignty which has never been extinguished.*" ...
>
> Indian tribes are, of course, no longer "possessed of the full attributes of sovereignty." *United States v. Kagama, supra,* at 381. Their incorporation within the territory of the United States, and their acceptance of its protection, necessarily divested them of some aspects of the sovereignty which they had previously exercised. By specific treaty provision they yielded up other sovereign powers; by statute, in the exercise of its plenary control, Congress has removed still others. ...
>
> In sum, Indian tribes still possess those aspects of sovereignty not withdrawn by treaty or statute, or *by implication as a necessary result of their dependent status.* ...
>
> The areas in which such *implicit divestiture* of sovereignty has been held to have occurred are those involving the relations between an Indian tribe and nonmembers of the tribe. Thus, Indian tribes can no longer freely alienate to non-Indians the land they occupy. ... They cannot enter into direct commercial or governmental relations with foreign nations. ... And, as we have recently held, they cannot try nonmembers in tribal courts. ...
>
> These limitations rest on the fact that the dependent status of Indian tribes within our territorial jurisdiction *is necessarily inconsistent* with their freedom independently to determine their *external* relations. [Emphasis added.]

[167] The US doctrine of domestic dependent nation differs in material respects from the proposals of our Royal Commission on Aboriginal Peoples. The concepts of merged sovereignty and shared sovereignty, which are said to be essential to the achievement of reconciliation as well as to the maintenance of diversity, are not reflected in the American jurisprudence. Under US law the powers of a tribal government (whatever its theoretical sovereignty) can be overridden by an ordinary law of Congress. Further, there is nothing that I am aware of in the US doctrine that extends the concept of self-government to claims to an independent self-sustaining economic base, as contemplated by the Royal Commission on Aboriginal Peoples (final report, vol. 2, *supra*, at p. 2). In any event, whatever be the differences and similarities, an international trading and mobility right, which necessarily involves "external relations," would appear *not* to be included in the attributes of a US-style "domestic dependent nation."

· · ·

[169] I refer to the US law only to alleviate any concern that addressing aspects of the sovereignty issue in the context of a claim to an international trading and mobility right would prejudice one way or the other a resolution of the much larger and more complex claim of First Nations in Canada to *internal* self-governing institutions. The United States has lived with internal tribal self-government within the framework of external relations

determined wholly by the United States government without doctrinal difficulties since *Johnson v. M'Intosh*, 21 US (8 Wheat.) 543 (1823), was decided almost 170 years ago.

• • •

[171] The question under consideration here is ... not about post-1982 extinguishment. It is about the *prior* question of whether the claimed international trading and mobility right could, as a matter of law, have arisen in the first place.

[172] It was, of course, an expression of sovereignty in 1982 to recognize existing aboriginal rights under s. 35(1) of the *Constitution Act, 1982*. However, if the claimed aboriginal right did not survive the transition to non-Mohawk sovereignty, there was nothing in existence in 1982 to which s. 35(1) protection of *existing* aboriginal rights could attach. It would have been, of course, quite within the sovereign's power to confer specific border privileges by treaty, but the respondent's claim to a treaty right was dismissed.

[173] In my respectful view the claimed aboriginal right never came into existence and it is unnecessary to consider the Crown's argument that whatever aboriginal rights in this respect may have existed were extinguished by border controls enforced by Canada prior to April 17, 1982.

Appeal allowed.

PART FIVE

Rights

CHAPTER FIFTEEN

Antecedents of the Charter

Most of the material about rights in this book involves the *Canadian Charter of Rights and Freedoms*, and doubtless much of the time in most constitutional law courses is spent on the Charter. Nonetheless, no one should assume that rights suddenly appeared in the Canadian Constitution on April 17, 1982. To explain this assertion, we take one example from a multitude. In his speech in 1864, on the Quebec Resolutions (about Confederation), John A. Macdonald said:

> We all feel the advantages we derive from our connection with England. So long as that alliance is maintained, we enjoy, under her protection, the privileges of constitutional liberty according to the British system. We will enjoy here that which is the great test of constitutional freedom—we will have the rights of the minority respected. In all countries the rights of the majority take care of themselves, but it is only in countries like England, enjoying constitutional liberty, and safe from the tyranny of a single despot or of an unbridled democracy, that the rights of minorities are regarded.

Macdonald probably had two different sets of ideas about rights in his mind. The first idea, probably more important to Macdonald, was the belief that the protection of individual rights was at the heart of the British constitution—the constitution that Canada would have—and that the most fundamental of these rights was liberty. The second relates to the extent to which a federal system of government can operate to safeguard rights and freedoms. To this we add a third, and that is the extent to which legislation can protect fundamental rights. Prior to the Charter's enactment, these three approaches to the protection of rights and freedoms formed part of the Canadian political landscape and, in different ways, continue to influence the Charter's development. This chapter is designed to introduce you to each of these important antecedents of the Charter, beginning with the idea of a common law constitution.

I. THE COMMON LAW CONSTITUTION

Macdonald shared with generations of British lawyers the belief that the British peoples had struggled since Anglo-Saxon times to defend their liberty against despotic rulers. In this struggle, individual rights had been established, which, by the late eighteenth century, were usually divided into two kinds. The first were political rights, which were rights to participate in government, especially responsible government, including rights of representation and voting. The second were civil rights, which were rights of individuals to liberty from restraint by government, especially freedoms of the person, speech, religion, and property. As well, in this struggle for liberty, the British peoples had established the basic principle of the rule of law. It had different meanings, but at its core was a claim that government and the people were bound equally by the law, and that the government must always obey the law. It was expressed in its classic form by Albert V. Dicey in 1885, in his great text *The Law of the Constitution*.

> **A.V. Dicey, *Introduction to the Study of the Law of the Constitution***
> (London: Macmillan, 1885), at 167

Two features have at all times since the Norman Conquest characterised the political institutions of England.

The first of these features is the omnipotence or undisputed supremacy throughout the whole country of the central government. This authority of the state or the nation was during the earlier periods of our history represented by the power of the Crown. ... This royal supremacy has now passed into [the] sovereignty of Parliament ... .

The second of these features, which is closely connected with the first, is the rule or supremacy of law. ...

When we say that the supremacy or the rule of law is a characteristic of the English constitution, we generally include under one expression at least three distinct though kindred conceptions.

We mean, in the first place, that no man is punishable or can be lawfully made to suffer in body or goods except for a distinct breach of law established in the ordinary legal manner before the ordinary Courts of the land. In this sense the rule of law is contrasted with every system of government based on the exercise by persons in authority of wide, arbitrary, or discretionary powers of constraint. ...

We mean in the second place, when we speak of the "rule of law" as a characteristic of our country, not only that with us no man is above the law, but (what is a different thing) that here every man, whatever be his rank or condition, is subject to the ordinary law of the realm and amenable to the jurisdiction of the ordinary tribunals.

In England the idea of legal equality, or of the universal subjection of all classes to one law administered by the ordinary Courts, has been pushed to its utmost limit. With us every official, from the Prime Minister down to a constable or a collector of taxes, is under the same responsibility for every act done without legal justification as any other citizen. ...

There remains yet a third and a different sense in which the "rule of law" or the predominance of the legal spirit may be described as a special attribute of English institutions. We may say that the constitution is pervaded by the rule of law on the ground that the general principles of the constitution (as for example the right to personal liberty, or the right of public meeting) are with us the result of judicial decisions determining the rights of private persons in particular cases brought before the Courts; whereas under many foreign constitutions the security (such as it is) given to the rights of individuals results, or appears to result, from the general principles of the constitution.

For Dicey and late nineteenth-century lawyers generally, individual rights and the rule of law were essentially common law rights, and the Constitution was a common law constitution. That is, these rights had been made, not in a revolution, not in the streets, and not in a code, but by judges, in an accumulation of decisions about individual cases. Moreover, the courts were the repository of rights and the means of enforcement. This common law constitution continues to be a part of our constitutional beliefs, but as a modern lawyer or law student reads Dicey, she or he asks, how can his two fundamental principles be reconciled? How can rights be protected in a constitution that also includes parliamentary sovereignty, and when they can be taken away by a simple statute?

There are two paths to be considered in answering this question. First, rights can be seen as a set of ideals that Parliament is constitutionally obligated to respect, even though parliamentary sovereignty precludes enforcement in the courts. Here, the security of rights depends greatly upon good faith and the effectiveness of representation, and although representation may have been central to the control of abuse of rights by the Crown, it may not be so effective security against a democratic majority. Some of these considerations return in Chapter 17, The Framework of the Charter.

A second path for thinking about protecting rights and the rule of law in a common law constitution is the ways courts have used them in interpreting statutes. Sometimes, according to the prevailing approach to interpretation, the words of statutes do not clearly specify one meaning; instead, there may be a range of possible meanings, some of which may intrude upon an individual's rights, and others not. In these situations, respect for rights pushes toward choosing benign interpretations, even though any of the rights can be abrogated by a statute that clearly has this effect. Much of this approach is expressed as presumptions—for example, presumptions about respecting established property interests. In *Roncarelli v. Duplessis*, the case that appears shortly, interpretation is the central issue: did the *Liquor Licence Act* give Duplessis authority to revoke Roncarelli's licence? In coming to the conclusion that it did not give the authority, Rand J invoked both the rule of law and common law rights.

Before we introduce *Roncarelli*, however, we must emphasize that interpretation in the name of the rule of law and common law rights has not always been benign. The common law has tended to value the individual more than the community, and liberty has been a banner that has been used to shield the established order from regulation and redistribution, to permit exploitation through the use of private power, and to protect the prestige and power of courts from encroachments by administrative agencies.

As well as an elegant and powerful example of interpretation protecting rights, *Roncarelli* is also an introduction to one of Canada's great judges, Ivan Rand, and another short look at another major Canadian lawyer, Frank Scott, who was introduced in Chapter 6, The 1930s: The Depression and the New Deal. The background of the case involves a long and complex story involving the Jehovah's Witnesses and the political and religious establishment in Quebec. This story is described in the following reading.

W. Kaplan, *State and Salvation:*
The Jehovah's Witnesses and Their Fight for Civil Rights
(Toronto: University of Toronto Press, 1989), at 232-37 and 245-48
(footnotes omitted)

At the end of the Second World War there were about ten thousand Jehovah's Witnesses in Canada, but fewer than five hundred in Quebec. The people of Quebec, the Jehovah's Witnesses believed, were "sitting in darkness" and were in urgent need of their attention. The Jehovah's Witnesses believed that Roman Catholics in Quebec were responsible for the wartime ban, and they were intent in the post-war period on revealing the hierarchy as an iniquitous institution. They also knew that Quebec, more than any other place in Canada, was hostile to their work, although whether or not this increased their enthusiasm for seeking converts in Quebec is difficult to say.

. . .

Many towns and municipalities ... passed by-laws making it an offence to distribute literature without a licence. Invariably, these by-laws were intended to keep Jehovah's Witnesses off city streets, but they were also employed from time to time to keep Baptist missionaries, Seventh-day Adventists, and assorted others from spreading their equally unwanted messages. In the years before the Second World War, approximately one hundred Jehovah's Witnesses were arrested every year. During the war these figures, as might be expected, increased. But it was after the war that the number of arrests showed exponential growth. More than eight hundred charges against Jehovah's Witnesses were filed in 1946. The explanation for the increase was simple enough. Duplessis believed that Witness activity in the province was a deliberate assault on values and virtues Quebeckers held dear. And like just about everything else, Witness conduct could be reduced to a question of provincial rights. If the federal government and the RCMP refused to discipline a seditious group that sought to destroy the Roman Catholic church then Duplessis, as attorney general, had no option but to intervene and defend the faith. As a result, he encouraged local authorities and provincial police to stamp out the sect.

The Jehovah's Witnesses did not respond to what they believed was another Satanic attack on God's work by turning the other cheek. Instead, they entered the lion's den. One of their ways of doing so was in print. *Quebec's Burning Hate* was issued first. The full title of the short leaflet, issued in the fall of 1946 in a first printing of 1.5 million copies, 500,000 of which were in French, was *Quebec's Burning Hate for God and Christ and Freedom Is the Shame of All Canada*. The tract painted a sordid and disturbing tableau.

Since the end of the war, *Quebec's Burning Hate* reported, the Jehovah's Witnesses had been the subject of province-wide persecution. From one parish to another, Witnesses had been beaten, arrested, and sentenced to jail. Civil authorities were involved, either by refusing Jehovah's Witnesses police protection or by passing by-laws directed against the sect, making distribution of their literature without a permit an offence, or usually by both. The church was behind it, the leaflet charged, goading the mobs and the local councils on, and sometimes parish priests led their flock in driving Witnesses out of town.

The Jehovah's Witnesses had not been sitting idly by. Montreal and Verdun were centres of activity against the sect, and the by-laws prohibiting Witness activity were challenged in court not long after the end of the war. Justice C. Gordon MacKinnon ordered writs of prohibition against the recorder's courts (which were equivalent to magistrates' courts elsewhere in Canada), in the two jurisdictions. Notwithstanding MacKinnon's finding that the by-laws in question were unconstitutional for their interference with free worship, charges continued to be laid. And the courts convicted more often than not.

The Quebec judiciary was, according to *Quebec's Burning Hate*, dominated by the church. Therefore, it was no accident to see the crucifix installed in all the province's courts, in the Legislative Assembly, and in government buildings throughout the province. The cardinal's personal chair, alongside that of the lieutenant-governor in the Legislative Assembly, was just further evidence of the diabolical church-state link. The province was priest-ridden and the priests, working in concert with the police and local authorities, were waging war against God, Christ, and Freedom, meaning, of course, the Jehovah's Witnesses. Quebec Catholics were not serving God by mobbing Jehovah's Witnesses; they were merely serving corrupt priests and dooming themselves to damnation. "Quebec," the leaflet concluded, "you have yielded yourself as an obedient servant of religious priests, and you have brought forth bumper crops of evil fruits." ...

If the Jehovah's Witnesses expected that *Quebec's Burning Hate* would bring what can only be described as religious persecution to an end, they soon found out otherwise. Premier Duplessis described the leaflet as "intolerable and seditious." The Jehovah's Witnesses saw things differently. "The Hierarchy," the Witnesses declared, "set up a howl of rage and counter-attacked; not with denial of the disgraceful account of her actions, but with her favourite weapons of slander, lies, violence and the pressure of Quebec's corrupt political machine upon the law enforcement bodies." In sixteen days, 260 arrests were made in the Montreal area alone, although not one arrest was made in any part of Canada outside of Quebec. "You bunch of crazy nuts," one judge boomed at some arrested Jehovah's Witnesses from the bench, "could at least have waited until the appeal of your judgment had been heard before resuming your activities." The Jehovah's Witnesses had no intention of doing so, and another leaflet, *Quebec: You Have Failed Your People*, this time in an edition of almost two million, was issued and distributed throughout the country. Readers could not help but be impressed with the case the Jehovah's Witnesses had made in detailing their persecution. All were invited to write the prime minister of Canada and tell him as much. Shouldn't Canadians, the leaflet asked, have freedom of religion? ...

Whatever the limits on these freedoms, Duplessis believed that they did not extend to sanctioning attacks on the Roman Catholic church. These attacks, not to mention the first real attempt by a religious organization to seek converts in the province, account for Duplessis's "war without mercy" on members of the sect. Between 1946 and 1953 he instigated 1,665 separate prosecutions against individual Jehovah's Witnesses. The charges ranged from trivial disturbances of the peace, such as handing out tracts on street corners without permits, to arrests and trials for sedition, a term which Duplessis twisted to mean almost any publicly spoken criticism of the established order. The result of the battle in the courts was a victory for both the Jehovah's Witnesses and for human rights. There are a number of cases that could be considered, but three of them stand out: *Boucher*, *Saumur*, and *Roncarelli*.

Aimé Boucher, a Jehovah Witness, was arrested in December 1946. A farmer in the rural St Germain Parish, Boucher was charged with sedition for distributing copies of *Quebec's Burning Hate*. There was a defence to the offence and Boucher relied on it. At trial he testified that he distributed the literature in good faith and in the hope that it would convince Quebeckers to stop persecuting Jehovah's Witnesses. Boucher was, however, convicted, an almost foregone result when the trial judge neglected to instruct the jury that it was up to it to decide whether or not Boucher had acted in good faith and was entitled to rely on the statutory defence. The Court of King's Bench denied Boucher's appeal. A dissent in the court of the appeal gave Boucher an entrée to the Supreme Court.

Boucher had been arrested in 1946 and convicted in 1947. By the time his case came to the Supreme Court of Canada, that court was supreme not just in name. As of 1949, it was no longer possible to appeal Canadian decisions to the Judicial Committee of the Privy Council in Great Britain (although criminal appeals to the JCPC had not been available for many years). In the context of a sedition charge, the *Boucher* case raised important questions about the scope of freedom of religion and freedom of speech. And it, along with the other Witness cases that followed, illustrated that the Supreme Court of Canada, in its first decade of independence, was of first rank. Credit for that rank belonged, in large measure, to recent appointee Ivan Rand. ... At that time, Rand had just been appointed to the Bench, but he brought with him the experience of a full life. The son of a railway mechanic, Rand studied law at Harvard where he became friends with Felix Frankfurter and came under the tutelage of Professor Louis Brandeis. Between 1913 and 1920 he practised law in Medicine Hat, a southern Alberta town, and then returned to his home town, Moncton, New Brunswick. A spell as attorney general of the province was enough to convince Rand that New Brunswick politics were not for him, and in 1926 he became corporate counsel to the Canadian National Railways. Mackenzie King appointed him a justice of the Supreme Court of Canada in 1943.

Rand immediately established a reputation for himself. He refused to give judicial approval to a government plan to deport Canada's Japanese and his extra-judicial duties included the settling of an important labour dispute in Windsor and a leading role in the UN Special Committee on Palestine. Unlike Frankfurter, Rand was committed to judicial activism in the search for social justice and he had no qualms about using the court in the pursuit of this goal. ...

[Justice Rand's decisions in *Saumur* and *Boucher* will be introduced later in this chapter. Here, the reading introduces *Roncarelli*, which came late in the story.]

Roncarelli was the owner of the Quaff Café in Montreal's west end. Disturbed by the treatment other Jehovah's Witnesses were receiving, Roncarelli arranged bail for some four hundred Witnesses arrested during the first part of Duplessis's "war without mercy" against the sect. When Duplessis learned about Roncarelli he was enraged. In late November 1946, Duplessis publicly warned him to stop posting bail. Roncarelli failed to heed the warning, and on 4 December 1946 Duplessis telephoned the chairman of the Quebec Liquor Commission, Judge Edouard Archambault, and instructed him to cancel Roncarelli's licence. Archambault did as he was told, and the police came and seized Roncarelli's stock. The next day Duplessis was quoted in *The Montreal Gazette*, explaining why: "A certain Mr Roncarelli has supplied bail for hundreds of Witnesses of Jehovah. The sympathy which this man has shown for the Witnesses in such an evident, repeated and audacious manner, is a provocation to public order, to the administration of justice and is definitely contrary to the aims of justice. He does not act, in this case, as a person posting bail for another person, but as a mass supplier of bails, whose great number by itself is most reprehensible." In fact, Roncarelli was put out of business because he had exercised a right given to him in law to post bail for persons accused of an offence. Especially interesting about the case was the public attention it drew.

News of these events was publicized in the press, and the public reacted. The closing of a business was an issue many people could sympathize with. More than twelve hundred McGill University students, for example, signed a petition demanding that the attorney general reverse his decision on the basis that Roncarelli had not violated any of the Quebec *Liquor Act* regulations. Other protesting groups included the McGill University Progressive Conservative Association, the Montreal Presbytery of the Presbyterian Church, and the Montreal Civil Liberties Committee, a group of both French- and English-speaking Montrealers.

· · ·

The Roncarelli issue returned to the public eye on 1 February 1947 when Roncarelli launched a suit against Judge Archambault in his capacity as head of the Quebec Liquor Commission. This suit, along with a subsequent one, failed as Quebec rules of civil procedure precluded legal actions of this kind. In a change of tactics, Roncarelli's lawyer, A.L. Stein of Montreal, made a bold move and sued Duplessis personally. There was no technical barrier to this claim. In the action Roncarelli asked for more than one hundred thousand dollars in damages. The suit precipitated a new wave of prosecutions against members of the sect, and Jehovah's Witnesses by the hundreds were taken into custody, including Laurier Saumur.

Throughout the province what can only be described as a reign of terror against the Jehovah's Witnesses began. Prayer meetings in private homes were broken up by the police, and Jehovah's Witnesses were taken into custody in the middle of the night and later released. Arrests were made and charges filed and then withdrawn. Men and women were sent to jail, or were chased out of towns and villages by screaming mobs as the police stood idly by. Witness literature was burned and Witness members beaten. It was the most extensive campaign of state-sponsored religious persecution ever undertaken in Canada.

In the meantime, A.L. Stein proceeded with Roncarelli's case. Stein held no brief for the Jehovah's Witnesses or their beliefs, but was personally offended by the action Duplessis had taken against Roncarelli. However, Stein needed some help, and he reasoned that the best co-counsel he could get would be a prominent French-Canadian, Roman Catholic lawyer. Of the half dozen or so whom he approached none would agree to help. F.R. Scott who was not French Canadian, however, agreed to assist. Together they fought a case that would take them to the Supreme Court of Canada and that, even today, tells us much about what is meant by the rule of law.

Roncarelli v. Duplessis
[1959] SCR 121, 16 DLR (2d) 689

[Roncarelli brought an action for damages against Duplessis, the premier of Quebec, for wrongful revocation of a licence to sell liquor. He succeeded at trial; the Quebec Court

of Appeal reversed; and Roncarelli's appeal to the Supreme Court was allowed by a majority of six to three. As the reading from Kaplan explains, the appeal was argued by
Frank Scott.]

RAND J (Judson J concurring): The material facts from which my conclusion is drawn
are these. The appellant was the proprietor of a restaurant in a busy section of Montreal
which in 1946 through its transmission to him from his father had been continuously licensed for the sale of liquor for approximately 34 years; he is of good education and repute
and the restaurant was of a superior class. On December 4 of that year, while his application for annual renewal was before the Liquor Commission, the existing licence was
cancelled and his application for renewal rejected, to which was added a declaration by
the respondent that no future licence would ever issue to him. These primary facts took
place in the following circumstances.

For some years the appellant had been an adherent of a rather militant Christian religious sect known as the Witnesses of Jehovah. Their ideology condemns the established
church institutions and stresses the absolute and exclusive personal relation of the individual to the Deity without human intermediation or intervention.

The first impact of their proselytizing zeal upon the Roman Catholic church and community in Quebec, as might be expected, produced a violent reaction. Meetings were
forcibly broken up, property damaged, individuals ordered out of communities, in one
case out of the province, and generally, within the cities and towns, bitter controversy
aroused. The work of the Witnesses was carried on both by word of mouth and by the
distribution of printed matter, the latter including two periodicals known as "The Watch
Tower" and "Awake" sold at a small price.

In 1945 the provincial authorities began to take steps to bring an end to what was
considered insulting and offensive to the religious beliefs and feelings of the Roman
Catholic population. Large scale arrests were made of young men and women, by whom
the publications mentioned were being held out for sale, under local by-laws requiring a
licence for peddling any kind of wares. Altogether almost one thousand of such charges
were laid. The penalty involved in Montreal, where most of the arrests took place, was a
fine of $40, and as the Witnesses disputed liability, bail was in all cases resorted to.

The appellant, being a person of some means, was accepted by the Recorder's Court
as bail without question, and up to November 12, 1946, he had gone security in about
380 cases, some of the accused being involved in repeated offences. Up to this time there
had been no suggestion of impropriety; the security of the appellant was taken as so satisfactory that at times, to avoid delay when he was absent from the city, recognizances were
signed by him in blank and kept ready for completion by the Court officials. The reason
for the accumulation of charges was the doubt that they could be sustained in law. Apparently the legal officers of Montreal, acting in concert with those of the Province, had
come to an agreement with the attorney for the Witnesses to have a test case proceeded
with. Pending that, however, there was no stoppage of the sale of the tracts and this became the annoying circumstance that produced the volume of proceedings.

On or about November 12 it was decided to require bail in cash for Witnesses so
arrested and the sum set ranged from $100 to $300. No such bail was furnished by the

appellant; his connection with giving security ended with this change of practice; and in the result, all of the charges in relation to which he had become surety were dismissed.

At no time did he take any part in the distribution of the tracts: he was an adherent of the group but nothing more. It was shown that he had leased to another member premises in Sherbrooke which were used as a hall for carrying on religious meetings: but it is unnecessary to do more than mention that fact to reject it as having no bearing on the issues raised. Beyond the giving of bail and being an adherent, the appellant is free from any relation that could be tortured into a badge of character pertinent to his fitness or unfitness to hold a liquor licence.

The mounting resistance that stopped the surety bail sought other means of crushing the propagandist invasion and among the circumstances looked into was the situation of the appellant. Admittedly an adherent, he was enabling these protagonists to be at large to carry on their campaign of publishing what they believed to be the Christian truth as revealed by the Bible; he was also the holder of a liquor licence, a "privilege" granted by the Province, the profits from which, as it was seen by the authorities, he was using to promote the disturbance of settled beliefs and arouse community disaffection generally. Following discussions between the then Mr. Archambault, as the personality of the Liquor Commission, and the chief prosecuting officer in Montreal, the former, on or about November 21, telephoned to the respondent, advised him of those facts, and queried what should be done. Mr. Duplessis answered that the matter was serious and that the identity of the person furnishing bail and the liquor licensee should be put beyond doubt. A few days later, that identity being established through a private investigator, Mr. Archambault again communicated with the respondent and, as a result of what passed between them, the licence, as of December 4, 1946, was revoked.

In the meantime, about November 25, 1946, a blasting answer had come from the Witnesses. In an issue of one of the periodicals, under the heading "Quebec's Burning Hate," was a searing denunciation of what was alleged to be the savage persecution of Christian believers. Immediately instructions were sent out from the department of the Attorney-General ordering the confiscation of the issue and proceedings were taken against one Boucher charging him with publication of a seditious libel.

It is then wholly as a private citizen, an adherent of a religious group, holding a liquor licence and furnishing bail to arrested persons for no other purpose than to enable them to be released from detention pending the determination of the charges against them, and with no other relevant considerations to be taken into account, that he is involved in the issues of this controversy.

The complementary state of things is equally free from doubt. From the evidence of Mr. Duplessis and Mr. Archambault alone, it appears that the action taken by the latter as the general manager and sole member of the Commission was dictated by Mr. Duplessis as Attorney-General and Prime Minister of the province; that that step was taken as a means of bringing to a halt the activities of the Witnesses, to punish the appellant for the part he had played not only by revoking the existing licence but in declaring him barred from one "forever," and to warn others that they similarly would be stripped of provincial "privileges" if they persisted in any activity directly or indirectly related to the Witnesses and to the objectionable campaign. The respondent felt that action to be his duty, something which his conscience demanded of him; and as representing the provincial government his decision became automatically that of Mr. Archambault and the Commission. ...

In these circumstances, when the *de facto* power of the Executive over its appointees at will to such a statutory public function is exercised deliberately and intentionally to destroy the vital business interests of a citizen, is there legal redress by him against the person so acting? This calls for an examination of the statutory provisions governing the issue, renewal and revocation of liquor licences and the scope of authority entrusted by law to the Attorney-General and the government in relation to the administration of the Act.

[An account of the legislation about liquor follows. Briefly, it created a commission, which had power to grant licences and to revoke them "at its discretion."]

The provisions of the statute, which may be supplemented by detailed regulations, furnish a code for the complete administration of the sale and distribution of alcoholic liquors directed by the Commission as a public service, for all legitimate purposes of the populace. It recognizes the association of wines and liquors as embellishments of food and its ritual and as an interest of the public. As put in Macbeth, the "sauce to meat is ceremony," and so we have restaurants, cafés, hotels and other places of serving food, specifically provided for in that association.

At the same time the issue of permits has a complementary interest in those so catering to the public. The continuance of the permit over the years, as in this case, not only recognizes its virtual necessity to a superior class restaurant but also its identification with the business carried on. The provisions for assignment of the permit are to this most pertinent and they were exemplified in the continuity of the business here. As its exercise continues, the economic life of the holder becomes progressively more deeply implicated with the privilege while at the same time his vocation becomes correspondingly dependent on it.

The field of licensed occupations and businesses of this nature is steadily becoming of greater concern to citizens generally. It is a matter of vital importance that a public administration that can refuse to allow a person to enter or continue a calling which, in the absence of regulation, would be free and legitimate, should be conducted with complete impartiality and integrity; and that the grounds for refusing or cancelling a permit should unquestionably be such and such only as are incompatible with the purposes envisaged by the statute: the duty of a commission is to serve those purposes and those only. A decision to deny or cancel such a privilege lies within the "discretion" of the Commission; but that means that decision is to be based upon a weighing of considerations pertinent to the object of the administration.

In public regulation of this sort there is no such thing as absolute and untrammelled "discretion," that is that action can be taken on any ground or for any reason that can be suggested to the mind of the administrator; no legislative Act can, without express language, be taken to contemplate an unlimited arbitrary power exercisable for any purpose, however capricious or irrelevant, regardless of the nature or purpose of the statute. Fraud and corruption in the Commission may not be mentioned in such statutes but they are always implied as exceptions. "Discretion" necessarily implies good faith in discharging public duty; there is always a perspective within which a statute is intended to operate;

and any clear departure from its lines or objects is just as objectionable as fraud or corruption. Could an applicant be refused a permit because he had been born in another province, or because of the colour of his hair? The ordinary language of the legislature cannot be so distorted.

To deny or revoke a permit because a citizen exercises an unchallengeable right totally irrelevant to the sale of liquor in a restaurant is equally beyond the scope of the discretion conferred. There was here not only revocation of the existing permit but a declaration of a future, definitive disqualification of the appellant to obtain one: it was to be "forever." This purports to divest his citizenship status of its incident of membership in the class of those of the public to whom such a privilege could be extended. Under the statutory language here, that is not competent to the Commission and *a fortiori* to the government or the respondent ... . There is here an administrative tribunal which, in certain respects, is to act in a judicial manner; ... what could be more malicious than to punish this licensee for having done what he had an absolute right to do in a matter utterly irrelevant to the *Liquor Act*? Malice in the proper sense is simply acting for a reason and purpose knowingly foreign to the administration, to which was added here the element of intentional punishment by what was virtually vocation outlawry.

It may be difficult if not impossible in cases generally to demonstrate a breach of this public duty in the illegal purpose served; there may be no means, even if proceedings against the Commission were permitted by the Attorney-General, as here they were refused, of compelling the Commission to justify a refusal or revocation or to give reasons for its action; on these questions I make no observation; but in the case before us that difficulty is not present: the reasons are openly avowed.

The act of the respondent through the instrumentality of the Commission brought about a breach of an implied public statutory duty toward the appellant; it was a gross abuse of legal power expressly intended to punish him for an act wholly irrelevant to the statute, a punishment which inflicted on him, as it was intended to do, the destruction of his economic life as a restaurant keeper within the province. Whatever may be the immunity of the Commission or its member from an action for damages, there is none in the respondent. He was under no duty in relation to the appellant and his act was an intrusion upon the functions of a statutory body. The injury done by him was a fault engaging liability within the principles of the underlying public law of Quebec. ... That, in the presence of expanding administrative regulation of economic activities, such a step and its consequences are to be suffered by the victim without recourse or remedy, that an administration according to law is to be superseded by action dictated by and according to the arbitrary likes, dislikes and irrelevant purposes of public officers acting beyond their duty, would signalize the beginning of disintegration of the rule of law as a fundamental postulate of our constitutional structure.

· · ·

The damages suffered involved the vocation of the appellant within the province. Any attempt at a precise computation or estimate must assume probabilities in an area of uncertainty and risk. The situation is one which the Court should approach as a jury would, in a view of its broad features; and in the best consideration I can give to them, the damages should be fixed at the sum of $25,000 plus that allowed by the trial court.

I would therefore allow the appeals, set aside the judgment of the Court of Queen's Bench and restore the judgment at trial modified by increasing the damages to the sum of $33,123.53.

[Martland J, with whom Kerwin CJC and Locke J concurred, and Abbot J gave judgments allowing the appeal for reasons similar to those of Rand J. Both Taschereau J and Fauteux J dissented, on the ground that the notice required by the Code of the Civil Procedure was not given. Cartwright J, dissenting, held that because of the extensive discretion given to the Commission, the courts could not inquire into the reasons for revocation.]

Appeal allowed.

II. RIGHTS AND FEDERALISM

Another antecedent of the Charter lies in the distinctively Canadian tangle of rights and federalism, and the ways in which rights have been protected (or ignored) in the structure of federalism and decisions about the division of powers. There are two themes in this tangle. The first is the ways that rights were protected in the basic idea of federalism itself and in the terms of the *British North America Act*, and the second is the ways that rights were protected (or ignored) in decisions about the division of powers.

At the bottom of the first theme is the idea that federalism may be a way of protecting rights by separating groups that might quarrel and seek to oppress each other if combined in the same state—that is, a group that shares a culture or tradition may share understandings of rights and the kinds of limitations on rights that are appropriate, and can, perhaps, debate and resolve differences about rights through public discourse.

Recall from the readings in Chapter 3, From Contact to Confederation, that one of the purposes of Confederation was to avoid conflict between the English-speaking Protestants in Ontario and the French-speaking Roman Catholics in Quebec. Each was given substantial power to govern its own affairs in its own province, especially in ss. 92(13) and 92(16), and in s. 93, which gave the power to each province "exclusively" to legislate "in relation to education." Yet in each province there was a minority, which feared oppression of its religion, its language, and its schools. At Confederation and later, much of the fear of these minorities centred on their schools, and s. 93 included two limitations designed to protect these schools. These limitations were complex, overlapping, and difficult to interpret and summarize, but their general nature can be suggested in these two propositions: (1) provincial legislation could not prejudicially affect religious schools established before Confederation, and (2) an appeal could be made to the federal cabinet against legislation prejudicially affecting schools established after Confederation. Similar, but not identical, limitations were imposed when other provinces joined Canada. Some of the issues about s. 93 and minority schools appear in Chapter 4, The Late Nineteenth Century: The Canadian Courts Under the Influence, and Chapter 19, Freedom of Religion.

This introductory note has been about the first theme in the tangle of rights and federalism. The second theme, the ways that rights were entangled in decisions about the division of powers, is considered in the next two sections.

A. Federalism and Race

This section presents notes and cases from a long history of racial discrimination against Chinese and Japanese persons in Canada. The Chinese began to come to Canada in the 1850s, coming from the western United States, as part of a northward shift in the search for gold. During the next decade, immigration from China began, and the Japanese began to arrive in the 1880s. From the 1870s onward their numbers were significant, although for the rest of the nineteenth century and well into the twentieth, they settled almost exclusively in the west, and mainly in British Columbia. At first, most were males, and worked in construction, especially in the construction of the transcontinental railway, mines, fishing, agriculture, and in domestic establishments.

From the 1870s until well into the twentieth century, these groups were targets of discriminatory legislation, most of it enacted by the western provinces, especially British Columbia. This legislation used a wide range of techniques: it restricted immigration—for example, by prohibitions, taxes, and language tests; it imposed taxes—for example, head taxes; it denied the franchise and restricted eligibility for public offices; and it restricted economic competition by imposing discriminatory licence requirements on businesses and prohibitions against employment.

The reasons for this discrimination are complex. One cluster was a belief in white superiority and fear of persons who were different and unknown. Another was economic; the willingness of the Chinese and Japanese to work long hours, efficiently, and for low wages, caused white workers to fear their competition. This attitude is described in this passage about the 1890s from P. Roy, *A White Man's Province* (Vancouver: University of British Columbia Press, 1989), at 65-66 (footnotes omitted):

> During much of the decade Asian immigration was not a major issue; the restriction of Asian labour already in the province, however, remained a lively subject. The Chinese head tax and sometimes unfavourable economic conditions contributed to a decline in the Chinese population; Japanese immigrants were not yet conspicuous except along the lower Fraser River. Occasionally, dramatic outbursts of opposition occurred. When Chinese were hired to clear land in Vancouver, a riot ensued; when Japanese fishermen helped break a strike, white fishermen pressed for laws to keep the Japanese out of the fisheries; when explosions killed 216 white and Chinese coal miners, the white miners claimed Chinese were a danger and pressed for their removal from the mines.
>
> Most agitation against Asian competition took place in the political arena. The question of restricting Asian competition was complicated by a fundamental division within British Columbia between capital and labour, that is, in this context, between those who believed "cheap" labour was essential for the development of the province and those who regarded "cheap" labour as a threat to their livelihoods. The presence of high-profile representatives of both camps in the legislature exacerbated the conflict. The dichotomy was especially clear in coal-mining and salmon-canning, industries in which Chinese and Japanese were extensively employed. The

contest was also evident in the perennial discussion of whether or not jobs created by new industries, especially railways and mines, should be reserved for men of "our own race" by including in their acts of incorporation a clause forbidding the employment of Chinese or Japanese. Nevertheless, the lines between those who opposed Asian labour and those who believed it was necessary were not always firmly drawn. On occasion, even sinophobes would set aside principles if they wanted a cheap labour supply quickly for a particular project. References to preserving British Columbia for "our own race" seem not so much to have reflected racist ideas as they did an attempt to broaden support for particular economic interests. Political expediency also influenced legislation. The legislature was more likely to pass anti-Asian measures just before an election than at any other time.

Union Colliery Co. v. Bryden
[1899] AC 580 (PC)

[The tensions described by Roy in the preceding passage became intense in the early 1880s. Proposals were made in the BC legislature to exclude Chinese workers from mines, often by claiming that inability to speak English caused dangers, especially below ground. In 1890, the *Coal Mines Regulation Act*, s. 4, was amended in response to this pressure, by adding the words "and no Chinaman" after the word "girl" in this prohibition: "no boy under the age of ten years and no woman or girl of any age shall be employed in or allowed to be for the purpose of employment in any mine to which the Act applies, below ground." The prohibition proved to be difficult to enforce; its constitutionality was questioned; and proposals were made throughout the 1890s to repeal it. Late in the decade, a shareholder of Union Colliery brought an action for a declaration that the mine was violating the prohibition, probably hoping that the prohibition would be declared *ultra vires*. The company appealed to the Privy Council from the BC Court of Appeal.]

LORD WATSON: ... [T]he question raised directly concerns the legislative authority of the legislature of British Columbia, which depends upon the construction of ss. 91 and 92 of the *British North America Act, 1867*. These clauses distribute all subjects of legislation between the Parliament of the Dominion and the several legislatures of the provinces. In assigning legislative power to the one or the other of these parliaments, it is not made a statutory condition that the exercise of such power shall be, in the opinion of a court of law, discreet. In so far as they possess legislative jurisdiction, the discretion committed to the parliaments, whether of the Dominion or of the provinces, is unfettered. It is the proper function of a court of law to determine what are the limits of the jurisdiction committed to them; but, when that point has been settled, courts of law have no right whatever to inquire whether their jurisdiction has been exercised wisely or not.

· · ·

There can be no doubt that, if s. 92 of the Act of 1867 had stood alone and had not been qualified by the provisions of the clause which precedes it, the provincial legislature of British Columbia would have had ample jurisdiction to enact s. 4 of the *Coal Mines Regulation Act*. The subject-matter of that enactment would clearly have been included in s. 92(10), which extends to provincial undertakings such as the coal mines of the appellant company. It would also have been included in s. 92(13), which embraces "Property and Civil Rights in the Province."

But s. 91(25) extends the exclusive legislative authority of the Parliament of Canada to "naturalization and aliens." Section 91 concludes with a proviso to the effect that "any matter coming within any of the classes of subjects enumerated in this section shall not be deemed to come within the class of matters of a local or private nature comprised in the enumeration of the classes of subjects by this Act assigned exclusively to the legislatures of the provinces."

Section 4 of the Provincial Act prohibits Chinamen who are of full age from employment in underground coal workings. Every alien when naturalized in Canada becomes, *ipso facto*, a Canadian subject of the Queen; and his children are not aliens, requiring to be naturalized, but are natural-born Canadians. It can hardly have been intended to give the Dominion Parliament the ʀ ᴄlusive right to legislate for the latter class of persons resident in Canada; but s. 91(25) might possibly be construed as conferring that power in the case of naturalized aliens after naturalization. The subject of "naturalization" seems prima facie to include the power of enacting what shall be the consequences of naturalization, or, in other words, what shall be the rights and privileges pertaining to residents in Canada after they have been naturalized. It does not appear to their Lordships to be necessary, in the present case, to consider the precise meaning which the term "naturalization" was intended to bear, as it occurs in s. 91(25). But it seems clear that the expression "aliens" occurring in that clause refers to, and, at least includes, all aliens who have not yet been naturalized; and the words "no Chinaman," as they are used in s. 4 of the Provincial Act, were probably meant to denote, and they certainly include, every adult Chinaman who has not been naturalized. ...

The provisions of which the validity has been thus affirmed by the Courts below are capable of being viewed in two different aspects, according to one of which they appear to fall within the subjects assigned to the provincial parliament by s. 92 of the *British North America Act, 1867*, whilst, according to the other, they clearly belong to the class of subjects exclusively assigned to the legislature of the Dominion by s. 91(25). They may be regarded as merely establishing a regulation applicable to the working of underground coal mines; and, if that were an exhaustive description of the substance of the enactments, it would be difficult to dispute that they were within the competency of the provincial legislature, by virtue either of s. 92(10), or s. 92(13). But the leading feature of the enactments consists in this—that they have, and can have, no application except to Chinamen who are aliens or naturalized subjects, and that they establish no rule or regulation except that these aliens or naturalized subjects shall not work, or be allowed to work, in underground coal mines within the Province of British Columbia.

Their Lordships see no reason to doubt that, by virtue of s. 91(25), the legislature of the Dominion is invested with exclusive authority in all matters which directly concern the rights, privileges, and disabilities of the class of Chinamen who are resident in the provinces of Canada. They are also of opinion that the whole pith and substance of the enactments of s. 4 of the *Coal Mines Regulation Act*, in so far as objected to by the appellant company, consists in establishing a statutory prohibition which affects aliens or naturalized subjects, and therefore trench upon the exclusive authority of the Parliament of Canada. ...

Their Lordships will therefore humbly advise Her Majesty to reverse the judgment appealed from; to find and declare that the provisions of s. 4 of the British Columbia *Coal Mines Regulation Act*, 1890, which are now embodied in chapter 138 of the Revised Statutes of British Columbia, 1897, were, in so far as they relate to Chinamen, *ultra vires* of the provincial legislature, and therefore illegal.

Appeal allowed.

Cunningham v. Tomey Homma
[1903] AC 151 (PC)

THE LORD CHANCELLOR (LORD HALSBURY): In this case a naturalized Japanese claims to be placed upon the register of voters for the electoral district of Vancouver City, and the objection which is made to his claim is that by the electoral law of the province it is enacted that no Japanese, whether naturalized or not, shall have his name placed on the register of voters or shall be entitled to vote. Application was made to the proper officer to enter the applicant's name on the register, but he refused to do so upon the ground that the enactment in question prohibited its being done. This refusal was overruled by the Chief Justice sitting in the county court, and the appeal from his decision to the Supreme Court of British Columbia was disallowed. The present appeal is from the decision of the Supreme Court.

There is no doubt that, if it is within the capacity of the province to enact the electoral law, the claimant is [dis]qualified by the express language of the statute; but it is contended that ss. 91 and 92 of the *British North America Act* have deprived the province of the power of making any such provision as to disqualify a naturalized Japanese from electoral privileges. It is maintained that s. 91(25), enacts that the whole subject of naturalization is reserved to the exclusive jurisdiction of the Dominion, while the *Naturalization Act of Canada* enacts that a naturalized alien shall within Canada be entitled to all political and other rights, powers, and privileges to which a natural-born British subject is entitled in Canada. To this it is replied that, by s. 92(1), the constitution of the province and any amendment of it are placed under the exclusive control of the provincial legislature. The question which their Lordships have to determine is which of these two views is the right one, and, in determining that question, the policy or impolicy of such an enactment as that which excludes a particular race from the franchise is not a topic which their Lordships are entitled to consider.

The first observation which arises is that the enactment, supposed to be ultra vires and to be impeached upon the ground of its dealing with alienage and naturalization, has not necessarily anything to do with either. A child of Japanese parentage born in Vancouver City is a natural-born subject of the King, and would be equally excluded from the possession of the franchise. ...

In the history of this country the right to the franchise has been granted and withheld on a great number of grounds, conspicuously upon grounds of religious faith, yet no one has ever suggested that a person excluded from the franchise was not under allegiance to the Sovereign.

Could it be suggested that the province of British Columbia could not exclude an alien from the franchise in that province? Yet, if the mere mention of alienage in the enactment could make the law ultra vires, such a construction of s. 91(25) would involve that absurdity. The truth is that the language of that section does not purport to deal with the consequences of either alienage or naturalization. It undoubtedly reserves these subjects for the exclusive jurisdiction of the Dominion—that is to say, it is for the Dominion to determine what shall constitute either the one or the other, but the question as to what consequences shall follow from either is not touched. The right of protection and the obligations of allegiance are necessarily involved in the nationality conferred by naturalization; but the privileges attached to it, where these depend upon residence, are quite independent of nationality.

This, indeed, seems to have been the opinion of the learned judges below; but they were under the impression that they were precluded from acting on their own judgment by the decision of this Board in the case of *Union Colliery Co. v. Bryden*, [1899] AC 580 (PC). That case depended upon totally different grounds. This Board, dealing with the particular facts of that case, came to the conclusion that the regulations there impeached were not really aimed at the regulation of coal mines at all, but were in truth devised to deprive the Chinese, naturalized or not, of the ordinary rights of the inhabitants of British Columbia and, in effect, to prohibit their earning their living in that province. It is obvious that such a decision can have no relation to the question whether any naturalized person has an inherent right to the suffrage within the province in which he resides.

For these reasons their Lordships will humbly advise His Majesty that the order of the Chief Justice in the country court and the order of the Supreme Court ought to be reversed.

Appeal allowed.

B. Ryder, "Racism and the Constitution: British Columbia Anti-Asian Legislation, 1872-1923" (unpublished, 1990) (footnotes omitted)

Beginning with the Privy Council's decision in *Cunningham v. Tomey Homma*, a revisionist understanding of the *Bryden* case emerged that removed any constitutional challenge to the racial status quo. The Privy Council in *Tomey Homma* abandoned the view expressed by Lord Watson in *Bryden* that s. 91(25) gave the Dominion government jurisdiction over all of the *consequences* of either alien or naturalized status. Rather, the Privy Council in *Tomey Homma* stated that s. 91(25) gave the Dominion jurisdiction only over the "ordinary rights" of the inhabitants of a province to reside and earn a living in the province. Post-*Bryden*, s. 91(25) was interpreted as prohibiting the provinces from passing laws that were intended to deprive a racial group of the right to reside and take up employment in wage labour in the province. Otherwise, provincial legislation imposing racial disabilities did not interfere with exclusive federal jurisdiction over aliens and naturalization. In this way the courts were able to follow Lord Watson's fusion of race with the s. 91(25) categories of federal jurisdiction while removing any potential that the *Bryden* principle had to disrupt the racial status quo.

This peculiar refashioning of judicial interpretation of s. 91(25) can be understood only in light of the network of racist assumptions and beliefs that sustained and justified a social order premised on racial hierarchy. Provincial laws imposing racial disabilities were held to be valid when they were believed to rest on accurate assumptions about racial difference. When it came to the right to reside and work in a province, provincial legislative disabilities were *ultra vires* because Chinese and Japanese workers were no different than European workers. Drake J, in dismissing a charge against a mine for employing Chinese underground, stated that a provincial legislature does not have the power "to exclude a large number of persons from earning a living in the manner they were brought up to do." (*R v. Priest*, (1904) 10 BCR 436, 437.) However, when it came to other rights, for example, rights as voters or employers rather than as labourers, racial differences provided a bona fide provincial legislative purpose that justified the imposition of disabilities on Chinese and Japanese by the provincial legislature. The acceptance of a racial difference grounded provincial laws in a provincial head of power, and removed the objection that the provincial law was in pith and substance imposing a disability on a racial group. ...

In this way, the post-*Bryden* jurisprudential accommodation used racial similarity and difference to ratify a social order premised on racial hierarchy.

In the 1870s and 1880s, before the Privy Council imposed its authority in *Bryden* and *Cunningham*, judges in British Columbia struck down some of the discriminatory legislation, openly protesting against the attitudes it expressed. These cases are discussed in McLaren, "The Early British Columbia Supreme Court and the 'Chinese Question': Echoes of the Rule of Law" (1991), 20 *Manitoba Law Review* 107. The full span of attitudes and legislation between 1884 and 1909, especially the role of the federal government and its use of the disallowance power, is discussed in Ryder, "Racism and the Constitution: The Constitutional Fate of British Columbia Anti-Asian Immigration Legislation, 1884-1909" (1991), 29 *Osgoode Hall Law Journal* 619.

Quong Wing v. The King
(1914), 49 SCR 440, 18 DLR 121

[In 1912, Saskatchewan enacted the *Female Employment Act*, which, in its entirety, read,

> 1. No person shall employ in any capacity any white woman or girl or permit any white woman or girl to reside or lodge in or to work in or, save as a *bona fide* customer in a public apartment thereof only, to frequent any restaurant, laundry or other place of business or amusement owned, kept or managed by any Japanese, Chinaman or other Oriental person.

> 2. Any employer guilty of any contravention or violation of this Act shall upon summary conviction be liable to a penalty not exceeding $100 and in default of payment to imprisonment for a term not exceeding two months.

The term "Chinaman" was not defined. The Dominion's *Naturalization Act*, RSC 1906, c. 77, s. 24, which was crucial to Idington J's dissent, provided:

> An alien to whom a certificate of naturalization is granted shall, within Canada, be entitled to all political and other rights, powers and privileges, and be subject to all obligations, to which a natural-born British subject is entitled or subject within Canada ... .

Quong Wing owned a restaurant and employed two white women as waitresses. When he was charged under the Act, he argued that the prohibition was *ultra vires*. He was convicted and appealed to the Supreme Court.]

DAVIES J: The question on this appeal is not one as to the policy or justice of the Act in question, but solely as to the power of the provincial legislature to pass it. There is no doubt that, as enacted, it seriously affects the civil rights of the Chinamen in Saskatchewan, whether they are aliens or naturalized British subjects. If the language of Lord Watson, in delivering the judgment of the Judicial Committee of the Privy Council in *Union Colliery Company of British Columbia v. Bryden*, [1899] AC 580, was to be accepted as the correct interpretation of the law defining the powers of the Dominion Parliament to legislate on the subject-matter of "naturalization and aliens" assigned to it by s. 91(25) of the *British North America Act, 1867*, I would feel some difficulty in upholding the legislation now under review. ...

If the "exclusive authority on all matters which directly concern the rights, privileges and disabilities of the class of Chinamen who are resident in the provinces of Canada" is vested in the Dominion Parliament by sub-section 25 of section 91 of the *British North America Act, 1867*, it would, to my mind, afford a strong argument that the legislation now in question should be held *ultra vires*.

But in the later case of *Cunningham v. Tomey Homma*, [1903] AC 151, the Judicial Committee modified the views of the construction of s. 91(25) stated in the *Union Colliery* decision.

Reading the *Union Colliery* case, therefore, as explained in this later case, and accepting their Lordships' interpretation of s. 91(25) that "its language does not purport to deal with the consequences of either alienage or naturalization," and that, while it exclusively reserves these subjects to the jurisdiction of the Dominion in so far as to determine what shall constitute either alienage or naturalization, it does not touch the question of what consequences shall follow from either, I am relieved from the difficulty I would otherwise feel.

The legislation under review does not, in this view, trespass upon the exclusive power of the Dominion legislature. It does deal with the subject-matter of "property and civil rights" within the province, exclusively assigned to the provincial legislatures, and so dealing cannot be held *ultra vires*, however harshly it may bear upon Chinamen, naturalized or not, residing in the province. There is no inherent right in any class of the community to employ women and children which the legislature may not modify or take away altogether. There is nothing in the *British North America Act* which says that such legislation may not be class legislation. Once it is decided that the subject-matter of the employment of white women is within the exclusive powers of the provincial legislature and does not infringe upon any of the enumerated subject-matters assigned to the Dominion, then such provincial powers are plenary.

What objects or motives may have controlled or induced the passage of the legislation in question I do not know. Once I find its subject-matter is not within the powers of the Dominion Parliament and is within that of the provincial legislature, I cannot inquire into its policy or justice or into the motives which prompted its passage.

But, in the present case, I have no reason to conclude that the legislation is not such as may be defended upon the highest grounds.

The regulations impeached in the *Union Colliery* case, were, as stated by the Judicial Committee, in the later case of *Tomey Homma*, at p. 157,

> not really aimed at the regulation of coal mines at all, but were in truth devised to deprive the Chinese, naturalized or not, of the ordinary rights of the inhabitants of British Columbia and, in effect, to prohibit their continued residence in that province, since it prohibited their earning their living in that province.

I think the pith and substance of the legislation now before us is entirely different. Its object and purpose is the protection of white women and girls; and the prohibition of their employment or residence, or lodging, or working, etc., in any place of business or amusement owned, kept or managed by any Chinaman is for the purpose of ensuring that protection. Such legislation does not, in my judgment, come within the class of legislation or regulation which the Judicial Committee held *ultra vires* of the provincial legislatures in the case of *The Union Collieries v. Bryden*.

The right to employ white women in any capacity or in any class of business is a civil right, and legislation upon that subject is clearly within the powers of the provincial legislatures. The right to guarantee and ensure their protection from a moral standpoint is, in my opinion, within such provincial powers and, if the legislation is *bona fide* for that purpose, it will be upheld even though it may operate prejudicially to one class or race of people.

There is no doubt in my mind that the prohibition is a racial one and that it does not cease to operate because a Chinaman becomes naturalized. It extends and was intended to extend to all Chinamen as such, naturalized or aliens. Questions which might arise in cases of mixed blood do not arise here.

The Chinaman prosecuted in this was found to have been born in China and of Chinese parents and, although, at the date of the offence charged, he had become a naturalized British subject, and had changed his political allegiance, he had not ceased to be a "Chinaman" within the meaning of that word as used in the statute. This would accord with the interpretation of the word "Chinaman" adopted by the judicial committee in the case of *The Union Colliery Company v. Bryden*. ...

The prohibition against the employment of white women was not aimed at alien Chinamen simply or at Chinamen having any political affiliation. It was against "any Chinaman" whether owing allegiance to the rulers of the Chinese Empire, or the United States Republic, or the British Crown. In other words, it was not aimed at any class of Chinamen, or at the political status of Chinamen, but at Chinamen as men of a particular race or blood, and whether aliens or naturalized.

For these reasons I would dismiss the appeal with costs.

IDINGTON J dissenting: ... It may well be argued that the highly prized gifts of equal freedom and equal opportunity before the law, are so characteristic of the tendency of all British modes of thinking and acting in relation thereto, that they are not to be impaired by the whims of a legislature; and that equality taken away unless and until forfeited for causes which civilized men recognize as valid.

For example, is it competent for a legislature to create a system of slavery and, above all, such a system as applied to naturalized British subjects? This legislation is but a piece of the product of the mode of thought that begot and maintained slavery; not so long ago fiercely claimed to be a laudable system of governing those incapable of governing themselves.

Again, it may also be well argued that, within the exclusive powers given to the Dominion Parliament over the subject of naturalization and aliens, there is implied the power to guarantee to all naturalized subjects that equality of freedom and opportunity to which I have adverted. And I ask, has it not done so by the foregoing provision of the *Naturalization Act*? ...

Canada, for example, is deeply interested as a whole and always has been in the colonization of its waste lands by aliens expecting to become British subjects and surely the power over naturalization must involve in its exercise many considerations relative to the future status of such people as invited to go there and accept the guarantees and inducements offered them. To define and forever determine beyond the power of any legislature to alter the status of such people and measure out their rights by that enjoyed by the native-born seems to me a power implied in the power over "naturalization and aliens." ...

The appellant having, under the *Naturalization Act* (as I think fair to infer), become a British subject, he has presumably been certified to as a man of good character and enjoying the assurance, conveyed in section thereof which I have quoted, of equal treatment with other British subjects, I shall not willingly impute an intention to the legislature to violate that assurance by this legislation specially aimed at his fellow-countrymen in origin. Indeed, in a piece of legislation alleged to have been promoted in the interests of morality, it would seem a strange thing to find it founded upon a breach of good faith which lies at the root of nearly all morality worth bothering one's head about. ...

Looked at from this point of view I am constrained to think that this Act must be construed as applicable only to those Chinamen who have not become naturalized British subjects, and is not applicable to the appellant who has become such.

Whether it is *ultra vires* or *intra vires* the alien Chinamen is a question with which, in this view, I have nothing to do. ...

DUFF J: ... The authority of the legislature of Saskatchewan to enact this statute now before us is disputed upon the ground that the Act is really and truly legislation in relation to a matter which falls within the subject assigned exclusively to the Dominion by s. 91(25), "aliens and naturalization," and to which, therefore, the jurisdiction of the province does not extend. This is said to be shewn by the decision of the Privy Council in *The Union Colliery Co. v. Bryden*. ...

I think that, on the proper construction of this Act (and this appears to me to be the decisive point), it applies to persons of the races mentioned without regard to nationality. According to the common understanding of the words "Japanese, Chinaman or other

Oriental person," they would embrace persons otherwise answering the description who, as being born in British territory (Singapore, Hong Kong, Victoria or Vancouver, for instance), are natural born subjects of His Majesty equally with persons of other nationalities. The terms Chinaman and Chinese, as generally used in Canadian legislation, point to a classification based upon origin, upon racial or personal characteristics and habits, rather than upon nationality or allegiance. The *Chinese Immigration Act*, for example, RSC 1906, ch. 15 (sec. 2(d) and sec. 7), particularly illustrates this; and the judgment of Mr. Justice Martin, *Re The Coal Mines Regulation Act*, 10 BCR 408, at pp. 421 and 428, gives other illustrations. Indeed, the presence of the phrase "other Oriental persons" seems to make it clear, even if there could otherwise have been any doubt upon the point, that the legislature is not dealing with these classes of persons according to nationality, but as persons of a certain origin or persons having certain common characteristics and habits sufficiently indicated by the language used.

Prima facie, therefore, the Act is not an Act dealing with aliens or with naturalized subjects as such. It seems also impossible to say that the Act is, in its practical operation, limited to aliens and naturalized subjects.

There is nothing in the Act itself to indicate that the legislature is doing anything more than attempting to deal according to its lights (as it is its duty to do) with a strictly local situation. In the sparsely inhabited Western provinces of this country the presence of Orientals in comparatively considerable numbers not infrequently raises questions for public discussion and treatment, and, sometimes in an acute degree, which in more thickly populated countries would excite little or no general interest. One can without difficulty figure to one's self the considerations which may have influenced the Saskatchewan Legislature in dealing with the practice of white girls taking employment in such circumstances as are within the contemplation of this Act; considerations, for example, touching the interests of immigrant European women, and considerations touching the effect of such a practice upon the local relations between Europeans and Orientals; to say nothing of considerations affecting the administration of the law.

[Fitzpatrick CJC gave a judgment essentially similar to the judgments of Davies and Duff JJ.]

Appeal dismissed.

Shortly after the outbreak of hostilities in the Pacific during World War II, the government began to impose controls on Japanese persons living in Canada, especially those living in British Columbia. At first, curfews were imposed and fishing boats were impounded, and in 1942, a comprehensive program of evacuation began. Japanese persons living in specified areas were moved to camps, most of which were in the interior of British Columbia, and the remainder on the prairies and in Ontario. Here, they worked on highway construction and sugar beet farms, often separated from their families, and much of their property was impounded.

These controls were imposed under the *War Measures Act*, which gave the government power to do whatever it considered "necessary or advisable for the security, defense, peace, order and welfare of Canada." This power was limited to the existence of "real or apprehended war, invasion, insurrection," and a proclamation by the government was to be conclusive evidence that these conditions existed. This general grant of power was followed by some particulars, which included, "arrest, detention, exclusion, and deportation." In 1945, the Dominion enacted the *National Emergency Transitional Powers Act, 1945,* which was designed to provide for the difficult transition following the war. It gave the government powers, like the *War Measures Act,* to do whatever it considered necessary during the continuing emergency. It included a power to continue orders made under the *War Measures Act,* and an appropriate order was made a few weeks later.

At the same time the government made provisions for deportation, which included power to deport specified groups of Japanese persons who were British subjects, either through birth or naturalization. This power was challenged, unsuccessfully, in *Co-operative Committee on Japanese Canadians v. AG Canada,* [1947] AC 87 (PC). The first part of this challenge was to the *War Measures Act* itself, and it prompted Lord Wright, who wrote the judgment of the Privy Council, to make a general comment about emergencies:

> Under the *British North America Act* property and civil rights in the several Provinces are committed to the Provincial legislatures, but the Parliament of the Dominion in a sufficiently great emergency, such as that arising out of war, has power to deal adequately with that emergency for the safety of the Dominion as a whole. The interests of the Dominion are to be protected and it rests with the Parliament of the Dominion to protect them. What those interests are the Parliament of the Dominion must be left with considerable freedom to judge. Again, if it be clear that an emergency has not arisen, or no longer exists, there can be no justification for the exercise or continued exercise of the exceptional powers. The rule of law as to the distribution of powers between the Parliaments of the Dominion and the Parliaments of the Provinces comes into play. But very clear evidence that an emergency has not arisen, or that the emergency no longer exists, is required to justify the judiciary, even though the question is one of ultra vires, in overruling the decision of the Parliament of the Dominion that exceptional measures were required or were still required. ... (at 101-2)

Several other arguments were made, and rejected, including one that the term "deportation" was limited to aliens. Lord Wright said at 104-5:

> On this argument it may be conceded that commonly it is only aliens who are made liable to deportation, and that in consequence, where reference is made to deportation, there is often imported the suggestion that aliens are under immediate consideration. The dictionaries, as might be expected, do not altogether agree as to the meaning of deportation, but the Oxford English Dictionary gives as its definition "The action of carrying away: 'forcible removal, especially into exile: transportation.'" As a matter of language, their Lordships take the view that "deportation" is not a word which is misused when applied to persons not aliens. Whether or not the word "deportation" is in its application to be confined to aliens or not remains therefore open as a matter of construction of the particular statute in which it is found. In the present case the Act is directed to dealing with emergencies; throughout it is in sweeping terms, and the word is found in the combination "arrest, detention, 'exclusion and deportation.'" As regards the first three of these words, nationality is obviously not a relevant consideration. The general nature of the Act and the collocation in which the word is found, establish, in their Lordships' view, that in this statute the word "deportation" is used in a general sense and as an action applicable to all persons irrespective of nationality. This being in their Lordships' judgment the

true construction of the Act, it must apply to all persons who are at the time subject to the laws of Canada. They may be so subject by the mere fact of being in Canada, whether they are aliens or British subjects or Canadian nationals. Nationality per se is not a relevant consideration. An order relating to deportation would not be unauthorized by reason that it related to Canadian nationals or British subjects. ...

B. The Implied Bill of Rights

This section is based on a series of cases about what has come to be called the "implied bill of rights." Prior to the enactment of the Charter, the Constitution did not expressly limit the legislative authority of Parliament or a province to interfere with fundamental freedoms, such as freedom of expression and freedom of religion. Generally speaking, the legislative authority to interfere with fundamental freedoms is distributed between the two levels of government, with the critical issue being whether the law in question is in relation to a subject matter assigned to the level of government that enacted it.

In the following cases, a number of provincial laws that interfered with fundamental freedoms were held to be *ultra vires*. As you read them, ask yourself whether they suggest that only Parliament, and not the provincial legislature in question, is authorized to enact a law that interferes with a fundamental freedom such as freedom of expression or religion, or whether the Constitution prevents both levels of government from enacting laws that interfere with the exercise of such freedoms.

The latter possibility is known as the "implied bill of rights," for it suggests that the Constitution itself, perhaps as a result of the preamble to the *BNA Act*, implies that there is a zone of liberty into which the state must not unjustifiably enter, regardless of whether the legislation in question is federal or provincial. This of course is the function that the *Charter of Rights and Freedoms* performs today, which is why the "implied bill of rights" doctrine is one of the Charter's antecedents.

Reference re Alberta Statutes
[1938] SCR 100, 2 DLR 81

[One of the most dramatic political events in the 1930s was the election of the Social Credit government in Alberta in 1937. Its monetary policies, which horrified the eastern establishment, especially its bankers, were vague and muddled, but the essential belief was that the total of the payments to individuals from all economic transactions was less than the total value of goods produced, and this shortfall was the cause of unemployment and depression. The solution was to impose public control over the banks, and provide each individual a "social credit," which he or she must spend to maintain the balance between payments and production. The newspaper accounts of the election victory and this economic policy were extensive and almost all hostile, and the hostility continued as the government began to implement its policies in 1936 and 1937. The government's response to this hostility was the Publication of Accurate News and Information Bill, which gave power to the Social Credit Board (which had been created by statute to implement the general program) to require newspapers to publish statements that it considered necessary to correct public misapprehension. The Bill also gave power to require disclosure of sources and the names of authors.

The Lieutenant Governor refused to assent to this Bill, and two others about economic policy. A reference was made to determine the extent of the powers of disallowance and reservation, which is of no interest here, and the powers of Alberta to enact the three reserved bills. The Supreme Court unanimously held that all three were *ultra vires*—and the statutes that had been enacted earlier were *ultra vires* as well.]

CANNON J: … The policy referred to in the preamble of the Press bill regarding which the people of the province are to be informed from the government standpoint, is undoubtedly the Social Credit policy of the government. The administration of the bill is in the hands of the Chairman of the Social Credit Board who is given complete and discretionary power by the bill. "Social Credit," according to s. 2(b) of *The Alberta Social Credit Amendment Act* is

> the power resulting from the belief inherent within society that its individual members in association can gain the objectives they desire;

and the objectives in which the people of Alberta must have a firm and unshaken belief are the monetization of credit and the creation of a provincial medium of exchange instead of money to be used for the purposes of distributing to Albertans loans without interest, per capita dividends and discount rates to purchase goods from retailers. This free distribution would be based on the unused capacity of the industries and people of the province of Alberta to produce goods and services, which capacity remains unused on account of the lack or absence of purchasing power in the consumers in the province. The purchasing power would equal or absorb this hitherto unused capacity to produce goods and services by the issue of Treasury Credit certificates against a Credit Fund or Provincial credit account established by the Commission each year representing the monetary value of this "unused capacity"—which is also called "Alberta credit."

It seems obvious that this kind of credit cannot succeed unless every one should be induced to believe in it and help it along. The word "credit" comes from the Latin: *credere*, to believe. It is, therefore, essential to control the sources of information of the people of Alberta, in order to keep them immune from any vacillation in their absolute faith in the plan of the government. The Social Credit doctrine must become, for the people of Alberta, a sort of religious dogma of which a free and uncontrolled discussion is not permissible. The bill aims to control any statement relating to any policy or activity of the government of the province and declares this object to be a matter of public interest. The bill does not regulate the relations of the newspapers' owners with private individual members of the public, but deals exclusively with expressions of opinion by the newspapers concerning government policies and activities. The pith and substance of the bill is to regulate the press of Alberta from the viewpoint of public policy by preventing the public from being misled or deceived as to any policy or activity of the Social Credit Government and by reducing any opposition to silence or bring upon it ridicule and public contempt.

I agree with the submission of the Attorney-General for Canada that this bill deals with the regulation of the press of Alberta, not from the viewpoint of private wrongs or civil injuries resulting from any alleged infringement or privation of civil rights which belong to individuals, considered as individuals, but from the viewpoint of public wrongs or crimes, i.e., involving a violation of the public rights and duties to the whole community, considered as a community, in its social aggregate capacity.

Do the provisions of this bill, as alleged by the Attorney-General for Canada, invade the domain of criminal law and trench upon the exclusive legislative jurisdiction of the Dominion in this regard?

The object of an amendment of the criminal law, as a rule, is to deprive the citizen of the right to do that, apart from the amendment, he could lawfully do. Sections 130 to 136 of the *Criminal Code* deal with seditious words and seditious publications; and s. 133(a) reads as follows:

No one shall be deemed to have a seditious intention only because he intends in good faith,—

(a) to show that His Majesty has been misled or mistaken in his measures; or

(b) to point out errors or defects in the *government* or constitution of the United Kingdom, or of any part of it, or of Canada or *any province thereof*, or *in any legislature*, or in the administration of justice; or to excite His Majesty's subjects to attempt to procure, by lawful means, the alteration of any matter of state; or

(c) to point out, in order to their removal, matters which are producing or have a tendency to produce feelings of hatred and ill-will between different classes of His Majesty's subjects.

It appears that in England, at first, criticism of any government policy was regarded as a crime involving severe penalties and punishable as such; but since the passing of *Fox's Libel Act* in 1792, the considerations now found in the above article of our criminal code that it is not criminal to point out errors in the Government of the country and to urge their removal by lawful means have been admitted as a valid defence in a trial for libel.

Now, it seems to me that the Alberta legislature by this retrograde Bill is attempting to revive the old theory of the crime of seditious libel by enacting penalties, confiscation of space in newspapers and prohibitions for actions which, after due consideration by the Dominion Parliament, have been declared innocuous and which, therefore, every citizen of Canada can do lawfully and without hindrance or fear of punishment. It is an attempt by the legislature to amend the *Criminal Code* in this respect and to deny the advantage of s. 133(a) to the Alberta newspaper publishers.

Under the British system, which is ours, no political party can erect a prohibitory barrier to prevent the electors from getting information concerning the policy of the government. Freedom of discussion is essential to enlighten public opinion in a democratic State; it cannot be curtailed without affecting the right of the people to be informed through sources independent of the government concerning matters of public interest. There must be an untrammelled publication of the news and political opinions of the political parties contending for ascendancy. As stated in the preamble of the *British North America Act*, our constitution is and will remain, unless radically changed, "similar in principle to that of the United Kingdom." At the time of Confederation, the United Kingdom was a democracy. Democracy cannot be maintained without its foundation: free public opinion and free discussion throughout the nation of all matters affecting the State within the limits set by the criminal code and the common law. Every inhabitant in

Alberta is also a citizen of the Dominion. The province may deal with his property and civil rights of a local and private nature within the province; but the province cannot interfere with his status as a Canadian citizen and his fundamental right to express freely his untrammelled opinion about government policies and discuss matters of public concern. The mandatory and prohibitory provisions of the Press Bill are, in my opinion, *ultra vires* of the provincial legislature. They interfere with the free working of the political organization of the Dominion. They have a tendency to nullify the political rights of the inhabitants of Alberta, as citizens of Canada, and cannot be considered as dealing with matters purely private and local in that province. The federal parliament is the sole authority to curtail, if deemed expedient and in the public interest, the freedom of the press in discussing public affairs and the equal rights in that respect of all citizens throughout the Dominion. These subjects were matters of criminal law before Confederation, have been recognized by Parliament as criminal matters and have been expressly dealt with by the *Criminal Code*. No province has the power to reduce in that province the political rights of its citizens as compared with those enjoyed by the citizens of other provinces of Canada. Moreover, citizens outside the province of Alberta have a vital interest in having full information and comment, favourable and unfavourable, regarding the policy of the Alberta government and concerning events in that province which would, in the ordinary course, be the subject of Alberta newspapers' news items and articles.

DUFF CJC:

[The first part of this judgment is omitted. It concluded that the Bill was *ultra vires* because it depended on the other bills, which were held to be invalid.]

This is sufficient for disposing of the question referred to us but, we think, there are some further observations upon the Bill which may properly be made. Under the constitution established by the *British North America Act*, legislative power for Canada is vested in one Parliament consisting of the sovereign, an upper house styled the Senate, and the House of Commons. Without entering in detail upon an examination of the enactments of the Act relating to the House of Commons, it can be said that these provisions manifestly contemplate a House of Commons which is to be, as the name itself implies, a representative body; constituted, that is to say, by members elected by such of the population of the united provinces as may be qualified to vote. The preamble of the statute, moreover, shows plainly enough that the constitution of the Dominion is to be similar in principle to that of the United Kingdom. The statute contemplates a parliament working under the influence of public opinion and public discussion. There can be no controversy that such institutions derive their efficacy from the free public discussion of affairs, from criticism and answer and counter-criticism, from attack upon policy and administration and defence and counter-attack; from the freest and fullest analysis and examination from every point of view of political proposals. This is signally true in respect of the discharge by Ministers of the Crown of their responsibility to Parliament, by members of Parliament of their duty to the electors, and by the electors themselves of their responsibilities in the election of their representatives.

The right of public discussion is, of course, subject to legal restrictions; those based upon considerations of decency and public order, and others conceived for the protection of various private and public interests with which, for example, the laws of defamation and sedition are concerned. In a word, freedom of discussion means, to quote the words of Lord Wright in *James v. Commonwealth*, "freedom governed by law."

Even within its legal limits, it is liable to abuse and grave abuse, and such abuse is constantly exemplified before our eyes; but it is axiomatic that the practice of this right of free public discussion of public affairs, notwithstanding its incidental mischiefs, is the breath of life for parliamentary institutions.

We do not doubt that (in addition to the power of disallowance vested in the Governor General) the Parliament of Canada possesses authority to legislate for the protection of this right. That authority rests upon the principle that the powers requisite for the protection of the constitution itself arise by necessary implication from the *British North America Act* as a whole (*Fort Frances Pulp & Power Co. Ltd. v. Manitoba Free Press Co. Ltd.*, [1923] AC 695 (PC)); and since the subject-matter in relation to which the power is exercised is not exclusively a provincial matter, it is necessarily vested in Parliament.

But this by no means exhausts the matter. Any attempt to abrogate this right of public debate or to suppress the traditional forms of the exercise of the right (in public meeting and through the press) would, in our opinion, be incompetent to the legislatures of the provinces, or to the legislature of any one of the provinces, as repugnant to the provisions of the *British North America Act*, by which the Parliament of Canada is established as the legislative organ of the people of Canada under the Crown, and Dominion legislation enacted pursuant to the legislative authority given by those provisions. The subject matter of such legislation could not be described as a provincial matter purely; as in substance exclusively a matter of property and civil rights within the province, or a matter private or local within the province. …

Some degree of regulation of newspapers everybody would concede to the provinces. Indeed, there is a very wide field in which the provinces undoubtedly are invested with legislative authority over newspapers; but the limit, in our opinion, is reached when the legislation effects such a curtailment of the exercise of the right of public discussion as substantially to interfere with the working of the parliamentary institutions of Canada as contemplated by the provisions of the *British North America Act* and the statutes of the Dominion of Canada.

[Davis J concurred with Duff CJC. Kerwin, Crocket, and Hudson JJ held that the Bill was invalid because it was dependent on the other bills and statutes, and expressly declined to discuss its validity on the grounds that Duff CJC and Cannon J adopted. An appeal was taken to the Privy Council about all three bills, but that body did not hear argument about this Bill, because the earlier statutes on which it depended had been repealed early in 1938: *AG Alberta v. AG Canada*, [1938] AC 294, [1938] 4 DLR 433 (PC).]

The next two cases return to the story of the struggle between the Jehovah's Witnesses and the Quebec government, which was the background for *Roncarelli*. You will recall that the excerpt from Kaplan, *State and Salvation*, introduced *Boucher v. The King*, [1951] SCR 265, [1950] 1 DLR 657 and Ivan Rand. Boucher, like many other Witnesses since the 1920s, was charged under s. 133 of the *Criminal Code* with publishing a seditious libel. After being convicted in the Quebec courts, he appealed to the Supreme Court, where the conviction was quashed. The core issue was the interpretation of s. 133, especially the definition of one of its crucial phrases, "seditious intent," which is obviously not within the topic of this chapter, but a comment by Rand J on freedom of speech (at DLR 682) can nonetheless usefully be included here.

> Freedom in thought and speech and disagreement in ideas and beliefs, on every conceivable subject, are of the essence of our life. The clash of critical discussion on political, social and religious subjects has too deeply become the stuff of daily experience to suggest that mere ill-will as a product of controversy can strike down the latter with illegality. A superficial examination of the word shows its insufficiency: what is the degree necessary to criminality? Can it ever, as mere subjective condition, be so? Controversial fury is aroused constantly by differences in abstract conceptions; heresy in some fields is again a mortal sin; there can be fanatical puritanism in ideas as well as in mortals; but our compact of free society accepts and absorbs these differences and they are exercised at large within the framework of freedom and order on broader and deeper uniformities as bases of social stability. Similarly in discontent, affection and hostility: as subjective incidents of controversy, they and the ideas which arouse them are part of our living which ultimately serve us in stimulation, in the clarification of thought and, as we believe, in the search for the constitution and truth of things generally.

Saumur v. City of Quebec
[1953] 2 SCR 299, [1953] 4 DLR 641

[Recall from Kaplan, *State and Salvation, supra,* that prosecutions under bylaws regulating the distribution of pamphlets in the streets was one of the principal ways in which the government sought to silence the Witnesses. Saumur, a Jehovah's Witness, was charged and convicted under a bylaw of this kind, and brought an action for a declaration that it was *ultra vires.* He eventually succeeded in the Supreme Court. All nine members of the Court sat, dividing five to four and reasoning in several different ways. Now, roughly fifty years later, our attention can be limited to parts of only two of these judgments.]

RAND J: The appellant seeks a declaration that by-law no. 184, of the City of Quebec, passed in October, 1933, is beyond the legislative power of the province:

> 1. It is by the present by-law forbidden to distribute in the streets of the City of Quebec any book, pamphlet, booklet, circular, or tract whatever without having previously obtained for so doing the written permission of the Chief of Police.

Contravention is punishable by fine, with imprisonment in default of payment. No question is raised that the by-law is not authorized by the city charter, and the grounds upon which it is challenged are that it infringes the freedom of religious worship, secured by a statute to which I shall later refer, and that it trenches upon the jurisdiction of the Dominion in restraining freedom of communication by writings.

The practice under it is undisputed and as stated to us by counsel is this: when a license is sought, a copy of the document or writing proposed to be distributed is brought to the police department and there the chief officer, acting with or without the city solicitor or others, or in his absence, an official representing him, peruses the writing; if there is nothing in it considered from any standpoint to be objectionable, the license issues; if there is, suggestions are made that the offending matter be removed, but if that is not done the license is refused.

As in all controversies of this nature, the first enquiry goes to the real nature and character of the by-law; in what substance and aspect of legislative matter is it enacted? and we must take its objects and purposes to be what its language fairly embraces. The by-law places no restriction on the discretion of the officer and none has been suggested. If, under cover of such a blanket authority, action may be taken which directly deals with matters beyond provincial powers, can the fact that the language may, at the same time, encompass action on matters within provincial authority preserve it from the taint of *ultra vires*? May a court enter upon a delineation of the limits and contours of the valid and invalid areas within it? Must the provision stand or fall as one or can it be severed or otherwise dealt with? These are the subsidiary questions to be answered.

What the practice under the by-law demonstrates is that the language comprehends the power of censorship. From its inception, printing has been recognized as an agency of tremendous possibilities, and virtually upon its introduction into Western Europe it was brought under the control and license of government. At that time, as now in despotisms, authority viewed with fear and wrath the uncensored printed word: it is and has been the bête noire of dogmatists in every field of thought; and the seat of its legislative control in this country becomes a matter of the highest moment.

The Christian religion, its practices and profession, exhibiting in Europe and America an organic continuity, stands in the first rank of social, political and juristic importance. ...

From 1760 to the present moment religious freedom has, in our legal system, been recognized as a principle of fundamental character; and although we have nothing in the nature of an established church, that the untrammelled affirmations of religious belief and its propagation, personal or institutional, remain as of the greatest constitutional significance throughout the Dominion is unquestionable. ...

The only powers given by s. 92 of the *Confederation Act* which have been suggested to extend to legislation in relation to religion are s. 92(13), Property and Civil Rights, and s. 92(16), Matters of a merely local or private nature in the province. The statutory history of the expression "Property and Civil Rights" already given exhibiting its parallel enactment with special provisions relating to religion shows indubitably that such matters as religious belief, duty and observances were never intended to be included within that collocation of powers. If it had not been so, the exceptional safeguards to Roman Catholics would have been redundant.

[An account of early statutes is omitted.]

Strictly speaking, civil rights arise from positive law; but freedom of speech, religion and the inviolability of the person, are original freedoms which are at once the necessary attributes and modes of self-expression of human beings and the primary conditions of their community life within a legal order. It is in the circumscription of these liberties by the creation of civil rights in persons who may be injured by their exercise, and by the sanctions of public law, that the positive law operates. What we realize is the residue inside that periphery. Their significant relation to our law lies in this, that under its principles to which there are only minor exceptions, there is no prior or antecedent restraint placed upon them: the penalties, civil or criminal, attach to results which their exercise may bring about, and apply as consequential incidents. So we have the civil rights against defamation, assault, false imprisonment and the like, and the punishments of the criminal law; but the sanctions of the latter lie within the exclusive jurisdiction of the Dominion. Civil rights of the same nature arise also as protection against infringements of these freedoms.

That legislation "in relation" to religion and its profession is not a local or private matter would seem to me to be self-evident: the dimensions of this interest are nationwide; it is even today embodied in the highest level of the constitutionalism of Great Britain; it appertains to a boundless field of ideas, beliefs and faiths with the deepest roots and loyalties; a religious incident reverberates from one end of this country to the other, and there is nothing to which the "body politic of the Dominion" is more sensitive.

There is, finally, the implication of s. 93 of the *Confederation Act* which deals with education. In this section appear the only references in the statute to religion. Subsec. (i) speaks of "*Denominational Schools*" and preserves their existing rights and privileges. Subsec. (ii) extends to the separate schools "of the Queen's Protestant and Roman Catholic subjects" in Quebec the same "powers, privileges and duties" then conferred and imposed upon the separate schools of the "Queen's Roman Catholic subjects" in Upper Canada. Subsec. (iii) provides for an appeal to the Governor-General in Council from any act or decision of a provincial authority "affecting any right or privilege of the Protestant or Roman Catholic minority of the Queen's subjects in relation to education." Subsec. (iv) declares that in the event of any failure on the part of the provincial authority to observe or enforce the provincial laws contemplated by the section, Parliament may provide for the execution of the provisions of the section. On the argument advanced, and apart from the question of criminal law, these vital constitutional provisions could be written off by the simple expedient of abolishing, as civil rights and by provincial legislation, the religious freedoms of minorities, and so, in legal contemplation, the minorities themselves.

So is it with freedom of speech. The *Confederation Act* recites the desire of the three provinces to be federally united into one Dominion "with a constitution similar in principle to that of the United Kingdom." Under that constitution, government is by parliamentary institutions, including popular assemblies elected by the people at large in both provinces and Dominion: government resting ultimately on public opinion reached by discussion and the interplay of ideas. If that discussion is placed under license, its basic condition is destroyed; the government, as licensor, becomes disjoined from the citizenry. The only security is steadily advancing enlightenment, for which the widest range of controversy is the *sine qua non.* ...

[A discussion of the *Alberta Press* case is omitted.]

What is proposed before us is that a newspaper, just as a religious, political or other tract or handbill, for the purposes of sale or distribution through use of streets, can be placed under the uncontrolled discretion of a municipal officer; that is, that the province, while permitting all others, could forbid a newspaper or any writing of a particular colour from being so disposed of. That public ways, in some circumstances the only practical means available for any appeal to the community generally, have from the most ancient times been the avenues for such communications, is demonstrated by the Bible itself: in the 6th verse of ch. xi of Jeremiah these words appear: "Proclaim all these words in the cities of Judah, and, in the streets of Jerusalem"; and a more objectionable interference, short of complete suppression, with that dissemination which is the "breath of life" of the political institutions of this country than that made possible by the by-law can scarcely be imagined.

But it is argued that the by-law relates not to religion or free speech at all but to the administration of streets. Undoubtedly the city may pass regulations for that purpose but within the general and neutral requirement of license by the by-law a number of equally plausible objects may be conjectured. No purpose whatever is indicated much less specified by the language; its sole effect is to create and vest in a functionary a power, to be exercised for any purpose or reason he sees fit, disclosed or undisclosed. The only practice actually followed is not remotely connected with street regulation: matters of traffic interference, of nuisance, of cleanliness or anything of like character would be within the city's authority, but these are no more to be inferred than others. A suggested possible purpose is to deal with writings that might provoke breaches of the peace by persons who dislike what they contain, but the same observation applies: that matter or purpose is not prescribed, and, assuming it to be within the provincial purview, on which I express no opinion, it would be only one of a number of objects of equal speculative inclusion within the enactment, some of which relate to matters beyond provincial powers. The alternatives of interpretation are whether of that group of objects, one being valid the by-law in its entirety is valid, or whether one being invalid, the by-law in its entirety falls; or shortly, can legislation embracing such a combination of unspecified possibilities be upheld?

It was urged by Mr. Beaulieu that the city as proprietor of the streets has authority to forbid or permit as it chooses, in the most unlimited and arbitrary manner, any action or conduct that takes place on them. The possibilities of such a proposition can be easily imagined. But it misconceives the relation of the province to the public highways. The public entitled to use them is that of the Dominion, whose citizens are not of this or that province but of Canada. What has been confided to the provinces is the regulation of their use by that public.

Conceding, as in the *Alberta Reference*, that aspects of the activities of religion and free speech may be affected by provincial legislation, such legislation, as in all other fields, must be sufficiently definite and precise to indicate its subject matter. In our political organization, as in federal structures generally, that is the condition of legislation by any authority within it: the courts must be able from its language and its relevant circumstances, to attribute an enactment to a matter *in relation to which* the legislature acting has been empowered to make laws. That principle inheres in the nature of federalism; otherwise, authority, in broad and general terms, could be conferred which would end the division of powers. Where the language is sufficiently specific and can fairly be interpreted as applying only to matter within the enacting jurisdiction, that attribution will be made; and where the requisite elements are present, there is the rule of severability. But to authorize action which may be related indifferently to a variety of incompatible matters by means of the device of a discretionary license cannot be brought within either of these mechanisms; and the Court is powerless, under general language that overlaps exclusive jurisdictions, to delineate and preserve valid power in a segregated form. If the purpose is street regulation, taxation, registration or other local object, the language must, with sufficient precision, define the matter and mode of administration; and by no expedient which ignores that requirement can constitutional limitations be circumvented.

I would, therefore, allow the appeal, direct judgment declaring the by-law invalid, and enjoin the respondent City from acting upon it. ...

RINFRET CJC dissenting (translation): ... Let us say at once that the by-law in dispute is nothing other than a police regulation; it is based primarily on the fact that the streets should not be used for the purpose of distributing documents. The normal use of the streets is that of circulation on foot or in vehicles.

It is not less clear that in the distribution it makes of legislative powers, the *BNA Act* by ss. 91 and 92, confers, upon the Legislature in each Province, the exclusive power to make laws relative to the municipal institutions in the Province (s. 92(8)), to property and civil rights in the Province (s. 92(13)), and generally to all matters of a purely local and private nature in the Province (s. 92(16)).

It would be really fantastic to maintain that some of the powers mentioned above and which are found in the *Cities and Towns Act* of the Province of Quebec, could belong to the federal field. I cannot easily picture the Federal Parliament undertaking to adopt laws on any of these matters. (See the judgment of the Privy Council in *Hodge v. The Queen* (1883), 9 App. Cas. 117 at pp. 131, 133-34.)

I do not understand, besides, that the appellant's attorney directs his argument in opposition to this general principle. He asks the Court to deviate from the text of the by-law and he seeks to find there a motive which would be that which he had already alleged in his declaration, "that this by-law had been passed specially for the purpose of limiting the activities of the plaintiff and of Jehovah's Witnesses."

It is to be noted that the by-law itself says nothing of the kind; it is applicable to all, whatever might be their nationality, their doctrine or their religion. But, what is more, the Judge of first instance decided in fact that it "has not been proved that this by-law had been passed specially for this purpose." On the other hand, in matters of exceeding powers, it is always at the "merit" (pith and substance) of the legislation that one must look. What the by-law is aiming at is solely the use of streets for purposes of distribution. Besides, as the Superior Court Judge has decided, no motive, no ulterior purpose was uncovered by the proof made at the trial; it is an erroneous idea to seek to attribute a motive to a law which does not mention it. A by-law may be valid even if the aim of the municipal council is bad. ...

The only question which the tribunals have to examine is that of finding out if the City of Quebec had the power to adopt this by-law. We do not have to search behind the text which it adopted to see what its aim could have been in making it. I will go even further, and say that the use of the streets of a municipality is unquestionably a question of the municipal field and a local question. I still can't see on what grounds one could pretend that this matter does not fall exclusively within the category of matters granted to the

Provinces in virtue of s. 92 of the *BNA Act*; and, in this case, even if it is admitted that freedom of worship is of the federal field, the power of control of the municipal streets, being a subject specifically attributed to the Provinces, would take precedence of the supposed power of the Federal Parliament to legislate on matters of worship. The jurisprudence is constant that from the moment a matter is specially granted to the provincial sphere by s. 92, it takes precedence and priority over every power which the federal claims to exercise, in virtue of the general powers mentioned in s. 91. ...

Here is in fact what we find in the testimony of Mr. Covington: ...

"Q. Do you consider necessary for your organization to attack the other religions, in fact, the Catholic, the Protestant and the Jews?   A. Indeed. The reason for that is because the Almighty God commands that error shall be exposed and not persons or nations."

The Court asked the same witness:

"Q. You are the only witnesses of the truth?   A. Jehovah's Witnesses are the only witnesses to the truth of Almighty God Jehovah ...   Q. Is the Roman Catholic a true church? A. No. ...   Q. It is an unclean woman?   A. It is pictured in the Bible as a whore, as having illicit relationship with the nations of this world, and history proves that fact, history that all have studied in school."

This same witness declared another point of view: "If obedience to a law of the state or nation would compel them (Jehovah's Witnesses) to thereby violate God's law, they will obey God rather than men." Which, he had already some time before affirmed in the course of his testimony to a question from the Court.

"Q. Notwithstanding the laws of the country to the contrary?   A. Notwithstanding the laws of the country to the contrary."

Who would dare to claim that pamphlets containing the preceding declarations, distributed in a city like Quebec, would not constitute a practice inconsistent with the peace and safety of the city or Province? What Court would condemn a municipal council for preventing the circulation of such statements? And I have chosen but a few passages from the books and tracts which are swarming with such affirmations. Besides, decency would command me not to cite any more of them. And that does not appear to me necessary to demonstrate that a municipality whose population is 90% Catholic not only has the right but the duty to prevent the dissemination of such infamies. ...

On the whole I have no hesitation in saying that the by-law attacked is legal, valid and constitutional and that the judgments which have declared such should be confirmed with costs.

[Recall that the Court divided five to four. Seven of the nine wrote judgments, and the tangle of reasonings and conclusions can best be described by beginning with three judges, Rinfret CJC and Kerwin and Taschereau JJ, even though they did not agree about the result. All three believed that the provinces could regulate religious practice under s. 92(13). Two of them, Rinfret CJC and Taschereau J, held that the bylaw was *intra vires* on this ground, and dissented. Kerwin J, though, reached a different result. He concluded that the bylaw conflicted with some early provincial statutes establishing freedom of religion—that is, he held that although the province had power to regulate religion, the legislation it had enacted rendered the bylaw invalid. This conclusion put Kerwin J among the majority, although it invited the Quebec legislature to amend the statutes. Cartwright J, with whom Fauteux J concurred, also wrote a dissenting judgment, holding that the pith and substance of the bylaw was regulation of use of the streets, a subject within provincial powers. As well, in response to the argument that the provinces could not legislate about religion, he said that even if the Dominion had the exclusive power to make laws about religion, a question he expressly declined to answer, legislation by a province about a subject over which it had jurisdiction could affect a subject within Dominion jurisdiction. The dissenters were, then, Rinfret CJC, and Taschereau, Cartwright, and Fauteux JJ. The majority was composed of Kerwin J, and the four others: Estey, Kellock, Locke, and Rand JJ. All of them, unlike Kerwin J, based their result solely on division of powers grounds, although they differed greatly in the details of their reasoning. All of them referred to the preamble of the *British North America Act*; Estey, Locke, and Kellock JJ considered s. 93 of the *British North America Act*; Locke and Rand JJ discussed the *Alberta Press* case; and Estey and Locke JJ concluded that religion could be regulated only by the Dominion's criminal law power.]

Appeal allowed.

Switzman v. Elbling
[1957] SCR 285, 7 DLR (2d) 337

[This action was essentially a challenge to the *"Padlock" Act*, which was enacted in 1937 by the Quebec legislature to control communism. Section 3, which was crucial, provided:

> It shall be illegal for any person, who possesses or occupies a house within the Province, to use it or allow any person to make use of it to propagate communism or bolshevism by any means whatsoever.

Switzman's landlord brought an action to evict him because he had used the leased premises for purposes prohibited by this section. His defence was that the section was *ultra vires*, and it succeeded in the Supreme Court, by a majority of eight to one.]

RAND J: The first ground on which the validity of s. 3 is supported is s. 92(13) of the *British North America Act*. "Property in the Province," and Mr. Beaulieu's contention goes in this manner: by that head the Province is vested with unlimited legislative power over property; it may, for instance, take land without compensation and generally may act as amply as if it were a sovereign state, untrammelled by constitutional limitation. The power being absolute can be used as an instrument or means to effect any purpose or object. Since the objective accomplishment under the statute here is an Act on property, its validity is self-evident and the question is concluded.

I am unable to agree that in our federal organization power absolute in such a sense resides in either legislature. The detailed distribution made by ss. 91 and 92 places limits to direct and immediate purposes of provincial action. Under s. 92(13) the purpose would, in general, be a "property" purpose either primary or subsidiary to another head of the same section. If such a purpose is foreign to powers vested in the Province by the Act, it will invade the field of the Dominion. For example, land could not be declared forfeited or descent destroyed by attainder on conviction of a crime, nor could the convicted person's right of access to provincial Courts be destroyed. These would trench upon both criminal law and citizenship status. The settled principle that calls for a determination of the "real character," the "pith and substance," of what purports to be enacted and whether it is "colourable" or is intended to effect its ostensible object, means that the true nature of the legislative act, its substance in purpose, must lie within s. 92 or some other endowment of provincial power. That a power ostensibly as here under a specific head cannot be exercised as a means directly and immediately to accomplish a purpose not within that endowment is demonstrated by the following decisions of the Judicial Committee: ...

[Discussion of several cases, including *Union Colliery v. Bryden*, is omitted.]

That the scene of study, discussion or dissemination of views or opinions on any matter has ever been brought under legal sanction in terms of nuisance is not suggested. For the past century and a half in both the United Kingdom and Canada, there has been a steady removal of restraints on this freedom, stopping only at perimeters where the foundation of the freedom itself is threatened. Apart from sedition, obscene writings and criminal libels, the public law leaves the literary, discursive and polemic use of language, in the broadest sense, free.

The object of the legislation here, as expressed by the title, is admittedly to prevent the propagation of communism and bolshevism, but it could just as properly have been the suppression of any other political, economic or social doctrine or theory; and the issue is whether that object is a matter "in relation to which" under s. 92 the Province may exclusively make laws. Two heads of the section are claimed to authorize it: s. 92(13), as a matter of "Civil Rights," and s. 92(16), "Local and Private Matters."

Mr. Tremblay in a lucid argument treated such a limitation of free discussion and the spread of ideas generally as in the same category as the ordinary civil restrictions of libel and slander. These obviously affect the matter and scope of discussion to the extent that it trenches upon the rights of individuals to reputation and standing in the community; and the line at which the restraint is drawn is that at which public concern for the discharge of legal or moral duties and government through rational persuasion, and that for private security, are found to be in rough balance.

But the analogy is not a true one. The ban is directed against the freedom or civil liberty of the actor; no civil right of anyone is affected nor is any civil remedy created. The aim of the statute is, by means of penalties, to prevent what is considered a poisoning of men's minds, to shield the individual from exposure to dangerous ideas, to protect him, in short, from his own thinking propensities. There is nothing of civil rights in this; it is to curtail or proscribe those freedoms which the majority so far consider to be the condition of social cohesion and its ultimate stabilizing force.

It is then said that the ban is a local matter under s. 92(16); that the social situation in Quebec is such that safeguarding its intellectual and spiritual life against subversive doctrines becomes a special need in contrast with that for a general regulation by Parliament. ...

Indicated by the opening words of the preamble in the Act of 1867, reciting the desire of the four Provinces to be united in a federal union with a constitution "similar in principle to that of the United Kingdom," the political theory which the Act embodies is that of parliamentary government, with all its social implications, and the provisions of the statute elaborate that principle in the institutional apparatus which they create or contemplate, whatever the deficiencies in its workings. Canadian government is in substance the will of the majority expressed directly or indirectly through popular assemblies. This means ultimately government by the free public opinion of an open society, the effectiveness of which, as events have not infrequently demonstrated, is undoubted.

But public opinion, in order to meet such a responsibility, demands the condition of a virtually unobstructed access to and diffusion of ideas. Parliamentary government postulates a capacity in men, acting freely and under self-restraints, to govern themselves; and that advance is best served in the degree achieved of individual liberation from subjective as well as objective shackles. Under that government, the freedom of discussion in Canada, as a subject-matter of legislation, has a unity of interest and significance extending equally to every part of the Dominion. With such dimensions it is *ipso facto* excluded from s. 92(16) as a local matter.

This constitutional fact is the political expression of the primary condition of social life, thought and its communication by language. Liberty in this is little less vital to man's mind and spirit than breathing is to his physical existence. As such an inherence in the individual it is embodied in his status of citizenship. Outlawry, for example, divesting civil standing and destroying citizenship, is a matter of Dominion concern. ...

Prohibition of any part of this activity as an evil would be within the scope of criminal law, as ss. 60, 61 and 62 of the *Criminal Code* dealing with sedition exemplify. Bearing in mind that the endowment of parliamentary institutions is one and entire for the Dominion, that Legislatures and Parliament are permanent features of our constitutional structure, and that the body of discussion is indivisible, apart from the incidence of criminal law and civil rights, and incidental effects of legislation in relation to other matters, the degree and nature of its regulation must await future consideration; for the purposes here it is sufficient to say that it is not a matter within the regulation of a Province.

I would, therefore, allow the appeal, set aside the judgments below, dismiss the action and direct a declaration on the intervention that the statute in its entirety is *ultra vires* of the Province.

ABBOTT J: The right of free expression of opinion and of criticism, upon matters of public policy and public administration, and the right to discuss and debate such matters, whether they be social, economic or political, are essential to the working of a parliamentary democracy such as ours ... .

This right cannot be abrogated by a Provincial Legislature, and the power of such Legislature to limit it is restricted to what may be necessary to protect purely private rights, such as for example provincial laws of defamation. It is obvious that the impugned statute does not fall within that category. It does not, in substance, deal with matters of property and civil rights or with a local or private matter within the Province and in my opinion is clearly *ultra vires*. Although it is not necessary, of course, to determine this question for the purposes of the present appeal, the Canadian constitution being declared to be similar in principle to that of the United Kingdom, I am also of opinion that as our constitutional Act now stands, Parliament itself could not abrogate this right of discussion and debate. The power of Parliament to limit it is, in my view, restricted to such powers as may be exercisable under its exclusive legislative jurisdiction with respect to criminal law and to make laws for the peace, order and good government of the nation.

TASCHEREAU J dissenting (translation): The appellant contends that this legislation is exclusive within the domain of the criminal law, and that consequently it is without the legislative competency of the provincial authority. I would willingly agree with him, if the Legislature had enacted that Communism was a crime punishable by law, because there would then be clearly an encroachment on the federal domain, which would make the legislation *ultra vires* of the Province. But such is not the case that we have before us. The Legislature did not say that any act constituted a crime, and it did not confer the character of criminality upon the Communistic doctrine. If the provincial Legislature has no power to create criminal offences, it has the right to legislate to prevent crimes, disorders, as treason, sedition, illegal public meetings, which are crimes under the *Criminal Code*, and to prevent conditions calculated to favour the development of crime. In order to achieve its aims, I entertain no doubt that it may validly legislate as to the possession and use of property, as this is exclusively within the domain of civil law, and is by virtue of s. 92(13) of the *BNA Act* within the provincial competency. ...

I am clearly of opinion that if a Province may validly legislate on all civil matters in relation to criminal law, *that it may enact laws calculated to suppress conditions favouring the development of crime*, and control properties in order to protect society against any illegal uses that may be made of them, if it has the undeniable right to supervise brokers in their financial transactions in order to protect the public against fraud, if, finally, it has the right to impose civil incapacities as a consequence of a criminal offence, I cannot see why it could not also have the power to enact that all those who extol doctrines, calculated to incite to treason, to the violation of official secrets, to sedition, etc., should be deprived of the enjoyment of the properties from where are spread these theories, the object of which is to undermine and overthrow the established order.

Experience, and it is within our power to take of it judicial notice, teaches us that Canadians, less than 10 years ago, in violation of their oath of allegiance, did not hesitate for the sake of Communism, to reveal official secrets and thus imperil the security of the state. The suppression of the spreading of these subversive doctrines by civil sanctions is, to my mind, as important as the suppression of disorderly houses. I remain convinced that the domain of criminal law, exclusively of federal competency, has not been encroached upon by the impugned legislation, and that *the latter merely establishes civil sanctions for the prevention of crime and the security of the country*.

It has also been contended that this legislation constituted an obstacle to the liberty of the press and the liberty of speech. I believe in those fundamental liberties; they are undeniable rights which, fortunately, the citizens of this country enjoy, but these liberties would cease to be a right and become a privilege if it were permitted to certain individuals to misuse them in order to propagate dangerous doctrines that are necessarily conducive to violations of the established order. These liberties which citizens and the press enjoy of expressing their beliefs, their thoughts and their doctrines without previous authorization or censure, do not constitute absolute rights. They are necessarily limited and must be exercised within the bounds of legality. When these limits are overstepped, these liberties become abusive, and the law must then necessarily intervene to exercise a repressive control in order to protect the citizens and society.

The same reasoning must serve to meet the objection raised by the appellant, to the effect that the impugned law is an obstacle to the free expression of all individuals, candidates in an election. Destructive ideas of social order and of established authority by dictatorial methods do not have more rights in electoral periods than in any other times. In the minds of many, this law may appear rigid (it is not within my province to judge of its wisdom), but the severity of a law adopted by a competent power does not brand it with unconstitutionality.

For all these reasons, I am of opinion that this appeal must be dismissed. ...

[Kerwin CJC and Cartwright, Fauteux, Locke, and Nolan JJ all held the Act *ultra vires* because it dealt, in substance, with criminal law. Kellock J concurred with Rand J.]

Appeal allowed.

Dupond v. City of Montreal et al.
[1978] 2 SCR 770, 84 DLR (3d) 420

[This case, which is also discussed in Chapter 11, Criminal Law, involved a challenge to a municipal bylaw imposing a 30-day prohibition on any public gatherings or assemblies. The bylaw was challenged on two grounds: (1) as an invasion of the federal criminal law power and (2) as an infringement of the fundamental freedoms of speech, assembly and association, the press, and religion. A majority of the Court, in a decision written by Beetz J, rejected both grounds of challenge and upheld the bylaw. Only the portions of the judgment dealing with the implied bill of rights argument are reproduced here.]

BEETZ J (Martland, Judson, Ritchie, and Pigeon JJ concurring): ...

IV

The second submission against the constitutionality of s. 5 and of the ordinance was that they are in relation to and in conflict with the fundamental freedoms of speech, of assembly and association, of the press and of religion which were inherited from the United Kingdom and made part of the Constitution by the preamble of the *British North America Act, 1867*, or which come under federal jurisdiction and are protected by the *Canadian Bill of Rights*. The *Alberta Press Act Case, Reference re Alberta Legislation*, [1938] 2 DLR 81, [1938] SCR 100 [aff'd. [1938] 4 DLR 433, [1939] AC 117, [1938] 3 WWR 337 (PC)] was relied upon.

I find it exceedingly difficult to deal with a submission couched in such general terms. What is it that distinguishes a right from a freedom and a fundamental freedom from a freedom which is not fundamental? Is there a correlation between freedom of speech and freedom of assembly on the one hand and, on the other, the right, if any, to hold a public meeting on a highway or in a park as opposed to a meeting open to the public on private land? How like or unlike each other are an assembly, a parade, a gathering, a demonstration, a procession? Modern parlance has fostered loose language upon lawyers. As was said by Sir Ivor Jennings, the English at least have no written constitution and so they may divide their law logically: W. Ivor Jennings, "The Right of Assembly in England," 9 *NYU Law Q Rev.* 217 (1931-32).

I am afraid I cannot avoid answering in kind appellants' submission. I believe I can state my position in a relatively small number of propositions which require little or no development for, difficult as it is at this level of abstraction, I must try not to say more than is necessary to dispose of the submission:

1. None of the freedoms referred to is so enshrined in the Constitution as to be above the reach of competent legislation.

2. None of those freedoms is a single matter coming within exclusive federal or provincial competence. Each of them is an aggregate of several matters which, depending on the aspect, come within federal or provincial competence. (This proposition is postulated in s. 5(3) of "An Act for the Recognition and Protection of Human Rights and Fundamental Freedoms," 1960 (Can.), c. 44, of which the *Canadian Bill of Rights* constitutes Part I.)

3. Freedoms of speech, of assembly and association, of the press and of religion are distinct and independent of the faculty of holding assemblies, parades, gatherings, demonstrations or processions on the public domain of a city. This is particularly so with respect to freedom of speech and freedom of the press as considered in the *Alberta Press Act* case, *supra.* Demonstrations are not a form of speech but of collective action. They are of the nature of a display of force rather than of that of an appeal to reason; their inarticulateness prevents them from becoming part of language and from reaching the level of discourse.

4. The right to hold public meetings on a highway or in a park is unknown to English law. Far from being the object of a right, the holding of a public meeting on a street or in a park may constitute a trespass against the urban authority in whom the ownership of the street is vested even though no one is obstructed and no injury is done; it may also amount to a nuisance: …

Being unknown to English law, the right to hold public meetings on the public domain of a city did not become part of the Canadian Constitution under the preamble of the *British North America Act, 1867.*

5. The holding of assemblies, parades or gatherings on the public domain is a matter which, depending on the aspect, comes under federal or provincial competence and falls to be governed by federal and provincial legislation such as the *Criminal Code,* laws relating to picketing, civil laws, municipal regulations and the like including s. 5 of the impugned by-law and the ordinance passed pursuant to it.

6. The *Canadian Bill of Rights,* assuming it has anything to do with the holding of assemblies, parades or gatherings on the public domain, does not apply to provincial and municipal legislation.

Appellants' second submission must also fail.

I would therefore dismiss both appeals.

Appeal dismissed.

Almost ten years later, Beetz J returned to this topic in *Ontario Public Service Employees' Union v. AG Ontario*, [1987] 2 SCR 2, 41 DLR (4th) 1, which has already been discussed in Chapter 8, Interpreting the Division of Powers. OPSEU challenged the *Ontario Public Service Act*, particularly its provisions that prohibited employees in the public service from participating in specified political activities—for example, being a candidate in a provincial or federal election, or soliciting funds for a provincial or federal party or candidate. The discussion in Chapter 8 was about interjurisdictional immunity. As well as this federalism challenge, OPSEU also made an argument based on the implied bill of rights cases. Beetz J said at 40 DLR:

> There is no doubt in my mind that the basic structure of our Constitution as established by the *Constitution Act, 1867* contemplates the existence of certain political institutions, including freely elected legislative bodies at the federal and provincial levels. In the words of Duff CJC in *Reference re Alberta Legislation* at p. 107 DLR, p. 133 SCR, "such institutions derive their efficacy from the free public discussions of affairs ..." and, in those of Abbott J in *Switzman v. Elbling* at p. 371 DLR, p. 328 SCR, neither a provincial legislature nor Parliament itself can "abrogate this right of discussion and debate." Speaking more generally, I hold that neither Parliament nor the provincial legislatures may enact legislation the effect of which would be to substantially interfere with the operation of this basic constitutional structure. On the whole, though, I am inclined to the view that the impugned legislation is in essence concerned with the constitution of the province and with regulating the provincial public service and affects federal and provincial elections only in an incidental way.
>
> I should perhaps add that issues like the last will in the future ordinarily arise for consideration in relation to the political rights guaranteed under the *Canadian Charter of Rights and Freedoms*, which, of course, gives broader protection to these rights and freedoms than is called for by the structural demands of the Constitution. However, it remains true that, quite apart from Charter considerations, the legislative bodies in this country must conform to these basic structural imperatives and can in no way override them. The present legislation does not go so far as to infringe upon the essential structure of free parliamentary institutions.

Dickson CJC and Lamer J, who also gave judgments, did not consider this argument.

The possibility that a system of representative government—even in the absence of a written charter of rights—implies some restriction on the authority of a legislature to interfere with certain fundamental rights or freedoms is not restricted to Canada, as noted by Professor Elliot (in "References, Structural Argumentation and the Organizing Principles of Canada's Constitution" (2001), 80 *Canadian Bar Review* 67, at 78 (footnotes omitted)):

> In recent years, the judges of the High Court of Australia have ... develop[ed] something of an implied bill of rights on the basis of that country's Constitution (although the High Court has preferred to characterize these rights, not as rights *per se*, but rather as limitations or restrictions on legislative power). The members of that Court are not in agreement as to the number of such rights that can properly be implied out of the Australian Constitution. For example, two members of the Court, Justices Deane and Toohey, have thus far been prepared to recognize a constitutional right to equality. However, there is clear consensus that, because it creates a system of "representative government," that country's Constitution protects such freedom of communication between the people concerning political or government matters as is necessary to

enable the people to exercise a free and informed choice as electors. And there also now appears to be majority support for the existence of additional rights to freedom of movement and association for political purposes; these rights are seen to be derivative of, and hence dependent upon, the right to freedom of public discussion.

III. THE CANADIAN BILL OF RIGHTS

In 1960, Parliament enacted the *Canadian Bill of Rights*. The immediate initiative came from Prime Minister John Diefenbaker, who had campaigned for constitutional protection for rights since becoming a member of Parliament in 1945, and had made it a principal platform promise during the elections of 1958. Much research and writing needs to be done about the context of the Bill and its shaping influences, but here are some tentative suggestions. Two external influences seem clear and important. The first was international declarations about rights, especially the Universal Declaration of Human Rights adopted by the United Nations in 1948. The second was the American *Bill of Rights*, and the liberal interpretations by the Supreme Court from the mid 1950s onward, especially *Brown v. Board of Education*, 347 US 483 (1954), a landmark decision about equality between blacks and whites. The influence of the American constitutional experience was probably heightened by the Cold War, and the sense that at its heart, it was a struggle for individual rights.

Within Canada, one large factor was probably the fears about regulation by legislatures and administrative agencies, which had expanded greatly during the war. For lawyers, this regulation threatened both legal values, especially the common law constitution, and political values, for most lawyers were hardly sympathetic to the politics of the regulatory state. Specific incidents also contributed. Both lawyers and the general public were troubled by denials of civil liberties in the treatment of the Japanese Canadians during the war, and by the conduct of an inquiry into espionage in 1946, which was widely criticized for curtailing the civil rights of individuals who were being investigated.

The Canadian Bill of Rights
RSC 1985, Appendix III

The Parliament of Canada, affirming that the Canadian Nation is founded upon principles that acknowledge the supremacy of God, the dignity and worth of the human person and the position of the family in a society of free men and free institutions;

Affirming also that men and institutions remain free only when freedom is founded upon respect for moral and spiritual values and the rule of law;

And being desirous of enshrining these principles and the human rights and fundamental freedoms derived from them, in a Bill of Rights which shall reflect the respect of Parliament for its constitutional authority and which shall ensure the protection of these rights and freedoms in Canada:

THEREFORE Her Majesty, by and with the advice and consent of the Senate and House of Commons of Canada, enacts as follows:

PART I
BILL OF RIGHTS

1. It is hereby recognized and declared that in Canada there have existed and shall continue to exist without discrimination by reason of race, national origin, colour, religion or sex, the following human rights and fundamental freedoms, namely,

(a) the right of the individual to life, liberty, security of the person and enjoyment of property, and the right not to be deprived thereof except by due process of law;

(b) the right of the individual to equality before the law and the protection of the law;

(c) freedom of religion;

(d) freedom of speech;

(e) freedom of assembly and association; and

(f) freedom of the press.

2. Every law of Canada shall, unless it is expressly declared by an Act of the Parliament of Canada that it shall operate notwithstanding the *Canadian Bill of Rights*, be so construed and applied as not to abrogate, abridge or infringe or to authorize the abrogation, abridgment or infringement of any of the rights or freedoms herein recognized and declared, and in particular, no law of Canada shall be construed or applied so as to

(a) authorize or effect the arbitrary detention, imprisonment or exile of any person;

(b) impose or authorize the imposition of cruel and unusual treatment or punishment;

(c) deprive a person who has been arrested or detained

(i) of the right to be informed promptly of the reason for his arrest or detention,

(ii) of the right to retain and instruct counsel without delay, or

(iii) of the remedy by way of *habeas corpus* for the determination of the validity of his detention and for his release if the detention is not lawful;

(d) authorize a court, tribunal, commission, board or other authority to compel a person to give evidence if he is denied counsel, protection against self incrimination or other constitutional safeguards;

(e) deprive a person of the right to a fair hearing in accordance with the principles of fundamental justice for the determination of his rights and obligations;

(f) deprive a person charged with a criminal offence of the right to be presumed innocent until proved guilty according to law in a fair and public hearing by an independent and impartial tribunal, or of the right to reasonable bail without just cause; or

(g) deprive a person of the right to the assistance of an interpreter in any proceedings in which he is involved or in which he is a party or a witness, before a court, commission, board or other tribunal, if he does not understand or speak the language in which such proceedings are conducted.

The *Bill of Rights* is simply a statute of Parliament, and not entrenched, like the *Constitution Act, 1982*. Two important consequences follow. First, it governs only matters within the federal government's power. During the 1950s, the possibility of including the provinces was discussed, but they were determined to protect their autonomy. Second, it can be amended like any other statute—although no significant amendments have been made.

In retrospect, the Bill presented two major problems for the courts. The first of these problems was its effect on other statutes. According to its own terms (s. 2), the Bill had no effect on a statute that contained a declaration that it was to be effective regardless of the Bill, but what about other statutes—ones that violated rights, but did not contain an express declaration? Consider a statute made before the Bill was enacted. Did the Bill prevail, and make a violation of rights in the earlier statute ineffective? Alternatively, was it no more than a guide to interpretation? If it was no more than a guide to interpretation, then any violation of rights in the earlier statute would continue to be effective, as long as it was express or otherwise clear. Now consider a statute made after the Bill, containing a provision that clearly denied some protected right. Because the Bill was simply a statute, did the later statute prevail, as a consequence of the general doctrine of parliamentary sovereignty? (A later statute is a repeal, express or implicit, of an earlier inconsistent one.) The second problem was more general: how should courts approach the Bill? Should its grants of rights be interpreted expansively or restrictively?

The decisions of the Supreme Court generally were disappointing to observers who had hoped that it would approach the Bill sympathetically, and interpret it liberally. Here is a short and selective account of its decisions, which deals first with the decisions about the effect of the Bill and second with the approach of the court.

The discussion of effect begins with a case that seemed to promise a different outcome, *R v. Drybones*, [1970] SCR 282, 9 DLR (3d) 473. Section 94(b) of the *Indian Act* provided that an Indian who was "intoxicated ... off a reserve" was guilty of an offence, and liable to a fine of a minimum of ten dollars (and a maximum of fifty dollars), or imprisonment for not more than three months. In contrast, the Liquor Ordinance of the Northwest Territories, which regulated liquor generally, provided in s. 94(6) that it was an offence for anyone to be "intoxicated ... in a public place," and specified a penalty of a fine, without any minimum amount, or imprisonment for no more than thirty days. (The crucial contrasts between these two statutes were first, the differences in the punishments, and second, the specifications of the location of the accused when he or she was intoxicated. The *Indian Act* specified anywhere off a reserve, and the Liquor Ordinance specified a public place.) Drybones, an Indian according to the definition in the *Indian Act*, was charged under the Act with being intoxicated off a reserve, and challenged the section because it violated his right to equality before the law under s. 1(b) of the Bill. The Supreme Court dismissed an appeal by the Crown from an acquittal in the lower courts, by a majority of six to three.

Ritchie J, writing the principal majority judgment, considered the argument that the Bill was simply a guide to interpretation, and said that it "appears to me to strike at the very foundations of the *Bill of Rights*, and convert it from its apparent character as a statutory declaration of the fundamental rights and freedoms which it recognizes, into little more than a rule for the construction of federal statutes" (at 293 SCR). He rejected this approach, relying primarily on the opening words of s. 2. The dissenters all believed that the courts should exercise more modest functions.

The section challenged in *Drybones*, the Liquor Ordinance, was enacted before the *Bill of Rights*, and therefore the outcome could be understood as a simple consequence of the general doctrine of parliamentary sovereignty. The problem of the effect of the Bill on statutes enacted after the Bill remained. For decades scholars had debated whether an earlier legislature could bind a later one. The most pressing question in this debate was whether a requirement of a particular procedure for making legislation (a "manner and form" requirement) specified in a statute would obligate later legislatures. If it did, the requirement in the Bill of a declaration that a statute "shall operate notwithstanding" would be an effective requirement, and any future statute that did not include such a declaration would be ineffective to the extent that it violated the protected rights. During the 1970s and 1980s, several members of the Supreme Court announced that the Bill, or provincial bills of rights like it, prevailed over later statutes, although their reasoning was not extensive. In *Curr v. R*, [1972] SCR 889, 26 DLR (3d) 603, Laskin J said, "federal law enacted after the date of the *Canadian Bill of Rights* as well as pre-existing federal law may be found to run foul of the prescriptions of the *Canadian Bill of Rights*" (at 893 SCR). More than a decade later, in considering the effect of the Manitoba *Human Rights Act*, in *Winnipeg School Division 1 v. Craton*, [1985] 2 SCR 150, 21 DLR (4th) 1, McIntyre J said: "It ... may not be altered, amended, or repealed, nor may exceptions be created to its provisions, save by clear legislative pronouncement. To adopt and apply any theory of implied repeal by later statutory enactment ... would be to rob it of its special nature and give scant protection to the rights it proclaims" (at 156 SCR). Last, in *Singh v. Minister of Employment and Immigration*, [1985] 1 SCR 177, 17 DLR (4th) 422 a unanimous Court upheld a challenge to procedures for determining refugee status. The six members divided equally about the grounds: three relied on the Charter, and three on the *Bill of Rights*. Beetz J speaking for three who invoked the Bill, said simply: "I do not see any reason not to apply the principle in the *Drybones* case to a provision enacted after the *Canadian Bill of Rights*" (at 239 SCR).

The Supreme Court's decisions about the effect of the Bill, therefore, seem sympathetic, if not fully reasoned. It was its approach to the interpretation of the rights that was disappointing. One pervasive question was the significance of the words "there have existed and shall continue to exist," in s. 1, and the words "herein recognized and declared," in s. 2. Did these words limit the courts to the nature of the specified rights as they stood in 1960? In *R v. Burnshine*, [1975] 1 SCR 693, 44 DLR (3d) 584, Martland J said: "The Bill ... declared and continued existing rights and freedoms. It was those existing rights and freedoms which were not to be infringed by any federal statute. Section 2 did not create new rights. Its purpose was to prevent infringement of existing rights" (at 705 SCR). This approach, named the "frozen rights" approach, was the dominant approach, and it seems to have been a manifestation of a general denial of expansive interpretation. Two examples are the interpretations of the provisions about equality and about procedures.

In *Drybones*, equality was at stake, and again, the result seemed to promise a different story. The Crown argued that the prohibition against being intoxicated off a reserve treated all Indians equally. Ritchie J, writing the principal majority judgment, rejected the argument, saying that it would permit "the most glaring discriminatory legislation against a racial group ... so long as all the other members are being discriminated against in the same way .... [N]o individual or group of individuals is to be treated more harshly than another under the law, and ... an individual is denied equality before the law if it is made an offence ... for him to do something which his fellow Canadians are free to do without having committed any offence" (at 297 SCR).

This formulation seemed generous (and perhaps unreasonably generous—did it really prohibit all distinctions between individuals and groups, including zoning bylaws and progressive taxes?), but the generosity seemed to be diminished two years later. In *AG Canada v. Lavell*, [1974] SCR 1349, 38 DLR (3d) 481, another part of the *Indian Act* was challenged. Section 12(1)(b) provided that an Indian woman who married a non-Indian man lost her registration under the Act, but there was no corresponding provision for an Indian man. By a majority of four to three, the Supreme Court rejected the challenge. Ritchie J declared that, "the meaning to be given to the language employed in the *Bill of Rights* is the meaning which it bore in Canada at the time when the Bill was enacted" (at 1365 SCR). For him, the phrase "equality before the law" did not express the "egalitarian" understandings he saw espoused by the Supreme Court of the United States. Instead, it was to be illuminated by the "rule of law," which was affirmed in the preamble to the Bill. This reference took him to Dicey's classic statement: equality means "equality before the law or the equal subjection of all classes to the ordinary law of the land." Ignoring the purpose and late nineteenth century context of Dicey's text, and the possibility that the twentieth century may have brought changes in understandings about equality that might have illuminated its meaning in 1960, Ritchie J asserted that the impugned section could be enforced without denying equality of treatment in the administration of the law.

In 1979, Ritchie J considered equality again, in *Bliss v. AG Canada*, [1979] 1 SCR 183, 92 DLR (3d) 417. The *Unemployment Insurance Act* established a program of benefits for women whose employment was interrupted because of pregnancy, but imposed a longer qualifying period for women claiming these benefits than it did for individuals claiming the regular benefits. As well, it excluded interruption of employment because of pregnancy from the categories of entitlements for the regular benefits. Bliss, whose employment was interrupted by pregnancy, claimed benefits, but she had not been employed for long enough to satisfy the qualifying period for the benefits specifically provided for women whose employment had been interrupted because of pregnancy, and she was excluded from the regular benefits by the specific exclusion of interruption because of pregnancy. Writing for a unanimous court, Ritchie J held that the Act did not discriminate against her on the specified ground of sex, saying that the sections creating the program of benefits were

> a complete code dealing exclusively with the entitlement of women to unemployment insurance benefits during the specified part of the period of pregnancy and childbirth; these provisions form an integral part of a legislative scheme enacted for valid federal objectives and they are concerned with conditions from which men are excluded. Any inequality between the sexes in this area is not created by legislation, but by nature.

He also held that the discrimination could not be grounded in the more general term "equality before the law":

> There is a wide difference between legislation which treats one section of the population more harshly than all others by reason of race as in the case of *Regina v. Drybones*, … and legislation providing additional benefits to one class of women, specifying the conditions which entitle a claimant to such benefits and defining a period during which no benefits are available. The one case involves the imposition of a penalty on a racial group to which other citizens are not subjected; the other involves a definition of the qualifications required for entitlement to benefits …

[T]here can be no doubt that [the longer qualifying period] is a relevant one for consideration in determining the conditions entitling pregnant women to benefits under a scheme of unemployment insurance enacted to achieve the valid federal objective imposed on Parliament by s. 91(2A) of the *British North America Act*.

Section 91(2A) gives the federal government power to legislate about "unemployment insurance." It was added in the late 1930s, in response to the *Unemployment Insurance Reference*, one of the New Deal cases considered in Chapter 6, The 1930s: The Depression and the New Deal. Ritchie J did not, though, explain the references in these passages to the valid objective. True, the Act as a whole had a valid purpose—to provide unemployment insurance, but this purpose could hardly justify denying Bliss any benefits at all. This case, more than any other, was a focus of protests by women during the debates about the *Charter of Rights and Freedoms* during the late 1970s and early 1980s.

The judgments about procedures and the phrases "due process" and "a fair hearing" were less dramatic, but just as narrow. Here is one example, from the many that might be given. There is a large body of common law, part of a body of law known as administrative law, that regulates the procedures of administrative agencies, and especially the procedures they must follow when they make decisions that affect individuals. The Supreme Court read these phrases as doing little more than incorporating this common law, and was unwilling to examine it to determine whether any particular requirement was as fair as it might have been according to some independent criteria of decency.

The *Bill of Rights* is still in force. Some of its terms are occasionally discussed, especially two sections that are wider than the corresponding sections of the Charter: s. 1(a), which specifically includes "property," and s. 2(e), which requires a "fair hearing" for determination of rights and obligations. See *Singh v. Minister of Employment and Immigration*, [1985] 1 SCR 177, 17 DLR (4th) 422. Even though it has occasionally been used as a ground for decision, it has been almost totally eclipsed by the *Charter of Rights and Freedoms*.

CHAPTER SIXTEEN

The Advent of the Charter

I. INTRODUCTION

In the introduction to this book, we described the constitutional renovation that Canada undertook in 1982. The 1982 amendments stand as the first major reconstruction of Canada's written constitution since 1867. Chief among the changes in 1982 was the adoption of the *Canadian Charter of Rights and Freedoms* (the Charter), which we begin to study in this chapter and which occupies the rest of the book. This chapter is composed of two topics: the first is an introduction to the history of the Charter's adoption. This material situates the Charter in its historical and political context, both domestic and international. It also introduces the division of opinion as to whether the Charter was a good idea and the ways in which this debate contributed to various substantive and institutional features of the Charter. The second topic gives an overview of the ongoing debate about the legitimacy of judicial enforcement of constitutionally guaranteed rights and freedoms.

II. THE ADOPTION OF THE CHARTER

The Charter project formally began at a federal-provincial first ministers' conference in January of 1968. Then Justice Minister Pierre Trudeau, at the beginning of his political career, tabled a document entitled "A Canadian Charter of Human Rights," an excerpt from which follows. Among other things, it traced the historical origins and evolution of modern conceptions of human rights.

The Honourable Pierre Elliott Trudeau, Minister of Justice, *A Canadian Charter of Human Rights*, January 1968

in Anne Bayefsky, *Canada's Constitution Act 1982 and Amendments: A Documentary History* (Toronto: McGraw-Hill Ryerson, 1989), at 51-53

Interest in human rights is as old as civilization itself. Once his primary requirements of security, shelter and nourishment have been satisfied, man has distinguished himself from other animals by directing his attention to those matters which affect his individual dignity.

In ancient times, and for centuries thereafter, these rights were known as "natural" rights; rights to which all men were entitled because they are endowed with a moral and rational nature. The denial of such rights was regarded as an affront to "natural" law—

those elementary principles of justice which apply to all human beings by virtue of their common possession of the capacity to reason. These natural rights were the origins of the western world's more modern concepts of individual freedom and equality.

Cicero said of natural law that it was "unchanging and everlasting," that it was "one eternal and unchangeable law ... valid for all nations and for all times."

In the Middle Ages, St. Thomas Aquinas emphasized that natural law was a law superior to man-made laws and that as a result all rulers were themselves subject to it.

The Reformation brought sharply to the fore the need for protection of freedom of religious belief.

As the concept of the social contract theory of government developed in the 18th century, still greater emphasis came to be given to the rights of the individual. Should a government fail to respect natural rights, wrote Locke and Rousseau, then disobedience and rebellion were justified. Thus was borne the modern notion of human rights. So responsive were men to this notion that the greatest social revolutions in the history of the western world took place—one in America and the other in France—in order to preserve for individuals the rights which they claimed belonged to them.

This deep-seated desire for recognition of human dignity is reflected in the memorable words of the American Declaration of Independence:

> We hold these truths to be self-evident, that all men are created equal, that they are endowed by their creator with certain unalienable rights, that among these are life, liberty and the pursuit of happiness. That to secure these rights Governments are instituted among men, deriving their just powers from the consent of the governed, that whenever any form of Government becomes destructive of these ends, it is the right of the people to alter or abolish it and institute new Government ... .

The *Bill of Rights* in the United States, enacted as an amendment to the Constitution, serves to safeguard the individual from governmental intolerance of the "unalienable rights."

In France, the 1789 Declaration of the Rights of Man and the Citizen sought to achieve similar results. "Men are born and remain free and equal in respect of rights" it said. "The purpose of all civil associations is the preservation of the natural and imprescriptible rights of man. These rights are liberty, property and resistance to oppression."

In both the United States and France, there was embodied the idea that men shall not be deprived of liberty or property except in accordance with the law. This is a manifestation of the belief that men should be ruled by laws, not men; that a government has no more power than the people have agreed to delegate to it.

Monarchies, as well as republics, are influenced by these principles; the authority of kings, as well as presidents, is limited. Many of the Commonwealth countries which inherited a tradition of parliamentary sovereignty have introduced constitutional restrictions, denying to the parliament as well as to the monarch the power to interfere with certain of the subjects' liberties. Constitutional checks on the exercise of governmental authority are a natural development in a democratic society.

The events of the Second World War were disturbing proof of the need to safeguard the rights of individuals. It is not by accident that an overwhelming number of newly independent states have included within their constitutions comprehensive bills of rights.

Since 1945 considerable discussion has taken place in Canada as well concerning similar constitutional measures. The topic has been considered by the Canadian Bar Association, by parliamentary committees, and by numerous commentators. While no constitutional step has been taken, some legislative enactments designed to protect human rights have been passed into law. Parliament in 1960 enacted the *Canadian Bill of Rights*—a step of considerable significance and one which prepares the way for a constitutional enactment. Several provinces have introduced human rights legislation, and a committee engaged in revision of the Quebec Civil Code has recently proposed that a declaration of civil rights be included in the revised code.

These measures are all evidence of the interest of the Canadian people in some form of safeguard of individual liberty. To date, however, there does not exist in Canada any form of guarantee (beyond those few contained in the *British North America Act*) which a provincial legislature or Parliament, as the case may be, cannot repeal as freely as any other statute it has enacted. In this sense, no Canadian has the benefit of a constitutional protection as exists in dozens of other countries.

An entrenched bill of rights would offer this constitutional protection, although at the price of some restriction on the theory of legislative supremacy. It is suggested that this is not too high a price to pay. In fact the theory of legislative supremacy is seldom pressed to its full extent. Indeed, even in England, the birthplace of parliamentary government, fundamental liberties have been protected not only through the common law but also by means of such historic documents as *Magna Carta* (1215), the *Petition of Right* (1628), and the *Bill of Rights* (1689). The purpose of an entrenched bill of rights is simple and straightforward. It has been described as serving "to withdraw certain subjects from the vicissitudes of political controversy, to place them beyond the reach of majorities and officials and to establish them as legal principles to be applied by the courts. One's right to life, liberty, and property, to free speech and a free press, freedom of worship and assembly, and other fundamental rights may not be submitted to vote; they depend on the outcome of no elections."

A constitutional bill of rights in Canada would guarantee the fundamental freedoms of the individual from interference, whether federal or provincial. It would as well establish that all Canadians, in every part of Canada, have equal rights. This would constitute a major first step towards basic constitutional reform.

Canada could not choose a more appropriate year than this one for the consideration of a constitutional bill of rights for Canadians. 1968 has been declared International Human Rights Year by the General Assembly of the United Nations. The General Assembly has done so as an acknowledgement that the centuries-old interest in human rights is now, in the mid-twentieth century, of universal scope. The preamble of the United Nations Charter declares that the peoples of the United Nations are determined "to reaffirm faith in fundamental human rights, in the dignity and worth of the human person, in the equal rights of men and women." As a reflection of this determination, the United Nations in 1948 adopted the Universal Declaration of Human Rights. Since that date some 15 separate conventions or treaties have been sponsored by the UN dealing with particular rights of a more specialized character. Only last year, however, were those rights which are generally regarded as "fundamental" formulated into two Covenants,

(The International Covenant on Economic, Social and Cultural Rights; The International Covenant on Civil and Political Rights) open for signature and ratification by all states.

It is the hopeful expectation of the General Assembly that in 1968 an aroused aware-ness by all peoples will result in government action everywhere. Canada has the oppor-tunity to take a lead in this respect.

A. Cairns, *Charter Versus Federalism: The Dilemmas of Constitutional Reform*
(Kingston: McGill-Queen's University Press, 1992), at 12-20 (footnotes omitted)

Interpretations of our recent constitutional discontents have focused overwhelmingly on domestic factors. Demands and responses, inputs and outputs, have been conceived in an insular fashion, almost as if Canadians inhabited a separate planet under their total control, and so minimal attention has been paid to our location in an international net-work of states and peoples. ...

In contrast, the pervasive international dimension to our struggles has received little concentrated attention.

The Erosion of Britishness

Few aspects of our recent constitutional evolution are more dramatic than the repudia-tion of the principle and practice of parliamentary supremacy by the adoption of the *Charter of Rights and Freedoms*. ...

For the Fathers of Confederation, parliamentary responsible government was a posi-tive heritage that differentiated Canada from the United States and gratifyingly confirmed the evolutionary nature of Canadian constitutional development. ... In the post-1945 period, the status of parliamentary government in Canada was weakened by the relative decline of the country of its origin—as a world power, as a centre of empire, and as an economic leader. ...

British parliamentary supremacy no longer seemed so central to Canadian identity as the prestige and status associated with connection to the United Kingdom eroded. Al-though as late as the 1950s, opposition to a growing support for a Canadian Bill of Rights could still be justified in terms of defending our British heritage, and by tarring a Bill of Rights with the stigma of Americanism, by the 1970s such arguments appeared strained. By the time of the 1980-1 Special Joint Committee of the Senate and of the House of Commons on the Constitution of Canada, dealing with the proposed constitutional reso-lution to be transmitted to Westminster, the remaining defenders of parliamentary su-premacy were clearly in retreat. The dominant thrust of the interveners was to strengthen the Charter. The once-imperial mother had lost the capacity to bestow sanctity on the parliamentary institutions that had been her most important nineteenth-century consti-tutional gift to her Canadian subjects. ...

Many of the new post-war immigrants, whose numbers steadily reduced the numeri-cal significance of the two founding European peoples, came from motherlands where the trusting attitude to the state implicit in the British parliamentary tradition would have been a mark of naïveté. Many of the visible minorities had little prior experience with constitutional government, British or other. As minorities, fearful of being singled out for negative treatment, they were naturally drawn toward the idea of judicially entrenched rights and away from parliamentary majoritarianism, whose deficiencies were less visible to those likely to wield majority power.

From a different perspective, a recurring argument in the early post-war years was that the influx of new immigrants of varying cultural and political backgrounds invalidated the historical belief that respect for rights could be left to a "natural," virtually automatic socialization into the British heritage. This trust in the implicit educative powers of tradition, aside from its questionable applicability to French Canada, did not extend to many of the new immigrants, for whom the educative effect of a visible written code was considered essential. ...

Growing support for a Charter in Canada was facilitated by removal of specific impediments. In this connection, the abolition of appeals to the Judicial Committee of the Privy Council in 1949 made a little-noticed indirect contribution to the lessening of support for parliamentary supremacy and to the provision of a positive environment in which Charter support could more easily grow. ...

More generally, national support for a Bill of Rights in the 1950s was part of the historic colony-to-nation movement that had propelled successive steps in Canadian independence from Great Britain. In contrast to the overtly political purpose of constraining centrifugal pressures that drove the federal government's support for a Charter in the late 1960s and the 1970s, the earlier support had "less to do with leashing the provinces and more to do with the evolution of the symbolic basis of the Canadian Constitution from the authority of the British Parliament to that of the people of Canada." ...

The capacity of parliamentary government to sustain a sense of Canadian distinctiveness in North America was conditioned by time and circumstance. It appears in retrospect that the traditional, positive evaluation of parliamentary government, unconstrained by entrenched rights, was intimately linked to the status of the United Kingdom as a great power and to the related tendency for many English Canadians to define themselves as British as long as significant domestic prestige continued to flow from the British connection. As that connection lost its instrumental value, Canadian support for the constitutional theory of parliamentary supremacy was weakened, along with a cluster of values, intellectual orientations, and practices that had previously given the Canadian constitution, and commentary on it, a distinctly British cast. ...

The weakened appreciation for this formerly potent symbol of Canadian constitutional identity created a gap in the constitutional symbolism of an almost completely autonomous nation. The Charter that emerged to fill that gap brought entrenched rights, judicial supremacy, and a greatly enhanced role for the written portion of the constitution—all of which further distanced Canadians from their British constitutional origins.

From the 1950s to the 1980s, the declining allegiance to the British parliamentary side of Canadian political life coincided with selective interest in and positive appraisal of American constitutional theory and practice.

International Sources of Politicized Ethnicity

The society to which the 1982 Charter was a response had undergone a profound trans-formation since the Second World War. That change was many-sided, but for our pur-poses its chief characteristic was a dramatic escalation of nationalism and ethnicity that affected not only francophones but also those who fell outside the charmed category of "founding peoples." ...

The ending of European empires and the resultant explosion of new states in Africa and Asia constituted decisive rejection of the ideology and practice of racial hierarchies based on a presumed European superiority. ...

This unpredicted world of race and ethnic nationalism has altered the ethnic composi-tion, cleavage structure, and politics of many Western societies, including Canada. ...

In general, the rhetoric and ideology of the emerging post-imperial international order reinforced ethnic and racial identities throughout the Western world and put on the defensive inequalities based on ascriptive criteria. The politicization of domestic cleavages, most obvious with respect to language, race, and ethnicity, also extended to the division between the sexes, to the disabled, to generational cleavages as youth emerged as a distinct category, and to multiple life-styles as sexual liberation movements extended the boundaries of the permissible and the legitimate. The movements behind the assertive self-confidence of these politicized social categories had an international component, a factor that explains their simultaneous emergence throughout the Western world. Diffusion of the new normative order was facilitated by the easy mobility of per-sons and ideas across national boundaries, especially in open societies. ...

The International Rights Dimension

In 1968, Maxwell Cohen attributed the novel and dramatic Canadian interest in "human rights" to transformed international and domestic beliefs which had "altered totally be-yond anything that could have been imagined two decades before." "Human rights," he continued, "became ... within the past twenty years, an important piece of 'debating' language ... part of the political dialogue, part of the debating experience of peoples in all parts of the world, even those in affluent societies."

The most influential catalyst of that transformed climate of Canadian and inter-national opinion was the United Nations, one of whose purposes has been to foster respect for fundamental freedoms and human rights. Its 1945 Charter, followed by the Universal Declaration of Human Rights, adopted as a unanimous resolution of the Gen-eral Assembly in 1948, and subsequent international covenants on Civil and Political Rights and on Economic, Social and Cultural Rights have been influential in channelling and stimulating a "rights" debate in Canada. ...

Initial Canadian responses to the inclusion of rights in the UN Charter, and to the subsequent Universal Declaration, were distinctly lukewarm. Canadian officials asserted the superior protection of rights under the British tradition, which they rather smugly contrasted with American experience, and also stressed the constitutional limitations of federalism in which some rights pertained to matters under provincial jurisdiction. Al-though the Special Joint Committee of the Senate and House of Commons of Canada on Human Rights and Fundamental Freedoms (1947-8) and the Special Committee of the

Senate on Human Rights and Fundamental Freedoms (1950) were explicit responses to the requirement for an analysis of Canadian practice in the light of the Charter and the Universal Declaration, they did not result in a Canadian version of the Charter. Nevertheless, it was standard practice for advocates of a Canadian Bill of Rights from the late 1940s on to cite the UN Charter and the Universal Declaration in support of their position, and the 1950 Senate committee did recommend a statutory Canadian Declaration of Human Rights derived in significant part from the Universal Declaration and limited to federal jurisdiction. Thirty years later, nearly all the civil liberties and human rights organizations that appeared before the Special Joint Committee of the Senate and of the House of Commons on the Constitution of Canada (1980-1) stressed Canadian obligations under UN international covenants. Human Rights Commissioner Gordon Fairweather, after citing various UN instruments, by means of which Canada has "increased her accountability to the world community" asserted that such obligations could not be met without an entrenched Charter binding on both orders of government.

Thus the direct and indirect proselytizing on behalf of rights by the United Nations challenged regimes practising federalism and employing parliamentary supremacy to modify their constitutional arrangements, as a Bill of Rights became an almost essential attribute of contemporary statehood. Accordingly, it is not surprising that a Bill of Rights has become virtually an automatic component of new constitutions, or that Bills of Rights have become increasingly comprehensive, or that an established state such as Canada, that had long existed without an entrenched Charter, has recently introduced one.

P. Russell, "The Political Purposes of the Canadian Charter of Rights and Freedoms"
(1983), 61 *Canadian Bar Review* 30 (footnotes omitted)

[This article explores two purposes of the Charter: (1) to contribute to national unity, and (2) to protect rights. The excerpt that follows is limited to the first purpose; it is included to give some understanding of the national political context of the making of the Charter.]

To understand the national unity rationale of the Charter, it is necessary to recall the context in which the federal government made a charter its number one priority for constitutional reform.

In the mid-1960's right up to the Confederation of Tomorrow Conference organized by the Premier of Ontario, John Robarts, in the fall of 1967, the Liberal Government in Ottawa was not interested in constitutional reform of any kind. Patriation with an amending formula had been very nearly achieved in 1964. Since then only Quebec had been pushing for constitutional change. But Quebec had drastically raised the stakes. The Lesage Liberals followed by Daniel Johnson's Union Nationale administration insisted that the price of Quebec's support for patriation of the Canadian Constitution would be agreement on substantive constitutional reform giving Quebec more recognition and power as the French Canadian homeland. This demand of Quebec provincial leaders for major constitutional change reflected a wholly new phase in Quebec nationalism. Historically the constitutional position of Quebec leaders had been profoundly conservative. Their prime concern had been to preserve the rights they believed had been acquired for Quebec and French Canada in the constitution of 1867. But now, under the impetus of Quebec's "quiet revolution," the province's leading politicians had become constitutional radicals. So long as these Quebec demands for radical change were the central preoccupation of constitutional debate, it was not in the federal government's interest to encourage the process of constitutional reform. The proposals likely to dominate such a debate, if they went far enough to placate Quebec nationalism, would either go too far in weakening the involvement of the federal government in the life of Quebec or else give Quebec representatives in federal institutions such a privileged place as to alienate opinion in the rest of the country. So the Pearson government at first tried to respond to Quebec through pragmatic adjustments in fiscal and administrative arrangements and took a dim view of Premier Robarts' constitutional initiative.

However, the very success of the Confederation of Tomorrow Conference in raising national expectations about both the necessity and the possibility of responding creatively to Quebec's constitutional discontents seemed to convince the Prime Minister and his Justice Minister, Pierre Trudeau, who was soon to succeed him, that a different strategy was needed. The constitutional issue could no longer be kept on the back burner. But if constitutional reform was to be seriously pursued, it was essential that Quebec's demands be countered by proposals designed to have a unifying effect on Canada. It was at this point that the federal government urged that a charter of rights be at the top of the constitutional reform agenda.

After the Confederation of Tomorrow Conference, Prime Minister Pearson suggested to the provincial governments "that first priority should be given to that part of the Constitution which should deal with the rights of the individual—both his rights as a citizen of a democratic federal state and his rights as a member of the linguistic community in which he has chosen to live." This was the position his government took at the Constitutional Conference in February 1968. Prime Minister Trudeau took exactly the same position. His government's paper prepared for the February 1969 Constitutional Conference repeated the commitment to a charter of rights as the first priority in constitutional change. "To reach agreement on common values," Trudeau argued, was "an essential first step" in any process of constitutional renewal. From this point until the final enactment of the *Constitution Act, 1982*, giving constitutional expression to fundamental rights including language rights was the Trudeau government's first constitutional priority. And throughout, the fundamental basic rationale for this constitutional strategy was the perceived value of such a measure as a popular and unifying counter to decentralizing provincial demands in the Canadian constitutional debate.

The Charter's attractiveness to the leaders of the federal Liberal Party as the centrepiece of their constitutional strategy was decisive in improving the political fortunes of the project of entrenching rights and freedoms in the Canadian constitution. Since World War II there had been a great deal of discussion of the Bill of Rights idea both within and outside Parliament. The prime stimulus of this discussion was international— the concern for human rights arising from the war against fascism and Canada's obligations under the United Nations Declaration of Human Rights. Domestic events also stimulated interest in a Bill of Rights. At the federal level, there was regret concerning the treatment of Japanese Canadians during the war and the denial of traditional legal rights in the investigation of a spy ring following the Gouzenko disclosures in 1946. At the provincial level the persecution of Jehovah's Witnesses by the Duplessis administration in Quebec, the treatment of Doukhabors and other religious minorities in the west and the repression of trade unionism in Newfoundland were major causes célèbres. There was also a touch of the national unity theme in the submissions made on a number of occasions to parliamentary committees on the implications of post-war immigration. The addition of such large numbers of new Canadians with no education or experience in liberal democratic values, it was argued, meant that Canada could no longer rely on the British method of protecting civil liberties. For such a heterogeneous population a written code was needed. Liberal leaders were not moved by these arguments for a Canadian Bill of Rights. The CCF was the only national party to commit itself to establishing a Bill of Rights. And it was under a Progressive Conservative government led by John Diefenbaker that a statutory Bill of Rights affecting only the federal level of government was enacted in 1960.

Pierre Trudeau, before he entered politics and joined the Liberal Party, expressed interest in a constitutional Bill of Rights. In 1965, as a legal academic writing a background paper on how to deal with the Quebec agitation for constitutional change, he placed a Bill of Rights in first place on his list of constitutional reform proposals. But the main thrust of his paper was to dissuade Quebecers from relying on constitutional reform to solve their problems of political and social modernization. His constitutional reform proposals were for "some day" in the future. Whenever a Bill of Rights was added to the constitution, he saw the abolition of the federal power of reservation and disallowance over provincial legislation as a logical quid pro quo. This emphasis on the connection between a constitutional Bill of Rights and the federal powers of reservation and disallowance underlines a constitutional charter's capacity for imposing national standards on the provinces. This link appeared again in the Trudeau government's 1978 constitutional initiative but was not part of the constitutional package which contained the new Charter. To have made a change in powers a quid pro quo for a charter of rights would not have fitted in very well with a political campaign in which the charter was being sold as part of a "people's package" and provincial premiers were being chastised for trying to swap rights for powers. In any event, by 1967 that distant day when constitutional reforms should be undertaken had suddenly arrived. Speaking to the Canadian Bar Association as Justice Minister in 1967 Trudeau announced his government's conclusion that a constitutional Bill of Rights proposal was "the best basis on which to begin a dialogue on constitution reform between the federal government and provincial governments," and he emphasized that in taking this approach: "Essentially we will be testing—and, hopefully, establishing—the unity of Canada."

After 1967 there were factors other than constitutional strategy which provided additional reasons for adopting a constitutional charter of rights. The application of the European Convention on Human Rights to the United Kingdom, Canada's accession to the International Covenant of Civil and Political Rights in 1976 and the enactment of human rights legislation by most of the Canadian provinces increased Canadian interest in a constitutional codification of basic rights. The invocation of the *War Measures Act* in 1970 and the excesses of the RCMP's Security Service stimulated civil libertarian interest in a constitutional Bill of Rights, as did the Supreme Court's generally narrow interpreta-tion of the "Diefenbaker" Bill. But I doubt that any of these developments had much to do with the Trudeau government's commitment to the Charter—except insofar as they indicated greater public support for such a measure.

Aside from the political and strategic advantages of the Charter, it may also have had some purely intellectual or even aesthetic attractions for Mr. Trudeau and some of his colleagues. Federal government position papers put forward the view that the rational approach to the constitution was to begin with a statement of the fundamental values of the Canadian political community. This notion of constitutional rationality, of the consti-tution as a logical construct built on an explicit formulation of first principles, may be a manifestation of French rationalism and the civil law tradition with its penchant for de-duction from codified principles in contrast with English empiricism and the inductive nature of common law. Even if there is some validity in this kind of ethnic stereotyping, it surely cannot account for the strength of the Trudeau government's political commit-ment to the Charter.

That commitment proved to be very strong indeed. A version of a constitutional Bill of Rights took pride of place in the Victoria Charter which Mr. Trudeau came so close to negotiating successfully with the provincial Premiers in 1971. Again in 1978 when, in response to the electoral victory of the separatists in Quebec, the federal government embarked on another serious programme of constitutional reform, a constitutional char-ter, albeit one which at first would not bind the provinces, was given a prominent position. But it was the inclusion of a constitutional Charter of Rights binding on the provinces in the package of constitutional change which Mr. Trudeau threatened to achieve, if neces-sary, unilaterally without provincial support that demonstrates how deeply he and his government believed in its benefits. At this point, when federal-provincial negotiations on the constitution were at an impasse, it would have been ever so much easier, from a political point of view, for the federal government to have proceeded simply with patria-tion and an amending formula. The insistence on coupling a constitutional charter with patriation shows how strongly the Trudeau government believed in the nation-building potential of a constitutional charter. They would risk dividing the country in order that it might become more united. This nation-building aspect of the Charter was the central thesis of Mr. Trudeau's final parliamentary speech on the Charter.

> Lest the forces of self-interest tear us apart, we must now define the common thread that binds us together.

L. Weinrib, "Of Diligence and Dice: Reconstituting Canada's Constitution"
(1992), 42 *University of Toronto Law Journal* 207
(modified extract; footnotes omitted)

The story [of the Charter] began in earnest in the early 1960s, when the project was sim-ply patriation with an amending formula in order to remove the last remaining legal vestige of colonial status—the exclusive power of the British Parliament at Westminster to amend the *British North America Act*. ...

The Report of the Royal Commission on Bilingualism and Biculturalism in 1967 broadened the agenda beyond patriation with an amending formula to include language rights in the political process, in government services at every level, and in minority language education. ... [T]his report ... precipitat[ed] the genesis of our current Charter in the form of a discussion paper, prepared under the name of then Minister of Justice Pierre Trudeau, for a federal–provincial meeting held in February 1968, proposing *A Canadian Charter of Human Rights*. ...

This stage of discussions culminated in a text prepared for the June 1971 First Ministers' Conference, in Victoria, British Columbia: the *Canadian Constitutional Charter, 1971*, known as the Victoria Charter. This effort failed. Although all provincial premiers reached unanimous consensus at the Conference, Premier Robert Bourassa of Quebec later withdrew his approval when he failed to achieve his desired resolution on the issue of social policy. Canada's adoption of a Charter was to await the passage of another decade.

A study of the Victoria Charter illuminates some of the distinctive features of the Charter as we know it. The range of rights in the Victoria Charter was more limited than Mr. Trudeau's initial proposal or the Charter's eventual formulation. The proposed text did not guarantee legal rights, economic rights, mobility rights or egalitarian rights. It extended protection to "political freedoms" only, including the fundamental freedoms of thought, conscience and religion; of opinion and expression; and peaceful assembly and association. The effect was to negate the exercise of government power rather than to require it. The text also affirmed universal suffrage and eligibility for elected office, free democratic elections, as well as other features of the parliamentary system. In addition, English and French were to become the official languages of Canada, with "status and protection" formulated in language rights in the political process, in the judicial system and in communication with government. There was, however, no provision for rights to minority language education.

· · ·

[There was also] an express provision for limitation of rights. This express limitation clause marked the text as one in the family of post second world war rights protecting instruments, which—unlike, for example, the *United States Bill of Rights*—set out express grounds for judicial limits upon otherwise protected interests:

· · ·

The momentum of constitutional reform lapsed until 1976, when the final push to the 1982 amendments began.

After unsuccessful attempts by Prime Minister Trudeau to secure provincial agreement on patriation, the federal government in June 1978 promulgated Bill C-60, the *Constitutional Amendment Bill*. This text ... expanded upon the Victoria Charter's fundamental freedoms to include, for example, protection for freedom of the press and other media; a right to life, liberty and security of the person; a right against deprivation of property contrary to law; a right to equality before the law and equal protection of the law. In addition, there was protection of a set of legal rights as well as rights of citizens, e.g., to mobility and to property holding and to pursue the gaining of a livelihood anywhere in Canada. These rights were to be enjoyed without discrimination because of race, national or ethnic origin, language, colour, religion, age or sex. The recommendations of the Royal Commission on Bilingualism and Biculturalism bore fruit in the creation of language rights guarantees for minority language education to citizens of Canada where numbers warranted.

Bill C-60 expanded the rights protected, but weakened the mode of protection. The Victoria Charter formulation [had] provided that "it is hereby recognized and declared that in Canada every person has the following fundamental freedoms … ." In contrast, s. 6 of Bill C-60 stated: "It is accordingly declared that, in Canada, every individual shall enjoy and continue to enjoy … ." The latter formulation improved upon the *Canadian Bill of Rights* in abandoning the statement that the rights "have existed," but its reference to continuity might have sustained retrospective rather than a new, legally enforceable content.

The Bill carried forward from the Victoria Charter the contrast between ideas of limitation and abrogation. Section 25, the limitation clause, provided:

> Nothing in this Charter shall be held to prevent such limitations on the exercise or enjoyment of any of the individual rights and freedoms declared by this Charter as are justifiable in a free and democratic society in the interests of public safety or health, the interests of the peace and security of the public, or the interests of the rights and freedoms of others, whether such limitations are imposed by law or by virtue of the construction or application of any law.

… The release of Bill C-60 set in train a flurry of constitutional drafting, primarily motivated by a desire to cut down the effect of the proposal.

L.E. Weinrib, "Canada's Charter of Rights: Paradigm Lost?"
(2002), 6 *Review of Constitutional Studies* 119, at 120, 132-40, 144-45, 147-48
(modified extract; footnotes omitted)

With the adoption of the *Canadian Charter of Rights and Freedoms, 1982*, Canada joined the family of nations operating under a postwar regime of rights-protection. This step marked the culmination of decades of discussion about the nature of rights and, as the debate matured, the institutional structure necessary to protect rights effectively in Canada. The challenge was to transform Canada's federal, parliamentary democracy into a modern, rights-protecting polity. Unlike other states making this transition, Canada did not create a special constitutional court or reconstruct its political institutions. It vested the new judicial review function in the existing courts, and, in addition, marked out an innovative constitutional role for the established legislatures.

· · ·

Proposals to add a system of rights protection, to stand supreme over the routine exercise of public authority, precipitated discussions as to the comparative competence of courts and legislatures to serve the desired end with extensive reference to the experience of other countries as well as to Canada's international obligations.

In the final stages of the debate, the draft text delineating these functions attracted a remarkable degree of attention precipitating what was, in effect, an intensive national seminar on the substantive content and institutional structure of the modern constitutional state. Politicians wary of any reduction in their powers found themselves pitted against individuals and groups intent on securing precisely such restrictions. The question of institutional legitimacy figured so prominently that the final text of the *Charter* includes a complex array of institutional directives. These directives mark one of the distinctive features of the *Charter*. They set it apart from older texts such as the *United States Bill of Rights*, which does not refer to judicial review, as well as from modern rights-protecting instruments, which do formally establish judicial review but set down less institutional detail. Other countries, deliberating later on the same questions in their own national contexts, have considered the Canadian *Charter* as a distinctive model. ...

The decades-long debate produced a fascinating series of proposals as to institutional role, some expansive and others restrictive. These rejected alternatives shed light on the final design. They demonstrate that in following a postwar trend, the *Charter* project did not ignore or dismiss concerns raised as to the legitimacy of judicial review of legislation in a democracy. On the contrary, those involved in the *Charter's* genesis took that controversy very seriously and responded to it. ...

The most important elements of the *Charter's* institutional structure are to be found in two companion clauses: s. 1, the guarantee and limitation clause, and s. 33, the notwithstanding or override clause. ...

The historical material illuminates the ideas and models that informed the *Charter's* distinctive institutional features. First, the limitation formula, following the postwar model of rights-protecting instruments, requires the state to formulate, as law, any exercise of power that limits guaranteed rights. The second is that the remedial aspirations for Canada's *Charter* adopt the postwar model of rights-protection, in which the normativity of the guaranteed rights offers only one level of constitutional guarantee. The other level is provided by the strict terms of the limitation formula, which carry the normative content of the guarantees into the strictures for permissible limitation. The third is that the legislative override or "notwithstanding" clause, which applies only to certain rights, ... gives legislatures the last word [for a maximum period of five years] unless the constitutional context is transformed or the extraordinary consensus necessary for constitutional amendment is satisfied. ...

The limitation and notwithstanding clauses ... mark the culmination of contentious federal-provincial negotiations seeking agreement on a constitutional text for inclusion by amendment into Canada's written constitution. The *Charter* project reflected Prime Minister Trudeau's dual commitment to liberal democracy under the rule of law and a national citizenship based on rights, including minority language rights, designed to counter Quebec nationalism. Only New Brunswick and Ontario supported this initiative. Combined in opposition, but not in motivation, were the remaining eight provinces, including Quebec. The so-called "gang of 8" joined forces to resist Trudeau's *Charter*, melding a provincial rights agenda, including the Quebec nationalist movement, to the desire to preserve legislative supremacy on the British model. Hoping that a consensus would emerge, Trudeau set in motion a deliberative process in which committees of federal and provincial officials worked toward a "best efforts" draft, pending political agreement on the project itself. ...

The drafting process became a natural battleground between the pro-*Charter* and anti-*Charter* camps. When objection to the project gained strength, opponents of the *Charter* secured agreement to remove rights, to diminish the force of their guarantee, and to negate their content through wide limitation clauses and provincial opt-out and/ or opt-in clauses. When the political balance shifted to those supporting rights protection, the rights proliferated and broadened, limitation clauses narrowed and the opt-in and opt-out conditions disappeared.

One element remained constant however. Every draft of the *Charter* included express limitation formulations, reflecting the fact that the legitimacy of the judicial role remained a strong concern. Sustained provincial opposition to the *Charter* initiative eventually produced a compromise draft that subordinated a range of rights to a single, expansive limitation clause:

> The *Canadian Charter of Rights and Freedoms* guarantees the rights and freedoms set out in it subject only to such reasonable limits as are generally accepted in a free and democratic society with a parliamentary system of government.

This version afforded marginal force to the rights guarantees. It did not even require that limits on rights have the form of law, which would have offered assurance that a measure restricting rights had passed through the legislative process or worked through the principled reasoning of the common law. Its vague language did not indicate any specific degree of "acceptance" beyond the vague word "general." What would this mean: passage by a legislature? long-standing application? presence in many of Canada's legal systems? presence in other legal systems? presence in systems that honoured rights? On any reading, this formulation failed to remedy the defects in the existing arrangements. Canadian experience offered numerous examples of the general acceptance of egregious rights infringements in their time and place. Indeed, it was precisely the past acceptance of these now wholly discredited policies—based on ignorance, prejudice, and tradition— that prompted widespread support for an entrenched *Charter*. In the Joint Committee hearings on the *Charter* described below, presenters dubbed this attempt at compromise the "Mack Truck clause," connoting the expansiveness of permissible limitation on rights with the image of a huge truck that could be driven at will through the *Charter*'s guarantees. The clause was also condemned as a "bathtub" section, enabling politicians to pull the plug on citizens' rights. ...

The Conservative Party, the official opposition in the national Parliament, hoping to give time for provincial efforts against the *Charter* project to consolidate, secured the Liberal government's reluctant agreement to put the *Charter* into a parliamentary committee for public hearings. ...

The Joint Committee of the Senate and House of Commons of 1980-81 created the opportunity for experts, representative groups and public interest associations to voice the strong public support for the *Charter* project that Trudeau's Liberals had been nurturing through intensive promotion of their "people's package" of reforms. ...

The experts as well as the large number of public interest associations dedicated to promoting equality and civil liberties submitted detailed critiques of the draft text. They proposed amendments, citing other rights-protecting systems as positive models and past failures to protect rights in the Canadian system as tests for the new *Charter* to meet. ...

This process resulted in dramatic changes to the guarantee-and-limitation clause. There was strong consensus among presenters that the "Mack Truck" formula would offer no effective protection of rights. As drafted, it would preserve legislative sovereignty at judicial prerogative. The record of the courts on the basic liberties and equality did not instill any more confidence than that of the legislatures. Revision of the limitation formula thus became a high priority, given that there would be no constitutional court to administer the *Charter* and no alteration of the existing political institutions. The limitation formula would therefore have to carry the burden of the transformation by providing a clear statement of the mode of institutional protection that the *Charter* would afford. …

The final changes to s. 1 marked acceptance of these concrete submissions. Justice Minister Chrétien quickly conceded the weaknesses of the "Mack Truck" limitation clause:

> … many witnesses and most members of the Committee have expressed concerns about Section 1 of the *Charter of Rights and Freedoms*. These concerns basically have to do with the argument that the clause as drafted leaves open the possibility that a great number of limits could be placed upon rights and freedoms in the *Charter* by the actions of Parliament or a legislature.
>
> … I am prepared on behalf of the government to accept an amendment similar to that suggested by Mr. Gordon Fairweather, Chief Commissioner of the Canadian Human Rights Commission and by Professor Walter Tarnopolsky, President of the Canadian Civil Liberties Association. The wording I am proposing is designed to make the limitation clause even *more stringent* than that recommended by Mr. Fairweather and Professor Tarnopolsky. I am proposing that Section 1 read as follows:
>
>> The *Canadian Charter of Rights and Freedoms* guarantees the rights and freedoms set out in it subject only to such reasonable limits prescribed by law as can be demonstrably justified in a free and democratic society.
>
> This will ensure that any limit on a right must be *not only* reasonable and prescribed by law, but must *also* be shown to be demonstrably justified. [Emphasis added.]
>
> • • •

Asked to comment on the extent of the judicial review power, Mr. Chrétien indicated that it is the role of the courts to interpret the law when citizens raise rights claims, as a check on what is otherwise the absolute and arbitrary power of legislatures … .

The *Charter*, removed from the crucible of federal-provincial politics by the public deliberations in the Joint Committee, reverted to negotiation among the first ministers. The politicians who opposed the *Charter* did not take up their old game of scaling down the rights and expanding the limitation formula. Instead, they left in place the guarantee and limitation clause as transformed in the Joint Committee. Perhaps they recognized that the revised text enjoyed profound legitimation by virtue of the unprecedented public participation in enlarging the content of many of the rights and narrowing the limitation clause, its strong popular support across the country, and the national television coverage of the Joint Committee proceedings.

As the price for acceptance of the *Charter* as redrafted in the Joint Committee, seven premiers exacted agreement to a fall-back mechanism in respect to the rights they considered most controversial, just in case the courts ventured too far beyond the politicians' tolerance for rights-protection. The first ministers created the legislative override or "notwithstanding" mechanism and made it applicable to the rights they believed should not rest for final determination in the courts: fundamental freedoms, legal rights, and equality rights. This mechanism enabled a legislature, within its legislative jurisdiction, to suppress guarantees it specified for up to five years, the maximum length of electoral office, by explicit enactment. Re-enactment of a lapsed overriding provision was permitted. Left to final judicial determination under the limitation provision, without recourse to the notwithstanding clause, were the democratic rights, the mobility rights, and the language rights. The politicians left these interests to the expertise of the independent judiciary, marking continuity with long established constitutional commitments to parliamentary democracy and federalism.

Quebec, which had mounted the strongest battle against the *Charter*, did not agree to this compromise. [This part of the story of the Charter's adoption is dealt with in the excerpt from M.E. Gold, below.]

The compromise on the notwithstanding clause did not emerge as a *deus ex machina* on the constitutional stage. It offered, in general form, the type of political flexibility that the opposing premiers had inserted in earlier drafts of the *Charter* as a complex set of opt-in and opt-out mechanisms for specific rights. The model for these clauses resided in various statutory rights-protecting instruments. They were considered safety valves for exceptional circumstances. And in fact the prototypes had all but never been used.

The "notwithstanding clause" materialized as a response to the *Charter* text that emerged from the Special Joint Committee proceedings. The new limitation provision made limits on rights the exception, rather than the rule. Without the "notwithstanding clause," the *Charter* created three possible outcomes to a successful *Charter* challenge: (i) the enjoyment of the rights as guaranteed, (ii) legally prescribed limits upon those rights as justified by governments in courts of law … or (iii) constitutional amendment. The notwithstanding clause added a fourth possibility: Parliament or a legislature could re-assert its primacy over specified *Charter* rights, for the duration of its electoral mandate, for whatever reason, by expressly indicating this desired result in legislation. Judicial affirmation of generally acceptable or merely reasonable limits on rights was not part of the final package … .

M.E. Gold, "The Mask of Objectivity: Politics and Rhetoric in the Supreme Court of Canada"
(1985), 7 *Supreme Court Law Review* 462, at 463-66 (footnotes omitted)

As is well known, the federal initiative initially attracted the support of only Ontario and New Brunswick and separate court challenges were launched by three of the provincial governments opposed to the federal plan. The Supreme Court ultimately ruled that, although legal, the federal proposal violated a constitutional convention requiring a "substantial measure of provincial consent" to amendments of this nature. The Court refused to specify precisely what measure of provincial consent would satisfy the convention, satisfied that the support of only two provinces was not sufficient.

The Court's decision made it politically impossible for the federal government to proceed; a breach of this constitutional convention would undermine the legitimacy of the Constitution. Furthermore, it appears that the initiative might well have foundered at

Westminster because of the paucity of provincial consent. Accordingly, another round of federal-provincial negotiations ensued.

Quebec had earlier agreed to form part of a common front against the federal initiative, joining with seven other provinces in holding out for a different amending formula and a revised Charter of Rights. In a well publicized news conference, this "gang of eight" had entered into a written agreement to oppose the federal government's plan. This was the first time in Canadian history that Quebec had tied its position on the amendment of the Constitution to the positions of other provinces, and the first time that a government of Quebec had agreed to support an amending formula that did not recognize a veto for Quebec.

The agreement was also politically important to the government of Quebec. Having been defeated in the 1980 referendum on sovereignty-association, the government wanted to demonstrate that it was honouring its referendum promise to respect the voters' judgment in good faith. By joining forces with seven other provinces, Quebec would not appear as the sole obstacle to constitutional change and could be seen as acting responsibly in opposing the federal plan.

The common front fell apart. Some have suggested that it was as a result of Premier Levesque's expressed interest in a referendum proposal floated by Prime Minister Trudeau at the beginning of the last round of federal–provincial negotiations. Quebec's apparent willingness to entertain a referendum option was anathema to certain provincial governments who considered the referendum a device to circumvent their role in the process of constitutional change. More generally, it could be argued that the common front was inherently unstable. Quebec was perceived to have joined the common front in the expectation that the front's proposals would never be accepted by the federal government, and it was natural for the provincial government to be wary of Quebec's motives. Rightly or wrongly, it was thought that the Parti Quebecois government could not allow any constitutional changes to be realized, as this would demonstrate the possibility of a renewed Canadian federalism.

The mistrust of Quebec ran so deep that the seven dissenting provinces held a secret meeting to discuss a revised package of amendments that they hoped would be acceptable to the federal government; the Quebec delegation was neither informed nor invited. This revised package was the basis of the agreement ultimately signed between the federal government and the nine provinces.

No one has explained adequately why the Quebec delegation was excluded from the meeting, although it seems clear why the other provinces were prepared to strike some deal with the federal government. Public opinion was shifting away from the provinces. Canadians supported the idea of patriation and favoured an entrenched Charter of Rights. The provincial governments were afraid to pay the political cost of appearing to act as obstructionists to a plan supported by a majority of their constituents. In any event, the Quebec delegation was kept in the dark about this crucial meeting and, to this day, no provincial official has explained the exclusion of Quebec to the government of Quebec itself. The inference is irresistible: the provinces were willing to abandon Quebec in the interest of securing a deal, but were embarrassed to confront the government of Quebec with this decision until after it had been reached.

The political consequences to the government of Quebec were considerable. The government had failed to safeguard Quebec's interests in negotiations and was condemned by the opposition Liberals in the National Assembly. Nonetheless, the event could be turned to some political advantage with the Quebec electorate. In its most innocent light, the result might convince the people of Quebec that they could not trust the other provinces (read English Canada) to respect the position of Quebec: only the government of Quebec could be relied upon to defend the interests of the province. More cynically perhaps, the exclusion of Quebec provided the Parti Quebecois government with a powerful new weapon in its drive to secure the independence of Quebec. Having been roundly assailed for having joined the common front and abandoning the claim for a constitutional veto, the Parti Quebecois was given a new lease on life. Whether fueled by a genuine sense of betrayal at the hands of the other provinces, motivated by partisan political considerations or most likely by both, the government of Quebec was not about to let events unravel passively.

As Lorraine Weinrib notes in "Canada's Charter of Rights: Paradigm Lost?," above:

> Quebec's opposition to the *Charter* did not reflect opposition to rights protection, to a formal bill of rights or to the type of institutional arrangements created by the *Charter*. The *Charter* had become one more battle ground in Canada's constitutional wars on division of powers generally and Quebec's place in Confederation. Quebec's *Charter of Human Rights and Freedoms* (*Charte des droits et libertés de la personne*), RSQ, c. C-12, originally enacted in 1975, has features and institutional arrangements similar to the Canadian *Charter*, although, as a provincial statute, it has different subject matter and application. Its array of protected rights is broader, including, for example, a right to rescue, rights to property, privacy, cultural rights, and economic and social rights. Its limitation clause, s. 9.1, applicable to the fundamental freedoms and rights, added in 1982, is similar to s. 1 of the Canadian *Charter* and shares the international human rights instruments as its model. Section 52 enables the National Assembly to expressly state that a later enacted law applies despite the *Charter*.

III. THE MERITS OF ENTRENCHMENT AND THE LEGITIMACY OF JUDICIAL REVIEW

As Lorraine Weinrib wrote in "Canada's Charter of Rights: Paradigm Lost?," above:

> [T]he *Charter* effected a revolutionary transformation of the Canadian polity from legislative supremacy to constitutional supremacy. The transformation changed the role of every public institution. The Supreme Court became the major agent of this transformation, mandated to bring the entire legal system into conformity with a complex new structure of rights-protection.

This transformation has not been without controversy. The following readings introduce you to the intense and prolific debate on the legitimacy of the Charter within Canada's democratic system of government. Some commentators reject the Charter altogether because it transforms the democratic structure of Canadian politics. Others praise it for the same reason.

These readings build on the introduction to judicial review and its legitimacy found in Chapter 2, Judicial Review and Constitutional Interpretation. Note the ways in which debates about the wisdom of entrenchment have turned into debates about the appropriate methodology for judicial interpretation of the Charter. Note as well the very different political orientations of the Charter critics—both the right and the left have mounted strong critiques of the Charter.

W. Bogart, *Courts and Country*
(Toronto: Oxford University Press, 1994), at 256-70 (footnotes omitted)

In bluntest terms, two very different models of democracy are at stake. The first recognizes the power of the ballot that is curbed by independent and tenured judges who ensure that rationality and principle are never ejected by impetuous legislatures, rigid bureaucracies, and a dulled citizenry. In this model, courts will shelter the disadvantaged, who will harness that rationality and principle. The second model places its confidence in those who can claim the power of the ballot. Realistic about democracy's foibles, it is even more reserved about using judicial intervention to solve them. In this model, judges' independence and tenure make them unaccountable, élitist, and, at present in any event, unrepresentative. The apprehension is that far from invigorating democracy, judicial review will sap it with regressive decisions, progressive decisions that nonetheless blunt popular responses to societal problems, and barriers to access because of the costs of litigation. In this second model, those who seek social reform may have the most to lose in the courts. ...

The Case for the Charter

A fundamental argument favouring an entrenched bill of rights is that such a document allows individuals, particularly those with minoirty interests, to seek vindication in an open, public, and responsive process as opposed to legislators who may be unresponsive and, in any event, are more attentive to majority concerns ... . Coupled with this argument is a claim that the coming of the Charter signals the full maturity of the Canadian legal system. This development, the end goal of which is an entrenched Charter, explains the Canadian courts' spotty record with the *Bill of Rights*. ...

Yet another justification for the Charter is its ability to unite Canadians. Before its entrenchment, the structure of Canadian society was significantly influenced by executive federalism, that élite form of accommodation dominated by a very small, unrepresentative handful of white males. Indeed, this tradition of structuring by a small group of men from the two dominant cultures was part of the pacts of 1982 and Meech Lake and was largely responsible for a momentous negative reaction, which, in the case of Meech Lake, was a large part of its undoing.

In contrast, the Charter has recognized "other" identities who can simultaneously gain strength and weaken the disjunctive tendencies of regionalism through their coalescence. No longer will the female Nova Scotian and the female British Columbian speak to each other through the tensions of regionalism; rather, they will be united by their gender.

Other more cautious bases for accepting the Charter stipulate certain conditions for its implementation. One condition rests on it being construed only to protect democracy's functioning and not to review substantive decisions made by elected officials. Fundamental to this view is the assertion that the Charter does not oblige a court "to test the substantive outcomes of the political process against some theory of the right or the good, but, instead, its focus is to assure the integrity of politics by buttressing the opportunities for public debate and collective deliberation." ...

Another condition to the acceptance and therefore justification of judicial review under the Charter is the existence and use of s. 33, which allows judicial decisions under most of the provisions of the Charter to be overridden by the competent legislative body. ...

The Case Against the Charter

In contrast, those who are opposed or at least indifferent to the Charter point out that the Charter and its accompanying judicial role did not come about because of the documentation of widespread abuse, nor did it arise from popular outcry. It was born as a device to shore up the centralizing tendencies that Pierre Trudeau believed were vital to enhance Quebec's stake in the nation and to check the forces of separatism led by his rival, René Lévesque. ...

Those who are opposed are hardly conspiratorial since many of them can agree about little else except their antagonism towards the document. The politics of many of them are left. For some of those so inclined, the vehemence against the judges arises because their role subverts any possibility of true democracy, which "means the greatest possible engagement by people in the greatest possible range of communal tasks and public action." In this conception, the Charter is a "reflection of the inherent contradiction of liberal ideology. ..."

What is the basis for this leeriness, which ranges from scepticism to unbridled antagonism? Though presented in different forms, the arguments can be summarized in three points. The first concerns substantive outcomes and claims that the elected members of government and their agencies have been the more effective vehicle for improving the lives of most Canadians in many circumstances. The second relates to process and asserts that the best chance for a vigorous, responsive, and respected democracy comes from elected representatives. The third is about the costs of access to the courts which privilege the powerful and organized and thus allow them disproportionate use of judicial review, either to dismantle legislation and programs or to shield themselves from attack by government or other groups. These three points are comparative. This is not to deny that courts have sometimes acted in admirable ways or that there have been some progressive—even visionary—judges: on the Supreme Court alone names such as Rand, Laskin, Dickson, and Wilson easily come to mind. Nor is it to claim that legislatures and their agents have always reached just outcomes by adequate processes. What is contended is that relatively, the chance for greatest justice will come from legislatures. ...

The first argument claims that assistance of the disadvantaged and the poor, as well as ordinary citizens, has more often happened because of legislative action. Whether in health, occupational safety, workers' rights, housing, peace and order in the streets, or other aspects of life, the advancement has come because of the popular support of political will.

In this view, government, while open to searing criticisms about waste and inefficiency, has also been the agent of civilizing and progressive change. It has mediated between those who wish *laissez-faire* and the enrichment of the few (regardless of the consequences) and those who insist upon a basic claim to entitlement for all. Conversely, this argument contends that the historical record reveals that courts, rather than achieving conditions to nurture and protect ordinary people in their everyday lives, have instead been uncaring or actively hostile. The explanation for this lies in an embrace of liberal ideology and an active suspicion of the political process as intrusion upon the purity of the judge-made common law that did not develop to meet these ends. State regulation and programs, designed to be responsive to the concerns of such people, have often been cut back under the guise of interpretation of statutes when in reality it was to allow the ideas of the judiciary to hold sway. ...

The second argument urges that for democracy not to be sapped but invigorated, basic decisions affecting the people must be made by elected representatives. This point does not suggest that such a process has not led to mistakes, sometimes horrible ones, such as our failure to save as many Jews as we could have in the Second World War. The tragedies that beset our Amerindians is surely another. Nor does it suggest that there are not major impediments to popular participation. What it argues is that concerted efforts should be exerted to eliminate them and that we should not rely upon a small unelected corps. Unlike the first argument, the concern here is not so much that judges will impose their views on a democratic majority. Rather, the worry is that critical, social, and political questions will be translated into legal issues that will be left to judges and lawyers instead of the citizenry working out acceptable and supportable solutions.

In this view, even a cycle of progressive and enlightened decisions entails costs, although the results may be desirable. There may be benefits, but they come from a small group of judges and lawyers who are bound together by a limited set of ideas and attitudes and who impose conclusions rather than persuade and build consensus among the electorate. The danger is that the basis for having citizens make their own decisions and face future issues will be eroded, and that the resentment felt by having solutions handed down will make future progress even more difficult and may even contribute to regressive backlash. ...

The third point focuses upon the costs of any court response. The contention is that whatever meaning is possible in interpreting the Charter, it will inevitably come to be slanted towards the rich and the organized. Obviously, access to the political and bureaucratic processes is imperfect, but it is not as expensive and complicated and is available without necessarily being mediated through the language of the law, a discourse largely available only to lawyers.

A. Petter, "Immaculate Deception: The Charter's Hidden Agenda"
(1987), 45 *The Advocate* 857, at 857-63 (footnotes omitted)

My purpose in this short essay is to put forward an argument that does not enjoy a great deal of currency on the "Charter circuit" these days. It is an argument that most lawyers do not wish to hear. And some may regard as downright impolite.

The argument is that, while sold to the public as part of a "people's package," the Canadian *Charter of Rights and Freedoms* is a regressive instrument more likely to undermine than to advance the interests of socially and economically disadvantaged Canadians. The reasons for this lie partly in the nature of the rights themselves and partly in the nature of the judicial system which is charged with their interpretation and enforcement.

I. The Nature of Charter Rights

The first thing that must be recognized about the Charter is that it is, at root, a 19th century liberal document set loose on a 20th century welfare state. The rights in the Charter are founded upon the belief that the main enemies of freedom are not disparities in wealth nor concentrations of private power, but the state. Thus one finds in the Charter little reference to positive economic or social entitlements, such as rights to employment, shelter or social services. Charter rights are predominantly negative in nature, aimed at protecting individuals from state interference or control with respect to this matter or that.

· · ·

The negative nature of the rights embodied within the Charter reflects what John Hart Ely refers to as a "systematic bias" in favour of the interests of the "upper middle-class, professional class from which most lawyers and judges, and for that matter most moral philosophers, are drawn." These people see their social and economic status most threatened by the regulatory and redistributive powers of the modern state. It is not surprising therefore that they regard as "fundamental" those values that afford them protection from such state powers. But, as Ely observes, "watch most fundamental-rights theorists start edging toward the door when someone mentions jobs, food or housing: those are important sure, but they aren't *fundamental*."

This "systematic bias" is reinforced by a highly selective view of what constitutes the state. The presumption underlying the Charter is that existing distributions of wealth and power are products of private initiative as opposed to state action. Never mind that these distributions depend for their existence and legitimacy upon a panoply of state sponsored laws and institutions. They are nevertheless viewed as outside politics and beyond the scope of Charter scrutiny. Thus far from being subject to Charter challenge, such distributions comprise the "natural" foundation upon which Charter rights are conferred and against which the constitutionality of "state action" is to be judged.

· · ·

The negative nature of Charter rights combined with this selective view of state action remove from Charter scrutiny the major source of inequality in our society—the unequal distribution of property entitlements among private parties. At the same time, they direct the restraining force of the Charter against the arm of the state best equipped to redress fundamental economic inequalities—the democratic arm, consisting of the legislature and the executive.

The irony of this will not be lost on those with a sense of history. The victories that have been won in this century on behalf of workers, the unemployed, women and other socially and economically disadvantaged Canadians are victories that have been achieved, for the most part, in the democratic arena. They are victories that have been won by harnessing the powers of the modern state to redistribute wealth and to place limits on the exercise of "private" economic power.

Thus workers have been granted the collective bargaining rights they now enjoy by virtue of legislation overriding common law rules that protected employers' liberty and privity of contract and that treated trade unions as illegal conspiracies. The economic benefits guaranteed to the unemployed flow from redistributive policies of modern government. The lot of women has been advanced, to the degree that it has, by means of legislative intervention in the form of labour standards legislation, minimum wage laws and human rights codes.

This is not to imply that these responses have been comprehensive or adequate. In my view they have not. The point is simply that where there has been progress, with few exceptions it has come in the democratic rather than the judicial arena. Such progress has been achieved through political action aimed at displacing the common law vision of unbridled individual autonomy with a countervision of collective social responsibility. Put simply, the negative conception of liberty imposed by the courts to protect the interests of the "haves" in society has been partially supplanted by a positive conception of liberty imposed by legislatures to further the interests of the "have-nots."

Yet the Charter now threatens to slow, or even reverse, this process. The rights and freedoms in the Charter are predicated on the same hostility to legislative action, and the same reverence for individual autonomy, that animated the common law. I am not suggesting that the present legislative regime of social and economic regulation will suddenly be eliminated under the Charter. The political costs of doing so are, thankfully, too great for the courts to contemplate. What the Charter is more likely to do is to enable the courts to chisel away at certain aspects of the regime, and to erect barriers to future innovation.

· · ·

This does not mean that there will be no "progressive" Charter decisions. Undoubtedly there will be some, although the bulk of such decisions will involve the courts in upholding legislation—in other words doing nothing. Additionally, there will be a few decisions in which the Charter is used to enhance legislative protections, for example by striking down an obsolete or inappropriate exemption in a regulatory regime. Such cases, however, will be the exception rather than the rule. Indeed, the very notion of looking to the courts to improve legislation is somewhat perverse. Most legislation, after all, was enacted to counteract the laissez-faire individualism of court-made, common law. Courts, even today, remain suspicious of, and at worst hostile to, the "eccentric principles of socialist philanthropy" upon which the welfare state is founded. Thus to look at the courts to repair flaws in the existing regulatory regime is a bit like taking one's car to be fixed by an auto wrecker.

In addition to eroding existing and stymieing future social and economic regulation, the Charter will serve to weaken the impetus for further legislative reform by diverting resources from the political to the judicial arena. Women's groups, for example, are raising millions of dollars to engage in Charter litigation, a considerable portion of which is being used to defend from Charter challenge legislation that is beneficial to women. The money, time and energy devoted by such groups to the Charter are money, time and energy that will be taken away from lobbying and other forms of political action.

II. The Nature of the Judicial System

The regressive impact of the Charter is exacerbated by the nature of the judicial system that is charged with its interpretation and enforcement. There are two features of this system that make it a particularly inappropriate forum for advancing the interests of the disadvantaged. The first is the cost of gaining access to the system; the second is the composition of the judiciary itself.

[T]he process of vindicating one's rights under the Charter is an extremely expensive one. ...

[Such costs] represent a major obstacle to disadvantaged Canadians who wish to pursue their Charter rights in court. ... [B]eyond the confines of criminal law, the effect of having chosen the courts as the adjudicative forum for resolving Charter claims is to favour those who command substantial economic resources.

The institutional barrier created by money not only denies the disadvantaged access to the courts; in doing so, it serves to shape the rights themselves. ...

If the issues raised in non-criminal Charter cases tend to represent the interests of those with economic resources in society, the interpretation of rights will necessarily respond to and, over time, will reflect those interests. ...

Consider ... the Charter right to freedom of expression. The opportunity to raise a claim concerning this right will be restricted to those who can command sufficient resources to bring an action in court and who consider it economically or politically worthwhile to do so. Litigation concerning this right is thus more likely to be brought by economically powerful interests in society, such as business interests, for whom the costs of litigation are small in relation to the potential economic gains. But if litigation relating to freedom of expression disproportionately represents the interests of business, the jurisprudence surrounding freedom of expression will come to reflect business concerns.

· · ·

There might be less cause for concern on this score if the judiciary had an equal understanding of, and empathy for, the problems of all segments of Canadian society. Unfortunately, there is no reason to suppose that this is the case. There are few public institutions in this country whose composition more poorly reflects, and whose members have less direct exposure to, the interests of the economically and socially disadvantaged. Canadian judges are "exclusively recruited from the small class of successful, middle-aged lawyers" and, if not of wealthy origin, most became wealthy or at least achieved a degree of affluence before accepting their judicial appointments. The majority made their name in private practice where they held themselves out as business people and shared business concerns. Furthermore, unless they practiced criminal or family law, much of their professional time was spent catering to the needs of the business community. In short, there is nothing about the Canadian judiciary to suggest that they possess the experience, the training or the disposition to comprehend the social impact of claims made to them under the Charter, let alone to resolve those claims in ways that promote, or even protect, the interests of lower income Canadians.

At a more fundamental level, the attitudes of lawyers and of judges tend to reflect the values of the legal system in which they were schooled and to which they owe their livelihood.

· · ·

From this perspective, one can see that property rights—the body of "natural" rules governing the ownership and exchange of property—is the core political value underlying the common law.

This does not imply that the desire to protect property is the sole force driving Canadian judiciary. What it does imply, however, is that deep in the judicial ethos there exists a special concern and reverence for property rights—a concern and reverence that over the course of time will guide and constrain judicial decision-making in Charter cases.

· · ·

The assumption of lawyers that property rights flow from a "natural" system of private ordering is also significant. This assumption reinforces the dichotomy between private and state action that underlies the Charter, thus making it more difficult for individuals to mobilize the Charter against underlying social disparities. Judges conceive their role under the Charter not as interest balancing, which they view as the preserve of politics, but rather as one of policing the boundary between the "natural" zone of individual autonomy (represented by the market) and the "unnatural" activities of the state (represented by the regulatory and redistributive instruments of modern governments). Thus the bias that judges bring to their task augments the bias of the Charter itself: "liberty" is represented by those things that expand the zone of individual autonomy by limiting the ability of the state to "interfere" in the lives of individual Canadians. The task of the judge is to interpret the Charter generously so as to "secur[e] for individuals the full benefit of the Charter's protection." Hence narrow Charter interpretations are "bad" while expansive interpretations are "good."

What is conveniently forgotten in all of this is that the liberty of many Canadians is better protected by the regulatory and redistributive policies of the state than by the market (assuming "liberty" includes the liberty to be clothed, housed and fed, and the liberty not to be preyed upon by those who command social and economic power).

As you read the Supreme Court of Canada's Charter decisions in subsequent chapters, consider whether the left critique of the Charter as articulated by Petter is justified. To what extent has the Court attempted to respond to this critique?

Further readings providing a critique from the left include Michael Mandel, *The Charter of Rights and the Legalization of Politics in Canada*, rev. ed. (Toronto: Thompson, 1994); Allan C. Hutchinson, *Waiting for Coraf: A Critique of Law and Rights* (Toronto: University of Toronto Press, 1995); and Joel Bakan, *Just Words: Constitutional Rights and Social Wrongs* (Toronto: University of Toronto Press, 1997).

L. Weinrib, "'Limitations on Rights' in a Constitutional Democracy"
(1996), 6 *Caribbean Law Review* 428, at 439-45 (footnotes omitted)

[This article describes two models for understanding the Charter and the role of the courts: the "majoritarian" model and the "supremacy of rights" model. The passage that follows is an account of the second, the "supremacy of rights" model.]

There is another possibility. A different model postulates that rights protection operates as a higher level of law—as supreme law. The foundation of this conception is a commitment to certain irreducible substantive values to which all other lawmaking, whether legislative or judicial, must conform. This model welcomes judicial protection of individual rights and their value structure as a correction for the perceived inadequacies of majoritarian politics. Underlying this model is respect for the equal dignity and autonomy of each member of the community. The individual must be able to espouse, follow, and modify his or her own conception of the good. Whatever the sources and trajectories of these commitments, the aim of collective political life is to create and preserve a structure in which each of us, to an equal extent, may pursue and act upon these commitments, either alone or in a given or chosen community. In interactions with the state, each individual is autonomous, equal to all others, an end and not a means to others' ends.

Far from standing opposed to the individual, political community in this model provides the necessary framework in which one conducts one's life in dignity and, if as desired, in group identity or communal life. The supreme law model is thus not antagonistic to the majoritarian apparatus that creates the positive law of the modern state. It merely recognizes that majority politics may lapse in its commitment to the initial human premises of the collective enterprise—the very premises that undergird democracy itself.

For one thing, the institutional operation of the political system often precludes effective examination of questions impinging on protected rights. Sometimes the political forum cannot foresee the implications of a policy for persons whose beliefs or commitments are unfamiliar or circumstances unusual. At other times, enduring legislative programs may have unexpected effects in new social and economic circumstances. There is no effective mechanism to alert the legislature to such consequences or to compel it, once informed, to act.

Alternatively, the dynamics of the political forum may not be receptive to the values embodied in rights. Legislative programs are forged in a chaotic melange of give and take, favour and obligation, dissimulation and frankness, long term objectives and crisis management, as government struggles to sustain and enlarge its base of support. In the rough and tumble of policy formation, those holding predominant ground in a society find their interests secured through regular politics because legislative representatives will share their claims. Politically adept and/or established minorities often fare almost as well. Others, however, cut off from political power by birth or belief or happenstance, must not only constantly monitor how particular policies may affect their vital interests, but also strive, usually without political representation and often without political connections or experience, to win accommodation for their unusual demands. Their position is less secure. Still less well-positioned are the criminally accused or incarcerated, who may suddenly find themselves beyond the pale of effective political action; and, similarly, those suffering physical or mental incapacities. ...

Within the model that accords rights legal supremacy, the representative branch of government exercises the powers of policy formation under the watchful eye of the judiciary. This model values independent, highly trained and educated judges as a means of tapping a deeper, long-term political voice. An independent judiciary unlocks the grip of day to day political deal-making and expediency, offers the politicians relief from final responsibility in an unknowable world, and lends legitimacy to a variety of legal operations, such as applying enacted law to particular circumstances, evolving judicial doctrines, constraining subordinate lawmakers to legislative direction and policing constitutional proprieties. Within this model, courts are important law creators, not merely servants to the legislative machine.

It is the affirmed task of the judiciary to elucidate the principled coherence of a legal system committed to the values basic to dignified human life. Guaranteed rights are an important part of this system, but even such specifically enumerated protection is not inviolate. For within the supreme law model, the rights-declaring text is but an imperfect crystallization of yet more abstract values. Because the text is the product of the historical moment in which the formulators drafted it, it is subject to the limits of their experience, vision and understanding, the difficulties of language, and the exigencies of their political context. Accordingly, the rights enumerated are not absolute; they must be read as conditional upon the preservation of the whole system of government committed to those underlying values.

The essential promise is thus general or abstract: assurance of a structure of government faithful to values inherent in dignified human life. Usually, this promise will be honoured by adherence to the specific, express guarantees that crystallize those values. Accordingly, in most circumstances, state action that infringes a guaranteed right will fall. On occasion, however, an act of state that encroaches upon an enumerated right must nonetheless prevail in the interest of fidelity to the general guarantee. *Thus while enumerated rights are absolute in neither model, the concession here marks an extension of the commitment to, rather than a departure from, rights-based values.*

It is therefore not accurate to say within this model, as one can in the majoritarian model, that rights are not absolute because they must bend to the majority's assertion of what is good for the individual, the group, or society at large. Instead, the enumerated rights are understood as the product of the supreme effort at articulating liberal democracy's bedrock values. If these rights must bend or give way, it is not because the rights protecting regime subordinates them to majority preferences. On the contrary, they cede only to the deeper principles of which they are but emanations.

In addition to the guarantee of the enumerated right, therefore, the right holder enjoys a deeper guarantee against all but a principled limit upon that right, consistent with the values for which all rights stand. This two-level guarantee imposes a distinctive task on the courts: to assure the enjoyment of the named rights or, failing that, to forward the interests for which rights stand. To serve this end, a court may have to resolve competing rights claims, stretch scarce resources over the array of rights guarantees, preserve the political community in times of external and internal threats to order and, on occasion, to preserve life and health in times of emergency. There is no call here to defer to majoritarian process or result *per se*. The democratic instruments of state policy formation subscribe to the same supreme values as the courts and must either honour the right or succeed in justifying, in terms of supreme law values, any departure from its strictures. Thus the judiciary need not emulate the legislature's mode of discourse or evaluation; it is freed from any formal inclination to defer.

In the rights-as-supreme-law model, both the courts and the legislatures, each working to its institutional strengths, mould society to its deepest commitments. The majoritarian function is therefore not a self-defining function; it is one of a number of institutional arrangements within the constitutional order. Through recognition that the same human values underpin both rights and their limits—supported by other organizing principles of the legal order—the courts oversee the functioning of a free and democratic society.

In the early years of the Charter, the main criticisms of entrenchment and judicial review came from the political left (as reflected in the piece by Petter, above), raising concerns that the Supreme Court of Canada would use the Charter to restrain socially desirable regulation and redistribution. More recently, however, vocal criticism about illegitimate "judicial activism" has come from the political right, with contentions that the Court is acting undemocratically by forcing unwilling majorities to accept the rights of unpopular minorities. An example of this new wave of criticism of judicial activism is found in F.L. Morton and R. Knopff, *The Charter Revolution and the Court Party* (Peterborough, ON: Broadview Press, 2000), discussed further below. In 1997, P. Hogg and A. Bushell, responding to these increasing charges of "judicial activism," added a new strand to the debates about the legitimacy of judicial review—the idea of judicial review under the Charter as a form of "dialogue" between courts and legislatures.

P.W. Hogg and A.A. Bushell, "The Charter Dialogue Between Courts and Legislatures (Or Perhaps the Charter of Rights Isn't Such a Bad Thing After All)"
(1997), 35 *Osgoode Hall Law Journal* 75, at 79-91 and 104-5 (footnotes omitted)

A. The Concept of Dialogue

The uninitiated might be excused for believing that, given the deluge of writing on the topic, everything useful that could possibly be said about the legitimacy of judicial review has now been said. However, one intriguing idea that has been raised in the literature seems to have been left largely unexplored. That is the notion that judicial review is part of a "dialogue" between judges and legislatures.

At first blush the word "dialogue" may not seem particularly apt to describe the relationship between the Supreme Court of Canada and the legislative bodies. After all, when the Court says what the Constitution requires, legislative bodies have to obey. Is it possible to have a dialogue between two institutions when one is so clearly subordinate to the other? Does dialogue not require a relationship between equals?

The answer, we suggest, is this. Where a judicial decision is open to legislative reversal, modification, or avoidance, then it is meaningful to regard the relationship between the Court and the competent legislative body as a dialogue. In that case, the judicial decision causes a public debate in which *Charter* values play a more prominent role than they would if there had been no judicial decision. The legislative body is in a position to devise a response that is properly respectful of the *Charter* values that have been identified by the Court, but which accomplishes the social or economic objectives that the judicial decision has impeded. Examples of this will be given later in this article.

B. *How Dialogue Works*

Where a judicial decision striking down a law on *Charter* grounds can be reversed, modified, or avoided by a new law, any concern about the legitimacy of judicial review is greatly diminished. To be sure, the Court may have forced a topic onto the legislative agenda that the legislative body would have preferred not to have to deal with. And, of course, the precise terms of any new law would have been powerfully influenced by the Court's decision. The legislative body would have been forced to give greater weight to the *Charter* values identified by the Court in devising the means of carrying out the objectives, or the legislative body might have been forced to modify its objectives to some extent to accommodate the Court's concerns. These are constraints on the democratic process, no doubt, but the final decision is the democratic one.

The dialogue that culminates in a democratic decision can only take place if the judicial decision to strike down a law can be reversed, modified, or avoided by the ordinary legislative process. Later in this article we will show that this is the normal situation. There is usually an alternative law that is available to the legislative body and that enables the legislative purpose to be substantially carried out, albeit by somewhat different means. Moreover, when the Court strikes down a law, it frequently offers a suggestion as to how the law could be modified to solve the constitutional problems. The legislative body often follows that suggestion, or devises a different law that also skirts the constitutional barriers. Indeed, our research, which surveyed sixty-five cases where legislation was invalidated for a breach of the *Charter*, found that in forty-four cases (two-thirds), the competent legislative body amended the impugned law. In most cases, relatively minor amendments were all that was required in order to respect the *Charter*, without compromising the objective of the original legislation.

Sometimes an invalid law is more restrictive of individual liberty than it needs to be to accomplish its purpose, and what is required is a narrower law. Sometimes a broader law is needed, because an invalid law confers a benefit, but excludes people who have a constitutional equality right to be included. Sometimes what is needed is a fairer procedure. But it is rare indeed that the constitutional defect cannot be remedied. Hence, as the subtitle of this article suggests, "perhaps the *Charter of Rights* isn't such a bad thing after all." The *Charter* can act as a catalyst for a two-way exchange between judiciary and legislature on the topic of human rights and freedoms, but it rarely raises an absolute barrier to the wishes of the democratic institutions.

. . .

A. *The Four Features [of the Charter] That Facilitate Dialogue*

Why is it usually possible for a legislature to overcome a judicial decision striking down a law for breach of the *Charter*? The answer lies in four features of the *Charter*: (1) section 33, which is the power of legislative override; (2) section 1, which allows for "reasonable limits" on guaranteed *Charter* rights; (3) the "qualified rights," in sections 7, 8, 9 and 12, which allow for action that satisfies standards of fairness and reasonableness; and (4) the guarantee of equality rights under section 15(1), which can be satisfied through a variety of remedial measures. Each of these features usually offers the competent legislative body room to advance its objectives, while at the same time respecting the requirements of the *Charter* as articulated by the courts.

· · ·

Section 33 of the *Charter* is commonly referred to as the power of legislative override. Under section 33, Parliament or a legislature need only insert an express notwithstanding clause into a statute and this will liberate the statute from the provisions of section 2 and sections 7–15 of the *Charter*. The legislative override is the most obvious and direct way of overcoming a judicial decision striking down a law for an infringement of *Charter* rights. Section 33 allows the competent legislative body to re-enact the original law without interference from the courts.

· · ·

When a law that impairs a *Charter* right fails to satisfy the least restrictive means standard of section 1 justification, the law is, of course, struck down. But the reviewing court will explain why the section 1 standard was not met, which will involve explaining the less restrictive alternative law that *would* have satisfied the section 1 standard. That alternative law is available to the enacting body and will generally be upheld. Even if the court has a weak grasp of the practicalities of the particular field of regulation, so that the court's alternative is not really workable, it will usually be possible for the policymakers to devise a less restrictive alternative that is practicable. With appropriate recitals in the legislation, and with appropriate evidence available if necessary to support the legislative choice, one can usually be confident that a carefully drafted "second attempt" will be upheld against any future *Charter* challenges.

· · ·

 Dialogue seems an apt description of the relationship between courts and legislative bodies [in these cases]. Certainly, it is hard to claim that an unelected court is thwarting the wishes of the people. In each case, the democratic process has been influenced by the reviewing court, but it has not been stultified.

[Hogg and Bushell do recognize that there are certain circumstances in which there are "barriers" to dialogue and in which courts will have the last word. These include situations where the court declares that the *objective* of the impugned legislation is unconstitutional and also those where, because the issue is so controversial, political forces make it impossible for the legislature to fashion a response to the court's Charter decision. An example they provide of the latter is the situation that arose after the Supreme Court of Canada's decision in *R v. Morgentaler*, [1988] 1 SCR 30, found in Chapter 22, Life, Liberty, and Security of the Person, which struck down the restrictions on abortion in the *Criminal Code*. Although the Court's decision left open the possibility that a less restrictive abortion law could be upheld, the divisiveness of the abortion issue precluded the formation of any democratic consensus, and no new legislation was enacted.

Hogg and Bushell then go on to discuss, in greater detail, their research in which they looked at the sequels to all cases (65 in number) in which laws had been struck down by the Supreme Court of Canada for violations of the Charter. They found that legislative action followed in the vast majority of cases, and that the typical outcome was new legislation that accomplished the same legislative objective, but which was more protective of rights. In two cases the Court's ruling was effectively reversed by the legislature, once by invoking s. 1, and once by invoking s. 33.]

D. Dialogue May Occur Even When Laws Are Upheld

This article focussed primarily on the legislative changes that have followed decisions striking down laws for a breach of the *Charter*. However, it should be noted that judicial decisions can occasionally have an impact on legislation even when the Court does not actually strike down any law.

. . .

[I]t is a mistake to view the *Charter* as giving non-elected judges a veto over the democratic will of competent legislative bodies. Canada's legislators are not indifferent to the equality and civil liberties concerns which are raised in *Charter* cases, and do not always wait for a court to "force" them to amend their laws before they are willing to consider fairer, less restrictive, or more inclusive laws. The influence of the *Charter* extends much further than the boundaries of what judges define as compulsory. *Charter* dialogue may continue outside the courts even when the courts hold that there is no *Charter* issue to talk about.

VI. Conclusion

Our conclusion is that the critique of the *Charter* based on democratic legitimacy cannot be sustained. To be sure, the Supreme Court of Canada is a non-elected, unaccountable body of middle-aged lawyers. To be sure, it does from time to time strike down statutes enacted by the elected, accountable, representative legislative bodies. But, the decisions of the Court almost always leave room for a legislative response, and they usually get a legislative response. In the end, if the democratic will is there, the legislative objective will still be able to be accomplished, albeit with some new safeguards to protect individual rights and liberty. Judicial review is not "a veto over the politics of the nation," but rather the beginning of a dialogue as to how best to reconcile the individualistic values of the *Charter* with the accomplishment of social and economic policies for the benefit of the community as a whole.

The concept of judicial review under the Charter as part of a democratic dialogue between courts and legislatures is further explored in K. Roach, *The Supreme Court on Trial: Judicial Activism or Democratic Dialogue* (Toronto: Irwin Law, 2001). He argues that the American debate about judicial activism has been inappropriately imported into Canada, without a recognition of the fundamental structural differences between the Charter (and other modern bills of rights) and the American *Bill of Rights*. In Canada, he argues, because of the presence of sections 1 and 33, which explicitly allow governments to limit and even override rights, judges do not have the last word on controversial issues of social policy. In Professor Roach's view, the Charter has created "a fertile and democratic middle ground between the extremes of legislative and judicial supremacy." He writes (at 295):

A constructive and democratic dialogue between courts and legislatures under a modern bill of rights such as the *Charter* can improve the performance of both institutions. The independent judiciary can be robust and fearless in its protection of rights and freedoms, knowing that it need not have the last word. The legislature will be encouraged to consider whether it can pursue its objectives in a manner more respectful of rights and to establish rules in legislation to authorize and justify the conduct of the police and other state officials. ... The democratic dialogue between courts and legislatures under a modern bill of rights such as the *Charter* can avoid the monologues and unchecked power that may be produced by either unfettered legislative supremacy or unfettered judicial supremacy. It is especially necessary to diffuse power in countries where the parliamentary system of government, combined with tight party discipline, gives governments more or less absolute power between elections. Strong courts are needed to balance the power of strong legislatures.

He worries, however, about the negative impact that allegations of excessive "judicial activism" may have on the important role courts must play in this "dialogue" (at 295-96):

The greatest danger in the dialogue between courts and legislatures is not excessive judicial activism, because legislatures can and will correct judicial overreaching on behalf of minorities and the unpopular. The result will be a self-critical and democratic dialogue, even if judicial decisions do not prevail. If, however, the Court is too weak in protecting the rights of minorities and the unpopular, it is less likely that elected governments will do more. The result can be a complacent and majoritarian monologue that is less truly democratic. Excessive judicial deference will allow legislatures and officials to act without being questioned by the Court about the effects of their actions on the most unpopular among us. The sense that courts will not challenge questionable laws may inhibit their reform, especially if those adversely affected by the law have little political power. The greatest danger of the judicial activism debate is that it may produce excessive judicial deference. If this happens—and there are signs that it may be happening in Canada, and that misperceptions about the Canadian experience have dampened enthusiasm for judicial review in other places—then the democratic and dialogue potential of the *Charter* will be squandered by the unnecessary importation of an American-style judicial activism debate based on the false dichotomy of judicial supremacy or legislative supremacy. This failure would be a tragedy not only for Canada but for other countries as well. It might mean that we will all continue to spin our wheels in the two-century American debate about judicial activism, one that ignores the potential under modern bills of rights with parliamentary forms of government to have the benefits and the responsibility of both judicial activism and legislative activism.

The answer to unacceptable judicial activism under a modern bill of rights is legislative activism and the assertion of democratic responsibility for limiting or overriding the Court's decisions. Citizens can enjoy the benefits of judicial activism without the costs of judicial supremacy.

In the *Vriend* decision, an excerpt from which follows, the Supreme Court of Canada directly addressed the issue of the legitimacy of judicial review, and in particular the allegation that it is anti-democratic, drawing in part on the concept of dialogue as presented by Hogg and Bushell. In this important case, which you will encounter many times in subsequent chapters (including Chapter 18, Application, Chapter 23, Equality Rights, and Chapter 25, Enforcement of Rights), the Supreme Court of Canada found that the omission of sexual orientation from the list of prohibited grounds in Alberta's human rights legislation constituted an unjustifiable violation of s. 15 of the Charter, the equality rights guarantee. Iacobucci J entered into the discussion of the appropriate relationship between courts and legislatures as he began to deal with the remedial issues raised by the case. His comments were part of joint reasons that he wrote with Cory J, and with which Lamer CJC and Gonthier, McLachlin, and Bastarache JJ concurred.

Vriend v. Alberta
[1998] 1 SCR 493, 156 DLR (4th) 385

IACOBUCCI J: ... [129] Having found the exclusion of sexual orientation from the *IRPA* to be an unjustifiable violation of the appellants' equality rights, I now turn to the question of remedy under s. 52 of the *Constitution Act, 1982*. Before discussing the jurisprudence on remedies, I believe it might be helpful to pause to reflect more broadly on the general issue of the relationship between legislatures and the courts in the age of the Charter.

[130] Much was made in argument before us about the inadvisability of the Court interfering with or otherwise meddling in what is regarded as the proper role of the legislature, which in this case was to decide whether or not sexual orientation would be added to Alberta's human rights legislation. Indeed, it seems that hardly a day goes by without some comment or criticism to the effect that under the Charter courts are wrongfully usurping the role of the legislatures. I believe this allegation misunderstands what took place and what was intended when our country adopted the Charter in 1981-82.

[131] When the Charter was introduced, Canada went, in the words of former Chief Justice Brian Dickson, from a system of Parliamentary supremacy to constitutional supremacy ("Keynote Address," in *The Cambridge Lectures 1985* (1985), at pp. 3-4). Simply put, each Canadian was given individual rights and freedoms which no government or legislature could take away. However, as rights and freedoms are not absolute, governments and legislatures could justify the qualification or infringement of these constitutional rights under s. 1 as I previously discussed. Inevitably, disputes over the meaning of the rights and their justification would have to be settled and here the role of the judiciary enters to resolve these disputes. ...

[132] We should recall that it was the deliberate choice of our provincial and federal legislatures in adopting the Charter to assign an interpretive role to the courts and to command them under s. 52 to declare unconstitutional legislation invalid.

[133] However, giving courts the power and commandment to invalidate legislation where necessary has not eliminated the debate over the "legitimacy" of courts taking such action. ... [J]udicial review, it is alleged, is illegitimate because it is anti-democratic in that unelected officials (judges) are overruling elected representatives (legislators) ... .

[134] To respond, it should be emphasized again that our Charter's introduction and the consequential remedial role of the courts were choices of the Canadian people through their elected representatives as part of a redefinition of our democracy. Our constitutional design was refashioned to state that henceforth the legislatures and executive must perform their roles in conformity with the newly conferred constitutional

people chose.

rights and freedoms. That the courts were the trustees of these rights insofar as disputes arose concerning their interpretation was a necessary part of this new design.

[135] So courts in their trustee or arbiter role must perforce scrutinize the work of the legislature and executive not in the name of the courts, but in the interests of the new social contract that was democratically chosen. All of this is implied in the power given to the courts under s. 24 of the Charter and s. 52 of the *Constitution Act, 1982*.

[136] Because the courts are independent from the executive and legislature, litigants and citizens generally can rely on the courts to make reasoned and principled decisions according to the dictates of the constitution even though specific decisions may not be universally acclaimed. In carrying out their duties, courts are not to second-guess legislatures and the executives; they are not to make value judgments on what they regard as the proper policy choice; this is for the other branches. Rather, the courts are to uphold the Constitution and have been expressly invited to perform that role by the Constitution itself. But respect by the courts for the legislature and executive role is as important as ensuring that the other branches respect each others' role and the role of the courts.

[137] This mutual respect is in some ways expressed in the provisions of our constitution as shown by the wording of certain of the constitutional rights themselves. For example, s. 7 of the Charter speaks of no denial of the rights therein except in accordance with the principles of fundamental justice, which include the process of law and legislative action. Section 1 and the jurisprudence under it are also important to ensure respect for legislative action and the collective or societal interests represented by legislation. In addition, as will be discussed below, in fashioning a remedy with regard to a Charter violation, a court must be mindful of the role of the legislature. Moreover, s. 33, the notwithstanding clause, establishes that the final word in our constitutional structure is in fact left to the legislature and not the courts (see Peter W. Hogg and Allison A. Bushell, "The Charter Dialogue Between Courts and Legislatures" (1997), 35 *Osgoode Hall LJ* 75).

[138] As I view the matter, the Charter has given rise to a more dynamic interaction among the branches of governance. This interaction has been aptly described as a "dialogue" by some (see Hogg and Bushell, *supra*). In reviewing legislative enactments and executive decisions to ensure constitutional validity, the courts speak to the legislative and executive branches. As has been pointed out, most of the legislation held not to pass constitutional muster has been followed by new legislation designed to accomplish similar objectives (see Hogg and Bushell, *supra*, at p. 82). By doing this, the legislature responds to the courts; hence the dialogue among the branches.

[139] To my mind, a great value of judicial review and this dialogue among the branches is that each of the branches is made somewhat accountable to the other. The work of the legislature is reviewed by the courts and the work of the court in its decisions can be reacted to by the legislature in the passing of new legislation (or even overarching laws under s. 33 of the Charter). This dialogue between and accountability of each of the branches has the effect of enhancing the democratic process, not denying it.

[140] There is also another aspect of judicial review that promotes democratic values. Although a court's invalidation of legislation usually involves negating the will of the majority, we must remember that the concept of democracy is broader than the notion of majority rule, fundamental as that may be. In this respect, we would do well to heed the words of Dickson CJ in [*R v.*] *Oakes* [[1986] 1 SCR 103, 26 DLR (4th) 200] at p. 136:

> The Court must be guided by the values and principles essential to a free and democratic society, which I believe to embody, to name but a few, respect for the inherent dignity of the human person, commitment to social justice and equality, accommodation of a wide variety of beliefs, respect for cultural and group identity, and faith in social and political institutions which enhance the participation of individuals and groups in society.
>
> [141] So, for example, when a court interprets legislation alleged to be a reasonable limitation in a free and democratic society as stated in s. 1 of the Charter, the court must inevitably delineate some of the attributes of a free and democratic society. ... [In this respect] Dickson CJ's comments remain instructive ... .
>
> [142] Democratic values and principles under the Charter demand that legislators and the executive take these into account; and if they fail to do so, courts should stand ready to intervene to protect these democratic values as appropriate. As others have so forcefully stated, judges are not acting undemocratically by intervening when there are indications that a legislative or executive decision was not reached in accordance with the democratic principles mandated by the Charter ... .
>
> [Iacobucci J went on to deal with the remedial issue, and concluded that the appropriate remedy was to "read in" discrimination on grounds of sexual orientation. That portion of the judgment can be found in Chapter 25, Enforcement of Rights.]

The Supreme Court of Canada also referred to and endorsed the "dialogue" theory of judicial review in *R v. Mills*, [1999] 3 SCR 668, 26 DLR (4th) 161. Peter Hogg describes the case as follows ("The Charter Revolution: Is It Undemocratic?" (2001/2002), 12 *Constitutional Forum* 1, at 7):

> A dramatic example of the acceptance by the Supreme Court of Canada of the notion of dialogue is the *Mills* case, decided after the Hogg and Bushell study. In that case, the Court upheld a new set of rules for confidentiality of records of sexual assaults that were more restrictive of the accused's right to make full answer and defence than had been stipulated in the earlier *O'Connor* decision [[1995] 45 CR 411]. The Court offered the idea of dialogue as a reason for deferring to Parliament's judgment as to the appropriate balance between the accused's right to make full answer and defence and the privacy right of the complainant.

K. Roach (*The Supreme Court on Trial*, above, at 281) is critical of the use of the dialogue metaphor in *Mills*, suggesting that Parliament should have used the override to reverse the earlier decision in *O'Connor*, and that the Supreme Court of Canada's decision upholding the legislation may actually inhibit further dialogue on the difficult issues involved in the legislation by legitimating the legislation as consistent with the Charter: "Upholding legislation as constitutional sends a message to the legislature and society that all is well, and it may actually discourage continued legislative debate and reform of this controversial and possibly unconstitutional law."

F.L. Morton and R. Knopff, strong critics of "judicial activism," have argued that the dialogue theory is flawed and does not remove their fundamental concerns about the undemocratic nature of judicial review. In their book *The Charter Revolution and the Court Party* (Peterborough, ON: Broadview Press, 2000), they describe as a "revolution" the active role that judges, in particular the judges of the Supreme Court of Canada, have assumed in policy making since the advent of the Charter. In their view, the Supreme Court has been far more "activist" in the exercise of its new role under the Charter than it should have been. One significant aspect of the "Charter revolution" is the way in which a cluster of interest groups, often funded by government, and which they refer to as the "Court Party," have used the Charter to advance their policy interests in the courts, seeking to constitutionalize policy preferences that could not easily be achieved through the legislative process. Included in the Court Party are various equality-seeking and civil libertarian groups—for example, organizations representing feminists, gays and lesbians, and other disadvantaged minorities.

In their view, Hogg's defence of judicial review as a form of dialogue between legislatures and courts is too simplistic because it fails to recognize the "staying power" of a new, judicially created policy *status quo*, "especially when the issue cuts across the normal lines of partisan cleavage and divides a government caucus." One example they give is the political aftermath of the 1988 *Morgentaler* decision, in which the Supreme Court struck down the restrictions on abortion in the *Criminal Code* on the basis that they violated s. 7 of the Charter. The government introduced new legislation recriminalizing abortion, but with less onerous requirements. The legislation was ultimately defeated in the Senate, however, because both the pro-choice and pro-life minorities voted against the compromise legislation.

For a direct response to Morton and Knopff's critique of the Charter revolution, see P. Hogg, "The Charter Revolution: Is It Undemocratic?" (2001-2), 12 *Constitutional Forum* 1. Here is Hogg's answer to their criticisms of the dialogue concept (at 5-7):

> The compatibility of the *Charter* with democracy is reinforced by the notion of judicial review as a "dialogue" between the Supreme Court of Canada and the legislatures. ...
>
> This idea of a dialogue between courts and legislatures is a serious challenge to the Morton-Knopff thesis. If *Charter* decisions are ultimately reviewable by elected legislative bodies, using the distinctively Canadian vehicles of sections 1 or 33, then it becomes much less significant whether the decisions have been achieved through the efforts of the Court Party or have been made in disregard of popular sentiment. In the last few pages of the book, the authors grapple with this problem. Professors Morton and Knopff acknowledge that the dialogue theory is "undoubtedly true in the abstract," but they say that it is "too simplistic." It is too simplistic because it "fails to recognize the staying power of a new, judicially created policy status quo." By this they mean that once the Court has spoken governments may find it expedient to leave the issue alone, thus preserving the judicial decision.
>
> One of the two examples Morton and Knopff provide of "the staying power of the new judicially-created policy status quo" is the aftermath to the *Morgentaler* decision, which struck down the therapeutic abortion provisions of the *Criminal Code* on the ground that they offended section 7 of the *Charter*. The Government of Canada introduced a new bill to recriminalize abortion, but with less onerous requirements for legal therapeutic abortions. The new bill was passed by the House of Commons and then defeated in the Senate on a tie vote. To be sure, the *status quo* created by the Supreme Court of Canada (no regulation of abortion) was preserved. But this example could as easily be treated as a case of dialogue since the Government did propose a substitute law for the one struck down and very nearly succeeded in enacting it.

The other example they provide is the aftermath of the *Vriend* decision, where the Supreme Court of Canada added sexual orientation to the grounds of discrimination for which a remedy was available under Alberta's *Human Rights, Citizenship and Multicultural Act*. The Government of Alberta mused publicly about restoring the old version of the statute by invoking section 33, but eventually decided not to do so, thus leaving the new ground of sexual orientation in the *Act*. The authors comment that the judicial ruling had "raised the political costs of saying no to the winning minority" and the Government concluded that "the safest thing was to do nothing." But what does this example show? Only that it is politically difficult to directly reverse a decision of the Supreme Court of Canada on an equality issue. Is that not as it should be? Reversal is possible in a case where there is a sufficiently strong popular revulsion of the Court's ruling, and this is an exceedingly important safeguard … .

… [T]he power to reverse a judicial ruling has in fact been exercised twice in Canada. It was done once by the National Assembly of Quebec, which reversed the *Ford* decision and restored its French-only law for commercial signs, and it was done once by the Parliament of Canada, which reversed the *Daviault* decision and restored the rule that intoxication is no defence to criminal offences of general intent. The decision of the Government of Alberta not to attempt to reverse the *Vriend* decision was probably based on a correct judgment that popular support was lacking for such a move. The fact that the move was legally possible and was seriously examined by the Government means that the sequel to *Vriend* could easily be regarded as an example of dialogue rather than as an example that contradicts the dialogue idea.

In any event, *Ford*, *Daviault* and *Vriend* are not typical cases. In the great majority of *Charter* cases, there is no political impulse to directly reverse the judicial decision. Usually, the attitude of the government whose law was struck down is not one of hostility to the Court's civil libertarian concern; rather, the issue for the government is (as it was after *Morgentaler*) the crafting of a new law that accommodates the Court's concerns while preserving the legislative objective … .

To return to the Morton-Knopff thesis, in the majority of *Charter* cases, the "staying power of a new judicially created policy status quo" is not very strong at all. In those rare cases where government simply cannot abide the Court's interpretation of the *Charter*, reversal is usually legally possible, and can be accomplished politically where public opinion is particularly strong, as *Ford* and *Daviault* demonstrate. Where public opinion is less strong or is divided, government may choose to leave the decision in place, as *Vriend* demonstrates.

The important point about the idea of dialogue is that judicial decisions striking down laws are not necessarily the last word on the issue, and are not usually the last word on the issue. The legislative process is influenced by but is not stopped in its tracks by a *Charter* decision. The ultimate outcome is normally up to the legislative body.

For other responses to Morton and Knopff, see R. Elliot, "The Charter Revolution and the Court Party: Sound Critical Analysis or Blinkered Political Polemic?" (2002), 35 *University of British Columbia Law Review* 271 and M. Smith, "Ghosts of the Judicial Committee of the Privy Council: Group Politics and Charter Litigation in Canadian Political Science" (2002), 35 *Canadian Journal of Political Science* 1.

CHAPTER SEVENTEEN

The Framework of the Charter

The Charter establishes a two-step process for the adjudication of rights claims. The first step is concerned with whether a Charter right has been breached by a state act. The court must define the protected interest or activity and determine whether it has been interfered with by the state. At this stage the burden of proof lies with the party claiming a breach of rights. The court will proceed to the second step of the adjudicative process only if it finds that a Charter right has been breached. This second step is concerned with the justification of limits on Charter rights. Section 1 of the Charter states that the protected rights and freedoms may be limited provided the limits are "prescribed by law," "reasonable," and "demonstrably justified." At this stage the burden of proof lies with the party seeking to uphold the limitation, usually the state.

This chapter will examine, in general terms, the two-step structure of Charter adjudication—the interpretation of rights and the justification of limits. It will also examine s. 33, the "notwithstanding clause" that enables the federal Parliament or provincial legislature to insulate a law from challenge on certain grounds. Other components of Charter analysis will be examined in subsequent chapters. The question of who is bound to respect Charter rights will be considered in Chapter 18, Application, and the question of what remedies are available to a court if it finds that a Charter right has been breached will be considered in Chapter 25, Enforcement of Rights.

I. INTERPRETING RIGHTS

The chapters that follow will deal in detail with the interpretation of specific Charter rights. The material here is intended to provide only a brief introduction to the courts' general approach to the interpretation of these rights.

A. The Purposive Approach

The courts have a adopted a "purposive approach" to the interpretation of Charter rights. In *Hunter v. Southam*, which follows, the Supreme Court of Canada stated that a judgment about the scope or value of a particular right can only be made after the court has "specif[ied] the purpose underlying" the right or "delineate[d] the nature of the interests it is meant to protect."

CHAPTER SEVENTEEN

The Framework of the Charter

The Charter establishes a two-step process for the adjudication of rights claims. The first step is concerned with whether a Charter right has been breached by a state act. The court must define the protected interest or activity and determine whether it has been interfered with by the state. At this stage the burden of proof lies with the party claiming a breach of rights. The court will proceed to the second step of the adjudicative process only if it finds that a Charter right has been breached. This second step is concerned with the justification of limits on Charter rights. Section 1 of the Charter states that the protected rights and freedoms may be limited provided the limits are "prescribed by law," "reasonable," and "demonstrably justified." At this stage the burden of proof lies with the party seeking to uphold the limitation, usually the state.

This chapter will examine, in general terms, the two-step structure of Charter adjudication—the interpretation of rights and the justification of limits. It will also examine s. 33, the "notwithstanding clause" that enables the federal Parliament or provincial legislature to insulate a law from challenge on certain grounds. Other components of Charter analysis will be examined in subsequent chapters. The question of who is bound to respect Charter rights will be considered in Chapter 18, Application, and the question of what remedies are available to a court if it finds that a Charter right has been breached will be considered in Chapter 25, Enforcement of Rights.

I. INTERPRETING RIGHTS

The chapters that follow will deal in detail with the interpretation of specific Charter rights. The material here is intended to provide only a brief introduction to the courts' general approach to the interpretation of these rights.

A. The Purposive Approach

The courts have a adopted a "purposive approach" to the interpretation of Charter rights. In *Hunter v. Southam*, which follows, the Supreme Court of Canada stated that a judgment about the scope or value of a particular right can only be made after the court has "specif[ied] the purpose underlying" the right or "delineate[d] the nature of the interests it is meant to protect."

757

Hunter v. Southam
[1984] 2 SCR 145, 11 DLR (4th) 641

[This early Charter case involved the s. 8 guarantee of freedom from unreasonable search and seizure. A search of newspaper offices was carried out by the Combines Investigation Branch. The statutory basis for the search did not require prior judicial authorization. In the following excerpt, Dickson CJC, writing for the Court, discussed Charter interpretation.]

DICKSON CJC (Ritchie, Beetz, Estey, McIntyre, Chouinard, Lamer, and Wilson JJ concurring): ... As is clear from the arguments of the parties as well as from the judgment of Prowse JA, the crux of this case is the meaning to be given to the term "unreasonable" in the s. 8 guarantee of freedom from unreasonable search or seizure. The guarantee is vague and open. The American courts have had the advantage of a number of specific prerequisites articulated in the Fourth Amendment to the United States Constitution, as well as a history of colonial opposition to certain Crown investigatory practices from which to draw out the nature of the interests protected by that Amendment and the kinds of conduct it proscribes. There is none of this in s. 8. There is no specificity in the section beyond the bare guarantee of freedom from "unreasonable" search and seizure; nor is there any particular historical, political or philosophic context capable of providing an obvious gloss on the meaning of the guarantee.

It is clear that the meaning of "unreasonable" cannot be determined by recourse to a dictionary, nor for that matter, by reference to the rules of statutory construction. The task of expounding a Constitution is crucially different from that of construing a statute. A statute defines present rights and obligations. It is easily enacted and as easily repealed. A Constitution, by contrast, is drafted with an eye to the future. Its function is to provide a continuing framework for the legitimate exercise of governmental power and, when joined by a Bill or a Charter of rights, for the unremitting protection of individual rights and liberties. Once enacted, its provisions cannot easily be repealed or amended. It must, therefore, be capable of growth and development over time to meet new social, political and historical realities often unimagined by its framers. The judiciary is the guardian of the Constitution and must, in interpreting its provisions, bear these considerations in mind. Professor Paul Freund expressed this idea aptly when he admonished the American courts "not to read the provisions of the Constitution like a last will and testament lest it become one."

The need for a broad perspective in approaching constitutional documents is a familiar theme in Canadian constitutional jurisprudence. It is contained in Viscount Sankey's classic formulation in *Re s. 24 of BNA Act; Edwards v. A-G Can.*, [1930] 1 DLR 98 at pp. 106-7, [1930] AC 124 at pp. 136-37, cited and applied in countless Canadian cases:

> The *BNA Act* planted in Canada a living tree capable of growth and expansion within its natural limits. The object of the Act was to grant a Constitution to Canada. ...
>
> Their Lordships do not conceive it to be the duty of this Board—it is certainly not their desire—to cut down the provisions of the Act by a narrow and technical construction, but rather to give it a large and liberal interpretation ... .

More recently, in *Minister of Home Affairs et al. v. Fisher et al.*, [1980] AC 319 at p. 329, dealing with the Bermudian Constitution, Lord Wilberforce reiterated that a constitution is a document "*sui generis*, calling for principles of interpretation of its own, suitable to its character," and that as such, a constitution incorporating a *Bill of Rights* calls for [at 328]: "a generous interpretation avoiding what has been called 'the austerity of tabulated legalism' suitable to give to individuals the full measure of the fundamental rights and freedoms referred to." Such a broad, purposive analysis, which interprets specific provisions of a constitutional document in the light of its larger objects, is also consonant with the classical principles of American constitutional construction enunciated by Chief Justice Marshall in *M'Culloch v. State of Maryland* (1819), 17 US (4 Wheaton) 316. It is, as well, the approach I intend to take in the present case.

I begin with the obvious. The *Canadian Charter of Rights and Freedoms* is a purposive document. Its purpose is to guarantee and to protect, within the limits of reason, the enjoyment of the rights and freedoms it enshrines. It is intended to constrain governmental action inconsistent with those rights and freedoms; it is not in itself an authorization for governmental action. In the present case this means, as Prowse JA pointed out, that in guaranteeing the right to be secure from unreasonable searches and seizures, s. 8 acts as a limitation on whatever powers of search and seizure the federal or provincial governments already and otherwise possess. It does not in itself confer any powers, even of "reasonable" search and seizure, on these governments. This leads, in my view, to the further conclusion that an assessment of the constitutionality of a search and seizure, or of a statute authorizing a search or seizure, must focus on its "reasonable" or "unreasonable" impact on the subject of the search or the seizure, and not simply on its rationality in furthering some valid government objective.

Since the proper approach to the interpretation of the *Canadian Charter of Rights and Freedoms* is a purposive one, before it is possible to assess the reasonableness or unreasonableness of the impact of a search or of a statute authorizing a search, it is first necessary to specify the purpose underlying s. 8: in other words, to delineate the nature of the interests it is meant to protect. ...

[Dickson CJC went on to determine that the US Supreme Court's understanding of the protection against search and seizure, as primarily property based, was inappropriate to the interpretation of s. 8. His analysis of the purpose for which security against unreasonable search and seizure is protected led him to conclude that s. 8 protects an individual's reasonable expectation of privacy. Accordingly he found invalid those provisions of the *Combines Investigation Act*, RSC 1970, c. C-23, ss. 10(1) and (3) that authorized the issuance of search warrants by officials whose functions were investigative, without any requirement for reasonable and probable grounds, based on sworn material, to believe that an offence had been committed and that the place of search would afford evidence of the commission of the offence.]

Appeal dismissed.

NOTES AND QUESTIONS

1. In *R v. Big M Drug Mart Ltd.*, [1985] 1 SCR 295, 18 DLR (4th) 321, another early Charter case, included in Chapter 19, Freedom of Religion, Dickson CJC reiterated the Court's commitment to a purposive approach:

> This Court has already, in some measure, set out the basic approach to be taken in interpreting the Charter. In *Hunter v. Southam Inc.*, [1984] 2 SCR 145 [11 DLR (4th) 641], this Court expressed the view that the proper approach to the definition of the rights and freedoms guaranteed by the Charter was a purposive one. The meaning of a right or freedom guaranteed by the Charter was to be ascertained by an analysis of the purpose of such a guarantee; it was to be understood, in other words, in the light of the interests it was meant to protect. In my view this analysis is to be undertaken, and the purpose of the right or freedom in question is to be sought by reference to the character and the larger objects of the Charter itself, to the language chosen to articulate the specific right or freedom, to the historical origins of the concepts enshrined, and where applicable, to the meaning and purpose of the other specific rights and freedoms with which it is associated within the text of the Charter. The interpretation should be, as the judgment in *Southam* emphasizes, a generous rather than a legalistic one, aimed at fulfilling the purpose of the guarantee and securing for individuals the full benefit of the Charter's protection. At the same time it is important not to overshoot the actual purpose of the right or freedom in question, but to recall that the Charter was not enacted in a vacuum, and must therefore, as this Court's decision in *Law Society of Upper Canada v. Skapinker*, [1984] 1 SCR 357 [9 DLR (4th) 161], illustrates, be placed in its proper linguistic, philosophic and historical contexts.

2. In *Hunter v. Southam* the Court stated that the task of interpreting the Constitution is "crucially different" from that of interpreting an ordinary statute. Do the courts not interpret statutes in light of the interests they are intended to protect? Are statutes not also forward looking? The Charter uses language that is more general than that which ordinarily appears in statutes. It entrenches abstract moral/political ideals, which are, in their elaboration or application, subject to significant disagreement. As you study specific rights in the chapters that follow, consider how much guidance the purposive approach gives the courts when defining the scope and limits of these rights. On the one hand, the court wants the attribution of a particular purpose to be relatively uncontroversial. (The attributed purpose sometimes sounds like a restatement of the right in equally abstract terms.) Yet, on the other hand, this attribution of purpose is meant to give real content to the right and to guide the court in the resolution of particular issues.

3. In *R v. Therens*, [1985] 1 SCR 613, 18 DLR (4th) 655, the Supreme Court of Canada observed that the inclusion of s. 1 in the Charter is conducive to a broad and purposive approach to the interpretation of particular rights: "[U]nder the Charter the right [to counsel] is made expressly subject by s. 1 to such reasonable limits as are demonstrably justified in a free and democratic society. Thus the right is expressly qualified in a way that permits more flexible treatment of it." Because competing interests can be recognized at the s. 1 stage, it is not necessary for the courts to read "internal" limits into the definition of a particular right—to narrow their understanding of the interests protected by the right.

The courts sometimes seem to use the expressions "purposive interpretation" and "generous interpretation" interchangeably. Is there a difference between them? Is it not possible that a purposive interpretation could result in limits being placed on the potential scope of a right?

4. The two-step structure of adjudication rests on the idea that there are two distinct issues to be addressed—the definition of the right and the justification of limits. The scope of the right is defined in terms of the interests it protects or advances. Any activity that advances the right's purpose falls within its scope. Other interests that compete or conflict with those that underlie the right may be taken into account under s. 1 as possible grounds for limitation. When you read the cases in later chapters consider whether the distinction between these different interests really is so straightforward—particularly if the purposive approach is unable to yield a bright line between activity that advances the purpose (and is protected) and activity that does not. How distinct are scope and limitations issues in the case of s. 2(a) and s. 2(b)? When you study rights such as s. 15, the right to equality, and s. 7, the right to fundamental justice, consider how much space the courts' interpretation of these rights leaves for the justification of limits under s. 1.

5. In its early Charter judgments, the Supreme Court of Canada seemed comfortable reviewing legislative and other forms of state action to ensure that it conformed with constitutional rights and freedoms. However, as you will see when you read more recent judgments, the Court (or at least some members of the Court) seems to have lost some of this initial confidence.

In *Reference re Section 94(2) of the Motor Vehicle Act (BC)*, [1985] 2 SCR 486, 24 DLR (4th) 536 (more fully extracted in Chapter 22, Life, Liberty, and Security of the Person), Lamer J stated:

> [The] argument [that the judiciary is not representative] was heard countless times prior to the entrenchment of the Charter but ... has in truth, for better or for worse, been settled by the very coming into force of the *Constitution Act, 1982*. It ought not to be forgotten that the historic decision to entrench the Charter in our Constitution was taken not by the courts but by the elected representatives of the people of Canada. It was those representatives who extended the scope of constitutional adjudication and entrusted the courts with this new and onerous responsibility. Adjudication under the Charter must be approached free of any lingering doubts as to its legitimacy.

There is a close link between the courts' perception of the legitimacy of their role and their general approach to rights adjudication. Despite the protests of Lamer J, concerns about the legitimacy of judicial review, and the competence of the courts to address complex social and political issues, have almost certainly affected their approach to the interpretation of particular rights and to the justification of limits under s. 1.

B. Aids to Interpretation

Purposive interpretation of Charter rights poses enormous challenges to courts. How does a judge go about determining the purpose of a particular Charter right? Dickson CJC offers some preliminary guidance in the passage from *Big M* found in note 1 above. What follows is a brief overview of some of the possible aids to Charter interpretation and the extent to which the courts have been willing to make use of them.

1. Interpretive Provisions in the Charter

The Charter includes several provisions that do not entrench a particular right, but instead affirm or highlight certain values that are to be taken into account when interpreting the entrenched rights and assessing the justification of limits under s. 1. These provisions include s. 27, which provides that the Charter "shall be interpreted in a manner consistent with the preservation and enhancement of the multicultural heritage of Canadians," and s. 28, which provides that "Notwithstanding anything in this Charter, the rights and freedoms referred to in it are guaranteed equally to male and female persons."

These sections are frequently referred to in Charter decisions. However, their impact in particular cases is difficult to measure. In *R v. Keegstra*, [1990] 3 SCR 697, 124 DLR (4th) 289, a decision concerning the constitutionality of a criminal ban on hate promotion (which is more fully extracted in Chapter 20, Freedom of Expression), Dickson CJC said about s. 27:

> This Court has where possible taken account of s. 27 and its recognition that Canada possesses a multicultural society in which the diversity and richness of various cultural groups is a value to be protected and enhanced. Section 27 has therefore been used in a number of judgments of this Court, both as an aid in interpreting the definition of Charter rights and freedoms ... and as an element of the s. 1 analysis.

2. Parliamentary and Committee Debates

In *Reference re Section 94(2) of the Motor Vehicle Act (BC)*, [1985] 2 SCR 486, 24 DLR (4th) 536, an early Charter case discussed in Chapter 22, Life, Liberty, and Security of the Person, the Court considered the relevance of the committee and Parliamentary debates, which preceded the enactment of the Charter, to the interpretation of the entrenched rights:

> LAMER J (Dickson CJC, Beetz, Chouinard, and Le Dain JJ concurring): ... If speeches and declarations by prominent figures are inherently unreliable and "speeches made in the Legislature at the time of enactment of the measure are inadmissible as having little evidential weight" ... the Minutes of the Proceedings of the Special Joint Committee, though admissible, and granted somewhat more weight than speeches should not be given too much weight. The inherent unreliability of such statements and speeches is not altered by the mere fact that they pertain to the Charter rather than a statute.
>
> Moreover, the simple fact remains that the Charter is not the product of a few individual public servants, however distinguished, but of a multiplicity of individuals who played major roles in the negotiating, drafting and adoption of the Charter. How can one say with any confidence that within this enormous multiplicity of actors, without forgetting the role of the provinces, the comments of a few federal civil servants can in any way be determinative? Were this Court to accord any significant weight to this testimony, it would in effect be assuming a fact which is nearly impossible of proof, i.e., the intention of the legislative bodies which adopted the Charter. In view of the indeterminate nature of the data, it would in my view be erroneous to give these materials anything but minimal weight.
>
> Another danger with casting the interpretation of s. 7 in terms of the comments made by those heard at the Special Joint Committee Proceedings is that, in so doing, the rights, freedoms and values embodied in the Charter in effect become frozen in time to the moment of

adoption with little or no possibility of growth, development and adjustment to changing societal needs. Obviously, in the present case, given the proximity in time of the Charter debates, such a problem is relatively minor, even though it must be noted that even at this early stage in the life of the Charter, a host of issues and questions have been raised which were largely unforeseen at the time of such proceedings. If the newly planted "living tree" which is the Charter is to have the possibility of growth and adjustment over time, care must be taken to ensure that historical materials, such as the Minutes of Proceedings and Evidence of the Special Joint Committee, do not stunt its growth.

3. Canadian Pre-Charter Jurisprudence

In several early Charter judgments, the Supreme Court of Canada signaled that decisions under the *Canadian Bill of Rights* (the pre-Charter rights-protecting statute of the federal government discussed in Chapter 15, Antecedents of the Charter) had only limited relevance in Charter cases, given the different constitutional status and structure of the Charter. In *R v. Therens*, [1985] 1 SCR 613, 18 DLR (4th) 655, Le Dain J stated that:

> In considering the relationship of a decision under the *Canadian Bill of Rights* to an issue arising under the Charter, a court cannot, in my respectful opinion, avoid bearing in mind an evident fact of Canadian judicial history, which must be squarely and frankly faced: that on the whole, with some notable exceptions, the courts have felt some uncertainty or ambivalence in the application of the *Canadian Bill of Rights* because it did not reflect a clear constitutional mandate to make judicial decisions having the effect of limiting or qualifying the traditional sovereignty of Parliament. The significance of the new constitutional mandate for judicial review provided by the Charter was emphasized by this Court in … *Hunter v. Southam.*

4. Comparative and International Sources

In seeking to give meaning to the Charter's rights and to determine whether the limits imposed on these rights by democratic institutions are reasonable and just, Canadian courts have drawn on international experience in rights protection. Even though much of the language of the Charter's text was new and "made in Canada," the drafters of the Charter had in many cases drawn on the text of other rights-protecting instruments. It made sense then that the Canadian courts would look to judgments in other jurisdictions interpreting these rights documents. The American *Bill of Rights* provides an obvious model for the Canadian courts. It is a centuries-old document that has generated a considerable body of case law.

While the Canadian courts often refer to American cases and commentary in their Charter decisions, they have said that these sources should be used with caution. In *R v. Keegstra*, [1990] 3 SCR 697, 124 DLR (4th) 289 (which dealt with the restriction of hate promotion and is found in Chapter 20, Freedom of Expression), Chief Justice Dickson noted that:

> In the United States, a collection of fundamental rights has been constitutionally protected for over two hundred years. The resulting practical and theoretical experience is immense, and should not be overlooked by Canadian courts. On the other hand, we must examine American constitutional law with a critical eye, and in this respect La Forest J has noted in *R v. Rahey*, [1987] 1 SCR 588 [39 DLR (4th) 481], at p. 639:

While it is natural and even desirable for Canadian courts to refer to American constitutional jurisprudence in seeking to elucidate the meaning of Charter guarantees that
have counterparts in the United States Constitution, they should be wary of drawing too
ready a parallel between constitutions born to different countries in different ages and in
very different circumstances ... .

Canada and the United States are not alike in every way, nor have the documents entrenching
human rights in our two countries arisen in the same context. It is only common sense to recognize that, just as similarities will justify borrowing from the American experience, differences
may require that Canada's constitutional vision depart from that endorsed in the United States.

More modern and more textually similar models are provided by international, post-
World War II instruments, notably the *International Covenant on Civil and Political Rights*
(adopted by the United Nations in 1966 and which came into force in 1976); the *International Covenant on Social, Economic and Cultural Rights* (adopted by the United Nations
in 1966 and which came into force in 1976); and the *European Convention for the Protection
of Human Rights and Fundamental Freedoms* (a rights document binding European countries, which came into force in 1953 and under which cases of infringement are brought before the European Court of Human Rights). In a wide range of cases, courts have looked to
international sources when interpreting the scope of Charter rights and assessing the justification of limits. According to Dickson CJC in *R v. Keegstra*, above, "[T]he international
human rights obligations taken on by Canada reflect the values and principles of a free and
democratic society, and thus those values and principles that underlie the Charter itself."
The following excerpt describes how the judiciary has relied on international instruments
and, in particular, the International Covenant on Economic, Social and Cultural Rights
(ICESCR) to interpret the terms of the Charter.

Patrick Macklem, "Social Rights in Canada"
in D. Barak-Erez and E. Gross, eds., *Exploring Social Rights: Between Theory and
Practice* (Oxford: Hart Publishing, 2007), 213, at 227-29 (footnotes omitted)

International law has become a prominent and significant feature of judicial interpretation by the Supreme Court of Canada of the nature and content of rights and freedoms
guaranteed by the *Charter of Rights and Freedoms*. In *Reference re Public Service Employee
Relations Act (Alberta)* [[1987] 1 SCR 313, 38 DLR (4th) 161, discussed in Chapter 21,
Freedom of Association], Dickson CJ, dissenting on other grounds, stated that

[t]he various sources of international human rights law—declarations, covenants, conventions, judicial and quasi-judicial decisions of international tribunals, customary norms—
must, in my opinion, be relevant and persuasive sources for interpretation of the Charter's
provisions.

In the same case, Dickson CJ also stated that "the Charter should generally be presumed to provide protection at least as great as that afforded by similar provisions in
international human rights documents which Canada has ratified." More recently, the
Court made reference to ILO jurisprudence on freedom of association and interpreted

the domestic constitutional guarantee of freedom of association as requiring legislative action to secure its protection. [*Health Services and Support v. British Columbia*, [2007] 2 SCR 391, 283 DLR (4th) 40 (discussed in Chapter 21, Freedom of Association).]

Recent cases have made it clear that the Court is not solely looking to treaties that Canada has ratified for guidance when interpreting the Charter. In *Suresh v. Canada (Minister of Citizenship and Immigration)* [[2002] 1 SCR 3, 208 DLR (4th) 1], for example, the Court relied on at least one international treaty to which Canada is not party to reach the conclusion "that international law rejects deportation to torture, even where national security interests are at stake," and that this norm "best informs the content of the principles of fundamental justice under s. 7 of the Charter."

Despite the fact that there are significant textual differences between the two instruments, Canada's international legal obligations under the ICESCR are therefore relevant to the interpretation of domestic constitutional guarantees. In *Canadian Egg Marketing Agency v. Richardson* [[1998] 3 SCR 157, 166 DLR (4th) 1 (discussed in Chapter 10, Economic Regulation)], for example, the Court relied on Article 6 of the ICESCR, which guarantees the right to work, in support of its conclusion that mobility rights enshrined in s. 6 of the Charter protect a right to pursue one's livelihood across provincial boundaries. In *R v. Advance Cutting & Coring* [[2001] 3 SCR 209, 205 DLR (4th) 385 (discussed in Chapter 21, Freedom of Association)], a minority of the Court, dissenting on other grounds, cited Article 8(1)(a) of the ICESCR, which guarantees the right to join a trade union of one's choice, to affirm that freedom of association as guaranteed by the Charter includes a negative right not to be compelled to belong to an association.

In addition, the ICESCR is relevant to determinations of determining what constitute reasonable limits on the exercise of a Charter right or freedom, specifically whether a legislative objective is sufficiently important to justify an infringement of a Charter guarantee. In *Slaight Communications* [[1989] 1 SCR 1038, 59 DLR (4th) 416 (discussed in Chapter 20, Freedom of Expression)], Dickson CJ, referring to Article 6 of the ICESCR, held that "the fact that a value has the status of an international human right, either in customary international law or under a treaty to which Canada is a State Party, should generally be indicative of a high degree of importance attached to that objective." Similarly, in *R v. Sharpe* [2001] 1 SCR 45, 194 DLR (4th) 1 [extracted in Chapter 20, Freedom of Expression)], Article 10(3) of the ICESCR, which calls on states to protect children "from economic and social exploitation," was invoked in support of the proposition that legislation criminalising the possession of child pornography possessed an objective sufficiently compelling to justify interfering with freedom of expression guaranteed by the Charter.

II. DEFINING LIMITATIONS: SECTION 1

This section introduces the two main structural components of s. 1: first, the requirement that all limits on rights be "prescribed by law" and second, the requirement that limits be "reasonable" and "demonstrably justified in a free and democratic society."

A. Prescribed by Law

Before the government (or any other party defending a Charter challenge) may argue that competing interests justify the limitation of a Charter right, it must first show that the limit is "prescribed by law." The requirement that a limit on a Charter right have the form of "law" serves a gatekeeper function, limiting the number of instances in which an infringement will be upheld under s. 1.

The European Court of Human Rights considered the term "prescribed by law," which is included in the *European Convention on Human Rights*, in *Sunday Times v. United Kingdom* (1979), 2 EHRR 271. The *Sunday Times* newspaper was prohibited by injunction from publishing an article about thalidomide-related birth defects on the grounds that such a publication might interfere with the course of lengthy, ongoing legal proceedings against the manufacturer of the drug. Breach of the injunction would constitute contempt of court. The *Sunday Times* argued that the injunction infringed its right to freedom of speech. The question arose whether the common law rule allowing a contempt action for breach of the injunction constituted a limit that was prescribed by law on the right to freedom of expression under the European Convention. The European Court made the following comments:

> In the Court's opinion, the following are two of the requirements that flow from the expression "prescribed by law." First, the law must be adequately accessible: the citizen must be able to have an indication that is adequate in the circumstances of the legal rules applicable to a given case. Secondly, a norm cannot be regarded as "law" unless it is formulated with sufficient precision to enable the citizen to regulate his conduct: he must be able—if need be with appropriate advice—to foresee, to a degree that is reasonable in the circumstances, the consequences which a given action may entail. Those consequences need not be foreseeable with absolute certainty: experience shows this to be unattainable. Again whilst certainty is highly desirable, it may bring in its train excessive rigidity and the law must be able to keep pace with changing circumstances. Accordingly, many laws are inevitably couched in terms which, to a greater or lesser extent, are vague and whose interpretation and application are questions of practice.

The two related values advanced by the "prescribed by law" requirement, according to the European Court, are accessibility and intelligibility to the citizen, the person subject to the law. Both of these values fall under the more general concept of notice to the citizen. Another justification offered for the "prescribed by law" requirement is the need to ensure public accountability for any restriction on a constitutional right. A commitment to public accountability precludes the legislature from granting broad discretion to administrative actors to limit protected rights.

In *R v. Therens*, [1985] 1 SCR 613, 18 DLR (4th) 655, Le Dain J stated that:

> The requirement that the limit be prescribed by law is chiefly concerned with the distinction between a limit imposed by law and one that is arbitrary. The limit will be prescribed by law within the meaning of s. 1 if it is expressly provided for by statute or regulation, or results by necessary implication from the terms of a statute or regulation or from its operating requirements. The limit may also result from the application of a common law rule.

In *Therens*, the accused had been required to accompany a police officer and take a breathalyzer test pursuant to s. 235 of the *Criminal Code*. The accused was not informed of his right to retain and instruct counsel. The Court held that the accused had been detained and that his s. 10(b) right to counsel had been breached. The Court went on to find that the limit on his right was not "prescribed by law." Section 235(1) of the *Criminal Code* stated that the motorist was required to supply a sample of breath at the time of the demand "or as soon thereafter as is practicable." Parliament did not purport to prescribe any limit on s. 10(b). The Court contrasted s. 235(1) with s. 234.1, which required that a motorist take a roadside breathalyzer test "forthwith" following a demand. The term "forthwith" could be understood as precluding the right to counsel.

Not surprisingly, the "rule of law" values that underlie the "prescribed by law" requirement appear in several other Charter contexts. For example, the courts have found that a law that interferes with life, liberty, or security of the person will not be in accordance with principles of fundamental justice under s. 7 if it is too vague. Concerns about vagueness or intelligibility are relevant considerations elsewhere in the courts' s. 1 analysis and in particular in their judgment as to whether a law restricts the right or freedom as little as is necessary to advance the law's pressing and substantial purpose.

The courts have been reluctant to set too high a standard for the prescribed by law requirement, concerned that an excessive emphasis on precision in language may unduly restrict legislatures in accomplishing their objectives. In *Irwin Toy Ltd. v. Quebec (Attorney General)*, [1989] 1 SCR 927, 58 DLR (4th) 577 (which is included in Chapter 20, Freedom of Expression), Dickson CJC and Lamer and Wilson JJ stated that:

> Absolute precision in the law exists rarely, if at all. The question is whether the legislature has provided an intelligible standard according to which the judiciary must do its work. The task of interpreting how that standard applies in particular instances might always be characterized as having a discretionary element, because the standard can never specify all the instances in which it applies. On the other hand, where there is no intelligible standard and where the legislature has given a plenary discretion to do whatever seems best in a wide set of circumstances, there is no "limit prescribed by law."

In *Irwin Toy*, a corporation brought a Charter challenge (principally on freedom of expression grounds) against a Quebec law, which prohibited commercial advertising directed at children under the age of 13. The law provided that in determining "whether or not an advertisement is directed at persons under thirteen years of age, account must be taken of the context of its presentation, and in particular of (a) the nature of the goods advertised; (b) the manner of presenting such advertisement; (c) the time and place it is shown." The Court found that the restriction was sufficiently clear to satisfy the prescribed by law standard, and then went on to uphold the law as a justified restriction on freedom of expression.

In many cases, courts have preferred to deal with the claim that a restriction is too vague or too broad in its grant of discretion at the second stage of its s. 1 analysis as part of a general (and contextual) balancing of competing interests. For example, in *Taylor v. Canadian Human Rights Commission*, [1990] 3 SCR 892, 75 DLR (4th) 577 (which is discussed in Chapter 20, Freedom of Expression), McLachlin J said:

> [T]he difficulty in ascribing a constant and universal meaning to the terms used [in the section being challenged] is a factor to be taken into account in assessing whether a law is "demonstrably justified in a free and democratic society." But I would be reluctant to circumvent the entire

balancing analysis of the s. 1 test by finding that the words used were so vague as not to constitute a "limit prescribed by law," unless the provision could truly be described as failing to offer
an intelligible standard.

While McLachlin J dissented from the final result in the case, there was no disagreement on
the issue of prescribed by law. In *Taylor* the entire Court held that a provision of the *Canadian Human Rights Act* (which provided that it was a discriminatory practice to use the telephone to communicate repeatedly any matter likely to expose persons to hatred or contempt
on certain grounds) was sufficiently precise to constitute a limit prescribed by law.

In *Osborne v. Canada (Treasury Board)*, [1991] 2 SCR 69, 82 DLR (4th) 321, Sopinka J
expressed a similar view:

> Vagueness can have constitutional significance in at least two ways in a s. 1 analysis. A law may
> be so uncertain as to be incapable of being interpreted so as to constitute any restraint on gov-
> ernmental power. The uncertainty may arise either from the generality of the discretion con-
> ferred on the donee of the power or from the use of language that is so obscure as to be incapable
> of interpretation with any degree of precision using the ordinary tools. In these circumstances,
> there is no "limit prescribed by law" and no s. 1 analysis is necessary as the threshold require-
> ment for its application is not met. The second way in which vagueness can play a constitutional
> role is in the analysis of s. 1. A law which passes the threshold test may, nevertheless, by reason
> of its imprecision, not qualify as a reasonable limit. Generality and imprecision of language may
> fail to confine the invasion of a Charter right within reasonable limits. In this sense vagueness
> is an aspect of overbreadth.
>
> This Court has shown a reluctance to disentitle a law to s. 1 scrutiny on the basis of vagueness
> which results in the granting of wide discretionary powers. Much of the activity of government
> is carried on under the aegis of laws which of necessity leave a broad discretion to government
> officials. ...
>
> Since it may very well be reasonable in the circumstances to confer a wide discretion, it is
> preferable in the vast majority of cases to deal with vagueness in the context of a s. 1 analysis
> rather than disqualifying the law *in limine*.

In *Osborne* the Court held that s. 33 of the federal *Public Service Employment Act*, which
prohibited federal public servants from "engaging in work" for or against a candidate or political party, violated s. 2(b). The Court went on to find that that the law could not be justified
under s. 1 because it restricted the right more than was necessary to advance the important
goal of ensuring public service neutrality. The Court held that the restriction of the freedom
of expression was prescribed by law. In the Court's view, even though the words "engage in
work" might be difficult to apply in specific situations, they were capable of interpretation.

The case that follows, *R v. Nova Scotia Pharmaceutical Society*, provides the Supreme
Court of Canada's most extensive discussion of the vagueness issue as it arises not only under
s. 1, but as well under s. 7 as part of a consideration of the principles of fundamental justice.

R v. Nova Scotia Pharmaceutical Society
[1992] 2 SCR 606, 93 DLR (4th) 36

[The accused were charged under the *Combines Investigation Act*, RSC 1970, c. C-23 with conspiring to lessen competition unduly in the sale of prescription drugs. They moved to quash the indictment, arguing that the provisions under which they were charged violated s. 7 on grounds of vagueness. The Supreme Court of Canada rejected their argument and dismissed the appeal.]

GONTHIER J (for the Court):

. . .

1. Vagueness can be raised under s. 7 of the Charter, since it is a principle of fundamental justice that laws may not be too vague. It can also be raised under s. 1 of the Charter *in limine*, on the basis that an enactment is so vague as not to satisfy the requirement that a limitation on Charter rights be "prescribed by law." Furthermore, vagueness is also relevant to the "minimal impairment" stage of the *Oakes* test (*R v. Morgentaler*, [1988] 1 SCR 30 [44 DLR (4th) 385]; *Irwin Toy*, [1989] 1 SCR 927 [58 DLR (4th) 577]; *Reference re ss. 193 & 195.1(1)(c) of the Criminal Code (Prostitution Reference)*, [1990] 1 SCR 1123).

2. The "doctrine of vagueness" is founded on the rule of law, particularly on the principles of fair notice to citizens and limitation of enforcement discretion: (*Prostitution Reference; Committee for the Commonwealth of Canada*, [1991] 1 SCR 139 [77 DLR (4th) 385]).

3. Factors to be considered in determining whether a law is too vague include (a) the need for flexibility and the interpretative role of the courts, (b) the impossibility of achieving absolute certainty, a standard of intelligibility being more appropriate and (c) the possibility that many varying judicial interpretations of a given disposition may exist and perhaps coexist (*Morgentaler; Irwin Toy; Prostitution Reference; R v. Taylor*, [1990] 3 SCR 892 [75 DLR (4th) 577]; *Osborne*, [1991] 2 SCR 69 [82 DLR (4th) 321]).

4. Vagueness, when raised under s. 7 or under s. 1 *in limine*, involves similar considerations (*Prostitution Reference; Committee for the Commonwealth of Canada*). On the other hand, vagueness as it relates to the "minimal impairment" branch of s. 1 merges with the related concept of overbreadth (*Committee for the Commonwealth of Canada; Osborne*).

5. The Court will be reluctant to find a disposition so vague as not to qualify as "law" under s. 1 *in limine*, and will rather consider the scope of this disposition under the "minimal impairment" test (*Taylor* and *Osborne*).

In order to give a more complete picture of issues of vagueness under the Charter, I will examine in turn the proper place of the doctrine of vagueness in Charter analysis and its content.

2. The Proper Place of the Doctrine of Vagueness in Charter Adjudication

… I would consider that the "doctrine of vagueness" is a single concept, whether invoked as a principle of fundamental justice under s. 7 of the Charter or as part of s. 1 of the Charter *in limine*. Indeed from a practical point of view this makes little difference in the analysis, since a consideration of s. 1 *in limine* would follow immediately the determination of whether s. 7 has been violated. No intermediate step is lost. From a theoretical perspective, the justifications invoked for the doctrine of vagueness under both s. 7 and s. 1 are similar. A reading of the aforementioned cases shows that the rationales of fair notice to the citizen and limitation of enforcement discretion are put forward in every discussion of vagueness, irrespective of where it occurs in the Charter analysis. I see no ground for distinguishing them.

Vagueness may be raised under the substantive sections of the Charter whenever these sections comprise some internal limitation. For example, under s. 7, it may be that the limitation on life, liberty and security of the person would not otherwise be objectionable, but for the vagueness of the impugned law. The doctrine of vagueness would then rank among the principles of fundamental justice. Outside of these cases, the proper place of a vagueness argument is under s. 1 *in limine*. …

3. The Content of the "Doctrine of Vagueness"

As was said by this Court in *Osborne* and *Butler* [1992] SCR 452 [89 DLR (4th) 449], the threshold for finding a law vague is relatively high. So far discussion of the content of the notion has evolved around intelligibility.

The two rationales of fair notice to the citizen and limitation of enforcement discretion have been adopted as the theoretical foundations of the doctrine of vagueness, here … as well as in the United States … and in Europe, as will be seen later. These two rationales have been broadly linked with the corpus of principles of government known as the "rule of law," which lies at the core of our political and constitutional tradition.

(a) Fair Notice to the Citizen

Fair notice to the citizen, as a guide to conduct and a contributing element to a full answer and defence, comprises two aspects.

First of all, there is the more formal aspect of notice, that is acquaintance with the actual text of a statute. … [G]iven that, as this Court has already recognized, case law applying and interpreting a particular section is relevant in determining whether the section is vague, formal notice is not a central concern in a vagueness analysis.

As Lamer J pointed out in *Re BC Motor Vehicle Act*, [1985] SCR 486 [24 DLR (4th) 536] principles of fundamental justice, such as the doctrine of vagueness, must have a substantive as well as procedural content. Indeed the idea of giving fair notice to citizens would be rather empty if the mere fact of bringing the text of the law to their attention was enough, especially when knowledge is presumed by law. There is also a substantive aspect to fair notice, which could be described as a notice, an understanding that some conduct comes under the law. …

Let me take homicide as an example. The actual provisions of the *Criminal Code* dealing with homicide are numerous ... . When one completes the picture of the *Code* with case law, both substantive and constitutional, the result is a fairly intricate body of rules. Notwithstanding formal notice, it can hardly be expected of the average citizen that he know the law of homicide in detail. Yet no one would seriously argue that there is no substantive fair notice here, or that the law of homicide is vague. It can readily be seen why this is so. First of all, everyone (or sadly, should I say, almost everyone) has an inherent knowledge that taking the life of another human being is wrong. There is a deeply-rooted perception that homicide cannot be tolerated, whether one comes to this perception from a moral, religious or sociological stance. Therefore it is expected that homicide will be punished by the State. Secondly, homicide is indeed punished by the State, and homicide trials and sentences receive a great deal of publicity.

I used homicide as an example, because it lies so at the core of our criminal law and our shared values that substantive notice is easy to demonstrate. Similar demonstrations could be made, at greater length, for other legal provisions. The substantive aspect of fair notice is therefore a subjective understanding that the law touches upon some conduct, based on the substratum of values underlying the legal enactment and on the role that the legal enactment plays in the life of the society.

I do not wish to suggest that the State can only intervene through law when some non-legal basis for intervention exists. Many enactments are relatively narrow in scope and echo little of society at large; this is the case with many regulatory enactments. The weakness or the absence of substantive notice before the enactment can be compensated by bringing to the attention of the public the actual terms of the law, so that substantive notice will be achieved. Merit point and driving license revocation schemes are prime examples of this; through publicity and advertisement these schemes have been "digested" by society. A certain connection between the formal and substantive aspects of fair notice can be seen here. ...

(b) Limitation of Law Enforcement Discretion

Lamer J in the *Prostitution Reference* used the phrase "standardless sweep," first coined by the United States Supreme Court in *Smith v. Goguen*, 415 US 566 (1974), at 575, to describe the limitation of enforcement discretion rationale for the doctrine of vagueness. It has become the prime concern in American constitutional law. ... Indeed today it has become paramount, given the considerable expansion in the discretionary powers of enforcement agencies that has followed the creation of the modern welfare state.

A law must not be so devoid of precision in its content that a conviction will automatically flow from the decision to prosecute. Such is the crux of the concern for limitation of enforcement discretion. When the power to decide whether a charge will lead to conviction or acquittal, normally the preserve of the judiciary, becomes fused with the power to prosecute because of the wording of the law, then a law will be unconstitutionally vague. ...

(c) European Court of Human Rights Case Law

I would also note that the European Court of Human Rights (hereinafter "ECHR") has adopted the same approach to issues of vagueness, in the course of its treatment of words such as "prescribed by law," found in many limitation clauses of the *European Convention for the Protection of Human Rights and Fundamental Freedoms* ... . The ECHR gave this phrase a substantive content, which went beyond a mere inquiry as to whether a law existed or not.

[An account of several ECHR cases is omitted, including the excerpt from the *Sunday Times* case that appeared above.]

(d) The Scope of Precision

This leads me to synthesize these remarks about vagueness. The substantive notice and limitation of enforcement discretion rationales point in the same direction: an unintelligible provision gives insufficient guidance for legal debate and is therefore unconstitutionally vague. ...

Legal rules only provide a framework, a guide as to how one may behave, but certainty is only reached in instant cases, where law is actualized by a competent authority. In the meanwhile, conduct is guided by approximation. The process of approximation sometimes results in quite a narrow set of options, sometimes in a broader one. Legal dispositions therefore delineate a risk zone, and cannot hope to do more, unless they are directed at individual instances.

By setting out the boundaries of permissible and non-permissible conduct, these norms give rise to legal debate. They bear substance, and they allow for a discussion as to their actualization. They therefore limit enforcement discretion by introducing boundaries, and they also sufficiently delineate an area of risk to allow for substantive notice to citizens.

Indeed no higher requirement as to certainty can be imposed on law in our modern State. Semantic arguments, based on a perception of language as an unequivocal medium, are unrealistic. Language is not the exact tool some may think it is. It cannot be argued that an enactment can and must provide enough guidance to predict the legal consequences of any given course of conduct in advance. All it can do is enunciate some boundaries, which create an area of risk. But it is inherent to our legal system that some conduct will fall along the boundaries of the area of risk; no definite prediction can then be made. Guidance, not direction, of conduct is a more realistic objective. The ECHR has repeatedly warned against a quest for certainty and adopted this "area of risk" approach in *Sunday Times* ... .

A vague provision does not provide an adequate basis for legal debate, that is for reaching a conclusion as to its meaning by reasoned analysis applying legal criteria. It does not sufficiently delineate any area of risk, and thus can provide neither fair notice to the citizen nor a limitation of enforcement discretion. Such a provision is not intelligible, to use the terminology of previous sufficient indications that could fuel a legal debate. It offers no grasp to the judiciary. This is an exacting standard, going beyond semantics. The term "legal debate" is used here not to express a new standard or one departing from that previously outlined by this Court. It is rather intended to reflect and encompass the same standard and criteria of fair notice and limitation of enforcement discretion viewed in the fuller context of an analysis of the quality and limits of human knowledge and understanding in the operation of the law.

(e) Vagueness and the Rule of Law

The criterion of absence of legal debate relates well to the rule of law principles that form the backbone of our polity. Here one must see the rule of law in the contemporary context. ...

One must move away from the non-interventionist attitude that surrounded the development of the doctrine of the rule of law to a more global conception of the State as an entity bound by and acting through law. The modern State intervenes in almost every field of human endeavour, and it plays a role that goes far beyond collecting taxes and policing. The State has entered fields where the positions are not so clear-cut; in the realm of social or economic policy, interests diverge, and the State does not seek to enforce a definite and limited social interest in public order, for instance, against an individual. Often the State attempts to realize a series of social objectives, some of which must be balanced against one another, and which sometimes conflict with the interests of individuals. The modern State, while still acting as an enforcer, assumes more and more of an arbitration role.

This arbitration must be done according to law, but often it reaches such a level of complexity that the corresponding enactment will be framed in relatively general terms. In my opinion the generality of these terms may entail a greater role for the judiciary, but unlike some authors ... . I fail to see a difference in kind between general provisions where the judiciary would assume part of the legislative role and "mechanical" provisions where the judiciary would simply apply the law. The judiciary always has a mediating role in the actualization of law, although the extent of this role may vary.

Indeed, as the ECHR has recognized ... laws that are framed in general terms may be better suited to the achievement of their objectives, inasmuch as in fields governed by public policy circumstances may vary widely in time and from one case to the other. A very detailed enactment would not provide the required flexibility, and it might furthermore obscure its purposes behind a veil of detailed provisions. The modern State intervenes today in fields where some generality in the enactments is inevitable. The substance of these enactments remains nonetheless intelligible. One must be wary of using the doctrine of vagueness to prevent or impede State action in furtherance of valid social objectives, by requiring the law to achieve a degree of precision to which the subject matter does not lend itself. A delicate balance must be maintained between societal interests and individual rights. A measure of generality also sometimes allows for greater respect for fundamental rights, since circumstances that would not justify the invalidation of a more precise enactment may be accommodated through the application of a more general one.

What becomes more problematic is not so much general terms conferring broad discretion, but terms failing to give direction as to how to exercise this discretion, so that this exercise may be controlled. Once more, an unpermissibly vague law will not provide a sufficient basis for legal debate; it will not give a sufficient indication as to how decisions must be reached, such as factors to be considered or determinative elements. In giving unfettered discretion, it will deprive the judiciary of means of controlling the exercise of this discretion. ...

The citizen is entitled to have the state abide by constitutional standards of precision whenever it enacts legal dispositions. In the criminal field, it may be thought that the terms of the legal debate should be outlined with special care by the State. In my opinion, however, once the minimal general standard has been met, any further arguments as to the precision of the enactments should be considered at the "minimal impairment" stage of s. 1 analysis.

Appeal dismissed.

B. Justification

1. *The Oakes Test*

The Supreme Court of Canada's first comprehensive treatment of the meaning of s. 1 came in *R v. Oakes*, which remains the primary referent for this second stage of Charter adjudication.

R v. Oakes
[1986] 1 SCR 103, 26 DLR (4th) 200

[Section 8 of the *Narcotic Control Act*, RSC 1970, c. N-1 created a "rebuttable presumption" that once the fact of possession of a narcotic had been proven, an intention to traffic would be inferred unless the accused established the absence of such an intention. In *Oakes* the accused challenged this "reverse onus" provision, arguing that it violated s. 11(d) of the Charter. After finding that s. 8 did violate s. 11(d) of the Charter, the Court then went on to discuss whether the limit could nonetheless be upheld under s. 1.]

DICKSON CJC (Chouinard, Lamer, Wilson, and Le Dain JJ concurring): ... It is important to observe at the outset that s. 1 has two functions: first, it constitutionally guarantees the rights and freedoms set out in the provisions which follow; and, second, it states explicitly the exclusive justificatory criteria (outside of s. 33 of the *Constitution Act, 1982*) against which limitations on those rights and freedoms must be measured. Accordingly, any s. 1 inquiry must be premised on an understanding that the impugned limit violates constitutional rights and freedoms—rights and freedoms which are part of the supreme law of Canada. As Wilson J stated in *Singh v. Minister of Employment and Immigration* [[1985] 1 SCR 177, at 218, 17 DLR (4th) 422]: "...it is important to remember that the courts are conducting this inquiry in light of a commitment to uphold the rights and freedoms set out in the other sections of the Charter."

A second contextual element of interpretation of s. 1 is provided by the words "free and democratic society." Inclusion of these words as the final standard of justification for limits on rights and freedoms refers the Court to the very purpose for which the Charter was originally entrenched in the Constitution: Canadian society is to be free and democratic. The Court must be guided by the values and principles essential to a free and democratic society which I believe embody, to name but a few, respect for the inherent dignity of the human person, commitment to social justice and equality, accommodation of a wide variety of beliefs, respect for cultural and group identity, and faith in social and political institutions which enhance the participation of individuals and groups in society. The underlying values and principles of a free and democratic society are the genesis of the rights and freedoms guaranteed by the Charter and the ultimate standard against which a limit on a right or freedom must be shown, despite its effect, to be reasonable and demonstrably justified.

The rights and freedoms guaranteed by the Charter are not, however, absolute. It may become necessary to limit rights and freedoms in circumstances where their exercise would be inimical to the realization of collective goals of fundamental importance. For this reason, s. 1 provides criteria of justification for limits on the rights and freedoms guaranteed by the Charter. These criteria impose a stringent standard of justification, especially when understood in terms of the two contextual considerations discussed above, namely, the violation of a constitutionally guaranteed right or freedom and the fundamental principles of a free and democratic society.

The onus of proving that a limit on a right or freedom guaranteed by the Charter is reasonable and demonstrably justified in a free and democratic society rests upon the party seeking to uphold the limitation. It is clear from the text of s. 1 that limits on the rights and freedoms enumerated in the Charter are exceptions to their general guarantee. The presumption is that the rights and freedoms are guaranteed unless the party invoking s. 1 can bring itself within the exceptional criteria which justify their being limited. This is further substantiated by the use of the word "demonstrably" which clearly indicates that the onus of justification is on the party seeking to limit: *Hunter v. Southam Inc.*, [[1984] 2 SCR 145, 11 DLR (4th) 641].

The standard of proof under s. 1 is the civil standard, namely, proof by a preponderance of probability. The alternative criminal standard, proof beyond a reasonable doubt, would, in my view, be unduly onerous on the party seeking to limit. Concepts such as "reasonableness," "justifiability" and "free and democratic society" are simply not amenable to such a standard. Nevertheless, the preponderance of probability test must be applied rigorously. Indeed, the phrase "demonstrably justified" in s. 1 of the Charter supports this conclusion. Within the broad category of the civil standard, there exist different degrees of probability depending on the nature of the case. ...

Having regard to the fact that s. 1 is being invoked for the purpose of justifying a violation of the constitutional rights and freedoms the Charter was designed to protect, a very high degree of probability will be, in the words of Lord Denning, "commensurate with the occasion." Where evidence is required in order to prove the constituent elements of a s. 1 inquiry, and this will generally be the case, it should be cogent and persuasive and make clear to the Court the consequences of imposing or not imposing the limit. ... A court will also need to know what alternative measures for implementing the objective were available to the legislators when they made their decisions. I should add, however, that there may be cases where certain elements of the s. 1 analysis are obvious or self-evident.

To establish that a limit is reasonable and demonstrably justified in a free and democrat-ic society, two central criteria must be satisfied. First, the objective, which the measures responsible for a limit on a Charter right or freedom are designed to serve, must be "of sufficient importance to warrant overriding a constitutionally protected right or freedom": *R v. Big M Drug Mart Ltd.*, [1985] 1 SCR 295 at 352, 18 DLR (4th) 321. The standard must be high in order to ensure that objectives which are trivial or discordant with the principles integral to a free and democratic society do not gain s. 1 protection. It is neces-sary, at a minimum, that an objective relate to concerns which are pressing and substantial in a free and democratic society before it can be characterized as sufficiently important.

Second, once a sufficiently significant objective is recognized, then the party invoking s. 1 must show that the means chosen are reasonable and demonstrably justified. This involves "a form of proportionality test": *R v. Big M Drug Mart Ltd.*, *supra*, at 352. Al-though the nature of the proportionality test will vary depending on the circumstances, in each case courts will be required to balance the interests of society with those of indi-viduals and groups. There are, in my view, three important components of a proportion-ality test. First, the measures adopted must be carefully designed to achieve the objective in question. They must not be arbitrary, unfair or based on irrational considerations. In short, they must be rationally connected to the objective. Second, the means, even if ra-tionally connected to the objective in this first sense, should impair "as little as possible" the right or freedom in question: *R v. Big M Drug Mart Ltd.*, *supra*, at 352. Third, there must be a proportionality between the effects of the measures which are responsible for limiting the Charter right or freedom, and the objective which has been identified as of "sufficient importance."

With respect to the third component, it is clear that the general effect of any measure impugned under s. 1 will be the infringement of a right or freedom guaranteed by the Charter; this is the reason why resort to s. 1 is necessary. The inquiry into effects must, however, go further. A wide range of rights and freedoms are guaranteed by the Charter, and an almost infinite number of factual situations may arise in respect of these. Some limits on rights and freedoms protected by the Charter will be more serious than others in terms of the nature of the right or freedom violated, the extent of the violation, and the degree to which the measures which impose the limit trench upon the integral principles of a free and democratic society. Even if an objective is of sufficient importance, and the first two elements of the proportionality test are satisfied, it is still possible that, because of the severity of the deleterious effects of a measure on individuals or groups, the meas-ure will not be justified by the purposes it is intended to serve. The more severe the dele-terious effects of a measure, the more important the objective must be if the measure is to be reasonable and demonstrably justified in a free and democratic society.

[The Court then went on to apply the above analysis to the reverse onus provision found in s. 8 of the *Narcotic Control Act*. The Court concluded that the objective of protecting society from the ills associated with drug trafficking was of sufficient importance to war-rant overriding a constitutionally protected right or freedom in certain cases and, more-over, that the seriousness of the problem was to a large extent self-evident. The federal government had submitted some evidence to establish the seriousness of the problem of drug trafficking. The evidence included several governmental reports on the problems of drug abuse and an International Protocol on the international trade in and use of opium that Canada had signed. However, the Court concluded that the means chosen to implement this objective—that is, the reverse onus—failed the first step of the proportionality test. The means were not rationally connected to the objective of curbing drug trafficking because there was no rational connection between possession of a small quantity of narcotics and an intent to traffic.]

Appeal dismissed.

NOTES AND QUESTIONS

1. *Pressing and Substantial Purpose.* As you read the cases in subsequent chapters you will see that courts rarely find that a restriction fails this first step of the *Oakes* test. *R v. Big M Drug Mart Ltd.*, [1985], 1 SCR 295, 18 DLR (4th) 321 (which is included in Chapter 19, Freedom of Religion) is an exceptional case. In *Big M* the Supreme Court of Canada found that the law's purpose, which was to compel a religious practice (observance of Sunday as the Sabbath), could not be considered "pressing and substantial." In the Court's view, such a purpose directly contradicted the constitutional commitment to religious freedom.

The courts seem prepared to regard almost any purpose (that is not a direct denial or contradiction of the right) as "pressing and substantial." They prefer to take account of the insubstantial character of a restriction's purpose at the proportionality stage of the *Oakes* test. Why do you think they have taken this approach?

In *Big M* the Court also said that in defending a law under s. 1 the government could not rely on a purpose different from that which animated the law at the time of its enactment. According to the Court: "Purpose is a function of the intent of those who drafted and enacted the legislation at the time, and not of any shifting variable." Any other view would mean that "[l]aws assumed valid on the basis of persuasive and powerful authority could be struck down as invalid. Not only would this create uncertainty in the law, but it would encourage re-litigation of the same issues and, it could be argued, provide the courts with a means by which to arrive at a result dictated by other than legal considerations." Are the Court's concerns justified? In *R v. Butler*, [1992] 1 SCR 452, 89 DLR (4th) 449 (found in Chapter 20, Freedom of Expression) the Court said that the rule against "shifting purpose" does not preclude a shift in the emphasis of the law's general purpose. When you read *Butler*, consider whether this distinction between "shifting purpose" and "permissible shift in emphasis" is workable.

2. *Rational Connection and Minimal Impairment.* While the first step of the *Oakes* test focuses on the purpose of the impugned law, the next two steps consider the means chosen to advance that purpose—their effectiveness and their scope. The rational connection and minimal impairment tests are closely related. A law that does not rationally advance the pressing and substantial purpose for which it was enacted can be described as unnecessarily restricting the right or freedom. Similarly, a law that restricts the right or freedom more than is necessary to advance its pressing purpose (that does not minimally impair the freedom) can be described as in part ineffective or irrational.

When a court finds that a restriction cannot be justified under s. 1, its decision is most often based on the minimal impairment requirement, and occasionally on the rational connection test. It is easy to understand why these tests have come to play such a central role in the courts' assessment of limits. Both tests can be presented as value-neutral—as involving a technical assessment of legislative means. A law may be struck down by the court not because its purpose is objectionable, but simply because the means chosen to advance that purpose are ineffective or will impair the protected freedom unnecessarily.

However, it is far from clear that these tests involve nothing more than an assessment of the effectiveness of means, divorced entirely from any judgment about the purpose of the law or the value of the restricted activity.

The rational connection test must require something more than that the law's means not be wholly irrational in relation to the law's ends—or wholly ineffective to achieve those ends. Indeed, it would be difficult to attribute to a law a purpose that seemed unconnected to its provisions. Instead, the rational connection test must involve some sort of effectiveness threshold—that the law reasonably advances the pressing and substantial purpose for which it was enacted. If rationality or effectiveness is a relative judgment, then there will be plenty of space for other factors, such as the importance of the law's objective and the value of the restricted activity, to affect the court's judgment that the law is (in)sufficiently effective or rational in the advancement of its purpose.

The intrusion of balancing seems even more difficult to avoid in the case of the minimal impairment test. It will be very rare that an alternative measure that is less rights restrictive will advance the law's substantial and compelling purpose as completely or as effectively. A law will fail the minimal impairment test when the court considers that a small or debatable decrease in the law's effectiveness in achieving its substantial and pressing purpose will significantly reduce its interference with the protected right.

The fact that judgments about rational connection and minimal impairment almost invariably involve a balancing or trade-off between competing interests may explain why the final "balancing" step of the *Oakes* test seldom plays more than a formal role in the s. 1 analysis.

3. *The Final Balance.* In *Dagenais v. Canadian Broadcasting Corp.*, [1994] 3 SCR 835, 120 DLR (4th) 12, Lamer CJC, writing for five members of the Court, added a refinement or clarification to the third part of the *Oakes* proportionality test. This last component of the *Oakes* test, which is referred to as the "deleterious effects" test or the "disproportionate effects" test, requires a proportionality between the effects of the measures that are responsible for limiting the Charter right or freedom, and the objective that has been identified as of "sufficient importance." The *Dagenais* refinement requires that in applying this test, courts consider not only the objective of the impugned law but also its salutary effects. The rationale for refining the test in this way is set out in the following extract:

> As Dickson CJ stated in *Oakes* ... "[e]ven if an objective is of sufficient importance, and the first two elements of the proportionality test are satisfied, it is still possible that, because of the severity of the deleterious effects of a measure on individuals or groups, the measure will not be justified by the purposes it is intended to serve." In many instances, the imposition of a measure will result in the full, or nearly full, realization of the legislative objective. In these situations, the third step of the proportionality test calls for an examination of the balance that has been struck between the objective in question and the deleterious effects on constitutionally protected rights arising from the means that have been employed to achieve this objective. At other

times, however, the measure at issue, while rationally connected to an important objective, will result in only the partial achievement of this object. In such cases, I believe that the third step of the second branch of the *Oakes* test requires both that the underlying *objective* of a measure and the *salutary effects* that actually result from its implementation be proportional to the deleterious effects the measure has on fundamental rights and freedoms. A legislative objective may be pressing and substantial, the means chosen may be rationally connected to that objective, and less rights-impairing alternatives may not be available. Nonetheless, even if the importance of the *objective itself* (when viewed in the abstract) outweighs the deleterious effects on protected rights, it is still possible that the actual *salutary effects* of the legislation will not be sufficient to justify these negative effects. ...

In my view, characterizing the third part of the second branch of the *Oakes* test as being concerned solely with the balance between the objective and the deleterious effects of a measure rests on too narrow a conception of proportionality. I believe that even if an objective is of sufficient importance, the first two elements of the proportionality test are satisfied, and the deleterious effects are proportional to the objectives, it is still possible that, because of a lack of proportionality between the deleterious effects and the salutary effects, a measure will not be reasonable and demonstrably justified in a free and democratic society. I would, therefore, rephrase the third part of the *Oakes* test as follows: there must be a proportionality between the deleterious effects of the measures which are responsible for limiting the rights or freedoms in question and the objective, *and there must be a proportionality between the deleterious and the salutary effects of the measures.*

The *Dagenais* requirement that the actual salutary effects of the law be considered may be relevant in cases where the challenged law may not be completely successful in achieving the objectives for which it was enacted. Such was the case in *Dagenais* itself, which involved a publication ban ordered for the purpose of guaranteeing a fair trial but which, in operation, was found to have only limited effect given the difficulty of effectively enforcing such bans in light of technological advances.

With respect to the overall structure of s. 1 analysis, the first step of the *Oakes* test involves a general judgment about the significance of the law's purpose. The next two steps involve a general assessment of the effectiveness of its means. At the final stage of the test the court is to look at the means and ends of the law together and compare the law's actual benefit or value (the value of what the law achieves and not simply the value of its general purpose) with its actual costs (based on the value of the restricted activity and not just the value of the right or freedom in the abstract). In actual practice, the courts have given relatively little weight to this final step of the *Oakes* test, and in the majority of cases the crucial s. 1 determinations are made at the minimal impairment stage of the *Oakes* test. The final step of the s. 1 analysis tends to be conclusory, with courts simply repeating earlier findings.

One notable, recent exception is *R v. Sharpe*, [2001] 1 SCR 45, 194 DLR (4th) 1 (which concerned the regulation of child pornography and is extracted in Chapter 20, Freedom of Expression). In *Sharpe*, McLachlin CJC, writing for a majority of the Court, found that part of the restriction at issue did not satisfy the final requirement of the s. 1 analysis:

> In the vast majority of the law's applications, the costs it imposes on freedom of expression are outweighed by the risk of harm to children. ... However, the prohibition also captures in its sweep materials that arguably pose little or no risk to children, and that deeply implicate the

freedoms guaranteed under s. 2(b). ... Consequently, the law's application to these materials, while peripheral to its objective, poses the most significant problems at the final stage of the proportionality analysis."

Could McLachlin CJC have reached the same result using the minimal impairment test? Is the Court signaling that it is going to be more explicit in its balancing of competing interests by making greater use of this final step of the *Oakes* test?

4. *Standard of Proof.* In *Oakes* the Court stated that the justification of a limit on a Charter right or freedom must be proved on a balance of probabilities, the civil rather than criminal standard of proof. This reference to standard of proof suggests that the limitation issue is (principally) a factual one. Is this true? The suggestion that factual determinations are key fits with the Court's focus on the rational connection and minimal impairment tests, both of which appear to involve judgments about the effectiveness rather than the value of the restriction. Yet most contemporary defences of judicial review regard the court as a "forum of principle," a place where basic value issues are addressed. If the key issues to be resolved under s. 1 are factual, should the courts not give significant space to the legislature's judgment? Or are the courts better equipped to make factual determinations?

In *Oakes*, Chief Justice Dickson indicated that it might not always be necessary for the government to provide evidence—"that there may be cases where certain elements of the s. 1 analysis are obvious or self-evident." Moreover, as will be discussed below, courts are often prepared to defer to the legislative reading of ambiguous social science evidence.

2. *The Subsequent Development of the Oakes Test: Context and Deference*

Two important and closely related developments in the Supreme Court of Canada's s. 1 analysis have occurred since the introduction of the *Oakes* test. The first is the emergence of the contextual approach to the assessment of limits under s. 1. This approach requires that courts assess the value or significance of the right and its restriction in their context rather than in the abstract. For example, when deciding whether a legislative restriction on hate speech is justified under s. 1, courts should not simply balance the value of the restriction's general purpose (that is, preventing the spread of hatred) against the value of free expression. Instead they should compare or balance the value of what the restriction achieves in practice—its likely impact on the spread of hatred—against its actual cost to freedom of expression values. Significantly, the Supreme Court of Canada has held that certain forms of expression such as hate promotion are less valuable (are less directly connected to the values underlying freedom of expression) than other forms of expression and that this lesser value is a relevant contextual factor in the balancing of interests under s. 1.

The second trend is the Court's willingness to defer in certain circumstances to the legislature's judgment about the need for, and effectiveness of, a particular limit on a Charter right. Deference is often linked to context, for the Court has held that deference is more appropriate in some contexts than in others.

As you will see when you read the case extracts in this section, there is significant disagreement among the members of the Supreme Court of Canada about when, and to what degree, the courts should defer to legislative judgments. There is not only disagreement about what contextual factors the courts should take into account when assessing limits under s. 1, but also about whether these factors should affect the application of the rational connection and minimal impairment stages of the *Oakes* test, or only the final balancing stage.

The origins of the "contextual" approach to s. 1 lie in *Edmonton Journal v. Alberta (Attorney General)*, an extract from which is reproduced below.

Edmonton Journal v. Alberta (Attorney General)
[1989] 2 SCR 1326, 64 DLR (4th) 577

[A newspaper challenged s. 30(1) of the Alberta *Judicature Act*, which limited the publication of information arising out of the court proceedings in matrimonial disputes, claiming that the provision was contrary to s. 2(b) of the Charter, the guarantee of freedom of expression. The Alberta attorney general argued that the law protected individual privacy. Although all members of the Court found that s. 30(1) violated freedom of expression, they were split on the justification issue. Four members of the Court ruled that the provision was not a reasonable limit under s. 1. Cory J wrote one decision supporting this result, with which Dickson CJC and Lamer J concurred. Wilson J wrote a separate concurring judgment. La Forest J wrote a dissenting judgment, with which L'Heureux-Dubé and Sopinka JJ concurred, in which he found that the limit on freedom of expression could be justified as a reasonable limit under s. 1. In her judgment, a portion of which has been extracted, Wilson J described a context-sensitive approach to s. 1 that was later adopted by the entire Court.]

WILSON J: ... In my view, this case raises an important issue regarding the proper method of application of the *Canadian Charter of Rights and Freedoms* to individual cases and, because my reasons for finding s. 30(1) of the Alberta *Judicature Act* unconstitutional reflect one of two possible approaches to the Charter's application, I thought it might be appropriate at the outset to say a word or two about the different approaches.

Of the two possible approaches to the Charter's application one might be described as the abstract approach and the other the contextual approach. While the mechanics of application, *i.e.*, the proper analytical steps to be taken, are the same under each, which one is adopted may tend to affect the result of the balancing process called for under s. 1.

Under each approach it is necessary to ascertain the underlying value which the right alleged to be violated was designed to protect. This is achieved through a purposive interpretation of Charter rights. It is also necessary under each approach to ascertain the legislative objective sought to be advanced by the impugned legislation. This is done by ascertaining the intention of the legislator in enacting the particular piece of legislation. When both the underlying value and the legislative objective have been identified, and it becomes clear that the legislative objective cannot be achieved without some infringement of the right, it must then be determined whether the impugned legislation constitutes a reasonable limit on the right which can be demonstrably justified in a free and democratic society.

It seems to me that under the abstract approach the underlying value sought to be protected by s. 2(b) of the Charter is determined at large as my colleague Cory J has done. He finds freedom of expression to have been fundamental to the historical development of our political, social and educational institutions in Canada. He emphasizes the seriousness of restricting the free exchange of ideas and opinions in a democratic form of society and concludes that it is difficult to imagine a more important right in a democracy than freedom of expression.

I do not disagree with my colleague that freedom of expression plays that vital role in a political democracy. The problem is that the values in conflict in the context of this particular case are the right of litigants to the protection of their privacy in matrimonial disputes and the right of the public to an open court process. Both cannot be fully respected. One must yield to the exigencies of the other. I ask myself therefore whether a contextual approach in balancing the right to privacy against freedom of the press under s. 1 is not more appropriate than an approach which assesses the relative importance of the competing values in the abstract or at large.

It is of interest to note in this connection that La Forest J completely agrees with Cory J about the importance of freedom of expression in the abstract. He acknowledges that it is fundamental in a democratic society. He sees the issue in the case, however, as being whether an open court process should prevail over the litigant's right to privacy. In other words, while not disputing the values which are protected by s. 2(b) as identified by Cory J, he takes a contextual approach to the definition of the conflict in this particular case. Notwithstanding the enormous importance of freedom of expression in a political context, he finds that it must yield in the context of this case to the litigant's right to privacy. The impugned legislation is accordingly, in his view, a reasonable limit on freedom of the press. Cory J reaches the converse conclusion and the concern raised is whether the difference in result may be conditioned by the methodology adopted in assessing the importance of the values in conflict.

One thing seems clear and that is that one should not balance one value at large and the conflicting value in its context. To do so could well be to pre-judge the issue by placing more weight on the value developed at large than is appropriate in the context of the case. Nor should one, it seems to me, balance a private interest, *i.e.*, litigant X's interest in his privacy against a public one, the public's interest in an open court process. Both interests must be seen as public interests, in this case the public interest in protecting the privacy of litigants generally in matrimonial cases against the public interest in an open court process. ...

One virtue of the contextual approach, it seems to me, is that it recognizes that a particular right or freedom may have a different value depending on the context. It may be, for example, that freedom of expression has greater value in a political context than it does in the context of disclosure of details of a matrimonial dispute. The contextual approach attempts to bring into sharp relief the aspect of the right or freedom which is truly at stake in the case as well as the relevant aspects of any values in competition with it. It seems to be more sensitive to the reality of the dilemma posed by the particular facts and therefore more conducive to finding a fair and just compromise between the two competing values under s. 1.

It is my view that a right or freedom may have different meanings in different contexts. Security of the person, for example, might mean one thing when addressed to the issue of overcrowding in prisons and something quite different when addressed to the issue of noxious fumes from industrial smokestacks. It seems entirely probable that the value to be attached to it in different contexts for the purpose of the balancing under s. 1 might also be different. It is for this reason that I believe that the importance of the right or freedom must be assessed in context rather than in the abstract and that its purpose must be ascertained in context. This having been done, the right or freedom must then, in accordance with the dictates of this court, be given a generous interpretation aimed at fulfilling that purpose and securing for the individual the full benefit of the guarantee.

The *Dagenais* modification to the *Oakes* test (discussed in note 3 in section II.B above) may be seen as a response to Wilson J's call, in *Edmonton Journal*, for a more contextual approach to limits under s. 1. Under the final step of the *Oakes* test courts are now required to compare the actual impact of the law on the affected right (for example, on the freedom of expression interests) with the actual contribution the law makes to its pressing and substantial purpose. However, the Court, or several of its members, seems also to have understood the call for a more contextual approach as requiring greater flexibility in the application of each of the steps of the *Oakes* test and greater deference to legislative judgment (in certain circumstances) when applying the test. The result has been a more deferential, reasonableness-based approach to the various strands in the s. 1 analysis in certain contexts.

Attorney General of Quebec v. Irwin Toy, which is extracted below, may represent the high water mark of judicial deference.

Irwin Toy Ltd. v. Quebec (Attorney General)
[1989] 1 SCR 927, 58 DLR (4th) 577

[This case, which involved restrictions on advertising directed at children, is found in Chapter 20, Freedom of Expression. Reproduced below is the portion of the judgment of Dickson CJC and Lamer and Wilson JJ in which they set out some of the circumstances in which deference to legislative judgment is appropriate.]

DICKSON CJC and LAMER and WILSON JJ: ... Where the legislature mediates between the competing claims of different groups in the community, it will inevitably be called upon to draw a line marking where one set of claims legitimately begins and the other fades away without access to complete knowledge as to its precise location. If the legislature has made a reasonable assessment as to where the line is most properly drawn, especially if that assessment involves weighing conflicting scientific evidence and allocating scarce resources on this basis, it is not for the court to second guess. That would only be to substitute one estimate for another. In dealing with inherently heterogeneous groups defined in terms of age or a characteristic analogous to age, evidence showing that a clear majority of the group requires the protection which the government has identified can help to establish that the group was defined reasonably. ...

... Thus, in matching means to ends and asking whether rights or freedoms are impaired as little as possible, a legislature mediating between the claims of competing groups will be forced to strike a balance without the benefit of absolute certainty concerning how that balance is best struck. Vulnerable groups will claim the need for protection by the government whereas other groups and individuals will assert that the government should not intrude. In [*Edwards Books and Art Ltd. v. The Queen*, [1986] 2 SCR 713, 35 DLR (4th) 1], Dickson CJ expressed an important concern about the situation of vulnerable groups (at p. 779):

> In interpreting and applying the Charter I believe that the courts must be cautious to ensure that it does not simply become an instrument of better situated individuals to roll back legislation which has as its object the improvement of the condition of less advantaged persons.

When striking a balance between the claims of competing groups, the choice of means, like the choice of ends, frequently will require an assessment of conflicting scientific evidence and differing justified demands on scarce resources. Democratic institutions are meant to let us all share in the responsibility for these difficult choices. Thus, as courts review the results of the legislature's deliberations, particularly with respect to the protection of vulnerable groups, they must be mindful of the legislature's representative function. For example, when "regulating industry or business it is open to the legislature to restrict its legislative reforms to sectors in which there appear to be particularly urgent concerns or to constituencies that seem especially needy" (*Edwards Books and Art Ltd.*, *supra*, at p. 772).

In other cases, however, rather than mediating between different groups, the government is best characterized as the singular antagonist of the individual whose right has been infringed. For example, in justifying an infringement of legal rights enshrined in ss. 7 to 14 of the Charter, the state, on behalf of the whole community, typically will assert its responsibility for prosecuting crime whereas the individual will assert the paramountcy of principles of fundamental justice. There might not be any further competing claims among different groups. In such circumstances, and indeed whenever the government's purpose relates to maintaining the authority and impartiality of the judicial system, the courts can assess with some certainty whether the "least drastic means" for achieving the purpose have been chosen, especially given their accumulated experience in dealing with such questions. ... The same degree of certainty may not be achievable in cases involving the reconciliation of claims of competing individuals or groups or the distribution of scarce government resources.

In the instant case, the Court is called upon to assess competing social science evidence respecting the appropriate means for addressing the problem of children's advertising. The question is whether the government had a reasonable basis, on the evidence tendered, for concluding that the ban on all advertising directed at children impaired freedom of expression as little as possible given the government's pressing and substantial objective.

In *Irwin Toy* the Court held that greater deference to legislative choice is appropriate in a variety of circumstances: where the government has sought to balance competing rights; to protect a socially vulnerable group; to balance the interests of various social groups competing for scarce resources; or to address conflicting social science evidence as to the cause of a social problem. Many themes emerge in the Court's discussion of the need for deference under s. 1. Social justice concerns that the Charter not be used as a tool to roll back legislative measures protecting socially vulnerable groups combine with more general institutional concerns about the inappropriateness of courts second-guessing legislative decisions on social policy—on grounds of both legitimacy and competence.

Irwin Toy introduced a distinction between those cases in which the government is seeking to mediate the interests of competing groups (where a more deferential application of s. 1 is appropriate) and those cases in which the government is the singular antagonist of the individual whose right has been infringed (where a more stringent application of s. 1 is warranted). How workable is this distinction?

In a variety of subsequent judgments, different members of the Court have argued that the *Oakes* test should be applied in a flexible manner. You will read many of these decisions in subsequent chapters. As R. Moon explains in "Justified Limits on Free Expression: The Collapse of the General Approach to Limits on Charter Rights" (2002), 40:3-4 *Osgoode Hall Law Journal* 337, there are at least three different ways in which a court can "defer" to legislative judgment or lower the standard of justification. The courts, however, do not always distinguish these different forms of deference. The first involves judicial deference to relevant findings of fact by the legislature (or a lowering by the court of the standard of proof that the legislature must meet when establishing the factual basis for its justification argument). For example, in *Irwin Toy*, there was little dispute that protecting children from manipulation was an objective important enough to justify restricting free expression. The more difficult issue was whether the government had proved that the restriction on advertising advanced this important end effectively, and without unnecessarily impairing freedom of expression. In seeking to justify the restriction on advertising directed at children up to the age of 13, the legislature relied on social science evidence that children were unable to assess advertisements critically. However, this evidence was not clear cut, particularly on the question of whether children over the age of 9 were subject to the manipulative impact of advertisements. The Court decided to defer to the government's reading of the social science evidence, perhaps because it recognized that it had limited competence in such matters, or no greater competence than the legislature.

The second form of deference by the courts is to the legislature's accommodation of competing values or interests. If the legislature has made an apparently reasonable judgment that concerns about the manipulation of children (or some other interest) justify a limited restriction on expression, then the courts may be reluctant to substitute their own judgment for that of the legislature. The reason for this form of deference may be the courts' lingering doubts about the legitimacy of second-guessing the value judgments of democratic institutions. A court's reluctance may be greater when it recognizes that the legislature is making a reasonable attempt to protect the interests of a vulnerable group or to accommodate competing "private" interests. In practice, these first two forms of deference are difficult to separate, particularly because the courts have tended to approach the question of justification under s. 1 as a factual issue.

The third form of deference is really a lowering of the standard of justification under s. 1. The courts recognize that a broad and inclusive definition of the scope of a right such as freedom of expression means that there may be significant variation in the value of different instances of the protected activity. The courts have held that a less substantial or significant competing interest may support the restriction of a less valuable form of expression, such as commercial advertising or hate promotion. In *Thomson Newspapers Co. v. Canada*, [1998] 1 SCR 877, 159 DLR (4th) 385 (discussed in Chapter 20, Freedom of Expression), Bastarache J acknowledged that different forms of expression protected under s. 2(b) of the Charter may have greater or lesser value under s. 1. In theory, at least, a court could lower the standard of justification (based on the lesser weight of the protected activity) without also deferring to the legislature's judgment that this standard has been satisfied (the standard of proof). In practice, however, this distinction may be impossible to draw. A judicial decision that the legislature may restrict a right or freedom on less than substantial or compelling grounds looks a lot like judicial deference to legislative judgment about the proper balance between competing interests, particularly if we are skeptical about the commensurability of competing values and the possibility of striking the perfect or correct balance between them.

In *R v. Lucas*, [1998] 1 SCR 439, 157 DLR (4th) 423, a majority of the Court upheld the defamatory libel provisions of the *Criminal Code* as a justified restriction on freedom of expression. McLachlin J argued that the lesser value of a particular form of expression should only play a role in the final stage of the proportionality analysis and should not affect the court's assessment of rational connection and minimal impairment. Her disagreement with judges such as Cory and La Forest JJ, who assume that the lesser value of the expression should affect the application of each of the proportionality tests in *Oakes*, may rest on a different understanding of what these tests involve. If the rational connection and minimal impairment tests involve a limited form of balancing of competing interests (as was suggested above) then they will also be affected by the judgment that a certain form of expression has greater or lesser value. If, on the other hand, as McLachlin J seems to believe, these tests are concerned exclusively with the effectiveness of the law in advancing its pressing and substantial purpose and are to be applied without any kind of balancing of competing interests, then the relative value of the restricted expression will be relevant only later at the third and final step of the *Oakes* proportionality analysis.

There may be another reason why the *Oakes* test remains vague and flexible. In *Oakes*, the Court sought to establish a generic approach to the assessment of limits under s. 1 of the Charter. Such an approach to limits rests on the idea that the rights protected in the Charter have the same basic structure—each right represents a zone of privacy or independence that should not be interfered with by the state except in very special circumstances. Yet, if the rights and freedoms in the Charter are more diverse in character, representing different aspects of human flourishing or human dignity, and do not all fit within a single liberty rights model, then the form or character of limits on these rights may differ in significant ways. The limits on different rights may not have a common structure. A limit on freedom of religion may be very different from a limit on the right to equality. While it may be possible to develop a reasonably clear or coherent set of standards or tests for the limitation of particular rights, the effort to develop standards applicable to all Charter rights may lead inevitably to ambiguity and inconsistency. It is worth noting that this understanding of limits provides a good reason for keeping this chapter of the book short. There may be limited value in examining the limitations issue in a general and preliminary way outside the context of particular Charter rights.

Consider the following account of the role of deference in the application of the *Oakes* test.

**Sujit Choudhry, "So What Is the Real Legacy of Oakes? Two Decades of
Proportionality Analysis Under the Canadian Charter's Section 1"**
(2006), 35 *Supreme Court Law Review* (2d) 501, at 503-4, 522-25, 527-30
(footnotes omitted)

There is a dominant narrative on what the true legacy of *Oakes* and the retreat from
Oakes are. The argument is that *Oakes* set out a uniform approach for assessing justifiable
limitations on Charter rights irrespective of differences in context, but that in the decade
following *Oakes*, the Court searched for criteria of deference, to reliably and predictably
categorize cases where deference was warranted and those where it was not. These categories were not applied consistently by the Court, and, indeed, produced disagreement
within the Court over how they should be applied in specific cases. Underlying both
trends were concerns regarding the cogency of the distinctions employed by the Court
to delineate the boundaries of these categories. The broader lesson of *Oakes* is the need
to tailor judicial review to the unique context of each case.

Although the dominant narrative captures much of *Oakes'* legacy, it misses much of
what is at stake in many recent section 1 cases, and by implication, what the true legacy
of *Oakes* and the retreat from *Oakes* are. In my view, *Oakes* created an enormous institutional dilemma for the Court, by setting up a conflict between the demand for definitive
proof to support each stage of the section 1 analysis, and the reality of policy making
under conditions of factual uncertainty. And so the legacy of *Oakes* is that the central
question of section 1 is how the Court should allocate the risk of factual uncertainty
when governments legislate under conditions of imperfect information. ... But not only
has the Court failed to recognize this as a central question; it has failed to adopt a consistent approach in how it answers it. ...

[W]ith 20 years of hindsight, it is questionable whether the Court was wise to strike
out as boldly as it did in *Oakes*. For in addition to setting up a stringent test of justification, *Oakes* also made empirics central to every stage of the *Oakes* test. As the Court said
in a largely ignored passage:

> Where evidence is required in order to prove the constituent elements of a s. 1 inquiry, and
> this will generally be the case, it should be cogent and persuasive and make clear to the
> Court the consequences of imposing or not imposing the limit.

This passage appears to have been largely overlooked in the academic literature. Moreover, it has been quoted infrequently by the Court—only in four Charter cases, whereas
Oakes has been cited by the Court in 152 subsequents judgments. But it is becoming increasingly central to the Court's jurisprudence. The justice most responsible for bringing
the Court's attention to this issue has been McLachlin CJ. As she explained in *RJR-Mac-
Donald* [*v. Canada (Attorney General)*, [1995] 3 SCR 199, 127 DLR (4th) 1, in which the
Court struck down a general ban on tobacco advertising (discussed in Chapter 20, Freedom of Expression)], the *Oakes* test

> sets up a process of "reasoned demonstration," as opposed to simply accepting the say-so of
> governments. By this, she meant that "[t]he s. 1 inquiry is by its very nature a fact-specific
> inquiry." ...

… [R]ights can only be justifiably limited in response to concrete, precise and real problems or harms whose existence can be demonstrated to the satisfaction of a court through the normal trial process.

Needless to say, in *Oakes* itself, no such factual record was before the Court, because the parties had no notice that they were required to produce one. To understand why *Oakes* may have been unwise, imagine if the Crown *had* known the requirements of the *Oakes* test in advance and attempted to adduce evidence sufficient to justify the challenged provision. Would it have been possible to provide evidence meeting the civil standard of proof mandated by *Oakes* with respect to each constituent element of the test? In particular, would it have been possible to definitely prove that the means chosen minimally impaired the right to be presumed innocent—*i.e.*, that other less intrusive means would not have been equally effective? Indeed, what *kind* of proof would have sufficed? The conundrum raised by this hypothetical is in fact a more general problem that has emerged as a central feature of Charter adjudication. Public policy is often based on approximations and extrapolations from the available evidence, inferences from comparative data, and, on occasion, even educated guesses. Absent a large-scale policy experiment, this is all the evidence that is likely to be available. Justice La Forest offered an observation in *McKinney* [*v. University of Guelph*, [1990] 3 SCR 229, 76 DLR (4th) 545], which rings true: "[d]ecisions on such matters must inevitably be the product of a mix of conjecture, fragmentary knowledge, general experience and knowledge of the needs, aspirations and resources of society."

In other words, *Oakes'* approach to interpreting section 1 has unwittingly created a major institutional dilemma for the Court, given the practical reality that public policy is often made on the basis of incomplete knowledge. In many important cases, disputes over justifiable limits on Charter rights have been *factual* disputes about the nature of social problems, and the effectiveness of government policy instruments in combating them. Although it has never been framed in this way, the basic question in these cases is the same: who should bear the risk of empirical uncertainty with respect to government activity that infringes Charter rights? This has become one of the unarticulated yet central questions in Charter litigation. It has given rise to an extensive jurisprudence, and is one of the principal legacies of *Oakes*.

One answer would be that in a constitutional, rights-based regime, in which rights are the rule and of presumptive importance, limitations on rights are the exception, governments bear the onus of justification in upholding rights-infringing measures, and the state bears the risk of empirical uncertainty. But to set such a high bar for governments may be to ask too much of them. It may simply be impossible to prove with scientific certainty that the means chosen to combat the problem actually will do so, and that other, less intrusive means to tackle the problem are equally effective. As La Forest J wrote in his dissenting judgment in *RJR-MacDonald* to require governments to bear the risk of empirical uncertainty "could have the effect of virtually paralyzing the operation of government … it will be impossible to govern … it would not be possible to make difficult but sometimes necessary legislative choices. There would be conferred on the courts a supervisory role over a state itself essentially inactive". And so another answer would be for the courts to not require governments to adduce much in the way of a factual record at all. But this would seem to read out the requirement that reasonable limits be "demonstrably justified," set out in the text of section 1 itself, and to ask courts to accept the say-so of governments on the existence of public policy problems, and the relative efficacy of policy instruments in dealing with them.

The Court has struck a compromise between these two extremes. In cases in which there is conflicting or inconclusive social science evidence, the question is whether the government has a "reasonable basis" for concluding that an actual problem exists, that the means chosen would address it, and that the means chosen infringes the right as little as possible. This standard is understood as expecting something less of governments than definitive, scientific proof. But an absolute lack of evidence is unacceptable; there must be some factual basis for the public policy.

· · ·

[A]lthough the Court has been unanimous in accepting the reasonable basis test to assess inconclusive social science evidence, and in permitting governments to rely on common sense or logic to surmount evidentiary gaps, there have been significant disagreements in recent cases over the boundaries of these doctrines. Significantly, these divisions on the Court have not turned on the sorts of problems which arose out of the categorical distinctions which it developed in *Irwin Toy* [*Ltd. v. Quebec (Attorney General)*, [1989] 1 SCR 927, 58 DLR (4th) 577] and other cases. For example, there is no disagreement in these cases over how to categorize the speech in question, or on whether to defer under minimal impairment.

So what is the basis of disagreement? In some cases, the disagreement has centred on what kinds of *inferences* governments are entitled to draw from inconclusive evidence. The most famous clash occurred in *RJR-MacDonald*, and centred on the link between tobacco advertising and consumption, given the absence of definitive evidence linking the two. The Court divided on whether governments were entitled to infer from the widespread use of "brand preference" and "informational" advertising by tobacco companies that such a link existed. Justice La Forest in dissent was willing to infer that by convincing smokers not to quit, these advertisements had the effect of sustaining levels of consumption, while McLachlin J refused to do so.

And the Court has also split on the circumstances in which it is appropriate to apply "logic" or "common sense" to surmount an absence of evidence. What is particularly interesting is that the Court has divided on this question in two cases concerning political expression, *Thomson Newspapers* [*Co. v. Canada (Attorney General)*, [1998] 1 SCR 877, 159 DLR (4th) 385] and *Harper* [*v. Canada (Attorney General)*, [2004] 1 SCR 827, 239 DLR (4th) 193 (both discussed in Chapter 20, Freedom of Expression)]. From the vantage point of the categories of deference set out in *Irwin Toy* and subsequent decisions, these were easy cases, because political expression lies at the core of section 2(b), and is a clear instance in which governments should be held to a strict standard of review. But although the Court agreed that political speech was at issue, it was nonetheless sharply divided over how to address the lack of definitive proof for the factual premises underlying the challenged laws. Although these cases have attracted minimal attention from constitutional scholars for their broader importance to the Court's understanding of the judicial role under the Charter, they are worthy of close attention because they tell us that there is another legacy of *Oakes*.

At the heart of the majority judgment in *Thomson Newspapers* was the concern that too broad an approach to bridging empirical gaps through judicial notice could undermine entirely the idea that governments can only justifiably limit constitutional rights to respond to real problems. The majority accordingly attempted to set some limits on when it could accept the existence of harm without evidence. It suggested that its common sense or logic approach to the existence of harm applied to hate speech and pornography because "the possibility of harm is within the everyday knowledge and experience of Canadians, or where factual determination and value judgments overlap". Thus the majority refused to infer from the fact that opinion polls influence voter choice in election campaigns that inaccurate polls mislead large numbers of voters and have a significant impact on the outcome of an election, "without more specific and conclusive evidence to that effect". It therefore found unconstitutional a publication ban on public opinion polls within the final three days of a federal election campaign. The message was that pornography and hate speech were in a special and narrow category.

But then in *Harper*, a divided Court disregarded this self-imposed limitation, and upheld restrictions on third party expenditures during election campaigns on the eve of the last federal vote. The justifications for the restrictions were to further the value of political equality (to equalize participation in political debate, to protect the outcome of an election from being distorted by third party expenditures, and to safeguard the public's confidence in the electoral process) and to protect the integrity of spending limits for candidates and political parties. The majority openly acknowledged that both the alleged harm and the efficacy of legislative responses to it were "difficult, if not impossible, to measure scientifically", but nonetheless was willing to reason both that the harm existed and that the cure was effective. The dissent, led by McLachlin CJ, argued that in the absence of evidence, "[t]he dangers posited are entirely hypothetical" and "unproven and speculative" and that "the legislation is an overreaction to a non-existent problem", and was completely unwilling to entertain the common sense argument. ...

For the last two decades, the Court has struggled to come to terms with the institutional task it set itself in *Oakes*. In response to the question of who bears the risk of empirical uncertainty with respect to government activity that infringes Charter rights, the rights-claimant or the government, the answer has been, in effect, both. But even though the Court has agreed on this compromise, deep disagreements persist along its ragged edges. The Court has yet to work out under what circumstances it will use common sense, reason or logic to bridge an absence of evidence, and to delineate when it will allow inferences to be drawn from inconclusive social science evidence.

III. THE OVERRIDE

Section 33 of the Charter, the "override," or "notwithstanding," clause, began as, and remains, a controversial part of the Charter. The Quebec sign law case, *Ford v. Quebec (Attorney General)* (an extract from which is reproduced below), is the only case in which the Supreme Court of Canada has been asked to review the exercise of the override power.

The history of the *Ford* case begins with the exclusion of the Parti Québécois government of Quebec from the final discussions and agreement that led to the amendment and "patriation" of the Constitution, which is dealt with in Chapter 16, The Advent of the Charter. In November 1981, the other ten governments agreed to a package of constitutional amendments that included the Charter of Rights.

As a way of protesting against a significant constitutional amendment to which it had not agreed and which did not, in its view, take adequate account of its interests, the Government of Quebec made use of s. 33 to shield its laws, as much as possible, from the Charter's application. (At the same time, the provincial government enacted the *Quebec Charter of Rights and Freedoms*, which gave legislative protection to many of the same rights included in the Charter.) In seeking to shield its laws from the operation of the Canadian Charter, the Quebec government used what came to be called a "standard override clause," which made reference to all the rights subject to the override:

> This Act shall operate notwithstanding the provisions of sections 2 and 7 to 15 of the *Constitution Act, 1982* (Schedule B of the *Canada Act*, chapter 11 in the 1982 volume of the *Act of Parliament of the United Kingdom*).

By an omnibus amendment enactment, the National Assembly repealed and re-enacted, with the addition of this standard clause, all pre-Charter provincial legislation. This technique insulated all existing provincial legislation from those Charter rights and freedoms to which the override applies. Then, statute by statute, it inserted the standard clause into all new enactments, including amending instruments.

The omnibus enactment came into force on June 23, 1982, three months after the Charter came into effect. However, by its terms the omnibus amendment was to be applied retroactively to April 17, 1982, the day the Charter came into force.

Ford v. Quebec (Attorney General)
[1988] 2 SCR 712, 54 DLR (4th) 577

[This case involved a challenge to those provisions of the *Quebec Charter of the French Language*, RSQ, c. C-11 (as amended) that required French-only in public signs, posters, and commercial advertising. The appellants challenged these provisions successfully under both the *Canadian Charter of Rights and Freedoms* and the *Quebec Charter of Human Rights and Freedoms*, RSQ, c. C-12, ss. 3 and 52. The extract here focuses on the question whether Quebec's standard clause, omnibus use of the override was valid. Another issue in the case, whether the French-only rule infringed freedom of expression, appears in Chapter 24, Language Rights.]

THE COURT (Dickson CJC, Beetz, Estey, McIntyre, Lamer, Wilson, and Le Dain JJ): ...

[The National Assembly of Quebec passed the following law in June 1982:]

> Sections 1, 2, 5, 6 and 7 of *An Act respecting the Constitution Act*, 1982, SQ 1982, c. 21, which was assented to on June 23, 1982, provide:

1. Each of the Acts adopted before 17 April 1982 is replaced by the text of each of them as they existed at that date, after being amended by the addition, at the end and as a separate section, of the following:

This Act shall operate notwithstanding the provisions of sections 2 and 7 to 15 of the *Constitution Act, 1982* (Schedule B of the *Canada Act*, chapter 11 in the 1982 volume of the Acts of the Parliament of the United Kingdom).

The text so amended of each of these Acts constitutes a separate Act.

No such Act is to be construed as new law except for the purposes of section 33 of the *Constitution Act, 1982*; for all other purposes, it has force of law as if it were a consolidation of the Act it replaces.

Every provision of such an Act shall have effect from the date the provision it replaces took effect or is to take effect.

Such an Act must be cited in the same manner as the Act it replaces.

2. Each of the Acts adopted between 17 April 1982 and 23 June 1982 is replaced by the text of each of them as they existed on 23 June 1982, after being amended by the addition, provision set out in the first paragraph of section 1.

The second, third, fourth and fifth paragraphs of section 1 apply, *mutatis mutandis*, to the Acts referred to in the first paragraph.

. . .

5. This Act shall operate notwithstanding the provision of sections 2 and 7 to 15 of the *Constitution Act, 1982*.

6. The sanction of this Act is valid for each of the Acts enacted under section 1 or 2.

7. This Act comes into force on the day of its sanction. However, section 1 and the first paragraph of section 3 have effect from 17 April 1982; section 2 and the second paragraph of section 3 have effect from the date from which each of the Acts replaced under section 2 came into force.

... The essential contention ... against the validity of the standard override provision, ... was that the provision did not sufficiently specify the guaranteed rights or freedoms which the legislation intended to override. In support of this contention reliance was placed not only on the wording of s. 33(1) and 33(2) of the Charter but on general considerations concerning the effectiveness of the democratic process. ...

It was contended that the words "a provision included in section 2 or sections 7 to 15 of this Charter" in s. 33(1) and the words "but for the provision of this Charter referred to in the declaration" in s. 33(2) indicate that in order to be valid, a declaration pursuant to s. 33 must specify the particular provision within a section of the Charter which Parliament or the legislature of a province intends to override. That is, the specific guaranteed right or freedom to be overridden must be referred to in the words of the Charter and not merely by the number of the section or paragraph in which it appears. The rationale underlying this contention is that the nature of the guaranteed right or freedom must be sufficiently drawn to the attention of the members of the legislature and of the public so that the relative seriousness of what is proposed may be perceived and reacted to through the democratic process. As the Attorney General for Ontario, who argued against the constitutionality of the standard override provision, put it, there must be a "political cost" for overriding a guaranteed right or freedom. ...

In the course of argument different views were expressed as to the constitutional perspective from which the meaning and application of s. 33 of the *Canadian Charter of Rights and Freedoms* should be approached: the one suggesting that it reflects the continuing importance of legislative supremacy, the other suggesting the seriousness of a legislative decision to override guaranteed rights and freedoms and the importance that such a decision be taken only as a result of a fully informed democratic process. These two perspectives are not, however, particularly relevant or helpful in construing the requirements of s. 33. Section 33 lays down requirements of form only, and there is no warrant for importing into it grounds for substantive review of the legislative policy in exercising the override authority in a particular case. The requirement of an apparent link or relationship between the overriding Act and the guaranteed rights or freedoms to be overridden seems to be a substantive ground of review. It appears to require that the legislature identify the provisions of the Act in question which might otherwise infringe specified guaranteed rights or freedoms. That would seem to require a *prima facie* justification of the decision to exercise the override authority rather than merely a certain formal expression of it. There is, however, no warrant in the terms of s. 33 for such a requirement. A legislature may not be in a position to judge with any degree of certainty what provisions of the *Canadian Charter of Rights and Freedoms* might be successfully invoked against various aspects of the Act in question. For this reason it must be permitted in a particular case to override more than one provision of the Charter and indeed all of the provisions which it is permitted to override by the terms of s. 33. The standard override provision in issue in this appeal is, therefore, a valid exercise of the authority conferred by s. 33 in so far as it purports to override all of the provisions in s. 2 and ss. 7 to 15 of the Charter. The essential requirement of form laid down by s. 33 is that the override declaration must be an express declaration that an Act or a provision of an Act shall operate notwithstanding a provision included in s. 2 or ss. 7 to 15 of the Charter. With great respect for the contrary view, this Court is of the opinion that a s. 33 declaration is sufficiently express if it refers to the number of the section, subsection or paragraph of the Charter which contains the provision or provisions to be overridden. Of course, if it is intended to override only a part of the provision or provisions contained in a section, subsection or paragraph then there would have to be a sufficient reference in words to the part to be overridden. In so far as requirements of the democratic process are relevant, this is the form of reference used in legislative drafting with respect to legislative provisions to be amended or repealed. There is no reason why more should be required under s. 33. A reference to the number of the section, subsection or paragraph containing the provisions or provisions to be overridden is a sufficient indication to those concerned of the relative seriousness of what is proposed. It cannot have been intended by the word "expressly" that a legislature should be required to encumber a s. 33 declaration by stating the provision or provisions to be overridden in the words of the Charter, which, in the case of the standard override provision in issue in the appeal, would be a very long recital indeed.

... [I]t remains to be considered whether the Court should exercise its discretion to rule on the other aspects of the validity of the standard override provision: ... the "omnibus" character of the enactment; and the retrospective effect given to the override provision. ...

The Court has concluded that although both of these provisions have ceased to have effect it is better that all questions concerning their validity should be settled in these appeals because of their possible continuing importance in other cases. Given the provision in the form indicated above is a valid exercise of the authority conferred by s. 33 of the *Canadian Charter of Rights and Freedoms*, this Court is of the opinion that the validity of its enactment is not affected by the fact that it was introduced into all Quebec statutes enacted prior to a certain date by a single enactment. That was an effective exercise of legislative authority that did not prevent the override declaration so enacted in each statute from being an express declaration within the meaning of s. 33 of the Canadian Charter. Counsel referred to this form of enactment as reflecting an impermissibly "routine" exercise of the override authority or even a "perversion" of it. It was even suggested that it amounted to an attempted amendment of the Charter. These are once again essentially submissions concerning permissible legislative policy in the exercise of the override authority rather than what constitutes a sufficiently express declaration of override. As has been stated, there is no warrant in s. 33 for such considerations as a basis of judicial review of a particular exercise of the authority conferred by s. 33. The Court is of a different view, however, concerning the retrospective effect given to the standard override provision. ... In this regard, the wording of s. 33(1) of the Canadian Charter is not without ambiguity. For purposes of clarity, we set out the relevant provision in both languages:

> 33.(1) Parliament or the legislature of a province may expressly declare in an Act of Parliament or of the legislature, as the case may be, that the Act or a provision thereof shall operate notwithstanding a provision included in section 2 or sections 7 to 15 of this Charter.
>
> 33.(1) Le Parlement ou la législature d'une province peut adopter une loi ou il est expressément déclaré que celle-ci ou une de ses dispositions a effet indépendamment d'une disposition donnée de l'article 2 ou des articles 7-15 de la présente charte.

In English, the critical phrase is "shall operate notwithstanding." Generally, the word "shall" may have either a prospective or an imperative meaning or both. Similarly, the French "a effet indépendamment" is susceptible of a valid interpretation in more than one tense. ...

Where, as here, an enabling provision is ambiguous as to whether it allows for retroactive legislation, the same rule of construction applies. In this case, s. 33(1) admits of two interpretations; one that allows Parliament or a legislature to enact retroactive override provisions, the other that permits prospective derogation only. We conclude that the latter and narrower interpretation is the proper one, and that s. 7 cannot give retrospective effect to the override provision. Section 7 of *An Act respecting the Constitution Act, 1982*, is to the extent of this inconsistency with s. 33 of the Canadian Charter, of no force or effect, with the result that the standard override provisions enacted by s. 1 of that Act came into force on June 23, 1982 in accordance with the first paragraph of s. 7.

Appeal dismissed.

NOTES AND QUESTIONS

1. As a general rule, one's view about s. 33 seems to depend on one's comfort or discomfort with the practice of judicial review. Those who see judicial review as an important and effective way to protect fundamental rights from the give and take of preference-based politics tend to view s. 33 as an undermining of the Charter's protection of individual rights. In their view, s. 33 allows governments to "override" fundamental rights. On the other hand, those who are troubled by the undemocratic practice of appointed judges second-guessing the policy and value judgments of elected legislatures seem to be untroubled by s. 33. In their view, s. 33 gives the legislature the final say on the appropriate scope and limits of certain basic rights. Section 33 simply permits the legislature to override the judicial interpretation of those rights (and their appropriate limits).

However, some supporters of judicial review take a more positive view of s. 33 as an important component of the Charter's complex institutional structure. Lorraine Weinrib, for example, argues that the notwithstanding clause may blunt the argument that judicial review under the Charter is anti-democratic and may give the courts greater confidence when reviewing legislation:

> Even when dormant, the [notwithstanding] clause insulates the judicial function from illegitimate political entanglement. The fact that legislatures may abrogate most Charter rights, as long as they do so expressly, means that judges can carry out their responsibilities without constantly looking over their shoulders. Their task is to protect the normative values for which rights stand, e.g., liberty, dignity, equality, on a case-by-case basis. This task is suited to the expertise, experience and independence of the judiciary. Judges should concentrate on providing the strongest support for their position to assist the legislators in performing their function.
>
> A government bent on disregarding Charter rights for the considerations of cost, convenience, expediency or tradition should take the heat in the legislature and beyond. Such positions have no place in the court-room, either as arguments against the recognition of the claimed right or freedom or as arguments as to the justified limitation on those guarantees. The notwithstanding clause designates the appropriate forum for realizing such preferences, the forum in which governments stand politically accountable to those whose rights are at stake. [Lorraine Weinrib, "The Notwithstanding Clause: The Loophole Cementing the Charter" (1998), XXVI *Cité Libre* 47, at 53.]

Has s. 33 had this effect? If not, why not?

2. Why do you think that s. 33 applies to some Charter rights but not to others? Is it not odd that s. 33 applies to a right such as freedom of expression, which is generally regarded as one of the most fundamental in the Charter? A not entirely satisfactory answer may be that rights that are less fundamental, or more accurately, that have been shaped by the country's history and politics, such as language rights or mobility rights, may be more vulnerable to (regional) government restriction. While there may be significant disagreement about the proper application of freedom of expression or the right to equality, citizens (and governments) across the country do not doubt their commitment to these (abstract) rights. However, the commitment to French language education may be less deeply or widely felt in many parts of the country. This explanation of why only some rights are subject to s. 33

assumes that legislatures use s. 33 not to override a right but rather to override the judicial interpretation of that right.

3. Outside of Quebec, s. 33 has been used on only two occasions: by the Saskatchewan government to immunize back to work legislation and by the Alberta government to immunize its legislative definition of marriage as an opposite sex relationship.

However, there have been several occasions in recent years when certain groups have vocally advocated its use. For example, following the Supreme Court of Canada's judgment in *Vriend v. Alberta*, [1998] 1 SCR 493 (discussed in Chapter 16, The Advent of the Charter and in Chapter 23, Equality Rights), in which the court ruled that the Alberta *Individual Rights Protection Act* violated s. 15 of the Charter because it failed to extend protection against discrimination to gays and lesbians, conservative forces in the province pressed the government to override the judgment using s. 33. The Conservative government of Alberta declined to do so.

Some have argued that s. 33 is politically unusable. Is this true? Why might this be so? Might the conditions that make s. 33 unusable change?

CHAPTER EIGHTEEN

Application

I. INTRODUCTION: THE DEBATE ABOUT APPLICATION TO PRIVATE ACTION

Before considering whether a Charter right or freedom has been infringed by an impugned course of action or inaction, we need to deal first with a threshold question: does the Charter even apply? Not all actions are subject to the Charter, and not all inaction gives rise to the possibility of a successful Charter claim. How do we know whether the Charter applies to a particular action or failure to act? The answer to this question lies in the interpretation of s. 32(1) of the Charter, which provides:

This Charter applies

(a) to the Parliament and government of Canada in respect of all matters within the authority of Parliament including all matters relating to the Yukon Territory and Northwest Territories; and

(b) to the legislature and government of each province in respect of all matters within the authority of the legislature of each province.

Does s. 32 limit the application of the Charter to the activities of governments and legislatures, leaving private actors free from an obligation to conform to Charter norms? Or was s. 32 added to the Charter as a cautionary measure simply to make it clear that the particular governmental bodies it identifies were to be bound, without restricting the Charter's application solely to governmental action?

In *Dolphin Delivery*, its first decision grappling with these issues, the Supreme Court of Canada concluded that the Charter does not apply directly to private actors.

Retail, Wholesale and Department Store Union, Local 580 v. Dolphin Delivery Ltd.
[1986] 2 SCR 573, 33 DLR (4th) 174

[At issue was the validity of a court order restraining the appellant union from picketing the premises of the respondent company, Dolphin Delivery. Union members were engaged in a labour dispute with their employer, Purolator, and they wished to picket Dolphin's premises on the grounds that the company was related to Purolator and was performing work for Purolator during the strike. Since the applicable labour legislation, the *Canada Labour Code*, did not regulate secondary picketing, the legality of the proposed picketing fell to be determined by the common law. Relying on the common law tort of inducing breach of contract, a BC court issued an injunction to restrain the picketing. On appeal, the union sought to have the injunction overturned on the ground that it violated its members' freedom of expression. The BC Court of Appeal dismissed the appeal and the union appealed to the Supreme Court of Canada.

Writing for the majority, McIntyre J held that peaceful picketing enjoyed protection pursuant to s. 2(b). He went on to conclude that Dolphin Delivery was not related to Purolator, and, therefore, an injunction to restrain the union from picketing Dolphin's premises was a reasonable limit on expressive freedoms that could be justified pursuant to s. 1. These aspects of the decision are dealt with further in Chapter 20, Freedom of Expression. While the conclusion on infringement of freedom of expression was sufficient to dismiss the appeal, McIntyre J went on to discuss whether the Charter even applied to the dispute in the first place.

He began by asking whether the Charter applied to the common law. Relying on the text of s. 52 of the *Constitution Act, 1982*, he gave this question an affirmative response:

> In my view, there can be no doubt that it does apply. ... The English text [of s. 52] provides that "any law that is inconsistent with the provisions of the Constitution is, to the extent of the inconsistency, of no force or effect." If this language is not broad enough to include the common law, it should be observed as well that the French text adds strong support to this conclusion in its employment of the words "elle rend inopérantes les dispositions incompatibles *de tout autre règle de droit.*" (Emphasis added.) To adopt a construction of s. 52(1) which would exclude from *Charter* application the whole body of the common law which in great part governs the rights and obligations of the individuals in society, would be wholly unrealistic and contrary to the clear language employed in s. 52(1) of the Act.

He then asked whether the Charter applied to litigation between private parties. After quoting from a number of commentators, and relying on the text of s. 32, he concluded in the excerpts below that it did not.]

McINTYRE J (Dickson CJC, Estey, Chouinard, and Le Dain JJ concurring): ... I am in agreement with the view that the *Charter* does not apply to private litigation. It is evident from the authorities and articles cited above that that approach has been adopted by most judges and commentators who have dealt with this question. In my view, s. 32 of the *Charter*, specifically dealing with the question of *Charter* application, is conclusive on this issue. ...(Section 32(1) refers to the Parliament and Government of Canada and to the legislatures and governments of the Provinces in respect of all matters within their respective authorities. In this, it may be seen that Parliament and the Legislatures are treated as separate or specific branches of government, distinct from the executive branch of government, and therefore where the word "government" is used in s. 32 it refers not to government in its generic sense—meaning the whole of the governmental apparatus of the state—but to a branch of government. The word "government," following as it does the words "Parliament" and "Legislature," must then, it would seem, refer to the executive or administrative branch of government. This is the sense in which one generally speaks of the Government of Canada or of a province. I am of the opinion that the word "government" is used in s. 32 of the *Charter* in the sense of the executive govern-

textual.

ment of Canada and the Provinces. This is the sense in which the words "Government of Canada" are ordinarily employed in other sections of the *Constitution Act, 1867*. Sections 12, 16, and 132 all refer to the Parliament and the Government of Canada as separate entities. The words "Government of Canada," particularly where they follow a reference to the word "Parliament," almost always refer to the executive government.

It is my view that s. 32 of the *Charter* specifies the actors to whom the *Charter* will apply. They are the legislative, executive and administrative branches of government. It will apply to those branches of government whether or not their action is invoked in public or private litigation. It would seem that legislation is the only way in which a legislature may infringe a guaranteed right or freedom. Action by the executive or administrative branches of government will generally depend upon legislation, that is, statutory authority. Such action may also depend, however, on the common law, as in the case of the prerogative. To the extent that it relies on statutory authority which constitutes or results in an infringement of a guaranteed right or freedom, the *Charter* will apply and it will be unconstitutional. The action will also be unconstitutional to the extent that it relies for authority or justification on a rule of the common law which constitutes or creates an infringement of a *Charter* right or freedom. In this way the *Charter* will apply to the common law, whether in public or private litigation. It will apply to the common law, however, only in so far as the common law is the basis of some governmental action which, it is alleged, infringes a guaranteed right or freedom.

The element of governmental intervention necessary to make the *Charter* applicable in an otherwise private action is difficult to define. We have concluded that the *Charter* applies to the common law but not between private parties. The problem here is that this is an action between private parties in which the appellant resists the common law claim of the respondent on the basis of a *Charter* infringement. The argument is made that the common law, which is itself subject to the *Charter*, creates the tort of civil conspiracy and that of inducing a breach of contract. The respondent has sued and has procured the injunction which has enjoined the picketing on the basis of the commission of these torts. The appellants say the injunction infringes their *Charter* right of freedom of expression under s. 2(b).

· · ·

I find the position [that the Charter applies to any court order based on the common law] troublesome and, in my view, it should not be accepted as an approach to this problem. While in political science terms it is probably acceptable to treat the courts as one of the three fundamental branches of Government, that is, legislative, executive, and judicial, I cannot equate for the purposes of *Charter* application the order of a court with an element of governmental action. This is not to say that the courts are not bound by the *Charter*. The courts are, of course, bound by the *Charter* as they are bound by all law. It is their duty to apply the law, but in doing so they act as neutral arbiters, not as contending parties involved in a dispute. To regard a court order as an element of governmental intervention necessary to invoke the *Charter* would, it seems to me, widen the scope of *Charter* application to virtually all private litigation. All cases must end, if carried to completion, with an enforcement order and if the *Charter* precludes the making of the order, where a *Charter* right would be infringed, it would seem that all private litigation would be subject to the *Charter*. In my view, this approach will not provide the answer to the question.

A more direct and a more precisely-defined connection between the element of government action and the claim advanced must be present before the *Charter* applies.

· · ·

[I]t is difficult and probably dangerous to attempt to define with narrow precision that
element of governmental intervention which will suffice to permit reliance on the *Charter* by private litigants in private litigation. ...

It would also seem that the *Charter* would apply to many forms of delegated legislation,
regulations, orders in council, possibly municipal by-laws, and by-laws and regulations of
other creatures of Parliament and the Legislatures. It is not suggested that this list is exhaustive. Where such exercise of, or reliance upon, governmental action is present and
where one private party invokes or relies upon it to produce an infringement of the *Charter* rights of another, the *Charter* will be applicable. Where, however, private party "A"
sues private party "B" relying on the common law and where no act of government is relied upon to support the action, the *Charter* will not apply. I should make it clear, however,
that this is a distinct issue from the question whether the judiciary ought to apply and develop the principles of the common law in a manner consistent with the fundamental values enshrined in the Constitution. The answer to this question must be in the affirmative.
In this sense, then, the *Charter* is far from irrelevant to private litigants whose disputes
fall to be decided at common law. But this is different from the proposition that one private party owes a constitutional duty to another, which proposition underlies the purported assertion of *Charter* causes of action or *Charter* defences between individuals.

· · ·

In the case at bar ... we have no offending statute. We have a rule of the common law
which renders secondary picketing tortious and subject to injunctive restraint, on the
basis that it induces a breach of contract. While, as we have found, the Charter applies to
the common law, we do not have in this litigation between purely private parties any
exercise of or reliance upon governmental action which would invoke the Charter. It follows then that the appeal must fail.

[Wilson and Beetz JJ each wrote concurring judgments in which they agreed with
McIntrye J's treatment of the application issue, but disagreed with his reasoning on freedom of expression. Beetz J would have found that the picketing in issue was not a form
of expression and that no question of an infringement of s. 2(b) could arise. Wilson J
would have reached a different result on the s. 1 analysis.]

Appeal dismissed.

NOTES AND QUESTIONS

1. The decision in *Dolphin Delivery* has spawned a great deal of criticism. While many
commentators support the basic premise of the decision—that is, that constitutions are intended to bind governments and that the Charter only applies to governmental action—they
are critical of the way in which the line between governmental and non-governmental action was drawn by the Court. Some of the criticism has focused on the anomalies created by
the decision's ruling that common law rules, when relied on by private litigants, are not sub-

ject to the Charter, whereas statutory rules governing private relationships are. The ruling creates the possibility of provincial variation in the application of the Charter depending upon whether a province has codified a particular area of law, such as, for example, libel law, or simply left the rules in common law form. As well, it raises the possibility of a significantly greater scope for the application of the Charter in Quebec than in the common law provinces, given that in Quebec the rules governing private relations are based on statute—the *Civil Code*. Numerous commentators have also pointed out the difficulty of maintaining that the courts are not bound by the Charter in the face of specific Charter guarantees that appear to be directed at courts. Others have argued that by leaving powerful private actors unchecked, the Charter cannot deliver on its promise of securing basic rights and liberties. See D. Beatty, "Constitutional Conceits: The Coercive Authority of Courts" (1987), 37 *University of Toronto Law Journal* 183; B. Slattery, "The Charter's Relevance to Private Litigation: Does Dolphin Deliver?" (1987), 32 *McGill Law Journal* 905; A. Hutchinson and A. Petter, "Private Rights/Public Wrongs: The Liberal Lie of the Charter" (1988), 38 *University of Toronto Law Journal* 278; and J. Bakan, *Just Words: Constitutional Rights and Social Wrongs* (Toronto: University of Toronto Press, 1997).

2. In "The Dolphin Delivery Case: The Application of the Charter to Private Action" (1987), 51 *Saskatchewan Law Review* 273, P. Hogg argues that although the Supreme Court was correct in holding that purely private action should be unconstrained by the Charter, it drew the line in the wrong place and should have subjected the common law to the Charter to the extent that the common law has "crystallized" into a rule that can be enforced by the courts. This is the approach taken in some US cases. US courts have interpreted their *Bill of Rights* as applying only when there has been "state action," but in some cases have found state action when a judicial order is sought that would support the infringement of rights. Thus, in *Shelley v. Kraemer*, 334 US 1 (1948), the court refused to enforce a racially discriminatory private agreement on the grounds that a judicial remedy to aid private discrimination would be state action in violation of the equal protection guarantee found in the Fourteenth Amendment. In *New York Times v. Sullivan*, 376 US 254 (1964), the common law of defamation was found to violate the First Amendment's guarantee of freedom of expression. Would this approach have been preferable to that adopted in *Dolphin Delivery*?

3. Is McIntyre J's narrow approach to the interpretation of s. 32 consistent with the "large and liberal" interpretive principle the Court has applied to the rights-conferring provisions of the Charter? If not, what explains the difference in approach?

As will be discussed below in section IV of this chapter, the significance of McIntyre J's ruling that the Charter does not apply directly to judges when developing and applying the common law has been significantly attenuated by subsequent rulings.

The conclusion that the Charter does not apply directly to private actors, on the other hand, is generally accepted. The Charter applies only to government. Defining government, however, is not an easy task. When can we say that an act or omission alleged to have infringed Charter rights or freedoms is the responsibility of government? The case law establishes that actions can qualify as governmental in two ways. First, obviously, if the actor itself is governmental, then its actions are subject to the Charter. Governmental actors include components and members of the legislative and executive branches of government, and other entities that are controlled by government or that are exercising governmental functions. Second, and less obviously, non-governmental actors may be subject to the Charter if they are engaged in governmental acts, such as implementing a governmental program or exercising a power of compulsion conferred by statute.

It is commonly asserted that the Charter applies to government *action*. This is true, but we should not forget that the Charter can also apply to government *inaction*. This is because the rights and freedoms set out in the Charter impose a mix of positive and negative obligations on governments. The Charter is not concerned purely with safeguarding negative liberty from active interference by the state. To the extent that the Charter imposes positive obligations on governments, it must also apply to government inaction to be coherent. For example, the right to minority language educational facilities in s. 23, or the right to an interpreter in s. 14, would be meaningless if the Charter did not apply to a failure by government to take steps to implement these rights. For this reason, the text of s. 32 does not refer to government action. Rather, it says the Charter applies to governments "in respect of all matters within [their] authority."

The material that follows begins, in section II, with an exploration of the different kinds of government action subject to the Charter. In this section we will look at the ways the courts have defined governmental actors and governmental acts. In section III, some circumstances in which the courts have applied the Charter to government inaction will be discussed. We will then, in section IV, turn our attention to the special problem of the application of the Charter to the courts and the common law. While the bulk of this chapter is concerned with determining who is subject to the burden of complying with obligations imposed by the Charter, the final part, section V, looks briefly at the application issue from the other side: who can claim the benefit of Charter rights and freedoms?

II. GOVERNMENTAL ACTION

A. Governmental Actors

If an entity is part of government, then the Charter will ordinarily apply to all of its actions. The references to Parliament and provincial legislatures in s. 32 of the Charter mean that when laws are passed by those bodies, they must comply with the Charter. Federal, provincial, and territorial statutes and regulations made thereunder are subject to the Charter. Moreover, the Charter applies to actions taken by a legislative assembly so long as those actions are not shielded from Charter scrutiny by constitutionally protected parliamentary privileges. See *New Brunswick Broadcasting Co. v. Nova Scotia*, [1993] 1 SCR 319, 100 DLR (4th) 212. In *Dolphin Delivery*, above, the Court held that the term "government" did not include the judiciary, although as we will see in section IV, below, this ruling has since been called into question. "Government" in s. 32 includes the executive branch of government, including cabinet (see *Operation Dismantle v. The Queen*, [1985] 1 SCR 441, 18 DLR (4th) 481), ministers, officials employed in government departments, police officers, and other public agencies or agents that are subject to ministerial control or charged with the performance of government responsibilities.

The case law makes clear that not all entities that have powers conferred on them by statute, that are controlled to some degree by government, or that receive public funding will qualify as "government" for the purposes of s. 32. What factors should courts emphasize in making a determination that governmental action is present: governmental approval or endorsement of the actions? the nature of the challenged actions—that is, whether they are regulatory or involve the performance of what may be thought of as a public function? To what extent will basic political intuitions about the kind of conduct that is inherently "private" influence the decision?

1. Entities Controlled by Government

McKinney v. University of Guelph
[1990] 3 SCR 229, 76 DLR (4th) 545

[Eight faculty members and a librarian challenged the mandatory retirement policies of four Ontario universities. They argued that the universities' policies violated the equality guarantees found in s. 15 of the Charter by discriminating on the basis of age. This argument raised the preliminary issue of whether the Charter was applicable to the actions of universities—that is, whether universities could be said to be government actors under s. 32 of the Charter. In the alternative, the challengers argued that the provincial human rights code, which only protected persons between the ages of 18 and 65 from age discrimination, violated s. 15 of the Charter by allowing discrimination against persons over 65. On the issue of the application of the Charter to universities, a majority of the court concluded that universities' mandatory retirement policies did not come within the concept of government action. The main judgment on the application issue was written by La Forest J.]

LA FOREST J (Dickson CJC and Gonthier J concurring): ... The exclusion of private activity from the Charter was not a result of happenstance. It was a deliberate choice which must be respected. We do not really know why this approach was taken, but several reasons suggest themselves. Historically, bills of rights, of which that of the United States is the great constitutional exemplar, have been directed at government. Government is the body that can enact and enforce rules and authoritatively impinge on individual freedom. Only government requires to be constitutionally shackled to preserve the rights of the individual. Others, it is true, may offend against the rights of individuals. This is especially true in a world in which economic life is largely left to the private sector where powerful private institutions are not directly affected by democratic forces. But government can either regulate these or create distinct bodies for the protection of human rights and the advancement of human dignity.

To open up all private and public action to judicial review could strangle the operation of society and, as put by counsel for the universities, "diminish the area of freedom within which individuals can act." ...

Opening up private activities to judicial review could impose an impossible burden on the courts. ...

The Court in *Dolphin Delivery* [*Retail, Wholesale and Department Store Union, Local 580 v. Dolphin Delivery Ltd.*, [1986] 2 SCR 573, 33 DLR (4th) 174] did not have to decide on the extent to which the Charter applies to the actions of subordinate bodies that are created and supported by Parliament or the legislatures, but it did leave open the possibility that such bodies could be governed by the Charter. ...

The appellants first argued that "universities constitute part of the legislature or government of the province within the meaning of s. 32 of the Charter, insofar as they are creatures of statute which exercise powers pursuant to statute and carry out a public function pursuant to statutory authority." Undoubtedly, as the Court of Appeal recognized, a statute providing for mandatory retirement in the universities would violate s. 15 of the Charter, and it is also true that the government could not do so in the exercise of a statutory power. That is because, as McIntyre J pointed out, they—the legislative, executive and administrative branches of government—are the actors to whom the Charter applies under s. 32(1).

But the mere fact that an entity is a creature of statute and has been given the legal attributes of a natural person is in no way sufficient to make its actions subject to the Charter. Such an entity may be established to facilitate the performance of tasks that those seeking incorporation wish to undertake and to control, not to facilitate the performance of tasks assigned to government. It would significantly undermine the obvious purpose of s. 32 to confine the application of the Charter to legislative and government action to apply it to private corporations, and it would fly in the face of the justifications for so confining the Charter to which I have already referred. ...

The appellants strongly relied on a statement by Professor Peter Hogg, *Constitutional Law of Canada*, 2d ed. (Scarborough, ON: Carswell, 1985), at p. 671 ... to the effect that Parliament and the legislatures cannot authorize action by others that would be in breach of the Charter.

[Hogg included universities within the group of governmental institutions exercising statutory power bound by the Charter.]

That statement would, no doubt, be true of a situation such as occurred in *Slaight Communications Inc. v. Davidson*, [1989] 1 SCR 1038 [59 DLR (4th) 416], where a statute authorizes a person to exercise a discretion in the course of performing a governmental objective. But the Charter was not intended to cover activities by non-governmental entities created by government for legally facilitating private individuals to do things of their own choosing without engaging governmental responsibility. ...

The Charter apart, there is no question of the power of the universities to negotiate contracts and collective agreements with their employees and to include within them provisions for mandatory retirement. These actions are not taken under statutory compulsion, so a Charter attack cannot be sustained on that ground. There is nothing to indicate that in entering into these arrangements, the universities were in any way following the dictates of the government. They were acting purely on their own initiative. Unless, then, it can be established that they form part of government, the universities' action here cannot fall within the ambit of the Charter. That cannot be answered by the mere fact that they are incorporated and perform an important public service. Many institutions in our society perform functions that are undeniably of an important public nature, but are undoubtedly not part of the government. These can include railroads and airlines, as well as symphonies and institutions of learning. And this may be so even though they are subjected to extensive governmental regulations and even assistance from the public purse. ... A public purpose test is simply inadequate. It is fraught with difficulty and uncertainty. It is simply not the test mandated by s. 32. ...

... [I]f the Charter covers municipalities, it is because "municipalities perform a quintessentially governmental function." They enact coercive laws binding on the public generally, for which offenders may be punished ... . The same can obviously not be said of universities. I hasten to add that ... the Charter is not limited to entities which discharge functions that are inherently governmental in nature. As to what other entities may be subject to the Charter by virtue of the functions they perform, I would think that more would have to be shown than that they engaged in activities or the provision of services that are subject to the legislative jurisdiction of either the federal or provincial governments. ...

The appellants also submit that the universities constitute part of the government under s. 32 of the Charter having regard to the nature of their relationship to the provincial government. The entire context must, they say, be looked at including the facts that they are established by statute which determines their powers, objects and governmental structures, that their historical development was as part of a public system of postsecondary education, that their survival depends on public funding, and that government structures largely coordinate and regulate their activities, through operating and capital grants, special funds, control over tuition fees and approval of new programmes.

There is no question that the relationship of government to Canadian universities has always been significantly different from that existing in Europe when communities of scholars first banded together to pursue learning. From the early days of this country, several of the provinces acted to establish provincial universities ... .

[The statutes establishing Ontario universities are then reviewed.]

... These statutes set out the universities' powers, functions, privileges and governing structure. While these vary from university to university, they are in general much the same. As well, the *University Expropriation Powers Act*, RSO 1980, c. 516, gives them expropriation powers, a matter not in issue here. The *Degree Granting Act*, SO 1983, c. 36, restricts the entities that can operate a university and grant university degrees.

There can be no doubt that the reshaping in the 1950s and 1960s of the universities of Ontario (a process that also occurred in other provinces) resulted from provincial policies aimed at promoting higher education. Nor did the Legislature confine itself to rationalizing the existing system. It heavily funds universities on an ongoing basis. The operating grants alone range, according to the evidence, between a low for York of 68.8% of its operating funds to a high for Guelph of 78.9%. The Ontario Council on University Affairs makes annual global funding recommendations to the government, but the latter assumes responsibility for determining the amounts. It also effectively defines tuition fees within a formula that limits the universities' discretion within a narrow scope. The province also provides most of the funds for capital expenditures, and provides special funds earmarked to meet specific policies. It exercises considerable control over new programs by requiring that they be specifically approved to be eligible for public funds.

It is evident from what has been recounted that the universities' fate is largely in the hands of government and that the universities are subjected to important limitations on what they can do, either by regulation or because of their dependence on government funds. It by no means follows, however, that the universities are organs of government. There are many other entities that receive government funding to accomplish policy objectives governments seek to promote. The fact is that each of the universities has its own governing body. Only a minority of its members (or in the case of York, none) are appointed by the Lieutenant-Governor in Council, and their duty is not to act at the direction of the government but in the interests of the university ... . The remaining members are officers of the Faculty, the students, the administrative staff and the alumni.

The government thus has no legal power to control the universities even if it wished to do so. Though the universities, like other private organizations, are subject to government regulations and in large measure depend on government funds, they manage their own affairs and allocate these funds, as well as those from tuition, endowment funds and other sources. ...

The legal autonomy of the universities is fully buttressed by their traditional position in society. Any attempt by government to influence university decisions, especially decisions regarding appointment, tenure and dismissal of academic staff, would be strenuously resisted by the universities on the basis that this could lead to breaches of academic freedom. In a word, these are not government decisions. Though the legislature may determine much of the environment in which universities operate, the reality is that they function as autonomous bodies within that environment. There may be situations in respect of specific activities where it can fairly be said that the decision is that of the government, or that the government sufficiently partakes in the decision as to make it an act of government, but there is nothing here to indicate any participation in the decision by the government and, as noted, there is no statutory requirement imposing mandatory retirement on the universities.

I should perhaps note that a similar approach has been followed in the United States. For example, in *Greenya v. George Washington University*, 512 F2d 556 (Dist. Col. Cir. 1975), the court refused to find the university to be a governmental entity, though it was incorporated by the state, was given tax exemption and received federal capital funding and funding for some of its programs. A similar approach has been followed in respect of other entities rendering public services that are heavily regulated by government (see *Jackson v. Metropolitan Edison Co.*, 419 US 345 (1974)—there a public utility) or that are heavily funded (see *Blum v. Yaretsky*, 457 US 991 (1982)—there a nursing school where virtually all the school's funds were derived from government funding).

It is true that there are some cases where United States courts did hold that significant government funding constitutes sufficient state involvement to trigger constitutional guarantees, but these were largely confined to cases of racial discrimination which was the prime target of the 14th Amendment ... . As Professor (now Mr. Justice) Tarnopolsky has noted ... these judicial intrusions, devised to meet a problem particular to the United States, should not be imported here; see "The Equality Rights in the Canadian Charter of Rights and Freedoms" (1983), 61 *Can. Bar Rev.* 242, at p. 256. ...

I, therefore, conclude that the respondent universities do not form part of the government apparatus, so their actions, as such, do not fall within the ambit of the Charter. Nor in establishing mandatory retirement for faculty and staff were they implementing a governmental policy. ...

[Both Sopinka and L'Heureux-Dubé JJ wrote short separate reasons concluding that universities were not part of government. Wilson J, writing in dissent (Cory J concurring), rejected the concept of the "minimal state" on which she saw La Forest J's decision resting, contrasting the Canadian attitude to government and its role with that of the United States. She instead opted for a broader view of government that is "sensitive ... to the wide variety of roles that government has come to play in our society and the need to ensure that in all of these roles it abides by the constitutional norms set out in the Charter." Wilson J then set out three tests to help identify the kinds of bodies that ought to be constrained by the Charter: (1) the "control" test, which asks whether the legislative, executive or administrative branch of government exercises general control over the entity in question; (2) the "government function" test, which asks whether the entity performs a traditional government function or a function that in more modern times is recognized as the responsibility of government; and (3) the "statutory authority and public interest" test, which asks whether the entity is one that acts pursuant to statutory authority specifically granted to it to enable it to further an objective that government seeks to promote in the broader public interest. She went on to find that universities satisfied all three tests.

Although the argument that the universities' mandatory retirement policies were subject to the Charter was rejected by a majority of the Court, the Court concluded that the provision in the Ontario *Human Rights Code* allowing mandatory retirement after age 65 was subject to Charter challenge. That provision was found to violate s. 15 of the Charter, but was upheld as a reasonable limit under s. 1.]

Appeal dismissed.

NOTES

1. At the same time as *McKinney*, the Supreme Court of Canada decided three other mandatory retirement cases, all of which also involved issues of application. *Harrison v. University of British Columbia*, [1990] 3 SCR 451, 77 DLR (4th) 55, like *McKinney*, involved a challenge to a university's mandatory retirement policy. A majority of the Court followed *McKinney* and ruled that the Charter was not directly applicable to a university's mandatory retirement policy.

Stoffman v. Vancouver General Hospital, [1990] 3 SCR 483, 76 DLR (4th) 700 involved a challenge by doctors at the Vancouver General Hospital to a hospital board regulation that established a policy of mandatory retirement at 65. Fourteen of the sixteen members of the board were appointed by the government. Moreover, the governing statute required that all regulations be approved by the Minister of Health Services and Hospital Insurance. Nonetheless, a majority of the Court concluded that the hospital was not part of government nor was the regulation in issue an act of the government. The majority emphasized that routine control of the hospital was in the hands of the hospital's board of trustees rather than in the hands of the provincial government. If routine or regular control of hospital policies was in the hands of government, or if the mandatory retirement policy had been dictated by government, the Charter would have applied. The majority also ruled that provision of a public service, even one as important as health care, did not qualify as a government function under s. 32. L'Heureux-Dubé J, who had concluded in *McKinney* that universities were not part of government, joined Wilson and Cory JJ in dissent in *Stoffman*, concluding that the hospital was acting as government. She found a greater degree of government involvement in this case than in *McKinney*, where in her view governmental involvement was primarily in the form of funding.

In *Douglas/Kwantlen Faculty Association v. Douglas College*, [1990] 3 SCR 570, 77 DLR (4th) 94, the Court reached a different result. This case involved a challenge to a mandatory retirement provision in a collective agreement between a college and a union. The affairs of the college were managed by a board appointed by the provincial government. The minister was allowed to establish and issue directions and approved all bylaws of the board. The Court was unanimous in concluding that the Charter applied to the actions of the college in the negotiation and administration of the collective agreement between itself and the association representing the teachers and librarians at the college. La Forest J distinguished the situation of the college from the universities in *McKinney* and *Harrison*:

> Though the government may choose to permit the college board to exercise a measure of discretion, the simple fact is that the board is not only appointed and removable at pleasure by the government; the government may at all times by law direct its operation. Briefly stated, it is simply part of the apparatus of government both in form and in fact. In carrying out its functions, therefore, the college is performing acts of government, and I see no reason why this should not include its actions in dealing with persons it employs in performing these functions. Its status is wholly different from the universities in the companion cases of *McKinney v. University of Guelph, supra*, and *Harrison v. University of British Columbia, supra*, which, though extensively regulated and funded by government, are essentially autonomous bodies. ...

Thus, because Ontario and BC universities enjoyed a significant measure of internal autonomy, while BC community colleges were subject to routine or regular government control, the colleges were subject to the Charter, while the universities were not. Does this distinction make sense?

2. In *Greater Vancouver Transportation Authority v. Canadian Federation of Students—British Columbia Component*, 2009 SCC 31, the Court had to decide whether the Greater Vancouver Transportation Authority ("TransLink") and British Columbia Transit ("BC Transit"), corporations that operated public transportation systems in British Columbia, had violated the Charter's guarantee of freedom of expression by refusing to accept political advertising to be placed on the sides of their buses. The Court found that TransLink and BC Transit were both bound by the Charter, and that their advertising policies had to be rewritten to comply with s. 2(b) of the Charter. The Court found that BC Transit

> is a statutory body designated by legislation as an "agent of the government," with a board of directors whose members are all appointed by the Lieutenant Governor in Council (*British Columbia Transit Act*, RSBC 1996, c. 38, ss. 2(5) and 4(1)). Moreover, the Lieutenant Governor in Council has the power to manage BC Transit's affairs and operations by means of regulations (s. 32(2)). BC Transit cannot thus be said to be operating autonomously from the provincial

government, because the latter has the power to exercise substantial control over its day-to-day activities. [para. 17]

The Court reached the same conclusion for TransLink. It based its conclusion on a close reading of the relevant legislation, which gave the municipality, itself part of the apparatus of government, substantial control over TransLink's day-to-day operations. Pursuant to statute, the municipality was required to appoint 12 of the 15 directors on TransLink's board and to ratify TransLink's strategic transportation plan and a variety of taxes and levies. Moreover, TransLink was required to prepare all its capital and service plans and policies and carry out all its activities and services in a manner that was consistent with its strategic transportation plan. Therefore, while TransLink was not itself part of the apparatus of government, it was governmental in the light of the substantial control that the municipality exercised over it. Deschamps J, writing for a unanimous Court on this issue, added:

> The conclusion that TransLink is a government entity is also supported by the principle enunciated by La Forest J in *Eldridge* [*v. British Columbia (Attorney General)*, [1997] 3 SCR 624, 151 DLR (4th) 577] (at para. 42) and *Godbout* [*v. Longueuil*, [1997] 3 SCR 844, 152 DLR (4th) 577] (at para. 48) that a government should not be able to shirk its *Charter* obligations by simply conferring its powers on another entity. The creation of TransLink by statute in 1998 and the partial vesting by the province of control over the region's public transit system in the GVRD [Greater Vancouver Regional District] was not a move towards the privatization of transit services, but an administrative restructuring designed to place more power in the hands of local governments (BCCA reasons, at paras. 75-79). The devolution of provincial responsibilities for public transit to the GVRD cannot therefore be viewed as having created a "Charter-free" zone for the public transit system in Greater Vancouver. [para. 22]

3. The Supreme Court of Canada has not yet ruled on the issue of whether public schools are subject to the Charter. Since the application of the Charter was conceded in *R v. M. (M.R.)*, [1998] 3 SCR 393, 166 DLR (4th) 261, the Court assumed, without deciding, that public schools are part of government. In *R v. A.M.*, 2008 SCC 119, [2008] 1 SCR 569, 293 DLR (4th) 187, a case involving a "sniffer-dog" search for drugs at a high school, the Court's analysis focused on the actions of police without directly addressing the question whether school authorities are subject to the Charter. Do schools or school boards enjoy the kind of internal autonomy possessed by the universities in *McKinney* and *Harrison*, or are they subject to routine or regular ministerial control like the college in *Douglas College* (see note 1, above)? Note that even if schools or school boards are not subject to routine or regular ministerial control, they may still be subject to the Charter on the ground that they exercise governmental functions. See *Godbout*, below.

4. Does the majority's insistence, in *McKinney* and the other three mandatory retirement rulings, as well as in *Greater Vancouver Transportation Authority*, on finding "routine or regular" or "substantial" governmental control unduly limit the scope of the Charter's application? Would a public function test or a public purpose test, as proposed by Wilson J, have been preferable?

5. In *McKinney*, La Forest J refers to US decisions under the state action doctrine. In some cases, US courts have applied the doctrine very broadly, with the result that the *Bill of Rights* has been found to apply to private entities that perform a public function or that are

connected to the state through funding and lease arrangements. Thus, in *Marsh v. Alabama*, 326 US 501 (1946), a company town was found subject to the First Amendment because it performed the same functions as a state-created municipality. And, in *Burton v. Wilmington Parking Authority*, 365 US 715 (1965), a private restaurant that leased premises from a parking authority that was an agency of the State of Delaware was held to be subject to the Fourteenth Amendment because (1) it leased premises in buildings that were owned and maintained by public funds, (2) there was mutual interdependence between the restaurant and the parking authority, and (3) the profits from discrimination contributed to the success of the governmental authority. As K. Swinton writes in "Application of the Canadian Charter of Rights and Freedoms," in W. Tarnopolsky and G. Beaudoin, eds., *The Canadian Charter of Rights and Freedoms: Commentary* (Scarborough, ON: Carswell, 1982), at 41:

> Some of the American tests are open to criticism, particularly those which seem to be based on leasing or financial support. Neither factor, alone, should convert private into public activity. If there is discrimination or restraint on freedoms by lessees or grant recipients, human rights codes or other legislation are likely to apply in Canada. Indeed, the state action doctrine developed, in part, because of the absence of comprehensive anti-discrimination legislation in many states and at the federal level, to restrain private action in the United States. It was not until 1964, with the enactment of the *Civil Rights Act*, that private discriminatory activity became subject to effective legislative restraint.

As Professor Swinton notes, the US state action doctrine is one that proceeds not on the basis of clearly articulated rules but, rather, on a case-by-case balancing of factors. In recent years, many of the cases have required a significant degree of state involvement in private activity before state action will be found. Thus in *Jackson v. Metropolitan Edison*, 419 US 345 (1974), referred to by La Forest J in *McKinney*, a private utility was found not to be a state actor and, hence, not subject to the due process guarantees, despite the fact of state licensing and approval of the company's tariff, its monopoly status, and the nature of the service provided.

6. The *Douglas College* ruling was followed in *Lavigne v. Ontario Public Service Employees Union*, [1991] 2 SCR 211, 81 DLR (4th) 545, which involved a Charter challenge by a faculty member at a community college to the union's expenditure of dues on political causes that he did not support. The collective agreement that had been entered into between the Ontario Council of Regents for Colleges of Applied Arts and Technology (which had exclusive statutory authority to negotiate collective agreements on behalf of all the community colleges in the province) and the union provided for the compulsory payment of union dues from all employees, whether or not they belonged to the union. The Supreme Court ruled that, although the Charter would not apply to the union's activities, it did apply to those of the Council of Regents. Like Douglas College, the Ontario Council of Regents was subject to "routine or regular control" by the Minister of Education. The Minister exercised "full control over all of the Council's activities," including collective bargaining with college employees. The Council was therefore an emanation of government for the purposes of s. 32. The provision in the collective agreement providing for the compulsory payment of union dues was found subject to the Charter, since the Council's agreement to it was government conduct. La Forest J rejected the submission that the Charter should apply only to the regulatory activities of government, leaving its commercial or contractual activities exempt. This proposition, he said, rested on an outdated understanding of government. Con-

temporary governments may pursue policies by engaging in commercial activities and should not be exempt from the Charter when they do so. *Lavigne* is dealt with more extensively in Chapter 21, Freedom of Association.

7. An issue that still remains unsettled is whether Crown corporations (such as the CBC or Canada Post) are subject to some aspects of the Charter. Should the fact of governmental ownership be a sufficient connection to government for the purposes of Charter application? Should designation as a Crown agent be determinative? Will the degree of ministerial control be examined? Will Crown corporations be found subject to the Charter with respect to some of their activities but not others? Before the Supreme Court of Canada's decision in *Lavigne*, for example, several lower courts had expressed the view that while some aspects of Canada Post's operations might be subject to the Charter, the collective bargaining relationship between it and its union was not. See *Canadian Union of Postal Workers v. Canada Post Corp.* (1987), 40 DLR (4th) 67 (Alta. QB) (holding that Canada Post security rules that required inspection of employees were open to review under the Charter); contrasted with *Canada Post Corp. v. CUPW* (1991), 84 DLR (4th) 150 (Ont. Gen. Div.) (holding that the Charter had no application to union picketing of a post office during a labour dispute). Note, however, that in *Lavigne*, discussed above in note 6, the Supreme Court of Canada disapproved of the attempt to distinguish between the public and commercial/private transactions of government.

Two decisions have found that the Charter does not apply to the CBC. Although recognizing that the CBC is a Crown agency whose functions are public in nature, the decisions went on to emphasize that the CBC has programming independence and its policy decisions are neither decisions of government nor subject to government influence or interference. See *National Party of Canada v. Canadian Broadcasting Corp.* (1993), 106 DLR (4th) 568 (Alta. QB); aff'd. (1993), 106 DLR (4th) 575 (Alta. CA); leave to appeal to SCC refused Oct. 4, 1993 (decision of CBC to produce and televise a leadership debate that did not include the participation of the leader of the applicant party not subject to Charter scrutiny); *Natural Law Party v. Canadian Broadcasting Corp.*, [1994] 1 FC 580 (TD) (to the same effect); and *Adbusters Media Foundation v. Canadian Broadcasting Corp.*, [1996] 2 WWR 698, 13 BCLR (3d) 265 (SC) (Charter not applicable to CBC's policy on advocacy advertising).

2. Entities Exercising Governmental Functions

Even if an entity is not part of the apparatus of government, because it is not subject to routine or regular ministerial control, it may nevertheless qualify as government for the purposes of s. 32 of the Charter if it is exercising governmental functions.

Godbout v. Longueuil (City)
[1997] 3 SCR 844, 152 DLR (4th) 577

[The city of Longueuil adopted a resolution requiring all new permanent employees to reside within its boundaries. As a condition of her employment, the respondent signed a declaration promising that she would establish her principal residence in the city and that she would continue to live there for as long as she remained in the city's employ. The declaration also provided that if she moved out of the city for any reason, she could be terminated without notice. When the respondent moved to a neighbouring municipality, her employment was terminated. The Supreme Court of Canada held unanimously that the city's residence requirement violated the right to respect for private life set out in s. 5 of Quebec's *Charter of Human Rights and Freedoms*. Six members of the Court found it unnecessary to consider arguments based on the Canadian Charter. In his concurring opinion, Justice La Forest concluded that the residence policy also violated the Charter, specifically s. 7, an aspect of the judgment that is discussed in Chapter 22, Life, Liberty, and Security of the Person. Before reaching this conclusion, however, La Forest J held that municipalities are subject to the Charter. His analysis of the application issue is excerpted below.]

LA FOREST J (McLachlin and L'Heureux-Dubé JJ concurring):

· · ·

[47] ... [Where] entities other than Parliament, the provincial legislatures or the federal or provincial governments ... are, in reality, "governmental" in nature—as evidenced by such things as the degree of government control exercised over them, or by the governmental quality of the functions they perform—they cannot escape *Charter* scrutiny. In other words, the ambit of s. 32 is wide enough to include all entities that are essentially governmental in nature and is not restricted merely to those that are formally part of the structure of the federal or provincial governments. This is not to say, of course, that the *Charter* applies *only* to those entities (other than Parliament, the provincial legislatures and the federal and provincial governments) that are, *by their nature*, governmental. Indeed, it may be that particular entities will be subject to *Charter* scrutiny in respect of certain governmental *activities* they perform, even if the entities themselves cannot accurately be described as "governmental" *per se*; see, e.g., *Re Klein and Law Society of Upper Canada* (1985), 50 OR (2d) 118 (Div. Ct.), at p. 157, where Callaghan J held for the majority that even though the Law Society of Upper Canada is not itself governmental in nature, it may nevertheless be subject to the *Charter* in performing what amount to governmental functions. Rather, it is simply to say that where an entity *can* accurately be described as "governmental in nature," it will be subject in its activities to *Charter* review. Thus, the *Charter* applied to Douglas College (in *Douglas*) [*Douglas/Kwantlen Faculty Association v. Douglas College*, [1990] 3 SCR 570, 77 DLR (4th) 94] and to the Council of Regents (in *Lavigne*) [*v. Ontario Public Service Employees Union*, [1991] 2 SCR 211, 81 DLR (4th) 545] because those bodies were wholly controlled by government and were, in essence, emanations of the provincial legislatures that created them. Since the same could not be said of the institutions under examination in *McKinney* [*v. University of Guelph*, [1990] 3 SCR 229, 76 DLR (4th) 545], *Harrison* [*v. University of British Columbia*, [1990] 3 SCR 451, 77 DLR (4th) 55] and *Stoffman* [*v. Vancouver General Hospital*, [1990] 3 SCR 483, 76 DLR (4th) 700] (and since none of those institutions was implementing a specific government policy or programme in adopting its mandatory retirement regulations), the *Charter* did not apply in those cases.

[48] The possibility that the Canadian *Charter* might apply to entities other than Parliament, the provincial legislatures and the federal or provincial governments is, of course, explicitly contemplated by the language of s. 32(1) inasmuch as entities that are controlled

by government or that perform truly governmental functions are themselves "matters within the authority" of the particular legislative body that created them. Moreover, interpreting s. 32 as including governmental entities other than those explicitly listed therein is entirely sensible from a practical perspective. Were the *Charter* to apply only to those bodies that are institutionally part of government but not to those that are—as a simple matter of fact—governmental in nature (or performing a governmental act), the federal government and the provinces could easily shirk their *Charter* obligations by conferring certain of their powers on other entities and having those entities carry out what are, in reality, governmental activities or policies. In other words, Parliament, the provincial legislatures and the federal and provincial executives could simply create bodies distinct from themselves, vest those bodies with the power to perform governmental functions and, thereby, avoid the constraints imposed upon their activities through the operation of the *Charter*. Clearly, this course of action would indirectly narrow the ambit of protection afforded by the *Charter* in a manner that could hardly have been intended and with consequences that are, to say the least, undesirable. Indeed, in view of their fundamental importance, *Charter* rights must be safeguarded from possible attempts to narrow their scope unduly or to circumvent altogether the obligations they engender.

[49] I pause here to reiterate an important observation made in the cases discussed earlier concerning how the notion of "government" is to be understood. The mere fact that an entity performs what may loosely be termed a "public function" will not by itself mean that the body under examination is "governmental" in nature. ... In order for the Canadian *Charter* to apply to institutions other than Parliament, the provincial legislatures and the federal and provincial governments, then, an entity must truly be acting in what can accurately be described as a "governmental"—as opposed to a merely "public"—capacity. The factors that might serve to ground a finding that an institution is performing "governmental functions" do not readily admit of any *a priori* elucidation. Nevertheless, and as I stated further on in *McKinney* (at p. 269), "[a] public purpose test is simply inadequate" and "is simply not the test mandated by s. 32."

[50] Having set out what I take to be the guiding principles, I turn now to examine directly the *Charter* application issues in this appeal. The main issue concerns whether the Canadian *Charter* applies to municipalities—like the appellant—at all. To my mind, the analysis I have undertaken thus far leads inexorably to the conclusion that it does. While this Court has never before expressly endorsed that proposition, we have done so inferentially, inasmuch as we have already applied the *Charter* to municipal by-laws without specifically engaging in an analysis of the application issue; see *Ramsden v. Peterborough (City)*, [1993] 2 SCR 1084 [106 DLR (4th) 233]. Moreover, the view that municipalities are subject to the *Charter* is not only sound, but also wholly consistent with the case law I have been discussing. Indeed, municipalities—though institutionally distinct from the provincial governments that create them—cannot but be described as "governmental entities." I base this finding on a number of considerations.

[51] First, municipal councils are democratically elected by members of the general public and are accountable to their constituents in a manner analogous to that in which Parliament and the provincial legislatures are accountable to the electorates they represent. To my mind, this itself is a highly significant (although perhaps not a decisive) *indicium* of "government" in the requisite sense. Secondly, municipalities possess a general taxing

power that, for the purposes of determining whether they can rightfully be described as "government," is indistinguishable from the taxing powers of Parliament or the provinces. Thirdly, and importantly, municipalities are empowered to make laws, to administer them and to enforce them within a defined territorial jurisdiction. ... Finally, and most significantly, municipalities derive their existence and law-making authority from the provinces; that is, they exercise powers conferred on them by provincial legislatures, powers and functions which they would otherwise have to perform themselves. Since the Canadian *Charter* clearly applies to the provincial legislatures and governments, it must, in my view, also apply to entities upon which they confer governmental powers within their authority. Otherwise, provinces could (in the manner outlined earlier) simply avoid the application of the *Charter* by devolving powers on municipal bodies.

· · ·

[54] The approach I have taken to the relation of municipalities to the provinces finds further support, I think, in the reasoning underlying this Court's decision in *Slaight Communications Inc. v. Davidson*, [1989] 1 SCR 1038 [59 DLR (4th) 416]. There, we had to decide, *inter alia*, whether the Canadian *Charter* applied to the discretionary orders of a statutorily appointed arbitrator. Speaking for the Court on this issue, Lamer J (as he then was) stated, at pp. 1077-78:

> *The fact that the Charter applies to the order made by the adjudicator in the case at bar is not, in my opinion, open to question. The adjudicator is a statutory creature: he is appointed pursuant to a legislative provision and derives all his powers from the statute.* As the Constitution is the supreme law of Canada and any law that is inconsistent with its provisions is, to the extent of the inconsistency, of no force or effect, it is impossible to interpret legislation conferring discretion as conferring a power to infringe the *Charter*, unless, of course, that power is expressly conferred or necessarily implied. ... Legislation conferring an imprecise discretion must therefore be interpreted as not allowing the *Charter* rights to be infringed. Accordingly, an adjudicator exercising delegated powers does not have the power to make an order that would result in an infringement of the *Charter* ... . [Emphasis added.]

While the application issues in *Slaight* and those in the present case are by no means identical, they can profitably be understood to share at least one salient feature; viz., both labour arbitrators (such as the one in *Slaight* itself) and municipalities (such as the appellant) exercise governmental powers conferred upon them by the appropriate legislative body. To be sure, the nature and scope of those powers is different. As regards the arbitrator in *Slaight*, the delegated power consisted in the discretion to make orders in the settlement of particular labour disputes. As regards municipalities, it consists in the much broader discretion to adopt and enforce coercive laws binding on a defined territory. In both cases, however, the ultimate source of authority is government *per se* and, consequently, the entity under scrutiny will be kept in check through the application of the *Charter*, just as government itself would be were it performing the functions conferred.

[55] For all these reasons, then, I am firmly of the opinion that the Canadian *Charter* applies to municipalities. But what of the appellant's submission that the *Charter* should not apply because the activity in question—i.e., the imposition of the residence requirement—is a "private" as opposed to a "governmental" act? As I have already suggested, I cannot accept this distinction. The particular modality a municipality chooses to adopt

in advancing its policies cannot shield its activities from *Charter* scrutiny. All the municipality's powers are derived from statute and all are of a governmental character; see the cited passage from *Slaight, supra*. An act performed by an entity that is governmental in nature is, to my mind, necessarily "governmental" and cannot properly be viewed as "private" at all.

NOTES

1. La Forest J's minority opinion in *Godbout* was the only one to address the application of the Charter. Six of the judges preferred to leave the issue for another day. Therefore, a majority of the Supreme Court has yet to determine explicitly whether municipalities are subject to the Charter. Lower courts have reached the same conclusion as La Forest J. See, for example, *Re McCutcheon and City of Toronto* (1983), 147 DLR (3d) 193 (Ont. HCJ); *Freitag v. Town of Penetanguishene* (1999), 179 DLR (4th) 140 (Ont. CA); *Moncton (City) v. Charlebois*, [2001] NBJ no. 480 (CA).

2. Are the territorial governments of the Yukon and the Northwest Territories subject to the Charter? On what basis? Is the government of Nunavut in the same position?

3. Are Aboriginal governments subject to the Charter? Section 32 does not mention Aboriginal governments; it refers to all matters within the authority of the federal and provincial governments. The issue is complicated by the different sources of Aboriginal governmental powers: they arise from inherent rights to self-government, treaty rights, and, in the case of band councils, the provisions of the *Indian Act*. The uncertain impact of s. 25 of the Charter complicates the issues further. For competing perspectives on the many unresolved issues regarding the interaction between Aboriginal governments and the Charter, see P. Macklem, *Indigenous Difference and the Constitution of Canada* (Toronto: University of Toronto Press, 2001), at 197-210 and K. McNeil, "Aboriginal Governments and the Canadian Charter of Rights and Freedoms," in *Emerging Justice: Essays on Indigenous Rights in Canada and Australia* (Saskatoon: Native Law Centre, 2001), at 215-48. Even if s. 32 does not make the Charter applicable to Aboriginal governments, the terms of a treaty may subject the exercise of Aboriginal governmental powers to Charter constraints. See, for example, the Nisga'a Final Agreement (1998), as discussed in section IX of Chapter 14, Aboriginal Peoples and the Constitution, which provides that the Charter applies to Nisga'a government in respect of all matters within its authority.

4. Does the Charter apply to professional bodies endowed with statutory powers of regulation? In *Re Klein and Law Society of Upper Canada* (1985), 16 DLR (4th) 489 (Ont. Div. Ct.), rules of the Law Society of Upper Canada with respect to lawyers' advertising were found to be subject to the Charter. The application of the Charter to law society rules was assumed without discussion by the Supreme Court in *Black and Co. v. Law Society of Alberta*, [1989] 1 SCR 591, 58 DLR (4th) 317 (law society rule prohibiting partnerships with non-resident lawyers violates the mobility rights in s. 6 of the Charter). What reasoning would you offer in support of the application of the Charter to the law societies in *Klein* and *Black*? Will the Charter apply to professional bodies in all of their activities, or only when they are exercising statutory powers of regulation?

B. Governmental Acts

1. Entities Implementing Government Programs

Eldridge v. British Columbia (Attorney General)
[1997] 3 SCR 624, 151 DLR (4th) 577

[Three individuals who were born deaf and whose preferred means of communication
was sign language sought a declaration that the failure to provide public funding for sign
language interpreters for the deaf when they received medical services violated s. 15 of
the Charter. According to the *Medical and Health Care Services Act*, the power to decide
whether a service is "medically required" and hence a "benefit" under the Act is delegated
to the Medical Services Commission. In the case of the *Hospital Insurance Act*, hospitals
were given discretion to determine which services should be provided free of charge. The
Commission and the hospitals did not make sign language interpretation available as an
insured service. The portion of the decision dealing with the s. 15 equality issue is found
in Chapter 23, Equality Rights. La Forest J's analysis of the application issue follows.]

LA FOREST J: ... [35] Having identified the sources of the alleged s. 15(1) violations, it
remains to be considered whether the Charter actually applies to them. At first blush, this
may seem to be a curious question. As I have discussed, it is a basic principle of constitutional theory that since legislatures may not enact laws that infringe the Charter, they
cannot authorize or empower another person or entity to do so; *Slaight* [*Communications
Inc. v. Davidson*, [1989] 1 SCR 1038, 59 DLR (4th) 416]. It is possible, however, for a legislature to give authority to a body that is not subject to the Charter. Perhaps the clearest
example of this is the power of incorporation. Private corporations are entirely creatures
of statute; they have no power or authority that does not derive from the legislation that
created them. The Charter does not apply to them, however, because legislatures have not
entrusted them to implement specific governmental policies. Of course, governments
may desire corporations to serve certain social and economic purposes, and may adjust
the terms of their existence to accord with those goals. Once brought into being, however, they are completely autonomous from government; they are empowered to exercise
only the same contractual and proprietary powers as are possessed by natural persons.
As a result, while the legislation creating corporations is subject to the Charter, corporations themselves are not part of "government" for the purposes of s. 32 of the Charter.

[36] Legislatures have created many other statutory entities, however, that are not as
clearly autonomous from government. There are myriad public or quasi-public institutions that may be independent from government in some respects, but in other respects
may exercise delegated governmental powers or be otherwise responsible for the implementation of government policy. When it is alleged that an action of one of these bodies,
and not the legislation that regulates them, violates the Charter, it must be established
that the entity, in performing that particular action, is part of "government" within the
meaning of s. 32 of the Charter.

[La Forest J's review of the case law is omitted.]

[40] In *Douglas [/Kwantlen Faculty Association v. Douglas College*, [1990] 3 SCR 570, 77 DLR (4th) 94] and *Lavigne [v. Ontario Public Service Employees Union*, [1991] 2 SCR 211, 81 DLR (4th) 545], the argument was made that even if the entities in question were generally part of "government" for the purposes of s. 32, the Charter should not apply to the "private" or "commercial" arrangements they engage in. In each case, the Court rejected this contention, holding that when an entity is determined to be part of the fabric of government, the Charter will apply to all its activities, including those that might in other circumstances be thought of as "private." The rationale for this principle is obvious: governments should not be permitted to evade their Charter responsibilities by implementing policy through the vehicle of private arrangements. ...

[41] While it is well established that the Charter applies to all the activities of government, whether or not those activities may be otherwise characterized as "private," this Court has also recognized that the Charter may apply to non-governmental entities in certain circumstances. ... It has been suggested, for example, that the Charter will apply to a private entity when engaged in activities that can in some way be attributed to government. ...

[42] It seems clear, then, that a private entity may be subject to the Charter in respect of certain inherently governmental actions. The factors that might serve to ground a finding that an activity engaged in by a private entity is "governmental" in nature do not readily admit of any *a priori* elucidation. *McKinney [v. University of Guelph*, [1990] 3 SCR 229, 76 DLR (4th) 545] makes it clear, however, that the Charter applies to private entities in so far as they act in furtherance of a specific governmental program or policy. In these circumstances, while it is a private actor that actually implements the program, it is government that retains responsibility for it. The rationale for this principle is readily apparent. Just as governments are not permitted to escape Charter scrutiny by entering into commercial contracts or other "private" arrangements, they should not be allowed to evade their constitutional responsibilities by delegating the implementation of their policies and programs to private entities ... .

[43] Two important points must be made with respect to this principle. First, the mere fact that an entity performs what may loosely be termed a "public function," or the fact that a particular activity may be described as "public" in nature, will not be sufficient to bring it within the purview of "government" for the purposes of s. 32 of the Charter. ... In order for the Charter to apply to a private entity, it must be found to be implementing a specific governmental policy or program. ...

[44] The second important point concerns the precise manner in which the Charter may be held to apply to a private entity. As the case law discussed above makes clear, the Charter may be found to apply to an entity on one of two bases. First, it may be determined that the entity is itself "government" for the purposes of s. 32. This involves an inquiry into whether the entity whose actions have given rise to the alleged Charter breach can, either by its very nature or in virtue of the degree of governmental control exercised over it, properly be characterized as "government" within the meaning of s. 32(1). In such cases, all of the activities of the entity will be subject to the Charter, regardless of whether the activity in which it is engaged could, if performed by a non-governmental actor, correctly be described as "private." Second, an entity may be found to attract Charter scrutiny with respect to a particular activity that can be ascribed to government. This

demands an investigation not into the nature of the entity whose activity is impugned but rather into the nature of the activity itself. In such cases, in other words, one must scrutinize the quality of the act at issue, rather than the quality of the actor. If the act is truly "governmental" in nature—for example, the implementation of a specific statutory scheme or a government program—the entity performing it will be subject to review under the Charter only in respect of that act, and not its other, private activities.

[45] In the present case, the controversy over the Charter's application centres on the question of hospitals. The respondents argue that if the failure to provide sign language interpreters does not flow from the Act but rather from the discretion of individual hospitals, then s. 15(1) is not engaged because the Charter does not apply to hospitals. Hospitals, they say, are not "government" for the purposes of s. 32 of the Charter. In their view, this result flows from a straightforward application of this Court's decision in *Stoffman* [*v. Vancouver General Hospital*, [1990] 3 SCR 483, 76 DLR (4th) 700].

[46] The foregoing analysis, however, establishes that it is not enough for the respondents to say that hospitals are not "government" for the purposes of s. 32 of the Charter. In *Stoffman*, the Court found that the Vancouver General Hospital was not part of the apparatus of government and that its adoption of a mandatory retirement policy did not implement a government policy. *Stoffman* made it clear that, as presently constituted, hospitals in British Columbia are non-governmental entities whose private activities are not subject to the Charter. It remains to be seen, however, whether hospitals effectively implement governmental policy in providing medical services under the *Hospital Insurance Act*.

[47] There is language in *Stoffman* that could be read as precluding the application of the Charter in the circumstances of the present case. There, I wrote, at p. 516, that "there can be no question of the Vancouver General's being held subject to the Charter on the ground that it performs a governmental function, for … the provision of a public service, even if it is one as important as health care, is not the kind of function which qualifies as a governmental function under s. 32." That statement, however, must be read in the context of the entire judgment. I determined only that the fact that an entity performs a "public function" in the broad sense does not render it "government" for the purposes of s. 32 and specifically left open the possibility that the Charter could be applied to hospitals in different circumstances. …

[48] [In *Stoffman*] the hospital's mandatory retirement policy, which was embodied in Medical Staff Regulation 5.04, was a matter of internal hospital management. Notwithstanding the requirement of ministerial approval, the Regulation was developed, written and adopted by hospital officials. It was not instigated by the government and did not reflect its mandatory retirement policy. Hospitals in British Columbia, moreover, exhibited great variety in their approaches to retirement. That each of these policies obtained ministerial approval reflected the large measure of managerial autonomy accorded to hospitals in this area.

[49] The situation in the present appeal is very different. The purpose of the *Hospital Insurance Act* is to provide particular services to the public. Although the benefits of that service are delivered and administered through private institutions—hospitals—it is the government, and not hospitals, that is responsible for defining both the content of the service to be delivered and the persons entitled to receive it. …

*Who got quality service
who can communicate to dr.*

[50] The structure of the *Hospital Insurance Act* reveals, therefore, that in providing medically necessary services, hospitals carry out a specific governmental objective. The Act is not, as the respondents contend, simply a mechanism to prevent hospitals from charging for their services. Rather, it provides for the delivery of a comprehensive social program. Hospitals are merely the vehicles the legislature has chosen to deliver this program. It is true that hospitals existed long before the statute, and have historically provided a full range of medical services. In recent decades, however, health care, including that generally provided by hospitals, has become a keystone tenet of governmental policy. The interlocking federal-provincial medicare system ... entitles all Canadians to essential medical services without charge. Although this system has retained some of the trappings of the private insurance model from which it derived, it has come to resemble more closely a government service than an insurance scheme. ...

[51] Unlike *Stoffman*, then, in the present case there is a "direct and ... precisely-defined connection" between a specific government policy and the hospital's impugned conduct. The alleged discrimination—the failure to provide sign language interpretation—is intimately connected to the medical service delivery system instituted by the legislation. The provision of these services is not simply a matter of internal hospital management; it is an expression of government policy. Thus, while hospitals may be autonomous in their day-to-day operations, they act as agents for the government in providing the specific medical services set out in the Act. The Legislature, upon defining its objective as guaranteeing access to a range of medical services, cannot evade its obligations under s. 15(1) of the Charter to provide those services without discrimination by appointing hospitals to carry out that objective. In so far as they do so, hospitals must conform with the Charter.

[52] The case of the Medical Services Commission is more straightforward. It was not contested that the Charter applies to the Commission in exercising its power to determine whether a service is a benefit pursuant to s. 4(1) of the *Medical and Health Care Services Act*. It is plain that in so doing, the Commission implements a government policy, namely, to ensure that all residents receive medically required services without charge. In lieu of setting out a comprehensive list of insured services in legislation, the government has delegated to the Commission the power to determine what constitutes a "medically required" service. There is no doubt, therefore, that in exercising this discretion the Commission acts in governmental capacity and is thus subject to the Charter. As there is no need to do so, I refrain from commenting on whether the Commission might be considered part of government for other purposes.

[La Forest J went on to find that the failure to provide funding for sign language interpretation violated the applicants' equality rights. For this portion of the ruling, see Chapter 23, Equality Rights.]

2. *Entities Exercising Statutory Powers of Compulsion*

In addition to government actors, and non-governmental actors implementing specific government programs, the Charter applies to non-governmental actors exercising coercive statutory powers. Thus, in *Slaight Communications Inc. v. Davidson*, [1989] 1 SCR 1038, 59

DLR (4th) 416, the Charter was held to apply to the order of an adjudicator acting pursuant to the *Canada Labour Code*, RSC 1970, c. L-1, because the adjudicator was exercising powers conferred by legislation. Lamer J, who wrote for the majority on the issue, reasoned as follows, at 1077 SCR, 444 DLR:

> The fact that the Charter applies to the order made by the adjudicator in the case at bar is not, in my opinion, open to question. The adjudicator is a statutory creature: he is appointed pursuant to a legislative provision and derives *all* his powers from the statute. As the Constitution is the supreme law of Canada and any law that is inconsistent with its provisions is, to the extent of the inconsistency, of no force or effect, it is impossible to interpret legislation conferring discretion as conferring a power to infringe the Charter, unless, of course, that power is expressly conferred or necessarily implied. Such an interpretation would require us to declare the legislation to be of no force or effect, unless it could be justified under s. 1. ... Legislation conferring an imprecise discretion must therefore be interpreted as not allowing the Charter rights to be infringed. Accordingly, an adjudicator exercising delegated powers does not have the power to make an order that would result in an infringement of the Charter, and he exceeds his jurisdiction if he does so.

On the facts of *Slaight*, the adjudicator's order requiring an employer, who had wrongfully dismissed an employee, to write a specific letter of reference for his employee was found to constitute a violation of freedom of expression, but one that could be upheld as a reasonable limit under s. 1. (The treatment of this issue will be discussed further in section III of Chapter 20, Freedom of Expression.) The result of the decision in *Slaight* is that some adjudicative bodies, such as administrative tribunals and labour adjudicators, are bound by the Charter, while courts, following *Dolphin Delivery*, are not, at least insofar as their orders are at the request of private litigants relying upon the common law. (See section IV below for discussion of further developments with respect to the application of the Charter to courts and the common law.)

NOTES

1. The *Eldridge* and *Slaight* rulings were followed in *Blencoe v. British Columbia (Human Rights Commission)*, [2000] 2 SCR 307, 190 DLR (4th) 513. At issue in the case was whether the lengthy delays resulting from the Human Rights Commission's processing of sexual harassment complaints against Blencoe had violated his rights under s. 7 of the Charter. On the application issue, it was argued that the Commission's independence from government rendered the Charter inapplicable to its actions. Bastarache J, writing for the majority, rejected this argument. Even though the Commission was not part of the apparatus of government, its acts could be subject to the Charter. First, like the Medical Services Commission and hospitals in *Eldridge*, the Human Rights Commission was charged with implementing a specific government policy or program. Second, the Commission exercised statutory powers of compulsion. The Commission's authority was not derived from the consent of the parties. The *Human Rights Code* granted various powers to the Commission to both investigate complaints and decide how to deal with such complaints. For these two reasons, the Charter applied to the Commission's acts in processing the complaint, although Bastarache J

went on to find no violation of Blencoe's Charter rights. That aspect of the judgment is discussed in Chapter 22, Life, Liberty, and Security of the Person.

2. When a private security guard or other non-governmental actor exercises a power of "citizen's arrest" pursuant to s. 494 of the *Criminal Code*, should the Charter apply to protect against arbitrary detentions, unreasonable searches, denials of the right to counsel, or other rights violations? The issue is unresolved, as some courts have decided that the Charter does apply to a citizen's arrest, and others have concluded that it does not. Which view is more consistent with *Slaight*, *Blencoe*, or the overall purposes of the Charter? See *R v. Lerke* (1986), 24 CCC (3d) 129 (Alta. CA) (Charter applies to arrest and search by tavern employees); *R v. Dean* (1991), 5 CR (4th) 176 (Ont. Ct. Gen. Div.) (arrest by security guard subject to Charter); *R v. Voege* (1997), 31 MVR (3d) 293 (Ont. Ct. Gen. Div.) (driver's actions during citizen's arrest of suspected drunk driver subject to the Charter); *R v. Parsons*, [2001] AJ no. 50 (QB) (citizen's arrest by special constables subject to Charter); *R v. J. (A.M.)*, (1999) 137 CCC (3d) 213 (BCCA) (person who makes citizen's arrest not required to give a Charter warning); and *R v. Shafie* (1989), 68 CR (3d) 259 (Ont. CA) (detention by private investigator not subject to the Charter).

III. GOVERNMENTAL INACTION

Section 32 provides that the Charter applies to all matters within the authority of the federal and provincial governments. If a Charter right or freedom requires the fulfillment of a positive obligation, the Charter will apply to inaction on the part of the government with jurisdiction to meet that obligation. Thus, for example, if a province fails to fund minority language educational facilities in accordance with its obligations pursuant to s. 23 of the Charter, its inaction will be subject to the Charter. See, for example, *Arsenault-Cameron v. Prince Edward Island*, [2000] 1 SCR 3, 181 DLR (4th) 1 and *Mahe v. Alberta*, [1990] 1 SCR 342, 68 DLR (4th) 69 in Chapter 24, Language Rights. Since most Charter provisions impose a mix of positive and negative obligations on government, inaction may be the subject of Charter scrutiny in a variety of contexts. The *Vriend* case, which follows, contains a discussion of the issue in the context of equality rights.

Vriend v. Alberta
[1998] 1 SCR 493, 156 DLR (4th) 385

[This case involved a challenge to the omission of sexual orientation from Alberta's *Individual's Rights Protection Act* ("the IRPA"). The general scheme of the IRPA, like similar legislation in all other provinces, was to prohibit discrimination in public life, and to establish a commission for enforcement. More particularly, it prohibited discrimination in public notices, public services, rentals, and employment or trade union membership on the basis of race, religious beliefs, colour, sex, marital status, age, and ancestry or place of origin. Sexual orientation was not included among the prohibited grounds, and the legislative history demonstrated clearly that the omission was deliberate.

Vriend was an employee of King's College, a Christian educational institution. His employers asked him about his sexual orientation, and dismissed him after he affirmed that he was gay. His attempt to file a complaint under the Act was rejected because of the omission. He then brought this action for a declaration that the omission offended the Charter, and he was joined by several supporting groups. The Supreme Court found that the omission violated Vriend's equality rights, and held that the words "sexual orientation" should be read into the relevant provisions of the Act. Below are excerpts from Cory J's discussion of why the Charter applies to the legislative omission at issue. Further discussion of the *Vriend* ruling can be found in Chapter 23, Equality Rights and Chapter 25, Enforcement of Rights.]

CORY J (Lamer CJC, Gonthier, McLachlin, Iacobucci, and Bastarache JJ concurring): ...
[50] Does s. 32 of the Charter prohibit consideration of a s. 15 violation when that issue arises from a legislative omission?

• • •

[52] This issue is resolved simply by determining whether the subject of the challenge in this case is one to which the Charter applies pursuant to s. 32. Questions relating to the nature of the legislature's decision, its effect, and whether it is neutral, are relevant instead to the s. 15 analysis. The threshold test demands only that there is some "matter within the authority of the legislature" which is the proper subject of a Charter analysis.
[53] Further confusion results when arguments concerning the respective roles of the legislature and the judiciary are introduced into the s. 32 analysis. These arguments put forward the position that courts must defer to a decision of the legislature not to enact a particular provision, and that the scope of Charter review should be restricted so that such decisions will be unchallenged. I cannot accept this position. Apart from the very problematic distinction it draws between legislative action and inaction, this argument seeks to substantially alter the nature of considerations of legislative deference in Charter analysis. The deference very properly due to the choices made by the legislature will be taken into account in deciding whether a limit is justified under s. 1 and again in determining the appropriate remedy for a Charter breach.

• • •

[59] The respondents contend that a deliberate choice not to legislate should not be considered government action and thus does not attract Charter scrutiny. This submission should not be accepted. They assert that there must be some "exercise" of "s. 32 authority" to bring the decision of the legislature within the purview of the Charter. Yet there is nothing either in the text of s. 32 or in the jurisprudence concerned with the application of the Charter which requires such a narrow view of the Charter's application.
[60] The relevant subsection, s. 32(1)(b), states that the Charter applies to "the legislature and government of each province in respect of all matters within the authority of the legislature of each province." There is nothing in that wording to suggest that a positive act encroaching on rights is required; rather the subsection speaks only of matters within the authority of the legislature. Dianne Pothier has correctly observed that s. 32 is "worded broadly enough to cover positive obligations on a legislature such that the Charter will be engaged even if the legislature refuses to exercise its authority" ("The Sounds of Silence: Charter Application When the Legislature Declines to Speak" (1996), 7 *Con-*

stitutional Forum 113, at p. 115). The application of the Charter is not restricted to situa tions where the government actively encroaches on rights.

[61] The *IRPA* is being challenged as unconstitutional because of its failure to protect Charter rights, that is to say its underinclusiveness. The mere fact that the challenged as pect of the Act is its underinclusiveness should not necessarily render the Charter inapplic able. If an omission were not subject to the Charter, underinclusive legislation which was worded in such a way as to simply omit one class rather than to explicitly exclude it would be immune from Charter challenge. If this position was accepted, the form, rather than the substance, of the legislation would determine whether it was open to challenge. This result would be illogical and more importantly unfair. Therefore, where, as here, the challenge concerns an Act of the legislature that is underinclusive as a result of an omis sion, s. 32 should not be interpreted as precluding the application of the Charter.

[62] It might also be possible to say in this case that the deliberate decision to omit sexual orientation from the provisions of the *IRPA* is an "act" of the Legislature to which the Charter should apply. This argument is strengthened and given a sense of urgency by the considered and specific positive actions taken by the government to ensure that those discriminated against on the grounds of sexual orientation were excluded from the pro tective procedures of the Human Rights Commission. However, it is not necessary to rely on this position in order to find that the Charter is applicable.

[63] It is also unnecessary to consider whether a government could properly be sub jected to a challenge under s. 15 of the Charter for failing to act at all, in contrast to a case such as this where it acted in an underinclusive manner. It has been held that certain provisions of the Charter, for example those dealing with minority language rights (s. 23), do indeed require a government to take positive actions to ensure that those rights are respected.

NOTES

1. The courts have held on a number of occasions that once government has decided to implement a policy or program, it must do so in a nondiscriminatory manner. Thus, *Vriend* can be seen as simply confirming the view that "underinclusive" government laws or pro grams can be subject to Charter review. See, for example, *Schachter v. Canada*, [1992] 2 SCR 679, 66 DLR (4th) 635; *Tétrault-Gadoury v. Canada*, [1991] 2 SCR 22, 81 DLR (4th) 358; and *Eldridge v. British Columbia (Attorney General)*, [1997] 3 SCR 624, 151 DLR (4th) 577. There is little judicial support for the view that s. 15 imposes positive obligations on governments to initiate action against inequalities. The question was left open in *Vriend* and *Eldridge*. An affirmative answer would mean that the Charter could apply to a failure to initiate programs to combat inequalities.

2. The courts have typically characterized the fundamental freedoms in s. 2 of the Char ter as being purely negative in character, imposing no positive obligations on the state. For example, the traditional view of freedom of expression is that it "prohibits gags, but does not compel the distribution of megaphones" (*Haig v. Canada*, [1993] 2 SCR 995, at 1035, 105 DLR (4th) 577 per L'Heureux-Dubé J). On this traditional view, the Charter will not apply to governmental inaction that is alleged to infringe civil liberties.

However, in *Dunmore v. Ontario (Attorney General)*, 2001 SCC 94, [2001] 3 SCR 1016, 207 DLR (4th) 193, found in Chapter 21, Freedom of Association, the Supreme Court departed to some degree from this traditional view. The Court suggested that governments may have positive obligations to protect the freedom of association of vulnerable groups. At issue in *Dunmore* was labour legislation that excluded agricultural workers from the right to form a trade union and bargain collectively with their employers. The Court found that the exclusion violated freedom of association. Bastarache J, writing for the majority, asked whether the vulnerability of workers meant that

> [20] ... in order to make the freedom to organize meaningful, s. 2(d) of the Charter imposes a positive obligation on the state to extend protective legislation to unprotected groups. More broadly, it may be asked whether the distinction between positive and negative state obligations ought to be nuanced in the context of labour relations, in the sense that excluding agricultural workers from a protective regime substantially contributes to the violation of protected freedoms.

He went on to reject the argument that the state has no obligation to facilitate the exercise of associational freedoms:

> [26] ... In this case, it is said that the inability to form an association is the result of private action and that mandating inclusion in a statutory regime would run counter to this Court's decision in *Dolphin Delivery* [*Retail, Wholesale and Department Store Union, Local 580 v. Dolphin Delivery Ltd.*, [1986] 2 SCR 573, 33 DLR (4th) 174]. However, it should be noted that this Court's understanding of "state action" has matured since the *Dolphin Delivery* case and may mature further in light of evolving Charter values. For example, this Court has repeatedly held that the contribution of private actors to a violation of fundamental freedoms does not immunize the state from Charter review; rather, such contributions should be considered part of the factual context in which legislation is reviewed. ... Moreover, this Court has repeatedly held in the s. 15(1) context that the Charter may oblige the state to extend underinclusive statutes to the extent underinclusion licenses private actors to violate basic rights and freedoms. ... Finally, there has been some suggestion that the Charter should apply to legislation which "permits" private actors to interfere with protected s. 2 activity, as in some contexts mere permission may function to encourage or support the act which is called into question. ... If we apply these general principles to s. 2(d), it is not a quantum leap to suggest that a failure to include someone in a protective regime may affirmatively permit restraints on the activity the regime is designed to protect. The rationale behind this is that underinclusive state action falls into suspicion not simply to the extent it discriminates against an unprotected class, but to the extent it substantially orchestrates, encourages or sustains the violation of fundamental freedoms.

Bastarache J was quick to add that his comments should not be taken as suggesting that the state is obliged to act where it has not already legislated:

> [29] ... One must always guard against reviewing legislative silence, particularly where no legislation has been enacted in the first place. By the same token, it must be remembered why the Charter applies to legislation that is underinclusive. Once the state has chosen to regulate a private relationship such as that between employer and employee, I believe it is unduly formalistic to consign that relationship to a "private sphere" that is impervious to Charter review.

Is the distinction Bastarache J draws between legislative silence and underinclusive legislation persuasive? If underinclusive legislation can substantially interfere with the freedom to organize of excluded groups, as Bastarache J held in *Dunmore*, why would a complete failure to recognize associational freedom be less damaging?

3. When a court finds that a legislative omission violates the Charter, as the Supreme Court did in *Vriend* and *Dunmore*, it is saying that the common law that operates in the absence of legislation needs to be revised to bring it into conformity with the Charter. For example, the ruling in *Vriend* requires that the common law of employment, which does not clearly prohibit discrimination on the basis of sexual orientation, must give way to the Charter's requirements. Recall that in *Dolphin Delivery*, above, the Court ruled that the Charter does not apply directly to the common law in private litigation. Yet, when a court subjects legislative omissions to the Charter, is it not applying the Charter to the common law? While the *Dolphin Delivery* ruling has not been overruled, cases like *Vriend* and *Dunmore*, and others described in the next section, show that the Supreme Court has steadily chipped away at its value as a precedent.

IV. APPLICATION OF THE CHARTER TO COURTS AND THE COMMON LAW

In *Dolphin Delivery*, above, the Supreme Court stated that the courts were not part of government for the purposes of s. 32(1) of the Charter. This proposition makes little sense. It has since been generally ignored. If the Charter did not apply to the courts, a number of the Charter's provisions, like the right to a fair trial within a reasonable time, would be difficult to enforce.

Dolphin Delivery also stands for the proposition that the Charter does not apply to the common law when relied upon by private litigants, nor does it apply to a court order issued at the conclusion of litigation between private parties resolved on the basis of the common law. These aspects of the ruling have been followed. Their significance, however, appears to be dwindling as the courts become more comfortable with the notion, also emanating from *Dolphin*, that the common law needs to be applied and developed in a manner consistent with Charter values.

A. Reliance by Government on Common Law

The Charter will apply to the common law when it is relied on in litigation involving a government party or in proceedings initiated for a public purpose. In *BCGEU v. British Columbia (A-G)*, [1988] 2 SCR 214, 53 DLR (4th) 1, for example, the Chief Justice of the Supreme Court of British Columbia, on his own motion, issued a temporary injunction restraining government employees on lawful strike from picketing a courthouse, on the ground that this interference with access to the courts constituted a contempt of court. The union challenged the injunction as a violation of their Charter rights of freedom of expression. Dickson CJC, writing for a majority of the Court, concluded, at 243-44 SCR, 22 DLR, that the Charter applied to the Chief Justice's order:

> As a preliminary matter, one must consider whether the order issued by McEachern CJSC is, or is not, subject to Charter scrutiny. … *Dolphin Delivery* … holds that the Charter does apply to the common law, although not where the common law is invoked with reference to a purely private dispute. At issue here is the validity of a common law breach of criminal law and ultimately the authority of the court to punish for breaches of that law. The court is acting on its own motion and not at the instance of any private party. The motivation for the court's action is entirely "public" in nature, rather than "private." The criminal law is being applied to vindicate the rule of law and the fundamental freedoms protected by the Charter. At the same time, however, this branch of the criminal law, like any other, must comply with the fundamental standards established by the Charter.

The Court concluded that the injunction did not violate the Charter.

Where a common law rule is relied upon by the Crown in criminal proceedings, the Charter applies as state prosecution provides the requisite element of governmental action. See *R v. Swain*, [1991] 1 SCR 933, 63 CCC (3d) 481 (common law rule permitting the Crown to raise the insanity defence over the objections of the accused found to violate the Charter) and *Dagenais v. Canadian Broadcasting Corp.*, [1994] 3 SCR 835, 120 DLR (4th) 12 (common law rules regarding publication bans reformulated to better protect freedom of expression).

In both *Swain* and *Dagenais*, the Court did not hesitate to reformulate the common law rules at issue to bring them into conformity with the Charter. As Lamer CJC wrote for the majority in *Swain*:

> Given that the common law rule was fashioned by judges and not by Parliament or a legislature, judicial deference to elected bodies is not an issue. If it is possible to reformulate a common law rule so that it will not conflict with the principles of fundamental justice, such a reformulation should be undertaken.

Same-sex couples have initiated a number of Charter challenges to the refusal of government officials to issue them marriage licences or to recognize the validity of their marriage ceremonies. These decisions are based on the common law rule that defines marriage as the union of a man and a woman. Does the Charter apply to the common law definition of marriage? If so, and assuming that denying the right to marry to same-sex couples violates their equality rights, should a court fashion a new common law rule, as in *Swain* and *Dagenais*, without deferring to the primary law-making role of Parliament?

B. Reliance on Common Law in Private Litigation

In private litigation resolved on the basis of the common law, the Charter does not apply directly, but it is still relevant. In *Dolphin Delivery*, the Court stated that "the judiciary ought to apply and develop the principles of the common law in a manner consistent with the fundamental values enshrined in the Constitution." This statement raised many questions, including whether the same results would be generated through a consideration of Charter values as by directly measuring the common law against the demands of Charter rights and freedoms. The Supreme Court of Canada's most sustained discussion of the relevance of the Charter values to the development of the common law in private litigation is found in the *Hill* case, which follows.

Hill v. Church of Scientology of Toronto
[1995] 2 SCR 1130, 126 DLR (4th) 129

[This case arose as a libel action brought by Crown Attorney Casey Hill against the Church of Scientology and its lawyer, Morris Manning. The action was brought in response to a press conference held by Church representatives and Manning to publicize criminal contempt proceedings, which they planned to commence against Hill. Their allegation was that Hill misled a judge of the Supreme Court of Ontario and breached orders sealing documents belonging to the Church of Scientology. These allegations were found to be untrue in the subsequent contempt proceedings.

In the libel action, Manning and Scientology were found liable at trial. Their appeal from this judgment was dismissed by a unanimous Court of Appeal, and the Supreme Court of Canada dismissed a further appeal. One of the main issues before the Supreme Court of Canada was whether the common law of defamation was inconsistent with the Charter guarantee of freedom of expression. Only the portions of the judgment dealing with the application of the Charter to libel law are included in the following extract.]

CORY J (La Forest, Gonthier, McLachlin, Iacobucci, and Major JJ concurring): ... The appellants have not challenged the constitutionality of any of the provisions of the *Libel and Slander Act*, RSO 1990, c. L.12. The question, then, is whether the common law of defamation can be subject to Charter scrutiny.

· · ·

It is clear from *Dolphin Delivery* [*Retail, Wholesale and Department Store Union, Local 580 v.*, [1986] 2 SCR 573, 33 DLR (4th) 174] that the common law must be interpreted in a manner which is consistent with Charter principles. This obligation is simply a manifestation of the inherent jurisdiction of the courts to modify or extend the common law in order to comply with prevailing social conditions and values. ...

Historically, the common law evolved as a result of the courts making those incremental changes which were necessary in order to make the law comply with current societal values. The Charter represents a restatement of the fundamental values which guide and shape our democratic society and our legal system. It follows that it is appropriate for the courts to make such incremental revisions to the common law as may be necessary to have it comply with the values enunciated in the Charter.

When determining how the Charter applies to the common law, it is important to distinguish between those cases in which the constitutionality of government action is challenged, and those in which there is no government action involved. It is important not to import into private litigation the analysis which applies in cases involving government action. ...

Private parties owe each other no constitutional duties and cannot found their cause of action upon a Charter right. The party challenging the common law cannot allege that the common law violates a Charter *right* because, quite simply, Charter rights do not exist in the absence of state action. The most that the private litigant can do is argue that the common law is inconsistent with Charter *values*. It is very important to draw this distinction between Charter rights and Charter values. Care must be taken not to expand the application of the Charter beyond that established by s. 32(1), either by creating new causes of action, or by subjecting all court orders to Charter scrutiny. Therefore, in the context of civil litigation involving only private parties, the Charter will "apply" to the common law only to the extent that the common law is found to be inconsistent with Charter values.

Courts have traditionally been cautious regarding the extent to which they will amend the common law. Similarly, they must not go further than is necessary when taking Charter values into account. Far-reaching changes to the common law must be left to the legislature.

When the common law is in conflict with Charter values, how should the competing principles be balanced? In my view, a traditional s. 1 framework for justification is not appropriate. It must be remembered that the Charter "challenge" in a case involving private litigants does not allege the violation of a Charter right. It addresses a conflict between principles. Therefore, the balancing must be more flexible than the traditional s. 1 analysis undertaken in cases involving governmental action cases. Charter values, framed in general terms, should be weighed against the principles which underlie the common law. The Charter values will then provide the guidelines for any modification to the common law which the court feels is necessary.

Finally, the division of onus which normally operates in a Charter challenge to government action should not be applicable in a private litigation Charter "challenge" to the common law. This is not a situation in which one party must prove a *prima facie* violation of a right while the other bears the onus of defending it. Rather, the party who is alleging that the common law is inconsistent with the Charter should bear the onus of proving both that the common law fails to comply with Charter values and that, when these values are balanced, the common law should be modified. In the ordinary situation, where government action is said to violate a Charter right, it is appropriate that the government undertake the justification for the impugned statute or common law rule. However, the situation is very different where two private parties are involved in a civil suit. One party will have brought the action on the basis of the prevailing common law which may have a long history of acceptance in the community. That party should be able to rely upon that law and should not be placed in the position of having to defend it. It is up to the party challenging the common law to bear the burden of proving not only that the common law is inconsistent with Charter values but also that its provisions cannot be justified.

[Cory J went on to discuss the importance of freedom of expression, and the protection of the reputation of the individual. He concluded that the common law of defamation reflected an appropriate balance between these competing interests. Therefore, it was consistent with the underlying values of the Charter and there was no need to amend or alter it.]

Appeal dismissed.

NOTES

1. In *R v. Salituro*, [1991] 3 SCR 654, 68 CCC (3d) 289, the Court considered the common law rule that prevents the spouse of an accused from testifying against him or her in criminal proceedings. The common law recognized no exception to the rule of spousal testimonial incompetence in circumstances where the spouses are irreconcilably separated and the witness spouse wishes to testify. The issue was whether the common law rule needed to be revised to conform to Charter values. Iacobucci J, writing for the Court, stated: "The Charter has played and will continue to play a central role in defining the legal and social fabric of this country ... even in the absence of legislation or government action." Courts, he wrote, should scrutinize common law rules closely to ensure that they are not out of step with the values enshrined in the Charter. At the same time, he expressed concern that the courts restrict themselves to incremental changes in the law; substantial exercises in law reform ought to be the prerogative of the legislative branch. He stated: "If it is possible to change the common law rule so as to make it consistent with Charter values, without upsetting the proper balance between judicial and legislative action that I have referred to above, then the rule ought to be changed." He concluded that the spousal incompetence rule was contrary to the dignity of witnesses who wished to testify, and that it was necessary to abrogate the rule where spouses are irreconcilably separated to better reflect Charter values.

2. In *RWDSU, Local 558 v. Pepsi-Cola Canada Beverages (West) Ltd.*, 2002 SCC 8, [2002] 1 SCR 156, 208 DLR (4th) 385, the Supreme Court applied the methodology set out in *Hill*, *supra*, to boldly revise the common law rules regarding secondary picketing. The respondent union was engaged in a lawful strike against Pepsi-Cola, and its picketing activities had spread to "secondary" locations, including retail outlets that sold Pepsi products and the residences of Pepsi management personnel. As in *Dolphin Delivery*, above, the validity of the secondary picketing fell to be determined by the common law. McLachlin CJC and LeBel J, in their joint judgment for the Court, began by affirming the importance of ensuring that the development of the common law is influenced by Charter values:

> The *Charter* constitutionally enshrines essential values and principles widely recognized in Canada, and more generally, within Western democracies. *Charter* rights, based on a long process of historical and political development, constitute a fundamental element of the Canadian legal order upon the patriation of the Constitution. The *Charter* must thus be viewed as one of the guiding instruments in the development of Canadian law.

They then embarked on a wide-ranging discussion of which approach to the regulation of secondary picketing would be consistent with the Charter value of freedom of expression. They rejected approaches that began with a presumption that secondary picketing is illegal. Instead, they adopted what they called a "wrongful action" model that treated secondary picketing as lawful unless it involves harmful conduct that amounts to a tort or a crime. Applying the new common law rules they fashioned to the facts of the picketing at issue, they concluded that the secondary picketing of retail outlets was lawful. The picketing of the homes of management personnel, on the other hand, was properly restrained, because the evidence showed that it amounted to the torts of intimidation and private nuisance.

Recall from *Dolphin Delivery* that McIntyre J found that the proposed picketing of secondary sites by the union would be illegal and an order restraining such picketing would not violate the Charter. McLachlin CJC and LeBel J distinguished the *Dolphin Delivery* rul-ing on the grounds that McIntyre J in that case had assumed that the proposed picketing would be tortious. In *Pepsi-Cola*, the Supreme Court refused to make any such presump-tion, insisting instead that Charter values required evidence of tortious or criminal conduct before secondary picketing could be restrained. Compared to *Dolphin Delivery*, the *Pepsi-Cola* decision takes a much more robust approach to protecting freedom of expression in labour disputes and to bringing the common law into line with Charter values. *Pepsi-Cola* is discussed further in section II of Chapter 20, Freedom of Expression.

3. In a number of other constitutional democracies, the development of law in private litigation is influenced by constitutional values. See A. Barak, "Constitutional Human Rights and Private Law" (1996), 3 *Review of Constitutional Studies* 218 and F. Raday, "Priva-tising Human Rights and the Abuse of Power" (2000), 13 *Canadian Journal of Law and Juris-prudence* 103. The German Constitutional Court has declared that no rule of private law may conflict with the system of constitutional values, and all such rules must be construed in accordance with the spirit of the Constitution. See K. Lewan, "The Significance of Consti-tutional Rights for Private Law: Theory and Practice in West Germany" (1968), 17 *Inter-national and Comparative Law Quarterly* 571; S. Oeter, "Fundamental Rights and Their Impact on Private Law—Doctrine and Practice Under the German Constitution" (1994), 12 *Tel Aviv Studies in Law* 7. The South African Constitution, in s. 35(3), states that, in the appli-cation and development of the common law and customary law, a court shall have due regard for the spirit, purport, and objects of the fundamental rights provisions. In Great Britain, the *Human Rights Act 1998* makes it unlawful for a public authority, including a court, to act in a way that is incompatible with the specified rights and freedoms under the European Convention of Human Rights and Fundamental Freedoms. See B. Markesinis, "Privacy, Freedom of Expression, and the Horizontal Effect of the Human Rights Bill: Lessons From Germany" (1999), 115 *Law Quarterly Review* 47. The application of the Charter to private law is further explored in L. Weinrib and E. Weinrib, "Constitutional Values and Private Law in Canada," in D. Friedman and D. Barak-Erez, eds., *Human Rights in Private Law* (Oxford: Hart Publishing, 2001), ch. 3.

V. TERRITORIAL LIMITS ON THE APPLICATION OF THE CHARTER

Foreign governments are not bound to comply with the Charter; see *R v. Harrer*, [1995] 3 SCR 562, 128 DLR (4th) 98 and *R v. Terry*, [1996] 2 SCR 207, 135 DLR (4th) 214 (US police not subject to the Charter when gathering evidence in the United States later used in Can-adian trials). But does the Charter apply to actions or decisions of Canadian governments outside Canada? Or does the Charter apply only to decisions taken by Canadian govern-ments on Canadian territory?

Section 32 of the Charter does not contain a territorial limitation: it simply provides that the Charter applies to "all matters within the authority" of Canadian governments. However, Canadian courts have not relied solely on the text of s. 32 to determine whether the Charter applies to Canadian government actions abroad. They have also sought to give effect to international law's prohibition against the extraterritorial application of domestic laws and to the principle of the comity of nations—that is, the deference and respect due by other states to the actions of a state legitimately taken within its territory. In the result, the courts have placed significant limitations on the application of the Charter to Canadian governments abroad.

In *R v. Cook*, [1998] 2 SCR 597, 164 DLR (4th) 1, Justices Cory and Iacobucci, writing for the majority, stated:

> [26] … [T]he scope of *Charter* application beyond Canadian territory cannot be determined merely by reference to s. 32(1). The analysis is further conditioned by the accepted principle of international law that "since states are sovereign and equal, it follows that one state may not exercise jurisdiction in a way that interferes with the rights of other states" (Hugh M. Kindred et al., *International Law: Chiefly as Interpreted and Applied in Canada* (5th ed. 1993), at p. 423). In essence, the principle of the sovereign equality of states generally prohibits extraterritorial application of domestic law since, in most instances, the exercise of jurisdiction beyond a state's territorial limits would constitute an interference under international law with the exclusive territorial jurisdiction of another state.

The general rule in public international law is that a state cannot enforce its law beyond its territory. The Charter, therefore, cannot be used to impose Canadian constitutional standards on foreign officials and procedures. However, the Court in *Cook* applied the Charter to the actions of Canadian detectives in the United States. Cook had been arrested on a warrant issued pursuant to an extradition request made by the Canadian government regarding a murder he was alleged to have committed in Vancouver. When detectives from the Vancouver Police Department interviewed Cook at a prison in New Orleans, they failed to provide him with a timely notification of his right to counsel as required by s. 10(b) of the Charter. Justices Cory and Iacobucci held that "the *Charter* applies on foreign territory in circumstances where the impugned act falls within the scope of s. 32(1) of the *Charter* on the jurisdictional basis of the nationality of the state law enforcement authorities engaged in governmental action, and where the application of *Charter* standards will not conflict with the concurrent territorial jurisdiction of the foreign state" (para. 48). Applying this principle, they concluded that the Charter applied:

> [49] … [W]e conclude that the *Charter* applies to the actions of the Vancouver detectives in New Orleans in the present case. First, both the appellant's arrest and detention and subsequent interrogation were actions initiated and carried out by Canadian law enforcement officials. The arrest warrant had been granted in response to an extradition request made by Canada. The interrogation was conducted by Canadian detectives, as opposed to foreign officials, in accordance with their powers of investigation as derived from Canadian law. Thus, the impugned action falls within the purview of s. 32(1) of the *Charter* and the first criterion is satisfied.
>
> [50] Second, in the particular circumstances of this case, the application of the *Charter* on the jurisdictional basis of nationality to the actions of the Canadian detectives abroad does not result in an interference with the territorial jurisdiction of the foreign state. In reaching this conclusion, we are relying in particular on the following factual elements: although the physical arrest was executed by a US official pursuant to US law, the arrest and the interrogation were initiated by a Canadian extradition request and related exclusively to an offence committed in Canada and to be prosecuted in Canada; the trial judge concluded at para. 15 that the United

States Marshal "took great care not to become involved in the Vancouver investigation and impair it in any way [and that h]e had no intention of questioning the accused or advising him in any way"; and the interview was conducted solely by Canadian officers deriving their investigatory powers from Canadian legislation. In these circumstances, Canadian criminal law standards are not being imposed on foreign officials. Further, the application of the *Charter* in the circumstances to the simple questioning of the appellant by Canadian authorities does not implicate or interfere with any criminal procedures engaged by or involving US authorities.

[51] In essence, the principle of state sovereignty is not violated by the application of the *Charter* to the taking of the appellant's statement by Canadian authorities in the United States. In this context, it is reasonable to expect the Canadian officers to comply with *Charter* standards. Furthermore, it is reasonable to permit the appellant, who is being made to adhere to Canadian criminal law and procedure, to claim Canadian constitutional rights relating to the interview conducted by the Canadian detectives in New Orleans.

More recently, in *R v. Hape*, [2007] 2 SCR 292, 280 DLR (4th) 385, the Supreme Court of Canada took a narrower approach than it did in *Cook* to the Charter's application abroad. While the Court did not expressly overrule *Cook* in *Hape*, it certainly has cast doubt on its precedential value. At issue in *Hape* was whether RCMP officers were subject to the Charter when conducting a search and seizure in the Turks and Caicos Islands in the course of an investigation of suspected money laundering activities of a Canadian businessman. The RCMP officers sought permission from the Turks and Caicos Islands authorities to conduct parts of their investigation on the Islands where the accused's investment company is located. The detective of the Turks and Caicos Police Force, who was in charge of criminal investigations on the Islands, agreed to allow the RCMP to continue the investigation on Turks and Caicos territory, but warned the officers that he would be in charge and that the RCMP would be working under his authority. In these circumstances, the Court found that the Charter did not apply. Justice LeBel, writing for the majority, put significant weight on the principle of comity:

[52] Comity means that when one state looks to another for help in criminal matters, it must respect the way in which the other state chooses to provide the assistance within its borders. That deference ends where clear violations of international law and fundamental human rights begin. If no such violations are in issue, courts in Canada should interpret Canadian law, and approach assertions of foreign law, in a manner respectful of the spirit of international co-operation and the comity of nations.

Justice LeBel undertook a lengthy analysis and critique of the Court's reasoning in *Cook*, which he described as giving rise "to a number of difficulties and criticisms, both theoretical and practical" (para. 83). In his revised approach, s. 32(1) of the Charter requires a consideration of two issues: first, whether the conduct of a Canadian state actor is at issue; and, second, if so, whether the challenged state action is in respect of a matter falling within the authority of the Canadian government. Because Canadian governments have no authority in a foreign jurisdiction, the Charter will generally not apply to their actions outside of Canada. Justice LeBel recognized two exceptions to the non-application of the Charter to Canadian governments abroad. The first, which he framed tentatively, relates to actions that violate international human rights:

[101] ... [T]here is an argument that comity cannot be invoked to allow Canadian author ities to participate in activities that violate Canada's international obligations. As a general rule, Canadian officers can participate in investigations abroad, but must do so under the laws of the foreign state. The permissive rule that allows Canadian officers to participate even when there is no obligation to do so derives from the principle of comity; the rule that foreign law governs derives from the principles of sovereign equality and non-intervention. But the principle of comity may give way where the participation of Canadian officers in investigative activities sanctioned by foreign law would place Canada in violation of its international obligations in respect of human rights. In such circumstances, the permissive rule might no longer apply and Canadian officers might be prohibited from participating. I would leave open the possibility that, in a future case, participation by Canadian officers in activities in another country that would violate Canada's international human rights obligations might justify a remedy under s. 24(1) of the *Charter* because of the impact of those activities on *Charter* rights in Canada.

The second exception is consent of the foreign state to the application of the Charter:

[106] In some cases, the evidence may establish that the foreign state consented to the exer cise of Canadian enforcement jurisdiction within its territory. The *Charter* can apply to the ac tivities of Canadian officers in foreign investigations where the host state consents. In such a case, the investigation would be a matter within the authority of Parliament and would fall within the scope of s. 32(1).

Applying this approach to the facts in *Hape*, the RCMP officers were clearly acting as agents of the Canadian state. However, LeBel J wrote, "since the search was carried out in Turks and Caicos, it is not a matter within the authority of Parliament" (para. 115). In the absence of evidence of Turks and Caicos consent to the extraterritorial application of Canadian en forcement jurisdiction (and, implicitly, in the absence of a violation of international human rights), LeBel J concluded that the Charter did not apply.

In *Canada (Justice) v. Khadr*, [2008] 2 SCR 125, 293 DLR (4th) 626, the Court gave effect to the international human rights exception to the general principle that the Charter does not apply extraterritorially. Canadian officials, including agents of the Canadian Security and Intelligence Service, had interviewed Omar Khadr, a Canadian citizen, while he was detained by US forces at Guantanamo Bay, Cuba. The Canadian officials shared the record of those interviews with US authorities. Khadr, facing murder and terrorism-related charges laid by the US government, sought to rely on the Charter to obtain disclosure, for the pur poses of his defence, of all relevant documents in the possession of the Canadian Crown. The Canadian government, relying on *Hape*, argued that Charter disclosure obligations did not apply extraterritorially. The Court rejected the Canadian government's position and or dered the disclosure of the records of the interviews in the possession of the Crown, as well as the disclosure of any other information given to US authorities that was obtained as a re sult of the interviews. In a unanimous opinion, the Court wrote as follows:

[18] In *Hape* ... the Court stated an important exception to the principle of comity. While not unanimous on all the principles governing extraterritorial application of the *Charter*, the Court was united on the principle that comity cannot be used to justify Canadian participation in activities of a foreign state or its agents that are contrary to Canada's international obligations. It was held that the deference required by the principle of comity "ends where clear violations

of international law and fundamental human rights begin" (*Hape*, at paras. 51, 52 and 101, *per* LeBel J). The Court further held that in interpreting the scope and application of the *Charter*, the courts should seek to ensure compliance with Canada's binding obligations under international law (para. 56, *per* LeBel J).

[19] If the Guantanamo Bay process under which Mr. Khadr was being held was in conformity with Canada's international obligations, the *Charter* has no application and Mr. Khadr's application for disclosure cannot succeed: *Hape*. However, if Canada was participating in a process that was violative of Canada's binding obligations under international law, the *Charter* applies to the extent of that participation.

[20] At this point, the question becomes whether the process at Guantanamo Bay at the time that CSIS handed the products of its interviews over to US officials was a process that violated Canada's binding obligations under international law.

[21] Issues may arise about whether it is appropriate for a Canadian court to pronounce on the legality of the process at Guantanamo Bay under which Mr. Khadr was held at the time that Canadian officials participated in that process. We need not resolve those issues in this case. The United States Supreme Court has considered the legality of the conditions under which the Guantanamo detainees were detained and liable to prosecution during the time Canadian officials interviewed Mr. Khadr and gave the information to US authorities, between 2002 and 2004. With the benefit of a full factual record, the United States Supreme Court held that the detainees had illegally been denied access to *habeas corpus* and that the procedures under which they were to be prosecuted violated the *Geneva Conventions*. Those holdings are based on principles consistent with the *Charter* and Canada's international law obligations. In the present appeal, this is sufficient to establish violations of these international law obligations, to which Canada subscribes.

[The Court's summary of the US Supreme Court rulings in *Rasul v. Bush*, 542 US 466 (2004) and *Hamdan v. Rumsfeld*, 126 S Ct. 2749 (2006) is omitted.]

[24] The violations of human rights identified by the United States Supreme Court are sufficient to permit us to conclude that the regime providing for the detention and trial of Mr. Khadr at the time of the CSIS interviews constituted a clear violation of fundamental human rights protected by international law.

[25] Canada is a signatory of the four *Geneva Conventions* of 1949, which it ratified in 1965 (Can. TS 1965 No. 20) and has incorporated into Canadian law with the *Geneva Conventions Act*, RSC 1985, c. G-3. The right to challenge the legality of detention by *habeas corpus* is a fundamental right protected both by the *Charter* and by international treaties. It follows that participation in the Guantanamo Bay process which violates these international instruments would be contrary to Canada's binding international obligations.

[26] We conclude that the principles of international law and comity that might otherwise preclude application of the *Charter* to Canadian officials acting abroad do not apply to the assistance they gave to US authorities at Guantanamo Bay. Given the holdings of the United States Supreme Court, the *Hape* comity concerns that would ordinarily justify deference to foreign law have no application here. The effect of the United States Supreme Court's holdings is that the conditions under which Mr. Khadr was held and was liable for prosecution were illegal under both US and international law at the time Canadian officials interviewed Mr. Khadr and gave the information to US authorities. Hence no question of deference to foreign law arises.

The *Charter* bound Canada to the extent that the conduct of Canadian officials involved it in a process that violated Canada's international obligations.

In *Amnesty International Canada v. Canada (National Defence)*, 2008 FCA 401, 305 DLR (4th) 741 (application for leave to appeal to the Supreme Court of Canada dismissed, 21 May 2009, [2009] SCCA No. 63), the Federal Court of Appeal considered the principles set out in *Hape* and *Khadr*. Amnesty International Canada and the BC Civil Liberties Association brought an application for judicial review with respect to Afghan detainees held by the Canadian Forces in Afghanistan and to the transfer of these individuals to Afghan authorities. The applicants alleged that formal arrangements between Canada and Afghanistan did not adequately safeguard against a substantial risk of torture, and sought various forms of relief, including a declaration that sections 7, 10, and 12 of the Charter apply to the detainees.

Justice Desjardins, writing for a unanimous Court, concluded that the Charter was not applicable to the Afghan detainees. In her view, the situation in *Khadr*, where a Canadian citizen was claiming access to all documents in the possession of Canadian authorities that were relevant to his defence in proceedings before a US military tribunal, "is miles apart from the situation where foreigners, with no attachment whatsoever to Canada or its laws, are held in Canadian Forces detention facilities in Afghanistan" (para. 14). While she acknowledged that the Supreme Court stated in *Hape* and *Khadr* that "deference and comity end where clear violations of international law and fundamental human rights begin,"

> ... [t]his does not mean that the Charter then applies as a consequence of these violations. Even though section 7 of the Charter applies to "Everyone ..." (compare with the words "Every citizen ..." in section 6 of the Charter) all the circumstances in a given situation must be examined before it can be said that the Charter applies [para. 20].

After finding that the Afghan government had not acquiesced to the extension of Canadian law over its nationals, and that the Canadian Forces were not in effective control of detention facilities, Desjardins JA concluded that the Charter did not apply to the Afghan detainees. This did not leave Afghan detainees in a legal vacuum, she noted, since "the applicable law is international humanitarian law" (para. 36).

Do you find the Federal Court of Appeal's ruling in *Amnesty International* persuasive? Or, following *Khadr*, would you have concluded that the Canadian Forces should be bound by the Charter extraterritorially if they are participating in processes that violate Canada's binding international law obligations? Following *Hape*, *Khadr*, and *Amnesty International*, how would you summarize the principles regarding the extraterritorial application of the Charter?

VI. WHO IS PROTECTED BY THE CHARTER?

This chapter has been concerned with the issue of who is bound by the Charter or, in other words, who is obligated to conform to the norms of the Charter. This final section will deal briefly with the other side of the application issue—that is, who may claim the protection of the Charter, a question often raised in the context of whether corporations can claim the benefit of the Charter. There is no general answer to this question, which must be resolved on a right-by-right basis having regard to the wording of the specific Charter provision and the nature of the right in issue. Thus, s. 2 of the Charter, which in guaranteeing the fundamental freedoms speaks of "everyone," has been interpreted as extending to corporations, but s. 15, the equality rights provision, which refers to "every individual," has been restricted to natural persons. Even some of the rights that are framed in terms of "everyone" have been held, because of their nature, to be inapplicable to corporations. Thus, with respect to the fundamental freedoms guaranteed in s. 2, corporations have been found capable of enjoying freedom of expression, but not freedom of religion. Similarly, while some Charter rights are expressly conferred on "citizens" (s. 3, voting rights; s. 6, mobility rights; and s .23, minority language education rights), non-citizens may claim the benefit of other rights and freedoms conferred on "everyone," "every individual," or "any person." These aspects of the application of the Charter will be dealt with as each of the rights is examined in turn in the chapters that follow.

It should be noted also that the rules of standing will in some circumstances allow a person (whether artificial or natural) whose rights have not been infringed to raise a Charter challenge to legislation based on the infringement of someone else's rights. Thus, a corporation, in defending a criminal charge, may base a Charter challenge to the legislation under which it is charged on rights that it is incapable of enjoying, such as freedom of religion or loss of liberty. The rules of standing in charter litigation are discussed in Chapter 25, Enforcement of Rights.

CHAPTER NINETEEN

Freedom of Religion

I. INTRODUCTION

This chapter begins the study of specific rights of the *Canadian Charter of Rights and Freedoms* ("the Charter"). The cases in this chapter pose some of the most difficult Charter questions: What is the relationship between the pre-Charter Constitution and the Charter? How does one ascertain the purpose and effect of legislation for the purposes of Charter analysis? Does the purpose of legislation remain stable over time, rooted in the understandings at the time of the legislation's enactment, or does it change as society changes and the legislation is retained? How does a court determine the nature and scope of a particular right? What place is there for traditional values originating in religious belief and practice, but now absorbed by the secular culture and considered to be secular in articulating the content of the right; in setting out a s. 1 justification of an infringement on a s. 2(a) right? What other values may be considered within a s. 1 analysis of justified limitation on a right to freedom of religion or conscience? To what extent does the Charter permit society to retain and forward the values or the practices and symbols of the majority religion as expressed through the work of majoritarian legislatures? To what extent does s. 2(a) protect members of minority religions in their beliefs and practices? Of what relevance are the laws decided under the *Canadian Bill of Rights*?

The text of the Charter reveals that religion is an important element in the understanding of the Canadian Constitution. Two of the stated rights make reference to religion. Section 2(a), leading off the list of fundamental freedoms, provides that "[e]veryone has the following fundamental freedoms ... freedom of conscience and religion." Section 15, the provision that sets out the Charter's equality guarantees, provides that the state cannot discriminate, *inter alia*, on the basis of religion. Section 15(2), which stipulates that it is not contrary to the equality guarantees set out in s. 15(1) for the state to ameliorate conditions of disadvantaged individuals or groups, includes mention of those disadvantaged because of religion. In addition, there are two interpretive provisions that are relevant to the subject of religion under the Charter. The preamble opens the Charter with the statement, "Whereas Canada is founded upon principles that recognize the supremacy of God and the rule of law." In addition, s. 27 mandates Charter interpretation "consistent with the multicultural heritage of Canadians."

Section 15 did not come into force until April 17, 1985, three years later than the rest of the Charter. As a result, the early cases litigated under s. 2(a) did not include explicit consideration of equality rights. This delay was provided to enable legislatures to bring their statute law into conformity with s. 15 to the extent possible. Many of the provinces and the federal government took up this opportunity. Cases such as *Big M Drug Mart*, *Edwards*

Books, and *Adler*, included in this chapter, highlight the close relationship between ideas of freedom of religion and guarantees against discrimination on the basis of religion.

The drafting of s. 2(a) of the Charter was a matter of stable consensus. The draft proposed in 1968 by the government of Canada contained, among the "human rights and fundamental freedoms" to be included, the "freedom of conscience and religion." This phrasing was expanded in a few versions before the final text to include "freedom of thought" and, on one occasion, reduced, at the urging of the provinces who objected to entrenchment of a bill of rights, to "religion" only. The most interesting proposal in respect to religion in the Charter's evolution was the federal Conservative Party's proposed amendment to s. 1 of the Charter, put forward in the House of Commons on April 23, 1981:

> Affirming that
>> (a) the Canadian nation is founded upon principles that acknowledge the supremacy of God, the dignity and worth of the human person and the position of the family in a society of free individuals and free institutions, and
>> (b) individuals and institutions remain free only when freedom is founded upon respect for moral and spiritual values and the rule of law,
> the *Canadian Charter of Rights and Freedoms* guarantees the rights and freedoms set out in it subject only to such reasonable limits prescribed by law as can be demonstrably justified in a free and democratic society.

As you read the cases included in this chapter, consider whether the analysis would have been different had this amendment been adopted. You might also want to keep this formulation in mind when you consider cases presented in later chapters that raise moral questions—for example, pornography, prostitution, abortion, assisted suicide, and the family (marriage and same-sex issues). For the development of the Charter's text, see A. Bayefsky, *Canada's Constitution Act 1982 and Amendment: A Documentary History* (Toronto: McGraw-Hill Ryerson, 1989) and L. Weinrib, "Of Diligence and Dice: Reconstituting Canada's Constitution" (1992), 42 *University of Toronto Law Journal* 207.

Religious freedom consists of two basic ideas. One idea is that the state cannot, in the exercise of its powers, impose the state's preferred religion on individuals or on groups. Extreme examples would include the establishment of a state religion to which all citizens must adhere, or the requirements of a particular religious affiliation for government employment. Less intrusive examples might involve the public celebration of certain religious holidays, the use of specific religious symbolism or prayer in state functions, or the provision of a religious curriculum in state-run schools. This idea goes under the name "establishment" of religion. Establishment refers to the imposition by the state of (usually) the majority's religion on the general population in some concrete or symbolic way. While state imposition of or support for a particular religion is usually an indication of reduced freedom of religion, that result is not always present. In England, where the Anglican church is the established church, there is considerable enjoyment of religious freedom. The separation of church and state forwards freedom of religion but is not the only way to realize such freedom.

A contrasting approach to freedom of religion gives emphasis to individual or group religious practice and stipulates that it is inappropriate for the state to interfere with religious belief or practice. This idea is called the protection of "free exercise" of religion. It is rare for a government to interfere with the religious belief or practice of the majority religion. Free exercise problems usually involve adherents of minority religions and, while intentional interference with minority religious practice may occur, it is more common for the interference to arise as the result of laws that had no such purpose but which nonetheless have this effect. Both establishment and free-exercise problems raise questions about the place of non-religion under the constitution: Can the state privilege religion over non-religion? Do claims to the free exercise of religion have a higher constitutional status than claims to be free of religion altogether? Does the guarantee of freedom of conscience, as well as religion, in s. 2(a) suggest ways to approach this question?

These classifications of religious freedom have evolved as an important component in the development of liberal democracy and some of that development is evident from the contrasts between the treatment of religion under the *Constitution Act, 1867* and the Charter. The pressing challenge for the Constitution to resolve in relation to religion in 1867 was the creation of a public school system acceptable to both the Catholic and the Protestant population. Section 93 of the *Constitution Act, 1867* provided the solution, taking advantage of the new federal structure to provide for religious coexistence. Ontario and Quebec each acquired a public system for the majority religion adherents as well as a state-funded minority system for its minority—that is, the Catholics in Ontario and the Protestants in Quebec. One hundred and twenty years later, this arrangement provided the basis for a series of Charter cases, some alleging impermissible establishment of religion and others alleging interference with free exercise of religion. These cases highlight the demographic transformation of Canada from its originally Catholic and Protestant population to a much more varied religious makeup today. They also highlight the transformation of the constitutional question from accommodation of different Christian beliefs and practices to the more multifaceted questions facing a multireligious country, with a wider range of beliefs and practices as well as ideas about the place of religion in public life. At the same time, these cases also demonstrate one constant: the importance of children to religious life and community and the perceived difficulties of raising children within a religious culture that is embedded in a larger context of varied religious and secular ways of life.

The more general question raised by the material in this chapter is the relationship of religion and law. For some, the best approach is to realize as much separation between the two as possible. For others, the secularization of the state is regrettable. As Perry Dane has argued (P. Dane, "Constitutional Law and Religion," in D. Patterson, ed., *A Companion to Philosophy of Law and Legal Theory* (Cambridge, MA: Blackwell, 1996)), the full complexity of the relationship requires that one appreciate the commonality and interaction between religion and law:

> Religion and law both have many layers. They are, for one, movements in human history—social, cultural, intellectual and institutional phenomena. In some societies, law and religion merge. Even when they are distinct, they grip each other. Religious values, directly or through the conduit of moral sensibility, obviously influence legal traditions. But legal doctrines also affect religious thought. In the Hebrew Bible, the covenant between God and Israel echoes ancient Near Eastern treaty law. Patristic accounts of the efficacy of Christ's redemptive sacrifice drew on the Roman legal doctrine of "satisfaction."
>
> The communal dramas of religion and law also mirror each other. Legal institutions take on religious trappings, to the point that they are sometimes accused of engaging in idolatry. Religious

institutions and communities not only take on legal trappings, but also often see themselves in juridical terms, and govern themselves through ecclesiastical law.

Nevertheless, in Western history, the effort of the legal order, in particular, to define itself as distinct from the religious order has long been a powerful theme. At its most realized, this effort helps mark the spirit of modernity. ...

At one level, the resemblance between law and religion as modes of thought is powerful. They are both hermeneutic activities. Both find efficacy in ritual. They each live a dialectic between a commitment to authority and tradition and a commitment to objective truth. They are both obsessed with questions of right and wrong, sin and crime. And both set that inquiry into a larger, structural, often hierarchical, frame.

A question for both law and religion, however, has been whether their resemblance implies a true bond, or is just a snare and a distraction. The question, whether asked from the perspective of religion or that of law, exposes deep debates about the nature of both.

It is difficult, if not impossible, to capture by exhaustive statement or precise definition the essence of religion. As philosopher William James has observed (*The Varieties of Religious Experience* (New York: New American Library of American Literature, 1953), at 39), the mere fact that there exist so many varied interpretations "proves that the word 'religion' cannot stand for any single principle or essence." Indeed, what may be perceived as secular to some may undoubtedly hold religious significance for others. As stated by Tarnopolsky JA of the Ontario Court of Appeal in *R v. Videoflicks* (1984), 14 DLR (4th) 10, at 36-37:

> [A]ll religions require their adherents to observe the basic tenets of that religion, which would appear to others to have a purely secular significance, such as not cutting one's hair and wearing turbans, or shaving one's head and wearing saffron robes, such as not eating certain foods or eating them on certain days and not others, such as not killing certain animals or consuming some and not others and, above all, such as not working or buying or selling goods or services on certain days specified as the sabbath. Such observations, when practised as part of a religious observance, have to be considered within the scope of one's religious freedom. This is so even though what is a religious practice for people of one religion is secular for those of another and *vice versa*.

By its guarantee of "freedom of conscience and religion," s. 2(a) of the *Canadian Charter of Rights and Freedoms* appears to offer protection not only to the free exercise of theocentric beliefs and practices, subject to justifiable limitations, but also to non-theistic systems of belief and morality. This is in keeping with provisions in other human rights documents such as art. 13 of the *International Covenant on Civil and Political Rights* and art. 9 of the *European Convention for the Protection of Human Rights and Fundamental Freedoms*, which recognize and affirm freedom of thought and conscience together with a guarantee of religious freedom. These ideas are captured in s. 2(b) of the Charter, which protects freedom of "thought, belief and opinion" as well as freedom of expression.

Many of the earliest Charter cases were litigated under s. 2(a); as a result, these cases provide an important grounding in the basic methodology used in judicial analysis of Charter rights claims. Many of the first s. 2(a) cases relitigated, with success, claims that had failed under the *Canadian Bill of Rights*. This early litigation reflected an important social fact: although the laws with religious content and meaning in Canada had remained stable for decades, the Canadian public had become much more diversified in their religious beliefs and practices and also more secularized. The early cases, therefore, produced a dramatic reduction in the religious framing of life in Canada that coincided with general societal trends.

You will also observe that the Supreme Court was more confident in its role as guardian of the constitutional order, including "large and liberal" rights protection, and more strict in its analysis of justifiable limits on rights under s. 1 of the Charter in the early cases. In later cases, the judges reveal deep disagreements on substantive and methodological grounds. It may be that the early cases appeared easier than those that followed because the rulings reflected widely held preferences for increased individual freedom from public policy infused with the religious preferences of the more homogeneous Canadian population in nineteenth-century Canada. Examples include religiously based Sunday closing laws (see Section II) and the requirement of religious instruction and prayer in the public schools (see Section IV).

Section III focuses on the claims of religious minorities who seek accommodation when the general rules that apply to their circumstances make it very difficult to live according to their sincerely held religious obligations. These cases are of particular interest because they demonstrate more of the complexity of claims under s. 2(a). Claims for accommodation can be brought by secular individuals who want to be free of state-imposed religious practices and preferences. They can also be brought by religious communities that seek protection by way of exemption or accommodation to facilitate their particular way of life. In addition, they can be brought by individuals whose commitment to a religious community may not include the community's full range of beliefs or practices.

Section IV, which deals with the structure and curriculum of the public school system is of particular interest in this regard. The nineteenth-century introduction of the public school system was premised on the condition that the classroom would not undermine the authority of the patriarchal family. In other words, the curriculum and activities would provide an extension of the religious and moral beliefs and practices of the home. The cases brought under s. 2(a) demonstrate a very different understanding of mandatory public education. These cases removed compulsory religious instruction and prayer to the extent possible, on the premise that the public school must educate children from a wide variety of traditions and belief systems as well as students being raised in more secular settings. Under the Charter, the idea of public education moved away from endorsement of the moral and spiritual beliefs and practices inculcated at home to provision of the opportunity for students to appreciate the diversity and democratic dynamic of Canadian society. It appears that the next wave of cases relating to religious freedom in the schools will be challenges brought by traditional families who fear that their children will be exposed to ideas and practices that are inconsistent with their faith-based teachings. Their concerns include classes on the history of religion and comparative religion. They also include sex education that regards adolescent sexuality, contraception, and same-sex relationships as acceptable possibilities.

Section V raises the difficult question of whether individuals can use Canadian law—for example, contract law—to secure protection of interests that have purely religious significance. The concern in such cases is that Canadian law should not become a tool of religious oppression. This issue was recently raised in Ontario in the debate on sharia arbitration. Members of the Muslim community had announced their intention to create sharia courts to enforce sharia law relating to personal status—for example, religious marriage and divorce—through Ontario's *Arbitration Act*. The proposal faltered when it became clear that its effect might undermine the ability of Muslim women to choose to have marital disputes settled under the more liberal arrangements afforded by provincial and federal statute. See L.E. Weinrib, "Ontario's Sharia Law Debate: Law and Politics Under the Charter," in R. Moon, ed., *Law and Religious Pluralism in Canada*, (Vancouver: UBC Press, 2008).

II. SUNDAY OBSERVANCE AND THE SCOPE OF SECTION 2(a)

We begin our study of s. 2(a) of the Charter with cases challenging Sunday closing laws, which were in place both at the federal and provincial level when the Charter came into force. These laws originated long ago in religious laws and cultural practices that prohibited work on one day of the week. Such prohibitions were common in both eastern and western societies. There were different ways of designating the special quality of particular days in various cultures. Sometimes the day attracted taboos based on the idea that performing the proscribed activities would attract supernatural punishment. Other cultures promoted celebration, religious rituals, and family on a particular day in conjunction with the day of rest from work. A different pattern is evident in the idea of special days dedicated to public business, markets, and festivities such as plays and circuses. The particular laws that we will study originated in laws that promoted the Christian Sunday Sabbath as a day on which to abstain from work as well as to participate in religious activity such as church attendance for prayer and religious instruction.

The historical development of these laws provides useful background for the cases that follow. In the sixteenth century, English law compelled church attendance and forbade business and labour. In the eighteenth century, laws began to ban public entertainment on Sundays. This approach to Sunday moved easily to North America. The Puritan settlers in the United States, for example, in the early seventeenth century, required church attendance and prohibited a wide array of activities beyond work, including travel and sports. The penalties demonstrated the seriousness of the prohibitions: loss of a week's provisions for the first offence, whipping for the second, and death for the third. These laws, with less stringent penalties of course, became a common feature of North American life. The advent of Saturday as a non-work day occurred in the late nineteenth and early twentieth centuries. Some of the pressure for a two-day weekend came from Jews, who observed both Friday evening and Saturday as a Sabbath involving no work. While the shorter work week appealed to workers, it might also have been generally attractive to provide time to engage in the commercial and cultural activity banned on Sunday. See W. Rybczynski, *Waiting for the Weekend* (New York: Viking, 1991), and the Ontario Law Reform Commission's study "Report on Sunday Observance Legislation, 1970."

In *R v. Big M Drug Mart Ltd.*, [1985] 1 SCR 295, 18 DLR (4th) 321, the Supreme Court of Canada struck down the federal *Lord's Day Act*, RSC 1970, c. L-13, on the ground that it unjustifiably interfered with freedom of conscience and religion as guaranteed by s. 2(a) of the Charter. The Act made it an offence, punishable on summary conviction, for anyone to engage in or carry on business on Sunday. The *Big M* case is important for its discussion of the foundations of religious freedom and more generally for its description of the way in which courts should approach the interpretation of the rights and freedoms guaranteed by the Charter.

R v. Big M Drug Mart Ltd.
[1985] 1 SCR 295, 18 DLR (4th) 321

DICKSON CJC (Beetz, McIntyre, Chouinard, and Lamer JJ concurring): Big M Drug Mart Ltd. was charged with unlawfully carrying on the sale of goods, on Sunday, May 30, 1982 in the City of Calgary, Alberta, contrary to the *Lord's Day Act*, RSC 1970, c. L-13.

Big M has challenged the constitutionality of the *Lord's Day Act*, both in terms of the division of powers and the *Canadian Charter of Rights and Freedoms*. Such challenge places in issue before this Court, for the first time, one of the fundamental freedoms protected by the Charter, the guarantee of "freedom of conscience and religion" entrenched in s. 2.

The constitutional validity of Sunday observance legislation has in the past been tested largely through the division of powers provided in ss. 91 and 92 of the *Constitution Act, 1867*. Freedom of religion has been seen to be a matter falling within federal legislative competence. Today, following the advent of the *Constitution Act, 1982*, we must address squarely the fundamental issues raised by individual rights and freedoms enshrined in the Charter, as well as those concerned with legislative powers. ...

An understanding of the scheme of [the *Lord's Day Act*] and its basic purpose and effect is integral to any analysis of its constitutional validity. Section 2 defines, *inter alia*, the Lord's Day:

> 2. ... "Lord's Day" means the period of time that begins at midnight on Saturday night and ends at midnight on the following night; ...

Section 4 contains the basic prohibition against any work or commercial activity upon the Lord's Day:

> 4. It is not lawful for any person on the Lord's Day, except as provided herein, or in any provincial Act or law in force on or after the 1st day of March 1907, to sell or offer for sale or purchase any goods, chattels, or other personal property, or any real estate, or to carry on or transact any business of his ordinary calling, or in connection with such calling, or for gain to do, or employ any other person to do, on that day, any work, business, or labour.

Section 5 provides that any worker, required to work by an employer operating on Sunday in conformity with the Act, be given a substitute day of rest; s. 6 prohibits any games or performances where an admission fee is charged; s. 7 prohibits any transportation operated for pleasure where a fee is charged; s. 8 prohibits any advertisement of anything prohibited by the Act; s. 9 prohibits any shooting of firearms; s. 10 prohibits any sale or distribution of a foreign newspaper.

It is important to note that any person may be exempted from the operation of ss. 4, 6, and 7 by provincial legislation or municipal charter. The following exemptions are also contained in the legislation: s. 3—the railways may be operated for passenger traffic; s. 11—any person may do any work of necessity or mercy which covers a broad range of activities listed in subss. (a) to (x).

The Act makes it an offence punishable on summary conviction for: any person to violate the Act (s. 12); any employer to direct any violation of the Act (s. 13); any corporation to authorize, direct or permit any violation of the Act (s. 14). ...

The Characterization of the Lord's Day Act

(A) The Problem

There are obviously two possible ways to characterize the purpose of Lord's Day legislation, the one religious, namely securing public observance of the Christian institution of
the Sabbath and the other secular, namely providing a uniform day of rest from labour.
It is undoubtedly true that both elements may be present in any given enactment, indeed
it is almost inevitable that they will be, considering that such laws combine a prohibition
of ordinary employment for one day out of seven with a specification that this day of rest
shall be the Christian Sabbath—Sunday.

[Dickson CJC observed that the English Sunday observance legislation, which originated
in 1677 and provided the model for the Federal *Lord's Day Act* in Canada, had a clear religious purpose—to ensure that the fourth commandment was followed: "Remember the
Sabbath day, to keep it holy." He also observed that the Canadian courts had previously
held that Sunday observance legislation was intended to protect public order and morality and was therefore criminal law falling within the exclusive jurisdiction of the federal
government.]

Purpose and Effect of Legislation

A finding that the *Lord's Day Act* has a secular purpose is, on the authorities, simply not
possible. Its religious purpose, in compelling sabbatical observance, has been long-
established and consistently maintained by the courts of this country.

The Attorney General for Alberta concedes that the Act is characterized by this religious purpose. He contends, however, that it is not the purpose but the effects of the Act
which are relevant. ... [He submits] that it is effects alone which must be assessed in determining whether legislation violates a constitutional guarantee of freedom of religion.

I cannot agree. In my view, both purpose and effect are relevant in determining constitutionality; either an unconstitutional purpose or an unconstitutional effect can invalidate legislation. All legislation is animated by an object the legislature intends to achieve.
This object is realized through the impact produced by the operation and application of
the legislation. Purpose and effect respectively, in the sense of the legislation's object and
its ultimate impact, are clearly linked, if not indivisible. Intended and actual effects have
often been looked to for guidance in assessing the legislation's object and thus, its
validity.

Moreover, consideration of the object of legislation is vital if rights are to be fully protected. The assessment by the courts of legislative purpose focuses scrutiny upon the
aims and objectives of the legislature and ensures they are consonant with the guarantees
enshrined in the Charter. The declaration that certain objects lie outside the legislature's
power checks governmental action at the first stage of unconstitutional conduct. Further,
it will provide more ready and more vigorous protection of constitutional rights by obviating the individual litigant's need to prove effects violative of Charter rights. It will also
allow courts to dispose of cases where the object is clearly improper, without inquiring
into the legislation's actual impact.

· · ·

If the acknowledged purpose of the *Lord's Day Act*, namely, the compulsion of sabbatical observance, offends freedom of religion, it is then unnecessary to consider the actual impact of Sunday closing upon religious freedom. Even if such effects were found inoffensive, as the Attorney General of Alberta urges, this could not save legislation whose purpose has been found to violate the Charter's guarantees. In any event, I would find it difficult to conceive of legislation with an unconstitutional purpose, where the effects would not also be unconstitutional.

· · ·

[T]he legislation's purpose is the initial test of constitutional validity and its effects are to be considered when the law under review has passed or, at least, has purportedly passed the purpose test. If the legislation fails the purpose test, there is no need to consider further its effects, since it has already been demonstrated to be invalid. Thus, if a law with a valid purpose interferes by its impact, with rights or freedoms, a litigant could still argue the effects of the legislation as a means to defeat its applicability and possibly its validity. In short, the effects test will only be necessary to defeat legislation with a valid purpose; effects can never be relied upon to save legislation with an invalid purpose.

... Both Stevenson, Prov. Ct. J, at trial, and the American Supreme Court, in its quartet on Sunday observance legislation [which sustained the legislation, finding no violation of either the free exercise or anti-establishment clauses of the American Constitution], suggest that the purpose of legislation may shift, or be transformed over time by changing social conditions. ... A number of objections can be advanced to this "shifting purpose" argument.

First, there are the practical difficulties. No legislation would be safe from a revised judicial assessment of purpose. Laws assumed valid on the basis of persuasive and powerful authority could, at any time, be struck down as invalid. Not only would this create uncertainty in the law, but it would encourage re-litigation of the same issues and, it could be argued, provide the courts with a means by which to arrive at a result dictated by other than legal considerations. It could effectively end the doctrine of *stare decisis* in division of power cases. ...

Furthermore, the theory of a shifting purpose stands in stark contrast to fundamental notions developed in our law concerning the nature of "Parliamentary intention." Purpose is a function of the intent of those who drafted and enacted the legislation at the time, and not of any shifting variable.

· · ·

While the effect of such legislation as the *Lord's Day Act* may be more secular today than it was in 1677 or in 1906, such a finding cannot justify a conclusion that its purpose has similarly changed. In result, therefore, the *Lord's Day Act* must be characterized as it has always been, a law the primary purpose of which is the compulsion of sabbatical observance.

Freedom of Religion

A truly free society is one which can accommodate a wide variety of beliefs, diversity of tastes and pursuits, customs and codes of conduct. A free society is one which aims at equality with respect to the enjoyment of fundamental freedoms and I say this without any reliance upon s. 15 of the Charter. Freedom must surely be founded in respect for the inherent dignity and the inviolable rights of the human person. The essence of the concept of freedom of religion is the right to entertain such religious beliefs as a person chooses, the right to declare religious beliefs openly and without fear of hindrance or reprisal, and the right to manifest religious belief by worship and practice or by teaching and dissemination. But the concept means more than that.

Freedom can primarily be characterized by the absence of coercion or constraint. If a person is compelled by the state or the will of another to a course of action or inaction which he would not otherwise have chosen, he is not acting of his own volition and he cannot be said to be truly free. One of the major purposes of the Charter is to protect, within reason, from compulsion or restraint. Coercion includes not only such blatant forms of compulsion as direct commands to act or refrain from acting on pain of sanction, coercion includes indirect forms of control which determine or limit alternative courses of conduct available to others. Freedom in a broad sense embraces both the absence of coercion and constraint, and the right to manifest beliefs and practices. Freedom means that, subject to such limitations as are necessary to protect public safety, order, health, or morals or the fundamental rights and freedoms of others, no one is to be forced to act in a way contrary to his beliefs or his conscience.

What may appear good and true to a majoritarian religious group, or to the state acting at their behest, may not, for religious reasons, be imposed upon citizens who take a contrary view. The Charter safeguards religious minorities from the threat of "the tyranny of the majority."

To the extent that it binds all to a sectarian Christian ideal, the *Lord's Day Act* works a form of coercion inimical to the spirit of the Charter and the dignity of all non-Christians. In proclaiming the standards of the Christian faith, the Act creates a climate hostile to, and gives the appearance of discrimination against, non-Christian Canadians. It takes religious values rooted in Christian morality and, using the force of the state, translates them into a positive law binding on believers and non-believers alike. The theological content of the legislation remains as a subtle and constant reminder to religious minorities within the country of their differences with, and alienation from, the dominant religious culture.

Non-Christians are prohibited for religious reasons from carrying out activities which are otherwise lawful, moral and normal. The arm of the state requires all to remember the Lord's day of the Christians and to keep it holy. The protection of one religion and the concomitant non-protection of others imports disparate impact destructive of the religious freedom of the collectivity.

I agree with the submission of the respondent that to accept that Parliament retains the right to compel universal observance of the day of rest preferred by one religion is not consistent with the preservation and enhancement of the multicultural heritage of Canadians. To do so is contrary to the expressed provisions of s. 27, which as earlier noted reads:

> 27. This Charter shall be interpreted in a manner consistent with the preservation and enhancement of the multicultural heritage of Canadians. ...

If I am a Jew or a Sabbatarian or a Muslim, the practice of my religion at least implies my right to work on a Sunday if I wish. It seems to me that any law purely religious in purpose, which denies me that right, must surely infringe my religious freedom.

. . .

(iii) The Purpose of Protecting Freedom of Conscience and Religion

This Court has already, in some measure, set out the basic approach to be taken in interpreting the Charter. In *Hunter v. Southam Inc.*, [1984] 2 SCR 145 [11 DLR (4th) 641], this Court expressed the view that the proper approach to the definition of the rights and freedoms guaranteed by the Charter was a purposive one. The meaning of a right or freedom guaranteed by the Charter was to be ascertained by an analysis of the purpose of such a guarantee; it was to be understood, in other words, in the light of the interests it was meant to protect.

In my view this analysis is to be undertaken, and the purpose of the right or freedom in question is to be sought by reference to the character and the larger objects of the Charter itself, to the language chosen to articulate the specific right or freedom, to the historical origins of the concepts enshrined, and where applicable, to the meaning and purpose of the other specific rights and freedoms with which it is associated within the text of the Charter. The interpretation should be, as the judgment in *Southam* emphasizes, a generous rather than a legalistic one, aimed at fulfilling the purpose of the guarantee and securing for individuals the full benefit of the Charter's protection. At the same time it is important not to overshoot the actual purpose of the right or freedom in question, but to recall that the Charter was not enacted in a vacuum, and must therefore ... be placed in its proper linguistic, philosophic and historical contexts.

With regard to freedom of conscience and religion, the historical context is clear. As they are relevant to the Charter, the origins of the demand for such freedom are to be found in the religious struggles in post-Reformation Europe. The spread of new beliefs, the changing religious allegiance of kings and princes, the shifting military fortunes of their armies and the consequent repeated redrawing of national and imperial frontiers led to situations in which large numbers of people—sometimes even the majority in a given territory—found themselves living under rulers who professed faiths different from, and often hostile to, their own and subject to laws aimed at enforcing conformity to religious beliefs and practices they did not share.

English examples of such laws, passed during the Tudor and Stuart periods, have been alluded to in the discussion above of the criminal law character of Sunday observance legislation. Opposition to such laws was confined at first to those who upheld the prohibited faiths and practices, and was designed primarily to avoid the disabilities and penalties to which these specific adherents were subject. As a consequence, when history or geography put power into the hands of these erstwhile victims of religious oppression the persecuted all too often became the persecutors.

Beginning, however, with the Independent faction within the Parliamentary party during the Commonwealth or Interregnum, many, even among those who shared the basic beliefs of the ascendant religion, came to voice opposition to the use of the State's coercive power to secure obedience to religious precepts and to extirpate non-conforming beliefs. The basis of this opposition was no longer simply a conviction that the State was enforcing the wrong set of beliefs and practices but rather the perception that belief itself was not amenable to compulsion. Attempts to compel belief or practice denied the reality of individual conscience and dishonoured the God that had planted it in His creatures. It is from these antecedents that the concepts of freedom of religion and freedom of conscience became associated, to form, as they do in s. 2(a) of our Charter, the single integrated concept of "freedom of conscience and religion."

What unites enunciated freedoms in the American First Amendment, in s. 2(a) of the Charter, and in the provisions of other human rights documents in which they are associated is the notion of the centrality of individual conscience and the inappropriateness of governmental intervention to compel or to constrain its manifestation. In *Hunter v. Southam Inc.*, *supra*, the purpose of the Charter was identified, at p. 155, as "the unremitting protection of individual rights and liberties." It is easy to see the relationship between respect for individual conscience and the valuation of human dignity that motivates such unremitting protection.

It should also be noted, however, that an emphasis on individual conscience and individual judgment also lies at the heart of our democratic political tradition. The ability of each citizen to make free and informed decisions is the absolute prerequisite for the legitimacy, acceptability, and efficacy of our system of self-government. It is because of the centrality of the rights associated with freedom of individual conscience both to basic beliefs about human worth and dignity and to a free and democratic political system that American jurisprudence has emphasized the primacy or "firstness" of the First Amendment. It is this same centrality that in my view underlies their designation in the *Canadian Charter of Rights and Freedoms* as "fundamental." They are the *sine qua non* of the political tradition underlying the Charter.

Viewed in this context, the purpose of freedom of conscience and religion becomes clear. The values that underlie our political and philosophic traditions demand that every individual be free to hold and to manifest whatever beliefs and opinions his or her conscience dictates, provided *inter alia* only that such manifestations do not injure his or her neighbours or their parallel rights to hold and manifest beliefs and opinions of their own. Religious belief and practice are historically prototypical and, in many ways, paradigmatic of conscientiously-held beliefs and manifestations and are therefore protected by the Charter. Equally protected, and for the same reasons, are expressions and manifestations of religious non-belief and refusals to participate in religious practice. It may perhaps be that freedom of conscience and religion extends beyond these principles to prohibit other sorts of governmental involvement in matters having to do with religion. For the present case it is sufficient in my opinion to say that whatever else freedom of conscience and religion may mean, it must at the very least mean this: government may not coerce individuals to affirm a specific religious belief or to manifest a specific religious practice for a sectarian purpose. I leave to another case the degree, if any, to which the government may, to achieve a vital interest or objective, engage in coercive action which s. 2(a) might otherwise prohibit. ...

In my view, the guarantee of freedom of conscience and religion prevents the government from compelling individuals to perform or abstain from performing otherwise harmless acts because of the religious significance of those acts to others. The element of religious compulsion is perhaps somewhat more difficult to perceive (especially for those whose beliefs are being enforced) when, as here, it is non-action rather than action that is being decreed, but in my view compulsion is nevertheless what it amounts to.

I would like to stress that nothing in these reasons should be read as suggesting any opposition to Sunday being spent as a religious day; quite the contrary. It is recognized that for a great number of Canadians, Sunday is the day when their souls rest in God, when the spiritual takes priority over the material, a day which, to them, gives security and meaning because it is linked to Creation and the Creator. It is a day which brings a balanced perspective to life, an opportunity for man to be in communion with man and with God. In my view, however, as I read the Charter, it mandates that the legislative preservation of a Sunday day of rest should be secular, the diversity of belief and non-belief, the diverse socio-cultural backgrounds of Canadians make it constitutionally incompetent for the federal Parliament to provide legislative preference for any one religion at the expense of those of another religious persuasion.

In an earlier time, when people believed in the collective responsibility of the community toward some deity, the enforcement of religious conformity may have been a legitimate object of government, but since the Charter, it is no longer legitimate. With the Charter, it has become the right of every Canadian to work out for himself or herself what his or her religious obligations, if any, should be and it is not for the state to dictate otherwise. The state shall not use the criminal sanctions at its disposal to achieve a religious purpose, namely, the uniform observance of the day chosen by the Christian religion as its day of rest.

On the authorities and for the reasons outlined, the true purpose of the *Lord's Day Act* is to compel the observance of the Christian Sabbath and I find the Act, and especially s. 4 thereof, infringes upon the freedom of conscience and religion guaranteed in s. 2(a) of the Charter. ...

Section 1 of the Charter

Is the *Lord's Day Act*, and especially s. 4 thereof, justified on the basis of s. 1 of the *Canadian Charter of Rights and Freedoms*?

. . .

At the outset, it should be noted that not every government interest or policy objective is entitled to s. 1 consideration. Principles will have to be developed for recognizing which government objectives are of sufficient importance to warrant overriding a constitutionally protected right or freedom. Once a sufficiently significant government interest is recognized then it must be decided if the means chosen to achieve this interest are reasonable—a form of proportionality test. The court may wish to ask whether the means adopted to achieve the end sought do so by impairing as little as possible the right or freedom in question.

Two reasons have been advanced to justify the legislation here in issue as a reasonable limit. It can be urged that the choice of the day of rest adhered to by the Christian majority is the most practical. This submission is really no more than an argument of convenience and expediency and is fundamentally repugnant because it would justify the law upon the very basis upon which it is attacked for violating s. 2(a).

The other more plausible argument is that everyone accepts the need and value of a universal day of rest from all work, business and labour and it may as well be the day traditionally observed in our society. I accept the secular justification for a day of rest in a Canadian context and the reasonableness of a day of rest has been clearly enunciated by the courts in the United States of America. The first and fatal difficulty with this argument is, as I have said, that it asserts an objective which has never been found by this Court to be the motivation for the legislation. It seems disingenuous to say that the legislation is valid criminal law and offends s. 2(a) because it compels the observance of a Christian religious duty, yet is still a reasonable limit demonstrably justifiable because it achieves the secular objective the legislators did not primarily intend. The appellant can no more assert under s. 1 a secular objective to validate legislation which in pith and substance involves a religious matter than it could assert a secular objective as the basis for the argument that the legislation does not offend s. 2(a). While there is no authority on this point, it seems clear that Parliament cannot rely upon an *ultra vires* purpose under s. 1 of the Charter. This use of s. 1 would invite colourability, allowing Parliament to do indirectly what it could not do directly.

The characterization of the purpose of the Act as one which compels religious observance renders it unnecessary to decide the question of whether s. 1 could validate such legislation whose purpose was otherwise or whether the evidence would be sufficient to discharge the onus upon the appellant to demonstrate the justification advanced.

... Were its purpose not religious but rather the secular goal of enforcing a uniform day of rest from labour, the Act would come under s. 92(12), property and civil rights in the province, and, hence, fall under provincial rather than federal competence.

[The *Lord's Day Act* was declared to be of no force or effect under s. 52 of the *Constitution Act, 1982*. Wilson J's separate concurring judgment has been omitted.]

Appeal dismissed.

NOTES AND QUESTIONS

In *Big M*, the Attorney General of Alberta argued that Big M did not have standing to challenge the law on freedom of religion grounds because a corporation, as a statutory creation, did not have a conscience and could not hold religious beliefs. Dickson CJC replied to this argument in the following way:

> Any accused, whether corporate or individual, may defend a criminal charge by arguing that the law under which the charge is brought is constitutionally invalid. Big M is arguing that the law under which it has been charged is inconsistent with section 2(a) of the Charter and ... is of no force and effect.
>
> Whether a corporation can enjoy or exercise freedom of religion is therefore irrelevant. [Big M] is arguing that the legislation is constitutionally invalid because it impairs freedom of religion—if the law impairs freedom of religion it does not matter whether the company can possess religious belief. ...

The argument that [Big M], by reason of being a corporation, is incapable of holding religious belief and therefore incapable of claiming rights under s. 2(a) of the Charter, confuses the nature of this appeal. A law which itself infringes religious freedom is, by that reason alone, inconsistent with s. 2(a) of the Charter. ... It is the nature of the law, not the status of the accused, that is in issue.

The rules of standing in Charter litigation are discussed further in Chapter 25, Enforcement of Rights.

Edwards Books and Art Ltd. v. The Queen, [1986] 2 SCR 713, 35 DLR (4th) 1 was decided by the Supreme Court of Canada a year after *Big M*. The case involved a challenge to the Ontario *Retail Business Holidays Act*, RSO 1980, c. 453, a provincial law that established a common day of rest for retail workers.

Edwards Books and Art Ltd. v. The Queen
[1986] 2 SCR 713, 35 DLR (4th) 1

DICKSON CJC (Chouinard and Le Dain JJ concurring): In this appeal the Court is called upon to consider the constitutional validity of Sunday closing legislation enacted by the Province of Ontario *sub nom. Retail Business Holidays Act*, RSO 1980, c. 453. Four Ontario retailers were charged in 1983 with failing to ensure that no goods were sold or offered for sale by retail on a holiday, contrary to s. 2 of the *Retail Business Holidays Act*. Each of the retailers admits that his store was open for business on a Sunday. In the Ontario Court of Appeal, in a decision reported *sub nom. R v. Videoflicks Ltd.* (1984), 48 OR (2d) 395, three of the retailers, the appellants, Edwards Books and Art Ltd., Longo Brothers Fruit Markets Ltd. et al., and Paul Magder, were convicted. In their appeals to this Court they challenge the constitutional validity of the *Retail Business Holidays Act*. The fourth, the respondent Nortown Foods Ltd., was acquitted. In answer to a Crown appeal, Nortown Foods Ltd. questions on constitutional grounds the applicability of the Act to its particular business. Nortown Foods Ltd. asks to be exempted from the Act, saying that otherwise its freedom of religion, or that of its owners, would be violated.

• • •

The Legislation

The scheme of the *Retail Business Holidays Act* is simple. Section 1 defines "holiday" to include Sundays and various other days, including some days which are of special significance to Christian denominations, and some which are clearly secular in nature [the other days include New Year's Day, Good Friday, Victoria Day, Dominion Day, Labour Day, Thanksgiving Day, Christmas Day, and Boxing Day.] ...

Sections 2 and 7 make it an offence to carry on a retail business on a holiday, punishable by a maximum fine of $10,000. ...

Sections 3 and 4 contain a diverse array of exceptions. Most "corner store" operations are exempted by s. 3(1). Pharmacies, gas stations, flower stores, and, during the summer months, fresh fruit and vegetable stores or stands are excluded by s. 3(2) and (3). Section 3(6) exempts educational, recreational or amusement services. Prepared meals, laundromat services, boat and vehicle rentals and service are permitted under s. 3(7). Section 3(8) and s. 4 allow a municipality to create its own scheme of exemptions where necessary for the promotion of the tourist industry.

A particularly controversial exemption is contained in s. 3(4). It applies to businesses which, on Sundays, have seven or fewer employees engaged in the service of the public and less than 5,000 square feet used for such service. Its effect is to exempt these businesses from having to close on Sunday if they closed on the previous Saturday.

· · ·

I agree with Tarnopolsky JA that the *Retail Business Holidays Act* was enacted with the intent of providing uniform holidays to retail workers. I am unable to conclude that the Act was a surreptitious attempt to encourage religious worship. The title and text of the Act, the legislative debates and the Ontario Law Reform Commission's *Report on Sunday Observance Legislation* (1970), all point to the secular purposes underlying the Act.

· · ·

Freedom of Conscience and Religion Under Section 2(a)

... The Act has a secular purpose which is not offensive to the Charter guarantee of freedom of conscience and religion.

The Court held, in the *Big M Drug Mart Ltd.* case [*R v.*, [1985] 1 SCR 295] ... that both the purposes and effects of legislation are relevant to determining its constitutionality. Even if a law has a valid purpose, it is still open to a litigant to argue that it interferes by its effects with a right or freedom guaranteed by the Charter. It will therefore be necessary to consider in some detail the impact of the *Retail Business Holidays Act*.

· · ·

A. The Constitutional Protection from State-Imposed Burdens on Religious Practices and Religious Non-Conformity

· · ·

The Court was concerned in [*Big M Drug Mart*] with a direct command, on pain of sanction, to conform to a particular religious precept. The appeals with which we are now concerned are alleged to involve two forms of coercion. First, it is argued that the *Retail Business Holidays Act* makes it more expensive for retailers and consumers who observe a weekly day of rest other than Sunday to practise their religious tenets. In this manner, it is said, the Act indirectly coerces these persons to forego the practice of a religious belief. Second, it is submitted that the Act has the direct effect of compelling non-believers to conform to majoritarian religious dogma, by requiring retailers to close their stores on Sunday.

The first question is whether indirect burdens on religious practice are prohibited by the constitutional guarantee of freedom of religion. In my opinion indirect coercion by the state is comprehended within the evils from which s. 2(a) may afford protection. The Court said as much in the *Big M Drug Mart Ltd.* case and any more restrictive interpretation would, in my opinion, be inconsistent with the Court's obligation under s. 27 to preserve and enhance the multicultural heritage of Canadians. ... It matters not, I believe, whether a coercive burden is direct or indirect, intentional or unintentional, foreseeable or unforeseeable. All coercive burdens on the exercise of religious beliefs are potentially within the ambit of s. 2(a).

This does not mean, however, that every burden on religious practices is offensive to the constitutional guarantee of freedom of religion. It means only that indirect or unintentional burdens will not be held to be outside the scope of Charter protection on that account alone. Section 2(a) does not require the legislatures to eliminate every minuscule state-imposed cost associated with the practice of religion. Otherwise the Charter would offer protection from innocuous secular legislation such as a taxation act that imposed a modest sales tax extending to all products, including those used in the course of religious worship. In my opinion, it is unnecessary to turn to s. 1 in order to justify legislation of that sort. The purpose of s. 2(a) is to ensure that society does not interfere with profoundly personal beliefs that govern one's perception of oneself, humankind, nature, and, in some cases, a higher or different order of being. These beliefs in turn govern one's conduct and practices. The Constitution shelters individuals and groups only to the extent that religious beliefs or conduct might reasonably or actually be threatened. For a state-imposed cost or burden to be proscribed by s. 2(a) it must be capable of interfering with religious belief or practice. In short, legislative or administrative action which increases the cost of practising or otherwise manifesting religious beliefs is not prohibited if the burden is trivial or insubstantial. ...

I propose, shortly, to apply the above principles to the legislation under review. First, however, I wish to consider the second form of religious coercion allegedly flowing from the Act. It is of a different nature entirely since it involves not the freedom affirmatively to practise one's religious beliefs, but rather the freedom to abstain from the religious practices of others. *The Retail Business Holidays Act* prevents some retailers from selling their products on Sundays. Longo Brothers submits that these effects are identical to those which flow from any other form of Sunday closing legislation, including the *Lord's Day Act*, and submits that the Act thereby requires retailers to conform to the religious practices of dominant Christian sects.

In *Big M Drug Mart Ltd.* this Court acknowledged that freedom of conscience and religion included the freedom to express and manifest religious non-belief and the freedom to refuse to participate in religious practice. ... These freedoms, which may compendiously be referred to as the freedom from conformity to religious dogma, are governed by somewhat different considerations than the freedom to manifest one's own religious beliefs. Religious freedom is inevitably abridged by legislation which has the effect of impeding conduct integral to the practice of a person's religion. But it is not necessarily impaired by legislation which requires conduct consistent with the religious beliefs of another person. One is not being compelled to engage in religious practices merely because a statutory obligation coincides with the dictates of a particular religion. I cannot accept, for example, that a legislative prohibition of criminal conduct such as theft and murder is a state-enforced compulsion to conform to religious practices, merely because some religions enjoin their members not to steal or kill. Reasonable citizens do not perceive the legislation as requiring them to pay homage to religious doctrine.

• • •

In my view, legislation with a secular inspiration does not abridge the freedom from conformity to religious dogma merely because statutory provisions coincide with the tenets of a religion. I leave open the possibility, however, that such legislation might limit the freedom of conscience and religion of persons whose conduct is governed by an intention to express or manifest his or her non-conformity with religious doctrine. None of the retail stores involved in the present appeals has established that it was open on Sunday for any purpose other than to make money. Accordingly, there is no evidentiary foundation to substantiate the contention of some of the retailers that their freedom from conforming to religious doctrine has been abridged. The second form of coercion allegedly flowing from the *Retail Business Holidays Act* has not been established in these appeals.

It therefore remains only to consider the impact of the Act with a view to determining whether it significantly impinges on the freedom to manifest or practise religious beliefs.

B. *The Impact of the Retail Business Holidays Act*

The Act has a different impact on persons with different religious beliefs. Four classes of persons might be differently affected: those not observing any religious day of rest, those observing Sundays, those observing Saturdays and those observing some other day of the week.

(i) *Non-Observers*

Consider, first, the persons who do not subscribe as a matter of faith to a duty to refrain from working or shopping on any specified day of the week. Included in this group are agnostics, adherents to faiths which do not prescribe a weekly day of rest, and persons who, although belonging to religious groups whose teachings may include the observance of a day of rest, do not personally feel a moral compulsion to conform to this particular religious injunction. For convenience, I refer to this varied constituency as the "non-observers."

The Act prevents non-observing retailers who cannot fit themselves within one of the statutory exemptions from doing business on Sundays. In the absence of the Act, these retailers would be able to transact business on seven days of the week, and they would have a competitive advantage in this respect relative to retailers whose religious beliefs required closing on Saturdays, Sundays, or any other day of the week. The adverse effects of the Act on non-observing retailers are not substantially reduced by s. 3(4): they must still close their businesses one day of each week.

For reasons which I have outlined above, however, the effects of the Act on non-observing retailers are generally secular in nature and do not impair or abridge their freedom of conscience or religion, at least in the absence of convincing evidence that the desire to remain open is motivated by dissentient religious purposes rather than purely business considerations.

(ii) Sunday Observers

The Act has a favourable impact on Sunday observers. By requiring some other retailers to refrain from trade on a day of special religious significance to Sunday observers, the latter are relieved of a loss of market share to retailers who would have been open for business on Sunday in the absence of the Act. The cost of religious observance has been decreased for Sunday observers by the enactment of the legislation.

(iii) Saturday Observers

There is evidence in the record that it is a religious tenet of the Jewish and Seventh-day Adventist faiths not to work or transact business on Saturdays. Other faiths may also observe Saturday as a religious day of rest, but for the purposes of the present appeals it is the effects on Jews and Seventh-day Adventists that will be considered.

The Attorney-General of Ontario submits that any disability suffered by Saturday-observing retailers is a consequence of their religious beliefs, and not of the Act. Even in the absence of the Act, devout Jews and Seventh-day Adventists would close on Saturdays. The effect of the Act is to require them and all other persons, subject to the exemptions but irrespective of religious persuasion, to close on Sundays. Consequently, it is argued, there is no nexus between the impugned law and the freedom of Saturday observers to exercise their religious beliefs. ... [The true effect of the Act, it is argued, is only to confer a benefit on Sunday observers.]

In view of the characteristics of the retail industry described in the [Ontario Law Reform Commission] *Report on Sunday Observance Legislation*, [1970] I find myself unable to draw such a neat distinction between benefits accruing to Sunday-observing retailers and burdens imposed on Saturday observers. The Report refers on numerous occasions to the highly competitive nature of the retail industry, such that an increase in sales by one individual retailer occasioned by that retailer's marketing practices tends to result in significant decreases in the sales of other retailers. It follows that if the Act confers an advantage on Sunday-observing retailers relative to Saturday-observing retailers, the latter are burdened by the legislation.

A careful comparison of the effects of Sunday closing legislation on different religious groups clearly demonstrates the manner in which the burden flows from the legislation. In the absence of legislative intervention, the Saturday observer and the Sunday observer would be on a roughly equal footing in competing for shares of the available consumer buying power. Both might operate for a maximum of six days each week. Both would be disadvantaged relative to non-observing retailers who would have the option of a seven-day week. On this account, however, they would have no complaint cognizable in law since the disability would be one flowing exclusively from their religious tenets: I agree ... that the state is normally under no duty under s. 2(a) to take affirmative action to eliminate the natural costs of religious practices. But, exemptions aside, the *Retail Business Holidays Act* has the effect of leaving the Saturday observer at the same natural disadvantage relative to the non-observer and adding the new, purely statutory disadvantage of being closed an extra day relative to the Sunday observer. Just as the Act makes it less costly for Sunday observers to practise their religious beliefs, it thereby makes it more expensive for some Jewish and Seventh-day Adventist retailers to practise theirs.

... I ... do not think that the competitive pressure on non-exempt retailers to abandon the observance of a Saturday Sabbath can be characterized as insubstantial or trivial. It follows that their freedom of religion is abridged by the Act.

It is important to recognize, however, that not all Saturday-observing retailers are detrimentally affected. The Act is not merely neutral in its impact on those Jewish and Seventh-day Adventist retailers who can practically comply with the employee and square-footage limits of s. 3(4). It confers a benefit by placing them on a roughly equal competitive footing with non-observing retailers, who, in the absence of legislative intervention, would be free to transact business seven days per week. The effect of the Act, far from producing a systematic discriminatory burden on all retailers of a particular faith, is to benefit some while burdening others.

Finally, I note that the Act also imposes a burden on Saturday-observing consumers. For single-parent families or two-parent families with both spouses working from Monday to Friday, the weekend is a time to do the things one did not have time to do during the week. The Act does not impair the ability of Sunday observers to go shopping or seek professional services on Saturdays, but it does circumscribe that of the Saturday observer on Sundays. Although there is no evidence before the Court of the degree to which shopping variety is restricted on Sundays, I am prepared to assume for the purposes of these appeals that the burden on Saturday-observing consumers is substantial and constitutes an abridgment of their religious freedom. I note that the burden may be particularly onerous on Jewish consumers who rely on retailers such as Nortown Foods Ltd. to supply them with foodstuffs that conform to religious dietary laws, although, once again, I must observe that there is no evidence regarding the degree to which Kosher foods can be purchased from smaller retailers on Sundays.

• • •

Section 1 of the Charter

• • •

I regard as self-evident the desirability of enabling parents to have regular days off from work in common with their child's day off from school, and with a day off enjoyed by most other family and community members. ... A family visit to an uncle or a grandmother, the attendance of a parent at a child's sports tournament, a picnic, a swim, or a hike in the park on a summer day, or a family expedition to a zoo, circus, or exhibition— these, and hundreds of other leisure activities are amongst the simplest but most profound joys that any of us can know. The aim of protecting workers, families and communities from a diminution of opportunity to experience the fulfilment offered by [family] activities, and from the alienation of the individual from his or her closest social bonds, is not one which I regard as unimportant or trivial. ... I am satisfied that the Act is aimed at a pressing and substantial concern. It therefore survives the first part of the inquiry under s. 1.

The requirement of rational connection calls for an assessment of how well the legislative garment has been tailored to suit its purpose. In the context of the *Retail Business Holidays Act* two questions are raised. First, is it acceptable for the legislature to have focused exclusively on the retail industry? Second, is the scheme of exemptions within the Act, as between types of retail business, justifiable?

... [T]he [Ontario] Law Reform Commission [perceived] that the retail industry presented a particularly pressing problem. It was in this industry that the Report told of competitive pressures forcing individual operators to extend their hours of business, largely against their wishes. The Report also documented the characteristics of the retail trade's labour force, including its low level of unionization, its high proportion of women, and its generally heterogeneous composition: p. 103. The Commission's conclusion that this labour force was especially vulnerable to subtle and overt pressure from its employers amply justified on the evidence the legislature's decision to single out the retail industry for special and immediate attention.

The exemptions for various types of business are also justifiable. ...

... [I]n regulating industry or business it is open to the legislature to restrict its legislative reforms to sectors in which there appear to be particularly urgent concerns or to constituencies that seem especially needy. ...

A more difficult question—and one which goes to the heart of this litigation—is whether the *Retail Business Holidays Act* abridges the freedom of religion of Saturday observers as little as is reasonably possible. Section 3(4) has the effect, and was intended to have the effect, of very substantially reducing the impact of the Act on those religious groups for whom Saturday is a Sabbath. What must be decided, however, is whether there is some reasonable alternative scheme which would allow the province to achieve its objective with fewer detrimental effects on religious freedom.

One suggestion was that the objective of protecting workers from involuntary Sunday labour could be achieved by legislation which focused on the employee rather than the employer. There could, for example, be an enactment conferring on workers a right to refuse Sunday work. But such a scheme would in my view fall far short of achieving the objectives of the *Retail Business Holidays Act*. It would fail to recognize the subtle coercive pressure which an employer can exert on an employee. The vulnerability of retail employees makes them an improbable group to resist such pressures. A scheme which requires an employee to assert his or her rights before a tribunal in order to obtain a Sunday holiday is an inadequate substitute for the regime selected by the Ontario legislature. Also a bilateral decision of individual retailers and employees to stay open and work on Sunday would pressure others to a similar decision and would ... place increased demands on ancillary services required to keep the stores open, such as wholesalers, truckers and public transportation.

The other alternative would be to retain the basic format of the *Retail Business Holidays Act*, but to replace s. 3(4) with a complete exemption from s. 2 for those retailers who have a sincerely held religious belief requiring them to close their stores on a day other than Sunday. ...

... I am unable to say whether one scheme results in a greater availability of Sunday shopping services to the Jewish or Seventh-day Adventist consumer than the other. In this context, I note that the *Report on Sunday Observance Legislation* (1970) at p. 98, Table V, discloses that only 8.1 percent of retail stores had ten or more employees at the time of the previous census in 1961. Since, subject to the square footage requirement, the exemption in s. 3(4) is available to any store provided that *at any given time on Sunday* the number of persons engaged in *serving the public* is fewer than eight, it appears that a very substantial variety of products, including specialty products such as Kosher foods, is available to Sunday shoppers, even if the proportion of large stores were to have doubled since 1961.

The most difficult questions stem from the different impacts of these exemptions on Saturday-observing retailers.

· · ·

[I]t is legitimate for legislatures to be concerned with minimizing the disruptive effect of any exemption on the scope and quality of the pause day, and ... it would be highly undesirable for such concern to find expression in a rule conditioning the availability of an exemption on the hiring by retailers of co-religionists. Because of their substantial share of total sales volume ... and their numerous employees, the operation of large retail outlets on Sundays would entail a substantial disruption of the quality of the pause day. It is, however, not so much the disruption of the quality of the pause day in terms of commercial activity that concerns me. What concerns me, rather, is the limitation of its *scope* in terms of the *employees* who would be denied the benefits which the Act was designed to provide them.

What cannot be forgotten is that the object of the legislation is to benefit retail employees by making available to them a weekly holiday which coincides with that enjoyed by most of the community. These employees do not constitute a powerful group in society. ...

The economic position of these employees affords them few choices in respect of their conditions of employment. It would ignore the realities faced by these workers to suggest that they stand up to their employer or seek a job elsewhere if they wish to enjoy a common day of rest with their families and friends. Although I have acknowledged that the legislation under review burdens the freedoms of Saturday-observing retailers, it must also be recognized that larger retailers have available to them options flowing from the resources at their disposal which are foreclosed to their employees. It is, perhaps, worth stating the obvious: a store with eight or more employees serving the public at any one time or with 5,000 square feet of retail space indeed constitutes a substantial retail operation. Such a store is not, by any stretch, a mere corner store staffed by the family. In interpreting and applying the Charter I believe that the courts must be cautious to ensure that it does not simply become an instrument of better situated individuals to roll back legislation which has as its object the improvement of the condition of less advantaged persons. When the interests of more than seven vulnerable employees in securing a Sunday holiday are weighed against the interests of their employer in transacting business on a Sunday, I cannot fault the legislature for determining that the protection of the employees ought to prevail. This is not to say that the legislature is constitutionally obligated to give effect to employee interests in preference to the interests of the store owner for large retail operations, but only that it may do so if it wishes.

I turn now to the second factor which, in my opinion, contributes to the justification of the legislation under review. ... The striking advantage of the Ontario Act is that it makes available an exemption to the small and mid-size retailer without the indignity of having to submit to ... an inquiry [into religious belief]. In my view, state-sponsored inquiries into any person's religion should be avoided wherever reasonably possible, since they expose an individual's most personal and private beliefs to public airing and testing in a judicial or quasi-judicial setting. The inquiry is all the worse when it is demanded only of members of a non-majoritarian faith, who may have good reason for reluctance about so exposing and articulating their non-conformity.

I do not mean to suggest that a judicial inquiry into the sincerity of religious beliefs is unconstitutional. To so hold would mean that the courts could never grant constitutional exemptions from legislation which impinged on the free exercise of religious beliefs. Judicial inquiries into religious beliefs are largely unavoidable if the constitutional freedoms guaranteed by s. 2(a) are to be asserted before the courts. We must live with the reality that such an inquiry is necessary in order for the same values to be given effect by the judicial system. Inquiries which are genuinely designed as a means of giving effect to religious freedoms will not therefore generally be unconstitutional. There will, however, be occasions when a substantial measure of religious freedom can be achieved without mandating a state-conducted inquiry into personal religious convictions and the legislatures ought to be encouraged to do so, if a fair balance is struck.

... In my view, there exists to some degree a trade-off between a scheme which provides complete relief from burdens on religious freedom to most Saturday-observing retailers by avoiding a distasteful inquiry, and, on the other hand, an alternative scheme which provides substantial relief from burdens on religious freedom to *all* Saturday-observing retailers. Both schemes provide incomplete relief for the class of Saturday-observing retailers as a whole, but the incompleteness is a necessary consequence of ensuring that as many employees as possible will realize the benefits of the common pause day legislation. Both schemes represent genuine and serious attempts to minimize the adverse effects of pause day legislation on Saturday observers. It is far from clear that one scheme is intrinsically better than the other.

In this context, I note that freedom of religion, perhaps unlike freedom of conscience, has both individual and collective aspects. Legislatures are justified in being conscious of the effects of legislation on religious groups as a whole, as well as on individuals. In some circumstances, it is open to balance the religious freedoms of the many members of any particular religious group against those of the few when differential treatment is based on a criterion, such as the size of one's retail business, which is not in itself offensive to constitutional provisions, principles, and purposes.

... In my view, the balancing of the interests of more than seven employees to a common pause day against the freedom of religion of those affected constitutes justification for the exemption scheme selected by the Province of Ontario, at least in a context wherein any satisfactory alternative scheme involves an inquiry into religious beliefs.

I might add that I do not believe there is any magic in the number seven as distinct from, say, five, ten, or fifteen employees as the cut-off point for eligibility for the exemption. In balancing the interests of retail employees to a holiday in common with their family and friends against the s. 2(a) interests of those affected the legislature engaged in the process envisaged by s. 1 of the Charter. A "reasonable limit" is one which, having regard to the principles enunciated in *Oakes* [*R v.*, [1986] 1 SCR 103, 26 DLR (4th) 200], it was reasonable for the legislature to impose. The courts are not called upon to substitute judicial opinions for legislative ones as to the place at which to draw a precise line.

Having said this, however, I do not share the views of the majority of the United States Supreme Court that no legislative effort need be made to accommodate the interests of any Saturday-observing retailers. In particular, I would be hard pressed to conceive of any justification for insisting that a small, family store which operates without any employees remain closed on Sundays when the tenets of the retailer's religion requires closing on Saturdays. In my view, the principles articulated in *Oakes* make it incumbent on a legislature which enacts Sunday closing laws to attempt very seriously to alleviate the effects of those laws on Saturday observers. The exemption in s. 3(4) of the Act under review in these appeals represents a satisfactory effort on the part of the legislature of Ontario to that end and is, accordingly, permissible. ...

I should emphasize that it is not the role of this Court to devise legislation that is constitutionally valid, or to pass on the validity of schemes which are not directly before it, or to consider what legislation might be the most desirable. The discussion of alternative legislative schemes that I have undertaken is directed to one end only, that is, to address the issue whether the existing scheme meets the requirements of the second limb of the test for the application of s. 1 of the Charter as set down in *Oakes*.

In view of the extent and quality of the abridgment of rights flowing from the legislation, I have little difficulty in applying the third element of the proportionality test. The infringement is not disproportionate to the legislative objectives. A serious effort has been made to accommodate the freedom of religion of Saturday observers, in so far as that is possible without undue damage to the scope and quality of the pause day objective. It follows that I would uphold the Act under s. 1. ...

BEETZ J (McIntyre J concurring): ... [I]n my respectful opinion, the impugned legislation does not violate the freedom of conscience and religion guaranteed by s. 2(a) of the Charter and, accordingly, is of full force and effect without any need to rely on s. 1 of the Charter.

• • •

In my respectful opinion [the reasoning in Dickson CJC's judgment] is flawed as it postulates that the economic burden imposed upon Saturday observers is the effect of the impugned legislation. That this is not the case is made clear when one looks at the situation which would prevail should all Sunday observance laws be repealed. A devout Saturday observer would close shop on Saturdays whereas most of his competitors would remain open all week. A Saturday observer would have to face the same dilemma in the absence of any Sunday observance law: he would have to choose between the observance of his religion and the opening of his business in order to meet competition.

The economic harm suffered by a Saturday observer who closes shop on Saturdays is not caused by the *Retail Business Holidays Act*. It is independent from this Act. It results from the deliberate choice of a tradesman who gives priority to the tenets of his religion over his financial benefit. It is accordingly erroneous to suggest that the effect of the Act is to induce a Saturday observer to choose between his religion and the requirements of business competition. ...

... [T]his Court has made it clear that in order to constitute a violation of the freedom of conscience and religion guaranteed by the Charter, the coercion must come from the state. ...

It may well be that the true reason why the constitutionality of the *Retail Business Holidays Act* was challenged is the apparent advantage that it may confer upon Sunday observers whose Sabbath coincides with the common pause day prescribed by the Act.

If this be the case, the challenge would then be based on s. 15 of the Charter and not on s. 2. … But, as I have already indicated, s. 15 did not have effect at the relevant time and I abstain from expressing any view on the merits of a challenge based on this provision.

• • •

WILSON J (dissenting in part): I agree with Dickson CJ that the *Retail Business Holidays Act*, RSO 1980, c. 453, is *intra vires* the Province of Ontario because its purpose is to establish a common pause day for those employed in retail business. I also agree with the Chief Justice that s. 2 of the statute infringes the freedom of religion of those who close on Saturdays for religious reasons because it attaches an economic penalty to their religious observance. It requires them to be closed two days in the week instead of one.

I part company with the Chief Justice, however, on the application of s. 1 of the Charter to the "Saturday exemption" contained in s. 3(4) of the Act. It seems to me that once it is accepted that s. 2 infringes the freedom of religion of those who close on Saturdays for religious reasons, the question becomes whether that infringement can be justified under s. 1 in order that a common pause day be established for retail workers. The Chief Justice finds that it can be justified in the case of large retailers but not in the case of small. He does so, as I understand his reasons, by reference to the number of persons the larger retailer employs, on the basis that a decision made by that retailer to stay open on Sundays would deprive a larger number of employees of their common pause day than would the same decision made by a smaller retailer. The Chief Justice finds that this disparate treatment of the members of the group whose religious freedom has been infringed can be justified on the basis that they are being differentiated on the ground of size which is not a prohibited ground of discrimination.

With respect, I do not think that a limit on freedom of religion which recognizes the freedom of some members of the group but not of other members of the same group can be reasonable and justified in a free and democratic society. The *effect* of the disparate treatment, characterized by the Chief Justice as being based on size, is that the religious freedom of some is respected by the legislation and the religious freedom of others is not. It is this *effect* which, in my view, makes the legislation vulnerable to attack on constitutional grounds.

• • •

[T]he legislature must decide whether to subordinate freedom of religion to the objective of a common pause day, one scheme of justice, or subordinate the common pause day to freedom of religion, the competing scheme of justice, and, having decided which scheme of justice to adopt, it must then apply it in all cases. It cannot decide to subordinate the freedom of religion of some members of the group to the objective of a common pause day and subordinate the common pause day to the freedom of religion of other members of the same group. Yet this is the effect of the distinction between the large and small retailer adopted by the legislature in this legislation. It is, in my view, "a compromised scheme of justice." It does not affirm a *principle* which is applicable to all. It reflects rather a failure on the part of the legislature to make up its mind which scheme of justice to adopt. The result is, in my opinion, what Professor Dworkin refers to as "checkerboard" legislation.

It follows from what I have said that, in my view, s. 3(4) cannot constitute a reasonable limit under s. 1 of the Charter or be justified in a free and democratic society. However, if I am wrong in this and disparate treatment of this kind can be justified under s. 1, it would, in my view, require much more compelling evidence than was adduced by the Crown in order to establish that the government objective of a common pause day required it. The Crown adduced no evidence to establish that permitting all retailers who close on Saturdays on religious grounds to stay open on Sundays would cause a substantial disruption of the common pause day. Nor was it established that retailers who were not motivated to close on Saturdays by religious considerations would elect under s. 3(4)(a) to close on Saturdays for the sole purpose of being open on Sundays. Economic considerations may well make such a choice unlikely.

[Wilson J concluded that the fault with the s. 3(4) exemption for stores that closed on Sunday was that it did not go far enough—"It did not protect the freedom of religion of all those who close on Saturdays for religious reasons." She would have severed those paragraphs that limited the scope of the exemption to smaller retailers.

La Forest J wrote a concurring judgment. He would have upheld the Act under s. 1 even if it had not contained the s. 3(4) exemption for smaller enterprises:

> In seeking to achieve a goal that is demonstrably justified in a free and democratic society ... a legislature must be given reasonable room to manoeuvre to meet these conflicting pressures. ... In a case like the present, it seems to me, the Legislature is caught between having to let the legislation place a burden on people who observe a day of worship other than Sunday or create exemptions which in their practical workings may substantially interfere with the goal the Legislature seeks to advance and which themselves result in imposing burdens on Sunday observers and possibly on others as well. That being so, it seems to me that the choice of having or not having an exemption for those who observe a day other than Sunday must remain, in essence, a legislative choice. That, barring equality considerations, is true as well of the compromises that must be made in creating religious exemptions. These choices require an in-depth knowledge of all the circumstances. They are choices a court is not in a position to make.]

Appeal dismissed.
Appeal by Crown allowed and conviction restored.

NOTES AND QUESTIONS

1. The claim that the Sunday-closing law *indirectly* restricted the religious practice of Saturday Sabbatarians raised two issues for the Court. The first concerned the type or degree of burden on religious practice that would breach religious freedom. If a law does not ban a religious practice outright, but simply makes engagement in the practice more difficult, then the impediment or burden could be either minor or substantial. As a practical matter, not every burden on religious practice can be treated as a violation of s. 2(a) that the government must justify under s. 1. How significant, then, must the burden or impediment be before a court will hold that it breaches s. 2(a)? The second and more fundamental question

concerned the state's responsibility for the "impact" on the religious practice of a law that advances an otherwise legitimate public purpose. When should the state be seen as responsible for the relative "burden on" the particular religious practice, and when should the disadvantage be seen simply as a "cost" of the practice, for which the state is not responsible?

2. The Court accepted that the objective of the legislature was not the enforcement of the Christian Sabbath, but was simply the establishment of a common pause day and that this represented a substantial and pressing purpose under s. 1. Did the Christian roots of this practice, and in particular the choice of Sunday as the pause day, contribute to the majority view that the law interfered with the religious practices of those who wished to keep Saturday as the Sabbath? In a subsequent Supreme Court decision, *Adler v. Ontario*, [1996] 3 SCR 609, 140 DLR (4th) 385, in Section V, below, Justice Sopinka stated that the unequal treatment of different religious practices was critical to the finding of a breach of s. 2(a) in *Edwards Books*.

3. *Edwards Books* is an important s. 1 case that introduced a more deferential, or "reasonableness," standard into the *Oakes* analysis (see Chapter 17, The Framework of the Charter). In applying the minimal impairment test, Dickson CJC framed the question as "whether there is some *reasonable* alternative scheme which would allow the province to achieve its objective with fewer detrimental effects on religious freedom" (emphasis added). At another point, discussing the cut-off point for the eligibility for the exemption, he stated: "A 'reasonable' limit is one which ... it was reasonable for the legislature to impose. The courts are not called upon to substitute judicial opinions for legislative ones as to the place at which to draw a precise line." One of the "contextual" factors triggering the more deferential approach in this case was that the government's objective was the protection of a vulnerable group—retail workers. In a frequently quoted passage Dickson CJC stated:

> In interpreting and applying the Charter I believe that the courts must be cautious to ensure that it does not simply become an instrument of better situated individuals to roll back legislation which has as its object the improvement of the condition of disadvantaged persons. When the interests of more than seven vulnerable employees in securing a Sunday holiday are weighed against the interests of their employer in transacting business on Sunday, I cannot fault the legislature for determining that the protection of employees ought to fail.

4. In February 1989, the *Retail Business Holidays Act*, RSO 1990, c. R.30 was amended to (1) include a municipal exemption from Sunday closing requirements, and (2) permit any retail store, regardless of its size, to open on Sunday provided it was closed for religious reasons on another day. The amended law was upheld by the Ontario Court of Appeal in *Peel v. Great Atlantic and Pacific Co.* (1991), 2 OR (3d) 65.

5. Does the statutory recognition of certain Christian holidays such as Christmas and Easter, along with the failure to recognize the holy days of other religions, violate s. 2(a)? In *Islamic Schools Federation of Ontario v. Ottawa Board of Education* (1997), 145 DLR (4th) 659 (Ont. Div. Ct.) an Islamic religious organization sought a declaration that the Ottawa Board of Education had acted improperly in refusing to close its schools on two major Muslim holidays. The court, in a judgment written by O'Leary J, held that the school calendar, which included Christmas and Easter holidays, did not have a religious *purpose*—that the Christmas and Easter holidays provide secular pause or rest days. Nor, in his view, did the calendar have the *effect* of infringing religious freedom since under the provincial *Education*

Act a Muslim student could be excused from attendance on a day regarded by his or her religion as a holy day.

The court also found that any breach of s. 15 was justified under s. 1:

> [I]n choosing school holidays that can be enjoyed by students and parents in common with the rest of the community [the common pause days recognized in other legislation such as the Ontario *Retail Business Holidays Act*], the legislature interfered the least it could with the holy days celebrated by various religions. ...
>
> I conclude, therefore, that the school holidays chosen are appropriate ones to meet the needs of the students and interfere as little as possible with the holy days of various religions. The only way adverse effect discrimination could be avoided would be to make every holy day of every student into a holiday. Even if that were possible, the new legislation would be invalid. Such legislation would provide for religious not secular holidays. ... Atheists, agnostics and those not affiliated with any religious denomination would have a legitimate complaint that their right to a sensible and convenient school calendar was being sacrificed in the interest of religion. ...
>
> [Nevertheless], I will assume that the [School] Board, or indeed the Ministry [of Education], has an obligation to take reasonable steps to accommodate the Muslims so as to undo the harm, namely two days missed from school, caused by the discrimination.

As noted in the introduction to this chapter, freedom of religion, as it emerges from the framework cases of *Big M* and *Edwards Books*, has as its central focus the protection against state "coercion." This freedom from coercion is understood to have two sides: (1) the protection of the individual's freedom *to* religion—that is, the freedom to engage in religious practice without restriction by the state; and (2) the protection of the individual's freedom *from* religion—that is, the freedom from being compelled by the state to engage in any form of religious practice. The materials that follow explore further developments with respect to each of these aspects of religious freedom: first, the restriction and accommodation of religious practice, and, second, state support for religion. As you will see, it is sometimes difficult to keep the two aspects of freedom of religion distinct—state efforts to accommodate religious practice may in some cases raise issues of state imposition of religion. In addition, you will see that there are other aspects of freedom of religion that are not completely captured by this two-pronged framework that focuses on state coercion of religious practice—in particular, the idea that the state should not become "entangled" in religion. This idea is explored in the last section of this chapter, which deals with religious families and communities and the relationship between secular and religious law.

Neither *Big M* nor *Edwards Books* explores in any detail the issues of how religion is defined and how religious and conscientious beliefs are distinguished from other beliefs and opinions. These are important issues because s. 2(a) protects not only the right to hold and express religious and conscientious beliefs (which even in the absence of s. 2(a) would be protected by s. 2(b), freedom of expression), but also the right to engage in *practices* associated with those beliefs. It was not until 2004, in the *Syndicat Northcrest v. Amselem* case, immediately below, that the Supreme Court of Canada addressed these issues. Thus *Amselem*, which is an important case on the accommodation of religious practice, has also come to be seen as a major part of the framework of s. 2(a), together with *Big M* and *Edwards Books*.

III. THE RESTRICTION AND ACCOMMODATION OF RELIGIOUS PRACTICE

In *Syndicat Northcrest v. Amselem*, below, the Supreme Court of Canada held that a condominium association's refusal to permit Orthodox Jewish unit owners to construct succahs on their balconies as part their celebration of the Jewish festival of Succot breached their freedom of religion under the *Quebec Charter of Human Rights and Freedoms*. Because the restriction on religious practice was imposed by a non-state actor, the *Canadian Charter of Rights and Freedoms* was not applicable. However, the majority judgment of Justice Iacobucci was clear in saying that "the principles ... applicable in cases where an individual alleges that his or her freedom of religion is infringed under the Quebec *Charter*" are also applicable to a claim under s. 2(a) of the Canadian Charter.

Syndicat Northcrest v. Amselem
[2004] 2 SCR 551, 2004 SCC 47, 241 DLR (4th) 1

IACOBUCCI J (McLachlin CJC, Iacobucci, Major, Arbour and Fish JJ concurring):

I. Introduction

[1] An important feature of our constitutional democracy is respect for minorities, which includes, of course, religious minorities: see *Reference re Secession of Quebec*, [1998] 2 SCR 217, at paras. 79-81 [161 DLR (4th) 385]. Indeed, respect for and tolerance of the rights and practices of religious minorities is one of the hallmarks of an enlightened democracy. But respect for religious minorities is not a stand-alone absolute right; like other rights, freedom of religion exists in a matrix of other correspondingly important rights that attach to individuals. Respect for minority rights must also coexist alongside societal values that are central to the make-up and functioning of a free and democratic society. This appeal requires the Court to deal with the interrelationship between fundamental rights both at a conceptual level and for a practical outcome.

[2] More specifically the cases which are the subject of this appeal involve a religious claim by the appellants for the setting up of a "succah" for nine days a year in the pursuit of their religious beliefs on their co-owned property under the Quebec *Charter of Human Rights and Freedoms*, RSQ, c. C-12 (the "Quebec *Charter*"). The Quebec courts denied the claim. With respect, I disagree and would allow the appeal.

[3] In particular, after defining the scope of freedom of religion and its infringement, I find that the appellants' religious freedom under the Quebec *Charter* has been infringed by the declaration of co-ownership. While the respondent has raised rights to enjoy property and personal security as justification for its refusal to allow a succah to be set up, I find that the impairment of the appellants' religious freedom is serious whereas I conclude that the intrusion on the respondent's rights is minimal. As such, I hold that the appellants must be permitted to set up succahs on their balconies, provided that the succahs remain only for the limited time necessary—in this case nine days, allow for an emergency access route, and conform, as much as possible, with the general aesthetics of

the property. I also find the argument that the appellants waived their religious rights cannot be maintained under the circumstances, nor did they implicitly agree not to set up succahs on their balconies by signing the declaration of co-ownership.

II. Background

[4] The appellants, all Orthodox Jews, are divided co-owners of residential units in "Place Northcrest," two luxury buildings forming part of "Le Sanctuaire du Mont-Royal" (the "Sanctuaire"), a larger complex in Montréal. ... Under the terms of the Sanctuaire's by-laws in the declaration of co-ownership, the balconies of individual units, although constituting [TRANSLATION] "common portions" of the immovable, are nonetheless reserved to the [TRANSLATION] "exclusive use" of the co-owners of the units to which they are attached.

[5] In late September 1996, Mr. Amselem, at the time a new resident of the Sanctuaire, set up a "succah" on his balcony for the purposes of fulfilling a biblically mandated obligation during the Jewish religious festival of Succot. A succah is a small enclosed temporary hut or booth, traditionally made of wood or other materials such as fastened canvas, and open to the heavens, in which, it has been acknowledged, Jews are commanded to "dwell" temporarily during the festival of Succot, which commences annually with nightfall on the fifteenth day of the Jewish month of Tishrei. This nine-day festival, which begins in late September or early-to mid-October, commemorates the 40-year period during which, according to Jewish tradition, the Children of Israel wandered in the desert, living in temporary shelters.

[6] Under the Jewish faith, in commemoration of the festival's historical connection and as a symbolic demonstration of their faith in the divine, Jews are obligated to dwell in these succahs, as their ancestors did in the desert. Orthodox Jews observe this biblically mandated commandment of "dwelling" in a succah by transforming the succah into the practitioner's primary residence for the entire holiday period. They are required to take all their meals in the succah; they customarily conduct certain religious ceremonies in the succah; they are required, weather permitting, to sleep in the succah; and they are otherwise required to generally make the succah their primary abode for the entirety of the festival period, health and weather permitting.

[7] Technically, a succah must minimally consist of a three-walled, open-roofed structure which must meet certain size specifications in order to fulfill the biblical commandment of dwelling in it properly according to the requirements of the Jewish faith. While a succah is usually festively decorated interiorly, there are no aesthetic requirements as to its exterior appearance.

[8] During the first two and last two days of the Succot holiday, as well as during any intermittent Saturday, Orthodox Jews are normally forbidden from inter alia turning electricity on or off and riding in cars or elevators. Similarly, during the Saturday(s) falling within the nine-day festival, Orthodox Jews are forbidden from carrying objects outside of their private domiciles in the absence of a symbolic enclosure, or eruv.

[9] After Mr. Amselem put up his succah in September 1996, the syndicate of co-ownership, Syndicat Northcrest (the "respondent" or "Syndicat"), requested its removal, claiming the succah was in violation of the Sanctuaire's by-laws as stated in the declara-

tion of co-ownership, which *inter alia* prohibited decorations, alterations and constructions on the Sanctuaire's balconies ... . None of the appellants had read the declaration of co-ownership prior to purchasing or occupying their individual units.

· · ·

[11] A year later, on October 6, 1997, and pursuant to the regulations in the declaration of co-ownership, Mr. Amselem requested permission from the Syndicat to set up a succah on, and thus enclose part of, his balcony to celebrate the same holiday of Succot. The Syndicat refused, invoking the restrictions in the declaration of co-ownership.

· · ·

[13] In a letter dated October 10, 1997, the Syndicat proposed to allow Mr. Amselem, in conjunction with the other Orthodox Jewish residents of the building, including the appellants Mr. Fonfeder and Mr. Klein, to set up a communal succah in the Sanctuaire's gardens.

[14] In their October 14, 1997 letter to the Syndicat, the appellants expressed their dissatisfaction with the respondent's proposed accommodation. They explained why a communal succah would not only cause extreme hardship with their religious observance, but would also be contrary to their personal religious beliefs which, they claimed, called for "their own succah, each on his own balcony."

[Despite the Syndicat's refusal of their request, the appellants each set up their own individual succahs. In response, the Syndicat filed an application for a permanent injunction prohibiting the appellants from setting up the succahs and, if necessary, permitting their demolition.]

III. Relevant Legislative Provisions

[18] Charter of Human Rights and Freedoms, RSQ, c. C-12

1. Every human being has a right to life, and to personal security, inviolability and freedom. He also possesses juridical personality.

3. Every person is the possessor of the fundamental freedoms, including freedom of conscience, freedom of religion, freedom of opinion, freedom of expression, freedom of peaceful assembly and freedom of association.

6. Every person has a right to the peaceful enjoyment and free disposition of his property, except to the extent provided by law.

9.1. In exercising his fundamental freedoms and rights, a person shall maintain a proper regard for democratic values, public order and the general well-being of the citizens of Québec. In this respect, the scope of the freedoms and rights, and limits to their exercise, may be fixed by law. ...

IV. Judicial History

[The trial judge, Rochon J, found that the impugned bylaws were not in violation of the Quebec Charter and issued the injunction requested by the Syndicat. The decision was upheld by the Quebec Court of Appeal.]

V. Issues

[35] In my view, the key issues before us are: (1) whether the clauses in the by-laws of the declaration of co-ownership, which contained a general prohibition against decorations or constructions on one's balcony, infringe the appellants' freedom of religion protected under the Quebec *Charter*; (2) if so, whether the refusal by the respondent to permit the setting up of a succah is justified by its reliance on the co-owners' rights to enjoy property under s. 6 of the Quebec *Charter* and their rights to personal security under s. 1 thereof; and (3) whether the appellants waived their rights to freedom of religion by signing the declaration of co-ownership.

VI. Analysis

· · ·

A. Freedom of Religion

[37] The analysis that follows sets out the principles that are applicable in cases where an individual alleges that his or her freedom of religion is infringed under the Quebec *Charter* or under the *Canadian Charter of Rights and Freedoms*. ...

(1) Definition of Religious Freedom

· · ·

[39] In order to define religious freedom, we must first ask ourselves what we mean by "religion." While it is perhaps not possible to define religion precisely, some outer definition is useful since only beliefs, convictions and practices rooted in religion, as opposed to those that are secular, socially based or conscientiously held, are protected by the guarantee of freedom of religion. Defined broadly, religion typically involves a particular and comprehensive system of faith and worship. Religion also tends to involve the belief in a divine, superhuman or controlling power. In essence, religion is about freely and deeply held personal convictions or beliefs connected to an individual's spiritual faith and integrally linked to one's self-definition and spiritual fulfilment, the practices of which allow individuals to foster a connection with the divine or with the subject or object of that spiritual faith.

[40] What then is the definition and content of an individual's protected right to religious freedom under the Quebec (or the Canadian) *Charter*? This Court has long articulated an expansive definition of freedom of religion, which revolves around the notion of personal choice and individual autonomy and freedom ... .

[Reference is then made to *R v. Big M Drug Mart Ltd.*, [1985] 1 SCR 295, 18 DLR (4th) 321 and *R v. Edwards Books and Art Ltd.*, [1986] 2 SCR 713, 35 DLR (4th) 1.]

[42] This understanding is consistent with a personal or subjective conception of freedom of religion, one that is integrally linked with an individual's self-definition and fulfilment and is a function of personal autonomy and choice, elements which undergird the right ... .

[43] The emphasis then is on personal choice of religious beliefs. In my opinion, these decisions and commentary should not be construed to imply that freedom of religion protects only those aspects of religious belief or conduct that are objectively recognized by religious experts as being obligatory tenets or precepts of a particular religion. Consequently, claimants seeking to invoke freedom of religion should not need to prove the objective validity of their beliefs in that their beliefs are objectively recognized as valid by other members of the same religion, nor is such an inquiry appropriate for courts to make … . In fact, this Court has indicated on several occasions that, if anything, a person must show "[s]incerity of belief" (*Edwards Books, supra*, at p. 735) and not that a particular belief is "valid."

• • •

[46] To summarize up to this point, our Court's past decisions and the basic principles underlying freedom of religion support the view that freedom of religion consists of the freedom to undertake practices and harbour beliefs, having a nexus with religion, in which an individual demonstrates he or she sincerely believes or is sincerely undertaking in order to connect with the divine or as a function of his or her spiritual faith, irrespective of whether a particular practice or belief is required by official religious dogma or is in conformity with the position of religious officials.

[47] But, at the same time, this freedom encompasses objective as well as personal notions of religious belief, "obligation," precept, "commandment," custom or ritual. Consequently, both obligatory as well as voluntary expressions of faith should be protected under the Quebec (and the Canadian) *Charter*. It is the religious or spiritual essence of an action, not any mandatory or perceived-as-mandatory nature of its observance, that attracts protection. An inquiry into the mandatory nature of an alleged religious practice is not only inappropriate, it is plagued with difficulties. …

• • •

[49] To require a person to prove that his or her religious practices are supported by a mandatory doctrine of faith, leaving it for judges to determine what those mandatory doctrines of faith are, would require courts to interfere with profoundly personal beliefs in a manner inconsistent with the principles set out by Dickson CJ in *Edwards Books, supra*, at p. 759:

> The purpose of s. 2(a) *is to ensure that society does not interfere* with profoundly personal beliefs that govern one's perception of oneself, humankind, nature, and, in some cases, a higher or different order of being. These beliefs, in turn, govern one's conduct and practices. [Emphasis added.]

[50] In my view, the State is in no position to be, nor should it become, the arbiter of religious dogma. Accordingly, courts should avoid judicially interpreting and thus determining, either explicitly or implicitly, the content of a subjective understanding of religious requirement, "obligation," precept, "commandment," custom or ritual. Secular judicial determinations of theological or religious disputes, or of contentious matters of religious doctrine, unjustifiably entangle the court in the affairs of religion.

[51] That said, while a court is not qualified to rule on the validity or veracity of any given religious practice or belief, or to choose among various interpretations of belief, it is qualified to inquire into the sincerity of a claimant's belief, where sincerity is in fact at

issue ... . It is important to emphasize, however, that sincerity of belief simply implies an honesty of belief ... .

[52] ... [T]he court's role in assessing sincerity is intended only to ensure that a presently asserted religious belief is in good faith, neither fictitious nor capricious, and that it is not an artifice. Otherwise, nothing short of a religious inquisition would be required to decipher the innermost beliefs of human beings.

[53] Assessment of sincerity is a question of fact that can be based on several non-exhaustive criteria, including the credibility of a claimant's testimony ... , as well as an analysis of whether the alleged belief is consistent with his or her other current religious practices. It is important to underscore, however, that it is inappropriate for courts rigorously to study and focus on the past practices of claimants in order to determine whether their current beliefs are sincerely held. Over the course of a lifetime, individuals change and so can their beliefs. Religious beliefs, by their very nature, are fluid and rarely static. A person's connection to or relationship with the divine or with the subject or object of his or her spiritual faith, or his or her perceptions of religious obligation emanating from such a relationship, may well change and evolve over time. Because of the vacillating nature of religious belief, a court's inquiry into sincerity, if anything, should focus not on past practice or past belief but on a person's belief at the time of the alleged interference with his or her religious freedom.

[54] A claimant may choose to adduce expert evidence to demonstrate that his or her belief is consistent with the practices and beliefs of other adherents of the faith. While such evidence may be relevant to a demonstration of sincerity, it is not necessary. Since the focus of the inquiry is not on what others view the claimant's religious obligations as being, but rather what the claimant views these personal religious "obligations" to be, it is inappropriate to require expert opinions to show sincerity of belief. An "expert" or an authority on religious law is not the surrogate for an individual's affirmation of what his or her religious beliefs are. Religious belief is intensely personal and can easily vary from one individual to another. Requiring proof of the established practices of a religion to gauge the sincerity of belief diminishes the very freedom we seek to protect.

[55] This approach to freedom of religion effectively avoids the invidious interference of the State and its courts with religious belief. The alternative would undoubtedly result in unwarranted intrusions into the religious affairs of the synagogues, churches, mosques, temples and religious facilities of the nation with value-judgment indictments of those beliefs that may be unconventional or not mainstream. As articulated by Professor Tribe [L.H. Tribe, *American Constitutional Law*, 2d ed. (Mineola, NY: Foundation Press, 1988)], at p. 1244, "an intrusive government inquiry into the nature of a claimant's beliefs would in itself threaten the values of religious liberty."

[56] Thus, at the first stage of a religious freedom analysis, an individual advancing an issue premised upon a freedom of religion claim must show the court that (1) he or she has a practice or belief, having a nexus with religion, which calls for a particular line of conduct, either by being objectively or subjectively obligatory or customary, or by, in general, subjectively engendering a personal connection with the divine or with the subject or object of an individual's spiritual faith, irrespective of whether a particular practice or belief is required by official religious dogma or is in conformity with the position

of religious officials; and (2) he or she is sincere in his or her belief. Only then will freedom of religion be triggered.

(2) Infringement of Religious Freedom

[57] Once an individual has shown that his or her religious freedom is triggered, as outlined above, a court must then ascertain whether there has been enough of an interference with the exercise of the implicated right so as to constitute an infringement of freedom of religion under the Quebec (or the Canadian) *Charter*.

[58] ... Section 2(a) of the Canadian *Charter* prohibits only burdens or impositions on religious practice that are non-trivial. This position was confirmed and adopted by Dickson CJ for the majority in *Edwards Books, supra*, at p. 759 ... .

[59] It consequently suffices that a claimant show that the impugned contractual or legislative provision (or conduct) interferes with his or her ability to act in accordance with his or her religious beliefs *in a manner that is more than trivial or insubstantial*. The question then becomes: what does this mean?

[60] At this stage, as a general matter, one can do no more than say that the context of each case must be examined to ascertain whether the interference is more than trivial or insubstantial. But it is important to observe what examining that context involves.

[61] In this respect, it should be emphasized that not every action will become summarily unassailable and receive automatic protection under the banner of freedom of religion. No right, including freedom of religion, is absolute: see, e.g., *Big M, supra*; ... *B.(R.) v. Children's Aid Society of Metropolitan Toronto*, [1995] 1 SCR 315 [122 DLR (4th) 1], at para. 226; *Trinity Western University v. British Columbia College of Teachers*, [2001] 1 SCR 772, 2001 SCC 31 [199 DLR (4th) 1], at para. 29. This is so because we live in a society of individuals in which we must always take the rights of others into account. ...

[62] Freedom of religion, as outlined above, quite appropriately reflects a broad and expansive approach to religious freedom under both the Quebec *Charter* and the Canadian *Charter* and should not be prematurely narrowly construed. However, our jurisprudence does not allow individuals to do absolutely anything in the name of that freedom. Even if individuals demonstrate that they sincerely believe in the religious essence of an action, for example, that a particular practice will subjectively engender a genuine connection with the divine or with the subject or object of their faith, and even if they successfully demonstrate non-trivial or non-insubstantial interference with that practice, they will still have to consider how the exercise of their right impacts upon the rights of others in the context of the competing rights of private individuals. Conduct which would potentially cause harm to or interference with the rights of others would not automatically be protected. The ultimate protection of any particular *Charter* right must be measured in relation to other rights and with a view to the underlying context in which the apparent conflict arises.

[63] Indeed, freedom of religion, like all other rights, applicable either as against the State or, under the Quebec *Charter*, in its private dimension as against another individual, may be made subject to overriding societal concerns. As with other rights, not every interference with religious freedom would be actionable, in accordance with the limitations on the exercise of fundamental rights recognized by the Quebec *Charter*.

· · ·

B. Application to the Facts

(1) Freedom of Religion and Infringement

(a) As Pertaining to Setting Up One's Own Succah

[65] As outlined above, the first step in successfully advancing a claim that an individual's freedom of religion has been infringed is for a claimant to demonstrate that he or she sincerely believes in a practice or belief that has a nexus with religion. The second step is to then demonstrate that the impugned conduct of a third party interferes with the individual's ability to act in accordance with that practice or belief in a manner that is non-trivial. At trial, Rochon J, relying primarily on the testimony of Rabbi Levy, whose testimony he found more compelling than that of Rabbi Ohana, found that the impugned clauses in the declaration of co-ownership did not infringe the appellants' rights to freedom of religion since, according to him, Judaism does not require its adherents to build their own succah (at p. 1909):

> [TRANSLATION] First of all, the court notes that practising Jews are not under a religious obligation to erect their own succahs. There is no commandment as to where they must be erected.

As a result, Rochon J believed that freedom of religion was not even triggered. Although Morin JA, in his concurring opinion, quite properly concluded that this was not the correct approach to take to freedom of religion, the majority of the Court of Appeal seemed to endorse the trial judge's reasoning. With respect, I believe their approach was mistaken.

[66] More particularly, the approach adopted by Rochon J at trial and Dalphond J for the majority of the Court of Appeal is inconsistent with the proper approach to freedom of religion. First, the trial judge's methodology was faulty in that he chose between two competing rabbinical authorities on a question of Jewish law. Second, he seems to have based his findings with respect to freedom of religion solely on what he perceived to be the objective obligatory requirements of Judaism. He thus failed to recognize that freedom of religion under the Quebec (and the Canadian) *Charter* does not require a person to prove that his or her religious practices are supported by any mandatory doctrine of faith.

[67] Furthermore, in my opinion, any incorporation of distinctions between "obligation" and "custom" or, as made by the respondent and the courts below, between "objective obligation" and "subjective obligation or belief" within the framework of a religious freedom analysis is dubious, unwarranted and unduly restrictive. In my view, when courts undertake the task of analysing religious doctrine in order to determine the truth or falsity of a contentious matter of religious law, or when courts attempt to define the very concept of religious "obligation," as has been suggested in the courts below, they enter forbidden domain. It is not within the expertise and purview of secular courts to adjudicate questions of religious doctrine.

[68] Similarly, to frame the right either in terms of objective religious "obligation" or even as the sincere subjective belief that an obligation exists and that the practice is *required* would lead to arbitrary and hierarchical determinations of religious "obligation," would exclude religious custom from protection, and would disregard the value of non-obligatory religious experiences by excluding those experiences from protection. Jewish

women, for example, strictly speaking, do not have a biblically mandated "obligation" to dwell in a succah during the Succot holiday. If a woman, however, nonetheless sincerely believes that sitting and eating in a succah brings her closer to her Maker, is that somehow less deserving of recognition simply because she has no strict "obligation" to do so? Is the Jewish yarmulke or Sikh turban worthy of less recognition simply because it may be borne out of religious custom, not obligation? Should an individual Jew, who may personally deny the modern relevance of literal biblical "obligation" or "commandment," be precluded from making a freedom of religion argument despite the fact that for some reason he or she sincerely derives a closeness to his or her God by sitting in a succah? Surely not.

[69] Rather, as I have stated above, regardless of the position taken by religious officials and in religious texts, provided that an individual demonstrates that he or she sincerely believes that a certain practice or belief is experientially religious in nature in that it is either objectively required by the religion, *or* that he or she subjectively believes that it is required by the religion, *or* that he or she sincerely believes that the practice engenders a personal, subjective connection to the divine or to the subject or object of his or her spiritual faith, and as long as that practice has a nexus with religion, it should trigger the protection of s. 3 of the Quebec *Charter* or that of s. 2(a) of the Canadian *Charter*, or both, depending on the context.

[70] On the question of sincerity, the respondent argues that the appellants do not sincerely believe that their religion requires them to build their own individual succahs on their balconies. That said, the trial judge did find that Mr. Amselem, at least, sincerely believed that he was obliged to set up a succah on his own property, thus triggering his freedom of religion protection according to the first step in our analysis.

[71] With respect to the appellants Mr. Klein and Mr. Fonfeder, Rochon J relied primarily on their past practices to question their sincerity and concluded that they must view the setting up of their own succah as a purely optional practice, which precluded their freedom of religion from being triggered. This conclusion is troublesome for a variety of reasons. First, Rochon J misconstrued the scope of freedom of religion. Given this mistaken approach, it is somewhat difficult to assess the sincerity of the appellants' religious beliefs regarding the setting up of succahs on their balconies. Second, I do not accept that one may conclude that a person's current religious belief is not sincere simply because he or she previously celebrated a religious holiday differently. Beliefs and observances evolve and change over time. If, as I have underscored, sincerity of belief at the relevant time is the governing standard to ensure that a claim is honest and not an artifice, then a rigorous examination of past conduct cannot be determinative of sincerity of belief.

[72] Furthermore, based on the above-discussed definition of freedom of religion, it appears that the trial judge applied the wrong test to the evidence adduced by the appellants in support of their belief. For if freedom of religion encompasses not only what adherents feel sincerely obliged to do, but also includes what an individual demonstrates he or she sincerely believes or is sincerely undertaking in order to engender a connection with the divine or with the subject or object of his or her spiritual faith, then the proper test would be whether the appellants sincerely believe that dwelling in or setting up their *own* individual succah is of religious significance to them, irrespective of whether they subjectively believe that their religion *requires* them to build their own succah. This is because it is hard to qualify the value of religious experience. Religious fulfilment is by

its very nature subjective and personal. To some, the religious and spiritual significance of building and eating in one's own succah could vastly outweigh the significance of a strict fulfilment of the biblical commandment of "dwelling" in a succah, and that, in and of itself, would suffice in grounding a claim of freedom of religion.

[73] When the appellants adduced Rabbi Ohana's expert testimony, they were submitting evidence of their sincere individual belief as to the inherently personal nature of fulfilling the commandment of dwelling in a succah. As expounded upon by Rabbi Ohana, according to Jewish law the obligation of "dwelling" must be complied with festively and joyously, without causing distress to the individual. Great distress, such as that caused by inclement weather, extreme cold or, in this case, the extreme unpleasantness rendered by forced relocation to a communal succah, with all attendant ramifications, for the entire nine-day period would not only preclude the acknowledged obligation of dwelling in a succah but would also render voluntary compliance wrongful and inappropriate, thus necessitating the setting up of a private succah. In light of our test for freedom of religion, such expert testimony, although not required, would in my view certainly support a positive finding of sincerity and honesty of the appellants' belief. As a result, all of the appellants have, in my opinion, successfully implicated freedom of religion.

[74] ... [I]n order for a triggered right of religious freedom to have been infringed, the interference with the right needs to be more than trivial or insubstantial ... . It is evident that in respect of Mr. Amselem the impugned clauses of the declaration of co-ownership interfere with his right in a substantial way. For if, as Rochon J himself found, Mr. Amselem sincerely believes that he is obligated by the Jewish religion to set up and dwell in his own succah, then a prohibition against setting up his own succah obliterates the substance of his right, let alone interferes with it in a non-trivial fashion. A communal succah is simply not an option. Thus, his right is definitely infringed.

[With respect to the other appellants, who did not hold a belief that they were *required* to build their own succah, Iacobucci J found that the evidence established that the distress that would be imposed on them by using a communal succah or by imposing on friends and family would detract significantly from the joyous celebration of the holiday, which was essential to its proper religious celebration, and would therefore constitute a non-trivial infringement of their freedom of religion.]

*(2) The Alleged Justification for the Limit on the Exercise of Freedom of Religion
    in This Case*

                                    • • •

[84] ... I am of the view that the alleged intrusions or deleterious effects on the respondent's rights or interests under the circumstances are, at best, minimal and thus cannot be reasonably considered as imposing valid limits on the exercise of the appellants' religious freedom.

[85] In practice, to what degree would the respondent be harmed were the appellants allowed to set up a succah for a period of 9 out of 365 days a year? The evidence before us does not provide a satisfactory answer. The respondent has simply not adduced enough evidence for us to conclude that allowing the appellants to set up such temporary succahs would cause the value of the units, or of the property, to decrease. Even if I were to con-

sider the possibility that the economic value of the property might decrease if a substantial number of co-owners were allowed to set up succahs on their balconies for a lengthy time period throughout the year, any drop in value caused by the presence of a small number of succahs for a period of nine days each year would undoubtedly be minimal. Consequently, in this case, the exercise of the appellants' freedom of religion, which I have concluded would be significantly impaired, would clearly outweigh the unsubstantiated concerns of the co-owners about the decrease in property value.

[86] Similarly, protecting the co-owners' enjoyment of the property by preserving the aesthetic appearance of the balconies and thus enhancing the harmonious external appearance of the building cannot be reconciled with a total ban imposed on the appellants' exercise of their religious freedom. Although residing in a building with a year-long uniform and harmonious external appearance might be the co-owners' preference, the potential annoyance caused by a few succahs being set up for a period of nine days each year would undoubtedly be quite trivial.

[87] In a multiethnic and multicultural country such as ours, which accentuates and advertises its modern record of respecting cultural diversity and human rights and of promoting tolerance of religious and ethnic minorities—and is in many ways an example thereof for other societies—the argument of the respondent that nominal, minimally intruded-upon aesthetic interests should outweigh the exercise of the appellants' religious freedom is unacceptable. Indeed, mutual tolerance is one of the cornerstones of all democratic societies. Living in a community that attempts to maximize human rights invariably requires openness to and recognition of the rights of others. ...

[88] Finally, the respondent alleges that banning succahs on the appellants' balconies, portions of which are subject under the by-laws to a right of servitude in cases of emergency, ensures that the balconies, as fire escape routes, would remain unobstructed in the case of emergency and, as such, the ban seeks to protect the co-owners' rights to personal security under s. 1 of the Quebec *Charter*. I agree that security concerns, if soundly established, would require appropriate recognition in ascertaining any limit on the exercise of the appellants' religious freedom.

[89] However, in their October 14, 1997 letter to the respondent, the appellants obviated any such concerns by all offering to set up their succahs "in such a way that they would not block any doors, would not obstruct fire lanes, [and] would pose no threat to safety or security in any way."

[90] Since the appellants have never claimed that the succah need have any exterior aesthetic religious component, the appellants should set up their succahs in a manner that conforms, as much as possible, with the general aesthetics of the property in order to respect the co-owners' property interests. Counsel for the appellants acknowledged this undertaking in oral argument.

. . .

[104] For the foregoing reasons, I would allow the appeal with costs throughout, set aside the decision of the Court of Appeal, and, in lieu thereof, declare that the appellants have a right to set up succahs on their balconies for the annual festival of Succot, subject to the undertakings they have given with regard to the size, placement, and general aesthetics of said succahs.

Appeal allowed.

NOTES AND QUESTIONS

1. The dissenting judgment of Bastarache J adopted a much narrower approach to the scope of freedom of religion. He argued that a practice is protected under s. 3 of the Quebec Charter and s. 2(a) of the Canadian Charter only if it is part of an established religious belief system and only if it is regarded by the individual claimant as a mandatory part of that system. In support of this narrower approach, Bastarache J emphasized that freedom of religion protects not just *beliefs* but also consequent religious *practices*:

> [137] … [T]here are in fact two elements to consider in analysing freedom of religion. First, there is the freedom to believe and profess one's beliefs; second, there is the right to manifest one's beliefs, primarily by observing rites, and by sharing one's faith by establishing places of worship and frequenting them. Thus, although private beliefs have a purely personal aspect, the other dimension of the right has genuine social significance and involves a relationship with others.

Thus, according to Bastarache J, individuals who claim that their *practices* fall within the guarantee of freedom of religion protection must show a "nexus" between their personal beliefs and the precepts of their religion. This connection between personal belief and established religious precepts that "constitute a body of objectively identifiable data" enabled Bastarche J to distinguish between "genuine religious beliefs and personal choices or practices that are unrelated to freedom of conscience." At para. 137 Bastarache J included the following passage in support of his argument that the right of freedom of religion has "genuine social significance and involves a relationship with others":

> Notwithstanding the wide variety of religious experience, no religion is or can be purely individual in its outlook, as ultimate concern is said to be. On the contrary, religions are necessarily collective endeavours. By the same token, no religion is or can be defined purely by an act of personal commitment, as the ultimate concerns of an individual are said to be. Instead, all religions demand a personal act of faith in relation to a set of beliefs that is historically derived and shared by the religious community. It follows that any genuine freedom of religion must protect, not only individual belief, but the institutions and practices that permit the collective development and expression of that belief.
>
> More fundamentally, while it is possible to understand religion in such a way as to include practices that would conventionally be regarded as secular, it is simply not possible to understand religion in such a way that the distinction between the religious and the secular collapses, for the religious and the secular exist in contradistinction to one another. Yet such a collapse is implicit in the view that the secular becomes religious as and when it becomes a matter of ultimate concern to any individual, for whether a practice is secular or religious would then be a purely subjective question. Any objective distinction between the two would disappear. [From T. Macklem, "Faith as a Secular Value" (2000), 45 *McGill LJ* 1, at 25.]

2. In his judgment Iacobucci J sought to distinguish religion from other belief systems. Why did he think it necessary to do this? The problem of distinguishing religious beliefs and practices from secular beliefs and practices, which has bedeviled the American courts, was something that Canadian courts and commentators thought section 2(a) had avoided by creating a single right to freedom of conscience and religion. Indeed, in *Big M*, Dickson CJC

had said that "freedom of conscience and religion" in s. 2(a) of the Charter formed a "single integrated concept." If freedom of conscience and religion are parts of a single, integrated right that protects deeply held commitments or beliefs about right and truth, why was it necessary for the court to embark on the difficult task of determining when a belief and/or practice is religious rather than secular?

3. Why do you think there are so few freedom of conscience cases under s. 2(a)? An exception is *Maurice v. Attorney General of Canada* (2002), 210 DLR (4th) 186, a decision of the Federal Court Trial Division, in which it was held that Correctional Service of Canada had a duty to provide vegetarian meals to an inmate who was ethically opposed to the consumption of meat.

4. Justice Iacobucci rejected the condominium association's argument that the appellants had waived their freedom of religion rights when they purchased their units and agreed to the bylaws. In his view, even if it were possible for an individual to waive his or her right to religious freedom, the appellants could not be understood to have done so in this case. While they signed the declaration of co-ownership, which included the bylaw restricting the use of the unit balconies, this did not amount to a waiver of their right to practice their religion. First, the waiver was not unconditional because the prohibition was subject to exemptions. Second, it was not voluntary because the appellants had no choice but to sign the declaration if they wanted to reside in the building. Moreover, they had not read the bylaws and so did not know what they were agreeing to. Third, the waiver was not explicit because it did not make specific reference to the affected Charter right.

Justice Binnie, dissenting, did not think it necessary for the association to establish that the appellants had *waived* their right to freedom of religion when they formally agreed to the condominium bylaws. In his view, when the appellants agreed to the bylaws, the other unit owners were entitled to conclude that the practice of their religion was compatible with these rules. He said: "[T]here is a vast difference between using freedom of religion as a shield against interference with religious freedoms by the State and as a sword against co-contractors in a private building." In holding the appellants to their agreement, Binnie J stressed the following factors: that the appellants were in the best position to determine, prior to their purchase of a unit in the building, what their religion required; that they could have purchased a unit in another building; that they had chosen not to read the bylaws when they entered into the contract with the other unit owners; and, finally, that they had rejected the accommodation of a communal succah, offered by the association, even though this accommodation was not inconsistent with their religious beliefs.

5. Iacobucci J, in setting out the framework for freedom of religion claims, notes (at para. 61) that

> not every action will become summarily unassailable and receive automatic protection under the banner of freedom of religion. No right, including freedom of religion, is absolute ... . This is so because we live in a society of individuals in which we must always take the rights of others into account.

One case he cites in support of this is *B.(R.) v. Children's Aid Society of Metropolitan Toronto*, [1995] 1 SCR 315, 122 DLR (4th) 1. *B.(R.)* involved Jehovah's Witness parents who refused to to consent to a blood transfusion for their critically ill infant child. The Children's Aid Society obtained a court order for wardship authority under the Ontario *Child Welfare Act*, which enabled the Society to consent to the transfusion. The parents challenged the order under the Charter. A majority of the Court held that because the law denied the parents the right to choose medical treatment for their infant according to their religious beliefs, their rights under s. 2(a) had been breached. However, the majority went on to find that this breach was justified under s. 1 because of the state interest in protecting children at risk and the carefully crafted legislative scheme that provided full procedural rights for parents wishing to challenge a state claim that their child was in need of protection. *B.(R.)* is discussed further below, in Section V, Religious Families and Religious Communities, and also in Chapter 22, Life, Liberty, and Security of the Person.

The minimal impairment analysis in the majority judgment in *Amselem* bears some similarities to the concept of "reasonable accommodation" that has developed in anti-discrimination law under human rights codes. That concept is examined in the following excerpt from the Bouchard-Taylor Report.

> **Gérard Bouchard and Charles Taylor,** *Building the Future:*
> *A Time for Reconciliation*
> Report of the Commission de consultation sur les pratiques d'accommodement
> reliées aux différences culturelles (Government of Quebec, 2008), at 160-62
> (emphases in original)

To start with, it is a good idea to ask ourselves from whence comes the general idea of harmonization [that is, accommodation]. *The question of the management of diversity inevitably arises in any society in which two or more cultures meet.* Until recently, it was usually resolved in an authoritarian manner: one more powerful culture attempted either to dominate the others by marginalizing them or to eliminate them through assimilation. Even so, practices aimed at relaxation or reconciliation have always existed, even in empires. However, for several decades, above all in the West, attitudes and the law have changed as the democratic nations have ... become more respectful of diversity. *This method of managing cohabitation that is taking shape is based on a general ideal of intercultural harmonization.*

· · ·

Through different approaches and at different paces, in fits and starts, [this ideal of intercultural harmonization] is now penetrating national cultures. In Québec, for example, our investigation reveals that harmonization measures are now part of the day-to-day life of public institutions, such as the public service, health care establishments, schools, universities and so on.

At the same time as this change (and perhaps in its wake), a new tradition has taken shape in the realm of law. The traditional conception of equality, which assumed uniform treatment, has given way to a conception that pays closer attention to differences. Little by little, the law has come to recognize that the rule of equality sometimes demands differential treatment. Over the past 25 years, this change has taken concrete form, in particular in the legal tool or provision called reasonable accommodation, which is basically dictated by the general principle of equality and fairness. In fact, the duty of accommodation seeks to make the rules fair in accordance with section 10 of the Québec Charter and article 15 of the Canadian Charter. The result is *a reconciliation ethic that encompasses all social intervenors* and, in particular, public and private managers.

Initially, the objective was to counteract certain forms of discrimination that courts described as indirect, which, without directly or explicitly excluding an individual or a group of people, nonetheless lead to adverse effect discrimination. This type of discrimination stems from the rigid application of a norm under certain circumstances in the realms of employment, public and private services, housing and so on. Since then, according to certain recent court judgments, some forms of direct discrimination can also lead to solutions that fall under reasonable accommodation. In short, the courts now focus on discriminatory impact, whether it is deliberate (direct) or fortuitous (indirect).

By way of illustration, consider the rule that prohibits students from bringing syringes into the classroom. A diabetic child's life could thus be endangered, which explains the relevance of the relaxation of the rule. Similar concerns guide the adjustment of certain rules in the workplace, e.g., the relaxation of a compulsory dress code for pregnant workers. The same principle applies to parking spaces, toilets and access ramps for the disabled.

In the absence of an adjustment of the rules, all of these individuals could be put at a disadvantage or excluded, which could jeopardize their right to equality. In these situations, *the duty of accommodation created by law does not require that a regulation or a statute be abrogated* but only that its discriminatory effects be mitigated in respect of certain individuals by making provision for an exception to the rule or a specific adaptation of it. In addition to prohibiting discrimination, the courts ask managers and employers to adopt a preventive attitude by seeking concrete measures likely to foster equality in society.

In accordance with the law, the harmonization measures requested or granted for religious reasons spring from the same logic. For example, let us mention the case of Jews or Muslims who have obtained leave to celebrate their religious holidays in the same way as Catholics, who, almost without exception, have always had permission to be absent from work on Sunday, Christmas Day and at Easter. Here, too, it is the rule of equality or fairness that prevails: what is legitimate for one faith is legitimate for the others. In this instance, as part of freedom of practice, more specifically the right of any citizen to exercise his religion, a secular State will fund the installation of chapels in detention centres because of the captive (in all senses of the term) nature of the prison population.

Each of these cases illustrates the logic inherent in harmonization. Sociologically speaking, we observe that *a number of apparently neutral or universal norms reproduce in actual fact worldviews, values, and implicit norms specific to the majority culture or population*, e.g., restaurant, airline or cafeteria menus, which, in bygone days, did not take into account vegetarians or individuals with food allergies. *Even if they do not exclude a priori any individual or group, these provisions can nonetheless lead to discrimination toward individuals because of specific traits* such as a temporary or permanent physical disability, age, or religious belief. It follows that *absolute rigour in the application of legislation and regulations does not always guarantee fairness*.

We can thus see that equality and freedom of religion do not necessarily have as a corollary uniformity or homogeneity. According to jurists, a given right may demand adjustments in treatment that must not be equated with privileges or exemptions since they remedy a flaw in the application of a statute or a regulation. As the experts have expressed it, *a treatment can be differential without being preferential*.

NOTE: MULTANI v. COMMISSION SCOLAIRE MARGUERITE-BOURGEOYS

The link between the minimal impairment analysis and the concept of reasonable accommodation was made explicit by the Court in a subsequent freedom of religion case, *Multani v. Commission scolaire Marguerite-Bourgeoys*, [2006] 1 SCR 256, 2006 SCC 6, 264 DLR (4th) 577. Charron J wrote for a majority of the Court:

> [53] … In relation to discrimination, the courts have held that there is a duty to make reasonable accommodation for individuals who are adversely affected by a policy or rule that is neutral on its face, and that this duty extends only to the point at which it causes undue hardship to the party who must perform it. Although it is not necessary to review all the cases on the subject, the analogy with the duty of reasonable accommodation seems to me to be helpful to explain the burden resulting from the minimal impairment test with respect to a particular individual, as in the case at bar.

Multani involved an orthodox Sikh student who was forbidden by a school board in Quebec from wearing his kirpan, or ceremonial dagger, to school pursuant to a rule forbidding all weapons in the school. After finding that there had been an infringement of freedom of religion, a majority of the Court went on to conclude that a total prohibition on the wearing of the kirpan was unreasonable and that reasonable accommodation would have consisted of allowing the kirpan to be worn to school if it were sealed and sewn into the student's clothing. In reaching this conclusion, the majority relied on evidence that, in Canada, there had never been a violent incident involving kirpans in the school. They also distinguished the school environment, where there are close, ongoing relationships between teachers and students, from courts and airlines, where prohibitions on kirpans have been upheld under human rights codes. The importance of creating an educational culture that instills values of tolerance and respect for minorities was also emphasized.

Congrégation des témoins de Jéhovah de St-Jérôme-Lafontaine v. Lafontaine (Village)
[2004] 2 SCR 650, 2004 SCC 48, 241 DLR (4th) 83

[The facts of the case are set out in the dissenting judgment of LeBEL J:]

> [39] … The appellants have been looking for a suitable parcel of land in [the Village of Lafontaine] on which to establish a place of worship, a "Kingdom Hall," since 1989 and have been seeking permission from the municipality to build such a facility since 1992.
>
> [40] The municipality's zoning by-law No. 362, as it read in 1992, allowed places of worship to be built in a regional community use zone designated as Zone P-3. As they felt that no land was available in this zone for the construction of their Kingdom Hall, the appellants made … [a] conditional offer on November 22, 1992 … to purchase a lot in Zone C-3, a commercial use zone. They then applied to the municipality a number of times for a zoning change that would permit them to build their place of worship on this lot. The municipality categorically refused to grant their application. There were then some heated exchanges with the municipality's lawyers, who justified the refusal to

amend the zoning by-law on the basis that lots were available in Zone P-3. On August 5, 1993, after the municipality refused to amend its zoning by-law, the appellants
bought the lot in Zone C-3.

[41] To obtain the necessary permits to build their place of worship on this lot, the appellants instituted a proceeding for mandamus. They based their proceeding on grounds
based primarily on constitutional law, alleging that the municipality's refusal to amend its
zoning by-law violated their freedom of religion under s. 2(a) of the *Charter* and under
the *Charter of Human Rights and Freedoms*, RSQ, c. C-12 (the "*Quebec Charter*"). They
also asked that the provisions of the *ALUPD* relating to the process for approving amendments to zoning by-laws by way of referendum be declared unconstitutional, because
such a public consultation, in their view, would violate their freedom of religion. ...

[The majority judgment of McLachlin CJC found that the municipality, in failing to provide reasons for its decision, breached basic standards of procedural fairness. The majority allowed the appeal and remitted the rezoning application to the municipality.

Justice LeBel, dissenting, declined to interfere with the judgment of the lower court
that there were available properties in areas zoned for churches. However, in the course
of his judgment he made the following comments about freedom of religion:]

[64] Freedom of religion is a fundamental right and represents a major triumph of our
democratic society. The philosophical and political values underpinning Canadian democracy recognize the need to respect the diverse opinions and beliefs that guide the con-
sciences and give direction to the lives of all members of our society. It is because of the
crucial importance of this fundamental right that this Court decided it was essential to
give it a liberal interpretation in *R v. Big M Drug Mart Ltd.*, [1985] 1 SCR 295 [18 DLR
(4th) 321], at p. 336:

> The essence of the concept of freedom of religion is the right to entertain such religious be-
> liefs as a person chooses, the right to declare religious beliefs openly and without fear of
> hindrance or reprisal, and the right to manifest religious belief by worship and practice or
> by teaching and dissemination.

[65] The concept of freedom of religion, which is not strictly limited to the above
definition, includes a positive aspect, that is, the right to believe or not believe what one
chooses, to declare one's beliefs openly, and to practice one's religion in accordance with
its tenets. This positive aspect also includes the right to proselytize, that is, to teach and
disseminate one's beliefs. Freedom of religion also has a negative aspect, that is, the right
not to be compelled to belong to a particular religion or to act in a manner contrary to
one's religious beliefs (J. Woehrling, "L'obligation d'accommodement raisonnable et
l'adaptation de la société à la diversité religieuse" (1998), 43 *McGill LJ* 325, at p. 371). This
fundamental freedom imposes on the state and public authorities, in relation to all religions and citizens, a duty of religious neutrality that assures individual or collective tolerance, thereby safeguarding the dignity of every individual and ensuring equality for all.

[66] The duty of neutrality appeared at the end of a long evolutionary process that is
part of the history of many countries that now share Western democratic traditions. Canada's history provides one example of this experience, which made it possible for the ties

between church and state to be loosened, if not dissolved. There were, of course, periods when there was a close union of ecclesiastical and secular authorities in Canada. European settlers introduced to Canada a political theory according to which the social order was based on an intimate alliance of the state and a single church, which the state was expected to promote within its borders. Throughout the history of New France, the Catholic church enjoyed the status of sole state religion. After the Conquest and the Treaty of Paris, the Anglican church became the official state religion, although social realities prompted governments to give official recognition to the status and role of the Catholic church and various Protestant denominations. This sometimes official, sometimes tacit recognition, which reflected the make-up of and trends in the society of the period, often inspired legislative solutions and certain policy choices. Thus, at the time of Confederation in 1867, the concept of religious neutrality implied primarily respect for Christian denominations. One illustration of this can be seen in the constitutional rules relating to educational rights originally found, *inter alia*, in s. 93 of the *Constitution Act, 1867*.

[67] Since then, the appearance and growing influence of new philosophical, political and legal theories on the organization and bases of civil society have gradually led to a dissociation of the functions of church and state; Canada's demographic evolution has also had an impact on this process, as have the urbanization and industrialization of the country. Although it has not excluded religions and churches from the realm of public debate, this evolution has led us to consider the practice of religion and the choices it implies to relate more to individuals' private lives or to voluntary associations (M.H. Ogilvie, *Religious Institutions and the Law in Canada* (2nd ed. 2003), at pp. 27 and 56). These societal changes have tended to create a clear distinction between churches and public authorities, placing the state under a duty of neutrality. Our Court has recognized this aspect of freedom of religion in its decisions, although it has in so doing not disregarded the various sources of our country's historical heritage. The concept of neutrality allows churches and their members to play an important role in the public space where societal debates take place, while the state acts as an essentially neutral intermediary in relations between the various denominations and between those denominations and civil society.

[68] In this context, it is no longer the state's place to give active support to any one particular religion, if only to avoid interfering in the religious practices of the religion's members. The state must respect a variety of faiths whose values are not always easily reconciled. As this Court observed in *Big M*, *supra*, "[w]hat may appear good and true to a majoritarian religious group, or to the state acting at their behest, may not, for religious reasons, be imposed upon citizens who take a contrary view" (p. 337; see also pp. 347 and 350-51). ... The guarantee of freedom of religion set out in s. 2(a) of the *Charter* prohibits the state from compelling an individual to adopt or renounce a particular belief or to practice a particular religion. This obligation remains essentially a negative one. As a general rule, the state refrains from acting in matters relating to religion. It is limited to setting up a social and legal framework in which beliefs are respected and members of the various denominations are able to associate freely in order to exercise their freedom of worship, which is a fundamental, collective aspect of freedom of religion, and to organize their churches or communities. In this context, the principle of neutrality must be taken into account in assessing the duty of public entities, such as municipalities, to actively help religious groups.

[69] A review of the various components of the concept of freedom of religion might suggest that the rights protected by s. 2(a) of the *Charter* are absolute, but such is not the case. This freedom is limited by the rights and freedoms of others. The diversity of opinions and convictions requires mutual tolerance and respect for others. Freedom of religion is also subject to limits necessary "to protect public safety, order, health, or morals." ... This Court has stressed that, in order to prove a violation of freedom of religion, it must be shown that the interference with the religious belief or practice in question is not trivial or insubstantial. Thus, churches and their members are not exempted from making any effort, or even sacrifice, *inter alia* in the exercise of their freedom of worship: ...

. . .

[71] As the municipality is required to be neutral in matters of religion, its by-laws must be structured in such a way as to avoid placing unnecessary obstacles in the way of the exercise of religious freedoms. However, it does not have to provide assistance of any kind to religious groups or actively help them resolve any difficulties they might encounter in their negotiations with third parties in relation to plans to establish a place of worship. In the case at bar, the municipality did not have to provide the appellants with access to a lot that corresponded better to their selection criteria. Such assistance would be incompatible with the municipality's duty of neutrality in that the municipality would be manipulating its regulatory standards in favour of a particular religion. Such support for a religious group could jeopardize the neutrality the municipality must adopt toward all such groups. Moreover, as this Court stated in *Edwards Books*, "[s]ection 2(a) does not require the legislatures to eliminate every minuscule state-imposed cost associated with the practice of religion" (p. 759). Although the very nature of the zoning by-law means that the appellants do not have absolute freedom to choose the location of their place of worship, this limit is necessary to protect safety and order, and ensure proper land use, in the municipality and does not constitute a violation of freedom of religion. Neither the purpose nor the effect of this by-law has been to infringe the appellants' freedom of religion.

[72] Since at least one lot remains available in Zone P-3 for the construction of their place of worship, the appellants must comply with the municipality's zoning by-law and build their place of worship in that zone, where such a use is authorized. Their religious beliefs and practices do not exempt them from complying with municipal by-laws. For this reason, I would dismiss the appeal. Having reached this conclusion, I could end my analysis here. However, for the sake of discussion only, and because of the nature of the debate that has taken place in the Quebec courts and in this Court and the importance of the constitutional issues raised, I propose to go on to review the parties' positions based on a different, fictitious premise. I will now consider what the legal consequences would have been had the evidence shown that no land was available in Zone P-3 for the appellants to establish a place of worship.

. . .

[73] [In this hypothetical case, the] appellants submit that, because no land is available in Zone P-3, the zoning by-law, as it is drafted, combined with the municipality's refusal to amend it, constitutes an infringement of their freedom of religion under s. 2(a) of the *Charter*. If no land were in fact available, I would agree with them. Thus, under the zoning by-law, places of worship may be established only in Zone P-3, but no land would be available there. The appellants would therefore be unable to build their place of worship anywhere within the boundaries of the municipality. Freedom of religion includes

the right to have a place of worship. Generally speaking, the establishment of a place of worship is necessary to the practice of a religion. Such facilities allow individuals to declare their religious beliefs, to manifest them and, quite simply, to practise their religion by worship, as well as to teach or disseminate it. In short, the construction of a place of worship is an integral part of the freedom of religion protected by s. 2(a) of the *Charter*.

[74] In the case at bar, the appellants have shown that their Kingdom Hall, a place of prayer and contemplation that serves as a venue for weddings and funerals, is necessary to the manifestation of their religious faith. They should therefore be free to establish such a facility within the boundaries of the municipality. If no land were available in Zone P-3, they would be prevented from doing so, in which case they would be unable to practise their religion, and their freedom guaranteed by s. 2(a) of the *Charter* would be infringed accordingly.

· · ·

[76] … As a general rule, the *Charter* does not require the state to take positive steps in support of the exercise of the fundamental freedoms provided for in s. 2(a) of the *Charter*. The principle of neutrality discussed above means that the state must even refrain from implementing measures that could favour one religion over another or that might simply have the effect of imposing one particular religion. However, there may be situations in which an absolute application of this principle unduly restricts the free exercise of religion. In some cases, an inflexible application of the principle of neutrality that fails to take the circumstances into account may prove to be inconsistent with the right to the free exercise of religion. …

[77] Our Court has noted on numerous occasions that it is not always enough for the state to adopt a posture of restraint. The Court has recognized that, in certain exceptional circumstances, positive government action may be required to make a fundamental freedom meaningful (*Delisle v. Canada (Deputy Attorney General)*, [1999] SCR 989 [176 DLR (4th) 513], at paras. 7 and 33; *Haig v. Canada*, [1993] 2 SCR 995 [105 DLR (4th) 577], at p. 1039; *Dunmore* [*v. Ontario (Attorney General)*, [2001] 3 SCR 1016, 207 DLR (4th) 193]).

NOTES AND QUESTIONS

1. What considerations do LeBel J's reasons add to the issue of reasonable accommodation of religious practices?

2. In the context of the recent "reasonable accommodation" debate, some Quebec scholars have noted that, due to its peculiar history and exposure to alternative cultural influences, societal attitudes about the appropriate relationship between the state and religion tend to be different in Quebec—incorporating a stronger conception of secularism—and that this difference is reflected in legal conceptions of that relation. See Sébastien Grammond, "Conceptions canadienne et québécoise des droits fondamentaux: convergence ou conflit?" (2009), 43 *Revue juridique Thémis* 83. Can Justice LeBel's dissenting judgment in *Lafontaine*, and Justice Deschamps dissent in *Bruker v. Marcovitz*, [2007] 3 SCR 607, 288 DLR (4th) 257, below in Section V, Religious Families and Religious Communities, be seen as reflecting, in part, this different conception of freedom of religion?

In the light of these different attitudes, some scholars have argued that Quebec's different historical understanding, with its stronger conception of secularism, could potentially be factored into the constitutional analysis of restrictions imposed by the Quebec government on certain religious practices, thereby recognizing a "provincial margin of appreciation" in the implementation of a fundamental freedom. See, *inter alia*, J. Woehrling, "Quelle place pour la religion dans les institutions publiques?," in J.-F. Gaudreault-DesBiens, ed., *La religion, le droit et le raisonnable: le fait religieux entre monisme étatique et pluralisme juridique* (Montreal: Éditions Thémis, 2009).

In evaluating the constitutionality of state restrictions on fundamental freedoms under s. 1 (or a functional equivalent), the Supreme Court has, on some occasions in the past, explicitly taken into consideration the particular societal fabric or historical evolution of the jurisdiction that has imposed the restriction. For example, in examining Quebec's language laws, it took into consideration the vulnerability of French in an overwhelmingly English-speaking continent and stated that a law making French predominant over other languages (without excluding them) could withstand a potential constitutional challenge (*Ford v. Quebec (Attorney General)*, [1988] 2 SCR 712, 54 DLR (4th) 577).

Do you think that the Supreme Court's case law concerning freedom of religion reflects a sensitivity to provincial or regional diffferences? Or is it instead informed by universalist assumptions about the existence of a monolithic Canadian community united in its attitude toward the appropriate balance to be struck between individual and collective religious rights, on the one hand, and the state, on the other? Think about *Multani*, above, and *Bruker v. Marcovitz*, [2007] 3 SCR 607, 288 DLR (4th) 257, below, Section V, Religious Families and Religious Communities.

To what extent should particular societal contexts be taken into consideration when adjudicating cases concerning fundamental freedoms? Are all such freedoms to be treated similarly; or is freedom of religion qualitatively different from other fundamental freedoms? How do you reconcile the sometimes significant cultural differences between Canadian provinces and regions in Charter adjudication? Can some degree of asymmetry be reconciled with the implementation of fundamental freedoms? Could provinces other than Quebec make a claim along the lines mentioned above?

The case that follows, *Alberta v. Hutterian Brethren of Wilson Colony*, is the Supreme Court of Canada's most recent freedom of religion decision. It is a significant decision not only on the issue of reasonable accommodation of religious minorities, but also on s. 1 of the Charter.

Alberta v. Hutterian Brethren of Wilson Colony
2009 SCC 37

[Regulations enacted pursuant to Alberta's *Traffic Safety Act*, RSA 2000, c. T-6 require all persons who drive motor vehicles on highways in the province to hold a driver's licence. Since 1974, each licence has borne a photograph of the licence holder, subject to exemptions for people who objected to having their photographs taken on religious grounds. At the registrar's discretion, religious objectors were granted a non-photo licence called a Condition Code G licence. In 2003, the province adopted a new regulation, which made the photo requirement universal. The photograph taken at the time of issuance of the licence is placed in the province's facial recognition data bank. There were about 450 Condition Code G licences in Alberta, 56 percent of which were held by members of Hutterian Brethren colonies. The Wilson Colony of Hutterian Brethren maintains a rural, communal lifestyle, carrying on a variety of commercial activities. They sincerely believe that the Second Commandment prohibits them from having their photograph willingly taken and thus objected to having their photographs taken on religious grounds. The province proposed two measures to lessen the impact of the universal photo requirement but, since these measures still required that a photograph be taken for placement in the province's facial recognition data bank, the members of the Wilson Colony rejected the measures. Instead, they proposed that no photograph be taken and that they be issued non-photo driver's licences marked, "Not to be used for identification purposes." Unable to reach an agreement with the province, the members of the Wilson Colony challenged the constitutionality of the regulation, alleging an unjustifiable breach of their religious freedom. The case proceeded on the basis that the universal photo requirement infringes s. 2(a) of the *Canadian Charter of Rights and Freedoms*. The claimants led evidence asserting that if members could not obtain driver's licences, the viability of their communal lifestyle would be threatened. The province, for its part, led evidence that the adoption of the universal photo requirement was connected to a new system aimed at minimizing identity theft associated with driver's licences and that the new facial recognition data bank was aimed at reducing the risk of this type of fraud. Both the chambers judge and the majority of the Court of Appeal held that the infringement of freedom of religion was not justified under s. 1 of the Charter.]

McLACHLIN CJC (Binnie, Deschamps, and Rothstein JJ concurring):

• • •

(1) The Nature of the Limit on the Section 2(a) Right

[29] The members of the Colony believe that permitting their photo to be taken violates the Second Commandment: "You shall not make for yourself an idol, or any likeness of what is in heaven above or on the earth beneath or in the water under the earth" (Exodus 20:4). They believe that photographs are "likenesses" within the meaning of the Second Commandment, and want nothing to do with their creation or use. The impact of having a photo taken might involve censure, such as being required to stand during religious services.

[30] Given these beliefs, the effect of the universal photo requirement is to place Colony members who wish to obtain driver's licences either in the position of violating their religious commitments, or of forgoing driver's licences. Without the ability of some members of the Colony to obtain driver's licences, Colony members argue that they will not be able to drive to local centres to do business and obtain the goods and services necessary to the Colony. The regulation, they argue, forces members to choose between obeying the Second Commandment and adhering to their rural communal lifestyle, thereby limiting their religious freedom and violating s. 2(a) of the *Charter*.

[31] My colleague Abella J notes at para. 130 that "freedom of religion has 'both individual and collective aspects.'" She asserts that "both ... are engaged in this case." While I agree that religious freedom has both individual and collective aspects, I think it is important to be clear about the relevance of those aspects at different stages of the analysis in this case. The broader impact of the photo requirement on the Wilson Colony community is relevant at the proportionality stage of the s. 1 analysis, specifically in weighing the deleterious and salutary effects of the impugned regulation. The extent to which the impugned law undermines the proper functioning of the community properly informs that comparison. Community impact does not, however, transform the essential claim—that of the individual claimants for photo-free licences—into an assertion of a group right.

[32] An infringement of s. 2(a) of the *Charter* will be made out where: (1) the claimant sincerely believes in a belief or practice that has a nexus with religion; and (2) the impugned measure interferes with the claimant's ability to act in accordance with his or her religious beliefs in a manner that is more than trivial or insubstantial: *Syndicat Northcrest v. Amselem*, 2004 SCC 47, [2004] 2 SCR 551, and *Multani* [*v. Commission scolaire Marguerite-Bourgeoys*, 2006 SCC 6, 1 SCR 256, 264 DLR (4th) 577]. ...

[33] The Province concedes the first element of this s. 2(a) test, sincere belief in a belief or practice that has a nexus with religion. ...

[34] The record does not disclose a concession on the second element of the test— whether the universal photo requirement interferes with Colony members' religious freedom in a manner that is more than trivial or insubstantial. ... [H]owever, the courts below seem to have proceeded on the assumption that this requirement was met. Given this assumption, I will proceed to consider whether the limit is a reasonable one, demonstrably justified in a free and democratic society.

(2) Is the Limit on the Section 2(a) Right Justified Under Section 1 of the Charter?

[35] This Court has recognized that a measure of leeway must be accorded to governments in determining whether limits on rights in public programs that regulate social and commercial interactions are justified under s. 1 of the *Charter*. Often, a particular problem or area of activity can reasonably be remedied or regulated in a variety of ways. The schemes are typically complex, and reflect a multitude of overlapping and conflicting interests and legislative concerns. They may involve the expenditure of government funds, or complex goals like reducing antisocial behaviour. The primary responsibility for making the difficult choices involved in public governance falls on the elected legislature and those it appoints to carry out its policies. Some of these choices may trench on constitutional rights.

[36] Freedom of religion presents a particular challenge in this respect because of the broad scope of the *Charter* guarantee. Much of the regulation of a modern state could be claimed by various individuals to have a more than trivial impact on a sincerely held religious belief. Giving effect to each of their religious claims could seriously undermine the universality of many regulatory programs, including the attempt to reduce abuse of driver's licences at issue here, to the overall detriment of the community.

[37] If the choice the legislature has made is challenged as unconstitutional, it falls to the courts to determine whether the choice falls within a range of reasonable alternatives. Section 1 of the *Charter* does not demand that the limit on the right be perfectly calibrated, judged in hindsight, but only that it be "reasonable" and "demonstrably justified." Where a complex regulatory response to a social problem is challenged, courts will generally take a more deferential posture throughout the s. 1 analysis than they will when the impugned measure is a penal statute directly threatening the liberty of the accused. ... The bar of constitutionality must not be set so high that responsible, creative solutions to difficult problems would be threatened. A degree of deference is therefore appropriate ... .

[38] With this in mind, I turn to the question of whether the limit on freedom of religion raised in this case has been shown to be justified under s. 1 of the *Charter*.

• • •

(b) Is the Purpose for Which the Limit Is Imposed Pressing and Substantial?

[41] The chambers judge defined the government's objective in imposing a universal photo requirement as being "to prevent identity theft or fraud and the various forms of mischief which identity theft may facilitate, and ... the harmonization of international and interprovincial standards for photo identification" (para. 10). This objective is part of the larger goal of ensuring the integrity of the system for licensing drivers. ...

[42] Maintaining the integrity of the driver's licensing system in a way that minimizes the risk of identity theft is clearly a goal of pressing and substantial importance, capable of justifying limits on rights. The purpose of a universal photo requirement is to have a complete digital data bank of facial photos to prevent wrongdoers from using driver's licences as breeder documents for purposes of identity theft. As discussed above (para. 10), the requirement permits the system to ensure that each licence in the system is connected to a single individual, and that no individual has more than one licence.

[43] The chambers judge found that the universal photo requirement was also aimed at harmonization of international and interprovincial standards for photo identification. The evidence supports the Province's contention that other provinces and nations are moving toward harmonization, and that a feature of this harmonization is likely to be a universal photo requirement for all licence holders. While the fact that other provinces have not yet moved to this requirement arguably undercuts the position that a universal photo requirement is necessary in Alberta now, governments are entitled to act in the present with a view to future developments. Accordingly, harmonization may be considered as a factor relevant to the Province's goal of ensuring the integrity of the licensing system by reducing identity theft associated with the system.

• • •

(c) Is the Means by Which the Goal Is Furthered Proportionate?

(i) IS THE LIMIT RATIONALLY CONNECTED TO THE PURPOSE?

• • •

[49] The government argues that a universal system of photo identification for drivers will be more effective in preventing identity theft than a system that grants exemptions to people who object to photos being taken on religious grounds. The affidavit evidence filed by the government supports this view.

· · ·

[52] I conclude that the Province has established that the universal photo requirement is rationally related to its goal of protecting the integrity of the driver's licensing system and preventing it from being used for purposes of identity theft.

(ii) DOES THE LIMIT MINIMALLY IMPAIR THE RIGHT?

[53] The question at this stage of the s. 1 proportionality analysis is whether the limit on the right is reasonably tailored to the pressing and substantial goal put forward to justify the limit. Another way of putting this question is to ask whether there are less harmful means of achieving the legislative goal. In making this assessment, the courts accord the legislature a measure of deference, particularly on complex social issues where the legislature may be better positioned than the courts to choose among a range of alternatives.

[54] In *RJR-MacDonald* [*Inc. v. Canada (Attorney General)*, [1995] 3 SCR 199, 127 DLR (4th) 1], the minimal impairment analysis was explained as follows, at para. 160:

As the second step in the proportionality analysis, *the government must show that the measures at issue impair the right of free expression as little as reasonably possible in order to achieve the legislative objective.* The impairment must be "minimal," that is, the law must be carefully tailored so that rights are impaired no more than necessary. The tailoring process seldom admits of perfection and the courts must accord some leeway to the legislator. If the law falls within a range of reasonable alternatives, the courts will not find it overbroad merely because they can conceive of an alternative which might better tailor objective to infringement. … On the other hand, if the government fails to explain why a significantly less intrusive and equally effective measure was not chosen, the law may fail. [Emphasis added; citations omitted.]

In this manner, the legislative goal, which has been found to be pressing and substantial, grounds the minimum impairment analysis. As Aharon Barak, former President of the Supreme Court of Israel, puts it, "the rational connection test and the least harmful measure [minimum impairment] test are essentially determined against the background of the proper objective, and are derived from the need to realize it": "Proportional Effect: The Israeli Experience" (2007), 57 *UTLJ* 369, at p. 374. President Barak describes this as the "internal limitation" in the minimum impairment test, which "prevents it [standing alone] from granting proper protection to human rights" (p. 373). The internal limitation arises from the fact that the minimum impairment test requires only that the government choose the least drastic means *of achieving its objective.* Less drastic means which do not actually achieve the government's objective are not considered at this stage.

[55] I hasten to add that in considering whether the government's objective could be achieved by other less drastic means, the court need not be satisfied that the alternative would satisfy the objective to *exactly* the same extent or degree as the impugned measure. In other words, the court should not accept an unrealistically exacting or precise formulation of the government's objective which would effectively immunize the law from scrutiny at the minimal impairment stage. The requirement for an "equally effective" alternative measure in the passage from *RJR-MacDonald*, quoted above, should not be taken to an impractical extreme. It includes alternative measures that give sufficient

protection, in all the circumstances, to the government's goal: *Charkaoui v. Canada (Citizenship and Immigration)*, 2007 SCC 9, [2007] 1 SCR 350 [276 DLR (4th) 594]. While the government is entitled to deference in formulating its objective, that deference is not blind or absolute. The test at the minimum impairment stage is whether there is an alternative, less drastic means of achieving the objective in a real and substantial manner. As I will explain, in my view the record in this case discloses no such alternative.

[56] The purpose of the limit in this case, I earlier concluded, is to maintain the integrity of the driver's licensing system by minimizing the risk of driver's licences being used for purposes of identity theft, so as to prevent fraud and various other misuses of the system. The regulation is part of a complex regulatory scheme and is aimed at an emerging and challenging problem. The question, therefore, is whether the means chosen to further its purpose—the universal photo requirement for all licensed drivers—is reasonably tailored to address the problem of identity theft associated with driver's licences.

[57] The Province proposes alternatives which maintain the universal photo requirement, but minimize its impact on Colony members by eliminating or alleviating the need for them to carry photos. This would permit the Province to achieve its goal of a maximally efficient photo recognition system to combat fraud associated with driver's licences, while reducing the impact on the members' s. 2(a) rights.

[58] However, the Hutterian claimants reject these proposals. For them, the only acceptable measure is one that entirely removes the limit on their s. 2(a) rights. They object to any photo being taken and held in a photo data bank. For them, the only alternative is a driver's licence issued without a photo, stamped with the words, "Not to be used for identification purposes."

[59] The problem with the claimants' proposal in the context of the minimum impairment inquiry is that it compromises the Province's goal of minimizing the risk of misuse of driver's licences for identity theft. The stamp "not to be used for identification purposes" might prevent a person who comes into physical possession of such a licence from using it as a breeder document, but it would not prevent a person from assuming the identity of the licence holder and producing a fake document, which could not be checked in the absence of a photo in the data bank. … [W]ithout the photo in the bank, the bank is neutralized and the risk that the identity of the holder can be stolen and used for fraudulent purposes is increased. The only way to reduce that risk as much as possible is through a universal photo requirement. The claimants' argument that the reduction in risk would be low, since few people are likely to request exemption from the photo requirement, assumes that some increase in risk and impairment of the government goal may occur, and hence does not assist at the stage of minimal impairment.

[60] The claimants' proposal, instead of asking what is minimally required to realize the legislative goal, asks the government to significantly compromise it. An exemption for an unspecified number of religious objectors would mean that the one-to-one correspondence between issued licences and photos in the data bank would be lost. As shown by the Province, this disparity could well be exploited by wrongdoers. Contrary to the suggestion of LeBel J (para. 201), the evidence discloses no alternative measures which would substantially satisfy the government's objective while allowing the claimants to avoid being photographed. In short, the alternative proposed by the claimants would

significantly compromise the government's objective and is therefore not appropriate for consideration at the minimal impairment stage.

[61] This is not to suggest the Colony members are acting improperly. Freedom of religion cases may often present this "all or nothing" dilemma. Compromising religious beliefs is something adherents may understandably be unwilling to do. And governments may find it difficult to tailor laws to the myriad ways in which they may trench on different people's religious beliefs and practices. The result may be that the justification of a limit on the right falls to be decided not at the point of minimal impairment, which proceeds on the assumption the state goal is valid, but at the stage of proportionality of effects, which is concerned about balancing the benefits of the measure against its negative effects.

[62] I conclude that the universal photo requirement minimally impairs the s. 2(a) right. It falls within a range of reasonable options available to address the goal of preserving the integrity of the driver's licensing system. All other options would significantly increase the risk of identity theft using driver's licences. The measure seeks to realize the legislative goal in a minimally intrusive way.

[63] Much has been made of the fact that over 700,000 Albertans do not hold driver's licences. The argument is that the risk posed by a few hundred potential religious objectors is minuscule as compared to the much larger group of unlicensed persons. This argument is accepted by the dissent. In my view, it rests on an overly broad view of the objective of the driver's licence photo requirement as being to eliminate all identity theft in the province. Casting the government objective in these broad terms, my colleague Abella J argues that the risk posed by a few religious dissenters is minimal, when compared to the general risk posed by unlicensed persons. But with respect, that is the wrong comparison. We must take the government's goal as it is. It is not the broad goal of eliminating all identity theft, but the more modest goal of maintaining the integrity of [the] driver's licensing system so as to minimize identity theft *associated with that system.* The question is whether, within that system, any exemptions, including for religious reasons, pose real risk to the integrity of the licensing system.

· · ·

[65] The courts below approached minimum impairment in a different fashion. First, they conducted the balancing inquiry at the stage of minimal impairment. Second, drawing on this Court's decision in *Multani*, the courts below applied a reasonable accommodation analysis instead of the *Oakes* test.

[66] In my view, a distinction must be maintained between the reasonable accommodation analysis undertaken when applying human rights laws, and the s. 1 justification analysis that applies to a claim that a law infringes the *Charter*. Where the validity of a law is at stake, the appropriate approach is a s. 1 *Oakes* analysis. Under this analysis, the issue at the stage of minimum impairment is whether the goal of the measure could be accomplished in a less infringing manner. The balancing of effects takes place at the third and final stage of the proportionality test. If the government establishes justification under the *Oakes* test, the law is constitutional. If not, the law is null and void under s. 52 insofar as it is inconsistent with the *Charter*.

[67] A different analysis applies where a government *action* or administrative *practice* is alleged to violate the claimant's *Charter* rights. If a *Charter* violation is found, the

court's remedial jurisdiction lies not under s. 52 of the *Constitution Act, 1982* but under s. 24(1) of the *Charter* ... . In such cases, the jurisprudence on the duty to accommodate, which applies to governments and private parties alike, may be helpful "to explain the burden resulting from the minimal impairment test *with respect to a particular individual*" (emphasis added): *Multani*, at para. 53, *per* Charron J.

[68] Minimal impairment and reasonable accommodation are conceptually distinct. Reasonable accommodation is a concept drawn from human rights statutes and jurisprudence. It envisions a dynamic process whereby the parties—most commonly an employer and employee—adjust the terms of their relationship in conformity with the requirements of human rights legislation, up to the point at which accommodation would mean undue hardship for the accommodating party. In *Multani*, Deschamps and Abella JJ explained:

> The process required by the duty of reasonable accommodation takes into account the specific details of the circumstances of the parties and allows for dialogue between them. This dialogue enables them to reconcile their positions and find common ground tailored to their own needs. [para. 131]

[69] A very different kind of relationship exists between a legislature and the people subject to its laws. By their very nature, laws of general application are not tailored to the unique needs of individual claimants. The legislature has no capacity or legal obligation to engage in such an individualized determination, and in many cases would have no advance notice of a law's potential to infringe *Charter* rights. It cannot be expected to tailor a law to every possible future contingency, or every sincerely held religious belief. Laws of general application affect the general public, not just the claimants before the court. The broader societal context in which the law operates must inform the s. 1 justification analysis. A law's constitutionality under s. 1 of the *Charter* is determined, not by whether it is responsive to the unique needs of every individual claimant, but rather by whether its infringement of *Charter* rights is directed at an important objective and is proportionate in its overall impact. While the law's impact on the individual claimants is undoubtedly a significant factor for the court to consider in determining whether the infringement is justified, the court's ultimate perspective is societal. The question the court must answer is whether the *Charter* infringement is justifiable in a free and democratic society, not whether a more advantageous arrangement for a particular claimant could be envisioned.

[70] Similarly, "undue hardship," a pivotal concept in reasonable accommodation, is not easily applicable to a legislature enacting laws. In the human rights context, hardship is seen as undue if it would threaten the viability of the enterprise which is being asked to accommodate the right. The degree of hardship is often capable of expression in monetary terms. By contrast, it is difficult to apply the concept of undue hardship to the cost of achieving or not achieving a legislative objective, especially when the objective is (as here) preventative or precautionary. Though it is possible to interpret "undue hardship" broadly as encompassing the hardship that comes with failing to achieve a pressing government objective, this attenuates the concept. Rather than strain to adapt "undue hardship" to the context of s. 1 of the *Charter*, it is better to speak in terms of minimal impairment and proportionality of effects.

[71] In summary, where the validity of a law of general application is at stake, reasonable accommodation is not an appropriate substitute for a proper s. 1 analysis based on the methodology of *Oakes*. ...

(iii) IS THE LAW PROPORTIONATE IN ITS EFFECT?

. . .

[73] [The] final question [is]: are the overall effects of the law on the claimants disproportionate to the government's objective? When one balances the harm done to the claimants' religious freedom against the benefits associated with the universal photo requirement for driver's licences, is the limit on the right proportionate in effect to the public benefit conferred by the limit?

. . .

[75] Despite the importance Dickson CJ accorded to this [third and final] stage of the justification analysis, it has not often been used. Indeed, Peter W. Hogg argues that the fourth branch of *Oakes* is actually redundant: *Constitutional Law of Canada* (5th ed. Supp.), vol. 2, at section 38.12. ...

[76] It may be questioned how a law which has passed the rigours of the first three stages of the proportionality analysis—pressing goal, rational connection, and minimum impairment—could fail at the final inquiry of proportionality of effects. The answer lies in the fact that the first three stages of *Oakes* are anchored in an assessment of the law's purpose. Only the fourth branch takes full account of the "severity of the deleterious effects of a measure on individuals or groups." As President Barak explains:

> Whereas the rational connection test and the least harmful measure test are essentially determined against the background of the proper objective, and are derived from the need to realize it, the test of proportionality (*stricto sensu*) examines whether the realization of this proper objective is commensurate with the deleterious effect upon the human right. ... It requires placing colliding values and interests side by side and balancing them according to their weight. [p. 374]

In my view, the distinction drawn by Barak is a salutary one, though it has not always been strictly followed by Canadian courts. Because the minimal impairment and proportionality of effects analyses involve different kinds of balancing, analytical clarity and transparency are well served by distinguishing between them. Where no alternative means are reasonably capable of satisfying the government's objective, the real issue is whether the impact of the rights infringement is disproportionate to the likely benefits of the impugned law. Rather than reading down the government's objective within the minimal impairment analysis, the court should acknowledge that no less drastic means are available and proceed to the final stage of *Oakes*.

. . .

[78] In my view, this is a case where the decisive analysis falls to be done at the final stage of *Oakes*. ...

1. Salutary Effects

[79] The first inquiry is into the benefits, or "salutary effects" associated with the legislative goal. Three salutary effects of the universal photo requirement were raised on the evidence: (1) enhancing the security of the driver's licensing scheme; (2) assisting in roadside safety and identification; and (3) eventually harmonizing Alberta's licensing scheme with those in other jurisdictions.

[80] The most important of these benefits and the one upon which Alberta principally relies is the enhancement of the security or integrity of the driver's licensing scheme. The photo requirement ensures both a "one-to-one" and "one-to-many" correspondence among licence holders. This makes it possible, through the use of computer software, to ensure that no person holds more than one licence. It is clear on the evidence that the universal photo requirement enhances the security of the licensing system and thus of Albertans. Mandatory photos represent a significant gain to the integrity and usefulness of the computer comparison system. In short, requiring that *all* licence holders are represented by a digital photo in the data bank will accomplish these security-related objectives more effectively than would an exemption for an as yet undetermined number of religious objectors. Any exemptions would undermine the certainty with which the government is able to say that a given licence corresponds to an identified individual and that no individual holds more than one licence. This evidence stands effectively uncontradicted.

[81] Though it is difficult to quantify in exact terms how much risk of fraud would result from permitted exemptions, it is clear that the internal integrity of the system would be compromised. In this respect, the present case may be contrasted with previous religious freedom cases where this Court has found that the potential risk was too speculative.

[Reference is then made to *Trinity Western University v. British Columbia College of Teachers*, 2001 SCC 31, [2001] 1 SCR 772, 199 DLR (4th) 1, which dealt with the risk of discriminatory conduct, and *Amselem*, which dealt with the risk of security concerns.]

[85] In summary, the salutary effects of the universal photo requirement for driver's licences are sufficient, subject to final weighing against the negative impact on the right, to support some restriction of the right. As discussed earlier, a government enacting social legislation is not required to show that the law will in fact produce the forecast benefits. Legislatures can only be asked to impose measures that reason and the evidence suggest will be beneficial. If legislation designed to further the public good were required to await proof positive that the benefits would in fact be realized, few laws would be passed and the public interest would suffer.

2. Deleterious Effects

[86] This brings us to the deleterious effects of the limit on Colony members' exercise of their s. 2(a) right. At this point, the seriousness of the effects of the limit on Colony members' freedom of religion falls to be addressed. Several points call for discussion.

. . .

[89] There is no magic barometer to measure the seriousness of a particular limit on a religious practice. Religion is a matter of faith, intermingled with culture. It is individual, yet profoundly communitarian. Some aspects of a religion, like prayers and the basic sacraments, may be so sacred that any significant limit verges on forced apostasy. Other practices may be optional or a matter of personal choice. Between these two extremes lies a vast array of beliefs and practices, more important to some adherents than to others.

[90] Because religion touches so many facets of daily life, and because a host of different religions with different rites and practices co-exist in our society, it is inevitable that some religious practices will come into conflict with laws and regulatory systems of general application. ... In judging the seriousness of the limit in a particular case, the perspective of the religious or conscientious claimant is important. However, this perspective must be considered in the context of a multicultural, multi-religious society where the duty of state authorities to legislate for the general good inevitably produces conflicts with individual beliefs. The bare assertion by a claimant that a particular limit curtails his or her religious practice does not, without more, establish the seriousness of the limit for purposes of the proportionality analysis. Indeed to end the inquiry with such an assertion would cast an impossibly high burden of justification on the state. We must go further and evaluate the degree to which the limit actually impacts on the adherent.

[91] The seriousness of a particular limit must be judged on a case-by-case basis. However, guidance can be found in the jurisprudence. Limits that amount to state compulsion on matters of belief are always very serious. ...

[92] Canadian law reflects the fundamental proposition that the state cannot by law directly compel religious belief or practice. [Reference is then made to a series of cases, including *Big M*.] To compel religious practice by force of law deprives the individual of the fundamental right to choose his or her mode of religious experience, or lack thereof. Such laws will fail at the first stage of *Oakes* and proportionality will not need to be considered.

[93] Cases of direct compulsion are straightforward. However, it may be more difficult to measure the seriousness of a limit on freedom of religion where the limit arises not from a direct assault on the right to choose, but as the result of incidental and unintended effects of the law. In many such cases, the limit does not preclude choice as to religious belief or practice, but it does make it more costly.

[94] The incidental effects of a law passed for the general good on a particular religious practice may be so great that they effectively deprive the adherent of a meaningful choice ... . Or the government program to which the limit is attached may be compulsory, with the result that the adherent is left with a stark choice between violating his or her religious belief and disobeying the law: *Multani*. The absence of a meaningful choice in such cases renders the impact of the limit very serious.

[95] However, in many cases, the incidental effects of a law passed for the general good on a particular religious practice may be less serious. The limit may impose costs on the religious practitioner in terms of money, tradition or inconvenience. However, these costs may still leave the adherent with a meaningful choice concerning the religious practice at issue. The *Charter* guarantees freedom of religion, but does not indemnify practitioners against all costs incident to the practice of religion. Many religious practices entail costs which society reasonably expect the adherents to bear. The inability to access conditional benefits or privileges conferred by law may be among such costs. A

limit on the right that exacts a cost but nevertheless leaves the adherent with a meaning-ful choice about the religious practice at issue will be less serious than a limit that effec-tively deprives the adherent of such choice.

[96] This returns us to the task at hand—assessing the seriousness of the limit on reli-gious practice imposed in this case by the regulation's universal photo requirement for driver's licences. This is not a case like *Edwards Books [and Art Ltd., R v.* [1986], 2 SCR 713, 35 DLR (4th) 1] or *Multani* where the incidental and unintended effect of the law is to de-prive the adherent of a meaningful choice as to the religious practice. The impugned regu-lation, in attempting to secure a social good for the whole of society—the regulation of driver's licences in a way that minimizes fraud—imposes a cost on those who choose not to have their photos taken: the cost of not being able to drive on the highway. But on the evidence before us, that cost does not rise to the level of depriving the Hutterian claim-ants of a meaningful choice as to their religious practice, or adversely impacting on other *Charter* values.

[97] The Hutterian claimants argue that the limit presents them with an invidious choice: the choice between some of its members violating the Second Commandment on the one hand, or accepting the end of their rural communal life on the other hand. How-ever, the evidence does not support the conclusion that arranging alternative means of highway transport would end the Colony's rural way of life. The claimants' affidavit says that it is necessary for at least some members to be able to drive from the Colony to nearby towns and back. It does not explain, however, why it would not be possible to hire people with driver's licences for this purpose, or to arrange third party transport to town for necessary services, like visits to the doctor. Many businesses and individuals rely on hired persons and commercial transport for their needs, either because they cannot drive or choose not to drive. Obtaining alternative transport would impose an additional eco-nomic cost on the Colony, and would go against their traditional self-sufficiency. But there is no evidence that this would be prohibitive.

[98] On the record before us, it is impossible to conclude that Colony members have been deprived of a meaningful choice to follow or not to follow the edicts of their reli-gion. The law does not compel the taking of a photo. It merely provides that a person who wishes to obtain a driver's licence must permit a photo to be taken for the photo identification data bank. Driving automobiles on highways is not a right, but a privilege. While most adult citizens hold driver's licences, many do not, for a variety of reasons.

. . .

3. *Weighing the Salutary and Deleterious Effects*

. . .

[101] The law has an important social goal—to maintain an effective driver's licence scheme that minimizes the risk of fraud to citizens as a whole. This is not a goal that should lightly be sacrificed. The evidence supports the conclusion that the universal photo requirement addresses a pressing problem and will reduce the risk of identity-related fraud, when compared to a photo requirement that permits exceptions.

[102] Against this important public benefit must be weighed the impact of the limit on the claimants' religious rights. While the limit imposes costs in terms of money and inconvenience as the price of maintaining the religious practice of not submitting to

photos, it does not deprive members of their ability to live in accordance with their beliefs. Its deleterious effects, while not trivial, fall at the less serious end of the scale.

[103] Balancing the salutary and deleterious effects of the law, I conclude that the impact of the limit on religious practice associated with the universal photo requirement for obtaining a driver's licence, is proportionate.

· · ·

ABELLA J (dissenting):

· · ·

[130] ... [I]t is important to recognize that freedom of religion has "both individual and collective aspects" (*Edwards Books*, at p. 781, *per* Dickson CJ). ... Both the individual and group aspects are engaged in this case.

[131] The group, or "community," aspect of religious freedom was discussed by the European Court of Human Rights in *Metropolitan Church of Bessarabia and Others v. Moldova*, no. 45701/99, ECHR 2001-XII:

> [T]he right of believers to freedom of religion, which includes the right to manifest one's religion in community with others, encompasses the expectation that believers will be allowed to associate freely, without arbitrary State intervention. Indeed, the autonomous existence of religious communities is indispensable for pluralism in a democratic society and is thus an issue at the very heart of the protection [of religious freedom]. ...
>
> In addition, one of the means of exercising the right to manifest one's religion, especially for a religious community, in its collective dimension, is the possibility of ensuring judicial protection of the community, its members and its assets. [para. 118]

[132] ... The nature of the religious right asserted will also be of relevance in balancing benefits and harms.

Section 1

· · ·

Minimal Impairment

[143] Where I start to part company with the majority, with respect, is at the minimal impairment stage of the analysis. This aspect of the s. 1 analysis has attracted judicial approaches of some elasticity, reflecting an understandable desire both to be respectful of the complexity of developing public policy, while at the same time ensuring that the infringing measure meets its policy objectives no more intrusively than necessary.

[144] As McLachlin J wrote in *RJR-MacDonald*, if the option chosen by the government "falls within a range of reasonable alternatives, the courts will not find it overbroad merely because they can conceive of an alternative which might better tailor objective to infringement" (para. 160). However, "if the government fails to explain why a significantly less intrusive and equally effective measure was not chosen, the law may fail" (para. 160).

[145] The government must therefore show that the measure impairs the right as little as reasonably possible in order to achieve the legislative objective. To be characterized as minimal, the impairment must be "carefully tailored so that rights are impaired no more than necessary" (*RJR-MacDonald*, at para. 160).

[146] In assessing whether Alberta's regulation satisfies the minimal impairment stage, the majority rejects the Colony's alternative proposal of a photoless licence stamped with an indication that it not be used for identification purposes, on the grounds that "[t]he only way to reduce that risk [of misusing driver's licences for identity theft] as much as possible is through a universal photo requirement" and "the alternative proposed by the claimants would *significantly* compromise the government's objective" (paras. 59-60 (emphasis in original)). But as discussed later in these reasons, there is no cogent or persuasive evidence [as required in *Oakes*] of any such dramatic interference with the government's objective.

[147] It is not difficult for the state to argue that only the measure it has chosen will *maximize* the attainment of the objective and that all other alternatives are substandard or less effective. And there is no doubt that the wider the use of the photographs, the greater the minimization of the risk. But at the minimal impairment stage, we do not assess whether the infringing measure fulfills the government's objective more perfectly than any other, but whether the means chosen impair the right no more than necessary to achieve the objective.

[148] In *RJR-MacDonald*, McLachlin J rejected a complete ban on advertising on the grounds that a full prohibition will only be constitutionally acceptable at the minimal impairment stage of the analysis if the government can show that only a full prohibition will enable it to achieve its goal. In this case, all of the alternatives presented by the government involve the taking of a photograph. This is the very act that offends the religious beliefs of the Wilson Colony members. The requirement therefore completely extinguishes the right, and is, accordingly, analogous to the complete ban in *RJR-MacDonald*. It is therefore difficult to conclude that it minimally impairs the Hutterites' religious rights.

[149] The minimal impairment stage should not, however, be seen to routinely end the s. 1 analysis. It is possible, for example, to have a law, which is not minimally impairing but may, on balance, given the importance of the government objective, be proportional. In my view, most of the heavy conceptual lifting and balancing ought to be done at the final step—proportionality. Proportionality is, after all, what s. 1 is about.

Proportionality

[150] It seems to me, with respect, that where the majority's s. 1 analysis fully flounders is in the final stage, where the negative effects of the infringement are balanced against the actual benefits derived from the legislative measure. ...

• • •

[153] Justice Bastarache wrote in *Thomson Newspapers* that the deleterious effects of the measure need to be assessed in light of the "values underlying the *Charter*" (para. 125). This was the approach, in fact, first enunciated by Dickson CJ in *Oakes*:

> The underlying *values and principles* of a free and democratic society are the genesis of the rights and freedoms guaranteed by the *Charter* and the *ultimate standard against which a limit on a right or freedom must be shown*, despite its effect, to be reasonable and demonstrably justified. [Emphasis added; p. 136.]

[154] Turning to the salutary effects in this case, in my view, the government has not discharged its evidentiary burden or demonstrated that the salutary effects in these circumstances are anything more than a web of speculation (Sujit Choudhry, "So What Is the Real Legacy of *Oakes*? Two Decades of Proportionality Analysis Under the Canadian *Charter*'s Section 1" (2006), 34 *SCLR* (2d) 501, at pp. 503-4).

[155] The positive impact of the mandatory photo requirement and the use of facial recognition technology is that it is a way to help ensure that individuals will not be able to commit identity theft. But the facial recognition technology is hardly fool-proof. Joseph Mark Pendleton, Director of the Special Investigations Unit of the Alberta Ministry of Government Services, acknowledged in his affidavit on behalf of the Government of Alberta, that "facial recognition software is not so advanced that it can make a definitive determination of whether two photographs are of the same person." The software merely narrows down potentially similar faces to a manageable number. A human investigator must still "eyeball" the pictures to determine if they are the same person.

[156] There is, in fact, no evidence from the government to suggest that the Condition Code G licences, in place for 29 years as an exemption to the photo requirement, caused any harm at all to the integrity of the licensing system. As a result, there is no basis for determining why the exemption is no longer feasible, or so dramatically obstructs the government's objective that it cannot be re-instated.

[157] In his affidavit, Mr. Pendleton noted that "[t]o date, we have been successful in making arrangements to accommodate the concerns of others who have religious reservations regarding a driver's licence photograph" (para. 42). The only example he provided of a problem involving a Condition Code G licence, was a "Caucasian man" who sought a Condition Code G licence, based upon his commitment to native spirituality. He was refused because he was not a member of any recognized organization or denomination that shared his beliefs. This singular example does not seem to me to represent "cogent and persuasive" evidence of the necessity of a mandatory photograph. ...

[158] [Seven hundred thousand] Albertans are without a driver's licence. That means that 700,000 Albertans have no photograph in the system that can be checked by facial recognition technology. While adding approximately 250 licence holders to the database will reduce some opportunity for identity theft, it is hard to see how it will make a significant impact on preventing it when there are already several hundred thousand unlicenced and therefore unphotographed Albertans. Since there are so many others who are not in the database, the benefit of adding the photographs of the few Hutterites who wish to drive, would be marginal.

[159] It is worth noting too that in Alberta, numerous documents are used for identity purposes, including birth certificates, social insurance cards and health cards—not all of which include a photograph. Nor has Alberta thought it necessary to introduce, for example, a universal identity card to prevent identity theft. This suggests that the risk is not sufficiently compelling to justify universality.

[160] The fact that Alberta is seemingly unengaged by the impact on identity theft of over 700,000 Albertans being without a driver's licence, makes it difficult to understand why it feels that the system cannot tolerate 250 or so more exemptions.

[161] The majority mentions two ancillary benefits of the mandatory photo requirement: the eventual harmonization of Alberta's licensing scheme with those of other

jurisdictions, and assistance in roadside safety and identification. There is no reason to anticipate that any such harmonized scheme would eliminate, rather than protect, religious exemptions. And as for the benefits to roadside identification and safety, Alberta conceded that this was not the purpose of the photo requirement and that any such benefits were minimal, as evidenced by the fact that this exemption has existed for the last 29 years without incident.

[162] The salutary effects of the infringing measure are, therefore, slight and largely hypothetical. The addition of the unphotographed Hutterite licence holders to the system seems only marginally useful to the prevention of identity theft.

[163] On the other hand, the harm to the religious rights of the Hutterites weighs more heavily. The majority assesses the Wilson Colony members' freedom of religion as being a choice between having their picture taken or not having a driver's licence which may have collateral effects on their way of life. This, with respect, is not a meaningful choice for the Hutterites.

[164] The chambers judge found that the mandatory photo requirement threatened the autonomous ability of the respondents to maintain their communal way of life, concluding that "it is essential to [the respondents'] continued existence as a community that some members operate motor vehicles" (para. 2). Conrad JA of the Alberta Court of Appeal similarly wrote that the "evidence shows that although the colonies attempt to be self-sufficient, certain members must drive regularly on Alberta highways in order to ... facilitate the sale of agricultural products, purchase raw materials from suppliers, transport colony members (including children) to medical appointments, and conduct the community's financial affairs" (para. 6).

[165] This self-sufficiency was explained in *Hofer v. Hofer*, [1970] SCR 958 [13 DLR (3d) 1], where Ritchie J wrote that "the Hutterite religious faith and doctrine permeates the whole existence of the members of any Hutterite Colony" (p. 968). Quoting the trial judge, he observed: "To a Hutterian the whole life is the Church. ... The tangible evidence of this spiritual community is the secondary or material community around them. They are not farming just to be farming—it is the type of livelihood that allows the greatest assurance of independence from the surrounding world" (p. 968). Justice Ritchie further noted that to the colonies, "the activities of the community were evidence of the living church" (p. 969).

• • •

[170] The mandatory photo requirement is a form of indirect coercion that places the Wilson Colony members in the untenable position of having to choose between compliance with their religious beliefs or giving up the self-sufficiency of their community, a community that has historically preserved its religious autonomy through its communal independence.

[171] I also have some discomfort with the majority's approach to assessing the seriousness of a religious infringement. It appears to suggest that there is a difference between the constitutional scrutiny of a government program that is "compulsory," and one that is "conditional" or a "privilege." This approach, with great respect, is troubling. It is both novel and inconsistent with the principle enunciated in *Eldridge v. British Columbia (Attorney General)*, [1997] 3 SCR 624 [151 DLR (4th) 577], that "once the state does provide a benefit, it is obliged to do so in a non-discriminatory manner" (para. 73).

[172] The question, it seems to me, is whether the government has acted constitutionally. This should not depend on whether it does so through a law, a regulation, or a licence. Moreover, I have difficulty understanding what is meant by a "privilege" in the context of the provision of government services. As long ago as *Roncarelli v. Duplessis*, [1959] SCR 121, this Court recognized the profound significance a licence may have on an individual's life or livelihood and that the government is required to exercise its power in administering the licensing system in a fair and constitutional manner.

· · ·

[176] Given the disproportion in this case between the harmful effects of the mandatory photo requirement on religious freedom, compared to the minimal salutary effects of requiring photographs from the Hutterites, the government has not discharged its burden of demonstrating that the infringement is justified under s. 1. This makes the mandatory photograph requirement for driver's licences, in the absence of the availability of an exemption on religious grounds, inconsistent with s. 2(a) of the *Charter*.

[177] I would therefore dismiss the appeal, but would suspend a declaration of invalidity for one year to give Alberta an opportunity to fashion a responsive amendment.

LeBEL J (dissenting) (Fish J concurring):

I. Introduction

[178] I have read the reasons of the Chief Justice and of my colleague Justice Abella. With respect for the other view, I agree with the comments of Justice Abella on the nature of the guarantee of freedom of religion under s. 2(a) of the *Canadian Charter of Rights and Freedoms*. I share her opinion that the impugned regulation that limits freedom of religion has not been properly justified by the appellant under s. 1 of the *Charter*. As a result, as she proposes, I would dismiss the appeal and uphold the declaration of invalidity of the regulation that requires the members of the Hutterite Colony to have their photos taken as a condition for the renewal or issuance of a driver's licence.

[179] After a few short comments on freedom of religion, I will focus my analysis on the interpretation and application of s. 1 of the *Charter*. I have some concerns as to how the reasons of the Chief Justice structure and apply the method of justification of s. 1, in other words, the *Oakes* test, as it is now known.

A. Freedom of Religion

[180] The constitutional guarantee of freedom of religion has triggered a substantial amount of litigation since the coming into force of the *Charter*. The present appeal illustrates enduring difficulties in respect of its interpretation and application. Perhaps, courts will never be able to explain in a complete and satisfactory manner the meaning of religion for the purposes of the *Charter*. One might have thought that the guarantee of freedom of opinion, freedom of conscience, freedom of expression and freedom of association could very well have been sufficient to protect freedom of religion. But the framers of the *Charter* thought fit to incorporate into the *Charter* an express guarantee of freedom of religion, which must be given meaning and effect.

[181] That decision reflects the complex and highly textured nature of freedom of religion. The latter is an expression of the right to believe or not. It also includes a right to manifest one's belief or lack of belief, or to express disagreement with the beliefs of others. It also incorporates a right to establish and maintain a community of faith that shares a common understanding of the nature of the human person, of the universe, and of their relationships with a Supreme Being in many religions, especially in the three major Abrahamic faiths, Judaism, Christianity and Islam.

[182] Religion is about religious beliefs, but also about religious relationships. The present appeal signals the importance of this aspect. It raises issues about belief, but also about the maintenance of communities of faith. We are discussing the fate not only of a group of farmers, but of a community that shares a common faith and a way of life that is viewed by its members as a way of living that faith and of passing it on to future generations. As Justice Abella points out, the regulatory measures have an impact not only on the respondents' belief system, but also on the life of the community. The reasons of the majority understate the nature and importance of this aspect of the guarantee of freedom of religion. This may perhaps explain the rather cursory treatment of the rights claimed by the respondents in the course of the s. 1 analysis. I will now turn to this aspect of the case.

B. Section 1: The Oakes Test

. . .

[184] In the context of the values of the democratic society of Canada, courts were assigned the responsibility of final adjudication in the case of conflicts between public authorities and citizens, subject to the derogation or notwithstanding clause in s. 33 (*Re BC Motor Vehicle Act*, [1985] 2 SCR 486 [24 DLR (4th) 536], at pp. 496-97). In its own way, the *Oakes* test is yet another attempt to determine why and how a law could be found to be just and whether it should be enforced. Many centuries ago, St. Thomas Aquinas put his mind to the same question. For him, a just law was one with a legitimate purpose which relied on reasonable or proportionate means to achieve it. Proportionate burdens should be imposed on citizens ... . In more modern times, the same idea informed the drafting of the European Convention of Human Rights. It inspired the approach of international law in domains like the laws of war ... . The principle of proportionality can even be found in Canadian criminal law. Self-defence, in s. 34 of the *Criminal Code*, RSC 1985, c. C-46, for example, is predicated on the legitimacy of the purpose and the proportionality of the means used to further that purpose.

[185] The *Oakes* test belongs to this legal and philosophical tradition. In essence, it is about purpose and means: the legitimacy of the purpose and the proportionality of the means. The use of proportionate means in order to achieve legitimate purposes will justify a limitation of rights under s. 1.

[The steps of the *Oakes* test are reviewed.]

[187] It has also been said, at times, that context should be considered at the outset of the analysis in order to determine the scope of the deference of courts to government when applying the *Oakes* test ... . One part of this context should not be forgotten: the

constitutional context itself. The *Charter* is designed to uphold and protect constitutional rights. The justification process under s. 1 is not designed to sidestep constitutional rights on every occasion. Rather, it seeks to define and reconcile these rights with other legitimate interests or even between themselves. The burden of justification rests on the state, although I will not attempt, within the limited scope of these reasons, to delve any further into the vexed question of what is sufficient evidence or demonstration of justification. The justification process also reflects the democratic life of a state like Canada, which operates under the rule of law, in the tradition of a parliamentary government, within the framework of a federal form of government. Section 1 and the *Oakes* test are designed to reach a proper equilibrium between the rule of law, the roles of courts, Parliament or legislatures, and executives, and the democratic life of our country. In the end, when conflict does arise and cannot be resolved, courts must try to strike a proper balance between competing demands, always mindful of their place within the constitutional and political sphere.

[188] In general, courts have only rarely questioned the purpose of a law or regulation in the course of a s. 1 analysis. The threshold of justification remains quite low and laws have almost never been struck down on the basis of an improper purpose (Hogg, at section 38.9(b)). The pressing and compelling purpose test amounts to a *prima facie* review of the legitimacy of the law's objective. Its flexibility reflects the need to avoid too close questioning of the policy reasons underlying a law. Such a review would be better left to the political and parliamentary process. The flexibility of the analysis at this stage results also from the abstract nature of the purpose, which can be expressed by the courts at "various levels of generality" (Hogg [above], at section 38.9(a); *Thomson Newspapers* [*sura*], at para. 125, *per* Bastarache J). Since this objective is often not expressed with much clarity in the law or regulation, its identification and definition at this stage of the analysis often amount to a judicial construct based on such evidence as is available. The nature of this part of the *Oakes* test should caution courts against treating the purpose with undue emphasis on its sanctity throughout the proportionality analysis, when its nature and effects will have to be more closely questioned.

[189] The first part of the *Oakes* test is closely connected to the proportionality analysis. The rational connection analysis requires the courts to determine, for a start, whether the means chosen will somehow advance the stated purpose of the law. At this stage too, courts have rarely found statutes and regulations wanting (Hogg, at section 38.10(a)).

[190] This acknowledgment of the realities of constitutional adjudication does not mean that courts will or should never intervene at these earlier stages. However, this situation confirms that, after almost a quarter century of s. 1 jurisprudence, the crux of the matter lies in what may be called the core of the proportionality analysis, the minimal impairment test and the balancing of effects. It is at these stages that the means are questioned and their relationship to the law's purpose is challenged and reviewed. It is also where the purpose itself must be reassessed with regard to the means chosen by Parliament or the legislature.

. . .

[192] It may be tempting to draw sharp analytical distinctions between the minimal impairment and balancing of effects parts of the *Oakes* test. But determining whether a

measure limiting a right successfully meets the justification test should lead to some questioning of the purpose in the course of the proportionality analysis, to determine not only whether an alternative solution could reach the goal, but also to what extent the goal itself ought to be realized. This part of the analysis may confirm the validity of alternative, less intrusive measures.

[193] The pull toward a sharp distinction between the two steps of the proportionality analysis, minimal impairment and balancing of effects, is perhaps intensified by semantic difficulties with the minimal impairment test. Courts still use the word "minimal" to characterize the acceptable level of rights impairment, in keeping with the original language used in *Oakes*. This is a strong word that seemed to suggest that, in the justification process, the state would have to show that the measure taken was really the least intrusive possible. It would have to demonstrate that no less drastic measure could be adopted that would achieve the stated legislative purpose. A literal application of such a test might lead, in essence, to courts adopting a libertarian perspective that the state should be constrained and its powers narrowly defined and limited. This understanding of the Constitution might have put Parliament and the legislature in a strait-jacket and would have crystallized constitutional arrangements essentially made up of negative rights.

[194] In practical terms, the jurisprudence of this Court confirms that minimal does not really mean minimal in the ordinary sense of the word. The *Oakes* test was quickly reinterpreted, so that the question, in the minimal impairment analysis, became whether the right was infringed "as little as is reasonably possible," within a range of reasonable options (*R v. Edwards Books and Art Ltd.*, [1986] 2 SCR 713, at p. 772 [35 DLR (4th) 1], *per* Dickson CJ). The analysis leaves a reasonable margin of action to the state (p. 795, *per* La Forest J). This is where we now stand, using words that, sometimes, no longer reflect the legal nature of a test.

[195] In order to determine whether the measure falls within a range of reasonable options, courts must weigh the purpose against the extent of the infringement. They must look at the range of options that are available within the bounds of a democratic Constitution. A deeper analysis of the purpose is in order at this stage of the proportionality analysis. The stated objective is not an absolute and should not be treated as a given. Moreover, alternative solutions should not be evaluated on a standard of maximal consistency with the stated objective. An alternative measure might be legitimate even if the objective could no longer be obtained in its complete integrity. At this stage of the proportionality analysis, the overall objective of the s. 1 analysis remains constant: to preserve constitutional rights, by looking for a solution that will reach a better balance, even if it demands a more restricted understanding of the scope and efficacy of the objectives of the measure. In this sense, courts must execute a holistic proportionality analysis with different legal and analytical components, which remain tightly woven.

· · ·

[197] For all practical purposes, the reasons of the Chief Justice treat the law's objective as if it were unassailable once the courts engage in the proportionality analysis. No means that would not allow the objective to be realized to its fullest extent could be considered as a reasonable alternative. In this respect, the reasons appear inconsistent. First, para. 54 states: "*[l]ess drastic means which do not actually achieve the government's objective are not considered at this stage ... ,*" i.e., the minimal impairment stage. Such an ap-

proach would severely restrict the ambit of court review of government action and would reduce it to an analysis of the alignment of means with purposes. At other times, however, I note that the reasons seem more alive to this problem. Thus, one may find in the reasons suggestions that *"achieving the objective"* might actually mean looking into whether there exists an alternative means of reaching the objective *"in a real and substantial manner"* (para. 55). What that would actually mean in practical terms may not be as clear as one could wish. Nevertheless, these words appear to signal that, even at the minimal impairment stage, the objective might have to be redefined and circumscribed.

[198] Indeed, one wonders how an objective could be satisfied in a real and substantial manner without being read down somewhat. A different approach to the interpretation and application of the *Oakes* test would seem hard to reconcile with previous pronouncements of our Court. Our recent judgment in *Charkaoui v. Canada (Citizenship and Immigration)*, 2007 SCC 9, [2007] 1 SCR 350 [276 DLR (4th) 594], offers a fine example of a different understanding of the nature of the proportionality analysis.

[199] In *Charkaoui*, our Court struck down in part, on s. 7 grounds, the security certificate regime set up under the *Immigration and Refugee Protection Act*, SC 2001, c. 27. It accepted that the security of Canada and the protection of intelligence sources were pressing and compelling objectives. Nevertheless, the Court found that alternative measures might give sufficient protection to confidential information. Important as they were, the objectives of the law were not treated as absolute goals, which had to be realized in their perfect integrity. The objectives were recast, in fact, at a lower level than the state might have wished. The Court assessed the objectives, the impugned means and the alternative means together, as necessary components of a seamless proportionality analysis (paras. 85-87).

II. Conclusion

[200] As to the outcome of this case, I agree with the reasons of Justice Abella and with the substance of her views on the lack of justification for the regulation under s. 1. Religious rights are certainly not unlimited. They may have to be restricted in the context of broader social values. But they are fundamental rights protected by the Constitution. The Government of Alberta had to prove that the limitations on the religious right were justified. Like Justice Abella, I believe that the Government of Alberta has failed to demonstrate that the regulation is a proportionate response to the identified societal problem of identity theft.

[201] Moreover, the driver's licence that it denies is not a privilege. It is not granted at the discretion of governments. Every would-be driver is entitled to a licence provided that he or she meets the required conditions and qualifications. Such a licence, as we know, is often of critical importance in daily life and is certainly so in rural Alberta. Other approaches to identity fraud might be devised that would fall within a reasonable range of options and that could establish a proper balance between the social and constitutional interests at stake. This balance cannot be obtained by belittling the impact of the measures on the beliefs and religious practices of the Hutterites and by asking them to rely on taxi drivers and truck rental services to operate their farms and to preserve their way of life. Absolute safety is probably impossible in a democratic society. A limited

restriction on the Province's objective of minimizing identity theft would not unduly compromise this aspect of the security of Alberta residents and might lie within the range of reasonable and constitutional alternatives. Indeed, the Province's stated purpose is not set in stone and does not need to be achieved at all costs. The infringing measure was implemented in order to reach a hypothetical objective of minimizing identity theft, by requiring driver's licences with photos. But a small number of people carrying a driver's licence without a photo will not significantly compromise the safety of the residents of Alberta. On the other hand, under the impugned regulation, a small group of people is being made to carry a heavy burden. The photo requirement was not a proportionate limitation of the religious rights at stake.

Appeal allowed.

A number of recent freedom of religion cases have required courts to address the tension or conflict between religious freedom and other Charter rights, such as equality rights. The Supreme Court of Canada dealt with this issue in *Trinity Western*, below.

Trinity Western University v. British Columbia College of Teachers
[2001] 1 SCR 772, 199 DLR (4th) 1

IACOBUCCI and BASTARACHE JJ (McLachlin CJC, Gonthier, Major, Binnie, Arbour, and LeBel JJ concurring): [1] Trinity Western University ("TWU") is a private institution located in Langley, British Columbia and incorporated under the laws of British Columbia. ... TWU is associated with the Evangelical Free Church of Canada. It is an accredited member of the Association of Universities and Colleges of Canada and the Council for Christian Colleges and Universities. TWU confers six baccalaureate degrees and offers four masters programs. ...

[2] In 1985, TWU established a teacher training program offering baccalaureate degrees in education upon completion of a five-year course, four years of which were spent at TWU, the fifth year being under the aegis of Simon Fraser University. In 1987, TWU applied to BC's Minister of Education for permission to assume full responsibility for the teacher education program. Although there appears to have been approval in principle in Cabinet, the Minister did not act on the request because of the creation in that year of the British Columbia College of Teachers ("BCCT") which would become the appropriate body to consider the application. TWU applied to the BCCT in January of 1988, but the College was not ready to consider the application. The application was therefore withdrawn and presented again in January of 1995. One of the reasons for assuming complete responsibility for the program was the desire of TWU to have the full program reflect the Christian world view of TWU.

[3] The philosophy of TWU is specifically described in a document entitled "Responsibilities of Membership in the Community of Trinity Western University." It is implemented through the adoption of "Community Standards" which are intended to reflect the preferred lifestyle of persons belonging to the TWU community; they apply both off

and on campus and are the object of a statement of acceptance by students, faculty and staff. An extract of the application made in 1995 is instructive:

> Trinity Western is a relatively unique Canadian university in that it offers academically responsible education within a distinctive Christian context. Its mission is to equip Christians to serve God and people throughout society. TWU's educational program, like those in public universities, is based on a particular worldview perspective. At TWU, that worldview is a Christian one. It includes (but is not limited to) a deep respect for integrity and authenticity, responsible stewardship of resources, the sanctity of human life, compassion for the disadvantaged, and justice for all. This provides a framework for the leadership development that is emphasized throughout TWU's program. Although its program is oriented towards those who profess the Christian faith, the university welcomes anyone who wishes to pursue a liberal arts education and is willing to be part of the Trinity Western community. While maintaining structural ties with its founding denomination, the Evangelical Free Church, the university serves the needs of the whole Christian community. Both the faculty and the student body represent a wide range of denominational backgrounds.

[4] The "Community Standards" document that students attending TWU must sign contains the following paragraph, which is at the root of the present controversy:

> REFRAIN FROM PRACTICES THAT ARE BIBLICALLY CONDEMNED. These include but are not limited to drunkenness (Eph. 5:18), swearing or use of profane language (Eph. 4:29, 5:4; Jas. 3:1-12), harassment (Jn 13:34-35; Rom. 12:9-21; Eph. 4:31), all forms of dishonesty including cheating and stealing (Prov. 12:22; Col. 3:9; Eph. 4:28), abortion (Ex. 20:13; Ps. 139:13-16), involvement in the occult (Acts 19:19; Gal. 5:19), and sexual sins including premarital sex, adultery, *homosexual behaviour*, and viewing of pornography (I Cor. 6:12-20; Eph. 4:17-24; I Thess. 4:3-8; Rom. 2:26-27; I Tim. 1:9-10). Furthermore married members of the community agree to maintain the sanctity of marriage and to take every positive step possible to avoid divorce. [Emphasis added.]

Faculty and staff are required to sign a "Community Standards" document that contains a similar paragraph, including the prohibition of homosexual behaviour.

[5] Following established policies, the BCCT appointed a program approval team ("PAT") to assess the TWU application. The PAT recommended the approval of the application for accreditation with conditions on March 21, 1996. On April 19, 1996, the Teacher Education Programs Committee ("TEPC") approved the PAT report but modified some of the conditions. On May 17, 1996, the Council of the BCCT rejected the report and recommendations. The motion was passed on two grounds: TWU did not meet the criteria stated in the BCCT bylaws and policies; and approval would not be in the public interest because of discriminatory practices of the institution. ... [Following a request for reconsideration, TWU's application was once again rejected.] ...

[6] The BCCT gave no written reasons explaining its initial denial of the application or rejection on reconsideration. The May 22, 1996 letter of the Registrar of the BCCT to TWU however refers to discriminatory practices and "specifically the requirement for students to sign a contract of 'Responsibilities of Membership in the Trinity Western University Community." The only other written explanation for denial of the application

comes from the Fall 1996 quarterly newsletter of the BCCT, where the whole matter becomes abundantly clear. The BCCT writes:

> Both the *Canadian Human Rights Act* and the *BC Human Rights Act* prohibit discrimination
> on the ground of sexual orientation. The *Charter of Rights* and the *Human Rights Acts* express the values which represent the public interest. Labelling homosexual behaviour as
> sinful has the effect of excluding persons whose sexual orientation is gay or lesbian. The
> Council believes and is supported by law in the belief that sexual orientation is no more
> separable from a person than colour. Persons of homosexual orientation, like persons of
> colour, are entitled to protection and freedom from discrimination under the law.

[TWU brought an application for judicial review of the decision of the BCCT. The BC Supreme Court found that it was not within the BCCT's jurisdiction to consider whether the program followed discriminatory practices and, furthermore, that there was no reasonable foundation to support the BCCT's decision with respect to discrimination. The Court issued an order requiring approval of the TWU proposed teacher education program for a five-year period subject to a number of conditions. The BC Court of Appeal, Rowles JA dissenting, found that the BCCT had jurisdiction to consider whether the program was discriminatory, but affirmed the trial judge's decision that on the facts of the case the finding of discrimination was not justified.]

Analysis

Is Consideration of Discriminatory Practices Within the Jurisdiction of the BCCT?

[11] The BCCT is empowered under s. 4 of the *Teaching Profession Act* (the "Act") to "establish, having regard to the public interest, standards for the education, professional responsibility and competence of its members, persons who hold certificates of qualification and applicants for membership and … to encourage the professional interest of its members … ." It is this reference to the public interest that is invoked by the BCCT as justification for considering the TWU admissions policy in deciding on the certification of its teacher education program. The BCCT argues that teaching programs must be offered in an environment that reflects human rights values and that those values can be used as a guide in the assessment of the impact of discriminatory practices on pedagogy. Although the BCCT did not take into account the existence of special institutions such as TWU in designing its bylaws and policies, it claims that all institutions who wish to train teachers for entry into the public education system must satisfy the BCCT that they will provide an institutional setting that appropriately prepares future teachers for the public school environment, and in particular for the diversity of public school students.

· · ·

[13] Our Court accepted in *Ross v. New Brunswick School District No. 15*, [1996] 1 SCR 825 [133 DLR (4th) 1], that teachers are a medium for the transmission of values. It is obvious that the pluralistic nature of society and the extent of diversity in Canada are important elements that must be understood by future teachers because they are the fabric of the society within which teachers operate and the reason why there is a need to respect and promote minority rights. The suitability for entrance into the profession of

teaching must therefore take into account all features of the education program at TWU. ... The power to establish standards provided for in s. 4 of the Act must be interpreted in light of the general purpose of the statute and in particular, the need to ensure that "the fulfilment of public functions is undertaken in a manner that does not undermine public trust and confidence" (*Ross*). Schools are meant to develop civic virtue and responsible citizenship, to educate in an environment free of bias, prejudice and intolerance. It would not be correct, in this context, to limit the scope of s. 4 to a determination of skills and knowledge.

[14] We are therefore of the view that the BCCT had jurisdiction to consider discriminatory practices in dealing with the TWU application. ...

Was the Decision of the BCCT Council Justified?

[Iacobucci and Bastarache JJ first considered the appropriate standard of review of a decision by the BCCT either to give or refuse approval to a teacher education program under the *Teaching Profession Act*, concluding that the appropriate standard was one of correctness.]

The Evidence of Discrimination

[20] There are in reality two elements to be considered under this heading: Are the internal documents of TWU illustrative of discriminatory practices? If so, are these discriminatory practices sufficient to establish a risk of discrimination sufficient to justify that graduates of TWU should not be admitted to teach in the public schools?

[21] The BCCT relied on the internal documents of TWU as evidence of discrimination against homosexuals. It concluded that the inclusion of homosexual behaviour in the list of biblically condemned practices demonstrates intolerance and that this cannot be overridden by the adoption of other values. Both the program and the practices of TWU, the declarations required of students and faculty in particular, were condemned because they reflected the beliefs of the signatories. According to the BCCT, discrimination against homosexuals had been institutionalized ... .

• • •

[27] The equality guarantees in the Charter and in BC's human rights legislation include protection against discrimination based on sexual orientation. In *Egan v. Canada*, [1995] 2 SCR 513 [124 DLR (4th) 609], this Court unanimously affirmed that sexual orientation is an analogous ground to those enumerated in s. 15(1) of the Charter. In addition, a majority of this Court explicitly recognized that gays and lesbians, "whether as individuals or couples, form an identifiable minority who have suffered and continue to suffer serious social, political and economic disadvantage." ... This statement was recently affirmed by a majority of this Court in *M. v. H.*, [1999] 2 SCR 3 [171 DLR (4th) 577] ... . See also *Vriend* [*v. Alberta*, [1998] 1 SCR 493, 156 DLR (4th) 385] and *Little Sisters Book and Art Emporium v. Canada (Minister of Justice)*, [2000] 2 SCR 1120 [193 DLR (4th) 193]. While the BCCT was not directly applying either the Charter or the province's human rights legislation when making its decision, it was entitled to look to these instruments to determine whether it would be in the public interest to allow public school teachers to be trained at TWU.

[28] At the same time, however, the BCCT is also required to consider issues of religious freedom. Section 15 of the Charter protects equally against "discrimination based on … religion." Similarly, s. 2(a) of the Charter guarantees that "[e]veryone has the following fundamental freedoms … freedom of conscience and religion." British Columbia's human rights legislation accommodates religious freedoms by allowing religious institutions to discriminate in their admissions policies on the basis of religion. … The issue at the heart of this appeal is how to reconcile the religious freedoms of individuals wishing to attend TWU with the equality concerns of students in BC's public school system, concerns that may be shared with their parents and society generally.

[29] In our opinion, this is a case where any potential conflict should be resolved through the proper delineation of the rights and values involved. In essence, properly defining the scope of the rights avoids a conflict in this case. Neither freedom of religion nor the guarantee against discrimination based on sexual orientation is absolute. As L'Heureux-Dubé J stated in *P.(D.) v. S.(C.)*, [1993] 4 SCR 141 [108 DLR (4th) 287], at p. 182, writing for the majority on this point:

> As the Court has reiterated many times, freedom of religion, like any freedom, is not absolute. *It is inherently limited by the rights and freedoms of others.* [Emphasis added.] …

[30] Similarly, Iacobucci and Major JJ concluded in *B.(R.) v. Children's Aid Society of Metropolitan Toronto*, [1995] 1 SCR 315 [122 DLR (4th) 1], at para. 226, that:

> there [are] limits to the scope of s. 2(a), especially so when this provision is called upon to protect activity that threatens the physical or psychological well-being of others. In other words, *although the freedom of belief may be broad, the freedom to act upon those beliefs is considerably narrower*, and it is the latter freedom at issue in this case. [Emphasis added.]

[31] In addition, the Charter must be read as a whole, so that one right is not privileged at the expense of another. As Lamer CJ stated for the majority of this Court in *Dagenais v. Canadian Broadcasting Corp.*, [1994] 3 SCR 835 [120 DLR (4th) 12], at p. 877:

> A hierarchical approach to rights, which places some over others, must be avoided, both when interpreting the Charter and when developing the common law. When the protected rights of two individuals come into conflict … Charter principles require a balance to be achieved that fully respects the importance of both sets of rights.

[32] Therefore, although the BCCT was right to evaluate the impact of TWU's admission policy on the public school environment, it should have considered more. The *Human Rights Code*, RSBC 1996, c. 210, specifically provides for exceptions in the case of religious institutions, and the legislature gave recognition to TWU as an institution affiliated to a particular church whose views were well known to it. While the BCCT says that it is not denying the right to TWU students and faculty to hold particular religious views, it has inferred without any concrete evidence that such views will limit consideration of social issues by TWU graduates and have a detrimental effect on the learning environment in public schools. There is no denying that the decision of the BCCT places a burden on members of a particular religious group and in effect, is preventing them from expressing freely their religious beliefs and associating to put them into practice. If TWU does not abandon its Community Standards, it renounces certification and full control

of a teacher education program permitting access to the public school system. Students are likewise affected because the affirmation of their religious beliefs and attendance at TWU will not lead to certification as public school teachers unless they attend a public university for at least one year. These are important considerations. What the BCCT was required to do was to determine whether the rights were in conflict in reality.

[33] TWU's Community Standards, which are limited to prescribing conduct of members while at TWU, are not sufficient to support the conclusion that the BCCT should anticipate intolerant behaviour in the public schools. Indeed, if TWU's Community Standards could be sufficient in themselves to justify denying accreditation, it is difficult to see how the same logic would not result in the denial of accreditation to members of a particular church. The diversity of Canadian society is partly reflected in the multiple religious organizations that mark the societal landscape and this diversity of views should be respected. The BCCT did not weigh the various rights involved in its assessment of the alleged discriminatory practices of TWU by not taking into account the impact of its decision on the right to freedom of religion of the members of TWU. Accordingly, this Court must.

[34] Consideration of human rights values in these circumstances encompasses consideration of the place of private institutions in our society and the reconciling of competing rights and values. Freedom of religion, conscience and association coexist with the right to be free of discrimination based on sexual orientation. Even though the requirement that students and faculty adopt the Community Standards creates unfavourable differential treatment since it would probably prevent homosexual students and faculty from applying, one must consider the true nature of the undertaking and the context in which this occurs. Many Canadian universities, including St. Francis Xavier University, Queen's University, McGill University and Concordia University College of Alberta, have traditions of religious affiliations. Furthermore, s. 93 of the *Constitution Act, 1867* enshrined religious public education rights into our Constitution, as part of the historic compromise which made Confederation possible. ...

[35] Another part of that context is the *Human Rights Act*, SBC 1984, c. 22, ... which provides, in s. 19 (now s. 41), that a religious institution is not considered to breach the Act where it prefers adherents of its religious constituency. It cannot be reasonably concluded that private institutions are protected but that their graduates are *de facto* considered unworthy of fully participating in public activities. In *Ontario Human Rights Commission v. Simpson-Sears Ltd.*, [1985] 2 SCR 536 [23 DLR (4th) 321], at p. 554, McIntyre J observed that a "natural corollary to the recognition of a right must be the social acceptance of a general duty to respect and to act within reason to protect it." In this particular case, it can reasonably be inferred that the BC legislature did not consider that training with a Christian philosophy was in itself against the public interest since it passed five bills in favour of TWU between 1969 and 1985. While homosexuals may be discouraged from attending TWU, a private institution based on particular religious beliefs, they will not be prevented from becoming teachers. In addition, there is nothing in the TWU Community Standards that indicates that graduates of TWU will not treat homosexuals fairly and respectfully. Indeed, the evidence to date is that graduates from the joint TWU-SFU teacher education program have become competent public school teachers, and there is no evidence before this Court of discriminatory conduct by any graduate. Although this

evidence is not conclusive, given that no students have yet graduated from a teacher education program taught exclusively at TWU, it is instructive. Students attending TWU are free to adopt personal rules of conduct based on their religious beliefs provided they do not interfere with the rights of others. Their freedom of religion is not accommodated if the consequence of its exercise is the denial of the right of full participation in society. Clearly, the restriction on freedom of religion must be justified by evidence that the exercise of this freedom of religion will, in the circumstances of this case, have a detrimental impact on the school system.

[36] Instead, the proper place to draw the line in cases like the one at bar is generally between belief and conduct. The freedom to hold beliefs is broader than the freedom to act on them. Absent concrete evidence that training teachers at TWU fosters discrimination in the public schools of BC, the freedom of individuals to adhere to certain religious beliefs while at TWU should be respected. The BCCT, rightfully, does not require public universities with teacher education programs to screen out applicants who hold sexist, racist or homophobic beliefs. For better or for worse, tolerance of divergent beliefs is a hallmark of a democratic society.

[37] Acting on those beliefs, however, is a very different matter. If a teacher in the public school system engages in discriminatory conduct, that teacher can be subject to disciplinary proceedings before the BCCT. Discriminatory conduct by a public school teacher when on duty should always be subject to disciplinary proceedings. This Court has held, however, that greater tolerance must be shown with respect to off-duty conduct. Yet disciplinary measures can still be taken when discriminatory off-duty conduct poisons the school environment. As La Forest J stated for a unanimous Court in *Ross*, *supra*, at para. 45:

> It is on the basis of the position of trust and influence that we hold the teacher to high standards both on and off duty, and it is an erosion of these standards that may lead to a loss in the community of confidence in the public school system. I do not wish to be understood as advocating an approach that subjects the entire lives of teachers to inordinate scrutiny on the basis of more onerous moral standards of behaviour. This could lead to a substantial invasion of the privacy rights and fundamental freedoms of teachers. However, where a "poisoned" environment within the school system is traceable to the off-duty conduct of a teacher that is likely to produce a corresponding loss of confidence in the teacher and the system as a whole, then the off-duty conduct of the teacher is relevant.

In this way, the scope of the freedom of religion and equality rights that have come into conflict in this appeal can be circumscribed and thereby reconciled.

[38] For the BCCT to have properly denied accreditation to TWU, it should have based its concerns on specific evidence. It could have asked for reports on student teachers, or opinions of school principals and superintendents. It could have examined discipline files involving TWU graduates and other teachers affiliated with a Christian school of that nature. Any concerns should go to risk, not general perceptions. ...

[L'Heureux-Dubé J dissented. Her judgment was informed by the view that teachers perform both a counselling as well as an educative function and a concern that the absence of a supportive classroom environment would mean that homosexual and bisexual students would be forced to remain invisible and would be reluctant to approach their teachers. In her view, even if there were no overt acts of discrimination by TWU graduates, there was sufficient justification for the BCCT's decision. The BCCT's decision not to accredit TWU was seen as a reasonable proactive measure designed to prevent any potential problems of student, parent, colleague, or staff perception of teachers.]

Appeal dismissed.

NOTES AND QUESTIONS

1. How realistic is the distinction between practice and belief that the Court draws in *Trinity Western*? Would such a distinction be made in the case of racist beliefs? See *Ross v. New Brunswick School District No. 15*, [1996] 1 SCR 825, 133 DLR (4th) 1, which involved a schoolteacher (Ross) who engaged in expression of anti-Semitic views outside of the classroom (through a number of published writings and appearances on television alleging an international Jewish conspiracy that was destroying Christian civilization). Ross had not made any anti-Semitic comments in the classroom. In a human rights complaint brought by a Jewish parent against Ross's employer, the school board, Ross's activities outside the classroom were found to have created a poisoned environment within the classroom that discriminated against Jewish students in the provision of educational services. In reaching this conclusion, the human rights tribunal relied on evidence of discriminatory conduct engaged in by some students. Although there was no evidence that anti-Jewish statements by students in the school were directly influenced by Ross's teachings, the tribunal concluded that it would nonetheless be reasonable to anticipate such an influence given the high degree of publicity surrounding Ross's publications. The tribunal ordered the school board to remove Ross from the classroom and to attempt to find him a non-teaching position. Ross was also permanently prohibited from publishing or distributing anti-Semitic writings as a condition of retaining employment with the school board. Ross appealed, arguing that the orders violated his freedom of expression under the Charter.

The Supreme Court of Canada upheld the order removing Ross from the classroom as a reasonable limit on freedom of expression and religion. In doing so, La Forest J, writing for the Court, stressed the importance of the educational context (at 32-33 DLR):

There can be no doubt that the attempt to foster equality, respect and tolerance in the Canadian educational system is a laudable goal. But the additional driving factor in this case is the nature of the educational services in question: we are dealing here with the education of young children. ... Young children are especially vulnerable to the messages conveyed by their teachers. They are less likely to make an intellectual distinction between comments a teacher makes in the school and those the teacher makes outside the school. They are, therefore, more likely to feel threatened and isolated by a teacher who makes comments that denigrate personal characteristics of a group to which they belong. Furthermore, they are unlikely to distinguish between falsehoods and truth and more likely to accept derogatory views espoused by a teacher. The importance of ensuring an equal and discrimination free educational environment, and the perception of fairness and tolerance in the classroom, are paramount in the education of young children. This helps foster self-respect and acceptance by others.

With respect to the freedom of religion claim, Justice La Forest concluded that an "attenuated level" of s. 1 justification was warranted, given the fact that the case raised religious beliefs that "denigrate[d] and defame[d] the religious beliefs of others" so as to erode "the very basis of the guarantee in s. 2(a)." In terms of rational connection, he concluded that it was sufficient for the board to reasonably anticipate a causal relationship between Ross's conduct and the poisoned educational environment in the school. Accordingly, it was necessary to remove him from the classroom. The minimal impairment argument also pivoted on the need to remove Ross from the classroom. The Court did not, however, uphold the permanent speech ban as a reasonable limit under s. 1, concluding that it was not reasonable to anticipate that Ross's writings would continue to produce a poisoned atmosphere in the classroom once he was in a non-teaching position.

2. In the case of *Kempling v. College of Teachers (British Columbia)*, 2005 BCCA 327, 255 DLR (4th) 169, the BC Court of Appeal upheld the decision of the BC College of Teachers to suspend the licence of a teacher who had written discriminatory letters about gays and lesbians to a local newspaper. The court noted that Mr. Kempling had stated clearly in his letters that he was writing as a teacher and that his views about homosexuality would govern his actions as a teacher.

3. In *Reference re Same-Sex Marriage*, [2004] 3 SCR 698, 2004 SCC 79, 246 DLR (4th) 193, the Supreme Court of Canada held that the extension of the right to civil marriage to same-sex couples would not breach the Charter guarantee of freedom of religion. The Court easily dismissed the argument that freedom of religion would be violated because the legalization of same-sex marriage would limit the freedom to hold religious views to the contrary. According to the Court, the purpose of the measure, "far from violating the *Charter*, flows from it. ... [T]he mere recognition of the equality rights of one group cannot, in itself, constitute a violation of the [Charter] rights of another." The Court went on to acknowledge that although

> the right to same-sex marriage conferred by the proposed legislation may potentially conflict with the right to freedom of religion if the legislation becomes law, conflicts of rights do not imply conflict with the *Charter*; rather, the resolution of such conflicts generally occurs within the ambit of the *Charter* itself by way of internal balancing and delineation. It has not been demonstrated in this reference that impermissible conflicts—conflicts incapable of resolution under s. 2(a)—will arise.

The Court also observed that "the guarantee of religious freedom in s. 2(a) of the *Charter* is broad enough to protect *religious officials* from being compelled by the state to perform civil or religious same-sex marriages that are contrary to their religious beliefs."

4. The more difficult issue, which the Court did not address in the *Reference* case, is the right of a *civil* marriage commissioner to refuse, for religious reasons, to perform a same-sex marriage. In *Goertzen v. Department of Justice (Saskatchewan)* (October 25, 2006), the Saskatchewan Human Rights Tribunal dismissed a complaint by a marriage commissioner that the provincial Justice Department's requirement that marriage commissioners perform same-sex marriages amounted to religious discrimination under the *Saskatchewan Human Rights Code*, SS 1979, c. S-24.1. In a subsequent ruling, in a complaint brought by a same-sex couple against another marriage commissioner who refused to marry them because of his religious convictions, the Tribunal found the marriage commissioner to have discriminated

against the couple and ordered him to pay a fine of $2,500 to the couple; see *M.J. v. Nichols* (May 23, 2008). The marriage commissioner appealed that decision, arguing that the order violated his freedom of religion under the Charter. His appeal was unsuccessful: *Nichols v. M.J.*, 2009 SKQB 299. The court concluded that, given Mr. Nichols's status as a government actor providing a public service, his freedom of religion could justifiably be limited to exclude discriminatory practices.

5. Section 293 of the *Criminal Code*, which bans polygamy, provides:

> 293(1) Every one who
>
>> (a) practises or enters into or in any manner agrees or consents to practise or enter
> into
>>> (i) any form of polygamy, or
>>> (ii) any kind of conjugal union with more than one person at the same time,
> whether or not it is by law recognized as a binding form of marriage, or
>> (b) celebrates, assists or is a party to a rite, ceremony, contract or consent that purports
> to sanction a relationship mentioned in subparagraph (a)(i) or (ii),
> is guilty of an indictable offence and liable to imprisonment for a term not exceeding five years.
>
> (2) Where an accused is charged with an offence under this section, no averment or proof of the method by which the alleged relationship was entered into, agreed to or consented to is necessary in the indictment or on the trial of the accused, nor is it necessary on the trial to prove that the persons who are alleged to have entered into the relationship had or intended to have sexual intercourse.

Polygamy is practised by members of a fundamentalist Mormon community in Bountiful, British Columbia. If charges were laid against members of the community, they would argue that s. 293 violates their freedom of religion under s. 2(a) of the Charter. What arguments would the federal government likely make in defending against the constitutional challenge? Based on the cases you have read, do you think the challenge would be successful?

IV. GOVERNMENT SUPPORT FOR RELIGION

This section explores the other aspect of freedom of religion identified by the Supreme Court of Canada—the right to be free from the coercive imposition of religion by the state. Recall that this was the aspect of freedom of religion at issue in *Big M* where the Supreme Court of Canada found that the Sunday closing requirement found in the federal *Lord's Day Act* violated s. 2(a) because its purpose was to impose observance of the Christian Sabbath. Because our constitution, unlike the US constitution, does not include an explicit anti-establishment clause, we have no explicit constitutional prohibition on state support for religion. What forms of state support for religion are precluded by s. 2(a)? When does state support for or facilitation of religion become a coercive imposition of religion? Is favouritism of one religion over others part of the concern under s. 2(a)? Or will state support for religion, even if even-handed, be seen in some circumstances as an imposition of religion on the non-religious? Some courts go beyond the concept of coercion and also draw on the idea of state neutrality toward religion. What does this mean? Is it an appropriate part of the legal framework for s. 2(a)?

The first two cases dealing with state imposition of religion found in this section—*Zylber-berg v. Sudbury Board of Education* and *Canadian Civil Liberties Assn. v. Ontario (Minister of Education)*—are early Charter decisions from the Ontario Court of Appeal that draw on the Supreme Court of Canada's ruling in *Big M*; both involved challenges to Christian prac-tices in public schools. The public or common schools that existed in most provinces at the time of their entry into Confederation were non-denominational. This does not mean that they were not religious. The curriculum was based on the general principles and practices shared by different Protestant groups in the community, and for the most part avoided mat-ters that were the subject of disagreement between the different denominations. In several provinces, a separate Catholic school system existed alongside the common public system. Later in this chapter we examine the constitutional position of the separate school system. State support for separate schools protected religious minority rights, but also helped to ensure the Protestant ethos of the common or public school system in provinces such as Ontario. With the growth of religious diversity and agnosticism, pressure grew to remove Protestant or Christian elements from the public school curriculum. Many non-Christians objected to what they saw as the imposition of Christian teachings and rituals. Some reli-gious adherents have responded to this objection, arguing that the removal of all religion from the public schools amounts to the establishment of a secular humanist world view in the public education system.

Zylberberg v. Sudbury Board of Education (Director)
(1988), 52 DLR (4th) 577, 65 OR (2d) 641 (CA)

BROOKE, BLAIR, GOODMAN, and ROBINS JJA: The issue in this appeal is whether reli-gious exercises, prescribed for the opening or closing of each school day in the public schools of this province, infringe the freedom of religion and conscience guaranteed by s. 2(a) of the *Canadian Charter of Rights and Freedoms*. ...

Statutes and Regulations

[Section 10(1), para. 18 of the *Education Act*, RSO 1980, c. 129 gives the minister of edu-cation the power to make regulations "governing the provisions of religious exercises and religious education in public and secondary schools and providing for the exemption of pupils from participating in such exercises and education and of a teacher from teaching, and a public school board or a secondary school board from providing, religious educa-tion in any school or class."]

Religious exercises in public schools are governed by s. 28 of RRO 1980, Reg. 262 (the Regulations), made pursuant to s. 10(1), the relevant parts of which provide:

RELIGIOUS EXERCISES AND RELIGIOUS EDUCATION IN THE PUBLIC SCHOOLS
    28(1) A public school shall be opened or closed each school day with religious exercises consisting of the *reading of the Scriptures or other suitable readings and the repeating of the Lord's Prayer or other suitable prayers.*

(2) The readings and prayers that form part of the religious exercises referred to in sub
section (1) shall be chosen from a list of selections approved for such purpose by the board
that operates the school where the board approves such a list and, where the board does not
approve such a list, the principal of the school shall select the readings and prayers after no-
tifying the board of his intention to do so, but his selection is subject to revision by the
board at any time.

(3) The religious exercises under subsection (1) may include the singing of one or more
hymns.

· · ·

(10) No pupil shall be required to take part in any religious exercises or be subject to any
instruction in religious education where his parent or, where the pupil is an adult, the pupil
applies to the principal of the school that the pupil attends for exemption of the pupil
therefrom.

(11) In public schools without suitable waiting rooms or other similar accommodation,
if the parent of a pupil or, where the pupil is an adult, the pupil applies to the principal of
the school for the exemption of the pupil from attendance while religious exercises are being
held or religious education given, such request shall be granted.

(12) Where a parent of a pupil, or a pupil who is an adult, objects to the pupil's taking
part in religious exercises or being subject to instruction in religious education, but requests
that the pupil remain in the classroom during the time devoted to religious exercises or instruction in religious education, the principal of the school that pupil attends shall permit
the pupil to do so, if he maintains decorous behavior. [Emphasis added.]

The appellants seek a declaration that s. 28(1) of the Regulations is of no force or effect
because it interferes with the appellants' freedom under s. 2(a) of the Charter ... . This necessarily would include s. 28(2) and (3).

· · ·

The Factual Background

This application [is made by three] parents of children attending elementary public
schools within the jurisdiction of the respondent school board in Sudbury [the Board]. ...
The three ... appellants were supported in argument by the three intervenors.

The Board's evidence was that the daily opening exercises in all its schools are brief
and include the singing of O Canada and the saying of the Lord's Prayer. The prayer is
either led by the class-room teacher or recited over the school's public address system. In
some schools, Scripture passages are also read.

At the request of a parent, a child is excused from the class-room during the exercises
or, if he or she remains in the room, is not required to participate. Arrangements are
made in every school for the care of children while they are excused from the class-room.
If they remain in the class-room, the Board's evidence is that they normally stand with
other students during the exercises but are not required to do so nor are they required to
bow their heads. The decision as to how best to accommodate a child excused from participation in the religious exercises is made in consultation with the parents. The Board
also permits students from different religious faiths to be absent from school at their
parents' request in order to observe religious holidays.

[One of the appellants] is of the Jewish religion and another is a Moslem. The third practises no religion but his wife is Roman Catholic and their children attend that church a few times a year. They decided to send their children to a public rather than a separate school in order to give them a secular education. One appellant made his objections to compulsory religious exercises known by letter to the Board but did not request an exemption from the exercises for his children although invited to do so. The other two appellants did not object before commencing these proceedings and did not request an exemption. The three appellants stated that they had not requested an exemption for their children because they did not want them singled out from their peers because of their religious beliefs.

There was a difference of expert opinion about the effect of religious exercises on non-Christian or non-participating children. An affidavit of a psychologist, filed by the appellants, expressed the view that such children would be placed under pressure to conform which, if resisted, would result in their being alienated from their peers. The affidavits of two psychologists, filed by the Board, asserted that children from minority religions were not harmed by the policy. They stated that pupils were routinely excused from other subjects and activities. They also claimed that religious exercises resulted in minority children "confronting the fact of their difference from the majority." This was said to be a normal and healthy part of growing up which would contribute to the development of religious tolerance and understanding which is important in view of the multicultural heritage of Canadians.

. . .

Does Section 28(1) Infringe the Charter Freedom of Conscience and Religion?

In Sudbury, the Board's application of s. 28(1) of the Regulations imposes Christian religious exercises in the schools. The Board has not exercised the option open to it under s. 28(1) of providing non-Christian prayers and non-Biblical readings. The possibility that the Board might exercise this option does not, however, affect the outcome in this case. The substantive issue here is whether s. 28(1), which makes it possible for the Board to prescribe Christian religious exercises, violates s. 2(a) of the Charter.

On its face, s. 28(1) infringes the freedom of conscience and religion guaranteed by s. 2(a) of the Charter. This was conceded by the respondents. Section 28(1) is antithetical to the Charter objective of promoting freedom of conscience and religion. The recitation of the Lord's Prayer, which is a Christian prayer, and the reading of Scriptures from the Christian Bible impose Christian observances upon non-Christian pupils and religious observances on non-believers.

The respondents, however, take the position that s. 28 viewed as a whole did not violate the freedoms of conscience and religion guaranteed by s. 2(a) of the Charter. They contend that the right to claim exemption from Christian religious exercises, conferred by s. 28(10), (11) and (12), eliminates any suggestion of pressure or compulsion on non-Christian pupils to participate in those exercises. Anderson J, as noted above, found it offensive to "logic and common sense" that the necessity of requesting an exemption was a form of "constraint, compulsion or coercion." At most, the Attorney-General submitted, the necessity of requesting an exemption might be an "embarrassment" but was not coercive in its effect.

From the majoritarian standpoint, the respondent's argument is understandable but, in our opinion, it does not reflect the reality of the situation faced by members of religious minorities. Whether or not there is pressure or compulsion must be assessed from their standpoint and, in particular, from the standpoint of pupils in the sensitive setting of a public school. ...

While the majoritarian view may be that s. 28 confers freedom of choice on the minority, the reality is that it imposes on religious minorities a compulsion to conform to the religious practices of the majority. The evidence in this case supports this view. The three appellants chose not to seek an exemption from religious exercises because of their concern about differentiating their children from other pupils. The peer pressure and the class-room norms to which children are acutely sensitive, in our opinion, are real and pervasive and operate to compel members of religious minorities to conform with majority religious practices. ...

We consider that s. 28(1) also infringes freedom of conscience and religion in a broader sense. The requirement that pupils attend religious exercises, unless exempt, compels students and parents to make a religious statement. ... [T]he effect of the exemption provisions is to discriminate against religious minorities. ...

... [T]he right to be excused from class, or to be exempted from participating, does not overcome the infringement of the Charter freedom of conscience and religion by the mandated religious exercises. On the contrary, the exemption provision imposes a penalty on pupils from religious minorities who utilize it by stigmatizing them as non-conformists and setting them apart from their fellow students who are members of the dominant religion. In our opinion, the conclusion is inescapable that the exemption provision fails to mitigate the infringement of freedom of conscience and religion by s. 28(1).

Other arguments were made for denying the applicability of s. 2(a) of the Charter to religious exercises. It was contended that they did no harm to pupils of minority religions. This assertion is not proven because, as earlier indicated, there was a difference of expert opinion on whether or not minority pupils were harmed. In any event, in our opinion, harm to individual pupils need not be proved by those who object to s. 28(1). It is irrelevant to the real issue which is whether the Charter freedom of conscience and religion is infringed. There is no burden on those objecting to s. 28(1) on this ground to prove, in addition, that it causes actual harm to individual pupils.

The effect of religious exercises cannot be glossed over with the comment that the exercises may be "good" for minority pupils. This view was expressed, as we indicated above, by a psychologist in supporting the Board's case who said that it was salutary for minority pupils to confront "the fact of their difference from the majority." This insensitive approach, in our opinion, not only depreciates the position of religious minorities but also fails to take into account the feelings of young children. It is also inconsistent with the multicultural nature of our society as recognized by s. 27 of the Charter. ...

· · ·

Can Section 1 Be Invoked to Justify the Charter Infringement?

. . .

The appellants contended that there was no saving secular purpose in s. 28(1). Its wording and, in the appellant's submission, its legislative background going back to the earliest times indicated that its purpose was religious and that, like the *Lord's Day Act* in *Big M* [*R v. Big M Drug Mart Ltd.*, [1985] 1 SCR 295, 18 DLR (4th) 321], it was incapable of justification under s. 1. The Attorney-General and the Board, on the other hand, asserted that s. 28(1) had paramount secular objectives, both educational and moral, and that the religious exercises served those purposes. ...

After a careful consideration of the Act, the Regulations, and other materials placed before us, we have concluded that the purpose of s. 28(1) is religious and that the exercises mandated by the Regulation were intended to be religious exercises. This is the only conclusion which can be drawn from the wording of the Act and the Regulations. ... It is clear that the exemption provision is included ... because the exercises were intended to serve religious and not secular purposes.

. . .

In this case it cannot be argued, as it was in *Big M, supra*, that over time the purpose of the impugned regulation had shifted from religious to secular objectives. ... The opening exercises may have secular moral and educational effects but these are, in our opinion, merely derivative from their religious objective. It is the purpose and not the impact of legislation which is determinative for constitutional purposes.

. . .

Could Section 28(1) Have Been Justified Under Section 1 of the Charter?

. . .

It is not necessary, in this case, to conduct a ritualistic step-by-step inquiry under each of the four elements of the *Oakes* test [*R v. Oakes*, [1986] 1 SCR 103, 26 DLR (4th) 200]. If the respondent fails under one element of the test, the Charter infringement cannot be justified. We propose, therefore, to consider the most vulnerable element of the test from the respondent's standpoint which is whether s. 28(1) impairs the appellants' freedoms under s. 2(a) "as little as possible." For the purposes of this inquiry we will assume, without deciding, that s. 28(1) could have been justified under the first two elements of the test as having an objective sufficiently important to warrant overriding the Charter freedom under s. 2(a) and as being rationally connected to the attainment of that objective.

The experience of the Toronto Board of Education convincingly demonstrates that there are less intrusive ways of imparting educational and moral values than those provided in s. 28. The Toronto experience ... shows that it is not necessary to give primacy to the Christian religion in school opening exercises and that they can be more appropriately founded upon the multicultural traditions of our society. In saying this we are not to be taken as passing a constitutional judgment on the opening exercises used in Toronto public schools. They were not in issue before us and we express no opinion as to whether they might give rise to Charter scrutiny. [The Toronto Board had produced a book of prayers and readings drawn from a number of sources including Buddhism, Confucianism, Hinduism, Islam, aboriginal beliefs, and Secular Humanism. The opening exercises in the Toronto schools began with the singing of *O Canada*, followed by the reading of one or more selections from the book and a moment of silence. The majority doubted that the Toronto program complied with s. 28(1), which required both prayers and readings.]

Conclusion

Since s. 28(1) infringes the appellants' Charter freedoms and could not, in any event, have been justified under s. 1, the appellants are entitled to the declaration they seek under s. 52 of the *Constitution Act, 1982* that s. 28(1) of the Regulations is of no force and effect. ...

Appeal allowed.

NOTES AND QUESTIONS

1. Justice Lacourciere, dissenting in *Zylberberg*, insisted that s. 2(a) did not prohibit state support for religion. He noted the omission from the Charter of any provision resembling the "Establishment Clause" of the US *Bill of Rights* and argued that s. 2(a) "does not prohibit all governmental aid to, or advancement of, religion *per se*." In his view, the prayer was simply a "state-created opportunity to participate in [a] religious activity." According to Lacourciere J, it could not reasonably be said that either the purpose or the effect of the regulation was to compel participation in a religious practice given the broad exemption granted to dissenters.

2. The same conclusion with respect to the constitutionality of the recitation of the Lord's Prayer in the public schools was reached *Russow v. BC (AG)* (1989), 62 DLR (4th) 98 (BCSC).

3. In *Canadian Civil Liberties Assn. v. Ontario (Minister of Education)* (1990), 65 DLR (4th) 1, the Ontario Court of Appeal held that s. 24(4) of Regulation 262 (a different subsection of the same regulation discussed in *Zylberberg*), which required that schools in the province devote two one-half hour periods each week to "religious education," had as its purpose the indoctrination of students in the Christian faith (rather than education about religions) and was therefore contrary to s. 2(a) of the Charter. In reaching this conclusion the Court noted that the regulation provided that the religious education could be provided by clergymen even though "such 'outsiders' were not authorized for any other part of the school programme." The Court found that "in the absence of evidence that clergymen are better equipped to teach comparative religions than they are skilled at indoctrination, the conclusion has to be that the purpose was indoctrination." The Court also noted that the subsection referred to clergymen of "different denominations" rather than of different religions or faiths, which suggested that the religious education was to be in "the Christian faith ... rather than many faiths." Finally, the Court reasoned that the exemption provision, s. 28(10) (which provided for the exemption of pupils from religious education), was only necessary if the instruction involved religious indoctrination.

As in *Zylberberg*, the Court found that the indoctrinating purpose of the regulation was not altered by the fact that students who did not want to participate in the religious education classes could be granted an exemption. Rather, the exemption was found to impose a penalty on those who used it "by stigmatizing them as non-conformists and setting them apart from their fellow students who are members of the dominant religion." The Court concluded:

> State-authorized religious indoctrination amounts to the imposition of majoritarian religious beliefs on minorities. Although s. 2(a) of the Charter is not infringed merely because education may be consistent with the religious beliefs of the majority of Canadians, ... teaching students Christian doctrine as if it were the exclusive means through which to develop moral thinking and behaviour amounts to religious coercion in the class-room. It creates a direct burden on religious minorities and non-believers who do not adhere to majoritarian beliefs. ... [T]his amounts to violation of s. 2(a) of the Charter.

Because the Court concluded that the purpose of the regulation was contrary to s. 2(a), it did not find it necessary to consider in any detail the effects of the regulation on religious freedom. However, the Court did go on to consider the constitutionality of the religious curriculum provided by the Elgin County School Board. The Court recognized that the line between religious indoctrination, which is contrary to s. 2(a), and education about religion, which is compatible with religious freedom, may sometimes be difficult to draw. Nevertheless based on the "general themes, lesson plans, teaching and resource materials and the manner of presentation of the course of study," the Court concluded that the curriculum (in both original and revised forms) "constituted religious indoctrination." The Court noted that the original curriculum was delivered by clergymen (or lay teachers designated by clergymen) and included verses from the Bible which were to be memorized and lesson plans that sought to teach students that salvation was through Jesus. The Court reached the same conclusion with regard to two later versions of the curriculum, which in the Court's view continued to be taught from a Christian perspective: "Notwithstanding the efforts which appear to have been made to effect changes in these curricula, it is our opinion that they contain sufficient indoctrinating material to preclude us from regarding it as trivial or inconsequential."

Finally, the Court held that neither violation of s. 2(a) was justified under s. 1. The curriculum could not be supported under s. 1 "because it does not constitute a limit prescribed by law," and the regulation could not be upheld because its "true purpose ... is to indoctrinate children in the Christian faith."

4. In *Zylberberg*, the Court takes a broad view of coercive pressure. Even though children can opt out of the prayer, the Court finds that they are under unacceptable pressure to conform. Does this apply only in the case of children? In *Freitag v. Penetanguishene* (1999), 47 OR (3d) 301, 179 DLR (4th) 150, the Ontario Court of Appeal held that the mayor's practice of opening town council meetings by inviting councillors (and, indirectly, members of the public) to rise with him and recite the Lord's Prayer violated s. 2(a) and could not be justified under s. 1. The following is an excerpt from the court's decision:

> [24] ... The appellant conceded that he did not feel forced to stand and recite the Lord's Prayer when others did. Others have observed that he does not stand, nor does he recite the prayer. They also note that he participates in meetings and that outwardly he does not appear to be uncomfortable. However he has deposed without challenge by cross-examination, that he feels great pressure to stand, and as a non-Christian, he feels intimidated by and uncomfortable with the practice of having the councillors stand and recite the prayer. ... .

[25] … Because the purpose of the practice, to impose a specifically Christian moral tone contravenes s. 2(a) of the Charter, there is no need to examine the effects of the practice. However, even if one does consider the effects, the application judge erred in finding that they are trivial and insubstantial.

• • •

[33] The main factor which distinguishes this case from *Zylberberg* is that the person who is seeking the relief in this case and who claims that he is being affected by the *Charter* breach is an adult citizen attending Town Council meetings, rather than children attending school, although in that case the rights of the parents of the affected children were also considered. Clearly the nature and potential effect of the coercion are much different for an adult who wishes to attend Town Council meetings than for children who are in the school environment all year with friends and teachers, and are subject to the pressures that those important relationships engender. …

[34] However, in my view, the fact that the applicants in *Zylberberg* may be perceived as more vulnerable than the appellant in this case is not determinative of the issue. Just as children are entitled to attend public school and be free from coercion or pressure to conform to the religious practices of the majority, so everyone is entitled to attend public local council meetings and to enjoy the same freedom.

• • •

[36] In this case there is no expert evidence on the effect of peer pressure on adults. There is, however, direct evidence, first from the appellant that he feels intimidation when he attends the meeting of his local Town Council. This does not mean he is so fearful that he does not participate. He does so, but as a citizen who is singled out as being not part of the majority recognized officially in the proceedings. Because of the exclusionary practice of the council, he has also been dissuaded from running for council in an election. Second, there is the evidence from the Town's witnesses that in fact the appellant is observed by others in attendance at the meetings and his actions are analyzed and made the subject of comment. Of course this is partly attributable to the fact that he has made an issue of the Town's practice. However, that fact further illustrates the significance of the situation. Someone who chooses to object to government action which is inclusive of the majority but forces the religious minority to conform or to accept exclusion, is then subjected to further scrutiny of his actions, together with the further pressure and intimidation which that may occasion.

• • •

[39] The "subtle and constant reminder" of his difference from the majority is what causes the appellant to feel intimidated and uncomfortable at council meetings. It has also deterred him from running for a council which proclaims and identifies itself as it does. In *Zylberberg*, this court also found an infringement of s. 2(a) in "a broader sense." It held, at p. 655, that the need to seek an exemption from attending the opening exercises "compels students *and parents* to make a religious statement" (emphasis added) so that the effect of the exemption provisions was to discriminate against religious minorities by stigmatizing them. The court concluded that the exemption provision, which was invoked to seek to avoid the compulsion of the infringing legislation, failed to mitigate the infringement.

[40] Similarly, the appellant is clearly stigmatized by his decision not to stand and recite the Lord's Prayer, so that the fact that he is not prohibited from making that choice does not save the Town's practice from infringing his *Charter* right.

[41] In my view, in the face of both the evidence in this case, as well as the well-established principles which have guided our courts in their interpretation and application of the freedom of religion guarantee, this is not a case where the effect of the *Charter* infringement is either trivial or insubstantial.

5. In *Allen v. Renfrew (County)* (2004), 69 OR (3d) 742 (Ont. SCJ), an Ontario judge held that a municipal council's practice of opening its meeting with an ecumenical prayer did not breach s. 2(a). The judge found that the prayer was not "in substance a religious observance, coercive or otherwise, and [did] not impose any burden on the applicant or any restriction on his exercise of his own beliefs." Despite the mention of God, the prayer was "broadly inclusive" and "non-denominational." Yet, if a Christian prayer excludes non-Christians, does an ecumenical prayer, which appeals explicitly to a divine creator, not, in the same way, exclude non-religious individuals—agnostics or atheists—or the followers of polytheistic or non-theistic belief systems? Is the state not favouring the practices of those who believe in a divine creator over those who do not? But if a court were to decide that the ecumenical prayer was objectionable because it excluded non-believers, would it then be favouring the beliefs or practices of agnostics and atheists over those of religious believers?

6. In 2008, a proposal by the government of Ontario to remove the Lord's Prayer from the opening ceremonies of the daily session of the legislative assembly was defeated following strong public reaction. The legislature's day now begins with a reading of the Lord's Prayer, followed by a second activity, such as another prayer, a recitation, or a moment of silence. Does this practice violate freedom of religion?

Is it a breach of religious freedom for the government to act on the basis of religious values? If so, how do we distinguish between religious and non-religious moral considerations? Is it reasonable to expect a religiously committed politician or voter to make decisions without relying on religious values? It is worth noting that religion has played a significant role in Canadian politics. The Social Gospel movement, for example, played an important role in the enactment of progressive legislation in the first half of the last century. In the United States, religious adherents and organizations played a central role in the civil rights movement.

In *Chamberlain v. Surrey School District*, the issue was whether a local school board acted outside its powers when it refused to approve, as supplementary teaching materials for the primary grades, three books depicting same-sex-parent families. The Supreme Court of Canada held that the decision to exclude the books was *ultra vires* the board because it was based on the belief, of parents and board members, that same-sex relationships are immoral and should not be affirmed, or even represented, to younger students. In the Court's view, the requirement in the BC *School Act* that the public schools operate according to "strictly secular principles" precluded the school board from supporting or enforcing a religious and or moral view that denies respect or recognition to another group or perspective in the community.

Chamberlain v. Surrey School District No. 36
[2002] 4 SCR 710, 2002 SCC 86, 221 DLR (4th) 156

McLACHLIN CJC (L'Heureux-Dubé, Iacobucci, Major, Binnie, and Arbour JJ concurring): [1] The Surrey, British Columbia, School Board passed a resolution refusing to authorize three books for classroom instruction on the ground that they depicted families in which both parents were either women or men—"same-sex parented families." The question on this appeal is whether that resolution was valid. The appellants have challenged the resolution on two grounds: first, that the Board acted outside its mandate under the *School Act*, RSBC 1996, c. 412, and second, that the resolution violates the *Canadian Charter of Rights and Freedoms*.

[2] I conclude that the resolution must be set aside on the first ground. The Board acted outside the mandate of the *School Act* by failing to apply the criteria required by the Act and by the Board's own regulation for approval of supplementary material.

[3] ... [T]he Board failed to conform to the requirements of the *School Act* and ... this rendered its decision unreasonable, requiring that the matter be remitted to the Board for consideration on the proper basis.

· · ·

[18] The *School Act*'s insistence on secularism and non-discrimination lies at the heart of this case. Section 76 of the *School Act* provides that "[a]ll schools and Provincial schools must be conducted on strictly secular and non-sectarian principles." It also emphasizes that "[t]he highest morality must be inculcated, but no religious dogma or creed is to be taught in a school or Provincial school."

[19] The Act's insistence on strict secularism does not mean that religious concerns have no place in the deliberations and decisions of the Board. Board members are entitled, and indeed required, to bring the views of the parents and communities they represent to the deliberation process. Because religion plays an important role in the life of many communities, these views will often be motivated by religious concerns. Religion is an integral aspect of people's lives, and cannot be left at the boardroom door. What secularism does rule out, however, is any attempt to use the religious views of one part of the community to exclude from consideration the values of other members of the community. A requirement of secularism implies that, although the Board is indeed free to address the religious concerns of parents, it must be sure to do so in a manner that gives equal recognition and respect to other members of the community. Religious views that deny equal recognition and respect to the members of a minority group cannot be used to exclude the concerns of the minority group. This is fair to both groups, as it ensures that each group is given as much recognition as it can consistently demand while giving the same recognition to others.

[20] The children attending BC's public schools come from many different types of families—"traditional" families parented by both biological parents; "single-parent" families, parented by either a man or a woman; families with step-parents; families with adopted children; foster families; interracial families; families with parents of different religious or cultural heritages; families in which siblings or members of the extended family live together; and same-sex parented families. Inevitably, some parents will view the cultural and family practices of certain other family types as morally questionable.

Yet if the school is to function in an atmosphere of tolerance and respect, in accordance with s. 76, the view that a certain lawful way of living is morally questionable cannot become the basis of school policy. Parents need not abandon their own commitments, or their view that the practices of others are undesirable. But where the school curriculum requires that a broad array of family models be taught in the classroom, a secular school system cannot exclude certain lawful family models simply on the ground that one group of parents finds them morally questionable.

· · ·

[25] In summary, the Act's requirement of strict secularism means that the Board must conduct its deliberations on all matters, including the approval of supplementary resources, in a manner that respects the views of all members of the school community. It cannot prefer the religious views of some people in its district to the views of other segments of the community. Nor can it appeal to views that deny the equal validity of the lawful lifestyles of some in the school community. The Board must act in a way that promotes respect and tolerance for all the diverse groups that it represents and serves.

· · ·

[28] ... [T]he Act makes it clear that the Board does not possess the same degree of autonomy as a legislature or a municipal council. It must act in a strictly secular manner. It must foster an atmosphere of tolerance and respect. It must not allow itself to be dominated by one religious or moral point of view, but must respect a diversity of views. It must adhere to the processes set out by the Act, which for approval of supplementary materials include acting according to a general regulation and considering the learning objectives of the provincial curriculum. ...

· · ·

[33] ... [A]lthough parental involvement is important, it cannot come at the expense of respect for the values and practices of all members of the school community. The requirement of secularism in s. 76 of the *School Act*, the emphasis on tolerance in the preamble, and the insistence of the curriculum on increasing awareness of a broad array of family types, all show, in my view, that parental concerns must be accommodated in a way that respects diversity. Parental views, however important, cannot override the imperative placed upon the British Columbia public schools to mirror the diversity of the community and teach tolerance and understanding of difference.

[34] The *School Act* confers on the Minister the power to approve basic educational resource materials to be used in teaching the curriculum, and confers on school boards the authority to approve supplementary educational resource material ... . The resolution at issue was made under the latter power.

[35] The purpose of supplementary learning resources is to enrich the educational experience in ways appropriate to the school community. It should be emphasized that approved supplementary materials are not *required* to be used in every classroom. Rather, the goal is to provide a range of materials from which teachers may *choose* to enrich the learning experience. ... Approval of the three books at issue in this case would therefore not have meant that all teachers were obliged to use them or even that they were strongly encouraged to use them. Rather, it would have meant that teachers *could* use them if this were required to meet the needs of the particular children in their classroom. However, without the Board's approval of these or equivalent materials, teachers who

have students from same-sex parented families might be left without resources to assist them in having their particular families discussed and understood.

· · ·

V. The Board's Decision

[43] The story begins in December 1996 and January 1997, when Mr. James Chamberlain, a Kindergarten teacher in the Surrey School District, asked for approval of the three books here in question.

· · ·

[50] On April 24, 1997, the Board passed the resolution here at issue declining to approve the three books. The resolution provides:

> THAT the Board, under Policy #8800—*Recommended Learning Resources and Library Resources*, not approve the use of the following three (3) learning resources:
>
> Grade Level K-1 Personal Planning
> - Elwin, R., & Paulse, M. (1990). *Asha's Mums.*
> - Newman, L. (1991). *Belinda's Bouquet.*
> - Valentine, J. (1994). *One Dad, Two Dads, Brown Dad, Blue Dads.*

The effect of this resolution was that the three books could not form part of the family life education curriculum taught in Kindergarten and Grade One classrooms.

[51] The chambers judge found that parental concern over the portrayal of same-sex parented families in the K-1 classroom was the overarching consideration in the Board's decision not to approve the books. She concluded that the Board's decision was based on concerns that the books would conflict with some parents' views on same-sex relationships ... . The Board's view was that addressing the subject of same sex relationships in Kindergarten and Grade One classes would raise sensitive issues for parents, and weight must be given to their concerns.

[52] More specifically, the Board was concerned that the use of the three books in the classroom might teach values to children divergent to those taught at home, confusing the children with inconsistent values. ...

[53] This argument, referred to as "cognitive dissonance," tied in with a second concern, "age appropriateness." The Board expressed the view that five- and six-year-old children in the K-1 classroom do not have the ability to resolve divergent moral lessons, and that children might be provoked to ask questions on subjects that parents feel should not be discussed at such a young age. For this reason, approving the three books would not be keeping with the best interests of the child.

· · ·

VI. Application of the Standard to the Impugned Decision

[56] Was the Board's decision not to approve the three books reasonable? As I discussed, the Board's decision will be unreasonable if the Board proceeded in a manner that took it outside the constraints intended by the legislature. In my view, the Board's decision was unreasonable in this sense.

· · ·

[58] The Board's first error was to violate the principles of secularism and tolerance in s. 76 of the *School Act*. Instead of proceeding on the basis of respect for all types of families, the Superintendent and the Board proceeded on an exclusionary philosophy. They acted on the concern of certain parents about the morality of same-sex relationships, without considering the interest of same-sex parented families and the children who belong to them in receiving equal recognition and respect in the school system. The Board was not permitted to reject the books simply because certain parents found the relationships depicted in them controversial or objectionable.

[59] As discussed earlier, the religious origin of the parents' objections is not in itself fatal to the Board's decision. The requirement of secularism in s. 76 does not preclude decisions motivated in whole or in part by religious considerations, provided they are otherwise within the Board's powers. It simply signals the need for educational decisions and policies, whatever their motivation, to respect the multiplicity of religious and moral views that are held by families in the school community. It follows that the fact that some parents and Board members may have been motivated by religious views is of no moment. What matters is whether the Board's decision was unreasonable in the context of the educational scheme mandated by the legislature.

[The Court found that the Board's second error was to depart from its own regulations made pursuant to ministerial order as to how decisions on supplementary resources should be made.]

[64] The argument based on cognitive dissonance essentially asserts that children should not be exposed to information and ideas with which their parents disagree. This claim stands in tension with the curriculum's objective of promoting an understanding of all types of families. The curriculum requires that all children be made aware of the array of family models that exist in our society, and that all be able to discuss their particular family model in the classroom.

· · ·

[66] Exposure to some cognitive dissonance is arguably necessary if children are to be taught what tolerance itself involves. As my colleague points out, the demand for tolerance cannot be interpreted as the demand to approve of another person's beliefs or practices. When we ask people to be tolerant of others, we do not ask them to abandon their personal convictions. We merely ask them to respect the rights, values and ways of being of those who may not share those convictions. The belief that others are entitled to equal respect depends, not on the belief that their values are right, but on the belief that they have a claim to equal respect regardless of whether they are right. Learning about tolerance is therefore learning that other people's entitlement to respect from us does not depend on whether their views accord with our own. Children cannot learn this unless they are exposed to views that differ from those they are taught at home.

[67] The Board's concern with age-appropriateness was similarly misplaced. The Board's regulation on appropriate selection criteria requires it to consider the age-appropriateness of proposed supplementary materials. However, here the curriculum itself designated the subject as age-appropriate by stating that *all* types of families found in the

community should be discussed by K-1 students, including same-sex parented families. The Board was not entitled to substitute its contrary view.

· · ·

[69] It is suggested that, while the message of the books may be unobjectionable, the books will lead children to ask questions of their parents that may be inappropriate for the K-1 level and difficult for parents to answer. Yet on the record before us, it is hard to see how the materials will raise questions which would not in any event be raised by the acknowledged existence of same-sex parented families in the K-1 parent population, or in the broader world in which these children live. The only *additional* message of the materials appears to be the message of tolerance. Tolerance is always age-appropriate.

· · ·

[73] I conclude that the Board's decision not to approve the proposed books depicting same-sex parented families was unreasonable because the Board failed to act in accordance with the *School Act*. ...

[74] I would allow the appeal with costs throughout to the appellants and remand the question of whether the books should be approved to the Board, to be considered according to the criteria laid out in the Board's own regulation, the curriculum guidelines and the broad principles of tolerance and non-sectarianism underlying the *School Act*.

[LeBel J wrote separate reasons concurring with the result reached by McLachlin CJC.]

GONTHIER and BASTARACHE JJ (dissenting): ... [76] Based on the nature of the decision being reviewed, the appropriate standard of review for such a decision and an examination of the totality of the context, I am of the view that this appeal ought to be dismissed. ... I am of the view that the decision was *intra vires* the School Board under the *School Act* and was clearly reasonable. The practice of approving or not approving books is clearly within the purview of the School Board's authority, the decision is consistent with a proper understanding of s. 76 of that Act (i.e. the decision accords with a correct understanding of "strictly secular and non-sectarian principles" and does not offend the requirement that "[t]he highest morality must be inculcated"), the considerations taken into account by the School Board were appropriate, and the decision is respectful of ss. 2(a), 2(b) and 15 of the *Canadian Charter of Rights and Freedoms*.

· · ·

[79] ... I am of the view that when one examines the totality of the context, the disagreement [between the parties] is actually about the appropriate way, in the K-1 classrooms of Surrey, BC, to teach and guarantee tolerance and non-discrimination of all persons in a way which respects the rights of parents to raise their children in accordance with their conscience, religious or otherwise. In my view, it is obvious that *Charter* values are to be respected in the school context generally. That context, however, involves a need to respect both the right of homosexual persons to be free from discrimination and parental rights to make the decisions they deem necessary to ensure the well-being and moral education of their children. ... Given ... that there is generally a shared commitment to *Charter* values and to actual non-discrimination in the school context more broadly, this case truly shows itself to be a question of balancing or accommodation, a question of choosing "ways and means" within policy implementation in a school context.

. . .

[81] The Surrey area is a culturally and religiously diverse community. It has large Protestant and Catholic Christian communities, including a large Evangelical Christian community. It also has a Sikh population of over 50,000 persons, the largest Muslim community in British Columbia, and a Hindu community.

. . .

[102] While this case specifically concerns the non-approval of particular books by an elected school board, it more generally raises contextual issues concerning the right of parents to raise their children in accordance with their conscience, religious or otherwise. In my view, the general nature of the interplay of the roles of parents and the state is clear: "The common law has long recognized that parents are in the best position to take care of their children and make all the decisions necessary to ensure their well-being": *B.(R.) v. Children's Aid Society of Metropolitan Toronto*, [1995] 1 SCR 315 [122 DLR (4th) 1], at para. 83. Thus, parents are clearly the primary actors, while the state plays a secondary, complementary role.

[Reflecting the paramount parental role, the Court has construed the nature of the authority that schools and teachers have over children as a delegated authority.]

[112] The notion of a school's authority being "delegated," if it permits the parental control response of removing a child from the public school system, also entails that parents must be guaranteed the role of having input with regard to the values which their children will receive in school. This is generally brought about by electing representatives who will develop consensus and govern on matters pertaining to public education, which may occur at the provincial level and at the local level. ...

. . .

[118] ... [T]he School Board, acting in the capacity of approving or not-approving "educational resource materials" which are complementary to the provincially approved materials, is acting as an elected representative body. As will be discussed below, the School Board's criteria for approving complementary "educational resource materials," not surprisingly, contained reference to concepts such as "age appropriateness" and envisaged that the existence of parental concern in the community would be a factor to be considered. These dimensions of the criteria obviously require the trustees to canvass local parental views as it is clear, from my discussion above, that parents are the best arbiters of what is in their children's best interests.

. . .

[122] ... [I]t would be inappropriate to embark upon a complete s. 15 analysis in the case at bar, as if to establish a direct breach of the *Charter* by the School Board. Although the appellants raise such issues before this Court, they were not addressed by the courts below, whose reasoning was based exclusively on the scope of the Board's authority under the Act. Thus, I would be reluctant, for instance, to deal with issues such as substantive discrimination under s. 15 and justification under s. 1 without the benefit of findings of fact specifically directed at them.

. . .

[125] ... I am of the view [however] that the relevant *Charter* values are incorporated in the requirements of the *School Act*, notably through the criterion of "highest morality" in s. 76. Therefore, I am satisfied that approaching this case as one of accommodation or balancing between competing *Charter* rights adequately addresses the impact of the *Charter*.

[126] The *Charter* reflects a commitment to equality, protects all persons from discrimination, protects the rights of all Canadians to exercise their religious freedom and freedom of conscience, and also protects freedom of expression. Thus, persons who believe that homosexual behaviour, manifest in the conduct of persons involved in same-sex relationships, is immoral or not morally equivalent to heterosexual behaviour, for religious or non-religious reasons, are entitled to hold and express that view. On the other hand, persons who believe that homosexual behaviour is morally equivalent to heterosexual behaviour are also entitled to hold and express that view. Both groups, however, are not entitled to act in a discriminatory manner. Thus, this case engages the s. 15, s. 2(a) and s. 2(b) rights of *both* the appellants and the parents who expressed their views to the School Board—and all must be considered as imported into the review of the School Board's decision. [Reference is then made to *Trinity Western University v. British Columbia College of Teachers*, [2001] 1 SCR 772, 199 DLR (4th) 1.]

[127] Many of the parents who signed affidavits supporting the respondent specifically stated that they do not discriminate and are not "homophobic." ... Adults in Canadian society who think that homosexual behaviour is immoral can still be staunchly committed to non-discrimination. In the case at bar, there is, in my view, no evidence that the parents who felt that the Three Books were inappropriate for five- and six-year-old children fostered discrimination against persons in any way. Many persons, religious and not, justify this distinction by drawing a line ... between beliefs held about persons and beliefs held about the conduct of persons.

· · ·

[129] This Court has recognized that there are many religious organizations within our Canadian community, and that their diversity must be respected. To this I add that there are many other organizations within civil society, including those such as GALE or the intervener EGALE, which espouse particular views about homosexuality which, while not being "religious" *per se*, are clearly particular normative claims about "beliefs." The views of these institutions of civil society must also be respected.

[130] ... In an instance where belief claims seem to conflict, there will be a need to strike a balance, either by defining the rights so as to avoid a conflict or within a s. 1 justification. In the case at bar, the recognition of the value of each rights claim is adequately respected in the balance or accommodation that was struck by the School Board: the Three Books portraying parents in same-sex relationships will not be employed in the two earliest grades, but this subject matter, like the issue of homosexuality as a general topic of human sexuality, is present in later aspects of the curriculum. Further, the failure to approve the Three Books does not necessarily preclude the issue of same-sex parents being discussed in the classroom ... .

· · ·

[133] It was submitted before this Court in the case at bar that the best interests of children includes education about "tolerance." I, obviously, agree. ... But to suggest that

"tolerance" requires the mandatory approval of the Three Books, which is what the appellants seek as a remedy, begs the question as to what the books portray and the capability of children to receive the messages in the books in a manner which is consistent with the parental determination of what is in their best interests. This is a question regarding which reasonable parents disagree. ...

[134] I also note that language espousing "tolerance" ought not be employed as a cloak for the means of obliterating disagreement. ... In my view, the relationship between s. 2 and s. 15 of the *Charter*, in a truly free society, must permit persons who respect the fundamental and inherent dignity of others and who do not discriminate, to still disagree with others and even disapprove of the conduct or beliefs of others. Otherwise, claims for "respect" or "recognition" or "tolerance," where such language becomes a constitutionally mandated proxy for "acceptance," tend to obliterate disagreement.

· · ·

[139] ... [I]n my view, the dual requirements that education be "secular" and "nonsectarian" refer to keeping the schools free from inculcation or indoctrination in the precepts of any religion, and do not prevent persons with religiously based moral positions on matters of public policy from participating in deliberations concerning moral education in public schools. Regardless of the personal convictions of individual members, the reasons invoked by the Board for refusing to approve the books—notably the fact that parents in the community held certain religious and moral views and the need to respect their constitutional right to freedom of religion and their primary role as educators of their children—raise secular concerns that could properly be considered by the Board.

· · ·

[141] ... [I]n the implementation of this general *School Act*-mandated policy of promoting tolerance, the need to strive for an appropriate balance between competing *Charter* rights—in the case at bar, the parents' freedom of religion under s. 2(a) and the right of same-sex couples and their children to equality under s. 15—remains a relevant consideration in the exercise by the School Board of its powers to approve complementary educational resources for local use. Thus, the question becomes whether the Board struck such an appropriate balance between these competing rights, taking into account the entire context, including the contents of the curriculum in its entirety, the framework established by the *School Act* and the nature of the Board's own authority as a delegate of the parents' right to educate their children. ...

· · ·

[156] The School Board had two choices: to approve or not to approve, that was the question. The appellants' argument seems to tend towards the conclusion that the School Board had no choice but to approve the books. What is a better educational choice, permit the Three Books to be taught in K-1 against the wishes of some parents and then provide for the exclusion of certain children from the class as suggested by the appellants, or to teach a general lesson about tolerance and respect for people by less controversial means and leave the issue of parents in same-sex relationships and homosexuality for a time when students are better positioned to address the issues involved and better positioned to reconcile the potentially incongruous messages they may be receiving on this subject matter? The choice is difficult. The choice, however, was *specifically intended to be made locally*, as the *School Act* envisages.

[Gonthier J went on to review the Ministerial directives dealing with the family life education curriculum and concluded that the considerations taken into account by the Board in reaching its decision not to approve the books were appropriate. He found that the totality of the context, including the Board's strong anti-discrimination policy, supported the conclusion that the Charter values of equality and non-discrimination were being fostered by the School Board.]

NOTES AND QUESTIONS

1. It is sometimes argued that religious values should be excluded from public debate and decision making because state law must be based on reasons that are accessible to all members of the community. Because religious beliefs rest on faith or family and cultural socialization, they lie beyond the scope of reasonable public debate and cannot provide a publicly acceptable basis for law making. Public action must then be based exclusively on non-religious values and concerns. Yet, because religion matters so deeply to its adherents and is the foundation for their views about justice and the collective good, it may be unreasonable or unrealistic to expect people to leave their beliefs behind when they participate in public life. It is sometimes argued that it is acceptable for a citizen or politician to be motivated by religious values when making public policy decisions provided that he or she is able to offer a secular reason for those decisions. Public decision-making about the rules of collective life is separated from personal commitment to spiritual truth or cultural identity by the requirement that the former be framed in non-religious terms. Is this fair or realistic?

2. The majority in *Chamberlain* based its decision to invalidate the school board's resolution on statutory interpretation—that is, on the wording of the BC *School Act* and, in particular, the requirement of adherence to strictly secular principles. The majority did not deal with the constitutional challenge to the resolution based on s. 2(b). How do you think the majority would have decided the freedom of religion claim apart from the statutory requirement of secularism in the BC *School Act*? Could the resolution be considered a coercive state imposition of religion? Under a Charter analysis, could other Charter claims also have come into play—for example, claims by same-sex parents and their children that the resolution violated their equality rights under s. 15 of the Charter; or claims by religious parents that the use of the books at issue in the classroom would violate their rights of freedom of religion? Note that Gonthier and Bastarache JJ, in their dissenting reasons upholding the resolution, did discuss the Charter values at stake and concluded that the resolution reflected an appropriate balance between the values of equality and freedom of religion.

3. The *B.(R.)* case relied on by the dissenting judges in *Chamberlain* to establish the right of parents to make important decisions about the rearing and education of their children is discussed further in the next section of this chapter, Section V, Religious Families and Religious Communities, and also in Chapter 22, Life, Liberty and Security of the Person.

4. In Canada, s. 93 of the *Constitution Act, 1867* provides for government-funded religious schools. What does the inclusion of this provision say about how state support for religion is dealt with in our constitutional framework? Section 93 will be explored in more detail in the next section of this chapter, Section V, which focuses on the issue of religious education.

V. RELIGIOUS FAMILIES AND RELIGIOUS COMMUNITIES

The accommodation issue becomes more complicated when the religious community is not simply seeking an exemption from a law that interferes with a *particular* religious practice, but is instead making a larger claim to govern its affairs according to its religious legal order, either with state support or, more often, simply without state interference. In Canada, many religious groups seek to regulate their internal affairs on the basis of their understanding of religious law, even when that law is inconsistent with state law or public values. Should the state interfere with the decisions religious parents make about how to educate and rear their children? Should it enforce a contract dealing with a religious subject, such as the obligation under Islamic law of a husband to pay *mahr* (a dowry) to his wife; or enforce arbitration decisions that are based on religious law? Should the state intervene when the husband in a Jewish marriage refuses to give his wife a *get*, a religious divorce, thereby preventing her from remarrying within the faith; or when someone is expelled from a Hutterite community, where all property is collectively held?

We will begin by looking at parental choices about the religious education of their children and the ways in which constitutional law has responded to those choices. It is not surprising that many of the leading freedom-of-religion cases involve the right of parents to make religiously based decisions concerning their children. The parent–child relationship exposes most clearly the tension in our conception of religious belief or commitment. Religious commitment is viewed as both a matter of choice—that is, something the individual chooses or adopts—and identity—that is, something that the individual is socialized into or nurtured within and that forms part of his or her identity or group membership. The education of children seems to give rise to some of the most contentious freedom-of-religion issues. It involves competing private and public interests or claims: on the one hand, the claim of parents to determine the basic upbringing of their children and to transmit their faith to their children and, on the other, the sometimes competing claim of the state, on behalf of the larger community, to teach children important community values such as tolerance and respect and to encourage children's development as thoughtful and informed citizens. The issues become even more complicated when we begin to think of children as having their own rights claims.

The issue of religion in the schools has a number of closely related parts. The first, discussed in the cases above, including *Chamberlain*, concerns the role of religion in the public or common schools. The second concerns state oversight of private schooling, and the third concerns public funding of religious schools.

The issue of state oversight of private education arose in *R v. Jones*, [1986] 2 SCR 284, 31 DLR (4th) 569. In that case, Alberta's *School Act* allowed children to be exempted from the requirement of compulsory public school attendance if either (1) they were attending a school approved by the provincial department of education, or (2) the department or school board certified that the pupil was under "efficient instruction" at home or elsewhere. Jones, a Baptist pastor who was educating his children in a small school in the basement of his church, refused to seek departmental approval of his school or to apply for a certificate that would exempt his children from compulsory public school attendance. He argued that applying to the state for permission to do what he was authorized to do by God violated his religious convictions and thus infringed his s. 2(a) right to freedom of religion. The Court dismissed his claim, with the majority finding a justified infringement of freedom of religion and Wilson J, in dissent, being unwilling to find even an infringement of freedom of religion.

Jones leaves many unanswered questions about state control of private education. Should parents be able to prevent their children from being exposed to values such as tolerance by withdrawing them from the public school system and placing them in a private school or schooling them at home? Does freedom of religion give parents the right to insulate their children from competing or critical views? What kind of intervention or supervision of private education by the state is appropriate or practical? Should the state intervene if a private school is teaching racist or homophobic beliefs? Should the state require private schools to teach sex education or evolution? Are the freedom-of-religion claims of children subsumed within those of their parents; or do children have independent rights that allow them, at least at some point in the future, to choose a different religious path from their parents? If so, can the state assert a claim to protect these rights by exposing children to different points of view in the course of their education?

The third aspect of religion and education, the public funding of religious schools, is dealt with in the material on s. 93 of the *Constitution Act, 1867* and in *Adler*, below.

NOTE: SECTION 93 OF THE CONSTITUTION ACT, 1867 AND THE PUBLIC FUNDING OF RELIGIOUS SCHOOLS

Section 93 of the *Constitution Act, 1867* provides as follows:

> 93. In and for each Province the Legislature may exclusively make Laws in relation to Education, subject and according to the following Provisions:
>
> (1) Nothing in any such Law shall prejudicially affect any Right or Privilege with respect to Denominational Schools which any Class of Persons have by Law in the Province at the Union:
>
> (2) All the Powers, Privileges and Duties at the Union by Law conferred and imposed in Upper Canada on the Separate Schools and School Trustees of the Queen's Roman Catholic Subjects shall be and the same are hereby extended to the Dissentient Schools of the Queen's Protestant and Roman Catholic Subjects in Quebec:
>
> (3) Where in any Province a System of Separate or Dissentient Schools exists by Law at the Union or is thereafter established by the Legislature of the Province, an Appeal shall lie to the Governor General in Council from any Act or Decision of any Provincial Authority affecting any Right or Privilege of the Protestant or Roman Catholic Minority of the Queen's Subjects in relation to Education:
>
> (4) In case any such Provincial Law as from Time to Time seems to the Governor General in Council requisite for the due Execution of the Provisions of this Section is not made, or in case any Decision of the Governor General in Council on any Appeal under this Section is not duly executed by the proper Provincial Authority in that Behalf, then and in every such Case, and as far only as the Circumstances of each Case require, the Parliament of Canada may make remedial Laws for the due Execution of the Provisions of this Section and of any Decision of the Governor General in Council under this Section.

While s. 93 gives the provinces general jurisdiction in relation to education, subsections (2), (3) and (4) limit that power by guaranteeing the rights and privileges of certain denominational schools.

In the following passage from *Trinity Western University v. British Columbia College of Teachers*, [2001] 1 SCR 772, 199 DLR (4th) 1, at SCR 813, the Supreme Court of Canada reiterated the view expressed in previous judgments that the protection of separate religious schools was a compromise or agreement necessary to bring about Confederation:

> [34] ... Furthermore, s. 93 of the *Constitution Act, 1867* enshrined religious public education rights into our Constitution, as part of the historic compromise which made Confederation possible. Section 17 of the *Alberta Act*, RSC 1985, App. II, No. 20, and *Saskatchewan Act*, RSC 1985, App. II, No. 21, s. 22 of the *Manitoba Act*, 1870, RSC 1985, App. II, No. 8, and Term 17 of the *Terms of Union of Newfoundland* with Canada as confirmed by the *Newfoundland Act*, RSC 1985, App. II, No. 32 were to the same effect.

As the Court notes, the rights of religious schools were altered by constitutional amendment in Newfoundland in 1998 and eliminated in Quebec in 1997. These rights remain in effect in Ontario, Alberta, Saskatchewan, and Manitoba. The early history of the treatment of denominational school rights in Manitoba is dealt with in Chapter 4, The Late Nineteenth Century: The Canadian Courts Under the Influence.

In Ontario at the time of Confederation a separate Roman Catholic school system was established by law alongside the much larger public system. In the early 1900s the public system was reorganized and extended to include high school grades or courses. However, the government of Ontario denied funding to the separate Catholic school system for the teaching of high school courses (and it prohibited the separate schools from teaching such courses). This refusal by the government was challenged in the courts by one of the separate school boards. The board argued that under s. 93(1) it had a right to teach these courses and to receive funding in the same manner as a public school board. This argument was rejected in *Tiny Roman Catholic Separate School Trustees v. The King*, [1928] AC 363, in which the Privy Council ruled that in 1867 the separate schools in Ontario had no existing legal right to funding for high school courses.

In 1986 the government of Ontario decided to extend funding to the separate school system to cover all the high school grades. In *Reference re Bill 30, an Act to amend the Education Act (Ontario)*, [1987] 1 SCR 1148; 40 DLR (4th) 18, the Supreme Court of Canada considered whether this extension of funding to the Catholic schools but not to other religious schools violated s. 2(a) and/or s. 15 of the Charter. Although s. 29 of the Charter provides that "[n]othing in this Charter abrogates from any rights or privileges guaranteed by or under the Constitution of Canada in respect of denominational, separate or dissentient schools," it was argued by those opposing the funding that s. 29 was not applicable in this case because, as had been established by the *Tiny* case, the separate school system did not have a constitutional right to funding for the later grades of high school. However, a majority of the Court thought that the *Tiny* decision was wrong and that "Roman Catholic separate school supporters had at Confederation a right or privilege by law, to have their children receive an appropriate education which could include instruction at the secondary school level and that such right or privilege is therefore constitutionally guaranteed under s. 93(1) of the *Constitution Act, 1867*." Moreover, all the members of the Court agreed that regardless of whether s. 93(1) guarantees secondary school funding to the separate schools, s. 93(3) specifically empowers the provincial government to grant new rights and privileges to separate or dissentient schools and that the exercise of this power could not be seen as a violation of the Charter. Wilson J wrote:

> [I think it is clear] that the rights or privileges protected by s. 93(1) are immune from Charter review under s. 29 of the Charter. ... What is less clear is whether s. 29 of the Charter was required in order to achieve that result. In my view, it was not. I believe it was put there simply to emphasize that the special treatment guaranteed by the constitution to denominational, separate or dissentient schools, even if it sits uncomfortably with the concept of equality embodied in the Charter because not available to other schools, is nevertheless not impaired by the Charter. It was never intended, in my opinion, that the Charter could be used to invalidate other provisions of the Constitution, particularly a provision such as s. 93 which represented a fundamental part of the Confederation compromise. Section 29, in my view, is present in the Charter only for greater certainty, at least in so far as the Province of Ontario is concerned.
>
> ... The s. 93(3) rights and privileges are not guaranteed in the sense that the s. 91(1) rights and privileges are guaranteed, *i.e.*, in the sense that the legislature which gave them cannot later pass laws which prejudicially affect them. But they are insulated from Charter attack as legislation enacted pursuant to the plenary power in relation to education granted to the provincial legislatures as part of the Confederation compromise. ... [T]he province is master of its own house when it legislates under its plenary power in relation to denominational, separate or dissentient schools. This was the agreement at Confederation and, in my view, it was not displaced by the enactment of the *Constitution Act, 1982.* ... I would conclude, therefore, that even if Bill 30 is supportable only under the province's plenary power and s. 93(3), it is insulated from Charter review.

Estey J made the point in this way:

> The power to establish or add to a system of Roman Catholic separate schools found in s. 93(3) expressly contemplates that the province may legislate with respect to a religion-based school system funded from the public treasury. Although the Charter is intended to constrain the exercise of legislative power conferred under the *Constitution Act, 1867* where the delineated rights of individual members of the community are adversely affected, it cannot be interpreted as rendering unconstitutional distinctions that are expressly permitted by the *Constitution Act, 1867.*

In the *Adler* case, which follows, the appellants, who were seeking the extension of public funding to other religious schools in Ontario, did not simply repeat the argument rejected in the *Reference re Bill 30* case that funding of Catholic schools but not other religious schools breached s. 2(a) and s. 15. They also argued that funding "secular" public schools but not religious schools breached s. 2(a) and/or s. 15.

Adler v. Ontario
[1996] 3 SCR 609, 140 DLR (4th) 385

IACOBUCCI J (Lamer CJC, La Forest, Gonthier, and Cory JJ concurring): This appeal involves the question of whether the current education funding scheme in the Province of Ontario violates the appellants' religious and equality rights as guaranteed by ss. 2(a) and 15 of the *Canadian Charter of Rights and Freedoms.* ...

Background

The appellants are parents who, by reason of religious or conscientious beliefs, send their children to private religious schools. The first five appellants (the "Adler appellants") are parents of children attending Jewish day schools. The "Elgersma appellants" are four parents whose children attend independent Christian schools, and a non-profit corporation, the Ontario Alliance of Christian School Societies ("OACSS"), which is active in the promotion of Christian elementary and secondary education.

The Adler appellants sought a declaration that the non-funding of Jewish day schools in Ontario was unconstitutional. Full-time Jewish day schools have existed in Ontario since 1949 and now have an enrolment of approximately 10,000 students. The schools provide Jewish religious instruction and Judaic studies in addition to secular studies at both the elementary and high school levels in conformity with Ministry of Education guidelines, although they receive no direct funding from the Government of Ontario. Their costs are met through tuition fees, funds raised by the schools, and other fund-raising activities of the Jewish community.

The Elgersma appellants sought, along with other relief, a declaration that the non-funding of independent Christian schools infringed their rights as guaranteed under the Charter. There are now 73 Christian schools in Ontario. Membership in each individual school society is open to all adult, active Christian church members who assent to the society's aims and confessional principles, who pay the prescribed membership fee, and who are willing to be actively involved in the work of the society. Most society members belong to the Christian Reformed Church. OACSS member schools, like Jewish day schools, do not receive government funding. Funds are obtained from parental tuition pledges, community donations, and other fund-raising activities.

· · ·

Analysis

As I see the issues before us, this case is to be resolved with reference to s. 93 of the *Constitution Act, 1867*. Section 93 grants to the provinces the power to legislate with regard to education. This grant is subject to certain restrictive conditions, among them s. 93(1) which provides that no law may prejudicially affect any right or privilege with respect to denominational schools which any class of persons had at the time of Union. The effect of this subsection is to entrench constitutionally a special status for such classes of persons, granting them rights which are denied to others.

The appellants advance, in essence, two Charter arguments. The first is that s. 2(a)'s guarantee of freedom of religion requires the Province of Ontario to provide public funding for independent religious schools. The second is that, by funding Roman Catholic separate schools and secular public schools at the same time as it denies funding to independent religious schools, the province is discriminating against the appellants on the basis of religion contrary to s. 15(1).

I propose to deal with these arguments in turn. As will be explained more fully below, it is my opinion that the s. 2(a) claim fails because any claim to public support for religious education must be grounded in s. 93(1) which is a "comprehensive code" of denominational school rights. With regard to the appellants' equality argument, this claim fails because the funding of Roman Catholic separate schools and public schools is within the contemplation of the terms of s. 93 and is, therefore, immune from Charter scrutiny.

A. The Appellants' Claims with Regard to Section 2(a) of the Charter

In my view, any analysis of denominational school rights must take as its starting point the guarantees contained in s. 93(1). If the rights claimed are not found in this subsection, I fail to see how other sections of the Constitution, in particular s. 2(a) of the Charter, can be used to enlarge upon s. 93's constitutionally blessed scheme for public funding of denominational schools.

Section 93 is the product of an historical compromise which was a crucial step along the road leading to Confederation. As Gonthier J said in *Reference re Education Act (Que.)*, [1993] 2 SCR 511 at p. 529, 105 DLR (4th) 266 (SCC):

> Section 93 is unanimously recognized as the expression of a desire for political compromise. It served to moderate religious conflicts which threatened the birth of the Union.

Without this "solemn pact," this "cardinal term" of Union, there would have been no Confederation. ...

As a child born of historical exigency, s. 93 does not represent a guarantee of fundamental freedoms. Beetz J stated, in *Greater Montreal Protestant School Board v. Quebec (Attorney-General)*, [1989] 1 SCR 377 at p. 401, 57 DLR (4th) 521:

> While it may be rooted in notions of tolerance and diversity, the exception in s. 93 is not a blanket affirmation of freedom of religion or freedom of conscience ... [and] should not be construed as a Charter human right or freedom or, to use the expression of Professor Peter Hogg, a "small bill of rights for the protection of minority religious groups" ... .
>
> • • •

Section 93(1) confers a ... privileged status on those religious minorities which, at the time of Confederation, enjoyed legal rights with respect to denominational schools. In *Reference re Bill 30 [an Act to amend the Education Act (Ont.)*, [1987] 1 SCR 1148, 40 DLR (4th) 18] Wilson J acknowledged at p. 1197 that this special status may "sit uncomfortably with the concept of equality embodied in the Charter," but it must nonetheless be respected.

• • •

[Section] 93 is a comprehensive code with respect to denominational school rights. As a result, s. 2(a) of the Charter cannot be used to enlarge this comprehensive code. Given that the appellants cannot bring themselves within the terms of s. 93's guarantees, they have no claim to public funding for their schools. To emphasize, in Ontario, s. 93(1) entrenches certain rights with respect to public funding of religious education. However, these rights are limited to those which were enjoyed at the time of Confederation. To decide otherwise by accepting the appellants' claim that s. 2(a) requires public funding of their religious schools would be to hold one section of the Constitution violative of another—a result which *Reference re Bill 30* tells us to avoid, as will be further discussed below.

B. The Appellants' Claims with Regard to Section 15(1) of the Charter

(a) Section 15(1) and Roman Catholic Separate Schools

In *Reference re Bill 30*, Wilson J, writing for the majority, upheld Ontario legislation which extended full funding to the province's Roman Catholic separate schools.

• • •

Wilson J ... address[ed] the claim that the government's choice to fund Roman Catholic separate schools but not other religious schools contravened s. 15(1) of the Charter. The Adler and Elgersma appellants are advancing what amounts to the same argument in the present case. Wilson J rejected this argument. ... [A summary of Wilson J's reasoning is found above in the note preceding the *Adler* case.]

Following the same line of reasoning used by Wilson J in the *Reference re Bill 30*, I find that public funding for the province's separate schools cannot form the basis for the appellants' Charter claim.

(b) The Appellants' Section 15(1) Claims and Public Schools

The appellants advanced a further argument which was that, even assuming that Roman Catholic separate schools are given a privileged place in our constitutional scheme, public schools are given no such protection. According to this argument, the fact that the government funds public schools but not private religious schools is analogous to the government funding, for example, private Christian schools but not private Islamic schools. As the reasoning goes, public schools are not a part of the scheme envisioned by s. 93 and are, thus, open to Charter challenge.

In my view, this argument is mistaken in supposing that public schools are not contemplated by the terms of s. 93, as it applies to Ontario. On the contrary, the public school system is an integral part of the s. 93 scheme. When the province funds public schools, it is, in the words of Wilson J in *Reference re Bill 30*, at p. 1198, legislating "pursuant to the plenary power in relation to education granted to the provincial legislatures as part of the Confederation compromise." A closer examination of s. 93, in particular s. 93(1), as it applies to the Province of Ontario, will help to illustrate that the public school system is impliedly, but nonetheless clearly, contemplated by the terms of that section.

In order to claim the protection of s. 93, it must be shown that there was a right or privilege with respect to denominational schooling which was enjoyed by a class of persons, by law, at the time of union. ... Thus, for Ontario, s. 93(1) requires an examination of the law as it stood in 1867, with regard to denominational schooling. ...

An Act to restore to Roman Catholics in Upper Canada certain rights in respect to Separate Schools, S. Prov. C. 1863 (2nd Sess.), c. 5 ("*Scott Act*"), was the last piece of legislation relating to denominational schools in Upper Canada enacted before Confederation. In essence, what this legislation did was to define the rights and privileges of Roman Catholic separate schools in terms of the rights and privileges of the province's common schools. The preamble reads:

WHEREAS it is just and proper to restore to Roman Catholics in Upper Canada certain rights which they formerly enjoyed in respect to Separate Schools, and *to bring the provi-*

sions of the Law respecting Separate Schools more in harmony with the provisions of the Law respecting Common Schools ... . [Emphasis added.]

... What the relevant pre-Confederation legislation did was to equate the rights and privileges of separate schools to those of public schools. The result is that public schools are part and parcel of s. 93's comprehensive code. Accordingly, as I noted above, public schools are impliedly but nonetheless clearly within the terms of the regime set up by s. 93. ...

... Therefore, the public school system is an integral part of the Confederation compromise and, consequently, receives a protection against constitutional or Charter attack.

This protection exists despite the fact that public school rights are not themselves constitutionally entrenched. It is the province's plenary power to legislate with regard to public schools, which are open to all members of society, without distinction, that is constitutionally entrenched. This is what creates the immunity from Charter scrutiny. To paraphrase Wilson J, in *Reference re Bill 30, supra*, at p. 1198, funding for public schools is insulated from Charter attack as legislation enacted pursuant to the plenary education power granted to the provincial legislatures as part of the Confederation compromise. If the plenary power is so insulated, then so is the proper exercise of it.

One thing should, however, be made clear. The province remains free to exercise its plenary power with regard to education in whatever way it sees fit, subject to the restrictions relating to separate schools imposed by s. 93(1). Section 93 grants to the province of Ontario the power to legislate with regard to public schools and separate schools. However, nothing in these reasons should be taken to mean that the province's legislative power is limited to these two school systems. In other words, the province could, if it so chose, pass legislation extending funding to denominational schools other than Roman Catholic schools without infringing the rights guaranteed to Roman Catholic separate schools under s. 93(1). ... However, an ability to pass such legislation does not amount to an obligation to do so. To emphasize, s. 93 defines the extent of the obligations of the province to set up and fund denominational schools when public schools are established. In this respect, it is a comprehensive code thereby excluding a different or broader obligation regarding denominational schools, while not restricting the plenary power of the province to establish and fund such other schools as it may decide.

Furthermore, it should be pointed out that all of this is not to say that no legislation in respect of public schools is subject to Charter scrutiny, just as this court's ruling in *Reference re Bill 30* did not hold that no legislation in respect of separate schools was subject to Charter scrutiny. Rather, it is merely the fact of their existence ... that is immune from Charter challenge. Whenever the government decides to go beyond the confines of this special mandate, the Charter could be successfully invoked to strike down the legislation in question.

For these reasons, I find that the funding of public schools coupled with the non-funding of private religious schools is immune from Charter attack and therefore does not violate s. 15(1) of the Charter. ...

SOPINKA J (Major J concurring): In this appeal the Adler appellants challenged the legislative scheme for the funding of public and Roman Catholic separate school education on two bases. First, they alleged that the funding of separate Roman Catholic schools creates a distinction and inequality that violates s. 2(a) and s. 15 of the *Canadian Charter of Rights and Freedoms*. Second, they submit that the funding of public schools while failing to fund independent religious schools constitutes a violation of these provisions. The Elgersma appellants limited their submissions to the second ground of attack.

With respect to the first ground advanced by the Adler appellants, the decision of this Court in the *Reference re Bill 30* ... is a complete answer. Legislation for the funding of separate schools is supported under both ss. 93(1) and 93(3) of the *Constitution Act, 1867*. In the *Reference re Bill 30*, this Court decided that legislation passed pursuant to these provisions was immune from Charter attack. On the other hand, legislation funding the public school system stands on a different footing. It is passed pursuant to the opening words of s. 93 conferring on the province a plenary power to legislate with respect to education. This power is no different from the heads of power contained in s. 92 of the *Constitution Act, 1867*. Like the latter, it is subject to the Charter. Nothing in the *Reference re Bill 30* suggests otherwise.

My colleague Justice Iacobucci would hold that s. 93 is a complete code with respect to denominational schools and that presumably the province is restricted to legislation that is mandated by s. 93(1) or permitted by s. 93(3). He concludes that this renders such legislation immune from s. 2(a) of the Charter but apparently not immune from s. 15. In my view, this wholly unwarranted restriction on the plenary power is supported by neither authority nor principle.

With respect to s. 15, my colleague finds that in certain respects and, in particular, with respect to funding, s. 93(1) can be interpreted to extend constitutional protection not only to "denominational schools" specified in the section but to public schools as well. I cannot agree with this proposition. My reasons, in summary, are as follows:

(1) The historic compromise which is embodied in s. 93 had as its purpose the protection of the religious schools of the minority, primarily Protestants in Quebec and Roman Catholics in Ontario. The majority schools needed no protection.

(2) Section 93 makes no mention of protection of the rights and privileges of the public schools.

(3) No decision of this Court or of any other court can be cited to support this proposition and all the authorities support the opposite conclusion.

(4) If s. 93 protects the rights and privileges of the public schools, then all rights and privileges enjoyed at Confederation must be included. There is no basis for concluding that while all rights and privileges of denominational schools are protected, the only privilege protected relating to public schools is funding.

(5) Entrenching rights and privileges of public schools relative to a benchmark of 1867 places the province in a strait-jacket which impedes the progressive reform of educational institutions.

· · ·

The Charter: Freedom of Religion

It is evident that there is some overlap between the claims based on s. 2(a) and s. 15 of the Charter. Under both sections, the appellants argue that the non-funding of private religious schools imposes an unfair burden on them. In both contexts, the argument is made that the appellants suffer an economic disadvantage in relation to parents who send their children to secular public schools. On the one hand, this economic burden is said to amount to an infringement of freedom of religion. On the other hand, this same burden is said to deny to the appellants the equal benefit of the law on grounds of religion, in breach of equality rights guaranteed under s. 15. During oral argument, it became increasingly difficult to identify whether a particular argument supported a claim under s. 2(a) or under s. 15.

. . .

[T]he appellants argue that the province's failure to fund private religious schools imposes an unconstitutional burden on their freedom of religion. It is thus the effect of the *Education Act* that is the source of the infringement. Much reliance is placed on *Edwards Books [and Art Ltd. v. The Queen*, [1986] 2 SCR 713, 35 DLR (4th) 1] in which Dickson CJC specified that s. 2(a) captures both indirect and direct coercion of religious beliefs.

In *Edwards Books* the purpose of Ontario's *Retail Business Holidays Act*, RSO 1980, c. 453, under challenge was to provide a common day of rest for retail workers, and therefore the purpose was not to coerce religious observance. However, this Court found that the *effect* of the Act imposed an economic burden on retailers whose sabbath was a day other than Sunday, relative to those retailers who observed a Sunday sabbath. In effect, the Act gave an advantage to Sunday sabbath observers by choosing their sabbath as a common day of rest, and burdened observers of a sabbath other than Sunday by forcing them to choose between closing their business an extra day or keeping their business open on their sabbath. ... [I]t is on the basis that the legislation had the effect of imposing different burdens on different religions vis-à-vis non-observers that a s. 2(a) infringement was found. ...

In the case of funding under the *Education Act*, private religious schools receive no state funding whereas public non-religious schools receive funding. By analogy to the situation in *Edwards Books*, then, all parents whose religion requires them to send their children to a private religious school charging tuition would be equally disadvantaged relative to parents who have the option of sending their children to state-funded public schools. All of the diverse religious groups represented by the appellants, and the many interveners on this appeal, suffer the same economic cost associated with sending their children to private religious schools. While a distinction is made between these religious groups and the separate Roman Catholic schools, this distinction is constitutionally mandated and cannot be the subject of a Charter attack. The legislation is not the source of any distinction amongst all the groups whose exercise of their religious freedom involves an economic cost. This situation is distinguishable from *Edwards Books*, where one religious group was suffering an additional burden not imposed on other religious groups vis-à-vis non-observers. On this account, the appellants have no complaint cognizable in law since the disadvantage they must bear is one flowing exclusively from their religious tenets.

In addition, failure to act in order to facilitate the practice of religion cannot be considered state interference with freedom of religion. The fact that no funding is provided for private religious education cannot be considered to infringe the appellants' freedom to educate their children in accordance with their religious beliefs where there is no restriction on religious schooling. As submitted by the intervener, the Canadian Civil Liberties Association, there are many spheres of government action which hold religious significance for religious believers. It does not follow that the government must pay for the religious dimensions of spheres in which it takes a role. If this flowed from s. 2(a), then religious marriages, religious corporations, and other religious community institutions such as churches and hospitals would all have a Charter claim to public funding. The same could also be said of the existing judicial system which is necessarily secular. The appellants' argument would lead to an obligation by the state to fund parallel religious justice systems founded on canon law or Talmudic law, for example. These are clearly untenable suggestions.

In conclusion, for the reasons given above, I am of the view that the failure to fund cannot constitute state interference with freedom of religion equivalent to a violation of s. 2(a) of the Charter. Moreover, the cost of sending their children to private religious schools is a natural cost of the appellants' religion and does not, therefore, constitute an infringement of their freedom of religion protected by s. 2(a) of the Charter.

[Sopinka J also rejected the s. 15 claim, finding that the *Education Act* did not draw a distinction, either directly or indirectly, on the basis of religion. He reasoned that although the appellants felt compelled to send their children to private school because of their religion and were thus unable to benefit from publicly funded schooling, this effect did not arise from the statute. Instead, it was a result of the appellant's religious beliefs in the face of a secular public school system mandated by s. 2(a) of the Charter.]

McLACHLIN J (dissenting in part): … I agree with Justice Iacobucci and Justice Sopinka that the lack of support to private schools violates neither [s. 2(a) nor s. 15], although for different reasons. …

A. Denial of Funding to Independent Religious Schools

1. Is Section 93 of the Constitution Act, 1867 an Answer to the Appellants' Charter Claim?

Before considering the Charter issues, it is necessary to determine whether s. 93 of the *Constitution Act, 1867* constitutes a code which ousts the operation of the Charter. I agree with Sopinka J that it does not. Section 93 requires Ontario to fund schools for the Roman Catholic minority in Ontario and requires Quebec to fund schools for the Protestant minority in Quebec. Neither its language nor its purpose suggests that it was intended to do more than guarantee school support for the Roman Catholic or Protestant minorities in the two provinces respectively. Provinces exercising their plenary powers to provide education services must, subject to this restriction, comply with the Charter.

2. Does the Failure to Fund Minority Religious Schools Constitute a Limit on the Guarantee of Freedom of Religion?

The appellants [argue] … that the failure to fund the minority religious schools imposes a burden on them not borne by persons of other religions or no religion, thereby infringing their freedom of religion.

· · ·

The argument rests on the proposition that the imposition of burdens on some religious minorities which people of other religions do not bear constitutes an infringement of freedom of religion. This Court's decisions in *R v. Big M Drug Mart Ltd.*, [1985] 1 SCR 295, 18 DLR (4th) 321 (SCC), and *R v. Edwards Books and Art Ltd.*, [1986] 2 SCR 713, 35 DLR (4th) 1 (SCC), contain statements that appear to support this proposition. ...

The burden complained of in this case is not one which constitutes an infringement of freedom of religion, in my view. The burden at issue in *Big M Drug Mart* and *Edwards Books* was a state prohibition on business operations which presented religious minorities with the option of either violating their religious tenets by operating on religious holidays or suffering the financial loss which would flow from closing their businesses on both their own religious holidays and the majoritarian holidays. Special burdens placed on religious minorities in the operation of their businesses have a venerable and infamous status in the annals of religious persecution. What was at stake in *Big M Drug Mart* and *Edwards Books* was nothing less than a state prohibition that put members of minority religions at a disadvantage in gaining their livelihood. This Court, looking at the history and context of such measures, concluded that they might indeed constitute an infringement of freedom of religion.

The burden at issue in the case at bar differs from that at issue in *Big M Drug Mart* and *Edwards Books* in two ways. First, it does not involve a state prohibition on otherwise lawful conduct. People remain free to educate their children whenever and however they choose, provided they meet prescribed standards. While this may impose costs on them not borne by parents of children attending public secular schools, the cost issue is more appropriately considered under the equality provision of the Charter, s. 15.

The second distinction between this case and the Sunday-closing cases is that the sort of absence of benefit complained of in this case has no history of recognition as a violation of freedom of religion. Absence of state funding for private religious practices, as distinct from prohibitions on such practices, has never been seen as religious persecution. In determining the content of the guarantees contained in the Charter, the courts must look to the history of values enshrined. That history provides no support for extending the guarantee of freedom of religion to the provision of equal funding for religious practices, like religious education. Never ... has it been suggested that freedom of religion entitles one to state support for one's religion.

I conclude that no infringement of the guarantee of freedom of religion has been established.

3. Does the Failure to Fund Independent Religious Schools Infringe the Equality Guarantee of the Charter?

Section 15 of the Charter provides that every person is entitled to equal benefit of the law and not to be discriminated against on grounds such as that of religion. Put in the context of this case, this means that the Province of Ontario may not enact an education law which deprives some people of benefits which others receive, on the ground of their religion.

· · ·

I conclude that while secular schooling is in theory available to all members of the public, the appellants' religious beliefs preclude them from sending their children to public schools. Therefore, they are adversely discriminated against by the lack of funding for schooling consistent with their religious beliefs. The fact that they may have chosen their religion and with it the need to send their children to religious schools does not negate the discrimination. This discrimination places a real and substantial financial burden on the appellants. The appellants are not treated as equal before and under the *Education Act* and do not receive equal benefit of the law. Therefore, the infringement of s. 15 is established.

4. Is the Infringement of Section 15 of the Charter Justified Under Section 1?

. . .

The Objective of the Denial of Funding

The decision to fully fund public secular schools while denying any funding to independent religious schools (other than the constitutionally mandated funding for Roman Catholic schools) is at base a political decision. Its objective, the record shows, is to foster a strong public secular school system attended by students of all cultural and religious groups. Canada in general and Ontario in particular is a multicultural, multi religious society. A multicultural multi religious society can only work, it is felt, if people of all groups understand and tolerate each other. According to the Shapiro Report (*Report of the Commission on Private Schools in Ontario* (Toronto, 1985)), submitted in evidence, "the public school context represents ... the most promising potential for realizing a more fully tolerant society." Children of all races and religions learn together and play together. No religion is touted over any other. The goal is to provide a forum for the development of respect for the beliefs and customs of all cultural groups and for their ethical and moral values. The strength of the public secular school system is its diversity—diversity which its supporters believe will lead to increased understanding and respect for different cultures and beliefs.

. . .

I conclude that the encouragement of a more tolerant harmonious multicultural society constitutes a pressing and substantial objective capable, provided its effect is duly proportionate, of justifying the infringement of s. 15.

Proportionality

(i) Rational Connection

. . .

The argument linking denial of funding for independent religious schools to the ultimate objective of a more tolerant society goes like this. By providing funding to secular schools where people of all religions are welcomed free of cost, the government encourages people of different cultures and creeds to educate their children together. If funding were provided for private religious schools many of those who now send their children to secular schools would instead send their children to independent religious schools. The public secular schools would lose some students from diverse backgrounds. These students, instead of being educated in public multicultural multireligious schools, would be educated with homogeneous groups of people of similar beliefs. In short, secular schools might become less diverse and the number of students receiving parochial educations would increase. The overall effect would be to diminish the multicultural exposure of children in schools. This lack of exposure, in turn, would diminish the mutual tolerance and understanding of Ontarians of diverse cultures and religions for one another.

[Relying on "common sense" rather than requiring a scientific demonstration of cause and effect, McLachlin J finds that the rational connection test is satisfied.]

(ii) Minimal Impairment

... Where social issues are at stake, courts approach the legislature's decision as to what infringement is required to achieve the desired end with considerable deference. ... As long as the measure falls within a range of acceptable solutions to the problem, it will pass the minimal impairment test. ... Again, common sense is the guide.

In the appeal at bar, it is impossible to say whether a less intrusive measure, such as partial funding for private religious schools, might achieve the same objective with less infringement of the guarantee of freedom of religion. The Ontario Legislature has chosen a measure that falls within the range of reasonable responses to the problem of promoting a more tolerant multicultural society.

(iii) Proportionality Between the Effect of the Infringing Measure and the Objective

...

In my view, the effect of denying funding to independent religious schools is proportionate to the objective sought. The goal of fostering multiracial and multicultural harmony is of great importance in a society as diverse as ours. Against this must be weighed the effect of the measure—to impose additional burdens upon parents whose religious beliefs preclude education of children in public secular schools. The denial of funding does not strike at the heart of the religion; indeed, I have concluded that it does not violate religious freedom at all. Even though it is true that the impugned scheme discriminates on the basis of religion, the record does not establish that the denial of funding compels anyone to violate their religious beliefs in a fashion which would violate s. 2(a) of the Charter. If the Act compelled attendance at public schools, then this might be argued to be the case. But the Act permits other alternatives, including home study. Such alternatives may impose burdens not carried by parents whose children attend publicly funded schools—therein lies the inequality that results in a finding of infringement of s. 15—but it does not preclude the state from attempting to justify its program on the ground of overarching public concern. ...

I conclude that while denial of funding for independent religious schools infringes the equality guarantee of the Charter, the infringement is justified under s. 1 of the Charter.

L'HEUREUX-DUBÉ J (dissenting): ...

[L'Heureux-Dubé J agrees with McLachlin J's findings that s. 93 does not provide the answer to the appellants' Charter claims and that the failure to fund independent religious schools does not violate the guarantee of freedom of religion.]

Dissentient minority religious groups have probably suffered most severely from the historic disadvantage which has adhered to religious identity. ... In today's secular society, it stands to reason that religious subgroups which have attempted to maintain a non-secular lifestyle are even more vulnerable to stereotype, social prejudice and marginalization.

These communities also constitute discrete and insular minorities, as their attempts to maintain a religious life leads them to distance themselves somewhat from the secular institutions of the larger society around them. While some may say this is their choice, we must remember that, in evaluating discriminatory effects of state action, we are concerned with its potential impact within the broader societal context. Insularity has become necessary to maintaining the religious lifestyle practised by the appellants by virtue of the powerful economic and other forces of secularization in society. Such insularity clearly carries with it the danger of such a group's interests being overlooked. ... [The appellants] constitute a group which is most clearly intended to receive Charter protection under s. 15.

· · ·

At issue here are the efforts of small, insular religious minority communities seeking to survive in a large, secular society. As such, the complete non-recognition of this group strikes at the very heart of the principles underlying s. 15. This provision, more than any other in the Charter, is intended to protect socially vulnerable groups from the discriminatory will of the majority as expressed through state action. The distinction created under the *Education Act* gives the clear message to these parents that their beliefs and practices are less worthy of consideration and value than those of the majoritarian secular society. They are not granted the same degree of concern, dignity and worth as other parents. I conclude that the *Education Act* funding scheme results in a *prima facie* violation of s. 15's guarantee of equal benefit of the law without discrimination.

· · ·

... A contextual approach in this case reveals the principal objectives of the legislation to be: first, to provide a large, publicly funded system of education intended to be universally open and free to all, without discrimination; and second, to foster the values of a pluralist, democratic society, including the values of cohesion, religious tolerance and understanding. ...

In [this] system, the objective of encouraging religious tolerance becomes linked to discouraging non-secular education. However, such a link is not inevitable. In fact, it is not the goal of encouraging social tolerance and understanding that creates a difficulty for the appellants, but rather the secular nature of the education. For example, as the Adler appellants submitted and one of the respondents' experts testified, the environment in the Jewish day schools was very conducive to social tolerance, successful integration, and acceptance of others.

· · ·

I agree with the Court of Appeal's finding in this case that the objectives of providing free public education and of fostering tolerance are clearly pressing and substantial in a democratic society. ... However, before discussing the proportionality element of the inquiry, I note that this same objective is no less pressing and substantial in the education systems in the five other provinces of Canada where independent religious schools receive partial funding, as indicated by the respondents' evidence.

. . .

The respondents have ... failed to discharge the burden of proving that the means used, in this case, a complete denial of funding, constitute a minimal impairment of the right in question. ...

In this case, the appellants made the alternate submission that partial funding should be provided to the independent schools. The respondents' evidence and argument nonetheless focused primarily on the potential effects of full funding to independent schools on the current system. This evidence consisted mainly of the opinion of expert witnesses and one study of the private school system in Ontario dating from 1985, the "Shapiro Report" (*Report of the Commission on Private Schools in Ontario* (Toronto, 1985)). Moreover, the evidence which they did lead as to the effects of partial funding points to a very limited impact on the current public system. In the evidence submitted by the respondents, estimates as to the increase in enrollment in independent schools in the event of partial funding ranged from 3% of the total enrollment in the public schools, to approximately 6%. ...

While partial funding is, on the evidence submitted by the respondents, a means for reasonably impairing the right in question, yet fulfilling the objectives of the legislation, this option was not implemented by the legislature. I thus cannot agree with the conclusion that it is impossible to say whether a less intrusive measure such as partial funding might achieve the same objective with less of an infringement. In fact, partial direct funding to independent religious schools is currently provided in five Canadian provinces, namely, Quebec, Manitoba, Saskatchewan, Alberta, and British Columbia. In these provinces, the minimum and maximum amounts of funding vary. Expressed as a percentage of the public school rate, the maximum rates of funding for independent religious schools in the provinces range from 50% to 75%. Partial funding would actually further the objective of providing a universally accessible education system and promote the value of religious tolerance in this context where some religious communities cannot be accommodated in the secular system.

Appeal dismissed.

NOTES

1. In *Waldman v. Canada* (1999), the United Nations Human Rights Committee ruled that the practice in Ontario of funding Catholic schools and no other religious schools was a breach of art. 26 of the *International Covenant on Civil and Political Rights*, the right against religious discrimination. The Committee observed that "the Covenant does not oblige States parties to fund schools that are established on a religious basis. However, if a State party chooses to provide public funding to religious schools, it should make this funding available without discrimination." The Committee was clear that simply because "a distinction [is] enshrined in the [Canadian] Constitution does not render it reasonable and objective" under the International Covenant. It is important to note, however, that the decisions of the Human Rights Committee are not automatically part of the domestic law of Canada.

2. Publicly funded Roman Catholic schools in Ontario are subject to the Charter, unless they are exercising a right or privilege granted to them under s. 93 of the *Constitution Act, 1867*. In *Hall (Litigation Guardian of) v. Powers* (2002), 213 DLR 4th 308, a judge found that there was a *prima facie* case that a Roman Catholic School in Ontario breached s. 15 of the Charter when it refused to permit a student to bring a same-sex date to the graduation dance, which was held off school property. The judge issued an interlocutory injunction prohibiting the school from preventing the student's attendance at the dance with his date.

NOTE: B.(R.) v. CHILDREN'S AID SOCIETY OF METROPOLITAN TORONTO

B.(R.) deals with the issue of the state's ability to interfere with the decisions that religious parents make about the medical care of their children. The case involved a court order for wardship authority granted to the Children's Aid Society under the Ontario *Child Welfare Act*. This order enabled the Children's Aid Society to consent to a blood transfusion for a one-month-old baby who was critically ill. The parents, who were Jehovah's Witnesses, had refused for religious reasons to consent to the transfusion. The parents challenged the order under the Charter. The principal argument was that the wardship order violated the parents' right to liberty under s. 7. That aspect of the case is dealt with in Chapter 22, Life, Liberty, and Security of the Person. However, the Supreme Court of Canada also addressed the argument that the order violated the parents' religious freedom. Five judges, in reasons written by La Forest J, held that because the law denied the parents the right to choose medical treatment for their infant according to their religious beliefs, their rights under s. 2(a) had been breached. However, these 5 judges went on to find that this breach was justified under s. 1 because of the state interest in protecting children at risk and the carefully crafted legislative scheme that provided full procedural rights for parents wishing to challenge a state claim that their child was in need of protection.

Four judges, in reasons written by Iacobucci and Major JJ, found no breach of the Charter guarantee of freedom of religion. In their view, the internal limits on freedom of religion articulated by Dickson J in *Big M* meant that the parents' freedom of religion would not include any actions that threatened their child's life or health. Iacobucci and Major JJ also considered the religious freedom of the child in their s. 2(a) analysis:

> The appellants proceed on the assumption that Sheena is of the same religion as they, and hence cannot submit to a blood transfusion. Yet, Sheena has never expressed any agreement with the Jehovah's Witness faith, nor, for that matter, with any religion, assuming any such agreement would be effective. There is thus an impingement on Sheena's freedom of conscience, which arguably includes the right to live long enough to make her own reasoned choice about the religion she wishes to follow as well as the right not to hold a religious belief. In fact, denying an infant necessary medical care could preclude that child from exercising any of her constitutional rights, because the child, due to parental beliefs, may not live long enough to make choices about the ideas she should like to express, the religion she should like to profess, or the associations she should like to join. "Freedom of religion" should not encompass activity that so categorically negates the "freedom of conscience" of another.

The Supreme Court of Canada was required to grapple with some of the difficult issues of how the state should deal with religious law in *Bruker v. Marcovitz*. A majority of the Supreme Court of Canada, in a judgment written by Abella J, held that a promise by a husband to give his consent to a religious divorce was enforceable as a contract and that damages could be awarded to remedy his breach of the promise. A strong dissent by Deschamps J raised concerns about inappropriate state "entanglement" in religion.

Bruker v. Marcovitz
[2007] 3 SCR 607, 2007 SCC 54, 288 DLR (4th) 257

ABELLA J (McLachlin CJC and Bastarache, Binnie, LeBel, Fish, and Rothstein JJ concurring):

· · ·

Background

[3] A *get* is a Jewish divorce. Only a husband can give one. A wife cannot obtain a *get* unless her husband agrees to give it. Under Jewish law, he does so by "releasing" his wife from the marriage and authorizing her to remarry. The process takes place before three rabbis in what is known as a *beth din*, or rabbinical court.

[4] The husband must voluntarily give the *get* and the wife consent to receive it. When he does not, she is without religious recourse, retaining the status of his wife and unable to remarry until he decides, in his absolute discretion, to divorce her. She is known as an *agunah* or "chained wife." Any children she would have on civil remarriage would be considered "illegitimate" under Jewish law.

[5] For an observant Jewish woman in Canada, this presents a dichotomous scenario: under Canadian law, she is free to divorce her husband regardless of his consent; under Jewish law, however, she remains married to him unless he gives his consent. This means that while she can remarry under Canadian law, she is prevented from remarrying in accordance with her religion. The inability to do so, for many Jewish women, results in the loss of their ability to remarry at all.

[6] The vast majority of Jewish husbands freely give their wives a *get*. Those who do not, however, represent a long-standing source of concern and frustration in Jewish communities ... .

[7] In response to these concerns, after consultation with the leaders of 50 religious groups in Canada and with the specific agreement of the Roman Catholic, Presbyterian and Anglican churches, in 1990 the then Minister of Justice, Doug Lewis, introduced amendments to the *Divorce Act*, RSC 1985, c. 3 (2nd Supp.), Bill C-61, giving a court discretionary authority to prevent a spouse from obtaining relief under the Act if that spouse refused to remove a barrier to religious remarriage (s. 21.1). ...

· · ·

[9] For many years, civil courts have attempted to remedy, or compensate for, the husband's recalcitrance in refusing to provide a *get* to his wife. They are often faced with assertions by the husband that such interventions are a violation of his freedom of religion.

[10] This is one such case. [In 1980,] the husband and wife, each represented by counsel, voluntarily negotiated and signed a "Consent to Corollary Relief" in order to settle their matrimonial disputes. One of the commitments made in the agreement [para. 12] was that they would attend before the rabbinical court to obtain a *get* [immediately after the granting of the civil divorce decree].

[11] The husband refused to do so for 15 years, challenging the very validity of the agreement he freely made, claiming that its religious aspect rendered it unenforceable under Quebec law, and arguing that he was entitled to be shielded by his right to freedom of religion from the consequences of refusing to comply with his commitment.

[12] The wife, on the other hand, asserted that the agreement to attend and obtain a *get* was part of the trade-offs negotiated by the parties (they signed mutual releases) and was consistent with Quebec law and values. She sought a remedy in the form of damages to compensate her for the husband's extended non-compliance. She did not seek an order of specific performance directing him to appear before the rabbis.

[The husband eventually gave the wife a *get* in 1995, when she used s. 21.2 of the *Divorce Act* to prevent him from seeking to rescind his child support obligation until he did so.]

[13] There are, therefore, two issues raised by this case. The first is whether the agreement in the Consent to give a *get* is a valid and binding contractual obligation under Quebec law. This first question involves examining the relevant provisions and principles of the *Civil Code of Québec*, SQ 1991, c. 64.

[14] If the commitment is a legally binding one under Quebec law, we must determine whether the husband can rely on freedom of religion to avoid the legal consequences of failing to comply with a lawful agreement. This inquiry takes place within the boundaries set by the provisions and principles of the Quebec *Charter of Human Rights and Freedoms*, RSQ c. C-12, where the claim of the husband to religious freedom is balanced against the claim of the wife that acceding to the husband's argument is disproportionately harmful to her personally, and, more generally, to democratic values and Quebec's best interests.

[15] The judicial role in balancing and reconciling competing interests and values when freedom of religion is raised is one that protects the tolerance Quebec endorsed in the Quebec *Charter*. Section 9.1 states that in exercising their fundamental freedoms and rights—including freedom of religion—persons "shall maintain a proper regard for democratic values, public order and the general well-being of the citizens of Québec." This provision is a legislative direction that the courts are to protect the rights of Quebec's citizens in a way that is balanced and reconciled with other public values.

[16] In my view, an agreement between spouses to take the necessary steps to permit each other to remarry in accordance with their own religions, constitutes a valid and binding contractual obligation under Quebec law. ... [S]uch agreements are consistent with public policy, our approach to marriage and divorce, and our commitment to eradicating gender discrimination.

[17] I am also persuaded that, applying the balancing mandated by s. 9.1 of the Quebec *Charter*, any harm to the husband's religious freedom in requiring him to pay damages for unilaterally breaching his commitment, is significantly outweighed by the harm caused by his unilateral decision not to honour it.

[18] This is not, as implied by the dissent, an unwarranted secular trespass into religious fields, nor does it amount to judicial sanction of the vagaries of an individual's religion. In deciding cases involving freedom of religion, the courts cannot ignore religion. To determine whether a particular claim to freedom of religion is entitled to protection, a court must take into account the particular religion, the particular religious right, and the particular personal and public consequences, including the religious consequences, of enforcing that right.

· · ·

[20] ... [T]he inquiry under the Quebec *Charter* is the application of a classic and cautious balancing that courts are required to undertake in determining whether a particular claim to religious freedom is sustainable, one case at a time, attempting always to be respectful of the complexity, sensitivity, and individuality inherent in these issues.

Prior Proceedings

· · ·

[31] At trial, Mass J held that once Mr. Marcovitz signed a civil agreement, the obligation to appear before the rabbinical authorities for the purpose of obtaining a *get* "moved into the realm of the civil courts" ... . He found that as a civil contract, notwithstanding that its purpose was partly to compel religious obligations, the Consent was valid and binding and that pursuant to Paragraph 12, Mr. Marcovitz had "a clear and unequivocal civil law obligation to appear 'immediately' before the Rabbinical authorities" ... .

[32] In his view, a claim for damages based on a breach of a civil obligation, even one with religious aspects, remains within the domain of the civil courts.

[33] Based on the expert evidence, Mass J concluded that had Mr. Marcovitz sought the *get* immediately, as he had agreed to do, it would have been granted by the rabbinical court. This meant that the breach of the obligation to appear before the rabbinical authorities was the cause of the damages claimed by Ms. Bruker. Finding that the failure of Mr. Marcovitz to grant the *get* had direct consequences on Ms. Bruker's life by depriving her "of the opportunity to marry within her community during this period" ... , Mass J ordered a total of $47,500 in damages: $2,500 for each of the 15 years between the Decree Nisi and the *get*, and $10,000 for Ms. Bruker's inability to have children considered "legitimate" under Jewish law.

· · ·

[36] The Court of Appeal allowed Mr. Marcovitz's appeal ... . Hilton JA, writing for a unanimous court, found that because "the substance of the ... obligation is religious in nature, irrespective of the form in which the obligation is stated" ... , the obligation was a moral one. It was therefore unenforceable by the courts. Requiring Mr. Marcovitz to pay damages in such circumstances would be inconsistent with the recognition of his right to exercise his religious beliefs as he saw fit without judicial intervention.

[37] In so deciding, the Court of Appeal relied in part on this Court's direction in *Syndicat Northcrest v. Amselem*, [2004] 2 SCR 551, 2004 SCC 47 [241 DLR (4th) 1], that

> the State is in no position to be, nor should it become, the arbiter of religious dogma. Accordingly, courts should avoid judicially interpreting and thus determining, either explicitly

or implicitly, the content of a subjective understanding of religious requirement, "obligation," precept, "commandment," custom or ritual. [para. 50]

· · ·

Analysis

A. Justiciability of the Agreement to Remove Religious Barriers to Remarriage

· · ·

[41] Unlike my colleague Justice Deschamps, with great respect, I see this case as one
properly attracting judicial attention. The fact that a dispute has a religious aspect does
not by itself make it non-justiciable. ...

· · ·

[43] The approach is correctly stated by the Canadian Civil Liberties Association in
its factum as follows:

> [N]o case goes so far as to hold that even in cases based upon a civil obligation, where the
> Court is not required to determine matters of religious doctrine, the Court should be pre-
> cluded from adjudicating disputes that involve obligations having a religious character.
> [para. 26]

[44] This is reflected in *McCaw v. United Church of Canada* (1991), 4 OR (3d) 481, a
case involving the dismissal of a minister from his church, where the religious aspect of
the dispute did not deter the Ontario Court of Appeal from deciding that the dispute was
justiciable. Even though the "law of the church as laid out in the provisions of the
[church] Manual" was at issue (p. 485), the court accepted jurisdiction and awarded the
minister damages for lost wages and benefits. ...

[45] Similarly, in *Lakeside Colony of Hutterian Brethren v. Hofer*, [1992] 3 SCR 165
[97 DLR (4th) 17], a Hutterite colony decided to expel some of its members from the
community without giving them an opportunity to respond to the decision. When the
members refused to leave, the colony asked the courts to enforce the expulsion and to
order the members to return all colony property to the colony. The members claimed
that they had a right to remain in the colony and that the courts could not enforce the
expulsion. Gonthier J, writing for the majority, noted that while the courts may not intervene in strictly doctrinal or spiritual matters, they will when civil or property rights
are engaged. Once the court takes jurisdiction over a dispute with religious components,
he continued, it must try "to come to the best understanding possible of the applicable
tradition and custom" (p. 191). Gonthier J held that, in the absence of a timely and adequate opportunity to make a response, the members could not be expelled.

[46] In the case before us, I find the dissenting reasons in *Re Morris and Morris*
(1973), 42 DLR (3d) 550 (Man. CA), compelling. While the issue in that case was the enforceability of a provision of a *ketubah*, or Jewish marriage contract, an issue we are not
called upon to consider, the language of Freedman CJM is nonetheless helpful:

> That the [marriage] contract is deeply affected by religious considerations is not determina-
> tive of the issue. That is the beginning and not the end of the matter. Some contracts rooted
> in the religion of a particular faith may indeed be contrary to public policy. Others may not.

Our task is to determine whether the rights and obligations flowing from the ... contract—specifically, the husband's obligation to give and the wife's right to receive a *get*—are contrary to public policy.

I find difficulty in pin-pointing the precise aspect of public policy which the [agreement to provide a *get*] may be said to offend. The attack upon it is on more general grounds. It appears that the real basis on which enforcement of the contract is being resisted is simply that it rests on religion, and that on grounds of public policy the Court should keep out of that field. But the law reports contain many instances of Courts dealing with disputes having a religious origin or basis. ... In each case some temporal right confronted the Court, and it did not hesitate to adjudicate thereon. [pp. 559-60]

[47] The fact that Paragraph 12 of the Consent had religious elements does not thereby immunize it from judicial scrutiny. We are not dealing with judicial review of doctrinal religious principles, such as whether a particular *get* is valid. Nor are we required to speculate on what the rabbinical court would do. The promise by Mr. Marcovitz to remove the religious barriers to remarriage by providing a *get* was negotiated between two consenting adults, each represented by counsel, as part of a voluntary exchange of commitments intended to have legally enforceable consequences. This puts the obligation appropriately under a judicial microscope.

B. Validity of the Agreement Under Quebec Law

• • •

[49] The civil law of Quebec recognizes three kinds of obligations: moral, civil (or legal) and natural. Only the first two are engaged in this case. ...

• • •

[51] I do not see the religious aspect of the obligation in Paragraph 12 of the Consent as a barrier to its civil validity. It is true that a party cannot be compelled to execute a moral duty, but there is nothing in the *Civil Code* preventing someone from transforming his or her moral obligations into legally valid and binding ones. Giving money to charity, for example, could be characterized as a moral and, therefore, legally unenforceable obligation. But if an individual enters into a contract with a particular charity agreeing to make a donation, the obligation may well become a valid and binding one if it complies with the requirements of a contract under the CCQ. If it does, it is transformed from a moral obligation to a civil one enforceable by the courts.

• • •

[54] Mr. Marcovitz argues, however, that, contrary to arts. 1412 and 1413 CCQ, the "object" of the contractual provision—the attendance of the parties before the rabbinical court to obtain a divorce in accordance with Jewish law to permit remarriage under that law—is against public order because it is a violation of his right to freedom of religion. ...

[55] The CCQ defines the object of a contract in art. 1412, which states that

> 1412. The object of a contract is the *juridical operation* envisaged by the parties at the time of its formation, as it emerges from all the rights and obligations created by the contract. ...

• • •

[58] With great respect, I see the concept of "juridical operation" (or object of the contract) in art. 1412 as attracting a much broader interpretation than the one proposed by Deschamps J, based largely on my view that art. 1412 is limited only by art. 1413, which states:

> 1413. A contract whose object is prohibited by law or contrary to public order is null.

[59] There are therefore only two limitations on the object of a contract: it cannot be prohibited by law or be contrary to public order. ...

· · ·

[62] I accept that there may well be agreements with religious aspects that would be against public order. It will obviously depend in each case on the nature of the undertaking and, in particular, on the extent to which the promise is consistent with our laws, policies, and democratic values. An agreement to resolve a custody dispute in a way that offends a child's best interests, or an agreement that violates our employment laws, for example, will likely be found to be contrary to public order.

[63] There is no doubt in my mind, however, about Mr. Marcovitz's agreement to provide a *get*. It is consistent with, not contrary to, public order. The 1990 *Divorce Act* amendments referred to earlier in these reasons contradict the argument that an agreement to grant a *get* breaches the principle of public order. On the contrary, Parliament manifested a clear intention to encourage the removal of religious barriers to remarriage. Moreover, as amplified later in these reasons, the enforceability of a promise by a husband to provide a *get* harmonizes with Canada's approach to religious freedom, to equality rights, to divorce and remarriage generally, and has been judicially recognized internationally.

[64] Accordingly, since the object is not contrary to public order, and since all the other requirements for a valid contract in accordance with Quebec law exist, the contractual obligation contained in Paragraph 12 is valid and legally binding under Quebec law.

C. Application of the Quebec Charter

[65] There remains Mr. Marcovitz's argument that he is exonerated by s. 3 of the Quebec *Charter* from the consequences of breaching Paragraph 12 of the Consent. He asserts that an award of damages would be a violation of his freedom of religion because it would condemn him *ex post facto* "for abiding by his religion in the first place." ...

[66] This Court's most recent decision examining the scope of this provision is *Amselem [Syndicat Northcrest v.*, [2004] 2 SCR 551]. ...

[67] The test applied by the majority in *Amselem* examines whether an individual's sincerely held and good faith religious belief is being unjustifiably limited to a non-trivial degree. Applying this test to the facts of this case, I see no *prima facie* infringement of Mr. Marcovitz's religious freedom.

[68] I start by querying whether Mr. Marcovitz, in good faith, sincerely believed that granting a *get* was an act to which he objected as a matter of religious belief or conscience. ...

[69] [The evidence suggests] that his refusal to provide the *get* was based less on religious conviction than on the fact that he was angry at Ms. Bruker. His religion does not

require him to refuse to give Ms. Bruker a *get*. The contrary is true. There is no doubt that at Jewish law he *could* refuse to give one, but that is very different from Mr. Marcovitz being prevented by a tenet of his religious beliefs from complying with a legal obligation he voluntarily entered into and of which he took the negotiated benefits.

[70] Even if requiring him to comply with his agreement to give a *get* can be said to conflict with a sincerely held religious belief and to have non-trivial consequences for him, both of which I have difficulty discerning, such a *prima facie* infringement does not survive the balancing mandated by this Court's jurisprudence and the Quebec *Charter*.

· · ·

[76] In Quebec, the fact that rights and freedoms, including freedom of religion, are limited by the extent to which their exercise is harmful to others, finds expression in s. 9.1 of the Quebec *Charter*. Only the first paragraph of s. 9.1 is engaged. It states:

> 9.1 In exercising his fundamental freedoms and rights, a person shall maintain a proper regard for democratic values, public order and the general well-being of the citizens of Québec.

[77] Section 9.1 confirms the principle that the assertion of a claim to religious freedom must be reconciled with countervailing rights, values, and harm. …

[78] Mr. Marcovitz's claim must therefore be weighed against the "democratic values, public order and the general well-being of the citizens of Québec" stipulated by s. 9.1. We thereby enter the complex, nuanced, fact-specific territory referred to at the outset of these reasons.

[79] Mr. Marcovitz, it seems to me, has little to put on the scales. To begin, he freely entered into a valid and binding contractual obligation and now seeks to have it set aside based on *ex post facto* religious compunctions. In my view, it is this attempt to resile from his binding promise, not the enforcement of the obligation, that offends public order.

[80] But the public policy benefit of preventing individuals from avoiding the usual legal consequences of their contractual breaches, is only one of the factors that weighs against his claim. The significant intrusions into our constitutionally and statutorily articulated commitments to equality, religious freedom and autonomous choice in marriage and divorce that flow from the breach of his legal obligation are what weigh most heavily against him.

[81] Section 21.1 of the *Divorce Act*, which gives a court discretionary authority to rebuff a spouse in civil proceedings who obstructs religious remarriage, is a clear indication that it is public policy in this country that such barriers are to be discouraged. … [T]hese amendments received overwhelming support from the Jewish community, including its more religious elements, reflecting a consensus that the refusal to provide a *get* was an unwarranted indignity imposed on Jewish women and, to the extent possible, one that should not be countenanced by Canada's legal system.

[82] We also accept the right of Canadians to decide for themselves whether their marriage has irretrievably broken down and we attempt to facilitate, rather than impede, their ability to continue their lives, including with new families. Moreover, under Canadian law, marriage and divorce are available equally to men and women. A *get*, on the other hand, can only be given under Jewish law by a husband. For those Jewish women

whose religious principles prevent them from considering remarriage unless they are able to do so in accordance with Jewish law, the denial of a *get* is the denial of the right to remarry. It is true that *get* also requires the consent of the wife, but ... the law has a disparate impact on women ... . The refusal of a husband to provide a *get*, therefore, arbitrarily denies his wife access to a remedy she independently has under Canadian law and denies her the ability to remarry and get on with her life in accordance with her religious beliefs.

[83] There is also support internationally for courts protecting Jewish women from husbands who refuse to provide a religious divorce.

[Justice Abella then reviewed judicial decisions from France, the United Kingdom, Australia, and the United States awarding damages or additional spousal support against husbands who refused to grant the *get* or ordering specific performance of an obligation in Jewish marriage contract to submit to the *beth din*.]

[89] Of particular interest is the judicial treatment of a husband's refusal to provide a *get* in Israel, where judges have awarded damages as compensation to a wife because of her husband's refusal to give her a *get*. In *Jane Doe v. John Doe*, Jerusalem Fam. Ct., No. 19270/03, December 21, 2004, Hacohen J recognized that "[t]he problem of *ghet* recalcitrance is one of the fundamental problems of Halakhic Judaism (Jewish Religious Law) and in Jewish family law" (para. 3). He observed that in HC 6751/04, *Sabag v. Supreme Rabbinical Court of Appeals*, 59(4) PD 817, the High Court of Justice stressed that it was imperative "to find effective solutions to this phenomenon ... in order to free couples ... and to allow them to begin new lives, and in that way to realize their right to independent lives in the area of personal status" (para. 3) (certified English translation). Noting the husband's argument that disputes of this nature should best be left to rabbinical courts because religious law applies to marriage and divorce in Israel, Hacohen J, who ordered the husband to pay 425,000 shekels in damages, including 100,000 shekels in aggravated damages, held:

> The rabbinical courts deal, at one tempo or another, with finding Halachic [religious law] solutions for the phenomenon of *get* recalcitrance and with the development of Halachic tools for exerting pressure on *get* withholders to consent to grant their wives the longed for *get*. However, in this suit the Court is not trespassing on this area. ... *The object of the relief applied for is to indemnify the wife for significant damages caused her by long years of aginut, loneliness and mental distress that were imposed on her by her husband.* [Emphasis added; para. 19.]

[90] This international perspective reinforces the view that judicial enforcement of an agreement to provide a Jewish divorce is consistent with public policy values shared by other democracies.

[91] Mr. Marcovitz cannot, therefore, rely on the Quebec *Charter* to avoid the consequences of failing to implement his legal commitment to provide the *get*.

[92] The public interest in protecting equality rights, the dignity of Jewish women in their independent ability to divorce and remarry, as well as the public benefit in enforcing valid and binding contractual obligations, are among the interests and values that

outweigh Mr. Marcovitz's claim that enforcing Paragraph 12 of the Consent would inter-fere with his religious freedom.

[93] Despite the moribund state of her marriage, Ms. Bruker remained, between the ages of 31 and 46, Mr. Marcovitz's wife under Jewish law, and dramatically restricted in the options available to her in her personal life. This represented an unjustified and se-vere impairment of her ability to live her life in accordance with this country's values and her Jewish beliefs. Any infringement of Mr. Marcovitz's freedom of religion is inconse-quential compared to the disproportionate disadvantaging effect on Ms. Bruker's ability to live her life fully as a Jewish woman in Canada.

[The trial judge's award of damages was upheld as appropriately compensating Ms. Bruker for what she had lost by Mr. Marcovitz's refusal to perform his obligation under the con-tract—the ability for 15 years to marry or have children in accordance with her religious beliefs.]

DESCHAMPS J (Charron J concurring) dissenting:

· · ·

2. Analysis

2.1 The Get from the Public Law Standpoint: Judicial Consideration of Claims with a Religious Basis

[120] Despite the religious foundations of Roman law and French civil law, from which Quebec civil law is derived, there should be no doubt today that in Quebec, the state is neutral where religion is concerned. A first break occurred at the time of the *Royal Proclamation* of 1763. Another step took place in the 20th century when Quebec opened up to the world and in the early 1960s, during the Quiet Revolution, when the state took charge of institutions controlled by religious communities. A more complete break oc-curred with the adoption by Canada of the policy of multiculturalism. (F.K. Comparato, *Essai d'analyse dualiste de l'obligation en droit privé* (1964), at pp. 135-36; *Congrégation des témoins de Jéhovah de St-Jérôme-Lafontaine v. Lafontaine (Village)*, [2004] 2 SCR 650, 2004 SCC 48, at paras. 66-68; and *Canadian Multiculturalism Act*, RSC 1985, c. 24 (4th Supp.).)

[121] This neutrality does not mean that the state never considers questions relating to religion. On the contrary, s. 2 of the *Canadian Charter of Rights and Freedoms* requires that the state respect freedom of religion. ...

[122] In Canadian law, a court is thus not barred from considering a question of a religious nature, provided that the claim is based on the violation of a rule recognized in positive law. ...

· · ·

[124] In every case, the parties and the court must refer to the relevant civil rules to determine whether the undertaking is binding. In the case at bar, the appellant is not questioning recourses that have already been recognized in order to find a solution to the problem of the *get*, but is seeking to create a new one.

[125] The appellant asks the courts to assess the impact the respondent's failure to consent to the *get* has had on her life. No civil rules provide for the consequences of the absence of a *get*. These consequences flow from religious rules. A wife who is not granted a *get* upon the dissolution of the civil marriage is considered an *agunah*, or "chained wife," and in the eyes of her religion, any children she has in the future will be *mamzerim*, or illegitimate children.

[126] The courts have long refused to intervene in the manner proposed by the appellant. The courts' role in matters of religion is neutral. It is limited to ensuring that laws are constitutional and, in the case of a private dispute, to identifying the point at which rights converge so as to ensure respect for freedom of religion. ...

. . .

[128] This Court's decision in *Ukrainian Greek Orthodox Church of Canada v. Trustees of the Ukrainian Greek Orthodox Cathedral of St. Mary the Protectress*, [1940] SCR 586, is ... clear. Crocket J wrote the following:

> ... [F]or it is well settled that, *unless some property or civil right is affected thereby, the civil courts of this country will not allow their process to be used for the enforcement of a purely ecclesiastical decree or order.* [Emphasis added; p. 591.]

He concluded, at p. 594, that "[t]he manifest and sole purpose of this claim, as that of the whole action, is to enforce obedience to a purely ecclesiastical sentence or decree. For that reason I am of opinion that the Court of Appeal was fully justified in dismissing the plaintiff's action."

[129] The requirements for issuing a *get* and the consequences of not having a religious divorce are governed by the rules of the Jewish religion. The state does not interfere in this area. ...

[130] I do not feel that the courts have reversed or qualified their approach to sanctioning purely religious obligations. Whether a court is asked to compel a party to appear before rabbinical authorities or to order the payment of money, the same principle is in issue: can the authority of the courts be based on a purely religious rule? I do not think it can. In *Lakeside Colony of Hutterian Brethren v. Hofer*, [1992] 3 SCR 165 [97 DLR (4th) 17], this Court reiterated the principle enunciated by Crocket J in *Ukrainian Greek Orthodox Church*. Its decision was based on the fact that, for members of the Hutterite colony, a voluntary association, the right to remain on land owned by the Lakeside Holding Co. was a contractual right (p. 174). That case, unlike the case at bar, concerned a validly formed contract between the parties. It cannot therefore be relied on to support an argument that the courts now intervene in religious disputes.

[131] Furthermore, this principle of non-intervention in religious practices was one of the most important bases for adoption of the subjective standard of sincere belief (*Syndicat Northcrest v. Amselem*, [2004] 2 SCR 551, 2004 SCC 47 [241 DLR (4th) 1]). The principle is an important one, since the circumstances in which the courts might be asked to intervene in religious disputes are manifold. The principle of non-intervention makes it possible to avoid situations in which the courts have to decide between various religious rules or between rules of secular law and religious rules. In the instant case, the appellant has not argued that her civil rights were infringed by a civil standard derived from positive law. Only her religious rights are in issue, and only as a result of religious

rules. Thus, she is not asking to be compensated because she could not remarry as a result of a civil rule. It was a rule of her religion that prevented her from doing so. She is not asking to be compensated because any children she might have given birth to would not have had the same civil rights as "legitimate" children. In Canadian law and in Quebec law, all children are equal whether they are born of a marriage or not. The ground for the appellant's claim for compensation conflicts with gains that are dear to civil society. Allowing the appellant's claim places the courts in conflict with the laws they are responsible for enforcing.

[132] It should be noted that the religious consequences of not having a *get* do not override secular law rules. Neither the *Divorce Act* nor the civil law has exclusionary rules like those related to *agunot* and *mamzerim*. Mosaic law—like canon law—has no influence on secular law. The reverse is also true: secular law has no effect in matters of religious law … . Where religion is concerned, the state leaves it to individuals to make their own choices. It is not up to the state to promote a religious norm. This is left to religious authorities.

· · ·

[165] The appellant submits that the obligation in issue arises from a *contract*. No other legal situation has been invoked, or even discussed. It must therefore be determined whether clause 12 constitutes a contract in Quebec law. …

· · ·

[170] The fourth condition of contract formation is the existence of an object. …

[171] Article 1412 specifies that the object of a contract is the *juridical operation* envisaged by the parties at the time of its formation. At this stage, the operation as a whole must be considered, and not just the obligations the parties are bound to perform. Identifying the object of the contract is important, because only the object makes it possible to determine the nature of the juridical operation the parties have agreed on. Contrary to what the majority assert, the review of the object is not limited to determining whether it is contrary to public order (art. 1413 CCQ). …

· · ·

[174] What operation was envisaged in the instant case? The parties envisaged the obtaining of a religious divorce. Considered as a whole, the purpose of the mutual undertakings to appear before the rabbinical authorities in order to obtain a religious divorce was to obtain a religious divorce. Is this a juridical operation? A juridical operation implies a mechanism capable of legal characterization; it must be capable of juridical consequences. Sale, service, lease and loan are some examples of juridical operations. Is the operation in the case at bar a juridical operation? Obtaining a religious divorce is not capable of legal characterization. The rabbinical authorities are not responsible for civil divorce in the way that certain religious authorities are for marriage. The act they perform or the judgment they render is not recognized in civil law. Neither the undertaking to consent to a religious divorce nor the religious divorce itself has civil consequences. I must therefore infer that, in clause 12 of the corollary relief agreement, the parties did not agree on an operation recognized in civil law. Since the parties did not envisage a juridical operation, it must be concluded that one of the essential elements of contract formation is missing.

[175] The undertaking to appear before the religious authorities is therefore not a contract as the appellant argues, and as the majority accept. But if the undertaking does

not flow from a contract, what did the parties do in agreeing to clause 12? What is the juridical nature of this undertaking? In the instant case, the undertaking to appear before the rabbinical authorities for a religious divorce, like an undertaking to go regularly to church, to synagogue or to a mosque, is based on a duty of conscience alone. The Court of Appeal was therefore right to view the undertaking in clause 12 as a purely moral obligation that may not be enforced civilly.

[176] Accordingly, as the Court of Appeal rightly noted, the undertaking to appear before the rabbinical authorities as incorporated into the corollary relief agreement could at most be considered a moral undertaking. Moreover, even if this moral undertaking had been actionable, determining the appropriate remedy would have been problematic. ...

[Deschamps J goes on to discuss the difficulties of enforcing religious obligations that are inconsistent with secular laws.]

Appeal allowed.

NOTES AND QUESTIONS

1. There are several reasons why the courts may hesitate or refuse to enforce agreements that are based on religious norms or deal with religious matters. First, the interpretation of such an agreement may draw the courts into disputes about the proper understanding of religious doctrine or practice. Second, legal enforcement may be inappropriate given the subject matter of the agreement (matters of faith or deep commitment) and the relationship between the parties (members of a community bound by a shared commitment to a set of values or practices, or to a way of life). Third, agreements between religious community members may be tainted by undue influence or unfair pressure.

2. Not far in the background of Justice Abella's judgment is the issue of the constitutionality of s. 21.1 of the *Divorce Act*, RSC 1985, c. 3 (2d Supp.), an issue that was specifically not pursued in the courts by Mr. Marcovitz, in part because the provision, which was enacted in 1990, was not in force when the parties divorced in 1980. Section 21.1 empowers a judge in a civil divorce case to exert pressure on a spouse who refuses to give his or her consent to a religious divorce by "dismissing any application by that spouse" and "strik[ing] out any other pleadings and affidavits filed by the spouse." See also the *Ontario Family Law Act*, RSO 1990, c. F.3, s. 2(5). While Justice Abella insisted that nothing in her reasons "purports in any way to decide the constitutionality of s. 21.1" (para. 35), her finding that Mr. Marcovitz's freedom of religion was not breached by the enforcement of his promise would seem to apply equally to this provision of the *Divorce Act*.

CHAPTER TWENTY

Freedom of Expression

I. INTRODUCTION: PURPOSES OF THE GUARANTEE

Numerous explanations have been offered for the importance accorded to freedom of expression. Some of the main rationales are reviewed by McLachlin J in the following excerpt from her judgment in *R v. Keegstra*. (Although the judgment was a dissenting opinion, the comments on freedom of expression were not the source of the disagreement.)

R v. Keegstra
[1990] 3 SCR 697, 61 CCC (3d) 1

McLACHLIN J: ... Various philosophical justifications exist for freedom of expression. Some of these posit free expression as a means to other ends. Others see freedom of expression as an end in itself.

Salient among the justifications for free expression in the first category is the postulate that the freedom is instrumental in promoting the free flow of ideas essential to political democracy and the functioning of democratic institutions. This is sometimes referred to as the political process rationale. ... The *locus classicus* of this rationale is A. Meiklejohn, *Free Speech and its Relation to Self-Government* (1948).

A corollary of the view that expression must be free because of its role in the political process is that only expression relating to the political process is worthy of constitutional protection. However, within these limits protection for expression is said to be absolute. The political process rationale has played a significant role in the development of First Amendment doctrine in the United States, and various justices of the US Supreme Court (though never a majority) have embraced its theory that protection of speech is absolute within these restricted bounds. Its importance has also been affirmed by Canadian courts, both before and since the advent of the Charter. ...

The validity of the political process rationale for freedom of expression is undeniable. It is, however, limited. It justifies only a relatively narrow sector of free expression—one much narrower than either the wording of the First Amendment or s. 2(b) of the Charter would suggest.

Another venerable rationale for freedom of expression (dating at least to Milton's *Areopagitica* in 1644) is that it is an essential precondition of the search for truth.

[Milton wrote:

> And though all the winds of doctrine were let loose to play upon the earth, so Truth be in the field, we do injuriously by licensing and prohibiting to misdoubt her strength. Let her and Falsehood grapple; who ever knew Truth put to the worse, in a free and open encounter?]

Like the political process model, this model is instrumental in outlook. Freedom of expression is seen as a means of promoting a "marketplace of ideas," in which competing ideas vie for supremacy to the end of attaining the truth. The "marketplace of ideas" metaphor was coined by Justice Oliver Wendell Holmes, in his famous dissent in *Abrams v. United States*, 250 US 616 (1919).

[The passage by Justice Holmes referred to reads as follows:

> Persecution for the expression of opinions seems to me perfectly logical. If you have no doubt of your premises or your power and want a certain result with all your heart, you naturally express your wishes in law and sweep away all opposition. To allow opposition by speech seems to indicate that you think the speech impotent, as when a man says that he has squared the circle, or that you do not care wholeheartedly for the result, or that you doubt either your power or your premises. But when men have realized that time has upset many fighting faiths, they may come to believe even more than they believe the very foundations of their own conduct that the ultimate good desired is better reached by free trade in ideas—that the best test of truth is the power of the thought to get itself accepted in the competition of the market, and that truth is the only ground upon which their wishes safely can be carried out. That at any rate is the theory of our Constitution.]

This approach, however, has been criticized on the ground that there is no guarantee that the free expression of ideas will in fact lead to the truth. Indeed, as history attests, it is quite possible that dangerous, destructive and inherently untrue ideas may prevail, at least in the short run.

Notwithstanding the cogency of this critique, it does not negate the essential validity of the notion of the value of the marketplace of ideas. While freedom of expression provides no guarantee that the truth will always prevail, it still can be argued that it assists in promoting the truth in ways which would be impossible without the freedom. One need only look to societies where free expression has been curtailed to see the adverse effects both on truth and on human creativity. It is no coincidence that in societies where freedom of expression is severely restricted truth is often replaced by the coerced propagation of ideas that may have little relevance to the problems which the society actually faces. Nor is it a coincidence that industry, economic development and scientific and artistic creativity may stagnate in such societies.

Moreover, to confine the justification for guaranteeing freedom of expression to the promotion of truth is arguably wrong, because however important truth may be, certain opinions are incapable of being proven either true or false. Many ideas and expressions which cannot be verified are valuable. Such considerations convince me that freedom of expression can be justified at least in part on the basis that it promotes the "marketplace of ideas" and hence a more relevant, vibrant and progressive society.

But freedom of expression may be viewed as more than a means to other ends. Many assert that free expression is an end in itself, a value essential to the sort of society we wish to preserve. This view holds that freedom of expression "derives from the widely accepted premise of Western thought that the proper end of man is the realization of his character and potentialities as a human being." It follows from this premise that all persons have the right to form their own beliefs and opinions, and to express them. "For expression is an integral part of the development of ideas, of mental exploration and of the affirmation of self": T.I. Emerson, "Toward a General Theory of the First Amendment" (1963), 72 *Yale LJ* 877, at p. 879. It is demeaning of freedom of expression and wrong, the proponents of this view argue, to conceive the right only in terms of the ends it may assist in achieving. "[I]t is not a general measure of the individual's right to freedom of expression that any particular exercise of the right may be thought to promote or retard other goals of the society" (p. 880). Freedom of expression is seen as worth preserving for its own intrinsic value.

Those who assert that freedom of expression is worth protecting for its intrinsic value to the self-realization of both speaker and listener tend to combine this rationale with others. ... On its own, this justification for free expression is arguably too broad and amorphous to found constitutional principle. Furthermore, it does not answer the question of why expression should be deserving of special constitutional status, while other self-fulfilling activities are not. Nevertheless, an emphasis on the intrinsic value of freedom of expression provides a useful supplement to the more utilitarian rationales, justifying, for example, forms of artistic expression which some might otherwise be tempted to exclude.

Arguments based on intrinsic value and practical consequences are married in the thought of F. Schauer (*Free Speech: A Philosophical Enquiry* (1982)). Rather than evaluating expression to see why it might be worthy of protection, Schauer evaluates the reasons why a government might attempt to limit expression. Schauer points out that throughout history, attempts to restrict expression have accounted for a disproportionate share of governmental blunders—from the condemnation of Galileo for suggesting the earth is round to the suppression as "obscene" of many great works of art. Professor Schauer explains this peculiar inability of censoring governments to avoid mistakes by the fact that, in limiting expression, governments often act as judge in their own cause. They have an interest in stilling criticism of themselves, or even in enhancing their own popularity by silencing unpopular expression. These motives may render them unable to carefully weigh the advantages and disadvantages of suppression in many instances. That is not to say that it is always illegitimate for governments to curtail expression, but government attempts to do so must *prima facie* be viewed with suspicion.

Schauer's approach reminds us that no one rationale provides the last word on freedom of expression. Indeed, it seems likely that theories about freedom of expression will continue to develop.

How do these diverse justifications of freedom of expression relate to s. 2(b) of the Charter? First, it may be noted that the broad wording of s. 2(b) of the Charter is arguably inconsistent with a justification based on a single facet of free expression. This suggests that there is no need to adopt any one definitive justification for freedom of expression. Different justifications for freedom of expression may assume varying degrees of importance in different fact situations. However, each of the above rationales is capable of providing guidance as to the scope and content of s. 2(b).

R. Moon, *The Constitutional Protection of Freedom of Expression*
(Toronto: University of Toronto Press, 2000), at 8, 3-4, and 24-26
(footnotes omitted)

There are many arguments for protecting freedom of expression, but all seem to focus on one or a combination of three values: truth, democracy and individual autonomy. Freedom of expression must be protected because it contributes to the public's recognition of truth or to the growth of public knowledge; or because it is necessary to the operation of a democratic form of government; or because it is important to individual self-realization; or because it is an important aspect of individual autonomy. Some arguments emphasize one value over the others. In these single value accounts the other values are seen as either derived from the primary value or as independent but of marginal significance only. However, most accounts assume that a commitment to freedom of expression, which extends protection to political, artistic, scientific and intimate expression, must rest on the contribution that freedom of expression makes to all three of these values. Freedom of expression, like other important rights, is supported by a number of overlapping justifications.

... While emphasising different values or concerns, these accounts [of the freedom's value] rest on a common recognition that human agency emerges in communicative interaction. ...

· · ·

Freedom of expression does not simply protect individual liberty from state interference. Rather, it protects the individual's freedom to communicate with others. The right of the individual is to participate in an activity that is deeply social in character that involves socially created languages and the use of community resources such as parks, streets, and broadcast stations. Yet the structure of constitutional adjudication, reinforced by an individual rights culture, tends to suppress the social or relational character of freedom of expression and its distributive demands (concern about the individual's effective opportunity to communicate with others).

Recognition of the social character of freedom of expression is critical to understanding both the value and potential harm of expression and to addressing questions about the freedom's scope and limits. Freedom of expression is valuable because human agency and identity emerge in discourse. We become individuals capable of thought and judgment and we develop as rational and feeling persons when we join in conversation with others. The social emergence of human thought, feeling, and identity can be expressed in the language of truth or individual autonomy or democratic self-government. Each of the traditional accounts of the value of freedom of expression (democratic-, truth-, and self-realization-based accounts) represents a particular perspective on, or dimension of, the constitution of human agency in community life. At the same time, the variety of these accounts reflects the diverse role that expression plays in the life of individual and community—that different relationships and different forms of communication contribute to the realization of human agency and the formation of individual identity. While the social character of human agency is seldom mentioned in the traditional accounts of the value of freedom of expression, it is the unstated premise of each. Each account is incomplete without some recognition that individual agency is realized in social interaction; this dimension has simply been pushed below the surface by the weight of the dominant individualist understanding of rights and agency.

Recognition that individual agency and identity emerge in communicative interaction is crucial to understanding not only the value of expression but also its potential for harm. Our dependence on expression means that words can sometimes be hurtful. Our identity is shaped by what we say and by what others say to us and about us. Expression can cause fear, it can harass, and it can undermine self-esteem. Expression can also be deceptive or manipulative. Human reflection and judgment are dependent on socially created languages, which give shape to thought and feeling. While language enables us to formulate and communicate our ideas and to understand the ideas of others, it is not a transparent vehicle, an instrument that lies within our perfect control.

• • •

The established accounts of the value of freedom of expression are described as either instrumental or intrinsic (or as result-oriented or process-oriented, or as concerned with the realization of a social goal or with protection of an individual right). Some accounts see freedom of expression as valuable in itself. The freedom is intrinsically valuable because it permits free and rational beings to express their ideas and feelings. Or it must be protected out of respect for the freedom and rationality of individuals. Other accounts see freedom of expression as important because it contributes to a valued state of affairs: freedom of expression is instrumental to the realization of social goods such as public knowledge or democratic government.

Intrinsic accounts assume that freedom of expression, like other rights, is an aspect of the individual's fundamental liberty or autonomy that should be insulated from the demands of collective welfare. Yet any account that regards freedom of expression as a liberty (as a right of the individual to be free from external interference) seems unable to explain the other-regarding or community-oriented character of the protected activity of expression—of individuals speaking and listening to others.

Instrumental accounts of freedom of expression recognize that the freedom protects an other-regarding or social activity and so must be concerned with something more than respect for individual autonomy, something more than individual "venting" or the exercise of individual reason. They assume that the freedom must be concerned with social goals that are in some way separate from, or beyond, the individual and his/her communicative actions, goals such as truth and democracy. Yet if freedom of expression is an instrumental right, its fundamental character seems less obvious. Its value is contingent on its contribution to the goals of truth and democracy. And there is no shortage of arguments that freedom of expression does not (always) advance these goals.

The value (and potential harm) of expression will remain unclear as long as discussion about freedom of expression is locked into the intrinsic/instrumental dichotomy, in which the freedom is concerned with either the good of the community or the right of the individual. The value of freedom of expression rests on the social nature of individuals and the constitutive character of public discourse. This understanding of the freedom, however, has been inhibited by the individualism that dominates contemporary thinking about rights—its assumptions about the pre-social individual and the instrumental value of community life. Once we recognize that individual agency and identity emerge in the social relationship of communication, the traditional split between intrinsic and instrumental accounts (or social and individual accounts) of the value of freedom of expression dissolves. Expression connects the individual (as speaker or listener) with others and in so doing contributes to her capacity for understanding and judgment, to her engagement in community life and to her participation in a shared culture and collective governance.

The arguments described as instrumental focus on the contribution of speech to the collective goals of truth and democracy. However, we value truth not as an abstract social achievement but rather as something that is consciously realized by members of the community, individually and collectively, in the process of public discussion. Similarly, freedom of expression is not simply a tool or instrument that contributes to democratic government. We value freedom of expression not simply because it provides individuals with useful political information but more fundamentally because it is the way in which citizens participate in collective self-governance. There is no way to separate the goal from the process or the individual good from the public good.

Attaching the label "intrinsic" to autonomy or self-realization accounts of the freedom seems also to misdescribe the value at stake. Communication is a joint or public process, in which individual participants realize their human capacities and their individual identities. The individual does not simply gain satisfaction from expressing his pre-existing views on things: an individual's views, and more broadly his judgment and identity, take shape in the communicative process.

Freedom of expression theories are also categorized as either "listener" or "speaker" centred. Listener-centred theories emphasize the right of the listener to hear and judge expression for herself. The listener's right is protected as a matter of respect for her autonomy as a rational agent or for its contribution to social goals such as the development of truth or the advancement of democratic government. Speaker-centred theories emphasize the value of self-expression. The individual's freedom to express himself is a part of his basic human autonomy or is critical to his ability to direct the development of his own personality. Each of these accounts recognizes the connection between speaking and listening, yet each values one or the other of these activities or, if it values them both, it values them as distinct or independent interests. Freedom of expression is valuable because it advances an important individual interest of the listener (or a more general social interest) and/or an important individual interest of the speaker.

The focus of these accounts on the different interests of the speaker and the listener, misses the central dynamic of the freedom, the communicative relationship, in which the interests of speaker and listener are tied. The activities of speaking and listening are part of a process and a relationship. This relationship is valuable because individual agency emerges and flourishes in the joint activity of creating meaning.

A central issue in many of the more contentious freedom of expression cases—for example, those involving the restriction of hate promotion, advertising, and pornography—is whether the restricted expression causes harm. As you will see below, under the Charter, these issues of harm are typically dealt with under s. 1 as issues justifying a limitation of the right. In most of these cases the court looks to social science evidence of the link between expression and harm. However, this evidence is often inconclusive and so the court sometimes falls back on a "common sense" recognition of the link between expression and harm or defers to the legislature's judgment that such a link exists, particularly when the restriction is meant to protect a vulnerable group in the community. What kind of harm does expression cause? How is this harm caused? As you read the cases in this chapter, consider how well the Court's approach to limits under s. 1 fits with the conventional view that individuals should be permitted to hear and assess competing positions and that the community must take the risk that they will sometimes make bad decisions.

Owen Fiss, in his book *Liberalism Divided: Freedom of Speech and the Many Uses of State Power* (Boulder, CO: Westview Press, 1996), at 4-6, suggests a way of looking at some of the issues with respect to limitation of freedom of expression:

The division within liberal circles prompted by the free speech controversies [about pornography, hate speech and election spending] of the [past few decades] is in part attributable to the maturation of liberalism as a political philosophy. Whereas liberalism in the nineteenth century was defined almost exclusively by the defense of individual liberty against state intrusion, today its mandate is more pluralistic. Contemporary liberalism is as devoted to furthering equality as it is to protecting liberty. ...

Equality has thus become one of the defining goals of liberalism. As a result, the traditional commitment of liberal theory to state minimalism necessarily has become compromised. The limited state may be an instrument furthering liberty, but, as many recognized, the pursuit of egalitarian objectives often requires strong exercises of state power, including curbs on speech or expressive activity. Those who support the regulation of pornography and hate speech, for example, have insisted that sometimes liberty must be sacrificed in order to protect disadvantaged groups from social stigmatization and subordination. Similar egalitarian sentiments inform the debates over campaign finance, access to shopping centers [and] regulation of mass media. ... The purpose of such state activity is to give the economically disadvantaged speech opportunities roughly comparable to those enjoyed by the rich. This intervention is defended by many liberals as a proper pursuit of egalitarianism even though it entails the sacrifice of individual liberty, specifically the freedom to decide how to deploy one's property or other economic resources to further political goals.

Formulated in these terms, the free speech controversy of the last two decades can be analyzed as one confronting liberals with a choice between transcendent values. Which shall be given priority, liberty or equality? Such a conflict is familiar in the history of political thought and even in the constitutional domain. For that reason, the present moment in the history of freedom of speech may be understood as nothing more than a transference of a familiar dilemma to a new realm. But I see within contemporary free speech controversies another problem. ... I see within these controversies not simply a conflict between liberty and equality but also, and perhaps more fundamental, a conflict between liberty and liberty. The division within liberalism arises not from its pluralistic commitments and inability to prioritize equality and liberty but rather, I maintain, from a dispute over the very meaning of freedom. What is at issue [are] two different ways of understanding liberty.

· · ·

Aside from the impact on the social status of disadvantaged groups such as women or minorities, some liberals support the regulation of pornography and hate speech on the hypothesis that these forms of expression silence disadvantaged groups and thus distort public debate. State regulation of private centers of power—say, shopping centers or the mass media—is advocated as a way of presenting the public with information from diverse, even antagonistic, sources. ...

Liberals' support for state interventions of the nature just outlined depends on contested empirical judgments—for example, about the silencing effect of pornography or the market's distortions of public debate. It also assumes that the state apparatus will not be captured by the powerful and used in the opposite way from that intended—not to enrich but to impoverish public debate.

But how does silencing occur? When should we regard the audience as something that expression "affects" or as something that expression "causes" to act in a particular way and when should we regard the audience as independent decision-makers capable of making judgments and of being responsible for the views they adopt and the actions they take?

II. THE SCOPE AND LIMITS OF FREEDOM OF EXPRESSION

In its early freedom of expression judgments, the Supreme Court of Canada adopted a broad view of the scope of s. 2(b). According to the Court, any (non-violent) activity that conveys a message is expression under s. 2(b). The Court held, for example, that labour picketing, communicating for the purposes of prostitution, commercial advertising, and language choice are all forms of expression protected by s. 2(b). In most freedom of expression cases, the Court finds, with little difficulty, that the restricted "expression" is protected under s. 2(b) and quickly moves on to s. 1, where the real debate seems to take place.

The first significant freedom of expression case to come before the Supreme Court of Canada, *Retail, Wholesale and Department Store Union, Local 580 v. Dolphin Delivery Ltd.*, [1986] 2 SCR 573, 33 DLR (4th) 174, concerned the constitutionality of an injunction against labour picketing. The striking employees of Purolator planned to set up a picket line at the workplace of Dolphin Delivery. They believed that Dolphin Delivery was doing work for Supercourier, a company related to Purolator that was carrying on Purolator's BC business during the strike. The Purolator workers hoped that the Dolphin Delivery workers would respect their picket line, putting pressure on Dolphin Delivery to stop doing Purolator work and, indirectly, on Purolator to settle the contract dispute.

Dolphin Delivery brought an application for an injunction against the Purolator union to prevent it from setting up the picket line. The injunction was granted by the Supreme Court of British Columbia on the grounds that a line by Purolator workers at the site of Dolphin Delivery would be a secondary picket meant to induce Dolphin Delivery to breach its contract with Supercourier and that this amounted to a common law tort.

The issue that came to the Supreme Court of Canada was whether the injunction violated freedom of expression under the Charter. In deciding whether or not the Charter had been breached, it was necessary for the Court to decide, first, whether or not an injunction issued under the common law rules concerning picketing was subject to review under the Charter second, whether picketing was a matter of freedom of expression protected by s. 2(b) and, finally, if picketing was expression, whether or not the restriction of picketing in this case was a justifiable limit under s. 1.

McIntyre J, writing for the majority of the Court, decided that the injunction was not government action subject to Charter review (and that portion of the judgment can be found in Chapter 18, Application). However, McIntyre J went on to consider the substantive Charter issues. The following excerpt from the case focuses on the freedom of expression claim made by the union.

Retail, Wholesale and Department Store Union, Local 580 v. Dolphin Delivery Ltd.
[1986] 2 SCR 573, 33 DLR (4th) 174

McINTYRE J (Dickson CJC and Estey, Chouinard, and Le Dain JJ concurring): This appeal raises the question of whether secondary picketing by members of a trade union in a labour dispute is a protected activity under s. 2(b) of the *Canadian Charter of Rights and Freedoms* and, accordingly, not the proper subject of an injunction to restrain it.

[After reviewing the decisions of the lower courts, McIntyre J made the following observations about the facts of the case.]

[T]he Chambers judge found that the purpose of the picketing was tortious and that the dominant purpose was to injure the plaintiff rather than the dissemination of information and protection of the defendant's interest. …
… In summary then, it has been found that the respondent was a third party, that the anticipated picketing would be tortious, that the purpose was to injure the plaintiff. It was assumed that the picketing would be peaceful, that some employees of the respondent and other trade union members of customers would decline to cross the picket lines, and that the business of the respondent would be disrupted to a considerable extent. …

Freedom of Expression

… Is freedom of expression involved in this case? In seeking an answer to this question, it must be observed at once that in any form of picketing there is involved at least some element of expression. The picketers would be conveying a message which at a very minimum would be classed as persuasion, aimed at deterring customers and prospective customers from doing business with the respondent. The question then arises. Does this expression in the circumstances of this case have Charter protection under the provisions of s. 2(b), and if it does, then does the injunction abridge or infringe such freedom?

The appellants argue strongly that picketing is a form of expression fully entitled to Charter protection and rely on various authorities to support the proposition. … They reject the American distinction between the concept of speech and that of conduct made in picketing cases, and they accept the view of Hutcheon JA in the Court of Appeal, in adopting the words of Freedman CJM in *Channel Seven Television Ltd. v. National Association of Broadcast Employees and Technicians*, [1971] 5 WWR 328, that "Peaceful picketing falls within freedom of speech."

The respondent contends for a narrower approach to the concept of freedom of expression. The position is summarized in the respondent's factum:

4. We submit that constitutional protection under section 2(b) should only be given to those forms of expression that warrant such protection. To do otherwise would trivialize freedom of expression generally and lead to a downgrading or dilution of this freedom.

Reliance is placed on the view of the majority in the Court of Appeal that picketing in a labour dispute is more than mere communication of information. It is also a signal to trade unionists not to cross the picket line. The respect accorded to picket lines by trade unionists is such that the result of the picketing would be to damage seriously the operation of the employer, not to communicate any information. Therefore, it is argued, since the picket line was not intended to promote dialogue or discourse (as would be the case where its purpose was the exercise of freedom of expression), it cannot qualify for protection under the Charter.

On the basis of the findings of fact that I have referred to above, it is evident that the purpose of the picketing in this case was to induce a breach of contract between the respondent and Supercourier and thus to exert economic pressure to force it to cease doing business with Supercourier. It is equally evident that, if successful, the picketing would have done serious injury to the respondent. There is nothing remarkable about this, however, because all picketing is designed to bring economic pressure on the person picketed and to cause economic loss for so long as the object of the picketing remains unfulfilled. There is, as I have earlier said, always some element of expression in picketing. The union is making a statement to the general public that it is involved in a dispute, that it is seeking to impose its will on the object of the picketing, and that it solicits the assistance of the public in honouring the picket line. Action on the part of the picketers will, of course, always accompany the expression, but not every action on the part of the picketers will be such as to alter the nature of the whole transaction and remove it from Charter protection for freedom of expression. That freedom, of course, would not extend to protect threats of violence or acts of violence. It would not protect the destruction of property, or assaults, or other clearly unlawful conduct. We need not, however, be concerned with such matters here because the picketing would have been peaceful. I am therefore of the view that the picketing sought to be restrained would have involved the exercise of the right of freedom of expression.

Section 1 of the Charter

… Can an injunction based on the common law tort of inducing a breach of contract, which has the effect of limiting the Charter right to freedom of expression, be sustained as a reasonable limit imposed by law in the peculiar facts of this case?

From the evidence, it may well be said that the concern of the respondent is pressing and substantial. It will suffer economically in the absence of an injunction to restrain picketing. On the other hand, the injunction has imposed a limitation upon a Charter freedom. A balance between the two competing concerns must be found. It may be argued that the concern of the respondent regarding economic loss would not be sufficient to constitute a reasonable limitation on the right of freedom of expression, but there is another basis upon which the respondent's position may be supported. This case involves secondary picketing—picketing of a third party not concerned in the dispute which underlies the picketing. The basis of our system of collective bargaining is the proposition that the parties themselves should, wherever possible, work out their own agreement. ...

When the parties do exercise the right to disagree, picketing and other forms of industrial conflict are likely to follow. The social cost is great, man-hours and wages are lost, production and services will be disrupted, and general tensions within the community may be heightened. Such industrial conflict may be tolerated by society but only as an inevitable corollary to the collective bargaining process. It is therefore necessary in the general social interest that picketing be regulated and sometimes limited. It is reasonable to restrain picketing so that the conflict will not escalate beyond the actual parties. While picketing is, no doubt, a legitimate weapon to be employed in a labour dispute by the employees against their employer, it should not be permitted to harm others. ...

I would say that the requirement of proportionality is also met, particularly when it is recalled that this is an interim injunction effective only until trial when the issues may be more fully canvassed on fuller evidence. It is my opinion then that a limitation on secondary picketing against a third party, that is, a non-ally, would be a reasonable limit in the facts of this case. I would therefore conclude that the injunction is "a reasonable limit prescribed by law which can be demonstrably justified in a free and democratic society." ...

Appeal dismissed.

NOTES AND QUESTIONS

1. In *Dolphin Delivery* the Court held that picketing is a form of expression protected by s. 2(b), but that it could be restricted in this case under s. 1 because it would cause (unnecessary) harm to the picketed business and to the larger community. However, since the picket line was pre-empted by the injunction there was no evidence of any physical intimidation or obstruction of the Dolphin Delivery employees. Even if the evidence had shown actual physical obstruction or intimidation, was the Court not required to consider whether this harm could have been prevented without a complete ban on picketing?

2. In determining whether a restriction on expression is justified under s. 1, is it enough simply to identify an injury or a loss that "results" from an act of expression? If someone pickets outside a store, encouraging people not to shop there because it sells goods manufactured in Burma, and if people listen to the message and decide not to shop at the store, or at least not to buy Burmese goods, is the store not being harmed? Is there a difference between this form of expression and labour picketing or between the harms caused by each?

3. In *UFCW, Local 1518 v. KMart Canada Ltd.*, [1999] 2 SCR 1083, 176 DLR (4th) 607 the Supreme Court of Canada distinguished between leafleting and picketing. The workers at several KMart stores, who had been locked out for six months while trying to negotiate a first collective agreement, distributed leaflets outside the entrances of several nonunionized KMart stores that were not directly involved in the labour dispute. The leaflets described the dispute and asked potential customers to boycott KMart. There was no interference with employees or with the delivery of supplies. Nor was public access to the stores impeded in any way. Nevertheless, the Labour Relations Board held that the distribution of leaflets at the nonunionized KMart stores fell within the definition of secondary picketing in the BC *Labour Relations Code*, SBC 1992, c. 82 and was therefore unlawful.

The Supreme Court of Canada ruled that the ban on secondary picketing in the BC *Labour Relations Code*, "which undoubtably encompass[es] leafleting," violated s. 2(b) and was not justified under s. 1. In reaching this conclusion the Court distinguished between labour picketing and consumer leafleting. Writing for the Court, Cory J held that:

> Consumer leafleting is very different from a picket line. It seeks to persuade members of the public to take a certain course of action. It does so through informed and rational discourse which is the very essence of freedom of expression. Leafleting does not trigger the "signal" effect inherent in the picket line and it certainly does not have the same coercive component.

Do you agree with the Court that leafleting and picketing are different? How workable is this distinction?

4. More recently, in *RWDSU, Local 558 v. Pepsi-Cola Canada Beverages (West) Ltd.*, 2002 SCC 8, 208 DLR (4th) 385, which is also discussed in Chapter 18, Application, the Supreme Court of Canada (re)interpreted the common law rules concerning secondary picketing in light of Charter values and held that "secondary picketing is generally lawful [under the common law] unless it involves tortious or criminal conduct." In a judgment written by McLachlin CJC and LeBel J, the Court rejected the suggestion that "expression in a labour context should be treated as fundamentally less important than expression in other contexts":

> [97] ... It is far from clear that union speech is more likely to elicit an irrational or reflexive response than, for example, speech by a political organization. If we say that the signalling effect justifies a special prohibition in the labour context, does it not follow that signalling in other contexts may also justify blanket prohibitions? Moreover, it seems clear that freedom of expression is not confined to "rational" speech. Irrationality may support according less protection to particular kinds of speech. But it does not justify denying all protection as a matter of principle.

The court understood tortious conduct to include inducing breach of contract. Is it obvious that expression should be restricted when it encourages an individual or corporation to breach a contract? (It is generally accepted that freedom of expression protects the right to argue in support of unlawful action.) Does the Court's willingness to uphold the tort of inducement to breach contract rest on an assumption that labour picketing has a "signalling effect"?

———————————————

The Supreme Court of Canada's second major decision on freedom of expression, *Ford v. Quebec (AG)*, [1988] 2 SCR 712, 54 DLR (4th) 577, involved a challenge to the provisions of the Quebec *Charter of the French Language*, which required that outdoor commercial signs be exclusively in French. The Supreme Court of Canada found that the legislation violated freedom of expression under s. 2(b) of the Charter and could not be upheld as a reasonable restriction under s. 1. The Court found that while the province was justified in requiring the use of French, it was not justified in prohibiting the use of other languages.

The Court rejected the distinction between message and medium put forward (ironically) by the Quebec Attorney General in support of the position that freedom of expression does not include the freedom to express oneself in the language of one's choice:

Language is so intimately related to the form and content of expression that there cannot be true freedom of expression by means of language if one is prohibited from using the language of one's choice. Language is not merely a means or medium of expression; it colours the content and meaning of expression. It is, as the preamble of the *Charter of the French Language* itself indicates, a means by which a people may express its cultural identity. It is also the means by which the individual expresses his or her personal identity and sense of individuality. That the concept of "expression" in s. 2(b) of the Canadian Charter ... goes beyond mere content is indicated by the specific protection accorded to "freedom of thought, belief [and] opinion" in s. 2. ... That suggests that "freedom of expression" is intended to extend to more than the content of expression in its narrow sense.

In *Ford*, the Supreme Court of Canada also held that commercial expression (that is, advertising) falls within the scope of s. 2(b):

Given the earlier pronouncements of this Court to the effect that the rights and freedoms guaranteed in the Canadian Charter should be given a large and liberal interpretation, there is no sound basis on which commercial expression can be excluded from the protection of s. 2(b) of the Charter. ... Over and above its intrinsic value as expression, commercial expression which, as has been pointed out, protects listeners as well as speakers, plays a significant role in enabling individuals to make informed economic choices, an important aspect of individual self-fulfillment and personal autonomy. The Court accordingly rejects the view that commercial expression serves no individual or societal value in a free and democratic society and for this reason is undeserving of any constitutional protection.

A more extensive extract from the *Ford* decision can be found in Chapter 24, Language Rights.

In *Irwin Toy*, below, the Court consolidated its earlier rulings in *Dolphin Delivery* and *Ford* and, in a comprehensive set of reasons, laid out the basic approach to be followed when freedom of expression claims are made.

Irwin Toy Ltd. v. Quebec (AG)
[1989] 1 SCR 927, 58 DLR (4th) 577

[This case involved a challenge to the provisions of Quebec's *Consumer Protection Act*, SQ 1978, c. 9 (CPA), and the relevant regulations governing children's advertising. Section 248 of the CPA provided that, subject to the regulations, "no person may make use of commercial advertising directed at persons under 13 years of age." Section 249 identified the factors to be considered in determining whether an advertisement is directed to persons under 13 years, including the nature and intended purpose of the goods advertised; the manner of presenting such advertisement; and the time and place it is shown. The regulations set out certain exemptions from the prohibition on children's advertising. Advertising in children's magazines was allowed, for example, as were announcements of children's programs or shows, subject to certain content restrictions, such as a prohibition on the use of a person or character known to children to promote goods and services. Irwin Toy broadcast messages that the Office de la protection du consommateur claimed were in contravention of ss. 248 and 249 of the Act. Irwin Toy then instituted an action for a declaration that the sections were *ultra vires* the province or inconsistent with the guarantee of freedom of expression found in s. 3 of the *Quebec Charter of Human Rights and Freedoms*, RSQ 1977, c. C-12. The trial judge dismissed the action. The Court of Appeal, having allowed Irwin Toy to amend its pleadings to raise the issue of inconsistency with the *Canadian Charter of Rights and Freedoms*, which had come into effect since the commencement of the action, concluded that the impugned sections violated s. 2(b) of the Charter and could not be justified under s. 1. At the Supreme Court of Canada, the issue of inconsistency with s. 7 of the Charter was also raised. Only the portions of the judgment dealing with s. 2(b) of the Charter (and the related s. 1 analysis) are reproduced below. The parallel analysis of s. 3 of the Quebec Charter (and s. 9.1, the equivalent of s. 1 of the Canadian Charter) has been omitted. The Supreme Court held that Irwin Toy could not rely on s. 7 to challenge the law since s. 7 did not protect corporations and other artificial entities that were incapable of enjoying life, liberty, and security of the person. On the federalism issue, the Court concluded that the provisions were *intra vires* the province as valid consumer protection legislation and did not constitute an intrusion into federal jurisdiction over broadcasting or criminal law.]

DICKSON CJC, LAMER and WILSON JJ:

. . .

VI. Whether Sections 248 and 249 Limit Freedom of Expression as Guaranteed by the Canadian and Quebec Charters

. . .

B. The First Step: Was the Plaintiff's Activity Within the Sphere of Conduct Protected by Freedom of Expression?

Does advertising aimed at children fall within the scope of freedom of expression? This question must be put even before deciding whether there has been a limitation of the guarantee. Clearly, not all activity is protected by freedom of expression, and governmental action restricting this form of advertising only limits the guarantee if the activity in issue was protected in the first place. ...

"Expression" has both a content and a form, and the two can be inextricably connected. Activity is expressive if it attempts to convey meaning. That meaning is its content. Freedom of expression was entrenched in our Constitution ... so as to ensure that everyone can manifest their thoughts, opinions, beliefs, indeed all expressions of the heart and mind, however unpopular, distasteful or contrary to the mainstream. Such protection is, in the words of both the Canadian and Quebec Charters, "fundamental" because in a free, pluralistic and democratic society we prize a diversity of ideas and opinions for their inherent value both to the community and to the individual. ...

We cannot, then, exclude human activity from the scope of guaranteed free expression on the basis of the content or meaning being conveyed. Indeed, if the activity conveys or attempts to convey a meaning, it has expressive content and *prima facie* falls within the scope of the guarantee. Of course, while most human activity combines expressive and physical elements, some human activity is purely physical and does not convey or attempt to convey meaning. It might be difficult to characterize certain day-to-day tasks, like parking a car, as having expressive content. To bring such activity within the protected sphere, the plaintiff would have to show that it was performed to convey a meaning. For example, an unmarried person might, as part of a public protest, park in a zone reserved for spouses of government employees in order to express dissatisfaction or outrage at the chosen method of allocating a limited resource. If that person could demonstrate that his activity did in fact have expressive content, he would, at this stage, be within the protected sphere and the s. 2(b) challenge would proceed.

The content of expression can be conveyed through an infinite variety of forms of expression: for example, the written or spoken word, the arts, and even physical gestures or acts. While the guarantee of free expression protects all content of expression, certainly violence as a form of expression receives no such protection. It is not necessary here to delineate precisely when and on what basis a form of expression chosen to convey a meaning falls outside the sphere of the guarantee. But it is clear, for example, that a murderer or rapist cannot invoke freedom of expression in justification of the form of expression he has chosen. ...

Thus, the first question remains: Does the advertising aimed at children fall within the scope of freedom of expression? Surely it aims to convey a meaning, and cannot be excluded as having no expressive content. Nor is there any basis for excluding the form of expression chosen from the sphere of protected activity. ...

Consequently, we must proceed to the second step of the inquiry and ask whether the purpose or effect of the government action in question was to restrict freedom of expression. ...

C. The Second Step: Was the Purpose or Effect of the Government Action to Restrict Freedom of Expression?

. . .

a. Purpose

When applying the purpose test to the guarantee of free expression, one must beware of drifting to either of two extremes. On the one hand, the greatest part of human activity has an expressive element and so one might find, on an objective test, that an aspect of the government's purpose is virtually always to restrict expression. On the other hand, the government can almost always claim that its subjective purpose was to address some real or purported social need, not to restrict expression. To avoid both extremes, the government's purpose must be assessed from the standpoint of the guarantee in question. ...

If the government's purpose is to restrict the content of expression by singling out particular meanings that are not to be conveyed, it necessarily limits the guarantee of free expression. If the government's purpose is to restrict a form of expression in order to control access by others to the meaning being conveyed or to control the ability of the one conveying the meaning to do so, it also limits the guarantee. On the other hand, where the government aims to control only the physical consequences of certain human activity, regardless of the meaning being conveyed, its purpose is not to control expression. Archibald Cox has described the distinction as follows (*Freedom of Expression* (1981), at pp. 59-60):

> The bold line ... between restrictions upon publication and regulation of the time, place and manner of expression tied to content, on the one hand, and regulation of time, place, or manner of expression regardless of content, on the other hand, reflects the difference between the state's usually impermissible effort to suppress "harmful" information, ideas, or emotions and the state's often justifiable desire to secure other interests against interference from the noise and the physical intrusions that accompany speech, regardless of the information, ideas, or emotions expressed.

Thus, for example, a rule against handing out pamphlets is a restriction on a manner of expression and is "tied to content," even if that restriction purports to control litter. The rule aims to control access by others to a meaning being conveyed as well as to control the ability of the pamphleteer to convey a meaning. To restrict this form of expression, handing out pamphlets, entails restricting its content. By contrast, a rule against littering is not a restriction "tied to content." It aims to control the physical consequences of certain conduct regardless of whether that conduct attempts to convey meaning. To restrict littering as a "manner of expression" need not lead inexorably to restricting a content. Of course, rules can be framed to appear neutral as to content even if their true purpose is to control attempts to convey a meaning. ...

In determining whether the government's purpose aims simply at harmful physical consequences, the question becomes: does the mischief consist in the meaning of the activity or the purported influence that meaning has on the behaviour of others, or does it consist, rather, only in the direct physical result of the activity.

b. Effects

Even if the government's purpose was not to control or restrict attempts to convey a meaning, the Court must still decide whether the effect of the government action was to restrict the plaintiff's free expression. Here, the burden is on the plaintiff to demonstrate that such an effect occurred. In order so to demonstrate, a plaintiff must state her claim with reference to the principles and values underlying the freedom.

We have already discussed the nature of the principles and values underlying the vigilant protection of free expression in a society such as ours. They were also discussed by the Court in *Ford v. Quebec (Attorney General)*, [1988] 2 SCR 712 (at pp. 765-67), and can be summarized as follows: (1) seeking and attaining the truth is an inherently good activity; (2) participation in social and political decision-making is to be fostered and encouraged; and (3) the diversity in forms of individual self-fulfillment and human flourishing ought to be cultivated in an essentially tolerant, indeed welcoming, environment not only for the sake of those who convey a meaning, but also for the sake of those to whom it is conveyed. In showing that the effect of the government's action was to restrict her free expression, a plaintiff must demonstrate that her activity promotes at least one of these principles. It is not enough that shouting, for example, has an expressive element. If the plaintiff challenges the effect of government action to control noise, presuming that action to have a purpose neutral as to expression, she must show that her aim was to convey a meaning reflective of the principles underlying freedom of expression. The precise and complete articulation of what kinds of activity promote these principles is, of course, a matter for judicial appreciation to be developed on a case-by-case basis.

But the plaintiff must at least identify the meaning being conveyed and how it relates to the pursuit of truth, participation in the community, or individual self-fulfillment and human flourishing. ...

In the instant case, the plaintiff's activity is not excluded from the sphere of conduct protected by freedom of expression. The government's purpose in enacting ss. 248 and 249 of the *Consumer Protection Act* and in promulgating ss. 87 to 91 of the *Regulation respecting the application of the Consumer Protection Act* was to prohibit particular content of expression in the name of protecting children. These provisions therefore constitute limitations to s. 2(b) of the Canadian Charter. ... They fall to be justified under s. 1 of the Canadian Charter. ...

VII. Whether the Limit on Freedom of Expression Imposed by Sections 248 and 249 Is Justified Under Section 9.1 of the Quebec Charter or Section 1 of the Canadian Charter

[The three judges then deal with the issue of whether the scheme put into place by ss. 248 and 249 is so vague as not to constitute a limit "prescribed by law." They conclude that there is nothing inherently confusing or contradictory about ss. 248 and 249 and that despite the element of discretion involved in the interpretation of the sections, the legislature had provided an intelligible standard. That aspect of the judgment is dealt with further in the discussion of "prescribed by law" and vagueness found in Chapter 17, The Framework of the Charter. The analysis then moves to the issue of justification under s. 1.]

The question becomes whether the evidence submitted by the government establishes that children under 13 are unable to make choices and distinctions respecting products advertised and whether this in turn justifies the restriction on advertising put into place. Studies subsequent to the enactment of the legislation can be used for this purpose.

[On the evidentiary issue, the three judges found that although it is not open to the government, under s. 1, to assert a legislative objective that did not animate the legislation at the time of enactment, in proving that the objective remains pressing and substantial the government is allowed to draw upon the best evidence currently available.]

. . .

a. Pressing and Substantial Objective

... In our view, the Attorney General of Quebec has demonstrated that the concern which prompted the enactment of the impugned legislation is pressing and substantial and that the purpose of the legislation is one of great importance. The concern is for the protection of a group which is particularly vulnerable to the techniques of seduction and manipulation abundant in advertising. In the words of the Attorney General of Quebec, [TRANSLATION] "Children experience most manifestly the kind of inequality and imbalance between producers and consumers which the legislature wanted to correct." The material given in evidence before this Court is indicative of a generalized concern in Western societies with the impact of media, and particularly but not solely televised advertising, on the development and perceptions of young children. ... Broadly speaking, the concerns which have motivated both legislative and voluntary regulation in this area are the particular susceptibility of young children to media manipulation, their inability to differentiate between reality and fiction and to grasp the persuasive intention behind the message, and the secondary effects of exterior influences on the family and parental authority. Responses to the perceived problems are as varied as the agencies and governments which have promulgated them. However the consensus of concern is high.

In establishing the factual basis for this generally identified concern, the Attorney General relied heavily upon the US Federal Trade Commission (FTC) Final Staff Report and Recommendation, "In the Matter of Children's Advertising," which contains a thorough review of the scientific evidence on the subject as at 1981. ... One of [the report's] principal conclusions is that young children (2-6) cannot distinguish fact from fiction or programming from advertising and are completely credulous when presented with advertising messages. ...

The report thus provides a sound basis on which to conclude that television advertising directed at young children is *per se* manipulative. Such advertising aims to promote products by convincing those who will always believe.

It is reasonable to extend this conclusion in two ways. First, it can be extended to advertising in other media. For example, the OECD Report [*Advertising Directed at Children: Endorsements in Advertising* (1982)] discusses children's advertising in all media including television, although the greatest body of evidence focuses on the persuasive force of television advertising. Second, it can be extended to advertising aimed at older children (7-13). The Attorney General filed a number of studies reaching somewhat different conclusions about the age at which children generally develop the cognitive ability to recognize the persuasive nature of advertising and to evaluate its comparative worth. The studies suggest that at some point between age seven and adolescence, children become as capable as adults of understanding and responding to advertisements. The majority in the Court of Appeal interpreted this evidence narrowly and found that it only justified the objective of regulating advertising aimed at children six or younger, not the regulation of advertising aimed at children between the ages of seven and thirteen. They concluded, and we agree, that the evidence was strongest with respect to the younger age category. Opinion is more divided when children in the older age category are involved. But the legislature was not obliged to confine itself solely to protecting the most clearly vulnerable group. It was only required to exercise a reasonable judgment in specifying the vulnerable group.

[Reference is then made to Dickson CJC's ruling in *Edwards Books and Art Ltd. v. The Queen*, [1986] 2 SCR 713, found in Chapter 19, Freedom of Religion, to the effect that s. 1 requires a "reasonable limit," with the result that "courts are not called upon to substitute judicial opinions for legislative ones as to the place at which to draw the line." The "line" in issue in *Edwards Books* was a legislative decision to exempt businesses having seven or fewer employees from a Sunday closing rule.]

The same can be said of evaluating competing credible scientific evidence and choosing thirteen, as opposed to ten or seven, as the upper age limit for the protected group here in issue. Where the legislature mediates between the competing claims of different groups in the community, it will inevitably be called upon to draw a line marking where one set of claims legitimately begins and the other fades away without access to complete knowledge as to its precise location. If the legislature has made a reasonable assessment as to where the line is most properly drawn, especially if that assessment involves weighing conflicting scientific evidence and allocating scarce resources on this basis, it is not for the court to second guess. That would only be to substitute one estimate for another. In dealing with inherently heterogeneous groups defined in terms of age or a characteristic analogous to age, evidence showing that a clear majority of the group requires the protection which the government has identified can help to establish that the group was defined reasonably. Here, the legislature has mediated between the claims of advertisers and those seeking commercial information on the one hand, and the claims of children and parents on the other. There is sufficient evidence to warrant drawing a line at age thirteen, and we would not presume to re-draw the line. ...

The s. 1 ... materials demonstrate, on the balance of probabilities, that children up to the age of thirteen are manipulated by commercial advertising and that the objective of protecting all children in this age group is predicated on a pressing and substantial concern. We thus conclude that the Attorney General has discharged the onus under the first part of the *Oakes* test.

b. Means Proportional to the Ends

[The rational connection test is easily found to have been satisfied. The analysis then moves to the issue of minimal impairment.]

... [I]n matching means to ends and asking whether rights or freedoms are impaired as little as possible, a legislature mediating between the claims of competing groups will be forced to strike a balance without the benefit of absolute certainty concerning how that balance is best struck. Vulnerable groups will claim the need for protection by the government whereas other groups and individuals will assert that the government should not intrude. In *Edwards Books*, *supra*, Chief Justice Dickson expressed an important concern about the situation of vulnerable groups (at p. 779):

> In interpreting and applying the Charter I believe that the courts must be cautious to ensure that it does not simply become an instrument of better situated individuals to roll back legislation which has as its object the improvement of the condition of less advantaged persons.

When striking a balance between the claims of competing groups, the choice of means, like the choice of ends, frequently will require an assessment of conflicting scientific evidence and differing justified demands on scarce resources. Democratic institutions are meant to let us all share in the responsibility for these difficult choices. Thus, as courts review the results of the legislature's deliberations, particularly with respect to the protection of vulnerable groups, they must be mindful of the legislature's representative function. ...

In other cases, however, rather than mediating between different groups, the government is best characterized as the singular antagonist of the individual whose right has been infringed. For example, in justifying an infringement of legal rights enshrined in ss. 7 to 14 of the Charter, the state, on behalf of the whole community, typically will assert its responsibility for prosecuting crime whereas the individual will assert the paramountcy of principles of fundamental justice. There might not be any further competing claims among different groups. In such circumstances, and indeed whenever the government's purpose relates to maintaining the authority and impartiality of the judicial system, the courts can assess with some certainty whether the "least drastic means" for achieving the purpose have been chosen, especially given their accumulated experience in dealing with such questions. ... The same degree of certainty may not be achievable in cases involving the reconciliation of claims of competing individuals or groups or the distribution of scarce government resources.

In the instant case, the Court is called upon to assess competing social science evidence respecting the appropriate means for addressing the problem of children's advertising. The question is whether the government had a reasonable basis, on the evidence tendered, for concluding that the ban on all advertising directed at children impaired freedom of expression as little as possible given the government's pressing and substantial objective.

The strongest evidence for the proposition that this ban impairs freedom of expression as little as possible comes from the FTC Report. Because the Report found that children are not equipped to identify the persuasive intent of advertising, content regulation could not address the problem. The Report concluded that the only effective means for dealing with advertising directed at children would be a ban on all such advertising because "[a]n informational remedy would not eliminate nor overcome the cognitive limitations that prevent young children from understanding advertising" (p. 36). However, the Report also concluded that such a ban could not be implemented either on the basis of audience composition data or on the basis of a definition of "advertising directed at children." It thus counselled against a ban. ...

Because the FTC Report focussed on the effect of advertising aimed at *young* children (2-6) and proceeded on the basis that advertising directed at *older* children (7-13) did not pose a problem, it concluded, reasonably enough, that no definition could distinguish adequately between advertising directed at young children and advertising directed at older children. ...

Sections 248 and 249 preserve the rationale for a ban contained in the FTC Report at the same time as overcoming the practical limitations suggested therein. The sections contemplate a larger age group than that envisaged by the FTC Report, and always allow advertising aimed at adults, thereby avoiding the difficulties identified in the Report both with a ban based on audience composition and with a ban based on the definition of "advertising directed to children." The *Guidelines for the application of sections 248 and 249* help to illustrate this. They specify a number of time periods during the day when, based on Bureau of Broadcast Measurement (BBM) statistics, over 15% of the audience is made up of children aged 2 to 11. It was possible to arrive at these time periods despite the FTC's arguments precisely because a larger target group was specified. Furthermore, using this larger target group, it was possible for the Office de la protection du consommateur to identify products and advertising methods aimed at children. ... By specifying categories of (1) products, (2) advertisements and (3) audience, the Guidelines allow for a sophisticated appraisal of when an advertisement is aimed at children. These three categories are drawn directly from s. 249 and their elaboration by the Office is an attempt to perform the same balancing test required of the courts. ... On this basis, the Guidelines set forth a table according to which different kinds of advertisements for the various product categories will be permitted depending upon audience composition. There is a system of pre-clearance run by a committee of the Office which helps advertisers to determine whether any given commercial is subject to the ban.

While ss. 248 and 249 do not incorporate all the details included in the Guidelines, they do put into place the framework for a practicable ban on advertising directed at children. ...

Of course, despite the FTC Report's conclusions to the contrary, the respondent argued that a ban was not the only effective means for dealing with the problem posed by children's advertising. In particular, it pointed to the self-regulation mechanism provided by the Broadcast Code for Advertising to Children as an obvious alternative and emphasized that Quebec was unique among industrialized countries in banning advertising aimed at children. ... The latter assertion must be qualified in two respects. First, as of 1984, Belgium, Denmark, Norway and Sweden did not allow any commercials on television and radio. Second, throughout Canada, as in Italy, the public network does not accept children's commercials (except, in the case of the CBC, during "family programs"). Consequently, Quebec's ban on advertising aimed at children is not out of proportion to measures taken in other jurisdictions. Nor is legislative action to protect vulnerable groups necessarily restricted to the least common denominator of actions taken elsewhere. Based on narrower objectives than those pursued by Quebec, some governments might reasonably conclude that self-regulation is an adequate mechanism for addressing the problem of children's advertising. But having identified advertising aimed at persons under thirteen as *per se* manipulative, the legislature of Quebec could conclude, just as reasonably, that the only effective statutory response was to ban such advertising.

In sum, the evidence sustains the reasonableness of the legislature's conclusion that a ban on commercial advertising directed to children was the minimal impairment of free expression consistent with the pressing and substantial goal of protecting children against manipulation through such advertising. While evidence exists that other less intrusive options reflecting more modest objectives were available to the government, there is evidence establishing the necessity of a ban to meet the objectives the government had reasonably set. This Court will not, in the name of minimal impairment, take a restrictive approach to social science evidence and require legislatures to choose the least ambitious means to protect vulnerable groups. There must nevertheless be a sound evidentiary basis for the government's conclusions. ...

iii. *Deleterious effects.* There is no suggestion here that the effects of the ban are so severe as to outweigh the government's pressing and substantial objective. Advertisers are always free to direct their message at parents and other adults. They are also free to participate in educational advertising. The real concern animating the challenge to the legislation is that revenues are in some degree affected. This only implies that advertisers will have to develop new marketing strategies for children's products. ...

[The impugned provisions are therefore upheld under s. 1 of the Charter.]

McINTYRE J (Beetz J concurring) dissenting: ... While I agree with [my colleagues] that ss. 248 and 249 of the *Consumer Protection Act* infringe s. 2(b) of the *Canadian Charter of Rights and Freedoms*. ... I do not agree that they may be justified under s. 1 of the Canadian Charter. ...

Can it be said that the welfare of children is at risk because of advertising directed at them? I am not satisfied that any case has been shown that it is. There was evidence that small children are incapable of distinguishing fact from fiction in advertising. This is hardly surprising: many adults have the same problem. Children, however, do not remain children. They grow up and, while advertising directed at children may well be a source of irritation to parents, no case has been shown here that children suffer harm. Children live in a world of fiction, imagination and make believe. Children's literature is based upon these concepts. As they mature, they make adjustments and can be expected to pass beyond the range of any ill which might be caused by advertising. In my view, no case has been made that children are at risk. Furthermore, even if I could reach another conclusion, I would be of the view that the restriction fails on the issue of proportionality. A total prohibition of advertising aimed at children below an arbitrarily fixed age makes no attempt at the achievement of proportionality.

In conclusion, I would say that freedom of expression is too important to be lightly cast aside or limited. It is ironic that most attempts to limit freedom of expression and hence freedom of knowledge and information are justified on the basis that the limitation is for the benefit of those whose rights will be limited. It was this proposition that motivated the early church in restricting access to information, even to prohibiting the promulgation and reading of the scriptures in a language understood by the people. The argument that freedom of expression was dangerous was used to oppose and restrict public education in earlier times. The education of women was greatly retarded on the basis that wider knowledge would only make them dissatisfied with their role in society. I do not suggest that the limitations imposed by ss. 248 and 249 are so earth shaking or that if sustained they will cause irremediable damage. I do say, however, that these limitations represent a small abandonment of a principle of vital importance in a free and democratic society and, therefore, even if it could be shown that some child or children have been adversely affected by advertising of the kind prohibited, I would still be of the opinion that the restriction should not be sustained. Our concern should be to recognize that in this century we have seen whole societies utterly corrupted by the suppression of free expression. We should not lightly take a step in that direction, even a small one.

... Freedom of expression, whether political, religious, artistic or commercial, should not be suppressed except in cases where urgent and compelling reasons exist and then only to the extent and for the time necessary for the protection of the community. ...

Appeal dismissed.

NOTES AND QUESTIONS

1. According to the Supreme Court of Canada, s. 2(b) protects any activity that "conveys or attempts to convey a message." The Court uses the example of illegal or unauthorized parking to illustrate the potential breadth of the category of protected expression. While

parking, illegal or otherwise, is not ordinarily an expressive act, if an individual parks his or her car illegally as a protest of some kind, then that act of parking will be considered expression and fall within the scope of s. 2(b).

An individual may communicate using symbolic forms such as spoken or written language, hand gestures, or wearing a black armband that may also be seen as conveying a message. Because the Supreme Court of Canada has defined expression so broadly that it includes all acts intended to convey a message, any act is potentially an act of expression. This also means that any law is potentially a restriction on expression. Has the Court defined the scope of s. 2(b) too broadly? Could it have been defined more narrowly?

2. In *Irwin Toy*, the Supreme Court introduced an exception to its broad definition of constitutionally protected expression: expressive activity that takes the form of violence is not included within the guarantee of freedom of expression. In *Retail, Wholesale and Department Store Union, Local 580 v. Dolphin Delivery Ltd.*, [1986] 2 SCR 573, 33 DLR (4th) 174, McIntyre J suggested that threats of violence might also be excluded, but in *R v. Keegstra*, [1990] 3 SCR 697, 61 CCC (3d) 1 (found below in this chapter), which was decided shortly after *Irwin Toy*, the Court held that threats of violence do not fall within the exception.

All acts of expression have some sort of direct physical consequences: if not a broken nose, then perhaps broken silence. When will the physical effects of an expressive act be considered violent, so that the act falls outside the scope of s. 2(b), and when will the act be protected under that section even though it causes injury to the interests of another—injury such as obstruction or harassment that might justify restriction under s. 1? In *Montréal (City) v. 2952-1366 Québec Inc.*, 2005 SCC 62, [2005] 3 SCR 141, 258 DLR (4th) 595 (an excerpt from which appears later in this chapter), the Supreme Court of Canada discussed the "violence exception." The majority judgment of McLachlin CJC and Deschamps J (Binnie J dissenting on another point) included the following observations:

> [60] Expressive activity may fall outside the scope of s. 2(b) protection because of how or where it is delivered. While all expressive *content* is worthy of protection (see *Irwin Toy*, at p. 969), the *method or location* of the expression may not be. For instance, this Court has found that violent expression is not protected by the *Canadian Charter*: *Irwin Toy*, at pp. 969-70. Violence is not excluded because of the message it conveys (no matter how hateful) but rather because the method by which the message is conveyed is not consonant with *Charter* protection.

> • • •

> [72] Expressive activity should be excluded from the protective scope of s. 2(b) only if its method or location clearly undermines the values that underlie the guarantee. Violent expression, which falls outside the scope of s. 2(b) by reason of its method, provides a useful analogy. Violent expression may be a means of political expression and may serve to enhance the self-fulfillment of the perpetrator. However, it is not protected by s. 2(b) because violent means and methods undermine the values that s. 2(b) seeks to protect. Violence prevents dialogue rather than fostering it. Violence prevents the self-fulfillment of the victim rather than enhancing it. And violence stands in the way of finding the truth rather than furthering it.

3. In *Irwin Toy* the Court introduces a distinction between laws that have as their purpose the control or restriction of expression and laws that merely have the effect of restricting expression. Where the law's purpose is to restrict protected expressive activity, the law will "automatically" violate s. 2(b). However, where the law simply has the effect of limiting

expressive activity, a violation of s. 2(b) will occur only if the plaintiff can establish that the restricted expression advances one of the values underlying the guarantee. Some commentators argue that this step in the analysis is redundant because any activity that conveys meaning will be found to serve the values underlying the guarantee. If a municipal noise bylaw has the effect of preventing me from communicating my political message using a megaphone at midnight in a residential neighbourhood, will it be difficult for me to show that my chosen form of expression advances freedom of expression values?

In introducing this distinction between purpose-based and effects-based restrictions on expression, the Court in *Irwin Toy* was clearly drawing on a distinction central to US First Amendment jurisprudence between content-based restrictions and content-neutral, "time, place and manner" restrictions. In the United States, government restrictions on the communication of particular messages are viewed as a serious threat to First Amendment values and are difficult to justify. On the other hand, time, place and manner restrictions, which seek to prevent harms caused by the form rather than the message of expression (for example, physical disruption of quiet or property use) will be upheld provided they are narrowly tailored and leave adequate alternative channels for communicative activity.

Is there any reason to differentiate between purpose-based and effects-based restrictions at the s. 2(b) stage? It is worth noting that on several occasions the Court has said that "time, place and manner" restrictions may be easier to justify under s. 1 than other types of restrictions.

4. As discussed above in Chapter 17, The Framework of the Charter, we also see in *Irwin Toy* the development of a more deferential, flexible, reasonableness-based approach to the various strands of the s. 1 test, and in particular the minimal impairment test. *Irwin Toy* builds upon the initial developments in this direction in *Edwards Books and Art Ltd. v. The Queen*, [1986] 2 SCR 713, 35 DLR (4th) 1, found in Chapter 19, Freedom of Religion. In *Irwin Toy*, this less stringent application of s. 1 is viewed as appropriate in cases classified as "regulatory"—that is, involving socioeconomic considerations where the government acts as the mediator between the claims of competing individuals or groups in the community. In contrast, a more rigorous application of s. 1 is warranted in criminal law cases where the government is the singular antagonist of the individual. Are the two kinds of cases as easily distinguished as the Court suggests?

A second theme is intertwined with the concerns expressed in *Irwin Toy* about the comparative institutional competence of courts and legislatures with respect to socioeconomic matters. There are also suggestions that the more deferential standard of review is particularly appropriate in circumstances where the government is acting to protect a vulnerable group—retail workers in *Edwards Books* and children in *Irwin Toy*. This second rationale for deference reflects a desire on the part of the Court to ensure that the Charter be used as a tool of social justice—that it be interpreted in such a way as to improve, or at least not worsen, the situation of the economically and socially disadvantaged.

In later judgments, the Supreme Court of Canada has indicated that a variety of factors may affect the standard of proof under s. 1, including (1) the nature of the harm and the inability to measure it, (2) the vulnerability of the group protected, (3) subjective fears and apprehension of harm, and (4) the nature of the infringed activity (Bastarache J in *R v. Bryan*, [2007] 1 SCR 527, at para. 10, 276 DLR (4th) 513).

5. For a review of many of the freedom of expression cases found in this chapter from the perspective of the s. 1 analysis and the evolution of the *Oakes* test, see Sujit Choudhry, "So What Is the Real Legacy of *Oakes*? Two Decades of Proportionality Analysis Under the Canadian Charter's Section 1" (2006), 34 *Supreme Court Law Review* (2d) 501-35, available online at http://www.law.utoronto.ca/documents/Choudhry/Oakes.pdf.

III. COMMERCIAL EXPRESSION

As noted above, in *Ford v. Quebec (AG)*, [1988] 2 SCR 712, 54 DLR (4th) 577, the Supreme Court of Canada held that commercial expression fell within the scope of s. 2(b):

> Over and above its intrinsic value as expression, commercial expression ... protects listeners as well as speakers, [and] plays a significant role in enabling individuals to make informed economic choices, an important aspect of individual self-fulfillment and personal autonomy.

Some commentators disagreed with this ruling, arguing that advertising is an instrumental form of expression undeserving of constitutional protection. For these critics, regulation of advertising is simply a form of economic regulation within the legitimate domain of the legislature: see, for example, A. Hutchinson, "Money Talk: Against Constitutionalizing (Commercial) Speech" (1990), 17 *Can. Bus. LJ* 2. In partial recognition of these concerns, the Court has said in subsequent judgments that, while commercial expression is protected under s. 2(b), its restriction may be more easily justified under s. 1 than the restriction of other forms of expression—that is, it may have less weight in the s. 1 balancing process because it is less directly connected to the values underlying our commitment to freedom of expression.

The distinction between core and marginal expression plays a significant role in the Supreme Court's approach to a variety of freedom of expression issues, including commercial advertising, hate promotion, and pornography. When the Court decides that a certain kind of expression has only a marginal connection to the values underlying freedom of expression, it applies some or all of the s. 1 steps in a more flexible or less rigorous way. When reading the various cases in this chapter, consider whether there is any basis for this distinction.

Rocket v. Royal College of Dental Surgeons, [1990] 2 SCR 232, 71 DLR (4th) 68 involved a challenge to a regulation enacted under the Ontario *Health Disciplines Act*, RSO 1980, c. 196 by the College of Dental Surgeons imposing stringent restrictions on advertising by dentists. The Supreme Court of Canada concluded that the regulation violated the Charter's guarantee of freedom of expression. In dealing with the s. 1 analysis, McLachlin J, writing for a unanimous court, noted that, although commercial expression had been included within the scope of the guarantee of freedom of expression, the commercial nature of the expression would be significant in the balancing exercise under s. 1. She suggested that because the motive behind the expression was primarily the pursuit of economic profit, rather than participation in the political process or spiritual or artistic self-fulfillment, "restrictions on expression of this kind might be easier to justify than other infringements of s. 2(b)." On the other hand, she also recognized the public interest served by such expression in enhancing the ability of consumers (or in this case, patients) to make informed choices. In the end, the court concluded that the regulation could not be justified under s. 1. While recognizing that the regulation of advertising might be necessary to protect members of the public (who would have difficulty judging claims of quality) and maintain standards of professionalism, the Court found that the regulation at issue failed the proportionality test because it precluded the advertising of information, such as hours of operation and language spoken, that would be useful to the public and would not mislead the public or undermine professionalism.

Another form of commercial expression, soliciting for the purposes of prostitution, was found to be protected by s. 2(b) of the Charter in *Reference re ss. 193 and 195.1(1)(c) of the Criminal Code*, [1990] 1 SCR 1123, 56 CCC (3d) 65. A majority of the Court concluded, however, that the *Criminal Code* provision prohibiting any communication in a public place for the purpose of engaging in prostitution could be upheld under s. 1 as a proportionate response to the nuisance created by street solicitation. The economic purpose motivating the expression was taken into account by Dickson CJC in the balancing process:

> [T]he expressive activity, as with any infringed Charter right, should also be analyzed in the particular context of the case. Here, the activity to which the impugned legislation is directed is expression with an economic purpose. It can hardly be said that communications regarding an economic transaction of sex for money lie at, or even near, the core of the guarantee of free-dom of expression.

The regulation of tobacco product advertising has been the subject of two significant freedom of expression cases. In the first, *RJR Macdonald*, a majority of the Supreme Court of Canada struck down a general ban on tobacco advertising. In the second the Court up-held a narrower ban. In the first judgment, Justice McLachlin, for the plurality, insisted that commercial expression was not less valuable than other forms of expression protected under s. 2(b).

RJR MacDonald Inc. v. Canada (Attorney General)
[1995] 3 SCR 199, 127 DLR (4th) 1

[The *Tobacco Products Control Act*, SC 1988, c. 20, enacted by Parliament in 1988, pro-hibited the advertising and promotion of tobacco products offered for sale in Canada, and required manufacturers to add to packages an unattributed warning about the dan-gers of smoking. The Act stated, in s. 3, that it was enacted to protect the health of Can-adians in light of evidence of the harmful effects of tobacco use. Two tobacco companies challenged the Act on both federalism and Charter grounds. During the litigation, the federal government refused to disclose policy documents revealing alternatives to a total ban on advertising that had been considered prior to the enactment of the legislation. The tobacco companies were successful at trial on both Charter and federalism grounds. The Quebec Court of Appeal allowed an appeal on both grounds, a majority of the Court concluding first, that the legislation was *intra vires* and second, that although the legisla-tion infringed freedom of expression under the Charter, it could be justified under s. 1. The tobacco manufacturers then appealed to the Supreme Court of Canada, a majority of which concluded that although the legislation was *intra vires* as a legitimate exercise of Parliament's criminal law power, its central provisions were of no force and effect as they unjustifiably infringed freedom of expression. Only those portions of the judgment dealing with the Charter issue have been reproduced below; those dealing with the federalism issue can be found in Chapter 11, Criminal Law.]

LA FOREST J (L'Heureux-Dubé, Gonthier, and Cory JJ concurring) dissenting: ...

[The government conceded that the prohibition on advertising constituted an infringement of freedom of expression under s. 2(b) of the Charter, although it did not include in this concession the requirement of the unattributed warning.]

The appellants have [also] conceded that the objective of protecting Canadians from the health risks associated with tobacco use, and informing them about these risks, is pressing and substantial. Rather than focusing upon the objective, the appellants submit that the measures employed under the Act are not proportional to the objective. In adopting this strategy, they rely heavily upon Chabot J's rigorous application of the proportionality requirement at trial. ...

It is my view that Chabot J's approach was not the correct one in the circumstances of these cases, and that he erred in deciding that the civil burden of proof must be "applied rigorously." As I will show, it is also my view that the Attorney General adduced sufficient evidence at trial to justify the limitation on freedom of expression entailed by this legislation, and that the appellants' argument accordingly fails. ...

The appropriate "test" to be applied in a s. 1 analysis is that found in s. 1 itself, which makes it clear that the court's role in applying that provision is to determine whether an infringement is reasonable and can be demonstrably justified in a "free and democratic society." In *R v. Oakes*, [1986] 1 SCR 103, this Court established a set of principles, or guidelines, intended to serve as a framework for making this determination. However, these guidelines should not be interpreted as a substitute for s. 1 itself. It is implicit in the wording of s. 1 that the courts must, in every application of that provision, strike a delicate balance between individual rights and community needs. Such a balance cannot be achieved in the abstract, with reference solely to a formalistic "test" uniformly applicable in all circumstances. ... *when flexibly — approve*

This Court has on many occasions affirmed that the *Oakes* requirements must be applied flexibly, having regard to the specific factual and social context of each case. The word "reasonable" in s. 1 necessarily imports flexibility. ...

This Court has on many occasions stated that the evidentiary requirements under s. 1 will vary substantially depending upon both the nature of the legislation and the nature of the right infringed. In the present cases, both these contextual elements are highly relevant to a proper application of the s. 1 analysis. ...

At trial and before this Court the Attorney General adduced copious evidence ... demonstrating that tobacco consumption is one of the leading causes of illness and death in our society. ...

[T]he nature and scope of the health problems raised by tobacco consumption are highly relevant to the s. 1 analysis, both in determining the appropriate standard of justification and in weighing the relevant evidence. In this respect, it is essential to keep in mind that tobacco addiction is a unique, and somewhat perplexing, phenomenon.

Despite the growing recognition of the detrimental health effects of tobacco use, close to a third of the population continues to use tobacco products on a regular basis. ... [D]espite the lack of definitive scientific explanations of the causes of tobacco addiction, clear evidence does exist of the detrimental social effects of tobacco consumption. ... [O]verwhelming evidence was introduced at trial that tobacco use is a principal cause of deadly cancers, heart disease and lung disease, and that tobacco is highly addictive. Perhaps the most distressing aspect of the evidence introduced at trial is that tobacco consumption is most widespread among the young and the less educated—those segments of the population who are least able to inform themselves about, and to protect themselves against, its hazards. ...

It appears, then, that there is a significant gap between our understanding of the health effects of tobacco consumption and of the root causes of tobacco consumption. In my view, this gap raises a fundamental institutional problem that must be taken into account in undertaking the s. 1 balancing. Simply put, a strict application of the proportionality analysis in cases of this nature would place an impossible onus on Parliament by requiring it to produce definitive social scientific evidence respecting the root causes of a pressing area of social concern every time it wishes to address its effects. This could have the effect of virtually paralyzing the operation of government in the socio-economic sphere.

[Reference is made to *McKinney v. University of Guelph*, [1990] 3 SCR 229, 76 DLR (4th) 545 in which a majority of the Supreme Court of Canada found mandatory retirement to be a reasonable limit on equality rights, taking the position that the complex nature of the socioeconomic problem in issue warranted a degree of judicial deference to legislative decisions.]

In several recent cases, this Court has recognized the need to attenuate the *Oakes* standard of justification when institutional constraints analogous to those in the present cases arise.

[Reference is made to cases, including *Irwin Toy Ltd. v. Quebec (AG)*, [1989] 1 SCR 927.]

In drawing a distinction between legislation aimed at "mediating between different groups," where a lower standard of s. 1 justification may be appropriate, and legislation where the state acts as the "singular antagonist of the individual," where a higher standard of justification is necessary, the Court in *Irwin Toy* was drawing upon the more fundamental institutional distinction between the legislative and judicial functions that lies at the very heart of our political and constitutional system. Courts are specialists in the protection of liberty and the interpretation of legislation and are, accordingly, well placed to subject criminal justice legislation to careful scrutiny. However, courts are not specialists in the realm of policy-making, nor should they be. This is a role properly assigned to the elected representatives of the people, who have at their disposal the necessary institutional resources to enable them to compile and assess social science evidence, to mediate between competing social interests and to reach out and protect vulnerable groups. In according a greater degree of deference to social legislation than to legislation in the criminal justice context, this Court has recognized these important institutional differences between legislatures and the judiciary.

In my view, the considerations addressed by this Court in *Irwin Toy* and *McKinney* ... are applicable to the present cases. In enacting this legislation, Parliament was facing a difficult policy dilemma. On the one hand, Parliament is aware of the detrimental health effects of tobacco use, and has a legitimate interest in protecting Canadians from, and in informing them about, the dangers of tobacco use. Health underlies many of our most cherished rights and values, and the protection of public health is one of the fundamental responsibilities of Parliament. On the other hand, however, it is clear that a prohibition on the manufacture, sale or use of tobacco products is unrealistic. Nearly seven million Canadians use tobacco products, which are highly addictive. Undoubtedly, a prohibition of this nature would lead to an increase in illegal activity, smuggling and, quite possibly, civil disobedience. Well aware of these difficulties, Parliament chose a less drastic, and more incremental, response to the tobacco health problem. In prohibiting the advertising and promotion of tobacco products, as opposed to their manufacture or sale, Parliament has sought to achieve a compromise among the competing interests of smokers, non-smokers and manufacturers, with an eye to protecting vulnerable groups in society. Given the fact that advertising, by its very nature, is intended to influence consumers and create demand, this was a reasonable policy decision. Moreover ... the Act is the product of a legislative process dating back to 1969, when the first report recommending a full prohibition on tobacco advertising was published. ...

Turning now to the nature of the right infringed under the Act, it is once again necessary to place the appellants' claim in context. ... [D]epending on its nature, expression will be entitled to varying levels of constitutional protection. ...

In *R v. Keegstra*, [1990] 3 SCR 697 ... Dickson CJC identified [the] fundamental or "core" values [served by freedom of expression] as including the search for political, artistic and scientific truth, the protection of individual autonomy and self-development, and the promotion of public participation in the democratic process. When state action places such values in jeopardy, this Court has been careful to subject it to a searching degree of scrutiny. However, when the form of expression placed in jeopardy falls farther from the "centre core of the spirit," this Court has ruled restrictions on such expression less difficult to justify. ...

[A discussion of *Keegstra*, which involved restrictions on hate speech, and *R v. Butler*, [1992] 1 SCR 452, which involved restrictions on pornography, has been omitted. Both cases are found below in this chapter.]

In my view, the harm engendered by tobacco, and the profit motive underlying its promotion, place this form of expression as far from the "core" of freedom of expression values as prostitution, hate mongering, or pornography, and thus entitle it to a very low degree of protection under s. 1. It must be kept in mind that tobacco advertising serves no political, scientific or artistic ends; nor does it promote participation in the political process. Rather, its sole purpose is to inform consumers about, and promote the use of, a product that is harmful, and often fatal, to the consumers who use it. The main, if not sole, motivation for this advertising is, of course, profit.

[La Forest J then provides an account of the profits of the tobacco companies that dominate the market and their expenditures on advertising.]

Proportionality

... In my view, Chabot J erred in finding that there was insufficient evidence to satisfy the proportionality requirement, and the majority of the Court of Appeal was correct to interfere with his findings and reevaluate the evidence. ...

[A discussion of the degree of deference owed by an appellate court to a trial judge's assessment of social science evidence is omitted. La Forest J concludes that while a trial judge is in a privileged position with respect to adjudicative fact finding, such is not the case with legislative or social fact finding, which involves the assessment of complex social science evidence and the drawing of general conclusions concerning the effect of legal rules on human behaviour. In the latter situation, appellate courts and legislatures are as well placed as trial judges to make findings, and an appellate court may interfere with a finding of a trial judge if it finds that the trial judge erred in the consideration or appreciation of the matter. The causal connection between tobacco advertising and consumption, or the lack thereof, is found to be a paradigm example of a legislative or social fact.]

Rational Connection

... As I explained in discussing the contextual nature of the s. 1 analysis, it is unnecessary ... for the government to demonstrate a rational connection according to a civil standard of proof. Rather, it is sufficient for the government to demonstrate that it had a reasonable basis for believing such a rational connection exists. ...

The appellants [argue] ... that there is no rational connection between the prohibition on advertising and promotion of tobacco products ... and the objective of reducing tobacco consumption. In my view, the appellants' argument fails. ...

I begin with what I consider to be a powerful common sense observation. Simply put, it is difficult to believe that Canadian tobacco companies would spend over 75 million dollars every year on advertising if they did not know that advertising increases the consumption of their product. In response to this observation, the appellants insist that their advertising is directed solely toward preserving and expanding brand loyalty among smokers, and not toward expanding the tobacco market by inducing non-smokers to start. In my view, the appellants' claim is untenable for two principal reasons. First, brand loyalty alone will not, and logically cannot, maintain the profit levels of these companies if the overall number of smokers declines. A proportionate piece of a smaller pie is still a smaller piece. ... Second, even if this Court were to accept the appellants' brand loyalty argument, the appellants have not adequately addressed the further problem that even commercials targeted solely at brand loyalty may also serve as inducements for smokers not to quit. The government's concern with the health effects of tobacco can quite reasonably extend not only to potential smokers who are considering starting, but also to current smokers who would prefer to quit but cannot.

I observe in passing, based upon the recent jurisprudence of this Court, that the foregoing common sense observation is sufficient in itself to establish a rational connection in these cases.

[La Forest J then refers to *Butler*, in which the court used a common sense analysis to presume a causal relationship between exposure to obscene material and changes in attitudes and beliefs about women.]

However, it is not necessary to rely solely upon common sense to reach this conclusion because there was, in any event, sufficient evidence adduced at trial to bear out the rational connection between advertising and consumption. ... This evidence can be conveniently subdivided into three categories: internal tobacco marketing documents, expert reports, and international materials. I will review each of these in turn.

Perhaps the most compelling evidence concerning the connection between advertising and consumption can be found in the internal marketing documents prepared by the tobacco manufacturers themselves. Although the appellants steadfastly argue that their marketing efforts are directed solely at maintaining and expanding brand loyalty among adult smokers, these documents show otherwise. In particular, the following general conclusions can be drawn from these documents: the tobacco companies are concerned about a shrinking tobacco market and recognize that an "advocacy thrust" is necessary to maintain the size of the overall market; the companies understand that, in order to maintain the overall numbers of smokers, they must reassure current smokers and make their product attractive to the young and to non-smokers; they also recognize that advertising is critical to maintaining the size of the market because it serves to reinforce the social acceptability of smoking by identifying it with glamour, affluence, youthfulness and vitality. ...

The internal marketing documents introduced at trial strongly suggest that the tobacco companies perceive advertising to be a cornerstone of their strategy to reassure current smokers and expand the market by attracting new smokers, primarily among the young. This conclusion is given added force by a number of reports introduced at trial, to which Chabot J made no reference, which attest to the causal connection between tobacco advertising and consumption.

[The account of this evidence, which consists of academic reports written by psychologists, historians, and professors of marketing, has been omitted.]

The views expressed in these reports are not, of course, definitive or conclusive. Indeed, there is currently a lively debate in the social sciences respecting the connection between advertising and consumption, a debate that has been carried on for years and will no doubt persist well into the near future. However, these reports attest, at the very least, to the existence of ... a "body of opinion" supporting the existence of a causal connection between advertising and consumption. Included in this "body of opinion" are a significant number of international health organizations, which support prohibitions on advertising as a viable strategy in the battle against tobacco consumption. ...

On the basis of the foregoing evidence, I conclude that there is a rational connection between the prohibition on advertising and consumption under ss. 4, 5, 6 and 8 of the Act and the reduction of tobacco consumption. ...

Minimal Impairment

... The appellants submit that Parliament has unjustifiably imposed a complete prohibition on tobacco advertising and promotion when it could have imposed a partial prohibition with equal effectiveness. They suggest that Parliament could have instituted a partial prohibition by forbidding "lifestyle" advertising (which seeks to promote an image by associating the consumption of the product with a particular lifestyle) or advertising directed at children, without at the same time prohibiting "brand preference" advertising (which seeks to promote one brand over another based on the colour and design of the package) or "informational" advertising (which seeks to inform the consumer about product content, taste and strength and the availability of different or new brands). According to the appellants, there is no need to prohibit brand preference or informational advertising because both are targeted solely at smokers, and serve a beneficial function by promoting consumer choice.

In my view, the appellants' argument fails for the same reasons that I have discussed throughout my s. 1 analysis. The relevance of context cannot be understated in s. 1 balancing, particularly at the minimal impairment stage. This Court has on many occasions stated that the degree of required fit between means and ends will vary depending upon both the nature of the right and the nature of the legislation. ...

Taking into account the legislative context, it is my view that the measures adopted under the Act satisfy the *Oakes* minimal impairment requirement. It must be kept in mind that the infringed right at issue in these cases is the right of tobacco corporations to advertise the only legal product sold in Canada which, when used precisely as directed, harms and often kills those who use it. As I discussed above, I have no doubt that Parliament could validly have employed the criminal law power to prohibit the manufacture and sale of tobacco products, and that such a prohibition would have been fully justifiable under the Charter. There is no right to sell harmful products in Canada, nor should there be. Thus, in choosing to prohibit solely the advertisement of tobacco products, it is clear that Parliament in fact adopted a relatively unintrusive legislative approach to the control of tobacco products. Indeed, the scope of conduct prohibited under the Act is narrow. Under the Act, tobacco companies continue to enjoy the right to manufacture and sell their products, to engage in public or private debate concerning the health effects of their products, and to publish consumer information on their product packages pertaining to the content of the products. The prohibition under this Act serves only to prevent these companies from employing sophisticated marketing and social psychology techniques to induce consumers to purchase their products. This type of expression, which is directed solely toward the pursuit of profit, is neither political nor artistic in nature, and therefore falls very far from the "core" of freedom of expression values discussed by this Court in *Keegstra*. ...

Furthermore, there was ample evidence introduced by the Attorney General at trial demonstrating that a full prohibition of tobacco advertising is justified and necessary. In enacting this legislation, Parliament came to the conclusion that all advertising stimulates consumption and that a full prohibition upon advertising is therefore necessary to reduce consumption effectively. Parliament reached this conclusion only after many years of careful study and reflection. ... [T]he measures adopted under the Act were the

product of an intensive 20-year public policy process, which involved extensive consultation with an array of national and international health groups and numerous studies, and
educational and legislative programs. Over the course of this 20-year period, the government adopted an incremental legislative approach by experimenting with a variety of less
intrusive measures before determining that a full prohibition on advertising was necessary. ... However, despite all these efforts, it was apparent by 1989 that close to one-third
of Canadians continued to smoke and that the decline in the numbers of smokers in
Canada since 1969 had been neither rapid nor substantial. Faced with this distressing sta-
tistic, and with the seeming ineffectiveness of the measures adopted up to that time, Parliament had more than reasonable grounds for concluding that the more robust measures
adopted under the Act were both necessary and a logical next step in the policy process.

The reasonableness of Parliament's decision to prohibit tobacco advertising has been
amply borne out by parallel developments in the international community before and
after the passage of the Act. It is of great significance, in my view, that over 20 democratic
nations have, in recent years, adopted complete prohibitions on tobacco advertising
similar to those adopted under the Act, including Australia, New Zealand, Norway, Fin-
land and France.

[La Forest J then discusses the issue of the government's failure to disclose documents
that may have contained information about alternative options that the government had
considered prior to the adoption of the Act, concluding that speculation about less intrusive options did not displace the overwhelming evidence that the total prohibition on
advertising was a reasonable one. He also notes evidence indicating that in countries that
have instituted partial prohibitions upon tobacco advertising, tobacco companies have
developed ingenious tactics to circumvent the restrictions.]

Thus, it appears that Parliament had compelling reasons for rejecting a partial prohibition on advertising and instituting a full prohibition. In this light, it would be highly
artificial for this Court to decide, on a purely abstract basis, that a partial prohibition on
advertising would be as effective as a full prohibition. In my view, this is precisely the
type of "line drawing" that this Court has identified as being within the institutional
competence of legislatures and not courts. ...

Proportionality Between the Effects of the Legislation and the Objective

... For the reasons I have given with respect to both the nature of the legislation and the
nature of the right infringed in these cases, it is my view that the deleterious effects of this
limitation, a restriction on the rights of tobacco companies to advertise products for profit
that are inherently dangerous and harmful, do not outweigh the legislative objective of
reducing the number of direct inducements for Canadians to consume these products.

The Unattributed Health Message Requirement

I now turn to the appellants' final argument, namely, that s. 9 of the Act constitutes an
unjustifiable infringement of their freedom of expression by compelling them to place on
tobacco packages an unattributed health message. I agree, to use Wilson J's phrase, that

if the effect of this provision is "to put a particular message into the mouth of the plain-tiff, as is metaphorically alleged to be the case here," the section runs afoul of s. 2(b) of the Charter; see *Lavigne v. Ontario Public Service Employees Union*, [1991] 2 SCR 211 at 267. ... I have ... problems accepting the appellants' contention that their s. 2(b) right was infringed by the requirement that a prescribed health warning must be placed on tobacco packages. It must be remembered that this statement is *unattributed* and I have some difficulty in seeing, in the context in which it was made, that it can in any real sense be considered to be attributed to the appellants. Simply because tobacco manufacturers are required to place unattributed warnings on their products does not mean that they must endorse these messages, or that they are perceived by consumers to endorse them. In a modern state, labelling of products, and especially products for human consumption, are subject to state regulation as a matter of course. It is common knowledge amongst the public at large that such statements emanate from the government, not the tobacco manufacturers. In this respect, there is an important distinction between messages directly attributed to tobacco manufacturers, which would create the impression that the message emanates from the appellants and would violate their right to silence, and the unattributed messages at issue in these cases, which emanate from the government and create no such impression. Seen in this way, the mandatory health warnings under s. 9 are no different from unattributed labelling requirements under the *Hazardous Products Act*, under which manufacturers of hazardous products are required to place unattributed warnings, such as "DANGER" or "POISON," and hazard symbols, such as skull and crossbones on their products. ...

Even if I were of the view that there was an infringement, I am firmly convinced that it is fully justifiable under s. 1. Once again, I stress the importance of context in the s. 1 analysis. The appellants are large corporations selling a product for profit which, on the basis of overwhelming evidence, is dangerous, yet maintain the right to engage in "counter-speech" against warnings which do nothing more than bring the dangerous nature of these products to the attention of consumers. Given that the objective of the unattributed health message requirement is simply to increase the likelihood that every literate consumer of tobacco products will be made aware of the risks entailed by the use of that product, and that these warnings have no political, social or religious content, it is clear that we are a long way in this context from cases where the state seeks to coerce a lone individual to make political, social or religious statements without a right to respond. I believe a lower level of constitutional scrutiny is justified in this context. ...

In my view, the requirement that health warnings must be unattributed is also proportional to the objective of informing consumers about the risks of tobacco use. Unattributed warnings are rationally connected to this objective because they increase the visual impact of the warning. It is not difficult to see that bold unattributed messages on a tobacco package (such as, for example, "SMOKING CAN KILL YOU") are more striking to the eye than messages cluttered by subtitles and attributions. Moreover, the attribution of the warnings also tends to dilute the factual impact of the messages. ...

McLACHLIN J (Sopinka and Major JJ concurring): ... I agree with La Forest J that the prohibition on advertising and promotion of tobacco products constitutes a violation of the right to free expression as the Attorney General conceded. Unlike La Forest J, I take

the view that s. 9 of the Act, which requires tobacco manufacturers to place an unattributed health warning on tobacco packages, also infringes the right of free expression. As
La Forest J notes … this Court has previously held that "freedom of expression necessarily
entails the right to say nothing or the right not to say certain things": *Slaight Communications Inc. v. Davidson*, [1989] 1 SCR 1038, at p. 1080, per Lamer J (as he then was). Under
s. 9(2), tobacco manufacturers are prohibited from displaying on their packages any
writing other than the name, brand name, trade mark, and other information required
by legislation. The combination of the unattributed health warnings and the prohibition
against displaying any other information which would allow tobacco manufacturers to
express their own views, constitutes an infringement of the right to free expression guaranteed by s. 2(b) of the Charter.

The only remaining question is whether these infringements of the right of free expression are saved under s. 1 of the Charter. …

While remaining sensitive to the social and political context of the impugned law and
allowing for difficulties of proof inherent in that context, the courts must nevertheless
insist that before the state can override constitutional rights, there be a reasoned demonstration of the good which the law may achieve in relation to the seriousness of the infringement. It is the task of the courts to maintain this bottom line if the rights conferred
by our constitution are to have force and meaning. The task is not easily discharged, and
may require the courts to confront the tide of popular public opinion. But that has always
been the price of maintaining constitutional rights. No matter how important Parliament's goal may seem, if the state has not demonstrated that the means by which it seeks
to achieve its goal are reasonable and proportionate to the infringement of rights, then
the law must perforce fail. …

The factors generally relevant to determining whether a violative law is reasonable
and demonstrably justified in a free and democratic society remain those set out in
Oakes. …

[La Forest J's] first point is that the *Oakes* test must be applied flexibly, having regard
to the factual and social context of each case. I agree. The need to consider the context of
the case has been accepted since Wilson J propounded it in *Edmonton Journal v. Alberta
(Attorney General)*, [1989] 2 SCR 1326. …

However, while the impugned law must be considered in its social and economic
context, nothing in the jurisprudence suggests that the contextual approach reduces the
obligation on the state to meet the burden of demonstrating that the limitation on rights
imposed by the law is reasonable and justified. Context is essential in determining legislative objective and proportionality, but it cannot be carried to the extreme of treating the
challenged law as a unique socioeconomic phenomenon, of which Parliament is deemed
the best judge. This would be to undercut the obligation on Parliament to justify limitations which it places on Charter rights and would be to substitute *ad hoc* judicial discretion for the reasoned demonstration contemplated by the Charter.

Related to context is the degree of deference which the courts should accord to Parliament. It is established that the deference accorded to Parliament or the legislatures may
vary with the social context in which the limitation on rights is imposed. For example, it
has been suggested that greater deference to Parliament or the Legislature may be appropriate if the law is concerned with the competing rights between different sectors of society

than if it is a contest between the individual and the state. .... However, such distinctions may not always be easy to apply. For example, the criminal law is generally seen as involving a contest between the state and the accused, but it also involves an allocation of priorities between the accused and the victim, actual or potential. The cases at bar provide a cogent example. We are concerned with a criminal law, which pits the state against the offender. But the social values reflected in this criminal law lead La Forest J to conclude that "the Act is the very type of legislation to which this Court has generally accorded a high degree of deference." ... This said, I accept that the situation which the law is attempting to redress may affect the degree of deference which the court should accord to Parliament's choice. The difficulty of devising legislative solutions to social problems which may be only incompletely understood may also affect the degree of deference that the courts accord to Parliament or the Legislature. ...

As with context, however, care must be taken not to extend the notion of deference too far. Deference must not be carried to the point of relieving the government of the burden which the Charter places upon it of demonstrating that the limits it has imposed on guaranteed rights are reasonable and justifiable. ...

Context and deference are related to a third concept in the s. 1 analysis: standard of proof. I agree with La Forest J that proof to the standard required by science is not required. Nor is proof beyond a reasonable doubt on the criminal standard required. As the s. 1 jurisprudence has established, the civil standard of proof on a balance of probabilities at all stages of the proportionality analysis is more appropriate. ... I thus disagree with La Forest J's conclusion ... that in these cases "it is unnecessary ... for the government to demonstrate a rational connection according to a civil standard of proof." Discharge of the civil standard does not require scientific demonstration; the balance of probabilities may be established by the application of common sense to what is known, even though what is known may be deficient from a scientific point of view. ...

In summary, while I agree with La Forest J that context, deference and a flexible and realistic standard of proof are essential aspects of the s. 1 analysis, these concepts should be used as they have been used by this Court in previous cases. They must not be attenuated to the point that they relieve the state of the burden the Charter imposes of demonstrating that the limits imposed on our constitutional rights and freedoms are reasonable and justifiable in a free and democratic society.

[McLachlin J's discussion of the degree of deference that appellate courts should accord to the findings of the trial judge under s. 1 of the Charter analysis is omitted. Although expressing some reservations about the distinction made by La Forest J between legislative and adjudicative facts, she accepts that more deference may be required to findings based on evidence of a purely factual nature and a lesser degree of deference when the trial judge has considered social science and other policy oriented evidence.]

Against this background, I return to the cases at bar and the factors for s. 1 justification discussed in *Oakes*.

The Objective of the Limit on Free Expression

... Care must be taken not to overstate the objective. The objective relevant to the s. 1 analysis is the objective of the infringing measure, since it is the infringing measure and nothing else which is sought to be justified. If the objective is stated too broadly, its importance may be exaggerated and the analysis compromised. As my colleague has noted, the *Tobacco Products Control Act* is but one facet of a complex legislative and policy scheme to protect Canadians from the health risks of tobacco use. However, the objective of the impugned measures themselves is somewhat narrower than this. The objective of the advertising ban ... must be to prevent people in Canada from being persuaded by advertising and promotion to use tobacco products. The objective of the mandatory package warning must be to discourage people who see the package from tobacco use. Both constitute important objectives, although the significance of the targeted decrease in consumption is reduced by the government's estimate that despite the ban, 65 percent of the Canadian magazine market will contain tobacco advertisements, given that the ban applies only to Canadian media and not to imported publications. ...

While the limited objective of reducing tobacco-associated health risks by reducing advertising-related consumption and providing warnings of dangers is less significant than the broad objective of protecting Canadians generally from the risks associated with tobacco use, it nevertheless constitutes an objective of sufficient importance to justify overriding the right of free expression guaranteed by the Charter. Even a small reduction in tobacco use may work a significant benefit to the health of Canadians and justify a properly proportioned limitation of right of free expression. ...

Rational Connection

... The causal relationship between the infringement of rights and the benefit sought may sometimes be proved by scientific evidence showing that as a matter of repeated observation, one affects the other. Where, however, legislation is directed at changing human behaviour, as in the case of the *Tobacco Products Control Act*, the causal relationship may not be scientifically measurable. In such cases, this Court has been prepared to find a causal connection between the infringement and benefit sought on the basis of reason or logic, without insisting on direct proof of a relationship between the infringing measure and the legislative objective.

[Reference is made to *Keegstra* and *Butler*.]

The trial judge in the cases at bar found that the government had not established a rational connection between the advertising ban and unattributed warnings and a reduction in tobacco use in the first, scientific sense.

[No reason is found for interfering with the trial judge's conclusions that the two items of "direct or scientific" evidence were not persuasive.]

This leaves the question of whether there is less direct evidence that suggests as a matter of "reason" or "logic" that advertising bans and package warnings lead to a reduction in tobacco use. The evidence relied upon by La Forest J in support of rational connection falls into this category. ...

The question is whether this evidence establishes that it is reasonable or logical to conclude that there is a causal link between tobacco advertising and unattributed health warnings and tobacco use. ...

[An account of the evidence considered by La Forest J is omitted.]

... All this taken together with the admittedly inconclusive scientific evidence is sufficient to establish on a balance of probabilities a link based on reason between certain forms of advertising, warnings and tobacco consumption. ...

Minimal Impairment

As the second step in the proportionality analysis, the government must show that the measures at issue impair the right of free expression as little as reasonably possible in order to achieve the legislative objective. The impairment must be "minimal," that is, the law must be carefully tailored so that rights are impaired no more than necessary. The tailoring process seldom admits of perfection and the courts must accord some leeway to the legislator. If the law falls within a range of reasonable alternatives, the courts will not find it overbroad merely because they can conceive of an alternative which might better tailor objective to infringement. ...

I turn first to the prohibition on advertising contained in s. 4 of the Act. It is, as has been observed, complete. It bans all forms of advertising of Canadian tobacco products while explicitly exempting all foreign advertising of non-Canadian products which are sold in Canada. It extends to advertising which arguably produces benefits to the consumer while having little or no conceivable impact on consumption. Purely informational advertising, simple reminders of package appearance, advertising for new brands and advertising showing relative tar content of different brands—all these are included in the ban. Smoking is a legal activity yet consumers are deprived of an important means of learning about product availability to suit their preferences and to compare brand content with an aim to reducing the risk to their health.

As this Court has observed before, it will be more difficult to justify a complete ban on a form of expression than a partial ban. ... A full prohibition will only be constitutionally acceptable under the minimal impairment stage of the analysis where the government can show that only a full prohibition will enable it to achieve its objective. Where, as here, no evidence is adduced to show that a partial ban would be less effective than a total ban, the justification required by s. 1 to save the violation of free speech is not established.

... [W]hile one may conclude as a matter of reason and logic that lifestyle advertising is designed to increase consumption, there is no indication that purely informational or brand preference advertising would have this effect. The government had before it a variety of less intrusive measures when it enacted the total ban on advertising, including: a partial ban which would allow information and brand preference advertising; a ban on lifestyle advertising only; measures such as those in Quebec's *Consumer Protection Act* ... to prohibit advertising aimed at children and adolescents; and labelling requirements only (which Health and Welfare believed would be preferable to an advertising ban ...). In my view, any of these alternatives would be a reasonable impairment of the right to free expression, given the important objective and the legislative context.

These considerations suggest that the advertising ban imposed by s. 4 of the Act may be more intrusive of freedom of expression than is necessary to accomplish its goals. Indeed, Health and Welfare proposed less-intrusive regulation instead of a complete prohibition on advertising. Why then, did the government adopt such a broad ban? The record provides no answer to this question. The government presented no evidence in defence of the total ban, no evidence comparing its effects to less invasive bans.

This omission is all the more glaring in view of the fact that the government carried out at least one study of alternatives to a total ban on advertising before enacting the total ban. The government has deprived the courts of the results of that study. ... In the face of this behaviour, one is hard-pressed not to infer that the results of the studies must undercut the government's claim that a less invasive ban would not have produced an equally salutary result.

Not only did the government present no evidence justifying its choice of a total ban, it also presented no argument before us on the point. ... [T]he Attorney General contented himself with the ... simple assertion that Parliament has the right to set such limits as it chooses. ...

Even on difficult social issues where the stakes are high, Parliament does not have the right to determine unilaterally the limits of its intrusion on the rights and freedoms guaranteed by the Charter. The Constitution, as interpreted by the courts, determines those limits. Section 1 specifically stipulates that the infringement may not exceed what is reasonable and "demonstrably justified in a free and democratic society," a test which embraces the requirement of minimal impairment, and places on the government the burden of demonstrating that Parliament has respected that limit. This the government has failed to do, notwithstanding that it had at least one study on the comparative effectiveness of a partial and complete ban. In the face of this omission, the fact that full bans have been imposed in certain other countries and the fact that opinions favouring total bans can be found, fall short of establishing minimal impairment.

[McLachlin J then goes on to deal with La Forest J's assessment of the low value of the speech in issue, which he used to justify a more deferential application of the minimal impairment test.]

... [C]are must be taken not to undervalue the expression at issue. Commercial speech, while arguably less important than some forms of speech, nevertheless should not be lightly dismissed. For example, in *Rocket* this Court struck down restrictions on dental advertising on the ground that the minimal impairment requirement had not been met. [The challenged legislation] prohibited forms of advertising which far from being unprofessional, might have benefited consumers and contributed to their health. The same may be said here. Tobacco consumption has not been banned in Canada. Yet the advertising ban deprives those who lawfully choose to smoke of information relating to price, quality and even health risks associated with different brands. It is no answer to suggest, as does my colleague ... that the tobacco companies have failed to establish the true benefits of such information. Under s. 1 of the Charter, the onus rests on the government to show why restrictions on these forms of advertising are required.

... La Forest J places a great deal of reliance on the fact that the appellants are motivated by profit. I note that the same may be said for many business persons or corporations that challenge a law as contrary to freedom of expression. While this Court has stated that restrictions on commercial speech may be easier to justify than other infringements, no link between the claimant's motivation and the degree of protection has been recognized. Book sellers, newspaper owners, toy sellers—all are linked by their shareholders' desire to profit from the corporation's business activity, whether the expression sought to be protected is closely linked to the core values of freedom of expression or not. In my view, motivation to profit is irrelevant to the determination of whether the government has established that the law is reasonable or justified as an infringement of freedom of expression.

It remains to consider whether the requirement that the warning be unattributed pursuant to s. 9 of the Act fails to meet the minimum impairment requirement of proportionality. The appellant corporations contend that a warning similar to that used in the United States, which identifies the author as the Surgeon General, would be equally effective while avoiding the inference some may draw that it is the corporations themselves who are warning of the danger. They object not only to being forced to say what they do not wish to say, but also to being required to do so in a way that associates them with the opinion in question. This impairs their freedom of expression, they contend, more than required to achieve the legislative goal.

The government is clearly justified in requiring the appellants to place warnings on tobacco packaging. The question is whether it was necessary to prohibit the appellants from attributing the message to the government and whether it was necessary to prevent the appellants from placing on their packaging any information other than that allowed by the regulations.

As with the advertising ban, it was for the government to show that the unattributed warning, as opposed to an attributed warning, was required to achieve its objective of reducing tobacco consumption among those who might read the warning. Similarly, it was for the government to show why permitting tobacco companies to place additional information on tobacco packaging, such as a statement announcing lower tar levels, would defeat the government's objective. This it has failed to do. ...

[Having concluded that the requirement of minimal impairment was not satisfied, McLachlin J found it unnecessary to proceed to the final stage of the proportionality analysis. The prohibitions against advertising and the requirement of the unattributed warning not being justified under s. 1, McLachlin J declared that they were of no force and effect.

Iaccobucci J wrote a concurring judgment. Although he agreed with La Forest J "that a contextual approach must be taken to s. 1 analysis" and that "the amount of legislative tailoring required to sustain minimal impairment analysis would not be very significant." In his view, however, "the government chose not to do any tailoring and, ultimately, this constitutes the lynch-pin of the Act's unconstitutionality."

He went on "to offer some indication of what sorts of measures would, in my mind, have survived Charter scrutiny. ... [I]t is clear that health warnings can and should be placed on the packages, but the strictures of the Charter necessitate that they be attributed to their author, in all likelihood Health and Welfare Canada. Regarding the advertising ban ... partial bans in the order of prohibitions on lifestyle advertising only and limitations on advertising aimed at adolescents could have been given more constructive attention."]

Appeal allowed.

NOTES AND QUESTIONS

1. McLachlin J was prepared to uphold a ban on lifestyle advertising because she accepted that this sort of advertising has the effect of increasing tobacco consumption. However, she concluded that informational and brand preference advertising should not be restricted because they do not encourage the smoking habit, but simply reinforce brand loyalty or encourage brand switching. Is there any real basis for this distinction between lifestyle advertising and brand preference or informational advertising? Can an ad reinforce brand loyalty without reinforcing the smoking habit? Can it encourage brand switching without encouraging smokers not to quit or non-smokers to start?

Both McLachlin J and La Forest J seemed to assume that cigarette advertising could be restricted if it was shown to be effective in persuading its audience to smoke, but that it could not be restricted if it was shown to be ineffective. Yet how can it be that the justification for restricting expression is stronger when the expression persuades its audience to start or continue smoking? If people have a legal right to perform a particular act, such as smoking, is it not wrong to prevent them from hearing expression that supports performance of that act? Does the Court's judgment rest on an assumption that at least some forms of tobacco advertising are manipulative or deceptive?

2. In *Rocket v. Royal College of Dental Surgeons*, [1990] 2 SCR 232, 71 DLR (4th) 68, McLachlin J noted that the motive behind commercial expression was "primarily economic" and that the loss caused by censorship of this form of expression "is merely loss of profit, and not loss of opportunity to participate in the political process or the marketplace of ideas, or to realize one's spirited or artistic self-fulfillment." For these reasons she decided that "restrictions on expression of this kind might be easier to justify than other infringements of s. 2(b)." However, in *RJR MacDonald*, McLachlin J argued that the profit motive or economic orientation should not lessen the claim of expression to constitutional protection: "In my view, motivation to profit is irrelevant to the determination of whether the government has established that the law is reasonable or justified as an infringement of freedom of expression." Did McLachlin J change her mind and accept that profit-motivated expression is no less valuable than other forms of expression?

3. McLachlin J found that the provision in the *Tobacco Products Act* requiring tobacco manufacturers to place unattributed health warnings on tobacco packages violated their freedom of expression and could not be justified under s. 1. Do all product labelling laws, including those that require the identification of poisons or the listing of food ingredients, violate the right to freedom of expression (and the Charter)? If not, why are cigarette health warnings different?

Freedom of expression is understood as entailing not just the right to express one's own ideas, but also the right not to speak. What is objectionable about compelled expression? Is it that the audience might mistakenly attribute the message to the speaker? In many or most cases in which individuals are compelled to express themselves the audience is aware that the message is compelled and is not the individual's own. Did the cigarette purchasers think that the health warnings on packages were the voluntarily expressed opinions of the manufacturers? Another view is that compelled expression is objectionable not because individuals will be incorrectly identified with views that are not their own, but because they will suffer the indignity of having to express such views. Does this sort of dignitary harm arise in the *RJR MacDonald* case?

In Canada, prior to *RJR MacDonald*, the right not to speak was recognized in *Slaight Communications Inc. v. Davidson*, [1989] 1 SCR 1038, 59 DLR (4th) 416. In that case a labour adjudicator, after finding that an employee had been wrongfully dismissed, ordered the employer, *inter alia*, to provide the employee with a letter of recommendation. The letter was to include specified information concerning the employee's sales performance and also a statement to the effect that the adjudicator had found the employee's termination to constitute unjust dismissal. The order was found to violate freedom of expression. However, it was upheld under s. 1. Central to the Court's s. 1 assessment was a recognition of the "unequal balance of power that normally exists between an employer and employee."

How far does the right not to speak extend? Does it prohibit the state from using, or allowing someone else to use, an individual's property to support expressive activity with which the individual does not agree? In *Lavigne v. Ontario Public Service Employees Union*, [1991] 2 SCR 211, 81 DLR (4th) 545, the Supreme Court of Canada addressed the issue of compulsory union dues and their expenditure by the union on political issues. Mr. Lavigne was an employee at a community college. As a member of the bargaining unit, but not of the union, he was subject to mandatory dues check-off. He challenged certain expenditures made by the union to the NDP, to pro-choice groups and to striking coal miners in the United Kingdom. He argued that his freedom of expression was violated when his compulsory payments to the union were spent on political matters not directly related to collective bargaining. All the members of the Court agreed that compelled union dues do not violate freedom of expression under s. 2(b). In reaching this conclusion the Court stressed that others were unlikely to attribute to Mr. Lavigne the views expressed by the union and that he had plenty of opportunity to disassociate himself from those views.

In 1997, the federal government passed new legislation regulating tobacco advertising and labelling. The *Tobacco Act*, SC 1997, c. 13 prohibits most tobacco advertising, but creates an exception for "information advertising" and "brand-preference advertising" contained in publications (primarily magazines) directed at an adult readership. All "lifestyle" advertising is banned. The legislation also requires the placement of health warnings, in a prescribed form and manner, on tobacco packages, but the warnings are attributed to a prescribed person or body. In the decision that follows, the Supreme Court of Canada upheld the legislation against a s. 2(b) challenge.

Canada (Attorney General) v. JTI-Macdonald Corp.
[2007], 2 SCR 610, 2007 SCC 30, 281 DLR (4th) 589

McLACHLIN CJC for the Court (Bastarache, Binnie, LeBel, Deschamps, Fish, Abella, Charron, and Rothstein JJ concurring):

I. Overview

[1] These appeals concern the constitutionality of Canada's laws on tobacco advertising and promotion, under the *Tobacco Act*, SC 1997, c. 13, and the *Tobacco Products Information Regulations*, SOR/2000-272 ("*TPIR*"). The main issue is whether the limits certain provisions impose on freedom of expression are justified as reasonable under s. 1 of the *Canadian Charter of Rights and Freedoms*.

[2] The case pits tobacco manufacturers against the Attorney General of Canada, who is supported by a number of provincial Attorneys General and the Canadian Cancer Society. The tobacco manufacturers, at this stage of the litigation, challenge six aspects of the legislative and regulatory scheme: (1) its effect on funded scientific publications; (2) its provisions dealing with false and erroneous promotion; (3) its provisions relating to advertising appealing to young persons; (4) its ban on lifestyle advertising; (5) its ban on sponsorship promotion; and (6) its regulatory requirement that health warning labels occupy 50 percent of tobacco packaging.

. . .

II. Background

. . .

[6] In 1995, this Court struck down the advertising provisions of the *Tobacco Products Control Act* (SC 1988, c. 20): *RJR-MacDonald Inc. v. Canada (Attorney General)*, [1995] 3 SCR 199. This Act broadly prohibited all advertising and promotion of tobacco products, subject to specific exceptions, and required affixing unattributed warning labels on tobacco product packaging. The majority of the Court in that case held that the provisions limited free expression and that the government had failed to justify the limitations under s. 1 of the *Charter*. In particular, the government, by failing to show that less intrusive measures were not available, had failed to establish that the limits met the requirement of minimal impairment developed in *R v. Oakes*, [1986] 1 SCR 103 ... . While the majority agreed that s. 1 justification on issues such as this does not require scientifically precise proof, it found that the absence of virtually any proof was fatal to the government's case. The trial judge had found that the requirements for justification were not met on the evidence. The majority concluded that on the record before it, there was no basis to interfere with the trial judge's conclusion.

[7] In response to the Court's decision in *RJR*, Parliament enacted the *Tobacco Act* and *Regulations* at issue on these appeals. The scheme of the new legislation, in broad terms, involved permitting information and brand-preference advertising, while forbidding lifestyle advertising and promotion, advertising appealing to young persons, and false or misleading advertising or promotion. In addition, the size of mandatory and attributed health warnings on packaging was increased from 33 percent to 50 percent of

the principal display surfaces. In general, the new scheme was more restrained and nuanced than its predecessor. It represented a genuine attempt by Parliament to craft controls on advertising and promotion that would meet its objectives as well as the concerns expressed by the majority of this Court in *RJR*.

[8] The government's response to the inevitable challenge to the new scheme, when it came, also reflected the Court's decision in *RJR*. The government presented detailed and copious evidence in support of its contention that where the new legislation posed limits on free expression, those limits were demonstrably justified under s. 1 of the *Charter*.

[9] Parliament was assisted in its efforts to craft and justify appropriately tailored controls on tobacco advertising and promotion by increased understanding of the means by which tobacco manufacturers seek to advertise and promote their products and by new scientific insights into the nature of tobacco addiction and its consequences. On the findings of the trial judge in the present case, tobacco is now irrefutably accepted as highly addictive and as imposing huge personal and social costs. We now know that half of smokers will die of tobacco-related diseases and that the costs to the public health system are enormous. We also know that tobacco addiction is one of the hardest addictions to conquer and that many addicts try to quit time and time again, only to relapse.

[10] Moreover, the international context has changed since 1995. Governments around the world are implementing anti-tobacco measures similar to and, in some cases, more restrictive than Canada's. The *WHO Framework Convention on Tobacco Control* (2003), 2302 UNTS 229, which Canada ratified in 2004, mandates a comprehensive ban on tobacco promotion, subject to state constitutional requirements. The Convention, with 168 signatories and 148 parties, is one of the most widely embraced of multilateral treaties. Domestically, governments now widely accept that protecting the public from second-hand smoke is a legitimate policy objective. Many provinces have banned smoking in enclosed public places, and some are legislating to recover health care costs from tobacco manufacturers and to restrict tobacco promotion even further than the federal *Tobacco Act*. The tobacco industry has been criticized for its use of "light" and "mild" cigarette designations, which the manufacturers agreed in 2006 to discontinue following an investigation by the Competition Bureau.

[11] None of these developments remove the burden on the Crown to show that limitations on free expression imposed by the legislation are demonstrably justified in a free and democratic society, as required by s. 1 of the *Charter*. The mere fact that the legislation represents Parliament's response to a decision of this Court does not militate for or against deference … . The legal template set out in *Oakes* and *RJR* remains applicable. However, when that template is applied to the evidence adduced by the government in this case more than a decade later, different conclusions may emerge. *RJR* was grounded in a different historical context and based on different findings supported by a different record at a different time. The *Tobacco Act* must be assessed in light of the knowledge, social conditions and regulatory environment revealed by the evidence presented in this case.

. . .

IV. The Legislative and Regulatory Scheme

[18] The purposes of the *Tobacco Act* are "to provide a legislative response to a national public health problem of substantial and pressing concern ..." and, more particularly, "to protect the health of Canadians in light of conclusive evidence implicating tobacco use in the incidence of numerous debilitating and fatal diseases"; "to protect young persons and others from inducements to use tobacco products and the consequent dependence on them"; " to protect the health of young persons by restricting access to tobacco products"; and "to enhance public awareness of the health hazards of using tobacco products": s. 4(a), (b), (c) and (d) ... .

. . .

[21] The basic structure of the limitations on advertising and promotion ... may be described as follows.

1. Promotion

[22] The starting point is a general prohibition on promoting tobacco products, except as authorized by the Act or regulations:

> 19. No person shall promote a tobacco product or a tobacco product-related brand element except as authorized by this Act or the regulations.

"Promotion" is defined in s. 18. The basic definition is broad:

> 18(1) In this Part, "promotion" means a representation about a product or service by any means, whether directly or indirectly, including any communication of information about a product or service and its price and distribution, that is likely to influence and shape attitudes, beliefs and behaviours about the product or service.

[23] Section 18(2) creates exceptions to this general prohibition. The first is an exception for representations of tobacco products in works of art or science, provided no consideration is given for the use or depiction in the work, production or performance: s. 18(2)(a). The second is an exception for "a report, commentary or opinion in respect of a tobacco product ... ," provided no consideration is given by a manufacturer or retailer for a reference to a tobacco product: s. 18(2)(b). ...

2. Specific Prohibitions: False Promotion; Lifestyle Advertising; Advertising Appealing to Young Persons

[24] Having broadly prohibited promotion subject to the specific exceptions within s. 18(2) and other provisions of the Act or regulations, the legislation goes on to make a number of specific prohibitions.

[25] The first is a broad blanket prohibition against false or deceptive promotion of tobacco products:

> 20. No person shall promote a tobacco product by any means, including by means of the packaging, that are false, misleading or deceptive or that are likely to create an erroneous impression about the characteristics, health effects or health hazards of the tobacco product or its emissions. ...

. . .

[27] In s. 22(1), the Act prohibits advertisements that depict "a tobacco product, its package or a brand element." However, in s. 22(2), it goes on to carve out an exception from this prohibition for information and brand-preference advertising in publications addressed and mailed to identified adults, in publications with an adult readership of not less than 85 percent, or in signs in places not frequented by young persons.

[28] The effect of s. 22(2) is to allow information or brand-preference advertising of tobacco products in publications and venues where adults will constitute the principal audience. However, presumably because Parliament was concerned that such advertising could still reach young people (for example, because publications with an 85 percent adult readership may nevertheless be read by large numbers of young persons), or could cross the line into lifestyle advertising, it further qualified this already restricted form of advertising:

> 22(3) Subsection (2) does not apply to lifestyle advertising or advertising that could be construed on reasonable grounds to be appealing to young persons.

"Lifestyle advertising" is defined in s. 22(4) as "advertising that associates a product with, or evokes a positive or negative emotion about or image of, a way of life such as one that includes glamour, recreation, excitement, vitality, risk or daring." No definition is provided of what might be appealing to young persons. The manufacturers argue that the prohibitions on lifestyle advertising and advertising appealing to young persons are vague and overbroad, and thus unconstitutional.

. . .

3. Sponsorships

[30] Section 24 of the *Tobacco Act* forbids the display of tobacco brand elements or manufacturers' names in any promotion "that is used, directly or indirectly, in the sponsorship of a person, entity, event, activity or permanent facility." Section 25 forbids display of brand elements or manufacturers' names on any "permanent facility," if this associates the element or name with a sports or cultural event or activity. ...

4. Warnings on Packaging

[31] Finally, the new regulations ... increase the required size of warning labels on packaging from 33 percent to 50 percent of the principal display surfaces (s. 5(2)(b)). ...

V. Analysis

. . .

[The Court engages in an overview of the s. 1 analysis, emphasizing the appropriateness of a certain measure of deference at both the rational connection and minimal impairment stages when the problem Parliament is tackling is a complex social problem, citing *Edwards Books* and *Irwin Toy* in support. The Court also notes that the minimal impairment analysis must take into account the possibility of potential overbreadth being resolved by statutory interpretation.]

[48] Against this background, I turn more specifically to the challenged provisions of the legislative and regulatory scheme.

1. Publication of Manufacturer-Sponsored Scientific Works

. . .

[The Court interpreted ss. 18 and 19 of the Act in such a way that these sections did not prohibit the publication of legitimate scientific research.]

2. False Promotion

[58] Section 20 bans "false, misleading or deceptive" promotion, as well as promotion "likely to create an erroneous impression about the characteristics, health effects or health hazards of the tobacco product or its emissions."

. . .

[60] Section 20 clearly infringes the guarantee of freedom of expression. The *Charter* is content-neutral and protects the expression of both truths and falsehoods. Consequently, the regulation of falsehoods must be justified under s. 1 of the *Charter*. See *R v. Zundel*, [1992] 2 SCR 731; *R v. Lucas*, [1998] 1 SCR 439.

[61] The s. 1 inquiry into the justification of the ban imposed by s. 20 of the Act must be set in the factual context of a long history of misleading and deceptive advertising by the tobacco industry. The creative ability of the manufacturers to send positive messages about a product widely known to be noxious is impressive. In recent years, for example, manufacturers have used labels such as "additive free" and "100% Canadian tobacco" to convey the impression that their product is wholesome and healthful. Technically, the labels may be true. But their intent and effect is to falsely lull consumers into believing, as they ask for the package behind the counter, that the product they will consume will not harm them, or at any rate will harm them less than would other tobacco products, despite evidence demonstrating that products bearing these labels are in fact no safer than other tobacco products. The wording chosen by Parliament in s. 20 and its justification must be evaluated with this context in mind. Parliament's concern was to combat misleading false inferences about product safety and to promote informed, enlightened consumer choice.

[62] The specific objection is to the phrase "or that are likely to create an erroneous impression" in s. 20. The manufacturers argue that this phrase is overbroad and vague, and introduces subjective considerations. How, they ask, can they predict what is "likely to create an erroneous impression"? The words false, misleading or deceptive, used as legal terms, generally refer to objectively ascertainable facts. If "likely to create an erroneous impression" adds something to "false, misleading or deceptive," as presumably was Parliament's intent, what is it?

[63] The answer is that the phrase "likely to create an erroneous impression" is directed at promotion that, while not literally false, misleading or deceptive in the traditional legal sense, conveys an erroneous impression about the effects of the tobacco product, in the sense of leading consumers to infer things that are not true. It represents an attempt to cover the grey area between demonstrable falsity and invitation to false inference that tobacco manufacturers have successfully exploited in the past.

[64] The industry practice of promoting tobacco consumption by inducing consumers to draw false inferences about the safety of the products is widespread. This suggests that it is viewed by the industry as effective. Parliament has responded by banning promotion that is "likely to create an erroneous impression." This constitutes a limit on free expression. The only question is whether the limit is justified under s. 1 of the *Charter*.

[65] Parliament's objective of combating the promotion of tobacco products by half-truths and by invitation to false inference constitutes a pressing and substantial objective, capable of justifying limits on the right of free expression. Prohibiting such forms of promotion is rationally connected to Parliament's public health and consumer protection purposes.

[66] The impugned phrase does not impair the right of free expression more than is necessary to achieve the objective. The words false, misleading or deceptive do not do the work assigned to the additional phrase, "likely to create an erroneous impression." Nor is it easy to find narrower words that would accomplish that task. ...

· · ·

[68] Finally, the impugned phrase meets the requirement of proportionality of effects. On the one hand, the objective is of great importance, nothing less than a matter of life or death for millions of people who could be affected, and the evidence shows that banning advertising by half-truths and by invitation to false inference may help reduce smoking. The reliance of tobacco manufacturers on this type of advertising attests to this. On the other hand, the expression at stake is of low value—the right to invite consumers to draw an erroneous inference as to the healthfulness of a product that, on the evidence, will almost certainly harm them. On balance, the effect of the ban is proportional.

· · ·

3. Advertising and Promotion Appealing to Young Persons

[70] The *Tobacco Act* uses three particular means of protecting young persons from tobacco advertising and promotion. The first consists of the placement restrictions, found in s. 22(2). The second is a ban on advertising that "could be construed on reasonable grounds to be appealing to young persons," found in s. 22(3). The third is a ban on the use of tobacco brand elements on non-tobacco products that are "associated with young persons or could be construed on reasonable grounds to be appealing to young persons": s. 27(a). The manufacturers challenge the second of these measures, the ban on advertising that "could be construed on reasonable grounds to be appealing to young persons": s. 22(3).

[71] The structure of the scheme at issue, broadly put, is this. As mentioned previously, s. 22(2) permits information and brand-preference advertising in certain media and certain locations. Brand-preference advertising is broadly defined as "advertising that promotes a tobacco product by means of its brand characteristics." Brand characteristics arguably may include elements that are directed at young persons. To remove these elements, s. 22(3) of the Act claws them back. The result is to ban this type of advertising.

[72] There is no doubt that this ban limits free expression and thus infringes s. 2(b) of the *Charter*. The only question is whether the ban is justified under s. 1 of the *Charter*. I conclude that it is.

[The Court rejected the manufacturer's argument that the provision banning advertising that could appeal to youth is too vague.]

[89] ... Section 22(3), thus interpreted, requires the prosecution in a given case to prove that there are reasonable grounds to believe that the advertisement of a tobacco product at issue could be appealing to young persons, in the sense that it could be particularly attractive and of interest to young persons, as distinguished from the general population.

[90] Having established the meaning of s. 22(3), I turn to the question of whether the incursion on free expression that it represents has been shown to be a reasonable limit demonstrably justified in a free and democratic society under s. 1 of the *Charter*.

[91] It is not disputed that Parliament's objective of preventing young people from being tempted to take up tobacco use and consequently becoming addicted is pressing and substantial. Nor is there doubt that a ban on advertising appealing to young persons is rationally connected to this goal.

[92] The manufacturers' claims that the provision is not minimally impairing by reason of vagueness and overbreadth, however, require close consideration. ... I conclude that s. 22(3), construed as I have suggested, is not vague. It does not impose a total ban on advertising. Information and brand-preference advertising is permitted, provided that it is not done in places that young persons are likely to frequent or publications not addressed to adults, and provided that it is not lifestyle advertising (considered below) or advertising that there are reasonable grounds to believe that it could be appealing to young people as a group.

[93] Is the ban on advertising that could appeal to young persons overbroad? Does it go farther than necessary to accomplish Parliament's purpose? It might be argued that it is enough to confine advertising to information and brand-preference and to impose placement restrictions, and that the further limit imposed by s. 22(3) is unnecessary. But this argument overlooks the breadth of Parliament's definition of brand-preference advertising, which may well permit advertising targeted at young persons. Information, too, can be packaged in many ways. These realities, coupled with the possibility that young persons may see or read that material permitted by the placement restrictions, justify a specific restriction on material that could be appealing to young persons. Brand-preference advertising is permitted in publications sent by mail to an identified adult (s. 22(2)(a)) or with an adult readership of at least 85 percent (s. 22(2)(b)). These publications may nevertheless be read by young persons. The purpose of s. 22(3), in this context, is to prevent advertising in these publications that "could be" appealing to young people, as opposed to the general adult population. Section 22(3) simply forbids presenting this type of advertising in a way that could have a particular appeal to young persons. Given the sophistication and subtlety of tobacco advertising practices in the past, as demonstrated by the record in this case, Parliament cannot be said to have gone farther than necessary in blocking advertising that might influence young persons to start smoking.

[94] Finally, s. 22(3) meets the requirement of proportionality of effects. The prohibited speech is of low value. Information about tobacco products and the characteristics of brands may have some value to the consumer who is already addicted to tobacco. But it is not great. On the other hand, the beneficial effects of the ban for young persons and

for society at large may be significant. The placement restrictions may mean that the majority of people seeing the advertising prohibited by s. 22(3) are adults. The restrictions may impose a cost in terms of the information and brand-preference advertising they may be able to receive. But that cost is small; all that is prohibited is advertising that could be specifically appealing to young people. Moreover, the vulnerability of the young may justify measures that privilege them over adults in matters of free expression. ...

[95] I conclude that the limit on free expression imposed by s. 22(3), properly interpreted, is justified as reasonable under s. 1 of the *Charter*.

4. *Lifestyle Advertising*

[96] Section 22(3) carves out from permitted information and brand-preference advertising under s. 22(2) two types of advertising: advertising that could appeal to young persons, just considered, and lifestyle advertising.

[97] Section 22(4) defines lifestyle advertising as follows:

> "lifestyle advertising" means advertising that associates a product with, or evokes a positive or negative emotion about or image of, a way of life such as one that includes glamour, recreation, excitement, vitality, risk or daring.

[98] It is agreed that this provision infringes the s. 2(b) guarantee of freedom of expression. The manufacturers, however, argue that it is overbroad and ask that it be struck down. ...

$$\cdots$$

[102] As with the other provisions challenged in these appeals, the first task is one of interpretation. Some background may be helpful. In *RJR*, the majority agreed that on the evidence presented in that case, a prohibition on lifestyle advertising (but not information and brand-preference advertising) could have been considered minimally impairing (*per* McLachlin J, at para. 164; *per* Iacobucci J, at para. 191). This was based on the understanding that lifestyle advertising invariably seeks to increase overall tobacco consumption, not just to inform existing smokers.

[103] The Attorney General of Canada asserts that s. 22 is Canada's response to the "guidelines" of the Court. However, the *Tobacco Act* departs in important respects from the template discussed in *RJR*, making direct comparisons inconclusive.

[104] First, the Act defines "lifestyle" differently than did the discussion in *RJR*. The definition of lifestyle advertising alluded to in *RJR* was broad, unencumbered by the references to "glamour, recreation, excitement, vitality, risk or daring" found in the Act. Moreover, the Court in *RJR* focused on advertising that "associates" a product with a way of life, and made no references to advertising that "evokes a positive or negative emotion about or image of" a way of life, as found in the *Tobacco Act*.

[105] Second, the *Tobacco Act* defines brand-preference advertising more broadly than the Court did in *RJR*. In *RJR*, brand-preference advertising was restricted in that it had to be aimed only at existing smokers, inducing them to switch brands, and was restricted to colour, design and package appearance (*per* La Forest J, relying on the definition used in the Court of Appeal ([1993] RJQ 375, 102 DLR (4th) 289), *per* Brossard JA). The *Tobacco Act*, by contrast, simply defines brand-preference advertising as "advertising

that promotes a tobacco product by means of its brand characteristics." This means that the window for permissible advertising opened by s. 22(2) is broader than it would have been had the narrower *RJR* definition of brand preference been adopted.

. . .

[107] How, then, is lifestyle advertising in s. 22(3) to be construed? ...

. . .

[110] ... Expressly including lifestyle advertising that evokes emotions and images makes it clear that even advertising that does not appear on its face to connect a lifestyle with a tobacco product is prohibited if it subliminally connects a tobacco product with a lifestyle.

[111] The phrase "evokes a positive or negative emotion or image" should not, however, be read so broadly as to encompass every perceptual impression. It should be interpreted in a way that leaves room for true information and brand-preference advertising, which s. 22(2) permits. This brings to mind the definition of brand-preference advertising used in *RJR*, which was confined to existing smokers and restricted to the colour, design and appearance of the packaging. It is possible to argue that a colour or image evokes an emotion in some highly abstract, artistic sense. Parliament, however, was concerned with emotions and images that may induce people to start to use or to increase their use of tobacco. Parliament used these terms in the context of its purpose—to prevent the increase of tobacco consumption through advertising and to confine permissible advertising to hard, factual data directed to confirmed smokers. The provision should be construed accordingly.

. . .

[114] ... As with the other challenged provisions, the pressing and substantial nature of Parliament's objective is beyond challenge. The record is replete with examples of lifestyle advertisements promoting tobacco products. It amply establishes the power of such advertisements to induce non-smokers to begin to smoke and to increase tobacco consumption among addicted smokers. It also establishes the sophistication and subtlety of such advertising. Lifestyle advertising spans the spectrum from the bold association of the Marlboro man with cowboy culture to the subtle suggestion emerging from a cup of coffee or a bath scene that evokes tobacco use through learned prior imagery.

[115] The sophistication and subtlety of lifestyle advertising are reflected in the means Parliament has chosen to deal with it. A ban on lifestyle advertising must catch not only clear associations, but subtle subliminal evocations. Hence the inclusion of advertising that "evokes a positive or negative emotion or image." There is a rational connection between this provision and Parliament's objective. Minimal impairment is also established. True information and brand-preference advertising continues to be permitted under s. 22(2). Such advertising crosses the line when it associates a product with a way of life or uses a lifestyle to evoke an emotion or image that may, by design or effect, lead more people to become addicted or lead people who are already addicted to increase their tobacco use. Finally, the proportionality of the effects is clear. The suppressed expression—the inducement of increased tobacco consumption—is of low value, compared with the significant benefits in lower rates of consumption and addiction that the ban may yield.

[116] The challenge of dealing with today's sophisticated advertising of tobacco products is not insignificant. The distinction between information and brand-preference

advertising directed to market share, on the one hand, and advertising directed to increased consumption and new smokers, on the other, is difficult to capture in legal terms. Parliament in its wisdom has chosen to take the task on. Properly interpreted, the law it has adopted meets the requirements of justification under s. 1 of the *Charter*.

5. *Sponsorships*

. . .

[The Court held that sponsorship promotion is essentially lifestyle advertising in disguise and can be restricted under s. 1 for the same reasons.]

6. *Health Warning Labels*

[130] The regulations pursuant to the Act (the *TPIR*) increased the minimum size of the mandatory health warnings on tobacco packaging from 33 percent under the old Act to 50 percent of the principal display surfaces. The question is whether this constitutes an infringement of s. 2(b) and, if so, whether that infringement is justified.

[131] The question of whether the mandatory warning requirement infringes s. 2(b) is not easily answered. The Attorney General argues that s. 2(b) is not infringed, claiming that it neither deprives the manufacturers of a vehicle for communicating their message, nor limits the form of expression. He relies on *Lavigne v. Ontario Public Service Employees Union*, [1991] 2 SCR 211, at pp. 279-80, where Wilson J stated: "If a law does not really deprive one of the ability to speak one's mind or does not effectively associate one with a message with which one disagrees, it is difficult to see how one's right to pursue truth, participate in the community, or fulfil oneself [the values protected by s. 2(b)] are denied." The regulations under the *TPIR* permit the manufacturers to present the health warnings, not as their messages, but as messages from Health Canada. The manufacturers still have half the package to convey such messages as they choose, and they are not confined to a particular size or style of package that might inhibit that ability. As a result, the Attorney General argues, the manufacturers have not shown that they are prevented from conveying messages of their choice on their packaging. Not having discharged this burden, they have not established a breach of their freedom of expression, he concludes.

[132] However, this Court has taken a broad view of "expressive activity" for s. 2(b) cases. In *Irwin Toy*, the Court went so far as to say that parking a car could be an expressive activity. In *Reference re ss. 193 and 195.1(1)(c) of the Criminal Code (Man.)*, [1990] 1 SCR 1123, at p. 1184, Lamer J stated that in some circumstances, silence could constitute expressive activity. To hold that minor restrictions or requirements with respect to packaging violate the s. 2(b) guarantee of freedom of expression might be to trivialize the guarantee. However, the requirement that manufacturers place the government's warning on one half of the surface of their package arguably rises to the level of interfering with how they choose to express themselves. I therefore conclude that s. 2(b) is infringed by the warning requirements in general, and specifically the requirement that 50 percent of the principal display surfaces of the package be devoted to the warnings.

[133] This leaves the question of whether the infringement is justified as a reasonable limit under s. 1 of the *Charter*. I conclude that it is.

. . .

[137] ... [T]he evidence established that bigger warnings may have a greater effect. Parliament is not required to implement less effective alternatives: *RJR*, at paras. 160 and 163.

Appeal allowed

NOTES AND QUESTIONS

In its practical application, how much narrower is the tobacco advertising restriction upheld in the *JTI MacDonald* decision than the restriction struck down in the *RJR MacDonald* case? In *RJR*, McLachlin CJC, in deciding that the general ban on tobacco advertising was overbroad, relied on the distinction between lifestyle advertising and other forms of advertising. Did this preclude her in *JTI* from deciding that the ban on lifestyle advertising in the new law was too vague? What does Chief Justice McLachlin mean in *JTI* when she writes that "*RJR* was grounded in a different historical context and based on different findings supported by a different record at a different time" (para. 11)?

R v. Guignard
[2002] 1 SCR 472, 2002 SCC 14, 209 DLR (4th) 549

[In many of its commercial speech cases, the Supreme Court of Canada has identified the informational interests of listeners as one of the reasons for protecting such expression. In *R v. Guignard,* the Court dealt with another aspect of commercial expression— "counteradvertising" by consumers—in the context of a challenge to a municipal bylaw that prohibited advertising signs in certain parts of a municipality. In a judgment authored by LeBel J, the Court struck down the bylaw.]

[3] In 1996, Guignard owned a property within the City of Saint-Hyacinthe. An insurance policy issued by a major company, the Commerce Group, covered the risks relating to this property. A loss occurred in May 1996 and the appellant claimed an indemnity from his insurer. Payment was delayed and Mr. Guignard eventually became impatient. He placed a sign on another of his buildings that eloquently expressed his dissatisfaction. On August 8, 1996, in response to a complaint, a municipal inspector ordered the appellant to remove the sign within 24 hours. According to the inspector, the sign contravened the zoning by-law of the City, which prohibited the erection of advertising signs outside an industrial area (*Règlement d'urbanisme nº 1200 de la Ville de Saint-Hyacinthe*, s. 14.1.5(p)). The sign read as follows:

[TRANSLATION]

DATE OF INCIDENT	10-05-96
DATE OF REPAIRS	10-13
DATE OF CLAIM	10-05-96
WHEN A CLAIM IS MADE,	
ONE FINDS OUT ABOUT	
POOR QUALITY INSURANCE	

COMMERCE GROUP
THE INCOMPETENT
INSURANCE COMPANY
HAS STILL NOT INDEMNIFIED ME

[4] When he refused to comply, the municipality charged Guignard with contravening the by-law. …

. . .

[23] The decisions of this Court accordingly recognize that commercial enterprises have a constitutional right to engage in activities to inform and promote, by advertising. As we know and can attest, sometimes with mixed feelings, the ubiquitous presence of advertising is a defining characteristic of western societies. Usually, it attempts to convey a positive message to potential consumers. However, it sometimes involves comparisons and may even be negative. On the other hand, consumers also have freedom of expression. This sometimes takes the form of "counter-advertising" to criticize a product or make negative comments about the services supplied. Within limits prescribed by the legal principles relating to defamation, every consumer enjoys this right. Consumers may express their frustration or disappointment with a product or service. Their freedom of expression in this respect is not limited to private communications intended solely for the vendor or supplier of the service. Consumers may share their concerns, worries or even anger with other consumers and try to warn them against the practices of a business. Given the tremendous importance of economic activity in our society, a consumer's "counter-advertising" assists in circulating information and protecting the interests of society just as much as does advertising or certain forms of political expression. This type of communication may be of considerable social importance, even beyond the merely commercial sphere.

[24] "Counter-advertising" is not merely a reaction to commercial speech, and is not a form of expression derived from commercial speech. Rather, it is a form of the expression of opinion that has an important effect on the social and economic life of a society. It is a right not only of consumers, but of citizens.

[25] In this respect, simple means of expression such as posting signs or distributing pamphlets or leaflets or, these days, posting messages on the Internet are the optimum means of communication for discontented consumers. The media are still often beyond their reach because of the cost. In *Ramsden v. Peterborough (City)*, [1993] 2 SCR 1084, this Court stressed the importance of signs as an effective and inexpensive means of communication for individuals and groups that do not have sufficient economic resources. Signs, which have been used for centuries to communicate political, artistic or economic information, sometimes convey forceful messages. Signs, in various forms, are thus a public, accessible and effective form of expressive activity for anyone who cannot undertake media campaigns. …

[26] By restricting the right to use this optimum means of expression to certain designated places, the impugned by-law directly infringes freedom of expression. This infringement impacts especially on the freedom of expression of a person who does not have access to substantial financial resources. A limitation of this nature can in fact deprive that person of the only means of expression that are truly accessible to him or her.

Even when a legislative or regulatory provision is neutral in appearance, it can have a major impact on the ability of a person or group to engage in expressive activity (see *Irwin Toy* at pp. 974-75).

. . .

[30] ... The by-law severely curtails Guignard's freedom to express his dissatisfaction with the practices of his insurance company publicly. It forces him to use advertising methods that presuppose the availability of adequate financial resources. Alternatively, it restricts him to private or virtually private communications such as distributing leaflets in the neighbourhood around his property, which is undoubtedly less effective, to convey to the public his opinion about the quality of his insurer's services.

. . .

[32] The only appropriate remedy in this case is a declaration that the provisions of the municipal by-law the appellant has challenged are invalid. ... A solution that applied solely and personally to the appellant would not satisfactorily resolve the legal problem before us. However, given the importance of the zoning by-law in municipal land use planning and the risk of creating acquired rights, during a period in which there was a legal vacuum, which could be set up against a subsequent by-law, that relief must be tempered by suspending the declaration of invalidity for a period of six months, to give the municipality an opportunity to revise its by-law.

NOTES AND QUESTIONS

1. In *Guignard*, reference is made to a previous decision of the Court, *Ramsden v. Peterborough (City)*, [1993] 2 SCR 1084 in which a municipal bylaw prohibiting postering on public signs was struck down as a violation of s. 2(b). *Ramsden* and other related cases are dealt with in Section VII, Access to Public Property, below, which deals with access to public property for expressive purposes.

2. Should a municipality be able to regulate billboards for aesthetic reasons? Can it regulate the size of signs or can it go further and simply ban all signs? See, for example, *Vann Niagara Ltd. v. Oakville*, [2003] 3 SCR 158, 234 DLR (4th) 118; *Vancouver v. Jaminer*, 2001 BCCA 240, 198 DLR (4th) 333; *Ontario (Minister of Transportation) v. Miracle* (2005), 249 DLR (4th) 680 (Ont. CA).

IV. HATE SPEECH

Hate speech in Canada is currently restricted or regulated by both federal and provincial laws. The *Criminal Code* of Canada prohibits the advocacy or promotion of genocide; the incitement of hatred against an identifiable group, when this incitement is likely to lead to a breach of the peace; and the wilful promotion of hatred against an identifiable group. The *Criminal Code* also includes a section that enables a court to order the seizure or erasure of material that the court determines to be "hate propaganda."

Section 13 of the *Canadian Human Rights Act*, SC 1976-77, c. 33 prohibits telephonic or Internet communication that is likely to expose the members of an identifiable group to hatred or contempt. The human rights codes of British Columbia, Alberta, Saskatchewan,

and the Northwest Territories include provisions similar to s. 13 of the CHRA, which prohibits signs, notices, and other representations that are likely to expose the members of an
identifiable group to hatred or contempt.

US courts have tended to view restrictions on hate speech as a violation of the First
Amendment. Hate speech is generally regarded as dissident political speech that advances
First Amendment values. According to the US courts, the injury caused by most hate speech
is simply the offence or upset experienced by the audience and is not sufficient to justify the
restriction of the fundamental right to free speech. Counterspeech, rather than censorship,
is seen as the appropriate response to offensive speech. Only speech that poses an imminent
danger of serious harm (in US constitutional language, a "clear and present danger") can be
suppressed on the basis of its content.

In *Keegstra*, which follows, and in its companion case, *Taylor*, discussed in the subsequent notes, the Supreme Court of Canada seems to have taken a different approach, one
that gives greater weight to equality values. As you read *Keegstra*, consider the following
questions: What is the harm caused by hate speech? Can a hate-speech law be drafted with
sufficient precision to catch only harmful speech? Should the promoters of hate be seen as
a persecuted minority, or as extreme representatives of the dominant culture? In answering
these questions, should we distinguish between different forms of hate speech—for example, between racist threats and insults directed at members of a particular racial and/or
ethnic group and racist claims meant to "persuade" members of the general community
about the undesirable characteristics of certain racial and/or ethnic groups?

R v. Keegstra
[1990] 3 SCR 697, 61 CCC (3d) 1

DICKSON CJC (Wilson, L'Heureux-Dubé, and Gonthier JJ concurring): ... Mr. James
Keegstra was a high school teacher in Eckville, Alberta from the early 1970s until his
dismissal in 1982. In 1984 Mr. Keegstra was charged under s. 319(2) (then 281.2(2)) of
the *Criminal Code* with unlawfully promoting hatred against an identifiable group by
communicating anti-Semitic statements to his students. He was convicted by a jury in a
trial before McKenzie J of the Alberta Court of Queen's Bench.

Mr. Keegstra's teachings attributed various evil qualities to Jews. He thus described
Jews to his pupils as "treacherous," "subversive," "sadistic," "money-loving," "power hungry" and "child killers." He taught his classes that Jewish people seek to destroy Christianity and are responsible for depressions, anarchy, chaos, wars and revolution. According
to Mr. Keegstra, Jews "created the Holocaust to gain sympathy" and, in contrast to the
open and honest Christians, were said to be deceptive, secretive and inherently evil.
Mr. Keegstra expected his students to reproduce his teachings in class and on exams. If
they failed to do so, their marks suffered.

Prior to his trial, Mr. Keegstra applied to the Court of Queen's Bench in Alberta for
an order quashing the charge on a number of grounds, the primary one being that
s. 319(2) of the *Criminal Code* unjustifiably infringed his freedom of expression as guaranteed by s. 2(b) of the Charter. Among the other grounds of appeal was the allegation
that the defence of truth found in s. 319(3)(a) of the *Code* violates the Charter's presump-

tion of innocence. The application was dismissed by Quigley J, and Mr. Keegstra was thereafter tried and convicted. He then appealed his conviction to the Alberta Court of Appeal, raising the same Charter issues. The Court of Appeal unanimously accepted his argument, and it is from this judgment that the Crown appeals. ...

[The relevant sections of the *Criminal Code* read:

319(2) Every one who, by communicating statements, other than in private conversation, wilfully promotes hatred against any identifiable group is guilty of

    (a) an indictable offence and is liable to imprisonment for a term not exceeding two years; or

    (b) an offence punishable on summary conviction.

(3) No person shall be convicted of an offence under subsection (2)

    (a) if he establishes that the statements communicated were true;

    (b) if, in good faith, he expressed or attempted to establish by argument an opinion upon a religious subject;

    (c) if the statements were relevant to any subject of public interest, the discussion of which was for the public benefit, and if on reasonable grounds he believed them to be true; or

    (d) if, in good faith, he intended to point out, for the purpose of removal, matters producing or tending to produce feelings of hatred towards an identifiable group in Canada.

. . .

(6) No proceeding for an offence under subsection (2) shall be instituted without the consent of the Attorney General.

(7) In this section,

"communicating" includes communicating by telephone, broadcasting or other audible or visible means;

"identifiable group" has the same meaning as in section 318;

"public place" includes any place to which the public have access as of right or by invitation, express or implied;

"statements" includes words spoken or written or recorded electronically or electromagnetically or otherwise, and gestures, signs or other visible representations.

. . .

318(4) In this section, "identifiable group" means any section of the public distinguished by colour, race, religion or ethnic origin.]

V. The History of Hate Propaganda Crimes in Canada

... Following the Second World War and revelation of the Holocaust, in Canada and throughout the world a desire grew to protect human rights, and especially to guard against discrimination. Internationally, this desire led to the landmark *Universal Declaration of Human Rights* in 1948, and, with reference to hate propaganda, was eventually manifested in two international human rights instruments. In Canada, the post-war mood saw an attempt to include anti-hate propaganda provisions in the 1953 revision of the *Criminal Code*, but most influential in changing the criminal law in order to prohibit hate propaganda was the appointment by Justice Minister Guy Favreau of a special committee to study problems associated with the spread of hate propaganda in Canada.

[The seven-person committee was chaired by Maxwell Cohen, who was Dean of the Faculty of Law at McGill University and included in its membership Pierre E. Trudeau, who was then an associate professor of law at the University of Montreal.]

The Special Committee on Hate Propaganda in Canada, usually referred to as the Cohen Committee, ... was a particularly strong Committee, and in 1966 it released the unanimous *Report of the Special Committee on Hate Propaganda in Canada*.

The tenor of the Report is reflected in the opening paragraph of its preface, which reads:

> This Report is a study in the power of words to maim, and what it is that a civilized society can do about it. Not every abuse of human communication can or should be controlled by law or custom. But every society from time to time draws lines at the point where the intolerable and the impermissible coincide. In a free society such as our own, where the privilege of speech can induce ideas that may change the very order itself, there is bias weighted heavily in favour of the maximum of rhetoric whatever the cost and consequences. But that bias stops this side of injury to the community itself and to individual members or identifiable groups innocently caught in verbal cross-fire that goes beyond legitimate debate.

In keeping with these remarks, the recurrent theme running throughout the Report is the need to prevent the dissemination of hate propaganda without unduly infringing the freedom of expression, a theme which led the Committee to recommend a number of amendments to the *Criminal Code*. These amendments were made, essentially along the lines suggested by the Committee, and covered the advocation of genocide (s. 318), the public incitement of hatred likely to lead to a breach of peace (s. 319(1)) and the provision challenged in this appeal and presently found in s. 319(2) of the Code, namely, the wilful promotion of hatred.

VI.   Section 2(b) of the Charter: Freedom of Expression

Having briefly set out the history of attempts to prohibit hate propaganda, I can now address ... whether the Charter guarantee of freedom of expression is infringed by s. 319(2) of the *Criminal Code*. ...

Communications which wilfully promote hatred against an identifiable group without doubt convey a meaning, and are intended to do so by those who make them. Because *Irwin Toy Ltd. v. Quebec (Attorney General)*, [1989] 1 SCR 927 stresses that the type of meaning conveyed is irrelevant to the question of whether s. 2(b) is infringed, that the expression covered by s. 319(2) is invidious and obnoxious is beside the point. It is enough that those who publicly and wilfully promote hatred convey or attempt to convey a meaning, and it must therefore be concluded that the first step of the *Irwin Toy* test is satisfied.

Moving to the second stage of the s. 2(b) inquiry, one notes that the prohibition in s. 319(2) aims directly at words—in this appeal, Mr. Keegstra's teachings—that have as their content and objective the promotion of racial or religious hatred. ... Section 319(2) therefore overtly seeks to prevent the communication of expression, and hence meets the second requirement of the *Irwin Toy* test.

... I thus find s. 319(2) to constitute an infringement of the freedom of expression guaranteed by s. 2(b) of the Charter.

[Dickson CJC then briefly canvasses and rejects two arguments that had been made to support the position that hate speech does not fall within the ambit of s. 2(b). He concludes first that hate speech is not a form of violence that would fall within the *Irwin Toy* exception, which he interprets narrowly as excluding from Charter protection only those activities where expression is communicated directly through the form of physical violence. Threats of violence, because they can only be classified by reference to the content of their meaning, are held not to fall within the exception. The argument that freedom of expression should be defined and limited by reference to other Charter provisions and Canada's international commitments, discussed below, with the result that s. 2(b) would not extend to communications that seriously undermine the equality, security, and dignity of others, is rejected in favour of an approach where freedom of expression is defined broadly and the consideration of other values is left to s. 1 of the Charter, which is viewed as especially well suited to the task of balancing.]

VII. Section 1 Analysis of S. 319(2)

A. General Approach to Section 1

... Obviously, a practical application of s. 1 requires more than an incantation of the words "free and democratic society." These words require some definition, an elucidation as to the values that they invoke. To a large extent, a free and democratic society embraces the very values and principles which Canadians have sought to protect and further by entrenching specific rights and freedoms in the Constitution, although the balancing exercise in s. 1 is not restricted to values expressly set out in the Charter. ...

[A] rigid or formalistic approach to the application of s. 1 must be avoided. The ability to use s. 1 as a gauge which is sensitive to the values and circumstances particular to an appeal has been identified as vital in past cases. ...

[Dickson CJC then discusses the relevance of the US constitutional jurisprudence with respect to hate propaganda. In the United States, the prevalent opinion is that the criminalization of hate propaganda violates the First Amendment. Initially this was not true. In *Beauharnais v. Illinois*, 343 US 250 (1952), the US Supreme Court upheld an Illinois criminal statute forbidding certain types of group defamation. Later cases weakened the authority of *Beauharnais*, however, to the extent that many regard it as overruled. The test that emerged for the restriction of speech was much stricter than the earlier formulations—that of a "clear and present danger" of violence or insurrection. Dickson CJC rejects the applicability of US constitutional doctrine in this area, noting that the Canadian Charter, unlike the US *Bill of Rights*, contains an express limitation clause. As well he posits that Canada's international law commitments, as well as the Charter's provisions with respect to equality and multiculturalism, suggest different pathways for the development of Canadian constitutional analysis.]

C. Objective of S. 319(2)

. . .

(i) Harm Caused by Expression Promoting the Hatred of Identifiable Groups

Looking to the legislation challenged in this appeal, one must ask whether the amount of hate propaganda in Canada causes sufficient harm to justify legislative intervention of some type. The Cohen Committee, speaking in 1965, found that the incidence of hate propaganda in Canada was not insignificant ... . In 1984, the House of Commons Special Committee on Participation of Visible Minorities in Canadian Society in its report, entitled *Equality Now!*, observed that increased immigration and periods of economic difficulty "have produced an atmosphere that may be ripe for racially motivated incidents." With regard to the dissemination of hate propaganda, the Special Committee found that the prevalence and scope of such material had risen since the Cohen Committee made its report. ...

[The report of the Special Committee noted that Canada had become a major source of supply of hate propaganda that finds its way to Europe, and especially West Germany.]

... [T]he presence of hate propaganda in Canada is sufficiently substantial to warrant concern. Disquiet caused by the existence of such material is not simply the product of its offensiveness, however, but stems from the very real harm which it causes. Essentially, there are two sorts of injury caused by hate propaganda. First, there is harm done to members of the target group. It is indisputable that the emotional damage caused by words may be of grave psychological and social consequence. ...

In my opinion, a response of humiliation and degradation from an individual targeted by hate propaganda is to be expected. A person's sense of human dignity and belonging to the community at large is closely linked to the concern and respect accorded to the groups to which he or she belongs ... . The derision, hostility and abuse encouraged by hate propaganda therefore have a severely negative impact on the individual's sense of self-worth and acceptance. ...

A second harmful effect of hate propaganda which is of pressing and substantial concern is its influence upon society at large. The Cohen Committee noted that individuals can be persuaded to believe "almost anything" if information or ideas are communicated using the right technique and in the proper circumstances ... . It is thus not inconceivable that the active dissemination of hate propaganda can attract individuals to its cause, and in the process create serious discord between various cultural groups in society. Moreover, the alteration of views held by the recipients of hate propaganda may occur subtly, and is not always attendant upon conscious acceptance of the communicated ideas. Even if the message of hate propaganda is outwardly rejected, there is evidence that its premise of racial or religious inferiority may persist in a recipient's mind as an idea that holds some truth, an incipient effect not to be entirely discounted. ...

(ii) International Human Rights Instruments

... I would also refer to international human rights principles ... for guidance with respect to assessing the legislative objective.

Generally speaking, the international human rights obligations taken on by Canada reflect the values and principles of a free and democratic society, and thus those values and principles that underlie the Charter itself .... Moreover, international human rights law and Canada's commitments in that area are of particular significance in assessing the importance of Parliament's objective under s. 1. ...

No aspect of international human rights has been given attention greater than that focused upon discrimination. ...

In 1966, the United Nations adopted the *International Convention on the Elimination of All Forms of Racial Discrimination*, Can. TS 1970, No. 28 (hereinafter CERD). The Convention, in force since 1969 and including Canada among its signatory members, contains a resolution that States Parties agree to:

> ... adopt all necessary measures for speedily eliminating racial discrimination in all its forms and manifestations, and to prevent and combat racist doctrines and practices in order to promote understanding between races and to build an international community free from all forms of racial segregation and racial discrimination. ...

Article 4 of the CERD is of special interest, providing that:

> States Parties condemn all propaganda and all organizations which are based on ideas or theories of superiority of one race or group of persons of one colour or ethnic origin, or which attempt to justify or promote racial hatred and discrimination in any form, and undertake to adopt immediate and positive measures designed to eradicate all incitement to, or acts of, such discrimination and, to this end, with due regard to the principles embodied in the *Universal Declaration of Human Rights* and the rights expressly set forth in article 5 of this Convention, *inter alia*:
>
> (a) Shall declare an offence punishable by law all dissemination of ideas based on racial superiority or hatred, incitement to racial discrimination, as well as all acts of violence or incitement to such acts against any race or group of persons of another colour or ethnic origin, and also the provision of any assistance to racist activities, including the financing thereof;

Further, the *International Covenant on Civil and Political Rights*, 999 UNTS 171 (1966) (hereinafter ICCPR), adopted by the United Nations in 1966 and in force in Canada since 1976 ... guarantees the freedom of expression [in art. 19] while simultaneously prohibiting the advocacy of hatred: ...

> Article 20
> 1. Any propaganda for war shall be prohibited by law.
> 2. Any advocacy of national, racial or religious hatred that constitutes incitement to discrimination, hostility or violence shall be prohibited by law.

· · ·

(iii) Other Provisions of the Charter

Significant indicia of the strength of the objective behind s. 319(2) are gleaned not only from the international arena, but are also expressly evident in various provisions of the Charter itself. ... Most importantly for the purposes of this appeal, ss. 15 and 27 represent a strong commitment to the values of equality and multiculturalism, and hence underline the great importance of Parliament's objective in prohibiting hate propaganda. ...

(iv) Conclusion Respecting Objective of Section 319(2)

In my opinion, it would be impossible to deny that Parliament's objective in enacting s. 319(2) is of the utmost importance. Parliament has recognized the substantial harm that can flow from hate propaganda, and in trying to prevent the pain suffered by target group members and to reduce racial, ethnic and religious tension in Canada has decided to suppress the wilful promotion of hatred against identifiable groups. ...

D. Proportionality

... [T]he interpretation of s. 2(b) under *Irwin Toy* gives protection to a very wide range of expression. Content is irrelevant to this interpretation, the result of a high value being placed upon freedom of expression in the abstract. This approach to s. 2(b) often operates to leave unexamined the extent to which the expression at stake in a particular case promotes freedom of expression principles. In my opinion, however, the s. 1 analysis of a limit upon s. 2(b) cannot ignore the nature of the expressive activity which the state seeks to restrict. While we must guard carefully against judging expression according to its popularity, it is equally destructive of free expression values, as well as the other values which underlie a free and democratic society, to treat all expression as equally crucial to those principles at the core of s. 2(b). ...

From the outset, I wish to make clear that in my opinion the expression prohibited by s. 319(2) is not closely linked to the rationale underlying s. 2(b). ...

At the core of freedom of expression lies the need to ensure that truth and the common good are attained, whether in scientific and artistic endeavors or in the process of determining the best course to take in our political affairs. Since truth and the ideal form of political and social organization can rarely, if at all, be identified with absolute certainty, it is difficult to prohibit expression without impeding the free exchange of potentially valuable information. ... Taken to its extreme, this argument would require us to permit the communication of all expression, it being impossible to know with absolute certainty which factual statements are true, or which ideas obtain the greatest good. The problem with this extreme position, however, is that the greater the degree of certainty that a statement is erroneous or mendacious, the less its value in the quest for truth. Indeed, expression can be used to the detriment of our search for truth; the state should not be the sole arbiter of truth, but neither should we overplay the view that rationality will overcome all falsehoods in the unregulated marketplace of ideas. There is very little chance that statements intended to promote hatred against an identifiable group are true, or that their vision of society will lead to a better world. To portray such statements as crucial to truth and the betterment of the political and social milieu is therefore misguided.

Another component central to the rationale underlying s. 2(b) concerns the vital role of free expression as a means of ensuring individuals the ability to gain self-fulfillment by developing and articulating thoughts and ideas as they see fit. It is true that s. 319(2) inhibits this process among those individuals whose expression it limits, and hence arguably works against freedom of expression values. On the other hand, such self-autonomy stems in large part from one's ability to articulate and nurture an identity derived from membership in a cultural or religious group. The message put forth by individuals who fall within the ambit of s. 319(2) represents a most extreme opposition to the idea that members of identifiable groups should enjoy this aspect of the s. 2(b) benefit. The extent to which the unhindered promotion of this message furthers free expression values must therefore be tempered insofar as it advocates with inordinate vitriol an intolerance and prejudice which views as execrable the process of individual self-development and human flourishing among all members of society.

Moving on to a third strain of thought said to justify the protection of free expression, one's attention is brought specifically to the political realm. The connection between freedom of expression and the political process is perhaps the linchpin of the s. 2(b) guarantee, and the nature of this connection is largely derived from the Canadian commitment to democracy. Freedom of expression is a crucial aspect of the democratic commitment, not merely because it permits the best policies to be chosen from among a wide array of proffered options, but additionally because it helps to ensure that participation in the political process is open to all persons. ...

The suppression of hate propaganda undeniably muzzles the participation of a few individuals in the democratic process, and hence detracts somewhat from free expression values, but the degree of this limitation is not substantial. I am aware that the use of strong language in political and social debate—indeed, perhaps even language intended to promote hatred—is an unavoidable part of the democratic process. Moreover, I recognize that hate propaganda is expression of a type which would generally be categorized as "political," thus putatively placing it at the very heart of the principle extolling freedom of expression as vital to the democratic process. Nonetheless, expression can work to undermine our commitment to democracy where employed to propagate ideas anathemic [*sic*] to democratic values. Hate propaganda works in just such a way, arguing as it does for a society in which the democratic process is subverted and individuals are denied respect and dignity simply because of racial or religious characteristics. This brand of expressive activity is thus wholly inimical to the democratic aspirations of the free expression guarantee.

Indeed, one may quite plausibly contend that it is through rejecting hate propaganda that the state can best encourage the protection of values central to freedom of expression, while simultaneously demonstrating dislike for the vision forwarded by hate-mongers. ...

(ii) Rational Connection

... [I]t would be difficult to deny that the suppression of hate propaganda reduces the harm such expression does to individuals who belong to identifiable groups and to relations between various cultural and religious groups in Canadian society.

Doubts have been raised, however, as to whether the actual effect of s. 319(2) is to undermine any rational connection between it and Parliament's objective. As stated in the reasons of McLachlin J, there are three primary ways in which the effect of the impugned legislation might be seen as an irrational means of carrying out the Parliamentary purpose. First, it is argued that the provision may actually promote the cause of hate-mongers by earning them extensive media attention. In this vein, it is also suggested that persons accused of intentionally promoting hatred often see themselves as martyrs, and may actually generate sympathy from the community in the role of underdogs engaged in battle against the immense powers of the state. Second, the public may view the suppression of expression by the government with suspicion, making it possible that such expression—even if it be hate propaganda—is perceived as containing an element of truth. Finally, it is often noted ... that Germany of the 1920s and 1930s possessed and used hate propaganda laws similar to those existing in Canada, and yet these laws did nothing to stop the triumph of a racist philosophy under the Nazis.

... I recognize that the effect of s. 319(2) is impossible to define with exact precision—the same can be said for many laws, criminal or otherwise. In my view, however, the position that there is no strong and evident connection between the criminalization of hate propaganda and its suppression is unconvincing. ...

It is undeniable that media attention has been extensive on those occasions when s. 319(2) has been used. Yet from my perspective, s. 319(2) serves to illustrate to the public the severe reprobation with which society holds messages of hate directed towards racial and religious groups. The existence of a particular criminal law, and the process of holding a trial when that law is used, is thus itself a form of expression, and the message sent out is that hate propaganda is harmful to target group members and threatening to a harmonious society. ...

In this context, it can also be said that government suppression of hate propaganda will not make the expression attractive and hence increase acceptance of its content. Similarly, it is very doubtful that Canadians will have sympathy for either propagators of hatred or their ideas. Governmental disapproval of hate propaganda does not invariably result in dignifying the suppressed ideology. Pornography is not dignified by its suppression, nor are defamatory statements against individuals seen as meritorious because the common law lends its support to their prohibition. Again, I stress my belief that hate propaganda legislation and trials are a means by which the values beneficial to a free and democratic society can be publicized. ...

As for the use of hate propaganda laws in pre-World War Two Germany ... [n]o one is contending that hate propaganda laws can in themselves prevent the tragedy of a Holocaust; conditions particular to Germany made the rise of Nazi ideology possible despite the existence and use of these laws. ... Rather, hate propaganda laws are one part of a free and democratic society's bid to prevent the spread of racism, and their rational connection to this objective must be seen in such a context. ... Indeed, this Court's attention has been drawn to the fact that a great many countries possess legislation similar to that found in Canada. ...

[I] therefore conclude that the first branch of the proportionality test has been met. ...

(iii) Minimal Impairment of the Section 2(b) Freedom

… The main argument of those who would strike down s. 319(2) is that it creates a real possibility of punishing expression that is not hate propaganda. It is thus submitted that the legislation is overbroad, its terms so wide as to include expression which does not relate to Parliament's objective, and also unduly vague, in that a lack of clarity and precision in its words prevents individuals from discerning its meaning with any accuracy. In either instance, it is said that the effect of s. 319(2) is to limit the expression of merely unpopular or unconventional communications. Such communications may present no risk of causing the harm which Parliament seeks to prevent, and will perhaps be closely associated with the core values of s. 2(b). This overbreadth and vagueness could consequently allow the state to employ s. 319(2) to infringe excessively the freedom of expression or, what is more likely, could have a chilling effect whereby persons potentially within s. 319(2) would exercise self-censorship. Accordingly, those attacking the validity of s. 319(2) contend that vigorous debate on important political and social issues, so highly valued in a society that prizes a diversity of ideas, is unacceptably suppressed by the provision. …

In order to … determine whether s. 319(2) minimally impairs the freedom of expression, the nature and impact of specific features of the provision must be examined in some detail. …

[Dickson CJC first notes that statements made in private conversation are excluded from s. 319(2), even if such statements are made in a public forum, indicating Parliament's concern not to intrude on the privacy of the individual. He then notes the demanding *mens rea* element entailed by the requirement that the promotion of hatred be "wilful," which has been interpreted as requiring that the accused have subjectively desired the promotion of hatred or have foreseen such a consequence as certain to result from the communication.]

It has been argued, however, that even a demanding *mens rea* component fails to give s. 319(2) a constitutionally acceptable breadth. The problem is said to lie in the failure of the offence to require proof of actual hatred resulting from a communication, the assumption being that only such proof can demonstrate a harm serious enough to justify limiting the freedom of expression under s. 1. It was largely because of this lack of need for proof of actual hatred that Kerans JA in the Court of Appeal held s. 319(2) to violate the Charter.

While mindful of the dangers identified by Kerans JA, I do not find them sufficiently grave to compel striking down s. 319(2). First, to predicate the limitation of free expression upon proof of actual hatred gives insufficient attention to the severe psychological trauma suffered by members of those identifiable groups targeted by hate propaganda. Second, it is clearly difficult to prove a causative link between a specific statement and hatred of an identifiable group. In fact, to require direct proof of hatred in listeners would severely debilitate the effectiveness of s. 319(2) in achieving Parliament's aim. It is well-accepted that Parliament can use the criminal law to prevent the risk of serious harms, a leading example being the drinking and driving provisions in the *Criminal Code*. The conclusions of the Cohen Committee and subsequent study groups show that the risk of hatred caused by hate propaganda is very real, and in view of the grievous harm to be avoided in the context of this appeal, I conclude that proof of actual hatred is not required in order to justify a limit under s. 1. ...

The meaning of "hatred" remains to be elucidated. ... [T]he word "hatred" [must] be defined according to the context in which it is found. A dictionary definition may be of limited aid to such an exercise, for by its nature a dictionary seeks to offer a panoply of possible usages, rather than the correct meaning of a word as contemplated by Parliament. Noting the purpose of s. 319(2), in my opinion the term "hatred" connotes emotion of an intense and extreme nature that is clearly associated with vilification and detestation. ... Hatred is predicated on destruction, and hatred against identifiable groups therefore thrives on insensitivity, bigotry and destruction of both the target group and of the values of our society. Hatred in this sense is a most extreme emotion that belies reason; an emotion that, if exercised against members of an identifiable group, implies that those individuals are to be despised, scorned, denied respect and made subject to ill-treatment on the basis of group affiliation. ...

The factors mentioned above suggest that s. 319(2) does not unduly restrict the s. 2(b) guarantee. The terms of the offence, as I have defined them, rather indicate that s. 319(2) possesses definitional limits which act as safeguards to ensure that it will capture only expressive activity which is openly hostile to Parliament's objective, and will thus attack only the harm at which the prohibition is targeted.

[Dickson CJC then reviews the defences found in s. 319(3) as further evidence of the narrow scope of s. 319(2). With respect to the defence of truth found in s. 319(3)(a), he expresses doubt as to whether even truthful statements communicated with an intention to promote hatred would be required to be free from criminal condemnation.]

... I should comment on a final argument marshalled in support of striking down s. 319(2) because of overbreadth or vagueness. It is said that the presence of the legislation has led authorities to interfere with a diverse range of political, educational and artistic expression, demonstrating only too well the way in which overbreadth and vagueness can result in undue intrusion and the threat of persecution. In this regard, a number of incidents are cited where authorities appear to have been overzealous in their interpretation of the law, including the arrest of individuals distributing pamphlets admonishing Americans to leave the country and the temporary holdup at the border of a film entitled *Nelson Mandela* and Salman Rushdie's novel *Satanic Verses* (1988) (... note that the latter two examples involve not s. 319(2), but similar wording found in the *Customs Tariff*, SC 1987, c. 49, s. 114, and Schedule VII, Code 9956(b)).

That s. 319(2) may in the past have led authorities to restrict expression offering valuable contributions to the arts, education or politics in Canada is surely worrying. I hope, however, that my comments as to the scope of the provision make it obvious that only the most intentionally extreme forms of expression will find a place within s. 319(2). In this light, one can safely say that the incidents mentioned above illustrate not over-expansive breadth and vagueness in the law, but rather actions by the state which cannot be lawfully taken pursuant to s. 319(2). The possibility of illegal police harassment clearly has minimal bearing on the proportionality of hate propaganda legislation to legitimate Parliamentary objectives, and hence the argument based on such harassment can be rejected.

C. ALTERNATIVE MODES OF FURTHERING PARLIAMENT'S OBJECTIVE

One of the strongest arguments supporting the contention that s. 319(2) unacceptably impairs the s. 2(b) guarantee posits that a criminal sanction is not necessary to meet Parliament's objective. ... [I]t is said that non-criminal responses can more effectively combat the harm caused by hate propaganda. Most generally, it is said that discriminatory ideas can best be met with information and education programmes extolling the merits of tolerance and cooperation between racial and religious groups. As for the prohibition of hate propaganda, human rights statutes are pointed to as being a less severe and more effective response than the criminal law. Such statutes not only subject the disseminator of hate propaganda to reduced stigma and punishment, but also take a less confrontational approach to the suppression of such expression. This conciliatory tack is said to be preferable to penal sanction because an incentive is offered the disseminator to cooperate with human rights tribunals and thus to amend his or her conduct.

Given the stigma and punishment associated with a criminal conviction and the presence of other modes of government response in the fight against intolerance, it is proper to ask whether s. 319(2) can be said to impair minimally the freedom of expression. With respect to the efficacy of criminal legislation in advancing the goals of equality and multicultural tolerance in Canada, I agree that the role of s. 319(2) will be limited. It is important, in my opinion, not to hold any illusions about the ability of this one provision to rid our society of hate propaganda and its associated harms. Indeed, to become overly complacent, forgetting that there are a great many ways in which to address the problem of racial and religious intolerance, could be dangerous. Obviously, a variety of measures need be employed in the quest to achieve such lofty and important goals.

In assessing the proportionality of a legislative enactment to a valid governmental objective, however, s. 1 should not operate in every instance so as to force the government to rely upon only the mode of intervention least intrusive of a Charter right or freedom. It may be that a number of courses of action are available in the furtherance of a pressing and substantial objective, each imposing a varying degree of restriction upon a right or freedom. In such circumstances, the government may legitimately employ a more restrictive measure, either alone or as part of a larger programme of action, if that measure is not redundant, furthering the objective in ways that alternative responses could not, and is in all other respects proportionate to a valid s. 1 aim. ...

I thus conclude that s. 319(2) of the *Criminal Code* does not unduly impair the freedom of expression. ...

[With respect to the third branch of the proportionality test, Dickson CJC emphasizes the enormous importance of the objective of s. 319(2): "Few concerns can be as central to the concept of a free and democratic society as the dissipation of racism, and the especially strong value which Canadian society attaches to this goal must never be forgotten in assessing the effects of an impugned legislative measure." He then concludes that in light of that objective, the effects of s. 319(2), "involving as they do the restriction of expression largely removed from the heart of free expression values, are not of such a deleterious nature as to outweigh any advantage gleaned from the limitation of s. 2(b)." The infringement of freedom of expression is therefore upheld as a reasonable limit under s. 1. Dickson CJC's discussion of s. 319(3)(a) and the presumption of innocence guaranteed under s. 11(d) of the Charter is omitted. He concludes that the presumption of innocence is infringed, but that the limitation of the right can be upheld under s. 1.]

McLACHLIN J (Sopinka J concurring; La Forest J concurring in part) dissenting: ... Hate literature presents a great challenge to our conceptions about the value of free expression. Its offensive content often constitutes a direct attack on many of the other principles which are cherished by our society. Tolerance, the dignity and equality of all individuals; these and other values are all adversely affected by the propagation of hateful sentiment. The problem is not peculiarly Canadian; it is universal. Wherever racially or culturally distinct groups of people live together, one finds people, usually a small minority of the population, who take it upon themselves to denigrate members of a group other than theirs. ...

The evil of hate propaganda is beyond doubt. It inflicts pain and indignity upon individuals who are members of the group in question. Insofar as it may persuade others to the same point of view, it may threaten social stability. And it is intrinsically offensive to people—the majority in most democratic countries—who believe in the equality of all people regardless of race or creed.

For these reasons, governments have legislated against the dissemination of propaganda directed against racial groups, and in some cases this legislation has been tested in the courts. Perhaps the experience most relevant to Canada is that of the United States, since its Constitution, like ours, places a high value on free expression, raising starkly the conflict between freedom of speech and the countervailing values of individual dignity and social harmony. ...

[McLachlin J reviews the treatment of hate propaganda under the US First Amendment and then goes on to discuss the approach adopted under international instruments.]

These international instruments embody quite a different conception of freedom of expression than the case law under the US First Amendment. The international decisions reflect the much more explicit priorities of the relevant documents regarding the relationship between freedom of expression and the objective of eradicating speech which advocates racial and cultural hatred. The approach seems to be to read down freedom of expression to the extent necessary to accommodate the legislation prohibiting the speech in question.

Both the American and international approach recognize that freedom of expression is not absolute, and must yield in some circumstances to other values. The divergence lies in the way the limits are determined. On the international approach, the objective of suppressing hatred appears to be sufficient to override freedom of expression. In the United States, it is necessary to go much further and show clear and present danger before free speech can be overridden.

The Charter follows the American approach in method, affirming freedom of expression as a broadly-defined and fundamental right, and contemplating balancing the values protected by and inherent in freedom of expression against the benefit conferred by the legislation limiting that freedom under s. 1 of the Charter.

This is in keeping with the strong liberal tradition favouring free speech in this country—a tradition which had led to conferring quasi-constitutional status on free expression in this country prior to any bill of rights or Charter. At the same time, the tests are not necessarily the same as in the United States. ...

[After finding that s. 319(2) infringes freedom of expression, McLachlin J proceeds to the s. 1 analysis. She easily concludes that the legislative goals of protecting social harmony and individual dignity are of a substantial nature. She then moves to the proportionality analysis.]

(b) Rational Connection

... [I]t is clear that the legislation does, at least at one level, further Parliament's objectives. Prosecutions of individuals for offensive material directed at a particular group may bolster its members' beliefs that they are valued and respected in their community, and that the views of a malicious few do not reflect those of the population as a whole. Such a use of the criminal law may well affirm certain values and priorities which are of a pressing and substantial nature.

It is necessary, however, to go further, and consider not only Parliament's intention, but whether, given the actual effect of the legislation, a rational connection exists between it and its objectives. Legislation designed to promote an objective may in fact impede that objective. ...

Section 319(2) may well have a chilling effect on defensible expression by law-abiding citizens. At the same time, it is far from clear that it provides an effective way of curbing hatemongers. Indeed, many have suggested it may promote their cause. Prosecutions under the *Criminal Code* for racist expression have attracted extensive media coverage. Zundel, prosecuted not under s. 319(2) but for the crime of spreading false news (s. 181), claimed that his court battle had given him "a million dollars worth of publicity": *The Globe and Mail*, March 1, 1985, p. P1. ...

Not only does the criminal process confer on the accused publicity for his dubious causes—it may even bring him sympathy. The criminal process is cast as a conflict between the accused and the state, a conflict in which the accused may appear at his most sympathetic. ...

The argument that criminal prosecutions for this kind of expression will reduce racism and foster multiculturalism depends on the assumption that some listeners are gullible enough to believe the expression if exposed to it. But if this assumption is valid, these listeners might be just as likely to believe that there must be some truth in the racist expression because the government is trying to suppress it. Theories of a grand conspiracy between government and elements of society wrongly perceived as malevolent can become all too appealing if government dignifies them by completely suppressing their utterance. ...

Historical evidence also gives reason to be suspicious of the claim that hate propaganda laws contribute to the cause of multiculturalism and equality.

[McLachlin J refers to evidence about the ineffectiveness of anti-hate laws in pre-Hitler Germany and the use of criminal prosecutions by the Nazis as platforms to propagate their message.]

Viewed from the point of view of actual effect, the rational connection between s. 319(2) and the goals it promotes may be argued to be tenuous. Certainly it cannot be said that there is a strong and evident connection between the criminalization of hate propaganda and its suppression.

(c) Minimum Impairment

… Despite the limitations found in s. 319(2), a strong case can be made that it is overbroad in that its definition of offending speech may catch many expressions which should be protected.

The first difficulty lies in the different interpretations which may be placed on the word "hatred." *The Shorter Oxford English Dictionary* defines "hatred" as: "The condition or state of relations in which one person hates another; the emotion of hate; active dislike, detestation; enmity, ill-will, malevolence." The wide range of diverse emotions which the word "hatred" is capable of denoting is evident from this definition. Those who defend its use in s. 319(2) of the *Criminal Code* emphasize one end of this range—hatred, they say, indicates the most powerful of virulent emotions lying beyond the bounds of human decency and limiting s. 319(2) to extreme materials. Those who object to its use point to the other end of the range, insisting that "active dislike" is not an emotion for the promotion of which a person should be convicted as a criminal. To state the arguments is to make the case; "hatred" is a broad term capable of catching a wide variety of emotion.

It is not only the breadth of the term "hatred" which presents dangers; it is its subjectivity. "Hatred" is proved by inference—the inference of the jury or the judge who sits as trier of fact—and inferences are more likely to be drawn when the speech is unpopular. The subjective and emotional nature of the concept of promoting hatred compounds the difficulty of ensuring that only cases meriting prosecution are pursued and that only those whose conduct is calculated to dissolve the social bonds of society are convicted.

But "hatred" does not stand alone. To convict, it must have been "wilfully promote[d]." Does this requirement sufficiently constrain the term to meet the claim that s. 319(2) is overbroad? …

It is argued that the requirement of "wilful promotion" eliminates from the ambit of s. 319(2) statements which are made for honest purposes such as telling a perceived truth or contributing to a political or social debate. The difficulty with this argument is that those purposes are compatible with the intention (or presumed intention by reason of foreseeability) of promoting hatred. A belief that what one says about a group is true and important to political and social debate is quite compatible with and indeed may inspire an intention to promote active dislike of that group. Such a belief is equally compatible with foreseeing that promotion of such dislike may stem from one's statements. The result is that people who make statements primarily for non nefarious reasons may be convicted of wilfully promoting hatred.

[McLachlin J refuses to place much weight on the absence of any requirement that actual harm or incitement to hatred be shown, recognizing the difficulty of assessing with any precision the effects that expression of a particular message will have on those who are ultimately exposed to it. She also acknowledges that the breadth of s. 319(2) is narrowed somewhat by the defences.]

The real answer to the debate about whether s. 319(2) is overbroad is provided by the section's track record. Although the section is of relatively recent origin, it has provoked many questionable actions on the part of the authorities. There have been no reported convictions, other than the instant appeals. But the record amply demonstrates that intemperate statements about identifiable groups, particularly if they represent an unpopular viewpoint, may attract state involvement or calls for police action. Novels such as Leon Uris' pro-Zionist novel, *The Haj* (1984), face calls for banning: *Toronto Star*, September 26, 1984, p. A6. Other works, such as Salman Rushdie's *Satanic Verses* (1988), are stopped at the border on the ground that they violate s. 319(2). Films may be temporarily kept out, as happened to a film entitled *Nelson Mandela*, ordered as an educational film by Ryerson Polytechnical Institute in 1986: *The Globe and Mail*, December 24, 1986, p. A14. Arrests are even made for distributing pamphlets containing the words "Yankee Go Home": *The Globe and Mail*, July 4, 1975, p. 1. Experience shows that many cases are winnowed out due to prosecutorial discretion and other factors. It shows equally, however, that initially quite a lot of speech is caught by s. 319(2).

Even where investigations are not initiated or prosecutions pursued, the vagueness and subjectivity inherent in s. 319(2) of the *Criminal Code* give ground for concern that the chilling effect of the law may be substantial. The more vague the language of the prohibition, the greater the danger that right-minded citizens may curtail the range of their expression against the possibility that they may run afoul of the law. The danger here is not so much that the legislation will deter those bent on promoting hatred—in so far as it does so (and of this I remain skeptical) it is arguably not overbroad. The danger is rather that the legislation may have a chilling effect on legitimate activities important to our society by subjecting innocent persons to constraints born out of a fear of the criminal process. Given the vagueness of the prohibition of expression in s. 319(2), one may ask how speakers are to know when their speech may be seen as encroaching on the forbidden area. The reaction is predictable. The combination of overbreadth and criminalization may well lead people desirous of avoiding even the slightest brush with the criminal law to protect themselves in the best way they can—by confining their expression to noncontroversial matters. Novelists may steer clear of controversial characterizations of ethnic characteristics, such as Shakespeare's portrayal of Shylock in *The Merchant of Venice*. Scientists may well think twice before researching and publishing results of research suggesting difference between ethnic or racial groups. Given the serious consequences of criminal prosecution, it is not entirely speculative to suppose that even political debate on crucial issues such as immigration, educational language rights, foreign ownership and trade may be tempered. These matters go to the heart of the traditional justifications for protecting freedom of expression.

This brings me to the second aspect of minimum impairment. The examples I have just given suggest that the very fact of criminalization itself may be argued to represent an excessive response to the problem of hate propagation. The procedures and sanctions associated with the criminal law are comparatively severe. Given the stigma that attaches and the freedom which is at stake, the contest between the individual and the state imposed by a criminal trial must be regarded as difficult and harrowing in the extreme. The seriousness of the imprisonment which may follow conviction requires no comment. Moreover, the chilling effect of prohibitions on expression is at its most severe where they are effected by means of the criminal law. It is this branch of the law more than any other which the ordinary, law-abiding citizen seeks to avoid. The additional sanction of the criminal law may pose little deterrent to a convinced hate-monger who may welcome the publicity it brings; it may, however, deter the ordinary individual.

Moreover, it is arguable whether criminalization of expression calculated to promote racial hatred is necessary. Other remedies are perhaps more appropriate and more effective. Discrimination on grounds of race and religion is worthy of suppression. Human rights legislation, focusing on reparation rather than punishment, has had considerable success in discouraging such conduct. ...

Finally, it can be argued that greater precision is required in the criminal law than, for example, in human rights legislation because of the different character of the two types of proceedings.

The consequences of alleging a violation of s. 319(2) of the *Criminal Code* are direct and serious in the extreme. Under the human rights process a tribunal has considerable discretion in determining what messages or conduct should be banned and by its order may indicate more precisely their exact nature, all of which occurs before any consequences inure to the alleged violator. ...

(d) Importance of the Right Versus Benefit Conferred

... Viewed from the perspective of our society as a whole, the infringement of the guarantee of freedom of expression before this Court is a serious one. Section 319(2) of the *Criminal Code* does not merely regulate the form or tone of expression—it strikes directly at its content and at the viewpoints of individuals. It strikes, moreover, at viewpoints in widely diverse domains, whether artistic, social or political. It is capable of catching not only statements like those at issue in this case, but works of art and the intemperate statement made in the heat of social controversy. While few may actually be prosecuted to conviction under s. 319(2), many fall within the shadow of its broad prohibition.

These dangers are exacerbated by the fact that s. 319(2) applies to all public expression. In short, the limitation on freedom of expression created by s. 319(2) of the *Criminal Code* invokes all of the values upon which s. 2(b) of the Charter rests. ...

The consequences of the infringement of freedom of speech imposed by s. 319(2) of the *Criminal Code* considered from the viewpoint of the individual caught within its net are equally serious. The exercise of the right of free speech contrary to its provisions may result in a criminal record and imprisonment of up to two years. No warning, other than the description in s. 319(2) itself (which necessarily includes subjective elements), is given as to what speech is liable to result in prosecution. And those individuals not caught may find their expression restricted by the fear of running afoul of a vague and subjective law. ...

I turn then to the other side of the scale and the benefit to be gained by maintenance of the limitation on freedom of expression effected by s. 319(2) of the *Criminal Code*. As indicated earlier, there is no question but that the objectives which underlie this legislation are of a most worthy nature. Unfortunately, the claims of gains to be achieved at the cost of the infringement of free speech represented by s. 319(2) are tenuous. It is far from clear that the legislation does not promote the cause of hate-mongering extremists and hinder the possibility of voluntary amendment of conduct more than it discourages the spread of hate propaganda. Accepting the importance to our society the goals of social harmony and individual dignity, of multiculturalism and equality, it remains difficult to see how s. 319(2) fosters them.

In my opinion, the result is clear. Any questionable benefit of the legislation is outweighed by the significant infringement on the constitutional guarantee of free expression effected by s. 319(2) of the *Criminal Code*. ...

[McLachlin J concludes that the limit on expression effected by s. 319(2) cannot be justified under s. 1. On the presumption of innocence issue, she found that s. 319(3) of the *Criminal Code* infringed the presumption of innocence and could not be upheld under s. 1. La Forest J agreed with McLachlin J on the freedom of expression issue, but found it unnecessary to deal with the issue respecting the right to be presumed innocent.]

Appeal allowed.

NOTES AND QUESTIONS

1. In *Mugesera v. Canada (Minister of Citizenship and Immigration)*, [2005] 2 SCR 100, 2005 SCC 40, 254 DLR (4th) 200, in the course of describing the elements of the s. 319(2) offence of wilfully promoting hatred, the Supreme Court of Canada noted that in determining whether speech conveys hatred, the court must take into account the character of the audience and the social and historical context of the speech.

2. In his s. 1 analysis, Chief Justice Dickson says that hate speech is low value, almost valueless, expression and that its restriction will be easier to justify than other forms of expression. Do you agree that hate speech is valueless or virtually so? Chief Justice Dickson's argument that hate speech has little value seems to rest on its harmful character. Is the Chief Justice "double counting"? Hate speech is low value because it causes harm and it should be restricted because it causes harm?

3. How does hate speech cause harm? Can hatred be caused or promoted by a single statement? Is the Chief Justice's skepticism about human judgment or reason compatible with the constitutional commitment to freedom of expression? Freedom of expression is said to be valuable because the free exchange of ideas is necessary to the formation of public opinion and to the realization/creation of individual and group identity. The standard freedom of expression position is that ideas cannot be censored simply because we fear that members

of the community may find them persuasive or that an individual's self-understanding or self-esteem may be negatively affected. According to this position we should respond to racist claims not with censorship, but by offering competing views that make the case for equal respect or by creating more avenues for marginalized groups to express themselves.

4. Dickson CJC argues that the ban on hate promotion is narrow in its scope. Do you agree?

5. One of the arguments raised against s. 319(2) of the *Criminal Code* in *Keegstra* was its so-called chilling effect, a term drawn from US First Amendment jurisprudence. The concern is that a broad and imprecisely worded restriction will deter or chill expression. Individuals may be reluctant to publish material, even valuable material, that should not, and possibly would not, be restricted because they are unwilling to take the risk that it might fall within a criminal prohibition that does not have a clear and uncontested scope.

Why does hate-speech regulation have a chilling effect? Can the problem be avoided by better drafting—by defining the prohibited activity more precisely?

In *Hill v. Church of Scientology of Toronto*, [1995] 2 SCR 1130, 126 DLR (4th) 129, which involved a challenge to defamation law, the Court appeared to give little weight to the argument that the traditional law of defamation, combined with high damage awards, chills criticism of public officials. At the Ontario Court of Appeal ((1994), 114 DLR (4th) 1, at 27) the court had been critical of the absence of evidence to establish a "libel chill":

> At a minimum some form of evidence is required to prove that libel chill exists which prevents publication of true comments in media reports and elsewhere; that there exists such a great societal interest in the criticism of public officials in Canada to warrant the propagation of falsehoods … . Without evidence of the deleterious effects of the law of defamation on freedom of expression, this court is faced with evaluating the Charter challenge in a factual vacuum and potentially delivering an ill-considered opinion without due consideration for the ramifications associated with accepting the primacy of freedom to criticize public officials over the individual's right to the protection of his or her reputation.

6. In *Taylor v. Canadian Human Rights Commission*, [1990] 3 SCR 892, 75 DLR (4th) 577, which was decided at the same time as *Keegstra*, the Supreme Court of Canada considered the constitutionality of s. 13 of the *Canadian Human Rights Act*, SC 1976-77, c. 33, which, as it then read, provided that it was a discriminatory practice for a person to use the telephone to repeatedly communicate messages "likely to expose a person or persons to hatred or contempt by reason of the fact that that person or those persons are identifiable on the basis of a prohibited ground of discrimination." (Section 13 was subsequently amended to extend to Internet communication.) Taylor and the Western Guard Party instituted a telephone message service with prerecorded messages on the theme of the Jewish conspiracy to control Canadian society. A complaint under s. 13(1) was brought against them. The tribunal that heard the complaint concluded that Taylor and the Western Guard had engaged in a discriminatory practice and issued a cease-and-desist order. The messages continued and Taylor and the Party were found to be in contempt. The Party was fined and Taylor was sentenced to imprisonment for one year. After his release from prison, Taylor resumed the messages. The Commission once again sought an order of committal against him. He responded by challenging s. 13(1) under s. 2(b) of the Charter (which had since come into force).

Chief Justice Dickson, writing for the majority, held that s. 13 of the *Canadian Human Rights Act* breached s. 2(b) of the Charter, but was a "reasonable" and "demonstrably justified" limit under s. 1. In defining the scope of s. 13, and more particularly the terms "hatred" and "contempt," the Chief Justice drew on the Canadian Human Rights Tribunal decision of *Nealy v. Johnson* (1989), 10 CHRR D/6450, at D/6469, which he quoted in his judgment:

> With "hatred" the focus is a set of emotions and feelings which involve extreme ill will towards another person or group of persons. To say that one "hates" another means in effect that one finds no redeeming qualities in the latter. It is a term, however, which does not necessarily involve the mental process of "looking down" on another or others. It is quite possible to "hate" someone who one feels is superior to one in intelligence, wealth or power. None of the synonyms used in the dictionary definition for "hatred" give any clues to the motivation for the ill will. "Contempt" is by contrast a term which suggests a mental process of "looking down" upon or treating as inferior the object of one's feelings. This is captured by the dictionary definition relied on in *Taylor* [the Canadian Human Rights Tribunal decision] ... in the use of the terms "despised," "dishonour" or "disgrace." Although the person can be "hated" (i.e. actively disliked) and treated with "contempt" (i.e. looked down upon), the terms are not fully coextensive, because "hatred" is in some instances the product of envy of superior qualities, which "contempt" by definition cannot be.

According to Dickson CJC, this interpretation of s. 13, which focuses on "unusually strong and deep-felt emotions of detestation, calumny and vilification" is not "particularly expansive." Dickson CJC noted, however, that "the nature of human rights legislation militates against an unduly narrow reading of s. 13(1)" and indicated that he had no "wish to transgress the well-established principle that the rights enumerated in such a code should be given their full recognition and effect through a fair, large and liberal interpretation." Even though "the section may impose a slightly broader limit upon freedom of expression than does s. 319(2) [the hate-promotion provision] of the *Criminal Code* ... the conciliatory bent of a human rights statute renders such a limit more acceptable than would be the case with a criminal provision." In his view, "as long as the Human Rights Tribunal continues to be well aware of the purpose of s. 13(1) and pays heed to the ardent and extreme nature of the feeling described in the phrase 'hatred or contempt', there is little danger that subjective opinion as to offensiveness will supplant the proper meaning of the section."

In her dissenting judgment in *Taylor*, McLachlin J argued that the "absence of any requirement of intent or foreseeability of the actual promotion of hatred or contempt," while "consistent with the remedial ... focus of human rights legislation," broadened the scope of the section so that it included communication that ought not to be prohibited. In response to this argument, that s. 13 is overly broad in its scope because it lacks an intention requirement, Chief Justice Dickson observed that the focus of the section "is solely upon likely effects, it being irrelevant whether an individual wishes to expose persons to hatred or contempt on the basis of their race or religion." According to Dickson CJC:

> The preoccupation with effects, and not with intent is readily explicable when one considers that systemic discrimination is much more widespread in our society than is intentional discrimination. To import a subjective intent requirement into human rights provisions, rather than allowing tribunals to focus solely upon effects, would thus defeat one of the primary goals

of anti-discrimination statutes. At the same time, however, it cannot be denied that to ignore intent in determining whether a discriminatory practice has taken place according to s. 13(1) increases the degree of restriction upon the constitutionally protected freedom of expression. This result flows from the realization that an individual open to condemnation and censure because his or her words may have an unintended effect will be more likely to exercise caution via self-censorship.

It is important to remember, wrote Dickson CJC, that, in contrast to criminal law, the purpose of human rights legislation is to "compensate and protect" the victim rather than to "stigmatize or punish" the person who has discriminated against him or her.

7. Section 12 of the *Canadian Human Rights Act*, another provision dealing with discriminatory speech, states that it is unlawful to display any notice, sign, symbol, emblem, or other representation that indicates discrimination or an intention to discriminate against an identifiable group. All provincial and territorial human rights laws, except for that in the Yukon Territory, include a provision similar to s. 12. When this provision was first enacted in Ontario, its purpose was to prohibit signs in store windows that indicated that members of certain racial or ethnic groups would not be served. However, in some jurisdictions the discriminatory sign provision has been interpreted broadly so that it extends to discriminatory speech that appears on signs and, in some provinces, that occurs in publications.

The human rights laws of some provinces—Alberta, British Columbia, Saskatchewan, and the Northwest Territories—have gone beyond the discriminatory signs provisions to include a provision similar to s. 13 of the *Canadian Human Rights Act* dealing directly with discriminatory speech. For example, s. 7 of the BC *Human Rights Code*, RSBC 1996, c. 210, provides that:

> A person may not publish, issue or display, or cause to be published, issued or displayed, any statement, publication, notice, sign, symbol, emblem or other representation that
>
> • • •
>
> (b) is likely to expose a person or a group of persons to hatred or contempt because of the race, colour, ancestry, place of origin, religion, marital status, family status, physical or mental disability, sex, sexual orientation or age of that person or that group or class of persons.

Section 14 of the *Saskatchewan Human Rights Code*, SS 1979, c. S-24.1, is potentially broader in its scope since it extends not simply to material that exposes or tends to expose the individual to hatred, but also to material that "ridicules, belittles, or otherwise affronts the dignity of" the person.

Guided by the Supreme Court of Canada's judgment in *Taylor*, the human rights tribunals in each of these provinces or territories have interpreted the relevant code sections narrowly as a ban on extreme expression that is hateful or contemptuous in character. The BC Human Rights Tribunal, for example, has developed a two-part test for determining whether the expression is caught by section 7:

> First, does the communication itself express hatred or contempt of a person or group on the basis of one or more of the listed grounds? Would a reasonable person understand this message as expressing hatred or contempt in the context of the expression? Second, assessed in this context, is the likely effect of the communication to make it more acceptable for others to mani-

fest hatred or contempt against the person or group concerned? Would a reasonable person consider it likely to increase the risk of exposure of target group members to hatred or contempt? (*Canadian Jewish Congress v. North Shore Press Ltd.*, [1997] BCHRTD No. 23)

The constitutionality of s. 14(1) of the Saskatchewan Code was considered in *Saskatchewan (Human Rights Commission) v. Bell* (1994), 114 DLR (4th) 370 (Sask. CA), a case in which a complaint was brought against a retailer who sold small stickers with caricatures of persons of black, Asian, and East Asian origin with a "not allowed" symbol over each caricature. The trial judge concluded that s. 14(1) of the Code could be upheld as a reasonable limit on freedom of expression under s. 1 of the Charter. The Court of Appeal, however, made a narrower ruling on the facts of the case. The Court held that because the stickers would tend to expose the groups they represented to hatred, it was not necessary to decide whether a broader ban on materials that "ridicule, belittle or otherwise affront the dignity" of persons would survive s. 1 scrutiny. The Court did suggest that if s. 14(1) were found to be overbroad, the provision might be read down to confine it to materials that promoted hatred.

In *Hellquist v. Owens* (2006), 267 DLR (4th) 733 (Sask. CA), Mr. Owens published an ad in a Saskatoon paper that depicted stick men holding hands with the prohibited line across the image. The ad also included references to biblical passages forbidding same-sex relations, such as Leviticus 18:22, which declares that men who lie together should be killed. Both the Board of Inquiry appointed under the Code and the Chambers judge found that the ad breached the hate speech provision of the Saskatchewan Code. However, this judgment was reversed by the Saskatchewan Court of Appeal. At paras. 67 and 68, the Court of Appeal noted that in applying s. 14(1)(b) of the Code it was important to consider the ad "in the context of the time and circumstances in which it was published," which "featured an active debate and discussion about the place of sexual identity in Canadian society." "In this context," said the court, the "advertisement tends to take on the character of a position advanced in a continuing public policy debate rather than the character of a message of hatred or ill will in the sense contemplated by *Bell*." The court also observed that, in contrast to *Bell*, the stickmen were presented "in a neutral and straightforward fashion" and not "in a way which suggests undesirable characteristics such as dangerousness, untrustworthiness, lack of cleanliness, dishonesty or deceit" (para. 70). Finally, the court thought that the Board of Inquiry and Chambers judge mistakenly "took these passages at face value, making no allowance for the fact they are ancient and fundamental religious text" (para. 77). The court observed that "the Bible as a whole is the source of more than one sort of message and, more specifically, is the source of messages involving themes of love, tolerance and forgiveness" (para. 78).

8. Human rights code regulation of hate speech has become the subject of public debate over the last few years. A controversy arose from complaints made to the Canadian Human Rights Commission and the BC Human Rights Tribunal against *Macleans* magazine for its publication of an article by Mark Steyn. In the article, "The Future Belongs to Islam" (October 2006), Steyn argued (among other things) that Muslims would come to dominate Europe through immigration and higher birth rates and that their goal is to make European countries into Muslim states that enforce *Sharia* law. He also argued that Muslims are generally supportive of violence to achieve this end. Both complaints were dismissed. Another well-publicized Canadian case involved a complaint made to the Alberta Human Rights Commission against Ezra Levant and the *Western Standard* magazine following the publication of the "Danish cartoons." The complaint was dismissed by the Commission and did not

proceed to adjudication before a tribunal. A report written by Richard Moon, "Report to the Canadian Human Rights Commission Concerning s. 13 of the CHRA and the Regulation of Hate Speech on the Internet" (Canadian Human Rights Commission, October 2008), recommended the repeal of s. 13.

9. Human rights codes prohibit racial and other forms of discrimination in the provision of employment, accommodation, and other services available to the public. This prohibition has been interpreted as covering acts that create a "negative environment" that adversely affects a person's ability to access and enjoy a particular service. Thus, certain forms of expression that contribute to the creation of such an environment may be found to constitute a discriminatory practice. An obvious example of expression that contributes to a negative environment is racial name-calling and verbal abuse directed at an individual in his or her workplace.

The issue of expression creating a negative environment was dealt with by the Supreme Court of Canada in *Ross v. New Brunswick School District No. 15*, [1996] 1 SCR 825, 133 DLR (4th) l. The case involved a school teacher (Ross) whose expression of anti-Semitic views outside of the classroom (in published writings and public appearances) was found by a human rights tribunal to have created a poisoned environment within the classroom. The tribunal found that the school board, in allowing Ross to continue to teach, was guilty of discrimination under the provincial human rights code. In reaching this conclusion, the human rights tribunal relied on evidence of discriminatory conduct engaged in by some students. Although there was no evidence that anti-Jewish statements by students in the school were directly influenced by Ross's teachings, the tribunal concluded that it was reasonable to anticipate such an influence given the high degree of publicity surrounding Ross's publications. The tribunal ordered the school board to remove Ross from the classroom and to make efforts to find him a non-teaching position. Ross was also permanently prohibited from publishing or distributing anti-Semitic writings as a condition of retaining employment with the school board. Ross appealed, arguing that the orders violated his freedom of expression under the Charter.

The Supreme Court of Canada upheld the order removing Ross from the classroom as a reasonable limit on freedom of expression. In doing so La Forest J, writing for the Court, stressed the importance of the educational context (at 32-33 DLR):

> There can be no doubt that the attempt to foster equality, respect and tolerance in the Canadian educational system is a laudable goal. But the additional driving factor in this case is the nature of the educational services in question: we are dealing here with the education of young children. ... Young children are especially vulnerable to the messages conveyed by their teachers. They are less likely to make an intellectual distinction between comments a teacher makes in the school and those the teacher makes outside the school. They are, therefore, more likely to feel threatened and isolated by a teacher who makes comments that denigrate personal characteristics of a group to which they belong. Furthermore, they are unlikely to distinguish between falsehoods and truth and more likely to accept derogatory views espoused by a teacher. The importance of ensuring an equal and discrimination free educational environment, and the perception of fairness and tolerance in the classroom, are paramount in the education of young children. This helps foster self-respect and acceptance by others.

The Court did not, however, uphold the permanent speech ban as a reasonable limit under s. 1. In the Court's view, once Ross was no longer in a teaching position, there was no reason to think that his writings would continue to produce a poisoned atmosphere in the classroom. See also the Court of Appeal decision in *Kempling v. College of Teachers (British Columbia)*, 2005 BCCA 327, 255 DLR (4th) 169, upholding the one-month suspension of a teacher for anti-homosexual statements published in a newspaper and dismissing Charter challenges based on ss. 2(a) and 2(b).

10. In the United States, the leading hate speech cases involve racist threats and insults against racial and/or ethnic groups. In *Collin v. Smith*, 578 F2d 1197 (7th Cir. 1978), a municipality sought to prevent a neo-Nazi march in a predominantly Jewish neighborhood that included a large number of Holocaust survivors. The Federal Court of Appeals held that the march was protected speech under the First Amendment. In *R.A.V. v. City of St. Paul*, 505 US 377 (1992), two young men who had planted a burning cross on the front lawn of the first black family to move into a previously all-white neighborhood were charged under an ordinance that prohibited the placing of racist symbols, such as swastikas and burning crosses, on public property. The US Supreme Court held that the municipal law, although directed at "fighting words," breached the First Amendment because it was not content neutral. The law prohibited racist symbols, but not the speech of antiracists and Justice Scalia said, "St. Paul has no such authority to license one side of a debate to fight freestyle, while requiring the other to follow Marquis of Queensberry rules" (at 392). In the more recent case of *Virginia v. Black*, 538 US 43 (2003), the US Supreme Court suggested that a state could prohibit cross-burning when it was intended to intimidate. The Court observed that cross-burnings had been used by the Ku Klux Klan to threaten and intimidate and had often been a prelude to violent action. The Court, however, struck down the Virginia cross-burning law. While the law formally prohibited the burning of a cross with the intent of intimidating any person or group, it included a provision that "[a]ny such burning ... shall be *prima facie* evidence of an intent to intimidate." The Court was concerned that this presumption might result in conviction even when the purpose behind the cross-burning was not to intimidate others but was instead to affirm "a statement of ideology" or "group solidarity" (at 365-66).

V. REGULATION OF SEXUALLY EXPLICIT EXPRESSION

The public justification for the censorship of sexually explicit representations no longer emphasizes the offensive or immoral character of such material. Censorship is now justified on the grounds that sexually explicit representations sometimes have harmful consequences. With this change in justification has come a shift in the focus of restriction from sexually explicit material in general to sexually explicit material that depicts violent or degrading activity and a change in the language used to describe the restricted material from obscenity to pornography.

The shift from obscenity to pornography is the consequence first of the rise of the harm principle: the idea that the prevention of harm is the only legitimate base for state coercion. This shift has been accelerated by the confrontation of censorship laws with the constitutional right to freedom of expression and the requirement that any restriction on expression be "demonstrably justified." Second, the shift from obscenity to pornography is the consequence of a growing awareness of the problems of sexual subordination and violence and a widely held belief that certain kinds of sexual representation contribute to these wrongs.

In its 1992 decision in *R v. Butler*, the Supreme Court of Canada reinterpreted the *Criminal Code* obscenity prohibition as a ban on *harmful* sexual representation and went on to uphold the law as a justified restriction on freedom of expression.

R v. Butler
[1992] 1 SCR 452, 89 DLR (4th) 449

[The accused, Butler, operated a shop that sold and rented what was described as "hard core pornography" in the form of videotapes, magazines, and sexual paraphernalia. He was charged with numerous offences contrary to the obscenity provisions of s. 163 of the *Criminal Code*, the majority of which related to the possession of obscene material for the purpose of sale. The trial judge found that all of the material was obscene within the meaning of s. 163 of the Code. In dealing with the Charter issue, he concluded that all of the material was protected by s. 2(b) of the Charter and that s. 1 of the Charter would only sustain the prohibition of sexual materials involving violence, cruelty, or dehumanization. The trial judge therefore dismissed the majority of the charges against the accused, upholding only those few charges relating to material falling within this category. The Manitoba Court of Appeal allowed the appeal of the Crown. Huband JA, writing for a three-person majority, concluded that s. 163 did not violate s. 2(b) of the Charter because obscene material fell outside the protection of the guarantee of freedom of expression. Obscene materials, which had as their purpose titillation, were found to constitute purely physical activity and to be devoid of meaning: "Sexual stimulation is not protected by s. 2(b) of the Charter. Intellectual rather than sensual arousal is what the Charter was intended to protect." Because of his reasoning on s. 2(b), Huband JA found it unnecessary to deal with s. 1. Twaddle JA and Helper JA dissented. Both found that obscene materials were protected by s. 2(b) of the Charter and that any prohibition must be justified under s. 1. Although their analyses of s. 1 differ, both essentially concluded that s. 1 would only sustain prohibitions of sexual material involving cruelty, violation, degradation, or dehumanization, and that s. 163 of the Code prohibited more material than could be justified under s. 1. Twaddle JA would have solved the problem of overbreadth by severing that part of s. 163 dealing with "undue exploitation of sex." Helper JA would have struck down s. 163 in its entirety as being too vague and overbroad.]

SOPINKA J (Lamer CJC, La Forest, Cory, McLachlin, Stevenson, and Iacobucci JJ concurring): ... [This] case requires the Court to address one of the most difficult and controversial of contemporary issues, that of determining whether, and to what extent, Parliament may legitimately criminalize obscenity. ...

[The relevant section of the *Criminal Code* reads:

> 163(1) Everyone commits an offence who,
>
> (a) makes, prints, publishes, distributes, circulates, or has in his possession for the purpose of publication, distribution or circulation any obscene written matter, picture, model, phonograph record or other thing whatever; or
>
> (b) makes, prints, publishes, distributes, sells or has in his possession for the purpose of publication, distribution or circulation a crime comic.
>
> (2) Every one commits an offence who knowingly, without lawful justification or excuse,
>
> (a) sells, exposes to public view or has in his possession for such a purpose any obscene written matter, picture, model, phonograph record or other thing whatever;
>
> (b) publicly exhibits a disgusting object or an indecent show;
>
> (c) offers to sell, advertises or publishes an advertisement of, or has for sale or disposal, any means, instructions, medicine, drug or article intended or represented as a method of causing abortion or miscarriage; or
>
> (d) advertises or publishes an advertisement of any means, instructions, medicine, drug or article intended or represented as a method for restoring sexual virility or curing venereal diseases or diseases of the generative organs.
>
> . . .
>
> (8) For the purposes of this Act, any publication a dominant characteristic of which is the undue exploitation of sex, or of sex and any one or more of the following subjects, namely, crime, horror, cruelty and violence, shall be deemed to be obscene.

Sopinka J indicates that the appeal will deal only with the constitutional validity of s. 163(8).]

4. Analysis

[Sopinka J begins with a review of the legislative history of the obscenity provisions, noting the focus of the earlier legislation on the "corruption of morals." Prior to the introduction of the current provision in 1959, which provided a statutory definition of "obscene," Canadian courts had based the definition on the test formulated in *R v. Hicklin* (1868), LR 3 QB 360, at 371: "[T]he test of obscenity is this, whether the tendency of the matter charged as obscenity is to deprave and corrupt those whose minds are open to such immoral influences, and into whose hands a publication of this sort may fall." The introduction of the statutory definition had the effect of replacing the *Hicklin* test with a series of rules developed by the courts, which Sopinka J then goes on to review.]

B. Judicial Interpretation of S. 163(8)

... In order for the work or material to qualify as "obscene," the exploitation of sex must not only be its dominant characteristic, but such exploitation must be "undue." In determining when the exploitation of sex will be considered "undue," the courts have attempted to formulate workable tests. The most important of these is the "community standard of tolerance" test.

In [*R v. Brodie*, [1962] SCR 681, 132 CCC 161], Judson J accepted the view espoused notably by the Australian and New Zealand courts that obscenity is to be measured against "community standards." He cited [at 182 CCC] the following passage in the judgment of Fullager J in *R v. Close*, [1948] VLR 445:

> There does exist in any community at all times—however the standard may vary from time to time—a general instinctive sense of what is decent and what is indecent, of what is clean and what is dirty, and when the distinction has to be drawn, I do not know that today there is any better tribunal than a jury to draw it. ... What is obscene is something which offends against those standards.

The community standards test has been the subject of extensive judicial analysis. ... Our Court was called upon to elaborate the community standards test in *Towne Cinema Theatres Ltd. v. The Queen*, [1985] 1 SCR 494. Dickson CJC reviewed the case law and found:

> The cases all emphasize that it is a standard of tolerance, not taste, that is relevant. What matters is not what Canadians think is right for themselves to see. What matters is what Canadians would not abide other Canadians seeing because it would be beyond the contemporary Canadian standard of tolerance to allow them to see it.

... There has been a growing recognition in recent cases that material which may be said to exploit sex in a "degrading or dehumanizing" manner will necessarily fail the community standards test. ...

Among other things, degrading or dehumanizing materials place women (and sometimes men) in positions of subordination, servile submission or humiliation. They run against the principles of equality and dignity of all human beings. In the appreciation of whether material is degrading or dehumanizing, the appearance of consent is not necessarily determinative. Consent cannot save materials that otherwise contain degrading or dehumanizing scenes. Sometimes the very appearance of consent makes the depicted acts even more degrading or dehumanizing.

This type of material would, apparently, fail the community standards test not because it offends against morals but because it is perceived by public opinion to be harmful to society, particularly to women. While the accuracy of this perception is not susceptible of exact proof, there is a substantial body of opinion that holds that the portrayal of persons being subjected to degrading or dehumanizing sexual treatment results in harm, particularly to women and therefore to society as a whole. ...

[T]he artistic defence is the last step in the analysis of whether the exploitation of sex is undue. Even material which by itself offends community standards will not be considered "undue," if it is required for the serious treatment of a theme. ...

Accordingly, the "internal necessities" test, or what has been referred to as the "artistic defence," has been interpreted to assess whether the exploitation of sex has a justifiable role in advancing the plot or the theme, and in considering the work as a whole, does not merely represent "dirt for dirt's sake" but has a legitimate role when measured by the internal necessities of the work itself. ...

This review of jurisprudence shows that it fails to specify the relationship of the tests one to another. Failure to do so with respect to the community standards test and the degrading or dehumanizing test, for example, raises a serious question as to the basis on which the community acts in determining whether the impugned material will be tolerated. With both these tests being applied to the same material and apparently independently, we do not know whether the community found the material to be intolerable because it was degrading or dehumanizing, because it offended against morals or on some other basis. In some circumstances a finding that the material is tolerable can be over-ruled by the conclusion by the court that it causes harm and is therefore undue. Moreover, is the internal necessities test dominant so that it will redeem material that would otherwise be undue or is it just one factor? Is this test applied by the community or is it determined by the court without regard for the community? This hiatus in the jurisprudence has left the legislation open to attack on the ground of vagueness and uncertainty. That attack is made in this case. This lacuna in the interpretation of the legislation must, if possible, be filled before subjecting the legislation to Charter scrutiny. ...

Pornography can be usefully divided into three categories: (1) explicit sex with violence, (2) explicit sex without violence but which subjects people to treatment that is degrading or dehumanizing, and (3) explicit sex without violence that is neither degrading nor dehumanizing. Violence in this context includes both actual physical violence and threats of physical violence. Relating these three categories to the terms of s. 163(8) of the Code, the first, explicit sex coupled with violence, is expressly mentioned. Sex coupled with crime, horror or cruelty will sometimes involve violence. Cruelty, for instance, will usually do so. But, even in the absence of violence, sex coupled with crime, horror or cruelty may fall within the second category. As for category (3), subject to the exception referred to below, it is not covered.

Some segments of society would consider that all three categories of pornography cause harm to society because they tend to undermine its moral fibre. Others would contend that none of the categories cause harm. Furthermore there is a range of opinion as to what is degrading or dehumanizing. See *Pornography and Prostitution in Canada: Report of the Special Committee on Pornography and Prostitution* (1985) (the Fraser Report), Vol. 1, at p. 51. Because this is not a matter that is susceptible of proof in the traditional way and because we do not wish to leave it to the individual tastes of judges, we must have a norm that will serve as an arbiter in determining what amounts to an undue exploitation of sex. That arbiter is the community as a whole.

The courts must determine as best they can what the community would tolerate others being exposed to on the basis of the degree of harm that may flow from such exposure. Harm in this context means that it predisposes persons to act in an anti-social manner as, for example, the physical or mental mistreatment of women by men, or, what is perhaps debatable, the reverse. Anti-social conduct for this purpose is conduct which society formally recognizes as incompatible with its proper functioning. The stronger the inference of a risk of harm the lesser the likelihood of tolerance. The inference may be drawn from the material itself or from the material and other evidence. Similarly, evidence as to the community standards is desirable but not essential.

In making this determination with respect to the three categories of pornography referred to above, the portrayal of sex coupled with violence will almost always constitute the undue exploitation of sex. Explicit sex which is degrading or dehumanizing may be undue if the risk of harm is substantial. Finally, explicit sex that is not violent and neither degrading nor dehumanizing is generally tolerated in our society and will not qualify as the undue exploitation of sex unless it employs children in its production. ...

The foregoing deals with the inter-relationship of the "community standards test" and "the degrading or dehumanizing" test. How does the "internal necessities" test fit into this scheme? The need to apply this test only arises if a work contains sexually explicit material that by itself would constitute the undue exploitation of sex. The portrayal of sex must then be viewed in context to determine whether that is the dominant theme of the work as a whole. Put another way, is undue exploitation of sex the main object of the work or is this portrayal of sex essential to a wider artistic, literary, or other similar purpose? Since the threshold determination must be made on the basis of community standards, that is, whether the sexually explicit aspect is undue, its impact when considered in context must be determined on the same basis. The court must determine whether the sexually explicit material when viewed in the context of the whole work would be tolerated by the community as a whole. Artistic expression rests at the heart of freedom of expression values and any doubt in this regard must be resolved in favour of freedom of expression.

C. Does Section 163 Violate Section 2(b) of the Charter?

The majority of the Court of Appeal in this case allowed the appeal of the Crown on the ground that s. 163 does not violate freedom of expression as guaranteed under s. 2(b) of the Charter. ...

In my view, the majority of the Manitoba Court of Appeal erred. ...

Huband JA misinterpreted the distinction between purely physical activity and activity having expressive content. The subject matter of the materials in this case is clearly "physical," but this does not mean that the materials do not convey or attempt to convey meaning such that they are without expressive content. ...

In light of our recent decision in *R v. Keegstra*, [1990] 3 SCR 697, the respondent, and most of the parties intervening in support of the respondent, do not take issue with the proposition that s. 163 of the *Criminal Code* violates s. 2(b) of the Charter. In *Keegstra*, we were unanimous in advocating a generous approach to the protection afforded by s. 2(b) of the Charter. ...

Meaning sought to be expressed need not be "redeeming" in the eyes of the court to merit the protection of s. 2(b) whose purpose is to ensure that thoughts and feelings may be conveyed freely in non-violent ways without fear of censure. ...

D. Is Section 163 Justified Under Section 1 of the Charter?

(a) Is Section 163 a Limit Prescribed by Law?

The appellant argues that the provision is so vague that it is impossible to apply it. Vagueness must be considered in relation to two issues in this appeal: (1) is the law so vague that it does not qualify as "a limit prescribed by law"; and (2) is it so imprecise that it is not a reasonable limit. Dealing with (1), the test is ... does the law provide "an intelligible standard according to which the judiciary must do its work" (*Irwin Toy Ltd. v. Quebec*

(Attorney General), [1989] 1 SCR 927 at p. 983; adopted in *Osborne v. Canada (Treasury Board)*, [1991] 2 SCR 69, at p. 96).

In assessing whether s. 163(8) prescribes an intelligible standard, consideration must be given to the manner in which the provision has been judicially interpreted. ...

Standards which escape precise technical definition, such as "undue," are an inevitable part of the law. The *Criminal Code* contains other such standards. ...

It is within the role of the judiciary to attempt to interpret these terms. If such interpretation yields an intelligible standard, the threshold test for the application of s. 1 is met. In my opinion, the interpretation of s. 163(8) in prior judgments which I have reviewed, as supplemented by these reasons, provides an intelligible standard.

(b) Objective

The respondent argues that there are several pressing and substantial objectives which justify overriding the freedom to distribute obscene materials. Essentially, these objectives are the avoidance of harm resulting from antisocial attitudinal changes that exposure to obscene material causes and the public interest in maintaining a "decent society." On the other hand, the appellant argues that the objective of s. 163 is to have the state act as "moral custodian" in sexual matters and to impose subjective standards of morality.

The obscenity legislation and jurisprudence prior to the enactment of s. 163 were evidently concerned with prohibiting the "immoral influences" of obscene publications and safeguarding the morals of individuals into whose hands such works could fall. The *Hicklin* philosophy posits that explicit sexual depictions, particularly outside the sanctioned contexts of marriage and procreation, threatened the morals or the fabric of society. ... In this sense, its dominant, if not exclusive, purpose was to advance a particular conception of morality. Any deviation from such morality was considered to be inherently undesirable, independently of any harm to society. ...

I agree with Twaddle JA of the Court of Appeal that this particular objective is no longer defensible in view of the Charter. To impose a certain standard of public and sexual morality, solely because it reflects the conventions of a given community, is inimical to the exercise and enjoyment of individual freedoms, which form the basis of our social contract. ... The prevention of "dirt for dirt's sake" is not a legitimate objective which would justify the violation of one of the most fundamental freedoms enshrined in the Charter.

On the other hand, I cannot agree with the suggestion of the appellant that Parliament does not have the right to legislate on the basis of some fundamental conception of morality for the purposes of safeguarding the values which are integral to a free and democratic society. ...

As the respondent and many of the interveners have pointed out, much of the criminal law is based on moral conceptions of right and wrong and the mere fact that a law is grounded in morality does not automatically render it illegitimate. In this regard, criminalizing the proliferation of materials which undermine another basic Charter right may indeed be a legitimate objective.

In my view, however, the overriding objective of s. 163 is not moral disapprobation but the avoidance of harm to society. In *Towne Cinema*, Dickson CJC stated: "It is harm to society from undue exploitation that is aimed at by the section, not simply lapses in propriety or good taste."

The harm was described in the following way in the *Report on Pornography by the Standing Committee on Justice and Legal Affairs* (MacGuigan Report) (1978):

> The clear and unquestionable danger of this type of material is that it reinforces some un-healthy tendencies in Canadian society. The effect of this type of material is to reinforce male–female stereotypes to the detriment of both sexes. It attempts to make degradation, humiliation, victimization, and violence in human relationships appear normal and accept-able. A society which holds that egalitarianism, non-violence, consensualism, and mutuality are basic to any human interaction, whether sexual or other, is clearly justified in controlling and prohibiting any medium of depiction, description or advocacy which violates these principles.

The appellant argues that to accept the objective of the provision as being related to the harm associated with obscenity would be to adopt the "shifting purpose" doctrine explicitly rejected in *R v. Big M Drug Mart Ltd.*, [1985] 1 SCR 295. ...

I do not agree that to identify the objective of the impugned legislation as the preven-tion of harm to society, one must resort to the "shifting purpose" doctrine. First, the no-tions of moral corruption and harm to society are not distinct, as the appellant suggests, but are inextricably linked. It is moral corruption of a certain kind which leads to the detrimental effect on society. Second, and more importantly, I am of the view that with the enactment of s. 163, Parliament explicitly sought to address the harms which are linked to certain types of obscene materials. The prohibition of such materials was based on a belief that they had a detrimental impact on individuals exposed to them and con-sequently on society as a whole. Our understanding of the harms caused by these materi-als has developed considerably since that time; however this does not detract from the fact that the purpose of this legislation remains, as it was in 1959, the protection of soci-ety from harms caused by the exposure to obscene materials. ...

A permissible shift in emphasis was built into the legislation when, as interpreted by the courts, it adopted the community standards test. Community standards as to what is harmful have changed since 1959.

This being the objective, is it pressing and substantial? Does the prevention of the harm associated with the dissemination of certain obscene materials constitute a suffi-ciently pressing and substantial concern to warrant a restriction on the freedom of ex-pression? In this regard, it should be recalled that in *Keegstra* this Court unanimously accepted that the prevention of the influence of hate propaganda on society at large was a legitimate objective. ...

This Court has thus recognized that the harm caused by the proliferation of materials which seriously offend the values fundamental to our society is a substantial concern which justifies restricting the otherwise full exercise of the freedom of expression. In my view, the harm sought to be avoided in the case of the dissemination of obscene materials is similar. In the words of Nemetz CJBC in *R v. Red Hot Video Ltd.* (1985), 45 CR (3d) 36 (BCCA), there is a growing concern that the exploitation of women and children, de-picted in publications and films can, in certain circumstances, lead to "abject and servile victimization" (at pp. 43-44). As Anderson JA also noted in that same case, if true equality between male and female persons is to be achieved, we cannot ignore the threat to equality resulting from exposure to audiences of certain types of violent and degrading material. Materials portraying women as a class as objects for sexual exploitation and abuse have a negative impact on "the individual's sense of self-worth and acceptance."

In reaching the conclusion that legislation proscribing obscenity is a valid objective which justifies some encroachment of the right to freedom of expression, I am persuaded in part that such legislation may be found in most free and democratic societies. ...

Finally, it should be noted that the burgeoning pornography industry renders the concern even more pressing and substantial than when the impugned provisions were first enacted. I would therefore conclude that the objective of avoiding the harm associated with the dissemination of pornography in this case is sufficiently pressing and substantial to warrant some restriction on full exercise of the right to freedom of expression. The analysis of whether the measure is proportional to the objective must, in my view, be undertaken in light of the conclusion that the objective of the impugned section is valid only insofar as it relates to the harm to society associated with obscene materials. Indeed, the section as interpreted in previous decisions and in these reasons is fully consistent with that objective. The objective of maintaining conventional standards of propriety, independently of any harm to society, is no longer justified in light of the values of individual liberty which underlie the Charter. ...

(c) Proportionality

(i) General

... In assessing whether the proportionality test is met, it is important to keep in mind the nature of expression which has been infringed. ...

The values which underlie the protection of freedom of expression relate to the search for truth, participation in the political process, and individual self-fulfillment. The Attorney General for Ontario argues that of these, only "individual self-fulfillment," and only in its most base aspect, that of physical arousal, is engaged by pornography. On the other hand, the civil liberties groups argue that pornography forces us to question conventional notions of sexuality and thereby launches us into an inherently political discourse. In their factum, the BC Civil Liberties Association adopts a passage from R. West, "The Feminist-Conservative Anti-Pornography Alliance and the 1986 Attorney General's Commission on Pornography Report" (1987), 4 *Am. Bar Found. Res. Jo.* 681, at p. 696:

> Good pornography has value because it validates women's will to pleasure. It celebrates female nature. It validates a range of female sexuality that is wider and truer than that legitimated by the non-pornographic culture. Pornography when it is good celebrates both female pleasure and male rationality.

A proper application of the test should not suppress what West refers to as "good pornography." The objective of the impugned provision is not to inhibit the celebration of human sexuality. However, it cannot be ignored that the realities of the pornography industry are far from the picture which the BC Civil Liberties Association would have us paint. Shannon J, in *R v. Wagner* (1985), 43 CR (3d) 318, 36 Alta. LR (2d) 301, described the materials more accurately when he observed:

Women, particularly, are deprived of unique human character or identity and are depicted as sexual playthings, hysterically and instantly responsive to male sexual demands. They worship male genitals and their own value depends upon the quality of their genitals and breasts.

In my view, the kind of expression which is sought to be advanced does not stand on equal footing with other kinds of expression which directly engage the "core" of the freedom of expression values.

This conclusion is further buttressed by the fact that the targeted material is expression which is motivated, in the overwhelming majority of cases, by economic profit. This Court held in *Rocket v. Royal College of Dental Surgeons of Ontario*, [1990] 2 SCR 232, at p. 247, that an economic motive for expression means that restrictions on the expression might "be easier to justify than other infringements."

I will now turn to an examination of the three basic aspects of the proportionality test.

(ii) Rational Connection

The message of obscenity which degrades and dehumanizes is analogous to that of hate propaganda. As the Attorney General of Ontario has argued in its factum, obscenity wields the power to wreak social damage in that a significant portion of the population is humiliated by its gross misrepresentations.

Accordingly, the rational link between s. 163 and the objective of Parliament relates to the actual causal relationship between obscenity and the risk of harm to society at large. On this point, it is clear that the literature of the social sciences remains subject to controversy. ...

The recent conclusions of the Fraser Report, *supra*, could not postulate any causal relationship between pornography and the commission of violent crimes, the sexual abuse of children, or the disintegration of communities and society. This is in contrast to the findings of the MacGuigan Report, *supra*.

While a direct link between obscenity and harm to society may be difficult, if not impossible, to establish, it is reasonable to presume that exposure to images bears a causal relationship to changes in attitudes and beliefs. The Meese Commission Report, (US, 1986), concluded in respect of sexually violent material:

> ... [T]he available evidence strongly supports the hypothesis that substantial exposure to sexually violent materials as described here bears a causal relationship to antisocial acts of sexual violence and, for some subgroups, possibly to unlawful acts of sexual violence.
>
> Although we rely for this conclusion on significant scientific empirical evidence, we feel it worthwhile to note the underlying logic of the conclusion. The evidence says simply that the images that people are exposed to bears a causal relationship to their behavior. This is hardly surprising. What would be surprising would be to find otherwise, and we have not so found. We have not, of course, found that the images people are exposed to are a greater cause of sexual violence than all or even many other possible causes the investigation of which has been beyond our mandate. Nevertheless, it would be strange indeed if graphic representations of a form of behavior, especially in a form that almost exclusively portrays such behavior as desirable, did not have at least some effect on patterns of behavior.

In the face of inconclusive social science evidence, the approach adopted by our Court in *Irwin Toy* is instructive. In that case, the basis for the legislation was that television advertising directed at young children is *per se* manipulative. The Court made it clear that in choosing its mode of intervention, it is sufficient that Parliament had a *reasonable basis*. ...

Similarly, in *Keegstra* the absence of proof of a causative link between hate propaganda and hatred of an identifiable group was discounted as a determinative factor in assessing the constitutionality of the hate literature provisions of the *Criminal Code*. ...

I am in agreement with Twaddle JA who expressed the view that Parliament was entitled to have a "reasoned apprehension of harm" resulting from the desensitization of individuals exposed to materials which depict violence, cruelty, and dehumanization in sexual relations.

Accordingly, I am of the view that there is a sufficiently rational link between the criminal sanction, which demonstrates our community's disapproval of the dissemination of materials which potentially victimize women and which restricts the negative influence which such materials have on changes in attitudes and behaviour, and the objective. ...

(iii) Minimal Impairment

In determining whether less intrusive legislation may be imagined, this Court [has] stressed ... that it is not necessary that the legislative scheme be the "perfect" scheme, but that it be appropriately tailored in the context of the infringed right. Furthermore, in *Irwin Toy* Dickson CJC, Lamer and Wilson JJ stated:

> This Court will not, in the name of minimal impairment, take a restrictive approach to social science evidence and require legislatures to choose the least ambitious means to protect vulnerable groups.

There are several factors which contribute to the finding that the provision minimally impairs the freedom which is infringed.

First, the impugned provision does not proscribe sexually explicit erotica without violence that is not degrading or dehumanizing. It is designed to catch material that creates a risk of harm to society. It might be suggested that proof of actual harm should be required. It is apparent from what I have said above that it is sufficient in this regard for Parliament to have a reasonable basis for concluding that harm will result and this requirement does not demand actual proof of harm.

Second, materials which have scientific, artistic or literary merit are not captured by the provision. As discussed above, the court must be generous in its application of the "artistic defence." ...

Third, in considering whether the provision minimally impairs the freedom in question, it is legitimate for the court to take into account Parliament's past abortive attempts to replace the definition with one that is more explicit. ... The attempt to provide exhaustive instances of obscenity has been shown to be destined to fail (Bill C-54, 2nd Sess., 33rd Parl.). It seems that the only practicable alternative is to strive towards a more abstract definition of obscenity which is contextually sensitive and responsive to progress in the knowledge and understanding of the phenomenon to which the legislation is directed. In my view, the standard of "undue exploitation" is therefore appropriate. The intractable nature of the problem and the impossibility of precisely defining a notion which is inherently elusive makes the possibility of a more explicit provision remote. In this light, it is appropriate to question whether, and at what cost, greater legislative precision can be demanded.

Fourth, while the discussion in this appeal has been limited to the definition portion of s. 163, I would note that the impugned section, with the possible exception of subs. 1 which is not in issue here, has been held by this Court not to extend its reach to the private use or viewing of obscene materials. ... Accordingly, it is only the public distribution and exhibition of obscene materials which is in issue here. ...

It is ... submitted [by the intervenors] that there are more effective techniques to promote the objectives of Parliament. For example, if pornography is seen as encouraging violence against women, there are certain activities which discourage it—counselling rape victims to charge their assailants, provision of shelter and assistance for battered women, campaigns for laws against discrimination on the grounds of sex, education to increase the sensitivity of law enforcement agencies and other governmental authorities. In addition, it is submitted that education is an under-used response.

It is noteworthy that many of the above suggested alternatives are in the form of responses to the harm engendered by negative attitudes against women. The role of the impugned provision is to control the dissemination of the very images that contribute to such attitudes. Moreover, it is true that there are additional measures which could alleviate the problem of violence against women. However, given the gravity of the harm, and the threat to the values at stake, I do not believe that the measure chosen by Parliament is equalled by the alternatives which have been suggested. Education, too, may offer a means of combating negative attitudes to women, just as it is currently used as a means of addressing other problems dealt with in the Code. However, there is no reason to rely on education alone. ... Serious social problems such as violence against women require multi-pronged approaches by government. Education and legislation are not alternatives but complements in addressing such problems. There is nothing in the Charter which requires Parliament to choose between such complementary measures.

(iv) Balance Between Effects of Limiting Measures and Legislative Objective

... The infringement on freedom of expression is confined to a measure designed to prohibit the distribution of sexually explicit materials accompanied by violence, and those without violence that are degrading or dehumanizing. As I have already concluded, this kind of expression lies far from the core of the guarantee of freedom of expression. It appeals only to the most base aspect of individual fulfillment, and it is primarily economically motivated.

The objective of the legislation, on the other hand, is of fundamental importance in a free and democratic society. It is aimed at avoiding harm, which Parliament has reasonably concluded will be caused directly or indirectly, to individuals, groups such as women and children, and consequently to society as a whole, by the distribution of these materials. It thus seeks to enhance respect for all members of society, and non-violence and equality in their relations with each other.

I therefore conclude that the restriction on freedom of expression does not outweigh the importance of the legislative objective. ...

I conclude that while s. 163(8) infringes s. 2(b) of the Charter, freedom of expression, it constitutes a reasonable limit and is saved by virtue of the provisions of s. 1.

[Gonthier J, L'Heureux-Dubé J concurring, wrote a concurring judgment in which he agreed with Sopinka J's disposition of the case, but differed somewhat in his understanding of s. 163 and its constitutional validity. He understands obscene materials as harmful because they "convey a distorted image of human sexuality, by making public and open elements of human nature which are usually hidden behind a veil of modesty and privacy. … This distorted image of human sexuality often comprises violence, cruelty, infliction of pain, [and] humiliation, among other elements of pornographic imagery." This conceptualization of the harm of obscene materials leads him to a different conclusion than Sopinka J with respect to the issue of whether s. 163 captures the third category of materials—explicit sex that is neither violent nor degrading nor dehumanizing. For Gonthier J, some public representations of explicit sexual activity, such as on a billboard rather than in a film or movie, may, because of the manner of the representation, trigger the application of s. 163, as they "contribute to the deformation of sexuality, through the loss of its humanity."]

Appeal allowed; new trial ordered.

NOTES AND QUESTIONS

1. *Shifting Purpose.* In *R v. Big M Drug Mart Ltd.*, [1985] 1 SCR 295, 18 DLR (4th) 321, it was held that the government, when seeking to justify a restriction under s. 1, could not put forward a "pressing and substantial" purpose different from that which originally animated the legislation. In *Butler*, does Sopinka J's reinterpretation of the objective of the obscenity provisions of the *Criminal Code* as the prevention of harm to women and children amount to an impermissible shift in purpose? Or does *Butler* simply involve a permissible shift in emphasis built into the wording of the legislation, as Sopinka J argued?

2. *Social Science Evidence and Proof of Harm.* In *Butler*, Sopinka J refers to the inconclusive social science evidence concerning the link between pornography and acts of sexual violence. Most of the empirical research concerns changes in the attitudes of men toward rape and sexual violence following exposure to violent pornography in a laboratory setting. However, these studies do not show that an individual's attitudes are changed over the long term or that it is more likely that he will act in a violent way after exposure to violent sexual imagery. The shortcomings of the empirical research are discussed in Daniel Linz, Steven D. Penrod, and Edward Donnerstein, "The Attorney General's Commission on Pornography: The Gaps Between 'Findings' and 'Facts,'" [1987] 4 *American Bar Foundation Research Journal* 713. The authors advocate caution in making generalizations about behaviour on the basis of laboratory experiments. They do say, however, that one of the things the studies show is that nudity is not the problem. Any attitudinal changes that may occur are the result of exposure to images of violence against women who may be naked or clothed.

Because the empirical evidence of harm was not clear-cut, Sopinka J found it necessary to rely on common sense (that it was "reasonable to presume that exposure to images bears a causal relationship to changes in attitudes and beliefs") and to defer to Parliament's reasonable judgment that pornography causes harm to women (even though it is not clear what sort of causal judgment Parliament made when it enacted this provision). When we express ourselves to others we want to affect their thinking and action. Is the state justified in restricting expression simply because it might persuade others to engage in harmful or wrongful action? Or is there something different about pornography, and the way it affects behaviour, that justifies its restriction?

3. *Other Forms of Expression Harmful to Women.* Why do we continue to focus on sexually explicit imagery? Images of women in television advertising, film, and fashion magazines often have the same structure as sexually explicit pornography and contribute to the social picture of women as subordinate. If the impact of representations of sexual violence or degradation does not depend on the nudity of the persons represented, then is there any reason to focus on sexually explicit material? Does the use of sexual explicitness as an essential element in the definition of the category of restricted material suggest that concerns about offence and public morals continue to affect our thinking about obscenity/pornography? Could the state successfully regulate these other forms of sexist expression, given Charter guarantees?

4. *Post-Butler Application of the Harm-Based Model of Obscenity.* Does Justice Sopinka's (re)interpretation of the *Criminal Code*'s obsenity prohibition, as a ban on "harmful" sexual representations, provide a manageable standard for identifying prohibited material? Does the community standards test help in any way? Do the concepts "degrading" and "dehumanizing" provide sufficient guidance to those administering the law, such as police officers and Customs officials? The Supreme Court of Canada has both affirmed and developed the harm test for obscenity in subsequent decisions: first in *Little Sisters Book and Art Emporium v. Canada (Minister of Justice)*, [2000] 2 SCR 1120, 193 DLR (4th) 193, which dealt with gay and lesbian sexual erotica; and, second, in *R v. Labaye*, [2005] 3 SCR 728, 2005 SCC 80, 260 DLR (4th) 595, which involved the interpretation of the related concept of indecency. Extracts from both of these decisions are found below.

5. *Child pornography.* Discussing the third category of pornography, explicit sex that is not violent and neither degrading nor dehumanizing, Sopinka J stated that it is "generally tolerated in our society and will not qualify as the undue exploitation of sex unless it employs children in its production." This suggests that a different understanding of harm will be operative in cases involving child pornography. The Supreme Court addressed this issue nine years later in *R v. Sharpe*, [2001] 1 SCR 45, 194 DLR (4th) 1, extracts from which are found below.

NOTE: LITTLE SISTERS BOOK AND ART EMPORIUM v. CANADA (MINISTER OF JUSTICE)

Censorship of both hate speech and obscene materials occurs under the *Customs Tariff*, SC 1997, c. 36 (formerly RSC 1985, c. 41 (3d Supp.)), which governs the importation of goods into Canada and dictates those materials that are not to be allowed entry. Section 136 of the *Customs Tariff* (formerly s. 114) prohibits the importation of goods, including goods referred to in Tariff item 9899.00.00 (formerly Code 9956 of Schedule VII of the Act), which reads in part:

Books, printed paper drawings, paintings, prints, photographs, or representations of any kind that:

(a) are deemed to be obscene under subsection 163(8) of the *Criminal Code*;

(b) constitute hate propaganda within the meaning of s. 320(8) of the *Criminal Code*;

(c) are of a treasonable character within the meaning of section 46 of the *Criminal Code*;

or

(d) are of a seditious character within the meaning of sections 59 and 60 of the *Criminal Code*.

Alleging that it was the victim of a longstanding Customs practice of targeting shipments destined for gay and lesbian bookstores, Little Sisters bookstore in Vancouver and its owners challenged the provisions of the Customs legislation that prohibited the importation of obscene publications. In *Little Sisters Book and Art Emporium v. Canada (Minister of Justice)*, [2000] 2 SCR 1120, 193 DLR (4th) 193, the Supreme Court, in a judgment written by Binnie J (Iacobucci, Arbour, and LeBel JJ dissenting in part) the Court held that these provisions restricted the appellants' freedom of expression, but that this restriction (with the exception of a reverse onus provision, which will be discussed further below) was justified under s. 1. However, the Court also found that the manner in which the legislation had been implemented by Customs officials violated the bookstore's rights and could not be justified under s. 1.

Under the *Customs Tariff*, Customs officials are empowered to determine whether imported materials are obscene. If material is classified as obscene, the importer may request a redetermination by a specialized Customs unit. A further appeal can be made to the Deputy Minister or his/her designate. Once these administrative procedures have been exhausted, the importer can appeal the prohibition to a judge of the superior court in the province where the material was seized, with a further appeal on a question of law to the Federal Court and with a final appeal (with leave) to the Supreme Court of Canada.

Binnie J noted that the trial judge had identified very high error rates in determinations respecting Little Sisters' imports at all levels of the Customs review procedure and had concluded that "[s]uch high rates of error indicate more than mere differences of opinion and suggest systemic causes" (para. 6). Specifically, the trial judge found that:

Many publications, particularly books, are ruled obscene without adequate evidence. This highlights perhaps the most serious defect in the present administration of code 9956(a), that is, that classifying officers are neither adequately trained to make decisions on obscenity nor are they routinely provided with the time and the evidence necessary to make such decisions. There is no formal procedure for placing evidence of artistic or literary merit before the classifying officers. Consequently, many publications are prohibited entry into Canada that would likely not be found to be obscene if full evidence were considered by officers properly trained to weigh and evaluate that evidence.

Binnie J found that Little Sisters bookstore had been "targeted as importers of obscene materials despite the absence of any evidence to suggest that gay and lesbian erotica is more likely to be obscene than heterosexual erotica, or that the appellants are likely offenders in this regard ... and that [i]n consequence of the targeting, [Little Sisters] have suffered excessive and unnecessary prejudice in terms of delays, cost and other losses in having their goods cleared (if at all) through Canada Customs" (para. 154). He concluded that the Customs authorities had exercised their legislative powers in a way that violated the appellants' s. 2(b) rights and could not be justified under s. 1. These constitutional violations were traced, in part, to under-staffing, inadequate training of Customs officials, the failure to provide proper guides and manuals and develop workable procedures, and the failure to establish internal deadlines.

Little Sisters, however, had sought more than just a declaration of unconstitutional application of the legislation to themselves. They had brought a challenge to the constitutionality of the legislation itself, seeking to have it declared invalid. In this they were largely unsuccessful. Their constitutional challenge to the Customs legislation was based on two grounds. As described by Binnie J, the first argument, or set of arguments, was that the decision in *Butler* to uphold the *Criminal Code* prohibition on obscene materials was incorrect and, "in any event, that the approach taken in *Butler* [to determining whether material is obscene] cannot be freely transferred from heterosexual erotica to gay and lesbian erotica." The second argument was that the procedure set out in the Customs legislation was so cumbersome and procedurally defective that it could not be administered in a way that respected the appellant's Charter rights.

Binnie J dismissed the first set of arguments concerning *Butler* and its applicability to gay and lesbian material:

> [53] [T]he appellants [Little Sisters bookstore and its owners] ... argue that in the context of the Customs legislation a "harm-based" approach which utilizes a single community standard across all regions and groups within society is insufficiently "contextual" or sensitive to specific circumstances to give effect to the equality rights of gays and lesbians. The appellants, supported by the interveners LEAF and EGALE, contend that homosexual erotica plays an important role in providing a positive self-image to gays and lesbians, who may feel isolated and rejected in the heterosexual mainstream. Erotica provides a positive celebration of what it means to be gay or lesbian. As such, it is argued that sexual speech in the context of gay and lesbian culture is a core value and *Butler* cannot legitimately be applied to locate it at the fringes of s. 2(b) expression. Erotica, they contend, plays a different role in a gay and lesbian community than it does in a heterosexual community, and the *Butler* approach based, they say, on heterosexual norms, is oblivious to this fact.

> • • •

> [55] The appellants contend that importing a majoritarian analysis into the definition of obscenity (e.g. what the broader Canadian community will tolerate) inevitably creates prejudice against non-mainstream, minority representations of sex and sexuality. They argue that the "national" community is by definition majoritarian and is more likely than the homosexual community itself to view gay and lesbian imagery as degrading and dehumanizing. The whole idea of a community standards test, they say, is incompatible with Charter values that were enacted to protect minority rights. ...

> [56] This line of criticism underestimates *Butler* ... . [The community standards] test was adopted to underscore the unacceptability of the trier of fact indulging personal biases. ... A concern for minority expression is one of the principal factors that led to adoption of the national community test in *Butler* in the first place. ...

> [57] ... [A] person's constitutionally protected space does not shrink by virtue of his or her geographical location or participation in a certain context or community, or indeed by the taste of a particular judge or jury.

. . .

[60] The appellants argue that the "degrading or dehumanizing" language in *Butler* is highly subjective and encouraged Customs, for example, to prohibit depictions of anal intercourse long after the Department of Justice advised Customs to the contrary. This argument seems to ignore that the phrase "degrading or dehumanizing" in *Butler* is qualified immediately by the words "if the risk of harm is substantial" ... . This makes it clear that not all sexually explicit erotica depicting adults engaged in conduct which is considered to be degrading or dehumanizing is obscene. The material must also create a substantial risk of harm which exceeds the community's tolerance. ... Parliament's concern was with behavioural changes in the voyeur that are potentially harmful in ways or to an extent that the community is not prepared to tolerate. There is no reason to restrict that concern to the heterosexual community.

. . .

[63] The intervener LEAF took the position that sado-masochism performs an emancipatory role in gay and lesbian culture and should therefore be judged by a different standard from that applicable to heterosexual culture. In support of this position LEAF points out that, by definition, gender discrimination is not an issue in "same-sex erotica." On the other hand, the intervener Equality Now took the view that gay and lesbian individuals have as much right as their heterosexual counterparts to be protected from depictions of sex with violence or sexual conduct that is dehumanizing or degrading in a way that can cause harm that exceeds community standards of tolerance.

[64] LEAF's argument seems to presuppose that the *Butler* test is exclusively gender-based. Violence against women was only one of several concerns, albeit an important one, that led to the formulation of the *Butler* harm-based test, which itself is gender neutral. While it would be quite open to the appellants to argue that a particular publication does not exceed the general community's tolerance of harm for various reasons, gay and lesbian culture as such does not constitute a general exemption from the *Butler* test.

. . .

[66] ... The trial judge ... relied on the conclusion of Professor Neil M. Malamuth that "homosexual pornography may have harmful effects even if it is distinct in certain ways from heterosexual pornography." Professor Malamuth further observed that:

> In recent years, [there] has been increasing scientific research indicating that some of the behaviors that might be related to exposure to some types of pornography are a serious problem within the gay community as well as within the heterosexual one. ... [T]here are studies suggesting that within homosexual interactions the frequency of sexually coercive acts as well as non-sexual aggression between intimates occurs at a frequency quite comparable to heterosexual interactions.

In adopting the *Butler* test to justify the prohibition on the importation of obscene material under s. 1, Binnie J also specifically rejected the appellants' argument that the restriction was too vague to satisfy the "prescribed by law" requirement:

> [146] Section 163 having been upheld in *Butler*, and the *Customs Tariff* having incorporated s. 163 and the related jurisprudence, it follows that the *Customs Tariff* prohibition is not void for vagueness or uncertainty, and is therefore validly "prescribed by law." The appellants argued that a legal standard which may be intelligible to a judge in a criminal trial surrounded with all the appropriate procedural protections is not necessarily intelligible to a Customs official

left to his or her own devices. ... I do not think "intelligibility" varies with the level of procedural sophistication. The standard set out in s. 163(8) of the *Criminal Code* either affords a reasonable guide to well-intentioned individuals seeking to keep themselves within the law or it does not. *Butler* held that it did. The standard is related to the community's tolerance of harm. It is the severity of the potential consequences that requires a judge to preside over a criminal trial, not the intelligibility of the "community tolerance" standard.

Binnie J also rejected Little Sisters' second argument that the Customs legislation failed to provide adequate procedural safeguards and was therefore unconstitutional:

> [71] The appellants say a regulatory structure that is open to the level of maladministration described in the trial judgment is unconstitutionally underprotective of their constitutional rights and should be struck down in its entirety. In effect they argue that Parliament was required to proceed by way of legislation rather than the creation of a delegated power of regulation in s. 164(1)(j), which authorizes the Governor in Council to "make regulations ... generally, to carry out the purposes and provisions of this Act," or by ministerial directive. My colleague Iacobucci J accepts the propositions that "[t]his Court's precedents demand sufficient safeguards in the legislative scheme itself to ensure that government action will not infringe constitutional rights" and because "the legislation makes no reasonable effort to ensure that it will be applied constitutionally to expressive materials" Code 9956 should be struck from the *Customs Tariff*. I do not think there is any constitutional rule that requires Parliament to deal with Customs' treatment of constitutionally protected expressive material by legislation (as the appellants contend) rather than by way of regulation (as Parliament contemplated in s. 164(1)(j)) or even by ministerial directive or departmental practice. Parliament is entitled to proceed on the basis that its enactments "will be applied constitutionally" by the public service.
>
> [72] ... [T]he appellants' complaint is about what Parliament did not enact rather than what it did enact. The imposition on Parliament of a constitutional obligation to deal itself with Charter-sensitive matters rather than by permitting Parliament the option of enacting a delegated regulation-making power has serious ramifications for the machinery of government. I do not agree that Parliament's options are so limited.

Binnie J examined the different procedures contained in the Customs legislation and concluded that, with one exception, they did not infringe any Charter rights. In his view, the problem was in the implementation of the legislated rules and procedures.

The one procedural provision that Binnie J found to be unconstitutional was a reverse onus clause. Section 152(3) of the *Customs Tariff*, which was applicable to "any proceeding under this Act," directed the decision maker to assume that Customs officials were right unless and until the importer proved them to be wrong. In the view of Binnie J:

> [101] ... [This] provision cannot constitutionally apply to put on the importer the onus of disproving obscenity. Otherwise entry of expressive materials could be denied by reason of the onus even where the standard of obscenity is not met, as for example, where an importer lacks the resources or the stamina to contest an initial determination. An importer has a Charter right to receive expressive material unless the state can justify its denial. It is not open to the state to put the onus on an individual to show why he or she should be allowed to exercise a Charter right. It is for the state to establish that a limitation on the Charter right is justified. ...

Iacobucci J (dissenting in part) would have struck down the restriction on the importation of obscene material, although he would have suspended the declaration of invalidity for an 18-month period. In his opinion:

[166] ... [T]he current procedures by which Customs enforces s. 163(8) at the border are grossly inadequate. With a few minor exceptions, expressive materials are classified when entering Canada in the same manner as mundane commercial goods. The Customs legislation lacks the most basic procedures necessary for a fair and accurate determination of whether something is obscene. Compounding these legislative deficiencies is the fact that Customs officers, while no doubt well-intentioned and conscientious civil servants, lack the training, time or resources to accomplish the task set for them. In my respectful opinion, the Customs legislation makes no meaningful accommodation for the expressive freedoms raised by this appeal. Such a regime cannot be demonstrably justified in a free and democratic society.

[167] The appropriate remedy for this violation of the appellants' constitutional rights is to strike down [the relevant provision of the Customs legislation]. ... Particularly in a case like the one before us, where there is an extensive record of the improper detention of non-obscene works, the only choice to ensure full protection of the constitutional rights at stake is to invalidate the legislation and invite Parliament to remedy the constitutional infirmities.

The portions of the judgment dealing with the appropriate remedy are found in Chapter 25, Enforcement of Rights.

R v. Labaye
[2005] 3 SCR 728, 2005 SCC 80, 260 DLR (4th) 595

[In this case, which concerned the meaning of "indecency" under s. 210(1) of the *Criminal Code*, the Supreme Court of Canada related indecency to obscenity and held that the courts should no longer look to community standards when determining whether actions are indecent or publications are obscene. The concept of "harm," which was central to the reasoning in *Butler*, was elaborated on. Note that this case concerned the proper meaning of the term "indecent" in the *Criminal Code*, and did not involve a constitutional challenge to the indecency provisions of the Code. On the facts, the accused owned a club that permitted couples and others to meet for group sex; a majority of the Court found that there was no basis for concluding that the sexual conduct in issue harmed individuals or society and the accused's conviction for keeping a common bawdy house for the purpose of the practice of acts of indecency was quashed.]

McLACHLIN CJC (Major, Binnie, Deschamps, Fish, Abella, and Charron JJ concurring):

4.1.1 The History of Criminal Indecency

· · ·

[17] In 1959, the Canadian Parliament introduced a new "undue exploitation of sex" test for obscene materials: s. 150(8) of the *Criminal Code*, SC 1953-54, c. 51 (added by SC 1959, c. 41, s. 11) (now s. 163(8)). In considering this test, the Supreme Court emphasized the failings of the previous test and the need for new criteria "which have some

certainty of meaning and are capable of objective application and which do not so much depend as before upon the idiosyncrasies and sensitivities of the tribunal of fact, whether judge or jury": *Brodie v. The Queen*, [1962] SCR 681, at p. 702, *per* Judson J.

[18] Borrowing on decisions from Australia and New Zealand emphasizing the foundation of criminal legislation on obscenity and indecency in societal norms, the Court adopted a test based on the community standard of tolerance. On its face, the test was objective, requiring the trier of fact to determine what the community would tolerate. Yet once again, in practice it proved difficult to apply in an objective fashion. How does one determine what the "community" would tolerate were it aware of the conduct or material? In a diverse, pluralistic society whose members hold divergent views, who is the "community"? And how can one objectively determine what the community, if one could define it, would tolerate, in the absence of evidence that community knew of and considered the conduct at issue? In practice, once again, the test tended to function as a proxy for the personal views of expert witnesses, judges and jurors. ...

[20] In 1985, the Supreme Court pursued the search for objectivity by introducing a two-part definition of community standards of tolerance in *Towne Cinema Theatres Ltd. v. The Queen*, [1985] 1 SCR 494. The first way to establish obscenity (undue exploitation of sex) was to show that the material violated the norm of tolerance of what Canadians would permit others, whose views they did not share, to do or see (p. 508). The second was to show that the material would have a harmful effect on others in society (p. 505). Although this notion of harm had been implicit in Cockburn CJ's definition of obscenity in *Hicklin* [*R v.* (1868), LR 3 QB 360], *Towne Cinema* marked the first clear articulation of the relationship between obscenity and harm in Canadian jurisprudence, and represented the beginning of a shift from a community standards test to a harm-based test.

[21] The shift to a harm-based rationale was completed by this Court's decisions in *R v. Butler*, [1992] 1 SCR 452, and *Little Sisters Book and Art Emporium v. Canada (Minister of Justice)*, [2000] 2 SCR 1120, 2000 SCC 69. In *Butler*, the two-part test for obscenity of *Towne Cinema* was resolved into a single test, in which the community standard of tolerance was determined by reference to the risk of harm entailed by the conduct:

> The courts must determine as best they can what the community would tolerate others being exposed to *on the basis of the degree of harm that may flow from such exposure.* Harm in this context means that it *predisposes persons to act in an anti-social manner* as, for example, the physical or mental mistreatment of women by men, or, what is perhaps debatable, the reverse. Anti-social conduct for this purpose is *conduct which society formally recognizes as incompatible with its proper functioning.* The stronger the inference of a risk of harm the lesser the likelihood of tolerance. [Emphasis added; p. 485, *per* Sopinka J.]

[22] The Court in *Little Sisters* confirmed that harm is an essential ingredient of obscenity. As Binnie J pointed out, "the phrase 'degrading or dehumanizing' in *Butler* is qualified immediately by the words '*if* the risk of harm is substantial'. ... This makes it clear that not all sexually explicit erotica depicting adults engaged in conduct which is considered to be degrading or dehumanizing is obscene. *The material must also create a substantial risk of harm which exceeds the community's tolerance*" (para. 60 (emphasis added)).

[23] In [*R v.*] *Mara* [[1997] 2 SCR 630], the Court affirmed that in cases of indecency, like obscenity, the community standard of tolerance test amounts to a test of harm incompatible with society's proper functioning.

[24] Grounding criminal indecency in harm represents an important advance in this difficult area of the law. Harm or significant risk of harm is easier to prove than a community standard. Moreover, the requirement of a risk of harm incompatible with the proper functioning of society brings this area of the law into step with the vast majority of criminal offences, which are based on the need to protect society from harm.

[25] However, it is not always clear precisely how the harm test for indecency applies in particular circumstances. New cases have raised questions as to the nature and degree of harm sufficient to establish indecency. Further definition is required in order to resolve cases like this, and to permit individuals to conduct themselves within the law and the police and courts to enforce the criminal sanction in an objective, fair way.

4.1.2 Toward a Theory of Harm

• • •

[28] The first step is to generically describe the type of harm targeted by the concept of indecent conduct under the *Criminal Code*. In *Butler* at p. 485 and *Little Sisters* at para. 59, this was described as "conduct which society formally recognizes as incompatible with its proper functioning."

[29] Two general requirements emerge from this description of the harm required for criminal indecency. First, the words "formally recognize" suggest that the harm must be grounded in norms which our society has recognized in its Constitution or similar fundamental laws. This means that the inquiry is not based on individual notions of harm, nor on the teachings of a particular ideology, but on what society, through its laws and institutions, has recognized as essential to its proper functioning. Second, the harm must be serious in degree. It must not only detract from proper societal functioning, but must be *incompatible* with it.

• • •

[31] I now turn to a more detailed consideration of each of the two requirements for establishing indecent acts for the purposes of s. 210 of the *Criminal Code*.

• • •

4.1.3 The Nature of the Harm: Harm to Individuals or Society Contrary to Society's Norms

[32] To ground criminal responsibility, the harm must be one which society *formally recognizes* as incompatible with its proper functioning: *Butler*, at p. 485.

[33] The requirement of formal societal recognition makes the test objective. The inquiry is not based on individual notions of harm, nor on the teachings of a particular ideology, but on what society, through its fundamental laws, has recognized as essential. Views about the harm that the sexual conduct at issue may produce, however widely held, do not suffice to ground a conviction. This is not to say that social values no longer have a role to play. On the contrary, to ground a finding that acts are indecent, the harm must be shown to be related to a fundamental value reflected in our society's Constitution or similar fundamental laws, like bills of rights, which constitutes society's formal

recognition that harm of the sort envisaged may be incompatible with its proper functioning. Unlike the community standard of tolerance test, the requirement of formal recognition inspires confidence that the values upheld by judges and jurors are truly those of Canadian society. Autonomy, liberty, equality and human dignity are among these values.

[34] The complexity of the guarantee of freedom of religion in this context requires further comment. The claim that particular sexual conduct violates particular religious rules or values does not alone suffice to establish this element of the test. The question is what values Canadian society has formally recognized. Canadian society through its Constitution and similar fundamental laws does not formally recognize particular religious views, but rather *the freedom to hold particular religious views*. This freedom does not endorse any particular religious view, but the right to hold a variety of diverse views.

[35] The requirement of formal endorsement ensures that people will not be convicted and imprisoned for transgressing the rules and beliefs of particular individuals or groups. To incur the ultimate criminal sanction, they must have violated values which Canadian society as a whole has formally endorsed.

[36] Three types of harm have thus far emerged from the jurisprudence as being capable of supporting a finding of indecency: (1) harm to those whose autonomy and liberty may be restricted by being confronted with inappropriate conduct; (2) harm to society by predisposing others to anti-social conduct; and (3) harm to individuals participating in the conduct. Each of these types of harm is grounded in values recognized by our Constitution and similar fundamental laws. The list is not closed; other types of harm may be shown in the future to meet the standards for criminality established by *Butler*. But thus far, these are the types of harm recognized by the cases.

[37] Reference to the fundamental values of our Constitution and similar fundamental laws also eliminates types of conduct that do *not* constitute a harm in the required sense. Bad taste does not suffice: *Towne Cinema*, at p. 507. Moral views, even if strongly held, do not suffice. Similarly, the fact that most members of the community might disapprove of the conduct does not suffice: *Butler*, at p. 492. In each case, more is required to establish the necessary harm for criminal indecency.

[38] A particular type of conduct may involve several types of harm; life does not fall into neatly tagged juridical boxes. But since each type of harm rests on its own set of values, it is useful to consider each independently. ...

4.1.3.1 THE HARM OF LOSS OF AUTONOMY AND LIBERTY THROUGH PUBLIC
         CONFRONTATION

[40] The first is the harm of public confrontation with unacceptable and inappropriate conduct. One reason for criminalizing indecent acts and displays is to protect the public from being confronted with acts and material that reduce their quality of life. Indecent acts are banned because they subject the public to unwanted confrontation with inappropriate conduct. This harm is conceptually akin to nuisance. Nevertheless, to call this the "eyesore" basis of criminalization of indecent acts is to trivialize the harm. The harm is not the aesthetic harm of a less attractive community, but the loss of autonomy and liberty that public indecency may impose on individuals in society, as they seek to

avoid confrontation with acts they find offensive and unacceptable. The value or interest protected is the autonomy and liberty of members of the public, to live within a zone that is free from conduct that deeply offends them.

[41] Much harm in this category does not rise to the levels of harm required by *Butler* and *Little Sisters*. Tolerance requires that only serious and deeply offensive moral assaults can be kept from public view on pain of criminal sanction. We live in an age when sexual images, some subtle and some not so subtle, are widely dispersed throughout our public space. However, this does not negate the fact that even in our emancipated society, there may be some kinds of sexual conduct the public display of which seriously impairs the livability of the environment and significantly constrains autonomy. Sexual relations are an intensely personal, religious and age-sensitive matter. People's autonomy and enjoyment of life can be deeply affected by being unavoidably confronted with debased public sexual displays. Even when avoidance is possible, the result may be diminished freedom to go where they wish or take their children where they want. Sexual conduct and material that presents a risk of seriously curtailing people's autonomy and liberty may justifiably be restricted. The loss of autonomy and liberty to ordinary people by in-your-face indecency is a potential harm to which the law is entitled to respond. If the risk of harm is significant enough, it may rise to the degree of the test for criminal indecency in *Butler*—conduct which society formally recognizes as incompatible with its proper functioning.

[42] Since the harm in this class of case is based on the public being confronted with unpalatable acts or material, it is essential that there be a risk that members of the public either will be unwillingly exposed to the conduct or material, or that they will be forced to significantly change their usual conduct to avoid being so exposed.

[43] This makes relevant the manner, place and audience of the acts alleged to be indecent. In this respect, indecency differs from obscenity, where an element of public exposure is presumed: *Butler*, at p. 485. As stated in *R v. Tremblay*, [1993] 2 SCR 932, at p. 960, "the place in which the acts take place and the composition of the audience" may affect whether acts are indecent.

. . .

4.1.3.2 THE HARM OF PREDISPOSING OTHERS TO ANTI-SOCIAL ACTS OR ATTITUDES

[45] The second source of harm is based on the danger that the conduct or material may predispose others to commit anti-social acts. As far back as *Hicklin*, Cockburn CJ spoke of using the criminal law to prevent material from depraving and corrupting susceptible people, into whose hands it may fall. The threshold for criminal indecency is higher under *Butler* than that envisioned by Cockburn CJ almost a century and a half ago, but the logic is the same: in some cases, the criminal law may limit conduct and expression in order to prevent people who may see it from becoming predisposed to acting in an anti-social manner: *Butler*, at p. 484. Indeed, a particular harm envisaged in *Butler* was the "predispos[ition of] persons to act in an anti-social manner as, for example, the physical or mental mistreatment of women by men, or, what is perhaps debatable, the reverse" (p. 485).

[46] This source of harm is not confined to explicit invitations or exhortations to commit anti-social acts. As discussed in *Butler*, the inquiry embraces attitudinal harm. Conduct or material that perpetuates negative and demeaning images of humanity is

likely to undermine respect for members of the targeted groups and hence to predispose others to act in an anti-social manner towards them. Such conduct may violate formally recognized societal norms, like the equality and dignity of all human beings, which is protected by the *Canadian Charter of Rights and Freedoms* and similar fundamental laws such as the provincial human rights codes.

[47] Because this source of harm involves members of the public being exposed to the conduct or material, here too it is relevant to inquire whether the conduct is private or public. This type of harm can arise only if members of the public may be exposed to the conduct or material in question.

4.1.3.3 HARM TO PARTICIPATING INDIVIDUALS

[48] A third source of harm is the risk of physical or psychological harm to individuals involved in the conduct at issue. Sexual activity is a positive source of human expression, fulfilment and pleasure. But some kinds of sexual activity may harm those involved. Women may be forced into prostitution or other aspects of the sex trade. They may be the objects of physical and psychological assault. Sometimes they may be seriously hurt or even killed. Similar harms may be perpetrated on children and men. Sexual conduct that risks this sort of harm may violate society's declared norms in a way that is incompatible with the proper functioning of society, and hence meet the *Butler* test for indecent conduct under the *Criminal Code*.

[49] The consent of the participant will generally be significant in considering whether this type of harm is established. However, consent may be more apparent than real. Courts must always be on the lookout for the reality of victimization. Where other aspects of debased treatment are clear, harm to participating individuals may be established despite apparent consent.

· · ·

4.1.3.4 THE DEGREE OF THE HARM: HARM INCOMPATIBLE WITH THE PROPER FUNCTIONING OF CANADIAN SOCIETY

[52] At this stage, the task is to examine the degree of the harm to determine whether it is incompatible with the proper functioning of society. The threshold is high. It proclaims that as members of a diverse society, we must be prepared to tolerate conduct of which we disapprove, short of conduct that can be objectively shown beyond a reasonable doubt to interfere with the proper functioning of society.

· · ·

[56] Incompatibility with the proper functioning of society is more than a test of tolerance. The question is not what individuals or the community think about the conduct, but whether permitting it engages a harm that threatens the basic functioning of our society. This ensures in part that the harm be related to a formally recognized value, at step one. But beyond this it must be clear beyond a reasonable doubt that the conduct, not only by its nature but also in degree, rises to the level of threatening the proper functioning of our society.

[57] Whether it does so must be determined by reference to the values engaged by the particular kind of harm at stake. If the harm is based on the threat to autonomy and liberty arising from unwanted confrontation by a particular kind of sexual conduct, for

example, the Crown must establish a real risk that the way people live will be significantly and adversely affected by the conduct. The number of people unwillingly exposed to the conduct and the circumstances in which they are exposed to it are critical under this head of harm. If the only people involved in or observing the conduct were willing participants, indecency on the basis of this harm will not be made out.

[58] If the harm is based on predisposing others to anti-social behaviour, a real risk that the conduct will have this effect must be proved. Vague generalizations that the sexual conduct at issue will lead to attitudinal changes and hence anti-social behaviour will not suffice. The causal link between images of sexuality and anti-social behaviour cannot be assumed. Attitudes in themselves are not crimes, however deviant they may be or disgusting they may appear. What is required is proof of links, first between the sexual conduct at issue and the formation of negative attitudes, and second between those attitudes and real risk of anti-social behaviour.

[59] Similarly, if the harm is based on physical or psychological injury to participants, it must again be shown that the harm has occurred or that there is a real risk that this will occur. Witnesses may testify as to actual harm. Expert witnesses may give evidence on the risks of potential harm. In considering psychological harm, care must be taken to avoid substituting disgust for the conduct involved, for proof of harm to the participants. In the case of vulnerable participants, it may be easier to infer psychological harm than in cases where participants operate on an equal and autonomous basis.

[60] These are matters that can and should be established by evidence, as a general rule. When the test was the community standard of tolerance, it could be argued that judges or jurors were in a position to gauge what the community would tolerate from their own experience in the community. But a test of harm or significant risk of harm incompatible with the proper functioning of society demands more. The judge and jurors are generally unlikely to be able to gauge the risk and impact of the harm, without assistance from expert witnesses. To be sure, there may be obvious cases where no one could argue that the conduct proved in evidence is compatible with the proper functioning of society, obviating the need for an expert witness. To kill in the course of sexual conduct, to take an obvious example, would on its face be repugnant to our law and the proper functioning of our society. But in most cases, expert evidence will be required to establish that the nature and degree of the harm makes it incompatible with the proper functioning of society. In every case, a conviction must be based on evidence establishing beyond a reasonable doubt actual harm or a significant risk of actual harm. ...

[61] Where actual harm is not established and the Crown is relying on risk, the test of incompatibility with the proper functioning of society requires the Crown to establish a significant risk. Risk is a relative concept. The more extreme the nature of the harm, the lower the degree of risk that may be required to permit use of the ultimate sanction of criminal law. Sometimes, a small risk can be said to be incompatible with the proper functioning of society. For example, the risk of a terrorist attack, although small, might be so devastating in potential impact that using the criminal law to counter the risk might be appropriate. However, in most cases, the nature of the harm engendered by sexual conduct will require at least a probability that the risk will develop to justify convicting and imprisoning those engaged in or facilitating the conduct.

4.1.5 Summary of the Test

[62] Indecent criminal conduct will be established where the Crown proves beyond a reasonable doubt the following two requirements:

1. That, by its *nature*, the conduct at issue causes harm or presents a significant risk of harm to individuals or society in a way that undermines or threatens to undermine a value reflected in and thus formally endorsed through the Constitution or similar fundamental laws by, for example:

    (a) confronting members of the public with conduct that significantly interferes with their autonomy and liberty; or

    (b) predisposing others to anti-social behaviour; or

    (c) physically or psychologically harming persons involved in the conduct, and

2. That the harm or risk of harm is of a *degree* that is incompatible with the proper functioning of society.

As the above makes clear, the categories of harm capable of satisfying the first branch of the inquiry are not closed, nor is any one of the listed categories in itself an integral part of the definition of harm. For example, predisposition to anti-social behaviour, while central to this Court's analysis in *Butler*, is but one illustration of the type of harm that undermines or threatens to undermine one of society's formally recognized values.

• • •

[Bastarache and LeBel JJ dissented. They reaffirmed the community standard of tolerance test for indecency. On the facts of the case, they found that the acts in issue failed to meet the minimum standards of public morality and were therefore indecent.]

NOTE: R v. SHARPE

In 1993, the federal government enacted amendments to the *Criminal Code* prohibiting not only the production, sale, and distribution of child pornography, but also its possession. Under s. 163.1 of the *Criminal Code*, child pornography is defined as

(a) a photographic, film, video, or other visual representation, whether or not it was made by electronic or mechanical means, (i) that shows a person who is or is depicted as being under the age of eighteen years and is engaged in or is depicted as engaged in explicit sexual activity or (ii) the dominant characteristic of which is the depiction, for a sexual purpose, of a sexual organ or the anal region of a person under the age of eighteen years; or

(b) any written material or visual representation that advocates or counsels sexual activity with a person under the age of eighteen years that would be an offence under this Act.

An exemption is provided for works that have artistic merit or an educational, scientific, or medical purpose, but the onus is on the accused to prove such.

The Supreme Court of Canada upheld the law, but read in two exceptions to its application. Chief Justice McLachlin, writing for the majority, held that the possession of child pornography is a form of expression protected by s. 2(b):

The possession of [expressive] material allows us to understand the thought of others or consolidate our own thought. Without the right to possess expressive material, freedom of thought, belief, opinion and expression would be compromised.

In her s. 1 analysis, McLachlin CJC accepted that the law's objective "to criminalize possession of child pornography that poses a reasoned risk of harm to children" (at para. 82) was pressing and substantial. She also found that the means chosen were rationally connected to the law's purpose. According to McLachlin CJC:

[89] The lack of unanimity in scientific evidence is not fatal. Complex human behaviour may not lend itself to precise scientific demonstration, and the courts cannot hold Parliament to a higher standard of proof than the subject matter admits of. Some studies suggest that child pornography, like other forms of pornography, will fuel fantasies and may incite offences in the case of certain individuals. This reasoned apprehension of harm demonstrates a rational connection between the law and the reduction of harm to children through child pornography.

· · ·

[94] ... [T]he social science evidence adduced in this case, buttressed by experience and common sense, amply meets the *Oakes* requirement of a rational connection between the purpose of the law and the means adopted to effect this purpose. Possession of child pornography increases the risk of child abuse. It introduces risk, moreover, that cannot be entirely targeted by laws prohibiting the manufacture, publication and distribution of child pornography. Laws against publication and distribution of child pornography cannot catch the private viewing of child pornography, yet private viewing may induce attitudes and arousals that increase the risk of offence. Nor do such laws catch the use of pornography to groom and seduce children. Only by extending the law to private possession can these harms be squarely attacked.

However, the Chief Justice found that

[99] ... the law may also capture the possession of material that one would not normally think of as "child pornography" and that raises little or no risk of harm to children: (i) written materials or visual representations created and held by the accused alone, exclusively for personal use; and (ii) visual recordings, created by or depicting the accused, that do not depict unlawful sexual activity and held by the accused exclusively for private use.

[100] Possession of material in these categories is less closely tied to harm to children than the vast majority of material caught by the law. ... [T]he risk [involved in permitting the possession of such material] is small, incidental and more tenuous than that associated with the vast majority of material targeted by s. 163.1(4). ... The bulk of the material in these two problematic classes, while engaging important values underlying the s. 2(b) guarantee, poses no reasoned risk of harm to children.

In applying the third and final step of the proportionality requirement, "the final balance," Chief Justice McLachlin concluded:

[110] ... [I]n broad impact and general application, the limits s. 163.1(4) imposes on free expression are justified by the protection the law affords children from exploitation and abuse. I cannot, however, arrive at the same conclusion in regard to the two problematic categories of materials described above. The legislation prohibits a person from articulating thoughts in

writing or visual images, even if the result is intended only for his or her own eyes. It further prohibits a teenager from possessing, again exclusively for personal use, sexually explicit photographs or videotapes of him—or herself alone or engaged with a partner in lawful sexual activity. The inclusion of these peripheral materials in the law's prohibition trenches heavily on freedom of expression while adding little to the protection the law provides children. To this extent, the law cannot be considered proportionate in its effects, and the infringement of s. 2(b) contemplated by the legislation is not demonstrably justifiable under s. 1.

Instead of nullifying "a law that is valid in most of its application," Chief Justice McLachlin decided "to read into the law an exclusion of the problematic applications of s. 163.1":

> [114] ... [I]n my view the appropriate remedy in this case is to read into the law an exclusion of the problematic applications of s. 163.1 following *Schachter v. Canada*, [1992] 2 SCR 679 (found in Chapter 25, Enforcement of Rights). *Schachter* suggests that the problem of peripheral unconstitutional provisions or applications of a law may be addressed by striking down the legislation, severing of the offending sections ... , reading down or reading in. The Court decides on the appropriate remedy on the basis of "twin guiding principles": respect for the role of Parliament, and respect for the purposes of the Charter. Applying these principles, I conclude that in the circumstances of the case reading in an exclusion is the appropriate remedy.

She thus went on to hold:

> [128] The guarantees provided in ss. 2(b) and 7 of the Charter require the recognition of two exemptions to s. 163.1(4) [and (2)], where the prohibition's intrusion into free expression and privacy is most pronounced and its benefits most attenuated:
>
> > (a) The first exception protects the possession of expressive material created through the efforts of a single person and held by that person alone, exclusively for his or her own personal use. This exception protects deeply private expression, such as personal journals and drawings intended solely for the eyes of their creator.
> > (b) The second exemption protects a person's possession of visual recordings created by or depicting that person, but only where these recordings do not depict unlawful sexual activity, are held only for private use, and were created with the consent of those persons depicted.

QUESTIONS

Why did the Court decide to "read in" these exemptions (or read out part of the law) instead of simply striking down the law? Was the Court engaging in judicial redrafting of the legislation? What other options did the Court have? The portions of McLachlin CJC's decision dealing with the choice of remedy are more fully extracted in Chapter 25, Enforcement of Rights.

VI. CONTROLS ON ELECTION SPENDING

The *Canada Elections Act*, SC 2000, c. 9 places limits on expenditures during an election campaign by parties, candidates, and "third parties." Limits on third-party spending have been the subject of several constitutional challenges—most recently the *Harper* case, which was brought by Stephen Harper when he was President of a lobby group, the National Citizens' Coalition.

Harper v. Canada (Attorney General)
[2004] 1 SCR 827, 2004 SCC 33, 239 DLR (4th) 193

. . .

McLACHLIN CJC and MAJOR J (dissenting in part) (Binnie J concurring): [1] This Court has repeatedly held that liberal democracy demands the free expression of political opinion, and affirmed that political speech lies at the core of the *Canadian Charter of Rights and Freedoms*' guarantee of free expression. It has held that the freedom of expression includes the right to attempt to persuade through peaceful interchange. And it has observed that the electoral process is the primary means by which the average citizen participates in the public discourse that shapes our polity. The question now before us is whether these high aspirations are fulfilled by a law that effectively denies the right of an ordinary citizen to give meaningful and effective expression to her political views during a federal election campaign.

[2] The law at issue sets advertising spending limits for citizens—called third parties—at such low levels that they cannot effectively communicate with their fellow citizens on election issues during an election campaign. The practical effect is that effective communication during the writ period is confined to registered political parties and their candidates. Both enjoy much higher spending limits. This denial of effective communication to citizens violates free expression where it warrants the greatest protection—the sphere of political discourse. As in *Libman v. Quebec (Attorney General)*, [1997] 3 SCR 569, the incursion essentially denies effective free expression and far surpasses what is required to meet the perceived threat that citizen speech will drown out other political discourse. It follows that the law is inconsistent with the guarantees of the Charter and, hence, invalid.

I. Citizen Spending Limits

A. What the Law Does

[3] The *Canada Elections Act*, SC 2000, c. 9, sets limits for spending on advertising for individuals and groups. It limits citizens to spending a maximum of $3,000 in each electoral district up to a total of $150,000 nationally. Section 350 provides:

> 350(1) A third party shall not incur election advertising expenses of a total amount of more than $150,000 during an election period in relation to a general election.

(2) Not more than $3,000 of the total amount referred to in subsection (1) shall be incurred to promote or oppose the election of one or more candidates in a given electoral district, including by

    (a) naming them;

    (b) showing their likenesses;

    (c) identifying them by their respective political affiliations; or

    (d) taking a position on an issue with which they are particularly associated.

Section 350(2)(d) is particularly restrictive. It prohibits individuals from spending more than the allowed amounts on any issue with which a candidate is "particularly associated." The candidates in an election are typically associated with a wide range of views on a wide range of issues. The evidence shows that the effect of the limits is to prevent citizens from effectively communicating their views on issues during an election campaign.

[4] The limits do not permit citizens to effectively communicate through the national media. The Chief Electoral Officer testified that it costs approximately $425,000 for a one-time full-page advertisement in major Canadian newspapers. ...

[5] Nor do the limits permit citizens to communicate through the mail. The Canada Post bulk mailing rate for some ridings amounts to more than $7,500, effectively prohibiting citizens from launching a mail campaign in these ridings without exceeding the $3,000 limit.

[6] The $3,000 riding limits are further reduced by the national limit of $150,000, which precludes citizens from spending the maximum amount in each of the 308 ridings in Canada. This effectively diminishes the $3,000 riding maximum. Quite simply, it puts effective radio and television communication within constituencies or throughout the country beyond the reach of "third party" citizens.

[7] Under the limits, a citizen may place advertisements in a local paper within her constituency. She may print some flyers and distribute them by hand or post them in conspicuous places. She may write letters to the editor of regional and national newspapers and hope they will be published. In these and other ways, she may be able to reach a limited number of people on the local level. But she cannot effectively communicate her position to her fellow citizens throughout the country in the ways those intent on communicating such messages typically do—through mail-outs and advertising in the regional and national media. The citizen's message is thus confined to minor local dissemination with the result that effective local, regional and national expression of ideas becomes the exclusive right of registered political parties and their candidates.

· · ·

[9] It is therefore clear that the *Canada Elections Act*'s advertising limits prevent citizens from effectively communicating their views on election issues to their fellow citizens, restricting them instead to minor local communication. As such, they represent a serious incursion on free expression in the political realm. The Attorney General raises three reasons why this restriction is justified as a reasonable limit in a free and democratic society under s. 1 of the Charter: to ensure the equality of each citizen in elections; to prevent the voices of the wealthy from drowning out those of others; and to preserve confidence in the electoral system. Whether that is so is the question in this appeal.

B. Is the Incursion on Free Speech Justified?

(1) The Significance of the Infringement

[10] One cannot determine whether an infringement of a right is justified without examining the seriousness of the infringement. Our jurisprudence on the guarantee of the freedom of expression establishes that some types of expression are more important and hence more deserving of protection than others. To put it another way, some restrictions on freedom of expression are easier to justify than others.

[11] Political speech, the type of speech here at issue, is the single most important and protected type of expression. It lies at the core of the guarantee of free expression. ...

[12] The right of the people to discuss and debate ideas forms the very foundation of democracy ... .

[13] Section 2(b) of the Charter aims not just to guarantee a voice to registered political parties, but an equal voice to *each citizen*. The right of *each citizen* to participate in democratic discussion was embraced by Iacobucci J, who elaborated on the scope of s. 3 for the Court in *Figueroa v. Canada (Attorney General)*, [2003] 1 SCR 912, 2003 SCC 37, at para. 26:

> Section 3 does not advert to the composition of Parliament subsequent to an election, but only to the right of each citizen to a certain level of participation in the electoral process. *On its very face, then, the central focus of s. 3 is the right of each citizen to participate in the electoral process. This signifies that the right of each citizen to participate in the political life of the country is one that is of fundamental importance in a free and democratic society and suggests that s. 3 should be interpreted in a manner that ensures that this right of participation embraces a content commensurate with the importance of individual participation in the selection of elected representatives in a free and democratic state.* Defining the purpose of s. 3 with reference to the right of *each citizen* to play a *meaningful* role in the electoral process, rather than the composition of Parliament subsequent to an election, better ensures that the right of participation that s. 3 explicitly protects is not construed too narrowly. [Emphasis added.]

[14] Permitting an effective voice for unpopular and minority views—views political parties may not embrace—is essential to deliberative democracy. The goal should be to bring the views of all citizens into the political arena for consideration, be they accepted or rejected at the end of the day. Free speech in the public square may not be curtailed merely because one might find the message unappetizing or the messenger distasteful (*Figueroa, supra*, at para. 28):

> Put simply, full political debate ensures that ours is an open society with the benefit of a broad range of ideas and opinions. ... This, in turn, ensures not only that policy makers are aware of a broad range of options, but also that the determination of social policy is sensitive to the needs and interests of a broad range of citizens.

Participation in political debate "is ... the primary means by which the average citizen participates in the open debate that animates the determination of social policy"; see *Figueroa*, at para. 29.

[15] The right to participate in political discourse is a right to *effective* participation—for each citizen to play a "meaningful" role in the democratic process, to borrow

again from the language of *Figueroa*. In *Committee for the Commonwealth* [*of Canada v. Canada*, [1991] 1 SCR 139], at p. 250, McLachlin J stated that s. 2(b) aspires to protect "the interest of the individual in *effectively communicating* his or her message to members of the public" (emphasis added). In the same case, Lamer CJ declared that "it must be understood that the individual has an interest in communicating his ideas in a place which, because of the presence of listeners, will favour *the effective dissemination* of what he has to say" (emphasis added); see *Committee for the Commonwealth*, at p. 154.

[16] The ability to engage in effective speech in the public square means nothing if it does not include the ability to attempt to persuade one's fellow citizens through debate and discussion. This is the kernel from which reasoned political discourse emerges. Freedom of expression must allow a citizen to give voice to her vision for her community and nation, to advocate change through the art of persuasion in the hope of improving her life and indeed the larger social, political and economic landscape ... .

[17] Freedom of expression protects not only the individual who speaks the message, but also the recipient. Members of the public—as viewers, listeners and readers—have a right to information on public governance, absent which they cannot cast an informed vote.... . Thus the *Charter* protects listeners as well as speakers; see *Ford v. Quebec (Attorney General)*, [1988] 2 SCR 712, at pp. 766-67.

· · ·

[19] The *Canada Elections Act* undercuts the right to listen by withholding from voters an ingredient that is critical to their individual and collective deliberation: substantive analysis and commentary on political issues of the day. The spending limits impede the ability of citizens to communicate with one another through public fora and media during elections and curtail the diversity of perspectives heard and assessed by the electorate. Because citizens cannot mount effective national television, radio and print campaigns, the only sustained messages voters see and hear during the course of an election campaign are from political parties.

[20] It is clear that the right here at issue is of vital importance to Canadian democracy. In the democracy of ancient Athens, all citizens were able to meet and discuss the issues of the day in person. In our modern democracy, we cannot speak personally with each of our fellow citizens. We can convey our message only through methods of mass communication. Advertising through mail-outs and the media is one of the most effective means of communication on a large scale. We need only look at the reliance of political parties on advertising to realize how important it is to actually reaching citizens—in a word, to effective participation. The ability to speak in one's own home or on a remote street corner does not fulfill the objective of the guarantee of freedom of expression, which is that each citizen be afforded the opportunity to present her views for public consumption and attempt to persuade her fellow citizens. Pell J's observation could not be more apt: "[s]peech without effective communication is not speech but an idle monologue in the wilderness"; see *United States v. Dellinger*, 472 F.2d 340 (7th Cir. 1972), at p. 415.

[21] This is the perspective from which we must approach the question whether the limitation on citizen spending is justified. It is no answer to say that the citizen can speak through a registered political party. The citizen may hold views not espoused by a registered party. The citizen has a right to communicate those views. The right to do so is essential to the effective debate upon which our democracy rests, and lies at the core of the

free expression guarantee. That does not mean that the right cannot be limited. But it does mean that limits on it must be supported by a clear and convincing demonstration that they are necessary, do not go too far, and enhance more than harm the democratic process.

(2) The Law's Objective: Is It Pressing and Substantial?

[22] …The Attorney General states that the objective of the legislation is to promote fair elections.

[23] In more concrete terms, the limits are purported to further three objectives: first, to favour equality, by preventing those with greater means from dominating electoral debate; second, to foster informed citizenship, by ensuring that some positions are not drowned out by others (this is related to the right to participate in the political process by casting an informed vote); third, to enhance public confidence by ensuring equality, a better informed citizenship and fostering the appearance and reality of fairness in the democratic process.

[24] These are worthy social purposes, endorsed as pressing and substantial by this Court in *Libman, supra*, at para. 47:

> Elections are fair and equitable only if all citizens are reasonably informed of all the possible choices and if parties and candidates are given a reasonable opportunity to present their positions so that election discourse is not dominated by those with access to greater financial resources.

. . .

[26] Common sense dictates that promoting electoral fairness is a pressing and substantial objective in our liberal democracy, even in the absence of evidence that past elections have been unfair … .

. . .

C. Proportionality

. . .

[31] The real question in this case … is whether the limits go too far in their incursion on free political expression.

. . .

[33] It is impossible to say whether an infringement is carefully tailored to the asserted goals without having some idea of the actual seriousness of the problem being addressed. The yardstick by which excessive interference with rights is measured is the need for the remedial infringement. If a serious problem is demonstrated, more serious measures may be needed to tackle it. Conversely, if a problem is only hypothetical, severe curtailments on an important right may be excessive.

[34] …The Attorney General presented no evidence that wealthier Canadians—alone or in concert—will dominate political debate during the electoral period absent limits. It offered only the hypothetical possibility that, without limits on citizen spending, problems could arise. If, as urged by the Attorney General, wealthy Canadians are poised to hijack this country's election process, an expectation of some evidence to that effect is reasonable. Yet none was presented. This minimizes the Attorney General's assertions of

necessity and lends credence to the argument that the legislation is an overreaction to a non-existent problem.

[35] On the other side of the equation, the infringement on the right is severe. We earlier reviewed the stringency of the limits. They prevent citizens from effectively communicating with their fellow citizens on election issues during a campaign. Any communication beyond the local level is effectively rendered impossible, and even at that level is seriously curtailed. The spending limits do not allow citizens to express themselves through mail-outs within certain ridings, radio and television media, nor the national press. Citizens are limited to 1.3 percent of the expenditures of registered political parties. This is significantly lower than other countries that have also imposed citizen spending limits. It is not an exaggeration to say that the limits imposed on citizens amount to a virtual ban on their participation in political debate during the election period. In actuality, the only space left in the marketplace of ideas is for political parties and their candidates. The right of each citizen to have her voice heard, so vaunted in *Figueroa, supra*, is effectively negated unless the citizen is able or willing to speak through a political party.

· · ·

[38] There is no demonstration that limits this draconian are required to meet the perceived dangers of inequality, an uninformed electorate and the public perception that the system is unfair. On the contrary, the measures may themselves exacerbate these dangers. Citizens who cannot effectively communicate with others on electoral issues may feel they are being treated unequally compared to citizens who speak through political parties. The absence of their messages may result in the public being less well informed than it would otherwise be. And a process that bans citizens from effective participation in the electoral debate during an election campaign may well be perceived as unfair. These fears may be hypothetical, but no more so than the fears conjured by the Attorney General in support of the infringement.

[39] This is not to suggest that election spending limits are never permissible. On the contrary, this Court in *Libman* has recognized that they are an acceptable, even desirable, tool to ensure fairness and faith in the electoral process. Limits that permit citizens to conduct effective and persuasive communication with their fellow citizens might well meet the minimum impairment test. The problem here is that the draconian nature of the infringement—to effectively deprive all those who do not or cannot speak through political parties of their voice during an election period—overshoots the perceived danger. Even recognizing that "[t]he tailoring process seldom admits of perfection" (*RJR-MacDonald [Inc. v. Canada (Attorney General)*, [1995] 3 SCR 199], at para. 160), and according Parliament a healthy measure of deference, we are left with the fact that nothing in the evidence suggests that a virtual ban on citizen communication through effective advertising is required to avoid the hypothetical evils of inequality, a misinformed public and loss of public confidence in the system.

[McLachlin CJC and Major J now move to the proportionality branch of the *Oakes* test.]

[41] Given the unproven and speculative nature of the danger the limits are said to address, the possible benefits conferred by the law are illusory. The smaller the danger, the less the benefit conferred. Yet the infringement is serious. It denies the citizen the

right of effective political communication except through a registered party. The denial is made all the more serious because political expression lies at the heart of the guarantee of free expression and underpins the very foundation of our democracy. The measures may actually cause more inequality, less civic engagement and greater disrepute than they avoid. In the absence of any evidence to the contrary, it cannot be said that the infringement does more good than harm.

[42] Having had the advantage of reviewing the reasons of Bastarache J, we believe it is important to make three observations. First, whether or not citizens dispose of sufficient funds to meet or exceed the existing spending limits is irrelevant. What is important is that citizens have the capacity, should they so choose, to exercise their right to free political speech. The spending limits as they currently stand do not allow this. Instead, they have a chilling effect on political speech, forcing citizens into a Hobson's choice between not expressing themselves at all or having their voice reduced to a mere whisper. Faced with such options, citizens could not be faulted for choosing the former.

[43] Second, it is important to recognize that the spending limits do not constrain the right of only a few citizens to speak. They constrain the political speech of all Canadians, be they of superior or modest means. Whether it is a citizen incurring expenditures of $3001 for leafleting in her riding or a group of citizens pooling 1501 individual contributions of $100 to run a national advertising campaign, the Charter protects the right to free political speech.

[44] Finally, even it *were* true that spending limits constrained the political speech rights of only a few citizens, it would be no answer to say, as suggests Bastarache J, at para. 112, that few citizens can afford to spend more than the limits anyway. This amounts to saying that even if the breach of s. 2(b) is not justified, it does not matter because it affects only a few people. Charter breaches cannot be justified on this basis. Moreover, one may question the premise that only a few people are affected by the spending limits. Indeed, if so few can afford to spend more than the existing limits, why, one may ask, are they needed?

· · ·

BASTARACHE J (Iacobucci, Arbour, LeBel, Deschamps, and Fish JJ concurring):

I. *Introduction*

[50] At issue in this appeal is whether the third party spending provisions of the *Canada Elections Act*, SC 2000, c. 9, violate ss. 2(b), 2(d) and 3 of the *Canadian Charter of Rights and Freedoms*. ...

V. *Analysis*

A. *Third Party Electoral Advertising Regime*

[55] Numerous groups and organizations participate in the electoral process as third parties. They do so to achieve three purposes. First, third parties may seek to influence the outcome of an election by commenting on the merits and faults of a particular candidate or political party. In this respect, the influence of third parties is most pronounced

in electoral districts with "marginal seats," in other words, in electoral districts where the incumbent does not have a significant advantage. Second, third parties may add a fresh perspective or new dimension to the discourse surrounding one or more issues associated with a candidate or political party. While third parties are true electoral participants, their role and the extent of their participation, like candidates and political parties, cannot be unlimited. Third, they may add an issue to the political debate and in some cases force candidates and political parties to address it.

[56] Third party spending limits in Canada have a long and litigious history. Limits on third party spending, together with limits on candidate and political party spending, were introduced in 1974 in the *Canada Elections Act*, pursuant to the recommendations of the Barbeau Committee (*Report of the Committee on Election Expenses* (1966)). Parliament prohibited all independent election spending that directly promoted or opposed a particular candidate or political party (Lortie Report, [Canada, Royal Commission on Electoral Reform and Party Financing, *Reforming Electoral Democracy: Final Report* (Ottawa, 1991)], at pp. 327-28). The constitutionality of this prohibition was successfully challenged in *National Citizens' Coalition Inc. v. Attorney General of Canada* (1984), 32 Alta. LR (2d) 249 (QB). Although the decision was binding only in Alberta, Elections Canada decided not to enforce the prohibition elsewhere in the country (Lortie Report, p. 332). Following the 1988 federal election, Parliament commissioned another Royal Commission, the Lortie Commission, and ultimately re-enacted third party spending limits; see ss. 259.1(1) and 259.2(2) of the *Canada Elections Act*, RSC 1985, c. E-2. The Alberta Court of Appeal declared these federal limits unconstitutional in *Somerville v. Canada (Attorney General)* (1996), 184 AR 241.

[57] Parliament enacted new third party spending limits as part of a larger third party electoral advertising regime in the 2000 *Canada Elections Act*. Part 17 of the Act, ss. 349 to 362, creates a scheme that limits the advertising expenses of individuals and groups who are not candidates or political parties. The scheme also requires such expenses to be reported to the Chief Electoral Officer. The regime can be broadly divided into four parts. First, s. 350 limits election advertising expenses to $3,000 in a given electoral district and $150,000 nationally. "[E]lection advertising" is defined in s. 319 of the Act as follows:

> "election advertising" means the transmission to the public by any means during an election period of an advertising message that promotes or opposes a registered party or the election of a candidate, including one that takes a position on an issue with which a registered party or candidate is associated. ...

Thus, the limits do not apply to third party advertising prior to the election period or to advertising which promotes an issue that is not associated with a candidate or political party. The second part of the regime is closely related to s. 350 as it prohibits individuals or groups from splitting or colluding for the purposes of circumventing the election advertising limits. Third, the attribution, registration and disclosure provisions (ss. 352 to 357, 359, 360 and 362) require a third party to identify itself in all of its election advertising and, under certain circumstances, to appoint financial agents and auditors who are required to record expenses, to register with, and to report to the Chief Electoral Officer who, in turn, makes this information available to the public. Finally, although s. 323 is not strictly part of the third party electoral advertising regime, third parties are also subject to the advertising blackout on polling day.

. . .

[59] This case represents the first opportunity for this Court to determine the constitutionality of the third party election advertising regime established by Parliament. This Court has however previously considered the constitutionality of limits on independent spending in the regulation of referendums in *Libman, supra*.

B. Libman v. Quebec (Attorney General)

[60] In *Libman*, the Court was asked to determine the constitutionality of the independent spending limits set out in Quebec's referenda legislation, the *Referendum Act*, RSQ, c. C-64.1. The impugned provisions of the *Referendum Act* circumscribed groups' or individuals' participation in a referendum campaign by requiring that they join the national committee supporting their position or by affiliating themselves with it. Only the national committees and the affiliated groups were permitted to incur "regulated expenses," which were effectively advertising expenses. Mr. Libman did not wish to endorse either position advocated by the national committee. Rather than supporting the "yes" or "no" position, Mr. Libman advocated in favour of abstaining from the vote. Mr. Libman argued that the impugned provisions infringed his rights to freedom of political expression and freedom of association because they restricted campaign expenditures conducted independently of the national committees.

[61] The Court agreed that the limits on independent spending set out in the *Referendum Act* were not justified. The Court did, however, endorse spending limits as an essential means of promoting fairness in referenda and elections which the Court held were parallel processes: *Libman*, at para. 46. The Court, relying on the Lortie Report, endorsed several principles applicable to the regulation of election spending generally and of independent or third party spending specifically. They include (at paras. 47-50):

[1] If the principle of fairness in the political sphere is to be preserved, it cannot be presumed that all persons have the same financial resources to communicate with the electorate. ... To ensure a right of equal participation in democratic government, laws limiting spending are needed to preserve the equality of democratic rights and ensure that one person's exercise of the freedom to spend does not hinder the communication opportunities of others. *Owing to the competitive nature of elections, such spending limits are necessary to prevent the most affluent from monopolizing election discourse and consequently depriving their opponents of a reasonable opportunity to speak and be heard* [equal dissemination of points of view].

[2] Spending limits are also necessary to guarantee the *right of electors to be adequately informed of all the political positions* advanced by the candidates and by the various political parties [free and informed vote]. ...

[3] For spending limits to be fully effective, *they must apply to all possible election expenses*, including those of independent individuals and groups [application to all-effectiveness of spending limits generally]. ...

[4] The actions of independent individuals and groups can [either] directly or indirectly support one of the parties or candidates, thereby resulting in an imbalance in the financial resources each candidate or political party is permitted. ... "At elections, *the advocacy of issue positions inevitably has consequences for election discourse and thus has partisan implications, either direct or indirect*: voters cast their ballots for candidates and not for issues" [issue advocacy vs partisan advocacy.] ...

[5] It is also important to *limit independent spending more strictly than spending by candidates or political parties*. ... [O]wing to their numbers, the impact of such spending on one of the candidates or political parties to the detriment of the others could be disproportionate [application to all-effectiveness of spending limits generally]. [Emphasis added.]

[62] The Court's conception of electoral fairness as reflected in the foregoing principles is consistent with the egalitarian model of elections adopted by Parliament as an essential component of our democratic society. This model is premised on the notion that individuals should have an equal opportunity to participate in the electoral process. Under this model, wealth is the main obstacle to equal participation; see C. Feasby, "*Libman v. Quebec (AG)* and the Administration of the Process of Democracy under the Charter: The Emerging Egalitarian Model" (1999), 44 *McGill* LJ 5. Thus, the egalitarian model promotes an electoral process that requires the wealthy to be prevented from controlling the electoral process to the detriment of others with less economic power. The state can equalize participation in the electoral process in two ways; see O.M. Fiss, *The Irony of Free Speech* (1996), at p. 4. First, the State can provide a voice to those who might otherwise not be heard. The Act does so by reimbursing candidates and political parties and by providing broadcast time to political parties. Second, the State can restrict the voices which dominate the political discourse so that others may be heard as well. In Canada, electoral regulation has focussed on the latter by regulating electoral spending through comprehensive election finance provisions. These provisions seek to create a level playing field for those who wish to engage in the electoral discourse. This, in turn, enables voters to be better informed; no one voice is overwhelmed by another. In contrast, the libertarian model of elections favours an electoral process subject to as few restrictions as possible.

[63] The current third party election advertising regime is Parliament's response to this Court's decision in *Libman*. The regime is clearly structured on the egalitarian model of elections. The overarching objective of the regime is to promote electoral fairness by creating equality in the political discourse. The regime promotes the equal dissemination of points of view by limiting the election advertising of third parties who, as this Court has recognized, are important and influential participants in the electoral process. The advancement of equality and fairness in elections ultimately encourages public confidence in the electoral system. Thus, broadly speaking, the third party election advertising regime is consistent with an egalitarian conception of elections and the principles endorsed by this Court in *Libman*.

· · ·

C. Election Advertising Expense Limits

(1) Freedom of Expression

[66] The appellant rightly concedes that the limits on election advertising expenses infringe s. 2(b) of the Charter. Most third party election advertising constitutes political expression and therefore lies at the core of the guarantee of free expression. As discussed below, in some circumstances, third party election advertising may be less deserving of constitutional protection where it seeks to manipulate voters.

[Bastarache J found that the section did not breach s. 3 of the Charter, the right to vote.]

(3) The Section 1 Justification Applicable to the Infringement of Freedom of Expression

[75] The central issue at this stage of the analysis is the nature and sufficiency of the evidence required for the Attorney General to demonstrate that the limits imposed on freedom of expression are reasonable and justifiable in a free and democratic society. The Attorney General of Canada alleges that the lower courts erred in requiring scientific proof that harm had actually occurred and, specifically, by requiring conclusive proof that third party advertising influences voters and election outcomes, rendering them unfair.

[76] This is not the first time the Court has addressed the standard of proof the Crown must satisfy in demonstrating possible harm. Nor is it the first time that the Court has been faced with conflicting social science evidence regarding the problem that Parliament seeks to address. Indeed, in *Thomson Newspapers* [*Co. v. Canada (Attorney General)*, [1998] 1 SCR 877], this Court addressed the nature and sufficiency of evidence required when Parliament adopts a regulatory regime to govern the electoral process. The context of the impugned provision determines the type of proof that a court will require of the legislature to justify its measures under s. 1; see *Thomson Newspapers*, at para. 88. As this pivotal issue affects the entire s. 1 analysis, it is helpful to consider the contextual factors at the outset.

(a) Contextual Factors

(i) THE NATURE OF THE HARM AND THE INABILITY TO MEASURE IT

[77] The legislature is not required to provide scientific proof based on concrete evidence of the problem it seeks to address in every case. Where the court is faced with inconclusive or competing social science evidence relating the harm to the legislature's measures, the court may rely on a reasoned apprehension of that harm.

[78] This Court has, in the absence of determinative scientific evidence, relied on logic, reason and some social science evidence in the course of the justification analysis in several cases; see *R v. Butler*, [1992] 1 SCR 452, at p. 503; *R v. Keegstra*, [1990] 3 SCR 697, at pp. 768 and 776; *RJR-MacDonald Inc. v. Canada (Attorney General)*, [1995] 3 SCR 199, at para. 137; *Thomson Newspapers, supra*, at paras. 104-7; *R v. Sharpe*, [2001] 1 SCR 45, 2001 SCC 2. In *RJR-MacDonald*, the Court held, in the absence of direct scientific evidence showing a causal link between advertising bans and a decrease in tobacco

consumption/use, that as a matter of logic advertising bans and package warnings lead to a reduction in tobacco use; see paras. 155-58. McLachlin J held, at para. 137, that:

> Discharge of the civil standard does not require scientific demonstration; the balance of probabilities may be established by the application of common sense to what is known, even though what is known may be deficient from a scientific point of view.

In *Thomson Newspapers*, the evidence as to the influence of polls on voter choice was uncertain. Nevertheless, the majority of the Court concluded, as a matter of logic assisted by some social science evidence, that the possible influence of polls on voter choice was a legitimate harm that Parliament could seek to remedy, and was thus a pressing and substantial objective; see paras. 104-107.

[79] Similarly, the nature of the harm and the efficaciousness of Parliament's remedy in this case is difficult, if not impossible, to measure scientifically. The harm which Parliament seeks to address can be broadly articulated as electoral unfairness. Several experts, as well as the Lortie Commission, concluded that unlimited third party advertising can undermine election fairness in several ways. First, it can lead to the dominance of the political discourse by the wealthy ... . Second, it may allow candidates and political parties to circumvent their own spending limits through the creation of third parties ... . Third, unlimited third party spending can have an unfair effect on the outcome of an election ... . Fourth, the absence of limits on third party advertising expenses can erode the confidence of the Canadian electorate who perceive the electoral process as being dominated by the wealthy. This harm is difficult, if not impossible, to measure because of the subtle ways in which advertising influences human behaviour; the influence of other factors such as the media and polls; and the multitude of issues, candidates and independent parties involved in the electoral process. In light of these difficulties, logic and reason assisted by some social science evidence is sufficient proof of the harm that Parliament seeks to remedy.

(ii) VULNERABILITY OF THE GROUP

[80] Third party spending limits seek to protect two groups. First, the limits seek to protect the Canadian electorate by ensuring that it is possible to hear from all groups and thus promote a more informed vote. Generally, the Canadian electorate "must be presumed to have a certain degree of maturity and intelligence"; see *Thomson Newspapers*, *supra*, at para. 101. Where, however, third party advertising seeks to systematically manipulate the voter, the Canadian electorate may be seen as more vulnerable; see *Thomson Newspapers*, at para. 114.

[81] The members of the second group protected by the legislation are candidates and political parties. The appellant argues that the provisions seek to ensure that candidates and political parties have an equal opportunity to present their positions to the electorate. As discussed in *Figueroa* [*v. Canada (Attorney General)*, [2003] 1 SCR 912], at para. 41, all political parties, whether large or small, are "capable of acting as a vehicle for the participation of individual citizens in the public discourse that animates the determination of social policy." Thus, regardless of their size, political parties are important to the democratic process. Nevertheless, neither candidates nor political parties can be said to be vulnerable.

(iii) SUBJECTIVE FEARS AND APPREHENSION OF HARM

[82] Perception is of utmost importance in preserving and promoting the electoral regime in Canada. Professor Aucoin emphasized that "[p]ublic *perceptions* are critical precisely because the legitimacy of the election regime depends upon how citizens assess the extent to which the regime advances the values of their electoral democracy" (emphasis in original). Electoral fairness is key. Where Canadians perceive elections to be unfair, voter apathy follows shortly thereafter.

[83] Several surveys indicate that Canadians view third party spending limits as an effective means of advancing electoral fairness. Indeed, in *Libman, supra*, at para. 52, the Court relied on the survey conducted by the Lortie Commission illustrating that 75 percent of Canadians supported limits on spending by interest groups to conclude that spending limits are important to maintain public confidence in the electoral system.

(iv) THE NATURE OF THE INFRINGED ACTIVITY: POLITICAL EXPRESSION

[84] Third party advertising is political expression. Whether it is partisan or issue-based, third party advertising enriches the political discourse (Lortie Report, *supra*, at p. 340). As such, the election advertising of third parties lies at the core of the expression guaranteed by the Charter and warrants a high degree of constitutional protection. ...

[85] In some circumstances, however, third party advertising will be less deserving of constitutional protection. Indeed, it is possible that third parties having access to significant financial resources can manipulate political discourse to their advantage through political advertising. In *Thomson Newspapers, supra*, at para. 94, the majority of the Court explained:

> [U]nder certain circumstances, the nature of the interests (i.e., a single party or faction with a great preponderance of financial resources) of the speakers could make the expression itself inimical to the exercise of a free and informed choice by others.

There is no evidence before the Court that indicates that third party advertising seeks to be manipulative. Nor is there any evidence that third parties wish to use their advertising dollars to *smear* candidates or engage in other forms of *non-political* discourse. Nevertheless, the danger that political advertising may manipulate or oppress the voter means that some deference to the means chosen by Parliament is warranted.

[86] The Attorney General of Canada argues that although the impugned provisions limit the political expression of some, the provisions enhance the political expression of others. This Court explored this dichotomy in *Libman, supra*, at para. 61:

> ... the legislature's objective, namely to enhance the exercise of the right to vote, must be borne in mind. Thus, while the impugned provisions do in a way restrict one of the most basic forms of expression, namely political expression, *the legislature must be accorded a certain deference to enable it to arbitrate between the democratic values of freedom of expression and referendum fairness.* The latter is related to the very values the Canadian Charter seeks to protect, in particular the political equality of citizens that is at the heart of a free and democratic society. *The impugned provisions impose a balance between the financial resources available to the proponents of each option* in order to ensure that the vote by the people will be free and informed and that the discourse of each option can be heard. *To attain this*

objective, the legislature had to try to strike a balance between absolute freedom of individual
expression and equality among the different expressions for the benefit of all. From this point
of view, the impugned provisions are therefore not purely restrictive of freedom of expression.
Their primary purpose is to promote political expression by ensuring an equal dissemination
of points of view and thereby truly respecting democratic traditions. [Emphasis added.]

Further, by limiting political expression, the spending limits bring greater balance to the
political discourse and allow for more meaningful participation in the electoral process.
Thus, the provisions also enhance a second Charter right, the right to vote.

[87] Under the egalitarian model of elections, Parliament must balance the rights and
privileges of the participants in the electoral process: candidates, political parties, third
parties and voters. Advertising expense limits may restrict free expression to ensure that
participants are able to meaningfully participate in the electoral process. For candidates,
political parties and third parties, meaningful participation means the ability to inform
voters of their position. For voters, meaningful participation means the ability to hear
and weigh many points of view. The difficulties of striking this balance are evident. Given
the right of Parliament to choose Canada's electoral model and the nuances inherent in
implementing this model, the Court must approach the justification analysis with deference. The lower courts erred in failing to do so (Paperny JA, at para. 135). In the end, the
electoral system, which regulates many aspects of an election, including its duration and
the control and reimbursement of expenses, reflects a political choice, the details of
which are better left to Parliament.

[88] On balance, the contextual factors favour a deferential approach to Parliament
in determining whether the third party advertising expense limits are demonstrably justified in a free and democratic society. Given the difficulties in measuring this harm, a
reasoned apprehension that the absence of third party election advertising limits will
lead to electoral unfairness is sufficient.

[Bastarache J rejects the argument that the third party advertising regime is too vague as
to constitute a limit prescribed by law.]

(c) Is the Objective Pressing and Substantial?

[91] The overarching objective of the third party election advertising limits is electoral fairness. Equality in the political discourse promotes electoral fairness and is
achieved, in part, by restricting the participation of those who have access to significant
financial resources. The more voices that have access to the political discourse, the more
voters will be empowered to exercise their right in a meaningful and informed manner.
Canadians understandably have greater confidence in an electoral system which ultimately encourages increased participation.

[92] ... More narrowly characterized, the objectives of the third party election advertising scheme are threefold: first, to promote equality in the political discourse; second, to protect the integrity of the financing regime applicable to candidates and parties;
and third, to ensure that voters have confidence in the electoral process.

[93] As discussed, the Attorney General of Canada does not need to provide evidence of actual harm to demonstrate that each objective is pressing and substantial; see

Butler, supra, Sharpe, supra; RJR-MacDonald, supra. The lower courts effectively required scientific proof that, in Canada, the absence of third party spending limits has rendered Canadian elections unfair. The lower courts sought evidence establishing that third party advertising influences the electorate in a disproportionate way ... . To require the Attorney General to produce definitive social science evidence establishing the causes of every area of social concern would be to place an unreasonably high onus on the Attorney General. In this case, the Attorney General adduced sufficient informed evidence of the importance of electoral regulation in our free and democratic society.

[94] In this case, the Lortie Report is the central piece of the evidentiary record establishing the possible harm engendered by uncontrolled third party advertising and justifying the limits set by Parliament on the advertising expenses of third parties.

• • •

[100] In my view, the findings of the Lortie Report can be relied upon in this appeal to determine whether the third party advertising limits are justified. ...

(i) TO PROMOTE EQUALITY IN THE POLITICAL DISCOURSE

[101] As discussed, the central component of the egalitarian model is equality in the political discourse; see *Libman*, at para. 61. Equality in the political discourse promotes full political debate and is important in maintaining both the integrity of the electoral process and the fairness of election outcomes; see *Libman*, at para. 47. Such concerns are always pressing and substantial "in any society that purports to operate in accordance with the tenets of a free and democratic society"; see *Harvey* [*v. New Brunswick (Attorney General)*, [1996] 2 SCR 876], at para. 38.

(ii) TO PROTECT THE INTEGRITY OF THE FINANCING REGIME APPLICABLE TO
    CANDIDATES AND PARTIES

[102] The primary mechanism by which the state promotes equality in the political discourse is through the electoral financing regime. The Court emphasized the importance of this regime in *Figueroa*, at para. 72:

> The systems and regulations that govern the process by which governments are formed should not be easily compromised. Electoral financing is an integral component of that process, and thus it is of great importance that the integrity of the electoral financing regime be preserved.

Accordingly, protecting the integrity of spending limits applicable to candidates and parties is a pressing and substantial objective.

(iii) TO MAINTAIN CONFIDENCE IN THE ELECTORAL PROCESS

[103] Maintaining confidence in the electoral process is essential to preserve the integrity of the electoral system which is the cornerstone of Canadian democracy. In *R v. Oakes*, [1986] 1 SCR 103, at p. 136, Dickson CJ concluded that faith in social and political institutions, which enhance the participation of individuals and groups in society, is of central importance in a free and democratic society. If Canadians lack confidence in the electoral system, they will be discouraged from participating in a meaningful way in the

electoral process. More importantly, they will lack faith in their elected representatives. Confidence in the electoral process is, therefore, a pressing and substantial objective.

(d) Rational Connection

[104] At this stage of the analysis, the Attorney General "must show a causal connection between the infringement and the benefit sought on the basis of reason or logic"; see *RJR-MacDonald, supra*, at para. 153. The lower courts erred by demanding too stringent a level of proof, in essence, by requiring the Attorney General to establish an empirical connection between third party spending limits and the objectives of s. 350. There is sufficient evidence establishing a rational connection between third party advertising expense limits and promoting equality in the political discourse, protecting the integrity of the financing regime applicable to candidates and parties, and maintaining confidence in the electoral process.

(i) TO PROMOTE EQUALITY IN THE POLITICAL DISCOURSE

[105] To establish that third party advertising expense limits promote equality in the political discourse, the Attorney General must establish, first, that political advertising influences voters, and second, that in the absence of regulation some voices could dominate and, in effect, drown others out.

[106] The majority of the Court of Appeal concluded, at para. 114, that the social science evidence of the impact of political advertising on voters was inconclusive. Professor Aucoin (in evidence) elucidated why there was a paucity of conclusive social science evidence:

> [T]here is no *prima facie* reason, or evidence, for the claim that the advertising of third parties can never have its desired effect. It is advertising like all other advertising: sometimes it works, in the sense that it has its intended effects; sometimes it does not (as in having no effect, or having a negative or perverse effect). As with candidate and political party spending on advertising, there are other factors at work and certain conditions must exist for advertising to have its intended effect. Third parties cannot simply spend on advertising and always expect to have influence, anymore than candidates or parties can expect to "buy" elections.

That political advertising influences voters accords with logic and reason. Surely, political parties, candidates, interest groups and corporations for that matter would not spend a significant amount of money on advertising if it was ineffective. Indeed, advertising is the primary expenditure of candidates and political parties.

[107] Where advertising influences the electorate, and those who have access to significant financial resources are able to purchase an unlimited amount of advertising, it follows that they will be able to dominate the electoral discourse to the detriment of others, both speakers and listeners. An upper limit on the amount that third parties can dedicate to political advertising curtails their ability to dominate the electoral debate. Thus, third party advertising expense limits are rationally connected to promoting equality in the political discourse.

(ii) TO PROTECT THE INTEGRITY OF THE FINANCING REGIME APPLICABLE TO
     CANDIDATES AND PARTIES

[108] Third party advertising can directly support a particular candidate or political party. Third party advertising can also indirectly support a candidate or political party by taking a position on an issue associated with that candidate or political party. In effect, third party advertising can create an imbalance between the financial resources of each candidate or political party; see *Libman, supra*, at para. 44. For candidate and political party spending limits to be truly effective, the advertising expenses of third parties must also be limited. Indeed, the Lortie Commission concluded that the electoral financing regime would be destroyed if third party advertising was not limited concomitantly with candidate and political party spending … . The Commission explained, at p. 327 of the Lortie Report:

> If individuals or groups were permitted to run parallel campaigns augmenting the spending of certain candidates or parties, those candidates or parties would have an unfair advantage over others not similarly supported. At the same time, candidates or parties who were the target of spending by individuals or groups opposed to their election would be put at a disadvantage compared with those who were not targeted. Should such activity become widespread, the purpose of the legislation would be destroyed, the reasonably equal opportunity the legislation seeks to establish would vanish, and the overall goal of restricting the role of money in unfairly influencing election outcomes would be defeated.

Thus, limiting third party advertising expenses is rationally connected with preserving the integrity of the financing regime set for candidates and parties.

(iii) TO MAINTAIN CONFIDENCE IN THE ELECTORAL PROCESS

[109] Limits on third party advertising expenses foster confidence in the electoral process in three ways. The limits address the perception that candidates and political parties can circumvent their spending limits through the creation of *special interest groups*. The limits also prevent the possibility that the wealthy can dominate the electoral discourse and dictate the outcome of elections. Finally, the limits assist in preventing overall advertising expenses from escalating. Thus, third party advertising expense limits advance the perception that access to the electoral discourse does not require wealth to be competitive with other electoral participants. Canadians, in turn, perceive the electoral process as substantively fair as it provides for a reasonable degree of equality between citizens who wish to participate in that process.

(e) Minimal Impairment

· · ·

[111] The contextual factors speak to the degree of deference to be accorded to the particular means chosen by Parliament to implement a legislative purpose; see *Thomson Newspapers, supra*, at para. 111. In this case, the contextual factors indicate that the Court should afford deference to the balance Parliament has struck between political expression and meaningful participation in the electoral process. As Berger JA in dissent aptly noted, at para. 268, "[t]he Court should not substitute judicial opinion for legislative

choice in the face of a genuine and reasonable attempt to balance the fundamental value
of freedom of expression against the need for fairness in the electoral process."

[112] The Chief Justice and Major J assert that short of spending well over $150,000
nationally and $3,000 in a given electoral district, citizens cannot effectively communi-
cate their views on election issues to their fellow citizens (para. 9). Respectfully, this ignores the fact that third party advertising is not restricted prior to the commencement
of the election period. Outside this time, the limits on third party intervention in political life do not exist. Any group or individual may freely spend money or advertise to
make its views known or to persuade others. In fact, many of these groups are not
formed for the purpose of an election but are already organized and have a continued
presence, mandate and political view which they promote. Many groups and individuals
will reinforce their message during an electoral campaign.

[113] The nature of Canada's political system must be considered when deciding
whether individuals and groups who engage in election advertising will be affected unduly by the limits set out in s. 350. First, as the Court discussed in *Figueroa*, there are few
obstacles for individuals to join existing political parties or to create their own parties to
facilitate individual participation in elections. Still, some will participate outside the
party affiliations; this explains why the existence of multiple organizations and parties of
varying sizes requires Parliament to balance their participation during the election period. Further, the reality in Canada is that regardless of the spending limits in the Act, the
vast majority of Canadian citizens simply cannot spend $150,000 nationally or $3,000 in
a given electoral district. What prevents most citizens from effectively exercising their
right of political free speech as defined by the Chief Justice and Major J is a lack of
means, not legislative restrictions. Contrary to what the Chief Justice and Major J say at
para. 44, I do not suggest that since the breach of s. 2(b) only affects a few people, it is
therefore justifiable. As discussed, the objective is to ensure the political discourse is not
dominated by those who have greater resources. The proper focus is on protecting the
right to meaningful participation of the entire electorate. Let me now examine in more
detail how this is achieved.

[114] Section 350 minimally impairs the right to free expression. The definition of
"election advertising" in s. 319 only applies to advertising that is associated with a candidate or party. Where an issue is not associated with a candidate or political party, third
parties may partake in an unlimited advertising campaign.

[115] The $3,000 limit per electoral district and $150,000 national limit allow for
meaningful participation in the electoral process while respecting the right to free expression. Why? First, because the limits established in s. 350 allow third parties to advertise in a limited way in some expensive forms of media such as television, newspaper and
radio. But, more importantly, the limits are high enough to allow third parties to engage
in a significant amount of low cost forms of advertising such as computer generated
posters or leaflets or the creation of a 1-800 number. In addition, the definition of "election advertising" in s. 319 does not apply to many forms of communication such as edi-
torials, debates, speeches, interviews, columns, letters, commentary, the news and the
Internet which constitute highly effective means of conveying information. Thus, as the
trial judge concluded, at para. 78, the limits allow for "modest, national, informational
campaigns and reasonable electoral district informational campaigns."

[116] Second, the limits set out in s. 350 are justifiably lower than the candidate and political party advertising limits, as recommended by the Lortie Commission. As this Court explained in *Libman*, *supra*, at paras. 49-50, the third party limit must be low enough to ensure that a particular candidate who is targeted by a third party has sufficient resources to respond. It cannot be forgotten that small political parties, who play an equally important role in the electoral process, may be easily overwhelmed by a third party having access to significant financial resources. The limits must also account for the fact that third parties generally have lower overall expenses than candidates and political parties. The limits must also appreciate that third parties tend to focus on one issue and may therefore achieve their objective less expensively. Thus, the limits seek to preserve a balance between the resources available to candidates and parties taking part in an election and those resources that might be available to third parties during this period. Professor Fletcher confirmed (in evidence) that the limits set out in s. 350 achieve this goal.

[117] The Chief Justice and Major J rely on the higher ratio of advertising spending limits for citizens to political parties in Britain as compared to Canada as evidence that the Canadian spending limits are too low (para. 8). In my view, this comparison is inappropriate. The British provisions apply to different categories of advertising and apply over different time periods.

[118] Certainly, one can conceive of less impairing limits. Indeed, any limit greater than $150,000 would be less impairing. Nevertheless, s. 350 satisfies this stage of the *Oakes* analysis. The limits allow third parties to inform the electorate of their message in a manner that will not overwhelm candidates, political parties or other third parties. The limits preclude the voices of the wealthy from dominating the political discourse, thereby allowing more voices to be heard. The limits allow for meaningful participation in the electoral process and encourage informed voting. The limits promote a free and democratic society.

(f) Proportionality

[119] The final stage of the *Oakes* analysis requires the Court to weigh the deleterious effects against the salutary effects.

[120] By ensuring that affluent groups or individuals do not dominate the political discourse, s. 350 promotes the political expression of those who are less affluent or less capable of obtaining access to significant financial resources and ensures that candidates and political parties who are subject to spending limits are not overwhelmed by third party advertising. Section 350 also protects the integrity of the candidate and political party spending limits by ensuring that these limits are not circumvented through the creation of phony third parties. Finally, s. 350 promotes fairness and accessibility in the electoral system and consequently increases Canadians' confidence in it.

[121] The deleterious effect of s. 350 is that the spending limits do not allow third parties to engage in unlimited political expression. That is, third parties are permitted to engage in informational but not necessarily persuasive campaigns, especially when acting alone. When weighed against the salutary effects of the legislation, the limits must be upheld. As the Court explained in *Libman*, *supra*, at para. 84:

> [P]rotecting the fairness of referendum campaigns is a laudable objective that will *necessarily* involve certain restrictions on freedom of expression. *Freedom of political expression, so*

*dear to our democratic tradition, would lose much value if it could only be exercised in a con-
text in which the economic power of the most affluent members of society constituted the ultimate guidepost of our political choices.* Nor would it be much better served by a system that
undermined the confidence of citizens in the referendum process. [First emphasis in original; second emphasis added.]

Accordingly, s. 350 should be upheld as a demonstrably justified limit in a free and
democratic society.

[The majority decision upheld other provisions of the *Canada Elections Act*, most notably the ban on transmitting election advertising on polling day.]

Appeal allowed.

NOTES AND QUESTIONS

1. In its earlier decision in *Libman*, the Supreme Court accepted that the third-party
spending ceilings in the Quebec referendum legislation restricted expression and so violated
s. 2(b). In the Court's view, "freedom of expression includes the right to employ any methods, other than violence, necessary for communication." However, the Court recognized
that under s. 1 there were substantial and compelling reasons for imposing spending limits,
including limits on third-party spending. Spending limits are needed to "guarantee the
democratic nature of referendums by promoting equality between the options" before the
public and to promote "free and informed voting." Unlimited spending would work against
"informed choice," allowing some positions to "bury" others. The Court recognized that the
spending limits imposed on the national "yes" and "no" committees would be ineffective if
third-party spending was not also limited. However, the Court thought that the law under
review was overly restrictive. In the Court's view, the *total* ban on third-party spending during a referendum campaign did not impair freedom of expression as little as was necessary
to protect the integrity of the election process. Claims that unlimited spending might enable
wealthier candidates to "drown out" or "bury" their less wealthy opponents are a familiar
part of the case for ceilings. Yet how do the voices of the wealthy "drown out" or "bury" the
voices of others? Why does unequal spending matter? How does it translate into unequal
campaign influence?

2. In *Thomson Newspapers Co. v. Canada*, [1998] 1 SCR 877, 159 DLR (4th) 385, the Supreme Court of Canada struck down the federal ban on the publication of election campaign polls during the final days of the campaign (s. 322.1 of the *Canada Elections Act*,
RSC 1985, c. E-2). The federal government argued that the ban was necessary "to prevent
the potentially distorting effect of public opinion survey results that are released late in the
election campaign leaving insufficient time to assess their validity."

Bastarache J, for the majority, dismissed this argument. He recognized that polls might
contain information useful to voters. Late poll results, in particular, might be useful to those
who want to vote strategically, that is, vote for their second choice if their first choice seems
to have no chance of winning. In any event, argued Bastarache J, it is up to voters to decide
what information they want to take into account when deciding how to vote: "If they feel

that their votes are better informed as a result of having this information, then the ban not only interferes with their freedom of expression, but with their perception of the freeness and validity of their vote."

We should not, said Bastarache J, underestimate the capacity of voters to assess polls. Voters are exposed to opinion polls throughout the campaign and are likely to spot a single inaccurate poll result. More generally, a commitment to democracy and to freedom of expression means that we must "presume" that the Canadian voter "is a rational actor who can learn from experience and make independent judgments about the value of particular sources of electoral information." Canadian voters must be "presumed to have a certain degree of maturity and intelligence." One cannot assume that "Canadians will become so mesmerized by the flurry of polls" in the media that they will forget about the real issues.

Gonthier J dissented. In his view the ban permitted timely discussion and careful scrutiny of all published poll results and so contributed to "the promotion of an informed vote over a misinformed vote."

3. In *R v. Bryan*, [2007] 1 SCR 527, 2007 SCC 12, 276 DLR (4th) 513, the Supreme Court of Canada dealt with a s. 2(b) challenge to s. 329 of the *Canada Elections Act*, SC 2000, c. 9, which prohibits the broadcasting of election results on election day until polling stations are closed in all parts of Canada. The facts involved the federal general election of November 27, 2000, during which the appellant transmitted the election results from Atlantic Canada while polling stations remained open in other parts of Canada by posting the results on a website. The results were therefore available to the public in every electoral district in Canada. The appellant had made his intention to do so public before the election, and the Commissioner of Canada Elections had warned him that such publication would be contrary to s. 329 of the *Canada Elections Act*. A majority of the Court held that while s. 329 infringed s. 2(b), the infringement was justified under s. 1. The pressing and substantial purpose of the provision was to ensure "informational equality" and to avoid the perception of unfairness that occurs when some voters have access to information that is not available to others and the possibility that access to that information will affect voter participation or choices.

VII. ACCESS TO PUBLIC PROPERTY

The courts have accepted that freedom of expression must include the right to communicate on state-owned property—that in the absence of any right to communicate on state-owned property, many individuals would be significantly limited in their ability to communicate with others. Yet the issue of communicative access to state property does not seem to fit neatly into the standard two-step model of freedom of expression adjudication. As you read the following cases, consider why this might be so.

The Supreme Court of Canada's first major decision on this issue was *Committee for the Commonwealth of Canada v. Canada*, [1991] 1 SCR 139, 77 DLR (4th) 385, in which a federal airport regulation that prohibited any advertising or soliciting in airports without the authorization of the minister was applied to preclude a group from distributing political leaflets. All members of the Court agreed that the group's freedom of expression under s. 2(b) of the Charter had been infringed in a way that could not be justified under s. 1. However, three different approaches to the issue of communicative access were put forward by the Court (as discussed in more detail in the notes below). The Court's second major decision on this issue was *Ramsden v. Peterborough (City)*, [1993] 2 SCR 1084, 106 DLR (4th) 233, in which all members of the Court once again agreed, without resolving the issue of the appropriate test, that a municipal bylaw that imposed an absolute prohibition on the affixing of posters (and which on the facts had been applied against a musician who affixed posters on hydro poles announcing an upcoming performance) should be struck down as an unjustifiable infringement of freedom of expression.

In the case that follows, the Court reviewed its prior decisions and attempted to articulate a single test for communicative access to public property. Do you think the Court has succeeded?

Montréal (City) v. 2952-1366 Québec Inc.
[2005] 3 SCR 141, 2005 SCC 62, 258 DLR (4th) 595

McLACHLIN CJC and DESCHAMPS J (Bastarache, LeBel, Abella, and Charron JJ concurring):

1. Introduction

[1] This appeal concerns the power of the city of Montréal ("City") to prohibit noise produced in the street by a loudspeaker located in the entrance of an establishment. Two arguments are raised, one based on the limits on the power to regulate and the other on the *Canadian Charter of Rights and Freedoms* ("*Canadian Charter*"). For the reasons that follow, these arguments must be rejected.

[2] In light of its scope, art. 9(1) of the *By-law concerning noise*, RBCM 1994, c. B-3 ("By-law"), was validly adopted by the City pursuant to its regulatory powers. Although this provision limits the freedom of expression guaranteed by s. 2(b) of the *Canadian Charter*, the limit is reasonable and can be justified within the meaning of s. 1 of the *Canadian Charter*.

2. Origins of the Case

[3] The respondent operates a club featuring female dancers in a commercial zone of downtown Montréal, in a building fronting Ste-Catherine Street. To attract customers and compete with a similar establishment located nearby, the respondent set up, in the main entrance to its club, a loudspeaker that amplified the music and commentary accompanying the show under way inside so that passers-by would hear them. Around midnight on May 14, 1996, a police officer on patrol on Ste-Catherine Street heard the music from a nearby intersection. The respondent was charged with producing noise that could be heard outside using sound equipment, in violation of arts. 9(1) and 11 of the By-law. These provisions read as follows:

> 9. In addition to the noise referred to in article 8, the following noises, where they can be heard from the outside, are specifically prohibited:
>
>> (1) noise produced by sound equipment, whether it is inside a building or installed or used outside;

· · ·

11. No noise specifically prohibited under articles 9 or 10 may be produced, whether or not it affects an inhabited place.

· · ·

3. Analysis

3.1 Does the City Have the Power to Adopt Art. 9(1) of the By-law?

[The majority held that, despite its general language, the bylaw applied only to sounds that stood out over environmental noise.]

[34] The historical and purposive analysis of the provision enabled us to determine that the lawmakers' purpose was to control noises that interfere with peaceful enjoyment of the urban environment. The immediate context of art. 9 indicates that the concept of noise that adversely affects the enjoyment of the environment is implicit in art. 9 and that the activities prohibited under it are activities that produce noises that can be detected as separate from the environmental noise. ...

[36] It is not in dispute that the City has the power to define and prohibit nuisances. In adopting art. 9(1) of the By-law, the City was targeting noises that constitute a nuisance. We accordingly conclude that the City had the power to adopt art. 9(1) of the By-law.

· · ·

3.2 Does Article 9(1) of the By-law Infringe Section 2(b) of the Canadian Charter?

· · ·

3.2.1 Expressive Content

[58] The first question is whether the noise emitted by a loudspeaker from inside the club had expressive content. The answer must be yes. The loudspeaker sent a message into the street about the show going on inside the club. The fact that the message may not, in the view of some, have been particularly valuable, or may even have been offensive, does not deprive it of s. 2(b) protection. Expressive activity is not excluded from the scope of the guarantee because of its particular message. ...

3.2.2 Excluded Expression

[60] Expressive activity may fall outside the scope of s. 2(b) protection because of how or where it is delivered. While all expressive *content* is worthy of protection (see *Irwin Toy* [*Ltd. v. Quebec (Attorney General)*, [1989] 1 SCR 927], at p. 969), the *method or location* of the expression may not be. For instance, this Court has found that violent expression is not protected by the Canadian Charter ... .

[61] This case raises the question of whether the *location* of the expression at issue causes the expression to be excluded from the scope of s. 2(b): see *Committee for the Commonwealth of Canada v. Canada*, [1991] 1 SCR 139, *per* Lamer CJ. Property may be private or public. Public property is government-owned. In this case, although the loudspeaker was located on the respondent's private property, the sound issued onto the street, a public space owned by the government. One aspect of free expression is the right

to express oneself in certain public spaces. Thus, the public square and the speakers' corner have by tradition become places of protected expression. The question here is whether s. 2(b) of the Canadian Charter protects not only what the appellants were doing, but their right to do it *in the place where they were doing it*, namely a public street.

[62] Section 2(b) protection does not extend to all places. Private property, for example, will fall outside the protected sphere of s. 2(b) absent state-imposed limits on expression, since state action is necessary to implicate the Canadian Charter. Public property, however, may be more problematic since, by definition, it implicates the state. Two countervailing arguments, both powerful, are pitted against each other where the issue is expression on public property.

[63] The argument for s. 2(b) protection on all public property focuses on ownership. It says the critical distinction is between government-owned places and other places. The government as the owner of property controls it. It follows that restrictions on the use of public property for expressive purposes are "government acts." Therefore, it is argued, the government is limiting the right to free expression guaranteed by s. 2(b) of the Canadian Charter and must justify this under s. 1.

[64] The argument against s. 2(b) protection on at least some government-owned property, by contrast, focuses on the distinction between public use of property and private use of property. Regardless of the fact that the government owns and hence controls its property, it is asserted, many government places are essentially private in use. Some areas of government-owned property have become recognized as public spaces in which the public has a right to express itself. But other areas, like private offices and diverse places of public business, have never been viewed as available spaces for public expression. It cannot have been the intention of the drafters of the Canadian Charter, the argument continues, to confer a *prima facie* right of free expression in these essentially private spaces and to cast the onus on the government to justify the exclusion of public expression from places that have always and unquestionably been off-limits to public expression and could not effectively function if they were open to the public.

[65] In *Committee for the Commonwealth of Canada*, six of seven judges endorsed the second general approach, although they adopted different tests for determining whether the government-owned property at issue was public or private in nature. Lamer CJ, supported by Sopinka and Cory JJ, advocated a test based on whether the primary function of the space was compatible with free expression. McLachlin J, supported by La Forest and Gonthier JJ, proposed a test based on whether expression in the place at issue served the values underlying the s. 2(b) free speech guarantee. L'Heureux-Dubé J opted for the first approach and went directly to s. 1.

[66] In this case, as in *Ramsden v. Peterborough (City)*, [1993] 2 SCR 1084, we are satisfied that on any of the tests proposed in *Committee for the Commonwealth of Canada*, the emission of noise onto a public street is protected by s. 2(b). The activity is expressive. The evidence does not establish that the method and location at issue here—a building-mounted amplifier emitting noise onto a public street—impede the function of city streets or fail to promote the values that underlie the free expression guarantee.

[67] This method of expression is not repugnant to the primary function of a public street, on the test of Lamer CJ Streets provide means of passing and accessing adjoining buildings. They also serve as venues of public communication. However one defines their

function, emitting noise produced by sound equipment onto public streets seems not in itself to interfere with it. If sound equipment were being used in a way that prevented people from using the street for passage or communication, the answer might be different … . However, the evidence here does not establish this.

[68] The method and location of the expression also arguably serve the values that underlie the guarantee of free expression, on the approach advocated by McLachlin J Amplified emissions of noise from buildings onto a public street could further democratic discourse, truth finding and self-fulfillment. Again, if the evidence showed that the amplification inhibited passage and communication on the street, the situation might be different. The argument that the emissions of noise onto a public street in this case did not serve the values underlying the freedom of expression rests on its content, and cannot be considered in addressing the issue of whether the method or location of the expression itself is inimical to s. 2(b).

[69] Finally, on the analysis of L'Heureux-Dubé J in *Committee for the Commonwealth of Canada*, the expressive content of the noise mandates the conclusion that it is protected by s. 2(b) and propels the analysis directly into s. 1, where justification is the issue.

[70] It follows that here, as in *Ramsden*, it is unnecessary to revisit the question of which of the divergent approaches to the issue of expression on public property should be adopted. However, since we are requested to clarify the test, we offer the following views.

[71] We agree with the view of the majority in *Committee for the Commonwealth of Canada* that the application of s. 2(b) is not attracted by the mere fact of government ownership of the place in question. There must be a further enquiry to determine if this is the *type* of public property which attracts s. 2(b) protection.

[72] Expressive activity should be excluded from the protective scope of s. 2(b) only if its method or location clearly undermines the values that underlie the guarantee. Violent expression, which falls outside the scope of s. 2(b) by reason of its method, provides a useful analogy. Violent expression may be a means of political expression and may serve to enhance the self-fulfillment of the perpetrator. However, it is not protected by s. 2(b) because violent means and methods undermine the values that s. 2(b) seeks to protect. Violence prevents dialogue rather than fostering it. Violence prevents the self-fulfillment of the victim rather than enhancing it. And violence stands in the way of finding the truth rather than furthering it. Similarly, in determining what public spaces fall outside s. 2(b) protection, we must ask whether free expression in a given place undermines the values underlying s. 2(b).

[73] We therefore propose the following test for the application of s. 2(b) to public property; it adopts a principled basis for method or location-based exclusion from s. 2(b) and combines elements of the tests of Lamer CJ and McLachlin J in *Committee for the Commonwealth of Canada*. The onus of satisfying this test rests on the claimant.

[74] The basic question with respect to expression on government-owned property is whether the place is a public place where one would expect constitutional protection for free expression on the basis that expression in that place does not conflict with the purposes which s. 2(b) is intended to serve, namely (1) democratic discourse, (2) truth finding and (3) self-fulfillment. To answer this question, the following factors should be considered:

(a) the historical or actual function of the place; and

(b) whether other aspects of the place suggest that expression within it would undermine the values underlying free expression.

[75] The historical function of a place for public discourse is an indicator that expression in that place is consistent with the purposes of s. 2(b). In places where free expression
has traditionally occurred, it is unlikely that protecting expression undermines the values
underlying the freedom. As a result, where historical use for free expression is made out,
the location of the expression as it relates to public property will be protected.

[76] Actual function is also important. Is the space in fact essentially private, despite
being government-owned, or is it public? Is the function of the space—the activity going
on there—compatible with open public expression? Or is the activity one that requires
privacy and limited access? Would an open right to intrude and present one's message by
word or action be consistent with what is done in the space? Or would it hamper the activity? Many government functions, from cabinet meetings to minor clerical functions,
require privacy. To extend a right of free expression to such venues might well undermine democracy and efficient governance.

[77] Historical and actual functions serve as markers for places where free expression
would have the effect of undermining the values underlying the freedom of expression.
The ultimate question, however, will always be whether free expression in the place at
issue would undermine the values the guarantee is designed to promote. Most cases will
be resolved on the basis of historical or actual function. However, we cannot discount the
possibility that other factors may be relevant. Changes in society and technology may affect the spaces where expression should be protected having regard to the values that
underlie the guarantee. The proposed test reflects this, by permitting factors other than
historical or actual function to be considered where relevant.

[78] The markers of historical and actual functions will provide ready answers in
most cases. However, we must accept that, on the difficult issue of whether free expression is protected in a given location, some imprecision is inevitable. As some scholars
point out, the public-private divide cannot be precisely defined in a way that will provide
an advance answer for all possible situations: see, e.g., R. Moon, *The Constitutional Protection of Freedom of Expression* (2000), at pp. 148 *et seq.* This said, the historical and actual functions of a place is something that can be established by evidence. As courts rule
on what types of spaces are inherently public, a central core of certainty may be expected
to evolve with respect to when expression in a public place will undermine the values
underlying the freedom of expression.

[79] Another concern is whether the proposed test screens out expression which
merits protection, on the one hand, or admits too much clearly unprotected expression
on the other. Our jurisprudence requires broad protection at the s. 2(b) stage, on the
understanding that governments can limit that protection if they can justify the limits
under s. 1 of the Canadian Charter. The proposed test reflects this. However, it also reflects the reality that some places must remain outside the protected sphere of s. 2(b).
People must know where they can and cannot express themselves and governments
should not be required to justify every exclusion or regulation of expression under s. 1. As
six of seven judges of this Court agreed in *Committee for the Commonwealth of Canada*,

the test must provide a preliminary screening process. Otherwise, uncertainty will prevail and governments will be continually forced to justify restrictions which, viewed from the perspective of history and common sense, are entirely appropriate. Restricted access to many government-owned venues is part of our history and our constitutional tradition. The Canadian Charter was not intended to turn this state of affairs on its head.

[80] A final concern is whether the proposed test is flexible enough to accommodate future developments. Changes in society will inevitably alter the specifics of the debate about the venues in which the guarantee of free expression will apply. Some say, for example, that the increasing privatization of government space will shift the debate to the private sector. Others say that the new spaces for communication created by electronic communication through the Internet will raise new questions on the issue of where the right to free speech applies. We do not suggest how the problems of the future will be answered. But it seems to us that a test that focuses on historical and actual functions as markers for public and private domains, adapted as necessary to accord with new situations and the values underlying the s. 2(b) guarantees, will be sufficiently flexible to meet the problems of the future.

[81] Applying the approach we propose to the case at bar confirms the conclusion reached earlier under the three *Committee for the Commonwealth of Canada* tests that the expression at issue in this case falls within the protected sphere of s. 2(b) of the Canadian Charter. The content, as already noted, is expressive. Viewed from the perspective of locus, the expression falls within the public domain. Streets are clearly areas of public, as opposed to private, concourse, where expression of many varieties has long been accepted. There is nothing to suggest that to permit this medium of expression would subvert the values of s. 2(b).

3.2.3 The Infringement

[82] This brings us to the third step of the *Irwin Toy* test. Having concluded that the expression falls within the protected scope of s. 2(b), we must ask whether the By-law impinges on protected expression, in purpose or effect.

[83] Here, the purpose of the By-law is benign. However, its effect is to restrict expression. Where the effect of a provision is to limit expression, a breach of s. 2(b) will be made out, provided the claimant shows that the expression at issue promotes one of the values underlying the freedom of expression: *Irwin Toy*, at p. 976.

[84] The electronically amplified noise at issue here encouraged passers-by to engage in the leisure activity of attending one of the performances held at the club. Generally speaking, engaging in lawful leisure activities promotes such values as individual self-fulfillment and human flourishing. The disputed value of particular expressions of self-fulfillment, like exotic dancing, does not negate this general proposition: *R v. Butler*, [1992] 1 SCR 452, at p. 489. It follows that the By-law has the effect of restricting expression which promotes one of the values underlying s. 2(b) of the Canadian Charter.

[85] We conclude that the City's ban on emitting amplified noise constitutes a limit on free expression under s. 2(b) of the Canadian Charter.

3.3 *Is the Limit Justified Under Section 1 of the Canadian Charter?*

. . .

[89] [Applying the test from *R v. Oakes*, [1986] 1 SCR 103] [w]e conclude that the objective of the limitation is pressing and substantial. The Superior Court judge, Boilard J, defined that objective as combatting noise pollution ... . Noise pollution is a serious problem in urban centers, and cities like Montréal are entitled to act reasonably and responsibly in seeking to curb it.

[90] This brings us to proportionality. Proportionality is concerned with the *means* chosen to meet the objective. Here the City chose a two-pronged attack on noise pollution. First, it prohibited noises exceeding a stipulated degree of loudness: art. 8. Second, it prohibited particular noises—namely noise that can be heard from the outside and is produced by sound equipment, whether it is inside a building or installed or used outside: art. 9. Noise targeted by art. 9 is prohibited regardless of whether it affects an inhabited place: art. 11. It is important, however, to note that art. 9 does not represent an absolute ban. Unlike *Ramsden*, where no relief from the restrictive by-law was possible, the scheme of the By-law in this case anticipates routine granting of licences as exceptions to the prohibition. Article 20 of the By-law provides that the City may authorize the use of sound equipment prohibited by arts. 9 and 11 in particular circumstances, as for special events, celebrations and demonstrations. The City has exercised this authority and granted permits to use sound equipment on hundreds of occasions ... . There is no evidence that it has exercised this authority arbitrarily or to curb democratic discourse. Moreover, as discussed above, in para. 34, a contextual reading of the impugned provision leads to the conclusion that art. 9(1) only captures noise that interferes with the peaceful use and enjoyment of the urban environment. This is the essence of the regulatory scheme the City put in place to deal with noise pollution on its streets.

[91] The first question is whether the limit on noise produced by sound equipment is rationally connected to the City's objective of limiting noise in the streets. Clearly it is. Amplified noise emitted into the street may interfere with the activities of people using the street and the buildings around it. People in urban neighbourhoods cannot expect to be free from the sounds of the many activities that go on around them. However, they can and do expect the level of this intrusion to be limited, so that they can enjoy a measure of peace and quiet. This was the City's objective. Presumptively prohibiting the emission of amplified noise was one of the means by which it sought to accomplish that objective.

[92] The second question, and the most difficult, is whether the measure impairs the right in a reasonably minimal way. ...

[94] First, in dealing with social issues like this one, where interests and rights conflict, elected officials must be accorded a measure of latitude. The Court will not interfere simply because it can think of a better, less intrusive way to manage the problem. What is required is that the City establish that it has tailored the limit to the exigencies of the problem in a reasonable way. This is particularly so on environmental issues, where views and interests conflict and precision is elusive ... .

[95] Second, it is far from clear that regulation by degree of loudness would effectively deal with the problem of noise pollution and the conflict between commercial concerns seeking to maximize commercial expression and citizens seeking a relatively peaceful

and calm environment. Boilard J erred in suggesting that the City could adequately deal with the problem of noise pollution by regulating the volume of noise measurable by sound level meter. Noise can be emitted randomly in unexpected places. Detecting and prosecuting violations could be difficult. Moreover, the regulation of sound levels alone would not prevent the possibility that multiple, simultaneous noises, each within the legal limit, could cumulatively exceed an acceptable sound level.

[96] Regulation by degree of loudness would not achieve the City's goal of eliminating, subject to exceptions, a certain *type* of sound—that produced by sound equipment. Moreover, regulation by sound level meters has definite limits. While some noises may be capable of being monitored in this way, some, like intermittent noises or random noises, cannot. Moreover, the suggestion was unrealistic. As Chamberland JA put it: [TRANSLATION] "[I]t would take a forest of sound level meters and an army of qualified technicians lying in waiting to monitor the noise produced by sound equipment at different times of day and night, everywhere in greater Montréal" (para. 119).

[97] Rights should never be sacrificed to mere administrative convenience. Here, however, the City contends that for a variety of reasons there was really no other practical way to deal with the complex problem it was facing. Accordingly, the City's measures do not go beyond what was reasonably necessary in the circumstances and, as a result, its regulatory plan is entitled to deference.

[98] It remains to consider whether the prejudicial effects on free expression flowing from the regulation of sound at issue are proportionate to the beneficial effects of the regulation. In our view, the test supports the conclusion that the By-law is valid.

[99] The expression limited by the By-law consists of noise produced by sound equipment that interferes with the peaceful use and enjoyment of the urban environment. This limitation therefore goes to the permitted forms of expression on city streets, regardless of content. Against this stand the benefits of reducing noise pollution on the street and in the neighbourhood. We acknowledge that in balancing the deleterious and positive effects of the By-law, account must be taken of the fact that the activity was taking place on a street with an active commercial nightlife in a large and sophisticated city. This does not, however, mean that its residents must necessarily be subjected to abuses of the enjoyment of their environment. As Chamberland JA put it, [TRANSLATION] "the citizens of a city, even a city the size of Montréal, are entitled to a healthy environment. Noise control is unquestionably part of what must be done to improve the quality of this environment" (para. 129). We conclude that the beneficial effects of the By-law outweigh its prejudicial effects. [We therefore conclude that the By-law is constitutional.]

[In a dissenting judgment, Binnie J found that the bylaw could not be interpreted as anything other than a ban on noise produced by sound equipment, regardless of its volume. In his view, the bylaw breached s. 2(b) and could not be justified under s. 1 because it went beyond what could be considered minimal impairment.]

Appeal allowed.

NOTES AND QUESTIONS

1. In 1984, officials at Dorval Airport in Montreal prevented three members of the Committee for the Republic of Canada from communicating their political views to passersby in the public areas of the airport. The Committee members were told that their activities—speaking with passersby and distributing leaflets—violated a federal airport regulation, which provided that "no person shall (1) conduct any business or undertaking, commercial or otherwise, at an airport; (2) advertise or solicit at an airport for the purpose of any business or undertaking" without the authorization of the Minister. The airport management indicated that the only exception made to the regulation was the sale of poppies by veterans every November. The Committee members brought a motion in the Federal Court seeking a declaration that under the Charter they had a right to express themselves in the public areas of the airport and that the airport regulation was an unjustified restriction on freedom of expression. The case was further appealed to the Supreme Court of Canada. In *Committee for the Commonwealth of Canada v. Canada*, [1991] 1 SCR 139, 77 DLR (4th) 385, which is discussed in the Montreal bylaw case, above, all members of the Court agreed that the airport authorities' interference with the respondents' communication of political views was a restriction on freedom of expression that could not be justified under s. 1. However, three different approaches to the issue of communicative access were put forward by the court:

a. Chief Justice Lamer took the position that the question of whether an individual has a right to communicate on state-owned property should be resolved under s. 2(b) and depend simply on whether the particular communication is consistent or compatible with the state's use of the property. A restriction that is based on the incompatibility of the particular form of expression with the state's property use does not violate s. 2(b) and so does not require special justification under s. 1.

b. McLachlin J adopted what she regarded as the reasonable "middle ground" on the issue of communicative access to state property, "between the extremes of the right to expression on all government property and the right to expression on none." According to McLachlin J, a restriction on communicative access to state-owned property that is based on the incompatibility of access with the state's use of its property, and not on the content of the communication, will violate s. 2(b) only if the restricted communication can be shown to advance the values underlying the constitutional protection of freedom of expression. The court should consider "whether the forum's relationship with the particular expressive activity invokes any of the values and principles underlying the guarantee." According to McLachlin J, constitutional protection of access should extend "to expression on some but not all government property." She thought that communicative access to certain state-owned properties—"private" state properties such as prison cells, judge's private chambers, private government offices, and publicly owned broadcasting facilities—would not advance the values of democracy, truth, and autonomy. She considered it self-evident that the purposes of freedom of expression would not be served by public expression in these places: "These are not places of public debate aimed at promoting either the truth or a better understanding of social and political issues. Nor is expression in these places related to the open and welcoming environment essential to the maximization of individual fulfillment and human flourishing." A restriction on communicative access to a private state-owned property will not violate s. 2(b) and so will not require justification under s. 1. On the other hand, McLachlin J considered that the purposes of the guarantee of free expression are served by protecting expression in public forums, "which have by tradition of designation been dedicated to public expressions." The use of these places for political, social, or artistic expression clearly seems to be linked to the values underlying the guarantee of free speech. A restriction on communicative access to a "public forum" will violate s. 2(b) and so will require justification under s. 1.

c. L'Heureux-Dubé J took the view that any time the state restricts expression on its property it violates s. 2(b) and must justify the restriction under s. 1. She thought that the balancing of competing individual and state interests should take place under s. 1. In her view, no other approach fits with the broad construction the Supreme Court has given to s. 2(b) in its earlier decisions. Any restriction of expression on state property must satisfy the rationality, minimal impairment, and proportionality standards of s. 1. She suggested, however, that these standards should not be applied strictly in access cases. When setting out what she believed should be the general approach to communicative access issues, L'Heureux-Dubé J called for a flexible balancing of competing state and individual interests under s. 1. She rejected the "rigid categorization" of the American public forum doctrine. In her view, "certain government restrictions cannot be automatically excised from the s. 2(b) guarantee strictly on the basis that they do not apply to locations traditionally associated with public expression."

On the other hand, L'Heureux-Dubé J thought that certain state properties could, as a matter of fact, be described as "public arenas" (a term she used to distinguish her approach from the American public forum doctrine), in the sense that they are generally open to the public and can easily accommodate public communication. She accepted that the public character of these properties was "relevant when evaluating what is a reasonable restriction on place" in the review of a time, place, and manner regulation under s. 1. L'Heureux-Dubé J also believed that a guarantee that encompasses all government property "is not necessary to fulfill the Charter's purposes or to avoid a stifling of free expression." In her view, "some but not all, government-owned property is constitutionally open to the public for engaging in expressive activity." More specifically, she said that "the Charter's framers did not intend internal government offices, air traffic control towers, prison cells and Judges' Chambers to be made available for leafletting or demonstrations. It is evident," she said, "that the right to freedom of expression under s. 2(b) of the Charter does not provide a right of access to all property whether public or private."

2. The American courts distinguish between two kinds of state-owned property: public forums (state-owned properties, such as parks and streets, that by tradition or designation are open to public communication and not simply to selected speakers) and non-public forums (state-owned properties to which the general public does not ordinarily have access), and they have set different rights of access to each. An individual has a general right to communicate on/in public forums. The state may restrict the content of speech in a public

forum only for substantial and compelling reasons and only if the restriction is narrowly drawn. Content-neutral restrictions (time, place, and manner restrictions) will be justified only if they serve an important state interest and leave open alternative channels of communication. However, in the case of a non-public forum, the state may restrict the content of communication provided the restriction is reasonable and is not simply based on the state's disagreement with the speaker's viewpoint.

Canadian courts initially assumed that they could address access claims by directly balancing competing state and individual interests (the individual's interest in communicative access and the state's interest in exclusion) and would not need to define general categories of property that were either open to, or insulated from, claims of public access. The complex American public forum doctrine was attributed to the absence of a limitations clause in the US *Bill of Rights*. When access was claimed, the Canadian courts would consider whether the state had a substantial reason to limit the individual's freedom to express himself or herself and whether the particular exclusion advanced the state's purpose rationally and with minimal impairment to the freedom. No claim of access would be rejected *a priori* on the basis of the state's use of the property or the classification of the property as a non-public forum. The Supreme Court of Canada, however, appears to have adopted a version of the public forum doctrine. Why do you think it has done this?

3. In *Ramsden v. Peterborough (City)*, [1993] 2 SCR 1084, 106 DLR (4th) 233, a musician affixed posters to hydro poles announcing an upcoming performance. He was charged with contravening a municipal bylaw that imposed an absolute prohibition on the affixing of posters on any public property. Without resolving the issue of the appropriate test for communicative access to public property, all members of the Court were agreed that the bylaw was an unjustifiable infringement of freedom of expression. In establishing a violation of freedom of expression, Iacobucci J, writing for the Court, noted that "posters have communicated political, cultural and social information for centuries. Postering on public property, including utility poles, increases the availability of those messages, and thereby fosters social and historical decision-making." Reference was made to the evidence of an art historian who testified that

> [p]osters have always been a medium of communication of revolutionary and unpopular ideas. They have been called "the circulating libraries of the poor." They have been not only a political weapon but also a means of communicating artistic, cultural, and commercial messages.

In the s. 1 analysis, the Court found that the municipality's concerns with litter and aesthetic blight, while legitimate, could be met in a manner far less restrictive than an absolute ban. It referred to such alternatives as

> regulating the use of [utility] poles for such purposes by specifiying or regulating the location, size of posters, the length of time that a poster might remain on any location, the type of substance used to affix posters, and requiring that the posters be removed after a certain specified time. If necessary, a reasonable fee could be imposed to defray costs of administering such a system.

4. In order to avoid harassment of both workers at abortion clinics and women seeking abortion services, a provincial legislature enacts access to abortion legislation creating access zones around the clinics. All anti-abortion protest activity is prohibited within the

access zones, including active protesting and sidewalk counselling as well as silent protests taking the form of displaying a sign. The access zones involve a maximum distance of 50 metres from the clinic. Violation of the legislation will result in a fine or imprisonment. Would protesters be able to raise a successful Charter challenge to the legislation on the grounds that the public streets and sidewalks outside abortion clinics should be available for their expressive activity, particularly given the symbolic significance of the venue? See *R v. Spratt* (2008), 298 DLR (4th) 317 (BCCA).

5. A public transit authority allows paid commercial advertisements to be carried on the outside of buses; however, its policies stated that no advertising would be accepted if it were "likely to cause offence or create controversy" and, furthermore, that no advertisement would be accepted if it advocated or opposed "any ideology or political philosophy, point of view, policy or action, or which conveys information about a political meeting, gathering or event, a political party or the candidacy of any person for a political position or public office." Two organizations that wished to have their political advertisements displayed on the outside of buses and were refused brought an action seeking a declaration that the advertising policies were unconstitutional because they unjustifiably infringed freedom of expression under s. 2(b) of the Charter. Will they be successful? See *Greater Vancouver Transportation Authority v. Canadian Federation of Students*, 2009 SCC 31, which is also discussed in Chapter 18, Application.

6. The materials in this section have largely dealt with situations where a speaker is claiming access to public property as a forum for speech. Another form of access right that may be grounded in freedom of expression is access to information related to the operation of government and issues of public policy. In the clearest application of this principle, s. 2(b) has been interpreted as including a *prima facie* right of public access, including the media, to judicial and quasi-judicial proceedings, with the result that legislative provisions for *in camera* proceedings are required to be justified under s. 1. See *Re Southam Inc. and The Queen (No. 1)* (1983), 146 DLR (3d) 408 (Ont. CA); *Pacific Press Ltd. v. Canada (Minister of Employment and Immigration)*, [1991] 2 FC 327 (CA); and *Canadian Broadcasting Corp. v. New Brunswick (Attorney General)*, [1996] 3 SCR 480, 139 DLR (4th) 385. In *Criminal Lawyers' Assn. v. Ontario (Ministry of Public Safety and Security)* (2007), 86 OR 259, 2007 ONCA 392, 280 DLR (4th) 193, the Ontario Court of Appeal held that in some circumstances s. 2(b) might give a right of access to government information. This case is on appeal to the Supreme Court of Canada.

7. The leading case on the related issue of publication bans (restrictions on the reporting of court proceedings) is *Dagenais v. Canadian Broadcasting Corp.*, [1994] 3 SCR 835, 120 DLR (4th) 12. In that case, the Supreme Court of Canada reformulated the common-law rule governing publication bans, taking into account freedom of expression interests. The Court stated that a publication ban should only be ordered when (1) such a ban is necessary in order to prevent a real and substantial risk to the fairness of a trial, because reasonably available alternative measures will not prevent the risk; and (2) the salutary effects of the publication ban outweigh the deleterious effects to the free expression of those affected by the ban.

VIII. STATE SUPPORT FOR EXPRESSION

To what extent does the constitutional guarantee of freedom of expression impose a positive obligation on the state to facilitate the expressive activity of citizens? As discussed above, freedom of expression requires government to permit public expression on some of its properties. Does the government have any other obligations to support expression? If a government chooses to facilitate expression, through funding or other means, do any constitutional obligations or constraints come into play?

The Canadian courts have been reluctant to impose on the state even a limited obligation to ensure that any support program it establishes is operated in an even-handed way. When the state supports or subsidizes expression it makes choices between different speakers or different messages, giving support to some and refusing support to others. We assume that the decision to give or deny support rests on state views about the relative value of different forms or instances of expression. Generally, this is not seen as problematic; it is accepted that the government is entitled to express, or lend its support to, particular views, such as national unity, the protection of Canadian culture, or the need for greater crime control.

Yet sometimes when the state declines to give support to particular speakers, or decides to withdraw support from them, we view the state decision not as a failure to support the speaker, which involves no constitutional wrong, but instead as a wrongful attempt to suppress or marginalize the speaker's viewpoint. When, if ever, should a refusal to give support (or the withdrawal of support) be treated as an interference with freedom of expression?

Haig v. Canada
[1993] 2 SCR 995, 105 DLR (4th) 577

[In October 1992, two referenda were held to solicit the opinions of Canadians with respect to the constitutional amendments proposed in the Charlottetown Accord: one held under provincial law in Quebec and one held under federal law in the rest of Canada. Because of different residency requirements in the federal and Quebec legislation, Haig, who had recently moved from Ontario to Quebec, was unable to vote. He did not satisfy the six-month residency requirement to vote in the Quebec referendum and was not ordinarily resident in a polling district in the rest of Canada as required by the federal legislation. Haig challenged the federal referendum legislation under the Charter, alleging a violation of his rights under ss. 2(b), 3, and 15, and sought a declaration that he was entitled to vote in the federal referendum. He was not successful in the lower courts and by the time his case was heard by the Supreme Court of Canada the referendum had taken place.]

L'HEUREUX-DUBÉ J (La Forest, Sopinka, Gonthier, and Major JJ concurring):

[L'Heureux-Dubé J first concludes that there is no violation of the right to vote guaranteed in s. 3 of the Charter as that provision is limited to the election of provincial and federal representatives. A referendum, which she characterizes as "basically a consultative process" that imposes no binding legal obligation on a government, is distinguished from an election.]

Mr. Haig also claims that the fact that he could not vote in the federal referendum infringed his freedom of expression. Expressing one's opinion on the Charlottetown Accord, according to Mr. Haig, is an attempt to convey meaning, the content of which relates to political discourse, which is at the core of s. 2(b) of the Charter and enjoys the highest degree of protection. The content of this expression, he says, cannot be meaningfully examined apart from its form, namely, participation in the referendum itself. Consequently, he urges the Court to find that the actual *casting of a ballot* in a federal referendum is a protected form of expression, asserting that s. 2(b) of the Charter mandates not only immunity from state interference, but also an affirmative role on the part of the state in providing this specific means of expression. ...

The casting of a ballot in a referendum is undoubtedly a means of expression. ...

At issue [however] is whether s. 2(b) of the Charter guarantees to all Canadians the right to vote in a referendum. In failing to ensure that each Canadian was provided with the opportunity to vote in the federal referendum, did the federal government infringe upon their freedom of expression guaranteed in s. 2(b) of the Charter? Does freedom of expression include a positive right to be provided with specific means of expression?

As a starting point, I would note that case law and doctrinal writings have generally conceptualized freedom of expression in terms of negative rather than positive entitlements. ...

Like its United States First Amendment counterpart, the Canadian s. 2(b) Charter jurisprudence has been shaped by these same foundational premises, focusing mainly on attempts by governments to place limitations on what can be expressed. The traditional question before courts has been: to what extent can freedom of expression be justifiably limited? ...

It has not yet been decided that, in circumstances such as the present ones, a government has a constitutional obligation under s. 2(b) of the Charter to provide *a particular platform* to facilitate the exercise of freedom of expression. The traditional view, in colloquial terms, is that the freedom of expression contained in s. 2(b) prohibits gags, but does not compel the distribution of megaphones. ...

However, it is these very premises that are being challenged by the appellants. While the basic theoretical framework underlying freedom of expression has remained unchanged over the past two hundred years, the appellants point out that the political, economic and social conditions under which the theory must be applied have changed significantly. They urge that true freedom of expression must be broader than simply the right to be free from interference, ... that the state "has a more affirmative role to play in the maintenance of a system of free expression in modern society."

I would agree, and it is well understood, that a philosophy of non-interference may not in all circumstances guarantee the optimal functioning of the marketplace of ideas. ...

Does this inevitably lead to the conclusion that the constitutional guarantees of freedom of expression may import more than the absence of government interference? Some people have suggested that it might. ... In *Reference re Public Service Employee Relations Act (Alta.)*, [1987] 1 SCR 313, a case dealing with the boundaries of freedom of association, Dickson CJ (dissenting) addressed this same concern at p. 361:

Section 2 of the Charter protects fundamental "freedoms" as opposed to "rights." Although
these two terms are sometimes used interchangeably, a conceptual distinction between the
two is often drawn. "Rights" are said to impose a corresponding duty or obligation on another party to ensure the protection of the right in question whereas "freedoms" are said to
involve simply an absence of interference or constraint. *This conceptual approach to the nature of "freedoms" may be too narrow since it fails to acknowledge situations where the absence
of government intervention may in effect substantially impede the enjoyment of fundamental
freedoms* (e.g., regulations limiting the monopolization of the press may be required to ensure freedom of expression and freedom of the press). [Emphasis added.]

... At this point, it is important to emphasize that, in talking about freedom of expression, a variety of vocabularies have been employed. People have sometimes used the language of negative and positive entitlements, sometimes focusing on distinctions between
rights and freedoms, other times on distinctions between "liberty to" and "liberty of." ...
There may be value to these conceptual distinctions as they provide frameworks which
can assist in an analysis of the issues, interests and values that shape a conclusion that a
right has or has not been violated.

However ... this language cannot be used in a dogmatic fashion. The distinctions between "freedoms" and "rights," and between positive and negative entitlements, are not
always clearly made, nor are they always helpful. One must not depart from the context
of the purposive approach articulated by this Court in *R v. Big M Drug Mart Ltd.*, [1985]
1 SCR 295. Under this approach, a situation might arise in which, in order to make a
fundamental freedom meaningful, a posture of restraint would not be enough, and positive governmental action might be required. This might, for example, take the form of
legislative intervention aimed at preventing certain conditions which muzzle expression,
or ensuring public access to certain kinds of information.

In the proper context, these may perhaps be relevant considerations leading a court
to conclude that positive governmental action is required. However, these considerations
do not arise in our case. The context here is a referendum whose legality and legitimacy
have been recognized. ... [T]he referendum itself, far from stifling expression, provided
a particular forum for such expression. ...

[T]here is no dispute concerning the importance of freedom of expression. Nor is it
disputed that voting is a form of expression. Further, in the context of legislative elections, it is clear that voting as a means of expression is constitutionally entrenched in s. 3
of the Charter. However, there is just as clearly no constitutionally entrenched right to
vote in a referendum.

A referendum is a creation of legislation. Independent of the legislation giving genesis
to a referendum, there is no right of participation. The right to vote in a referendum is a
right accorded by statute, and the statute governs the terms and conditions of participation. The Court is being asked to find that this statutorily created platform for expression
has taken on constitutional status. In my view, though a referendum is undoubtedly a
platform for expression, s. 2(b) of the Charter does not impose upon a government,
whether provincial or federal, any positive obligation to consult its citizens through the
particular mechanism of a referendum. Nor does it confer upon all citizens the right to
express their opinions in a referendum. A government is under no constitutional obliga-

tion to extend this platform of expression to *anyone*, let alone to *everyone*. A referendum as a platform of expression is, in my view, a matter of legislative policy and not of constitutional law.

The following caveat is, however, in order here. While s. 2(b) of the Charter does not include the right to any particular means of expression, where a government chooses to provide one, it must do so in a fashion that is consistent with the Constitution. The traditional rules of Charter scrutiny continue to apply. Thus, while the government may extend such a benefit to a limited number of persons, it may not do so in a discriminatory fashion, and particularly not on ground prohibited under s. 15 of the Charter. ...

In *Schachter v. Canada*, [1992] 2 SCR 679, the Court said that s. 15 of the Charter is indeed a hybrid of positive and negative protection, and that a government may be required to take positive steps to ensure the equality of people or groups who come within the scope of s. 15. It might well be that, in the context of a particular equality claim, those positive steps may involve the provision of means of expression to certain groups or individuals. ...

[L'Heureux-Dubé J went on to find that the exclusion of citizens who could not satisfy the residency requirements did not constitute a violation of s. 15.]

IACOBUCCI J (Lamer CJC concurring) dissenting: ... [I]n my view, the appellant's rights under s. 2(b) of the *Canadian Charter of Rights and Freedoms* were violated by the effect of the *Referendum Act*, SC 1992, c. 30 ("*Referendum Act*"), and such violation cannot, in the absence of evidence on the point, be saved under s. 1 of the Charter. In the result, I would allow the appeal.

In a technical or formal sense, it is correct to observe, as L'Heureux-Dubé J does, that two referenda were held in the circumstances of this case: one by the province of Quebec and one by the federal government in the rest of Canada. ...

In my opinion, focusing on the technicalities of separate referenda obscures the national character of the referendum. ... [T]he reality was that Parliament intended the country to have a national referendum which would be conducted by the holding of a federal referendum in conjunction with one or more provincial referenda. ...

[T]he federal legislation was aimed at a national referendum; to accomplish that end, it was coordinated with the Quebec referendum. As my colleague L'Heureux-Dubé J observes, the appellant unfortunately fell between the legislative cracks and was neither able to participate in the national referendum directly, nor was he able to participate indirectly through the Quebec referendum.

The question which then arises is whether his inability to participate in the referendum process amounts to a violation of his rights under the Charter, and it is to that question I now turn.

I agree with the view that the federal government is not legally obligated to hold referenda, nor is it legally bound by the results of any referenda it conducts. However, if the government chooses to conduct a referendum, it must do so in compliance with the Charter. The *Referendum Act* provided a legislative framework to allow Canadian citizens to express their political opinions. The referendum was an important expressive activity relating to constitutional change in this country. ...

Although Parliament was under no *legal* obligation to follow the results of the referendum, apparently a *political* obligation to do so had been assumed. Despite the absence of such a legal obligation, nevertheless, the referendum was exceedingly important expressive activity that is worthy of Charter protection. ...

The right to express opinions in social and political decision-making clearly attracts the protection of s. 2(b). ... Casting a referendum ballot is an important form of expression which is worthy of constitutional protection. In my view, the appellant Haig's right to express his political views by participating in the referendum was guaranteed by s. 2(b) of the Charter. He was denied the right to participate and thus his s. 2(b) rights were violated.

Although the appellant Haig was free to express his views as he wished on the Charlottetown Accord prior to the vote, he was denied the ability to participate in the most important expressive activity, that of voting in the referendum. While the purpose of the *Referendum Act* was to include all voters, the effect was to deprive those residents of Quebec who were ordinarily resident in another province in the six-month period prior to the referendum of the ability to participate in expressive activity, which is clearly protected under the Charter.

As the respondent Attorney General of Canada did not introduce any evidence on s. 1, the violation of the appellant's s. 2(b) rights has not been justified under s. 1.

[Both Cory and McLachlin JJ wrote concurring judgments in which they generally agreed with L'Heureux-Dubé J's reasons on the constitutional issues.]

Appeal dismissed.

NOTES AND QUESTIONS

A referendum is not only a process for gauging public reaction to a state initiative, but also for gaining democratic legitimacy for that initiative. The significance of a referendum depends on its being broadly democratic. The government may not have excluded Mr. Haig because it disagreed with his political views. Nevertheless, Mr. Haig was denied an expressive opportunity (or at least an opportunity to participate in a collective expression of opinion) that was available to other citizens. Was he not justified in seeing this denial as an interference with his freedom of expression?

Native Women's Assn. of Canada v. Canada
[1994] 3 SCR 627, 119 DLR (4th) 224

[During 1991 and 1992, the federal government established a constitutional review process (which ultimately led to the *Charlottetown Accord*) to deal with a set of proposed constitutional amendments, including a proposal to entrench a right to aboriginal self-government. The federal government gave funding to four national aboriginal organizations and consulted them in the review process, which included their attendance at constitutional conferences. Part of the funds allocated to the four groups were earmarked for women's issues. The Native Women's Association of Canada (NWAC), concerned that the aboriginal organizations selected by the federal government were male-dominated and would not effectively represent the interests of aboriginal women, and in particular their interest in the continued application of the Charter and its equality guarantees to aboriginal self-government, requested that the federal government recognize them as a distinct group and grant them funding and rights of participation equivalent to those of other groups. After the federal government refused their request, NWAC sought, *inter alia*, a declaration that the government's failure to provide them with funding and rights of participation violated their rights under ss. 2(b), 15, and 28 of the Charter. At the Federal Court of Appeal, while the claim based on s. 15 was rejected, the Court concluded that the government's actions had violated NWAC's rights under ss. 2(b) and 28 by according the advocates of male-dominated self-government a preferred position in the exercise of expressive activity. The Court was, however, unwilling to go so far as to require funding equal to that provided to the other designated groups and simply ordered a declaration that freedom of expression had been violated. The federal government appealed to the Supreme Court of Canada.]

SOPINKA J (Lamer CJC, La Forest, Gonthier, Cory, Iacobucci, and Major JJ concurring): ... The main contention of the respondents is that the Government's provision of funding to [the four aboriginal organizations] along with the opportunity to participate in the constitutional discussions, required the Government to bestow upon NWAC an equal chance for expression of its views. ...

In order to determine whether the assertions of the respondents are valid, it is necessary to consider the scope of the freedom of expression as guaranteed by s. 2(b) of the Charter. In particular, it must be determined whether there is any positive duty on the Government to provide funding to NWAC in these circumstances. This case does not involve the typical situation of government action restricting or interfering with freedom of expression in the negative sense. Rather, the respondents claim that the Charter requires the Government of Canada to provide them with a forum for expression equal to that of the other Aboriginal organizations. ...

The conclusions reached in *Haig v. Canada*, [1993] 2 SCR 995 have application to the case at bar. Similar to a referendum, the Government of Canada was engaging in a consultative process to secure the public opinion with respect to potential constitutional amendments. To further this goal, a parallel process of consultation was established within the Aboriginal community. It cannot be claimed that NWAC has a constitutional right to receive government funding aimed at promoting participation in the constitutional conferences. The respondents conceded as much ... . Furthermore, the provision of funding and the invitation to participate in constitutional discussions facilitated and enhanced the expression of Aboriginal groups. It did not stifle expression.

However, the respondents rely on *Haig* for the proposition that the Government cannot provide a platform of expression in a discriminatory fashion or in a way which otherwise violates the Charter. They state that this result is clearly mandated by s. 28 of the Charter. ...

Haig establishes the principle that generally the government is under no obligation to fund or provide a specific platform of expression to an individual or a group. However, the decision in *Haig* leaves open the possibility that, in certain circumstances, positive governmental action may be required in order to make the freedom of expression meaningful. Furthermore, in some circumstances where the government does provide such a platform, it must not do so in a discriminatory fashion contrary to the Charter. It is this last proposition upon which the respondents rely in conjunction with s. 28 of the Charter to support their position that their rights under s. 2(b) of the Charter were violated in that they did not receive an equal platform to express their views.

At this point, I should add that it cannot be said that every time the Government of Canada chooses to fund or consult a certain group, thereby providing a platform upon which to convey certain views, that the Government is also required to fund a group purporting to represent the opposite point of view. Otherwise, the implications of this proposition would be untenable. For example, if the Government chooses to fund a women's organization to study the issue of abortion to assist in drafting proposed legislation, can it be argued that the Government is bound by the Constitution to provide equal funding to a group purporting to represent the rights of fathers? If this was the intended scope of s. 2(b) of the Charter, the ramifications on government spending would be far reaching indeed.

Although care must be taken when referring to American authority with respect to the First Amendment, the American version of freedom of expression, I find the comments of O'Connor J of the United States Supreme Court in *Minnesota State Board for Community Colleges v. Knight*, 465 US 271 (1984) at p. 285, apposite:

> Government makes so many policy decisions affecting so many people that it would likely grind to a halt were policymaking constrained by constitutional requirements on whose voices must be heard. "There must be a limit to individual argument in such matters if government is to go on." [Cite omitted.] Absent statutory restrictions, the State must be free to consult or not to consult whomever it pleases.

... With respect to the argument that allowing the participation of one group while not equally permitting the same forum to another group amplifies the former's voice, O'Connor J remarked as follows (at p. 288):

> Amplification of the sort claimed is inherent in government's freedom to choose its advisers. A person's right to speak is not infringed when government simply ignores that person while listening to others.

Therefore, while it may be true that the Government cannot provide a particular means of expression that has the effect of discriminating against a group, it cannot be said that merely by consulting an organization, or organizations, purportedly representing a male or female point of view, the Government must automatically consult groups representing the opposite perspective. It will be rare indeed that the provision of a platform or funding to one or several organizations will have the effect of suppressing another's freedom of speech.

Although it appears that the respondents' arguments relate more closely to an equality argument under s. 15 of the Charter, the respondents devoted much of their energy addressing s. 2(b). In either case, regardless of how the arguments are framed, it will be seen that the evidence does not support the conclusions urged by the respondents.

There is no question here of the Government of Canada attempting to suppress NWAC's expression of its point of view with respect to the Constitution. The s. 2(b) argument advanced is dependent on a finding that the funding of and participation by NWAC were essential to provide an equal voice for the rights of women. A corollary to this submission is that the funded groups are not representative of Native women because they advocate a male-dominated aboriginal self-government. This is the submission that was accepted by the Court of Appeal and is the foundation of its judgment. A review of the factual record reveals that there was no evidence to support the contention that the funded groups were less representative of the viewpoint of women with respect to the Constitution. Nor was there any evidence with respect to the level of support of NWAC by women as compared to the funded groups. As well, the evidence does not support the contention that the funded groups advocate a male-dominated form of self-government. ...

It is evident from the record that NWAC had the opportunity to express its ideas both directly to the Government as well as through the four Aboriginal representative organizations. The trial judge made the following statement regarding NWAC's participation in the process (at pp. 479-80):

> On the facts it is evident that the Native Women's Association of Canada has had and will continue to have many opportunities to express its views, both to the appropriate political authorities, to the public and even to the groups which will participate in the Conference, some at least of whom share the Native Women's Association of Canada's concern respecting the continued application of the Charter to aboriginal people. Undoubtedly the more money placed at their disposal the louder their voice could be heard, but it certainly cannot be said that they are being deprived of the right of freedom of speech in contravention of the Charter.

An example of NWAC's public participation in the process is found in its submissions to the Beaudoin-Dobbie Committee. The 1992 *Report of the Special Joint Committee on a Renewed Canada* ... made specific reference to the submissions made by NWAC and incorporated into the report NWAC's recommendation that the Charter apply to Aboriginal self-government.

The evidence is also indicative of the fact that Aboriginal women, including members of NWAC, did have a direct voice regarding the position of the funded groups with respect to the constitutional discussions. NWAC participated in the parallel process set up by the four national Aboriginal organizations to discuss constitutional reform. ...

Furthermore, NWAC also received some of the Government funding under the Contribution Agreements, as all four groups were required to direct a portion of the funds received specifically to address women's issues. ...

Rather than illustrate that the funded groups advocated male-dominated Aboriginal self-government, the evidence discloses that the four funded groups made efforts to include the viewpoint of women. As well, there was no evidence to suggest that NWAC enjoyed any higher level of support amongst Aboriginal women as compared to the funded Aboriginal groups. ...

Even assuming that in certain extreme circumstances, the provision of a platform of expression to one group may infringe the expression of another and thereby require the Government to provide an equal opportunity for the expression of that group, there was

no evidence in this case to suggest that the funding or consultation of the four Aboriginal groups infringed the respondents' equal right of freedom of expression. The four Aboriginal groups invited to discuss possible constitutional amendments are all *bona fide* national representatives of Aboriginal people in Canada and, based on the facts in this case, there was no requirement under s. 2(b) of the Charter to also extend an invitation and funding directly to the respondents. …

[Sopinka J also finds that the s. 15 argument fails for lack of an evidentiary basis to support the claim of discrimination.]

L'HEUREUX-DUBÉ J: … Although I am in general agreement with my colleague Sopinka J's reasons as well as with the result he reaches … I cannot agree [with his statement] that *Haig* "establishes the principle that generally the government is under no obligation to fund or provide a specific platform of expression to an individual or a group" … . In my view, *Haig* rather stands for the proposition that the government *in that particular case* was under no constitutional obligation to provide for the right to a referendum under s. 2(b) of the Charter, but that if and when the government does decide to provide a specific platform of expression, it must do so in a manner consistent with the Charter.

This Court has always fostered a broad approach to the interpretation of s. 2(b) of the Charter, freedom of expression being an important aspect of the healthy functioning of the democratic process … . *Haig* is consistent with this approach in that it underlines the possible consequences of disparate financing of viewpoints and the importance of promoting a variety of views. It is also recognised in *Haig* … "that a philosophy of non-interference may not *in all circumstances* guarantee the optimal functioning of the marketplace of ideas" (emphasis added).

The approach in *Haig* is one that in fact affords significant relevance to circumstances, and this is why I am of the view that in certain ones, funding or consultation may be mandated by the Constitution by virtue of the fact that when the government does decide to facilitate the expression of views, it must do so in a manner that is mindful of the Charter. In this respect, one must note that the circumstances in which the government may be held to a positive obligation in terms of providing a specific platform of expression invariably depend on the nature of the evidence presented by the parties.

In the present case, the evidence demonstrates that the complainant organization was not prevented from expressing its views, albeit not in the way it would have desired. I would therefore agree that on its facts, this case does not give rise to a positive obligation analogous to the type referred to in *Haig* since not providing the complainant organization with the funding and constitutional voice requested did not amount to a breach of its freedom of expression. However … the outcome of the present case should in no way be interpreted as limiting the proposition for which *Haig* stands.

[McLachlin J wrote a brief concurring judgment holding that the freedom of governments to choose and fund their advisors is not constrained by the Charter. She distinguished policy consultations from a formal electoral vote of the type at issue in *Haig*.]

Appeal allowed.

Baier v. Alberta
[2007] 2 SCR 673, 2007 SCC 31, 283 DLR (4th) 1

ROTHSTEIN J (McLachlin CJC and Binnie, Deschamps, and Charron JJ concurring):

· · ·

[3] The *Local Authorities Election Act*, RSA 2000, c. L-21 ("LAEA"), governs the proceedings for election to municipal councils and school boards in Alberta. The LAEA sets out the qualifications required to be a candidate for school trustee. A person may be nominated as a candidate if he or she is eligible to vote [and] meets certain residency requirements … .

· · ·

[5] … [However], a person is not eligible to be nominated as a candidate for election as a trustee of *any* school board if that person is employed by *any* school district or division, charter school, or private school in Alberta [unless she/he is on a leave of absence]. If a school employee is ultimately elected as a school trustee, s. 22(9) of the *LAEA* is engaged, which deems the school employee to have resigned his or her position of employment in order to carry out the role of school trustee. There is therefore a deemed resignation even when a school employee is elected to a school board which is not his or her employer.

· · ·

[21] In *Haig* [*v. Canada*, [1993] 2 SCR 995], this Court considered whether freedom of expression includes a positive right to be provided with a specific means of expression. L'Heureux-Dubé J for the majority, noted that freedom of expression has typically been conceptualized in terms of negative rights rather than positive entitlements:

> The traditional view, in colloquial terms, is that the freedom of expression contained in
> s. 2(b) prohibits gags, but does not compel the distribution of megaphones. [at 1035]

[22] That case arose in the context of federal and Quebec referenda concerning proposed constitutional amendments in 1992. Mr. Haig had moved from Ontario to Quebec and was unable to vote in either the federal or Quebec referendum because of different residency requirements in the federal and provincial legislation. He challenged the federal legislation as violating his freedom of expression. The majority held that the right to vote in the referendum was governed by the *Referendum Act*, SC 1992, c. 30, and s. 2(b) did not require the government to extend that right to all. L'Heureux-Dubé J stated:

> The Court is being asked to find that this *statutorily created platform* for expression has taken
> on constitutional status. In my view, though a referendum is undoubtedly a platform for ex-
> pression, *s. 2(b) of the Charter does not impose upon a government, whether provincial or*
> *federal, any positive obligation* to consult its citizens through the particular mechanism of a
> referendum. Nor does it confer upon all citizens the right to express their opinions in a ref-
> erendum. *A government is under no constitutional obligation to extend this platform of ex-*
> *pression to anyone, let alone to everyone.* A referendum as a platform of expression is, in my
> view, a matter of legislative policy and not of constitutional law. [Emphasis added; p. 1041.]

[23] The statutory platform analysis in *Haig* has been followed in a number of subsequent cases which have held that underinclusive legislative schemes or government action did not infringe s. 2. In *Native Women's Assn. of Canada v. Canada*, [1994] 3 SCR

627 ("NWAC"), the Native Women's Association of Canada alleged that the government's funding of some Aboriginal organizations, along with the opportunity to participate in constitutional discussions, required the government to bestow upon the Association an equal chance for expression of its views, and funding to enable it to do so. The Court determined that there was no positive duty on the government to provide funding to the Association in the circumstances. Sopinka J, for the majority, stated:

> [I]t cannot be said that every time the Government of Canada chooses to fund or consult a certain group, thereby providing a platform upon which to convey certain views, that the Government is also required to fund a group purporting to represent the opposite point of view. [at 656]

and

> The freedom of expression guaranteed by s. 2(b) of the Charter does not guarantee any particular means of expression or place a positive obligation upon the Government to consult anyone. [at 663]

[24] In *Siemens v. Manitoba (Attorney General)*, [2003] 1 SCR 6, 2003 SCC 3, the Court considered legislation, the *Gaming Control Local Option (VLT) Act*, SM 1999, c. 44, enabling municipalities to hold binding plebiscites on prohibiting video lottery terminals ("VLTs"). The legislation also deemed a previous non-binding plebiscite in the Town of Winkler, in which the residents had voted to prohibit VLTs, to be binding. The appellants, owners of the Winkler Inn who relied on VLTs for revenue, claimed that the effect of the "deemed vote" was to deny them the right to vote in a plebiscite under the Act, and therefore violated their freedom of expression. Following *Haig*, the Court held there was no breach of s. 2(b). A municipal plebiscite, like a referendum, was a creation of legislation, and any right to vote in it must be found within the language of that legislation.

[25] The statutory platform analysis in *Haig* has also been applied in cases raising claims under Charter s. 2(d) freedom of association. In *Delisle [v. Canada (Deputy Attorney General)*, [1999] 2 SCR 989], the Court considered whether underinclusive labour legislation offended s. 2(d) or 2(b). Bastarache J, for the majority, found that neither s. 2(d) or 2(b) required that RCMP officers be included in a statutory labour regime. He made clear that underinclusive legislation would generally not offend s. 2:

> The structure of s. 2 of the Charter is very different from that of s. 15 and it is important not to confuse them. While s. 2 defines the specific fundamental freedoms Canadians enjoy, s. 15 provides they are equal before and under the law and have the right to equal protection and equal benefit of the law. The only reason why s. 15 may from time to time be invoked when a statute is underinclusive, that is, when it does not offer the same protection or the same benefits to a person on the basis of an enumerated or analogous ground (on this issue, see *Schachter v. Canada*, [1992] 2 SCR 679), is because this is contemplated in the wording itself of s. 15. ... However, while the letter and spirit of the right to equality sometimes dictate a requirement of inclusion in a statutory regime, the same cannot be said of the individual freedoms set out in s. 2, which generally requires only that the state not interfere and does not call upon any comparative standard. [at para. 25]

Citing Dickson J's definition of "freedom" as "the absence of coercion or constraint" (*R v. Big M Drug Mart Ltd.*, [1985] 1 SCR 295, at p. 336), Bastarache J went on to state at para. 26:

> It is because of the very nature of freedom that s. 2 generally imposes a negative obligation on the government and not a positive obligation of protection or assistance.

As Bastarache J stated at para. 27 of *Delisle*, except in exceptional circumstances, ss. 2(d) and 2(b) require only that Parliament not interfere with these fundamental freedoms.

[26] While *Haig*, *NWAC*, *Siemens* and *Delisle*, found s. 2 was not offended by under-inclusive legislation or underinclusive government action and that there was no right to a particular platform for expression, the Court left open the possibility that, in exceptional cases, positive action by government may be called for under s. 2. In *Haig*, for example, L'Heureux-Dubé J left the door open to positive government action being required in some cases. At p. 1039, she stated:

> ... a situation might arise in which, in order to make a fundamental freedom meaningful, a posture of restraint would not be enough, and positive governmental action might be required. This might, for example, take the form of legislative intervention aimed at preventing certain conditions which muzzle expression, or ensuring public access to certain kinds of information.

[27] In *Dunmore v. Ontario (Attorney General)*, [2001] 3 SCR 1016, 2001 SCC 94, a majority of the Court found such an exception to the general rule that s. 2 does not require positive government action. Labour legislation excluding agricultural workers from a protective regime was found to infringe s. 2(d). Bastarache J, for the majority, considered the factors relevant to establishing an exception:

(1) Claims of underinclusion should be grounded in fundamental Charter freedoms rather than in access to a particular statutory regime (para. 24).

(2) The claimant must meet an evidentiary burden of demonstrating that exclusion from a statutory regime permits a substantial interference with activity protected under s. 2 (para. 25), or that the purpose of the exclusion was to infringe such activity (paras. 31-33). The exercise of a fundamental freedom need not be impossible, but the claimant must seek more than a particular channel for exercising his or her fundamental freedoms (para. 25).

(3) The state must be accountable for the inability to exercise the fundamental freedom: "[U]nderinclusive state action falls into suspicion not simply to the extent it discriminates against an unprotected class, but to the extent it substantially orchestrates, encourages or sustains the violation of fundamental freedoms" (para. 26).

[28] In *Dunmore*, these factors were met. The appellant agricultural workers sought protection for the freedom to establish and maintain an employee association. They were substantially incapable of exercising their fundamental freedom to organize without protective legislation. Furthermore, their exclusion from the legislative regime

"function[ed] not simply to permit private interference with their fundamental freedoms, but to substantially reinforce such interferences" (para. 35). Agricultural workers were distinguished from the RCMP officers in *Delisle* because RCMP officers were capable of associating despite exclusion from a protective regime. Unlike agricultural workers, for RCMP officers, inclusion in a statutory regime would serve to enhance rather than safeguard their exercise of a fundamental freedom.

[29] While *Dunmore* concerned freedom of association rather than freedom of expression, the three factors for challenging underinclusive legislation were described as applicable to s. 2 in general. As Bastarache J noted, *Haig*, *NWAC* and *Delisle* circumscribed, but did not foreclose, the possibility of challenging underinclusion under s. 2 of the Charter. Thus, *Dunmore* makes clear that while claims of underinclusion may raise concerns under Charter s. 15 equality rights, in certain cases, underinclusion may offend s. 2 itself.

[30] In cases where a government defending a Charter challenge alleges, or the Charter claimant concedes, that a positive rights claim is being made under s. 2(b), a court must proceed in the following way. First it must consider whether the activity for which the claimant seeks s. 2(b) protection is a form of expression. If so, then second, the court must determine if the claimant claims a positive entitlement to government action, or simply the right to be free from government interference. If it is a positive rights claim, then third, the three *Dunmore* factors must be considered. As indicated above, these three factors are (1) that the claim is grounded in a fundamental freedom of expression rather than in access to a particular statutory regime; (2) that the claimant has demonstrated that exclusion from a statutory regime has the effect of a substantial interference with s. 2(b) freedom of expression, or has the purpose of infringing freedom of expression under s. 2(b); and (3) that the government is responsible for the inability to exercise the fundamental freedom. If the claimant cannot satisfy these criteria then the s. 2(b) claim will fail. If the three factors are satisfied then s. 2(b) has been infringed and the analysis will shift to s. 1.

[31] ... [In this case] [t]he respondent concedes that seeking nomination for school trustee and some of the activities of school trustees may be characterized as having an expressive nature. ...

[33] ... Expressive activity is in issue, although what is restricted is the platform on which that expression may take place rather than the content of the expression. I find that the expressive aspects of school trustee candidacy and school trusteeship are sufficient to continue consideration of whether s. 2(b) is violated.

· · ·

[44] ... The appellants' claim, as they have articulated it, is grounded in access to the particular statutory regime of school trusteeship. As such it would not meet the first of the *Dunmore* criteria.

· · ·

[48] In my view, the appellants have not established that their practical exclusion from school trusteeship substantially interferes with their ability to express themselves on matters relating to the education system. The *LAEA* Amendments may deprive them of one particular means of expression, but it has not been demonstrated that absent in-

clusion in this statutory scheme, they are unable to express themselves on education issues. ...

[49] [T]the appellants' ability to be a candidate and serve as a school trustee *is* significantly impaired by the legislation. But school trusteeship in itself is not a protected freedom.

. . .

[53] The chambers judge found "the purpose of the *LAEA* Amendments ... does not infringe s. 2(b) as the legislation is meant to protect the democratic process by ensuring the business of school boards can be carried on without concerns about conflicts of interest" (para. 79). ... I would not interfere with the findings of the chambers judge on this point.

[54] The appellants have not met the evidentiary burden of demonstrating that exclusion from the statutory regime permits a substantial interference with their freedom of expression on school board issues or education generally. Rather they seek a particular channel of expression. Nor have the appellants proved that the purpose of the LAEA Amendments was to infringe their freedom of expression. Therefore, their claim does not meet the second *Dunmore* factor. Because the appellants have not established a substantial interference with their ability to exercise their freedom of expression, it is unnecessary to consider the third *Dunmore* factor.

[55] In finding against the appellants here, I leave open the possibility that there may be exceptional situations where exclusion from a statutory platform interferes substantially with fundamental freedom of expression and meets the *Dunmore* criteria. While s. 2(b) does not give a right to a specific statutory platform, so that restricting access to such a platform will not generally offend s. 2(b), and while *Dunmore* itself was decided under s. 2(d) rather than s. 2(b), there may be exceptional cases where exclusion from a platform so substantially interferes with freedom of expression that it may infringe s. 2(b). However, the case at bar is not such a case.

. . .

[60] The consistent approach of this Court has been to characterize a claim such as the appellants' as a claim to a platform for expression, which engages s. 2(b). The platform approach strikes an appropriate balance by maintaining this Court's traditional broad approach to freedom of expression, without constitutionalizing a positive obligation on governments to provide platforms of expression except in unusual circumstances. I have found that such unusual circumstances are not present in the appellants' case.

[LeBel J (Bastarache and Abella JJ concurring) wrote a concurring judgment in which he found that the constitutional guarantee of freedom of expression does not protect a right to run for office as a school trustee and, if elected, to take part in the management of the school board. In his view, the appellants' claim concerned a democratic right—that is, the right to be elected to a management role in the local education system—that the Charter does not protect. He found that the ban on school employees running for office and serving as school trustees did not prevent them from expressing views on any subject, let alone education.

NOTES AND QUESTIONS

Given the negative rulings in *Haig*, *Native Women's Association of Canada*, and *Baier*, are there any situations where the courts might impose a positive obligation on the government to facilitate or support expression? Consider the example of the police officer who declines to protect a speaker from an angry mob because he or she also objects to the message being communicated. The failure to enforce ordinary assault laws in such a case would be experienced by the speaker as state censorship or, at least, as state support for censorship. The individual reasonably expects state protection from unlawful interference with individual expression. Assault laws are part of the basic framework within which public discourse takes place. Furthermore, protection from assault rests on concerns or values that are unrelated to the speaker's viewpoint. For these reasons, a state decision not to protect an individual speaker from assault would be viewed as suppression of expression and not simply as a failure to support or protect expression. How far can this approach be extended?

CHAPTER TWENTY-ONE

Freedom of Association

I. INTRODUCTION

The readings in this chapter are testimony to the fact that freedom of association is intimately connected to the history of labour relations in Canada. The common law of employment, generally speaking, is hostile to efforts by employees to improve their terms and conditions of work by collective means. With the rise of collective bargaining legislation, employees generally are entitled to join together for the purposes of collective bargaining with their employer and, if necessary and under strict conditions, to strike for the purposes of improving their working conditions. Thus, the history of labour relations in Canada, in many ways, is a history of efforts by employees to expand their freedom of association. With the enactment of s. 2(d) of the Charter, the judiciary became vested with the authority to rule on the constitutionality of laws that regulate relations between employers and employees. The constitutional guarantee of freedom of association raises critical questions concerning the extent to which governments can restrict the ability of employees to form unions, bargain collectively, and strike. It also raises questions about whether employees can be required to belong or contribute to trade unions and participate in their lawful activities.

Yet it would be a mistake to think of freedom of association as significant solely in the context of labour relations. John Stuart Mill wrote that "from the liberty of each individual follows the liberty, within the same limits of combination among individuals; freedom to unite, for any purpose not involving harm to others." Dicey, emphasizing the unique quality of group identity, wrote that "[w]hen a body of twenty or two thousand men bind themselves together to act in a particular way for some common purpose, they create a body which by no fiction of law, but by the very nature of things, differs from the individuals of which it is constituted." Other theorists stress the importance of "intermediate associations" between the state and the individual to democratic values and civic society. Associational activity is central to individual, communal, and national identities that reach well beyond the context of work. When you read through the following materials, try to extrapolate from the labour relations setting to other settings, such as the family, religious institutions, political activity, and ethnic and cultural ties. What are the implications of the Court's approach for other spheres of social and political life that manifest associational activity? How should freedom of association relate to other constitutional guarantees, such as equality or freedom of religion?

In the Court's first decision under section 2(d), the *Alberta Reference*, below, one of three decisions known collectively as the *Labour Trilogy*, the majority of the Court, per McIntyre and Le Dain JJ, defined the scope of freedom of association narrowly, an interpretation which governed subsequent cases until the *Dunmore* decision, below, in 2001 in which the majority adopted some of Dickson CJC's dissenting views in the *Alberta Reference*. More recently, in *Health Services and Support v. British Columbia*, [2007] 2 SCR 391, 283 DLR (4th) 40, the Court dramatically overturned much of what remained of its approach in the *Alberta Reference*, ushering in an expansive conception of freedom of association in the context of work.

II. THE RIGHT TO ASSOCIATE WITH OTHERS

NOTE ON THE LABOUR TRILOGY

In *Reference re Public Service Employee Relations Act (Alta.)*, [1987] 1 SCR 313, 38 DLR (4th) 161, the Government of Alberta had referred three statutes to the Alberta Court of Appeal, the opinion of which the Government subsequently appealed to the Supreme Court of Canada. The statutes were the *Public Service Employee Relations Act*, RSA 1980, c. P-33, the *Labour Relations Act*, RSA 1980, c. L-1.1, and the *Police Officers Collective Bargaining Act*, SA 1983, c. P-12.05, all of which removed the right to strike of selected government employees (police, firefighters, hospital employees, and public servants) and replaced that right with a scheme of compulsory arbitration. The provisions governing interest arbitration also limited the matters that could be arbitrated and included criteria to guide arbitral decision making. The legal issue presented to the judiciary was whether the right to strike and the right to bargain collectively are constitutionally protected under s. 2(d) of the Charter, which guarantees freedom of association. A majority of the Court of Appeal decided that s. 2(d) of the Charter did not include the right to strike and thus declared the three statutes valid.

McIntyre J of the Supreme Court of Canada identified freedom of association as "one of the most fundamental rights in a free society," as indicated by "the fact that historically the conqueror, seeking to control foreign peoples, invariably strikes first at freedom of association in order to eliminate effective opposition. Meetings are forbidden, curfews are enforced, trade and commerce is suppressed and rigid controls are imposed to isolate and thus debilitate the individual." In defining the scope of freedom of association under section 2(d) of the Charter, McIntyre J stated:

> Freedom of association then serves the interest of the individual, strengthens the general social order, and supports the healthy functioning of democratic government.
>
> In considering the constitutional position of freedom of association, it must be recognized that while it advances many group interests and, of course, cannot be exercised alone, it is none the less a freedom belonging to the individual and not to the group formed through its exercise. ... People, by merely combining together, cannot create an entity which has greater constitutional rights and freedoms than they, as individuals, possess. Freedom of association cannot therefore vest independent rights in the group. ...
>
> The recognition of this principle in the case at bar is of great significance. The only basis on which it is contended that the Charter enshrines a right to strike is that of freedom of association. Collective bargaining is a group concern, a group activity, but the group can exercise only the constitutional rights of its individual members on behalf of those members. If the right asserted is not found in the Charter for the individual, it cannot be implied for the group merely

by the fact of association. It follows as well that the rights of the individual members of the group cannot be enlarged merely by the fact of association.

McIntyre J examined six theories about the meaning of freedom of association. The first is that freedom of association is limited to the right to associate with others, but that neither the objects nor the actions of the group are protected. Under the second approach, freedom of association protects the right to engage collectively in activities that are constitutionally protected for the individual. The third approach protects the organization in doing whatever the individual could lawfully do alone (that is, individuals can do together that which they can lawfully do alone). The fourth approach protects collective activities considered to be fundamental to our culture (such as marriage or gaining a livelihood). The fifth extends protection to all activities necessary for the association to achieve its lawful goals (this was the approach taken by the Ontario Divisional Court in *Re Service Employees' Int'l Union, Loc. 204 and Broadway Manor Nursing Home* (1983), 4 DLR (4th) 231, 44 OR (2d) 392, 10 CRR 37, which held that freedom of association included the right to bargain collectively and to strike). The sixth approach is the broadest, encompassing all acts done in association, subject to limitation under s. 1 of the Charter.

McIntyre J rejected both the fifth and sixth approaches. The fifth, he said, "rejects the individual nature of freedom of association" and "confer[s] greater constitutional rights upon members of the association than upon non-members." The sixth approach would give constitutional status to activities simply because they were performed in association, even when some of the activities might not be protected when performed by individuals. He also rejected the fourth approach because it too focuses on the activity and not on the purpose of the right, which, in his view, is to ensure that goals can be pursued collectively as well as individually.

He then considered the remaining three approaches. The first, under which individuals are able to join together to engage in lawful activities and to establish and maintain organizations, reflects the pre-Charter scope of freedom of association and should be recognized under the Charter. In addition, freedom of association should protect not only the collective exercise of rights that are constitutionally protected for the individual, as under the second approach, but activities that the individual may *lawfully* pursue, as permitted by the third approach. Although the legislature could restrict otherwise lawful individual activity, it could not restrict the same activity by associations if it did not limit the same activity when carried on by individuals.

Since the right belongs to individuals and is dependent on the lawful or constitutional rights in which individuals can engage, it does not encompass activities that can be engaged in only by more than one person. Accordingly, as McIntyre J explained:

> When this definition of freedom of association is applied, it is clear that it does not guarantee the right to strike. Since the right to strike is not independently protected under the Charter, it can receive protection under freedom of association only if it is an activity which is permitted by law to an individual. Accepting this conclusion, the appellants argue that freedom of association must guarantee the right to strike because individuals may lawfully refuse to work. This position, however, is untenable for two reasons. First, it is not correct to say that it is lawful for an individual employee to cease work during the currency of his contract of employment. ...

The second reason is simply that there is no analogy whatever between the cessation of work by a single employee and a strike conducted in accordance with modern labour legislation. The individual has, by reason of the cessation of work, either breached or terminated his contract of employment. It is true that the law will not compel the specific performance of the contract by ordering him back to work as this would reduce "the employee to a state tantamount to slavery": I. Christie, *Employment Law in Canada* (Toronto: Butterworths, 1980), p. 268. But, this is markedly different from a lawful strike. An employee who ceases work does not contemplate a return to work, while employees on strike always contemplate a return to work. In recognition of this fact, the law does not regard a strike as either a breach of contract or a termination of employment. Every province and the federal Parliament has enacted legislation which preserves the employer-employee relationship during a strike: ...

In addition to finding that freedom of association does not include a right to strike, McIntyre J gave several other reasons based on the nature of the Charter that support that conclusion. It is consistent with the general approach of the Charter, which, in his view, recognizes individual rights rather, with some exceptions, than group rights and which, again with a few exceptions, does not protect economic rights. Furthermore, he pointed out, although the framers were aware that strikes were "commonplace" in Canada, and inclusion of a right to strike in the Charter was discussed, no Charter resolution was proposed before the Special Joint Committee of the Senate and of the House of Commons on the Constitution of Canada to include protection for the right. Even though strikes may be commonplace, legislation has only recently recognized the right to strike and therefore it has not attained the status of "an immutable, fundamental right, firmly embedded in our traditions, our political and social philosophy."

McIntyre J bolstered these reasons with a justification grounded in the policy that labour law is best determined by the legislatures:

... Labour law, as we have seen, is a fundamentally important as well as an extremely sensitive subject. It is based upon a political and economic compromise between organized labour—a very powerful socio-economic force—on the one hand, and the employers of labour—an equally powerful socio-economic force—on the other. The balance between the two forces is delicate and the public at large depends for its security and welfare upon the maintenance of that balance. One group concedes certain interests in exchange for concessions from the other. There is clearly no correct balance which may be struck giving permanent satisfaction to the two groups as well as securing the public interest. The whole process is inherently dynamic and unstable. Care must be taken then in considering whether constitutional protection should be given to one aspect of this dynamic and evolving process while leaving the others subject to the social pressures of the day. Great changes—economic, social and industrial—are afoot, not only in Canada and in North America, but as well in other parts of the world. Changes in the Canadian national economy, the decline in resource-based as well as heavy industries, the changing patterns of international trade and industry, have resulted in great pressure to reassess the traditional approaches to economic and industrial questions, including questions of labour law and policy ... . [I]t is obvious that the immediate direction of labour policy is unclear. It is, however, clear that labour policy can only be developed step by step with, in this country, the provinces playing their "classic federal role as laboratories for legal experimentation with our industrial relations ailments": Paul Weiler, *Reconcilable Differences: New Directions in Canadian Labour*

Law (Scarborough, ON: Carswell, 1980), p. 11). The fulfilment of this role in the past has resulted in the growth and development of the body of labour law which now prevails in Canada. The fluid and constantly changing conditions of modern society demand that it continue. To intervene in that dynamic process at this early stage of Charter development by implying constitutional protection for a right to strike would, in my view, give to one of the contending forces an economic weapon removed from and made immune, subject to s. 1, to legislative control which could go far towards freezing the development of labour relations and curtailing that process of evolution necessary to meet the changing circumstances of a modern society in a modern world. This, I repeat, is not to say that a right to strike does not exist at law or that it should be abolished. It merely means that at this stage of our Charter development such a right should not have constitutional status which would impair the process of future development in legislative hands. ...

To constitutionalize a particular feature of labour relations by entrenching a right to strike would have other adverse effects. Our experience with labour relations has shown that the courts, as a general rule, are not the best arbiters of disputes which arise from time to time. Labour legislation has recognized this fact and has created other procedures and other tribunals for the more expeditious and efficient settlement of labour problems. Problems arising in labour matters frequently involve more than legal questions. Political, social and economic questions frequently dominate in labour disputes. ... In my view, it is scarcely contested that specialized labour tribunals are better suited than courts for resolving labour problems, except for the resolution of purely legal questions. If the right to strike is constitutionalized, then its application, its extent and any questions of its legality, become matters of law. This would inevitably throw the courts back into the field of labour relations and much of the value of specialized labour tribunals would be lost. ...

Justice McIntyre's understanding of judicial restraint in the labour relations arena is reinforced by his concern that courts would be required, under s. 1, to assess whether a service is essential, whether arbitration is an appropriate substitute for the right to strike, or whether it is justifiable to postpone collective bargaining. According to McIntyre J, "[n]one of these issues is amenable to principled resolution" and should be determined by the legislatures.

It was not clear from McIntyre J's opinion in the *Alberta Reference* whether he also had concluded that collective bargaining was not protected by freedom of association. Le Dain J (Beetz and La Forest JJ concurring) agreed with McIntyre J's conclusion, but viewed it as stating that the right to bargain collectively was not protected under freedom of association. Le Dain J emphasized that freedom of association will be applied to "a wide range of associations or organizations of a political, religious, social or economic nature, with a wide variety of objects, as well as activity by which the objects may be pursued," and therefore it is important to be restrained in granting constitutional protection to activities in which associations engage.

Dickson CJC (Wilson J concurring) took a different view of the scope of freedom of association, which he described as "the cornerstone of modern labour relations." He considered two approaches to the scope of the freedom, the constitutive and the derivative, both of which he rejected in favour of an interpretation that recognized that individuals are sometimes able to engage in activities through associations that they are unable to engage in solely as individuals:

A wide variety of alternative interpretations of freedom of association has been advanced in the jurisprudence summarized above and in argument before this court.

At one extreme is a purely constitutive definition whereby freedom of association entails only a freedom to belong to or form an association. On this view, the constitutional guarantee does not extend beyond protecting the individual's *status* as a member of an association. It would not protect his or her associational *actions*.

In the trade union context, then, a constitutive definition would find a *prima facie* violation of s. 2(d) of the Charter in legislation such as s. 2(1) of the *Police Officers Act*, which prohibits membership in any organization affiliated with a trade union. But it could find no violation of s. 2(d) in respect of legislation which prohibited a concerted refusal to work. Indeed, a wide variety of trade union activities, ranging from the organization of social activities for its members, to the establishment of union pension plans, to the discussion of collective bargaining strategy, could be prohibited by the State without infringing s. 2(d).

The essentially formal nature of a constitutive approach to freedom of association is equally apparent when one considers other types of associational activity in our society. While the constitutive approach might find a possible violation of s. 2(d) in a legislative enactment which prohibited marriage for certain classes of people, it would hold inoffensive an enactment which precluded the same people from engaging in the activities integral to a marriage, such as cohabiting and raising children together. If freedom of association only protects the joining together of persons for common purposes, but not the pursuit of the very activities for which the association was formed, then the freedom is indeed legalistic, ungenerous, indeed vapid.

In my view, while it is unquestionable that s. 2(d), at a minimum, guarantees the liberty of persons to *be* in association or belong to an organization, it must extend beyond a concern for associational status to give effective protection to the interests to which the constitutional guarantee is directed. In this respect, it is important to consider the purposive approach to constitutional interpretation mandated by this court in *R v. Big M Drug Mart Ltd.* ...

A second approach, the derivative approach, prevalent in the United States, embodies a somewhat more generous definition of freedom of association than the formal, constitutive approach. In the Canadian context, it is suggested by some that associational action which relates specifically to one of the other freedoms enumerated in s. 2 is constitutionally protected, but other associational activity is not.

I am unable, however, to accept that freedom of association should be interpreted so restrictively. Section 2(d) of the Charter provides an explicit and independent guarantee of freedom of association. In this respect it stands in marked contrast to the First Amendment to the American Constitution. The derivative approach would, in my view, largely make surplusage of s. 2(d). The associational or collective dimensions of s. 2(a) and (b) have already been recognized by this court in *R v. Big M Drug Mart Ltd.* without resort to s. 2(d). The associational aspect of s. 2(c) clearly finds adequate protection in the very expression of a freedom of peaceful assembly. What is to be learnt from the United States jurisprudence is not that freedom of association must be restricted to associational activities involving independent constitutional rights but, rather, that the express conferral of a freedom of association is unnecessary if all that is intended is to give effect to the collective enjoyment of other individual freedoms.

· · ·

Freedom of association is most essential in those circumstances where the individual is liable to be prejudiced by the actions of some larger and more powerful entity, like the government or an employer. Association has always been the means through which political, cultural and racial minorities, religious groups and workers have sought to attain their purposes and fulfil their aspirations; it has enabled those who would otherwise be vulnerable and ineffective to meet on more equal terms the power and strength of those with whom their interests interact and, perhaps, conflict. ...

The Chief Justice accepted that the guarantee protects the collective exercise of lawful individual activities, but pointed out that there will be situations "when no analogy involving individuals can be found for associational activity, or when a comparison between groups and individuals fails to capture the essence of a possible violation of associational rights." This is the case with the right to strike, since, in his view, there is no individual parallel to the collective action of striking.

Finally, Dickson CJC distinguished between associational activity with economic objectives, such as earning a livelihood or dignity in the workplace, and "concerns of an exclusively pecuniary nature," the former of which he believed should receive constitutional protection, while protection of the latter is more debatable. He concluded, therefore, that collective bargaining and the right to strike are encompassed by freedom of association:

> The role of association has always been vital as a means of protecting the essential needs and interests of working people. Throughout history, workers have associated to overcome their vulnerability as individuals to the strength of their employers. The capacity to bargain collectively has long been recognized as one of the integral and primary functions of associations of working people. While trade unions also fulfil other important social, political and charitable functions, collective bargaining remains vital to the capacity of individual employees to participate in ensuring fair wages, health and safety protections and equitable and humane working conditions.
>
> • • •
>
> Closely related to collective bargaining, at least in our existing industrial relations context, is the freedom to strike. ...
>
> The Woods Task Force Report at p. 129 identifies the work stoppage as the essential ingredient in collective bargaining:
>
> > Strikes and lockouts are an indispensable part of the Canadian industrial relations system and are likely to remain so in our present socio-economic-political society.
>
> • • •
>
> I am satisfied, in sum, that whether or not freedom of association generally extends to protecting associational activity for the pursuit of exclusively pecuniary ends—a question on which I express no opinion—collective bargaining protects important employee interests which cannot be characterized as merely pecuniary in nature. Under our existing system of industrial relations, effective constitutional protection of the associational interests of employees in the collective bargaining process requires concomitant protection of their freedom to withdraw collectively their services, subject to s. 1 of the Charter.

Dickson CJC found that the restrictions under the impugned legislation were not justified under s. 1 of the Charter because they inadequately defined the essential services that could be exempted from the right to strike, they were overbroad in their application to certain workers, and the arbitration system was not an adequate replacement for the right to strike.

The Court delivered reasons in two companion cases at the same time as it rendered judgment in the *Alberta Reference*. In *Retail, Wholesale and Department Store Union v. Saskatchewan*, [1987] 1 SCR 460, 38 DLR (4th) 277, the first of the two companion cases, the respondent union had been negotiating a contract with Palm Dairies Ltd. After negotiations had broken off, the union notified the dairy that it would commence a series of rotating strikes. Before the strikes had begun, the dairy chose to lock out the entire workforce. The Government of Saskatchewan responded with *The Dairy Workers (Maintenance of Operations) Act*, which prevented the union from striking and the dairy from locking out workers. The union then brought an action in the Court of Queen's Bench seeking a declaration that the Act violated s. 2(d) of the Charter. The application was denied, but on appeal to the Saskatchewan Court of Appeal, the application was granted. The government subsequently appealed to the Supreme Court of Canada, which allowed the appeal, Wilson J dissenting. The decisions of Beetz, Le Dain, La Forest, and McIntyre JJ are the same as those outlined in the majority in the *Alberta Reference*.

Dickson CJC wrote separate concurring reasons. Although he held that s. 2(d) of the Charter guarantees the right to strike and bargain collectively, he held that, under the circumstances before him, the Act was saved by s. 1 because of the need to protect dairy farmers from grave economic harm should a strike or lockout occur. The arbitration provisions in the Act were held to be fair, since either party could invoke them and there were no restrictions on arbitrable subjects.

Wilson J dissented. She felt that the evidence of economic harm to the dairy industry was not sufficient to warrant restraint of the type imposed. Moreover, the government's strike and lockout ban was not sufficiently tailored to meet the objective of preventing harm. She suggested a partial ban should have been imposed.

In *PSAC v. Canada*, [1987] 1 SCR 424, 38 DLR (4th) 249, the second companion case to the *Alberta Reference*, at issue was the constitutional validity of the *Public Sector Compensation Restraint Act* (Can.). This statute implemented the federal government's "six and five program" and, in effect, imposed fixed wage increases on federal government employees for two years. The legislation removed the right to strike and the right to alter the compensation scheme through collective bargaining for the two-year period. Changes to the noncompensation provisions of a contract or collective agreement could be negotiated by agreement.

The Public Service Alliance of Canada, a union that represents a large number of federal government employees, brought an action seeking a declaration that the Act violated s. 2(d) of the Charter and s. 1(b) of the Canadian Bill of Rights (the guarantee of equality before the law).

At trial, Madame Justice Reed of the Federal Court ruled that s. 2(d) of the Charter does not guarantee the right to bargain collectively. On appeal, the Federal Court of Appeal held that s. 2(d) of the Charter does not guarantee the objects or means of an association, only the right to associate itself.

On further appeal to the Supreme Court of Canada, the Court upheld the decision of the Federal Court of Appeal (Wilson J dissenting, Dickson CJC dissenting in part). In very brief reasons, McIntyre and Le Dain JJ repeated their reasoning in the *Alberta Reference*. (Again, Le Dain J wrote for the majority.)

Dickson CJC dissented in part. While he felt that the limitation on collective bargaining over monetary issues was reasonable under s. 1 in order to provide an example or model for private sector restraint, he was also of the view that it was not justifiable to limit bargaining to issues not related to compensation. Wilson J also dissented and argued that the Act could not be saved by s. 1. Although the objective of controlling inflation was valid, the means chosen (restraints on federal public sector employees) were completely arbitrary.

On the Canadian Bill of Rights issue, the court decided 5 to 1 (Wilson J dissenting) that the Act did not violate s. 1(b) of the Bill of Rights. Even if the right defined by the Bill had been breached, the majority viewed reducing inflation as a valid federal objective authorizing the infringement.

In the *Alberta Reference*, Dickson CJC's dissent proposes a different test for determining the scope of freedom of association from that proposed by either McIntyre or Le Dain JJ. What are the differences among the three tests? Do they suggest different understandings of constitutional guarantees?

NOTES ON PROFESSIONAL INSTITUTE OF THE PUBLIC SERVICE OF CANADA v. NORTHWEST TERRITORIES

1. While it was clear from the decisions rendered in the *Labour Trilogy* that freedom of association did not include a right to strike, what was less evident in the wake of these judgments was the constitutional status of collective bargaining. It will be recalled in *PSAC v. Canada*, above, that this issue was left largely unresolved as only three of the six justices held that the right to bargain collectively could not be found within the guarantee of freedom of association. Yet in *Professional Institute of the Public Service of Canada v. Northwest Territories*, [1990] 2 SCR 367, 72 DLR (4th) 1 (*PIPSC*), three years after the *Labour Trilogy*, a majority of the court dismissed an appeal that would have entrenched the right to bargain collectively within the meaning of s. 2(d) of the Charter.

At issue in *PIPSC* was the constitutionality of a statutory collective bargaining regime adopted by the government of the Northwest Territories. Under the provisions of the scheme, unions were required to secure legislative permission by way of statutory incorporation (accomplished by s. 42 of the *Public Service Act*) before they could bargain collectively in the Territories and hold the government to good faith negotiations. The Professional Institute, which had previously been the bargaining agent for 32 nurses before they were transferred to the employ of the territorial government, sought legislative permission under the scheme but was denied incorporation, thereby rendering it incapable of acting as the bargaining agent of the nurses. Subsequently, the Institute sought a declaration that s. 42 of the *Public Service Act* interfered with s. 2(d) of the Charter.

After the Institute scored an initial victory in the Supreme Court of the Northwest Territories, the decision was reversed by the Court of Appeal, setting the stage for an appeal to the Supreme Court of Canada. The appeal was dismissed by a majority of the Court.

Justice Sopinka, who wrote the plurality judgment, drawing from a review of the *Alberta Reference*, outlined the doctrinal approach in addressing violations of s. 2(d) of the Charter. In his view, the *Alberta Reference* stood for four propositions:

> [F]irst, that s. 2(d) protects the freedom to establish, belong to and maintain an association; second, that s. 2(d) does not protect an activity solely on the ground that the activity is a foundational or essential purpose of an association; third, that s. 2(d) protects the exercise in

association of the constitutional rights and freedoms of individuals; and fourth, that s. 2(d) protects the exercise in association of the lawful rights of individuals.

In applying this framework to the right to bargain collectively, Sopinka J found that although such activity was an integral function of trade unions, it was nevertheless beyond the protection afforded by s. 2(d) of the Charter. It was, he maintained, no longer an "open question" as to whether the scope of s. 2(d) extended to protect essential or integral purposes of an association. This was definitively answered in the negative by the decisions of the *Labour Trilogy*. Thus, while s. 42 of the *Public Service Act* may restrict the activity of collective bargaining, it did not interfere with the ability of individuals to join or form associations that is needed to engage s. 2(d) protection. Moreover, in keeping with the individualized approach to freedom of association articulated by McIntyre J in the *Alberta Reference*, Sopinka J held that, given there exists no individual analogue to the right to bargain collectively over conditions of employment, it was impossible to rationalize this right in terms of the constitutional guarantees of freedom of association. Dickson CJC, and L'Heureux-Dubé and La Forest JJ, wrote separate reasons concurring with Sopinka J.

Cory J dissenting, with whom Wilson and Gonthier JJ concurred, argued that the regime put in place by the government necessarily interfered with an individual's right to choose and form a trade union because it vested in the government an "unfettered discretion to choose which association will be incorporated as a collective bargaining agent." To the extent that this discretion interferes with an individual's ability to join a trade union of their choice, it violates s. 2(d) of the Charter. Accordingly, given the existence of more traditional certification regimes in other jurisdictions, the system enacted by the government of the Territories, in Justice Cory's view, could not be saved under s. 1 of the Charter.

2. Do you agree with Cory J's argument that once a legislature has created a regime for the collective negotiation of terms and conditions of work, employees ought to be free to determine among themselves which group or entity will represent them?

3. In *Delisle v. Canada (Deputy Attorney General)*, [1999] 2 SCR 989, 176 DLR (4th) 513, the Court addressed the constitutionality of a provision in the *Public Service Staff Relations Act* that expressly excluded members of the Royal Canadian Mounted Police from the application of the Act, which established a collective bargaining regime for most civil servants and protected the right to form and join a union by prohibiting specific forms of managerial interference. Bastarache J, for a majority of the Court (Cory and Iacobucci JJ dissenting), relying on *PIPSC*, held there to be no violation of freedom of association. He added that "the fundamental freedoms protected by s. 2 of the Charter do not impose a positive obligation of protection or inclusion on Parliament or the government, except perhaps in exceptional circumstances which are not at issue in the present case" (para. 33).

P. Macklem, "Developments in Employment Law: The 1990-91 Term"
(1992), 3 *Supreme Court Law Review* (2d) 227, at 239-41 (footnotes omitted)

Justice Sopinka's majority judgment in *PIPS* perhaps represents the final curtain on the constitutional guarantee of freedom of association in the context of work. Unless there is a major doctrinal reversal, the combined effect of the *Labour Trilogy* and *PIPS* is to strip the constitutional guarantee of freedom of association of any substantive meaning in the context of union power. As a result of the *Labour Trilogy*, the Charter does not constitutionally recognize the freedom of workers to collectively withdraw their labour even when they are under no contractual obligation to continue to work for an employer. As a result of *PIPS*, the Charter does not recognize the freedom of employees to band together for the purpose of bargaining collectively with their employers. In the words of Justice Cory: "The fact that the people who form the association (the union) may still meet together without interference from the state has no meaning if this association cannot be recognized under the relevant labour legislation."

As stated, the invocation of Justice McIntyre's test in the *Labour Trilogy* was defended by reference to an individualistic vision of constitutional guarantees. By the time *PIPS* was decided, the test was a matter of precedent and was presented as an incontrovertible feature of the constitutional landscape. The indeterminacy of the guarantee was made to disappear. Alternative visions of freedom of association were not even introduced for discussion. Even Chief Justice Dickson accepted the now-dominant understanding of the guarantee. The interpretive function took on an apolitical, objective veneer. Moreover, in applying the test that now has fixed the meaning of freedom of association, arguments were ignored that would have led to the protection of the very activity that the Court excluded from section 2(d). As a result of the *Labour Trilogy* and *PIPS*, freedom of association is rendered barren, protecting nothing of positive importance to the union movement.

Whatever one thinks of the institutional competence of the judiciary in second-guessing substantive policy choices of legislatures, or of the progressive potential of Charter litigation, the combined effect of the *Labour Trilogy* and *PIPS* is a national embarrassment. As stated previously, scholars disagree on the reasons why freedom of association is valuable in a democratic state. Some stress the fact that associational activity is critical to the self-realization of the individual, in that it is necessary in many cases to combine together to secure sufficient power to offset countervailing institutional forces that threaten individual autonomy and freedom. Others view associational activity as part of what it means to be human, in that an important component of human personality only obtains expression by association with others, and that such activity ought to be cherished and protected against the individuating tendencies of the modern state. Whatever the reason ultimately underpinning commitments to freedom of association, the important fact is that this freedom ought to be valued highly as a critical component of a democratic state.

Blinded by individualism, the Court treats freedom of association as though it potentially amounts to a threat to democracy. In contrast to the "large and liberal" approach to defining the scope and content of constitutional guarantees that the Court has been proud to articulate in relation to other constitutional rights, the Court appears determined to provide as minimal a content to freedom of association as possible. *Alberta Reference*'s premise and conclusion is that the Constitution does not protect the essential purposes of some associations from state interference, yet no argument that does more than reiterate this view is given by the Court. In *PIPS*, no argument is necessary: precedent rules the day. The real reason for the Court's position appears to be a combination of conservatism and fear. It cannot be denied that groups can be powerful, nor can it be denied that the judiciary is not the most competent or legitimate institution to assess the relative merits of different types of associational activity. But these facts should go to the level of deference that the judiciary ought to accord to certain state initiatives, not to the definition of freedom of association itself. Workers deserve more from the judiciary than a jurisprudence of fear.

Dunmore v. Ontario (Attorney General)
[2001] 3 SCR 1016, 2001 SCC 94, 207 DLR (4th) 193

[In 1994, the Ontario legislature enacted the *Agricultural Labour Relations Act, 1994* (ALRA), which extended trade union and collective bargaining rights to agricultural workers. Prior to the adoption of this legislation, agricultural workers had always been excluded from Ontario's labour relations regime. A year later, following a change in government, the legislature, by virtue of s. 80 of the *Labour Relations and Employment Statute Law Amendment Act, 1995* (LRESLAA), repealed the ALRA in its entirety. The effect was thus to subject agricultural workers to s. 3(b) of the *Labour Relations Act, 1995* (LRA), which excluded them from the labour relations regime set out in the LRA. Section 80 also terminated any certification rights of trade unions under the ALRA, as well as any collective agreements certified thereunder. The appellants brought an application challenging the repeal of the ALRA and their exclusion from the *LRA* on the basis that it infringed their rights under ss. 2(d) and 15(1) of the *Canadian Charter of Rights and Freedoms*. Both the Ontario Court (General Division) and the Ontario Court of Appeal upheld the challenged legislation.]

BASTARACHE J (McLachlin CJC and Gonthier, Iacobucci, Binnie, Arbour, and LeBel J concurring):

[16] ... [T]he purpose of s. 2(d) commands a single inquiry: has the state precluded activity *because* of its associational nature, thereby discouraging the collective pursuit of common goals? In my view, while the four-part test [outlined in *Professional Institute of Public Service of Canada v. Northwest Territories (Commissioner)*, [1990] 2 SCR 367, 72 DLR (4th) 1 ("*PIPSC*")] for freedom of association sheds light on this concept, it does not capture the full range of activities protected by s. 2(d). In particular, there will be occasions where a given activity does not fall within the third and fourth rules ... , but where the state has nevertheless prohibited that activity solely because of its associational nature. These occasions will involve activities which 1) are not protected under any other constitutional freedom, and 2) cannot, for one reason or another, be understood as the lawful activities of individuals. As discussed by Dickson CJC in the *Alberta Reference* [*re Public Service Employee Relations Act (Alta.)*, [1987] 1 SCR 313, 38 DLR (4th) 161], such activities may be *collective* in nature, in that they cannot be performed by individuals acting alone. [This aspect of Dickson CJC's reasons,] which was not explicitly rejected by the majority in the *Alberta Reference* or in *PIPSC*, recognizes that the collective is "qualitatively" distinct from the individual: individuals associate not simply because there is strength in numbers, but because communities can embody objectives that individuals cannot. For example, a "majority view" cannot be expressed by a lone individual, but a group of individuals can form a constituency and distill their views into a single platform. ... In-

deed, this is the essential purpose of joining a political party, participating in a class action or certifying a trade union. To limit s. 2(d) to activities that are performable by individuals would, in my view, render futile these fundamental initiatives. At best, it would encourage s. 2(d) claimants to contrive individual analogs for inherently associational activities, a process which this Court clearly resisted in the labour trilogy, in *Egg Marketing* [*Canadian Egg Marketing Agency v. Richardson*, [1998] 3 SCR 157, 166 DLR (4th) 1] and in its jurisprudence on union security clauses and the right not associate. ...

[17] As I see it, the very notion of "association" recognizes the qualitative differences between individuals and collectivities. It recognizes that the press differs qualitatively from the journalist, the language community from the language speaker, the union from the worker. In all cases, the community assumes a life of its own and develops needs and priorities that differ from those of its individual members. Thus, for example, a language community cannot be nurtured if the law protects only the individual's right to speak (see *R v. Beaulac*, [1999] 1 SCR 768 [173 DLR (4th) 193], at para. 20). Similar reasoning applies, albeit in a limited fashion, to the freedom to organize: because trade unions develop needs and priorities that are distinct from those of their members individually, they cannot function if the law protects exclusively what might be "the lawful activities of individuals." Rather, the law must recognize that certain union activities—making collective representations to an employer, adopting a majority political platform, federating with other unions—may be central to freedom of association even though they are inconceivable on the individual level. This is not to say that all such activities are protected by s. 2(d), nor that all collectivities are worthy of constitutional protection; indeed, this Court has repeatedly excluded the right to strike and collectively bargain from the protected ambit of s. 2(d). ... It is to say, simply, that certain collective activities must be recognized if the freedom to form and maintain an association is to have any meaning. As one author puts it, the *per se* exclusion of collective action reduces employee collectives to mere "aggregate[s] of economically self-interested individuals" rather than "co-operative undertakings where individual flourishing can be encouraged through membership in and co-operation with the community of fellow workers" (see L. Harmer, "The Right to Strike: Charter Implications and Interpretations" (1989), 47 *UT Fac. L Rev.* 420, at pp. 434-35). This would surely undermine the purpose of s. 2(d), which is to allow the achievement of individual potential through interpersonal relationships and collective action (see, e.g., *Lavigne* [*v. Ontario Public Service Employees Union*, [1991] 2 SCR 211, 81 DLR (4th) 545] *per* McLachlin J, at pp. 343-44, *per* La Forest J, at pp. 327-28).

• • •

[19] The content of the freedom to organize having been discussed, the next question that arises is the scope of state responsibility in respect of this freedom. This responsibility is generally characterized as "negative" in nature, meaning that Parliament and the provincial legislatures need only refrain from interfering (either in purpose or effect) with protected associational activity. Conversely, the *Charter* does not oblige the state to take affirmative action to safeguard or facilitate the exercise of fundamental freedoms.

[20] However, history has shown, and Canada's legislatures have uniformly recognized, that a posture of government restraint in the area of labour relations will expose most workers not only to a range of unfair labour practices, but potentially to legal liability under common law inhibitions on combinations and restraints of trade. Knowing this

would foreclose the effective exercise of the freedom to organize, Ontario has provided a statutory freedom to organize in its *LRA* (s. 5), as well as protections against denial of access to property (s. 13), employer interference with trade union activity (s. 70), discrimination against trade unionists (s. 72), intimidation and coercion (s. 76), alteration of working conditions during the certification process (s. 86), coercion of witnesses (s. 87), and removal of Board notices (s. 88). In this context, it must be asked whether, in order to make the freedom to organize meaningful, s. 2(d) of the *Charter* imposes a positive obligation on the state to extend protective legislation to unprotected groups. More broadly, it may be asked whether the distinction between positive and negative state obligations ought to be nuanced in the context of labour relations, in the sense that excluding agricultural workers from a protective regime substantially contributes to the violation of protected freedoms.

· · ·

[22] … Where a group is denied a statutory benefit accorded to others, as is the case in this appeal, the normal course is to review this denial under s. 15(1) of the *Charter*, not s. 2(d) (see *Haig v. Canada*, [1993] 2 SCR 995 [105 DLR (4th) 577]; *Native Women's Assn. of Canada v. Canada*, [1994] 3 SCR 627 [119 DLR (4th) 224] ("*NWAC*"); *Delisle* [*v. Canada (Deputy Attorney General)*, [1999] 2 SCR 989, 176 DLR (4th) 513]). … However, it seems to me that apart from any consideration of a claimant's dignity interest, exclusion from a protective regime may in some contexts amount to an affirmative interference with the effective exercise of a protected freedom. In such a case, it is not so much the differential treatment that is at issue, but the fact that the government is creating conditions which in effect substantially interfere with the exercise of a constitutional right; it has been held in the s. 2(a) context, for example, that "protection of one religion and the concomitant non-protection of others imports disparate impact destructive of the religious freedom of the collectivity" (see *Big M Drug Mart* [*Ltd., R v.*, [1985] 1 SCR 295, 18 DLR (4th) 321] at p. 337). This does not mean that there is a constitutional right to protective legislation *per se*; it means legislation that is *underinclusive* may, in unique contexts, substantially impact the exercise of a constitutional freedom.

[23] This brings me to the central question of this appeal: can excluding agricultural workers from a statutory labour relations regime, without expressly or intentionally prohibiting association, constitute a substantial interference with freedom of association?

· · ·

[28] … [W]hile it is generally desirable to confine claims of underinclusion to s. 15(1), it will not be appropriate to do so where the underinclusion results in the effective denial of a fundamental freedom such as the right of association itself. This is not to say that such claims will be common: they are constrained by both s. 32 of the *Charter*, which demands a minimum of state action before the *Charter* can be invoked, as well as by the factors discussed above. However, a claim for inclusion should not, in my view, automatically fail a s. 2(d) analysis: depending on the circumstances, freedom of association may, for example, prohibit the selective exclusion of a group from whatever protections are necessary to form and maintain an association, even though there is no constitutional right to such statutory protection *per se*. In this sense, the burden imposed by s. 2(d) of the *Charter* differs from that imposed by s. 15(1): while the latter focuses on the effects of underinclusion on human dignity (*Law v. Canada (Minister of Employment and Im-*

migration), [1999] 1 SCR 497 [170 DLR (4th) 1]), the former focuses on the effects of underinclusion on the ability to exercise a fundamental freedom. This distinction is contemplated by the wording of the *Charter* itself and is supported by subsequent jurisprudence of this Court (see, e.g., *Delisle, supra*, at para. 25).

[Bastarache J's discussion of *Retail, Wholesale and Department Store Union, Local 580 v. Dolphin Delivery Ltd.*, [1986] 2 SCR 573, 33 DLR (4th) 174, and the application of the *Charter* to private action can be found in Chapter 18, Application.]

[29] ... [T]he above doctrine does not, on its own, oblige the state to act where it has not already legislated in respect of a certain area. One must always guard against reviewing legislative silence, particularly where no legislation has been enacted in the first place. By the same token, it must be remembered why the *Charter* applies to legislation that is underinclusive. Once the state has chosen to regulate a private relationship such as that between employer and employee, I believe it is unduly formalistic to consign that relationship to a "private sphere" that is impervious to *Charter* review. As Dean P.W. Hogg has stated, "[t]he effect of the governmental action restriction is that there is a private realm in which people are not obliged to subscribe to 'state' values, and into which constitutional norms do not intrude. The boundaries of that realm are marked, not by an *a priori* definition of what is 'private,' but by the absence of statutory or other governmental intervention" (see *Constitutional Law of Canada* (loose-leaf ed.), at p. 34-27). I am not prepared to say that the relationship between farmers and their employees falls within that boundary. If, by investigating the effects of a statute that regulates this sphere, this Court is imposing "positive" obligations on the state, that is only because such imposition is justified in the circumstances.

· · ·

[Justice Bastarache held that conflicting claims concerning the meaning of troubling comments in the legislature make it impossible to conclude that the exclusion of agricultural workers from the *LRA* was intended to infringe their freedom to organize, but the effect of the exclusion in s. 3(b) of the *LRA* is to infringe their right to freedom of association. When discussing the effects of the exclusion, he made the following observations.]

[38] By protecting the freedom to organize, s. 2(d) of the *Charter* recognizes the dynamic and evolving role of the trade union in Canadian society. In addition to permitting the collective expression of employee interests, trade unions contribute to political debate. At the level of national policy, unions advocate on behalf of disadvantaged groups and present views on fair industrial policy. These functions, when viewed globally, affect all levels of society and constitute "an important subsystem in a democratic market-economy system" (see K. Sugeno, "Unions as social institutions in democratic market economies" (1994), 133 *Int'l Lab. Rev.* 511, at p. 519). For these reasons, the notion that minimum legislative protection cannot be extended to agricultural workers without extending full collective bargaining rights is misguided. Equally misguided is the notion that inherent difficulties in the formation of trade unions, or the fact that unions are in some cases experiencing a decline in membership, diminishes their social and political

significance. On the contrary, unions remain core voluntary associations based on the principle of freedom of association. ...

[39] The fact that a regime aims to safeguard a fundamental freedom does not, of course, mean that exclusion from that regime automatically gives rise to a *Charter* violation. [A] group that proves capable of associating despite its exclusion from a protective regime will be unable to meet the evidentiary burden required of a *Charter* claim. In such a case, inclusion in a statutory regime cannot be said to safeguard, but rather to enhance, the exercise of a fundamental freedom. In this case, by contrast, the appellants contend that total exclusion from the *LRA* creates a situation whereby they are substantially incapable of exercising their constitutional right to associate.

• • •

[41] ... Not only have agricultural workers proved unable to form employee associations in provinces which deny them protection but, unlike the RCMP officers in *Delisle*, they argue that their relative status and lack of statutory protection all but guarantee this result. Distinguishing features of agricultural workers are their political impotence, their lack of resources to associate without state protection and their vulnerability to reprisal by their employers; as noted [below] by Sharpe J, agricultural workers are "poorly paid, face difficult working conditions, have low levels of skill and education, low status and limited employment mobility" (p. 216). Moreover, unlike RCMP officers, agricultural workers are not employed by the government and therefore cannot access the *Charter* directly to suppress an unfair labour practice (*Delisle*, para. 32). It is no wonder, therefore, according to the appellants, that agricultural workers have failed to associate in any meaningful way in Ontario, while RCMP officers have successfully created independent employee associations in several provinces across Canada (*Delisle*, para. 31). ...

[42] ... As stated earlier in these reasons, it is only the right to associate that is at issue here, not the right to collective bargaining. Nevertheless, to suggest that s. 2(d) of the *Charter* is respected where an association is reduced to *claiming* a right to unionize would, in my view, make a mockery of freedom of association. The record shows that, but for the brief period covered by the *ALRA*, there has never been an agricultural workers' union in Ontario. Agricultural workers have suffered repeated attacks on their efforts to unionize. Conversely, in those provinces where labour relations rights have been extended to agricultural workers, union density is higher than in Ontario (see Statistics Canada, *Annual Report of the Minister of Industry, Science and Technology under the Corporations and Labour Unions Returns Act, Part II, Labour Unions* (1992), at pp. 38-41). The respondents do not contest this evidence, nor do they deny that legislative protection is absolutely crucial if agricultural workers wish to unionize. Indeed, to suggest otherwise would contradict a widespread consensus among Parliament and the provincial legislatures that without certain minimum protections, the somewhat limited freedom to organize itself would be a hollow freedom. For these reasons, I readily conclude that the evidentiary burden has been met in this case: the appellants have brought this litigation because there is no possibility for association as such without minimum statutory protection. ...

[43] Their freedom to organize having been substantially impeded by exclusion from protective legislation, it is still incumbent on the appellants to link this impediment to state, not just private action (see *Dolphin Delivery, supra*). On this point, the respondent argues that since agricultural workers are isolated, seasonal and relatively under-educated, this,

along with the unfair labour practices of their employers, is what explains the difficulty in creating associations rather than the underinclusiveness of the legislation. On the other hand, the appellants argue that the above conditions are reinforced by legislation which fails to provide minimum protection of their freedom to organize and further isolates agricultural workers by excluding them from the general regime of labour relations.

[44] In my view, the appellants' argument must prevail. What the legislature has done by reviving the *LRA* is not simply allow private circumstances to subsist; it has reinforced those circumstances by excluding agricultural workers from the only available channel for associational activity (see *Vriend* [*v. Alberta*, [1998] 1 SCR 493, 156 DLR (4th) 385], at paras. 99-103). ...

[45] The most palpable effect of the *LRESLAA* and the *LRA* is, in my view, to place a chilling effect on non-statutory union activity. By extending statutory protection to just about every class of worker in Ontario, the legislature has essentially discredited the organizing efforts of agricultural workers. This is especially true given the relative status of agricultural workers in Canadian society. In *Delisle, supra*, I linked RCMP officers' ability to associate to their relative status, comparing them with the armed forces, senior executives in the public service and judges. The thrust of this argument was that if the *PSSRA* sought to discourage RCMP officers from associating, it could not do so in light of their relative status, their financial resources and their access to constitutional protection. By contrast, it is hard to imagine a more discouraging legislative provision than s. 3(b) of the *LRA*. The evidence is that the ability of agricultural workers to associate is only as great as their access to legal protection, and such protection exists neither in statutory nor constitutional form. Moreover, agricultural workers already possess a limited sense of entitlement as a result of their exclusion from other protective legislation related to employment standards and occupational health and safety. ... In this context, the effect of s. 3(b) of the *LRA* is not simply to perpetuate an existing inability to organize, but to exert the precise chilling effect I declined to recognize in *Delisle, supra*. ...

[46] Conversely, the didactic effects of labour relations legislation on employers must not be underestimated. It is widely accepted that labour relations laws function not only to provide a forum for airing specific grievances, but for fostering dialogue in an otherwise adversarial workplace. As P. Weiler has written, unionization introduces a form of political democracy into the workplace, subjecting employer and employee alike to the "rule of law" (see P. Weiler, *Reconcilable Differences: New Directions in Canadian Labour Law* (1980), at pp. 31-32). In this context, the wholesale exclusion of agricultural workers from a labour relations regime can only be viewed as a stimulus to interfere with organizing activity. The exclusion suggests that workplace democracy has no place in the agricultural sector and, moreover, that agricultural workers' efforts to associate are illegitimate. As surely as *LRA* protection would foster the "rule of law" in a unionized workplace, exclusion from that protection privileges the will of management over that of the worker. Again, a contrast to *Delisle, supra*, is apposite: a government employer is less likely than a private employer to take exclusion from protective legislation as a green light to commit unfair labour practices, as its employees have direct recourse to the *Charter*.

• • •

[48] In sum, I believe it is reasonable to conclude that the exclusion of agricultural workers from the *LRA* substantially interferes with their fundamental freedom to organize.

The inherent difficulties of organizing farm workers, combined with the threats of economic reprisal from employers, form only part of the reason why association is all but
impossible in the agricultural sector in Ontario. Equally important is the message sent
by s. 3(b) of the *LRA*, which delegitimizes associational activity and thereby ensures its
ultimate failure. Given these known and foreseeable effects of s. 3(b), I conclude that the
provision infringes the freedom to organize and thus violates s. 2(d) of the *Charter*.

[With respect to the s. 1 analysis, Bastarache J held that the evidence establishes that
many farms in Ontario are family-owned and -operated, and that the protection of the
family farm is a pressing enough objective to warrant the infringement of s. 2(d) of the
Charter. The economic objective of ensuring farm productivity is also important. Agriculture occupies a volatile and highly competitive part of the private sector economy, experiences disproportionately thin profit margins, and, due to its seasonal character, is
particularly vulnerable to strikes and lockouts. However, the wholesale exclusion of agricultural workers from Ontario's labour relations regime does not minimally impair
their right to freedom of association. The categorical exclusion of agricultural workers is
unjustified where no satisfactory effort has been made to protect their basic right to form
associations. The exclusion is overly broad as it denies the right of association to every
sector of agriculture without distinction. The reliance on the family farm justification ignores an increasing trend in Canada toward corporate farming and complex agribusiness
and does not justify the unqualified and total exclusion of all agricultural workers from
Ontario's labour relations regime.

He held further that the appropriate remedy in this case is to declare the *LRESLAA*
unconstitutional to the extent that it gives effect to the exclusion clause found in s. 3(b)
of the *LRA*, and to declare s. 3(b) of the *LRA* to be unconstitutional. The declarations
should be suspended for 18 months, thereby allowing amending legislation to be passed
if the legislature sees fit to do so. Section 2(d) of the Charter only requires the legislature
to provide a statutory framework that is consistent with the principles established in this
case. At a minimum, these principles require that the statutory freedom to organize in
s. 5 of the *LRA* be extended to agricultural workers, along with protections judged essential to its meaningful exercise, such as freedom to assemble, freedom from interference,
coercion and discrimination, and freedom to make representations and to participate in
the lawful activities of the association. The appropriate remedy does not require or forbid
the inclusion of agricultural workers in a full collective bargaining regime, whether it be
the *LRA* or a special regime applicable only to agricultural workers.

L'Heureux-Dubé J concurred in separate reasons, adding that the occupational status
of agricultural workers constitutes an "analogous ground" for the purposes of an analysis
under s. 15(1). Major J dissented, arguing that s. 2(d) does not impose a positive obligation of protection or inclusion on the state.]

Health Services and Support-Facilities Subsector Bargaining Assn. v.
British Columbia
[2007] 2 SCR 391, 2007 SCC 27, 283 DLR (4th) 40

[*The Health and Social Services Delivery Improvement Act* was designed to restructure labour relations in BC's health care system. Part 2 of the Act introduced changes to transfers and multi-worksite assignment rights (ss. 4 and 5), contracting out (s. 6), the status of contracted-out employees (s. 6), job security programs (ss. 7 and 8), and layoffs and bumping rights (s. 9). It gave health care employers greater flexibility to organize their relations with their employees as they see fit and, in some cases, in ways that would not have been permissible under existing collective agreements and without adhering to requirements of consultation and notice that would otherwise obtain. It invalidated important provisions of collective agreements then in force and effectively precluded meaningful collective bargaining on a number of specific issues. Furthermore, s. 10 voided any part of a collective agreement, past or future, that was inconsistent with Part 2 and any collective agreement purporting to modify these restrictions. The appellants—unions and members of the unions representing the nurses, facilities, or community subsectors—challenged the constitutional validity of Part 2 of the Act as a violation of ss. 2(d) and 15 of the Charter. Adhering to the precedent of the *Labour Trilogy*, both the trial judge and the Court of Appeal upheld the constitutionality of Part 2 of the Act.]

McLACHLIN CJC and LeBEL J (Bastarache, Binnie, Fish, and Abella JJ concurring):

I. Introduction

. . .

[4] The [*Health and Social Services Delivery Improvement*] *Act* was adopted as a response to challenges facing British Columbia's health care system. Demand for health care and the cost of providing needed health care services had been increasing significantly for years. For example, in the period from 1991 to 2001, the growth rate of health care costs in British Columbia was three times that of the provincial economy. As a result, the government of British Columbia found itself struggling to provide health care services to its citizens. The government characterized the state of affairs in 2001 as a "crisis of sustainability" in the health care system … .

[5] The goals of the Act were to reduce costs and to facilitate the efficient management of the workforce in the health care sector. Not wishing to decrease employees' wages, the government attempted to achieve these goals in more sustainable ways. According to the government, the Act was designed in particular to focus on permitting health care employers to reorganize the administration of the labour force and on making operational changes to enhance management's ability to restructure service delivery … .

[6] The Act was quickly passed. It came into force three days after receiving a first reading as Bill 29 before the British Columbia legislature.

[7] There was no meaningful consultation with unions before it became law. The government was aware that some of the areas affected by Bill 29 were of great concern to the unions and had expressed a willingness to consult. However, in the end, consultation

was minimal. A few meetings were held between representatives of the unions and the government on general issues relating to health care. These did not deal specifically with Bill 29 and the changes that it proposed. Union representatives expressed their desire to be further consulted. The Minister of Health Services telephoned a union representative 20 minutes before Bill 29 was introduced in the legislative assembly to inform the union that the government would be introducing legislation dealing with employment security and other provisions of existing collective agreements. This was the only consultation with unions before the Act was passed. ...

[10] Only Part 2 of the Act is at issue in the current appeal. It introduced changes to transfers and multi-worksite assignment rights (ss. 4 and 5), contracting out (s. 6), the status of employees under contracting-out arrangements (s. 6), job security programs (ss. 7 and 8), and layoffs and bumping rights (s. 9).

[11] Part 2 gave health care employers greater flexibility to organize their relations with their employees as they see fit, and in some cases, to do so in ways that would not have been permissible under existing collective agreements and without adhering to requirements of consultation and notice that would otherwise obtain. It invalidated important provisions of collective agreements then in force, and effectively precluded meaningful collective bargaining on a number of specific issues. Section 10 invalidated any part of a collective agreement, past or future, which was inconsistent with Part 2, and any collective agreement purporting to modify these restrictions. In the words of the Act, s. 10: "Part [2] prevails over collective agreements." It is not open to the employees (or the employer) to contract out of Part 2 or to rely on a collective agreement inconsistent with Part 2. ...

III. Analysis

. . .

[19] At issue in the present appeal is whether the guarantee of freedom of association in s. 2(d) of the Charter protects collective bargaining rights. We conclude that s. 2(d) of the Charter protects the capacity of members of labour unions to engage, in association, in collective bargaining on fundamental workplace issues. This protection does not cover all aspects of "collective bargaining," as that term is understood in the statutory labour relations regimes that are in place across the country. Nor does it ensure a particular outcome in a labour dispute, or guarantee access to any particular statutory regime. What is protected is simply the right of employees to associate in a process of collective action to achieve workplace goals. If the government substantially interferes with that right, it violates s. 2(d) of the Charter: *Dunmore* [*v. Ontario (Attorney General)*, [2001] 3 SCR 1016, 207 DLR (4th) 193]. We note that the present case does not concern the right to strike, which was considered in earlier litigation on the scope of the guarantee of freedom of association.

[20] Our conclusion that s. 2(d) of the Charter protects a process of collective bargaining rests on four propositions. First, a review of the s. 2(d) jurisprudence of this Court reveals that the reasons evoked in the past for holding that the guarantee of freedom of association does not extend to collective bargaining can no longer stand. Second, an interpretation of s. 2(d) that precludes collective bargaining from its ambit is inconsistent with Canada's historic recognition of the importance of collective bargaining to

freedom of association. Third, collective bargaining is an integral component of freedom of association in international law, which may inform the interpretation of Charter guarantees. Finally, interpreting s. 2(d) as including a right to collective bargaining is consistent with, and indeed, promotes, other Charter rights, freedoms and values.

· · ·

[22] In earlier decisions, the majority view in the Supreme Court of Canada was that the guarantee of freedom of association did not extend to collective bargaining. *Dunmore* opened the door to reconsideration of that view. We conclude that the grounds advanced in the earlier decisions for the exclusion of collective bargaining from the Charter's protection of freedom of association do not withstand principled scrutiny and should be rejected.

· · ·

[24] In [the *Labour Trilogy* and *Professional Institute of the Public Service of Canada v. Northwest Territories (Commissioner)*, [1990] 2 SCR 367, 72 DLR (4th) 1 [*PIPSC*]], different members of the majorities put forth five main reasons in support of the contention that collective bargaining does not fall within s. 2(d)'s protection.

[25] The first suggested reason was that the rights to strike and to bargain collectively are "modern rights" created by legislation, not "fundamental freedoms" (*Alberta Reference* [*Re Public Service Employees Relations Act (Alta.)*, [1987] 1 SCR 313, 38 DLR (4th) 161] per Le Dain J, writing on behalf of himself, Beetz and La Forest JJ, at p. 391). The difficulty with this argument is that it fails to recognize the history of labour relations in Canada. As developed more thoroughly in the next section of these reasons, the fundamental importance of collective bargaining to labour relations was the very reason for its incorporation into statute. Legislatures throughout Canada have historically viewed collective bargaining rights as sufficiently important to immunize them from potential interference. The statutes they passed did not create the right to bargain collectively. Rather, they afforded it protection. There is nothing in the statutory entrenchment of collective bargaining that detracts from its fundamental nature.

[26] The second suggested reason was that recognition of a right to collective bargaining would go against the principle of judicial restraint in interfering with government regulation of labour relations (*Alberta Reference*, at p. 391). The regulation of labour relations, it is suggested, involves policy decisions best left to government. This argument again fails to recognize the fact that worker organizations historically had the right to bargain collectively outside statutory regimes and takes an overbroad view of judicial deference. It may well be appropriate for judges to defer to legislatures on policy matters expressed in particular laws. But to declare a judicial "no go" zone for an entire right on the ground that it may involve the courts in policy matters is to push deference too far. Policy itself should reflect Charter rights and values.

[27] The third suggested reason for excluding collective bargaining from s. 2(d) of the Charter rested on the view that freedom of association protects only those activities performable by an individual (see *PIPSC*, per L'Heureux-Dubé and Sopinka JJ). This view arises from a passage in which Sopinka J set out the scope of s. 2(d) in four oft-quoted propositions (at pp. 402-3): (1) s. 2(d) protects the freedom to establish, belong to and maintain an association; (2) it does not protect an activity solely on the ground that the activity is foundational or essential to the association; (3) it protects the exercise

in association of the constitutional rights and freedoms of individuals; and (4) it protects the exercise in association of the lawful rights of individuals. If this framework and the premise that s. 2(d) covers only activities performable by an individual is accepted, it follows that collective bargaining cannot attract the protection of s. 2(d) because collective bargaining cannot be performed by an individual.

[28] This narrow focus on individual activities has been overtaken by *Dunmore*, where this Court rejected the notion that freedom of association applies only to activities capable of performance by individuals. Bastarache J held that "[t]o limit s. 2(d) to activities that are performable by individuals would ... render futile these fundamental initiatives" (para. 16), since, as Dickson CJ noted in his dissent in the *Alberta Reference*, some collective activities may, by their very nature, be incapable of being performed by an individual. Bastarache J provided the example of expressing a majority viewpoint as being an inherently collective activity without an individual analogue (para. 16). He concluded that:

> As I see it, the very notion of "association" recognizes the qualitative differences between individuals and collectivities. It recognizes that the press differs qualitatively from the journalist, the language community from the language speaker, the union from the worker. In all cases, the community assumes a life of its own and develops needs and priorities that differ from those of its individual members. ... [B]ecause trade unions develop needs and priorities that are distinct from those of their members individually, they cannot function if the law protects exclusively what might be "the lawful activities of individuals." *Rather, the law must recognize that certain union activities—making collective representations to an employer, adopting a majority political platform, federating with other unions—may be central to freedom of association even though they are inconceivable on the individual level.* This is not to say that all such activities are protected by s. 2(d), nor that all collectivities are worthy of constitutional protection; indeed, this Court has repeatedly excluded the right to strike and collectively bargain from the protected ambit of s. 2(d). ... It is to say, simply, that *certain collective activities must be recognized if the freedom to form and maintain an association is to have any meaning.* [Emphasis added; para. 17.]

[29] The fourth reason advanced for excluding collective bargaining rights from s. 2(d) was the suggestion of L'Heureux-Dubé J that s. 2(d) was not intended to protect the "objects" or goals of an association (see *PIPSC*, at pp. 391-93). This argument overlooks the fact that it will always be possible to characterize the pursuit of a particular activity in concert with others as the "object" of that association. Recasting collective bargaining as an "object" begs the question of whether or not the activity is worthy of constitutional protection. L'Heureux-Dubé J's underlying concern—that the Charter not be used to protect the substantive outcomes of any and all associations—is a valid one. However, "collective bargaining" as a procedure has always been distinguishable from its final outcomes (e.g., the results of the bargaining process, which may be reflected in a collective agreement). Professor Bora Laskin (as he then was) aptly described collective bargaining over 60 years ago as follows:

> Collective bargaining is the procedure through which the views of the workers are made known, expressed through representatives chosen by them, not through representatives selected or nominated or approved by employers. More than that, it is a procedure through

which terms and conditions of employment may be settled by negotiations between an employer and his employees on the basis of a comparative equality of bargaining strength. ("Collective Bargaining in Canada: In Peace and in War" (1941), 2:3 *Food for Thought*, at p. 8.)

In our view, it is entirely possible to protect the "procedure" known as collective bargaining without mandating constitutional protection for the fruits of that bargaining process. Thus, the characterization of collective bargaining as an association's "object" does not provide a principled reason to deny it constitutional protection.

[30] An overarching concern is that the majority judgments in the *Alberta Reference* and *PIPSC* adopted a decontextualized approach to defining the scope of freedom of association, in contrast to the purposive approach taken to other Charter guarantees. The result was to forestall inquiry into the purpose of that Charter guarantee. The generic approach of the earlier decisions to s. 2(d) ignored differences between organizations. Whatever the organization—be it trade union or book club—its freedoms were treated as identical. The unfortunate effect was to overlook the importance of collective bargaining—both historically and currently—to the exercise of freedom of association in labour relations.

[31] We conclude that the reasons provided by the majorities in the *Alberta Reference* and *PIPSC* should not bar reconsideration of the question of whether s. 2(d) applies to collective bargaining. This is manifestly the case since this Court's decision in *Dunmore*, which struck down a statute that effectively prohibited farm workers from engaging in collective bargaining by denying them access to the Province's labour relations regime, as violating of s. 2(d) of the Charter. *Dunmore* clarified three developing aspects of the law: what constitutes interference with the "associational aspect" of an activity; the need for a contextual approach to freedom of association; and the recognition that s. 2(d) can impose positive obligations on government.

[32] *Dunmore* accepted the conclusion of the majority in *Canadian Egg Marketing Agency v. Richardson*, [1998] 3 SCR 157 [166 DLR (4th) 1], that only the "associational aspect" of an activity and not the activity itself are protected under s. 2(d). It clarified, however, that equal legislative treatment of individuals and groups does not mean that the "associational aspect" of an activity has not been interfered with. A prohibition on an individual may not raise associational concerns, while the same prohibition on the collective may do so. *Dunmore* concluded:

> In sum, a purposive approach to s. 2(d) demands that we "distinguish between the associational aspect of the activity and the activity itself," a process mandated by this Court in the *Alberta Reference* [p. 1043] (see *Egg Marketing, supra*, per Iacobucci and Bastarache JJ, at para. 111). Such an approach begins with the existing framework established in that case, which enables a claimant to show that a group activity is permitted for individuals in order to establish that its regulation targets the association per se (see *Alberta Reference, supra*, per Dickson CJ, at p. 367). Where this burden cannot be met, however, it may still be open to a claimant to show, by direct evidence or inference, that the legislature has targeted associational conduct because of its concerted or associational nature. (Per Bastarache J, at para. 18.)

[33] Second, *Dunmore* correctly advocated a more contextual analysis than had hitherto prevailed. Showing that a legislature has targeted associational conduct because of its "concerted or associational nature" requires a more contextual assessment than found in the early s. 2(d) cases. This contextual approach was foreshadowed by the dissenting reasons of Bastarache J in *R v. Advance Cutting and Coring Ltd.*, [2001] 3 SCR 209, 2001 SCC 70 [205 DLR (4th) 385], expressing the view that to define the limits of s. 2(d), "the whole context of the right must be considered" (para. 9).

[34] Finally, *Dunmore* recognized that, in certain circumstances, s. 2(d) may place positive obligations on governments to extend legislation to particular groups. Under-inclusive legislation may, "in unique contexts, substantially impact the exercise of a constitutional freedom" (para. 22). This will occur where the claim of underinclusion is grounded in the fundamental Charter freedom and not merely in access to a statutory regime (para. 24); where a proper evidentiary foundation is provided to create a positive obligation under the Charter (para. 25); and where the state can truly be held accountable for any inability to exercise a fundamental freedom (para. 26). There must be evidence that the freedom would be next to impossible to exercise without positively recognizing a right to access a statutory regime.

[35] Bastarache J reconciled the holding in *Dunmore* of a positive obligation on government to permit farm workers to join together to bargain collectively in an effective manner with the conclusion in *Delisle v. Canada (Deputy Attorney General)*, [1999] 2 SCR 989 [176 DLR (4th) 513], that the federal government was not under a positive obligation to provide RCMP officers with access to collective bargaining by distinguishing the effects of the legislation in the two cases. Unlike the RCMP members in *Delisle*, farm workers faced barriers that made them substantially incapable of exercising their right to form associations outside the statutory framework (per Bastarache J, at paras. 39, 41 and 48). The principle affirmed was clear: Government measures that substantially interfere with ... the ability of individuals to associate with a view to promoting work-related interests violate the guarantee of freedom of association under s. 2(d) of the Charter.

[36] In summary, a review of the jurisprudence leads to the conclusion that the holdings in the *Alberta Reference* and *PIPSC* excluding collective bargaining from the scope of s. 2(d) can no longer stand. None of the reasons provided by the majorities in those cases survive scrutiny, and the rationale for excluding inherently collective activities from s. 2(d)'s protection has been overtaken by *Dunmore*.

• • •

[39] The general purpose of the Charter guarantees and the language of s. 2(d) are consistent with at least a measure of protection for collective bargaining. The language of s. 2(d) is cast in broad terms and devoid of limitations. However, this is not conclusive. To answer the question before us, we must consider the history of collective bargaining in Canada, collective bargaining in relation to freedom of association in the larger international context, and whether Charter values favour an interpretation of s. 2(d) that protects a process of collective bargaining: *R v. Big M Drug Mart Ltd.*, [1985] 1 SCR 295 [18 DLR (4th) 321], at p. 344, per Dickson J. Evaluating the scope of s. 2(d) of the Charter through these tools leads to the conclusion that s. 2(d) does indeed protect workers' rights to a process of collective bargaining.

[40] Association for purposes of collective bargaining has long been recognized as a fundamental Canadian right which predated the Charter. This suggests that the framers of the Charter intended to include it in the protection of freedom of association found in s. 2(d) of the Charter.

[41] The respondent argues that the right to collective bargaining is of recent origin and is merely a creature of statute. This assertion may be true if collective bargaining is equated solely to the framework of rights of representation and collective bargaining now recognized under federal and provincial labour codes. However, the origin of a right to collective bargaining in the sense given to it in the present case (i.e., a procedural right to bargain collectively on conditions of employment), precedes the adoption of the present system of labour relations in the 1940s. The history of collective bargaining in Canada reveals that long before the present statutory labour regimes were put in place, collective bargaining was recognized as a fundamental aspect of Canadian society. This is the context against which the scope of the s. 2(d) must be considered.

[The Chief Justice and LeBel J reviewed the history of legal regulation of labour relations in Canada and summarized it in the following terms:]

[63] ... [W]orkers in Canada began forming collectives to bargain over working conditions with their employers as early as the 18th century. However, the common law cast a shadow over the rights of workers to act collectively. When Parliament first began recognizing workers' rights, trade unions had no express statutory right to negotiate collectively with employers. Employers could simply ignore them. However, workers used the powerful economic weapon of strikes to gradually force employers to recognize unions and to bargain collectively with them. By adopting the *Wagner Act* model [which authorizes employees to form unions, bargain collectively, and strike], governments across Canada recognized the fundamental need for workers to participate in the regulation of their work environment. This legislation confirmed what the labour movement had been fighting for over centuries and what it had access to in the *laissez-faire* era through the use of strikes—the right to collective bargaining with employers.

· · ·

[66] Collective bargaining, despite early discouragement from the common law, has long been recognized in Canada. Indeed, historically, it emerges as the most significant collective activity through which freedom of association is expressed in the labour context. In our opinion, the concept of freedom of association under s. 2(d) of the Charter includes this notion of a procedural right to collective bargaining.

[67] This established Canadian right to collective bargaining was recognized in the Parliamentary hearings that took place before the adoption of the Charter. The acting Minister of Justice, Mr. Robert Kaplan, explained why he did not find necessary a proposed amendment to have the freedom to organize and bargain collectively expressly included under s. 2(d). These rights, he stated, were already implicitly recognized in the words "freedom of association":

> Our position on the suggestion that there be specific reference to freedom to organize and bargain collectively is that that is already covered in the freedom of association that is provided

already in the Declaration or in the Charter; and that by singling out association for bargaining one might tend to d[i]minish all the other forms of association which are contemplated—church associations; associations of fraternal organizations or community organizations. (Special Joint Committee of the Senate and of the House of Commons on the Constitution of Canada, Minutes of Proceedings and Evidence, Issue No. 43, January 22, 1981, at pp. 69-70)

. . .

[70] Canada's adherence to international documents recognizing a right to collective bargaining supports recognition of the right in s. 2(d) of the Charter. As Dickson CJ observed in the *Alberta Reference*, at p. 349, the Charter should be presumed to provide at least as great a level of protection as is found in the international human rights documents that Canada has ratified.

[71] The sources most important to the understanding of s. 2(d) of the Charter are the *International Covenant on Economic, Social and Cultural Rights*, 993 UNTS 3 ("*ICESCR*"), the *International Covenant on Civil and Political Rights*, 999 UNTS 171 ("*ICCPR*"), and the International Labour Organization's (ILO's) *Convention (No. 87) Concerning Freedom of Association and Protection of the Right to Organize*, 68 UNTS 17 ("Convention No. 87"). Canada has endorsed all three of these documents, acceding to both the *ICESCR* and the *ICCPR*, and ratifying *Convention No. 87* in 1972. This means that these documents reflect not only international consensus, but also principles that Canada has committed itself to uphold.

[72] The *ICESCR*, the *ICCPR* and *Convention No. 87* extend protection to the functioning of trade unions in a manner suggesting that a right to collective bargaining is part of freedom of association. The interpretation of these conventions, in Canada and internationally, not only supports the proposition that there is a right to collective bargaining in international law, but also suggests that such a right should be recognized in the Canadian context under s. 2(d).

. . .

[81] Human dignity, equality, liberty, respect for the autonomy of the person and the enhancement of democracy are among the values that underly the Charter: *R v. Zundel*, [1992] 2 SCR 731 [95 DLR (4th) 202]; *Corbiere v. Canada (Minister of Indian and Northern Affairs)*, [1999] 2 SCR 203, at para. 100; *R v. Oakes*, [1986] 1 SCR 103 [26 DLR (4th) 200]. All of these values are complemented and indeed, promoted, by the protection of collective bargaining in s. 2(d) of the Charter.

[82] The right to bargain collectively with an employer enhances the human dignity, liberty and autonomy of workers by giving them the opportunity to influence the establishment of workplace rules and thereby gain some control over a major aspect of their lives, namely their work … . As explained by P.C. Weiler in *Reconcilable Differences* (1980):

> Collective bargaining is not simply an instrument for pursuing external ends, whether these be mundane monetary gains or the erection of a private rule of law to protect dignity of the worker in the face of managerial authority. Rather, collective bargaining is intrinsically valuable as an experience in self-government. It is the mode in which employees participate in setting the terms and conditions of employment, rather than simply accepting what their employer chooses to give them … . [p. 33]

. . .

[84] Collective bargaining also enhances the Charter value of equality. One of the fundamental achievements of collective bargaining is to palliate the historical inequality between employers and employees: see *Wallace v. United Grain Growers Ltd.* [[1997] 3 SCR 701, 152 DLR (4th) 8], per Iacobucci J. In 1889, the Royal Commission on Capital and Labour appointed by the Macdonald government to make inquiries into the subject of labour and its relation to capital, stated that "Labour organizations are necessary to enable working men to deal on equal terms with their employers" (quoted in Glenday and Schrenk [Daniel Glenday and Christopher Schrenk, "Trade Unions and the State: An Interpretive Essay on the Historical Development of Class and State Relations in Canada, 1889-1949" (1978), 2 Alternate Routes 114], at p. 121; see also G. Kealey, ed., *Canada investigates industrialism: The Royal Commission on the Relations of Labor and Capital, 1889* (abridged) (1973)). Similarly, Dickson CJ rightly emphasized this concern about equality in the *Alberta Reference*:

> Freedom of association is the cornerstone of modern labour relations. Historically, workers have combined to overcome the inherent inequalities of bargaining power in the employment relationship and to protect themselves from unfair, unsafe, or exploitative working conditions. As the United States Supreme Court stated in *N.L.R.B. v. Jones & Laughlin Steel Corp.*, 301 US 1 (1937), at p. 33:
>
>> Long ago we stated the reason for labor organizations. We said that they were organized out of the necessities of the situation; that a single employee was helpless in dealing with an employer; that he was dependent ordinarily on his daily wage for the maintenance of himself and family; that if the employer refused to pay him the wages that he thought fair, he was nevertheless unable to leave the employ and resist arbitrary and unfair treatment; ...
>>
>> The "necessities of the situation" go beyond, of course, the fairness of wages and remunerative concerns, and extend to matters such as health and safety in the work place, hours of work, sexual equality, and other aspects of work fundamental to the dignity and personal liberty of employees. [pp. 334-35]

[85] Finally, a constitutional right to collective bargaining is supported by the Charter value of enhancing democracy. Collective bargaining permits workers to achieve a form of workplace democracy and to ensure the rule of law in the workplace. Workers gain a voice to influence the establishment of rules that control a major aspect of their lives ... .

[86] We conclude that the protection of collective bargaining under s. 2(d) of the Charter is consistent with and supportive of the values underlying the Charter and the purposes of the Charter as a whole. Recognizing that workers have the right to bargain collectively as part of their freedom to associate reaffirms the values of dignity, personal autonomy, equality and democracy that are inherent in the Charter.

. . .

[89] The scope of the right to bargain collectively ought to be defined bearing in mind the pronouncements of *Dunmore*, which stressed that s. 2(d) does not apply solely to individual action carried out in common, but also to associational activities themselves. The scope of the right properly reflects the history of collective bargaining and the

international covenants entered into by Canada. Based on the principles developed in *Dunmore* and in this historical and international perspective, the constitutional right to collective bargaining concerns the protection of the ability of workers to engage in associational activities, and their capacity to act in common to reach shared goals related to workplace issues and terms of employment. In brief, the protected activity might be described as employees banding together to achieve particular work-related objectives. Section 2(d) does not guarantee the particular objectives sought through this associational activity. However, it guarantees the process through which those goals are pursued. It means that employees have the right to unite, to present demands to health sector employers collectively and to engage in discussions in an attempt to achieve workplace-related goals. Section 2(d) imposes corresponding duties on government employers to agree to meet and discuss with them. It also puts constraints on the exercise of legislative powers in respect of the right to collective bargaining, which we shall discuss below.

[90] Section 2(d) of the Charter does not protect all aspects of the associational activity of collective bargaining. It protects only against "substantial interference" with associational activity, in accordance with a test crafted in *Dunmore* by Bastarache J, which asked whether "excluding agricultural workers from a statutory labour relations regime, without expressly or intentionally prohibiting association, [can] constitute a substantial interference with freedom of association" (para. 23). Or to put it another way, does the state action target or affect the associational activity, "thereby discouraging the collective pursuit of common goals"? (*Dunmore*, at para. 16) Nevertheless, intent to interfere with the associational right of collective bargaining is not essential to establish breach of s. 2(d) of the Charter. It is enough if the effect of the state law or action is to substantially interfere with the activity of collective bargaining, thereby discouraging the collective pursuit of common goals. It follows that the state must not substantially interfere with the ability of a union to exert meaningful influence over working conditions through a process of collective bargaining conducted in accordance with the duty to bargain in good faith. Thus the employees' right to collective bargaining imposes corresponding duties on the employer. It requires both employer and employees to meet and to bargain in good faith, in the pursuit of a common goal of peaceful and productive accommodation.

[91] The right to collective bargaining thus conceived is a limited right. First, as the right is to a process, it does not guarantee a certain substantive or economic outcome. Moreover, the right is to a general process of collective bargaining, not to a particular model of labour relations, nor to a specific bargaining method. ... Finally, and most importantly, the interference, as *Dunmore* instructs, must be substantial—so substantial that it interferes not only with the attainment of the union members' objectives (which is not protected), but with the very process that enables them to pursue these objectives by engaging in meaningful negotiations with the employer.

[92] To constitute substantial interference with freedom of association, the intent or effect must seriously undercut or undermine the activity of workers joining together to pursue the common goals of negotiating workplace conditions and terms of employment with their employer that we call collective bargaining. Laws or actions that can be characterized as "union breaking" clearly meet this requirement. But less dramatic interference with the collective process may also suffice. In *Dunmore*, denying the union access to the labour laws of Ontario designed to support and give a voice to unions was enough.

Acts of bad faith, or unilateral nullification of negotiated terms, without any process of meaningful discussion and consultation may also significantly undermine the process of collective bargaining. The inquiry in every case is contextual and fact-specific. The question in every case is whether the process of voluntary, good faith collective bargaining between employees and the employer has been, or is likely to be, significantly and adversely impacted.

[93] Generally speaking, determining whether a government measure affecting the protected process of collective bargaining amounts to substantial interference involves two inquiries. The first inquiry is into the importance of the matter affected to the process of collective bargaining, and more specifically, to the capacity of the union members to come together and pursue collective goals in concert. The second inquiry is into the manner in which the measure impacts on the collective right to good faith negotiation and consultation.

[94] Both inquiries are necessary. If the matters affected do not substantially impact on the process of collective bargaining, the measure does not violate s. 2(d) and, indeed, the employer may be under no duty to discuss and consult. There will be no need to consider process issues. If, on the other hand, the changes substantially touch on collective bargaining, they will still not violate s. 2(d) if they preserve a process of consultation and good faith negotiation.

[95] Turning to the first inquiry, the essential question is whether the subject matter of a particular instance of collective bargaining is such that interfering with bargaining over that issue will affect the ability of unions to pursue common goals collectively. It may help to clarify why the importance of the subject matter of bargaining is relevant to the s. 2(d) inquiry. As we have stated, one requirement for finding a breach of s. 2(d) is that the state has "precluded activity because of its associational nature, thereby discouraging the collective pursuit of common goals" (*Dunmore*, at para. 16 (emphasis deleted)). Interference with collective bargaining over matters of lesser importance to the union and its capacity to pursue collective goals in concert may be of some significance to workers. However, interference with collective bargaining over these less important matters is more likely to fall short of discouraging the capacity of union members to come together and pursue common goals in concert. Therefore, if the subject matter is of lesser importance to the union, then it is less likely that the s. 2(d) right to bargain collectively is infringed. The importance of an issue to the union and its members is not itself determinative, but will bear on the "single inquiry" prescribed in *Dunmore* as it applies in the particular context of collective bargaining: does interference with collective bargaining over certain subject matter affect the ability of the union members to come together and pursue common goals? The more important the matter, the more likely that there is substantial interference with the s. 2(d) right. Conversely, the less important the matter to the capacity of union members to pursue collective goals, the less likely that there is substantial interference with the s. 2(d) right to collective bargaining.

[96] While it is impossible to determine in advance exactly what sorts of matters are important to the ability of union members to pursue shared goals in concert, some general guidance may be apposite. Laws or state actions that prevent or deny meaningful discussion and consultation about working conditions between employees and their employer may substantially interfere with the activity of collective bargaining, as may

laws that unilaterally nullify significant negotiated terms in existing collective agreements. By contrast, measures affecting less important matters such as the design of uniform, the lay out and organization of cafeterias, or the location or availability of parking
lots, may be far less likely to constitute significant interference with the s. 2(d) right of
freedom of association. This is because it is difficult to see how interfering with collective
bargaining over these matters undermines the capacity of union members to pursue
shared goals in concert. Thus, an interference with collective bargaining over these issues
is less likely to meet the requirements set out in *Dunmore* for a breach of s. 2(d).

[97] Where it is established that the measure impacts on subject matter important to
collective bargaining and the capacity of the union members to come together and pursue common goals, the need for the second inquiry arises: does the legislative measure
or government conduct in issue respect the fundamental precept of collective bargaining—the duty to consult and negotiate in good faith? If it does, there will be no violation
of s. 2(d), even if the content of the measures might be seen as being of substantial importance to collective bargaining concerns, since the process confirms the associational
right of collective bargaining.

[The Chief Justice and LeBel J addressed the nature and scope of the duty to bargain in
good faith and concluded that one of its basic elements is an obligation to actually meet
and to commit time to the process. The parties have a duty to engage in meaningful dialogue, to exchange and explain their positions and to make a reasonable effort to arrive
at an acceptable contract. However, the duty to bargain in good faith does not impose on
the parties an obligation to conclude a collective agreement, nor does it include a duty to
accept any particular contractual provisions. In considering whether the legislative provisions impinge on the collective right to good faith negotiations and consultation, regard
must be had for the circumstances surrounding their adoption. Situations of exigency
and urgency may affect the content and the modalities of the duty to bargain in good
faith. Different situations may demand different processes and timelines. Moreover, failure to comply with the duty to consult and bargain in good faith should not be lightly
found, and should be clearly supported on the record.

They went on to conclude that ss. 4 and 5 of the Act could not be said to amount to a
substantial interference with the union's ability to engage in collective bargaining so as to
attract the protection under s. 2(d) of the Charter. However, they concluded that the
provisions dealing with contracting out (ss. 6(2) and 6(4)); layoffs (ss. 9(a), 9(b), and
9(c)); and bumping (s. 9(d)) infringe the right to bargain collectively that is protected by
s. 2(d). These provisions deal with matters central to the freedom of association and
amount to substantial interference with associational activities. Furthermore, these provisions did not preserve the processes of collective bargaining. Although the government
was facing a situation of exigency, the measures it adopted constituted a virtual denial of
the s. 2(d) right to a process of good faith bargaining and consultation.

They also held that these infringements are not justified under s. 1 of the Charter.
While the government established that the Act's main objective of improving the delivery
of health care services and subordinate objectives were pressing and substantial, and while
it could logically and reasonably be concluded that there was a rational connection between the means adopted by the Act and the objectives, it was not shown that the Act

minimally impaired the employees' s. 2(d) right of collective bargaining. The record disclosed no consideration by the government of whether it could reach its goal by less intrusive measures. A range of options were on the table, but the government presented no evidence as to why this particular solution was chosen and why there was no meaningful consultation with the unions about the range of options open to it. This was an important and significant piece of labour legislation that had the potential to affect the rights of employees dramatically and unusually. Yet, it was adopted rapidly with full knowledge that the unions were strongly opposed to many of the provisions, without consideration of alternative ways to achieve the government objective, and without explanation of the government's choices.

Deschamps J, dissenting in part, disagreed with the "substantial interference" standard proposed by the majority for determining whether a government measure amounts to an infringement of s. 2(d). In her view, a more appropriate test for determining whether s. 2(d) has been infringed is as follows: Laws or state actions that prevent or deny meaningful discussion and consultation about significant workplace issues between employees and their employer may interfere with the activity of collective bargaining, as may laws that unilaterally nullify negotiated terms on significant workplace issues in existing collective agreements. The first inquiry is into whether the process of negotiation between employers and employees or their representatives is interfered with in any way. If so, the court should then turn to the second inquiry and consider whether the issues involved are significant. Only interference with significant workplace issues is relevant to s. 2(d). She held further that ss. 4, 5, 6(2), 6(4), and 9 of the Act infringed freedom of association but that, with the exception of s. 6(4), they were justified under s. 1 of the Charter.]

Appeal allowed in part.

NOTES

1. Note that the Court's decision in *BC Health Services* does not address the holding in the *Labour Trilogy* that s. 2(d) does not include a right to strike. How might you conclude that the Court's test from *BC Health Services* for determining whether freedom of association protects certain activities dictates that s. 2(d) protects striking?

2. As stated in the introduction to this chapter, the readings thus far illustrate that the nature and scope of freedom of association has been debated largely in the context of labour disputes. Yet a number of cases before both the Supreme Court of Canada and lower courts have addressed the guarantee in non-labour settings, adding greater depth and texture to the developing jurisprudence on freedom of association.

In *Black and Co. v. Law Society of Alberta*, [1989] 1 SCR 591, 58 DLR (4th) 317, for example, the Supreme Court of Canada assessed the constitutionality of two regulations adopted by the Law Society of Alberta that, in effect, prevented the formation of partnerships between resident and non-resident members of the law society. While the majority of the Court held the provisions to be an unjustifiable interference with the respondents' mobility rights as guaranteed under s. 6 of the Charter, Justice McIntyre, dissenting in part, with whom Wilson J concurred, found the restrictions offensive, not with respect to mobility rights, but with the respondents' freedom to associate, thereby implicating s. 2(d) of the

Charter. In Justice McIntyre's view, the provision preventing the forming of a partnership or association between active member residents and active member non-residents (r. 154) amounted to an infringement of s. 2(d), which could not be saved under s. 1. With respect to r. 75B, which prevented members of the Society from being partners in more than one firm, McIntyre J found this provision to offend s. 2(d) of the Charter, but upheld the restriction under s. 1 as necessary to ensure and maintain the ethical practice of law in Alberta.

In *Canadian Egg Marketing Agency v. Richardson*, [1998] 3 SCR 157, 166 DLR (4th) 1, referred to in *BC Health Services*, the Canadian Egg Marketing Agency sought an injunction to prevent egg producers in the Northwest Territories from selling their eggs in interprovincial trade in the absence of federal quota authorizing such trade. The producers challenged the constitutionality of the federal regulatory scheme, arguing *inter alia* that it violated their freedom of association. Consider the following reasons by Iacobucci and Bastarache JJ for a majority of the Court:

> [104] … Since it is impossible to "market eggs by oneself" (p. 224), considering the legality of the activity if performed alone is an inappropriate litmus test for determining whether this associational activity is comprehended by s. 2(d). If it is necessary to associate with others to do something, then the right in s. 2(d) reaches beyond protecting the act of associating to protect the very activity for which the association is formed, an activity which is described as "foundational" to the association. The problem with this argument is that in this case it is not so much the activity that is foundational to the association as it is the association that is foundational to the activity. It is the activity that the respondents seek to cloak with the protection of s. 2(d); any association with others is merely a means to an end.
>
> [105] The fact that the association is but a means to an end is not immediately fatal to the respondents' case, because associations normally are a means to an end. As McIntyre J noted in *Reference re Public Service Employee Relations Act (Alta.)*, … the right protected by s. 2(d) derives from the fact that "the attainment of individual goals, through the exercise of individual rights, is generally impossible without the aid and cooperation of others" (p. 395). However, underlying the cases on s. 2(d) is the proposition that freedom of association protects only the associational aspect of activities, not the activity itself. If the activity is to be protected by the Constitution, that protection must be found elsewhere than in s. 2(d).
>
> • • •
>
> [109] … It cannot be said that freedom of contract and trade is a modern notion. Nevertheless, the regulation of trade, and in particular, trade in agricultural commodities, is an exercise that involves a balance of competing interests that requires specialized expertise. Yet the effect of the respondents' submissions would be to constitutionalize all commercial relationships under the rubric of freedom of association. There is no trade or profession that can be exercised entirely by oneself.

III. THE FREEDOM NOT TO ASSOCIATE WITH OTHERS

While most of the freedom of association cases involve the right to associate, the Supreme Court of Canada has also interpreted s. 2(d) as including a right not to associate. As you read the following decisions, ask yourself whether the Court's account of the right not to associate is consistent with the reasons it offered in *BC Health Services* in support of its holding that freedom of association includes a right to bargain collectively.

The first case in which the Court squarely addressed the issue of whether freedom of association includes a right not to associate, or what is also described as a negative right of association, was *Lavigne v. Ontario Public Service Employees Union*, [1991] 2 SCR 211, 81 DLR (4th) 545, which involved a challenge to mandatory dues checkoff. The appellant Lavigne taught at a community college in Ontario. The Ontario Public Service Employees Union (OPSEU) was the bargaining agent for community college faculty members, including the appellant. Sections 51, 52, and 53 of the Ontario *Colleges Collective Bargaining Act*, RSO 1980, c. 74 authorized the inclusion of what is known as a "Rand formula"—requiring all employees to pay dues to a trade union regardless of whether they are members of the union—in collective agreements governing terms and conditions of employment at community colleges. The appellant objected to certain expenditures by OPSEU, including contributions to the following: a campaign against cruise missile testing; a campaign opposing the expenditure of municipal funds for the SkyDome stadium in Toronto; the National Union of Mine Workers in the United Kingdom; and the New Democratic Party. He also opposed contributions required by OPSEU's constitution to the National Union of Provincial Government Employees (NUPGE), which in turn pays dues to the Canadian Labour Congress. Both of these organizations also make a number of contributions of an economic, social, and political nature.

The appellant brought an application seeking a declaration that ss. 51, 52, and 53 of the Act infringe ss. 2(b) and 2(d) of the Charter. White J of the Supreme Court of Ontario found in favour of the appellant, holding that the Charter applies to Crown agencies in certain circumstances and that the appellant's freedom of association was unjustifiably infringed by the union's use of dues unrelated to the purpose justifying their imposition. The Court of Appeal allowed an appeal and set aside the orders of the trial judge. A further appeal was dismissed by a unanimous Supreme Court of Canada.

The issue of the Charter's application is discussed in Chapter 18, Application. Briefly, La Forest J (Sopinka, Gonthier, Cory, and McLachlin JJ concurring) held that the Council of Regents, which is the entity responsible for negotiating a collective agreement with the union, is a part of government, because it is a Crown agent, and the provincial Ministry of Colleges and Universities exercises full control of the Council's activities. In his view, the Council's agreement to the Rand formula constituted government action sufficient to trigger Charter scrutiny. Wilson J (L'Heureux-Dubé J concurring) gave separate concurring reasons substantially similar to the views expressed by Justice La Forest on this issue.

With respect to the claim that compelled payment of dues interferes with the appellant's freedom of expression, Justice La Forest (Sopinka and Gonthier JJ concurring) held that the payment of dues to the union does not amount to an attempt to convey meaning, and the union's uses of his dues cannot be regarded as an expression of the appellant's views. Wilson J (L'Heureux-Dubé and Cory JJ concurring) essentially agreed with Justice La Forest on this point, but added that even if compelled payment of dues amounts to an infringement of freedom of expression, it can be justified in the light of its purpose—that is, to foster collective bargaining.

Justices La Forest (Sopinka and Gonthier JJ concurring), Wilson (L'Heureux-Dubé and Cory JJ concurring), and McLachlin also dismissed the argument that compelled payment of dues unjustifiably interferes with freedom of association. McLachlin J held that s. 2(d) protects against compelled association of an individual with ideas and values to which he or she does not voluntarily subscribe. In her view, the compelled payment does not violate freedom of association, because there is no link between the mandatory payment and conformity with the ideas and values to which the appellant objected.

La Forest J (Sopinka and Gonthier JJ concurring) explained that the Rand formula can be challenged only if it interferes with the freedom not to associate with others—that is, the negative aspect of freedom of association. He therefore identified the issue as whether s. 2(d) encompasses the freedom not to be forced to associate with others, and concluded that it does:

> In my view, the answer is clearly yes. Forced association will stifle the individual's potential for self-fulfillment and realization as surely as voluntary association will develop it. Moreover, society cannot expect meaningful contribution from groups or organizations that are not truly representative of their memberships' convictions and free choice. Instead, it can expect that such groups and organizations will, overall, have a negative effect on the development of the larger community. One need only think of the history of social stagnation in Eastern Europe and of the role played in its development and preservation by officially established "free" trade unions, peace movements and cultural organizations to appreciate the destructive effect forced association can have upon the body politic. Recognition of the freedom of the individual to refrain from association is a necessary counterpart of meaningful association in keeping with democratic ideals.
>
> Furthermore, this is in keeping with our conception of freedom as guaranteed by the Charter. In *R v. Big M Drug Mart Ltd.* (1985), 18 DLR (4th) 321 at p. 354, 18 CCC (3d) 385, [1985] 1 SCR 295, Dickson J had this to say:

> > Freedom can primarily be characterized by the absence of coercion or constraint. *If a person is compelled by the State or the will of another to a course of action or inaction which he would not otherwise have chosen, he is not acting of his own volition and he cannot be said to be truly free.* One of the major purposes of the Charter is to protect, within reason, from compulsion or restraint. Coercion includes not only such blatant forms of compulsion as direct commands to act or refrain from acting on pain or sanction, coercion includes indirect forms of control which determine or limit alternative courses of conduct available to others. *Freedom in a broad sense embraces both the absence of coercion and constraint*, and the right to manifest beliefs and practices. Freedom means that, subject to such limitations as are necessary to protect public safety, order, health, or morals or the fundamental rights and freedoms of others, no one is to be forced to act in a way contrary to his beliefs or his conscience. [Emphasis added.]

> It is clear that a conception of freedom of association that did not include freedom from forced association would not truly be "freedom" within the meaning of the Charter.
>
> This brings into focus the critical point that freedom from forced association and freedom to associate should not be viewed in opposition, one "negative" and the other "positive." These are not distinct rights, but two sides of a bilateral freedom which has as its unifying purpose the advancement of individual aspirations. The bilateral nature of the associational right is explicitly recognized in art. 20 of the United Nations *Universal Declaration of Human Rights*, 1948, which provides as follows:

1. Everyone has the right to freedom of peaceful assembly and association.
2. No one may be compelled to belong to an association.

In Justice La Forest's view, the fact that some aspects of freedom of association may also be protected by other guarantees does not mean that s. 2(d) should not be given its full meaning, nor that all forms of association are protected under s. 2(d): s. 2(d) is not "a right to isolation" because "certain associations ... are accepted because they are integral to the very structure of society." In considering the test for determining whether there has been an infringement of the right not to associate, La Forest J focused on the role of freedom of association in enhancing the autonomy of the individual. In Lavigne's case, therefore, it is not sufficient that other people may not assume that he agrees with the union's position on various causes just because he is required to pay dues that are given to those causes. He is entitled to object to his dues being allocated to causes with which he disagrees. La Forest J found that the payment of dues (which are used to further the objects of the union) constitutes association. Lavigne had conceded that the requirement he pay dues for collective bargaining purposes is constitutional, and thus the only issue was whether it was constitutional to require him to pay dues to causes not directly related to collective bargaining or the workplace more generally.

After having found that the forced payment of dues constitutes a *prima facie* violation of an individual's rights under s. 2(d) of the Charter, La Forest J proceeded to uphold the infringement under s. 1. In his view, the fundamental importance of trade unions in democratizing the workplace, as well as their broader societal role in promoting democratic principles, would be undermined if the courts were to find agency shop provisions unconstitutional. Thus, at the minimal impairment stage of the *Oakes* test, he rejects the possibility of an "opting out" formula in the payment of dues as a feasible alternative. Such a formula, he argues, would not only strike at a union's financial base, rendering it less fit to fulfill its role, but would also undermine the solidarity that "is so important to the emotional and symbolic underpinnings of unionism." For La Forest J, the agency shop provisions represent a justifiable limit on freedom of association.

Wilson J (L'Heureux-Dubé and Cory JJ concurring) disagreed that freedom to associate encompasses a freedom from compelled association. Recognizing a freedom not to associate, in her view, "would be 'to overshoot the actual purpose of the right or freedom in question'" and "would set the scene for contests between the positive associational rights of union members and the negative associational rights of non-members." Thus "[t]o construe the section in this way would place the court in the impossible position of having to choose whose s. 2(d) rights should prevail." Furthermore, an individual who does not wish to associate with a particular group would be able to bring the claim under s. 2(b) or s. 7 of the Charter. Wilson J concluded that Lavigne's positive right to associate had not been contravened and that, even if there were a negative right, it had not been contravened because it would encompass the same narrow scope as the positive right pursuant to the *Alberta Reference*. Accordingly, she held that Lavigne's challenge did not fall within s. 2(d).

The application of the negative freedom of association arises not only in the context of dues payment, but also, perhaps more directly, in the context of mandatory union membership. The Supreme Court of Canada addressed this issue in its decision in *Advance Cutting & Coring*, in which the Court was divided on the application of the negative right.

R v. Advance Cutting & Coring Ltd.
[2001] 3 SCR 209, 2001 SCC 70, 205 DLR (4th) 385

[Section 119.1 of the Quebec *Act Respecting Labour Relations, Vocational Training and Manpower Management in the Construction Industry* required construction workers to obtain a competency certificate before they could work on a project. Before they could obtain a certificate, they had to join one of five union groups listed in s. 28 of the Act. Section 30 of the Act also required the Commission de la construction du Québec to prepare a list of workers who were eligible to take part in a mandatory vote by which the workers would choose which of the five union groups would represent them. The appellants were contractors and real estate promoters who had been charged with hiring employees who did not have competency certificates and construction workers who had been charged with working without competency certificates. They challenged the legislative provisions on the ground that requiring the workers to become members of the union groups in order to obtain competency certificates contravened s. 2(d) of the Charter, freedom of association, which they argued included the freedom *not* to associate. At the Supreme Court of Canada, in an opinion written by Bastarache J, four justices held that the provisions contravened the Charter and were not justified under s. 1 of the Charter; four justices held that the provisions did not contravene the Charter (of whom three, per LeBel J, found that the negative freedom of association was not infringed and one, L'Heureux-Dubé J, held that s. 2(d) did not encompass a negative freedom of association). Since the ninth justice, Iacobucci J, found a contravention, but considered that it was justifiable under s. 1, the provisions were upheld by a narrow margin.]

LeBEL J (Gonthier and Arbour JJ concurring): ... [163] The case at bar offers the possibility for an evolution in the relationship between the Charter and labour law. [T]he present case involves an attack on some forms of union security clauses. Under many shapes and forms, such arrangements often provide for an obligation to obtain or maintain union membership in order to retain or obtain employment. They may also address the financing of union activities. They may combine provisions relating to the checking off of union dues with others concerning the maintenance of union membership. A well known and common form of union security, the Rand formula, which was discussed in the *Lavigne* case [*Lavigne v. Ontario Public Service Employees Union*, [1991] 2 SCR 211, 81 DLR (4th) 545], has even become a standard part of the labour laws of some provinces, for example, under the Quebec *Labour Code*, RSQ, c. C-27, s. 47. Under this formula, union dues are withheld from the pay of an employee, whether or not he or she belongs to the union.

· · ·

[205] The present case presents a more difficult problem than the application of the Rand formula canvassed in *Lavigne*. The *Construction Act* imposes an obligation to join one of five unions. The question becomes whether this fact *per se* triggers the negative component and becomes a breach of s. 2(d) of the Charter that must be justified under s. 1. If we adopt this route, it might well mean that all forms of compulsory membership provided for or even authorized under statute would be open to challenge under the Charter.

[206] A proper analysis of *Lavigne* and of the nature of the constitutional guarantee does not allow for such a result. Although differing in some respects, McLachlin J's and La Forest J's reasons both refused to view the negative right as a simple mirror-image of the positive right of association. Both Justices accepted that the nature of a workplace and the status of the persons participating in its life and experience created associations that became unavoidable or "compelled." The use of the notion of ideological conformity by McLachlin J or La Forest J's concerns for the safeguarding of broad liberty interests acknowledged the need for association, as well as the need to join, which may be required in some aspects of life in the workplace. At the same time, they intended to meet the need to safeguard democratic values and to foster them in the area of labour relations. Their reasons reflect the view that some forms of compelled association might breach s. 2(d) of the Charter if the fact of association imposes on an individual values and views of the world antithetical to his or her own.

[207] The Court found a balance in *Lavigne*. This balance is now at stake in the present case. The majority of the Court in *Lavigne* found that there was a negative right not to associate. Although it acknowledged the need for such a right, it accepted a democratic rationale for putting internal limits on the right not to associate. La Forest J regarded the Constitution's presumption of democracy as a reason for concluding that forced associations which flow from the functioning of democracy cannot be severed with the aid of the Charter (at pp. 317 and 320-21). Democracy is not primarily about withdrawal, but fundamentally about participation in the life and management of democratic institutions like unions.

[208] An approach that fails to read in some inner limits and restrictions to a right not to associate would deny the individual the benefits arising from an association. This Court has maintained, since the labour law trilogy of 1987, that the right of association intends to foster individual autonomy and attaches to individuals. At the same time, the exercise of the right of association also reinforces the ability of an individual to convey ideas and opinions, through a group voice, as the Court acknowledged in the *Libman* case [*Libman v. Quebec (Attorney General)*, [1997] 3 SCR 569, 151 DLR (4th) 385, discussed in Chapter 20, Freedom of Expression], while discussing political and ideological associations. It should not be viewed as an inferior right, barely tolerated and narrowly circumscribed.

· · ·

[218] The *Construction Act* imposes an obligation to join a union group. The obligation remains, nevertheless, a very limited one. It boils down to the obligation to designate a collective bargaining representative, to belong to it for a given period of time, and to pay union dues. The Act does not require more. At the same time, the Act provides protection against past, present and potential abuses of union power. ... The law allows any construction worker to change his or her union affiliation, at the appropriate time. As it stands, the law does not impose on construction workers much more than the bare obligation to belong to a union. It does not create any mechanism to enforce ideological conformity.

· · ·

[220] ... No witness came forward to assert that he felt or believed that joining a union associated him with activities he disapproved of, or with opinions he did not share. In order to trigger the negative guarantee in this case, ideological conformity or breach of another liberty interest would have to be found in the fact that unions, as other groups

belonging to or participating in a democratic society, sometimes engage in public debate, take positions on issues concerning their members, or comment on broad social or political questions.

[221] Our Court would have to presume that, because they take part in social debate, unions in Quebec or elsewhere act in breach of the democratic values of our society, and of the liberty interests and the freedom of opinion and expression of their members. Still, if union members assert such a concern, it may have to be addressed. Accommodation may become necessary to safeguard the democratic character of unions and of the society within which they operate.

. . .

[223] No evidence was introduced about union practices that would impose values or opinions on their members. No evidence was offered about the internal life of construction unions or about the constraints they might seek to impose upon members. There was no indication that free expression is limited by union activities of such a nature that forced association would trigger the guarantee of s. 2(d). The nature of a particular legislative or regulatory system, in an important part of the economy like the construction industry, may certainly be subject to criticisms or political discussions. Nevertheless, personal disagreements with the extent of a strict regulatory system do not suffice to mount a successful Charter challenge. It should now be clear that the mere fact of compelled association will not, by itself, involve a breach of the Charter. More is needed in order to trigger the negative component of s. 2(d).

[LeBel J then addressed the issue of whether the Court could infer or presume that workers were subject to ideological coercion.]

[224] May the Court presume ideological coercion from the fact that, at times, Quebec unions, like other groups, have advocated particular causes? ...

[225] In order to reach such a result, the Court would have to take judicial notice of the presumed ideological bent of Quebec unions. The Court would have to judicially notice that ideological orientations or the adoption of social and political causes within the union movement mean that a form of intellectual conformity is being imposed by unions on their members, and that the liberty interests of those members are being jeopardized. Judicial notice certainly has its place in constitutional adjudication. ...

[226] The fact that unions intervene in political social debate is well known and well documented and might be the object of judicial notice. Indeed, our Court acknowledged the importance of this role in the *Lavigne* case. Several ideological currents have crisscrossed the history of the Quebec labour movement. ...

[227] Taking judicial notice of the fact that Quebec unions have a constant ideology, act in constant support of a particular cause or policy, and seek to impose that ideology on their members seems far more controversial. It would require a leap of faith and logic, absent a proper factual record on the question. The assertion seems to rest on the tenuous line that, although we do not have any evidence to this effect, coercion on the individuals should be inferred from "ideological" trends present in the labour movement. This "fact" is unlike issues of notorious discrimination against certain groups in Canadian society, and unlike the disadvantage experienced by women and children after a di-

vorce, both facts of which this Court has taken judicial notice (see *R v. Williams*, [1998] 1 SCR 1128, and *Willick v. Willick*, [1994] 3 SCR 670). In this case, it cannot be said that some form of politicization and ideological conformity which allegedly flows from the political and social orientation of the labour movement is self-evident. Instead, such views evidence stereotypes about the union movement as authoritarian and undemocratic, and conjure images of workers marching in lock step without any free choice or free will, under the watchful eyes of union bosses and their goon squads.

[228] In fact, democracy undergirds the particular form of union security provided for by the *Construction Act*. Throughout the conflicts and difficulties that marred the history of the construction industry, a critical flaw of the regime appeared to be the lack of participation in the life of unions and the need to reestablish and maintain member control over their affairs. ... Affiliation means that he or she has, at least, gained the ability to influence the life of the association whether or not he or she decides to exercise this right.

[229] In the case of the construction unions, a heightened degree of participation in the life of the associations appeared necessary in order to foster union democracy. At the same time, the legislative formula left workers a choice among the various groups active in the construction industry. These groups had held widely different views on the role of labour unions in society. Their orientations represented a broad spectrum of opinions, both about the orientation of society and about the functions of unions. The legislative solution represented an answer to some of the pressing problems that the Quebec construction industry had been confronted with during several years. The degree of relative peace and equilibrium reached by the time the present case started bears witness to the basic soundness of this legislative choice, which expresses a deep concern for democratic values. One might think that an absolute right to withdraw at will, even with payment of service fees for unions, would not preserve and develop the internal democracy of union groups in the same manner. It would deprive the dues-paying worker of any influence on the life of the union and on the determination of working conditions meant to be extended to the entire industry or a sector thereof, as rules of public order. ...

[230] Union members seem to act very independently from their union when it comes to the expression of their political choices and, even more so, to their voting preferences, come election time. Existence of attempted ideological conformity, let alone its realization, seems highly doubtful. ...

[231] In this context, there is simply no evidence to support judicial notice of Quebec unions ideologically coercing their members. Such an inference presumes that unions hold a single ideology and impose it on their rank and file, including the complainants in this case. Such an inference would amount to little more than an unsubstantiated stereotype.

• • •

BASTARACHE J dissenting (McLachlin CJC and Major and Binnie JJ concurring): ...

• • •

[3] The test relied upon by LeBel J is based primarily upon the decision of McLachlin J (as she then was) in *Lavigne [supra]*. According to LeBel J, for ideological conformity to exist, there must be evidence of an imposition of union values or opinions on the member.

evidence of a limitation of the member's free expression, or evidence that the union participates in causes and activities of which the member disapproves. … In other words, LeBel J's interpretation of ideological conformity is a narrow one where, in order to exist, there must be some impact on the member's moral convictions. This test, as formulated by LeBel J, is, in my opinion, too narrow and results in a negative right that is too constrained. I do not agree that McLachlin J's opinion in *Lavigne* need be interpreted so restrictively. In my view, the interpretation of ideological conformity must be broader and take place in context. In this case, this context would take into account the true nature of unions as participatory bodies holding political and economic roles in society which, in turn, translates into the existence of ideological positions. To mandate that an individual adhere to such a union is ideological conformity. …

[Justice Bastarache referred to the concerns about association prior to the Charter as reflected in the Rand formula whereby a worker will be required to pay union dues but can choose not to join the union that represents the employees in a workplace. The infringement in the current case is more significant, he said, and therefore requires greater justification.]

[17] … To suggest that the unions in the present case are not associated with any ideological cause is to ignore the history of the union movement itself. Although it has been accepted that freedom of association protects an activity by an association that is permitted by an individual, this does not mean that there is no distinctive function for an association, or that associational analogues to individual rights need be ignored. The collective character of the right to associate is undeniable because collective activity is not equivalent to the addition of individual activities. It is important, however, that belonging to important social institutions be free; this is how democracy will be enhanced. …

[Justice Bastarache then considered whether the negative right is infringed. He discussed the political role played by unions, including their support of the New Democratic Party, their participation in the sovereignty issue in Quebec, and the general political representation of their members.]

[27] … Furthermore, membership has meaning. Membership is about sharing values, joining to pursue goals in common, expressing views reflecting the position of a particular group in society. … It is because of the collective force produced by membership that unions can be a potent force in public debate, that they can influence Parliament and the legislatures in their functions, that they can bargain effectively. This force must be constituted democratically to conform to s. 2(d).

· · ·

[29] In the present case, workers objected to being forced to join a union and objected generally to the compulsory unionization scheme, which is, in my view, ideological in nature.

· · ·

[31] This is a case where the freedom not to associate is markedly infringed. ... This is a clear situation of government coercion, the result of which mandates that workers in the construction industry in Quebec group together in a few unions which are specified and approved by government. The fact that there are five unions from which workers can choose in no way negates this infringement for it remains government-mandated group affiliation. Self-realization of the worker is violated in many ways. He or she must unionize. Within the prescribed regime, democracy is further restricted by limited choice. There is no guarantee that a majority of voters will exercise their right. A default provision can determine the outcome of elections. Those voting for minority associations may be left out of future negotiations.

. . .

[34] As I have said, ideological conformity is engaged in particular because the members of the associations necessarily participate in and indirectly support a system of forced association and state control over work opportunity. This is a situation whereby the democratic rights of workers are taken away. Being forced to accept and participate in a system that severely limits the democratic principle in the area of labour relations is a form of coercion that cannot be segregated totally from ideological conformity. If Parliament provided that a person must belong to a specific political party to work in the public service of Canada, the situation would be analogous. Some would argue that one does not have to believe, simply that one has to belong; ... I believe there would still be clear ideological conformity.

[35] Since ideological conformity is part of the broader test to which I subscribe, I conclude that the challenged statutory provisions infringe the negative right which forms part of s. 2(d).

[36] ... There is also a distinction to be made with the requirements of professional associations such as medical associations and law societies, where the need for protection of the public may require a forced association which is justified under s. 1 of the *Charter*. In this case, the provisions are not based on the protection of the public by way of assuring the competency of workers. To receive certification, a worker must be a member of one of the five chosen unions; to become a member, he or she must have been a resident of Quebec in the previous year, have worked a set number of hours in that year and must be under 50 years of age. Without having met these requirements, a worker is unable to work in Quebec regardless of his or her actual competence or experience in his or her chosen trade. The conditions related to forced association have nothing to do with the protection of the public. As stated by Bonin J of the Court of Québec, "[TRANSLATION] [t]he certificate's main purpose was to maintain hiring priority." As such, a s. 1 justification is required. Before considering s. 1, however, I turn next to the examination of the positive right which is also part of s. 2(d).

[Bastarache J found that s. 30 of the Act, which establishes the conditions under which a competency card can be obtained (workers have to be resident in Quebec in the previous year during which they had to have worked 300 hours and be under 50 years old), and the regional quota requirements limiting the right to be placed on the union lists breaches the positive right to associate. The conditions affect workers inside and outside Quebec and "severely" restrict their ability to join one of the unions. He concluded that, under s. 1 of the Charter, these requirements were disproportionate to their their stated objectives.

Iacobucci J agreed that s. 2(d) includes a negative right to be free from compelled association. He held that the legislation infringed that right, but that it was justified under s. 1 of the Charter. He disagreed with both LeBel J and Bastarache J, however, that the test for whether the negative right has been infringed relies on a finding of ideological conformity, preferring the test of whether the association poses a threat to a specific liberty interest enunciated by La Forest J in *Lavigne*. Indicating that forced association with respect to professional or skilled organizations will usually be valid because it reflects competence, he found that the forced membership in the construction unions is not contingent on competency. It also impaired the liberty interest of those who are opposed to joining a union and those who would choose a different union than one of the five recognized unions. He adopted LeBel J's s. 1 analysis to find the contravention justified.

L'Heureux-Dubé J held that *Lavigne* does not support a clear statement of a constitutional right not to associate and that since freedom from ideological conformity can be addressed through s. 2(b) or 7 of the Charter, it is not appropriate to develop new constitutional tools. She did not recognize a negative right of association and therefore held that there was no contravention of s. 2(d). She further expressed concern that "the impetus for efforts to establish the negative right to association has historically originated with those opposed to the establishment or maintenance of labour associations. Such a tainted pedigree raises the question of whether we should constitutionalize an initiative whose purpose was to defeat the right to associate."]

Appeal dismissed.

CHAPTER TWENTY-TWO

Life, Liberty, and Security of the Person

I. INTRODUCTION

Section 7 of the *Canadian Charter of Rights and Freedoms*, guaranteeing that "[e]veryone has the right to life, liberty and security of the person and the right not to be deprived thereof except in accordance with the principles of fundamental justice," contains powerful words that have been at the centre of our constitutional tradition for centuries, especially liberty and justice. To introduce readers to the nature and scope of the guarantee, we begin with an account of two topics that may, at first blush, seem to have little relevance. The first is *Lochner v. New York*, 198 US 45 (1905), a landmark case in American constitutional law; the second relates to Canadian administrative law.

In *Lochner*, the US Supreme Court struck down a New York statute that set maximum hours of work for bakers on the ground that it violated the due process clause of the Bill of Rights, which prohibits state governments from taking away a person's "liberty" without "due process." The liberty the court saw violated was the liberty of employees to make contracts about hours of work. This result and others like it are called "substantive due process," which protects substantive values such as freedom of contract, in contrast to "procedural due process," which protects values associated with procedural fairness.

Lochner has been a landmark of American constitutional thought throughout this century, although, like most landmarks, it has been interpreted in different ways by different generations. The dominant understanding has been that the Supreme Court imposed its own laissez-faire ideology, frustrating the efforts of progressive legislatures to reform working conditions, and defying the terms and history of the Bill of Rights and the preferences of the majority of Americans. In the past couple of decades, American legal historians have presented different readings of *Lochner*, showing how both the result and the reasoning were shaped by older themes of American constitutional beliefs, but these revisions are not part of the story that concerns us here. Instead, it is the dominant, earlier understanding that is significant. In this reading, the case is a paradigm example of the need for judicial restraint and the danger that arises when judges read their own personal economic and social values into the terms of constitutional guarantees. Scholars wrote endlessly on the topic, brandishing the spectre of *Lochner* and admonishing judges to eschew "substantive due process." In the 1930s, the Supreme Court committed itself to a much more restrained standard of review for economic and social legislation, requiring only a "rational basis."

Our second topic in these preliminary comments is a doctrine about administrative law—in particular, a body of doctrine for which "natural justice" is one of the more common titles (another is fairness). An individual who will be affected in some distinctive or particular way by a proposed administrative action or decision by the government is entitled to "natural justice"—that is, to have a hearing and to have the decision made by officials who are impartial and independent. The phrase "some distinctive or particular way" refers to the effect of a wide range of decisions, all of them contrasted to the making of general policy. For example, if the governing body of a profession proposes to discipline a member for misconduct or negligence, it must give a hearing, because the decision will affect the member alone. Whether natural justice is required for making a zoning bylaw, a standard for toxic emission levels, or a tariff schedule depends greatly on the context. The hearing that is required if a decision meets this threshold requirement is a reasonable opportunity to know what is being contemplated and to participate in the decision through the presentation of evidence and arguments. Depending on the context, natural justice may range from an informal interview or written submissions to a formal proceeding that is much like a trial.

The requirement of impartiality and independence, the other element of the entitlement to natural justice, is a simple, general principle. Some examples of the absence of impartiality and independence are a financial interest in the outcome of the decision, personal animosity or friendship toward a party, and participation in both the prosecution and the adjudication of an issue. More difficult examples depend on the context. A member of an environmental assessment tribunal may have, and may even be expected to have, some experience and attitudes that shape her perception of the decisions she must make, but a member of a tribunal dealing with professional discipline must be much more free from predispositions. This body of doctrine, "natural justice," together with the procedural protections in the criminal law, stands as one of the large elements of the common law protections of constitutional liberty in the British tradition.

How do *Lochner* and natural justice bear on the nature and scope of s. 7? Both were part of the stock of common knowledge of the lawyers who participated in drafting s. 7, and of the lawyers and judges who sought to interpret it. It is reasonably apparent that the drafters felt an acute need to avoid the dangers represented by *Lochner*. The word property, for example, was not included in the phrase "life, liberty and security of the person," and several proposals to include it afterward have perished. The drafters of s. 7 also tended to assume, often expressly, that fundamental justice meant only rules designed to secure procedural fairness or natural justice, as opposed to rules vindicating substantive values that may or may not find expression elsewhere in the Constitution. Later, when the courts were asked to interpret fundamental justice, they were told that if the term was not limited to procedures, the only alternative was substantive review along the lines of *Lochner*. In response, the judiciary rejected interpreting "liberty" as including "liberty of contract." In *Reference re ss. 193 and 195.1(1)(c) of the Criminal Code*, [1990] 1 SCR 1123, 24 DLR (4th) 536 ("Prostitution Reference"), for example, Lamer CJC stated:

> I … reject the application of the American line of cases that suggest that liberty under the Fourteenth Amendment includes liberty of contract. … [T]hese cases have a specific historical context, a context that incorporated into the American jurisprudence certain laissez-faire principles that may not have a corresponding application to the interpretation of the Charter in the present day. There is also a significant difference in the wording of s. 7 and the Fourteenth Amendment. The American provision speaks specifically of a protection of property interests

while our framers did not choose to similarly protect property rights (see *Irwin Toy Ltd. v. Quebec (Attorney General)*, [1989] 1 SCR 927, at p. 1003).

Although the courts have been careful to disclaim any attraction to *Lochner*'s temptations, as we shall see, the Supreme Court has interpreted fundamental justice to mean more than procedural protections for life, liberty, and security of the person.

The following case, often referred to as the *BC Motor Vehicle Reference*, was the first major decision of the Supreme Court of Canada addressing the nature and scope of s. 7. At issue was s. 94(2) of the *Motor Vehicle Act*, RSBC 1979, c. 288, which imposed a fine and imprisonment on a driver for driving while his or her licence was suspended, regardless of knowledge of the suspension or intent. Because the Court regarded imprisonment as a clear deprivation of liberty, much of the decision addressed the meaning of fundamental justice. The decision nonetheless also provides valuable insight on how life, liberty, and security of the person relate to each other, to principles of fundamental justice, and to other rights and freedoms guaranteed in the Charter. While reading it, keep in mind that the structure of s. 7 authorizes the state to violate the right to life, liberty, and security of the person if it does so in a manner that conforms with a principle of fundamental justice, and that a law that does not comply with fundamental justice may amount to a reasonable limit under s. 1 of the Charter. This structure thus requires a court to determine, first, the nature and scope of the right to life, liberty, and security of the person; second, the nature and scope of fundamental justice; and third, the applicability of s. 1 of the Charter.

Reference re Section 94(2) of the Motor Vehicle Act (BC)
[1985] 2 SCR 486, 24 DLR (4th) 536

LAMER J (Dickson CJC, Chouinard, and Le Dain JJ concurring): ...

The Nature and Legitimacy of Constitutional Adjudication Under the Charter

• • •

[I]n the context of s. 7, and in particular of the interpretation of "principles of fundamental justice" there has prevailed in certain quarters an assumption that all but a narrow construction of s. 7 will inexorably lead the courts to question the wisdom of enactments, to adjudicate upon the merits of public policy.

From this have sprung warnings of the dangers of a judicial "super-legislature" beyond the reach of Parliament, the provincial legislatures and the electorate. ...

This is an argument which was heard countless times prior to the entrenchment of the Charter but which has in truth, for better or for worse, been settled by the very coming into force of the *Constitution Act, 1982*. It ought not to be forgotten that the historic decision to entrench the Charter in our Constitution was taken not by the courts but by the elected representatives of the people of Canada. It was those representatives who extended the scope of constitutional adjudication and entrusted the courts with this new and onerous responsibility. Adjudication under the Charter must be approached free of any lingering doubts as to its legitimacy.

The concerns with the bounds of constitutional adjudication explain the characterization of the issue in a narrow and restrictive fashion, i.e., whether the term "principles of fundamental justice" has a substantive or merely procedural content. In my view, the characterization of the issue in such fashion preempts an open-minded approach to determining the meaning of "principles of fundamental justice."

The substantive/procedural dichotomy narrows the issue almost to an all-or-nothing proposition. Moreover, it is largely bound up in the American experience with substantive and procedural due process. It imports into the Canadian context American concepts, terminology and jurisprudence, all of which are inextricably linked to problems concerning the nature and legitimacy of adjudication under the US Constitution. That Constitution, it must be remembered, has no s. 52 nor has it the internal checks and balances of ss. 1 and 33. We would, in my view, do our own Constitution a disservice to simply allow the American debate to define the issue for us, all the while ignoring the truly fundamental structural differences between the two constitutions. Finally, the dichotomy creates its own set of difficulties by the attempt to distinguish between two concepts whose outer boundaries are not always clear and often tend to overlap. Such difficulties can and should, when possible, be avoided.

. . .

The Principles of Fundamental Justice

. . .

In the framework of a purposive analysis, designed to ascertain the purpose of the s. 7 guarantee and "the interests it was meant to protect" (*R v. Big M Drug Mart Ltd.*, [1985] 1 SCR 295 [18 DLR (4th) 321]), it is clear to me that the interests which are meant to be protected by the words "and the right not to be deprived thereof except in accordance with the principles of fundamental justice" of s. 7 are the life, liberty and security of the person. The principles of fundamental justice, on the other hand, are not a protected interest, but rather a qualifier of the right not to be deprived of life, liberty and security of the person.

... [The meaning of] the phrase "principles of fundamental justice" ... must, in my view, be determined by reference to the interests which those words of the section are designed to protect and the particular role of the phrase within the section. As a qualifier, the phrase serves to establish the parameters of the interests but it cannot be interpreted so narrowly as to frustrate or stultify them. For the narrower the meaning given to "principles of fundamental justice" the greater will be the possibility that individuals may be deprived of these most basic rights. This latter result is to be avoided given that the rights involved are as fundamental as those which pertain to the life, liberty and security of the person. ...

For these reasons, I am of the view that it would be wrong to interpret the term "fundamental justice" as being synonymous with natural justice as the Attorney General of British Columbia and others have suggested. To do so would strip the protected interests of much, if not most, of their content and leave the "right" to life, liberty and security of the person in a sorely emaciated state. Such a result would be inconsistent with the broad, affirmative language in which those rights are expressed and equally inconsistent with the approach adopted by this Court toward the interpretation of Charter rights. ...

It would mean that the right to liberty would be narrower than the right not to be arbitrarily detained or imprisoned (s. 9), that the right to security of the person would have less content than the right to be secure against unreasonable search or seizure (s. 8). Such an interpretation would give the specific expressions of the "right to life, liberty and security of the person" which are set forth in ss. 8 to 14 greater content than the general concept from which they originate.

Sections 8 to 14, in other words, address specific deprivations of the "right" to life, liberty and security of the person in breach of the principles of fundamental justice, and as such, violations of s. 7. They are designed to protect, in a specific manner and setting, the right to life, liberty and security of the person set forth in s. 7. It would be incongruous to interpret s. 7 more narrowly than the rights in ss. 8 to 14. ...

Sections 8 to 14 are illustrative of deprivations of those rights to life, liberty and security of the person in breach of the principles of fundamental justice. For they, in effect, illustrate some of the parameters of the "right" to life, liberty and security of the person; they are examples of instances in which the "right" to life, liberty and security of the person would be violated in a manner which is not in accordance with the principles of fundamental justice. To put matters in a different way, ss. 7 to 14 could have been fused into one section, with inserted between the words of s. 7 and the rest of those sections the oft utilised provision in our statutes, "and, without limiting the generality of the foregoing (s. 7) the following shall be deemed to be in violation of a person's rights under this section." Clearly, some of those sections embody principles that are beyond what could be characterized as "procedural."

Thus, ss. 8 to 14 provide an invaluable key to the meaning of "principles of fundamental justice." Many have been developed over time as presumptions of the common law, others have found expression in the international conventions on human rights. All have been recognized as essential elements of a system for the administration of justice which is founded upon a belief in "the dignity and worth of the human person" (preamble to the *Canadian Bill of Rights*, RSC 1970, App. III) and on "the rule of law" (preamble to the *Canadian Charter of Rights and Freedoms*).

It is this common thread which, in my view, must guide us in determining the scope and content of "principles of fundamental justice." In other words, the principles of fundamental justice are to be found in the basic tenets of our legal system. They do not lie in the realm of general public policy but in the inherent domain of the judiciary as guardian of the justice system. Such an approach to the interpretation of "principles of fundamental justice" is consistent with the wording and structure of s. 7, the context of the section, i.e., ss. 8 to 14, and the character and larger objects of the Charter itself. It provides meaningful content for the s. 7 guarantee all the while avoiding adjudication of policy matters.

Thus, it seems to me that to replace "fundamental justice" with the term "natural justice" misses the mark entirely. It was, after all, clearly open to the legislator to use the term natural justice, a known term of art, but such was not done. We must, as a general rule, be loath to exchange the terms actually used with terms so obviously avoided.

Whatever may have been the degree of synonymy between the two expressions in the past (which in any event has not been clearly demonstrated by the parties and interveners), as of the last few decades this country has given a precise meaning to the words natural justice for the purpose of delineating the responsibility of adjudicators (in the wide sense of the word) in the field of administrative law.

It is, in my view, that precise and somewhat narrow meaning that the legislator avoided, clearly indicating thereby a will to give greater content to the words "principles of fundamental justice," the limits of which were left for the courts to develop but within, of course, the acceptable sphere of judicial activity.

. . .

We should not be surprised to find that many of the principles of fundamental justice are procedural in nature. Our common law has largely been a law of remedies and procedures and, as Frankfurter J wrote in *McNabb v. United States*, 318 US 332 (1942), at p. 347, "the history of liberty has largely been the history of observance of procedural safeguards." This is not to say, however, that the principles of fundamental justice are limited solely to procedural guarantees. Rather, the proper approach to the determination of the principles of fundamental justice is quite simply one in which, as Professor L. Tremblay has written, "future growth will be based on historical roots" ("Section 7 of the Charter: Substantive Due Process?" (1984), 18 *UBCL Rev.* 201, at p. 254).

[Lamer J concluded that absolute liability offended fundamental justice, deriving this conclusion from the basic principle that the innocent should not be punished. He also concluded that absolute liability could not be justified under s. 1. Even though it was highly desirable that bad drivers be kept off the road, and that drivers who scorned licence requirements be severely punished, the government had not demonstrated that the risk of imprisoning innocent persons was a reasonable limit when weighed against the alternative of a statute that imposed strict liability coupled with a defence of due diligence. Wilson and McIntyre JJ wrote separate reasons agreeing with Lamer J.]

Appeal dismissed.

II. SECTION 7 AND BODILY INTEGRITY

Because imprisonment has been held to constitute a deprivation of liberty, s. 7 has been invoked in many challenges to *Criminal Code* provisions, especially challenges about procedures and about standards of fault. The result is a large body of doctrine, most of which we have omitted on the assumption that it is dealt with in criminal law courses. Some laws, however, also threaten interests associated with the integrity of the human body in addition to or in the absence of any threat to liberty by imprisonment, and thus require a closer examination of the interests that s. 7 is designed to protect. The following two cases involve criminal prohibitions that interfere with bodily integrity.

R v. Morgentaler
[1988] 1 SCR 30, 44 DLR (4th) 385

[Section 251(1) of the *Criminal Code* provided that anyone who took steps to cause an abortion was guilty of an indictable offence and liable to imprisonment for life. Section 251(2) provided that a pregnant female who sought to cause her own abortion was guilty of an indictable offence and liable to imprisonment for two years. Section 251(4) created an exception to s. 251(1) for abortions performed "in an accredited or approved hospital ... if ... the therapeutic abortion committee for that ... hospital ... has by certificate in writing stated that in its opinion the continuation of the pregnancy ... would or would be likely to endanger her life or health," and if the abortion was performed by "a qualified medical practitioner who was not a member of the committee." (The reference to "an accredited or approved hospital" was to hospitals that had been approved by a provincial minister of health for the purpose of performing abortions and accredited by the Canadian Council on Hospital Accreditation.) The prohibition in s. 251(1) had been in the Code since the late nineteenth century, continuing a longstanding common law prohibition. The exception in s. 251(2) was enacted in 1969.

Dr. Morgentaler and two colleagues established and operated an abortion clinic in Toronto, clearly violating s. 251(1), because the clinic was not approved, and because they did not obtain a certificate from a committee. Charged under s. 251(1), they argued that the provision violated s. 7 of the Charter. The Ontario Court of Appeal allowed an appeal from an acquittal at trial, ordering a new trial. Morgentaler appealed to the Supreme Court.]

DICKSON CJC (Lamer J concurring): ...

Security of the Person

The law has long recognized that the human body ought to be protected from interference by others. At common law, for example, any medical procedure carried out on a person without that person's consent is an assault. Only in emergency circumstances does the law allow others to make decisions of this nature. Similarly, art. 19 of the *Civil Code of Lower Canada* provides that "The human person is inviolable" and that "No person may cause harm to the person of another without his consent or without being authorized by law to do so." "Security of the person," in other words, is not a value alien to our legal landscape. With the advent of the Charter, security of the person has been elevated to the status of a constitutional norm. This is not to say that the various forms of protection accorded to the human body by the common and civil law occupy a similar status. "Security of the person" must be given content in a manner sensitive to its constitutional position. The above examples are simply illustrative of our respect for individual physical integrity. (See R. Macdonald, "Procedural Due Process in Canadian Constitutional Law" (1987), 39 *U Fla. L Rev.* 217, at 248.) Nor is it to say that the state can never impair personal security interests. There may well be valid reasons for interfering with security of the person. It is to say, however, that if the state does interfere with security of the person, the Charter requires such interference to conform with the principles of fundamental justice.

The appellants submitted that the "security of the person" protected by the Charter is an explicit right to control one's body and to make fundamental decisions about one's life. The Crown contended that "security of the person" is a more circumscribed interest and that, like all of the elements of s. 7, it at most relates to the concept of physical control, simply protecting the individual's interest in his or her bodily integrity.

· · ·

It may well be that constitutional protection of the above interests is specific to, and is only triggered by, the invocation of our system of criminal justice. It must not be forgotten, however, that s. 251 of the *Code*, subject to s-s. (4), makes it an indictable offence for a person to procure the miscarriage and provides a maximum sentence of two years in the case of the woman herself, and a maximum sentence of life imprisonment in the cases of another person. Like Justice Beetz, I do not find it necessary to decide how s. 7 would apply in other cases.

The case law leads me to the conclusion that state interference with bodily integrity and serious state-imposed psychological stress, at least in the criminal law context, constitute a breach of security of the person. It is not necessary in this case to determine whether the right extends further, to protect either interests central to personal autonomy, such as a right to privacy, or interests unrelated to criminal justice.

I wish to reiterate that finding a violation of security of the person does not end the s. 7 inquiry. Parliament could choose to infringe security of the person if it did so in a manner consistent with the principles of fundamental justice. The present discussion should therefore be seen as a threshold inquiry and the conclusions do not dispose definitively of all the issues relevant to s. 7. With that caution, I have no difficulty in concluding that the encyclopedic factual submissions addressed to us by counsel in the present appeal establish beyond any doubt that s. 251 of the *Criminal Code* is *prima facie* a violation of the security of the person of thousands of Canadian women who have made the difficult decision that they do not wish to continue with a pregnancy.

At the most basic, physical and emotional level, every pregnant woman is told by the section that she cannot submit to a generally safe medical procedure that might be of clear benefit to her unless she meets criteria entirely unrelated to her own priorities and aspirations. Not only does the removal of decision-making power threaten women in a physical sense; the indecision of knowing whether an abortion will be granted inflicts emotional stress. Section 251 clearly interferes with a woman's bodily integrity in both a physical and emotional sense. Forcing a woman, by threat of criminal sanction, to carry a foetus to term unless she meets certain criteria unrelated to her own priorities and aspirations, is a profound interference with a woman's body and thus a violation of security of the person. Section 251, therefore, is required by the Charter to comport with the principles of fundamental justice.

Although this interference with physical and emotional integrity is sufficient in itself to trigger a review of s. 251 against the principles of fundamental justice, the operation of the decision-making mechanism set out in s. 251 creates additional glaring breaches of security of the person. The evidence indicates that s. 251 causes a certain amount of delay for women who are successful in meeting its criteria. In the context of abortion, any unnecessary delay can have profound consequences on the woman's physical and emotional well-being.

[Dickson CJC then reviewed evidence about the relationship between delay in access to abortion and health risks.]

It is no doubt true that the overall complication and mortality rates for women who undergo abortions are very low, but the increasing risks caused by delay are so clearly established that I have no difficulty in concluding that the delay in obtaining therapeutic abortions caused by the mandatory procedures of s. 251 is an infringement of the purely physical aspect of the individual's right to security of the person. I should stress that the marked contrast between the relative speed with which abortions can be obtained at the government-sponsored community clinics in Quebec and in hospitals under the s. 251 procedure was established at trial. The evidence indicated that at the government-sponsored clinics in Quebec, the maximum delay was less than a week. One must conclude, and perhaps underline, that the delay experienced by many women seeking a therapeutic abortion, be it of one, two, four, or six weeks' duration, is caused in large measure by the requirements of s. 251 itself.

The above physical interference caused by the delays created by s. 251, involving a clear risk of damage to the physical well-being of a woman, is sufficient, in my view, to warrant inquiring whether s. 251 comports with the principles of fundamental justice. However, there is yet another infringement of security of the person. It is clear from the evidence that s. 251 harms the psychological integrity of women seeking abortions. A 1985 report of the Canadian Medical Association, discussed in the Powell Report [*Report on Therapeutic Abortion Services in Ontario* (Toronto: Ontario Ministry of Health, 1987)], at 15, emphasized that the procedure involved in s. 251, with the concomitant delays, greatly increases the stress levels of patients and that this can lead to more physical complications associated with abortion.

· · ·

In summary, s. 251 is a law which forces women to carry a foetus to term contrary to their own priorities and aspirations and which imposes serious delay causing increased physical and psychological trauma to those women who meet its criteria. It must, therefore, be determined whether that infringement is accomplished in accordance with the principles of fundamental justice, thereby saving s. 251 under the second part of s. 7.

· · ·

The Principles of Fundamental Justice

[After describing s. 251, Dickson CJC considered its practical operation. He relied heavily on the Badgley report (*The Report of the Committee on the Operation of the Abortion Law*), a report made in 1977 by a committee established by the federal government to determine whether the abortion provisions were operating "equitably." The report demonstrated that the "procedural and administrative requirements" had created substantial inconsistencies and obstacles that greatly limited the number of hospitals performing abortions. Section 251 implicitly required at least three doctors for a committee, and because none of them could perform the abortion, a fourth was needed. Only about 75 percent of the hospitals in Canada met this minimum requirement. As well, the accreditation requirement excluded about 60 percent, and only about 50 percent of the remainder had chosen to establish a committee. The combined effect of these constraints was that in 1976 only about 20 percent of the hospitals in Canada performed abortions, and the provinces could, by regulation, impose even more restrictive requirements for approval, and even eliminate the exception provided in s. 251(4).]

A further flaw with the administrative system established in s. 251(4) is the failure to provide an adequate standard for therapeutic abortion committees which must determine when a therapeutic abortion should, as a matter of law, be granted. Subsection (4) states simply that a therapeutic abortion committee may grant a certificate when it determines that a continuation of a pregnancy would be likely to endanger the "life or health" of the pregnant woman. It was noted above that "health" is not defined for the purposes of the section. The Crown admitted in its supplementary factum that the medical witnesses at trial testified uniformly that the health standard was ambiguous, but the Crown derives comfort from the fact that "the medical witnesses were unanimous in their approval of the broad World Health Organization definition of health." The World Health Organization defines "health" not merely as the absence of disease or infirmity, but as a state of physical, mental and social well-being. ...

... Various expert doctors testified at trial that therapeutic abortion committees apply widely differing definitions of health. For some committees, psychological health is a justification for therapeutic abortion; for others it is not. Some committees routinely refuse abortions to married women unless they are in physical danger, while for other committees it is possible for a married woman to show that she would suffer psychological harm if she continued with a pregnancy, thereby justifying an abortion. It is not typically possible for women to know in advance what standards of health will be applied by any given committee. ...

It is no answer to say that "health" is a medical term and that doctors who sit on therapeutic abortion committees must simply exercise their professional judgment. A therapeutic abortion committee is a strange hybrid, part medical committee and part legal committee. ...

When the decision of the therapeutic abortion committee is so directly laden with consequences, the absence of any clear legal standard to be applied by the committee in reaching its decision is a serious procedural flaw.

The combined effect of all of these problems with the procedure stipulated in s. 251 for access to therapeutic abortions is a failure to comply with the principles of fundamental justice. In *Motor Vehicle Act Reference*, [1985] 2 SCR 486 [24 DLR (4th) 536], Lamer J held, at 503, that "the principles of fundamental justice are to be found in the basic tenets of our legal system." One of the basic tenets of our system of criminal justice is that when Parliament creates a defence to a criminal charge, the defence should not be illusory or so difficult to attain as to be practically illusory. The criminal law is a very special form of governmental regulation, for it seeks to express our society's collective disapprobation of certain acts and omissions. When a defence is provided, especially a specifically-tailored defence to a particular charge, it is because the legislator has determined that the disapprobation of society is not warranted when the conditions of the defence are met.

Consider then the case of a pregnant married woman who wishes to apply for a therapeutic abortion certificate because she fears that her psychological health would be impaired seriously if she carried the foetus to term. The uncontroverted evidence reveals that there are many areas in Canada where such a woman would simply not have access to a therapeutic abortion. She may live in an area where no hospital has four doctors; no therapeutic abortion committee can be created. Equally, she may live in a place where the treatment functions of the nearby hospitals do not satisfy the definition of "accredited hospital" in s. 251(6). Or she may live in a province where the provincial government has imposed such stringent requirements on hospitals seeking to create therapeutic abortion committees that no hospital can qualify. Alternatively, our hypothetical woman may confront a therapeutic abortion committee in her local hospital which defines "health" in purely physical terms or which refuses to countenance abortions for married women. In each of these cases, it is the administrative structures and procedures established by s. 251 itself that would in practice prevent the woman from gaining the benefit of the defence held out to her in s. 251(4).

[The Crown argued that women could travel to hospitals that performed abortions, but the enormous emotional and financial burden of travelling was itself an obstacle, and one created by the Code. As well, some hospitals imposed geographic limitations.]

Parliament must be given room to design an appropriate administrative and procedural structure for bringing into operation a particular defence to criminal liability. But if that structure is "so manifestly unfair, having regard to the decisions it is called upon to make, as to violate the principles of *fundamental* justice," that structure must be struck down. In the present case, the structure [of] the system regulating access to therapeutic abortions is manifestly unfair. It contains so many potential barriers to its own operation that the defence it creates will in many circumstances be practically unavailable to women who would *prima facie* qualify for the defence, or at least would force such women to travel great distances at substantial expense and inconvenience in order to benefit from a defence that is held out to be generally available.

I conclude that the procedures created in s. 251 of the *Criminal Code* for obtaining a therapeutic abortion do not comport with the principles of fundamental justice. It is not necessary to determine whether s. 7 also contains a substantive content leading to the conclusion that, in some circumstances at least, the deprivation of a pregnant woman's right to security of the person can never comport with fundamental justice. Simply put, assuming Parliament can act, it must do so properly. For the reasons given earlier, the deprivation of security of the person caused by s. 251 as a whole is not in accordance with the second clause of s. 7.

[Dickson CJC held further that s. 251 could not be justified under s. 1 of the Charter because its procedures impair s. 7 rights far more than is necessary in that they hold out an illusory defence to many women who would *prima facie* qualify under the exculpatory provisions of s. 251(4). Many women whom Parliament professes not to wish to subject to criminal liability will nevertheless be forced by the practical unavailability of the supposed defence to risk liability or to suffer other harm such as a traumatic late abortion caused by the delay inherent in the s. 251 system. Finally, the effects of the limitation upon the s. 7 rights of many pregnant women are out of proportion to the objective sought to be achieved. To the extent that s. 251(4) is designed to protect the life and health of women, the procedures it establishes may actually defeat that objective. In his opinion, the administrative structures of s. 251(4) are so cumbersome that women whose health is endangered by pregnancy may not be able to gain a therapeutic abortion, at least without great trauma, expense, and inconvenience.]

BEETZ J (Estey J concurring): A pregnant woman's person cannot be said to be secure if, when her life or health is in danger, she is faced with a rule of criminal law which precludes her from obtaining effective and timely medical treatment.

· · ·

If a rule of criminal law precludes a person from obtaining appropriate medical treatment when his or her life or health is in danger, then the state has intervened and this intervention constitutes a violation of that man's or that woman's security of the person. "Security of the person" must include a right of access to medical treatment for a condition representing a danger to life or health without fear of criminal sanction. If an act of Parliament forces a person whose life or health is in danger to choose between, on the one hand, the commission of a crime to obtain effective and timely medical treatment and, on the other hand, inadequate treatment or no treatment at all, the right to security of the person has been violated.

This interpretation of s. 7 of the Charter is sufficient to measure the content of s. 251 of the *Criminal Code* against that of the Charter in order to dispose of this appeal. While I agree with McIntyre J that a breach of a right to security must be "based upon an infringement of some interest which would be of such nature and such importance as to warrant constitutional protection," I am of the view that the protection of life or health is an interest of sufficient importance in this regard. Under the *Criminal Code*, the only way in which a pregnant woman can legally secure an abortion when the continuation of the pregnancy would or would be likely to endanger her life or health is to comply with the procedure set forth in s. 251(4). Where the continued pregnancy does constitute a danger to life or health, the pregnant woman faces a choice: (1) she can endeavour to follow the s. 251(4) procedure, which, as we shall see, creates an additional medical risk given its inherent delays and the possibility that the danger will not be recognized by the state-imposed therapeutic abortion committee; or (2) she can secure medical treatment without respecting s. 251(4) and subject herself to criminal sanction under s. 251(2).

· · ·

The evidence reveals that the actual workings of s. 251(4) are the source of certain delays which create an additional medical risk for many pregnant women whose medical condition already meets the standard of s. 251(4)(c). Stated simply, when pregnant women suffer from a condition which represents a danger to their life or health, their efforts to conform to the procedure set forth for obtaining lawful abortions in the *Criminal Code* often create an additional risk to their health. They may have to choose between bearing the burden of these risks by accepting delayed medical treatment, and committing a crime by seeking timely medical treatment outside s. 251(4). Given that the proccdurc in s. 251(4) is the source of this additional risk, it constitutes a violation of the pregnant woman's security of the person. ...

While only administrative inefficiencies that are caused by the rules in s. 251 are relevant to the evaluation of the constitutionality of the legislation under s. 7 of the Charter, the evidence which relates to the availability of therapeutic abortions under the *Criminal Code* reveals three sorts of delay, *all of which can be traced to the requirements of s. 251 itself*: (1) the absence of hospitals with therapeutic abortion committees in many parts of Canada; (2) the quotas which some hospitals with committees impose on the number of therapeutic abortions which they perform; and (3) the committee requirement itself each create delays for pregnant women who seek timely and effective medical treatment.

· · ·

The delays which a pregnant woman may have to suffer as a result of the requirements of s. 251(4) must undermine the security of her person in order that there be a violation of this element of s. 7 of the Charter. As I said earlier, s. 7 cannot be invoked simply because a woman's pregnancy amounts to a medically dangerous condition. If, however, the delays occasioned by s. 251(4) of the *Criminal Code* result in an additional danger to the pregnant woman's health, then the state has intervened and this intervention constitutes a violation of that woman's security of the person. By creating this additional risk, s. 251 prevents access to effective and timely medical treatment for the continued pregnancy which would or would be likely to endanger her life or health. If an effective and timely therapeutic abortion may only be obtained by committing a crime, then s. 251 violates the pregnant woman's right to security of the person.

The evidence reveals that the delays caused by s. 251(4) result in at least three broad types of additional medical risks. The risk of post-operative complications increases with delay. Secondly, there is a risk that the pregnant woman requires a more dangerous means of procuring a miscarriage because of the delay. Finally, since a pregnant woman knows her life or health is in danger, the delay created by the s. 251(4) procedure may result in an additional psychological trauma.

· · ·

I turn now to a consideration of the manner in which pregnant women are deprived of their right to security of the person by s. 251. Section 7 of the Charter states that everyone has the right not to be deprived of security of the person except in accordance with the principles of fundamental justice. As I will endeavour to demonstrate, s. 251(4) does not accord with the principles of fundamental justice.

[Unlike Dickson CJC, Beetz J held that the requirement for an independent medical opinion as to the danger to the life or health of the pregnant woman does not offend principles of fundamental justice.]

The assertion that an independent medical opinion, distinct from that of the pregnant woman and her practising physician, does not offend the principles of fundamental justice would need to be reevaluated if a right of access to abortion is founded upon the right to "liberty" in s. 7 of the Charter. I am of the view that there would still be circumstances in which the state interest in the protection of the foetus would require an independent medical opinion as to the danger to the life or health of the pregnant woman. Assuming without deciding that a right of access to abortion can be founded upon the right to "liberty," would be a point in time at which the state interest in the foetus would become compelling. From this point in time, Parliament would be entitled to limit abortions to those required by therapeutic reasons and therefore require an independent opinion as to the health exception.

· · ·

Some delay is inevitable in connection with any system which purports to limit to therapeutic reasons the grounds upon which an abortion can be performed lawfully. Any statutory mechanism for ensuring an independent confirmation as to the state of the woman's life or health, adopted pursuant to the objective of assuring the protection of the foetus, will inevitably result in a delay which would exceed whatever delay would be encountered if an independent opinion was not required. Furthermore, rules promoting the safety of abortions designed to protect the interest of the pregnant woman will also cause some unavoidable delay. It is only insofar as the administrative structure creates delays which are unnecessary that the structure can be considered to violate the principles of fundamental justice.

[Beetz J, however, argued that the requirement that abortions be performed in hospitals, the power to appoint a committee of more than three members, and the exclusion of doctors who performed therapeutic abortions were all unnecessary and thus violated the principles of fundamental justice and, as a result, s. 251 could not be saved under s. 1 of the Charter.]

WILSON J: At the heart of this appeal is the question whether a pregnant woman can, as a constitutional matter, be compelled by law to carry the foetus to term. The legislature has proceeded on the basis that she can be so compelled and, indeed, has made it a criminal offence punishable by imprisonment under s. 251 of the *Criminal Code* for her or her physician to terminate the pregnancy unless the procedural requirements of the section are complied with.

My colleagues, the Chief Justice and Justice Beetz, have attacked those requirements in reasons which I have had the privilege of reading. They have found that the requirements do not comport with the principles of fundamental justice in the procedural sense and have concluded that, since they cannot be severed from the provisions creating the substantive offence, the whole of s. 251 must fall.

With all due respect, I think that the Court must tackle the primary issue first. A consideration as to whether or not the procedural requirements for obtaining or performing an abortion comport with fundamental justice is purely academic if such requirements cannot as a constitutional matter be imposed at all. If a pregnant woman cannot, as a constitutional matter, be compelled by law to carry the foetus to term against her will, a review of the procedural requirements by which she may be compelled to do so seems pointless. Moreover, it would, in my opinion, be an exercise in futility for the legislature to expend its time and energy in attempting to remedy the defects in the procedural requirements unless it has some assurance that this process will, at the end of the day, result in the creation of a valid criminal offence. I turn, therefore, to what I believe is the central issue that must be addressed.

1. The Right of Access to Abortion

. . .

It seems to me ... that to commence the analysis with the premise that the s. 7 right encompasses only a right to physical and psychological security and to fail to deal with the right to liberty in the context of "life, liberty and security of the person" begs the central issue in the case. If either the right to liberty or the right to security of the person or a combination of both confers on the pregnant woman the right to decide for herself (with the guidance of her physician) whether or not to have an abortion, then we have to examine the legislative scheme not only from the point of view of fundamental justice in the procedural sense but in the substantive sense as well. I think, therefore, that we must answer the question: what is meant by the right to liberty in the context of the abortion issue? Does it ... give the pregnant woman control over decisions affecting her own body? If not, does her right to security of the person give her such control? I turn first to the right to liberty.

(a) The Right to Liberty

. . .

The Charter is predicated on a particular conception of the place of the individual in society. An individual is not a totally independent entity disconnected from the society in which he or she lives. Neither, however, is the individual a mere cog in an impersonal machine in which his or her values, goals and aspirations are subordinated to those of the collectivity. The individual is a bit of both. The Charter reflects this reality by leaving a wide range of activities and decisions open to legitimate government control while at the same time placing limits on the proper scope of that control. Thus, the rights guaranteed in the Charter erect around each individual, metaphorically speaking, an invisible fence over which the state will not be allowed to trespass. The role of the courts is to map out, piece by piece, the parameters of the fence.

The Charter and the right to individual liberty guaranteed under it are inextricably tied to the concept of human dignity.

. . .

The idea of human dignity finds expression in almost every right and freedom guaranteed in the Charter. Individuals are afforded the right to choose their own religion and their own philosophy of life, the right to choose with whom they will associate and how they will express themselves, the right to choose where they will live and what occupation they will pursue. These are all examples of the basic theory underlying the Charter, namely that the state will respect choices made by individuals and, to the greatest extent possible, will avoid subordinating these choices to any one conception of the good life.

Thus, an aspect of the respect for human dignity on which the Charter is founded is the right to make fundamental personal decisions without interference from the state. This right is a critical component of the right to liberty. Liberty ... is a phrase capable of a broad range of meaning. In my view, this right, properly construed, grants the individual a degree of autonomy in making decisions of fundamental personal importance.

... Liberty in a free and democratic society does not require the state to approve the personal decisions made by its citizens; it does, however, require the state to respect them.

This conception of the proper ambit of the right to liberty under our Charter is consistent with the American jurisprudence on the subject.

[An account of the American doctrine is omitted.]

In my opinion, the respect for individual decision-making in matters of fundamental personal importance reflected in the American jurisprudence also informs the *Canadian Charter*. Indeed, as the Chief Justice pointed out in *R v. Big M Drug Mart Ltd.*, [[1985] 1 SCR 295, 18 DLR (4th) 321] beliefs about human worth and dignity "are the *sine qua non* of the political tradition underlying the Charter." I would conclude, therefore, that the right to liberty contained in s. 7 guarantees to every individual a degree of personal autonomy over important decisions intimately affecting their private lives.

The question then becomes whether the decision of a woman to terminate her pregnancy falls within this class of protected decisions. I have no doubt that it does. This decision is one that will have profound psychological, economic and social consequences for the pregnant woman. The circumstances giving rise to it can be complex and varied and there may be, and usually are, powerful considerations militating in opposite directions. It is a decision that deeply reflects the way the woman thinks about herself and her relationship to others and to society at large. It is not just a medical decision; it is a profound social and ethical one as well. Her response to it will be the response of the whole person.

It is probably impossible for a man to respond, even imaginatively, to such a dilemma not just because it is outside the realm of his personal experience (although this is, of course, the case) but because he can relate to it only by objectifying it, thereby eliminating the subjective elements of the female psyche which are at the heart of the dilemma. As Noreen Burrows, Lecturer in European Law at the University of Glasgow, has pointed out in her essay on "International Law and Human Rights: The Case of Women's Rights," in *Human Rights: From Rhetoric to Reality* (1986), the history of the struggle for human rights from the eighteenth century on has been the history of men struggling to assert their dignity and common humanity against an overbearing state apparatus. The more recent struggle for women's rights has been a struggle to eliminate discrimination, to achieve a place for women in a man's world, to develop a set of legislative reforms in order to place women in the same position as men (at 81-82). It has not been a struggle to define the rights of women in relation to their special place in the societal structure and in relation to the biological distinction between the two sexes. Thus, women's needs and aspirations are only now being translated into protected rights. The right to reproduce or not to reproduce which is in issue in this case is one such right and is properly perceived as an integral part of modern woman's struggle to assert her dignity and worth as a human being.

Given then that the right to liberty guaranteed by s. 7 of the Charter gives a woman the right to decide for herself whether or not to terminate her pregnancy, does s. 251 of the *Criminal Code* violate this right? Clearly it does. The purpose of the section is to take the decision away from the woman and give it to a committee. Furthermore, as the Chief Justice correctly points out, at 56, the committee bases its decision on "criteria entirely unrelated to [the pregnant woman's] priorities and aspirations." The fact that the decision whether a woman will be allowed to terminate her pregnancy is in the hands of a committee is just as great a violation of the woman's right to personal autonomy in decisions of an intimate and private nature as it would be if a committee were established to decide whether a woman should be allowed to continue her pregnancy. Both these arrangements violate the woman's right to liberty by deciding for her something that she has the right to decide for herself.

(b) The Right to Security of the Person

Section 7 of the Charter also guarantees everyone the right to security of the person. Does this ... extend to the right of control over one's own body?

I agree with the Chief Justice and with Beetz J that the right to "security of the person" under s. 7 of the Charter protects both the physical and psychological integrity of the individual. State enforced medical or surgical treatment comes readily to mind as an obvious invasion of physical integrity. ... I believe, however, that the flaw in the present legislative scheme goes much deeper than that. In essence, what it does is assert that the woman's capacity to reproduce is not to be subject to her own control. It is to be subject to the control of the state. She may not choose whether to exercise her existing capacity or not to exercise it. This is not, in my view, just a matter of interfering with her right to liberty in the sense (already discussed) of her right to personal autonomy in decision-making, it is a direct interference with her physical person as well. She is truly being treated as ... a means to an end which she does not desire but over which she has no control. She is the passive recipient of a decision made by others as to whether her body is to be used to nurture a new life. Can there be anything that comports less with human dignity and self-respect? How can a woman in this position have any sense of security with respect to her person? I believe that s. 251 of the *Criminal Code* deprives the pregnant woman of her right to security of the person as well as her right to liberty.

[Wilson J concluded that s. 251 deprives women of their right to liberty and security of the person in a manner that does not accord with the principles of fundamental justice. Further, she held that the deprivation of a s. 7 right, which has the effect of infringing a right guaranteed elsewhere in the Charter, cannot be in accordance with the principles of fundamental justice. Section 251 results in a deprivation of a s. 7 right in a manner that offends s. 2(a) of the Charter, which guarantees everyone freedom of conscience and religion. Finally, Wilson J concluded that s. 251 is not a reasonable limit under s. 1 because it took the decision away from the woman at *all* stages of her pregnancy and was not sufficiently tailored to its objective.]

McINTYRE J (La Forest J concurring) dissenting: ...

The Right to Abortion and Section 7 of the Charter

The judgment of my colleague, Wilson J, is based upon the proposition that a pregnant woman has a right, under s. 7 of the Charter, to have an abortion. The same concept underlies the judgment of the Chief Justice. ... He has not said in specific terms that the pregnant woman has the right to an abortion, whether therapeutic or otherwise. In my view, however, his whole position depends for its validity upon that proposition and that interference with the right constitutes an infringement of her right to security of the person. It is said that a law which forces a woman to carry a foetus to term unless she meets certain criteria unrelated to her own priorities and aspirations interferes with security of her person. If compelling a woman to complete her pregnancy interferes with security of her person, it can only be because the concept of security of her person includes a right not to be compelled to carry the child to completion of her pregnancy. This, then, is simply to say that she has a right to have an abortion. It follows, then, that if no such right can be shown, it cannot be said that security of her person has been infringed by state action or otherwise.

All laws, it must be noted, have the potential for interference with individual priorities and aspirations. In fact, the very purpose of most legislation is to cause such interference. It is only when such legislation goes beyond interfering with priorities and aspirations, and abridges rights, that courts may intervene. …

The proposition that women enjoy a constitutional right to have an abortion is devoid of support in the language of s. 7 of the Charter or any other section. While some human rights documents, such as the *American Convention on Human Rights, 1969* (Article 4(1)), expressly address the question of abortion, the Charter is entirely silent on the point. It may be of some significance that the Charter uses specific language in dealing with other topics, such as voting rights, religion, expression and such controversial matters as mobility rights, language rights and minority rights, but remains silent on the question of abortion which, at the time the Charter was under consideration, was as much a subject of public controversy as it is today. Furthermore, it would appear that the history of the constitutional text of the Charter affords no support for the appellants' proposition.

. . .

It cannot be said that the history, traditions and underlying philosophies of our society would support the proposition that a right to abortion could be implied in the Charter.

[An account of the history of the common law and legislation about abortion is omitted.]

There has always been clear recognition of a public interest in the protection of the unborn and there has been no evidence or indication of any general acceptance of the concept of abortion at will in our society. It is to be observed as well that at the time of adoption of the Charter the sole provision for an abortion in Canadian law was that to be found in s. 251 of the *Criminal Code*. It follows then, in my view, that the interpretive approach to the Charter, which has been accepted in this Court, affords no support for the entrenchment of a constitutional right of abortion.

As to an asserted right to be free from any state interference with bodily integrity and serious state-imposed psychological stress, I would say that to be accepted, as a constitutional right, it would have to be based on something more than the mere imposition, by the State, of such stress and anxiety. It must, surely, be evident that many forms of government action deemed to be reasonable, and even necessary in our society, will cause stress and anxiety to many, while at the same time being acceptable exercises of government power in pursuit of socially desirable goals. …

To invade the s. 7 right of security of the person, there would have to be more than state-imposed stress or strain. A breach of the right would have to be based upon an infringement of some interest which would be of such nature and such importance as to warrant constitutional protection. This, it would seem to me, would be limited to cases where the state-action complained of, in addition to imposing stress and strain, also infringed another right, freedom or interest which was deserving of protection under the concept of security of the person. For the reasons outlined above, the right to have an abortion—given the language, structure and history of the Charter and given the history, traditions and underlying philosophies of our society—is not such an interest.

Appeal allowed; acquittals restored.

NOTE ON ABORTION: SOME OTHER ISSUES

In 1978, a different challenge was made to s. 251, by Joseph Borowski, who claimed that the foetus was protected by both ss. 7 and 15. In a major case about standing, he was permitted to proceed simply as a concerned citizen, because the issue was an important one and since there was no other reasonably effective way it was likely to be brought to court. (For a discussion of standing, see Section III, Triggering Judicial Review and Procedural Issues, in Chapter 2, Judicial Review and Constitutional Interpretation.) Both the Manitoba Court of Queen's Bench and the Manitoba Court of Appeal dismissed his claim, holding that the foetus did not come within the meaning of "everyone" in s. 7 or within the meaning of "every individual" in s. 15. Borowski appealed to the Supreme Court, but before the appeal was heard, the court decided *Morgentaler*. The Supreme Court then dismissed Borowski's appeal on the grounds of mootness: the basis of his action disappeared when s. 251 was struck down. (See *Borowski v. AG Canada*, [1989] 1 SCR 342, 57 DLR (4th) 231.)

In *Daigle v. Tremblay*, [1989] 2 SCR 530, 62 DLR (4th) 634, a prospective father asked the Quebec courts to prevent the mother, his former partner, from obtaining an abortion. An injunction that was granted by the trial judge and affirmed by the Court of Appeal was set aside on appeal by the Supreme Court, on the ground that neither the foetus nor the father had a right to be protected. The Court held that the foetus was not a "human being" under the Quebec Charter. It did not, though, undertake to answer the question whether the foetus was included in the term "everyone" in s. 7 of the Canadian Charter, because s. 7 did not apply: the action was one between two private individuals. The prospective father, in contrast to the foetus, had no right to participate in the mother's decisions.

The *Morgentaler* judgment left a legislative void with respect to federal regulation of the practice of abortion. In 1990, the government introduced Bill C-43, which was drafted with a view to eliminating the constitutional infirmities that had plagued the previous *Criminal Code* provisions. As a result of a tie vote in the Senate, the bill was defeated. Its major section was as follows:

Every person who induces an abortion on a female person is guilty of an indictable offence and liable to imprisonment for a term not exceeding two years, unless the abortion is induced by or under the direction of a medical practitioner who is of the opinion that, if the abortion were not induced, the health or life of the female person would be likely to be threatened.

"Health" was defined as including "physical, mental and psychological health." If the bill had been enacted, would it have survived a challenge under s. 7? What about a requirement of a waiting period, or, for prospective mothers under the age of 16, parental consent?

Provincial legislative power to regulate abortion as a matter of health is circumscribed by federal jurisdiction over the criminal law. Thus, a province cannot enact legislation to reduce or eliminate abortion on the ground that it is morally repugnant. In *R v. Morgentaler*, [1993] 3 SCR 463, 107 DLR (4th) 537, reproduced in Chapter 8, Interpreting the Division of Powers, the Supreme Court of Canada declared *ultra vires* a Nova Scotia statute prohibiting the performance of certain medical procedures, including abortion, outside of accredited hospitals, and denying medical insurance coverage to abortions that were performed in contravention of the statute. The province contended that the purpose of the statute was to ensure a single, uniform, high-quality health care system. The Court held that the true object was to prevent the establishment of abortion clinics, and that the statute was, in pith and substance, an exercise of criminal law jurisdiction and thus *ultra vires*.

Rodriguez v. British Columbia (Attorney General)
[1993] 3 SCR 519, 107 DLR (4th) 342

[Rodriguez, the appellant, was terminally ill, suffering from amyotrophic lateral sclerosis, or Lou Gherig's disease, a progressive degeneration of the motor neurons. Although this disease would likely not affect her mind, its ineluctable course would destroy her ability to control her body. Within months or, at most, a few years, she would become bedridden and unable to speak or to care for herself. She sought a declaration that she was entitled to have assistance in committing suicide when, in her judgment, her condition became unbearable and if she was then unable to commit suicide without assistance. The obstacle was s. 241(b) of the *Criminal Code*, which provided that "[e]very one who ... aids or abets a person to commit suicide, whether suicide ensues or not, is guilty of an indictable offence and liable to imprisonment for a term not exceeding fourteen years." She appealed to the Supreme Court after her application was dismissed by the both Supreme Court of British Columbia and the BC Court of Appeal.]

SOPINKA J (La Forest, Gonthier, Iacobucci, and Major JJ concurring): ... The most substantial issue in this appeal is whether s. 241(b) infringes s. 7 in that it inhibits the appellant in controlling the timing and manner of her death. I conclude that while the section impinges on the security interest of the appellant, any resulting deprivation is not contrary to the principles of fundamental justice. I would come to the same conclusion with respect to any liberty interest which may be involved.

· · ·

The appellant argues that, by prohibiting anyone from assisting her to end her life when her illness has rendered her incapable of terminating her life without such assistance, by threat of criminal sanction, s. 241(b) deprives her of both her liberty and her security of the person. The appellant asserts that her application is based upon (a) the right to live her remaining life with the inherent dignity of a human person; (b) the right to control what happens to her body while she is living; and (c) the right to be free from governmental interference in making fundamental personal decisions concerning the terminal stages of her life. The first two of these asserted rights can be seen to invoke both liberty and security of the person; the latter is more closely associated with only the liberty interest.

Life, Liberty and Security of the Person

The appellant seeks a remedy which would assure her some control over the time and manner of her death. While she supports her claim on the ground that her liberty and security of the person interests are engaged, a consideration of these interests cannot be divorced from the sanctity of life, which is one of the three Charter values protected by s. 7.

None of these values prevail *a priori* over the others. All must be taken into account in determining the content of the principles of fundamental justice and there is no basis for imposing a greater burden on the propounder of one value as against that imposed on another.

· · ·

As a threshold issue, I do not accept the submission that the appellant's problems are due to her physical disabilities caused by her terminal illness, and not by governmental action. There is no doubt that the prohibition in s. 241(b) will contribute to the appellant's distress if she is prevented from managing her death in the circumstances which she fears will occur. ...

I find more merit in the argument that security of the person, by its nature, cannot encompass a right to take action that will end one's life as security of the person is intrinsically concerned with the well-being of the living person. This argument focuses on the generally held and deeply rooted belief in our society that human life is sacred or inviolable (which terms I use in the non-religious sense described by Ronald Dworkin, *Life's Dominion: An Argument About Abortion, Euthanasia, and Individual Freedom* (New York: Knopf, 1993), to mean that human life is seen to have a deep intrinsic value of its own.) As members of a society based upon respect for the intrinsic value of human life and on the inherent dignity of every human being, can we incorporate within the Constitution, which embodies our most fundamental values, a right to terminate one's own life in any circumstances? This question in turn evokes other queries of fundamental importance such as the degree to which our conception of the sanctity of life includes notions of quality of life as well.

Sanctity of life, as we will see, has been understood historically as excluding freedom of choice in the self-infliction of death and certainly in the involvement of others in carrying out that choice. At the very least, no new consensus has emerged in society opposing the right of the state to regulate the involvement of others in exercising power over individuals ending their lives.

The appellant suggests that for the terminally ill, the choice is one of time and manner of death rather than death itself since the latter is inevitable. I disagree. Rather it is one of choosing death instead of allowing natural forces to run their course. The time and precise manner of death remain unknown until death actually occurs. There can be no certainty in forecasting the precise circumstances of a death. Death is, for all mortals, inevitable.

Even when death appears imminent, seeking to control the manner and timing of one's death constitutes a conscious choice of death over life. It follows that life as a value is engaged even in the case of the terminally ill who seek to choose death over life.

Indeed, it has been abundantly pointed out that such persons are particularly vulnerable as to their life and will to live and great concern has been expressed as to their adequate protection, as will be further set forth.

I do not draw from this that in such circumstances life as a value must prevail over security of person or liberty as these have been understood under the Charter, but that it is one of the values engaged in the present case.

· · ·

In my view, then, the judgments of this Court in [*R v.*] *Morgentaler* [[1988] 1 SCR 30, 44 DLR (4th) 385] can be seen to encompass a notion of personal autonomy involving, at the very least, control over one's bodily integrity free from state interference and freedom from state-imposed psychological and emotional stress. In *Reference re: ss. 193 and 195.1(1)(c) of Criminal Code (Man.)*, [1985] 2 SCR 486, 24 DLR (4th) 536, Lamer J (as he then was) also expressed this view, stating at p. 106 that "[s]ection 7 is also implicated when the state restricts individuals' security of the person by interfering with, or removing from them, control over their physical or mental integrity." There is no question, then, that personal autonomy, at least with respect to the right to make choices concerning one's own body, control over one's physical and psychological integrity, and basic human dignity are encompassed within security of the person, at least to the extent of freedom from criminal prohibitions which interfere with these.

The effect of the prohibition in s. 241(b) is to prevent the appellant from having assistance to commit suicide when she is no longer able to do so on her own. She fears that she will be required to live until the deterioration from her disease is such that she will die as a result of choking, suffocation or pneumonia caused by aspiration of food or secretions. She will be totally dependent upon machines to perform her bodily functions and completely dependent upon others. Throughout this time, she will remain mentally competent and able to appreciate all that is happening to her. Although palliative care may be available to ease the pain and other physical discomfort which she will experience, the appellant fears the sedating effects of such drugs and argues, in any event, that they will not prevent the psychological and emotional distress which will result from being in a situation of utter dependence and loss of dignity. That there is a right to choose how one's body will be dealt with, even in the context of beneficial medical treatment, has long been recognized by the common law. To impose medical treatment on one who refuses it constitutes battery, and our common law has recognized the right to demand that medical treatment which would extend life be withheld or withdrawn. In my view, these considerations lead to the conclusion that the prohibition in s. 241(b) deprives the appellant of autonomy over her person and causes her physical pain and psychological stress in a manner which impinges on the security of her person. The appellant's security interest (considered in the context of the life and liberty interest) is, therefore, engaged, and it is necessary to determine whether there has been any deprivation thereof that is not in accordance with the principles of fundamental justice.

The Principles of Fundamental Justice

. . .

In this case, it is not disputed that in general s. 241(b) is valid and desirable legislation which fulfils the government's objectives of preserving life and protecting the vulnerable. The complaint is that the legislation is over-inclusive because it does not exclude from the reach of the prohibition those in the situation of the appellant who are terminally ill, mentally competent, but cannot commit suicide on their own. It is also argued that the extension of the prohibition to the appellant is arbitrary and unfair as suicide itself is not unlawful, and the common law allows a physician to withhold or withdraw life-saving or life-maintaining treatment on the patient's instructions and to administer palliative care which has the effect of hastening death. The issue is whether, given this legal context, the existence of a criminal prohibition on assisting suicide for one in the appellant's situation is contrary to principles of fundamental justice.

Discerning the principles of fundamental justice with which deprivation of life, liberty or security of the person must accord, in order to withstand constitutional scrutiny, is not an easy task. A mere common law rule does not suffice to constitute a principle of fundamental justice, rather, as the term implies, principles upon which there is some consensus that they are vital or fundamental to our societal notion of justice are required. Principles of fundamental justice must not, however, be so broad as to be no more than vague generalizations about what our society considers to be ethical or moral. They must be capable of being identified with some precision and applied to situations in a manner which yields an understandable result. They must also, in my view, be legal principles. ...

This court has often stated that in discerning the principles of fundamental justice governing a particular case, it is helpful to look at the common law and legislative history of the offence in question: *Reference re: s. 94(2) of Motor Vehicle Act*, [1985] 2 SCR 486 [24 DLR (4th) 536], and *Morgentaler, supra*, and *R v. Swain*, [1991] 1 SCR 933. It is not sufficient, however, merely to conduct a historical review and conclude that because neither Parliament nor the various medical associations had ever expressed a view that assisted suicide should be decriminalized, that to prohibit it could not be said to be contrary to the principles of fundamental justice. Such an approach would be problematic for two reasons. First, a strictly historical analysis will always lead to the conclusion, in a case such as this, that the deprivation is in accordance with fundamental justice, as the legislation will not have kept apace with advances in medical technology. Secondly, such reasoning is somewhat circular, in that it relies on the continuing existence of the prohibition to find the prohibition to be fundamentally just.

The way to resolve these problems is not to avoid the historical analysis, but to make sure that one is looking not just at the existence of the practice itself (*i.e.*, the continued criminalization of assisted suicide) but at the rationale behind that practice and the principles which underlie it.

The appellant asserts that it is a principle of fundamental justice that the human dignity and autonomy of individuals be respected, and that to subject her to needless suffering in this manner is to rob her of her dignity. ...

That respect for human dignity is one of the underlying principles upon which our society is based is unquestioned. I have difficulty, however, in characterizing this in itself as a principle of fundamental justice within the meaning of s. 7. While respect for human dignity is the genesis for many principles of fundamental justice, not every law that fails to accord such respect runs afoul of these principles. To state that "respect for human dignity and autonomy" is a principle of fundamental justice, then, is essentially to state that the deprivation of the appellant's security of the person is contrary to principles of fundamental justice because it deprives her of security of the person. This interpretation would equate security of the person with a principle of fundamental justice and render the latter redundant.

I cannot subscribe to the opinion expressed by my colleague, McLachlin J, that the state interest is an inappropriate consideration in recognizing the principles of fundamental justice in this case. This court has affirmed that in arriving at these principles, a balancing of the interest of the state and the individual is required. ...

Where the deprivation of the right in question does little or nothing to enhance the state's interest (whatever it may be), it seems to me that a breach of fundamental justice will be made out, as the individual's rights will have been deprived for no valid purpose. This is, to my mind, essentially the type of analysis which E. Colvin advocates in his article "Section Seven of the Canadian Charter of Rights and Freedoms" (1989), 68 *Can. Bar Rev.* 560, and which was carried out in *Morgentaler*. That is, both Dickson CJC and Beetz J were of the view that at least some of the restrictions placed upon access to abortion had no relevance to the state objective of protecting the foetus while protecting the life and health of the mother. In that regard the restrictions were arbitrary or unfair. It follows that before one can determine that a statutory provision is contrary to fundamental justice, the relationship between the provision and the state interest must be considered. One cannot conclude that a particular limit is arbitrary because (in the words of my colleague, McLachlin J) "it bears no relation to, or is inconsistent with, the objective that lies behind" the legislation without considering the state interest and the societal concerns which it reflects.

The issue here, then, can be characterized as being whether the blanket prohibition on assisted suicide is arbitrary or unfair in that it is unrelated to the state's interest in protecting the vulnerable, and that it lacks a foundation in the legal tradition and societal beliefs which are said to be represented by the prohibition.

Section 241(b) has as its purpose the protection of the vulnerable who might be induced in moments of weakness to commit suicide. This purpose is grounded in the state interest in protecting life and reflects the policy of the state that human life should not be depreciated by allowing life to be taken. This policy finds expression not only in the provisions of our *Criminal Code* which prohibit murder and other violent acts against others notwithstanding the consent of the victim, but also in the policy against capital punishment and, until its repeal, attempted suicide. This is not only a policy of the state, however, but is part of our fundamental conception of the sanctity of human life.

[Sopinka J reviewed the history of common law and legislative protection of the terminally ill, and continued.]

What the preceding review demonstrates is that Canada and other western democracies recognize and apply the principle of the sanctity of life as a general principle which is subject to limited and narrow exceptions in situations in which notions of personal autonomy and dignity must prevail. However, these same societies continue to draw distinctions between passive and active forms of intervention in the dying process, and with very few exceptions, prohibit assisted suicide in situations akin to that of the appellant. The task then becomes to identify the rationales upon which these distinctions are based and to determine whether they are constitutionally supportable.

The distinction between withdrawing treatment upon a patient's request ... on the one hand, and assisted suicide on the other has been criticized as resting on a legal fiction—that is, the distinction between active and passive forms of treatment. The criticism is based on the fact that the withdrawal of life supportive measures is done with the knowledge that death will ensue, just as is assisting suicide, and that death does in fact ensue as a result of the action taken. ...

Other commentators, however, uphold the distinction on the basis that in the case of withdrawal of treatment, the death is "natural"—the artificial forces of medical technology which have kept the patient alive are removed and nature takes its course. In the case of assisted suicide or euthanasia, however, the course of nature is interrupted, and death results *directly* from the human action taken. ...

Whether or not one agrees that the active versus passive distinction is maintainable, however, the fact remains that under our common law, the physician has no choice but to accept the patient's instructions to discontinue treatment. To continue to treat the patient when the patient has withdrawn consent to that treatment constitutes battery .... The doctor is, therefore, not required to make a choice which will result in the patient's death as he would be if he chose to assist a suicide or to perform active euthanasia.

The fact that doctors may deliver palliative care to terminally ill patients without fear of sanction, it is argued, attenuates to an even greater degree any legitimate distinction which can be drawn between assisted suicide and what are currently acceptable forms of medical treatment. The administration of drugs designed for pain control in dosages which the physician knows will hasten death constitutes active contribution to death by any standard. However, the distinction drawn here is one based upon intention—in the case of palliative care the intention is to ease pain, which has the effect of hastening death, while in the case of assisted suicide, the intention is undeniably to cause death. The Law Reform Commission, although it recommended the continued criminal prohibition of both euthanasia and assisted suicide, stated, at p. 70 of the Working Paper, that a doctor should never refuse palliative care to a terminally ill person only because it may hasten death. In my view, distinctions based upon intent are important, and in fact form the basis of our criminal law. While factually the distinction may, at times, be difficult to draw, legally it is clear. The fact that in some cases, the third party will, under the guise of palliative care, commit euthanasia or assist in suicide and go unsanctioned due to the difficulty of proof, cannot be said to render the existence of the prohibition fundamentally unjust.

The principles of fundamental justice cannot be created for the occasion to reflect the court's dislike or distaste of a particular statute. While the principles of fundamental justice are concerned with more than process, reference must be made to principles which are "fundamental" in the sense that they would have general acceptance among reasonable people. From the review that I have conducted above, I am unable to discern anything approaching unanimity with respect to the issue before us. Regardless of one's personal views as to whether the distinctions drawn between withdrawal of treatment and palliative care, on the one hand, and assisted suicide on the other, are practically compelling, the fact remains that these distinctions are maintained and can be persuasively defended. To the extent that there is a consensus, it is that human life must be respected and we must be careful not to undermine the institutions that protect it.

This consensus finds legal expression in our legal system which prohibits capital punishment. This prohibition is supported, in part, on the basis that allowing the state to kill will cheapen the value of human life and thus the state will serve in a sense as a role model for individuals in society. The prohibition against assisted suicide serves a similar purpose. In upholding the respect for life, it may discourage those who consider that life is unbearable at a particular moment, or who perceive themselves to be a burden upon others, from committing suicide. To permit a physician to lawfully participate in taking life would send a signal that there are circumstances in which the state approves of suicide.

I also place some significance in the fact that the official position of various medical associations is against decriminalizing assisted suicide (Canadian Medical Association, British Medical Association, Council of Ethical and Judicial Affairs of the American Medical Association, World Medical Association and the American Nurses Association). Given the concerns about abuse that have been expressed and the great difficulty in creating appropriate safeguards to prevent these, it cannot be said that the blanket prohibition on assisted suicide is arbitrary or unfair, or that it is not reflective of fundamental values at play in our society. I am thus unable to find that any principle of fundamental justice is violated by s. 241(b).

[Sopinka J also concluded that s. 241 did not violate s. 12, which gives "everyone a right not be subjected to any cruel and unusual treatment or punishment." As well, he concluded that if it violated s. 15, it was saved by s. 1.]

McLACHLIN J (L'Heureux-Dubé J concurring) dissenting: ... In my view, the denial to Sue Rodriguez of a choice available to others cannot be justified. The potential for abuse is amply guarded against by existing provisions in the *Criminal Code*, as supplemented by the condition of judicial authorization, and ultimately, it is hoped, revised legislation. I cannot agree that the failure of Parliament to address the problem of the terminally ill is determinative of this appeal. Nor do I agree that the fact that medically assisted suicide has not been widely accepted elsewhere bars Sue Rodriguez's claim. Since the advent of the Charter, this court has been called upon to decide many issues which formerly lay fallow. If a law offends the Charter, this court has no choice but to so declare.

... In the present case, Parliament has put into force a legislative scheme which does not bar suicide but criminalizes the act of assisting suicide. The effect of this is to deny to some people the choice of ending their lives solely because they are physically unable to do so. This deprives Sue Rodriguez of her security of the person (the right to make decisions concerning her own body, which affect only her own body) in a way that offends the principles of fundamental justice, thereby violating s. 7 of the Charter. The violation cannot be saved under s. 1. This is precisely the logic which led the majority of this court to strike down the abortion provisions of the *Criminal Code* in *Morgentaler*. In that case, Parliament had set up a scheme authorizing therapeutic abortion. The effect of the provisions was in fact to deny or delay therapeutic abortions to some women. This was held to violate s. 7 because it deprived some women of the right to deal with their own bodies as they chose thereby infringing their security of the person, in a manner which did not comport with the principles of fundamental justice. Parliament could not advance an interest capable of justifying this arbitrary legislative scheme, and accordingly, the law was not saved under s. 1 of the Charter.

. . .

Section 7 of the Charter mandates that if the state limits what people do with their bodies, the state must do so in a way which does not violate the principles of fundamental justice. … It requires the court to inquire into whether the manner in which the state has chosen to limit what one does with one's body violates the principles of fundamental justice. The question on this appeal is whether, having chosen to limit the right to do with one's body what one chooses by s. 241(b) of the *Criminal Code*, Parliament has acted in a manner which comports with the principles of fundamental justice.

This brings us to the next question: what are the principles of fundamental justice? … Without defining the entire content of the phrase "principles of fundamental justice," it is sufficient for the purposes of this case to note that a legislative scheme which limits the right of a person to deal with her body as she chooses may violate the principles of fundamental justice under s. 7 of the Charter if the limit is arbitrary. A particular limit will be arbitrary if it bears no relation to, or is inconsistent with, the objective that lies behind the legislation. This was the foundation of the decision of the majority of this court in *Morgentaler, supra*.

This brings us to the critical issue in the case. Does the fact that the legal regime which regulates suicide denies to Sue Rodriguez the right to commit suicide because of her physical incapacity, render the scheme arbitrary and, hence, in violation of s. 7? Under the scheme Parliament has set up, the physically able person is legally allowed to end his or her life; he or she cannot be criminally penalized for attempting or committing suicide. But the person who is physically unable to accomplish the act is not similarly allowed to end her life. This is the effect of s. 241(b) of the *Criminal Code*, which criminalizes the act of assisting a person to commit suicide and which may render the person who desires to commit suicide a conspirator to that crime. Assuming without deciding that Parliament *could* criminalize all suicides, whether assisted or not, does the fact that suicide is not criminal make the criminalization of all assistance in suicide arbitrary?

My colleague Sopinka J has noted that the decriminalization of suicide reflects parliament's decision that the matter is best left to sciences outside the law. He suggests that it does not reveal any consensus that the autonomy interest of those who wish to end their lives is paramount to a state interest in protecting life. I agree. But this conclusion begs the question. What is the difference between suicide and assisted suicide that justifies making the one lawful and the other a crime, that justifies allowing some this choice, while denying it to others?

The answer to this question depends on whether the denial to Sue Rodriguez of what is available to others can be justified. It is argued that the denial to Sue Rodriguez of the capacity to treat her body in a way available to the physically able is justified because to permit assisted suicide will open the doors, if not the floodgates, to the killing of disabled persons who may not truly consent to death. The argument is essentially this. There may be no reason on the facts of Sue Rodriguez's case for denying to her the choice to end her life, a choice that those physically able have available to them. Nevertheless, she must be denied that choice because of the danger that other people may wrongfully abuse the power they have over the weak and ill, and may end the lives of these persons against their consent. Thus, Sue Rodriguez is asked to bear the burden of the chance that other people in other situations may act criminally to kill others or improperly sway them to suicide. She is asked to serve as a scapegoat.

The merits of this argument may fall for consideration at the next stage of the analysis, where the question is whether a limit imposed contrary to the principles of fundamental justice may nevertheless, be saved under s. 1 of the Charter as a limit, demonstrably justified in a free and democratic society. But they have no place in the s. 7 analysis that must be undertaken on this appeal. When one is considering whether a law breaches the principles of fundamental justice under s. 7 by reason of arbitrariness, the focus is on whether a legislative scheme infringes a particular person's protected interests in a way that cannot be justified having regard to the objective of this scheme. The principles of fundamental justice require that each person, considered individually, be treated fairly by the law. The fear that abuse may arise if an individual is permitted that which she is wrongly denied, plays no part at this initial stage. In short, it does not accord with the principles of fundamental justice that Sue Rodriguez be disallowed what is available to others merely because it is possible that other people, at some other time, may suffer, not what she seeks, but an act of killing without true consent. ... I add that it is not generally appropriate that the complainant be obliged to negate societal interests at the s. 7 stage, where the burden lies upon her, but that the matter be left for s. 1, where the burden lies on the state.

. . .

It is also argued that Sue Rodriguez must be denied the right to treat her body as others are permitted to do, because the state has an interest in absolutely forbidding anyone to help end the life of another. As my colleague Sopinka J would have it: "... active participation by one individual in the death of another is intrinsically morally and legally wrong." The answer to this is that Parliament has not exhibited a consistent intention to criminalize acts which cause the death of another. Individuals are not subject to criminal penalty when their omissions cause the death of another. Those who are under a legal duty to provide the "necessaries of life" are not subject to criminal penalty where a breach of this duty causes death, if a lawful excuse is made out, for instance the consent of the party who dies, or incapacity to provide: see *Criminal Code*, s. 215. Again, killing in self-defence is not culpable. Thus there is no absolute rule that causing or assisting in the death of another is criminally wrong. Criminal culpability depends on the circumstances in which the death is brought about or assisted. The law has long recognized that if there is a valid justification for bringing about someone's death, the person who does so will not be held criminally responsible. In the case of Sue Rodriguez, there is arguably such a justification—the justification of giving her the capacity to end her life which able-bodied people have as a matter of course, and the justification of her clear consent and desire to end her life at a time when, in her view, it makes no sense to continue living it.

So the argument, that the prohibition on assisted suicide is justified because the state has an interest in absolutely criminalizing any wilful act which contributes to the death of another, is of no assistance.

This conclusion meets the contention that only passive assistance—the withdrawal of support necessary to life—should be permitted. If the justification for helping someone to end life is established, I cannot accept that it matters whether the act is "passive"—the withdrawal of support necessary to sustain life—or "active"—the provision of a means to permit a person of sound mind to choose to end his or her life with dignity.

Certain of the interveners raise the concern that the striking down of s. 241(b) might demean the value of life. But what value is there in life without the choice to do what one wants with one's life, one might counter. one's life includes one's death. Different people hold different views on life and on what devalues it. For some, the choice to end one's life with dignity is infinitely preferable to the inevitable pain and diminishment of a long, slow decline. Section 7 protects that choice against arbitrary state action which would remove it.

In summary, the law draws a distinction between suicide and assisted suicide. The latter is criminal, the former is not. The effect of the distinction is to prevent people like Sue Rodriguez from exercising the autonomy over their bodies available to other people. The distinction, to borrow the language of the Law Reform Commission of Canada, "is difficult to justify on grounds of logic alone": Working Paper 28, *Euthanasia, Aiding Suicide and the Cessation of Treatment* (Ottawa: Minister of Supply and Services Canada, 1982), at p. 53. In short, it is arbitrary. The objective that motivates the legislative scheme that Parliament has enacted to treat suicide is not reflected in its treatment of assisted suicide. It follows that the s. 241(b) prohibition violates the fundamental principles of justice and that s. 7 is breached. ...

A law which violates the principles of fundamental justice under s. 7 of the Charter may be saved under s. 1 of the Charter if the state proves that it is "reasonable ... [and] demonstrably justified in a free and democratic society."

The first thing which the state must show is that the law serves an objective important enough to outweigh the seriousness of the infringement of individual liberties. What then is the objective of the provision of the *Criminal Code* which criminalizes the act of assisting another to commit suicide? It cannot be the prevention of suicide, since Parliament has decriminalized suicide. It cannot be the prevention of the physical act of assisting in bringing about death, since, as discussed above, in many circumstances that act is not a crime. The true objective, it seems, is a practical one. It is the fear that if people are allowed to assist other people in committing suicide, the power will be abused in a way that may lead to the killing of those who have not truly and of their free will consented to death. ...

This justification for s. 241(b) embraces two distinct concerns. The first is the fear that unless assisted suicide is prohibited, it will be used as cloak, not for suicide, but for murder. Viewed thus, the objective of the prohibition is not to prohibit what it purports to prohibit, namely assistance in suicide, but to prohibit another crime, murder or other forms of culpable homicide.

I entertain considerable doubt whether a law which infringes the principles of fundamental justice can be found to be reasonable and demonstrably justified on the sole ground that crimes other than those which it prohibits may become more frequent if it is not present. In Canada, it is not clear that such a provision is necessary; there is a sufficient remedy in the offences of culpable homicide. Nevertheless, the fear cannot be dismissed cavalierly; there is some evidence from foreign jurisdictions indicating that legal codes which permit assisted suicide may be linked to cases of involuntary deaths of the aging and disabled.

The second concern is that even where consent to death is given, the consent may not in fact be voluntary. There is concern that individuals will, for example, consent while in the grips of transitory depression. There is also concern that the decision to end one's life may have been influenced by others. It is argued that to permit assisted suicide will permit people, some well intentioned, some malicious, to bring undue influence to bear on the vulnerable person, thereby provoking a suicide which would otherwise not have occurred.

The obvious response to this concern is that the same dangers are present in any suicide. People are led to commit suicide while in the throes of depression and it is not regarded as criminal conduct. Moreover, this appeal is concerned with s. 241(b) of the *Criminal Code*. Section 241(a), which prohibits counselling in suicide, remains in force even if it is found that s. 241(b) is unconstitutional. But bearing in mind the peculiar vulnerability of the physically disabled, it might be facile to leave the question there. The danger of transitory or improperly induced consent must be squarely faced.

The concern for deaths produced by outside influence or depression centre on the concept of consent. If a person of sound mind, fully aware of all relevant circumstances, comes to the decision to end her life at a certain point, as Sue Rodriguez has, it is difficult to argue that the criminal law should operate to prevent her, given that it does not so operate in the case of others throughout society. The fear is that a person who does not consent may be murdered, or that the consent of a vulnerable person may be improperly procured.

. . .

In my view, the existing provisions in the *Criminal Code* go a considerable distance to meeting the concerns of lack of consent and improperly obtained consent. A person who causes the death of an ill or handicapped person without that person's consent can be prosecuted under the provisions for culpable homicide. The cause of death having been established, it will be for the person who administered the cause to establish that the death was really a suicide, to which the deceased consented. The existence of a criminal penalty for those unable to establish this should be sufficient to deter killings without consent or where consent is unclear. As noted above, counselling suicide would also remain a criminal offence under s. 241(a). Thus the bringing of undue influence upon a vulnerable person would remain prohibited.

These provisions may be supplemented, by way of a remedy on this appeal, by a further stipulation requiring court orders to permit the assistance of suicide in a particular case. The judge must be satisfied that the consent is freely given with a full appreciation of all the circumstances. This will ensure that only those who truly desire to bring their lives to an end obtain assistance. While this may be to ask more of Ms Rodriguez than is asked of the physically able person who seeks to commit suicide, the additional precautions are arguably justified by the peculiar vulnerability of the person who is physically unable to take her own life.

· · ·

It was strenuously argued that it was the role of Parliament to deal with assisted suicide and that the court should not enter on the question. These arguments echo the views of the justices of the majority of the Court of Appeal below. Hollinrake JA stated: "it is my view in areas with public opinion at either extreme, and which involve basically philosophical and not legal considerations, it is proper that the matter be left in the hands of Parliament as historically has been the case" (p. 177). Proudfoot JA added: "On the material available to us, we are in no position to assess the consensus in Canada with respect to assisted suicide ... . I would leave to Parliament the responsibility of taking the pulse of the nation" (p. 186).

Were the task before me that of taking the pulse of the nation, I too should quail, although as a matter of constitutional obligation, a court faced with a Charter breach may not enjoy the luxury of choosing what it will and will not decide. I do not, however, see this as the task which faces the court in this case. We were not asked to second guess parliament's objective of criminalizing the assistance of suicide. Our task was the much more modest one of determining whether, given the legislative scheme regulating suicide which Parliament has put in place, the denial to Sue Rodriguez of the ability to end her life is arbitrary and, hence, amounts to a limit on her security of the person which does not comport with the principles of fundamental justice. Parliament in fact has chosen to legislate on suicide. It has set up a scheme which makes suicide lawful, but which makes assisted suicide criminal. The only question is whether Parliament, having chosen to act in this sensitive area, touching the autonomy of people over their bodies, has done so in a way which is fundamentally fair to all. The focus is not on why Parliament has acted, but on the way in which it has acted.

[Lamer CJC also dissented, arguing that s. 241(b) infringed s. 15 of the Charter by discriminating on the basis of physical disability, and could not be justified under s. 1 because it was an absolute prohibition indifferent to individual circumstances. Cory J also dissented, agreeing in substance with both Lamer CJC and McLachlin J.]

Appeal dismissed.

NOTES

1. Since *Morgentaler* and *Rodriguez*, a number of cases have explored the psychological dimensions of bodily integrity as an interest underlying security of the person. In *New Brunswick (Minister of Health and Community Services) v. G.(J.)*, [1999] 3 SCR 46, 177 DLR (4th) 124, for example, at issue was whether indigent parents have a constitutional right to be provided with state-funded counsel when the state seeks a judicial order suspending such parents' custody of their children pursuant to child welfare legislation. The decision not to provide the appellant with legal aid was made pursuant to a policy in force at the time of her application that stipulated that no legal aid certificates would be issued to respondents in custody applications made by the Minister of Health and Community Services. The Court

held that the failure to provide the appellant with legal aid violated her right to security of the person and was not justifiable under s. 1 of the Charter. The following excerpt is from the majority judgment of Lamer CJC addressing the psychological dimensions of bodily integrity.

[59] Delineating the boundaries protecting the individual's psychological integrity from state interference is an inexact science. Dickson CJ in [R v.] Morgentaler [[1988] 1 SCR 30, 44 DLR (4th) 385], at p. 56, suggested that security of the person would be restricted through serious state-imposed psychological stress (emphasis added). Dickson CJ was trying to convey something qualitative about the type of state interference that would rise to the level of an infringement of this right. It is clear that the right to security of the person does not protect the individual from the ordinary stresses and anxieties that a person of reasonable sensibility would suffer as a result of government action. If the right were interpreted with such broad sweep, countless government initiatives could be challenged on the ground that they infringe the right to security of the person, massively expanding the scope of judicial review, and, in the process, trivializing what it means for a right to be constitutionally protected. Nor will every violation of a fundamental freedom guaranteed in s. 2 of the Charter amount to a restriction of security of the person. I do not believe it can be seriously argued that a law prohibiting certain kinds of commercial expression in violation of s. 2(b), for example, will necessarily result in a violation of the psychological integrity of the person. This is not to say, though, that there will never be cases where a violation of s. 2 will also deprive an individual of security of the person.

[60] For a restriction of security of the person to be made out, then, the impugned state action must have a serious and profound effect on a person's psychological integrity. The effects of the state interference must be assessed objectively, with a view to their impact on the psychological integrity of a person of reasonable sensibility. This need not rise to the level of nervous shock or psychiatric illness, but must be greater than ordinary stress or anxiety.

[61] I have little doubt that state removal of a child from parental custody pursuant to the state's parens patriae jurisdiction constitutes a serious interference with the psychological integrity of the parent. The parental interest in raising and caring for a child is, as La Forest J held in B.(R.) [v. Children's Aid Society of Metropolitan Toronto, [1995] 1 SCR 315, 122 DLR (4th) 1], at para. 83, "an individual interest of fundamental importance in our society." Besides the obvious distress arising from the loss of companionship of the child, direct state interference with the parent–child relationship, through a procedure in which the relationship is subject to state inspection and review, is a gross intrusion into a private and intimate sphere. Further, the parent is often stigmatized as "unfit" when relieved of custody. As an individual's status as a parent is often fundamental to personal identity, the stigma and distress resulting from a loss of parental status is a particularly serious consequence of the state's conduct.

• • •

[63] Not every state action which interferes with the parent–child relationship will restrict a parent's right to security of the person. For example, a parent's security of the person is not restricted when, without more, his or her child is sentenced to jail or conscripted into the army. Nor is it restricted when the child is negligently shot and killed by a police officer: see Augustus v. Gosset, [1996] 3 SCR 268 [138 DLR (4th) 617].

[64] While the parent may suffer significant stress and anxiety as a result of the interference with the relationship occasioned by these actions, the quality of the injury to the parent is distinguishable from that in the present case. In the aforementioned examples, the state is making

no pronouncement as to the parent's fitness or parental status, nor is it usurping the parental role or prying into the intimacies of the relationship. In short, the state is not directly interfering with the psychological integrity of the parent *qua* parent. The different effect on the psychological integrity of the parent in the above examples leads me to the conclusion that no constitutional rights of the parent are engaged.

In *Blencoe v. British Columbia (Human Rights Commission)*, [2000] 2 SCR 307, 190 DLR (4th) 513, at issue was psychological harm suffered by a minister in the government of British Columbia by virtue of accusations of sexual harassment levelled against him. Following the allegations, Mr. Blencoe suffered from severe depression. He did not stand for re-election, and considered himself "unemployable" due to the outstanding complaints. He commenced judicial review proceedings to stay complaints brought before the BC Human Rights Commission, arguing that the Commission lost jurisdiction due to unreasonable delay, and that the delay caused serious prejudice to him and his family that amounted to an abuse of process and a denial of natural justice. A majority of the BC Court of Appeal held that his rights under s. 7 of the Charter were violated by the delay and ordered a stay of proceedings. The Commission appealed. The Supreme Court of Canada, per Bastarache J, allowed the appeal on the basis that the harm to the respondent was neither, in the words of Dickson CJ in *Morgentaler*, "state-imposed," because it occurred before the commencement of proceedings before the Commission, nor, in Bastarache J's words, "seriously exacerbated by the delays." The following except from Bastarache J's reasons address the seriousness of the threat posed to the respondent's psychological integrity.

> [96] I do not doubt that parties in human rights sex discrimination proceedings experience some level of stress and disruption of their lives as a consequence of allegations of complainants. Even accepting that the stress and anxiety experienced by the respondent in this case was linked to delays in the proceedings, I cannot conclude that the scope of his security of the person protected by s. 7 of the Charter covers such emotional effects nor that they can be equated with the kind of stigma contemplated in *Mills* [*v. The Queen*, [1986] 1 SCR 863, 29 DLR (4th) 161], of an overlong and vexatious pending criminal trial or in [*New Brunswick (Minister of Health and Community Services) v.*] *G.(J.)* [[1999] 3 SCR 46, 177 DLR (4th) 124], where the state sought to remove a child from his or her parents. If the purpose of the impugned proceedings is to provide a vehicle or act as an arbiter for redressing private rights, some amount of stress and stigma attached to the proceedings must be accepted. This will also be the case when dealing with the regulation of a business, profession, or other activity. A civil suit involving fraud, defamation or the tort of sexual battery will also be "stigmatizing." The Commission's investigations are not public, the respondent is asked to provide his version of events, and communication goes back and forth. While the respondent may be vilified by the press, there is no "stigmatizing" state pronouncement as to his "fitness" that would carry with it serious consequences such as those in *G.(J.)*. There is thus no constitutional right or freedom against such stigma protected by the s. 7 rights to "liberty" or "security of the person."

2. Recall that in *Morgentaler*, both Dickson CJC and Lamer J were careful to restrict their s. 7 analyses to the criminal law context. In both *G.(J.)* and *Blencoe*, the Court was willing to extend s. 7 beyond the criminal law context to an individual's interaction with the justice system more broadly. In *G.(J.)*, Lamer CJC described this extension in the following terms:

[65] I now turn to the question of whether the right to security of the person extends beyond the criminal law context. In both *Reference re ss. 193 and 195.1(1)(c) of the Criminal Code* [[1990] 1 SCR 1123, 24 DLR (4th) 536], and *B.(R.)* [*v. Children's Aid Society of Metropolitan Toronto*, [1995] 1 SCR 315, 122 DLR (4th) 1], I held that the restrictions on liberty and security of the person that s. 7 is concerned with are those that occur as a result of an individual's interaction with the justice system and its administration. In other words, the subject matter of s. 7 is the state's conduct in the course of enforcing and securing compliance with the law, where the state's conduct deprives an individual of his or her right to life, liberty, or security of the person. I hastened to add, however, that s. 7 is not limited solely to purely criminal or penal matters. There are other ways in which the government, in the course of the administration of justice, can deprive a person of their s. 7 rights to liberty and security of the person, i.e., civil committal to a mental institution: see *B.(R.)*, *supra*, at para. 22.

[66] A child custody application is an example of state action which directly engages the justice system and its administration. The *Family Services Act* provides that a judicial hearing must be held in order to determine whether a parent should be relieved of custody of his or her child.

III. LIFE, LIBERTY, AND SECURITY OF THE PERSON AND DECISIONAL AUTONOMY

Morgentaler and *Rodriguez* demonstrate that the phrase "life, liberty and security of the person" implicates interests associated with the integrity of the human body. However, Wilson J, in her concurring decision in *Morgentaler*, spoke of s. 7 (and the Charter more broadly) in terms of a commitment to the ideal of human dignity, and was of the view that s. 7 accordingly secures "a degree of autonomy in making decisions of fundamental personal importance." Several cases have explored the capacity of s. 7 to protect interests associated with personal autonomy and human dignity beyond the realm of bodily integrity and outside of the criminal law context.

In *Godbout v. Longueuil*, [1997] 3 SCR 844, 152 DLR (4th) 577, for example, an extract from which appears in Chapter 18, Application, at issue was the constitutionality of a municipal resolution requiring all new permanent employees to reside within its boundaries. La Forest J, writing for three members of the Court, held that the right to liberty in s. 7 goes beyond the notion of mere freedom from physical constraint and protects within its scope a narrow sphere of personal autonomy wherein individuals may make inherently private choices free from state interference. He concluded that the right to choose where to establish one's home falls within the scope of this liberty interest, and that the municipal resolution violated the right to liberty in a manner that did not accord with the principles of fundamental justice and was not saved by s. 1. A majority of the Court (Lamer CJC, Cory, Iacobucci, Sopinka, Major, and Gonthier JJ) held that the resolution unjustifiably violated the Quebec Charter, and thus that there was no need to consider the application of s. 7 of the Canadian Charter.

In *R v. Jones*, [1986] 2 SCR 284, 31 DLR (4th) 569, discussed in Chapter 19, Freedom of Religion, a minister of a fundamentalist congregation refused to send his children to public school. Instead, guided by his religious faith, he educated them himself in a school in the church. Charged with truancy, he claimed that both ss. 2(a) and 7 gave him the right to de-

termine the education of his children. In the consideration of s. 7, La Forest J for the majority avoided deciding whether there was a violation of life, liberty, and security of the person,
because he believed that even if there had been a violation, fundamental justice had been
given. Wilson J, however, asserted that liberty included the right of parents to educate their
children in accordance with their religious beliefs. She invoked US doctrine about privacy
and Dickson CJC's exposition of the values of a free and democratic society in *R v. Oakes*,
[1986] 1 SCR 103, saying:

> I believe that the framers of the Constitution in guaranteeing liberty as a fundamental value in
> a free and democratic society had in mind the freedom of the individual to develop and realize
> his potential to the full, to plan his own life to suit his own character, to make his own choices
> for good or ill, to be non-conformist, idiosyncratic and even eccentric—to be, in to-day's par-
> lance, "his own person" and accountable as such.

B.(R.) v. Children's Aid Society of Metropolitan Toronto
[1995] 1 SCR 315, 122 DLR (4th) 1

[At issue in this case was an order pursuant to the Ontario *Child Welfare Act*, RSO 1980,
c. 66, granting a children's aid society wardship of a child born with severe medical problems. The wardship order was sought to give the society the authority to consent to a
blood transfusion opposed by the child's parents who were both devout Jehovah's Witnesses. The parents subsequently challenged the wardship order, arguing that it violated
their right to choose medical treatment for their child in accordance with the tenets of
their religion. They based their claim on both ss. 2(a) and 7 of the Charter. The Supreme
Court dismissed the parents' claim for a wide range of reasons. With respect to the s. 7
claim, La Forest J, writing for four members of the Court, found that the parents' right to
liberty had been violated, but that fundamental justice had been observed. His decision,
an excerpt from which follows, has had a significant influence on subsequent doctrinal
developments with respect to s. 7's protection of rights to decisional autonomy. The
s. 2(a) aspect of the case is discussed in a note in Chapter 19, Freedom of Religion.]

LA FOREST J (L'Heureux-Dubé, Gonthier, and McLachlin JJ, concurring):

· · ·

On the one hand, liberty does not mean unconstrained freedom. ... Freedom of the individual to do what he or she wishes must, in any organized society, be subjected to numerous constraints for the common good. The state undoubtedly has the right to impose
many types of restraints on individual behaviour, and not all limitations will attract
Charter scrutiny. On the other hand, liberty does not mean mere freedom from physical
restraint. In a free and democratic society, the individual must be left room for personal
autonomy to live his or her own life and to make decisions that are of fundamental personal importance.

· · ·

　　Where to draw the line between interests and regulatory powers falling within the accepted ambit of state authority will often raise difficulty. But much on either side of the

line is clear enough. On that basis, I would have thought it plain that the right to nurture a child, to care for its development, and to make decisions for it in fundamental matters such as medical care, are part of the liberty interest of a parent. ... The common law has long recognized that parents are in the best position to take care of their children and make all the decisions necessary to ensure their well-being. ... Although the philosophy underlying state intervention has changed over time, most contemporary statutes dealing with child protection matters, and in particular the Ontario Act, while focusing on the best interest of the child, favour minimal intervention. In recent years, courts have expressed some reluctance to interfere with parental rights, and state intervention has been tolerated only when necessity was demonstrated. This only serves to confirm that the parental interest in bringing up, nurturing and caring for a child, including medical care and moral upbringing, is an individual interest of fundamental importance to our society.

· · ·

... This liberty interest is not a parental right tantamount to a right of property in children. (Fortunately, we have distanced ourselves from the ancient juridical conception of children as chattels of their parents.) The state is now actively involved in a number of areas traditionally conceived of as properly belonging to the private sphere. Nonetheless, our society is far from having repudiated the privileged role parents exercise in the upbringing of their children. This role translates into a protected sphere of parental decision-making which is rooted in the presumption that parents should make important decisions affecting their children both because parents are more likely to appreciate the best interests of their children and because the state is ill-equipped to make such decisions itself. Moreover, individuals have a deep personal interest as parents in fostering the growth of their own children. This is not to say that the state cannot intervene when it considers it necessary to safeguard the child's autonomy or health. But such intervention must be justified. In other words, parental decision-making must receive the protection of the *Charter* in order for state interference to be properly monitored by the courts, and be permitted only when it conforms to the values underlying the *Charter*.

The respondents also argued that the infant's rights were paramount to those of the appellants and, on that basis alone, state intervention was justified. ... Children undeniably benefit from the *Charter*, most notably in its protection of their rights to life and to the security of their person. As children are unable to assert these, our society presumes that parents will exercise their freedom of choice in a manner that does not offend the rights of their children. If one considers the multitude of decisions parents make daily, it is clear that in practice, state interference in order to balance the rights of parents and children will arise only in exceptional cases. In fact, we must accept that parents can, at times, make decisions contrary to their children's wishes—and rights—as long as they do not exceed the threshold dictated by public policy, in its broad conception. For instance, it would be difficult to deny that a parent can dictate to his or her child the place where he or she will live, or which school he or she will attend. However, the state can properly intervene in situations where parental conduct falls below the socially acceptable threshold. But in doing so, the state is limiting the constitutional rights of parents rather then vindicating the constitutional rights of children.

· · ·

Once it is decided that the parents have a liberty interest, further balancing of parents' and children's rights should be done in the course of determining whether state interference conforms to the principles of fundamental justice, rather than when defining the scope of the liberty interest. Even assuming that the rights of children can qualify the liberty interest of their parents, that interest exists nonetheless. In the case at bar, the application of the Act deprived the appellants of their right to decide which medical treatment should be administered to their infant. In so doing, the Act has infringed upon the parental "liberty" protected in s. 7 of the *Charter*. I now propose to determine whether this deprivation was made in accordance with the principles of fundamental justice.

[La Forest J concluded that the general procedure under the *Child Welfare Act* for granting orders of wardship met the standards of fundamental justice. In coming to this conclusion, he stressed the provisions about notice; the hearing before a judge, at which the parents had ample opportunity to present their concerns and preferences; and the onus on the applicant. Sopinka J finessed the question of whether there was a violation of life, liberty, and security of the person by reasoning that, whether or not there had been a violation, fundamental justice had been observed. Iacobucci and Cory JJ found no violation of the parents' right to liberty under s. 7. Taking the position that the child's s. 7 rights to life and security of the person had to be considered, they found that an exercise of parental liberty that seriously endangers the survival of the child falls outside s. 7. Lamer CJC also found that there was no violation of life, liberty, and security of the person, but for different reasons, connected to his belief that it would inappropriately expand the scope of s. 7 to extend the interests protected beyond those of physical liberty.]

Blencoe v. British Columbia (Human Rights Commission), [2000] 2 SCR 307, 190 DLR (4th) 513, it will be recalled, dealt with a human rights inquiry into sexual harassment allegations. In the course of his decision, Bastarache J, writing for a majority of the Court, provided an overview of the scope of s. 7 and set out the relationship between s. 7 and decisional autonomy in the following terms:

[49] The liberty interest protected by s. 7 of the *Charter* is no longer restricted to mere freedom from physical restraint. Members of this Court have found that "liberty" is engaged where state compulsions or prohibitions affect important and fundamental life choices. This applies for example where persons are compelled to appear at a particular time and place for fingerprinting (*R v. Beare*, [1988] 2 SCR 387); to produce documents or testify (*Thomson Newspapers Ltd. v. Canada (Director of Investigation and Research, Restrictive Trade Practices Commission)*, [1990] 1 SCR 425); and not to loiter in particular areas (*R v. Heywood*, [1994] 3 SCR 761). In our free and democratic society, individuals are entitled to make decisions of fundamental importance free from state interference.

. . .

[86] Few interests are as compelling as, and basic to individual autonomy than, a woman's choice to terminate her pregnancy, an individual's decision to terminate his or her life, the right to raise one's children, and [as in *R v. O'Connor*, [1995] 4 SCR 411] the ability of sexual assault victims to seek therapy without fear of their private records being disclosed. Such interests are indeed basic to individual dignity. But the alleged right to be free from stigma associated with a

human rights complaint does not fall within this narrow sphere. The state has not interfered with the respondent's right to make decisions that affect his fundamental being. The prejudice to the respondent in this case, as recognized by Lowry J, at para. 10, is essentially confined to his personal hardship. He is not "employable" as a politician, he and his family have moved residences twice, his financial resources are depleted, and he has suffered physically and psychologically. However, the state has not interfered with the respondent and his family's ability to make essential life choices. To accept that the prejudice suffered by the respondent in this case amounts to state interference with his security of the person would be to stretch the meaning of this right.

In *R v. Malmo-Levine; R v. Caine*, 2003 SCC 74, [2003] 3 SCR 571, 233 DLR (4th) 415, which involved a Charter challenge to the provisions in the *Narcotics Control Act*, RSC 1985, c. N-1 criminalizing the possession of marijuana, the Supreme Court emphasized the limits placed on the s. 7 liberty right to decisional autonomy:

GONTHIER and BINNIE JJ (McLachlin CJC, Iacobucci, Major, and Bastarache JJ concurring):

· · ·

[84] We say at once that the availability of imprisonment for the offence of simple possession is sufficient to trigger s. 7 scrutiny ... . However, Malmo-Levine's position ... requires us to address whether broader considerations of personal autonomy, short of imprisonment, are also sufficient to invoke s. 7 protection. The appellant Caine, whose factum talks of the "fun" or "social" use of cannabis, writes, at para. 30:

> It is submitted that a decision whether or not to possess and consume Cannabis (marijuana), even if potentially harmful to the user, is analogous to the decision by an individual as to what food to eat or not eat and whether or not to eat fatty foods, and as such is a decision of fundamental personal importance involving a choice made by the individual involving that individual's personal autonomy.

[85] In *Morgentaler* [[1988] 1 SCR 30], Wilson J suggested that liberty "grants the individual a degree of autonomy in making decisions of fundamental personal importance," "without interference from the state." Liberty accordingly means more than freedom from physical restraint. It includes "the right to an irreducible sphere of personal autonomy wherein individuals may make inherently private choices free from state interference": *Godbout v. Longueuil (City)*, [1997] 3 SCR 844, 152 DLR (4th) 577, at para. 66; *B.(R.) v. Children's Aid Society of Metropolitan Toronto*, [1995] 1 SCR 315, 122 DLR (4th)1, at para. 80. This is true only to the extent that such matters "can properly be characterized as fundamentally or inherently personal such that, by their very nature, they implicate basic choices going to the core of what it means to enjoy individual dignity and independence": *Godbout, supra*, at para. 66. See also *Blencoe v. British Columbia (Human Rights Commission)*, [2000] 2 SCR 307, 170 DLR (4th) 344, at para. 54. ...

[86] While we accept Malmo-Levine's statement that smoking marihuana is central to his lifestyle, the Constitution cannot be stretched to afford protection to whatever activity an individual chooses to define as central to his or her lifestyle. One individual chooses to smoke marihuana; another has an obsessive interest in golf; a third is addicted to gambling. The appellant Caine invokes a taste for fatty foods. A society that extended constitutional protection to any and all such lifestyles would be ungovernable. Lifestyle choices of this order are not, we think, "basic choices going to the core of what it means to enjoy individual dignity and independence" (*Godbout, supra*, at para. 66).

[87] In our view, with respect, Malmo-Levine's desire to build a lifestyle around the recreational use of marihuana does not attract Charter protection. There is no free-standing constitutional right to smoke "pot" for recreational purposes.

Arbour, LeBel, and Deschamps JJ dissented in part, but their disagreement was with respect to the reasoning of the majority on fundamental justice and not with the interpretation of the liberty interest at stake.

IV. SECTION 7 AND SOCIAL CITIZENSHIP

Should interests associated with social citizenship—for example, social security, adequate food, housing, education, and health care—receive constitutional protection in the form of a right to life, liberty, and security of the person? The following two cases discuss this question. As you read them, ask yourself to what extent they are consistent with one another.

Gosselin v. Quebec (Attorney General)
[2002] 4 SCR 429

[Under Quebec's social assistance scheme, found in the *Social Aid Act*, RSQ, c. A-16 and accompanying regulations, between 1984 and 1989 the base amount of money payable to claimants under the age of 30 was one-third of that payable to those 30 and over. Those under 30 could increase their welfare payments to either the same as or slightly less than the amount received by those 30 and over by participating in an educational or work experience program. The age-based distinction was removed in 1989. Gosselin brought a class action on behalf of all those who had been under 30 and affected by the old scheme before 1989. (Until 1987 the scheme was protected by Quebec's invocation of the s. 33 "notwithstanding" clause.) Arguments were based on both ss. 15 and 7 of the Charter. Reproduced below are the Court's opinions on whether the legislation violated s. 7 of the Charter. A discussion of the Court's reasoning on the s. 15 issue can be found in a note in Section VI.D of Chapter 23, Equality Rights.]

McLACHLIN CJC (Gonthier, Iacobucci, Major and Binnie JJ concurring): ...
[75] ... The appellant argues that the s. 7 right to security of the person includes the right to receive a particular level of social assistance from the state adequate to meet basic needs. She argues that the state deprived her of this right by providing inadequate welfare benefits, in a way that violated the principles of fundamental justice. There are three elements to this claim: (1) that the legislation affects an interest protected by the right to life, liberty and security of the person within the meaning of s. 7; (2) that providing inadequate benefits constitutes a "deprivation" by the state; and (3) that, if deprivation of a right protected by s. 7 is established, this was not in accordance with the principles of fundamental justice. The factual record is insufficient to support this claim. Nevertheless, I will examine these three elements.

· · ·

[78] This Court has indicated in its s. 7 decisions that the administration of justice does not refer exclusively to processes operating in the criminal law. ... Rather, our decisions recognize that the administration of justice can be implicated in a variety of circumstances: see *Blencoe* [*v. British Columbia (Human Rights Commission)*, [2000] 2 SCR 307, 190 DLR (4th) 513] (human rights process); *B.(R.)* [*v. Children's Aid Society of Metropolitan Toronto*, [1995] 1 SCR 315, 122 DLR (4th) 1] (parental rights in relation to state-imposed medical treatment); [*New Brunswick (Minister of Health and Community Services) v.*] *G.(J.)* [[1999] 3 SCR 46, 177 DLR (4th) 124] (parental rights in the custody process); *Winnipeg Child and Family Services (Northwest Area) v. G.(D.F)*, [1997] 3 SCR 925 [152 DLR (4th) 193] (liberty to refuse state-imposed addiction treatment). Bastarache J argues that s. 7 applies only in an adjudicative context. With respect, I believe that this conclusion may be premature. An adjudicative context might be sufficient, but we have not yet determined that one is *necessary* in order for s. 7 to be implicated.

[79] In my view, it is both unnecessary and undesirable to attempt to state an exhaustive definition of the administration of justice at this stage, delimiting all circumstances in which the administration of justice might conceivably be implicated. The meaning of the administration of justice, and more broadly the meaning of s. 7, should be allowed to develop incrementally, as heretofore unforeseen issues arise for consideration. The issue here is not whether the administration of justice is implicated—plainly it is not—but whether the Court ought to apply s. 7 despite this fact.

[80] Can s. 7 apply to protect rights or interests wholly unconnected to the administration of justice? The question remains unanswered. In *R v. Morgentaler*, [1988] 1 SCR 30 [44 DLR (4th) 385], at p. 56, Dickson CJ, for himself and Lamer J entertained (without deciding on) the possibility that the right to security of the person extends "to protect either interests central to personal autonomy, such as a right to privacy." Similarly, in *Irwin Toy Ltd. v. Quebec (Attorney General)*, [1989] 1 SCR 927 [58 DLR (4th) 577], at p. 1003, Dickson CJ, for the majority, left open the question of whether s. 7 could operate to protect "economic rights fundamental to human ... survival." Some cases, while on their facts involving the administration of justice, have described the rights protected by s. 7 without explicitly linking them to the administration of justice. ...

[81] Even if s. 7 could be read to encompass economic rights, a further hurdle emerges. Section 7 speaks of the right not to be deprived of life, liberty and security of the person, except in accordance with the principles of fundamental justice. Nothing in the jurisprudence thus far suggests that s. 7 places a positive obligation on the state to ensure that each person enjoys life, liberty or security of the person. Rather, s. 7 has been interpreted as restricting the state's ability to deprive people of these. Such a deprivation does not exist in the case at bar.

[82] One day s. 7 may be interpreted to include positive obligations. To evoke Lord Sankey's celebrated phrase in *Edwards v. Attorney-General for Canada*, [1930] AC 124 (PC), at p. 136, the Canadian Charter must be viewed as [a] "living tree capable of growth and expansion within its natural limits." ... It would be a mistake to regard s. 7 as frozen, or its content as having been exhaustively defined in previous cases. ... The question therefore is not whether s. 7 has ever been—or will ever be—recognized as creating positive rights. Rather, the question is whether the present circumstances warrant a novel application of s. 7 as the basis for a positive state obligation to guarantee adequate living standards.

[83] I conclude that they do not. With due respect for the views of my colleague Arbour J, ... I do not believe that there is sufficient evidence in this case to support the proposed interpretation of s. 7. I leave open the possibility that a positive obligation to sustain life, liberty, or security of person may be made out in special circumstances. However, this is not such a case. The impugned program contained compensatory "workfare" provisions and the evidence of actual hardship is wanting. The frail platform provided by the facts of this case cannot support the weight of a positive state obligation of citizen support.

[Bastarache J reached the same result as the majority on s. 7, but for different reasons, which focused on the restriction of s. 7 to situations involving interaction with the justice system and its administration. LeBel J, who dissented on the s. 15 issue, found it unnecessary to consider the effect of s. 7 beyond stating that, while no violation of s. 7 was established, he agreed with that part of McLachlin CJC's reasons stating that it is inappropriate to rule out the possibility that s. 7 might be applied in the future to circumstances unrelated to the justice system.]

ARBOUR J (dissenting): ...
[308] I would allow this appeal on the basis of the appellant's s. 7 Charter claim. In doing so, I conclude that the s. 7 rights to "life, liberty and security of the person" include a positive dimension. Few would dispute that an advanced modern welfare state like Canada has a positive moral obligation to protect the life, liberty and security of its citizens. There is considerably less agreement, however, as to whether this positive moral obligation translates into a legal one. Some will argue that there are interpretive barriers to the conclusion that s. 7 imposes a positive obligation on the state to offer such basic protection.

[309] In my view these barriers are all less real and substantial than one might assume. This Court has never ruled, nor does the language of the Charter itself require, that we must reject any positive claim against the state—as in this case—for the most basic positive protection of life and security. This Court has consistently chosen instead to leave open the possibility of finding certain positive rights to the basic means of subsistence within s. 7. In my view, far from resisting this conclusion, the language and structure of the Charter—and of s. 7 in particular—actually *compel* it. Before demonstrating all of this it will be necessary to deconstruct the various firewalls that are said to exist around s. 7, precluding this Court from reaching in this case what I believe to be an inevitable and just outcome.

· · ·

II. Analysis of Section 7 of the Charter

· · ·

[336] ... I set out s. 7 in its entirety:

7. Everyone has the right to life, liberty and security of the person *and* the right not to be deprived thereof except in accordance with the principles of fundamental justice. [Emphasis added.]

I have drawn attention to the conjunction in s. 7 ... .

[337] ... My reasons for emphasizing this ... are straightforward. Past judicial treatments of the section have habitually read out of the English version of s. 7 the conjunction and, with it, the entire first clause. The result is that we typically speak about s. 7 guaranteeing only the right not to be deprived of life, liberty and security of the person except in accordance with the principles of fundamental justice. ...

• • •

[340] ... [But] only by ignoring the structure of s. 7—by effectively reading out the conjunction and, with it, the first clause—is it possible to conclude that it protects exclusively "the right not to be deprived of life, liberty or security of the person except in accordance with the principles of fundamental justice." There may be some question as to how far, precisely, the protection of s. 7 extends beyond this, but that the section's first clause affords some additional protection seems, as a purely textual matter, beyond reasonable objection.

• • •

[355] ... Charter rights and freedoms find protection in s. 1, not only because they are guaranteed in that section, but because limitations on some rights are required by the positive protection of others. This approach to s. 1 justification, which invokes the values that underpin the Charter as the only suitable basis for limiting those rights, confirms that Charter rights contain a positive dimension. Constitutional rights are not simply a shield against state interference with liberty; they place a positive obligation on the state to arbitrate competing demands arising from the liberty and rights of others.

[356] In other words, the justificatory mechanism in place in s. 1 of the Charter reflects the existence of a positive right to Charter protection asserted in support of alleged interference by the state with the rights of others. If such positive rights exist in that form in s. 1, they must, *a fortiori*, exist in the various Charter provisions articulating the existence of the rights. For instance, if one's right to life, liberty and security of the person can be limited under s. 1 by the need to protect the life, liberty or security of others, it can only be because the right is not merely a negative right but a positive one, calling for the state not only to abstain from interfering with life, liberty and security of the person but also to actively secure that right in the face of competing demands.

[357] This concludes my interpretive analysis of s. 7. In my view, the results are unequivocal: every suitable approach to Charter interpretation, including textual analysis, purposive analysis, and contextual analysis, mandates the conclusion that the s. 7 rights of life, liberty and security of the person include a positive dimension.

[358] It remains to show that the interest claimed in this case falls within the range of entitlements that the state is under a positive obligation to provide under s. 7. In one sense it seems obvious that it does. ... [A] minimum level of welfare is so closely connected to issues relating to one's basic health (or security of the person), and potentially even to one's survival (or life interest), that it appears inevitable that a positive right to life, liberty and security of the person must provide for it. Indeed in this case the legislature has in fact chosen to legislate in respect of welfare rights. Thus determining the applicability of the foregoing general principles to the case at bar requires only that we analyse this case through the lens of the underinclusiveness line of cases ... .

• • •

III. Application to the Case at Bar

. . .

[365] *Dunmore* [*v. Ontario (Attorney General)*, [2001 SCC 94, [2001] 3 SCR 1016, 207 DLR (4th) 193] articulated the criteria necessary for making a Charter claim based on underinclusion outside the context of s. 15. In my view, these criteria are satisfied in this case. They are as follows:

1. The claim must be grounded in a fundamental Charter right or freedom rather than in access to a particular statutory regime … .
2. A proper evidentiary foundation must be provided, before creating a positive obligation under the Charter, by demonstrating that exclusion from the regime constitutes a substantial interference with the exercise and fulfillment of a protected right … .
3. It must be determined whether the state can truly be held accountable for any inability to exercise the right or freedom in question … .

A. Is the Claim Grounded in an Appropriate Charter Right?

[367] … Under s. 7, [the claimants argue] not that exclusion from the statutory regime is illicit *per se*, but that it violates their self-standing right to security of the person (and potentially their right to life as well). As in *Dunmore*, this right exists independently of any statutory enactment.

[368] The distinction between the s. 7 claim and the s. 15 claim can be illustrated as follows: if it were the case that the claimants could meet their basic needs through means outside of the *Social Aid Act*—for instance through an independent government program providing for subsidized housing, food vouchers, etc., in exchange for the performance of works of public service—their s. 7 claim would entirely disappear, but their s. 15 claim would potentially remain intact inasmuch as it would still be open to them to argue that being forced to resort to these alternative means somehow violated their human dignity. The problem in this case, by way of contrast, is that exclusion from this statutory regime effectively excludes the claimants from any real possibility of having their basic needs met through any means whatsoever. Thus, it is not exclusion from the *particular* statutory regime that is at stake but, more basically, the claimants' fundamental rights to security of the person and life itself.

B. Is There a Sufficient Evidentiary Basis to Establish That Exclusion from the Social Aid Act Substantially Interfered with the Fulfilment and Exercise of the Claimants' Fundamental Right to Security of the Person?

[370] … [O]ne must avoid placing undue emphasis on whatever (often remote) possibility there might have been that the claimants could have satisfied their basic needs through private means, whether in the open market or with the assistance of other private actors such as family members or charitable groups. There is simply no requirement that they prove they exhausted all other avenues of relief before turning to public assistance. On the contrary, all that is required is that the claimants show that the lack of government intervention "substantially impede[d]" the enjoyment of their s. 7 rights. This

requirement is best put in language that mirrors that used by L'Heureux-Dubé J in *Haig* [*v. Canada*, [1993] 2 SCR 995] that the claimants must show that government intervention was necessary in order to render their s. 7 rights meaningful.

[371] There is ample evidence in this case that the legislated exclusion of young adults from the full benefits of the social assistance regime substantially interfered with their s. 7 rights, in particular their right to security of the person. Welfare recipients under the age of 30 were allowed $170/month. The various remedial programs put in place in 1984 simply did not work: a startling 88.8 percent of the young adults who were eligible to participate in the programs were unable to increase their benefits to the level payable to adults 30 and over. In these conditions, the physical and psychological security of young adults was severely compromised during the period at issue. This was compellingly illustrated by the appellant's own testimony and by that of her four witnesses: a social worker, a psychologist, a dietician and a community physician. The sizeable volume of the appellant's record prohibits an exhaustive exposé of the dismal conditions in which many young welfare recipients lived. I will nevertheless outline the evidence illustrating how the exclusion of young adults from the full benefits of the social assistance regime amounted to a substantial interference with their fundamental right to security of the person and drove them to resort to other demeaning and often dangerous means to ensure their survival.

[372] On $170/month, paying rent is impossible. Indeed, in 1987, the rent for a bachelor apartment in the Montreal Metropolitan Area was approximately $237 to $412/month, depending on the location. Two-bedroom apartments went for about $368 to $463/month. As a result, while some welfare recipients were able to live with parents, many became homeless. During the period at issue, it is estimated that over 5,000 young adults lived on the streets of the Montreal Metropolitan Area. Arthur Sandborn, a social worker, testified that young welfare recipients would often combine their funds and share a small apartment. After paying rent however, very little money was left to pay for the other basic necessities of life, including hot water, electricity and food. No telephone meant further marginalization and made job hunting very difficult, as did the inability to afford suitable clothes and transportation.

(1) Interference with Physical Security of the Person

[373] The exclusion of welfare recipients under the age of 30 from the full benefits of the social assistance regime severely interfered with their physical integrity and security. First, there are the health risks that flow directly from the dismal living conditions that $170/month afford. Obviously, the inability to pay for adequate clothing, electricity, hot water or, in the worst cases, for any shelter whatsoever, dramatically increases one's vulnerability to such ailments as the common cold or influenza. According to Dr. Christine Colin, persons living in poverty are six times more likely to develop diseases like bronchial infections, asthma and emphysema than persons who live in decent conditions. Dr. Colin also testified that the poor not only develop more health problems, but are also more severely affected by their ailments than those who live in more favourable conditions.

[374] Second, the malnourishment and undernourishment of young welfare recipients also result in a plethora of health problems. In 1987, the cost of proper nourishment

for a single person was estimated at $152/month, that is 89 percent of the $170/month allowance. Jocelyne Leduc-Gauvin, a dietician, gave detailed evidence of the effects of poor and insufficient nourishment. Malnourished young adults suffer from lethargy and from various chronic problems such as obesity, anxiety, hypertension, infections, ulcers, fatigue and an increased sensitivity to pain. Malnourished women are prone to gyneco-logical disorders, high rates of miscarriage and abnormal pregnancies. Children born to malnourished mothers tend to be smaller and are often afflicted by congenital deficien-cies such as poor vision and learning disorders. Like many welfare recipients under the age of 30, the appellant suffered the consequences of malnutrition. As noted by Ms. Leduc-Gauvin, there is a sad irony in the fact that those who were left to fend for themselves on a lean $170/month—young adults aged 18 to 29—in fact required a higher daily intake of calories and nutrients than older adults.

[375] In order to eat, many young welfare recipients benefited from food banks, soup kitchens and like charitable organizations. But since these could not be relied upon con-sistently other avenues had to be pursued. While some resorted to theft, others turned to prostitution. Dumpsters and garbage cans were scavenged in search of edible morsels of food, exposing the hungry youths to the risks of food poisoning and contamination. In one particular case reported by Mr. Sandborn, two young adults paid a restauranteur $10/month for the right to sit in his kitchen and eat whatever patrons left in their plates.

(2) Interference with Psychological Security of the Person

[376] The psychological and social consequences of being excluded from the full benefits of the social assistance regime were equally devastating. The hardships and mar-ginalization of poverty propel the individual into a spiral of isolation, depression, humili-ation, low self-esteem, anxiety, stress and drug addiction. According to a 1987 enquiry by Santé Québec, one out of five indigent young adults attempted suicide or had suicidal thoughts. The situation was even more alarming among homeless youths in Montreal, 50 percent of whom reportedly attempted to take their own lives.

[377] In my view, this evidence overwhelmingly demonstrates that the exclusion of young adults from the full benefits of the social assistance regime substantially interfered with their fundamental right to security of the person and, at the margins, perhaps with their right to life as well. Freedom from state interference with bodily or psychological integrity is of little consolation to those who, like the claimants in this case, are faced with a daily struggle to meet their most basic bodily and psychological needs. To them, such a purely negative right to security of the person is essentially meaningless: theirs is a world in which the primary threats to security of the person come not from others, but from their own dire circumstances. In such cases, one can reasonably conclude that posi-tive state action is what is required in order to breathe purpose and meaning into their s. 7 guaranteed rights.

C. Can the State Be Held Accountable for the Claimants' Inability to Exercise Their Section 7 Rights?

[378] In one sense, there appears to be considerable overlap between this third criterion for making out a successful underinclusion claim and the second criterion just discussed. In fact, once one establishes in accordance with the second criterion that a claimant's fundamental rights cannot be effectively exercised without government intervention, it is difficult to see what more would be required in order to demonstrate state accountability.

[379] The absence of a direct, positive action by the state may appear to create particular problems of causation. Of course, state accountability in this context cannot be conceived of along the same lines of causal responsibility as where there is affirmative state action that causally contributes to, and in some cases even determines, the infringement. By contrast, positive rights are violable by mere inaction on the part of the state. This may mean that one should not search for the same kind of causal nexus tying the state to the claimants' inability to exercise their fundamental freedoms. Such a nexus could only ever be established by pointing to some positive state action giving rise to the claimants' aggrieved condition. While this focus on state action is appropriate where one is considering the violation of a negative right, it imports a requirement that is inimical to the very idea of positive rights.

[380] Among the immediate implications of this is that the claimants in this case need not establish, in order to satisfy the third criterion, that the state can be held causally responsible for the socio-economic environment in which their s. 7 rights were threatened, nor do they need to establish that the government's inaction worsened their plight. Here, as in all claims asserting the infringement of a positive right, the focus is on whether the state is under an obligation of performance to alleviate the claimants' condition, and not on whether it can be held causally responsible for that condition in the first place.

[381] All of which indicates that government accountability in the context of claims of underinclusion is to be understood simply in terms of the existence of a positive state obligation to redress conditions for which the state may or may not be causally responsible. On this view, the third criterion serves the purpose of ensuring not only that government intervention is needed to secure the effective exercise of a claimant's fundamental rights or freedoms, but also that it is obligatory. ... . In conceiving of state accountability in terms of the breach of a positive duty of performance, it becomes possible for the first time to recognize how underinclusive legislation can violate a fundamental right by effectively turning a blind eye to, or *sustaining*, independently existing threats to that right.

[382] A focus on state obligation was also the driving force behind this Court's finding in *Dunmore* that the government could be held accountable for the violation of the claimants' s. 2(d) rights in that case. It led to the search for a "minimum of state action" ... that would bring the government within reach of the Charter by engaging s. 32. Ultimately, the minimum of state action was satisfied in *Dunmore* by the mere fact that the government had chosen to legislate over matters of association. In this Court's view, that choice triggered a state obligation that invoked Charter scrutiny and removed any possibility of the state claiming lack of responsibility for the violation of associational rights (at para. 29):

> Once the state has chosen to regulate a private relationship such as that between employer and employee ... it is unduly formalistic to consign that relationship to a "private sphere" that is impervious to Charter review ... .

There can be no doubt that these dicta apply with equal force to the instant appeal.

[383] The *Social Aid Act* is quite clearly directed at addressing basic needs relating to the personal security and survival of indigent members of society. It is almost a cliché that the modern welfare state has developed in response to an obvious failure on the part of the free market economy to provide these basic needs for everyone. Were it necessary, this Court could take judicial notice of this fact in assessing the relevance of the *Social Aid Act* to the claimants' s. 7 rights. As it happens, any such necessity is mitigated by the fact that s. 6 of the Act explicitly sets out its objective: to provide supplemental aid to those who fall below a *subsistence level*.

[384] Additional support for the proposition that the *Social Aid Act* is directed at securing the interests that s. 7 of the Charter was meant to protect can be found in various statements made by the Quebec government in a policy paper that ultimately led to the reform of the social assistance regime in 1989, putting an end to the differential treatment between younger and older welfare recipients. This paper was published in 1987 by the government of Quebec ... . In it, the Quebec government unequivocally states that it "recognizes its duty and obligation to provide for the essential needs of persons who are unable to work." It then goes on to state that it must ... "resolutely tackle the deficiencies" of the social assistance programs, which, it admits, "remain barriers to the autonomy and emancipation of welfare recipients." On the same page, the government specifically identifies the difference in treatment between younger and older welfare recipients as such a deficiency, describing it as a ... "problem."

[385] At the very least, these statements indicate that the *Social Aid Act* constituted an excursion into regulating the field of interests that generally fall within the rubric of s. 7 of the Charter. Legislative intervention aimed at providing for essential needs touching on the personal security and survival of indigent members of society is sufficient to satisfy whatever "minimum state action" requirement might be necessary in order to engage s. 32 of the Charter. ... I must conclude that this effective lack of government intervention constituted a violation of their s. 7 rights.

[Arbour J concluded that the government had not demonstrated that the violation could be saved by it. L'Heureux-Dubé J concurred with Arbour J's reasoning on the s. 7 issue.]

Chaoulli v. Quebec (Attorney General)
[2005] 1 SCR 791, 254 DLR (4th) 577

[Suffering from various health problems, Mr. Zeliotis found the waiting times in Quebec's public health care system untenable. Dr. Chaoulli, a physician, was unsuccessful in having his home-delivered medical activities recognized and in obtaining a licence to operate an independent private hospital. Their situations had come about as a result of a statutory prohibition on private health insurance for health care services available in the public system (the prohibition was found in the *Health Insurance Act* (HEIA) and the *Hospital Insurance Act* (HOIA). Having joined forces, Zeliotis and Chaoulli challenged the validity of this prohibition, contending that it deprived them of access to services that do not come with the waiting times inherent in the public system. This, in their view, violated both their rights under s. 7 of the *Canadian Charter of Rights and Freedoms* and s. 1 of the *Quebec Charter of Human Rights and Freedoms*. The trial court dismissed the motion for a declaratory judgment on the basis that even though Zeliotis and Chaoulli had demonstrated a deprivation of the rights to life, liberty, and security of the person guaranteed by s. 7 of the Canadian Charter, this deprivation was in accordance with the principles of fundamental justice. The Court of Appeal affirmed that decision. A majority of the Supreme Court of Canada allowed the appeal.

Note that Deschamps J's judgment, one of the two judgments that together form the majority ruling, was based strictly on the *Quebec Charter of Human Rights and Freedoms*. Having concluded that this Charter had been violated, she found it unnecessary to consider arguments based on the Canadian Charter. Section 1 of the Quebec Charter provides that "[e]very human being has a right to life, and to personal security, inviolability and freedom." It is thus a functional equivalent of s. 7 of the Canadian Charter, subject to the absence in it of any qualification, such as that found in s. 7, of the rights guaranteed therein through a reference to principles of fundamental justice. This makes s. 1's scope of application broader than that of s. 7. Deschamps J's judgment is thus relevant to s. 7 of the Canadian Charter for its general characterization of the issue at stake and for its interpretation of the right to life and security of the person. Moreover, although the wording of the Quebec Charter's limitation clause, s. 9.1, is different from that of s. 1 of the Canadian Charter, Deschamps J nevertheless applied the Canadian Charter's *Oakes* test to s. 9.1, which reads as follows: "In exercising his fundamental freedoms and rights, a person shall maintain a proper regard for democratic values, public order and the general well-being of the citizens of Québec. In this respect, the scope of the freedoms and rights, and limits to their exercise, may be fixed by law." Her comments on the circumstances where deference should, or should not, be shown to legislative choices are relevant to the Canadian Charter's limitation clause.]

[1] DESCHAMPS J: Quebeckers are prohibited from taking out insurance to obtain in the private sector services that are available under Quebec's public health care plan. Is this prohibition justified by the need to preserve the integrity of the plan?

[2] As we enter the 21st century, health care is a constant concern. The public health care system, once a source of national pride, has become the subject of frequent and sometimes bitter criticism. This appeal does not question the appropriateness of the state making health care available to all Quebeckers. On the contrary, all the parties stated that they support this kind of role for the government. Only the state can make available to all Quebeckers the social safety net consisting of universal and accessible health care. The demand for health care is constantly increasing, and one of the tools used by governments to control this increase has been the management of waiting lists. The choice of waiting lists as a management tool falls within the authority of the state and not of the courts. The appellants do not claim to have a solution that will eliminate waiting lists.

Rather, they submit that the delays resulting from waiting lists violate their rights under [both the Quebec and Canadian Charters]. ...

[4] In essence, the question is whether Quebeckers who are prepared to spend money to get access to health care that is, in practice, not accessible in the public sector because of waiting lists may be validly prevented from doing so by the state. For the reasons that follow, I find that the prohibition infringes the right to personal inviolability and that it is not justified by a proper regard for democratic values, public order and the general well-being of the citizens of Quebec.

. . .

[14] As I mentioned at the beginning of my reasons, no one questions the need to preserve a sound public health care system. The central question raised by the appeal is whether the prohibition is justified by the need to preserve the integrity of the public system. In this regard, when my colleagues ask whether Quebec has the power under the Constitution to discourage the establishment of a parallel health care system, I can only agree with them that it does. But that is not the issue in the appeal. The appellants do not contend that they have a constitutional right to private insurance. Rather, they contend that the waiting times violate their rights to life and security. It is the measure chosen by the government that is in issue, not Quebeckers' need for a public health care system.

. . .

I. Legislative Context

[16] ... The debate about the effectiveness of public health care has become an emotional one. The Romanow Report [Canada, Commission on the Future of Health Care in Canada, *Building on Values: The Future of Health Care in Canada* (Ottawa, 2002)] stated that the *Canada Health Act* [RSC 1985, c. C-6] has achieved an iconic status that makes it untouchable by politicians ... . The tone adopted by my colleagues Binnie and LeBel JJ is indicative of this type of emotional reaction. It leads them to characterize the debate as pitting rich against poor when the case is really about determining whether a specific measure is justified under either the *Quebec Charter* or the *Canadian Charter*. I believe that it is essential to take a step back and consider these various reactions objectively. The *Canada Health Act* does not prohibit private health care services, nor does it provide benchmarks for the length of waiting times that might be regarded as consistent with the principles it lays down, and in particular with the principle of real accessibility.

[17] In reality, a large proportion of health care is delivered by the private sector. First, there are health care services in respect of which the private sector acts, in a sense, as a subcontractor and is paid by the state. There are also many services that are not delivered by the state, such as home care or care provided by professionals other than physicians. ... In the case of private sector services that are not covered by the public plan, Quebeckers may take out private insurance without the spectre of the two-tier system being evoked. The *Canada Health Act* is therefore only a general framework that leaves considerable latitude to the provinces. In analysing the justification for the prohibition, I will have occasion to briefly review some of the provisions of Canada's provincial plans. The range of measures shows that there are many ways to deal with the public sector/private sector dynamic without resorting to a ban.

. . .

V. Infringement of the Rights Protected by Section 1 of the Quebec Charter

[37] The appellant Zeliotis argues that the prohibition infringes Quebeckers' right to life. Some patients die as a result of long waits for treatment in the public system when they could have gained prompt access to care in the private sector. Were it not for [the impugned provisions], they could buy private insurance and receive care in the private sector.

[38] The Superior Court judge stated [TRANSLATION] "that there [are] serious problems in certain sectors of the health care system" (at p. 823). The evidence supports that assertion. After meticulously analysing the evidence, she found that the right to life and liberty protected by s. 7 of the Canadian Charter had been infringed. ... [T]he trial judge's findings of fact concerning the infringement of the right to life and liberty protected by s. 7 of the *Canadian Charter* apply to the right protected by s. 1 of the Quebec Charter.

[39] Not only is it common knowledge that health care in Quebec is subject to waiting times, but a number of witnesses acknowledged that the demand for health care is potentially unlimited and that waiting lists are a more or less implicit form of rationing ... . Waiting lists are therefore real and intentional. ...

[40] [Because of a monthly rise in the risk of mortality due, according to a physician witness, to waiting times], [t]he right to life is therefore affected by the delays that are the necessary result of waiting lists. ...

· · ·

[44] In the opinion of my colleagues Binnie and LeBel JJ, there is an internal mechanism that safeguards the public health system. According to them, Quebeckers may go outside the province for treatment where services are not available in Quebec. This possibility is clearly not a solution for the system's deficiencies. The evidence did not bring to light any administrative mechanism that would permit Quebeckers suffering as a result of waiting times to obtain care outside the province. The possibility of obtaining care outside Quebec is case-specific and is limited to crisis situations.

[45] I find that the trial judge did not err in finding that the prohibition on insurance for health care already insured by the state constitutes an infringement of the right to life and security. ... Quebeckers are denied a solution that would permit them to avoid waiting lists, which are used as a tool to manage the public plan. ...

VI. Justification for the Prohibition

· · ·

A. Purpose of the Statute

[49] ... The general objective of [the impugned] statutes is to promote health care of the highest possible quality for all Quebeckers regardless of their ability to pay. Quality of care and equality of access are two inseparable objectives under the statutes.

· · ·

[52] The *HOIA* and the *HEIA* provide that, within the framework they establish, the state is responsible for the provision and funding of health services. ... [A detailed review of the legislation and its administration is omitted.]

[53] It can be seen from this brief review of the legislation governing health services that such services are controlled almost entirely by the state.

. . .

[55] Section 11 *HOIA* and s. 15 *HEIA* convey [very clearly the intention of the Quebec legislature to limit the provision of private services outside the public plan]. They render any proposal to develop private professional services almost illusory. The prohibition on private insurance creates an obstacle that is practically insurmountable for people with average incomes. Only the very wealthy can reasonably afford to pay for entirely private services. ... These effects must not be confused with the objective of the legislation. According to the Attorney General of Quebec, the purpose of the prohibition is to preserve the integrity of the public health care system. From this perspective, the objective appears at first glance to be pressing and substantial. Its pressing and substantial nature can be confirmed by considering the historical context.

[56] Government involvement in health care came about gradually. Initially limited to extreme cases, such as epidemics or infectious diseases, the government's role has expanded to become a safety net that ensures that the poorest people have access to basic health care services. The enactment of the first legislation providing for universal health care was a response to a need for social justice. ... Since the government passed legislation based on its view that it had to be the principal actor in the health care sphere, it is easy to understand its distrust of the private sector. At the stage of analysis of the objective of the legislation, I believe that preserving the public plan is a pressing and substantial purpose.

B. Proportionality

(1) Rational Connection

. . .

[58] ... Although the effect of a measure is not always indicative of a rational connection between the measure and its objective, in the instant case the consequences show an undeniable connection between the objective and the measure. The public plan is preserved because it has a quasi-monopoly.

(2) Minimal Impairment

. . .

(a) The Experts Who Testified at Trial and Whose Evidence Was Accepted by the Superior Court Judge

. . .

(i) HUMAN REACTIONS

. . .

[64] It is apparent from this summary that for each threat mentioned, no study was produced or discussed in the Superior Court. While it is true that scientific or empirical evidence is not always necessary, witnesses in a case in which the arguments are supposedly based on logic or common sense should be able to cite specific facts in support of their conclusions. The human reactions described by the experts, many of whom came from outside Quebec, do not appear to me to be very convincing, particularly in the context of Quebec legislation. Participation in the public plan is mandatory and there is

no risk that the Quebec public will abandon the public plan. The state's role is not being called into question. As well, the *HEIA* contains a clear provision authorizing the Minister of Health to ensure that the public plan is not jeopardized by having too many physicians opt for the private system (s. 30 *HEIA*). The evidence that the existence of the health care system would be jeopardized by human reactions to the emergence of a private system carries little weight.

(ii) IMPACT ON THE PUBLIC PLAN

. . .

[68] ... [T]he [trial] judge's finding that the appellants had failed to show that the scope of the prohibition was excessive and that the principles of fundamental justice had not been violated was based solely on the "fear" of an erosion of resources or a [TRANSLATION] "threat [to] the integrity" of the system (at p. 827; emphasis deleted). But the appellants did not have the burden of disproving every fear or every threat. The onus was on the Attorney General of Quebec to justify the prohibition. Binnie and LeBel JJ rely on a similar test in asserting that private health care would likely have an impact on the public plan. This standard does not meet the requirement of preponderance under s. 9.1 of the *Quebec Charter*. It can be seen from the evidence that the Attorney General of Quebec failed to discharge his burden of proving that a total prohibition on private insurance met the minimal impairment test.

[69] There is other evidence in the record that might be of assistance in the justification analysis. In this regard, it is useful to observe the approaches of the other Canadian provinces because they also operate within the financial framework established by the *Canada Health Act*.

(b) Overview of Other Provincial Plans

[70] The approach to the role of the private sector taken by the other nine provinces of Canada is by no means uniform. In addition to Quebec, six other provinces have adopted measures to discourage people from turning to the private sector. The other three, in practice, give their residents free access to the private sector.

. . .

[74] Even if it were assumed that the prohibition on private insurance could contribute to preserving the integrity of the system, the variety of measures implemented by different provinces shows that prohibiting insurance contracts is by no means the only measure a state can adopt to protect the system's integrity. In fact, because there is no indication that the public plans of the three provinces that are open to the private sector suffer from deficiencies that are not present in the plans of the other provinces, it must be deduced that the effectiveness of the measure in protecting the integrity of the system has not been proved. The example illustrated by a number of other Canadian provinces casts doubt on the argument that the integrity of the public plan depends on the prohibition against private insurance. Obviously, since Quebec's public plan is in a quasi-monopoly position, its predominance is assured. Also, the regimes of the provinces where a private system is authorized demonstrate that public health services are not threatened by private insurance. It can therefore be concluded that the prohibition is not necessary to guarantee the integrity of the public plan.

[75] In the context of s. 9.1 of the Quebec Charter, I must conclude that a comparison with the plans of the other Canadian provinces does not support the position of the Attorney General of Quebec.

. . .

(c) Overview of Practices in Certain OECD Countries

. . .

[82] It can be seen from the systems in these various OECD countries that a number of governments have taken measures to protect their public plans from abuse. The measures vary from country to country depending on the nature of their specific systems. ...

[83] As can be seen from the evolution of public plans in the few OECD countries that have been examined in studies produced in the record, there are a wide range of measures that are less drastic, and also less intrusive in relation to the protected rights. ... A measure as drastic as prohibiting private insurance contracts appears to be neither essential nor determinative.

[84] It cannot therefore be concluded from the evidence relating to the Quebec plan or the plans of the other provinces of Canada, or from the evolution of the systems in place in various OECD countries, that the Attorney General of Quebec has discharged his burden of proof under s. 9.1 of the Quebec Charter. A number of measures are available to him to protect the integrity of Quebec's health care plan. The choice of prohibiting private insurance contracts is not justified by the evidence. However, is this a case in which the Court should show deference?

(d) Level of Deference Required

[85] ... [A]s can be seen from the large number of interveners in this appeal, differences of views over the emergence of a private health care plan have a polarizing effect on the debate, and the question of the deference owed to the government by the courts must be addressed. Some of the interveners urge the courts to step in, while others argue that this is the role of the state. It must be possible to base the criteria for judicial intervention on legal principles and not on a socio-political discourse that is disconnected from reality.

. . .

[89] The courts have a duty to rise above political debate. They leave it to the legislatures to develop social policy. But when such social policies infringe rights that are protected by the charters, the courts cannot shy away from considering them. The judicial branch plays a role that is not played by the legislative branch. [As K. Roach has stated in "Dialogic Judicial Review and Its Critics" (2004), 23 *Supreme Court Law Review* 49, at 71:]

> Judges can add value to societal debates about justice by listening to claims of injustice and by promoting values and perspectives that may not otherwise be taken seriously in the legislative process.

. . .

[91] To refuse to exercise the power set out in s. 52 of the Quebec Charter [that Charter's primacy clause] would be to deny that provision its real meaning and to deprive Quebeckers of the protection to which they are entitled.

[92] In a given case, a court may find that evidence could not be presented for reasons that it considers valid, be it due to the complexity of the evidence or to some other factor. However, the government cannot argue that the evidence is too complex without explaining why it cannot be presented. If such an explanation is given, the court may show greater deference to the government. Based on the extent of the impairment and the complexity of the evidence considered to be necessary, the court can determine whether the government has discharged its burden of proof.

· · ·

[95] In short, a court must show deference where the evidence establishes that the government has assigned proper weight to each of the competing interests. Certain factors favour greater deference, such as the prospective nature of the decision, the impact on public finances, the multiplicity of competing interests, the difficulty of presenting scientific evidence and the limited time available to the state. This list is certainly not exhaustive. It serves primarily to highlight the facts that it is up to the government to choose the measure, that the decision is often complex and difficult, and that the government must have the necessary time and resources to respond. ...

[96] The instant case is a good example of a case in which the courts have all the necessary tools to evaluate the government's measure. Ample evidence was presented. The government had plenty of time to act. Numerous commissions have been established ... , and special or independent committees have published reports .... Governments have promised on numerous occasions to find a solution to the problem of waiting lists. Given the tendency to focus the debate on a sociopolitical philosophy, it seems that governments have lost sight of the urgency of taking concrete action. The courts are therefore the last line of defence for citizens.

[97] For many years, the government has failed to act; the situation continues to deteriorate. This is not a case in which missing scientific data would allow for a more informed decision to be made. The principle of prudence that is so popular in matters relating to the environment and to medical research cannot be transposed to this case. Under the Quebec plan, the government can control its human resources in various ways, whether by using the time of professionals who have already reached the maximum for payment by the state, by applying the provision that authorizes it to compel even non-participating physicians to provide services (s. 30 *HEIA*) or by implementing less restrictive measures, like those adopted in the four Canadian provinces that do not prohibit private insurance or in the other OECD countries. While the government has the power to decide what measures to adopt, it cannot choose to do nothing in the face of the violation of Quebeckers' right to security. The government has not given reasons for its failure to act. Inertia cannot be used as an argument to justify deference.

[98] In the instant case, the effectiveness of the prohibition has by no means been established. The government has not proved, by the evidence in the record, that the measure minimally impairs the protected rights. Moreover, the evidence shows that a wide variety of measures are available to governments, as can be seen from the plans of other provinces and other countries.

· · ·

McLACHLIN CJC and MAJOR J (Bastarache J concurring): [Agreeing with Deschamps J's conclusion as to the invalidity of the impugned provisions in respect of the *Quebec Charter of Human Rights and Freedoms*, McLachlin CJC and Major J focused their analysis on the *Canadian Charter of Rights and Freedoms*.]

[103] The appellants do not seek an order that the government spend more money on health care, nor do they seek an order that waiting times for treatment under the public health care scheme be reduced. They only seek a ruling that because delays in the public system place their health and security at risk, they should be allowed to take out insurance to permit them to access private services.

[104]] The Charter does not confer a freestanding constitutional right to health care. However, where the government puts in place a scheme to provide health care, that scheme must comply with the Charter. ...

[106] The *Canada Health Act*, the *Health Insurance Act*, and the *Hospital Insurance Act* do not expressly prohibit private health services. However, they limit access to private health services by removing the ability to contract for private health care insurance to cover the same services covered by public insurance. The result is a virtual monopoly for the public health scheme. The state has effectively limited access to private health care except for the very rich, who can afford private care without need of insurance. This virtual monopoly, on the evidence, results in delays in treatment that adversely affect the citizen's security of the person. Where a law adversely affects life, liberty or security of the person, it must conform to the principles of fundamental justice. This law, in our view, fails to do so.

[107] While the decision about the type of health care system Quebec should adopt falls to the Legislature of that province, the resulting legislation, like all laws, is subject to constitutional limits, including those imposed by s. 7 of the Charter. The fact that the matter is complex, contentious or laden with social values does not mean that the courts can abdicate the responsibility vested in them by our Constitution to review legislation for Charter compliance when citizens challenge it. ...

[108] ... The question in this case, however, is not whether single-tier health care is preferable to two-tier health care. Even if one accepts the government's goal, the legal question raised by the appellants must be addressed: is it a violation of s. 7 of the Charter to prohibit private insurance for health care, when the result is to subject Canadians to long delays with resultant risk of physical and psychological harm? The mere fact that this question may have policy ramifications does not permit us to avoid answering it.

I. Section 7 of the Charter

. . .

A. Deprivation of Life, Liberty or Security of the Person

[110] The issue at this stage is whether the prohibition on insurance for private medical care deprives individuals of their life, liberty or security of the person protected by s. 7 of the Charter.

[111] The appellants have established that many Quebec residents face delays in treatment that adversely affect their security of the person and that they would not sustain but

for the prohibition on medical insurance. It is common ground that the effect of the prohibition on insurance is to allow only the very rich, who do not need insurance, to secure
private health care in order to avoid the delays in the public system. Given the ban on insurance, most Quebeckers have no choice but to accept delays in the medical system and
their adverse physical and psychological consequences.

[After reviewing the evidence adduced at trial, McLachlin CJC and Major J reached the
same conclusion as Deschamps J, emphasizing both the physical and psychological consequences of waiting times on patients.]

[118] [Reference is made to *R v. Morgentaler*, [1988] 1 SCR 30, 44 DLR (4th) 385.] The
jurisprudence of this Court holds that delays in obtaining medical treatment which affect
patients physically and psychologically trigger the protection of s. 7 of the Charter. ...

[119] In this appeal, delays in treatment giving rise to psychological and physical
suffering engage the s. 7 protection of security of the person just as they did in *Morgentaler*. In *Morgentaler*, as in this case, the problem arises from a legislative scheme that offers health services. In *Morgentaler*, as in this case, the legislative scheme denies people
the right to access alternative health care. (That the sanction in *Morgentaler* was criminal
prosecution while the sanction here is administrative prohibition and penalties is irrelevant. The important point is that in both cases, care outside the legislatively provided
system is effectively prohibited.) In *Morgentaler* the result of the monopolistic scheme
was delay in treatment with attendant physical risk and psychological suffering. In *Morgentaler*, as here, people in urgent need of care face the same prospect: unless they fall
within the wealthy few who can pay for private care, typically outside the country, they
have no choice but to accept the delays imposed by the legislative scheme and the adverse
physical and psychological consequences this entails. As in *Morgentaler*, the result is
interference with security of the person under s. 7 of the Charter.

. . .

[121] The issue in *Morgentaler* was whether a system for obtaining approval for
abortions (as an exception to a prohibition) that in practice imposed significant delays
in obtaining medical treatment unjustifiably violated s. 7 of the Charter. Parliament had
established a mandatory system for obtaining medical care in the termination of pregnancy. The sanction by which the mandatory public system was maintained differed:
criminal in *Morgentaler*, "administrative" in the case at bar. Yet the consequences for the
individual in both cases are serious. In *Morgentaler*, as here, the system left the individual
facing a lack of critical care with no choice but to travel outside the country to obtain the
required medical care at her own expense. It was this constraint on s. 7 security, taken
from the perspective of the woman facing the health care system, and not the criminal
sanction, that drove the majority analysis in *Morgentaler*. We therefore conclude that the
decision provides guidance in the case at bar.

. . .

[123] Not every difficulty rises to the level of adverse impact on security of the person under s. 7. The impact, whether psychological or physical, must be serious. However,
because patients may be denied timely health care for a condition that is clinically signifi-

cant to their current and future health, s. 7 protection of security of the person is engaged. Access to a waiting list is not access to health care. As we noted above, there is unchallenged evidence that in some serious cases, patients die as a result of waiting lists for public health care. Where lack of timely health care can result in death, s. 7 protection of life itself is engaged. The evidence here demonstrates that the prohibition on health insurance results in physical and psychological suffering that meets this threshold requirement of seriousness.

[124] We conclude, based on the evidence, that prohibiting health insurance that would permit ordinary Canadians to access health care, in circumstances where the government is failing to deliver health care in a reasonable manner, thereby increasing the risk of complications and death, interferes with life and security of the person as protected by s. 7 of the Charter.

. . .

B. Deprivation in Accordance with the Principles of Fundamental Justice

. . .

(1) Laws Shall Not Be Arbitrary: A Principle of Fundamental Justice

[129] It is a well-recognized principle of fundamental justice that laws should not be arbitrary: see, e.g., *Malmo-Levine* [2003 SCC 74, [2003] 3 SCR 571, 233 DLR (4th) 415], at para. 135; *Rodriguez* [[1993] 3 SCR 519], at p. 594. ...

[130] A law is arbitrary where "it bears no relation to, or is inconsistent with, the objective that lies behind [it]." To determine whether this is the case, it is necessary to consider the state interest and societal concerns that the provision is meant to reflect: *Rodriguez*, at pp. 594-95.

[131] In order not to be arbitrary, the limit on life, liberty and security requires not only a theoretical connection between the limit and the legislative goal, but a real connection on the facts. The onus of showing lack of connection in this sense rests with the claimant. The question in every case is whether the measure is arbitrary in the sense of bearing no real relation to the goal and hence being manifestly unfair. The more serious the impingement on the person's liberty and security, the more clear must be the connection. Where the individual's very life may be at stake, the reasonable person would expect a clear connection, in theory and in fact, between the measure that puts life at risk and the legislative goals.

. . .

[133] ... Beetz J's concurring reasons in *Morgentaler* ... serve as an example of how the rule against arbitrariness may be implicated in the particular context of access to health care. The fact that Dickson CJ, Lamer J concurring, found that the scheme offended a different principle of fundamental justice, namely that defences to criminal charges must not be illusory, does not detract from the proposition adopted by Beetz J that rules that endanger health arbitrarily do not comply with the principles of fundamental justice.

(2) Whether the Prohibition on Private Medical Insurance Is Arbitrary

. . .

[135] The government argues that the interference with security of the person caused by denying people the right to purchase private health insurance is necessary to providing effective health care under the public health system. It argues that if people can purchase private health insurance, they will seek treatment from private doctors and hospitals, which are not banned under the Act. According to the government's argument, this will divert resources from the public health system into private health facilities, ultimately reducing the quality of public care.

. . .

[137] The appellants ... disagreed and offered their own conflicting "common sense" argument for the proposition that prohibiting private health insurance is neither necessary nor related to maintaining high quality in the public health care system. Quality public care, they argue, depends not on a monopoly, but on money and management. They testified that permitting people to buy private insurance would make alternative medical care more accessible and reduce the burden on the public system. The result, they assert, would be better care for all. The appellants reinforce this argument by pointing out that disallowing private insurance precludes the vast majority of Canadians (middle-income and low-income earners) from accessing additional care, while permitting it for the wealthy who can afford to travel abroad or pay for private care in Canada.

[138] To this point, we are confronted with competing but unproven "common sense" arguments, amounting to little more than assertions of belief. We are in the realm of theory. But as discussed above, a theoretically defensible limitation may be arbitrary if in fact the limit lacks a connection to the goal.

[139] This brings us to the evidence called by the appellants at trial on the experience of other developed countries with public health care systems which permit access to private health care. The experience of these countries suggests that there is no real connection in fact between prohibition of health insurance and the goal of a quality public health system.

[140] The evidence adduced at trial establishes that many western democracies that do not impose a monopoly on the delivery of health care have successfully delivered to their citizens medical services that are superior to and more affordable than the services that are presently available in Canada. This demonstrates that a monopoly is not necessary or even related to the provision of quality public health care.

. . .

[149] In summary, the evidence on the experience of other western democracies refutes the government's theoretical contention that a prohibition on private insurance is linked to maintaining quality public health care.

[150] Binnie and LeBel JJ suggest that the experience of other countries is of little assistance. With respect, we cannot agree. This evidence was properly placed before the trial judge and, unless discredited, stands as the best guide with respect to the question of whether a ban on private insurance is necessary and relevant to the goal of providing quality public health care. The task of the courts, on s. 7 issues as on others, is to evaluate the issue in the light, not just of common sense or theory, but of the evidence. This is

supported by our jurisprudence, according to which the experience of other western democracies may be relevant in assessing alleged arbitrariness. ...

[151] Binnie and LeBel JJ also suggest that the government's continued commitment to a monopoly on the provision of health insurance cannot be arbitrary because it is rooted in reliance on "a series of authoritative reports [that analysed] health care in this country and in other countries" (para. 258); ... . We observe in passing that the import of these reports, which differ in many of their conclusions, is a matter of some debate, as attested by our earlier reference to the Kirby Report [Canada Senate, Standing Committee on Social Affairs, Science and Technology, *The Health of Canadians—The Federal Role*, Final Report, 2002]. But the conclusions of other bodies on other material cannot be determinative of this litigation. They cannot relieve the courts of their obligation to review government action for consistency with the Charter on the evidence before them.

[152] When we look to the evidence rather than to assumptions, the connection between prohibiting private insurance and maintaining quality public health care vanishes. The evidence before us establishes that where the public system fails to deliver adequate care, the denial of private insurance subjects people to long waiting lists and negatively affects their health and security of the person. The government contends that this is necessary in order to preserve the public health system. The evidence, however, belies that contention.

[153] We conclude that on the evidence adduced in this case, the appellants have established that in the face of delays in treatment that cause psychological and physical suffering, the prohibition on private insurance jeopardizes the right to life, liberty and security of the person of Canadians in an arbitrary manner, and is therefore not in accordance with the principles of fundamental justice.

II. *Section 1 of the Charter*

• • •

[155] The government undeniably has an interest in protecting the public health regime. However, given the absence of evidence that the prohibition on the purchase and sale of private health insurance protects the health care system, the rational connection between the prohibition and the objective is not made out. Indeed, we question whether an arbitrary provision, which by reason of its arbitrariness cannot further its stated objective, will ever meet the rational connection test under *R v. Oakes*, [1986] 1 SCR 103.

[156] In addition, the resulting denial of access to timely and effective medical care to those who need it is not proportionate to the beneficial effects of the prohibition on private insurance to the health system as a whole. On the evidence here and for the reasons discussed above, the prohibition goes further than necessary to protect the public system: it is not minimally impairing.

[157] Finally, the benefits of the prohibition do not outweigh the deleterious effects. Prohibiting citizens from obtaining private health care insurance may, as discussed, leave people no choice but to accept excessive delays in the public health system. The physical and psychological suffering and risk of death that may result outweigh whatever benefit (and none has been demonstrated to us here) there may be to the system as a whole.

• • •

BINNIE and LeBEL JJ (dissenting) (Fish J concurring):

I. Introduction

[161] The question in this appeal is whether the province of Quebec not only has the constitutional authority to establish a comprehensive single-tier health plan, but to discourage a second (private) tier health sector by prohibiting the purchase and sale of private health insurance. The appellants argue that timely access to needed medical service is not being provided in the publicly funded system and that the province cannot therefore deny to those Quebeckers (who can qualify) the right to purchase private insurance to pay for medical services whenever and wherever such services can be obtained for a fee, *i.e.*, in the private sector. ... We are unable to agree with our four colleagues who would allow the appeal that such a debate can or should be resolved as a matter of law by judges. ...

[163] The Court recently held in *Auton (Guardian ad litem of) v. British Columbia (Attorney General)*, [2004] 3 SCR 657[245 DLR (4th) 411], 2004 SCC 78, that the government was not required to fund the treatment of autistic children. It did not on that occasion address in constitutional terms the scope and nature of "reasonable" health services. Courts will now have to make that determination. What, then, are constitutionally required "reasonable health services"? What is treatment "within a reasonable time"? What are the benchmarks? How short a waiting list is short enough? How many MRIs does the Constitution require? The majority does not tell us. The majority lays down no manageable constitutional standard. The public cannot know, nor can judges or governments know, how much health care is "reasonable" enough to satisfy s. 7 of the *Canadian Charter of Rights and Freedoms* ("Canadian Charter") and s. 1 of the *Charter of Human Rights and Freedoms*, RSQ c. C-12 ("Quebec Charter"). It is to be hoped that we will know it when we see it.

[164] The policy of the *Canada Health Act*, RSC 1985, c. C-6, and its provincial counterparts is to provide health care based on need rather than on wealth or status. The evidence certainly established that the public health care system put in place to implement this policy has serious and persistent problems. This does not mean that the courts are well placed to perform the required surgery. The resolution of such a complex fact-laden policy debate does not fit easily within the institutional competence or procedures of courts of law. The courts can use s. 7 of the Canadian Charter to pre-empt the ongoing public debate only if the current health plan violates an established "principle of fundamental justice." Our colleagues McLachlin CJ and Major J argue that Quebec's enforcement of a single-tier health plan meets this legal test because it is "arbitrary." In our view, with respect, the prohibition against private health insurance is a rational consequence of Quebec's commitment to the goals and objectives of the *Canada Health Act*.

[165] ... [I]t must be recognized that the liberty and security of Quebeckers who do *not* have the money to afford private health insurance, or who cannot qualify for it, or who are not employed by establishments that provide it, are not put at risk by the absence of "upper tier" health care. It is Quebeckers who have the money to afford private medical insurance and can qualify for it who will be the beneficiaries of the appellants' constitutional challenge.

[166] The Quebec government views the prohibition against private insurance as essential to preventing the current single-tier health system from disintegrating into a *de*

facto two-tier system. The trial judge found, and the evidence demonstrated, that there is good reason for this fear. The trial judge concluded that a private health sector fuelled by private insurance would frustrate achievement of the objectives of the *Canada Health Act*. She thus found no *legal* basis to intervene, and declined to do so. This raises the issue of *who* it is that *should* resolve these important and contentious issues. … [T]he debate is about *social* values. It is not about constitutional law. …

[167] We believe our colleagues the Chief Justice and Major J have extended too far the strands of interpretation under the *Canadian Charter* laid down in some of the earlier cases, in particular the ruling on abortion in *R v. Morgentaler*, [1988] 1 SCR 30 [44 DLR (4th) 385] (which involved criminal liability, not public health policy). We cannot find in the constitutional law of Canada a "principle of fundamental justice" dispositive of the problems of waiting lists in the Quebec health system. In our view, the appellants' case does not rest on constitutional law but on their disagreement with the Quebec government on aspects of its social policy. The proper forum to determine the social policy of Quebec in this matter is the National Assembly.

[168] … There is nothing in the evidence to justify our colleagues' disagreement with [the trial judge's] conclusion that the general availability of health insurance will lead to a significant expansion of the private health sector to the detriment of the public health sector. While no one doubts that the Quebec health plan is under sustained and heavy criticism, … [a]s a matter of law, we see no reason to interfere with [lower courts'] collective and unanimous judgment on this point. Whatever else it might be, the prohibition is not arbitrary.

[169] We can all support the vague objective of "public health care of a reasonable standard within a reasonable time." Most people have opinions, many of them conflicting, about how to achieve it. A legislative policy is not "arbitrary" just because we may disagree with it. As our colleagues the Chief Justice and Major J fully recognize, the legal test of "arbitrariness" is quite well established in the earlier case law. … Suffice it to say at this point that in our view, the appellants' argument about "arbitrariness" is based largely on generalizations about the public system drawn from fragmentary experience, an overly optimistic view of the benefits offered by private health insurance, an oversimplified view of the adverse effects on the public health system of permitting private sector health services to flourish and an overly interventionist view of the role the courts should play in trying to supply a "fix" to the failings, real or perceived, of major social programs.

A. The Argument About Adding an "Upper Tier" to the Quebec Health Plan

[170] … It is evident, of course, that neither Quebec nor any of the other provinces has a "pure" single-tier system. In the area of *un*insured medical services, for example, the private sector is the dominant supplier. In other cases, the private sector may perform the service but is paid by the state. The issue here, as it is so often in social policy debates, is where to draw the line. One can rarely say in such matters that one side of a line is "right" and the other side of a line is "wrong." Still less can we say that the boundaries of the Quebec health plan are dictated by the Constitution. Drawing the line around social programs properly falls within the legitimate exercise of the democratic mandates of people elected for such purposes, preferably after a public debate.

B. Background to the Health Policy Debate

[171] Prior to 1961, only 53 per cent of Canadians were covered by some form of health insurance, leaving approximately 8 million Canadians without insurance coverage ... . At that time, health care costs were the number one cause of personal bankruptcy in Canada.

[172] In these circumstances, the people of Quebec, through their elected representatives, opted for a need-based, rather than a wealth-based, health care system. ...

[173] ... Both the Kirby Report and the Romanow Report contained extensive investigations into the operations and problems of the current public health systems across Canada. They acknowledged that the financing of health care is putting a growing stress on public finances and national resources. ... Whether this growing level of expenditure is sustainable, justified or wise is a matter on which we all have opinions. In the absence of a violation of a recognized "principle of fundamental justice," the opinions that prevail should be those of the legislatures.

[174] Not all Canadian provinces prohibit private health insurance, but all of them (with the arguable exception of Newfoundland) take steps to protect the public health system by discouraging the private sector, whether by prohibiting private insurance (Quebec, Ontario, Manitoba, British Columbia, Alberta and Prince Edward Island) or by prohibiting doctors who opt out of the public sector, from billing their private patients more than the public sector tariff, thereby dulling the incentive to opt out (Ontario, Manitoba and Nova Scotia), or eliminating any form of cross-subsidy from the public to the private sector (Quebec, British Columbia, Alberta, Prince Edward Island, Saskatchewan and New Brunswick). The mixture of deterrents differs from province to province, but the underlying policies flow from the *Canada Health Act* and are the same: i.e. as a matter of principle, health care should be based on need, not wealth, and as a matter of practicality the provinces judge that growth of the private sector will undermine the strength of the public sector and its ability to achieve the objectives of the *Canada Health Act*.

[175] The argument for a "two-tier system" is that it will enable "ordinary" Canadians to access private health care. Indeed, this is the view taken by our colleagues the Chief Justice and Major J ... . This way of putting the argument suggests that the Court has a mandate to save middle-income and low-income Quebeckers from themselves ... . Our colleagues rely in part on the experience in the United States (para. 148) and the fact that public funding in that country accounts for only 45 per cent of total health care spending. But if we look at the practical reality of the US system, the fact is that 15.6 per cent of the American population (*i.e.*, about 45 million people) had no health insurance coverage at all in 2003, including about 8.4 million children. As to making health care available to medium and low-income families, the effect of "two-tier" health coverage in the US is much worse for minority groups than for the majority. Hispanics had an uninsured rate of 32.7 per cent, and African Americans had an uninsured rate of 19.4 per cent. For 45 million Americans, as for those "ordinary" Quebeckers who cannot afford private medical insurance or cannot obtain it because they are deemed to be "bad risks," it is a matter of public health care or no care at all ... .

[176] It would be open to Quebec to adopt a US-style health care system. No one suggests that there is anything in our Constitution to prevent it. But to do so would be contrary

to the policy of the Quebec National Assembly, and its policy in that respect is shared by the other provinces and the federal Parliament. As stated, Quebec further takes the view that significant growth in the private health care system (which the appellants advocate) would inevitably damage the public system. Our colleagues the Chief Justice and Major J disagree with this assessment, but governments are entitled to act on a reasonable apprehension of risk of such damage. ... While the existence of waiting times is undoubted, and their management a matter of serious public concern, the proposed constitutional right to a two-tier health system for those who can afford private medical insurance would precipitate a seismic shift in health policy for Quebec. We do not believe that such a seismic shift is compelled by either the Quebec Charter or the Canadian Charter.

II. Analysis

• • •

[180] Our colleagues the Chief Justice and Major J agree with the appellants that there is a violation of s. 7 of the Canadian Charter. As mentioned earlier, their opinion rests in substantial part on observations made by various members of this Court in *Morgentaler*. At issue in that case was the criminal liability of doctors and their patients under s. 251 of the *Criminal Code*, R.S.C. 1970, c. C-34, for performing abortions. The nub of the legal challenge was that in creating the abortion offence Parliament had qualified the charge with a "therapeutic abortion" defence, but the defence was not working. The factual and legal issues raised in that criminal law problem are, we think, far removed from the debate over a two-tiered health system. *Morgentaler* applied a "manifest unfairness" test which has never been adopted by the Court outside the criminal law, and certainly not in the context of the design of social programs. The *Morgentaler* judgment fastened on internal inconsistencies in s. 251 of the [*Criminal*] *Code*, which find no counterpart here. In our view, with respect, *Morgentaler* provides no support for the appellants in this case, as we discuss commencing at para. 259.

[181] As stated, we accept the finding of the courts below that a two-tier health care system would likely have a negative impact on the integrity, functioning and viability of the public system ... . Although this finding is disputed by our colleagues the Chief Justice and Major J (a point to which we will return), it cannot be contested that as a matter of *principle*, access to *private* health care based on wealth rather than need contradicts one of the key social policy objectives expressed in the *Canada Health Act*. The state has established its interest in promoting the *equal* treatment of its citizens in terms of health care. The issue of arbitrariness relates only to the validity of the *means* adopted to achieve that policy objective. ... While Quebec does not outlaw private health care, which is therefore accessible to those with cash on hand, it wishes to discourage its growth. Failure to stop the few people with ready cash does not pose a structural threat to the Quebec health plan. Failure to stop private health insurance will, as the trial judge found, do so. Private insurance is a condition precedent to, and aims at promoting, a flourishing parallel private health care sector. For Dr. Chaoulli in particular, that is the whole point of this proceeding.

• • •

B. The Canadian Charter of Rights and Freedoms

· · ·

(1) The Application of Section 7 to Matters Not Falling Within the Administration of Justice

· · ·

[195] The present challenge does not arise out of an adjudicative context or one involving the administration of justice. ... Section 11 is a *civil* prohibition against the making or renewing of a contract for insurance for "insured services" and against the payment under such a contract for "insured services." Any contract entered into in contravention of s. 11 and s. 15 would be absolutely null and unenforceable because it is contrary to the general interest: art. 1417 of the *Civil Code of Québec*, S.Q. 1991, c. 64. Although small fines may be imposed for the breach of these provisions, we think that regulations providing for such fines, which are wholly incidental to the regulatory purpose, would not create a sufficient nexus with the adjudicative context to ground the application of s. 7 on that basis.

[196] It will likely be a rare case where s. 7 will apply in circumstances entirely unrelated to adjudicative or administrative proceedings.

· · ·

[199] Claimants whose life, liberty or security of the person is put at risk are entitled to relief only to the extent that their complaint arises from a breach of an identifiable principle of fundamental justice. *The real control over the scope and operation of s. 7 is to be found in the requirement that the applicant identify a violation of a principle of fundamental justice.* The further a challenged state action lies from the traditional adjudicative context, the more difficult it will be for a claimant to make that essential link. As will become clear, that is precisely the difficulty encountered by the claimants here: they are unable to demonstrate that any principle of fundamental justice has been contravened.

(2) Which Section 7 Interests Are Engaged?

[200] Section 7 interests are enumerated as life, liberty and security of the person. As stated, we accept the trial judge's finding that the current state of the Quebec health system, linked to the prohibition against health insurance for insured services, is capable, at least in the cases of *some* individuals on *some* occasions, of putting at risk their life or security of the person.

[201] We do not agree with the appellants, however, that the *Quebec Health Plan* puts the "liberty" of Quebeckers at risk. The argument that "liberty" includes freedom of contract (in this case to contract for private medical insurance) is novel in Canada, where economic rights are not included in the Charter and discredited in the United States. In that country, the liberty of individuals (mainly employers) to contract out of social and economic programs was endorsed by the Supreme Court in the early decades of the 20th century on the theory that laws that prohibited employers from entering into oppressive contracts with employees violated their "liberty" of contract; see, e.g., *Lochner v. New York*, 198 US 45 (1905) ... .

[202] Nor do we accept that s. 7 of the Canadian Charter guarantees Dr. Chaoulli the "liberty" to deliver health care in a private context. ... The fact that state action constrains an individual's freedom by eliminating career choices that would otherwise be available does not in itself attract the protection of the liberty interest under s. 7. The liberty interest does not, for example, include the right to transact business whenever one wishes: *R v. Edwards Books and Art Ltd.*, [1986] 2 SCR 713, at p. 786. Nor does it protect the right to exercise one's chosen profession: *Prostitution Reference* [[1990] 1 SCR 1123, 24 DLR (4th) 536], at p. 1179, per Lamer J. We would therefore reject Dr. Chaoulli's claim on behalf of care providers that their liberty interest under either the Canadian Charter or the Quebec Charter has been infringed by Quebec's single-tier public health system.

(3) Is There a Constitutional Right to Spend Money?

[203] ... While we do not accept that there is a constitutional right "to spend money," which would be a property right, we agree that if the public system fails to deliver life-saving care and an individual is simultaneously prevented from seeking insurance to cover the cost of that care in a private facility, then the individual is potentially caught in a situation that may signal a deprivation of his or her security of the person.

[204] This is not to say that every encounter with a waiting list will trigger the application of s. 7. The interference with one's mental well-being must not be trivial. It must rise above the ordinary anxiety caused by the vicissitudes of life, but it need not be so grave as to lead to serious mental anguish or nervous breakdown. *Some* individuals that meet this test are to be found entangled in the Quebec health system. The fact such individuals do not include the appellants personally is not fatal to their challenge because they come here as plaintiffs purporting to represent the public interest.

[205] The Court has found a deprivation of one's psychological integrity sufficient to ground a s. 7 claim in a range of cases. ...

[206] It may also be that a lack of timely medical intervention will put the physical security of the patient at risk. The condition of a cardiac or cancer patient, for example, may seriously deteriorate if treatment is not available quickly.

[207] As stated, the principal legal hurdle to the appellants' Charter challenge is not the preliminary step of identifying a s. 7 interest potentially affected in the case of some Quebeckers in some circumstances. The hurdle lies in their failure to find a fundamental principle of justice that is violated by the Quebec health plan so as to justify the Court in striking down the prohibition against private insurance for what the government has identified as "insured services."

C. Principles of Fundamental Justice

[208] For a principle to be one of fundamental justice, it must count among the basic tenets of our *legal* system: *Re BC Motor Vehicle Act* [[1985] 2 SCR 486, 24 DLR (4th) 536], at p. 503. It must generally be accepted as such among reasonable people. ...

[209] Thus, the formal requirements for a principle of fundamental justice are threefold. First, it must be a *legal* principle. Second, the reasonable person must regard it as vital to our societal notion of justice, which implies a significant *societal consensus*. Third, it

must be capable of being *identified with precision* and applied in a manner that yields *predictable results*. These requirements present insurmountable hurdles to the appellants. The aim of "health care to a reasonable standard within reasonable time" is not a *legal* principle. There is no "societal consensus" about what it means or how to achieve it. It cannot be "identified with precision." As the testimony in this case showed, a level of care that is considered perfectly reasonable by some doctors is denounced by others. Finally, we think it will be very difficult for those designing and implementing a health plan to predict when its provisions cross the line from what is "reasonable" into the forbidden territory of what is "unreasonable," and how the one is to be distinguished from the other.

• • •

[211] The case history of the appellant Zeliotis illustrates why rationing of health services is necessary and how it works. The trial judge, having heard all the evidence, concluded that the delays Mr. Zeliotis experienced in obtaining hip surgery were caused not by excessive waiting lists but by a number of other factors, including his pre-existing depression and his indecision and unfounded medical complaints ... . Mr. Zeliotis sought a second opinion, which he was entitled to do, and this further delayed his surgery. More importantly, his physician believed that Mr. Zeliotis was not an "ideal candidate" for the surgery because he had suffered a heart attack and undergone bypass surgery earlier that year. Accordingly, neither the mere existence of waiting lists, nor the fact that certain individuals like Mr. Zeliotis feel unfairly dealt with, necessarily points to a constitutional problem with the public health system as a whole.

• • •

[212] A review of the expert evidence and the medical literature suggests that there is no consensus regarding guidelines for timely medical treatment. ... There are currently no national standards for timely treatment ... .

[Binnie and LeBel JJ note that the bulk of expert evidence adduced and accepted by the trial judge is reliable and credible.]

[217] How serious is the waiting-list problem? No doubt it is serious; but how serious? The first major evidentiary difficulty for the appellants is the lack of accurate data. The major studies concluded that the real picture concerning waiting lists in Canada is subject to contradictory evidence and conflicting claims ... .

• • •

[220] It is even more difficult to generalize about the potential impact of a waiting list on a particular patient. ... [After examining the literature, Binnie and LeBel JJ comment:] In other words, waiting lists may be serious in some cases, but in how many cases and how serious?

• • •

[221] Waiting times are not only found in public systems. They are found in all health care systems, be they single-tier private, single-tier public, or the various forms of two-tier public/private ... . The consequence of a quasi-unlimited demand for health care coupled with limited resources, be they public or private, is to ration services. ...

• • •

[223] In a public system founded on the values of equity, solidarity and collective responsibility, rationing occurs on the basis of clinical need rather than wealth and social status ... . As a result, there exists in Canada a phenomenon of "static queues" whereby a group of persons may remain on a waiting list for a considerable time if their situation is not pressing. ... In general, the evidence suggests that patients who need immediate medical care receive it. There are of course exceptions, and these exceptions are properly the focus of controversy, but in our view they can and should be addressed on a case-by-case basis.

. . .

[224] Section 10 of the *Health Insurance Act* provides that in certain circumstances Quebeckers will be reimbursed for the cost of "insured services" rendered outside Quebec but in Canada (*Regulation respecting the application of the Health Insurance Act*, RRQ 1981, s. 23.1), or outside Canada altogether (s. 23.2). There is no doubt that the power of reimbursement is exercised sparingly, and on occasion unlawfully ... . The reimbursement scheme for out-of-province services exists as a form of safety valve for situations in which Quebec facilities are unable to respond. As Stein shows, there are lapses of judgment, as there will be in the administration of any government plan. The existence of the individual remedy, however, introduces an important element of flexibility, if administered properly.

. . .

[225] ... [O]ur colleagues write, "patients die while on waiting lists" (para. 112). This, too, is true. But our colleagues are not advocating an overbuilt system with enough idle capacity to eliminate waiting lists, and such generalized comments provided no guidance for what in practical terms would constitute an appropriate level of resources to meet their suggested standard of "public health care of a reasonable standard within reasonable time" (para. 105).

[226] We have similar concerns about the use made by the appellants of various reports in connection with other OECD countries. ... We think the Court is sufficiently burdened with conflicting evidence about our own health system without attempting a detailed investigation of the merits of trade-offs made in other countries, for their own purposes. ...

[Binnie and LeBel JJ go on to criticize what they perceive as McLachlin CJC and Major J's selective use of evidence about the situation in foreign states.]

[229] We are not to be taken as disputing the undoubted fact that there are serious problems with the single-tier health plan in Canada. Our point is simply that bits of evidence must be put in context. With respect, it is particularly dangerous to venture selectively into aspects of foreign health care systems with which we, as Canadians, have little familiarity. At the very least such information should be filtered and analysed at trial through an expert witness.

. . .

(2) Arbitrariness

[231] Our colleagues the Chief Justice and Major J take the view that a law which arbitrarily violates life or security of the person is unconstitutional. We agree that this is a principle of fundamental justice. We do not agree that it applies to the facts of this case.

[232] A deprivation of a right will be arbitrary and will thus infringe s. 7 if it bears no relation to, or is inconsistent with, the state interest that lies behind the legislation: *Rodriguez* [[1993] 3 SCR 519], at pp. 619-20; *Malmo-Levine* [2003 SCC 74, [2003] 3 SCR 571, 233 DLR (4th) 415], at para. 135. ...

[233] We agree with our colleagues the Chief Justice and Major J that a law is arbitrary if "it bears no relation to, or is inconsistent with, the objective that lies behind [the legislation]" (para. 130). We do not agree with the Chief Justice and Major J that the prohibition against private health insurance "bears no relation to, or is inconsistent with" the preservation of access to a health system based on need rather than wealth in accordance with the *Canada Health Act*. We also do not agree with our colleagues' expansion of the *Morgentaler* principle to invalidate a prohibition simply because a court believes it to be "unnecessary" for the government's purpose. There must be more than that to sustain a valid objection.

[234] The accepted definition in *Rodriguez* states that a law is arbitrary only where "it bears no relation to, or is inconsistent with, the objective that lies behind the legislation." To substitute the term "unnecessary" for "inconsistent" is to substantively alter the meaning of the term "arbitrary." "Inconsistent" means that the law logically contradicts its objectives, whereas "unnecessary" simply means that the objective could be met by other means. It is quite apparent that the latter is a much broader term that involves a policy choice. If a court were to declare unconstitutional every law impacting "security of the person" that the court considers unnecessary, there would be much greater scope for intervention under s. 7 than has previously been considered by this Court to be acceptable. ... The courts might find themselves constantly second-guessing the validity of governments' public policy objectives based on subjective views of the necessity of particular means used to advance legitimate government action as opposed to other means which critics might prefer.

[235] ... We approach the issue of arbitrariness in three steps ... .

(a) What Is the "State Interest" Sought to Be Protected?

[236] Quebec's legislative objective is to provide high quality health care, at a reasonable cost, for as many people as possible in a manner that is consistent with principles of efficiency, equity and fiscal responsibility. Quebec (along with the other provinces and territories) subscribes to the policy objectives of the *Canada Health Act*, which include (i) the equal provision of medical services to all residents, regardless of status, wealth or personal insurability, and (ii) fiscal responsibility. An overbuilt health system is seen as no more in the larger public interest than a system that on occasion falls short. The legislative task is to strike a balance among competing interests.

[237] The appellants do not challenge the constitutional validity of the objectives set out in the *Canada Health Act*. Thus our job as judges is not to agree or disagree with

these objectives but simply to determine whether the means adopted by Quebec to implement these objectives are arbitrary.

(b) What Is the Relationship Between the "State Interest" Thus Identified and
    the Prohibition Against Private Health Insurance?

[238] The relationship lies both in principle and in practicality.

[239] In *principle*, Quebec wants a health system where access is governed by need rather than wealth or status. Quebec does not want people who are uninsurable to be left behind. To accomplish this objective endorsed by the *Canada Health Act*, Quebec seeks to discourage the growth of private-sector delivery of "insured" services based on wealth and insurability. We believe the prohibition is rationally connected to Quebec's objective and is not inconsistent with it.

[240] In *practical terms*, Quebec bases the prohibition on the view that private insurance, and a consequent major expansion of private health services, would have a harmful effect on the public system.

. . .

(c) Have the Appellants Established That the Prohibition Bears No Relation to,
    or Is Inconsistent with, the State Interest?

[242] The trial judge considered all the evidence and concluded that the expansion of private health care would undoubtedly have a negative impact on the public health system ... . The trial judge relied on the reports available to her in rejecting the appellants' constitutional challenge, and none of the material that has since been added (such as the Romanow Report) changes or modifies the correctness of her conclusion, in our view. We therefore agree with the trial judge and the Quebec Court of Appeal that the appellants failed to make out a case of "arbitrariness" on the evidence. Indeed the evidence proves the contrary. ...

[Binnie and LeBel JJ summarize the extrinsic and expert evidence under the following headings:

  (i) A Parallel Private Regime Will Have a Negative Impact on Waiting Times in the
       Public System
  (ii) The Impact of a Parallel Private Regime on Government Support for a Public
        System
  (iii) Private Insurers May "Skim the Cream" and Leave the Difficult and Costly Care
        to the Public Sector
  (iv) The US Two-Tier System of Health Coverage
  (v) Moreover the Government's Interest in Fiscal Responsibility and Efficiency May
       Best Be Served by a Single-Tier System]
  (vi) Conclusion on "Arbitrariness"]

[256] For all these reasons, we agree ... that in light of the legislative objectives of the *Canada Health Act* it is not "arbitrary" for Quebec to discourage the growth of private sector health care. Prohibition of private health insurance is directly related to Quebec's

interest in promoting a need-based system and in ensuring its viability and efficiency. Prohibition of private insurance is not "inconsistent" with the state interest; still less is it "unrelated" to it.

[257] In short, it cannot be said that the prohibition against private health insurance "bears no relation to, or is inconsistent with" preservation of a health system predominantly based on need rather than wealth or status, as required by the *Rodriguez* test, at pp. 594-95.

[258] As to our colleagues' dismissal of the factual basis for Quebec's legislative choice, the public has invested very large sums of money in a series of authoritative reports to analyse health care in this country and in other countries. The reports uniformly recommend the retention of single-tier medicine. People are free to challenge (as do the appellants) the government's reliance on those reports but such reliance cannot be dismissed as "arbitrary." People are also free to dispute Quebec's strategy, but in our view it cannot be said that a single-tier health system, and the prohibition on private health insurance designed to protect it, is a legislative choice that has been adopted "arbitrarily" by the Quebec National Assembly as that term has been understood to date in the Canadian Charter jurisprudence.

· · ·

[264] The safety valve (however imperfectly administered) of allowing Quebec residents to obtain essential health care outside the province when they are unable to receive the care in question at home in a timely way is of importance. If, as the appellants claim, this safety valve is opened too sparingly, the courts are available to supervise enforcement of the rights of those patients who are directly affected by the decision on a case-by-case basis. Judicial intervention at this level on a case-by-case basis is preferable to acceptance of the appellants' global challenge to the entire single-tier health plan. It is important to emphasize that rejection of the appellants' global challenge to Quebec's health plan would not foreclose individual patients from seeking individual relief tailored to their individual circumstances.

(4) Conclusion Under Section 7 of the Canadian Charter

[265] For the foregoing reasons, even accepting (as we do) the trial judge's conclusion that the claimants have established a deprivation of the life and security of *some* Quebec residents occasioned in *some* circumstances by waiting list delays, the deprivation would not violate any *legal* principle of fundamental justice within the meaning of s. 7 of the *Canadian Charter*. ...

Appeal allowed.

NOTES

1. In *Flora v. Ontario Health Insurance Plan*, 2008 ONCA 538, 295 DLR (4th) 309, the appellant was diagnosed with liver cancer in 1999. After consulting several Ontario doctors, he was told that he was not a suitable candidate for a liver transplant and was given approximately six to eight months to live. Eventually, at a cost of about $450,000, he underwent

chemoembolization to contain the growth and decrease the size of his existing tumours, and a living-related liver transplantation (LRLT), a procedure involving the transfer of part of a living donor's liver to the patient, at a hospital in London, England. These procedures saved the appellant's life. Mr. Flora applied to the Ontario Health Insurance Plan (OHIP) for reimbursement of his medical expenses. When his reimbursement request was rejected by the respondent, the general manager of OHIP, he sought a review of OHIP's decision before the Health Services Appeal and Review Board. The majority of the Board upheld OHIP's denial of reimbursement on the basis that the treatment received by the appellant in England was not an "insured service" within the meaning of the *Health Insurance Act*, RSO 1990, c. H.6 (the Act) and s. 28.4(2) of RRO 1990, Reg. 552 (the Regulation). Mr. Flora's subsequent appeals to the Divisional Court and the Court of Appeal were dismissed. The following is an excerpt from the Court of Appeal's decision addressing an alleged violation of s. 7 of the Charter:

> [101] … In contrast to the legislative provisions at issue in *Chaoulli*, *Morgentaler* and *Rodriguez*, s. 28.4(2) of the Regulation does not prohibit or impede anyone from seeking medical treatment. Section 28.4(2) neither prescribes nor limits the types of medical services available to Ontarians. Nor does it represent governmental interference with an existing right or other coercive state action. Quite the opposite. Section 28.4(2) provides a defined benefit for out-of-country medical treatment that is not otherwise available to Ontarians—the right to obtain public funding for certain specific out-of-country medical treatments. By not providing funding for *all* out-of-country medical treatments, it does not deprive an individual of the rights protected by s. 7 of the Charter.

2. In *New Brunswick (Minister of Health and Community Services) v. G.(J.)*, [1999] 3 SCR 46, 177 DLR (4th) 124, discussed above, the Court held that the failure to provide legal aid to an indigent parent violated s. 7 of the Charter, and it ordered the New Brunswick government to provide the parent with state-funded legal cousel. How does the Court's holding in *G.(J.)* square with its decisions in *Gosselin* and *Chaoulli*?

3. In *Victoria (City) v. Adams*, 2008 BCSC 1363, 299 DLR (4th) 193, at issue was a civil injunction, sought by the city of Victoria, British Columbia, against a group of homeless people who had erected a tent city in a park. The injunction required them to vacate pursuant to a city bylaw that made it an offence for anyone to "take up a temporary abode overnight" or "erect or construct, or cause to be erected or constructed, a tent, building or structure, including a temporary structure such as a tent, in a park." Madame Justice Ross of the BC Supreme Court struck down the bylaw, holding it in violation of s. 7 of the Charter. In her words, "the uncontradicted expert evidence establishes that exposure to the elements without adequate shelter, and in particular without overhead protection, can result in a number of serious and life-threatening conditions, most notably hypothermia." Because Victoria's emergency shelters were insufficient to house the city's homeless population, she concluded that some homeless people were invariably forced to seek public shelter in a way that exposed them to significant health and safety risks. Justice Ross held further that the deprivation to life, liberty, and security of the person violated two principles of fundamental justice because the bylaw was both arbitrary and overbroad. The purposes of the prohibition were to ensure that use of public spaces was open to all members of society, to protect the natural environment from damage, and to address public health and safety concerns. But

the specific ban on setting up a tent in a park was not tailored to any of these purposes. Noting the Supreme Court of Canada's decision in *Gosselin*, Ross J did not declare that s. 7 imposes a positive obligation on the government to provide adequate housing. Instead, relying on the Court's decision in *Chaoulli*, she concluded that the government violated a negative obligation to not deprive individuals of their s. 7 rights.

CHAPTER TWENTY-THREE

Equality Rights

Equality is a complex and highly contested concept. Many academic disciplines reflect on equality, but no common terminology has emerged to capture the many ideas and distinctions considered. Legal systems, at both the national and international levels, have not developed a common vocabulary either. Canadian jurisprudence on equality rights has its own distinctive conceptual structure, shaped in no small measure by the text of s. 15 of the Charter. The drafting history of s. 15 reveals a desire to move beyond the limited understandings of equality that courts brought to the interpretation of the "equality before the law" clause in the *Canadian Bill of Rights*. The *Canadian Bill of Rights* jurisprudence on equality was shaped by the work of the British constitutional theorist A.V. Dicey, who conceptualized equality in terms of "the rule of law." Dicey comprehended equality as a normative commitment to equal treatment in the administration and enforcement of the law—a commitment central to the aspiration that society be governed by law, but one that provides no capacity to assess the constitutionality of the exercise of legislative power itself. Those who contributed to the formulation of s. 15 sought to ensure that it would not suffer the same interpretive fate as the equality guarantee in the *Canadian Bill of Rights*. Section I of this chapter introduces Dicey's conception of equality, and the universally repudiated pre-Charter approach to equality under the *Canadian Bill of Rights*, as well as an overview of some of the models, both positive and negative, for the drafting and interpretation of the Charter's equality clause. Subsequent sections trace major jurisprudential shifts in the Supreme Court of Canada's approach to the structure of an equality claim, and then delve into specific elements of the various tests the Court has elaborated to give meaning to equality rights in the Charter.

I. THE CONSTITUTIONAL HISTORY OF EQUALITY

The history of equality rights in Canada prior to the Charter is a long and protracted story, beginning in the late 1940s in the aftermath of World War II. For a detailed account leading up to the adoption and interpretation of the *Canadian Bill of Rights*—a federal statute that requires federal laws to be interpreted in a manner consistent with its terms—see W.S. Tarnopolsky, *The Canadian Bill of Rights*, 2d ed., rev. (Toronto: McClelland & Stewart, 1975). We pick up the story by first setting out Dicey's conception of equality and its impact on judicial interpretation of the *Canadian Bill of Rights* and then turning to debates over the drafting of s. 15 in the Special Joint Committee on the Constitution.

W.S. Tarnopolsky, "The Equality Rights"
in Walter S. Tarnopolsky and Gerald-A. Beaudoin, eds., *The Canadian Charter of
Rights and Freedoms* (Scarborough, ON: Carswell, 1982), at 399-401
(footnotes omitted)

Equality Before the Law in United Kingdom Constitutional Law

The classic statement of "equality before the law," as one of the fundamental characteristics of the United Kingdom Constitution, is that of Dicey. He proposed it as one of three meanings of a fundamental principle of the United Kingdom constitution known as the "rule of law." This meaning he explained in the following terms:

> [E]quality before the law, or the equal subjection of all classes to the ordinary law of the land, administered by the ordinary law courts; the "rule of law" in this sense excludes the idea of any exemption of officials or others from the duty of obedience to the law which governs other citizens or from the jurisdiction of the ordinary tribunals ...

Dicey went on to point out that, as a result, the United Kingdom knew nothing of "administrative law" or "administrative tribunals," as did France. In other words, his reference to "equality before the law" as part of the "rule of law" was for the purpose of showing that, unlike the continental situation, in the United Kingdom the government and its servants were not to be dealt with by special official bodies, but rather within the sphere of civil courts. Although the subsequent development of "administrative law," both in the United Kingdom and in Canada, have disproved this distinction, his limitation on the "equality before the law" clause has continued to find favour, even in our Supreme Court as recently as 1973.

A more modern, although somewhat closely related variant of the Dicey definition of "equality before the law," is that suggested by Marshall, i.e., that the doctrine implies "equality of state and individual before the law." Although the state and citizen cannot really be equals, and while state servants might in fact be given specific powers, nevertheless, the doctrine requires that rules granting powers to officials should be precise, and that it is the duty of the courts to hold an equal balance between citizens and officials.

One of the most famous applications of this view of "equality before the law" as part of "the rule of law" was the decision of the Supreme Court of Canada in *Roncarelli v. Duplessis* [[1959] SCR 121, 16 DLR (2d) 689]. The essence of this decision was probably most concisely set out by one of Roncarelli's counsel, Frank Scott, who suggested that the essence of the "rule of law," which includes "equality before the law," could be stated in "two basic rules underlying our constitutional structure, which entitles us to say that we live in a free society":

> The first is that the individual may do anything he pleases, in any circumstances anywhere, unless there is some provision of law prohibiting him. Freedom is thus presumed, and is the general rule. All restrictions are exceptions. The second rule defines the authority of the state, and places the public official (including the policeman) in exactly the opposite situation from the private individual: the public officer can do nothing in his public capacity unless the law permits it. His incapacity is presumed, and authority to act is an exception.

Duplessis, for instance, could not find any legal authority to justify his order to cancel Roncarelli's liquor licence: so he paid personally.

Some of Dicey's modern critics, for example Sir Ivor Jennings, have extended this concept somewhat, to require a basic procedural equality in the sense that there shall be impartiality before the ordinary law courts as well as other adjudicatory tribunals. Sir Ivor described "equality before the Law" thus:

> It assumes that among equals the laws should be equal and should be equally administered, that like should be treated alike. The right to sue and be sued, to prosecute and be prosecuted, for the same kind of action should be the same for all citizens of full age and understanding, and without distinction of race, religion, wealth, social status or political influence.

Nevertheless, even this view of "equality before the law" basically restricts it to a procedural concept relating only to the even-handed operation of the legal system in its application and enforcement of the law.

W.S. Tarnopolsky, "The Equality Rights in the Canadian Charter of Rights and Freedoms"
(1983), 61 *Canadian Bar Review* 242, at 247-53 (footnotes omitted)

From Section 1 of the Canadian Bill of Rights to Section 15 of the Charter

Section 1 of the *Canadian Bill of Rights* includes both a non-discrimination clause and one on "equality before the law."

• • •

The main focus of the Supreme Court was on the "equality before the law" clause. ...

The only case in which the Supreme Court held that a federal provision contravened the "equality before the law" clause and was therefore inoperative, was *Regina v. Drybones* [[1970] SCR 282, 9 DLR (3d) 473]. In this case Mr. Justice Ritchie, on behalf of the majority of the Supreme Court, held that the provision in the *Indian Act* which made it an offence for Indians to be intoxicated off a reserve contravened the "equality before the law" clause, and gave that clause the following meaning:

> ... I think that s. 1(b) means at least that no individual or group of individuals is to be treated more harshly than another under that law, and I am therefore of the opinion that an individual is denied equality before the law if it is made an offence punishable at law, on account of his race, for him to do something which his fellow Canadians are free to do without having committed any offence or having been made subject to any penalty.

However, in the *Lavell* case, [1974] SCR 1349, 38 DLR (3d) 481, Mr. Justice Ritchie held that section 12(1)(b) of the *Indian Act*, which provides that an Indian woman who married someone who is not an Indian would thereby lose her band membership, whereas an Indian man not only did not lose his band membership, but gave it to his spouse, did not contravene the "equality before the law" clause. In doing so he made two assertions which have had a clear effect upon the formulation of section 15 of the Charter. The first was that he rejected any "egalitarian concept exemplified by the Fourteenth Amendment of the US Constitution as interpreted by the courts of that country." Rather, and this was his second assertion, he purported to apply the concept of "equality before the law" as it would have been understood at the time the *Bill of Rights* was enacted, and adopted Dicey's definition of "equal subjection of all classes to the ordinary law of the land administered by the ordinary courts" …

Therefore, to the extent that he … rejected any possible references to the American "egalitarian" conception, section 15 now includes the "equal protection of the law" clause. To the extent that he adopted the Dicey definition and suggested that *Lavell* could be distinguished from *Drybones* on the basis that in the former case no "inequality of treatment between Indian men and women flows as a necessary result of the application of section 12(1)(b) of the *Indian Act*," or, in other words, to the extent that he implied there was a distinction between clauses like "equality before the law" and "unequal treatment *under* the law," section 15 now includes a reference to equality "*under* the law."

In order to understand the motivation behind the addition of the fourth equality clause, namely "equal *benefit* of the law," it is necessary to recall the *Bliss* case [[1979] 1 SCR 183, 92 DLR (3d) 417]. Stella Bliss was a pregnant woman who had worked long enough to have qualified for ordinary unemployment benefits, that is eight weeks, but not the ten weeks necessary to qualify for maternity benefits. However, she could not claim ordinary benefits because it was assumed that during the maternity period women are not capable of and available for work. She, therefore, challenged section 46, the relevant provision in the *Unemployment Insurance Act*, 1971 [SC 1970-71-72, c. 48], on the ground that it contravened the "equality before the law" clause in the *Canadian Bill of Rights*. In the Federal Court of Appeal Pratte J held that this was not discrimination because of sex, but rather a distinction between pregnant women and all other unemployed persons, male or female. When the case reached the Supreme Court of Canada, Ritchie J gave the unanimous decision upholding the judgment of Pratte J and, in addition, suggested that there was no contravention of "equality before the law" because section 46 did not involve denial of equality of treatment in the administration and enforcement of the law before the ordinary courts of the land:

> … There is a wide difference between legislation which treats one section of the population more harshly than all others by reason of race as in the case of *R v. Drybones* (1969), 9 DLR (3d) 473, [1970] 3 CCC 355, [1970] SCR 282 and legislation providing additional benefits to one class of women, specifying the conditions which entitle a claimant to such benefits and defining a period during which no benefits are available. The one case involves the imposition of a penalty on a racial group to which other citizens are not subjected; the other involves a definition of the qualifications required for entitlement to benefits. …

Since this assertion implied a distinction between "equality before the law" or "equal *protection* of the law," on the one hand, and "equal *benefit* of the law," on the other, this presumed gap, too, has now been covered in section 15 of the Canadian Charter.

This very brief survey of how majority decisions on the Supreme Court of Canada limited the "equality before the law" clause in the *Canadian Bill of Rights*, and how these limitations led directly to the incorporation of four equality clauses in section 15(1), also explains, partly, why various women's groups lobbied so hard, both before and after the November 1981 Accord, for the inclusion of section 28. Although one might have expected that the equality clauses, particularly since section 15(1) lists "sex" as one of the forbidden grounds of discrimination, must require equality between men and women, there was sufficient suspicion amongst women, based upon the Supreme Court judgments referred to above, to press for an "equal rights amendment" in the Charter.

NOTE: THE EQUAL PROTECTION CLAUSE IN THE US CONSTITUTION

The experience in the United States, which has a broader constitutional guarantee of legal equality that extends beyond equal treatment in the enforcement and administration of the law, influenced the drafting of the Charter in both positive and negative ways. Section 15(1) of the Charter employs the same phrase, "equal protection of the law," that appears in the Fourteenth Amendment of the US Constitution. The equal protection clause does not contain a list of prohibited grounds of discrimination, and its silence on affirmative action has provoked intense controversy about the constitutionality of programs designed to ameliorate the condition of disadvantaged groups. The text of s. 15(1) attempts to avoid some of the uncertainties produced by the Fourteenth Amendment.

There was no mention of equality in the original American Constitution or *Bill of Rights*. The equal protection clause was adopted after the Civil War in an effort to abolish government discrimination against African-Americans. For many years, the Fourteenth Amendment had little impact on racial discrimination. The courts upheld racial segregation, relying on the notorious "separate but equal" doctrine; see *Plessy v. Ferguson*, 163 US 537 (1896). The US Supreme Court began to bring more searching scrutiny to the legal edifice of racial inequality in the mid-20th century. In its landmark unanimous opinion in *Brown v. Board of Education*, 347 US 483 (1954), the Court declared that "separate but equal" is "inherently unequal" and "has no place" in the field of public education.

Modern equal protection jurisprudence is characterized by a three-tiered approach to the review of legal classifications. Under the first tier, known as strict scrutiny, courts will strike down any legislative classification that is not necessary to achieving a compelling government objective. Strict scrutiny is applied to legislation that classifies on the basis of race or alienage, or that burdens fundamental rights. Most legislation reviewed by the Supreme Court under the strict scrutiny standard has been invalidated. The second or intermediate tier of scrutiny is applied to classifications on the basis of gender. Legislation will not survive intermediate scrutiny unless the government can demonstrate that the classification is substantially related to an important societal interest. The third tier is known as minimal scrutiny. The courts will uphold a law on this approach so long as the classification is reasonably related to a legitimate government interest. Most laws regulating social and economic matters are reviewed and upheld by courts using this minimal level of scrutiny. In summary, constitutional equality in the United States poses a serious challenge to all legal classifications on the basis of immutable characteristics such as race or sex, but does not interfere with most of the ways governments draw distinctions in their laws.

The Special Joint Committee effected dramatic changes to many parts of the Charter, including s. 15. The following brief account sketches the intense lobbying effort by women's groups to make the equality guarantee more effective.

D. Gibson, *The Law of the Charter: Equality Rights*
(Scarborough, ON: Carswell, 1990), at 42-45 (footnotes omitted)

The equality provisions came in for especially intense consideration from the public during [the hearings of the Special Joint Committee]. ... The Committee recommended major changes in the provisions as a result. ...

The alterations made by the Committee included:

(a) Expanding the guarantee to include equality "under the law," and, even more significantly, "equal benefit of the law."

(b) Adding disability to the expressly prohibited grounds of discrimination.

(c) Making unmistakable provision for other, unspecified, forms of unconstitutional discrimination ["in particular"].

(d) Elaborating the affirmative action proviso to ensure that the criteria of "disadvantage" include those that form the basis for prohibited discrimination.

(e) Altering the description of those entitled to the right from "everyone" to "every individual," with the apparent purpose of denying the right to corporations.

A related amendment, which ended up as section 27 of the Charter, required all Charter provisions to be interpreted "in a manner consistent with the preservation and enhancement of the multicultural heritage of Canadians."

Lobbying efforts by women's organizations after the final report of the Joint Parliamentary Committee resulted in Government sponsorship of an additional equality provision, the constitutional import of which was not altogether clear:

> 28. Notwithstanding anything in this Charter, the rights and freedoms referred to in it are guaranteed equally to male and female persons.

The wording of sections 15, 27 and 28 emerged intact from the politico-legal maelstrom that raged during the Charter's final year of gestation, although section 28 came close to being a casualty. ...

The debate over section 28 was part of a much larger controversy caused by the First Ministers' addition to the Charter, as a crucial element of the federal–provincial compromise, of section 33, permitting Parliament and the Legislatures to avoid most Charter rights by means of a simple legislative declaration that particular statutes should apply "notwithstanding" the Charter. While section 28 ended up being exempted from that provision, the general equality guarantee in section 15 was not.

As mentioned previously, section 32(2) of the Charter postponed the coming into force of section 15 until 17th April 1985—three years after the rest of the Charter came into operation. ...

The purpose of the delay was to enable federal and provincial governments to house-clean. It gave them three years to study their statute books and their policies and practices, with a view to dealing pre-emptively with any equality violations [that] those laws, policies or practices might involve, rather than waiting for challenges to be raised in the courts. This purpose was fulfilled in part. ... The exercise was far from whole-hearted, however. ... The result was to leave all but a tiny fraction of Canada's constitutional equality problems for the courts to resolve.

II. EARLY INTERPRETATION AND APPLICATION OF SECTION 15: THE ANDREWS TEST AND THE 1995 TRILOGY

As the above readings make clear, the drafting history of s. 15 reveals a desire to move beyond the limited understandings of equality found in the common law and under the *Canadian Bill of Rights*. As you read through the Supreme Court of Canada cases in this chapter, consider the extent to which the text of s. 15 has had a strong influence on interpretation. Would those whose ideas were encapsulated in the text of s. 15 be pleased with the analysis offered by the Court? Should Charter text have a strong influence on the Court's interpretive choices? Should that influence abate as the time or context of drafting recedes?

Because the implementation of s. 15 was delayed until three years after the rest of the Charter came into force, it was not until 1989 that the Supreme Court of Canada decided its first case interpreting and applying the equality guarantees, in *Andrews*, which follows. In *Andrews*, the Court set out the contours of its approach to s. 15 in a three-part test requiring (1) a distinction in treatment (2) that results in the imposition of a burden or denial of a benefit (3) on the basis of an expressly prohibited ground or one analogous thereto. The *Andrews* ruling was the leading case through the first decade of s. 15 jurisprudence, although the judgments that followed *Andrews* gave rise to questions about the extent to which the Court had remained faithful to the approach it originally set out. As we will see in the next section, 10 years after *Andrews*, in its decision in *Law v. Canada (Minister of Employment and Immigration)*, [1999] 1 SCR 497, 170 DLR (4th) 1, the Supreme Court of Canada reformulated the *Andrews* test, stating that burdensome differences in treatment on the basis of prohibited grounds are discriminatory only if they can reasonably be said to violate the human dignity of the claimant. Nine years later, however, the Court repudiated this focus on human dignity in *R v. Kapp*, [2008] 2 SCR 483, 294 DLR (4th) 1, and reverted to a version of the approach it adopted in *Andrews*.

Andrews v. Law Society of British Columbia
[1989] 1 SCR 143, 56 DLR (4th) 1

[Andrews, a British subject permanently resident in Canada, brought an action for a declaration that the Canadian citizenship requirement for admission to the Law Society of British Columbia violated s. 15 of the Charter. Andrews was otherwise qualified to practise law in the province. In accepting his claim, the Supreme Court evaluated three possible approaches to s. 15 and selected the one that seemed to make the most sense of its language and history, as well as the relationship between ss. 15 and 1.

The Supreme Court held unanimously that the citizenship requirement violated s. 15. Justice McIntyre wrote the principal opinion on the interpretation of s. 15. Justice Wilson (Dickson CJC and L'Heureux-Dubé J concurring) and Justice La Forest wrote separate opinions in which they agreed with Justice McIntyre's approach to s. 15. They parted company with Justice McIntyre on the s. 1 issue—in their view, the citizenship requirement was not closely linked to candidates' ability to effectively practise law. McIntyre J would have upheld the citizenship requirement pursuant to s. 1 by introducing a deferential approach to the state's burden of justifying s. 15 violations. Thus, while Justice McIntyre's opinion was ultimately the dissent in a 4 to 2 ruling, it represents the Court's unanimous position on the interpretation of s. 15.]

McINTYRE J (Lamer J concurring) dissenting: This appeal raises only one question. Does the citizenship requirement for entry into the legal profession contained in s. 42 of the *Barristers and Solicitors Act*, RSBC 1979, c. 26, ... contravene s. 15(1) of the *Canadian Charter of Rights and Freedoms*?

. . .

The Concept of Equality

Section 15(1) of the Charter provides for every individual a guarantee of equality before and under the law, as well as the equal protection and equal benefit of the law without discrimination. This is not a general guarantee of equality; it does not provide for equality between individuals or groups within society in a general or abstract sense, nor does it impose on individuals or groups an obligation to accord equal treatment to others. It is concerned with the application of the law. No problem regarding the scope of the word "law," as employed in s. 15(1), can arise in this case because it is an Act of the Legislature which is under attack. Whether other governmental or quasi-governmental regulations, rules, or requirements may be termed laws under s. 15(1) should be left for cases in which the issue arises.

The concept of equality has long been a feature of Western thought. As embodied in s. 15(1) of the Charter, it is an elusive concept and, more than any of the other rights and freedoms guaranteed in the Charter, it lacks precise definition. ... It is a comparative concept, the condition of which may only be attained or discerned by comparison with the condition of others in the social and political setting in which the question arises. It must be recognized at once, however, that every difference in treatment between individuals under the law will not necessarily result in inequality and, as well, that identical treatment may frequently produce serious inequality. ...

[The thought that inequality may result from equal treatment] has been expressed in this Court in the context of s. 2(a) of the Charter in *R v. Big M Drug Mart Ltd.*, [1985] 1 SCR 295, where Dickson CJC said at p. 347:

> The equality necessary to support religious freedom does not require identical treatment of all religions. In fact, the interests of true equality may well require differentiation in treatment.

... Recognizing that there will always be an infinite variety of personal characteristics, capacities, entitlements and merits among those subject to a law, there must be accorded, as nearly as may be possible, an equality of benefit and protection and no more of the restrictions, penalties or burdens imposed upon one than another. In other words, the admittedly unattainable ideal should be that a law expressed to bind all should not because of irrelevant personal differences have a more burdensome or less beneficial impact on one than another.

... The similarly situated test is a restatement of the Aristotelian principle of formal equality—that "things that are alike should be treated alike, while things that are unalike should be treated unalike in proportion to their unalikeness" (*Ethica Nichomaceu*, trans. W. Ross, Book V3, at p. 1131a-6 (1925)).

The test as stated, however, is seriously deficient in that it excludes any consideration of the nature of the law. If it were to be applied literally, it could be used to justify the Nuremberg laws of Adolf Hitler. Similar treatment was contemplated for all Jews.

. . .

[T]he [similarly situated] test cannot be accepted as a fixed rule or formula for the resolution of equality questions arising under the Charter. Consideration must be given to the content of the law, to its purpose, and its impact upon those to whom it applies, and also upon those whom it excludes from its application. The issues which will arise from case to case are such that it would be wrong to attempt to confine these considerations within such a fixed and limited formula.

It is not every distinction or differentiation in treatment at law which will transgress the equality guarantees of s. 15 of the Charter. It is, of course, obvious that legislatures may—and to govern effectively must—treat different individuals and groups in different ways. Indeed, such distinctions are one of the main preoccupations of legislatures. The classifying of individuals and groups, the making of different provisions respecting such groups, the application of different rules, regulations, requirements and qualifications to different persons is necessary for the governance of modern society. As noted above, for the accommodation of differences, which is the essence of true equality, it will frequently be necessary to make distinctions. What kinds of distinctions will be acceptable under s. 15(1) and what kinds will violate its provisions? ...

It is clear that the purpose of s. 15 is to ensure equality in the formulation and application of the law. The promotion of equality entails the promotion of a society in which all are secure in the knowledge that they are recognized at law as human beings equally deserving of concern, respect and consideration. It has a large remedial component. ... It must be recognized, however, as well, that the promotion of equality under s. 15 has a much more specific goal than the mere elimination of distinctions. If the Charter was intended to eliminate all distinctions, then there would be no place for sections such as 27 (multicultural heritage); 2(a) (freedom of conscience and religion); 25 (aboriginal rights and freedoms); and other such provisions designed to safeguard certain distinctions. Moreover, the fact that identical treatment may frequently produce serious inequality is recognized in s. 15(2), which states that the equality rights in s. 15(1) do "not preclude any law, program or activity that has as its object the amelioration of conditions of disadvantaged individuals or groups." ...

Discrimination

The right to equality before and under the law, and the rights to the equal protection and benefit of the law contained in s. 15, are granted with the direction contained in s. 15 itself that they be without discrimination. Discrimination is unacceptable in a democratic society because it epitomizes the worst effects of the denial of equality, and discrimination reinforced by law is particularly repugnant. The worst oppression will result from discriminatory measures having the force of law. It is against this evil that s. 15 provides a guarantee.

Discrimination as referred to in s. 15 of the Charter must be understood in the context of pre-Charter history. Prior to the enactment of s. 15(1), the Legislatures of the various provinces and the federal Parliament had passed during the previous fifty years what may be generally referred to as Human Rights Acts. ...

What does discrimination mean? The question has arisen most commonly in a consideration of the Human Rights Acts and the general concept of discrimination under those enactments has been fairly well settled. There is little difficulty, drawing upon the cases in this Court, in isolating an acceptable definition. In *Ontario (Human Rights Commission) v. Simpsons-Sears Ltd.*, [1985] 2 SCR 536, at p. 551, discrimination (in that case adverse effect discrimination) was described in these terms:

> It arises where an employer ... adopts a rule or standard ... which has a discriminatory effect upon a prohibited ground on one employee or group of employees in that it imposes, because of some special characteristic of the employee or group, obligations, penalties, or restrictive conditions not imposed on other members of the work force.

It was held in that case, as well, that no intent was required as an element of discrimination, for it is in essence the impact of the discriminatory act or provision upon the person affected which is decisive in considering any complaint. ... I would say then that discrimination may be described as a distinction, whether intentional or not but based on grounds relating to personal characteristics of the individual or group, which has the effect of imposing burdens, obligations, or disadvantages on such individual or group not imposed upon others, or which withholds or limits access to opportunities, benefits, and advantages available to other members of society. Distinctions based on personal characteristics attributed to an individual solely on the basis of association with a group will rarely escape the charge of discrimination, while those based on an individual's merits and capacities will rarely be so classed. ...

[McIntyre J discussed three approaches that had been adopted with respect to the interpretation of s. 15. The first, advanced by Peter Hogg in *Constitutional Law of Canada*, 2d ed. (1985) would treat every distinction made by the law as discriminatory and thus justifiable only pursuant to s. 1. He rejected this approach, saying it trivialized the notion of discrimination and denied any role to s. 15. The second approach would define discrimination as unfair or unreasonable differences in treatment. He rejected this approach because it left no role to s. 1. McIntyre J adopted the third view, that s. 15 is limited to prohibiting differences in treatment on the basis of prohibited grounds.]

The third or "enumerated and analogous grounds" approach most closely accords with the purposes of s. 15 and the definition of discrimination outlined above and leaves questions of justification to s. 1. However, in assessing whether a complainant's rights have been infringed under s. 15(1), it is not enough to focus only on the alleged ground of discrimination and decide whether or not it is an enumerated or analogous ground. The effect of the impugned distinction or classification on the complainant must be considered. Once it is accepted that not all distinctions and differentiations created by law are discriminatory, then a role must be assigned to s. 15(1) which goes beyond the mere recognition of a legal distinction. A complainant under s. 15(1) must show not only that he or she is not receiving equal treatment before and under the law or that the law has a differential impact on him or her in the protection or benefit accorded by law but, in addition, must show that the legislative impact of the law is discriminatory.

Where discrimination is found a breach of s. 15(1) has occurred and—where s. 15(2) is not applicable—any justification, any consideration of the reasonableness of the enactment; indeed, any consideration of factors which could justify the discrimination and support the constitutionality of the impugned enactment would take place under s. 1. This approach would conform with the directions of this Court in earlier decisions concerning the application of s. 1 and at the same time would allow for the screening out of the obviously trivial and vexatious claim. In this, it would provide a workable approach to the problem.

It would seem to me apparent that a legislative distinction has been made by s. 42 of the *Barristers and Solicitors Act* between citizens and non-citizens with respect to the practice of law. The distinction would deny admission to the practice of law to non-citizens who in all other respects are qualified. Have the respondents because of s. 42 of the Act been denied equality before and under the law or the equal protection of the law? In practical terms it should be noted that the citizenship requirement affects only those non-citizens who are permanent residents. The permanent resident must wait for a minimum of three years from the date of establishing permanent residence status before citizenship may be acquired. The distinction therefore imposes a burden in the form of some delay on permanent residents who have acquired all or some of their legal training abroad and is, therefore, discriminatory.

The rights guaranteed in s. 15(1) apply to all persons whether citizens or not. A rule which bars an entire class of persons from certain forms of employment, solely on the grounds of a lack of citizenship status and without consideration of educational and professional qualifications or the other attributes or merits of individuals in the group, would, in my view, infringe s. 15 equality rights. Non-citizens, lawfully permanent residents of Canada, are, in the words of the US Supreme Court in *United States v. Carolene Products Co.*, 304 US 144 (1938), at pp. 152-53, n. 4, subsequently affirmed in *Graham v. Richardson*, 403 US 365 (1971), at p. 372, a good example of a "discrete and insular minority" who come within the protection of s. 15.

[Wilson J and La Forest J wrote separate opinions concurring with McIntyre J's approach to the interpretation of s. 15. Wilson J agreed that noncitizens should have access to s. 15. Like McIntyre J, she borrowed a famous phrase from American equal protection law: she stated that noncitizens are a "discrete and insular minority" vulnerable to having their interests overlooked in the legislative process. As she explained:

> Relative to citizens, non-citizens are a group lacking in political power and as such vulnerable to having their interests overlooked and their rights to equal concern and respect violated. ...
> I would conclude therefore that non-citizens fall into an analogous category to those specifically enumerated in s. 15. I emphasize, moreover, that this is a determination which is not to be made only in the context of the law which is subject to challenge but rather in the context of the place of the group in the entire social, political and legal fabric of our society. While legislatures must inevitably draw distinctions among the governed, such distinctions

should not bring about or reinforce the disadvantage of certain groups and individuals by denying them the rights freely accorded to others.

La Forest J agreed that citizenship should be treated as an analogous ground of discrimination. In addition to the relative lack of political power emphasized by McIntyre J and Wilson J, he mentioned two other considerations that supported recognizing citizenship as an analogous ground. First, he noted that citizenship, like most of the enumerated grounds of discrimination, is immutable or beyond the control of the individual. It is, "at least temporarily, a characteristic of personhood not alterable by conscious action and in some cases not alterable except on the basis of unacceptable costs." Second, he noted that citizenship is generally irrelevant to the legitimate work of government and to the assessment of an individual's ability to perform or contribute to society.

While the judges agreed on the approach to s. 15, they split sharply on the appropriate role of s. 1 in equality cases. McIntyre J, dissenting in the result, favoured relaxing the *Oakes* test because "the section 15(1) guarantee is the broadest of all guarantees" and should not unduly hinder government from making the "innumerable legislative distinctions and categorizations" that are an unavoidable aspect of governing. He suggested that the "pressing and substantial objective" requirement of *Oakes* was "too stringent" in the context of equality claims. He favoured upholding violations of equality rights if governments are pursuing sound objectives in a reasonable manner. Applying this approach to the citizenship requirement at issue, McIntyre J concluded that it was a reasonable means of ensuring that members of the legal profession are qualified.

The majority judgments of Wilson J and La Forest J disagreed with McIntyre J's approach to s. 1. Wilson J stated that the *Oakes* test

> remains an appropriate standard when it is recognized that not every distinction between individuals and groups will violate s. 15. If every distinction between individuals and groups gave rise to a violation of s. 15, then this standard might well be too stringent for application in all cases and might deny the community at large the benefits associated with sound and desirable social and economic legislation. This is not a concern, however, once the position that every distinction drawn by law constitutes discrimination is rejected as indeed it is in the judgment of my colleague, McIntyre J. Given that s. 15 is designed to protect those groups who suffer social, political and legal disadvantage in our society, the burden resting on government to justify the type of discrimination against such groups is appropriately an onerous one.

La Forest J wrote that, in contrast to McIntyre J's departure from *Oakes*, he preferred "to think in terms of a single test for s. 1," although it "must be approached in a flexible manner." In the end, both Wilson J and La Forest J concluded that the citizenship requirement was not closely tailored to the objective of ensuring that candidates for admission to the bar had a sufficient understanding of, and commitment to, Canadian institutions.]

Appeal dismissed.

NOTES

1. Although it was the Supreme Court's first decision to grapple with the meaning of s. 15 of the Charter, the *Andrews* ruling established a number of principles that continue to frame Canadian discussions of constitutional equality. First, the Court emphasized that equality cannot be reduced to sameness of treatment. Equality sometimes requires that differences be taken into account. Therefore, differential treatment does not necessarily amount to legal discrimination. Similarly, laws that treat everyone the same—laws that are "facially neutral"—may be discriminatory in their impact. This is referred to as "adverse effects discrimination." Second, McIntyre J rejected the similarly situated test, or the notion of formal equality, as a reliable guide to the interpretation of s. 15 because, in his view, "[c]onsideration must be given to the content of the law, to its purpose, and its impact upon those to whom it applies, and also upon those whom it excludes from its application." Third, the actual effects of a challenged law or practice should be the focus of the analysis. It is not necessary to establish intentional or purposeful discrimination. Fourth, to make out a violation of s. 15, the claimant must establish differential treatment that amounts to discrimination on the basis of a personal characteristic that is either listed as a prohibited ground of discrimination in s. 15 ("enumerated") or that is analogous to the listed grounds. A discriminatory law, for McIntyre J, is one that, in purpose or effect, attributes personal characteristics to an individual solely on the basis of association with a group. In contrast, Wilson J's reasons appear to equate discrimination with the production or reinforcement of disadvantage of certain groups and individuals. Fifth, a personal characteristic will be accepted as an analogous ground if it shares the essential features of the personal characteristics listed in s. 15. La Forest J argues that what makes a ground analogous to those listed in s. 15 is that it refers to a personal characteristic that is "immutable or beyond the control of the individual," whereas Wilson and McIntyre JJ suggest that what unites enumerated and analogous grounds is that they refer to personal characteristics of groups "lacking in political power."

2. Many commentators applauded the Court for moving beyond the similarly situated approach and reaching for a substantive conception of equality. See, for example, C. Sheppard, "Recognition of the Disadvantaging of Women: The Promise of Andrews v. Law Society of British Columbia" (1989), 35 *McGill Law Journal* 207 and W. Black and L. Smith, "The Equality Rights," in G.-A. Beaudoin and E. Mendes, eds., *The Canadian Charter of Rights and Freedoms*, 3d ed. (Scarborough, ON: Carswell, 1996), at 14-19. Others argued that the Court was too quick to reject the similarly situated test, or that the Court did not understand its potential rigour. Some insisted that courts cannot avoid a "similarly situated" analysis since equality, as the Court noted, is an inherently comparative concept. Therefore, courts will inevitably have to decide whether there are differences between two groups that justify differential treatment. See, for example, M. Gold, "Comment: Andrews v. Law Society of British Columbia" (1989), 34 *McGill Law Journal* 1063 and D. Gibson, *The Law of the Charter: Equality Rights* (Scarborough, ON: Carswell, 1990), at 72. For further reading on *Andrews*, see R. Moon, "A Discrete and Insular Right to Equality: Comment on Andrews v. Law Society of British Columbia" (1989), 21 *Ottawa Law Review* 563 and D.M. Beatty, "The Canadian Conception of Equality" (1996), 46 *University of Toronto Law Journal* 349.

3. The phrase "discrete and insular minority" is misleading if taken literally. When coined by Mr. Justice Stone of the United States Supreme Court in 1938, it was an attempt

to describe the social conditions of groups, like African-Americans, that made them vulnerable to the prejudices of those in power. But vulnerable groups are not necessarily discrete and insular. They may be diffuse and difficult to identify. The phrase is best understood, then, as a way of describing those groups, like noncitizens, that suffer a relative lack of political power. See D. Gibson, *The Law of the Charter: Equality Rights* (Scarborough, ON: Carswell, 1990), at 151.

4. The *Andrews* ruling limited s. 15's role to combatting discrimination based on listed or analogous grounds of discrimination. As a result, *Andrews* had the effect of closing the doors to many challenges to allegedly arbitrary or irrational laws making their way through the courts at the time. These cases failed unless the claimants could link the challenged laws to personal characteristics associated with common prejudices, stereotypes, or certain patterns of disadvantage.

For example, in *Reference re Validity of Sections 32 and 34 of the Workers' Compensation Act*, [1989] 1 SCR 922, 56 DLR (4th) 765, the Court held that s. 15 was not violated by provisions of the *Newfoundland Workers' Compensation Act*, which provided a statutory right to compensation for workplace injuries in lieu of all tort rights to which a worker or his or her dependents might otherwise have been entitled. According to La Forest J, in a brief oral judgment for the Court, there was no discrimination within the meaning of s. 15, since "[t]he situation of the workers and dependents here is in no way analogous to those listed in s. 15(1), as a majority in *Andrews* stated was required to permit recourse to s. 15(1)." Unfortunately, La Forest J did not explain why the situation of workers was "in no way analogous" to that of, say, noncitizens in *Andrews*. Can you formulate persuasive reasons in support of La Forest J's conclusion?

In lower courts, attacks on a wide range of grounds, including differential limitation periods and restraints on public service collective bargaining, were rejected following *Andrews*. See, for example, *Mirhadizadeh v. Ontario* (1989), 69 OR (2d) 422, 60 DLR (4th) 597 (CA); *Jones v. Ontario (Attorney General); Rheaume v. Ontario (Attorney General)* (1992), 7 OR (3d) 22, 89 DLR (4th) 11 (CA).

5. The divisions on the Court regarding s. 1, so apparent in the *Andrews* opinions, have not disappeared from the subsequent equality jurisprudence. Some majority judgments in s. 15 cases have relaxed the burden of justification imposed on governments by s. 1 in a manner similar to McIntyre J's dissent in *Andrews*. See, for example, *McKinney v. University of Guelph*, [1990] 3 SCR 229, 76 DLR (4th) 545, per La Forest J and *Egan v. Canada*, [1995] 2 SCR 513, 124 DLR (4th) 609, per Sopinka J.

Differences of opinion regarding s. 1 resurfaced more recently in *Lavoie v. Canada*, [2002] 1 SCR 769, 210 DLR (4th) 193. The case involved a challenge to a federal law that gave preferential treatment to citizens in competitions for federal public service jobs. A 6 to 3 majority of the Court found that the citizenship preference did not violate the Charter.

Four members of the majority, in an opinion written by Bastarache J (Gonthier, Iacobucci, and Major JJ concurring), upheld the law as a reasonable limit on s. 15 rights. The burden that Bastarache J placed on the government under s. 1 has more in common with McIntyre J's dissenting approach to s. 1 in *Andrews* than it does with Wilson J's emphasis on an "onerous" test. Bastarache J defined the objectives of the law as enhancing "the meaning of citizenship as a unifying symbol" and encouraging permanent residents to take out citizenship. These objectives, he concluded, were sufficiently important to justify overriding equality rights. He went on to conclude that the law was sufficiently well tailored to the achievement of these objectives. Bastarache J suggested that deference to Parliament's ability to assess competing policy options was appropriate, "particularly given the delicate balancing that is required in this area of the law."

The two other members of the majority in favour of upholding the law, Arbour and LeBel JJ, distinguished *Andrews* and, applying the test for discrimination set out in *Law v. Canada (Minister of Employment and Immigration)* (reproduced in Section IV, below), found no violation of s. 15. But Arbour J was sharply critical of the judgment of Bastarache J for conducting a s. 1 inquiry that, in her view, risked depriving the equality guarantee of any meaningful content. She argued in favour of a narrow understanding of discrimination and a s. 1 analysis conducted with "uncompromising rigour":

> Lack of care can only result in the creation of an equality guarantee that is far-reaching but wafer-thin, an expansive but insubstantial shield with which to fend off state incursions on our dignity and freedom. This of course is precisely the paradox that so exercised this Court in *Andrews*. It is a paradox that will prove inescapable if we are too quick to find s. 15(1) violations on the basis of a discrimination inquiry devoid of real content. For we shall then be forced in almost every case to turn to a justificatory analysis under s. 1 which, although suitably rigorous in other contexts, will inevitably become diluted in the s. 15(1) context. The *Oakes* test was not designed to bear the considerable strain of salvaging under s. 1 a plethora of laws that would otherwise offend a s. 15(1) analysis essentially lacking consideration for the existence of objectively discernible discrimination. Yet this is exactly what s. 1 is asked to do, on pain of unravelling the legislative process, when s. 15(1) infringements are too easily found. In response, courts are forced to engage in a s. 1 analysis that pays an undue amount of deference to the legislatures, both in the objectives they choose to pursue and in the means they adopt in pursuing them. For it is only by continually loosening the strictures imposed under the *Oakes* test that s. 1 can discharge the onerous burden that it has been placed under. The problem is that in thus discharging its burden s. 1 effectively denudes the equality rights guaranteed under s. 15(1) of their meaning and content while paying lip service to a broad and generous concept of equality.

The jointly written dissent of L'Heureux-Dubé J and McLachlin CJC (Binnie J concurring) found that, on the authority of *Andrews*, the citizenship preference violated s. 15. As for s. 1, they repeated Wilson J's view that the burden of justification in cases involving violations of s. 15 should be "onerous." Cases of justifiable discrimination, they said, should be rare. In this case, they found that the law in question was not rationally connected to its objectives of enhancing citizenship and encouraging naturalization. They argued that discriminatory laws do not enhance the value of Canadian citizenship. They further pointed out that there was no evidence that the law had an impact on naturalization rates.

A 5 to 4 majority of the Court in *Lavoie* favoured a strict approach to the government's burden of justifying violations of equality rights pursuant to s. 1, just as a 4 to 2 majority had rejected McIntyre J's deferential approach to s. 1 in *Andrews*. However, the end result was different in *Lavoie*, with a 6 to 3 majority rejecting the equality claim. The combination in *Lavoie* of Arbour J's narrow view of discrimination and Bastarache J's deference to Parliament in the s. 1 analysis leaves the impression that the equality rights of non-citizens are now in a more vulnerable state than they were following *Andrews*.

6. A notable absence from the opinions in *Andrews* was the failure to articulate the purpose of equality rights in accordance with the purposive approach to Charter interpretation recommended by the Court in *R v. Big M Drug Mart Ltd.*, [1985] 1 SCR 295. Different formulations of s. 15's purpose have appeared in the case law in the decade following *Andrews*. In *R v. Turpin*, [1989] 1 SCR 1296, 48 CCC (3d) 8, Wilson J ventured the Court's first attempt to describe s. 15's purpose. The case involved two persons charged with murder in Ontario who argued that the *Criminal Code* discriminated against them by denying them the choice of a trial by judge alone, a choice open to accused persons in Alberta. Justice Wilson, writing for the unanimous Court, rejected the claim. She insisted on the need to examine s. 15 claims in their wider social, political, and legal contexts:

> In determining whether there is discrimination on grounds relating to the personal characteristics of the individual or group, it is important to look not only at the impugned legislation which has created a distinction that violates the right to equality but also to the larger social, political and legal context. ... It is only by examining the larger context that a court can determine whether differential treatment results in equality or whether, contrariwise, it would be identical treatment which would in the particular context result in equality or foster disadvantage. A finding that there is discrimination will, I think, in most but perhaps not all cases, necessarily entail a search for disadvantage that exists apart from and independent of the particular legal distinction being challenged.

Wilson J concluded that it would be "stretching the imagination" to characterize persons charged with a crime outside of Alberta as members of a "discrete and insular minority." The interest they raised in being treated no less favourably than persons accused of crime elsewhere in the country was not the kind of interest that s. 15 of the Charter was designed to protect. The purpose of s. 15 was to remedy or prevent "discrimination against groups suffering social, political, and legal disadvantage in our society."

Wilson J's version of s. 15's purpose—overcoming group-based disadvantage—raised the question of whether someone who would be understood to hold "membership" in a relatively advantaged group would be able to successfully argue an infringement of s. 15. One concern was that the approach as stated would preclude s. 15 claims by men, given that so much of the background of the equality provisions took up the case of women as long experiencing social, economic, and political disadvantage in Canada. Other concerns appear relevant as well: how reliable are the ideas of "membership" and "groups" engaged in the analysis? What about the situation of the relative advantage of various "members" of disadvantaged groups? (And what if that relative advantage is secured at the cost of the group's less advantaged?) How well could courts deal with the wide variety of individual and group characteristics that might be put forward for consideration?

7. One of the implications of *Turpin*—that membership in a disadvantaged group might be a precondition to bringing a s. 15 claim—was rejected in *R v. Hess; R v. Nguyen*, [1990] 2 SCR 906, 59 CCC (3d) 161. Two accused persons challenged the validity of the now repealed "statutory rape" provision of the *Criminal Code*, which made it a crime for a "male person" to have "sexual intercourse with a female person" under the age of 14. The majority opinion of Wilson J struck down the provision as a violation of s. 7 of the Charter. Both Wilson J, and McLachlin J in dissent, considered the s. 15 claims of the two accused men.

Wilson J found that the "statutory rape" provision did not violate the equality rights of boys or men since the acts in question can, as a matter of "biological reality," be committed only by men. McLachlin J stated that one need not be a member of a disadvantaged group to suffer discrimination. She found that the offence violated s. 15 because it burdens men as it does not burden women. She would have upheld the law pursuant to s. 1 since "only males can cause pregnancies" and "only females are likely to become pregnant."

Justice Wilson's opinion in *Hess* has been criticized for invoking "biological realities" to insulate the statutory rape offence from more searching s. 15 scrutiny. While governments need to take biological differences into account in framing laws, they have not always done so in a benign manner. Indeed, "biological realities" have been invoked to justify oppressive laws relating, for example, to pregnancy and women's reproductive capacities. Some commentators have suggested that the key question from an equality perspective is whether laws taking into account biological differences have done so in a manner that ameliorates or exacerbates group-based disadvantage. See W. Black and I. Grant, "Equality and Biological Differences" (1990), 79 CR (3d) 372. See also C. Boyle, "The Role of Equality in Criminal Law" (1994), 58 *Saskatchewan Law Review* 203.

8. Another case in which, as in *Hess*, the Supreme Court held that differential treatment based on sex did not violate the Charter is *Weatherall v. Canada (Attorney General)*, [1993] 2 SCR 872, 105 DLR (4th) 210. The claimant argued that allowing male penitentiary inmates to be frisk searched by female guards was discriminatory, since female inmates were not subject to being searched by male guards. In a brief ruling, La Forest J rejected this argument:

> The jurisprudence of this court is clear: equality does not necessarily connote identical treatment and, in fact, different treatment may be called for in certain cases to promote equality. Given the historical, biological and sociological differences between men and women, equality does not demand that practices which are forbidden where male officers guard female inmates must also be banned where female officers guard male inmates. The reality of the relationship between the sexes is such that the historical trend of violence perpetrated by men against women is not matched by a comparable trend pursuant to which men are the victims and women the aggressors. Biologically, a frisk search or surveillance of a man's chest area conducted by a female guard does not implicate the same concerns as the same practice by a male guard in relation to a female inmate. Moreover, women generally occupy a disadvantaged position in society in relation to men. Viewed in this light, it becomes clear that the effect of cross-gender searching is different and more threatening for women than for men. The different treatment to which the appellant objects thus may not be discrimination at all.

Even if s. 15(1) were violated by the different search practices, which he doubted, La Forest J said the violation would be a reasonable limit on the equality rights of male inmates, since hiring women as officers in male penitentiaries promoted inmate rehabilitation, security, and employment equity.

III. THE "EQUALITY TRILOGY OF 1995"

In the equality cases decided between 1989 and 1995, members of the Supreme Court did not call into question the three-stage test articulated in *Andrews* for determining whether government had breached s. 15(1). They agreed that the issue was whether the claimant could establish (1) differential treatment (2) on the basis of an enumerated or analogous ground (3) that had the effect of imposing a disadvantage. In a trilogy of equality rulings released in 1995, this consensus collapsed. The Court fragmented into three different camps on the interpretation of s. 15(1). Set out below is a brief description of the results in the three cases, followed by a summary of the three perspectives that emerged in them.

In *Miron v. Trudel*, [1995] 2 SCR 418, 124 DLR (4th) 693, the Court held, by a five to four majority, that the denial of automobile accident benefits to an unmarried opposite-sex couple constituted discrimination on the basis of marital status, contrary to s. 15. The majority held that the discrimination could not be justified pursuant to s. 1. Some means, more accurate than marriage, had to be found to identify the economically interdependent family relationships relevant to the legislative objective.

In *Egan v. Canada*, [1995] 2 SCR 513, 124 DLR (4th) 609, the Court held, again by a 5 to 4 majority, that the denial of an old age spousal allowance to same-sex couples did not violate the Charter. The monthly benefit could be claimed by persons between the ages of 60 and 65 so long as they were widowed or the spouse of an old age pensioner. The legislation defined spouse as a husband or wife of a pensioner, or a person of the opposite sex to the pensioner who lived with him or her for at least one year in a conjugal relationship. Egan and his partner Nesbitt had lived together for over forty years, but Nesbitt was denied the monthly allowance to which he would otherwise have been entitled because he did not meet the opposite-sex component of the definition of spouse. Five judges found that the legislation discriminated on the basis of sexual orientation. The legislation was upheld when Justice Sopinka broke ranks with the s. 15 majority at the s. 1 stage of analysis, leaving it to Parliament to determine when it had the financial means to extend spousal pension benefits to same-sex couples.

In *Thibaudeau v. Canada*, [1995] 2 SCR 513, 124 DLR (4th) 449, the Court dismissed a challenge to the "inclusion-deduction" rules in the *Income Tax Act*, which, at that time, permitted the parent who paid spousal and child support to deduct it from income while requiring the parent receiving support to add the amount to income. The government defended the scheme on the ground that it delivered a subsidy to children of divorce. The assumption was that the payor was in a higher tax bracket than the custodial parent and that by taxing support payments in the lower income-earner's hands, benefits would accrue to the child(ren) though the operation of the family law system. The inequality claim, based on sex, arose because 98 percent of the payors were men and 98 percent receiving support were women. Thibaudeau was a divorced woman with custody of her children. She argued that women were penalized by the scheme since the impact of taxation was frequently neglected or inaccurately considered by the family law system when the amount of support was established. A majority of the Court dismissed her claim on the grounds that the scheme confers a benefit on the post-divorce "family unit." L'Heureux-Dubé and McLachlin JJ, in dissent, found there was a violation of s. 15 because the *Income Tax Act* imposed a disadvantage upon a significant proportion of (mostly female) custodial parents, while providing a tax saving to the (mostly male) noncustodial parents.

Three approaches to s. 15 emerged in the 1995 trilogy. The first approach, supported by McLachlin, Cory, Iacobucci, and Sopinka JJ, looked for differential treatment on the basis of a prohibited ground that had the effect of imposing a real disadvantage in the social and political context of the claim. This group characterized the "overall purpose of the equality guarantee" as the prevention of "the violation of human dignity and freedom by imposing limitations, disadvantages or burdens through the stereotypical application of presumed group characteristics rather than on the basis of individual merit, capacity or circumstance" (per McLachlin J in *Miron*). On this approach, the laws at issue in *Miron* and *Egan* were found to be discriminatory, since they were premised on the stereotype that opposite-sex common law relationships and same-sex relationships are not "lasting, caring, mutually supportive relationships" characterized by "economic interdependence" (per Cory J in *Egan*).

Another group of four judges—Lamer CJC, Gonthier, La Forest, and Major JJ—added a new layer to the s. 15 analysis. To the three requirements of the *Andrews* test, they added a fourth precondition to a finding of discrimination: the personal characteristic at issue must be irrelevant to the functional values underlying the challenged law. On their view, since the functional value underlying the laws at issue in *Miron* and *Egan* was the support of marriage, it followed that marital status and sexual orientation were relevant and the laws therefore were not discriminatory. The addition of the "relevance" test represented a minority view that was harshly criticized by the other five members of the Court.

The third position, espoused by L'Heureux-Dubé J alone, recommended that the focus on grounds of discrimination be abandoned. For Justice L'Heureux-Dubé,

> at the heart of s. 15 is the promotion of a society in which all are secure in the knowledge that they are recognized at law as equal human beings, equally capable, and equally deserving. A person or group of persons has been discriminated against within the meaning of s. 15 of the Charter when members of that group have been made to feel, by virtue of the impugned legislative distinction, that they are less capable, or less worthy of recognition or value as human beings or as members of Canadian society, equally deserving of concern, respect, and consideration. These are the core elements of a definition of "discrimination"—a definition that focuses on impact (i.e. discriminatory effect) rather than on constituent elements (i.e. the grounds of the distinction).

In her view, a focus on grounds of discrimination distracted from the essential issues. The solution, she suggested, was to drop the search for an enumerated or analogous ground as a necessary precondition to a finding of discrimination. Instead, the analysis should focus on the nature of the group and the nature of the interest adversely affected by the challenged law. The more vulnerable the affected group, and the more fundamental the interest at stake, the more likely that a difference in treatment will be discriminatory. Applying this approach in the trilogy, L'Heureux-Dubé J concluded that the laws challenged in *Miron*, *Egan*, and *Thibaudeau* were all discriminatory.

In the first four equality rulings issued following the trilogy, members of the Supreme Court agreed on the result without resolving the differences in approach that had so fractured the Court in 1995. See *Eaton v. Brant County Board of Education*, [1997] 1 SCR 241, 142 DLR (4th) 385; *Benner v. Canada (Secretary of State)*, [1997] 1 SCR 358, 143 DLR (4th) 577; *Eldridge v. British Columbia (Attorney General)*, [1997] 3 SCR 624, 151 DLR (4th) 577; and *Vriend v. Alberta*, [1998] 1 SCR 493, 156 DLR (4th) 385. It was not until the decision in

Law v. Canada, released in 1999, that members of the Court were able to agree again on the interpretation of s. 15. The *Law* ruling replaced *Andrews* as the leading case on s. 15 until 2008, when the Court rendered its decision in *R v. Kapp*, [2008] 2 SCR 483, 294 DLR (4th) 1. As you read the excerpts below, consider the extent to which the ruling was faithful to McIntyre J's opinion in *Andrews*, and the extent to which Iacobucci J's compromise position borrowed from each of the three approaches articulated in the 1995 trilogy.

IV. THE LAW TEST

Law v. Canada (Minister of Employment and Immigration)
[1999] 1 SCR 497, 170 DLR (4th) 1

[The Canada Pension Plan (CPP) is a compulsory social insurance scheme that provides wage-earning contributors and their families with reasonable minimum levels of income upon the retirement, disability, or death of contributors. One of the benefits available under the CPP is the survivor's pension—a monthly benefit paid to a surviving spouse whose deceased partner has made sufficient contributions to the CPP. A claimant who is over the age of 45 at the time of the contributor's death, or is maintaining dependent children of the deceased contributor, or is (or becomes) disabled is entitled to receive the survivor's pension at the full rate. However, the legislation gradually reduces that pension for able-bodied surviving spouses without dependent children who are between the ages of 35 and 45, with the result that surviving spouses who are under 35 at the time of the death of the contributor are not entitled to a survivor's pension until they reach the age of 65.

The appellant, Nancy Law, was 30 years old when her husband died in 1991. At the time of his death, he was 50 and had contributed to the CPP for 22 years. The couple had no children. Law's request for survivor's benefits under the CPP was denied as she was under the age of 35 at the time of her husband's death, was not disabled, and did not have dependent children. She appealed on the ground that the age distinctions in the CPP discriminated against her on the basis of age contrary to s. 15(1) of the Charter. The Pension Appeal Board dismissed her appeal, ruling that the age distinctions did not violate s. 15(1) of the Charter and, even if they did, they would be justified under s. 1. A subsequent appeal to the Federal Court of Appeal was dismissed. Law then appealed to the Supreme Court of Canada. Justice Iacobucci, writing for a unanimous Court, dismissed the appeal.]

IACOBUCCI J for the Court (Lamer CJC, L'Heureux-Dubé, Gonthier, Cory, McLachlin, Major, Bastarache, and Binnie JJ):

I. *Introduction and Overview*

[1] … In my view, a purposive reading and application of s. 15(1) results in the conclusion that the appellant has not established discrimination within the meaning of the Charter.

[2] Section 15 of the Charter guarantees to every individual the right to equal treat ment by the state without discrimination. It is perhaps the Charter's most conceptually difficult provision. In this Court's first s. 15 case, *Andrews v. Law Society of British Columbia*, [1989] 1 SCR 143, at p. 164, McIntyre J noted that, as embodied in s. 15(1) of the Charter, the concept of equality is "an elusive concept," and that "more than any of the other rights and freedoms guaranteed in the Charter, it lacks precise definition." Part of the difficulty in defining the concept of equality stems from its exalted status. The quest for equality expresses some of humanity's highest ideals and aspirations, which are by their nature abstract and subject to differing articulations. The challenge for the judiciary in interpreting and applying s. 15(1) of the Charter is to transform these ideals and aspirations into practice in a manner which is meaningful to Canadians and which accords with the purpose of the provision.

· · ·

[5] Throughout [the brief history of this Court's interpretation of s. 15(1) of the Charter], although there have been differences of opinion among the members of this Court as to the appropriate interpretation of s. 15(1), I believe it is fair to say that there has been and continues to be general consensus regarding the basic principles relating to the purpose of s. 15(1) and the proper approach to equality analysis. In my view, the present case is a useful juncture at which to summarize and comment upon these basic principles, in order to provide a set of guidelines for courts that are called upon to analyze a discrimination claim under the Charter.

[6] In accordance with McIntyre J's caution in *Andrews, supra*, I think it is sensible to articulate the basic principles under s. 15(1) as guidelines for analysis, and not as a rigid test which might risk being mechanically applied. Equality analysis under the Charter must be purposive and contextual. The guidelines which I review below are just that— points of reference which are designed to assist a court in identifying the relevant contextual factors in a particular discrimination claim, and in evaluating the effect of those factors in light of the purpose of s. 15(1).

· · ·

VI. Analysis

A. Approach to Section 15(1)

[Iacobucci J reviewed McIntyre J's opinion in *Andrews*.]

[30] [T]he *Andrews* decision established that there are three key elements to a discrimination claim under s. 15(1) of the Charter: differential treatment, an enumerated or analogous ground, and discrimination in a substantive sense involving factors such as prejudice, stereotyping, and disadvantage. Of fundamental importance, as stressed repeatedly by all of the judges who wrote, the determination of whether each of these elements exists in a particular case is always to be undertaken in a purposive manner, taking into account the full social, political, and legal context of the claim.

· · ·

[31] The general approach adopted in *Andrews* was regularly applied in subsequent decisions of the Court.

· · ·

[35] Each of the elements of the approach to s. 15(1) articulated by the Court in *Andrews* and confirmed in later cases has developed and been enriched by the subsequent jurisprudence.

[36] In *Eaton* [*v. Brant County Board of Education*, [1997] 1 SCR 241, 142 DLR (4th) 385], at paras. 66-67, Sopinka J for the full Court elaborated upon the point made by McIntyre J in *Andrews* that, although in many cases a claimant will be able to establish substantively differential treatment by pointing to a formal distinction drawn by the impugned legislation, there are other ways to establish differential treatment. In particular, Sopinka J noted that an approach which requires proof of an express legislative distinction is not necessarily applicable where a claim of "adverse effects" discrimination is made. In such cases, it is the legislation's failure to take into account the true characteristics of a disadvantaged person or group within Canadian society (i.e., by treating all persons in a formally identical manner), and not the express drawing of a distinction, which triggers s. 15(1). ...

[37] In a similar vein, relating to the issue of enumerated and analogous grounds, the Court has had the opportunity to develop the principles relating to the indicia of an analogous ground. ... Notably, in *Symes* [*v. Canada*, [1993] 4 SCR 695, 110 DLR (4th) 470], this Court recognized that, although *Andrews* spoke of differential treatment being based upon one enumerated or analogous ground, it is open to a s. 15(1) claimant to articulate a discrimination claim on the basis of more than one ground. As is discussed in more detail below, the claimant may place the evidentiary focus of the claim upon a person or subgroup identified by several grounds. ...

[38] In the same way, the jurisprudence of the Court has affirmed and clarified McIntyre J's emphasis in *Andrews* upon the necessity of establishing discrimination in a substantive or purposive sense, beyond mere proof of a distinction on enumerated or analogous grounds. ...

[39] ... [A] court that is called upon to determine a discrimination claim under s. 15(1) should make the following three broad inquiries. First, does the impugned law (a) draw a formal distinction between the claimant and others on the basis of one or more personal characteristics, or (b) fail to take into account the claimant's already disadvantaged position within Canadian society resulting in substantively differential treatment between the claimant and others on the basis of one or more personal characteristics? If so, there is differential treatment for the purpose of s. 15(1). Second, was the claimant subject to differential treatment on the basis of one or more of the enumerated and analogous grounds? And third, does the differential treatment discriminate in a substantive sense, bringing into play the purpose of s. 15(1) of the Charter in remedying such ills as prejudice, stereotyping, and historical disadvantage? The second and third inquiries are concerned with whether the differential treatment constitutes discrimination in the substantive sense intended by s. 15(1).

B. The Purpose of Section 15(1)

[40] … [T]he proper approach to the definition of rights guaranteed by the Charter is a purposive one. …

[41] Since the beginning of its s. 15(1) jurisprudence, this Court has recognized that the existence of a conflict between an impugned law and the purpose of s. 15(1) is essential in order to found a discrimination claim. This principle holds true with respect to each element of a discrimination claim. The determination of whether legislation fails to take into account existing disadvantage, or whether a claimant falls within one or more of the enumerated and analogous grounds, or whether differential treatment may be said to constitute discrimination within the meaning of s. 15(1), must all be undertaken in a purposive and contextual manner.

[42] What is the purpose of the s. 15(1) equality guarantee? There is great continuity in the jurisprudence of this Court on this issue. …

[A review of the cases, including *Andrews*, *Turpin*, *Weatherall*, *Eaton*, *Egan*, and *Miron*, is omitted.]

[51] All of these statements share several key elements. It may be said that the purpose of s. 15(1) is to prevent the violation of essential human dignity and freedom through the imposition of disadvantage, stereotyping, or political or social prejudice, and to promote a society in which all persons enjoy equal recognition at law as human beings or as members of Canadian society, equally capable and equally deserving of concern, respect and consideration. Legislation which effects differential treatment between individuals or groups will violate this fundamental purpose where those who are subject to differential treatment fall within one or more enumerated or analogous grounds, and where the differential treatment reflects the stereotypical application of presumed group or personal characteristics, or otherwise has the effect of perpetuating or promoting the view that the individual is less capable, or less worthy of recognition or value as a human being or as a member of Canadian society. Alternatively, differential treatment will not likely constitute discrimination within the purpose of s. 15(1) where it does not violate the human dignity or freedom of a person or group in this way, and in particular where the differential treatment also assists in ameliorating the position of the disadvantaged within Canadian society.

[52] As noted above, one of the difficulties in defining the concepts of "equality" and "discrimination" is the abstract nature of the words and the similarly abstract nature of words used to explain them. No single word or phrase can fully describe the content and purpose of s. 15(1). However, in the articulation of the purpose of s. 15(1) just provided on the basis of past cases, a focus is quite properly placed upon the goal of assuring human dignity by the remedying of discriminatory treatment.

[53] What is human dignity? There can be different conceptions of what human dignity means. For the purpose of analysis under s. 15(1) of the Charter, however, the jurisprudence of this Court reflects a specific, albeit non-exhaustive, definition. As noted by Lamer CJ in *Rodriguez v. British Columbia (Attorney General)*, [1993] 3 SCR 519, at p. 554, the equality guarantee in s. 15(1) is concerned with the realization of personal

autonomy and self-determination. Human dignity means that an individual or group feels self-respect and self-worth. It is concerned with physical and psychological integrity and empowerment. Human dignity is harmed by unfair treatment premised upon personal traits or circumstances which do not relate to individual needs, capacities, or merits. It is enhanced by laws which are sensitive to the needs, capacities, and merits of different individuals, taking into account the context underlying their differences. Human dignity is harmed when individuals and groups are marginalized, ignored, or devalued, and is enhanced when laws recognize the full place of all individuals and groups within Canadian society. Human dignity within the meaning of the equality guarantee does not relate to the status or position of an individual in society per se, but rather concerns the manner in which a person legitimately feels when confronted with a particular law. Does the law treat him or her unfairly, taking into account all of the circumstances regarding the individuals affected and excluded by the law?

[54] The equality guarantee in s. 15(1) of the Charter must be understood and applied in light of the above understanding of its purpose. The overriding concern with protecting and promoting human dignity in the sense just described infuses all elements of the discrimination analysis.

[55] In order to determine whether the fundamental purpose of s. 15(1) is brought into play in a particular claim, it is essential to engage in a comparative analysis which takes into consideration the surrounding context of the claim and the claimant. I now propose to comment briefly on the nature of the comparative approach, and then to examine some of the contextual factors that a court should consider in determining whether s. 15(1) has been infringed. Each factor may be more or less relevant depending upon the circumstances of the case.

C. The Comparative Approach

[56] As discussed above, McIntyre J emphasized in *Andrews*, *supra*, that the equality guarantee is a comparative concept. Ultimately, a court must identify differential treatment as compared to one or more other persons or groups. Locating the appropriate comparator is necessary in identifying differential treatment and the grounds of the distinction. Identifying the appropriate comparator will be relevant when considering many of the contextual factors in the discrimination analysis.

[57] To locate the appropriate comparator, we must consider a variety of factors, including the subject-matter of the legislation. The object of a s. 15(1) analysis is not to determine equality in the abstract; it is to determine whether the impugned legislation creates differential treatment between the claimant and others on the basis of enumerated or analogous grounds, which results in discrimination. Both the purpose and the effect of the legislation must be considered in determining the appropriate comparison group or groups. Other contextual factors may also be relevant. The biological, historical, and sociological similarities or dissimilarities may be relevant in establishing the relevant comparator in particular, and whether the legislation effects discrimination in a substantive sense more generally. ...

[58] When identifying the relevant comparator, the natural starting point is to consider the claimant's view. It is the claimant who generally chooses the person, group, or

groups with whom he or she wishes to be compared for the purpose of the discrimination inquiry, thus setting the parameters of the alleged differential treatment that he or she wishes to challenge. However, the claimant's characterization of the comparison may not always be sufficient. It may be that the differential treatment is not between the groups identified by the claimant, but rather between other groups. Clearly a court cannot, *ex proprio motu*, evaluate a ground of discrimination not pleaded by the parties and in relation to which no evidence has been adduced. ... However, within the scope of the ground or grounds pleaded, I would not close the door on the power of a court to refine the comparison presented by the claimant where warranted.

D. Establishing Discrimination in a Purposive Sense: Contextual Factors

(1) The Appropriate Perspective

[59] The determination of the appropriate comparator, and the evaluation of the contextual factors which determine whether legislation has the effect of demeaning a claimant's dignity must be conducted from the perspective of the claimant. As applied in practice in several of this Court's equality decisions, and as neatly discussed by L'Heureux-Dubé J in *Egan* [*v. Canada*, [1995] 2 SCR 513, 124 DLR (4th) 609], at para. 56, the focus of the discrimination inquiry is both subjective and objective: subjective in so far as the right to equal treatment is an individual right, asserted by a specific claimant with particular traits and circumstances; and objective in so far as it is possible to determine whether the individual claimant's equality rights have been infringed only by considering the larger context of the legislation in question, and society's past and present treatment of the claimant and of other persons or groups with similar characteristics or circumstances. The objective component means that it is not sufficient, in order to ground a s. 15(1) claim, for a claimant simply to assert, without more, that his or her dignity has been adversely affected by a law.

[60] As stated by L'Heureux-Dubé J in *Egan*, *supra*, at para. 56, the relevant point of view is that of the reasonable person, dispassionate and fully apprised of the circumstances, possessed of similar attributes to, and under similar circumstances as, the claimant. Although I stress that the inquiry into whether legislation demeans the claimant's dignity must be undertaken from the perspective of the claimant and from no other perspective, a court must be satisfied that the claimant's assertion that differential treatment imposed by legislation demeans his or her dignity is supported by an objective assessment of the situation. All of that individual's or that group's traits, history, and circumstances must be considered in evaluating whether a reasonable person in circumstances similar to those of the claimant would find that the legislation which imposes differential treatment has the effect of demeaning his or her dignity.

. . .

(2) Contextual Factors

[62] There is a variety of factors which may be referred to by a s. 15(1) claimant in order to demonstrate that legislation has the effect of demeaning his or her dignity, as dignity is understood for the purpose of the Charter equality guarantee. In these reasons

I discuss four such factors in particular, although, as I discuss below, there are undoubtedly others, and not all four factors will necessarily be relevant in every case.

a. PRE-EXISTING DISADVANTAGE

[63] As has been consistently recognized throughout this Court's jurisprudence, probably the most compelling factor favouring a conclusion that differential treatment imposed by legislation is truly discriminatory will be, where it exists, pre-existing disadvantage, vulnerability, stereotyping, or prejudice experienced by the individual or group. ... These factors are relevant because, to the extent that the claimant is already subject to unfair circumstances or treatment in society by virtue of personal characteristics or circumstances, persons like him or her have often not been given equal concern, respect, and consideration. It is logical to conclude that, in most cases, further differential treatment will contribute to the perpetuation or promotion of their unfair social characterization, and will have a more severe impact upon them, since they are already vulnerable.

[64] One consideration which the Court has frequently referred to with respect to the issue of pre-existing disadvantage is the role of stereotypes. A stereotype may be described as a misconception whereby a person or, more often, a group is unfairly portrayed as possessing undesirable traits, or traits which the group, or at least some of its members, do not possess. In my view, probably the most prevalent reason that a given legislative provision may be found to infringe s. 15(1) is that it reflects and reinforces existing inaccurate understandings of the merits, capabilities and worth of a particular person or group within Canadian society, resulting in further stigmatization of that person or the members of the group or otherwise in their unfair treatment. This view accords with the emphasis placed by this Court ever since *Andrews*, *supra*, upon the role of s. 15(1) in overcoming prejudicial stereotypes in society. However, proof of the existence of a stereotype in society regarding a particular person or group is not an indispensable element of a successful claim under s. 15(1). Such a restriction would unduly constrain discrimination analysis, when there is more than one way to demonstrate a violation of human dignity. I emphasize, then, that any demonstration by a claimant that a legislative provision or other state action has the effect of perpetuating or promoting the view that the individual is less capable, or less worthy of recognition or value as a human being or as a member of Canadian society (whether or not it involves a demonstration that the provision or other state action corroborates or exacerbates an existing prejudicial stereotype), will suffice to establish an infringement of s. 15(1).

[65] It should be stressed that, while it is helpful to demonstrate the existence of historic disadvantage, it is of course not necessary to show such disadvantage in order to establish a s. 15(1) violation, for at least two distinct reasons. On the one hand, this Court has stated several times that, although a distinction drawn on such a basis is an important indicium of discrimination, it is not determinative. ... A member of any of the more advantaged groups in society is clearly entitled to bring a s. 15(1) claim which, in appropriate cases, will be successful.

[66] On the other hand, it may be misleading or inappropriate in some cases to speak about "membership" within a group for the purpose of a s. 15(1) claim. The Charter guarantees equality rights to individuals. In this respect, it must be made clear that the s. 15(1) claimant is not required to establish membership in a sociologically recognized group in

order to be successful. It will always be helpful to the claimant to be able to identify a pattern of discrimination against a class of persons with traits similar to the claimant, i.e., a group, of which the claimant may consider herself or himself a member. Nonetheless, an infringement of s. 15(1) may be established by other means, and may exist even if there is no one similar to the claimant who is experiencing the same unfair treatment.

[67] At the same time, I also do not wish to suggest that the claimant's association with a group which has historically been more disadvantaged will be conclusive of a violation under s. 15(1), where differential treatment has been established. This may be the result, but whether or not it is the result will depend upon the circumstances of the case and, in particular, upon whether or not the distinction truly affects the dignity of the claimant. There is no principle or evidentiary presumption that differential treatment for historically disadvantaged persons is discriminatory.

[68] Moreover, in line with my earlier comment, in referring to groups which, historically, have been more or less disadvantaged, I do not wish to imply the existence of a strict dichotomy of advantaged and disadvantaged groups, within which each claimant must be classified. I mean to identify simply the social reality that a member of a group which historically has been more disadvantaged in Canadian society is less likely to have difficulty in demonstrating discrimination. Since *Andrews*, it has been recognized in the jurisprudence of this Court that an important, though not exclusive, purpose of s. 15(1) is the protection of individuals and groups who are vulnerable, disadvantaged, or members of "discrete and insular minorities." The effects of a law as they relate to this purpose should always be a central consideration in the contextual s. 15(1) analysis.

b. RELATIONSHIP BETWEEN GROUNDS AND THE CLAIMANT'S CHARACTERISTICS
   OR CIRCUMSTANCES

[69] What are some factors other than an individual's or a group's pre-existing disadvantage which may be referred to by a s. 15(1) claimant in order to demonstrate a negative effect upon the claimant's dignity? One factor in some circumstances may be the relationship between the ground upon which the claim is based and the nature of the differential treatment. Some of the enumerated and analogous grounds have the potential to correspond with need, capacity, or circumstances. As was recognized in *Eaton, supra*, and in *Eldridge* [*v. British Columbia (Attorney General)*, [1997] 3 SCR 624, 151 DLR (4th) 577], one of these grounds is disability, where the avoidance of discrimination will frequently require distinctions be made to take into account the actual personal characteristics of disabled persons. Another ground is sex, as was recognized by this Court in *Weatherall* [*v. Canada (Attorney General)*, [1993] 2 SCR 872, 105 DLR (4th) 210], and, in the context of a statutory human rights code, in *Brooks v. Canada Safeway*, [1989] 1 SCR 1219 [59 DLR (4th) 321]. A further such ground is age, where need, capacity, or circumstances may again correspond with the ground.

[70] It is thus necessary to analyze in a purposive manner the ground upon which the s. 15(1) claim is based when determining whether discrimination has been established. As a general matter, ... legislation which takes into account the actual needs, capacity, or circumstances of the claimant and others with similar traits in a manner that respects their value as human beings and members of Canadian society will be less likely to have a negative effect on human dignity. This is not to say that the mere fact of impugned

legislation's having to some degree taken into account the actual situation of persons like the claimant will be sufficient to defeat a s. 15(1) claim. The focus must always remain upon the central question of whether, viewed from the perspective of the claimant, the differential treatment imposed by the legislation has the effect of violating human dignity. The fact that the impugned legislation may achieve a valid social purpose for one group of individuals cannot function to deny an equality claim where the effects of the legislation upon another person or group conflict with the purpose of the s. 15(1) guarantee. ... I mean simply to state that it will be easier to establish discrimination to the extent that impugned legislation fails to take into account a claimant's actual situation, and more difficult to establish discrimination to the extent that legislation properly accommodates the claimant's needs, capacities, and circumstances.

[71] Examples are prevalent in the jurisprudence of this Court of legislation or other state action which either failed to take into account the actual situation of a claimant, or alternatively quite properly treated a claimant differently on the basis of actual personal differences between individuals. In *Eldridge, supra*, for example, a provincial government's failure to provide limited funding for sign language interpreters for deaf persons when receiving medical services was found to violate s. 15(1), in part on the basis that the government's failure to take into account the actual needs of deaf persons infringed their human dignity. Conversely, in *Weatherall, supra*, it was stated that the decision to permit cross-gender prison searches of male prisoners but not of female prisoners likely did not violate s. 15(1), because such a difference in treatment was appropriate in light of the historical, biological and sociological differences between men and women.

c. AMELIORATIVE PURPOSE OR EFFECTS

[72] Another possibly important factor will be the ameliorative purpose or effects of impugned legislation or other state action upon a more disadvantaged person or group in society. As stated by Sopinka J in *Eaton, supra*, at para. 66: "the purpose of s. 15(1) of the Charter is not only to prevent discrimination by the attribution of stereotypical characteristics to individuals, but also to ameliorate the position of groups within Canadian society who have suffered disadvantage by exclusion from mainstream society." An ameliorative purpose or effect which accords with the purpose of s. 15(1) of the Charter will likely not violate the human dignity of more advantaged individuals where the exclusion of these more advantaged individuals largely corresponds to the greater need or the different circumstances experienced by the disadvantaged group being targeted by the legislation. I emphasize that this factor will likely only be relevant where the person or group that is excluded from the scope of ameliorative legislation or other state action is more advantaged in a relative sense. Underinclusive ameliorative legislation that excludes from its scope the members of an historically disadvantaged group will rarely escape the charge of discrimination: see *Vriend* [*v. Alberta*, [1998] 1 SCR 493, 156 DLR (4th) 385], at paras. 94-104, per Cory J.

[73] At the same time, I would not wish to be taken as foreclosing the possibility that a member of society could be discriminated against by laws aimed at ameliorating the situation of others, requiring the court to consider justification under s. 1, or the operation of s. 15(2). The possibility of new forms of discrimination denying essential human worth cannot be foreclosed. This said, the ameliorative aim and effect of the law is a fac-

tor to be considered in determining whether discrimination is present. Conversely, where the impugned legislation does not have a purpose or effect which is ameliorative in s. 15(1) terms, this factor may be of some assistance, depending upon the circumstances, in establishing a s. 15(1) infringement.

d. NATURE OF THE INTEREST AFFECTED

[74] A further contextual factor which may be relevant in appropriate cases in determining whether the claimant's dignity has been violated will be the nature and scope of the interest affected by the legislation. This point was well explained by L'Heureux-Dubé J in *Egan*, *supra*, at paras. 63-64. As she noted, at para. 63, "[i]f all other things are equal, the more severe and localized the ... consequences on the affected group, the more likely that the distinction responsible for these consequences is discriminatory within the meaning of s. 15 of the Charter." L'Heureux-Dubé J explained, at para. 64, that the discriminatory calibre of differential treatment cannot be fully appreciated without evaluating not only the economic but also the constitutional and societal significance attributed to the interest or interests adversely affected by the legislation in question. Moreover, it is relevant to consider whether the distinction restricts access to a fundamental social institution, or affects "a basic aspect of full membership in Canadian society," or "constitute[s] a complete non-recognition of a particular group."

[75] There are other factors which may be referred to by a s. 15(1) claimant in order to establish an infringement of equality rights in a purposive sense, but they are not directly relevant to the inquiry in the present appeal. Guidance as to these other factors may be found in previous decisions of this Court, and through analogy to the factors listed above. The general theme, though, may be simply stated. An infringement of s. 15(1) of the Charter exists if it can be demonstrated that, from the perspective of a reasonable person in circumstances similar to those of the claimant who takes into account the contextual factors relevant to the claim, the legislative imposition of differential treatment has the effect of demeaning his or her dignity: see *Egan*, *supra*, at para. 56, per L'Heureux-Dubé J. Demonstrating the existence of discrimination in this purposive sense will require a claimant to advert to factors capable of supporting an inference that the purpose of s. 15(1) of the Charter has been infringed by the legislation.

[Iacobucci J went on to comment on the nature and extent of the claimant's burden under s. 15(1). He noted that while data and other kinds of social science evidence may help establish a violation of the claimant's dignity, this kind of evidence is not necessary, and that a court may often, where appropriate, make a determination of whether impugned legislation violates s. 15(1) on the basis of judicial notice and logical reasoning alone. He also emphasized that the claimant need not prove that the intent of the impugned government decision was discriminatory.]

[84] ... I have reviewed in these reasons the general approach taken to s. 15(1) by this Court, which involves three broad elements, namely (1) the existence of differential treatment, (2) the presence of enumerated or analogous grounds, and (3) discrimination which brings into play the purpose of s. 15(1). However, it is possible to understand the third element of the s. 15(1) inquiry as really being a restatement of the requirement that

there be substantive rather than merely formal inequality in order for an infringement of
s. 15(1) to have been made out. Under this alternative view, the definition of "substantive
inequality" is "discrimination" within the meaning of the Charter, bringing into play the
claimant's human dignity. No substantive inequality would exist where the claimant's
human dignity was not brought into play by his or her treatment by the state.

[85] I agree with the general idea that, in practice in some cases, it may well be duplicative to determine first whether differential treatment exists, and then to determine
whether the purpose of s. 15(1) has been brought into play ... [T]his will particularly be
the case where adverse effects discrimination is at issue, since the analysis of whether the
claimant's difference has been effectively ignored by an impugned law will usually bring
into play issues of human dignity. In such cases, there may be no real difference in analysis or result regardless of whether one or the other approach is used.

· · ·

E. Summary of Guidelines

[88] Before moving on to apply the principles that I have just discussed to the facts
of this case, I believe it would be useful to summarize some of the main guidelines for
analysis under s. 15(1) to be derived from the jurisprudence of this Court, as reviewed in
these reasons. As I stated above, these guidelines should not be seen as a strict test, but
rather should be understood as points of reference for a court that is called upon to decide whether a claimant's right to equality without discrimination under the Charter has
been infringed. Inevitably, the guidelines summarized here will need to be supplemented
in practice by the explanation of these guidelines in these reasons and those of previous
cases, and by a full appreciation of the context surrounding the specific s. 15(1) claim at
issue. It goes without saying that as our s. 15 jurisprudence evolves it may well be that
further elaborations and modifications will emerge.

General Approach

1. It is inappropriate to attempt to confine analysis under s. 15(1) of the Charter to
    a fixed and limited formula. A purposive and contextual approach to discrimina-
    tion analysis is to be preferred, in order to permit the realization of the strong re-
    medial purpose of the equality guarantee, and to avoid the pitfalls of a formalistic
    or mechanical approach.

2. The approach adopted and regularly applied by this Court to the interpretation
    of s. 15(1) focuses upon three central issues:

    A. whether a law imposes differential treatment between the claimant and
        others, in purpose or effect;

    B. whether one or more enumerated or analogous grounds of discrimination
        are the basis for the differential treatment; and

    C. whether the law in question has a purpose or effect that is discriminatory
        within the meaning of the equality guarantee.

The first issue is concerned with the question of whether the law causes differential treatment. The second and third issues are concerned with whether the differential treatment constitutes discrimination in the substantive sense intended by s. 15(1).

3. Accordingly, a court that is called upon to determine a discrimination claim under s. 15(1) should make the following three broad inquiries:

    A. Does the impugned law (a) draw a formal distinction between the claimant and others on the basis of one or more personal characteristics, or (b) fail to take into account the claimant's already disadvantaged position within Canadian society resulting in substantively differential treatment between the claimant and others on the basis of one or more personal characteristics?

    B. Is the claimant subject to differential treatment based on one or more enumerated and analogous grounds?

and

    C. Does the differential treatment discriminate, by imposing a burden upon or withholding a benefit from the claimant in a manner which reflects the stereotypical application of presumed group or personal characteristics, or which otherwise has the effect of perpetuating or promoting the view that the individual is less capable or worthy of recognition or value as a human being or as a member of Canadian society, equally deserving of concern, respect, and consideration?

Purpose

4. In general terms, the purpose of s. 15(1) is to prevent the violation of essential human dignity and freedom through the imposition of disadvantage, stereotyping, or political or social prejudice, and to promote a society in which all persons enjoy equal recognition at law as human beings or as members of Canadian society, equally capable and equally deserving of concern, respect and consideration.

5. The existence of a conflict between the purpose or effect of an impugned law and the purpose of s. 15(1) is essential in order to found a discrimination claim. The determination of whether such a conflict exists is to be made through an analysis of the full context surrounding the claim and the claimant.

Comparative Approach

6. The equality guarantee is a comparative concept, which ultimately requires a court to establish one or more relevant comparators. The claimant generally chooses the person, group, or groups with whom he or she wishes to be compared for the purpose of the discrimination inquiry. However, where the claimant's characterization of the comparison is insufficient, a court may, within the scope of the ground or grounds pleaded, refine the comparison presented by the claimant where warranted. Locating the relevant comparison group requires an

examination of the subject-matter of the legislation and its effects, as well as a full appreciation of context.

Context

7. The contextual factors which determine whether legislation has the effect of demeaning a claimant's dignity must be construed and examined from the perspective of the claimant. The focus of the inquiry is both subjective and objective. The relevant point of view is that of the reasonable person, in circumstances similar to those of the claimant, who takes into account the contextual factors relevant to the claim.

8. There is a variety of factors which may be referred to by a s. 15(1) claimant in order to demonstrate that legislation demeans his or her dignity. The list of factors is not closed. Guidance as to these factors may be found in the jurisprudence of this Court, and by analogy to recognized factors.

9. Some important contextual factors influencing the determination of whether s. 15(1) has been infringed are, among others:

   A. Pre-existing disadvantage, stereotyping, prejudice, or vulnerability experienced by the individual or group at issue. The effects of a law as they relate to the important purpose of s. 15(1) in protecting individuals or groups who are vulnerable, disadvantaged, or members of "discrete and insular minorities" should always be a central consideration. Although the claimant's association with an historically more advantaged or disadvantaged group or groups is not per se determinative of an infringement, the existence of these pre-existing factors will favour a finding that s. 15(1) has been infringed.

   B. The correspondence, or lack thereof, between the ground or grounds on which the claim is based and the actual need, capacity, or circumstances of the claimant or others. Although the mere fact that the impugned legislation takes into account the claimant's traits or circumstances will not necessarily be sufficient to defeat a s. 15(1) claim, it will generally be more difficult to establish discrimination to the extent that the law takes into account the claimant's actual situation in a manner that respects his or her value as a human being or member of Canadian society, and less difficult to do so where the law fails to take into account the claimant's actual situation.

   C. The ameliorative purpose or effects of the impugned law upon a more disadvantaged person or group in society. An ameliorative purpose or effect which accords with the purpose of s. 15(1) of the Charter will likely not violate the human dignity of more advantaged individuals where the exclusion of these more advantaged individuals largely corresponds to the greater need or the different circumstances experienced by the disadvantaged group being targeted by the legislation. This factor is more relevant where the s. 15(1) claim is brought by a more advantaged member of society.

and

    D. The nature and scope of the interest affected by the impugned law. The more severe and localized the consequences of the legislation for the affected group, the more likely that the differential treatment responsible for these consequences is discriminatory within the meaning of s. 15(1).

10. Although the s. 15(1) claimant bears the onus of establishing an infringement of his or her equality rights in a purposive sense through reference to one or more contextual factors, it is not necessarily the case that the claimant must adduce evidence in order to show a violation of human dignity or freedom. Frequently, where differential treatment is based on one or more enumerated or analogous grounds, this will be sufficient to found an infringement of s. 15(1) in the sense that it will be evident on the basis of judicial notice and logical reasoning that the distinction is discriminatory within the meaning of the provision.

F. Application to the Case at Bar

[Iacobucci J found that the impugned provisions of the CPP draw a distinction on the basis of an enumerated ground, age, that results in unequal treatment in the form of either a delay or reduction of benefits. He rejected the government's argument that because entitlement to the survivor's pension depends upon the interplay of three factors, namely, age, disability and responsibility for dependent children, the legislation could not be said to draw a distinction based on age. He stated that in an appropriate case a discrimination claim positing an intersection of grounds might be understood as analogous to, or as a synthesis of, the grounds listed in s. 15(1).

    Iacobucci J then turned to the third stage of the s. 15 analysis: whether the differential treatment of widows in Nancy Law's situation amounted to discrimination.]

Discrimination

[95] The central question in the present case is whether the age distinctions drawn by ss. 44(1)(d) and 58 of the CPP impose a disadvantage upon the appellant as a younger adult in a manner which constitutes discrimination under s. 15(1) of the Charter. The appellant is asserting her claim solely on the basis of age—specifically, on the basis of being an adult under the age of 45. Relatively speaking, adults under the age of 45 have not been consistently and routinely subjected to the sorts of discrimination faced by some of Canada's discrete and insular minorities. For this reason, it will be more difficult as a practical matter for this Court to reason, from facts of which the Court may appropriately take judicial notice, that the legislative distinction at issue violates the human dignity of the appellant.

[96] The appellant argues that the impugned CPP provisions infringe s. 15(1) of the Charter in both their purpose and their effect. She submits that the original intent underlying the distinctions created by ss. 44(1)(d) and 58 was to provide benefits to those surviving spouses most in need, based on an assumed correlation between, among other things, increased age and one's ability to enter or re-enter the workforce following the

death of one's spouse. The appellant argues that this assumed correlation is faulty because, in fact, young people generally, and the appellant in particular, have difficulty in obtaining employment, and the legislation's assumptions to the contrary are based on false stereotypes regarding the advantages of youth. The appellant submits that there is no evidence establishing a direct link between a survivor's age at the time of the spouse's death and the need for benefits. She suggests that the effect of the impugned provisions is to demean the dignity of adults under the age of 45 and to treat them as being less worthy than older adults, by stereotyping them as being less in need.

· · ·

[98] In reply, the respondent maintains that, although the age distinctions in the survivor's pension provisions of the CPP might initially have been based upon assumptions, the accuracy of those assumptions are also today reflected in statistical data, other legislation, and several decisions of this Court. The respondent also emphasizes that the assumptions underlying the impugned CPP provisions concern, not the relatively immediate financial needs of surviving spouses, but their long-term financial needs.

[99] The questions, to take up the dignity-related concerns discussed above, may be put in the following terms. Do the impugned CPP provisions, in purpose or effect, violate essential human dignity and freedom through the imposition of disadvantage, stereotyping, or political or social prejudice? Does the law, in purpose or effect, conform to a society in which all persons enjoy equal recognition as human beings or as members of Canadian society, equally capable and equally deserving of concern, respect, and consideration? Does the law, in purpose or effect, perpetuate the view that people under 45 are less capable or less worthy of recognition or value as human beings or as members of Canadian society?

[100] ... [The appellant] has not demonstrated that either the purpose or the effect of the impugned legislative provisions violates her human dignity in the sense discussed above so as to constitute discrimination. I agree with the appellant that surviving spouses of all ages are vulnerable, economically and otherwise, immediately following the death of a spouse. However, as both the appellant and respondent acknowledged in their submissions before this Court, the purpose and function of the impugned CPP provisions is not to remedy the immediate financial need experienced by widows and widowers, but rather to enable older widows and widowers to meet their basic needs during the longer term.

[101] As the appellant states, reflected in the age distinctions in the survivor's pension provisions of the CPP appears to be the notion that young persons experience fewer impediments to long-term labour force participation and are generally in a better position than older persons to replace independently over the long run as a working member of Canadian society the income of a deceased spouse. It seems to me that the increasing difficulty with which one can find and maintain employment as one grows older is a matter of which a court may appropriately take judicial notice ... .

[102] ... The law on its face treats ... younger people differently, but the differential treatment does not reflect or promote the notion that they are less capable or less deserving of concern, respect, and consideration, when the dual perspectives of long-term security and the greater opportunity of youth are considered. Nor does the differential treatment perpetuate the view that people in this class are less capable or less worthy of recognition or value as human beings or as members of Canadian society. Given the con-

temporary and historical context of the differential treatment and those affected by it, the legislation does not stereotype, exclude, or devalue adults under 45. The law functions not by the device of stereotype, but by distinctions corresponding to the actual situation of individuals it affects. By being young, the appellant, *a fortiori*, has greater prospect of long-term income replacement.

[103] Another factor supporting the view that the impugned CPP provisions do not violate essential human dignity is the clear ameliorative purpose of the pension scheme for older surviving spouses. Older surviving spouses, like surviving spouses who are disabled or who care for dependent children, are more economically vulnerable to the long-term effects of the death of a spouse. Parliament's intent in enacting a survivor's pension scheme with benefits allocated according to age appears to have been to allocate funds to those persons whose ability to overcome need was weakest … . Given that the appellant is more advantaged in a relative sense, and that the legislative distinctions in the present case largely correspond to the greater long-term need and different circumstances experienced by the more disadvantaged group being targeted by the legislation, I find it difficult to perceive in the purpose or effects of the impugned legislation a violation of the appellant's dignity.

[104] The challenged legislation simply reflects the fact that people in the appellant's position are more able to overcome long-term need because of the nature of a human being's life cycle. … Young people are inherently better able to initiate and maintain long-term labour force participation, and as such the impugned CPP provisions cannot be said to impose a discriminatory disadvantage upon them. In such narrow circumstances, where legislation does not demean the dignity of those it excludes in either its purpose or its effects, it is open to the legislature to use age as a proxy for long-term need.

[105] In referring to the existence of a correspondence between a legislative distinction in treatment and the actual situation of different individuals or groups, I do not wish to imply that legislation must always correspond perfectly with social reality in order to comply with s. 15(1) of the Charter. The determination of whether a legislative provision infringes a claimant's dignity must in every case be considered in the full context of the claim. In the present case, the appellant is more advantaged by virtue of her young age. She is challenging the validity of legislation with an egalitarian purpose and function whose provisions correspond to a very large degree with the needs and circumstances of the persons whom the legislation targets. There are no other factors suggesting that her dignity as a younger adult is demeaned by the legislation, either in its purpose or in its effects.

[106] Under these circumstances, the fact that the legislation is premised upon informed statistical generalizations which may not correspond perfectly with the long-term financial need of all surviving spouses does not affect the ultimate conclusion that the legislation is consonant with the human dignity and freedom of the appellant. Parliament is entitled, under these limited circumstances at least, to premise remedial legislation upon informed generalizations without running afoul of s. 15(1) of the Charter and being required to justify its position under s. 1. I emphasize, though, that under other circumstances a more precise correspondence will undoubtedly be required in order to comply with s. 15(1). In particular, a more precise correspondence will likely be important where the individual or group which is excluded by the legislation is already disadvantaged or vulnerable within Canadian society.

[107] In conclusion with respect to the particular circumstances of the appellant's case, I would also note that people in the position of the appellant are not completely excluded from obtaining a survivor's pension, although it is delayed until the person reaches age 65 unless they become disabled before then. The availability of the pension to the appellant strengthens the conclusion that the law does not reflect a view of the appellant that suggests she is undeserving or less worthy as a person, only that the distribution of the benefit to her will be delayed until she is at a different point in her life cycle, when she reaches retirement age.

[108] In these circumstances, recalling the purposes of s. 15(1), I am at a loss to locate any violation of human dignity. The impugned distinctions in the present case do not stigmatize young persons, nor can they be said to perpetuate the view that surviving spouses under age 45 are less deserving of concern, respect or consideration than any others. Nor do they withhold a government benefit on the basis of stereotypical assumptions about the demographic group of which the appellant happens to be a member. I must conclude that, when considered in the social, political, and legal context of the claim, the age distinctions in ss. 44(1)(d) and 58 of the CPP are not discriminatory.

. . .

[110] I conclude, then, that this is one of the rare cases contemplated in *Andrews*, *supra*, in which differential treatment based on one or more of the enumerated or analogous grounds in s. 15(1) is not discriminatory. It is important to identify such cases through a purposive analysis of s. 15(1), in order to ensure that analysis under s. 15(1) does not become mechanistic, but rather addresses the true social, political and legal context underlying each and every equality claim.

1. Section 1 of the Charter

[111] As I have found no violation of s. 15(1) of the Charter, it is not necessary to turn to s. 1.

Appeal dismissed.

NOTES AND QUESTIONS

1. The Court distinguished between a rule-bound, formal, rigid, and mechanical formula for equality, which it rejected, and a flexible, nuanced, adaptive, contextual, purposive, and remedial set of guidelines. What is at stake in this differentiation? Do you think that the Court worked with the situation of the claimant and the terms of the legislation in as much detail as was warranted? If you think that deeper analysis was called for on some questions, is this a failure to contextualize sufficiently?

2. The Court told Nancy Law that the benefit she claimed was unavailable to her because of her age, which stands as a proxy for her ability to re-enter the job market or remarry. Assuming that these are real statistical possibilities, they do not seem to be the kind of transitions that one can take quickly and easily after the loss of a spouse. This seems to be the type of situation that requires short-term, rather than long-term, assistance. The likelihood of re-establishing financial security and/or remarrying may be different for men and women

in the under-45 age bracket. Should these considerations have been taken into account in the Court's Charter analysis?

3. After members of the Court had presented three different approaches to the interpretation of s. 15 in the 1995 trilogy of decisions, the *Law* ruling signalled a welcome return to a single approach favoured by a unanimous Court. Unanimity, however, was purchased at some cost to clarity and predictability, and by adding to the claimant's burden in establishing a s. 15 violation. Iacobucci J presented the *Law* guidelines as simply a summary of the *Andrews* test as refined in subsequent jurisprudence. But most commentators were of the view that *Law* significantly modified the s. 15 test. Previously, the dominant approach was that a claimant established a violation of s. 15 if she or he could show differential and disadvantageous treatment based on a prohibited ground of discrimination. According to *Law*, such treatment is discriminatory only if the claimant can also establish that it implicates his or her human dignity in terms of the four contextual factors outlined by the Court.

4. Commentators criticized the human dignity standard introduced in *Law* as being vague and malleable, and for shifting to the s. 15 analysis a balancing of individual rights and social objectives that ought to take place pursuant to s. 1, where the government rather than the claimant has the burden of proof. See S. Martin, "Balancing Individual Rights to Equality and Social Goals" (2001), 80 *Canadian Bar Review* 299, at 329-32; P.W. Hogg, *Constitutional Law of Canada*, 4th ed., looseleaf (Scarborough, ON: Carswell, 1997), at 52-53; and J. Ross, "A Flawed Synthesis of the Law" (2000), 11 *Constitutional Forum* 74. Donna Greschner shared the view that the Court achieved consensus at a high level of abstraction in *Law*. Nevertheless, she defended the *Law* test as more likely to promote substantive equality than any of the alternatives. See D. Greschner, "Does Law Advance the Cause of Equality?" (2001), 27 *Queen's Law Journal* 299.

5. In *Law*, the Court did not refer to the irrelevant personal characteristics test applied by four judges in the 1995 trilogy, led by La Forest J in *Egan* and Gonthier J in *Miron*. Because Iacobucci J's discussion of earlier s. 15 jurisprudence was comprehensive, it could be assumed that this test had been abandoned. But it is also possible to read *Law* as giving life to this approach, with the Court concluding, in essence, that age was relevant to the values and objectives underlying the CPP: see B. Baines, "Law v. Canada: Formatting Equality" (2000), 11 *Constitutional Forum* 65. In particular, the "correspondence" factor seems to invite the "relevance" analysis.

6. Was Iacobucci J right to suggest that cases like *Law*, where the Court finds that differential treatment based on a prohibited ground is not discriminatory in a substantive sense, will be "rare"? Such cases have figured repeatedly in the Court's s. 15 jurisprudence, both before *Law* and even more so after. These cases will be examined in Section VI.D, Disadvantage/Discrimination, below. An analysis of the first five years of s. 15 cases after *Law* showed a pattern of unsuccessful s. 15 claims failing more often at the s. 15(1) stage rather than under s. 1; see B. Ryder, C.C. Faria, and E. Lawrence, "What's Law Good For? An Empirical Overview of Charter Equality Rights Decisions" (2004), 24 *Supreme Court Law Review* (2d) 103.

V. THE KAPP TEST

In *R v. Kapp*, below, the Court jettisoned its commitment in *Law* to conditioning an infringe-ment of s. 15 on a violation of human dignity. In its place, the Court reverted to a version of the approach proposed by McIntyre J in *Andrews*. It did so in the context of a challenge to a program that, according to the Court, fell within the meaning of s. 15(2) of the Charter, which provides that s. 15(1) "does not preclude any law, program or activity that has as its object the amelioration of conditions of disadvantaged individuals or groups including those that are disadvantaged because of race, national or ethnic origin, colour, religion, sex, age or mental or physical disability." As you read the decision, ask yourself whether you agree with the reasons the Court offers for reverting to McIntyre J's approach in *Andrews*.

R v. Kapp
[2008] 2 SCR 483, 294 DLR (4th) 1

McLACHLIN CJC and ABELLA J (Binnie, LeBel, Deschamps, Fish, Charron, and Roth-stein JJ concurring): [1] The appellants are commercial fishers, mainly non-aboriginal, who assert that their equality rights under s. 15 of the *Canadian Charter of Rights and Freedoms* were violated by a communal fishing licence granting members of three ab-original bands the exclusive right to fish for salmon in the mouth of the Fraser River for a period of 24 hours on August 19-20, 1998.

. . .

[7] [The federal government has pursued various policies with a view to increasing Aboriginal involvement in the commercial fishery. These policies are] united under the umbrella of the "Aboriginal Fisheries Strategy," [which] has three stated objectives: ensur-ing the rights recognized by the *Sparrow* decision are respected; providing aboriginal communities with a larger role in fisheries management and increased economic bene-fits; and minimizing the disruption of non-aboriginal fisheries (1994 Gardner Pinfold Report). In response to consultations with stakeholders carried out since its inception, the Aboriginal Fisheries Strategy has been reviewed and adjusted periodically in order to achieve these goals. A significant part of the Aboriginal Fisheries Strategy was the intro-duction of three pilot sales programs, one of which resulted in the issuance of the communal fishing licence at issue in this case. [Under the *Aboriginal Communal Fishing Licences Regulations*, SOR/93-332 (ACFLR), an "Aboriginal organization," including an Indian band, can receive a communal licence and can authorize individuals to fish under that licence.]

[8] The licence with which we are concerned permitted fishers designated by the bands to fish for sockeye salmon between 7:00 a.m on August 19, 1998 and 7:00 a.m. on August 20, 1998, and to use the fish caught for food, social and ceremonial purposes, and for sale. Some of the fishers designated by the bands to fish under the communal fishing licence were also licensed commercial fishers entitled to fish at other openings for com-mercial fishers.

[9] The appellants are all commercial fishers who were excluded from the fishery during the 24 hours allocated to the aboriginal fishery under the communal fishing li-

cence. [They were] charged with fishing at a prohibited time. In defence of the charges, they filed notice of a constitutional question seeking declarations that the communal fishing licence, the ACFLR and related regulations and the Aboriginal Fisheries Strategy were unconstitutional.

[The Provincial Court ruled that the exclusive communal fishing licence violated s. 15 of the Charter and was not justified under s. 1. It stayed the charges against the appellants. The BC Supreme Court allowed an appeal by the Crown, entering convictions against the appellants. The BC Court of Appeal dismissed the appellants' appeal.]

C. Analysis

. . .

1. The Purpose of Section 15

[14] Nearly 20 years have passed since the Court handed down its first s. 15 decision in the case of *Andrews v. Law Society of British Columbia*, [1989] 1 SCR 143. *Andrews* set the template for this Court's commitment to substantive equality—a template which subsequent decisions have enriched but never abandoned.

[15] Substantive equality, as contrasted with formal equality, is grounded in the idea that: "The promotion of equality entails the promotion of a society in which all are secure in the knowledge that they are recognized at law as human beings equally deserving of concern, respect and consideration": *Andrews*, at p. 171, per McIntyre J, for the majority on the s. 15 issue. [McIntyre J pointed] out that the concept of equality does not necessarily mean identical treatment and that the formal "like treatment" model of discrimination may in fact produce inequality ... . An insistence on substantive equality has remained central to the Court's approach to equality claims.

[16] Sections 15(1) and 15(2) work together to promote the vision of substantive equality that underlies s. 15 as a whole. Section 15(1) is aimed at preventing discriminatory distinctions that impact adversely on members of groups identified by the grounds enumerated in s. 15 and analogous grounds. This is one way of combatting discrimination. However, governments may also wish to combat discrimination by developing programs aimed at helping disadvantaged groups improve their situation. Through s. 15(2), the Charter preserves the right of governments to implement such programs, without fear of challenge under s. 15(1). This is made apparent by the existence of s. 15(2). Thus s. 15(1) and s. 15(2) work together to confirm s. 15's purpose of furthering substantive equality.

[17] The template in *Andrews*, as further developed in a series of cases culminating in *Law v. Canada (Minister of Employment and Immigration)*, [1999] 1 SCR 497, established in essence a two-part test for showing discrimination under s. 15(1): (1) Does the law create a distinction based on an enumerated or analogous ground? (2) Does the distinction create a disadvantage by perpetuating prejudice or stereotyping? These were divided, in *Law*, into three steps, but in our view the test is, in substance, the same.

[18] In *Andrews*, McIntyre J viewed discriminatory impact through the lens of two concepts: (1) the perpetuation of prejudice or disadvantage to members of a group on the basis of personal characteristics identified in the enumerated and analogous grounds;

and (2) stereotyping on the basis of these grounds that results in a decision that does not correspond to a claimant's or group's actual circumstances and characteristics. *Andrews*, for example, was decided on the second of these concepts; it was held that the prohibition against non-citizens practising law was based on a stereotype that non-citizens could not properly discharge the responsibilities of a lawyer in British Columbia—a view that denied non-citizens a privilege, not on the basis of their merits and capabilities, but on the basis of ... "attributed rather than actual characteristics." Additionally, McIntyre J emphasized that a finding of discrimination might be grounded in the fact that the impact of a particular law or program was to perpetuate the disadvantage of a group defined by enumerated or analogous s. 15 grounds. In this context, he said (at p. 174):

> I would say then that discrimination may be described as a distinction, whether intentional or not but based on grounds relating to personal characteristics of the individual or group, which has the effect of imposing burdens, obligations, or disadvantages on such individual or group not imposed upon others, or which withholds or limits access to opportunities, benefits, and advantages available to other members of society.

[19] A decade later, in *Law*, this Court suggested that discrimination should be defined in terms of the impact of the law or program on the "human dignity" of members of the claimant group, having regard to four contextual factors: (1) pre-existing disadvantage, if any, of the claimant group; (2) degree of correspondence between the differential treatment and the claimant group's reality; (3) whether the law or program has an ameliorative purpose or effect; and (4) the nature of the interest affected (paras. 62-75).

[20] The achievement of *Law* was its success in unifying what had become, since *Andrews*, a division in this Court's approach to s. 15. *Law* accomplished this by reiterating and confirming *Andrews*'s interpretation of s. 15 as a guarantee of substantive, and not just formal, equality. Moreover, *Law* made an important contribution to our understanding of the conceptual underpinnings of substantive equality.

[21] At the same time, several difficulties have arisen from the attempt in *Law* to employ human dignity as a legal test. There can be no doubt that human dignity is an essential value underlying the s. 15 equality guarantee. In fact, the protection of all of the rights guaranteed by the Charter has as its lodestar the promotion of human dignity. ...

[22] But as critics have pointed out, human dignity is an abstract and subjective notion that, even with the guidance of the four contextual factors, cannot only become confusing and difficult to apply; it has also proven to be an *additional* burden on equality claimants, rather than the philosophical enhancement it was intended to be. Criticism has also accrued for the way *Law* has allowed the formalism of some of the Court's post-*Andrews* jurisprudence to resurface in the form of an artificial comparator analysis focussed on treating likes alike.

[23] The analysis in a particular case, as *Law* itself recognizes, more usefully focuses on the factors that identify impact amounting to discrimination. The four factors cited in *Law* are based on and relate to the identification in *Andrews* of perpetuation of disadvantage and stereotyping as the primary indicators of discrimination. Pre-existing disadvantage and the nature of the interest affected (factors one and four in *Law*) go to perpetuation of disadvantage and prejudice, while the second factor deals with stereotyping. The ameliorative purpose or effect of a law or program (the third factor in *Law*) goes to whether

the purpose is remedial within the meaning of s. 15(2). (We would suggest, without deciding here, that the third *Law* factor might also be relevant to the question under s. 15(1) as to whether the effect of the law or program is to perpetuate disadvantage.)

[24] Viewed in this way, *Law* does not impose a new and distinctive test for discrimination, but rather affirms the approach to substantive equality under s. 15 set out in *Andrews* and developed in numerous subsequent decisions. The factors cited in *Law* should not be read literally as if they were legislative dispositions, but as a way of focussing on the central concern of s. 15 identified in *Andrews*—combatting discrimination, defined in terms of perpetuating disadvantage and stereotyping.

[25] The central purpose of combatting discrimination, as discussed, underlies both s. 15(1) and s. 15(2). Under s. 15(1), the focus is on *preventing* governments from making distinctions based on the enumerated or analogous grounds that: have the effect of perpetuating group disadvantage and prejudice; or impose disadvantage on the basis of stereotyping. Under s. 15(2), the focus is on *enabling* governments to pro-actively combat existing discrimination through affirmative measures.

· · ·

2. *Section 15(2)*

[27] Under *Andrews*, as previously noted, s. 15 does not mean identical treatment. McIntyre J explained that "every difference in treatment between individuals under the law will not necessarily result in inequality," and that "identical treatment may frequently produce serious inequality" (p. 164). …

[28] Rather than requiring identical treatment for everyone, in *Andrews*, McIntyre J distinguished between difference and discrimination and adopted an approach to equality that acknowledged and accommodated differences. McIntyre J proposed the following model, at p. 182:

> … A complainant under s. 15(1) must show not only that he or she is not receiving equal treatment before and under the law or that the law has a differential impact on him or her in the protection or benefit accorded by law but, in addition, must show that the legislative impact of the law is discriminatory.

In other words, not every distinction is discriminatory. By their very nature, programs designed to ameliorate the disadvantage of one group will inevitably exclude individuals from other groups. This does not necessarily make them either unconstitutional or "reverse discrimination." *Andrews* requires that discriminatory conduct entail more than *different* treatment. As McIntyre J declared at p. 167, a law will not "necessarily be bad because it makes distinctions."

[29] In our view, the appellants have established that they were treated differently based on an enumerated ground, race. Because the government argues that the program ameliorated the conditions of a disadvantaged group, we must take a more detailed look at s. 15(2).

[30] The question that arises is whether the program that targeted the aboriginal bands falls under s. 15(2) in the sense that it is a "law, program or activity that has as its object the amelioration of conditions of disadvantaged individuals or groups." As noted, the communal fishing licence authorizing the three bands to fish for sale on August 19-20

was issued pursuant to an enabling statute and regulations—namely the ACFLR. This qualifies as a "law, program or activity" within the meaning of s. 15(2). The more complex issue is whether the program fulfills the remaining criteria of s. 15(2)—that is, whether the program "has as its object the amelioration of conditions of disadvantaged individuals or groups."

[31] Even before the enactment of the Charter, this Court in *Athabasca Tribal Council v. Amoco Canada Petroleum Company Ltd.*, [1981] 1 SCR 699, recognized that ameliorative programs targeting a disadvantaged group do not constitute discrimination. [In that case, a concurring opinion by Ritchie J concluded that certain proposed affirmative action programs were not discriminatory within the meaning of *The Individual's Rights Protection Act of Alberta, 1972*, SA 1972, c. 2.]

· · ·

[34] This Court dealt explicitly with the relationship between s. 15(1) and s. 15(2) in *Lovelace v. Ontario*, [2000] 1 SCR 950, 2000 SCC 37. The Court, per Iacobucci J, appeared unwilling at that time to give s. 15(2) independent force, but left the door open for that possibility, at para. 108:

> [A]t this stage of the jurisprudence, I see s. 15(2) as confirmatory of s. 15(1) and, in that respect, claimants arguing equality claims in the future should first be directed to s. 15(1) since that subsection can embrace ameliorative programs of the kind that are contemplated by s. 15(2). By doing that one can ensure that the program is subject to the full scrutiny of the discrimination analysis, as well as the possibility of a s. 1 review. *However ... we may well wish to reconsider this matter at a future time in the context of another case.* [Emphasis added.]

[35] Iacobucci J in *Lovelace* perceived two possible approaches to the interpretation of s. 15(2). He believed that the Supreme Court could either read s. 15(2) as an interpretive aid to s. 15(1) (the approach adopted in *Lovelace*) or read it as an exception or exemption from the operation of s. 15(1).

[36] He favoured the interpretive aid approach, while acknowledging that the exemption approach had some support. ...

[37] In our view, there is a third option: if the government can demonstrate that an impugned program meets the criteria of s. 15(2), it may be unnecessary to conduct a s. 15(1) analysis at all. As discussed at the outset of this analysis, s. 15(1) and s. 15(2) should be read as working together to promote substantive equality. The focus of s. 15(1) is on *preventing* governments from making distinctions based on enumerated or analogous grounds that have the effect of perpetuating disadvantage or prejudice or imposing disadvantage on the basis of stereotyping. The focus of s. 15(2) is on *enabling* governments to pro-actively combat discrimination. Read thus, the two sections are confirmatory of each other. Section 15(2) supports a full expression of equality, rather than derogating from it. "Under a substantive definition of equality, different treatment in the service of equity for disadvantaged groups is an expression of equality, not an exception to it": P.W. Hogg, *Constitutional Law of Canada* (5th ed. 2007), vol. 2, at p. 55-53.

[38] But this confirmatory purpose does not preclude an independent role for s. 15(2). Section 15(2) is more than a hortatory admonition. It tells us, in simple clear language, that s. 15(1) cannot be read in a way that finds an ameliorative program aimed at combatting disadvantage to be discriminatory and in breach of s. 15.

[39] Here the appellants claim discrimination on the basis of s. 15(1). The source of that discrimination the very essence of their complaint is a program that may be ameliorative. This leaves but one conclusion: if the government establishes that the program falls under s. 15(2), the appellants' claim must fail.

[40] In other words, once the s. 15 claimant has shown a distinction made on an enumerated or analogous ground, it is open to the government to show that the impugned law, program or activity is ameliorative and, thus, constitutional. This approach has the advantage of avoiding the symbolic problem of finding a program discriminatory before "saving" it as ameliorative, while also giving independent force to a provision that has been written as distinct and separate from s. 15(1). Should the government fail to demonstrate that its program falls under s. 15(2), the program must then receive full scrutiny under s. 15(1) to determine whether its impact is discriminatory.

[41] We would therefore formulate the test under s. 15(2) as follows. A program does not violate the s. 15 equality guarantee if the government can demonstrate that: (1) the program has an ameliorative or remedial purpose; and (2) the program targets a disadvantaged group identified by the enumerated or analogous grounds. In proposing this test, we are mindful that future cases may demand some adjustment to the framework in order to meet the litigants' particular circumstances. However, at this early stage in the development of the law surrounding s. 15(2), the test we have described provides a basic starting point—one that is adequate for determining the issues before us on this appeal, but leaves open the possibility for future refinement.

[42] We build our analysis of s. 15(2) and its operation around three key phrases in the provision. The subsection protects "any law, program or activity that *has as its object* the *amelioration* of conditions of *disadvantaged* individuals or groups." While there is some overlap in the considerations raised by each of these terms, it may be useful to consider each of them individually.

a) "Has as Its Object"

[43] In interpreting this phrase, two issues arise. The first is whether courts should look to the *purpose* or to the *effect* of legislation. The second is whether, in order to qualify for s. 15(2) protection, a program must have an ameliorative purpose as its sole object, or whether having such a goal as one of several objectives is sufficient.

[44] The language of s. 15(2) suggests that legislative goal rather than actual effect is the paramount consideration in determining whether or not a program qualifies for s. 15(2) protection. Michael Peirce defends this view, which he refers to as the "subjective" approach, because it adheres more closely to the language of the provision and avoids potentially inappropriate judicial intervention in government programs ("A Progressive Interpretation of Subsection 15(2) of the Charter" (1993), 57 *Sask. L Rev.* 263). Scholars have nonetheless disagreed about the appropriate approach, often using the "subjective" (goal-based) and "objective" (effect-based) language.

[45] Scholars and judges who have supported judicial examination of the actual effect of a program offer one primary argument to defend their view. They express concern that a "subjective" test will permit the government to defeat a discrimination claim by declaring that the impugned law has an ameliorative purpose. ... [The argument is] that "if ameliorative legislative purpose were the sole test under section 15(2), a legislature could

easily circumvent the egalitarian requirements under section 15(1) by including in any potentially discriminatory legislation a clause which provides that 'this Act has as its object the amelioration of the conditions of … a disadvantaged group.'" [citation omitted]

[46] In our opinion, this concern can be easily addressed. There is nothing to suggest that a test focussed on the goal of legislation must slavishly accept the government's characterization of its purpose. Courts could well examine legislation to ensure that the declared purpose is genuine. …

[47] In that vein, proponents of the approach that focusses on the ameliorative goal of the program, rather than its effect, argue that doing so will prevent courts from unduly interfering in ameliorative programs created by the legislature. They note that Canadian Charter drafters wished to avoid the American experience, whereby judges overturned affirmative action programs under the banner of equality. The purpose-driven approach also reflects the language of the provision itself, which focuses on the "object" of the program, law or activity rather than its impact. Moreover, the effects of a program in its fledgling stages cannot always be easily ascertained. The law or program may be experimental. If the sincere purpose is to promote equality by ameliorating the conditions of a disadvantaged group, the government should be given some leeway to adopt innovative programs, even though some may ultimately prove to be unsuccessful. The government may learn from such failures and revise equality-enhancing programs to make them more effective.

[48] Given the language of the provision and its goal of enabling governments to pro-actively combat discrimination, we believe the "purpose"-based approach is more appropriate than the "effect"-based approach: where a law, program or activity creates a distinction based on an enumerated or analogous ground, was the government's goal in creating that distinction to improve the conditions of a group that is disadvantaged? In examining purpose, courts may therefore find it necessary to consider not only statements made by the drafters of the program but also whether the legislature chose means rationally related to that ameliorative purpose, in the sense that it appears at least plausible that the program may indeed advance the stated goal of combatting disadvantage. …

[49] Analysing the means employed by the government can easily turn into assessing the *effect* of the program. As a result, to preserve an intent-based analysis, courts could be encouraged to frame the analysis as follows: Was it rational for the state to conclude that the means chosen to reach its ameliorative goal would contribute to that purpose? For the distinction to be rational, there must be a correlation between the program and the disadvantage suffered by the target group. Such a standard permits significant deference to the legislature but allows judicial review where a program nominally seeks to serve the disadvantaged but in practice serves other non-remedial objectives.

[50] The next issue is whether the program's ameliorative purpose needs to be its exclusive objective. Programs frequently serve more than one purpose or attempt to meet more than one goal. Must the ameliorative object be the sole object, or may it be one of several?

[51] We can find little justification for requiring the ameliorative purpose to be the sole object of a program. It seems unlikely that a single purpose will motivate any particular program; any number of goals are likely to be subsumed within a single scheme. To prevent such programs from earning s. 15(2) protection on the grounds that they contain other objectives seems to undermine the goal of s. 15(2).

[52] The importance of the ameliorative purpose within the scheme may help determine the scope of s. 15(2) protection, however. Consider that an ameliorative program may coexist with or interact with a larger legislative scheme. If only the program has an ameliorative purpose, does s. 15(2) extend to protect the wider legislative scheme? We offer as a tentative guide that s. 15(2) precludes from s. 15(1) review distinctions made on enumerated or analogous grounds that serve and are necessary to the ameliorative purpose.

b) "Amelioration"

[53] Section 15(2) protects programs that aim to "ameliorate" the condition of disadvantaged groups identified by the enumerated or analogous grounds. Although the word does not at first seem liable to misunderstanding, courts have previously understood the term (and s. 15(2)) to apply in surprising circumstances. In *R v. Music Explosion Ltd.* (1989), 62 Man. R (2d) 189, the Manitoba Court of Queen's Bench upheld a Winnipeg bylaw that restricted young people under 16 from operating an amusement device without the consent of a guardian or a parent on the grounds that it was protected by s. 15(2). Smith J declared that the bylaw "is obviously for the benefit of the special needs of young persons" (para. 21). On appeal, the decision was reversed. The Court of Appeal explained: "[T]his legislation does not confer special benefits upon young people, but rather imposes a limitation. Nor is the purpose of the legislation the amelioration of their condition" ((1990), 68 Man. R (2d) 203, at para. 18). ...

[54] These precedents suggest that the meaning of "amelioration" deserves careful attention in evaluating programs under s. 15(2). We would suggest that laws designed to restrict or punish behaviour would not qualify for s. 15(2) protection. Nor, as already discussed, should the focus be on the effect of the law. This said, the fact that a law has no plausible or predictable ameliorative effect may render suspect the state's ameliorative purpose. Governments, as discussed above, are not permitted to protect discriminatory programs on colourable pretexts.

c) "Disadvantaged"

[55] The interpretation of "disadvantaged," explored in *Andrews*, *Miron v. Trudel*, [1995] 2 SCR 418, and *Law*, and other cases in the context of s. 15(1), requires little further elaboration here. "Disadvantage" under s. 15 connotes vulnerability, prejudice and negative social characterization. Section 15(2)'s purpose is to protect government programs targeting the conditions of a specific and identifiable disadvantaged group, as contrasted with broad societal legislation, such as social assistance programs. Not all members of the group need to be disadvantaged, as long as the group as a whole has experienced discrimination.

3. *Application of Section 15(2) to This Case*

[56] The appellants have argued they were denied a benefit on the basis of race, a ground enumerated in s. 15 of the Charter. As discussed above, once the appellants have demonstrated such a distinction, the government may attempt to show the program is protected under s. 15(2). The government conferred the communal fishing licence valid

for August 19-20 to particular aboriginal bands. Therefore, we are satisfied that the appellants have demonstrated a distinction imposed on the basis of race, an enumerated ground under s. 15.

[57] We have earlier suggested that a distinction based on the enumerated or analogous grounds in a government program will not constitute discrimination under s. 15 if, under s. 15(2), (1) the program has an ameliorative or remedial purpose; and (2) the program targets a disadvantaged group identified by the enumerated or analogous grounds. The question is whether the program at issue on this appeal meets these conditions.

[58] The first issue is whether the program that excluded Mr. Kapp and other non-band fishers from the fishery had an ameliorative or remedial purpose. The Crown describes numerous objectives for the impugned pilot sales program. These include negotiating solutions to aboriginal fishing rights claims, providing economic opportunities to native bands and supporting their progress towards self-sufficiency. The impugned fishing licence relates to all of these goals. The pilot sales program was part of an attempt—albeit a small part—to negotiate a solution to aboriginal fishing rights claims. The communal fishing licence provided economic opportunities, through sale or trade, to the bands. Through these endeavours, the government was pursuing the goal of promoting band self-sufficiency. In these ways, the government was hoping to redress the social and economic disadvantage of the targeted bands. The means chosen to achieve the purpose (special fishing privileges for aboriginal communities, constituting a benefit) are rationally related to serving that purpose. It follows that the Crown has established a credible ameliorative purpose for the program.

[59] The government's aims correlate to the actual economic and social disadvantage suffered by members of the three aboriginal bands. The disadvantage of aboriginal people is indisputable. In *Corbiere v. Canada (Minister of Indian and Northern Affairs)*, [1999] 2 SCR 203, the Court noted "the legacy of stereotyping and prejudice against Aboriginal peoples" (para. 66). The Court has also acknowledged that "Aboriginal peoples experience high rates of unemployment and poverty, and face serious disadvantages in the areas of education, health and housing" (*Lovelace*, at para. 69). More particularly, the evidence shows in this case that the bands granted the benefit were in fact disadvantaged in terms of income, education and a host of other measures. This disadvantage, rooted in history, continues to this day. The communal fishing licence, by addressing long-term goals of self-sufficiency and, more immediately, by providing additional sources of income and employment, relates to the social and economic disadvantage suffered by the bands. The fact that some individual members of the bands may not experience personal disadvantage does not negate the group disadvantage suffered by band members.

[60] Mr. Kapp suggests that the focus must be on the particular forms of disadvantage suffered by the bands who received the benefit, and argues that this program did not offer a benefit that effectively tackled the problems faced by these bands. As discussed above, what is required is a correlation between the program and the disadvantage suffered by the target group. If the target group is socially and economically disadvantaged, as is the case here, and the program may rationally address that disadvantage, then the necessary correspondence is established.

[61] We conclude that the government program here at issue is protected by s. 15(2) as a program that "has as its object the amelioration of conditions of disadvantaged indi-

viduals or groups." It follows that the program does not violate the equality guarantee of s. 15 of the Charter.

...

D. Conclusion

[66] We would dismiss the appeal on the ground that breach of the s. 15 equality guarantee has not been established.

[Bastarache J wrote separate reasons concurring in the result.]

Appeal dismissed.

NOTES

1. The impact of *Kapp*'s abandonment of *Law*'s focus on human dignity on the discrimination analysis under s. 15(1) remains to be seen. What role will *Law*'s four contextual factors continue to play in the analysis? Will *Kapp* reduce the impact of the "correspondence" factor? Two post-*Kapp* cases, *Ermineskin Indian Band and Nation v. Canada*, 2009 SCC 9 and *AC v. Manitoba (Director of Child and Family Services)*, 2009 SCC 30, are discussed in Section VI.D, below.

2. In addition to abandoning *Law*'s focus on human dignity, *Kapp* redefines the relationship between ss. 15(1) and 15(2) of the Charter. Recall that in *Law* the Court held that the ameliorative purpose (or effect) of a law is a factor that weighs against concluding that it is discriminatory. In *Lovelace v. Ontario*, [2000] 1 SCR 950, 188 DLR (4th) 193, the Court had made clear what the *Law* test implied with respect to the relationship between s. 15(1) and s. 15(2) of the Charter. At issue in *Lovelace* was an agreement between the Ontario government and Indian bands—First Nations regulated by the federal *Indian Act*—in the province dealing with the proceeds of Casino Rama, a commercial casino located on Rama First Nation's reserve. The purpose of the agreement was to improve the socioeconomic conditions of band members, and the casino's net revenues were to be distributed to a First Nation Fund, which would benefit all bands in Ontario. The applicants in *Lovelace* represented Ontario's Métis and non-status Indians—that is, Aboriginal communities not registered as bands under the *Indian Act*. They applied for a declaration that they were entitled to share in the profits of the casino. The Supreme Court of Canada, per Iacobucci J, held there to be no violation of s. 15(1), in no small measure because of the ameliorative purpose of the program. According to Iacobucci J, s. 15(2) is "confirmatory of s. 15(1) and, in that respect, claimants arguing equality claims in the future should first be directed to s. 15(1) since that subsection can embrace ameliorative programs of the kind that are contemplated by s. 15(2)."

Kapp reverses the structure of analysis outlined in *Lovelace*, directing parties first to the question of whether the law, program, or activity in question falls under s. 15(2). If the government can establish this to be the case, then it is "exempted" from s. 15(1) scrutiny. *Kapp*'s reorientation of the relationship between s. 15(1) and s. 15(2) effectively transforms one of the four "contextual factors" outlined in *Law* used to ascertain whether a law is discriminatory—the presence of an ameliorative purpose—into an absolute defence against a claim of a s. 15(1) violation.

As a result of this reversal, the test for determining whether a law, program, or activity falls within s. 15(2) now occupies centre stage in claims alleging a violation of equality rights. McLachlin CJC and Abella J state this test in the following terms:

> [41] … A program does not violate the s. 15 equality guarantee if the government can demonstrate that: (1) the program has an ameliorative or remedial purpose; and (2) the program targets a disadvantaged group identified by the enumerated or analogous grounds. In proposing this test, we are mindful that future cases may demand some adjustment to the framework in order to meet the litigants' particular circumstances. However, at this early stage in the development of the law surrounding s. 15(2), the test we have described provides a basic starting point—one that is adequate for determining the issues before us on this appeal, but leaves open the possibility for future refinement.

Note that this test focuses solely on the purpose of the program in question and not on its effects. According to the Court, such a focus should include an inquiry into whether it was "rational for the state to conclude that the means chosen to reach its ameliorative goal would contribute to that purpose" (para. 49). By "rational," the Court means that there exists "a correlation between the program and the disadvantage suffered by the target group" (*ibid.*) such that "it appears at least plausible that the program may indeed advance the stated goal of combatting disadvantage" (para. 40). Moreover, the ameliorative purpose of a program need not be its sole object for it to be exempted from s. 15(1) scrutiny; according to the Court, "[i]t seems unlikely that a single purpose will motivate any particular program; any number of goals are likely to be subsumed within a single scheme" (para. 51).

3. McLachin CJC and Abella J defend this relaxed stance to s. 15(2) by pointing to the text of s. 15(2), the desire to avoid the US experience of strict scrutiny of "affirmative action" programs, and the need to defer to the government. Do you agree that s. 15(2) should be interpreted so broadly? McLachlin CJC and Abella J note that "[b]y their very nature, programs designed to ameliorate the disadvantage of one group will inevitably exclude individuals from other groups" (para. 28). But should this immunize all such programs from s. 15(1) scrutiny? What if a program designed to ameliorate the conditions of one group identified by an enumerated or analogous ground exacerbates the disadvantaged conditions on a group identified by another enumerated or analogous ground?

4. In his discussion of the third contextual factor ("ameliorative purpose or effects") in *Law*, Iacobucci J suggested that the exclusion of more advantaged individuals from ameliorative programs will not likely violate s. 15, whereas underinclusive ameliorative legislation that excludes members of a disadvantaged group "will rarely escape the charge of discrimination." In *Lovelace*, Iacobucci J appeared to pull back to some degree from this approach, stating (at para. 84) that "ameliorative legislation designed to benefit the population in general, yet which excludes historically disadvantaged claimants," will rarely escape this charge, suggesting by implication that it may be difficult for challenges brought by members of disadvantaged groups to targeted programs, as opposed to universal ameliorative programs, to succeed. This is consistent with David Schneiderman's assessment of equality rights litigation that "claims based upon what the Court considers to be universalistic schemes—schemes which seemingly are intended to embrace everyone, including the middle class—are more likely to be successful than are claims seeking access to targeted or means-tested plans, where fundamental distinctions between classes, as emphasised by the Court, are built into

the very structure of the program"; see D. Schneiderman, "Universality vs Particularity: Litigating Middle Class Values under Section 15," in S. Rodgers and S. McIntyre, eds, *Diminishing Returns: Inequality and the Canadian Charter of Rights and Freedoms* (Markham, ON: LexisNexis Butterworths, 2006). As a result of *Kapp*, are targeted or means-based ameliorative programs now completely exempt from s. 15(1) scrutiny?

5. In concurring reasons, Bastarache J approached the dispute in *Kapp* through the lens of s. 25 of the Charter:

> 25. The guarantee in this Charter of certain rights and freedoms shall not be construed so as to abrogate or derogate from any aboriginal, treaty or other rights or freedoms that pertain to the aboriginal peoples of Canada including
>
> (a) any rights or freedoms that have been recognized by the Royal Proclamation of October 7, 1763; and
>
> (b) any rights or freedoms that now exist by way of land claims agreements or may be so acquired.

In Bastarache J's view,

> [103] … the reference to "aboriginal and treaty rights" suggests that the focus of the provision is the uniqueness of those persons or communities mentioned in the Constitution; the rights protected are those that are unique to them because of their special status. As argued by Macklem [P. Macklem, *Indigenous Difference and the Constitution of Canada* (Toronto: University of Toronto Press, 2001)], s. 25 "protects federal, provincial and aboriginal initiatives that seek to further interests associated with indigenous difference from Charter scrutiny": see p. 225. Accordingly, legislation that distinguishes between aboriginal and non-aboriginal people in order to protect interests associated with aboriginal culture, territory, sovereignty or the treaty process deserves to be shielded from Charter scrutiny.
>
> . . .
>
> [105] Laws adopted under the s. 91(24) power would normally fall into this category, the power being in relation to the aboriginal peoples as such, but not laws that fall under s. 88 of the *Indian Act*, because they are by definition laws of general application. "[O]ther rights or freedoms" comprise statutory rights which seek to protect interests associated with aboriginal culture, territory, self-government, as mentioned above, and settlement agreements that are a replacement for treaty and aboriginal rights. But private rights of individual Indians held in a private capacity as ordinary Canadian citizens would not be protected.

Given that they found no violation of s. 15, McLachlin CJC and Abella J held it unnecessary to consider the effect of s. 25 on the appellants' claim. They did, however, note (at para. 63) that

> the wording of s. 25 and the examples given therein—aboriginal rights, treaty rights, and "other rights or freedoms," such as rights derived from the *Royal Proclamation* or from land claims agreements—suggest that not every aboriginal interest or program falls within the provision's scope. Rather, only rights of a constitutional character are likely to benefit from s. 25. If so, we would question, without deciding, whether the fishing licence is a s. 25 right or freedom.

VI. EQUALITY'S THREE STEPS

The analysis under s. 15(1) involves many steps. *Kapp* speaks of a two-part test for showing discrimination under s. 15(1): (1) Does the law in question create a distinction based on an enumerated or analogous ground? (2) Does the distinction create a disadvantage by perpetuating prejudice or stereotyping? (Under *Law*, this step had been formulated as "Does the differential treatment discriminate?") Case law on s. 15 demonstrates that the first part of this test actually contains two inquiries. The first asks whether the law creates a distinction, and the second asks whether this distinction is based on an enumerated or an analogous ground. Thus, s. 15(1) really involves three steps of analysis. As well, *Law* highlighted the comparative nature of equality and the need to structure all steps of the s. 15 analysis around a "comparator group." The choice of the appropriate comparator group has come to be seen as an important, initial analytic step in its own right before the third step, determining whether the distinction creates disadvantage, is addressed.

There is extensive jurisprudence on each of these steps which will be examined in the material that follows. Complicating this picture is the fact that some of these decisions were rendered before *Law* proposed that human dignity be the central organizing principle of s. 15, some were rendered after the *Law* decision, and some were rendered after *Kapp* excised human dignity from the s. 15 analysis.

A. Differential Treatment

The first step in the s. 15(1) analysis is to determine whether the impugned government action or inaction has produced differential treatment. A difference in treatment most often will be apparent on the face of the challenged law or policy. For example, the law at issue in *Andrews* explicitly made citizenship a requirement for being called to the bar and thus treated citizens and non-citizens differently. This is an example of what is referred to as "direct discrimination." On other occasions, no difference in treatment will be apparent on the face of the challenged law or policy. Differential treatment could nevertheless result from the effects of the law. When a "facially neutral" law has a differential impact on the basis of a prohibited ground of discrimination, the result is referred to as "adverse effects" discrimination.

Andrews, *Law*, and *Kapp* all emphasized that discrimination can lie in the effects of a law. The *Eldridge* case, excerpted below, was decided before *Law*. It provides a good example of a successful s. 15 claim based on differential treatment resulting from a facially neutral policy.

Eldridge v. British Columbia (Attorney General)
[1997] 3 SCR 624, 151 DLR (4th) 577

[Three individuals who were born deaf and whose preferred means of communication was sign language sought a declaration that the failure to provide public funding for sign language interpreters for the deaf when they received medical services violated s. 15 of the Charter. According to the *Medical and Health Care Services Act*, the power to decide whether a service is "medically required" and hence a "benefit" under the Act is delegated to the Medical Services Commission. In the case of the *Hospital Insurance Act*, hospitals were given discretion to determine which services should be provided free of charge. The Commission and the hospitals did not make sign language interpretation available as an insured service. The s. 32 issue of whether the Charter applies to hospital or Commission funding decisions is discussed in Chapter 18, Application. The portions of La Forest J's judgment excerpted below focus on the question of whether the failure to provide funding for sign language interpretation violated s. 15.]

LA FOREST J (Lamer CJC, L'Heureux-Dubé, Sopinka, Gonthier, Cory, McLachlin, Iacobucci, and Major JJ concurring): ... [53] Having concluded that the Charter applies to the failure of hospitals and the Medical Services Commission to provide sign language interpreters, it remains to be determined whether that failure infringes the appellants' equality rights under s. 15(1) of the Charter. ... I emphasize at the outset that s. 15(1), like other Charter rights, is to be generously and purposively interpreted ... .

[54] In the case of s. 15(1), this Court has stressed that it serves two distinct but related purposes. First, it expresses a commitment—deeply ingrained in our social, political and legal culture—to the equal worth and human dignity of all persons. ... Secondly, it instantiates a desire to rectify and prevent discrimination against particular groups "suffering social, political and legal disadvantage in our society" ... . While this Court has confirmed that it is not necessary to show membership in a historically disadvantaged group in order to establish a s. 15(1) violation, the fact that a law draws a distinction on such a ground is an important indicium of discrimination ... .

[55] As deaf persons, the appellants belong to an enumerated group under s. 15(1)— the physically disabled. ...

[56] It is an unfortunate truth that the history of disabled persons in Canada is largely one of exclusion and marginalization. Persons with disabilities have too often been excluded from the labour force, denied access to opportunities for social interaction and advancement, subjected to invidious stereotyping and relegated to institutions ... . This historical disadvantage has to a great extent been shaped and perpetuated by the notion that disability is an abnormality or flaw. As a result, disabled persons have not generally been afforded the "equal concern, respect and consideration" that s. 15(1) of the Charter demands. Instead, they have been subjected to paternalistic attitudes of pity and charity, and their entrance into the social mainstream has been conditional upon their emulation of able-bodied norms ... . One consequence of these attitudes is the persistent social and economic disadvantage faced by the disabled. Statistics indicate that persons with disabilities, in comparison to non-disabled persons, have less education, are more likely to be outside the labour force, face much higher unemployment rates, and are concentrated at the lower end of the pay scale when employed ... .

[57] Deaf persons have not escaped this general predicament. Although many of them resist the notion that deafness is an impairment and identify themselves as members of a distinct community with its own language and culture, this does not justify their compelled exclusion from the opportunities and services designed for and otherwise available to the hearing population. For many hearing persons, the dominant perception of deafness is one of silence. This perception has perpetuated ignorance of the needs of deaf persons and has resulted in a society that is for the most part organized as though

everyone can hear ... . Not surprisingly, therefore, the disadvantage experienced by deaf persons derives largely from barriers to communication with the hearing population.

[La Forest J then reviewed the general analytic framework to s. 15 and the different approaches adopted by various members of the Court in the 1995 trilogy.]

[59] In my view, in the present case the same result is reached regardless of which of these approaches is applied ... . There is no question that the distinction here is based on a personal characteristic that is irrelevant to the functional values underlying the health care system. Those values consist of the promotion of health and the prevention and treatment of illness and disease, and the realization of those values through the vehicle of a publicly funded health care system. There could be no personal characteristic less relevant to these values than an individual's physical disability.

[60] The only question in this case, then, is whether the appellants have been afforded "equal benefit of the law without discrimination" within the meaning of s. 15(1) of the Charter. On its face, the medicare system in British Columbia applies equally to the deaf and hearing populations. It does not make an explicit "distinction" based on disability by singling out deaf persons for different treatment. Both deaf and hearing persons are entitled to receive certain medical services free of charge. The appellants nevertheless contend that the lack of funding for sign language interpreters renders them unable to benefit from this legislation to the same extent as hearing persons. Their claim, in other words, is one of "adverse effects" discrimination.

[61] This Court has consistently held that s. 15(1) of the Charter protects against this type of discrimination. In [*Law Society of British Columbia v.*] *Andrews* [[1989] 1 SCR 143], McIntyre J found that facially neutral laws may be discriminatory. ... Section 15(1), the Court held, was intended to ensure a measure of substantive, and not merely formal equality.

[62] As a corollary to this principle, this Court has also concluded that a discriminatory purpose or intention is not a necessary condition of a s. 15(1) violation ... . A legal distinction need not be motivated by a desire to disadvantage an individual or group in order to violate s. 15(1). It is sufficient if the effect of the legislation is to deny someone the equal protection or benefit of the law. ... In this the Court has staked out a different path than the United States Supreme Court, which requires a discriminatory intent in order to ground an equal protection claim under the Fourteenth Amendment of the Constitution ... .

[63] This Court first addressed the concept of adverse effects discrimination in the context of provincial human rights legislation. In [*Ontario (Human Rights Commission) v.*] *Simpson-Sears* [[1985] 2 SCR 536], the Court was faced with the question of whether a rule requiring employees to be available for work on Friday evenings and Saturdays discriminated against those observing a Saturday Sabbath. Though this rule was neutral on its face in that it applied equally to all employees, the Court nevertheless found it to be discriminatory. Writing for the Court, McIntyre J commented as follows, at p. 551:

> A distinction must be made between what I would describe as direct discrimination and the concept already referred to as adverse effect discrimination in connection with employ-

ment. Direct discrimination occurs in this connection where an employer adopts a practice or rule which on its face discriminates on a prohibited ground. For example, "No Catholics or no women or no blacks employed here." ... On the other hand, there is the concept of adverse effect discrimination. It arises where an employer for genuine business reasons adopts a rule or standard which is on its face neutral, and which will apply equally to all employees, but which has a discriminatory effect upon a prohibited ground on one employee or group of employees in that it imposes, because of some special characteristic of the employee or group, obligations, penalties, or restrictive conditions not imposed on other members of the work force.

I note that in *Andrews*, McIntyre J made it clear that the equality principles developed by the Court in human rights cases are equally applicable in s. 15(1) cases. ...

[64] Adverse effects discrimination is especially relevant in the case of disability. The government will rarely single out disabled persons for discriminatory treatment. More common are laws of general application that have a disparate impact on the disabled. ...

[65] The Court elaborated upon this principle in its recent decision in *Eaton* [*v. Brant County Board of Education*, [1997] 1 SCR 241, 142 DLR (4th) 385]. Although Eaton involved direct discrimination, Sopinka J observed that in the case of disabled persons, it is often the failure to take into account the adverse effects of generally applicable laws that results in discrimination. He remarked, at paras. 66-67:

> The principles that not every distinction on a prohibited ground will constitute discrimination and that, in general, distinctions based on presumed rather than actual characteristics are the hallmarks of discrimination have particular significance when applied to physical and mental disability. Avoidance of discrimination on this ground will frequently require distinctions to be made taking into account the actual personal characteristics of disabled persons. In *Andrews v. Law Society of British Columbia*, [1989] 1 SCR 143, at p. 169, McIntyre J stated that the "accommodation of differences ... is the essence of true equality." This emphasizes that the purpose of s. 15(1) of the Charter is not only to prevent discrimination by the attribution of stereotypical characteristics to individuals, but also to ameliorate the position of groups within Canadian society who have suffered disadvantage by exclusion from mainstream society as has been the case with disabled persons.

> The principal object of certain of the prohibited grounds is the elimination of discrimination by the attribution of untrue characteristics based on stereotypical attitudes relating to immutable conditions such as race or sex. In the case of disability, this is one of the objectives. The other equally important objective seeks to take into account the true characteristics of this group which act as headwinds to the enjoyment of society's benefits and to accommodate them. Exclusion from the mainstream of society results from the construction of a society based solely on "mainstream" attributes to which disabled persons will never be able to gain access. Whether it is the impossibility of success at a written test for a blind person, or the need for ramp access to a library, the discrimination does not lie in the attribution of untrue characteristics to the disabled individual. The blind person cannot see and the person in a wheelchair needs a ramp. Rather, it is the failure to make reasonable accommodation, to fine-tune society so that its structures and assumptions do not result in the relegation and banishment of disabled persons from participation, which results in discrimination against them.

The discrimination inquiry which uses "the attribution of stereotypical characteristics" reasoning as commonly understood is simply inappropriate here. It may be seen rather as a case
of reverse stereotyping which, by not allowing for the condition of a disabled individual, ignores his or her disability and forces the individual to sink or swim within the mainstream
environment. It is recognition of the actual characteristics, and reasonable accommodation
of these characteristics which is the central purpose of s. 15(1) in relation to disability.

[66] Unlike in *Simpsons-Sears* ... , in the present case the adverse effects suffered by
deaf persons stem not from the imposition of a burden not faced by the mainstream
population, but rather from a failure to ensure that they benefit equally from a service
offered to everyone. It is on this basis that the trial judge and the majority of the Court
of Appeal found that the failure to provide medically related sign language interpretation
was not discriminatory. Their analyses presuppose that there is a categorical distinction
to be made between state-imposed burdens and benefits, and that the government is not
obliged to ameliorate disadvantage that it has not helped to create or exacerbate. Before
attempting to evaluate these assumptions, it will be helpful to relate the reasoning of the
courts below in more detail.

[67] As previously noted, both the trial judge and majority of the Court of Appeal
determined that, while the access of deaf people to medical services is limited to a certain
extent by their communication handicap, this limitation does not result from the denial
of any benefit of the law within the meaning of s. 15(1) of the Charter. They were able to
come to this conclusion because of the manner in which they characterized sign language interpretation. Interpretation services, they held, are not medically required.
Rather, they are "ancillary services," which, like other non-medical services such as
transportation to a doctor's office or hospital, are not publicly funded.

[68] Having determined that sign language interpretation is a discrete, non-medical
"ancillary" service, the courts below were able to conclude that the appellants were not
denied a benefit available to the hearing population. As the majority of the Court of Appeal explained, prior to the introduction of a universal medicare system, deaf and hearing
persons were each required to pay their doctors. When necessary for effective communication, deaf persons were also obliged to pay for sign language translators. The Medical
Services Plan, the court observed, removes the responsibility of both hearing and deaf
persons to pay their physicians. Deaf persons, of course, remain responsible for the payment of translators in order to receive equivalent medical services as hearing persons, as
they would be in the absence of the legislation. In the court's view, however, any resulting
inequality exists independently of the benefit provided by the state.

[69] While this approach has a certain formal, logical coherence, in my view it seriously
mischaracterizes the practical reality of health care delivery. Effective communication is
quite obviously an integral part of the provision of medical services. At trial, the appellants presented evidence that miscommunication can lead to misdiagnosis or a failure to
follow a recommended treatment. This risk is particularly acute in emergency situations,
as illustrated by the appellant Linda Warren's experience during the premature birth of
her twin daughters. That adequate communication is essential to proper medical care is
surely so incontrovertible that the Court could, if necessary, take judicial notice of it.

. . .

[71] If there are circumstances in which deaf patients cannot communicate effectively with their doctors without an interpreter, how can it be said that they receive the same level of medical care as hearing persons? Those who hear do not receive communication as a distinct service. For them, an effective means of communication is routinely available, free of charge, as part of every health care service. In order to receive the same quality of care, deaf persons must bear the burden of paying for the means to communicate with their health care providers, despite the fact that the system is intended to make ability to pay irrelevant. Where it is necessary for effective communication, sign language interpretation should not therefore be viewed as an "ancillary" service. On the contrary, it is the means by which deaf persons may receive the same quality of medical care as the hearing population.

[72] Once it is accepted that effective communication is an indispensable component of the delivery of medical services, it becomes much more difficult to assert that the failure to ensure that deaf persons communicate effectively with their health care providers is not discriminatory. In their effort to persuade this Court otherwise, the respondents and their supporting interveners maintain that s. 15(1) does not oblige governments to implement programs to alleviate disadvantages that exist independently of state action. Adverse effects only arise from benefit programs, they aver, when those programs exacerbate the disparities between the group claiming a s. 15(1) violation and the general population. They assert, in other words, that governments should be entitled to provide benefits to the general population without ensuring that disadvantaged members of society have the resources to take full advantage of those benefits.

[73] In my view, this position bespeaks a thin and impoverished vision of s. 15(1). It is belied, more importantly, by the thrust of this Court's equality jurisprudence. It has been suggested that s. 15(1) of the Charter does not oblige the state to take positive actions, such as provide services to ameliorate the symptoms of systemic or general inequality … . Whether or not this is true in all cases, and I do not purport to decide the matter here, the question raised in the present case is of a wholly different order. This Court has repeatedly held that once the state does provide a benefit, it is obliged to do so in a non-discriminatory manner … . In many circumstances, this will require governments to take positive action, for example by extending the scope of a benefit to a previously excluded class of persons.

· · ·

[77] This Court has consistently held, then, that discrimination can arise both from the adverse effects of rules of general application as well as from express distinctions flowing from the distribution of benefits. Given this state of affairs, I can think of no principled reason why it should not be possible to establish a claim of discrimination based on the adverse effects of a facially neutral benefit scheme. Section 15(1) expressly states, after all, that "[e]very individual is equal before and under the law and has the right to the equal protection and equal benefit of the law without discrimination …" (emphasis added). The provision makes no distinction between laws that impose unequal burdens and those that deny equal benefits. If we accept the concept of adverse effect discrimination, it seems inevitable, at least at the s. 15(1) stage of analysis, that the government will be required to take special measures to ensure that disadvantaged groups are able to benefit equally from government services. As I will develop below, if

there are policy reasons in favour of limiting the government's responsibility to ameliorate disadvantage in the provision of benefits and services, those policies are more appropriately considered in determining whether any violation of s. 15(1) is saved by s. 1 of the Charter.

[78] The principle that discrimination can accrue from a failure to take positive steps to ensure that disadvantaged groups benefit equally from services offered to the general public is widely accepted in the human rights field.

· · ·

[80] In my view, therefore, the failure of the Medical Services Commission and hospitals to provide sign language interpretation where it is necessary for effective communication constitutes a *prima facie* violation of the s. 15(1) rights of deaf persons. This failure denies them the equal benefit of the law and discriminates against them in comparison with hearing persons.

[La Forest J went on to find that the s. 15 violation could not be justified pursuant to s. 1. He held that "the government has manifestly failed to demonstrate that it had a reasonable basis for concluding that a total denial of medical interpretation services for the deaf constituted a minimum impairment of their rights." The government did not demonstrate that the negative impact on deaf persons' access to health care "must be tolerated in order to achieve the objective of limiting health care expenditures. Stated differently, the government has not made a 'reasonable accommodation' of the appellants' disability." In the result, he issued a declaration that the failure to fund sign language interpretation violated s. 15(1). The government was given six months to ensure that "sign language interpreters will be provided where necessary for effective communication in the delivery of medical services."]

Appeal allowed.

NOTES

1. Another example of a successful claim of "adverse effects" discrimination is *Vriend v. Alberta*, [1998] 1 SCR 493, 156 DLR (4th) 385. The appellant was fired from a Bible college when he revealed that he was gay. He attempted to file a complaint with the Alberta Human Rights Commission alleging discrimination on the basis of sexual orientation, but the Commission would not accept the complaint because sexual orientation was not a prohibited ground of discrimination in the Alberta human rights legislation. Vriend then initiated a court action arguing that the omission of protection against discrimination on the basis of sexual orientation was a violation of his equality rights. The government of Alberta argued that the exclusion of sexual orientation did not amount to differential treatment; it constituted a "neutral silence." In response, Cory J stated that the exclusion amounted to differential treatment directly and in terms of its adverse effects:

[81] It is clear that the [Act], by reason of its underinclusiveness, does create a distinction. The distinction is simultaneously drawn along two different lines. The first is the distinction between homosexuals, on one hand, and other disadvantaged groups which are protected

under the Act, on the other. Gays and lesbians do not even have formal equality with reference to other protected groups, since those other groups are explicitly included and they are not.

[82] The second distinction, and, I think, the more fundamental one, is between homosexuals and heterosexuals. This distinction may be more difficult to see because there is, on the surface, a measure of formal equality: gay or lesbian individuals have the same access as heterosexual individuals to the protection of the *IRPA* in the sense that they could complain to the Commission about an incident of discrimination on the basis of any of the grounds currently included. However, the exclusion of the ground of sexual orientation, considered in the context of the social reality of discrimination against gays and lesbians, clearly has a disproportionate impact on them as opposed to heterosexuals. Therefore the *IRPA* in its underinclusive state denies substantive equality to the former group. This was well expressed by W.N. Renke, "Case Comment: Vriend v. Alberta: Discrimination, Burdens of Proof, and Judicial Notice" (1996), 34 *Alta. L Rev.* 925, at pp. 942-43:

> If both heterosexuals and homosexuals equally suffered discrimination on the basis of sexual orientation, neither might complain of unfairness if the *IRPA* extended no remedies for discrimination on the basis of sexual orientation. A person belonging to one group would be treated like a person belonging to the other. Where, though, discrimination is visited virtually exclusively against persons with one type of sexual orientation, an absence of legislative remedies for discrimination based on sexual orientation has a differential impact. The absence of remedies has no real impact on heterosexuals, since they have no complaints to make concerning sexual orientation discrimination. The absence of remedies has a real impact on homosexuals, since they are the persons discriminated against on the basis of sexual orientation. Furthermore, a heterosexual has recourse to all the currently available heads of discrimination, should a complaint be necessary. A homosexual, it is true, may also have recourse to those heads of discrimination, but the only type of discrimination he or she may suffer may be sexual orientation discrimination. He or she would have no remedy for this type of discrimination. Seen in this way, the *IRPA* does distinguish between homosexuals and heterosexuals.

See also Pothier [D. Pothier, "The Sounds of Silence: Charter Application When the Legislature Declines to Speak" (1996), 7 *Constitutional Forum* 113], at p. 119. It is possible that a heterosexual individual could be discriminated against on the ground of sexual orientation. Yet this is far less likely to occur than discrimination against a homosexual or lesbian on that same ground. It thus is apparent that there is a clear distinction created by the disproportionate impact which arises from the exclusion of the ground from the *IRPA*.

Further extracts from *Vriend* are found in Chapter 16, The Advent of the Charter; Chapter 18, Application; and Chapter 25, Enforcement of Rights.

2. *Eldridge* and *Vriend* both involved facially neutral rules that had a more burdensome impact on all members of minority groups: the hearing impaired in *Eldridge*, and gays and lesbians in *Vriend*. The adverse effect consisted of the greater burden imposed on deaf persons by a rule denying funding for translation services in health care, and the greater burden imposed on sexual minorities by the denial of protection against discrimination on the basis of sexual orientation. A different kind of adverse effect arises when a facially neutral, burdensome rule has a statistically disproportionate impact on members of a disadvantaged

group. Such a rule imposes equal burdens on all to whom it applies, but the population to whom it applies is composed disproportionately of members of disadvantaged groups. This kind of statistical adverse effect is typically more difficult to prove than claims based on disproportionate burdens. The evidence required may be more complex, and courts may be uncomfortable with the potentially far-reaching implications of the claims. Although the Supreme Court has indicated its acceptance of the concept, it has yet to find a s. 15(1) violation based on statistical adverse effects.

3. An example of a failed claim based on statistical adverse effects is *Symes v. Canada*, [1993] 4 SCR 695, 110 DLR (4th) 470. The case involved a challenge brought by a female lawyer to provisions of the *Income Tax Act* that did not permit the full deduction of childcare expenses as a business expense. Iacobucci J concluded that the claimant had not established that the challenged provisions had a disproportionate impact on women. He noted that an abundance of information had been placed before the Court that "conclusively demonstrates that women bear a disproportionate share of the child care burden in Canada." But to establish that the limited deductibility of childcare expenses amounts to differential treatment on the basis of sex, he said, "it is not sufficient for the appellant to show that women disproportionately bear the burden of *child care* in society. Rather, she must show that women disproportionately *pay child care expenses*." Iacobucci J went on to suggest that "a different sub-group of women with a different evidentiary focus," such as single mothers, "might well be able to demonstrate the adverse effects required by s. 15(1)."

4. Another s. 15(1) claim based on statistical adverse effects that failed is *Thibaudeau v. Canada*, [1995] 2 SCR 627, 124 DLR (4th) 449, also discussed above in Section III. A divorced mother with custody of the child from the marriage challenged the *Income Tax Act* rules that, at that time, required custodial parents who receive spousal and child support payments to include such payments in their income, and permitted the payors to deduct those payments from their income. The government defended the "inclusion/deduction" scheme on the ground that taxing spousal and child support in the hands of the lower income earner meant that such income was taxed at a lower marginal tax rate, resulting in a tax saving that would flow to the advantage of the children of divorce. Thibaudeau argued that, in practice, the rules penalized custodial parents because the family law system consistently failed to take the tax impact into account. Since 98 percent of the recipients of child support were women, the fact that the rules had a statistically disparate impact on the basis of sex was evident. Nevertheless, a majority of the Supreme Court found that the rules did not have a negative impact on custodial parents; rather, the rules operated to the overall advantage of the post-divorce family unit.

In the article excerpted below, Colleen Sheppard discusses the need to develop further the concept of adverse effects discrimination. Sheppard's discussion revolves around the Supreme Court's ruling in the case of Tracey Meiorin (*British Columbia (Public Service Employee Relations Commission) v. BCGSEU*, [1999] 3 SCR 3, 176 DLR (4th) 1), a BC firefighter who successfully argued that she was discriminated against on the basis of sex when she was dismissed from her employment for failing an aerobics test. *Meiorin* and a number of the other cases Sheppard discusses involve the interpretation of statutory human rights codes, but the ideas developed in them are applicable to the interpretation of s. 15 of the Charter.

C. Sheppard, "Of Forest Fires and Systemic Discrimination: A Review of British Columbia (Public Service Employee Relations Commission) v. BCGSEU"
(2001), 46 *McGill Law Journal* 533, at 542-49 (footnotes omitted)

[T]he distinction [between direct and adverse effects discrimination] remains critically important for identifying the adverse effects of apparently neutral policies, practices, and procedures on the socially disadvantaged groups accorded protection against discrimination in human rights documents. Moreover, despite its path-breaking recognition of adverse effect discrimination in *Ontario (Human Rights Commission) v. Simpsons-Sears* [[1985] 2 SCR 536, also referred to as the *O'Malley* case], the Court has not provided any significant elaboration of how to identify adverse effect discrimination in its more recent jurisprudence. Rather than moving away from the albeit challenging task of elaborating on the concept of adverse effect discrimination, more in-depth legal analysis of the concept is needed.

Why is it so critical to expand on our understanding of adverse effect discrimination? If we do not, there is a significant risk that discrimination embedded in apparently neutral institutional policies, rules, or procedures will not be recognized as discriminatory. This risk is accentuated by the necessity in anti-discrimination law to connect the experience of exclusion, harm, prejudice, or disadvantage to a recognized ground of discrimination. Thus, for example, it is not enough to claim that one is excluded because of a height and weight standard; it is necessary to link the apparently neutral standard to the recognized ground of sex or race discrimination. While the analogous grounds in subsection 15(1) of the Charter mean that direct discrimination against domestic workers, for example, could be recognized as constituting discrimination against a new analogous ground (that of domestic workers), adverse effect analysis allows us to make the conceptual link between discrimination against domestic workers and sexism and racism. While making that conceptual link may be self-evident in some cases, in others it will be invisible and unacknowledged, especially for those who do not experience the disadvantage. We need a sophisticated and coherent theory of adverse effect discrimination to assist claimants, lawyers, and adjudicators with the complexities of the manifestations of systemic discrimination. While I do not endeavour here to articulate a complete theory of adverse effect discrimination, I offer a few preliminary ideas about potential avenues for clarification.

Eliminating Intent from Discrimination Analysis

First, it is necessary to dispense with the intent problem. When anti-discrimination laws first emerged, the general understanding was that discrimination was rooted in the intentional exclusion or mistreatment of individuals on the basis of their group membership. Indeed, early forays into the legal prohibition of discrimination relied on a criminal law model, including the requirement of a mens rea or a discriminatory intent. This approach to anti-discrimination law was premised on deeply rooted ideas in criminal law and tort law that individuals should only be held legally accountable if they are at fault or if they intentionally cause harm to others. When the concept of adverse effect discrimination first emerged, it ushered in a growing recognition of the possibility of legal accountability based on the victim's experience of harm even in the absence of any intent to discriminate. Human rights law was to be a remedial law that compensated victims of discrimination. Its focus diverged from its criminal law antecedents and shifted away from the earlier perpetrator perspective. As Dickson CJC notes in *Action travail des femmes* [*Canadian National Railway Co. v. Canada (Canadian Human Rights Commission),* [1987] 1 SCR 1114, 40 DLR (4th) 193], "The purpose of the [*Canadian Human Rights*] *Act* is not to punish wrongdoing but to prevent discrimination."

Adverse effect discrimination, as an emerging category of discrimination, was understood as the dichotomous opposite of direct discrimination. Direct discrimination involved differential treatment. Adverse effect discrimination resulted in unequal effects in the wake of similar or facially neutral treatment. Intent was explicitly eliminated as a component of adverse effect discrimination. By default, intent appeared to be a necessary component of direct discrimination. Surely, so the argument went, if individuals were being treated differently based on their group membership there was an intent to discriminate.

Intent, however, is a problematic concept that is difficult to apply in direct discrimination cases as well. In *Action travail des femmes* Dickson CJC recognizes the analytical quagmire of the intent requirement, observing "a continuing confusion of the notions of 'intent' and 'malice.'" Intent was understood in anti-discrimination cases to entail some moral blameworthiness rather than the "simple willing of a consequence." Adverse effect discrimination often arose inadvertently and did not signal moral blameworthiness on the part of the policy-makers who introduced the facially neutral rule. The hard hat policy at issue in *Bhinder* [*v. Canadian National Railway Co.,* [1985] 2 SCR 5, 23 DLR (4th) 481] is a good example. It was clearly not introduced to exclude Sikhs, but rather to advance occupational health and safety. Direct discrimination may or may not involve an intent to discriminate. It clearly involves an intent to treat individuals differently based on group membership; however, the differential treatment may not have been designed to cause discriminatory effects. If it does, it should be actionable under human rights laws regardless of whether or not the discriminator realized or had an intent to discriminate. While it may be important to recognize intent to underscore the human agency behind both direct and adverse effect discrimination, or possibly as an element that would justify some aggravated damages for deterrence reasons, intent should not normally be accorded legal significance in either direct or indirect discrimination cases. ...

When Are Disparate Effects Discriminatory?

Second, we need an understanding of when and how adverse effects cause discrimination. Our paradigm for thinking about adverse effect discrimination is religion and employment. Many of the leading cases on adverse effect discrimination involve discrimination against employees of minority religions. In these cases, the adverse effect analysis is relatively straightforward because of the complete (or 100 percent) exclusion or disadvantage that results. That is, everyone in the minority religion is potentially affected. The individual litigant provides a living example of the absolute exclusionary effects and harm caused by employment policies, rules, or practices not designed for the minority religion. For example, in O'Malley, an employment rule that requires store clerks to work on Saturdays has an absolute exclusionary impact on Seventh Day Adventists who cannot work on their Saturday Sabbath. Disability cases also entail virtually absolute exclusion in their discriminatory effects.

It is in adverse impact cases dealing with race or gender that the disparate effects are often not so straightforward. In this domain, the effects may not be absolute or result in 100 percent exclusion of women or racial minorities. And yet, in many cases the patterns of exclusion and disadvantage can and should be understood to result from sex or race discrimination. The leading decision in the *United States, Griggs v. Duke Power Corporation* [401 US 424 (1971)], involved not an absolute exclusion of black employees from promotions and hiring, but a disproportionate exclusion resulting from a standardized employment test.

Meiorin [*British Columbia (Public Service Employee Relations Commission) v. British Columbia Government Service Employees' Union*, [1999] 3 SCR 3, 176 DLR (4th) 1] provides us with an interesting factual basis for understanding adverse effect discrimination that is based predominantly on a statistical disparity. In explaining the gender inequity of the aerobic standard, McLachlin J writes:

> Evidence accepted by the arbitrator demonstrated that, owing to physiological differences, most women have lower aerobic capacity than most men. Even with training, most women cannot increase their aerobic capacity to the level required by the aerobic standard, although training can allow most men to meet it. The arbitrator also heard evidence that 65% to 70% of male applicants pass the Tests on their initial attempts, while only 35% of female applicants have similar success. Of the 800 to 900 Initial Attack Crew members employed by the Government in 1995, only 100 to 150 were female.

Although there was expert evidence put forward by the government that "most women can achieve the aerobic standard with training," McLachlin J notes that the arbitrator considered this evidence to be "anecdotal" and "not supported by scientific data." McLachlin J then concludes that Ms. Meiorin had established a prima facie case of discrimination. One finds no discussion in the judgment of the amount of statistical disparity required to satisfy an allegation of sex discrimination. Of note, however, is that 35 percent of women pass the test on their initial attempt. And yet, 65 percent of women fail in contrast to the 30 to 35 percent failure rate for men—a discrepancy that discloses a fairly stark gender-based disparity. It would have been helpful if McLachlin J had elaborated even slightly on the Court's conclusion that the facts disclosed a prima facie case of discrimination. When does a statistical disparity reveal discrimination? Is an adverse impact affecting only 51 percent of a disadvantaged group enough to ground a claim of discrimination, or would it be necessary to show a greater disproportionate impact of 55 or 60 percent? In *Meiorin* the Court endorses a finding of prima facie discrimination based on a 65 to 70 percent disparity.

From a statistics perspective, it is generally thought that discrimination can be deduced from a disparate pattern of exclusion or harm that is statistically significant and not simply the result of chance. ...

While statistical clarity is important, the hidden biases of statistics and the extent to which statistical evidentiary requirements seem to increase the complexities and thus the costs of human rights litigation may make us reluctant to elaborate any fixed quantitative requirements for proving adverse effect discrimination. Moreover, it is often difficult to isolate the quantitative dimensions of discrimination from the larger qualitative aspects of inequality. A lower statistical disparity combined with significant qualitative factors may well substantiate a discrimination claim in some cases.

In *Symes v. Canada* [[1993] 4 SCR 695, 110 DLR (4th) 470], one of the few judgments to discuss adverse effect discrimination, Iacobucci J also raises a causation requirement. The adverse impact must be directly caused or related to the impugned provision and not be due to other factors:

> If the adverse effects analysis is to be coherent, it must not assume that a statutory provision has an effect which is not proved. We must take care to distinguish between effects which are wholly caused, or are contributed to, by an impugned provision, and those social circumstances which exist independently of such a provision.

In *Symes* Iacobucci J concludes that both parents had an obligation to pay for child care under law and that there was no proof that women assumed a greater proportion of this financial burden. The proof adduced focussed on gender inequalities in the assumption of child care work.

Thus, beyond questions of the degree of disparity, the proof must reveal a causal link or connection between the discriminatory effects and the rule or policy. ...

Recognizing Different Types of Adverse Effect Discrimination

A third, further dimension of our understanding of adverse effect discrimination relates to the need to distinguish between a facially neutral rule or policy applied to everyone and a facially neutral distinction. ...

As noted, the numerous complexities that surround the concept of adverse effect discrimination require more, not less, legal analysis. One starting point for discussing the various components of adverse effect discrimination would be a more precise typology of adverse effect discrimination. It could include the following:

1. *Facially Neutral Policy, Practice, or Standard*: A standard rule, test, practice, or policy that is applied to everyone in the same way. The adverse effects may affect (a) all members of a group protected by human rights law (100 percent exclusion or harm—e.g. religion or disability); or (b) a disproportionate number of members of a group protected under human rights law;

2. *Facially Neutral Distinction or Categorization*: Harmful differential treatment, categorization, or direct distinction that corresponds to a prohibited ground of discrimination in human rights law because of the preponderance of individuals from particular social groups affected by the facially neutral distinction or category (e.g. domestic workers, immigrant spouses).

Auton (Guardian ad litem of) v. British Columbia (Attorney General)
[2004] 3 SCR 657, 245 DLR (4th) 1

[Autistic children and their parents brought an action against the province of British Columbia, alleging that its failure to fund a particular treatment—applied behavioural therapy—for all autistic children between the ages of 3 and 6 violated s. 15(1) of the *Canadian Charter of Rights and Freedoms*. The government funded a number of programs for autistic children, but did not establish funding for applied behavioural therapy because of, *inter alia*, financial constraints and the emergent and controversial nature of this therapy. The trial judge found that the failure to fund applied behavioural therapy violated the petitioners' equality rights. The Court of Appeal upheld the judgment. In a unanimous judgment authored by McLachlin CJC, the Supreme Court of Canada allowed the appeal, finding that there had been no violation of equality rights. Surprisingly, the s. 15 analysis failed at the very first step—that of establishing differential treatment under the law.]

McLACHLIN CJC (Major, Bastarache, Binnie, LeBel, Deschamps, and Fish JJ concurring):

I. Introduction

[1] This case raises the issue of whether the Province of British Columbia's refusal to fund a particular treatment for preschool-aged autistic children violates the right to equality under the *Canadian Charter of Rights and Freedoms*. The petitioners are autistic children and their parents. They argue that the government's failure to fund applied behavioural therapy for autism unjustifiably discriminated against them. In the background lies the larger issue of when, if ever, a province's public health plan under the *Canada Health Act*, RSC 1985, c. C-6 ("CHA"), is required to provide a particular health treatment outside the "core" services administered by doctors and hospitals.

[2] One sympathizes with the petitioners, and with the decisions below ordering the public health system to pay for their therapy. However, the issue before us is not what the public health system should provide, which is a matter for Parliament and the legislature. The issue is rather whether the British Columbia Government's failure to fund these services under the health plan amounted to an unequal and discriminatory denial of benefits under that plan, contrary to s. 15 of the Charter. Despite their forceful argument, the petitioners fail to establish that the denial of benefits violated the Charter.

[3] The government must provide the services authorized by law in a non-discriminatory manner. Here, however, discrimination has not been established. First, the claim for discrimination is based on the erroneous assumption that the CHA and the relevant British Columbia legislation provided the benefit claimed. Second, on the facts here and applying the appropriate comparator, it is not established that the government excluded autistic children on the basis of disability. For these reasons, the claim fails and the appeal is allowed.

. . .

(1) Is the Claim for a Benefit Provided by Law?

[27] In order to succeed, the claimants must show unequal treatment under the law—more specifically that they failed to receive a benefit that the law provided, or was saddled with a burden the law did not impose on someone else. The primary and oft-stated goal of s. 15(1) is to combat discrimination and ameliorate the position of disadvantaged groups within society. Its specific promise, however, is confined to benefits and burdens "of the law." Combatting discrimination and ameliorating the position of members of disadvantaged groups is a formidable task and demands a multi-pronged response. Section 15(1) is part of that response. Section 15(2)'s exemption for affirmative action programs is another prong of the response. Beyond these lie a host of initiatives that governments, organizations and individuals can undertake to ameliorate the position of members of disadvantaged groups.

[28] The specific role of s. 15(1) in achieving this objective is to ensure that when governments choose to enact benefits or burdens, they do so on a non-discriminatory basis. This confines s. 15(1) claims to benefits and burdens imposed by law. ...

[29] Most s. 15(1) claims relate to a clear statutory benefit or burden. Consequently, the need for the benefit claimed or burden imposed to emanate from law has not been much discussed. Nevertheless, the language of s. 15(1) as well as the jurisprudence demand that it be met before a s. 15(1) claim can succeed.

[30] In this case, the issue of whether the benefit claimed is one conferred by law does arise, and must be carefully considered. The claim, as discussed, is for funding for a "medically necessary" treatment. The unequal treatment is said to lie in funding medically required treatments for non-disabled Canadian children or adults with mental illness, while refusing to fund medically required ABA/IBI therapy to autistic children. The decisions under appeal proceeded on this basis. The trial judge, affirmed by the Court of Appeal, ruled that the discrimination lay in denying a "medically necessary" service to a disadvantaged group while providing "medically necessary" services for others. Thus the benefit claimed, in essence, is funding for all medically required treatment.

[31] This raises the question of whether the legislative scheme in fact provides anyone with all medically required treatment. An examination of the scheme shows that it does not: see Appendix A (Relevant Legislative and Regulatory Provisions) and Appendix B (Interaction of the Relevant Legislative and Regulatory Provisions).

[32] The scheme designates two distinct categories of funded treatment based on service. First, the scheme provides complete funding for services delivered by medical practitioners, referred to as "core" services. This is required by the CHA. Many medically necessary or required services, including ABA/IBI therapy for autistic children, fall outside this core.

[33] Secondly, the CHA permits the provinces at their discretion to fund non-core medical services—services that are not delivered by physicians. British Columbia does this by naming classes of "health care practitioners" whose services may be partially funded. It then falls to the Medical Services Commission, an administrative body, to designate particular practitioners and procedures within these categories for funding.

[34] It was suggested that the reference by the *Medicare Protection Act*, RSBC 1996, c. 286 ("MPA"), to "medically required" services is an indication that all medically re-

quired or necessary non-core services must be funded. However, the Act does not say this. Section 1 uses the phrase "medically required services" in conjunction with the services of doctors or "medical practitioners" or an "approved diagnostic facility" (s. 1 "benefits," paras. (a) and (c)). Only these services are funded on the basis of being "medically required." "Medically required" in the MPA does not touch the services of "health care practitioners" which are funded only if the Province chooses to place a class of health care practitioner on an "enrolled" list by legislation or regulation: MPA, s. 1 "benefits," para. (b).

[35] In summary, the legislative scheme does not promise that any Canadian will receive funding for all medically required treatment. All that is conferred is core funding for services provided by medical practitioners, with funding for non-core services left to the Province's discretion. Thus, the benefit here claimed—funding for all medically required services—was not provided for by the law.

[36] More specifically, the law did not provide funding for ABA/IBI therapy for autistic children. The British Columbia MPA authorized partial funding for the services of the following health care practitioners: chiropractors, dentists, optometrists, podiatrists, physical therapists, massage therapists and naturopathic doctors. In addition, provincial regulations authorized funding for the services of physical therapists, massage therapists and nurses. At the time of trial, the Province had not named providers of ABA/IBI therapy as "health care practitioners," whose services could be funded under the plan.

[37] It followed that the Medical Services Commission, charged with administration of the MPA, had no power to order funding for ABA/IBI therapy. The Commission, as an administrative body, had no authority to enlarge the class of "health care practitioners." That could be done only by the government. Since the government had not designated ABA/IBI therapists as "health care practitioners," the Commission was not permitted to list their services for funding. This is how things stood at the time of trial. British Columbia's law governing non-core benefits did not provide the benefit that the petitioners were seeking.

[38] The petitioners rely on *Eldridge* [*v. British Columbia (Attorney General)*, [1997] 3 SCR 624, 151 DLR (4th) 577] in arguing for equal provision of medical benefits. … *Eldridge* was concerned with unequal access to a benefit that the law conferred and with applying a benefit-granting law in a non-discriminatory fashion. By contrast, this case is concerned with access to a benefit that the law has not conferred. For this reason, *Eldridge* does not assist the petitioners.

[39] However, this does not end the inquiry. Courts should look to the reality of the situation to see whether the claimants have been denied benefits of the legislative scheme other than those they have raised. This brings up the broader issue of whether the legislative scheme is discriminatory, since it provides non-core services to some groups while denying funding for ABA/IBI therapy to autistic children. The allegation is that the scheme is itself discriminatory, by funding some non-core therapies while denying equally necessary ABA/IBI therapy.

[40] This argument moves beyond the legislative definition of "benefit." As pointed out in *Hodge* [*v. Canada (Minister of Human Resources Development)*, [2004] 3 SCR 357, 244 DLR (4th) 257], at para. 25:

... the legislative definition, being the subject matter of the equality rights challenge, is not the last word. Otherwise, a survivor's pension restricted to white protestant males could be defended on the ground that all surviving white protestant males were being treated equally.

We must look behind the words and ask whether the statutory definition is itself a means of perpetrating inequality rather than alleviating it. Section 15(1) requires not merely formal equality, but substantive equality: *Andrews* [*v. Law Society of British Columbia*, [1989] 1 SCR 143, 56 DLR (4th) 1], at p. 166.

[41] It is not open to Parliament or a legislature to enact a law whose policy objectives and provisions single out a disadvantaged group for inferior treatment: *Corbiere v. Canada (Minister of Indian and Northern Affairs)*, [1999] 2 SCR 203. On the other hand, a legislative choice not to accord a particular benefit absent demonstration of discriminatory purpose, policy or effect does not offend this principle and does not give rise to s. 15(1) review. This Court has repeatedly held that the legislature is under no obligation to create a particular benefit. It is free to target the social programs it wishes to fund as a matter of public policy, provided the benefit itself is not conferred in a discriminatory manner: *Granovsky v. Canada (Minister of Employment and Immigration)*, [2000] 1 SCR 703, 2000 SCC 28, at para. 61; *Nova Scotia (Attorney General) v. Walsh*, [2002] 4 SCR 325, 2002 SCC 83, at para. 55; *Hodge, supra*, at para. 16.

[42] A statutory scheme may discriminate either directly, by adopting a discriminatory policy or purpose, or indirectly, by effect. Direct discrimination on the face of a statute or in its policy is readily identifiable and poses little difficulty. Discrimination by effect is more difficult to identify. Where stereotyping of persons belonging to a group is at issue, assessing whether a statutory definition that excludes a group is discriminatory, as opposed to being the legitimate exercise of legislative power in defining a benefit, involves consideration of the purpose of the legislative scheme which confers the benefit and the overall needs it seeks to meet. If a benefit program excludes a particular group in a way that undercuts the overall purpose of the program, then it is likely to be discriminatory: it amounts to an arbitrary exclusion of a particular group. If, on the other hand, the exclusion is consistent with the overarching purpose and scheme of the legislation, it is unlikely to be discriminatory. Thus, the question is whether the excluded benefit is one that falls within the general scheme of benefits and needs which the legislative scheme is intended to address.

[43] The legislative scheme in the case at bar, namely the CHA and the MPA, does not have as its purpose the meeting of all medical needs. As discussed, its only promise is to provide full funding for core services, defined as physician-delivered services. Beyond this, the provinces may, within their discretion, offer specified non-core services. It is, by its very terms, a partial health plan. It follows that exclusion of particular non-core services cannot, without more, be viewed as an adverse distinction based on an enumerated ground. Rather, it is an anticipated feature of the legislative scheme. It follows that one cannot infer from the fact of exclusion of ABA/IBI therapy for autistic children from non-core benefits that this amounts to discrimination. There is no discrimination by effect.

[44] The correctness of this conclusion may be tested by considering the consequences to the legislative scheme of obliging provinces to provide non-core medical services re-

quired by disabled persons and people associated with other enumerated and analogous grounds, like gender and age. Subject to a finding of no discrimination at the third step, a class of people legally entitled to non-core benefits would be created. This would effectively amend the medicare scheme and extend benefits beyond what it envisions—core physician-provided benefits plus non-core benefits at the discretion of the Province.

[45] Had the situation been different, the petitioners might have attempted to frame their legal action as a claim to the benefit of equal application of the law by the Medical Services Commission. This would not have been a substantive claim for funding for particular medical services, but a procedural claim anchored in the assertion that benefits provided by the law were not distributed in an equal fashion. Such a claim, if made out, would be supported by *Eldridge, supra*. The argument would be that the Medical Services Commission violated s. 15(1) by approving non-core services for non-disabled people, while denying equivalent services to autistic children and their families.

[46] Such a claim depends on a prior showing that there is a benefit provided by law. There can be no administrative duty to distribute non-existent benefits equally. Had the legislature designated ABA/IBI therapists (or a broader group of therapists which included them) as "health care practitioners" under the MPA at the time of trial, this would have amounted to a legislated benefit, which the Commission would be charged with implementing. The Commission would then have been obliged to implement that benefit in a non-discriminatory fashion. However, this is not the case. Here, the legislature had not legislated funding for the benefit in question, and the Commission had no power to deal with it.

[47] I conclude that the benefit claimed, no matter how it is viewed, is not a benefit provided by law. This is sufficient to end the inquiry.

[The Court also rejected the comparator groups chosen by the petitioners and, using what it determined was the appropriate comparator group, found that the exclusion of autistic children from the funding scheme under the province's public health plan was not on the basis of mental disability. This part of McLachlin CJ's reasons can be found below in Section VI.C.]

B. Enumerated and Analogous Grounds

The second stage of the s. 15(1) analysis is to determine whether the differential treatment at issue is on the basis of a personal characteristic that is either listed in s. 15(1) or analogous to those listed. Beginning in *Andrews*, the Supreme Court has restricted the role of s. 15 to combatting discrimination on an enumerated or analogous ground. The grounds limitation on the reach of s. 15(1) has been criticized by those who believe that equality rights should protect individuals from all arbitrary or irrational laws. The grounds have also been criticized for distorting and compartmentalizing people's complex experiences of discrimination, and for obscuring the asymmetrical and unequal experience of discrimination between the groups targeted by the specific grounds. See N. Iyer, "Categorical Denials: Equality Rights and the Shaping of Social Identity" (1993), 19 *Queen's Law Journal* 179; C. Sheppard, "Grounds of Discrimination: Towards an Inclusive and Contextual Approach" (2001), 80 *Canadian Bar Review* 893. As mentioned above in Section III, L'Heureux-Dubé J took the position in the 1995 trilogy that the courts could better analyze people's experience of discrimination if they dropped the requirement of grounds. Others, like Pothier in the excerpt below, have defended the role of grounds in focusing attention on the history and social reality of unequal power relations.

D. Pothier, "Connecting Grounds of Discrimination to Real People's Real Experiences"
(2001), 13 *Canadian Journal of Women and the Law* 37, at 40-45 and 57-58
(footnotes omitted)

Justice L'Heureux-Dubé's concern, which was expressed in *Egan*, that a focus on grounds risks "being distanced and desensitised from real people's real experiences" assumes that grounds are disconnected from real people's real experiences. In contrast, I would contend, along with Celina Romany, that grounds are an important means of providing the necessary history and context of discrimination. This point is relevant with respect to both long-established and newly recognized grounds of discrimination. When, in *Egan*, Justice John Sopinka described the recognition of same-sex relationships as "novel," thereby justifying non-intervention by the Court, he was indeed "distanced and desensitised from real people's real experiences." However, the distance and insensitivity of his judgment is not because sexual orientation is disconnected from the lives of lesbians and gay men. Rather, it reflects the fact that sexual orientation has for so long been either constrained by, or invisible to, the law.

Grounds of discrimination are not a purely legal construct. They reflect a political and social reality to which the law has, belatedly, given recognition. Discrimination was a fact of life long before the law decided that it should intervene to prohibit it. It is the grounds of discrimination that separate people who experience discrimination from those who do not. The focus on why something counts as a ground of discrimination should be a constant reminder of why discrimination is, legislatively and/or constitutionally, prohibited. Without a thorough understanding of the pertinent ground or grounds of discrimination, the discrimination analysis will be inadequate.

· · ·

[I]t is grounds of discrimination that serve as a reminder of the link to history and context. ... In light of the ongoing reality of discrimination, and as long as people and institutions factor in grounds both intentionally and structurally, legal analysis must pay close attention to grounds in order to remain relevant. While Justice L'Heureux-Dubé and other critics of a grounds approach contend that grounds result in individual circumstances being improperly overlooked, I content that the problem is exactly the opposite—that a de-emphasis on grounds makes it too easy to validate generalizations and/or categorical distinctions.

· · ·

The essence of the critique of grounds is the claim that they are an artificial compartmentalization, which obscure the complex reality of real life. In contrast, the defence of grounds is based on the contention that they serve to focus attention on the real sources of discrimination.

. . .

Grounds of discrimination are obviously only one element of the analysis. Although, in theory, it would be possible to be attentive to the dynamics of such phenomena as racism and sexism without making grounds a separate element of analysis, in practice, it is attention to grounds that can help ensure that the history and context of discrimination do not simply fade into the background. Grounds of discrimination, as a legal construct, are markers of the dynamics of power. The exercise of identifying new analogous grounds forces an inquiry into the complexities of the dynamics of power. Although there are certain commonalities across different kinds of discrimination, discrimination operates in different ways in the context of different grounds of discrimination. It is through an understanding of the different ways in which discrimination operates that a more complex and comprehensive appreciation of equality can emerge.

The *Andrews* case indicated that a personal characteristic will be recognized as an analogous ground of discrimination if it shares the essential features of the enumerated grounds of discrimination. In *Andrews*, the Court recognized citizenship as an analogous ground of discrimination. Recall that in *Andrews*, LaForest J argued that what makes a ground analogous to those listed in s. 15 is that it refers to a personal characteristic that is "immutable or beyond the control of the individual," whereas Wilson and McIntyre JJ suggested that what unites enumerated and analogous grounds is that they refer to personal characteristics of groups "lacking in political power."

Since *Andrews*, the Court has recognized three more analogous grounds of discrimination. In *Egan v. Canada*, [1995] 2 SCR 513, 124 DLR (4th) 609, the Court held that sexual orientation is an analogous ground of discrimination. La Forest J, writing for four members of the Court, stated that sexual orientation "is a deeply personal characteristic that is either unchangeable or changeable only at unacceptable personal costs, and so falls within the ambit of s. 15 protection as being analogous to the enumerated grounds." Cory J, writing for another four members of the Court, did not mention immutability. He focused on the relationship between sexual orientation and stereotyping, historical disadvantage and vulnerability to political and social prejudice. Noting that gays and lesbians have long been subject to harassment, violence, discrimination, and stigmatization, he concluded that they "form an identifiable minority who have suffered and continue to suffer serious social, political and economic disadvantage." For other rulings treating sexual orientation as a prohibited ground of discrimination, see *Vriend v. Alberta*, [1998] 1 SCR 493, 156 DLR (4th) 385 and *M. v. H.*, [1999] 2 SCR 3, 171 DLR (4th) 577.

In *Miron v. Trudel*, [1995] 2 SCR 418, 124 DLR (4th) 693, the Court found that marital status is an analogous ground of discrimination and, by a five to four majority, held that the denial of automobile insurance benefits to unmarried opposite-sex couples violated the Charter. McLachlin J, writing for four members of the majority, examined a range of factors before concluding that marital status is an analogous ground. First, she said, marital status touches matters that are related to "the essential dignity and worth of the individual"— namely, "the individual's freedom to live life with the mate of one's choice in the fashion of one's choice." Second, marital status is associated with patterns of historical disadvantage and prejudice. Third, marital status may not be immutable in a strong sense, but it is a designation over which "the individual exercises limited but not exclusive control." In response to the argument that marital status cannot be a ground of discrimination because marriage is a "good" or even "sacred" institution, she stated:

> The fallacy in the argument is the assumption that the grounds of discrimination are evil. Discrimination is evil. But the grounds upon which it rests are not. Consider the enumerated grounds—race, national or ethnic origin, colour, religion, sex, age and mental or physical disability. None of these are evil in themselves. Indeed, people rightfully take pride in their race and ethnic origin; they find identity in their colour and their sex. Even mental and physical disabilities should be regarded not as deficiencies, but differences—differences which, while they will make some aspects of life more difficult, do not affect others, and may, moreover, contribute to society's richness and texture. What is evil is not the ground of discrimination, but its inappropriate use to deny equal protection and benefit to people who are members of the marked groups—not on the basis of their true abilities or circumstance, but on the basis of the group to which they belong. The argument that marital status cannot be an analogous ground because it is good cannot succeed. The issue is not whether marriage is good, but rather whether it may be used to deny equal treatment to people on grounds which have nothing to do with their true worth or entitlement due to circumstance.

McLachlin J concluded that the denial of automobile insurance benefits to unmarried couples was discriminatory because marriage was an inaccurate marker of the relationships characterized by financial interdependence that were relevant to the objectives of legislation.

In dissent, Gonthier J was wary of stating rules that might hinder governments' ability to support marriage as an important social institution. In his analysis, analogous grounds are irrelevant personal characteristics associated with historical disadvantage and stereotyping. He concluded that marital status may be an analogous ground in some circumstances, but not when the benefits and burdens that the law attaches to marriage are at issue.

Finally, in *Corbière*, excerpted below, the Court recognized the status of being an off-reserve member of a First Nation regulated as an Indian band by the *Indian Act* as an analogous ground of discrimination.

Corbière v. Canada (Minister of Indian and Northern Affairs)
[1999] 2 SCR 203, 173 DLR (4th) 1

[The case concerned s. 77(1) of the *Indian Act*, which requires band members to be "ordinarily resident" on their reserve in order to be eligible to vote in band elections. Non-resident band members brought a challenge under s. 15, alleging that residence was an irrelevant personal characteristic on which to deprive them of a voice in decisions that could deeply affect them—for instance, the sale of band-owned land or the expenditure of band-controlled moneys. While the entire Court agreed that the impugned provision violated s. 15, the interpretation of the "analogous grounds" doctrine differed significantly in the two judgments. Excerpted below are the portions of the judgments that deal with the issue of analogous grounds.]

McLACHLIN and BASTARACHE JJ (Lamer CJC, Cory, and Major JJ concurring): ...

[3] The narrow issue raised in this appeal is whether the exclusion of off-reserve members of an Indian band from the right to vote in band elections pursuant to s. 77(1) of the *Indian Act*, RSC 1985, c. I-5, is inconsistent with s. 15(1). ...

[4] The first step is to determine whether the impugned law makes a distinction that denies equal benefit or imposes an unequal burden. The *Indian Act*'s exclusion of off-reserve band members from voting privileges on band governance satisfies this requirement.

[5] The next step is to determine whether the distinction is discriminatory. The first inquiry is whether the distinction is made on the basis of an enumerated ground or a ground analogous to it. The answer to this question will be found in considering the general purpose of s. 15(1), i.e. to prevent the violation of human dignity through the imposition of disadvantage based on stereotyping and social prejudice, and to promote a society where all persons are considered worthy of respect and consideration.

[6] We agree with L'Heureux-Dubé J that Aboriginality-residence (off-reserve band member status) constitutes a ground of discrimination analogous to the enumerated grounds. However, we wish to comment on two matters: (1) the suggestion by some that the same ground may or may not be analogous depending on the circumstances; and (2) the criteria that identify an analogous ground.

[7] The enumerated grounds function as legislative markers of suspect grounds associated with stereotypical, discriminatory decision making. They are a legal expression of a general characteristic, not a contextual, fact-based conclusion about whether discrimination exists in a particular case. As such, the enumerated grounds must be distinguished from a finding that discrimination exists in a particular case. Since the enumerated grounds are only indicators of suspect grounds of distinction, it follows that decisions on these grounds are not always discriminatory; if this were otherwise, it would be unnecessary to proceed to the separate examination of discrimination at the third stage of our analysis discussed in *Law* [*v. Canada (Minister of Employment and Immigration)*, [1999] 1 SCR 497, 170 DLR (4th) 1], per Iacobucci J.

[8] The same applies to the grounds recognized by the courts as "analogous" to the grounds enumerated in s. 15. To say that a ground of distinction is an analogous ground is merely to identify a type of decision making that is suspect because it often leads to discrimination and denial of substantive equality. Like distinctions made on enumerated grounds, distinctions made on analogous grounds may well not be discriminatory. But this does not mean that they are not analogous grounds or that they are analogous grounds only in some circumstances. Just as we do not speak of enumerated grounds existing in one circumstance and not another, we should not speak of analogous grounds existing in one circumstance and not another. The enumerated and analogous grounds stand as constant markers of suspect decision making or potential discrimination. What varies is whether they amount to discrimination in the particular circumstances of the case.

[9] We therefore disagree with the view that a marker of discrimination can change from case to case, depending on the government action challenged. It seems to us that it is not the *ground* that varies from case to case, but the determination of whether a distinction on the basis of a constitutionally cognizable ground is *discriminatory*. Sex will

always be a ground, although sex-based legislative distinctions may not always be discriminatory. To be sure, *R v. Turpin*, [1989] 1 SCR 1296, suggested that residence *might*
be an analogous ground in certain contexts. But in view of the synthesis of previous cases
suggested in *Law*, *supra*, it is more likely that today the same result, dismissal of the
claim, would be achieved either by finding no analogous ground or no discrimination in
fact going to essential human dignity.

[10] If it is the intention of L'Heureux-Dubé J's reasons to affirm contextual dependency of the enumerated and analogous grounds, we must respectfully disagree. If
"Aboriginality-residence" is to be an analogous ground (and we agree with L'Heureux-
Dubé J that it should), then it must always stand as a constant marker of potential legislative discrimination, whether the challenge is to a governmental tax credit, a voting
right, or a pension scheme. This established, the analysis moves to the third stage:
whether the distinction amounts, in purpose or effect, to discrimination on the facts of
the case.

[11] Maintaining the distinction in *Law*, *supra*, between the enumerated or analogous
ground analysis and the third-stage contextual discrimination analysis, offers several
advantages. Both stages are concerned with discrimination and the violation of the presumption of the equal dignity and worth of every human being. But they approach it from
different perspectives. The analogous grounds serve as jurisprudential markers for suspect
distinctions. They function conceptually to identify the sorts of claims that properly fall
under s. 15. By screening out other cases, they avoid trivializing the s. 15 equality guarantee and promote the efficient use of judicial resources. And they permit the development
over time of a conceptual jurisprudence of the sorts of distinctions that fall under the s. 15
guarantee, without foreclosing new cases of discrimination. A distinction on an enumerated or analogous ground established, the contextual and fact-specific inquiry proceeds to
whether the distinction amounts to discrimination in the context of the particular case.

[12] Our second concern relates to the manner in which a new analogous ground
may be identified. In our view, conflation of the second and third stages of the *Law*
framework is to be avoided. To be sure, *Law* is meant to provide a set of guidelines and
not a formalistic straitjacket, but the second and third stages are unquestionably distinct:
the former asks whether the distinction is on the basis of an enumerated or analogous
ground, the latter whether that distinction on the facts of the case affronts s. 15. Affirmative answers to *both* inquiries are a precondition to establishing a constitutional claim.

[13] What then are the criteria by which we identify a ground of distinction as analogous? The obvious answer is that we look for grounds of distinction that are analogous
or like the grounds enumerated in s. 15—race, national or ethnic origin, colour, religion,
sex, age, or mental or physical disability. It seems to us that what these grounds have in
common is the fact that they often serve as the basis for stereotypical decisions made not
on the basis of merit but on the basis of a personal characteristic that is immutable or
changeable only at unacceptable cost to personal identity. This suggests that the thrust of
identification of analogous grounds at the second stage of the *Law* analysis is to reveal
grounds based on characteristics that we cannot change or that the government has no
legitimate interest in expecting us to change to receive equal treatment under the law. To
put it another way, s. 15 targets the denial of equal treatment on grounds that are actually
immutable, like race, or constructively immutable, like religion. Other factors identified

in the cases as associated with the enumerated and analogous grounds, like the fact that the decision adversely impacts on a discrete and insular minority or a group that has been historically discriminated against, may be seen to flow from the central concept of immutable or constructively immutable personal characteristics, which too often have served as illegitimate and demeaning proxies for merit-based decision making.

[14] L'Heureux-Dubé J ultimately concludes that "Aboriginality-residence" as it pertains to whether an Aboriginal band member lives on or off the reserve is an analogous ground. We agree. L'Heureux-Dubé J's discussion makes clear that the distinction goes to a personal characteristic essential to a band member's personal identity, which is no less constructively immutable than religion or citizenship. Off-reserve Aboriginal band members can change their status to on-reserve band members only at great cost, if at all.

[15] Two brief comments on this new analogous ground are warranted. First, reserve status should not be confused with residence. The ordinary "residence" decisions faced by the average Canadians should not be confused with the profound decisions Aboriginal band members make to live on or off their reserves, assuming choice is possible. The reality of their situation is unique and complex. Thus no new water is charted, in the sense of finding residence, in the generalized abstract, to be an analogous ground. Second, we note that the analogous ground of off-reserve status or Aboriginality-residence is limited to a subset of the Canadian population, while s. 15 is directed to everyone. In our view, this is no impediment to its inclusion as an analogous ground under s. 15. Its demographic limitation is no different, for example, from pregnancy, which is a distinct, but fundamentally interrelated form of discrimination from gender. "Embedded" analogous grounds may be necessary to permit meaningful consideration of intra-group discrimination. ...

L'HEUREUX-DUBÉ J (Gonthier, Iacobucci, and Binnie JJ concurring):

[After determining that the legislation imposed differential treatment, L'Heureux-Dubé J turned to the issue of analogous grounds.]

[59] The analysis at the analogous grounds stage involves considering whether differential treatment of those defined by that characteristic or combination of traits has the potential to violate human dignity in the sense underlying s. 15(1). ... The analogous grounds inquiry, like the other two stages of analysis, must be undertaken in a purposive and contextual manner: *Law, supra,* at para. 41. The "nature and situation of the individual or group at issue, and the social, political, and legal history of Canadian society's treatment of that group" must be considered: *Law, supra,* at para. 93 ... .

[60] Various contextual factors have been recognized in the case law that may demonstrate that the trait or combination of traits by which the claimants are defined has discriminatory potential. An analogous ground may be shown by the fundamental nature of the characteristic: whether from the perspective of a reasonable person in the position of the claimant, it is important to their identity, personhood, or belonging. The fact that a characteristic is immutable, difficult to change, or changeable only at unacceptable personal cost may also lead to its recognition as an analogous ground: *Miron v. Trudel,* [1995] 2 SCR 418 [124 DLR (4th) 693], at para. 148; *Vriend v. Alberta,* [1998] 1 SCR 493

[156 DLR (4th) 385], at para. 90. It is also central to the analysis if those defined by the characteristic are lacking in political power, disadvantaged, or vulnerable to becoming disadvantaged or having their interests overlooked: *Andrews* [*v. Law Society of British Columbia*, [1989] 1 SCR 143, 56 DLR (4th) 1], at p. 152; *Law, supra*, at para. 29. Another indicator is whether the ground is included in federal and provincial human rights codes: *Miron, supra*, at para. 148. Other criteria, of course, may also be considered in subsequent cases, and none of the above indicators are necessary for the recognition of an analogous ground or combination of grounds: *Miron, supra*, at para. 149.

[61] I should also note that if indicia of an analogous ground are not present in general, or among a certain group in Canadian society, they may nevertheless be present in another social or legislative context, within a different group in Canadian society, or in a given geographic area, to give only a few examples. Here, to illustrate, the nature of the decisions band members make about whether to live on or off a reserve are different from those made by many other Canadians in relation to their place of residence. So are other factors related to the analogous grounds analysis that still affect them. The second stage must therefore be flexible enough to adapt to stereotyping, prejudice, or denials of human dignity and worth that might occur in specific ways for specific groups of people, to recognize that personal characteristics may overlap or intersect (such as race, band membership, and place of residence in this case), and to reflect changing social phenomena or new or different forms of stereotyping or prejudice. As this Court unanimously held in *Law, supra*, at para. 73: "The possibility of new forms of discrimination denying essential human worth cannot be foreclosed."

[62] Here, several factors lead to the conclusion that recognizing off-reserve band member status as an analogous ground would accord with the purposes of s. 15(1). From the perspective of off-reserve band members, the choice of whether to live on- or off-reserve, if it is available to them, is an important one to their identity and personhood, and is therefore fundamental. It involves choosing whether to live with other members of the band to which they belong, or apart from them. It relates to a community and land that have particular social and cultural significance to many or most band members. Also critical is the fact that as discussed below during the third stage of analysis, band members living off-reserve have generally experienced disadvantage, stereotyping, and prejudice, and form part of a "discrete and insular minority" defined by race and place of residence. In addition, because of the lack of opportunities and housing on many reserves, and the fact that the *Indian Act*'s rules formerly removed band membership from various categories of band members, residence off the reserve has often been forced upon them, or constitutes a choice made reluctantly or at high personal cost. For these reasons, the second stage of analysis has been satisfied, and "off-reserve band member status" is an analogous ground. It will hereafter be recognized as an analogous ground in any future case involving this combination of traits. I note that in making this determination, I make no findings about "residence" as an analogous ground in contexts other than as it affects band members who do not live on the reserve of the band to which they belong. ...

[All members of the Court agreed, at the third stage of the *Law* analysis, that the distinction drawn by s. 77(1) of the *Indian Act* discriminated against off-reserve band members, and perpetuated the historic disadvantage experienced by off-reserve band members. The distinction did not correspond with the characteristics of off-reserve band members in a way that respected their dignity and difference. Although some of the decisions of band councils related to matters of purely local interest, the complete denial to off-reserve members of the right to vote and participate in governance treated them as less worthy and deserving than other band members. The distinction was based on a stereotype that presumed that Aboriginals living off-reserve were not interested in maintaining meaningful participation in the band or preserving their cultural identity. Finally, the interests affected were fundamental as they related to the preservation of cultural identity on the part of Aboriginals living off-reserve. As well, band councils had the power to make important decisions with respect to the surrender of lands, the allocation of land to band members, and the raising of funds and the making of expenditures for the benefit of all band members that could have a significant effect on the interests of off-reserve band members.

All members of the Court also agreed that s. 77(1) of the *Indian Act*, having been found to violate s. 15, could not be justified under s. 1. Although the restriction on voting was rationally connected to the objective of giving a voice in the affairs of the reserve only to the persons most directly affected by the decisions of the band council, it was not minimally impairing of equality rights. The government had not demonstrated that a complete denial of the right of band members living off-reserve to participate in the affairs of the band was necessary. More specifically, the government had led no evidence of the costs and administrative difficulties associated with other schemes that would give off-reserve members some role in band governance.

With respect to remedy, the words "and is ordinarily resident" were struck from the statute, but the order was delayed for a period of eighteen months to allow the parties to create an electoral structure that would conform to the requirements of the Charter.]

NOTES

1. In *Corbière*, the joint judgment of McLachlin and Bastarache JJ appears to take issue with L'Heureux-Dubé J on whether the recognition of a personal characteristic as an analogous ground will be context-specific. McLachlin and Bastarache JJ take the position that once a personal characteristic is recognized or rejected as an analogous ground, that determination will hold across all legal contexts. L'Heureux-Dubé J, like Gonthier J in *Miron v. Trudel*, [1995] 2 SCR 418, 124 DLR (4th) 693, seems to suggest that the answer could vary from context to context. The Court has since united behind McLachlin and Bastarache JJ's view. See *Lavoie v. Canada*, [2002] 1 SCR 769, 210 DLR (4th) 193, at para. 2, per McLachlin CJC and L'Heureux-Dubé J, and para. 41, per Bastarache J ("once a ground is found to be analogous, it is permanently enrolled as analogous for other cases").

2. In *Corbière*, McLachlin and Bastarache JJ argued that the common feature of the enumerated grounds, and thus the defining feature of an analogous ground, is immutability. As they put it, analogous grounds are personal characteristics "that we cannot change or that the government has no legitimate interest in expecting us to change to receive equal treatment under the law." Other factors identified in the case law, they said, "may be seen to flow from the central concept of immutable or constructively immutable personal characteristics." L'Heureux-Dubé J, by contrast, stated that a range of factors, none of them necessary,

should be considered when determining whether a personal characteristic deserves to be recognized as an analogous ground. In this regard, L'Heureux-Dubé J was following the approach articulated by McLachlin J in *Miron*, above. What are the implications of the apparent shift from *Miron* to *Corbière* from a broader, more flexible inquiry to one that focuses on the single requirement of immutability?

3. The Court has ruled that the following personal characteristics do not qualify as analogous grounds: employment status or occupation (*Re Workers' Compensation Act*, [1989] 1 SCR 922, 56 DLR (4th) 765; *Delisle v. Canada (Deputy Attorney General)*, [1999] 2 SCR 989, 176 DLR (4th) 513, with respect to the RCMP; and *Health Services and Support-Facilities Subsector Bargaining Assn. v. BC*, [2007] 2 SCR 391, 283 DLR (4th), with respect to health care workers; but see *Dunmore v. Ontario (Attorney General)*, 2001 SCC 94, 207 DLR (4th) 513, per L'Heureux-Dubé J, who alone would have found agricultural workers to be an analogous group); province of residence (*R v. Turpin*, [1989] 1 SCR 1296, 48 CCC (3d) 8; *Haig v. Canada*, [1993] 2 SCR 995, 105 DLR (4th) 577); persons charged with war crimes or crimes against humanity outside of Canada (*R v. Finta*, [1994] 1 SCR 701, 112 DLR (4th) 513); persons bringing a claim against the Crown (*Rudolph Wolff & Co. v. Canada*, [1990] 1 SCR 695, 69 DLR (4th) 392); and marijuana users (*R v. Malmo-Levine*, [2003] 3 SCR 571, 2003 SCC 74, 233 DLR (4th) 415).

4. Apart from citizenship, sexual orientation, marital status, and Aboriginality-residence, what other personal characteristics ought to be recognized by the courts as analogous grounds of discrimination? Should family status be recognized? See *Thibaudeau v. Canada*, [1995] 2 SCR 627, 124 DLR (4th) 449, per McLachlin J (separated or divorced custodial parenthood an analogous ground) and *Schafer v. Canada (Attorney General)*, (1997) 149 DLR (4th) 704 (Ont. CA), application for leave to appeal to SCC dismissed (whether adoptive parent status an analogous ground). Should language be recognized? Or would its recognition undermine the integrity of the constitutional scheme of language rights? See *Lalonde v. Ontario (Commission de restructuration des services de santé)* (2001), 56 OR (3d) 505 (CA). Should poverty, or social condition, be recognized? Or would its recognition involve the courts in adjudicating issues with complex socioeconomic and political dimensions best left to legislatures? See M. Jackman, "Constitutional Contact with the Disparities in the World: Poverty as a Prohibited Ground of Discrimination Under the Canadian Charter and Human Rights Law" (1994), 2 *Review of Constitutional Studies* 76; *Masse v. Ontario (Ministry of Community and Social Services)* (1996), 134 DLR (4th) 20 (Ont. Div. Ct.); application for leave to appeal to SCC dismissed (recipients of social assistance not a protected or analogous group); *Falkiner v. Ontario (Director, Income Maintenance Branch, Ministry of Community and Social Services)* (2002), 212 DLR (4th) 633 (Ont. CA) (receipt of social assistance recognized as an analogous ground; "spouse in the house" rule imposed on social assistance recipients found to discrinate on the basis of three grounds: receipt of social assistance, sex, and marital status); *R v. Banks* (2007), 275 DLR (4th) 640 (Ont. CA), leave to appeal to SCC dismissed (law prohibiting "squeegeeing" does not violate s. 15, poverty not an analogous ground); and *Boulter v. Nova Scotia Power Inc.*, 2009 NSCA 17, 307 DLR (4th) 293 (poverty not an analogous ground; provision in *Public Utilities Act* requiring that rates be set the same for all customers and precluding the setting of lower rates for low income consumers does not violate s. 15). Several provincial human rights codes recognize social condition as a prohibited ground of discrimination. See the Quebec *Charter of Human Rights and Free-*

doms, RSQ, c. C-12, s. 10 ("social condition") and *Human Rights Code*, RSO 1990, c. H.19, s. 2 ("receipt of social assistance").

C. The Appropriate Comparator Group

In *Law*, the Supreme Court of Canada emphasized that equality is a comparative concept and that establishing differential treatment on the basis of an enumerated or analogous ground involves comparing the treatment of the claimant under the law or government action in issue to that of other persons or groups. Locating the "appropriate comparator" has thus become part of the s. 15 analysis:

> [56] ... McIntyre J emphasized in *Andrews* ... that the equality guarantee is a comparative concept. Ultimately, a court must identify differential treatment *as compared* to one or more other persons or groups. Locating the appropriate comparator is necessary in identifying differential treatment and the grounds of the distinction. Identifying the appropriate comparator will be relevant when considering many of the contextual factors in the discrimination analysis.
>
> [57] To locate the appropriate comparator, we must consider a variety of factors, including the subject-matter of the legislation. The object of a s. 15(1) analysis is not to determine equality in the abstract; it is to determine whether the impugned legislation creates differential treatment between the claimant and others on the basis of enumerated or analogous grounds, which results in discrimination. Both the purpose and the effect of the legislation must be considered in determining the appropriate comparison group or groups. Other contextual factors may also be relevant. The biological, historical, and sociological similarities or dissimilarities may be relevant in establishing the relevant comparator in particular, and whether the legislation effects discrimination in a substantive sense more generally ... .
>
> [58] When identifying the relevant comparator, the natural starting point is to consider the claimant's view. It is the claimant who generally chooses the person, group, or groups with whom he or she wishes to be compared for the purpose of the discrimination inquiry, thus setting the parameters of the alleged differential treatment that he or she wishes to challenge. However, the claimant's characterization of the comparison may not always be sufficient. It may be that the differential treatment is not between the groups identified by the claimant, but rather between other groups. Clearly a court cannot, ex proprio motu, evaluate a ground of discrimination not pleaded by the parties and in relation to which no evidence has been adduced ... . However, within the scope of the ground or grounds pleaded, I would not close the door on the power of a court to refine the comparison presented by the claimant where warranted.

The issue of whether the claimant has chosen the appropriate comparator group is typically addressed in the initial stages of the s. 15 analysis, before the analysis of disadvantage and/or discrimination.

Hodge v. Canada (Minister of Human Resources Development)
[2004] 3 SCR 357, 244 DLR (4th) 257

[This case involved a woman (Hodge) who had lived together with a man for many years in a common law relationship. Both had contributed over the years to the *Canada Pension Plan* ("CPP"). After approximately 21 years, the relationship ended in February 1994. The man died, bankrupt, in July 1994 and, on his death, Hodge immediately applied under the CPP for a survivor's pension. The pension application was denied on the grounds that she was no longer a spouse. At that time, the definition of spouse in the *Canada Pension Plan* read as follows:

> 2.(1) ...
> "Spouse," in relation to a contributor, means,
>> (a) except in or in relation to section 55,
>>> (i) if there is no person described in subparagraph (ii), a person who is married to the contributor at the relevant time, or
>>> (ii) a person of the opposite sex who is cohabiting with the contributor in a conjugal relationship at the relevant time, having so cohabited with the contributor for a continuous period of at least one year ...

Hodge appealed, arguing that the definition of spouse constituted discrimination on the basis of marital status, thus violating s. 15 of the Charter. In framing her argument, Hodge compared the situation of married spouses who were living separate and apart at the time of the contributor's death (who were treated as spouses until divorced or until the contributor entered a common law relationship) and common law spouses who were separated and living apart at the time of the contributor's death (who were not treated as spouses). Although Hodge was successful at several stages as her case made its way through a series of tribunals and lower courts, the Supreme Court of Canada, in a unanimous judgment written by Binnie J, dismissed her claim, finding no violation of s. 15. The central issue in the case, in the Court's view, was the appropriate comparator group, on which the Court provided an extended analysis.]

BINNIE J (McLACHLIN CJC and Major, Bastarache, LeBel, Deschamps, and Fish JJ concurring):

• • •

A. The Role of the Court in Determining the Appropriate Comparator Group

[20] The outcome of a s. 15(1) claim cannot be skewed by a claimant attempting to associate himself or herself with a group whose relevant characteristics do not reflect the claimant's actual circumstances, or by targeting the benefits of a group whose relevant characteristics are simply not comparable. The role of the court in scrutinizing the claimant's choice of comparator group was addressed in *Law* [*v. Canada (Minister of Employment and Immigration)*, [1999] 1 SCR 497, 170 DLR (4th) 1], at para. 58:

> When identifying the relevant comparator, the natural *starting point* is to consider the claimant's view. It is the claimant who generally chooses the person, group, or groups with

whom he or she wishes to be compared for the purpose of the discrimination inquiry, thus setting the parameters of the alleged differential treatment that he or she wishes to challenge. However, the claimant's characterization of the comparison may not always be sufficient. *It may be that the differential treatment is not between the groups identified by the claimant, but rather between other groups.* [Emphasis added.]

[21] In my view, with respect, the Federal Court of Appeal erred in concluding that a court is required to "adopt the comparator group chosen by the applicant unless it can be shown that there is a paucity of evidence or a failure to plead that comparator" (para. 23). While it is up to the claimant to make an initial choice of "the person, group, or groups with whom he or she *wishes* to be compared" (emphasis added), the correctness of that choice is a matter of law for the court to determine … .

[22] Where "the differential treatment is not between the groups identified by the claimant, but rather between other groups" … it is the duty of the court to step in and measure the claim to equality rights in the proper context and against the proper standard.

B. The Criteria for Identifying the Appropriate Comparator Group

[23] The appropriate comparator group is the one which mirrors the characteristics of the claimant (or claimant group) relevant to the benefit or advantage sought except that the statutory definition includes a personal characteristic that is offensive to the Charter or omits a personal characteristic in a way that is offensive to the Charter. An example of the former is the requirement that spouses be of the opposite sex; *M. v. H.*, [[1999] 2 SCR 3, 171 DLR (4th) 577]. An example of the latter is the omission of sexual orientation from the *Alberta Individual's Rights Protection Act; Vriend v. Alberta*, [1998] 1 SCR 493 [156 DLR (4th) 385].

[24] The usual starting point is an analysis of the legislation (or state conduct) that denied the benefit or imposed the unwanted burden. While we are dealing in this appeal with access to a government benefit, and the starting point is thus the purpose of the legislative provisions, a similar exercise is required where a claim is based on the effect of an impugned law or state action. Thus, in *Little Sisters Book and Art Emporium v. Canada (Minister of Justice)*, [2000] 2 SCR 1120 [221 DLR (4th) 257], the terms of the powers given to customs officers to intercept incoming publications were neutral, but the appellant, a Vancouver bookstore, claimed that their shipments of books and magazines were targeted by customs officials in a discriminatory way because the store catered to gay and lesbian clients. It was clear that customs officials had systematically delayed and denied entry to lawful materials. Thus, the comparator group, defined by reference to the effect of the impugned conduct of customs officials, was "other individuals importing comparable publications of a heterosexual nature" (para. 120).

[25] In either case, the universe of people potentially entitled to equal treatment in relation to the subject matter of the claim must be identified. I use the phrase "potentially entitled" because the legislative definition, being the subject matter of the equality rights challenge, is not the last word. Otherwise, a survivor's pension restricted to white Protestant males could be defended on the ground that all surviving white protestant males were being treated equally. The objective of s. 15(1) is not just "formal" equality but substantive

equality (*Andrews v. Law Society of British Columbia*, [1989] 1 SCR 143 [56 DLR (4th) 1], at p. 166).

[26] Nevertheless, in a government benefits case, the initial focus is on what the legislature is attempting to accomplish. It is not open to the court to rewrite the terms of the legislative program except to the extent the benefit is being made available or the burden is being imposed on a discriminatory basis.

[27] In *Lovelace* [*v. Ontario*, [2000] 1 SCR 950, 188 DLR (4th) 193], for example, some disappointed aboriginal claimants challenged the distribution of the profits from Casino Rama amongst the First Nations in Ontario. The claimants were non-status Indians who considered themselves discriminated against by a provincial government program favouring status Indians. However, the Court held that the Casino Rama fund, for legitimate public policy reasons, targeted aboriginal *communities*, not aboriginal *individuals*. It was not the Court's role to rewrite the policy objectives of a program that were not in themselves discriminatory (i.e., individual versus community). The program was aimed at supporting "a government-to-government relationship" (para. 74), and the potential universe of claimants was therefore limited to "band and non-band aboriginal *communities*" (para. 64 (emphasis added), per Iacobucci J).

[28] Similarly, in [*Nova Scotia (Workers' Compensation Board) v.*] *Martin* [[2003] 2 SCR 504, 231 DLR (4th) 385, 2003 SCC 54], chronic pain sufferers alleging discriminatory neglect by the Nova Scotia Workers' Compensation Board attempted to compare themselves to chronic pain sufferers whose injuries were not employment related. Such people were free to go to court to claim appropriate compensation for their chronic pain. However Gonthier J held, at para. 72, that tort claimants could not constitute a proper comparator group. There was no proper alignment between the benefit sought and the ground of discrimination alleged. The asserted comparator group shared the personal characteristic on which the s. 15(1) claim was based (chronic pain disability), but the benefits under the *Workers' Compensation Act* were by definition not available to people who had suffered their injuries outside the workplace in circumstances altogether outside the scope of the statutory compensation plan.

[29] A more straightforward example is *Trociuk v. British Columbia (Attorney General)*, [2003] 1 SCR 835 [226 DLR(4th) 1], 2003 SCC 34, where the impugned legislation permitted mothers to "unacknowledge" fathers by excluding their particulars from the birth registration. This meant fathers could be prevented from participating in naming their children. The choice to unacknowledge was at the mother's discretion. Fathers had no recourse. The relevant universe of potential claimants were biological parents. Mr. Trociuk claimed discrimination on the basis of sex, since his biological relationship to the child was equivalent to that of the mother in all relevant respects. His claim succeeded.

· · ·

[31] *Lavoie v. Canada*, [2002] 1 SCR 769 [210 DLR (4th) 193], dealt with a hiring preference in the federal public service for Canadian citizens. The relevant universe of potential claimants were applicants who were qualified for public service jobs. The distinction complained about was made between those who were Canadian citizens, and those who were otherwise qualified but were not Canadian citizens. Applying the proper

comparator group, a majority of the Court found an infringement of s. 15(1), although the infringement was ultimately justified under s. 1.

[32] Similarly, in *Granovsky* [*v. Canada (Minister of Employment and Immigration)*, [2000] 1 SCR 703, 2000 SCC 28, 186 DLR (4th) 1], the subject matter of the claim was a disability pension. The claimant was not eligible for two reasons: firstly, his disability was temporary rather than permanent; and secondly, he had not made the required CPP contributions. He contended that the proper comparator group consisted of able-bodied workers who were able to keep up their CPP contributions because they were *not* disabled. He was unable to do so because of his disability. The Court rejected his choice of comparator group because it ignored the basis of the benefit he was seeking, i.e., able-bodied workers are not within the universe of persons potentially eligible for a disability pension. If and when they did qualify, it would be because they were no longer able-bodied. In other words, the benefit sought by the claimant did not correspond with the personal characteristic of the comparator group that he asserted to be the basis of his s. 15(1) claim. The proper comparator group was the *permanently* disabled CPP contributors with whom Granovsky could not properly demand equal treatment.

[33] If the claim to equality is to succeed, the ground has to be a personal characteristic enumerated or analogous to those listed in s. 15(1). This too is occasionally lost sight of. In *Martin*, the excluded chronic pain sufferers at one point attempted to compare themselves to another group of chronic pain sufferers who had suffered workplace injuries at an earlier date. The earlier group had obtained greater benefits under the *Workers' Compensation Act* than the later group of sufferers, but in the interim the benefit the earlier group had received had been terminated and the group grandfathered. Gonthier J rejected the group of earlier sufferers as a relevant comparator group because what differentiated them from the claimants was not the type of disability but simply the date of their respective workplace accidents, which was not a prohibited ground of discrimination.

[34] In this respect, the facts in *Martin* and the facts in this case may usefully be compared with those in *Corbiere v. Canada (Minister of Indian and Northern Affairs)*, [1999] 2 SCR 203 [173 DLR (4th) 1]. In that case, the subject matter of the impugned legislation was the right to vote, which the legislature extended to band members (which included the claimants) but drew a distinction between band members living *off* the reserve (who were denied the vote) and band members living *on* the reserve (who received it). The claimants were able to demonstrate that in every way relevant to the benefit (the vote) they were comparable to those who were favoured by the legislation except that they lived off the reserve. Unlike one of the claimed comparisons in *Martin*, the claimants in *Corbiere* belonged to the proposed comparator group at the same time.

[35] The claimants in *Corbiere* would have found themselves in the position of the respondent here if they had altogether ceased being members of the band prior to the vote being called.

[36] In *Gosselin* [*v. Quebec (Attorney Genereal)*, [2002] 4 SCR 429, 221 DLR (4th) 257], McLachlin CJ for the majority noted, at para. 28:

> The Regulation at issue made a distinction on the basis of an enumerated ground, age. People under 30 were subject to a different welfare regime than people 30 and over.

[37] Much of the claimant's argument in *Gosselin* was rejected because it put the focus on the disadvantages attaching to welfare recipients as a class rather than differentiating within that general class between the two age groups. The evidence of discrimination was therefore not properly aligned with the alleged ground of discrimination.

[The Court went on to find that Hodge had not chosen the appropriate comparator group in framing her s. 15 argument. The appropriate comparator group was married spouses who had divorced rather than separated married spouses. In the Court's view, at the time of the contributor's death, Hodge was not a separated common law spouse, but a former common law spouse. Former spouses, whether married or common law, did not qualify for a survivor's pension under the relevant provisions of the CPP. Since former married spouses and former common law spouses were treated the same, there was no distinction based on marital status, and thus no discrimination. Central to the reasoning was the Court's view of common law relationships as informal relationships based on cohabitation, which terminate when cohabitation ceases, in contrast to marital relationships which begin and end with formal legal acts.]

Auton (Guardian ad litem of) v. British Columbia (Attorney General)
[2004] 3 SCR 657, 245 DLR (4th) 1

[The facts of *Auton* are set out above in Section VI.A of this chapter. Recall that the dispute centred on the fact that British Columbia funded a number of programs for autistic children but did not establish funding for applied behavioral therapy because of, *inter alia*, financial constraints and the emergent and controversial nature of this therapy. Recall also the Court's reasons for its main holding that there was no denial of the right to equal benefit of the law. In the following excerpt, the Court rules, in the alternative, that the claim incorrectly identified the relevant comparator group.]

McLACHLIN CJC (Major, Bastarache, Binnie, LeBel, Deschamps, and Fish JJ concurring):

· · ·

(2) Denial of a Benefit Granted to a Comparator Group, on an Enumerated or Analogous Ground

[48] This question first requires us to determine the appropriate comparator group, and then to ask whether, as compared with people in that group, the petitioners have been denied a benefit.

[49] The first task is to determine the appropriate comparator group. The petitioners suggested that they should be compared with non-disabled children and their parents, as well as adult persons with mental illness. A closer look reveals problems with both suggested comparators.

· · ·

[55] Applying [the criteria identified in *Hodge* [*v. Canada (Minister of Human Resources Development)*, [2004] 3 SCR 357, 244 DLR (4th) 257], I conclude that the appro-

priate comparator for the petitioners is a non-disabled person or a person suffering a disability other than a mental disability (here autism) seeking or receiving funding for a non-core therapy important for his or her present and future health, which is emergent and only recently becoming recognized as medically required. It will be recalled that in many jurisdictions ABA/IBI therapy remained unfunded at the time of trial. Indeed, it was only in the year preceding the trial that two Canadian provinces had authorized funding for ABA/IBI therapy to autistic children. The comparators, as noted, must be like the claimants in all ways save for characteristics relating to the alleged ground of discrimination. People receiving well-established non-core therapies are not in the same position as people claiming relatively new non-core benefits. Funding may be legitimately denied or delayed because of uncertainty about a program and administrative difficulties related to its recognition and implementation. This has nothing to do with the alleged ground of discrimination. It follows that comparison with those receiving established therapies is inapt.

[56] The petitioners' comparators were deficient in that they focussed on the non-existent medical benefit of medically required care, as discussed above. However, even if I were to assume that the benefit is one provided by law—more particularly, that the BC legislation had listed ABA/IBI therapists as "health care practitioners" whose services could be considered funded benefits—the petitioners' comparators would still be deficient, because they have left the recent and emergent nature of ABA/IBI therapy out of the equation. This error was replicated in the decisions below.

[57] The remaining question is whether, applying the appropriate comparator, the claimant or claimant group was denied a benefit made available to the comparator group. Differential treatment having regard to the appropriate comparator may be established either by showing an explicit distinction (direct discrimination) or by showing that the effect of the government action amounted to singling the claimant out for less advantageous treatment on the basis of the alleged ground of discrimination (indirect discrimination). In indirect discrimination, the terms on which the claimants are denied the benefit operate as a proxy for their group status. For example, in *British Columbia (Public Service Employee Relations Commission) v. BCGSEU*, [1999] 3 SCR 3 [176 DLR (4th) 1], facially neutral physical requirements for firefighters were set at aerobic levels not generally attainable by female firefighters—levels, moreover, which were not required for performance of the job. The specified aerobic levels made no mention of gender. On their face, they did not discriminate. Yet, in effect, they excluded women, not on the basis of ability to do the job, but on the basis of gender. The aerobic levels served as a proxy for gender. Hence, they were held to discriminate on the basis of gender.

[58] As discussed, the appropriate comparator in this case is a member of a non-disabled group or a person suffering a disability other than a mental disability that requests or receives funding for non-core therapy important to present and future health, but which is emergent and only recently becoming recognized as medically required. On the evidence adduced here, differential treatment either directly or by effect is not established. There was no evidence of how the Province had responded to requests for new therapies or treatments by non-disabled or otherwise disabled people. We know that it was slow in responding to the demands for ABA/IBI funding for autistic children. But we do not know whether it acted in a similar manner with respect to other new therapies.

[59] Indeed, the conduct of the government considered in the context of the emergent nature of ABA/IBI therapy for autistic children raises doubts about whether there was a real denial or differential treatment of autistic children. The government put in place a number of programs, albeit not intensive ABA/IBI therapy, directed to helping autistic children and their families. In the year before the trial, the government had announced an Autism Action Plan and an Autism Action Implementation Plan which acknowledged the importance of early intervention, diagnosis and assessment. The government's failing was to delay putting in place what was emerging in the late-1990s as the most, indeed the only known, effective therapy for autism, while continuing to fund increasingly discredited treatments.

[60] As discussed earlier, the delay in providing funding for ABA/IBI therapy seems to have been related to three factors. The first was the inauspicious decision to transfer child and youth mental health from the Ministry of Health to the Ministry of Children and Families, which meant that the decision makers lacked medical and psychiatric expertise and viewed autism from a social rather than medical perspective. The second was financial concerns and competing claims on insufficient resources. The third was the emergent nature of the recognition that ABA/IBI therapy was appropriate and medically required.

[61] With hindsight, it is possible to say that the government should have moved more quickly. But on the evidence before us, it is difficult to say that the government in purpose or effect put autistic children and their families "on the back burner" when compared to non-disabled or otherwise disabled groups seeking emergent therapies. Rather, to use the trial judge's phrase, the government's failing was that its actions to that point did not meet the "gold standard of scientific methodology" ((2000), 78 BCLR (3d) 55, at para. 66).

[62] The issue, however, is not whether the government met the gold standard of scientific methodology, but whether it denied autistic people benefits it accorded to others in the same situation, save for mental disability. There is no evidence suggesting that the government's approach to ABA/IBI therapy was different than its approach to other comparable, novel therapies for non-disabled persons or persons with a different type of disability. In the absence of such evidence, a finding of discrimination cannot be sustained.

NOTES AND QUESTIONS

1. In cases such as *Hodge* and *Auton*, the Court's reformulation of the appropriate comparator group resulted in a finding that there was no differential treatment based on an enumerated or analogous ground. In other cases, the choice of the comparator group will influence the analysis of whether the differential treatment is discriminatory in the third step of the s. 15(1) analysis. One example is *Granovsky v. Canada (Minister of Employment and Immigration)*, [2000] 1 SCR 703, 186 DLR (4th) 1. In *Granovsky*, the appellant challenged the rules regarding eligibility for a *Canada Pension Plan* disability pension. To qualify for a disability pension, a claimant was required to meet a "recency of contributions" test: she or he must have made contributions in five of the last ten years, or two of the last three years. These rules were relaxed by a "drop-out" provision under which periods of disability are not counted in the recency of contributions calculations. The drop-out provision applied

to persons with permanent disabilities. As a person considered to be temporarily disabled, the appellant was denied the advantage of the drop-out provision. He was subject to the same recency of contributions test as able-bodied persons, and, as a result, did not qualify for a pension. Binnie J, for a unanimous Court, acknowledged that the law treated the appellant differently on the basis of the nature of his disability. The appellant argued that the appropriate comparison was between able-bodied persons and persons like himself with temporary disabilities. Binnie J disagreed, saying that the appropriate comparison was between persons with temporary disabilities and "the body of CPP contributors who suffered a severe and permanent disability in the years of their respective contribution histories and who therefore did benefit from the drop-out provision to which the appellant claims entitlement on the basis of his equality rights." Binnie J's identification of the comparator group was a key move in his reasoning. If he had accepted the appellant's suggested comparison, the failure of the legislation to accommodate the different circumstances of the temporarily disabled stood out. By comparing Granovsky's situation to that of more seriously disabled persons, it was easier for Binnie J to argue that the differential treatment was not discriminatory. A reasonable person, he concluded, would not consider that limiting the advantages of the drop-out provision to persons with greater disabilities demeaned other disabled persons' sense of worth and dignity.

2. In *Kapp*, McLachlin CJC acknowledged the criticisms that have been leveled at the analysis of comparator groups following *Law*:

> [22] … Criticism has also accrued for the way *Law* has allowed the formalism of some of the Court's post-*Andrews* jurisprudence to resurface in the form of an artificial comparator analysis focussed on treating likes alike.

What are the problems with the way in which the Court has conducted the comparator group analysis? Does *Kapp* offer any alternatives? For a discussion of the ways in which the comparator group analysis relates to larger questions about the way in which equality is conceptualized, see the extract from Sophia R. Moreau, "The Wrongs of Unequal Treatment" (2004), 54 *University of Toronto Law Journal* 291, found below at the end of Section VI.D.

D. Disadvantage/Discrimination

M. v. H.
[1999] 2 SCR 3, 171 DLR (4th) 577

[Two women, M. and H., cohabited in a same-sex relationship from 1982 to 1992. H. was in a financially stronger position than M. during the relationship. The parties lived in a house owned by H. and started their own advertising business. H.'s contributions to the business were greater than those of M., who devoted more of her time to domestic tasks than to the business. When the business failed because of a dramatic downturn in the economy, H. was able to find other employment, but M. was not. After the breakup of their relationship in 1992, M., who was at that time unemployed, commenced an action against H., advancing a number of claims, including a claim for support pursuant to Part III of the *Family Law Act*, RSO 1990, c. F.3 (the "FLA"). Section 29 of the Act extended the definition of "spouse" governing support applications beyond married persons to include a man and a woman who were not married to each other and had cohabited continuously for a period of not less than three years. M. asserted that the definition of "spouse" found in s. 29 was unconstitutional by virtue of its exclusion of same-sex couples, and that the appropriate remedy was an extension of the definition to include same-sex couples. On a motion by H. for a determination of the constitutional issues prior to trial, the exclusion of same-sex couples by s. 29 of the FLA was found to violate the right to equality guaranteed by s. 15 of the *Canadian Charter of Rights and Freedoms* in a way that could not be justified under s. 1. The definition of "spouse" was extended through an order reading out the words "a man and woman" from the definition and reading in the words "two persons." H. appealed, joined by the attorney general of Ontario, who had intervened on the motion below. The Ontario Court of Appeal upheld the decision of the motions judge, but suspended the order for one year to give the legislature time to amend the FLA. Leave to appeal to the Supreme Court was granted to the attorney general.

Members of the Court agreed that the first two steps of the s. 15 analysis were satisfied: the definition of spouse resulted in differential treatment on the basis of sexual orientation, a prohibited ground of discrimination. Excerpted below are the portions of the judgments addressing the issue of whether the differentiation amounted to discrimination.]

CORY and IACOBUCCI JJ (Lamer CJC, L'Heureux-Dubé, McLachlin, and Binnie JJ concurring): [In their joint reasons, Cory J addressed the s. 15 issue.]

CORY J: ...

[65] The determination of whether differential treatment imposed by legislation on an enumerated or analogous ground is discriminatory within the meaning of s. 15(1) of the Charter is to be undertaken in a purposive and contextual manner. The relevant inquiry is whether the differential treatment imposes a burden upon or withholds a benefit from the claimant in a manner that reflects the stereotypical application of presumed group or personal characteristics, or which otherwise has the effect of perpetuating or promoting the view that the individual is less capable or worthy of recognition or value as a human being or as a member of Canadian society, equally deserving of concern, respect, and consideration: *Law* [*v. Canada (Minister of Employment and Immigration)*, [1999] 1 SCR 497], at para. 88.

[66] ... [T]he spousal support provisions of the FLA help protect the economic interests of individuals in intimate relationships. When a relationship breaks down, the support provisions help to ensure that a member of a couple who has contributed to the couple's welfare in intangible ways will not find himself or herself utterly abandoned. This protective aspect of the spousal support provisions is properly considered in relation to s. 15(1). Thus it is appropriate to conclude that s. 29 of the FLA creates a distinction that withholds a benefit from the respondent M. The question is whether this denial of a benefit violates the purpose of s. 15(1).

[67] In *Law*, Iacobucci J explained that there are a variety of contextual factors that may be referred to by a s. 15(1) claimant in order to demonstrate that legislation demeans his or her dignity. The list of factors is not closed, and there is no specific formula that must be considered in every case. In *Law* itself, Iacobucci J listed four important

contextual factors in particular which may influence the determination of whether s. 15(1) has been infringed. He emphasized, at paras. 59-61, that in examining these contextual factors, a court must adopt the point of view of a reasonable person, in circumstances similar to those of the claimant, who takes into account the contextual factors relevant to the claim.

[68] One factor which may demonstrate that legislation that treats the claimant differently has the effect of demeaning the claimant's dignity is the existence of preexisting disadvantage, stereotyping, prejudice, or vulnerability experienced by the individual or group at issue ... .

[69] In this case, there is significant preexisting disadvantage and vulnerability, and these circumstances are exacerbated by the impugned legislation. The legislative provision in question draws a distinction that prevents persons in a same-sex relationship from gaining access to the court enforced and protected support system. This system clearly provides a benefit to unmarried heterosexual persons who come within the definition set out in s. 29, and thereby provides a measure of protection for their economic interests. This protection is denied to persons in a same-sex relationship who would otherwise meet the statute's requirements, and as a result, a person in the position of the claimant is denied a benefit regarding an important aspect of life in today's society. Neither common law nor equity provides the remedy of maintenance that is made available by the FLA. The denial of that potential benefit, which may impose a financial burden on persons in the position of the claimant, contributes to the general vulnerability experienced by individuals in same-sex relationships.

[70] A second contextual factor that was discussed in *Law* as being potentially relevant to the s. 15(1) inquiry is the correspondence, or the lack of it, between the ground on which a claim is based and the actual need, capacity, or circumstances of the claimant or others: para. 70. Iacobucci J nonetheless cautioned that the mere fact that the impugned legislation take into account the claimant's actual situation will not necessarily defeat a s. 15(1) claim, as the focus of the inquiry must always remain upon the central question of whether, viewed from the perspective of the claimant, the differential treatment imposed by the legislation has the effect of violating human dignity. However, the legislation at issue in the current appeal fails to take into account the claimant's actual situation. As I have already discussed, access to the court enforced spousal support regime provided in the FLA is given to individuals in conjugal relationships of a specific degree of permanence. Being in a same-sex relationship does not mean that it is an impermanent or a nonconjugal relationship.

[71] A third contextual factor referred to by Iacobucci J in *Law, supra*, at para. 72, is the question of whether the impugned legislation has an ameliorative purpose or effect for a group historically disadvantaged in the context of the legislation ... . [T]he existence of an ameliorative purpose or effect may help to establish that human dignity is not violated where the person or group that is excluded is more advantaged with respect to the circumstances addressed by the legislation. Gonthier J [in dissent] argues that the legislation under scrutiny in the present appeal is just such ameliorative legislation—that it is meant to target women in married or opposite-sex relationships. He proceeds to argue that in this legal context, women in same-sex relationships are not similarly disadvantaged. For the reasons expressed elsewhere, we disagree with this characterization of

the legislation. Accordingly, we reject the idea that the allegedly ameliorative purpose of this legislation does anything to lessen the charge of discrimination in this case.

[72] A fourth contextual factor specifically adverted to by Iacobucci J in *Law*, at para. 74, was the nature of the interest affected by the impugned legislation. ... In the present case, the interest protected by s. 29 of the FLA is fundamental, namely the ability to meet basic financial needs following the breakdown of a relationship characterized by intimacy and economic dependence. Members of same-sex couples are entirely ignored by the statute, notwithstanding the undeniable importance to them of the benefits accorded by the statute.

[73] The societal significance of the benefit conferred by the statute cannot be over-emphasized. The exclusion of same-sex partners from the benefits of s. 29 of the FLA promotes the view that M., and individuals in same-sex relationships generally, are less worthy of recognition and protection. It implies that they are judged to be incapable of forming intimate relationships of economic interdependence as compared to opposite-sex couples, without regard to their actual circumstances. As the intervener EGALE submitted, such exclusion perpetuates the disadvantages suffered by individuals in same-sex relationships and contributes to the erasure of their existence.

[74] Therefore I conclude that an examination of the four factors outlined above, in the context of the present appeal, indicate that the human dignity of individuals in same-sex relationships is violated by the impugned legislation. In light of this, I conclude that the definition of spouse in s. 29 of the FLA violates s. 15(1).

[Iacobucci J wrote the s. 1 portion of the opinion he co-authored with Cory J. He began by considering the objectives of the spousal support provisions of the FLA, and of the omission of same-sex couples from the scheme. He concluded that the objectives are "the equitable resolution of economic disputes that arise when intimate relationships between individuals who have been financially interdependent break down" and the alleviation of "the burden on the public purse by shifting the obligation to provide support for needy persons to those parents and spouses who have the capacity to provide support to these individuals." The exclusion of same-sex couples was not rationally connected to these objectives. "If anything," Iacobucci J commented, "the goals of the legislation are undermined by the impugned exclusion." In the result, he declared s. 29 of the FLA to be of no force or effect, but temporarily suspended the effect of the declaration for six months to give the legislature an opportunity to rectify the constitutional defect.

Major and Bastarache JJ each wrote separate judgments concurring in the result reached by Cory and Iacobucci JJ. In his short judgment, Major J found that the purpose of the spousal support provisions "is to allow persons who become financially dependent on one another in the course of a lengthy 'conjugal' relationship some relief from financial hardship resulting from the breakdown of that relationship." He stated that excluding same-sex couples serves no purpose and in fact undermines the legislative objective by increasing burdens on the public purse. In his concurring judgment, Bastarache J agreed that the legislation violated s. 15. The exclusion suggested that same-sex unions are not worthy of recognition or protection. In his lengthy s. 1 analysis, Bastarache J stated that the primary legislative purpose in extending support obligations was to address the disadvantaged economic position of women in nonmarital, opposite-sex relationships. He found that this objective was pressing and substantial. However, Bastarache J emphasized that it was necessary to also examine the reasons for excluding same-sex couples from the law. He could find no pressing and substantial reason for the exclusion. Even if the purposes of the exclusion were to promote the traditional family or economic equality in family relationships, the exclusion of same-sex couples bore no rational connection to these objectives.]

GONTHIER J (dissenting):

[Gonthier J began by reviewing the approach to analyzing the s. 15(1) claims set out in *Law*. He then examined the history of spousal support generally and the support regime legislated in Ontario specifically. The story he told is one of the gradual emancipation of women from legal impediments to full equality. Gonthier J's reading of the recent legislative history acknowledged that the reforms were based on the premise that formal equality between spouses should be the legal norm in Ontario. He stressed, however, that the legislature enacted the spousal support provisions fully aware of the economic and social realities of women and the need to ameliorate the position of women who had become dependent on their partners in both married and conjugal opposite-sex relationships. In his view,

> [t]he primary purpose of the FLA is to recognize the social function specific to opposite-sex couples and their position as a fundamental unit in society, and to address the dynamic of dependence unique to men and women in opposite-sex relationships. This dynamic of dependence stems from this specific social function, the roles regularly taken by one member of that relationship, the biological reality of the relationship, and the pre-existing economic disadvantage that is usually, but not exclusively, suffered by women. This purpose is apparent from the text of the provision, the preamble to the legislation, and the legislative history of the provision.

Turning to the analysis of the s. 15(1) claim, Gonthier J agreed that the legislation imposed differential treatment on the basis of sexual orientation and that the differential treatment resulted in the withholding of a benefit. The final question in the s. 15(1) analysis was whether the difference in treatment amounted to discrimination.]

[221] Having established that the legislation confers a benefit, we must then turn to the question of whether the benefit is withheld "in a manner which reflects the stereotypical application of presumed group or personal characteristics, or which otherwise has the effect of perpetuating or promoting the view that the individual is less capable or worthy of recognition or value as a human being or as a member of Canadian society, equally deserving of concern, respect, and consideration": *Law, supra*, at para. 88. As I explain below, the concept of "stereotyping" often is linked to the contextual factor of "correspondence." Where the legislation takes into account the actual need, capacity or circumstances of the claimant and the comparator, then it is unlikely to rest on a stereotype.

• • •

[227] The contextual factor of correspondence is critical for determining the central issue in this appeal, whether the analogous ground of sexual orientation nourishes a

challenge to the definition of "spouse" and renders the exclusion of gay and lesbian persons from that definition discriminatory under s. 15(1) of the Charter. The definition of "spouse," as I have already suggested, is an extension of marriage. To be a spouse is, in essence, to be as if married, whether or not one is actually married. Spouse-hood is a social and cultural institution, not merely an instrument of economic policy. The concept of "spouse," while a social construct, is one with deep roots in our history. It informs our legal system: the status of "spouse" is defined, recognized, and regulated by the Legislature. ... It is rooted in Western history, in which the concept of "spouse" has always referred to a member of a cohabiting opposite-sex couple. That is what it means to be a spouse. ... That well-recognized definition does not discriminate on the basis of sexual orientation, any more than the status of "child" or "adult" discriminates on the basis of age, or "male" or "female" discriminates on the basis of sex.

• • •

[230] Legislation such as Part III of the FLA, which provides differing economic and legal treatment for married couples and opposite-sex common law couples is premised on certain assumptions about the nature of the economic, social, and legal dynamic of the relationships those individuals have. That economic, social, and legal dynamic, I should emphasize, is a multi-faceted one, and some of its features will be shared by other relationships, including some long-term same-sex relationships. One of the central questions, therefore, is whether those underlying assumptions, embodied in the distinction drawn in s. 29, are based on stereotypes ... .

• • •

[232] The Legislative Assembly has restricted the meaning of "spouse" in Part III of the FLA. However, it is critical to see that the restriction has not been made on the basis of stereotypical assumptions regarding group or personal characteristics. ... To the contrary, s. 29's definition of "spouse" corresponds with an accurate account of the actual needs, capacity and circumstances of opposite-sex couples as compared to others, including same-sex couples. Those differences stem, in part, from the biological reality that only opposite-sex couples can bear children. That biological reality means that opposite-sex couples play a unique social role. That social role often leads to the well-established economic vulnerability of women in long-term opposite-sex relationships, often (though not always) stemming from the decision to bear and raise children.

[233] Cohabiting opposite-sex couples are the natural and most likely site for the procreation and raising of children. This is their specific, unique role ... .

[234] This unique social role of opposite-sex couples has two related features. First, it is notorious ... that "women bear a disproportionate share of the child care burden in Canada," and that this burden is borne both by working mothers and mothers who stay at home with their children. The second feature is that one partner (most often the woman) tends to become economically dependent upon the other.

• • •

[241] It is this dynamic of dependence that the legislature has sought to address by way of Part III of the FLA. ... [t]he dependency of women in long-term opposite-sex relationships arises precisely because they are opposite-sex relationships. There is simply no evidence that same-sex couples in long-term relationships exhibit this type of dependency in any significant numbers.

|242| Indeed, the evidence before us is to the contrary. [The citations to the numerous social science studies referred to have been omitted.] That evidence indicates that lesbian relationships are characterized by a more even distribution of labour, a rejection of stereotypical gender roles, and a lower degree of financial interdependence than is prevalent in opposite-sex relationships. ... Same-sex couples are much less likely to adopt traditional sex roles than are opposite-sex couples ... . Indeed, "research shows that most lesbians and gay men actively reject traditional husband-wife or masculine-feminine roles as a model for enduring relationships" ... .

[243] The evidence before us also indicates that partners in a lesbian couple are more likely to each pursue a career and to work outside the home than are partners in an opposite-sex couple ... . As members of same-sex couples are, obviously, of the same sex, they are more likely than members of opposite-sex couples to earn similar incomes, because no male-female income differential is present. For the same reason, the gendered division of domestic and child-care responsibilities that continues to characterize opposite-sex relationships simply has no purchase in same-sex relationships.

[244] Undoubtedly, in some same-sex relationships, one partner may become financially dependent on the other. This may happen for any number of reasons, including explicit or implicit agreement, differences in age, health, or education, and so on. However, no pattern of dependence emerges. Put another way, dependence in same-sex relationships is not systemic: it does not exhibit the gendered dependency characteristic of many cohabiting opposite-sex relationships. Due to the high degree of equality observed in lesbian relationships, very few women were dependent on their same-sex partners for financial support, and even differences in income between same-sex partners did not affect women's perception of their financial dependence on one another in same-sex relationships ... .

[245] ... [T]he legislation takes into account the claimant's actual need, capacity and circumstances as compared with individuals in opposite-sex couples and by doing so it does not violate human dignity.

. . .

[252] ... The distinction drawn by s. 29 does not discriminate because it does not involve the stereotypical application of presumed group or personal characteristics, and it does not otherwise have the effect of perpetuating or promoting the view that individuals in same-sex relationships are less deserving of concern, respect, and consideration. The evidence bears out the contention that the legislative distinction is drawn on the basis of a true appreciation of the facts. As I see it, the key question is whether there is a correspondence between the ground on which the claim is based and the actual need, capacity, or circumstances of the claimant or others. I am convinced that there is. The one feature that distinguishes the two types of relationship is that which is addressed by the FLA: the necessarily gendered nature of the relationship, which in a great many cases leads to economic dependency based on gender, often (though not always) due to the presence of children. Moreover, the economic disparity between men and women in relationships only occurs in opposite-sex relationships. By definition, a same-sex relationship cannot exhibit these features. Dependency may arise in some same-sex relationships, to be sure, but it must by necessity stem from a different cause, and as I have discussed, it is much less likely to occur. Where a legislative distinction is drawn on the basis of an accurate

picture of capacity and circumstance (no one suggests that merit is at issue here), there is no stereotype, and discrimination is unlikely: *Law, supra; Miron* [*v. Trudel*, [1995] 2 SCR 418], at para. 132 (per McLachlin J).

[Gonthier J went on to consider the other contextual factors outlined in *Law*. He argued that same-sex couples do not suffer from pre-existing disadvantage in the area of family law, because, in his view, their relationships do not carry the same burden of unequal social roles, systemic dependence, and structural wage differentials that frequently characterize opposite-sex relationships. The legislation, he said, has an ameliorative purpose (assisting women). Finally, Gonthier J stated that the consequences of the exclusion were not severe, because same-sex couples were relieved of the burden of support obligations and were free to formulate contracts to impose support obligations on themselves. The result, he concluded, was that a reasonable person would see that the legislation takes into account accurate differences in a manner that respects the claimant's dignity, and therefore s. 15(1) was not violated. The majority, having found an unjustifiable infringement of s. 15, declared the definition of "spouse" in the FLA to be of no force and effect, subject to six months' delayed declaration of invalidity, as opposed to reading out the words "a man and a woman" and replacing them with the words "two persons," the remedy adopted in the courts below. That portion of the decision can be found in Chapter 25, Enforcement of Rights.]

Appeal dismissed; remedy modified.

NOTES AND QUESTIONS

1. The majority and dissent in *M. v. H.* divide on the question of the purpose behind the spousal support scheme, and this leads them to disagree on the second contextual factor in *Law*—namely, whether there is a correspondence between the actual needs and circumstances of same-sex couples and their exclusion from the legislation. Is there some way to secure a stable methodology for ascertaining purpose so that the s. 15(1) analysis does not deteriorate into a result-oriented exercise?

2. In the 1995 rulings in *Miron* and *Egan*, Gonthier J joined with three other members of the Court in concluding that laws employing marital status and sexual orientation to define the rights of spouses were not discriminatory because these grounds were relevant to the legislative objectives of supporting the traditional family. The *Law* ruling, by ignoring this approach, appeared to spell the end of the "relevance" test in the s. 15(1) jurisprudence. Is there, however, any significant difference between Gonthier J's emphasis on the correspondence between the aims of the legislation and the exclusion of same-sex couples in *M. v. H.*, and the approach he took in the 1995 trilogy?

3. In the principal majority judgment, Cory J emphasized that the appeal was concerned with the equal treatment of unmarried conjugal couples; it had "nothing to do with marriage *per se.*" Gonthier J, on the other hand, expressed concern about the "far-reaching effects" of the Court's ruling, and seemed anxious to prevent constitutional law from undermining the opposite-sex definition of marriage and marriage-like relationships. Same-sex couples

launched a number of constitutional challenges, based on s. 15 of the Charter, to the opposite-sex requirement of the legal definition of marriage shortly after the ruling in *M. v. H.*

A number of lower courts agreed: *see EGALE Canada Inc. v. Canada (Attorney General)* (2003), 225 DLR (4th) 472, 2003 BCCA 251; *Halpern v. Canada (Attorney General)* (2003), 65 OR (3d) 161 (CA); and *Hendricks v. Québec (Procureur général)*, [2002] RJQ 2506 (Sup. Ct.). This led the federal government to request an advisory opinion from the Supreme Court of Canada on whether legislation that extends the legal capacity to marry to persons of the same sex is consistent with the Charter. In *Reference re Same-Sex Marriage*, [2004] 3 SCR 698, 246 DLR (4th) 193, the Court answered in the affirmative, stating (at para. 32) that the "government's policy stance in relation to the s. 15(1) concerns of same-sex couples ... combined with the circumstances giving rise to [the proposed legislation] points unequivocally to a purpose which, far from violating the Charter, flows from it." The Court, however, declined to rule on whether an opposite-sex requirement for marriage was also consistent with the Charter. In its view, such a ruling would be inappropriate given that the federal government had stated its intention to enact the proposed legislation; the parties to previous litigation had relied on the finality of lower court decisions and acquired rights that were, in the Court's opinion, entitled to protection; and such a ruling might undermine the goal of ensuring uniformity of the law.

4. Following the release of the Court's opinion in the *Same-Sex Reference*, the federal government introduced legislation providing for legal recognition of same-sex marriage. After an extremely difficult and contentious passage through both the House of Commons and Senate, Bill C-38 received Royal Assent and the *Civil Marriage Act*, SC 2005, c. 33 came into force on July 20, 2005. The Act is very brief, with the main body of the legislation, apart from a lengthy preamble and a series of consequential amendments to other federal laws, consisting of only four sections:

> 2. *Marriage—certain aspects of capacity.* Marriage, for civil purposes, is the lawful union of two persons to the exclusion of all others.
>
> 3. *Religious officials.* It is recognized that officials of religious groups are free to refuse to perform marriages that are not in accordance with their religious beliefs.
>
> 3.1 *Freedom of conscience and religion and expression of beliefs.* For greater certainty, no person or organization shall be deprived of any benefit, or be subject to any obligation or sanction, under any law of the Parliament of Canada solely by reason of their exercise, in respect of marriage between persons of the same sex, of the freedom of conscience and religion guaranteed under the *Canadian Charter of Rights and Freedoms* or the expression of their beliefs in respect of marriage as the union of a man and woman to the exclusion of all others based on that guaranteed freedom.
>
> 4. *Marriage not void or voidable.* For greater certainty, a marriage is not void or voidable by reason only that the spouses are of the same sex.

The issue that has become the focus of attention since the legalization of same-sex marriage is the scope of the protection afforded to freedom of religion/conscience. This issue is addressed in ss. 3 and 3.1 of the *Civil Marriage Act* and also in provincial human rights codes and legislation relating to solemnization of marriage. In Ontario, for example, the following subsections were added to s. 20 of the *Marriage Act*, RSO 1990, c. M.3, which deals with religious officials registered to perform marriages:

20(6) *Rights of Persons Registered.* A person registered under this section is not required to solemnize a marriage, to allow a sacred place to be used for solemnizing a marriage or for an event related to the solemnization of a marriage, or to otherwise assist in the solemnization of a marriage, if to do so would be contrary to,

> (a) a person's religious beliefs; or
>
> (b) the doctrines, rites, usages or customs of the religious body to which the person belongs.

(7) *Definition.* In subsection (6),

"sacred place" includes a place of worship and any ancillary or accessory facilities.

Many questions will undoubtedly arise of how far the protection for religious officials/institutions goes. As well, there will be many questions of the accommodation of religious beliefs in the secular context—for example, can civil marriage commissioners rely on freedom of conscience and religion to be exempted from an obligation to perform same-sex marriages? These issues are discussed further in Chapter 19, Freedom of Religion.

5. Another successful s. 15 challenge was *Trociuk v. BC (Attorney General)*, [2003] 1 SCR 835, 226 DLR (4th) 1, which involved a provision in British Columbia's *Vital Statistics Act*, RSBC 1996, c. 479, that allowed the mother of a newborn child who either did not know the father or who refused to acknowledge the father to include only her particulars on the birth registration and to choose the child's surname. The differential treatment based on sex was found to discriminate against fathers, allowing mothers to arbitrarily exclude fathers from the birth registration and the naming of their children and sending the message that a father's relationship with his children was less worthy than that between a mother and her children. The discrimination could not be justified under s. 1. While ensuring the accurate and prompt recording of births was an important objective, the legislation did not satisfy the minimal impairment test. The legislation did not distinguish between cases where there were good reasons to exclude the father from the registration and naming processes and those where he was unjustifiably excluded. Nor was there any mechanism to allow unjustifiably excluded fathers to apply for an after-the-fact amendment of the birth registration.

6. Many s. 15 claims where differential treatment on an enumerated or analogous ground has been established have failed at the disadvantage/discrimination stage of the analysis, some before *Law* and many after. Some of these cases where there has been no finding of discrimination have involved differential treatment on the basis of sex: *R v. Hess; R v. Nguyen*, [1990] 2 SCR 906, 59 CCC (3d) 161; *Weatherall v. Canada (Attorney General)*, [1993] 2 SCR 872, 210 DLR (4th) 193 (both discussed in the notes following *Andrews*, above in Section II). Many have involved disability: see *Eaton v. Brant County Board of Education*, [1997] 1 SCR 241, 143 DLR (4th) 577 (discussed above in the excerpt from *Eldridge*, in Section VI.A); *Granovsky v. Canada (Minister of Employment and Immigration)*, [2000] 1 SCR 703, 186 DLR (4th) 1 (discussed above in Section VI.C); and *Winko v. British Columbia (Forensic Psychiatric Institute)*, [1999] 2 SCR 625, 175 DLR (4th) 193. In *Winko*, the Court rejected a Charter challenge to the provisions of the *Criminal Code* dealing with the disposition of accused persons found to be "not criminally responsible" (NCR) because of a mental disability. The provisions granted to a review board the power to discharge an accused absolutely or conditionally, or to detain an accused indefinitely in a hospital if necessary to protect the public. Even though the NCR provisions treated accused persons differently on

the basis of mental disability, the Court concluded that they were not discriminatory. In the principal majority judgment, McLachlin J argued that the impugned provisions did not involve the stereotypical application of group characteristics. To the contrary, she said, the NCR provisions put in place a process that involves an individualized assessment that is "the antithesis of the logic of stereotype." The scheme moves beyond formal equality and sameness of treatment by recognizing "the NCR accused's disability, incapacity and particular personal situation and, based upon that recognition, creates a system of individualized assessment and treatment that deliberately undermines the invidious stereotype of the mentally ill as dangerous." For this reason, she concluded, the scheme did not discriminate in a substantive sense.

7. Many s. 15 claims involving differential treatment on the basis of age have also failed at the third step of the analysis. *Law* itself is one example. Two others are *Gosselin v. Quebec (Attorney General)*, [2002] 4 SCR 429, 229 DLR (4th) 156 and *Canadian Foundation for Children, Youth and the Law v. Canada (Attorney General)*, [2004] 1 SCR 76, 234 DLR (4th) 257, both dealt with in notes below.

NOTE: GOSSELIN v. QUEBEC (ATTORNEY GENERAL)

At issue in *Gosselin v. Quebec (Attorney General)*, 2002 SCC 84, [2002] 4 SCR 429, 229 DLR (4th) 156, were provisions in Quebec's *Social Aid Act*, RSQ, c. A-16 and accompanying regulations, governing the period between 1984 and 1989, which stipulated that the base amount of social assistance payable to people under the age of 30 was one-third of that payable to those 30 and over. Those under 30 could increase their welfare payments, to either the same as or slightly less than those 30 and over, by participating in an educational or work experience program. There was evidence that many young persons fell between the cracks and were unable to participate in these programs. In 1989 the age-based distinction was removed. Gosselin brought a class action on behalf of all those who been under 30 and affected by the old scheme before 1989. (Until 1987 the scheme was protected by Quebec's invocation of the s. 33 "notwithstanding" clause.) Arguments were based on both s. 15 and s. 7 of the Charter. The Court's opinions on whether the legislation violated s. 7 of the Charter are found in Chapter 22, Life, Liberty, and Security of the Person.

With respect to the s. 15 claim, all of the opinions offered by the Court relied on *Law*'s four contextual factors to assess whether the provisions discriminated on the basis of age. McLachlin CJC, for a majority of the Court, held that they did not. She found no impairment of the dignity of younger people because, in providing those under 30 with significantly less social assistance than what it provided older recipients, the government was attempting to create incentives for younger people to enter the labour force. L'Heureux-Dubé J, dissenting, held that "Ms. Gosselin would have reasonably felt that she was being less valued as a member of society than people 30 and over and that she was being treated as less deserving of respect" (at para 133). Bastarache J, dissenting, argued that the distinction in question "was made simply on the basis of age, not need, opportunity or personal circumstances" and for this and other reasons it offended human dignity.

What arguments would you mount to support the claim that the provisions are discriminatory based on the Court's decision in *Kapp*? Are provisions such as these now exempt from s. 15(1) scrutiny as a result of *Kapp*'s approach to s. 15(2) of the Charter?

NOTE: CANADIAN FOUNDATION FOR CHILDREN, YOUTH AND THE LAW
v. CANADA (ATTORNEY GENERAL)

Canadian Foundation for Children, Youth and the Law v. Canada (Attorney General), 2004
SCC 4, [2004] 1 SCR 76, 234 DLR (4th) 257, the so-called "spanking case," involved a challenge to s. 43 of the *Criminal Code*, which justifies the reasonable use of force by way of
correction by parents and teachers against children in their care. The Foundation sought a
declaration that s. 43 violated ss. 7 and 15 of the Charter. The s. 7 challenge focused on the
violation of children's bodily integrity. The s. 15 challenge was based on the argument that,
as a result of s. 43, children received less protection against assault under the *Criminal Code*
than adults, and that this constituted discrimination on the basis of age. The trial judge and
the Court of Appeal rejected the Foundation's contentions and refused to issue the declaration requested. A majority of the Supreme Court of Canada agreed. The Court's reasoning
on the s. 7 issue is discussed in Chapter 22, Life, Liberty, and Security of the Person.

With respect to the s. 15(1) challenge, McLachlin CJC, writing for a majority of the
Court, found no violation of s. 15(1), largely because of the correspondence between the
age-based distinction found in s. 43 and the actual needs and circumstances of children. In
the view of the majority, while children need a safe environment, they also depend on parents for guidance and discipline, to protect them from harm and to promote their healthy
development. Section 43 was seen to represent Parliament's attempt to accommodate both
of these needs, allowing parents the ability to carry out the reasonable education of their
children without the threat of sanction of the criminal law. The decision not to criminalize
reasonable corrective actions by parents was grounded not in a devaluation of children, but
rather in a concern that criminalizing such conduct risks ruining lives and breaking up
families—a burden that in large part would be borne by children.

Binnie J, dissenting in part, found a violation of s. 15(1). In his view, denying children the
protection of the criminal law against the infliction of physical force that would be criminal
assault if used against an adult was disrespectful of a child's dignity and turned the child into
a second-class citizen. Protection of physical integrity against the use of unlawful force was
a fundamental value applicable to all. He saw the majority's application of the correspondence
factor as inappropriately moving into s. 15(1) factors relevant to the s.1 analysis. Binnie J went
on, however, to uphold s. 43 as a reasonable limit under s. 1, concluding that it was a proportionate measure directed at limiting the intrusion of the *Criminal Code* into family life.

Deschamps J, dissenting, found a violation of s. 15(1), concluding that s. 43, far from
corresponding to the actual needs and circumstances of children, compounded their pre-
existing disadvantage as a vulnerable and often powerless group whose access to legal redress was already restricted. Furthermore, she found that the infringement of s. 15 could
not be justified under s. 1, largely because the provision was overbroad and could have been
tailored to apply only to very minor applications of force rather than being broad enough to
capture more serious assaults on a child's body.

NOTE: THE IMPLICATIONS OF R v. KAPP FOR THE
DISADVANTAGE/DISCRIMINATION ANALYSIS

Has *R v. Kapp* significantly changed the reasoning or the likely results under the third step of the s. 15(1) analysis? Recall that in *Kapp*, the Court abandoned its commitment in *Law* to human dignity as a legal test for determining whether a law is discriminatory. In its place, the Court held that the perpetuation of prejudice or stereotyping renders a distinction discriminatory. However, its reasons are unclear as to whether the perpetuation of *prejudice* or *stereotyping* is the only way in which a distinction can amount to discrimination, or whether a distinction that perpetuates *disadvantage* in other ways can amount to discrimination (the "broader interpretation"). McLachlin CJC and Abella J write (at para. 37) that "the focus of s. 15(1) is on preventing governments from making distinctions based on enumerated or analogous grounds that have the effect of perpetuating disadvantage or prejudice or imposing disadvantage on the basis of stereotyping." They suggest, in other words, that distinctions that have the effect of perpetuating disadvantage in ways other than perpetuating prejudice or stereotyping can also constitute discrimination.

In *Ermineskin Indian Band and Nation v. Canada*, 2009 SCC 9, [2009] 1 SCR 222, 302 DLR (4th) 577, however, the Court, without explicit discussion of the issue, applied a narrower interpretation of the *Kapp* definition of discrimination. In *Ermineskin*, at issue was the failure by the Crown to invest oil and gas royalties received on behalf of First Nations as a prudent investor would—that is, to invest the royalties in a diversified portfolio. One of the several unsuccessful arguments put to the Court on behalf of the First Nations was that the inability of the Crown to invest resulted in lower returns than those available to non-Indians, and that this amounted to discrimination within the meaning of s. 15(1) of the Charter. The Court acknowledged that the statutory scheme in place applied only to status Indians and therefore constituted a distinction between Indians and non-Indians but that this distinction did not amount to discrimination. Assuming that the failure by the Crown to invest disadvantaged the First Nations, the Court held that this disadvantage did not perpetuate prejudice or stereotyping; it did not explore the possibility that the provisions in question perpetuated disadvantage in other ways.

At the same time, however, the reasons the Court offered in in *Ermineskin* in support of this conclusion suggest a willingness to understand "prejudice" in fiscal or financial terms. The Court noted that the statutory provisions in question "do not preclude investment, provided the investments are made by the bands or trustees on their behalf after expenditure of funds from the CRF [Consolidated Revenue Fund] to the bands and the release of the Crown from further responsibility with respect to the royalties," and that, "until the funds are expended by the Crown for the purposes of investment by the bands or trustees on their behalf, they are held by the Crown in the CRF and the bands are provided with liquidity and a return on the royalties" [ibid.]. This suggests that the Court might have viewed the provisions as discriminatory had the First Nations in fact been financially prejudiced by their operation.

In *AC v. Manitoba (Director of Child and Family Services)*, 2009 SCC 30, another post-*Kapp* decision, the issue was the constitutionality of the Manitoba *Child and Family Services Act*, CCSM c. C80, by which the court may authorize treatment that it considers to be in a child's best interests. Section 25(9) of the Act presumes that the best interests of a child 16 or over will be most effectively promoted by allowing the child's views to be determinative, unless it can be shown that the child does not understand the decision or appreciate its consequences. Where the child is under 16, however, no such presumption exists. Applying the test in *Kapp*, a majority of the Court, per Abella J, held (at para. 152) that the provisions do not violate s. 15

> because the distinction drawn by the Act between minors under 16 and those 16 and over is ameliorative, not invidious. First, it aims at protecting the interests of minors as a vulnerable group. Second, it protects the members of the targeted group—children under 16—in a way that gives the individual child a degree of input into the ultimate decision on treatment. In my view, this is sufficient to demonstrate that the distinction drawn by the Act, while based on an enumerated ground, is not discriminatory within the meaning of s. 15.

S.R. Moreau, "The Wrongs of Unequal Treatment"
(2004), 54 *University of Toronto Law Journal* 291, at 303-13 (footnotes omitted)

[In the following excerpt, Sophia Moreau argues that unequal treatment wrongs individuals in four different ways. The Court's decision in *R v. Kapp* only appears to recognize one of these four ways—namely, when unequal treatment is based on prejudice or stereotyping. Moreau provides an extensive analysis of this type of wrong. One of her conclusions (at p. 303) is that when the wrong of unequal treatment is understood as based on stereotype or prejudice, it is incorrect to suppose that the assessment of an individual's claim requires the establishment of a "comparator group." This is because the wrong in question does not arise from a "comparative fact—that is, any fact that depends on a comparison between the situation of these individuals and that of the groups who have received the benefit." A second conclusion she reaches is that "a stereotype is no less a stereotype because the law that employs it also works to improve the plight of others; this fact about their situation does not make the denial of the benefit any less arbitrary from the perspective of those who are stereotyped, nor any less of a threat to their autonomy." From this it follows that the presence of an "ameliorative purpose," which *Kapp* currently treats as weighing against a violation of s. 15, should not "weigh against it when the wrong is understood as based upon stereotype or prejudice."

Moreau goes on to identify three additional wrongs that render unequal treatment discriminatory. As you read this excerpt, ask yourself whether the definition of discrimination that the Court advances in *Kapp* should be expanded to comprehend the wrongs that Moreau identifies. Ask, too, what her analysis might mean for the Court's understanding of the relationship between ss. 15(1) and (2) of the Charter.]

III ... *Unequal treatment wrongs individuals when ...*

B. *It perpetuates oppressive power relations*

A different reason that unequal treatment may wrong individuals ... is that it may perpetuate oppressive power relations. It may, that is, have the effect of further entrenching or reinforcing power imbalances that are unacceptably large and that leave certain individuals without sufficient social or political influence. What amounts to an "unacceptably large" imbalance or a "sufficient" influence in this context is, of course, a question that different theorists have answered in different ways; but, as my arguments need not presuppose one answer or another, I shall leave the question open.

It may seem that any conception of the wrong of unequal treatment that locates it in the perpetuation of oppressive power relations could not be significantly different from the conception we have just considered. When the denial of a certain benefit perpetuates oppressive power relations, is this not precisely because the denial was based upon a stereotype or a prejudice? Not necessarily. It need not involve prejudicial motives because, as recent literature on systemic discrimination has taught us, oppressive power relations are often the indirect effect of institutional structures—structures that were not deliberately designed to harm the individuals in question, or to express contempt for them, but nevertheless perpetuate the social or political domination of certain groups. Nor does oppression always involve stereotyping. As Amartya Sen has noted, it is sometimes a sign of extreme oppression that the oppressed person or group has come to fit the image that has been defined for them by the dominant social group and has come to lack all motivation for a change in identity. In such cases, the generalization that we make about these individuals may in fact be accurate, and the oppressed individuals may have adopted the generalization for themselves, as an accurate depiction of themselves. So the generalization will not be a "stereotype" in the sense we considered above: it will not be inaccurate, and the individuals to whom it is applied would indeed themselves assent to it, as a description of themselves. But this does not mean that the denial of a certain benefit to the individuals to whom this generalization applies does not have the effect of perpetuating objectionable forms of domination. Moreover, even in cases where there is no such extreme oppression, the denial of the benefit may not involve the application of a generalization at all but may simply result from an omission in a certain scheme of protection or from a policy with unforeseen side effects on a particular group. Hence, there can be denials of benefits that perpetuate oppressive power relations without involving stereotypes or prejudices.

An example of such a case might help to make this point more forcefully. Consider the treatment received by the claimant in *Vriend v. Alberta* [[1998] 1 SCR 493, 156 DLR (4th) 385]. Delwin Vriend was barred from bringing a complaint of discrimination on the basis of sexual orientation against his employer under Alberta's *Individual's Rights Protection Act* [IRPA] because, at the time, it did not include "sexual orientation" among its list of prohibited grounds. The Alberta legislature had omitted this ground simply because it believed the issue was "too controversial." It seems implausible to suggest that members of the legislature could not have believed that the controversial nature of this ground was a good reason for omitting it from the legislation unless motivated by prejudice or by stereotypes about homosexuals. It seems more likely that they simply made a judgement about which decision would yield the most popular support. Yet it is clear that the denial of this benefit to Vriend perpetuated oppressive power relations—in particular, between homosexuals as a group and those who disparage their sexual orientation.

One might suggest, however, that even if stereotyping and prejudice are not present in such cases, nevertheless what makes the perpetuation of oppression wrong is essentially the same as one of the elements—indeed, the main element—that made unequal treatment on the basis of stereotyping and prejudice wrong: namely, harm to the victim's autonomy. This certainly seems to be part of the reason that oppressive power relations are objectionable: if other individuals exert significant control over me, I will be less able to shape my own life in accordance with my choices. But I am not certain that this is the heart of the wrong done through the perpetuation of oppression. When some individuals are oppressed by others, certain goods are denied to them—such as the opportunity to participate as equals in public political argument, the opportunity to have equal influence in certain social contexts, and the opportunity to contribute to a genuinely collective self-determination. These goods have value in and of themselves, quite apart from their instrumental value in promoting individual autonomy. So it seems plausible to hold that, merely by virtue of being deprived of these goods, the individual has been wronged, quite apart from whether this has also lessened his autonomy.

Unlike the good of autonomy, the goods listed above are all relational: they concern the individual's standing and opportunities in relation to those of others, and they can be assessed only through a comparison of the individual with others. This leads to one important difference between the wrong of being denied a benefit where this perpetuates oppressive power relations and the wrong of being denied a benefit on the basis of stereotype or prejudice. We saw above that the latter wrong is not essentially relational: the wrong of being denied a benefit on the basis of a stereotype or prejudice is dependent solely upon facts about this individual's treatment and its effects upon her, considered quite apart from others. By contrast, one must engage in comparative judgements to ascertain whether differential treatment in fact perpetuates oppressive power relations. And when it does, this amounts to a wrong largely because it denies the individual access to certain relational goods.

This wrong, then, is essentially comparative. It is important to note, however, that the relevant comparator group is not the group that has been given the benefit in question but the group or groups who exercise oppressive amounts of power over those who have been denied the benefit. This is because, in order to ascertain whether the denial of a benefit genuinely perpetuates oppressive power relations, one needs to focus not on the group that has been given the benefit but, rather, on whether or not there is indeed some group that exercises an undue amount of power over those who are denied the benefit and on whether the denial of the benefit will perpetuate these unacceptable power relations. The group that dominates may indeed be coextensive with the class of people who have been given the benefit. But it will not always be so. Certainly in *Vriend*, the benefits of the IRPA in an employment context were obtained mainly by employees, whereas the group that exercised undue amounts of power over individuals such as Vriend consisted of some, but not all, employees and some employers—namely, any who disparaged homosexuals as unworthy of human rights protection. And even in cases where the group that receives the benefit is indeed coextensive with the group that exercises unacceptable domination over those denied the benefit, what is relevant about the comparator group is not their receipt of the benefit but their oppression of those who have been denied it.

A further implication of this conception of the wrong is that, although it is relational, the wrong is not lessened or eliminated by the fact that the law resulting in the denial of the benefit has an ameliorative purpose. Even if a law aims to eliminate the oppression of some other group—perhaps a group that, in absolute terms, was much worse off than those denied the benefit—this does not eliminate or diminish the oppression of those to whom the benefit is denied.

This is not to say that the fact that a law has an ameliorative purpose is of no relevance at all. The presence of an ameliorative purpose may indeed be relevant to the question of whether the law is justified, all things considered (in legal terms, this is the question asked in s. 1 analysis). But because it does not lessen the oppression of those who are denied the benefit, it seems implausible to treat it as relevant to whether the unequal treatment that these individuals have received is unfair to them, or amounts to a wrong to them, in the sense relevant to s. 15 analysis. And, indeed, *Vriend* is a good illustration of this. Anti-discrimination legislation is inherently remedial: the IRPA was specifically designed by the Alberta legislature to try to eliminate the oppression of other groups—for instance, working women and various ethnic minorities. Yet the fact that the legislation had this purpose was quite properly not treated by the Court as a factor weighing against the conclusion that Vriend had been treated unfairly.

C. It leaves some individuals without access to basic goods

Much of the recent philosophical work on equality has aimed to show that, in many cases, our concern over unequal treatment is not ultimately a concern that some people have unfairly been given less than others but, rather, a concern that these people do not have enough, when their situation is considered on its own, in absolute terms. Harry Frankfurt, for instance, has argued that inequalities are morally problematic only when they result in certain people having less than what is "sufficient." He writes that

> When we consider people who are substantially worse off than ourselves, we do very commonly find that we are morally disturbed by their circumstances. What directly touches us in cases of this kind, however, is not a quantitative discrepancy but a qualitative condition.

That is to say, what is of moral importance to us, in Frankfurt's view, is not the relative difference between those who have more and those who have less but the absolute condition of those who are worse off. It is whether those who are worse off lack sufficient goods. (What amounts to "sufficient goods" depends on what, in a moral context, one takes to be morally relevant, or, in a legal context, legally relevant. It may be "goods sufficient to maintain one's life," or "goods sufficient for a life in which one has time to do more than stay alive"; or it may be a set of goods that is important not because of their contribution to the individual's own well-being, but because they are "goods necessary for the individual to function as an equal in society." I shall consider these alternatives presently.)

Derek Parfit has drawn a similar distinction between a concern for eliminating inequalities *per se* and the aim of giving priority to those who are "worse off." And he, too, has questioned whether the moral value of equality does not inhere entirely in the aim of improving the situation of those who are worse off—not because it matters that they are worse off than others but simply because it matters that, in absolute terms, they are so badly off.

For a variety of reasons, one might think that although this concern for the situation of those who are badly off may ground some of our moral objections to inequality, it cannot be the basis for a legal complaint about unequal treatment—or, at least, cannot be the

basis for a s. 15 challenge. First, one might hold that our concern for those who lack access
to basic goods can only be interpreted as the view that the government is under a positive
duty to provide certain basic goods to all citizens, and one might doubt whether any section of the Charter can plausibly be construed as imposing such a positive duty. Second,
and alternatively, one might maintain, as Madam Justice Arbour did in *Gosselin* [*v. Quebec (Attorney General)*, [2002] 4 SCR 429, 229 DLR (4th) 156], that although there can
be a positive duty on the government to ensure that individuals have access to certain
basic goods, the proper way to understand this positive duty is as an implication of the
s. 7 right not to be deprived of "security of the person" except in accordance with "principles of fundamental justice." This duty is best understood in terms of s. 7, one might
claim, because our concern that all individuals have access to basic goods is ultimately a
concern for their physical and psychological security. Moreover, one might argue, unlike
s. 7, s. 15 protects only against wrongs that are inherently comparative in nature. And the
wrong of being deprived of access to basic goods is clearly not comparative. So if any
section of the Charter protects against this wrong, it must be s. 7; it cannot be s. 15.

However, each of these lines of reasoning can be questioned. First, it is not clear that
our concern here must be construed as an insistence that the government is under a
positive duty to provide certain basic goods to all. Some theories of the nature and justification of the Charter and the rights it guarantees imply that it cannot impose positive
duties on governments to provide certain benefits; similarly, certain theories of the appropriate roles of the courts and the legislatures imply that courts simply do not have the
institutional mandate to interpret the Charter as imposing positive duties on governments. My aim here is not to take a stand on the adequacy of these theories. It is, rather,
to suggest that the claims that these theories make about the indefensibility of positive
rights under the Charter could quite coherently limit, and help to give shape to, our concern for the absolute level of those who are badly off. ... [W]e might [thus] treat [this]
concern [as] limited by the need to defer to the government's choice of whether or not to
legislate in a particular area and to provide particular benefits to the public. ... [O]ur
concern will take the form of an objection to the way in which the government sometimes acts once it has chosen to legislate in a certain area. The objection will be that if the
government chooses to make a certain benefit available to the public—for instance, government pensions, unemployment insurance, or a certain level of welfare payment that
it deems sufficient for basic survival—then it wrongs individuals if it denies them these
benefits and this denial leaves them without access to a relevant basic good. Hence, if the
government wishes to legislate over a certain matter and to provide certain benefits, it
must do so in a way does not leave the most disadvantaged groups in our society without
access to the relevant basic goods.

But it may also choose not to legislate over these areas, and in this case, even those
who are very badly off can have no equality-based objection. ...

[Another] reason ... for thinking that our concern for those who lack access to basic
goods is best understood in terms of s. 7 rights to security of the person [is] that this
concern is essentially a concern for the security of those who are worse off—that is, a
concern to ensure that they have all of the goods necessary for basic health and survival.
This is certainly one way of understanding the concern. But there are other ways. It may
be a concern that they be given goods sufficient for a life that includes more than simply

working to survive. Or it may be the concern that Anderson foregrounds—namely, that each individual have sufficient resources to be able to participate in and enjoy the goods of society and to participate in democratic self-government. We need not decide this issue here. What is important for our purposes is to note that there are other, equally plausible ways of understanding the concern. We need not see it as the type of concern that can be adequately addressed only through s. 7.

[As for the argument that s. 15 only protects against wrongs that are inherently comparative in nature, Moreau draws on her earlier analysis of the wrong of differential treatment based on prejudice or stereotype and her argument that these wrongs are not inherently comparative.]

I have now tried to counter various arguments purporting to show that it is inappropriate to consider s. 15 as protecting against the wrong of denying individuals a benefit in a manner that leaves them without access to basic goods. I want now to argue, further, that in a number of s. 15 cases, this is the most plausible way of making sense of the wrong that was alleged by the claimants and recognized as a wrong by at least some members of the Supreme Court. Consider first the case of *Eldridge v. British Columbia (AG)*, [[1997] 3 SCR 624, 151 DLR (4th) 577]. The case concerned the failure of the British Columbia government to provide funding for sign language interpreters for individuals requiring medical services. The Supreme Court held that this did constitute a violation of the claimants' equality rights. Their reasoning was that effective communication with one's medical practitioners is an essential, not an ancillary, part of medical service—and the British Columbia government had chosen to fund essential medical services. In other words, the denial of this benefit left deaf persons lacking a basic good that was relevant to the area in which the government had chosen to legislate.

The Court's objection to the treatment of deaf persons in *Eldridge* is, I believe, misconstrued if construed simply as an objection to the difference between the effective communication available to hearing persons and the difficulties experienced by deaf persons in the absence of interpreters. If it were simply an objection to this difference, then it would be adequately met by eliminating the difference in the levels of communication with medical personnel enjoyed by hearing persons and by deaf persons. But it would not matter, for the purposes of s. 15, how this difference was eliminated—and, in particular, it would not matter whether the government eliminated the difference by raising the level of communicative efficacy enjoyed by the deaf or simply by lowering the level enjoyed by the hearing. Suppose, fancifully, that the government had attempted to eliminate the difference in this case by "levelling down" and ensuring that hearing persons found communication with medical staff just as difficult as deaf persons. (Imagine, for example, that the government required medical staff to address hearing persons only in languages other than their own.) This would hardly remove the unfairness to deaf persons, even though it would eliminate the difference between their situation and that of those with normal hearing. It would also, of course, result in an irrational legislative agenda: choosing to provide funding for essential medical services and yet denying all individuals the effective communication that they must have if they are to take full advantage of these services. But that is a separate objection. What is relevant for our purposes is simply that, in such a situation, the original objection of deaf persons would remain: whatever other objections could be made to this new scheme, they could still object that they were treated unfairly by the government. They were denied access to a relevant basic good, even though the government had chosen to legislate in this area.

Two more recent cases in which this is a plausible way of construing one of the main wrongs alleged by the claimant are *Gosselin* and *Canadian Foundation for Children, Youth and the Law v. Canada (AG)*, or the "*Spanking Case*" [[2004] 1 SCR 76, 234 DLR (4th) 257]. Louise Gosselin's complaint pertained to Quebec's social assistance scheme, which for a time set the base welfare payment for those under age thirty at one-third of the amount, viewed by the government as the basic survival amount, that was payable to those aged thirty and above. The scheme stipulated that under-thirties could receive an amount comparable to that received by those aged thirty and above only if they participated in designated work activity or education programs. One aspect of the wrong alleged by Gosselin pertained to the stereotypes that she viewed as underlying the restrictions on the amount payable to those under thirty: she held that they were based upon an inaccurate view of young persons as better able to find employment than those older, as less needy, and as able to rely upon parents for additional support. But only part of her objection was to the unfairness of being denied the full benefit on the basis of a stereotype. Her complaint was also that she was not, under the scheme, given enough to live on: the amount she received left her unable to pay for adequate shelter, food, and clothing. And this aspect of her complaint seems best understood in terms of the wrong of being denied access to a basic good relevant to the area in which the government had chosen to legislate. Similarly, part of the complaint of *Canadian Foundation for Children, Youth and the Law* was that the exclusion from the crime of assault of "reasonable" force exerted "by way of correction" left children without a basic good—namely, protection against intentional physical force. As Mr Justice Binnie wrote in dissent, quoting Peter Newell, "Children are people, and hitting people is wrong." What is objectionable is not the mere difference between the treatment received by adults and the treatment received by children but, rather, the fact that, as a result of the exemption for reasonable corrective force, children were left without access to the basic good of protection from intentional infliction of physical force.

I have now tried to show that this way of construing the wrong of unequal treatment has some plausibility. Before we turn to consider the final conception that I shall discuss, we should note two implications of this conception. First, as we have seen, this conception of the wrong renders it non-comparative. Consequently, when a claimant is alleging this type of wrong, there is no need to locate a relevant comparator group; we need only ask whether the government has legislated in the area in question and whether the denial of a benefit to these individuals results in their lacking access to a relevant basic good. Second, it is once again irrelevant whether the law in question aims to ameliorate the position of some other group. For recall that the claim of those who have been denied the benefit is not, on this conception of the wrong, dependent on their being the worst off of any group in society; it simply depends on the fact that they lack access to a relevant basic good, and this fact is not changed by the way in which the legislation affects others.

D. *It diminishes individuals' feelings of self-worth*

A further way of understanding the wrong of unequal treatment is in terms of injury to a person's sense of self-worth. This way of understanding the wrong appeals to a subjective conception of dignity. That is, it is concerned not with the objective idea of individual worth that we earlier saw was central to the abstract ideal of equal concern and respect for dignity, but with the individual's own perception of her self-worth—with whether the individual believes herself to have worth as a human being or feels as though she is worthless. This subjective conception of dignity is essentially a conception of self-respect. Hence, this way of understanding the wrong of unequal treatment is as an injury to the individual's self-respect. The individual has been made to feel as though she is worthless.

As Scanlon has argued, however, many quite legitimate policies that recognize and reward some individuals' initiative or labour will make others feel that they are of lesser worth. For instance, a law firm's policy of giving bonuses to lawyers who bill over and above the target hours will inevitably result in certain other lawyers feeling as though they are of lesser worth, even if the policy is applied in a manner that seems wholly fair and unobjectionable. The feelings of inferiority generated in the lawyers who do not receive the bonus will seem to us simply an unfortunate side effect of the policy, not grounds for thinking that it wrongs these individuals.

What examples like this suggest is that the mere fact that unequal treatment decreases the self-respect of those who are denied the benefit is not sufficient to render that treatment unfair. It follows, therefore, that this way of understanding the wrong of unequal treatment cannot stand on its own as a complete explanation of why certain forms of differential treatment are objectionable. We will deem a person's feelings of inferiority an appropriate object of redress, as a matter of equality rights, only if we have already determined that the differential treatment of this person was unfair, or amounted to a wrong, in light of one of the other conceptions of the wrong that is done by unequal treatment. It may be that, once the differential treatment has been shown to amount to a wrong of one or another of the types examined above, then the claimant can show that he has suffered a further wrong by losing his sense of self-worth as a result. But merely having one's sense of self-respect injured cannot, on its own, render unequal treatment unfair.

As we shall see, this has significant implications. For it suggests that, to the extent that the *Law* test reduces "dignity" to an experiential good (albeit one that is assessed from the perspective of a reasonable person in the claimant's position), it mistakenly tries to treat what can be at most one of the wrongs involved in discrimination as a full and complete account of these wrongs. And it thereby conceals the more important work that is done by the explanation of why the differential treatment is unfair in the first place— an explanation that cannot itself be provided by an appeal to the way in which the treatment has affected the claimant's feelings of self-respect.

CHAPTER TWENTY-FOUR

Language Rights

I. INTRODUCTION

Language has been a matter of the highest importance at every stage of Canadian constitutional development. Surprisingly, this preoccupation with language does not appear explicitly in those parts of the Constitution where one might expect to find reference. For example, ss. 91 and 92 of the *Constitution Act, 1867* contain no specific allocation of the subject of language to Parliament or to the legislatures. Instead, language is treated as an ancillary matter, which allows both levels of government to legislate with respect to language, subject to any specific limitations in the Constitution.

Section 133 of the *Constitution Act, 1867* marks an important compromise facilitating Confederation by setting down rules for language use in government and judicial activity at the federal level and in Quebec. As noted in Chapter 4, The Late Nineteenth Century: The Canadian Courts Under the Influence, similar guarantees were inserted in the *Manitoba Act, 1870*.

The Charter provisions relating to language (ss. 16 to 23) mark a more modern understanding of Canadian citizenship entitlements for those who are members of French and English minority language communities. This pattern is reflected in the amendment provisions of the *Constitution Act, 1982*, which make special provision for changes to the Constitution in respect to language in ss. 41(c) and 43(b).

In addition to these specific provisions, more general provisions may also be applicable. While language is not included in the prohibited grounds of discrimination in the equality guarantee in s. 15 of the Charter, it may someday be treated as an analogous ground, and language cases have arisen as division of powers concerns, as well as freedom of expression claims under the Charter.

Before turning to language rights litigation in our courts, the readings provide an introduction to the values and history underlying claims to constitutional protection of language rights. When you read the decisions of the Supreme Court of Canada, you will see that the Court, at times, affords protection to language claims as if they were fundamental human rights. On other occasions, the Court has taken the view that language rights are less fundamental and universal than other constitutional rights, and accordingly attract a less purposive mode of interpretation. This approach is based on the idea that language rights are rooted in historical, political compromises particular to Canada. While language rights may involve individuals, consider, as well, whether they are a form of group rights.

1337

A. Braën, "Language Rights"
in Michel Bastarache et al., eds., *Language Rights in Canada*
(Montreal: Les Éditions Yvon Blais, 1987) 3, at 25-30 (footnotes omitted)

The language issue has always been a dominant theme in Canadian life. Indeed, it was raised during the colonial period, from the first contacts between the French and English settlers and the native populations. ...

The French language arrived in this country at the beginning of the colonial period, with the first settlers from France. Contacts were quickly established between the French and English settlers who, in disregard of the native inhabitants, were in conflict over the possession of the territory. In 1713, by the *Treaty of Utrecht*, France surrendered to England its territory of Acadia which comprised, at that time, a large part of what are today the Maritime Provinces. The treaty preserved the freedom of the catholic religion, subject to the laws of England. No provision of the treaty referred to the language question but by the change in sovereignty, English became the language of administration. The English language rapidly became, especially after the Deportation of 1755, the only language of legislation and of the courts in the Maritime Provinces.

In Canada, with the surrender of Quebec in 1759, the evolution was different. The *Articles of Capitulation of Quebec* guaranteed the freedom of exercise of the catholic religion but did not refer to the question of language. Section 42 of the *Articles of Capitulation of Montreal, 1760*, provided for the continuation of the customs of the French population. Did this terminology form the basis for a certain protection of the French language? In any event, General Amherst merely stated that the inhabitants had become subjects of the king. Under the military government, caution seems to have been the guiding principle. The government allowed the use of the French language in the courts and in the drafting of ordinances. Indeed, this constitutes the origin of functional bilingualism in the legislation and in the administration of justice in Quebec.

In 1763, the *Treaty of Paris* officially ceded Canada to England. As in the former documents, freedom of exercise of the catholic religion is guaranteed but nothing is said on the issue of language. The *Royal Proclamation of October 7, 1763, Murray's Commission* on November 21, 1763 and the *Instructions to Governor Murray*, December 7, 1763 granted full scope to the Governor to introduce English private law and to promote the assimilation of the francophone population. This policy of assimilation, however, was rapidly overcome by the authorization to use the French language in the administration of justice. Increasing discontent on the part of the French-speaking population, political disturbances in the New England colonies and the desire to gain the trust of the francophone population of Canada resulted in the adoption by the British Parliament of the *Quebec Act* of 1774. This Act re-established French private law and guaranteed freedom of exercise of the catholic religion. None of its provisions dealt with language. At that time, however, language and religion were closely related. The debates and statutory registers of the legislative council were drafted in French and in English, as were the ordinances; bilingualism became established as a matter of course in the administration of justice.

After the Rebellion of 1837-1838, the constitution of 1791 was suspended. Lord Durham was appointed to conduct an inquiry. In his report he recommended, *inter alia*, the establishment of responsible government and the union of both provinces to ensure that the francophone population became a minority, in order to hasten its assimilation. In 1840, London adopted the *Act of Union*. Section 41 of that imperial Act abolished French as a language of legislation and provided that English be the only official language. The United Parliament mitigated this measure by adopting in 1848 an Act designed to establish a process of translation and of publication of the laws in both languages. The British Parliament repealed section 41 in 1848 and the courts seemed to pursue, during this period, a bilingual tradition. This system continued until Confederation, in 1867. Noting the fact, the Royal Commission on Bilingualism and Biculturalism has stated that Ontario, during 18 years, experienced a bilingual system.

The *Constitution Act, 1867*, contains only one provision granting language rights, section 93 of this Act having been held not germane to this issue. Section 133 specifies that everyone has a right to use the French or the English language in the debates or the business of the houses of Parliament of Canada and of Quebec. It provides moreover that the records and journals of those assemblies must be kept in both languages. Finally, everyone is entitled to the use of French or English before the courts established under the authority of the Parliament of Canada or that of Quebec. These provisions constitute, at the most, what has been termed "seminal official bilingualism."

Manitoba was created in 1870. Section 23 of the *Manitoba Act, 1870* is analogous to section 133. Despite this, the French-speaking population having become a minority, the Legislative Assembly of that province adopted in 1890 an Act declaring English to be the only official language of legislation and the courts. The same year, the system of confessional schools was abolished and replaced by a public school system where the language of instruction was English. Except during a brief period where the Greenway-Laurier compromise was applied, that system was maintained. Only since the recent judicial challenges of the Act of 1890 has there been any important movement on the language question in that province.

The Northwest Territories and part of Rupert's Land were integrated with Canada in 1870 and placed under the authority of the Canadian Parliament. In 1877, the latter instituted bilingualism in the council and courts of those territories. A campaign on the part of opponents of the French fact incited the Canadian Parliament to amend its legislation in 1891 in order to enable the council to regulate its debate and records. Soon after that, in 1892 English unilingualism was decreed.

Saskatchewan and Alberta were admitted into the Union in 1905. The acts creating these provinces provide that the laws in force in those territories shall continue to apply thus making it arguable that the French language is endowed with some legal status. Recent judicial decisions have confirmed this point of view.

In Ontario, anti-catholic and anti-French pressure resulted in the adoption in 1912-1913, of regulation 17 which reduced to insignificant proportions the use of French as a language of instruction. Apart from the issue of official bilingualism, language in the educational context continued to be a problem in that province even after the adoption of the *Constitutional Act, 1982*. In 1986 a bill concerning government services in French was introduced.

Following the Laurendeau-Dunton report, the Canadian Parliament adopted, in 1969, its *Official Languages Act*. The Act was severely tested at the time of the air controllers' crisis in 1976. Also inspired by that report and directed by the Robichaud Government,

New Brunswick, in 1968, adopted French and English as its two official languages. In 1981, an Act went as far as to recognize the equality of both official language communities. Despite this, the establishment of true bilingualism in that province appears a difficult objective, judging by the reactions to a recent report *Towards Equality of Official Languages in New Brunswick* (Bastarache-Poirier report).

On many occasions, Quebec has legislated in matters of language. However, the national question took on a new dimension with the adoption of the *French Language Charter* (Loi 101), in 1977. This Act provides that French be the only official language of legislation, of the administration of justice and of public administration. Even if the language rights of the English-speaking minority are generally recognized, in particular its educational rights, some aspects of that Act are heavily criticized, such as the provisions dealing with the language of business signs and the language of instruction of new immigrants. An impressive series of court challenges has partly dismantled this legislative scheme.

Patriation of the Canadian constitution was effected by the adoption of the *Constitution Act, 1982*. Sections 16 to 22 of this Act set out the language guarantees of Canadians with respect to the Federal Government and the Government of New Brunswick. Section 23 affirms the right to instruction in an official minority language and to minority administered educational facilities. Since then, a number of court challenges have attempted to determine the scope of this section.

P.A. Coulombe, *Language Rights in French Canada*
(New York: Peter Lang, 1995), at 90-94 (endnotes omitted)

Justifying Strong Language Rights

Whether we are talking about official bilingualism at the federal level, Quebec's Bill 101, or New Brunswick's Bill 88, community rights such as these are often perceived as illiberal attacks on universal moral rights that protect autonomy. While it is true that an important strand of democratic tradition is conceived along those lines, it tends to obfuscate the justifications for these rights. Anglophones living in North America do not need to think about protecting the English language simply because market forces always privilege the dominant linguistic group. Moreover, allophone immigrants will choose to learn English as the dominant language in order to maximize their chances of integration and upward mobility. This process guarantees a continued supply (so to speak) of new anglophones and brings further pressures to assimilate all linguistic minorities, including French. Given these demolinguistic conditions, how could the Quebec state afford to be culturally neutral? How could the New Brunswick government not recognize community rights for Acadia? The rationale for state intervention in linguistic matters is no different from the rationale for intervening in matters such as social welfare, education, the environment and security: market forces benefit the powerful and, in this particular case, are incapable of sustaining linguistic minorities and of fostering proper relations between the various language groups of a given polity.

Many will object to such arguments, invoking the danger that strong language rights pose to individual freedoms. Language rights, they will say, should be limited to the protection of some of the conditions for personal autonomy, such as the right to freedom of action within one's own private affairs. These would include the rights against undue interference in private language use and against discrimination on the basis of language. Few are those who will deny us the right to speak our language at home and on the streets, to use it in letters and on the telephone, to keep our native names and surnames, to use our language within our cultural and religious institutions, newspapers, radio stations, and community centres. We could also add to this list the right to an interpreter in judicial proceedings, a language right derived from the right to a fair trial.

Why are these language rights more easily defensible? Because they are typically associated with state tolerance, or, put differently, they are rights *against* state interference rather than ones that require a positive state intervention. The right not to be interfered with within one's private sphere of language activity and that of not being discriminated against on the basis of language are derived from the right to privacy and fairness, respectively. They can be grounded in the interests of all citizens of a liberal polity, regardless of their particular community status. Were I the last person speaking my language, I would still have the right against undue interference and discrimination. For our purposes such rights can be called negative language rights, for the duties they involve are negative duties: *not* interfering in a person's language use, and treating everyone equally *regardless* of the language spoken.

Negative language rights are recognized in the *International Covenant on Civil and Political Rights*. Section 26 reads as follows:

> All persons are equal before the law and are entitled without any discrimination to equal protection of the law. In this respect the law shall prohibit any discrimination and guarantee to all persons equal and effective protection against discrimination on any ground such as race, color, sex, *language*, religion, political or other opinion, national or social origin, birth or other status. [my emphasis]

Moreover, section 27 states:

> In those States in which ethnic, religious or linguistic minorities exist, persons belonging to such minorities shall not be denied the right, *in community with the other members of their group*, to enjoy their own culture, to profess and practise their own religion, or to use their own language. [my emphasis]

… Positive state intervention is necessary to promote minority languages, for their vulnerability in a free market environment cannot be disputed. Unrestrained competition between languages will not bring about linguistic harmony, but a subordination of minority languages to the dominant language, and a subordination of the minority community to the dominant community. The idea of state neutrality is deceitful in this context, for laissez-faire de facto prejudices the dominant language in terms of its use and status. …

As far as Quebec is concerned, the reasons for active state language planning are many, but most are primarily socioeconomic: despite its solid majority status—approximately 80% of the Quebecois have had French as a mother tongue during this century—French was long subordinate to English, especially in the economy where English was the language of those who held economic power. Before state intervention, French was

used in the lower echelons of economic life, while English was used in the upper echelons, and so bilingualism was experienced differently depending if one was French- or
English-speaking: "The social pressures for using French as a language of communication at work are more strongly felt by lower status anglophones, while the pressures to
use English increases as francophones rise in the corporate world." In this cultural division of labour, the subordinate position of the French language and the subordinate position of French Canadians appeared as two sides of the same coin since francophones and
anglophones were not equals in the economic realm. In short, French would tend to be
relegated to the private sphere, in the homes, schools, and churches. …

This situation was compounded by the widely held belief that even in French-speaking
Quebec English is the language of prestige. As Gerard Bergeron notes, it was natural to
believe so when generations after generations saw that all important things happen in
English, and that knowing English opens the doors to the good life. Moreover, a study
comparing French- and English-speakers of equal education and job status revealed that
English-speakers were perceived by both anglophones *and* francophones as being more
intelligent, having a better job and a higher education. The inferiority complex of French
Canadians, reflecting a low self-esteem, led some to despise their origins and to identify
with the Anglo-American lifestyle. There was some truth to the idea that capital spoke
English and labour spoke French, and linguistic identity and self-esteem were certain to
suffer from it. Not surprisingly, diagnosing this disequilibrium motivated a corresponding state intervention.

Another reason for state language planning remains the need to respond to demolinguistic factors which threaten Quebec's relative weight in the federation, not to
mention French Canada's cultural security within Quebec itself. The decline of Quebec's
population relative to the Canadian whole translates itself into a greater minority status
for Quebec within the federation. Quebec's share of members of Parliament went from
33.5% in 1867 to 25.4% in 1990, and is expected to go down to 20% or less in about a
century. In addition to weakening Quebec's political power in the federation, the demographic decline of the Quebecois population of French origins creates a cultural insecurity insofar as traditional cultural traits are lost.

Jacques Henripin cites three demographic challenges facing Quebec. First, the birth
rate of the Quebecois (1.6 children per couple) is inferior to the required rate for replacing generations (2 children per couple); as a result, the population is growing old. A second problem is the high emigration rate towards other provinces. Anglophones leave
Quebec at a rate fifteen times higher than francophones, allophones (those who have
neither French nor English as a mother tongue) at a rate five times higher. This means
that immigration, despite what is often believed, contributes little to counteracting the
low birth rate since Quebec must accept three immigrants in order to keep one. A third
problem relates to the difficult integration of immigrants in Montreal, in part because of
the attraction that the English language has there. English is still the language which
most immigrants adopt, although the situation is improving.

Before Bill 101, immigrant parents, especially those living in Montreal, would often
choose English as the language of schooling for their children. In 1970, 8.3% of students
in Montreal's English schools were French, while only 1.9% of students in French schools
were English. Significantly, 22.5% of students in English schools were allophones, com-

pared to merely 0.9% in French schools. And in 1961, language transfers of allophones toward French were in the proportion of 23.2% in Montreal, as compared with 56.6% in the rest of Quebec. Between 1945 and 1966, 80% of immigrants integrated into the anglophone community of Quebec, the great majority of them in Montreal.

Various studies and governmental reports have concurred that these concerns were and still are legitimate and, thus, that there are grounds for taking steps to ensure that the French language is protected in Quebec, namely by sending an unequivocal message to immigrants: French, not English, is the majority language in Quebec. Even the Supreme Court of Canada argued that the circumstances discussed above "favored the use of the English language despite the predominance in Quebec of a francophone population … prior to the enactment of the legislation at issue [Bill 101] … ." No one seriously challenges the difficulties French is facing in Quebec; what is debated is the scope of language legislation and its impact on other language rights.

As can be expected, Acadians also have had to face major sociodemographic obstacles, but with little or no collective means at their disposal. Assimilation has reached high levels in Prince Edward Island and Nova Scotia, where by 1961 the majority of those of French extraction no longer declared French as their mother tongue. And of those who could still speak French, less than 40% spoke it at home by 1971.

II. LANGUAGE RIGHTS AND THE CONSTITUTION

A. The Federal Bargain

As noted earlier, while federalism as a system of government was adopted in part to deal with the claims of French-speaking Canadians, ss. 91 and 92 of the *Constitution Act, 1867* are silent in respect to language. As noted in Chapter 3, From Contact to Confederation, it was the opportunity that federalism offered for French-speakers to form a majority in Quebec and, thus, to make laws on a wide range of subjects, rather than the content of the division of powers as between the federal and provincial governments in respect to language specifically, that made the 1867 arrangements acceptable to many Quebecois.

Section 133 of the *Constitution Act, 1867* is the provision that embodies the express, original constitutional bargain in respect to language. The section addresses the language issue in the context of parliamentary debate, legislative enactment, and court proceedings. It establishes entitlements to the use of English and French in legislative and judicial proceedings at the federal level and in Quebec only. No such language requirements are imposed on the other original provinces by the *Constitution Act, 1867*. Section 133 provides:

> Either the English or the French Language may be used by any Person in the Debates of the Houses of the Parliament of Canada and of the Houses of the Legislature of Quebec; and both those Languages shall be used in the respective Records and Journals of those Houses; and either of those Languages may be used by any Person or in any Pleading or Process in or issuing from any Court of Canada established under this Act, and in or from all or any of the Courts of Quebec.
>
> The Acts of the Parliament of Canada and of the Legislature of Quebec shall be printed and published in both those Languages.

This final version of s. 133 was more stringent than its earlier drafts, which had merely permitted, rather than mandated, publication of legislative journals and laws in both English and French. The mandated use of both languages prevailed in order to preclude the possibility that the majority in the federal or Quebec legislatures might choose to publish parliamentary proceedings and enactments only in its own language and thus prejudice the minority language group.

Jones v. AG New Brunswick, [1975] 2 SCR 182, 45 DLR (3d) 583 addressed the ability of the federal Parliament to enact the *Official Languages Act* [now RSC 1985, c. 31 (4th Supp.)], which made English and French the official languages of Canada within federal institutions, such as Parliament and the courts under federal jurisdiction. The Supreme Court of Canada upheld the federal Act, as well as New Brunswick legislation (enacted under the s. 92(14) class of subject "Administration of Justice in the Province"), which similarly stipulated that both French and English were the official languages of the courts of that province. The Court made clear that s. 133 of the *Constitution Act, 1867* set down minimum constitutional protection for language, but this did not preclude Parliament or a legislature from conferring additional "rights or privileges" or imposing additional "obligations" in respect to the English and French languages. The only proviso was that the enacting legislature must conform to the rules of the division of powers.

The Court returned to the question of general legislative jurisdiction in respect to language in *Devine v. AG Quebec*, [1988] 2 SCR 790, 55 DLR (4th) 641. One question before the Court was the legislative jurisdiction of the National Assembly to enact those parts of Quebec's *Charter of the French Language* that mandated the use of French, and in some instances French only, in commercial dealings. In a unanimous judgment, the Court ruled that this legislation fell within provincial legislative jurisdiction:

> In order to be valid, provincial legislation with respect to language must be truly in relation to an institution or activity that is otherwise within provincial legislative jurisdiction. ...
>
> It is true, as the preamble of the *Charter of the French Language* indicates, that one of its objects is "to make of French the language of ... commerce and business" but that object necessarily involves the regulation of an aspect of commerce and business within the province, whatever the nature of the effect of such regulation may be. The purpose and effect of the challenged provisions of Chapter VII of the *Charter of the French Language* entitled "The Language of Commerce and Business" is to regulate an aspect of the manner in which commerce and business in the province may be carried on and as such they are in relation to such commerce and business. That the overall object of the *Charter of the French Language* is the enhancement of the status of the French language in Quebec does not make the challenged provisions any less an intended regulation of an aspect of commerce within the province. As such, they fall within provincial legislative jurisdiction under the *Constitution Act, 1867*.

The 1867 language strictures set down in s. 133 were applicable only to the federal government and to Quebec. Similar requirements were applied later to Manitoba, Saskatchewan, and Alberta when they entered Confederation. The *Manitoba Act, 1870*, SC 1870, c. 3, s. 23, passed by Parliament and confirmed by the UK Parliament, applied the s. 133 type requirements to the new province of Manitoba. (See *British North America Act, 1871*, ss. 5 and 6.) The *North-West Territories Act*, RSC 1886, c. 50, s. 110, a non-entrenched enactment, provided similar language guarantees for the territory that would become Saskatchewan and Alberta. These provisions reflected the fact that the population of these provinces at the time was largely French-speaking and was expected to stay that way.

In deliberate contradiction to the terms of the *Manitoba Act, 1870* requiring the use of both languages, Manitoba passed the *Official Language Act* in 1890, which set down that English only would be the language of the legislature and the courts. Lower court rulings in 1892, 1909, and 1976 invalidated this enactment, finding it inconsistent with the requirements of the entrenched *Manitoba Act*. The Manitoba governments at the time of these court rulings did not treat these decisions as authoritative, although they did not appeal. One might have expected that these decisions, and the failure of the Manitoba government to comply or appeal, would have become the subject of intense political debate, both in Manitoba and nationally. The demographic makeup of the province had changed so much in the intervening decades, however, that the French-speaking minority lacked the political clout to press their cause further. Moreover, as described in Chapter 4, The Late Nineteenth Century: The Canadian Courts Under the Influence, the energy of that community was at the time directed at opposing provincial policies diminishing the opportunity for education in French in the denominational schools.

The question of the validity of the 1890 legislation finally reached the Supreme Court of Canada in *AG Manitoba v. Forest*, [1979] 2 SCR 1032, 101 DLR (3d) 385. The Court ruled that the entrenched *Manitoba Act* provisions prevailed over the provincial enactment. This ruling raised the possibility that all the enactments of the Manitoba legislature since 1890 were invalid, because they had been enacted only in English. In *Reference re Manitoba Language Rights*, [1985] 1 SCR 721, 19 DLR (4th) 1 (*Manitoba Language Reference*), the Supreme Court considered this possibility. It characterized the strictures of the *Manitoba Act*, requiring the enactment of all legislation in both English and French, as mandatory and not merely directory—with the consequence that the body of Manitoba legislation passed in breach of the language enactment requirement was invalid. To avoid a legal vacuum, the Court went on to recognize the temporary validity of these laws until the language requirements could be satisfied by translation, through a temporary suspension of the declaration of invalidity. (This aspect of the decision is discussed further in Chapter 25, Enforcement of Rights.) The Court identified the purpose of both s. 133 of the *Constitution Act, 1867* and of the *Manitoba Act, 1870* as "to ensure full and equal access to the legislatures, the laws and the courts for francophones and anglophones alike." The Court stated:

> The importance of language rights is grounded in the essential role that language plays in human existence, development and dignity. It is through language that we are able to form concepts; to structure and order the world around us. Language bridges the gap between isolation and community, allowing humans to delineate the rights and duties they hold in respect of one another, and thus to live in society.

Similar litigation arose in Saskatchewan and Alberta, in respect to the availability of French language court proceedings. In *Mercure v. AG Saskatchewan*, [1988] 1 SCR 234, 48 DLR (4th) 1, the accused applied to have the provincial court proceed with his trial in French on the basis of s. 110 of the *North-West Territories Act*. The Supreme Court found that this Act was continued in force by s. 16 of the *Saskatchewan Act, 1905*. Section 110 provided language rights substantially the same as s. 133 of the *Constitution Act, 1867*. However, the Court differentiated the legal regime of language requirements in Saskatchewan from that in Manitoba. The *Manitoba Act* was constitutionally entrenched and bound the legislature of Manitoba; the Saskatchewan legislature, however, was free to alter the terms of the *North-West Territories Act*, because it was not entrenched. Following this ruling, the Saskatchewan legislature enacted legislation dispensing with the language stipulations mirroring s. 133— in part to avoid the necessity of having to translate and re-enact all its statutes passed only in English (*Language Act*, SS 1988, c. L-6.1).

A similar holding with regard to Alberta, in *R v. Paquette*, [1990] 2 SCR 1103, 73 DLR (4th) 575, led to similar legislation in that province (*Languages Act*, SA 1988, c. L-7.5).

B. Charter Language Rights

As discussed earlier in Chapter 16, The Advent of the Charter, many commentators view language rights as the original core of the Charter project. Whether or not this historical view is correct, ss. 16 to 23 of the Charter constitute strong recognition of the major importance of language in Canadian constitutionalism. These sections recognize the official, equal status of English and French in the business of the federal and New Brunswick governments and also provide guarantees to minority language education throughout Canada in certain circumstances. The detail and range of these provisions reflect fidelity to the idea of Canada as a country founded by English- and French-speaking people. With respect to minority language education, at least, the Constitution also espouses a form of "personality principle" of language, rather than a solely territorial one—provinces cannot opt for unilingualism, and an individual's right to French or English education can be exercised throughout the country.

The provisions pose interesting questions about the continuing role of this idea of Canada in the context of a country that today possesses a dramatically different demographic makeup than it did in 1867, as well as greater sensitivity to both the historical and the current claims of its Aboriginal inhabitants.

Sections 16 to 23 contain a number of striking features. For example, s. 16 introduces the language of equality into the formulation of language entitlements: "English and French are the official languages of Canada and have equality of status and equal rights and privileges as to their use in all institutions of the Parliament and government of Canada." Sections 16(2), 17(2), 18(2), 19(2), and 20(2) bring New Brunswick into the regime of institutional bilingualism, discussed earlier in reference to the prairie provinces. Added to the legislative and judicial contexts is the availability of communication with federal and New Brunswick government institutions in either English or French. Considerable pressure was brought to bear upon Ontario to take on these constitutional strictures as well, but the Ontario government has resisted on the grounds that incremental, statutory adherence to institutional bilingualism was more acceptable in the prevailing political climate.

A further section concerning linguistic rights in New Brunswick was added on April 7, 1993, when the *Constitution Act, 1982* was amended (under s. 43 of that Act) to include the following:

> 16.1(1) The English linguistic community and the French linguistic community in New Brunswick have equality of status and equal rights and privileges, including the right to distinct educational institutions and such distinct cultural institutions as are necessary for the preservation and promotion of those communities.

(2) The role of the legislature and government of New Brunswick to preserve and promote the status, rights and privileges referred to in subsection (1) is affirmed.

III. INTERPRETING LANGUAGE RIGHTS

As you read the cases that follow, note the different approaches taken by the Supreme Court of Canada in the interpretation of language rights. The first case deals with s. 133, while those following interpret Charter provisions.

AG Quebec v. Blaikie (No. 1)
[1979] 2 SCR 1016, 101 DLR (3d) 394

[*Blaikie* raised three issues regarding the interpretation of s. 133 of the *Constitution Act, 1867* in the context of Quebec's *Charter of the French Language*, which made French the official language of the province. The first issue was the content of s. 133's requirement that "Acts" of "the Legislature of Quebec" (that is, the Quebec National Assembly) "be printed and published" in both English and French. The Supreme Court determined that the National Assembly of Quebec did not comply with s. 133 when it produced merely unofficial English translations of its enactments, including subordinate legislation. The second issue was whether regulations issued under the authority of Quebec statutes were held to be "Acts" within s. 133; the Court held that they were. The excerpt below deals with the third issue—whether the right to use English or French before "any of the Courts of Quebec" extended to adjudicative tribunals.]

THE COURT (Laskin CJC, Martland, Ritchie, Pigeon, Dickson, Beetz, Estey, Pratte, and McIntyre JJ): ... [T]he reference in s. 133 to "any of the Courts of Quebec" ought to be considered broadly as including not only so-called s. 96 [of the *Constitution Act, 1867*] Courts but also Courts established by the Province and administered by provincially appointed Judges. It is not a long distance from this latter class of tribunal to those which exercise judicial power, although they are not courts in the traditional sense. If they are statutory agencies which are adjudicative, applying legal principles to the assertion of claims under their constituent legislation, rather than settling issues on grounds of expediency or administrative policy, they are judicial bodies, however some of their procedures may differ not only from those of Courts but also from those of other adjudicative bodies. In the rudimentary state of administrative law in 1867, it is not surprising that there was no reference to non-curial adjudicative agencies. Today, they play a significant role in the control of a wide range of individual and corporate activities, subjecting them to various norms of conduct which are at the same time limitations on the jurisdiction of the agencies and on the legal position of those caught by them. The guarantee given for the use of French or English in Court proceedings should not be liable to curtailment by provincial substitution of adjudicative agencies for Courts to such extent as is compatible with s. 96 of the *British North America Act, 1867.*

Two judgments of the Privy Council, which wrestled with similar questions of principle in the construction of the *British North America Act, 1867* are, to some degree, apposite here. In *Edwards v. Attorney General of Canada*, [1930] AC 124, the "persons" case (respecting the qualification of women for appointment to the Senate under s. 24), there are observations by Lord Sankey of the need to give the *British North America Act* a broad interpretation attuned to changing circumstances: "The *British North America Act*," he said, at p. 136, "planted in Canada a living tree capable of growth and expansion within its natural limits." Dealing, as this Court is here, with a constitutional guarantee, it would be overly technical to ignore the modern development of non-curial adjudicative agencies which play so important a role in our society, and to refuse to extend to proceedings before them the guarantee to the right to use either French or English by those subject to their jurisdiction.

In *Attorney General of Ontario v. Attorney General of Canada*, [1947] AC 127 (the *Privy Council Appeals Reference*), Viscount Jowitt said in the course of his discussion of the issues, that "it is, as their Lordships think, irrelevant that the question is one that might have seemed unreal at the date of the *British North America Act*. To such an organic statute the flexible interpretation must be given which changing circumstances require" (at p. 154).

Although there are clear points of distinction between these two cases and the issue of the scope of s. 133, in its reference to the Courts of Quebec, they nonetheless lend support to what is to us the proper approach to an entrenched provision, that is, to make it effective through the range of institutions which exercise judicial power, be they called courts or adjudicative agencies. In our opinion, therefore, the guarantee and requirements of s. 133 extend to both.

It follows that the guarantee in s. 133 of the use of either French or English "by any person or in any pleading or process in or issuing from ... all or any of the Courts of Quebec" applies to both ordinary Courts and other adjudicative tribunals. Hence, not only is the option to use either language given to any person involved in proceedings before the Courts of Quebec or its other adjudicative tribunals (and this covers both written and oral submissions) but documents emanating from such bodies or issued in their name or under their authority may be in either language, and this option extends to the issuing and publication of judgments or other orders.

NOTES

1. In *AG Quebec v. Blaikie (No. 2)*, [1981] 1 SCR 312, 123 DLR (3d) 15, the Court further elaborated on its earlier pronouncement by finding that subordinate legislation made by non-governmental officials or bodies, but subject to government approval, fell within the requirements of enactment in both English and French as did the rules of practice in the courts. In contrast, municipal bylaws and school board bylaws fell outside the requirements of s. 133, because those regulations did not require governmental approval to be legally effective. In reaching these conclusions, the Court rejected the argument put forward by Quebec that its authority to amend its provincial constitution, under then s. 92(1) of the *Constitution Act, 1867*, extended to alteration of the provisions of s. 133 applicable to the province. A similar argument was rejected in the companion case, *AG Manitoba v. Forest*, [1979] 2 SCR 1032, 101 DLR (3d) 385 with respect to the *Manitoba Act*.

2. The case that follows, *Société des Acadiens*, deals with language rights under s. 19(2) of the Charter in court proceedings. It was decided on the same day as *MacDonald v. City of Montreal*, [1986] 1 SCR 688, 27 DLR (4th) 321, which interpreted s. 133 of the *Constitution Act, 1867*. In *Société des Acadiens*, the appellants objected that a member of the New Brunswick Court of Appeal, who sat on a leave to appeal application, did not have sufficient knowledge of French to understand their argument in that language, and thus their rights under s. 19(2) of the Charter were infringed. In *MacDonald*, the appellant relied on s. 133 of the *Constitution Act, 1867* to object to the validity of a summons issued only in French by the Municipal Court of Montreal. Both cases reached the same result—the provisions guarantee the litigant the right to choose to use French or English in the course of judicial proceedings, but they do not guarantee that the proceedings themselves will be conducted in the language that he or she chooses.

Société des Acadiens du Nouveau-Brunswick Inc. v. Association of Parents for Fairness in Education
[1986] 1 SCR 460, 27 DLR (4th) 406

BEETZ J (Estey, Chouinard, Lamer, and Le Dain JJ concurring): ... It is my view that the rights guaranteed by s. 19(2) of the Charter are of the same nature and scope as those guaranteed by s. 133 of the *Constitution Act, 1867* with respect to the courts of Canada and the courts of Quebec. As was held by the majority at pp. 40-5 (DLR) in *MacDonald*, these are essentially language rights unrelated to and not to be confused with the requirements of natural justice. These language rights are the same as those which are guaranteed by s. 17 of the Charter with respect to parliamentary debates. They vest in the speaker or in the writer or issuer of court processes and give the speaker or the writer the constitutionally protected power to speak or to write in the official language of his choice. And there is no language guarantee, either under s. 133 of the *Constitution Act, 1867,* or s. 19 of the Charter, any more than under s. 17 of the Charter, that the speaker will be heard or understood, or that he has the right to be heard or understood in the language of his choice.

I am reinforced in this view by the contrasting wording of s. 20 of the Charter. Here, the Charter has expressly provided for the right to communicate in either official language with some offices of an institution of the Parliament or Government of Canada and with any office of an institution of the Legislature or Government of New Brunswick. The right to communicate in either language postulates the right to be heard or understood in either language.

I am further reinforced in this view by the fact that those who drafted the Charter had another explicit model they could have used had they been so inclined, namely s. 13(1) of the *Official Languages of New Brunswick Act*, RSNB 1973, c. O-1:

> 13(1) Subject to section 15, in any proceeding before a court, any person appearing or giving evidence may be heard in the official language of his choice and such choice is not to place that person at any disadvantage.

Here again, s. 13(1) of the Act, unlike the Charter, has expressly provided for the right to be heard in the official language of one's choice. Those who drafted s. 19(2) of the

Charter and agreed to it could easily have followed the language of s. 13(1) of the *Official Languages of New Brunswick Act* instead of that of s. 133 of the *Constitution Act, 1867*. That they did not do so is a clear signal that they wanted to provide for a different effect, namely the effect of s. 133. If the people of the Province of New Brunswick were agreeable to have a provision like s. 13(1) of the *Official Languages of New Brunswick Act* as part of their law, they did not agree to see it entrenched in the Constitution. I do not think it should be forced upon them under the guise of constitutional interpretation.

The only other provision, apart from s. 20, in that part of the Charter entitled "Official Languages of Canada," which ensures communication or understanding in both official languages is that of s. 18. It provides for bilingualism at the legislative level. In *MacDonald* one can read the following passage, in the reasons of the majority, at pp. 37-8 (DLR):

> Section 133 has not introduced a comprehensive scheme or system of official bilingualism, even potentially, but a limited form of compulsory bilingualism at the legislative level, combined with an even more limited form of optional unilingualism at the option of the speaker in Parliamentary debates and at the option of the speaker, writer or issuer in judicial proceedings or processes. Such a limited scheme can perhaps be said to facilitate communication and understanding, up to a point, but only as far as it goes and it does not guarantee that the speaker, writer or issuer of proceedings or processes will be understood in the language of his choice by those he is addressing.

The scheme has now been made more comprehensive in the Charter with the addition of New Brunswick to Quebec—and Manitoba—and with new provisions such as s. 20. But where the scheme deliberately follows the model of s. 133 of the *Constitution Act, 1867*, as it does in s. 19(2), it should, in my opinion, be similarly construed.

I must again cite a passage of the reasons of the majority, at p. 44, in *MacDonald* relating to s. 133 of the *Constitution Act, 1867* but which is equally applicable, *a fortiori*, to the official languages provisions of the Charter:

> This is not to put the English and the French languages on the same footing as other languages. Not only are the English and the French languages placed in a position of equality, they are also given a preferential position over all other languages. And this equality as well as this preferential position are both constitutionally protected by s. 133 of the *Constitution Act, 1867*. Without the protection of this provision, one of the two official languages could, by simple legislative enactment, be given a degree of preference over the other as was attempted in Chapter III of Title 1 of the *Charter of the French Language*, invalidated in *Blaikie No. 1*. English unilingualism, French unilingualism and, for that matter, unilingualism in any other language could also be imposed by simple legislative enactment. Thus it can be seen that, if s. 133 guarantees but a minimum, this minimum is far from being insubstantial.

The common law right of the parties to be heard and understood by a court and the right to understand what is going on in court is not a language right but an aspect of the right to a fair hearing. It is a broader and more universal right than language rights. It extends to everyone including those who speak or understand neither official language. It belongs to the category of rights which in the Charter are designated as legal rights and indeed it is protected at least in part by provisions such as those of ss. 7 and 14 of the Charter ... .

The fundamental nature of this common law right to a fair hearing was stressed in *MacDonald*, in the reasons of the majority, at p. 43:

> It should be absolutely clear however that this common law right to a fair hearing, including the right of the defendant to understand what is going on in court and to be understood is a fundamental right deeply and firmly embedded in the very fabric of the Canadian legal system. That is why certain aspects of this right are entrenched in general as well as specific provisions of the *Charter* such as s. 7, relating to life, liberty and security of the person and s. 14, relating to the assistance of an interpreter. While Parliament or the Legislature of a province may, pursuant to s. 33 of the *Charter*, expressly declare that an Act or a provision thereof shall operate notwithstanding a provision included in s. 2 or ss. 7 to 15 of the *Charter*, it is almost inconceivable that they would do away altogether with the fundamental common law right itself, assuming that they could do so.

While legal rights as well as language rights belong to the category of fundamental rights,

> [i]t would constitute an error either to import the requirements of natural justice into ... language rights ... or vice versa, or to relate one type of right to the other ... . Both types of rights are conceptually different ... . To link these two types of rights is to risk distorting both rather than re-enforcing either.

> ... Unlike language rights which are based on political compromise, legal rights tend to be seminal in nature because they are rooted in principle. Some of them, such as the one expressed in s. 7 of the Charter, are so broad as to call for frequent judicial determination.

> Language rights, on the other hand, although some of them have been enlarged and incorporated into the Charter, remain nonetheless founded on political compromise.

> This essential difference between the two types of rights dictates a distinct judicial approach with respect to each. More particularly, the courts should pause before they decide to act as instruments of change with respect to language rights. This is not to say that language rights provisions are cast in stone and should remain immune altogether from judicial interpretation. But, in my opinion, the courts should approach them with more restraint than they would in construing legal rights.

> Such an attitude of judicial restraint is in my view compatible with s. 16 of the Charter, the introductory section of the part entitled "Official Languages of Canada."

> Section 19(2) being the substantive provision which governs the case at bar, we need not concern ourselves with the substantive content of s. 16, whatever it may be. But something should be said about the interpretative effect of s. 16 as well as the question of the equality of the two official languages.

> I think it is accurate to say that s. 16 of the Charter does contain a principle of advancement or progress in the equality of status or use of the two official languages. I find it highly significant however that this principle of advancement is linked with the legislative process referred to in s. 16(3), which is a codification of the rule in *Jones v. Attorney General of New Brunswick*, [1975] 2 SCR 182. The legislative process, unlike the judicial one, is a political process and hence particularly suited to the advancement of rights founded on political compromise.

One should also take into consideration the constitutional amending formula with respect to the use of official languages. Under s. 41(c) of the *Constitution Act, 1982*, the unanimous consent of the Senate and House of Commons and of the legislative assembly of each province is required for that purpose but "subject to section 43." Section 43 provides for the constitutional amendment of provisions relating to some but not all provinces and requires the "resolutions of the Senate and House of Commons and of the legislative assembly of each province to which the amendment applies." It is public knowledge that some provinces other than New Brunswick—and apart from Quebec and Manitoba—were expected ultimately to opt into the constitutional scheme or part of the constitutional scheme prescribed by ss. 16 to 22 of the Charter, and a flexible form of constitutional amendment was provided to achieve such an advancement of language rights. But again, this is a form of advancement brought about through a political process, not a judicial one.

If however the provinces were told that the scheme provided by ss. 16 to 22 of the Charter was inherently dynamic and progressive, apart from legislation and constitutional amendment, and that the speed of progress of this scheme was to be controlled mainly by the courts, they would have no means to know with relative precision what it was that they were opting into. This would certainly increase their hesitation in so doing and would run contrary to the principle of advancement contained in s. 16(3).

In my opinion, s. 16 of the Charter confirms the rule that the courts should exercise restraint in their interpretation of language rights provisions.

I do not think the interpretation I adopt for s. 19(2) of the Charter offends the equality provision of s. 16. Either official language may be used by anyone in any court of New Brunswick or written by anyone in any pleading in or process issuing from any such court. The guarantee of language equality is not, however, a guarantee that the official language used will be understood by the person to whom the pleading or process is addressed.

Before I leave this question of equality however, I wish to indicate that if one should hold that the right to be understood in the official language used in court is a language right governed by the equality provision of s. 16, one would have gone a considerable distance towards the adoption of a constitutional requirement which could not be met except by a bilingual judiciary. Such a requirement would have far reaching consequences and would constitute a surprisingly roundabout and implicit way of amending the judicature provisions of the Constitution of Canada. ...

[Dickson CJC and Wilson J each wrote separate reasons concurring in the conclusion that the appeal should be dismissed. However, both took the view that the right to use either English or French in court included the right to be understood by the judge or judges hearing the case. Dickson CJC left open the question of what techniques might satisfy this obligation—for example, the use of interpreters or simultaneous translation. Wilson J held that the judge's level of understanding "must be such that the full flavour of the argument can be appreciated" (at 474 DLR).]

NOTES

1. Whose interests are understood to be protected by s. 19(2) of the Charter in this case, or by s. 133 in *MacDonald*? Is the Court's approach to interpretation here consistent with its earlier approach in *Blaikie*?

2. What is the significance of this characterization of language rights as forged by historic political compromise? Is this characterization valid? Is the interpretive posture that flows from it inevitable?

3. The restrictive approach taken by *Société des Acadiens* and *MacDonald* to the interpretation of language rights attracted the criticism of the Court in two recent judgments. The first is *R v. Beaulac*, [1999] 1 SCR 768, 173 DLR (4th) 193. That case concerned the interpretation of ss. 530(1) and (4) of the *Criminal Code*, RSC 1985, c. C-46, which govern the language of criminal trials. In discussing the correct interpretation to be given to those provisions, Bastarache J (speaking for seven members of the Court) stated in *obiter* that "the existence of a political compromise is without consequence with regard to the scope of language rights," that "[l]anguage rights must in all cases be interpreted purposively, in a manner consistent with the preservation and development of official language communities in Canada," and that "[t]o the extent that *Société des Acadiens du Nouveau-Brunswick* stands for a restrictive interpretation of language rights, it is to be rejected" (citation omitted). Lamer CJC and Binnie J, although concurring in Bastarache J's interpretation of the relevant provisions of the Criminal Code, expressly distanced themselves from this aspect of Bastarache J's judgment, stating that "[a] re-assessment of the Court's approach to *Charter* language rights developed in *Société des Acadiens* and reiterated in subsequent cases is not necessary or desirable in this appeal." However, in *Arsenault-Cameron v. Prince Edward Island*, [2000] 1 SCR 3, 181 DLR (4th) 1, a case arising under s. 23 of the Charter (discussed below), the Court unanimously approved Bastarache J's statements in *Beaulac*, stating that "the fact that constitutional language rights resulted from a political compromise is not unique to language rights and does not affect their scope." Neither *Beaulac* nor *Arsenault-Cameron* dealt squarely with s. 19(2) of the Charter or s. 133 of the *Constitution Act, 1867*, the two constitutional provisions at issue in *Société des Acadiens* and *MacDonald*, and so the specific holdings in those decisions have not been overruled. But in light of *Beaulac* and *Arsenault-Cameron*, would those cases be decided the same way today?

4. Michael MacMillan notes that there are two ways to justify language rights: on the theoretical basis that they share the essential elements of human rights, and on a more empirical or inductive basis that supports language rights on the basis of public attitudes and social practices ("Linking Theory to Practice: Comments on 'The Constitutional Protection of Language,'" in D. Schneiderman, ed., *Language and the State: The Law and Politics of Identity* (Cowansville: Yvon Blais, 1991), at 59.

5. In *MacDonald*, Beetz J made a distinction between language rights and legal rights, explaining their interaction in the following quotation:

> Suppose that a person is charged with a criminal offence drafted in either the French or the English language and that person does not understand the language of the charge. It goes without saying that this person cannot be asked to plead and be tried upon the charge in these circumstances. What will happen as a matter of practice as well as of law is that the judge will call upon a sworn interpreter to translate the charge into a language that the accused can understand. But

this is so whether the accused speaks only German or Cantonese and has nothing to do with what s. 133 stands for. Provision is made for this different purpose by other enactments relating for instance to interpreters and under other principles of law some of which are now enshrined in the provisions of distinct constitutional or quasi-constitutional instruments, such as s. 2(g) of the *Canadian Bill of Rights* and s. 14 of the Charter, also relating to interpreters. ...

It is axiomatic that everyone has a common law right to a fair hearing, including the right to be informed of the case one has to meet and the right to make full answer and defence. Where the defendant cannot understand the proceedings because he is unable to understand the language in which they are being conducted, or because he is deaf, the effective exercise of these rights may well impose a consequential duty upon the court to provide adequate translation. But the right of the defendant to understand what is going on in court and to be understood is not a separate right, nor a language right, but an aspect of the right to a fair hearing.

The constitutional right to an interpreter in s. 14 of the Charter is discussed in *R v. Tran*, [1994] 2 SCR 951, 117 DLR (4th) 7.

Does the above discussion of English and French, as differentiated from other languages, reflect the special place of English and French in the history of the Canadian Constitution, or does it depart from that history in recognition of Canada as a multicultural—and thus multilingual—society?

6. Section 23 of the Charter contains the minority language education guarantees. It is distinctive in that it imposes obligations on all provinces, unlike the institutional bilingualism provisions that currently apply to Quebec, New Brunswick, and Manitoba. But not all of s. 23 applies in Quebec. By virtue of s. 59 of the *Constitution Act, 1982*, s. 23(1)(a) does not come into effect in Quebec until authorized by the "legislative assembly or government of Quebec." This provision reflects Quebec's concern that immigrants have tended to gravitate to the anglophone community. Therefore, access to English language education in Quebec depends on the parents being citizens who received primary school instruction in English in Canada.

Section 23 was the focus of one of the earliest Charter cases to reach the Supreme Court of Canada, *AG Quebec v. Quebec Association of Protestant School Boards*, [1984] 2 SCR 66, 10 DLR (4th) 321. The Court struck down the portions of Quebec's *Charter of the French Language* that gave access to English language schools only to the children of persons who had been educated in English *in Quebec*. This provision, known as the "Quebec clause," clashed with the "Canada clause" contained in s. 23(1)(b), which offered minority language schooling in Quebec to the children of parents who had received primary instruction in English not just in Quebec, but in any other part of Canada. The judgment of the Court characterized the legislation as having the purpose of ousting the Canada clause of the Charter, rather than limiting its reach. Therefore, s. 1 of the Charter could not save it.

7. The major Supreme Court judgment on s. 23 of the Charter is *Mahe v. Alberta*, which follows. For the Court, this case was the first attempt at determining the scope of the rights to educational facilities for minority language groups. Note how the Court tries to set out some general principles for application in this and the many other fact situations that will arise across the country—in effect, initiating an ongoing dialogue between courts and legislatures about the appropriate design of minority language educational systems.

Mahe v. Alberta
[1990] 1 SCR 342, 68 DLR (4th) 69

DICKSON CJC (Wilson, La Forest, L'Heureux-Dubé, Sopinka, Gonthier, and Cory JJ concurring): ... Section 23 is one component in Canada's constitutional protection of the official languages. The section is especially important in this regard, however, because of the vital role of education in preserving and encouraging linguistic and cultural vitality. It thus represents a linchpin in this nation's commitment to the values of bilingualism and biculturalism.

The appellants claim that their rights under s. 23 are not satisfied by the existing educational system in Edmonton nor by the legislation under which it operates, resulting in an erosion of their cultural heritage, contrary to the spirit and intent of the Charter. In particular, the appellants argue that s. 23 guarantees the right, in Edmonton, to the "management and control" of a minority-language school—that is, to a Francophone school run by a Francophone school board. Our task then is to determine the meaning of s. 23 of the Charter. ...

The appellants Jean-Claude Mahe and Paul Dubé are parents whose first language learned and still understood is French. The appellant Angeline Martel is a parent who received her primary school instruction in French. All three have school age children, and thus qualify under s. 23(1) of the Charter as persons who, subject to certain limitations, "have the right to have their children receive primary and secondary school instruction" in the language of the linguistic minority population of the province—in this case, the French language. They may therefore conveniently be called "s. 23 parents," and their children "s. 23 students." ...

At the heart of this appeal is the claim of the appellants that the term "minority language educational facilities" referred to in s. 23(3)(b) includes administration by distinct school boards. The respondent takes the position that the word "facilities" means a school building. The respondent submits that the rights of the Francophone minority in metropolitan Edmonton have not been denied because those rights are being met with current Francophone educational facilities. ...

The primary issue raised by this appeal is the degree, if any, of "management and control" of a French language school which should be accorded to s. 23 parents in Edmonton. (The phrase "management and control," it should be noted, is not a term of art: it appears to have been introduced in earlier s. 23 cases and has now gained such currency that it was utilized by all the groups in this appeal.) The appellants appear to accept that, with a few exceptions, the government has provided whatever other services or rights might be mandated in Edmonton under s. 23: their fundamental complaint is that they do not have the exclusive management and control of the existing Francophone schools. ...

There are two general questions which must be answered in order to decide this appeal: (1) do the rights which s. 23 mandates, depending upon the numbers of students, include a right to management and control; and (2) if so, is the number of students in Edmonton sufficient to invoke this right? I will begin with the first question.

It appeared to be common ground between the parties that if a right to management and control is provided by s. 23, it must be found in the right to "minority language educational facilities" set out in subs. (3)(b). Before this particular subsection can be examined, however, it is essential to consider two general matters: (1) the purpose of s. 23; and (2) the relationship between the different subsections and paragraphs which comprise s. 23. In interpreting s. 23, as in interpreting any provision of the Charter, it is crucial to consider the underlying purpose of the section. As to the second matter, the structure of s. 23 makes it imperative that each part of the section be read in the context of all of the constituent parts.

(1) The Purpose of Section 23

The general purpose of s. 23 is clear: it is to preserve and promote the two official languages of Canada, and their respective cultures, by ensuring that each language flourishes, as far as possible, in provinces where it is not spoken by the majority of the population. The section aims at achieving this goal by granting minority language educational rights to minority language parents throughout Canada.

My reference to cultures is significant: it is based on the fact that any broad guarantee of language rights, especially in the context of education, cannot be separated from a concern for the culture associated with the language. Language is more than a mere means of communication, it is part and parcel of the identity and culture of the people speaking it. It is the means by which individuals understand themselves and the world around them. The cultural importance of language was recognized by this Court in *Ford v. Attorney General (Quebec)*, [1988] 2 SCR 712, at pp. 748-49:

> Language is not merely a means or medium of expression; it colours the content and meaning of expression. It is, as the preamble of the *Charter of the French Language* itself indicates, *a means by which a people may express its cultural identity*. [Emphasis added.]

Similar recognition was granted by the Royal Commission on Bilingualism and Biculturalism, itself a major force in the eventual entrenchment of language rights in the Charter. At page 8 of Book II of its report, the Commission stated:

> Language is also the key to cultural development. Language and culture are not synonymous, but the vitality of the language is a necessary condition for the complete preservation of a culture.

And at p. 19, in a comment on the role of minority language schools, the Commission added:

> These schools are essential for the development of both official languages and cultures; ... the aim must be to provide for members of the minority an education appropriate to their *linguistic and cultural identity* ... . [Emphasis added.]

In addition, it is worth noting that minority schools themselves provide community centres where the promotion and preservation of minority language culture can occur; they provide needed locations where the minority community can meet and facilities which they can use to express their culture.

A further important aspect of the purpose of s. 23 is the role of the section as a remedial provision. It was designed to remedy an existing problem in Canada, and hence to alter the status quo. ...

In my view the appellants are fully justified in submitting that "history reveals that s. 23 was designed to correct, on a national scale, the progressive erosion of minority of ficial language groups and to give effect to the concept of the 'equal partnership' of the two official language groups in the context of education."

The remedial aspect of s. 23 was indirectly questioned by the respondent and several of the interveners in an argument which they put forward for a "narrow construction" of s. 23.

[Reference to Beetz J's comments on the political nature of language rights and the restrictive role of the courts in their interpretation is omitted.]

I do not believe that these words support the proposition that s. 23 should be given a particularly narrow construction, or that its remedial purpose should be ignored. Beetz J makes it clear in this quotation that language rights are not cast in stone nor immune from judicial interpretation. … Beetz J's warning that courts should be careful in interpreting language rights is a sound one. Section 23 provides a perfect example of why such caution is advisable. The provision provides for a novel form of legal right, quite different from the type of legal rights which courts have traditionally dealt with. Both its genesis and its form are evidence of the unusual nature of s. 23. Section 23 confers upon a group a right which places positive obligations on government to alter or develop major institutional structures. Careful interpretation of such a section is wise: however, this does not mean that courts should not "breathe life" into the expressed purpose of the section, or avoid implementing the possibly novel remedies needed to achieve that purpose.

(2) The Context of Section 23(3)(b): An Overview of Section 23

The proper way of interpreting s. 23, in my opinion, is to view the section as providing a general right to minority language instruction. Paragraphs (a) and (b) of subs. (3) qualify this general right: para. (a) adds that the right to instruction is only guaranteed where the "number of children" warrants, while para. (b) further qualifies the general right to instruction by adding that where numbers warrant it includes a right to "minority language educational facilities." In my view, subs. (3)(b) is included in order to indicate the upper range of possible institutional requirements which may be mandated by s. 23 (the government may, of course, provide more than the minimum required by s. 23).

Another way of expressing the above interpretation of s. 23 is to say that s. 23 should be viewed as encompassing a "sliding scale" of requirement, with subs. (3)(b) indicating the upper level of this range and the term "instruction" in subs. (3)(a) indicating the lower level. The idea of a sliding scale is simply that s. 23 guarantees whatever type and level of rights and services is appropriate in order to provide minority language instruction for the particular number of students involved.

The sliding scale approach can be contrasted with that which views s. 23 as only encompassing two rights—one with respect to instruction and one with respect to facilities—each providing a certain level of services appropriate for one of two numerical thresholds. On this interpretation of s. 23, which could be called the "separate rights" approach, a specified number of s. 23 students would trigger a particular level of instruction, while a greater, specified number of students would require, in addition, a particular level of minority language educational facilities. Where the number of students fell between the two threshold numbers, only the lower level of instruction would be required.

The sliding scale approach is preferable to the separate rights approach, not only because it accords with the text of s. 23, but also because it is consistent with the purpose of s. 23. The sliding scale approach ensures that the minority group receives the full amount of protection that its numbers warrant. Under the separate rights approach, if it were accepted, for example, that "X" number of students ensured a right to full management and control, then presumably "X – 1" students would not bring about any rights to management and control or even to a school building. Given the variety of possible means of fulfilling the purpose of s. 23, such a result is unacceptable. Moreover, the separate rights approach places parties like the appellants in the paradoxical position of forwarding an argument which, if accepted, might ultimately harm the overall position of minority language students in Canada. If, for instance, the appellants succeeded in persuading this Court that s. 23 mandates a completely separate school board—as opposed to some sort of representation on an existing board—then other groups of s. 23 parents with slightly fewer numbers might find themselves without a right to any degree of management and control—even though their numbers might justify granting them some degree of management and control.

The only way to avoid the weaknesses of the separate rights approach would be to lower the numbers requirement—with the result that it would be impractical to require governments to provide more than the minimum level of minority language educational services. In my view, it is more sensible, and consistent with the purpose of s. 23, to interpret s. 23 as requiring whatever minority language educational protection the number of students in any particular case warrants. Section 23 simply mandates that governments do whatever is practical in the situation to preserve and promote minority language education.

There are outer limits to the sliding scale of s. 23. In general, s. 23 may not require that anything be done in situations where there are a small number of minority language students. There is little that governments can be required to do, for instance, in the case of a solitary, isolated minority language student. Section 23 requires, at a minimum, that "instruction" take place in the minority language: if there are too few students to justify a programme which qualifies as "minority language instruction," then s. 23 will not require any programmes be put in place. However, the question of what is the "minimum" programme which could constitute "instruction," and the further question of how many students might be required in order to warrant such a programme, are not at issue in this appeal and I will not be addressing them. The question at issue here concerns only the "upper level" of the possible range of requirements under s. 23—that is, the requirements where there are a relatively large number of s. 23 students. ...

In my view, the words of s. 23(3)(b) are consistent with and supportive of the conclusion that s. 23 mandates, where the numbers warrant, a measure of management and control. Consider, first, the words of subs. (3)(b) in the context of the entire section. Instruction must take place somewhere and accordingly the right to "instruction" includes an implicit right to be instructed in facilities. If the term "minority language educational facilities" is not viewed as encompassing a degree of management and control, then there would not appear to be any purpose in including it in s. 23. This common sense conclusion militates against interpreting "facilities" as a reference to physical structures. Indeed, once the sliding scale approach is accepted it becomes unnecessary to focus too intently upon the word "facilities." Rather, the text of s. 23 supports viewing the entire term "minority language educational facilities" as setting out an upper level of management and control. ...

The foregoing textual analysis of s. 23(3)(b) is strongly supported by a consideration of the overall purpose of s. 23. That purpose, as discussed earlier, is to preserve and promote minority language and culture throughout Canada. In my view, it is essential, in order to further this purpose, that, where the numbers warrant, minority language parents possess a measure of management and control over the educational facilities in which their children are taught. Such management and control is vital to ensure that their language and culture flourish. It is necessary because a variety of management issues in education, *e.g.*, curricula, hiring, expenditures, can affect linguistic and cultural concerns. I think it incontrovertible that the health and survival of the minority language and culture can be affected in subtle but important ways by decisions relating to these issues. To give but one example, most decisions pertaining to curricula clearly have an influence on the language and culture of the minority students.

Furthermore, as the historical context in which s. 23 was enacted suggests, minority language groups cannot always rely upon the majority to take account of all of their linguistic and cultural concerns. Such neglect is not necessarily intentional: the majority cannot be expected to understand and appreciate all of the diverse ways in which educational practices may influence the language and culture of the minority. ...

Section 23 clearly encompasses a right to management and control. On its own, however, the phrase "management and control" is imprecise and requires further specification. This can be accomplished by considering what type of management and control is needed in order to fulfill the purpose of s. 23.

The appellants argue for a completely independent Francophone school board. Much is to be said in support of this position and indeed it may be said to reflect the ideal. ...

Historically, separate or denominational boards have been the principal bulwarks of minority language education in the absence of any provision for minority representation and authority within public or common school boards. Such independent boards constitute, for the minority, institutions which it can consider its own with all this entails in terms of opportunity of working in its own language and of sharing a common culture, interests and understanding and being afforded the fullest measure of representation and control. These are particularly important in setting overall priorities and responding to the special educational needs of the minority.

In some circumstances an independent Francophone school board is necessary to meet the purpose of s. 23. However, where the number of students enrolled in minority schools is relatively small, the ability of an independent board to fulfill this purpose may be reduced and other approaches may be appropriate whereby the minority is able to identify with the school but has the benefit of participating in a larger organization through representation and a certain exclusive authority within the majority school board. Under these circumstances, such an arrangement avoids the isolation of an independent school district from the physical resources which the majority school district enjoys and facilitates the sharing of resources with the majority board, something which can be crucial for smaller minority schools. By virtue of having a larger student population, it can be expected that the majority board would have greater access to new educational developments and resources. Where the number of s. 23 students is not sufficiently large, a complete isolation of the minority schools would tend to frustrate the purpose of s. 23 because, in the long run, it would contribute to a decline in the status of the minority language group and its educational facilities. Graduates of the minority schools would be less well-prepared (thus hindering career opportunities for the minority) and potential students would be disinclined to enter minority language schools. ...

Perhaps the most important point to stress is that completely separate school boards are not necessarily the best means of fulfilling the purpose of s. 23. What is essential, however, to satisfy that purpose is that the minority language group have control over those aspects of education which pertain to or have an effect upon their language and culture. This degree of control can be achieved to a substantial extent by guaranteeing representation of the minority on a shared school board and by giving these representatives exclusive control over all of the aspects of minority education which pertain to linguistic and cultural concerns.

To give but one example, the right to tax (which would accompany the creation of an independent school district), is not, in my view, essential to satisfy the concerns of s. 23 with linguistic and cultural security. Section 23 guarantees that minority schools shall receive public funds, but it is not necessary that the funds be derived through a separate tax base provided adequate funding is otherwise assured. Similar observations can be made in respect of other features of separate school districts.

It is not possible to give an exact description of what is required in every case in order to ensure that the minority language group has control over those aspects of minority language education which pertain to or have an effect upon minority language and culture. Imposing a specific form of educational system in the multitude of different circumstances which exist across Canada would be unrealistic and self-defeating. The problems with mandating "specific modalities" have been recognized by all of the courts in Canada which have considered s. 23. At this stage of early development of s. 23 jurisprudence, the appropriate response for the courts is to describe in general terms the requirements mandated. It is up to the public authorities to satisfy these general requirements. Where there are alternative ways of satisfying the requirements, the public authorities may choose the means of fulfilling their duties. In some instances this approach may result in further litigation to determine whether the general requirements mandated by the court have been implemented. I see no way to avoid this result, as the alternative of a uniform detailed order runs the real risk of imposing impractical solutions. Section 23 is a new type of legal right in Canada and thus requires new responses from the courts. ...

In my view, the measure of management and control required by s. 23 of the Charter may, depending on the numbers of students to be served, warrant an independent school board. Where numbers do not warrant granting this maximum level of management and control, however, they may nonetheless be sufficient to require linguistic minority representation on an existing school board. In this latter case:

(1) The representation of the linguistic minority on local boards or other public authorities which administer minority language instruction or facilities should be guaranteed;

(2) The number of minority language representatives on the board should be, at a minimum, proportional to the number of minority language students in the school district, *i.e.*, the number of minority language students for whom the board is responsible;

(3) The minority language representatives should have exclusive authority to make decisions relating to the minority language instruction and facilities, including:

(a) expenditures of funds provided for such instruction and facilities;

(b) appointment and direction of those responsible for the administration of such instruction and facilities;

(c) establishment of programs of instruction;

(d) recruitment and assignment of teachers and other personnel; and

(e) making of agreements for education and services for minority language pupils.

I do not doubt that in future cases courts will have occasion to expand upon or refine these words. It is impossible at this stage in the development of s. 23 to foresee all of the circumstances relevant to its implementation.

There are a few general comments I wish to add in respect of the above description. First, the matter of the quality of education to be provided to the minority students was not dealt with above because, strictly speaking, it does not pertain to the issue of management and control. It is, of course, an important issue and one which was raised in this appeal. I think it should be self-evident that in situations where the above degree of management and control is warranted the quality of education provided to the minority should in principle be on a basis of equality with the majority. This proposition follows directly from the purpose of s. 23. However, the specific form of educational system provided to the minority need not be identical to that provided to the majority. The different circumstances under which various schools find themselves, as well as the demands of a minority language education itself, make such a requirement impractical and undesirable. It should be stressed that the funds allocated for the minority language schools must be at least equivalent on a per student basis to the funds allocated to the majority schools. Special circumstances may warrant an allocation for minority language schools that exceeds the per capita allocation for majority schools. I am confident that this will be taken into account not only in the enabling legislation, but in budgetary discussions of the board.

With respect to funding, the reference point for determining the number of students will normally be the pupils actually receiving minority language education. During the period in which a minority language education programme is getting started, however, it would seem reasonable to budget for the number of students who can realistically be seen as attending the school once operations are well established. This may be one example of a special circumstance which calls for a higher allocation of funds for minority education programmes. It could also be seen, however, as a consideration which would equally be extended to a majority language programme during its start-up period.

Second, provincial and local authorities may, of course, give minority groups a greater degree of management and control than that described above. Section 23 only mandates a minimum level of management and control in a given situation; it does not set a ceiling.

Third, there are a variety of different forms of institutional structures which will satisfy the above guidelines. I have stressed this aspect of the flexibility of s. 23 before, but this feature bears repeating. The constant in any acceptable scheme of minority representation, however, will be the granting of representation proportional to the number of minority language students who fall under the responsibility of the particular school board.

Fourth, the persons who will exercise the measure of management and control described above are "s. 23 parents" or persons such parents designate as their representatives. I appreciate that because of the wording of s. 23 these parents may not be culturally a part of the minority language group. This could occasionally result in persons who are not, strictly speaking, members of the minority language group exercising some control over minority language education. This would be a rare occurrence, and is not reason to lessen the degree of management and control given to s. 23 parents.

Fifth, I wish to emphasize that the above description is only meant to cover the degree of management and control which, short of a separate school board, is required under s. 23 where the number of s. 23 students is significant enough to warrant moving towards the upper level of the sliding scale. Other degrees of management and control may be required in situations where the numbers do not justify granting full rights of management and control. What is required in any case will turn on what the "numbers warrant."

Finally, it should be noted that the management and control accorded to s. 23 parents does not preclude provincial regulation. The province has an interest both in the content and the qualitative standards of educational programmes. Such programmes can be imposed without infringing s. 23, in so far as they do not interfere with the linguistic and cultural concerns of the minority. ...

Appeal allowed.

D. Réaume and L. Green, "Education and Linguistic Security in the Charter"
(1989), 34 *McGill Law Journal* 777 (footnotes omitted)

I. *The Value of Linguistic Security*

Two mischievous notions about language rights have some currency in Canada. The first is that language rights are a mere product of political compromise and have no foundation in principle. The second contradicts the first. According to it, language rights are founded on the principle of survival: governments have a duty to ensure that minority languages continue into the future. These are not politically innocent notions, for each has implications for the way in which language rights should be interpreted and the weight they should be given. But they are both founded on mistakes.

The first confuses the *genesis* of constitutional rights with their *justification*. All rights entrenched in positive law have a particular form that attempts to make concrete certain abstract values which the law prizes. Every constitutional right thus marks a kind of compromise between competing interpretations of the values it protects; every one strikes some balance between legislative sovereignty and minority protections; every one can be protected only by a combination of non-interference and positive action on the part of government. Because these are features of all constitutional rights, they do not distinguish language rights from the rest and therefore provide no ground for interpreting them differently. That is why the Supreme Court of Canada, to whom this first mistake is due, has not been able to draw the proposed distinction between "compromise- and principle-based" rights in a consistent and persuasive way. Such truth as there is in the idea amounts to this: the courts must give effect to the terms of a constitutional agreement without, under the guise of interpretation, amending them. That claim is as harmless as it is sound. It does nothing to show what those terms are, nor how courts should proceed when they are equivocal. Thus, the claim that they originate in a compromise does not in fact justify the Court's recent policy of reading some language rights restrictively.

The second view, according to which minority language rights are rooted in the principle of survival, makes a different error. It confuses the *justification* of a right with the likely *by-product* of its exercise. Minority languages are under threat from a variety of sources, but they die out for a common reason: they are abandoned by their speakers. Language rights aim to protect speakers from certain pressures to abandon their languages. When linguistic choices are made in a secure environment, roughly, one without unfair pressure to conform to majority practices, they will in fact typically lead to a higher rate of survival. Does it follow, then, that the aim of language rights is to protect the endangered species of the linguistic world?

We can test that hypothesis by considering some policies aimed at ensuring language survival. Suppose, for example, that one of the majority English provinces required all French speakers to send their children to French schools and denied them access to English instruction. Or suppose that by residential zoning it attempted to reduce exogamy among declining minorities. Set aside the question of whether these measures would violate other rights, and let us ask simply whether *as far as language goes*, they are aimed in the right direction. Could they be said to take at least one step towards justice? On reflection that seems dubious. The problem is not simply that language rights and other liberties are here in conflict, but that moral rights to language use are *themselves* violated by the policies in question. Prohibiting the minorities from learning the majority language and banning minority-language instruction offend common principles: they attack linguistic security by creating unfair pressures to conform. These pressures do not become acceptable when they are inflicted on a minority within the minority community itself. Draconian measures to promote minority languages may evince a kind of concern for the health of the languages, but they do not give appropriate concern for the interests of their speakers.

That security and not survival is the root value is suggested by considering the importance of language. Apart from its instrumental value in communication, language is also an important marker of identity. Those who wish to use minority languages do so partly as an expression of belonging to and identifying with a community. But language use has this valuable expressive dimension only if rooted in a free and fair context. Those who are forced to use a particular language cannot be thought thereby to express their identity. That does not mean that language must be consciously chosen. Language is only partially a realm of free choice. Children have a mother tongue long before they develop the capacity for reflective and informed choice about ethnic identification, and parents typically transmit their mother tongues as a matter of course. But these normal processes of social development contribute value to their outcomes only in circumstances which are fair and unbiased. Thus, while facilitating minority language education and requiring it both promote the survival of minority languages, this equivalence in consequences does not establish an equivalence in aim. The point of language rights is to give speakers a secure environment in which to make choices about language use, and in which ethnic identification can have positive value.

The confusion of survival and security is easily made, for the conditions threatening security also make survival less likely. Evidence of assimilation and decline among the francophone minorities made it clear that the lack of adequate protection in the 1867 constitution had exacerbated their demographic fragility, and the desire to remedy this was a driving force of the language rights provisions. Nonetheless, the decline of the minorities is a symptom and not itself a disease. It is presumptive evidence that there is strong and potentially unfair social pressure to abandon their language. But this evidence is rebuttable. It is possible (though not probable under normal circumstances) that even in a completely secure environment, some members of minority language groups would still make free and informed decisions to integrate with a majority community. The need to identify with a community may be deeply rooted in human nature, but we know that there is nonetheless much flexibility regarding the community with which one identifies.

These considerations suggest that it is not the survival of languages but the security of their speakers that justifies language rights. To have linguistic security in the fullest sense is to have the opportunity, without serious impediments, to live a full life in a community of people who share one's language. This opportunity is taken for granted by those in linguistically homogeneous societies and by those who speak the majority language in multilingual societies. Through sheer numbers they enjoy *de facto* linguistic security without need for special legal protections. No doors are closed, and no aspects of human fulfillment are unavailable on account of language. Abandoning one's mother tongue (oneself or on behalf of one's children) is of course a conceivable option for them, but not one to which they are driven by force of social circumstance and not one which will even be considered in the normal course of life. It is otherwise for members of linguistic minorities. Without special protections, minority language speakers are inevitably placed under strong pressures to abandon their mother tongue. Because of its central role in every aspect of human co-operation, people share a common interest in communicating with others. To be excluded from this is to be denied most of what is valued in life. The more restricted the existence available in one's mother tongue the more rational it becomes to take up the language that offers greater opportunities. This does not mean that the minority language speakers do not value their language or communities, any more than the decision of hold-up victims to part with their wallets means that they do not value their money. It means simply that there are some burdens that outweigh it, and some costs that it is unjust to expect them to bear. ...

The role of government in protecting linguistic security is thus easily explained. The familiar official language rights serve the interests of linguistic security by facilitating participation in activities under government control. Participation in political life involves communication with officials. A community that could not participate in the political life of its country would be severely handicapped, and, if participation must be on the majority's terms, then the incentive to assimilate is obvious. Similarly, the denial of government services, whether the court system or the kind of everyday help and advice that many government departments provide, turns the use of one's mother tongue into a handicap and sometimes even a source of shame. But, unlike ethnic groups, government has no mother tongue of its own. The choice of its working languages is a matter over which the government has complete control. Participation can therefore be guaranteed in one's own language without sacrificing the legitimate interests of others. How does education fit into the emerging picture?

The system of education, particularly at the primary and secondary levels, makes major contributions to the security of one's linguistic environment. Provision for minority language education is a complex good with many different facets. For convenience, we distinguish two main aspects. There are powerful *individual benefits* of children being able to learn in their mother-tongue: it is easier to master other subjects when one knows the language and feels socially at ease in the class-room. It also opens doors to participation in one's community and fosters a positive attitude towards it. The absence of minority language education is quite obviously a powerful assimilative force. Children grow up with a grasp of their mother tongue which is inadequate for the kind of adult pursuits which require strong communication skills. In such circumstances it is hardly surprising that people abandon their first language and do not teach it to their children. Before long, such a community ceases to be viable and its language, if it persists at all, has merely folkloric status.

Education cannot however be fully understood as an individual good. Minority language instruction benefits the linguistic group as well. It has *collective benefits* which flow from the language being a vehicle of instruction. For example, it provides and renews cultural capital. This is true at the level of both "high" and "popular" culture: the productive and appreciative capacities must be nurtured and trained through a comprehensive education. Musicians, writers, artists obviously depend on and draw on common cultural capital in representing and contesting the life of the community. But even folk and oral traditions, sporting culture, *etc.*, all draw on a stock of common forms and images. In modern societies this capital is largely controlled by the educational system.

Other direct collective benefits are more instrumental: the education system provides jobs for members of the minority community. There are also indirect collective benefits which flow from the existence and administration of minority-language instruction. For one thing, a community with public institutions will have greater visibility and status. More importantly, an educational facility such as a neighbourhood school is an important focus of social and cultural activities for the community, especially in smaller towns. And managing a school system by electing trustees, hiring teachers, setting policy, *etc.* are all important parts of the political life of such communities and contribute to their richness and vitality.

These are only some of the ways in which minority-language education enters the collective life of the community. Many of them exhibit interesting structural features. Some collective benefits are *public goods* in the economists' sense: none can be excluded from their benefits and they do not diminish with consumption. This is clearly the case with respect to the diffuse effects of a minority language education system on the security, status, and vitality of the community. And, where publicly funded education is the norm, it is true of educational options themselves: they become available to any parents who wish to take advantage of them. Moreover, the existence of these schools makes the entire community more vital in diffuse ways which generate benefits even for those who do not directly participate in its activities. For example, the increased use of minority languages obviously increases the instrumental value of being able to speak them, and this benefit accrues to all.

But minority-language instruction has further collective benefits which, though excludable, are social and non-rival. Where these flow from the inherent value of participating with others in some social activity, we call them *participatory goods*. A school plays a significant role in fostering human relationships, teaching co-operation, and imparting other social skills in a way that could not be achieved under a system of private individual tuition. Public education is the central means by which children are introduced to and can participate in the cultural traditions of their community. Management and control of an education system, similarly, provides a forum in which parents can exercise and develop skills of self-government. In all these ways, minority language education has a significant social role.

NOTES

1. *Mahe*, in effect, sets up a dialogue between the legislative and judicial branches on the meaning of s. 23, as governments attempt to implement the section. For further discussion by the Supreme Court of Canada, see *Reference re Public Schools Act (Man.), ss. 79(3), (4), and (7)*, [1993] 1 SCR 839, 100 DLR (4th) 723, where the Court was asked to determine the meaning of s. 23(3)(b), the right to receive instruction in "minority language educational facilities." The Court concluded that s. 23 requires that the educational facilities be of or belong to the minority group, and includes a right to a distinct physical setting. However, as in *Mahe*, it declined to elaborate on what this might mean in a given fact situation. Again, the Court emphasized that the determination of whether facilities are appropriate can only be undertaken on the basis of a distinct geographic region. The Court also determined that the Manitoba *Public Schools Act* did not meet the province's constitutional obligations. Given the number of potential French-language students, s. 23 required the establishment of an independent French-language school board under the exclusive management and control of the French-speaking language minority.

2. For a critique of the *Mahe* decision on the grounds that it is overly activist and a departure from the appropriate judicial reading of history, legislative purpose, and constitutional text, see R.G. Richards, "Mahe v. Alberta: Management and Control of Minority Language Education" (1991), 36 *McGill Law Journal* 216:

> The Court chose to overlook a fundamental point when it said that management and control must be read into section 23 because the historical absence of these rights had led to a failure to provide minority language education. Section 23 *itself* guarantees minority language instruction and facilities. Minority language groups no longer need political influence or control of school boards to get instruction and facilities. They have a constitutional right to them which can be enforced in court if necessary. The very purpose of section 23 is to break the link be-

tween the availability of minority language education and political control of school boards or legislatures.

Thus, it seems clear that the purpose and focus of section 23 would have been more appropriately stated in more concrete and specific terms than those chosen by the Chief Justice. As the section itself says, it is aimed at guaranteeing rights to primary and secondary education in the official minority language of each province. The preservation of cultural and linguistic integrity is not the *direct* object of section 23. The availability of minority language education will have an impact on assimilation but that is the *effect* of the section rather than its immediate purpose. Section 23 can easily become over-inflated if it is seen as being aimed directly at guaranteeing linguistic and cultural vitality.

3. Joseph Magnet, in *Official Language of Canada* (Cowansville, QC: Yvon Blais, 1995), at 80-83, is critical of the principle of linguistic security discussed by Green and Réaume, above. He argues that to create true linguistic security for minority language communities, government would have to intervene in language policy in a very ambitious manner—and this is an unrealistic expectation. Moreover, he criticizes their attempt to justify language rights on a single basis because this approach ignores the complexity of the issue. For example, he identifies an additional justificaiton for language rights, namely, that they manage conflict between Canada's linguistic communities.

4. *Mahe* was applied by the Supreme Court in *Arsenault-Cameron* (discussed above), in which the Court held that the right of a minority language community to management and control encompassed a right to control over the location of minority language instruction and facilities. In that case, parents from Summerside, Prince Edward Island, and its environs challenged the decision of the provincial Minister of Education to provide bus transportation to a French-language school in a neighbouring district, as opposed to establishing a school in the Summerside area. The Court held that this decision was for the minority language community (in that case, acting through a French-language school board) to make, because it would likely be based on "cultural or linguistic considerations" that are better understood by the minority language community itself. In addition to this purposive argument, the Court also pointed to the text of s. 23, in particular the term "wherever in the province" in s. 23(3)(a), to support the conclusion that the right to management and control included a right to choice of location. Do you agree? The Court, however, stated that the right to choice of location is "subject to objective provincial norms and guidelines that are consistent with s. 23," for example, those regarding "[s]chool size, facilities, transportation and assembly of students."

5. In both *Mahe* and the *Manitoba Language Reference* above, the Court gave only declaratory relief that set out guidelines for future action by government in consultation with the minority language population. In other cases, plaintiffs have sought structural remedies. Indeed, the majority of claims for structural relief under the Charter have arisen in the context of minority language education rights. For example, in *Marchand v. Simcoe County Board of Education* (1986), 29 DLR (4th) 596 (Ont. HCJ), Sirois J ordered the defendant school board to provide the facilities and funding necessary to achieve instruction and facilities in the French-language secondary school equivalent to those in the English stream, and to establish industrial arts and shop programs at the French-language secondary school equivalent to those in the English schools. In *Doucet-Boudreau v. Nova Scotia (Minister of*

Education), [2003] 3 SCR 3, 232 DLR (4th) 17, found in Chapter 25, Enforcement of Rights, a majority of the Court found that a trial judge was justified in retaining jurisdiction over the case and requiring the government to report back to the court and the parties on its progress in making minority language schools available after the judge had issued a declaration that the s. 23 minority language educational rights of francophones in Nova Scotia had been violated.

6. *Lalonde v. Ontario (Commission de restructuration des services de santé)* (2001), 56 OR (3d) 505 (CA) presents an interesting variation on the language rights cases discussed above. In that decision, the Ontario Court of Appeal struck down the decision of the Ontario Health Services Restructuring Commission to close the Montfort Hospital. The hospital was the only hospital in the province where French-language services were available on a full-time basis. Moreover, because the working language of the hospital was French, it was the only hospital in the province where health care professionals were trained in French. The Court rejected constitutional challenges to the discussion to close the hospital, on the basis of ss. 15 and 16(3). However, the Court found that the Commission had exercised its statutory discretion unreasonably by failing to consider, and to justify, any departure from the unwritten constitutional principle of the "protection of minorities" laid down by the Supreme Court in the *Reference re Secession of Quebec*, [1998] 2 SCR 217, found in Chapter 1, Introduction. On February 1, 2002, Ontario announced its decision to not appeal this judgment.

7. The legislative measures in the *Ford* case that follows could be seen as an example of Quebec's vigorous efforts to protect linguistic security for francophones. Its importance in this chapter is to show how the Supreme Court has extended language rights protection beyond the explicit guarantees described so far and how it has tried to reconcile the interests of different linguistic communities when they come into conflict.

In interpreting s. 2(b), the guarantee of freedom of expression, to include protection against the suppression of one's language by the state, the Court has given added protection not only to English and French minorities, but to other linguistic communities as well. Note, though, that there is a difference between s. 2(b) and the language rights described so far, since the latter confer positive rights whereas the guarantee in s. 2(b) has been understood in primarily negative terms, restricting the state's ability to prevent the use of a language, but not requiring that the state confer services. As well, the language rights guaranteed through s. 2(b) are vulnerable to legislative override under s. 33.

Ford v. Quebec (AG)
[1988] 2 SCR 712, 54 DLR (4th) 577

[This case involved a challenge to ss. 58 and 69 of the Quebec *Charter of the French Language* that required that signs, posters, and commercial advertising be solely in the French language and that only the French version of a firm name be used. The legislation was attacked under both the *Canadian Charter of Rights and Freedoms* and the Quebec *Charter of Human Rights and Freedoms*. The editing here emphasizes the former. The override power found in s. 33 of the Charter was also involved, and the parts of the judgment dealing with that issue are found in Chapter 17, The Framework of the Charter.]

THE COURT (Dickson CJC, Beetz, McIntyre, Lamer, and Wilson JJ): ...

VII *Whether the Freedom of Expression Guaranteed by s. 2(b) of the Canadian Charter of Rights and Freedoms and by s. 3 of the Quebec Charter of Human Rights and Freedoms Includes the Freedom to Express Oneself in the Language of One's Choice*

Insofar as this issue is concerned, the words "freedom of expression" in s. 2(b) of the Canadian Charter and s. 3 of the Quebec Charter should be given the same meaning. As indicated above, both the Superior Court and the Court of Appeal held that freedom of expression includes the freedom to express oneself in the language of one's choice. ...

The conclusion of the Superior Court and the Court of Appeal on this issue is correct. Language is so intimately related to the form and content of expression that there cannot be true freedom of expression by means of language if one is prohibited from using the language of one's choice. Language is not merely a means or medium of expression; it colours the content and meaning of expression. It is, as the preamble of the *Charter of the French Language* itself indicates, a means by which a people may express its cultural identity. It is also the means by which the individual expresses his or her personal identity and sense of individuality. That the concept of "expression" in s. 2(b) of the Canadian Charter and s. 3 of the Quebec Charter goes beyond mere content is indicated by the specific protection accorded to "freedom of thought, belief [and] opinion" in s. 2 and to "freedom of conscience" and "freedom of opinion" in s. 3. That suggests that "freedom of expression" is intended to extend to more than the content of expression in its narrow sense.

The Attorney-General of Quebec made several submissions against the conclusion reached by the Superior Court and the Court of Appeal on this issue, the most important of which may be summarized as follows: (a) in determining the meaning of freedom of expression the court should apply the distinction between the message and the medium which must have been known to the framers of the Canadian and Quebec Charters; (b) the express provision for the guarantee of language rights in ss. 16 to 23 of the Canadian Charter indicate that it was not intended that a language freedom should result incidentally from the guarantee of freedom of expression in s. 2(b); (c) the recognition of a freedom to express oneself in the language of one's choice under s. 2(b) of the Canadian Charter and s. 3 of the Quebec Charter would undermine the special and limited constitutional position of the specific guarantees of language rights in s. 133 of the *Constitution Act, 1867* and ss. 16 to 23 of the Canadian Charter that was emphasized by the Court in *MacDonald v. City of Montreal*, [1986] 1 SCR 460; 27 DLR (4th) 321 and *Société des Acadiens du Nouveau-Brunswick Inc. v. Association of Parents for Fairness in Education, Grand Rapids Falls District 50 Branch* (1986), [1986] 1 SCR 549; 27 DLR (4th) 406; and (d) the recognition that freedom of expression includes the freedom to express oneself in the language of one's choice would be contrary to the views expressed on this issue by the European Commission of Human Rights and the European Court of Human Rights.

The distinction between the message and the medium was applied by Dugas J of the Superior Court in *Devine v. A-G Que.*, [1982] Que. SC 355; aff'd. 36 DLR (4th) 321, [1987] RJQ 50, in holding that freedom of expression does not include freedom to express oneself in the language of one's choice. It has already been indicated why that distinction is inappropriate as applied to language as a means of expression because of the intimate relationship between language and meaning. As one of the authorities on language quoted by the appellant Singer in the *Devine* appeal, J. Fishman, *The Sociology of Language* (Rowley, Mass.: Newbury House Publishers, 1972), at p. 4, puts it:

> ... language is not merely a *means* of interpersonal communication and influence. It is not merely a *carrier* of content, whether latent or manifest. Language itself *is* content, a reference for loyalties and animosities, an indicator of social statuses and personal relationships, a marker of situations and topics as well as of the societal goals and the large-scale value-laden arenas of interaction that typify every speech community.

As has been noted this quality or characteristic of language is acknowledged by the *Charter of the French Language* itself where, in the first paragraph of its preamble, it states:

> Whereas the French language, the distinctive language of a people that is in the majority French-speaking, is the instrument by which that people has articulated its identity;

The second and third of the submissions of the Attorney-General of Quebec, which have been summarized above, with reference to the implications for this issue of the express or specific guarantees of language rights in s. 133 of the *Constitution Act, 1867*, and ss. 16 to 23 of the *Canadian Charter of Rights and Freedoms*, are closely related and may be addressed together. These special guarantees of language rights do not, by implication, preclude a construction of freedom of expression that includes the freedom to express oneself in the language of one's choice. A general freedom to express oneself in the language of one's choice and the special guarantees of language rights in certain areas of governmental activity or jurisdiction—the legislature and administration, the courts and education—are quite different things. The latter have, as this court has indicated in *MacDonald, supra*, and *Société des Acadiens, supra*, their own special historical, political and constitutional basis. The central unifying feature of all of the language rights given explicit recognition in the Constitution of Canada is that they pertain to governmental institutions and for the most part they oblige the government to provide for, or at least tolerate, the use of both official languages. In this sense they are more akin to rights, properly understood, than freedoms. They grant entitlement to a specific benefit from the government or in relation to one's dealing with the government. Correspondingly, the government is obliged to provide certain services or benefits in both languages or at least permit use of either language by persons conducting certain affairs with the government. They do not ensure, as does a guaranteed freedom, that within a given broad range of private conduct, an individual will be free to choose his or her own course of activity. The language rights in the Constitution impose obligations on government and governmental institutions that are in the words of Beetz J in *MacDonald*, a "precise scheme," providing specific opportunities to use English or French, or to receive services in English or French, in concrete, readily ascertainable and limited circumstances. In contrast, what the respondents seek in this case is a freedom as that term was explained by Dickson J (as he then was) in *R v. Big M Drug Mart Ltd.*, [1985] 1 SCR 295 at p. 336, 18 DLR (4th) 321 at p. 354:

Freedom can primarily be characterized by the absence of coercion or constraint. If a person is compelled by the State or the will of another to a course of action or inaction which he would not otherwise have chosen, he is not acting of his own volition and he cannot be said to be truly free. One of the major purposes of the Charter is to protect, within reason, from compulsion or constraint.

The respondents seek to be free of the state imposed requirement that their commercial signs and advertising be in French only, and seek the freedom, in the entirely private or non-governmental realm of commercial activity, to display signs and advertising in the language of their choice as well as that of French. Manifestly the respondents are not seeking to use the language of their choice in any form of direct relations with any branch of government and are not seeking to oblige government to provide them any services or other benefits in the language of their choice. In this sense the respondents are asserting a freedom, the freedom to express oneself in the language of one's choice in an area of non-governmental activity, as opposed to a language right of the kind guaranteed in the Constitution. The recognition that freedom of expression includes the freedom to express oneself in the language of one's choice does not undermine or run counter to the special guarantees of official language rights in areas of governmental jurisdiction or responsibility. The legal structure, function and obligations of government institutions with respect to the English and French languages are in no way affected by the recognition that freedom of expression includes the freedom to express oneself in the language of one's choice in areas outside of those for which the special guarantees of language have been provided.

The decisions of the European Commission of Human Rights and the European Court of Human Rights on which the Attorney-General of Quebec relied are all distinguishable on the same basis, apart from the fact that, as Bisson JA observed in the Court of Appeal, they arose in an entirely different constitutional context. They all involved claims to language rights in relations with government that would have imposed some obligation on government. ...

[The discussion of whether the guarantee of freedom of expression extends to commercial expression has been omitted. The Court concluded that the fact that the signs in issue had a commercial purpose did not remove the expression contained therein from the scope of protected freedom. Having found an infringement of freedom of expression, the Court turned to s. 1 of the Canadian Charter and s. 9.1 of the Quebec Charter.]

The s. 1 and s. 9.1 materials consist of some fourteen items ranging in nature from the general theory of language policy and planning to statistical analysis of the position of the French language in Quebec and Canada. The material deals with two matters of particular relevance to the issue in the appeal: (1) the vulnerable position of the French language in Quebec and Canada, which is the reason for the language policy reflected in the *Charter of the French Language*; and (2) the importance attached by language planning theory to the role of language in the public domain, including the communication or expression by language contemplated by the challenged provisions of the *Charter of the French Language*. As to the first, the material amply establishes the importance of the legislative purpose reflected in the *Charter of the French Language* and that it is a response to a substantial and pressing need. Indeed, this was conceded by the respondents both in the Court of Appeal and in this court. The vulnerable position of the French language in Quebec and Canada was described in a series of reports by commissions of inquiry beginning with the Report of the Royal Commission on Bilingualism and Biculturalism in 1969 and continuing with the Parent Commission and the Gendron Commission. It is reflected in statistics referred to in these reports and in later studies forming part of the materials, with due adjustment made in the light of the submissions of the appellant Singer in *Devine* with respect to some of the later statistical material. The causal factors for the threatened position of the French language that have generally been identified are: (a) the declining birth rate of Quebec francophones resulting in a decline in the Quebec francophone proportion of the Canadian population as a whole; (b) the decline of the francophone population outside Quebec as a result of assimilation; (c) the greater rate of assimilation of immigrants to Quebec by the anglophone community of Quebec; and (d) the continuing dominance of English at the higher levels of the economic sector. These factors have favoured the use of the English language despite the predominance in Quebec of a francophone population. Thus, in the period prior to the enactment of the legislation at issue, the "visage linguistique" of Quebec often gave the impression that English had become as significant as French. This "visage linguistique" reinforced the concern among francophones that English was gaining in importance, that the French language was threatened and that it would ultimately disappear. It strongly suggested to young and ambitious francophones that the language of success was almost exclusively English. It confirmed to anglophones that there was no great need to learn the majority language. And it suggested to immigrants that the prudent course lay in joining the anglophone community. The aim of such provisions as ss. 58 and 69 of the *Charter of the French Language* was, in the words of its preamble, "to see the quality and influence of the French language assured." The threat to the French language demonstrated to the government that it should, in particular, take steps to assure that the "visage linguistique" of Quebec would reflect the predominance of the French language.

The s. 1 and s. 9.1 materials establish that the aim of the language policy underlying the *Charter of the French Language* was a serious and legitimate one. They indicate the concern about the survival of the French language and the perceived need for an adequate legislative response to the problem. Moreover, they indicate a rational connection between protecting the French language and assuring that the reality of Quebec society is communicated through the "visage linguistique." The s. 1 and s. 9.1 materials do not, however, demonstrate that the requirement of the use of French only is either necessary for the achievement of the legislative objective or proportionate to it. That specific question is simply not addressed by the materials. Indeed, in his factum and oral argument the Attorney-General of Quebec did not attempt to justify the requirement of the exclusive use of French. He concentrated on the reasons for the adoption of the *Charter of the French Language* and the earlier language legislation, which, as was noted above, were conceded by the respondents. The Attorney-General of Quebec relied on what he referred to as the general democratic legitimacy of Quebec language policy without referring explicitly to the requirement of the exclusive use of French. Insofar as proportionality is concerned, the Attorney-General of Quebec referred to the American jurisprudence with respect to commercial speech, presumably as indicating the judicial deference that should be paid to the legislative choice of means to serve an admittedly legitimate legislative purpose, at least in the area of commercial expression. He did, however, refer in justification of the requirement of the exclusive use of French to the attenuation of this requirement reflected in ss. 59 to 62 of the *Charter of the French Language* and the regulations. He submitted that these exceptions to the requirement of the exclusive use of French indicate the concern for carefully designed measures and for interfering as little as possible with commercial expression. The qualifications of the requirement of the exclusive use of French in other provisions of the *Charter of the French Language* and the regulations do not make ss. 58 and 69 any less prohibitions of the use of any language other than French as applied to the respondents. The issue is whether any such prohibition is justified. In the opinion of this court it has not been demonstrated that the prohibition of the use of any language other than French in ss. 58 and 69 of the *Charter of the French Language* is necessary to the defence and enhancement of the status of the French language in Quebec or that it is proportionate to that legislative purpose. Since the evidence put to us by the government showed that the predominance of the French language was not reflected in the "visage linguistique" of Quebec, the governmental response could well have been tailored to meet that specific problem and to impair freedom of expression minimally. Thus, whereas requiring the predominant display of the French language, even its marked predominance, would be proportional to the goal of promoting and maintaining a French "visage linguistique" in Quebec and therefore justified under s. 9.1 of the Quebec Charter and s. 1 of the Canadian Charter, requiring the exclusive use of French has not been so justified. French could be required in addition to any other language or it could be required to have greater visibility than that accorded to other languages. Such measures would ensure that the "visage linguistique" reflected the demography of Quebec: the predominant language is French. This reality should be communicated to all citizens and non-citizens alike, irrespective of their mother tongue. But exclusivity for the French language has not survived the scrutiny of a proportionality test and does not reflect the reality of Quebec society. Accordingly, we are of the view that the limit imposed on freedom of expression by s. 58 of the *Charter of the French Language* respecting the exclusive use of French on public signs and posters and in commercial advertising is not justified under s. 9.1 of the Quebec Charter. In like measure, the limit imposed on freedom of expression by s. 69 of the *Charter of the French Language* respecting the exclusive use of the French version of a firm name is not justified under either s. 9.1 of the Quebec Charter or s. 1 of the Canadian Charter.

Appeal dismissed.

NOTES

When Quebec enacted new legislation restricting the use of English in outdoor signs—and protected it from Charter scrutiny through the use of s. 33 of the Charter—several anglophones from Quebec brought a complaint under the *International Covenant on Civil and Political Rights*. Their argument, *inter alia*, was that the sign law violated art. 19 of the Covenant, which reads in part:

2. Everyone shall have the right to freedom of expression; this right shall include freedom to seek, receive and impart information and ideas of all kinds, regardless of frontiers, either orally, in writing or in print, in the form of art, or through any other media of his choice.

3. The exercise of the rights provided for in paragraph 2 of this Article carries with it special duties and responsibilities. It may therefore be subject to certain restrictions, but these shall only be such as are provided by law and are necessary:

(a) For respect of the rights or reputations of others;

(b) For the protection of national security or of public order (ordre public), or of public health and morals.

The United Nations Human Rights Committee took a position similar to the Supreme Court of Canada (*Ballantyne et al. v. Canada*, 359/1989, 385/1989), stating:

11.4 Any restriction of the freedom of expression must cumulatively meet the following conditions: it must be provided for by law, it must address one of the aims enumerated in paragraphs 3(a) and (b) of article 19, and must be necessary to achieve the legitimate purpose. While the restrictions on outdoor advertising are indeed provided for by law, the issue to be addressed is whether they are necessary for the respect of the rights of others. The rights of others could only be the rights of the francophone minority within Canada under article 27. This is the right to use their own language, which is not jeopardized by the freedom of others to advertise in other than the French language. Nor does the Committee have reason to believe that public order would be jeopardized by commercial advertising outdoors in a language other than French. The Committee notes that the State party does not seek to defend Bill 178 on these grounds. Any constraints under paragraphs 3(a) and 3(b) of article 19 would in any event have to be shown to be necessary. The Committee believes that it is not necessary, in order to protect the vulnerable position in Canada of the francophone group, to prohibit commercial advertising in English. This protection may be achieved in other ways that do not preclude the freedom of expression, in a language of their choice, of those engaged in such fields as trade. For example, the law could have required that advertising be in both French and English. A state may choose one or more official languages, but it may not exclude, outside the spheres of public life, the freedom to express oneself in a language of one's choice. The Committee accordingly concludes that there has been a violation of article 19, paragraph 2.

In 1993, Quebec changed its language legislation once again so as to permit the use of English on signs, provided French was predominant (*Charter of the French Language*, RSQ 1985, c. C-11, s. 58, as amended by SQ 1993, c. 40). The override of the Charter, enacted in 1988 (SQ 1988, c. 54, s. 10), was not renewed. A constitutional challenge to s. 58, on the basis of, *inter alia*, s. 2(b), was recently rejected by the Quebec Court of Appeal in *R c. W.F.H. Enterprises Ltée*, [2001] JQ no. 5021 (CA). The controversial aspect of the decision is that the court permitted the Quebec government to rely on the factual findings of the trial court in *Ford*, instead of requiring it to adduce new evidence.

IV. PROPOSALS FOR CONSTITUTIONAL AMENDMENT

As discussed in Chapter 12, Instruments of Flexibility in the Federal System, there have been two major efforts to amend the Constitution since 1982. Neither constitutional round included explicit provisions dealing with language. However, both the Meech Lake Accord (the 1987-1990 round) and the Charlottetown Accord (the 1991-1992 round) proposed amendments to recognize Quebec as a distinct society. These clauses proved very controversial politically, which contributed to the demise of both proposals.

The Charlottetown Accord's distinct society clause was part of the "Canada clause" that was to be added to the *Constitution Act, 1867*:

> 2(1) The Constitution of Canada, including the *Canadian Charter of Rights and Freedoms*, shall be interpreted in a manner consistent with the following fundamental characteristics:
>
> (a) Canada is a democracy committed to a parliamentary and federal system of government and to the rule of law;
>
> (b) the Aboriginal peoples of Canada, being the first peoples to govern this land, have the right to promote their languages, cultures and traditions and to ensure the integrity of their societies, and their governments constitute one of the three orders of government in Canada;
>
> (c) Quebec constitutes within Canada a distinct society, which includes a French-speaking majority, a unique culture and a civil law tradition;
>
> (d) Canadians and their governments are committed to the vitality and development of official language minority communities throughout Canada;
>
> (e) Canadians are committed to racial and ethnic equality in a society that includes citizens from many lands who have contributed, and continue to contribute, to the building of a strong Canada that reflects its cultural and racial diversity;
>
> (f) Canadians are committed to a respect for individual and collective human rights and freedoms of all people;
>
> (g) Canadians are committed to the equality of female and male persons; and
>
> (h) Canadians confirm the principle of the equality of the provinces at the same time as recognizing their diverse characteristics.
>
> (2) The role of the legislature and Government of Quebec to preserve and promote the distinct society of Quebec is affirmed.
>
> (3) Nothing in this section derogates from the powers, rights or privileges of the Parliament or the Government of Canada, or of the legislatures or governments of the provinces, or of the legislative bodies or governments of the Aboriginal peoples of Canada, including any powers, rights or privileges relating to language and, for greater certainty, nothing in this section derogates from the aboriginal and treaty rights of the Aboriginal peoples of Canada.

Opinion on the possible legal effect of the distinct society clauses was divided. Proponents variously indicated that the clauses would have only, or mainly, symbolic effect. Some argued that the clause did no more than affirm what the Supreme Court had said in *Ford*, above; that Quebec, with a French-speaking majority constituting a minority in North America, might take special steps to protect its distinctive language and culture.

Critics viewed the clauses as designed to undermine the commitment to individual rights, including freedom of choice in the use of language, embodied in the Charter. Some critics were apprehensive that the clauses would create a hierarchy of more favoured rights at the expense of other rights and freedoms.

For discussion of the history of constitutional amendments, including these controversial provisions, see Peter Russell, *Constitutional Odyssey*, 3d ed. (Toronto: University of Toronto Press, 2004).

Following the narrow defeat of the sovereignty proposal in the October 1995 Quebec referendum, the federal Parliament, on December 6, 1995 (*House of Commons Debates, First Session—Thirty-Fifth Parliament*, at 17288), passed a resolution on the distinct society in the following terms:

> That whereas the people of Quebec have expressed the desire for recognition of Quebec's distinct society:
>
> - The House recognize that Quebec's is a distinct society within Canada;
> - The House recognize that Quebec's distinct society includes its French-speaking majority, unique culture and civil law tradition;
> - The House undertake to be guided by this reality;
> - The House encourage all components of the legislative and executive branches of government to take note of this recognition and be guided in their conduct accordingly.

CHAPTER TWENTY-FIVE

Enforcement of Rights

This chapter focuses on the remedial issues that arise after a breach of Charter rights has been established. It also deals, briefly, with two other issues, closely related to remedies, which arise in enforcing Charter rights—that of standing to seek remedies for breach of Charter rights and that of the jurisdictional competence of various courts and tribunals to deal with Charter issues and grant the remedies sought. Although related conceptually to remedies, both of these issues arise at a very different stage of a Charter case—that is, at the very beginning—and must be determined before the case can be heard.

I. REMEDIES

A. Introduction

Fundamental human rights and freedoms are meaningless absent effective means for their enforcement. In contrast to the *Canadian Bill of Rights*, the Charter includes, in s. 24, an explicit remedial provision. Section 24(1) reads as follows:

> Anyone whose rights or freedoms, as guaranteed by this Charter, have been infringed or denied may apply to a court of competent jurisdiction to obtain such remedy as the court considers appropriate and just in the circumstances.

Section 24(2) goes on to make explicit provision for the remedy of exclusion of evidence obtained in violation of Charter rights, a remedy that will often be sought in the criminal law context, but which will not be further considered in this chapter.

In addition to s. 24 of the Charter, s. 52(1) of the *Constitution Act, 1982*, which applies to the entire Constitution, is also available for enforcement of Charter rights. Section 52(1) reads:

> The Constitution of Canada is the supreme law of Canada, and any law that is inconsistent with the provisions of the Constitution is, to the extent of the inconsistency, of no force or effect.

The relationship between s. 24(1) of the Charter and s. 52(1) of the *Constitution Act, 1982* has been the source of some confusion. Initially, some believed that s. 24 was the exclusive source of remedial relief for Charter infringements, including declarations of invalidity. This view was rejected by the Supreme Court of Canada in *R v. Big M Drug Mart Ltd.*, [1985] 1 SCR 295, 18 DLR (4th) 321, excerpted in Chapter 19, Freedom of Religion, where it concluded that s. 52 was available in cases where the constitutionality of the legislation was at issue and a declaration of invalidity was sought. Dickson CJC, for the majority, commented at 336 DLR:

Section 24(1) sets out a remedy for individuals (whether real persons or artificial ones such as corporations) whose rights under the Charter have been infringed. It is not, however, the only recourse in the face of unconstitutional legislation. Where, as here, the challenge is based on the unconstitutionality of the legislation, recourse to s. 24 is unnecessary and the particular effect on the challenging party is irrelevant.

(One of the implications of the availability of relief for Charter violations under s. 52 is that standing to raise Charter issues may be extended beyond those whose rights have been directly infringed. Such occurred in *Big M* where a corporation defending a criminal charge was allowed to challenge the constitutionality of the law under which it had been charged although it could not allege any violation of its own Charter rights. Issues of standing in Charter litigation are discussed further in Section II, below.)

While some of the finer issues with respect to the relationship between s. 24 of the Charter and s. 52 of the *Constitution Act, 1982* remain unresolved, it is now generally understood that declarations of legislative invalidity, including declarations of partial invalidity (see below, Section I.B, are granted pursuant to s. 52; s. 24 provides for a broad range of individualized remedies, which include, in addition to the exclusion of evidence expressly provided for by s. 24(2), declarations that the rights of an individual or group have been infringed; damages; and injunctions (both prohibitory and mandatory). There has been some question about whether s. 24(1) might also allow for the remedy of what have been called constitutional exemptions—that is, orders exempting an individual from the application of a particular law (see further discussion below, Section I.B.5). However, in *R v. Ferguson*, [2008] 1 SCR 96, 2008 SCC 6, where the issue was relief from a mandatory sentence, the Supreme Court of Canada cast doubt on this and indicated that such relief was only available under s. 52(1) and not under s. 24(1). Note that while s. 52 relief is available only where *laws* (including delegated legislation) are being challenged, s. 24 remedies are available in cases where the Charter infringement is the result of the actions of public officials, including the police, who are operating outside the legitimate—that is, constitutional—scope of their authority. As a general rule, an individual remedy under s. 24(1)—for example, damages—will not be available when a declaration of invalidity has been granted under s. 52(1), although the Supreme Court has not completely precluded the possibility of combining remedies under ss. 24(1) and 52(1): see *Mackin v. New Brunswick*, [2002] 1 SCR 405, 2002 SCC 13.

As discussed in the extract immediately below, the Charter, with its extensive array of remedial possibilities, has focused attention on the large degree of judicial discretion involved in the choice of constitutional remedies. This has prompted discussion of a sort hitherto largely absent from our constitutional tradition about the factors that should influence that choice.

K. Roach, *Constitutional Remedies in Canada*
(Aurora, ON: Canada Law Book, 1994), at 3-1 to 3-3, and 3-35 to 3-37
(footnotes omitted)

Not surprisingly, debates in legal theory about the proper role of law and judicial review echo through constitutional remedies. Constitutional remedies can have different purposes and are bounded by a variety of constraints. The main purposes of constitutional remedies outlined in this chapter are the correction of constitutional violations and the regulation of governmental behaviour. The constraints examined are the need to balance the interests affected by remedies and to respect appropriate institutional roles. ...

In some contexts, different purposes and constraints may be more relevant than others. When responding to an overcrowded prison, a deficient minority language school system or a discriminatory workplace, for example, it may be impossible for a court to correct the harmful effects of a violation fully or immediately. In such institutional contexts, declarations and injunctions may be issued in order to change governmental behaviour while, at the same time, balancing the interests affected by the remedy and respecting limits on the role of the judiciary. A remedy need not serve only one purpose or recognize one constraint.

Disagreements about the appropriate role of the judiciary lie at the heart of debate about remedial purposes and constraints. The goal of correcting constitutional violations is associated with a classical model of adjudication in which judges provide remedies for those who have suffered violations and attempt to restore victims to the position they occupied before the violation. Under corrective theory, judges are only justified and competent to order remedies to the extent that they repair harms caused by a government's violation. Judges should leave more robust remedial ambitions to "the legislative and administrative direction of the community as the pursuit of distributive justice." On the other hand, when a violation is proven, they should insist on full correction without attempting either to balance the affected interests or change governmental behaviour in the future. If a court focuses on correcting harms caused by proven violations, it will not have to worry about infringing the role of other branches of government to pursue distributive justice.

Constitutional remedies that attempt to regulate governmental behaviour are associated with a public model of adjudication which stresses that remedial decision-making is a more instrumental and contingent process than determining violations of constitutional rights. ... [On this model] judges do not attempt to deduce remedies from the nature of the violation but rather fashion them to achieve compliance with the Constitution in the future. Courts can invoke the breadth of their remedial powers at equity to justify ordering remedies that respond to harms and conditions that may not be causally connected to proven violations and also to balance all the interests affected by the remedy. Courts are concerned with implementing their decisions, and to this end, they can delay and supervise the remedial process and rely on negotiations between the affected interests to win acceptance for their remedies. ...

Regard for the limits of the judicial role and the appropriate roles of legislatures is an important social interest that is often considered when devising remedies. Even though they are granted explicit mandates in s. 24 of the Charter and s. 52(1) *Constitution Act, 1982* to provide constitutional remedies, Canadian courts have been concerned about not exceeding their role when devising constitutional remedies.

One perhaps paradoxical effect of the concern not to intrude on the role of legislatures has been an inclination for Canadian courts to strike unconstitutional laws down in their entirety rather than attempting to save them by reading in terms or granting limited constitutional exemptions. ... Another consequence of the concern not to invade the role of the legislature is a preference for general forms of declaratory relief as opposed to specific or mandatory remedies. ... [As well,] although remedies can and do affect budgets, courts hesitate to interfere unduly with budgetary priorities.

Most constitutional cases in Canada contemplate a dialogue between the courts and the legislature. A judicial ruling is rarely final because the legislature can respond with new legislation to be justified under s. 1 or even exempted from certain Charter rights by s. 33. In some cases, Canadian courts have invited a legislative reply by suspending a declaration of invalidity and allowing the legislature an opportunity to devise constitutional legislation before the court's declaration of invalidity takes effect.

The material that follows will provide a more detailed examination, first, of the variants on the declaration of invalidity available under s. 52(1) of the *Constitution Act, 1982* and, second, of the individual remedies that may be ordered under s. 24(1) of the Charter. For further discussion of the remedial issues raised by the Charter, see Kent Roach, *Constitutional Remedies in Canada*, looseleaf ed. (Aurora, ON: Canada Law Book, 1994).

B. Remedies Under Section 52(1) of the Constitution Act, 1982

1. Introduction and Overview

The focus of this section will be on the use of the declaration of invalidity under s. 52 as a remedy for violations of rights under the Charter. As courts have faced the new forms of constitutional infringements that arise under the Charter, they have begun to develop and utilize variations on the standard declaration of invalidity familiar from federalism.

A declaration that a law is invalid in its entirety may constitute an overly broad remedy in cases where only some parts of the law or some of its applications infringe the Charter. There are a variety of ways to structure more limited remedies that will save the permissible applications of the law and simply preclude those that are impermissible. Partial invalidation of laws may be accomplished through the techniques of *severance, reading down, reading in*, and *constitutional exemptions*.

A declaration of invalidity may also be a problematic remedy in the case of so-called underinclusive laws, where the problem with the law is that benefits being provided to some individuals are not being provided to others, creating a situation that violates the equality guarantees found in s. 15 of the Charter. Striking down the law will have the result of depriving those who are currently entitled to benefits, as well as providing no benefit to the person challenging the law. In cases of underinclusive laws, extension of benefits is a possible remedy that may be achieved either through severance of an explicit limitation on the operation of the law or by *reading in* an extension of benefits.

While these new remedial possibilities under the Charter have the advantage of preserving many socially useful laws and avoiding the creation of large legislative gaps, they also raise concerns about judicial usurpation of the legislative role. At what point do courts become subject to the charge that they are engaging in the rewriting or drafting of legislation, a task more appropriately left to the legislature?

Another remedial option, which avoids the legislative void created by the immediate nullification of a law and does not involve the judiciary in reshaping a new law that will meet the dictates of the Charter, is the *temporary suspension of a declaration of invalidity* for a period of time to allow Parliament or the provincial legislature to fill the void. While attractive from the perspective of maintaining an appropriate judicial role, this remedy may fail to provide adequate redress for a violation of Charter rights as it allows a state of affairs that has been found to violate the Charter to persist for a period of time despite the violation.

The first comprehensive treatment by the Supreme Court of Canada of the remedial issues raised by the Charter and in particular constitutionally underinclusive legislation, is found in *Schachter v. Canada*, reproduced below.

Schachter v. Canada
[1992] 2 SCR 679, 93 DLR (4th) 1

[At the time this case was litigated, the *Unemployment Insurance Act* provided mothers who had given birth with 15 weeks of maternity benefits (s. 30) and adoptive parents with 15 weeks of parenting leave, following the placement of their child with them, the benefits to be shared between the two parents according to their wishes (s. 32). A father, whose claim for "paternity benefits" following the birth of his child was dismissed as not falling within the provisions of the Act, challenged the decision as a violation of his rights to equality under s. 15 of the Charter. At trial, Strayer J found a violation of s. 15 of the Charter in that s. 32 discriminated between natural parents and adoptive parents with respect to parental leave. (No s. 1 argument was made.) With respect to the issue of the appropriate remedy, Strayer J granted declaratory relief under s. 24(1), extending to natural parents the same benefits as were granted to adoptive parents under s. 32, without affecting a woman's right to maternity benefits. On appeal to the Federal Court of Appeal, the parties conceded a violation of s. 15 of the Charter, and the only issue appealed was the jurisdiction of the trial judge to order the remedy granted. The Court of Appeal upheld Strayer J's decision. An appeal was taken to the Supreme Court of Canada.]

LAMER CJC (Sopinka, Gonthier, Cory, and McLachlin JJ concurring): ...

I. *Reading In as a Remedial Option Under Section 52*

A court has flexibility in determining what course of action to take following a violation of the Charter which does not survive s. 1 scrutiny. Section 52 of the *Constitution Act, 1982* mandates the striking down of any law that is inconsistent with the provisions of the Constitution, but only "to the extent of the inconsistency." Depending upon the circumstances, a court may simply strike down, it may strike down and temporarily suspend the declaration of invalidity, or it may resort to the techniques of reading down or reading in. In addition, s. 24 of the Charter extends to any court of competent jurisdiction the power to grant an "appropriate and just" remedy to "[a]nyone whose [Charter] rights and freedoms ... have been infringed or denied." In choosing how to apply s. 52 or s. 24 a court will determine its course of action with reference to the nature of the violation and the context of the specific legislation under consideration.

A. The Doctrine of Severance

The flexibility of the language of s. 52 is not a new development in Canadian constitutional law. The courts have always struck down laws only to the extent of the inconsistency using the doctrine of severance or "reading down." Severance is used by the courts so as to interfere with the laws adopted by the legislature as little as possible. Generally speaking, when only a part of a statute or provision violates the Constitution, it is common sense that only the offending portion should be declared to be of no force or effect, and the rest should be spared. ...

[A]s Rogerson has pointed out [in "The Judicial Search for Appropriate Remedies Under the Charter: The Examples of Overbreadth and Vagueness," in Sharpe, ed., *Charter Litigation* (1987), at 250-52], it is logical to expect that severance would be a more prominent technique under the Charter than it has been in division of powers cases. In division of powers cases the question of constitutional validity often turns on an overall examination of the pith and substance of the legislation rather than on an examination of the effects of particular portions of the legislation on individual rights. Where a statute violates the division of powers, it tends to do so as a whole. This is not so of violations of the Charter where the offending portion tends to be more limited.

Where the offending portion of a statute can be defined in a limited manner it is consistent with legal principles to declare inoperative only that limited portion. In that way, as much of the legislative purpose as possible may be realized. However, there are some cases in which to sever the offending portion would actually be more intrusive to the legislative purpose than the alternate course of striking down provisions which are not themselves offensive but which are closely connected with those that are. This concern is reflected in the classic statement of the test for severance in *Attorney-General for Alberta v. Attorney-General for Canada*, [1947] AC 503 (PC), at p. 518:

> The real question is whether what remains is so inextricably bound up with the part declared invalid that what remains cannot independently survive or, as it has sometimes been put, whether on a fair review of the whole matter it can be assumed that the legislature would have enacted what survives without enacting the part that is ultra vires at all.

This test recognizes that the seemingly laudable purpose of retaining the parts of the legislative scheme which do not offend the Constitution rests on an assumption that the legislature would have passed the constitutionally sound part of the scheme without the unsound part. In some cases this assumption will not be a safe one. In those cases it will be necessary to go further and declare inoperative portions of the legislation which are not themselves unsound. ...

B. Reading In as Akin to Severance

This same approach should be applied to the question of reading in since extension by way of reading in is closely akin to the practice of severance. The difference is the manner in which the extent of the inconsistency is defined. In the usual case of severance the inconsistency is defined as something improperly included in the statute which can be severed and struck down. In the case of reading in the inconsistency is defined as what the statute wrongly excludes rather than what it wrongly includes. Where the inconsistency is defined as what the statute excludes, the logical result of declaring inoperative that inconsistency may be to include the excluded group within the statutory scheme. This has the effect of extending the reach of the statute by way of reading in rather than reading down.

A statute may be worded in such a way that it gives a benefit or right to one group (inclusive wording) [for example, "A benefits"] or it may be worded to give a right or benefit to everyone except a certain group (exclusive wording) [for example, "Everyone benefits except B"]. It would be an arbitrary distinction to treat inclusively and exclusively worded statutes differently. To do so would create a situation where the style of drafting would be the single critical factor in the determination of a remedy. ...

The first example would require the court to "read in" the words "and B," while the second example would require the court to "strike out" the words "except B." In each case, the result would be identical.

Accordingly, whether a court "reads in" or "strikes out" words from a challenged law, the focus of the court should be on the appropriate remedy in the circumstances and not on the label used to arrive at the result.

There is nothing in s. 52 of the *Constitution Act, 1982* to suggest that the court should be restricted to the verbal formula employed by the legislature in defining the inconsistency between a statute and the Constitution. Section 52 does not say that the words expressing a law are of no force or effect to the extent that they are inconsistent with the Constitution. It says that a law is of no force or effect to the extent of the inconsistency. Therefore, the inconsistency can be defined as what is left out of the verbal formula as well as what is wrongly included. ...

C. The Purposes of Reading In and Severance

(i) Respect for the Role of the Legislature

The logical parallels between reading in and severance are mirrored by their parallel purposes. Reading in is as important a tool as severance in avoiding undue intrusion into the legislative sphere. As with severance, the purpose of reading in is to be as faithful as possible within the requirements of the Constitution to the scheme enacted by the Legislature. Rogerson makes this observation at p. 288:

> Courts should certainly go as far as required to protect rights, but no further. Interference with legitimate legislative purposes should be minimized and laws serving such purposes should be allowed to remain operative to the extent that rights are not violated. Legislation which serves desirable social purposes may give rise to entitlements which themselves deserve some protection.

Of course, reading in will not always constitute the lesser intrusion for the same reason that severance sometimes does not. In some cases, it will not be a safe assumption that the legislature would have enacted the constitutionally permissible part of its enactment without the impermissible part. For example, in a benefits case, it may not be a safe assumption that the legislature would have enacted a benefits scheme if it were impermissible to exclude particular parties from entitlement under that scheme.

(ii) Respect for the Purposes of the Charter

Just as reading in is sometimes required in order to respect the purposes of the legislature, it is also sometimes required in order to respect the purposes of the Charter. The absolute unavailability of reading in would mean that the standards developed under the Charter would have to be applied in certain cases in ways which would derogate from the deeper social purposes of the Charter. ... [E]ven in situations where the standards of the Charter allow for more than one remedial response, the purposes of the Charter may encourage one kind of response more strongly than another.

This is best illustrated by the case of *Attorney-General of Nova Scotia v. Phillips* (1986), 34 DLR (4th) 633 (NS CA). In that case, a form of welfare benefit was available to single mothers but not single fathers. This was held to violate s. 15 of the Charter since benefits should be available to single mothers and single fathers equally. However, the court held that s. 15 merely required equal benefit, so that the Charter would be equally satisfied whether the benefit was available to both mothers and fathers or to neither. Given this and the court's conclusion that it could not extend benefits, the only available course was to nullify the benefits to single mothers. The irony of this result is obvious.

Perhaps in some cases s. 15 does simply require relative equality and is just as satisfied with equal graveyards as equal vineyards, as it has sometimes been put (see [E.] Caminker ["A Norm-Based Remedial Model for Underinclusive Statutes" (1986), 95 *Yale Law Journal* 1185], at p. 1186). Yet the nullification of benefits to single mothers does not sit well with the overall purpose of s. 15 of the Charter and for s. 15 to have such a result clearly amounts to "equality with a vengeance," as LEAF [Women's Legal Action and Education Fund], one of the intervenors in this case, has suggested. While s. 15 may not absolutely require that benefits be available to single mothers, surely it at least encourages such action to relieve the disadvantaged position of persons in those circumstances. In cases of this kind, reading in allows the court to act in a manner more consistent with the basic purposes of the Charter.

Reading in should therefore be recognized as a legitimate remedy akin to severance and should be available under s. 52 in cases where it is an appropriate technique to fulfil the purposes of the Charter and at the same time minimize the interference of the court with the parts of legislation that do not themselves violate the Charter.

II. Choice of Remedial Options Under Section 52

A. Defining the Extent of the Inconsistency

The first step in choosing a remedial course under s. 52 is defining the extent of the inconsistency which must be struck down. Usually, the manner in which the law violates the Charter and the manner in which it fails to be justified under s. 1 will be critical to this determination. ...

In some circumstances, s. 52(1) mandates defining the inconsistent portion which must be struck down very broadly. This will almost always be the case where the legislation or legislative provision does not meet the first part of the *Oakes* test, in that the purpose is not sufficiently pressing or substantial to warrant overriding a Charter right. ... *R v. Big M Drug Mart Ltd.*, [1985] 1 SCR 295, 18 DLR (4th) 321, provides a clear example. ...

Where the purpose of the legislation or legislative provision is deemed to be pressing and substantial, but the means used to achieve this objective are found not to be rationally connected to it, the inconsistency to be struck down will generally be the whole of the portion of the legislation which fails the rational connection test. ...

Where the second and/or third elements of the proportionality test are not met, there is more flexibility in defining the extent of the inconsistency. For instance, if the legislative provision fails because it is not carefully tailored to be a minimal intrusion, or because it has effects disproportionate to its purpose, the inconsistency could be defined as being the provisions left out of the legislation which would carefully tailor it, or would avoid a disproportionate effect. According to the logic outlined above, such an inconsistency could be declared inoperative with the result that the statute was extended by way of reading in.

Striking down, severing or reading in may be appropriate in cases where the second and/or third elements of the proportionality test are not met. The choice of remedy will be guided by the following considerations.

B. Deciding Whether Severance or Reading In Is Appropriate

Having determined what the extent of the inconsistency is, the next question is whether that inconsistency may be dealt with by way of severance, or in some cases reading in, or whether an impugned provision must be struck down in its entirety.

(i) Remedial Precision

While reading in is the logical counterpart of severance, and serves the same purposes, there is one important distinction between the two practices which must be kept in mind. In the case of severance, the inconsistent part of the statutory provision can be defined with some precision on the basis of the requirements of the Constitution. This will not always be so in the case of reading in. In some cases, the question of how the statute ought to be extended in order to comply with the Constitution cannot be answered with a sufficient degree of precision on the basis of constitutional analysis. In such a case, it is the legislature's role to fill in the gaps, not the court's. This point is made most clearly in *Hunter v. Southam Inc.*, [1984] 2 SCR 145, 11 DLR (4th) 641, at p. 169 [SCR]:

> While the courts are guardians of the Constitution and of individuals' rights under it, it is the legislature's responsibility to enact legislation that embodies appropriate safeguards to comply with the Constitution's requirements. It should not fall to the courts to fill in the details that will render legislative lacunae constitutional.

In *Hunter*, the Court decided that the scheme for authorizing searches under the relevant legislation did not withstand Charter scrutiny. In such a circumstance, it would theoretically be possible to characterize the "extent of the inconsistency" as the absence of certain safeguards. Thus, in the abstract, the absence of appropriate safeguards could have been declared of no force or effect, which would have led to the establishment of the appropriate safeguards. However, this approach would have been inappropriate, because this would have required establishing a new scheme, the details of which would have been up to the Court to determine. ...

[T]he Court should not read in in cases where there is no manner of extension which flows with sufficient precision from the requirements of the Constitution. In such cases, to read in would amount to making *ad hoc* choices from a variety of options, none of which was pointed to with sufficient precision by the interaction between the statute in question and the requirements of the Constitution. This is the task of the legislature, not the courts.

(ii) Interference with the Legislative Objective

... The degree to which a particular remedy intrudes into the legislative sphere can only be determined by giving careful attention to the objective embodied in the legislation in question.

[Lamer CJC goes on to state that the legislature's choice of means to implement its objective must also be examined. If the choice of means is unequivocal, to further the objective of the legislative scheme through different means would constitute an unwarranted intrusion into the legislative domain.]

Even where extension by way of reading in can be used to further the legislative objective through the very means the legislature has chosen, to do so may, in some cases, involve an intrusion into budgetary decisions which cannot be supported. This Court has held, and rightly so, that budgetary considerations cannot be used to justify a violation under s. 1. However, such considerations are clearly relevant once a violation which does not survive s. 1 has been established, s. 52 is determined to have been engaged and the Court turns its attention to what action should be taken thereunder.

Any remedy granted by a court will have some budgetary repercussions whether it be a saving of money or an expenditure of money. Striking down or severance may well lead to an expenditure of money. ... In determining whether reading in is appropriate then, the question is not whether courts can make decisions that impact on budgetary policy, it is to what degree they can appropriately do so. A remedy which entails an intrusion into this sphere so substantial as to change the nature of the legislative scheme in question is clearly inappropriate.

(iii) The Change in Significance of the Remaining Portion

Another way of asking whether to read in or sever would be an illegitimate intrusion into the legislative sphere is to ask whether the significance of the part which would remain is substantially changed when the offending part is excised. ...

In cases where the issue is whether to extend benefits to a group not included in the statute, the question of the change in significance of the remaining portion sometimes focuses on the relative size of the two relevant groups. For instance, in *Knodel, supra*, Rowles J extended the provision of benefits to spouses to include same-sex spouses. She considered this course to be far less intrusive to the intention of the legislature than striking down the benefits to heterosexual spouses since the group to be added was much smaller than the group already benefitted ... .

Where the group to be added is smaller than the group originally benefitted, this is an indication that the assumption that the legislature would have enacted the benefit in any case is a sound one. When the group to be added is much larger than the group originally benefitted, this could indicate that the assumption is not safe. This is not because of the numbers *per se*. Rather, the numbers may indicate that for budgetary reasons, or simply because it constitutes a marked change in the thrust of the original program, it cannot be assumed that the legislature would have passed the benefit without the exclusion. In some contexts, the fact that the group to be added is much larger than the original group will not lead to these conclusions. ...

(iv) The Significance of the Remaining Portion

Other cases have focused on the significance or longstanding nature of the remaining portion. ...

It is sensible to consider the significance of the remaining portion when asking whether the assumption that the legislature would have enacted the remaining portion is a safe one. If the remaining portion is very significant, or of a long standing nature, it strengthens the assumption that it would have been enacted without the impermissible portion.

The significance of the remaining portion may be enhanced where the Constitution specifically encourages that sort of provision. ...

The fact that the permissible part of a provision is encouraged by the purposes of the Constitution, even if not mandated by it, strengthens the assumption that the legislature would have enacted it without the impermissible portion.

[Human rights codes, and in particular the case of *Re Blainey and Ontario Hockey Association* (1986), 54 OR (2d) 513 (CA), are given as an example. *Blainey* involved a situation where the Ontario *Human Rights Code* contained a general prohibition on discrimination on the grounds of sex, but created an exemption for athletic activities. After finding a violation of s. 15 of the Charter, the court severed the exemption, thereby in effect extending the benefits of the Code's protection against sex discrimination to athletic activities. Lamer CJC views this as the correct result given that it would be safe to assume that the legislature would have passed the general prohibition on discrimination even if it could not limit its application in the area of athletics.]

(v) Conclusion

It should be apparent from this analysis that there is no easy formula by which a court may decide whether severance or reading in is appropriate in a given case. While respect for the role of the legislature and the purposes of the Charter are the twin guiding principles, these principles can only be fulfilled with respect to the variety of considerations set out above which require careful attention in each case.

C. Whether to Temporarily Suspend the Declaration of Invalidity

Having identified the extent of the inconsistency, and having determined whether that inconsistency should be dealt with by way of striking down, severance or reading in, the court has identified what portion must be struck down. The final step is to determine whether the declaration of invalidity of that portion should be temporarily suspended.

A court may strike down legislation or a legislative provision but suspend the effect of that declaration until Parliament or the provincial legislature has had an opportunity to fill the void. This approach is clearly appropriate where the striking down of a provision poses a potential danger to the public (*R v. Swain*, [[1991] 1 SCR 933]) or otherwise threatens the rule of law (*Reference re Manitoba Language Rights*, [1985] 1 SCR 721, 19 DLR (4th) 1). It may also be appropriate in cases of underinclusiveness as opposed to overbreadth. For example, in this case some of the interveners argued that in cases where a denial of equal benefit of the law is alleged, the legislation in question is not usually problematic in and of itself. It is its underinclusiveness that is problematic so striking down the law immediately would deprive deserving persons of benefits without providing them to the applicant. At the same time, if there is no obligation on the government to provide the benefits in the first place, it may be inappropriate to go ahead and extend them. The logical remedy is to strike down but suspend the declaration of invalidity to allow the government to determine whether to cancel or extend the benefits.

I would emphasize that the question of whether to delay the effect of a declaration is an entirely separate question from whether reading in or nullification is the appropriate route under s. 52. While delayed declarations are appropriate in some cases, they are not a panacea for the problem of interference with the institution of the legislature under s. 52 of the *Constitution Act, 1982*.

A delayed declaration is a serious matter from the point of view of the enforcement of the Charter. A delayed declaration allows a state of affairs which has been found to violate standards embodied in the Charter to persist for a time despite the violation. There may be good pragmatic reasons to allow this in particular cases. However, reading in is much preferable where it is appropriate, since it immediately reconciles the legislation in question with the requirements of the Charter.

Furthermore, the fact that the court's declaration is delayed is not really relevant to the question of which course of action, reading in or nullification, is less intrusive upon the institution of the legislature. By deciding upon nullification or reading in, the court has already chosen the less intrusive path. If reading in is less intrusive than nullification in a particular case, then there is no reason to think that a delayed nullification would be any better. To delay nullification forces the matter back onto the legislative agenda at a time not of the choosing of the legislature, and within time limits under which the legislature would not normally be forced to act. This is a serious interference in itself with the institution of the legislature. Where reading in is appropriate, the legislature may consider the issue in its own good time and take whatever action it wishes. Thus delayed declarations of nullity should not be seen as preferable to reading in in cases where reading in is appropriate.

The question whether to delay the application of a declaration of nullity should therefore turn not on considerations of the role of the courts and the legislature, but rather on considerations listed earlier relating to the effect of an immediate declaration on the public. ...

IV. Remedial Options Appropriate to This Case

A. The Nature of the Right Involved

The right which was determined to be violated here is a positive right: the right to equal benefit of the law. Positive rights by their very nature tend to carry with them special considerations in the remedial context. It will be a rare occasion when a benefit conferring scheme is found to have an unconstitutional purpose. Cases involving positive rights are more likely to fall into the remedial classifications of reading down/reading in or striking down and suspending the operation of the declaration of invalidity than to mandate an immediate striking down. Indeed, if the benefit which is being conferred is itself constitutionally guaranteed (for example, the right to vote), reading in may be mandatory. For a court to deprive persons of a constitutionally guaranteed right by striking down underinclusive legislation would be absurd. Certainly the intrusion into the legislative sphere of extending a constitutionally guaranteed benefit is warranted when the benefit was itself guaranteed by the legislature through constitutional amendment.

Other rights will be more in the nature of "negative" rights, which merely restrict the government. However, even in those cases, the rights may have certain positive aspects. For instance, the right to life, liberty and security of the person is in one sense a negative right, but the requirement that the government respect the "fundamental principles of justice" may provide a basis for characterizing s. 7 as a positive right in some circumstances. Similarly, the equality right is a hybrid of sorts since it is neither purely positive nor purely negative. In some contexts it will be proper to characterize s. 15 as providing positive rights.

The benefit with which we are concerned here is a monetary benefit for parents under the *Unemployment Insurance Act, 1971*, not one which Parliament is constitutionally obliged to provide to the included group or the excluded group. What Parliament is obliged to do, by virtue of the conceded s. 15 violation, is equalize the provision of that benefit. The benefit itself is not constitutionally prohibited; it is simply underinclusive. Thus striking down the provision immediately would be inappropriate as such a course of action would deprive eligible persons of a benefit without providing any relief to the respondent. Such a situation demands, at the very least, that the operation of any declaration of invalidity be suspended to allow Parliament time to bring the provision into line with constitutional requirements. ... The question which remains is whether this is a case in which it is appropriate to go further and read the excluded group into the legislation. ...

B. The Context of the Unemployment Insurance Act, 1971

It is not difficult to discern the legislative objective of this scheme as a whole. ... It is, however, not as simple to discern the objective of the particular provision. It is not clear on the text of the provision alone that the purpose of it is to extend benefits to parents of newborns caring for them at home, a purpose which reading in the excluded group would further. Indeed, on the express language of the provision, one could quickly conclude that the benefits were only intended to be conferred on adoptive parents and that natural parents were deliberately excluded. One could postulate that the provision was specifically aimed at responding to circumstances peculiar to adoptive parents. Certainly, this possibility cannot be ruled out on the basis of the text of the provision alone, and we have not been provided with the further assistance of a s. 1 argument here or in the courts below.

Without a mandate based on a clear legislative objective, it would be imprudent for me to take the course of reading the excluded group into the legislation. A consideration of the budgetary implications of such a course of action further underlines this conclusion. ... Here, the excluded group sought to be included likely vastly outnumbers the group to whom the benefits were already extended.

Given the nature of the benefit and the size of the group to whom it is sought to be extended, to read in natural parents would in these circumstances constitute a substantial intrusion into the legislative domain. This intrusion would be substantial enough to change potentially the nature of the scheme as a whole. If this Court were to dictate that the same benefits conferred on adoptive parents under s. 32 be extended to natural parents, the ensuing financial shake-up could mean that other benefits to other disadvantaged groups would have to be done away with to pay for the extension. Parliament and the provincial legislatures are much better equipped to assess the whole picture in formulating solutions in cases such as these. Clearly, the appropriate action for the Court to take is to declare the provision invalid but to suspend that declaration to allow the legislative body in question to weigh all the relevant factors in amending the legislation to meet constitutional requirements.

I think it significant and worthy of mention that in this case Parliament did amend the impugned provision following the launching of this action, and that that amendment was not the one that reading in would have imposed. Parliament equalized the benefits given to adoptive parents and natural parents but not on the same terms as they were originally conferred by s. 32. The two groups now receive equal benefits for ten weeks rather than the original fifteen. This situation provides a valuable illustration of the dangers associated with reading in when legislative intention with respect to budgetary issues is not clear. In this case, reading in would not necessarily further the legislative objective and it would definitely interfere with budgetary decisions in that it would mandate the expenditure of a greater sum of money than Parliament is willing or able to allocate to the program in question. ...

Disposition

In the result, the appeal is allowed and the judgment of the trial judge set aside. Normally, I would order that s. 32 of the *Unemployment Insurance Act, 1971* ... be struck down pursuant to s. 52 and be declared to be of no force or effect, and I would further suspend the operation of this declaration to allow Parliament to amend the legislation to bring it into line with its constitutional obligations. There is, however, no need for a declaration of invalidity or a suspension thereof at this stage of this matter given the November 1990 repeal and replacement of the impugned provision.

[La Forest J, with whom L'Heureux-Dubé J concurred, wrote a brief judgment in which he concurred with the result reached by Lamer CJC, but distanced himself somewhat from the broader pronouncements with respect to the assessment of when reading in or reading down should be utilized. La Forest J cautioned that a mechanistic approach, such as may be encouraged by tying the process too closely to the *Oakes* checklist, must be avoided, and that the factual context may be an important consideration. He suggested, for example, that there may be more room for judicial rewriting of social assistance schemes than of laws that impinge on the liberty of subjects, where rewriting would have the effect of enhancing police powers.]

Appeal allowed.

2. Underinclusive Laws and Reading In

The two cases that follow, *Vriend v. Alberta* and *M. v. H.*, illustrate different remedial responses to underinclusive laws through application of the factors laid out in *Schachter*. It should be noted that while these cases, like *Schachter*, both involved equality rights under s. 15 of the Charter, issues of underinclusiveness may also arise in other contexts where the right in issue is understood as imposing positive obligations on government; see, for example, *Dunmore v. Ontario (Attorney General)*, [2001] 3 SCR 1016, 2001 SCC 94, 207 DLR (4th) 193, found in Chapter 21, Freedom of Association.

Vriend v. Alberta
[1998] 1 SCR 493, 156 DLR (4th) 385

[In this case, which is also discussed in Chapter 18, Application, and Chapter 23, Equality Rights, the Supreme Court of Canada found that the omission of sexual orientation from the list of prohibited grounds of discrimination found in Alberta's human rights legislation—the *Individual's Rights Protection Act* (IRPA)—constituted an unjustifiable violation of s. 15 of the Charter. The legislative history showed that the omission of sexual orientation was deliberate. The facts of the case, which are drawn upon to some extent in the discussion of the appropriate remedy, involved a gay employee of a religious college who had been fired when his homosexuality was discovered. Unable to bring a complaint of discrimination under the IRPA because of the legislation's failure to protect against discrimination on the grounds of sexual orientation, he challenged the omission as a violation of s. 15 of the Charter. From a remedial perspective, *Vriend* is significant as one of the few cases in which the Supreme Court has extended constitutionally underinclusive legislation by reading in rather than striking it down. As will be seen, however, the use of this remedy was not without controversy and dissent.]

IACOBUCCI J (Lamer CJC, Gonthier, Cory, McLachlin, and Bastarache JJ concurring): [129] Having found the exclusion of sexual orientation from the *IRPA* to be an unjustifiable violation of the appellants' equality rights, I now turn to the question of remedy under s. 52 of the *Constitution Act, 1982*.

· · ·

[144] The leading case on constitutional remedies is *Schachter* [*v. Canada*, [1992] 2 SCR 679]. Writing on behalf of the majority in *Schachter*, Lamer CJ stated that the first step in selecting a remedial course under s. 52 is to define the extent of the Charter

inconsistency which must be struck down. In the present case, that inconsistency is the exclusion of sexual orientation from the protected grounds of the *IRPA*. As I have concluded above, this exclusion is an unjustifiable infringement upon the equality rights guaranteed in s. 15 of the Charter.

[145] Once the Charter inconsistency has been identified, the next step is to determine which remedy is appropriate. In *Schachter*, this Court noted that, depending upon the circumstances, there are several remedial options available to a court in dealing with a Charter violation that was not saved by s. 1. These include striking down the legislation, severance of the offending sections, striking down or severance with a temporary suspension of the declaration of invalidity, reading down, and reading provisions into the legislation.

[146] Because the Charter violation in the instant case stems from an omission, the remedy of reading down is simply not available. Further, I note that given the considerable number of sections at issue in this case and the important roles they play in the scheme of the *IRPA* as a whole, severance of these sections from the remainder of the Act would be akin to striking down the entire Act.

. . .

[148] In *Schachter*, Lamer CJ noted that when determining whether the remedy of reading in is appropriate, courts must have regard to the "twin guiding principles," namely, respect for the role of the legislature and respect for the purposes of the Charter ... . Turning first to the role of the legislature, Lamer CJ stated at p. 700 that reading in is an important tool in "avoiding undue intrusion into the legislative sphere. ... [T]he purpose of reading in is to be as faithful as possible within the requirements of the Constitution to the scheme enacted by the Legislature."

. . .

[150] As I discussed above, the purpose of the *IRPA* is the recognition and protection of the inherent dignity and inalienable rights of Albertans through the elimination of discriminatory practices. It seems to me that the remedy of reading in would minimize interference with this clearly legitimate legislative purpose and thereby avoid excessive intrusion into the legislative sphere whereas striking down the *IRPA* would deprive all Albertans of human rights protection and thereby unduly interfere with the scheme enacted by the Legislature.

[151] I find support for my position in *Haig* [*v. Canada* (1992), 9 OR (3d) 495 (CA)], where the Ontario Court of Appeal read the words "sexual orientation" into s. 3(1) of the *Canadian Human Rights Act*, RSC 1985, c. H-6. At p. 508, Krever JA, writing for a unanimous court, stated that it was

> inconceivable ... that Parliament would have preferred no human rights Act over one that included sexual orientation as a prohibited ground of discrimination. To believe otherwise would be a gratuitous insult to Parliament.

[152] Turning to the second of the twin guiding principles, the respondents suggest that the facts of this case are illustrative of a conflict between two grounds, namely, religion and sexual orientation. If sexual orientation were simply read into the *IRPA*, the respondents contend that this would undermine the ability of the *IRPA* to provide protection against discrimination based on religion, one of the fundamental goals of that legislation. This result is alleged to be "inconsistent with the deeper social purposes of the Charter."

[153] I concluded above that the internal balancing mechanisms of the *IRPA* were an adequate means of disposing of any conflict that might arise between religion and sexual orientation. [The internal balancing mechanisms included a general defence that the discrimination was "reasonable and justifiable in the circumstances" and an exemption for *bona fide* occupational requirements.] Thus, I cannot accept the respondents' assertion that the reading in approach does not respect the purposes of the Charter. In fact, as I see the matter, reading sexual orientation into the *IRPA* as a further ground of prohibited discrimination can only enhance those purposes. The Charter, like the *IRPA*, is concerned with the promotion and protection of inherent dignity and inalienable rights. Thus, expanding the list of prohibited grounds of discrimination in the *IRPA* allows this Court to act in a manner which, consistent with the purposes of the Charter, would augment the scope of the *IRPA*'s protections. In contrast, striking down or severing parts of the *IRPA* would deny all Albertans protection from marketplace discrimination. In my view, this result is clearly antithetical to the purposes of the Charter.

[154] In *Schachter, supra*, Lamer CJ noted that the twin guiding principles can only be fulfilled if due consideration is given to several additional criteria which further inform the determination as to whether the remedy of reading in is appropriate. These include remedial precision, budgetary implications, effects on the thrust of the legislation, and interference with legislative objectives.

[155] As to the first of the above listed criteria, the court must be able to define with a "sufficient degree of precision" how the statute ought to be extended in order to comply with the Constitution. I do not believe that the present case is one in which this Court has been improperly called upon to fill in large gaps in the legislation. ...

[156] In her reasons in this case, Hunt JA concluded that there was insufficient remedial precision to justify the remedy of reading in. She expressed two concerns. Firstly, she held that adequate precision likely would not be possible without a definition of the term "sexual orientation." With respect, I cannot agree. Although the term "sexual orientation" has been defined in the human rights legislation of the Yukon Territory, it appears undefined in the *Canadian Human Rights Act*, the human rights legislation of Nova Scotia, New Brunswick, Quebec, Ontario, Manitoba, Saskatchewan, British Columbia, and s. 718.2(a)(i) of the *Criminal Code*, RSC 1985, c. C-46, as amended by SC 1995, c. 22, s. 6. In addition, "sexual orientation" was not defined when it was recognized by this Court in *Egan* [*v. Canada*, [1995] 2 SCR 513] as an analogous ground under s. 15 of the Charter. In my opinion, "sexual orientation" is a commonly used term with an easily discernible common sense meaning.

. . .

[158] Hunt JA was also troubled by the possible impact of reading in upon s. 7(2) of the *IRPA*. This section states that s. 7(1) (employment), as regards age and marital status, "does not affect the operation of any bona fide retirement or pension plan or the terms or conditions of any bona fide group or employee insurance plan." As the Court of Appeal heard no argument on this point and as there was no evidence before the court to explain the rationale behind this provision, Hunt JA held that, if the protections of the *IRPA* were to be extended to gay men and lesbians, it would be necessary to decide whether this group would be included or excluded from s. 7(2). She found that this was something the court was in no position to do. In light of this difficulty, Hunt JA was concerned that the

reading in remedy "would engage the court in the kind of 'filling in of details' against which Lamer CJC cautions in *Schachter* [above]" (p. 69).

[159] In my view, whether gay men and lesbians are included or excluded from s. 7(2) is a peripheral issue which does not deprive the reading in remedy of the requisite precision. I agree with K. Roach who noted that the legislature "can always subsequently intervene on matters of detail that are not dictated by the Constitution" (*Constitutional Remedies in Canada* (Aurora, Ont.: Canada Law Book, 1994) (loose-leaf), at p. 14-64.1). I therefore conclude on this point that, in the present case, there is sufficient remedial precision to justify the remedy of reading in.

[160] Turning to budgetary repercussions, in the circumstances of the present appeal, such considerations are not sufficiently significant to warrant avoiding the reading in approach. On this issue, the trial judge stated (at p. 18):

> There will undoubtedly be some budgetary impact on the Human Rights Commission as a result of the addition of sexual orientation as a prohibited ground of discrimination. But, unlike *Schachter* [*supra*], it would not be substantial enough to change the nature of the scheme of the legislation.

[161] As to the effects on the thrust of the legislation, it is difficult to see any deleterious impact. All persons covered under the current scope of the *IRPA* would continue to benefit from the protection provided by the Act in the same manner as they had before the reading in of sexual orientation. Thus, I conclude that it is reasonable to assume that, if the Legislature had been faced with the choice of having no human rights statute or having one that offered protection on the ground of sexual orientation, the latter option would have been chosen. As the inclusion of sexual orientation in the *IRPA* does not alter the legislation to any significant degree, it is reasonable to assume that the Legislature would have enacted it in any event.

[162] In addition, in *Schachter, supra*, Lamer CJ noted that, in cases where the issue is whether to extend benefits to a group excluded from the legislation, the question of the effects on the thrust of the legislation will sometimes focus on the size of the group to be added as compared to the group originally benefited. ...

[163] Lamer CJ went on to note that, "[w]here the group to be added is smaller than the group originally benefitted, this is an indication that the assumption that the legislature would have enacted the benefit in any case is a sound one" (p. 712). In the present case, gay men and lesbians are clearly a smaller group than those already benefited by the *IRPA*. Thus, in my view, reading in remains the less intrusive option.

[164] The final criterion to examine is interference with the legislative objective. In *Schachter*, Lamer CJ commented upon this factor as follows (at pp. 707-8):

> The degree to which a particular remedy intrudes into the legislative sphere can only be determined by giving careful attention to the objective embodied in the legislation in question. ... A second level of legislative intention may be manifest in the means chosen to pursue that objective.

[165] With regard to the first level of legislative intention, as I discussed above, it is clear that reading sexual orientation into the *IRPA* would not interfere with the objective of the legislation. Rather, in my view, it can only enhance that objective. However, at first

blush, it appears that reading in might interfere with the second level of legislative intention identified by Lamer CJ

[166] As the Alberta Legislature has expressly chosen to exclude sexual orientation from the list of prohibited grounds of discrimination in the *IRPA*, the respondents argue that reading in would unduly interfere with the will of the Government. McClung JA shares this view. In his opinion, the remedy of reading in will never be appropriate where a legislative omission reflects a deliberate choice of the legislating body. He states that if a statute is unconstitutional, "the preferred consequence should be its return to the sponsoring legislature for representative, constitutional overhaul" (p. 35). However, as I see the matter, by definition, Charter scrutiny will always involve some interference with the legislative will.

[167] Where a statute has been found to be unconstitutional, whether the court chooses to read provisions into the legislation or to strike it down, legislative intent is necessarily interfered with to some extent. Therefore, the closest a court can come to respecting the legislative intention is to determine what the legislature would likely have done if it had known that its chosen measures would be found unconstitutional. As I see the matter, a deliberate choice of means will not act as a bar to reading in save for those circumstances in which the means chosen can be shown to be of such centrality to the aims of the legislature and so integral to the scheme of the legislation, that the legislature would not have enacted the statute without them.

[168] Indeed, as noted by the intervener Canadian Jewish Congress, if reading in is always deemed an inappropriate remedy where a government has expressly chosen a course of action, this amounts to the suggestion that whenever a government violates a Charter right, it ought to do so in a deliberate manner so as to avoid the remedy of reading in. In my view, this is a wholly unacceptable result.

[169] In the case at bar, the means chosen by the legislature, namely, the exclusion of sexual orientation from the *IRPA*, can hardly be described as integral to the scheme of that Act. Nor can I accept that this choice was of such centrality to the aims of the legislature that it would prefer to sacrifice the entire *IRPA* rather than include sexual orientation as a prohibited ground of discrimination, particularly for the reasons I will now discuss.

[170] As mentioned by my colleague Cory J, in 1993, the Alberta Legislature appointed the Alberta Human Rights Review Panel to conduct a public review of the *IRPA* and the Alberta Human Rights Commission. The Panel issued a report making several recommendations including the inclusion of sexual orientation as a prohibited ground of discrimination in all areas covered by the Act. The Government responded to this recommendation by deferring the decision to the judiciary: "This recommendation will be dealt with through the current court case *Vriend* ... ."

[171] In my opinion, this statement is a clear indication that, in light of the controversy surrounding the protection of gay men and lesbians under the *IRPA*, it was the intention of the Alberta Legislature to defer to the courts on this issue. Indeed, I interpret this statement to be an express invitation for the courts to read sexual orientation into the *IRPA* in the event that its exclusion from the legislation is found to violate the provisions of the Charter. Therefore, primarily because of this and contrary to the assertions of the respondents, I believe that, in these circumstances, the remedy of reading in is entirely consistent with the legislative intention.

[172] In addition to the comments which I outlined above, McClung JA also criticizes the remedy of reading in on a more fundamental level. He views the reading of provisions into a statute as an unacceptable intrusion of the courts into the legislative process. Commenting upon the trial judge's decision to read sexual orientation into the *IRPA* he stated (at pp. 29-30):

> To amend and extend it, by reading up to include "sexual orientation" was a sizeable judicial intervention into the affairs of the community and, at a minimum, an undesirable arrogation of legislative power by the court. ... [T]o me it is an extravagant exercise for any s. 96 judge to use the enormous review power of his or her office in this way in order to wean competent legislatures from their "errors."

...

[174] With respect ... I do not accept that extending the legislation in this case is an undemocratic exercise of judicial power.

...

[176] ... [T]he concept of democracy means more than majority rule as Dickson CJ so ably reminded us in *Oakes* [*R v.*, [1986] 1 SCR 103]. In my view, a democracy requires that legislators take into account the interests of majorities and minorities alike, all of whom will be affected by the decisions they make. Where the interests of a minority have been denied consideration, especially where that group has historically been the target of prejudice and discrimination, I believe that judicial intervention is warranted to correct a democratic process that has acted improperly.

...

[178] ... When a court remedies an unconstitutional statute by reading in provisions, no doubt this constrains the legislative process and therefore should not be done needlessly, but only after considered examination. However, in my view, the "parliamentary safeguards" remain. Governments are free to modify the amended legislation by passing exceptions and defences which they feel can be justified under s. 1 of the Charter. Thus, when a court reads in, this is not the end of the legislative process because the legislature can pass new legislation in response, as I outlined above (see also Hogg and Bushell ["The Charter Dialogue Between Courts and Legislature" (1997), 35 *Osgoode Hall Law Journal* 75]). Moreover, the legislators can always turn to s. 33 of the Charter, the override provision, which in my view is the ultimate "parliamentary safeguard."

[179] On the basis of the foregoing analysis, I conclude that reading sexual orientation into the impugned provisions of the *IRPA* is the most appropriate way of remedying this underinclusive legislation. The appellants suggest that this remedy should have immediate effect. I agree. There is no risk in the present case of harmful unintended consequences upon private parties or public funds. ... Further, the mechanisms to deal with complaints of discrimination on the basis of sexual orientation are already in place and require no significant adjustment.

MAJOR J (dissenting in part on the issue of remedy):

[194] With respect to remedy, Iacobucci J relies on the reasoning in *Schachter v. Canada*, [1992] 2 SCR 679, to support his conclusion that the words "sexual orientation" ought to be read into the *IRPA*. In my view, the analysis in *Schachter* with respect to read-

ing in is not compelling here. The Court there decided that the appropriate remedy was to strike down the relevant legislation but temporarily suspend the declaration of invalidity. The directions on "reading in" were not as the Chief Justice stated at p. 719, intended "as hard and fast rules to be applied regardless of factual context."

[195] In my opinion, *Schachter* did not contemplate the circumstances that pertain here, that is, where the Legislature's opposition to including sexual orientation as a prohibited ground of discrimination is abundantly clear on the record. Reading in may be appropriate where it can be safely assumed that the legislature itself would have remedied the underinclusiveness by extending the benefit or protection to the previously excluded group. That assumption cannot be made in this appeal.

[196] The issue may be that the Legislature would prefer no human rights act over one that includes sexual orientation as a prohibited ground of discrimination, or the issue may be how the legislation ought to be amended to bring it into conformity with the Charter. That determination is best left to the Legislature. As was stated in *Hunter v. Southam Inc.*, [1984] 2 SCR 145, at p. 169:

> While the courts are guardians of the Constitution and of individuals' rights under it, *it is the legislature's responsibility to enact legislation that embodies appropriate safeguards to comply with the Constitution's requirements. It should not fall to the courts to fill in the details that will render legislative lacunae constitutional.* [Emphasis added.]

[197] There are numerous ways in which the legislation could be amended to address the underinclusiveness. Sexual orientation may be added as a prohibited ground of discrimination to each of the impugned provisions. In so doing, the Legislature may choose to define the term "sexual orientation," or it may devise constitutional limitations on the scope of protection provided by the IRPA. As an alternative, the Legislature may choose to override the Charter breach by invoking s. 33 of the Charter. ... Given the persistent refusal of the Legislature to protect against discrimination on the basis of sexual orientation, it may be that it would choose to invoke s. 33 in these circumstances. In any event it should lie with the elected Legislature to determine this issue. They are answerable to the electorate of that province and it is for them to choose the remedy whether it is changing the legislation or using the notwithstanding clause. That decision in turn will be judged by the voters.

[198] The responsibility of enacting legislation that accords with the rights guaranteed by the Charter rests with the legislature. Except in the clearest of cases, courts should not dictate how underinclusive legislation must be amended. Obviously, the courts have a role to play in protecting Charter rights by deciding on the constitutionality of legislation. Deference and respect for the role of the legislature come into play in determining how unconstitutional legislation will be amended where various means are available.

[199] Given the apparent legislative opposition to including sexual orientation in the *IRPA*, I conclude that this is not an appropriate case for reading in. It is preferable to declare the offending sections invalid and provide the Legislature with an opportunity to rectify them. ...

[200] The only remaining issue is whether the declaration of invalidity ought to be temporarily suspended. In *Schachter*, Lamer CJ stated that a declaration of invalidity may be temporarily suspended where the legislation is deemed unconstitutional because of

underinclusiveness rather than overbreadth, and striking down the legislation would result in the deprivation of benefits from deserving persons without thereby benefitting the individual whose rights have been violated.

[201] There is no intention to deprive individuals in Alberta of the protection afforded by the *IRPA*, but only to ensure that the legislation is brought into conformity with the Charter while simultaneously respecting the role of the legislature. I would therefore order that the declaration of invalidity be suspended for one year to allow the Legislature an opportunity to bring the impugned provisions into line with its constitutional obligations.

M. v. H.
[1999] 2 SCR 3, 171 DLR (4th) 577

[In the portion of this case found in Chapter 23, Equality Rights, the Supreme Court of Canada found that the exclusion of same-sex couples from the definition of "spouse" in s. 29 of Ontario's *Family Law Act* (FLA)—the definition which governed the right to claim spousal support—was an unjustifiable infringement of s. 15 of the Charter. Thus, like *Vriend*, *M. v. H.* involved legislation that was constitutionally underinclusive because of the omission of gays and lesbians. However, on the issue of remedy, the Court distinguished *Vriend* and chose to strike down the underinclusive legislation, subject to a six-month delayed declaration of invalidity, instead of utilizing the technique of reading in to extend the definition of spouse to include same-sex couples.]

IACOBUCCI J (Lamer CJC, Cory, and McLachlin JJ concurring):

VI. Remedy

[136] Having found that the exclusion of same-sex couples from s. 29 of the *FLA* is unconstitutional and cannot be saved under s. 1 of the Charter, I must now consider the issue of remedy under s. 52 of the *Constitution Act, 1982*. In the court below, the words "a man and woman" were read out of the definition of "spouse" in s. 29 of the *FLA* and replaced with the words "two persons." The application of the order was suspended for a period of one year. With respect, I am not convinced that that is a suitable remedy in the circumstances of the present case.

[137] In the leading case on constitutional remedies, *Schachter v. Canada*, [1992] 2 SCR 679, and more recently in *Vriend* [*v. Alberta*, [1998] 1 SCR 493], this Court stated that the first step in selecting the appropriate remedial course is to determine the extent of the inconsistency between the impugned legislation and the Charter. In the case at bar, the inconsistency emanates from the underinclusive definition of "spouse" in s. 29 of the *FLA*. As I have concluded above, the exclusion of same-sex partners from this definition violates the equality rights guaranteed in s. 15 of the Charter and cannot survive any of the stages of review that comprise the s. 1 analysis.

[138] Having identified the extent of the inconsistency, the Court must determine the appropriate remedy. *Schachter* provides several options in the present case: (1) "striking down": the Court may hold that the *FLA* in its entirety is of no force or effect; or (2) "severance": the Court may hold that only the offending portion of the statute, namely, s. 29

is of no force or effect and that the rest of the Act remains in force; or (3) "reading in/ reading down": the Court may engage in some combination of reading in and reading down so as to replace the offending words with language that will include the wrongly excluded group (as the inconsistency in the instant case stems from an omission, reading down alone is inappropriate); or (4) striking down, severance, or reading in/reading down with a temporary suspension of the Court's order so that the government has an opportunity to enact a constitutionally valid spousal support scheme.

[139] In determining whether the reading in/reading down option is more appropriate than either striking down or severance, the Court must consider how precisely the remedy can be stated, budgetary implications, the effect the remedy would have on the remaining portion of the legislation, the significance or long-standing nature of the remaining portion and the extent to which a remedy would interfere with legislative objectives ... . As to the first of these criteria, the remedy of reading in is only available where the Court can direct with a sufficient degree of precision what is to be read in to comply with the Constitution. Remedial precision requires that the insertion of a handful of words will, without more, ensure the validity of the legislation and remedy the constitutional wrong ... .

[140] In the present case, the defect in the definition of "spouse" can be precisely traced to the use of the phrase "a man and woman," which has the effect of excluding same-sex partners from the spousal support scheme under the *FLA*. I recognize that there is remedial precision in so far as reading down this phrase and reading in the words "two persons" will, without more "remedy the constitutional wrong." However, I am not persuaded that reading in will also "ensure the validity of the legislation."

[141] If the remedy adopted by the court below is allowed to stand, s. 29 of the *FLA* will entitle members of same-sex couples who otherwise qualify under the definition of "spouse" to apply for spousal support. However, any attempt to opt out of this regime by means of a cohabitation agreement provided for in s. 53 or a separation agreement set out in s. 54 would not be recognized under the Act. Both ss. 53 and 54 extend to common-law cohabitants but apply only to agreements entered into between "a man and woman." Any extension of s. 29 of the Act would have no effect upon these Part IV domestic contract provisions of the *FLA*, which do not rely upon the Part III definition of "spouse." Thus, same-sex partners would find themselves in the anomalous position of having no means of opting out of the default system of support rights. As this option is available to opposite-sex couples, and protects the ability of couples to choose to order their own affairs in a manner reflecting their own expectations, reading in would in effect remedy one constitutional wrong only to create another, and thereby fail to ensure the validity of the legislation.

[142] In addition, reading into the definition of "spouse" in s. 29 of the Act will have the effect of including same-sex couples in Part V of the *FLA* (Dependants' Claim for Damages), as that part of the Act relies upon the definition of "spouse" as it is defined in Part III. In my opinion, where reading in to one part of a statute will have significant repercussions for a separate and distinct scheme under that Act, it is not safe to assume that the legislature would have enacted the statute in its altered form. In such cases, reading in amounts to the making of *ad hoc* choices, which Lamer CJ in *Schachter*, *supra*, at p. 707, warned is properly the task of the legislatures, not the courts.

[143] In cases where reading in is inappropriate, the court must choose between striking down the legislation in its entirety and severing only the offending portions of the statute. As noted by Lamer CJ in *Schachter*, at p. 697, "[w]here the offending portion of a statute can be defined in a limited manner it is consistent with legal principles to declare inoperative only that limited portion. In that way, as much of the legislative purpose as possible may be realized."

[144] In the case at bar, striking down the whole of the *FLA* would be excessive as only the definition of "spouse" in Part III of the Act has been found to violate the Charter. This is not a case where the parts of the legislative scheme which do offend the Charter are so inextricably bound up with the non-offending portions of the statute that what remains cannot independently survive. As a result, it would be safe to assume that the legislature would have passed the constitutionally sound parts of the statute without the unsound parts. See *Attorney-General for Alberta v. Attorney-General for Canada*, [1947] AC 503, at p. 518; *Schachter, supra*, at p. 697.

[145] On the basis of the foregoing, I conclude that severing s. 29 of the Act such that it alone is declared of no force or effect is the most appropriate remedy in the present case. This remedy should be temporarily suspended for a period of six months. Although we have been advised against the imposition of a suspension by both the appellant and the respondent, for the reasons which follow, I find that a suspension is necessary.

[146] In *Egan* [*v. Canada*, [1995] 2 SCR 513], at para. 226, writing in dissent on behalf of myself and Cory J, I would have granted a suspension of the remedy on the basis that "the extension of the spousal allowance, while certainly a legal issue, is also a concern of public policy." In this respect, I noted that "some latitude ought to be given to Parliament to address the issue and devise its own approach to ensuring that the spousal allowance be distributed in a manner that conforms with the equality guarantees of the Charter." These same concerns arise in the case at bar with respect to the spousal support scheme under the *FLA*.

[147] In addition, I note that declaring s. 29 of the *FLA* to be of no force or effect may well affect numerous other statutes that rely upon a similar definition of the term "spouse." The legislature may wish to address the validity of these statutes in light of the unconstitutionality of s. 29 of the *FLA*. On this point, I agree with the majority of the Court of Appeal which noted that if left up to the courts, these issues could only be resolved on a case-by-case basis at great cost to private litigants and the public purse. Thus, I believe the legislature ought to be given some latitude in order to address these issues in a more comprehensive fashion.

NOTES AND QUESTIONS

Can the Court's remedial decisions in *Vriend* and *M. v. H.* be adequately reconciled? In *M. v. H.*, was the Court overly concerned about the kind of "remedial detail" that had not deterred it in *Vriend* from using the remedy of reading in? Is it possible that the remedial choice in *M. v. H.* was influenced by a concern that, in the wake of the decision, many other statutes denying benefits to same-sex couples would be open to constitutional challenge and that legislatures could provide more comprehensive solutions than any judicial remedy of reading in? Within the six-month period contemplated in *M. v. H.*, the Ontario legislature in fact introduced legislation amending over 60 pieces of legislation in response to *M. v. H.* This legislation did not, however, define same-sex couples as "spouses," but rather as "same-sex partners." Was this part of the dialogue between courts and legislatures? See K. Roach, *The Supreme Court on Trial: Judicial Activism or Democratic Dialogue* (Toronto: Irwin Law, 2001).

3. Limits on the Availability of Retroactive Relief and the Justification for Prospective Relief

The next case deals with the question of the consequences of a remedy under s. 52(1) and, in particular, whether departures from the remedial norm of retroactive relief can ever be justified.

As a result of the Court's decision in *M. v. H.*, Parliament amended legislation to allow same-sex partners to receive survivor benefits under the self-funded *Canada Pension Plan*. Parliament, however, provided prospective relief only as of 2000, the date of the amendments. It did not provide fully retroactive benefits to 1985, the date at which the equality rights under s. 15 of the Charter came into force. The appellants, representing a class of same-sex survivors, challenged s. 72(1) of the *Canada Pension Plan*, RSC 1985, c. C-30 (2nd Supp.), which limited retroactive pension payments to 12 months after an application was received. The Supreme Court held that it was not necessary to decide whether this provision violated s. 15 of the Charter because of its adverse effects on same-sex couples, because the Court would not issue relief in the form of pension arrears retroactive to 1985.

Canada (Attorney General) v. Hislop
[2007] 1 SCR 429, 2007 SCC 10, 278 DLR (4th) 385

LeBEL and ROTHSTEIN JJ (McLachlin CJC and Binnie, Deschamps, and Abella JJ concurring):

· · ·

[79] In substance, the position of the appellants is predicated on the traditional—often called Blackstonian—view that judges never make law, but merely discover it. In this perspective, the courts are said to apply the law as it really was or has been rediscovered. As a consequence of the declaration of nullity, the appellants claim that they are entitled to the full benefits of the law, in conformity with an understanding of the Constitution, which is deemed to have never changed.

[80] The supremacy clause, now enshrined at s. 52, is silent about the remedies which may flow from a declaration of nullity. Does it mean that such a declaration is always both prospective and retroactive? This does not appear to have been the position of our Court throughout the incremental development of the law of constitutional remedies after the adoption of the Charter. A body of jurisprudence now accepts the legitimacy of limiting the retroactive effect of a declaration of nullity and of fashioning prospective remedies in appropriate circumstances.

· · ·

[86] ... Because courts are adjudicative bodies that, in the usual course of things, are called upon to decide the legal consequences of past happenings, they generally grant

remedies that are retroactive to the extent necessary to ensure that successful litigants will have the benefit of the ruling: see S. Choudhry and K. Roach, "Putting the Past Behind Us? Prospective Judicial and Legislative Constitutional Remedies" (2003), 21 *Supreme Court Law Review* (2d) 205, at pp. 211 and 218. There is, however, an important difference between saying that judicial decisions are *generally* retroactive and that they are *necessarily* retroactive. When the law changes through judicial intervention, courts operate outside of the Blackstonian paradigm. In those situations, it may be appropriate for the court to issue a prospective rather than retroactive remedy. The question then becomes what kind of change and which conditions will justify the crafting of judicial prospective remedies.

. . .

[90] … [T]he Court has held that providing immediate and retroactive judicial remedies may be "inappropriate" when "doing so would create a lacuna in the regime before Parliament would have a chance to act": *R v. Demers*, [2004] 2 SCR 489, 2004 SCC 46, at para. 57. In such cases, the Court has temporarily suspended the declaration of invalidity of the unconstitutional legislation to avoid creating a "legal vacuum" or "legal chaos" before Parliament or the Legislature has the opportunity to enact something in place of the unconstitutional legislation: *Reference re Language Rights Under s. 23 of Manitoba Act, 1870 & s. 133 of Constitution Act, 1867*, [1985] 1 SCR 721 (*"Manitoba Language Rights Reference"*), at p. 747; *Schachter* [*v. Canada*, [1992] 2 SCR 679]. In *Schachter*, this Court held that the suspended declaration of invalidity was appropriate when giving immediate retroactive effect to the Court's declaration of invalidity would (a) "pose a danger to the public"; (b) "threaten the rule of law"; or (c) "result in the deprivation of benefits from deserving persons," such as when the legislation was "deemed unconstitutional because of underinclusiveness rather than overbreadth" … .

[91] Like transition periods and other purely prospective remedies, the suspended declaration of invalidity is not fully consistent with the declaratory approach. By suspending the declaration of invalidity, the Court allows the constitutional infirmity to continue temporarily so that the legislature can fix the problem. In other words, the Court extends the life of a law, which, on the Blackstonian view, never existed.

[92] Although if the legislature fails to comply with the Court's order within the period of suspension, the Court's declaration would apply retroactively, the purpose of a suspended declaration of invalidity can be to facilitate the legislature's function in crafting a prospective remedy. The temporal delay in striking down the law also has the effect of extending the life of an unconstitutional law. In such cases, to allow the claimants to recover concurrent retroactive relief would be at cross-purposes with the Court's decision to grant a suspended declaration of invalidity: *Schachter*, at p. 720.

[93] The determination of whether to limit the retroactive effect of a s. 52(1) remedy and grant a purely prospective remedy will be largely determined by whether the Court is operating inside or outside the Blackstonian paradigm. When the Court is declaring the law as it has existed, then the Blackstonian approach is appropriate and retroactive relief should be granted. On the other hand, when a court is developing new law within the broad confines of the Constitution, it may be appropriate to limit the retroactive effect of its judgment.

[94] The approach which our Court has adopted in respect of the crafting of constitutional remedies also flows from its understanding of the process of constitutional interpretation, which the "living tree" metaphor neatly describes. From the time Lord Sankey LC used these words to characterize the nature of the Canadian Constitution, courts have relied on this expression to emphasize the ability of the Constitution to develop with our country (*Edwards v. Canada (Attorney General)* (1929), [1930] AC 124 (Canada PC), at p. 136). This Court has often stated that the Canadian Constitution should not be viewed as a static document but as an instrument capable of adapting with the times by way of a process of evolutionary interpretation, within the natural limits of the text, which "accommodates and addresses the realities of modern life ... ."

[95] It is true that the "living tree" doctrine is not wedded to a particular model of the judicial function. At times, its application may reflect the fact that, in a case, the Court is merely declaring the law of the country as it has stood and that a retroactive remedy is then generally appropriate. In other circumstances, its use recognizes that the law has changed, that the change must be acknowledged and that, from a given point in time, the new law or the new understanding of some legal principle will prevail.

[96] The question is no longer the legitimacy of prospective remedies, but rather when, why and how judges may rule prospectively or restrict the retroactive effect of their decisions in constitutional matters. The key question becomes the nature and effect of the legal change at issue in order to determine whether a prospective remedy is appropriate. The legitimacy of its use turns on the answer to this question.

. . .

[99] Change in the law occurs in many ways. "Clear break with the past" catches some of its diversity. It can be best identified with those situations where, in Canadian law, the Supreme Court departs from its own jurisprudence by expressly overruling or implicitly repudiating a prior decision. Such clear situations would justify recourse to prospective remedies in a proper context. But other forms of substantial change may be as relevant, especially in constitutional adjudication, where courts must give content to broad, but previously undefined, rights, principles or norms. The definition of a yet undetermined standard or the recognition that a situation is now covered by a constitutional guarantee also often expresses a substantial change in the law. The right may have been there, but it finds an expression in a new or newly recognized technological or social environment. Such a legal response to these developments properly grounds the use of prospective remedies, when the appropriate circumstances are met. A substantial change in the law is necessary, not sufficient, to justify purely prospective remedies. Hence, we must now turn to what else must be considered once legal change has been established.

[100] Although the list of such factors should not be considered as closed, some of them appear more clearly compelling. They may include reasonable or in good faith reliance by governments (*Miron* [*v. Trudel*, [1995] 2 SCR 418], at para. 173; *Mackin v. New Brunswick (Minister of [Finance])*, [2002] 1 SCR 405, 2002 SCC 13, at para. 78), or the fairness of the limitation of the retroactivity of the remedy to the litigants. Courts ought also consider whether a retroactive remedy would unduly interfere with the constitutional role of legislatures and democratic governments in the allocation of public resources (*Benner* [*v. Canada (Secretary of State)*, [1997] 1 SCR 358], at para. 103; *Schachter*, at p. 710).

[101] A careful consideration of reliance interests is critical to this analytical process. Although legal mechanisms, such as the *de facto* doctrine, *res judicata* or the law of limitations, may mitigate the consequences of declaratory rulings in certain circumstances, they do not address every situation. Fully retroactive remedies might prove highly disruptive in respect of government action, which, on the basis of settled or broadly held views of the law as it stood, framed budgets or attempted to design social programs. Persons and public authorities could then become liable under a new legal norm. Neither governments nor citizens could be reasonably assured of the legal consequences of their actions at the time they are taken.

[102] The strict declaratory approach also hardly appears reconcilable with the well established doctrine of qualified immunity in respect of the adoption of unconstitutional statutes which our Court applied, for example, in cases such as *Mackin* and *Guimond v. Québec (Procureur général)*, [1996] 3 SCR 347. Where legislation is found to be invalid as a result of a judicial shift in the law, it will not generally be appropriate to impose liability on the government. As Gonthier J wrote in *Mackin*, it is a general rule of public law that "absent conduct that is clearly wrong, in bad faith or an abuse of power, the courts will not award damages for the harm suffered as a result of the mere enactment or application of a law that is subsequently declared to be unconstitutional" (para. 78). The rationale for this qualified immunity, which applies equally to actions for damages based on the general law of civil liability and to claims for damages under s. 24(1) of the Charter, was aptly expressed by Gonthier J:

> Thus, the government and its representatives are required to exercise their powers in good faith and to respect the "established and indisputable" laws that define the constitutional rights of individuals. However, if they act in good faith and without abusing their power under prevailing law and only subsequently are their acts found to be unconstitutional, they will not be liable. Otherwise, the effectiveness and efficiency of government action would be excessively constrained. Laws must be given their full force and effect as long as they are not declared invalid. Thus it is only in the event of conduct that is clearly wrong, in bad faith or an abuse of power that damages may be awarded … . [para. 79]

The same principles will apply in respect of claims for retroactive benefits under s. 15 of the Charter. Whether framed as a remedy under s. 52 or s. 24(1), it may be tantamount to a claim for compensatory damages flowing from the underinclusiveness of the legislation.

[103] People generally conduct their affairs based on their understanding of what the law requires. Governments in this country are no different. Every law they pass or administrative action they take must be performed with an eye to what the Constitution requires. Just as ignorance of the law is no excuse for an individual who breaks the law, ignorance of the Constitution is no excuse for governments. But where a judicial ruling changes the existing law or creates new law, it may, under certain conditions, be inappropriate to hold the government retroactively liable. An approach to constitutional interpretation that makes it possible to identify, in appropriate cases, a point in time when the law changed, makes it easier to ensure that persons and legislatures who relied on the former legal rule while it prevailed will be protected. In this way, a balance is struck between the legitimate reliance interests of actors who make decisions based on a reason-

able assessment of the state of the law at the relevant time on one hand and the need to allow constitutional jurisprudence to evolve over time on the other.

[104] Having regard to the above-mentioned criteria, it is possible to distinguish this case from some cases where fully retroactive remedies were granted. *Miron* provides an example of when it would *not* be appropriate for courts to limit the retroactive effect of a s. 52(1) remedy. In *Miron*, the appellant was injured while a passenger in a vehicle driven by an uninsured driver. He made a claim for accident benefits against the insurance policy of his unmarried partner but his claim was denied on the basis that the policy covered only legally married spouses. Writing for the majority, McLachlin J (as she then was) held that the distinction based on marital status was discriminatory under s. 15(1) of the Charter. She concluded that retroactive reading up of the legislation was an appropriate remedy, which entitled the appellant to the retroactive benefit of his partner's insurance policy.

[105] In *Miron*, it would not have been appropriate for the Court to limit the retroactive effect of the remedy and grant a purely prospective remedy. First, the government did not meet the threshold factor of showing a substantial change from the existing law. As early as 1980, the Ontario Legislature was able to agree on a formula to extend death benefits to certain unmarried persons. And in 1981, in the context of the Ontario *Human Rights Code*, the Legislature agreed on a definition of "spouse" as the person to whom a person of the opposite sex is married or with whom the person is living in a conjugal relationship outside marriage. In other words, Ontario's vehicle insurance legislation was out of step with the evolving understanding of "spouse" as it existed in other Ontario statutes. Therefore, the Court's holding in *Miron*—that the vehicle insurance legislation's definition of spouse violated s. 15—was not a substantial change from the existing law. To the contrary, it reflected an understanding of s. 15 of the Charter that was already understood by the Ontario Legislature in the context of the Ontario *Human Rights Code* and other provincial legislation. Because the finding of a s. 15 infringement in *Miron* did not represent a substantial change in the law, it would have been inappropriate to limit the retroactive effect of its decision.

[106] However, even if the government had succeeded in meeting the substantial change requirement, other factors militated against limiting the retroactive effect of the remedy. In reaching her conclusion, McLachlin J drew support from three observations. First, she observed that the legislature had, since the accident occurred, amended the applicable legislation to include unmarried partners, thus allaying any concerns about interfering unduly with legislative objectives. The amended legislation provided "the best possible evidence of what the Legislature would have done had it been forced to face the problem the appellants raise[d]" (para. 180). Second, considerations of fairness to the successful litigant also weighed in favour of retroactivity, as providing a retroactive remedy in this case was the only means of "cur[ing] an injustice which might otherwise go unremedied": *ibid.* Third, McLachlin J noted that the distinction based on marital status was unreasonable, *even at the time the impugned legislation was enacted* (para. 173). Because the Legislature ought to have known that the vehicle insurance legislation was out of step with a modern understanding of "spouse," it could not reasonably exclude common law spouses from insurance coverage.

[107] It should be noted that, in *Miron*, all of the factors discussed above—good faith reliance by governments, fairness to the litigants and the need to respect the constitutional role of legislatures—favoured a retroactive remedy. In a number of cases, however, these factors may pull in different directions, with some factors favouring a retroactive remedy and others favouring a purely prospective remedy. In such cases, once the "substantial change" threshold criterion is met, it may be appropriate to limit the retroactive effect of the remedy based on a *balancing* of these other factors. This balance must be struck on a case-by-case basis.

[108] A second situation that must be distinguished was considered by this Court in its recent judgment in *Kingstreet Investments Ltd. v. New Brunswick (Department of Finance)*, [2007] 1 SCR 3, 2007 SCC 1, wherein it held that taxes collected pursuant to an *ultra vires* regulation are recoverable by the taxpayer. The difference between the result in *Kingstreet* and the type of situation in the present case may be understood in terms of a basic distinction between cases involving moneys collected by the government and benefits cases. Where the government has collected taxes in violation of the Constitution, there can be only one possible remedy: restitution to the taxpayer. In contrast, where a scheme for benefits falls foul of the s. 15 guarantee of equal benefit under the law, we normally do not know what the legislature would have done had it known that its benefits scheme failed to comply with the *Charter*. In benefits cases, a range of options is open to government. The excluded group could simply be included in the existing benefit scheme as was the result in *Tétreault-Gadoury v. Canada (Employment & Immigration Commission)*, [1991] 2 SCR 22. It could also be included in a modified benefit scheme, adopted by legislative amendments, as occurred in *Schachter*. Also, in *Schachter*, the Court alluded to the possibility of an elimination of the benefit (p. 702). In our political system, choosing between those options remains the domain of governments. This principle points towards limiting the retroactive effect of remedies in s. 15 benefits cases in which the other above-mentioned criteria are met.

(2) The Appropriate Remedy in This Case

(a) Limits on the Retroactive Effect of the Remedy in the Context of This Case

[109] Same-sex equality jurisprudence since 1985 is illustrative of the sort of legal shift that gives rise to new law and justifies consideration of prospective remedies. The factors mentioned above also weigh in favour of limiting the retroactive effect of the remedy in the context of this case.

(i) The Substantial Change in the Law

[110] This Court's decision in *M. v. H.* [[1999] 2 SCR 3] marked a departure from pre-existing jurisprudence on same-sex equality rights. In 1995, a majority of this Court upheld the exclusion of same-sex partners from old age security legislation in *Egan* [*v. Canada*, [1995] 2 SCR 513], with four judges finding no s. 15(1) violation, and one judge concluding that the scheme was contrary to s. 15(1) but that it could be justified under s. 1. Four years later in *M. v. H.*, eight members of this Court held that the exclusion of same-sex partners from the spousal support provisions under the *Family Law Act* was

contrary to s. 15(1) and could not be saved under s. 1. *M. v. H.* thus marks a clear shift in the jurisprudence of the Court, where it moved away from the plurality's holding in *Egan* and came to a new understanding of the scope of equality rights.

[111] Bastarache J disagrees with our conclusion on the nature of the change brought about by *M. v. H.* He cites lower court decisions rendered prior to *Egan* and before *M. v. H.* to show that the law on same-sex equality rights remained unsettled until *M. v. H.* However, in our system, the Supreme Court has the final word on the interpretation of the Constitution: *Manitoba Language Rights Reference*, at p. 745. A majority of the Court in *Egan* rejected the appellants' claim for equal benefits under the law. It was a fact that this Court held in *Egan* that the Constitution did not require equal benefits for same-sex couples. This fact changed only after *M. v. H.* when this Court held that it was unconstitutional to exclude same-sex couples from the definition of spouse in the *Family Law Act.* The threshold requirement for limiting the retroactive effect of the remedy has been satisfied. The Court must now consider other relevant factors. In this case, reliance interests, fairness concerns, the government's good faith, and the need to respect Parliament's legislative role all weigh in favour of limiting retroactive relief.

(ii) Reasonable Reliance

[112] Given the state of the jurisprudence prior to *M. v. H.*, the exclusion of same-sex partners from the former *CPP* was based on a reasonable understanding of the state of s. 15(1) jurisprudence as it existed after *Egan* and before *M. v. H.* Admittedly, the Court in *Egan* was divided over whether to extend old age security benefits to same-sex couples, with four judges dissenting. After *M. v. H.*, it became apparent that the *Egan* dissent had prevailed. However, the benefit of hindsight does not undermine the government's reasonableness in relying on *Egan*.

[113] In holding that the government reasonably relied on the pre-*M. v. H.* jurisprudence, we do not seek to justify the slowness of legislatures and courts alike in recognizing Charter rights. Rather, we acknowledge the fact that although the Constitution embodies the supreme law and the enduring values of this country, it is up to the courts to interpret and apply those provisions. In *Manitoba Language Rights Reference*, this Court held:

> The Constitution of a country is a statement of the will of the people to be governed in accordance with certain principles held as fundamental and certain prescriptions restrictive of the powers of the legislature and government. It is, as s. 52 of the *Constitution Act, 1982* declares, the "supreme law" of the nation, unalterable by the normal legislative process, and unsuffering of laws inconsistent with it. The duty of the judiciary is to interpret and apply the laws of Canada and each of the provinces, and it is thus our duty to ensure that the constitutional law prevails. [p. 745]

[114] The text of the Constitution establishes the broad confines of the supreme law, but it is up to the courts to interpret and apply the Constitution in any given context. The inviolability of the Constitution ensures that our nation's most cherished values are preserved, while the role of the courts in applying the Constitution ensures that the law is sufficiently flexible to change over time to reflect advances in human understanding. But it also means that the Constitution, at any snapshot in time, is only as robust as the court

interpreting it. If the judiciary errs or is slow to recognize that previous interpretations of the Constitution no longer correspond to social realities, it must change the law. However, in breaking with the past, the Court does not create an automatic right to redress for the Court's prior ruling. Where the government's reliance on the unconstitutional law was reasonable because it was relying on this Court's jurisprudence, it will be less likely that a right to retroactive relief will flow from a subsequent declaration of invalidity of the unconstitutional law.

(iii) Good Faith

[115] Our comments above indicate that the government did not act in bad faith in failing to extend survivors' benefits to same-sex couples prior to *M. v. H.* It is significant that the survivors' benefit scheme under the former *CPP* was never struck down by a court of competent jurisdiction. Rather, recognizing the likely implications of this Court's ruling in *M. v. H.* for that scheme, Parliament endeavoured to pre-emptively correct the constitutional deficiencies therein by enacting remedial legislation. Because the government acted in good faith by attempting pre-emptively to correct a constitutional infirmity soon after it was discovered, it would be inappropriate to reach back further in time and impose a retroactive remedy.

(iv) Fairness to Litigants

[116] In seeking payment of arrears back as far as 1985, the Hislop class effectively asks this Court to overlook the evolution in the jurisprudence of same-sex equality rights that has taken place and to declare that the understanding to which we have come over that period of time was in fact the law in 1985. This position cannot be sustained. Although *M. v. H.* declares what the Constitution requires, it does not give rise to an automatic right to every government benefit that might have been paid out had the Court always interpreted the Constitution in accordance with its present-day understanding of it. *M. v. H.* was not a case like *Miron* where limiting the retroactive effect of the s. 52(1) remedy would have granted the "successful" claimant a hollow victory. In contrast, a *purely prospective remedy* in *M. v. H.* was not meaningless. *M. v. H.* resulted in wide scale amendments to federal and provincial legislation across the country to extend government benefits to same-sex couples. Equally important, *M. v. H.* helped usher in a new era of understanding of the equal human dignity of same-sex couples. One could not say that *M. v. H.* granted those litigants only a Pyrrhic victory.

(v) Respecting Parliament's Role

[117] Achieving an appropriate balance between fairness to individual litigants and respecting the legislative role of Parliament may mean that Charter remedies will be directed more toward government action in the future and less toward the correction of past wrongs. In the present case, the Hislop class' claim for a retroactive remedy is tantamount to a claim for compensatory damages flowing from the underinclusiveness of the former *CPP*. Imposing that sort of liability on the government, absent bad faith, unreasonable reliance or conduct that is clearly wrong, would undermine the important

balance between the protection of constitutional rights and the need for effective govern-ment that is struck by the general rule of qualified immunity. A retroactive remedy in the instant case would encroach unduly on the inherently legislative domain of the distribu-tion of government resources and of policy making in respect of this process.

(vi) Conclusion

[118] For the foregoing reasons, the retroactive relief sought by the Hislop class is unavailable under the law applicable to constitutional remedies. It is not therefore neces-sary to carry out a s. 15(1) analysis in respect of s. 72(1).

NOTES AND QUESTIONS

Bastarache J wrote separate concurring reasons that stressed that the denial of retroactive relief should depend on a general balance of interest and not on whether there was a sub-stantial change in the law. He also indicated that, in his view, the Court's decision in *M. v. H.* did not constitute a substantial change in the law. Do you agree with the majority that a substantial change in the law can justify a departure from retroactive relief? If so, is the Court's distinction between the recognition of same-sex spousal rights in *M. v. H.* as a sub-stantial change in the law and the recognition of common-law spousal rights in *Miron* as not a substantial change in the law persuasive? Should courts refuse, as in *Hislop*, to decide whether rights were violated because the remedy of retroactive relief is not available? What does this tell us about the relationship between rights and remedies?

4. Severance and Reading Down

As noted in *Schachter*, severance is a remedy familiar from federalism cases and one that involves partial invalidation of the law. See, for example, *Reference re Validity of Section 5(a) of the Dairy Industry Act (Margarine Reference)*, [1949] SCR 1, 1 DLR 433, which can be found in Chapter 11, Criminal Law. The Supreme Court has indicated that severance can be used to fulfill the purposes of the Charter while preserving those parts of the legislation that do not violate the Charter. It was used in *Tétreault-Gadoury v. Canada (Employment and Immigration Commission)*, [1991] 2 SCR 22, 81 DLR (4th) 358, in which, after finding a vio-lation of s. 15, the Court deleted the age 65 bar to unemployment insurance benefits. Is there any difference between this form of judicial amendment of laws, involving deletion of language, and reading in as discussed in *Schachter* and used in *Vriend*?

Reading down is also a remedy that has been used in federalism cases to avoid declaring a law to be of no force or effect. Reading down permits courts to save from invalidity a law that would be unconstitutional if given its broadest interpretation by giving the law a nar-rower interpretation that would preclude unconstitutional applications. For an example of reading down in the federalism context see *McKay v. The Queen*, [1965] SCR 798, 53 DLR (2d) 532, which can be found in Chapter 8, Interpreting the Division of Powers. In that case, a municipal bylaw prohibiting the placement of signs on residential properties was inter-preted so as not to apply to federal election signs. The Court concluded that such an applica-tion would have been *ultra vires*.

Reading down need not only be thought of as a remedy for invalidity; it also functions as a technique of interpretation to avoid invalidity. As such, the doctrine of reading down is rooted in notions of legislative intent: the narrowing interpretation is placed on the law because of a presumption that the legislature intended to act within the bounds of the Constitution. For an example of reading down as a technique of interpretation see *R v. Butler*, [1992] 1 SCR 452, 89 DLR (4th) 449, which can be found in Chapter 20, Freedom of Expression. In *Butler* the Court chose to place a narrow, constitutional reading on the obscenity provisions of the *Criminal Code*, thereby avoiding any finding of a Charter violation. Reading down was thus used in its traditional form as a preliminary interpretive device to keep the law within constitutional bounds, rather than as an explicit remedy after a finding of a constitutional violation.

Stronger forms of reading down can also be used as a remedy for possible invalidity and can involve reading limitations into legislation. The Supreme Court of Canada was originally reluctant to save legislation through strong forms of reading in. In *Hunter v. Southam*, [1984] 2 SCR 145, 11 DLR (4th) 641, after finding that the broad search and seizure powers under the *Combines Investigation Act* violated s. 8 of the Charter (freedom from unreasonable search and seizure), Justice Dickson, writing for a unanimous Court, rejected the federal government's request that the procedures required by s. 8 of the Charter be read into the legislation, stating: "While the courts are guardians of the Constitution and of individuals' rights under it, it is the Legislature's responsibility to enact legislation that embodies appropriate safeguards to comply with the Constitution's requirements. It should not fall to the courts to fill in the details that will render legislative lacunae constitutional."

In *R v. Sharpe*, [2001] 1 SCR 45, 194 DLR (4th) 1, which is also excerpted in Chapter 20, Freedom of Expression, the Supreme Court of Canada used an explicit and strong remedy of reading in to save potentially overbroad legislation prohibiting the possession of child pornography. Certain exemptions were read into the law to narrow its scope and cure the potential overbreadth. McLachlin CJC stated:

> [111] Confronted with a law that is substantially constitutional and peripherally problematic, the Court may consider a number of alternatives. One is to strike out the entire law. This was the choice of the trial judge and the majority of the British Columbia Court of Appeal. The difficulty with this remedy is that it nullifies a law that is valid in most of its applications. Until Parliament can pass another law, the evil targeted goes unremedied. Why one might well ask, should a law that is substantially constitutional be struck down simply because the accused can point to a hypothetical application that is far removed from his own case which might not be constitutional?
>
> [112] Another alternative might be to hold that the law as it applies to the case at bar is valid, declining to find it unconstitutional on the basis of a hypothetical scenario that has not yet arisen. In the United States, courts have frequently declined to strike out laws on the basis of hypothetical situations not before the court, although less so in First Amendment (free expression) cases. While the Canadian jurisprudence on the question is young, thus far it suggests that laws may be struck out on the basis of hypothetical situations, provided they are "reasonable."
>
> [113] Yet another alternative might be to uphold the law on the basis that it is constitutionally valid in the vast majority of its applications and stipulate that if and when unconstitutional applications arise, the accused may seek a constitutional exemption.

[114] I find it unnecessary to canvass any of these suggestions further because in my view the appropriate remedy in this case is to read into the law an exclusion of the problematic applications of s. 163.1, following *Schachter v. Canada*, [1992] 2 SCR 679. *Schachter* suggests that the problem of peripheral unconstitutional provisions or applications of a law may be addressed by striking down the legislation, severing of the offending sections (with or without a temporary suspension of invalidity), reading down, or reading in. The Court decides on the appropriate remedy on the basis of "twin guiding principles": respect for the role of Parliament, and respect for the purposes of the Charter (p. 715). Applying these principles, I conclude that in the circumstances of the case reading in an exclusion is the appropriate remedy.

[115] To assess the appropriateness of reading in as a remedy, we must identify a distinct provision that can be read into the existing legislation to preserve its constitutional balance. In this case, s. 163.1 might be read as incorporating an exception for the possession of:

1. *Self-created expressive material: i.e.*, any written material or visual representation created by the accused alone, and held by the accused alone, exclusively for his or her own personal use; and

2. *Private recordings of lawful sexual activity: i.e.*, any visual recording, created by or depicting the accused, provided it does not depict unlawful sexual activity and is held by the accused exclusively for private use.

· · ·

[121] *Schachter, supra*, holds that reading in will be appropriate only where (1) the legislative objective is obvious and reading in would further that objective or constitute a lesser interference with that objective than would striking down the legislation; (2) the choice of means used by the legislature to further the legislation's objective is not so unequivocal that reading in would constitute an unacceptable intrusion into the legislative domain; and (3) reading in would not require an intrusion into legislative budgetary decisions so substantial as to change the nature of the particular legislative enterprise. The third requirement is not of concern here. The first two inquiries—conformity with legislative objective and avoidance of unacceptable law-making—require more discussion.

[122] The first question is whether the legislative objective of s. 163.1(4) is evident. In my view it is. The purpose of the legislation is to protect children from exploitation and abuse by prohibiting possession of material that presents a reasoned risk of harm to children. This question leads to a second: whether reading in will further that objective. In other words, will precluding the offending applications of the law better conform to Parliament's objective than striking down the whole law? Again the answer is clearly yes. The applications of the law that pose constitutional problems are exactly those whose relation to the objective of the legislation is most remote. Carving out those applications by incorporating the proposed exception will not undermine the force of the law; rather, it will preserve the force of the statute while also recognizing the purposes of the Charter. The defects of the section are not so great that their exclusion amounts to impermissible redrafting ... . The new exceptions resemble those that Parliament has already created and are consistent with its overall approach of catching mainstream child pornography reasonably linked to harm while excluding peripheral material that engages free speech values. Moreover, since the problematic applications lie on the periphery of the material targeted by Parliament, carving them out will not create an exception-riddled provision bearing little resemblance to the provision envisioned by Parliament. This suggests

that excluding the offending applications of the law will not subvert Parliament's object. On the other hand, striking down the statute altogether would assuredly undermine Parliament's object, making it impossible to combat the lawfully targeted harms until it can pass new legislation.

· · ·

[124] The second prong of *Schachter*, *supra*, is directed to the possibility that reading in, though recognizing the objective of the legislation, may nonetheless undermine legislative intent by substituting one means of effecting that intent with another. As we noted in *Vriend v. Alberta*, [1998] 1 SCR 493, the relevant question is "what the legislature would ... have done if it had known that its chosen measures would be found unconstitutional" (para. 167). If it is not clear that the legislature would have enacted the legislation without the problematic provisions or aspects, then reading in a term may not provide the appropriate remedy. This concern has more relevance where the legislature has made a "deliberate choice of means" by which to reach its objective. Even in such a case, however, "a deliberate choice of means will not act as a bar to reading in save for those circumstances in which the means chosen can be shown to be of such centrality to the aims of the legislature and so integral to the scheme of the legislation, that the legislature would not have enacted the statute without them": *Vriend*, *supra*, at para. 167.

[125] In the present case it cannot be said that the legislature has made a deliberate choice of means in the sense that phrase was used in *Vriend*, *supra*. ... I see no evidence ... that Parliament saw the statute's application to the two problematic categories of materials (*i.e.*, self-created expressive materials and private recordings that do not depict unlawful sexual activity) as an integral part of the legislative scheme. On the contrary, given that the risk to children posed by materials falling within these two categories is relatively remote, it seems reasonable to conclude that such materials are caught incidentally, not deliberately, and that Parliament would have excluded these two categories from the purview of the law had it been seized of the difficulty raised by their inclusion.

5. *Constitutional Exemptions*

When a constitutional exemption is granted, the law remains in force, but it is declared inapplicable to individuals or groups whose Charter rights are infringed by its effects. In *R v. Ferguson*, [2008] 1 SCR 96, 2008 SCC 6, 290 DLR (4th) 17, the Supreme Court ruled that a constitutional exemption could only be formulated as a remedy under s. 52(1) of the *Constitution Act, 1982*. Chief Justice McLachlin stated (at para. 64) for the Court:

> The highly discretionary language in s. 24(1), "such remedy as the court considers appropriate and just in the circumstances," is appropriate for control of unconstitutional acts. By contrast, s. 52(1) targets the unconstitutionality of laws in a direct non-discretionary way: laws are of no force or effect to the extent that they are unconstitutional.

The Court held (at para. 56) that it would be inappropriate to fashion a constitutional exemption for a mandatory sentence under the *Criminal Code* because

> [t]o allow constitutional exemptions for mandatory minimum sentences is, in effect, to read in a discretion to a provision where Parliament clearly intended to exclude discretion. ... It cannot be assumed that Parliament would have enacted the mandatory minimum sentencing scheme

with the discretion that allowing constitutional exemptions would create. For the Court to introduce such a discretion would thus represent an inappropriate intrusion into the legislative
sphere.

How can this restrictive approach to constitutional exemptions be reconciled with the
Court's willingness to consider using a reading-in remedy in *Schachter* or *Vriend*, or its use
of strong reading-down remedies in *Sharpe*?

6. *Temporary Suspension of the Declaration of Invalidity*

The immediate nullification of a law that results from a declaration of invalidity creates a
legislative void. As the Supreme Court recognized in *Schachter*, in some cases it may be appropriate to suspend temporarily the effect of the declaration for a period of time in order to
allow Parliament or the provincial legislature to fill the void. The Court cautioned, however,
that the remedy should not be used indiscriminately, as it allows a state of affairs that has
been found to violate the Charter to persist for a period of time despite the violation. The
criteria suggested in *Schachter* for a delayed declaration of invalidity are: potential danger to
the public, a threat to the constitutional order, or an underinclusive law where striking
down would deprive deserving persons of benefits without providing them to the individual
whose rights have been violated.

The case that introduced the temporary suspension of a declaration of invalidity into
Canadian constitutional law was *Reference re Manitoba Language Rights*, [1985] 1 SCR 721,
19 DLR (4th) 1 (*Manitoba Language Reference*), in which the Supreme Court of Canada
found that Manitoba's failure to meet the requirements for bilingual enactment and publication of its statutes constituted a violation of s. 23 of the constitution of the province, the
Manitoba Act, 1870. As a result, most of the statutes enacted by the province between 1890
and 1985 were found to be invalid and of no force or effect. Recognizing that such a large
scale invalidation of legislation would create legal chaos and undermine the fundamental
constitutional principle of the rule of law, the Court declared the invalid legislation temporarily valid for the minimum period of time required for translation and re-enactment of the
laws in both French and English. This use of the suspension of the declaration of invalidity
was clearly endorsed in *Schachter*.

In *Dixon v. British Columbia (Attorney-General)* (1989), 60 DLR (4th) 445 (BCSC), British
Columbia's scheme of electoral boundaries was found to violate the right to vote guaranteed
by s. 3 of the Charter because the population variations between constituencies resulted in
too extreme a deviation from the principle of relative equality of voting power. Recognizing
that the result of a declaration of invalidity under s. 52 of the *Constitution Act, 1982* would be
the disappearance of the province's electoral districts, the Court concluded that the appropriate remedy was to specify a temporary period during which the legislation would remain
valid to allow the legislature an opportunity to enact an apportionment scheme complying
with the Charter. The Court also referred to the fact that the chosen remedy would facilitate
an appropriate division of labour between the courts and the legislature, allowing the legislature to choose between the range of policy choices available in devising electoral boundaries that would satisfy the requirements of the Constitution. Does *Dixon* satisfy the criteria
for a suspension of the declaration of invalidity referred to in *Schachter*? Did invalidation

threaten a constitutional emergency? Does *Schachter* allow the institutional factors referred to by the court to be taken into account? Should they be relevant?

If the court decides that a temporary suspension of the declaration of invalidity is the appropriate remedy because redrafting the law (so as to include, for example, appropriate exemptions) is a task that requires complex legislative choices, the result is that the individual before the court whose rights have been infringed and who would clearly fall within any exemption drafted by the legislature is denied relief. Would it be possible for the court to grant individuals constitutional exemptions under s. 24(1) on a case-by-case basis during the period of suspension? (See *Rodriguez v. British Columbia (Attorney General)*, [1993] 3 SCR 519, 107 DLR (4th) 342, found in Chapter 22, Life, Liberty, and Security of the Person, in which four members of the Court would have granted such a remedy.)

What is the appropriate length of a delayed or suspended declaration of invalidity? In *M. v. H.*, above, the Supreme Court issued a six-month delayed declaration of invalidity. In other cases, however, it has issued suspensions as long as 18 months; see *Corbière v. Canada*, [1999] 2 SCR 203, 173 DLR (4th) 1, found in Chapter 23, Equality Rights and *Dunmore v. Ontario (Attorney General)*, [2001] 3 SCR 1016, 2001 SCC 94, 207 DLR (4th) 193, found in Chapter 21, Freedom of Association. In the *Manitoba Language Reference*, above, the period of delay lasted the number of years required to translate Manitoba's unilingual laws. What factors should be relevant in determining the duration of a suspended declaration of invalidity? For arguments that suspended declarations of invalidity deprive litigants of effective remedies, see B. Ryder, "Suspending the Charter" (2003), 21 *Supreme Court Law Review* (2d) 267. For arguments that they can be an instrument of dialogue, see K. Roach, "Remedial Consensus and Challenge: General Declarations and Delayed Declarations of Invalidity" (2002), 35 *UBC L Rev.* 211.

Another issue is whether a declaration issued under s. 24(1) can also be delayed. See *Eldridge v. British Columbia (Attorney General)*, [1997] 3 SCR 624, 151 DLR (4th) 577, found in Chapter 23, Equality Rights, in which a declaration of entitlement to sign language interpretation services was delayed for a six-month period.

C. Remedies Under Section 24(1) of the Charter

In *Little Sisters*, excerpted below, a majority of the Supreme Court of Canada issued a declaration, under s. 24(1) of the Charter, that the applicants' Charter rights had been violated because of the unconstitutional application of the challenged law, rather than the remedy requested—namely, striking down the law in its entirety under s. 52 of the *Constitution Act, 1982*. As the minority reasons show, however, the majority's remedial choice was not uncontroversial.

The case, which is discussed in Chapter 20, Freedom of Expression, involved a challenge, on the basis of ss. 2(b) and 15 of the Charter, to provisions in the federal Customs legislation that prohibited the importation of obscene publications and empowered Customs officials to make the necessary determination of obscenity. The challenge was brought by a bookstore, Little Sisters, which alleged a Customs practice of targeting material destined for gay and lesbian bookstores. Little Sisters had sought not only a recognition that its own rights had been violated because of the way in which the law had been applied to them, but also a declaration of the law's invalidity on the ground, *inter alia*, that the procedure for determining obscenity was so cumbersome and procedurally defective that it could not be administered in a way that respected Charter rights. With the exception of a reverse onus clause, a majority of the Court, in a judgment written by Binnie J, found no constitutional flaw in the legislation itself. Any problems were found to lie in the administration of the law, the appropriate remedy for which was a declaration under s. 24(1) of the Charter. The majority also refused Little Sisters' request for an injunction restraining Customs from applying the law so long as any risk of unconstitutional administration existed.

Little Sisters Book and Art Emporium v. Canada
[2000] 2 SCR 1120, 193 DLR (4th) 193

BINNIE J (McLachlin CJC, L'Heureux-Dubé, Gonthier, Major, and Bastarache JJ concurring):

. . .

[154] In my view, the appellants have established that:

1. Section 152(3) of the *Customs Act* should not be construed and applied so as to place the onus on an importer to establish that goods are not obscene within the meaning of s. 163(8) of the *Criminal Code*. The burden of proving obscenity rests on the Crown or other person who alleges it.

2. The rights of the appellants under s. 2(b) and s. 15(1) of the Charter have been infringed in the following respects:

   (a) They have been targeted as importers of obscene materials despite the absence of any evidence to suggest that gay and lesbian erotica is more likely to be obscene than heterosexual erotica, or that the appellants are likely offenders in this regard;

   (b) In consequence of the targeting, the appellants have suffered excessive and unnecessary prejudice in terms of delays, cost and other losses in having their goods cleared (if at all) through Canada Customs;

   (c) The reasons for this excessive and unnecessary prejudice include:

      (i) failure by Customs to devote a sufficient number of officials to carry out the review of the appellants' publications in a timely way;

      (ii) the inadequate training of the officials assigned to the task;

      (iii) the failure to place at the disposal of these officials proper guides and manuals, failure to update Memorandum D9-1-1 and its accompanying illustrative manual in a timely way, and the failure to develop workable procedures to deal with books consisting mostly or wholly of written text;

      (iv) failure to establish internal deadlines and related criteria for the expeditious review of expressive materials;

(v) failure to incorporate into departmental guides and manuals relevant advice received from time to time from the Department of Justice;

(vi) failure to provide the appellants in a timely way with notice of the basis for detention of publications, the opportunity to make meaningful submissions on a re-determination, and reasonable access to the disputed materials for that purpose; and

(vii) failure to extend to the appellants the equal benefit of fair and expeditious treatment of their imported goods without discrimination based on sexual orientation.

[155] It is apparent that this catalogue particularizes in greater detail the declaration issued by the trial judge, namely:

> THIS COURT DECLARES that Tariff Code 9956(a) of Schedule VII and s. 114 of the *Customs Tariff*, SC 1987, c. 41 (3rd Supplement) and ss. 58 and 71 of the *Customs Act*, SC 1986, c. 1 (2nd Supplement) have at times been construed and applied in a manner contrary to s. 2(b) and s. 15(1) of the *Canadian Charter of Rights and Freedoms*.

• • •

[157] Having rejected that s. 52 argument, except as to the reverse onus provision, the remaining question is whether the Court should attempt to fashion a more structured s. 24(1) remedy. I conclude, with some hesitation, that it is not practicable to do so. The trial concluded on December 20, 1994. We are told that in the past six years, Customs has addressed the institutional and administrative problems encountered by the appellants. In the absence of more detailed information as to what precisely has been done, and the extent to which (if at all) it has remedied the situation, I am not prepared to endorse my colleague's conclusion that these measures are "not sufficient" (para. 262) and have offered "little comfort" (para. 265). Equally, however, we have not been informed by the appellants of the specific measures (short of declaring the legislation invalid or inoperative) that in the appellants' view would remedy any continuing problems.

[158] The most detailed suggestion the appellants have made in the way of a s. 24(1) remedy is the following request:

> ... in the final alternative an injunction restraining Customs from applying and administering the *Customs Tariff*, SC 1987, c. 41 (3rd Supplement) s. 114, Schedule VII, Code 9956(a) and the *Customs Act*, SC 1986 (2nd Supp.), s. 58 and s. 71, as amended, permanently or until such time as there is no risk that the unconstitutional administration will continue.

The first branch of the proposed injunction ("permanently") amounts to a s. 52 declaration of inoperability, which I do not consider justified. The second branch ("until such time") sets an unrealistic standard ("no risk"). If diluted to a call for constitutional behaviour, the result would add little to the general duty that falls on any government official to act in accordance with the Constitution, injunction or no injunction, and would scarcely advance the objectives of either clarity or enforceability. A more structured s. 24(1) remedy might well be helpful but it would serve the interests of none of the parties for this Court to issue a formal declaratory order based on six-year-old evidence supplemented by conflicting oral submissions and speculation on the current state of affairs. The views of the Court on the merits of the appellants' complaints as the situation stood at the end of 1994 are recorded in these reasons and those of my colleague Iacobucci J. These findings should provide the appellants with a solid platform from which to launch any further action in the Supreme Court of British Columbia should they consider that further action is necessary.

IACOBUCCI J (Arbour and LeBel JJ concurring) dissenting in part:

[253] Given Smith J's finding that there were "grave systemic problems" in the administration of the law—a conclusion with which I wholeheartedly agree—the primarily declaratory remedy relied on by Binnie J is simply inadequate. Systemic problems call for systemic solutions. I believe that Customs' history of improper censorship, coupled with its inadequate response to the declarations of the courts below, confirms that only striking down the legislation in question will guarantee vindication of the appellants' constitutional rights. Having concluded that the law must fall, I will offer some broad guidelines for future reform.

(i) Legislation Must Ensure Constitutional Application

[254] ... In this case, it is true that nothing in the Customs legislation itself forces Customs to ignore evidence of literary and artistic merit; to make decisions without even allowing written submissions from the parties affected; and to discriminate against gay and lesbian materials. However, the legislation does call for prior restraint by an investigatory rather than adjudicatory body, and does not provide for any meaningful safeguards aimed at preventing the inevitable flaws that result from such a system.

[255] Effectively, the respondents call on this Court to trust them. Indeed, when questioned at oral arguments about what guarantee we have that the mistakes of the past will not continue, counsel for the respondent Canada replied, "what may have occurred then, I trust will not occur now." ...

[256] In fact, the respondents' approach would mean that every unconstitutional law requires no more than a declaratory remedy; after all, Parliament is fully capable of amending a law to bring it into compliance with the Constitution at any time. I therefore disagree with Binnie J's conclusion that, with the exception of s. 152(3) of the *Customs Act*, a declaratory remedy is sufficient in this case. While the government is free to delegate powers, it must do so in a way that ensures—or at the very least attempts to ensure—that Charter rights will be respected.

...

(ii) Declaratory Relief Is Insufficient

[258] The need to strike down the Customs legislation as it applies to expressive materials is reinforced by comparison with the alternate remedy adopted by both the courts below, and by Binnie J in this Court. Declarations are, in many cases, an appropriate constitutional remedy. As Kent Roach has summarized in his *Constitutional Remedies in Canada* (loose-leaf ed.), at para. 12.30, declarations are often preferable to injunctive relief because they are more flexible, require less supervision, and are more deferential to the other branches of government. However, declarations can suffer from vagueness,

insufficient remedial specificity, an inability to monitor compliance, and an ensuing need for subsequent litigation to ensure compliance: see *ibid.*, at para. 12.320.

[259] *Mahe v. Alberta*, [1990] 1 SCR 342, illustrates the appropriate role of declaratory relief. In that case the Court held that Edmonton's school system violated s. 23 of the Charter because it did not grant sufficient "management and control" over French-language education to the linguistic minority. In determining the appropriate remedy, Dickson CJ recognized, at pp. 391-92, that the impugned provisions of the *School Act* were " 'permissive' provisions, that is, they do not prevent authorities from acting in accordance with the Charter, but neither do they guarantee that such compliance will occur." The Chief Justice declined to strike down the legislation, instead choosing to issue a declaration. He feared that "the result of a declaration of invalidity would be to create a legislative vacuum" (p. 392), which would potentially leave the appellants worse off. The Court therefore simply issued "a declaration in respect of the concrete rights which are due to the minority language parents in Edmonton under s. 23" (p. 392). Similarly, in *Eldridge [v. British Columbia (Attorney General)*, [1997] 3 SCR 624] the Court simply declared that services must be provided to the deaf instead of striking down the entire legislative scheme.

[260] The rationale behind the remedial choice in those cases does not apply to the present appeal. Striking down the applicability of the Customs legislation to expressive materials will not make the appellants worse off; it will fully vindicate their rights. While the appellants are admittedly not entitled to any particular legislative scheme, they are entitled to a remedy that will prevent further systematic and consistent violations of their constitutional rights. Only invalidating the impugned Customs legislation will achieve that goal.

[261] A final reason that declaratory relief is inappropriate in this case is the difficulties the appellants face in enforcing it. This case has been a massive undertaking for the appellants. Proving the constitutional violations recognized by Smith J required the production of an enormous record. Unfortunately, if the appellants are unsatisfied with the government's compliance with the declaration affirmed by this Court, they have little choice but to try to assemble a similar record documenting the enforcement of the Customs regime since the declaration was made. This is obviously a heavy burden, and indeed unfair. A stronger remedy is necessary to vindicate the appellants' rights. ...

[262] In my respectful opinion, declaratory relief has already proven ineffective. As Roach, *supra*, at para. 13.884 has noted, "declaratory relief does not facilitate continued judicial supervision and may not be effective where governments do not take prompt and good faith steps to comply with the declaration." While obviously we lack evidence of the enforcement of the Customs regime since Smith J's declaration, I believe that the reforms thus far are not sufficient.

[Iacobucci J then reviews the reforms, concluding that: "With respect, I am not satisfied that these measures will remedy the 'grave systemic problems' found by Smith J. They are largely hortatory or permissive."]

[266] ... [B]oth constitutional precedent and common sense suggest that when a government agency has systematically violated constitutional rights, structural reforms are

necessary. In [*R v.*] *Morgentaler* [[1988] 1 SCR 30] the Court could also have simply issued a declaration. The various federal and provincial ministries could have approved more hospitals, eliminated quotas, and otherwise solved the problems identified by this Court. However, the Court recognized that such a solution was inappropriate. Where the problems are a direct result of flaws in the legislation itself, as I believe is the case here, patchwork measures aimed at various symptoms will not cure the underlying ailment. As Smith J found, and as I have endeavoured to demonstrate in these reasons, the flaws in the Customs regime are systemic. They flow from the very nature of prior restraint, and require careful consideration by Parliament. Declaratory relief, in my opinion, is not appropriate.

[267] The need for structural reform is reinforced by Customs' long history of excessive, inappropriate censorship. ...

[268] These are not the kinds of problems that can be solved by simply directing Customs to behave themselves. In all the circumstances, further indulgence misses the mark; what is needed is the firm guidance that only new legislation from Parliament can provide. Striking down the applicability of the Customs legislation to expressive materials is consistent with the "Charter Dialogue Between Courts and Legislatures," as it was described by Peter Hogg and Allison Bushell: (1997), 35 *Osgoode Hall Law Journal* 75. This Court has frequently recognized the importance of fostering a dialogue between courts and legislatures ... . Particularly where, as here, it appears that Parliament has not turned its mind to the issue at hand, striking down the legislation may encourage much needed changes. ...

[Iacobucci J makes several recommendations for reform including the enactment of new legislation with appropriate safeguards for timely decisions and freedom of expression, the creation of a specialized administrative tribunal and reliance on criminal prosecutions for obscenity.]

[281] No doubt there are many other steps that could be taken to improve the current system. I put these suggestions forward to show that there is a variety of approaches available to Parliament to underscore the importance of ensuring Canadians have access to as many expressive materials as possible while realizing the practical constraints that are involved. Because the present regime essentially treats books like any other commodity, I hope that Parliament will review and revise the current Customs legislation to reflect the seminal importance of freedom of expression in our Canadian democracy. ...

[282] In conclusion, I respectfully cannot agree with my colleague Binnie J that the only amendment needed to the existing legislation is to shift the onus from the importer to the government. Without the opportunity for importers to make effective representations and a statutory guarantee that decisions will be made in a timely fashion, I question the significance of a shift in onus. In my opinion, the record in this appeal amply bears out Smith J's conclusion that there are "grave systemic" flaws in the enforcement of the Customs legislation. But I cannot agree that the remedy is simply to issue a declaration and take it on faith that Canada Customs—an agency which, it bears repeating, has a long and ignominious record of excessive censorship throughout this century—will reform its ways.

[283] I would therefore allow the appeal, set aside the judgment of the British Columbia Court of Appeal and declare, pursuant to s. 52 of the *Constitution Act, 1982*, that Schedule VII, Tariff Code 9956(a) (now Tariff Item 9989.00.00) is of no force and effect. I would
suspend this declaration of invalidity for a period of 18 months to allow the government
time to choose the preferred remedial option described in these reasons, and to take the
related steps necessary to make the implementation of the chosen option effective.

NOTES AND QUESTIONS

1. Does the majority's judgment suggest that the Court might be inclined to sanction the
use of structural injunctions (discussed below) in appropriate cases? What does the majority's judgment suggest about how such injunctions should be constructed and when they
will be appropriate?

2. Is the minority's judgment an example of a court approving a structural injunction; or
is it a case of recognizing the limitations of declarations as a remedy and inviting Parliament, as opposed to a court, to engage in structural reform?

NOTE ON STRUCTURAL INJUNCTIONS

In drafting remedies for constitutional violations, US courts have made extensive use of
complex supervisory orders called "structural injunctions" or "civil rights injunctions," the
goal of which is to restructure institutions that have operated unconstitutionally in the past,
resulting in systemic violations of rights. Such orders have resulted in US courts redrawing
electoral boundaries, desegregating school systems by redrawing school boundaries and
ordering the busing of children, and running prisons and mental hospitals. The civil rights
injunction is a controversial remedy and has been criticized for allowing judges to exercise
legislative and administrative powers. See R.J. Sharpe, "Injunctions and the Charter" (1984),
22 *Osgoode Hall Law Journal* 474 for the argument that, while institutional advantages
clearly favour legislators and administrators in the task of designing structural changes in
institutions to meet the demands of the Charter, if they fail to respond positively, the courts
will be required to act. The majority of requests for structural remedies under the Charter
thus far have arisen in the context of the minority language education rights guaranteed by
s. 23 of the Charter, and are discussed in Chapter 24, Language Rights. For further discussion of the structural injunction under the Charter, see, in addition to Professor Sharpe's
article, N. Gillespie, "Charter Remedies: The Structural Injunction" (1990), 11 *Advocates'
Quarterly* 190; G. Otis, "La Charte et la modification des programmes gouvernementaux"
(1991), 36 *McGill Law Journal* 1348; C. Manfredi, "Appropriate and Just in the Circumstances" (1994), 27 *Canadian Journal of Political Science* 435; and K. Roach, *Constitutional
Remedies in Canada*, looseleaf ed. (Aurora, ON: Canada Law Book, 1994), ch. 13.

The next case concerns whether a trial judge was justified in retaining jurisdiction over
a case and requiring the government to report back to the court and the parties on its progress in making minority language schools available after the judge had issued a declaration
that the s. 23 minority language educational rights of francophones in Nova Scotia had been
violated.

Doucet-Boudreau v. Nova Scotia (Minister of Education)
[2003] 3 SCR 3, 2003 SCC 62, 232 DLR (4th) 17

IACOBUCCI and ARBOUR JJ (McLachlin CJC, Gonthier, and Bastarache JJ concurring):

[41] Section 24(1) entrenches in the Constitution a remedial jurisdiction for infringements or denials of Charter rights and freedoms. The respondent makes various arguments suggesting that LeBlanc J exceeded his jurisdiction by violating constitutional norms, statutory provisions, and common law rules. We will first deal with the extent of the remedial jurisdiction in s. 24(1) and the constitutional limits to that jurisdiction proposed by the respondent. Later we will discuss how statutes and common law rules might be relevant to the choice of remedy under s. 24(1).

. . .

[43] A remedy under s. 24(1) is available where there is some government action, beyond the enactment of an unconstitutional statute or provision, that infringes a person's Charter rights ... . In the present appeal, the difficulty does not lie with the legislation: no provision or omission in the *Education Act* prevented the government from providing minority language education as required by the *Constitution Act, 1982*. On the contrary, the *Education Act*, as amended in 1996, establishes a French-language school board to provide homogeneous French-language education to children of s. 23 entitled parents. Neither is the problem rooted in any particular government action; rather, the problem was *inaction* on the part of the provincial government, particularly its failure to mobilize resources to provide school facilities in a timely fashion, as required by s. 23 of the Charter. Section 24(1) is available to remedy this failure.

. . .

[51] The power of the superior courts under s. 24(1) to make appropriate and just orders to remedy infringements or denials of Charter rights is part of the supreme law of Canada. It follows that this remedial power cannot be strictly limited by statutes or rules of the common law. We note, however, that statutes and common law rules may be helpful to a court choosing a remedy under s. 24(1) insofar as the statutory provisions or common law rules express principles that are relevant to determining what is "appropriate and just in the circumstances."

(3) The Meaning of "Appropriate and Just in the Circumstances"

[52] What, then, is meant in s. 24(1) by the words "appropriate and just in the circumstances"? Clearly, the task of giving these words meaning in particular cases will fall to the courts ordering the remedies since s. 24(1) specifies that the remedy should be such as *the court considers* appropriate and just. Deciding on an appropriate and just remedy in particular circumstances calls on the judge to exercise a discretion based on his or her careful perception of the nature of the right and of the infringement, the facts of the case, and the application of the relevant legal principles. Once again, we emphasize McIntyre J's words in *Mills* [*v. The Queen*, [1986] 1 SCR 863], at p. 965:

> It is difficult to imagine language which could give the court a wider and less fettered discretion. It is impossible to reduce this wide discretion to some sort of binding formula for

general application in all cases, and it is not for appellate courts to pre-empt or cut down this wide discretion.

[53] With respect, the approach to s. 24 reflected in the reasons of LeBel and Deschamps JJ would tend to pre-empt and reduce this wide discretion. Their approach would also, in this case, pre-empt and devalue the constitutional promise respecting language rights in s. 23. In our view, judicial restraint and metaphors such as "dialogue" must not be elevated to the level of strict constitutional rules to which the words of s. 24 can be subordinated. The same may be said of common law procedural principles such as *functus officio* which may to some extent be incorporated in statutes. Rather, as LeBel and Deschamps JJ appear to recognize at paras. 135 and following, there are situations in which our Constitution requires special remedies to secure the very order it envisages.

[54] While it would be unwise at this point to attempt to define, in detail, the words "appropriate and just" or to draw a rigid distinction between the two terms, there are some broad considerations that judges should bear in mind when evaluating the appropriateness and justice of a potential remedy. These general principles may be informed by jurisprudence relating to remedies outside the Charter context, such as cases discussing the doctrine of *functus* and overly vague remedies, although, as we have said, that jurisprudence does not apply strictly to orders made under s. 24(1).   •

[55] First, an appropriate and just remedy in the circumstances of a Charter claim is one that meaningfully vindicates the rights and freedoms of the claimants. Naturally, this will take account of the nature of the right that has been violated and the situation of the claimant. A meaningful remedy must be relevant to the experience of the claimant and must address the circumstances in which the right was infringed or denied. An ineffective remedy, or one which was "smothered in procedural delays and difficulties," is not a meaningful vindication of the right and therefore not appropriate and just ... .

[56] Second, an appropriate and just remedy must employ means that are legitimate within the framework of our constitutional democracy. ... [A] court ordering a Charter remedy must strive to respect the relationships with and separation of functions among the legislature, the executive and the judiciary. This is not to say that there is a bright line separating these functions in all cases. A remedy may be appropriate and just notwithstanding that it might touch on functions that are principally assigned to the executive. The essential point is that the courts must not, in making orders under s. 24(1), depart unduly or unnecessarily from their role of adjudicating disputes and granting remedies that address the matter of those disputes.

[57] Third, an appropriate and just remedy is a judicial one which vindicates the right while invoking the function and powers of a court. It will not be appropriate for a court to leap into the kinds of decisions and functions for which its design and expertise are manifestly unsuited. The capacities and competence of courts can be inferred, in part, from the tasks with which they are normally charged and for which they have developed procedures and precedent.

[58] Fourth, an appropriate and just remedy is one that, after ensuring that the right of the claimant is fully vindicated, is also fair to the party against whom the order is made. The remedy should not impose substantial hardships that are unrelated to securing the right.

[59] Finally, it must be remembered that s. 24 is part of a constitutional scheme for the vindication of fundamental rights and freedoms enshrined in the Charter. As such, s. 24 because of its broad language and the myriad of roles it may play in cases should be allowed to evolve to meet the challenges and circumstances of those cases. That evolution may require novel and creative features when compared to traditional and historical remedial practice because tradition and history cannot be barriers to what reasoned and compelling notions of appropriate and just remedies demand. In short, the judicial approach to remedies must remain flexible and responsive to the needs of a given case.

(4) Application to This Case: The Remedy Ordered by the Trial Judge Was Appropriate and Just in the Circumstances

(a) The Reporting Order Effectively Vindicated the Rights of the Parents

[60] LeBlanc J exercised his discretion to select an effective remedy that meaningfully vindicated the s. 23 rights of the appellants in the context of serious rates of assimilation and a history of delay in the provision of French-language education in Kingston (Greenwood, Chéticamp, Île Madame-Arichat (Petit de Grat), Argyle, and Clare). The facts as found by LeBlanc J disclosed that continued delay could imperil the already vulnerable s. 23 rights, their exercise depending as it does on the numbers of potential students. As Freeman JA noted in dissent in the Court of Appeal, the reporting hearings were aimed at identifying difficulties with the timely implementation of the trial judge's order as they arose, instead of requiring fresh applications by the appellants every time it appeared that a party was not using its best efforts to comply with the judge's order.

[61] In the absence of reporting hearings, the appellant parents would have been forced to respond to any new delay by amassing a factual record by traditional means disclosing whether the parties were nonetheless using their best efforts. A new proceeding would be required and this might be heard by another judge less familiar with the case than LeBlanc J. All of this would have taken significant time and resources from parents who had already waited too long and dedicated much energy to the cause of realizing their s. 23 rights. The order of reporting hearings was, as Freeman JA wrote "a pragmatic approach to getting the job done expeditiously" (para. 74). LeBlanc J's order is a creative blending of remedies and processes already known to the courts in order to give life to the right in s. 23.

[62] In assessing the extent to which LeBlanc J's remedy was appropriate and just in the circumstances, it is useful to examine the options before the trial judge. In doing so we are not intending to usurp the role and discretion of the trial judge but only to gain a fuller understanding of the situation he faced. LeBlanc J could have limited the remedy to a declaration of the rights of the parties, as the Court considered prudent in *Mahe* [*v. Alberta*, [1990] 1 SCR 342], at pp. 392-93. In *Mahe*, however, the primary issues before the Court concerned the scope and content of s. 23 of the *Charter*, including the degree of management of control of schools to be accorded to s. 23 parents, and the determination of when the numbers are sufficient to warrant given programs and facilities. After clarifying the content and scope of the s. 23 rights at issue, the Court chose the remedy of ordering a declaration of those rights. It did so to allow the government the greatest flexibility to fashion a response suited to the circumstances (p. 393). The assumption

underlying this choice of remedy is that governments will comply with the declaration promptly and fully.

[63] After *Mahe*, litigation to vindicate minority language education rights has entered a new phase. The general content of s. 23 in many cases is now largely settled ... . In the present case, for example, it was clear to and accepted by the parties from the start that the government was required to provide the homogeneous French-language facilities at issue. The entitled parents sought the assistance of the court in enforcing the *full and prompt* vindication of their rights after a lengthy history of government inaction.

[64] Our colleagues LeBel and Deschamps JJ state at para. 140 of their reasons that the trial judge was not faced with a government which had understood its obligations but refused to comply with them. Our colleagues suggest that there was some issue as to what s. 23 demanded in the situation. With respect, this portrayal is directly at odds with the findings of fact made by the trial judge. At para. 198 of his reasons, the trial judge wrote:

> It is apparent that the real issue between the parties is the date on which these programs and facilities are to be implemented. The Department, in its submissions, does not challenge the applicants' right and entitlement to these programs and facilities but point [*sic*] to a number of factors which ought to satisfy the applicants. The Conseil opposes the applicants' claim for an earlier implementation of the transition plan but supports the applicants in its [*sic*] demand for declaration that the Department ought to be directed to provide homogeneous facilities.

[65] LeBlanc J further noted that the Department of Education did not provide either statistical or financial evidence with respect to the "numbers warrant" test and that, in any case, the number of children of s. 23 parents were greater than the number in the case of *Mahe*, *supra*, decided by this Court (paras. 200-201). Instead, the government argued at trial that it should be allowed to delay its obligations because of a lack of consensus in the Acadian and Francophone communities (para. 202) and because the political compromise in s. 23 required a "go-slowly approach" (para. 214). According to the trial judge, the government did not deny the existence or content of the s. 23 rights of the parents but rather failed to prioritize those rights and delayed fulfilling its obligations. The government "did not give sufficient priority to the serious rate of assimilation occurring among Acadians and Francophones in Nova Scotia and the fact that rights established in s. 23 are individual rights" (para. 204) despite clear reports showing that assimilation was "reaching critical levels" (para. 215). These are the findings of fact which can only be made by a judge who has heard all the evidence at trial. These findings are not on appeal and it is not open for appellate judges to reverse these findings without proper justification. LeBlanc J properly took account of the factual circumstances within which he exercised his discretion to select a remedy which was appropriate and just.

[66] LeBlanc J obviously considered that, given the Province's failure to give due priority to the s. 23 rights of its minority Francophone populations in the five districts despite being well aware of them, there was a significant risk that such a declaration would be an ineffective remedy. Parents such as the appellants should not be forced continually to seek declarations that are essentially restatements of the declaration in *Mahe*. Where governments have failed to comply with their well understood constitutional obligations to take positive action in support of the right in s. 23, the assumption underlying a pref-

erence for declarations may be undermined. In *Mahe, supra*, at p. 393, Dickson CJ recognized this possibility:

> As the Attorney General for Ontario submits, the government should have the widest possible discretion in selecting the institutional means by which its s. 23 obligations are to be met; the courts should be loath to interfere and impose what will be necessarily procrustean standards, *unless that discretion is not exercised at all, or is exercised in such a way as to deny a constitutional right.* Once the Court has declared what is required in Edmonton, then the government can and must do whatever is necessary to ensure that these appellants, and other parents in their situation, receive what they are due under s. 23. [Emphasis added.]

This Court's judgment in *Mahe* speaks to all provincial and territorial governments. LeBlanc J was entitled to conclude that he was not limited to declaring the appellant parents' rights and could take into consideration that the case before him was different from those in which declarations had been considered appropriate and just.

[67] Our colleagues LeBel and Deschamps JJ suggest that the reporting order in this case was not called for since any violation of a simple declaratory remedy could be dealt with in contempt proceedings against the Crown. We do not doubt that contempt proceedings may be available in appropriate cases. The threat of contempt proceedings is not, in our view, inherently more respectful of the executive than simple reporting hearings in which a linguistic minority could discover in a timely way what progress was being made towards the fulfilment of their s. 23 rights. More importantly, given the critical rate of assimilation found by the trial judge, it was appropriate for him to grant a remedy that would in his view lead to prompt compliance. Viewed in this light, LeBlanc J selected a remedy that reduced the risk that the minority language education rights would be smothered in additional procedural delay.

(b) The Reporting Order Respected the Framework of our Constitutional Democracy

[68] The remedy granted by LeBlanc J took into account, and did not depart unduly or unnecessarily from, the role of the courts in our constitutional democracy. LeBlanc J considered the government's progress toward providing the required schools and services (see, e.g., paras. 233-34). Some flexibility was built into the "best efforts" order to allow for unforeseen difficulties. It was appropriate for LeBlanc J to preserve and reinforce the Department of Education's role in providing school facilities as mandated by s. 88 of the *Education Act*, as this could be done without compromising the entitled parents' rights to the prompt provision of school facilities.

[69] To some extent, the legitimate role of the court *vis-à-vis* various institutions of government will depend on the circumstances. In these circumstances, it was appropriate for LeBlanc J to craft the remedy so that it vindicated the rights of the parents while leaving the detailed choices of means largely to the executive.

[70] Our colleagues LeBel and Deschamps JJ appear to consider that the issuance of an injunction against the government under s. 24(1) is constitutionally suspect and represents a departure from a consensus about *Charter* remedies (see para. 134 of the dissent). With respect, it is clear that a court may issue an injunction under s. 24(1) of the

Charter. The power of courts to issue injunctions against the executive is central to s. 24(1) of the *Charter* which envisions more than declarations of rights. Courts do take actions to ensure that rights are enforced, and not merely declared. Contempt proceedings in the face of defiance of court orders, as well as coercive measures such as garnishments, writs of seizure and sale and the like are all known to courts. In this case, it was open to the trial judge in all the circumstances to choose the injunctive remedy on the terms and conditions that he prescribed.

(c) The Reporting Order Called on the Function and Powers of a Court

[71] Although it may not be common in the context of *Charter* remedies, the reporting order issued by LeBlanc J was judicial in the sense that it called on the functions and powers known to courts. In several different contexts, courts order remedies that involve their continuing involvement in the relations between the parties … . Superior courts, which under the *Judicature Acts* possess the powers of common law courts and courts of equity, have "assumed active and even managerial roles in the exercise of their traditional equitable powers" (K. Roach, *Constitutional Remedies in Canada* (loose-leaf), at para. 13.60). A panoply of equitable remedies are now available to courts in support of the litigation process and the final adjudication of disputes. For example, prejudgment remedies [such as *Mareva* injunctions and *Anton Pillar* orders, developed by the courts] involve the court in the preservation of evidence and the management of parties' assets prior to trial. In bankruptcy and receivership matters, courts may be called on to supervise fairly complex and ongoing commercial transactions relating to debtors' assets. Court-appointed receivers may report to and seek guidance from the courts and in some cases must seek the permission of the courts before disposing of property … . Similarly, the courts' jurisdiction in respect of trusts and estates may sometimes entail detailed and continuing supervision and support of their administration … . Courts may also retain an ongoing jurisdiction in family law cases to order alterations in maintenance payments or parenting arrangements as circumstances change. Finally, this Court has in the past remained seized of a matter so as to facilitate the implementation of constitutional language rights … .

[72] The difficulties of ongoing supervision of parties by the courts have sometimes been advanced as a reason that orders for specific performance and mandatory injunctions should not be awarded. Nonetheless, courts of equity have long accepted and overcome this difficulty of supervision where the situations demanded such remedies … .

[73] As academic commentators have pointed out, the range of remedial orders available to courts in civil proceedings demonstrates that constitutional remedies involving some degree of ongoing supervision do not represent a radical break with the past practices of courts … . The change announced by s. 24 of the *Charter* is that the flexibility inherent in an equitable remedial jurisdiction may be applied to orders addressed to government to vindicate constitutionally entrenched rights.

[74] The order in this case was in no way inconsistent with the judicial function. There was never any suggestion in this case that the court would, for example, improperly take over the detailed management and co-ordination of the construction projects.

Hearing evidence and supervising cross-examinations on progress reports about the construction of schools are not beyond the normal capacities of courts.

. . .

(d) The Reporting Order Vindicated the Right by Means That Were Fair

[83] In the context, the reporting order was one which, after vindicating the entitled parents' rights, was not unfair to the respondent government. The respondent argues that it was subject to an overly vague remedy. In our opinion, the reporting order was not vaguely worded so as to render it invalid. While, in retrospect, it would certainly have been advisable for LeBlanc J to provide more guidance to the parties as to what they could expect from the reporting sessions, his order was not incomprehensible or impossible to follow. In our view, the "reporting" element of LeBlanc J remedy was not unclear in a way that would render it invalid.

[84] Doubtless, as LeBel and Deschamps JJ point out, the initial retention of jurisdiction by LeBlanc J could have been more specific in its terms so as to give parties a precise understanding of the procedure at reporting sessions. Nonetheless, the respondent knew it was required to present itself to the court to report on the status of its efforts to provide the facilities as ordered by LeBlanc J. LeBlanc J's written order is satisfactory and clearly communicates that the obligation on government was simply to report. The fact that this was the subject of questions later in the process suggests that future orders of this type could be more explicit and detailed with respect to the jurisdiction retained and the procedure at reporting hearings.

[85] It should be remembered that LeBlanc J was crafting a fairly original remedy in order to provide flexibility to the executive while vindicating the s. 23 right. It may be expected that in future cases judges will be in a better position to ensure that the contents of their orders are clearer. In addition, the reporting order chosen by LeBlanc J is not the only tool of its kind. It may be more helpful in some cases for the trial judge to seek submissions on whether to specify a timetable with a right of the government to seek variation where just and appropriate to do so.

[86] Once again, we emphasize that s. 24(1) gives a court the discretion to fashion the remedy that *it considers* just and appropriate in the circumstances. The trial judge is not required to identify the single best remedy, even if that were possible. In our view, the trial judge's remedy was clearly appropriate and just in the circumstances.

(5) Conclusion

[87] Section 24(1) of the Charter requires that courts issue effective, responsive remedies that guarantee full and meaningful protection of Charter rights and freedoms. The meaningful protection of Charter rights, and in particular the enforcement of s. 23 rights, may in some cases require the introduction of novel remedies. A superior court may craft any remedy that it considers appropriate and just in the circumstances. In doing so, courts should be mindful of their roles as constitutional arbiters and the limits of their institutional capacities. Reviewing courts, for their part, must show considerable deference to trial judges' choice of remedy, and should refrain from using hindsight to

perfect a remedy. A reviewing court should only interfere where the trial judge has committed an error of law or principle.

[88] The remedy crafted by LeBlanc J meaningfully vindicated the rights of the appellant parents by encouraging the Province's prompt construction of school facilities, without drawing the court outside its proper role. The Court of Appeal erred in wrongfully interfering with and striking down the portion of LeBlanc J's order in which he retained jurisdiction to hear progress reports on the status of the Province's efforts in providing school facilities by the required dates. ...

· · ·

LeBEL and DESCHAMPS JJ (dissenting) (Major and Binnie JJ concurring):

· · ·

[91] The devil is in the details. Awareness of the critical importance of effectively enforcing constitutional rights should not lead to forgetfulness about the need to draft pleadings, orders and judgments in a sound manner, consonant with the basic rules of legal writing, and with an understanding of the proper role of courts and of the organizing principles of the legal and political order of our country. Court orders should be written in such a way that parties are put on notice of what is expected of them. Courts should not unduly encroach on areas which should remain the responsibility of public administration and should avoid turning themselves into managers of the public service. Judicial interventions should end when and where the case of which a judge is seized is brought to a close.

[92] In our respectful view, without putting in any doubt the desire of the trial judge to fashion an effective remedy to address the consequences of a long history of neglect of the rights of the Francophone minority in Nova Scotia, the drafting of his so-called reporting order was seriously flawed. It gave the parties no clear notice of their obligations, the nature of the reports or even the purpose of the reporting hearings. In addition, the reporting order assumed that the judge could retain jurisdiction at will, after he had finally disposed of the matter of which he had been seized, thereby breaching the constitutional principle of separation of powers. The order did so by reason of the way it was framed and the manner in which it was implemented. In our opinion, the reporting order was void, as the Court of Appeal of Nova Scotia found, and the appeal should be dismissed.

· · ·

[97] The drafting of applications asking for injunctive relief, or of orders granting such remedies, can be a serious challenge for counsel and judges. The exercise of the court power to grant injunctions may lead, from time to time, to situations of non-compliance where it may be necessary to call upon the drastic exercise of courts' powers to impose civil or criminal penalties, including imprisonment ... . Therefore, proper notice to the parties of the obligations imposed upon them and clarity in defining the standard of compliance expected of them must be essential requirements of a court's intervention. Vague or ambiguous language should be strictly avoided ... .

[98] Unfortunately, the drafting of the present reporting order was anything but clear. Its brevity and apparent simplicity belie its actual complexity and the state of confusion and uncertainty in which it left not only all of the parties, but the trial judge himself at times. This order was final, not interim, and it was tied to the "best efforts order," which

was not couched in terms liable to shed much light on the nature of the obligations of the respondents. Given that this part of the order was not challenged on appeal, we will not discuss it at length, but instead, will focus exclusively on the reporting order which is the object of this appeal.

[99] At first, when judgment was rendered, the reporting order read, at para. 245:

> The applicants have requested that I should maintain jurisdiction. I agree to do so. I am scheduling a further appearance for Thursday, July 27, 2000 at 1:30 p.m., and at that time the respondents will report on the status of their efforts. I am requesting the respondents to utilize their best efforts to comply with this decision.

This drafting was slightly modified in the final order, dated December 14, 2000:

> The Court shall retain jurisdiction to hear reports from the respondents respecting the respondents' compliance with this Order. The respondents shall report to this Court on March 23, 2001 at 9:30 a.m., or on such other date as the Court may determine.

[100] As Flinn JA observed in his reasons in the Court of Appeal ((2001), 194 NSR (2d) 323, 2001 NSCA 104), nobody knew the exact nature of these reports. Their form and content were undefined. There was no indication as to whether they should be delivered orally or in writing or both nor as to how detailed they should be and what kind of supporting documents, if any, would be needed. The order also provided for hearings, but again, it left the parties in the dark as to the procedure, purpose or nature of these sessions of the court. The parties learned only shortly before these hearings that affidavits needed to be filed and deponents made available for cross-examination. Further, there seemed to be little direction, if any at all, as to what sort of evidence was required to be included for the purpose of the hearings. The nature of these hearings, as the process developed, appeared to become a cross between a mini-trial, an informal meeting with the judge and some kind of mediation session, for the purpose of monitoring the execution of the school-building program for Francophone students.

[101] The trial judge himself seemed unsure about the nature of the hearings he had ordered and of the process he had initiated. At first, he appeared to lean towards the view that those hearings were regular sessions of the court, that he had not issued a final order and that additional relief could be requested. For example, in the July 27, 2000 hearing, the trial judge stated that in the hearings, he "would have the opportunity to determine if the Respondents were indeed making every or best efforts to comply" (appellants' record, at p. 762). This a reiteration of a claim made earlier in that hearing (appellants' record, at p. 720). Similarly, in the August 9, 2000 hearing, the trial judge stated: "the amount of room I have with respect to a decision or direction or comment is very limited" (appellants' record, at pp. 997-98); this statement implies that the trial judge had the power, albeit limited, to make orders. However, after the setting down of his formal order, at the last hearing in March 2001, he commented that he could not grant further relief, that he had fully disposed of the matter in his order and accompanying reasons, which were released the previous summer. He added that the sessions had a solely informational purpose.

[102] In the meantime, schools were built or renovated and made available to Francophone students. It is difficult to determine whether those sessions accomplished anything

in this respect. What these sessions certainly did was sow confusion, doubt and uncertainty about the obligations of the respondents and about the nature of a process that went on over several months. The trial judge appeared to view this process as open ended and indeterminate, with more sessions being scheduled as he wished. Nobody really knew when it all would come to an end.

[103] The uncertainty engendered by the reporting order was not merely inconvenient for the parties. In our view it amounted to a breach of the parties' interest in procedural fairness. One essential feature of a fair procedural rule is that its contents are clearly defined, and known in advance by the parties subject to it. ...

IV. The Appropriate Role of the Judiciary

[105] While superior courts' powers to craft Charter remedies may not be constrained by statutory or common law limits, they are nonetheless bound by rules of fundamental justice, as we have shown above, and by constitutional boundaries, as we shall see below. In the context of constitutional remedies, courts fulfill their proper function by issuing orders precise enough for the parties to know what is expected of them, and by permitting the parties to execute those orders. Such orders are final. A court purporting to retain jurisdiction to oversee the implementation of a remedy, after a final order has been issued, will likely be acting inappropriately on two levels. First, by attempting to extend the court's jurisdiction beyond its proper role, it will breach the separation of powers principle. Second, by acting after exhausting its jurisdiction, it will breach the *functus officio* doctrine. We will look at each of these breaches in turn.

1. The Separation of Powers

[106] Courts are called upon to play a fundamental role in the Canadian constitutional regime. When needed, they must be assertive in enforcing constitutional rights. At times, they have to grant such relief as will be required to safeguard basic constitutional rights and the rule of law, despite the sensitivity of certain issues or circumstances and the reverberations of their decisions in their societal environment. Despite—or, perhaps, because of—the critical importance of their functions, courts should be wary of going beyond the proper scope of the role assigned to them in the public law of Canada. In essence, this role is to declare what the law is, contribute to its development and to give claimants such relief in the form of declarations, interpretation and orders as will be needed to remedy infringements of constitutional and legal rights by public authorities. Beyond these functions, an attitude of restraint remains all the more justified, given that, as the majority reasons acknowledge, Canada has maintained a tradition of compliance by governments and public servants with judicial interpretations of the law and court orders.

. . .

[110] ... Aside from their duties to supervise administrative tribunals created by the executive and to act as vigilant guardians of constitutional rights and the rule of law, courts should, as a general rule, avoid interfering in the management of public administration.

[111] More specifically, once they have rendered judgment, courts should resist the temptation to directly oversee or supervise the administration of their orders. They

should generally operate under a presumption that judgments of courts will be executed with reasonable diligence and good faith. Once they have declared what the law is, issued their orders and granted such relief as they think is warranted by circumstances and relevant legal rules, courts should take care not to unnecessarily invade the province of public administration. To do otherwise could upset the balance that has been struck between our three branches of government.

[112] This is what occurred in the present case. When the trial judge attempted to oversee the implementation of his order, he not only assumed jurisdiction over a sphere traditionally outside the province of the judiciary, but also acted beyond the jurisdiction with which he was legitimately charged as a trial judge. In other words, he was *functus officio* and breached an important principle which reflects the nature and function of the judiciary in the Canadian constitutional order ... .

· · ·

[115] If a court is permitted to continually revisit or reconsider final orders simply because it has changed its mind or wishes to continue exercising jurisdiction over a matter, there would never be finality to a proceeding ... .

· · ·

[117] In addition to this concern with finality, the question of whether a court is clothed with the requisite authority to act raises concerns related to the separation of powers, a principle that transcends procedural and common law rules. In our view, if a court intervenes, as here, in matters of administration properly entrusted to the executive, it exceeds its proper sphere and thereby breaches the separation of powers. By crossing the boundary between judicial acts and administrative oversight, it acts illegitimately and without jurisdiction. Such a crossing of the boundary cannot be characterized as relief that is "appropriate and just in the circumstances" within the meaning of s. 24(1) of the *Charter*.

V. Application of the Relevant Principles to the Present Case

[118] When the above principles are applied to the present facts, it is evident that McIntyre J's admonition in *R v. Mills*, [1986] 1 SCR 863, that s. 24(1) "was not intended to turn the Canadian legal system upside down" is *à propos* (p. 953). In our view, the trial judge's remedy undermined the proper role of the judiciary within our constitutional order, and unnecessarily upset the balance between the three branches of government. As a result, the trial judge in the present circumstances acted inappropriately, and contrary to s. 24(1).

[119] As we noted above, the trial judge equivocated on the question of whether his purported retention of jurisdiction empowered him to make further orders. Regardless of which position is taken, the separation of powers was still breached. On the one hand, if he did purport to be able to make further orders, based on the evidence presented at the reporting hearings, he was *functus officio*. We find it difficult to imagine how any subsequent order would not have resulted in a change to the original final order. This necessarily falls outside the narrow exceptions provided by *functus officio*, and breaches that rule.

[120] Such a breach would also have resulted in a violation of the separation of powers principle. By purporting to be able to make subsequent orders, the trial judge would
have assumed a supervisory role which included administrative functions that properly
lie in the sphere of the executive. These functions are beyond the capacities of courts. The
judiciary is ill equipped to make polycentric choices or to evaluate the wide-ranging
consequences that flow from policy implementation. This Court has recognized that
courts possess neither the expertise nor the resources to undertake public administration. In *Eldridge v. British Columbia (Attorney General)*, [1997] 3 SCR 624, at para. 96, it
was held that in light of the "myriad options" available to the government to rectify the
unconstitutionality of the impugned system, it was "not this Court's role to dictate how
this is to be accomplished."

[121] In addition, if he purported to adopt a managerial role, the trial judge undermined the norm of co-operation and mutual respect that not only describes the relationship between the various actors in the constitutional order, but defines its particularly
Canadian nature, and invests each branch with legitimacy. In *Vriend v. Alberta*, [1998] 1
SCR 493, Iacobucci J noted that "respect by the courts for the legislature and the executive role is as important as ensuring that the other branches respect each others' role and
the role of the courts" (para. 136). He discussed the wording of provisions of the Charter
that expressed this norm of mutual respect (para. 137), and remarked that this norm has
"the effect of enhancing the democratic process" (para. 139).

[122] Similarly, McLachlin J (as she then was) in the 1990 Weir Memorial Lecture
reviewed the elements of our legal culture—including our political climate, our tradition
of judicial restraint, and the system of references—that have contributed to a spirit of co-
operation, rather than confrontation among the branches of government (B.M. McLachlin,
"The Charter: A New Role for the Judiciary?" (1991), 29 *Alta. L Rev.* 540, at pp. 554-56).
Moreover, referring to her reasons in *Dixon v. British Columbia (Attorney General)*
(1989), 59 DLR (4th) 247 (BCSC), she spoke to the importance of considerations of institutional legitimacy for a court crafting a remedy (at p. 557):

> It was not for me, I felt, to dictate to the Legislature what sort of law they should enact; that
> was the responsibility of the elected representatives. But, again following a time-honoured
> judicial tradition, I offered advice on what limits on the principle of one person-one vote,
> might be acceptable.

· · ·

[124] Therefore, just as the legislature should, after a judicial finding of a Charter
breach retain independence in writing its legislative response, the executive should after
a judicial finding of a breach, retain autonomy in administering government policy that
conforms with the Charter. In our constitutional order, the legislature and the executive
are intimately interrelated and are the principal loci of democratic will. Judicial respect
for that will should extend to both branches.

[125] Thus, if the trial judge's initial suggestion that he could continue to make
orders, and thereby effectively engage in administrative supervision and decision making
accurately characterizes the nature of the reporting sessions, the order for reporting sessions breached the constitutional principle of separation of powers. Since no part of the
Constitution can be interpreted to conflict with another, that order cannot be considered

appropriate and just in the circumstances, under s. 24(1). The trial judge's order for reporting sessions should also be considered inappropriate because it put into question the Canadian tradition of mutual respect between the judiciary and the institutions that are the repository of democratic will.

[126] If, however, the trial judge's statement in the last session that he could not make further orders correctly characterized his remedial order, then he breached the separation of powers in another way. When considered in light of this constitutional principle and applied to the present facts, McLachlin CJ's proposition that "s. 24 should not be read so broadly that it endows courts and tribunals with powers that they were never intended to exercise" (*Ontario v. 974649 Ontario Inc.*, [2001] 3 SCR 575, 2001 SCC 81 ("*Dunedin*"), at para. 22) leads to the conclusion that the trial judge's remedy was not appropriate and just in the circumstances.

[127] The appellants argued that the trial judge retained jurisdiction *only* to hear reports, and that these hearings had purely "suasive" value. They also argued that the hearings were designed to hold "the Province's feet to the fire" (SCC hearing transcripts). They further suggested that the threat of having to report to the trial judge functioned as an incentive for the government to comply with the best efforts order. In the words of the appellants:

> Is it a coincidence that, after a nine month delay (October 1999 to July 2000) the Province called for tenders eight days before the reporting hearing and "fast tracked" the school? The Province knew it would have to report on July 27. The Province ensured that a call for tenders and a construction schedule were in place for July 27.

[128] If this characterization of the trial judge's activity is accurate, then the order for reporting sessions did not result in the exercise of adjudicative, or any other, functions that traditionally define the ambit of a court's proper sphere. Moreover, it resulted in activity that can be characterized as political. According to the appellants' characterization, a primary purpose of the hearings was to put public pressure on the government to act. This kind of pressure is paradigmatically associated with political actors. Indeed, the practice of publicly questioning a government on its performance, without having any legal power to compel it to alter its behaviour, is precisely that undertaken by an opposition party in the legislature during question period.

[129] In the above, we reasoned that the trial judge, by breaching the separation of powers, would have put in question the norm of co-operation that defines the relationship between the branches of government in Canada. We will presently demonstrate how the trial judge, by improperly altering the relationship between the judiciary and the executive, would have breached the separation of powers.

[130] In *Provincial Court Judges Reference* [*Reference re Remuneration of Judges of the Provincial Court of Prince Edward Island*, [1997] 3 SCR 3], Lamer CJ described the separation of powers as providing that "the relationships between the different branches of government should have a particular *character*" (para. 139 (emphasis in original)). In particular, according to him, the separation of powers doctrine requires that these relationships be *depoliticized* (para. 140 (emphasis in original)).

[131] In that case, Lamer CJ remarked that the legislature and the executive cannot exert, and cannot appear to exert political pressure on the judiciary (para. 140). The

reciprocal proposition applies to the immediate case. With the reporting hearings, the trial judge may have sought to exert political or public pressure on the executive, and at least appeared to do so. In our view, such action would tend to politicize the relationship between the executive and the judiciary.

[132] If the reporting hearings were intended to hold "the Province's feet to the fire," the character of the relationship between the judiciary and the executive was improperly altered and, as per the *Provincial Court Judges Reference*, the constitutional principle of separation of powers was breached. Once again, since no part of the Constitution can conflict with another, the trial judge's order for reporting hearings cannot be interpreted as appropriate and just under s. 24(1).

[133] We would reiterate, at this point, the importance of clarity and certainty in the provisions of a court order. If the trial judge had precisely defined the terms of the remedy, *in advance*, then the ensuing confusion surrounding his role may not have occurred. Moreover, by complying with this essential element of fair procedure, he may have been able to avoid the constitutional breach of the separation of powers that followed.

VI. Neither a Breach of Procedural Fairness Nor of the Separation of Powers Was Appropriate

[134] We noted above that this Court in *Eldridge* recognized the appropriateness of judicial restraint in issuing a remedy under s. 24(1), given the variety of choices open to the executive in administering policy. Implicit in the declaratory remedy ordered in that case was the presumption that the government will act in good faith in rectifying Charter wrongs and the recognition that legislatures and executives, not the courts, are in the best position to decide exactly how this should be done. Turning to the present case then, the trial judge's decision to provide injunctive relief already represented a departure from the cooperative norm that defines and shapes the relationships among the branches of the Canadian constitutional order. We do not deny that in the appropriate factual circumstances, injunctive relief may become necessary. However, the trial judge's order for reporting sessions then purported to go even further, and breached both a fundamental principle of procedural fairness and the constitutional principle of separation of powers.

· · ·

[139] … The facts here do not require us to decide whether previous government non-compliance can ever justify remedial orders that breach principles of procedural fairness and the separation of powers. The Government of Nova Scotia did not refuse to comply with either a prior remedial order or a declaration with respect to its particular obligations in the fact-situation at hand. No such order was made and it is impossible to determine whether the government would have responded in the present case to either a declaration of rights, or the injunction to meet the deadline as these measures were combined with the order purporting to retain jurisdiction to oversee the reporting sessions. Therefore, it cannot be asserted that the trial judge's order has succeeded where less intrusive remedial measures failed.

[140] Moreover, what was required by the Government of Nova Scotia to comply with its obligations pursuant to s. 23 was not self-evident at trial. The trial judge was not faced with a government which was cognizant of how it should fulfill its obligations, but

refused to do so. Indeed, at issue before the trial judge was precisely the question of what compliance with s. 23 involved. The present order, therefore, did not overcome governmental recalcitrance in the face of a clear understanding of what s. 23 required in the circumstances of the case. Remedies must be chosen in light of the nature and structure of the Canadian constitutional order, an important feature of which is the presumption of co-operation between the branches of government. Therefore, unless it is established that this constitutional balance has been upset by the executive's clear defiance of a directly applicable judicial order, increased judicial intervention in public administration will rarely be appropriate.

. . .

[143] In the present case, refusing superior courts the power to order reporting hearings clearly would not deny claimants' access to a recognized Charter remedy, as such an order is entirely idiosyncratic. More importantly, refusing superior courts this power would not deprive claimants of access to that which they are guaranteed by s. 23, namely, the timely provision of minority language instruction facilities. Indeed, if the appellants' characterization of the reporting hearings' purpose is correct, it is difficult to see how they could have been more effective than the construction deadline coupled with the possibility of a contempt order. ...

VII. Conclusion

[145] In the result, the trial judge breached both a principle of procedural fairness and the constitutional principle of separation of powers, and it is not clear that alternative, less-intrusive remedial measures, would not have achieved the ends sought. While a trial judge's decisions with respect to remedies are owed deference, we believe that this must be tempered when fundamental legal principles are threatened. In light of these principles, and in the presence of untested alternative remedies, we would find that the present trial judge's retention of jurisdiction was not appropriate and just under s. 24(1). The Court of Appeal was correct in declaring that the order to retain jurisdiction for the purposes of reporting sessions was of no force and effect.

[146] In closing, we recur to the underlying purpose of s. 24(1), by referring to a passage in *Mills*, *supra*, at pp. 952-53, in which McIntyre J wrote:

> To begin with, it must be recognized that the jurisdiction of the various courts of Canada is fixed by the Legislatures of the various provinces and by the Parliament of Canada. It is not for the judge to assign jurisdiction in respect of any matters to one court or another. This is wholly beyond the judicial reach. ...
>
> The absence of jurisdictional provisions and directions in the *Charter* confirms the view that the *Charter* was not intended to turn the Canadian legal system upside down. What is required rather is that it be fitted into the existing scheme of Canadian legal procedure.

[147] The proper development of the law of constitutional remedies requires that courts reconcile their duty to act within proper jurisdictional limits with the need to give full effect to the rights of a claimant. To read into s. 24(1) a judicial *carte blanche* would not only "turn the Canadian legal system upside down," but would also be an injustice to the parties who come before the court to have their disputes resolved in accordance with

basic legal principles. In our view, proper consideration of the principles of procedural
fairness and the separation of powers is required to establish the requisite legitimacy and
certainty essential to an appropriate and just remedy under s. 24(1) of the *Charter*.

Appeal allowed.

NOTES AND QUESTIONS

1. Do you agree with the majority that the trial judge's order was fair and within his
power? Or do you agree with the minority that it was unfair and exceeded the trial judge's
powers?

2. The majority stressed the particular context of the history of denial of minority language education rights in Nova Scotia. To what extent is the remedial approach taken in this
case based on the particular nature of rights to minority language schools? Could a similar
approach ever be justified, as has been done in other countries, in relation to conditions of
confinement in custodial institutions or with respect to health care rights? For a comparison
of *Doucet-Boudreau* with a leading case from the South African Constitutional Court on
structural interdicts to require governments to supply drugs to prevent mother-to-child
HIV transmission, see K. Roach and G. Budlender, "Mandatory Relief and Supervisory
Jurisdiction: When Is It Appropriate, Just, and Equitable" (2005), 122 *South African Law
Journal* 325.

3. Although the Court disagreed about the particular remedy devised in this case, it
agreed that s. 24(1) of the Charter provides a basis for an injunction against the government. Would this have changed the remedy in *Little Sisters*? If a judge is prepared to issue
injunctive relief under s. 24(1), what considerations should guide his or her exercise of remedial discretion? What will be the likely effect of the stress that the minority places on the
clarity of the order and its enforceability? Should contempt powers ever be used to enforce
a constitutional remedy? For commentary on this case, see D. MacAlister, "Case Comment"
(2004), 16 *NJCL* 153; K. Roach, "Principled Remedial Decision Making Under the Charter"
(2004), 25 *Supreme Court Law Review* (2d) 101; Hon. P. Rouleau, S. Bhattacharjee, and
N. Rouleau, "Revisiting Doucet-Boudreau: Perspectives on Remedies in Section 23 Cases"
(2006), 32 *Supreme Court Law Review* (2d) 301.

NOTE ON DAMAGES

Although damages are a possible remedy for Charter violations, such claims to date remain
a rarity, with only a very few having been successful. Although the Supreme Court of Canada has not directly ruled on the issue, there have been indications in several judgments of
the Court that retroactive relief in the form of a s. 24(1) remedy, including a claim for damages, will not ordinarily be available where a statutory provision has been struck down pursuant to s. 52 of the *Constitution Act, 1982*. In *Schachter v. Canada*, [1992] 2 SCR 679, for
example, Lamer CJC commented:

> An individual remedy under s. 24(1) of the Charter will rarely be available in conjunction with
> an action under s. 52 of the *Constitution Act, 1982*. Ordinarily, where a provision is declared

unconstitutional and immediately struck down pursuant to s. 52 that will be the end of the matter. No retroactive s. 24 remedy will be available.

(See also *Guimond v. Quebec (Attorney General)*, [1996] 3 SCR 347, 138 DLR (4th) 647, and *Mackin v. New Brunswick*, [2002] 1 SCR 405, at para. 82, establishing that the award of damages under s. 24(1) of the Charter can only be combined with a declaration of invalidity under s. 52(1) of the Constitution in cases where the government "acted negligently, in bad faith or by abusing its powers.")

Claims for damages will, therefore, typically be brought against public officials alleged to have violated Charter rights in the course of exercising their statutory powers and, in that context, courts have generally refused to award damages if public officials have acted in good faith—that is, on the belief that the law authorizing their actions was valid. In *Ferri v. Ontario*, 2007 ONCA 79, 279 DLR (4th) 643, the Ontario Court of Appeal has applied the requirement of some form of fault as contemplated in *Guimond* and *Mackin* to damage actions under s. 24(1) of the Charter, as distinguished from actions that do not require the invalidation of legislation under s. 52(1). The BC Court of Appeal, however, has rejected a requirement of fault in a case where a lawyer was arrested and subjected to an unconstitutional strip search in *Ward v. British Columbia*, 2009 BCCA 23, 304 DLR (4th) 653. Because a majority of the claims for damages arise in the criminal law context, involving, for example, unconstitutional arrests, searches, or assaults, the issue will not be examined in these materials. For a full discussion of the issue see K.D. Cooper-Stevenson, *Charter Damage Claims* (Calgary: Carswell, 1990) and K. Roach, *Constitutional Remedies in Canada*, looseleaf ed. (Aurora, ON: Canada Law Book, 1994).

II. STANDING: WHO CAN RAISE CHARTER ISSUES?

Remedies and standing are closely intertwined issues. The availability of remedies for Charter violations under s. 24 of the Charter and s. 52(1) of the *Constitution Act, 1982* raises the issue of who can claim such remedies. These materials will not deal extensively with issues of standing, but merely provide a brief overview of the main ways in which standing to raise Charter issues may be claimed. Reference should also be made to the introductory discussion of standing in constitutional litigation found in Chapter 2, Judicial Review and Constitutional Interpretation.

It is clear that anyone whose Charter rights have been violated has standing to raise the Charter issue and seek a remedy under either s. 24 or s. 52(1), depending on the nature of the relief desired. The issue of Charter infringement may be raised in two ways. First, it can be raised as a collateral issue in ongoing criminal or civil proceedings, for example, as a defence to a criminal charge or a claim of civil liability. Alternatively, an independent action may be commenced seeking declaratory relief or other remedies.

The more difficult question is whether a person whose own rights are not in issue will nonetheless be allowed to challenge legislation as infringing another person's Charter rights. This issue frequently arises in situations where a corporation wishes to have a law to which it is subject declared invalid, but the Charter right that the law is alleged to infringe is not one that a corporation is capable of enjoying, for example, s. 2(a) (freedom of religion) or s. 7 (life, liberty and security of the person). To challenge the law, the corporation seeks to argue the infringement of someone else's Charter rights. To what extent has this been allowed?

The starting point for answering this question is *R v. Big M Drug Mart Ltd.*, [1985] 1 SCR 295, 18 DLR (4th) 321, excerpted in Chapter 19, Freedom of Religion. In that case, a corporation that had been charged with violating Sunday closing legislation wished to challenge the law as a violation of freedom of religion. Dickson CJC, in a passage partially reproduced earlier in the introductory discussion of remedies, found that the corporation had standing to raise the Charter issue, stating at 336 DLR:

> Section 24(1) sets out a remedy for individuals (whether real persons or artificial ones such as corporations) whose rights under the Charter have been infringed. It is not, however, the only recourse in the face of unconstitutional legislation. Where, as here, the challenge is based on the unconstitutionality of the legislation, recourse to s. 24 is unnecessary and the particular effect on the challenging party is irrelevant.
>
> Section 52 sets out the fundamental principle of constitutional law that the Constitution is supreme. The undoubted corollary to be drawn from this principle is that no one can be convicted of an offence under an unconstitutional law. ...
>
> Any accused ... may defend a criminal charge by arguing that the law under which the charge is brought is constitutionally invalid. Big M is urging that the law under which it has been charged is inconsistent with s. 2(a) of the Charter and by reason of s. 52 of the *Constitution Act, 1982*, it is of no force or effect.

Thus, a declaration of invalidity sought under s. 52 is governed by more generous standing requirements than the relief available under s. 24(1). Following this ruling in *Big M*, corporations have been allowed, in the context of criminal prosecutions, to make s. 7 Charter challenges to the legislation under which they have been charged (see, for example, *R v. Wholesale Travel Group*, [1991] 3 SCR 154, 67 CCC (3d) 193, where a corporation was allowed to challenge the false advertising provisions of the federal *Competition Act* under which it had been charged).

The Supreme Court has, however, placed some limits on the *Big M* expansion of standing. Corporations that cannot claim an infringement of their own Charter rights have not been allowed to bring independent civil actions seeking declarations of a law's invalidity, despite the fact that they are subject to regulation under the law in issue and to possible criminal or penal sanctions should they violate it (see *Irwin Toy Ltd. v. Quebec (Attorney General)*, [1989] 1 SCR 927, 58 DLR (4th) 577, and *Hy and Zel's Inc. v. Ontario (Attorney General)*, [1993] 3 SCR 675, 107 DLR (4th) 634). This is in contrast to federalism cases where the fact that a corporation's interests are directly affected by a law is sufficient to ground standing and, indeed, in *Irwin Toy*, the corporation was granted standing to bring a federalism challenge. Opinion is divided on this restriction of standing in Charter cases—for some it is an unjustifiable limitation on judicial review; for others it is a positive attempt to prevent the Charter, intended to protect individual rights and dignity, from being used to benefit corporate, economic interests. These issues of standing are further discussed in J. Ross, "Standing in Charter Declaratory Actions" (1995), 33 *Osgoode Hall Law Journal* 151.

Another way in which individuals or corporations may be allowed to argue the violation of another person's Charter rights, in addition to reliance on the *Big M* standing rule, is through a grant of public interest standing under the rules developed in the *Thorson-McNeil-Borowski* trilogy, discussed in Chapter 2, Judicial Review and Constitutional Interpretation.

III. JURISDICTION: WHERE CAN CHARTER ISSUES BE RAISED?

This section brings our attention back to a basic question: In which adjudicative forum does one bring a Charter claim? This discussion will provide a brief overview of the relevant considerations.

Recall that s. 24 of the Charter sets down the rules for those who initiate Charter claims. It directs the plaintiff or applicant to "a court of competent jurisdiction." The Supreme Court of Canada has indicated that s. 24 confers no new jurisdiction on courts. To grant relief under s. 24, a court must have jurisdiction, independent of the Charter, over (1) the parties, (2) the subject matter of the application, and (3) the remedy sought.

The choice of court is usually obvious, but complications do arise. The main consideration to keep in mind is that some courts have inherent jurisdiction and others have statutory jurisdiction. The superior (or Queen's Bench) courts in Canada have inherent jurisdiction. That means that they can hear cases concerning any area of law except those specifically reserved by legislation for lower courts. For this reason, one assumes that they have jurisdiction. Other courts, such as the Divisional Court in Ontario, which deals with review of the work of administrative tribunals and some appeals from their decisions, are statutory courts. A statutory court has only the jurisdiction vested in it by statute. The Federal Court of Canada is also a statutory court, established by federal statute, with jurisdiction to hear matters arising under federal legislation, regulations, and common law. The designation of the proper court for a Charter claim arises within this framework and should be kept in mind as you read cases from the various courts.

Another concern is whether an administrative tribunal is empowered to deliberate on Charter claims. The Supreme Court of Canada has ruled that the principle of the supremacy of the Constitution, embodied in s. 52 of the *Constitution Act, 1982*, means that any court or tribunal with the power to determine questions of law is thereby authorized to consider the Constitution as well as the other relevant law in its deliberations. After a number of cases laid out the foundation for resolving this question, the Court recently set down its fullest account of the principles and rules for determining whether a particular administrative tribunal has jurisdiction to deliberate a Charter claim in *Nova Scotia (Workers Compensation Board) v. Martin*, [2003] 2 SCR 504, 2003 SCC 54, 231 DLR (4th) 504.

The Court's analysis in *Martin* reflects the competing considerations engaged in. On the one hand, administrative tribunals provide an expeditious, inexpensive, expert, and informal forum for deliberation on alleged breach of Charter rights. Duplicative proceedings are avoided and the specialized competence of the tribunal may provide assistance to the reviewing court by preparing a full factual record and applying subject matter expertise. On the other hand, the informal processes of some tribunals and their lack of legal expertise or training may render them unsuitable for dealing with constitutional issues, which call for a different kind of knowledge, expertise, and value structure. More generally, our legal system traditionally reserved questions that relate to individual rights to courts of law because of

their independence, expertise, and stature. This idea is rooted in the constitutional principles of the rule of law and the separation of powers. Because constitutional law constrains
the exercise of political authority, it has been considered appropriate for judges, rather than
officials appointed by government for limited purposes for limited terms, to determine
constitutional questions.

What follows are some portions from the Court's unanimous judgment in *Martin*, written
by Gonthier J, where it lays out the relevant considerations and doctrinal rules that pertain
to the deliberation by administrative tribunals and official tribunals over Charter claims.

[28] First, and most importantly, the Constitution is, under s. 52(1) of the *Constitution Act,
1982*, "the supreme law of Canada, and any law that is inconsistent with the provisions of the
Constitution is, to the extent of the inconsistency, of no force or effect." The invalidity of a legislative provision inconsistent with the Charter does not arise from the fact of its being declared
unconstitutional by a court, but from the operation of s. 52(1). Thus, in principle, such a provision is invalid from the moment it is enacted, and a judicial declaration to this effect is but one
remedy amongst others to protect those whom it adversely affects. ... Courts may not apply invalid laws, and the same obligation applies to every level and branch of government, including
the administrative organs of the state. Obviously, it cannot be the case that every government
official has to consider and decide for herself the constitutional validity of every provision she
is called upon to apply. If, however, she is endowed with the power to consider questions of law
relating to a provision, that power will normally extend to assessing the constitutional validity
of that provision. ...

[29] From this principle of constitutional supremacy also flows, as a practical corollary, the
idea that Canadians should be entitled to assert the rights and freedoms that the Constitution
guarantees them in the most accessible forum available, without the need for parallel proceedings before the courts ... . This accessibility concern is particularly pressing given that many
administrative tribunals have exclusive initial jurisdiction over disputes relating to their enabling legislation, so that forcing litigants to refer Charter issues to the courts would result in
costly and time-consuming bifurcation of proceedings. ...

[30] Second, Charter disputes do not take place in a vacuum. They require a thorough
understanding of the objectives of the legislative scheme being challenged, as well as of the
practical constraints it faces and the consequences of proposed constitutional remedies. This
need is heightened when, as is often the case, it becomes necessary to determine whether a
prima facie violation of a *Charter* right is justified under s. 1. In this respect, the factual findings
and record compiled by an administrative tribunal, as well as its informed and expert view of
the various issues raised by a constitutional challenge, will often be invaluable to a reviewing
court ... .

[31] Third, administrative tribunal decisions based on the Charter are subject to judicial
review on a correctness standard ... . An error of law by an administrative tribunal interpreting
the Constitution can always be reviewed fully by a superior court. In addition, the constitutional remedies available to administrative tribunals are limited and do not include general
declarations of invalidity. A determination by a tribunal that a provision of its enabling statute
is invalid pursuant to the Charter is not binding on future decision makers, within or outside
the tribunal's administrative scheme. Only by obtaining a formal declaration of invalidity by a
court can a litigant establish the general invalidity of a legislative provision for all future cases.

Therefore, allowing administrative tribunals to decide Charter issues does not undermine the role of the courts as final arbiters of constitutionality in Canada.

• • •

[33] … When a case brought before an administrative tribunal involves a challenge to the constitutionality of a provision of its enabling statute, the tribunal is asked to interpret the relevant Charter right, apply it to the impugned provision, and if it finds a breach and concludes that the provision is not saved under s. 1, to disregard the provision on constitutional grounds and rule on the applicant's claim as if the impugned provision were not in force.

• • •

[35] In each case, the first question to be addressed is whether the administrative tribunal at issue has jurisdiction, explicit or implied, to decide questions of law arising under the challenged provision. … The question is not whether Parliament or the legislature intended the tribunal to apply the Charter. As has often been pointed out, such an attribution of intent would be artificial, given that many of the relevant enabling provisions pre-date the *Charter* … .

[36] … [O]ne must ask whether the empowering legislation implicitly or explicitly grants to the tribunal the jurisdiction to interpret or decide *any* question of law. If it does, then the tribunal will be presumed to have the concomitant jurisdiction to interpret or decide that question in light of the Charter, unless the legislator has removed that power from the tribunal. Thus, an administrative tribunal that has the power to decide questions of law arising under a particular legislative provision will be presumed to have the power to determine the constitutional validity of that provision.

• • •

[41] Absent an explicit grant, it becomes necessary to consider whether the legislator intended to confer upon the tribunal implied jurisdiction to decide questions of law arising under the challenged provision. Implied jurisdiction must be discerned by looking at the statute as a whole. Relevant factors will include the statutory mandate of the tribunal in issue and whether deciding questions of law is necessary to fulfilling this mandate effectively; the interaction of the tribunal in question with other elements of the administrative system; whether the tribunal is adjudicative in nature; and practical considerations, including the tribunal's capacity to consider questions of law. …

[42] Once this presumption has been raised, either by an explicit or implicit grant of authority to decide questions of law, the second question that arises is whether it has been rebutted. The burden of establishing this lies on the party who alleges that the administrative body at issue lacks jurisdiction to apply the Charter. In general terms, the presumption may only be rebutted by an explicit withdrawal of authority to decide constitutional questions or by a clear implication to the same effect, arising from the statute itself rather than from external considerations. The question to be asked is whether an examination of the statutory provisions clearly leads to the conclusion that the legislature intended to exclude the Charter, or more broadly, a category of questions of law encompassing the Charter, from the scope of the questions of law to be addressed by the tribunal. For instance, an express conferral of jurisdiction to another administrative body to consider Charter issues or certain complex questions of law deemed too difficult or time-consuming for the initial decision maker, along with a procedure allowing such issues to be efficiently redirected to such body, could give rise to a clear implication that the initial decision maker was not intended to decide constitutional questions.

• • •

[44] I refrain, however, from expressing any opinion as to the constitutionality of a provision that would place procedural barriers in the way of claimants seeking to assert their rights in a timely and effective manner, for instance by removing Charter jurisdiction from a tribunal without providing an effective alternative administrative route for Charter claims.

NOTES AND QUESTIONS

1. Does the framework set down in *Martin* resolve the competing considerations adequately? Does it provide a clear set of directives or does it invite further litigation to settle contested questions in specific instances?

2. In paragraph 44, McLachlin CJC raises the possibility that legislation that removed Charter jurisdiction from a tribunal might be constitutionally invalid if it made no provision for an alternate administrative disposition of the Charter issue. What would be the basis of a finding of invalidity? Would the provision of a special tribunal for resolving Charter issues in the administrative context be consistent with the considerations that animated the analysis in *Martin*?

3. In *Cooper v. Canada (Human Rights Commission)*, [1996] 3 SCR 854, 140 DLR (4th) 393, at para. 70, McLachlin J (as she then was) made this comment in the context of deliberating on the concerns that were later resolved in *Martin*:

> The Charter is not some holy grail which only judicial initiates of the superior courts may touch. The Charter belongs to the people. All law and law-makers that touch the people must conform to it. Tribunals and commissions charged with deciding legal issues are no exception. Many more citizens have their rights determined by these tribunals than by the courts. If the Charter is to be meaningful to ordinary people, then it must find its expression in the decisions of these tribunals.

Does this statement lie at the heart of her resolution of the competing considerations in *Martin*?

4. The Court later applied its analysis in *Martin* to Aboriginal rights claims made under s. 35(1) before provincial administrative tribunals: see *Paul v. British Columbia (Forest Appeals Commission)*, [2003] 2 SCR 585, 2003 SCC 55, 231 DLR (4th) 449. For an example of provincial legislation precluding consideration of a constitutional claim by an administrative tribunal, see *Tranchemontagne v. Ontario (Director, Disability Support Program)*, [2006] 1 SCR 513, 2006 SCC 14, 266 DLR (4th) 287.

5. Further discussion of the jurisdiction of various courts with respect to constitutional issues may be found in Chapter 13, The Judicial Function.